This yOuth Quest StUdy Bible

was given

To _____

On _____

By _____

yOur wOrd is a Lamp fOr my feet, a Light On my path.

PSaLm 119:105

NEW INTERNATIONAL VERSION

yOuth Quest StUdy Bible

NEW INTERNATIONAL VERSION

youth
Quest
Study Bible

Published by Zondervan
Grand Rapids, Michigan 49530, USA

www.zondervan.com

Library of Congress Catalog Card Number 2011932302

11 12 13 14 15 16 17 18 19 20 /DSC/ 15 14 13 12 11 10 9 8 7 6 5 4 3 2 1

A portion of the purchase price of your NIV® Bible is provided to Biblica so together we support the mission of *Transforming lives through God's Word.*

Biblica provides God's Word to people through translation, publishing and Bible engagement in Africa, Asia Pacific, Europe, Latin America, Middle East, and North America. Through its worldwide reach, Biblica engages people with God's Word so that their lives are transformed through a relationship with Jesus Christ.

Contents

Contents

Welcome to the Youth Quest Study Bible

Your word is a lamp for my feet,
a light for my path.

—PSALM 119:105

GOD'S WORD
The text of the Bible itself is the most important feature of this book. God reveals himself to us through his Holy Word. The New International Version (NIV) is the most read, most trusted modern English translation.

BOOK INTRODUCTIONS
At the beginning of each book of the Bible, you will find helpful information answering questions like: Who wrote the book? What purpose did the author have in mind? What is the historical background? What are the main sections of the book? Time lines are also included.

SIDE-COLUMN NOTES
Because the Bible describes events that took place a long time ago, modern readers often have questions about the meaning of some parts of the Bible. There are about 4,000 questions and answers in the side column to help you better understand the Bible by explaining words or ideas that may not be clear. The answers sometimes include some historical information that the Bible doesn't mention, and they often tell how modern Bible scholars interpret different passages.

ARTICLES
There are about 100 articles scattered throughout this Bible that go into more depth to give answers to questions that young people often ask. These articles sometimes deal with difficult topics, and they often suggest that you speak to a parent, teacher, or minister about your own faith questions.

MAPS
Small two-color maps are included at various points to help you see where the events took place. Several full-color maps are located in the back of the Bible to help you find some of the important places at different times in the Bible's story.

SUBJECT INDEX
This index will help you locate Bible passages that refer to important themes.

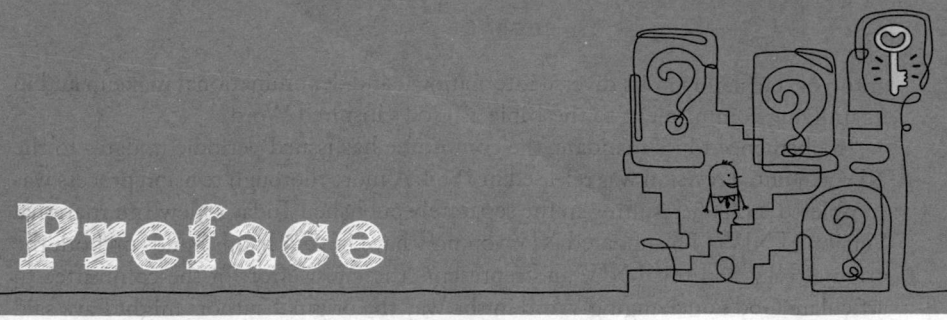

Preface

The goal of the New International Version (NIV) is to enable English-speaking people from around the world to read and hear God's eternal Word in their own language. Our work as translators is motivated by our conviction that the Bible is God's Word in written form. We believe that the Bible contains the divine answer to the deepest needs of humanity, sheds unique light on our path in a dark world and sets forth the way to our eternal well-being. Out of these deep convictions, we have sought to recreate as far as possible the experience of the original audience—blending transparency to the original text with accessibility for the millions of English speakers around the world. We have prioritized accuracy, clarity and literary quality with the goal of creating a translation suitable for public and private reading, evangelism, teaching, preaching, memorizing and liturgical use. We have also sought to preserve a measure of continuity with the long tradition of translating the Scriptures into English.

The complete NIV Bible was first published in 1978. It was a completely new translation made by over a hundred scholars working directly from the best available Hebrew, Aramaic and Greek texts. The translators came from the United States, Great Britain, Canada, Australia and New Zealand, giving the translation an international scope. They were from many denominations and churches—including Anglican, Assemblies of God, Baptist, Brethren, Christian Reformed, Church of Christ, Evangelical Covenant, Evangelical Free, Lutheran, Mennonite, Methodist, Nazarene, Presbyterian, Wesleyan and others. This breadth of denominational and theological perspective helped to safeguard the translation from sectarian bias. For these reasons, and by the grace of God, the NIV has gained a wide readership in all parts of the English-speaking world.

The work of translating the Bible is never finished. As good as they are, English translations must be regularly updated so that they will continue to communicate accurately the meaning of God's Word. Updates are needed in order to reflect the latest developments in our understanding of the biblical world and its languages and to keep pace with changes in English usage. Recognizing, then, that the NIV would retain its ability to communicate God's Word accurately only if it were regularly updated, the original translators established The Committee on Bible Translation (CBT). The committee is a self-perpetuating group of biblical scholars charged with keeping abreast of advances in biblical scholarship and changes in English and issuing periodic updates to the NIV. CBT is an independent, self-governing body and has sole responsibility for the NIV text. The committee mirrors the original group of translators in its diverse international and denominational makeup and in its unifying commitment to the Bible as God's inspired Word.

In obedience to its mandate, the committee has issued periodic updates to the NIV. An initial revision was released in 1984. A more thorough revision process was completed in 2005, resulting in the separately published Today's New International Version (TNIV). The updated NIV you now have in your hands builds on both the original NIV and the TNIV and represents the latest effort of the committee to articulate God's unchanging Word in the way the original authors might have said it had they been speaking in English to the global English-speaking audience today.

The first concern of the translators has continued to be the accuracy of the translation and its faithfulness to the intended meaning of the biblical writers. This has moved the translators to go beyond a formal word-for-word rendering of the original texts. Because thought patterns and syntax differ from language to language, accurate communication of the meaning of the biblical authors demands constant regard for varied contextual uses of words and idioms and for frequent modifications in sentence structures.

As an aid to the reader, sectional headings have been inserted. They are not to be regarded as part of the biblical text and are not intended for oral reading. It is the committee's hope that these headings may prove more helpful to the reader than the traditional chapter divisions, which were introduced long after the Bible was written.

For the Old Testament the standard Hebrew text, the Masoretic Text as published in the latest edition of *Biblia Hebraica*, has been used throughout. The Masoretic Text tradition contains marginal notations that offer variant readings. These have sometimes been followed instead of the text itself. Because such instances involve variants within the Masoretic tradition, they have not been indicated in the textual notes. In a few cases, words in the basic consonantal text have been divided differently than in the Masoretic Text. Such cases are usually indicated in the textual footnotes. The Dead Sea Scrolls contain biblical texts that represent an earlier stage of the transmission of the Hebrew text. They have been consulted, as have been the Samaritan Pentateuch and the ancient scribal traditions concerning deliberate textual changes. The translators also consulted the more important early versions—the Greek Septuagint, Aquila, Symmachus and Theodotion, the Latin Vulgate, the Syriac Peshitta, the Aramaic Targums and, for the Psalms, the *Juxta Hebraica* of Jerome. Readings from these versions, the Dead Sea Scrolls and the scribal traditions were occasionally followed where the Masoretic Text seemed doubtful and where accepted principles of textual criticism showed that one or more of these textual witnesses appeared to provide the correct reading. In rare cases, the committee has emended the Hebrew text where it appears to have become corrupted at an even earlier stage of its transmission. These departures from the Masoretic Text are also indicated in the textual footnotes. Sometimes the vowel indicators (which are later additions to the basic consonantal text) found in the Masoretic Text did not, in the judgment of the committee, represent the correct vowels for the original text. Accordingly, some words have been read with a different set of vowels. These instances are usually not indicated in the footnotes.

The Greek text used in translating the New Testament is an eclectic one, based on the latest editions of the Nestle-Aland/United Bible Societies' Greek New Testament. The committee has made its choices among the variant readings in accordance with widely accepted principles of New Testament textual criticism. Footnotes call attention to places where uncertainty remains.

The New Testament authors, writing in Greek, often quote the Old Testament from its ancient Greek version, the Septuagint. This is one reason why some of the Old Testament quotations in the NIV New Testament are not identical to the corresponding passages in the NIV Old Testament. Such quotations in the New Testament are indicated with the footnote "(see Septuagint)."

Other footnotes in this version are of several kinds, most of which need no explanation. Those giving alternative translations begin with "Or" and generally introduce the alternative with the last word preceding it in the text, except when it is a single-word alternative. When poetry is quoted in a footnote, a slash mark indicates a line division.

It should be noted that references to diseases, minerals, flora and fauna, architectural details, clothing, jewelry, musical instruments and other articles cannot always be identified with precision. Also, linear measurements and measures of capacity can only be approximated (see the Table of Weights and Measures). Although *Selah*, used mainly in the Psalms, is probably a musical term, its meaning is uncertain. Since it may interrupt reading and distract the reader, this word has not been kept in the English text, but every occurrence has been signaled by a footnote.

One of the main reasons the task of Bible translation is never finished is the change in our own language, English. Although a basic core of the language remains relatively stable, many diverse and complex linguistic factors continue to bring about subtle shifts in the meanings and/or connotations of even old, well-established words and phrases. One of the shifts that creates particular challenges to writers and translators alike is the manner in which gender is presented. The original NIV (1978) was published in a time when "a man" would naturally be understood, in many contexts, to be referring to a person, whether male or female. But most English speakers today tend to hear a distinctly male connotation in this word. In recognition of this change in English, this edition of the NIV, along with almost all other recent English translations, substitutes other expressions when the original text intends to refer generically to men and women equally. Thus, for instance, the NIV (1984) rendering of 1 Corinthians 8:3, "But the man who loves God is known by God" becomes in this edition "But whoever loves God is known by God." On the other hand, "man" and "mankind," as ways of denoting the human race, are still widely used. This edition of the NIV therefore continues to use these words, along with other expressions, in this way.

A related shift in English creates a greater challenge for modern translations: the move away from using the third-person masculine singular pronouns—"he/him/his"—to refer to men and women equally. This usage does persist at a low level in some forms of English, and this revision therefore occasionally uses these pronouns in a generic sense. But the tendency, recognized in day-to-day usage and confirmed by extensive research, is away from the generic use of "he," "him" and "his." In recognition of this shift in language and in an effort to translate into the "common"

English that people are actually using, this revision of the NIV generally uses other constructions when the biblical text is plainly addressed to men and women equally. The reader will frequently encounter a "they," "them" or "their" to express a generic singular idea. Thus, for instance, Mark 8:36 reads: "What good is it for someone to gain the whole world, yet forfeit their soul?" This generic use of the "indefinite" or "singular" "they/them/their" has a venerable place in English idiom and has quickly become established as standard English, spoken and written, all over the world. Where an individual emphasis is deemed to be present, "anyone" or "everyone" or some other equivalent is generally used as the antecedent of such pronouns.

Sometimes the chapter and/or verse numbering in English translations of the Old Testament differs from that found in published Hebrew texts. This is particularly the case in the Psalms, where the traditional titles are often included in the Hebrew verse numbering. Such differences are indicated in the footnotes at the bottom of the page. In the New Testament, verse numbers that marked off portions of the traditional English text not supported by the best Greek manuscripts now appear in brackets, with a footnote indicating the text that has been omitted (see, for example, Matthew 17:[21]).

Mark 16:9–20 and John 7:53–8:11, although long accorded virtually equal status with the rest of the Gospels in which they stand, have a very questionable—and confused—standing in the textual history of the New Testament, as noted in the bracketed annotations with which they are set off. A different typeface has been chosen for these passages to indicate even more clearly their uncertain status.

Basic formatting of the text, such as lining the poetry, paragraphing (both prose and poetry), setting up of (administrative-like) lists, indenting letters and lengthy prayers within narratives and the insertion of sectional headings, has been the work of the committee. However, the choice between single-column and double-column formats has been left to the publishers. Also the issuing of "red-letter" editions is a publisher's choice—one the committee does not endorse.

The committee has again been reminded that every human effort is flawed— including this revision of the NIV. We trust, however, that many will find in it an improved representation of the Word of God, through which they hear his call to faith in our Lord Jesus Christ and to service in his kingdom. We offer this version of the Bible to him in whose name and for whose glory it has been made.

The Committee on Bible Translation
September 2010

Old Testament

Genesis

INTRODUCTION

Who wrote this book?	There is some debate about who wrote Genesis. However, many scholars believe Moses wrote it.
Why was this book written?	Genesis tells how God created the universe and human beings. It also covers the special promises God made to Abraham.
What do we learn about God in this book?	God created all things. He loves people, but he will punish sin. God promises, however, to save people who trust him.
Who are the key people in this book?	The most important people in this book are Adam and Eve, Noah, Abraham and Sarah, Isaac and Rebekah, Jacob and Rachel, and Joseph.
Where did this happen?	Genesis 1–11 happened in Mesopotamia. Genesis 12–36 took place in Canaan, which is also called the promised land. The rest of Genesis took place in Egypt. (See the map on the next page.)

What are some of the stories in this book?		
	God creates the universe	Genesis 1
	God creates Adam and Eve	Genesis 2
	Adam and Eve sin	Genesis 3
	Noah builds an ark	Genesis 6
	God sends a flood to punish sin	Genesis 7–8
	God gives promises to Abraham	Genesis 12
	Abraham prays for a city	Genesis 18
	Jacob steals Esau's blessing	Genesis 27
	Jacob's name is changed	Genesis 32
	Joseph's brothers sell him into slavery	Genesis 37
	Joseph becomes a ruler	Genesis 39–41

When did these things happen?

	2200 BC	2100	2000	1900	1800	1700	1600	1500	1400
CREATION, FALL									
THE FLOOD									
THE TOWER OF BABEL									
ABRAHAM'S LIFE (ABOUT 2166–1991 BC)									
ISAAC'S LIFE (ABOUT 2066–1886 BC)									
JACOB'S LIFE (ABOUT 2006–1859 BC)									
JOSEPH'S LIFE (ABOUT 1915–1805 BC)									
BOOK OF GENESIS WRITTEN (ABOUT 1446–1406 BC)									

Was God the only one in the beginning? (1:1)
Yes, he was the only one. Although everything else has a beginning, God has always been around, and the Bible describes him as everlasting or eternal.

How did God say things into being? (1:3)
Just by his creative word, God brought all things into being.

Were the six days of creation actual 24-hour days? (1:5)
They could have been 24-hour days, or this could have been a figure of speech. Since the sun wasn't created until the fourth day, some Christians think that the six days of creation were long periods of time rather than 24 hours each.

THE BEGINNING

1 In the beginning God created the heavens and the earth. [2] Now the earth was formless and empty, darkness was over the surface of the deep, and the Spirit of God was hovering over the waters.

[3] And God said, "Let there be light," and there was light. [4] God saw that the light was good, and he separated the light from the darkness. [5] God called the light "day," and the darkness he called "night." And there was evening, and there was morning—the first day.

[6] And God said, "Let there be a vault between the waters to separate water from water." [7] So God made the vault and separated the water under the vault from the water above it. And it was so. [8] God called the vault "sky." And there was evening, and there was morning—the second day.

[9] And God said, "Let the water under the sky be gathered to one place, and let dry ground appear." And it was so. [10] God called the dry ground "land," and the gathered waters he called "seas." And God saw that it was good.

[11] Then God said, "Let the land produce vegetation: seed-bearing plants and trees on the land that bear fruit with seed in it, according to their various kinds." And it was so. [12] The land produced vegetation: plants bearing seed according to their kinds and trees bearing fruit with seed in it according to their kinds. And God saw

SETTING OF GENESIS

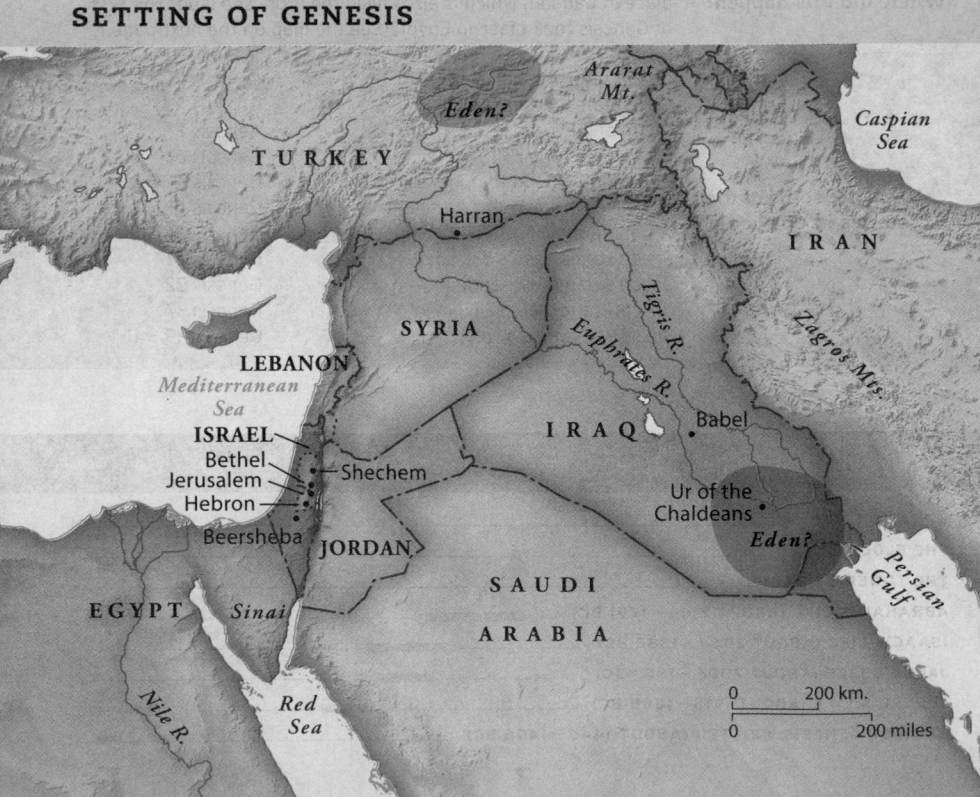

that it was good. [13] And there was evening, and there was morning—the third day.

[14] And God said, "Let there be lights in the vault of the sky to separate the day from the night, and let them serve as signs to mark sacred times, and days and years, [15] and let them be lights in the vault of the sky to give light on the earth." And it was so. [16] God made two great lights—the greater light to govern the day and the lesser light to govern the night. He also made the stars. [17] God set them in the vault of the sky to give light on the earth, [18] to govern the day and the night, and to separate light from darkness. And God saw that it was good. [19] And there was evening, and there was morning—the fourth day.

[20] And God said, "Let the water teem with living creatures, and let birds fly above the earth across the vault of the sky." [21] So God created the great creatures of the sea and every living thing with which the water teems and that moves about in it, according to their kinds, and every winged bird according to its kind. And God saw that it was good. [22] God blessed them and said, "Be fruitful and increase in number and fill the water in the seas, and let the birds increase on the earth." [23] And there was evening, and there was morning—the fifth day.

[24] And God said, "Let the land produce living creatures according to their kinds: the livestock, the creatures that move along the ground, and the wild animals, each according to its kind." And it was so. [25] God made the wild animals according to their kinds, the livestock according to their kinds, and all the creatures that move along the ground according to their kinds. And God saw that it was good.

[26] Then God said, "Let us make mankind in our image, in our likeness, so that they may rule over the fish in the sea and the birds in the sky, over the livestock and all the wild animals,[a] and over all the creatures that move along the ground."

[a] 26 Probable reading of the original Hebrew text (see Syriac); Masoretic Text the earth

Why does the Bible say that "God saw that it was good" after each day of creation? (1:10, 12, 18, 21, 25)
Everything God created was perfect. The Bible emphasizes this when God declared it "very good" (verse 31).

Was there an order to creation? (1:3–31)
On the first three days God *formed* creation with light, water and sky, land and vegetation. On the final three days God *filled* creation with light givers, fish and birds, and animals and humans.

What does it mean he created animals "according to their kinds"? (1:21, 24–25)
Both creation and reproduction are orderly. God created plants and animals with distinct attributes and patterns of development true to their families and species.

Did God create dinosaurs too? (1:24)
Although dinosaurs are not mentioned specifically, they were probably created on the sixth day. It is possible what the Bible describes as a *monster* (Psalm 74:13), *dragon* (Revelation 12:3), or *behemoth* (Job 40:15–19) may be dinosaurs.

Did God really create the universe, or did everything just happen?

GENESIS 1

The very first verse of the Bible tells us that in the beginning God created the heavens and the earth. Many people have wondered how God did that.

Many scientists today think that the Big Bang theory is the best explanation for how the universe came into being. According to this theory, the universe began billions of years ago instantly as a small, dense, hot entity. It then began to quickly expand and cool, eventually clustering into planets, stars, and galaxies. Many Christians think that this is a good explanation because it takes into account the scientific evidence and because it claims that the universe came into existence instantly when there had been nothing before. Other Christians, however, believe that the universe began about 6,000 years ago. They believe that the days of creation were literal 24-hour days.

Even though Christians have a wide range of opinions about the beginning of the universe, all can agree that God was the Creator. Not only that, but he created a perfect universe filled with stars and planets and a perfect earth filled with an amazing variety of plants and animals. And God continues to care for this world even though creation has experienced the effects of sin.

How was the creation of human beings special? (1:27) People are different from everything else God made because they are made in his image. That means human beings share some of God's characteristics, such as intelligence, love, and creativity. Since humans are made in God's image, every person is important to God.

What does it mean when God told humans to "fill the earth and subdue it"? (1:28) God wants people to be caretakers of creation and use its resources responsibly.

Why did God rest on the seventh day? (2:2–3) God did not need to rest because he was tired. He rested because his creation work was finished. God wants us to follow his example and rest one day each week and to set one day apart as holy.

Why did God make the first man out of dust? (2:7) Both animals and people were created out of the ground with God's breath of life. And we will return to dust when we die.

[27] So God created mankind in his own image,
     in the image of God he created them;
     male and female he created them.

[28] God blessed them and said to them, "Be fruitful and increase in number; fill the earth and subdue it. Rule over the fish in the sea and the birds in the sky and over every living creature that moves on the ground."

[29] Then God said, "I give you every seed-bearing plant on the face of the whole earth and every tree that has fruit with seed in it. They will be yours for food. [30] And to all the beasts of the earth and all the birds in the sky and all the creatures that move along the ground—everything that has the breath of life in it—I give every green plant for food." And it was so.

[31] God saw all that he had made, and it was very good. And there was evening, and there was morning—the sixth day.

2 Thus the heavens and the earth were completed in all their vast array.

[2] By the seventh day God had finished the work he had been doing; so on the seventh day he rested from all his work. [3] Then God blessed the seventh day and made it holy, because on it he rested from all the work of creating that he had done.

ADAM AND EVE

[4] This is the account of the heavens and the earth when they were created, when the LORD God made the earth and the heavens.

[5] Now no shrub had yet appeared on the earth[a] and no plant had yet sprung up, for the LORD God had not sent rain on the earth and there was no one to work the ground, [6] but streams[b] came up from the earth and watered the whole surface of the ground. [7] Then the LORD God formed a man[c]

[a] 5 Or *land*; also in verse 6   [b] 6 Or *mist*   [c] 7 The Hebrew for *man (adam)* sounds like and may be related to the Hebrew for *ground (adamah)*; it is also the name *Adam* (see verse 20).

What does the creation story teach us about our responsibility to the environment?

GENESIS 2

After God had created everything else, he created human beings. God first created Adam and "put him in the Garden of Eden to work it and take care of it" (Genesis 2:15). God did not intend for human beings to simply sit back and bask in all the beauty of the world that God had given them. Instead, they were supposed to be caretakers or stewards of creation.

After Adam and Eve sinned, there were consequences for them and for all of creation. One effect of sin was that thorns and weeds replaced many of the perfect plants that God had placed in his world. Another result of sin was that many people stopped caring about creation.

Pollution is a serious problem. Christians should be concerned about protecting the environment and using natural resources wisely. It is true that God gave plants, animals, minerals, land, and water for people to use, but not for them to waste or destroy. Christians should care for the environment, not just for the sake of future generations, but as part of their obedient service to God. As Psalm 24:1 says, "The earth is the LORD's, and everything in it, the world, and all who live in it."

from the dust of the ground and breathed into his nostrils the breath of life, and the man became a living being.

[8]Now the LORD God had planted a garden in the east, in Eden; and there he put the man he had formed. [9]The LORD God made all kinds of trees grow out of the ground—trees that were pleasing to the eye and good for food. In the middle of the garden were the tree of life and the tree of the knowledge of good and evil.

[10]A river watering the garden flowed from Eden; from there it was separated into four headwaters. [11]The name of the first is the Pishon; it winds through the entire land of Havilah, where there is gold. [12](The gold of that land is good; aromatic resin[a] and onyx are also there.) [13]The name of the second river is the Gihon; it winds through the entire land of Cush.[b] [14]The name of the third river is the Tigris; it runs along the east side of Ashur. And the fourth river is the Euphrates.

[15]The LORD God took the man and put him in the Garden of Eden to work it and take care of it. [16]And the LORD God commanded the man, "You are free to eat from any tree in the garden; [17]but you must not eat from the tree of the knowledge of good and evil, for when you eat from it you will certainly die."

[18]The LORD God said, "It is not good for the man to be alone. I will make a helper suitable for him."

[19]Now the LORD God had formed out of the ground all the wild animals and all the birds in the sky. He brought them to the man to see what he would name them; and whatever the man called each living creature, that was its name. [20]So the man gave names to all the livestock, the birds in the sky and all the wild animals.

But for Adam[c] no suitable helper was found. [21]So the LORD God caused the man to fall into a deep sleep; and while he was sleeping, he took one of the man's ribs[d] and then closed up the place with flesh. [22]Then the LORD God made a woman from the rib[e] he had taken out of the man, and he brought her to the man.

[23]The man said,

"This is now bone of my bones
    and flesh of my flesh;
she shall be called 'woman,'
    for she was taken out of man."

[24]That is why a man leaves his father and mother and is united to his wife, and they become one flesh.

[25]Adam and his wife were both naked, and they felt no shame.

THE FALL

3 Now the serpent was more crafty than any of the wild animals the LORD God had made. He said to the woman, "Did God really say, 'You must not eat from any tree in the garden'?"

---

[a] 12 Or good; pearls   [b] 13 Possibly southeast Mesopotamia   [c] 20 Or the man   [d] 21 Or took part of the man's side   [e] 22 Or part

---

Where was Eden? (2:8, 10–14)
Eden was probably in what is now the country of Iraq. The location of the rivers tells us that it could be an area that also extends through Egypt and Ethiopia.

What was the tree of life? (2:9)
This tree was in the middle of the Garden of Eden. Its fruit was special because those who ate it would live forever. God gave Adam and Eve access to the tree of life because he intended for them to have eternal life.

Is it bad to know about good and evil? (2:17)
When God warned them not to eat from the tree of the knowledge of good and evil, Adam and Eve already knew right from wrong. But *knowing evil* means experiencing it. God was testing their obedience. When they *experienced* evil, they brought sin and death into the world.

Why did Adam need a helper? (2:18, 20)
All of God's other creatures had been created in pairs, but Adam was alone. Eve would provide friendship and help for Adam, and together they would carry on the human race.

What does it mean to become one flesh? (2:24)
God sees two people who marry each other as one unit. Marriage is a serious, lifetime commitment, an intimate relationship filled with love and friendship.

Who was the serpent? (3:1)
Satan, or the devil, took the form of a snake to tempt Adam and Eve.

How did the serpent convince them to eat from the tree of the knowledge of good and evil? (3:4)
The serpent told them that their eyes would be opened and they would become like God. He said they would know good from evil. In fact, their eyes were opened, but the outcome was different from what the serpent promised.

If Eve was the one who talked to the serpent, isn't she responsible for the fall? (3:6)
It seems from verse six that Adam was with Eve. If he wasn't there, then he made the decision to disobey without the pressure from the serpent. He is just as guilty as she is.

Did God actually walk in the garden? (3:8)
We don't know, but this is probably written in a way for humans to understand. God is a spirit and doesn't have a body like humans. God really was present, however, and God did communicate with Adam and Eve.

What did Adam and Eve say when God confronted them? (3:12–13)
Adam blamed Eve, and Eve blamed the serpent. Neither took responsibility for their actions.

²The woman said to the serpent, "We may eat fruit from the trees in the garden, ³but God did say, 'You must not eat fruit from the tree that is in the middle of the garden, and you must not touch it, or you will die.'"

⁴"You will not certainly die," the serpent said to the woman. ⁵"For God knows that when you eat from it your eyes will be opened, and you will be like God, knowing good and evil."

⁶When the woman saw that the fruit of the tree was good for food and pleasing to the eye, and also desirable for gaining wisdom, she took some and ate it. She also gave some to her husband, who was with her, and he ate it. ⁷Then the eyes of both of them were opened, and they realized they were naked; so they sewed fig leaves together and made coverings for themselves.

⁸Then the man and his wife heard the sound of the LORD God as he was walking in the garden in the cool of the day, and they hid from the LORD God among the trees of the garden. ⁹But the LORD God called to the man, "Where are you?"

¹⁰He answered, "I heard you in the garden, and I was afraid because I was naked; so I hid."

¹¹And he said, "Who told you that you were naked? Have you eaten from the tree that I commanded you not to eat from?"

¹²The man said, "The woman you put here with me—she gave me some fruit from the tree, and I ate it."

¹³Then the LORD God said to the woman, "What is this you have done?"

The woman said, "The serpent deceived me, and I ate."

¹⁴So the LORD God said to the serpent, "Because you have done this,

"Cursed are you above all livestock
    and all wild animals!
You will crawl on your belly
    and you will eat dust
    all the days of your life.
¹⁵ And I will put enmity
    between you and the woman,
    and between your offspring*ᵃ* and hers;

ᵃ 15 Or *seed*

If God knew that Adam and Eve were going to sin, why did he give them the choice to obey or not?   GENESIS 3

God could foresee that Adam and Eve would disobey his commandment about not eating the fruit from the tree of the knowledge of good and evil. And if God had wanted to, he could have created Adam and Eve in such a way that it was impossible for them to sin. However, God wanted Adam and Even to have a free choice about serving God. If they weren't even able to sin, they would have simply been like robots rather than creatures who might gladly choose to love God and obey him. Making humans like robots would have been easy for God, but this would have meant creating man and woman without freedom and creativity.

God wanted his creatures and all of creation to be completely devoted to him and to serve him perfectly. In order for that to happen, Adam and Eve had to have the ability to choose, but unfortunately, they made the wrong decision.

he will crush^a your head,
 and you will strike his heel."

¹⁶To the woman he said,

"I will make your pains in childbearing very severe;
 with painful labor you will give birth to children.
Your desire will be for your husband,
 and he will rule over you."

¹⁷To Adam he said, "Because you listened to your wife and ate fruit from the tree about which I commanded you, 'You must not eat from it,'

"Cursed is the ground because of you;
 through painful toil you will eat food from it
 all the days of your life.
¹⁸It will produce thorns and thistles for you,
 and you will eat the plants of the field.
¹⁹By the sweat of your brow
 you will eat your food
until you return to the ground,
 since from it you were taken;
for dust you are
 and to dust you will return."

²⁰Adam^b named his wife Eve,^{c} because she would become the mother of all the living.
²¹The Lᴏʀᴅ God made garments of skin for Adam and his wife and clothed them. ²²And the Lᴏʀᴅ God said, "The man has now become like one of us, knowing good and evil. He must not be allowed to reach out his hand and take also from the tree of life and eat, and live forever." ²³So the Lᴏʀᴅ God banished him from the Garden of Eden to work the ground from which he had been taken. ²⁴After he drove the man out, he placed on the east side^d of the Garden of Eden cherubim and a flaming sword flashing back and forth to guard the way to the tree of life.

CAIN AND ABEL

4 Adam^b made love to his wife Eve, and she became pregnant and gave birth to Cain.^{e} She said, "With the help of the Lᴏʀᴅ I have brought forth^f a man." ²Later she gave birth to his brother Abel.

Now Abel kept flocks, and Cain worked the soil. ³In the course of time Cain brought some of the fruits of the soil as an offering to the Lᴏʀᴅ. ⁴And Abel also brought an offering—fat portions from some of the firstborn of his flock. The Lᴏʀᴅ looked with favor on Abel and his offering, ⁵but on Cain and his offering he did not look with favor. So Cain was very angry, and his face was downcast.

⁶Then the Lᴏʀᴅ said to Cain, "Why are you angry? Why is your face downcast? ⁷If you do what is right, will you not be accepted? But if you do not do what is right, sin is crouching at your door; it desires to have you, but you must rule over it."

What was the meaning of God's curse on the serpent? (3:14–15)
God cursed the serpent to crawl on its belly and fight with humans. The promise that the offspring of the woman would crush the serpent's head hints at salvation through Jesus' death on the cross. (See Romans 16:20.)

What did God's words to Adam mean? (3:17–19)
God told Adam that because of sin, work to get food would become difficult and painful. And God said that when Adam died, he would go back to the dust from which he was created.

What are cherubim? (3:24)
Cherubim are winged angels who exist to glorify God. Here they are guarding the entrance to the Garden of Eden so Adam and Eve cannot return. Now the tree of life is only available to humans through Christ's redemption.

Why was Abel's offering better than Cain's offering? (4:3–4)
Both a plant offering and an animal offering were acceptable, but Cain's offering was not made with a pure heart. Abel pleased God because he offered his best animals.

---

^{a} 15 Or strike ^{b} 20,1 Or The man ^{c} 20 Eve probably means living.
^{d} 24 Or placed in front ^{e} 1 Cain sounds like the Hebrew for brought forth or acquired. ^{f} 1 Or have acquired

⁸Now Cain said to his brother Abel, "Let's go out to the field."^a While they were in the field, Cain attacked his brother Abel and killed him.

⁹Then the Lord said to Cain, "Where is your brother Abel?"

"I don't know," he replied. "Am I my brother's keeper?"

¹⁰The Lord said, "What have you done? Listen! Your brother's blood cries out to me from the ground. ¹¹Now you are under a curse and driven from the ground, which opened its mouth to receive your brother's blood from your hand. ¹²When you work the ground, it will no longer yield its crops for you. You will be a restless wanderer on the earth."

¹³Cain said to the Lord, "My punishment is more than I can bear. ¹⁴Today you are driving me from the land, and I will be hidden from your presence; I will be a restless wanderer on the earth, and whoever finds me will kill me."

¹⁵But the Lord said to him, "Not so^b; anyone who kills Cain will suffer vengeance seven times over." Then the Lord put a mark on Cain so that no one who found him would kill him. ¹⁶So Cain went out from the Lord's presence and lived in the land of Nod,^c east of Eden.

¹⁷Cain made love to his wife, and she became pregnant and gave birth to Enoch. Cain was then building a city, and he named it after his son Enoch. ¹⁸To Enoch was born Irad, and Irad was the father of Mehujael, and Mehujael was the father of Methushael, and Methushael was the father of Lamech.

¹⁹Lamech married two women, one named Adah and the other Zillah. ²⁰Adah gave birth to Jabal; he was the father of those who live in tents and raise livestock. ²¹His brother's name was Jubal; he was the father of all who play stringed instruments and pipes. ²²Zillah also had a son, Tubal-Cain, who forged all kinds of tools out of^d bronze and iron. Tubal-Cain's sister was Naamah.

²³Lamech said to his wives,

"Adah and Zillah, listen to me;
    wives of Lamech, hear my words.
I have killed a man for wounding me,
    a young man for injuring me.
²⁴If Cain is avenged seven times,
    then Lamech seventy-seven times."

²⁵Adam made love to his wife again, and she gave birth to a son and named him Seth,^e saying, "God has granted me another child in place of Abel, since Cain killed him." ²⁶Seth also had a son, and he named him Enosh.

At that time people began to call on^f the name of the Lord.

FROM ADAM TO NOAH

5 This is the written account of Adam's family line.

When God created mankind, he made them in the likeness of God. ²He created them male and female and blessed

---

How did God curse Cain? (4:11–12)
Cain had made his living as a farmer, but now the ground was symbolically soaked with his brother's blood and would no longer produce any crops. Instead of staying with his family, Cain was forced to wander the earth.

What kind of mark did God place on Cain? (4:15)
The Bible doesn't say. We do know that it was a warning sign to protect him from anyone wanting to kill him.

Was it okay to marry two women? (4:19)
Having more than one wife was common in ancient times, but it goes against God's original plan for marriage to be between one man and one woman. Having more than one wife sometimes caused problems for husbands in Old Testament times.

---

^a 8 Samaritan Pentateuch, Septuagint, Vulgate and Syriac; Masoretic Text does not have *"Let's go out to the field."*   ^b 15 Septuagint, Vulgate and Syriac; Hebrew *Very well*   ^c 16 *Nod* means *wandering* (see verses 12 and 14).   ^d 22 Or *who instructed all who work in*   ^e 25 *Seth* probably means *granted.*   ^f 26 Or *to proclaim*

them. And he named them "Mankind"*a* when they were created.

³When Adam had lived 130 years, he had a son in his own likeness, in his own image; and he named him Seth. ⁴After Seth was born, Adam lived 800 years and had other sons and daughters. ⁵Altogether, Adam lived a total of 930 years, and then he died.

⁶When Seth had lived 105 years, he became the father*b* of Enosh. ⁷After he became the father of Enosh, Seth lived 807 years and had other sons and daughters. ⁸Altogether, Seth lived a total of 912 years, and then he died.

⁹When Enosh had lived 90 years, he became the father of Kenan. ¹⁰After he became the father of Kenan, Enosh lived 815 years and had other sons and daughters. ¹¹Altogether, Enosh lived a total of 905 years, and then he died.

¹²When Kenan had lived 70 years, he became the father of Mahalalel. ¹³After he became the father of Mahalalel, Kenan lived 840 years and had other sons and daughters. ¹⁴Altogether, Kenan lived a total of 910 years, and then he died.

¹⁵When Mahalalel had lived 65 years, he became the father of Jared. ¹⁶After he became the father of Jared, Mahalalel lived 830 years and had other sons and daughters. ¹⁷Altogether, Mahalalel lived a total of 895 years, and then he died.

¹⁸When Jared had lived 162 years, he became the father of Enoch. ¹⁹After he became the father of Enoch, Jared lived 800 years and had other sons and daughters. ²⁰Altogether, Jared lived a total of 962 years, and then he died.

²¹When Enoch had lived 65 years, he became the father of Methuselah. ²²After he became the father of Methuselah, Enoch walked faithfully with God 300 years and had other sons and daughters. ²³Altogether, Enoch lived a total of 365 years. ²⁴Enoch walked faithfully with God; then he was no more, because God took him away.

²⁵When Methuselah had lived 187 years, he became the father of Lamech. ²⁶After he became the father of Lamech, Methuselah lived 782 years and had other sons and daughters. ²⁷Altogether, Methuselah lived a total of 969 years, and then he died.

²⁸When Lamech had lived 182 years, he had a son. ²⁹He named him Noah*c* and said, "He will comfort us in the labor and painful toil of our hands caused by the ground the LORD has cursed." ³⁰After Noah was born, Lamech lived 595 years and had other sons and daughters. ³¹Altogether, Lamech lived a total of 777 years, and then he died.

³²After Noah was 500 years old, he became the father of Shem, Ham and Japheth.

WICKEDNESS IN THE WORLD

6 When human beings began to increase in number on the earth and daughters were born to them, ²the sons of God saw that the daughters of humans were beautiful, and they married any of them they chose. ³Then the LORD said,

How could people live such long lives? (5:5–32)
God's original plan was that people would live forever. When Adam and Eve sinned, death was a result, and the length of human life gradually shortened.

Did Enoch die? (5:24)
No. Enoch had a very close, intimate relationship with God, and the Bible tells us that his life on earth ended in a very unusual way: God took him without Enoch experiencing death.

Why did Noah's father think that he would comfort God's people? (5:29)
God may have inspired him to say this because Noah would eventually save God's people from the flood by building an ark.

---

a 2 Hebrew *adam*   *b* 6 *Father* may mean *ancestor*; also in verses 7-26.
c 29 *Noah* sounds like the Hebrew for *comfort.*

"My Spirit will not contend with[a] humans forever, for they are mortal[b]; their days will be a hundred and twenty years."

⁴The Nephilim were on the earth in those days—and also afterward—when the sons of God went to the daughters of humans and had children by them. They were the heroes of old, men of renown.

⁵The Lord saw how great the wickedness of the human race had become on the earth, and that every inclination of the thoughts of the human heart was only evil all the time. ⁶The Lord regretted that he had made human beings on the earth, and his heart was deeply troubled. ⁷So the Lord said, "I will wipe from the face of the earth the human race I have created—and with them the animals, the birds and the creatures that move along the ground—for I regret that I have made them." ⁸But Noah found favor in the eyes of the Lord.

NOAH AND THE FLOOD

⁹This is the account of Noah and his family.

Noah was a righteous man, blameless among the people of his time, and he walked faithfully with God. ¹⁰Noah had three sons: Shem, Ham and Japheth.

¹¹Now the earth was corrupt in God's sight and was full of violence. ¹²God saw how corrupt the earth had become, for all the people on earth had corrupted their ways. ¹³So God said to Noah, "I am going to put an end to all people, for the earth is filled with violence because of them. I am surely going to destroy both them and the earth. ¹⁴So make yourself an ark of cypress[c] wood; make rooms in it and coat it with pitch inside and out. ¹⁵This is how you are to build it: The ark is to be three hundred cubits long, fifty cubits wide and thirty cubits high.[d] ¹⁶Make a roof for it, leaving below the roof an opening one cubit[e] high all around.[f] Put a door in the side of the ark and make lower, middle and upper decks. ¹⁷I am going to bring floodwaters on the earth to destroy all life under the heavens, every creature that has the breath of life in it. Everything on earth will perish. ¹⁸But I will establish my covenant with you, and you will enter the ark—you and your sons and your wife and your sons' wives with you. ¹⁹You are to bring into the ark two of all living creatures, male and female, to keep them alive with you. ²⁰Two of every kind of bird, of every kind of animal and of every kind of creature that moves along the ground will come to you to be kept alive. ²¹You are to take every kind of food that is to be eaten and store it away as food for you and for them."

²²Noah did everything just as God commanded him.

7 The Lord then said to Noah, "Go into the ark, you and your whole family, because I have found you righteous in this generation. ²Take with you seven pairs of every kind of clean animal, a male and its mate, and one pair of every kind of unclean animal, a male and its mate, ³and also seven

ᵃ 3 Or *My spirit will not remain in*   ᵇ 3 Or *corrupt*   ᶜ 14 The meaning of the Hebrew for this word is uncertain.   ᵈ 15 That is, about 450 feet long, 75 feet wide and 45 feet high or about 135 meters long, 23 meters wide and 14 meters high   ᵉ 16 That is, about 18 inches or about 45 centimeters   ᶠ 16 The meaning of the Hebrew for this clause is uncertain.

Who were the Nephilim? (6:4)
They were people who were very tall, strong, and powerful. They were known as heroes because of their power as rulers.

Why did God destroy other creatures beside humans with the flood? (6:7)
Human sin had contaminated everything God had made. So the animal world also shared in God's judgment.

What is an ark? (6:14)
This ark is the ship God told Noah to build. It was about 450 feet long, 75 feet wide, and 45 feet high.

Noah's Ark

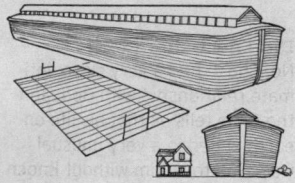

What makes an animal clean or unclean? (7:2)
God declared that some animals were ceremonially unclean or impure. God gave his people laws about what to eat. The laws don't make sense to us today, but they would have made sense then. (See Leviticus 5:2 and Leviticus 11.)

Why did they need to bring more clean animals on the ark? (7:2-3)
In addition to repopulating the earth after the flood, the clean animals were also used as food while on the ark and afterwards as sacrifices to God.

pairs of every kind of bird, male and female, to keep their various kinds alive throughout the earth. [4]Seven days from now I will send rain on the earth for forty days and forty nights, and I will wipe from the face of the earth every living creature I have made."

[5]And Noah did all that the LORD commanded him.

[6]Noah was six hundred years old when the floodwaters came on the earth. [7]And Noah and his sons and his wife and his sons' wives entered the ark to escape the waters of the flood. [8]Pairs of clean and unclean animals, of birds and of all creatures that move along the ground, [9]male and female, came to Noah and entered the ark, as God had commanded Noah. [10]And after the seven days the floodwaters came on the earth.

[11]In the six hundredth year of Noah's life, on the seventeenth day of the second month—on that day all the springs of the great deep burst forth, and the floodgates of the heavens were opened. [12]And rain fell on the earth forty days and forty nights.

[13]On that very day Noah and his sons, Shem, Ham and Japheth, together with his wife and the wives of his three sons, entered the ark. [14]They had with them every wild animal according to its kind, all livestock according to their kinds, every creature that moves along the ground according to its kind and every bird according to its kind, everything with wings. [15]Pairs of all creatures that have the breath of life in them came to Noah and entered the ark. [16]The animals going in were male and female of every living thing, as God had commanded Noah. Then the LORD shut him in.

[17]For forty days the flood kept coming on the earth, and as the waters increased they lifted the ark high above the earth. [18]The waters rose and increased greatly on the earth, and the ark floated on the surface of the water. [19]They rose greatly on the earth, and all the high mountains under the entire heavens were covered. [20]The waters rose and covered the mountains to a depth of more than fifteen cubits.[a,b] [21]Every

[a] 20 That is, about 23 feet or about 6.8 meters   [b] 20 Or *rose more than fifteen cubits, and the mountains were covered*

How did Noah get all those animals on board the ark? (7:9)

The Bible tells us the animals came to Noah. We don't know for sure, but maybe God gave the animals instincts to know that a disaster was coming.

Did the flood cover the entire earth or was it more local?

GENESIS 7

There are two opinions about the extent of the flood.

The language in chapters 6–9 suggests that the flood was universal, covering the whole globe. For example, in Genesis 6:17 God said, "I am going to bring floodwaters on the earth to destroy all life under the heavens, every creature that has the breath of life in it. Everything on earth will perish." Those who believe that the flood was universal also believe that it changed the geography of the earth, pushing up mountains and carving out valleys. Some think that fossils around the earth confirm the fact that the flood was worldwide.

Others think that the flood was local, covering only the part of the earth where people lived at that time. A limited flood would have been enough to accomplish God's purpose of destroying all the wicked people, while saving Noah and his family. The language about destroying the whole earth and all life on it could refer to the part of the world where Noah lived, which would have been his perception of what the whole world consisted of.

In either case, the flood was a historical event that God used to punish the wicked and save those who believed in him.

Were fish and other sea animals destroyed with the flood? (7:23)
The Bible says only animals that lived on land and birds were destroyed.

How does the story change at this point? (8:1)
Until now, the flood story has been about God's judgment. Now the story becomes one of redemption. When the Bible says that God *remembered* Noah, it doesn't mean that God had forgotten him and his family. Instead, it means that he honored his promise to Noah.

Where are the mountains of Ararat? (8:4)
This mountain range was north of Mesopotamia and east of modern Turkey.

Why did Noah send out a dove? (8:8–12)
The raven he sent out first didn't give him a clear answer. The dove ate only leaves, so it could better tell Noah that land and vegetation had reappeared.

Why is an olive leaf special? (8:11)
Olive trees grow at lower elevation, and the fresh leaf told Noah that the water had receded enough for them to grow again. This story is the source for the modern symbol for peace—a dove with an olive branch.

What is a burnt offering? (8:20)
Animals and birds were cooked as a sacrifice to thank God for taking care of them. Sacrifices were an important part of worship during Old Testament times.

living thing that moved on land perished—birds, livestock, wild animals, all the creatures that swarm over the earth, and all mankind. ²²Everything on dry land that had the breath of life in its nostrils died. ²³Every living thing on the face of the earth was wiped out; people and animals and the creatures that move along the ground and the birds were wiped from the earth. Only Noah was left, and those with him in the ark.

²⁴The waters flooded the earth for a hundred and fifty days.

8 But God remembered Noah and all the wild animals and the livestock that were with him in the ark, and he sent a wind over the earth, and the waters receded. ²Now the springs of the deep and the floodgates of the heavens had been closed, and the rain had stopped falling from the sky. ³The water receded steadily from the earth. At the end of the hundred and fifty days the water had gone down, ⁴and on the seventeenth day of the seventh month the ark came to rest on the mountains of Ararat. ⁵The waters continued to recede until the tenth month, and on the first day of the tenth month the tops of the mountains became visible.

⁶After forty days Noah opened a window he had made in the ark ⁷and sent out a raven, and it kept flying back and forth until the water had dried up from the earth. ⁸Then he sent out a dove to see if the water had receded from the surface of the ground. ⁹But the dove could find nowhere to perch because there was water over all the surface of the earth; so it returned to Noah in the ark. He reached out his hand and took the dove and brought it back to himself in the ark. ¹⁰He waited seven more days and again sent out the dove from the ark. ¹¹When the dove returned to him in the evening, there in its beak was a freshly plucked olive leaf! Then Noah knew that the water had receded from the earth. ¹²He waited seven more days and sent the dove out again, but this time it did not return to him.

¹³By the first day of the first month of Noah's six hundred and first year, the water had dried up from the earth. Noah then removed the covering from the ark and saw that the surface of the ground was dry. ¹⁴By the twenty-seventh day of the second month the earth was completely dry.

¹⁵Then God said to Noah, ¹⁶"Come out of the ark, you and your wife and your sons and their wives. ¹⁷Bring out every kind of living creature that is with you—the birds, the animals, and all the creatures that move along the ground—so they can multiply on the earth and be fruitful and increase in number on it."

¹⁸So Noah came out, together with his sons and his wife and his sons' wives. ¹⁹All the animals and all the creatures that move along the ground and all the birds—everything that moves on land—came out of the ark, one kind after another.

²⁰Then Noah built an altar to the LORD and, taking some of all the clean animals and clean birds, he sacrificed burnt offerings on it. ²¹The LORD smelled the pleasing aroma and said in his heart: "Never again will I curse the ground because of humans, even though*ᵃ* every inclination of the human

---

ᵃ 21 Or *humans, for*

heart is evil from childhood. And never again will I destroy all living creatures, as I have done.

22 "As long as the earth endures,
   seedtime and harvest,
   cold and heat,
   summer and winter,
   day and night
   will never cease."

GOD'S COVENANT WITH NOAH

9 Then God blessed Noah and his sons, saying to them, "Be fruitful and increase in number and fill the earth. 2 The fear and dread of you will fall on all the beasts of the earth, and on all the birds in the sky, on every creature that moves along the ground, and on all the fish in the sea; they are given into your hands. 3 Everything that lives and moves about will be food for you. Just as I gave you the green plants, I now give you everything.

4 "But you must not eat meat that has its lifeblood still in it. 5 And for your lifeblood I will surely demand an accounting. I will demand an accounting from every animal. And from each human being, too, I will demand an accounting for the life of another human being.

6 "Whoever sheds human blood,
   by humans shall their blood be shed;
   for in the image of God
   has God made mankind.

7 As for you, be fruitful and increase in number; multiply on the earth and increase upon it."

8 Then God said to Noah and to his sons with him: 9 "I now establish my covenant with you and with your descendants after you 10 and with every living creature that was with you—the birds, the livestock and all the wild animals, all those that came out of the ark with you—every living creature on earth. 11 I establish my covenant with you: Never again will all life be destroyed by the waters of a flood; never again will there be a flood to destroy the earth."

12 And God said, "This is the sign of the covenant I am making between me and you and every living creature with you, a covenant for all generations to come: 13 I have set my rainbow in the clouds, and it will be the sign of the covenant between me and the earth. 14 Whenever I bring clouds over the earth and the rainbow appears in the clouds, 15 I will remember my covenant between me and you and all living creatures of every kind. Never again will the waters become a flood to destroy all life. 16 Whenever the rainbow appears in the clouds, I will see it and remember the everlasting covenant between God and all living creatures of every kind on the earth."

17 So God said to Noah, "This is the sign of the covenant I have established between me and all life on the earth."

THE SONS OF NOAH

18 The sons of Noah who came out of the ark were Shem, Ham and Japheth. (Ham was the father of Canaan.) 19 These

---

Why did God promise to never again destroy all living things? (8:21–22)
God was pleased with Noah's sacrifice, but he knew that humans would continue to sin no matter what. He was showing forgiveness and grace for life on earth. He promised that the normal cycles of nature would continue until the end of time.

What instructions did God give to Noah and his family? (9:1, 7)
God renewed his original call to be fruitful and multiply and take care of the earth. (See Genesis 1:28.)

Why would animals fear humans? (9:2–3)
Sin brought violence into the world. God reaffirmed that humankind would rule over all creation, including the animal world. God also gave Noah permission to eat animal meat.

What was wrong with bloody meat? (9:4)
The blood of the animal represented its life. Since life is a gift from God, it must be honored. To honor that life, people were required to drain the blood from the meat they were eating.

Why is God's judgment on a murderer so severe? (9:5–6)
God created human beings in his own image, so human life is sacred.

Why did God give his people the sign of the rainbow? (9:12–16)
God knows that people tend to forget things, even important things like his faithfulness. God said the rainbow reminds people that God will keep his promise to never again destroy the world with a flood.

were the three sons of Noah, and from them came the people who were scattered over the whole earth.

²⁰Noah, a man of the soil, proceeded*ᵃ* to plant a vineyard. ²¹When he drank some of its wine, he became drunk and lay uncovered inside his tent. ²²Ham, the father of Canaan, saw his father naked and told his two brothers outside. ²³But Shem and Japheth took a garment and laid it across their shoulders; then they walked in backward and covered their father's naked body. Their faces were turned the other way so that they would not see their father naked.

²⁴When Noah awoke from his wine and found out what his youngest son had done to him, ²⁵he said,

"Cursed be Canaan!
    The lowest of slaves
    will he be to his brothers."

²⁶He also said,

"Praise be to the LORD, the God of Shem!
    May Canaan be the slave of Shem.
²⁷May God extend Japheth's*ᵇ* territory;
    may Japheth live in the tents of Shem,
    and may Canaan be the slave of Japheth."

²⁸After the flood Noah lived 350 years. ²⁹Noah lived a total of 950 years, and then he died.

THE TABLE OF NATIONS

10 This is the account of Shem, Ham and Japheth, Noah's sons, who themselves had sons after the flood.

THE JAPHETHITES

²The sons*ᶜ* of Japheth:
    Gomer, Magog, Madai, Javan, Tubal, Meshek and Tiras.
³The sons of Gomer:
    Ashkenaz, Riphath and Togarmah.
⁴The sons of Javan:
    Elishah, Tarshish, the Kittites and the Rodanites.*ᵈ*
    ⁵(From these the maritime peoples spread out into their territories by their clans within their nations, each with its own language.)

THE HAMITES

⁶The sons of Ham:
    Cush, Egypt, Put and Canaan.
⁷The sons of Cush:
    Seba, Havilah, Sabtah, Raamah and Sabteka.
The sons of Raamah:
    Sheba and Dedan.

⁸Cush was the father*ᵉ* of Nimrod, who became a mighty

What was wrong with what Ham did to Noah? (9:22)
Ham did not show respect for his father, Noah. Instead of covering his father's nakedness as his brothers did, Ham told others about his father's drunkenness and nakedness.

Why did Noah curse his grandson Canaan instead of Ham? (9:25)
It was common for children to be punished for their fathers' sins. Canaan's descendants may have been punished because Noah already saw even worse sins committed by Ham's children.

Why are these lists of names included in the Bible? (10:1–32)
Genealogies were important in ancient times as a way to record people's history and show how families were connected to the community. People were identified by their relatives. Many family trees in the Bible point forward and backward—forward to Jesus and backward to the people from whom he descended.

ᵃ *20 Or soil, was the first*   ᵇ *27 Japheth sounds like the Hebrew for extend.*
ᶜ *2 Sons may mean descendants or successors or nations; also in verses 3, 4, 6, 7, 20-23, 29 and 31.*   ᵈ *4 Some manuscripts of the Masoretic Text and Samaritan Pentateuch (see also Septuagint and 1 Chron. 1:7); most manuscripts of the Masoretic Text Dodanites*   ᵉ *8 Father may mean ancestor or predecessor or founder; also in verses 13, 15, 24 and 26.*

warrior on the earth. ⁹He was a mighty hunter before the
LORD; that is why it is said, "Like Nimrod, a mighty hunter
before the LORD." ¹⁰The first centers of his kingdom were
Babylon, Uruk, Akkad and Kalneh, in*ᵃ* Shinar.*ᵇ* ¹¹From that
land he went to Assyria, where he built Nineveh, Rehoboth
Ir,*ᶜ* Calah ¹²and Resen, which is between Nineveh and Calah—which is the great city.

¹³Egypt was the father of
the Ludites, Anamites, Lehabites, Naphtuhites,
¹⁴Pathrusites, Kasluhites (from whom the Philistines
came) and Caphtorites.
¹⁵Canaan was the father of
Sidon his firstborn,*ᵈ* and of the Hittites, ¹⁶Jebusites,
Amorites, Girgashites, ¹⁷Hivites, Arkites, Sinites,
¹⁸Arvadites, Zemarites and Hamathites.

Later the Canaanite clans scattered ¹⁹and the borders of
Canaan reached from Sidon toward Gerar as far as Gaza,

ᵃ 10 Or Uruk and Akkad—all of them in   *ᵇ 10 That is, Babylonia*
ᶜ 11 Or Nineveh with its city squares   *ᵈ 15 Or of the Sidonians, the foremost*

NATIONS DESCENDED FROM NOAH'S SONS (10:1)

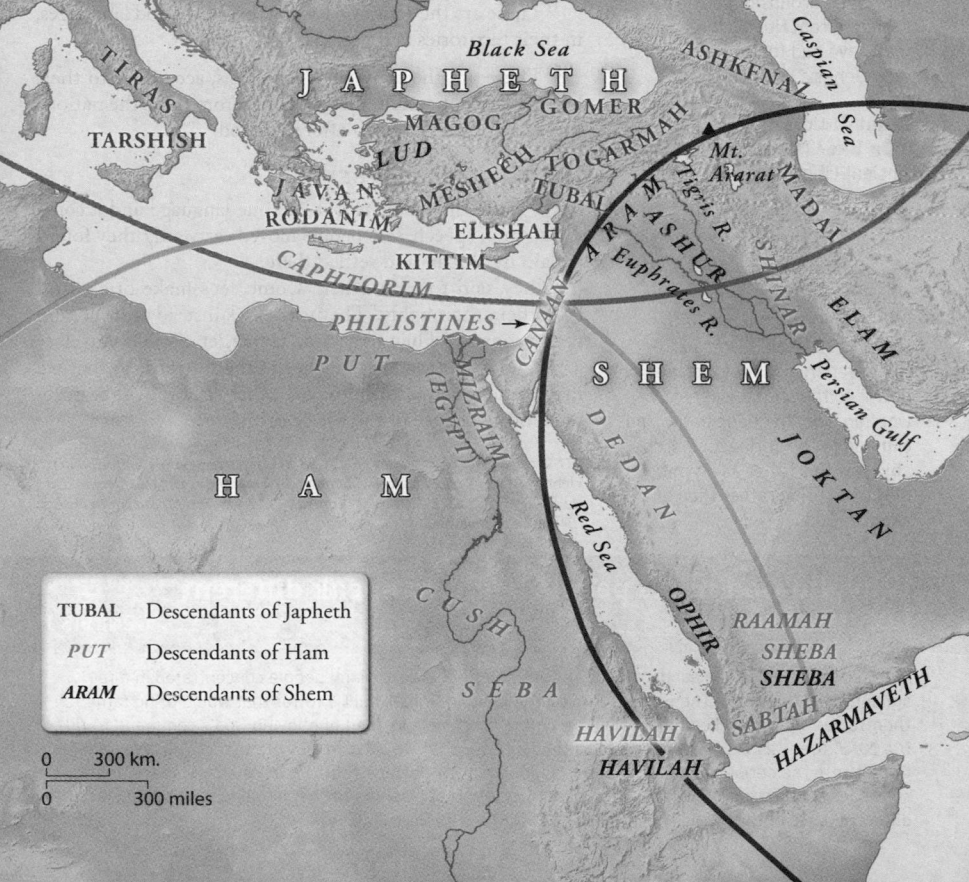

TUBAL	Descendants of Japheth
PUT	Descendants of Ham
ARAM	Descendants of Shem

0   300 km.

0   300 miles

and then toward Sodom, Gomorrah, Admah and Zeboyim, as far as Lasha.

²⁰These are the sons of Ham by their clans and languages, in their territories and nations.

THE SEMITES

²¹Sons were also born to Shem, whose older brother was[a] Japheth; Shem was the ancestor of all the sons of Eber.

²²The sons of Shem:
Elam, Ashur, Arphaxad, Lud and Aram.

²³The sons of Aram:
Uz, Hul, Gether and Meshek.[b]

²⁴Arphaxad was the father of[c] Shelah,
and Shelah the father of Eber.

²⁵Two sons were born to Eber:
One was named Peleg,[d] because in his time the earth was divided; his brother was named Joktan.

²⁶Joktan was the father of
Almodad, Sheleph, Hazarmaveth, Jerah, ²⁷Hadoram, Uzal, Diklah, ²⁸Obal, Abimael, Sheba, ²⁹Ophir, Havilah and Jobab. All these were sons of Joktan.

³⁰The region where they lived stretched from Mesha toward Sephar, in the eastern hill country.

³¹These are the sons of Shem by their clans and languages, in their territories and nations.

³²These are the clans of Noah's sons, according to their lines of descent, within their nations. From these the nations spread out over the earth after the flood.

THE TOWER OF BABEL

11 Now the whole world had one language and a common speech. ²As people moved eastward,[e] they found a plain in Shinar[f] and settled there.

³They said to each other, "Come, let's make bricks and bake them thoroughly." They used brick instead of stone, and tar for mortar. ⁴Then they said, "Come, let us build ourselves a city, with a tower that reaches to the heavens, so that we may make a name for ourselves; otherwise we will be scattered over the face of the whole earth."

[a] 21 Or *Shem, the older brother of*   [b] 23 See Septuagint and 1 Chron. 1:17; Hebrew *Mash.*   [c] 24 Hebrew; Septuagint *father of Cainan, and Cainan was the father of*   [d] 25 *Peleg* means *division.*   [e] 2 Or *from the east;* or *in the east*   [f] 2 That is, Babylonia

How was the earth divided? (10:25)
The earth was divided into separate nations, probably when God confused the languages at the tower of Babel (11:8 – 9).

Before the tower of Babel, what was the "one language"? (11:1)
No one knows for sure. Although people could understand each other, the groups of people descended from Noah's three sons may have had their own dialects. (See Genesis 10:5, 20, 31.)

What did the tower of Babel look like? (11:4)
Ancient cities were built around a central temple complex. The typical Mesopotamian temple tower, called a ziggurat, had a square base and sloping, stepped sides that led to a shrine on the top. Ziggurats were meant to serve as staircases from earth to heaven. A god could "come down" to the shrine and receive worship from the people who had climbed to the shrine. God probably saw this tower as a symbol of human pride rather than of glory to God.

Why did God make people begin to speak different languages?

GENESIS 11

As the population on the earth grew after the flood, there were many people concentrated in a fairly small part of the world. The people living on the plain in Shinar built a tower that would bring fame to themselves and would keep them from becoming scattered. Instead of obeying God's command to *fill the earth* (Genesis 1:28), they decided to build a tower that would give glory to their own achievements. God caused the people to speak different languages so that they would be forced to separate themselves into different groups with different languages. This also meant that people would spread out into different parts of the earth, which was part of God's plan for the world.

[5] But the LORD came down to see the city and the tower the people were building. [6] The LORD said, "If as one people speaking the same language they have begun to do this, then nothing they plan to do will be impossible for them. [7] Come, let us go down and confuse their language so they will not understand each other."

[8] So the LORD scattered them from there over all the earth, and they stopped building the city. [9] That is why it was called Babel[a]—because there the LORD confused the language of the whole world. From there the LORD scattered them over the face of the whole earth.

FROM SHEM TO ABRAM

[10] This is the account of Shem's family line.

Two years after the flood, when Shem was 100 years old, he became the father[b] of Arphaxad. [11] And after he became the father of Arphaxad, Shem lived 500 years and had other sons and daughters.

[12] When Arphaxad had lived 35 years, he became the father of Shelah. [13] And after he became the father of Shelah, Arphaxad lived 403 years and had other sons and daughters.[c]

[14] When Shelah had lived 30 years, he became the father of Eber. [15] And after he became the father of Eber, Shelah lived 403 years and had other sons and daughters.

[16] When Eber had lived 34 years, he became the father of Peleg. [17] And after he became the father of Peleg, Eber lived 430 years and had other sons and daughters.

[18] When Peleg had lived 30 years, he became the father of Reu. [19] And after he became the father of Reu, Peleg lived 209 years and had other sons and daughters.

[20] When Reu had lived 32 years, he became the father of Serug. [21] And after he became the father of Serug, Reu lived 207 years and had other sons and daughters.

[22] When Serug had lived 30 years, he became the father of Nahor. [23] And after he became the father of Nahor, Serug lived 200 years and had other sons and daughters.

[24] When Nahor had lived 29 years, he became the father of Terah. [25] And after he became the father of Terah, Nahor lived 119 years and had other sons and daughters.

[26] After Terah had lived 70 years, he became the father of Abram, Nahor and Haran.

ABRAM'S FAMILY

[27] This is the account of Terah's family line.

Terah became the father of Abram, Nahor and Haran. And Haran became the father of Lot. [28] While his father Terah was still alive, Haran died in Ur of the Chaldeans, in the land of his birth. [29] Abram and Nahor both married. The name of

A Ziggurat

The Tower of Babel (11:4)

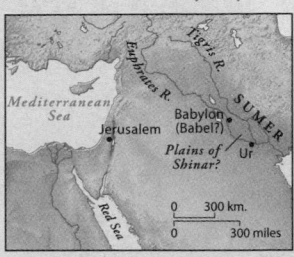

Why did God want to scatter the people? (11:9)
Building the tower was a symbol for the people developing great power for the wrong purpose. God may have been scattering the people for their own good, to stop their destructive behavior.

---

[a] 9 That is, Babylon; *Babel* sounds like the Hebrew for *confused.*
[b] 10 *Father* may mean *ancestor*; also in verses 11-25.   [c] 12,13 Hebrew; Septuagint (see also Luke 3:35, 36 and note at Gen. 10:24) *35 years, he became the father of Cainan.* [13] *And after he became the father of Cainan, Arphaxad lived 430 years and had other sons and daughters, and then he died. When Cainan had lived 130 years, he became the father of Shelah. And after he became the father of Shelah, Cainan lived 330 years and had other sons and daughters*

Abram's wife was Sarai, and the name of Nahor's wife was Milkah; she was the daughter of Haran, the father of both Milkah and Iskah. ³⁰Now Sarai was childless because she was not able to conceive.

³¹Terah took his son Abram, his grandson Lot son of Haran, and his daughter-in-law Sarai, the wife of his son Abram, and together they set out from Ur of the Chaldeans to go to Canaan. But when they came to Harran, they settled there.

³²Terah lived 205 years, and he died in Harran.

THE CALL OF ABRAM

12 The LORD had said to Abram, "Go from your country, your people and your father's household to the land I will show you.

²"I will make you into a great nation,
　　and I will bless you;
　I will make your name great,
　　and you will be a blessing.ᵃ
³I will bless those who bless you,
　　and whoever curses you I will curse;
　and all peoples on earth
　　will be blessed through you."ᵇ

⁴So Abram went, as the LORD had told him; and Lot went with him. Abram was seventy-five years old when he set out from Harran. ⁵He took his wife Sarai, his nephew Lot, all the possessions they had accumulated and the people they had acquired in Harran, and they set out for the land of Canaan, and they arrived there.

⁶Abram traveled through the land as far as the site of the great tree of Moreh at Shechem. At that time the Canaanites were in the land. ⁷The LORD appeared to Abram and said, "To your offspringᶜ I will give this land." So he built an altar there to the LORD, who had appeared to him.

⁸From there he went on toward the hills east of Bethel and pitched his tent, with Bethel on the west and Ai on the east. There he built an altar to the LORD and called on the name of the LORD.

⁹Then Abram set out and continued toward the Negev.

ABRAM IN EGYPT

¹⁰Now there was a famine in the land, and Abram went down to Egypt to live there for a while because the famine was severe. ¹¹As he was about to enter Egypt, he said to his wife Sarai, "I know what a beautiful woman you are. ¹²When the Egyptians see you, they will say, 'This is his wife.' Then they will kill me but will let you live. ¹³Say you are my sister, so that I will be treated well for your sake and my life will be spared because of you."

¹⁴When Abram came to Egypt, the Egyptians saw that Sarai was a very beautiful woman. ¹⁵And when Pharaoh's officials saw her, they praised her to Pharaoh, and she was

What does God's promise to Abram mean? (12:3)
God's promise to Abram was to save humankind through one of his descendants, Jesus. In time, Jesus would offer deliverance to the entire world.

Abram's Journeys (12:4)

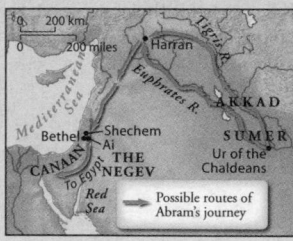

Was it wrong for Abram to lie about his wife? (12:13)
Abram probably thought he had a good reason to justify the lie, but it showed his lack of trust in God's protection.

ᵃ 2 Or *be seen as blessed*　　ᵇ 3 Or *earth / will use your name in blessings* (see 48:20)　　ᶜ 7 Or *seed*

taken into his palace. ¹⁶He treated Abram well for her sake, and Abram acquired sheep and cattle, male and female donkeys, male and female servants, and camels.

¹⁷But the LORD inflicted serious diseases on Pharaoh and his household because of Abram's wife Sarai. ¹⁸So Pharaoh summoned Abram. "What have you done to me?" he said. "Why didn't you tell me she was your wife? ¹⁹Why did you say, 'She is my sister,' so that I took her to be my wife? Now then, here is your wife. Take her and go!" ²⁰Then Pharaoh gave orders about Abram to his men, and they sent him on his way, with his wife and everything he had.

ABRAM AND LOT SEPARATE

13 So Abram went up from Egypt to the Negev, with his wife and everything he had, and Lot went with him. ²Abram had become very wealthy in livestock and in silver and gold.

³From the Negev he went from place to place until he came to Bethel, to the place between Bethel and Ai where his tent had been earlier ⁴and where he had first built an altar. There Abram called on the name of the LORD.

⁵Now Lot, who was moving about with Abram, also had flocks and herds and tents. ⁶But the land could not support them while they stayed together, for their possessions were so great that they were not able to stay together. ⁷And quarreling arose between Abram's herders and Lot's. The Canaanites and Perizzites were also living in the land at that time.

⁸So Abram said to Lot, "Let's not have any quarreling between you and me, or between your herders and mine, for we are close relatives. ⁹Is not the whole land before you? Let's part company. If you go to the left, I'll go to the right; if you go to the right, I'll go to the left."

¹⁰Lot looked around and saw that the whole plain of the Jordan toward Zoar was well watered, like the garden of the LORD, like the land of Egypt. (This was before the LORD destroyed Sodom and Gomorrah.) ¹¹So Lot chose for himself the whole plain of the Jordan and set out toward the east. The two men parted company: ¹²Abram lived in the land of Canaan, while Lot lived among the cities of the plain and pitched his tents near Sodom. ¹³Now the people of Sodom were wicked and were sinning greatly against the LORD.

¹⁴The LORD said to Abram after Lot had parted from him, "Look around from where you are, to the north and south, to the east and west. ¹⁵All the land that you see I will give to you and your offspring*a* forever. ¹⁶I will make your offspring like the dust of the earth, so that if anyone could count the dust, then your offspring could be counted. ¹⁷Go, walk through the length and breadth of the land, for I am giving it to you."

¹⁸So Abram went to live near the great trees of Mamre at Hebron, where he pitched his tents. There he built an altar to the LORD.

a 15 Or seed; also in verse 16

How did Pharaoh figure out that Sarai was Abram's wife? (12:17–18)
Ancient people believed anything bad that happened was because they had displeased the gods. Pharaoh may have realized that the serious diseases that his family was suffering began when he took Sarai into his household.

Why did Abram let Lot choose his land first? (13:9, 14–17)
Abram remembered God's promise that all the land would eventually belong to Abram and his descendants. So Abram placed his confidence in God by giving Lot the first choice.

Why did God compare Abram's offspring to the dust of the earth? (13:16)
This was a poetic way of saying that the number of Abram's descendants would be so large that it would be as hard to count them as it would be to count the grains of sands on the earth.

ABRAM RESCUES LOT

14 At the time when Amraphel was king of Shinar,[a] Arioch king of Ellasar, Kedorlaomer king of Elam and Tidal king of Goyim, [2]these kings went to war against Bera king of Sodom, Birsha king of Gomorrah, Shinab king of Admah, Shemeber king of Zeboyim, and the king of Bela (that is, Zoar). [3]All these latter kings joined forces in the Valley of Siddim (that is, the Dead Sea Valley). [4]For twelve years they had been subject to Kedorlaomer, but in the thirteenth year they rebelled.

[5]In the fourteenth year, Kedorlaomer and the kings allied with him went out and defeated the Rephaites in Ashteroth Karnaim, the Zuzites in Ham, the Emites in Shaveh Kiriathaim [6]and the Horites in the hill country of Seir, as far as El Paran near the desert. [7]Then they turned back and went to En Mishpat (that is, Kadesh), and they conquered the whole territory of the Amalekites, as well as the Amorites who were living in Hazezon Tamar.

[8]Then the king of Sodom, the king of Gomorrah, the king of Admah, the king of Zeboyim and the king of Bela (that is, Zoar) marched out and drew up their battle lines in the Valley of Siddim [9]against Kedorlaomer king of Elam, Tidal king of Goyim, Amraphel king of Shinar and Arioch king of Ellasar—four kings against five. [10]Now the Valley of Siddim was full of tar pits, and when the kings of Sodom and Gomorrah fled, some of the men fell into them and the rest fled to the hills. [11]The four kings seized all the goods of Sodom and Gomorrah and all their food; then they went away. [12]They also carried off Abram's nephew Lot and his possessions, since he was living in Sodom.

[13]A man who had escaped came and reported this to Abram the Hebrew. Now Abram was living near the great trees of Mamre the Amorite, a brother[b] of Eshkol and Aner, all of whom were allied with Abram. [14]When Abram heard that his relative had been taken captive, he called out the 318 trained men born in his household and went in pursuit as far as Dan. [15]During the night Abram divided his men to attack them and he routed them, pursuing them as far as Hobah, north of Damascus. [16]He recovered all the goods and brought back his relative Lot and his possessions, together with the women and the other people.

[17]After Abram returned from defeating Kedorlaomer and the kings allied with him, the king of Sodom came out to meet him in the Valley of Shaveh (that is, the King's Valley).

[18]Then Melchizedek king of Salem brought out bread and wine. He was priest of God Most High, [19]and he blessed Abram, saying,

"Blessed be Abram by God Most High,
    Creator of heaven and earth.
[20]And praise be to God Most High,
    who delivered your enemies into your hand."

Then Abram gave him a tenth of everything.

a 1 That is, Babylonia; also in verse 9   *b 13* Or *a relative;* or *an ally*

What are tar pits? (14:10)
A black, tarry substance like asphalt had been dug out of this area to be used as a construction material. The kings may have fallen into these pits.

Why is Abram called the Hebrew? (14:13)
Abram, the father of the Hebrew people, is the first person in the Bible to be called a Hebrew. The word refers to Semitic people, the descendants of Noah's son, Shem.

Abram Rescues Lot (14:14)

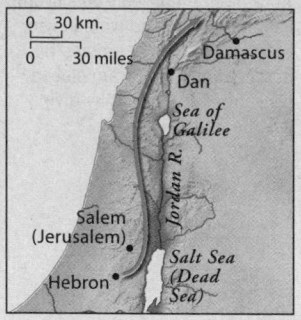

Why did Abram give a tenth of everything to Melchizedek? (14:20)
A tenth, or tithe, was known as the king's share. This is the first time the Bible refers to tithing. Abram showed gratitude to God for his victory by giving a tenth of the goods to God's priest, Melchizedek.

²¹The king of Sodom said to Abram, "Give me the people and keep the goods for yourself."

²²But Abram said to the king of Sodom, "With raised hand I have sworn an oath to the Lᴏʀᴅ, God Most High, Creator of heaven and earth, ²³that I will accept nothing belonging to you, not even a thread or the strap of a sandal, so that you will never be able to say, 'I made Abram rich.' ²⁴I will accept nothing but what my men have eaten and the share that belongs to the men who went with me—to Aner, Eshkol and Mamre. Let them have their share."

THE LORD'S COVENANT WITH ABRAM

15 After this, the word of the Lᴏʀᴅ came to Abram in a vision:

"Do not be afraid, Abram.
   I am your shield,[a]
   your very great reward.[b]"

²But Abram said, "Sovereign Lᴏʀᴅ, what can you give me since I remain childless and the one who will inherit[c] my estate is Eliezer of Damascus?" ³And Abram said, "You have given me no children; so a servant in my household will be my heir."

⁴Then the word of the Lᴏʀᴅ came to him: "This man will not be your heir, but a son who is your own flesh and blood will be your heir." ⁵He took him outside and said, "Look up at the sky and count the stars—if indeed you can count them." Then he said to him, "So shall your offspring[d] be."

⁶Abram believed the Lᴏʀᴅ, and he credited it to him as righteousness.

⁷He also said to him, "I am the Lᴏʀᴅ, who brought you out of Ur of the Chaldeans to give you this land to take possession of it."

⁸But Abram said, "Sovereign Lᴏʀᴅ, how can I know that I will gain possession of it?"

⁹So the Lᴏʀᴅ said to him, "Bring me a heifer, a goat and a ram, each three years old, along with a dove and a young pigeon."

¹⁰Abram brought all these to him, cut them in two and arranged the halves opposite each other; the birds, however, he did not cut in half. ¹¹Then birds of prey came down on the carcasses, but Abram drove them away.

¹²As the sun was setting, Abram fell into a deep sleep, and a thick and dreadful darkness came over him. ¹³Then the Lᴏʀᴅ said to him, "Know for certain that for four hundred years your descendants will be strangers in a country not their own and that they will be enslaved and mistreated there. ¹⁴But I will punish the nation they serve as slaves, and afterward they will come out with great possessions. ¹⁵You, however, will go to your ancestors in peace and be buried at a good old age. ¹⁶In the fourth generation your descendants will come back here, for the sin of the Amorites has not yet reached its full measure."

---

[a] 1 Or *sovereign*   [b] 1 Or *shield; / your reward will be very great*
[c] 2 The meaning of the Hebrew for this phrase is uncertain.   [d] 5 Or *seed*

Why did Abram choose a servant to be his heir? (15:2) In ancient times, a childless man could adopt a servant as his heir. The servant would inherit the possessions and carry on the family name.

Why did God compare Abram's offspring to the stars? (15:5) This is a poetic way of saying that the number of Abram's descendants would be so large that there would be too many to count, like the stars.

Why did Abram cut the animals in half? (15:10) This was an ancient custom used when covenants or promises were made. The people making the agreement would walk between the animal halves to show that they would die, just as the animals had died, if they broke the agreement.

Why did God wait four generations before giving Abram's descendants the land? (15:16) God wanted the Amorites, who lived in the land, to have plenty of time to repent of their sins. God is compassionate and even deals with sinners in a fair way.

Why did a smoking firepot with a blazing torch appear? (15:17)
The smoking firepot with a blazing torch symbolized the presence of God. It was like his signature on the contract he had made with Abram.

Why did Sarai offer her maid to Abram? (16:2)
Since Sarai was unable to have children, she could not fulfill her primary role in the marriage. The custom was to have a maid become a second wife to bear a child, who would become the heir. Sarai was impatient for God to fulfill his promise to Abram.

Why did Sarai blame Abram for Hagar's hatred? (16:5)
Sarai acted rudely because she felt hurt. Since Abram was the head of the family, she blamed him for her situation.

Who was the angel of the LORD? (16:7)
The angel was God's messenger, and some believe it was the human form in which God appeared to his people.

Why was Hagar's son compared to a wild donkey? (16:12)
Ishmael would roam the desert like a wild donkey, far away from other people and hostile toward others.

[17]When the sun had set and darkness had fallen, a smoking firepot with a blazing torch appeared and passed between the pieces. [18]On that day the LORD made a covenant with Abram and said, "To your descendants I give this land, from the Wadi[a] of Egypt to the great river, the Euphrates— [19]the land of the Kenites, Kenizzites, Kadmonites, [20]Hittites, Perizzites, Rephaites, [21]Amorites, Canaanites, Girgashites and Jebusites."

HAGAR AND ISHMAEL

16 Now Sarai, Abram's wife, had borne him no children. But she had an Egyptian slave named Hagar; [2]so she said to Abram, "The LORD has kept me from having children. Go, sleep with my slave; perhaps I can build a family through her."

Abram agreed to what Sarai said. [3]So after Abram had been living in Canaan ten years, Sarai his wife took her Egyptian slave Hagar and gave her to her husband to be his wife. [4]He slept with Hagar, and she conceived.

When she knew she was pregnant, she began to despise her mistress. [5]Then Sarai said to Abram, "You are responsible for the wrong I am suffering. I put my slave in your arms, and now that she knows she is pregnant, she despises me. May the LORD judge between you and me."

[6]"Your slave is in your hands," Abram said. "Do with her whatever you think best." Then Sarai mistreated Hagar; so she fled from her.

[7]The angel of the LORD found Hagar near a spring in the desert; it was the spring that is beside the road to Shur. [8]And he said, "Hagar, slave of Sarai, where have you come from, and where are you going?"

"I'm running away from my mistress Sarai," she answered.

[9]Then the angel of the LORD told her, "Go back to your mistress and submit to her." [10]The angel added, "I will increase your descendants so much that they will be too numerous to count."

[11]The angel of the LORD also said to her:

"You are now pregnant
    and you will give birth to a son.
You shall name him Ishmael,[b]
    for the LORD has heard of your misery.
[12]He will be a wild donkey of a man;
    his hand will be against everyone
    and everyone's hand against him,
and he will live in hostility
    toward[c] all his brothers."

[13]She gave this name to the LORD who spoke to her: "You are the God who sees me," for she said, "I have now seen[d] the One who sees me." [14]That is why the well was called Beer Lahai Roi[e]; it is still there, between Kadesh and Bered.

[15]So Hagar bore Abram a son, and Abram gave the name Ishmael to the son she had borne. [16]Abram was eighty-six years old when Hagar bore him Ishmael.

---

[a] 18 Or river   [b] 11 Ishmael means God hears.   [c] 12 Or live to the east / of
[d] 13 Or seen the back of   [e] 14 Beer Lahai Roi means well of the Living One who sees me.

THE COVENANT OF CIRCUMCISION

17 When Abram was ninety-nine years old, the LORD appeared to him and said, "I am God Almighty*a*; walk before me faithfully and be blameless. ²Then I will make my covenant between me and you and will greatly increase your numbers."

³Abram fell facedown, and God said to him, ⁴"As for me, this is my covenant with you: You will be the father of many nations. ⁵No longer will you be called Abram*b*; your name will be Abraham,*c* for I have made you a father of many nations. ⁶I will make you very fruitful; I will make nations of you, and kings will come from you. ⁷I will establish my covenant as an everlasting covenant between me and you and your descendants after you for the generations to come, to be your God and the God of your descendants after you. ⁸The whole land of Canaan, where you now reside as a foreigner, I will give as an everlasting possession to you and your descendants after you; and I will be their God."

⁹Then God said to Abraham, "As for you, you must keep my covenant, you and your descendants after you for the generations to come. ¹⁰This is my covenant with you and your descendants after you, the covenant you are to keep: Every male among you shall be circumcised. ¹¹You are to undergo circumcision, and it will be the sign of the covenant between me and you. ¹²For the generations to come every male among you who is eight days old must be circumcised, including those born in your household or bought with money from a foreigner—those who are not your offspring. ¹³Whether born in your household or bought with your money, they must be circumcised. My covenant in your flesh is to be an everlasting covenant. ¹⁴Any uncircumcised male, who has not been circumcised in the flesh, will be cut off from his people; he has broken my covenant."

¹⁵God also said to Abraham, "As for Sarai your wife, you are no longer to call her Sarai; her name will be Sarah. ¹⁶I will bless her and will surely give you a son by her. I will bless her so that she will be the mother of nations; kings of peoples will come from her."

¹⁷Abraham fell facedown; he laughed and said to himself, "Will a son be born to a man a hundred years old? Will Sarah bear a child at the age of ninety?" ¹⁸And Abraham said to God, "If only Ishmael might live under your blessing!"

¹⁹Then God said, "Yes, but your wife Sarah will bear you a son, and you will call him Isaac.*d* I will establish my covenant with him as an everlasting covenant for his descendants after him. ²⁰And as for Ishmael, I have heard you: I will surely bless him; I will make him fruitful and will greatly increase his numbers. He will be the father of twelve rulers, and I will make him into a great nation. ²¹But my covenant I will establish with Isaac, whom Sarah will bear to you by this time next year." ²²When he had finished speaking with Abraham, God went up from him.

Why did God change Abram's name to Abraham? (17:5)
In ancient Hebrew culture, names signified a person's status and could be changed as status changed. Abraham means "father of many." By giving him this name, God was renewing and strengthening his promise to make a great nation of Abram's descendants.

What is circumcision? (17:10)
Circumcision is a procedure in which the foreskin of the penis is removed, usually on the eighth day after birth. It was a sign of the covenant with God and a physical reminder of the special, spiritual relationship between God and his chosen people.

Why was Sarai's name changed to Sarah? (17:15)
Both names mean "princess." The renaming stressed that she was to be the mother of nations and kings and that God intended to fulfill his promise to Abraham through her.

Why did God choose the name Isaac? (17:19)
The name means "he laughs." The name may be a reminder of Sarah's laughter when God said she would have a baby in her old age.

---

a 1 Hebrew *El-Shaddai*   *b* 5 *Abram* means *exalted father.*   *c* 5 *Abraham* probably means *father of many.*   *d* 19 *Isaac* means *he laughs.*

²³On that very day Abraham took his son Ishmael and all those born in his household or bought with his money, every male in his household, and circumcised them, as God told him. ²⁴Abraham was ninety-nine years old when he was circumcised, ²⁵and his son Ishmael was thirteen; ²⁶Abraham and his son Ishmael were both circumcised on that very day. ²⁷And every male in Abraham's household, including those born in his household or bought from a foreigner, was circumcised with him.

THE THREE VISITORS

18 The Lord appeared to Abraham near the great trees of Mamre while he was sitting at the entrance to his tent in the heat of the day. ²Abraham looked up and saw three men standing nearby. When he saw them, he hurried from the entrance of his tent to meet them and bowed low to the ground.

³He said, "If I have found favor in your eyes, my lord,ᵃ do not pass your servant by. ⁴Let a little water be brought, and then you may all wash your feet and rest under this tree. ⁵Let me get you something to eat, so you can be refreshed and then go on your way—now that you have come to your servant."

"Very well," they answered, "do as you say."

⁶So Abraham hurried into the tent to Sarah. "Quick," he said, "get three seahsᵇ of the finest flour and knead it and bake some bread."

⁷Then he ran to the herd and selected a choice, tender calf and gave it to a servant, who hurried to prepare it. ⁸He then brought some curds and milk and the calf that had been prepared, and set these before them. While they ate, he stood near them under a tree.

⁹"Where is your wife Sarah?" they asked him.

"There, in the tent," he said.

¹⁰Then one of them said, "I will surely return to you about this time next year, and Sarah your wife will have a son."

Now Sarah was listening at the entrance to the tent, which was behind him. ¹¹Abraham and Sarah were already very old, and Sarah was past the age of childbearing. ¹²So Sarah laughed to herself as she thought, "After I am worn out and my lord is old, will I now have this pleasure?"

¹³Then the Lord said to Abraham, "Why did Sarah laugh and say, 'Will I really have a child, now that I am old?' ¹⁴Is anything too hard for the Lord? I will return to you at the appointed time next year, and Sarah will have a son."

¹⁵Sarah was afraid, so she lied and said, "I did not laugh."

But he said, "Yes, you did laugh."

ABRAHAM PLEADS FOR SODOM

¹⁶When the men got up to leave, they looked down toward Sodom, and Abraham walked along with them to see them on their way. ¹⁷Then the Lord said, "Shall I hide from Abraham what I am about to do? ¹⁸Abraham will surely become a great and powerful nation, and all nations on earth will be blessed

---

ᵃ 3 Or *eyes, Lord*   ᵇ 6 That is, probably about 36 pounds or about 16 kilograms

---

How did God appear to Abraham? (18:1)

God appeared to Abraham in many ways. Sometimes he came to Abraham in dreams or visions. Other times he spoke to him. And on rare occasions God even took on a physical body. God has many ways of communicating with his people.

What was a seah? (18:6)

A *seah* was a dry measurement of about seven quarts. Three seahs would be about 20 quarts or 22 liters.

Is anything too hard for God? (18:14)

God didn't mean for Abraham to answer this question. The obvious answer is no. Sarah's laughter showed she thought it was impossible, but she did have a child. This was also true for her descendants Mary and Elizabeth (see Luke 1:34–37). God is all-powerful, and he can accomplish his will even if it doesn't seem possible.

Why did God share his plans with Abraham? (18:17–19)

God wanted Abraham to direct his children to do what was right. God also gave Abraham the opportunity to ask for mercy for the people of Sodom and Gomorrah.

through him.ª ¹⁹For I have chosen him, so that he will direct his children and his household after him to keep the way of the LORD by doing what is right and just, so that the LORD will bring about for Abraham what he has promised him."

²⁰Then the LORD said, "The outcry against Sodom and Gomorrah is so great and their sin so grievous ²¹that I will go down and see if what they have done is as bad as the outcry that has reached me. If not, I will know."

²²The men turned away and went toward Sodom, but Abraham remained standing before the LORD.ᵇ ²³Then Abraham approached him and said: "Will you sweep away the righteous with the wicked? ²⁴What if there are fifty righteous people in the city? Will you really sweep it away and not spareᶜ the place for the sake of the fifty righteous people in it? ²⁵Far be it from you to do such a thing—to kill the righteous with the wicked, treating the righteous and the wicked alike. Far be it from you! Will not the Judge of all the earth do right?"

²⁶The LORD said, "If I find fifty righteous people in the city of Sodom, I will spare the whole place for their sake."

²⁷Then Abraham spoke up again: "Now that I have been so bold as to speak to the Lord, though I am nothing but dust and ashes, ²⁸what if the number of the righteous is five less than fifty? Will you destroy the whole city for lack of five people?"

"If I find forty-five there," he said, "I will not destroy it."

²⁹Once again he spoke to him, "What if only forty are found there?"

He said, "For the sake of forty, I will not do it."

³⁰Then he said, "May the Lord not be angry, but let me speak. What if only thirty can be found there?"

He answered, "I will not do it if I find thirty there."

³¹Abraham said, "Now that I have been so bold as to speak to the Lord, what if only twenty can be found there?"

He said, "For the sake of twenty, I will not destroy it."

³²Then he said, "May the Lord not be angry, but let me speak just once more. What if only ten can be found there?"

He answered, "For the sake of ten, I will not destroy it."

³³When the LORD had finished speaking with Abraham, he left, and Abraham returned home.

SODOM AND GOMORRAH DESTROYED

19 The two angels arrived at Sodom in the evening, and Lot was sitting in the gateway of the city. When he saw them, he got up to meet them and bowed down with his face to the ground. ²"My lords," he said, "please turn aside to your servant's house. You can wash your feet and spend the night and then go on your way early in the morning."

"No," they answered, "we will spend the night in the square."

³But he insisted so strongly that they did go with him and entered his house. He prepared a meal for them, baking bread without yeast, and they ate. ⁴Before they had gone to

Why did God go down and see what the situation was like in Sodom and Gomorrah? (18:21)
God knows everything. He already knew the situation, but this is a way of describing in human terms what God did. This wording emphasizes that God doesn't act out of ignorance or give judgment without knowing all of the facts.

Why did Abraham say that he was nothing but dust and ashes? (18:27)
This phrase refers to the fact that the human body is made from ordinary chemical elements. For example, Adam was created from the dust of the earth. The phrase emphasizes how great God is and how insignificant human beings are in comparison.

Was Abraham bargaining or pleading with God? (18:27–32)
In a way, Abraham was negotiating with God, but he wasn't selfishly asking for himself; he was asking for the sake of others. He was praying for the city and for the few righteous people who might be found there.

Why did Abraham stop at ten? (18:32)
Perhaps he stopped at ten because he thought there could be that many righteous people: Lot, his wife, possibly two sons, at least two daughters and their husbands, and possibly two unmarried daughters. (See Genesis 19:12–16.)

ª 18 Or will use his name in blessings (see 48:20)   ᵇ 22 Masoretic Text; an ancient Hebrew scribal tradition but the LORD remained standing before Abraham   ᶜ 24 Or forgive; also in verse 26

bed, all the men from every part of the city of Sodom—both young and old—surrounded the house. [5]They called to Lot, "Where are the men who came to you tonight? Bring them out to us so that we can have sex with them."

[6]Lot went outside to meet them and shut the door behind him [7]and said, "No, my friends. Don't do this wicked thing. [8]Look, I have two daughters who have never slept with a man. Let me bring them out to you, and you can do what you like with them. But don't do anything to these men, for they have come under the protection of my roof."

[9]"Get out of our way," they replied. "This fellow came here as a foreigner, and now he wants to play the judge! We'll treat you worse than them." They kept bringing pressure on Lot and moved forward to break down the door.

[10]But the men inside reached out and pulled Lot back into the house and shut the door. [11]Then they struck the men who were at the door of the house, young and old, with blindness so that they could not find the door.

[12]The two men said to Lot, "Do you have anyone else here—sons-in-law, sons or daughters, or anyone else in the city who belongs to you? Get them out of here, [13]because we are going to destroy this place. The outcry to the LORD against its people is so great that he has sent us to destroy it."

[14]So Lot went out and spoke to his sons-in-law, who were pledged to marry[a] his daughters. He said, "Hurry and get out of this place, because the LORD is about to destroy the city!" But his sons-in-law thought he was joking.

[15]With the coming of dawn, the angels urged Lot, saying, "Hurry! Take your wife and your two daughters who are here, or you will be swept away when the city is punished."

[16]When he hesitated, the men grasped his hand and the hands of his wife and of his two daughters and led them safely out of the city, for the LORD was merciful to them. [17]As soon as they had brought them out, one of them said, "Flee for your lives! Don't look back, and don't stop anywhere in the plain! Flee to the mountains or you will be swept away!"

[18]But Lot said to them, "No, my lords,[b] please! [19]Your[c] servant has found favor in your[c] eyes, and you[c] have shown great kindness to me in sparing my life. But I can't flee to the mountains; this disaster will overtake me, and I'll die. [20]Look, here is a town near enough to run to, and it is small. Let me flee to it—it is very small, isn't it? Then my life will be spared."

[21]He said to him, "Very well, I will grant this request too; I will not overthrow the town you speak of. [22]But flee there quickly, because I cannot do anything until you reach it." (That is why the town was called Zoar.[d])

[23]By the time Lot reached Zoar, the sun had risen over the land. [24]Then the LORD rained down burning sulfur on Sodom and Gomorrah—from the LORD out of the heavens. [25]Thus he overthrew those cities and the entire plain, destroying all those living in the cities—and also the vegetation in the land. [26]But Lot's wife looked back, and she became a pillar of salt.

---

[a] 14 Or were married to　[b] 18 Or No, Lord; or No, my lord
[c] 19 The Hebrew is singular.　[d] 22 Zoar means small.

How did Lot show hospitality to his guests? (19:6–9)
Lot not only invited the strangers to stay with him and prepared a meal for them, but he also tried to save them from the mob. He even went so far as to offer his daughters to the men of the city. This shows the extent of his hospitality, but it doesn't reflect well on his attitude toward his daughters. Perhaps Lot was simply making the offer impulsively or out of desperation.

Why did Lot's sons-in-law ignore his warnings? (19:14)
The Bible says they thought he was joking. Perhaps they could not imagine that God really would send his judgment and destroy the city. Like many other people, they underestimated the extent of God's outrage at disobedience and his judgment on sin.

Where did the burning sulfur come from that fell on the city? (19:24)
There may have been an earthquake that spewed asphalt on the city. There still are deposits of asphalt and sulfur in the area where Sodom and Gomorrah were located.

Why was Lot's wife turned into a pillar of salt? (19:26)
Lot and his wife found it difficult to leave their home. When they had to get out of the city, Lot wanted to stay in a nearby town. Lot's wife took one last look of longing at the world she was leaving, even though one of the angels had told her not to (19:17).

²⁷ Early the next morning Abraham got up and returned to the place where he had stood before the LORD. ²⁸ He looked down toward Sodom and Gomorrah, toward all the land of the plain, and he saw dense smoke rising from the land, like smoke from a furnace.

²⁹ So when God destroyed the cities of the plain, he remembered Abraham, and he brought Lot out of the catastrophe that overthrew the cities where Lot had lived.

LOT AND HIS DAUGHTERS

³⁰ Lot and his two daughters left Zoar and settled in the mountains, for he was afraid to stay in Zoar. He and his two daughters lived in a cave. ³¹ One day the older daughter said to the younger, "Our father is old, and there is no man around here to give us children — as is the custom all over the earth. ³² Let's get our father to drink wine and then sleep with him and preserve our family line through our father."

³³ That night they got their father to drink wine, and the older daughter went in and slept with him. He was not aware of it when she lay down or when she got up.

³⁴ The next day the older daughter said to the younger, "Last night I slept with my father. Let's get him to drink wine again tonight, and you go in and sleep with him so we can preserve our family line through our father." ³⁵ So they got their father to drink wine that night also, and the younger daughter went in and slept with him. Again he was not aware of it when she lay down or when she got up.

³⁶ So both of Lot's daughters became pregnant by their father. ³⁷ The older daughter had a son, and she named him Moabᵃ; he is the father of the Moabites of today. ³⁸ The younger daughter also had a son, and she named him Ben-Ammiᵇ; he is the father of the Ammonitesᶜ of today.

ABRAHAM AND ABIMELEK

20 Now Abraham moved on from there into the region of the Negev and lived between Kadesh and Shur. For a while he stayed in Gerar, ² and there Abraham said of his wife Sarah, "She is my sister." Then Abimelek king of Gerar sent for Sarah and took her.

³ But God came to Abimelek in a dream one night and said to him, "You are as good as dead because of the woman you have taken; she is a married woman."

⁴ Now Abimelek had not gone near her, so he said, "Lord, will you destroy an innocent nation? ⁵ Did he not say to me, 'She is my sister,' and didn't she also say, 'He is my brother'? I have done this with a clear conscience and clean hands."

⁶ Then God said to him in the dream, "Yes, I know you did this with a clear conscience, and so I have kept you from sinning against me. That is why I did not let you touch her. ⁷ Now return the man's wife, for he is a prophet, and he will pray for you and you will live. But if you do not return her, you may be sure that you and all who belong to you will die."

ᵃ 37 *Moab* sounds like the Hebrew for *from father.*   ᵇ 38 *Ben-Ammi* means *son of my father's people.*   ᶜ 38 Hebrew *Bene-Ammon*

Why was Lot saved? (19:29)
God answered Abraham's prayer that Lot would be saved.

Why did Abraham lie about his wife again? (20:2)
It's surprising that Abraham would fall back into an old habit (see Genesis 12:13), but even people who have strong faith can experience times of weakness when they don't put all their trust in God. Abraham was trying to get out of a difficult situation on his own rather than relying on God.

How did God communicate with Abimelek? (20:3)
God spoke to him through a dream. The dream was powerful enough to persuade Abimelek to plead his innocence to God, return Sarah to Abraham, and give gifts to Abraham.

Was Abraham more at fault than Abimelek? (20:7)
Yes. Abraham's dishonesty is what led Abimelek to take Sarah as a wife. But even though Abimelek's motives were innocent, there were still consequences for his actions.

Was Abraham a prophet? (20:7)
God called him a prophet. A biblical prophet was mainly a preacher of God's will. That didn't necessarily mean they predicted the future. God shared his plans with Abraham. He showed future generations the importance of believing in and trusting God.

Why did Abimelek give
Abraham money? (20:16)
He probably hoped that the money would show that he hadn't meant to cause harm or shame. This was his way of apologizing for his mistake. He also probably hoped that the gift would help him gain favor with Abraham and with Abraham's God.

Why was Isaac circumcised?
(21:4)
Abraham was obeying God's command that all males in his household be circumcised. (See Genesis 17:10.)

Why did Abraham host
a feast when Isaac was
weaned? (21:8)
In ancient times, weaning was an important milestone. Weaning introduces a child to an adult diet without the mother's milk. If a child lived to this age, the child could be expected to survive to adulthood. Since Isaac was the promised son, this was a reason for Abraham and Sarah to celebrate.

Why did God provide for
Ishmael and Hagar? (21:13)
Even though God would fulfill his promise to Abraham through his son Isaac, God showed love and mercy to Abraham by taking care of Ishmael and promising that he also would be the father of a nation.

[8]Early the next morning Abimelek summoned all his officials, and when he told them all that had happened, they were very much afraid. [9]Then Abimelek called Abraham in and said, "What have you done to us? How have I wronged you that you have brought such great guilt upon me and my kingdom? You have done things to me that should never be done." [10]And Abimelek asked Abraham, "What was your reason for doing this?"

[11]Abraham replied, "I said to myself, 'There is surely no fear of God in this place, and they will kill me because of my wife.' [12]Besides, she really is my sister, the daughter of my father though not of my mother; and she became my wife. [13]And when God had me wander from my father's household, I said to her, 'This is how you can show your love to me: Everywhere we go, say of me, "He is my brother."'"

[14]Then Abimelek brought sheep and cattle and male and female slaves and gave them to Abraham, and he returned Sarah his wife to him. [15]And Abimelek said, "My land is before you; live wherever you like."

[16]To Sarah he said, "I am giving your brother a thousand shekels[a] of silver. This is to cover the offense against you before all who are with you; you are completely vindicated."

[17]Then Abraham prayed to God, and God healed Abimelek, his wife and his female slaves so they could have children again, [18]for the LORD had kept all the women in Abimelek's household from conceiving because of Abraham's wife Sarah.

THE BIRTH OF ISAAC

21 Now the LORD was gracious to Sarah as he had said, and the LORD did for Sarah what he had promised. [2]Sarah became pregnant and bore a son to Abraham in his old age, at the very time God had promised him. [3]Abraham gave the name Isaac[b] to the son Sarah bore him. [4]When his son Isaac was eight days old, Abraham circumcised him, as God commanded him. [5]Abraham was a hundred years old when his son Isaac was born to him.

[6]Sarah said, "God has brought me laughter, and everyone who hears about this will laugh with me." [7]And she added, "Who would have said to Abraham that Sarah would nurse children? Yet I have borne him a son in his old age."

HAGAR AND ISHMAEL SENT AWAY

[8]The child grew and was weaned, and on the day Isaac was weaned Abraham held a great feast. [9]But Sarah saw that the son whom Hagar the Egyptian had borne to Abraham was mocking, [10]and she said to Abraham, "Get rid of that slave woman and her son, for that woman's son will never share in the inheritance with my son Isaac."

[11]The matter distressed Abraham greatly because it concerned his son. [12]But God said to him, "Do not be so distressed about the boy and your slave woman. Listen to whatever Sarah tells you, because it is through Isaac that your offspring[c] will be reckoned. [13]I will make the son of the slave into a nation also, because he is your offspring."

[a] 16 That is, about 25 pounds or about 12 kilograms　　[b] 3 Isaac means he laughs.　[c] 12 Or seed

¹⁴Early the next morning Abraham took some food and a skin of water and gave them to Hagar. He set them on her shoulders and then sent her off with the boy. She went on her way and wandered in the Desert of Beersheba.

¹⁵When the water in the skin was gone, she put the boy under one of the bushes. ¹⁶Then she went off and sat down about a bowshot away, for she thought, "I cannot watch the boy die." And as she sat there, she*ª* began to sob.

¹⁷God heard the boy crying, and the angel of God called to Hagar from heaven and said to her, "What is the matter, Hagar? Do not be afraid; God has heard the boy crying as he lies there. ¹⁸Lift the boy up and take him by the hand, for I will make him into a great nation."

¹⁹Then God opened her eyes and she saw a well of water. So she went and filled the skin with water and gave the boy a drink.

²⁰God was with the boy as he grew up. He lived in the desert and became an archer. ²¹While he was living in the Desert of Paran, his mother got a wife for him from Egypt.

THE TREATY AT BEERSHEBA

²²At that time Abimelek and Phicol the commander of his forces said to Abraham, "God is with you in everything you do. ²³Now swear to me here before God that you will not deal falsely with me or my children or my descendants. Show to me and the country where you now reside as a foreigner the same kindness I have shown to you."

²⁴Abraham said, "I swear it."

²⁵Then Abraham complained to Abimelek about a well of water that Abimelek's servants had seized. ²⁶But Abimelek said, "I don't know who has done this. You did not tell me, and I heard about it only today."

²⁷So Abraham brought sheep and cattle and gave them to Abimelek, and the two men made a treaty. ²⁸Abraham set apart seven ewe lambs from the flock, ²⁹and Abimelek asked Abraham, "What is the meaning of these seven ewe lambs you have set apart by themselves?"

³⁰He replied, "Accept these seven lambs from my hand as a witness that I dug this well."

³¹So that place was called Beersheba,*ᵇ* because the two men swore an oath there.

³²After the treaty had been made at Beersheba, Abimelek and Phicol the commander of his forces returned to the land of the Philistines. ³³Abraham planted a tamarisk tree in Beersheba, and there he called on the name of the LORD, the Eternal God. ³⁴And Abraham stayed in the land of the Philistines for a long time.

ABRAHAM TESTED

22 Some time later God tested Abraham. He said to him, "Abraham!"

"Here I am," he replied.

²Then God said, "Take your son, your only son, whom you

ª 16 Hebrew; Septuagint the child   ᵇ 31 Beersheba can mean well of seven and well of the oath.

How did Hagar support herself and Ishmael? (21:17–21) Although they lived in the desert, God provided them with water. God cared for Ishmael and his mother. And Abraham probably supported them since Ishmael was his son. God promised that Ishmael would lead a great nation.

What did the gift of animals represent in the treaty with Abimelek? (21:27–30) In ancient times there were no written contracts. Instead, a treaty was guaranteed with a gift of animals. Because there were no courts or police or lawyers, people guaranteed their agreements by giving a valuable gift.

Why did God tell Abraham to sacrifice his son? (22:1) God was giving Abraham an extremely difficult test to confirm his faith and prove his commitment. Naturally Abraham did not want to sacrifice his son, who represented the promises of God. That is why the test was so difficult. Abraham answered God as a servant when he said, "Here I am."

love—Isaac—and go to the region of Moriah. Sacrifice him there as a burnt offering on a mountain I will show you."

³Early the next morning Abraham got up and loaded his donkey. He took with him two of his servants and his son Isaac. When he had cut enough wood for the burnt offering, he set out for the place God had told him about. ⁴On the third day Abraham looked up and saw the place in the distance. ⁵He said to his servants, "Stay here with the donkey while I and the boy go over there. We will worship and then we will come back to you."

⁶Abraham took the wood for the burnt offering and placed it on his son Isaac, and he himself carried the fire and the knife. As the two of them went on together, ⁷Isaac spoke up and said to his father Abraham, "Father?"

"Yes, my son?" Abraham replied.

"The fire and wood are here," Isaac said, "but where is the lamb for the burnt offering?"

⁸Abraham answered, "God himself will provide the lamb for the burnt offering, my son." And the two of them went on together.

⁹When they reached the place God had told him about, Abraham built an altar there and arranged the wood on it. He bound his son Isaac and laid him on the altar, on top of the wood. ¹⁰Then he reached out his hand and took the knife to slay his son. ¹¹But the angel of the LORD called out to him from heaven, "Abraham! Abraham!"

"Here I am," he replied.

¹²"Do not lay a hand on the boy," he said. "Do not do anything to him. Now I know that you fear God, because you have not withheld from me your son, your only son."

¹³Abraham looked up and there in a thicket he saw a ram[a] caught by its horns. He went over and took the ram and sacrificed it as a burnt offering instead of his son. ¹⁴So Abraham called that place The LORD Will Provide. And to this day it is said, "On the mountain of the LORD it will be provided."

¹⁵The angel of the LORD called to Abraham from heaven a second time ¹⁶and said, "I swear by myself, declares the LORD, that because you have done this and have not withheld your son, your only son, ¹⁷I will surely bless you and make your descendants as numerous as the stars in the sky and as the sand on the seashore. Your descendants will take possession of the cities of their enemies, ¹⁸and through your offspring[b] all nations on earth will be blessed,[c] because you have obeyed me."

¹⁹Then Abraham returned to his servants, and they set off together for Beersheba. And Abraham stayed in Beersheba.

NAHOR'S SONS

²⁰Some time later Abraham was told, "Milkah is also a mother; she has borne sons to your brother Nahor: ²¹Uz the firstborn, Buz his brother, Kemuel (the father of Aram),

Didn't Abraham have a responsibility to care for Isaac? (22:8)
Abraham was showing how great his faith in God was. He believed God would keep the promise he made that, through Isaac, Abraham would have many descendants. Abraham truly believed that God would provide a substitute or even raise Isaac from the dead. (See Hebrews 11:19.)

How does this story point to Jesus? (22:16)
This is the first time that substituting one life for another is mentioned in the Bible. As the ram died in Isaac's place, so also Jesus gave his life for many. Abraham's willingness to sacrifice his son points toward God sending his Son to be a sacrifice.

Why did God restate his promises to Abraham? (22:16–18)
God honored Abraham's obedience by taking the most powerful oath possible: swearing by his own name. He renewed his promises to Abraham, including the promise that all nations would be blessed through Abraham's descendant Jesus.

---

[a] 13 Many manuscripts of the Masoretic Text, Samaritan Pentateuch, Septuagint and Syriac; most manuscripts of the Masoretic Text *a ram behind him*   [b] 18 Or *seed*   [c] 18 Or *and all nations on earth will use the name of your offspring in blessings* (see 48:20)

²² Kesed, Hazo, Pildash, Jidlaph and Bethuel." ²³ Bethuel became the father of Rebekah. Milkah bore these eight sons to Abraham's brother Nahor. ²⁴ His concubine, whose name was Reumah, also had sons: Tebah, Gaham, Tahash and Maakah.

THE DEATH OF SARAH

23 Sarah lived to be a hundred and twenty-seven years old. ² She died at Kiriath Arba (that is, Hebron) in the land of Canaan, and Abraham went to mourn for Sarah and to weep over her.

³ Then Abraham rose from beside his dead wife and spoke to the Hittites.ᵃ He said, ⁴ "I am a foreigner and stranger among you. Sell me some property for a burial site here so I can bury my dead."

⁵ The Hittites replied to Abraham, ⁶ "Sir, listen to us. You are a mighty prince among us. Bury your dead in the choicest of our tombs. None of us will refuse you his tomb for burying your dead."

⁷ Then Abraham rose and bowed down before the people of the land, the Hittites. ⁸ He said to them, "If you are willing to let me bury my dead, then listen to me and intercede with Ephron son of Zohar on my behalf ⁹ so he will sell me the cave of Machpelah, which belongs to him and is at the end of his field. Ask him to sell it to me for the full price as a burial site among you."

¹⁰ Ephron the Hittite was sitting among his people and he replied to Abraham in the hearing of all the Hittites who had come to the gate of his city. ¹¹ "No, my lord," he said. "Listen to me; I giveᵇ you the field, and I giveᵇ you the cave that is in it. I giveᵇ it to you in the presence of my people. Bury your dead."

¹² Again Abraham bowed down before the people of the land ¹³ and he said to Ephron in their hearing, "Listen to me, if you will. I will pay the price of the field. Accept it from me so I can bury my dead there."

¹⁴ Ephron answered Abraham, ¹⁵ "Listen to me, my lord; the land is worth four hundred shekelsᶜ of silver, but what is that between you and me? Bury your dead."

¹⁶ Abraham agreed to Ephron's terms and weighed out for him the price he had named in the hearing of the Hittites: four hundred shekels of silver, according to the weight current among the merchants.

¹⁷ So Ephron's field in Machpelah near Mamre—both the field and the cave in it, and all the trees within the borders of the field—was deeded ¹⁸ to Abraham as his property in the presence of all the Hittites who had come to the gate of the city. ¹⁹ Afterward Abraham buried his wife Sarah in the cave in the field of Machpelah near Mamre (which is at Hebron) in the land of Canaan. ²⁰ So the field and the cave in it were deeded to Abraham by the Hittites as a burial site.

ISAAC AND REBEKAH

24 Abraham was now very old, and the LORD had blessed him in every way. ² He said to the senior

---

ᵃ 3 Or the descendants of Heth; also in verses 5, 7, 10, 16, 18 and 20
ᵇ 11 Or sell   ᶜ 15 That is, about 10 pounds or about 4.6 kilograms

---

Where were Abraham and Sarah buried? (23:9)
Both Abraham and Sarah were buried in the cave of Machpelah.

Did Ephron really intend to give the property to Abraham? (23:11)
No, this offer was not meant to be taken seriously. This type of courtesy was customary in ancient trading practices. Ephron knew that Abraham would not accept a gift, especially because he was a rich man.

How much was 400 shekels of silver? (23:15)
A shekel was a measurement of weight. The 400 shekels would have weighed about 10 pounds (about 4.5 kilograms). The term *shekel* is also used as a name for currency in modern Israel.

Without a written contract, how did Ephron deed the cave to Abraham? (23:17)
Contracts were not usually written down, so they were finalized at the main gateway of a city with many witnesses from the community. If either party tried to break the contract, the citizens could be called as witnesses.

Why did Abraham tell his servant to put a hand under his thigh? (24:2)
This may have been an ancient custom that indicates a great amount of trust that the oath represented. (See Genesis 47:29.)

Why did Abraham want Isaac to marry a relative? (24:4)
Abraham wanted Isaac to marry within his own clan — which was customary in those days. Perhaps Abraham did not want Isaac to marry someone who worshiped false gods.

Why didn't Abraham want Isaac to return to his native country? (24:6–8)
God had promised Abraham and his descendants that they would inherit the land of Canaan. Sending Isaac back to his native land was not part of God's plan.

Why did Abraham's servant ask God to give him a sign? (24:14)
The servant had to make a major decision for Isaac — finding him a wife. He gave the decision to God, asking him to make it clear who would be the right woman.

How was Rebekah related to Isaac? (24:15)
Rebekah was the granddaughter of Isaac's uncle.

How did Rebekah show her kindness to Abraham's servant? (24:19–20)
The servant asked for only a small drink for himself, but she brought water for him and for his ten camels. Camels could drink a lot, so watering ten camels was a big gesture of hospitality.

Why did the servant give Rebekah jewelry? (24:22)
The nose ring and bracelets probably indicated that he was there to arrange a marriage.

servant in his household, the one in charge of all that he had, "Put your hand under my thigh. [3]I want you to swear by the LORD, the God of heaven and the God of earth, that you will not get a wife for my son from the daughters of the Canaanites, among whom I am living, [4]but will go to my country and my own relatives and get a wife for my son Isaac."

[5]The servant asked him, "What if the woman is unwilling to come back with me to this land? Shall I then take your son back to the country you came from?"

[6]"Make sure that you do not take my son back there," Abraham said. [7]"The LORD, the God of heaven, who brought me out of my father's household and my native land and who spoke to me and promised me on oath, saying, 'To your offspring[a] I will give this land'—he will send his angel before you so that you can get a wife for my son from there. [8]If the woman is unwilling to come back with you, then you will be released from this oath of mine. Only do not take my son back there." [9]So the servant put his hand under the thigh of his master Abraham and swore an oath to him concerning this matter.

[10]Then the servant left, taking with him ten of his master's camels loaded with all kinds of good things from his master. He set out for Aram Naharaim[b] and made his way to the town of Nahor. [11]He had the camels kneel down near the well outside the town; it was toward evening, the time the women go out to draw water.

[12]Then he prayed, "LORD, God of my master Abraham, make me successful today, and show kindness to my master Abraham. [13]See, I am standing beside this spring, and the daughters of the townspeople are coming out to draw water. [14]May it be that when I say to a young woman, 'Please let down your jar that I may have a drink,' and she says, 'Drink, and I'll water your camels too'— let her be the one you have chosen for your servant Isaac. By this I will know that you have shown kindness to my master."

[15]Before he had finished praying, Rebekah came out with her jar on her shoulder. She was the daughter of Bethuel son of Milkah, who was the wife of Abraham's brother Nahor. [16]The woman was very beautiful, a virgin; no man had ever slept with her. She went down to the spring, filled her jar and came up again.

[17]The servant hurried to meet her and said, "Please give me a little water from your jar."

[18]"Drink, my lord," she said, and quickly lowered the jar to her hands and gave him a drink.

[19]After she had given him a drink, she said, "I'll draw water for your camels too, until they have had enough to drink." [20]So she quickly emptied her jar into the trough, ran back to the well to draw more water, and drew enough for all his camels. [21]Without saying a word, the man watched her closely to learn whether or not the LORD had made his journey successful.

[22]When the camels had finished drinking, the man took out a gold nose ring weighing a beka[c] and two gold bracelets

[a] 7 Or seed   [b] 10 That is, Northwest Mesopotamia   [c] 22 That is, about 1/5 ounce or about 5.7 grams

weighing ten shekels.[a] [23]Then he asked, "Whose daughter are you? Please tell me, is there room in your father's house for us to spend the night?"

[24]She answered him, "I am the daughter of Bethuel, the son that Milkah bore to Nahor." [25]And she added, "We have plenty of straw and fodder, as well as room for you to spend the night."

[26]Then the man bowed down and worshiped the LORD, [27]saying, "Praise be to the LORD, the God of my master Abraham, who has not abandoned his kindness and faithfulness to my master. As for me, the LORD has led me on the journey to the house of my master's relatives."

[28]The young woman ran and told her mother's household about these things. [29]Now Rebekah had a brother named Laban, and he hurried out to the man at the spring. [30]As soon as he had seen the nose ring, and the bracelets on his sister's arms, and had heard Rebekah tell what the man said to her, he went out to the man and found him standing by the camels near the spring. [31]"Come, you who are blessed by the LORD," he said. "Why are you standing out here? I have prepared the house and a place for the camels."

[32]So the man went to the house, and the camels were unloaded. Straw and fodder were brought for the camels, and water for him and his men to wash their feet. [33]Then food was set before him, but he said, "I will not eat until I have told you what I have to say."

"Then tell us," Laban said.

[34]So he said, "I am Abraham's servant. [35]The LORD has blessed my master abundantly, and he has become wealthy. He has given him sheep and cattle, silver and gold, male and female servants, and camels and donkeys. [36]My master's wife Sarah has borne him a son in her old age, and he has given him everything he owns. [37]And my master made me swear an oath, and said, 'You must not get a wife for my son from the daughters of the Canaanites, in whose land I live, [38]but go to my father's family and to my own clan, and get a wife for my son.'

[39]"Then I asked my master, 'What if the woman will not come back with me?'

[40]"He replied, 'The LORD, before whom I have walked faithfully, will send his angel with you and make your journey a success, so that you can get a wife for my son from my own clan and from my father's family. [41]You will be released from my oath if, when you go to my clan, they refuse to give her to you—then you will be released from my oath.'

[42]"When I came to the spring today, I said, 'LORD, God of my master Abraham, if you will, please grant success to the journey on which I have come. [43]See, I am standing beside this spring. If a young woman comes out to draw water and I say to her, "Please let me drink a little water from your jar," [44]and if she says to me, "Drink, and I'll draw water for your camels too," let her be the one the LORD has chosen for my master's son.'

[45]"Before I finished praying in my heart, Rebekah came

How much is a beka? (24:22)
A beka is half a shekel, a measurement of weight equal to about one-fifth of an ounce.

Why is the story repeated here? (24:34–49)
An old storytelling technique is to repeat important elements so listeners could memorize the story. This part of the story is repeated to stress God's role in the events.

[a] *22 That is, about 4 ounces or about 115 grams*

out, with her jar on her shoulder. She went down to the spring and drew water, and I said to her, 'Please give me a drink.'

⁴⁶"She quickly lowered her jar from her shoulder and said, 'Drink, and I'll water your camels too.' So I drank, and she watered the camels also.

⁴⁷"I asked her, 'Whose daughter are you?'

"She said, 'The daughter of Bethuel son of Nahor, whom Milkah bore to him.'

"Then I put the ring in her nose and the bracelets on her arms, ⁴⁸ and I bowed down and worshiped the LORD. I praised the LORD, the God of my master Abraham, who had led me on the right road to get the granddaughter of my master's brother for his son. ⁴⁹ Now if you will show kindness and faithfulness to my master, tell me; and if not, tell me, so I may know which way to turn."

⁵⁰ Laban and Bethuel answered, "This is from the LORD; we can say nothing to you one way or the other. ⁵¹ Here is Rebekah; take her and go, and let her become the wife of your master's son, as the LORD has directed."

⁵² When Abraham's servant heard what they said, he bowed down to the ground before the LORD. ⁵³ Then the servant brought out gold and silver jewelry and articles of clothing and gave them to Rebekah; he also gave costly gifts to her brother and to her mother. ⁵⁴ Then he and the men who were with him ate and drank and spent the night there.

When they got up the next morning, he said, "Send me on my way to my master."

⁵⁵ But her brother and her mother replied, "Let the young woman remain with us ten days or so; then youᵃ may go."

⁵⁶ But he said to them, "Do not detain me, now that the LORD has granted success to my journey. Send me on my way so I may go to my master."

⁵⁷ Then they said, "Let's call the young woman and ask her about it." ⁵⁸ So they called Rebekah and asked her, "Will you go with this man?"

"I will go," she said.

⁵⁹ So they sent their sister Rebekah on her way, along with her nurse and Abraham's servant and his men. ⁶⁰ And they blessed Rebekah and said to her,

"Our sister, may you increase
    to thousands upon thousands;
may your offspring possess
    the cities of their enemies."

⁶¹ Then Rebekah and her attendants got ready and mounted the camels and went back with the man. So the servant took Rebekah and left.

⁶² Now Isaac had come from Beer Lahai Roi, for he was living in the Negev. ⁶³ He went out to the field one evening to meditate,ᵇ and as he looked up, he saw camels approaching. ⁶⁴ Rebekah also looked up and saw Isaac. She got down from her camel ⁶⁵ and asked the servant, "Who is that man in the field coming to meet us?"

Why did the servant give so many gifts to Rebekah and her family? (24:53)
The rich gifts he gave indicated the wealth of the household into which she was marrying. In an arranged marriage, the family wanted to know their daughter was joining a good family that would care for her.

Why did Abraham's servant want to leave so quickly? (24:56)
He was probably excited to complete the job that seemed to be going well, according to God's plan. He may also have wanted to get back before Abraham died.

Why did Rebekah cover herself with a veil when she saw Isaac? (24:65)
It was the custom for a woman to cover herself in the presence of her future husband.

ᵃ 55 Or *she*   ᵇ 63 The meaning of the Hebrew for this word is uncertain.

"He is my master," the servant answered. So she took her veil and covered herself.

⁶⁶Then the servant told Isaac all he had done. ⁶⁷Isaac brought her into the tent of his mother Sarah, and he married Rebekah. So she became his wife, and he loved her; and Isaac was comforted after his mother's death.

THE DEATH OF ABRAHAM

25 Abraham had taken another wife, whose name was Keturah. ²She bore him Zimran, Jokshan, Medan, Midian, Ishbak and Shuah. ³Jokshan was the father of Sheba and Dedan; the descendants of Dedan were the Ashurites, the Letushites and the Leummites. ⁴The sons of Midian were Ephah, Epher, Hanok, Abida and Eldaah. All these were descendants of Keturah.

⁵Abraham left everything he owned to Isaac. ⁶But while he was still living, he gave gifts to the sons of his concubines and sent them away from his son Isaac to the land of the east.

⁷Abraham lived a hundred and seventy-five years. ⁸Then Abraham breathed his last and died at a good old age, an old man and full of years; and he was gathered to his people. ⁹His sons Isaac and Ishmael buried him in the cave of Machpelah near Mamre, in the field of Ephron son of Zohar the Hittite, ¹⁰the field Abraham had bought from the Hittites.ᵃ There Abraham was buried with his wife Sarah. ¹¹After Abraham's death, God blessed his son Isaac, who then lived near Beer Lahai Roi.

ISHMAEL'S SONS

¹²This is the account of the family line of Abraham's son Ishmael, whom Sarah's slave, Hagar the Egyptian, bore to Abraham.

¹³These are the names of the sons of Ishmael, listed in the order of their birth: Nebaioth the firstborn of Ishmael, Kedar, Adbeel, Mibsam, ¹⁴Mishma, Dumah, Massa, ¹⁵Hadad, Tema, Jetur, Naphish and Kedemah. ¹⁶These were the sons of Ishmael, and these are the names of the twelve tribal rulers according to their settlements and camps. ¹⁷Ishmael lived a hundred and thirty-seven years. He breathed his last and died, and he was gathered to his people. ¹⁸His descendants settled in the area from Havilah to Shur, near the eastern border of Egypt, as you go toward Ashur. And they lived in hostility towardᵇ all the tribes related to them.

JACOB AND ESAU

¹⁹This is the account of the family line of Abraham's son Isaac.

Abraham became the father of Isaac, ²⁰and Isaac was forty years old when he married Rebekah daughter of Bethuel the Aramean from Paddan Aramᶜ and sister of Laban the Aramean.

²¹Isaac prayed to the LORD on behalf of his wife, because

ᵃ 10 Or the descendants of Heth   ᵇ 18 Or lived to the east of   ᶜ 20 That is, Northwest Mesopotamia

How did the marriage become legal? (24:67)
The marriage became legal after the two families agreed to the marriage. The ceremony consisted of the bride moving from her father's house to the home of her husband. Then a week-long celebration took place.

How were Abraham and Keturah's sons different from Isaac? (25:1–5)
None of these sons shared Isaac's special status as the child through whom God would bless the rest of the nations. Their mother was a concubine, and they would not inherit Abraham's wealth or blessings.

What was a concubine? (25:6)
A concubine is like a second wife who is more of a servant. Her primary purpose was to bear children. The taking of concubines was common in ancient cultures.

Why did Abraham send away the sons of his concubines? (25:6)
By sending them out of the land that God had promised him, Abraham was showing that Isaac was his sole heir.

What did God's words tell Rebekah? (25:23)
She was to give birth to twin boys whose descendants would grow into two great nations. Under ordinary circumstances, the younger would serve the older, but here God reversed this custom to fulfill his will.

What does the name *Jacob* mean? (25:26)
The name means "he grasps the heel." Jacob was grasping Esau's heel when he was born. Because of Jacob's behavior, it later came to mean "he deceives."

What is a birthright? (25:31)
During this time, special rights were given to the firstborn son. When his father died, he would become leader of the family and inherit most of the family's land and herds of animals. Esau did not care much about this position, but Jacob wanted it badly.

Why does it say Esau despised his birthright? (25:34)
He did not value it or the covenant promises from God that the birthright represented.

Why did God tell Isaac to remain in the land of Gerar? (26:2–3)
God repeated his earlier promise to Abraham. God promised to bless Isaac with many children and land. God wanted Isaac to trust in him even though there was a famine.

Why did God compare Isaac's descendants to stars? (26:4)
This is a poetic way of saying that the number of Isaac's descendants would be so large that there would be too many to count, like the stars.

Why did Isaac pretend his wife was his sister? (26:7)
Isaac was afraid someone would kill him in order to marry his beautiful wife. Like his father, Isaac did not trust in God's protection.

she was childless. The LORD answered his prayer, and his wife Rebekah became pregnant. ²²The babies jostled each other within her, and she said, "Why is this happening to me?" So she went to inquire of the LORD.
²³The LORD said to her,

"Two nations are in your womb,
    and two peoples from within you will be separated;
one people will be stronger than the other,
    and the older will serve the younger."

²⁴When the time came for her to give birth, there were twin boys in her womb. ²⁵The first to come out was red, and his whole body was like a hairy garment; so they named him Esau.ᵃ ²⁶After this, his brother came out, with his hand grasping Esau's heel; so he was named Jacob.ᵇ Isaac was sixty years old when Rebekah gave birth to them.

²⁷The boys grew up, and Esau became a skillful hunter, a man of the open country, while Jacob was content to stay at home among the tents. ²⁸Isaac, who had a taste for wild game, loved Esau, but Rebekah loved Jacob.

²⁹Once when Jacob was cooking some stew, Esau came in from the open country, famished. ³⁰He said to Jacob, "Quick, let me have some of that red stew! I'm famished!" (That is why he was also called Edom.ᶜ)

³¹Jacob replied, "First sell me your birthright."

³²"Look, I am about to die," Esau said. "What good is the birthright to me?"

³³But Jacob said, "Swear to me first." So he swore an oath to him, selling his birthright to Jacob.

³⁴Then Jacob gave Esau some bread and some lentil stew. He ate and drank, and then got up and left.

So Esau despised his birthright.

ISAAC AND ABIMELEK

26 Now there was a famine in the land—besides the previous famine in Abraham's time—and Isaac went to Abimelek king of the Philistines in Gerar. ²The LORD appeared to Isaac and said, "Do not go down to Egypt; live in the land where I tell you to live. ³Stay in this land for a while, and I will be with you and will bless you. For to you and your descendants I will give all these lands and will confirm the oath I swore to your father Abraham. ⁴I will make your descendants as numerous as the stars in the sky and will give them all these lands, and through your offspringᵈ all nations on earth will be blessed,ᵉ ⁵because Abraham obeyed me and did everything I required of him, keeping my commands, my decrees and my instructions." ⁶So Isaac stayed in Gerar.

⁷When the men of that place asked him about his wife, he said, "She is my sister," because he was afraid to say, "She is my wife." He thought, "The men of this place might kill me on account of Rebekah, because she is beautiful."

⁸When Isaac had been there a long time, Abimelek king

ᵃ 25 *Esau* may mean *hairy*.   ᵇ 26 *Jacob* means *he grasps the heel*, a Hebrew idiom for *he deceives*.   ᶜ 30 *Edom* means *red*.   ᵈ 4 Or *seed*   ᵉ 4 Or *and all nations on earth will use the name of your offspring in blessings* (see 48:20)

of the Philistines looked down from a window and saw Isaac caressing his wife Rebekah. ⁹So Abimelek summoned Isaac and said, "She is really your wife! Why did you say, 'She is my sister'?"

Isaac answered him, "Because I thought I might lose my life on account of her."

¹⁰Then Abimelek said, "What is this you have done to us? One of the men might well have slept with your wife, and you would have brought guilt upon us."

¹¹So Abimelek gave orders to all the people: "Anyone who harms this man or his wife shall surely be put to death."

¹²Isaac planted crops in that land and the same year reaped a hundredfold, because the LORD blessed him. ¹³The man became rich, and his wealth continued to grow until he became very wealthy. ¹⁴He had so many flocks and herds and servants that the Philistines envied him. ¹⁵So all the wells that his father's servants had dug in the time of his father Abraham, the Philistines stopped up, filling them with earth.

¹⁶Then Abimelek said to Isaac, "Move away from us; you have become too powerful for us."

¹⁷So Isaac moved away from there and encamped in the Valley of Gerar, where he settled. ¹⁸Isaac reopened the wells that had been dug in the time of his father Abraham, which the Philistines had stopped up after Abraham died, and he gave them the same names his father had given them.

¹⁹Isaac's servants dug in the valley and discovered a well of fresh water there. ²⁰But the herders of Gerar quarreled with those of Isaac and said, "The water is ours!" So he named the well Esek,ᵃ because they disputed with him. ²¹Then they dug another well, but they quarreled over that one also; so he named it Sitnah.ᵇ ²²He moved on from there and dug another well, and no one quarreled over it. He named it Rehoboth,ᶜ saying, "Now the LORD has given us room and we will flourish in the land."

²³From there he went up to Beersheba. ²⁴That night the LORD appeared to him and said, "I am the God of your father Abraham. Do not be afraid, for I am with you; I will bless you and will increase the number of your descendants for the sake of my servant Abraham."

²⁵Isaac built an altar there and called on the name of the LORD. There he pitched his tent, and there his servants dug a well.

²⁶Meanwhile, Abimelek had come to him from Gerar, with Ahuzzath his personal adviser and Phicol the commander of his forces. ²⁷Isaac asked them, "Why have you come to me, since you were hostile to me and sent me away?"

²⁸They answered, "We saw clearly that the LORD was with you; so we said, 'There ought to be a sworn agreement between us'—between us and you. Let us make a treaty with you ²⁹that you will do us no harm, just as we did not harm you but always treated you well and sent you away peacefully. And now you are blessed by the LORD."

³⁰Isaac then made a feast for them, and they ate and drank.

ᵃ 20 Esek means dispute.   ᵇ 21 Sitnah means opposition.   ᶜ 22 Rehoboth means room.

Why did Abimelek's men fill in the wells? (26:15)
They were jealous of Isaac's wealth and knew that his wealth depended on providing water for his many herds of animals. Because water was scarce in this region, disputes over water were common.

Why did Abimelek ask Isaac to move away? (26:16)
As God blessed Isaac with wealth and servants, Abimelek became afraid of Isaac's power. The king saw Isaac's great wealth and power as a threat to his own land and people.

Why did Isaac build an altar and call on God's name? (26:25)
Altars were built to give sacrifices in thanks to God. By calling on God's name, Isaac may have been following a custom used in sealing a covenant, similar to swearing on the Bible in court today.

Why were Esau's new wives a source of grief to his parents? (26:35)
Isaac and Rebekah wanted Esau to marry within his own clan or ethnic group. Perhaps they did not want Esau married to someone who worshiped false gods.

Why was Isaac's deathbed blessing important? (27:4)
Spoken deathbed blessings had legal standing in the ancient Middle East. Although Esau had sold his birthright to Jacob, Isaac's spoken blessing would have reinstated Esau as his heir. Jacob knew Isaac could give only one blessing, and Jacob wanted it to secure the birthright he had bought from Esau.

Why did Rebekah help Jacob deceive his father? (27:5-10)
She wanted her favorite son to get the blessing from Isaac. She probably thought of the promise God gave her before the twins were born—that Esau would serve his brother (25:23). She might even have used God's promise to tell herself that it was all right to take matters into her own hands.

Was getting the blessing worth risking a curse? (27:12-13)
Jacob was fearful of receiving a curse. Instead of giving a blessing for prosperity, Isaac could have pronounced a curse on Jacob. Rebekah was willing to take that risk. However, she may have simply been saying that she would be the one to risk Isaac's anger.

Why did Isaac ask Jacob so many questions? (27:18-24)
To the very end, Isaac remained suspicious. Because he was blind, Isaac asked his son his name and how he had made the food so quickly. Isaac also asked to feel his skin, and finally asked if he was really Esau.

[31] Early the next morning the men swore an oath to each other. Then Isaac sent them on their way, and they went away peacefully.

[32] That day Isaac's servants came and told him about the well they had dug. They said, "We've found water!" [33] He called it Shibah,[a] and to this day the name of the town has been Beersheba.[b]

JACOB TAKES ESAU'S BLESSING

[34] When Esau was forty years old, he married Judith daughter of Beeri the Hittite, and also Basemath daughter of Elon the Hittite. [35] They were a source of grief to Isaac and Rebekah.

27 When Isaac was old and his eyes were so weak that he could no longer see, he called for Esau his older son and said to him, "My son."

"Here I am," he answered.

[2] Isaac said, "I am now an old man and don't know the day of my death. [3] Now then, get your equipment—your quiver and bow—and go out to the open country to hunt some wild game for me. [4] Prepare me the kind of tasty food I like and bring it to me to eat, so that I may give you my blessing before I die."

[5] Now Rebekah was listening as Isaac spoke to his son Esau. When Esau left for the open country to hunt game and bring it back, [6] Rebekah said to her son Jacob, "Look, I overheard your father say to your brother Esau, [7] 'Bring me some game and prepare me some tasty food to eat, so that I may give you my blessing in the presence of the LORD before I die.' [8] Now, my son, listen carefully and do what I tell you: [9] Go out to the flock and bring me two choice young goats, so I can prepare some tasty food for your father, just the way he likes it. [10] Then take it to your father to eat, so that he may give you his blessing before he dies."

[11] Jacob said to Rebekah his mother, "But my brother Esau is a hairy man while I have smooth skin. [12] What if my father touches me? I would appear to be tricking him and would bring down a curse on myself rather than a blessing."

[13] His mother said to him, "My son, let the curse fall on me. Just do what I say; go and get them for me."

[14] So he went and got them and brought them to his mother, and she prepared some tasty food, just the way his father liked it. [15] Then Rebekah took the best clothes of Esau her older son, which she had in the house, and put them on her younger son Jacob. [16] She also covered his hands and the smooth part of his neck with the goatskins. [17] Then she handed to her son Jacob the tasty food and the bread she had made.

[18] He went to his father and said, "My father."

"Yes, my son," he answered. "Who is it?"

[19] Jacob said to his father, "I am Esau your firstborn. I have done as you told me. Please sit up and eat some of my game, so that you may give me your blessing."

---

[a] 33 *Shibah* can mean *oath* or *seven.*   [b] 33 *Beersheba* can mean *well of the oath* and *well of seven.*

²⁰Isaac asked his son, "How did you find it so quickly, my son?"

"The LORD your God gave me success," he replied.

²¹Then Isaac said to Jacob, "Come near so I can touch you, my son, to know whether you really are my son Esau or not."

²²Jacob went close to his father Isaac, who touched him and said, "The voice is the voice of Jacob, but the hands are the hands of Esau." ²³He did not recognize him, for his hands were hairy like those of his brother Esau; so he proceeded to bless him. ²⁴"Are you really my son Esau?" he asked.

"I am," he replied.

²⁵Then he said, "My son, bring me some of your game to eat, so that I may give you my blessing."

Jacob brought it to him and he ate; and he brought some wine and he drank. ²⁶Then his father Isaac said to him, "Come here, my son, and kiss me."

²⁷So he went to him and kissed him. When Isaac caught the smell of his clothes, he blessed him and said,

> "Ah, the smell of my son
>   is like the smell of a field
>   that the LORD has blessed.
> ²⁸May God give you heaven's dew
>   and earth's richness—
>   an abundance of grain and new wine.
> ²⁹May nations serve you
>   and peoples bow down to you.
> Be lord over your brothers,
>   and may the sons of your mother bow down to you.
> May those who curse you be cursed
>   and those who bless you be blessed."

³⁰After Isaac finished blessing him, and Jacob had scarcely left his father's presence, his brother Esau came in from hunting. ³¹He too prepared some tasty food and brought it to his father. Then he said to him, "My father, please sit up and eat some of my game, so that you may give me your blessing."

³²His father Isaac asked him, "Who are you?"

"I am your son," he answered, "your firstborn, Esau."

³³Isaac trembled violently and said, "Who was it, then, that hunted game and brought it to me? I ate it just before you came and I blessed him—and indeed he will be blessed!"

³⁴When Esau heard his father's words, he burst out with a loud and bitter cry and said to his father, "Bless me—me too, my father!"

³⁵But he said, "Your brother came deceitfully and took your blessing."

³⁶Esau said, "Isn't he rightly named Jacob*? This is the second time he has taken advantage of me: He took my birthright, and now he's taken my blessing!" Then he asked, "Haven't you reserved any blessing for me?"

³⁷Isaac answered Esau, "I have made him lord over you and have made all his relatives his servants, and I have sustained

---

What did Jacob's kiss fore-shadow? (27:27)
In trying to get the covenant blessing, Jacob betrayed his brother with a kiss. In a way, this points toward Jesus, Jacob's descendant, who ultimately obtained the blessing for his people after he was betrayed by a kiss. (See Matthew 26:48.)

Why would God bless Jacob when Jacob lied to get the blessing? (27:35)
God's choice of Jacob was made before he was even born; it was not based on whether he was a good person or not. God's blessings are always unexpected. We are never deserving of his grace.

ᵃ 36 Jacob means he grasps the heel, a Hebrew idiom for he takes advantage of or he deceives.

Couldn't Isaac bless Esau too? (27:38)
In this culture only one son could receive the family blessing. Moreover, the predicted Messiah could only be born from one of the brother's family lines.

What were the results of Rebekah's role in tricking Isaac? (27:42–43)
Through her actions, Rebekah created a feud between her sons. She cheated Esau and betrayed Isaac's trust. Rebekah sent her favorite son away from the family in order to save his life.

Why was this additional blessing important? (28:4)
This blessing passed on God's promise to Abraham, that Jacob and his descendants would inherit the land in which they were living. Abraham realized God would use Jacob to keep his promise.

Why did Esau marry a daughter of Ishmael? (28:9)
Esau was trying to please his father by also marrying a descendant of Abraham. However, since Ishmael was not included in the promise God made to Abraham and Isaac, this marriage would not help him receive that promise.

Jacob's Journeys (28:10)

Why did Jacob use a stone for his pillow? (28:11)
In ancient times headrests were often quite hard, sometimes even made of metal. People were used to sleeping on the ground, so this was not an unusual way to sleep.

him with grain and new wine. So what can I possibly do for you, my son?"

[38]Esau said to his father, "Do you have only one blessing, my father? Bless me too, my father!" Then Esau wept aloud.

[39]His father Isaac answered him,

"Your dwelling will be
    away from the earth's richness,
    away from the dew of heaven above.
[40]You will live by the sword
    and you will serve your brother.
But when you grow restless,
    you will throw his yoke
    from off your neck."

[41]Esau held a grudge against Jacob because of the blessing his father had given him. He said to himself, "The days of mourning for my father are near; then I will kill my brother Jacob."

[42]When Rebekah was told what her older son Esau had said, she sent for her younger son Jacob and said to him, "Your brother Esau is planning to avenge himself by killing you. [43]Now then, my son, do what I say: Flee at once to my brother Laban in Harran. [44]Stay with him for a while until your brother's fury subsides. [45]When your brother is no longer angry with you and forgets what you did to him, I'll send word for you to come back from there. Why should I lose both of you in one day?"

[46]Then Rebekah said to Isaac, "I'm disgusted with living because of these Hittite women. If Jacob takes a wife from among the women of this land, from Hittite women like these, my life will not be worth living."

28 So Isaac called for Jacob and blessed him. Then he commanded him: "Do not marry a Canaanite woman. [2]Go at once to Paddan Aram,[a] to the house of your mother's father Bethuel. Take a wife for yourself there, from among the daughters of Laban, your mother's brother. [3]May God Almighty[b] bless you and make you fruitful and increase your numbers until you become a community of peoples. [4]May he give you and your descendants the blessing given to Abraham, so that you may take possession of the land where you now reside as a foreigner, the land God gave to Abraham." [5]Then Isaac sent Jacob on his way, and he went to Paddan Aram, to Laban son of Bethuel the Aramean, the brother of Rebekah, who was the mother of Jacob and Esau.

[6]Now Esau learned that Isaac had blessed Jacob and had sent him to Paddan Aram to take a wife from there, and that when he blessed him he commanded him, "Do not marry a Canaanite woman," [7]and that Jacob had obeyed his father and mother and had gone to Paddan Aram. [8]Esau then realized how displeasing the Canaanite women were to his father Isaac; [9]so he went to Ishmael and married Mahalath, the sister of Nebaioth and daughter of Ishmael son of Abraham, in addition to the wives he already had.

[a] 2 That is, Northwest Mesopotamia; also in verses 5, 6 and 7   [b] 3 Hebrew El-Shaddai

JACOB'S DREAM AT BETHEL

[10]Jacob left Beersheba and set out for Harran. [11]When he reached a certain place, he stopped for the night because the sun had set. Taking one of the stones there, he put it under his head and lay down to sleep. [12]He had a dream in which he saw a stairway resting on the earth, with its top reaching to heaven, and the angels of God were ascending and descending on it. [13]There above it[a] stood the LORD, and he said: "I am the LORD, the God of your father Abraham and the God of Isaac. I will give you and your descendants the land on which you are lying. [14]Your descendants will be like the dust of the earth, and you will spread out to the west and to the east, to the north and to the south. All peoples on earth will be blessed through you and your offspring.[b] [15]I am with you and will watch over you wherever you go, and I will bring you back to this land. I will not leave you until I have done what I have promised you."

[16]When Jacob awoke from his sleep, he thought, "Surely the LORD is in this place, and I was not aware of it." [17]He was afraid and said, "How awesome is this place! This is none other than the house of God; this is the gate of heaven."

[18]Early the next morning Jacob took the stone he had placed under his head and set it up as a pillar and poured oil on top of it. [19]He called that place Bethel,[c] though the city used to be called Luz.

[20]Then Jacob made a vow, saying, "If God will be with me and will watch over me on this journey I am taking and will give me food to eat and clothes to wear [21]so that I return safely to my father's household, then the LORD[d] will be my God [22]and[e] this stone that I have set up as a pillar will be God's house, and of all that you give me I will give you a tenth."

JACOB ARRIVES IN PADDAN ARAM

29 Then Jacob continued on his journey and came to the land of the eastern peoples. [2]There he saw a well in the open country, with three flocks of sheep lying near it because the flocks were watered from that well. The stone over the mouth of the well was large. [3]When all the flocks were gathered there, the shepherds would roll the stone away from the well's mouth and water the sheep. Then they would return the stone to its place over the mouth of the well.

[4]Jacob asked the shepherds, "My brothers, where are you from?"

"We're from Harran," they replied.

[5]He said to them, "Do you know Laban, Nahor's grandson?"

"Yes, we know him," they answered.

[6]Then Jacob asked them, "Is he well?"

"Yes, he is," they said, "and here comes his daughter Rachel with the sheep."

[7]"Look," he said, "the sun is still high; it is not time for

---

Are dreams messages from God? (28:12–15)
They can be, though they are not always. In this dream God told Jacob he would receive the promises made to his ancestors. If God speaks to us in a dream, it will correspond to the teaching of the Bible. Dreams are not God's normal way of revealing his will.

Why did the dream include a stairway reaching to heaven? (28:12)
The angels going up and down the stairway were a sign that the Lord offered to be Jacob's God and be with him on his journey.

Why did Jacob pour oil on the pillar after his dream? (28:18)
He created the pillar as a memorial to honor God, saying that the spot where God talked to him was holy. Oil was used symbolically to dedicate the spot to God.

Was Jacob making a bargain with God? (28:20)
It's possible that Jacob was bargaining with God for the very thing that God had just promised him. Or it may have been a general promise that Isaac made in thankfulness to God. Jacob accepted the God of Abraham and Isaac as his own.

Why did Jacob promise a tenth to God? (28:22)
A tenth, or tithe, was known as the king's share. It was Jacob's way of saying the Lord was his God and King.

Why was a large stone covering the well? (29:2–3)
The stone protected the water from being polluted or tampered with, and it may have been placed there to prevent anyone from falling in. When Jacob rolled the stone away by himself (verse 10), it was a feat of unusual strength because the stone was so large.

---

[a] 13 Or *There beside him*   [b] 14 Or *will use your name and the name of your offspring in blessings* (see 48:20)   [c] 19 *Bethel* means *house of God.*
[d] 20,21 Or *Since God . . . father's household, the* LORD   [e] 21,22 Or *household, and the* LORD *will be my God,* [22]*then*

the flocks to be gathered. Water the sheep and take them back to pasture."

[8] "We can't," they replied, "until all the flocks are gathered and the stone has been rolled away from the mouth of the well. Then we will water the sheep."

[9] While he was still talking with them, Rachel came with her father's sheep, for she was a shepherd. [10] When Jacob saw Rachel daughter of his uncle Laban, and Laban's sheep, he went over and rolled the stone away from the mouth of the well and watered his uncle's sheep. [11] Then Jacob kissed Rachel and began to weep aloud. [12] He had told Rachel that he was a relative of her father and a son of Rebekah. So she ran and told her father.

[13] As soon as Laban heard the news about Jacob, his sister's son, he hurried to meet him. He embraced him and kissed him and brought him to his home, and there Jacob told him all these things. [14] Then Laban said to him, "You are my own flesh and blood."

JACOB MARRIES LEAH AND RACHEL

After Jacob had stayed with him for a whole month, [15] Laban said to him, "Just because you are a relative of mine, should you work for me for nothing? Tell me what your wages should be."

[16] Now Laban had two daughters; the name of the older was Leah, and the name of the younger was Rachel. [17] Leah had weak[a] eyes, but Rachel had a lovely figure and was beautiful. [18] Jacob was in love with Rachel and said, "I'll work for you seven years in return for your younger daughter Rachel."

[19] Laban said, "It's better that I give her to you than to some other man. Stay here with me." [20] So Jacob served seven years to get Rachel, but they seemed like only a few days to him because of his love for her.

[21] Then Jacob said to Laban, "Give me my wife. My time is completed, and I want to make love to her."

[22] So Laban brought together all the people of the place and gave a feast. [23] But when evening came, he took his daughter Leah and brought her to Jacob, and Jacob made love to her. [24] And Laban gave his servant Zilpah to his daughter as her attendant.

[25] When morning came, there was Leah! So Jacob said to Laban, "What is this you have done to me? I served you for Rachel, didn't I? Why have you deceived me?"

[26] Laban replied, "It is not our custom here to give the younger daughter in marriage before the older one. [27] Finish this daughter's bridal week; then we will give you the younger one also, in return for another seven years of work."

[28] And Jacob did so. He finished the week with Leah, and then Laban gave him his daughter Rachel to be his wife. [29] Laban gave his servant Bilhah to his daughter Rachel as her attendant. [30] Jacob made love to Rachel also, and his love for Rachel was greater than his love for Leah. And he worked for Laban another seven years.

[a] 17 Or *delicate*

Why did Jacob kiss Rachel and cry? (29:11)
Jacob was probably overcome with emotion at finding a relative in a faraway land. He was weeping for joy and in gratitude to God for guiding him here. This kiss between relatives was part of the culture and not a sign of romantic love.

Why did Jacob work for seven years? (29:18)
Jacob worked for seven years as his gift to Laban to show that he valued Laban's daughter. It was how he compensated Laban for taking away a valuable worker.

Why didn't Jacob recognize Leah on his wedding night? (29:25)
The darkness in the tent or a veil may have hidden Leah's face. Or perhaps Jacob had drunk too much wine at his own wedding celebration.

Why did Laban deceive Jacob? (29:26–27)
Laban was following the custom that the elder daughter be married first. It seems that he found a way to trick Jacob into more service. This was ironic since Jacob, the deceiver, was deceived himself.

What was a bridal week? (29:27)
It was a wedding feast that usually lasted seven days.

Why did Laban give Rachel his servant girl to be her maid? (29:29)
Rachel received Bilhah as a wedding gift from her father. This was a wedding custom common in many ancient marriage contracts.

JACOB'S CHILDREN

³¹When the LORD saw that Leah was not loved, he enabled her to conceive, but Rachel remained childless. ³²Leah became pregnant and gave birth to a son. She named him Reuben,^a for she said, "It is because the LORD has seen my misery. Surely my husband will love me now."

³³She conceived again, and when she gave birth to a son she said, "Because the LORD heard that I am not loved, he gave me this one too." So she named him Simeon.^b

³⁴Again she conceived, and when she gave birth to a son she said, "Now at last my husband will become attached to me, because I have borne him three sons." So he was named Levi.^c

³⁵She conceived again, and when she gave birth to a son she said, "This time I will praise the LORD." So she named him Judah.^d Then she stopped having children.

30 When Rachel saw that she was not bearing Jacob any children, she became jealous of her sister. So she said to Jacob, "Give me children, or I'll die!"

²Jacob became angry with her and said, "Am I in the place of God, who has kept you from having children?"

³Then she said, "Here is Bilhah, my servant. Sleep with her so that she can bear children for me and I too can build a family through her."

⁴So she gave him her servant Bilhah as a wife. Jacob slept with her, ⁵and she became pregnant and bore him a son. ⁶Then Rachel said, "God has vindicated me; he has listened to my plea and given me a son." Because of this she named him Dan.^e

⁷Rachel's servant Bilhah conceived again and bore Jacob a second son. ⁸Then Rachel said, "I have had a great struggle with my sister, and I have won." So she named him Naphtali.^f

⁹When Leah saw that she had stopped having children, she took her servant Zilpah and gave her to Jacob as a wife. ¹⁰Leah's servant Zilpah bore Jacob a son. ¹¹Then Leah said, "What good fortune!"^g So she named him Gad.^h

¹²Leah's servant Zilpah bore Jacob a second son. ¹³Then Leah said, "How happy I am! The women will call me happy." So she named him Asher.ⁱ

¹⁴During wheat harvest, Reuben went out into the fields and found some mandrake plants, which he brought to his mother Leah. Rachel said to Leah, "Please give me some of your son's mandrakes."

¹⁵But she said to her, "Wasn't it enough that you took away my husband? Will you take my son's mandrakes too?"

"Very well," Rachel said, "he can sleep with you tonight in return for your son's mandrakes."

¹⁶So when Jacob came in from the fields that evening, Leah went out to meet him. "You must sleep with me," she

---

^a *32 Reuben sounds like the Hebrew for he has seen my misery; the name means see, a son.* ^b *33 Simeon probably means one who hears.* ^c *34 Levi sounds like and may be derived from the Hebrew for attached.* ^d *35 Judah sounds like and may be derived from the Hebrew for praise.* ^e *6 Dan here means he has vindicated.* ^f *8 Naphtali means my struggle.* ^g *11 Or "A troop is coming!"* ^h *11 Gad can mean good fortune or a troop.* ⁱ *13 Asher means happy.*

Why did God give children only to Leah? (29:31)
God was comforting Leah, the unloved wife. She became the mother of Jacob's first four sons, including Judah, who would be the ancestor of David and ultimately Jesus.

Why did Leah name her sons as she did? (29:32–35)
Sometimes a name is prophetic, indicating God's plan for a child. In this case, the sons were named for the circumstance of their births.

How did Bilhah's child become Rachel's? (30:3–6)
Since Rachel was unable to have children, she could not fulfill her primary role in the marriage. The custom was then to have a maid become like a second wife (called a concubine) to bear a child who would then be adopted by the wife.

Why did Rachel want the mandrake plants? (30:14)
The mandrake plant has fleshy, forked roots that look like the lower part of a human body. Eating the roots was thought to increase the chance of getting pregnant. Rachel believed this superstition and was hoping to still become pregnant.

Did Rachel become pregnant because of the mandrakes? (30:16–24)
No. Even though Rachel tried to get what she wanted by magical means, God listened to her prayers and enabled her to have a child.

said. "I have hired you with my son's mandrakes." So he slept with her that night.

[17] God listened to Leah, and she became pregnant and bore Jacob a fifth son. [18] Then Leah said, "God has rewarded me for giving my servant to my husband." So she named him Issachar.[a]

[19] Leah conceived again and bore Jacob a sixth son. [20] Then Leah said, "God has presented me with a precious gift. This time my husband will treat me with honor, because I have borne him six sons." So she named him Zebulun.[b]

[21] Some time later she gave birth to a daughter and named her Dinah.

[22] Then God remembered Rachel; he listened to her and enabled her to conceive. [23] She became pregnant and gave birth to a son and said, "God has taken away my disgrace." [24] She named him Joseph,[c] and said, "May the LORD add to me another son."

JACOB'S FLOCKS INCREASE

[25] After Rachel gave birth to Joseph, Jacob said to Laban, "Send me on my way so I can go back to my own homeland. [26] Give me my wives and children, for whom I have served you, and I will be on my way. You know how much work I've done for you."

[27] But Laban said to him, "If I have found favor in your eyes, please stay. I have learned by divination that the LORD has blessed me because of you." [28] He added, "Name your wages, and I will pay them."

[29] Jacob said to him, "You know how I have worked for you and how your livestock has fared under my care. [30] The little you had before I came has increased greatly, and the LORD has blessed you wherever I have been. But now, when may I do something for my own household?"

[31] "What shall I give you?" he asked.

"Don't give me anything," Jacob replied. "But if you will do this one thing for me, I will go on tending your flocks and watching over them: [32] Let me go through all your flocks today and remove from them every speckled or spotted sheep, every dark-colored lamb and every spotted or speckled goat. They will be my wages. [33] And my honesty will testify for me in the future, whenever you check on the wages you have paid me. Any goat in my possession that is not speckled or spotted, or any lamb that is not dark-colored, will be considered stolen."

[34] "Agreed," said Laban. "Let it be as you have said." [35] That same day he removed all the male goats that were streaked or spotted, and all the speckled or spotted female goats (all that had white on them) and all the dark-colored lambs, and he placed them in the care of his sons. [36] Then he put a three-day journey between himself and Jacob, while Jacob continued to tend the rest of Laban's flocks.

[37] Jacob, however, took fresh-cut branches from poplar, almond and plane trees and made white stripes on them by

Why did Dinah's birth seem unimportant? (30:21)
Families in Bible times did not value daughters as much they did sons. A daughter would marry and leave to help her husband's family, and she would not carry on the family name.

What was Rachel's disgrace? (30:23)
Being unable to have children was considered to be shameful and a sign of God's disfavor.

What was divination? (30:27)
Divination was an attempt to receive messages from the spirit world. People in the pagan world often believed they would know their god's will by examining a sacrificial animal's internal organs or by looking for pictures in water. Laban claimed he had received a message from God through these means.

Why did Laban agree to Jacob's plan and then remove the flocks? (30:35)
Laban pretended to agree with Jacob, but then he tried to outsmart him. He secretly took the animals that should have been Jacob's wage and sent them far away so Jacob wouldn't find them or know he had been cheated.

Did the striped sticks really cause more and better animals to be born? (30:37–43)
Jacob believed that what the animal saw when mating affected the offspring. Jacob's trick worked, not because of his theory, but because God made it happen.

[a] 18 Issachar sounds like the Hebrew for reward.   [b] 20 Zebulun probably means honor.   [c] 24 Joseph means may he add.

peeling the bark and exposing the white inner wood of the branches. ³⁸Then he placed the peeled branches in all the watering troughs, so that they would be directly in front of the flocks when they came to drink. When the flocks were in heat and came to drink, ³⁹they mated in front of the branches. And they bore young that were streaked or speckled or spotted. ⁴⁰Jacob set apart the young of the flock by themselves, but made the rest face the streaked and dark-colored animals that belonged to Laban. Thus he made separate flocks for himself and did not put them with Laban's animals. ⁴¹Whenever the stronger females were in heat, Jacob would place the branches in the troughs in front of the animals so they would mate near the branches, ⁴²but if the animals were weak, he would not place them there. So the weak animals went to Laban and the strong ones to Jacob. ⁴³In this way the man grew exceedingly prosperous and came to own large flocks, and female and male servants, and camels and donkeys.

JACOB FLEES FROM LABAN

31 Jacob heard that Laban's sons were saying, "Jacob has taken everything our father owned and has gained all this wealth from what belonged to our father." ²And Jacob noticed that Laban's attitude toward him was not what it had been.

³Then the LORD said to Jacob, "Go back to the land of your fathers and to your relatives, and I will be with you."

⁴So Jacob sent word to Rachel and Leah to come out to the fields where his flocks were. ⁵He said to them, "I see that your father's attitude toward me is not what it was before, but the God of my father has been with me. ⁶You know that I've worked for your father with all my strength, ⁷yet your father has cheated me by changing my wages ten times. However, God has not allowed him to harm me. ⁸If he said, 'The speckled ones will be your wages,' then all the flocks gave birth to speckled young; and if he said, 'The streaked ones will be your wages,' then all the flocks bore streaked young. ⁹So God has taken away your father's livestock and has given them to me.

¹⁰"In breeding season I once had a dream in which I looked up and saw that the male goats mating with the flock were streaked, speckled or spotted. ¹¹The angel of God said to me in the dream, 'Jacob.' I answered, 'Here I am.' ¹²And he said, 'Look up and see that all the male goats mating with the flock are streaked, speckled or spotted, for I have seen all that Laban has been doing to you. ¹³I am the God of Bethel, where you anointed a pillar and where you made a vow to me. Now leave this land at once and go back to your native land.'"

¹⁴Then Rachel and Leah replied, "Do we still have any share in the inheritance of our father's estate? ¹⁵Does he not regard us as foreigners? Not only has he sold us, but he has used up what was paid for us. ¹⁶Surely all the wealth that God took away from our father belongs to us and our children. So do whatever God has told you."

How did Laban's attitude toward Jacob change? (31:2) Jacob had worked hard for his father-in-law for 20 years, but during the last 6 years Jacob had grown extremely rich. Laban and his sons thought that Jacob had taken advantage of them and were worried about what would be left of their inheritance.

If Jacob credited God with making him prosper, why did he scheme? (31:9) Jacob's faith was not perfect. His scheme to increase his livestock worked, but he admitted it was because of God's power and not his own superstition.

How do we know if a dream is from God? (31:11) Sometimes God speaks to people in dreams. But not all dreams are from God. We have God's Word to us in the Bible, so we know that dreams that are from God will not contradict his Word.

What vow did Jacob make when he anointed the pillar? (31:13) Jacob vowed that the Lord would be his God if God kept his promise that Jacob and his descendants would inherit the land of Canaan. (See Genesis 28:13, 20–22.)

Why did Rachel and Leah say their father sold them? (31:15) Though Laban did a lot of questionable things, he didn't actually sell his daughters. When he agreed to let Jacob marry his daughters, Jacob was required to pay Laban for the legal custody that protected the women. It was a type of business deal and was very common for this culture and time period.

¹⁷Then Jacob put his children and his wives on camels, ¹⁸and he drove all his livestock ahead of him, along with all the goods he had accumulated in Paddan Aram,^a to go to his father Isaac in the land of Canaan.

¹⁹When Laban had gone to shear his sheep, Rachel stole her father's household gods. ²⁰Moreover, Jacob deceived Laban the Aramean by not telling him he was running away. ²¹So he fled with all he had, crossed the Euphrates River, and headed for the hill country of Gilead.

LABAN PURSUES JACOB

²²On the third day Laban was told that Jacob had fled. ²³Taking his relatives with him, he pursued Jacob for seven days and caught up with him in the hill country of Gilead. ²⁴Then God came to Laban the Aramean in a dream at night and said to him, "Be careful not to say anything to Jacob, either good or bad."

²⁵Jacob had pitched his tent in the hill country of Gilead when Laban overtook him, and Laban and his relatives camped there too. ²⁶Then Laban said to Jacob, "What have you done? You've deceived me, and you've carried off my daughters like captives in war. ²⁷Why did you run off secretly and deceive me? Why didn't you tell me, so I could send you away with joy and singing to the music of timbrels and harps? ²⁸You didn't even let me kiss my grandchildren and my daughters goodbye. You have done a foolish thing. ²⁹I have the power to harm you; but last night the God of your father said to me, 'Be careful not to say anything to Jacob, either good or bad.' ³⁰Now you have gone off because you longed to return to your father's household. But why did you steal my gods?"

³¹Jacob answered Laban, "I was afraid, because I thought you would take your daughters away from me by force. ³²But if you find anyone who has your gods, that person shall not live. In the presence of our relatives, see for yourself whether there is anything of yours here with me; and if so, take it." Now Jacob did not know that Rachel had stolen the gods.

³³So Laban went into Jacob's tent and into Leah's tent and into the tent of the two female servants, but he found nothing. After he came out of Leah's tent, he entered Rachel's tent. ³⁴Now Rachel had taken the household gods and put them inside her camel's saddle and was sitting on them. Laban searched through everything in the tent but found nothing.

³⁵Rachel said to her father, "Don't be angry, my lord, that I cannot stand up in your presence; I'm having my period." So he searched but could not find the household gods.

³⁶Jacob was angry and took Laban to task. "What is my crime?" he asked Laban. "How have I wronged you that you hunt me down? ³⁷Now that you have searched through all my goods, what have you found that belongs to your household? Put it here in front of your relatives and mine, and let them judge between the two of us.

³⁸"I have been with you for twenty years now. Your sheep

^a *18* That is, Northwest Mesopotamia

Why did Rachel steal her father's idols? (31:19)
Perhaps she still believed the pagan gods would protect and bless her. Or perhaps she knew that having these idols would help her claim an inheritance from her father.

Why did God forbid Laban from saying anything to Jacob? (31:24)
Perhaps God was warning Laban to keep his anger in check. Maybe God did not want Laban to prevent Jacob from returning to Canaan.

Why did Rachel remain seated? (31:35)
Women in her time showed respect to men by standing when the men entered the room. If a woman was having her menstrual period, she was excused from standing. Rachel was deceiving her father in order to keep her theft from being discovered.

Was Jacob at fault in his dealings with Laban? (31:36–37)
Jacob had deceived Laban about his departure, but his prosperity was a result of God being with him. God kept Jacob and his family safe.

and goats have not miscarried, nor have I eaten rams from your flocks. [39]I did not bring you animals torn by wild beasts; I bore the loss myself. And you demanded payment from me for whatever was stolen by day or night. [40]This was my situation: The heat consumed me in the daytime and the cold at night, and sleep fled from my eyes. [41]It was like this for the twenty years I was in your household. I worked for you fourteen years for your two daughters and six years for your flocks, and you changed my wages ten times. [42]If the God of my father, the God of Abraham and the Fear of Isaac, had not been with me, you would surely have sent me away empty-handed. But God has seen my hardship and the toil of my hands, and last night he rebuked you."

[43]Laban answered Jacob, "The women are my daughters, the children are my children, and the flocks are my flocks. All you see is mine. Yet what can I do today about these daughters of mine, or about the children they have borne? [44]Come now, let's make a covenant, you and I, and let it serve as a witness between us."

[45]So Jacob took a stone and set it up as a pillar. [46]He said to his relatives, "Gather some stones." So they took stones and piled them in a heap, and they ate there by the heap. [47]Laban called it Jegar Sahadutha, and Jacob called it Galeed.[a]

[48]Laban said, "This heap is a witness between you and me today." That is why it was called Galeed. [49]It was also called Mizpah,[b] because he said, "May the LORD keep watch between you and me when we are away from each other. [50]If you mistreat my daughters or if you take any wives besides my daughters, even though no one is with us, remember that God is a witness between you and me."

[51]Laban also said to Jacob, "Here is this heap, and here is this pillar I have set up between you and me. [52]This heap is a witness, and this pillar is a witness, that I will not go past this heap to your side to harm you and that you will not go past this heap and pillar to my side to harm me. [53]May the God of Abraham and the God of Nahor, the God of their father, judge between us."

So Jacob took an oath in the name of the Fear of his father Isaac. [54]He offered a sacrifice there in the hill country and invited his relatives to a meal. After they had eaten, they spent the night there.

[55]Early the next morning Laban kissed his grandchildren and his daughters and blessed them. Then he left and returned home.[c]

JACOB PREPARES TO MEET ESAU

32[d] Jacob also went on his way, and the angels of God met him. [2]When Jacob saw them, he said, "This is the camp of God!" So he named that place Mahanaim.[e]

[3]Jacob sent messengers ahead of him to his brother Esau in the land of Seir, the country of Edom. [4]He instructed

---

[a] 47 The Aramaic *Jegar Sahadutha* and the Hebrew *Galeed* both mean *witness heap*.   [b] 49 Mizpah means *watchtower*.   [c] 55 In Hebrew texts this verse (31:55) is numbered 32:1.   [d] In Hebrew texts 32:1-32 is numbered 32:2-33.   [e] 2 Mahanaim means *two camps*.

Why is God called *the Fear of Isaac*? (31:42)
This is another name for God. The Hebrew word suggests *kinsman* and stresses the close relationship between God and Isaac.

What did the stone heap and pillar mean? (31:45–53)
They were a sign of the promise made between Jacob and Laban under God's watchful eyes.

Why did Laban not want Jacob to marry again? (31:50)
Laban was trying to protect his daughters and their children. He did not want Jacob's wealth shared with other wives.

Why did God send angels to Jacob? (32:1–2)
Jacob was entering the land God had promised him and the land of the brother he had deceived. God sent the angels as a sign that God was with Jacob, as he had promised.

How did Jacob try to make amends with Esau? (32:4, 13–15)
Jacob was humble and called himself Esau's servant. He sent people ahead with gifts of livestock for Esau. Most importantly, he prayed to God to save him from his brother.

Why did Esau bring 400 men with him? (32:6)
This was a large number of warriors. Twenty years earlier Esau had vowed revenge because Jacob had taken his birthright and blessing. He may have intended to kill Jacob and his family and take back his inheritance.

Who wrestled with Jacob? (32:24–30)
The stranger wrestled with Jacob for hours without getting tired. Then he was able to dislocate Jacob's hip while barely touching him. Jacob realized eventually that it was God himself in the form of an angel.

Why did Jacob ask a blessing from someone who had just hurt him? (32:26)
Jacob wanted the stranger's blessing as a kind of certainty that he would be able to overcome his brother's anger. Jacob really believed the stranger was God. The angel could have easily killed him. But he showed Jacob compassion, a trait God embodies.

them: "This is what you are to say to my lord Esau: 'Your servant Jacob says, I have been staying with Laban and have remained there till now. [5]I have cattle and donkeys, sheep and goats, male and female servants. Now I am sending this message to my lord, that I may find favor in your eyes.'"

[6]When the messengers returned to Jacob, they said, "We went to your brother Esau, and now he is coming to meet you, and four hundred men are with him."

[7]In great fear and distress Jacob divided the people who were with him into two groups,[a] and the flocks and herds and camels as well. [8]He thought, "If Esau comes and attacks one group,[b] the group[b] that is left may escape."

[9]Then Jacob prayed, "O God of my father Abraham, God of my father Isaac, LORD, you who said to me, 'Go back to your country and your relatives, and I will make you prosper,' [10]I am unworthy of all the kindness and faithfulness you have shown your servant. I had only my staff when I crossed this Jordan, but now I have become two camps. [11]Save me, I pray, from the hand of my brother Esau, for I am afraid he will come and attack me, and also the mothers with their children. [12]But you have said, 'I will surely make you prosper and will make your descendants like the sand of the sea, which cannot be counted.'"

[13]He spent the night there, and from what he had with him he selected a gift for his brother Esau: [14]two hundred female goats and twenty male goats, two hundred ewes and twenty rams, [15]thirty female camels with their young, forty cows and ten bulls, and twenty female donkeys and ten male donkeys. [16]He put them in the care of his servants, each herd by itself, and said to his servants, "Go ahead of me, and keep some space between the herds."

[17]He instructed the one in the lead: "When my brother Esau meets you and asks, 'Who do you belong to, and where are you going, and who owns all these animals in front of you?' [18]then you are to say, 'They belong to your servant Jacob. They are a gift sent to my lord Esau, and he is coming behind us.'"

[19]He also instructed the second, the third and all the others who followed the herds: "You are to say the same thing to Esau when you meet him. [20]And be sure to say, 'Your servant Jacob is coming behind us.'" For he thought, "I will pacify him with these gifts I am sending on ahead; later, when I see him, perhaps he will receive me." [21]So Jacob's gifts went on ahead of him, but he himself spent the night in the camp.

JACOB WRESTLES WITH GOD

[22]That night Jacob got up and took his two wives, his two female servants and his eleven sons and crossed the ford of the Jabbok. [23]After he had sent them across the stream, he sent over all his possessions. [24]So Jacob was left alone, and a man wrestled with him till daybreak. [25]When the man saw that he could not overpower him, he touched the socket of Jacob's hip so that his hip was wrenched as he wrestled with the man. [26]Then the man said, "Let me go, for it is daybreak."

[a] 7 Or *camps*   [b] 8 Or *camp*

But Jacob replied, "I will not let you go unless you bless me."

²⁷The man asked him, "What is your name?"

"Jacob," he answered.

²⁸Then the man said, "Your name will no longer be Jacob, but Israel,^a because you have struggled with God and with humans and have overcome."

²⁹Jacob said, "Please tell me your name."

But he replied, "Why do you ask my name?" Then he blessed him there.

³⁰So Jacob called the place Peniel,^b saying, "It is because I saw God face to face, and yet my life was spared."

³¹The sun rose above him as he passed Peniel,^c and he was limping because of his hip. ³²Therefore to this day the Israelites do not eat the tendon attached to the socket of the hip, because the socket of Jacob's hip was touched near the tendon.

JACOB MEETS ESAU

33 Jacob looked up and there was Esau, coming with his four hundred men; so he divided the children among Leah, Rachel and the two female servants. ²He put the female servants and their children in front, Leah and her children next, and Rachel and Joseph in the rear. ³He himself went on ahead and bowed down to the ground seven times as he approached his brother.

⁴But Esau ran to meet Jacob and embraced him; he threw his arms around his neck and kissed him. And they wept. ⁵Then Esau looked up and saw the women and children. "Who are these with you?" he asked.

Jacob answered, "They are the children God has graciously given your servant."

⁶Then the female servants and their children approached and bowed down. ⁷Next, Leah and her children came and bowed down. Last of all came Joseph and Rachel, and they too bowed down.

⁸Esau asked, "What's the meaning of all these flocks and herds I met?"

"To find favor in your eyes, my lord," he said.

⁹But Esau said, "I already have plenty, my brother. Keep what you have for yourself."

¹⁰"No, please!" said Jacob. "If I have found favor in your eyes, accept this gift from me. For to see your face is like seeing the face of God, now that you have received me favorably. ¹¹Please accept the present that was brought to you, for God has been gracious to me and I have all I need." And because Jacob insisted, Esau accepted it.

¹²Then Esau said, "Let us be on our way; I'll accompany you."

¹³But Jacob said to him, "My lord knows that the children are tender and that I must care for the ewes and cows that are nursing their young. If they are driven hard just one day, all the animals will die. ¹⁴So let my lord go on ahead of his

Why was Jacob's name changed to Israel? (32:28) Israel means "he struggles with God." Later it would also be the name of the nation that descended from Jacob. In ancient times, a person's name was changed to mark something important in that person's life.

Was there a reason Jacob put his family in this order? (33:2) Jacob wanted to keep his favorite wife and child away from possible danger. If Esau killed the first groups, those in the back would have a chance to escape.

Why was seeing Esau like seeing the face of God? (33:10) Esau's face was probably so warm and accepting that Jacob knew God had changed his brother's heart and his feelings toward him.

---

^a 28 *Israel* probably means *he struggles with God.*   ^b 30 *Peniel* means *face of God.*   ^c 31 Hebrew *Penuel,* a variant of *Peniel*

servant, while I move along slowly at the pace of the flocks and herds before me and the pace of the children, until I come to my lord in Seir."

¹⁵Esau said, "Then let me leave some of my men with you."

"But why do that?" Jacob asked. "Just let me find favor in the eyes of my lord."

¹⁶So that day Esau started on his way back to Seir. ¹⁷Jacob, however, went to Sukkoth, where he built a place for himself and made shelters for his livestock. That is why the place is called Sukkoth.ᵃ

¹⁸After Jacob came from Paddan Aram,ᵇ he arrived safely at the city of Shechem in Canaan and camped within sight of the city. ¹⁹For a hundred pieces of silver,ᶜ he bought from the sons of Hamor, the father of Shechem, the plot of ground where he pitched his tent. ²⁰There he set up an altar and called it El Elohe Israel.ᵈ

DINAH AND THE SHECHEMITES

34 Now Dinah, the daughter Leah had borne to Jacob, went out to visit the women of the land. ²When Shechem son of Hamor the Hivite, the ruler of that area, saw her, he took her and raped her. ³His heart was drawn to Dinah daughter of Jacob; he loved the young woman and spoke tenderly to her. ⁴And Shechem said to his father Hamor, "Get me this girl as my wife."

⁵When Jacob heard that his daughter Dinah had been defiled, his sons were in the fields with his livestock; so he did nothing about it until they came home.

⁶Then Shechem's father Hamor went out to talk with Jacob. ⁷Meanwhile, Jacob's sons had come in from the fields as soon as they heard what had happened. They were shocked and furious, because Shechem had done an outrageous thing inᵉ Israel by sleeping with Jacob's daughter—a thing that should not be done.

⁸But Hamor said to them, "My son Shechem has his heart set on your daughter. Please give her to him as his wife. ⁹Intermarry with us; give us your daughters and take our daughters for yourselves. ¹⁰You can settle among us; the land is open to you. Live in it, tradeᶠ in it, and acquire property in it."

¹¹Then Shechem said to Dinah's father and brothers, "Let me find favor in your eyes, and I will give you whatever you ask. ¹²Make the price for the bride and the gift I am to bring as great as you like, and I'll pay whatever you ask me. Only give me the young woman as my wife."

¹³Because their sister Dinah had been defiled, Jacob's sons replied deceitfully as they spoke to Shechem and his father Hamor. ¹⁴They said to them, "We can't do such a thing; we can't give our sister to a man who is not circumcised. That would be a disgrace to us. ¹⁵We will enter into an agreement with you on one condition only: that you become like us

Why did Jacob set up an altar on this land? (33:20)
After finally returning to the promised land, Jacob set up this altar to show he was making this place his permanent home. The name of the altar means *God, the God of Israel* and includes Jacob's new name, Israel.

Why didn't Shechem suggest marriage himself? (34:4)
It was the custom in the ancient Middle East to have marriages arranged by the parents, especially for members of different clans or nations. Besides, it is unlikely that Dinah would agree to marry the man who had just raped her.

What does it mean that Dinah had been defiled? (34:5)
Shechem forced himself sexually on Dinah (against her will).

Why was Hamor so eager to have his people intermarry with Jacob's clan? (34:9, 23)
The Canaanites wanted to benefit from the wealth and blessings Jacob had received from the Lord. But marrying people from another nation was a threat to Jacob's descendants, who were God's people.

Was it wrong for Dinah's brothers to demand circumcision? (34:15)
Yes. They were using a sacred ceremony for a sinful purpose. Circumcision (removal of the foreskin of the penis) was a sign of their covenant with God. Dinah's brothers were using circumcision as part of their plot to punish these Canaanites for Dinah's rape, not to introduce them to God.

ᵃ 17 *Sukkoth* means *shelters.*   ᵇ 18 That is, Northwest Mesopotamia
ᶜ 19 Hebrew *hundred kesitahs*; a kesitah was a unit of money of unknown weight and value.   ᵈ 20 *El Elohe Israel* can mean *El is the God of Israel* or *mighty is the God of Israel.*   ᵉ 7 Or *against*   ᶠ 10 Or *move about freely*; also in verse 21

by circumcising all your males. ¹⁶Then we will give you our daughters and take your daughters for ourselves. We'll settle among you and become one people with you. ¹⁷But if you will not agree to be circumcised, we'll take our sister and go."

¹⁸Their proposal seemed good to Hamor and his son Shechem. ¹⁹The young man, who was the most honored of all his father's family, lost no time in doing what they said, because he was delighted with Jacob's daughter. ²⁰So Hamor and his son Shechem went to the gate of their city to speak to the men of their city. ²¹"These men are friendly toward us," they said. "Let them live in our land and trade in it; the land has plenty of room for them. We can marry their daughters and they can marry ours. ²²But the men will agree to live with us as one people only on the condition that our males be circumcised, as they themselves are. ²³Won't their livestock, their property and all their other animals become ours? So let us agree to their terms, and they will settle among us."

²⁴All the men who went out of the city gate agreed with Hamor and his son Shechem, and every male in the city was circumcised.

²⁵Three days later, while all of them were still in pain, two of Jacob's sons, Simeon and Levi, Dinah's brothers, took their swords and attacked the unsuspecting city, killing every male. ²⁶They put Hamor and his son Shechem to the sword and took Dinah from Shechem's house and left. ²⁷The sons of Jacob came upon the dead bodies and looted the city where[a] their sister had been defiled. ²⁸They seized their flocks and herds and donkeys and everything else of theirs in the city and out in the fields. ²⁹They carried off all their wealth and all their women and children, taking as plunder everything in the houses.

³⁰Then Jacob said to Simeon and Levi, "You have brought trouble on me by making me obnoxious to the Canaanites and Perizzites, the people living in this land. We are few in number, and if they join forces against me and attack me, I and my household will be destroyed."

³¹But they replied, "Should he have treated our sister like a prostitute?"

JACOB RETURNS TO BETHEL

35 Then God said to Jacob, "Go up to Bethel and settle there, and build an altar there to God, who appeared to you when you were fleeing from your brother Esau."

²So Jacob said to his household and to all who were with him, "Get rid of the foreign gods you have with you, and purify yourselves and change your clothes. ³Then come, let us go up to Bethel, where I will build an altar to God, who answered me in the day of my distress and who has been with me wherever I have gone." ⁴So they gave Jacob all the foreign gods they had and the rings in their ears, and Jacob buried them under the oak at Shechem. ⁵Then they set out, and the terror of God fell on the towns all around them so that no one pursued them.

[a] 27 Or *because*

Why did Jacob's sons kill all the men in the city? (34:25)
If they had killed only Shechem, the men of the city would have come after them for revenge. During that time, an entire clan or community might be held responsible for one person's crime.

Why was Dinah staying in Shechem's house? (34:26)
Since Dinah had been raped, the proper but humiliating response was to stay in Shechem's tent until the marriage ceremony took place.

Why did Jacob's family have foreign gods? (35:2)
Rachel had brought her father's household idols with her, probably as a type of good-luck charm. The captives from Shechem's city probably had their idols with them, too. Jacob's children may have accepted some of the religious beliefs of the pagans in the surrounding cultures.

Why did they also give Jacob their earrings? (35:4)
As part of a pagan religious custom, the earrings were worn as charms to ward off evil or bring good luck.

[6]Jacob and all the people with him came to Luz (that is, Bethel) in the land of Canaan. [7]There he built an altar, and he called the place El Bethel,[a] because it was there that God revealed himself to him when he was fleeing from his brother.

[8]Now Deborah, Rebekah's nurse, died and was buried under the oak outside Bethel. So it was named Allon Bakuth.[b]

[9]After Jacob returned from Paddan Aram,[c] God appeared to him again and blessed him. [10]God said to him, "Your name is Jacob,[d] but you will no longer be called Jacob; your name will be Israel.[e]" So he named him Israel.

[11]And God said to him, "I am God Almighty[f]; be fruitful and increase in number. A nation and a community of nations will come from you, and kings will be among your descendants. [12]The land I gave to Abraham and Isaac I also give to you, and I will give this land to your descendants after you." [13]Then God went up from him at the place where he had talked with him.

[14]Jacob set up a stone pillar at the place where God had talked with him, and he poured out a drink offering on it; he also poured oil on it. [15]Jacob called the place where God had talked with him Bethel.[g]

THE DEATHS OF RACHEL AND ISAAC

[16]Then they moved on from Bethel. While they were still some distance from Ephrath, Rachel began to give birth and had great difficulty. [17]And as she was having great difficulty in childbirth, the midwife said to her, "Don't despair, for you have another son." [18]As she breathed her last—for she was dying—she named her son Ben-Oni.[h] But his father named him Benjamin.[i]

[19]So Rachel died and was buried on the way to Ephrath (that is, Bethlehem). [20]Over her tomb Jacob set up a pillar, and to this day that pillar marks Rachel's tomb.

[21]Israel moved on again and pitched his tent beyond Migdal Eder. [22]While Israel was living in that region, Reuben went in and slept with his father's concubine Bilhah, and Israel heard of it.

Jacob had twelve sons:
[23]The sons of Leah:
    Reuben the firstborn of Jacob,
    Simeon, Levi, Judah, Issachar and Zebulun.
[24]The sons of Rachel:
    Joseph and Benjamin.
[25]The sons of Rachel's servant Bilhah:
    Dan and Naphtali.
[26]The sons of Leah's servant Zilpah:
    Gad and Asher.
These were the sons of Jacob, who were born to him in Paddan Aram.

---

[a] 7 *El Bethel* means *God of Bethel*.   [b] 8 *Allon Bakuth* means *oak of weeping*.   [c] 9 That is, Northwest Mesopotamia; also in verse 26   [d] 10 *Jacob* means *he grasps the heel*, a Hebrew idiom for *he deceives*.   [e] 10 *Israel* probably means *he struggles with God*.   [f] 11 Hebrew *El-Shaddai*   [g] 15 *Bethel* means *house of God*.   [h] 18 *Ben-Oni* means *son of my trouble*.   [i] 18 *Benjamin* means *son of my right hand*.

What is a drink offering? (35:14)
Wine or oil was poured out sometimes as a sacrifice to honor and thank God.

Why would Reuben sleep with one of Jacob's concubines? (35:22)
As eldest son, Reuben would inherit his father's concubines, but only when his father died. This act was probably impulsive and would be considered adultery. This shameful offense against his father resulted in Reuben losing his legal status as the firstborn heir. (See Genesis 49:3–4.)

Why did Jacob have so many wives? (35:23–26)
The practice of taking many wives (polygamy) was common in the ancient Middle East. It was a sign of wealth and rank because only those rich enough to pay the bride price could afford more than one wife. Polygamy goes against God's original plan for marriage to be between one man and one woman.

²⁷Jacob came home to his father Isaac in Mamre, near Kiriath Arba (that is, Hebron), where Abraham and Isaac had stayed. ²⁸Isaac lived a hundred and eighty years. ²⁹Then he breathed his last and died and was gathered to his people, old and full of years. And his sons Esau and Jacob buried him.

ESAU'S DESCENDANTS

36 This is the account of the family line of Esau (that is, Edom).

²Esau took his wives from the women of Canaan: Adah daughter of Elon the Hittite, and Oholibamah daughter of Anah and granddaughter of Zibeon the Hivite— ³also Basemath daughter of Ishmael and sister of Nebaioth.

⁴Adah bore Eliphaz to Esau, Basemath bore Reuel, ⁵and Oholibamah bore Jeush, Jalam and Korah. These were the sons of Esau, who were born to him in Canaan.

⁶Esau took his wives and sons and daughters and all the members of his household, as well as his livestock and all his other animals and all the goods he had acquired in Canaan, and moved to a land some distance from his brother Jacob. ⁷Their possessions were too great for them to remain together; the land where they were staying could not support them both because of their livestock. ⁸So Esau (that is, Edom) settled in the hill country of Seir.

⁹This is the account of the family line of Esau the father of the Edomites in the hill country of Seir.

¹⁰These are the names of Esau's sons:
Eliphaz, the son of Esau's wife Adah, and Reuel, the son of Esau's wife Basemath.
¹¹The sons of Eliphaz:
Teman, Omar, Zepho, Gatam and Kenaz.
¹²Esau's son Eliphaz also had a concubine named Timna, who bore him Amalek. These were grandsons of Esau's wife Adah.
¹³The sons of Reuel:
Nahath, Zerah, Shammah and Mizzah. These were grandsons of Esau's wife Basemath.
¹⁴The sons of Esau's wife Oholibamah daughter of Anah and granddaughter of Zibeon, whom she bore to Esau:
Jeush, Jalam and Korah.

¹⁵These were the chiefs among Esau's descendants:
The sons of Eliphaz the firstborn of Esau:
Chiefs Teman, Omar, Zepho, Kenaz, ¹⁶Korah,ᵃ Gatam and Amalek. These were the chiefs descended from Eliphaz in Edom; they were grandsons of Adah.
¹⁷The sons of Esau's son Reuel:
Chiefs Nahath, Zerah, Shammah and Mizzah. These were the chiefs descended from Reuel in Edom; they were grandsons of Esau's wife Basemath.

Why list all of Esau's descendants? (36:1–43)
Genealogies were important to people in ancient times to record their history and also to show how they were connected to the community. This genealogy shows how God fulfilled his promise to Sarah to become the mother of nations. (See Genesis 17:16.)

Why were Esau's wives Canaanites? (36:2)
He probably married them because the Canaanites lived nearby. He may not have valued the covenant with Abraham, or he was just trying to create a peaceful relationship with the local people.

Why did Jacob and Esau live far apart? (36:7)
The land where they lived didn't have enough water to support all their livestock. They decided to keep their herds spread out and separate so there would be enough land and water for both.

ᵃ 16 Masoretic Text; Samaritan Pentateuch (also verse 11 and 1 Chron. 1:36) does not have *Korah*.

[18]The sons of Esau's wife Oholibamah:

Chiefs Jeush, Jalam and Korah. These were the chiefs descended from Esau's wife Oholibamah daughter of Anah.

[19]These were the sons of Esau (that is, Edom), and these were their chiefs.

[20]These were the sons of Seir the Horite, who were living in the region:

Lotan, Shobal, Zibeon, Anah, [21]Dishon, Ezer and Dishan. These sons of Seir in Edom were Horite chiefs.

[22]The sons of Lotan:

Hori and Homam.[a] Timna was Lotan's sister.

[23]The sons of Shobal:

Alvan, Manahath, Ebal, Shepho and Onam.

[24]The sons of Zibeon:

Aiah and Anah. This is the Anah who discovered the hot springs[b] in the desert while he was grazing the donkeys of his father Zibeon.

[25]The children of Anah:

Dishon and Oholibamah daughter of Anah.

[26]The sons of Dishon[c]:

Hemdan, Eshban, Ithran and Keran.

[27]The sons of Ezer:

Bilhan, Zaavan and Akan.

[28]The sons of Dishan:

Uz and Aran.

[29]These were the Horite chiefs:

Lotan, Shobal, Zibeon, Anah, [30]Dishon, Ezer and Dishan. These were the Horite chiefs, according to their divisions, in the land of Seir.

THE RULERS OF EDOM

[31]These were the kings who reigned in Edom before any Israelite king reigned:

[32]Bela son of Beor became king of Edom. His city was named Dinhabah.

[33]When Bela died, Jobab son of Zerah from Bozrah succeeded him as king.

[34]When Jobab died, Husham from the land of the Temanites succeeded him as king.

[35]When Husham died, Hadad son of Bedad, who defeated Midian in the country of Moab, succeeded him as king. His city was named Avith.

[36]When Hadad died, Samlah from Masrekah succeeded him as king.

[37]When Samlah died, Shaul from Rehoboth on the river succeeded him as king.

[38]When Shaul died, Baal-Hanan son of Akbor succeeded him as king.

[39]When Baal-Hanan son of Akbor died, Hadad[d] succeeded him as king. His city was named Pau, and his

---

Why were hot springs so valuable? (36:24)
Finding water of any kind in a desert was very important for supporting livestock. Hot water was especially rare, and it increased the value of the land.

---

[a] 22 Hebrew *Hemam,* a variant of *Homam* (see 1 Chron. 1:39)
[b] 24 Vulgate; Syriac *discovered water;* the meaning of the Hebrew for this word is uncertain.   [c] 26 Hebrew *Dishan,* a variant of *Dishon*   [d] 39 Many manuscripts of the Masoretic Text, Samaritan Pentateuch and Syriac (see also 1 Chron. 1:50); most manuscripts of the Masoretic Text *Hadar*

wife's name was Mehetabel daughter of Matred, the daughter of Me-Zahab.

⁴⁰These were the chiefs descended from Esau, by name, according to their clans and regions:

Timna, Alvah, Jetheth, ⁴¹Oholibamah, Elah, Pinon, ⁴²Kenaz, Teman, Mibzar, ⁴³Magdiel and Iram. These were the chiefs of Edom, according to their settlements in the land they occupied.

This is the family line of Esau, the father of the Edomites.

JOSEPH'S DREAMS

37 Jacob lived in the land where his father had stayed, the land of Canaan.

²This is the account of Jacob's family line.

Joseph, a young man of seventeen, was tending the flocks with his brothers, the sons of Bilhah and the sons of Zilpah, his father's wives, and he brought their father a bad report about them.

³Now Israel loved Joseph more than any of his other sons, because he had been born to him in his old age; and he made an ornate*a* robe for him. ⁴When his brothers saw that their father loved him more than any of them, they hated him and could not speak a kind word to him.

⁵Joseph had a dream, and when he told it to his brothers, they hated him all the more. ⁶He said to them, "Listen to this dream I had: ⁷We were binding sheaves of grain out in the field when suddenly my sheaf rose and stood upright, while your sheaves gathered around mine and bowed down to it."

⁸His brothers said to him, "Do you intend to reign over us? Will you actually rule us?" And they hated him all the more because of his dream and what he had said.

⁹Then he had another dream, and he told it to his brothers. "Listen," he said, "I had another dream, and this time the sun and moon and eleven stars were bowing down to me."

¹⁰When he told his father as well as his brothers, his father rebuked him and said, "What is this dream you had? Will your mother and I and your brothers actually come and bow down to the ground before you?" ¹¹His brothers were jealous of him, but his father kept the matter in mind.

JOSEPH SOLD BY HIS BROTHERS

¹²Now his brothers had gone to graze their father's flocks near Shechem, ¹³and Israel said to Joseph, "As you know, your brothers are grazing the flocks near Shechem. Come, I am going to send you to them."

"Very well," he replied.

¹⁴So he said to him, "Go and see if all is well with your brothers and with the flocks, and bring word back to me." Then he sent him off from the Valley of Hebron.

When Joseph arrived at Shechem, ¹⁵a man found him

a 3 The meaning of the Hebrew for this word is uncertain; also in verses 23 and 32.

Why is this section of Genesis introduced as the account of Jacob? (37:2) The final section of Genesis tells the story of Jacob's descendants. The story of Joseph receives the most attention because what eventually happened to the twelve tribes of Israel depended on Joseph's story.

What bad report did Joseph make to his father? (37:2) The Bible doesn't say what the bad report was. Maybe the brothers were not doing their jobs well or were scheming against their father. In any case, the brothers' hatred for Joseph grew because Joseph had reported on them and because Jacob showed such favoritism toward Joseph.

What did Joseph's robe look like? (37:3) The Bible doesn't give specific details, but it probably was very bright in color. Dying a robe would have taken a lot of time and money, clearly showing Jacob's favoritism. Joseph's brothers, on the other hand, probably wore simple, natural colored robes, which would have cost less.

When Joseph told his brothers his dreams, was he taunting them? (37:5) Joseph knew that he was his father's favorite. As a teenager, he may have been proud of his special status. But it's also possible that he was simply acting as a prophet, sharing the truth of God that had been revealed to him.

What were the reactions to Joseph's dreams? (37:11) Neither the brothers nor Jacob actually thought that they would one day bow down to Joseph. The brothers became more jealous, but Jacob kept the dreams in mind. When they eventually came true, he may have remembered these predictions.

Why did Reuben try to save Joseph? (37:21)

As Jacob's firstborn son, Reuben probably felt a special responsibility for Joseph. But he didn't really stand up to his brothers because he suggested that they put Joseph into a cistern—a covered pit cut into rock to store rainwater.

Who were the Ishmaelites? (37:25)

These groups of people were also called Midianites and Medanites. The tribal groups were interrelated since Midian and Medan, like Ishmael, were sons of Abraham. These traders were probably second or third cousins to Joseph and his brothers. These merchants were involved in the profitable business of slave trading.

Joseph Sold Into Egypt (37:28)

Why did Reuben go along with the cover-up? (37:29–32)

Reuben didn't participate in selling Joseph to the slave traders, but he would have been held responsible for it by Jacob because he was the oldest son. Since he was already out of favor with this father, he didn't want to risk more anger.

wandering around in the fields and asked him, "What are you looking for?"

[16] He replied, "I'm looking for my brothers. Can you tell me where they are grazing their flocks?"

[17] "They have moved on from here," the man answered. "I heard them say, 'Let's go to Dothan.'"

So Joseph went after his brothers and found them near Dothan. [18] But they saw him in the distance, and before he reached them, they plotted to kill him.

[19] "Here comes that dreamer!" they said to each other. [20] "Come now, let's kill him and throw him into one of these cisterns and say that a ferocious animal devoured him. Then we'll see what comes of his dreams."

[21] When Reuben heard this, he tried to rescue him from their hands. "Let's not take his life," he said. [22] "Don't shed any blood. Throw him into this cistern here in the wilderness, but don't lay a hand on him." Reuben said this to rescue him from them and take him back to his father.

[23] So when Joseph came to his brothers, they stripped him of his robe—the ornate robe he was wearing— [24] and they took him and threw him into the cistern. The cistern was empty; there was no water in it.

[25] As they sat down to eat their meal, they looked up and saw a caravan of Ishmaelites coming from Gilead. Their camels were loaded with spices, balm and myrrh, and they were on their way to take them down to Egypt.

[26] Judah said to his brothers, "What will we gain if we kill our brother and cover up his blood? [27] Come, let's sell him to the Ishmaelites and not lay our hands on him; after all, he is our brother, our own flesh and blood." His brothers agreed.

[28] So when the Midianite merchants came by, his brothers pulled Joseph up out of the cistern and sold him for twenty shekels[a] of silver to the Ishmaelites, who took him to Egypt.

[29] When Reuben returned to the cistern and saw that Joseph was not there, he tore his clothes. [30] He went back to his brothers and said, "The boy isn't there! Where can I turn now?"

[31] Then they got Joseph's robe, slaughtered a goat and dipped the robe in the blood. [32] They took the ornate robe back to their father and said, "We found this. Examine it to see whether it is your son's robe."

[33] He recognized it and said, "It is my son's robe! Some ferocious animal has devoured him. Joseph has surely been torn to pieces."

[34] Then Jacob tore his clothes, put on sackcloth and mourned for his son many days. [35] All his sons and daughters came to comfort him, but he refused to be comforted. "No," he said, "I will continue to mourn until I join my son in the grave." So his father wept for him.

[36] Meanwhile, the Midianites[b] sold Joseph in Egypt to Potiphar, one of Pharaoh's officials, the captain of the guard.

<hr />

[a] 28 That is, about 8 ounces or about 230 grams　　[b] 36 Samaritan Pentateuch, Septuagint, Vulgate and Syriac (see also verse 28); Masoretic Text *Medanites*

JUDAH AND TAMAR

38 At that time, Judah left his brothers and went down to stay with a man of Adullam named Hirah. ²There Judah met the daughter of a Canaanite man named Shua. He married her and made love to her; ³she became pregnant and gave birth to a son, who was named Er. ⁴She conceived again and gave birth to a son and named him Onan. ⁵She gave birth to still another son and named him Shelah. It was at Kezib that she gave birth to him.

⁶Judah got a wife for Er, his firstborn, and her name was Tamar. ⁷But Er, Judah's firstborn, was wicked in the LORD's sight; so the LORD put him to death.

⁸Then Judah said to Onan, "Sleep with your brother's wife and fulfill your duty to her as a brother-in-law to raise up offspring for your brother." ⁹But Onan knew that the child would not be his; so whenever he slept with his brother's wife, he spilled his semen on the ground to keep from providing offspring for his brother. ¹⁰What he did was wicked in the LORD's sight; so the LORD put him to death also.

¹¹Judah then said to his daughter-in-law Tamar, "Live as a widow in your father's household until my son Shelah grows up." For he thought, "He may die too, just like his brothers." So Tamar went to live in her father's household.

¹²After a long time Judah's wife, the daughter of Shua, died. When Judah had recovered from his grief, he went up to Timnah, to the men who were shearing his sheep, and his friend Hirah the Adullamite went with him.

¹³When Tamar was told, "Your father-in-law is on his way to Timnah to shear his sheep," ¹⁴she took off her widow's clothes, covered herself with a veil to disguise herself, and then sat down at the entrance to Enaim, which is on the road to Timnah. For she saw that, though Shelah had now grown up, she had not been given to him as his wife.

¹⁵When Judah saw her, he thought she was a prostitute, for she had covered her face. ¹⁶Not realizing that she was his daughter-in-law, he went over to her by the roadside and said, "Come now, let me sleep with you."

"And what will you give me to sleep with you?" she asked.

¹⁷"I'll send you a young goat from my flock," he said.

"Will you give me something as a pledge until you send it?" she asked.

¹⁸He said, "What pledge should I give you?"

"Your seal and its cord, and the staff in your hand," she answered. So he gave them to her and slept with her, and she became pregnant by him. ¹⁹After she left, she took off her veil and put on her widow's clothes again.

²⁰Meanwhile Judah sent the young goat by his friend the Adullamite in order to get his pledge back from the woman, but he did not find her. ²¹He asked the men who lived there, "Where is the shrine prostitute who was beside the road at Enaim?"

"There hasn't been any shrine prostitute here," they said.

²²So he went back to Judah and said, "I didn't find her. Besides, the men who lived there said, 'There hasn't been any shrine prostitute here.'"

How did Onan sin? (38:8–10)
If a man died without children, it was his brother's duty to raise heirs with his widow. Onan refused to carry out this responsibility, perhaps because he did not want to risk his own estate.

Why did Judah blame Tamar? (38:11)
Judah may have thought that Tamar was in some way responsible for the deaths of two of his sons. He told her to wait to marry his next son, Shelah, until he had grown up. Judah had no intention of actually allowing Tamar to marry Shelah.

What were widow's clothes? (38:14)
Widows were supposed to dress in a modest fashion. They usually dressed in sackcloth or torn garments. They left their hair unbound and their feet bare. Also, since it was the community's job to care for widows, special clothing made it easy to identify those who needed help.

²³Then Judah said, "Let her keep what she has, or we will become a laughingstock. After all, I did send her this young goat, but you didn't find her."

²⁴About three months later Judah was told, "Your daughter-in-law Tamar is guilty of prostitution, and as a result she is now pregnant."

Judah said, "Bring her out and have her burned to death!"

²⁵As she was being brought out, she sent a message to her father-in-law. "I am pregnant by the man who owns these," she said. And she added, "See if you recognize whose seal and cord and staff these are."

²⁶Judah recognized them and said, "She is more righteous than I, since I wouldn't give her to my son Shelah." And he did not sleep with her again.

²⁷When the time came for her to give birth, there were twin boys in her womb. ²⁸As she was giving birth, one of them put out his hand; so the midwife took a scarlet thread and tied it on his wrist and said, "This one came out first." ²⁹But when he drew back his hand, his brother came out, and she said, "So this is how you have broken out!" And he was named Perez.^a ³⁰Then his brother, who had the scarlet thread on his wrist, came out. And he was named Zerah.^b

JOSEPH AND POTIPHAR'S WIFE

39 Now Joseph had been taken down to Egypt. Potiphar, an Egyptian who was one of Pharaoh's officials, the captain of the guard, bought him from the Ishmaelites who had taken him there.

²The Lord was with Joseph so that he prospered, and he lived in the house of his Egyptian master. ³When his master saw that the Lord was with him and that the Lord gave him success in everything he did, ⁴Joseph found favor in his eyes and became his attendant. Potiphar put him in charge of his household, and he entrusted to his care everything he owned. ⁵From the time he put him in charge of his household and of all that he owned, the Lord blessed the household of the Egyptian because of Joseph. The blessing of the Lord was on everything Potiphar had, both in the house and in the field. ⁶So Potiphar left everything he had in Joseph's care; with Joseph in charge, he did not concern himself with anything except the food he ate.

Now Joseph was well-built and handsome, ⁷and after a while his master's wife took notice of Joseph and said, "Come to bed with me!"

⁸But he refused. "With me in charge," he told her, "my master does not concern himself with anything in the house; everything he owns he has entrusted to my care. ⁹No one is greater in this house than I am. My master has withheld nothing from me except you, because you are his wife. How then could I do such a wicked thing and sin against God?" ¹⁰And though she spoke to Joseph day after day, he refused to go to bed with her or even be with her.

¹¹One day he went into the house to attend to his duties, and none of the household servants was inside. ¹²She caught

Why did Tamar want to have a child even though she no longer had a husband? (38:26)
Barrenness was cause for great shame in the ancient Middle East. It was more dishonorable to be a barren woman and not fulfill what society considered a woman's duty (to have children) than to be unmarried with a child.

What type of official was Potiphar? (39:1)
Potiphar's job was to help carry out all of Pharaoh's decrees, including supervising prisons and executing people. These responsibilities fell under the title of captain of the guard.

What were Joseph's responsibilities? (39:4–6)
Potiphar gave Joseph full responsibility for his household. Later Joseph would have responsibility in prison and later still in all of Egypt. This growing responsibility was evidence of God's blessing.

---

^a 29 Perez means breaking out.   ^b 30 Zerah can mean scarlet or brightness.

him by his cloak and said, "Come to bed with me!" But he left his cloak in her hand and ran out of the house.

[13] When she saw that he had left his cloak in her hand and had run out of the house, [14] she called her household servants. "Look," she said to them, "this Hebrew has been brought to us to make sport of us! He came in here to sleep with me, but I screamed. [15] When he heard me scream for help, he left his cloak beside me and ran out of the house."

[16] She kept his cloak beside her until his master came home. [17] Then she told him this story: "That Hebrew slave you brought us came to me to make sport of me. [18] But as soon as I screamed for help, he left his cloak beside me and ran out of the house."

[19] When his master heard the story his wife told him, saying, "This is how your slave treated me," he burned with anger. [20] Joseph's master took him and put him in prison, the place where the king's prisoners were confined.

But while Joseph was there in the prison, [21] the LORD was with him; he showed him kindness and granted him favor in the eyes of the prison warden. [22] So the warden put Joseph in charge of all those held in the prison, and he was made responsible for all that was done there. [23] The warden paid no attention to anything under Joseph's care, because the LORD was with Joseph and gave him success in whatever he did.

THE CUPBEARER AND THE BAKER

40 Some time later, the cupbearer and the baker of the king of Egypt offended their master, the king of Egypt. [2] Pharaoh was angry with his two officials, the chief cupbearer and the chief baker, [3] and put them in custody in the house of the captain of the guard, in the same prison where Joseph was confined. [4] The captain of the guard assigned them to Joseph, and he attended them.

After they had been in custody for some time, [5] each of the two men — the cupbearer and the baker of the king of Egypt, who were being held in prison — had a dream the same night, and each dream had a meaning of its own.

[6] When Joseph came to them the next morning, he saw that they were dejected. [7] So he asked Pharaoh's officials who were in custody with him in his master's house, "Why do you look so sad today?"

[8] "We both had dreams," they answered, "but there is no one to interpret them."

Then Joseph said to them, "Do not interpretations belong to God? Tell me your dreams."

[9] So the chief cupbearer told Joseph his dream. He said to him, "In my dream I saw a vine in front of me, [10] and on the vine were three branches. As soon as it budded, it blossomed, and its clusters ripened into grapes. [11] Pharaoh's cup was in my hand, and I took the grapes, squeezed them into Pharaoh's cup and put the cup in his hand."

[12] "This is what it means," Joseph said to him. "The three branches are three days. [13] Within three days Pharaoh will lift up your head and restore you to your position, and you will put Pharaoh's cup in his hand, just as you used to do

What was prison like for the king's prisoners? (39:20)
The king's prisoners were treated much better than the normal prisoners. They were still guarded, and could be subjected to worse punishment, but they were not forced to do manual labor like regular prisoners.

How did Joseph's situation change again? (39:21–23)
Joseph's life was like a roller-coaster ride. After being falsely accused and thrown into prison, Joseph was again blessed by God, and he was given the authority to supervise the other prisoners.

What was a cupbearer? (40:2)
Cupbearers were servants who sampled the king's wine to test it for poison. The Pharaohs placed great trust in their cupbearers, and these servants often became very powerful politically.

Why did they pay so much attention to dreams? (40:8)
In the ancient world, dreams were thought to come from the gods and should be analyzed to guide people about actions they should take. A ruler's dreams would be especially important. People consulted experts and books to interpret their dreams. Joseph, a dreamer himself, relied on God for his interpretations, but his explanations followed the typical Egyptian pattern for similar symbols.

when you were his cupbearer. ¹⁴But when all goes well with you, remember me and show me kindness; mention me to Pharaoh and get me out of this prison. ¹⁵I was forcibly carried off from the land of the Hebrews, and even here I have done nothing to deserve being put in a dungeon."

¹⁶When the chief baker saw that Joseph had given a favorable interpretation, he said to Joseph, "I too had a dream: On my head were three baskets of bread.ᵃ ¹⁷In the top basket were all kinds of baked goods for Pharaoh, but the birds were eating them out of the basket on my head."

¹⁸"This is what it means," Joseph said. "The three baskets are three days. ¹⁹Within three days Pharaoh will lift off your head and impale your body on a pole. And the birds will eat away your flesh."

²⁰Now the third day was Pharaoh's birthday, and he gave a feast for all his officials. He lifted up the heads of the chief cupbearer and the chief baker in the presence of his officials: ²¹He restored the chief cupbearer to his position, so that he once again put the cup into Pharaoh's hand— ²²but he impaled the chief baker, just as Joseph had said to them in his interpretation.

²³The chief cupbearer, however, did not remember Joseph; he forgot him.

PHARAOH'S DREAMS

41 When two full years had passed, Pharaoh had a dream: He was standing by the Nile, ²when out of the river there came up seven cows, sleek and fat, and they grazed among the reeds. ³After them, seven other cows, ugly and gaunt, came up out of the Nile and stood beside those on the riverbank. ⁴And the cows that were ugly and gaunt ate up the seven sleek, fat cows. Then Pharaoh woke up.

⁵He fell asleep again and had a second dream: Seven heads of grain, healthy and good, were growing on a single stalk. ⁶After them, seven other heads of grain sprouted—thin and scorched by the east wind. ⁷The thin heads of grain swallowed up the seven healthy, full heads. Then Pharaoh woke up; it had been a dream.

⁸In the morning his mind was troubled, so he sent for all the magicians and wise men of Egypt. Pharaoh told them his dreams, but no one could interpret them for him.

⁹Then the chief cupbearer said to Pharaoh, "Today I am reminded of my shortcomings. ¹⁰Pharaoh was once angry with his servants, and he imprisoned me and the chief baker in the house of the captain of the guard. ¹¹Each of us had a dream the same night, and each dream had a meaning of its own. ¹²Now a young Hebrew was there with us, a servant of the captain of the guard. We told him our dreams, and he interpreted them for us, giving each man the interpretation of his dream. ¹³And things turned out exactly as he interpreted them to us: I was restored to my position, and the other man was impaled."

¹⁴So Pharaoh sent for Joseph, and he was quickly brought from the dungeon. When he had shaved and changed his clothes, he came before Pharaoh.

ᵃ 16 Or *three wicker baskets*

Why would God allow Joseph to be forgotten by the cupbearer? (40:23)
Even though people may forget, God never forgets his people. God may have been using this time in prison to allow Joseph to grow spiritually. As in the other events in Joseph's life — positive or negative — God was in control, and he would accomplish his plan.

The Nile (41:1-3)

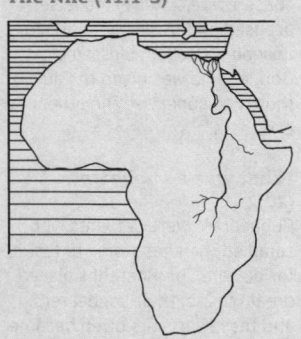

Why did Pharaoh call for magicians to interpret his dreams? (41:8)
Magicians were often used as advisers to kings because they seemed to have some supernatural power.

Why did Joseph shave before coming before Pharaoh? (41:14)
Egyptians were normally smooth-shaven, while Palestinians wore beards. So Joseph was identifying himself as an Egyptian, even though he was a foreigner.

¹⁵Pharaoh said to Joseph, "I had a dream, and no one can interpret it. But I have heard it said of you that when you hear a dream you can interpret it."

¹⁶"I cannot do it," Joseph replied to Pharaoh, "but God will give Pharaoh the answer he desires."

¹⁷Then Pharaoh said to Joseph, "In my dream I was standing on the bank of the Nile, ¹⁸when out of the river there came up seven cows, fat and sleek, and they grazed among the reeds. ¹⁹After them, seven other cows came up—scrawny and very ugly and lean. I had never seen such ugly cows in all the land of Egypt. ²⁰The lean, ugly cows ate up the seven fat cows that came up first. ²¹But even after they ate them, no one could tell that they had done so; they looked just as ugly as before. Then I woke up.

²²"In my dream I saw seven heads of grain, full and good, growing on a single stalk. ²³After them, seven other heads sprouted—withered and thin and scorched by the east wind. ²⁴The thin heads of grain swallowed up the seven good heads. I told this to the magicians, but none of them could explain it to me."

²⁵Then Joseph said to Pharaoh, "The dreams of Pharaoh are one and the same. God has revealed to Pharaoh what he is about to do. ²⁶The seven good cows are seven years, and the seven good heads of grain are seven years; it is one and the same dream. ²⁷The seven lean, ugly cows that came up afterward are seven years, and so are the seven worthless heads of grain scorched by the east wind: They are seven years of famine.

²⁸"It is just as I said to Pharaoh: God has shown Pharaoh what he is about to do. ²⁹Seven years of great abundance are coming throughout the land of Egypt, ³⁰but seven years of famine will follow them. Then all the abundance in Egypt will be forgotten, and the famine will ravage the land. ³¹The abundance in the land will not be remembered, because the famine that follows it will be so severe. ³²The reason the dream was given to Pharaoh in two forms is that the matter has been firmly decided by God, and God will do it soon.

³³"And now let Pharaoh look for a discerning and wise man and put him in charge of the land of Egypt. ³⁴Let Pharaoh appoint commissioners over the land to take a fifth of the harvest of Egypt during the seven years of abundance. ³⁵They should collect all the food of these good years that are coming and store up the grain under the authority of Pharaoh, to be kept in the cities for food. ³⁶This food should be held in reserve for the country, to be used during the seven years of famine that will come upon Egypt, so that the country may not be ruined by the famine."

³⁷The plan seemed good to Pharaoh and to all his officials. ³⁸So Pharaoh asked them, "Can we find anyone like this man, one in whom is the spirit of God*?"

³⁹Then Pharaoh said to Joseph, "Since God has made all this known to you, there is no one so discerning and wise as you. ⁴⁰You shall be in charge of my palace, and all my people are to submit to your orders. Only with respect to the throne will I be greater than you."

*38 Or *of the gods*

Why did Joseph say, "I cannot do it"? (41:16)
Joseph relied on God throughout his life. He did not want to claim credit for himself for interpreting the dream. Instead, he wanted to emphasize that his interpretation came from God.

Would seven years of famine be unusual? (41:27)
Long famines were rare in Egypt because the Nile River overflowed every year, providing irrigation for crops.

Did Pharaoh believe in the true God? (41:37–39)
Probably not. He thought that Joseph had suggested a good plan for dealing with the famine, and so he complimented him by saying that Joseph had the spirit of God in him. Pharaoh respected Joseph, but that does not mean that he became a believer.

What were a leader's symbols of power? (41:40–43)
The three symbols of power in the ancient Middle East were the signet ring, the robe, and the gold chain. Pharaoh put Joseph in charge as administrative head of Egypt. Joseph was now second only to Pharaoh in his authority over the kingdom.

Why did Pharaoh change Joseph's name? (41:45)
He changed his name to show that Joseph was completely accepted as a member of Pharaoh's court. The name change also showed Pharaoh's complete authority over Joseph, along with Joseph's allegiance to Egypt and his break from his past.

Why did Joseph name his first son Manasseh? (41:51)
The name means "forget." The name was a reminder that Joseph had forgotten his troubles caused by his family members because of God's blessings.

What happened to Manasseh and Ephraim? (41:51–52)
They each received an inheritance when Jacob died because he adopted them. Because Jacob treated them as if they were his sons, their children inherited the promised land.

Why didn't Jacob send Benjamin to Egypt along with his other sons? (42:4)
Rachel had died, and Jacob thought Joseph was dead. He didn't want anything to happen to the only remaining son of his favorite wife.

JOSEPH IN CHARGE OF EGYPT

[41] So Pharaoh said to Joseph, "I hereby put you in charge of the whole land of Egypt." [42] Then Pharaoh took his signet ring from his finger and put it on Joseph's finger. He dressed him in robes of fine linen and put a gold chain around his neck. [43] He had him ride in a chariot as his second-in-command,[a] and people shouted before him, "Make way[b]!" Thus he put him in charge of the whole land of Egypt.

[44] Then Pharaoh said to Joseph, "I am Pharaoh, but without your word no one will lift hand or foot in all Egypt." [45] Pharaoh gave Joseph the name Zaphenath-Paneah and gave him Asenath daughter of Potiphera, priest of On,[c] to be his wife. And Joseph went throughout the land of Egypt.

[46] Joseph was thirty years old when he entered the service of Pharaoh king of Egypt. And Joseph went out from Pharaoh's presence and traveled throughout Egypt. [47] During the seven years of abundance the land produced plentifully. [48] Joseph collected all the food produced in those seven years of abundance in Egypt and stored it in the cities. In each city he put the food grown in the fields surrounding it. [49] Joseph stored up huge quantities of grain, like the sand of the sea; it was so much that he stopped keeping records because it was beyond measure.

[50] Before the years of famine came, two sons were born to Joseph by Asenath daughter of Potiphera, priest of On. [51] Joseph named his firstborn Manasseh[d] and said, "It is because God has made me forget all my trouble and all my father's household." [52] The second son he named Ephraim[e] and said, "It is because God has made me fruitful in the land of my suffering."

[53] The seven years of abundance in Egypt came to an end, [54] and the seven years of famine began, just as Joseph had said. There was famine in all the other lands, but in the whole land of Egypt there was food. [55] When all Egypt began to feel the famine, the people cried to Pharaoh for food. Then Pharaoh told all the Egyptians, "Go to Joseph and do what he tells you."

[56] When the famine had spread over the whole country, Joseph opened all the storehouses and sold grain to the Egyptians, for the famine was severe throughout Egypt. [57] And all the world came to Egypt to buy grain from Joseph, because the famine was severe everywhere.

JOSEPH'S BROTHERS GO TO EGYPT

42 When Jacob learned that there was grain in Egypt, he said to his sons, "Why do you just keep looking at each other?" [2] He continued, "I have heard that there is grain in Egypt. Go down there and buy some for us, so that we may live and not die."

[3] Then ten of Joseph's brothers went down to buy grain from Egypt. [4] But Jacob did not send Benjamin, Joseph's

---

[a] 43 Or *in the chariot of his second-in-command*; or *in his second chariot*
[b] 43 Or *Bow down* [c] 45 That is, Heliopolis; also in verse 50
[d] 51 *Manasseh* sounds like and may be derived from the Hebrew for *forget*.
[e] 52 *Ephraim* sounds like the Hebrew for *twice fruitful*.

brother, with the others, because he was afraid that harm might come to him. [5] So Israel's sons were among those who went to buy grain, for there was famine in the land of Canaan also.

[6] Now Joseph was the governor of the land, the person who sold grain to all its people. So when Joseph's brothers arrived, they bowed down to him with their faces to the ground. [7] As soon as Joseph saw his brothers, he recognized them, but he pretended to be a stranger and spoke harshly to them. "Where do you come from?" he asked.

"From the land of Canaan," they replied, "to buy food."

[8] Although Joseph recognized his brothers, they did not recognize him. [9] Then he remembered his dreams about them and said to them, "You are spies! You have come to see where our land is unprotected."

[10] "No, my lord," they answered. "Your servants have come to buy food. [11] We are all the sons of one man. Your servants are honest men, not spies."

[12] "No!" he said to them. "You have come to see where our land is unprotected."

[13] But they replied, "Your servants were twelve brothers, the sons of one man, who lives in the land of Canaan. The youngest is now with our father, and one is no more."

[14] Joseph said to them, "It is just as I told you: You are spies! [15] And this is how you will be tested: As surely as Pharaoh lives, you will not leave this place unless your youngest brother comes here. [16] Send one of your number to get your brother; the rest of you will be kept in prison, so that your words may be tested to see if you are telling the truth. If you are not, then as surely as Pharaoh lives, you are spies!" [17] And he put them all in custody for three days.

[18] On the third day, Joseph said to them, "Do this and you will live, for I fear God: [19] If you are honest men, let one of your brothers stay here in prison, while the rest of you go and take grain back for your starving households. [20] But you must bring your youngest brother to me, so that your words may be verified and that you may not die." This they proceeded to do.

[21] They said to one another, "Surely we are being punished because of our brother. We saw how distressed he was when he pleaded with us for his life, but we would not listen; that's why this distress has come on us."

[22] Reuben replied, "Didn't I tell you not to sin against the boy? But you wouldn't listen! Now we must give an accounting for his blood." [23] They did not realize that Joseph could understand them, since he was using an interpreter.

[24] He turned away from them and began to weep, but then came back and spoke to them again. He had Simeon taken from them and bound before their eyes.

[25] Joseph gave orders to fill their bags with grain, to put each man's silver back in his sack, and to give them provisions for their journey. After this was done for them, [26] they loaded their grain on their donkeys and left.

[27] At the place where they stopped for the night one of them opened his sack to get feed for his donkey, and he saw

Why did Joseph recognize his brothers when they didn't recognize him? (42:8) When the brothers sold Joseph into slavery, he was a teenager. In the 20 or more years since then, their appearance hadn't changed as much as Joseph's. Also, he was in a position of authority, was dressed as an Egyptian, and spoke through an interpreter.

Why did Joseph's brothers call themselves his servants? (42:10) This was the way people usually spoke to powerful leaders. Without knowing it, they were fulfilling his dreams in Genesis 37:5 – 9.

Why did Jacob want to test his brothers? (42:15) On the surface, he was trying to see if their story was true. But he also might have wanted to find out if the brothers would leave Simeon to slavery as they had left Joseph.

Why did the brothers think that they were being punished? (42:21) They must have still felt guilty about what they had done to Joseph, and they thought this was how they were being punished.

his silver in the mouth of his sack. ²⁸"My silver has been returned," he said to his brothers. "Here it is in my sack."

Their hearts sank and they turned to each other trembling and said, "What is this that God has done to us?"

²⁹When they came to their father Jacob in the land of Canaan, they told him all that had happened to them. They said, ³⁰"The man who is lord over the land spoke harshly to us and treated us as though we were spying on the land. ³¹But we said to him, 'We are honest men; we are not spies. ³²We were twelve brothers, sons of one father. One is no more, and the youngest is now with our father in Canaan.'

³³"Then the man who is lord over the land said to us, 'This is how I will know whether you are honest men: Leave one of your brothers here with me, and take food for your starving households and go. ³⁴But bring your youngest brother to me so I will know that you are not spies but honest men. Then I will give your brother back to you, and you can trade*ᵃ* in the land.'"

³⁵As they were emptying their sacks, there in each man's sack was his pouch of silver! When they and their father saw the money pouches, they were frightened. ³⁶Their father Jacob said to them, "You have deprived me of my children. Joseph is no more and Simeon is no more, and now you want to take Benjamin. Everything is against me!"

³⁷Then Reuben said to his father, "You may put both of my sons to death if I do not bring him back to you. Entrust him to my care, and I will bring him back."

³⁸But Jacob said, "My son will not go down there with you; his brother is dead and he is the only one left. If harm comes to him on the journey you are taking, you will bring my gray head down to the grave in sorrow."

THE SECOND JOURNEY TO EGYPT

43 Now the famine was still severe in the land. ²So when they had eaten all the grain they had brought from Egypt, their father said to them, "Go back and buy us a little more food."

³But Judah said to him, "The man warned us solemnly, 'You will not see my face again unless your brother is with you.' ⁴If you will send our brother along with us, we will go down and buy food for you. ⁵But if you will not send him, we will not go down, because the man said to us, 'You will not see my face again unless your brother is with you.'"

⁶Israel asked, "Why did you bring this trouble on me by telling the man you had another brother?"

⁷They replied, "The man questioned us closely about ourselves and our family. 'Is your father still living?' he asked us. 'Do you have another brother?' We simply answered his questions. How were we to know he would say, 'Bring your brother down here'?"

⁸Then Judah said to Israel his father, "Send the boy along with me and we will go at once, so that we and you and our children may live and not die. ⁹I myself will guarantee his safety; you can hold me personally responsible for him. If I

Why did Reuben guarantee Benjamin's safety? (42:37)
He was Jacob's oldest son, and he was the one who had tried to save Joseph's life when the other brothers wanted to kill him. Now he wanted to protect Jacob's youngest son.

ᵃ 34 Or move about freely

do not bring him back to you and set him here before you, I will bear the blame before you all my life. [10] As it is, if we had not delayed, we could have gone and returned twice."

[11] Then their father Israel said to them, "If it must be, then do this: Put some of the best products of the land in your bags and take them down to the man as a gift — a little balm and a little honey, some spices and myrrh, some pistachio nuts and almonds. [12] Take double the amount of silver with you, for you must return the silver that was put back into the mouths of your sacks. Perhaps it was a mistake. [13] Take your brother also and go back to the man at once. [14] And may God Almighty[a] grant you mercy before the man so that he will let your other brother and Benjamin come back with you. As for me, if I am bereaved, I am bereaved."

[15] So the men took the gifts and double the amount of silver, and Benjamin also. They hurried down to Egypt and presented themselves to Joseph. [16] When Joseph saw Benjamin with them, he said to the steward of his house, "Take these men to my house, slaughter an animal and prepare a meal; they are to eat with me at noon."

[17] The man did as Joseph told him and took the men to Joseph's house. [18] Now the men were frightened when they were taken to his house. They thought, "We were brought here because of the silver that was put back into our sacks the first time. He wants to attack us and overpower us and seize us as slaves and take our donkeys."

[19] So they went up to Joseph's steward and spoke to him at the entrance to the house. [20] "We beg your pardon, our lord," they said, "we came down here the first time to buy food. [21] But at the place where we stopped for the night we opened our sacks and each of us found his silver — the exact weight — in the mouth of his sack. So we have brought it back with us. [22] We have also brought additional silver with us to buy food. We don't know who put our silver in our sacks."

[23] "It's all right," he said. "Don't be afraid. Your God, the God of your father, has given you treasure in your sacks; I received your silver." Then he brought Simeon out to them.

[24] The steward took the men into Joseph's house, gave them water to wash their feet and provided fodder for their donkeys. [25] They prepared their gifts for Joseph's arrival at noon, because they had heard that they were to eat there.

[26] When Joseph came home, they presented to him the gifts they had brought into the house, and they bowed down before him to the ground. [27] He asked them how they were, and then he said, "How is your aged father you told me about? Is he still living?"

[28] They replied, "Your servant our father is still alive and well." And they bowed down, prostrating themselves before him.

[29] As he looked about and saw his brother Benjamin, his own mother's son, he asked, "Is this your youngest brother, the one you told me about?" And he said, "God be gracious to you, my son." [30] Deeply moved at the sight of his brother,

Why did Jacob send gifts for the brothers to take to Egypt? (43:11)
That was the common practice when someone approached a person of greater superiority. Jacob referred to the gifts as the best products of the land.

Why were the brothers frightened when they were invited to dinner? (43:18)
They thought they were going to be imprisoned for stealing the silver. It was also rare for nomadic people to be invited to a royal person's house.

[a] 14 Hebrew *El-Shaddai*

Joseph hurried out and looked for a place to weep. He went into his private room and wept there.

[31] After he had washed his face, he came out and, controlling himself, said, "Serve the food."

[32] They served him by himself, the brothers by themselves, and the Egyptians who ate with him by themselves, because Egyptians could not eat with Hebrews, for that is detestable to Egyptians. [33] The men had been seated before him in the order of their ages, from the firstborn to the youngest; and they looked at each other in astonishment. [34] When portions were served to them from Joseph's table, Benjamin's portion was five times as much as anyone else's. So they feasted and drank freely with him.

A SILVER CUP IN A SACK

44 Now Joseph gave these instructions to the steward of his house: "Fill the men's sacks with as much food as they can carry, and put each man's silver in the mouth of his sack. [2] Then put my cup, the silver one, in the mouth of the youngest one's sack, along with the silver for his grain." And he did as Joseph said.

[3] As morning dawned, the men were sent on their way with their donkeys. [4] They had not gone far from the city when Joseph said to his steward, "Go after those men at once, and when you catch up with them, say to them, 'Why have you repaid good with evil? [5] Isn't this the cup my master drinks from and also uses for divination? This is a wicked thing you have done.'"

[6] When he caught up with them, he repeated these words to them. [7] But they said to him, "Why does my lord say such things? Far be it from your servants to do anything like that! [8] We even brought back to you from the land of Canaan the silver we found inside the mouths of our sacks. So why would we steal silver or gold from your master's house? [9] If any of your servants is found to have it, he will die; and the rest of us will become my lord's slaves."

[10] "Very well, then," he said, "let it be as you say. Whoever is found to have it will become my slave; the rest of you will be free from blame."

[11] Each of them quickly lowered his sack to the ground and opened it. [12] Then the steward proceeded to search, beginning with the oldest and ending with the youngest. And the cup was found in Benjamin's sack. [13] At this, they tore their clothes. Then they all loaded their donkeys and returned to the city.

[14] Joseph was still in the house when Judah and his brothers came in, and they threw themselves to the ground before him. [15] Joseph said to them, "What is this you have done? Don't you know that a man like me can find things out by divination?"

[16] "What can we say to my lord?" Judah replied. "What can we say? How can we prove our innocence? God has uncovered your servants' guilt. We are now my lord's slaves—we ourselves and the one who was found to have the cup."

[17] But Joseph said, "Far be it from me to do such a thing!

Why did the brothers sit separately from the Egyptians? (43:32)
The Egyptians considered the Hebrew people to be ritually unclean because they didn't worship the Egyptian gods.

Why were the brothers astonished that they were seated according to their ages? (43:33)
It was common to seat people in order of their ages. The oldest would be regarded to have the highest rank. The brothers were astonished that anyone at this table could know what their birth order was. They were also surprised that Benjamin's portion was the largest.

Why did Joseph continue to test his brothers? (44:1)
He created a situation where Benjamin was at risk, and he wanted to see how the brothers would respond. He wanted to see if they would abandon a brother again.

Why did they tear their clothes? (44:13)
This was a sign of grief and distress.

Only the man who was found to have the cup will become my slave. The rest of you, go back to your father in peace."

¹⁸ Then Judah went up to him and said: "Pardon your servant, my lord, let me speak a word to my lord. Do not be angry with your servant, though you are equal to Pharaoh himself. ¹⁹ My lord asked his servants, 'Do you have a father or a brother?' ²⁰ And we answered, 'We have an aged father, and there is a young son born to him in his old age. His brother is dead, and he is the only one of his mother's sons left, and his father loves him.'

²¹ "Then you said to your servants, 'Bring him down to me so I can see him for myself.' ²² And we said to my lord, 'The boy cannot leave his father; if he leaves him, his father will die.' ²³ But you told your servants, 'Unless your youngest brother comes down with you, you will not see my face again.' ²⁴ When we went back to your servant my father, we told him what my lord had said.

²⁵ "Then our father said, 'Go back and buy a little more food.' ²⁶ But we said, 'We cannot go down. Only if our youngest brother is with us will we go. We cannot see the man's face unless our youngest brother is with us.'

²⁷ "Your servant my father said to us, 'You know that my wife bore me two sons. ²⁸ One of them went away from me, and I said, "He has surely been torn to pieces." And I have not seen him since. ²⁹ If you take this one from me too and harm comes to him, you will bring my gray head down to the grave in misery.'

³⁰ "So now, if the boy is not with us when I go back to your servant my father, and if my father, whose life is closely bound up with the boy's life, ³¹ sees that the boy isn't there, he will die. Your servants will bring the gray head of our father down to the grave in sorrow. ³² Your servant guaranteed the boy's safety to my father. I said, 'If I do not bring him back to you, I will bear the blame before you, my father, all my life!'

³³ "Now then, please let your servant remain here as my lord's slave in place of the boy, and let the boy return with his brothers. ³⁴ How can I go back to my father if the boy is not with me? No! Do not let me see the misery that would come on my father."

JOSEPH MAKES HIMSELF KNOWN

45 Then Joseph could no longer control himself before all his attendants, and he cried out, "Have everyone leave my presence!" So there was no one with Joseph when he made himself known to his brothers. ² And he wept so loudly that the Egyptians heard him, and Pharaoh's household heard about it.

³ Joseph said to his brothers, "I am Joseph! Is my father still living?" But his brothers were not able to answer him, because they were terrified at his presence.

⁴ Then Joseph said to his brothers, "Come close to me." When they had done so, he said, "I am your brother Joseph, the one you sold into Egypt! ⁵ And now, do not be distressed and do not be angry with yourselves for selling me here,

How did Judah retell the story of their return? (44:18–34)
Even though most of the details are familiar, there are some new elements. He mentions Jacob's favoritism toward Joseph and Benjamin, he pleads for Benjamin to be spared, and he offers to become a slave for the sake of his brother.

Why were Joseph's brothers terrified? (45:3)
They were shocked at not only finding Joseph alive, but finding him in a position of such power. Joseph's brothers were afraid of what he would do to them.

Why was Joseph able to forgive his brothers? (45:5–7)
Joseph knew that his brothers' cruel act had accomplished God's purpose: to place him in Egypt, where he could save his family from starvation and preserve God's chosen people.

because it was to save lives that God sent me ahead of you. [6] For two years now there has been famine in the land, and for the next five years there will be no plowing and reaping. [7] But God sent me ahead of you to preserve for you a remnant on earth and to save your lives by a great deliverance. [a]

[8] "So then, it was not you who sent me here, but God. He made me father to Pharaoh, lord of his entire household and ruler of all Egypt. [9] Now hurry back to my father and say to him, 'This is what your son Joseph says: God has made me lord of all Egypt. Come down to me; don't delay. [10] You shall live in the region of Goshen and be near me—you, your children and grandchildren, your flocks and herds, and all you have. [11] I will provide for you there, because five years of famine are still to come. Otherwise you and your household and all who belong to you will become destitute.'

[12] "You can see for yourselves, and so can my brother Benjamin, that it is really I who am speaking to you. [13] Tell my father about all the honor accorded me in Egypt and about everything you have seen. And bring my father down here quickly."

[14] Then he threw his arms around his brother Benjamin and wept, and Benjamin embraced him, weeping. [15] And he kissed all his brothers and wept over them. Afterward his brothers talked with him.

[16] When the news reached Pharaoh's palace that Joseph's brothers had come, Pharaoh and all his officials were pleased. [17] Pharaoh said to Joseph, "Tell your brothers, 'Do this: Load your animals and return to the land of Canaan, [18] and bring your father and your families back to me. I will give you the best of the land of Egypt and you can enjoy the fat of the land.'

[19] "You are also directed to tell them, 'Do this: Take some carts from Egypt for your children and your wives, and get your father and come. [20] Never mind about your belongings, because the best of all Egypt will be yours.'"

[21] So the sons of Israel did this. Joseph gave them carts, as Pharaoh had commanded, and he also gave them provisions for their journey. [22] To each of them he gave new clothing, but to Benjamin he gave three hundred shekels [b] of silver and five sets of clothes. [23] And this is what he sent to his father: ten donkeys loaded with the best things of Egypt, and ten female donkeys loaded with grain and bread and other provisions for his journey. [24] Then he sent his brothers away, and as they were leaving he said to them, "Don't quarrel on the way!"

[25] So they went up out of Egypt and came to their father Jacob in the land of Canaan. [26] They told him, "Joseph is still alive! In fact, he is ruler of all Egypt." Jacob was stunned; he did not believe them. [27] But when they told him everything Joseph had said to them, and when he saw the carts Joseph had sent to carry him back, the spirit of their father Jacob revived. [28] And Israel said, "I'm convinced! My son Joseph is still alive. I will go and see him before I die."

How could Joseph be father to Pharaoh? (45:8)
The term *father* was used to show honor and respect.

Why did Joseph want his family to move to Egypt? (45:10)
Joseph wanted his family close not only because he could provide and protect them if they were closer, but because of Goshen's geographical location. Next to the Nile Delta, this area had better land because of its nearness to a water source.

Why did Joseph give Benjamin more than the other brothers? (45:22)
Joseph gave Benjamin five sets of clothes and about seven and a half pounds of silver. He favored Benjamin because they had the same mother, while the other brothers were stepbrothers.

Why did Joseph tell his brothers not to argue? (45:24)
He didn't want anything to delay their return. He wanted them to avoid fighting about the past and who was at fault. Perhaps Joseph was hoping this incident might bring harmony among them.

---

[a] 7 Or *save you as a great band of survivors*   [b] 22 That is, about 7 1/2 pounds or about 3.5 kilograms

JACOB GOES TO EGYPT

46 So Israel set out with all that was his, and when he reached Beersheba, he offered sacrifices to the God of his father Isaac.

[2] And God spoke to Israel in a vision at night and said, "Jacob! Jacob!"

"Here I am," he replied.

[3] "I am God, the God of your father," he said. "Do not be afraid to go down to Egypt, for I will make you into a great nation there. [4] I will go down to Egypt with you, and I will surely bring you back again. And Joseph's own hand will close your eyes."

[5] Then Jacob left Beersheba, and Israel's sons took their father Jacob and their children and their wives in the carts that Pharaoh had sent to transport him. [6] So Jacob and all his offspring went to Egypt, taking with them their livestock and the possessions they had acquired in Canaan. [7] Jacob brought with him to Egypt his sons and grandsons and his daughters and granddaughters—all his offspring.

[8] These are the names of the sons of Israel (Jacob and his descendants) who went to Egypt:

Reuben the firstborn of Jacob.
[9] The sons of Reuben:
Hanok, Pallu, Hezron and Karmi.
[10] The sons of Simeon:
Jemuel, Jamin, Ohad, Jakin, Zohar and Shaul the son of a Canaanite woman.
[11] The sons of Levi:
Gershon, Kohath and Merari.
[12] The sons of Judah:
Er, Onan, Shelah, Perez and Zerah (but Er and Onan had died in the land of Canaan).
The sons of Perez:
Hezron and Hamul.
[13] The sons of Issachar:
Tola, Puah,[a] Jashub[b] and Shimron.
[14] The sons of Zebulun:
Sered, Elon and Jahleel.

[15] These were the sons Leah bore to Jacob in Paddan Aram,[c] besides his daughter Dinah. These sons and daughters of his were thirty-three in all.

[16] The sons of Gad:
Zephon,[d] Haggi, Shuni, Ezbon, Eri, Arodi and Areli.
[17] The sons of Asher:
Imnah, Ishvah, Ishvi and Beriah.
Their sister was Serah.
The sons of Beriah:
Heber and Malkiel.

---

[a] 13 Samaritan Pentateuch and Syriac (see also 1 Chron. 7:1); Masoretic Text *Puvah*   [b] 13 Samaritan Pentateuch and some Septuagint manuscripts (see also Num. 26:24 and 1 Chron. 7:1); Masoretic Text *Iob*   [c] 15 That is, Northwest Mesopotamia   [d] 16 Samaritan Pentateuch and Septuagint (see also Num. 26:15); Masoretic Text *Ziphion*

Why did Jacob offer a sacrifice at Beersheba? (46:1)
Beersheba was the place that Abraham and Isaac had also worshiped the Lord.

What does "Joseph's own hand will close your eyes" mean? (46:4)
God was promising to be with Jacob when he left his homeland just as he had before. (See Genesis 28:10–16.) He wanted Jacob to know that Joseph would be with him when he died.

Didn't Jacob have his own carts? (46:5)
Apparently not. Pharaoh was showing his generosity by providing what were probably two-wheeled oxcarts to transport the elderly and the young.

Why is it important to list all these names? (46:8–25)
Genealogies were important to people in ancient times to record their history and also to show how they were connected to the community. This was a complete list of descendants rather than only a list of those who entered Egypt.

[18] These were the children born to Jacob by Zilpah, whom Laban had given to his daughter Leah—sixteen in all.

[19] The sons of Jacob's wife Rachel:
Joseph and Benjamin. [20] In Egypt, Manasseh and Ephraim were born to Joseph by Asenath daughter of Potiphera, priest of On.[a]
[21] The sons of Benjamin:
Bela, Beker, Ashbel, Gera, Naaman, Ehi, Rosh, Muppim, Huppim and Ard.
[22] These were the sons of Rachel who were born to Jacob—fourteen in all.

[23] The son of Dan:
Hushim.
[24] The sons of Naphtali:
Jahziel, Guni, Jezer and Shillem.
[25] These were the sons born to Jacob by Bilhah, whom Laban had given to his daughter Rachel—seven in all.

[26] All those who went to Egypt with Jacob—those who were his direct descendants, not counting his sons' wives—numbered sixty-six persons. [27] With the two sons[b] who had been born to Joseph in Egypt, the members of Jacob's family, which went to Egypt, were seventy[c] in all.

[28] Now Jacob sent Judah ahead of him to Joseph to get directions to Goshen. When they arrived in the region of Goshen, [29] Joseph had his chariot made ready and went to Goshen to meet his father Israel. As soon as Joseph appeared before him, he threw his arms around his father[d] and wept for a long time.

[30] Israel said to Joseph, "Now I am ready to die, since I have seen for myself that you are still alive."

[31] Then Joseph said to his brothers and to his father's household, "I will go up and speak to Pharaoh and will say to him, 'My brothers and my father's household, who were living in the land of Canaan, have come to me. [32] The men are shepherds; they tend livestock, and they have brought along their flocks and herds and everything they own.' [33] When Pharaoh calls you in and asks, 'What is your occupation?' [34] you should answer, 'Your servants have tended livestock from our boyhood on, just as our fathers did.' Then you will be allowed to settle in the region of Goshen, for all shepherds are detestable to the Egyptians."

47 Joseph went and told Pharaoh, "My father and brothers, with their flocks and herds and everything they own, have come from the land of Canaan and are now in Goshen." [2] He chose five of his brothers and presented them before Pharaoh.

[3] Pharaoh asked the brothers, "What is your occupation?"

"Your servants are shepherds," they replied to Pharaoh, "just as our fathers were." [4] They also said to him, "We have come to live here for a while, because the famine is severe in

Why was the number 70 so important? (46:26–27)
Seventy was also the number of nations that formed after the flood in Noah's time.

Was it unusual for a grown man to cry so much? (46:29)
Joseph seems to have been a sensitive and emotional person who cried often. When Joseph saw his father after so many years, he wept for a long time. Tears show you are human.

Why didn't Joseph present all his brothers to Pharaoh? (47:2)
Because Egyptians were suspicious of foreigners, Joseph probably thought his large clan might be too intimidating. He also emphasized their occupations as livestock herders who would not interfere with Egypt's politics or economy.

---

[a] 20 That is, Heliopolis   [b] 27 Hebrew; Septuagint *the nine children*
[c] 27 Hebrew (see also Exodus 1:5 and note); Septuagint (see also Acts 7:14) *seventy-five*   [d] 29 Hebrew *around him*

Canaan and your servants' flocks have no pasture. So now, please let your servants settle in Goshen."

⁵Pharaoh said to Joseph, "Your father and your brothers have come to you, ⁶and the land of Egypt is before you; settle your father and your brothers in the best part of the land. Let them live in Goshen. And if you know of any among them with special ability, put them in charge of my own livestock."

⁷Then Joseph brought his father Jacob in and presented him before Pharaoh. After Jacob blessed*a* Pharaoh, ⁸Pharaoh asked him, "How old are you?"

⁹And Jacob said to Pharaoh, "The years of my pilgrimage are a hundred and thirty. My years have been few and difficult, and they do not equal the years of the pilgrimage of my fathers." ¹⁰Then Jacob blessed*b* Pharaoh and went out from his presence.

¹¹So Joseph settled his father and his brothers in Egypt and gave them property in the best part of the land, the district of Rameses, as Pharaoh directed. ¹²Joseph also provided his father and his brothers and all his father's household with food, according to the number of their children.

JOSEPH AND THE FAMINE

¹³There was no food, however, in the whole region because the famine was severe; both Egypt and Canaan wasted away because of the famine. ¹⁴Joseph collected all the money that was to be found in Egypt and Canaan in payment for the grain they were buying, and he brought it to Pharaoh's palace. ¹⁵When the money of the people of Egypt and Canaan was gone, all Egypt came to Joseph and said, "Give us food. Why should we die before your eyes? Our money is all gone."

¹⁶"Then bring your livestock," said Joseph. "I will sell you food in exchange for your livestock, since your money is gone." ¹⁷So they brought their livestock to Joseph, and he gave them food in exchange for their horses, their sheep and goats, their cattle and donkeys. And he brought them through that year with food in exchange for all their livestock.

¹⁸When that year was over, they came to him the following year and said, "We cannot hide from our lord the fact that since our money is gone and our livestock belongs to you, there is nothing left for our lord except our bodies and our land. ¹⁹Why should we perish before your eyes—we and our land as well? Buy us and our land in exchange for food, and we with our land will be in bondage to Pharaoh. Give us seed so that we may live and not die, and that the land may not become desolate."

²⁰So Joseph bought all the land in Egypt for Pharaoh. The Egyptians, one and all, sold their fields, because the famine was too severe for them. The land became Pharaoh's, ²¹and Joseph reduced the people to servitude,*c* from one end of Egypt to the other. ²²However, he did not buy the land of the priests, because they received a regular allotment from

---

a 7 Or *greeted*   *b 10* Or *said farewell to*   *c 21* Samaritan Pentateuch and Septuagint (see also Vulgate); Masoretic Text *and he moved the people into the cities*

Why did Jacob refer to his life as a pilgrimage? (47:9) A pilgrimage is a journey, especially to a sacred place. Jacob's life was made up of many journeys as he waited for the fulfillment of God's promise.

Who was Rameses? (47:11) Rameses was a future Pharaoh —Rameses II. The district of Rameses is a later name for the region of Goshen. (See the map at Exodus 13:17.)

How did Joseph change the system of land ownership in Egypt? (47:20–21) Joseph brought about a permanent change in the system of land ownership in Egypt. Almost all the land became the property of Pharaoh, and the previous owners became his tenants.

Does God use unbelievers to accomplish his will? (47:13–27) God is in control of all things and also works through people who have no faith in him. God had a plan for the nation of Egypt and used the Egyptians, along with Joseph, to accomplish his purposes.

Pharaoh and had food enough from the allotment Pharaoh gave them. That is why they did not sell their land.

23 Joseph said to the people, "Now that I have bought you and your land today for Pharaoh, here is seed for you so you can plant the ground. 24 But when the crop comes in, give a fifth of it to Pharaoh. The other four-fifths you may keep as seed for the fields and as food for yourselves and your households and your children."

25 "You have saved our lives," they said. "May we find favor in the eyes of our lord; we will be in bondage to Pharaoh."

26 So Joseph established it as a law concerning land in Egypt—still in force today—that a fifth of the produce belongs to Pharaoh. It was only the land of the priests that did not become Pharaoh's.

27 Now the Israelites settled in Egypt in the region of Goshen. They acquired property there and were fruitful and increased greatly in number.

28 Jacob lived in Egypt seventeen years, and the years of his life were a hundred and forty-seven. 29 When the time drew near for Israel to die, he called for his son Joseph and said to him, "If I have found favor in your eyes, put your hand under my thigh and promise that you will show me kindness and faithfulness. Do not bury me in Egypt, 30 but when I rest with my fathers, carry me out of Egypt and bury me where they are buried."

"I will do as you say," he said.

31 "Swear to me," he said. Then Joseph swore to him, and Israel worshiped as he leaned on the top of his staff. [a]

MANASSEH AND EPHRAIM

48 Some time later Joseph was told, "Your father is ill." So he took his two sons Manasseh and Ephraim along with him. 2 When Jacob was told, "Your son Joseph has come to you," Israel rallied his strength and sat up on the bed.

3 Jacob said to Joseph, "God Almighty [b] appeared to me at Luz in the land of Canaan, and there he blessed me 4 and said to me, 'I am going to make you fruitful and increase your numbers. I will make you a community of peoples, and I will give this land as an everlasting possession to your descendants after you.'

5 "Now then, your two sons born to you in Egypt before I came to you here will be reckoned as mine; Ephraim and Manasseh will be mine, just as Reuben and Simeon are mine. 6 Any children born to you after them will be yours; in the territory they inherit they will be reckoned under the names of their brothers. 7 As I was returning from Paddan, [c] to my sorrow Rachel died in the land of Canaan while we were still on the way, a little distance from Ephrath. So I buried her there beside the road to Ephrath" (that is, Bethlehem).

8 When Israel saw the sons of Joseph, he asked, "Who are these?"

9 "They are the sons God has given me here," Joseph said to his father.

Where did Jacob want to be buried? (47:30)
He wanted to be buried with his ancestors in the cave of Machpelah, in Canaan, the land the Lord had promised to him and his descendants. (See Genesis 23:9.)

Where was Luz? (48:3)
Luz was an old name for Bethel (Genesis 28:19). Jacob was referring to the place where God had first appeared to him in a dream with angels ascending and descending a stairway to heaven. This is where God made his covenant with Jacob that God would give him the land of Canaan and his descendants would be too many to count.

Why did Jacob claim Joseph's two sons as his own? (48:5)
Jacob adopted them in order to change their inheritance. The firstborn son normally received a double portion, and then other sons received equal portions of the remainder. Jacob was increasing Joseph's inheritance.

Why didn't Jacob recognize his grandsons? (48:8, 10)
Because Jacob was old, perhaps his eyesight was failing and he couldn't see them clearly. Also he may have never met them before.

---

[a] 31 Or *Israel bowed down at the head of his bed*   [b] 3 Hebrew *El-Shaddai*
[c] 7 That is, Northwest Mesopotamia

Then Israel said, "Bring them to me so I may bless them."

[10] Now Israel's eyes were failing because of old age, and he could hardly see. So Joseph brought his sons close to him, and his father kissed them and embraced them.

[11] Israel said to Joseph, "I never expected to see your face again, and now God has allowed me to see your children too."

[12] Then Joseph removed them from Israel's knees and bowed down with his face to the ground. [13] And Joseph took both of them, Ephraim on his right toward Israel's left hand and Manasseh on his left toward Israel's right hand, and brought them close to him. [14] But Israel reached out his right hand and put it on Ephraim's head, though he was the younger, and crossing his arms, he put his left hand on Manasseh's head, even though Manasseh was the firstborn.

[15] Then he blessed Joseph and said,

"May the God before whom my fathers
    Abraham and Isaac walked faithfully,
the God who has been my shepherd
    all my life to this day,
[16] the Angel who has delivered me from all harm
    —may he bless these boys.
May they be called by my name
    and the names of my fathers Abraham and Isaac,
and may they increase greatly
    on the earth."

[17] When Joseph saw his father placing his right hand on Ephraim's head he was displeased; so he took hold of his father's hand to move it from Ephraim's head to Manasseh's head. [18] Joseph said to him, "No, my father, this one is the firstborn; put your right hand on his head."

[19] But his father refused and said, "I know, my son, I know. He too will become a people, and he too will become great. Nevertheless, his younger brother will be greater than he, and his descendants will become a group of nations." [20] He blessed them that day and said,

"In your*a* name will Israel pronounce this blessing:
    'May God make you like Ephraim and Manasseh.'"

So he put Ephraim ahead of Manasseh.

[21] Then Israel said to Joseph, "I am about to die, but God will be with you*b* and take you*b* back to the land of your*b* fathers. [22] And to you I give one more ridge of land*c* than to your brothers, the ridge I took from the Amorites with my sword and my bow."

JACOB BLESSES HIS SONS

49 Then Jacob called for his sons and said: "Gather around so I can tell you what will happen to you in days to come.

[2] "Assemble and listen, sons of Jacob;
    listen to your father Israel.

a 20 The Hebrew is singular.   *b 21* The Hebrew is plural.
c 22 The Hebrew for *ridge of land* is identical with the place name Shechem.

Why did Jacob cross his arms to put his right hand on Ephraim's head? (48:13–14)
In the ancient Middle East, the right hand was the hand of strength and privilege. It was a sign of honor to sit to the right of someone. He was giving more honor to the younger son.

Why was Joseph displeased? (48:17–18)
He thought Jacob made a mistake. Joseph expected his older son to receive the special blessing. But Jacob said that the younger brother would be greater. Through Jacob, God was reminding Joseph that he doesn't always do things in the expected ways.

Was Jacob right to put the younger son ahead of the older son? (48:20)
Yes. He was demonstrating that blessing is not a right but a gift. For four generations, the younger brother received the family blessing: Isaac rather than Ishmael; Jacob rather than Esau; Joseph rather than Reuben; and now Ephraim rather than Manasseh.

Did Jacob really know the future? (49:1)
No, but even people today are interested in a dying person's last words.

Why did Jacob scold Reuben? (49:3–4)
Reuben had lost his rights as firstborn by sleeping with his father's concubine (see Genesis 35:22).

Why did Jacob curse Simeon and Levi? (49:7)
He cursed their anger rather than the sons themselves. Perhaps he hoped that when they heard his warning, they would be blessed by correcting their faults.

Why did Jacob describe his sons as animals? (49:9–27)
A common practice in the Bible, Jacob was using a metaphor to compare his son's characteristics to animals. A lion, for instance, symbolized strength and strong leadership, so Jacob told Judah he was a good leader. For the other animals, the donkey equaled submission; the serpent represented craftiness; the doe symbolized swiftness with skills; and the wolf embodied persistence.

What did the scepter and ruler's staff represent? (49:10)
These were signs of royalty. Judah's clan became the most important tribal group, and this was Jacob's way of confirming Judah as leader of the family.

³ "Reuben, you are my firstborn,
  my might, the first sign of my strength,
  excelling in honor, excelling in power.
⁴ Turbulent as the waters, you will no longer excel,
  for you went up onto your father's bed,
  onto my couch and defiled it.

⁵ "Simeon and Levi are brothers—
  their swords[a] are weapons of violence.
⁶ Let me not enter their council,
  let me not join their assembly,
  for they have killed men in their anger
  and hamstrung oxen as they pleased.
⁷ Cursed be their anger, so fierce,
  and their fury, so cruel!
I will scatter them in Jacob
  and disperse them in Israel.

⁸ "Judah,[b] your brothers will praise you;
  your hand will be on the neck of your enemies;
  your father's sons will bow down to you.
⁹ You are a lion's cub, Judah;
  you return from the prey, my son.
Like a lion he crouches and lies down,
  like a lioness—who dares to rouse him?
¹⁰ The scepter will not depart from Judah,
  nor the ruler's staff from between his feet,[c]
until he to whom it belongs[d] shall come
  and the obedience of the nations shall be his.
¹¹ He will tether his donkey to a vine,
  his colt to the choicest branch;
he will wash his garments in wine,
  his robes in the blood of grapes.
¹² His eyes will be darker than wine,
  his teeth whiter than milk.[e]

¹³ "Zebulun will live by the seashore
  and become a haven for ships;
  his border will extend toward Sidon.

¹⁴ "Issachar is a rawboned[f] donkey
  lying down among the sheep pens.[g]
¹⁵ When he sees how good is his resting place
  and how pleasant is his land,
he will bend his shoulder to the burden
  and submit to forced labor.

¹⁶ "Dan[b] will provide justice for his people
  as one of the tribes of Israel.
¹⁷ Dan will be a snake by the roadside,
  a viper along the path,
that bites the horse's heels
  so that its rider tumbles backward.

---

a 5 The meaning of the Hebrew for this word is uncertain.   *b 8 Judah* sounds like and may be derived from the Hebrew for *praise.*   *c 10* Or *from his descendants*   *d 10* Or *to whom tribute belongs*; the meaning of the Hebrew for this phrase is uncertain.   *e 12* Or *will be dull from wine, / his teeth white from milk*   *f 14* Or *strong*   *g 14* Or *the campfires*; or *the saddlebags*   *b 16 Dan* here means *he provides justice.*

18 "I look for your deliverance, LORD.

19 "Gad*a* will be attacked by a band of raiders,
  but he will attack them at their heels.

20 "Asher's food will be rich;
  he will provide delicacies fit for a king.

21 "Naphtali is a doe set free
  that bears beautiful fawns.*b*

22 "Joseph is a fruitful vine,
  a fruitful vine near a spring,
  whose branches climb over a wall.*c*

23 With bitterness archers attacked him;
  they shot at him with hostility.

24 But his bow remained steady,
  his strong arms stayed*d* limber,
 because of the hand of the Mighty One of Jacob,
  because of the Shepherd, the Rock of Israel,

25 because of your father's God, who helps you,
  because of the Almighty,*e* who blesses you
 with blessings of the skies above,
  blessings of the deep springs below,
  blessings of the breast and womb.

26 Your father's blessings are greater
  than the blessings of the ancient mountains,
  than*f* the bounty of the age-old hills.
 Let all these rest on the head of Joseph,
  on the brow of the prince among*g* his brothers.

27 "Benjamin is a ravenous wolf;
  in the morning he devours the prey,
  in the evening he divides the plunder."

28 All these are the twelve tribes of Israel, and this is what
their father said to them when he blessed them, giving each
the blessing appropriate to him.

THE DEATH OF JACOB

29 Then he gave them these instructions: "I am about to be
gathered to my people. Bury me with my fathers in the cave
in the field of Ephron the Hittite, 30 the cave in the field of
Machpelah, near Mamre in Canaan, which Abraham bought
along with the field as a burial place from Ephron the Hittite. 31 There Abraham and his wife Sarah were buried, there
Isaac and his wife Rebekah were buried, and there I buried
Leah. 32 The field and the cave in it were bought from the
Hittites.*h*"

33 When Jacob had finished giving instructions to his sons,
he drew his feet up into the bed, breathed his last and was
gathered to his people.

---

a 19 Gad sounds like the Hebrew for *attack* and also for *band of raiders.*
b 21 Or *free; / he utters beautiful words*   *c 22* Or *Joseph is a wild colt, / a wild
colt near a spring, / a wild donkey on a terraced hill*   *d 23,24* Or *archers will
attack . . . will shoot . . . will remain . . . will stay*   *e 25* Hebrew *Shaddai*
f 26 Or *of my progenitors, / as great as*   *g 26* Or *of the one separated from*
h 32 Or *the descendants of Heth*

**Does this attack refer to the
time when Joseph's brothers
attacked him? (49:23)**
It may refer to the original attack
on Joseph by his brothers, but
it could also mean the ordeals
Joseph endured in Egypt.

**Why wasn't Jacob buried
with his favorite wife,
Rachel? (49:31)**
Jacob followed the tradition of
being buried in the family burial
grounds with his first wife. Although Rachel was his favorite,
she was his second wife and was
buried elsewhere.

What is embalming?
(50:2–3)
Embalming is a process of preserving the body after death. After embalming, the body was wrapped in linen and placed in a wooden case. The philosophy behind the Egyptian practice of embalming was the belief that the body should be preserved as a place for the soul to occupy after death.

Why did so many Egyptians mourn a foreigner? (50:7)
Because of Joseph's importance and out of respect, the Egyptians held a grand funeral procession for his father. They also extended the mourning period to 70 days, which indicated how Joseph was held in high regard.

What is a threshing floor?
(50:10)
A threshing floor was a flat circular surface located on a high open area. The wheat was beaten on this surface in order to separate the kernels of grain from the plant. The wind carried away the lighter waste, and the heavy grain was picked up.

50 Joseph threw himself on his father and wept over him and kissed him. [2] Then Joseph directed the physicians in his service to embalm his father Israel. So the physicians embalmed him, [3] taking a full forty days, for that was the time required for embalming. And the Egyptians mourned for him seventy days.

[4] When the days of mourning had passed, Joseph said to Pharaoh's court, "If I have found favor in your eyes, speak to Pharaoh for me. Tell him, [5] 'My father made me swear an oath and said, "I am about to die; bury me in the tomb I dug for myself in the land of Canaan." Now let me go up and bury my father; then I will return.'"

[6] Pharaoh said, "Go up and bury your father, as he made you swear to do."

[7] So Joseph went up to bury his father. All Pharaoh's officials accompanied him—the dignitaries of his court and all the dignitaries of Egypt— [8] besides all the members of Joseph's household and his brothers and those belonging to his father's household. Only their children and their flocks and herds were left in Goshen. [9] Chariots and horsemen[a] also went up with him. It was a very large company.

[10] When they reached the threshing floor of Atad, near the Jordan, they lamented loudly and bitterly; and there Joseph observed a seven-day period of mourning for his father. [11] When the Canaanites who lived there saw the mourning at the threshing floor of Atad, they said, "The Egyptians are holding a solemn ceremony of mourning." That is why that place near the Jordan is called Abel Mizraim.[b]

[12] So Jacob's sons did as he had commanded them: [13] They carried him to the land of Canaan and buried him in the cave in the field of Machpelah, near Mamre, which Abraham had bought along with the field as a burial place from Ephron the Hittite. [14] After burying his father, Joseph returned to Egypt, together with his brothers and all the others who had gone with him to bury his father.

JOSEPH REASSURES HIS BROTHERS

[15] When Joseph's brothers saw that their father was dead, they said, "What if Joseph holds a grudge against us and pays us back for all the wrongs we did to him?" [16] So they sent

[a] 9 Or *charioteers*   [b] 11 *Abel Mizraim* means *mourning of the Egyptians.*

How does God care for his people even when things seem to be going wrong? GENESIS 50

The story of Joseph is just one example of many in the Bible where followers of God experience hardship, pain, or misfortune. Joseph's brothers sold him into slavery, he was imprisoned in Egypt, and things did not seem very promising. However, God led Joseph to Pharaoh's court, and he became second in command over the kingdom. He also developed a plan for storing crops to help the people get through several years of famine.

God frequently uses people who seem to be unlikely to accomplish his purposes. The classic summary of this is found in Genesis 50:19–20, where Joseph speaks to his brothers: "Don't be afraid. Am I in the place of God? You intended to harm me, but God intended it for good to accomplish what is now being done, the saving of many lives."

word to Joseph, saying, "Your father left these instructions before he died: [17]'This is what you are to say to Joseph: I ask you to forgive your brothers the sins and the wrongs they committed in treating you so badly.' Now please forgive the sins of the servants of the God of your father." When their message came to him, Joseph wept.

[18]His brothers then came and threw themselves down before him. "We are your slaves," they said.

[19]But Joseph said to them, "Don't be afraid. Am I in the place of God? [20]You intended to harm me, but God intended it for good to accomplish what is now being done, the saving of many lives. [21]So then, don't be afraid. I will provide for you and your children." And he reassured them and spoke kindly to them.

THE DEATH OF JOSEPH

[22]Joseph stayed in Egypt, along with all his father's family. He lived a hundred and ten years [23]and saw the third generation of Ephraim's children. Also the children of Makir son of Manasseh were placed at birth on Joseph's knees.[a]

[24]Then Joseph said to his brothers, "I am about to die. But God will surely come to your aid and take you up out of this land to the land he promised on oath to Abraham, Isaac and Jacob." [25]And Joseph made the Israelites swear an oath and said, "God will surely come to your aid, and then you must carry my bones up from this place."

[26]So Joseph died at the age of a hundred and ten. And after they embalmed him, he was placed in a coffin in Egypt.

Why did Joseph say God would come to their aid to leave Egypt? (50:24)
Joseph predicted that God would help the Hebrews return to Canaan in order to fulfill his promise to Joseph's ancestors. Joseph had no idea at this time that several generations later, his descendants would be slaves to the Egyptians and would truly need God's help. (See Exodus 1.)

Why was Joseph's burial place so important to him? (50:25)
Joseph wanted to stay true to God's original promise to Abraham of a homeland (see Genesis 12:1–3). His desire to be buried in Canaan was an expression of faith that God would keep his promise.

---

[a] 23 That is, were counted as his

Exodus

INTRODUCTION

Who wrote this book?	Moses.
Why was this book written?	Exodus shows how God used his power to rescue the Israelites from slavery.
What happens in this book?	God brings ten terrible plagues on Egypt. He forces Pharaoh to let God's people go. God gives the Israelites the Ten Commandments and other laws by which to live.
What do we learn about God in this book?	God uses his power to rescue helpless people. God expects his people to live moral and righteous lives.
Who are the key people in this book?	The most important people in this book are Moses and Aaron.
Where did this happen?	Exodus 1–12 took place in Egypt. Most other events took place at Mount Sinai. (See the map at the back of this Bible to find Mount Sinai.)
What are some of the stories in this book?	Baby Moses — Exodus 2 A burning bush — Exodus 3 The ten plagues — Exodus 7–11 The Passover — Exodus 12 Crossing the Red Sea — Exodus 14 The Ten Commandments — Exodus 20 Building the tabernacle — Exodus 25–27 The golden calf — Exodus 32

When did these things happen?

2200 BC 2100 2000 1900 1800 1700 1600 1500 1400

MOSES' BIRTH (C. 1526 BC)

THE PLAGUES; THE PASSOVER (C. 1446 BC)

THE EXODUS (C. 1446 BC)

DESERT WANDERINGS (C. 1446 – 1406 BC)

THE TEN COMMANDMENTS (C. 1445 BC)

BOOK OF EXODUS WRITTEN (C. 1440 BC)

MOSES DIES; JOSHUA BECOMES LEADER (C. 1406 BC)

ISRAELITES ENTER CANAAN (C. 1406 BC)

THE ISRAELITES OPPRESSED

1 These are the names of the sons of Israel who went to Egypt with Jacob, each with his family: ²Reuben, Simeon, Levi and Judah; ³Issachar, Zebulun and Benjamin; ⁴Dan and Naphtali; Gad and Asher. ⁵The descendants of Jacob numbered seventy*a* in all; Joseph was already in Egypt.

⁶Now Joseph and all his brothers and all that generation died, ⁷but the Israelites were exceedingly fruitful; they multiplied greatly, increased in numbers and became so numerous that the land was filled with them.

⁸Then a new king, to whom Joseph meant nothing, came to power in Egypt. ⁹"Look," he said to his people, "the Israelites have become far too numerous for us. ¹⁰Come, we must deal shrewdly with them or they will become even more numerous and, if war breaks out, will join our enemies, fight against us and leave the country."

¹¹So they put slave masters over them to oppress them with forced labor, and they built Pithom and Rameses as store cities for Pharaoh. ¹²But the more they were oppressed, the more they multiplied and spread; so the Egyptians came to dread the Israelites ¹³and worked them ruthlessly. ¹⁴They made their lives bitter with harsh labor in brick and mortar and with all kinds of work in the fields; in all their harsh labor the Egyptians worked them ruthlessly.

¹⁵The king of Egypt said to the Hebrew midwives, whose names were Shiphrah and Puah, ¹⁶"When you are helping the Hebrew women during childbirth on the delivery stool, if you see that the baby is a boy, kill him; but if it is a girl, let her live." ¹⁷The midwives, however, feared God and did not do what the king of Egypt had told them to do; they let the boys live. ¹⁸Then the king of Egypt summoned the midwives and asked them, "Why have you done this? Why have you let the boys live?"

¹⁹The midwives answered Pharaoh, "Hebrew women are not like Egyptian women; they are vigorous and give birth before the midwives arrive."

²⁰So God was kind to the midwives and the people increased and became even more numerous. ²¹And because the midwives feared God, he gave them families of their own.

²²Then Pharaoh gave this order to all his people: "Every Hebrew boy that is born you must throw into the Nile, but let every girl live."

THE BIRTH OF MOSES

2 Now a man of the tribe of Levi married a Levite woman, ²and she became pregnant and gave birth to a son. When she saw that he was a fine child, she hid him for three months. ³But when she could hide him no longer, she got a papyrus basket*b* for him and coated it with tar and pitch. Then she placed the child in it and put it among the reeds along the bank of the Nile. ⁴His sister stood at a distance to see what would happen to him.

---

a 5 Masoretic Text (see also Gen. 46:27); Dead Sea Scrolls and Septuagint (see also Acts 7:14 and note at Gen. 46:27) *seventy-five*   *b 3* The Hebrew can also mean *ark*, as in Gen. 6:14.

Why didn't the new king of Egypt know about Joseph? (1:8)
Many years and many generations had passed since Joseph died. The Egyptians forgot Joseph's role in saving their people from starving.

Why did the king want to "deal shrewdly" with the Israelites? (1:9–10)
The king saw that the Israelites were growing in number, and he was afraid they would recognize their power and rebel against the people in charge. He thought it would be wise to plan ahead and to make them slaves so they would be powerless.

What were Egyptian bricks like? (1:14)
Ancient bricks were generally square and measured about 13 x 13 x 3.5 inches (33 x 33 x 9 cm). Before the bricks were baked, they were often stamped with the name of the ruler.

What is a midwife? (1:15)
A midwife is a woman who helps other women give birth to their babies.

Was it morally acceptable for the midwives to lie to the king? (1:19–20)
Because the king's command was evil and contradicted God's law, the midwives were obeying a higher authority: God himself.

Did Moses' mother obey the king's command? (2:3)
In a way, yes. She did put her son in the river as commanded, but instead of *throwing* him into the Nile River, she made a waterproof papyrus basket for him and placed it along the shore where Pharaoh's daughter bathed.

[5]Then Pharaoh's daughter went down to the Nile to bathe, and her attendants were walking along the riverbank. She saw the basket among the reeds and sent her female slave to get it. [6]She opened it and saw the baby. He was crying, and she felt sorry for him. "This is one of the Hebrew babies," she said.

[7]Then his sister asked Pharaoh's daughter, "Shall I go and get one of the Hebrew women to nurse the baby for you?"

[8]"Yes, go," she answered. So the girl went and got the baby's mother. [9]Pharaoh's daughter said to her, "Take this baby and nurse him for me, and I will pay you." So the woman took the baby and nursed him. [10]When the child grew older, she took him to Pharaoh's daughter and he became her son. She named him Moses,[a] saying, "I drew him out of the water."

MOSES FLEES TO MIDIAN

[11]One day, after Moses had grown up, he went out to where his own people were and watched them at their hard labor. He saw an Egyptian beating a Hebrew, one of his own people. [12]Looking this way and that and seeing no one, he killed the Egyptian and hid him in the sand. [13]The next day he went out and saw two Hebrews fighting. He asked the one in the wrong, "Why are you hitting your fellow Hebrew?"

[14]The man said, "Who made you ruler and judge over us? Are you thinking of killing me as you killed the Egyptian?" Then Moses was afraid and thought, "What I did must have become known."

[15]When Pharaoh heard of this, he tried to kill Moses, but Moses fled from Pharaoh and went to live in Midian, where he sat down by a well. [16]Now a priest of Midian had seven daughters, and they came to draw water and fill the troughs to water their father's flock. [17]Some shepherds came along and drove them away, but Moses got up and came to their rescue and watered their flock.

[18]When the girls returned to Reuel their father, he asked them, "Why have you returned so early today?"

[19]They answered, "An Egyptian rescued us from the shepherds. He even drew water for us and watered the flock."

[20]"And where is he?" Reuel asked his daughters. "Why did you leave him? Invite him to have something to eat."

[21]Moses agreed to stay with the man, who gave his daughter Zipporah to Moses in marriage. [22]Zipporah gave birth to a son, and Moses named him Gershom,[b] saying, "I have become a foreigner in a foreign land."

[23]During that long period, the king of Egypt died. The Israelites groaned in their slavery and cried out, and their cry for help because of their slavery went up to God. [24]God heard their groaning and he remembered his covenant with Abraham, with Isaac and with Jacob. [25]So God looked on the Israelites and was concerned about them.

[a] 10 Moses sounds like the Hebrew for *draw out.*   [b] 22 Gershom sounds like the Hebrew for *a foreigner there.*

How long did Moses' mother take care of him? (2:9–10)
Moses' mother was paid to nurse him, probably for at least his first two years of life and possibly for even three or four years.

Did the princess actually adopt Moses? (2:10)
Yes; some people believe that slave adoption was a common practice for Egyptian nobility. The princess gave Moses an Egyptian name and raised Moses as an Egyptian, not as a Hebrew. Her royal status put her above the law others had to follow—to kill male Hebrew babies.

Was it right for Moses to kill the Egyptian? (2:12)
No. Moses showed he knew it was wrong when he looked around to see if anyone was watching and when he buried the body.

Moses Flees to Midian (2:15)

Who was this priest of Midian? (2:16)
The Midianites had descended from Abraham through one of his concubines (see Genesis 25:1–2). In addition to serving a religious role, the priest was probably the tribal chief. He took Moses in and gave him his daughter to marry.

MOSES AND THE BURNING BUSH

3 Now Moses was tending the flock of Jethro his father-in-law, the priest of Midian, and he led the flock to the far side of the wilderness and came to Horeb, the mountain of God. [2]There the angel of the LORD appeared to him in flames of fire from within a bush. Moses saw that though the bush was on fire it did not burn up. [3]So Moses thought, "I will go over and see this strange sight—why the bush does not burn up."

[4]When the LORD saw that he had gone over to look, God called to him from within the bush, "Moses! Moses!"

And Moses said, "Here I am."

[5]"Do not come any closer," God said. "Take off your sandals, for the place where you are standing is holy ground." [6]Then he said, "I am the God of your father,[a] the God of Abraham, the God of Isaac and the God of Jacob." At this, Moses hid his face, because he was afraid to look at God.

[7]The LORD said, "I have indeed seen the misery of my people in Egypt. I have heard them crying out because of their slave drivers, and I am concerned about their suffering. [8]So I have come down to rescue them from the hand of the Egyptians and to bring them up out of that land into a good and spacious land, a land flowing with milk and honey—the home of the Canaanites, Hittites, Amorites, Perizzites, Hivites and Jebusites. [9]And now the cry of the Israelites has reached me, and I have seen the way the Egyptians are oppressing them. [10]So now, go. I am sending you to Pharaoh to bring my people the Israelites out of Egypt."

[11]But Moses said to God, "Who am I that I should go to Pharaoh and bring the Israelites out of Egypt?"

[12]And God said, "I will be with you. And this will be the sign to you that it is I who have sent you: When you have brought the people out of Egypt, you[b] will worship God on this mountain."

[13]Moses said to God, "Suppose I go to the Israelites and say to them, 'The God of your fathers has sent me to you,' and they ask me, 'What is his name?' Then what shall I tell them?"

[14]God said to Moses, "I AM WHO I AM.[c] This is what you are to say to the Israelites: 'I AM has sent me to you.'"

[15]God also said to Moses, "Say to the Israelites, 'The LORD,[d] the God of your fathers—the God of Abraham, the God of Isaac and the God of Jacob—has sent me to you.'

"This is my name forever,
    the name you shall call me
    from generation to generation.

[16]"Go, assemble the elders of Israel and say to them, 'The LORD, the God of your fathers—the God of Abraham, Isaac and Jacob—appeared to me and said: I have watched over you and have seen what has been done to you in Egypt.

Why did Moses take off his sandals before he approached the burning bush? (3:5)
This was holy ground because God spoke to Moses there. Bare feet were a symbol of respect for God.

Why would God make the tribes living in Canaan leave? (3:8)
The Canaanites were living on the land that God had promised to Moses' ancestors (see Genesis 12:7). God promised they would get back the land they had left behind. In addition, God wanted to punish the pagan Canaanite tribes for their idolatry.

Why would using God's name convince the Israelites? (3:14)
Many scholars think that the names *I AM WHO I AM* or *I AM* were the most holy names for God. When Moses spoke this name, it probably reminded the Israelites of God's absolute supremacy and his promise to them.

---

[a] 6 Masoretic Text; Samaritan Pentateuch (see Acts 7:32) *fathers*
[b] 12 The Hebrew is plural.   [c] 14 Or *I WILL BE WHAT I WILL BE*
[d] 15 The Hebrew for LORD sounds like and may be related to the Hebrew for *I AM* in verse 14.

¹⁷ And I have promised to bring you up out of your misery in Egypt into the land of the Canaanites, Hittites, Amorites, Perizzites, Hivites and Jebusites — a land flowing with milk and honey.'

¹⁸ "The elders of Israel will listen to you. Then you and the elders are to go to the king of Egypt and say to him, 'The LORD, the God of the Hebrews, has met with us. Let us take a three-day journey into the wilderness to offer sacrifices to the LORD our God.' ¹⁹ But I know that the king of Egypt will not let you go unless a mighty hand compels him. ²⁰ So I will stretch out my hand and strike the Egyptians with all the wonders that I will perform among them. After that, he will let you go.

²¹ "And I will make the Egyptians favorably disposed toward this people, so that when you leave you will not go empty-handed. ²² Every woman is to ask her neighbor and any woman living in her house for articles of silver and gold and for clothing, which you will put on your sons and daughters. And so you will plunder the Egyptians."

SIGNS FOR MOSES

4 Moses answered, "What if they do not believe me or listen to me and say, 'The LORD did not appear to you'?" ² Then the LORD said to him, "What is that in your hand?"

"A staff," he replied.

³ The LORD said, "Throw it on the ground."

Moses threw it on the ground and it became a snake, and he ran from it. ⁴ Then the LORD said to him, "Reach out your hand and take it by the tail." So Moses reached out and took hold of the snake and it turned back into a staff in his hand. ⁵ "This," said the LORD, "is so that they may believe that the LORD, the God of their fathers — the God of Abraham, the God of Isaac and the God of Jacob — has appeared to you."

⁶ Then the LORD said, "Put your hand inside your cloak." So Moses put his hand into his cloak, and when he took it out, the skin was leprous^a — it had become as white as snow.

⁷ "Now put it back into your cloak," he said. So Moses put his hand back into his cloak, and when he took it out, it was restored, like the rest of his flesh.

⁸ Then the LORD said, "If they do not believe you or pay attention to the first sign, they may believe the second. ⁹ But if they do not believe these two signs or listen to you, take some water from the Nile and pour it on the dry ground. The water you take from the river will become blood on the ground."

¹⁰ Moses said to the LORD, "Pardon your servant, Lord. I have never been eloquent, neither in the past nor since you have spoken to your servant. I am slow of speech and tongue."

¹¹ The LORD said to him, "Who gave human beings their mouths? Who makes them deaf or mute? Who gives them sight or makes them blind? Is it not I, the LORD? ¹² Now go; I will help you speak and will teach you what to say."

What wonders was God referring to? (3:20)
God's wonders were the plagues he would send against Egypt.

Why would the Egyptians hand over their jewelry? (3:21–22)
It was the Egyptian custom to provide freed slaves with gifts to help them get started on their own. By the time the Israelites left Egypt after the plagues, the Egyptians were probably more than happy to see them go (See Exodus 12:33–36).

Why did God choose these signs to show the Egyptians through Moses that he was God? (4:1–9)
The staff and the snake may have been Egyptian symbols of power and life; the signs symbolized that God was more powerful than the Egyptians and their gods. The leprous hand warned Pharaoh that Moses, with the power of God, had the power to make people sick. Because the Egyptians worshiped the Nile River, the blood demonstrated that God had power over the Egyptian gods.

---

^a 6 The Hebrew word for *leprous* was used for various diseases affecting the skin.

¹³But Moses said, "Pardon your servant, Lord. Please send someone else."

¹⁴Then the LORD's anger burned against Moses and he said, "What about your brother, Aaron the Levite? I know he can speak well. He is already on his way to meet you, and he will be glad to see you. ¹⁵You shall speak to him and put words in his mouth; I will help both of you speak and will teach you what to do. ¹⁶He will speak to the people for you, and it will be as if he were your mouth and as if you were God to him. ¹⁷But take this staff in your hand so you can perform the signs with it."

MOSES RETURNS TO EGYPT

¹⁸Then Moses went back to Jethro his father-in-law and said to him, "Let me return to my own people in Egypt to see if any of them are still alive."

Jethro said, "Go, and I wish you well."

¹⁹Now the LORD had said to Moses in Midian, "Go back to Egypt, for all those who wanted to kill you are dead." ²⁰So Moses took his wife and sons, put them on a donkey and started back to Egypt. And he took the staff of God in his hand.

²¹The LORD said to Moses, "When you return to Egypt, see that you perform before Pharaoh all the wonders I have given you the power to do. But I will harden his heart so that he will not let the people go. ²²Then say to Pharaoh, 'This is what the LORD says: Israel is my firstborn son, ²³and I told you, "Let my son go, so he may worship me." But you refused to let him go; so I will kill your firstborn son.'"

²⁴At a lodging place on the way, the LORD met Moses[a] and was about to kill him. ²⁵But Zipporah took a flint knife, cut off her son's foreskin and touched Moses' feet with it.[b] "Surely you are a bridegroom of blood to me," she said. ²⁶So the LORD let him alone. (At that time she said "bridegroom of blood," referring to circumcision.)

²⁷The LORD said to Aaron, "Go into the wilderness to meet Moses." So he met Moses at the mountain of God and kissed him. ²⁸Then Moses told Aaron everything the LORD had sent him to say, and also about all the signs he had commanded him to perform.

²⁹Moses and Aaron brought together all the elders of the Israelites, ³⁰and Aaron told them everything the LORD had said to Moses. He also performed the signs before the people, ³¹and they believed. And when they heard that the LORD was concerned about them and had seen their misery, they bowed down and worshiped.

BRICKS WITHOUT STRAW

5 Afterward Moses and Aaron went to Pharaoh and said, "This is what the LORD, the God of Israel, says: 'Let my people go, so that they may hold a festival to me in the wilderness.'"

²Pharaoh said, "Who is the LORD, that I should obey him and let Israel go? I do not know the LORD and I will not let Israel go."

[a] 24 Hebrew him   [b] 25 The meaning of the Hebrew for this clause is uncertain.

Why did God call Israel his firstborn son? (4:22)
This is a figure of speech indicating Israel's special relationship with God. This language symbolizes how God will repay Pharaoh for keeping the Israelites in bondage.

Why did God want to kill Moses? (4:24)
God's people were told to circumcise their sons (remove the foreskin of the penis). Moses had not done this (maybe because his wife did not believe in the practice). Because Moses had disobeyed God, God was ready to kill him. God wanted Moses and his wife to take care of this before Moses faced Pharaoh.

Why was Pharaoh unimpressed by the Israelites' God? (5:2)
He didn't know their God and thought his gods were more important than the God of the lower-class people he ruled.

Why would they need to travel into the desert to make sacrifices? (5:3)
The Egyptians considered the Hebrew people to be ritually unclean because they didn't worship the Egyptian gods. The Israelites would need to make animal sacrifices where the Egyptians couldn't see them because the Egyptians would find the sacrifices detestable. (See Genesis 43:32.)

Why didn't Moses and Aaron perform God's signs for Pharaoh? (5:3)
On the first visit, they were giving Pharaoh the opportunity to do the right thing without force.

Why was straw needed to make the bricks? (5:7)
Egyptian brick was made of clay and sand mixed with water; straw was added as a binder to make the bricks hold together better. The bricks were shaped by hand or poured into molds.

Why did Pharaoh think the Israelites were lying? (5:9)
Pharaoh believed these religious observances were the excuses of lazy people who wanted a holiday.

Why did Moses blame God for the trouble? (5:22)
Moses had been reluctant to carry out this mission, and now it had turned out to be worse than failure. He blamed God because speaking in the Lord's name had brought even more trouble for his people.

³Then they said, "The God of the Hebrews has met with us. Now let us take a three-day journey into the wilderness to offer sacrifices to the LORD our God, or he may strike us with plagues or with the sword."

⁴But the king of Egypt said, "Moses and Aaron, why are you taking the people away from their labor? Get back to your work!" ⁵Then Pharaoh said, "Look, the people of the land are now numerous, and you are stopping them from working."

⁶That same day Pharaoh gave this order to the slave drivers and overseers in charge of the people: ⁷"You are no longer to supply the people with straw for making bricks; let them go and gather their own straw. ⁸But require them to make the same number of bricks as before; don't reduce the quota. They are lazy; that is why they are crying out, 'Let us go and sacrifice to our God.' ⁹Make the work harder for the people so that they keep working and pay no attention to lies."

¹⁰Then the slave drivers and the overseers went out and said to the people, "This is what Pharaoh says: 'I will not give you any more straw. ¹¹Go and get your own straw wherever you can find it, but your work will not be reduced at all.'" ¹²So the people scattered all over Egypt to gather stubble to use for straw. ¹³The slave drivers kept pressing them, saying, "Complete the work required of you for each day, just as when you had straw." ¹⁴And Pharaoh's slave drivers beat the Israelite overseers they had appointed, demanding, "Why haven't you met your quota of bricks yesterday or today, as before?"

¹⁵Then the Israelite overseers went and appealed to Pharaoh: "Why have you treated your servants this way? ¹⁶Your servants are given no straw, yet we are told, 'Make bricks!' Your servants are being beaten, but the fault is with your own people."

¹⁷Pharaoh said, "Lazy, that's what you are—lazy! That is why you keep saying, 'Let us go and sacrifice to the LORD.' ¹⁸Now get to work. You will not be given any straw, yet you must produce your full quota of bricks."

¹⁹The Israelite overseers realized they were in trouble when they were told, "You are not to reduce the number of bricks required of you for each day." ²⁰When they left Pharaoh, they found Moses and Aaron waiting to meet them, ²¹and they said, "May the LORD look on you and judge you! You have made us obnoxious to Pharaoh and his officials and have put a sword in their hand to kill us."

GOD PROMISES DELIVERANCE

²²Moses returned to the LORD and said, "Why, Lord, why have you brought trouble on this people? Is this why you sent me? ²³Ever since I went to Pharaoh to speak in your name, he has brought trouble on this people, and you have not rescued your people at all."

6 Then the LORD said to Moses, "Now you will see what I will do to Pharaoh: Because of my mighty hand he will let them go; because of my mighty hand he will drive them out of his country."

²God also said to Moses, "I am the LORD. ³I appeared to Abraham, to Isaac and to Jacob as God Almighty,ᵃ but by my name the LORDᵇ I did not make myself fully known to them. ⁴I also established my covenant with them to give them the land of Canaan, where they resided as foreigners. ⁵Moreover, I have heard the groaning of the Israelites, whom the Egyptians are enslaving, and I have remembered my covenant.

⁶"Therefore, say to the Israelites: 'I am the LORD, and I will bring you out from under the yoke of the Egyptians. I will free you from being slaves to them, and I will redeem you with an outstretched arm and with mighty acts of judgment. ⁷I will take you as my own people, and I will be your God. Then you will know that I am the LORD your God, who brought you out from under the yoke of the Egyptians. ⁸And I will bring you to the land I swore with uplifted hand to give to Abraham, to Isaac and to Jacob. I will give it to you as a possession. I am the LORD.'"

⁹Moses reported this to the Israelites, but they did not listen to him because of their discouragement and harsh labor.

¹⁰Then the LORD said to Moses, ¹¹"Go, tell Pharaoh king of Egypt to let the Israelites go out of his country."

¹²But Moses said to the LORD, "If the Israelites will not listen to me, why would Pharaoh listen to me, since I speak with faltering lipsᶜ?"

FAMILY RECORD OF MOSES AND AARON

¹³Now the LORD spoke to Moses and Aaron about the Israelites and Pharaoh king of Egypt, and he commanded them to bring the Israelites out of Egypt.

¹⁴These were the heads of their familiesᵈ:

The sons of Reuben the firstborn son of Israel were Hanok and Pallu, Hezron and Karmi. These were the clans of Reuben.

¹⁵The sons of Simeon were Jemuel, Jamin, Ohad, Jakin, Zohar and Shaul the son of a Canaanite woman. These were the clans of Simeon.

¹⁶These were the names of the sons of Levi according to their records: Gershon, Kohath and Merari. Levi lived 137 years.

¹⁷The sons of Gershon, by clans, were Libni and Shimei.

¹⁸The sons of Kohath were Amram, Izhar, Hebron and Uzziel. Kohath lived 133 years.

¹⁹The sons of Merari were Mahli and Mushi.

These were the clans of Levi according to their records.

²⁰Amram married his father's sister Jochebed, who bore him Aaron and Moses. Amram lived 137 years.

²¹The sons of Izhar were Korah, Nepheg and Zikri.

²²The sons of Uzziel were Mishael, Elzaphan and Sithri.

ᵃ 3 Hebrew *El-Shaddai*   ᵇ 3 See note at 3:15.   ᶜ 12 Hebrew *I am uncircumcised of lips*; also in verse 30   ᵈ 14 The Hebrew for *families* here and in verse 25 refers to units larger than clans.

Why was God's name to Moses different than it was to Abraham? (6:3)
Before this, God's name meant that he was a provider and sustainer. Now he says his name is the LORD, which means *I AM WHO I AM*. This name may have signaled the beginning of God's more personal relationship with Israel and his intention to save his people.

What does it mean that God will redeem the Israelites with "an outstretched arm"? (6:6)
God means that he will take an active role in freeing the Israelites and judging the Egyptians.

What does it mean that God swore with "uplifted hand"? (6:8)
An uplifted hand is palm forward with fingers pointing up. This is a symbol of a promise or oath, just as you see people today raise their hand in court. God made a promise to Abraham to give the land to his children.

Why was the family tree of Moses and Aaron included here? (6:14–27)
This family record verifies Moses' and Aaron's positions as Israel's leaders.

²³ Aaron married Elisheba, daughter of Amminadab and sister of Nahshon, and she bore him Nadab and Abihu, Eleazar and Ithamar. ²⁴ The sons of Korah were Assir, Elkanah and Abiasaph. These were the Korahite clans. ²⁵ Eleazar son of Aaron married one of the daughters of Putiel, and she bore him Phinehas.

These were the heads of the Levite families, clan by clan.

²⁶ It was this Aaron and Moses to whom the LORD said, "Bring the Israelites out of Egypt by their divisions." ²⁷ They were the ones who spoke to Pharaoh king of Egypt about bringing the Israelites out of Egypt—this same Moses and Aaron.

AARON TO SPEAK FOR MOSES

²⁸ Now when the LORD spoke to Moses in Egypt, ²⁹ he said to him, "I am the LORD. Tell Pharaoh king of Egypt everything I tell you."

³⁰ But Moses said to the LORD, "Since I speak with faltering lips, why would Pharaoh listen to me?"

7 Then the LORD said to Moses, "See, I have made you like God to Pharaoh, and your brother Aaron will be your prophet. ² You are to say everything I command you, and your brother Aaron is to tell Pharaoh to let the Israelites go out of his country. ³ But I will harden Pharaoh's heart, and though I multiply my signs and wonders in Egypt, ⁴ he will not listen to you. Then I will lay my hand on Egypt and with mighty acts of judgment I will bring out my divisions, my people the Israelites. ⁵ And the Egyptians will know that I am the LORD when I stretch out my hand against Egypt and bring the Israelites out of it."

⁶ Moses and Aaron did just as the LORD commanded them. ⁷ Moses was eighty years old and Aaron eighty-three when they spoke to Pharaoh.

AARON'S STAFF BECOMES A SNAKE

⁸ The LORD said to Moses and Aaron, ⁹ "When Pharaoh says to you, 'Perform a miracle,' then say to Aaron, 'Take your staff and throw it down before Pharaoh,' and it will become a snake."

¹⁰ So Moses and Aaron went to Pharaoh and did just as the LORD commanded. Aaron threw his staff down in front of Pharaoh and his officials, and it became a snake. ¹¹ Pharaoh then summoned wise men and sorcerers, and the Egyptian magicians also did the same things by their secret arts: ¹² Each one threw down his staff and it became a snake. But Aaron's staff swallowed up their staffs. ¹³ Yet Pharaoh's heart became hard and he would not listen to them, just as the LORD had said.

THE PLAGUE OF BLOOD

¹⁴ Then the LORD said to Moses, "Pharaoh's heart is unyielding; he refuses to let the people go. ¹⁵ Go to Pharaoh in the morning as he goes out to the river. Confront him on the

How did God make Moses "like God to Pharaoh"? (7:1)
God spoke to Pharaoh through Moses. Pharaoh himself was worshiped as a god, so he would understand that Moses was speaking for God. Pharaoh didn't see it at first, but eventually he feared the power that Moses represented.

Why did God harden Pharaoh's heart? (7:3)
Sometimes God hardens a person's heart to accomplish his purposes, as he did here to show his power and release the Israelites. Pharaoh "hardened his heart" toward God and the Israelites even in the face of the terrible plagues.

Why did God choose such old men to be leaders? (7:7)
Moses didn't start leading at 80 years old; he had been preparing most of his life for this moment. Since Moses lived to be 120, he was more like a middle-aged man today.

What message was God sending when Aaron's staff swallowed the others? (7:12)
It showed that the power of Israel's God was greater than any power that Pharaoh had. It also predicted disaster for Egypt: God's snake had defeated one of Egypt's national symbols, an animal considered to be sacred.

Was the water really blood? (7:20)
God could have turned the water into actual blood. Some people think the river was polluted with red dirt during flooding that turned the water into the color of blood. Others think the water really turned into blood.

bank of the Nile, and take in your hand the staff that was changed into a snake. [16]Then say to him, 'The LORD, the God of the Hebrews, has sent me to say to you: Let my people go, so that they may worship me in the wilderness. But until now you have not listened. [17]This is what the LORD says: By this you will know that I am the LORD: With the staff that is in my hand I will strike the water of the Nile, and it will be changed into blood. [18]The fish in the Nile will die, and the river will stink; the Egyptians will not be able to drink its water.'"

[19]The LORD said to Moses, "Tell Aaron, 'Take your staff and stretch out your hand over the waters of Egypt—over the streams and canals, over the ponds and all the reservoirs—and they will turn to blood.' Blood will be everywhere in Egypt, even in vessels[a] of wood and stone."

[20]Moses and Aaron did just as the LORD had commanded. He raised his staff in the presence of Pharaoh and his officials and struck the water of the Nile, and all the water was changed into blood. [21]The fish in the Nile died, and the river smelled so bad that the Egyptians could not drink its water. Blood was everywhere in Egypt.

[22]But the Egyptian magicians did the same things by their secret arts, and Pharaoh's heart became hard; he would not listen to Moses and Aaron, just as the LORD had said. [23]Instead, he turned and went into his palace, and did not take even this to heart. [24]And all the Egyptians dug along the Nile to get drinking water, because they could not drink the water of the river.

THE PLAGUE OF FROGS

8[b] [25]Seven days passed after the LORD struck the Nile. [1]Then the LORD said to Moses, "Go to Pharaoh and say to him, 'This is what the LORD says: Let my people go, so that they may worship me. [2]If you refuse to let them go, I will send a plague of frogs on your whole country. [3]The Nile will teem with frogs. They will come up into your palace and your bedroom and onto your bed, into the houses of your officials and on your people, and into your ovens and kneading troughs. [4]The frogs will come up on you and your people and all your officials.'"

[5]Then the LORD said to Moses, "Tell Aaron, 'Stretch out your hand with your staff over the streams and canals and ponds, and make frogs come up on the land of Egypt.'"

[6]So Aaron stretched out his hand over the waters of Egypt, and the frogs came up and covered the land. [7]But the magicians did the same things by their secret arts; they also made frogs come up on the land of Egypt.

[8]Pharaoh summoned Moses and Aaron and said, "Pray to the LORD to take the frogs away from me and my people, and I will let your people go to offer sacrifices to the LORD."

[9]Moses said to Pharaoh, "I leave to you the honor of setting the time for me to pray for you and your officials and your people that you and your houses may be rid of the frogs, except for those that remain in the Nile."

---

[a] 19 Or *even on their idols*   [b] In Hebrew texts 8:1-4 is numbered 7:26-29, and 8:5-32 is numbered 8:1-28.

Why was this plague so devastating? (7:21)
The Nile's life-giving water was the source of Egypt's greatness as a civilization, and the Egyptians worshiped it. An attack on the Nile was nothing less than an attack on Egypt and its gods.

Why would Pharaoh's magicians recreate the plagues and bring further harm on their own people? (7:22)
By copying Moses' and Aaron's miracle, they were trying to prove they were as powerful as the Israelites' God.

Why did the Egyptians dig along the Nile for drinking water? (7:24)
The Nile's water was undrinkable. They hoped to dig wells and tap into springs that were separate from the contaminated river water.

Why did God choose to use frogs as a plague? (8:5)
God may have chosen frogs because the Egyptians worshiped the goddess Heqt, a frog-headed woman. This plague showed the power of Israel's God over the gods of Egypt. Pharaoh probably thought Israel was mocking this god.

How were the Egyptian magicians able to copy God's miracles? (8:7)
The Bible says they used "secret arts." Some of the magicians used illusions, hypnosis, or sleight-of-hand to make it look as if they were duplicating God's miracles. Other magicians may have used power from the devil.

Why did Moses want Pharaoh to choose the time? (8:9)
Moses was offering further proof that prayers to his God were powerful and the circumstances of the plague were no coincidence.

Why would Pharaoh want the plague to end tomorrow instead of immediately? (8:10)
Perhaps Pharaoh wanted to test Moses and God by naming tomorrow instead of the expected answer.

Why did Pharaoh break his promise? (8:15)
He had everything to lose if he released the Israelites: he would look weak if he gave in to the challenge to his authority as ruler of Egypt; he didn't want to admit that the power of his gods was less than Moses' God; and losing his slaves would weaken his country's economy.

Did the dust actually turn into gnats? (8:17)
God may have created gnats from the dust just as he had made Adam from dust. (See Genesis 2:7.) Or the gnats were as numerous as the dust of the earth. But it is most probable that the gnats came up out of the dust.

Why did the magicians call the miracle of gnats "the finger of God"? (8:19)
The magicians admitted their failure in trying to copy the plague of gnats. Their tricks or demonic powers could no longer reproduce the plagues sent by Israel's God.

Why did God make an exception of Goshen? (8:22)
God offered further proof to Pharaoh that it was Israel's God sending the plagues. God protected the Israelites in Goshen from the plague while judging Egypt with this plague and others.

[10] "Tomorrow," Pharaoh said.

Moses replied, "It will be as you say, so that you may know there is no one like the LORD our God. [11] The frogs will leave you and your houses, your officials and your people; they will remain only in the Nile."

[12] After Moses and Aaron left Pharaoh, Moses cried out to the LORD about the frogs he had brought on Pharaoh. [13] And the LORD did what Moses asked. The frogs died in the houses, in the courtyards and in the fields. [14] They were piled into heaps, and the land reeked of them. [15] But when Pharaoh saw that there was relief, he hardened his heart and would not listen to Moses and Aaron, just as the LORD had said.

THE PLAGUE OF GNATS

[16] Then the LORD said to Moses, "Tell Aaron, 'Stretch out your staff and strike the dust of the ground,' and throughout the land of Egypt the dust will become gnats." [17] They did this, and when Aaron stretched out his hand with the staff and struck the dust of the ground, gnats came on people and animals. All the dust throughout the land of Egypt became gnats. [18] But when the magicians tried to produce gnats by their secret arts, they could not.

Since the gnats were on people and animals everywhere, [19] the magicians said to Pharaoh, "This is the finger of God." But Pharaoh's heart was hard and he would not listen, just as the LORD had said.

THE PLAGUE OF FLIES

[20] Then the LORD said to Moses, "Get up early in the morning and confront Pharaoh as he goes to the river and say to him, 'This is what the LORD says: Let my people go, so that they may worship me. [21] If you do not let my people go, I will send swarms of flies on you and your officials, on your people and into your houses. The houses of the Egyptians will be full of flies; even the ground will be covered with them.

[22] "'But on that day I will deal differently with the land of Goshen, where my people live; no swarms of flies will be there, so that you will know that I, the LORD, am in this land. [23] I will make a distinction[a] between my people and your people. This sign will occur tomorrow.'"

[24] And the LORD did this. Dense swarms of flies poured into Pharaoh's palace and into the houses of his officials; throughout Egypt the land was ruined by the flies.

[25] Then Pharaoh summoned Moses and Aaron and said, "Go, sacrifice to your God here in the land."

[26] But Moses said, "That would not be right. The sacrifices we offer the LORD our God would be detestable to the Egyptians. And if we offer sacrifices that are detestable in their eyes, will they not stone us? [27] We must take a three-day journey into the wilderness to offer sacrifices to the LORD our God, as he commands us."

[28] Pharaoh said, "I will let you go to offer sacrifices to the LORD your God in the wilderness, but you must not go very far. Now pray for me."

---

[a] 23 Septuagint and Vulgate; Hebrew *will put a deliverance*

29 Moses answered, "As soon as I leave you, I will pray to the Lord, and tomorrow the flies will leave Pharaoh and his officials and his people. Only let Pharaoh be sure that he does not act deceitfully again by not letting the people go to offer sacrifices to the Lord."

30 Then Moses left Pharaoh and prayed to the Lord, 31 and the Lord did what Moses asked. The flies left Pharaoh and his officials and his people; not a fly remained. 32 But this time also Pharaoh hardened his heart and would not let the people go.

THE PLAGUE ON LIVESTOCK

9 Then the Lord said to Moses, "Go to Pharaoh and say to him, 'This is what the Lord, the God of the Hebrews, says: "Let my people go, so that they may worship me." 2 If you refuse to let them go and continue to hold them back, 3 the hand of the Lord will bring a terrible plague on your livestock in the field—on your horses, donkeys and camels and on your cattle, sheep and goats. 4 But the Lord will make a distinction between the livestock of Israel and that of Egypt, so that no animal belonging to the Israelites will die.'"

5 The Lord set a time and said, "Tomorrow the Lord will do this in the land." 6 And the next day the Lord did it: All the livestock of the Egyptians died, but not one animal belonging to the Israelites died. 7 Pharaoh investigated and found that not even one of the animals of the Israelites had died. Yet his heart was unyielding and he would not let the people go.

THE PLAGUE OF BOILS

8 Then the Lord said to Moses and Aaron, "Take handfuls of soot from a furnace and have Moses toss it into the air in the presence of Pharaoh. 9 It will become fine dust over the whole land of Egypt, and festering boils will break out on people and animals throughout the land."

10 So they took soot from a furnace and stood before Pharaoh. Moses tossed it into the air, and festering boils broke out on people and animals. 11 The magicians could not stand before Moses because of the boils that were on them and on all the Egyptians. 12 But the Lord hardened Pharaoh's heart and he would not listen to Moses and Aaron, just as the Lord had said to Moses.

THE PLAGUE OF HAIL

13 Then the Lord said to Moses, "Get up early in the morning, confront Pharaoh and say to him, 'This is what the Lord, the God of the Hebrews, says: Let my people go, so that they may worship me, 14 or this time I will send the full force of my plagues against you and against your officials and your people, so you may know that there is no one like me in all the earth. 15 For by now I could have stretched out my hand and struck you and your people with a plague that would have wiped you off the earth. 16 But I have raised you up[a] for this very purpose, that I might show you my power and that my name might be proclaimed in all the earth.

a 16 Or have spared you

Why was the plague on livestock especially offensive? (9:3)
The Egyptians worshiped many animals, including a bull-god, a cow-god, and a ram-god. The plague mocked the Egyptian religion and showed God to be more powerful.

Why did God use ashes for the plague of boils? (9:8)
The boils of the sixth plague probably came from the soot of kilns that fired bricks made by the Israelite slaves. God was showing his power by using these kilns against the Egyptians, perhaps judging them for their treatment of the Israelites.

Were the boils contagious? (9:11)
The Bible says they were on men and animals. Some doctors think the boils were a result of a bacterial infection, which would have meant they were contagious. Only herbal remedies were available to people at this time.

What does it mean that God raised up Pharaoh? (9:16)
This means God spared Pharaoh. He could have wiped him and all his people out, but God used Pharaoh for God's own purposes. By continuing to send plagues, God used Pharaoh's stubbornness to showcase his power.

Were all the livestock killed in the plague of hail? (9:19–20)
No, some were taken to a place of shelter. Some Egyptian officials believed Moses and saved their slaves and livestock by bringing them in from the fields, out of danger.

[17]You still set yourself against my people and will not let them go. [18]Therefore, at this time tomorrow I will send the worst hailstorm that has ever fallen on Egypt, from the day it was founded till now. [19]Give an order now to bring your livestock and everything you have in the field to a place of shelter, because the hail will fall on every person and animal that has not been brought in and is still out in the field, and they will die.'"

[20]Those officials of Pharaoh who feared the word of the Lord hurried to bring their slaves and their livestock inside. [21]But those who ignored the word of the Lord left their slaves and livestock in the field.

[22]Then the Lord said to Moses, "Stretch out your hand toward the sky so that hail will fall all over Egypt—on people and animals and on everything growing in the fields of Egypt." [23]When Moses stretched out his staff toward the sky, the Lord sent thunder and hail, and lightning flashed down to the ground. So the Lord rained hail on the land of Egypt; [24]hail fell and lightning flashed back and forth. It was the worst storm in all the land of Egypt since it had become a nation. [25]Throughout Egypt hail struck everything in the fields—both people and animals; it beat down everything growing in the fields and stripped every tree. [26]The only place it did not hail was the land of Goshen, where the Israelites were.

[27]Then Pharaoh summoned Moses and Aaron. "This time I have sinned," he said to them. "The Lord is in the right, and I and my people are in the wrong. [28]Pray to the Lord, for we have had enough thunder and hail. I will let you go; you don't have to stay any longer."

[29]Moses replied, "When I have gone out of the city, I will spread out my hands in prayer to the Lord. The thunder will stop and there will be no more hail, so you may know that the earth is the Lord's. [30]But I know that you and your officials still do not fear the Lord God."

[31](The flax and barley were destroyed, since the barley had headed and the flax was in bloom. [32]The wheat and spelt, however, were not destroyed, because they ripen later.)

[33]Then Moses left Pharaoh and went out of the city. He spread out his hands toward the Lord; the thunder and hail stopped, and the rain no longer poured down on the land. [34]When Pharaoh saw that the rain and hail and thunder had stopped, he sinned again: He and his officials hardened their hearts. [35]So Pharaoh's heart was hard and he would not let the Israelites go, just as the Lord had said through Moses.

What is spelt? (9:32)
Spelt is a species of wheat. It grows well in poorer and drier soil and requires less fertilizer than wheat.

How was Moses safe walking out into the hailstorm? (9:33)
It is possible the hail storms were in the countryside, destroying the harvest. Or Moses may have walked between the cloudbursts or was protected by God in the same way the land of Goshen had been spared.

THE PLAGUE OF LOCUSTS

10 Then the Lord said to Moses, "Go to Pharaoh, for I have hardened his heart and the hearts of his officials so that I may perform these signs of mine among them [2]that you may tell your children and grandchildren how I dealt harshly with the Egyptians and how I performed my signs among them, and that you may know that I am the Lord."

[3]So Moses and Aaron went to Pharaoh and said to him, "This is what the Lord, the God of the Hebrews, says: 'How

long will you refuse to humble yourself before me? Let my people go, so that they may worship me. ⁴If you refuse to let them go, I will bring locusts into your country tomorrow. ⁵They will cover the face of the ground so that it cannot be seen. They will devour what little you have left after the hail, including every tree that is growing in your fields. ⁶They will fill your houses and those of all your officials and all the Egyptians—something neither your parents nor your ancestors have ever seen from the day they settled in this land till now.'"Then Moses turned and left Pharaoh.

⁷Pharaoh's officials said to him, "How long will this man be a snare to us? Let the people go, so that they may worship the Lord their God. Do you not yet realize that Egypt is ruined?"

⁸Then Moses and Aaron were brought back to Pharaoh. "Go, worship the Lord your God," he said. "But tell me who will be going."

⁹Moses answered, "We will go with our young and our old, with our sons and our daughters, and with our flocks and herds, because we are to celebrate a festival to the Lord."

¹⁰Pharaoh said, "The Lord be with you—if I let you go, along with your women and children! Clearly you are bent on evil.ᵃ ¹¹No! Have only the men go and worship the Lord, since that's what you have been asking for."Then Moses and Aaron were driven out of Pharaoh's presence.

¹²And the Lord said to Moses, "Stretch out your hand over Egypt so that locusts swarm over the land and devour everything growing in the fields, everything left by the hail."

¹³So Moses stretched out his staff over Egypt, and the Lord made an east wind blow across the land all that day and all that night. By morning the wind had brought the locusts; ¹⁴they invaded all Egypt and settled down in every area of the country in great numbers. Never before had there been such a plague of locusts, nor will there ever be again. ¹⁵They covered all the ground until it was black. They devoured all that was left after the hail—everything growing in the fields and the fruit on the trees. Nothing green remained on tree or plant in all the land of Egypt.

¹⁶Pharaoh quickly summoned Moses and Aaron and said, "I have sinned against the Lord your God and against you. ¹⁷Now forgive my sin once more and pray to the Lord your God to take this deadly plague away from me."

¹⁸Moses then left Pharaoh and prayed to the Lord. ¹⁹And the Lord changed the wind to a very strong west wind, which caught up the locusts and carried them into the Red Sea.ᵇ Not a locust was left anywhere in Egypt. ²⁰But the Lord hardened Pharaoh's heart, and he would not let the Israelites go.

THE PLAGUE OF DARKNESS

²¹Then the Lord said to Moses, "Stretch out your hand toward the sky so that darkness spreads over Egypt—darkness that can be felt." ²²So Moses stretched out his hand toward the sky, and total darkness covered all Egypt for three days. ²³No one could see anyone else or move about for three days. Yet all the Israelites had light in the places where they lived.

ᵃ 10 Or *Be careful, trouble is in store for you!*   ᵇ 19 Or *the Sea of Reeds*

What are locusts? (10:4)
Locusts are grasshoppers in a swarming phase. A swarm is caused by grasshopper overcrowding. It would only take a few minutes for an army of these insects to destroy an entire field of crops. In the ancient world, locust plagues were greatly feared and became a symbol of divine judgment.

How badly had Egypt been damaged by the plagues? (10:7)
The plagues devastated the Egyptian economy. It would take years to recover from the economic losses of crops and livestock. In addition, people were hurt by boils and biting insects and polluted water. But the greatest damage was the humiliation to their religious system. The plagues showed the inferiority of all their gods to the God of Israel.

Why did Pharaoh say that only the men could go? (10:11)
Generally it was only men who participated in worship, and Pharaoh probably wanted the women and children to stay behind so he could be assured the men would return.

What was the plague of darkness? (10:21–23)
Like the third and sixth plagues, the ninth plague was unannounced. It was possibly caused by a severe *khamsin*, a sandstorm that blows in from the desert each spring. The darkness was an insult to the Egyptian sun god Ra.

Why didn't Moses accept Pharaoh's offer to leave? (10:24–26)
Pharaoh and Moses both knew that if the Israelites left for worship, they would be leaving Egypt permanently. Pharaoh may have wanted to keep the Israelites' livestock to help Egypt recover from the plagues. In any case, Moses was not willing to compromise; if they went, they would take all of their animals with them.

What was the plague on the firstborn sons? (11:4–5)
Firstborn sons had special status, and their deaths would have caused great sadness among the people. In addition, judgment on the firstborn represented judgment on the entire community.

Why did God send ten plagues instead of just one? (11:9–10)
Maybe Pharaoh needed more convincing than one plague could have produced. Each plague showed how much more powerful God was over all of the Egyptian gods.

Why were the Passover requirements so detailed? (12:1–27)
God gave detailed instructions to ensure the safety of his people, to guide their successful departure, to bring the people together, and to test their trust in him. The Passover was one of the most important events in the history of Israel, and the details were symbolic.

Why were the people told to sacrifice a lamb? (12:3–11)
The lamb was a symbol of innocence sacrificed to save someone else. This foreshadowed salvation through Jesus Christ. The Israelites painted this lamb's blood on their doorframe. This was a symbol that this house should be passed over when God kills the firstborn sons of Egypt.

²⁴Then Pharaoh summoned Moses and said, "Go, worship the LORD. Even your women and children may go with you; only leave your flocks and herds behind."

²⁵But Moses said, "You must allow us to have sacrifices and burnt offerings to present to the LORD our God. ²⁶Our livestock too must go with us; not a hoof is to be left behind. We have to use some of them in worshiping the LORD our God, and until we get there we will not know what we are to use to worship the LORD."

²⁷But the LORD hardened Pharaoh's heart, and he was not willing to let them go. ²⁸Pharaoh said to Moses, "Get out of my sight! Make sure you do not appear before me again! The day you see my face you will die."

²⁹"Just as you say," Moses replied. "I will never appear before you again."

THE PLAGUE ON THE FIRSTBORN

11 Now the LORD had said to Moses, "I will bring one more plague on Pharaoh and on Egypt. After that, he will let you go from here, and when he does, he will drive you out completely. ²Tell the people that men and women alike are to ask their neighbors for articles of silver and gold." ³(The LORD made the Egyptians favorably disposed toward the people, and Moses himself was highly regarded in Egypt by Pharaoh's officials and by the people.)

⁴So Moses said, "This is what the LORD says: 'About midnight I will go throughout Egypt. ⁵Every firstborn son in Egypt will die, from the firstborn son of Pharaoh, who sits on the throne, to the firstborn son of the female slave, who is at her hand mill, and all the firstborn of the cattle as well. ⁶There will be loud wailing throughout Egypt—worse than there has ever been or ever will be again. ⁷But among the Israelites not a dog will bark at any person or animal.' Then you will know that the LORD makes a distinction between Egypt and Israel. ⁸All these officials of yours will come to me, bowing down before me and saying, 'Go, you and all the people who follow you!' After that I will leave." Then Moses, hot with anger, left Pharaoh.

⁹The LORD had said to Moses, "Pharaoh will refuse to listen to you—so that my wonders may be multiplied in Egypt." ¹⁰Moses and Aaron performed all these wonders before Pharaoh, but the LORD hardened Pharaoh's heart, and he would not let the Israelites go out of his country.

THE PASSOVER AND THE FESTIVAL OF UNLEAVENED BREAD

12 The LORD said to Moses and Aaron in Egypt, ²"This month is to be for you the first month, the first month of your year. ³Tell the whole community of Israel that on the tenth day of this month each man is to take a lamb*a* for his family, one for each household. ⁴If any household is too small for a whole lamb, they must share one with their nearest neighbor, having taken into account the number of people there are. You are to determine the amount of lamb

---

*a 3 The Hebrew word can mean *lamb* or *kid*; also in verse 4.

needed in accordance with what each person will eat. [5] The animals you choose must be year-old males without defect, and you may take them from the sheep or the goats. [6] Take care of them until the fourteenth day of the month, when all the members of the community of Israel must slaughter them at twilight. [7] Then they are to take some of the blood and put it on the sides and tops of the doorframes of the houses where they eat the lambs. [8] That same night they are to eat the meat roasted over the fire, along with bitter herbs, and bread made without yeast. [9] Do not eat the meat raw or boiled in water, but roast it over a fire—with the head, legs and internal organs. [10] Do not leave any of it till morning; if some is left till morning, you must burn it. [11] This is how you are to eat it: with your cloak tucked into your belt, your sandals on your feet and your staff in your hand. Eat it in haste; it is the LORD's Passover.

[12] "On that same night I will pass through Egypt and strike down every firstborn of both people and animals, and I will bring judgment on all the gods of Egypt. I am the LORD. [13] The blood will be a sign for you on the houses where you are, and when I see the blood, I will pass over you. No destructive plague will touch you when I strike Egypt.

[14] "This is a day you are to commemorate; for the generations to come you shall celebrate it as a festival to the LORD—a lasting ordinance. [15] For seven days you are to eat bread made without yeast. On the first day remove the yeast from your houses, for whoever eats anything with yeast in it from the first day through the seventh must be cut off from Israel. [16] On the first day hold a sacred assembly, and another one on the seventh day. Do no work at all on these days, except to prepare food for everyone to eat; that is all you may do.

[17] "Celebrate the Festival of Unleavened Bread, because it was on this very day that I brought your divisions out of Egypt. Celebrate this day as a lasting ordinance for the generations to come. [18] In the first month you are to eat bread made without yeast, from the evening of the fourteenth day until the evening of the twenty-first day. [19] For seven days no yeast is to be found in your houses. And anyone, whether foreigner or native-born, who eats anything with yeast in it must be cut off from the community of Israel. [20] Eat nothing made with yeast. Wherever you live, you must eat unleavened bread."

[21] Then Moses summoned all the elders of Israel and said to them, "Go at once and select the animals for your families and slaughter the Passover lamb. [22] Take a bunch of hyssop, dip it into the blood in the basin and put some of the blood on the top and on both sides of the doorframe. None of you shall go out of the door of your house until morning. [23] When the LORD goes through the land to strike down the Egyptians, he will see the blood on the top and sides of the doorframe and will pass over that doorway, and he will not permit the destroyer to enter your houses and strike you down.

[24] "Obey these instructions as a lasting ordinance for you and your descendants. [25] When you enter the land that the

Why were the people told to make bread without yeast? (12:15)
The bread without yeast could be made quickly, which was essential. It also symbolized purity because baking bread with yeast used sour dough.

What does it mean to be cut off from Israel? (12:15)
This may have meant banishment or shunning. It may even have meant execution. In any case, the penalty for disobedience was very severe.

What is hyssop? (12:22)
Hyssop is a bushy herb with a straight stalk and white flowers. The hairy surface of the leaves and branches hold liquids well, making it useful for sprinkling liquids and cleaning holy places.

Who was the destroyer? (12:23)
The destroyer was a type of spirit to bring judgment and punish the Egyptians. This may have been an angel (or a group of angels).

Why did all the firstborn have to die? (12:29)
God planned to save the Israelites from slavery in Egypt, but Pharaoh was stubborn through many trials. The final plague of killing all the firstborn sons convinced Pharaoh to free the Israelites — probably because it was such an obvious punishment by God that could not be seen as coincidence. Earlier God told Pharaoh that Israel was his firstborn, and he would repay Egypt for holding his firstborn hostage. (See Exodus 4:22 – 23.)

Why were the Egyptians willing to give their valuable possessions to the Israelites? (12:35 – 36)
Some people think that the Israelites took advantage of the Egyptians, but it's more likely that this was part of the custom symbolizing the move from slavery to freedom. The Egyptians were probably glad to be rid of the Israelites who had caused them so much pain.

How many Israelites left Egypt? (12:37)
The total number could have been well over two million people.

Why did some Egyptians go with them? (12:38)
Some Egyptians probably wanted to leave the disaster area. Others may have been moved to faith because of God's mighty acts. Still others may have been friends of the Israelites.

Why did God wait so long to free his people? (12:40)
We don't know the reason God planned things the way he did, but we do know that the Israelites weren't slaves the entire 430 years they were in Egypt. Their slavery probably began about 125 years before they were freed. The important message is that God did not abandon his people. (See Exodus 2:24.)

Lord will give you as he promised, observe this ceremony. ²⁶ And when your children ask you, 'What does this ceremony mean to you?' ²⁷ then tell them, 'It is the Passover sacrifice to the Lord, who passed over the houses of the Israelites in Egypt and spared our homes when he struck down the Egyptians.'" Then the people bowed down and worshiped. ²⁸ The Israelites did just what the Lord commanded Moses and Aaron.

²⁹ At midnight the Lord struck down all the firstborn in Egypt, from the firstborn of Pharaoh, who sat on the throne, to the firstborn of the prisoner, who was in the dungeon, and the firstborn of all the livestock as well. ³⁰ Pharaoh and all his officials and all the Egyptians got up during the night, and there was loud wailing in Egypt, for there was not a house without someone dead.

THE EXODUS

³¹ During the night Pharaoh summoned Moses and Aaron and said, "Up! Leave my people, you and the Israelites! Go, worship the Lord as you have requested. ³² Take your flocks and herds, as you have said, and go. And also bless me."

³³ The Egyptians urged the people to hurry and leave the country. "For otherwise," they said, "we will all die!" ³⁴ So the people took their dough before the yeast was added, and carried it on their shoulders in kneading troughs wrapped in clothing. ³⁵ The Israelites did as Moses instructed and asked the Egyptians for articles of silver and gold and for clothing. ³⁶ The Lord had made the Egyptians favorably disposed toward the people, and they gave them what they asked for; so they plundered the Egyptians.

³⁷ The Israelites journeyed from Rameses to Sukkoth. There were about six hundred thousand men on foot, besides women and children. ³⁸ Many other people went up with them, and also large droves of livestock, both flocks and herds. ³⁹ With the dough the Israelites had brought from Egypt, they baked loaves of unleavened bread. The dough was without yeast because they had been driven out of Egypt and did not have time to prepare food for themselves.

⁴⁰ Now the length of time the Israelite people lived in Egypt[a] was 430 years. ⁴¹ At the end of the 430 years, to the very day, all the Lord's divisions left Egypt. ⁴² Because the Lord kept vigil that night to bring them out of Egypt, on this night all the Israelites are to keep vigil to honor the Lord for the generations to come.

PASSOVER RESTRICTIONS

⁴³ The Lord said to Moses and Aaron, "These are the regulations for the Passover meal:

"No foreigner may eat it. ⁴⁴ Any slave you have bought may eat it after you have circumcised him, ⁴⁵ but a temporary resident or a hired worker may not eat it.

⁴⁶ "It must be eaten inside the house; take none of the meat outside the house. Do not break any of the bones. ⁴⁷ The whole community of Israel must celebrate it.

---

a 40 Masoretic Text; Samaritan Pentateuch and Septuagint *Egypt and Canaan*

48 "A foreigner residing among you who wants to celebrate the Lord's Passover must have all the males in his household circumcised; then he may take part like one born in the land. No uncircumcised male may eat it. 49 The same law applies both to the native-born and to the foreigner residing among you."

50 All the Israelites did just what the Lord had commanded Moses and Aaron. 51 And on that very day the Lord brought the Israelites out of Egypt by their divisions.

CONSECRATION OF THE FIRSTBORN

13 The Lord said to Moses, 2 "Consecrate to me every firstborn male. The first offspring of every womb among the Israelites belongs to me, whether human or animal."

3 Then Moses said to the people, "Commemorate this day, the day you came out of Egypt, out of the land of slavery, because the Lord brought you out of it with a mighty hand. Eat nothing containing yeast. 4 Today, in the month of Aviv, you are leaving. 5 When the Lord brings you into the land of the Canaanites, Hittites, Amorites, Hivites and Jebusites — the land he swore to your ancestors to give you, a land flowing with milk and honey — you are to observe this ceremony in this month: 6 For seven days eat bread made without yeast and on the seventh day hold a festival to the Lord. 7 Eat unleavened bread during those seven days; nothing with yeast in it is to be seen among you, nor shall any yeast be seen anywhere within your borders. 8 On that day tell your son, 'I do this because of what the Lord did for me when I came out of Egypt.' 9 This observance will be for you like a sign on your hand and a reminder on your forehead that this law of the Lord is to be on your lips. For the Lord brought you out of Egypt with his mighty hand. 10 You must keep this ordinance at the appointed time year after year.

11 "After the Lord brings you into the land of the Canaanites and gives it to you, as he promised on oath to you and your ancestors, 12 you are to give over to the Lord the first offspring of every womb. All the firstborn males of your livestock belong to the Lord. 13 Redeem with a lamb every firstborn donkey, but if you do not redeem it, break its neck. Redeem every firstborn among your sons.

14 "In days to come, when your son asks you, 'What does this mean?' say to him, 'With a mighty hand the Lord brought us out of Egypt, out of the land of slavery. 15 When Pharaoh stubbornly refused to let us go, the Lord killed the firstborn of both people and animals in Egypt. This is why I sacrifice to the Lord the first male offspring of every womb and redeem each of my firstborn sons.' 16 And it will be like a sign on your hand and a symbol on your forehead that the Lord brought us out of Egypt with his mighty hand."

CROSSING THE SEA

17 When Pharaoh let the people go, God did not lead them on the road through the Philistine country, though that was shorter. For God said, "If they face war, they might change

Why did the people "consecrate" the firstborn males? (13:2)
Consecrated means "given to God." God killed the firstborn male in every Egyptian household. The Israelites could have fallen to the same fate. But God spared them. As a way to show their gratitude and to pay God back for his kindness, animals were killed as substitutes and given to the priests as sacrifices.

What were the signs on the hand and forehead? (13:9, 16)
The Passover was a sign that showed how God is powerful and caring. In later times, Jews obeyed this command by wearing little boxes containing words of Scripture strapped to the arm or forehead.

Why were the Israelites armed for battle? (13:17–18)
Armed for battle meant being prepared to defend the freedom God gave them. God wanted the people to see themselves as a free nation belonging to him. They were not looking for conflict, but they were prepared in case they were attacked. The former slaves probably carried spears, bows, and slings as added precaution. They also probably marched as a unit in an orderly manner.

Why did they take the bones of Joseph? (13:19)

The place of burial was important to the Israelites. Joseph had made his children swear an oath to return his remains to the burial place of his ancestors Abraham, Isaac, and Jacob.

How did God guide his people? (13:21–22)

The people didn't see God face-to-face, but he comforted them and guided them with his presence in a pillar of cloud and fire.

Did God want Pharaoh to go after the Israelites? (14:4)

God could see that Pharaoh did not have a change of heart, and God led Pharaoh into a trap to gain glory for himself.

their minds and return to Egypt." ¹⁸So God led the people around by the desert road toward the Red Sea.ᵃ The Israelites went up out of Egypt ready for battle.

¹⁹Moses took the bones of Joseph with him because Joseph had made the Israelites swear an oath. He had said, "God will surely come to your aid, and then you must carry my bones up with you from this place."ᵇ

²⁰After leaving Sukkoth they camped at Etham on the edge of the desert. ²¹By day the Lord went ahead of them in a pillar of cloud to guide them on their way and by night in a pillar of fire to give them light, so that they could travel by day or night. ²²Neither the pillar of cloud by day nor the pillar of fire by night left its place in front of the people.

14 Then the Lord said to Moses, ²"Tell the Israelites to turn back and encamp near Pi Hahiroth, between Migdol and the sea. They are to encamp by the sea, directly opposite Baal Zephon. ³Pharaoh will think, 'The Israelites are wandering around the land in confusion, hemmed in by the desert.' ⁴And I will harden Pharaoh's heart, and he will pursue them. But I will gain glory for myself through Pharaoh and all his army, and the Egyptians will know that I am the Lord." So the Israelites did this.

ᵃ 18 Or *the Sea of Reeds*   ᵇ 19 See Gen. 50:25.

THE EXODUS (13:17)

⁵When the king of Egypt was told that the people had fled, Pharaoh and his officials changed their minds about them and said, "What have we done? We have let the Israelites go and have lost their services!" ⁶So he had his chariot made ready and took his army with him. ⁷He took six hundred of the best chariots, along with all the other chariots of Egypt, with officers over all of them. ⁸The LORD hardened the heart of Pharaoh king of Egypt, so that he pursued the Israelites, who were marching out boldly. ⁹The Egyptians— all Pharaoh's horses and chariots, horsemenᵃ and troops— pursued the Israelites and overtook them as they camped by the sea near Pi Hahiroth, opposite Baal Zephon.

¹⁰As Pharaoh approached, the Israelites looked up, and there were the Egyptians, marching after them. They were terrified and cried out to the LORD. ¹¹They said to Moses, "Was it because there were no graves in Egypt that you brought us to the desert to die? What have you done to us by bringing us out of Egypt? ¹²Didn't we say to you in Egypt, 'Leave us alone; let us serve the Egyptians'? It would have been better for us to serve the Egyptians than to die in the desert!"

¹³Moses answered the people, "Do not be afraid. Stand firm and you will see the deliverance the LORD will bring you today. The Egyptians you see today you will never see again. ¹⁴The LORD will fight for you; you need only to be still."

¹⁵Then the LORD said to Moses, "Why are you crying out to me? Tell the Israelites to move on. ¹⁶Raise your staff and stretch out your hand over the sea to divide the water so that the Israelites can go through the sea on dry ground. ¹⁷I will harden the hearts of the Egyptians so that they will go in after them. And I will gain glory through Pharaoh and all his army, through his chariots and his horsemen. ¹⁸The Egyptians will know that I am the LORD when I gain glory through Pharaoh, his chariots and his horsemen."

¹⁹Then the angel of God, who had been traveling in front of Israel's army, withdrew and went behind them. The pillar of cloud also moved from in front and stood behind them, ²⁰coming between the armies of Egypt and Israel. Throughout the night the cloud brought darkness to the one side and light to the other side; so neither went near the other all night long.

²¹Then Moses stretched out his hand over the sea, and all that night the LORD drove the sea back with a strong east wind and turned it into dry land. The waters were divided, ²²and the Israelites went through the sea on dry ground, with a wall of water on their right and on their left.

²³The Egyptians pursued them, and all Pharaoh's horses and chariots and horsemen followed them into the sea. ²⁴During the last watch of the night the LORD looked down from the pillar of fire and cloud at the Egyptian army and threw it into confusion. ²⁵He jammedᵇ the wheels of their chariots so that they had difficulty driving. And the Egyptians said, "Let's get away from the Israelites! The LORD is fighting for them against Egypt."

²⁶Then the LORD said to Moses, "Stretch out your hand

Did the Israelites really want to stay in Egypt? (14:12)
Probably not, but they were probably afraid of the unknown ahead of them. They were frustrated when they faced hardship. The Israelites often complained about their time in the desert.

How did the pillar of cloud help the Israelites? (14:19)
The pillar of cloud hid the Israelites from the Egyptians, and it provided light to guide them at night. It was a pillar of light for the Israelites and a pillar of darkness for the Egyptians.

Can a wind push back the sea to make walls of water? (14:21–22)
A strong hurricane-like wind known as a *sirocco* could displace large amounts of water and cause the land to dry up. But the miracle at the Red Sea was not a natural occurrence. The water was divided on the left and on the right.

How could the people know what the Egyptians said? (14:25)
Some of the Israelites may have been close enough to hear them. Or they could have read the Egyptians' body language and inferred what they were saying.

ᵃ 9 Or *charioteers*; also in verses 17, 18, 23, 26 and 28   ᵇ 25 See Samaritan Pentateuch, Septuagint and Syriac; Masoretic Text *removed*

Is there any historical record of this event? (14:28)
No documents have been found about this event, except for the account in the Bible. That's not surprising because Egyptians did not usually record their defeats in battle.

over the sea so that the waters may flow back over the Egyptians and their chariots and horsemen." [27] Moses stretched out his hand over the sea, and at daybreak the sea went back to its place. The Egyptians were fleeing toward[a] it, and the LORD swept them into the sea. [28] The water flowed back and covered the chariots and horsemen—the entire army of Pharaoh that had followed the Israelites into the sea. Not one of them survived.

[29] But the Israelites went through the sea on dry ground, with a wall of water on their right and on their left. [30] That day the LORD saved Israel from the hands of the Egyptians, and Israel saw the Egyptians lying dead on the shore. [31] And when the Israelites saw the mighty hand of the LORD displayed against the Egyptians, the people feared the LORD and put their trust in him and in Moses his servant.

THE SONG OF MOSES AND MIRIAM

15 Then Moses and the Israelites sang this song to the LORD:

"I will sing to the LORD,
    for he is highly exalted.
Both horse and driver
    he has hurled into the sea.

[2] "The LORD is my strength and my defense[b];
    he has become my salvation.
He is my God, and I will praise him,
    my father's God, and I will exalt him.
[3] The LORD is a warrior;
    the LORD is his name.
[4] Pharaoh's chariots and his army
    he has hurled into the sea.
The best of Pharaoh's officers
    are drowned in the Red Sea.[c]
[5] The deep waters have covered them;
    they sank to the depths like a stone.
[6] Your right hand, LORD,
    was majestic in power.
Your right hand, LORD,
    shattered the enemy.

[7] "In the greatness of your majesty
    you threw down those who opposed you.
You unleashed your burning anger;
    it consumed them like stubble.
[8] By the blast of your nostrils
    the waters piled up.
The surging waters stood up like a wall;
    the deep waters congealed in the heart of the sea.
[9] The enemy boasted,
    'I will pursue, I will overtake them.
I will divide the spoils;
    I will gorge myself on them.
I will draw my sword
    and my hand will destroy them.'

---

[a] 27 Or *from*   [b] 2 Or *song*   [c] 4 Or *the Sea of Reeds*; also in verse 22

¹⁰ But you blew with your breath,
　　and the sea covered them.
They sank like lead
　　in the mighty waters.
¹¹ Who among the gods
　　is like you, LORD?
Who is like you—
　　majestic in holiness,
awesome in glory,
　　working wonders?

¹² "You stretch out your right hand,
　　and the earth swallows your enemies.
¹³ In your unfailing love you will lead
　　the people you have redeemed.
In your strength you will guide them
　　to your holy dwelling.
¹⁴ The nations will hear and tremble;
　　anguish will grip the people of Philistia.
¹⁵ The chiefs of Edom will be terrified,
　　the leaders of Moab will be seized with trembling,
the people*a* of Canaan will melt away;
¹⁶　　terror and dread will fall on them.
By the power of your arm
　　they will be as still as a stone—
until your people pass by, LORD,
　　until the people you bought*b* pass by.
¹⁷ You will bring them in and plant them
　　on the mountain of your inheritance—
the place, LORD, you made for your dwelling,
　　the sanctuary, Lord, your hands established.

¹⁸ "The LORD reigns
　　for ever and ever."

¹⁹ When Pharaoh's horses, chariots and horsemen*c* went into the sea, the LORD brought the waters of the sea back over them, but the Israelites walked through the sea on dry ground. ²⁰ Then Miriam the prophet, Aaron's sister, took a timbrel in her hand, and all the women followed her, with timbrels and dancing. ²¹ Miriam sang to them:

"Sing to the LORD,
　　for he is highly exalted.
Both horse and driver
　　he has hurled into the sea."

THE WATERS OF MARAH AND ELIM

²² Then Moses led Israel from the Red Sea and they went into the Desert of Shur. For three days they traveled in the desert without finding water. ²³ When they came to Marah, they could not drink its water because it was bitter. (That is why the place is called Marah.*d*) ²⁴ So the people grumbled against Moses, saying, "What are we to drink?"
²⁵ Then Moses cried out to the LORD, and the LORD

---

a 15 Or *rulers*　　*b 16* Or *created*　　*c 19* Or *charioteers*　　*d 23 Marah* means *bitter.*

Who were the chiefs of Edom? (15:15)
The Edomites were the children and descendents of Jacob's brother, Esau. The chiefs of Edom were their leaders.

What was Miriam's role as a prophet? (15:20)
Miriam, Moses and Aaron's sister, was also a leader of Israel. God spoke through her, and she led the people in worship after the victory over the Egyptians.

What type of dancing was this? (15:20)
Dancing was usually performed by women, with one woman leading. Dancing usually took place outside and was often accompanied by responsive singing.

How did the water become sweet? (15:25)
Maybe God's power improved the water, or maybe God showed Moses which wood or plants to use to sweeten the water. Either way, God performed this miracle after Moses called out to God for help.

showed him a piece of wood. He threw it into the water, and the water became fit to drink.

There the LORD issued a ruling and instruction for them and put them to the test. ²⁶He said, "If you listen carefully to the LORD your God and do what is right in his eyes, if you pay attention to his commands and keep all his decrees, I will not bring on you any of the diseases I brought on the Egyptians, for I am the LORD, who heals you."

²⁷Then they came to Elim, where there were twelve springs and seventy palm trees, and they camped there near the water.

MANNA AND QUAIL

16 The whole Israelite community set out from Elim and came to the Desert of Sin, which is between Elim and Sinai, on the fifteenth day of the second month after they had come out of Egypt. ²In the desert the whole community grumbled against Moses and Aaron. ³The Israelites said to them, "If only we had died by the LORD's hand in Egypt! There we sat around pots of meat and ate all the food we wanted, but you have brought us out into this desert to starve this entire assembly to death."

⁴Then the LORD said to Moses, "I will rain down bread from heaven for you. The people are to go out each day and gather enough for that day. In this way I will test them and see whether they will follow my instructions. ⁵On the sixth day they are to prepare what they bring in, and that is to be twice as much as they gather on the other days."

⁶So Moses and Aaron said to all the Israelites, "In the evening you will know that it was the LORD who brought you out of Egypt, ⁷and in the morning you will see the glory of the LORD, because he has heard your grumbling against him. Who are we, that you should grumble against us?" ⁸Moses also said, "You will know that it was the LORD when he gives you meat to eat in the evening and all the bread you want in the morning, because he has heard your grumbling against him. Who are we? You are not grumbling against us, but against the LORD."

⁹Then Moses told Aaron, "Say to the entire Israelite community, 'Come before the LORD, for he has heard your grumbling.'"

¹⁰While Aaron was speaking to the whole Israelite community, they looked toward the desert, and there was the glory of the LORD appearing in the cloud.

¹¹The LORD said to Moses, ¹²"I have heard the grumbling of the Israelites. Tell them, 'At twilight you will eat meat, and in the morning you will be filled with bread. Then you will know that I am the LORD your God.'"

¹³That evening quail came and covered the camp, and in the morning there was a layer of dew around the camp. ¹⁴When the dew was gone, thin flakes like frost on the ground appeared on the desert floor. ¹⁵When the Israelites saw it, they said to each other, "What is it?" For they did not know what it was.

Moses said to them, "It is the bread the LORD has given

How did God test the Israelites? (16:4)
God gave specific instructions for collecting the bread. If they didn't follow God's directions, the bread turned bad. God promised to provide what they needed in the desert. Because they lacked faith, God taught them to trust through this process of testing.

What does the phrase *bread from heaven* refer to? (16:4)
This was manna, the food that God sent for his people in the desert. Jesus called himself "the true bread from heaven" (John 6:32) and "the bread of life" (John 6:48). In this way he was reminding people of the way God had cared for Israel in the desert.

Why was it wrong for the people to grumble? (16:7)
The people's grumbling showed that they lacked gratitude for all that God had done for them and that they didn't trust in his promises.

you to eat. [16] This is what the LORD has commanded: 'Everyone is to gather as much as they need. Take an omer[a] for each person you have in your tent.'"

[17] The Israelites did as they were told; some gathered much, some little. [18] And when they measured it by the omer, the one who gathered much did not have too much, and the one who gathered little did not have too little. Everyone had gathered just as much as they needed.

[19] Then Moses said to them, "No one is to keep any of it until morning."

[20] However, some of them paid no attention to Moses; they kept part of it until morning, but it was full of maggots and began to smell. So Moses was angry with them.

[21] Each morning everyone gathered as much as they needed, and when the sun grew hot, it melted away. [22] On the sixth day, they gathered twice as much — two omers[b] for each person — and the leaders of the community came and reported this to Moses. [23] He said to them, "This is what the LORD commanded: 'Tomorrow is to be a day of sabbath rest, a holy sabbath to the LORD. So bake what you want to bake and boil what you want to boil. Save whatever is left and keep it until morning.'"

[24] So they saved it until morning, as Moses commanded, and it did not stink or get maggots in it. [25] "Eat it today," Moses said, "because today is a sabbath to the LORD. You will not find any of it on the ground today. [26] Six days you are to gather it, but on the seventh day, the Sabbath, there will not be any."

[27] Nevertheless, some of the people went out on the seventh day to gather it, but they found none. [28] Then the LORD said to Moses, "How long will you[c] refuse to keep my commands and my instructions? [29] Bear in mind that the LORD has given you the Sabbath; that is why on the sixth day he gives you bread for two days. Everyone is to stay where they are on the seventh day; no one is to go out." [30] So the people rested on the seventh day.

[31] The people of Israel called the bread manna.[d] It was white like coriander seed and tasted like wafers made with honey. [32] Moses said, "This is what the LORD has commanded: 'Take an omer of manna and keep it for the generations to come, so they can see the bread I gave you to eat in the wilderness when I brought you out of Egypt.'"

[33] So Moses said to Aaron, "Take a jar and put an omer of manna in it. Then place it before the LORD to be kept for the generations to come."

[34] As the LORD commanded Moses, Aaron put the manna with the tablets of the covenant law, so that it might be preserved. [35] The Israelites ate manna forty years, until they came to a land that was settled; they ate manna until they reached the border of Canaan.

[36] (An omer is one-tenth of an ephah.)

---

[a] 16 That is, possibly about 3 pounds or about 1.4 kilograms; also in verses 18, 32, 33 and 36   [b] 22 That is, possibly about 6 pounds or about 2.8 kilograms   [c] 28 The Hebrew is plural.   [d] 31 Manna sounds like the Hebrew for What is it? (see verse 15).

What is the Sabbath? (16:23)
The Sabbath is a day of rest on the seventh day of the week. The idea of a day of rest is in the creation story (Genesis 2), but this is the first time it is mentioned as a requirement for the Israelites to rest on the seventh day.

What exactly was manna? (16:31)
Manna came at night, resembling frost and dropping with the dew. It was white and sweet, and the Israelites said it looked a little like coriander seed. There is no other substance today that exactly matches the description of manna. It was provided by God for his people in a miraculous way. Later, when other food became available, God stopped sending manna.

How could this manna be saved for generations without spoiling? (16:32)
Manna was sent as a miracle, and God was able to control how it was preserved. It only lasted for one day during the week, but it lasted for two days over the Sabbath. In this case, God preserved a small amount to serve as a sign for future generations of his people.

How much was an omer? (16:36)
An omer was approximately 2 quarts (1.9 liters).

Why was it wrong for the Israelites to want water? (17:2)
Not trusting God and doubting his power is a sin, not simply wanting water. The people resisted Moses' leadership and doubted God, even though God had already shown them that he would provide water and food.

WATER FROM THE ROCK

17 The whole Israelite community set out from the Desert of Sin, traveling from place to place as the LORD commanded. They camped at Rephidim, but there was no water for the people to drink. ²So they quarreled with Moses and said, "Give us water to drink."

Moses replied, "Why do you quarrel with me? Why do you put the LORD to the test?"

³But the people were thirsty for water there, and they grumbled against Moses. They said, "Why did you bring us up out of Egypt to make us and our children and livestock die of thirst?"

⁴Then Moses cried out to the LORD, "What am I to do with these people? They are almost ready to stone me."

⁵The LORD answered Moses, "Go out in front of the people. Take with you some of the elders of Israel and take in your hand the staff with which you struck the Nile, and go. ⁶I will stand there before you by the rock at Horeb. Strike the rock, and water will come out of it for the people to drink." So Moses did this in the sight of the elders of Israel. ⁷And he called the place Massah*a* and Meribah*b* because the Israelites quarreled and because they tested the LORD saying, "Is the LORD among us or not?"

THE AMALEKITES DEFEATED

⁸The Amalekites came and attacked the Israelites at Rephidim. ⁹Moses said to Joshua, "Choose some of our men and go out to fight the Amalekites. Tomorrow I will stand on top of the hill with the staff of God in my hands."

¹⁰So Joshua fought the Amalekites as Moses had ordered, and Moses, Aaron and Hur went to the top of the hill. ¹¹As long as Moses held up his hands, the Israelites were winning, but whenever he lowered his hands, the Amalekites were winning. ¹²When Moses' hands grew tired, they took a stone and put it under him and he sat on it. Aaron and Hur held his hands up—one on one side, one on the other—so that his hands remained steady till sunset. ¹³So Joshua overcame the Amalekite army with the sword.

¹⁴Then the LORD said to Moses, "Write this on a scroll as something to be remembered and make sure that Joshua hears it, because I will completely blot out the name of Amalek from under heaven."

¹⁵Moses built an altar and called it The LORD is my Banner. ¹⁶He said, "Because hands were lifted up against*c* the throne of the LORD,*d* the LORD will be at war against the Amalekites from generation to generation."

Who were the Amalekites? (17:8)
They were ruthless nomads who were enemies of the Israelites. They were descendants of a grandson of Esau, Jacob's brother.

Who was Hur? (17:10)
Hur may have been Moses' and Aaron's brother-in-law. He was likely married to their sister, Miriam. He supported Moses during the battle with the Amalekites, and later he and Aaron took responsibility for the people while Moses went up to Mount Sinai. (See Exodus 24:14.)

What were scrolls? (17:14)
Scrolls were long strips of leather or papyrus on which scribes wrote in columns, sometimes on both sides. Egyptian scrolls were sometimes longer than 100 feet (30.5 meters), but most biblical scrolls were under 30 feet (9 meters). Reading a scroll involved unrolling it with one hand while rolling it back up with the other.

JETHRO VISITS MOSES

18 Now Jethro, the priest of Midian and father-in-law of Moses, heard of everything God had done for Moses and for his people Israel, and how the LORD had brought Israel out of Egypt.

---

a 7 *Massah* means *testing.*   *b* 7 *Meribah* means *quarreling.*   *c* 16 Or *to*
d 16 The meaning of the Hebrew for this clause is uncertain.

² After Moses had sent away his wife Zipporah, his father-in-law Jethro received her ³ and her two sons. One son was named Gershom,ᵃ for Moses said, "I have become a foreigner in a foreign land"; ⁴ and the other was named Eliezer,ᵇ for he said, "My father's God was my helper; he saved me from the sword of Pharaoh."

⁵ Jethro, Moses' father-in-law, together with Moses' sons and wife, came to him in the wilderness, where he was camped near the mountain of God. ⁶ Jethro had sent word to him, "I, your father-in-law Jethro, am coming to you with your wife and her two sons."

⁷ So Moses went out to meet his father-in-law and bowed down and kissed him. They greeted each other and then went into the tent. ⁸ Moses told his father-in-law about everything the LORD had done to Pharaoh and the Egyptians for Israel's sake and about all the hardships they had met along the way and how the LORD had saved them.

⁹ Jethro was delighted to hear about all the good things the LORD had done for Israel in rescuing them from the hand of the Egyptians. ¹⁰ He said, "Praise be to the LORD, who rescued you from the hand of the Egyptians and of Pharaoh, and who rescued the people from the hand of the Egyptians. ¹¹ Now I know that the LORD is greater than all other gods, for he did this to those who had treated Israel arrogantly." ¹² Then Jethro, Moses' father-in-law, brought a burnt offering and other sacrifices to God, and Aaron came with all the elders of Israel to eat a meal with Moses' father-in-law in the presence of God.

¹³ The next day Moses took his seat to serve as judge for the people, and they stood around him from morning till evening. ¹⁴ When his father-in-law saw all that Moses was doing for the people, he said, "What is this you are doing for the people? Why do you alone sit as judge, while all these people stand around you from morning till evening?"

¹⁵ Moses answered him, "Because the people come to me to seek God's will. ¹⁶ Whenever they have a dispute, it is brought to me, and I decide between the parties and inform them of God's decrees and instructions."

¹⁷ Moses' father-in-law replied, "What you are doing is not good. ¹⁸ You and these people who come to you will only wear yourselves out. The work is too heavy for you; you cannot handle it alone. ¹⁹ Listen now to me and I will give you some advice, and may God be with you. You must be the people's representative before God and bring their disputes to him. ²⁰ Teach them his decrees and instructions, and show them the way they are to live and how they are to behave. ²¹ But select capable men from all the people — men who fear God, trustworthy men who hate dishonest gain — and appoint them as officials over thousands, hundreds, fifties and tens. ²² Have them serve as judges for the people at all times, but have them bring every difficult case to you; the simple cases they can decide themselves. That will make your load lighter, because they will share it with you. ²³ If you do

---

ᵃ 3 *Gershom* sounds like the Hebrew for *a foreigner there.*   ᵇ 4 *Eliezer* means *my God is helper.*

Why did Moses send his wife and children away? (18:2)
This is the first time we hear that his wife wasn't with him. He may have sent her back to her father before the plagues started or before the exodus. Or maybe he sent her home after they reached Sinai so that she could take her father Jethro back with her.

Did Jethro worship other gods? (18:11)
Jethro finally accepted that God is the one and only true God, and he showed God how sincere his faith was by offering up a sacrifice. He may have worshiped many tribal gods before, so God was pleased when he gave them up.

How did Moses know God's laws? (18:15-16)
God revealed his laws to Moses through various cases in his time as leader of Israel.

Why did Jethro suggest that Moses select other judges? (18:21-22)
Moses took on a huge workload serving as the only judge over all the Israelites. Jethro convinced him to share the responsibility. If Moses did his work with a team of people, he would not be so exhausted and much more would be accomplished.

Would God take away his promised land if the Israelites didn't obey him? (19:5)
God had made an unconditional covenant with Abraham to bless him and his descendants. Because of this covenant, God led Israel out of Egypt. When God gave laws to Israel, the people were called to obey because God had saved them, not so that he would save them. Although God's blessing may depend on keeping God's law, salvation does not.

What did it mean for Israel to be a kingdom of priests? (19:6)
As God's kingdom, Israel was to be wholly consecrated to God, just as priests were consecrated to God's service. (See Exodus 19:14.)

Why couldn't the people of Israel touch the mountain? (19:12–13)
The whole mountain became holy because of God's presence. The people were unclean, and they had to follow the process of becoming clean before they touched the holy mountain.

What does it mean that Moses had to consecrate the people? (19:14)
To be consecrated means to be set apart for God's use. Moses had to make sure the people washed themselves and their clothes so they were pure before God.

Why were the people told not to have sex for three days? (19:15)
The Israelites had to focus on preparing to meet with God. Sex itself was not wrong, but it would make the participants ceremonially unclean and would distract them from their focus.

Why were Moses and Aaron able to approach God? (19:20–24)
Moses and Aaron were ambassadors from God to his people. God gave them special permission to approach the mountain.

this and God so commands, you will be able to stand the strain, and all these people will go home satisfied."

24 Moses listened to his father-in-law and did everything he said. 25 He chose capable men from all Israel and made them leaders of the people, officials over thousands, hundreds, fifties and tens. 26 They served as judges for the people at all times. The difficult cases they brought to Moses, but the simple ones they decided themselves.

27 Then Moses sent his father-in-law on his way, and Jethro returned to his own country.

AT MOUNT SINAI

19 On the first day of the third month after the Israelites left Egypt—on that very day—they came to the Desert of Sinai. 2 After they set out from Rephidim, they entered the Desert of Sinai, and Israel camped there in the desert in front of the mountain.

3 Then Moses went up to God, and the LORD called to him from the mountain and said, "This is what you are to say to the descendants of Jacob and what you are to tell the people of Israel: 4 'You yourselves have seen what I did to Egypt, and how I carried you on eagles' wings and brought you to myself. 5 Now if you obey me fully and keep my covenant, then out of all nations you will be my treasured possession. Although the whole earth is mine, 6 you*a* will be for me a kingdom of priests and a holy nation.' These are the words you are to speak to the Israelites."

7 So Moses went back and summoned the elders of the people and set before them all the words the LORD had commanded him to speak. 8 The people all responded together, "We will do everything the LORD has said." So Moses brought their answer back to the LORD.

9 The LORD said to Moses, "I am going to come to you in a dense cloud, so that the people will hear me speaking with you and will always put their trust in you." Then Moses told the LORD what the people had said.

10 And the LORD said to Moses, "Go to the people and consecrate them today and tomorrow. Have them wash their clothes 11 and be ready by the third day, because on that day the LORD will come down on Mount Sinai in the sight of all the people. 12 Put limits for the people around the mountain and tell them, 'Be careful that you do not approach the mountain or touch the foot of it. Whoever touches the mountain is to be put to death. 13 They are to be stoned or shot with arrows; not a hand is to be laid on them. No person or animal shall be permitted to live.' Only when the ram's horn sounds a long blast may they approach the mountain."

14 After Moses had gone down the mountain to the people, he consecrated them, and they washed their clothes. 15 Then he said to the people, "Prepare yourselves for the third day. Abstain from sexual relations."

16 On the morning of the third day there was thunder and lightning, with a thick cloud over the mountain, and a very loud trumpet blast. Everyone in the camp trembled. 17 Then

a 5,6 Or possession, for the whole earth is mine. 6 You

Moses led the people out of the camp to meet with God, and they stood at the foot of the mountain. ¹⁸Mount Sinai was covered with smoke, because the LORD descended on it in fire. The smoke billowed up from it like smoke from a furnace, and the whole mountain*ᵃ* trembled violently. ¹⁹As the sound of the trumpet grew louder and louder, Moses spoke and the voice of God answered him.*ᵇ*

²⁰The LORD descended to the top of Mount Sinai and called Moses to the top of the mountain. So Moses went up ²¹and the LORD said to him, "Go down and warn the people so they do not force their way through to see the LORD and many of them perish. ²²Even the priests, who approach the LORD, must consecrate themselves, or the LORD will break out against them."

²³Moses said to the LORD, "The people cannot come up Mount Sinai, because you yourself warned us, 'Put limits around the mountain and set it apart as holy.'"

²⁴The LORD replied, "Go down and bring Aaron up with you. But the priests and the people must not force their way through to come up to the LORD, or he will break out against them."

²⁵So Moses went down to the people and told them.

THE TEN COMMANDMENTS

20 And God spoke all these words:

²"I am the LORD your God, who brought you out of Egypt, out of the land of slavery.

³"You shall have no other gods before*ᶜ* me.

⁴"You shall not make for yourself an image in the form of anything in heaven above or on the earth beneath or in the waters below. ⁵You shall not bow down to them or worship them; for I, the LORD your God, am a jealous God, punishing the children for the sin of the parents to the third and fourth generation of those who hate me, ⁶but showing love to a thousand generations of those who love me and keep my commandments.

⁷"You shall not misuse the name of the LORD your God, for the LORD will not hold anyone guiltless who misuses his name.

⁸"Remember the Sabbath day by keeping it holy. ⁹Six days you shall labor and do all your work, ¹⁰but the seventh day is a sabbath to the LORD your God. On it you shall not do any work, neither you, nor your son or daughter, nor your male or female servant, nor your animals, nor any foreigner residing in your towns. ¹¹For in six days the LORD made the heavens and the earth, the sea, and all that is in them, but he rested on the seventh day. Therefore the LORD blessed the Sabbath day and made it holy.

ᵃ 18 Most Hebrew manuscripts; a few Hebrew manuscripts and Septuagint *and all the people*   *ᵇ 19* Or *and God answered him with thunder*
ᶜ 3 Or *besides*

Stone Tablets (20:1–17)

Do the Ten Commandments appear anywhere else in the Bible? (20:1–17)
When the people of Israel were about to enter the promised land, Moses repeated the commandments to them. (See Deuteronomy 5:6–21.)

What does it mean that God is jealous? (20:5)
This means that God will not tolerate anything that comes between him and his people. God demands that his people worship only him. God will judge all those who oppose him. And God will save and protect his people.

Why do the commandments include consequences for future generations? (20:5–6)
This language is like what was used in ancient treaties. If people broke the treaty, the effects would be felt by entire families down into future generations. If the people obeyed the treaty, their ancestors would be rewarded.

Why did Moses tell the people to not be afraid? (20:20)
Moses wanted the people to know that God had not come to frighten them. To fear God doesn't mean to be afraid of him. It means to have great respect for him and for what he does. God had come to his people to make a covenant with them as their heavenly King.

Why did God require sacrifices? (20:24)
The Old Testament is filled with sacrifices. Various animals were killed and offered to God, and the people brought to God gifts of grain, oil, and wine. Why were they important? First, sacrifices reminded people that God would not ignore sin; someone had to pay the price so that God would forgive the sin. Second, sacrifices showed that the innocent can substitute for the guilty. In this way, Old Testament sacrifices pointed toward Jesus, who sacrificed himself to redeem his people. Third, sacrifices involved offering something valuable to God because he deserved the best. Fourth, the system of sacrifices served to bring the community together, often around meals.

Why was slavery permitted? (21:2)
The people of Israel had known cruel slavery in Egypt. They were familiar with hard work and could offer their services as a way to repay debts or to make up for

12 "Honor your father and your mother, so that you may live long in the land the LORD your God is giving you.

13 "You shall not murder.

14 "You shall not commit adultery.

15 "You shall not steal.

16 "You shall not give false testimony against your neighbor.

17 "You shall not covet your neighbor's house. You shall not covet your neighbor's wife, or his male or female servant, his ox or donkey, or anything that belongs to your neighbor."

18 When the people saw the thunder and lightning and heard the trumpet and saw the mountain in smoke, they trembled with fear. They stayed at a distance 19 and said to Moses, "Speak to us yourself and we will listen. But do not have God speak to us or we will die."

20 Moses said to the people, "Do not be afraid. God has come to test you, so that the fear of God will be with you to keep you from sinning."

21 The people remained at a distance, while Moses approached the thick darkness where God was.

IDOLS AND ALTARS

22 Then the LORD said to Moses, "Tell the Israelites this: 'You have seen for yourselves that I have spoken to you from heaven: 23 Do not make any gods to be alongside me; do not make for yourselves gods of silver or gods of gold.

24 "'Make an altar of earth for me and sacrifice on it your burnt offerings and fellowship offerings, your sheep and goats and your cattle. Wherever I cause my name to be honored, I will come to you and bless you. 25 If you make an altar of stones for me, do not build it with dressed stones, for you will defile it if you use a tool on it. 26 And do not go up to my altar on steps, or your private parts may be exposed.'

21

"These are the laws you are to set before them:

HEBREW SERVANTS

2 "If you buy a Hebrew servant, he is to serve you for six years. But in the seventh year, he shall go free, without paying anything. 3 If he comes alone, he is to go free alone; but if he has a wife when he comes, she is to go with him. 4 If his

Do we still need to obey the 10 Commandments? EXODUS 20

For Christians today, God's laws serve several purposes. First, they show what God expects as the right way to behave. When God gave the commandments to Moses, he wanted his people to obey them, but they constantly rebelled against God and broke his laws.

Second, God's laws show us how sinful we are; ever since Adam and Eve first sinned in the Garden of Eden, human beings have been unable to keep all of the commandments perfectly. God loved his people and sent Jesus to bring salvation to his people because they could never earn it themselves.

Third, the commandments show Christians how to live their lives in thankfulness to God for his great love. Even though we aren't able to keep the law perfectly, God's law still shows us how we should try to live our lives in thankful obedience to him.

master gives him a wife and she bears him sons or daughters, the woman and her children shall belong to her master, and only the man shall go free.

5 "But if the servant declares, 'I love my master and my wife and children and do not want to go free,' 6 then his master must take him before the judges.[a] He shall take him to the door or the doorpost and pierce his ear with an awl. Then he will be his servant for life.

7 "If a man sells his daughter as a servant, she is not to go free as male servants do. 8 If she does not please the master who has selected her for himself,[b] he must let her be redeemed. He has no right to sell her to foreigners, because he has broken faith with her. 9 If he selects her for his son, he must grant her the rights of a daughter. 10 If he marries another woman, he must not deprive the first one of her food, clothing and marital rights. 11 If he does not provide her with these three things, she is to go free, without any payment of money.

PERSONAL INJURIES

12 "Anyone who strikes a person with a fatal blow is to be put to death. 13 However, if it is not done intentionally, but God lets it happen, they are to flee to a place I will designate. 14 But if anyone schemes and kills someone deliberately, that person is to be taken from my altar and put to death.

15 "Anyone who attacks[c] their father or mother is to be put to death.

16 "Anyone who kidnaps someone is to be put to death, whether the victim has been sold or is still in the kidnapper's possession.

17 "Anyone who curses their father or mother is to be put to death.

18 "If people quarrel and one person hits another with a stone or with their fist[d] and the victim does not die but is confined to bed, 19 the one who struck the blow will not be held liable if the other can get up and walk around outside with a staff; however, the guilty party must pay the injured person for any loss of time and see that the victim is completely healed.

20 "Anyone who beats their male or female slave with a rod must be punished if the slave dies as a direct result, 21 but they are not to be punished if the slave recovers after a day or two, since the slave is their property.

22 "If people are fighting and hit a pregnant woman and she gives birth prematurely[e] but there is no serious injury, the offender must be fined whatever the woman's husband demands and the court allows. 23 But if there is serious injury, you are to take life for life, 24 eye for eye, tooth for tooth, hand for hand, foot for foot, 25 burn for burn, wound for wound, bruise for bruise.

26 "An owner who hits a male or female slave in the eye and destroys it must let the slave go free to compensate for the eye. 27 And an owner who knocks out the tooth of a male or female slave must let the slave go free to compensate for the tooth.

something they did wrong. Moses allowed this type of slavery but with strict rules so it had limits.

Why would a father sell his daughter as a servant? (21:7 – 11)
The practice provided protection from mistreatment. This servant/marriage contract was especially important when a man could have more than one wife. A father would insist on this contract so he knew his daughter would always be cared for (have food and clothing and other rights) or she would be set free.

Why would someone who killed be killed? (21:12)
Human life is sacred because God created human beings in his own image. Taking a human life was like attacking the image of God. This was worthy of the most severe punishment, offering the murderer's life back to God.

Why would someone be executed for cursing a parent? (21:17)
People are made in God's image. A curse was considered an attack on the part of the person that is in God's image. Sending harm toward a person in this way was equivalent to murder.

What was the principle of an "eye for eye, tooth for tooth"? (21:23 – 25)
This is the idea that the punishment was equal to the harm caused (the same was done to you that you did). This balanced approach to punishment was an improvement over the other legal codes in the ancient Middle East. It limited the damages that had to be repaid and discouraged revenge.

---

[a] 6 Or before God   [b] 8 Or master so that he does not choose her   [c] 15 Or kills
[d] 18 Or with a tool   [e] 22 Or she has a miscarriage

Why couldn't the bull be eaten? (21:28)
A bull that was stoned to death would be ceremonially unclean. Moreover, if a bull gored someone, it should be killed and no value should come out of the bull. Eating the meat of a bull that had killed someone would take attention away from the loss of human life.

[28] "If a bull gores a man or woman to death, the bull is to be stoned to death, and its meat must not be eaten. But the owner of the bull will not be held responsible. [29] If, however, the bull has had the habit of goring and the owner has been warned but has not kept it penned up and it kills a man or woman, the bull is to be stoned and its owner also is to be put to death. [30] However, if payment is demanded, the owner may redeem his life by the payment of whatever is demanded. [31] This law also applies if the bull gores a son or daughter. [32] If the bull gores a male or female slave, the owner must pay thirty shekels[a] of silver to the master of the slave, and the bull is to be stoned to death.

[33] "If anyone uncovers a pit or digs one and fails to cover it and an ox or a donkey falls into it, [34] the one who opened the pit must pay the owner for the loss and take the dead animal in exchange.

[35] "If anyone's bull injures someone else's bull and it dies, the two parties are to sell the live one and divide both the money and the dead animal equally. [36] However, if it was known that the bull had the habit of goring, yet the owner did not keep it penned up, the owner must pay, animal for animal, and take the dead animal in exchange.

PROTECTION OF PROPERTY

Why was killing a thief different in the day from in the night? (22:2-3)
During the day, there is light to see if a thief is armed. When it is dark outside, it's harder to tell if a thief is threatening. Self-defense is more justifiable than outright killing.

22[b] "Whoever steals an ox or a sheep and slaughters it or sells it must pay back five head of cattle for the ox and four sheep for the sheep.

[2] "If a thief is caught breaking in at night and is struck a fatal blow, the defender is not guilty of bloodshed; [3] but if it happens after sunrise, the defender is guilty of bloodshed.

"Anyone who steals must certainly make restitution, but if they have nothing, they must be sold to pay for their theft. [4] If the stolen animal is found alive in their possession— whether ox or donkey or sheep—they must pay back double.

[5] "If anyone grazes their livestock in a field or vineyard and lets them stray and they graze in someone else's field, the offender must make restitution from the best of their own field or vineyard.

[6] "If a fire breaks out and spreads into thornbushes so that it burns shocks of grain or standing grain or the whole field, the one who started the fire must make restitution.

Why were the people given such detailed laws about ownership of property? (22:7-9)
The laws were given to help the community maintain peace and goodwill. The extensive detail would help resolve conflicts in Israelite society.

[7] "If anyone gives a neighbor silver or goods for safekeeping and they are stolen from the neighbor's house, the thief, if caught, must pay back double. [8] But if the thief is not found, the owner of the house must appear before the judges, and they must[c] determine whether the owner of the house has laid hands on the other person's property. [9] In all cases of illegal possession of an ox, a donkey, a sheep, a garment, or any other lost property about which somebody says, 'This is mine,' both parties are to bring their cases before the judges.[d] The one whom the judges declare[e] guilty must pay back double to the other.

---

[a] 32 That is, about 12 ounces or about 345 grams   [b] In Hebrew texts 22:1 is numbered 21:37, and 22:2-31 is numbered 22:1-30.   [c] 8 Or before God, and he will   [d] 9 Or before God   [e] 9 Or whom God declares

[10]"If anyone gives a donkey, an ox, a sheep or any other animal to their neighbor for safekeeping and it dies or is injured or is taken away while no one is looking, [11]the issue between them will be settled by the taking of an oath before the LORD that the neighbor did not lay hands on the other person's property. The owner is to accept this, and no restitution is required. [12]But if the animal was stolen from the neighbor, restitution must be made to the owner. [13]If it was torn to pieces by a wild animal, the neighbor shall bring in the remains as evidence and shall not be required to pay for the torn animal.

[14]"If anyone borrows an animal from their neighbor and it is injured or dies while the owner is not present, they must make restitution. [15]But if the owner is with the animal, the borrower will not have to pay. If the animal was hired, the money paid for the hire covers the loss.

SOCIAL RESPONSIBILITY

[16]"If a man seduces a virgin who is not pledged to be married and sleeps with her, he must pay the bride-price, and she shall be his wife. [17]If her father absolutely refuses to give her to him, he must still pay the bride-price for virgins.

[18]"Do not allow a sorceress to live.

[19]"Anyone who has sexual relations with an animal is to be put to death.

[20]"Whoever sacrifices to any god other than the LORD must be destroyed.[a]

[21]"Do not mistreat or oppress a foreigner, for you were foreigners in Egypt.

[22]"Do not take advantage of the widow or the fatherless. [23]If you do and they cry out to me, I will certainly hear their cry. [24]My anger will be aroused, and I will kill you with the sword; your wives will become widows and your children fatherless.

[25]"If you lend money to one of my people among you who is needy, do not treat it like a business deal; charge no interest. [26]If you take your neighbor's cloak as a pledge, return it by sunset, [27]because that cloak is the only covering your neighbor has. What else can they sleep in? When they cry out to me, I will hear, for I am compassionate.

[28]"Do not blaspheme God[b] or curse the ruler of your people.

[29]"Do not hold back offerings from your granaries or your vats.[c]

"You must give me the firstborn of your sons. [30]Do the same with your cattle and your sheep. Let them stay with their mothers for seven days, but give them to me on the eighth day.

[31]"You are to be my holy people. So do not eat the meat of an animal torn by wild beasts; throw it to the dogs.

LAWS OF JUSTICE AND MERCY

23 "Do not spread false reports. Do not help a guilty person by being a malicious witness.

---

[a] 20 The Hebrew term refers to the irrevocable giving over of things or persons to the LORD, often by totally destroying them.   [b] 28 Or Do not revile the judges   [c] 29 The meaning of the Hebrew for this phrase is uncertain.

Why is this section entitled Social Responsibility? (22:16–31)
This section of laws reflects the close connection between social concerns and matters of proper worship. For Israel all life was rooted in worship, and the quality of people's worship was partly demonstrated by the way they behaved toward other people.

Why was a man who seduced a young woman required to pay a bride-price? (22:16–17)
Because marriages were arranged by contract, a young woman had economic value to her father. Her father could not get the full price for her marriage if she was not a virgin. The man who seduced her would have to pay the father for his loss.

What was a sorceress? (22:18)
A sorceress was a woman who tried to gain power from something other than God. She may have held séances or cast spells on people.

Why couldn't the Israelites charge interest? (22:25)
God wanted the Israelites to be compassionate and help the poor by giving interest-free loans. This law doesn't rule out charging interest or earning money from investments. The focus is on the way to treat poor people. Jesus told his followers to make interest free loans to the poor. The loans were to be treated as gifts. The people should not expect anything in return for helping. (See Luke 6:34–35.)

How were people expected to act toward their enemies? (23:4–5)
God commanded to treat all people with the same consideration, whether they were friends or enemies. Later, Jesus told his followers, "Love your enemies" (Matthew 5:44).

Why was no one supposed to come to God empty-handed? (23:15)
This verse is about giving thanks for what God has done for his people. The Israelites brought something of value as a sign of their thankfulness.

What was the Festival of Unleavened Bread? (23:15)
This feast was celebrated at the beginning of the barley harvest in memory of the exodus from Egypt.

What was the Festival of Harvest? (23:16)
This feast celebrated the first harvested crops and was also called the Festival of Weeks because it was held seven weeks after the Festival of Unleavened Bread. In the New Testament this feast was called Pentecost.

What was the Festival of Ingathering? (23:16)
This feast celebrated the harvest of the orchards and vines and recalled the desert wanderings after the exodus. People built temporary shelters to remind them of the shelters they lived in when God brought them out of Egypt. It was also called the Festival of Tabernacles or the Festival of Booths.

Why were they forbidden to cook a goat in its mother's milk? (23:19)
This was one of the practices of pagan religions that God wanted his people to avoid. The pagans thought the milk had magical powers for increasing fertility, and they used it on crops and vineyards to make them more productive.

²"Do not follow the crowd in doing wrong. When you give testimony in a lawsuit, do not pervert justice by siding with the crowd, ³and do not show favoritism to a poor person in a lawsuit.

⁴"If you come across your enemy's ox or donkey wandering off, be sure to return it. ⁵If you see the donkey of someone who hates you fallen down under its load, do not leave it there; be sure you help them with it.

⁶"Do not deny justice to your poor people in their lawsuits. ⁷Have nothing to do with a false charge and do not put an innocent or honest person to death, for I will not acquit the guilty.

⁸"Do not accept a bribe, for a bribe blinds those who see and twists the words of the innocent.

⁹"Do not oppress a foreigner; you yourselves know how it feels to be foreigners, because you were foreigners in Egypt.

SABBATH LAWS

¹⁰"For six years you are to sow your fields and harvest the crops, ¹¹but during the seventh year let the land lie unplowed and unused. Then the poor among your people may get food from it, and the wild animals may eat what is left. Do the same with your vineyard and your olive grove.

¹²"Six days do your work, but on the seventh day do not work, so that your ox and your donkey may rest, and so that the slave born in your household and the foreigner living among you may be refreshed.

¹³"Be careful to do everything I have said to you. Do not invoke the names of other gods; do not let them be heard on your lips.

THE THREE ANNUAL FESTIVALS

¹⁴"Three times a year you are to celebrate a festival to me.

¹⁵"Celebrate the Festival of Unleavened Bread; for seven days eat bread made without yeast, as I commanded you. Do this at the appointed time in the month of Aviv, for in that month you came out of Egypt.

"No one is to appear before me empty-handed.

¹⁶"Celebrate the Festival of Harvest with the firstfruits of the crops you sow in your field.

"Celebrate the Festival of Ingathering at the end of the year, when you gather in your crops from the field.

¹⁷"Three times a year all the men are to appear before the Sovereign Lord.

¹⁸"Do not offer the blood of a sacrifice to me along with anything containing yeast.

"The fat of my festival offerings must not be kept until morning.

¹⁹"Bring the best of the firstfruits of your soil to the house of the Lord your God.

"Do not cook a young goat in its mother's milk.

GOD'S ANGEL TO PREPARE THE WAY

²⁰"See, I am sending an angel ahead of you to guard you along the way and to bring you to the place I have prepared.

[21] Pay attention to him and listen to what he says. Do not rebel against him; he will not forgive your rebellion, since my Name is in him. [22] If you listen carefully to what he says and do all that I say, I will be an enemy to your enemies and will oppose those who oppose you. [23] My angel will go ahead of you and bring you into the land of the Amorites, Hittites, Perizzites, Canaanites, Hivites and Jebusites, and I will wipe them out. [24] Do not bow down before their gods or worship them or follow their practices. You must demolish them and break their sacred stones to pieces. [25] Worship the LORD your God, and his blessing will be on your food and water. I will take away sickness from among you, [26] and none will miscarry or be barren in your land. I will give you a full life span.

[27] "I will send my terror ahead of you and throw into confusion every nation you encounter. I will make all your enemies turn their backs and run. [28] I will send the hornet ahead of you to drive the Hivites, Canaanites and Hittites out of your way. [29] But I will not drive them out in a single year, because the land would become desolate and the wild animals too numerous for you. [30] Little by little I will drive them out before you, until you have increased enough to take possession of the land.

[31] "I will establish your borders from the Red Sea[a] to the Mediterranean Sea,[b] and from the desert to the Euphrates River. I will give into your hands the people who live in the land, and you will drive them out before you. [32] Do not make a covenant with them or with their gods. [33] Do not let them live in your land or they will cause you to sin against me, because the worship of their gods will certainly be a snare to you."

THE COVENANT CONFIRMED

24 Then the LORD said to Moses, "Come up to the LORD, you and Aaron, Nadab and Abihu, and seventy of the elders of Israel. You are to worship at a distance, [2] but Moses alone is to approach the LORD; the others must not come near. And the people may not come up with him."

[3] When Moses went and told the people all the LORD's words and laws, they responded with one voice, "Everything the LORD has said we will do." [4] Moses then wrote down everything the LORD had said.

He got up early the next morning and built an altar at the foot of the mountain and set up twelve stone pillars representing the twelve tribes of Israel. [5] Then he sent young Israelite men, and they offered burnt offerings and sacrificed young bulls as fellowship offerings to the LORD. [6] Moses took half of the blood and put it in bowls, and the other half he splashed against the altar. [7] Then he took the Book of the Covenant and read it to the people. They responded, "We will do everything the LORD has said; we will obey."

[8] Moses then took the blood, sprinkled it on the people and said, "This is the blood of the covenant that the LORD has made with you in accordance with all these words."

[9] Moses and Aaron, Nadab and Abihu, and the seventy elders of Israel went up [10] and saw the God of Israel. Under

[a] 31 Or *the Sea of Reeds*   [b] 31 Hebrew *to the Sea of the Philistines*

Why did God tell the Israelites to destroy the Canaanites? (23:24)
The Canaanites were immoral people who worshiped pagan gods and would have corrupted the Israelites. God judged them harshly and wanted them destroyed.

Why didn't God drive out all the Canaanites at once? (23:27–30)
God helped them take over all the land gradually so they had time to build up and train the army to manage the new land. If they drove out all the enemy at once, there would be a lot of unoccupied territory, and wild animals would multiply and cause problems for the settlers.

Who were Nadab and Abihu? (24:1)
They were Aaron's two oldest sons. They both became priests. (Read more about them in Leviticus 10:1–2.)

Why was blood used to confirm the covenant? (24:6–8)
Blood was used to seal the covenant. The blood on the altar symbolized God's forgiveness. The blood on the people symbolized their promise to follow God.

What was the Book of the Covenant? (24:7)
The Book of the Covenant was written by Moses and made up of the terms God set out for his people. The Book of the Covenant immediately follows the Ten Commandments. The official book was in Genesis 20:22–23:19.

How was it possible for Moses to see God and live? (24:9–11)
It wasn't possible for a person to see God and live, so Moses and Aaron and Aaron's sons probably only were given a glancing look at God's awesomeness.

his feet was something like a pavement made of lapis lazuli, as bright blue as the sky. [11]But God did not raise his hand against these leaders of the Israelites; they saw God, and they ate and drank.

[12]The LORD said to Moses, "Come up to me on the mountain and stay here, and I will give you the tablets of stone with the law and commandments I have written for their instruction."

[13]Then Moses set out with Joshua his aide, and Moses went up on the mountain of God. [14]He said to the elders, "Wait here for us until we come back to you. Aaron and Hur are with you, and anyone involved in a dispute can go to them."

[15]When Moses went up on the mountain, the cloud covered it, [16]and the glory of the LORD settled on Mount Sinai. For six days the cloud covered the mountain, and on the seventh day the LORD called to Moses from within the cloud. [17]To the Israelites the glory of the LORD looked like a consuming fire on top of the mountain. [18]Then Moses entered the cloud as he went on up the mountain. And he stayed on the mountain forty days and forty nights.

OFFERINGS FOR THE TABERNACLE

25 The LORD said to Moses, [2]"Tell the Israelites to bring me an offering. You are to receive the offering for me from everyone whose heart prompts them to give. [3]These are the offerings you are to receive from them: gold, silver and bronze; [4]blue, purple and scarlet yarn and fine linen; goat hair; [5]ram skins dyed red and another type of durable leather[a]; acacia wood; [6]olive oil for the light; spices for the anointing oil and for the fragrant incense; [7]and onyx stones and other gems to be mounted on the ephod and breastpiece.

[8]"Then have them make a sanctuary for me, and I will dwell among them. [9]Make this tabernacle and all its furnishings exactly like the pattern I will show you.

THE ARK

[10]"Have them make an ark[b] of acacia wood—two and a half cubits long, a cubit and a half wide, and a cubit and a half high.[c] [11]Overlay it with pure gold, both inside and out, and make a gold molding around it. [12]Cast four gold rings for it and fasten them to its four feet, with two rings on one side and two rings on the other. [13]Then make poles of acacia wood and overlay them with gold. [14]Insert the poles into the rings on the sides of the ark to carry it. [15]The poles are to remain in the rings of this ark; they are not to be removed. [16]Then put in the ark the tablets of the covenant law, which I will give you.

[17]"Make an atonement cover of pure gold—two and a half cubits long and a cubit and a half wide. [18]And make two cherubim out of hammered gold at the ends of the cover. [19]Make one cherub on one end and the second cherub on

Why were the colors blue, purple, and scarlet used? (25:4)
These were royal colors. Blue and purple dyes were made from various shellfish in the Mediterranean Sea. The dyeing industry was so important that the promised land was known as Canaan (which means "land of purple"). Scarlet dye was made from the eggs and carcasses of a worm that attached itself to the holly plant.

Why would a chest be called an ark? (25:10)
The word *ark* comes from the same Hebrew word that means chest or coffin. The English word *ark* has been used to describe a sort of boat.

What was the purpose of this ark? (25:10–22)
It was like a portable miniature temple that symbolized God's presence wherever it was carried. It held objects that represented God's work: the stone tablets, a pot of manna, and Aaron's staff.

What are cherubim? (25:18)
Cherubim are angels who praise God. Golden cherubim decorated the ark and reminded people to worship God. They were not idols to be worshiped.

[a] 5 Possibly the hides of large aquatic mammals   [b] 10 That is, a chest
[c] 10 That is, about 3 3/4 feet long and 2 1/4 feet wide and high or about 1.1 meters long and 68 centimeters wide and high; similarly in verse 17

the other; make the cherubim of one piece with the cover, at the two ends. ²⁰The cherubim are to have their wings spread upward, overshadowing the cover with them. The cherubim are to face each other, looking toward the cover. ²¹Place the cover on top of the ark and put in the ark the tablets of the covenant law that I will give you. ²²There, above the cover between the two cherubim that are over the ark of the covenant law, I will meet with you and give you all my commands for the Israelites.

THE TABLE

²³"Make a table of acacia wood—two cubits long, a cubit wide and a cubit and a half high.ᵃ ²⁴Overlay it with pure gold and make a gold molding around it. ²⁵Also make around it a rim a handbreadthᵇ wide and put a gold molding on the rim. ²⁶Make four gold rings for the table and fasten them to the four corners, where the four legs are. ²⁷The rings are to be close to the rim to hold the poles used in carrying the table. ²⁸Make the poles of acacia wood, overlay them with gold and carry the table with them. ²⁹And make its plates and dishes of pure gold, as well as its pitchers and bowls for the pouring out of offerings. ³⁰Put the bread of the Presence on this table to be before me at all times.

ᵃ *23* That is, about 3 feet long, 1 1/2 feet wide and 2 1/4 feet high or about 90 centimeters long, 45 centimeters wide and 68 centimeters high   ᵇ *25* That is, about 3 inches or about 7.5 centimeters

What was the bread of the Presence? (25:30)
This was an offering of twelve loaves of bread that represented the twelve tribes of Israel. To show the devotion of the tribes, the bread was refreshed weekly so the offering was always fresh and in the presence of God.

TABERNACLE FURNISHINGS

The symbolism of God's redemptive covenant was preserved in the tabernacle, making each element an object lesson for the worshiper. Reconstruction of the furnishings is possible because of extremely detailed descriptions and precise measurements recorded in Exodus 25 – 40.

1. ARK OF THE COVENANT

Inside the ark of the covenant (or ark of the covenant law) were kept the Ten Commandments (Dt 10:1–2), a jar of manna (Ex 16:32–34) and Aaron's staff that budded (Nu 17:10–11; compare Heb 9:4).

2. LAMPSTAND

3. TABLE

The table holding the bread of the Presence was made of wood covered with thin sheets of gold. All of the objects were portable and fitted with rings and carrying poles.

4. INCENSE ALTAR

5. BRONZE ALTAR

The altar of burnt offering was made of wood overlaid with bronze.

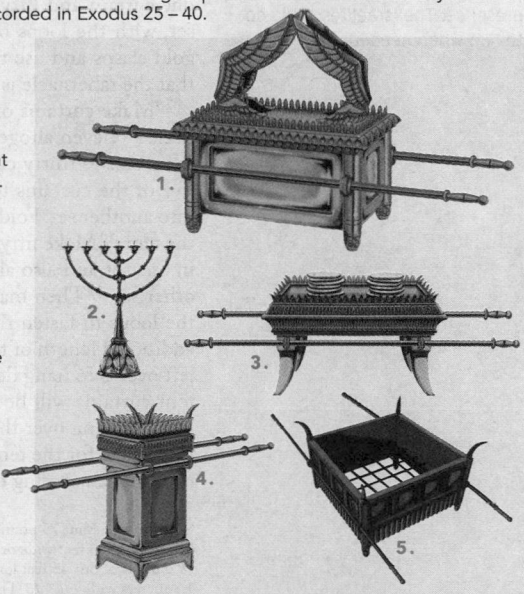

Why was so much gold used? (25:31)
Because gold was one of the most valuable metals on earth, its use showed honor and respect for God.

What was the tabernacle? (26:1)
The tabernacle was a large structure that was a holy place of worship more permanent than the tents of meeting. It was the place where God showed himself to the Israelites. The tabernacle gave God the appearance of a physical presence. The Israelites could go to him when needed.

THE LAMPSTAND

³¹"Make a lampstand of pure gold. Hammer out its base and shaft, and make its flowerlike cups, buds and blossoms of one piece with them. ³²Six branches are to extend from the sides of the lampstand—three on one side and three on the other. ³³Three cups shaped like almond flowers with buds and blossoms are to be on one branch, three on the next branch, and the same for all six branches extending from the lampstand. ³⁴And on the lampstand there are to be four cups shaped like almond flowers with buds and blossoms. ³⁵One bud shall be under the first pair of branches extending from the lampstand, a second bud under the second pair, and a third bud under the third pair—six branches in all. ³⁶The buds and branches shall all be of one piece with the lampstand, hammered out of pure gold.

³⁷"Then make its seven lamps and set them up on it so that they light the space in front of it. ³⁸Its wick trimmers and trays are to be of pure gold. ³⁹A talent*ᵃ* of pure gold is to be used for the lampstand and all these accessories. ⁴⁰See that you make them according to the pattern shown you on the mountain.

THE TABERNACLE

26 "Make the tabernacle with ten curtains of finely twisted linen and blue, purple and scarlet yarn, with cherubim woven into them by a skilled worker. ²All the curtains are to be the same size—twenty-eight cubits long and four cubits wide.*ᵇ* ³Join five of the curtains together, and do the same with the other five. ⁴Make loops of blue material along the edge of the end curtain in one set, and do the same with the end curtain in the other set. ⁵Make fifty loops on one curtain and fifty loops on the end curtain of the other set, with the loops opposite each other. ⁶Then make fifty gold clasps and use them to fasten the curtains together so that the tabernacle is a unit.

⁷"Make curtains of goat hair for the tent over the tabernacle—eleven altogether. ⁸All eleven curtains are to be the same size—thirty cubits long and four cubits wide.*ᶜ* ⁹Join five of the curtains together into one set and the other six into another set. Fold the sixth curtain double at the front of the tent. ¹⁰Make fifty loops along the edge of the end curtain in one set and also along the edge of the end curtain in the other set. ¹¹Then make fifty bronze clasps and put them in the loops to fasten the tent together as a unit. ¹²As for the additional length of the tent curtains, the half curtain that is left over is to hang down at the rear of the tabernacle. ¹³The tent curtains will be a cubit*ᵈ* longer on both sides; what is left will hang over the sides of the tabernacle so as to cover it. ¹⁴Make for the tent a covering of ram skins dyed red, and over that a covering of the other durable leather.*ᵉ*

ᵃ 39 That is, about 75 pounds or about 34 kilograms   *ᵇ 2* That is, about 42 feet long and 6 feet wide or about 13 meters long and 1.8 meters wide   *ᶜ 8* That is, about 45 feet long and 6 feet wide or about 13.5 meters long and 1.8 meters wide   *ᵈ 13* That is, about 18 inches or about 45 centimeters   *ᵉ 14* Possibly the hides of large aquatic mammals (see 25:5)

¹⁵"Make upright frames of acacia wood for the tabernacle. ¹⁶Each frame is to be ten cubits long and a cubit and a half wide,ᵃ ¹⁷with two projections set parallel to each other. Make all the frames of the tabernacle in this way. ¹⁸Make twenty frames for the south side of the tabernacle ¹⁹and make forty silver bases to go under them—two bases for each frame, one under each projection. ²⁰For the other side, the north side of the tabernacle, make twenty frames ²¹and forty silver bases—two under each frame. ²²Make six frames for the far end, that is, the west end of the tabernacle, ²³and make two frames for the corners at the far end. ²⁴At these two corners they must be double from the bottom all the way to the top and fitted into a single ring; both shall be like that. ²⁵So there will be eight frames and sixteen silver bases—two under each frame.

²⁶"Also make crossbars of acacia wood: five for the frames on one side of the tabernacle, ²⁷five for those on the other side, and five for the frames on the west, at the far end of the tabernacle. ²⁸The center crossbar is to extend from end to end at the middle of the frames. ²⁹Overlay the frames with gold and make gold rings to hold the crossbars. Also overlay the crossbars with gold.

³⁰"Set up the tabernacle according to the plan shown you on the mountain.

³¹"Make a curtain of blue, purple and scarlet yarn and finely twisted linen, with cherubim woven into it by a skilled worker. ³²Hang it with gold hooks on four posts of acacia wood overlaid with gold and standing on four silver bases. ³³Hang the curtain from the clasps and place the ark of the covenant law behind the curtain. The curtain will separate the Holy Place from the Most Holy Place. ³⁴Put the atonement cover on the ark of the covenant law in the Most Holy Place. ³⁵Place the table outside the curtain on the north side of the tabernacle and put the lampstand opposite it on the south side.

³⁶"For the entrance to the tent make a curtain of blue, purple and scarlet yarn and finely twisted linen—the work of an embroiderer. ³⁷Make gold hooks for this curtain and five posts of acacia wood overlaid with gold. And cast five bronze bases for them.

THE ALTAR OF BURNT OFFERING

27 "Build an altar of acacia wood, three cubitsᵇ high; it is to be square, five cubits long and five cubits wide.ᶜ ²Make a horn at each of the four corners, so that the horns and the altar are of one piece, and overlay the altar with bronze. ³Make all its utensils of bronze—its pots to remove the ashes, and its shovels, sprinkling bowls, meat forks and firepans. ⁴Make a grating for it, a bronze network, and make a bronze ring at each of the four corners of the network. ⁵Put it under the ledge of the altar so that it is halfway up the altar. ⁶Make poles of acacia wood for the altar and overlay them

---

ᵃ 16 That is, about 15 feet long and 2 1/4 feet wide or about 4.5 meters long and 68 centimeters wide   ᵇ 1 That is, about 4 1/2 feet or about 1.4 meters   ᶜ 1 That is, about 7 1/2 feet or about 2.3 meters long and wide

Why was it important to use acacia wood? (26:15)
The acacia tree provided hard wood that was durable and resistant to wood-eating insects. The thorns of the acacia tree may also have been a good symbol for God's intimidating majesty.

Where did the Israelites get all the materials for the tabernacle? (26:31–37)
The people donated materials from the supplies they had brought out of Egypt.

What was the function of the curtain? (26:31–33)
The curtain divided the tabernacle into two rooms: the Holy Place and the Most Holy Place. The Most Holy Place was enclosed with linen curtains embroidered with cherubim, and it contained only the ark. It represented God's throne room.

The Tabernacle

What were the horns on the altar for? (27:2)
The horns projected from each corner of the altar. They were symbols of help and refuge. They also symbolized the power of the ark in atoning for sin; some of the blood was put on the horns of the altar before the rest was poured out at the base.

with bronze. [7] The poles are to be inserted into the rings so they will be on two sides of the altar when it is carried. [8] Make the altar hollow, out of boards. It is to be made just as you were shown on the mountain.

THE COURTYARD

[9] "Make a courtyard for the tabernacle. The south side shall be a hundred cubits[a] long and is to have curtains of finely twisted linen, [10] with twenty posts and twenty bronze bases and with silver hooks and bands on the posts. [11] The north side shall also be a hundred cubits long and is to have curtains, with twenty posts and twenty bronze bases and with silver hooks and bands on the posts.

[12] "The west end of the courtyard shall be fifty cubits[b] wide and have curtains, with ten posts and ten bases. [13] On the east end, toward the sunrise, the courtyard shall also be fifty cubits wide. [14] Curtains fifteen cubits[c] long are to be on one side of the entrance, with three posts and three bases, [15] and curtains fifteen cubits long are to be on the other side, with three posts and three bases.

[16] "For the entrance to the courtyard, provide a curtain twenty cubits[d] long, of blue, purple and scarlet yarn and finely twisted linen—the work of an embroiderer—with four posts and four bases. [17] All the posts around the courtyard are to have silver bands and hooks, and bronze bases. [18] The courtyard shall be a hundred cubits long and fifty cubits wide,[e] with curtains of finely twisted linen five cubits[f] high, and with bronze bases. [19] All the other articles used in the service of the tabernacle, whatever their function, including all the tent pegs for it and those for the courtyard, are to be of bronze.

OIL FOR THE LAMPSTAND

[20] "Command the Israelites to bring you clear oil of pressed olives for the light so that the lamps may be kept burning. [21] In the tent of meeting, outside the curtain that shields the ark of the covenant law, Aaron and his sons are to keep the lamps burning before the LORD from evening till morning. This is to be a lasting ordinance among the Israelites for the generations to come.

THE PRIESTLY GARMENTS

28 "Have Aaron your brother brought to you from among the Israelites, along with his sons Nadab and Abihu, Eleazar and Ithamar, so they may serve me as priests. [2] Make sacred garments for your brother Aaron to give him dignity and honor. [3] Tell all the skilled workers to whom I have given wisdom in such matters that they are to make garments for Aaron, for his consecration, so he may serve me

---

What was finely twisted linen? (27:16)
This was something made by an embroiderer out of high-quality cotton. It would have been like silk in its softness, beauty, and strength.

What type of oil was burned? (27:20)
The oil came from unripe olives that were crushed in a mortar. The pulpy mass was then placed in a cloth basket, and the oil dripped out the bottom. This produced a clear fuel that burned with little or no smoke.

Why did God want the lamps to burn all night? (27:20–21)
God is always with his people, and the lamps were always to be kept burning as a reminder.

Why were the priests' garments so elaborate? (28:1–40)
The elaborate designs impressed the people. God wanted the priests' garments to display their dignity and honor, and they helped the people see the worship of God as an awesome and special privilege.

---

[a] 9 That is, about 150 feet or about 45 meters; also in verse 11   [b] 12 That is, about 75 feet or about 23 meters; also in verse 13   [c] 14 That is, about 23 feet or about 6.8 meters; also in verse 15   [d] 16 That is, about 30 feet or about 9 meters   [e] 18 That is, about 150 feet long and 75 feet wide or about 45 meters long and 23 meters wide   [f] 18 That is, about 7 1/2 feet or about 2.3 meters

as priest. [4]These are the garments they are to make: a breast-piece, an ephod, a robe, a woven tunic, a turban and a sash. They are to make these sacred garments for your brother Aaron and his sons, so they may serve me as priests. [5]Have them use gold, and blue, purple and scarlet yarn, and fine linen.

THE EPHOD

[6]"Make the ephod of gold, and of blue, purple and scarlet yarn, and of finely twisted linen—the work of skilled hands. [7]It is to have two shoulder pieces attached to two of its corners, so it can be fastened. [8]Its skillfully woven waistband is to be like it—of one piece with the ephod and made with gold, and with blue, purple and scarlet yarn, and with finely twisted linen.

[9]"Take two onyx stones and engrave on them the names of the sons of Israel [10]in the order of their birth—six names on one stone and the remaining six on the other. [11]Engrave the names of the sons of Israel on the two stones the way a gem cutter engraves a seal. Then mount the stones in gold filigree settings [12]and fasten them on the shoulder pieces of the ephod as memorial stones for the sons of Israel. Aaron is to bear the names on his shoulders as a memorial before the Lord. [13]Make gold filigree settings [14]and two braided chains of pure gold, like a rope, and attach the chains to the settings.

THE BREASTPIECE

[15]"Fashion a breastpiece for making decisions—the work of skilled hands. Make it like the ephod: of gold, and of blue, purple and scarlet yarn, and of finely twisted linen. [16]It is to be square—a span[a] long and a span wide—and folded double. [17]Then mount four rows of precious stones on it. The first row shall be carnelian, chrysolite and beryl; [18]the second row shall be turquoise, lapis lazuli and emerald; [19]the third row shall be jacinth, agate and amethyst; [20]the fourth row shall be topaz, onyx and jasper.[b] Mount them in gold filigree settings. [21]There are to be twelve stones, one for each of the names of the sons of Israel, each engraved like a seal with the name of one of the twelve tribes.

[22]"For the breastpiece make braided chains of pure gold, like a rope. [23]Make two gold rings for it and fasten them to two corners of the breastpiece. [24]Fasten the two gold chains to the rings at the corners of the breastpiece, [25]and the other ends of the chains to the two settings, attaching them to the shoulder pieces of the ephod at the front. [26]Make two gold rings and attach them to the other two corners of the breastpiece on the inside edge next to the ephod. [27]Make two more gold rings and attach them to the bottom of the shoulder pieces on the front of the ephod, close to the seam just above the waistband of the ephod. [28]The rings of the breastpiece are to be tied to the rings of the ephod with blue cord, connecting it to the waistband, so that the breastpiece will not swing out from the ephod.

[a] 16 That is, about 9 inches or about 23 centimeters   [b] 20 The precise identification of some of these precious stones is uncertain.

What was an ephod? (28:6)
The ephod was sleeveless clothing made of fine linen and was worn by the high priest.

What was the purpose of the engraved stones worn on the shoulders of the ephod? (28:12)
Aaron wore the names of the 12 sons of Israel on his shoulders to show that in his role as high priest he represented all of the people.

29 "Whenever Aaron enters the Holy Place, he will bear the names of the sons of Israel over his heart on the breastpiece of decision as a continuing memorial before the LORD. 30 Also put the Urim and the Thummim in the breastpiece, so they may be over Aaron's heart whenever he enters the presence of the LORD. Thus Aaron will always bear the means of making decisions for the Israelites over his heart before the LORD.

OTHER PRIESTLY GARMENTS

31 "Make the robe of the ephod entirely of blue cloth, 32 with an opening for the head in its center. There shall be a woven edge like a collar^a around this opening, so that it will not tear. 33 Make pomegranates of blue, purple and scarlet yarn around the hem of the robe, with gold bells between them. 34 The gold bells and the pomegranates are to alternate around the hem of the robe. 35 Aaron must wear it when he ministers. The sound of the bells will be heard when he enters the Holy Place before the LORD and when he comes out, so that he will not die.

36 "Make a plate of pure gold and engrave on it as on a seal: HOLY TO THE LORD. 37 Fasten a blue cord to it to attach it to the turban; it is to be on the front of the turban. 38 It will be on Aaron's forehead, and he will bear the guilt involved in the sacred gifts the Israelites consecrate, whatever their gifts may be. It will be on Aaron's forehead continually so that they will be acceptable to the LORD.

39 "Weave the tunic of fine linen and make the turban of fine linen. The sash is to be the work of an embroiderer. 40 Make tunics, sashes and caps for Aaron's sons to give them dignity and honor. 41 After you put these clothes on your brother Aaron and his sons, anoint and ordain them. Consecrate them so they may serve me as priests.

42 "Make linen undergarments as a covering for the body, reaching from the waist to the thigh. 43 Aaron and his sons must wear them whenever they enter the tent of meeting or approach the altar to minister in the Holy Place, so that they will not incur guilt and die.

"This is to be a lasting ordinance for Aaron and his descendants.

CONSECRATION OF THE PRIESTS

29 "This is what you are to do to consecrate them, so they may serve me as priests: Take a young bull and two rams without defect. 2 And from the finest wheat flour make round loaves without yeast, thick loaves without yeast and with olive oil mixed in, and thin loaves without yeast and brushed with olive oil. 3 Put them in a basket and present them along with the bull and the two rams. 4 Then bring Aaron and his sons to the entrance to the tent of meeting and wash them with water. 5 Take the garments and dress Aaron with the tunic, the robe of the ephod, the ephod itself and the breastpiece. Fasten the ephod on him by its skillfully woven waistband. 6 Put the turban on his head and attach the sacred emblem to the turban. 7 Take the anointing oil

---

^a 32 The meaning of the Hebrew for this word is uncertain.

What were the Urim and Thummim that Aaron wore on his breastpiece? (28:30)
The Urim and Thummim may have been small metal objects or stones or sticks inscribed with symbols and used like dice to get a simple yes or no answer from God. The symbols may have been the 22 letters of the Hebrew alphabet. (*Urim* is the first letter and *Thummim* is the last letter of the Hebrew alphabet.)

Why did the high priest wear bells and linen undergarments? (28:35, 42–43)
The bells and linen undergarments were part of the high priest's robe that set him apart. These details apparently symbolized his spiritual purity. Without them he was unfit to serve in the presence of God.

What if the bells stopped sounding when the priest was in the Holy Place? (28:35)
According to Jewish tradition, one end of a length of rope was tied to the priest's ankle. When he moved around, people outside of the Holy Place would be able to hear the sound of the bells. If they stopped hearing the sound of the bells, someone could pull gently on the rope to see if the priest had died.

Why make the bread and cakes without yeast? (29:2)
Yeast wasn't used in the original Passover meal because the people had to prepare their food quickly so they could leave Egypt. Over time, yeast became a symbol of corruption.

and anoint him by pouring it on his head. [8]Bring his sons and dress them in tunics [9]and fasten caps on them. Then tie sashes on Aaron and his sons.[a] The priesthood is theirs by a lasting ordinance.

"Then you shall ordain Aaron and his sons.

[10]"Bring the bull to the front of the tent of meeting, and Aaron and his sons shall lay their hands on its head. [11]Slaughter it in the LORD's presence at the entrance to the tent of meeting. [12]Take some of the bull's blood and put it on the horns of the altar with your finger, and pour out the rest of it at the base of the altar. [13]Then take all the fat on the internal organs, the long lobe of the liver, and both kidneys with the fat on them, and burn them on the altar. [14]But burn the bull's flesh and its hide and its intestines outside the camp. It is a sin offering.[b]

[15]"Take one of the rams, and Aaron and his sons shall lay their hands on its head. [16]Slaughter it and take the blood and splash it against the sides of the altar. [17]Cut the ram into pieces and wash the internal organs and the legs, putting them with the head and the other pieces. [18]Then burn the entire ram on the altar. It is a burnt offering to the LORD, a pleasing aroma, a food offering presented to the LORD.

[19]"Take the other ram, and Aaron and his sons shall lay their hands on its head. [20]Slaughter it, take some of its blood and put it on the lobes of the right ears of Aaron and his sons, on the thumbs of their right hands, and on the big toes of their right feet. Then splash blood against the sides of the altar. [21]And take some blood from the altar and some of the anointing oil and sprinkle it on Aaron and his garments and on his sons and their garments. Then he and his sons and their garments will be consecrated.

[22]"Take from this ram the fat, the fat tail, the fat on the internal organs, the long lobe of the liver, both kidneys with the fat on them, and the right thigh. (This is the ram for the ordination.) [23]From the basket of bread made without yeast, which is before the LORD, take one round loaf, one thick loaf with olive oil mixed in, and one thin loaf. [24]Put all these in the hands of Aaron and his sons and have them wave them before the LORD as a wave offering. [25]Then take them from their hands and burn them on the altar along with the burnt offering for a pleasing aroma to the LORD, a food offering presented to the LORD. [26]After you take the breast of the ram for Aaron's ordination, wave it before the LORD as a wave offering, and it will be your share.

[27]"Consecrate those parts of the ordination ram that belong to Aaron and his sons: the breast that was waved and the thigh that was presented. [28]This is always to be the perpetual share from the Israelites for Aaron and his sons. It is the contribution the Israelites are to make to the LORD from their fellowship offerings.

[29]"Aaron's sacred garments will belong to his descendants so that they can be anointed and ordained in them. [30]The son who succeeds him as priest and comes to the tent of meeting to minister in the Holy Place is to wear them seven days.

[a] 9 Hebrew; Septuagint *on them*   [b] 14 Or *purification offering*; also in verse 36

Why was oil poured over Aaron's head? (29:7)
Anointing with oil symbolized setting someone apart to serve God for a special purpose. Aaron was anointed, and so was the tabernacle.

Why were there specific instructions about various animal parts? (29:13–14)
In a sacrifice, each action had a symbolic meaning. The best parts of the animal were given to God. Other parts of the animal associated with sin weren't even eaten. They were taken out of the camp and burned.

Why was blood spread on the priests' right ears, thumbs, and feet? (29:20)
This ceremony may have symbolized cleansing and directing the priests' life for God. The ears may have symbolized sensitivity to God and hearing his Word, while the hands and feet may have symbolized a life of service to others on God's behalf.

What was a wave offering? (29:22–28)
A wave offering got its name because it was waved before God as it was offered to him. This was part of a peace offering. The priest ate the offering after it was presented to God.

³¹"Take the ram for the ordination and cook the meat in a sacred place. ³²At the entrance to the tent of meeting, Aaron and his sons are to eat the meat of the ram and the bread that is in the basket. ³³They are to eat these offerings by which atonement was made for their ordination and consecration. But no one else may eat them, because they are sacred. ³⁴And if any of the meat of the ordination ram or any bread is left over till morning, burn it up. It must not be eaten, because it is sacred.

³⁵"Do for Aaron and his sons everything I have commanded you, taking seven days to ordain them. ³⁶Sacrifice a bull each day as a sin offering to make atonement. Purify the altar by making atonement for it, and anoint it to consecrate it. ³⁷For seven days make atonement for the altar and consecrate it. Then the altar will be most holy, and whatever touches it will be holy.

³⁸"This is what you are to offer on the altar regularly each day: two lambs a year old. ³⁹Offer one in the morning and the other at twilight. ⁴⁰With the first lamb offer a tenth of an ephah^a of the finest flour mixed with a quarter of a hin^b of oil from pressed olives, and a quarter of a hin of wine as a drink offering. ⁴¹Sacrifice the other lamb at twilight with the same grain offering and its drink offering as in the morning—a pleasing aroma, a food offering presented to the LORD.

⁴²"For the generations to come this burnt offering is to be made regularly at the entrance to the tent of meeting, before the LORD. There I will meet you and speak to you; ⁴³there also I will meet with the Israelites, and the place will be consecrated by my glory.

⁴⁴"So I will consecrate the tent of meeting and the altar and will consecrate Aaron and his sons to serve me as priests. ⁴⁵Then I will dwell among the Israelites and be their God. ⁴⁶They will know that I am the LORD their God, who brought them out of Egypt so that I might dwell among them. I am the LORD their God.

THE ALTAR OF INCENSE

30 "Make an altar of acacia wood for burning incense. ²It is to be square, a cubit long and a cubit wide, and two cubits high^c—its horns of one piece with it. ³Overlay the top and all the sides and the horns with pure gold, and make a gold molding around it. ⁴Make two gold rings for the altar below the molding—two on each of the opposite sides—to hold the poles used to carry it. ⁵Make the poles of acacia wood and overlay them with gold. ⁶Put the altar in front of the curtain that shields the ark of the covenant law—before the atonement cover that is over the tablets of the covenant law—where I will meet with you.

⁷"Aaron must burn fragrant incense on the altar every morning when he tends the lamps. ⁸He must burn incense again when he lights the lamps at twilight so incense will

^a 40 That is, probably about 3 1/2 pounds or about 1.6 kilograms
^b 40 That is, probably about 1 quart or about 1 liter   ^c 2 That is, about 1 1/2 feet long and wide and 3 feet high or about 45 centimeters long and wide and 90 centimeters high

Why did it take seven days to ordain the priests? (29:35) Seven was a symbolic number in the Bible that started with the seven days of creation. Just as it took seven days to make a perfect world, it took seven days to make the priests holy and set them apart for God's service.

How did God speak to the Israelites? (29:42–43) God may have spoken out of the cloud, or perhaps he spoke only to Moses.

What was incense made of? (30:7) Incense was a sweet-smelling substance made of various gums and spices. It was used only for worship, not for ordinary purposes. If it was mixed incorrectly, it was rejected. The fragrant smoke of incense symbolized the prayers of God's people.

burn regularly before the LORD for the generations to come. [9] Do not offer on this altar any other incense or any burnt offering or grain offering, and do not pour a drink offering on it. [10] Once a year Aaron shall make atonement on its horns. This annual atonement must be made with the blood of the atoning sin offering[a] for the generations to come. It is most holy to the LORD."

ATONEMENT MONEY

[11] Then the LORD said to Moses, [12] "When you take a census of the Israelites to count them, each one must pay the LORD a ransom for his life at the time he is counted. Then no plague will come on them when you number them. [13] Each one who crosses over to those already counted is to give a half shekel,[b] according to the sanctuary shekel, which weighs twenty gerahs. This half shekel is an offering to the LORD. [14] All who cross over, those twenty years old or more, are to give an offering to the LORD. [15] The rich are not to give more than a half shekel and the poor are not to give less when you make the offering to the LORD to atone for your lives. [16] Receive the atonement money from the Israelites and use it for the service of the tent of meeting. It will be a memorial for the Israelites before the LORD, making atonement for your lives."

BASIN FOR WASHING

[17] Then the LORD said to Moses, [18] "Make a bronze basin, with its bronze stand, for washing. Place it between the tent of meeting and the altar, and put water in it. [19] Aaron and his sons are to wash their hands and feet with water from it. [20] Whenever they enter the tent of meeting, they shall wash with water so that they will not die. Also, when they approach the altar to minister by presenting a food offering to the LORD, [21] they shall wash their hands and feet so that they will not die. This is to be a lasting ordinance for Aaron and his descendants for the generations to come."

ANOINTING OIL

[22] Then the LORD said to Moses, [23] "Take the following fine spices: 500 shekels[c] of liquid myrrh, half as much (that is, 250 shekels) of fragrant cinnamon, 250 shekels[d] of fragrant calamus, [24] 500 shekels of cassia—all according to the sanctuary shekel—and a hin[e] of olive oil. [25] Make these into a sacred anointing oil, a fragrant blend, the work of a perfumer. It will be the sacred anointing oil. [26] Then use it to anoint the tent of meeting, the ark of the covenant law, [27] the table and all its articles, the lampstand and its accessories, the altar of incense, [28] the altar of burnt offering and all its utensils, and the basin with its stand. [29] You shall consecrate them so they will be most holy, and whatever touches them will be holy.

[30] "Anoint Aaron and his sons and consecrate them so they

Why did the Israelites have to pay a ransom during the census? (30:12)
The census may have been a part of a military draft or to create an official roll. When the people were counted, they paid a small ransom. The money was used to support the tabernacle service.

Why did the rich and poor pay the same offering to the LORD? (30:15)
The half shekel offering was small enough that anyone could afford it. The point of the ransom was that both rich and poor are equal in God's eyes.

Why would people die in the tent of meeting? (30:20-21)
God's people were sinful, and they needed to cleanse themselves and serve God with respect in the face of his holiness. If people were careless in God's presence, there were severe consequences.

---

[a] 10 Or purification offering   [b] 13 That is, about 1/5 ounce or about 5.8 grams; also in verse 15   [c] 23 That is, about 12 1/2 pounds or about 5.8 kilograms; also in verse 24   [d] 23 That is, about 6 1/4 pounds or about 2.9 kilograms   [e] 24 That is, probably about 1 gallon or about 3.8 liters

may serve me as priests. ³¹Say to the Israelites, 'This is to be my sacred anointing oil for the generations to come. ³²Do not pour it on anyone else's body and do not make any other oil using the same formula. It is sacred, and you are to consider it sacred. ³³Whoever makes perfume like it and puts it on anyone other than a priest must be cut off from their people.'"

INCENSE

³⁴Then the Lord said to Moses, "Take fragrant spices— gum resin, onycha and galbanum—and pure frankincense, all in equal amounts, ³⁵and make a fragrant blend of incense, the work of a perfumer. It is to be salted and pure and sacred. ³⁶Grind some of it to powder and place it in front of the ark of the covenant law in the tent of meeting, where I will meet with you. It shall be most holy to you. ³⁷Do not make any incense with this formula for yourselves; consider it holy to the Lord. ³⁸Whoever makes incense like it to enjoy its fragrance must be cut off from their people."

BEZALEL AND OHOLIAB

31 Then the Lord said to Moses, ²"See, I have chosen Bezalel son of Uri, the son of Hur, of the tribe of Judah, ³and I have filled him with the Spirit of God, with wisdom, with understanding, with knowledge and with all kinds of skills— ⁴to make artistic designs for work in gold, silver and bronze, ⁵to cut and set stones, to work in wood, and to engage in all kinds of crafts. ⁶Moreover, I have appointed Oholiab son of Ahisamak, of the tribe of Dan, to help him. Also I have given ability to all the skilled workers to make everything I have commanded you: ⁷the tent of meeting, the ark of the covenant law with the atonement cover on it, and all the other furnishings of the tent— ⁸the table and its articles, the pure gold lampstand and all its accessories, the altar of incense, ⁹the altar of burnt offering and all its utensils, the basin with its stand— ¹⁰and also the woven garments, both the sacred garments for Aaron the priest and the garments for his sons when they serve as priests, ¹¹and the anointing oil and fragrant incense for the Holy Place. They are to make them just as I commanded you."

THE SABBATH

¹²Then the Lord said to Moses, ¹³"Say to the Israelites, 'You must observe my Sabbaths. This will be a sign between me and you for the generations to come, so you may know that I am the Lord, who makes you holy.

¹⁴"'Observe the Sabbath, because it is holy to you. Anyone who desecrates it is to be put to death; those who do any work on that day must be cut off from their people. ¹⁵For six days work is to be done, but the seventh day is a day of sabbath rest, holy to the Lord. Whoever does any work on the Sabbath day is to be put to death. ¹⁶The Israelites are to observe the Sabbath, celebrating it for the generations to come as a lasting covenant. ¹⁷It will be a sign between me and the Israelites forever, for in six days the Lord made the heavens and the earth, and on the seventh day he rested and was refreshed.'"

Why was Bezalel chosen to be filled with the Spirit of God? (31:1–5)
God often gave a special anointing of his Spirit to individuals to engage in arts and crafts, such as working in gold, setting stones, and working in wood. Bezalel was anointed to create furnishings for the tent of meeting.

How was observing the Sabbath a sign? (31:13)
The Israelites were God's holy people, so they observed the Sabbath as a reminder. It also strengthened their already special relationship with God.

What were the two tablets of the covenant law? (31:18)
They were two copies of the same document, one copy for the people and one copy for God. Both were kept inside the ark.

[18] When the LORD finished speaking to Moses on Mount Sinai, he gave him the two tablets of the covenant law, the tablets of stone inscribed by the finger of God.

THE GOLDEN CALF

32 When the people saw that Moses was so long in coming down from the mountain, they gathered around Aaron and said, "Come, make us gods[a] who will go before us. As for this fellow Moses who brought us up out of Egypt, we don't know what has happened to him."

[2] Aaron answered them, "Take off the gold earrings that your wives, your sons and your daughters are wearing, and bring them to me." [3] So all the people took off their earrings and brought them to Aaron. [4] He took what they handed him and made it into an idol cast in the shape of a calf, fashioning it with a tool. Then they said, "These are your gods,[b] Israel, who brought you up out of Egypt."

[5] When Aaron saw this, he built an altar in front of the calf and announced, "Tomorrow there will be a festival to the LORD." [6] So the next day the people rose early and sacrificed burnt offerings and presented fellowship offerings. Afterward they sat down to eat and drink and got up to indulge in revelry.

[7] Then the LORD said to Moses, "Go down, because your people, whom you brought up out of Egypt, have become corrupt. [8] They have been quick to turn away from what I commanded them and have made themselves an idol cast in the shape of a calf. They have bowed down to it and sacrificed to it and have said, 'These are your gods, Israel, who brought you up out of Egypt.'

[9] "I have seen these people," the LORD said to Moses, "and they are a stiff-necked people. [10] Now leave me alone so that my anger may burn against them and that I may destroy them. Then I will make you into a great nation."

[11] But Moses sought the favor of the LORD his God. "LORD," he said, "why should your anger burn against your people, whom you brought out of Egypt with great power and a mighty hand? [12] Why should the Egyptians say, 'It was with evil intent that he brought them out, to kill them in the mountains and to wipe them off the face of the earth'? Turn from your fierce anger; relent and do not bring disaster on your people. [13] Remember your servants Abraham, Isaac and Israel, to whom you swore by your own self: 'I will make your descendants as numerous as the stars in the sky and I will give your descendants all this land I promised them, and it will be their inheritance forever.'" [14] Then the LORD relented and did not bring on his people the disaster he had threatened.

[15] Moses turned and went down the mountain with the two tablets of the covenant law in his hands. They were inscribed on both sides, front and back. [16] The tablets were the work of God; the writing was the writing of God, engraved on the tablets.

[17] When Joshua heard the noise of the people shouting, he said to Moses, "There is the sound of war in the camp."

---

[a] 1 Or *a god*; also in verses 23 and 31   [b] 4 Or *This is your god*; also in verse 8

What did it mean that the tablets were "inscribed by the finger of God"? (31:18)
God is a Spirit and does not have physical fingers. The phrase means that the covenants and covenant rules came directly from God.

Why did the Israelites want to have a god that they could see? (32:1)
The Egyptian gods were visible. The Israelites were used to images that represented gods. While Moses was on the mountain, the people needed reassurance that God was near. Ancient people saw an idol as an earthly representation of a god, not as the god itself. The Israelites may have seen the calf as the throne of God.

What did the golden calf look like? (32:4)
The idol may have been carved from wood and covered with gold plating. Or it may have been cast in solid gold and then shaped with a tool.

The Golden Calf

Was God serious about destroying his chosen people? (32:10)
Yes. He was ready to destroy them and start over. But Moses prayed for the people, and God listened to Moses and did not destroy them. In his role as a mediator between God and human beings, Moses foreshadowed the future work of Jesus.

¹⁸Moses replied:

"It is not the sound of victory,
it is not the sound of defeat;
it is the sound of singing that I hear."

¹⁹When Moses approached the camp and saw the calf and the dancing, his anger burned and he threw the tablets out of his hands, breaking them to pieces at the foot of the mountain. ²⁰And he took the calf the people had made and burned it in the fire; then he ground it to powder, scattered it on the water and made the Israelites drink it.

²¹He said to Aaron, "What did these people do to you, that you led them into such great sin?"

²²"Do not be angry, my lord," Aaron answered. "You know how prone these people are to evil. ²³They said to me, 'Make us gods who will go before us. As for this fellow Moses who brought us up out of Egypt, we don't know what has happened to him.' ²⁴So I told them, 'Whoever has any gold jewelry, take it off.' Then they gave me the gold, and I threw it into the fire, and out came this calf!"

²⁵Moses saw that the people were running wild and that Aaron had let them get out of control and so become a laughingstock to their enemies. ²⁶So he stood at the entrance to the camp and said, "Whoever is for the LORD, come to me." And all the Levites rallied to him.

²⁷Then he said to them, "This is what the LORD, the God of Israel, says: 'Each man strap a sword to his side. Go back and forth through the camp from one end to the other, each killing his brother and friend and neighbor.'" ²⁸The Levites did as Moses commanded, and that day about three thousand of the people died. ²⁹Then Moses said, "You have been set apart to the LORD today, for you were against your own sons and brothers, and he has blessed you this day."

³⁰The next day Moses said to the people, "You have committed a great sin. But now I will go up to the LORD; perhaps I can make atonement for your sin."

³¹So Moses went back to the LORD and said, "Oh, what a great sin these people have committed! They have made themselves gods of gold. ³²But now, please forgive their sin—but if not, then blot me out of the book you have written."

Why wasn't Aaron punished for making the golden calf? (32:21–25)
Aaron sinned in making the calf, but God spared him because of Moses' prayers on Aaron's behalf.

Why did Moses tell the Levites to kill their family members, friends, and neighbors? (32:27)
Moses asked who was still for the Lord. It was the Levites who stepped forward. Moses ordered them to kill all those who had obviously been sinning, even if they were friends or family members. God's justice demanded that the wrongdoers be punished.

What does it mean that the Levites were "set apart"? (32:29)
They were set apart to serve God in a special way. They would later help the priests and care for the tabernacle.

Can our prayers cause God to change his mind?   EXODUS 32

There are several stories in the Bible where God seems to change his mind based on the prayers of his people. But we also know that God does not change and that he holds the past, present, and future in his hands.

Sometimes it seems as if God changes his mind, but that is from our human perspective. What it may really mean is that God knew all along what he would do, but we imagine that he changed course or direction. Certainly God wants us to pray and to ask him for the things that are important to us, such as comfort or healing or direction for our lives.

God does not change his will just because a large number of people ask him for something. At the same time, God hears our prayers, and sometimes—from our perspective—it seems as if he adjusts his plans. However, it's important to remember that God is always in charge and always in control. As the old hymn says, "He's got the whole world in his hands."

³³The LORD replied to Moses, "Whoever has sinned against me I will blot out of my book. ³⁴Now go, lead the people to the place I spoke of, and my angel will go before you. However, when the time comes for me to punish, I will punish them for their sin."

³⁵And the LORD struck the people with a plague because of what they did with the calf Aaron had made.

33 Then the LORD said to Moses, "Leave this place, you and the people you brought up out of Egypt, and go up to the land I promised on oath to Abraham, Isaac and Jacob, saying, 'I will give it to your descendants.' ²I will send an angel before you and drive out the Canaanites, Amorites, Hittites, Perizzites, Hivites and Jebusites. ³Go up to the land flowing with milk and honey. But I will not go with you, because you are a stiff-necked people and I might destroy you on the way."

⁴When the people heard these distressing words, they began to mourn and no one put on any ornaments. ⁵For the LORD had said to Moses, "Tell the Israelites, 'You are a stiff-necked people. If I were to go with you even for a moment, I might destroy you. Now take off your ornaments and I will decide what to do with you.'" ⁶So the Israelites stripped off their ornaments at Mount Horeb.

THE TENT OF MEETING

⁷Now Moses used to take a tent and pitch it outside the camp some distance away, calling it the "tent of meeting." Anyone inquiring of the LORD would go to the tent of meeting outside the camp. ⁸And whenever Moses went out to the tent, all the people rose and stood at the entrances to their tents, watching Moses until he entered the tent. ⁹As Moses went into the tent, the pillar of cloud would come down and stay at the entrance, while the LORD spoke with Moses. ¹⁰Whenever the people saw the pillar of cloud standing at the entrance to the tent, they all stood and worshiped, each at the entrance to their tent. ¹¹The LORD would speak to Moses face to face, as one speaks to a friend. Then Moses would return to the camp, but his young aide Joshua son of Nun did not leave the tent.

MOSES AND THE GLORY OF THE LORD

¹²Moses said to the LORD, "You have been telling me, 'Lead these people,' but you have not let me know whom you will send with me. You have said, 'I know you by name and you have found favor with me.' ¹³If you are pleased with me, teach me your ways so I may know you and continue to find favor with you. Remember that this nation is your people."

¹⁴The LORD replied, "My Presence will go with you, and I will give you rest."

¹⁵Then Moses said to him, "If your Presence does not go with us, do not send us up from here. ¹⁶How will anyone know that you are pleased with me and with your people unless you go with us? What else will distinguish me and your people from all the other people on the face of the earth?"

What does God mean when he says the Israelites are stiff-necked people? (33:3) God means they are difficult to deal with. They continue to complain and disobey even after all the times God has helped them and forgiven them.

How could Moses speak to the Lord face to face? (33:11) This phrase is meant as a metaphor. No one could see God's face and live. God spoke to Moses in a straightforward way, like a friend.

What does it mean that God found favor with Moses? (33:12) Moses was very faithful to God. He did not earn God's favor, but he did not reject the gift of grace through disobedience or unfaithfulness.

Why did Moses want Israel to be seen as different from other nations? (33:16) Moses wanted some sign or mark to let other nations know that they should not attack Israel because of Israel's special status with God.

¹⁷And the LORD said to Moses, "I will do the very thing you have asked, because I am pleased with you and I know you by name."

¹⁸Then Moses said, "Now show me your glory."

¹⁹And the LORD said, "I will cause all my goodness to pass in front of you, and I will proclaim my name, the LORD, in your presence. I will have mercy on whom I will have mercy, and I will have compassion on whom I will have compassion. ²⁰But," he said, "you cannot see my face, for no one may see me and live."

²¹Then the LORD said, "There is a place near me where you may stand on a rock. ²²When my glory passes by, I will put you in a cleft in the rock and cover you with my hand until I have passed by. ²³Then I will remove my hand and you will see my back; but my face must not be seen."

THE NEW STONE TABLETS

34 The LORD said to Moses, "Chisel out two stone tablets like the first ones, and I will write on them the words that were on the first tablets, which you broke. ²Be ready in the morning, and then come up on Mount Sinai. Present yourself to me there on top of the mountain. ³No one is to come with you or be seen anywhere on the mountain; not even the flocks and herds may graze in front of the mountain."

⁴So Moses chiseled out two stone tablets like the first ones and went up Mount Sinai early in the morning, as the LORD had commanded him; and he carried the two stone tablets in his hands. ⁵Then the LORD came down in the cloud and stood there with him and proclaimed his name, the LORD. ⁶And he passed in front of Moses, proclaiming, "The LORD, the LORD, the compassionate and gracious God, slow to anger, abounding in love and faithfulness, ⁷maintaining love to thousands, and forgiving wickedness, rebellion and sin. Yet he does not leave the guilty unpunished; he punishes the children and their children for the sin of the parents to the third and fourth generation."

⁸Moses bowed to the ground at once and worshiped. ⁹"Lord," he said, "if I have found favor in your eyes, then let the Lord go with us. Although this is a stiff-necked people, forgive our wickedness and our sin, and take us as your inheritance."

¹⁰Then the LORD said: "I am making a covenant with you. Before all your people I will do wonders never before done in any nation in all the world. The people you live among will see how awesome is the work that I, the LORD, will do for you. ¹¹Obey what I command you today. I will drive out before you the Amorites, Canaanites, Hittites, Perizzites, Hivites and Jebusites. ¹²Be careful not to make a treaty with those who live in the land where you are going, or they will be a snare among you. ¹³Break down their altars, smash their sacred stones and cut down their Asherah poles.ᵃ ¹⁴Do not worship any other god, for the LORD, whose name is Jealous, is a jealous God.

ᵃ 13 That is, wooden symbols of the goddess Asherah

Why did Moses make replacement tablets? (34:1)
God told Moses to make replacement tablets, and God wrote the Ten Commandments on them. The tablets were later placed in the ark of the covenant.

Why would future generations be punished for the sins of their fathers and grandfathers? (34:7)
Families were regarded as a unit, and both blessings and curses could affect several generations of a family.

What were Asherah poles? (34:13)
Asherah was the name of the wife of El, the chief Canaanite god. Wooden poles, possibly carved with her image, were often set up in her honor and placed near other pagan objects of worship.

15 "Be careful not to make a treaty with those who live in the land; for when they prostitute themselves to their gods and sacrifice to them, they will invite you and you will eat their sacrifices. 16 And when you choose some of their daughters as wives for your sons and those daughters prostitute themselves to their gods, they will lead your sons to do the same.

17 "Do not make any idols.

18 "Celebrate the Festival of Unleavened Bread. For seven days eat bread made without yeast, as I commanded you. Do this at the appointed time in the month of Aviv, for in that month you came out of Egypt.

19 "The first offspring of every womb belongs to me, including all the firstborn males of your livestock, whether from herd or flock. 20 Redeem the firstborn donkey with a lamb, but if you do not redeem it, break its neck. Redeem all your firstborn sons.

"No one is to appear before me empty-handed.

21 "Six days you shall labor, but on the seventh day you shall rest; even during the plowing season and harvest you must rest.

22 "Celebrate the Festival of Weeks with the firstfruits of the wheat harvest, and the Festival of Ingathering at the turn of the year.ᵃ 23 Three times a year all your men are to appear before the Sovereign LORD, the God of Israel. 24 I will drive out nations before you and enlarge your territory, and no one will covet your land when you go up three times each year to appear before the LORD your God.

25 "Do not offer the blood of a sacrifice to me along with anything containing yeast, and do not let any of the sacrifice from the Passover Festival remain until morning.

26 "Bring the best of the firstfruits of your soil to the house of the LORD your God.

"Do not cook a young goat in its mother's milk."

27 Then the LORD said to Moses, "Write down these words, for in accordance with these words I have made a covenant with you and with Israel." 28 Moses was there with the LORD forty days and forty nights without eating bread or drinking water. And he wrote on the tablets the words of the covenant—the Ten Commandments.

THE RADIANT FACE OF MOSES

29 When Moses came down from Mount Sinai with the two tablets of the covenant law in his hands, he was not aware that his face was radiant because he had spoken with the LORD. 30 When Aaron and all the Israelites saw Moses, his face was radiant, and they were afraid to come near him. 31 But Moses called to them; so Aaron and all the leaders of the community came back to him, and he spoke to them. 32 Afterward all the Israelites came near him, and he gave them all the commands the LORD had given him on Mount Sinai.

33 When Moses finished speaking to them, he put a veil over his face. 34 But whenever he entered the LORD's presence

ᵃ 22 That is, in the autumn

Why did God want Israel to remain separate from the Canaanite people? (34:15–16)
God knew the pagan people would invite the people of Israel to participate in their pagan worship practices. The pagan people led Israel astray more often than Israel led the pagan people to God.

Why was Moses' face radiant? (34:29)
Moses had asked to see God's glory, and perhaps his radiant face was a reflection of God's glory. The first time he came down from the mountain, Moses was so angry there was no glory on his face.

Why did Moses put a veil over his face? (34:33)
Moses knew the radiance would fade. He didn't want people to see this. If they did, Moses thought they could lose faith or question his position as God's representative. (See 2 Corinthians 3:13.)

to speak with him, he removed the veil until he came out. And when he came out and told the Israelites what he had been commanded, [35] they saw that his face was radiant. Then Moses would put the veil back over his face until he went in to speak with the LORD.

SABBATH REGULATIONS

35 Moses assembled the whole Israelite community and said to them, "These are the things the LORD has commanded you to do: [2] For six days, work is to be done, but the seventh day shall be your holy day, a day of sabbath rest to the LORD. Whoever does any work on it is to be put to death. [3] Do not light a fire in any of your dwellings on the Sabbath day."

MATERIALS FOR THE TABERNACLE

[4] Moses said to the whole Israelite community, "This is what the LORD has commanded: [5] From what you have, take an offering for the LORD. Everyone who is willing is to bring to the LORD an offering of gold, silver and bronze; [6] blue, purple and scarlet yarn and fine linen; goat hair; [7] ram skins dyed red and another type of durable leather*; acacia wood; [8] olive oil for the light; spices for the anointing oil and for the fragrant incense; [9] and onyx stones and other gems to be mounted on the ephod and breastpiece.

[10] "All who are skilled among you are to come and make everything the LORD has commanded: [11] the tabernacle with its tent and its covering, clasps, frames, crossbars, posts and bases; [12] the ark with its poles and the atonement cover and the curtain that shields it; [13] the table with its poles and all its articles and the bread of the Presence; [14] the lampstand that is for light with its accessories, lamps and oil for the light; [15] the altar of incense with its poles, the anointing oil and the fragrant incense; the curtain for the doorway at the entrance to the tabernacle; [16] the altar of burnt offering with its bronze grating, its poles and all its utensils; the bronze basin with its stand; [17] the curtains of the courtyard with its posts and bases, and the curtain for the entrance to the courtyard; [18] the tent pegs for the tabernacle and for the courtyard, and their ropes; [19] the woven garments worn for ministering in the sanctuary—both the sacred garments for Aaron the priest and the garments for his sons when they serve as priests."

[20] Then the whole Israelite community withdrew from Moses' presence, [21] and everyone who was willing and whose heart moved them came and brought an offering to the LORD for the work on the tent of meeting, for all its service, and for the sacred garments. [22] All who were willing, men and women alike, came and brought gold jewelry of all kinds: brooches, earrings, rings and ornaments. They all presented their gold as a wave offering to the LORD. [23] Everyone who had blue, purple or scarlet yarn or fine linen, or goat hair, ram skins dyed red or the other durable leather brought them. [24] Those presenting an offering of silver or

---

*7 Possibly the hides of large aquatic mammals; also in verse 23

Why were the people told not to light a fire on the Sabbath? (35:3)
Lighting a fire was a great deal of work in those days and included cutting and carrying wood and sparking a flame. The Sabbath was a day of rest with no work. The people used the fires from the day before.

Were the people required to give materials for the building of the tabernacle? (35:5)
No. Moses said that *everyone who is willing* should contribute to the project. There was an emphasis on the voluntary nature of the offering.

Why is there so much repetition of the instructions? (35:5–39:43)
Repetition was a common feature of ancient Middle Eastern literature and was meant to fix the details of a narrative in the listener's mind.

bronze brought it as an offering to the LORD, and everyone who had acacia wood for any part of the work brought it. [25] Every skilled woman spun with her hands and brought what she had spun—blue, purple or scarlet yarn or fine linen. [26] And all the women who were willing and had the skill spun the goat hair. [27] The leaders brought onyx stones and other gems to be mounted on the ephod and breastpiece. [28] They also brought spices and olive oil for the light and for the anointing oil and for the fragrant incense. [29] All the Israelite men and women who were willing brought to the LORD freewill offerings for all the work the LORD through Moses had commanded them to do.

BEZALEL AND OHOLIAB

[30] Then Moses said to the Israelites, "See, the LORD has chosen Bezalel son of Uri, the son of Hur, of the tribe of Judah, [31] and he has filled him with the Spirit of God, with wisdom, with understanding, with knowledge and with all kinds of skills— [32] to make artistic designs for work in gold, silver and bronze, [33] to cut and set stones, to work in wood and to engage in all kinds of artistic crafts. [34] And he has given both him and Oholiab son of Ahisamak, of the tribe of Dan, the ability to teach others. [35] He has filled them with skill to do all kinds of work as engravers, designers, embroiderers in blue, purple and scarlet yarn and fine linen, and weavers—all

36 of them skilled workers and designers. [1] So Bezalel, Oholiab and every skilled person to whom the LORD has given skill and ability to know how to carry out all the work of constructing the sanctuary are to do the work just as the LORD has commanded."

[2] Then Moses summoned Bezalel and Oholiab and every skilled person to whom the LORD had given ability and who was willing to come and do the work. [3] They received from Moses all the offerings the Israelites had brought to carry out the work of constructing the sanctuary. And the people continued to bring freewill offerings morning after morning. [4] So all the skilled workers who were doing all the work on the sanctuary left what they were doing [5] and said to Moses, "The people are bringing more than enough for doing the work the LORD commanded to be done."

[6] Then Moses gave an order and they sent this word throughout the camp: "No man or woman is to make anything else as an offering for the sanctuary." And so the people were restrained from bringing more, [7] because what they already had was more than enough to do all the work.

THE TABERNACLE

[8] All those who were skilled among the workers made the tabernacle with ten curtains of finely twisted linen and blue, purple and scarlet yarn, with cherubim woven into them by expert hands. [9] All the curtains were the same size—twenty-eight cubits long and four cubits wide.[a] [10] They joined five of the curtains together and did the same with the other five.

Why did the people give so freely to build the tabernacle? (36:4–7)
The people may have been impressed with God's power and afraid of his punishment. They also may have been inspired by the radiance of Moses when he spoke to God. In any case, they gave so much that Moses told the people not to bring more.

---

[a] 9 That is, about 42 feet long and 6 feet wide or about 13 meters long and 1.8 meters wide

[11] Then they made loops of blue material along the edge of the end curtain in one set, and the same was done with the end curtain in the other set. [12] They also made fifty loops on one curtain and fifty loops on the end curtain of the other set, with the loops opposite each other. [13] Then they made fifty gold clasps and used them to fasten the two sets of curtains together so that the tabernacle was a unit.

[14] They made curtains of goat hair for the tent over the tabernacle—eleven altogether. [15] All eleven curtains were the same size—thirty cubits long and four cubits wide.[a] [16] They joined five of the curtains into one set and the other six into another set. [17] Then they made fifty loops along the edge of the end curtain in one set and also along the edge of the end curtain in the other set. [18] They made fifty bronze clasps to fasten the tent together as a unit. [19] Then they made for the tent a covering of ram skins dyed red, and over that a covering of the other durable leather.[b]

[20] They made upright frames of acacia wood for the tabernacle. [21] Each frame was ten cubits long and a cubit and a half wide,[c] [22] with two projections set parallel to each other. They made all the frames of the tabernacle in this way. [23] They made twenty frames for the south side of the tabernacle [24] and made forty silver bases to go under them—two bases for each frame, one under each projection. [25] For the other side, the north side of the tabernacle, they made twenty frames [26] and forty silver bases—two under each frame. [27] They made six frames for the far end, that is, the west end of the tabernacle, [28] and two frames were made for the corners of the tabernacle at the far end. [29] At these two corners the frames were double from the bottom all the way to the top and fitted into a single ring; both were made alike. [30] So there were eight frames and sixteen silver bases—two under each frame.

[31] They also made crossbars of acacia wood: five for the frames on one side of the tabernacle, [32] five for those on the other side, and five for the frames on the west, at the far end of the tabernacle. [33] They made the center crossbar so that it extended from end to end at the middle of the frames. [34] They overlaid the frames with gold and made gold rings to hold the crossbars. They also overlaid the crossbars with gold.

[35] They made the curtain of blue, purple and scarlet yarn and finely twisted linen, with cherubim woven into it by a skilled worker. [36] They made four posts of acacia wood for it and overlaid them with gold. They made gold hooks for them and cast their four silver bases. [37] For the entrance to the tent they made a curtain of blue, purple and scarlet yarn and finely twisted linen—the work of an embroiderer; [38] and they made five posts with hooks for them. They overlaid the tops of the posts and their bands with gold and made their five bases of bronze.

---

[a] 15 That is, about 45 feet long and 6 feet wide or about 14 meters long and 1.8 meters wide   [b] 19 Possibly the hides of large aquatic mammals (see 35:7)   [c] 21 That is, about 15 feet long and 2 1/4 feet wide or about 4.5 meters long and 68 centimeters wide

THE ARK

37 Bezalel made the ark of acacia wood—two and a half cubits long, a cubit and a half wide, and a cubit and a half high.[a] [2]He overlaid it with pure gold, both inside and out, and made a gold molding around it. [3]He cast four gold rings for it and fastened them to its four feet, with two rings on one side and two rings on the other. [4]Then he made poles of acacia wood and overlaid them with gold. [5]And he inserted the poles into the rings on the sides of the ark to carry it.

[6]He made the atonement cover of pure gold—two and a half cubits long and a cubit and a half wide. [7]Then he made two cherubim out of hammered gold at the ends of the cover. [8]He made one cherub on one end and the second cherub on the other; at the two ends he made them of one piece with the cover. [9]The cherubim had their wings spread upward, overshadowing the cover with them. The cherubim faced each other, looking toward the cover.

The Ark of the Covenant
(37:1–9)

THE TABLE

[10]They[b] made the table of acacia wood—two cubits long, a cubit wide and a cubit and a half high.[c] [11]Then they overlaid it with pure gold and made a gold molding around it. [12]They also made around it a rim a handbreadth[d] wide and put a gold molding on the rim. [13]They cast four gold rings for the table and fastened them to the four corners, where the four legs were. [14]The rings were put close to the rim to hold the poles used in carrying the table. [15]The poles for carrying the table were made of acacia wood and were overlaid with gold. [16]And they made from pure gold the articles for the table—its plates and dishes and bowls and its pitchers for the pouring out of drink offerings.

---

[a] 1 That is, about 3 3/4 feet long and 2 1/4 feet wide and high or about 1.1 meters long and 68 centimeters wide and high; similarly in verse 6   [b] 10 Or *He*; also in verses 11–29   [c] 10 That is, about 3 feet long, 1 1/2 feet wide and 2 1/4 feet high or about 90 centimeters long, 45 centimeters wide and 68 centimeters high   [d] 12 That is, about 3 inches or about 7.5 centimeters

What was the ark of the covenant and what happened to it?
EXODUS 37

The ark was a chest-like box made of acacia wood and was covered with gold inside and out. There were two rings on each side of the ark, so that the priests could slip poles through them in order to carry the ark. On the top were golden sculptures of two cherubim facing each other. Inside the ark were the stone tablets with the law that God had given to Moses, a jar of manna, and Aaron's rod that had budded. The ark was a symbol of God's glory and his presence with his people.

The ark was carried by the priests as they led the people into the promised land. When they had conquered the land, the ark was placed in the tabernacle. The Philistines captured the ark and took it from Shiloh, the ark's first home in Canaan. Then it was briefly taken to Beth Shemesh. From there it was transferred to Abinidab in Kiriath Jearim, where it stayed for 20 years. After it was moved briefly to the house of Obed-Edom, David took it to the tabernacle in Jerusalem where it stayed until the temple was built. When Solomon built the temple in Jerusalem, the ark was placed in the Most Holy Place, which only the high priest was permitted to enter. There is no record of what happened to the ark after Nebuchadnezzar destroyed Jerusalem and the temple in 586 B.C.

THE LAMPSTAND

[17] They made the lampstand of pure gold. They hammered out its base and shaft, and made its flowerlike cups, buds and blossoms of one piece with them. [18] Six branches extended from the sides of the lampstand — three on one side and three on the other. [19] Three cups shaped like almond flowers with buds and blossoms were on one branch, three on the next branch and the same for all six branches extending from the lampstand. [20] And on the lampstand were four cups shaped like almond flowers with buds and blossoms. [21] One bud was under the first pair of branches extending from the lampstand, a second bud under the second pair, and a third bud under the third pair — six branches in all. [22] The buds and the branches were all of one piece with the lampstand, hammered out of pure gold.

[23] They made its seven lamps, as well as its wick trimmers and trays, of pure gold. [24] They made the lampstand and all its accessories from one talent[a] of pure gold.

THE ALTAR OF INCENSE

[25] They made the altar of incense out of acacia wood. It was square, a cubit long and a cubit wide and two cubits high[b] — its horns of one piece with it. [26] They overlaid the top and all the sides and the horns with pure gold, and made a gold molding around it. [27] They made two gold rings below the molding — two on each of the opposite sides — to hold the poles used to carry it. [28] They made the poles of acacia wood and overlaid them with gold.

[29] They also made the sacred anointing oil and the pure, fragrant incense — the work of a perfumer.

THE ALTAR OF BURNT OFFERING

38 They[c] built the altar of burnt offering of acacia wood, three cubits[d] high; it was square, five cubits long and five cubits wide.[e] [2] They made a horn at each of the four corners, so that the horns and the altar were of one piece, and they overlaid the altar with bronze. [3] They made all its utensils of bronze — its pots, shovels, sprinkling bowls, meat forks and firepans. [4] They made a grating for the altar, a bronze network, to be under its ledge, halfway up the altar. [5] They cast bronze rings to hold the poles for the four corners of the bronze grating. [6] They made the poles of acacia wood and overlaid them with bronze. [7] They inserted the poles into the rings so they would be on the sides of the altar for carrying it. They made it hollow, out of boards.

THE BASIN FOR WASHING

[8] They made the bronze basin and its bronze stand from the mirrors of the women who served at the entrance to the tent of meeting.

What were the mirrors of the women? (38:8)
These were pieces of bronze polished so that they provided a reflection, like a glass mirror today. The women donated the generous gifts to help make the basin of bronze.

Who were the women who served at the entrance of the tent of meeting? (38:8)
Unlike pagan temples where prostitutes could be found, these women were there to serve God. They may have been musicians and provided music. Or they may have had some responsibilities for caring for or cleaning the tent of meeting.

---

[a] 24 That is, about 75 pounds or about 34 kilograms   [b] 25 That is, about 1 1/2 feet long and wide and 3 feet high or about 45 centimeters long and wide and 90 centimeters high   [c] 1 Or He; also in verses 2-9   [d] 1 That is, about 4 1/2 feet or about 1.4 meters   [e] 1 That is, about 7 1/2 feet or about 2.3 meters long and wide

THE COURTYARD

⁹Next they made the courtyard. The south side was a hundred cubits* long and had curtains of finely twisted linen, ¹⁰with twenty posts and twenty bronze bases, and with silver hooks and bands on the posts. ¹¹The north side was also a hundred cubits long and had twenty posts and twenty bronze bases, with silver hooks and bands on the posts.

¹²The west end was fifty cubits* wide and had curtains, with ten posts and ten bases, with silver hooks and bands on the posts. ¹³The east end, toward the sunrise, was also fifty cubits wide. ¹⁴Curtains fifteen cubits* long were on one side of the entrance, with three posts and three bases, ¹⁵and curtains fifteen cubits long were on the other side of the entrance to the courtyard, with three posts and three bases. ¹⁶All the curtains around the courtyard were of finely twisted linen. ¹⁷The bases for the posts were bronze. The hooks and bands on the posts were silver, and their tops were overlaid with silver; so all the posts of the courtyard had silver bands.

¹⁸The curtain for the entrance to the courtyard was made of blue, purple and scarlet yarn and finely twisted linen—the work of an embroiderer. It was twenty cubits* long and, like the curtains of the courtyard, five cubits* high, ¹⁹with four posts and four bronze bases. Their hooks and bands were silver, and their tops were overlaid with silver. ²⁰All the tent pegs of the tabernacle and of the surrounding courtyard were bronze.

THE MATERIALS USED

²¹These are the amounts of the materials used for the tabernacle, the tabernacle of the covenant law, which were recorded at Moses' command by the Levites under the direction of Ithamar son of Aaron, the priest. ²²(Bezalel son of Uri, the son of Hur, of the tribe of Judah, made everything the LORD commanded Moses; ²³with him was Oholiab son of Ahisamak, of the tribe of Dan—an engraver and designer, and an embroiderer in blue, purple and scarlet yarn and fine linen.) ²⁴The total amount of the gold from the wave offering used for all the work on the sanctuary was 29 talents and 730 shekels,ᶠ according to the sanctuary shekel.

²⁵The silver obtained from those of the community who were counted in the census was 100 talentsᵍ and 1,775 shekels,ʰ according to the sanctuary shekel— ²⁶one beka per person, that is, half a shekel,ⁱ according to the sanctuary shekel, from everyone who had crossed over to those counted, twenty years old or more, a total of 603,550 men. ²⁷The 100 talents of silver were used to cast the bases for the sanctuary and for the curtain—100 bases from the 100 talents, one talent for each base. ²⁸They used the 1,775 shekels to make the hooks

---

ᵃ 9 That is, about 150 feet or about 45 meters   *ᵇ 12* That is, about 75 feet or about 23 meters   *ᶜ 14* That is, about 22 meters or about 6.8 meters
ᵈ 18 That is, about 30 feet or about 9 meters   *ᵉ 18* That is, about 7 1/2 feet or about 2.3 meters   *ᶠ 24* The weight of the gold was a little over a ton or about 1 metric ton.   *ᵍ 25* That is, about 3 3/4 tons or about 3.4 metric tons; also in verse 27   *ʰ 25* That is, about 44 pounds or about 20 kilograms; also in verse 28   *ⁱ 26* That is, about 1/5 ounce or about 5.7 grams

---

How were the Levites able to carry so much weight? (38:24–29)
The weight of the gold, silver, and bronze was over 7.25 tons, but there were thousands of Levites to share the load. We learn in Numbers 3:39 that there were 22,000 Levites, including children, at the time God talked to Moses on Mount Sinai. There are 2000 pounds in a ton, and with 7.25 tons, the weight equaled 14,500 pounds. That's less than a pound to carry per person.

What was the value of all this gold, silver, and bronze? (38:24–29)
Ancient Israel did not have a money-based economy, so it is difficult to estimate a value. But the weight of the gold alone would be worth millions of dollars today.

Did the priests wear fruit on their garments? (39:24–26)
These pomegranates attached to the hems were not actually fruit but were made of yarn twisted or knotted as trim to look like pomegranates.

for the posts, to overlay the tops of the posts, and to make their bands. [29] The bronze from the wave offering was 70 talents and 2,400 shekels.[a] [30] They used it to make the bases for the entrance to the tent of meeting, the bronze altar with its bronze grating and all its utensils, [31] the bases for the surrounding courtyard and those for its entrance and all the tent pegs for the tabernacle and those for the surrounding courtyard.

THE PRIESTLY GARMENTS

39 From the blue, purple and scarlet yarn they made woven garments for ministering in the sanctuary. They also made sacred garments for Aaron, as the LORD commanded Moses.

THE EPHOD

[2] They[b] made the ephod of gold, and of blue, purple and scarlet yarn, and of finely twisted linen. [3] They hammered out thin sheets of gold and cut strands to be worked into the blue, purple and scarlet yarn and fine linen—the work of skilled hands. [4] They made shoulder pieces for the ephod, which were attached to two of its corners, so it could be fastened. [5] Its skillfully woven waistband was like it—of one piece with the ephod and made with gold, and with blue, purple and scarlet yarn, and with finely twisted linen, as the LORD commanded Moses.

[6] They mounted the onyx stones in gold filigree settings and engraved them like a seal with the names of the sons of Israel. [7] Then they fastened them on the shoulder pieces of the ephod as memorial stones for the sons of Israel, as the LORD commanded Moses.

THE BREASTPIECE

[8] They fashioned the breastpiece—the work of a skilled craftsman. They made it like the ephod: of gold, and of blue, purple and scarlet yarn, and of finely twisted linen. [9] It was square—a span[c] long and a span wide—and folded double. [10] Then they mounted four rows of precious stones on it. The first row was carnelian, chrysolite and beryl; [11] the second row was turquoise, lapis lazuli and emerald; [12] the third row was jacinth, agate and amethyst; [13] the fourth row was topaz, onyx and jasper.[d] They were mounted in gold filigree settings. [14] There were twelve stones, one for each of the names of the sons of Israel, each engraved like a seal with the name of one of the twelve tribes.

[15] For the breastpiece they made braided chains of pure gold, like a rope. [16] They made two gold filigree settings and two gold rings, and fastened the rings to two of the corners of the breastpiece. [17] They fastened the two gold chains to the rings at the corners of the breastpiece, [18] and the other ends of the chains to the two settings, attaching them to the shoulder pieces of the ephod at the front. [19] They made two

---

[a] *29* The weight of the bronze was about 2 1/2 tons or about 2.4 metric tons.
[b] *2* Or *He*; also in verses 7, 8 and 22　　[c] *9* That is, about 9 inches or about 23 centimeters　　[d] *13* The precise identification of some of these precious stones is uncertain.

gold rings and attached them to the other two corners of the breastpiece on the inside edge, next to the ephod. [20]Then they made two more gold rings and attached them to the bottom of the shoulder pieces on the front of the ephod, close to the seam just above the waistband of the ephod. [21]They tied the rings of the breastpiece to the rings of the ephod with blue cord, connecting it to the waistband so that the breastpiece would not swing out from the ephod—as the LORD commanded Moses.

OTHER PRIESTLY GARMENTS

[22]They made the robe of the ephod entirely of blue cloth—the work of a weaver— [23]with an opening in the center of the robe like the opening of a collar,[a] and a band around this opening, so that it would not tear. [24]They made pomegranates of blue, purple and scarlet yarn and finely twisted linen around the hem of the robe. [25]And they made bells of pure gold and attached them around the hem between the pomegranates. [26]The bells and pomegranates alternated around the hem of the robe to be worn for ministering, as the LORD commanded Moses.

[27]For Aaron and his sons, they made tunics of fine linen—the work of a weaver— [28]and the turban of fine linen, the linen caps and the undergarments of finely twisted linen. [29]The sash was made of finely twisted linen and blue, purple and scarlet yarn—the work of an embroiderer—as the LORD commanded Moses.

[30]They made the plate, the sacred emblem, out of pure gold and engraved on it, like an inscription on a seal: HOLY TO THE LORD. [31]Then they fastened a blue cord to it to attach it to the turban, as the LORD commanded Moses.

MOSES INSPECTS THE TABERNACLE

[32]So all the work on the tabernacle, the tent of meeting, was completed. The Israelites did everything just as the LORD commanded Moses. [33]Then they brought the tabernacle to Moses: the tent and all its furnishings, its clasps, frames, crossbars, posts and bases; [34]the covering of ram skins dyed red and the covering of another durable leather[b] and the shielding curtain; [35]the ark of the covenant law with its poles and the atonement cover; [36]the table with all its articles and the bread of the Presence; [37]the pure gold lampstand with its row of lamps and all its accessories, and the olive oil for the light; [38]the gold altar, the anointing oil, the fragrant incense, and the curtain for the entrance to the tent; [39]the bronze altar with its bronze grating, its poles and all its utensils; the basin with its stand; [40]the curtains of the courtyard with its posts and bases, and the curtain for the entrance to the courtyard; the ropes and tent pegs for the courtyard; all the furnishings for the tabernacle, the tent of meeting; [41]and the woven garments worn for ministering in the sanctuary, both the sacred garments for Aaron the priest and the garments for his sons when serving as priests.

---

[a] 23 The meaning of the Hebrew for this word is uncertain.   [b] 34 Possibly the hides of large aquatic mammals

What was the "sacred emblem"? (39:30)
This was a decorative crown or headband that was a sign of royalty. They affixed it to a turban to show that the priest was set apart as holy to the LORD.

What was this "other durable leather"? (39:34)
This was possibly leather from sea cows—mammals related to manatees. They lived in the Red Sea and grew to a length of 8 to 15 feet (2.5 – 4.5 meters) and weighed up to 1,500 pounds (680 kilograms).

[42]The Israelites had done all the work just as the LORD had commanded Moses. [43]Moses inspected the work and saw that they had done it just as the LORD had commanded. So Moses blessed them.

SETTING UP THE TABERNACLE

40 Then the LORD said to Moses: [2]"Set up the tabernacle, the tent of meeting, on the first day of the first month. [3]Place the ark of the covenant law in it and shield the ark with the curtain. [4]Bring in the table and set out what belongs on it. Then bring in the lampstand and set up its lamps. [5]Place the gold altar of incense in front of the ark of the covenant law and put the curtain at the entrance to the tabernacle.

[6]"Place the altar of burnt offering in front of the entrance to the tabernacle, the tent of meeting; [7]place the basin between the tent of meeting and the altar and put water in it. [8]Set up the courtyard around it and put the curtain at the entrance to the courtyard.

[9]"Take the anointing oil and anoint the tabernacle and everything in it; consecrate it and all its furnishings, and it will be holy. [10]Then anoint the altar of burnt offering and all its utensils; consecrate the altar, and it will be most holy. [11]Anoint the basin and its stand and consecrate them.

[12]"Bring Aaron and his sons to the entrance to the tent of meeting and wash them with water. [13]Then dress Aaron in the sacred garments, anoint him and consecrate him so he may serve me as priest. [14]Bring his sons and dress them in tunics. [15]Anoint them just as you anointed their father, so they may serve me as priests. Their anointing will be to a priesthood that will continue throughout their generations." [16]Moses did everything just as the LORD commanded him.

[17]So the tabernacle was set up on the first day of the first month in the second year. [18]When Moses set up the tabernacle, he put the bases in place, erected the frames, inserted the crossbars and set up the posts. [19]Then he spread the tent over the tabernacle and put the covering over the tent, as the LORD commanded him.

[20]He took the tablets of the covenant law and placed them in the ark, attached the poles to the ark and put the atonement cover over it. [21]Then he brought the ark into the tabernacle and hung the shielding curtain and shielded the ark of the covenant law, as the LORD commanded him.

[22]Moses placed the table in the tent of meeting on the north side of the tabernacle outside the curtain [23]and set out the bread on it before the LORD, as the LORD commanded him.

[24]He placed the lampstand in the tent of meeting opposite the table on the south side of the tabernacle [25]and set up the lamps before the LORD, as the LORD commanded him.

[26]Moses placed the gold altar in the tent of meeting in front of the curtain [27]and burned fragrant incense on it, as the LORD commanded him.

[28]Then he put up the curtain at the entrance to the tabernacle. [29]He set the altar of burnt offering near the entrance

How long did it take to build the tabernacle? (40:17) It probably took about six months to build the tabernacle.

to the tabernacle, the tent of meeting, and offered on it burnt offerings and grain offerings, as the LORD commanded him.

30 He placed the basin between the tent of meeting and the altar and put water in it for washing, 31 and Moses and Aaron and his sons used it to wash their hands and feet. 32 They washed whenever they entered the tent of meeting or approached the altar, as the LORD commanded Moses.

33 Then Moses set up the courtyard around the tabernacle and altar and put up the curtain at the entrance to the courtyard. And so Moses finished the work.

THE GLORY OF THE LORD

34 Then the cloud covered the tent of meeting, and the glory of the LORD filled the tabernacle. 35 Moses could not enter the tent of meeting because the cloud had settled on it, and the glory of the LORD filled the tabernacle.

36 In all the travels of the Israelites, whenever the cloud lifted from above the tabernacle, they would set out; 37 but if the cloud did not lift, they did not set out—until the day it lifted. 38 So the cloud of the LORD was over the tabernacle by day, and fire was in the cloud by night, in the sight of all the Israelites during all their travels.

Who was allowed to enter the tent of meeting? (40:35) The priests were the only ones who could enter the tabernacle. Even Moses could not enter because he wasn't a priest.

Leviticus

INTRODUCTION

Who wrote this book?	Moses.
Why was this book written?	Leviticus shows the Israelites how to worship God and live a holy life.
What happens in this book?	Moses gives the people and the priests of Israel God's instructions.
What do we learn about God in this book?	God is holy and expects his people to be holy. God accepts sacrifices and forgives people who sin.
Who are the key people in this book?	The most important people in this book are Moses and Aaron.
Where did this happen?	The Israelites were camped at Mount Sinai when these instructions were given. (See the map index at the back of this Bible to see where Mount Sinai is.)

What are some of the stories in this book?		
	Aaron is ordained high priest	Leviticus 8
	Aaron's sons disobey God	Leviticus 10
	God sets special holidays	Leviticus 23

When did these things happen?

2200 BC 2100 2000 1900 1800 1700 1600 1500 1400

MOSES' BIRTH (C. 1526 BC)

THE PLAGUES; THE PASSOVER (C. 1446 BC)

THE EXODUS (C. 1446 BC)

DESERT WANDERINGS (C. 1446 – 1406 BC)

THE TEN COMMANDMENTS (C. 1445 BC)

BOOK OF LEVITICUS WRITTEN (C. 1440 BC)

MOSES DIES; JOSHUA BECOMES LEADER (C. 1406 BC)

ISRAELITES ENTER CANAAN (C. 1406 BC)

THE BURNT OFFERING

1 The Lord called to Moses and spoke to him from the tent of meeting. He said, ²"Speak to the Israelites and say to them: 'When anyone among you brings an offering to the Lord, bring as your offering an animal from either the herd or the flock.

³"'If the offering is a burnt offering from the herd, you are to offer a male without defect. You must present it at the entrance to the tent of meeting so that it will be acceptable to the Lord. ⁴You are to lay your hand on the head of the burnt offering, and it will be accepted on your behalf to make atonement for you. ⁵You are to slaughter the young bull before the Lord, and then Aaron's sons the priests shall bring the blood and splash it against the sides of the altar at the entrance to the tent of meeting. ⁶You are to skin the burnt offering and cut it into pieces. ⁷The sons of Aaron the priest are to put fire on the altar and arrange wood on the fire. ⁸Then Aaron's sons the priests shall arrange the pieces, including the head and the fat, on the wood that is burning on the altar. ⁹You are to wash the internal organs and the legs with water, and the priest is to burn all of it on the altar. It is a burnt offering, a food offering, an aroma pleasing to the Lord.

¹⁰"'If the offering is a burnt offering from the flock, from either the sheep or the goats, you are to offer a male without defect. ¹¹You are to slaughter it at the north side of the altar before the Lord, and Aaron's sons the priests shall splash its blood against the sides of the altar. ¹²You are to cut it into pieces, and the priest shall arrange them, including the head and the fat, on the wood that is burning on the altar. ¹³You are to wash the internal organs and the legs with water, and the priest is to bring all of them and burn them on the altar. It is a burnt offering, a food offering, an aroma pleasing to the Lord.

¹⁴"'If the offering to the Lord is a burnt offering of birds, you are to offer a dove or a young pigeon. ¹⁵The priest shall bring it to the altar, wring off the head and burn it on the altar; its blood shall be drained out on the side of the altar. ¹⁶He is to remove the crop and the feathers*a* and throw them down east of the altar where the ashes are. ¹⁷He shall tear it open by the wings, not dividing it completely, and then the priest shall burn it on the wood that is burning on the altar. It is a burnt offering, a food offering, an aroma pleasing to the Lord.

THE GRAIN OFFERING

2 "'When anyone brings a grain offering to the Lord, their offering is to be of the finest flour. They are to pour olive oil on it, put incense on it ²and take it to Aaron's sons the priests. The priest shall take a handful of the flour and oil, together with all the incense, and burn this as a memorial*b* portion on the altar, a food offering, an aroma pleasing to the Lord. ³The rest of the grain offering belongs to Aaron and his sons; it is a most holy part of the food offerings presented to the Lord.

---

a 16 Or *crop with its contents*; the meaning of the Hebrew for this word is uncertain.   *b 2* Or *representative*; also in verses 9 and 16

How many types of offerings were there? (1:2)
There were five different types of offerings: burnt, grain, fellowship, sin, and guilt. Each offering had a different purpose.

What was the purpose of burnt offerings? (1:3–17)
The purpose of the burnt offering was atonement — paying the price for sin in order to make a person right with God. Burning the entire animal symbolized the complete devotion of the worshiper to the Lord.

Why did they have to wash the animal parts before they burned them? (1:9)
This removed any dirt or excrement from the animal's inner parts and legs in order to make it perfect for God. The clean animal symbolized the purity of heart required by God.

Was God as pleased with a bird as with a flock animal? (1:14)
God was pleased with the offering if the intent was sincere. Israelites who couldn't afford a sheep or goat could substitute a bird.

What was the purpose of a grain offering? (2:1–16)
Unlike animal offerings that were given to ask God for forgiveness, grain offerings showed God how devoted the people were to him.

OLD TESTAMENT SACRIFICES

SACRIFICE	OLD TESTAMENT REFERENCES	ELEMENTS	PURPOSE
Burnt Offering	Lev 1; 6:8–13; 8:18–21; 16:24	Bull, ram or male bird (dove or young pigeon for the poor); wholly consumed; no defect	Voluntary act of worship; atonement for unintentional sin in general; expression of devotion, commitment and complete surrender to God
Grain Offering	Lev 2; 6:14–23	Grain, fine flour, olive oil, incense, baked bread (cakes or wafers), salt; no yeast or honey; accompanied burnt offering and fellowship offering (along with drink offering)	Voluntary act of worship; recognition of God's goodness and provisions; devotion to God
Fellowship Offering	Lev 3; 7:11–34	Any animal without defect from herd or flock; variety of breads	Voluntary act of worship; thanksgiving and fellowship (it included a communal meal)
Sin Offering	Lev 4:1—5:13; 6:24–30; 8:14–17; 16:3–22	1. Young bull: for high priest and congregation 2. Male goat: for leader 3. Female goat or lamb: for common person 4. Dove or pigeon: for the poor 5. Tenth of an ephah of fine flour: for the very poor	Mandatory atonement for specific unintentional sin; confession of sin; forgiveness of sin; cleansing from defilement
Guilt Offering	Lev 5:14—6:7; 7:1–6	Ram	Mandatory atonement for unintentional sin requiring restitution; cleansing from defilement; make restitution; pay 20% fine

When more than one kind of offering was presented (as in Nu 7:16,17), the procedure was usually as follows: (1) sin offering or guilt offering, (2) burnt offering, (3) fellowship offering and grain offering (along with a drink offering). This sequence furnishes part of the spiritual significance of the sacrificial system. First, sin had to be dealt with (sin offering or guilt offering). Second, the worshipers committed themselves completely to God (burnt offering and grain offering). Third, fellowship or communion between the Lord, the priest and the worshiper was established (fellowship offering). To state it another way, there were sacrifices of expiation (sin offerings and guilt offerings), consecration (burnt offerings and grain offerings) and communion (fellowship offerings—these included vow offerings, thank offerings and freewill offerings).

⁴"'If you bring a grain offering baked in an oven, it is to consist of the finest flour: either thick loaves made without yeast and with olive oil mixed in or thin loaves made without yeast and brushed with olive oil. ⁵If your grain offering is prepared on a griddle, it is to be made of the finest flour mixed with oil, and without yeast. ⁶Crumble it and pour oil on it; it is a grain offering. ⁷If your grain offering is cooked in a pan, it is to be made of the finest flour and some olive oil. ⁸Bring the grain offering made of these things to the LORD; present it to the priest, who shall take it to the altar. ⁹He shall take out the memorial portion from the grain offering and burn it on the altar as a food offering, an aroma pleasing to the LORD. ¹⁰The rest of the grain offering belongs to Aaron and his sons; it is a most holy part of the food offerings presented to the LORD.

¹¹"'Every grain offering you bring to the LORD must be made without yeast, for you are not to burn any yeast or honey in a food offering presented to the LORD. ¹²You may bring them to the LORD as an offering of the firstfruits, but they are not to be offered on the altar as a pleasing aroma. ¹³Season all your grain offerings with salt. Do not leave the salt of the covenant of your God out of your grain offerings; add salt to all your offerings.

¹⁴"'If you bring a grain offering of firstfruits to the LORD, offer crushed heads of new grain roasted in the fire. ¹⁵Put oil and incense on it; it is a grain offering. ¹⁶The priest shall burn the memorial portion of the crushed grain and the oil, together with all the incense, as a food offering presented to the LORD.

THE FELLOWSHIP OFFERING

3 "'If your offering is a fellowship offering, and you offer an animal from the herd, whether male or female, you are to present before the LORD an animal without defect. ²You are to lay your hand on the head of your offering and slaughter it at the entrance to the tent of meeting. Then Aaron's sons the priests shall splash the blood against the sides of the altar. ³From the fellowship offering you are to bring a food offering to the LORD: the internal organs and all the fat that is connected to them, ⁴both kidneys with the fat on them near the loins, and the long lobe of the liver, which you will remove with the kidneys. ⁵Then Aaron's sons are to burn it on the altar on top of the burnt offering that is lying on the burning wood; it is a food offering, an aroma pleasing to the LORD.

⁶"'If you offer an animal from the flock as a fellowship offering to the LORD, you are to offer a male or female without defect. ⁷If you offer a lamb, you are to present it before the LORD, ⁸lay your hand on its head and slaughter it in front of the tent of meeting. Then Aaron's sons shall splash its blood against the sides of the altar. ⁹From the fellowship offering you are to bring a food offering to the LORD: its fat, the entire fat tail cut off close to the backbone, the internal organs and all the fat that is connected to them, ¹⁰both kidneys with the fat on them near the loins, and the long lobe of the liver, which you will remove with the kidneys. ¹¹The priest shall burn them on the altar as a food offering presented to the LORD.

What was a memorial portion? (2:9)
A memorial portion was used to ask the Lord to bless the people making the offering.

Did it matter how the grain was cooked? (2:4–7, 11–12)
Any method was acceptable as long as the grain was mixed with oil and had no yeast or honey. The process of cooking showed that the worshiper took special care. The oil represented joy and thankfulness. Yeast and honey were not to be used because they were associated with making an alcoholic drink.

Why was salt so important? (2:13)
In ancient times salt was very costly, but it was an important part of the diet. Salt served as a preservative in food, so it probably symbolized God's everlasting love.

What was a fellowship offering? (3:1–17)
This was the only offering of which the worshiper was allowed to eat some. Because it symbolized eating a meal of gratitude and fellowship with God, this was originally known as a peace offering. Worshipers often shared the meat with neighbors in need. In this way it provided fellowship among neighbors.

Why would food be burned as sacrifices? (3:11, 16)
The Israelites knew God wasn't actually going to eat their offerings. They were offered up to ask God for forgiveness, express thanks, and show gratitude. God appreciated all of these offerings.

¹²"'If your offering is a goat, you are to present it before the Lord, ¹³lay your hand on its head and slaughter it in front of the tent of meeting. Then Aaron's sons shall splash its blood against the sides of the altar. ¹⁴From what you offer you are to present this food offering to the Lord: the internal organs and all the fat that is connected to them, ¹⁵both kidneys with the fat on them near the loins, and the long lobe of the liver, which you will remove with the kidneys. ¹⁶The priest shall burn them on the altar as a food offering, a pleasing aroma. All the fat is the Lord's.

¹⁷"'This is a lasting ordinance for the generations to come, wherever you live: You must not eat any fat or any blood.'"

THE SIN OFFERING

4 The Lord said to Moses, ²"Say to the Israelites: 'When anyone sins unintentionally and does what is forbidden in any of the Lord's commands—

³"'If the anointed priest sins, bringing guilt on the people, he must bring to the Lord a young bull without defect as a sin offering[a] for the sin he has committed. ⁴He is to present the bull at the entrance to the tent of meeting before the Lord. He is to lay his hand on its head and slaughter it there before the Lord. ⁵Then the anointed priest shall take some of the bull's blood and carry it into the tent of meeting. ⁶He is to dip his finger into the blood and sprinkle some of it seven times before the Lord, in front of the curtain of the sanctuary. ⁷The priest shall then put some of the blood on the horns of the altar of fragrant incense that is before the Lord in the tent of meeting. The rest of the bull's blood he shall pour out at the base of the altar of burnt offering at the entrance to the tent of meeting. ⁸He shall remove all the fat from the bull of the sin offering—all the fat that is connected to the internal organs, ⁹both kidneys with the fat on them near the loins, and the long lobe of the liver, which he will remove with the kidneys— ¹⁰just as the fat is removed from the ox[b] sacrificed as a fellowship offering. Then the priest shall burn them on the altar of burnt offering. ¹¹But the hide of the bull and all its flesh, as well as the head and

---

[a] 3 Or purification offering; here and throughout this chapter
[b] 10 The Hebrew word can refer to either male or female.

What was a lasting ordinance? (3:17)
An ordinance is a rule, and the lasting ordinance indicates that the rules about sacrifices were important and must be followed as long as God's covenant lasted. Today, most Christians believe that the laws about sacrifices no longer apply because of Christ's sacrifice for sin.

Why did sacrifices have to be made for unintentional sins? (4:2)
In this context *unintentional* means "wandering away." This type of sin was made out of weakness of character rather than active rebellion.

Why were the people guilty for a priest's sin? (4:3)
In the Old Testament, the priest represented the people to God. If he was not pure, he became a flawed representative, and God viewed the people through the priest's sins as being guilty and unclean.

Why was the blood sprinkled seven times? (4:5–7)
Seven is a number with significant symbolism. It's the number of days God took to create the world. Seven represents God's perfection and purity.

Why did God require so many sacrifices from his people?
LEVITICUS 1—7

God required animal sacrifices in order to satisfy the requirements of the covenant and to provide a way for his people to offer thanks and seek forgiveness. There were several types of sacrifices for different purposes, for different occasions, and with different requirements.

The sacrifices reminded God's people of their relationship to him. Some sacrifices were specifically offered for the forgiveness of sins. The animal that was sacrificed symbolically took on the guilt of the sin. Other sacrifices were made as an offering or a voluntary act of worship. People would bring perfect animals or crops and offer them to God as a form of thanksgiving. Still other sacrifices were a form of fellowship or communion among the Lord, the priest, and the worshiper.

We no longer offer sacrifices because Jesus came to earth and became the perfect sacrifice by taking all the sins of the world on himself and dying in order to redeem the world.

legs, the internal organs and the intestines— ¹²that is, all the rest of the bull—he must take outside the camp to a place ceremonially clean, where the ashes are thrown, and burn it there in a wood fire on the ash heap.

¹³"If the whole Israelite community sins unintentionally and does what is forbidden in any of the Lord's commands, even though the community is unaware of the matter, when they realize their guilt ¹⁴and the sin they committed becomes known, the assembly must bring a young bull as a sin offering and present it before the tent of meeting. ¹⁵The elders of the community are to lay their hands on the bull's head before the Lord, and the bull shall be slaughtered before the Lord. ¹⁶Then the anointed priest is to take some of the bull's blood into the tent of meeting. ¹⁷He shall dip his finger into the blood and sprinkle it before the Lord seven times in front of the curtain. ¹⁸He is to put some of the blood on the horns of the altar that is before the Lord in the tent of meeting. The rest of the blood he shall pour out at the base of the altar of burnt offering at the entrance to the tent of meeting. ¹⁹He shall remove all the fat from it and burn it on the altar, ²⁰and do with this bull just as he did with the bull for the sin offering. In this way the priest will make atonement for the community, and they will be forgiven. ²¹Then he shall take the bull outside the camp and burn it as he burned the first bull. This is the sin offering for the community.

²²"When a leader sins unintentionally and does what is forbidden in any of the commands of the Lord his God, when he realizes his guilt ²³and the sin he has committed becomes known, he must bring as his offering a male goat without defect. ²⁴He is to lay his hand on the goat's head and slaughter it at the place where the burnt offering is slaughtered before the Lord. It is a sin offering. ²⁵Then the priest shall take some of the blood of the sin offering with his finger and put it on the horns of the altar of burnt offering and pour out the rest of the blood at the base of the altar. ²⁶He shall burn all the fat on the altar as he burned the fat of the fellowship offering. In this way the priest will make atonement for the leader's sin, and he will be forgiven.

²⁷"If any member of the community sins unintentionally and does what is forbidden in any of the Lord's commands, when they realize their guilt ²⁸and the sin they have committed becomes known, they must bring as their offering for the sin they committed a female goat without defect. ²⁹They are to lay their hand on the head of the sin offering and slaughter it at the place of the burnt offering. ³⁰Then the priest is to take some of the blood with his finger and put it on the horns of the altar of burnt offering and pour out the rest of the blood at the base of the altar. ³¹They shall remove all the fat, just as the fat is removed from the fellowship offering, and the priest shall burn it on the altar as an aroma pleasing to the Lord. In this way the priest will make atonement for them, and they will be forgiven.

³²"If someone brings a lamb as their sin offering, they are to bring a female without defect. ³³They are to lay their hand

Why was the rest of the bull burned outside the camp? (4:12)
The bull sacrifice represented atonement for sin. After the blood was offered and specific parts were burned on the altar, the rest of the bull was carried outside of the camp. This symbolized cleansing the person of their sin.

What were sin offerings? (4:1–35)
Sin offerings were given to cover various types of sins. Sin offerings were made for the whole congregation on all of the feast days, especially on the Day of Atonement.

on its head and slaughter it for a sin offering at the place where the burnt offering is slaughtered. [34] Then the priest shall take some of the blood of the sin offering with his finger and put it on the horns of the altar of burnt offering and pour out the rest of the blood at the base of the altar. [35] They shall remove all the fat, just as the fat is removed from the lamb of the fellowship offering, and the priest shall burn it on the altar on top of the food offerings presented to the LORD. In this way the priest will make atonement for them for the sin they have committed, and they will be forgiven.

5 "'If anyone sins because they do not speak up when they hear a public charge to testify regarding something they have seen or learned about, they will be held responsible.

[2] "'If anyone becomes aware that they are guilty—if they unwittingly touch anything ceremonially unclean (whether the carcass of an unclean animal, wild or domestic, or of any unclean creature that moves along the ground) and they are unaware that they have become unclean, but then they come to realize their guilt; [3] or if they touch human uncleanness (anything that would make them unclean) even though they are unaware of it, but then they learn of it and realize their guilt; [4] or if anyone thoughtlessly takes an oath to do anything, whether good or evil (in any matter one might carelessly swear about) even though they are unaware of it, but then they learn of it and realize their guilt— [5] when anyone becomes aware that they are guilty in any of these matters, they must confess in what way they have sinned. [6] As a penalty for the sin they have committed, they must bring to the LORD a female lamb or goat from the flock as a sin offering[a]; and the priest shall make atonement for them for their sin.

[7] "'Anyone who cannot afford a lamb is to bring two doves or two young pigeons to the LORD as a penalty for their sin—one for a sin offering and the other for a burnt offering. [8] They are to bring them to the priest, who shall first offer the one for the sin offering. He is to wring its head from its neck, not dividing it completely, [9] and is to splash some of the blood of the sin offering against the side of the altar; the rest of the blood must be drained out at the base of the altar. It is a sin offering. [10] The priest shall then offer the other as a burnt offering in the prescribed way and make atonement for them for the sin they have committed, and they will be forgiven.

[11] "'If, however, they cannot afford two doves or two young pigeons, they are to bring as an offering for their sin a tenth of an ephah[b] of the finest flour for a sin offering. They must not put olive oil or incense on it, because it is a sin offering. [12] They are to bring it to the priest, who shall take a handful of it as a memorial[c] portion and burn it on the altar on top of the food offerings presented to the LORD. It is a sin offering. [13] In this way the priest will make atonement for them for any of these sins they have committed, and they will be forgiven. The rest of the offering will belong to the priest, as in the case of the grain offering.'"

What did it mean to be ceremonially unclean? (5:2)
This meant that something was impure in a religious sense. It didn't mean it was literally dirty. God made the rules about what was clean and unclean.

How could someone take an oath and not know it? (5:4)
Taking an oath without knowing it means taking an oath before thinking about the consequences. Breaking an oath was a crime not to be taken lightly, especially if the oath was made to God, so it was important to think of all the aftereffects before making a promise.

---

[a] 6 Or *purification offering*; here and throughout this chapter   [b] 11 That is, probably about 3 1/2 pounds or about 1.6 kilograms   [c] 12 Or *representative*

THE GUILT OFFERING

¹⁴The Lord said to Moses: ¹⁵"When anyone is unfaithful to the Lord by sinning unintentionally in regard to any of the Lord's holy things, they are to bring to the Lord as a penalty a ram from the flock, one without defect and of the proper value in silver, according to the sanctuary shekel.ᵃ It is a guilt offering. ¹⁶They must make restitution for what they have failed to do in regard to the holy things, pay an additional penalty of a fifth of its value and give it all to the priest. The priest will make atonement for them with the ram as a guilt offering, and they will be forgiven.

¹⁷"If anyone sins and does what is forbidden in any of the Lord's commands, even though they do not know it, they are guilty and will be held responsible. ¹⁸They are to bring to the priest as a guilt offering a ram from the flock, one without defect and of the proper value. In this way the priest will make atonement for them for the wrong they have committed unintentionally, and they will be forgiven. ¹⁹It is a guilt offering; they have been guilty ofᵇ wrongdoing against the Lord."

6ᶜ The Lord said to Moses: ²"If anyone sins and is unfaithful to the Lord by deceiving a neighbor about something entrusted to them or left in their care or about something stolen, or if they cheat their neighbor, ³or if they find lost property and lie about it, or if they swear falsely about any such sin that people may commit— ⁴when they sin in any of these ways and realize their guilt, they must return what they have stolen or taken by extortion, or what was entrusted to them, or the lost property they found, ⁵or whatever it was they swore falsely about. They must make restitution in full, add a fifth of the value to it and give it all to the owner on the day they present their guilt offering. ⁶And as a penalty they must bring to the priest, that is, to the Lord, their guilt offering, a ram from the flock, one without defect and of the proper value. ⁷In this way the priest will make atonement for them before the Lord, and they will be forgiven for any of the things they did that made them guilty."

THE BURNT OFFERING

⁸The Lord said to Moses: ⁹"Give Aaron and his sons this command: 'These are the regulations for the burnt offering: The burnt offering is to remain on the altar hearth throughout the night, till morning, and the fire must be kept burning on the altar. ¹⁰The priest shall then put on his linen clothes, with linen undergarments next to his body, and shall remove the ashes of the burnt offering that the fire has consumed on the altar and place them beside the altar. ¹¹Then he is to take off these clothes and put on others, and carry the ashes outside the camp to a place that is ceremonially clean. ¹²The fire on the altar must be kept burning; it must not go out. Every morning the priest is to add firewood and arrange the burnt offering on the fire and burn the fat of the fellowship offerings on it. ¹³The fire must be kept burning on the altar continuously; it must not go out.

ᵃ *15 That is, about 2/5 ounce or about 12 grams*   ᵇ *19 Or offering; atonement has been made for their*   ᶜ In Hebrew texts 6:1-7 is numbered 5:20-26, and 6:8-30 is numbered 6:1-23.

What were the Lord's holy things? (5:15)
Holy things could refer to anything dedicated to God. One committed a violation of the Lord's holy things by eating food dedicated for the priests or by failing to pay a vow or a tithe.

What was the purpose of the guilt offerings? (5:15, 19)
The guilt offering was a special kind of sin offering that restored the sinner, taking the guilt away. There were only some offenses, such as sins against sacred property, for which the sinner could have his conscience restored.

Why did the priests wear linen underwear while making the burnt offering? (6:10)
Linen underwear was part of the uniform priests wore when working inside the temple. The uniform helped separate daily tasks from those considered sacred.

Why did God want the offering fire to burn continuously? (6:12–13)
God wanted the fire to burn nonstop to show the Israelites how he is always with his people.

THE GRAIN OFFERING

14 "'These are the regulations for the grain offering: Aaron's sons are to bring it before the LORD, in front of the altar. 15 The priest is to take a handful of the finest flour and some olive oil, together with all the incense on the grain offering, and burn the memorial[a] portion on the altar as an aroma pleasing to the LORD. 16 Aaron and his sons shall eat the rest of it, but it is to be eaten without yeast in the sanctuary area; they are to eat it in the courtyard of the tent of meeting. 17 It must not be baked with yeast; I have given it as their share of the food offerings presented to me. Like the sin offering[b] and the guilt offering, it is most holy. 18 Any male descendant of Aaron may eat it. For all generations to come it is his perpetual share of the food offerings presented to the LORD. Whatever touches them will become holy.[c]'"

19 The LORD also said to Moses, 20 "This is the offering Aaron and his sons are to bring to the LORD on the day he[d] is anointed: a tenth of an ephah[e] of the finest flour as a regular grain offering, half of it in the morning and half in the evening. 21 It must be prepared with oil on a griddle; bring it well-mixed and present the grain offering broken[f] in pieces as an aroma pleasing to the LORD. 22 The son who is to succeed him as anointed priest shall prepare it. It is the LORD's perpetual share and is to be burned completely. 23 Every grain offering of a priest shall be burned completely; it must not be eaten."

THE SIN OFFERING

24 The LORD said to Moses, 25 "Say to Aaron and his sons: 'These are the regulations for the sin offering: The sin offering is to be slaughtered before the LORD in the place the burnt offering is slaughtered; it is most holy. 26 The priest who offers it shall eat it; it is to be eaten in the sanctuary area, in the courtyard of the tent of meeting. 27 Whatever touches any of the flesh will become holy, and if any of the blood is spattered on a garment, you must wash it in the sanctuary area. 28 The clay pot the meat is cooked in must be broken; but if it is cooked in a bronze pot, the pot is to be scoured and rinsed with water. 29 Any male in a priest's family may eat it; it is most holy. 30 But any sin offering whose blood is brought into the tent of meeting to make atonement in the Holy Place must not be eaten; it must be burned up.

THE GUILT OFFERING

7 "'These are the regulations for the guilt offering, which is most holy: 2 The guilt offering is to be slaughtered in the place where the burnt offering is slaughtered, and its blood is to be splashed against the sides of the altar. 3 All its fat shall be offered: the fat tail and the fat that covers the internal organs, 4 both kidneys with the fat on them near the loins, and the long lobe of the liver, which is to be removed

Why did they have to break the clay cooking pots? (6:28) Clay pots are hard to clean and leftover fat and juice could easily be left in the pot, or worse, absorbed. Breaking the pots was a way to make sure none of the sacrifice was left behind. New pots would ensure that everything would be clean for the next offering.

---

[a] 15 Or representative   [b] 17 Or purification offering; also in verses 25 and 30
[c] 18 Or Whoever touches them must be holy; similarly in verse 27
[d] 20 Or each   [e] 20 That is, probably about 3 1/2 pounds or about 1.6 kilograms   [f] 21 The meaning of the Hebrew for this word is uncertain.

with the kidneys. ⁵The priest shall burn them on the altar as a food offering presented to the Lord. It is a guilt offering. ⁶Any male in a priest's family may eat it, but it must be eaten in the sanctuary area; it is most holy.

⁷"'The same law applies to both the sin offering*a* and the guilt offering: They belong to the priest who makes atonement with them. ⁸The priest who offers a burnt offering for anyone may keep its hide for himself. ⁹Every grain offering baked in an oven or cooked in a pan or on a griddle belongs to the priest who offers it, ¹⁰and every grain offering, whether mixed with olive oil or dry, belongs equally to all the sons of Aaron.

THE FELLOWSHIP OFFERING

¹¹"'These are the regulations for the fellowship offering anyone may present to the Lord:

¹²"'If they offer it as an expression of thankfulness, then along with this thank offering they are to offer thick loaves made without yeast and with olive oil mixed in, thin loaves made without yeast and brushed with oil, and thick loaves of the finest flour well-kneaded and with oil mixed in. ¹³Along with their fellowship offering of thanksgiving they are to present an offering with thick loaves of bread made with yeast. ¹⁴They are to bring one of each kind as an offering, a contribution to the Lord; it belongs to the priest who splashes the blood of the fellowship offering against the altar. ¹⁵The meat of their fellowship offering of thanksgiving must be eaten on the day it is offered; they must leave none of it till morning.

¹⁶"'If, however, their offering is the result of a vow or is a freewill offering, the sacrifice shall be eaten on the day they offer it, but anything left over may be eaten on the next day. ¹⁷Any meat of the sacrifice left over till the third day must be burned up. ¹⁸If any meat of the fellowship offering is eaten on the third day, the one who offered it will not be accepted. It will not be reckoned to their credit, for it has become impure; the person who eats any of it will be held responsible.

¹⁹"'Meat that touches anything ceremonially unclean must not be eaten; it must be burned up. As for other meat, anyone ceremonially clean may eat it. ²⁰But if anyone who is unclean eats any meat of the fellowship offering belonging to the Lord, they must be cut off from their people. ²¹Anyone who touches something unclean—whether human uncleanness or an unclean animal or any unclean creature that moves along the ground*b*—and then eats any of the meat of the fellowship offering belonging to the Lord must be cut off from their people.'"

EATING FAT AND BLOOD FORBIDDEN

²²The Lord said to Moses, ²³"Say to the Israelites: 'Do not eat any of the fat of cattle, sheep or goats. ²⁴The fat of an animal found dead or torn by wild animals may be used

How could they offer cakes made with yeast if yeast was forbidden? (7:13)
Because these cakes were not burned, offering a cake baked with yeast did not contradict any of the previous guidelines.

Why did the meat have to be eaten the same day? (7:15)
With no refrigerators, there was no way to keep meat cold. It spoiled quickly in Canaan, and spoiled meat was considered ceremonially impure.

What would make a person unclean? (7:20)
Like cleanliness, uncleanliness was also contagious. A person could become unclean simply by touching an unclean object like sick people, the dead, or unclean animals. To become clean again, a person would have to take part in a purification ritual.

What does it mean to "be cut off from their people"? (7:20)
This often means death. It is a judgment from God in which a person was removed physically from the covenant people.

a 7 Or purification offering; also in verse 37   b 21 A few Hebrew manuscripts, Samaritan Pentateuch, Syriac and Targum (see 5:2); most Hebrew manuscripts any unclean, detestable thing

What was wrong with eating blood? (7:26–27)
Blood was used in offerings to ask for forgiveness. It wasn't meant to be food. (See Leviticus 17:11.) The punishment for a person who ate the life of a creature was to be cut off from his people.

for any other purpose, but you must not eat it. ²⁵ Anyone who eats the fat of an animal from which a food offering may be*a* presented to the LORD must be cut off from their people. ²⁶ And wherever you live, you must not eat the blood of any bird or animal. ²⁷ Anyone who eats blood must be cut off from their people.'"

THE PRIESTS' SHARE

²⁸ The LORD said to Moses, ²⁹ "Say to the Israelites: 'Anyone who brings a fellowship offering to the LORD is to bring part of it as their sacrifice to the LORD. ³⁰ With their own hands they are to present the food offering to the LORD; they are to bring the fat, together with the breast, and wave the breast before the LORD as a wave offering. ³¹ The priest shall burn the fat on the altar, but the breast belongs to Aaron and his sons. ³² You are to give the right thigh of your fellowship offerings to the priest as a contribution. ³³ The son of Aaron who offers the blood and the fat of the fellowship offering shall have the right thigh as his share. ³⁴ From the fellowship offerings of the Israelites, I have taken the breast that is waved and the thigh that is presented and have given them to Aaron the priest and his sons as their perpetual share from the Israelites.'"

³⁵ This is the portion of the food offerings presented to the LORD that were allotted to Aaron and his sons on the day they were presented to serve the LORD as priests. ³⁶ On the day they were anointed, the LORD commanded that the Israelites give this to them as their perpetual share for the generations to come.

³⁷ These, then, are the regulations for the burnt offering, the grain offering, the sin offering, the guilt offering, the ordination offering and the fellowship offering, ³⁸ which the LORD gave Moses at Mount Sinai in the Desert of Sinai on the day he commanded the Israelites to bring their offerings to the LORD.

THE ORDINATION OF AARON AND HIS SONS

8 The LORD said to Moses, ² "Bring Aaron and his sons, their garments, the anointing oil, the bull for the sin offering,*b* the two rams and the basket containing bread made without yeast, ³ and gather the entire assembly at the entrance to the tent of meeting." ⁴ Moses did as the LORD commanded him, and the assembly gathered at the entrance to the tent of meeting.

⁵ Moses said to the assembly, "This is what the LORD has commanded to be done." ⁶ Then Moses brought Aaron and his sons forward and washed them with water. ⁷ He put the tunic on Aaron, tied the sash around him, clothed him with the robe and put the ephod on him. He also fastened the ephod with a decorative waistband, which he tied around him. ⁸ He placed the breastpiece on him and put the Urim and Thummim in the breastpiece. ⁹ Then he placed the turban on Aaron's head and set the gold plate, the sacred emblem, on the front of it, as the LORD commanded Moses.

Why did a priest have to wear all of this elaborate clothing? (8:7–9)
The priest was God's representative, and the priestly garments gave dignity and honor to the position of priest.

a 25 Or *offering is*   *b* 2 Or *purification offering*; also in verse 14

¹⁰Then Moses took the anointing oil and anointed the tabernacle and everything in it, and so consecrated them. ¹¹He sprinkled some of the oil on the altar seven times, anointing the altar and all its utensils and the basin with its stand, to consecrate them. ¹²He poured some of the anointing oil on Aaron's head and anointed him to consecrate him. ¹³Then he brought Aaron's sons forward, put tunics on them, tied sashes around them and fastened caps on them, as the LORD commanded Moses.

¹⁴He then presented the bull for the sin offering, and Aaron and his sons laid their hands on its head. ¹⁵Moses slaughtered the bull and took some of the blood, and with his finger he put it on all the horns of the altar to purify the altar. He poured out the rest of the blood at the base of the altar. So he consecrated it to make atonement for it. ¹⁶Moses also took all the fat around the internal organs, the long lobe of the liver, and both kidneys and their fat, and burned it on the altar. ¹⁷But the bull with its hide and its flesh and its intestines he burned up outside the camp, as the LORD commanded Moses.

¹⁸He then presented the ram for the burnt offering, and Aaron and his sons laid their hands on its head. ¹⁹Then Moses slaughtered the ram and splashed the blood against the sides of the altar. ²⁰He cut the ram into pieces and burned the head, the pieces and the fat. ²¹He washed the internal organs and the legs with water and burned the whole ram on the altar. It was a burnt offering, a pleasing aroma, a food offering presented to the LORD, as the LORD commanded Moses.

²²He then presented the other ram, the ram for the ordination, and Aaron and his sons laid their hands on its head. ²³Moses slaughtered the ram and took some of its blood and put it on the lobe of Aaron's right ear, on the thumb of his right hand and on the big toe of his right foot. ²⁴Moses also brought Aaron's sons forward and put some of the blood on the lobes of their right ears, on the thumbs of their right hands and on the big toes of their right feet. Then he splashed blood against the sides of the altar. ²⁵After that, he took the fat, the fat tail, all the fat around the internal organs, the long lobe of the liver, both kidneys and their fat and the right thigh. ²⁶And from the basket of bread made without yeast, which was before the LORD, he took one thick loaf, one thick loaf with olive oil mixed in, and one thin loaf, and he put these on the fat portions and on the right thigh. ²⁷He put all these in the hands of Aaron and his sons, and they waved them before the LORD as a wave offering. ²⁸Then Moses took them from their hands and burned them on the altar on top of the burnt offering as an ordination offering, a pleasing aroma, a food offering presented to the LORD. ²⁹Moses also took the breast, which was his share of the ordination ram, and waved it before the LORD as a wave offering, as the LORD commanded Moses.

³⁰Then Moses took some of the anointing oil and some of the blood from the altar and sprinkled them on Aaron and his garments and on his sons and their garments. So he consecrated Aaron and his garments and his sons and their garments.

If Moses wasn't a priest, why could he offer sacrifices? (8:15 – 19)
Moses served as the temporary high priest. As soon as Aaron and his sons became priests, they offered the sacrifices.

What is ordination? (8:22)
The word ordination meant "to fill the hand." The ram of ordination was placed in the priests' hands. Today ordination means to give official authority, and the ordination of ministers comes from the ritual described here.

Why were the priests' right ears, thumbs, and big toes special? (8:23)
These body parts are considered special because of the abilities they represent. Ears symbolize hearing, thumbs represent working, and toes symbolize walking.

Why was Aaron, who was sinful, made a high priest? (8:30)
Every person sins and no one is perfect. Although Aaron made the golden calf, he also helped Moses confront Pharaoh. Aaron was consecrated — cleansed and set apart — for his important work as high priest.

[31] Moses then said to Aaron and his sons, "Cook the meat at the entrance to the tent of meeting and eat it there with the bread from the basket of ordination offerings, as I was commanded: 'Aaron and his sons are to eat it.' [32] Then burn up the rest of the meat and the bread. [33] Do not leave the entrance to the tent of meeting for seven days, until the days of your ordination are completed, for your ordination will last seven days. [34] What has been done today was commanded by the LORD to make atonement for you. [35] You must stay at the entrance to the tent of meeting day and night for seven days and do what the LORD requires, so you will not die; for that is what I have been commanded."

[36] So Aaron and his sons did everything the LORD commanded through Moses.

THE PRIESTS BEGIN THEIR MINISTRY

9 On the eighth day Moses summoned Aaron and his sons and the elders of Israel. [2] He said to Aaron, "Take a bull calf for your sin offering*a* and a ram for your burnt offering, both without defect, and present them before the LORD. [3] Then say to the Israelites: 'Take a male goat for a sin offering, a calf and a lamb—both a year old and without defect—for a burnt offering, [4] and an ox*b* and a ram for a fellowship offering to sacrifice before the LORD, together with a grain offering mixed with olive oil. For today the LORD will appear to you.'"

[5] They took the things Moses commanded to the front of the tent of meeting, and the entire assembly came near and stood before the LORD. [6] Then Moses said, "This is what the LORD has commanded you to do, so that the glory of the LORD may appear to you."

[7] Moses said to Aaron, "Come to the altar and sacrifice your sin offering and your burnt offering and make atonement for yourself and the people; sacrifice the offering that is for the people and make atonement for them, as the LORD has commanded."

[8] So Aaron came to the altar and slaughtered the calf as a sin offering for himself. [9] His sons brought the blood to him, and he dipped his finger into the blood and put it on the horns of the altar; the rest of the blood he poured out at the base of the altar. [10] On the altar he burned the fat, the kidneys and the long lobe of the liver from the sin offering, as the LORD commanded Moses; [11] the flesh and the hide he burned up outside the camp.

[12] Then he slaughtered the burnt offering. His sons handed him the blood, and he splashed it against the sides of the altar. [13] They handed him the burnt offering piece by piece, including the head, and he burned them on the altar. [14] He washed the internal organs and the legs and burned them on top of the burnt offering on the altar.

[15] Aaron then brought the offering that was for the people. He took the goat for the people's sin offering and slaughtered it and offered it for a sin offering as he did with the first one. [16] He brought the burnt offering and offered it in the

Did the sacrifices make God appear? (9:4)
No. It was God's decision to appear in front of them.

---

a 2 Or *purification offering;* here and throughout this chapter   *b 4* The Hebrew word can refer to either male or female; also in verses 18 and 19.

prescribed way. [17]He also brought the grain offering, took a handful of it and burned it on the altar in addition to the morning's burnt offering.

[18]He slaughtered the ox and the ram as the fellowship offering for the people. His sons handed him the blood, and he splashed it against the sides of the altar. [19]But the fat portions of the ox and the ram — the fat tail, the layer of fat, the kidneys and the long lobe of the liver — [20]these they laid on the breasts, and then Aaron burned the fat on the altar. [21]Aaron waved the breasts and the right thigh before the LORD as a wave offering, as Moses commanded.

[22]Then Aaron lifted his hands toward the people and blessed them. And having sacrificed the sin offering, the burnt offering and the fellowship offering, he stepped down.

[23]Moses and Aaron then went into the tent of meeting. When they came out, they blessed the people; and the glory of the LORD appeared to all the people. [24]Fire came out from the presence of the LORD and consumed the burnt offering and the fat portions on the altar. And when all the people saw it, they shouted for joy and fell facedown.

THE DEATH OF NADAB AND ABIHU

10 Aaron's sons Nadab and Abihu took their censers, put fire in them and added incense; and they offered unauthorized fire before the LORD, contrary to his command. [2]So fire came out from the presence of the LORD and consumed them, and they died before the LORD. [3]Moses then said to Aaron, "This is what the LORD spoke of when he said:

"'Among those who approach me
  I will be proved holy;
in the sight of all the people
  I will be honored.'"

Aaron remained silent.

[4]Moses summoned Mishael and Elzaphan, sons of Aaron's uncle Uzziel, and said to them, "Come here; carry your cousins outside the camp, away from the front of the sanctuary." [5]So they came and carried them, still in their tunics, outside the camp, as Moses ordered.

[6]Then Moses said to Aaron and his sons Eleazar and Ithamar, "Do not let your hair become unkempt[a] and do not tear your clothes, or you will die and the LORD will be angry with the whole community. But your relatives, all the Israelites, may mourn for those the LORD has destroyed by fire. [7]Do not leave the entrance to the tent of meeting or you will die, because the LORD's anointing oil is on you." So they did as Moses said.

[8]Then the LORD said to Aaron, [9]"You and your sons are not to drink wine or other fermented drink whenever you go into the tent of meeting, or you will die. This is a lasting ordinance for the generations to come, [10]so that you can distinguish between the holy and the common, between the unclean and the clean, [11]and so you can teach the Israelites all the decrees the LORD has given them through Moses."

[a] 6 Or *Do not uncover your heads*

Why was the fire unauthorized? (10:1)
Aaron's sons Nadab and Abihu were killed because they did not follow the correct manner for making an offering to God. God punished them for not following his specific instructions.

Why would the priests die if they left the tent of meeting with oil on them? (10:7)
Moses said they still had the anointing oil on them, and they were still consecrated to God's service. He wanted them to stay distanced from the sin of Nadab and Abihu.

[12]Moses said to Aaron and his remaining sons, Eleazar and Ithamar, "Take the grain offering left over from the food offerings prepared without yeast and presented to the LORD and eat it beside the altar, for it is most holy. [13]Eat it in the sanctuary area, because it is your share and your sons' share of the food offerings presented to the LORD; for so I have been commanded. [14]But you and your sons and your daughters may eat the breast that was waved and the thigh that was presented. Eat them in a ceremonially clean place; they have been given to you and your children as your share of the Israelites' fellowship offerings. [15]The thigh that was presented and the breast that was waved must be brought with the fat portions of the food offerings, to be waved before the LORD as a wave offering. This will be the perpetual share for you and your children, as the LORD has commanded."

[16]When Moses inquired about the goat of the sin offering[a] and found that it had been burned up, he was angry with Eleazar and Ithamar, Aaron's remaining sons, and asked, [17]"Why didn't you eat the sin offering in the sanctuary area? It is most holy; it was given to you to take away the guilt of the community by making atonement for them before the LORD. [18]Since its blood was not taken into the Holy Place, you should have eaten the goat in the sanctuary area, as I commanded."

[19]Aaron replied to Moses, "Today they sacrificed their sin offering and their burnt offering before the LORD, but such things as this have happened to me. Would the LORD have been pleased if I had eaten the sin offering today?" [20]When Moses heard this, he was satisfied.

CLEAN AND UNCLEAN FOOD

11 The LORD said to Moses and Aaron, [2]"Say to the Israelites: 'Of all the animals that live on land, these are the ones you may eat: [3]You may eat any animal that has a divided hoof and that chews the cud.

[4]"'There are some that only chew the cud or only have a divided hoof, but you must not eat them. The camel, though it chews the cud, does not have a divided hoof; it is ceremonially unclean for you. [5]The hyrax, though it chews the cud, does not have a divided hoof; it is unclean for you. [6]The rabbit, though it chews the cud, does not have a divided hoof; it is unclean for you. [7]And the pig, though it has a divided hoof, does not chew the cud; it is unclean for you. [8]You must not eat their meat or touch their carcasses; they are unclean for you.

[9]"'Of all the creatures living in the water of the seas and the streams you may eat any that have fins and scales. [10]But all creatures in the seas or streams that do not have fins and scales—whether among all the swarming things or among all the other living creatures in the water—you are to regard as unclean. [11]And since you are to regard them as unclean, you must not eat their meat; you must regard their carcasses as unclean. [12]Anything living in the water that does not have fins and scales is to be regarded as unclean by you.

Why was Moses angry with Eleazar and Ithamar for burning the offering? (10:16–19)
The priests were supposed to eat a portion of the offering to symbolize removing the guilt of the people. This meant God had not accepted the offering, and he might judge them harshly again for their carelessness.

Why didn't Aaron and his sons eat the offering? (10:19–20)
Aaron and his sons were not being careless or deliberately disobedient. Perhaps the deaths of Nadab and Abihu had caused them to lose their appetite. Moses could see that they were physically unable to eat the offering.

What was the difference between clean and unclean foods? (11:1–47)
Over the years, people have suggested many possible reasons for why God designated some creatures as clean and others as unclean for food. The Bible does not give the answer, but these food laws helped the Israelites eat a healthy diet and maintain their identity as his covenant people. Obeying these food laws consecrated the Israelites, setting them apart as holy.

---

[a] 16 Or *purification offering*; also in verses 17 and 19

13 "'These are the birds you are to regard as unclean and not eat because they are unclean: the eagle,[a] the vulture, the black vulture, 14 the red kite, any kind of black kite, 15 any kind of raven, 16 the horned owl, the screech owl, the gull, any kind of hawk, 17 the little owl, the cormorant, the great owl, 18 the white owl, the desert owl, the osprey, 19 the stork, any kind of heron, the hoopoe and the bat.

20 "'All flying insects that walk on all fours are to be regarded as unclean by you. 21 There are, however, some flying insects that walk on all fours that you may eat: those that have jointed legs for hopping on the ground. 22 Of these you may eat any kind of locust, katydid, cricket or grasshopper. 23 But all other flying insects that have four legs you are to regard as unclean.

24 "'You will make yourselves unclean by these; whoever touches their carcasses will be unclean till evening. 25 Whoever picks up one of their carcasses must wash their clothes, and they will be unclean till evening.

26 "'Every animal that does not have a divided hoof or that does not chew the cud is unclean for you; whoever touches the carcass of any of them will be unclean. 27 Of all the animals that walk on all fours, those that walk on their paws are unclean for you; whoever touches their carcasses will be unclean till evening. 28 Anyone who picks up their carcasses must wash their clothes, and they will be unclean till evening. These animals are unclean for you.

29 "'Of the animals that move along the ground, these are unclean for you: the weasel, the rat, any kind of great lizard, 30 the gecko, the monitor lizard, the wall lizard, the skink and the chameleon. 31 Of all those that move along the ground, these are unclean for you. Whoever touches them when they are dead will be unclean till evening. 32 When one of them dies and falls on something, that article, whatever its use, will be unclean, whether it is made of wood, cloth, hide or sackcloth. Put it in water; it will be unclean till evening, and then it will be clean. 33 If one of them falls into a clay pot, everything in it will be unclean, and you must break the pot. 34 Any food you are allowed to eat that has come into contact with water from any such pot is unclean, and any liquid that is drunk from such a pot is unclean. 35 Anything that one of their carcasses falls on becomes unclean; an oven or cooking pot must be broken up. They are unclean, and you are to regard them as unclean. 36 A spring, however, or a cistern for collecting water remains clean, but anyone who touches one of these carcasses is unclean. 37 If a carcass falls on any seeds that are to be planted, they remain clean. 38 But if water has been put on the seed and a carcass falls on it, it is unclean for you.

39 "'If an animal that you are allowed to eat dies, anyone who touches its carcass will be unclean till evening. 40 Anyone who eats some of its carcass must wash their clothes, and they will be unclean till evening. Anyone who picks up the carcass must wash their clothes, and they will be unclean till evening.

[a] 13 The precise identification of some of the birds, insects and animals in this chapter is uncertain.

Don't most insects have six legs? (11:20)
Today, insects have six legs, but in ancient times it's possible that insects looked different; however, it's more likely that the Israelites simply did not count the insects' hind legs. The back two legs on the insect were used for jumping, so they have a different function and they look different than the other four legs on the upper part of the body.

Why would the Israelites be unclean until evening if they touched the carcass of an unclean animal? (11:24)
Evening marked the end of one day and the beginning of a new one. This new beginning gave the individual a "clean slate" to resume worshiping God.

⁴¹"'Every creature that moves along the ground is to be regarded as unclean; it is not to be eaten. ⁴²You are not to eat any creature that moves along the ground, whether it moves on its belly or walks on all fours or on many feet; it is unclean. ⁴³Do not defile yourselves by any of these creatures. Do not make yourselves unclean by means of them or be made unclean by them. ⁴⁴I am the LORD your God; consecrate yourselves and be holy, because I am holy. Do not make yourselves unclean by any creature that moves along the ground. ⁴⁵I am the LORD, who brought you up out of Egypt to be your God; therefore be holy, because I am holy.

⁴⁶"'These are the regulations concerning animals, birds, every living thing that moves about in the water and every creature that moves along the ground. ⁴⁷You must distinguish between the unclean and the clean, between living creatures that may be eaten and those that may not be eaten.'"

PURIFICATION AFTER CHILDBIRTH

12 The LORD said to Moses, ²"Say to the Israelites: 'A woman who becomes pregnant and gives birth to a son will be ceremonially unclean for seven days, just as she is unclean during her monthly period. ³On the eighth day the boy is to be circumcised. ⁴Then the woman must wait thirty-three days to be purified from her bleeding. She must not touch anything sacred or go to the sanctuary until the days of her purification are over. ⁵If she gives birth to a daughter, for two weeks the woman will be unclean, as during her period. Then she must wait sixty-six days to be purified from her bleeding.

⁶"'When the days of her purification for a son or daughter are over, she is to bring to the priest at the entrance to the tent of meeting a year-old lamb for a burnt offering and a young pigeon or a dove for a sin offering.^a ⁷He shall offer them before the LORD to make atonement for her, and then she will be ceremonially clean from her flow of blood.

"'These are the regulations for the woman who gives birth to a boy or a girl. ⁸But if she cannot afford a lamb, she is to bring two doves or two young pigeons, one for a burnt offering and the other for a sin offering. In this way the priest will make atonement for her, and she will be clean.'"

REGULATIONS ABOUT DEFILING SKIN DISEASES

13 The LORD said to Moses and Aaron, ²"When anyone has a swelling or a rash or a shiny spot on their skin that may be a defiling skin disease,^b they must be brought to Aaron the priest or to one of his sons^c who is a priest. ³The priest is to examine the sore on the skin, and if the hair in the sore has turned white and the sore appears to be more than skin deep, it is a defiling skin disease. When the priest examines that person, he shall pronounce them ceremonially

---

Would following these laws automatically make the Israelites holy? (11:44–47)
No. Of course God wanted his people to follow the rules he set out for them, but they had to have heartfelt faith in order to be truly holy.

Why would giving birth make a woman ceremonially unclean? (12:1–5)
The baby didn't make a woman unclean. A baby's birth is always to be celebrated. The ancient Israelites thought the blood associated with the birth was unclean.

Why would a woman's purification time be longer if she had a girl? (12:4)
This might sound strange to us now, but the cultural ideologies were much different in ancient times. God may have made this rule based on those ideas at the time.

If childbirth isn't a bad thing, then why was an offering necessary? (12:7)
One of the purposes of a burnt offering was to worship God, so this offering might have been a way for the parents to praise God for the new life and to serve as a promise to raise their child according to his commandments. The sin offering served to get rid of the uncleanness associated with the birth.

Why did people come to the priests when they had skin infections? (13:2–3)
The priests were not doctors, but they could determine if a rash was infectious. An infection made the person ceremonially unclean, so it was the priest's job to decide whether the person was considered unclean. The unclean person then had to be isolated until they were better.

---

^a 6 Or *purification offering*; also in verse 8   ^b 2 The Hebrew word for *defiling skin disease*, traditionally translated "leprosy," was used for various diseases affecting the skin; here and throughout verses 3–46.
^c 2 Or *descendants*

unclean. ⁴If the shiny spot on the skin is white but does not appear to be more than skin deep and the hair in it has not turned white, the priest is to isolate the affected person for seven days. ⁵On the seventh day the priest is to examine them, and if he sees that the sore is unchanged and has not spread in the skin, he is to isolate them for another seven days. ⁶On the seventh day the priest is to examine them again, and if the sore has faded and has not spread in the skin, the priest shall pronounce them clean; it is only a rash. They must wash their clothes, and they will be clean. ⁷But if the rash does spread in their skin after they have shown themselves to the priest to be pronounced clean, they must appear before the priest again. ⁸The priest is to examine that person, and if the rash has spread in the skin, he shall pronounce them unclean; it is a defiling skin disease.

⁹"When anyone has a defiling skin disease, they must be brought to the priest. ¹⁰The priest is to examine them, and if there is a white swelling in the skin that has turned the hair white and if there is raw flesh in the swelling, ¹¹it is a chronic skin disease and the priest shall pronounce them unclean. He is not to isolate them, because they are already unclean.

¹²"If the disease breaks out all over their skin and, so far as the priest can see, it covers all the skin of the affected person from head to foot, ¹³the priest is to examine them, and if the disease has covered their whole body, he shall pronounce them clean. Since it has all turned white, they are clean. ¹⁴But whenever raw flesh appears on them, they will be unclean. ¹⁵When the priest sees the raw flesh, he shall pronounce them unclean. The raw flesh is unclean; they have a defiling disease. ¹⁶If the raw flesh changes and turns white, they must go to the priest. ¹⁷The priest is to examine them, and if the sores have turned white, the priest shall pronounce the affected person clean; then they will be clean.

¹⁸"When someone has a boil on their skin and it heals, ¹⁹and in the place where the boil was, a white swelling or reddish-white spot appears, they must present themselves to the priest. ²⁰The priest is to examine it, and if it appears to be more than skin deep and the hair in it has turned white, the priest shall pronounce that person unclean. It is a defiling skin disease that has broken out where the boil was. ²¹But if, when the priest examines it, there is no white hair in it and it is not more than skin deep and has faded, then the priest is to isolate them for seven days. ²²If it is spreading in the skin, the priest shall pronounce them unclean; it is a defiling disease. ²³But if the spot is unchanged and has not spread, it is only a scar from the boil, and the priest shall pronounce them clean.

²⁴"When someone has a burn on their skin and a reddish-white or white spot appears in the raw flesh of the burn, ²⁵the priest is to examine the spot, and if the hair in it has turned white, and it appears to be more than skin deep, it is a defiling disease that has broken out in the burn. The priest shall pronounce them unclean; it is a defiling skin disease. ²⁶But if the priest examines it and there is no white hair in the spot and if it is not more than skin deep and has faded,

What kinds of diseases are being described? (13:1–38)
There are several possible skin diseases that seem to fit the descriptions. They include chronic dermatitis, chronic skin infection, psoriasis, and skin cancer.

Why was a person with completely white flesh declared cured? (13:13)
This may refer to the healed flesh after a rash. If it was unhealed and still infectious, it would have appeared red or bleeding.

then the priest is to isolate them for seven days. [27]On the seventh day the priest is to examine that person, and if it is spreading in the skin, the priest shall pronounce them unclean; it is a defiling skin disease. [28]If, however, the spot is unchanged and has not spread in the skin but has faded, it is a swelling from the burn, and the priest shall pronounce them clean; it is only a scar from the burn.

[29]"If a man or woman has a sore on their head or chin, [30]the priest is to examine the sore, and if it appears to be more than skin deep and the hair in it is yellow and thin, the priest shall pronounce them unclean; it is a defiling skin disease on the head or chin. [31]But if, when the priest examines the sore, it does not seem to be more than skin deep and there is no black hair in it, then the priest is to isolate the affected person for seven days. [32]On the seventh day the priest is to examine the sore, and if it has not spread and there is no yellow hair in it and it does not appear to be more than skin deep, [33]then the man or woman must shave themselves, except for the affected area, and the priest is to keep them isolated another seven days. [34]On the seventh day the priest is to examine the sore, and if it has not spread in the skin and appears to be no more than skin deep, the priest shall pronounce them clean. They must wash their clothes, and they will be clean. [35]But if the sore does spread in the skin after they are pronounced clean, [36]the priest is to examine them, and if he finds that the sore has spread in the skin, he does not need to look for yellow hair; they are unclean. [37]If, however, the sore is unchanged so far as the priest can see, and if black hair has grown in it, the affected person is healed. They are clean, and the priest shall pronounce them clean.

[38]"When a man or woman has white spots on the skin, [39]the priest is to examine them, and if the spots are dull white, it is a harmless rash that has broken out on the skin; they are clean.

[40]"A man who has lost his hair and is bald is clean. [41]If he has lost his hair from the front of his scalp and has a bald forehead, he is clean. [42]But if he has a reddish-white sore on his bald head or forehead, it is a defiling disease breaking out on his head or forehead. [43]The priest is to examine him, and if the swollen sore on his head or forehead is reddish-white like a defiling skin disease, [44]the man is diseased and is unclean. The priest shall pronounce him unclean because of the sore on his head.

[45]"Anyone with such a defiling disease must wear torn clothes, let their hair be unkempt,[a] cover the lower part of their face and cry out, 'Unclean! Unclean!' [46]As long as they have the disease they remain unclean. They must live alone; they must live outside the camp.

REGULATIONS ABOUT DEFILING MOLDS

[47]"As for any fabric that is spoiled with a defiling mold— any woolen or linen clothing, [48]any woven or knitted material of linen or wool, any leather or anything made of leather— [49]if the affected area in the fabric, the leather, the

[a] 45 Or clothes, uncover their head

What were the requirements for people with infectious diseases? (13:45)
They were to wear torn clothes, let their hair go wild, cover their lower face, and identify themselves as unclean by shouting, "Unclean! Unclean!" The torn clothes, unkempt hair, and covered face were all signs of mourning. This appearance warned people to stay away.

Why were people with diseases excluded from the camp? (13:46)
Keeping diseased people away from the tabernacle kept it from becoming unclean. These rules also protected the rest of the camp by keeping disease from spreading.

woven or knitted material, or any leather article, is greenish or reddish, it is a defiling mold and must be shown to the priest. [50]The priest is to examine the affected area and isolate the article for seven days. [51]On the seventh day he is to examine it, and if the mold has spread in the fabric, the woven or knitted material, or the leather, whatever its use, it is a persistent defiling mold; the article is unclean. [52]He must burn the fabric, the woven or knitted material of wool or linen, or any leather article that has been spoiled; because the defiling mold is persistent, the article must be burned.

[53]"But if, when the priest examines it, the mold has not spread in the fabric, the woven or knitted material, or the leather article, [54]he shall order that the spoiled article be washed. Then he is to isolate it for another seven days. [55]After the article has been washed, the priest is to examine it again, and if the mold has not changed its appearance, even though it has not spread, it is unclean. Burn it, no matter which side of the fabric has been spoiled. [56]If, when the priest examines it, the mold has faded after the article has been washed, he is to tear the spoiled part out of the fabric, the leather, or the woven or knitted material. [57]But if it reappears in the fabric, in the woven or knitted material, or in the leather article, it is a spreading mold; whatever has the mold must be burned. [58]Any fabric, woven or knitted material, or any leather article that has been washed and is rid of the mold, must be washed again. Then it will be clean."

[59]These are the regulations concerning defiling molds in woolen or linen clothing, woven or knitted material, or any leather article, for pronouncing them clean or unclean.

CLEANSING FROM DEFILING SKIN DISEASES

14 The Lord said to Moses, [2]"These are the regulations for any diseased person at the time of their ceremonial cleansing, when they are brought to the priest: [3]The priest is to go outside the camp and examine them. If they have been healed of their defiling skin disease,[a] [4]the priest shall order that two live clean birds and some cedar wood, scarlet yarn and hyssop be brought for the person to be cleansed. [5]Then the priest shall order that one of the birds be killed over fresh water in a clay pot. [6]He is then to take the live bird and dip it, together with the cedar wood, the scarlet yarn and the hyssop, into the blood of the bird that was killed over the fresh water. [7]Seven times he shall sprinkle the one to be cleansed of the defiling disease, and then pronounce them clean. After that, he is to release the live bird in the open fields.

[8]"The person to be cleansed must wash their clothes, shave off all their hair and bathe with water; then they will be ceremonially clean. After this they may come into the camp, but they must stay outside their tent for seven days. [9]On the seventh day they must shave off all their hair; they must shave their head, their beard, their eyebrows and the rest of their hair. They must wash their clothes and bathe themselves with water, and they will be clean.

---

[a] 3 The Hebrew word for *defiling skin disease*, traditionally translated "leprosy," was used for various diseases affecting the skin; also in verses 7, 32, 54 and 57.

Why was mildew so bad? (13:47 – 52)
Mildew (translated as infectious skin disease) on fabric could be evidence of infectious disease, or it could be harmless. The procedure helped to determine what type of mildew it was. Objects with mildew may have been condemned because they appeared impure and were not permitted to remain in the camp with a holy God.

What was the meaning of the ritual with the birds? (14:4 – 7)
This is a cleansing ritual for the person who was healed from an infectious disease. The two clean birds may have represented the person being cleansed.

Why did the returning person have to live outside his tent? (14:8)
This was the second stage of restoration in the cleansing ritual. He or she was not yet clean enough to fully participate in the community life.

Why were offerings necessary after the person was healed from the skin disease? (14:10–12)
Although sickness was not a sin, sickness made the camp unsuitable for God's presence. After accepting the individual's sacrifice, God allowed the person to join in worship and fellowship again.

[10] "On the eighth day they must bring two male lambs and one ewe lamb a year old, each without defect, along with three-tenths of an ephah[a] of the finest flour mixed with olive oil for a grain offering, and one log[b] of oil. [11] The priest who pronounces them clean shall present both the one to be cleansed and their offerings before the LORD at the entrance to the tent of meeting.

[12] "Then the priest is to take one of the male lambs and offer it as a guilt offering, along with the log of oil; he shall wave them before the LORD as a wave offering. [13] He is to slaughter the lamb in the sanctuary area where the sin offering[c] and the burnt offering are slaughtered. Like the sin offering, the guilt offering belongs to the priest; it is most holy. [14] The priest is to take some of the blood of the guilt offering and put it on the lobe of the right ear of the one to be cleansed, on the thumb of their right hand and on the big toe of their right foot. [15] The priest shall then take some of the log of oil, pour it in the palm of his own left hand, [16] dip his right forefinger into the oil in his palm, and with his finger sprinkle some of it before the LORD seven times. [17] The priest is to put some of the oil remaining in his palm on the lobe of the right ear of the one to be cleansed, on the thumb of their right hand and on the big toe of their right foot, on top of the blood of the guilt offering. [18] The rest of the oil in his palm the priest shall put on the head of the one to be cleansed and make atonement for them before the LORD.

[19] "Then the priest is to sacrifice the sin offering and make atonement for the one to be cleansed from their uncleanness. After that, the priest shall slaughter the burnt offering [20] and offer it on the altar, together with the grain offering, and make atonement for them, and they will be clean.

[21] "If, however, they are poor and cannot afford these, they must take one male lamb as a guilt offering to be waved to make atonement for them, together with a tenth of an ephah[d] of the finest flour mixed with olive oil for a grain offering, a log of oil, [22] and two doves or two young pigeons, such as they can afford, one for a sin offering and the other for a burnt offering.

[23] "On the eighth day they must bring them for their cleansing to the priest at the entrance to the tent of meeting, before the LORD. [24] The priest is to take the lamb for the guilt offering, together with the log of oil, and wave them before the LORD as a wave offering. [25] He shall slaughter the lamb for the guilt offering and take some of its blood and put it on the lobe of the right ear of the one to be cleansed, on the thumb of their right hand and on the big toe of their right foot. [26] The priest is to pour some of the oil into the palm of his own left hand, [27] and with his right forefinger sprinkle some of the oil from his palm seven times before the LORD. [28] Some of the oil in his palm he is to put on the same places he put the blood of the guilt offering — on the lobe of the right ear of the one to be cleansed, on the thumb of

[a] *10* That is, probably about 11 pounds or about 5 kilograms   [b] *10* That is, about 1/3 quart or about 0.3 liter; also in verses 12, 15, 21 and 24
[c] *13* Or *purification offering*; also in verses 19, 22 and 31   [d] *21* That is, probably about 3 1/2 pounds or about 1.6 kilograms

their right hand and on the big toe of their right foot. ²⁹ The rest of the oil in his palm the priest shall put on the head of the one to be cleansed, to make atonement for them before the LORD. ³⁰ Then he shall sacrifice the doves or the young pigeons, such as the person can afford, ³¹ one as a sin offering and the other as a burnt offering, together with the grain offering. In this way the priest will make atonement before the LORD on behalf of the one to be cleansed."

³² These are the regulations for anyone who has a defiling skin disease and who cannot afford the regular offerings for their cleansing.

CLEANSING FROM DEFILING MOLDS

³³ The LORD said to Moses and Aaron, ³⁴ "When you enter the land of Canaan, which I am giving you as your possession, and I put a spreading mold in a house in that land, ³⁵ the owner of the house must go and tell the priest, 'I have seen something that looks like a defiling mold in my house.' ³⁶ The priest is to order the house to be emptied before he goes in to examine the mold, so that nothing in the house will be pronounced unclean. After this the priest is to go in and inspect the house. ³⁷ He is to examine the mold on the walls, and if it has greenish or reddish depressions that appear to be deeper than the surface of the wall, ³⁸ the priest shall go out the doorway of the house and close it up for seven days. ³⁹ On the seventh day the priest shall return to inspect the house. If the mold has spread on the walls, ⁴⁰ he is to order that the contaminated stones be torn out and thrown into an unclean place outside the town. ⁴¹ He must have all the inside walls of the house scraped and the material that is scraped off dumped into an unclean place outside the town. ⁴² Then they are to take other stones to replace these and take new clay and plaster the house.

⁴³ "If the defiling mold reappears in the house after the stones have been torn out and the house scraped and plastered, ⁴⁴ the priest is to go and examine it and, if the mold has spread in the house, it is a persistent defiling mold; the house is unclean. ⁴⁵ It must be torn down — its stones, timbers and all the plaster — and taken out of the town to an unclean place.

⁴⁶ "Anyone who goes into the house while it is closed up will be unclean till evening. ⁴⁷ Anyone who sleeps or eats in the house must wash their clothes.

⁴⁸ "But if the priest comes to examine it and the mold has not spread after the house has been plastered, he shall pronounce the house clean, because the defiling mold is gone. ⁴⁹ To purify the house he is to take two birds and some cedar wood, scarlet yarn and hyssop. ⁵⁰ He shall kill one of the birds over fresh water in a clay pot. ⁵¹ Then he is to take the cedar wood, the hyssop, the scarlet yarn and the live bird, dip them into the blood of the dead bird and the fresh water, and sprinkle the house seven times. ⁵² He shall purify the house with the bird's blood, the fresh water, the live bird, the cedar wood, the hyssop and the scarlet yarn. ⁵³ Then he is to release the live bird in the open fields outside the town. In this way he will make atonement for the house, and it will be clean."

Why did God send spreading mildew in Canaan? (14:34)
Unlike the plagues in Exodus, the mildew was not sent as punishment on the people. Rather, it seems that God contaminated a house to remind the people of his power.

Why did the house need atonement? (14:53)
Any imperfections, even in the buildings, made the Israelites unfit for God's presence. Just as the Israelites wanted their bodies to be pure, their homes needed to be pure as well.

⁵⁴These are the regulations for any defiling skin disease, for a sore, ⁵⁵for defiling molds in fabric or in a house, ⁵⁶and for a swelling, a rash or a shiny spot, ⁵⁷to determine when something is clean or unclean.

These are the regulations for defiling skin diseases and defiling molds.

DISCHARGES CAUSING UNCLEANNESS

15 The LORD said to Moses and Aaron, ²"Speak to the Israelites and say to them: 'When any man has an unusual bodily discharge, such a discharge is unclean. ³Whether it continues flowing from his body or is blocked, it will make him unclean. This is how his discharge will bring about uncleanness:

⁴"'Any bed the man with a discharge lies on will be unclean, and anything he sits on will be unclean. ⁵Anyone who touches his bed must wash their clothes and bathe with water, and they will be unclean till evening. ⁶Whoever sits on anything that the man with a discharge sat on must wash their clothes and bathe with water, and they will be unclean till evening.

⁷"'Whoever touches the man who has a discharge must wash their clothes and bathe with water, and they will be unclean till evening.

⁸"'If the man with the discharge spits on anyone who is clean, they must wash their clothes and bathe with water, and they will be unclean till evening.

⁹"'Everything the man sits on when riding will be unclean, ¹⁰and whoever touches any of the things that were under him will be unclean till evening; whoever picks up those things must wash their clothes and bathe with water, and they will be unclean till evening.

¹¹"'Anyone the man with a discharge touches without rinsing his hands with water must wash their clothes and bathe with water, and they will be unclean till evening.

¹²"'A clay pot that the man touches must be broken, and any wooden article is to be rinsed with water.

¹³"'When a man is cleansed from his discharge, he is to count off seven days for his ceremonial cleansing; he must wash his clothes and bathe himself with fresh water, and he will be clean. ¹⁴On the eighth day he must take two doves or two young pigeons and come before the LORD to the entrance to the tent of meeting and give them to the priest. ¹⁵The priest is to sacrifice them, the one for a sin offering*ª* and the other for a burnt offering. In this way he will make atonement before the LORD for the man because of his discharge.

¹⁶"'When a man has an emission of semen, he must bathe his whole body with water, and he will be unclean till evening. ¹⁷Any clothing or leather that has semen on it must be washed with water, and it will be unclean till evening. ¹⁸When a man has sexual relations with a woman and there is an emission of semen, both of them must bathe with water, and they will be unclean till evening.

ª 15 Or purification offering; also in verse 30

Why did God give these laws about personal cleanliness? (15:1–33)
Not only did these laws help keep the people clean and help prevent sickness, they were also a way for God to differentiate his people from others.

What was a bodily discharge in this case? (15:2–3)
This might refer to diarrhea or a discharge from the genitals caused by an infection.

Where did people living in the desert find water for bathing and washing clothes? (15:5–13)
Ritual bathing would not have required a lot of water. So even if they could only draw a little bit from wells or cisterns that collect rainfall, it would be enough.

Why did natural functions cause uncleanness? (15:16–24)
Any type of discharge was considered unclean and therefore required some sort of cleansing. There is nothing sinful about sexual intercourse (within marriage) or a woman's menstrual cycle.

¹⁹"'When a woman has her regular flow of blood, the impurity of her monthly period will last seven days, and anyone who touches her will be unclean till evening.

²⁰"'Anything she lies on during her period will be unclean, and anything she sits on will be unclean. ²¹Anyone who touches her bed will be unclean; they must wash their clothes and bathe with water, and they will be unclean till evening. ²²Anyone who touches anything she sits on will be unclean; they must wash their clothes and bathe with water, and they will be unclean till evening. ²³Whether it is the bed or anything she was sitting on, when anyone touches it, they will be unclean till evening.

²⁴"'If a man has sexual relations with her and her monthly flow touches him, he will be unclean for seven days; any bed he lies on will be unclean.

²⁵"'When a woman has a discharge of blood for many days at a time other than her monthly period or has a discharge that continues beyond her period, she will be unclean as long as she has the discharge, just as in the days of her period. ²⁶Any bed she lies on while her discharge continues will be unclean, as is her bed during her monthly period, and anything she sits on will be unclean, as during her period. ²⁷Anyone who touches them will be unclean; they must wash their clothes and bathe with water, and they will be unclean till evening.

²⁸"'When she is cleansed from her discharge, she must count off seven days, and after that she will be ceremonially clean. ²⁹On the eighth day she must take two doves or two young pigeons and bring them to the priest at the entrance to the tent of meeting. ³⁰The priest is to sacrifice one for a sin offering and the other for a burnt offering. In this way he will make atonement for her before the LORD for the uncleanness of her discharge.

³¹"'You must keep the Israelites separate from things that make them unclean, so they will not die in their uncleanness for defiling my dwelling place,ᵃ which is among them.'"

³²These are the regulations for a man with a discharge, for anyone made unclean by an emission of semen, ³³for a woman in her monthly period, for a man or a woman with a discharge, and for a man who has sexual relations with a woman who is ceremonially unclean.

THE DAY OF ATONEMENT

16 The LORD spoke to Moses after the death of the two sons of Aaron who died when they approached the LORD. ²The LORD said to Moses: "Tell your brother Aaron that he is not to come whenever he chooses into the Most Holy Place behind the curtain in front of the atonement cover on the ark, or else he will die. For I will appear in the cloud over the atonement cover.

³"This is how Aaron is to enter the Most Holy Place: He must first bring a young bull for a sin offeringᵇ and a ram for a burnt offering. ⁴He is to put on the sacred linen tunic,

ᵃ 31 Or *my tabernacle*   ᵇ 3 Or *purification offering*; here and throughout this chapter

Why could being close to God cause Aaron to die? (16:2)
The priests had the responsibility of approaching God on behalf of his people. This was a very serious responsibility. Unless Aaron was properly prepared, God's glory in the Most Holy Place would kill him.

What was the atonement cover? (16:2)
The atonement cover was the lid of the ark of the covenant. This is the place where God appeared. (See Exodus 25:22.)

What was a scapegoat? (16:7–10, 20–22)
A sacrifice was a substitute for the sinner that symbolically received the consequences of sin in place of someone else. The scapegoat was a goat, a living sacrifice, which symbolically carried away the guilt of the people far from camp.

What were the "tablets of the covenant law"? (16:13)
They were the Ten Commandments; the tablets on which they were subscribed were in the ark of the covenant.

with linen undergarments next to his body; he is to tie the linen sash around him and put on the linen turban. These are sacred garments; so he must bathe himself with water before he puts them on. ⁵ From the Israelite community he is to take two male goats for a sin offering and a ram for a burnt offering.

⁶ "Aaron is to offer the bull for his own sin offering to make atonement for himself and his household. ⁷ Then he is to take the two goats and present them before the LORD at the entrance to the tent of meeting. ⁸ He is to cast lots for the two goats — one lot for the LORD and the other for the scapegoat.ᵃ ⁹ Aaron shall bring the goat whose lot falls to the LORD and sacrifice it for a sin offering. ¹⁰ But the goat chosen by lot as the scapegoat shall be presented alive before the LORD to be used for making atonement by sending it into the wilderness as a scapegoat.

¹¹ "Aaron shall bring the bull for his own sin offering to make atonement for himself and his household, and he is to slaughter the bull for his own sin offering. ¹² He is to take a censer full of burning coals from the altar before the LORD and two handfuls of finely ground fragrant incense and take them behind the curtain. ¹³ He is to put the incense on the fire before the LORD, and the smoke of the incense will conceal the atonement cover above the tablets of the covenant law, so that he will not die. ¹⁴ He is to take some of the bull's blood and with his finger sprinkle it on the front of the atonement cover; then he shall sprinkle some of it with his finger seven times before the atonement cover.

¹⁵ "He shall then slaughter the goat for the sin offering for the people and take its blood behind the curtain and do with it as he did with the bull's blood: He shall sprinkle it on the atonement cover and in front of it. ¹⁶ In this way he will make atonement for the Most Holy Place because of the uncleanness and rebellion of the Israelites, whatever their sins have been. He is to do the same for the tent of meeting, which is among them in the midst of their uncleanness. ¹⁷ No one is to be in the tent of meeting from the time Aaron goes in to make atonement in the Most Holy Place until he comes out, having made atonement for himself, his household and the whole community of Israel.

¹⁸ "Then he shall come out to the altar that is before the LORD and make atonement for it. He shall take some of the bull's blood and some of the goat's blood and put it on all the horns of the altar. ¹⁹ He shall sprinkle some of the blood on it with his finger seven times to cleanse it and to consecrate it from the uncleanness of the Israelites.

²⁰ "When Aaron has finished making atonement for the Most Holy Place, the tent of meeting and the altar, he shall bring forward the live goat. ²¹ He is to lay both hands on the head of the live goat and confess over it all the wickedness and rebellion of the Israelites — all their sins — and put them on the goat's head. He shall send the goat away into the wilderness in the care of someone appointed for the task. ²² The

ᵃ *8* The meaning of the Hebrew for this word is uncertain; also in verses 10 and 26.

goat will carry on itself all their sins to a remote place; and
the man shall release it in the wilderness.

²³"Then Aaron is to go into the tent of meeting and take
off the linen garments he put on before he entered the Most
Holy Place, and he is to leave them there. ²⁴He shall bathe
himself with water in the sanctuary area and put on his regular garments. Then he shall come out and sacrifice the burnt
offering for himself and the burnt offering for the people, to
make atonement for himself and for the people. ²⁵He shall
also burn the fat of the sin offering on the altar.

²⁶"The man who releases the goat as a scapegoat must
wash his clothes and bathe himself with water; afterward
he may come into the camp. ²⁷The bull and the goat for the
sin offerings, whose blood was brought into the Most Holy
Place to make atonement, must be taken outside the camp;
their hides, flesh and intestines are to be burned up. ²⁸The
man who burns them must wash his clothes and bathe himself with water; afterward he may come into the camp.

²⁹"This is to be a lasting ordinance for you: On the tenth
day of the seventh month you must deny yourselves*ᵃ* and not
do any work—whether native-born or a foreigner residing
among you— ³⁰because on this day atonement will be made
for you, to cleanse you. Then, before the LORD, you will be
clean from all your sins. ³¹It is a day of sabbath rest, and you
must deny yourselves; it is a lasting ordinance. ³²The priest
who is anointed and ordained to succeed his father as high
priest is to make atonement. He is to put on the sacred linen
garments ³³and make atonement for the Most Holy Place,
for the tent of meeting and the altar, and for the priests and
all the members of the community.

³⁴"This is to be a lasting ordinance for you: Atonement
is to be made once a year for all the sins of the Israelites."

And it was done, as the LORD commanded Moses.

EATING BLOOD FORBIDDEN

17 The LORD said to Moses, ²"Speak to Aaron and his
sons and to all the Israelites and say to them: 'This
is what the LORD has commanded: ³Any Israelite who sacrifices an ox,*ᵇ* a lamb or a goat in the camp or outside of it
⁴instead of bringing it to the entrance to the tent of meeting
to present it as an offering to the LORD in front of the tabernacle of the LORD—that person shall be considered guilty
of bloodshed; they have shed blood and must be cut off from
their people. ⁵This is so the Israelites will bring to the LORD
the sacrifices they are now making in the open fields. They
must bring them to the priest, that is, to the LORD, at the entrance to the tent of meeting and sacrifice them as fellowship
offerings. ⁶The priest is to splash the blood against the altar
of the LORD at the entrance to the tent of meeting and burn
the fat as an aroma pleasing to the LORD. ⁷They must no
longer offer any of their sacrifices to the goat idols*ᶜ* to whom
they prostitute themselves. This is to be a lasting ordinance
for them and for the generations to come.'

---

*ᵃ 29 Or must fast; also in verse 31   ᵇ 3 The Hebrew word can refer to either
male or female.   ᶜ 7 Or the demons*

**Why was a day of atone-
ment needed? (16:29–30)**
In order for God to remain with
the Israelites, they had to atone
for all of their sins, even the ones
they weren't aware they committed. Sacrifices on the day of
atonement cleansed the whole
nation of all sins. Christ's death
was the final day of atonement,
making sacrifices unnecessary
thereafter.

**Why did God require the
Israelites to make their
sacrifice in front of the
tabernacle? (17:3–4)**
Unlike the pagans who worshipped their gods at numerous
shrines, God wanted his people
to be focused on him at one
spot at the tent of meeting. This
would help set them apart from
the ungodly practices of the
pagans.

**Why waste the meat of a
dead animal? (17:5)**
God gave the Israelites very
strict rules about what they
could and could not eat. One
important rule was to not eat
anything that was unclean. A
dead animal would be considered
unclean because the blood was
not properly drained from its
carcass.

**What were the goat idols
they were told not to sacrifice to? (17:7)**
They may have been idols in the
shape of a goat, like calf idols,
that were worshiped in Egypt. Or
they may have been some type
of demon.

[8]"Say to them: 'Any Israelite or any foreigner residing among them who offers a burnt offering or sacrifice [9]and does not bring it to the entrance to the tent of meeting to sacrifice it to the LORD must be cut off from the people of Israel.

[10]"'I will set my face against any Israelite or any foreigner residing among them who eats blood, and I will cut them off from the people. [11]For the life of a creature is in the blood, and I have given it to you to make atonement for yourselves on the altar; it is the blood that makes atonement for one's life.[a] [12]Therefore I say to the Israelites, "None of you may eat blood, nor may any foreigner residing among you eat blood."

[13]"'Any Israelite or any foreigner residing among you who hunts any animal or bird that may be eaten must drain out the blood and cover it with earth, [14]because the life of every creature is its blood. That is why I have said to the Israelites, "You must not eat the blood of any creature, because the life of every creature is its blood; anyone who eats it must be cut off."

[15]"'Anyone, whether native-born or foreigner, who eats anything found dead or torn by wild animals must wash their clothes and bathe with water, and they will be ceremonially unclean till evening; then they will be clean. [16]But if they do not wash their clothes and bathe themselves, they will be held responsible.'"

UNLAWFUL SEXUAL RELATIONS

18 The LORD said to Moses, [2]"Speak to the Israelites and say to them: 'I am the LORD your God. [3]You must not do as they do in Egypt, where you used to live, and you must not do as they do in the land of Canaan, where I am bringing you. Do not follow their practices. [4]You must obey my laws and be careful to follow my decrees. I am the LORD your God. [5]Keep my decrees and laws, for the person who obeys them will live by them. I am the LORD.

[6]"'No one is to approach any close relative to have sexual relations. I am the LORD.

[7]"'Do not dishonor your father by having sexual relations with your mother. She is your mother; do not have relations with her.

[8]"'Do not have sexual relations with your father's wife; that would dishonor your father.

[9]"'Do not have sexual relations with your sister, either your father's daughter or your mother's daughter, whether she was born in the same home or elsewhere.

[10]"'Do not have sexual relations with your son's daughter or your daughter's daughter; that would dishonor you.

[11]"'Do not have sexual relations with the daughter of your father's wife, born to your father; she is your sister.

[12]"'Do not have sexual relations with your father's sister; she is your father's close relative.

[13]"'Do not have sexual relations with your mother's sister, because she is your mother's close relative.

[14]"'Do not dishonor your father's brother by approaching his wife to have sexual relations; she is your aunt.

Why is it specifically the blood that atones for sin? (17:11)
Blood is necessary for life. When the animal's blood was shed, it was paying the price for the sinner with its life.

Why were there so many rules that start with "Do not"? (18:7–24)
By using the negative language, the rules clearly state the expected behavior. These rules communicated clearly what was right and wrong.

---

[a] 11 Or *atonement by the life in the blood*

¹⁵"Do not have sexual relations with your daughter-in-law. She is your son's wife; do not have relations with her.

¹⁶"Do not have sexual relations with your brother's wife; that would dishonor your brother.

¹⁷"Do not have sexual relations with both a woman and her daughter. Do not have sexual relations with either her son's daughter or her daughter's daughter; they are her close relatives. That is wickedness.

¹⁸"Do not take your wife's sister as a rival wife and have sexual relations with her while your wife is living.

¹⁹"Do not approach a woman to have sexual relations during the uncleanness of her monthly period.

²⁰"Do not have sexual relations with your neighbor's wife and defile yourself with her.

²¹"Do not give any of your children to be sacrificed to Molek, for you must not profane the name of your God. I am the LORD.

²²"Do not have sexual relations with a man as one does with a woman; that is detestable.

²³"Do not have sexual relations with an animal and defile yourself with it. A woman must not present herself to an animal to have sexual relations with it; that is a perversion.

²⁴"Do not defile yourselves in any of these ways, because this is how the nations that I am going to drive out before you became defiled. ²⁵Even the land was defiled; so I punished it for its sin, and the land vomited out its inhabitants. ²⁶But you must keep my decrees and my laws. The native-born and the foreigners residing among you must not do any of these detestable things, ²⁷for all these things were done by the people who lived in the land before you, and the land became defiled. ²⁸And if you defile the land, it will vomit you out as it vomited out the nations that were before you.

²⁹"Everyone who does any of these detestable things — such persons must be cut off from their people. ³⁰Keep my requirements and do not follow any of the detestable customs that were practiced before you came and do not defile yourselves with them. I am the LORD your God.'"

VARIOUS LAWS

19 The LORD said to Moses, ²"Speak to the entire assembly of Israel and say to them: 'Be holy because I, the LORD your God, am holy.

³"Each of you must respect your mother and father, and you must observe my Sabbaths. I am the LORD your God.

⁴"Do not turn to idols or make metal gods for yourselves. I am the LORD your God.

⁵"When you sacrifice a fellowship offering to the LORD, sacrifice it in such a way that it will be accepted on your behalf. ⁶It shall be eaten on the day you sacrifice it or on the next day; anything left over until the third day must be burned up. ⁷If any of it is eaten on the third day, it is impure and will not be accepted. ⁸Whoever eats it will be held responsible because they have desecrated what is holy to the LORD; they must be cut off from their people.

Why were parents told not to sacrifice their children? (18:21)
It seems obvious that parents wouldn't do this, but sacrificing children was part of pagan worship. God made it clear that he did not approve of this practice.

Why was homosexual behavior called detestable? (18:22)
Homosexuality is a departure from God's design that sex be reserved for marriage between a man and a woman.

How could the Israelites control what the foreigners and others living among them did? (18:26)
The Israelites could enforce God's laws in the land even though they could not control the consciences of the people living there.

Did God expect his followers to be perfect? (19:2)
He doesn't expect them to be perfect, but he expects them to be holy. To be holy means to be set apart for God's purposes. Holiness is the central theme of the book of Leviticus.

9 "'When you reap the harvest of your land, do not reap to the very edges of your field or gather the gleanings of your harvest. 10 Do not go over your vineyard a second time or pick up the grapes that have fallen. Leave them for the poor and the foreigner. I am the LORD your God.

11 "'Do not steal.

"'Do not lie.

"'Do not deceive one another.

12 "'Do not swear falsely by my name and so profane the name of your God. I am the LORD.

13 "'Do not defraud or rob your neighbor.

"'Do not hold back the wages of a hired worker overnight.

14 "'Do not curse the deaf or put a stumbling block in front of the blind, but fear your God. I am the LORD.

15 "'Do not pervert justice; do not show partiality to the poor or favoritism to the great, but judge your neighbor fairly.

16 "'Do not go about spreading slander among your people.

"'Do not do anything that endangers your neighbor's life. I am the LORD.

17 "'Do not hate a fellow Israelite in your heart. Rebuke your neighbor frankly so you will not share in their guilt.

18 "'Do not seek revenge or bear a grudge against anyone among your people, but love your neighbor as yourself. I am the LORD.

19 "'Keep my decrees.

"'Do not mate different kinds of animals.

"'Do not plant your field with two kinds of seed.

"'Do not wear clothing woven of two kinds of material.

20 "'If a man sleeps with a female slave who is promised to another man but who has not been ransomed or given her freedom, there must be due punishment.[a] Yet they are not to be put to death, because she had not been freed. 21 The man, however, must bring a ram to the entrance to the tent of meeting for a guilt offering to the LORD. 22 With the ram of the guilt offering the priest is to make atonement for him before the LORD for the sin he has committed, and his sin will be forgiven.

23 "'When you enter the land and plant any kind of fruit tree, regard its fruit as forbidden.[b] For three years you are to consider it forbidden[b]; it must not be eaten. 24 In the fourth year all its fruit will be holy, an offering of praise to the LORD. 25 But in the fifth year you may eat its fruit. In this way your harvest will be increased. I am the LORD your God.

26 "'Do not eat any meat with the blood still in it.

"'Do not practice divination or seek omens.

27 "'Do not cut the hair at the sides of your head or clip off the edges of your beard.

28 "'Do not cut your bodies for the dead or put tattoo marks on yourselves. I am the LORD.

29 "'Do not degrade your daughter by making her a prostitute, or the land will turn to prostitution and be filled with wickedness.

30 "'Observe my Sabbaths and have reverence for my sanctuary. I am the LORD.

[a] 20 Or be an inquiry   [b] 23 Hebrew uncircumcised

Why were workers supposed to be paid every day? (19:13)
This rule was probably for the benefit of the poor, who needed money each day in order to survive.

Why is the phrase, "I am the LORD" repeated so many times in these chapters? (19:16)
The phrase is repeated so many times in order to show how these rules are legitimate. These rules did not originate from a human's mind or stem from pagan religion; God stood behind them.

Why were there laws about hairstyles and tattoos? (19:27 – 28)
The rules were meant to keep the Israelites from copying rituals performed by pagans. Some pagan people would apply tattoos, cut themselves, or cut their beards. If the Israelites were to do these things, it would show respect for the pagan gods and disrespect for God.

³¹"'Do not turn to mediums or seek out spiritists, for you will be defiled by them. I am the Lᴏʀᴅ your God.

³²"'Stand up in the presence of the aged, show respect for the elderly and revere your God. I am the Lᴏʀᴅ.

³³"'When a foreigner resides among you in your land, do not mistreat them. ³⁴The foreigner residing among you must be treated as your native-born. Love them as yourself, for you were foreigners in Egypt. I am the Lᴏʀᴅ your God.

³⁵"'Do not use dishonest standards when measuring length, weight or quantity. ³⁶Use honest scales and honest weights, an honest ephah*ᵃ* and an honest hin.*ᵇ* I am the Lᴏʀᴅ your God, who brought you out of Egypt.

³⁷"'Keep all my decrees and all my laws and follow them. I am the Lᴏʀᴅ.'"

PUNISHMENTS FOR SIN

20 The Lᴏʀᴅ said to Moses, ²"Say to the Israelites: 'Any Israelite or any foreigner residing in Israel who sacrifices any of his children to Molek is to be put to death. The members of the community are to stone him. ³I myself will set my face against him and will cut him off from his people; for by sacrificing his children to Molek, he has defiled my sanctuary and profaned my holy name. ⁴If the members of the community close their eyes when that man sacrifices one of his children to Molek and if they fail to put him to death, ⁵I myself will set my face against him and his family and will cut them off from their people together with all who follow him in prostituting themselves to Molek.

⁶"'I will set my face against anyone who turns to mediums and spiritists to prostitute themselves by following them, and I will cut them off from their people.

⁷"'Consecrate yourselves and be holy, because I am the Lᴏʀᴅ your God. ⁸Keep my decrees and follow them. I am the Lᴏʀᴅ, who makes you holy.

⁹"'Anyone who curses their father or mother is to be put to death. Because they have cursed their father or mother, their blood will be on their own head.

¹⁰"'If a man commits adultery with another man's wife— with the wife of his neighbor—both the adulterer and the adulteress are to be put to death.

¹¹"'If a man has sexual relations with his father's wife, he has dishonored his father. Both the man and the woman are to be put to death; their blood will be on their own heads.

¹²"'If a man has sexual relations with his daughter-in-law, both of them are to be put to death. What they have done is a perversion; their blood will be on their own heads.

¹³"'If a man has sexual relations with a man as one does with a woman, both of them have done what is detestable. They are to be put to death; their blood will be on their own heads.

¹⁴"'If a man marries both a woman and her mother, it is wicked. Both he and they must be burned in the fire, so that no wickedness will be among you.

ᵃ 36 An ephah was a dry measure having the capacity of about 3/5 of a bushel or about 22 liters.   *ᵇ 36* A hin was a liquid measure having the capacity of about 1 gallon or about 3.8 liters.

What were an ephah and a hin? (19:36)
An ephah was a dry measure of approximately 3/5 of a bushel (22 liters). A hin was a liquid measure of approximately one gallon.

What did it mean for God to set his face against someone? (20:5)
This is an intimidating picture of God deciding to bring judgment on someone.

What is a *medium*? (20:6)
A medium is a person who claims to have the ability to communicate with the spiritual world. They are different from priests or prophets who gain their wisdom from God. Mediums do not have God's guidance. God told his people that consulting with a medium is a sin. They should turn to God for help, not anyone else.

Why was the punishment for cursing a parent so extreme? (20:9)
Cursing a parent went beyond saying bad words. It showed hatred for parents, which went against God's commandment to honor parents.

Why was sorcery wrong? (20:6, 27)
Trusting in sorcery and witchcraft was a problem because these things teach that there is something more powerful than God—which there isn't. God is the only all-powerful being who has the power to change the future. Followers of God should place their trust in him to guide the course of the future.

¹⁵ "'If a man has sexual relations with an animal, he is to be put to death, and you must kill the animal.

¹⁶ "'If a woman approaches an animal to have sexual relations with it, kill both the woman and the animal. They are to be put to death; their blood will be on their own heads.

¹⁷ "'If a man marries his sister, the daughter of either his father or his mother, and they have sexual relations, it is a disgrace. They are to be publicly removed from their people. He has dishonored his sister and will be held responsible.

¹⁸ "'If a man has sexual relations with a woman during her monthly period, he has exposed the source of her flow, and she has also uncovered it. Both of them are to be cut off from their people.

¹⁹ "'Do not have sexual relations with the sister of either your mother or your father, for that would dishonor a close relative; both of you would be held responsible.

²⁰ "'If a man has sexual relations with his aunt, he has dishonored his uncle. They will be held responsible; they will die childless.

²¹ "'If a man marries his brother's wife, it is an act of impurity; he has dishonored his brother. They will be childless.

²² "'Keep all my decrees and laws and follow them, so that the land where I am bringing you to live may not vomit you out. ²³ You must not live according to the customs of the nations I am going to drive out before you. Because they did all these things, I abhorred them. ²⁴ But I said to you, "You will possess their land; I will give it to you as an inheritance, a land flowing with milk and honey." I am the LORD your God, who has set you apart from the nations.

²⁵ "'You must therefore make a distinction between clean and unclean animals and between unclean and clean birds. Do not defile yourselves by any animal or bird or anything that moves along the ground—those that I have set apart as unclean for you. ²⁶ You are to be holy to me because I, the LORD, am holy, and I have set you apart from the nations to be my own.

²⁷ "'A man or woman who is a medium or spiritist among you must be put to death. You are to stone them; their blood will be on their own heads.'"

RULES FOR PRIESTS

21 The LORD said to Moses, "Speak to the priests, the sons of Aaron, and say to them: 'A priest must not make himself ceremonially unclean for any of his people who die, ² except for a close relative, such as his mother or father, his son or daughter, his brother, ³ or an unmarried sister who is dependent on him since she has no husband—for her he may make himself unclean. ⁴ He must not make himself unclean for people related to him by marriage,^a and so defile himself.

⁵ "'Priests must not shave their heads or shave off the edges of their beards or cut their bodies. ⁶ They must be holy to their God and must not profane the name of their God. Because they present the food offerings to the LORD, the food of their God, they are to be holy.

^a 4 Or *unclean as a leader among his people*

Is it always wrong for a man to marry his brother's wife? (20:21)
This law states that a man cannot marry his brother's wife while the brother is still living. But if a man died and the widow was childless, the brother was supposed to marry the widow.

Why was shaving unholy? (21:5–6)
Canaanites who worshiped other gods often shaved to express their sadness when someone died. God wanted his people to avoid all pagan practices in order to remain holy, set apart for him.

What was the food of God? (21:6, 8)
Unlike pagans who fed their gods, the Israelites knew God does not need actual food and water. This is a metaphor for offerings that the people could easily understand.

⁷"'They must not marry women defiled by prostitution or divorced from their husbands, because priests are holy to their God. ⁸Regard them as holy, because they offer up the food of your God. Consider them holy, because I the Lord am holy—I who make you holy.

⁹"'If a priest's daughter defiles herself by becoming a prostitute, she disgraces her father; she must be burned in the fire.

¹⁰"'The high priest, the one among his brothers who has had the anointing oil poured on his head and who has been ordained to wear the priestly garments, must not let his hair become unkempt*a* or tear his clothes. ¹¹He must not enter a place where there is a dead body. He must not make himself unclean, even for his father or mother, ¹²nor leave the sanctuary of his God or desecrate it, because he has been dedicated by the anointing oil of his God. I am the Lord.

¹³"'The woman he marries must be a virgin. ¹⁴He must not marry a widow, a divorced woman, or a woman defiled by prostitution, but only a virgin from his own people, ¹⁵so that he will not defile his offspring among his people. I am the Lord, who makes him holy.'"

¹⁶The Lord said to Moses, ¹⁷"Say to Aaron: 'For the generations to come none of your descendants who has a defect may come near to offer the food of his God. ¹⁸No man who has any defect may come near: no man who is blind or lame, disfigured or deformed; ¹⁹no man with a crippled foot or hand, ²⁰or who is a hunchback or a dwarf, or who has any eye defect, or who has festering or running sores or damaged testicles. ²¹No descendant of Aaron the priest who has any defect is to come near to present the food offerings to the Lord. He has a defect; he must not come near to offer the food of his God. ²²He may eat the most holy food of his God, as well as the holy food; ²³yet because of his defect, he must not go near the curtain or approach the altar, and so desecrate my sanctuary. I am the Lord, who makes them holy.'"

²⁴So Moses told this to Aaron and his sons and to all the Israelites.

22 The Lord said to Moses, ²"Tell Aaron and his sons to treat with respect the sacred offerings the Israelites consecrate to me, so they will not profane my holy name. I am the Lord.

³"Say to them: 'For the generations to come, if any of your descendants is ceremonially unclean and yet comes near the sacred offerings that the Israelites consecrate to the Lord, that person must be cut off from my presence. I am the Lord.

⁴"'If a descendant of Aaron has a defiling skin disease*b* or a bodily discharge, he may not eat the sacred offerings until he is cleansed. He will also be unclean if he touches something defiled by a corpse or by anyone who has an emission of semen, ⁵or if he touches any crawling thing that makes him unclean, or any person who makes him unclean, whatever the uncleanness may be. ⁶The one who touches any such

---

a 10 Or *not uncover his head*   *b 4* The Hebrew word for *defiling skin disease,* traditionally translated "leprosy," was used for various diseases affecting the skin.

thing will be unclean till evening. He must not eat any of the sacred offerings unless he has bathed himself with water. [7] When the sun goes down, he will be clean, and after that he may eat the sacred offerings, for they are his food. [8] He must not eat anything found dead or torn by wild animals, and so become unclean through it. I am the LORD.

[9] "'The priests are to perform my service in such a way that they do not become guilty and die for treating it with contempt. I am the LORD, who makes them holy.

[10] "'No one outside a priest's family may eat the sacred offering, nor may the guest of a priest or his hired worker eat it. [11] But if a priest buys a slave with money, or if slaves are born in his household, they may eat his food. [12] If a priest's daughter marries anyone other than a priest, she may not eat any of the sacred contributions. [13] But if a priest's daughter becomes a widow or is divorced, yet has no children, and she returns to live in her father's household as in her youth, she may eat her father's food. No unauthorized person, however, may eat it.

[14] "'Anyone who eats a sacred offering by mistake must make restitution to the priest for the offering and add a fifth of the value to it. [15] The priests must not desecrate the sacred offerings the Israelites present to the LORD [16] by allowing them to eat the sacred offerings and so bring upon them guilt requiring payment. I am the LORD, who makes them holy.'"

UNACCEPTABLE SACRIFICES

[17] The LORD said to Moses, [18] "Speak to Aaron and his sons and to all the Israelites and say to them: 'If any of you—whether an Israelite or a foreigner residing in Israel—presents a gift for a burnt offering to the LORD, either to fulfill a vow or as a freewill offering, [19] you must present a male without defect from the cattle, sheep or goats in order that it may be accepted on your behalf. [20] Do not bring anything with a defect, because it will not be accepted on your behalf. [21] When anyone brings from the herd or flock a fellowship offering to the LORD to fulfill a special vow or as a freewill offering, it must be without defect or blemish to be acceptable. [22] Do not offer to the LORD the blind, the injured or the maimed, or anything with warts or festering or running sores. Do not place any of these on the altar as a food offering presented to the LORD. [23] You may, however, present as a freewill offering an ox[a] or a sheep that is deformed or stunted, but it will not be accepted in fulfillment of a vow. [24] You must not offer to the LORD an animal whose testicles are bruised, crushed, torn or cut. You must not do this in your own land, [25] and you must not accept such animals from the hand of a foreigner and offer them as the food of your God. They will not be accepted on your behalf, because they are deformed and have defects.'"

[26] The LORD said to Moses, [27] "When a calf, a lamb or a goat is born, it is to remain with its mother for seven days. From the eighth day on, it will be acceptable as a food offering presented to the LORD. [28] Do not slaughter a cow or a sheep and its young on the same day.

[a] 23 The Hebrew word can refer to either male or female.

Why did God make so many requirements for the priests with such severe penalties? (22:9)
The penalties were more severe for priests because they had greater responsibility to the community. They were to set an example for the others to follow. Harsh punishments would help the priests understand the seriousness of their position.

What was the difference between a freewill offering and a vow? (22:23)
Unlike a vow that was based on a preexisting promise or agreement, a freewill offering was voluntary, so there were fewer rules about it.

Why did an animal have to be at least eight days old before it could be sacrificed? (22:27)
Rather than an act of compassion for the baby animal, this law was meant to ensure the value of the sacrifice. Killing an animal at birth did not symbolize the sacrifice of a life because birth and death were too close together.

²⁹"When you sacrifice a thank offering to the LORD, sacrifice it in such a way that it will be accepted on your behalf. ³⁰It must be eaten that same day; leave none of it till morning. I am the LORD.

³¹"Keep my commands and follow them. I am the LORD. ³²Do not profane my holy name, for I must be acknowledged as holy by the Israelites. I am the LORD, who made you holy ³³and who brought you out of Egypt to be your God. I am the LORD."

THE APPOINTED FESTIVALS

23 The LORD said to Moses, ²"Speak to the Israelites and say to them: 'These are my appointed festivals, the appointed festivals of the LORD, which you are to proclaim as sacred assemblies.

THE SABBATH

³"'There are six days when you may work, but the seventh day is a day of sabbath rest, a day of sacred assembly. You are not to do any work; wherever you live, it is a sabbath to the LORD.

THE PASSOVER AND THE FESTIVAL OF UNLEAVENED BREAD

⁴"'These are the LORD's appointed festivals, the sacred assemblies you are to proclaim at their appointed times: ⁵The LORD's Passover begins at twilight on the fourteenth day of the first month. ⁶On the fifteenth day of that month the LORD's Festival of Unleavened Bread begins; for seven days you must eat bread made without yeast. ⁷On the first day hold a sacred assembly and do no regular work. ⁸For seven days present a food offering to the LORD. And on the seventh day hold a sacred assembly and do no regular work.'"

OFFERING THE FIRSTFRUITS

⁹The LORD said to Moses, ¹⁰"Speak to the Israelites and say to them: 'When you enter the land I am going to give you and you reap its harvest, bring to the priest a sheaf of the first grain you harvest. ¹¹He is to wave the sheaf before the LORD so it will be accepted on your behalf; the priest is to wave it on the day after the Sabbath. ¹²On the day you wave the sheaf, you must sacrifice as a burnt offering to the LORD a lamb a year old without defect, ¹³together with its grain offering of two-tenths of an ephah[a] of the finest flour mixed with olive oil—a food offering presented to the LORD, a pleasing aroma—and its drink offering of a quarter of a hin[b] of wine. ¹⁴You must not eat any bread, or roasted or new grain, until the very day you bring this offering to your God. This is to be a lasting ordinance for the generations to come, wherever you live.

THE FESTIVAL OF WEEKS

¹⁵"'From the day after the Sabbath, the day you brought the sheaf of the wave offering, count off seven full weeks.

Why were there so many festivals and feasts? (23:1–44)
The feasts brought people together in joyful celebration. The feasts ensured that the practice was communal rather than private and joyful rather than an obligation. The traditions of the feasts lasted for generations, tying the past to the present and giving hope to the future.

Why was the Sabbath the first on the list of festivals? (23:3)
The weekly Sabbath was celebrated by families and other small groups of people who gathered to worship the Lord. The pattern of Sabbath rest and worship was established by God on the seventh day of creation.

Why did the Israelites have to present the first grain harvested to the Lord? (23:9–10)
This offering showed that all the products of the land came from God and demonstrated thankfulness for his goodness.

What were drink offerings? (23:13)
Wine could be offered along with a grain offering, accompanying burnt offerings. Drink offerings amounted to a quarter of a hin (about 1 quart or 1 liter) of wine.

---

a 13 That is, probably about 7 pounds or about 3.2 kilograms; also in verse 17
b 13 That is, about 1 quart or about 1 liter

OLD TESTAMENT FESTIVALS AND OTHER SACRED DAYS

NAME	OT REFERENCES	TIME	DESCRIPTION	NT REFERENCES
Sabbath	Ex 20:8–11; 31:12–17; Lev 23:3; Dt 5:12–15	7th day	Day of rest; no work	Mt 12:1–14; Mk 2:23—3:5; Lk 4:16–30; 6:1–10; 13:10–16; 14:1–5; Jn 5:1–15; 9:1–34; Ac 13:14–48; 17:2; 18:4; Heb 4:1–11
Sabbath Year	Ex 23:10–11; Lev 25:1–7	7th year	Year of rest; fallow fields	
Year of Jubilee	Lev 25:8–55; 27:17–24; Nu 36:4	50th year	Canceled debts; liberation of slaves and indentured servants; land returned to original family owners	
Passover	Ex 12:1–14; Lev 23:5; Nu 9:1–14; 28:16; Dt 16:1–7	1st month (Abib) 14	Slaying and eating a lamb, together with bitter herbs and bread made without yeast in every household	Mt 26:1–2,17–29; Mk 14:12–26; Lk 22:7–38; Jn 2:13–25; 11:55–56; 13:1–30; 1Co 5:7
Unleavened Bread	Ex 12:15–20; 13:3–10; 23:15; Lev 23:6–8; Nu 28:17–25; Dt 16:3–4,8	1st month (Abib) 15–21	Eating bread made without yeast; holding several assemblies; making designated offerings	Mt 26:17; Mk 14:1,12; Lk 22:1,7; Ac 12:3; 20:6; 1Co 5:6–8
Firstfruits	Leviticus 23:9–14	1st month (Abib) 16	Presenting a sheaf of the first of the barley harvest as a wave offering; making a burnt offering and a grain offering	Ro 8:23; 1Co 15:20–23
Weeks (Pentecost) (Harvest)	Ex 23:16a; 34:22a; Lev 23:15–21; Nu 28:26–31; Dt 16:9–12	3rd month (Sivan) 6	A festival of joy; mandatory and voluntary offerings, including the firstfruits of the wheat harvest	Ac 2:1–41; 20:16; 1Co 16:8
Trumpets (Later: Rosh Hashanah— New Year's Day)	Lev 23:23–25; Nu 29:1–6	7th month (Tishri) 1	An assembly on a day of rest commemorated with trumpet blasts and sacrifices	
Day of Atonement (Yom Kippur)	Lev 16:1–34; 23:26–32; Nu 29:7–11	7th month (Tishri) 10	A day of rest, fasting and sacrifices of atonement for priests and people and atonement for the tabernacle and altar	Ac 27:9; Ro 3:24–26; Heb 9:1–14,23–26; 10:19–22
Tabernacles (Booths) (Ingathering)	Ex 23:16b; 34:22b; Lev 23:33–36;39–43; Nu 29:12–34; Dt 16:13–15	7th month (Tishri) 15–21	A week of celebration for the harvest; living in booths and offering sacrifices	Jn 7:2–37
Sacred Assembly	Lev 23:36; Nu 29:35–38	7th month (Tishri) 22	A day of convocation, rest and offering sacrifices	Jn 7:37–44
Dedication		9th month (Tebeth)	A commemoration of the purification of the temple in the Maccabean era (166–160 BC)	Jn 10:22–39
Purim	Est 9:18–32	12th month (Adar) 14,15	A day of joy and feasting and giving presents	

¹⁶Count off fifty days up to the day after the seventh Sabbath, and then present an offering of new grain to the LORD. ¹⁷From wherever you live, bring two loaves made of two-tenths of an ephah of the finest flour, baked with yeast, as a wave offering of firstfruits to the LORD. ¹⁸Present with this bread seven male lambs, each a year old and without defect, one young bull and two rams. They will be a burnt offering to the LORD, together with their grain offerings and drink offerings—a food offering, an aroma pleasing to the LORD. ¹⁹Then sacrifice one male goat for a sin offering*ᵃ* and two lambs, each a year old, for a fellowship offering. ²⁰The priest is to wave the two lambs before the LORD as a wave offering, together with the bread of the firstfruits. They are a sacred offering to the LORD for the priest. ²¹On that same day you are to proclaim a sacred assembly and do no regular work. This is to be a lasting ordinance for the generations to come, wherever you live.

²²"'When you reap the harvest of your land, do not reap to the very edges of your field or gather the gleanings of your harvest. Leave them for the poor and for the foreigner residing among you. I am the LORD your God.'"

THE FESTIVAL OF TRUMPETS

²³The LORD said to Moses, ²⁴"Say to the Israelites: 'On the first day of the seventh month you are to have a day of sabbath rest, a sacred assembly commemorated with trumpet blasts. ²⁵Do no regular work, but present a food offering to the LORD.'"

THE DAY OF ATONEMENT

²⁶The LORD said to Moses, ²⁷"The tenth day of this seventh month is the Day of Atonement. Hold a sacred assembly and deny yourselves,*ᵇ* and present a food offering to the LORD. ²⁸Do not do any work on that day, because it is the Day of Atonement, when atonement is made for you before the LORD your God. ²⁹Those who do not deny themselves on that day must be cut off from their people. ³⁰I will destroy from among their people anyone who does any work on that day. ³¹You shall do no work at all. This is to be a lasting ordinance for the generations to come, wherever you live. ³²It is a day of sabbath rest for you, and you must deny yourselves. From the evening of the ninth day of the month until the following evening you are to observe your sabbath."

THE FESTIVAL OF TABERNACLES

³³The LORD said to Moses, ³⁴"Say to the Israelites: 'On the fifteenth day of the seventh month the LORD's Festival of Tabernacles begins, and it lasts for seven days. ³⁵The first day is a sacred assembly; do no regular work. ³⁶For seven days present food offerings to the LORD, and on the eighth day hold a sacred assembly and present a food offering to the LORD. It is the closing special assembly; do no regular work.

³⁷("'These are the LORD's appointed festivals, which you are to proclaim as sacred assemblies for bringing food offerings to the LORD—the burnt offerings and grain offerings,

---

ᵃ 19 Or *purification offering*   *ᵇ 27* Or *and fast*; similarly in verses 29 and 32

sacrifices and drink offerings required for each day. [38]These offerings are in addition to those for the LORD's Sabbaths and[a] in addition to your gifts and whatever you have vowed and all the freewill offerings you give to the LORD.)

[39]"'So beginning with the fifteenth day of the seventh month, after you have gathered the crops of the land, celebrate the festival to the LORD for seven days; the first day is a day of sabbath rest, and the eighth day also is a day of sabbath rest. [40]On the first day you are to take branches from luxuriant trees—from palms, willows and other leafy trees—and rejoice before the LORD your God for seven days. [41]Celebrate this as a festival to the LORD for seven days each year. This is to be a lasting ordinance for the generations to come; celebrate it in the seventh month. [42]Live in temporary shelters for seven days: All native-born Israelites are to live in such shelters [43]so your descendants will know that I had the Israelites live in temporary shelters when I brought them out of Egypt. I am the LORD your God.'"

[44]So Moses announced to the Israelites the appointed festivals of the LORD.

OLIVE OIL AND BREAD SET BEFORE THE LORD

24 The LORD said to Moses, [2]"Command the Israelites to bring you clear oil of pressed olives for the light so that the lamps may be kept burning continually. [3]Outside the curtain that shields the ark of the covenant law in the tent of meeting, Aaron is to tend the lamps before the LORD from evening till morning, continually. This is to be a lasting ordinance for the generations to come. [4]The lamps on the pure gold lampstand before the LORD must be tended continually.

[5]"Take the finest flour and bake twelve loaves of bread, using two-tenths of an ephah[b] for each loaf. [6]Arrange them in two stacks, six in each stack, on the table of pure gold before the LORD. [7]By each stack put some pure incense as a memorial[c] portion to represent the bread and to be a food offering presented to the LORD. [8]This bread is to be set out before the LORD regularly, Sabbath after Sabbath, on behalf of the Israelites, as a lasting covenant. [9]It belongs to Aaron and his sons, who are to eat it in the sanctuary area, because it is a most holy part of their perpetual share of the food offerings presented to the LORD."

A BLASPHEMER PUT TO DEATH

[10]Now the son of an Israelite mother and an Egyptian father went out among the Israelites, and a fight broke out in the camp between him and an Israelite. [11]The son of the Israelite woman blasphemed the Name with a curse; so they brought him to Moses. (His mother's name was Shelomith, the daughter of Dibri the Danite.) [12]They put him in custody until the will of the LORD should be made clear to them.

[13]Then the LORD said to Moses: [14]"Take the blasphemer

Did Aaron have to spend all night at the tabernacle? (24:3)
Aaron had to make sure the special gold lamps in the tent of meeting would burn throughout the night. He didn't have to stay there all night, but he had to make sure they stayed lit.

---

[a] 38 Or *These festivals are in addition to the LORD's Sabbaths, and these offerings are*   [b] 5 That is, probably about 7 pounds or about 3.2 kilograms
[c] 7 Or *representative*

outside the camp. All those who heard him are to lay their hands on his head, and the entire assembly is to stone him. [15] Say to the Israelites: 'Anyone who curses their God will be held responsible; [16] anyone who blasphemes the name of the LORD is to be put to death. The entire assembly must stone them. Whether foreigner or native-born, when they blaspheme the Name they are to be put to death.

[17] "'Anyone who takes the life of a human being is to be put to death. [18] Anyone who takes the life of someone's animal must make restitution — life for life. [19] Anyone who injures their neighbor is to be injured in the same manner: [20] fracture for fracture, eye for eye, tooth for tooth. The one who has inflicted the injury must suffer the same injury. [21] Whoever kills an animal must make restitution, but whoever kills a human being is to be put to death. [22] You are to have the same law for the foreigner and the native-born. I am the LORD your God.'"

[23] Then Moses spoke to the Israelites, and they took the blasphemer outside the camp and stoned him. The Israelites did as the LORD commanded Moses.

THE SABBATH YEAR

25 The LORD said to Moses at Mount Sinai, [2] "Speak to the Israelites and say to them: 'When you enter the land I am going to give you, the land itself must observe a sabbath to the LORD. [3] For six years sow your fields, and for six years prune your vineyards and gather their crops. [4] But in the seventh year the land is to have a year of sabbath rest, a sabbath to the LORD. Do not sow your fields or prune your vineyards. [5] Do not reap what grows of itself or harvest the grapes of your untended vines. The land is to have a year of rest. [6] Whatever the land yields during the sabbath year will be food for you — for yourself, your male and female servants, and the hired worker and temporary resident who live among you, [7] as well as for your livestock and the wild animals in your land. Whatever the land produces may be eaten.

THE YEAR OF JUBILEE

[8] "'Count off seven sabbath years — seven times seven years — so that the seven sabbath years amount to a period of forty-nine years. [9] Then have the trumpet sounded everywhere on the tenth day of the seventh month; on the Day of Atonement sound the trumpet throughout your land.

What did the principle of "eye for eye, tooth for tooth" mean? (24:20)
The principle was that the penalty should fit the crime but not exceed it. The same principle was outlined in Exodus 21:23 – 25.

If they didn't plant crops, what would they eat during the Sabbath year? (25:4 – 7, 21)
Every seventh year the Israelites were to give the land a "sabbath rest" when everyone would live off the land, eating the crops that sprouted on their own, taking just enough to live on. God also promised to bless their harvest during the sixth year so there would be enough left over to see them through.

Is it really so bad to swear?

Swearing can refer to taking an oath, but it can also refer to using God's name in a wrong way by cursing. God is holy, and he expects us to honor him. When we misuse his name as a way of expressing anger or frustration, or if we ask God to curse someone with whom we are angry, we are dishonoring God. In ancient times, God's people were so careful to respect God's name that they did not speak it aloud or write it out completely. Today, people often swear very casually. One of the most common misuses of God's name is the expression "Oh, my God." Most of the time when people say this, they are simply expressing surprise or excitement rather than giving thanks to the Creator of the universe.

Using God's name incorrectly or without respect is offensive to God, and it harms our Christian witness. Believers should always remember to honor God's name as holy.

What was the Jubilee? (25:10)
In Israel every 50th year was a Year of Jubilee. It was a special year that God set aside for the Israelites so that slaves could be freed, debts could be canceled, and all people could return to their home property. The rules that God made for this year kept the people from taking advantage of one another and kept every family's land in their family.

Why did the Year of Jubilee affect the value of the land? (25:15–16)
The value of the land was greatest when there were many years of harvesting before Jubilee. All land that had been purchased was returned to the original owners in the Year of Jubilee. Land sales were temporary, similar to leasing or renting the property. This helped people remember that God was the real landowner.

What does redemption of the land mean? (25:24)
It was the right of the original landowner to repurchase the land he had sold in order to keep it in the family. A relative of the original landowner had the right to buy back the land, or the landowner himself could buy it back, basing the purchase price on the value of the crops until the Year of Jubilee. Otherwise, the land would return to the original family without cost during the Year of Jubilee.

Who were foreigners and temporary residents? (25:35)
A foreigner was someone living in Israel who was not an Israelite. A temporary resident could be either an Israelite or a foreigner, but they did not own property. Both groups of people were typically very poor and had to work off debts. God made rules so the Israelites would treat them fairly.

Why was it wrong to charge interest? (25:36–37)
This law shows God's concern for the poor. Paying interest on

10 Consecrate the fiftieth year and proclaim liberty throughout the land to all its inhabitants. It shall be a jubilee for you; each of you is to return to your family property and to your own clan. 11 The fiftieth year shall be a jubilee for you; do not sow and do not reap what grows of itself or harvest the untended vines. 12 For it is a jubilee and is to be holy for you; eat only what is taken directly from the fields.

13 "In this Year of Jubilee everyone is to return to their own property.

14 "If you sell land to any of your own people or buy land from them, do not take advantage of each other. 15 You are to buy from your own people on the basis of the number of years since the Jubilee. And they are to sell to you on the basis of the number of years left for harvesting crops. 16 When the years are many, you are to increase the price, and when the years are few, you are to decrease the price, because what is really being sold to you is the number of crops. 17 Do not take advantage of each other, but fear your God. I am the LORD your God.

18 "Follow my decrees and be careful to obey my laws, and you will live safely in the land. 19 Then the land will yield its fruit, and you will eat your fill and live there in safety. 20 You may ask, "What will we eat in the seventh year if we do not plant or harvest our crops?" 21 I will send you such a blessing in the sixth year that the land will yield enough for three years. 22 While you plant during the eighth year, you will eat from the old crop and will continue to eat from it until the harvest of the ninth year comes in.

23 "The land must not be sold permanently, because the land is mine and you reside in my land as foreigners and strangers. 24 Throughout the land that you hold as a possession, you must provide for the redemption of the land.

25 "If one of your fellow Israelites becomes poor and sells some of their property, their nearest relative is to come and redeem what they have sold. 26 If, however, there is no one to redeem it for them but later on they prosper and acquire sufficient means to redeem it themselves, 27 they are to determine the value for the years since they sold it and refund the balance to the one to whom they sold it; they can then go back to their own property. 28 But if they do not acquire the means to repay, what was sold will remain in the possession of the buyer until the Year of Jubilee. It will be returned in the Jubilee, and they can then go back to their property.

29 "Anyone who sells a house in a walled city retains the right of redemption a full year after its sale. During that time the seller may redeem it. 30 If it is not redeemed before a full year has passed, the house in the walled city shall belong permanently to the buyer and the buyer's descendants. It is not to be returned in the Jubilee. 31 But houses in villages without walls around them are to be considered as belonging to the open country. They can be redeemed, and they are to be returned in the Jubilee.

32 "The Levites always have the right to redeem their houses in the Levitical towns, which they possess. 33 So the property of the Levites is redeemable—that is, a house sold

in any town they hold—and is to be returned in the Jubilee, because the houses in the towns of the Levites are their property among the Israelites. ³⁴But the pastureland belonging to their towns must not be sold; it is their permanent possession.

³⁵"If any of your fellow Israelites become poor and are unable to support themselves among you, help them as you would a foreigner and stranger, so they can continue to live among you. ³⁶Do not take interest or any profit from them, but fear your God, so that they may continue to live among you. ³⁷You must not lend them money at interest or sell them food at a profit. ³⁸I am the LORD your God, who brought you out of Egypt to give you the land of Canaan and to be your God.

³⁹"If any of your fellow Israelites become poor and sell themselves to you, do not make them work as slaves. ⁴⁰They are to be treated as hired workers or temporary residents among you; they are to work for you until the Year of Jubilee. ⁴¹Then they and their children are to be released, and they will go back to their own clans and to the property of their ancestors. ⁴²Because the Israelites are my servants, whom I brought out of Egypt, they must not be sold as slaves. ⁴³Do not rule over them ruthlessly, but fear your God.

⁴⁴"Your male and female slaves are to come from the nations around you; from them you may buy slaves. ⁴⁵You may also buy some of the temporary residents living among you and members of their clans born in your country, and they will become your property. ⁴⁶You can bequeath them to your children as inherited property and can make them slaves for life, but you must not rule over your fellow Israelites ruthlessly.

⁴⁷"If a foreigner residing among you becomes rich and any of your fellow Israelites become poor and sell themselves to the foreigner or to a member of the foreigner's clan, ⁴⁸they retain the right of redemption after they have sold themselves. One of their relatives may redeem them: ⁴⁹An uncle or a cousin or any blood relative in their clan may redeem them. Or if they prosper, they may redeem themselves. ⁵⁰They and their buyer are to count the time from the year they sold themselves up to the Year of Jubilee. The price for their release is to be based on the rate paid to a hired worker for that number of years. ⁵¹If many years remain, they must pay for their redemption a larger share of the price paid for them. ⁵²If only a few years remain until the Year of Jubilee, they are to compute that and pay for their redemption accordingly. ⁵³They are to be treated as workers hired from year to year; you must see to it that those to whom they owe service do not rule over them ruthlessly.

⁵⁴"Even if someone is not redeemed in any of these ways, they and their children are to be released in the Year of Jubilee, ⁵⁵for the Israelites belong to me as servants. They are my servants, whom I brought out of Egypt. I am the LORD your God.

REWARD FOR OBEDIENCE

26 "Do not make idols or set up an image or a sacred stone for yourselves, and do not place a carved stone in your land to bow down before it. I am the LORD your God.

borrowed money or food would have been really hard for the poor who were barely able to afford the necessities.

Why didn't God allow the Israelites to become slaves? (25:39)
God wanted his people to be treated as temporary residents or as hired workers, not slaves. God brought the Israelites out of the land of Egypt where they had been slaves. He saved them from slavery.

Why did God permit slavery of the Canaanites? (25:44–46)
God would not allow his own people to be ruled over as slaves, but he permitted slaves to be bought from the pagan nations around them. God modified the custom of slavery of that time rather than eliminating it. His laws greatly improved the lives of slaves by setting up restrictions the Israelites were to follow.

How could slaves be freed? (25:47–49)
Sometimes poor people sold themselves into slavery when they couldn't pay money they owed. To free a slave, a relative paid money to the slave's owner. The price of redemption was decided by how many years remained until the Year of Jubilee. During the Year of Jubilee, regardless of any debt the slave still owed, the slave owner set all slaves free. Christians use the same language of redemption: "We used to be 'slaves' to sin, and Jesus redeemed us when he died on the cross."

Why were the Israelites not allowed to create idols? (26:1)
God forbid idol worship because God is the only one we are to worship. Even if the idol is made in God's image or is used to represent God, it would be tempting to worship the idol and not God.

2 "'Observe my Sabbaths and have reverence for my sanctuary. I am the LORD.

3 "'If you follow my decrees and are careful to obey my commands, 4 I will send you rain in its season, and the ground will yield its crops and the trees their fruit. 5 Your threshing will continue until grape harvest and the grape harvest will continue until planting, and you will eat all the food you want and live in safety in your land.

6 "'I will grant peace in the land, and you will lie down and no one will make you afraid. I will remove wild beasts from the land, and the sword will not pass through your country. 7 You will pursue your enemies, and they will fall by the sword before you. 8 Five of you will chase a hundred, and a hundred of you will chase ten thousand, and your enemies will fall by the sword before you.

9 "'I will look on you with favor and make you fruitful and increase your numbers, and I will keep my covenant with you. 10 You will still be eating last year's harvest when you will have to move it out to make room for the new. 11 I will put my dwelling place*a* among you, and I will not abhor you. 12 I will walk among you and be your God, and you will be my people. 13 I am the LORD your God, who brought you out of Egypt so that you would no longer be slaves to the Egyptians; I broke the bars of your yoke and enabled you to walk with heads held high.

PUNISHMENT FOR DISOBEDIENCE

14 "'But if you will not listen to me and carry out all these commands, 15 and if you reject my decrees and abhor my laws and fail to carry out all my commands and so violate my covenant, 16 then I will do this to you: I will bring on you sudden terror, wasting diseases and fever that will destroy your sight and sap your strength. You will plant seed in vain, because your enemies will eat it. 17 I will set my face against you so that you will be defeated by your enemies; those who hate you will rule over you, and you will flee even when no one is pursuing you.

18 "'If after all this you will not listen to me, I will punish you for your sins seven times over. 19 I will break down your stubborn pride and make the sky above you like iron and the ground beneath you like bronze. 20 Your strength will be spent in vain, because your soil will not yield its crops, nor will the trees of your land yield their fruit.

21 "'If you remain hostile toward me and refuse to listen to me, I will multiply your afflictions seven times over, as your sins deserve. 22 I will send wild animals against you, and they will rob you of your children, destroy your cattle and make you so few in number that your roads will be deserted.

23 "'If in spite of these things you do not accept my correction but continue to be hostile toward me, 24 I myself will be hostile toward you and will afflict you for your sins seven times over. 25 And I will bring the sword on you to avenge the breaking of the covenant. When you withdraw into your cities, I will send a plague among you, and you will be given

a 11 Or my tabernacle

What does it mean that God had a dwelling place among the people? (26:11)
Because God is spirit, he is everywhere. His presence was with the Israelites in a special way in the tabernacle, which means *dwelling place*.

Why would God punish them seven times? (26:18, 21, 24)
The number seven has significant symbolism and special meaning in the Bible. Since the time of creation it often meant something complete or perfect.

Are afflictions always punishment from God? (26:24)
God's covenant with Israel promised prosperity and blessings for obedience and suffering for disobedience. God often let the Israelites know that evil things happened because he was punishing them for their sin. The New Testament teaches that obedience doesn't guarantee an absence of physical problems. Tragic events and illness are not punishment from God, but when they happen, God may use them as a way to test his people and strengthen their faith (see James 1:2 — 4:1).

into enemy hands. ²⁶When I cut off your supply of bread, ten women will be able to bake your bread in one oven, and they will dole out the bread by weight. You will eat, but you will not be satisfied.

²⁷"'If in spite of this you still do not listen to me but continue to be hostile toward me, ²⁸then in my anger I will be hostile toward you, and I myself will punish you for your sins seven times over. ²⁹You will eat the flesh of your sons and the flesh of your daughters. ³⁰I will destroy your high places, cut down your incense altars and pile your dead bodiesᵃ on the lifeless forms of your idols, and I will abhor you. ³¹I will turn your cities into ruins and lay waste your sanctuaries, and I will take no delight in the pleasing aroma of your offerings. ³²I myself will lay waste the land, so that your enemies who live there will be appalled. ³³I will scatter you among the nations and will draw out my sword and pursue you. Your land will be laid waste, and your cities will lie in ruins. ³⁴Then the land will enjoy its sabbath years all the time that it lies desolate and you are in the country of your enemies; then the land will rest and enjoy its sabbaths. ³⁵All the time that it lies desolate, the land will have the rest it did not have during the sabbaths you lived in it.

³⁶"'As for those of you who are left, I will make their hearts so fearful in the lands of their enemies that the sound of a windblown leaf will put them to flight. They will run as though fleeing from the sword, and they will fall, even though no one is pursuing them. ³⁷They will stumble over one another as though fleeing from the sword, even though no one is pursuing them. So you will not be able to stand before your enemies. ³⁸You will perish among the nations; the land of your enemies will devour you. ³⁹Those of you who are left will waste away in the lands of their enemies because of their sins; also because of their ancestors' sins they will waste away.

⁴⁰"'But if they will confess their sins and the sins of their ancestors—their unfaithfulness and their hostility toward me, ⁴¹which made me hostile toward them so that I sent them into the land of their enemies—then when their uncircumcised hearts are humbled and they pay for their sin, ⁴²I will remember my covenant with Jacob and my covenant with Isaac and my covenant with Abraham, and I will remember the land. ⁴³For the land will be deserted by them and will enjoy its sabbaths while it lies desolate without them. They will pay for their sins because they rejected my laws and abhorred my decrees. ⁴⁴Yet in spite of this, when they are in the land of their enemies, I will not reject them or abhor them so as to destroy them completely, breaking my covenant with them. I am the LORD their God. ⁴⁵But for their sake I will remember the covenant with their ancestors whom I brought out of Egypt in the sight of the nations to be their God. I am the LORD.'"

⁴⁶These are the decrees, the laws and the regulations that the LORD established at Mount Sinai between himself and the Israelites through Moses.

ᵃ 30 Or *your funeral offerings*

What is an uncircumcised heart? (26:41)
This is a figurative way to talk about the sinful hearts of the people. In physical circumcision the foreskin is removed; similarly, the people needed to cut sinful impurities from their lives.

What did it mean to "dedicate a person to the LORD"?
(27:2)
Sometimes people made a vow
to God (in exchange for a request) and gave a child, a slave,
or themselves in service to the
tabernacle. Hannah dedicated
her son Samuel to God, and he
lived and worked in the temple.
(See 1 Samuel 1:11.)

Why were men worth more
than women and the middle-
aged worth more than the
elderly? (27:3–8)
The priests expected heavier
physical labor and more productivity from middle-aged men than
from women or the young and
the elderly. These amounts did
not reflect someone's value as
a person but someone's ability
and experience in working at the
tabernacle.

REDEEMING WHAT IS THE LORD'S

27 The LORD said to Moses, [2]"Speak to the Israelites and say to them: 'If anyone makes a special vow to dedicate a person to the LORD by giving the equivalent value, [3]set the value of a male between the ages of twenty and sixty at fifty shekels[a] of silver, according to the sanctuary shekel[b]; [4]for a female, set her value at thirty shekels[c]; [5]for a person between the ages of five and twenty, set the value of a male at twenty shekels[d] and of a female at ten shekels[e]; [6]for a person between one month and five years, set the value of a male at five shekels[f] of silver and that of a female at three shekels[g] of silver; [7]for a person sixty years old or more, set the value of a male at fifteen shekels[h] and of a female at ten shekels. [8]If anyone making the vow is too poor to pay the specified amount, the person being dedicated is to be presented to the priest, who will set the value according to what the one making the vow can afford.

[9]"If what they vowed is an animal that is acceptable as an offering to the LORD, such an animal given to the LORD becomes holy. [10]They must not exchange it or substitute a good one for a bad one, or a bad one for a good one; if they should substitute one animal for another, both it and the substitute become holy. [11]If what they vowed is a ceremonially unclean animal—one that is not acceptable as an offering to the LORD—the animal must be presented to the priest, [12]who will judge its quality as good or bad. Whatever value the priest then sets, that is what it will be. [13]If the owner wishes to redeem the animal, a fifth must be added to its value.

[14]"If anyone dedicates their house as something holy to the LORD, the priest will judge its quality as good or bad. Whatever value the priest then sets, so it will remain. [15]If the one who dedicates their house wishes to redeem it, they must add a fifth to its value, and the house will again become theirs.

[16]"If anyone dedicates to the LORD part of their family land, its value is to be set according to the amount of seed required for it—fifty shekels of silver to a homer[i] of barley seed. [17]If they dedicate a field during the Year of Jubilee, the value that has been set remains. [18]But if they dedicate a field after the Jubilee, the priest will determine the value according to the number of years that remain until the next Year of Jubilee, and its set value will be reduced. [19]If the one who dedicates the field wishes to redeem it, they must add a fifth to its value, and the field will again become theirs. [20]If, however, they do not redeem the field, or if they have sold it to someone else, it can never be redeemed. [21]When the field is released in the Jubilee, it will become holy, like a field devoted to the LORD; it will become priestly property. [22]"If anyone dedicates to the LORD a field they have

---

[a] 3 That is, about 1 1/4 pounds or about 575 grams; also in verse 16
[b] 3 That is, about 2/5 ounce or about 12 grams; also in verse 25   [c] 4 That is, about 12 ounces or about 345 grams   [d] 5 That is, about 8 ounces or about 230 grams   [e] 5 That is, about 4 ounces or about 115 grams; also in verse 7   [f] 6 That is, about 2 ounces or about 58 grams   [g] 6 That is, about 1 1/4 ounces or about 35 grams   [h] 7 That is, about 6 ounces or about 175 grams   [i] 16 That is, probably about 300 pounds or about 135 kilograms

bought, which is not part of their family land, [23] the priest will determine its value up to the Year of Jubilee, and the owner must pay its value on that day as something holy to the LORD. [24] In the Year of Jubilee the field will revert to the person from whom it was bought, the one whose land it was. [25] Every value is to be set according to the sanctuary shekel, twenty gerahs to the shekel.

[26] "'No one, however, may dedicate the firstborn of an animal, since the firstborn already belongs to the LORD; whether an ox[a] or a sheep, it is the LORD's. [27] If it is one of the unclean animals, it may be bought back at its set value, adding a fifth of the value to it. If it is not redeemed, it is to be sold at its set value.

[28] "'But nothing that a person owns and devotes[b] to the LORD—whether a human being or an animal or family land—may be sold or redeemed; everything so devoted is most holy to the LORD.

[29] "'No person devoted to destruction[c] may be ransomed; they are to be put to death.

[30] "'A tithe of everything from the land, whether grain from the soil or fruit from the trees, belongs to the LORD; it is holy to the LORD. [31] Whoever would redeem any of their tithe must add a fifth of the value to it. [32] Every tithe of the herd and flock—every tenth animal that passes under the shepherd's rod—will be holy to the LORD. [33] No one may pick out the good from the bad or make any substitution. If anyone does make a substitution, both the animal and its substitute become holy and cannot be redeemed.'"

[34] These are the commands the LORD gave Moses at Mount Sinai for the Israelites.

What was the difference between "devoting" and "dedicating" something to the LORD? (27:26–28)
Devotion is more of a commitment than dedication. When something was devoted to God, it was holy and could only be used in a way that would glorify God and not its original purpose. In contrast, a dedication could be redeemed through payment or other means.

What does devoted to destruction mean? (27:29)
A person who made a serious violation of the law, such as idolatry or murder, could not be redeemed. The person who committed this violation was "devoted to destruction" and must pay for the sin with their death.

What was a tithe? (27:30)
A tithe is a tenth. Here the tithe referred to giving one-tenth of one's crops and livestock to the Lord as a type of vow.

---

[a] 26 The Hebrew word can refer to either male or female.
[b] 28 The Hebrew term refers to the irrevocable giving over of things or persons to the LORD.   [c] 29 The Hebrew term refers to the irrevocable giving over of things or persons to the LORD, often by totally destroying them.

Numbers

INTRODUCTION

Who wrote this book?	Moses.
Why was this book written?	Numbers tells how Israel's disobedience kept the Israelites from entering the promised land.
What happens in this book?	The Israelites are frightened by the power of the Canaanites. They disobey when God tells them to attack Canaan. The Israelites wander in the desert for 40 years, until all the adults who disobeyed God have died.
What do we learn about God in this book?	God will not bless people who refuse to trust and obey him.
Who are the key people in this book?	The most important people in this book are Moses and Aaron.
Where did this happen?	Numbers 1–10 happened at Mount Sinai. Numbers 11–14 happened just outside Canaan. The rest of the book took place in the wilderness and on the way back to Canaan 40 years later. (See the map index at the back of this Bible to see where Canaan was.)
What are some of the stories in this book?	The Israelites complain — Numbers 11 Aaron and Miriam turn against Moses — Numbers 12 Spies explore Canaan — Numbers 13 The Israelites disobey God — Numbers 14 Korah leads a rebellion — Numbers 16 Aaron's staff buds — Numbers 17 Balaam tries to curse Israel — Numbers 22–24 Israel defeats the Midianites — Numbers 31

When did these things happen? 2200 BC · 2100 · 2000 · 1900 · 1800 · 1700 · 1600 · 1500 · 1400

MOSES' BIRTH (C. 1526 BC) —————————————————————————

THE PLAGUES; THE PASSOVER (C. 1446 BC) ———————————————

THE EXODUS (C. 1446 BC) —————————————————————————

DESERT WANDERINGS (C. 1446 – 1406 BC) ——————————————

EXPLORATION OF CANAAN (C. 1443 BC) ———————————————

BOOK OF NUMBERS WRITTEN (C. 1406 BC) —————————————

MOSES DIES; JOSHUA BECOMES LEADER (C. 1406 BC) ——————

ISRAELITES ENTER CANAAN (C. 1406 BC) ——————————————

THE CENSUS

1 The LORD spoke to Moses in the tent of meeting in the Desert of Sinai on the first day of the second month of the second year after the Israelites came out of Egypt. He said: ²"Take a census of the whole Israelite community by their clans and families, listing every man by name, one by one. ³You and Aaron are to count according to their divisions all the men in Israel who are twenty years old or more and able to serve in the army. ⁴One man from each tribe, each of them the head of his family, is to help you. ⁵These are the names of the men who are to assist you:

from Reuben, Elizur son of Shedeur;
⁶from Simeon, Shelumiel son of Zurishaddai;
⁷from Judah, Nahshon son of Amminadab;
⁸from Issachar, Nethanel son of Zuar;
⁹from Zebulun, Eliab son of Helon;
¹⁰from the sons of Joseph:
from Ephraim, Elishama son of Ammihud;
from Manasseh, Gamaliel son of Pedahzur;
¹¹from Benjamin, Abidan son of Gideoni;
¹²from Dan, Ahiezer son of Ammishaddai;
¹³from Asher, Pagiel son of Okran;
¹⁴from Gad, Eliasaph son of Deuel;
¹⁵from Naphtali, Ahira son of Enan."

¹⁶These were the men appointed from the community, the leaders of their ancestral tribes. They were the heads of the clans of Israel.

¹⁷Moses and Aaron took these men whose names had been specified, ¹⁸and they called the whole community together on the first day of the second month. The people registered their ancestry by their clans and families, and the men twenty years old or more were listed by name, one by one, ¹⁹as the LORD commanded Moses. And so he counted them in the Desert of Sinai:

²⁰From the descendants of Reuben the firstborn son of Israel:
All the men twenty years old or more who were able to serve in the army were listed by name, one by one, according to the records of their clans and families. ²¹The number from the tribe of Reuben was 46,500.

²²From the descendants of Simeon:
All the men twenty years old or more who were able to serve in the army were counted and listed by name, one by one, according to the records of their clans and families. ²³The number from the tribe of Simeon was 59,300.

²⁴From the descendants of Gad:
All the men twenty years old or more who were able to serve in the army were listed by name, according to the records of their clans and families. ²⁵The number from the tribe of Gad was 45,650.

²⁶From the descendants of Judah:
All the men twenty years old or more who were able

Why is it important that the Lord spoke to Moses? (1:1)
A significant message in Numbers is that the LORD spoke to Moses and through Moses to Israel. This is stated over 150 times and in more than 20 ways in this book.

How did God speak to Moses? (1:1)
At times Moses seemed to have actually heard the voice of God (see Numbers 7:89 and Exodus 33:11). At other times he may have experienced an inner conversation or conviction.

What is a census? (1:1–3)
A census is an official population count. This census did not include women and children because its purpose was to count those who would serve in the army — only men ages 20 and over were counted.

What is the pattern of this list? (1:20–43)
For each tribe there are two verses giving the name of the tribe, the information about those numbered, the name of the tribe again, and the total count for the tribe. The same numbers are given for each tribe again in chapter two.

to serve in the army were listed by name, according to the records of their clans and families. **27**The number from the tribe of Judah was 74,600.

28 From the descendants of Issachar:

All the men twenty years old or more who were able to serve in the army were listed by name, according to the records of their clans and families. **29**The number from the tribe of Issachar was 54,400.

30 From the descendants of Zebulun:

All the men twenty years old or more who were able to serve in the army were listed by name, according to the records of their clans and families. **31**The number from the tribe of Zebulun was 57,400.

32 From the sons of Joseph:

From the descendants of Ephraim:

All the men twenty years old or more who were able to serve in the army were listed by name, according to the records of their clans and families. **33**The number from the tribe of Ephraim was 40,500.

34 From the descendants of Manasseh:

All the men twenty years old or more who were able to serve in the army were listed by name, according to the records of their clans and families. **35**The number from the tribe of Manasseh was 32,200.

36 From the descendants of Benjamin:

All the men twenty years old or more who were able to serve in the army were listed by name, according to the records of their clans and families. **37**The number from the tribe of Benjamin was 35,400.

38 From the descendants of Dan:

All the men twenty years old or more who were able to serve in the army were listed by name, according to the records of their clans and families. **39**The number from the tribe of Dan was 62,700.

40 From the descendants of Asher:

All the men twenty years old or more who were able to serve in the army were listed by name, according to the records of their clans and families. **41**The number from the tribe of Asher was 41,500.

42 From the descendants of Naphtali:

All the men twenty years old or more who were able to serve in the army were listed by name, according to the records of their clans and families. **43**The number from the tribe of Naphtali was 53,400.

44These were the men counted by Moses and Aaron and the twelve leaders of Israel, each one representing his family. **45**All the Israelites twenty years old or more who were able to serve in Israel's army were counted according to their families. **46**The total number was 603,550.

47The ancestral tribe of the Levites, however, was not counted along with the others. **48**The LORD had said to Moses: **49**"You must not count the tribe of Levi or include them

How many Israelites left Egypt? (1:46)
The Israelite population probably grew to more than two million people in Egypt.

Why was the tribe of Levi excluded from the census? (1:47 – 49)
The census was a count and list of the Israelite army. The Levites could not serve in the army because they already had a special job. God chose them to guard the tabernacle and offer sacrifices for the Israelites.

in the census of the other Israelites. ⁵⁰Instead, appoint the Levites to be in charge of the tabernacle of the covenant law—over all its furnishings and everything belonging to it. They are to carry the tabernacle and all its furnishings; they are to take care of it and encamp around it. ⁵¹Whenever the tabernacle is to move, the Levites are to take it down, and whenever the tabernacle is to be set up, the Levites shall do it. Anyone else who approaches it is to be put to death. ⁵²The Israelites are to set up their tents by divisions, each of them in their own camp under their standard. ⁵³The Levites, however, are to set up their tents around the tabernacle of the covenant law so that my wrath will not fall on the Israelite community. The Levites are to be responsible for the care of the tabernacle of the covenant law."

⁵⁴The Israelites did all this just as the LORD commanded Moses.

THE ARRANGEMENT OF THE TRIBAL CAMPS

2 The LORD said to Moses and Aaron: ²"The Israelites are to camp around the tent of meeting some distance from it, each of them under their standard and holding the banners of their family."

³On the east, toward the sunrise, the divisions of the camp of Judah are to encamp under their standard. The leader of the people of Judah is Nahshon son of Amminadab. ⁴His division numbers 74,600.

⁵The tribe of Issachar will camp next to them. The leader of the people of Issachar is Nethanel son of Zuar. ⁶His division numbers 54,400.

⁷The tribe of Zebulun will be next. The leader of the people of Zebulun is Eliab son of Helon. ⁸His division numbers 57,400.

⁹All the men assigned to the camp of Judah, according to their divisions, number 186,400. They will set out first.

¹⁰On the south will be the divisions of the camp of Reuben under their standard. The leader of the people of Reuben is Elizur son of Shedeur. ¹¹His division numbers 46,500.

¹²The tribe of Simeon will camp next to them. The leader of the people of Simeon is Shelumiel son of Zurishaddai. ¹³His division numbers 59,300.

¹⁴The tribe of Gad will be next. The leader of the people of Gad is Eliasaph son of Deuel.ᵃ ¹⁵His division numbers 45,650.

¹⁶All the men assigned to the camp of Reuben, according to their divisions, number 151,450. They will set out second.

¹⁷Then the tent of meeting and the camp of the Levites will set out in the middle of the camps. They will set out in the same order as they encamp, each in their own place under their standard.

ᵃ 14 Many manuscripts of the Masoretic Text, Samaritan Pentateuch and Vulgate (see also 1:14); most manuscripts of the Masoretic Text *Reuel*

What was the "covenant law"? (1:50)
This was the Ten Commandments written on stone tablets, which were placed in the ark.

Why would someone be put to death for going near the tabernacle? (1:51–53)
The Hebrew word that is translated here as *anyone else* is often translated as *stranger, alien,* or *foreigner.* God wanted to emphasize that his covenant was with his chosen people.

What were the banners and standards? (2:2)
Each tribe had its own banner, and each group of three tribes had its own standard. These were like flags that were carried into battle. Jewish tradition suggests that the tribal banners had colors corresponding to the stones in the breastplate of the high priest (see Exodus 28:15–21) and that the standard of the group of three tribes led by Judah had the figure of a lion; Reuben, the figure of a man; Ephraim, the figure of an ox; and Dan, the figure of an eagle.

Why was Judah listed first? (2:3–4)
The tribe of Judah was honored above the other tribes (see Genesis 49:8). Although Judah was Jacob's fourth son, the Messiah would come from the tribe of Judah.

Why are these details about the camp and travel arrangements included in the Bible? (2:17-34)
These details show that God valued a well-ordered society. By organizing the camp around the tabernacle, the Lord was closer to his people. Also, God wanted his people to be safe. The instructions kept the Israelites from arguing among themselves about setting up camp and gave them the discipline and organization needed for battle.

¹⁸On the west will be the divisions of the camp of Ephraim under their standard. The leader of the people of Ephraim is Elishama son of Ammihud. ¹⁹His division numbers 40,500.

²⁰The tribe of Manasseh will be next to them. The leader of the people of Manasseh is Gamaliel son of Pedahzur. ²¹His division numbers 32,200.

²²The tribe of Benjamin will be next. The leader of the people of Benjamin is Abidan son of Gideoni. ²³His division numbers 35,400.

²⁴All the men assigned to the camp of Ephraim, according to their divisions, number 108,100. They will set out third.

²⁵On the north will be the divisions of the camp of Dan under their standard. The leader of the people of Dan is Ahiezer son of Ammishaddai. ²⁶His division numbers 62,700.

²⁷The tribe of Asher will camp next to them. The leader of the people of Asher is Pagiel son of Okran. ²⁸His division numbers 41,500.

²⁹The tribe of Naphtali will be next. The leader of the people of Naphtali is Ahira son of Enan. ³⁰His division numbers 53,400.

³¹All the men assigned to the camp of Dan number 157,600. They will set out last, under their standards.

³²These are the Israelites, counted according to their families. All the men in the camps, by their divisions, number 603,550. ³³The Levites, however, were not counted along with the other Israelites, as the LORD commanded Moses.

³⁴So the Israelites did everything the LORD commanded Moses; that is the way they encamped under their standards, and that is the way they set out, each of them with their clan and family.

THE LEVITES

3 This is the account of the family of Aaron and Moses at the time the LORD spoke to Moses at Mount Sinai.

²The names of the sons of Aaron were Nadab the firstborn and Abihu, Eleazar and Ithamar. ³Those were the names of Aaron's sons, the anointed priests, who were ordained to serve as priests. ⁴Nadab and Abihu, however, died before the LORD when they made an offering with unauthorized fire before him in the Desert of Sinai. They had no sons, so Eleazar and Ithamar served as priests during the lifetime of their father Aaron.

⁵The LORD said to Moses, ⁶"Bring the tribe of Levi and present them to Aaron the priest to assist him. ⁷They are to perform duties for him and for the whole community at the tent of meeting by doing the work of the tabernacle. ⁸They are to take care of all the furnishings of the tent of meeting, fulfilling the obligations of the Israelites by doing the work of the tabernacle. ⁹Give the Levites to Aaron and his sons;

Who were Nadab and Abihu? (3:4)
Nadab and Abihu were Aaron's sons who ignored God's commands about how to make an offering with fire. In order to be close to God's holiness, priests had to obey God's commands. (See Leviticus 10:1-3.)

they are the Israelites who are to be given wholly to him.[a] [10] Appoint Aaron and his sons to serve as priests; anyone else who approaches the sanctuary is to be put to death."

[11] The LORD also said to Moses, [12] "I have taken the Levites from among the Israelites in place of the first male offspring of every Israelite woman. The Levites are mine, [13] for all the firstborn are mine. When I struck down all the firstborn in Egypt, I set apart for myself every firstborn in Israel, whether human or animal. They are to be mine. I am the LORD."

[14] The LORD said to Moses in the Desert of Sinai, [15] "Count the Levites by their families and clans. Count every male a month old or more." [16] So Moses counted them, as he was commanded by the word of the LORD.

[17] These were the names of the sons of Levi:

Gershon, Kohath and Merari.

[18] These were the names of the Gershonite clans:

Libni and Shimei.

[19] The Kohathite clans:

Amram, Izhar, Hebron and Uzziel.

[20] The Merarite clans:

Mahli and Mushi.

These were the Levite clans, according to their families.

[21] To Gershon belonged the clans of the Libnites and Shimeites; these were the Gershonite clans. [22] The number of all the males a month old or more who were counted was 7,500. [23] The Gershonite clans were to camp on the west, behind the tabernacle. [24] The leader of the families of the Gershonites was Eliasaph son of Lael. [25] At the tent of meeting the Gershonites were responsible for the care of the tabernacle and tent, its coverings, the curtain at the entrance to the tent of meeting, [26] the curtains of the courtyard, the curtain at the entrance to the courtyard surrounding the tabernacle and altar, and the ropes—and everything related to their use.

[27] To Kohath belonged the clans of the Amramites, Izharites, Hebronites and Uzzielites; these were the Kohathite clans. [28] The number of all the males a month old or more was 8,600.[b] The Kohathites were responsible for the care of the sanctuary. [29] The Kohathite clans were to camp on the south side of the tabernacle. [30] The leader of the families of the Kohathite clans was Elizaphan son of Uzziel. [31] They were responsible for the care of the ark, the table, the lampstand, the altars, the articles of the sanctuary used in ministering, the curtain, and everything related to their use. [32] The chief leader of the Levites was Eleazar son of Aaron, the priest. He was appointed over those who were responsible for the care of the sanctuary.

[33] To Merari belonged the clans of the Mahlites and the Mushites; these were the Merarite clans. [34] The number of all

Why did firstborn sons get special treatment? (3:12–13)
The firstborn son was honored in this time and culture. God used this custom to claim the Levites as his priests.

Why would God change his mind and order Moses to count the Levites? (3:15, see 1:47–49).
God didn't change his mind. The reason for this census was different than the last. The last census was to count all of the men were who old enough and able to serve in the military. This census counted all of the people who could help with priestly duties. And since only men could serve in the military or become a priest, women weren't included in either count.

What was the purpose of all of the curtains? (3:25–26)
All three curtains acted as covering screens for the tabernacle.

---

[a] 9 Most manuscripts of the Masoretic Text; some manuscripts of the Masoretic Text, Samaritan Pentateuch and Septuagint (see also 8:16) *to me*
[b] 28 Hebrew; some Septuagint manuscripts *8,300*

the males a month old or more who were counted was 6,200. [35] The leader of the families of the Merarite clans was Zuriel son of Abihail; they were to camp on the north side of the tabernacle. [36] The Merarites were appointed to take care of the frames of the tabernacle, its crossbars, posts, bases, all its equipment, and everything related to their use, [37] as well as the posts of the surrounding courtyard with their bases, tent pegs and ropes.

[38] Moses and Aaron and his sons were to camp to the east of the tabernacle, toward the sunrise, in front of the tent of meeting. They were responsible for the care of the sanctuary on behalf of the Israelites. Anyone else who approached the sanctuary was to be put to death.

[39] The total number of Levites counted at the LORD's command by Moses and Aaron according to their clans, including every male a month old or more, was 22,000.

[40] The LORD said to Moses, "Count all the firstborn Israelite males who are a month old or more and make a list of their names. [41] Take the Levites for me in place of all the firstborn of the Israelites, and the livestock of the Levites in place of all the firstborn of the livestock of the Israelites. I am the LORD." [42] So Moses counted all the firstborn of the Israelites, as the LORD commanded him. [43] The total number of firstborn males a month old or more, listed by name, was 22,273.

[44] The LORD also said to Moses, [45] "Take the Levites in place of all the firstborn of Israel, and the livestock of the Levites in place of their livestock. The Levites are to be mine. I am the LORD. [46] To redeem the 273 firstborn Israelites who exceed the number of the Levites, [47] collect five shekels[a] for each one, according to the sanctuary shekel, which weighs twenty gerahs. [48] Give the money for the redemption of the additional Israelites to Aaron and his sons."

[49] So Moses collected the redemption money from those who exceeded the number redeemed by the Levites. [50] From the firstborn of the Israelites he collected silver weighing 1,365 shekels,[b] according to the sanctuary shekel. [51] Moses gave the redemption money to Aaron and his sons, as he was commanded by the word of the LORD.

THE KOHATHITES

4 The LORD said to Moses and Aaron: [2] "Take a census of the Kohathite branch of the Levites by their clans and families. [3] Count all the men from thirty to fifty years of age who come to serve in the work at the tent of meeting.

[4] "This is the work of the Kohathites at the tent of meeting: the care of the most holy things. [5] When the camp is to move, Aaron and his sons are to go in and take down the shielding curtain and put it over the ark of the covenant law. [6] Then they are to cover the curtain with a durable leather,[c] spread a cloth of solid blue over that and put the poles in place.

---

[a] 47 That is, about 2 ounces or about 58 grams   [b] 50 That is, about 35 pounds or about 16 kilograms   [c] 6 Possibly the hides of large aquatic mammals; also in verses 8, 10, 11, 12, 14 and 25

Why did God claim the Levites in place of the firstborn from other tribes? (3:45)
By choosing one tribe to serve as priests, families and clans were able to stay together. It may have been less confusing to have just one tribe of priests.

What was a sanctuary shekel? (3:47)
This was a unit of weight equal to about 11 grams. That's close to the weight of two nickels.

Why were there such detailed directions for each Levite clan? (4:1–48)
Organizing the tasks made it easier to get the work done quickly and correctly.

Why did God command the Israelites to move the tabernacle so carefully? (4:1–48)
God wanted to stress the importance of the sacredness of the tabernacle. Everything associated with the tabernacle remained holy, even when moving it around.

Who could see the ark of the covenant law? (4:5)
Only the high priest could see the ark of the covenant law or even enter the Most Holy Place, the place where the ark was kept, once each year. Even when the tabernacle was moved, the priests covered the ark with the sheltering curtain so no one could see it.

What animal was this "durable leather" from? (4:6)
It may have come from sea cows, large mammals related to manatees, found in the Red Sea and other tropical areas. They grow to a length of 8 to 15 feet (2.5–4.5 meters) and weigh up to 1,500 pounds (680 kilograms).

⁷"Over the table of the Presence they are to spread a blue cloth and put on it the plates, dishes and bowls, and the jars for drink offerings; the bread that is continually there is to remain on it. ⁸They are to spread a scarlet cloth over them, cover that with the durable leather and put the poles in place.

⁹"They are to take a blue cloth and cover the lampstand that is for light, together with its lamps, its wick trimmers and trays, and all its jars for the olive oil used to supply it. ¹⁰Then they are to wrap it and all its accessories in a covering of the durable leather and put it on a carrying frame.

¹¹"Over the gold altar they are to spread a blue cloth and cover that with the durable leather and put the poles in place.

¹²"They are to take all the articles used for ministering in the sanctuary, wrap them in a blue cloth, cover that with the durable leather and put them on a carrying frame.

¹³"They are to remove the ashes from the bronze altar and spread a purple cloth over it. ¹⁴Then they are to place on it all the utensils used for ministering at the altar, including the firepans, meat forks, shovels and sprinkling bowls. Over it they are to spread a covering of the durable leather and put the poles in place.

¹⁵"After Aaron and his sons have finished covering the holy furnishings and all the holy articles, and when the camp is ready to move, only then are the Kohathites to come and do the carrying. But they must not touch the holy things or they will die. The Kohathites are to carry those things that are in the tent of meeting.

¹⁶"Eleazar son of Aaron, the priest, is to have charge of the oil for the light, the fragrant incense, the regular grain offering and the anointing oil. He is to be in charge of the entire tabernacle and everything in it, including its holy furnishings and articles."

¹⁷The LORD said to Moses and Aaron, ¹⁸"See that the Kohathite tribal clans are not destroyed from among the Levites. ¹⁹So that they may live and not die when they come near the most holy things, do this for them: Aaron and his sons are to go into the sanctuary and assign to each man his work and what he is to carry. ²⁰But the Kohathites must not go in to look at the holy things, even for a moment, or they will die."

THE GERSHONITES

²¹The LORD said to Moses, ²²"Take a census also of the Gershonites by their families and clans. ²³Count all the men from thirty to fifty years of age who come to serve in the work at the tent of meeting.

²⁴"This is the service of the Gershonite clans in their carrying and their other work: ²⁵They are to carry the curtains of the tabernacle, that is, the tent of meeting, its covering and its outer covering of durable leather, the curtains for the entrance to the tent of meeting, ²⁶the curtains of the courtyard surrounding the tabernacle and altar, the curtain for the entrance to the courtyard, the ropes and all the equipment used in the service of the tent. The Gershonites are to do all that needs to be done with these things. ²⁷All their service, whether carrying or doing other work, is to be done

How large were the holy articles? (4:15)
The ark of the covenant and the altar of incense were about the size of a living-room chair today. The outer court's 60 wooden pillars were each about 7.5 feet high (2.3 meters).

Why would God kill people for looking at the holy things? (4:20)
Spiritual things are not to be taken lightly; God wanted to emphasize that. Disrespect would not be tolerated.

under the direction of Aaron and his sons. You shall assign to them as their responsibility all they are to carry. ²⁸This is the service of the Gershonite clans at the tent of meeting. Their duties are to be under the direction of Ithamar son of Aaron, the priest.

THE MERARITES

²⁹"Count the Merarites by their clans and families. ³⁰Count all the men from thirty to fifty years of age who come to serve in the work at the tent of meeting. ³¹As part of all their service at the tent, they are to carry the frames of the tabernacle, its crossbars, posts and bases, ³²as well as the posts of the surrounding courtyard with their bases, tent pegs, ropes, all their equipment and everything related to their use. Assign to each man the specific things he is to carry. ³³This is the service of the Merarite clans as they work at the tent of meeting under the direction of Ithamar son of Aaron, the priest."

THE NUMBERING OF THE LEVITE CLANS

³⁴Moses, Aaron and the leaders of the community counted the Kohathites by their clans and families. ³⁵All the men from thirty to fifty years of age who came to serve in the work at the tent of meeting, ³⁶counted by clans, were 2,750. ³⁷This was the total of all those in the Kohathite clans who served at the tent of meeting. Moses and Aaron counted them according to the LORD's command through Moses.

³⁸The Gershonites were counted by their clans and families. ³⁹All the men from thirty to fifty years of age who came to serve in the work at the tent of meeting, ⁴⁰counted by their clans and families, were 2,630. ⁴¹This was the total of those in the Gershonite clans who served at the tent of meeting. Moses and Aaron counted them according to the LORD's command.

⁴²The Merarites were counted by their clans and families. ⁴³All the men from thirty to fifty years of age who came to serve in the work at the tent of meeting, ⁴⁴counted by their clans, were 3,200. ⁴⁵This was the total of those in the Merarite clans. Moses and Aaron counted them according to the LORD's command through Moses.

⁴⁶So Moses, Aaron and the leaders of Israel counted all the Levites by their clans and families. ⁴⁷All the men from thirty to fifty years of age who came to do the work of serving and carrying the tent of meeting ⁴⁸numbered 8,580. ⁴⁹At the LORD's command through Moses, each was assigned his work and told what to carry.

Thus they were counted, as the LORD commanded Moses.

THE PURITY OF THE CAMP

5 The LORD said to Moses, ²"Command the Israelites to send away from the camp anyone who has a defiling skin disease*ᵃ* or a discharge of any kind, or who is ceremonially unclean because of a dead body. ³Send away male and female alike; send them outside the camp so they will not

---

ᵃ 2 The Hebrew word for *defiling skin disease*, traditionally translated "leprosy," was used for various diseases affecting the skin.

How is this chapter arranged? (5:1–31)
This chapter focuses on purity. The first paragraph is concerned with impurities that are obvious and visible. The second paragraph is about more secret faults that harm relationships. The third section is about even more private matters connected with intimate relationships.

Why were people with skin diseases or discharges banished from the camp? (5:2–3)
The banishment was not meant as a punishment. The important issue was God's holiness, and skin diseases and discharges made the camp ceremonially unclean. These rules also protected the rest of the camp by keeping disease from spreading. Often banishment was not permanent. If a priest considered the person healed, he or she could return back to camp.

defile their camp, where I dwell among them." ⁴The Israelites did so; they sent them outside the camp. They did just as
the Lord had instructed Moses.

RESTITUTION FOR WRONGS

⁵The Lord said to Moses, ⁶"Say to the Israelites: 'Any
man or woman who wrongs another in any way*ᵃ* and so is
unfaithful to the Lord is guilty ⁷and must confess the sin
they have committed. They must make full restitution for the
wrong they have done, add a fifth of the value to it and give
it all to the person they have wronged. ⁸But if that person
has no close relative to whom restitution can be made for the
wrong, the restitution belongs to the Lord and must be giv-
en to the priest, along with the ram with which atonement
is made for the wrongdoer. ⁹All the sacred contributions the
Israelites bring to a priest will belong to him. ¹⁰Sacred things
belong to their owners, but what they give to the priest will
belong to the priest.'"

THE TEST FOR AN UNFAITHFUL WIFE

¹¹Then the Lord said to Moses, ¹²"Speak to the Israelites
and say to them: 'If a man's wife goes astray and is unfaithful to him ¹³so that another man has sexual relations with
her, and this is hidden from her husband and her impurity
is undetected (since there is no witness against her and she
has not been caught in the act), ¹⁴and if feelings of jealousy
come over her husband and he suspects his wife and she is
impure—or if he is jealous and suspects her even though she
is not impure— ¹⁵then he is to take his wife to the priest.
He must also take an offering of a tenth of an ephah*ᵇ* of barley flour on her behalf. He must not pour olive oil on it or
put incense on it, because it is a grain offering for jealousy, a
reminder-offering to draw attention to wrongdoing.

¹⁶"'The priest shall bring her and have her stand before the
Lord. ¹⁷Then he shall take some holy water in a clay jar and
put some dust from the tabernacle floor into the water. ¹⁸After
the priest has had the woman stand before the Lord, he shall
loosen her hair and place in her hands the reminder-offering,
the grain offering for jealousy, while he himself holds the bitter
water that brings a curse. ¹⁹Then the priest shall put the woman under oath and say to her, "If no other man has had sexual
relations with you and you have not gone astray and become
impure while married to your husband, may this bitter water
that brings a curse not harm you. ²⁰But if you have gone astray
while married to your husband and you have made yourself
impure by having sexual relations with a man other than your
husband"— ²¹here the priest is to put the woman under this
curse—"may the Lord cause you to become a curse*ᶜ* among
your people when he makes your womb miscarry and your abdomen swell. ²²May this water that brings a curse enter your
body so that your abdomen swells or your womb miscarries."

"'Then the woman is to say, "Amen. So be it."

ᵃ 6 Or *woman who commits any wrong common to mankind*   *ᵇ 15* That is,
probably about 3 1/2 pounds or about 1.6 kilograms   *ᶜ 21* That is, may he
cause your name to be used in cursing (see Jer. 29:22); or, may others see that
you are cursed; similarly in verse 27.

**Why would an innocent
woman go through this test
just because her husband
was suspicious? (5:14–31)**
This test protected an innocent
woman who was falsely accused
of having an affair. In this time
and culture, men often beat their
wives if they were suspected of
being unfaithful. Without the
test, a jealous husband might
harm his wife. The test also assured that the people were pure
like God intended.

**Where did this holy water
come from? (5:17)**
This was water which had been
purified and then stored in a special container. It was dedicated to
God, so it could only be used in
service to God.

**Why would the priest
"loosen" the woman's hair?
(5:18)**
Unbound hair on a woman was a
sign of openness. If the woman
was guilty, this gesture would
represent the judgment of the
community.

**What was the meaning of a
swollen abdomen? (5:22)**
This is a poetic way of saying the
woman would not be able to have
children.

23 "'The priest is to write these curses on a scroll and then wash them off into the bitter water. 24 He shall make the woman drink the bitter water that brings a curse, and this water that brings a curse and causes bitter suffering will enter her. 25 The priest is to take from her hands the grain offering for jealousy, wave it before the LORD and bring it to the altar. 26 The priest is then to take a handful of the grain offering as a memorial[a] offering and burn it on the altar; after that, he is to have the woman drink the water. 27 If she has made herself impure and been unfaithful to her husband, this will be the result: When she is made to drink the water that brings a curse and causes bitter suffering, it will enter her, her abdomen will swell and her womb will miscarry, and she will become a curse. 28 If, however, the woman has not made herself impure, but is clean, she will be cleared of guilt and will be able to have children.

29 "'This, then, is the law of jealousy when a woman goes astray and makes herself impure while married to her husband, 30 or when feelings of jealousy come over a man because he suspects his wife. The priest is to have her stand before the LORD and is to apply this entire law to her. 31 The husband will be innocent of any wrongdoing, but the woman will bear the consequences of her sin.'"

THE NAZIRITE

6 The LORD said to Moses, 2 "Speak to the Israelites and say to them: 'If a man or woman wants to make a special vow, a vow of dedication to the LORD as a Nazirite, 3 they must abstain from wine and other fermented drink and must not drink vinegar made from wine or other fermented drink. They must not drink grape juice or eat grapes or raisins. 4 As long as they remain under their Nazirite vow, they must not eat anything that comes from the grapevine, not even the seeds or skins.

5 "'During the entire period of their Nazirite vow, no razor may be used on their head. They must be holy until the period of their dedication to the LORD is over; they must let their hair grow long.

6 "'Throughout the period of their dedication to the LORD, the Nazirite must not go near a dead body. 7 Even if their own father or mother or brother or sister dies, they must not make themselves ceremonially unclean on account of them, because the symbol of their dedication to God is on their head. 8 Throughout the period of their dedication, they are consecrated to the LORD.

9 "'If someone dies suddenly in the Nazirite's presence, thus defiling the hair that symbolizes their dedication, they must shave their head on the seventh day—the day of their cleansing. 10 Then on the eighth day they must bring two doves or two young pigeons to the priest at the entrance to the tent of meeting. 11 The priest is to offer one as a sin offering[b] and the other as a burnt offering to make atonement for the Nazirite because they sinned by being in the presence of the dead body. That same day they are to consecrate

Why wasn't there a test for unfaithfulness for men? (5:31)
The woman's test protected her from her husband's abuse. In this time and culture, because women typically didn't beat their husbands for adultery, the men didn't need the same kind of laws for protection.

What was a Nazirite? (6:2)
A Nazirite was a man or woman who made a vow to be more devoted to the Lord for a time. A typical vow was for 30 days, but sometimes the vow was for a lifetime of service.

Why would a Nazirite not cut his or her hair? (6:5)
The long hair of a Nazirite would be a visible symbol of the person's devotion to the Lord.

Why was any contact with the dead prohibited? (6:6–12)
Contact with the dead would make a Nazirite ceremonially unclean. The restriction applied even to close family members who died. Even accidental contact would make the Nazirite ceremonially unclean.

a 26 Or *representative*   *b 11* Or *purification offering*; also in verses 14 and 16

their head again. [12]They must rededicate themselves to the
LORD for the same period of dedication and must bring a
year-old male lamb as a guilt offering. The previous days do
not count, because they became defiled during their period
of dedication.

[13]"'Now this is the law of the Nazirite when the period
of their dedication is over. They are to be brought to the
entrance to the tent of meeting. [14]There they are to present
their offerings to the LORD: a year-old male lamb without
defect for a burnt offering, a year-old ewe lamb without defect for a sin offering, a ram without defect for a fellowship
offering, [15]together with their grain offerings and drink offerings, and a basket of bread made with the finest flour and
without yeast—thick loaves with olive oil mixed in, and thin
loaves brushed with olive oil.

[16]"'The priest is to present all these before the LORD and
make the sin offering and the burnt offering. [17]He is to present the basket of unleavened bread and is to sacrifice the
ram as a fellowship offering to the LORD, together with its
grain offering and drink offering.

[18]"'Then at the entrance to the tent of meeting, the Nazirite must shave off the hair that symbolizes their dedication.
They are to take the hair and put it in the fire that is under
the sacrifice of the fellowship offering.

[19]"'After the Nazirite has shaved off the hair that symbolizes their dedication, the priest is to place in their hands
a boiled shoulder of the ram, and one thick loaf and one
thin loaf from the basket, both made without yeast. [20]The
priest shall then wave these before the LORD as a wave offering; they are holy and belong to the priest, together with
the breast that was waved and the thigh that was presented.
After that, the Nazirite may drink wine.

[21]"'This is the law of the Nazirite who vows offerings to
the LORD in accordance with their dedication, in addition to
whatever else they can afford. They must fulfill the vows they
have made, according to the law of the Nazirite.'"

THE PRIESTLY BLESSING

[22]The LORD said to Moses, [23]"Tell Aaron and his sons,
'This is how you are to bless the Israelites. Say to them:

[24]"'"The LORD bless you
    and keep you;
[25]the LORD make his face shine on you
    and be gracious to you;
[26]the LORD turn his face toward you
    and give you peace."'

[27]"So they will put my name on the Israelites, and I will
bless them."

OFFERINGS AT THE DEDICATION
OF THE TABERNACLE

7 When Moses finished setting up the tabernacle, he
anointed and consecrated it and all its furnishings. He
also anointed and consecrated the altar and all its utensils.
[2]Then the leaders of Israel, the heads of families who were the

**What did the Nazirite have
to do after completing the
vow? (6:13–20)**
After completing the vow, the
Nazirite had to offer many
expensive sacrifices. These sacrifices represented the total commitment that the Nazirite had
made to the Lord. The Nazirite
also burned his or her hair, which
had grown as a sign of the vow.

**Why would a person become
a Nazirite? (6:21)**
There were many reasons for
taking the Nazirite vows. A parent might take these vows before
the birth of a child. Someone
in trouble or someone who was
extremely thankful for God's
blessings might also take the
vows. So might a woman who
was suspected of being unfaithful
until the suspicion could be removed. Women and slaves could
only become Nazirites if they had
the permission of their husbands
or their masters.

**What did Moses do to conse-
crate the tabernacle? (7:1)**
Oil was used to consecrate—
dedicate to God—people and
things for God's service. Moses
probably poured or wiped special
olive oil on the tabernacle and
other holy things.

194

tribal leaders in charge of those who were counted, made offerings. ³They brought as their gifts before the LORD six covered carts and twelve oxen—an ox from each leader and a cart from every two. These they presented before the tabernacle.

⁴The LORD said to Moses, ⁵"Accept these from them, that they may be used in the work at the tent of meeting. Give them to the Levites as each man's work requires."

⁶So Moses took the carts and oxen and gave them to the Levites. ⁷He gave two carts and four oxen to the Gershonites, as their work required, ⁸and he gave four carts and eight oxen to the Merarites, as their work required. They were all under the direction of Ithamar son of Aaron, the priest. ⁹But Moses did not give any to the Kohathites, because they were to carry on their shoulders the holy things, for which they were responsible.

¹⁰When the altar was anointed, the leaders brought their offerings for its dedication and presented them before the altar. ¹¹For the LORD had said to Moses, "Each day one leader is to bring his offering for the dedication of the altar."

¹²The one who brought his offering on the first day was Nahshon son of Amminadab of the tribe of Judah.

¹³His offering was one silver plate weighing a hundred and thirty shekels[a] and one silver sprinkling bowl weighing seventy shekels,[b] both according to the sanctuary shekel, each filled with the finest flour mixed with olive oil as a grain offering; ¹⁴one gold dish weighing ten shekels,[c] filled with incense; ¹⁵one young bull, one ram and one male lamb a year old for a burnt offering; ¹⁶one male goat for a sin offering[d]; ¹⁷and two oxen, five rams, five male goats and five male lambs a year old to be sacrificed as a fellowship offering. This was the offering of Nahshon son of Amminadab.

¹⁸On the second day Nethanel son of Zuar, the leader of Issachar, brought his offering.

¹⁹The offering he brought was one silver plate weighing a hundred and thirty shekels and one silver sprinkling bowl weighing seventy shekels, both according to the sanctuary shekel, each filled with the finest flour mixed with olive oil as a grain offering; ²⁰one gold dish weighing ten shekels, filled with incense; ²¹one young bull, one ram and one male lamb a year old for a burnt offering; ²²one male goat for a sin offering; ²³and two oxen, five rams, five male goats and five male lambs a year old to be sacrificed as a fellowship offering. This was the offering of Nethanel son of Zuar.

²⁴On the third day, Eliab son of Helon, the leader of the people of Zebulun, brought his offering.

²⁵His offering was one silver plate weighing a hundred and thirty shekels and one silver sprinkling bowl

Why are the identical offerings listed in such detail? (7:12–83)
Over twelve days of the dedication, each tribe in turn brought an identical offering. The point of listing the offerings multiple times is probably to emphasize the splendor of this great ceremony.

Why were all these different kinds of animals sacrificed? (7:15–83)
This was a very special offering that only happened once a year. In order to show their gratitude to the Lord for all he had given them, the number of sacrifices the Israelites offered was very large.

Did the large number of animals waiting to be sacrificed cause problems? (7:15–83)
It's possible that so many animals could have been problematic, but all of the animals were probably brought to the temple at different times.

---

[a] 13 That is, about 3 1/4 pounds or about 1.5 kilograms; also elsewhere in this chapter   [b] 13 That is, about 1 3/4 pounds or about 800 grams; also elsewhere in this chapter   [c] 14 That is, about 4 ounces or about 115 grams; also elsewhere in this chapter   [d] 16 Or *purification offering*; also elsewhere in this chapter

weighing seventy shekels, both according to the sanctuary shekel, each filled with the finest flour mixed with olive oil as a grain offering; 26 one gold dish weighing ten shekels, filled with incense; 27 one young bull, one ram and one male lamb a year old for a burnt offering; 28 one male goat for a sin offering; 29 and two oxen, five rams, five male goats and five male lambs a year old to be sacrificed as a fellowship offering. This was the offering of Eliab son of Helon.

30 On the fourth day Elizur son of Shedeur, the leader of the people of Reuben, brought his offering.

31 His offering was one silver plate weighing a hundred and thirty shekels and one silver sprinkling bowl weighing seventy shekels, both according to the sanctuary shekel, each filled with the finest flour mixed with olive oil as a grain offering; 32 one gold dish weighing ten shekels, filled with incense; 33 one young bull, one ram and one male lamb a year old for a burnt offering; 34 one male goat for a sin offering; 35 and two oxen, five rams, five male goats and five male lambs a year old to be sacrificed as a fellowship offering. This was the offering of Elizur son of Shedeur.

36 On the fifth day Shelumiel son of Zurishaddai, the leader of the people of Simeon, brought his offering.

37 His offering was one silver plate weighing a hundred and thirty shekels and one silver sprinkling bowl weighing seventy shekels, both according to the sanctuary shekel, each filled with the finest flour mixed with olive oil as a grain offering; 38 one gold dish weighing ten shekels, filled with incense; 39 one young bull, one ram and one male lamb a year old for a burnt offering; 40 one male goat for a sin offering; 41 and two oxen, five rams, five male goats and five male lambs a year old to be sacrificed as a fellowship offering. This was the offering of Shelumiel son of Zurishaddai.

42 On the sixth day Eliasaph son of Deuel, the leader of the people of Gad, brought his offering.

43 His offering was one silver plate weighing a hundred and thirty shekels and one silver sprinkling bowl weighing seventy shekels, both according to the sanctuary shekel, each filled with the finest flour mixed with olive oil as a grain offering; 44 one gold dish weighing ten shekels, filled with incense; 45 one young bull, one ram and one male lamb a year old for a burnt offering; 46 one male goat for a sin offering; 47 and two oxen, five rams, five male goats and five male lambs a year old to be sacrificed as a fellowship offering. This was the offering of Eliasaph son of Deuel.

48 On the seventh day Elishama son of Ammihud, the leader of the people of Ephraim, brought his offering.

49 His offering was one silver plate weighing a hundred and thirty shekels and one silver sprinkling bowl weighing seventy shekels, both according to the sanctuary shekel, each filled with the finest flour mixed with

olive oil as a grain offering; ⁵⁰one gold dish weighing ten shekels, filled with incense; ⁵¹one young bull, one ram and one male lamb a year old for a burnt offering; ⁵²one male goat for a sin offering; ⁵³and two oxen, five rams, five male goats and five male lambs a year old to be sacrificed as a fellowship offering. This was the offering of Elishama son of Ammihud.

⁵⁴On the eighth day Gamaliel son of Pedahzur, the leader of the people of Manasseh, brought his offering.

⁵⁵His offering was one silver plate weighing a hundred and thirty shekels and one silver sprinkling bowl weighing seventy shekels, both according to the sanctuary shekel, each filled with the finest flour mixed with olive oil as a grain offering; ⁵⁶one gold dish weighing ten shekels, filled with incense; ⁵⁷one young bull, one ram and one male lamb a year old for a burnt offering; ⁵⁸one male goat for a sin offering; ⁵⁹and two oxen, five rams, five male goats and five male lambs a year old to be sacrificed as a fellowship offering. This was the offering of Gamaliel son of Pedahzur.

⁶⁰On the ninth day Abidan son of Gideoni, the leader of the people of Benjamin, brought his offering.

⁶¹His offering was one silver plate weighing a hundred and thirty shekels and one silver sprinkling bowl weighing seventy shekels, both according to the sanctuary shekel, each filled with the finest flour mixed with olive oil as a grain offering; ⁶²one gold dish weighing ten shekels, filled with incense; ⁶³one young bull, one ram and one male lamb a year old for a burnt offering; ⁶⁴one male goat for a sin offering; ⁶⁵and two oxen, five rams, five male goats and five male lambs a year old to be sacrificed as a fellowship offering. This was the offering of Abidan son of Gideoni.

⁶⁶On the tenth day Ahiezer son of Ammishaddai, the leader of the people of Dan, brought his offering.

⁶⁷His offering was one silver plate weighing a hundred and thirty shekels and one silver sprinkling bowl weighing seventy shekels, both according to the sanctuary shekel, each filled with the finest flour mixed with olive oil as a grain offering; ⁶⁸one gold dish weighing ten shekels, filled with incense; ⁶⁹one young bull, one ram and one male lamb a year old for a burnt offering; ⁷⁰one male goat for a sin offering; ⁷¹and two oxen, five rams, five male goats and five male lambs a year old to be sacrificed as a fellowship offering. This was the offering of Ahiezer son of Ammishaddai.

⁷²On the eleventh day Pagiel son of Okran, the leader of the people of Asher, brought his offering.

⁷³His offering was one silver plate weighing a hundred and thirty shekels and one silver sprinkling bowl weighing seventy shekels, both according to the sanctuary shekel, each filled with the finest flour mixed with olive oil as a grain offering; ⁷⁴one gold dish weighing ten shekels, filled with incense; ⁷⁵one young bull, one

ram and one male lamb a year old for a burnt offering; [76] one male goat for a sin offering; [77] and two oxen, five rams, five male goats and five male lambs a year old to be sacrificed as a fellowship offering. This was the offering of Pagiel son of Okran.

[78] On the twelfth day Ahira son of Enan, the leader of the people of Naphtali, brought his offering.

[79] His offering was one silver plate weighing a hundred and thirty shekels and one silver sprinkling bowl weighing seventy shekels, both according to the sanctuary shekel, each filled with the finest flour mixed with olive oil as a grain offering; [80] one gold dish weighing ten shekels, filled with incense; [81] one young bull, one ram and one male lamb a year old for a burnt offering; [82] one male goat for a sin offering; [83] and two oxen, five rams, five male goats and five male lambs a year old to be sacrificed as a fellowship offering. This was the offering of Ahira son of Enan.

[84] These were the offerings of the Israelite leaders for the dedication of the altar when it was anointed: twelve silver plates, twelve silver sprinkling bowls and twelve gold dishes. [85] Each silver plate weighed a hundred and thirty shekels, and each sprinkling bowl seventy shekels. Altogether, the silver dishes weighed two thousand four hundred shekels,[a] according to the sanctuary shekel. [86] The twelve gold dishes filled with incense weighed ten shekels each, according to the sanctuary shekel. Altogether, the gold dishes weighed a hundred and twenty shekels.[b] [87] The total number of animals for the burnt offering came to twelve young bulls, twelve rams and twelve male lambs a year old, together with their grain offering. Twelve male goats were used for the sin offering. [88] The total number of animals for the sacrifice of the fellowship offering came to twenty-four oxen, sixty rams, sixty male goats and sixty male lambs a year old. These were the offerings for the dedication of the altar after it was anointed.

[89] When Moses entered the tent of meeting to speak with the LORD, he heard the voice speaking to him from between the two cherubim above the atonement cover on the ark of the covenant law. In this way the LORD spoke to him.

SETTING UP THE LAMPS

8 The LORD said to Moses, [2] "Speak to Aaron and say to him, 'When you set up the lamps, see that all seven light up the area in front of the lampstand.'"

[3] Aaron did so; he set up the lamps so that they faced forward on the lampstand, just as the LORD commanded Moses. [4] This is how the lampstand was made: It was made of hammered gold—from its base to its blossoms. The lampstand was made exactly like the pattern the LORD had shown Moses.

THE SETTING APART OF THE LEVITES

[5] The LORD said to Moses: [6] "Take the Levites from among all the Israelites and make them ceremonially clean.

[a] 85 That is, about 60 pounds or about 28 kilograms   [b] 86 That is, about 3 pounds or about 1.4 kilograms

Was the ark of the testimony the same as the ark of the covenant law? (7:89)
Yes. The ark had many names: *ark of the covenant, ark of the Lord, ark of God,* and *ark of the testimony.*

Did God actually speak to Moses? (7:89)
Moses was incredibly blessed. He actually heard God's voice. Most prophets communicated with God in other ways.

**How were the Levites conse-
crated? (8:5–14)**
The Levites were helpers to the
priests, so their consecration
was somewhat different from
that of the priests. The priests
were made holy; the Levites were
made clean. The priests were
anointed and washed; the Levites
were sprinkled. The priests were
given new garments; the Levites
washed theirs. And blood was applied to the priests; it was waved
over the Levites.

**Why was ritual purification
important? (8:7)**
This ceremony prepared a person
to participate in the worship
of God. Being clean was very
important to the Israelites. This
ritual of washing and praying
helped make the person spiritually clean.

**Why did the Israelites lay
their hands on the Levites?
(8:10)**
By laying their hands on the Levites, the Israelites symbolically
showed that the Levites were
substitutes for the whole nation.

**Why did God impose age
restrictions on those who
served as priests? (8:24–25)**
This was not a job to be taken
lightly. Serving in the tabernacle
was hard work. It required a lot
of dedication. A minimum age
would help ensure the worker
would be mature enough to
handle the tasks. An age limit
also helped make sure the priest
was in good physical shape. They
had to do a lot of lifting to move
and set up the tabernacle.

[7] To purify them, do this: Sprinkle the water of cleansing on
them; then have them shave their whole bodies and wash
their clothes. And so they will purify themselves. [8] Have
them take a young bull with its grain offering of the finest flour mixed with olive oil; then you are to take a second
young bull for a sin offering.[a] [9] Bring the Levites to the front
of the tent of meeting and assemble the whole Israelite community. [10] You are to bring the Levites before the LORD, and
the Israelites are to lay their hands on them. [11] Aaron is to
present the Levites before the LORD as a wave offering from
the Israelites, so that they may be ready to do the work of
the LORD.

[12] "Then the Levites are to lay their hands on the heads
of the bulls, using one for a sin offering to the LORD and
the other for a burnt offering, to make atonement for the
Levites. [13] Have the Levites stand in front of Aaron and his
sons and then present them as a wave offering to the LORD.
[14] In this way you are to set the Levites apart from the other
Israelites, and the Levites will be mine.

[15] "After you have purified the Levites and presented them
as a wave offering, they are to come to do their work at the
tent of meeting. [16] They are the Israelites who are to be given
wholly to me. I have taken them as my own in place of the
firstborn, the first male offspring from every Israelite woman. [17] Every firstborn male in Israel, whether human or animal, is mine. When I struck down all the firstborn in Egypt,
I set them apart for myself. [18] And I have taken the Levites in
place of all the firstborn sons in Israel. [19] From among all the
Israelites, I have given the Levites as gifts to Aaron and his
sons to do the work at the tent of meeting on behalf of the
Israelites and to make atonement for them so that no plague
will strike the Israelites when they go near the sanctuary."

[20] Moses, Aaron and the whole Israelite community did
with the Levites just as the LORD commanded Moses. [21] The
Levites purified themselves and washed their clothes. Then
Aaron presented them as a wave offering before the LORD
and made atonement for them to purify them. [22] After that,
the Levites came to do their work at the tent of meeting under the supervision of Aaron and his sons. They did with the
Levites just as the LORD commanded Moses.

[23] The LORD said to Moses, [24] "This applies to the Levites:
Men twenty-five years old or more shall come to take part in
the work at the tent of meeting, [25] but at the age of fifty, they
must retire from their regular service and work no longer.
[26] They may assist their brothers in performing their duties
at the tent of meeting, but they themselves must not do the
work. This, then, is how you are to assign the responsibilities
of the Levites."

THE PASSOVER

9 The LORD spoke to Moses in the Desert of Sinai in the
first month of the second year after they came out of
Egypt. He said, [2] "Have the Israelites celebrate the Passover
at the appointed time. [3] Celebrate it at the appointed time, at

---

[a] 8 Or *purification offering*; also in verse 12

twilight on the fourteenth day of this month, in accordance with all its rules and regulations."

⁴So Moses told the Israelites to celebrate the Passover, ⁵and they did so in the Desert of Sinai at twilight on the fourteenth day of the first month. The Israelites did everything just as the LORD commanded Moses.

⁶But some of them could not celebrate the Passover on that day because they were ceremonially unclean on account of a dead body. So they came to Moses and Aaron that same day ⁷and said to Moses, "We have become unclean because of a dead body, but why should we be kept from presenting the LORD's offering with the other Israelites at the appointed time?"

⁸Moses answered them, "Wait until I find out what the LORD commands concerning you."

⁹Then the LORD said to Moses, ¹⁰"Tell the Israelites: 'When any of you or your descendants are unclean because of a dead body or are away on a journey, they are still to celebrate the LORD's Passover, ¹¹but they are to do it on the fourteenth day of the second month at twilight. They are to eat the lamb, together with unleavened bread and bitter herbs. ¹²They must not leave any of it till morning or break any of its bones. When they celebrate the Passover, they must follow all the regulations. ¹³But if anyone who is ceremonially clean and not on a journey fails to celebrate the Passover, they must be cut off from their people for not presenting the LORD's offering at the appointed time. They will bear the consequences of their sin.

¹⁴"'A foreigner residing among you is also to celebrate the LORD's Passover in accordance with its rules and regulations. You must have the same regulations for both the foreigner and the native-born.'"

THE CLOUD ABOVE THE TABERNACLE

¹⁵On the day the tabernacle, the tent of the covenant law, was set up, the cloud covered it. From evening till morning the cloud above the tabernacle looked like fire. ¹⁶That is how it continued to be; the cloud covered it, and at night it looked like fire. ¹⁷Whenever the cloud lifted from above the tent, the Israelites set out; wherever the cloud settled, the Israelites encamped. ¹⁸At the LORD's command the Israelites set out, and at his command they encamped. As long as the cloud stayed over the tabernacle, they remained in camp. ¹⁹When the cloud remained over the tabernacle a long time, the Israelites obeyed the LORD's order and did not set out. ²⁰Sometimes the cloud was over the tabernacle only a few days; at the LORD's command they would encamp, and then at his command they would set out. ²¹Sometimes the cloud stayed only from evening till morning, and when it lifted in the morning, they set out. Whether by day or by night, whenever the cloud lifted, they set out. ²²Whether the cloud stayed over the tabernacle for two days or a month or a year, the Israelites would remain in camp and not set out; but when it lifted, they would set out. ²³At the LORD's command they encamped, and at the LORD's command they set out. They obeyed the LORD's order, in accordance with his command through Moses.

THE SILVER TRUMPETS

10 The LORD said to Moses: ²"Make two trumpets of hammered silver, and use them for calling the community together and for having the camps set out. ³When both are sounded, the whole community is to assemble before you at the entrance to the tent of meeting. ⁴If only one is sounded, the leaders—the heads of the clans of Israel—are to assemble before you. ⁵When a trumpet blast is sounded, the tribes camping on the east are to set out. ⁶At the sounding of a second blast, the camps on the south are to set out. The blast will be the signal for setting out. ⁷To gather the assembly, blow the trumpets, but not with the signal for setting out.

⁸"The sons of Aaron, the priests, are to blow the trumpets. This is to be a lasting ordinance for you and the generations to come. ⁹When you go into battle in your own land against an enemy who is oppressing you, sound a blast on the trumpets. Then you will be remembered by the LORD your God and rescued from your enemies. ¹⁰Also at your times of rejoicing—your appointed festivals and New Moon feasts—you are to sound the trumpets over your burnt offerings and fellowship offerings, and they will be a memorial for you before your God. I am the LORD your God."

THE ISRAELITES LEAVE SINAI

¹¹On the twentieth day of the second month of the second year, the cloud lifted from above the tabernacle of the covenant law. ¹²Then the Israelites set out from the Desert of Sinai and traveled from place to place until the cloud came to rest in the Desert of Paran. ¹³They set out, this first time, at the LORD's command through Moses.

¹⁴The divisions of the camp of Judah went first, under their standard. Nahshon son of Amminadab was in command. ¹⁵Nethanel son of Zuar was over the division of the tribe of Issachar, ¹⁶and Eliab son of Helon was over the division of the tribe of Zebulun. ¹⁷Then the tabernacle was taken down, and the Gershonites and Merarites, who carried it, set out.

¹⁸The divisions of the camp of Reuben went next, under their standard. Elizur son of Shedeur was in command. ¹⁹Shelumiel son of Zurishaddai was over the division of the tribe of Simeon, ²⁰and Eliasaph son of Deuel was over the division of the tribe of Gad. ²¹Then the Kohathites set out, carrying the holy things. The tabernacle was to be set up before they arrived.

²²The divisions of the camp of Ephraim went next, under their standard. Elishama son of Ammihud was in command. ²³Gamaliel son of Pedahzur was over the division of the tribe of Manasseh, ²⁴and Abidan son of Gideoni was over the division of the tribe of Benjamin.

²⁵Finally, as the rear guard for all the units, the divisions of the camp of Dan set out under their standard. Ahiezer son of Ammishaddai was in command. ²⁶Pagiel son of Okran was over the division of the tribe of Asher, ²⁷and Ahira son of Enan was over the division of the tribe of Naphtali.

What were these trumpets like? (10:1–10)
They looked different than what trumpets look like today. These were long, straight, slender metal tubes with flared ends.

Why did God need to "remember" the Israelites? (10:9)
This did not mean that God had forgotten them. God never forgets his people, not even for a second. Instead, it means that God was ready to take action.

Why are the names of the tribes and their leaders listed again? (10:14–27)
This is the fourth time in the book of Numbers that the tribes and leaders' names are listed. The names are probably repeated to remind the Israelites that God saved the descendants of the sons of Jacob.

How could the tabernacle be set up before the Kohathites arrived? (10:21)
When the Israelites moved to a new location, the entire group didn't travel together. Part of the group left before the others so that the tabernacle was set up by the time the rest of the group arrived.

²⁸This was the order of march for the Israelite divisions as they set out.

²⁹Now Moses said to Hobab son of Reuel the Midianite, Moses' father-in-law, "We are setting out for the place about which the Lord said, 'I will give it to you.' Come with us and we will treat you well, for the Lord has promised good things to Israel."

³⁰He answered, "No, I will not go; I am going back to my own land and my own people."

³¹But Moses said, "Please do not leave us. You know where we should camp in the wilderness, and you can be our eyes. ³²If you come with us, we will share with you whatever good things the Lord gives us."

³³So they set out from the mountain of the Lord and traveled for three days. The ark of the covenant of the Lord went before them during those three days to find them a place to rest. ³⁴The cloud of the Lord was over them by day when they set out from the camp.

³⁵Whenever the ark set out, Moses said,

"Rise up, Lord!
    May your enemies be scattered;
    may your foes flee before you."

³⁶Whenever it came to rest, he said,

"Return, Lord,
    to the countless thousands of Israel."

FIRE FROM THE LORD

11 Now the people complained about their hardships in the hearing of the Lord, and when he heard them his anger was aroused. Then fire from the Lord burned among them and consumed some of the outskirts of the camp. ²When the people cried out to Moses, he prayed to the Lord and the fire died down. ³So that place was called Taberah,ᵃ because fire from the Lord had burned among them.

QUAIL FROM THE LORD

⁴The rabble with them began to crave other food, and again the Israelites started wailing and said, "If only we had meat to eat! ⁵We remember the fish we ate in Egypt at no cost—also the cucumbers, melons, leeks, onions and garlic. ⁶But now we have lost our appetite; we never see anything but this manna!"

⁷The manna was like coriander seed and looked like resin. ⁸The people went around gathering it, and then ground it in a hand mill or crushed it in a mortar. They cooked it in a pot or made it into loaves. And it tasted like something made with olive oil. ⁹When the dew settled on the camp at night, the manna also came down.

¹⁰Moses heard the people of every family wailing at the entrance to their tents. The Lord became exceedingly angry, and Moses was troubled. ¹¹He asked the Lord, "Why have you brought this trouble on your servant? What have I done

ᵃ 3 Taberah means burning.

Why did the Israelites' complaints make the Lord angry? (11:1)
God had repeatedly shown that he would care for his people. He was angry because they were ungrateful and did not have faith in him. God brought them out of Egypt and gave them what they needed to survive in the desert. When the people complained about their hardships, the Lord became angry about how little faith they had.

Why were the Israelites unhappy? (11:4)
They didn't put all of their trust in God. God promised he would take care of them, but instead of believing him and heading straight for the promised land, they wandered around in the desert and spent a lot of time at the foot of a mountain. They were worried because while they were slaves in Egypt, though difficult, they knew what to expect. In the desert, they did not know what dangers they would face. It might have been difficult, but they needed to have complete faith in God.

What are coriander seeds and resin? (11:7)
Coriander seeds come from a plant closely related to parsley. Some people think coriander seeds taste similar to parsley, with a flavor slightly like citrus. Resin is a waxy substance. Although the Israelites compared manna to familiar objects, no one knows exactly what it was.

Why was Moses frustrated? (11:10–15)
The Israelites kept complaining, and they blamed Moses for their hardships. Moses complained to God because he must have felt like he was carrying the whole nation on his back. He was so unhappy that he asked God to put him to death. Instead, God appointed elders to help Moses govern the people.

to displease you that you put the burden of all these people on me? [12] Did I conceive all these people? Did I give them birth? Why do you tell me to carry them in my arms, as a nurse carries an infant, to the land you promised on oath to their ancestors? [13] Where can I get meat for all these people? They keep wailing to me, 'Give us meat to eat!' [14] I cannot carry all these people by myself; the burden is too heavy for me. [15] If this is how you are going to treat me, please go ahead and kill me—if I have found favor in your eyes—and do not let me face my own ruin."

[16] The LORD said to Moses: "Bring me seventy of Israel's elders who are known to you as leaders and officials among the people. Have them come to the tent of meeting, that they may stand there with you. [17] I will come down and speak with you there, and I will take some of the power of the Spirit that is on you and put it on them. They will share the burden of the people with you so that you will not have to carry it alone.

[18] "Tell the people: 'Consecrate yourselves in preparation for tomorrow, when you will eat meat. The LORD heard you when you wailed, "If only we had meat to eat! We were better off in Egypt!" Now the LORD will give you meat, and you will eat it. [19] You will not eat it for just one day, or two days, or five, ten or twenty days, [20] but for a whole month—until it comes out of your nostrils and you loathe it—because you have rejected the LORD, who is among you, and have wailed before him, saying, "Why did we ever leave Egypt?"'"

[21] But Moses said, "Here I am among six hundred thousand men on foot, and you say, 'I will give them meat to eat for a whole month!' [22] Would they have enough if flocks and herds were slaughtered for them? Would they have enough if all the fish in the sea were caught for them?"

[23] The LORD answered Moses, "Is the LORD's arm too short? Now you will see whether or not what I say will come true for you."

[24] So Moses went out and told the people what the LORD had said. He brought together seventy of their elders and had them stand around the tent. [25] Then the LORD came down in the cloud and spoke with him, and he took some of the power of the Spirit that was on him and put it on the seventy elders. When the Spirit rested on them, they prophesied—but did not do so again.

[26] However, two men, whose names were Eldad and Medad, had remained in the camp. They were listed among the elders, but did not go out to the tent. Yet the Spirit also rested on them, and they prophesied in the camp. [27] A young man ran and told Moses, "Eldad and Medad are prophesying in the camp."

[28] Joshua son of Nun, who had been Moses' aide since youth, spoke up and said, "Moses, my lord, stop them!"

[29] But Moses replied, "Are you jealous for my sake? I wish that all the LORD's people were prophets and that the LORD would put his Spirit on them!" [30] Then Moses and the elders of Israel returned to the camp.

[31] Now a wind went out from the LORD and drove quail

Why were the 70 elders given the gift of prophecy? (11:25)
This showed that God's Spirit was with these leaders. Their ability to prophesy showed the rest of the people that they had been chosen by God.

Shouldn't Eldad and Medad have been punished for not going to the tent? (11:26)
These two men may not have been among the 70 elders that Moses called to the tent. Clearly they had the gift of God's Spirit, so punishing them for receiving a gift from God would not have made sense.

Why didn't the quail fly away when the Israelites got close to them? (11:31)
Large numbers of quail migrated each year across the Sinai Peninsula on their way from Africa to Europe and Asia. The birds had heavy bodies and did not fly well, so they depended on winds to help them fly. After crossing large bodies of water, they were probably weak and exhausted, so it was easy for the Israelites to catch them.

in from the sea. It scattered them up to two cubits*a* deep all around the camp, as far as a day's walk in any direction. ³²All that day and night and all the next day the people went out and gathered quail. No one gathered less than ten homers.*b* Then they spread them out all around the camp. ³³But while the meat was still between their teeth and before it could be consumed, the anger of the LORD burned against the people, and he struck them with a severe plague. ³⁴Therefore the place was named Kibroth Hattaavah,*c* because there they buried the people who had craved other food.

³⁵From Kibroth Hattaavah the people traveled to Hazeroth and stayed there.

MIRIAM AND AARON OPPOSE MOSES

12 Miriam and Aaron began to talk against Moses because of his Cushite wife, for he had married a Cushite. ²"Has the LORD spoken only through Moses?" they asked. "Hasn't he also spoken through us?" And the LORD heard this.

³(Now Moses was a very humble man, more humble than anyone else on the face of the earth.)

⁴At once the LORD said to Moses, Aaron and Miriam, "Come out to the tent of meeting, all three of you." So the three of them went out. ⁵Then the LORD came down in a pillar of cloud; he stood at the entrance to the tent and summoned Aaron and Miriam. When the two of them stepped forward, ⁶he said, "Listen to my words:

"When there is a prophet among you,
    I, the LORD, reveal myself to them in visions,
    I speak to them in dreams.
⁷But this is not true of my servant Moses;
    he is faithful in all my house.
⁸With him I speak face to face,
    clearly and not in riddles;
    he sees the form of the LORD.
Why then were you not afraid
    to speak against my servant Moses?"

⁹The anger of the LORD burned against them, and he left them.

¹⁰When the cloud lifted from above the tent, Miriam's skin was leprous*d*—it became as white as snow. Aaron turned toward her and saw that she had a defiling skin disease, ¹¹and he said to Moses, "Please, my lord, I ask you not to hold against us the sin we have so foolishly committed. ¹²Do not let her be like a stillborn infant coming from its mother's womb with its flesh half eaten away."

¹³So Moses cried out to the LORD, "Please, God, heal her!"

¹⁴The LORD replied to Moses, "If her father had spit in her face, would she not have been in disgrace for seven days? Confine her outside the camp for seven days; after that she

Why were Miriam and Aaron cruelly gossiping about Moses' Cushite wife? (12:1–2) Aaron and Miriam envied Moses because he was God's special spokesperson. They may have thought it was safer to vent their frustration on Moses' wife rather than on Moses.

Why was Miriam singled out for God's displeasure when Aaron was just as much to blame as she was? (12:10–15) It may seem unfair to an outsider, but remember that God is always just. Perhaps Miriam started the whole thing, or maybe God spared Aaron because he was the high priest.

Why did the father spit in his daughter's face? (12:14) Spitting was a public punishment.

---

a 31 That is, about 3 feet or about 90 centimeters   *b 32* That is, possibly about 1 3/4 tons or about 1.6 metric tons   *c 34 Kibroth Hattaavah* means *graves of craving.*   *d 10* The Hebrew for *leprous* was used for various diseases affecting the skin.

can be brought back."[15] So Miriam was confined outside the camp for seven days, and the people did not move on till she was brought back.

[16] After that, the people left Hazeroth and encamped in the Desert of Paran.

EXPLORING CANAAN

13 The LORD said to Moses, [2]"Send some men to explore the land of Canaan, which I am giving to the Israelites. From each ancestral tribe send one of its leaders."

[3] So at the LORD's command Moses sent them out from the Desert of Paran. All of them were leaders of the Israelites. [4] These are their names:

from the tribe of Reuben, Shammua son of Zakkur;
[5] from the tribe of Simeon, Shaphat son of Hori;
[6] from the tribe of Judah, Caleb son of Jephunneh;
[7] from the tribe of Issachar, Igal son of Joseph;
[8] from the tribe of Ephraim, Hoshea son of Nun;
[9] from the tribe of Benjamin, Palti son of Raphu;
[10] from the tribe of Zebulun, Gaddiel son of Sodi;
[11] from the tribe of Manasseh (a tribe of Joseph), Gaddi son of Susi;
[12] from the tribe of Dan, Ammiel son of Gemalli;
[13] from the tribe of Asher, Sethur son of Michael;
[14] from the tribe of Naphtali, Nahbi son of Vophsi;
[15] from the tribe of Gad, Geuel son of Maki.

[16] These are the names of the men Moses sent to explore the land. (Moses gave Hoshea son of Nun the name Joshua.)

[17] When Moses sent them to explore Canaan, he said, "Go up through the Negev and on into the hill country. [18] See what the land is like and whether the people who live there are strong or weak, few or many. [19] What kind of land do they live in? Is it good or bad? What kind of towns do they live in? Are they unwalled or fortified? [20] How is the soil? Is it fertile or poor? Are there trees in it or not? Do your best to bring back some of the fruit of the land." (It was the season for the first ripe grapes.)

[21] So they went up and explored the land from the Desert of Zin as far as Rehob, toward Lebo Hamath. [22] They went up through the Negev and came to Hebron, where Ahiman, Sheshai and Talmai, the descendants of Anak, lived. (Hebron had been built seven years before Zoan in Egypt.) [23] When they reached the Valley of Eshkol,[a] they cut off a branch bearing a single cluster of grapes. Two of them carried it on a pole between them, along with some pomegranates and figs. [24] That place was called the Valley of Eshkol because of the cluster of grapes the Israelites cut off there. [25] At the end of forty days they returned from exploring the land.

REPORT ON THE EXPLORATION

[26] They came back to Moses and Aaron and the whole Israelite community at Kadesh in the Desert of Paran. There they reported to them and to the whole assembly and

---

Why were explorers sent into the land? (13:1–2)
The LORD commanded the Israelites to scout out the promised land. This was a test of their faith. If they would have had faith in God they would have been rewarded with land flowing with milk and honey. Instead, the explorers had very few positive things to say about their journey.

Exploring Canaan (13:2)

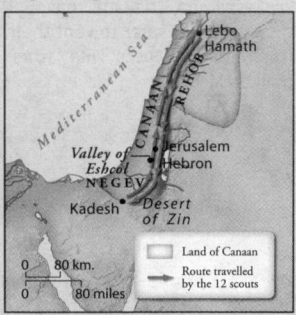

Why did Moses change Hoshea's name to Joshua? (13:16)
The names are closely related. *Hoshea* means *salvation. Joshua* means *the Lord saves.* This emphasized Joshua's future role as God's leader of the Israelites.

Who were the Anakites? (13:22, 28, 33)
The descendants of Anak were giant men. The Israelite spies were so afraid of the Anakites and their immense strength that they spread a bad report about the land God had promised to them.

---

[a] 23 *Eshkol* means *cluster*; also in verse 24.

showed them the fruit of the land. ²⁷They gave Moses this account: "We went into the land to which you sent us, and it does flow with milk and honey! Here is its fruit. ²⁸But the people who live there are powerful, and the cities are fortified and very large. We even saw descendants of Anak there. ²⁹The Amalekites live in the Negev; the Hittites, Jebusites and Amorites live in the hill country; and the Canaanites live near the sea and along the Jordan."

³⁰Then Caleb silenced the people before Moses and said, "We should go up and take possession of the land, for we can certainly do it."

³¹But the men who had gone up with him said, "We can't attack those people; they are stronger than we are." ³²And they spread among the Israelites a bad report about the land they had explored. They said, "The land we explored devours those living in it. All the people we saw there are of great size. ³³We saw the Nephilim there (the descendants of Anak come from the Nephilim). We seemed like grasshoppers in our own eyes, and we looked the same to them."

THE PEOPLE REBEL

14 That night all the members of the community raised their voices and wept aloud. ²All the Israelites grumbled against Moses and Aaron, and the whole assembly said to them, "If only we had died in Egypt! Or in this wilderness! ³Why is the LORD bringing us to this land only to let us fall by the sword? Our wives and children will be taken as plunder. Wouldn't it be better for us to go back to Egypt?" ⁴And they said to each other, "We should choose a leader and go back to Egypt."

⁵Then Moses and Aaron fell facedown in front of the whole Israelite assembly gathered there. ⁶Joshua son of Nun and Caleb son of Jephunneh, who were among those who had explored the land, tore their clothes ⁷and said to the entire Israelite assembly, "The land we passed through and explored is exceedingly good. ⁸If the LORD is pleased with us, he will lead us into that land, a land flowing with milk and honey, and will give it to us. ⁹Only do not rebel against the LORD. And do not be afraid of the people of the land, because we will devour them. Their protection is gone, but the LORD is with us. Do not be afraid of them."

¹⁰But the whole assembly talked about stoning them.

How did the Israelites react to the report of the spies? (14:1–4)
The people were frightened and upset. Once again they complained to Moses and Aaron about leaving Egypt. They seemed to have forgotten all the miraculous ways that the LORD had cared for them since they left Egypt.

Why did Joshua and Caleb tear their clothes? (14:6)
This was a traditional sign of mourning. They were sad and upset that the Israelites were so willing to believe the bad report about the promised land.

Why did the Israelites consider stoning their leaders? (14:10)
Moses, Aaron, Caleb, and Joshua urged the Israelites to enter a dangerous area, and the people thought they were threatening the community's existence. Stoning was public execution for a major offense against God or the community, so the people thought this was a fitting punishment.

Does God punish children for what their parents do?
NUMBERS 14

Throughout history God's people often turned away from God and disobeyed him. When this happened, God would often punish the whole nation. (This is sometimes called corporate sin, where a large group of people sin against God and the effects are far reaching.) For example, the Israelites had to wander in the wilderness for an extra 40 years because of the sins of their leaders. Sin has consequences that sometimes carry on through the generations.

By Jesus' time, the rabbis had developed a theory that if someone suffered from a physical ailment, that person's parents or grandparents must have sinned, or that the person himself or herself had eve sinned before being born. Jesus provided a new way of thinking in John 9:2. Just because some fers does not mean that God is directly punishing that person for their sin or the sin of th

Then the glory of the LORD appeared at the tent of meeting to all the Israelites. [11]The LORD said to Moses, "How long will these people treat me with contempt? How long will they refuse to believe in me, in spite of all the signs I have performed among them? [12]I will strike them down with a plague and destroy them, but I will make you into a nation greater and stronger than they."

[13]Moses said to the LORD, "Then the Egyptians will hear about it! By your power you brought these people up from among them. [14]And they will tell the inhabitants of this land about it. They have already heard that you, LORD, are with these people and that you, LORD, have been seen face to face, that your cloud stays over them, and that you go before them in a pillar of cloud by day and a pillar of fire by night. [15]If you put all these people to death, leaving none alive, the nations who have heard this report about you will say, [16]'The LORD was not able to bring these people into the land he promised them on oath, so he slaughtered them in the wilderness.'

[17]"Now may the Lord's strength be displayed, just as you have declared: [18]'The LORD is slow to anger, abounding in love and forgiving sin and rebellion. Yet he does not leave the guilty unpunished; he punishes the children for the sin of the parents to the third and fourth generation.' [19]In accordance with your great love, forgive the sin of these people, just as you have pardoned them from the time they left Egypt until now."

[20]The LORD replied, "I have forgiven them, as you asked. [21]Nevertheless, as surely as I live and as surely as the glory of the LORD fills the whole earth, [22]not one of those who saw my glory and the signs I performed in Egypt and in the wilderness but who disobeyed me and tested me ten times— [23]not one of them will ever see the land I promised on oath to their ancestors. No one who has treated me with contempt will ever see it. [24]But because my servant Caleb has a different spirit and follows me wholeheartedly, I will bring him into the land he went to, and his descendants will inherit it. [25]Since the Amalekites and the Canaanites are living in the valleys, turn back tomorrow and set out toward the desert along the route to the Red Sea.*"

[26]The LORD said to Moses and Aaron: [27]"How long will this wicked community grumble against me? I have heard the complaints of these grumbling Israelites. [28]So tell them, 'As surely as I live, declares the LORD, I will do to you the very thing I heard you say: [29]In this wilderness your bodies will fall—every one of you twenty years old or more who was counted in the census and who has grumbled against me. [30]Not one of you will enter the land I swore with uplifted hand to make your home, except Caleb son of Jephunneh and Joshua son of Nun. [31]As for your children that you said would be taken as plunder, I will bring them in to enjoy the land you have rejected. [32]But as for you, your bodies will fall in this wilderness. [33]Your children will be shepherds here for forty years, suffering for your unfaithfulness, until the last of your bodies lies in the wilderness. [34]For forty years—one year for each of the forty days you explored the land—you

Why was Moses concerned about the Egyptians' opinion? (14:13)
Moses wanted to protect the LORD's reputation. If the Israelites died in the desert, the Egyptians may have thought the plagues were just a coincidence rather than an act of God.

What other reason did Moses give for sparing the people of Israel? (14:17–19)
After arguing to protect God's reputation, Moses spoke about God's character. Moses reminded God of his loyal love for his people.

If the people died, does that mean that God didn't really forgive the people for their sins? (14:20–35)
No. God definitely forgave these people. However, the consequences of sin may still happen. God did not kill them, but they were not allowed to enter the promised land.

---

a 25 Or *the Sea of Reeds*

will suffer for your sins and know what it is like to have me against you.' ³⁵I, the Lord, have spoken, and I will surely do these things to this whole wicked community, which has banded together against me. They will meet their end in this wilderness; here they will die."

³⁶So the men Moses had sent to explore the land, who returned and made the whole community grumble against him by spreading a bad report about it— ³⁷these men who were responsible for spreading the bad report about the land were struck down and died of a plague before the Lord. ³⁸Of the men who went to explore the land, only Joshua son of Nun and Caleb son of Jephunneh survived.

³⁹When Moses reported this to all the Israelites, they mourned bitterly. ⁴⁰Early the next morning they set out for the highest point in the hill country, saying, "Now we are ready to go up to the land the Lord promised. Surely we have sinned!"

⁴¹But Moses said, "Why are you disobeying the Lord's command? This will not succeed! ⁴²Do not go up, because the Lord is not with you. You will be defeated by your enemies, ⁴³for the Amalekites and the Canaanites will face you there. Because you have turned away from the Lord, he will not be with you and you will fall by the sword."

⁴⁴Nevertheless, in their presumption they went up toward the highest point in the hill country, though neither Moses nor the ark of the Lord's covenant moved from the camp. ⁴⁵Then the Amalekites and the Canaanites who lived in that hill country came down and attacked them and beat them down all the way to Hormah.

SUPPLEMENTARY OFFERINGS

15 The Lord said to Moses, ²"Speak to the Israelites and say to them: 'After you enter the land I am giving you as a home ³and you present to the Lord food offerings from the herd or the flock, as an aroma pleasing to the Lord—whether burnt offerings or sacrifices, for special vows or freewill offerings or festival offerings— ⁴then the person who brings an offering shall present to the Lord a grain offering of a tenth of an ephah*a* of the finest flour mixed with a quarter of a hin*b* of olive oil. ⁵With each lamb for the burnt offering or the sacrifice, prepare a quarter of a hin of wine as a drink offering.

⁶"'With a ram prepare a grain offering of two-tenths of an ephah*c* of the finest flour mixed with a third of a hin*d* of olive oil, ⁷and a third of a hin of wine as a drink offering. Offer it as an aroma pleasing to the Lord.

⁸"'When you prepare a young bull as a burnt offering or sacrifice, for a special vow or a fellowship offering to the Lord, ⁹bring with the bull a grain offering of three-tenths of an ephah*e* of the finest flour mixed with half a hin*f* of olive

What was the significance of 40 years? (14:34–35)
The Israelites had to spend one year in the desert for each day the spies spent in Canaan.

Why did the Israelites decide to go into Canaan after Moses told them they would die in the desert? (14:40–45)
They might not have believed that God would let them die in the desert. Their lack of faith in God was replaced by a belief that they could somehow force God to change his mind.

Why would the aroma please God? (15:3)
The offerings showed God the people's willingness to follow him, and it was the offerings that produced the smell. The obedience was what pleased God, not the actual smell.

What was a drink offering? (15:5)
The purpose of a drink offering was to thank and honor God for his greatness. Wine or oil was usually offered up by pouring it out.

---

a 4 That is, probably about 3 1/2 pounds or about 1.6 kilograms   *b 4* That is, about 1 quart or about 1 liter; also in verse 5   *c 6* That is, probably about 7 pounds or about 3.2 kilograms   *d 6* That is, about 1 1/3 quarts or about 1.3 liters; also in verse 7   *e 9* That is, probably about 11 pounds or about 5 kilograms   *f 9* That is, about 2 quarts or about 1.9 liters; also in verse 10

oil, [10]and also bring half a hin of wine as a drink offering. This will be a food offering, an aroma pleasing to the LORD. [11]Each bull or ram, each lamb or young goat, is to be prepared in this manner. [12]Do this for each one, for as many as you prepare.

[13]"'Everyone who is native-born must do these things in this way when they present a food offering as an aroma pleasing to the LORD. [14]For the generations to come, whenever a foreigner or anyone else living among you presents a food offering as an aroma pleasing to the LORD, they must do exactly as you do. [15]The community is to have the same rules for you and for the foreigner residing among you; this is a lasting ordinance for the generations to come. You and the foreigner shall be the same before the LORD: [16]The same laws and regulations will apply both to you and to the foreigner residing among you.'"

[17]The LORD said to Moses, [18]"Speak to the Israelites and say to them: 'When you enter the land to which I am taking you [19]and you eat the food of the land, present a portion as an offering to the LORD. [20]Present a loaf from the first of your ground meal and present it as an offering from the threshing floor. [21]Throughout the generations to come you are to give this offering to the LORD from the first of your ground meal.

OFFERINGS FOR UNINTENTIONAL SINS

[22]"'Now if you as a community unintentionally fail to keep any of these commands the LORD gave Moses— [23]any of the LORD's commands to you through him, from the day the LORD gave them and continuing through the generations to come— [24]and if this is done unintentionally without the community being aware of it, then the whole community is to offer a young bull for a burnt offering as an aroma pleasing to the LORD, along with its prescribed grain offering and drink offering, and a male goat for a sin offering.[a] [25]The priest is to make atonement for the whole Israelite community, and they will be forgiven, for it was not intentional and they have presented to the LORD for their wrong a food offering and a sin offering. [26]The whole Israelite community and the foreigners residing among them will be forgiven, because all the people were involved in the unintentional wrong.

[27]"'But if just one person sins unintentionally, that person must bring a year-old female goat for a sin offering. [28]The priest is to make atonement before the LORD for the one who erred by sinning unintentionally, and when atonement has been made, that person will be forgiven. [29]One and the same law applies to everyone who sins unintentionally, whether a native-born Israelite or a foreigner residing among you.

[30]"'But anyone who sins defiantly, whether native-born or foreigner, blasphemes the LORD and must be cut off from the people of Israel. [31]Because they have despised the LORD's word and broken his commands, they must surely be cut off; their guilt remains on them.'"

---

[a] 24 Or *purification offering*; also in verses 25 and 27

Why did sacrifices have to be made for unintentional sins? (15:22–29)
Even if they didn't commit the sin intentionally, the Israelites believed there was still guilt associated with the sin. In order to rid themselves of this guilt, sacrifices were made.

Who decided whether a sin was intentional or not? (15:22–29)
A person would tell the priest about the sin. The priest would decide whether or not the sin was intentional. A sin due to weakness had a different penalty than sin caused by choosing to rebel against God.

THE SABBATH-BREAKER PUT TO DEATH

³²While the Israelites were in the wilderness, a man was found gathering wood on the Sabbath day. ³³Those who found him gathering wood brought him to Moses and Aaron and the whole assembly, ³⁴and they kept him in custody, because it was not clear what should be done to him. ³⁵Then the LORD said to Moses, "The man must die. The whole assembly must stone him outside the camp." ³⁶So the assembly took him outside the camp and stoned him to death, as the LORD commanded Moses.

TASSELS ON GARMENTS

³⁷The LORD said to Moses, ³⁸"Speak to the Israelites and say to them: 'Throughout the generations to come you are to make tassels on the corners of your garments, with a blue cord on each tassel. ³⁹You will have these tassels to look at and so you will remember all the commands of the LORD, that you may obey them and not prostitute yourselves by chasing after the lusts of your own hearts and eyes. ⁴⁰Then you will remember to obey all my commands and will be consecrated to your God. ⁴¹I am the LORD your God, who brought you out of Egypt to be your God. I am the LORD your God.'"

KORAH, DATHAN AND ABIRAM

16 Korah son of Izhar, the son of Kohath, the son of Levi, and certain Reubenites—Dathan and Abiram, sons of Eliab, and On son of Peleth—became insolent*ᵃ* ²and rose up against Moses. With them were 250 Israelite men, well-known community leaders who had been appointed members of the council. ³They came as a group to oppose Moses and Aaron and said to them, "You have gone too far! The whole community is holy, every one of them, and the LORD is with them. Why then do you set yourselves above the LORD's assembly?"

⁴When Moses heard this, he fell facedown. ⁵Then he said to Korah and all his followers: "In the morning the LORD will show who belongs to him and who is holy, and he will have that person come near him. The man he chooses he will cause to come near him. ⁶You, Korah, and all your followers are to do this: Take censers ⁷and tomorrow put burning coals and incense in them before the LORD. The man the LORD chooses will be the one who is holy. You Levites have gone too far!"

⁸Moses also said to Korah, "Now listen, you Levites! ⁹Isn't it enough for you that the God of Israel has separated you from the rest of the Israelite community and brought you near himself to do the work at the LORD's tabernacle and to stand before the community and minister to them? ¹⁰He has brought you and all your fellow Levites near himself, but now you are trying to get the priesthood too. ¹¹It is against the LORD that you and all your followers have banded together. Who is Aaron that you should grumble against him?"

ᵃ *1 Or Peleth—took men*

Why was this man stoned for gathering wood on the Sabbath? (15:32–36)
God established the death penalty for breaking the Sabbath in Exodus 31:12–17 and 35:1–3. And his rules are to be obeyed. The stoning showed in a strong way that God was serious.

How would tassels help the people obey God's laws? (15:38–40)
All of the Jews wore tassels on their clothing. When they looked at the tassel they were reminded of their promise to be faithful to God's commands. The blue cord probably represented royalty as a reminder that God was ruler over all.

What did Korah and his followers accuse Moses and Aaron of doing? (16:3)
Korah, Dathan, Abiram, and On claimed that since all of God's people were holy, Moses and Aaron weren't the only ones qualified to lead Israel. They said that Moses and Aaron had misused their positions as leaders.

Weren't all the Levites priests? (16:10)
No. All the Levites served God, but not all the Levites were priests. They all had jobs related to the priests and the holy things, but only descendants of Aaron could be priests.

What was the land flowing with milk and honey? (16:13)
This phrase described Canaan (see Exodus 3:8 and Number 13:27), but Dathan and Abiram used it to describe Egypt.

What test was to be given to the rebels? (16:18–21)
The trial was to be by fire. Which men would the Lord accept as priests in the holy tabernacle? The 250 men with Korah came with their censers of fire to challenge Moses and Aaron at the entrance to the tent of meeting. The Lord told Moses and Aaron to separate themselves from the rebellious men.

How were the people of Israel supposed to know that this judgment was from the Lord? (16:30)
If the Lord sent Moses, the men who rebelled would die in an unusual way, like being swallowed by the earth. That's exactly what happened.

¹²Then Moses summoned Dathan and Abiram, the sons of Eliab. But they said, "We will not come! ¹³Isn't it enough that you have brought us up out of a land flowing with milk and honey to kill us in the wilderness? And now you also want to lord it over us! ¹⁴Moreover, you haven't brought us into a land flowing with milk and honey or given us an inheritance of fields and vineyards. Do you want to treat these men like slavesᵃ? No, we will not come!"

¹⁵Then Moses became very angry and said to the Lord, "Do not accept their offering. I have not taken so much as a donkey from them, nor have I wronged any of them."

¹⁶Moses said to Korah, "You and all your followers are to appear before the Lord tomorrow—you and they and Aaron. ¹⁷Each man is to take his censer and put incense in it—250 censers in all—and present it before the Lord. You and Aaron are to present your censers also." ¹⁸So each of them took his censer, put burning coals and incense in it, and stood with Moses and Aaron at the entrance to the tent of meeting. ¹⁹When Korah had gathered all his followers in opposition to them at the entrance to the tent of meeting, the glory of the Lord appeared to the entire assembly. ²⁰The Lord said to Moses and Aaron, ²¹"Separate yourselves from this assembly so I can put an end to them at once."

²²But Moses and Aaron fell facedown and cried out, "O God, the God who gives breath to all living things, will you be angry with the entire assembly when only one man sins?"

²³Then the Lord said to Moses, ²⁴"Say to the assembly, 'Move away from the tents of Korah, Dathan and Abiram.'"

²⁵Moses got up and went to Dathan and Abiram, and the elders of Israel followed him. ²⁶He warned the assembly, "Move back from the tents of these wicked men! Do not touch anything belonging to them, or you will be swept away because of all their sins." ²⁷So they moved away from the tents of Korah, Dathan and Abiram. Dathan and Abiram had come out and were standing with their wives, children and little ones at the entrances to their tents.

²⁸Then Moses said, "This is how you will know that the Lord has sent me to do all these things and that it was not my idea: ²⁹If these men die a natural death and suffer the fate of all mankind, then the Lord has not sent me. ³⁰But if the Lord brings about something totally new, and the earth opens its mouth and swallows them, with everything that belongs to them, and they go down alive into the realm of the dead, then you will know that these men have treated the Lord with contempt."

³¹As soon as he finished saying all this, the ground under them split apart ³²and the earth opened its mouth and swallowed them and their households, and all those associated with Korah, together with their possessions. ³³They went down alive into the realm of the dead, with everything they owned; the earth closed over them, and they perished and were gone from the community. ³⁴At their cries, all the Israelites around them fled, shouting, "The earth is going to swallow us too!"

ᵃ 14 Or *to deceive these men*; Hebrew *Will you gouge out the eyes of these men*

[35] And fire came out from the LORD and consumed the 250 men who were offering the incense.

[36] The LORD said to Moses, [37] "Tell Eleazar son of Aaron, the priest, to remove the censers from the charred remains and scatter the coals some distance away, for the censers are holy— [38] the censers of the men who sinned at the cost of their lives. Hammer the censers into sheets to overlay the altar, for they were presented before the LORD and have become holy. Let them be a sign to the Israelites."

[39] So Eleazar the priest collected the bronze censers brought by those who had been burned to death, and he had them hammered out to overlay the altar, [40] as the LORD directed him through Moses. This was to remind the Israelites that no one except a descendant of Aaron should come to burn incense before the LORD, or he would become like Korah and his followers.

[41] The next day the whole Israelite community grumbled against Moses and Aaron. "You have killed the LORD's people," they said.

[42] But when the assembly gathered in opposition to Moses and Aaron and turned toward the tent of meeting, suddenly the cloud covered it and the glory of the LORD appeared. [43] Then Moses and Aaron went to the front of the tent of meeting, [44] and the LORD said to Moses, [45] "Get away from this assembly so I can put an end to them at once." And they fell facedown.

[46] Then Moses said to Aaron, "Take your censer and put incense in it, along with burning coals from the altar, and hurry to the assembly to make atonement for them. Wrath has come out from the LORD; the plague has started." [47] So Aaron did as Moses said, and ran into the midst of the assembly. The plague had already started among the people, but Aaron offered the incense and made atonement for them. [48] He stood between the living and the dead, and the plague stopped. [49] But 14,700 people died from the plague, in addition to those who had died because of Korah. [50] Then Aaron returned to Moses at the entrance to the tent of meeting, for the plague had stopped.[a]

THE BUDDING OF AARON'S STAFF

17[b] The LORD said to Moses, [2] "Speak to the Israelites and get twelve staffs from them, one from the leader of each of their ancestral tribes. Write the name of each man on his staff. [3] On the staff of Levi write Aaron's name, for there must be one staff for the head of each ancestral tribe. [4] Place them in the tent of meeting in front of the ark of the covenant law, where I meet with you. [5] The staff belonging to the man I choose will sprout, and I will rid myself of this constant grumbling against you by the Israelites."

[6] So Moses spoke to the Israelites, and their leaders gave him twelve staffs, one for the leader of each of their ancestral tribes, and Aaron's staff was among them. [7] Moses placed the staffs before the LORD in the tent of the covenant law.

[a] 50 In Hebrew texts 16:36-50 is numbered 17:1-15.   [b] In Hebrew texts 17:1-13 is numbered 17:16-28.

What is a censer? (16:37)
A censer is a small container that incense is burned in.

Why did the Israelites grumble about what had happened? (16:41)
By the next day already the Israelites were complaining to Moses and Aaron. Their rebellious attitude was so intense that they would not see or admit that God was the one who had judged Korah and the others.

How did burning incense atone for the sins of the people? (16:46)
Incense was part of the atonement process (the way to make the relationship right between God and men) described in Leviticus 16:12-13. God created this way of satisfying his anger when Israel sinned.

⁸The next day Moses entered the tent and saw that Aaron's staff, which represented the tribe of Levi, had not only sprouted but had budded, blossomed and produced almonds. ⁹Then Moses brought out all the staffs from the Lord's presence to all the Israelites. They looked at them, and each of the leaders took his own staff.

¹⁰The Lord said to Moses, "Put back Aaron's staff in front of the ark of the covenant law, to be kept as a sign to the rebellious. This will put an end to their grumbling against me, so that they will not die." ¹¹Moses did just as the Lord commanded him.

¹²The Israelites said to Moses, "We will die! We are lost, we are all lost! ¹³Anyone who even comes near the tabernacle of the Lord will die. Are we all going to die?"

DUTIES OF PRIESTS AND LEVITES

18 The Lord said to Aaron, "You, your sons and your family are to bear the responsibility for offenses connected with the sanctuary, and you and your sons alone are to bear the responsibility for offenses connected with the priesthood. ²Bring your fellow Levites from your ancestral tribe to join you and assist you when you and your sons minister before the tent of the covenant law. ³They are to be responsible to you and are to perform all the duties of the tent, but they must not go near the furnishings of the sanctuary or the altar. Otherwise both they and you will die. ⁴They are to join you and be responsible for the care of the tent of meeting—all the work at the tent—and no one else may come near where you are.

⁵"You are to be responsible for the care of the sanctuary and the altar, so that my wrath will not fall on the Israelites again. ⁶I myself have selected your fellow Levites from among the Israelites as a gift to you, dedicated to the Lord to do the work at the tent of meeting. ⁷But only you and your sons may serve as priests in connection with everything at the altar and inside the curtain. I am giving you the service of the priesthood as a gift. Anyone else who comes near the sanctuary is to be put to death."

OFFERINGS FOR PRIESTS AND LEVITES

⁸Then the Lord said to Aaron, "I myself have put you in charge of the offerings presented to me; all the holy offerings the Israelites give me I give to you and your sons as your portion, your perpetual share. ⁹You are to have the part of the most holy offerings that is kept from the fire. From all the gifts they bring me as most holy offerings, whether grain or sin[a] or guilt offerings, that part belongs to you and your sons. ¹⁰Eat it as something most holy; every male shall eat it. You must regard it as holy.

¹¹"This also is yours: whatever is set aside from the gifts of all the wave offerings of the Israelites. I give this to you and your sons and daughters as your perpetual share. Everyone in your household who is ceremonially clean may eat it.

Why were the Israelites overcome with fear? (17:12) They finally realized that God caused the disaster, and not Moses or Aaron. They feared for their lives.

Why would the priests be punished if the Levites went near the furnishings of the sanctuary or the altar? (18:3) It was a holy place, and only priests were permitted to be there. If a priest allowed a Levite, or any other person who was not a priest, into the holy places, both were guilty of breaking God's commandment.

Why was being a priest considered a gift? (18:7) The priests had a special relationship with God. They were important to the Israelites because they were able to save the people from God's anger.

---

[a] 9 Or *purification*

¹²"I give you all the finest olive oil and all the finest new wine and grain they give the LORD as the firstfruits of their harvest. ¹³All the land's firstfruits that they bring to the LORD will be yours. Everyone in your household who is ceremonially clean may eat it.

¹⁴"Everything in Israel that is devoted[a] to the LORD is yours. ¹⁵The first offspring of every womb, both human and animal, that is offered to the LORD is yours. But you must redeem every firstborn son and every firstborn male of unclean animals. ¹⁶When they are a month old, you must redeem them at the redemption price set at five shekels[b] of silver, according to the sanctuary shekel, which weighs twenty gerahs.

¹⁷"But you must not redeem the firstborn of a cow, a sheep or a goat; they are holy. Splash their blood against the altar and burn their fat as a food offering, an aroma pleasing to the LORD. ¹⁸Their meat is to be yours, just as the breast of the wave offering and the right thigh are yours. ¹⁹Whatever is set aside from the holy offerings the Israelites present to the LORD I give to you and your sons and daughters as your perpetual share. It is an everlasting covenant of salt before the LORD for both you and your offspring."

²⁰The LORD said to Aaron, "You will have no inheritance in their land, nor will you have any share among them; I am your share and your inheritance among the Israelites.

²¹"I give to the Levites all the tithes in Israel as their inheritance in return for the work they do while serving at the tent of meeting. ²²From now on the Israelites must not go near the tent of meeting, or they will bear the consequences of their sin and will die. ²³It is the Levites who are to do the work at the tent of meeting and bear the responsibility for any offenses they commit against it. This is a lasting ordinance for the generations to come. They will receive no inheritance among the Israelites. ²⁴Instead, I give to the Levites as their inheritance the tithes that the Israelites present as an offering to the LORD. That is why I said concerning them: 'They will have no inheritance among the Israelites.'"

²⁵The LORD said to Moses, ²⁶"Speak to the Levites and say to them: 'When you receive from the Israelites the tithe I give you as your inheritance, you must present a tenth of that tithe as the LORD's offering. ²⁷Your offering will be reckoned to you as grain from the threshing floor or juice from the winepress. ²⁸In this way you also will present an offering to the LORD from all the tithes you receive from the Israelites. From these tithes you must give the LORD's portion to Aaron the priest. ²⁹You must present as the LORD's portion the best and holiest part of everything given to you.'

³⁰"Say to the Levites: 'When you present the best part, it will be reckoned to you as the product of the threshing floor or the winepress. ³¹You and your households may eat the rest of it anywhere, for it is your wages for your work at the tent of meeting. ³²By presenting the best part of it you will not be guilty in this matter; then you will not defile the holy offerings of the Israelites, and you will not die.'"

[a] 14 The Hebrew term refers to the irrevocable giving over of things or persons to the LORD.   [b] 16 That is, about 2 ounces or about 58 grams

Why were oil, wine, and grain important? (18:12)
These were the main foods in the Israelites' diet. God's people gave their finest produce to the Lord.

Why couldn't the Levites own land? (18:20, 23)
The Levites needed to focus on serving God rather than their own interests. Owning land was a big responsibility and would have distracted them from serving God.

Were the Levites expected to tithe also? (18:26–32)
Yes. Even though they depended on the tithes and offerings of the people, the Levites were supposed to worship God by giving one-tenth of what they received to Aaron. They were supposed to make sure that the best part was given to honor the Lord.

Why was a red heifer killed? (19:2–3)
The young female calf was killed and burned. The ashes from the calf were needed to make the "water of cleansing" used to show that a person was washing away their sin. The red color of the calf represented blood, while using a female calf symbolized new life.

Why were the third and seventh days special? (19:12)
The numbers three and seven symbolize fullness or completeness.

THE WATER OF CLEANSING

19 The LORD said to Moses and Aaron: ²"This is a requirement of the law that the LORD has commanded: Tell the Israelites to bring you a red heifer without defect or blemish and that has never been under a yoke. ³Give it to Eleazar the priest; it is to be taken outside the camp and slaughtered in his presence. ⁴Then Eleazar the priest is to take some of its blood on his finger and sprinkle it seven times toward the front of the tent of meeting. ⁵While he watches, the heifer is to be burned—its hide, flesh, blood and intestines. ⁶The priest is to take some cedar wood, hyssop and scarlet wool and throw them onto the burning heifer. ⁷After that, the priest must wash his clothes and bathe himself with water. He may then come into the camp, but he will be ceremonially unclean till evening. ⁸The man who burns it must also wash his clothes and bathe with water, and he too will be unclean till evening.

⁹"A man who is clean shall gather up the ashes of the heifer and put them in a ceremonially clean place outside the camp. They are to be kept by the Israelite community for use in the water of cleansing; it is for purification from sin. ¹⁰The man who gathers up the ashes of the heifer must also wash his clothes, and he too will be unclean till evening. This will be a lasting ordinance both for the Israelites and for the foreigners residing among them.

¹¹"Whoever touches a human corpse will be unclean for seven days. ¹²They must purify themselves with the water on the third day and on the seventh day; then they will be clean. But if they do not purify themselves on the third and seventh days, they will not be clean. ¹³If they fail to purify themselves after touching a human corpse, they defile the LORD's tabernacle. They must be cut off from Israel. Because the water of cleansing has not been sprinkled on them, they are unclean; their uncleanness remains on them.

¹⁴"This is the law that applies when a person dies in a tent: Anyone who enters the tent and anyone who is in it will be unclean for seven days, ¹⁵and every open container without a lid fastened on it will be unclean.

¹⁶"Anyone out in the open who touches someone who has been killed with a sword or someone who has died a natural death, or anyone who touches a human bone or a grave, will be unclean for seven days.

¹⁷"For the unclean person, put some ashes from the burned purification offering into a jar and pour fresh water over them. ¹⁸Then a man who is ceremonially clean is to take some hyssop, dip it in the water and sprinkle the tent and all the furnishings and the people who were there. He must also sprinkle anyone who has touched a human bone or a grave or anyone who has been killed or anyone who has died a natural death. ¹⁹The man who is clean is to sprinkle those who are unclean on the third and seventh days, and on the seventh day he is to purify them. Those who are being cleansed must wash their clothes and bathe with water, and that evening they will be clean. ²⁰But if those who are unclean do not purify themselves, they must be cut off from the community,

because they have defiled the sanctuary of the LORD. The water of cleansing has not been sprinkled on them, and they are unclean. ²¹This is a lasting ordinance for them.

"The man who sprinkles the water of cleansing must also wash his clothes, and anyone who touches the water of cleansing will be unclean till evening. ²²Anything that an unclean person touches becomes unclean, and anyone who touches it becomes unclean till evening."

WATER FROM THE ROCK

20 In the first month the whole Israelite community arrived at the Desert of Zin, and they stayed at Kadesh. There Miriam died and was buried.

²Now there was no water for the community, and the people gathered in opposition to Moses and Aaron. ³They quarreled with Moses and said, "If only we had died when our brothers fell dead before the LORD! ⁴Why did you bring the LORD's community into this wilderness, that we and our livestock should die here? ⁵Why did you bring us up out of Egypt to this terrible place? It has no grain or figs, grapevines or pomegranates. And there is no water to drink!"

⁶Moses and Aaron went from the assembly to the entrance to the tent of meeting and fell facedown, and the glory of the LORD appeared to them. ⁷The LORD said to Moses, ⁸"Take the staff, and you and your brother Aaron gather the assembly together. Speak to that rock before their eyes and it will pour out its water. You will bring water out of the rock for the community so they and their livestock can drink."

⁹So Moses took the staff from the LORD's presence, just as he commanded him. ¹⁰He and Aaron gathered the assembly together in front of the rock and Moses said to them, "Listen, you rebels, must we bring you water out of this rock?" ¹¹Then Moses raised his arm and struck the rock twice with his staff. Water gushed out, and the community and their livestock drank.

¹²But the LORD said to Moses and Aaron, "Because you did not trust in me enough to honor me as holy in the sight of the Israelites, you will not bring this community into the land I give them."

¹³These were the waters of Meribah,ᵃ where the Israelites quarreled with the LORD and where he was proved holy among them.

EDOM DENIES ISRAEL PASSAGE

¹⁴Moses sent messengers from Kadesh to the king of Edom, saying:

"This is what your brother Israel says: You know about all the hardships that have come on us. ¹⁵Our ancestors went down into Egypt, and we lived there many years. The Egyptians mistreated us and our ancestors, ¹⁶but when we cried out to the LORD, he heard our cry and sent an angel and brought us out of Egypt.

"Now we are here at Kadesh, a town on the edge of

ᵃ *13 Meribah* means *quarreling.*

Why did the people of Israel continue to complain after God had showed his power? (20:3–4)
This happened 40 years after Korah and his followers had revolted. Most of these people had not seen God's response to that rebellion.

How did Moses disobey God? (20:11)
The LORD had told Moses to speak to the rock and it would produce water. But Moses was so angry with the people that he hit the rock twice with his staff. Moses did not trust God that speaking would be enough to make water come from the rock.

How did the LORD show that he was holy? (20:12–13)
Even though God chose Moses and Aaron, God punished them for disobeying. But God also provided water for his people even though their leaders had not been obedient to him.

Why did the Israelites consider the Edomites to be their brothers? (20:14)
They shared a common ancestor. The Edomites were descended from Isaac's son Esau. The Israelites were descended from Esau's twin brother, Jacob, who was later given the name Israel. Through Jacob, the Israelites inherited God's promises to Abraham. Esau, the slightly older brother, would normally have received the promises instead. (See Genesis 27:1–40.) There was still tension between the Israelites and the Edomites.

What was the King's Highway? (20:17)
This was the major north-south trade route, extending from Arabia to Damascus.

Why did Edom refuse to allow the Israelites to pass through the land? (20:20–21)
The Edomites were afraid that a neighboring country, already at war with their allies, would attack the Israelites and start a war while they traveled through Edom.

How did the Israelites mourn for 30 days? (20:29)
After Aaron died (the Bible says he was "gathered to his people"), the Israelites honored him by mourning his death for a month. They mourned by spending a short time each day remembering their great leader.

Why did the Canaanite cities have to be completely destroyed? (21:2)
Destroying the cities got rid of all traces of pagan worship. The Israelites were not as tempted to be unfaithful to God when the pagan places of worship were gone.

Journey to Moab (21:4)

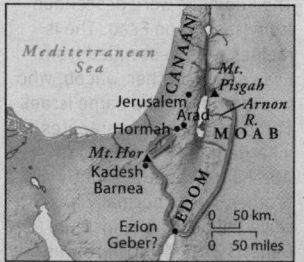

your territory. ¹⁷ Please let us pass through your country. We will not go through any field or vineyard, or drink water from any well. We will travel along the King's Highway and not turn to the right or to the left until we have passed through your territory."

¹⁸ But Edom answered:

"You may not pass through here; if you try, we will march out and attack you with the sword."

¹⁹ The Israelites replied:

"We will go along the main road, and if we or our livestock drink any of your water, we will pay for it. We only want to pass through on foot—nothing else."

²⁰ Again they answered:

"You may not pass through."

Then Edom came out against them with a large and powerful army. ²¹ Since Edom refused to let them go through their territory, Israel turned away from them.

THE DEATH OF AARON

²² The whole Israelite community set out from Kadesh and came to Mount Hor. ²³ At Mount Hor, near the border of Edom, the LORD said to Moses and Aaron, ²⁴ "Aaron will be gathered to his people. He will not enter the land I give the Israelites, because both of you rebelled against my command at the waters of Meribah. ²⁵ Get Aaron and his son Eleazar and take them up Mount Hor. ²⁶ Remove Aaron's garments and put them on his son Eleazar, for Aaron will be gathered to his people; he will die there."

²⁷ Moses did as the LORD commanded: They went up Mount Hor in the sight of the whole community. ²⁸ Moses removed Aaron's garments and put them on his son Eleazar. And Aaron died there on top of the mountain. Then Moses and Eleazar came down from the mountain, ²⁹ and when the whole community learned that Aaron had died, all the Israelites mourned for him thirty days.

ARAD DESTROYED

21 When the Canaanite king of Arad, who lived in the Negev, heard that Israel was coming along the road to Atharim, he attacked the Israelites and captured some of them. ² Then Israel made this vow to the LORD: "If you will deliver these people into our hands, we will totally destroy* their cities." ³ The LORD listened to Israel's plea and gave the Canaanites over to them. They completely destroyed them and their towns; so the place was named Hormah.*

THE BRONZE SNAKE

⁴ They traveled from Mount Hor along the route to the Red Sea,* to go around Edom. But the people grew impatient

---

a 2 The Hebrew term refers to the irrevocable giving over of things or persons to the LORD, often by totally destroying them; also in verse 3. *b 3 Hormah* means *destruction.* *c 4 Or the Sea of Reeds*

on the way; [5] they spoke against God and against Moses, and said, "Why have you brought us up out of Egypt to die in the wilderness? There is no bread! There is no water! And we detest this miserable food!"

[6] Then the LORD sent venomous snakes among them; they bit the people and many Israelites died. [7] The people came to Moses and said, "We sinned when we spoke against the LORD and against you. Pray that the LORD will take the snakes away from us." So Moses prayed for the people.

[8] The LORD said to Moses, "Make a snake and put it up on a pole; anyone who is bitten can look at it and live." [9] So Moses made a bronze snake and put it up on a pole. Then when anyone was bitten by a snake and looked at the bronze snake, they lived.

THE JOURNEY TO MOAB

[10] The Israelites moved on and camped at Oboth. [11] Then they set out from Oboth and camped in Iye Abarim, in the wilderness that faces Moab toward the sunrise. [12] From there they moved on and camped in the Zered Valley. [13] They set out from there and camped alongside the Arnon, which is in the wilderness extending into Amorite territory. The Arnon is the border of Moab, between Moab and the Amorites. [14] That is why the Book of the Wars of the LORD says:

". . . Zahab[a] in Suphah and the ravines,
    the Arnon [15] and[b] the slopes of the ravines
that lead to the settlement of Ar
    and lie along the border of Moab."

[16] From there they continued on to Beer, the well where the LORD said to Moses, "Gather the people together and I will give them water."

[17] Then Israel sang this song:

"Spring up, O well!
    Sing about it,
[18] about the well that the princes dug,
    that the nobles of the people sank—
    the nobles with scepters and staffs."

Then they went from the wilderness to Mattanah, [19] from Mattanah to Nahaliel, from Nahaliel to Bamoth, [20] and from Bamoth to the valley in Moab where the top of Pisgah overlooks the wasteland.

DEFEAT OF SIHON AND OG

[21] Israel sent messengers to say to Sihon king of the Amorites:

[22] "Let us pass through your country. We will not turn aside into any field or vineyard, or drink water from any well. We will travel along the King's Highway until we have passed through your territory."

[23] But Sihon would not let Israel pass through his territory. He mustered his entire army and marched out into the

Why was God angry with the people for complaining? (21:5 – 6)
When the Israelites complained, they were showing disrespect, disobedience, and lack of trust in God.

What was the Book of the Wars of the LORD? (21:14)
This book is mentioned only once in the Old Testament. It was probably a collection of songs of war in praise of God.

What song did the people sing after God gave them water? (21:17 – 18)
This "song of the well" may have also come from the Book of the Wars of the LORD.

---

[a] 14 Septuagint; Hebrew *Waheb*   [b] 14,15 Or *"I have been given from Suphah and the ravines / of the Arnon* [15] *to*

What does the phrase "its surrounding settlements" mean? (21:25)
Small villages were protected by nearby cities. People in villages would provide payment to the cities for protection from nomads. The "surrounding settlements" were the villages that a city protected.

What was this song? (21:27–30)
The third ancient poem in this chapter was an Amorite song about their earlier victory over Moab. To mock their victims, the Amorites would sing this song. The Israelites used the same song to mock the Amorites, but added their own ending.

Defeat of Sihon and Og (21:23–35)

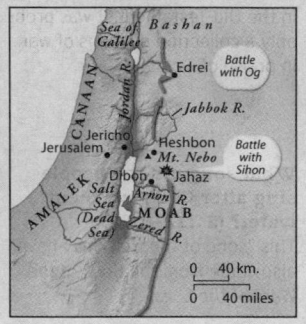

Who was Balaam? (22:5)
Balaam was a famous prophet who made his living tricking people into believing he could predict the future and interpret dreams. Since Balaam was known for casting spells and acting evil, Balak asked him to pronounce a curse on Israel. Balak tried to fight Israel through fortunetelling because he didn't think Israel could be defeated by his army.

wilderness against Israel. When he reached Jahaz, he fought with Israel. ²⁴Israel, however, put him to the sword and took over his land from the Arnon to the Jabbok, but only as far as the Ammonites, because their border was fortified. ²⁵Israel captured all the cities of the Amorites and occupied them, including Heshbon and all its surrounding settlements. ²⁶Heshbon was the city of Sihon king of the Amorites, who had fought against the former king of Moab and had taken from him all his land as far as the Arnon.

²⁷That is why the poets say:

"Come to Heshbon and let it be rebuilt;
    let Sihon's city be restored.
²⁸"Fire went out from Heshbon,
    a blaze from the city of Sihon.
It consumed Ar of Moab,
    the citizens of Arnon's heights.
²⁹Woe to you, Moab!
    You are destroyed, people of Chemosh!
He has given up his sons as fugitives
    and his daughters as captives
to Sihon king of the Amorites.
³⁰"But we have overthrown them;
    Heshbon's dominion has been destroyed all the way
        to Dibon.
We have demolished them as far as Nophah,
    which extends to Medeba."

³¹So Israel settled in the land of the Amorites. ³²After Moses had sent spies to Jazer, the Israelites captured its surrounding settlements and drove out the Amorites who were there. ³³Then they turned and went up along the road toward Bashan, and Og king of Bashan and his whole army marched out to meet them in battle at Edrei.

³⁴The LORD said to Moses, "Do not be afraid of him, for I have delivered him into your hands, along with his whole army and his land. Do to him what you did to Sihon king of the Amorites, who reigned in Heshbon."

³⁵So they struck him down, together with his sons and his whole army, leaving them no survivors. And they took possession of his land.

BALAK SUMMONS BALAAM

22 Then the Israelites traveled to the plains of Moab and camped along the Jordan across from Jericho.

²Now Balak son of Zippor saw all that Israel had done to the Amorites, ³and Moab was terrified because there were so many people. Indeed, Moab was filled with dread because of the Israelites.

⁴The Moabites said to the elders of Midian, "This horde is going to lick up everything around us, as an ox licks up the grass of the field."

So Balak son of Zippor, who was king of Moab at that time, ⁵sent messengers to summon Balaam son of Beor, who was at Pethor, near the Euphrates River, in his native land. Balak said:

"A people has come out of Egypt; they cover the face of the land and have settled next to me. ⁶Now come and put a curse on these people, because they are too powerful for me. Perhaps then I will be able to defeat them and drive them out of the land. For I know that whoever you bless is blessed, and whoever you curse is cursed."

⁷The elders of Moab and Midian left, taking with them the fee for divination. When they came to Balaam, they told him what Balak had said.

⁸"Spend the night here," Balaam said to them, "and I will report back to you with the answer the LORD gives me." So the Moabite officials stayed with him.

⁹God came to Balaam and asked, "Who are these men with you?"

¹⁰Balaam said to God, "Balak son of Zippor, king of Moab, sent me this message: ¹¹'A people that has come out of Egypt covers the face of the land. Now come and put a curse on them for me. Perhaps then I will be able to fight them and drive them away.'"

¹²But God said to Balaam, "Do not go with them. You must not put a curse on those people, because they are blessed."

¹³The next morning Balaam got up and said to Balak's officials, "Go back to your own country, for the LORD has refused to let me go with you."

¹⁴So the Moabite officials returned to Balak and said, "Balaam refused to come with us."

¹⁵Then Balak sent other officials, more numerous and more distinguished than the first. ¹⁶They came to Balaam and said:

"This is what Balak son of Zippor says: Do not let anything keep you from coming to me, ¹⁷because I will reward you handsomely and do whatever you say. Come and put a curse on these people for me."

¹⁸But Balaam answered them, "Even if Balak gave me all the silver and gold in his palace, I could not do anything great or small to go beyond the command of the LORD my God. ¹⁹Now spend the night here so that I can find out what else the LORD will tell me."

²⁰That night God came to Balaam and said, "Since these men have come to summon you, go with them, but do only what I tell you."

BALAAM'S DONKEY

²¹Balaam got up in the morning, saddled his donkey and went with the Moabite officials. ²²But God was very angry when he went, and the angel of the LORD stood in the road to oppose him. Balaam was riding on his donkey, and his two servants were with him. ²³When the donkey saw the angel of the LORD standing in the road with a drawn sword in his hand, it turned off the road into a field. Balaam beat it to get it back on the road.

²⁴Then the angel of the LORD stood in a narrow path through the vineyards, with walls on both sides. ²⁵When the

Why would a pagan prophet claim to have insight from God? (22:8)
The language here and in verse 18 ("the LORD my God") has led some people to believe that Balaam worshiped God. However, it is more likely that he wanted to be seen as a spokesman for any god, or that he was trying to steal God's power from Israel for his own use.

Why was God angry with Balaam for going with the men of Moab? (22:20–22)
God allowed Balaam to go with the Moabites, but only if he would follow God's direction. When Balaam went with the men of Moab, God knew that Balaam planned to disobey him and curse Israel.

Were donkeys ridden with saddles? (22:21)
Although the verse says that Balaam "saddled his donkey," donkeys were not actually ridden with saddles. Instead, a donkey carrying a heavy burden was fitted with a thick cushion on its back to protect the donkey's back.

donkey saw the angel of the LORD, it pressed close to the wall, crushing Balaam's foot against it. So he beat the donkey again.

²⁶Then the angel of the LORD moved on ahead and stood in a narrow place where there was no room to turn, either to the right or to the left. ²⁷When the donkey saw the angel of the LORD, it lay down under Balaam, and he was angry and beat it with his staff. ²⁸Then the LORD opened the donkey's mouth, and it said to Balaam, "What have I done to you to make you beat me these three times?"

²⁹Balaam answered the donkey, "You have made a fool of me! If only I had a sword in my hand, I would kill you right now."

³⁰The donkey said to Balaam, "Am I not your own donkey, which you have always ridden, to this day? Have I been in the habit of doing this to you?"

"No," he said.

³¹Then the LORD opened Balaam's eyes, and he saw the angel of the LORD standing in the road with his sword drawn. So he bowed low and fell facedown.

³²The angel of the LORD asked him, "Why have you beaten your donkey these three times? I have come here to oppose you because your path is a reckless one before me.ᵃ ³³The donkey saw me and turned away from me these three times. If it had not turned away, I would certainly have killed you by now, but I would have spared it."

³⁴Balaam said to the angel of the LORD, "I have sinned. I did not realize you were standing in the road to oppose me. Now if you are displeased, I will go back."

³⁵The angel of the LORD said to Balaam, "Go with the men, but speak only what I tell you." So Balaam went with Balak's officials.

³⁶When Balak heard that Balaam was coming, he went out to meet him at the Moabite town on the Arnon border, at the edge of his territory. ³⁷Balak said to Balaam, "Did I not send you an urgent summons? Why didn't you come to me? Am I really not able to reward you?"

³⁸"Well, I have come to you now," Balaam replied. "But I can't say whatever I please. I must speak only what God puts in my mouth."

³⁹Then Balaam went with Balak to Kiriath Huzoth. ⁴⁰Balak sacrificed cattle and sheep, and gave some to Balaam and the officials who were with him. ⁴¹The next morning Balak took Balaam up to Bamoth Baal, and from there he could see the outskirts of the Israelite camp.

BALAAM'S FIRST MESSAGE

23 Balaam said, "Build me seven altars here, and prepare seven bulls and seven rams for me." ²Balak did as Balaam said, and the two of them offered a bull and a ram on each altar.

³Then Balaam said to Balak, "Stay here beside your offering while I go aside. Perhaps the LORD will come to meet with me. Whatever he reveals to me I will tell you." Then he went off to a barren height.

ᵃ *32* The meaning of the Hebrew for this clause is uncertain.

Why did God use a donkey to communicate with Balaam? (22:28)
God wanted Balaam to obey him, and he used a humble donkey to humiliate Balaam.

Did Balak offer sacrifices to God? (22:40)
It's possible that Balak offered sacrifices to the gods of Moab; however, it's equally as probable that he offered sacrifices to the God of Israel in order to gain God's favor.

Why did Balaam want to build seven altars and use seven bulls and seven rams? (23:1)
Semitic people in general had a high regard for the number seven, which symbolized completeness.

What is an oracle? (23:1 — 24:25)
An oracle is an announcement or message from God.

Balaam's Message (23:3)

⁴God met with him, and Balaam said, "I have prepared seven altars, and on each altar I have offered a bull and a ram."

⁵The LORD put a word in Balaam's mouth and said, "Go back to Balak and give him this word."

⁶So he went back to him and found him standing beside his offering, with all the Moabite officials. ⁷Then Balaam spoke his message:

"Balak brought me from Aram,
    the king of Moab from the eastern mountains.
'Come,' he said, 'curse Jacob for me;
    come, denounce Israel.'
⁸How can I curse
    those whom God has not cursed?
How can I denounce
    those whom the LORD has not denounced?
⁹From the rocky peaks I see them,
    from the heights I view them.
I see a people who live apart
    and do not consider themselves one of the nations.
¹⁰Who can count the dust of Jacob
    or number even a fourth of Israel?
Let me die the death of the righteous,
    and may my final end be like theirs!"

¹¹Balak said to Balaam, "What have you done to me? I brought you to curse my enemies, but you have done nothing but bless them!"

¹²He answered, "Must I not speak what the LORD puts in my mouth?"

BALAAM'S SECOND MESSAGE

¹³Then Balak said to him, "Come with me to another place where you can see them; you will not see them all but only the outskirts of their camp. And from there, curse them for me." ¹⁴So he took him to the field of Zophim on the top of Pisgah, and there he built seven altars and offered a bull and a ram on each altar.

¹⁵Balaam said to Balak, "Stay here beside your offering while I meet with him over there."

¹⁶The LORD met with Balaam and put a word in his mouth and said, "Go back to Balak and give him this word."

¹⁷So he went to him and found him standing beside his offering, with the Moabite officials. Balak asked him, "What did the LORD say?"

¹⁸Then he spoke his message:

"Arise, Balak, and listen;
    hear me, son of Zippor.
¹⁹God is not human, that he should lie,
    not a human being, that he should change
        his mind.
Does he speak and then not act?
Does he promise and not fulfill?
²⁰I have received a command to bless;
    he has blessed, and I cannot change it.

What is the meaning of "God is not human, that he should lie"? (23:19)
This verse speaks about God's character. He is described as being completely truthful. The verse goes on to speak about God's consistency: he does not change his mind. Because God had blessed Israel, no human power such as Balaam's could take away or change this blessing.

Why was Israel compared to a wild ox? (23:22)
A wild ox ("aurochs" or "oryx") was a traditional image of power in the ancient Middle East.

Why was Israel compared to a lioness? (23:24)
Israel was about to rise up and devour its enemies like a lioness on a hunt.

[21] "No misfortune is seen in Jacob,
    no misery observed[a] in Israel.
The LORD their God is with them;
    the shout of the King is among them.
[22] God brought them out of Egypt;
    they have the strength of a wild ox.
[23] There is no divination against[b] Jacob,
    no evil omens against[b] Israel.
It will now be said of Jacob
    and of Israel, 'See what God has done!'
[24] The people rise like a lioness;
    they rouse themselves like a lion
that does not rest till it devours its prey
    and drinks the blood of its victims.'"

[25] Then Balak said to Balaam, "Neither curse them at all nor bless them at all!"

[26] Balaam answered, "Did I not tell you I must do whatever the LORD says?"

BALAAM'S THIRD MESSAGE

[27] Then Balak said to Balaam, "Come, let me take you to another place. Perhaps it will please God to let you curse them for me from there." [28] And Balak took Balaam to the top of Peor, overlooking the wasteland.

[29] Balaam said, "Build me seven altars here, and prepare seven bulls and seven rams for me." [30] Balak did as Balaam had said, and offered a bull and a ram on each altar.

Did God approve of Balaam's use of sorcery? (24:1)
Sorcery was strictly forbidden by God. But God used Balaam for his own good purpose — to bless Israel — in spite of Balaam's pagan practices.

How did the Spirit of God come upon Balaam? (24:2)
The actual process is not clear, but God somehow made Balaam aware of what he was revealing to him so that he could see into the future.

How did Balaam describe the life of Israel in the promised land? (24:6–7)
Balaam described the wonderful life that Israel would experience in the promised land; the richness of their blessing from the Lord would resemble Eden.

24 Now when Balaam saw that it pleased the LORD to bless Israel, he did not resort to divination as at other times, but turned his face toward the wilderness. [2] When Balaam looked out and saw Israel encamped tribe by tribe, the Spirit of God came on him [3] and he spoke his message:

"The prophecy of Balaam son of Beor,
    the prophecy of one whose eye sees clearly,
[4] the prophecy of one who hears the
        words of God,
    who sees a vision from the Almighty,[c]
    who falls prostrate, and whose eyes are opened:

[5] "How beautiful are your tents, Jacob,
    your dwelling places, Israel!

[6] "Like valleys they spread out,
    like gardens beside a river,
like aloes planted by the LORD,
    like cedars beside the waters.
[7] Water will flow from their buckets;
    their seed will have abundant water.

"Their king will be greater than Agag;
    their kingdom will be exalted.

[8] "God brought them out of Egypt;
    they have the strength of a wild ox.

---

[a] 21 Or *He has not looked on Jacob's offenses / or on the wrongs found*
[b] 23 Or *in*   [c] 4 Hebrew *Shaddai*; also in verse 16

They devour hostile nations
    and break their bones in pieces;
    with their arrows they pierce them.
⁹ Like a lion they crouch and lie down,
    like a lioness—who dares to rouse them?

"May those who bless you be blessed
    and those who curse you be cursed!"

¹⁰Then Balak's anger burned against Balaam. He struck his hands together and said to him, "I summoned you to curse my enemies, but you have blessed them these three times. ¹¹ Now leave at once and go home! I said I would reward you handsomely, but the LORD has kept you from being rewarded."

¹²Balaam answered Balak, "Did I not tell the messengers you sent me, ¹³'Even if Balak gave me all the silver and gold in his palace, I could not do anything of my own accord, good or bad, to go beyond the command of the LORD—and I must say only what the LORD says'? ¹⁴Now I am going back to my people, but come, let me warn you of what this people will do to your people in days to come."

BALAAM'S FOURTH MESSAGE

¹⁵Then he spoke his message:

"The prophecy of Balaam son of Beor,
    the prophecy of one whose eye sees clearly,
¹⁶ the prophecy of one who hears the words of God,
    who has knowledge from the Most High,
who sees a vision from the Almighty,
    who falls prostrate, and whose eyes are opened:

¹⁷"I see him, but not now;
    I behold him, but not near.
A star will come out of Jacob;
    a scepter will rise out of Israel.
He will crush the foreheads of Moab,
    the skulls*ᵃ* of*ᵇ* all the people of Sheth.*ᶜ*
¹⁸ Edom will be conquered;
    Seir, his enemy, will be conquered,
    but Israel will grow strong.
¹⁹ A ruler will come out of Jacob
    and destroy the survivors of the city."

BALAAM'S FIFTH MESSAGE

²⁰Then Balaam saw Amalek and spoke his message:

"Amalek was first among the nations,
    but their end will be utter destruction."

BALAAM'S SIXTH MESSAGE

²¹Then he saw the Kenites and spoke his message:

"Your dwelling place is secure,
    your nest is set in a rock;
²² yet you Kenites will be destroyed
    when Ashur takes you captive."

ᵃ 17 Samaritan Pentateuch (see also Jer. 48:45); the meaning of the word in the Masoretic Text is uncertain.   *ᵇ* 17 Or possibly *Moab, / batter*
ᶜ 17 Or *all the noisy boasters*

Who is described in this prophecy? (24:17)
This prophecy was partially fulfilled by David, a later ruler who delivered Israel from its enemies. But the language also described the Messiah, who would deliver his people from the powers of sin and death.

Who were the sons of Sheth? (24:17)
They may have been the early inhabitants of Moab. Ancient Egyptian documents refer to them as the Shutu people.

BALAAM'S SEVENTH MESSAGE

²³Then he spoke his message:

"Alas! Who can live when God does this?ᵃ
²⁴   Ships will come from the shores of Cyprus;
they will subdue Ashur and Eber,
    but they too will come to ruin."

²⁵Then Balaam got up and returned home, and Balak went his own way.

MOAB SEDUCES ISRAEL

25 While Israel was staying in Shittim, the men began to indulge in sexual immorality with Moabite women, ²who invited them to the sacrifices to their gods. The people ate the sacrificial meal and bowed down before these gods. ³So Israel yoked themselves to the Baal of Peor. And the LORD's anger burned against them.

⁴The LORD said to Moses, "Take all the leaders of these people, kill them and expose them in broad daylight before the LORD, so that the LORD's fierce anger may turn away from Israel."

⁵So Moses said to Israel's judges, "Each of you must put to death those of your people who have yoked themselves to the Baal of Peor."

⁶Then an Israelite man brought into the camp a Midianite woman right before the eyes of Moses and the whole assembly of Israel while they were weeping at the entrance to the tent of meeting. ⁷When Phinehas son of Eleazar, the son of Aaron, the priest, saw this, he left the assembly, took a spear in his hand ⁸and followed the Israelite into the tent. He drove the spear into both of them, right through the Israelite man and into the woman's stomach. Then the plague against the Israelites was stopped; ⁹but those who died in the plague numbered 24,000.

¹⁰The LORD said to Moses, ¹¹"Phinehas son of Eleazar, the son of Aaron, the priest, has turned my anger away from the Israelites. Since he was as zealous for my honor among them as I am, I did not put an end to them in my zeal. ¹²Therefore tell him I am making my covenant of peace with him. ¹³He and his descendants will have a covenant of a lasting priesthood, because he was zealous for the honor of his God and made atonement for the Israelites."

¹⁴The name of the Israelite who was killed with the Midianite woman was Zimri son of Salu, the leader of a Simeonite family. ¹⁵And the name of the Midianite woman who was put to death was Kozbi daughter of Zur, a tribal chief of a Midianite family.

¹⁶The LORD said to Moses, ¹⁷"Treat the Midianites as enemies and kill them. ¹⁸They treated you as enemies when they deceived you in the Peor incident involving their sister Kozbi, the daughter of a Midianite leader, the woman who was killed when the plague came as a result of that incident."

ᵃ 23 Masoretic Text; with a different word division of the Hebrew *The people from the islands will gather from the north.*

Why did the Israelite men sleep with Moabite women? (25:1–2)
The Midianites and Moabites planned to sabotage Israel (see Numbers 22:4, 7). They wanted Israel to disobey their God, which would cause him to take away his protection. Their plan was to invite Israelite men to their fertility festival, where people worshiped their god Baal and had sex with temple prostitutes. Some of the Israelite men participated in these pagan practices. God was furious with their disobedience.

Why would someone be so bold about sinning? (25:6)
Zimri (see verse 14) had little respect for God and his laws, and his sin cost him his life.

Why did God punish people who didn't worship Baal? (25:9)
The whole community was responsible for the sin because they didn't try to stop their people from worshiping Baal. Because the sin was the responsibility of the community, the plague killed people throughout the community.

THE SECOND CENSUS

26 After the plague the LORD said to Moses and Eleazar son of Aaron, the priest, ²"Take a census of the whole Israelite community by families—all those twenty years old or more who are able to serve in the army of Israel." ³So on the plains of Moab by the Jordan across from Jericho, Moses and Eleazar the priest spoke with them and said, ⁴"Take a census of the men twenty years old or more, as the LORD commanded Moses."

These were the Israelites who came out of Egypt:

⁵The descendants of Reuben, the firstborn son of Israel, were:

    through Hanok, the Hanokite clan;
    through Pallu, the Palluite clan;
    ⁶through Hezron, the Hezronite clan;
    through Karmi, the Karmite clan.

⁷These were the clans of Reuben; those numbered were 43,730.

⁸The son of Pallu was Eliab, ⁹and the sons of Eliab were Nemuel, Dathan and Abiram. The same Dathan and Abiram were the community officials who rebelled against Moses and Aaron and were among Korah's followers when they rebelled against the LORD. ¹⁰The earth opened its mouth and swallowed them along with Korah, whose followers died when the fire devoured the 250 men. And they served as a warning sign. ¹¹The line of Korah, however, did not die out.

¹²The descendants of Simeon by their clans were:

    through Nemuel, the Nemuelite clan;
    through Jamin, the Jaminite clan;
    through Jakin, the Jakinite clan;
    ¹³through Zerah, the Zerahite clan;
    through Shaul, the Shaulite clan.

¹⁴These were the clans of Simeon; those numbered were 22,200.

¹⁵The descendants of Gad by their clans were:

    through Zephon, the Zephonite clan;
    through Haggi, the Haggite clan;
    through Shuni, the Shunite clan;
    ¹⁶through Ozni, the Oznite clan;
    through Eri, the Erite clan;
    ¹⁷through Arodi,ᵃ the Arodite clan;
    through Areli, the Arelite clan.

¹⁸These were the clans of Gad; those numbered were 40,500.

¹⁹Er and Onan were sons of Judah, but they died in Canaan. ²⁰The descendants of Judah by their clans were:

    through Shelah, the Shelanite clan;
    through Perez, the Perezite clan;
    through Zerah, the Zerahite clan.

²¹The descendants of Perez were:

      through Hezron, the Hezronite clan;
      through Hamul, the Hamulite clan.

Why was there another census? (26:2)
Israel was about to enter the promised land, so a census was important for deciding how to divide up the territory among the tribes. But a more imminent concern was the war against the Midianites that God had just announced. The census would count the number of men eligible to serve as soldiers. Also, the population changed a lot since the last census almost 40 years earlier.

Why is this list of names included in the Bible? (26:4–61)
This helped to strengthen the people's faith and helped them see how they were connected to earlier generations of God's people. One of the things that they, and we, can remember is that God asked Abraham to place his trust in God and travel to a strange land a thousand miles away. Some 500 years later, this census showed that God kept his promises to Abraham and made his descendants into a great nation.

ᵃ 17 Samaritan Pentateuch and Syriac (see also Gen. 46:16); Masoretic Text *Arod*

²²These were the clans of Judah; those numbered were 76,500.

²³The descendants of Issachar by their clans were:
through Tola, the Tolaite clan;
through Puah, the Puite^a clan;
²⁴through Jashub, the Jashubite clan;
through Shimron, the Shimronite clan.
²⁵These were the clans of Issachar; those numbered were 64,300.

²⁶The descendants of Zebulun by their clans were:
through Sered, the Seredite clan;
through Elon, the Elonite clan;
through Jahleel, the Jahleelite clan.
²⁷These were the clans of Zebulun; those numbered were 60,500.

²⁸The descendants of Joseph by their clans through Manasseh and Ephraim were:

²⁹The descendants of Manasseh:
through Makir, the Makirite clan (Makir was the father of Gilead);
through Gilead, the Gileadite clan.
³⁰These were the descendants of Gilead:
through Iezer, the Iezerite clan;
through Helek, the Helekite clan;
³¹through Asriel, the Asrielite clan;
through Shechem, the Shechemite clan;
³²through Shemida, the Shemidaite clan;
through Hepher, the Hepherite clan.
³³(Zelophehad son of Hepher had no sons; he had only daughters, whose names were Mahlah, Noah, Hoglah, Milkah and Tirzah.)
³⁴These were the clans of Manasseh; those numbered were 52,700.

³⁵These were the descendants of Ephraim by their clans:
through Shuthelah, the Shuthelahite clan;
through Beker, the Bekerite clan;
through Tahan, the Tahanite clan.
³⁶These were the descendants of Shuthelah:
through Eran, the Eranite clan.
³⁷These were the clans of Ephraim; those numbered were 32,500.

These were the descendants of Joseph by their clans.

³⁸The descendants of Benjamin by their clans were:
through Bela, the Belaite clan;
through Ashbel, the Ashbelite clan;
through Ahiram, the Ahiramite clan;
³⁹through Shupham,^b the Shuphamite clan;
through Hupham, the Huphamite clan.

Why are so few daughters named in this genealogy? (26:33)
This particular list, and many like it, generally did not name daughters because the purpose of this genealogy was to record the numbers of men who could fight in the army. Other genealogies that had different purposes list daughters. (See 1 Chronicles 2 and 7.)

^a 23 Samaritan Pentateuch, Septuagint, Vulgate and Syriac (see also 1 Chron. 7:1); Masoretic Text *through Puvah, the Punite*   ^b 39 A few manuscripts of the Masoretic Text, Samaritan Pentateuch, Vulgate and Syriac (see also Septuagint); most manuscripts of the Masoretic Text *Shephupham*

[40] The descendants of Bela through Ard and Naaman were:

through Ard,[a] the Ardite clan;

through Naaman, the Naamite clan.

[41] These were the clans of Benjamin; those numbered were 45,600.

[42] These were the descendants of Dan by their clans:

through Shuham, the Shuhamite clan.

These were the clans of Dan: [43] All of them were Shuhamite clans; and those numbered were 64,400.

[44] The descendants of Asher by their clans were:

through Imnah, the Imnite clan;

through Ishvi, the Ishvite clan;

through Beriah, the Beriite clan;

[45] and through the descendants of Beriah:

through Heber, the Heberite clan;

through Malkiel, the Malkielite clan.

[46] (Asher had a daughter named Serah.)

[47] These were the clans of Asher; those numbered were 53,400.

[48] The descendants of Naphtali by their clans were:

through Jahzeel, the Jahzeelite clan;

through Guni, the Gunite clan;

[49] through Jezer, the Jezerite clan;

through Shillem, the Shillemite clan.

[50] These were the clans of Naphtali; those numbered were 45,400.

[51] The total number of the men of Israel was 601,730.

[52] The LORD said to Moses, [53] "The land is to be allotted to them as an inheritance based on the number of names. [54] To a larger group give a larger inheritance, and to a smaller group a smaller one; each is to receive its inheritance according to the number of those listed. [55] Be sure that the land is distributed by lot. What each group inherits will be according to the names for its ancestral tribe. [56] Each inheritance is to be distributed by lot among the larger and smaller groups."

[57] These were the Levites who were counted by their clans:

through Gershon, the Gershonite clan;

through Kohath, the Kohathite clan;

through Merari, the Merarite clan.

[58] These also were Levite clans:

the Libnite clan,

the Hebronite clan,

the Mahlite clan,

the Mushite clan,

the Korahite clan.

(Kohath was the forefather of Amram; [59] the name of Amram's wife was Jochebed, a descendant of Levi, who was born to the Levites[b] in Egypt. To Amram she bore Aaron, Moses and their sister Miriam. [60] Aaron was the

How accurate were the census numbers? (26:41) The totals for the various clans appear to be round numbers, rounded to the nearest hundred (except for the tribe of Reuben).

Why was Asher's daughter included in the census? (26:46) It isn't clear why this daughter was singled out. Serah may have been Jacob's only granddaughter.

How had the Israelite population changed since the first census just after they escaped from Egypt? (26:51) The first census taken when they started traveling in the desert recorded a total of 603,550 while this one had a total of 601,730. Even with all of the misfortunes in the desert, the population stayed nearly the same, fulfilling God's promise to make Abraham's descendants a great nation.

[a] 40 Samaritan Pentateuch and Vulgate (see also Septuagint); Masoretic Text does not have *through Ard*.   [b] 59 Or *Jochebed, a daughter of Levi, who was born to Levi*

father of Nadab and Abihu, Eleazar and Ithamar. [61]But Nadab and Abihu died when they made an offering before the LORD with unauthorized fire.)

[62]All the male Levites a month old or more numbered 23,000. They were not counted along with the other Israelites because they received no inheritance among them.

[63]These are the ones counted by Moses and Eleazar the priest when they counted the Israelites on the plains of Moab by the Jordan across from Jericho. [64]Not one of them was among those counted by Moses and Aaron the priest when they counted the Israelites in the Desert of Sinai. [65]For the LORD had told those Israelites they would surely die in the wilderness, and not one of them was left except Caleb son of Jephunneh and Joshua son of Nun.

ZELOPHEHAD'S DAUGHTERS

27 The daughters of Zelophehad son of Hepher, the son of Gilead, the son of Makir, the son of Manasseh, belonged to the clans of Manasseh son of Joseph. The names of the daughters were Mahlah, Noah, Hoglah, Milkah and Tirzah. They came forward [2]and stood before Moses, Eleazar the priest, the leaders and the whole assembly at the entrance to the tent of meeting and said, [3]"Our father died in the wilderness. He was not among Korah's followers, who banded together against the LORD, but he died for his own sin and left no sons. [4]Why should our father's name disappear from his clan because he had no son? Give us property among our father's relatives."

[5]So Moses brought their case before the LORD, [6]and the LORD said to him, [7]"What Zelophehad's daughters are saying is right. You must certainly give them property as an inheritance among their father's relatives and give their father's inheritance to them.

[8]"Say to the Israelites, 'If a man dies and leaves no son, give his inheritance to his daughter. [9]If he has no daughter, give his inheritance to his brothers. [10]If he has no brothers, give his inheritance to his father's brothers. [11]If his father had no brothers, give his inheritance to the nearest relative in his clan, that he may possess it. This is to have the force of law for the Israelites, as the LORD commanded Moses.'"

JOSHUA TO SUCCEED MOSES

[12]Then the LORD said to Moses, "Go up this mountain in the Abarim Range and see the land I have given the Israelites. [13]After you have seen it, you too will be gathered to your people, as your brother Aaron was, [14]for when the community rebelled at the waters in the Desert of Zin, both of you disobeyed my command to honor me as holy before their eyes." (These were the waters of Meribah Kadesh, in the Desert of Zin.)

[15]Moses said to the LORD, [16]"May the LORD, the God who gives breath to all living things, appoint someone over this community [17]to go out and come in before them, one who will lead them out and bring them in, so the LORD's people will not be like sheep without a shepherd."

Why were Levites who were younger than 20 years old included in the census? (26:62)
This census not only counted soldiers — where men had to be 20 to serve — it also counted the men who were eligible to be priests. Priests could fulfill their duties younger than a soldier could serve in the army.

What was surprising about the actions of the daughters of Zelophehad? (27:1–11)
The law was that only sons had the right to inherit, and the firstborn son was to receive a double portion of the family estate. The daughters of Zelophehad, a man who had no sons, were concerned about their rights of inheritance and about preserving their father's name. By approaching Moses with their request, they demonstrated courage and conviction.

How did Moses make decisions? (27:5–7)
Although God had given Moses basic laws, they didn't cover everything that could happen. When the people asked Moses to solve new or unusual problems, Moses usually asked God for help.

Why was Moses not allowed to enter the promised land? (27:12–16)
Moses had sinned when he struck the rock with his staff at Meribah (Numbers 20:1–13). Because of this sin against the Lord, he was not allowed to go into the promised land.

¹⁸So the LORD said to Moses, "Take Joshua son of Nun, a man in whom is the spirit of leadership,^a and lay your hand on him. ¹⁹Have him stand before Eleazar the priest and the entire assembly and commission him in their presence. ²⁰Give him some of your authority so the whole Israelite community will obey him. ²¹He is to stand before Eleazar the priest, who will obtain decisions for him by inquiring of the Urim before the LORD. At his command he and the entire community of the Israelites will go out, and at his command they will come in."

²²Moses did as the LORD commanded him. He took Joshua and had him stand before Eleazar the priest and the whole assembly. ²³Then he laid his hands on him and commissioned him, as the LORD instructed through Moses.

DAILY OFFERINGS

28 The LORD said to Moses, ²"Give this command to the Israelites and say to them: 'Make sure that you present to me at the appointed time my food offerings, as an aroma pleasing to me.' ³Say to them: 'This is the food offering you are to present to the LORD: two lambs a year old without defect, as a regular burnt offering each day. ⁴Offer one lamb in the morning and the other at twilight, ⁵together with a grain offering of a tenth of an ephah^b of the finest flour mixed with a quarter of a hin^c of oil from pressed olives. ⁶This is the regular burnt offering instituted at Mount Sinai as a pleasing aroma, a food offering presented to the LORD. ⁷The accompanying drink offering is to be a quarter of a hin of fermented drink with each lamb. Pour out the drink offering to the LORD at the sanctuary. ⁸Offer the second lamb at twilight, along with the same kind of grain offering and drink offering that you offer in the morning. This is a food offering, an aroma pleasing to the LORD.

SABBATH OFFERINGS

⁹"'On the Sabbath day, make an offering of two lambs a year old without defect, together with its drink offering and a grain offering of two-tenths of an ephah^d of the finest flour mixed with olive oil. ¹⁰This is the burnt offering for every Sabbath, in addition to the regular burnt offering and its drink offering.

MONTHLY OFFERINGS

¹¹"'On the first of every month, present to the LORD a burnt offering of two young bulls, one ram and seven male lambs a year old, all without defect. ¹²With each bull there is to be a grain offering of three-tenths of an ephah^e of the finest flour mixed with oil; with the ram, a grain offering of two-tenths of an ephah of the finest flour mixed with oil; ¹³and with each lamb, a grain offering of a tenth of an ephah of the finest flour mixed with oil. This is for a burnt

Did Sabbath offerings count toward daily offerings? (28:9)
No. Sabbath offerings had to be made in addition to the daily offering.

How did the Israelites know when a month started? (28:11)
The Hebrews based their calendar system on the phases of the moon.

---

^a 18 Or *the Spirit*   ^b 5 That is, probably about 3 1/2 pounds or about 1.6 kilograms; also in verses 13, 21 and 29   ^c 5 That is, about 1 quart or about 1 liter; also in verses 7 and 14   ^d 9 That is, probably about 7 pounds or about 3.2 kilograms; also in verses 12, 20 and 28   ^e 12 That is, probably about 11 pounds or about 5 kilograms; also in verses 20 and 28

What was a hin? (28:14)
A hin was a liquid measurement
of about 4 quarts (4 liters).

offering, a pleasing aroma, a food offering presented to the
LORD. [14]With each bull there is to be a drink offering of half
a hin[a] of wine; with the ram, a third of a hin[b]; and with each
lamb, a quarter of a hin. This is the monthly burnt offering
to be made at each new moon during the year. [15]Besides the
regular burnt offering with its drink offering, one male goat
is to be presented to the LORD as a sin offering.[c]

THE PASSOVER

[16]"'On the fourteenth day of the first month the LORD's
Passover is to be held. [17]On the fifteenth day of this month
there is to be a festival; for seven days eat bread made without yeast. [18]On the first day hold a sacred assembly and
do no regular work. [19]Present to the LORD a food offering
consisting of a burnt offering of two young bulls, one ram
and seven male lambs a year old, all without defect. [20]With
each bull offer a grain offering of three-tenths of an ephah
of the finest flour mixed with oil; with the ram, two-tenths;
[21]and with each of the seven lambs, one-tenth. [22]Include
one male goat as a sin offering to make atonement for you.
[23]Offer these in addition to the regular morning burnt offering. [24]In this way present the food offering every day for
seven days as an aroma pleasing to the LORD; it is to be offered in addition to the regular burnt offering and its drink
offering. [25]On the seventh day hold a sacred assembly and
do no regular work.

THE FESTIVAL OF WEEKS

[26]"'On the day of firstfruits, when you present to the
LORD an offering of new grain during the Festival of Weeks,
hold a sacred assembly and do no regular work. [27]Present a
burnt offering of two young bulls, one ram and seven male
lambs a year old as an aroma pleasing to the LORD. [28]With
each bull there is to be a grain offering of three-tenths of
an ephah of the finest flour mixed with oil; with the ram,
two-tenths; [29]and with each of the seven lambs, one-tenth.
[30]Include one male goat to make atonement for you. [31]Offer
these together with their drink offerings, in addition to the
regular burnt offering and its grain offering. Be sure the animals are without defect.

Why did animals offered as
sacrifices have to be perfect?
(28:31)
A clean and perfect animal symbolizes the purity that God, who
is holy, requires.

What was a sacred assem-
bly? (29:1)
These were times when the
whole community worshiped and
celebrated together.

THE FESTIVAL OF TRUMPETS

29 "'On the first day of the seventh month hold a sacred
assembly and do no regular work. It is a day for you
to sound the trumpets. [2]As an aroma pleasing to the LORD,
offer a burnt offering of one young bull, one ram and seven
male lambs a year old, all without defect. [3]With the bull offer a grain offering of three-tenths of an ephah[d] of the finest
flour mixed with olive oil; with the ram, two-tenths[e]; [4]and
with each of the seven lambs, one-tenth.[f] [5]Include one male

[a] *14* That is, about 2 quarts or about 1.9 liters   [b] *14* That is, about 1 1/3
quarts or about 1.3 liters   [c] *15* Or *purification offering*; also in verse 22
[d] *3* That is, probably about 11 pounds or about 5 kilograms; also in verses 9
and 14   [e] *3* That is, probably about 7 pounds or about 3.2 kilograms; also
in verses 9 and 14   [f] *4* That is, probably about 3 1/2 pounds or about 1.6
kilograms; also in verses 10 and 15

goat as a sin offering[a] to make atonement for you. [6] These are in addition to the monthly and daily burnt offerings with their grain offerings and drink offerings as specified. They are food offerings presented to the LORD, a pleasing aroma.

THE DAY OF ATONEMENT

[7] "'On the tenth day of this seventh month hold a sacred assembly. You must deny yourselves[b] and do no work. [8] Present as an aroma pleasing to the LORD a burnt offering of one young bull, one ram and seven male lambs a year old, all without defect. [9] With the bull offer a grain offering of three-tenths of an ephah of the finest flour mixed with oil; with the ram, two-tenths; [10] and with each of the seven lambs, one-tenth. [11] Include one male goat as a sin offering, in addition to the sin offering for atonement and the regular burnt offering with its grain offering, and their drink offerings.

THE FESTIVAL OF TABERNACLES

[12] "'On the fifteenth day of the seventh month, hold a sacred assembly and do no regular work. Celebrate a festival to the LORD for seven days. [13] Present as an aroma pleasing to the LORD a food offering consisting of a burnt offering of thirteen young bulls, two rams and fourteen male lambs a year old, all without defect. [14] With each of the thirteen bulls offer a grain offering of three-tenths of an ephah of the finest flour mixed with oil; with each of the two rams, two-tenths; [15] and with each of the fourteen lambs, one-tenth. [16] Include one male goat as a sin offering, in addition to the regular burnt offering with its grain offering and drink offering.

[17] "'On the second day offer twelve young bulls, two rams and fourteen male lambs a year old, all without defect. [18] With the bulls, rams and lambs, offer their grain offerings and drink offerings according to the number specified. [19] Include one male goat as a sin offering, in addition to the regular burnt offering with its grain offering, and their drink offerings.

[20] "'On the third day offer eleven bulls, two rams and fourteen male lambs a year old, all without defect. [21] With the bulls, rams and lambs, offer their grain offerings and drink offerings according to the number specified. [22] Include one male goat as a sin offering, in addition to the regular burnt offering with its grain offering and drink offering.

[23] "'On the fourth day offer ten bulls, two rams and fourteen male lambs a year old, all without defect. [24] With the bulls, rams and lambs, offer their grain offerings and drink offerings according to the number specified. [25] Include one male goat as a sin offering, in addition to the regular burnt offering with its grain offering and drink offering.

[26] "'On the fifth day offer nine bulls, two rams and fourteen male lambs a year old, all without defect. [27] With the bulls, rams and lambs, offer their grain offerings and drink offerings according to the number specified. [28] Include one

How were the Israelites supposed to deny themselves? (29:7)
As a way to show they were sorry for their sins and wanted to be forgiven, on the day of atonement the people denied themselves by not eating.

What was the day of atonement? (29:7–11)
The sacrifices on the Day of Atonement were for the sins of the whole community, both known and unknown sins. These sins needed to be removed so God (who is holy) could remain with them. (See Leviticus 16.)

What was the festival of tabernacles? (29:12–39)
During this feast the Israelites built temporary shelters to remind them of the shelters they lived in when God brought them out of Egypt (see Leviticus 23:33–43).

---

[a] 5 Or *purification offering*; also elsewhere in this chapter   [b] 7 Or *must fast*

male goat as a sin offering, in addition to the regular burnt offering with its grain offering and drink offering.

29 " 'On the sixth day offer eight bulls, two rams and fourteen male lambs a year old, all without defect. 30 With the bulls, rams and lambs, offer their grain offerings and drink offerings according to the number specified. 31 Include one male goat as a sin offering, in addition to the regular burnt offering with its grain offering and drink offering.

32 " 'On the seventh day offer seven bulls, two rams and fourteen male lambs a year old, all without defect. 33 With the bulls, rams and lambs, offer their grain offerings and drink offerings according to the number specified. 34 Include one male goat as a sin offering, in addition to the regular burnt offering with its grain offering and drink offering.

35 " 'On the eighth day hold a closing special assembly and do no regular work. 36 Present as an aroma pleasing to the Lord a food offering consisting of a burnt offering of one bull, one ram and seven male lambs a year old, all without defect. 37 With the bull, the ram and the lambs, offer their grain offerings and drink offerings according to the number specified. 38 Include one male goat as a sin offering, in addition to the regular burnt offering with its grain offering and drink offering.

39 " 'In addition to what you vow and your freewill offerings, offer these to the Lord at your appointed festivals: your burnt offerings, grain offerings, drink offerings and fellowship offerings.' "

40 Moses told the Israelites all that the Lord commanded him.[a]

VOWS

30[b] Moses said to the heads of the tribes of Israel: "This is what the Lord commands: 2 When a man makes a vow to the Lord or takes an oath to obligate himself by a pledge, he must not break his word but must do everything he said.

3 "When a young woman still living in her father's household makes a vow to the Lord or obligates herself by a pledge 4 and her father hears about her vow or pledge but says nothing to her, then all her vows and every pledge by which she obligated herself will stand. 5 But if her father forbids her when he hears about it, none of her vows or the pledges by which she obligated herself will stand; the Lord will release her because her father has forbidden her.

6 "If she marries after she makes a vow or after her lips utter a rash promise by which she obligates herself 7 and her husband hears about it but says nothing to her, then her vows or the pledges by which she obligated herself will stand. 8 But if her husband forbids her when he hears about it, he nullifies the vow that obligates her or the rash promise by which she obligates herself, and the Lord will release her.

9 "Any vow or obligation taken by a widow or divorced woman will be binding on her.

Why did Moses tell the people "all that the Lord commanded him"? (29:40)
Moses gave the instructions about the festivals once more as part of the transfer of power from Moses to Joshua.

Why are there so many vows? (30:2–15)
During this time, a vow was like a contract. Since writers and writing materials were scarce, vows were witnessed by others. The witnesses then held people to their word.

What was the difference between a vow and a pledge to God? (30:2)
A vow was a promise to do something for God while a pledge was a promise to stop doing something or give up something. Vows and pledges were ways people could show their devotion to God.

---

[a] 40 In Hebrew texts this verse (29:40) is numbered 30:1.   [b] In Hebrew texts 30:1-16 is numbered 30:2-17.

¹⁰"If a woman living with her husband makes a vow or obligates herself by a pledge under oath ¹¹and her husband hears about it but says nothing to her and does not forbid her, then all her vows or the pledges by which she obligated herself will stand. ¹²But if her husband nullifies them when he hears about them, then none of the vows or pledges that came from her lips will stand. Her husband has nullified them, and the LORD will release her. ¹³Her husband may confirm or nullify any vow she makes or any sworn pledge to deny herself.ᵃ ¹⁴But if her husband says nothing to her about it from day to day, then he confirms all her vows or the pledges binding on her. He confirms them by saying nothing to her when he hears about them. ¹⁵If, however, he nullifies them some time after he hears about them, then he must bear the consequences of her wrongdoing."

¹⁶These are the regulations the LORD gave Moses concerning relationships between a man and his wife, and between a father and his young daughter still living at home.

VENGEANCE ON THE MIDIANITES

31 The LORD said to Moses, ²"Take vengeance on the Midianites for the Israelites. After that, you will be gathered to your people."

³So Moses said to the people, "Arm some of your men to go to war against the Midianites so that they may carry out the LORD's vengeance on them. ⁴Send into battle a thousand men from each of the tribes of Israel." ⁵So twelve thousand men armed for battle, a thousand from each tribe, were supplied from the clans of Israel. ⁶Moses sent them into battle, a thousand from each tribe, along with Phinehas son of Eleazar, the priest, who took with him articles from the sanctuary and the trumpets for signaling.

⁷They fought against Midian, as the LORD commanded Moses, and killed every man. ⁸Among their victims were Evi, Rekem, Zur, Hur and Reba—the five kings of Midian. They also killed Balaam son of Beor with the sword. ⁹The Israelites captured the Midianite women and children and took all the Midianite herds, flocks and goods as plunder. ¹⁰They burned all the towns where the Midianites had settled, as well as all their camps. ¹¹They took all the plunder and spoils, including the people and animals, ¹²and brought the captives, spoils and plunder to Moses and Eleazar the priest and the Israelite assembly at their camp on the plains of Moab, by the Jordan across from Jericho.

¹³Moses, Eleazar the priest and all the leaders of the community went to meet them outside the camp. ¹⁴Moses was angry with the officers of the army—the commanders of thousands and commanders of hundreds—who returned from the battle.

¹⁵"Have you allowed all the women to live?" he asked them. ¹⁶"They were the ones who followed Balaam's advice and enticed the Israelites to be unfaithful to the LORD in the Peor incident, so that a plague struck the LORD's people. ¹⁷Now kill all the boys. And kill every woman who has slept

Why send a thousand men from each tribe? (31:4)
It wouldn't be fair or advantageous to send all the men from one tribe. This way, the burden of war—the casualties—was split evenly between all of the tribes.

Why were the Israelites sometimes allowed to keep plunder from battles? (31:9)
God told them to take the Midianites' wealth. But when the Israelites fought against the king of Arad (Numbers 21:1–3), they had made a vow that they would destroy everything if they were successful in the battle.

ᵃ *13* Or *to fast*

Why were these girls saved? (31:18)
The Midianite women who seduce Israelite men into worshiping Baal and being sexually immoral had to be punished. But the virgins of Midian, who had not been part of this plan, were saved.

How could soldiers who were obeying God's commandments become unclean? (31:19)
Anyone who touched a dead body was ceremonially unclean. The soldiers would have had contact with dead people. Even though God had commanded the killing, they would have to complete a process of cleansing.

with a man, [18]but save for yourselves every girl who has never slept with a man.

[19]"Anyone who has killed someone or touched someone who was killed must stay outside the camp seven days. On the third and seventh days you must purify yourselves and your captives. [20]Purify every garment as well as everything made of leather, goat hair or wood."

[21]Then Eleazar the priest said to the soldiers who had gone into battle, "This is what is required by the law that the LORD gave Moses: [22]Gold, silver, bronze, iron, tin, lead [23]and anything else that can withstand fire must be put through the fire, and then it will be clean. But it must also be purified with the water of cleansing. And whatever cannot withstand fire must be put through that water. [24]On the seventh day wash your clothes and you will be clean. Then you may come into the camp."

DIVIDING THE SPOILS

[25]The LORD said to Moses, [26]"You and Eleazar the priest and the family heads of the community are to count all the people and animals that were captured. [27]Divide the spoils equally between the soldiers who took part in the battle and the rest of the community. [28]From the soldiers who fought in the battle, set apart as tribute for the LORD one out of every five hundred, whether people, cattle, donkeys or sheep. [29]Take this tribute from their half share and give it to Eleazar the priest as the LORD's part. [30]From the Israelites' half, select one out of every fifty, whether people, cattle, donkeys, sheep or other animals. Give them to the Levites, who are responsible for the care of the LORD's tabernacle." [31]So Moses and Eleazar the priest did as the LORD commanded Moses.

[32]The plunder remaining from the spoils that the soldiers took was 675,000 sheep, [33]72,000 cattle, [34]61,000 donkeys [35]and 32,000 women who had never slept with a man. [36]The half share of those who fought in the battle was:

337,500 sheep, [37]of which the tribute for the LORD was 675;
[38]36,000 cattle, of which the tribute for the LORD was 72;
[39]30,500 donkeys, of which the tribute for the LORD was 61;
[40]16,000 people, of whom the tribute for the LORD was 32.

[41]Moses gave the tribute to Eleazar the priest as the LORD's part, as the LORD commanded Moses.

[42]The half belonging to the Israelites, which Moses set apart from that of the fighting men— [43]the community's half—was 337,500 sheep, [44]36,000 cattle, [45]30,500 donkeys [46]and 16,000 people. [47]From the Israelites' half, Moses selected one out of every fifty people and animals, as the LORD commanded him, and gave them to the Levites, who were responsible for the care of the LORD's tabernacle.

[48]Then the officers who were over the units of the army— the commanders of thousands and commanders of hundreds—went to Moses [49]and said to him, "Your servants have counted the soldiers under our command, and not one

How could every one of the 12,000 Israelites soldiers survive the war? (31:49)
God was with the Israelite army and protected them.

is missing. [50] So we have brought as an offering to the LORD the gold articles each of us acquired — armlets, bracelets, signet rings, earrings and necklaces — to make atonement for ourselves before the LORD."

[51] Moses and Eleazar the priest accepted from them the gold — all the crafted articles. [52] All the gold from the commanders of thousands and commanders of hundreds that Moses and Eleazar presented as a gift to the LORD weighed 16,750 shekels.[a] [53] Each soldier had taken plunder for himself. [54] Moses and Eleazar the priest accepted the gold from the commanders of thousands and commanders of hundreds and brought it into the tent of meeting as a memorial for the Israelites before the LORD.

THE TRANSJORDAN TRIBES

32 The Reubenites and Gadites, who had very large herds and flocks, saw that the lands of Jazer and Gilead were suitable for livestock. [2] So they came to Moses and Eleazar the priest and to the leaders of the community, and said, [3] "Ataroth, Dibon, Jazer, Nimrah, Heshbon, Elealeh, Sebam, Nebo and Beon — [4] the land the LORD subdued before the people of Israel — are suitable for livestock, and your servants have livestock. [5] If we have found favor in your eyes," they said, "let this land be given to your servants as our possession. Do not make us cross the Jordan."

[6] Moses said to the Gadites and Reubenites, "Should your fellow Israelites go to war while you sit here? [7] Why do you discourage the Israelites from crossing over into the land the LORD has given them? [8] This is what your fathers did when I sent them from Kadesh Barnea to look over the land. [9] After they went up to the Valley of Eshkol and viewed the land, they discouraged the Israelites from entering the land the LORD had given them. [10] The LORD's anger was aroused that day and he swore this oath: [11] 'Because they have not followed me wholeheartedly, not one of those who were twenty years old or more when they came up out of Egypt will see the land I promised on oath to Abraham, Isaac and Jacob — [12] not one except Caleb son of Jephunneh the Kenizzite and Joshua son of Nun, for they followed the LORD wholeheartedly.' [13] The LORD's anger burned against Israel and he made them wander in the wilderness forty years, until the whole generation of those who had done evil in his sight was gone.

[14] "And here you are, a brood of sinners, standing in the place of your fathers and making the LORD even more angry with Israel. [15] If you turn away from following him, he will again leave all this people in the wilderness, and you will be the cause of their destruction."

[16] Then they came up to him and said, "We would like to build pens here for our livestock and cities for our women and children. [17] But we will arm ourselves for battle[b] and go ahead of the Israelites until we have brought them to their place. Meanwhile our women and children will live in fortified cities, for protection from the inhabitants of the land.

[a] 52 That is, about 420 pounds or about 190 kilograms   [b] 17 Septuagint; Hebrew *will be quick to arm ourselves*

Why did the Reubenites and Gadites ask if they could stay in this place? (32:1–5) There was a great deal of fertile land in this location, and they had large herds and flocks that could graze on this land.

Why did Moses at first deny their request? (32:6–14) Moses was afraid that if some tribes began settling down away from the rest of the community, the other Israelites would be content with land that had not been promised to them by God. But when the leaders of the tribes promised to lead the rest of the Israelites in conquering Canaan, the promised land, Moses let them live on the east side of the Jordan River.

What does "fortified cities" mean? (32:17) These cities usually had walls built around them for protection, and sometimes they were built on steep hills to make them difficult to attack and conquer.

[18]We will not return to our homes until each of the Israelites has received their inheritance. [19]We will not receive any inheritance with them on the other side of the Jordan, because our inheritance has come to us on the east side of the Jordan."

[20]Then Moses said to them, "If you will do this—if you will arm yourselves before the LORD for battle [21]and if all of you who are armed cross over the Jordan before the LORD until he has driven his enemies out before him— [22]then when the land is subdued before the LORD, you may return and be free from your obligation to the LORD and to Israel. And this land will be your possession before the LORD.

[23]"But if you fail to do this, you will be sinning against the LORD; and you may be sure that your sin will find you out. [24]Build cities for your women and children, and pens for your flocks, but do what you have promised."

[25]The Gadites and Reubenites said to Moses, "We your servants will do as our lord commands. [26]Our children and wives, our flocks and herds will remain here in the cities of Gilead. [27]But your servants, every man who is armed for battle, will cross over to fight before the LORD, just as our lord says."

[28]Then Moses gave orders about them to Eleazar the priest and Joshua son of Nun and to the family heads of the Israelite tribes. [29]He said to them, "If the Gadites and Reubenites, every man armed for battle, cross over the Jordan with you before the LORD, then when the land is subdued before you, you must give them the land of Gilead as their possession. [30]But if they do not cross over with you armed, they must accept their possession with you in Canaan."

[31]The Gadites and Reubenites answered, "Your servants will do what the LORD has said. [32]We will cross over before the LORD into Canaan armed, but the property we inherit will be on this side of the Jordan."

[33]Then Moses gave to the Gadites, the Reubenites and the half-tribe of Manasseh son of Joseph the kingdom of Sihon king of the Amorites and the kingdom of Og king of Bashan—the whole land with its cities and the territory around them.

[34]The Gadites built up Dibon, Ataroth, Aroer, [35]Atroth Shophan, Jazer, Jogbehah, [36]Beth Nimrah and Beth Haran as fortified cities, and built pens for their flocks. [37]And the Reubenites rebuilt Heshbon, Elealeh and Kiriathaim, [38]as well as Nebo and Baal Meon (these names were changed) and Sibmah. They gave names to the cities they rebuilt.

[39]The descendants of Makir son of Manasseh went to Gilead, captured it and drove out the Amorites who were there. [40]So Moses gave Gilead to the Makirites, the descendants of Manasseh, and they settled there. [41]Jair, a descendant of Manasseh, captured their settlements and called them Havvoth Jair.[a] [42]And Nobah captured Kenath and its surrounding settlements and called it Nobah after himself.

STAGES IN ISRAEL'S JOURNEY

33 Here are the stages in the journey of the Israelites when they came out of Egypt by divisions under the

[a] 41 Or them the settlements of Jair

What did Moses mean when he said, "your sin will find you out"? (32:23)
Moses agreed to the proposal of the Reubenites and Gadites, but he warned them to keep their promise to help the rest of the Israelites conquer the land of Canaan. If they didn't keep their word, there would be severe penalties.

What happened to all of these cities? (32:34–36)
The Israelites lived there after they made repairs on the city walls.

What does "came out ... by divisions" mean? (33:1)
It probably means each tribe was divided into groups to make traveling more organized. Because "divisions" often relates to an army, the groups may have been protected by armed men.

leadership of Moses and Aaron. [2] At the LORD's command Moses recorded the stages in their journey. This is their journey by stages:

[3] The Israelites set out from Rameses on the fifteenth day of the first month, the day after the Passover. They marched out defiantly in full view of all the Egyptians, [4] who were burying all their firstborn, whom the LORD had struck down among them; for the LORD had brought judgment on their gods.

[5] The Israelites left Rameses and camped at Sukkoth.

[6] They left Sukkoth and camped at Etham, on the edge of the desert.

[7] They left Etham, turned back to Pi Hahiroth, to the east of Baal Zephon, and camped near Migdol.

[8] They left Pi Hahiroth[a] and passed through the sea into the desert, and when they had traveled for three days in the Desert of Etham, they camped at Marah.

[9] They left Marah and went to Elim, where there were twelve springs and seventy palm trees, and they camped there.

[10] They left Elim and camped by the Red Sea.[b]

[11] They left the Red Sea and camped in the Desert of Sin.

[12] They left the Desert of Sin and camped at Dophkah.

[13] They left Dophkah and camped at Alush.

[14] They left Alush and camped at Rephidim, where there was no water for the people to drink.

[15] They left Rephidim and camped in the Desert of Sinai.

[16] They left the Desert of Sinai and camped at Kibroth Hattaavah.

[17] They left Kibroth Hattaavah and camped at Hazeroth.

[18] They left Hazeroth and camped at Rithmah.

[19] They left Rithmah and camped at Rimmon Perez.

[20] They left Rimmon Perez and camped at Libnah.

[21] They left Libnah and camped at Rissah.

[22] They left Rissah and camped at Kehelathah.

[23] They left Kehelathah and camped at Mount Shepher.

[24] They left Mount Shepher and camped at Haradah.

[25] They left Haradah and camped at Makheloth.

[26] They left Makheloth and camped at Tahath.

[27] They left Tahath and camped at Terah.

[28] They left Terah and camped at Mithkah.

[29] They left Mithkah and camped at Hashmonah.

[30] They left Hashmonah and camped at Moseroth.

[31] They left Moseroth and camped at Bene Jaakan.

[32] They left Bene Jaakan and camped at Hor Haggidgad.

[33] They left Hor Haggidgad and camped at Jotbathah.

---

[a] 8 Many manuscripts of the Masoretic Text, Samaritan Pentateuch and Vulgate; most manuscripts of the Masoretic Text *left from before Hahiroth*
[b] 10 Or *the Sea of Reeds*; also in verse 11

³⁴They left Jotbathah and camped at Abronah.

³⁵They left Abronah and camped at Ezion Geber.

³⁶They left Ezion Geber and camped at Kadesh, in the Desert of Zin.

³⁷They left Kadesh and camped at Mount Hor, on the border of Edom. ³⁸At the LORD's command Aaron the priest went up Mount Hor, where he died on the first day of the fifth month of the fortieth year after the Israelites came out of Egypt. ³⁹Aaron was a hundred and twenty-three years old when he died on Mount Hor.

⁴⁰The Canaanite king of Arad, who lived in the Negev of Canaan, heard that the Israelites were coming.

⁴¹They left Mount Hor and camped at Zalmonah.

⁴²They left Zalmonah and camped at Punon.

⁴³They left Punon and camped at Oboth.

⁴⁴They left Oboth and camped at Iye Abarim, on the border of Moab.

⁴⁵They left Iye Abarim and camped at Dibon Gad.

⁴⁶They left Dibon Gad and camped at Almon Diblathaim.

⁴⁷They left Almon Diblathaim and camped in the mountains of Abarim, near Nebo.

⁴⁸They left the mountains of Abarim and camped on the plains of Moab by the Jordan across from Jericho.

⁴⁹There on the plains of Moab they camped along the Jordan from Beth Jeshimoth to Abel Shittim.

⁵⁰On the plains of Moab by the Jordan across from Jericho the LORD said to Moses, ⁵¹"Speak to the Israelites and say to them: 'When you cross the Jordan into Canaan, ⁵²drive out all the inhabitants of the land before you. Destroy all their carved images and their cast idols, and demolish all their high places. ⁵³Take possession of the land and settle in it, for I have given you the land to possess. ⁵⁴Distribute the land by lot, according to your clans. To a larger group give a larger inheritance, and to a smaller group a smaller one. Whatever falls to them by lot will be theirs. Distribute it according to your ancestral tribes.

⁵⁵"'But if you do not drive out the inhabitants of the land, those you allow to remain will become barbs in your eyes and thorns in your sides. They will give you trouble in the land where you will live. ⁵⁶And then I will do to you what I plan to do to them.'"

BOUNDARIES OF CANAAN

34 The LORD said to Moses, ²"Command the Israelites and say to them: 'When you enter Canaan, the land that will be allotted to you as an inheritance is to have these boundaries:

³"'Your southern side will include some of the Desert of Zin along the border of Edom. Your southern boundary will start in the east from the southern end of the Dead Sea, ⁴cross south of Scorpion Pass, continue on to Zin and go south of Kadesh Barnea. Then it will go to Hazar Addar and

---

What does "high places" mean? (33:52)

High places, often on hilltops, were places where idols were worshipped. Sometimes worship of these pagan gods included human sacrifice.

over to Azmon, [5]where it will turn, join the Wadi of Egypt and end at the Mediterranean Sea.

[6]"'Your western boundary will be the coast of the Mediterranean Sea. This will be your boundary on the west.

[7]"'For your northern boundary, run a line from the Mediterranean Sea to Mount Hor [8]and from Mount Hor to Lebo Hamath. Then the boundary will go to Zedad, [9]continue to Ziphron and end at Hazar Enan. This will be your boundary on the north.

[10]"'For your eastern boundary, run a line from Hazar Enan to Shepham. [11]The boundary will go down from Shepham to Riblah on the east side of Ain and continue along the slopes east of the Sea of Galilee.[a] [12]Then the boundary will go down along the Jordan and end at the Dead Sea.

"'This will be your land, with its boundaries on every side.'"

[13]Moses commanded the Israelites: "Assign this land by lot as an inheritance. The LORD has ordered that it be given to the nine and a half tribes, [14]because the families of the tribe of Reuben, the tribe of Gad and the half-tribe of Manasseh have received their inheritance. [15]These two and a half tribes have received their inheritance east of the Jordan across from Jericho, toward the sunrise."

[16]The LORD said to Moses, [17]"These are the names of the men who are to assign the land for you as an inheritance: Eleazar the priest and Joshua son of Nun. [18]And appoint one leader from each tribe to help assign the land. [19]These are their names:

Caleb son of Jephunneh,
    from the tribe of Judah;
[20]Shemuel son of Ammihud,
    from the tribe of Simeon;
[21]Elidad son of Kislon,
    from the tribe of Benjamin;
[22]Bukki son of Jogli,
    the leader from the tribe of Dan;
[23]Hanniel son of Ephod,
    the leader from the tribe of Manasseh son of Joseph;
[24]Kemuel son of Shiphtan,
    the leader from the tribe of Ephraim son of Joseph;
[25]Elizaphan son of Parnak,
    the leader from the tribe of Zebulun;
[26]Paltiel son of Azzan,
    the leader from the tribe of Issachar;
[27]Ahihud son of Shelomi,
    the leader from the tribe of Asher;
[28]Pedahel son of Ammihud,
    the leader from the tribe of Naphtali."

[29]These are the men the LORD commanded to assign the inheritance to the Israelites in the land of Canaan.

TOWNS FOR THE LEVITES

35 On the plains of Moab by the Jordan across from Jericho, the LORD said to Moses, [2]"Command the

[a] 11 Hebrew *Kinnereth*

What was the Wadi of Egypt? (34:5)
A valley that is dry except during the rainy seasons of the year is called a wadi. This wadi was probably southwest of the Dead Sea, ending at the Mediterranean Sea.

Boundaries of Canaan (34:2–12)

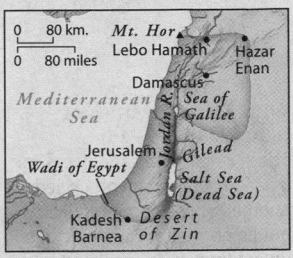

Why were only nine and a half assignments made? (34:13–15)
The tribes of Reuben, Gad, and half of the tribe of Manasseh were going to settle in the Transjordan region on the east side of the Jordan River.

Where was Jericho? (35:1)
The city of Jericho was located seven miles west of the Jordan River and north of the Dead Sea.

Why couldn't the Levites own land? (35:2)
The Levites needed to focus on serving God rather than their own interests. Owning land was a big responsibility and would have distracted them from serving God.

What were the cities of refuge? (35:6, 9–15)
These cities were safe places for a person who accidently killed another. These people could not be harmed within the cities unless they were convicted in a trial. The Levites owned and managed the six cities of refuge.

Who was the avenger of blood? (35:19)
The avenger of blood was the nearest male relative, related by blood, to the person who had died.

Israelites to give the Levites towns to live in from the inheritance the Israelites will possess. And give them pasturelands around the towns. ³Then they will have towns to live in and pasturelands for the cattle they own and all their other animals.

⁴"The pasturelands around the towns that you give the Levites will extend a thousand cubits*a* from the town wall. ⁵Outside the town, measure two thousand cubits*b* on the east side, two thousand on the south side, two thousand on the west and two thousand on the north, with the town in the center. They will have this area as pastureland for the towns.

CITIES OF REFUGE

⁶"Six of the towns you give the Levites will be cities of refuge, to which a person who has killed someone may flee. In addition, give them forty-two other towns. ⁷In all you must give the Levites forty-eight towns, together with their pasturelands. ⁸The towns you give the Levites from the land the Israelites possess are to be given in proportion to the inheritance of each tribe: Take many towns from a tribe that has many, but few from one that has few."

⁹Then the LORD said to Moses: ¹⁰"Speak to the Israelites and say to them: 'When you cross the Jordan into Canaan, ¹¹select some towns to be your cities of refuge, to which a person who has killed someone accidentally may flee. ¹²They will be places of refuge from the avenger, so that anyone accused of murder may not die before they stand trial before the assembly. ¹³These six towns you give will be your cities of refuge. ¹⁴Give three on this side of the Jordan and three in Canaan as cities of refuge. ¹⁵These six towns will be a place of refuge for Israelites and for foreigners residing among them, so that anyone who has killed another accidentally can flee there.

¹⁶"'If anyone strikes someone a fatal blow with an iron object, that person is a murderer; the murderer is to be put to death. ¹⁷Or if anyone is holding a stone and strikes someone a fatal blow with it, that person is a murderer; the murderer is to be put to death. ¹⁸Or if anyone is holding a wooden object and strikes someone a fatal blow with it, that person is a murderer; the murderer is to be put to death. ¹⁹The avenger of blood shall put the murderer to death; when the avenger comes upon the murderer, the avenger shall put the murderer to death. ²⁰If anyone with malice aforethought shoves another or throws something at them intentionally so that they die ²¹or if out of enmity one person hits another with their fist so that the other dies, that person is to be put to death; that person is a murderer. The avenger of blood shall put the murderer to death when they meet.

²²"'But if without enmity someone suddenly pushes another or throws something at them unintentionally ²³or, without seeing them, drops on them a stone heavy enough to kill them, and they die, then since that other person was not an enemy and no harm was intended, ²⁴the assembly

---

*a 4 That is, about 1,500 feet or about 450 meters   b 5 That is, about 3,000 feet or about 900 meters

must judge between the accused and the avenger of blood according to these regulations. ²⁵The assembly must protect the one accused of murder from the avenger of blood and send the accused back to the city of refuge to which they fled. The accused must stay there until the death of the high priest, who was anointed with the holy oil.

²⁶"'But if the accused ever goes outside the limits of the city of refuge to which they fled ²⁷and the avenger of blood finds them outside the city, the avenger of blood may kill the accused without being guilty of murder. ²⁸The accused must stay in the city of refuge until the death of the high priest; only after the death of the high priest may they return to their own property.

²⁹"'This is to have the force of law for you throughout the generations to come, wherever you live.

³⁰"'Anyone who kills a person is to be put to death as a murderer only on the testimony of witnesses. But no one is to be put to death on the testimony of only one witness.

³¹"'Do not accept a ransom for the life of a murderer, who deserves to die. They are to be put to death.

³²"'Do not accept a ransom for anyone who has fled to a city of refuge and so allow them to go back and live on their own land before the death of the high priest.

³³"'Do not pollute the land where you are. Bloodshed pollutes the land, and atonement cannot be made for the land on which blood has been shed, except by the blood of the one who shed it. ³⁴Do not defile the land where you live and where I dwell, for I, the LORD, dwell among the Israelites.'"

INHERITANCE OF ZELOPHEHAD'S DAUGHTERS

36 The family heads of the clan of Gilead son of Makir, the son of Manasseh, who were from the clans of the descendants of Joseph, came and spoke before Moses and the leaders, the heads of the Israelite families. ²They said, "When the LORD commanded my lord to give the land as an inheritance to the Israelites by lot, he ordered you to give the inheritance of our brother Zelophehad to his daughters. ³Now suppose they marry men from other Israelite tribes; then their inheritance will be taken from our ancestral inheritance and added to that of the tribe they marry into. And so part of the inheritance allotted to us will be taken away. ⁴When the Year of Jubilee for the Israelites comes, their inheritance will be added to that of the tribe into which they marry, and their property will be taken from the tribal inheritance of our ancestors."

⁵Then at the LORD's command Moses gave this order to the Israelites: "What the tribe of the descendants of Joseph is saying is right. ⁶This is what the LORD commands for Zelophehad's daughters: They may marry anyone they please as long as they marry within their father's tribal clan. ⁷No inheritance in Israel is to pass from one tribe to another, for every Israelite shall keep the tribal inheritance of their ancestors. ⁸Every daughter who inherits land in any Israelite tribe must marry someone in her father's tribal clan, so that every Israelite will possess the inheritance of their ancestors.

Did all women have to marry within their own tribe? (36:3)
No, only women who inherited land had to marry within their own tribe. Land was very important to the Israelites. If a woman married a man from another tribe, she became part of her husband's tribe. If she also owned land, the land would belong to her new tribe, and the tribal boundaries would change.

What was the Year of Jubilee? (36:4)
The Year of Jubilee happened once every 50 years. During that year, all of the land was given back to the original owners, and no one planted the fields. People were told to forgive others from their debt, and slaves were granted their freedom.

⁹"No inheritance may pass from one tribe to another, for each Israelite tribe is to keep the land it inherits."

¹⁰So Zelophehad's daughters did as the LORD commanded Moses. ¹¹Zelophehad's daughters — Mahlah, Tirzah, Hoglah, Milkah and Noah — married their cousins on their father's side. ¹²They married within the clans of the descendants of Manasseh son of Joseph, and their inheritance remained in their father's tribe and clan.

¹³These are the commands and regulations the LORD gave through Moses to the Israelites on the plains of Moab by the Jordan across from Jericho.

Deuteronomy

INTRODUCTION

Who wrote this book?
Moses.

Why was this book written?
Deuteronomy tells a new generation of Israelites how to please God, so that God will bless them.

What happens in this book?
Moses speaks to the Israelites. He tells what God has done for them and reviews God's rules for holy living. The Israelites promise to obey God.

What do we learn about God in this book?
God helps people because he loves them. God's rules for living are given in love, and he blesses people who keep his rules.

Who is the key person in this book?
The most important person in this book is Moses.

Where did this happen?
During this time the Israelites were camped across the Jordan River from Canaan, the promised land. (See the next page to see where the Jordan River is.)

What are some of the stories in this book?

Moses tells of Israel's journey	Deuteronomy 1–3
Moses tells of the golden calf	Deuteronomy 9
Moses gives instructions for an altar	Deuteronomy 27
Israel promises to obey God	Deuteronomy 29
Moses dies	Deuteronomy 34

When did these things happen?

2200 BC 2100 2000 1900 1800 1700 1600 1500 1400

MOSES' BIRTH (C. 1526 BC) _____

THE PLAGUES; THE PASSOVER (C. 1446 BC) _____

THE EXODUS (C. 1446 BC) _____

DESERT WANDERINGS (C. 1446 – 1406 BC) _____

THE TEN COMMANDMENTS (C. 1445 BC) _____

BOOK OF DEUTERONOMY WRITTEN (C. 1406 BC) _____

MOSES DIES; JOSHUA BECOMES LEADER (C. 1406 BC) _____

ISRAELITES ENTER CANAAN (C. 1406 BC) _____

Where was the Arabah? (1:1)
This was an area east of the Jordan River, a wasteland in the Jordan Valley. The word *Arabah* means "dry or burnt up."

Setting of Deuteronomy (1:1)

What was the "fortieth year"? (1:3)
This was the fortieth year after the Israelites had left Egypt.

Why did Moses retell this history of the Israelites? (1:5–46)
The people were about to enter the promised land after 40 years of wandering in the desert. Many of the people present had not been alive through the whole experience, so Moses wanted to make God's role clear. He explained about God's redemption and faithfulness. He also told them about the faithlessness of the people and challenged the listeners to obey God.

THE COMMAND TO LEAVE HOREB

1 These are the words Moses spoke to all Israel in the wilderness east of the Jordan — that is, in the Arabah — opposite Suph, between Paran and Tophel, Laban, Hazeroth and Dizahab. ²(It takes eleven days to go from Horeb to Kadesh Barnea by the Mount Seir road.)

³In the fortieth year, on the first day of the eleventh month, Moses proclaimed to the Israelites all that the LORD had commanded him concerning them. ⁴This was after he had defeated Sihon king of the Amorites, who reigned in Heshbon, and at Edrei had defeated Og king of Bashan, who reigned in Ashtaroth.

⁵East of the Jordan in the territory of Moab, Moses began to expound this law, saying:

⁶The LORD our God said to us at Horeb, "You have stayed long enough at this mountain. ⁷Break camp and advance into the hill country of the Amorites; go to all the neighboring peoples in the Arabah, in the mountains, in the western foothills, in the Negev and along the coast, to the land of the Canaanites and to Lebanon, as far as the great river, the Euphrates. ⁸See, I have given you this land. Go in and take possession of the land the LORD swore he would give to your fathers — to Abraham, Isaac and Jacob — and to their descendants after them."

THE APPOINTMENT OF LEADERS

⁹At that time I said to you, "You are too heavy a burden for me to carry alone. ¹⁰The LORD your God has increased your numbers so that today you are as numerous as the stars in the sky. ¹¹May the LORD, the God of your ancestors, increase you a thousand times and bless you as he has promised! ¹²But how can I bear your problems and your burdens and your disputes all by myself? ¹³Choose some wise, understanding and respected men from each of your tribes, and I will set them over you."

¹⁴You answered me, "What you propose to do is good."

¹⁵So I took the leading men of your tribes, wise and respected men, and appointed them to have authority over you — as commanders of thousands, of hundreds, of fifties and of tens and as tribal officials. ¹⁶And I charged your judges at that time, "Hear the disputes between your people and judge fairly, whether the case is between two Israelites or between an Israelite and a foreigner residing among you. ¹⁷Do not show partiality in judging; hear both small and great alike. Do not be afraid of anyone, for judgment belongs to God. Bring me any case too hard for you, and I will hear it." ¹⁸And at that time I told you everything you were to do.

SPIES SENT OUT

¹⁹Then, as the LORD our God commanded us, we set out from Horeb and went toward the hill country of the Amorites through all that vast and dreadful wilderness that you have seen, and so we reached Kadesh Barnea. ²⁰Then I said to you, "You have reached the hill country of the Amorites, which the LORD our God is giving us. ²¹See, the LORD your

God has given you the land. Go up and take possession of it as the LORD, the God of your ancestors, told you. Do not be afraid; do not be discouraged."

²²Then all of you came to me and said, "Let us send men ahead to spy out the land for us and bring back a report about the route we are to take and the towns we will come to."

²³The idea seemed good to me; so I selected twelve of you, one man from each tribe. ²⁴They left and went up into the hill country, and came to the Valley of Eshkol and explored it. ²⁵Taking with them some of the fruit of the land, they brought it down to us and reported, "It is a good land that the LORD our God is giving us."

REBELLION AGAINST THE LORD

²⁶But you were unwilling to go up; you rebelled against the command of the LORD your God. ²⁷You grumbled in your tents and said, "The LORD hates us; so he brought us out of Egypt to deliver us into the hands of the Amorites to destroy us. ²⁸Where can we go? Our brothers have made our hearts melt in fear. They say, 'The people are stronger and taller than we are; the cities are large, with walls up to the sky. We even saw the Anakites there.'"

²⁹Then I said to you, "Do not be terrified; do not be afraid of them. ³⁰The LORD your God, who is going before you, will fight for you, as he did for you in Egypt, before your very eyes, ³¹and in the wilderness. There you saw how the LORD your God carried you, as a father carries his son, all the way you went until you reached this place."

³²In spite of this, you did not trust in the LORD your God, ³³who went ahead of you on your journey, in fire by night and in a cloud by day, to search out places for you to camp and to show you the way you should go.

³⁴When the LORD heard what you said, he was angry and solemnly swore: ³⁵"No one from this evil generation shall see the good land I swore to give your ancestors, ³⁶except Caleb son of Jephunneh. He will see it, and I will give him and his descendants the land he set his feet on, because he followed the LORD wholeheartedly."

³⁷Because of you the LORD became angry with me also and said, "You shall not enter it, either. ³⁸But your assistant, Joshua son of Nun, will enter it. Encourage him, because he will lead Israel to inherit it. ³⁹And the little ones that you said would be taken captive, your children who do not yet know good from bad—they will enter the land. I will give it to them and they will take possession of it. ⁴⁰But as for you, turn around and set out toward the desert along the route to the Red Sea.ᵃ"

⁴¹Then you replied, "We have sinned against the LORD. We will go up and fight, as the LORD our God commanded us." So every one of you put on his weapons, thinking it easy to go up into the hill country.

⁴²But the LORD said to me, "Tell them, 'Do not go up and fight, because I will not be with you. You will be defeated by your enemies.'"

ᵃ 40 Or the Sea of Reeds

Who were the Anakites? (1:28)
The descendants of Anak were very strong and tall. The Israelite spies were so afraid they convinced themselves that the Anakites were related to the Nephilim, a race of giants.

Did God punish Moses for the Israelites' lack of faith? (1:37)
No. God punished Moses for his sin. He sinned when he angrily struck the rock with his staff at Meribah (Numbers 20:1–13). Because of this sin against God, he was not allowed to go into the promised land.

43 So I told you, but you would not listen. You rebelled against the LORD's command and in your arrogance you marched up into the hill country. **44** The Amorites who lived in those hills came out against you; they chased you like a swarm of bees and beat you down from Seir all the way to Hormah. **45** You came back and wept before the LORD, but he paid no attention to your weeping and turned a deaf ear to you. **46** And so you stayed in Kadesh many days—all the time you spent there.

WANDERINGS IN THE WILDERNESS

2 Then we turned back and set out toward the wilderness along the route to the Red Sea,*a* as the LORD had directed me. For a long time we made our way around the hill country of Seir.

2 Then the LORD said to me, **3** "You have made your way around this hill country long enough; now turn north. **4** Give the people these orders: 'You are about to pass through the territory of your relatives the descendants of Esau, who live in Seir. They will be afraid of you, but be very careful. **5** Do not provoke them to war, for I will not give you any of their land, not even enough to put your foot on. I have given Esau the hill country of Seir as his own. **6** You are to pay them in silver for the food you eat and the water you drink.'"

7 The LORD your God has blessed you in all the work of your hands. He has watched over your journey through this vast wilderness. These forty years the LORD your God has been with you, and you have not lacked anything.

8 So we went on past our relatives the descendants of Esau, who live in Seir. We turned from the Arabah road, which comes up from Elath and Ezion Geber, and traveled along the desert road of Moab.

9 Then the LORD said to me, "Do not harass the Moabites or provoke them to war, for I will not give you any part of their land. I have given Ar to the descendants of Lot as a possession."

10 (The Emites used to live there—a people strong and numerous, and as tall as the Anakites. **11** Like the Anakites, they too were considered Rephaites, but the Moabites called them Emites. **12** Horites used to live in Seir, but the descendants of Esau drove them out. They destroyed the Horites from before them and settled in their place, just as Israel did in the land the LORD gave them as their possession.)

13 And the LORD said, "Now get up and cross the Zered Valley." So we crossed the valley.

14 Thirty-eight years passed from the time we left Kadesh Barnea until we crossed the Zered Valley. By then, that entire generation of fighting men had perished from the camp, as the LORD had sworn to them. **15** The LORD's hand was against them until he had completely eliminated them from the camp.

16 Now when the last of these fighting men among the people had died, **17** the LORD said to me, **18** "Today you are to pass by the region of Moab at Ar. **19** When you come to the

a 1 Or the Sea of Reeds

Why wouldn't God accept the people's repentance? (1:45)
The people were not sincere with their repentance. They disobeyed God repeatedly. When they were defeated, they were sorry, but God was not impressed by this show of repentance that came too late.

Why were Esau's descendants afraid of the Israelites? (2:4–5)
It's likely that they had heard about Israel's great victories, and they knew God was on Israel's side because of his promise to Abraham. Even though they shared common ancestors with the Israelites, they were afraid that Israel might overtake them.

Why did the Lord protect Esau's descendants? (2:5–6)
God promised Esau and his descendants the hill country. Long ago, when Jacob returned home with Rachel and Leah, Esau welcomed him with love even though Jacob had tricked their father into blessing him and giving him Esau's birthright (see Genesis 33:1–9).

Why did God watch over the Israelites when they were being punished? (2:7)
God watched over his people for the 40 years they were punished in the desert. When they were finally ready to enter the promised land, God knew the Israelites had learned that they could trust God to keep his promises.

Ammonites, do not harass them or provoke them to war, for I will not give you possession of any land belonging to the Ammonites. I have given it as a possession to the descendants of Lot."

²⁰(That too was considered a land of the Rephaites, who used to live there; but the Ammonites called them Zamzummites. ²¹They were a people strong and numerous, and as tall as the Anakites. The LORD destroyed them from before the Ammonites, who drove them out and settled in their place. ²²The LORD had done the same for the descendants of Esau, who lived in Seir, when he destroyed the Horites from before them. They drove them out and have lived in their place to this day. ²³And as for the Avvites who lived in villages as far as Gaza, the Caphtorites coming out from Caphtor*ᵃ* destroyed them and settled in their place.)

DEFEAT OF SIHON KING OF HESHBON

²⁴"Set out now and cross the Arnon Gorge. See, I have given into your hand Sihon the Amorite, king of Heshbon, and his country. Begin to take possession of it and engage him in battle. ²⁵This very day I will begin to put the terror and fear of you on all the nations under heaven. They will hear reports of you and will tremble and be in anguish because of you."

²⁶From the Desert of Kedemoth I sent messengers to Sihon king of Heshbon offering peace and saying, ²⁷"Let us pass through your country. We will stay on the main road; we will not turn aside to the right or to the left. ²⁸Sell us food to eat and water to drink for their price in silver. Only let us pass through on foot— ²⁹as the descendants of Esau, who live in Seir, and the Moabites, who live in Ar, did for us—until we cross the Jordan into the land the LORD our God is giving us." ³⁰But Sihon king of Heshbon refused to let us pass through. For the LORD your God had made his spirit stubborn and his heart obstinate in order to give him into your hands, as he has now done.

³¹The LORD said to me, "See, I have begun to deliver Sihon and his country over to you. Now begin to conquer and possess his land."

³²When Sihon and all his army came out to meet us in battle at Jahaz, ³³the LORD our God delivered him over to us and we struck him down, together with his sons and his whole army. ³⁴At that time we took all his towns and completely destroyed*ᵇ* them—men, women and children. We left no survivors. ³⁵But the livestock and the plunder from the towns we had captured we carried off for ourselves. ³⁶From Aroer on the rim of the Arnon Gorge, and from the town in the gorge, even as far as Gilead, not one town was too strong for us. The LORD our God gave us all of them. ³⁷But in accordance with the command of the LORD our God, you did not encroach on any of the land of the Ammonites, neither the land along the course of the Jabbok nor that around the towns in the hills.

ᵃ 23 That is, Crete   *ᵇ 34* The Hebrew term refers to the irrevocable giving over of things or persons to the LORD, often by totally destroying them.

Why were some nations spared and others defeated? (2:24)
These other nations were sinful and worthy of judgment, but God dealt with each nation differently. To some he showed his mercy, while others become tools of punishment to Israel. Some nations, such as the Amorites, were given years of chances to turn away from evil before he destroyed them.

How did God put the terror and fear of Israel on its enemies? (2:25)
Even pagan cultures view military victory as divine intervention. When they heard reports of Israel being freed from Egypt, they knew it was a result of God's work. They feared Israel because they knew Israel's God was mightier than their own gods.

Why were some nations completely destroyed? (2:34)
Some nations were so wicked that God wanted to wipe them out completely. The Israelites would destroy everything and everyone that could be destroyed. Objects made of gold, silver, and bronze were put in a secure place as God's possessions. Total destruction represented giving the whole evil nation over to the LORD.

DEFEAT OF OG KING OF BASHAN

3 Next we turned and went up along the road toward Bashan, and Og king of Bashan with his whole army marched out to meet us in battle at Edrei. ²The LORD said to me, "Do not be afraid of him, for I have delivered him into your hands, along with his whole army and his land. Do to him what you did to Sihon king of the Amorites, who reigned in Heshbon."

³So the LORD our God also gave into our hands Og king of Bashan and all his army. We struck them down, leaving no survivors. ⁴At that time we took all his cities. There was not one of the sixty cities that we did not take from them—the whole region of Argob, Og's kingdom in Bashan. ⁵All these cities were fortified with high walls and with gates and bars, and there were also a great many unwalled villages. ⁶We completely destroyed*a* them, as we had done with Sihon king of Heshbon, destroying*a* every city—men, women and children. ⁷But all the livestock and the plunder from their cities we carried off for ourselves.

⁸So at that time we took from these two kings of the Amorites the territory east of the Jordan, from the Arnon Gorge as far as Mount Hermon. ⁹(Hermon is called Sirion by the Sidonians; the Amorites call it Senir.) ¹⁰We took all the towns on the plateau, and all Gilead, and all Bashan as far as Salekah and Edrei, towns of Og's kingdom in Bashan. ¹¹(Og king of Bashan was the last of the Rephaites. His bed was decorated with iron and was more than nine cubits long and four cubits wide.*b* It is still in Rabbah of the Ammonites.)

DIVISION OF THE LAND

¹²Of the land that we took over at that time, I gave the Reubenites and the Gadites the territory north of Aroer by the Arnon Gorge, including half the hill country of Gilead, together with its towns. ¹³The rest of Gilead and also all of Bashan, the kingdom of Og, I gave to the half-tribe of Manasseh. (The whole region of Argob in Bashan used to be known as a land of the Rephaites. ¹⁴Jair, a descendant of Manasseh, took the whole region of Argob as far as the border of the Geshurites and the Maakathites; it was named after him, so that to this day Bashan is called Havvoth Jair.*c*) ¹⁵And I gave Gilead to Makir. ¹⁶But to the Reubenites and the Gadites I gave the territory extending from Gilead down to the Arnon Gorge (the middle of the gorge being the border) and out to the Jabbok River, which is the border of the Ammonites. ¹⁷Its western border was the Jordan in the Arabah, from Kinnereth to the Sea of the Arabah (that is, the Dead Sea), below the slopes of Pisgah.

¹⁸I commanded you at that time: "The LORD your God has given you this land to take possession of it. But all your able-bodied men, armed for battle, must cross over ahead of the other Israelites. ¹⁹However, your wives, your children and

---

What were the gates and bars that fortified the city? (3:5)
This was a system of primitive locks used to fasten city gates. They were made of heavy beams of wood that were placed into slots on either side of the city's gate to secure it.

Why was Og's bed so huge? (3:11)
This 14 by 6 foot bed probably wasn't his actual bed for sleeping. It may have been a sarcophagus, a stone coffin. This was very large for a sarcophagus of the time.

---

a 6 The Hebrew term refers to the irrevocable giving over of things or persons to the LORD, often by totally destroying them.   *b 11* That is, about 14 feet long and 6 feet wide or about 4 meters long and 1.8 meters wide
c 14 Or *called the settlements of Jair*

your livestock (I know you have much livestock) may stay in the towns I have given you, [20]until the LORD gives rest to your fellow Israelites as he has to you, and they too have taken over the land that the LORD your God is giving them across the Jordan. After that, each of you may go back to the possession I have given you."

MOSES FORBIDDEN TO CROSS THE JORDAN

[21]At that time I commanded Joshua: "You have seen with your own eyes all that the LORD your God has done to these two kings. The LORD will do the same to all the kingdoms over there where you are going. [22]Do not be afraid of them; the LORD your God himself will fight for you."

[23]At that time I pleaded with the LORD: [24]"Sovereign LORD, you have begun to show to your servant your greatness and your strong hand. For what god is there in heaven or on earth who can do the deeds and mighty works you do? [25]Let me go over and see the good land beyond the Jordan—that fine hill country and Lebanon."

[26]But because of you the LORD was angry with me and would not listen to me. "That is enough," the LORD said. "Do not speak to me anymore about this matter. [27]Go up to the top of Pisgah and look west and north and south and east. Look at the land with your own eyes, since you are not going to cross this Jordan. [28]But commission Joshua, and encourage and strengthen him, for he will lead this people across and will cause them to inherit the land that you will see." [29]So we stayed in the valley near Beth Peor.

OBEDIENCE COMMANDED

4 Now, Israel, hear the decrees and laws I am about to teach you. Follow them so that you may live and may go in and take possession of the land the LORD, the God of your ancestors, is giving you. [2]Do not add to what I command you and do not subtract from it, but keep the commands of the LORD your God that I give you.

[3]You saw with your own eyes what the LORD did at Baal Peor. The LORD your God destroyed from among you everyone who followed the Baal of Peor, [4]but all of you who held fast to the LORD your God are still alive today.

[5]See, I have taught you decrees and laws as the LORD my God commanded me, so that you may follow them in the land you are entering to take possession of it. [6]Observe them carefully, for this will show your wisdom and understanding to the nations, who will hear about all these decrees and say, "Surely this great nation is a wise and understanding people." [7]What other nation is so great as to have their gods near them the way the LORD our God is near us whenever we pray to him? [8]And what other nation is so great as to have such righteous decrees and laws as this body of laws I am setting before you today?

[9]Only be careful, and watch yourselves closely so that you do not forget the things your eyes have seen or let them fade from your heart as long as you live. Teach them to your children and to their children after them. [10]Remember the day

Were women and children left unprotected when the army went away to fight? (3:18–20)
No. Some men stayed with the women and children. The young men (under 20) and older men stayed behind. And some men were excused from fighting if they had obligations at home (such as new crops or were recently married).

Why did God tell Moses to climb Pisgah? (3:27)
Moses wanted to see the promised land. God would not let him cross the Jordan, but he told Moses to climb this mountain and see it from this viewpoint.

Why would the Israelites be tempted to worship idols? (4:15–19)
People at that time were used to worshiping statues or other objects that represented one of their gods. The Israelites had heard God's voice, but God had not allowed his people to see him in a physical form. So they may have been tempted to worship something that they could see.

How were the Israelites the "people of his inheritance"? (4:20)
They were God's inheritance because they were the people God had chosen to be his very own. The Israelites also received an inheritance from God — their land and their knowledge of the true God that no other nation had.

Was Moses blaming the people for his sin? (4:21)
Moses wasn't blaming them or denying that he had sinned, but he was recalling the facts. God was angry with Moses when he struck the rock at Meribah to get water. The rebellion of the Israelites put Moses in a situation that resulted in his sinning against the Lord, but Moses was responsible for his actions, and now he was being punished.

How is God a consuming fire? (4:24)
This image of a fire showed how deep God's anger would be if his people were disloyal to him by serving idols. God's righteous jealousy would totally consume like a fire anyone who undermined his holiness or complete devotion.

Why did God call heaven and earth as witnesses? (4:26)
In ancient treaties, each party to an agreement called upon their gods as witnesses, because they believed their gods had the power to enforce the treaty. Since no one is above God, he called heaven and earth as witnesses. This

you stood before the LORD your God at Horeb, when he said to me, "Assemble the people before me to hear my words so that they may learn to revere me as long as they live in the land and may teach them to their children." [11] You came near and stood at the foot of the mountain while it blazed with fire to the very heavens, with black clouds and deep darkness. [12] Then the LORD spoke to you out of the fire. You heard the sound of words but saw no form; there was only a voice. [13] He declared to you his covenant, the Ten Commandments, which he commanded you to follow and then wrote them on two stone tablets. [14] And the LORD directed me at that time to teach you the decrees and laws you are to follow in the land that you are crossing the Jordan to possess.

IDOLATRY FORBIDDEN

[15] You saw no form of any kind the day the LORD spoke to you at Horeb out of the fire. Therefore watch yourselves very carefully, [16] so that you do not become corrupt and make for yourselves an idol, an image of any shape, whether formed like a man or a woman, [17] or like any animal on earth or any bird that flies in the air, [18] or like any creature that moves along the ground or any fish in the waters below. [19] And when you look up to the sky and see the sun, the moon and the stars — all the heavenly array — do not be enticed into bowing down to them and worshiping things the LORD your God has apportioned to all the nations under heaven. [20] But as for you, the LORD took you and brought you out of the iron-smelting furnace, out of Egypt, to be the people of his inheritance, as you now are.

[21] The LORD was angry with me because of you, and he solemnly swore that I would not cross the Jordan and enter the good land the LORD your God is giving you as your inheritance. [22] I will die in this land; I will not cross the Jordan; but you are about to cross over and take possession of that good land. [23] Be careful not to forget the covenant of the LORD your God that he made with you; do not make for yourselves an idol in the form of anything the LORD your God has forbidden. [24] For the LORD your God is a consuming fire, a jealous God.

[25] After you have had children and grandchildren and have lived in the land a long time — if you then become corrupt and make any kind of idol, doing evil in the eyes of the LORD your God and arousing his anger, [26] I call the heavens and the earth as witnesses against you this day that you will quickly perish from the land that you are crossing the Jordan to possess. You will not live there long but will certainly be destroyed. [27] The LORD will scatter you among the peoples, and only a few of you will survive among the nations to which the LORD will drive you. [28] There you will worship man-made gods of wood and stone, which cannot see or hear or eat or smell. [29] But if from there you seek the LORD your God, you will find him if you seek him with all your heart and with all your soul. [30] When you are in distress and all these things have happened to you, then in later days you will return to the LORD your God and obey him. [31] For the LORD your God is a merciful God; he will not abandon or destroy

you or forget the covenant with your ancestors, which he confirmed to them by oath.

THE LORD IS GOD

[32] Ask now about the former days, long before your time, from the day God created human beings on the earth; ask from one end of the heavens to the other. Has anything so great as this ever happened, or has anything like it ever been heard of? [33] Has any other people heard the voice of God[a] speaking out of fire, as you have, and lived? [34] Has any god ever tried to take for himself one nation out of another nation, by testings, by signs and wonders, by war, by a mighty hand and an outstretched arm, or by great and awesome deeds, like all the things the LORD your God did for you in Egypt before your very eyes?

[35] You were shown these things so that you might know that the LORD is God; besides him there is no other. [36] From heaven he made you hear his voice to discipline you. On earth he showed you his great fire, and you heard his words from out of the fire. [37] Because he loved your ancestors and chose their descendants after them, he brought you out of Egypt by his Presence and his great strength, [38] to drive out before you nations greater and stronger than you and to bring you into their land to give it to you for your inheritance, as it is today.

[39] Acknowledge and take to heart this day that the LORD is God in heaven above and on the earth below. There is no other. [40] Keep his decrees and commands, which I am giving you today, so that it may go well with you and your children after you and that you may live long in the land the LORD your God gives you for all time.

CITIES OF REFUGE

[41] Then Moses set aside three cities east of the Jordan, [42] to which anyone who had killed a person could flee if they had unintentionally killed a neighbor without malice aforethought. They could flee into one of these cities and save their life. [43] The cities were these: Bezer in the wilderness plateau, for the Reubenites; Ramoth in Gilead, for the Gadites; and Golan in Bashan, for the Manassites.

INTRODUCTION TO THE LAW

[44] This is the law Moses set before the Israelites. [45] These are the stipulations, decrees and laws Moses gave them when they came out of Egypt [46] and were in the valley near Beth Peor east of the Jordan, in the land of Sihon king of the Amorites, who reigned in Heshbon and was defeated by Moses and the Israelites as they came out of Egypt. [47] They took possession of his land and the land of Og king of Bashan, the two Amorite kings east of the Jordan. [48] This land extended from Aroer on the rim of the Arnon Gorge to Mount Sirion[b] (that is, Hermon), [49] and included all the Arabah east of the Jordan, as far as the Dead Sea,[c] below the slopes of Pisgah.

[a] 33 Or of a god   [b] 48 Syriac (see also 3:9); Hebrew Siyon   [c] 49 Hebrew the Sea of the Arabah

---

also reminded the Israelites that if they broke the covenant, they would be threatened by natural disasters and bad harvests.

Why did God pick these people instead of others? (4:33)
God made it clear that the Israelites were his chosen people, but not because they were special or deserved God's favor more than any other nation. Choosing them may have been a matter of God's timing. God used the Israelites as a means to bring his blessings to the whole world.

Did Israel keep this land for all time? (4:40)
No. God gave them the land as long as they obeyed his commands. Unfortunately, Israel disobeyed God and they ended up losing the land.

What were the cities of refuge? (4:41–43)
These cities were used as a holding place for people accused of a crime. The accused lived and worked here until they were put on trial. (See Numbers 35:6–34.)

Why did Moses repeat the Ten Commandments? (5:1)
Before the Israelites entered the promised land, Moses wanted to review the law and explain it further, especially to the next generation of Israelites.

What did it mean that the covenant was made "not with our ancestors ... but with us"? (5:3)
The covenant was first made with the people who were present at Sinai, but the covenant was made with all future generations as well.

Where else in the Bible are the Ten Commandments recorded?
They are also listed in Exodus 20:1–17.

Must Christians still obey the Ten Commandments? (5:6–21)
For Christians today, God's laws serve several purposes. First, they show what God expects as correct behavior. Second, they show us how sinful we are; human beings can never keep all of the commandments perfectly. Jesus has brought salvation to his people, because they could never earn it themselves. Third, the commandments show Christians how to live their lives in thankfulness to God for his great love.

THE TEN COMMANDMENTS

5 Moses summoned all Israel and said:

Hear, Israel, the decrees and laws I declare in your hearing today. Learn them and be sure to follow them. [2]The LORD our God made a covenant with us at Horeb. [3]It was not with our ancestors[a] that the LORD made this covenant, but with us, with all of us who are alive here today. [4]The LORD spoke to you face to face out of the fire on the mountain. [5](At that time I stood between the LORD and you to declare to you the word of the LORD, because you were afraid of the fire and did not go up the mountain.) And he said:

[6]"I am the LORD your God, who brought you out of Egypt, out of the land of slavery.

[7]"You shall have no other gods before[b] me.

[8]"You shall not make for yourself an image in the form of anything in heaven above or on the earth beneath or in the waters below. [9]You shall not bow down to them or worship them; for I, the LORD your God, am a jealous God, punishing the children for the sin of the parents to the third and fourth generation of those who hate me, [10]but showing love to a thousand generations of those who love me and keep my commandments.

[11]"You shall not misuse the name of the LORD your God, for the LORD will not hold anyone guiltless who misuses his name.

[12]"Observe the Sabbath day by keeping it holy, as the LORD your God has commanded you. [13]Six days you shall labor and do all your work, [14]but the seventh day is a sabbath to the LORD your God. On it you shall not do any work, neither you, nor your son or daughter, nor your male or female servant, nor your ox, your donkey or any of your animals, nor any foreigner residing in your towns, so that your male and female servants may rest, as you do. [15]Remember that you were slaves in Egypt and that the

---

[a] 3 Or *not only with our parents*   [b] 7 Or *besides*

What did it mean to observe the Sabbath?   DEUTERONOMY 5

The Sabbath, or seventh day of the week, was set aside as a day which people were to keep as holy by not doing any work. This followed the pattern of creation in which God created the universe in six days and rested on the seventh. Since God is all-powerful, he did not need to rest because he was tired. This was a sign that his creation work was finished. Resting on the seventh day is a pattern that God wants us to follow, setting one day apart as holy to the Lord.

By Jesus' time, the religious leaders had built up so many rules and regulations about the Sabbath that they had forgotten the real purpose of it. The Pharisees accused Jesus and his disciples of breaking some of these rules by picking grain to eat and healing those who were sick. Jesus challenged them by describing some times when the Sabbath rules had been broken to accomplish a greater good. The rules for the Sabbath had become so specific and numerous that people had lost sight of the original purpose of the Sabbath, which was for humans to experience physical, mental, and spiritual restoration (see Mark 2:27).

Since the time of Christ, Christians have set aside Sunday, the first day of the week, as a special day that has the same function as the Sabbath.

LORD your God brought you out of there with a mighty hand and an outstretched arm. Therefore the LORD your God has commanded you to observe the Sabbath day.

16 "Honor your father and your mother, as the LORD your God has commanded you, so that you may live long and that it may go well with you in the land the LORD your God is giving you.

17 "You shall not murder.

18 "You shall not commit adultery.

19 "You shall not steal.

20 "You shall not give false testimony against your neighbor.

21 "You shall not covet your neighbor's wife. You shall not set your desire on your neighbor's house or land, his male or female servant, his ox or donkey, or anything that belongs to your neighbor."

22 These are the commandments the LORD proclaimed in a loud voice to your whole assembly there on the mountain from out of the fire, the cloud and the deep darkness; and he added nothing more. Then he wrote them on two stone tablets and gave them to me.

23 When you heard the voice out of the darkness, while the mountain was ablaze with fire, all the leaders of your tribes and your elders came to me. 24 And you said, "The LORD our God has shown us his glory and his majesty, and we have heard his voice from the fire. Today we have seen that a person can live even if God speaks with them. 25 But now, why should we die? This great fire will consume us, and we will die if we hear the voice of the LORD our God any longer. 26 For what mortal has ever heard the voice of the living God speaking out of fire, as we have, and survived? 27 Go near and listen to all that the LORD our God says. Then tell us whatever the LORD our God tells you. We will listen and obey."

28 The LORD heard you when you spoke to me, and the LORD said to me, "I have heard what this people said to you. Everything they said was good. 29 Oh, that their hearts would be inclined to fear me and keep all my commands always, so that it might go well with them and their children forever!

30 "Go, tell them to return to their tents. 31 But you stay here with me so that I may give you all the commands, decrees and laws you are to teach them to follow in the land I am giving them to possess."

32 So be careful to do what the LORD your God has commanded you; do not turn aside to the right or to the left. 33 Walk in obedience to all that the LORD your God has commanded you, so that you may live and prosper and prolong your days in the land that you will possess.

LOVE THE LORD YOUR GOD

6 These are the commands, decrees and laws the LORD your God directed me to teach you to observe in the land that you are crossing the Jordan to possess, 2 so that you, your children and their children after them may fear the LORD your God as long as you live by keeping all his decrees

Why do the commandments include consequences for future generations? (5:9–10) This language is like the language used in ancient treaties. If people broke the treaty, the effects would be felt by entire families even into future generations. If the people obeyed the treaty, their ancestors would be rewarded.

and commands that I give you, and so that you may enjoy long life. ³Hear, Israel, and be careful to obey so that it may go well with you and that you may increase greatly in a land flowing with milk and honey, just as the LORD, the God of your ancestors, promised you.

⁴Hear, O Israel: The LORD our God, the LORD is one.ᵃ ⁵Love the LORD your God with all your heart and with all your soul and with all your strength. ⁶These commandments that I give you today are to be on your hearts. ⁷Impress them on your children. Talk about them when you sit at home and when you walk along the road, when you lie down and when you get up. ⁸Tie them as symbols on your hands and bind them on your foreheads. ⁹Write them on the doorframes of your houses and on your gates.

¹⁰When the LORD your God brings you into the land he swore to your fathers, to Abraham, Isaac and Jacob, to give you — a land with large, flourishing cities you did not build, ¹¹houses filled with all kinds of good things you did not provide, wells you did not dig, and vineyards and olive groves you did not plant — then when you eat and are satisfied, ¹²be careful that you do not forget the LORD, who brought you out of Egypt, out of the land of slavery.

¹³Fear the LORD your God, serve him only and take your oaths in his name. ¹⁴Do not follow other gods, the gods of the peoples around you; ¹⁵for the LORD your God, who is among you, is a jealous God and his anger will burn against you, and he will destroy you from the face of the land. ¹⁶Do not put the LORD your God to the test as you did at Massah. ¹⁷Be sure to keep the commands of the LORD your God and the stipulations and decrees he has given you. ¹⁸Do what is right and good in the LORD's sight, so that it may go well with you and you may go in and take over the good land the LORD promised on oath to your ancestors, ¹⁹thrusting out all your enemies before you, as the LORD said.

²⁰In the future, when your son asks you, "What is the meaning of the stipulations, decrees and laws the LORD our God has commanded you?" ²¹tell him: "We were slaves of Pharaoh in Egypt, but the LORD brought us out of Egypt with a mighty hand. ²²Before our eyes the LORD sent signs and wonders — great and terrible — on Egypt and Pharaoh and his whole household. ²³But he brought us out from there to bring us in and give us the land he promised on oath to our ancestors. ²⁴The LORD commanded us to obey all these decrees and to fear the LORD our God, so that we might always prosper and be kept alive, as is the case today. ²⁵And if we are careful to obey all this law before the LORD our God, as he has commanded us, that will be our righteousness."

DRIVING OUT THE NATIONS

7 When the LORD your God brings you into the land you are entering to possess and drives out before you many nations — the Hittites, Girgashites, Amorites, Canaanites, Perizzites, Hivites and Jebusites, seven nations larger and

---

What does it mean that "the LORD is one"? (6:4)
The words mean that there is only one God. This God is unique — one of a kind.

What is special about these five verses? (6:4–9)
These verses are known as the *Shema*, the Hebrew word for *hear*. This has become the Jewish confession of faith, and it is still recited by Jewish people today.

Why did Israel take over the land and property of other people? (6:10–11)
This was punishment on the wicked Amorites, but more importantly, it was God's way of fulfilling the promise that he had made to Abraham. God gave his people the land so long as they were faithful to him. Later when the Israelites turned away from God, their land was taken from them.

What happened at Massah? (6:16)
This was one of the places where the Israelites complained to Moses about the lack of water. The people did not trust that God would take care of them, even though he had brought them out of Egypt and had provided for their needs in the desert. So God told Moses to strike the rock with his staff, and water gushed out.

ᵃ *4 Or The LORD our God is one LORD; or The LORD is our God, the LORD is one; or The LORD is our God, the LORD alone*

stronger than you— ²and when the LORD your God has delivered them over to you and you have defeated them, then you must destroy them totally.ᵃ Make no treaty with them, and show them no mercy. ³Do not intermarry with them. Do not give your daughters to their sons or take their daughters for your sons, ⁴for they will turn your children away from following me to serve other gods, and the LORD's anger will burn against you and will quickly destroy you. ⁵This is what you are to do to them: Break down their altars, smash their sacred stones, cut down their Asherah polesᵇ and burn their idols in the fire. ⁶For you are a people holy to the LORD your God. The LORD your God has chosen you out of all the peoples on the face of the earth to be his people, his treasured possession.

⁷The LORD did not set his affection on you and choose you because you were more numerous than other peoples, for you were the fewest of all peoples. ⁸But it was because the LORD loved you and kept the oath he swore to your ancestors that he brought you out with a mighty hand and redeemed you from the land of slavery, from the power of Pharaoh king of Egypt. ⁹Know therefore that the LORD your God is God; he is the faithful God, keeping his covenant of love to a thousand generations of those who love him and keep his commandments. ¹⁰But

> those who hate him he will repay to their face by
>   destruction;
>   he will not be slow to repay to their face those who
>   hate him.

¹¹Therefore, take care to follow the commands, decrees and laws I give you today.

¹²If you pay attention to these laws and are careful to follow them, then the LORD your God will keep his covenant of love with you, as he swore to your ancestors. ¹³He will love you and bless you and increase your numbers. He will bless the fruit of your womb, the crops of your land—your grain, new wine and olive oil—the calves of your herds and the lambs of your flocks in the land he swore to your ancestors to give you. ¹⁴You will be blessed more than any other people; none of your men or women will be childless, nor will any of your livestock be without young. ¹⁵The LORD will keep you free from every disease. He will not inflict on you the horrible diseases you knew in Egypt, but he will inflict them on all who hate you. ¹⁶You must destroy all the peoples the LORD your God gives over to you. Do not look on them with pity and do not serve their gods, for that will be a snare to you.

¹⁷You may say to yourselves, "These nations are stronger than we are. How can we drive them out?" ¹⁸But do not be afraid of them; remember well what the LORD your God did to Pharaoh and to all Egypt. ¹⁹You saw with your own eyes the great trials, the signs and wonders, the mighty hand and outstretched arm, with which the LORD your God brought

Why did the Lord tell the Israelites to show no mercy? (7:2–6)
God wanted his people to stay away from pagan religious practices, so he told them to destroy the Canaanites. This warned the Israelites of the punishment for turning from God.

What were Asherah poles? (7:5)
Asherah was the name of the wife of El, the chief Canaanite god. Asherah poles were wooden poles set up in her honor and placed near other pagan objects of worship.

Why were the Israelites told to feel no pity? (7:16)
They were acting as God's agents of judgment. They had to show God's determination and their commitment to God's purposes.

ᵃ 2 The Hebrew term refers to the irrevocable giving over of things or persons to the LORD, often by totally destroying them; also in verse 26.   ᵇ 5 That is, wooden symbols of the goddess Asherah; here and elsewhere in Deuteronomy

you out. The Lord your God will do the same to all the peoples you now fear. ²⁰Moreover, the Lord your God will send the hornet among them until even the survivors who hide from you have perished. ²¹Do not be terrified by them, for the Lord your God, who is among you, is a great and awesome God. ²²The Lord your God will drive out those nations before you, little by little. You will not be allowed to eliminate them all at once, or the wild animals will multiply around you. ²³But the Lord your God will deliver them over to you, throwing them into great confusion until they are destroyed. ²⁴He will give their kings into your hand, and you will wipe out their names from under heaven. No one will be able to stand up against you; you will destroy them. ²⁵The images of their gods you are to burn in the fire. Do not covet the silver and gold on them, and do not take it for yourselves, or you will be ensnared by it, for it is detestable to the Lord your God. ²⁶Do not bring a detestable thing into your house or you, like it, will be set apart for destruction. Regard it as vile and utterly detest it, for it is set apart for destruction.

DO NOT FORGET THE LORD

8 Be careful to follow every command I am giving you today, so that you may live and increase and may enter and possess the land the Lord promised on oath to your ancestors. ²Remember how the Lord your God led you all the way in the wilderness these forty years, to humble and test you in order to know what was in your heart, whether or not you would keep his commands. ³He humbled you, causing you to hunger and then feeding you with manna, which neither you nor your ancestors had known, to teach you that man does not live on bread alone but on every word that comes from the mouth of the Lord. ⁴Your clothes did not wear out and your feet did not swell during these forty years. ⁵Know then in your heart that as a man disciplines his son, so the Lord your God disciplines you.

⁶Observe the commands of the Lord your God, walking in obedience to him and revering him. ⁷For the Lord your God is bringing you into a good land—a land with brooks, streams, and deep springs gushing out into the valleys and hills; ⁸a land with wheat and barley, vines and fig trees, pomegranates, olive oil and honey; ⁹a land where bread will not be scarce and you will lack nothing; a land where the rocks are iron and you can dig copper out of the hills.

¹⁰When you have eaten and are satisfied, praise the Lord your God for the good land he has given you. ¹¹Be careful that you do not forget the Lord your God, failing to observe his commands, his laws and his decrees that I am giving you this day. ¹²Otherwise, when you eat and are satisfied, when you build fine houses and settle down, ¹³and when your herds and flocks grow large and your silver and gold increase and all you have is multiplied, ¹⁴then your heart will become proud and you will forget the Lord your God, who brought you out of Egypt, out of the land of slavery. ¹⁵He led you through the vast and dreadful wilderness, that thirsty and waterless land, with its venomous snakes and scorpions. He brought

Why was it necessary to burn the idols? (7:25)
Because the metal had been used for making an image of a false god, even the metal itself was corrupted in God's eyes.

Why did God test the Israelites? (8:2)
As an omnipotent ruler, God already knew what was in their hearts. He tested them in the desert so that they could see their true nature and have the desire to change.

What does it mean that "man does not live on bread alone"? (8:3)
Food is important for human beings, but life is God's gift. In the desert God taught the Israelites that they were totally dependent on him by protecting them and providing them with food and water. God's truths are even more important than food. Jesus quoted this verse when he was tempted by Satan (see Matthew 4:4 and Luke 4:4).

What does "the rocks are iron" mean? (8:9)
Valuable metals, such as copper, tin, bronze, and iron were available in Canaan. Since iron was valuable, saying "the rocks are iron" was a metaphor for how abundant the land was.

you water out of hard rock. [16]He gave you manna to eat in the wilderness, something your ancestors had never known, to humble and test you so that in the end it might go well with you. [17]You may say to yourself, "My power and the strength of my hands have produced this wealth for me." [18]But remember the LORD your God, for it is he who gives you the ability to produce wealth, and so confirms his covenant, which he swore to your ancestors, as it is today.

[19]If you ever forget the LORD your God and follow other gods and worship and bow down to them, I testify against you today that you will surely be destroyed. [20]Like the nations the LORD destroyed before you, so you will be destroyed for not obeying the LORD your God.

NOT BECAUSE OF ISRAEL'S RIGHTEOUSNESS

9 Hear, Israel: You are now about to cross the Jordan to go in and dispossess nations greater and stronger than you, with large cities that have walls up to the sky. [2]The people are strong and tall—Anakites! You know about them and have heard it said: "Who can stand up against the Anakites?" [3]But be assured today that the LORD your God is the one who goes across ahead of you like a devouring fire. He will destroy them; he will subdue them before you. And you will drive them out and annihilate them quickly, as the LORD has promised you.

[4]After the LORD your God has driven them out before you, do not say to yourself, "The LORD has brought me here to take possession of this land because of my righteousness." No, it is on account of the wickedness of these nations that the LORD is going to drive them out before you. [5]It is not because of your righteousness or your integrity that you are going in to take possession of their land; but on account of the wickedness of these nations, the LORD your God will drive them out before you, to accomplish what he swore to your fathers, to Abraham, Isaac and Jacob. [6]Understand, then, that it is not because of your righteousness that the LORD your God is giving you this good land to possess, for you are a stiff-necked people.

THE GOLDEN CALF

[7]Remember this and never forget how you aroused the anger of the LORD your God in the wilderness. From the day you left Egypt until you arrived here, you have been rebellious against the LORD. [8]At Horeb you aroused the LORD's wrath so that he was angry enough to destroy you. [9]When I went up on the mountain to receive the tablets of stone, the tablets of the covenant that the LORD had made with you, I stayed on the mountain forty days and forty nights; I ate no bread and drank no water. [10]The LORD gave me two stone tablets inscribed by the finger of God. On them were all the commandments the LORD proclaimed to you on the mountain out of the fire, on the day of the assembly.

[11]At the end of the forty days and forty nights, the LORD gave me the two stone tablets, the tablets of the covenant. [12]Then the LORD told me, "Go down from here at once, because your people whom you brought out of Egypt have

Why did God hold the other nations accountable for not worshiping him? (9:4)
God had revealed himself to people from the beginning of the world, but these groups of people willfully rebelled against him.

How were the Israelites a stiff-necked people? (9:6)
This expression meant that the Israelites were stubborn and not worthy of God's favor. The term was originally used to describe an ox or a horse that refused to respond when its rope was tugged.

Why were there two tablets of the law? (9:10)
One tablet was made for each party involved in the agreement, a standard practice in ancient Middle Eastern culture. The Israelites kept their copy along with God's copy inside the ark of the covenant.

become corrupt. They have turned away quickly from what I commanded them and have made an idol for themselves."

¹³And the LORD said to me, "I have seen this people, and they are a stiff-necked people indeed! ¹⁴Let me alone, so that I may destroy them and blot out their name from under heaven. And I will make you into a nation stronger and more numerous than they."

¹⁵So I turned and went down from the mountain while it was ablaze with fire. And the two tablets of the covenant were in my hands. ¹⁶When I looked, I saw that you had sinned against the LORD your God; you had made for yourselves an idol cast in the shape of a calf. You had turned aside quickly from the way that the LORD had commanded you. ¹⁷So I took the two tablets and threw them out of my hands, breaking them to pieces before your eyes.

¹⁸Then once again I fell prostrate before the LORD for forty days and forty nights; I ate no bread and drank no water, because of all the sin you had committed, doing what was evil in the LORD's sight and so arousing his anger. ¹⁹I feared the anger and wrath of the LORD, for he was angry enough with you to destroy you. But again the LORD listened to me. ²⁰And the LORD was angry enough with Aaron to destroy him, but at that time I prayed for Aaron too. ²¹Also I took that sinful thing of yours, the calf you had made, and burned it in the fire. Then I crushed it and ground it to powder as fine as dust and threw the dust into a stream that flowed down the mountain.

²²You also made the LORD angry at Taberah, at Massah and at Kibroth Hattaavah.

²³And when the LORD sent you out from Kadesh Barnea, he said, "Go up and take possession of the land I have given you." But you rebelled against the command of the LORD your God. You did not trust him or obey him. ²⁴You have been rebellious against the LORD ever since I have known you.

²⁵I lay prostrate before the LORD those forty days and forty nights because the LORD had said he would destroy you. ²⁶I prayed to the LORD and said, "Sovereign LORD, do not destroy your people, your own inheritance that you redeemed by your great power and brought out of Egypt with a mighty hand. ²⁷Remember your servants Abraham, Isaac and Jacob. Overlook the stubbornness of this people, their wickedness and their sin. ²⁸Otherwise, the country from which you brought us will say, 'Because the LORD was not able to take them into the land he had promised them, and because he hated them, he brought them out to put them to death in the wilderness.' ²⁹But they are your people, your inheritance that you brought out by your great power and your outstretched arm."

TABLETS LIKE THE FIRST ONES

10 At that time the LORD said to me, "Chisel out two stone tablets like the first ones and come up to me on the mountain. Also make a wooden ark.ᵃ ²I will write on the tablets the words that were on the first tablets, which you broke. Then you are to put them in the ark."

ᵃ 1 That is, a chest

Why did the Israelites worship a calf? (9:16)
A calf was a familiar symbol of an idol at the time. The Israelites must have been familiar with the Egyptian bull-god Apis. A calf or bull was also a symbol of the Canaanite god Baal, who was the god of fertility and strength.

Did Moses' prayer change God's mind? (9:25–29)
It seems as if God was ready to destroy the Israelites until Moses begged God to spare them. This may be a way of explaining God's actions in human terms rather than actually meaning that Moses changed God's mind.

What was this wooden ark? (10:1)
This was the ark of the covenant (see Exodus 25:10–12).

³So I made the ark out of acacia wood and chiseled out two stone tablets like the first ones, and I went up on the mountain with the two tablets in my hands. ⁴The LORD wrote on these tablets what he had written before, the Ten Commandments he had proclaimed to you on the mountain, out of the fire, on the day of the assembly. And the LORD gave them to me. ⁵Then I came back down the mountain and put the tablets in the ark I had made, as the LORD commanded me, and they are there now.

⁶(The Israelites traveled from the wells of Bene Jaakan to Moserah. There Aaron died and was buried, and Eleazar his son succeeded him as priest. ⁷From there they traveled to Gudgodah and on to Jotbathah, a land with streams of water. ⁸At that time the LORD set apart the tribe of Levi to carry the ark of the covenant of the LORD, to stand before the LORD to minister and to pronounce blessings in his name, as they still do today. ⁹That is why the Levites have no share or inheritance among their fellow Israelites; the LORD is their inheritance, as the LORD your God told them.)

¹⁰Now I had stayed on the mountain forty days and forty nights, as I did the first time, and the LORD listened to me at this time also. It was not his will to destroy you. ¹¹"Go," the LORD said to me, "and lead the people on their way, so that they may enter and possess the land I swore to their ancestors to give them."

FEAR THE LORD

¹²And now, Israel, what does the LORD your God ask of you but to fear the LORD your God, to walk in obedience to him, to love him, to serve the LORD your God with all your heart and with all your soul, ¹³and to observe the LORD's commands and decrees that I am giving you today for your own good?

¹⁴To the LORD your God belong the heavens, even the highest heavens, the earth and everything in it. ¹⁵Yet the LORD set his affection on your ancestors and loved them, and he chose you, their descendants, above all the nations—as it is today. ¹⁶Circumcise your hearts, therefore, and do not be stiff-necked any longer. ¹⁷For the LORD your God is God of gods and Lord of lords, the great God, mighty and awesome, who shows no partiality and accepts no bribes. ¹⁸He defends the cause of the fatherless and the widow, and loves the foreigner residing among you, giving them food and clothing. ¹⁹And you are to love those who are foreigners, for you yourselves were foreigners in Egypt. ²⁰Fear the LORD your God and serve him. Hold fast to him and take your oaths in his name. ²¹He is the one you praise; he is your God, who performed for you those great and awesome wonders you saw with your own eyes. ²²Your ancestors who went down into Egypt were seventy in all, and now the LORD your God has made you as numerous as the stars in the sky.

LOVE AND OBEY THE LORD

11 Love the LORD your God and keep his requirements, his decrees, his laws and his commands always. ²Remember today that your children were not the ones who saw

What did it mean to circumcise their hearts? (10:16)
This means that people served God from their hearts. Physical circumcision (removal of the foreskin on the penis) was a sign of the covenant between God and his people (see Genesis 17:9–14). This spiritual circumcision required an action of the heart to commit to God.

What does "God of gods and Lord of lords" mean? (10:17)
This exalted language means that God is God in the most absolute sense. God is above human understanding, leaving people in awe of him. Moses did not mean to imply that there actually were other gods, but he used poetic language to emphasize God's majesty.

What do the words requirements, decrees, laws, and commands refer to? (11:1)
All of these words refer to God's laws for his people as they prepared to enter Canaan.

Who were Dathan and Abiram? (11:6)
They joined Korah's rebellion and challenged Moses' authority. God judged them for this sin by having the earth open up and swallow them along with their households and possessions (see Numbers 16:1–34).

How was Canaan different from Egypt? (11:10–14)
In Egypt the Israelites had to water their crops by digging irrigation ditches. But in Canaan the people would depend on God to provide rain for the crops. The rainy season in Palestine begins in October and ends in April.

How did the Israelites place God's words on their arms and foreheads? (11:18)
They obeyed this commandment by wearing phylacteries. These were little boxes strapped to the arm or the forehead that contained parchment strips with words of Scripture written on them (see Exodus 13:9).

How did the people write God's words on their doorframes and gates? (11:20)
They inscribed key words or letters from the law on the wooden doorframes as a reminder of God's law. A mezuzah is a box containing a small parchment scroll with the words of Deuteronomy 6:4–9 and 11:13–21 on it. Today, some Jews place a mezuzah on their doorframe rather than writing on the doorframe.

and experienced the discipline of the LORD your God: his majesty, his mighty hand, his outstretched arm; ³the signs he performed and the things he did in the heart of Egypt, both to Pharaoh king of Egypt and to his whole country; ⁴what he did to the Egyptian army, to its horses and chariots, how he overwhelmed them with the waters of the Red Sea*a* as they were pursuing you, and how the LORD brought lasting ruin on them. ⁵It was not your children who saw what he did for you in the wilderness until you arrived at this place, ⁶and what he did to Dathan and Abiram, sons of Eliab the Reubenite, when the earth opened its mouth right in the middle of all Israel and swallowed them up with their households, their tents and every living thing that belonged to them. ⁷But it was your own eyes that saw all these great things the LORD has done.

⁸Observe therefore all the commands I am giving you today, so that you may have the strength to go in and take over the land that you are crossing the Jordan to possess, ⁹and so that you may live long in the land the LORD swore to your ancestors to give to them and their descendants, a land flowing with milk and honey. ¹⁰The land you are entering to take over is not like the land of Egypt, from which you have come, where you planted your seed and irrigated it by foot as in a vegetable garden. ¹¹But the land you are crossing the Jordan to take possession of is a land of mountains and valleys that drinks rain from heaven. ¹²It is a land the LORD your God cares for; the eyes of the LORD your God are continually on it from the beginning of the year to its end.

¹³So if you faithfully obey the commands I am giving you today—to love the LORD your God and to serve him with all your heart and with all your soul— ¹⁴then I will send rain on your land in its season, both autumn and spring rains, so that you may gather in your grain, new wine and olive oil. ¹⁵I will provide grass in the fields for your cattle, and you will eat and be satisfied.

¹⁶Be careful, or you will be enticed to turn away and worship other gods and bow down to them. ¹⁷Then the LORD's anger will burn against you, and he will shut up the heavens so that it will not rain and the ground will yield no produce, and you will soon perish from the good land the LORD is giving you. ¹⁸Fix these words of mine in your hearts and minds; tie them as symbols on your hands and bind them on your foreheads. ¹⁹Teach them to your children, talking about them when you sit at home and when you walk along the road, when you lie down and when you get up. ²⁰Write them on the doorframes of your houses and on your gates, ²¹so that your days and the days of your children may be many in the land the LORD swore to give your ancestors, as many as the days that the heavens are above the earth.

²²If you carefully observe all these commands I am giving you to follow—to love the LORD your God, to walk in obedience to him and to hold fast to him— ²³then the LORD will drive out all these nations before you, and you will dispossess nations larger and stronger than you. ²⁴Every place where you set your foot will be yours: Your territory will

a 4 Or the Sea of Reeds

extend from the desert to Lebanon, and from the Euphrates River to the Mediterranean Sea. ²⁵ No one will be able to stand against you. The LORD your God, as he promised you, will put the terror and fear of you on the whole land, wherever you go.

²⁶ See, I am setting before you today a blessing and a curse— ²⁷ the blessing if you obey the commands of the LORD your God that I am giving you today; ²⁸ the curse if you disobey the commands of the LORD your God and turn from the way that I command you today by following other gods, which you have not known. ²⁹ When the LORD your God has brought you into the land you are entering to possess, you are to proclaim on Mount Gerizim the blessings, and on Mount Ebal the curses. ³⁰ As you know, these mountains are across the Jordan, westward, toward the setting sun, near the great trees of Moreh, in the territory of those Canaanites living in the Arabah in the vicinity of Gilgal. ³¹ You are about to cross the Jordan to enter and take possession of the land the LORD your God is giving you. When you have taken it over and are living there, ³² be sure that you obey all the decrees and laws I am setting before you today.

THE ONE PLACE OF WORSHIP

12 These are the decrees and laws you must be careful to follow in the land that the LORD, the God of your ancestors, has given you to possess—as long as you live in the land. ² Destroy completely all the places on the high mountains, on the hills and under every spreading tree, where the nations you are dispossessing worship their gods. ³ Break down their altars, smash their sacred stones and burn their Asherah poles in the fire; cut down the idols of their gods and wipe out their names from those places.

⁴ You must not worship the LORD your God in their way. ⁵ But you are to seek the place the LORD your God will choose from among all your tribes to put his Name there for his dwelling. To that place you must go; ⁶ there bring your burnt offerings and sacrifices, your tithes and special gifts, what you have vowed to give and your freewill offerings, and the firstborn of your herds and flocks. ⁷ There, in the presence of the LORD your God, you and your families shall eat and shall rejoice in everything you have put your hand to, because the LORD your God has blessed you.

⁸ You are not to do as we do here today, everyone doing as they see fit, ⁹ since you have not yet reached the resting place and the inheritance the LORD your God is giving you. ¹⁰ But you will cross the Jordan and settle in the land the LORD your God is giving you as an inheritance, and he will give you rest from all your enemies around you so that you will live in safety. ¹¹ Then to the place the LORD your God will choose as a dwelling for his Name—there you are to bring everything I command you: your burnt offerings and sacrifices, your tithes and special gifts, and all the choice possessions you have vowed to the LORD. ¹² And there rejoice before the LORD your God—you, your sons and daughters, your male and female servants, and the Levites from your towns who

A Mezuzah

Why were these commands about worship given first? (12:4–7)
This shows the importance of establishing permanent practices of worship as they get settled in the new land. Obeying God's laws about worship would unify the people and preserve their purity before God.

What was the place that the LORD chose to put his Name? (12:5)
This referred to God's dwelling place—the tabernacle and, later on, the temple—located reliably in a central place. The Canaanites worshiped their gods wherever they thought the gods might be. God wanted to keep the Israelites away from these pagan practices by commanding that worship take place only at God's house.

have no allotment or inheritance of their own. [13]Be careful not to sacrifice your burnt offerings anywhere you please. [14]Offer them only at the place the LORD will choose in one of your tribes, and there observe everything I command you.

[15]Nevertheless, you may slaughter your animals in any of your towns and eat as much of the meat as you want, as if it were gazelle or deer, according to the blessing the LORD your God gives you. Both the ceremonially unclean and the clean may eat it. [16]But you must not eat the blood; pour it out on the ground like water. [17]You must not eat in your own towns the tithe of your grain and new wine and olive oil, or the first-born of your herds and flocks, or whatever you have vowed to give, or your freewill offerings or special gifts. [18]Instead, you are to eat them in the presence of the LORD your God at the place the LORD your God will choose—you, your sons and daughters, your male and female servants, and the Levites from your towns—and you are to rejoice before the LORD your God in everything you put your hand to. [19]Be careful not to neglect the Levites as long as you live in your land.

[20]When the LORD your God has enlarged your territory as he promised you, and you crave meat and say, "I would like some meat," then you may eat as much of it as you want. [21]If the place where the LORD your God chooses to put his Name is too far away from you, you may slaughter animals from the herds and flocks the LORD has given you, as I have command-ed you, and in your own towns you may eat as much of them as you want. [22]Eat them as you would gazelle or deer. Both the ceremonially unclean and the clean may eat. [23]But be sure you do not eat the blood, because the blood is the life, and you must not eat the life with the meat. [24]You must not eat the blood; pour it out on the ground like water. [25]Do not eat it, so that it may go well with you and your children after you, be-cause you will be doing what is right in the eyes of the LORD. [26]But take your consecrated things and whatever you have vowed to give, and go to the place the LORD will choose. [27]Present your burnt offerings on the altar of the LORD your God, both the meat and the blood. The blood of your sacri-fices must be poured beside the altar of the LORD your God, but you may eat the meat. [28]Be careful to obey all these reg-ulations I am giving you, so that it may always go well with you and your children after you, because you will be doing what is good and right in the eyes of the LORD your God.

[29]The LORD your God will cut off before you the nations you are about to invade and dispossess. But when you have driven them out and settled in their land, [30]and after they have been destroyed before you, be careful not to be ensnared by inquiring about their gods, saying, "How do these nations serve their gods? We will do the same." [31]You must not wor-ship the LORD your God in their way, because in worshiping their gods, they do all kinds of detestable things the LORD hates. They even burn their sons and daughters in the fire as sacrifices to their gods.

[32]See that you do all I command you; do not add to it or take away from it.[a]

[a] 32 In Hebrew texts this verse (12:32) is numbered 13:1.

What was a tithe? (12:17)
A tithe is a tenth. Here the tithe referred to giving one-tenth of one's crops and livestock to the LORD. The tithe was given to sup-port the Levites in their service as priests and also those in need (see Leviticus 27:30–32). The Levites also offered a tithe of what they received as their sacri-fice to God.

Why did the Israelites have to leave their towns to eat the tithe? (12:17)
The tithe was not ordinary food. It must be eaten in the presence of the LORD in the place the LORD chooses.

Why did God warn his people about sacrificing their children? (12:31)
Pagan worship sometimes includ-ed human sacrifices, even sacri-fices of children. God wanted his people to completely avoid these practices that were designed to win favor with the pagan gods.

WORSHIPING OTHER GODS

13[a] If a prophet, or one who foretells by dreams, appears among you and announces to you a sign or wonder, [2] and if the sign or wonder spoken of takes place, and the prophet says, "Let us follow other gods" (gods you have not known) "and let us worship them," [3] you must not listen to the words of that prophet or dreamer. The LORD your God is testing you to find out whether you love him with all your heart and with all your soul. [4] It is the LORD your God you must follow, and him you must revere. Keep his commands and obey him; serve him and hold fast to him. [5] That prophet or dreamer must be put to death for inciting rebellion against the LORD your God, who brought you out of Egypt and redeemed you from the land of slavery. That prophet or dreamer tried to turn you from the way the LORD your God commanded you to follow. You must purge the evil from among you.

[6] If your very own brother, or your son or daughter, or the wife you love, or your closest friend secretly entices you, saying, "Let us go and worship other gods" (gods that neither you nor your ancestors have known, [7] gods of the peoples around you, whether near or far, from one end of the land to the other), [8] do not yield to them or listen to them. Show them no pity. Do not spare them or shield them. [9] You must certainly put them to death. Your hand must be the first in putting them to death, and then the hands of all the people. [10] Stone them to death, because they tried to turn you away from the LORD your God, who brought you out of Egypt, out of the land of slavery. [11] Then all Israel will hear and be afraid, and no one among you will do such an evil thing again.

[12] If you hear it said about one of the towns the LORD your God is giving you to live in [13] that troublemakers have arisen among you and have led the people of their town astray, saying, "Let us go and worship other gods" (gods you have not known), [14] then you must inquire, probe and investigate it thoroughly. And if it is true and it has been proved that this detestable thing has been done among you, [15] you must certainly put to the sword all who live in that town. You must destroy it completely,[b] both its people and its livestock. [16] You are to gather all the plunder of the town into the middle of the public square and completely burn the town and all its plunder as a whole burnt offering to the LORD your God. That town is to remain a ruin forever, never to be rebuilt, [17] and none of the condemned things[b] are to be found in your hands. Then the LORD will turn from his fierce anger, will show you mercy, and will have compassion on you. He will increase your numbers, as he promised on oath to your ancestors— [18] because you obey the LORD your God by keeping all his commands that I am giving you today and doing what is right in his eyes.

CLEAN AND UNCLEAN FOOD

14 You are the children of the LORD your God. Do not cut yourselves or shave the front of your heads for

---

Why did God test his people? (13:3)
God was warning them not to be tricked by false prophets into worshiping false gods. Testing them taught them what they needed to know about themselves, and showed whether they would remain faithful to God. Resisting false prophets strengthened their love and obedience to God.

Why was the punishment of a false prophet death? (13:5)
The false prophet preached rebellion against God. God wanted to eliminate the evildoer as well as the evil itself.

Was there no religious freedom? (13:10)
They had freedom to choose, but if the Israelites rejected God, they would pay for their actions. They were in a unique relationship with the Lord, and if they rejected God, they were breaking the promise they had made.

Why did they have to kill everything, even animals? (13:15)
Destroying people, animals, and objects made them useless to the Israelites and put them in the hands of God. Everything was burned as an offering to God. This severe punishment showed how serious God was about his people not worshiping other gods.

Why would people cut themselves or shave their heads? (14:1)
These were pagan religious customs. People slashed themselves as a sign of grief, and shaving the forehead was also a practice of mourners in Canaan.

---

[a] In Hebrew texts 13:1-18 is numbered 13:2-19.   [b] 15,17 The Hebrew term refers to the irrevocable giving over of things or persons to the LORD, often by totally destroying them.

Why were some meats unacceptable to eat? (14:3–21)
Over the years, people have suggested many possible reasons for why God designated some creatures as clean and others as unclean for food. The Bible does not give the answer, but these food laws helped the Israelites eat a healthy diet and maintain their identity as his covenant people. Obeying these food laws consecrated the Israelites, setting them apart as holy.

Do Jews today still follow these food laws? (14:3–21)
These laws are still followed by Orthodox Jews; they are not kept by all Jews. Food that is prepared according to these laws is called *kosher*.

Why couldn't they cook a goat in its mother's milk? (14:21)
This was one of the practices of pagan religions that God wanted his people to avoid. The pagans thought the milk had magical powers for increasing fertility, and they used it on crops and vineyards to make them more productive.

What are fermented drinks? (14:26)
Fermented drinks are alcoholic drinks. It was acceptable for Israelites to drink alcohol and wine, but not to get drunk.

the dead, ²for you are a people holy to the LORD your God. Out of all the peoples on the face of the earth, the LORD has chosen you to be his treasured possession.

³Do not eat any detestable thing. ⁴These are the animals you may eat: the ox, the sheep, the goat, ⁵the deer, the gazelle, the roe deer, the wild goat, the ibex, the antelope and the mountain sheep.ᵃ ⁶You may eat any animal that has a divided hoof and that chews the cud. ⁷However, of those that chew the cud or that have a divided hoof you may not eat the camel, the rabbit or the hyrax. Although they chew the cud, they do not have a divided hoof; they are ceremonially unclean for you. ⁸The pig is also unclean; although it has a divided hoof, it does not chew the cud. You are not to eat their meat or touch their carcasses.

⁹Of all the creatures living in the water, you may eat any that has fins and scales. ¹⁰But anything that does not have fins and scales you may not eat; for you it is unclean.

¹¹You may eat any clean bird. ¹²But these you may not eat: the eagle, the vulture, the black vulture, ¹³the red kite, the black kite, any kind of falcon, ¹⁴any kind of raven, ¹⁵the horned owl, the screech owl, the gull, any kind of hawk, ¹⁶the little owl, the great owl, the white owl, ¹⁷the desert owl, the osprey, the cormorant, ¹⁸the stork, any kind of heron, the hoopoe and the bat.

¹⁹All flying insects are unclean to you; do not eat them. ²⁰But any winged creature that is clean you may eat.

²¹Do not eat anything you find already dead. You may give it to the foreigner residing in any of your towns, and they may eat it, or you may sell it to any other foreigner. But you are a people holy to the LORD your God.

Do not cook a young goat in its mother's milk.

TITHES

²²Be sure to set aside a tenth of all that your fields produce each year. ²³Eat the tithe of your grain, new wine and olive oil, and the firstborn of your herds and flocks in the presence of the LORD your God at the place he will choose as a dwelling for his Name, so that you may learn to revere the LORD your God always. ²⁴But if that place is too distant and you have been blessed by the LORD your God and cannot carry your tithe (because the place where the LORD will choose to put his Name is so far away), ²⁵then exchange your tithe for silver, and take the silver with you and go to the place the LORD your God will choose. ²⁶Use the silver to buy whatever you like: cattle, sheep, wine or other fermented drink, or anything you wish. Then you and your household shall eat there in the presence of the LORD your God and rejoice. ²⁷And do not neglect the Levites living in your towns, for they have no allotment or inheritance of their own.

²⁸At the end of every three years, bring all the tithes of that year's produce and store it in your towns, ²⁹so that the Levites (who have no allotment or inheritance of their own) and the foreigners, the fatherless and the widows who live

---

ᵃ 5 The precise identification of some of the birds and animals in this chapter is uncertain.

in your towns may come and eat and be satisfied, and so that the LORD your God may bless you in all the work of your hands.

THE YEAR FOR CANCELING DEBTS

15 At the end of every seven years you must cancel debts. ²This is how it is to be done: Every creditor shall cancel any loan they have made to a fellow Israelite. They shall not require payment from anyone among their own people, because the LORD's time for canceling debts has been proclaimed. ³You may require payment from a foreigner, but you must cancel any debt your fellow Israelite owes you. ⁴However, there need be no poor people among you, for in the land the LORD your God is giving you to possess as your inheritance, he will richly bless you, ⁵if only you fully obey the LORD your God and are careful to follow all these commands I am giving you today. ⁶For the LORD your God will bless you as he has promised, and you will lend to many nations but will borrow from none. You will rule over many nations but none will rule over you.

⁷If anyone is poor among your fellow Israelites in any of the towns of the land the LORD your God is giving you, do not be hardhearted or tightfisted toward them. ⁸Rather, be openhanded and freely lend them whatever they need. ⁹Be careful not to harbor this wicked thought: "The seventh year, the year for canceling debts, is near," so that you do not show ill will toward the needy among your fellow Israelites and give them nothing. They may then appeal to the LORD against you, and you will be found guilty of sin. ¹⁰Give generously to them and do so without a grudging heart; then because of this the LORD your God will bless you in all your work and in everything you put your hand to. ¹¹There will always be poor people in the land. Therefore I command you to be openhanded toward your fellow Israelites who are poor and needy in your land.

FREEING SERVANTS

¹²If any of your people—Hebrew men or women—sell themselves to you and serve you six years, in the seventh year you must let them go free. ¹³And when you release them, do not send them away empty-handed. ¹⁴Supply them liberally from your flock, your threshing floor and your winepress. Give to them as the LORD your God has blessed you. ¹⁵Remember that you were slaves in Egypt and the LORD your God redeemed you. That is why I give you this command today.

¹⁶But if your servant says to you, "I do not want to leave you," because he loves you and your family and is well off with you, ¹⁷then take an awl and push it through his earlobe into the door, and he will become your servant for life. Do the same for your female servant.

¹⁸Do not consider it a hardship to set your servant free, because their service to you these six years has been worth twice as much as that of a hired hand. And the LORD your God will bless you in everything you do.

Why were debts canceled and slaves freed every seventh year? (15:1, 12)
The number seven is linked with the seven days of creation, when the world was finished. Every seventh year was a Sabbath year. By forgiving debts and freeing slaves every seven years, Israel helped the poor become more successful in society.

Why did foreigners have to pay their debts? (15:3)
They did not enjoy the rights of citizens. They also were not required to let their fields lie fallow during the seventh year as the Israelites were, so they would be able to pay their debts.

What should a believer's attitude be toward the poor? (15:11)
God's command is to be generous in helping those who are poor. The Bible is filled with statements that show God's concern for poor people.

Why did they pierce a servant's earlobe? (15:17)
The servant who chose to become a servant for life agreed to listen to the commands of his master. Piercing the ear was a symbol of the decision to listen.

THE FIRSTBORN ANIMALS

[19] Set apart for the Lord your God every firstborn male of your herds and flocks. Do not put the firstborn of your cows to work, and do not shear the firstborn of your sheep. [20] Each year you and your family are to eat them in the presence of the Lord your God at the place he will choose. [21] If an animal has a defect, is lame or blind, or has any serious flaw, you must not sacrifice it to the Lord your God. [22] You are to eat it in your own towns. Both the ceremonially unclean and the clean may eat it, as if it were gazelle or deer. [23] But you must not eat the blood; pour it out on the ground like water.

THE PASSOVER

16 Observe the month of Aviv and celebrate the Passover of the Lord your God, because in the month of Aviv he brought you out of Egypt by night. [2] Sacrifice as the Passover to the Lord your God an animal from your flock or herd at the place the Lord will choose as a dwelling for his Name. [3] Do not eat it with bread made with yeast, but for seven days eat unleavened bread, the bread of affliction, because you left Egypt in haste — so that all the days of your life you may remember the time of your departure from Egypt. [4] Let no yeast be found in your possession in all your land for seven days. Do not let any of the meat you sacrifice on the evening of the first day remain until morning.

[5] You must not sacrifice the Passover in any town the Lord your God gives you [6] except in the place he will choose as a dwelling for his Name. There you must sacrifice the Passover in the evening, when the sun goes down, on the anniversary[a] of your departure from Egypt. [7] Roast it and eat it at the place the Lord your God will choose. Then in the morning return to your tents. [8] For six days eat unleavened bread and on the seventh day hold an assembly to the Lord your God and do no work.

THE FESTIVAL OF WEEKS

[9] Count off seven weeks from the time you begin to put the sickle to the standing grain. [10] Then celebrate the Festival of Weeks to the Lord your God by giving a freewill offering in proportion to the blessings the Lord your God has given you. [11] And rejoice before the Lord your God at the place he will choose as a dwelling for his Name — you, your sons and daughters, your male and female servants, the Levites in your towns, and the foreigners, the fatherless and the widows living among you. [12] Remember that you were slaves in Egypt, and follow carefully these decrees.

THE FESTIVAL OF TABERNACLES

[13] Celebrate the Festival of Tabernacles for seven days after you have gathered the produce of your threshing floor and your winepress. [14] Be joyful at your festival — you, your sons and daughters, your male and female servants, and the Levites, the foreigners, the fatherless and the widows who live in your towns. [15] For seven days celebrate the festival to the

---

What was the month of Aviv? (16:1)
Aviv on the Jewish calendar is the about the same time as March/April on the modern calendar. It marks the beginning of the religious year.

Why was unleavened bread called the bread of affliction? (16:3)
Affliction means great suffering, so unleavened bread reminded the Israelites of the hardships in Egypt. When they fled Egypt, they had to leave so quickly that the bread didn't have time to rise (see Exodus 12:34 – 39).

---

[a] 6 Or *down, at the time of day*

LORD your God at the place the LORD will choose. For the LORD your God will bless you in all your harvest and in all the work of your hands, and your joy will be complete.

[16] Three times a year all your men must appear before the LORD your God at the place he will choose: at the Festival of Unleavened Bread, the Festival of Weeks and the Festival of Tabernacles. No one should appear before the LORD empty-handed: [17] Each of you must bring a gift in proportion to the way the LORD your God has blessed you.

JUDGES

[18] Appoint judges and officials for each of your tribes in every town the LORD your God is giving you, and they shall judge the people fairly. [19] Do not pervert justice or show partiality. Do not accept a bribe, for a bribe blinds the eyes of the wise and twists the words of the innocent. [20] Follow justice and justice alone, so that you may live and possess the land the LORD your God is giving you.

WORSHIPING OTHER GODS

[21] Do not set up any wooden Asherah pole beside the altar you build to the LORD your God, [22] and do not erect a sacred stone, for these the LORD your God hates.

17 Do not sacrifice to the LORD your God an ox or a sheep that has any defect or flaw in it, for that would be detestable to him.

[2] If a man or woman living among you in one of the towns the LORD gives you is found doing evil in the eyes of the LORD your God in violation of his covenant, [3] and contrary to my command has worshiped other gods, bowing down to them or to the sun or the moon or the stars in the sky, [4] and this has been brought to your attention, then you must investigate it thoroughly. If it is true and it has been proved that this detestable thing has been done in Israel, [5] take the man or woman who has done this evil deed to your city gate and stone that person to death. [6] On the testimony of two or three witnesses a person is to be put to death, but no one is to be put to death on the testimony of only one witness. [7] The hands of the witnesses must be the first in putting that person to death, and then the hands of all the people. You must purge the evil from among you.

LAW COURTS

[8] If cases come before your courts that are too difficult for you to judge—whether bloodshed, lawsuits or assaults—take them to the place the LORD your God will choose. [9] Go to the Levitical priests and to the judge who is in office at that time. Inquire of them and they will give you the verdict. [10] You must act according to the decisions they give you at the place the LORD will choose. Be careful to do everything they instruct you to do. [11] Act according to whatever they teach you and the decisions they give you. Do not turn aside from what they tell you, to the right or to the left. [12] Anyone who shows contempt for the judge or for the priest who stands ministering there to the LORD your God is to be put

Why did they execute people in public for idol worship? (17:7)
Worshiping idols violated God's covenant with his people. They had to work together to get rid of this evil from the whole community.

to death. You must purge the evil from Israel. [13] All the people will hear and be afraid, and will not be contemptuous again.

THE KING

[14] When you enter the land the LORD your God is giving you and have taken possession of it and settled in it, and you say, "Let us set a king over us like all the nations around us," [15] be sure to appoint over you a king the LORD your God chooses. He must be from among your fellow Israelites. Do not place a foreigner over you, one who is not an Israelite. [16] The king, moreover, must not acquire great numbers of horses for himself or make the people return to Egypt to get more of them, for the LORD has told you, "You are not to go back that way again." [17] He must not take many wives, or his heart will be led astray. He must not accumulate large amounts of silver and gold.

[18] When he takes the throne of his kingdom, he is to write for himself on a scroll a copy of this law, taken from that of the Levitical priests. [19] It is to be with him, and he is to read it all the days of his life so that he may learn to revere the LORD his God and follow carefully all the words of this law and these decrees [20] and not consider himself better than his fellow Israelites and turn from the law to the right or to the left. Then he and his descendants will reign a long time over his kingdom in Israel.

OFFERINGS FOR PRIESTS AND LEVITES

18 The Levitical priests—indeed, the whole tribe of Levi—are to have no allotment or inheritance with Israel. They shall live on the food offerings presented to the LORD, for that is their inheritance. [2] They shall have no inheritance among their fellow Israelites; the LORD is their inheritance, as he promised them.

[3] This is the share due the priests from the people who sacrifice a bull or a sheep: the shoulder, the internal organs and the meat from the head. [4] You are to give them the first-fruits of your grain, new wine and olive oil, and the first wool from the shearing of your sheep, [5] for the LORD your God has chosen them and their descendants out of all your tribes to stand and minister in the LORD's name always.

[6] If a Levite moves from one of your towns anywhere in Israel where he is living, and comes in all earnestness to the place the LORD will choose, [7] he may minister in the name of the LORD his God like all his fellow Levites who serve there in the presence of the LORD. [8] He is to share equally in their benefits, even though he has received money from the sale of family possessions.

OCCULT PRACTICES

[9] When you enter the land the LORD your God is giving you, do not learn to imitate the detestable ways of the nations there. [10] Let no one be found among you who sacrifices their son or daughter in the fire, who practices divination or sorcery, interprets omens, engages in witchcraft, [11] or casts

If God didn't want the Israelites to have a king, why did he give instructions for appointing one? (17:15)
God knew that the people would want to have a king, just as other nations did. If they were to have a king, God wanted them to choose someone from their own nation who would be a good ruler.

Why did God make rules about what a king could own? (17:16–17)
God wanted the Israelite's king to be humble and focused on God's will. If the king was interested in power and money, he might make deals that were in his own self-interest.

Why would the king have to write his own copy of the law? (17:8)
This would be a sign of the king's submission to the LORD as *his* King. This was a common requirement in the ancient world for vassal kings who served under other kings.

Why didn't the priests get any inheritance other than the offerings? (18:1–2)
The Levites were supposed to devote themselves entirely to the LORD and his work, caring for the tabernacle and offering sacrifices, not land and other possessions (see 1 Samuel 2:12–17).

What were these detestable practices? (18:9–13)
This section describes the practices of the pagan religions to try to be like God.

spells, or who is a medium or spiritist or who consults the dead. ¹²Anyone who does these things is detestable to the LORD; because of these same detestable practices the LORD your God will drive out those nations before you. ¹³You must be blameless before the LORD your God.

THE PROPHET

¹⁴The nations you will dispossess listen to those who practice sorcery or divination. But as for you, the LORD your God has not permitted you to do so. ¹⁵The LORD your God will raise up for you a prophet like me from among you, from your fellow Israelites. You must listen to him. ¹⁶For this is what you asked of the LORD your God at Horeb on the day of the assembly when you said, "Let us not hear the voice of the LORD our God nor see this great fire anymore, or we will die."

¹⁷The LORD said to me: "What they say is good. ¹⁸I will raise up for them a prophet like you from among their fellow Israelites, and I will put my words in his mouth. He will tell them everything I command him. ¹⁹I myself will call to account anyone who does not listen to my words that the prophet speaks in my name. ²⁰But a prophet who presumes to speak in my name anything I have not commanded, or a prophet who speaks in the name of other gods, is to be put to death."

²¹You may say to yourselves, "How can we know when a message has not been spoken by the LORD?" ²²If what a prophet proclaims in the name of the LORD does not take place or come true, that is a message the LORD has not spoken. That prophet has spoken presumptuously, so do not be alarmed.

CITIES OF REFUGE

19 When the LORD your God has destroyed the nations whose land he is giving you, and when you have driven them out and settled in their towns and houses, ²then set aside for yourselves three cities in the land the LORD your God is giving you to possess. ³Determine the distances involved and divide into three parts the land the LORD your

What is the difference between prophecy and divination? (18:14–15)
Divination was a method people used for trying to predict the future. Prophecy was one method that God used to communicate with his people.

How can people tell if a message is from a false prophet? (18:21–22)
God made his will clearly known. If a prophesy contradicted God's will or proved wrong, it must have come from a false prophet.

What is the purpose of the cities of refuge? (19:1–7)
Three cities, centrally located in the promised land, offered a safe place for people to go who accidentally killed someone. In the city of refuge, the person was removed from his own home, but was safe from the revenge of the family of the person who died. Today we still distinguish murder from accidental killing, known as manslaughter.

Is fortune telling always wrong?   DEUTERONOMY 18

People use different methods to try to predict the future. Sometimes they look at the creases in a person's palm; sometimes they use special cards that they lay out in different ways on a table; sometimes they use tea leaves or other materials to try to tell what the future holds.

Throughout the Bible it is clear that God is in control. He knows what has happened in the past and what will happen in the future. That is a source of comfort for believers because we can rely on God's grace and providence to care for us in whatever situation we find ourselves. The only people that God allowed to predict the future were the prophets, and they usually did not predict what would happen to individuals. Instead, they talked about the major events that would occur for God's people, such as the coming of the Messiah.

However, some people are so curious about the future that they try to use different methods to find out what will happen to them in the future. Even if this is just done as a game or for fun, it still is wrong because it goes against God's commandments and because it denies that God alone can see into the future.

God is giving you as an inheritance, so that a person who kills someone may flee for refuge to one of these cities.

⁴This is the rule concerning anyone who kills a person and flees there for safety—anyone who kills a neighbor unintentionally, without malice aforethought. ⁵For instance, a man may go into the forest with his neighbor to cut wood, and as he swings his ax to fell a tree, the head may fly off and hit his neighbor and kill him. That man may flee to one of these cities and save his life. ⁶Otherwise, the avenger of blood might pursue him in a rage, overtake him if the distance is too great, and kill him even though he is not deserving of death, since he did it to his neighbor without malice aforethought. ⁷This is why I command you to set aside for yourselves three cities.

⁸If the Lord your God enlarges your territory, as he promised on oath to your ancestors, and gives you the whole land he promised them, ⁹because you carefully follow all these laws I command you today—to love the Lord your God and to walk always in obedience to him—then you are to set aside three more cities. ¹⁰Do this so that innocent blood will not be shed in your land, which the Lord your God is giving you as your inheritance, and so that you will not be guilty of bloodshed.

¹¹But if out of hate someone lies in wait, assaults and kills a neighbor, and then flees to one of these cities, ¹²the killer shall be sent for by the town elders, be brought back from the city, and be handed over to the avenger of blood to die. ¹³Show no pity. You must purge from Israel the guilt of shedding innocent blood, so that it may go well with you.

¹⁴Do not move your neighbor's boundary stone set up by your predecessors in the inheritance you receive in the land the Lord your God is giving you to possess.

WITNESSES

¹⁵One witness is not enough to convict anyone accused of any crime or offense they may have committed. A matter must be established by the testimony of two or three witnesses.

¹⁶If a malicious witness takes the stand to accuse someone of a crime, ¹⁷the two people involved in the dispute must stand in the presence of the Lord before the priests and the judges who are in office at the time. ¹⁸The judges must make a thorough investigation, and if the witness proves to be a liar, giving false testimony against a fellow Israelite, ¹⁹then do to the false witness as that witness intended to do to the other party. You must purge the evil from among you. ²⁰The rest of the people will hear of this and be afraid, and never again will such an evil thing be done among you. ²¹Show no pity: life for life, eye for eye, tooth for tooth, hand for hand, foot for foot.

GOING TO WAR

20 When you go to war against your enemies and see horses and chariots and an army greater than yours, do not be afraid of them, because the Lord your God, who brought you up out of Egypt, will be with you. ²When you are about to go into battle, the priest shall come forward and

Who was an avenger of blood? (19:6)
This was the closest male relative of a person who had been killed. That person must take revenge on the person who killed his family member.

What was a boundary stone? (19:14)
This was a stone that marked the boundary of a person's property. Moving a stone was forbidden because it was a way to steal land.

What did the principle of "eye for eye, tooth for tooth" mean? (19:21)
The principle was that the penalty should fit the crime but not exceed it. The same principle was outlined in Exodus 21:23–25 and Leviticus 24:20.

address the army. ³He shall say: "Hear, Israel: Today you are going into battle against your enemies. Do not be fainthearted or afraid; do not panic or be terrified by them. ⁴For the LORD your God is the one who goes with you to fight for you against your enemies to give you victory."

⁵The officers shall say to the army: "Has anyone built a new house and not yet begun to live in it? Let him go home, or he may die in battle and someone else may begin to live in it. ⁶Has anyone planted a vineyard and not begun to enjoy it? Let him go home, or he may die in battle and someone else enjoy it. ⁷Has anyone become pledged to a woman and not married her? Let him go home, or he may die in battle and someone else marry her." ⁸Then the officers shall add, "Is anyone afraid or fainthearted? Let him go home so that his fellow soldiers will not become disheartened too." ⁹When the officers have finished speaking to the army, they shall appoint commanders over it.

¹⁰When you march up to attack a city, make its people an offer of peace. ¹¹If they accept and open their gates, all the people in it shall be subject to forced labor and shall work for you. ¹²If they refuse to make peace and they engage you in battle, lay siege to that city. ¹³When the LORD your God delivers it into your hand, put to the sword all the men in it. ¹⁴As for the women, the children, the livestock and everything else in the city, you may take these as plunder for yourselves. And you may use the plunder the LORD your God gives you from your enemies. ¹⁵This is how you are to treat all the cities that are at a distance from you and do not belong to the nations nearby.

¹⁶However, in the cities of the nations the LORD your God is giving you as an inheritance, do not leave alive anything that breathes. ¹⁷Completely destroy[a] them—the Hittites, Amorites, Canaanites, Perizzites, Hivites and Jebusites—as the LORD your God has commanded you. ¹⁸Otherwise, they will teach you to follow all the detestable things they do in worshiping their gods, and you will sin against the LORD your God.

¹⁹When you lay siege to a city for a long time, fighting against it to capture it, do not destroy its trees by putting an ax to them, because you can eat their fruit. Do not cut them down. Are the trees people, that you should besiege them?[b] ²⁰However, you may cut down trees that you know are not fruit trees and use them to build siege works until the city at war with you falls.

ATONEMENT FOR AN UNSOLVED MURDER

21 If someone is found slain, lying in a field in the land the LORD your God is giving you to possess, and it is not known who the killer was, ²your elders and judges shall go out and measure the distance from the body to the neighboring towns. ³Then the elders of the town nearest the body shall take a heifer that has never been worked and has never

---

a 17 The Hebrew term refers to the irrevocable giving over of things or persons to the LORD, often by totally destroying them.   *b 19* Or *down to use in the siege, for the fruit trees are for the benefit of people.*

Why were there so many reasons for sending soldiers home? (20:5–8)
Soldiers could be excused from military service for a variety of reasons. Only soldiers who were ready and willing were supposed to fight in the army, because if they weren't focused, they could put other soldiers at risk.

Why would God approve of taking women and children as plunder? (20:14)
It was common at that time to take prisoners of war. God expected Israel to treat these people fairly. God even provided a way for women to leave their old ways and become part of the covenant through marriage (see 21:10–14).

Why is there a note about saving the trees? (20:19)
When they captured a city, they were told to save the trees that could support them with food. Other nations destroyed everything and left the land worthless, but God wanted his people to have fruit once they took possession of the land.

Why did they follow this ritual for an unsolved murder? (21:1–9)
This ritual with the heifer symbolically purified the polluted land after a murder since there was no one to punish for it.

worn a yoke ⁴and lead it down to a valley that has not been plowed or planted and where there is a flowing stream. There in the valley they are to break the heifer's neck. ⁵The Levitical priests shall step forward, for the LORD your God has chosen them to minister and to pronounce blessings in the name of the LORD and to decide all cases of dispute and assault. ⁶Then all the elders of the town nearest the body shall wash their hands over the heifer whose neck was broken in the valley, ⁷and they shall declare: "Our hands did not shed this blood, nor did our eyes see it done. ⁸Accept this atonement for your people Israel, whom you have redeemed, LORD, and do not hold your people guilty of the blood of an innocent person." Then the bloodshed will be atoned for, ⁹and you will have purged from yourselves the guilt of shedding innocent blood, since you have done what is right in the eyes of the LORD.

MARRYING A CAPTIVE WOMAN

¹⁰When you go to war against your enemies and the LORD your God delivers them into your hands and you take captives, ¹¹if you notice among the captives a beautiful woman and are attracted to her, you may take her as your wife. ¹²Bring her into your home and have her shave her head, trim her nails ¹³and put aside the clothes she was wearing when captured. After she has lived in your house and mourned her father and mother for a full month, then you may go to her and be her husband and she shall be your wife. ¹⁴If you are not pleased with her, let her go wherever she wishes. You must not sell her or treat her as a slave, since you have dishonored her.

THE RIGHT OF THE FIRSTBORN

¹⁵If a man has two wives, and he loves one but not the other, and both bear him sons but the firstborn is the son of the wife he does not love, ¹⁶when he wills his property to his sons, he must not give the rights of the firstborn to the son of the wife he loves in preference to his actual firstborn, the son of the wife he does not love. ¹⁷He must acknowledge the son of his unloved wife as the firstborn by giving him a double share of all he has. That son is the first sign of his father's strength. The right of the firstborn belongs to him.

A REBELLIOUS SON

¹⁸If someone has a stubborn and rebellious son who does not obey his father and mother and will not listen to them when they discipline him, ¹⁹his father and mother shall take hold of him and bring him to the elders at the gate of his town. ²⁰They shall say to the elders, "This son of ours is stubborn and rebellious. He will not obey us. He is a glutton and a drunkard." ²¹Then all the men of his town are to stone him to death. You must purge the evil from among you. All Israel will hear of it and be afraid.

VARIOUS LAWS

²²If someone guilty of a capital offense is put to death and their body is exposed on a pole, ²³you must not leave the

Was it okay for an Israelite man to send his foreign wife away if he wasn't pleased with her? (21:14)
This rule actually protected a woman from becoming a slave or mistreated. Letting her go where she wanted was much more humane than how other nations treated women captives.

What were the rights of the firstborn? (21:15–17)
The firstborn son owned the birthright (the right to a double share of his father's possessions), and it was his duty to care for the women in the family.

body hanging on the pole overnight. Be sure to bury it that same day, because anyone who is hung on a pole is under God's curse. You must not desecrate the land the LORD your God is giving you as an inheritance.

22 If you see your fellow Israelite's ox or sheep straying, do not ignore it but be sure to take it back to its owner. ²If they do not live near you or if you do not know who owns it, take it home with you and keep it until they come looking for it. Then give it back. ³Do the same if you find their donkey or cloak or anything else they have lost. Do not ignore it.

⁴If you see your fellow Israelite's donkey or ox fallen on the road, do not ignore it. Help the owner get it to its feet.

⁵A woman must not wear men's clothing, nor a man wear women's clothing, for the LORD your God detests anyone who does this.

⁶If you come across a bird's nest beside the road, either in a tree or on the ground, and the mother is sitting on the young or on the eggs, do not take the mother with the young. ⁷You may take the young, but be sure to let the mother go, so that it may go well with you and you may have a long life.

⁸When you build a new house, make a parapet around your roof so that you may not bring the guilt of bloodshed on your house if someone falls from the roof.

⁹Do not plant two kinds of seed in your vineyard; if you do, not only the crops you plant but also the fruit of the vineyard will be defiled.ᵃ

¹⁰Do not plow with an ox and a donkey yoked together.

¹¹Do not wear clothes of wool and linen woven together.

¹²Make tassels on the four corners of the cloak you wear.

MARRIAGE VIOLATIONS

¹³If a man takes a wife and, after sleeping with her, dislikes her ¹⁴and slanders her and gives her a bad name, saying, "I married this woman, but when I approached her, I did not find proof of her virginity," ¹⁵then the young woman's father and mother shall bring to the town elders at the gate proof that she was a virgin. ¹⁶Her father will say to the elders, "I gave my daughter in marriage to this man, but he dislikes her. ¹⁷Now he has slandered her and said, 'I did not find your daughter to be a virgin.' But here is the proof of my daughter's virginity." Then her parents shall display the cloth before the elders of the town, ¹⁸and the elders shall take the man and punish him. ¹⁹They shall fine him a hundred shekelsᵇ of silver and give them to the young woman's father, because this man has given an Israelite virgin a bad name. She shall continue to be his wife; he must not divorce her as long as he lives.

²⁰If, however, the charge is true and no proof of the young woman's virginity can be found, ²¹she shall be brought to the door of her father's house and there the men of her town shall stone her to death. She has done an outrageous thing in Israel by being promiscuous while still in her father's house. You must purge the evil from among you.

Why was there a law about harming a mother bird? (22:6–7)
If they left the mother bird alive, then she could lay more eggs. This guaranteed food source meant more food for the people.

Why was it wrong to mix seeds, types of cloth, and animals that weren't the same? (22:9–11)
This was probably a sign of purity or a symbol of undivided loyalty, but it probably had practical applications too. For example, a hybrid plant does not regenerate.

ᵃ 9 Or *be forfeited to the sanctuary*   ᵇ 19 That is, about 2 1/2 pounds or about 1.2 kilograms

Why was adultery punished by death? (22:22–25)
God intended marriage to be permanent, and he expected husbands and wives to remain faithful to each other. One possible reason for such a harsh penalty was to keep people from having illegitimate children who could wrongly receive the family's inheritance.

Why would a girl have to marry a man who raped her? (22:29)
Young women were considered property of their fathers. After the rape, she would be considered damaged. Her father could not get the full price for her, and she may not get a marriage contract. This law forced the man to pay the price for something he tried to take without obligation.

Why couldn't the Israelites be friends with the Ammonites and Moabites? (23:3–6)
These groups did not help the Israelites when they left Egypt. God's punishment is they may not enter the assembly of the LORD.

[22]If a man is found sleeping with another man's wife, both the man who slept with her and the woman must die. You must purge the evil from Israel.

[23]If a man happens to meet in a town a virgin pledged to be married and he sleeps with her, [24]you shall take both of them to the gate of that town and stone them to death—the young woman because she was in a town and did not scream for help, and the man because he violated another man's wife. You must purge the evil from among you.

[25]But if out in the country a man happens to meet a young woman pledged to be married and rapes her, only the man who has done this shall die. [26]Do nothing to the woman; she has committed no sin deserving death. This case is like that of someone who attacks and murders a neighbor, [27]for the man found the young woman out in the country, and though the betrothed woman screamed, there was no one to rescue her.

[28]If a man happens to meet a virgin who is not pledged to be married and rapes her and they are discovered, [29]he shall pay her father fifty shekels[a] of silver. He must marry the young woman, for he has violated her. He can never divorce her as long as he lives.

[30]A man is not to marry his father's wife; he must not dishonor his father's bed.[b]

EXCLUSION FROM THE ASSEMBLY

23[c] No one who has been emasculated by crushing or cutting may enter the assembly of the LORD.

[2]No one born of a forbidden marriage[d] nor any of their descendants may enter the assembly of the LORD, not even in the tenth generation.

[3]No Ammonite or Moabite or any of their descendants may enter the assembly of the LORD, not even in the tenth generation. [4]For they did not come to meet you with bread and water on your way when you came out of Egypt, and they hired Balaam son of Beor from Pethor in Aram Naharaim[e] to pronounce a curse on you. [5]However, the LORD your God would not listen to Balaam but turned the curse into a blessing for you, because the LORD your God loves you. [6]Do not seek a treaty of friendship with them as long as you live.

[7]Do not despise an Edomite, for the Edomites are related to you. Do not despise an Egyptian, because you resided as foreigners in their country. [8]The third generation of children born to them may enter the assembly of the LORD.

UNCLEANNESS IN THE CAMP

[9]When you are encamped against your enemies, keep away from everything impure. [10]If one of your men is unclean because of a nocturnal emission, he is to go outside the camp and stay there. [11]But as evening approaches he is to wash himself, and at sunset he may return to the camp.

---

[a] 29 That is, about 1 1/4 pounds or about 575 grams   [b] 30 In Hebrew texts this verse (22:30) is numbered 23:1.   [c] In Hebrew texts 23:1-25 is numbered 23:2-26.   [d] 2 Or one of illegitimate birth   [e] 4 That is, Northwest Mesopotamia

¹²Designate a place outside the camp where you can go to relieve yourself. ¹³As part of your equipment have something to dig with, and when you relieve yourself, dig a hole and cover up your excrement. ¹⁴For the LORD your God moves about in your camp to protect you and to deliver your enemies to you. Your camp must be holy, so that he will not see among you anything indecent and turn away from you.

MISCELLANEOUS LAWS

¹⁵If a slave has taken refuge with you, do not hand them over to their master. ¹⁶Let them live among you wherever they like and in whatever town they choose. Do not oppress them.

¹⁷No Israelite man or woman is to become a shrine prostitute. ¹⁸You must not bring the earnings of a female prostitute or of a male prostitute*a* into the house of the LORD your God to pay any vow, because the LORD your God detests them both.

¹⁹Do not charge a fellow Israelite interest, whether on money or food or anything else that may earn interest. ²⁰You may charge a foreigner interest, but not a fellow Israelite, so that the LORD your God may bless you in everything you put your hand to in the land you are entering to possess.

²¹If you make a vow to the LORD your God, do not be slow to pay it, for the LORD your God will certainly demand it of you and you will be guilty of sin. ²²But if you refrain from making a vow, you will not be guilty. ²³Whatever your lips utter you must be sure to do, because you made your vow freely to the LORD your God with your own mouth.

²⁴If you enter your neighbor's vineyard, you may eat all the grapes you want, but do not put any in your basket. ²⁵If you enter your neighbor's grainfield, you may pick kernels with your hands, but you must not put a sickle to their standing grain.

24 If a man marries a woman who becomes displeasing to him because he finds something indecent about her, and he writes her a certificate of divorce, gives it to her and sends her from his house, ²and if after she leaves his house she becomes the wife of another man, ³and her second husband dislikes her and writes her a certificate of divorce, gives it to her and sends her from his house, or if he dies, ⁴then her first husband, who divorced her, is not allowed to marry her again after she has been defiled. That would be detestable in the eyes of the LORD. Do not bring sin upon the land the LORD your God is giving you as an inheritance.

⁵If a man has recently married, he must not be sent to war or have any other duty laid on him. For one year he is to be free to stay at home and bring happiness to the wife he has married.

⁶Do not take a pair of millstones — not even the upper one — as security for a debt, because that would be taking a person's livelihood as security.

⁷If someone is caught kidnapping a fellow Israelite and treating or selling them as a slave, the kidnapper must die. You must purge the evil from among you.

ᵃ 18 Hebrew of a dog

Who were shrine prostitutes? (23:17)
These were pagan men and women who performed sexual acts in the temple as part of their religious practices. God hated this sin.

What was wrong with charging interest on loans? (23:19)
God did not want his people to take advantage of each other by charging interest. The law also reduced the problem of poverty. However, the Israelites were allowed to charge interest on loans made to foreigners. (See also Psalm 15:5 and Matthew 25:27.)

Was it okay to eat other people's crops? (23:24–25)
The Bible says you may eat fruit or grain while you stand in your neighbor's field, but you may not carry it away in a basket or cut it down. This may have been a way to share with poor people, while limiting the amount that could be taken.

Was divorce something that God allowed? (24:1–4)
God permitted divorce in some circumstances, but it could not be based on frivolous or trivial reasons. Because the family unit was considered so important, divorce was uncommon among the Hebrews.

Why were Israelites required to return some pledges? (24:10–13)
This law was meant to protect the poor. If all that a person had to offer as a pledge was his coat, he was probably extremely poor. God showed his care for the poor by commanding that a poor person's coat should be returned as needed so that he would have some covering at night.

How did God want the Israelites to provide for the poor? (24:19–22)
God instructed the people to leave some of their crops behind for poor people to glean. This also would keep the farmers from becoming too greedy and from thinking that the land and crops belonged to them rather than to the Lord.

Why did God place a limit on the number of beatings that could be given? (25:2–3)
Lashing was a common form of punishment in the ancient world. God imposed a limit on the number of lashes that could be given to keep the punishment from becoming overly abusive and inhumane.

Why were oxen not to be muzzled when they were treading out the grain? (25:4)
This was a simple, humane command in keeping with the kind spirit of much of the law.

Why did a man have to marry his brother's widow? (25:5–10)
The widow's children should carry on the name of her husband. If she married someone outside of the family and had children, it brought shame to the first husband's name. If she already had a son, this wasn't necessary.

⁸In cases of defiling skin diseases,ᵃ be very careful to do exactly as the Levitical priests instruct you. You must follow carefully what I have commanded them. ⁹Remember what the Lord your God did to Miriam along the way after you came out of Egypt.

¹⁰When you make a loan of any kind to your neighbor, do not go into their house to get what is offered to you as a pledge. ¹¹Stay outside and let the neighbor to whom you are making the loan bring the pledge out to you. ¹²If the neighbor is poor, do not go to sleep with their pledge in your possession. ¹³Return their cloak by sunset so that your neighbor may sleep in it. Then they will thank you, and it will be regarded as a righteous act in the sight of the Lord your God.

¹⁴Do not take advantage of a hired worker who is poor and needy, whether that worker is a fellow Israelite or a foreigner residing in one of your towns. ¹⁵Pay them their wages each day before sunset, because they are poor and are counting on it. Otherwise they may cry to the Lord against you, and you will be guilty of sin.

¹⁶Parents are not to be put to death for their children, nor children put to death for their parents; each will die for their own sin.

¹⁷Do not deprive the foreigner or the fatherless of justice, or take the cloak of the widow as a pledge. ¹⁸Remember that you were slaves in Egypt and the Lord your God redeemed you from there. That is why I command you to do this.

¹⁹When you are harvesting in your field and you overlook a sheaf, do not go back to get it. Leave it for the foreigner, the fatherless and the widow, so that the Lord your God may bless you in all the work of your hands. ²⁰When you beat the olives from your trees, do not go over the branches a second time. Leave what remains for the foreigner, the fatherless and the widow. ²¹When you harvest the grapes in your vineyard, do not go over the vines again. Leave what remains for the foreigner, the fatherless and the widow. ²²Remember that you were slaves in Egypt. That is why I command you to do this.

25 When people have a dispute, they are to take it to court and the judges will decide the case, acquitting the innocent and condemning the guilty. ²If the guilty person deserves to be beaten, the judge shall make them lie down and have them flogged in his presence with the number of lashes the crime deserves, ³but the judge must not impose more than forty lashes. If the guilty party is flogged more than that, your fellow Israelite will be degraded in your eyes.

⁴Do not muzzle an ox while it is treading out the grain.

⁵If brothers are living together and one of them dies without a son, his widow must not marry outside the family. Her husband's brother shall take her and marry her and fulfill the duty of a brother-in-law to her. ⁶The first son she bears shall carry on the name of the dead brother so that his name will not be blotted out from Israel.

⁷However, if a man does not want to marry his brother's wife, she shall go to the elders at the town gate and say, "My

---

ᵃ 8 The Hebrew word for *defiling skin diseases*, traditionally translated "leprosy," was used for various diseases affecting the skin.

husband's brother refuses to carry on his brother's name in Israel. He will not fulfill the duty of a brother-in-law to me." [8]Then the elders of his town shall summon him and talk to him. If he persists in saying, "I do not want to marry her," [9]his brother's widow shall go up to him in the presence of the elders, take off one of his sandals, spit in his face and say, "This is what is done to the man who will not build up his brother's family line." [10]That man's line shall be known in Israel as The Family of the Unsandaled.

[11]If two men are fighting and the wife of one of them comes to rescue her husband from his assailant, and she reaches out and seizes him by his private parts, [12]you shall cut off her hand. Show her no pity.

[13]Do not have two differing weights in your bag—one heavy, one light. [14]Do not have two differing measures in your house—one large, one small. [15]You must have accurate and honest weights and measures, so that you may live long in the land the LORD your God is giving you. [16]For the LORD your God detests anyone who does these things, anyone who deals dishonestly.

[17]Remember what the Amalekites did to you along the way when you came out of Egypt. [18]When you were weary and worn out, they met you on your journey and attacked all who were lagging behind; they had no fear of God. [19]When the LORD your God gives you rest from all the enemies around you in the land he is giving you to possess as an inheritance, you shall blot out the name of Amalek from under heaven. Do not forget!

FIRSTFRUITS AND TITHES

26 When you have entered the land the LORD your God is giving you as an inheritance and have taken possession of it and settled in it, [2]take some of the firstfruits of all that you produce from the soil of the land the LORD your God is giving you and put them in a basket. Then go to the place the LORD your God will choose as a dwelling for his Name [3]and say to the priest in office at the time, "I declare today to the LORD your God that I have come to the land the LORD swore to our ancestors to give us." [4]The priest shall take the basket from your hands and set it down in front of the altar of the LORD your God. [5]Then you shall declare before the LORD your God: "My father was a wandering Aramean, and he went down into Egypt with a few people and lived there and became a great nation, powerful and numerous. [6]But the Egyptians mistreated us and made us suffer, subjecting us to harsh labor. [7]Then we cried out to the LORD, the God of our ancestors, and the LORD heard our voice and saw our misery, toil and oppression. [8]So the LORD brought us out of Egypt with a mighty hand and an outstretched arm, with great terror and with signs and wonders. [9]He brought us to this place and gave us this land, a land flowing with milk and honey; [10]and now I bring the firstfruits of the soil that you, LORD, have given me." Place the basket before the LORD your God and bow down before him. [11]Then you and the Levites and the foreigners residing

Why would the woman meet the elders at the town gates? (25:7)
Since people worked their fields or cared for their flocks on land surrounding the city, many people walked through the city gates every day. Because there was so much traffic passing through the gates, it became a meeting place and a place of business.

Why was the punishment so severely for injuring a man's sexual organs? (25:11–12)
Producing children was valued highly in Israelite society. Damaging a man's sexual organs could prevent a man from becoming a father, so this punishment was aimed at reducing the risk of injury.

What were firstfruits? (26:2)
These were the first crops to ripen. They were given to God to show that he is their first priority.

Who was the wandering Aramean? (26:5)
This was a reference to Jacob, who had wandered from southern Canaan to Haran and back and had later migrated to Egypt.

Why was the third year called the year of the tithe? (26:12)
Every third year the Israelites offered their tithe (one-tenth of their produce) within their own towns instead of to Jerusalem. The food was given to poor people who had no land.

Why did God call Israel his treasured possession? (26:18)
God had chosen Israel to receive his special blessing and participate in the covenant. Israel's responsibility was to share their knowledge and worship of the one true God. Jesus extended this covenant relationship to all believers.

What were the Israelites supposed to do as soon as they entered the promised land? (27:1–8)
On Mount Ebal they were to set up stones for an altar and stones on which they had written God's laws. Writing laws on stones (or even on mountainsides) was common in the ancient Middle East.

What was the purpose of burnt offerings? (27:6)
The burnt offering could represent an act of worship and love for God, or it could be a request for forgiveness for sins.

What was a fellowship offering? (27:7)
This type of offering was meant to express thankfulness. It was also called a peace offering.

among you shall rejoice in all the good things the Lord your God has given to you and your household.

^{12}When you have finished setting aside a tenth of all your produce in the third year, the year of the tithe, you shall give it to the Levite, the foreigner, the fatherless and the widow, so that they may eat in your towns and be satisfied. ^{13}Then say to the Lord your God: "I have removed from my house the sacred portion and have given it to the Levite, the foreigner, the fatherless and the widow, according to all you commanded. I have not turned aside from your commands nor have I forgotten any of them. ^{14}I have not eaten any of the sacred portion while I was in mourning, nor have I removed any of it while I was unclean, nor have I offered any of it to the dead. I have obeyed the Lord my God; I have done everything you commanded me. ^{15}Look down from heaven, your holy dwelling place, and bless your people Israel and the land you have given us as you promised on oath to our ancestors, a land flowing with milk and honey."

FOLLOW THE LORD'S COMMANDS

^{16}The Lord your God commands you this day to follow these decrees and laws; carefully observe them with all your heart and with all your soul. ^{17}You have declared this day that the Lord is your God and that you will walk in obedience to him, that you will keep his decrees, commands and laws — that you will listen to him. ^{18}And the Lord has declared this day that you are his people, his treasured possession as he promised, and that you are to keep all his commands. ^{19}He has declared that he will set you in praise, fame and honor high above all the nations he has made and that you will be a people holy to the Lord your God, as he promised.

THE ALTAR ON MOUNT EBAL

27 Moses and the elders of Israel commanded the people: "Keep all these commands that I give you today. ^{2}When you have crossed the Jordan into the land the Lord your God is giving you, set up some large stones and coat them with plaster. ^{3}Write on them all the words of this law when you have crossed over to enter the land the Lord your God is giving you, a land flowing with milk and honey, just as the Lord, the God of your ancestors, promised you. ^{4}And when you have crossed the Jordan, set up these stones on Mount Ebal, as I command you today, and coat them with plaster. ^{5}Build there an altar to the Lord your God, an altar of stones. Do not use any iron tool on them. ^{6}Build the altar of the Lord your God with fieldstones and offer burnt offerings on it to the Lord your God. ^{7}Sacrifice fellowship offerings there, eating them and rejoicing in the presence of the Lord your God. ^{8}And you shall write very clearly all the words of this law on these stones you have set up."

CURSES FROM MOUNT EBAL

^{9}Then Moses and the Levitical priests said to all Israel, "Be silent, Israel, and listen! You have now become the people of the Lord your God. ^{10}Obey the Lord your God and follow his commands and decrees that I give you today."

¹¹On the same day Moses commanded the people:

¹²When you have crossed the Jordan, these tribes shall stand on Mount Gerizim to bless the people: Simeon, Levi, Judah, Issachar, Joseph and Benjamin. ¹³And these tribes shall stand on Mount Ebal to pronounce curses: Reuben, Gad, Asher, Zebulun, Dan and Naphtali.

¹⁴The Levites shall recite to all the people of Israel in a loud voice:

¹⁵"Cursed is anyone who makes an idol—a thing detestable to the LORD, the work of skilled hands—and sets it up in secret."

Then all the people shall say, "Amen!"

¹⁶"Cursed is anyone who dishonors their father or mother."

Then all the people shall say, "Amen!"

¹⁷"Cursed is anyone who moves their neighbor's boundary stone."

Then all the people shall say, "Amen!"

¹⁸"Cursed is anyone who leads the blind astray on the road."

Then all the people shall say, "Amen!"

¹⁹"Cursed is anyone who withholds justice from the foreigner, the fatherless or the widow."

Then all the people shall say, "Amen!"

²⁰"Cursed is anyone who sleeps with his father's wife, for he dishonors his father's bed."

Then all the people shall say, "Amen!"

²¹"Cursed is anyone who has sexual relations with any animal."

Then all the people shall say, "Amen!"

²²"Cursed is anyone who sleeps with his sister, the daughter of his father or the daughter of his mother."

Then all the people shall say, "Amen!"

²³"Cursed is anyone who sleeps with his mother-in-law."

Then all the people shall say, "Amen!"

²⁴"Cursed is anyone who kills their neighbor secretly."

Then all the people shall say, "Amen!"

²⁵"Cursed is anyone who accepts a bribe to kill an innocent person."

Then all the people shall say, "Amen!"

²⁶"Cursed is anyone who does not uphold the words of this law by carrying them out."

Then all the people shall say, "Amen!"

BLESSINGS FOR OBEDIENCE

28 If you fully obey the LORD your God and carefully follow all his commands I give you today, the LORD your God will set you high above all the nations on earth. ²All these blessings will come on you and accompany you if you obey the LORD your God:

³You will be blessed in the city and blessed in the country.

⁴The fruit of your womb will be blessed, and the

What does it mean to lead the blind astray? (27:18)
People with disabilities were easy to take advantage of. This law says it is a crime to mistreat people with disabilities such as blindness. In this verse, God showed his love for people who were weak or powerless.

Does God see sins that are done secretly? (27:15, 24)
Yes, God sees all sins, even the ones done secretly.

If you obey God, are you going to receive these blessings? (28:2–6)
The promise of these blessings was made to the nation of Israel, not to individuals. Bad things still happen to good people, but God wanted Israel to be a powerful nation to show surrounding nations that Israel served the one true God.

crops of your land and the young of your livestock—the calves of your herds and the lambs of your flocks. ⁵Your basket and your kneading trough will be blessed.

⁶You will be blessed when you come in and blessed when you go out.

⁷The LORD will grant that the enemies who rise up against you will be defeated before you. They will come at you from one direction but flee from you in seven.

⁸The LORD will send a blessing on your barns and on everything you put your hand to. The LORD your God will bless you in the land he is giving you.

⁹The LORD will establish you as his holy people, as he promised you on oath, if you keep the commands of the LORD your God and walk in obedience to him. ¹⁰Then all the peoples on earth will see that you are called by the name of the LORD, and they will fear you. ¹¹The LORD will grant you abundant prosperity—in the fruit of your womb, the young of your livestock and the crops of your ground—in the land he swore to your ancestors to give you.

¹²The LORD will open the heavens, the storehouse of his bounty, to send rain on your land in season and to bless all the work of your hands. You will lend to many nations but will borrow from none. ¹³The LORD will make you the head, not the tail. If you pay attention to the commands of the LORD your God that I give you this day and carefully follow them, you will always be at the top, never at the bottom. ¹⁴Do not turn aside from any of the commands I give you today, to the right or to the left, following other gods and serving them.

CURSES FOR DISOBEDIENCE

¹⁵However, if you do not obey the LORD your God and do not carefully follow all his commands and decrees I am giving you today, all these curses will come on you and overtake you:

¹⁶You will be cursed in the city and cursed in the country.

¹⁷Your basket and your kneading trough will be cursed.

¹⁸The fruit of your womb will be cursed, and the crops of your land, and the calves of your herds and the lambs of your flocks.

What was a kneading trough? (28:5)
A kneading trough was a household tool used for the preparation of food, particularly bread.

Why was it important that Israel was called by the name of the LORD? (28:10)
When a person gave his own name to another, it meant they were joined in close unity. When God gave his name to Israel, it meant they were his chosen people.

Why are the blessings repeated as curses? (28:16–19)
This agreement between God and Israel was very much like other legal agreements of that time. It was common to repeat curses as the opposite of blessings.

Does God ever want us to feel anxious?   DEUTERONOMY 28

God told the Israelites that if they did not obey his law there would be consequences. They would be punished for their disobedience with attacks from foreign nations, with plagues, with diseases, with exile, and with worry. Those who do not believe in God or who do not obey him have good reason to worry because they are offending God and putting their souls at risk.

But even Christians often have fears and worries. These are natural emotions, and they are not punishments from God. When we are afraid or worried, we can pray to God and ask for his help. We can read the Bible and find many Scripture passages that comfort us with descriptions of God's constant love. We can also share our fears with other Christians—friends, parents, pastors—who can help us by listening to our concerns, comforting us, and praying with us.

¹⁹You will be cursed when you come in and cursed when you go out.

²⁰The LORD will send on you curses, confusion and rebuke in everything you put your hand to, until you are destroyed and come to sudden ruin because of the evil you have done in forsaking him.ᵃ ²¹The LORD will plague you with diseases until he has destroyed you from the land you are entering to possess. ²²The LORD will strike you with wasting disease, with fever and inflammation, with scorching heat and drought, with blight and mildew, which will plague you until you perish. ²³The sky over your head will be bronze, the ground beneath you iron. ²⁴The LORD will turn the rain of your country into dust and powder; it will come down from the skies until you are destroyed.

²⁵The LORD will cause you to be defeated before your enemies. You will come at them from one direction but flee from them in seven, and you will become a thing of horror to all the kingdoms on earth. ²⁶Your carcasses will be food for all the birds and the wild animals, and there will be no one to frighten them away. ²⁷The LORD will afflict you with the boils of Egypt and with tumors, festering sores and the itch, from which you cannot be cured. ²⁸The LORD will afflict you with madness, blindness and confusion of mind. ²⁹At midday you will grope about like a blind person in the dark. You will be unsuccessful in everything you do; day after day you will be oppressed and robbed, with no one to rescue you.

³⁰You will be pledged to be married to a woman, but another will take her and rape her. You will build a house, but you will not live in it. You will plant a vineyard, but you will not even begin to enjoy its fruit. ³¹Your ox will be slaughtered before your eyes, but you will eat none of it. Your donkey will be forcibly taken from you and will not be returned. Your sheep will be given to your enemies, and no one will rescue them. ³²Your sons and daughters will be given to another nation, and you will wear out your eyes watching for them day after day, powerless to lift a hand. ³³A people that you do not know will eat what your land and labor produce, and you will have nothing but cruel oppression all your days. ³⁴The sights you see will drive you mad. ³⁵The LORD will afflict your knees and legs with painful boils that cannot be cured, spreading from the soles of your feet to the top of your head.

³⁶The LORD will drive you and the king you set over you to a nation unknown to you or your ancestors. There you will worship other gods, gods of wood and stone. ³⁷You will become a thing of horror, a byword and an object of ridicule among all the peoples where the LORD will drive you.

³⁸You will sow much seed in the field but you will harvest little, because locusts will devour it. ³⁹You will plant vineyards and cultivate them but you will not drink the wine or gather the grapes, because worms will eat them. ⁴⁰You will have olive trees throughout your country but you will not use the oil, because the olives will drop off. ⁴¹You will have sons

Why would the sky be bronze and the ground like iron? (28:23)
Moses was talking about a curse of a severe drought. Without rain, the sun would bake the land and make the ground extremely dry and hard, like iron. Plants and all vegetation would die.

ᵃ 20 Hebrew *me*

and daughters but you will not keep them, because they will go into captivity. ⁴²Swarms of locusts will take over all your trees and the crops of your land.

⁴³The foreigners who reside among you will rise above you higher and higher, but you will sink lower and lower. ⁴⁴They will lend to you, but you will not lend to them. They will be the head, but you will be the tail.

⁴⁵All these curses will come on you. They will pursue you and overtake you until you are destroyed, because you did not obey the LORD your God and observe the commands and decrees he gave you. ⁴⁶They will be a sign and a wonder to you and your descendants forever. ⁴⁷Because you did not serve the LORD your God joyfully and gladly in the time of prosperity, ⁴⁸therefore in hunger and thirst, in nakedness and dire poverty, you will serve the enemies the LORD sends against you. He will put an iron yoke on your neck until he has destroyed you.

⁴⁹The LORD will bring a nation against you from far away, from the ends of the earth, like an eagle swooping down, a nation whose language you will not understand, ⁵⁰a fierce-looking nation without respect for the old or pity for the young. ⁵¹They will devour the young of your livestock and the crops of your land until you are destroyed. They will leave you no grain, new wine or olive oil, nor any calves of your herds or lambs of your flocks until you are ruined. ⁵²They will lay siege to all the cities throughout your land until the high fortified walls in which you trust fall down. They will besiege all the cities throughout the land the LORD your God is giving you.

⁵³Because of the suffering your enemy will inflict on you during the siege, you will eat the fruit of the womb, the flesh of the sons and daughters the LORD your God has given you. ⁵⁴Even the most gentle and sensitive man among you will have no compassion on his own brother or the wife he loves or his surviving children, ⁵⁵and he will not give to one of them any of the flesh of his children that he is eating. It will be all he has left because of the suffering your enemy will inflict on you during the siege of all your cities. ⁵⁶The most gentle and sensitive woman among you—so sensitive and gentle that she would not venture to touch the ground with the sole of her foot—will begrudge the husband she loves and her own son or daughter ⁵⁷the afterbirth from her womb and the children she bears. For in her dire need she intends to eat them secretly because of the suffering your enemy will inflict on you during the siege of your cities.

⁵⁸If you do not carefully follow all the words of this law, which are written in this book, and do not revere this glorious and awesome name—the LORD your God— ⁵⁹the LORD will send fearful plagues on you and your descendants, harsh and prolonged disasters, and severe and lingering illnesses. ⁶⁰He will bring on you all the diseases of Egypt that you dreaded, and they will cling to you. ⁶¹The LORD will also bring on you every kind of sickness and disaster not recorded in this Book of the Law, until you are destroyed. ⁶²You who were as numerous as the stars in the sky will be left but few in

What was an iron yoke? (28:48)
A yoke was a wooden frame fitting the neck and shoulders of a person or animal for carrying heavy loads. It was a symbol of slavery. An iron yoke represented a scarier and longer lasting form of slavery.

What nation from far away will swoop down and destroy them? (28:49)
The "eagle swooping down" may have been a symbol of the speed and power of Assyria and Babylon. The languages of these countries were related to Hebrew but were not understood by the average Israelite.

Was Moses predicting cannibalism? (28:53)
Yes, this curse came to pass during a siege in Israel (see 2 Kings 6:24–29).

What were the diseases of Egypt? (28:60)
The diseases that were brought on the Egyptians during the plagues included boils, tumors, diseases of the bowels, loss of sight, mental illness, and skin diseases.

number, because you did not obey the LORD your God. ⁶³Just as it pleased the LORD to make you prosper and increase in number, so it will please him to ruin and destroy you. You will be uprooted from the land you are entering to possess.

⁶⁴Then the LORD will scatter you among all nations, from one end of the earth to the other. There you will worship other gods—gods of wood and stone, which neither you nor your ancestors have known. ⁶⁵Among those nations you will find no repose, no resting place for the sole of your foot. There the LORD will give you an anxious mind, eyes weary with longing, and a despairing heart. ⁶⁶You will live in constant suspense, filled with dread both night and day, never sure of your life. ⁶⁷In the morning you will say, "If only it were evening!" and in the evening, "If only it were morning!"—because of the terror that will fill your hearts and the sights that your eyes will see. ⁶⁸The LORD will send you back in ships to Egypt on a journey I said you should never make again. There you will offer yourselves for sale to your enemies as male and female slaves, but no one will buy you.

RENEWAL OF THE COVENANT

29 ᵃ These are the terms of the covenant the LORD commanded Moses to make with the Israelites in Moab, in addition to the covenant he had made with them at Horeb.

²Moses summoned all the Israelites and said to them:

Your eyes have seen all that the LORD did in Egypt to Pharaoh, to all his officials and to all his land. ³With your own eyes you saw those great trials, those signs and great wonders. ⁴But to this day the LORD has not given you a mind that understands or eyes that see or ears that hear. ⁵Yet the LORD says, "During the forty years that I led you through the wilderness, your clothes did not wear out, nor did the sandals on your feet. ⁶You ate no bread and drank no wine or other fermented drink. I did this so that you might know that I am the LORD your God."

⁷When you reached this place, Sihon king of Heshbon and Og king of Bashan came out to fight against us, but we defeated them. ⁸We took their land and gave it as an inheritance to the Reubenites, the Gadites and the half-tribe of Manasseh.

⁹Carefully follow the terms of this covenant, so that you may prosper in everything you do. ¹⁰All of you are standing today in the presence of the LORD your God—your leaders and chief men, your elders and officials, and all the other men of Israel, ¹¹together with your children and your wives, and the foreigners living in your camps who chop your wood and carry your water. ¹²You are standing here in order to enter into a covenant with the LORD your God, a covenant the LORD is making with you this day and sealing with an oath, ¹³to confirm you this day as his people, that he may be your God as he promised you and as he swore to your fathers, Abraham, Isaac and Jacob. ¹⁴I am making this covenant, with

ᵃ In Hebrew texts 29:1 is numbered 28:69, and 29:2-29 is numbered 29:1-28.

Why would it please God to destroy Israel? (28:63)
God did not want to punish his people, but he would make sure justice was done.

Why did God plan to give his people anxious minds? (28:65)
This means they would not have peace. They would desire peace and forgiveness because of their sins.

Why did God need to make a new covenant? (29:1)
God made many covenants in the Bible. Forty years had passed since the first covenant God had made with Moses at Mount Sinai (see Exodus 19:5), and since Joshua was about to become the new leader of Israel, it was time to update the agreement.

its oath, not only with you [15]who are standing here with us today in the presence of the LORD our God but also with those who are not here today.

[16]You yourselves know how we lived in Egypt and how we passed through the countries on the way here. [17]You saw among them their detestable images and idols of wood and stone, of silver and gold. [18]Make sure there is no man or woman, clan or tribe among you today whose heart turns away from the LORD our God to go and worship the gods of those nations; make sure there is no root among you that produces such bitter poison.

[19]When such a person hears the words of this oath and they invoke a blessing on themselves, thinking, "I will be safe, even though I persist in going my own way," they will bring disaster on the watered land as well as the dry. [20]The LORD will never be willing to forgive them; his wrath and zeal will burn against them. All the curses written in this book will fall on them, and the LORD will blot out their names from under heaven. [21]The LORD will single them out from all the tribes of Israel for disaster, according to all the curses of the covenant written in this Book of the Law.

[22]Your children who follow you in later generations and foreigners who come from distant lands will see the calamities that have fallen on the land and the diseases with which the LORD has afflicted it. [23]The whole land will be a burning waste of salt and sulfur—nothing planted, nothing sprouting, no vegetation growing on it. It will be like the destruction of Sodom and Gomorrah, Admah and Zeboyim, which the LORD overthrew in fierce anger. [24]All the nations will ask: "Why has the LORD done this to this land? Why this fierce, burning anger?"

[25]And the answer will be: "It is because this people abandoned the covenant of the LORD, the God of their ancestors, the covenant he made with them when he brought them out of Egypt. [26]They went off and worshiped other gods and bowed down to them, gods they did not know, gods he had not given them. [27]Therefore the LORD's anger burned against this land, so that he brought on it all the curses written in this book. [28]In furious anger and in great wrath the LORD uprooted them from their land and thrust them into another land, as it is now."

[29]The secret things belong to the LORD our God, but the things revealed belong to us and to our children forever, that we may follow all the words of this law.

PROSPERITY AFTER TURNING TO THE LORD

30 When all these blessings and curses I have set before you come on you and you take them to heart wherever the LORD your God disperses you among the nations, [2]and when you and your children return to the LORD your God and obey him with all your heart and with all your soul according to everything I command you today, [3]then the LORD your God will restore your fortunes[a] and have compassion on you and gather you again from all the nations where

---

Was there a sin that God would not forgive? (29:18–20)
God wanted to protect the whole community from one person's sin of disobedience. A person who turned away from God to worship pagan gods would not be forgiven.

What were Admah and Zeboyim? (29:23)
These two cities, along with Sodom and Gomorrah, were destroyed for their wickedness when God rained down burning sulfur on them.

What were the secret things that belonged to God? (29:29)
They were the hidden events of Israel's future. Only God knew whether Israel would obey and be blessed, but Israel knew the laws. The Israelites could determine their own future if they obeyed God's law.

---

[a] 3 Or *will bring you back from captivity*

he scattered you. [4]Even if you have been banished to the most distant land under the heavens, from there the LORD your God will gather you and bring you back. [5]He will bring you to the land that belonged to your ancestors, and you will take possession of it. He will make you more prosperous and numerous than your ancestors. [6]The LORD your God will circumcise your hearts and the hearts of your descendants, so that you may love him with all your heart and with all your soul, and live. [7]The LORD your God will put all these curses on your enemies who hate and persecute you. [8]You will again obey the LORD and follow all his commands I am giving you today. [9]Then the LORD your God will make you most prosperous in all the work of your hands and in the fruit of your womb, the young of your livestock and the crops of your land. The LORD will again delight in you and make you prosperous, just as he delighted in your ancestors, [10]if you obey the LORD your God and keep his commands and decrees that are written in this Book of the Law and turn to the LORD your God with all your heart and with all your soul.

THE OFFER OF LIFE OR DEATH

[11]Now what I am commanding you today is not too difficult for you or beyond your reach. [12]It is not up in heaven, so that you have to ask, "Who will ascend into heaven to get it and proclaim it to us so we may obey it?" [13]Nor is it beyond the sea, so that you have to ask, "Who will cross the sea to get it and proclaim it to us so we may obey it?" [14]No, the word is very near you; it is in your mouth and in your heart so you may obey it.

[15]See, I set before you today life and prosperity, death and destruction. [16]For I command you today to love the LORD your God, to walk in obedience to him, and to keep his commands, decrees and laws; then you will live and increase, and the LORD your God will bless you in the land you are entering to possess.

[17]But if your heart turns away and you are not obedient, and if you are drawn away to bow down to other gods and worship them, [18]I declare to you this day that you will certainly be destroyed. You will not live long in the land you are crossing the Jordan to enter and possess.

[19]This day I call the heavens and the earth as witnesses against you that I have set before you life and death, blessings and curses. Now choose life, so that you and your children may live [20]and that you may love the LORD your God, listen to his voice, and hold fast to him. For the LORD is your life, and he will give you many years in the land he swore to give to your fathers, Abraham, Isaac and Jacob.

JOSHUA TO SUCCEED MOSES

31 Then Moses went out and spoke these words to all Israel: [2]"I am now a hundred and twenty years old and I am no longer able to lead you. The LORD has said to me, 'You shall not cross the Jordan.' [3]The LORD your God himself will cross over ahead of you. He will destroy these nations before you, and you will take possession of their land.

What's the difference between heart and soul? (30:6)
Heart often meant the mind or intellect, and *soul* usually meant human desire or will. Only when the people cleansed their hearts of sin could they fully love God with their hearts (mind) and souls (will).

Was it possible to perfectly obey the Old Testament law? (30:11)
No. Even though Moses said that obeying the law was not difficult or beyond their reach, sin kept people from keeping God's law perfectly. The only one who was ever able to obey the law without sin was Jesus.

What did it mean to choose life? (30:19–20)
The law, the LORD, and life were all bound together. So when the Israelites chose to follow the LORD and his laws, their lives would become filled with blessings.

Joshua also will cross over ahead of you, as the LORD said. ⁴And the LORD will do to them what he did to Sihon and Og, the kings of the Amorites, whom he destroyed along with their land. ⁵The LORD will deliver them to you, and you must do to them all that I have commanded you. ⁶Be strong and courageous. Do not be afraid or terrified because of them, for the LORD your God goes with you; he will never leave you nor forsake you."

⁷Then Moses summoned Joshua and said to him in the presence of all Israel, "Be strong and courageous, for you must go with this people into the land that the LORD swore to their ancestors to give them, and you must divide it among them as their inheritance. ⁸The LORD himself goes before you and will be with you; he will never leave you nor forsake you. Do not be afraid; do not be discouraged."

PUBLIC READING OF THE LAW

⁹So Moses wrote down this law and gave it to the Levitical priests, who carried the ark of the covenant of the LORD, and to all the elders of Israel. ¹⁰Then Moses commanded them: "At the end of every seven years, in the year for canceling debts, during the Festival of Tabernacles, ¹¹when all Israel comes to appear before the LORD your God at the place he will choose, you shall read this law before them in their hearing. ¹²Assemble the people—men, women and children, and the foreigners residing in your towns—so they can listen and learn to fear the LORD your God and follow carefully all the words of this law. ¹³Their children, who do not know this law, must hear it and learn to fear the LORD your God as long as you live in the land you are crossing the Jordan to possess."

ISRAEL'S REBELLION PREDICTED

¹⁴The LORD said to Moses, "Now the day of your death is near. Call Joshua and present yourselves at the tent of meeting, where I will commission him." So Moses and Joshua came and presented themselves at the tent of meeting.

¹⁵Then the LORD appeared at the tent in a pillar of cloud, and the cloud stood over the entrance to the tent. ¹⁶And the LORD said to Moses: "You are going to rest with your ancestors, and these people will soon prostitute themselves to the foreign gods of the land they are entering. They will forsake me and break the covenant I made with them. ¹⁷And in that day I will become angry with them and forsake them; I will hide my face from them, and they will be destroyed. Many disasters and calamities will come on them, and in that day they will ask, 'Have not these disasters come on us because our God is not with us?' ¹⁸And I will certainly hide my face in that day because of all their wickedness in turning to other gods.

¹⁹"Now write down this song and teach it to the Israelites and have them sing it, so that it may be a witness for me against them. ²⁰When I have brought them into the land flowing with milk and honey, the land I promised on oath to their ancestors, and when they eat their fill and thrive, they will turn to other gods and worship them, rejecting me and breaking my covenant. ²¹And when many disasters and

How could the people remember the law if it was only read every seven years? (31:11)
The public reading of the law during the Sabbath year was a special time for the people to hear and think about the law together. But the law was read much more often in smaller gatherings so that the people could commit it to memory.

Why did God teach them a song? (31:19–22)
It is easier to remember information when it is turned into a song. This song was meant to remind the Israelites not to disobey God.

Was the land literally flowing with milk and honey? (31:20)
This was an image used to describe Canaan's rich soil and excellent climate. The land had great potential, and the Israelites would be blessed if they obeyed God.

calamities come on them, this song will testify against them, because it will not be forgotten by their descendants. I know what they are disposed to do, even before I bring them into the land I promised them on oath." [22] So Moses wrote down this song that day and taught it to the Israelites.

[23] The LORD gave this command to Joshua son of Nun: "Be strong and courageous, for you will bring the Israelites into the land I promised them on oath, and I myself will be with you."

[24] After Moses finished writing in a book the words of this law from beginning to end, [25] he gave this command to the Levites who carried the ark of the covenant of the LORD: [26] "Take this Book of the Law and place it beside the ark of the covenant of the LORD your God. There it will remain as a witness against you. [27] For I know how rebellious and stiff-necked you are. If you have been rebellious against the LORD while I am still alive and with you, how much more will you rebel after I die! [28] Assemble before me all the elders of your tribes and all your officials, so that I can speak these words in their hearing and call the heavens and the earth to testify against them. [29] For I know that after my death you are sure to become utterly corrupt and to turn from the way I have commanded you. In days to come, disaster will fall on you because you will do evil in the sight of the LORD and arouse his anger by what your hands have made."

THE SONG OF MOSES

[30] And Moses recited the words of this song from beginning to end in the hearing of the whole assembly of Israel:

32 Listen, you heavens, and I will speak;
hear, you earth, the words of my mouth.
[2] Let my teaching fall like rain
and my words descend like dew,
like showers on new grass,
like abundant rain on tender plants.

[3] I will proclaim the name of the LORD.
Oh, praise the greatness of our God!
[4] He is the Rock, his works are perfect,
and all his ways are just.
A faithful God who does no wrong,
upright and just is he.

[5] They are corrupt and not his children;
to their shame they are a warped and crooked
generation.
[6] Is this the way you repay the LORD,
you foolish and unwise people?
Is he not your Father, your Creator,[a]
who made you and formed you?

[7] Remember the days of old;
consider the generations long past.
Ask your father and he will tell you,
your elders, and they will explain to you.

How were the Israelites no longer his children? (32:5) Israel could surrender its birthright (God's covenant) in exchange for comfort or lack of faith. But God continued to love his people and called them to come back to him.

---

[a] 6 Or *Father, who bought you*

How were the Israelites the apple of God's eye? (32:10)
This is a metaphor for the pupil of the eye. The pupil is necessary for sight and therefore must be protected at all costs.

How could honey come from a rock? (32:13)
This is a poetic image of God caring for his people by providing food and other care in places where it would not normally be found. It didn't necessarily literally mean the honey came from a rock, though in Canaan, bees sometimes built their hives in the spaces between groups of rocks. Travelers would eat the honey and gain strength for their journey.

Why would God become jealous? (32:21)
God expected his people to worship only him. He was angry at his people for turning away from him and worshiping images made of wood and stone.

[8] When the Most High gave the nations their
     inheritance,
   when he divided all mankind,
 he set up boundaries for the peoples
     according to the number of the sons of Israel.[a]
[9] For the LORD's portion is his people,
   Jacob his allotted inheritance.

[10] In a desert land he found him,
    in a barren and howling waste.
  He shielded him and cared for him;
    he guarded him as the apple of his eye,
[11] like an eagle that stirs up its nest
    and hovers over its young,
  that spreads its wings to catch them
    and carries them aloft.
[12] The LORD alone led him;
    no foreign god was with him.

[13] He made him ride on the heights of the land
    and fed him with the fruit of the fields.
  He nourished him with honey from the rock,
    and with oil from the flinty crag,
[14] with curds and milk from herd and flock
    and with fattened lambs and goats,
  with choice rams of Bashan
    and the finest kernels of wheat.
  You drank the foaming blood of the grape.

[15] Jeshurun[b] grew fat and kicked;
    filled with food, they became heavy and sleek.
  They abandoned the God who made them
    and rejected the Rock their Savior.
[16] They made him jealous with their foreign gods
    and angered him with their detestable idols.
[17] They sacrificed to false gods, which are not God—
    gods they had not known,
    gods that recently appeared,
    gods your ancestors did not fear.
[18] You deserted the Rock, who fathered you;
    you forgot the God who gave you birth.

[19] The LORD saw this and rejected them
    because he was angered by his sons
        and daughters.
[20] "I will hide my face from them," he said,
    "and see what their end will be;
  for they are a perverse generation,
    children who are unfaithful.
[21] They made me jealous by what is no god
    and angered me with their worthless idols.
  I will make them envious by those who are
        not a people;
    I will make them angry by a nation that has
        no understanding.

[a] 8 Masoretic Text; Dead Sea Scrolls (see also Septuagint) *sons of God*
[b] 15 *Jeshurun* means *the upright one*, that is, Israel.

²² For a fire will be kindled by my wrath,
    one that burns down to the realm of the dead below.
It will devour the earth and its harvests
    and set afire the foundations of the mountains.

²³ "I will heap calamities on them
    and spend my arrows against them.
²⁴ I will send wasting famine against them,
    consuming pestilence and deadly plague;
I will send against them the fangs of wild beasts,
    the venom of vipers that glide in the dust.
²⁵ In the street the sword will make them childless;
    in their homes terror will reign.
The young men and young women will perish,
    the infants and those with gray hair.
²⁶ I said I would scatter them
    and erase their name from human memory,
²⁷ but I dreaded the taunt of the enemy,
    lest the adversary misunderstand
and say, 'Our hand has triumphed;
    the Lord has not done all this.'"

²⁸ They are a nation without sense,
    there is no discernment in them.
²⁹ If only they were wise and would understand this
    and discern what their end will be!
³⁰ How could one man chase a thousand,
    or two put ten thousand to flight,
unless their Rock had sold them,
    unless the Lord had given them up?
³¹ For their rock is not like our Rock,
    as even our enemies concede.
³² Their vine comes from the vine of Sodom
    and from the fields of Gomorrah.
Their grapes are filled with poison,
    and their clusters with bitterness.
³³ Their wine is the venom of serpents,
    the deadly poison of cobras.

³⁴ "Have I not kept this in reserve
    and sealed it in my vaults?
³⁵ It is mine to avenge; I will repay.
    In due time their foot will slip;
their day of disaster is near
    and their doom rushes upon them."

³⁶ The Lord will vindicate his people
    and relent concerning his servants
when he sees their strength is gone
    and no one is left, slave or free.ᵃ
³⁷ He will say: "Now where are their gods,
    the rock they took refuge in,
³⁸ the gods who ate the fat of their sacrifices
    and drank the wine of their drink offerings?
Let them rise up to help you!
    Let them give you shelter!

ᵃ 36 Or *and they are without a ruler or leader*

Who was the Rock? (32:30)
The word *Rock* was a metaphor for God.

What was sealed in vaults? (32:34–35)
This means that the Lord's plans for the future are fixed and as certain as if they are locked in a vault. Sin would be punished when God decided that the time was right.

39 "See now that I myself am he!
    There is no god besides me.
I put to death and I bring to life,
    I have wounded and I will heal,
    and no one can deliver out of my hand.
40 I lift my hand to heaven and solemnly swear:
    As surely as I live forever,
41 when I sharpen my flashing sword
    and my hand grasps it in judgment,
I will take vengeance on my adversaries
    and repay those who hate me.
42 I will make my arrows drunk with blood,
    while my sword devours flesh:
the blood of the slain and the captives,
    the heads of the enemy leaders."

43 Rejoice, you nations, with his people,[a,b]
    for he will avenge the blood of his servants;
he will take vengeance on his enemies
    and make atonement for his land and people.

44 Moses came with Joshua[c] son of Nun and spoke all the words of this song in the hearing of the people. 45 When Moses finished reciting all these words to all Israel, 46 he said to them, "Take to heart all the words I have solemnly declared to you this day, so that you may command your children to obey carefully all the words of this law. 47 They are not just idle words for you—they are your life. By them you will live long in the land you are crossing the Jordan to possess."

MOSES TO DIE ON MOUNT NEBO

48 On that same day the Lord told Moses, 49 "Go up into the Abarim Range to Mount Nebo in Moab, across from Jericho, and view Canaan, the land I am giving the Israelites as their own possession. 50 There on the mountain that you have climbed you will die and be gathered to your people, just as your brother Aaron died on Mount Hor and was gathered to his people. 51 This is because both of you broke faith with me in the presence of the Israelites at the waters of Meribah Kadesh in the Desert of Zin and because you did not uphold my holiness among the Israelites. 52 Therefore, you will see the land only from a distance; you will not enter the land I am giving to the people of Israel."

MOSES BLESSES THE TRIBES

33 This is the blessing that Moses the man of God pronounced on the Israelites before his death. 2 He said:

"The Lord came from Sinai
    and dawned over them from Seir;
he shone forth from Mount Paran.
He came with[d] myriads of holy ones
    from the south, from his mountain slopes.[e]

a 43 Or Make his people rejoice, you nations   b 43 Masoretic Text; Dead Sea Scrolls (see also Septuagint) people, / and let all the angels worship him, /   c 44 Hebrew Hoshea, a variant of Joshua   d 2 Or from   e 2 The meaning of the Hebrew for this phrase is uncertain.

³ Surely it is you who love the people;
　　all the holy ones are in your hand.
At your feet they all bow down,
　　and from you receive instruction,
⁴ the law that Moses gave us,
　　the possession of the assembly of Jacob.
⁵ He was king over Jeshurun*
　　when the leaders of the people assembled,
　　along with the tribes of Israel.

⁶ "Let Reuben live and not die,
　　nor* his people be few."

⁷ And this he said about Judah:

"Hear, Lord, the cry of Judah;
　　bring him to his people.
With his own hands he defends his cause.
　　Oh, be his help against his foes!"

⁸ About Levi he said:

"Your Thummim and Urim belong
　　to your faithful servant.
You tested him at Massah;
　　you contended with him at the waters
　　　　of Meribah.
⁹ He said of his father and mother,
　　'I have no regard for them.'
He did not recognize his brothers
　　or acknowledge his own children,
but he watched over your word
　　and guarded your covenant.
¹⁰ He teaches your precepts to Jacob
　　and your law to Israel.
He offers incense before you
　　and whole burnt offerings on your altar.
¹¹ Bless all his skills, Lord,
　　and be pleased with the work of his hands.
Strike down those who rise against him,
　　his foes till they rise no more."

¹² About Benjamin he said:

"Let the beloved of the Lord rest secure in him,
　　for he shields him all day long,
　　and the one the Lord loves rests between his
　　　　shoulders."

¹³ About Joseph he said:

"May the Lord bless his land
　　with the precious dew from heaven above
　　and with the deep waters that lie below;
¹⁴ with the best the sun brings forth
　　and the finest the moon can yield;
¹⁵ with the choicest gifts of the ancient mountains
　　and the fruitfulness of the everlasting hills;

What were the Urim and Thummim? (33:8)
The Urim and Thummim may have been small metal objects or stones or sticks inscribed with symbols. Most likely the Urim and Thummim were like dice, giving yes or no answers from God (see Exodus 28:30).

Did God expect those who served him to completely ignore their families? (33:9)
This is an example of exaggeration to emphasize the Levites' total commitment to God's law. Protecting the law was so important to them that no other commitments compared in strength.

---

a 5 *Jeshurun* means *the upright one,* that is, Israel; also in verse 26.
b 6 Or *but let*

What were the best gifts of the earth? (33:16)
Under the LORD's blessing, Joseph's land in central Canaan was to be unusually fertile and productive.

16 with the best gifts of the earth and its fullness
   and the favor of him who dwelt in the
      burning bush.
Let all these rest on the head of Joseph,
   on the brow of the prince among[a] his brothers.
17 In majesty he is like a firstborn bull;
   his horns are the horns of a wild ox.
With them he will gore the nations,
   even those at the ends of the earth.
Such are the ten thousands of Ephraim;
   such are the thousands of Manasseh."

18 About Zebulun he said:

"Rejoice, Zebulun, in your going out,
   and you, Issachar, in your tents.
19 They will summon peoples to the mountain
   and there offer the sacrifices of the righteous;
they will feast on the abundance of the seas,
   on the treasures hidden in the sand."

20 About Gad he said:

"Blessed is he who enlarges Gad's domain!
   Gad lives there like a lion,
   tearing at arm or head.
21 He chose the best land for himself;
   the leader's portion was kept for him.
When the heads of the people assembled,
   he carried out the LORD's righteous will,
   and his judgments concerning Israel."

22 About Dan he said:

"Dan is a lion's cub,
   springing out of Bashan."

23 About Naphtali he said:

"Naphtali is abounding with the favor
     of the LORD
   and is full of his blessing;
he will inherit southward to the lake."

24 About Asher he said:

"Most blessed of sons is Asher;
   let him be favored by his brothers,
   and let him bathe his feet in oil.
25 The bolts of your gates will be iron and bronze,
   and your strength will equal your days.

26 "There is no one like the God of Jeshurun,
   who rides across the heavens to help you
   and on the clouds in his majesty.
27 The eternal God is your refuge,
   and underneath are the everlasting arms.
He will drive out your enemies before you,
   saying, 'Destroy them!'

What was special about bathing feet in oil? (33:24)
In the desert, feet became dry and hard. Oil was a luxury because it was expensive, and it would have felt soothing on rough, dry, tired feet.

---

[a] 16 Or *of the one separated from*

28 So Israel will live in safety;
  Jacob will dwell[a] secure
in a land of grain and new wine,
  where the heavens drop dew.
29 Blessed are you, Israel!
  Who is like you,
    a people saved by the LORD?
He is your shield and helper
  and your glorious sword.
Your enemies will cower before you,
  and you will tread on their heights."

THE DEATH OF MOSES

34 Then Moses climbed Mount Nebo from the plains
of Moab to the top of Pisgah, across from Jericho.
There the LORD showed him the whole land—from Gilead
to Dan, 2 all of Naphtali, the territory of Ephraim and Manasseh, all the land of Judah as far as the Mediterranean Sea,
3 the Negev and the whole region from the Valley of Jericho,
the City of Palms, as far as Zoar. 4 Then the LORD said to
him, "This is the land I promised on oath to Abraham, Isaac
and Jacob when I said, 'I will give it to your descendants.' I
have let you see it with your eyes, but you will not cross over
into it."

5 And Moses the servant of the LORD died there in Moab,
as the LORD had said. 6 He buried him[b] in Moab, in the valley
opposite Beth Peor, but to this day no one knows where his
grave is. 7 Moses was a hundred and twenty years old when
he died, yet his eyes were not weak nor his strength gone.
8 The Israelites grieved for Moses in the plains of Moab thirty days, until the time of weeping and mourning was over.

9 Now Joshua son of Nun was filled with the spirit[c] of
wisdom because Moses had laid his hands on him. So the
Israelites listened to him and did what the LORD had commanded Moses.

10 Since then, no prophet has risen in Israel like Moses,
whom the LORD knew face to face, 11 who did all those signs
and wonders the LORD sent him to do in Egypt—to Pharaoh and to all his officials and to his whole land. 12 For no
one has ever shown the mighty power or performed the awesome deeds that Moses did in the sight of all Israel.

**Why was Israel so blessed?
(33:29)**
Israel was not blessed because
they were righteous or especially
good. They were blessed because
God chose them to be a model of
his love to the rest of the world.

**Why was Moses buried in a
secret grave? (34:6)**
It was a Canaanite practice to
worship the dead. Moses' grave
was probably hidden so nobody
would make a shrine out of it.

**How did the Israelites
mourn for 30 days? (34:8)**
The Israelites may have expressed grief by tearing their
clothes, wailing and crying loudly, putting ashes on their heads,
wearing rough clothes, and singing funeral songs.

**What did it mean for Moses
to lay his hands on Joshua?
(34:9)**
In ancient cultures this was an
important act that symbolized
the transfer of leadership. It was
also a symbol of God's approval
of Joshua as leader.

---

a 28 Septuagint; Hebrew *Jacob's spring is*   b 6 Or *He was buried*
c 9 Or *Spirit*

Joshua

INTRODUCTION

Who wrote this book?
The author of Joshua is not named but probably was someone who witnessed the events described.

Why was this book written?
The book of Joshua tells how God helped the Israelites defeat the Canaanites.

What happens in this book?
Joshua becomes Israel's leader. Joshua leads Israel's armies to victory. Joshua assigns land to Israel's 12 tribes.

What do we learn about God in this book?
God will give victory to his people when they obey him.

Who is the key person in this book?
The most important person in this book is Joshua.

Where did this happen?
The events in this book happened in the land of Canaan. Today we call that land Israel. (See the map index at the back of this Bible to see where Israel is.)

What are some of the stories in this book?

The Lord instructs Joshua	Joshua 1
Rahab protects the spies	Joshua 2
Israel crosses the Jordan	Joshua 3 – 4
Jericho's walls fall down	Joshua 6
Achan's sin brings defeat	Joshua 7
The Gibeonites fool Joshua	Joshua 9
The sun stands still	Joshua 10
Joshua says good-bye	Joshua 24

When did these things happen?

1400 BC 1300 1200 1100 1000 900 800 700 600 500 400

ISRAELITES ENTER CANAAN (C. 1406 BC)

CONQUEST OF CANAAN (C. 1406 – 1375 BC)

BOOK OF JOSHUA WRITTEN (C. 1390 BC)

JOSHUA'S DEATH (C. 1390 BC)

JUDGES BEGIN TO RULE (C. 1375 BC)

SAUL NAMED KING (1050 BC)

DAVID NAMED KING (1010 BC)

DIVISION OF THE KINGDOM (930 BC)

JOSHUA INSTALLED AS LEADER

1 After the death of Moses the servant of the LORD, the LORD said to Joshua son of Nun, Moses' aide: ²"Moses my servant is dead. Now then, you and all these people, get ready to cross the Jordan River into the land I am about to give to them—to the Israelites. ³I will give you every place where you set your foot, as I promised Moses. ⁴Your territory will extend from the desert to Lebanon, and from the great river, the Euphrates—all the Hittite country—to the Mediterranean Sea in the west. ⁵No one will be able to stand against you all the days of your life. As I was with Moses, so I will be with you; I will never leave you nor forsake you. ⁶Be strong and courageous, because you will lead these people to inherit the land I swore to their ancestors to give them.

⁷"Be strong and very courageous. Be careful to obey all the law my servant Moses gave you; do not turn from it to the right or to the left, that you may be successful wherever you go. ⁸Keep this Book of the Law always on your lips; meditate on it day and night, so that you may be careful to do everything written in it. Then you will be prosperous and successful. ⁹Have I not commanded you? Be strong and courageous. Do not be afraid; do not be discouraged, for the LORD your God will be with you wherever you go."

¹⁰So Joshua ordered the officers of the people: ¹¹"Go through the camp and tell the people, 'Get your provisions ready. Three days from now you will cross the Jordan here to go in and take possession of the land the LORD your God is giving you for your own.'"

¹²But to the Reubenites, the Gadites and the half-tribe of Manasseh, Joshua said, ¹³"Remember the command that Moses the servant of the LORD gave you after he said, 'The LORD your God will give you rest by giving you this land.' ¹⁴Your wives, your children and your livestock may stay in the land that Moses gave you east of the Jordan, but all your fighting men, ready for battle, must cross over ahead of your fellow Israelites. You are to help them ¹⁵until the LORD gives them rest, as he has done for you, and until they too have taken possession of the land the LORD your God is giving them. After that, you may go back and occupy your own land, which Moses the servant of the LORD gave you east of the Jordan toward the sunrise."

¹⁶Then they answered Joshua, "Whatever you have commanded us we will do, and wherever you send us we will go. ¹⁷Just as we fully obeyed Moses, so we will obey you. Only may the LORD your God be with you as he was with Moses. ¹⁸Whoever rebels against your word and does not obey it, whatever you may command them, will be put to death. Only be strong and courageous!"

RAHAB AND THE SPIES

2 Then Joshua son of Nun secretly sent two spies from Shittim. "Go, look over the land," he said, "especially Jericho." So they went and entered the house of a prostitute named Rahab and stayed there.

²The king of Jericho was told, "Look, some of the Israelites have come here tonight to spy out the land." ³So the king

---

Did God really speak out loud to Joshua? (1:1)
We aren't sure. Perhaps Joshua heard God's voice, or maybe God impressed his words on Joshua's mind. In any case, he communicated directly with Joshua, giving instructions for entering the promised land.

How hard would it have been to cross the Jordan River? (1:2)
The flow of the Jordan River was light during most of the year; it was only 80 to 100 feet (24.5 – 30.5 meters) wide. But during its flood stage, the river was more than a mile (1.6 kilometers) across and would have been difficult to cross. The Israelites crossed the river during its flood stage. (For details of the crossing, see chapter 3.)

Was it right for the Israelites to take land belonging to others? (1:4)
The Israelites were following God's orders. God took the land away from the Canaanites as punishment for their sins. Later, when Israel turned away from God, he took the land away from them.

Why did the spies visit the house of a prostitute? (2:1)
This was probably a good place to find out information. Also, if they were discovered, it would be easy to quickly escape because of the location of the house.

Why did the city of Jericho have a king? (2:2)
The major cities in Canaan were actually small kingdoms, and each one was ruled by a king.

Did God bless Rahab for lying? (2:4–5)

God's law forbids lying, but God blessed Rahab for hiding the men and then sending them away safely. Rahab believed in the God of Israel (verses 10–13), and she was rewarded for her faith.

of Jericho sent this message to Rahab: "Bring out the men who came to you and entered your house, because they have come to spy out the whole land."

[4] But the woman had taken the two men and hidden them. She said, "Yes, the men came to me, but I did not know where they had come from. [5] At dusk, when it was time to close the city gate, they left. I don't know which way they went. Go after them quickly. You may catch up with them." [6] (But she had taken them up to the roof and hidden them under the stalks of flax she had laid out on the roof.) [7] So the men set out in pursuit of the spies on the road that leads to the fords of the Jordan, and as soon as the pursuers had gone out, the gate was shut.

[8] Before the spies lay down for the night, she went up on the roof [9] and said to them, "I know that the LORD has given you this land and that a great fear of you has fallen on us, so that all who live in this country are melting in fear because of you. [10] We have heard how the LORD dried up the water of the Red Sea[a] for you when you came out of Egypt, and what you did to Sihon and Og, the two kings of the Amorites east of the Jordan, whom you completely destroyed.[b] [11] When we heard of it, our hearts melted in fear and everyone's courage failed because of you, for the LORD your God is God in heaven above and on the earth below.

[12] "Now then, please swear to me by the LORD that you will show kindness to my family, because I have shown kindness to you. Give me a sure sign [13] that you will spare the lives of my father and mother, my brothers and sisters, and all who belong to them—and that you will save us from death."

[14] "Our lives for your lives!" the men assured her. "If you don't tell what we are doing, we will treat you kindly and faithfully when the LORD gives us the land."

[15] So she let them down by a rope through the window, for the house she lived in was part of the city wall. [16] She said to them, "Go to the hills so the pursuers will not find you. Hide yourselves there three days until they return, and then go on your way."

Were houses actually built on the city walls? (2:15)

Cities like Jericho often had two walls, a higher and a lower one. People in these cities sometimes built their houses between the walls with the lower wall forming the back of the house. This would have given the spies a chance to easily escape.

[a] 10 Or *the Sea of Reeds*   [b] 10 The Hebrew term refers to the irrevocable giving over of things or persons to the LORD, often by totally destroying them.

Would God ever want someone to disobey one of his commandments?

JOSHUA 2

God is righteous, and he expects his people to obey the laws that he has given. People have often asked questions like these: Is it wrong to steal a loaf of bread in order to feed a starving child? Is it wrong to lie to a criminal in order to keep him from hurting you? These are situations where two of God's laws come into conflict. In this story Rahab lied in order to protect the lives of the spies. In reward for her faith, the Israelites saved her and her family when the city of Jericho was destroyed. She was not necessarily rewarded for lying but rather for her faith, as Hebrews 11:31 points out: "By faith the prostitute Rahab, because she welcomed the spies, was not killed with those who were disobedient."

Jesus was accused by the Pharisees of breaking the law about working on the Sabbath (see Matthew 12:3–12). In response, he asked the Pharisees if they would work by pulling one of their sheep out of a pit that it fell into on the Sabbath.

When two principles come into conflict, it is important to prayerfully ask for wisdom about what to do.

¹⁷Now the men had said to her, "This oath you made us swear will not be binding on us ¹⁸unless, when we enter the land, you have tied this scarlet cord in the window through which you let us down, and unless you have brought your father and mother, your brothers and all your family into your house. ¹⁹If any of them go outside your house into the street, their blood will be on their own heads; we will not be responsible. As for those who are in the house with you, their blood will be on our head if a hand is laid on them. ²⁰But if you tell what we are doing, we will be released from the oath you made us swear."

²¹"Agreed," she replied. "Let it be as you say."

So she sent them away, and they departed. And she tied the scarlet cord in the window.

²²When they left, they went into the hills and stayed there three days, until the pursuers had searched all along the road and returned without finding them. ²³Then the two men started back. They went down out of the hills, forded the river and came to Joshua son of Nun and told him everything that had happened to them. ²⁴They said to Joshua, "The LORD has surely given the whole land into our hands; all the people are melting in fear because of us."

CROSSING THE JORDAN

3 Early in the morning Joshua and all the Israelites set out from Shittim and went to the Jordan, where they camped before crossing over. ²After three days the officers went throughout the camp, ³giving orders to the people: "When you see the ark of the covenant of the LORD your God, and the Levitical priests carrying it, you are to move out from your positions and follow it. ⁴Then you will know which way to go, since you have never been this way before. But keep a distance of about two thousand cubits*a* between you and the ark; do not go near it."

⁵Joshua told the people, "Consecrate yourselves, for tomorrow the LORD will do amazing things among you."

⁶Joshua said to the priests, "Take up the ark of the covenant and pass on ahead of the people." So they took it up and went ahead of them.

⁷And the LORD said to Joshua, "Today I will begin to exalt you in the eyes of all Israel, so they may know that I am with you as I was with Moses. ⁸Tell the priests who carry the ark of the covenant: 'When you reach the edge of the Jordan's waters, go and stand in the river.'"

⁹Joshua said to the Israelites, "Come here and listen to the words of the LORD your God. ¹⁰This is how you will know that the living God is among you and that he will certainly drive out before you the Canaanites, Hittites, Hivites, Perizzites, Girgashites, Amorites and Jebusites. ¹¹See, the ark of the covenant of the Lord of all the earth will go into the Jordan ahead of you. ¹²Now then, choose twelve men from the tribes of Israel, one from each tribe. ¹³And as soon as the priests who carry the ark of the LORD—the Lord of all the earth—set foot in the Jordan, its waters flowing downstream will be cut off and stand up in a heap."

a 4 That is, about 3,000 feet or about 900 meters

Why did the spies tell Rahab to use a scarlet cord? (2:18)
This cord was probably a decorative rope. Its red color is a reminder of the blood spread on doorposts during the first Passover. Those who put blood on their doorposts were spared from the final plague in Egypt.

Why did the people have to keep their distance from the ark? (3:4)
The ark represented God's holiness and presence. Only the priests could come close to the ark because they represented the link between the people and God.

How did the Israelites consecrate themselves? (3:5)
The people consecrated, or symbolically dedicated themselves to God, by washing their clothes and themselves with water. This was one way to become ceremonially pure before they crossed the river.

When did the Israelites
cross the Jordan River? (3:15)
It was during the time of the
grain harvest (April and May),
when the river would have been
at its flood stage. The river was
probably 10 to 12 feet (3 to 3.5
meters) deep.

How did God stop the flow of
the river? (3:16)
We don't know. No matter what
method God used, it was a
miracle that was a reminder of
the way the Israelites had left
Egypt by crossing the Red Sea on
dry ground.

Why did Joshua tell the
people to make a stone
monument? (4:5 – 7)
Stone monuments were com-
mon during Old Testament
times to help future generations
remember the great things God
had done for his people. The 12
stones would also remind the
Israelites of their unity as a nation of 12 tribes.

Building a Stone Monument
(4:4 – 9)

¹⁴So when the people broke camp to cross the Jordan, the
priests carrying the ark of the covenant went ahead of them.
¹⁵Now the Jordan is at flood stage all during harvest. Yet as
soon as the priests who carried the ark reached the Jordan
and their feet touched the water's edge, ¹⁶the water from
upstream stopped flowing. It piled up in a heap a great distance away, at a town called Adam in the vicinity of Zarethan, while the water flowing down to the Sea of the Arabah
(that is, the Dead Sea) was completely cut off. So the people
crossed over opposite Jericho. ¹⁷The priests who carried the
ark of the covenant of the LORD stopped in the middle of
the Jordan and stood on dry ground, while all Israel passed
by until the whole nation had completed the crossing on
dry ground.

4 When the whole nation had finished crossing the Jordan, the LORD said to Joshua, ²"Choose twelve men
from among the people, one from each tribe, ³and tell them
to take up twelve stones from the middle of the Jordan, from
right where the priests are standing, and carry them over
with you and put them down at the place where you stay
tonight."

⁴So Joshua called together the twelve men he had appointed from the Israelites, one from each tribe, ⁵and said
to them, "Go over before the ark of the LORD your God into
the middle of the Jordan. Each of you is to take up a stone
on his shoulder, according to the number of the tribes of the
Israelites, ⁶to serve as a sign among you. In the future, when
your children ask you, 'What do these stones mean?' ⁷tell
them that the flow of the Jordan was cut off before the ark
of the covenant of the LORD. When it crossed the Jordan,
the waters of the Jordan were cut off. These stones are to be
a memorial to the people of Israel forever."

⁸So the Israelites did as Joshua commanded them. They
took twelve stones from the middle of the Jordan, according
to the number of the tribes of the Israelites, as the LORD had
told Joshua; and they carried them over with them to their
camp, where they put them down. ⁹Joshua set up the twelve
stones that had been*a* in the middle of the Jordan at the spot
where the priests who carried the ark of the covenant had
stood. And they are there to this day.

¹⁰Now the priests who carried the ark remained standing in the middle of the Jordan until everything the LORD
had commanded Joshua was done by the people, just as Moses had directed Joshua. The people hurried over, ¹¹and as
soon as all of them had crossed, the ark of the LORD and
the priests came to the other side while the people watched.
¹²The men of Reuben, Gad and the half-tribe of Manasseh
crossed over, ready for battle, in front of the Israelites, as
Moses had directed them. ¹³About forty thousand armed
for battle crossed over before the LORD to the plains of Jericho for war.

¹⁴That day the LORD exalted Joshua in the sight of all Israel; and they stood in awe of him all the days of his life, just
as they had stood in awe of Moses.

a 9 Or Joshua also set up twelve stones

[15]Then the Lord said to Joshua, [16]"Command the priests carrying the ark of the covenant law to come up out of the Jordan."

[17]So Joshua commanded the priests, "Come up out of the Jordan."

[18]And the priests came up out of the river carrying the ark of the covenant of the Lord. No sooner had they set their feet on the dry ground than the waters of the Jordan returned to their place and ran at flood stage as before.

[19]On the tenth day of the first month the people went up from the Jordan and camped at Gilgal on the eastern border of Jericho. [20]And Joshua set up at Gilgal the twelve stones they had taken out of the Jordan. [21]He said to the Israelites, "In the future when your descendants ask their parents, 'What do these stones mean?' [22]tell them, 'Israel crossed the Jordan on dry ground.' [23]For the Lord your God dried up the Jordan before you until you had crossed over. The Lord your God did to the Jordan what he had done to the Red Sea[a] when he dried it up before us until we had crossed over. [24]He did this so that all the peoples of the earth might know that the hand of the Lord is powerful and so that you might always fear the Lord your God."

5 Now when all the Amorite kings west of the Jordan and all the Canaanite kings along the coast heard how the Lord had dried up the Jordan before the Israelites until they[b] had crossed over, their hearts melted in fear and they no longer had the courage to face the Israelites.

CIRCUMCISION AND PASSOVER AT GILGAL

[2]At that time the Lord said to Joshua, "Make flint knives and circumcise the Israelites again." [3]So Joshua made flint knives and circumcised the Israelites at Gibeath Haaraloth.[c]

[4]Now this is why he did so: All those who came out of Egypt—all the men of military age—died in the wilderness on the way after leaving Egypt. [5]All the people that came out had been circumcised, but all the people born in the wilderness during the journey from Egypt had not. [6]The Israelites had moved about in the wilderness forty years until all the men who were of military age when they left Egypt had died, since they had not obeyed the Lord. For the Lord had sworn to them that they would not see the land he had solemnly promised their ancestors to give us, a land flowing with milk and honey. [7]So he raised up their sons in their place, and these were the ones Joshua circumcised. They were still uncircumcised because they had not been circumcised on the way. [8]And after the whole nation had been circumcised, they remained where they were in camp until they were healed.

[9]Then the Lord said to Joshua, "Today I have rolled away the reproach of Egypt from you." So the place has been called Gilgal[d] to this day.

[10]On the evening of the fourteenth day of the month,

What type of calendar did the Israelites use? (4:19) Israel used two calendars, one sacred and one agricultural. The sacred calendar is referred to in this passage. In the sacred calendar, Aviv (March-April) is the first month, and it is a reminder of the deliverance from Egypt. In the agricultural calendar, Ethanim (or Tishri: September-October) is the first month.

Why did Joshua have to circumcise the Israelites? (5:2–3) This was the sign of the covenant God made with his people. It symbolized the fact that the old life was being cut off and a new life was beginning with God (see Genesis 17:13).

What was the reproach of Egypt? (5:9) If the Israelites had died in the wilderness, the people of Egypt would have mocked the Israelites. Now that the Israelites had crossed into the promised land, the possibility of that reproach was over.

---

[a] 23 Or *the Sea of Reeds*   [b] 1 Another textual tradition *we*   [c] 3 *Gibeath Haaraloth* means *the hill of foreskins.*   [d] 9 *Gilgal* sounds like the Hebrew for *roll.*

Why did God stop sending manna? (5:12)
God had provided manna to the Israelites when they were in the desert and didn't have other sources for food. When they arrived in the land that God had promised them, they no longer needed manna.

Who was the commander of the army of the LORD? (5:14)
This was either an angel or God himself appearing in a human form.

Why did God speak as if the victory had already happened? (6:2)
In the Old Testament, predictions about the future were sometimes stated in the present or even the past tense. God knew the outcome, and the Israelites were guaranteed the victory.

Why did God tell the Israelites to march around the city? (6:3)
In ancient times, circling a city was a common practice before attacking. The people of Jericho became afraid when the Israelites marched around the city because they knew a fight was coming.

What kind of trumpets were these? (6:4)
These trumpets were made from the horns of rams. They were designed to send signals for military and religious purposes.

Why was the ark carried around the city? (6:9)
The ark was a symbol of God's presence among his people.

while camped at Gilgal on the plains of Jericho, the Israelites celebrated the Passover. ¹¹The day after the Passover, that very day, they ate some of the produce of the land: unleavened bread and roasted grain. ¹²The manna stopped the day after*a* they ate this food from the land; there was no longer any manna for the Israelites, but that year they ate the produce of Canaan.

THE FALL OF JERICHO

¹³Now when Joshua was near Jericho, he looked up and saw a man standing in front of him with a drawn sword in his hand. Joshua went up to him and asked, "Are you for us or for our enemies?"

¹⁴"Neither," he replied, "but as commander of the army of the LORD I have now come." Then Joshua fell facedown to the ground in reverence, and asked him, "What message does my Lord*b* have for his servant?"

¹⁵The commander of the LORD's army replied, "Take off your sandals, for the place where you are standing is holy." And Joshua did so.

6 Now the gates of Jericho were securely barred because of the Israelites. No one went out and no one came in.

²Then the LORD said to Joshua, "See, I have delivered Jericho into your hands, along with its king and its fighting men. ³March around the city once with all the armed men. Do this for six days. ⁴Have seven priests carry trumpets of rams' horns in front of the ark. On the seventh day, march around the city seven times, with the priests blowing the trumpets. ⁵When you hear them sound a long blast on the trumpets, have the whole army give a loud shout; then the wall of the city will collapse and the army will go up, everyone straight in."

⁶So Joshua son of Nun called the priests and said to them, "Take up the ark of the covenant of the LORD and have seven priests carry trumpets in front of it." ⁷And he ordered the army, "Advance! March around the city, with an armed guard going ahead of the ark of the LORD."

⁸When Joshua had spoken to the people, the seven priests carrying the seven trumpets before the LORD went forward, blowing their trumpets, and the ark of the LORD's covenant followed them. ⁹The armed guard marched ahead of the priests who blew the trumpets, and the rear guard followed the ark. All this time the trumpets were sounding. ¹⁰But Joshua had commanded the army, "Do not give a war cry, do not raise your voices, do not say a word until the day I tell you to shout. Then shout!" ¹¹So he had the ark of the LORD carried around the city, circling it once. Then the army returned to camp and spent the night there.

¹²Joshua got up early the next morning and the priests took up the ark of the LORD. ¹³The seven priests carrying the seven trumpets went forward, marching before the ark of the LORD and blowing the trumpets. The armed men went ahead of them and the rear guard followed the ark of the LORD, while the trumpets kept sounding. ¹⁴So on the second

---

a 12 Or *the day*   *b 14* Or *lord*

day they marched around the city once and returned to the camp. They did this for six days.

¹⁵On the seventh day, they got up at daybreak and marched around the city seven times in the same manner, except that on that day they circled the city seven times. ¹⁶The seventh time around, when the priests sounded the trumpet blast, Joshua commanded the army, "Shout! For the LORD has given you the city! ¹⁷The city and all that is in it are to be devoted*ᵃ* to the LORD. Only Rahab the prostitute and all who are with her in her house shall be spared, because she hid the spies we sent. ¹⁸But keep away from the devoted things, so that you will not bring about your own destruction by taking any of them. Otherwise you will make the camp of Israel liable to destruction and bring trouble on it. ¹⁹All the silver and gold and the articles of bronze and iron are sacred to the LORD and must go into his treasury."

²⁰When the trumpets sounded, the army shouted, and at the sound of the trumpet, when the men gave a loud shout, the wall collapsed; so everyone charged straight in, and they took the city. ²¹They devoted the city to the LORD and destroyed with the sword every living thing in it — men and women, young and old, cattle, sheep and donkeys.

²²Joshua said to the two men who had spied out the land, "Go into the prostitute's house and bring her out and all who belong to her, in accordance with your oath to her." ²³So the young men who had done the spying went in and brought out Rahab, her father and mother, her brothers and sisters and all who belonged to her. They brought out her entire family and put them in a place outside the camp of Israel.

²⁴Then they burned the whole city and everything in it, but they put the silver and gold and the articles of bronze and iron into the treasury of the LORD's house. ²⁵But Joshua spared Rahab the prostitute, with her family and all who belonged to her, because she hid the men Joshua had sent as spies to Jericho — and she lives among the Israelites to this day.

²⁶At that time Joshua pronounced this solemn oath: "Cursed before the LORD is the one who undertakes to rebuild this city, Jericho:

ᵃ 17 The Hebrew term refers to the irrevocable giving over of things or persons to the LORD, often by totally destroying them; also in verses 18 and 21.

Why was the number seven so special? (6:13–15)
God created all things in six days and rested on the seventh day. Jericho was defeated on the seventh day. The number seven represented completion and perfection.

How was the city "devoted to the LORD"? (6:17)
Items devoted to the LORD were sometimes destroyed (see Deuteronomy 20:16–18). For example, animals were given to the LORD as sacrifices. So destroying a sinful city was a way of devoting it to the LORD.

The Battle of Jericho (6:20)

Why did God tell us not to kill, yet the Old Testament is full of stories about battles?
JOSHUA 6

In the Ten Commandments God says you shall not murder. Jesus extends that concept by saying that hating another person is also breaking the commandment. The focus is on individual acts of murder, malice, revenge, and hatred.

But in the Bible God often commanded his people to go to war against other countries that opposed them because God was trying to accomplish something good by punishing evil nations, eliminating idol worship, or clearing the land so that the people had a good place to live.

God spoke directly to his people in Old Testament times commanding them to go to war. It's much more complicated today to decide what God's will is concerning war. Christians probably should not condemn all wars, but they should also be very careful to determine if a particular war is justified according to biblical principles.

"At the cost of his firstborn son
   he will lay its foundations;
at the cost of his youngest
   he will set up its gates."

²⁷ So the LORD was with Joshua, and his fame spread throughout the land.

ACHAN'S SIN

7 But the Israelites were unfaithful in regard to the devoted things*; Achan son of Karmi, the son of Zimri,* the son of Zerah, of the tribe of Judah, took some of them. So the LORD's anger burned against Israel.

² Now Joshua sent men from Jericho to Ai, which is near Beth Aven to the east of Bethel, and told them, "Go up and spy out the region." So the men went up and spied out Ai.

³ When they returned to Joshua, they said, "Not all the army will have to go up against Ai. Send two or three thousand men to take it and do not weary the whole army, for only a few people live there." ⁴ So about three thousand went up; but they were routed by the men of Ai, ⁵ who killed about thirty-six of them. They chased the Israelites from the city gate as far as the stone quarries and struck them down on the slopes. At this the hearts of the people melted in fear and became like water.

⁶ Then Joshua tore his clothes and fell facedown to the ground before the ark of the LORD, remaining there till evening. The elders of Israel did the same, and sprinkled dust on their heads. ⁷ And Joshua said, "Alas, Sovereign LORD, why did you ever bring this people across the Jordan to deliver us into the hands of the Amorites to destroy us? If only we had been content to stay on the other side of the Jordan! ⁸ Pardon your servant, Lord. What can I say, now that Israel has been routed by its enemies? ⁹ The Canaanites and the other people of the country will hear about this and they will surround us and wipe out our name from the earth. What then will you do for your own great name?"

¹⁰ The LORD said to Joshua, "Stand up! What are you doing down on your face? ¹¹ Israel has sinned; they have violated my covenant, which I commanded them to keep. They have taken some of the devoted things; they have stolen, they have lied, they have put them with their own possessions. ¹² That is why the Israelites cannot stand against their enemies; they turn their backs and run because they have been made liable to destruction. I will not be with you anymore unless you destroy whatever among you is devoted to destruction.

¹³ "Go, consecrate the people. Tell them, 'Consecrate yourselves in preparation for tomorrow; for this is what the LORD, the God of Israel, says: There are devoted things among you, Israel. You cannot stand against your enemies until you remove them.

Why did Joshua tear his clothes and lie face down on the ground? (7:6)
Joshua was alarmed and sad that God had abandoned them in the battle against Ai. Ancient people expressed their grief in extreme ways such as this.

Why did all the people have to suffer for one person's sin? (7:11)
The Israelites thought that if one person sinned, the whole community was guilty. Since Achan broke God's law, the whole nation suffered the consequences.

What does "liable to destruction" mean? (7:12)
God threatened to destroy the Israelites unless they destroyed everything that was supposed to have been dedicated to God.

ᵃ 1 The Hebrew term refers to the irrevocable giving over of things or persons to the LORD, often by totally destroying them; also in verses 11, 12, 13 and 15.
ᵇ 1 See Septuagint and 1 Chron. 2:6; Hebrew *Zabdi*; also in verses 17 and 18.

¹⁴"In the morning, present yourselves tribe by tribe. The tribe the Lord chooses shall come forward clan by clan; the clan the Lord chooses shall come forward family by family; and the family the Lord chooses shall come forward man by man. ¹⁵Whoever is caught with the devoted things shall be destroyed by fire, along with all that belongs to him. He has violated the covenant of the Lord and has done an outrageous thing in Israel!'"

¹⁶Early the next morning Joshua had Israel come forward by tribes, and Judah was chosen. ¹⁷The clans of Judah came forward, and the Zerahites were chosen. He had the clan of the Zerahites come forward by families, and Zimri was chosen. ¹⁸Joshua had his family come forward man by man, and Achan son of Karmi, the son of Zimri, the son of Zerah, of the tribe of Judah, was chosen.

¹⁹Then Joshua said to Achan, "My son, give glory to the Lord, the God of Israel, and honor him. Tell me what you have done; do not hide it from me."

²⁰Achan replied, "It is true! I have sinned against the Lord, the God of Israel. This is what I have done: ²¹When I saw in the plunder a beautiful robe from Babylonia,ᵃ two hundred shekelsᵇ of silver and a bar of gold weighing fifty shekels,ᶜ I coveted them and took them. They are hidden in the ground inside my tent, with the silver underneath."

²²So Joshua sent messengers, and they ran to the tent, and there it was, hidden in his tent, with the silver underneath. ²³They took the things from the tent, brought them to Joshua and all the Israelites and spread them out before the Lord.

²⁴Then Joshua, together with all Israel, took Achan son of Zerah, the silver, the robe, the gold bar, his sons and daughters, his cattle, donkeys and sheep, his tent and all that he had, to the Valley of Achor. ²⁵Joshua said, "Why have you brought this trouble on us? The Lord will bring trouble on you today."

Then all Israel stoned him, and after they had stoned the rest, they burned them. ²⁶Over Achan they heaped up a large pile of rocks, which remains to this day. Then the Lord turned from his fierce anger. Therefore that place has been called the Valley of Achorᵈ ever since.

AI DESTROYED

8 Then the Lord said to Joshua, "Do not be afraid; do not be discouraged. Take the whole army with you, and go up and attack Ai. For I have delivered into your hands the king of Ai, his people, his city and his land. ²You shall do to Ai and its king as you did to Jericho and its king, except that you may carry off their plunder and livestock for yourselves. Set an ambush behind the city."

³So Joshua and the whole army moved out to attack Ai. He chose thirty thousand of his best fighting men and sent them out at night ⁴with these orders: "Listen carefully. You

How could confessing sin give glory to God? (7:19)
By confessing sin, the sinner acknowledged that what they did was wrong, and that God was ultimately right.

Why were Achan's sons and daughters punished for his sin? (7:24–25)
By his sin, Achan made everyone in his family guilty. Because of the community mentality of the Israelites, his sin made everyone associated with him sinful as well. In order to purify the whole nation, God destroyed everything that belonged to Achan, including his children.

Why did the Lord tell Joshua to not be afraid? (8:1)
Now that Israel had been cleansed of Achan's sin, the Lord reassured Joshua that he would be with them.

Why could the Israelites take plunder from Ai? (8:2)
Obtaining goods by force was common practice in the ancient world. Things taken from the defeated city helped to resupply the army with food and equipment. Jericho was an exception, where the people had been commanded to dedicate — meaning destroy — everything to the Lord.

ᵃ 21 Hebrew *Shinar*   ᵇ 21 That is, about 5 pounds or about 2.3 kilograms
ᶜ 21 That is, about 1 1/4 pounds or about 575 grams   ᵈ 26 *Achor* means *trouble.*

The Battle of Ai (8:1–29)

are to set an ambush behind the city. Don't go very far from it. All of you be on the alert. ⁵I and all those with me will advance on the city, and when the men come out against us, as they did before, we will flee from them. ⁶They will pursue us until we have lured them away from the city, for they will say, 'They are running away from us as they did before.' So when we flee from them, ⁷you are to rise up from ambush and take the city. The Lord your God will give it into your hand. ⁸When you have taken the city, set it on fire. Do what the Lord has commanded. See to it; you have my orders."

⁹Then Joshua sent them off, and they went to the place of ambush and lay in wait between Bethel and Ai, to the west of Ai—but Joshua spent that night with the people.

¹⁰Early the next morning Joshua mustered his army, and he and the leaders of Israel marched before them to Ai. ¹¹The entire force that was with him marched up and approached the city and arrived in front of it. They set up camp north of Ai, with the valley between them and the city. ¹²Joshua had taken about five thousand men and set them in ambush between Bethel and Ai, to the west of the city. ¹³So the soldiers took up their positions—with the main camp to the north of the city and the ambush to the west of it. That night Joshua went into the valley.

¹⁴When the king of Ai saw this, he and all the men of the city hurried out early in the morning to meet Israel in battle at a certain place overlooking the Arabah. But he did not know that an ambush had been set against him behind the city. ¹⁵Joshua and all Israel let themselves be driven back before them, and they fled toward the wilderness. ¹⁶All the men of Ai were called to pursue them, and they pursued Joshua and were lured away from the city. ¹⁷Not a man remained in Ai or Bethel who did not go after Israel. They left the city open and went in pursuit of Israel.

¹⁸Then the Lord said to Joshua, "Hold out toward Ai the javelin that is in your hand, for into your hand I will deliver the city." So Joshua held out toward the city the javelin that was in his hand. ¹⁹As soon as he did this, the men in the ambush rose quickly from their position and rushed forward. They entered the city and captured it and quickly set it on fire.

²⁰The men of Ai looked back and saw the smoke of the city rising up into the sky, but they had no chance to escape in any direction; the Israelites who had been fleeing toward the wilderness had turned back against their pursuers. ²¹For when Joshua and all Israel saw that the ambush had taken the city and that smoke was going up from it, they turned around and attacked the men of Ai. ²²Those in the ambush also came out of the city against them, so that they were caught in the middle, with Israelites on both sides. Israel cut them down, leaving them neither survivors nor fugitives. ²³But they took the king of Ai alive and brought him to Joshua.

²⁴When Israel had finished killing all the men of Ai in the fields and in the wilderness where they had chased them, and when every one of them had been put to the sword, all the Israelites returned to Ai and killed those who were in it.

²⁵Twelve thousand men and women fell that day—all the people of Ai. ²⁶For Joshua did not draw back the hand that held out his javelin until he had destroyed^a all who lived in Ai. ²⁷But Israel did carry off for themselves the livestock and plunder of this city, as the Lord had instructed Joshua.

²⁸So Joshua burned Ai^b and made it a permanent heap of ruins, a desolate place to this day. ²⁹He impaled the body of the king of Ai on a pole and left it there until evening. At sunset, Joshua ordered them to take the body from the pole and throw it down at the entrance of the city gate. And they raised a large pile of rocks over it, which remains to this day.

THE COVENANT RENEWED AT MOUNT EBAL

³⁰Then Joshua built on Mount Ebal an altar to the Lord, the God of Israel, ³¹as Moses the servant of the Lord had commanded the Israelites. He built it according to what is written in the Book of the Law of Moses—an altar of uncut stones, on which no iron tool had been used. On it they offered to the Lord burnt offerings and sacrificed fellowship offerings. ³²There, in the presence of the Israelites, Joshua wrote on stones a copy of the law of Moses. ³³All the Israelites, with their elders, officials and judges, were standing on both sides of the ark of the covenant of the Lord, facing the Levitical priests who carried it. Both the foreigners living among them and the native-born were there. Half of the people stood in front of Mount Gerizim and half of them in front of Mount Ebal, as Moses the servant of the Lord had formerly commanded when he gave instructions to bless the people of Israel.

³⁴Afterward, Joshua read all the words of the law—the blessings and the curses—just as it is written in the Book of the Law. ³⁵There was not a word of all that Moses had commanded that Joshua did not read to the whole assembly of Israel, including the women and children, and the foreigners who lived among them.

THE GIBEONITE DECEPTION

9 Now when all the kings west of the Jordan heard about these things—the kings in the hill country, in the western foothills, and along the entire coast of the Mediterranean Sea as far as Lebanon (the kings of the Hittites, Amorites, Canaanites, Perizzites, Hivites and Jebusites)— ²they came together to wage war against Joshua and Israel.

³However, when the people of Gibeon heard what Joshua had done to Jericho and Ai, ⁴they resorted to a ruse: They went as a delegation whose donkeys were loaded^c with worn-out sacks and old wineskins, cracked and mended. ⁵They put worn and patched sandals on their feet and wore old clothes. All the bread of their food supply was dry and moldy. ⁶Then they went to Joshua in the camp at Gilgal and said to him

---

^a 26 The Hebrew term refers to the irrevocable giving over of things or persons to the Lord, often by totally destroying them.   ^b 28 Ai means the ruin.   ^c 4 Most Hebrew manuscripts; some Hebrew manuscripts, Vulgate and Syriac (see also Septuagint) They prepared provisions and loaded their donkeys

Why was the altar made of uncut stones? (8:31)
The law said the altar would be defiled, or become unclean, if a tool was used to make it (see Exodus 20:25). This may have been because the pagans used iron tools to make altars to their gods. God wanted this to be a clear distinction between a pagan altar and an altar used to worship him. Also, since the Israelites did not have iron tools of their own, it would have been wrong to use tools taken from the pagan nations to make an altar for the true God.

Why did Joshua make another copy of the law? (8:32)
Stone would last longer than any other material. It was important to keep the commandments around as a reminder of how important God's laws are.

Why were these two mountains significant? (8:33–34)
Mount Gerizim represented the blessings for obeying God's law. Mount Ebal represented the opposite. This mountain represented the curses for disobeying the law (see Deuteronomy 11:29).

Who were the foreigners living with the Israelites? (8:35)
The foreigners included Rahab and her family and other people who had come into the Israelites' camp for food or shelter. The group of foreigners also included some Egyptians who had gone with the Israelites when they left Egypt in Moses' time.

and the Israelites, "We have come from a distant country; make a treaty with us."

⁷The Israelites said to the Hivites, "But perhaps you live near us, so how can we make a treaty with you?"

⁸"We are your servants," they said to Joshua.

But Joshua asked, "Who are you and where do you come from?"

⁹They answered: "Your servants have come from a very distant country because of the fame of the LORD your God. For we have heard reports of him: all that he did in Egypt, ¹⁰and all that he did to the two kings of the Amorites east of the Jordan—Sihon king of Heshbon, and Og king of Bashan, who reigned in Ashtaroth. ¹¹And our elders and all those living in our country said to us, 'Take provisions for your journey; go and meet them and say to them, "We are your servants; make a treaty with us."' ¹²This bread of ours was warm when we packed it at home on the day we left to come to you. But now see how dry and moldy it is. ¹³And these wineskins that we filled were new, but see how cracked they are. And our clothes and sandals are worn out by the very long journey."

¹⁴The Israelites sampled their provisions but did not inquire of the LORD. ¹⁵Then Joshua made a treaty of peace with them to let them live, and the leaders of the assembly ratified it by oath.

¹⁶Three days after they made the treaty with the Gibeonites, the Israelites heard that they were neighbors, living near them. ¹⁷So the Israelites set out and on the third day came to their cities: Gibeon, Kephirah, Beeroth and Kiriath Jearim. ¹⁸But the Israelites did not attack them, because the leaders of the assembly had sworn an oath to them by the LORD, the God of Israel.

The whole assembly grumbled against the leaders, ¹⁹but all the leaders answered, "We have given them our oath by the LORD, the God of Israel, and we cannot touch them now. ²⁰This is what we will do to them: We will let them live, so that God's wrath will not fall on us for breaking the oath we swore to them." ²¹They continued, "Let them live, but let them be woodcutters and water carriers in the service of the whole assembly." So the leaders' promise to them was kept.

²²Then Joshua summoned the Gibeonites and said, "Why did you deceive us by saying, 'We live a long way from you,' while actually you live near us? ²³You are now under a curse: You will never be released from service as woodcutters and water carriers for the house of my God."

²⁴They answered Joshua, "Your servants were clearly told how the LORD your God had commanded his servant Moses to give you the whole land and to wipe out all its inhabitants from before you. So we feared for our lives because of you, and that is why we did this. ²⁵We are now in your hands. Do to us whatever seems good and right to you."

²⁶So Joshua saved them from the Israelites, and they did not kill them. ²⁷That day he made the Gibeonites woodcutters and water carriers for the assembly, to provide for the needs of the altar of the LORD at the place the LORD would choose. And that is what they are to this day.

Did the Gibeonites believe in the LORD? (9:9)
They did not really believe, but they understood how great and powerful God was. They wanted to make a treaty with the Israelites so that they would not be destroyed.

Why did the people complain? (9:18)
The people were probably upset that their leaders had been fooled by the Gibeonites. They also may have wondered what would happen if they didn't follow God's command to destroy all the Canaanites.

Why did the leaders feel obligated to honor an oath they had been tricked into making? (9:19)
Even though the Israelites had been tricked into making a treaty with Gibeon (a violation of Exodus 34:12), it would have been wrong to break their oath with the Gibeonites, who respected Israel and their God.

Did the Gibeonites act in a way that pleased God? (9:25–27)
Not at first. The Gibeonites used trickery to avoid being harmed, which was wrong. However, they admitted their trickery and submitted to the Israelites. Since Joshua kept them from being killed and made them servants, God probably was not entirely displeased with them.

THE SUN STANDS STILL

10 Now Adoni-Zedek king of Jerusalem heard that Joshua had taken Ai and totally destroyed[a] it, doing to Ai and its king as he had done to Jericho and its king, and that the people of Gibeon had made a treaty of peace with Israel and had become their allies. [2]He and his people were very much alarmed at this, because Gibeon was an important city, like one of the royal cities; it was larger than Ai, and all its men were good fighters. [3]So Adoni-Zedek king of Jerusalem appealed to Hoham king of Hebron, Piram king of Jarmuth, Japhia king of Lachish and Debir king of Eglon. [4]"Come up and help me attack Gibeon," he said, "because it has made peace with Joshua and the Israelites."

[5]Then the five kings of the Amorites—the kings of Jerusalem, Hebron, Jarmuth, Lachish and Eglon—joined forces. They moved up with all their troops and took up positions against Gibeon and attacked it.

[6]The Gibeonites then sent word to Joshua in the camp at Gilgal: "Do not abandon your servants. Come up to us quickly and save us! Help us, because all the Amorite kings from the hill country have joined forces against us."

[7]So Joshua marched up from Gilgal with his entire army, including all the best fighting men. [8]The LORD said to Joshua, "Do not be afraid of them; I have given them into your hand. Not one of them will be able to withstand you."

[9]After an all-night march from Gilgal, Joshua took them by surprise. [10]The LORD threw them into confusion before Israel, so Joshua and the Israelites defeated them completely at Gibeon. Israel pursued them along the road going up to Beth Horon and cut them down all the way to Azekah and Makkedah. [11]As they fled before Israel on the road down from Beth Horon to Azekah, the LORD hurled large hailstones down on them, and more of them died from the hail than were killed by the swords of the Israelites.

[12]On the day the LORD gave the Amorites over to Israel, Joshua said to the LORD in the presence of Israel:

"Sun, stand still over Gibeon,
    and you, moon, over the Valley of Aijalon."
[13]So the sun stood still,
    and the moon stopped,
    till the nation avenged itself on[b] its enemies,

as it is written in the Book of Jashar.

The sun stopped in the middle of the sky and delayed going down about a full day. [14]There has never been a day like it before or since, a day when the LORD listened to a human being. Surely the LORD was fighting for Israel!

[15]Then Joshua returned with all Israel to the camp at Gilgal.

FIVE AMORITE KINGS KILLED

[16]Now the five kings had fled and hidden in the cave at Makkedah. [17]When Joshua was told that the five kings had

---

[a] 1 The Hebrew term refers to the irrevocable giving over of things or persons to the LORD, often by totally destroying them; also in verses 28, 35, 37, 39 and 40.   [b] 13 Or *nation triumphed over*

The Battle of Gibeon (10:5)

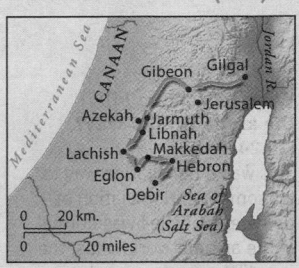

Why did Israel have to defend Gibeon? (10:6–7)
Allies were required to help each other because of the treaties they had made. Joshua may have also thought it was a part of God's plan to get the armies of the five cities working together. Fighting one battle against all of them would be easier than fighting five separate battles.

Did Joshua speak to the sun and the moon? (10:12)
Pagans prayed to the sun and moon, which they thought were gods. Joshua prayed to the LORD because he could help his people. The sun and the moon could not.

How did the sun stop? (10:13–14)
Like the other miracles in the Bible, we don't know how God did this. Some believe that the sun stayed in the sky longer that day. Others think that it may only have seemed to be an extra long day. The important thing is that the LORD intervened and gave the victory to the Israelites.

What is the Book of Jashar? (10:13)
This book, now lost, was a collection of songs and historical notes about Israel's wars.

been found hiding in the cave at Makkedah, [18]he said, "Roll large rocks up to the mouth of the cave, and post some men there to guard it. [19]But don't stop; pursue your enemies! Attack them from the rear and don't let them reach their cities, for the LORD your God has given them into your hand."

[20]So Joshua and the Israelites defeated them completely, but a few survivors managed to reach their fortified cities. [21]The whole army then returned safely to Joshua in the camp at Makkedah, and no one uttered a word against the Israelites.

[22]Joshua said, "Open the mouth of the cave and bring those five kings out to me." [23]So they brought the five kings out of the cave—the kings of Jerusalem, Hebron, Jarmuth, Lachish and Eglon. [24]When they had brought these kings to Joshua, he summoned all the men of Israel and said to the army commanders who had come with him, "Come here and put your feet on the necks of these kings." So they came forward and placed their feet on their necks.

[25]Joshua said to them, "Do not be afraid; do not be discouraged. Be strong and courageous. This is what the LORD will do to all the enemies you are going to fight." [26]Then Joshua put the kings to death and exposed their bodies on five poles, and they were left hanging on the poles until evening.

[27]At sunset Joshua gave the order and they took them down from the poles and threw them into the cave where they had been hiding. At the mouth of the cave they placed large rocks, which are there to this day.

SOUTHERN CITIES CONQUERED

[28]That day Joshua took Makkedah. He put the city and its king to the sword and totally destroyed everyone in it. He left no survivors. And he did to the king of Makkedah as he had done to the king of Jericho.

[29]Then Joshua and all Israel with him moved on from Makkedah to Libnah and attacked it. [30]The LORD also gave that city and its king into Israel's hand. The city and everyone in it Joshua put to the sword. He left no survivors there. And he did to its king as he had done to the king of Jericho.

[31]Then Joshua and all Israel with him moved on from Libnah to Lachish; he took up positions against it and attacked it. [32]The LORD gave Lachish into Israel's hands, and Joshua took it on the second day. The city and everyone in it he put to the sword, just as he had done to Libnah. [33]Meanwhile, Horam king of Gezer had come up to help Lachish, but Joshua defeated him and his army—until no survivors were left.

[34]Then Joshua and all Israel with him moved on from Lachish to Eglon; they took up positions against it and attacked it. [35]They captured it that same day and put it to the sword and totally destroyed everyone in it, just as they had done to Lachish.

[36]Then Joshua and all Israel with him went up from Eglon to Hebron and attacked it. [37]They took the city and put it to the sword, together with its king, its villages and everyone in it. They left no survivors. Just as at Eglon, they totally destroyed it and everyone in it.

Why did Joshua kill the kings in this way? (10:24–26)
This was a humiliating way to kill someone. Humiliation of defeated enemies was normal in the ancient world. Plus, the Israelites were engaged in a war that had been commanded by God. God ordered them to kill their enemies, and they obeyed. Joshua also wanted to remind the Israelites that God was helping them.

³⁸Then Joshua and all Israel with him turned around and attacked Debir. ³⁹They took the city, its king and its villages, and put them to the sword. Everyone in it they totally destroyed. They left no survivors. They did to Debir and its king as they had done to Libnah and its king and to Hebron.

⁴⁰So Joshua subdued the whole region, including the hill country, the Negev, the western foothills and the mountain slopes, together with all their kings. He left no survivors. He totally destroyed all who breathed, just as the LORD, the God of Israel, had commanded. ⁴¹Joshua subdued them from Kadesh Barnea to Gaza and from the whole region of Goshen to Gibeon. ⁴²All these kings and their lands Joshua conquered in one campaign, because the LORD, the God of Israel, fought for Israel.

⁴³Then Joshua returned with all Israel to the camp at Gilgal.

NORTHERN KINGS DEFEATED

11 When Jabin king of Hazor heard of this, he sent word to Jobab king of Madon, to the kings of Shimron and Akshaph, ²and to the northern kings who were in the mountains, in the Arabah south of Kinnereth, in the western foothills and in Naphoth Dor on the west; ³to the Canaanites in the east and west; to the Amorites, Hittites, Perizzites and Jebusites in the hill country; and to the Hivites below Hermon in the region of Mizpah. ⁴They came out with all their troops and a large number of horses and chariots—a huge army, as numerous as the sand on the seashore. ⁵All these kings joined forces and made camp together at the Waters of Merom to fight against Israel.

⁶The LORD said to Joshua, "Do not be afraid of them, because by this time tomorrow I will hand all of them, slain, over to Israel. You are to hamstring their horses and burn their chariots."

⁷So Joshua and his whole army came against them suddenly at the Waters of Merom and attacked them, ⁸and the LORD gave them into the hand of Israel. They defeated them and pursued them all the way to Greater Sidon, to Misrephoth Maim, and to the Valley of Mizpah on the east, until no survivors were left. ⁹Joshua did to them as the LORD had directed: He hamstrung their horses and burned their chariots.

¹⁰At that time Joshua turned back and captured Hazor and put its king to the sword. (Hazor had been the head of all these kingdoms.) ¹¹Everyone in it they put to the sword. They totally destroyed*a* them, not sparing anyone that breathed, and he burned Hazor itself.

¹²Joshua took all these royal cities and their kings and put them to the sword. He totally destroyed them, as Moses the servant of the LORD had commanded. ¹³Yet Israel did not burn any of the cities built on their mounds—except Hazor, which Joshua burned. ¹⁴The Israelites carried off for

---

a 11 The Hebrew term refers to the irrevocable giving over of things or persons to the LORD, often by totally destroying them; also in verses 12, 20 and 21.

Why did these kings join forces? (11:1–5)
Canaan was made up of independent city-states that were usually hostile to one another. But the victories of the Israelites led these kings to combine their armies. This was the most challenging enemy for the Israelites because of all the horses and chariots. The Israelites only had foot soldiers.

The Battle of Hazor (11:1–8)

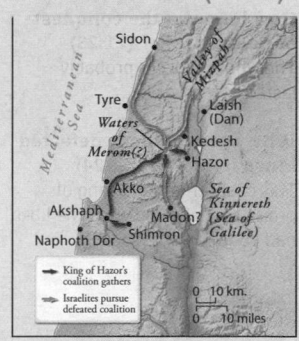

Why was Joshua supposed to cripple the captured horses? (11:6)
God wanted his people to trust him rather than put their trust in horses and chariots.

themselves all the plunder and livestock of these cities, but all the people they put to the sword until they completely destroyed them, not sparing anyone that breathed. [15]As the LORD commanded his servant Moses, so Moses commanded Joshua, and Joshua did it; he left nothing undone of all that the LORD commanded Moses.

[16]So Joshua took this entire land: the hill country, all the Negev, the whole region of Goshen, the western foothills, the Arabah and the mountains of Israel with their foothills, [17]from Mount Halak, which rises toward Seir, to Baal Gad in the Valley of Lebanon below Mount Hermon. He captured all their kings and put them to death. [18]Joshua waged war against all these kings for a long time. [19]Except for the Hivites living in Gibeon, not one city made a treaty of peace with the Israelites, who took them all in battle. [20]For it was the LORD himself who hardened their hearts to wage war against Israel, so that he might destroy them totally, exterminating them without mercy, as the LORD had commanded Moses.

[21]At that time Joshua went and destroyed the Anakites from the hill country: from Hebron, Debir and Anab, from all the hill country of Judah, and from all the hill country of Israel. Joshua totally destroyed them and their towns. [22]No Anakites were left in Israelite territory; only in Gaza, Gath and Ashdod did any survive.

[23]So Joshua took the entire land, just as the LORD had directed Moses, and he gave it as an inheritance to Israel according to their tribal divisions. Then the land had rest from war.

LIST OF DEFEATED KINGS

12 These are the kings of the land whom the Israelites had defeated and whose territory they took over east of the Jordan, from the Arnon Gorge to Mount Hermon, including all the eastern side of the Arabah:

[2]Sihon king of the Amorites, who reigned in Heshbon. He ruled from Aroer on the rim of the Arnon Gorge—from the middle of the gorge—to the Jabbok River, which is the border of the Ammonites. This included half of Gilead. [3]He also ruled over the eastern Arabah from the Sea of Galilee[a] to the Sea of the Arabah (that is, the Dead Sea), to Beth Jeshimoth, and then southward below the slopes of Pisgah.

[4]And the territory of Og king of Bashan, one of the last of the Rephaites, who reigned in Ashtaroth and Edrei. [5]He ruled over Mount Hermon, Salekah, all of Bashan to the border of the people of Geshur and Maakah, and half of Gilead to the border of Sihon king of Heshbon.

[6]Moses, the servant of the LORD, and the Israelites conquered them. And Moses the servant of the LORD gave their land to the Reubenites, the Gadites and the half-tribe of Manasseh to be their possession.

[a] 3 Hebrew *Kinnereth*

Why did the Israelites leave some pagan peoples undefeated? (11:22–23)
They were probably tired of fighting and stopped before all of the people were defeated. If they had continued the war they would have received control over the whole region as God had promised.

How long did the conquest of Canaan take? (11:23)
The whole process probably lasted seven years.

Why were all these defeated kings listed? (12:1–24)
This chapter is like a song of praise that showed what the LORD had done for his people.

⁷Here is a list of the kings of the land that Joshua and the Israelites conquered on the west side of the Jordan, from Baal Gad in the Valley of Lebanon to Mount Halak, which rises toward Seir. Joshua gave their lands as an inheritance to the tribes of Israel according to their tribal divisions. ⁸The lands included the hill country, the western foothills, the Arabah, the mountain slopes, the wilderness and the Negev. These were the lands of the Hittites, Amorites, Canaanites, Perizzites, Hivites and Jebusites. These were the kings:

CONQUEST OF CANAAN (12:1)

[9] the king of Jericho	one
the king of Ai (near Bethel)	one
[10] the king of Jerusalem	one
the king of Hebron	one
[11] the king of Jarmuth	one
the king of Lachish	one
[12] the king of Eglon	one
the king of Gezer	one
[13] the king of Debir	one
the king of Geder	one
[14] the king of Hormah	one
the king of Arad	one
[15] the king of Libnah	one
the king of Adullam	one
[16] the king of Makkedah	one
the king of Bethel	one
[17] the king of Tappuah	one
the king of Hepher	one
[18] the king of Aphek	one
the king of Lasharon	one
[19] the king of Madon	one
the king of Hazor	one
[20] the king of Shimron Meron	one
the king of Akshaph	one
[21] the king of Taanach	one
the king of Megiddo	one
[22] the king of Kedesh	one
the king of Jokneam in Carmel	one
[23] the king of Dor (in Naphoth Dor)	one
the king of Goyim in Gilgal	one
[24] the king of Tirzah	one

thirty-one kings in all.

LAND STILL TO BE TAKEN

13 When Joshua had grown old, the LORD said to him, "You are now very old, and there are still very large areas of land to be taken over.

[2] "This is the land that remains: all the regions of the Philistines and Geshurites, [3] from the Shihor River on the east of Egypt to the territory of Ekron on the north, all of it counted as Canaanite though held by the five Philistine rulers in Gaza, Ashdod, Ashkelon, Gath and Ekron; the territory of the Avvites [4] on the south; all the land of the Canaanites, from Arah of the Sidonians as far as Aphek and the border of the Amorites; [5] the area of Byblos; and all Lebanon to the east, from Baal Gad below Mount Hermon to Lebo Hamath.

[6] "As for all the inhabitants of the mountain regions from Lebanon to Misrephoth Maim, that is, all the Sidonians, I myself will drive them out before the Israelites. Be sure to allocate this land to Israel for an inheritance, as I have instructed you, [7] and divide it as an inheritance among the nine tribes and half of the tribe of Manasseh."

Had the Israelites conquered all of Canaan? (13:1–6)
The Israelites had taken the less-desirable hill country, but the Canaanites still controlled most of the fertile plains and cities. Because the Israelites had not wiped out the Canaanites, this meant that the Israelites lived as neighbors with them. This led them to often combine worship of God with worship of the pagan gods.

The Unconquered Land (13:1)

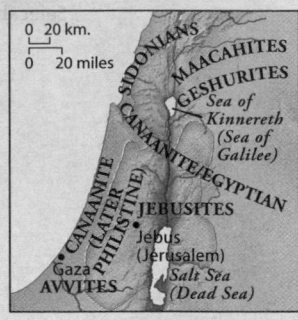

Why was the land divided before all of it had been conquered? (13:6–7)
As leader, it was Joshua's responsibility to divide the land before he died. And because he was growing old, he knew he needed to act sooner rather than later. No single leader took Joshua's place, so each tribe developed its own leadership and military forces.

DIVISION OF THE LAND EAST OF THE JORDAN

[8] The other half of Manasseh,[a] the Reubenites and the Gadites had received the inheritance that Moses had given them east of the Jordan, as he, the servant of the Lord, had assigned it to them.

[9] It extended from Aroer on the rim of the Arnon Gorge, and from the town in the middle of the gorge, and included the whole plateau of Medeba as far as Dibon, [10] and all the towns of Sihon king of the Amorites, who ruled in Heshbon, out to the border of the Ammonites. [11] It also included Gilead, the territory of the people of Geshur and Maakah, all of Mount Hermon and all Bashan as far as Salekah— [12] that is, the whole kingdom of Og in Bashan, who had reigned in Ashtaroth and Edrei. (He was the last of the Rephaites.) Moses had defeated them and taken over their land. [13] But the Israelites did not drive out the people of Geshur and Maakah, so they continue to live among the Israelites to this day.

[14] But to the tribe of Levi he gave no inheritance, since the food offerings presented to the Lord, the God of Israel, are their inheritance, as he promised them.

[15] This is what Moses had given to the tribe of Reuben, according to its clans:

[16] The territory from Aroer on the rim of the Arnon Gorge, and from the town in the middle of the gorge, and the whole plateau past Medeba [17] to Heshbon and all its towns on the plateau, including Dibon, Bamoth Baal, Beth Baal Meon, [18] Jahaz, Kedemoth, Mephaath, [19] Kiriathaim, Sibmah, Zereth Shahar on the hill in the valley, [20] Beth Peor, the slopes of Pisgah, and Beth Jeshimoth— [21] all the towns on the plateau and the entire realm of Sihon king of the Amorites, who ruled at Heshbon. Moses had defeated him and the Midianite chiefs, Evi, Rekem, Zur, Hur and Reba—princes allied with Sihon—who lived in that country. [22] In addition to those slain in battle, the Israelites had put to the sword Balaam son of Beor, who practiced divination. [23] The boundary of the Reubenites was the bank of the Jordan. These towns and their villages were the inheritance of the Reubenites, according to their clans.

[24] This is what Moses had given to the tribe of Gad, according to its clans:

[25] The territory of Jazer, all the towns of Gilead and half the Ammonite country as far as Aroer, near Rabbah; [26] and from Heshbon to Ramath Mizpah and Betonim, and from Mahanaim to the territory of Debir; [27] and in the valley, Beth Haram, Beth Nimrah, Sukkoth and Zaphon with the rest of the realm of Sihon king of Heshbon (the east side of the Jordan, the territory up to the end of the Sea of Galilee[b]). [28] These towns and their

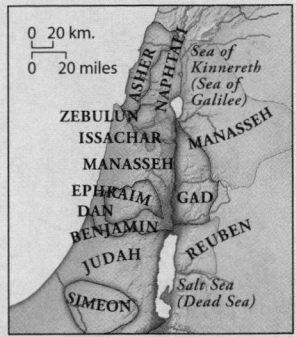

Dividing the Land (13:8 — 19:51)

0   20 km.
0   20 miles

ASHER
NAPHTALI
Sea of Kinnereth (Sea of Galilee)
ZEBULUN
ISSACHAR
MANASSEH
MANASSEH
EPHRAIM   GAD
DAN
BENJAMIN
JUDAH   REUBEN
SIMEON   Salt Sea (Dead Sea)

---

[a] 8 Hebrew *With it* (that is, with the other half of Manasseh)   [b] 27 Hebrew *Kinnereth*

villages were the inheritance of the Gadites, according to their clans.

²⁹This is what Moses had given to the half-tribe of Manasseh, that is, to half the family of the descendants of Manasseh, according to its clans:

³⁰The territory extending from Mahanaim and including all of Bashan, the entire realm of Og king of Bashan — all the settlements of Jair in Bashan, sixty towns, ³¹half of Gilead, and Ashtaroth and Edrei (the royal cities of Og in Bashan). This was for the descendants of Makir son of Manasseh — for half of the sons of Makir, according to their clans.

³²This is the inheritance Moses had given when he was in the plains of Moab across the Jordan east of Jericho. ³³But to the tribe of Levi, Moses had given no inheritance; the LORD, the God of Israel, is their inheritance, as he promised them.

DIVISION OF THE LAND WEST OF THE JORDAN

14 Now these are the areas the Israelites received as an inheritance in the land of Canaan, which Eleazar the priest, Joshua son of Nun and the heads of the tribal clans of Israel allotted to them. ²Their inheritances were assigned by lot to the nine and a half tribes, as the LORD had commanded through Moses. ³Moses had granted the two and a half tribes their inheritance east of the Jordan but had not granted the Levites an inheritance among the rest, ⁴for Joseph's descendants had become two tribes — Manasseh and Ephraim. The Levites received no share of the land but only towns to live in, with pasturelands for their flocks and herds. ⁵So the Israelites divided the land, just as the LORD had commanded Moses.

ALLOTMENT FOR CALEB

⁶Now the people of Judah approached Joshua at Gilgal, and Caleb son of Jephunneh the Kenizzite said to him, "You know what the LORD said to Moses the man of God at Kadesh Barnea about you and me. ⁷I was forty years old when Moses the servant of the LORD sent me from Kadesh Barnea to explore the land. And I brought him back a report according to my convictions, ⁸but my fellow Israelites who went up with me made the hearts of the people melt in fear. I, however, followed the LORD my God wholeheartedly. ⁹So on that day Moses swore to me, 'The land on which your feet have walked will be your inheritance and that of your children forever, because you have followed the LORD my God wholeheartedly.'ᵃ

¹⁰"Now then, just as the LORD promised, he has kept me alive for forty-five years since the time he said this to Moses, while Israel moved about in the wilderness. So here I am today, eighty-five years old! ¹¹I am still as strong today as the day Moses sent me out; I'm just as vigorous to go out to battle now as I was then. ¹²Now give me this hill country

ᵃ 9 Deut. 1:36

What did the Levites inherit? (13:33)
The Levites did not inherit land, but God honored them by giving them responsibility for priestly duties. They also received offerings and tithes from the other tribes.

Why did Caleb ask Joshua to give him land if his tribe already had a place? (14:6–14)
After Joshua and Caleb had explored the land of Canaan more than 40 years earlier, God had promised Caleb land because of the good report he brought back (see Numbers 14:24). Joshua granted him Hebron as his inheritance.

that the LORD promised me that day. You yourself heard then that the Anakites were there and their cities were large and fortified, but, the LORD helping me, I will drive them out just as he said."

¹³Then Joshua blessed Caleb son of Jephunneh and gave him Hebron as his inheritance. ¹⁴So Hebron has belonged to Caleb son of Jephunneh the Kenizzite ever since, because he followed the LORD, the God of Israel, wholeheartedly. ¹⁵(Hebron used to be called Kiriath Arba after Arba, who was the greatest man among the Anakites.)

Then the land had rest from war.

ALLOTMENT FOR JUDAH

15 The allotment for the tribe of Judah, according to its clans, extended down to the territory of Edom, to the Desert of Zin in the extreme south.

²Their southern boundary started from the bay at the southern end of the Dead Sea, ³crossed south of Scorpion Pass, continued on to Zin and went over to the south of Kadesh Barnea. Then it ran past Hezron up to Addar and curved around to Karka. ⁴It then passed along to Azmon and joined the Wadi of Egypt, ending at the Mediterranean Sea. This is their*ᵃ* southern boundary.

⁵The eastern boundary is the Dead Sea as far as the mouth of the Jordan.

The northern boundary started from the bay of the sea at the mouth of the Jordan, ⁶went up to Beth Hoglah and continued north of Beth Arabah to the Stone of Bohan son of Reuben. ⁷The boundary then went up to Debir from the Valley of Achor and turned north to Gilgal, which faces the Pass of Adummim south of the gorge. It continued along to the waters of En Shemesh and came out at En Rogel. ⁸Then it ran up the Valley of Ben Hinnom along the southern slope of the Jebusite city (that is, Jerusalem). From there it climbed to the top of the hill west of the Hinnom Valley at the northern end of the Valley of Rephaim. ⁹From the hilltop the boundary headed toward the spring of the waters of Nephtoah, came out at the towns of Mount Ephron and went down toward Baalah (that is, Kiriath Jearim). ¹⁰Then it curved westward from Baalah to Mount Seir, ran along the northern slope of Mount Jearim (that is, Kesalon), continued down to Beth Shemesh and crossed to Timnah. ¹¹It went to the northern slope of Ekron, turned toward Shikkeron, passed along to Mount Baalah and reached Jabneel. The boundary ended at the sea.

¹²The western boundary is the coastline of the Mediterranean Sea.

These are the boundaries around the people of Judah by their clans.

¹³In accordance with the LORD's command to him, Joshua gave to Caleb son of Jephunneh a portion in Judah — Kiriath Arba, that is, Hebron. (Arba was the forefather of Anak.)

ᵃ 4 Septuagint; Hebrew your

¹⁴From Hebron Caleb drove out the three Anakites—Sheshai, Ahiman and Talmai, the sons of Anak. ¹⁵From there he marched against the people living in Debir (formerly called Kiriath Sepher). ¹⁶And Caleb said, "I will give my daughter Aksah in marriage to the man who attacks and captures Kiriath Sepher." ¹⁷Othniel son of Kenaz, Caleb's brother, took it; so Caleb gave his daughter Aksah to him in marriage.

¹⁸One day when she came to Othniel, she urged him^a to ask her father for a field. When she got off her donkey, Caleb asked her, "What can I do for you?"

¹⁹She replied, "Do me a special favor. Since you have given me land in the Negev, give me also springs of water." So Caleb gave her the upper and lower springs.

²⁰This is the inheritance of the tribe of Judah, according to its clans:

²¹The southernmost towns of the tribe of Judah in the Negev toward the boundary of Edom were:

Kabzeel, Eder, Jagur, ²²Kinah, Dimonah, Adadah, ²³Kedesh, Hazor, Ithnan, ²⁴Ziph, Telem, Bealoth, ²⁵Hazor Hadattah, Kerioth Hezron (that is, Hazor), ²⁶Amam, Shema, Moladah, ²⁷Hazar Gaddah, Heshmon, Beth Pelet, ²⁸Hazar Shual, Beersheba, Biziothiah, ²⁹Baalah, Iyim, Ezem, ³⁰Eltolad, Kesil, Hormah, ³¹Ziklag, Madmannah, Sansannah, ³²Lebaoth, Shilhim, Ain and Rimmon—a total of twenty-nine towns and their villages.

³³In the western foothills:

Eshtaol, Zorah, Ashnah, ³⁴Zanoah, En Gannim, Tappuah, Enam, ³⁵Jarmuth, Adullam, Sokoh, Azekah, ³⁶Shaaraim, Adithaim and Gederah (or Gederothaim)^b—fourteen towns and their villages.

³⁷Zenan, Hadashah, Migdal Gad, ³⁸Dilean, Mizpah, Joktheel, ³⁹Lachish, Bozkath, Eglon, ⁴⁰Kabbon, Lahmas, Kitlish, ⁴¹Gederoth, Beth Dagon, Naamah and Makkedah—sixteen towns and their villages.

⁴²Libnah, Ether, Ashan, ⁴³Iphtah, Ashnah, Nezib, ⁴⁴Keilah, Akzib and Mareshah—nine towns and their villages.

⁴⁵Ekron, with its surrounding settlements and villages; ⁴⁶west of Ekron, all that were in the vicinity of Ashdod, together with their villages; ⁴⁷Ashdod, its surrounding settlements and villages; and Gaza, its settlements and villages, as far as the Wadi of Egypt and the coastline of the Mediterranean Sea.

⁴⁸In the hill country:

Shamir, Jattir, Sokoh, ⁴⁹Dannah, Kiriath Sannah (that is, Debir), ⁵⁰Anab, Eshtemoh, Anim, ⁵¹Goshen, Holon and Giloh—eleven towns and their villages.

⁵²Arab, Dumah, Eshan, ⁵³Janim, Beth Tappuah, Aphekah, ⁵⁴Humtah, Kiriath Arba (that is, Hebron) and Zior—nine towns and their villages.

How could the daughter just be given away? (15:17)
Israelite girls were treated like property. They had very little rights of their own, so they could be awarded as a prize to a man for a military victory. This practice continued for at least another 400 years.

Why did Aksah have to ask for water? (15:19)
She first asked her husband, Othniel, to ask her father for some land. When her father, Caleb, agreed, he overlooked the fact that the land did not have water on it. Then Caleb gave her two springs of water.

What is a wadi? (15:47)
A *wadi* is a valley that is completely dry except for a short season during the year. The Wadi of Egypt was probably located in the northeastern part of the Sinai Peninsula.

---

^a 18 Hebrew and some Septuagint manuscripts; other Septuagint manuscripts (see also note at Judges 1:14) *Othniel, he urged her*   ^b 36 Or *Gederah and Gederothaim*

⁵⁵Maon, Carmel, Ziph, Juttah, ⁵⁶Jezreel, Jokdeam, Zanoah, ⁵⁷Kain, Gibeah and Timnah — ten towns and their villages.

⁵⁸Halhul, Beth Zur, Gedor, ⁵⁹Maarath, Beth Anoth and Eltekon — six towns and their villages.ᵃ

⁶⁰Kiriath Baal (that is, Kiriath Jearim) and Rabbah — two towns and their villages.

⁶¹In the wilderness:

Beth Arabah, Middin, Sekakah, ⁶²Nibshan, the City of Salt and En Gedi — six towns and their villages.

⁶³Judah could not dislodge the Jebusites, who were living in Jerusalem; to this day the Jebusites live there with the people of Judah.

ALLOTMENT FOR EPHRAIM AND MANASSEH

16 The allotment for Joseph began at the Jordan, east of the springs of Jericho, and went up from there through the desert into the hill country of Bethel. ²It went on from Bethel (that is, Luz),ᵇ crossed over to the territory of the Arkites in Ataroth, ³descended westward to the territory of the Japhletites as far as the region of Lower Beth Horon and on to Gezer, ending at the Mediterranean Sea. ⁴So Manasseh and Ephraim, the descendants of Joseph, received their inheritance.

⁵This was the territory of Ephraim, according to its clans:

The boundary of their inheritance went from Ataroth Addar in the east to Upper Beth Horon ⁶and continued to the Mediterranean Sea. From Mikmethath on the north it curved eastward to Taanath Shiloh, passing by it to Janoah on the east. ⁷Then it went down from Janoah to Ataroth and Naarah, touched Jericho and came out at the Jordan. ⁸From Tappuah the border went west to the Kanah Ravine and ended at the Mediterranean Sea. This was the inheritance of the tribe of the Ephraimites, according to its clans. ⁹It also included all the towns and their villages that were set aside for the Ephraimites within the inheritance of the Manassites.

¹⁰They did not dislodge the Canaanites living in Gezer; to this day the Canaanites live among the people of Ephraim but are required to do forced labor.

17 This was the allotment for the tribe of Manasseh as Joseph's firstborn, that is, for Makir, Manasseh's firstborn. Makir was the ancestor of the Gileadites, who had received Gilead and Bashan because the Makirites were great soldiers. ²So this allotment was for the rest of the people of Manasseh — the clans of Abiezer, Helek, Asriel, Shechem, Hepher and Shemida. These are the other male descendants of Manasseh son of Joseph by their clans.

³Now Zelophehad son of Hepher, the son of Gilead, the son of Makir, the son of Manasseh, had no sons but only daughters, whose names were Mahlah, Noah, Hoglah,

Why couldn't Judah drive out the Jebusites? (15:63) The Israelites got impatient and decided that settling the land was more important than removing the people. They tolerated their enemies rather than push them out of the territory.

ᵃ 59 The Septuagint adds another district of eleven towns, including Tekoa and Ephrathah (Bethlehem).   ᵇ 2 Septuagint; Hebrew *Bethel to Luz*

What rights did women have? (17:3–4)
Women had relatively few rights compared to today. Normally women couldn't own land, but in some cases, women could inherit their father's land when they had no brothers. Laws were put in place so women could not be wrongfully divorced.

Milkah and Tirzah. ⁴They went to Eleazar the priest, Joshua son of Nun, and the leaders and said, "The LORD commanded Moses to give us an inheritance among our relatives." So Joshua gave them an inheritance along with the brothers of their father, according to the LORD's command. ⁵Manasseh's share consisted of ten tracts of land besides Gilead and Bashan east of the Jordan, ⁶because the daughters of the tribe of Manasseh received an inheritance among the sons. The land of Gilead belonged to the rest of the descendants of Manasseh.

⁷The territory of Manasseh extended from Asher to Mikmethath east of Shechem. The boundary ran southward from there to include the people living at En Tappuah. ⁸(Manasseh had the land of Tappuah, but Tappuah itself, on the boundary of Manasseh, belonged to the Ephraimites.) ⁹Then the boundary continued south to the Kanah Ravine. There were towns belonging to Ephraim lying among the towns of Manasseh, but the boundary of Manasseh was the northern side of the ravine and ended at the Mediterranean Sea. ¹⁰On the south the land belonged to Ephraim, on the north to Manasseh. The territory of Manasseh reached the Mediterranean Sea and bordered Asher on the north and Issachar on the east.

¹¹Within Issachar and Asher, Manasseh also had Beth Shan, Ibleam and the people of Dor, Endor, Taanach and Megiddo, together with their surrounding settlements (the third in the list is Naphoth[a]).
¹²Yet the Manassites were not able to occupy these towns, for the Canaanites were determined to live in that region. ¹³However, when the Israelites grew stronger, they subjected the Canaanites to forced labor but did not drive them out completely.

Why did Joseph's descendants ask for more land? (17:14)
They claimed that because there were so many of them, the land they were given would not support them all. Joshua told them to clear some of the nearby forests to get more land.

¹⁴The people of Joseph said to Joshua, "Why have you given us only one allotment and one portion for an inheritance? We are a numerous people, and the LORD has blessed us abundantly."

¹⁵"If you are so numerous," Joshua answered, "and if the hill country of Ephraim is too small for you, go up into the forest and clear land for yourselves there in the land of the Perizzites and Rephaites."

Why would the tribes have to fight individually? (17:17–18)
Since no leader would take Joshua's place when he died, each tribe would have its own leader. The individual tribes would then need to learn to fight their own battles. Joshua assured them that they were strong enough to drive out the Canaanites.

¹⁶The people of Joseph replied, "The hill country is not enough for us, and all the Canaanites who live in the plain have chariots fitted with iron, both those in Beth Shan and its settlements and those in the Valley of Jezreel."

¹⁷But Joshua said to the tribes of Joseph—to Ephraim and Manasseh—"You are numerous and very powerful. You will have not only one allotment ¹⁸but the forested hill country as well. Clear it, and its farthest limits will be yours; though the Canaanites have chariots fitted with iron and though they are strong, you can drive them out."

DIVISION OF THE REST OF THE LAND

18 The whole assembly of the Israelites gathered at Shiloh and set up the tent of meeting there. The country

What was the tent of meeting? (18:1)
It was the tent that held the sacred ark of the covenant, and it was the place where God met with his people (see Exodus 25:8–22).

a 11 That is, Naphoth Dor

was brought under their control, ²but there were still seven Israelite tribes who had not yet received their inheritance.

³So Joshua said to the Israelites: "How long will you wait before you begin to take possession of the land that the LORD, the God of your ancestors, has given you? ⁴Appoint three men from each tribe. I will send them out to make a survey of the land and to write a description of it, according to the inheritance of each. Then they will return to me. ⁵You are to divide the land into seven parts. Judah is to remain in its territory on the south and the tribes of Joseph in their territory on the north. ⁶After you have written descriptions of the seven parts of the land, bring them here to me and I will cast lots for you in the presence of the LORD our God. ⁷The Levites, however, do not get a portion among you, because the priestly service of the LORD is their inheritance. And Gad, Reuben and the half-tribe of Manasseh have already received their inheritance on the east side of the Jordan. Moses the servant of the LORD gave it to them."

⁸As the men started on their way to map out the land, Joshua instructed them, "Go and make a survey of the land and write a description of it. Then return to me, and I will cast lots for you here at Shiloh in the presence of the LORD." ⁹So the men left and went through the land. They wrote its description on a scroll, town by town, in seven parts, and returned to Joshua in the camp at Shiloh. ¹⁰Joshua then cast lots for them in Shiloh in the presence of the LORD, and there he distributed the land to the Israelites according to their tribal divisions.

ALLOTMENT FOR BENJAMIN

¹¹The first lot came up for the tribe of Benjamin according to its clans. Their allotted territory lay between the tribes of Judah and Joseph:

¹²On the north side their boundary began at the Jordan, passed the northern slope of Jericho and headed west into the hill country, coming out at the wilderness of Beth Aven. ¹³From there it crossed to the south slope of Luz (that is, Bethel) and went down to Ataroth Addar on the hill south of Lower Beth Horon.

¹⁴From the hill facing Beth Horon on the south the boundary turned south along the western side and came out at Kiriath Baal (that is, Kiriath Jearim), a town of the people of Judah. This was the western side.

¹⁵The southern side began at the outskirts of Kiriath Jearim on the west, and the boundary came out at the spring of the waters of Nephtoah. ¹⁶The boundary went down to the foot of the hill facing the Valley of Ben Hinnom, north of the Valley of Rephaim. It continued down the Hinnom Valley along the southern slope of the Jebusite city and so to En Rogel. ¹⁷It then curved north, went to En Shemesh, continued to Geliloth, which faces the Pass of Adummim, and ran down to the Stone of Bohan son of Reuben. ¹⁸It continued to the northern slope of Beth Arabah*a* and on down into the

a 18 Septuagint; Hebrew *slope facing the Arabah*

Why had seven tribes still not taken possession of the land? (18:1–3)
Boundaries could not be drawn until they knew where water and the most fertile land were located. They had to survey the land in order to make sure that it would be divided up fairly.

How did they cast lots? (18:10)
Like drawing names out of a hat, they probably placed small marked stones in a jar and drew them out one at a time. The Israelites relied on God to control the outcome of the lots.

What was the Stone of Bohan? (18:17)
Large stones were often used as boundary markers. It was probably somewhere southeast of Jericho. We don't know who Bohan was, only that this boundary stone was named for him.

Arabah. [19] It then went to the northern slope of Beth Hoglah and came out at the northern bay of the Dead Sea, at the mouth of the Jordan in the south. This was the southern boundary.

[20] The Jordan formed the boundary on the eastern side.

These were the boundaries that marked out the inheritance of the clans of Benjamin on all sides.

[21] The tribe of Benjamin, according to its clans, had the following towns:

Jericho, Beth Hoglah, Emek Keziz, [22] Beth Arabah, Zemaraim, Bethel, [23] Avvim, Parah, Ophrah, [24] Kephar Ammoni, Ophni and Geba — twelve towns and their villages.

[25] Gibeon, Ramah, Beeroth, [26] Mizpah, Kephirah, Mozah, [27] Rekem, Irpeel, Taralah, [28] Zelah, Haeleph, the Jebusite city (that is, Jerusalem), Gibeah and Kiriath — fourteen towns and their villages.

This was the inheritance of Benjamin for its clans.

ALLOTMENT FOR SIMEON

19 The second lot came out for the tribe of Simeon according to its clans. Their inheritance lay within the territory of Judah. [2] It included:

Beersheba (or Sheba),[a] Moladah, [3] Hazar Shual, Balah, Ezem, [4] Eltolad, Bethul, Hormah, [5] Ziklag, Beth Markaboth, Hazar Susah, [6] Beth Lebaoth and Sharuhen — thirteen towns and their villages;

[7] Ain, Rimmon, Ether and Ashan — four towns and their villages — [8] and all the villages around these towns as far as Baalath Beer (Ramah in the Negev).

This was the inheritance of the tribe of the Simeonites, according to its clans. [9] The inheritance of the Simeonites was taken from the share of Judah, because Judah's portion was more than they needed. So the Simeonites received their inheritance within the territory of Judah.

ALLOTMENT FOR ZEBULUN

[10] The third lot came up for Zebulun according to its clans:

The boundary of their inheritance went as far as Sarid. [11] Going west it ran to Maralah, touched Dabbesheth, and extended to the ravine near Jokneam. [12] It turned east from Sarid toward the sunrise to the territory of Kisloth Tabor and went on to Daberath and up to Japhia. [13] Then it continued eastward to Gath Hepher and Eth Kazin; it came out at Rimmon and turned toward Neah. [14] There the boundary went around on the north to Hannathon and ended at the Valley of Iphtah El. [15] Included were Kattath, Nahalal, Shimron, Idalah and Bethlehem. There were twelve towns and their villages.

[16] These towns and their villages were the inheritance of Zebulun, according to its clans.

[a] 2 Or *Beersheba, Sheba*; 1 Chron. 4:28 does not have *Sheba*.

Why was Simeon's land inside the territory of Judah? (19:1)
This fulfilled Jacob's prophecy that Simeon's descendants would be scattered among the rest of the nation because some of Judah's cities were given to the tribe of Simeon.

Why did the tribe of Judah receive more territory than they needed? (19:9)
Because they had been quick to take up the fight against the Canaanites, they received their territory before the final seven tribes received theirs. After defeating the Canaanites, they had been the first to stake out a claim to the land and apparently took more than they needed.

How could a town have a village? (19:15)
Larger, walled towns usually had small villages scattered around them. It was more convenient for villagers to live close to their fields. When the villagers feared an enemy attack, they gathered in the central town, where they could be protected by the town's walls and people.

ALLOTMENT FOR ISSACHAR

[17]The fourth lot came out for Issachar according to its clans. [18]Their territory included:

Jezreel, Kesulloth, Shunem, [19]Hapharaim, Shion, Anaharath, [20]Rabbith, Kishion, Ebez, [21]Remeth, En Gannim, En Haddah and Beth Pazzez. [22]The boundary touched Tabor, Shahazumah and Beth Shemesh, and ended at the Jordan. There were sixteen towns and their villages.

[23]These towns and their villages were the inheritance of the tribe of Issachar, according to its clans.

ALLOTMENT FOR ASHER

[24]The fifth lot came out for the tribe of Asher according to its clans. [25]Their territory included:

Helkath, Hali, Beten, Akshaph, [26]Allammelek, Amad and Mishal. On the west the boundary touched Carmel and Shihor Libnath. [27]It then turned east toward Beth Dagon, touched Zebulun and the Valley of Iphtah El, and went north to Beth Emek and Neiel, passing Kabul on the left. [28]It went to Abdon,[a] Rehob, Hammon and Kanah, as far as Greater Sidon. [29]The boundary then turned back toward Ramah and went to the fortified city of Tyre, turned toward Hosah and came out at the Mediterranean Sea in the region of Akzib, [30]Ummah, Aphek and Rehob. There were twenty-two towns and their villages.

[31]These towns and their villages were the inheritance of the tribe of Asher, according to its clans.

> **What was a fortified city? (19:29)**
> It was a well protected city usually surrounded by walls. Such cities were often built on steep hills to provide further protection from an enemy attack.

ALLOTMENT FOR NAPHTALI

[32]The sixth lot came out for Naphtali according to its clans:

[33]Their boundary went from Heleph and the large tree in Zaanannim, passing Adami Nekeb and Jabneel to Lakkum and ending at the Jordan. [34]The boundary ran west through Aznoth Tabor and came out at Hukkok. It touched Zebulun on the south, Asher on the west and the Jordan[b] on the east. [35]The fortified towns were Ziddim, Zer, Hammath, Rakkath, Kinnereth, [36]Adamah, Ramah, Hazor, [37]Kedesh, Edrei, En Hazor, [38]Iron, Migdal El, Horem, Beth Anath and Beth Shemesh. There were nineteen towns and their villages.

[39]These towns and their villages were the inheritance of the tribe of Naphtali, according to its clans.

ALLOTMENT FOR DAN

[40]The seventh lot came out for the tribe of Dan according to its clans. [41]The territory of their inheritance included:

Zorah, Eshtaol, Ir Shemesh, [42]Shaalabbin, Aijalon, Ithlah, [43]Elon, Timnah, Ekron, [44]Eltekeh, Gibbethon, Baalath, [45]Jehud, Bene Berak, Gath Rimmon, [46]Me Jarkon and Rakkon, with the area facing Joppa.

[a] 28 Some Hebrew manuscripts (see also 21:30); most Hebrew manuscripts Ebron   [b] 34 Septuagint; Hebrew *west, and Judah, the Jordan,*

Why did the Danites occupy
a different territory? (19:47)
The Danites were unable to defeat the enemies living in their
territory. They solved their problem by moving farther north,
where they were able to defeat
the city of Leshem more easily.
Though God had not told them to
go elsewhere, he had not prohibited them either.

Why wasn't Joshua's land
decided by casting lots?
(19:49–50)
Of the 12 men sent on a spying
mission to Canaan, Caleb and
Joshua were the only ones who
believed in God's promise that Israel would conquer the land (see
Numbers 13:1–33). God rewarded
them for their faithful service by
allowing them to choose their
own land.

What were the cities of
refuge? (20:2)
Six cities functioned as jails without walls for people who were
waiting to be tried and for those
who were found guilty of accidentally killing someone. They
provided a safe place to live and
work under the supervision of
the Levites.

Were cities of refuge common in the ancient world?
(20:2–3)
Cities of refuge were not the
typical way of handling accidental death. The Israelite law held a
high view of human life and established a principle of "innocent
until proven guilty" not seen in
other cultures at this time.

What did the avenger of
blood do? (20:3)
Also called the kinsman-redeemer, the avenger of blood was the
nearest male blood relative to
the person who had been killed.
He was obligated to even the
score for the loss of life in his
clan. The avenger did not put the
killer to death out of revenge,
however. His aim was to restore
the balance of life in society.

47 (When the territory of the Danites was lost to them,
they went up and attacked Leshem, took it, put it to the
sword and occupied it. They settled in Leshem and named it
Dan after their ancestor.)
48 These towns and their villages were the inheritance of the
tribe of Dan, according to its clans.

ALLOTMENT FOR JOSHUA

49 When they had finished dividing the land into its allotted portions, the Israelites gave Joshua son of Nun an
inheritance among them, 50 as the LORD had commanded.
They gave him the town he asked for—Timnath Serah[a] in
the hill country of Ephraim. And he built up the town and
settled there.
51 These are the territories that Eleazar the priest, Joshua son of Nun and the heads of the tribal clans of Israel
assigned by lot at Shiloh in the presence of the LORD at
the entrance to the tent of meeting. And so they finished
dividing the land.

CITIES OF REFUGE

20 Then the LORD said to Joshua: 2 "Tell the Israelites
to designate the cities of refuge, as I instructed you
through Moses, 3 so that anyone who kills a person accidentally and unintentionally may flee there and find protection
from the avenger of blood. 4 When they flee to one of these
cities, they are to stand in the entrance of the city gate and
state their case before the elders of that city. Then the elders
are to admit the fugitive into their city and provide a place
to live among them. 5 If the avenger of blood comes in pursuit, the elders must not surrender the fugitive, because the
fugitive killed their neighbor unintentionally and without
malice aforethought. 6 They are to stay in that city until they
have stood trial before the assembly and until the death of
the high priest who is serving at that time. Then they may go
back to their own home in the town from which they fled."
7 So they set apart Kedesh in Galilee in the hill country
of Naphtali, Shechem in the hill country of Ephraim, and
Kiriath Arba (that is, Hebron) in the hill country of Judah.
8 East of the Jordan (on the other side from Jericho) they
designated Bezer in the wilderness on the plateau in the tribe
of Reuben, Ramoth in Gilead in the tribe of Gad, and Golan
in Bashan in the tribe of Manasseh. 9 Any of the Israelites
or any foreigner residing among them who killed someone
accidentally could flee to these designated cities and not be
killed by the avenger of blood prior to standing trial before
the assembly.

TOWNS FOR THE LEVITES

21 Now the family heads of the Levites approached Eleazar the priest, Joshua son of Nun, and the heads of the
other tribal families of Israel 2 at Shiloh in Canaan and said to
them, "The LORD commanded through Moses that you give

[a] 50 Also known as *Timnath Heres* (see Judges 2:9)

us towns to live in, with pasturelands for our livestock." [3] So, as the LORD had commanded, the Israelites gave the Levites the following towns and pasturelands out of their own inheritance:

[4] The first lot came out for the Kohathites, according to their clans. The Levites who were descendants of Aaron the priest were allotted thirteen towns from the tribes of Judah, Simeon and Benjamin. [5] The rest of Kohath's descendants were allotted ten towns from the clans of the tribes of Ephraim, Dan and half of Manasseh.

[6] The descendants of Gershon were allotted thirteen towns from the clans of the tribes of Issachar, Asher, Naphtali and the half-tribe of Manasseh in Bashan.

[7] The descendants of Merari, according to their clans, received twelve towns from the tribes of Reuben, Gad and Zebulun.

[8] So the Israelites allotted to the Levites these towns and their pasturelands, as the LORD had commanded through Moses.

[9] From the tribes of Judah and Simeon they allotted the following towns by name [10] (these towns were assigned to the descendants of Aaron who were from the Kohathite clans of the Levites, because the first lot fell to them):

[11] They gave them Kiriath Arba (that is, Hebron), with its surrounding pastureland, in the hill country of Judah. (Arba was the forefather of Anak.) [12] But the fields and villages around the city they had given to Caleb son of Jephunneh as his possession.

[13] So to the descendants of Aaron the priest they gave Hebron (a city of refuge for one accused of murder), Libnah, [14] Jattir, Eshtemoa, [15] Holon, Debir, [16] Ain, Juttah and Beth Shemesh, together with their pasturelands—nine towns from these two tribes.

[17] And from the tribe of Benjamin they gave them Gibeon, Geba, [18] Anathoth and Almon, together with their pasturelands—four towns.

[19] The total number of towns for the priests, the descendants of Aaron, came to thirteen, together with their pasturelands.

[20] The rest of the Kohathite clans of the Levites were allotted towns from the tribe of Ephraim:

[21] In the hill country of Ephraim they were given Shechem (a city of refuge for one accused of murder) and Gezer, [22] Kibzaim and Beth Horon, together with their pasturelands—four towns.

[23] Also from the tribe of Dan they received Eltekeh, Gibbethon, [24] Aijalon and Gath Rimmon, together with their pasturelands—four towns.

[25] From half the tribe of Manasseh they received Taanach and Gath Rimmon, together with their pasturelands—two towns.

[26] All these ten towns and their pasturelands were given to the rest of the Kohathite clans.

[27] The Levite clans of the Gershonites were given:

from the half-tribe of Manasseh,
Golan in Bashan (a city of refuge for one accused of

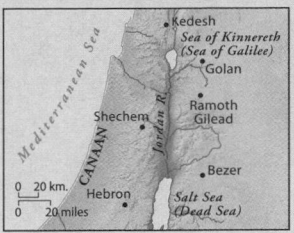

Cities of Refuge (20:7–9)

Were these towns unoccupied? (21:3)
No. Some cities were occupied by Israelites and others by Canaanites. The Canaanites would have been forced out, just as they were in other locations.

Why were the Levites scattered among the tribes? (21:3)
When Israel entered the promised land, the tribe of Levi was very small. The scattering among the other tribes fulfilled Jacob's curse on Levi for his part in the massacre at Shechem (see Genesis 49:7). But through Moses and Aaron, the Levites became a blessing to the whole nation in their role as priests.

Why were the towns of the Levites listed? (21:8–42)
Because the Levites did not inherit their own land and were spread throughout the tribes, the Israelites could pay their tithes to them. The Levites were symbols of God's presence. Giving part of what they earned from the land to the Levites reminded the Israelites that the land belonged to God.

murder) and Be Eshterah, together with their pasturelands—two towns;
²⁸from the tribe of Issachar,
    Kishion, Daberath, ²⁹Jarmuth and En Gannim, togeth-
    er with their pasturelands—four towns;
³⁰from the tribe of Asher,
    Mishal, Abdon, ³¹Helkath and Rehob, together with
    their pasturelands—four towns;
³²from the tribe of Naphtali,
    Kedesh in Galilee (a city of refuge for one accused of
    murder), Hammoth Dor and Kartan, together with
    their pasturelands—three towns.
³³The total number of towns of the Gershonite clans came
to thirteen, together with their pasturelands.

³⁴The Merarite clans (the rest of the Levites) were given:
from the tribe of Zebulun,
    Jokneam, Kartah, ³⁵Dimnah and Nahalal, together with
    their pasturelands—four towns;
³⁶from the tribe of Reuben,
    Bezer, Jahaz, ³⁷Kedemoth and Mephaath, together with
    their pasturelands—four towns;
³⁸from the tribe of Gad,
    Ramoth in Gilead (a city of refuge for one accused of
    murder), Mahanaim, ³⁹Heshbon and Jazer, together
    with their pasturelands—four towns in all.
⁴⁰The total number of towns allotted to the Merarite clans,
who were the rest of the Levites, came to twelve.

⁴¹The towns of the Levites in the territory held by the
Israelites were forty-eight in all, together with their pasturelands. ⁴²Each of these towns had pasturelands surrounding
it; this was true for all these towns.

⁴³So the LORD gave Israel all the land he had sworn to
give their ancestors, and they took possession of it and settled there. ⁴⁴The LORD gave them rest on every side, just as
he had sworn to their ancestors. Not one of their enemies
withstood them; the LORD gave all their enemies into their
hands. ⁴⁵Not one of all the LORD's good promises to Israel
failed; every one was fulfilled.

EASTERN TRIBES RETURN HOME

22 Then Joshua summoned the Reubenites, the Gadites and the half-tribe of Manasseh ²and said to
them, "You have done all that Moses the servant of the LORD
commanded, and you have obeyed me in everything I commanded. ³For a long time now—to this very day—you have
not deserted your fellow Israelites but have carried out the
mission the LORD your God gave you. ⁴Now that the LORD
your God has given them rest as he promised, return to your
homes in the land that Moses the servant of the LORD gave
you on the other side of the Jordan. ⁵But be very careful to
keep the commandment and the law that Moses the servant
of the LORD gave you: to love the LORD your God, to walk in
obedience to him, to keep his commands, to hold fast to him
and to serve him with all your heart and with all your soul."

**How did the LORD hand
their enemies over to them?
(21:44)**
God offered the land, but the
Israelites did not do their part.
They did not completely wipe out
the Canaanites.

**How long did the Israelites
spend taking over the land?
(22:3)**
The conquest of Canaan took
about seven years.

⁶Then Joshua blessed them and sent them away, and they went to their homes. ⁷(To the half-tribe of Manasseh Moses had given land in Bashan, and to the other half of the tribe Joshua gave land on the west side of the Jordan along with their fellow Israelites.) When Joshua sent them home, he blessed them, ⁸saying, "Return to your homes with your great wealth—with large herds of livestock, with silver, gold, bronze and iron, and a great quantity of clothing—and divide the plunder from your enemies with your fellow Israelites."

⁹So the Reubenites, the Gadites and the half-tribe of Manasseh left the Israelites at Shiloh in Canaan to return to Gilead, their own land, which they had acquired in accordance with the command of the LORD through Moses.

¹⁰When they came to Geliloth near the Jordan in the land of Canaan, the Reubenites, the Gadites and the half-tribe of Manasseh built an imposing altar there by the Jordan. ¹¹And when the Israelites heard that they had built the altar on the border of Canaan at Geliloth near the Jordan on the Israelite side, ¹²the whole assembly of Israel gathered at Shiloh to go to war against them.

¹³So the Israelites sent Phinehas son of Eleazar, the priest, to the land of Gilead—to Reuben, Gad and the half-tribe of Manasseh. ¹⁴With him they sent ten of the chief men, one from each of the tribes of Israel, each the head of a family division among the Israelite clans.

¹⁵When they went to Gilead—to Reuben, Gad and the half-tribe of Manasseh—they said to them: ¹⁶"The whole assembly of the LORD says: 'How could you break faith with the God of Israel like this? How could you turn away from the LORD and build yourselves an altar in rebellion against him now? ¹⁷Was not the sin of Peor enough for us? Up to this very day we have not cleansed ourselves from that sin, even though a plague fell on the community of the LORD! ¹⁸And are you now turning away from the LORD?

"'If you rebel against the LORD today, tomorrow he will be angry with the whole community of Israel. ¹⁹If the land you possess is defiled, come over to the LORD's land, where the LORD's tabernacle stands, and share the land with us. But do not rebel against the LORD or against us by building an altar for yourselves, other than the altar of the LORD our God. ²⁰When Achan son of Zerah was unfaithful in regard to the devoted things,ᵃ did not wrath come on the whole community of Israel? He was not the only one who died for his sin.'"

²¹Then Reuben, Gad and the half-tribe of Manasseh replied to the heads of the clans of Israel: ²²"The Mighty One, God, the LORD! The Mighty One, God, the LORD! He knows! And let Israel know! If this has been in rebellion or disobedience to the LORD, do not spare us this day. ²³If we have built our own altar to turn away from the LORD and to offer burnt offerings and grain offerings, or to sacrifice fellowship offerings on it, may the LORD himself call us to account.

ᵃ 20 The Hebrew term refers to the irrevocable giving over of things or persons to the LORD, often by totally destroying them.

Why were the Israelites willing to go to war over an altar? (22:10–12)
They interpreted the altar as competition for the LORD's altar in Shiloh. The other Israelites felt that if the tribes east of the Jordan River departed from the LORD, God would judge the whole nation.

What was the sin of Peor? (22:17)
At Peor, some of the Israelite men had become involved with women of Moab and Midian and had worshiped the god Baal with them. Even though God had sent a plague, this didn't remove their tendency to sin.

Why did the accused tribes repeat God's names? (22:22)
Calling on God in this way was like taking an oath. Each of the three names highlighted a different aspect of who God was.

Why did they think the Jordan River might one day mark the border of the LORD's territory? (22:25)
The eastern tribes were afraid that one day the western tribes would see the natural boundary of the river as marking the outer limit of God's territory.

Was this all a misunderstanding? (22:26–29)
Yes. The eastern tribes had not built the altar as a place to offer sacrifices. Instead, they had built a replica of God's altar to serve as a visible symbol that they worshiped the same God as the rest of the Israelites.

²⁴"No! We did it for fear that some day your descendants might say to ours, 'What do you have to do with the LORD, the God of Israel? ²⁵The LORD has made the Jordan a boundary between us and you—you Reubenites and Gadites! You have no share in the LORD.' So your descendants might cause ours to stop fearing the LORD.

²⁶"That is why we said, 'Let us get ready and build an altar—but not for burnt offerings or sacrifices.' ²⁷On the contrary, it is to be a witness between us and you and the generations that follow, that we will worship the LORD at his sanctuary with our burnt offerings, sacrifices and fellowship offerings. Then in the future your descendants will not be able to say to ours, 'You have no share in the LORD.'

²⁸"And we said, 'If they ever say this to us, or to our descendants, we will answer: Look at the replica of the LORD's altar, which our ancestors built, not for burnt offerings and sacrifices, but as a witness between us and you.'

²⁹"Far be it from us to rebel against the LORD and turn away from him today by building an altar for burnt offerings, grain offerings and sacrifices, other than the altar of the LORD our God that stands before his tabernacle."

³⁰When Phinehas the priest and the leaders of the community—the heads of the clans of the Israelites—heard what Reuben, Gad and Manasseh had to say, they were pleased. ³¹And Phinehas son of Eleazar, the priest, said to Reuben, Gad and Manasseh, "Today we know that the LORD is with us, because you have not been unfaithful to the LORD in this matter. Now you have rescued the Israelites from the LORD's hand."

³²Then Phinehas son of Eleazar, the priest, and the leaders returned to Canaan from their meeting with the Reubenites and Gadites in Gilead and reported to the Israelites. ³³They were glad to hear the report and praised God. And they talked no more about going to war against them to devastate the country where the Reubenites and the Gadites lived.

³⁴And the Reubenites and the Gadites gave the altar this name: A Witness Between Us—that the LORD is God.

JOSHUA'S FAREWELL TO THE LEADERS

23 After a long time had passed and the LORD had given Israel rest from all their enemies around them, Joshua, by then a very old man, ²summoned all Israel—their elders, leaders, judges and officials—and said to them: "I am very old. ³You yourselves have seen everything the LORD your God has done to all these nations for your sake; it was the LORD your God who fought for you. ⁴Remember how I have allotted as an inheritance for your tribes all the land of the nations that remain—the nations I conquered—between the Jordan and the Mediterranean Sea in the west. ⁵The LORD your God himself will push them out for your sake. He will drive them out before you, and you will take possession of their land, as the LORD your God promised you.

⁶"Be very strong; be careful to obey all that is written in the Book of the Law of Moses, without turning aside to the

right or to the left. ⁷Do not associate with these nations that remain among you; do not invoke the names of their gods or swear by them. You must not serve them or bow down to them. ⁸But you are to hold fast to the LORD your God, as you have until now.

⁹"The LORD has driven out before you great and powerful nations; to this day no one has been able to withstand you. ¹⁰One of you routs a thousand, because the LORD your God fights for you, just as he promised. ¹¹So be very careful to love the LORD your God.

¹²"But if you turn away and ally yourselves with the survivors of these nations that remain among you and if you intermarry with them and associate with them, ¹³then you may be sure that the LORD your God will no longer drive out these nations before you. Instead, they will become snares and traps for you, whips on your backs and thorns in your eyes, until you perish from this good land, which the LORD your God has given you.

¹⁴"Now I am about to go the way of all the earth. You know with all your heart and soul that not one of all the good promises the LORD your God gave you has failed. Every promise has been fulfilled; not one has failed. ¹⁵But just as all the good things the LORD your God has promised you have come to you, so he will bring on you all the evil things he has threatened, until the LORD your God has destroyed you from this good land he has given you. ¹⁶If you violate the covenant of the LORD your God, which he commanded you, and go and serve other gods and bow down to them, the LORD's anger will burn against you, and you will quickly perish from the good land he has given you."

THE COVENANT RENEWED AT SHECHEM

24 Then Joshua assembled all the tribes of Israel at Shechem. He summoned the elders, leaders, judges and officials of Israel, and they presented themselves before God.

²Joshua said to all the people, "This is what the LORD, the God of Israel, says: 'Long ago your ancestors, including Terah the father of Abraham and Nahor, lived beyond the Euphrates River and worshiped other gods. ³But I took your father Abraham from the land beyond the Euphrates and led him throughout Canaan and gave him many descendants. I gave him Isaac, ⁴and to Isaac I gave Jacob and Esau. I assigned the hill country of Seir to Esau, but Jacob and his family went down to Egypt.

⁵"'Then I sent Moses and Aaron, and I afflicted the Egyptians by what I did there, and I brought you out. ⁶When I brought your people out of Egypt, you came to the sea, and the Egyptians pursued them with chariots and horsemen*a* as far as the Red Sea.*b* ⁷But they cried to the LORD for help, and he put darkness between you and the Egyptians; he brought the sea over them and covered them. You saw with your own eyes what I did to the Egyptians. Then you lived in the wilderness for a long time.

What was the message behind the "snares and traps" and "thorns" for Israel? (23:13)
Traps made of nets were used to capture birds and other wild animals. Snares sprang shut with flexible branches or ropes that someone pulled. The words showed how Israel was tangled up with other nations and their idols. And before land could be used for farming, it had to be cleared of thorns and thistles. In the process, a person could be scratched, and the eye was especially sensitive. Because they hadn't cleared the Canaanites from the land, the Israelites couldn't "see" clearly, and they fell into sin.

---

a 6 Or *charioteers*   *b* 6 Or *the Sea of Reeds*

Did God actually send out hornets? (24:12)
It is possible. It's also possible that the term could refer to Egyptian troops, since the bee or hornet was one of Pharaoh's symbols. The Egyptians raided Canaan frequently, and this may have weakened Canaan before the Israelites arrived.

Why had the Israelites kept the idols belonging to their forefathers? (24:14, 23)
Israel had generally stayed faithful to God. But there had been times when the Israelites were influenced by their neighbors to worship other gods. Perhaps they kept the idols as something to fall back on if God failed to take care of them.

Why was Joshua so negative after the Israelites promised to serve the LORD? (24:19)
Joshua scolded the people for responding so quickly and confidently. Joshua wanted them to see that they were spiritually weak and unable to please a holy and jealous God. He wanted them to realize that they needed to depend on God.

Why did the people need new decrees and laws? (24:25)
They didn't. Joshua did not add to or change the Law that Moses had given. Instead, he was reconfirming the covenant.

What was the "holy place of the LORD"? (24:26)
This may have been the site of an old altar that stood in Shechem near an oak tree. This same oak tree appears in other Old Testament passages.

8 " 'I brought you to the land of the Amorites who lived east of the Jordan. They fought against you, but I gave them into your hands. I destroyed them from before you, and you took possession of their land. 9 When Balak son of Zippor, the king of Moab, prepared to fight against Israel, he sent for Balaam son of Beor to put a curse on you. 10 But I would not listen to Balaam, so he blessed you again and again, and I delivered you out of his hand.

11 " 'Then you crossed the Jordan and came to Jericho. The citizens of Jericho fought against you, as did also the Amorites, Perizzites, Canaanites, Hittites, Girgashites, Hivites and Jebusites, but I gave them into your hands. 12 I sent the hornet ahead of you, which drove them out before you—also the two Amorite kings. You did not do it with your own sword and bow. 13 So I gave you a land on which you did not toil and cities you did not build; and you live in them and eat from vineyards and olive groves that you did not plant.'

14 "Now fear the LORD and serve him with all faithfulness. Throw away the gods your ancestors worshiped beyond the Euphrates River and in Egypt, and serve the LORD. 15 But if serving the LORD seems undesirable to you, then choose for yourselves this day whom you will serve, whether the gods your ancestors served beyond the Euphrates, or the gods of the Amorites, in whose land you are living. But as for me and my household, we will serve the LORD."

16 Then the people answered, "Far be it from us to forsake the LORD to serve other gods! 17 It was the LORD our God himself who brought us and our parents up out of Egypt, from that land of slavery, and performed those great signs before our eyes. He protected us on our entire journey and among all the nations through which we traveled. 18 And the LORD drove out before us all the nations, including the Amorites, who lived in the land. We too will serve the LORD, because he is our God."

19 Joshua said to the people, "You are not able to serve the LORD. He is a holy God; he is a jealous God. He will not forgive your rebellion and your sins. 20 If you forsake the LORD and serve foreign gods, he will turn and bring disaster on you and make an end of you, after he has been good to you."

21 But the people said to Joshua, "No! We will serve the LORD."

22 Then Joshua said, "You are witnesses against yourselves that you have chosen to serve the LORD."

"Yes, we are witnesses," they replied.

23 "Now then," said Joshua, "throw away the foreign gods that are among you and yield your hearts to the LORD, the God of Israel."

24 And the people said to Joshua, "We will serve the LORD our God and obey him."

25 On that day Joshua made a covenant for the people, and there at Shechem he reaffirmed for them decrees and laws. 26 And Joshua recorded these things in the Book of the Law of God. Then he took a large stone and set it up there under the oak near the holy place of the LORD.

27 "See!" he said to all the people. "This stone will be a

witness against us. It has heard all the words the LORD has
said to us. It will be a witness against you if you are untrue
to your God."

²⁸Then Joshua dismissed the people, each to their own
inheritance.

BURIED IN THE PROMISED LAND

²⁹After these things, Joshua son of Nun, the servant of the
LORD, died at the age of a hundred and ten. ³⁰And they buried him in the land of his inheritance, at Timnath Serah*ᵃ* in
the hill country of Ephraim, north of Mount Gaash.

³¹Israel served the LORD throughout the lifetime of Joshua
and of the elders who outlived him and who had experienced
everything the LORD had done for Israel.

³²And Joseph's bones, which the Israelites had brought up
from Egypt, were buried at Shechem in the tract of land that
Jacob bought for a hundred pieces of silver*ᵇ* from the sons of
Hamor, the father of Shechem. This became the inheritance
of Joseph's descendants.

³³And Eleazar son of Aaron died and was buried at Gibeah, which had been allotted to his son Phinehas in the hill
country of Ephraim.

**Why had the people carried
the bones of Joseph with
them? (24:32)**
Before Joseph died, he made
the sons of Israel take an oath to
bury him in the promised land.
His wish to be buried in Canaan
showed his faith that God would
keep his promise to his people
(see Genesis 50:24 – 26).

ᵃ 30 Also known as *Timnath Heres* (see Judges 2:9)   *ᵇ 32* Hebrew *hundred
kesitahs*; a kesitah was a unit of money of unknown weight and value.

Judges

INTRODUCTION

Who wrote this book?
No one knows for sure. Many people think Samuel is the author.

Why was this book written?
The book of Judges shows what happened when the Israelites abandoned God to worship idols.

What happens in this book?
God's people sin again and again. God lets Israel's enemies win. When the Israelites suffer, they turn to God. Then God sends a "judge" to defeat the enemy and lead Israel.

What do we learn about God in this book?
God is eager to forgive and help people who have sinned if only they will turn to him.

Who are the key people in this book?
The most important people in this book are Deborah, Gideon, Jephthah, and Samson.

Where did this happen?
The events of this book happened in different parts of Canaan.

What are some of the stories in this book?

Deborah leads Israel	Judges 4-5
Gideon asks God for a sign	Judges 6
Gideon defeats the Midianites	Judges 7
Jephthah defeats the Ammonites	Judges 11-12
Samson's special birth	Judges 13
Samson's marriage	Judges 14
Samson's revenge	Judges 15
Samson and Delilah	Judges 16

When did these things happen?

1400 BC 1300 1200 1100 1000 900 800 700 600 500 400

ISRAELITES ENTER CANAAN (C. 1406 BC)

DEBORAH'S RULE (C. 1209 – 1169 BC)

GIDEON'S RULE (C. 1162 – 1122 BC)

SAMUEL'S BIRTH (C. 1105 BC)

JEPHTHAH'S RULE (C. 1078 – 1072 BC)

SAMSON'S RULE (C. 1075 – 1055 BC)

BOOK OF JUDGES WRITTEN (C. 1000 BC)

DIVISION OF THE KINGDOM (930 BC)

ISRAEL FIGHTS THE REMAINING CANAANITES

1 After the death of Joshua, the Israelites asked the LORD, "Who of us is to go up first to fight against the Canaanites?"

²The LORD answered, "Judah shall go up; I have given the land into their hands."

³The men of Judah then said to the Simeonites their fellow Israelites, "Come up with us into the territory allotted to us, to fight against the Canaanites. We in turn will go with you into yours." So the Simeonites went with them.

⁴When Judah attacked, the LORD gave the Canaanites and Perizzites into their hands, and they struck down ten thousand men at Bezek. ⁵It was there that they found Adoni-Bezek and fought against him, putting to rout the Canaanites and Perizzites. ⁶Adoni-Bezek fled, but they chased him and caught him, and cut off his thumbs and big toes.

⁷Then Adoni-Bezek said, "Seventy kings with their thumbs and big toes cut off have picked up scraps under my table. Now God has paid me back for what I did to them." They brought him to Jerusalem, and he died there.

⁸The men of Judah attacked Jerusalem also and took it. They put the city to the sword and set it on fire.

⁹After that, Judah went down to fight against the Canaanites living in the hill country, the Negev and the western foothills. ¹⁰They advanced against the Canaanites living in Hebron (formerly called Kiriath Arba) and defeated Sheshai, Ahiman and Talmai. ¹¹From there they advanced against the people living in Debir (formerly called Kiriath Sepher).

¹²And Caleb said, "I will give my daughter Aksah in marriage to the man who attacks and captures Kiriath Sepher." ¹³Othniel son of Kenaz, Caleb's younger brother, took it; so Caleb gave his daughter Aksah to him in marriage.

¹⁴One day when she came to Othniel, she urged him*a* to ask her father for a field. When she got off her donkey, Caleb asked her, "What can I do for you?"

¹⁵She replied, "Do me a special favor. Since you have given me land in the Negev, give me also springs of water." So Caleb gave her the upper and lower springs.

¹⁶The descendants of Moses' father-in-law, the Kenite, went up from the City of Palms*b* with the people of Judah to live among the inhabitants of the Desert of Judah in the Negev near Arad.

¹⁷Then the men of Judah went with the Simeonites their fellow Israelites and attacked the Canaanites living in Zephath, and they totally destroyed*c* the city. Therefore it was called Hormah.*d* ¹⁸Judah also took*e* Gaza, Ashkelon and Ekron—each city with its territory.

¹⁹The LORD was with the men of Judah. They took possession of the hill country, but they were unable to drive the people from the plains, because they had chariots fitted with iron. ²⁰As Moses had promised, Hebron was given to Caleb, who

---

a 14 Hebrew; Septuagint and Vulgate *Othniel, he urged her*   *b 16* That is, Jericho   *c 17* The Hebrew term refers to the irrevocable giving over of things or persons to the LORD, often by totally destroying them.
d 17 Hormah means *destruction.*   *e 18* Hebrew; Septuagint *Judah did not take*

How did the Israelites hear from God? (1:1–2)
The priest used the Urim and Thummim to receive yes or no answers from God (see Exodus 28:30).

Judah's Fight for Land (1:4)

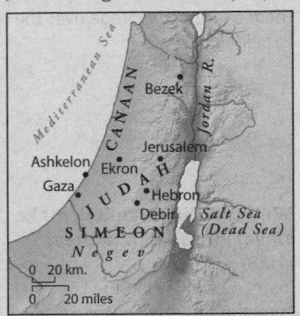

Why did they cut off the king's thumbs and big toes? (1:6)
This practice was common in the ancient Middle East. Cutting off a prisoner's thumbs would make him unable to hold a weapon. Cutting off his toes would make him unable to run in battle. The defeated king understood his punishment because he had done the same thing to prisoners his army had taken.

Why would Caleb give his daughter away? (1:12–13)
Traditionally, a groom paid a bride-price to the father when he married one of his daughters. This helped cover the cost of losing the daughter, who was valued for her work. Because Caleb wanted to achieve a victory, he dropped the bride-price and offered his daughter Aksah to the man who defeated the city of Kiriath Sepher.

What was the City of Palms? (1:16)
This was another name for Jericho.

What was so special about iron chariots? (1:19)
Chariots were difficult to fight against because they could travel fast and maneuver quickly. When they had iron parts, such as

axles, they were almost unbeatable. During the shift from the bronze to the iron age (around 1200 BC), the Canaanites guarded the secrets of metal-making and iron became as valuable as gold and silver. The Philistines also had iron weapons, which gave them a large advantage over the Israelites.

Why did the Israelites make slaves of the Canaanites? (1:28)
Instead of following the LORD's command to drive out the Canaanites, the Israelites turned them into slaves. Having servants to do the work made the Israelites' life easier, but there would be negative consequences later on.

drove from it the three sons of Anak. [21] The Benjamites, however, did not drive out the Jebusites, who were living in Jerusalem; to this day the Jebusites live there with the Benjamites. [22] Now the tribes of Joseph attacked Bethel, and the LORD was with them. [23] When they sent men to spy out Bethel (formerly called Luz), [24] the spies saw a man coming out of the city and they said to him, "Show us how to get into the city and we will see that you are treated well." [25] So he showed them, and they put the city to the sword but spared the man and his whole family. [26] He then went to the land of the Hittites, where he built a city and called it Luz, which is its name to this day.

[27] But Manasseh did not drive out the people of Beth Shan or Taanach or Dor or Ibleam or Megiddo and their surrounding settlements, for the Canaanites were determined to live in that land. [28] When Israel became strong, they pressed the Canaanites into forced labor but never drove them out completely. [29] Nor did Ephraim drive out the Canaanites living in Gezer, but the Canaanites continued to live there among them. [30] Neither did Zebulun drive out the Canaanites living in Kitron or Nahalol, so these Canaanites lived among them, but Zebulun did subject them to forced labor. [31] Nor did Asher drive out those living in Akko or Sidon or Ahlab or Akzib or Helbah or Aphek or Rehob. [32] The Asherites lived among the Canaanite inhabitants of the land because they did not drive them out. [33] Neither did Naphtali drive out those living in Beth Shemesh or Beth Anath; but the Naphtalites too lived among the Canaanite inhabitants of the land, and those living in Beth Shemesh and Beth Anath became forced laborers for them. [34] The Amorites confined the Danites to the hill country, not allowing them to come down into the plain. [35] And the Amorites were determined also to hold out in Mount Heres, Aijalon and Shaalbim, but when the power of the tribes of Joseph increased, they too were pressed into forced labor. [36] The boundary of the Amorites was from Scorpion Pass to Sela and beyond.

THE ANGEL OF THE LORD AT BOKIM

2 The angel of the LORD went up from Gilgal to Bokim and said, "I brought you up out of Egypt and led you into the land I swore to give to your ancestors. I said, 'I will never break my covenant with you, [2] and you shall not make a covenant with the people of this land, but you shall break down their altars.' Yet you have disobeyed me. Why have you done this? [3] And I have also said, 'I will not drive them out before you; they will become traps for you, and their gods will become snares to you.'"

[4] When the angel of the LORD had spoken these things to all the Israelites, the people wept aloud, [5] and they called that place Bokim.[a] There they offered sacrifices to the LORD.

DISOBEDIENCE AND DEFEAT

[6] After Joshua had dismissed the Israelites, they went to take possession of the land, each to their own inheritance.

What was the angel of the LORD? (2:1, 4)
Some think this was God in human form. Others think that it was an angel or spirit sent by God or perhaps a prophet or a priest.

Why did the people offer sacrifices? (2:5)
It may have been to show their sorrow for their sins, or by doing so they may have hoped to avoid the predicted trouble with the Canaanites.

---

[a] 5 *Bokim* means *weepers*.

[7]The people served the LORD throughout the lifetime of Joshua and of the elders who outlived him and who had seen all the great things the LORD had done for Israel.

[8]Joshua son of Nun, the servant of the LORD, died at the age of a hundred and ten. [9]And they buried him in the land of his inheritance, at Timnath Heres[a] in the hill country of Ephraim, north of Mount Gaash.

[10]After that whole generation had been gathered to their ancestors, another generation grew up who knew neither the LORD nor what he had done for Israel. [11]Then the Israelites did evil in the eyes of the LORD and served the Baals. [12]They forsook the LORD, the God of their ancestors, who had brought them out of Egypt. They followed and worshiped various gods of the peoples around them. They aroused the LORD's anger [13]because they forsook him and served Baal and the Ashtoreths. [14]In his anger against Israel the LORD gave them into the hands of raiders who plundered them. He sold them into the hands of their enemies all around, whom they were no longer able to resist. [15]Whenever Israel went out to fight, the hand of the LORD was against them to defeat them, just as he had sworn to them. They were in great distress.

[16]Then the LORD raised up judges,[b] who saved them out of the hands of these raiders. [17]Yet they would not listen to their judges but prostituted themselves to other gods and worshiped them. They quickly turned from the ways of their ancestors, who had been obedient to the LORD's commands. [18]Whenever the LORD raised up a judge for them, he was with the judge and saved them out of the hands of their enemies as long as the judge lived; for the LORD relented because of their groaning under those who oppressed and afflicted them. [19]But when the judge died, the people returned to ways even more corrupt than those of their ancestors, following other gods and serving and worshiping them. They refused to give up their evil practices and stubborn ways.

[20]Therefore the LORD was very angry with Israel and said, "Because this nation has violated the covenant I ordained for their ancestors and has not listened to me, [21]I will no longer drive out before them any of the nations Joshua left when he died. [22]I will use them to test Israel and see whether they will keep the way of the LORD and walk in it as their

[a] 9 Also known as *Timnath Serah* (see Joshua 19:50 and 24:30)
[b] 16 Or *leaders*; similarly in verses 17–19

How could a whole generation not know the LORD? (2:10)
The Israelites had failed to teach their children about God, in spite of his frequent reminders that parents were to tell their children about the great things he had done. The Israelites became too comfortable with their Canaanite neighbors' beliefs and gradually forgot about God.

Who was Baal? (2:13)
Baal was the god worshiped by the Canaanites and Phoenicians. As the god of fertility, he was pictured as standing on a bull, a symbol of strength. The worship of Baal often involved prostitution and even child sacrifice.

Who were the Ashtoreths? (2:13)
These were female gods such as Ashtoreth and Asherah. Ashtoreth was the goddess of war and fertility. The worship of these goddesses often included immoral practices.

Why did the people need judges to help them stay faithful to God? (2:19)
Without strong leadership, the people of Israel stopped following the LORD and adopted the practices of their pagan neighbors. Though most of the judges were strong military leaders, they lacked the spiritual knowledge that a high priest or prophet possessed. But when a judge died after liberating the people, the people fell back into idolatry.

What pattern or cycle took place during the time of the judges?
JUDGES 2

The pattern had four parts and is summed up in Judges 2:16–19. First, the Israelites would fall away from God. They would forget about God's covenant with them, and they would disobey God's law by worshiping pagan gods. Second, God would be angry with the Israelites and would punish them by allowing the Canaanites to attack and oppress them. Third, the Israelites would ask God to deliver them from the other tribes. They would also repent of their sin of worshiping pagan gods, and they would turn back to God and ask him to forgive them. Finally, God would send a judge who would deliver them from their difficult situation. After things settled down, the people would become comfortable and forget what happened when they broke God's laws, so the cycle would start all over again.

Why did God want them to learn warfare? (3:2)
The LORD taught the Israelites how to protect themselves from their enemies and to test their obedience.

What were the signs that God had appointed Othniel as judge? (3:10)
Othniel probably displayed outstanding leadership abilities. The people could tell that God had given him wisdom, courage, and strength.

How did Ehud manage to kill the king? (3:15–21)
Because he was left-handed, Ehud strapped a dagger to his right leg. When the guards checked him before he went in to the king's room, they probably looked at his left leg, which is where right-handed people would strap a weapon.

What were the stone images near Gilgal? (3:19)
They may have been stone statues of King Eglon that marked the boundaries of his land. They may also have been the stones Joshua set up after the Israelites crossed the Jordan River (see Joshua 4:19–24).

ancestors did." ²³The LORD had allowed those nations to remain; he did not drive them out at once by giving them into the hands of Joshua.

3 These are the nations the LORD left to test all those Israelites who had not experienced any of the wars in Canaan ²(he did this only to teach warfare to the descendants of the Israelites who had not had previous battle experience): ³the five rulers of the Philistines, all the Canaanites, the Sidonians, and the Hivites living in the Lebanon mountains from Mount Baal Hermon to Lebo Hamath. ⁴They were left to test the Israelites to see whether they would obey the LORD's commands, which he had given their ancestors through Moses.

⁵The Israelites lived among the Canaanites, Hittites, Amorites, Perizzites, Hivites and Jebusites. ⁶They took their daughters in marriage and gave their own daughters to their sons, and served their gods.

OTHNIEL

⁷The Israelites did evil in the eyes of the LORD; they forgot the LORD their God and served the Baals and the Asherahs. ⁸The anger of the LORD burned against Israel so that he sold them into the hands of Cushan-Rishathaim king of Aram Naharaim,ᵃ to whom the Israelites were subject for eight years. ⁹But when they cried out to the LORD, he raised up for them a deliverer, Othniel son of Kenaz, Caleb's younger brother, who saved them. ¹⁰The Spirit of the LORD came on him, so that he became Israel's judgeᵇ and went to war. The LORD gave Cushan-Rishathaim king of Aram into the hands of Othniel, who overpowered him. ¹¹So the land had peace for forty years, until Othniel son of Kenaz died.

EHUD

¹²Again the Israelites did evil in the eyes of the LORD, and because they did this evil the LORD gave Eglon king of Moab power over Israel. ¹³Getting the Ammonites and Amalekites to join him, Eglon came and attacked Israel, and they took possession of the City of Palms.ᶜ ¹⁴The Israelites were subject to Eglon king of Moab for eighteen years.

¹⁵Again the Israelites cried out to the LORD, and he gave them a deliverer—Ehud, a left-handed man, the son of Gera the Benjamite. The Israelites sent him with tribute to Eglon king of Moab. ¹⁶Now Ehud had made a double-edged sword about a cubitᵈ long, which he strapped to his right thigh under his clothing. ¹⁷He presented the tribute to Eglon king of Moab, who was a very fat man. ¹⁸After Ehud had presented the tribute, he sent on their way those who had carried it. ¹⁹But on reaching the stone images near Gilgal he himself went back to Eglon and said, "Your Majesty, I have a secret message for you."

The king said to his attendants, "Leave us!" And they all left.

ᵃ 8 That is, Northwest Mesopotamia   ᵇ 10 Or leader   ᶜ 13 That is, Jericho   ᵈ 16 That is, about 18 inches or about 45 centimeters

²⁰Ehud then approached him while he was sitting alone in the upper room of his palace*ᵃ* and said, "I have a message from God for you." As the king rose from his seat, ²¹Ehud reached with his left hand, drew the sword from his right thigh and plunged it into the king's belly. ²²Even the handle sank in after the blade, and his bowels discharged. Ehud did not pull the sword out, and the fat closed in over it. ²³Then Ehud went out to the porch*ᵇ*; he shut the doors of the upper room behind him and locked them.

²⁴After he had gone, the servants came and found the doors of the upper room locked. They said, "He must be relieving himself in the inner room of the palace." ²⁵They waited to the point of embarrassment, but when he did not open the doors of the room, they took a key and unlocked them. There they saw their lord fallen to the floor, dead.

²⁶While they waited, Ehud got away. He passed by the stone images and escaped to Seirah. ²⁷When he arrived there, he blew a trumpet in the hill country of Ephraim, and the Israelites went down with him from the hills, with him leading them.

²⁸"Follow me," he ordered, "for the LORD has given Moab, your enemy, into your hands." So they followed him down and took possession of the fords of the Jordan that led to Moab; they allowed no one to cross over. ²⁹At that time they struck down about ten thousand Moabites, all vigorous and strong; not one escaped. ³⁰That day Moab was made subject to Israel, and the land had peace for eighty years.

SHAMGAR

³¹After Ehud came Shamgar son of Anath, who struck down six hundred Philistines with an oxgoad. He too saved Israel.

DEBORAH

4 Again the Israelites did evil in the eyes of the LORD, now that Ehud was dead. ²So the LORD sold them into the hands of Jabin king of Canaan, who reigned in Hazor. Sisera, the commander of his army, was based in Harosheth Haggoyim. ³Because he had nine hundred chariots fitted with iron and had cruelly oppressed the Israelites for twenty years, they cried to the LORD for help.

⁴Now Deborah, a prophet, the wife of Lappidoth, was leading*ᶜ* Israel at that time. ⁵She held court under the Palm of Deborah between Ramah and Bethel in the hill country of Ephraim, and the Israelites went up to her to have their disputes decided. ⁶She sent for Barak son of Abinoam from Kedesh in Naphtali and said to him, "The LORD, the God of Israel, commands you: 'Go, take with you ten thousand men of Naphtali and Zebulun and lead them up to Mount Tabor. ⁷I will lead Sisera, the commander of Jabin's army, with his chariots and his troops to the Kishon River and give him into your hands.'"

ᵃ 20 The meaning of the Hebrew for this word is uncertain; also in verse 24.
ᵇ 23 The meaning of the Hebrew for this word is uncertain.
ᶜ 4 Traditionally judging

Who was Shamgar? (3:31)
There is only one verse describing this judge. He killed 600 Philistines with an oxgoad, a long, wooden rod (sometimes with a metal tip) used to drive animals. The word *oxgoad* means "an instrument of learning."

How did the LORD sell his people? (4:1–2)
By letting them be defeated by a pagan tribe, the LORD "sold them" by allowing them to become slaves to Jabin.

Deborah Defeats King Jabin (4:2)

How did a woman become a judge in this male-dominated society? (4:4)
Deborah probably had strong leadership abilities. Even though it was rare for a woman to have a position like this, God had not forbidden it. In fact, God blessed her for her trust in him. Deborah is the only judge described as a prophet.

Why did Barak ask Deborah to go with him? (4:8)

It was a known fact that Deborah could hear the voice of God. In order to ensure that God would be with them and help them defeat their enemies, Barak thought it would be a good idea for her to come with him.

Who were the Kenites? (4:11)

The Kenites were descendants of Hobab, the brother-in-law of Moses. When the Israelites left Sinai, Moses invited Hobab to come with them to act as a guide (see Numbers 10:29–32). Hobab's descendants were friendly with Israel and traveled with Judah from Jericho (see 1:16).

Why was Jael's tent a good hiding place? (4:18)

Ancient custom prohibited any man other than a woman's father or husband from entering her tent. No one would have thought to look for Sisera there.

Why was Deborah's song included in a book of history? (5:1)

The song of Deborah and Barak praised God for their victory. It applauded the tribes that allied with Israel, and looked down on those that did not. Songs were often used throughout Israel's history and were an excellent teaching tool.

⁸Barak said to her, "If you go with me, I will go; but if you don't go with me, I won't go."

⁹"Certainly I will go with you," said Deborah. "But because of the course you are taking, the honor will not be yours, for the LORD will deliver Sisera into the hands of a woman." So Deborah went with Barak to Kedesh. ¹⁰There Barak summoned Zebulun and Naphtali, and ten thousand men went up under his command. Deborah also went up with him.

¹¹Now Heber the Kenite had left the other Kenites, the descendants of Hobab, Moses' brother-in-law,ᵃ and pitched his tent by the great tree in Zaanannim near Kedesh.

¹²When they told Sisera that Barak son of Abinoam had gone up to Mount Tabor, ¹³Sisera summoned from Harosheth Haggoyim to the Kishon River all his men and his nine hundred chariots fitted with iron.

¹⁴Then Deborah said to Barak, "Go! This is the day the LORD has given Sisera into your hands. Has not the LORD gone ahead of you?" So Barak went down Mount Tabor, with ten thousand men following him. ¹⁵At Barak's advance, the LORD routed Sisera and all his chariots and army by the sword, and Sisera got down from his chariot and fled on foot.

¹⁶Barak pursued the chariots and army as far as Harosheth Haggoyim, and all Sisera's troops fell by the sword; not a man was left. ¹⁷Sisera, meanwhile, fled on foot to the tent of Jael, the wife of Heber the Kenite, because there was an alliance between Jabin king of Hazor and the family of Heber the Kenite.

¹⁸Jael went out to meet Sisera and said to him, "Come, my lord, come right in. Don't be afraid." So he entered her tent, and she covered him with a blanket.

¹⁹"I'm thirsty," he said. "Please give me some water." She opened a skin of milk, gave him a drink, and covered him up.

²⁰"Stand in the doorway of the tent," he told her. "If someone comes by and asks you, 'Is anyone in there?' say 'No.'"

²¹But Jael, Heber's wife, picked up a tent peg and a hammer and went quietly to him while he lay fast asleep, exhausted. She drove the peg through his temple into the ground, and he died.

²²Just then Barak came by in pursuit of Sisera, and Jael went out to meet him. "Come," she said, "I will show you the man you're looking for." So he went in with her, and there lay Sisera with the tent peg through his temple—dead.

²³On that day God subdued Jabin king of Canaan before the Israelites. ²⁴And the hand of the Israelites pressed harder and harder against Jabin king of Canaan until they destroyed him.

THE SONG OF DEBORAH

5 On that day Deborah and Barak son of Abinoam sang this song:

²"When the princes in Israel take the lead,
   when the people willingly offer themselves—
      praise the LORD!

ᵃ 11 Or father-in-law

³ "Hear this, you kings! Listen, you rulers!
　　I, even I, will sing to^a the LORD;
　　I will praise the LORD, the God of Israel, in song.

⁴ "When you, LORD, went out from Seir,
　　when you marched from the land of Edom,
　the earth shook, the heavens poured,
　　the clouds poured down water.
⁵ The mountains quaked before the LORD,
　　　the One of Sinai,
　　before the LORD, the God of Israel.

⁶ "In the days of Shamgar son of Anath,
　　in the days of Jael, the highways
　　　were abandoned;
　　travelers took to winding paths.
⁷ Villagers in Israel would not fight;
　　they held back until I, Deborah, arose,
　　until I arose, a mother in Israel.
⁸ God chose new leaders
　　when war came to the city gates,
　but not a shield or spear was seen
　　among forty thousand in Israel.
⁹ My heart is with Israel's princes,
　　with the willing volunteers among the people.
　　Praise the LORD!

¹⁰ "You who ride on white donkeys,
　　sitting on your saddle blankets,
　　and you who walk along the road,
　consider ¹¹ the voice of the singers^b at the watering
　　　places.
　　They recite the victories of the LORD,
　　the victories of his villagers in Israel.

　"Then the people of the LORD
　　went down to the city gates.
¹² 'Wake up, wake up, Deborah!
　　Wake up, wake up, break out in song!
　Arise, Barak!
　　Take captive your captives, son of Abinoam.'

¹³ "The remnant of the nobles came down;
　　the people of the LORD came down to me against
　　　the mighty.
¹⁴ Some came from Ephraim, whose roots were in
　　　Amalek;
　　Benjamin was with the people who followed you.
　From Makir captains came down,
　　from Zebulun those who bear a
　　　commander's^b staff.
¹⁵ The princes of Issachar were with Deborah;
　　yes, Issachar was with Barak,
　　sent under his command into the valley.
　In the districts of Reuben
　　there was much searching of heart.

^a 3 Or of　　^b 11,14 The meaning of the Hebrew for this word is uncertain.

Why were the roads abandoned? (5:6)
Life had become difficult and violent. Travelers took the back paths rather than the main roads in order to avoid robbers.

How did village life cease? (5:7)
The farmers who lived in small, unprotected villages would not have been safe. So they either went into hiding or moved to walled towns for safety.

If the Israelites didn't have swords or spears, how did they fight? (5:8)
Israel's enemies tried to disarm them by taking away their weapons and by forbidding blacksmiths from working so they couldn't make spears or swords. The song may be an exaggeration because some of the Israelites probably had hidden weapons or had created makeshift ones.

Why didn't all the tribes fight? (5:15–17)
Although some of the tribes joined forces with Deborah and Barak, several others did not. Deborah was not pleased by their refusal to help. By not fighting with Deborah and Barak, the other tribes showed their true mentality. They did not consider all of the tribes a single nation. They selfishly only cared about the well-being of their own tribe.

16 Why did you stay among the sheep pens[a]
    to hear the whistling for the flocks?
In the districts of Reuben
    there was much searching of heart.
17 Gilead stayed beyond the Jordan.
    And Dan, why did he linger by the ships?
Asher remained on the coast
    and stayed in his coves.
18 The people of Zebulun risked their very lives;
    so did Naphtali on the terraced fields.

19 "Kings came, they fought,
    the kings of Canaan fought.
At Taanach, by the waters of Megiddo,
    they took no plunder of silver.
20 From the heavens the stars fought,
    from their courses they fought
        against Sisera.
21 The river Kishon swept them away,
    the age-old river, the river Kishon.
March on, my soul; be strong!
22 Then thundered the horses' hooves—
    galloping, galloping go his mighty steeds.
23 'Curse Meroz,' said the angel of the LORD.
    'Curse its people bitterly,
because they did not come to help the LORD,
    to help the LORD against the mighty.'

24 "Most blessed of women be Jael,
    the wife of Heber the Kenite,
    most blessed of tent-dwelling women.
25 He asked for water, and she gave him milk;
    in a bowl fit for nobles she brought him curdled
        milk.
26 Her hand reached for the tent peg,
    her right hand for the workman's hammer.
She struck Sisera, she crushed his head,
    she shattered and pierced his temple.
27 At her feet he sank,
    he fell; there he lay.
At her feet he sank, he fell;
    where he sank, there he fell—dead.

28 "Through the window peered Sisera's mother;
    behind the lattice she cried out,
'Why is his chariot so long in coming?
    Why is the clatter of his chariots delayed?'
29 The wisest of her ladies answer her;
    indeed, she keeps saying to herself,
30 'Are they not finding and dividing the spoils:
    a woman or two for each man,
colorful garments as plunder for Sisera,
    colorful garments embroidered,
highly embroidered garments for my neck—
    all this as plunder?'

---

[a] 16 Or the campfires; or the saddlebags

Where did the battle take place? (5:19–23)
Sisera chose the Valley of Jezreel along the Kishon River as the place for battle so that his chariots would have room to maneuver. But God fought from heaven, using a storm and a flood to defeat Sisera.

Why does the song mention Sisera's mother? (5:28–30)
This is a poetic account of how Sisera's mother may have reacted. It was meant to contrast the grief of the defeated enemies with the joy of the victorious Israelites.

³¹"So may all your enemies perish, LORD!
    But may all who love you be like the sun
        when it rises in its strength."

Then the land had peace forty years.

GIDEON

6 The Israelites did evil in the eyes of the LORD, and for seven years he gave them into the hands of the Midianites. ²Because the power of Midian was so oppressive, the Israelites prepared shelters for themselves in mountain clefts, caves and strongholds. ³Whenever the Israelites planted their crops, the Midianites, Amalekites and other eastern peoples invaded the country. ⁴They camped on the land and ruined the crops all the way to Gaza and did not spare a living thing for Israel, neither sheep nor cattle nor donkeys. ⁵They came up with their livestock and their tents like swarms of locusts. It was impossible to count them or their camels; they invaded the land to ravage it. ⁶Midian so impoverished the Israelites that they cried out to the LORD for help.

⁷When the Israelites cried out to the LORD because of Midian, ⁸he sent them a prophet, who said, "This is what the LORD, the God of Israel, says: I brought you up out of Egypt, out of the land of slavery. ⁹I rescued you from the hand of the Egyptians. And I delivered you from the hand of all your oppressors; I drove them out before you and gave you their land. ¹⁰I said to you, 'I am the LORD your God; do not worship the gods of the Amorites, in whose land you live.' But you have not listened to me."

¹¹The angel of the LORD came and sat down under the oak in Ophrah that belonged to Joash the Abiezrite, where his son Gideon was threshing wheat in a winepress to keep it from the Midianites. ¹²When the angel of the LORD appeared to Gideon, he said, "The LORD is with you, mighty warrior."

¹³"Pardon me, my lord," Gideon replied, "but if the LORD is with us, why has all this happened to us? Where are all his wonders that our ancestors told us about when they said, 'Did not the LORD bring us up out of Egypt?' But now the LORD has abandoned us and given us into the hand of Midian."

¹⁴The LORD turned to him and said, "Go in the strength you have and save Israel out of Midian's hand. Am I not sending you?"

¹⁵"Pardon me, my lord," Gideon replied, "but how can I save Israel? My clan is the weakest in Manasseh, and I am the least in my family."

¹⁶The LORD answered, "I will be with you, and you will strike down all the Midianites, leaving none alive."

¹⁷Gideon replied, "If now I have found favor in your eyes, give me a sign that it is really you talking to me. ¹⁸Please do not go away until I come back and bring my offering and set it before you."

And the LORD said, "I will wait until you return."

¹⁹Gideon went inside, prepared a young goat, and from

Why did the Midianites destroy Israel's crops? (6:4)
This common wartime practice weakened the Israelites, who struggled to survive. Without food, the Israelites would be too weak to fight back. The Midianites also may have taken some of the crops for themselves.

Why was Gideon threshing wheat in a winepress? (6:11)
The winepress would have been a very tight space, but Gideon probably felt safer threshing in secret than in a more open area.

Was this visitor an angel or the LORD? (6:11, 14)
Both terms are used to describe the visitor. God appeared in human or angelic form several times during the Old Testament in order to communicate directly with human beings.

Why did Gideon think he would not be able to save Israel? (6:15)
Gideon said his clan was the weakest of his tribe, and he was one of the least important members of the clan. But the LORD chose him, just as the LORD often chose people who were poor or appeared unqualified to carry out his work.

Why did Gideon ask for a sign? (6:17)
Gideon wanted to be sure that the message was truly from God and that the things the messenger had said would come true. The LORD agreed to give him a sign.

an ephah*ᵃ* of flour he made bread without yeast. Putting the meat in a basket and its broth in a pot, he brought them out and offered them to him under the oak.

²⁰The angel of God said to him, "Take the meat and the unleavened bread, place them on this rock, and pour out the broth." And Gideon did so. ²¹Then the angel of the LORD touched the meat and the unleavened bread with the tip of the staff that was in his hand. Fire flared from the rock, consuming the meat and the bread. And the angel of the LORD disappeared. ²²When Gideon realized that it was the angel of the LORD, he exclaimed, "Alas, Sovereign LORD! I have seen the angel of the LORD face to face!"

²³But the LORD said to him, "Peace! Do not be afraid. You are not going to die."

²⁴So Gideon built an altar to the LORD there and called it The LORD Is Peace. To this day it stands in Ophrah of the Abiezrites.

²⁵That same night the LORD said to him, "Take the second bull from your father's herd, the one seven years old.*ᵇ* Tear down your father's altar to Baal and cut down the Asherah pole*ᶜ* beside it. ²⁶Then build a proper kind of*ᵈ* altar to the LORD your God on the top of this height. Using the wood of the Asherah pole that you cut down, offer the second*ᵉ* bull as a burnt offering."

²⁷So Gideon took ten of his servants and did as the LORD told him. But because he was afraid of his family and the townspeople, he did it at night rather than in the daytime.

²⁸In the morning when the people of the town got up, there was Baal's altar, demolished, with the Asherah pole beside it cut down and the second bull sacrificed on the newly built altar!

²⁹They asked each other, "Who did this?"

When they carefully investigated, they were told, "Gideon son of Joash did it."

³⁰The people of the town demanded of Joash, "Bring out your son. He must die, because he has broken down Baal's altar and cut down the Asherah pole beside it."

³¹But Joash replied to the hostile crowd around him, "Are you going to plead Baal's cause? Are you trying to save him? Whoever fights for him shall be put to death by morning! If Baal really is a god, he can defend himself when someone breaks down his altar." ³²So because Gideon broke down Baal's altar, they gave him the name Jerub-Baal*ᶠ* that day, saying, "Let Baal contend with him."

³³Now all the Midianites, Amalekites and other eastern peoples joined forces and crossed over the Jordan and camped in the Valley of Jezreel. ³⁴Then the Spirit of the LORD came on Gideon, and he blew a trumpet, summoning the Abiezrites to follow him. ³⁵He sent messengers throughout Manasseh, calling them to arms, and also into Asher, Zebulun and Naphtali, so that they too went up to meet them.

Why did God choose someone whose family worshiped Baal? (6:25)
Gideon's family worshiped God along with pagan gods. Unfortunately, this was common in Israel during this time. Gideon was uncertain he was the right person to lead the Israelites. He knew he had his weaknesses and shortcomings. But God gave him the ability to be a courageous leader.

ᵃ 19 That is, probably about 36 pounds or about 16 kilograms
ᵇ 25 Or *Take a full-grown, mature bull from your father's herd*   *ᶜ 25* That is, a wooden symbol of the goddess Asherah; also in verses 26, 28 and 30
ᵈ 26 Or *build with layers of stone an*   *ᵉ 26* Or *full-grown*; also in verse 28
ᶠ 32 Jerub-Baal probably means *let Baal contend*.

³⁶Gideon said to God, "If you will save Israel by my hand as you have promised— ³⁷look, I will place a wool fleece on the threshing floor. If there is dew only on the fleece and all the ground is dry, then I will know that you will save Israel by my hand, as you said." ³⁸And that is what happened. Gideon rose early the next day; he squeezed the fleece and wrung out the dew—a bowlful of water.

³⁹Then Gideon said to God, "Do not be angry with me. Let me make just one more request. Allow me one more test with the fleece, but this time make the fleece dry and let the ground be covered with dew." ⁴⁰That night God did so. Only the fleece was dry; all the ground was covered with dew.

GIDEON DEFEATS THE MIDIANITES

7 Early in the morning, Jerub-Baal (that is, Gideon) and all his men camped at the spring of Harod. The camp of Midian was north of them in the valley near the hill of Moreh. ²The LORD said to Gideon, "You have too many men. I cannot deliver Midian into their hands, or Israel would boast against me, 'My own strength has saved me.' ³Now announce to the army, 'Anyone who trembles with fear may turn back and leave Mount Gilead.'" So twenty-two thousand men left, while ten thousand remained.

⁴But the LORD said to Gideon, "There are still too many men. Take them down to the water, and I will thin them out for you there. If I say, 'This one shall go with you,' he shall go; but if I say, 'This one shall not go with you,' he shall not go."

⁵So Gideon took the men down to the water. There the LORD told him, "Separate those who lap the water with their tongues as a dog laps from those who kneel down to drink." ⁶Three hundred of them drank from cupped hands, lapping like dogs. All the rest got down on their knees to drink.

⁷The LORD said to Gideon, "With the three hundred men that lapped I will save you and give the Midianites into your hands. Let all the others go home." ⁸So Gideon sent the rest of the Israelites home but kept the three hundred, who took over the provisions and trumpets of the others.

Now the camp of Midian lay below him in the valley. ⁹During that night the LORD said to Gideon, "Get up, go down against the camp, because I am going to give it into your hands. ¹⁰If you are afraid to attack, go down to the camp with your servant Purah ¹¹and listen to what they are saying. Afterward, you will be encouraged to attack the camp." So he and Purah his servant went down to the outposts of the camp. ¹²The Midianites, the Amalekites and all the other eastern peoples had settled in the valley, thick as locusts. Their camels could no more be counted than the sand on the seashore.

¹³Gideon arrived just as a man was telling a friend his dream. "I had a dream," he was saying. "A round loaf of barley bread came tumbling into the Midianite camp. It struck the tent with such force that the tent overturned and collapsed." ¹⁴His friend responded, "This can be nothing other than the sword of Gideon son of Joash, the Israelite. God has given the Midianites and the whole camp into his hands."

Did Gideon have a strong faith? (6:36–40)
Gideon lacked confidence to do what he was being asked to do. God had assured him of his presence (6:12) and had promised to use Gideon to deliver Israel. God had also given him a sign by setting fire to his offering. Now Gideon wanted further proof by setting out the fleece — twice. The Bible is filled with people whose faith was sometimes weak. God showed patience by giving them the confidence they needed.

Gideon's Victory (7:1)

What was important about the way the men drank water? (7:5–6)
The drinking test may have had no special significance. It was simply a way for God to reduce the size of the army to 300.

Why were these 300 soldiers selected? (7:7)
There is no evidence to show that these were the best fighters. God simply chose this small band of soldiers to show that he was the one who would win the battle.

What was the significance of this dream and its interpretation? (7:13–14)
It showed Gideon that the Midianites were fearful of the Israelites. God used this conversation as another way of convincing Gideon that he would give him the victory.

**How could Gideon under-
stand their language? (7:15)**
Even though the Midianite
language was not identical to
Hebrew, there were enough similarities that Gideon could understand their conversation.

**What were the watches of
the night? (7:19)**
These were the divisions into
which the 12 hours of darkness
were divided. The Israelites divided night into 3 watches, so the
middle watch would have been
from 10:00 P.M. until 2:00 A.M.

**What did it mean to "seize
the waters of the Jordan"?
(7:24)**
This was a very common war
strategy. People used the river as
an escape route. But if the Israelites had control over the river
and were watching where they
knew the river could be crossed,
they could stop the Midianites
from running away and escaping.

**Why did these towns refuse
to help their fellow Israelites? (8:6, 8)**
Gideon's army was so small that
people didn't believe it would
provide long-term protection and
safety. The people of these towns
thought they would be safer if
they maintained good relations
with the Midianites.

¹⁵When Gideon heard the dream and its interpretation, he bowed down and worshiped. He returned to the camp of Israel and called out, "Get up! The LORD has given the Midianite camp into your hands." ¹⁶Dividing the three hundred men into three companies, he placed trumpets and empty jars in the hands of all of them, with torches inside.

¹⁷"Watch me," he told them. "Follow my lead. When I get to the edge of the camp, do exactly as I do. ¹⁸When I and all who are with me blow our trumpets, then from all around the camp blow yours and shout, 'For the LORD and for Gideon.'"

¹⁹Gideon and the hundred men with him reached the edge of the camp at the beginning of the middle watch, just after they had changed the guard. They blew their trumpets and broke the jars that were in their hands. ²⁰The three companies blew the trumpets and smashed the jars. Grasping the torches in their left hands and holding in their right hands the trumpets they were to blow, they shouted, "A sword for the LORD and for Gideon!" ²¹While each man held his position around the camp, all the Midianites ran, crying out as they fled.

²²When the three hundred trumpets sounded, the LORD caused the men throughout the camp to turn on each other with their swords. The army fled to Beth Shittah toward Zererah as far as the border of Abel Meholah near Tabbath. ²³Israelites from Naphtali, Asher and all Manasseh were called out, and they pursued the Midianites. ²⁴Gideon sent messengers throughout the hill country of Ephraim, saying, "Come down against the Midianites and seize the waters of the Jordan ahead of them as far as Beth Barah."

So all the men of Ephraim were called out and they seized the waters of the Jordan as far as Beth Barah. ²⁵They also captured two of the Midianite leaders, Oreb and Zeeb. They killed Oreb at the rock of Oreb, and Zeeb at the winepress of Zeeb. They pursued the Midianites and brought the heads of Oreb and Zeeb to Gideon, who was by the Jordan.

ZEBAH AND ZALMUNNA

8 Now the Ephraimites asked Gideon, "Why have you treated us like this? Why didn't you call us when you went to fight Midian?" And they challenged him vigorously.

²But he answered them, "What have I accomplished compared to you? Aren't the gleanings of Ephraim's grapes better than the full grape harvest of Abiezer? ³God gave Oreb and Zeeb, the Midianite leaders, into your hands. What was I able to do compared to you?" At this, their resentment against him subsided.

⁴Gideon and his three hundred men, exhausted yet keeping up the pursuit, came to the Jordan and crossed it. ⁵He said to the men of Sukkoth, "Give my troops some bread; they are worn out, and I am still pursuing Zebah and Zalmunna, the kings of Midian."

⁶But the officials of Sukkoth said, "Do you already have the hands of Zebah and Zalmunna in your possession? Why should we give bread to your troops?"

⁷Then Gideon replied, "Just for that, when the LORD has given Zebah and Zalmunna into my hand, I will tear your flesh with desert thorns and briers."

⁸From there he went up to Peniel*a* and made the same request of them, but they answered as the men of Sukkoth had. ⁹So he said to the men of Peniel, "When I return in triumph, I will tear down this tower."

¹⁰Now Zebah and Zalmunna were in Karkor with a force of about fifteen thousand men, all that were left of the armies of the eastern peoples; a hundred and twenty thousand swordsmen had fallen. ¹¹Gideon went up by the route of the nomads east of Nobah and Jogbehah and attacked the unsuspecting army. ¹²Zebah and Zalmunna, the two kings of Midian, fled, but he pursued them and captured them, routing their entire army.

¹³Gideon son of Joash then returned from the battle by the Pass of Heres. ¹⁴He caught a young man of Sukkoth and questioned him, and the young man wrote down for him the names of the seventy-seven officials of Sukkoth, the elders of the town. ¹⁵Then Gideon came and said to the men of Sukkoth, "Here are Zebah and Zalmunna, about whom you taunted me by saying, 'Do you already have the hands of Zebah and Zalmunna in your possession? Why should we give bread to your exhausted men?'" ¹⁶He took the elders of the town and taught the men of Sukkoth a lesson by punishing them with desert thorns and briers. ¹⁷He also pulled down the tower of Peniel and killed the men of the town.

¹⁸Then he asked Zebah and Zalmunna, "What kind of men did you kill at Tabor?"

"Men like you," they answered, "each one with the bearing of a prince."

¹⁹Gideon replied, "Those were my brothers, the sons of my own mother. As surely as the LORD lives, if you had spared their lives, I would not kill you." ²⁰Turning to Jether, his oldest son, he said, "Kill them!" But Jether did not draw his sword, because he was only a boy and was afraid.

²¹Zebah and Zalmunna said, "Come, do it yourself. 'As is the man, so is his strength.'" So Gideon stepped forward and killed them, and took the ornaments off their camels' necks.

GIDEON'S EPHOD

²²The Israelites said to Gideon, "Rule over us—you, your son and your grandson—because you have saved us from the hand of Midian."

²³But Gideon told them, "I will not rule over you, nor will my son rule over you. The LORD will rule over you." ²⁴And he said, "I do have one request, that each of you give me an earring from your share of the plunder." (It was the custom of the Ishmaelites to wear gold earrings.)

²⁵They answered, "We'll be glad to give them." So they spread out a garment, and each of them threw a ring from his plunder onto it. ²⁶The weight of the gold rings he asked for came to seventeen hundred shekels,*b* not counting the

How could desert thorns and briers teach a lesson? (8:16) The people of Succoth learned to support Gideon when they saw their elders suffer a painful death. They had been beaten with whips made of thorns and briers.

Was this extreme punishment justified? (8:17) Gideon had promised that the people of Succoth would suffer severe consequences for not helping him. By refusing to help him in battle, it was as if they were committing treason.

What were these ornaments? (8:21) The ornaments were crescent moon-shaped necklaces that implied reverence for a popular moon god.

---

a 8 Hebrew *Penuel*, a variant of *Peniel*; also in verses 9 and 17   *b 26* That is, about 43 pounds or about 20 kilograms

What was Gideon's ephod?
(8:27)
The original ephod was worn
by the high priest (see Exodus
39:1–26). In Gideon's case, it
could have been a garment or
a statue. The problem was not
with the ephod itself but with
the fact that the people later
worshiped it.

**Why did Gideon have so
many wives?** (8:30)
Perhaps because he was seen
as a hero among the Israelites,
Gideon was able to marry many
women. Though this practice was
common during Old Testament
times, it was not God's plan for
marriage. It sometimes caused
family problems.

**How could Jotham be heard
by the people without being
killed?** (9:7)
Jotham climbed the slopes of
Mount Gerizim, possibly shouting down from the top of a cliff
or out of a hiding place behind
some rocks or a cave. The walls
of the valley may have amplified
his voice.

What did this story mean?
(9:8–15)
This story is an analogy for
Abimelek and Gideon's sons. The
harmful thorn bush represents
Abimelek. Though the trees,
who represent the Shechemites,
wanted him to be king, they
would regret their decision. The
olive tree, the fig tree, and the
vine would have made better
kings. They could have provided
for their people as the plants
produce olives, figs, and wine.

ornaments, the pendants and the purple garments worn by
the kings of Midian or the chains that were on their camels' necks. ²⁷Gideon made the gold into an ephod, which he
placed in Ophrah, his town. All Israel prostituted themselves
by worshiping it there, and it became a snare to Gideon and
his family.

GIDEON'S DEATH

²⁸Thus Midian was subdued before the Israelites and did
not raise its head again. During Gideon's lifetime, the land
had peace forty years.

²⁹Jerub-Baal son of Joash went back home to live. ³⁰He
had seventy sons of his own, for he had many wives. ³¹His
concubine, who lived in Shechem, also bore him a son, whom
he named Abimelek. ³²Gideon son of Joash died at a good
old age and was buried in the tomb of his father Joash in
Ophrah of the Abiezrites.

³³No sooner had Gideon died than the Israelites again
prostituted themselves to the Baals. They set up Baal-Berith
as their god.³⁴and did not remember the LORD their God,
who had rescued them from the hands of all their enemies
on every side. ³⁵They also failed to show any loyalty to the
family of Jerub-Baal (that is, Gideon) in spite of all the good
things he had done for them.

ABIMELEK

9 Abimelek son of Jerub-Baal went to his mother's brothers in Shechem and said to them and to all his mother's
clan, ²"Ask all the citizens of Shechem, 'Which is better for
you: to have all seventy of Jerub-Baal's sons rule over you, or
just one man?' Remember, I am your flesh and blood."

³When the brothers repeated all this to the citizens of
Shechem, they were inclined to follow Abimelek, for they
said, "He is related to us." ⁴They gave him seventy shekels*ᵃ* of silver from the temple of Baal-Berith, and Abimelek
used it to hire reckless scoundrels, who became his followers.
⁵He went to his father's home in Ophrah and on one stone
murdered his seventy brothers, the sons of Jerub-Baal. But
Jotham, the youngest son of Jerub-Baal, escaped by hiding.
⁶Then all the citizens of Shechem and Beth Millo gathered beside the great tree at the pillar in Shechem to crown
Abimelek king.

⁷When Jotham was told about this, he climbed up on the
top of Mount Gerizim and shouted to them, "Listen to me,
citizens of Shechem, so that God may listen to you. ⁸One
day the trees went out to anoint a king for themselves. They
said to the olive tree, 'Be our king.'

⁹"But the olive tree answered, 'Should I give up my oil,
by which both gods and humans are honored, to hold sway
over the trees?'

¹⁰"Next, the trees said to the fig tree, 'Come and be our
king.'

¹¹"But the fig tree replied, 'Should I give up my fruit, so
good and sweet, to hold sway over the trees?'

ᵃ 4 That is, about 1 3/4 pounds or about 800 grams

¹²"Then the trees said to the vine, 'Come and be our king.'

¹³"But the vine answered, 'Should I give up my wine, which cheers both gods and humans, to hold sway over the trees?'

¹⁴"Finally all the trees said to the thornbush, 'Come and be our king.'

¹⁵"The thornbush said to the trees, 'If you really want to anoint me king over you, come and take refuge in my shade; but if not, then let fire come out of the thornbush and consume the cedars of Lebanon!'

¹⁶"Have you acted honorably and in good faith by making Abimelek king? Have you been fair to Jerub-Baal and his family? Have you treated him as he deserves? ¹⁷Remember that my father fought for you and risked his life to rescue you from the hand of Midian. ¹⁸But today you have revolted against my father's family. You have murdered his seventy sons on a single stone and have made Abimelek, the son of his female slave, king over the citizens of Shechem because he is related to you. ¹⁹So have you acted honorably and in good faith toward Jerub-Baal and his family today? If you have, may Abimelek be your joy, and may you be his, too! ²⁰But if you have not, let fire come out from Abimelek and consume you, the citizens of Shechem and Beth Millo, and let fire come out from you, the citizens of Shechem and Beth Millo, and consume Abimelek!"

²¹Then Jotham fled, escaping to Beer, and he lived there because he was afraid of his brother Abimelek.

²²After Abimelek had governed Israel three years, ²³God stirred up animosity between Abimelek and the citizens of Shechem so that they acted treacherously against Abimelek. ²⁴God did this in order that the crime against Jerub-Baal's seventy sons, the shedding of their blood, might be avenged on their brother Abimelek and on the citizens of Shechem, who had helped him murder his brothers. ²⁵In opposition to him these citizens of Shechem set men on the hilltops to ambush and rob everyone who passed by, and this was reported to Abimelek.

²⁶Now Gaal son of Ebed moved with his clan into Shechem, and its citizens put their confidence in him. ²⁷After they had gone out into the fields and gathered the grapes and trodden them, they held a festival in the temple of their god. While they were eating and drinking, they cursed Abimelek. ²⁸Then Gaal son of Ebed said, "Who is Abimelek, and why should we Shechemites be subject to him? Isn't he Jerub-Baal's son, and isn't Zebul his deputy? Serve the family of Hamor, Shechem's father! Why should we serve Abimelek? ²⁹If only this people were under my command! Then I would get rid of him. I would say to Abimelek, 'Call out your whole army!'"ᵃ

³⁰When Zebul the governor of the city heard what Gaal son of Ebed said, he was very angry. ³¹Under cover he sent messengers to Abimelek, saying, "Gaal son of Ebed and his clan have come to Shechem and are stirring up the city

What did this fire refer to? (9:20)
This was a prediction that Abimelek and the people of Shechem would destroy each other by fire. Jotham's curse came true three years later (see verses 49 and 57).

Why was Shechem so torn by conflict? (9:22–24, 45)
Shechem was supposed to be a city of refuge, a safe place for those accused of murder, but it became a place of violence because of the people living there.

ᵃ 29 Septuagint; Hebrew *him." Then he said to Abimelek, "Call out your whole army!"*

against you. ³²Now then, during the night you and your men should come and lie in wait in the fields. ³³In the morning at sunrise, advance against the city. When Gaal and his men come out against you, seize the opportunity to attack them."

³⁴So Abimelek and all his troops set out by night and took up concealed positions near Shechem in four companies. ³⁵Now Gaal son of Ebed had gone out and was standing at the entrance of the city gate just as Abimelek and his troops came out from their hiding place.

³⁶When Gaal saw them, he said to Zebul, "Look, people are coming down from the tops of the mountains!"

Zebul replied, "You mistake the shadows of the mountains for men."

³⁷But Gaal spoke up again: "Look, people are coming down from the central hill,[a] and a company is coming from the direction of the diviners' tree."

³⁸Then Zebul said to him, "Where is your big talk now, you who said, 'Who is Abimelek that we should be subject to him?' Aren't these the men you ridiculed? Go out and fight them!"

³⁹So Gaal led out[b] the citizens of Shechem and fought Abimelek. ⁴⁰Abimelek chased him all the way to the entrance of the gate, and many were killed as they fled. ⁴¹Then Abimelek stayed in Arumah, and Zebul drove Gaal and his clan out of Shechem.

⁴²The next day the people of Shechem went out to the fields, and this was reported to Abimelek. ⁴³So he took his men, divided them into three companies and set an ambush in the fields. When he saw the people coming out of the city, he rose to attack them. ⁴⁴Abimelek and the companies with him rushed forward to a position at the entrance of the city gate. Then two companies attacked those in the fields and struck them down. ⁴⁵All that day Abimelek pressed his attack against the city until he had captured it and killed its people. Then he destroyed the city and scattered salt over it.

⁴⁶On hearing this, the citizens in the tower of Shechem went into the stronghold of the temple of El-Berith. ⁴⁷When Abimelek heard that they had assembled there, ⁴⁸he and all his men went up Mount Zalmon. He took an ax and cut off some branches, which he lifted to his shoulders. He ordered the men with him, "Quick! Do what you have seen me do!" ⁴⁹So all the men cut branches and followed Abimelek. They piled them against the stronghold and set it on fire with the people still inside. So all the people in the tower of Shechem, about a thousand men and women, also died.

⁵⁰Next Abimelek went to Thebez and besieged it and captured it. ⁵¹Inside the city, however, was a strong tower, to which all the men and women—all the people of the city—had fled. They had locked themselves in and climbed up on the tower roof. ⁵²Abimelek went to the tower and attacked it. But as he approached the entrance to the tower to set it on fire, ⁵³a woman dropped an upper millstone on his head and cracked his skull.

What kind of tower could hold a thousand people? (9:46, 49)
It might have been a tower built into the city walls. Or it might have been a fortress.

How did the people in this tower defend themselves? (9:52-53)
While the men used bows, arrows, and spears, the women helped to defend the tower by dropping heavy stones on the attackers.

---

[a] 37 The Hebrew for this phrase means *the navel of the earth.*   [b] 39 Or *Gaal went out in the sight of*

⁵⁴Hurriedly he called to his armor-bearer, "Draw your sword and kill me, so that they can't say, 'A woman killed him.'" So his servant ran him through, and he died. ⁵⁵When the Israelites saw that Abimelek was dead, they went home.

⁵⁶Thus God repaid the wickedness that Abimelek had done to his father by murdering his seventy brothers. ⁵⁷God also made the people of Shechem pay for all their wickedness. The curse of Jotham son of Jerub-Baal came on them.

TOLA

10 After the time of Abimelek, a man of Issachar named Tola son of Puah, the son of Dodo, rose to save Israel. He lived in Shamir, in the hill country of Ephraim. ²He led^a Israel twenty-three years; then he died, and was buried in Shamir.

JAIR

³He was followed by Jair of Gilead, who led Israel twenty-two years. ⁴He had thirty sons, who rode thirty donkeys. They controlled thirty towns in Gilead, which to this day are called Havvoth Jair.^b ⁵When Jair died, he was buried in Kamon.

JEPHTHAH

⁶Again the Israelites did evil in the eyes of the LORD. They served the Baals and the Ashtoreths, and the gods of Aram, the gods of Sidon, the gods of Moab, the gods of the Ammonites and the gods of the Philistines. And because the Israelites forsook the LORD and no longer served him, ⁷he became angry with them. He sold them into the hands of the Philistines and the Ammonites, ⁸who that year shattered and crushed them. For eighteen years they oppressed all the Israelites on the east side of the Jordan in Gilead, the land of the Amorites. ⁹The Ammonites also crossed the Jordan to fight against Judah, Benjamin and Ephraim; Israel was in great distress. ¹⁰Then the Israelites cried out to the LORD, "We have sinned against you, forsaking our God and serving the Baals."

¹¹The LORD replied, "When the Egyptians, the Amorites, the Ammonites, the Philistines, ¹²the Sidonians, the Amalekites and the Maonites^c oppressed you and you cried to me for help, did I not save you from their hands? ¹³But you have forsaken me and served other gods, so I will no longer save you. ¹⁴Go and cry out to the gods you have chosen. Let them save you when you are in trouble!"

¹⁵But the Israelites said to the LORD, "We have sinned. Do with us whatever you think best, but please rescue us now." ¹⁶Then they got rid of the foreign gods among them and served the LORD. And he could bear Israel's misery no longer.

¹⁷When the Ammonites were called to arms and camped in Gilead, the Israelites assembled and camped at Mizpah. ¹⁸The leaders of the people of Gilead said to each other, "Whoever will take the lead in attacking the Ammonites will be head over all who live in Gilead."

What was the significance of 30 sons, 30 donkeys, and 30 towns? (10:4)
This showed how wealthy and powerful Jair was. Riding on a donkey was a mark of prestige and power. Horses were not available until later when Solomon imported them.

Why did the Israelites keep repeating the same mistakes? (10:6)
Even though the LORD had repeatedly saved them when they called, as soon as things settled down, they fell back into old patterns and began to worship the gods of their neighbors, the Canaanites. They seemed unable to resist the temptation to worship false gods.

---

^a 2 Traditionally *judged*; also in verse 3   ^b 4 Or *called the settlements of Jair*
^c 12 Hebrew; some Septuagint manuscripts *Midianites*

11 Jephthah the Gileadite was a mighty warrior. His father was Gilead; his mother was a prostitute. ²Gilead's wife also bore him sons, and when they were grown up, they drove Jephthah away. "You are not going to get any inheritance in our family," they said, "because you are the son of another woman." ³So Jephthah fled from his brothers and settled in the land of Tob, where a gang of scoundrels gathered around him and followed him.

⁴Some time later, when the Ammonites were fighting against Israel, ⁵the elders of Gilead went to get Jephthah from the land of Tob. ⁶"Come," they said, "be our commander, so we can fight the Ammonites."

⁷Jephthah said to them, "Didn't you hate me and drive me from my father's house? Why do you come to me now, when you're in trouble?"

⁸The elders of Gilead said to him, "Nevertheless, we are turning to you now; come with us to fight the Ammonites, and you will be head over all of us who live in Gilead."

⁹Jephthah answered, "Suppose you take me back to fight the Ammonites and the LORD gives them to me—will I really be your head?"

¹⁰The elders of Gilead replied, "The LORD is our witness; we will certainly do as you say." ¹¹So Jephthah went with the elders of Gilead, and the people made him head and commander over them. And he repeated all his words before the LORD in Mizpah.

¹²Then Jephthah sent messengers to the Ammonite king with the question: "What do you have against me that you have attacked my country?"

¹³The king of the Ammonites answered Jephthah's messengers, "When Israel came up out of Egypt, they took away my land from the Arnon to the Jabbok, all the way to the Jordan. Now give it back peaceably."

¹⁴Jephthah sent back messengers to the Ammonite king, ¹⁵saying:

> "This is what Jephthah says: Israel did not take the land of Moab or the land of the Ammonites. ¹⁶But when they came up out of Egypt, Israel went through the wilderness to the Red Sea*ᵃ* and on to Kadesh. ¹⁷Then Israel sent messengers to the king of Edom, saying, 'Give us permission to go through your country,' but the king of Edom would not listen. They sent also to the king of Moab, and he refused. So Israel stayed at Kadesh.
>
> ¹⁸"Next they traveled through the wilderness, skirted the lands of Edom and Moab, passed along the eastern side of the country of Moab, and camped on the other side of the Arnon. They did not enter the territory of Moab, for the Arnon was its border.
>
> ¹⁹"Then Israel sent messengers to Sihon king of the Amorites, who ruled in Heshbon, and said to him, 'Let us pass through your country to our own place.' ²⁰Sihon, however, did not trust Israel*ᵇ* to pass through his territory.

Why did the elders pick an outcast to lead them? (11:4–6)
Because there was a crisis, they did not worry about Jephthah's background (he was the illegitimate son of Gilead). While he was in exile, Jephthah had shown that he was an effective leader. So when no one else volunteered to be leader at Mizpah, the elders recruited him (see 10:17–18).

ᵃ 16 Or the Sea of Reeds   ᵇ 20 Or however, would not make an agreement for Israel

He mustered all his troops and encamped at Jahaz and fought with Israel.

²¹"Then the Lord, the God of Israel, gave Sihon and his whole army into Israel's hands, and they defeated them. Israel took over all the land of the Amorites who lived in that country, ²²capturing all of it from the Arnon to the Jabbok and from the desert to the Jordan.

²³"Now since the Lord, the God of Israel, has driven the Amorites out before his people Israel, what right have you to take it over? ²⁴Will you not take what your god Chemosh gives you? Likewise, whatever the Lord our God has given us, we will possess. ²⁵Are you any better than Balak son of Zippor, king of Moab? Did he ever quarrel with Israel or fight with them? ²⁶For three hundred years Israel occupied Heshbon, Aroer, the surrounding settlements and all the towns along the Arnon. Why didn't you retake them during that time? ²⁷I have not wronged you, but you are doing me wrong by waging war against me. Let the Lord, the Judge, decide the dispute this day between the Israelites and the Ammonites."

²⁸The king of Ammon, however, paid no attention to the message Jephthah sent him.

²⁹Then the Spirit of the Lord came on Jephthah. He crossed Gilead and Manasseh, passed through Mizpah of Gilead, and from there he advanced against the Ammonites. ³⁰And Jephthah made a vow to the Lord: "If you give the Ammonites into my hands, ³¹whatever comes out of the door of my house to meet me when I return in triumph from the Ammonites will be the Lord's, and I will sacrifice it as a burnt offering."

³²Then Jephthah went over to fight the Ammonites, and the Lord gave them into his hands. ³³He devastated twenty towns from Aroer to the vicinity of Minnith, as far as Abel Keramim. Thus Israel subdued Ammon.

³⁴When Jephthah returned to his home in Mizpah, who should come out to meet him but his daughter, dancing to the sound of timbrels! She was an only child. Except for her he had neither son nor daughter. ³⁵When he saw her, he tore his clothes and cried, "Oh no, my daughter! You have brought me down and I am devastated. I have made a vow to the Lord that I cannot break."

³⁶"My father," she replied, "you have given your word to the Lord. Do to me just as you promised, now that the Lord has avenged you of your enemies, the Ammonites. ³⁷But grant me this one request," she said. "Give me two months to roam the hills and weep with my friends, because I will never marry."

³⁸"You may go," he said. And he let her go for two months. She and her friends went into the hills and wept because she would never marry. ³⁹After the two months, she returned to her father, and he did to her as he had vowed. And she was a virgin.

From this comes the Israelite tradition ⁴⁰that each year the young women of Israel go out for four days to commemorate the daughter of Jephthah the Gileadite.

What showed that the Spirit of the Lord had given Jephthah the power to lead? (11:29)
As Jephthah headed to battle, troops from the tribes of Gad and Manasseh joined him, showing that there was a shared sense of responsibility.

Why did Jephthah make such a rash vow? (11:29–31)
Even though Jephthah was empowered by God's Spirit, he was still a person with faults. This impulsive oath would have serious consequences for his daughter.

Why did Jephthah's daughter roam the hills for two months? (11:37)
Her retreat to the mountains may have been personal, or it may have been a local custom. She was mourning the fact that she would never marry or have children.

JEPHTHAH AND EPHRAIM

12 The Ephraimite forces were called out, and they crossed over to Zaphon. They said to Jephthah, "Why did you go to fight the Ammonites without calling us to go with you? We're going to burn down your house over your head."

² Jephthah answered, "I and my people were engaged in a great struggle with the Ammonites, and although I called, you didn't save me out of their hands. ³ When I saw that you wouldn't help, I took my life in my hands and crossed over to fight the Ammonites, and the LORD gave me the victory over them. Now why have you come up today to fight me?"

⁴ Jephthah then called together the men of Gilead and fought against Ephraim. The Gileadites struck them down because the Ephraimites had said, "You Gileadites are renegades from Ephraim and Manasseh." ⁵ The Gileadites captured the fords of the Jordan leading to Ephraim, and whenever a survivor of Ephraim said, "Let me cross over," the men of Gilead asked him, "Are you an Ephraimite?" If he replied, "No," ⁶ they said, "All right, say 'Shibboleth.'" If he said, "Sibboleth," because he could not pronounce the word correctly, they seized him and killed him at the fords of the Jordan. Forty-two thousand Ephraimites were killed at that time.

⁷ Jephthah led*ᵃ* Israel six years. Then Jephthah the Gileadite died and was buried in a town in Gilead.

IBZAN, ELON AND ABDON

⁸ After him, Ibzan of Bethlehem led Israel. ⁹ He had thirty sons and thirty daughters. He gave his daughters away in marriage to those outside his clan, and for his sons he brought in thirty young women as wives from outside his clan. Ibzan led Israel seven years. ¹⁰ Then Ibzan died and was buried in Bethlehem.

¹¹ After him, Elon the Zebulunite led Israel ten years. ¹² Then Elon died and was buried in Aijalon in the land of Zebulun.

¹³ After him, Abdon son of Hillel, from Pirathon, led Israel. ¹⁴ He had forty sons and thirty grandsons, who rode on seventy donkeys. He led Israel eight years. ¹⁵ Then Abdon son of Hillel died and was buried at Pirathon in Ephraim, in the hill country of the Amalekites.

THE BIRTH OF SAMSON

13 Again the Israelites did evil in the eyes of the LORD, so the LORD delivered them into the hands of the Philistines for forty years.

² A certain man of Zorah, named Manoah, from the clan of the Danites, had a wife who was childless, unable to give birth. ³ The angel of the LORD appeared to her and said, "You are barren and childless, but you are going to become pregnant and give birth to a son. ⁴ Now see to it that you drink no wine or other fermented drink and that you do not eat anything unclean. ⁵ You will become pregnant and have a son whose head is never to be touched by a razor because the

Why were the men of Ephraim so angry? (12:1)
Not being invited to participate in battle was an insult. Ephraim claimed responsibility for all the northern tribes and those living east of the Jordan River.

Why was the word Shibboleth chosen as a test? (12:6)
The people west of the Jordan River had a difficult time pronouncing the *sh* sound because it was not part of their natural dialect. So the Israelites chose the word *Shibboleth*, meaning *floods*, as a password.

Were marriages to outsiders unusual? (12:9)
It was permissible to marry outside one's clan or tribe as long as the spouse was an Israelite. But marrying a foreigner, a person who wasn't an Israelite, was forbidden (see Exodus 34:15 – 17 and Deuteronomy 7:1 – 4).

ᵃ 7 Traditionally judged; also in verses 8-14

boy is to be a Nazirite, dedicated to God from the womb.
He will take the lead in delivering Israel from the hands of
the Philistines."

⁶Then the woman went to her husband and told him, "A
man of God came to me. He looked like an angel of God,
very awesome. I didn't ask him where he came from, and he
didn't tell me his name. ⁷But he said to me, 'You will become
pregnant and have a son. Now then, drink no wine or other
fermented drink and do not eat anything unclean, because
the boy will be a Nazirite of God from the womb until the
day of his death.'"

⁸Then Manoah prayed to the LORD: "Pardon your servant,
Lord. I beg you to let the man of God you sent to us come
again to teach us how to bring up the boy who is to be born."

⁹God heard Manoah, and the angel of God came again
to the woman while she was out in the field; but her husband Manoah was not with her. ¹⁰The woman hurried to
tell her husband, "He's here! The man who appeared to me
the other day!"

¹¹Manoah got up and followed his wife. When he came to
the man, he said, "Are you the man who talked to my wife?"

"I am," he said.

¹²So Manoah asked him, "When your words are fulfilled,
what is to be the rule that governs the boy's life and work?"

¹³The angel of the LORD answered, "Your wife must do all
that I have told her. ¹⁴She must not eat anything that comes
from the grapevine, nor drink any wine or other fermented
drink nor eat anything unclean. She must do everything I
have commanded her."

¹⁵Manoah said to the angel of the LORD, "We would like
you to stay until we prepare a young goat for you."

¹⁶The angel of the LORD replied, "Even though you detain
me, I will not eat any of your food. But if you prepare a burnt
offering, offer it to the LORD." (Manoah did not realize that
it was the angel of the LORD.)

¹⁷Then Manoah inquired of the angel of the LORD, "What
is your name, so that we may honor you when your word
comes true?"

¹⁸He replied, "Why do you ask my name? It is beyond un-
derstanding.ᵃ" ¹⁹Then Manoah took a young goat, together
with the grain offering, and sacrificed it on a rock to the
LORD. And the LORD did an amazing thing while Manoah
and his wife watched: ²⁰As the flame blazed up from the
altar toward heaven, the angel of the LORD ascended in the
flame. Seeing this, Manoah and his wife fell with their faces
to the ground. ²¹When the angel of the LORD did not show
himself again to Manoah and his wife, Manoah realized that
it was the angel of the LORD.

²²"We are doomed to die!" he said to his wife. "We have
seen God!"

²³But his wife answered, "If the LORD had meant to kill
us, he would not have accepted a burnt offering and grain
offering from our hands, nor shown us all these things or
now told us this."

ᵃ 18 Or is wonderful

What was a Nazirite? (13:5)
A Nazirite was a person who
made a special vow to the LORD.
A typical vow was for 30 days,
but sometimes the vow was for
a lifetime of service, and a parent could make a vow on behalf
of a child. A Nazirite couldn't
eat or drink grape products and
couldn't cut his or her hair. These
were visible symbols of devotion
to God. A Nazirite also could not
go near a dead body (see Numbers 6:1–21).

**What is wrong with grapes
and wine? (13:14)**
Grapes and wine were considered
delicacies, but to a Nazirite they
had spiritual significance.

**Why did Manoah offer to
prepare a young goat as a
meal? (13:15)**
A young goat was considered
a special delicacy. Hospitality
of this sort was common and
expected in the ancient Middle
East.

**How was the angel's name
beyond understanding?
(13:18)**
Literally, his name was *wonderful*. This meant he was not an
ordinary messenger, but somehow linked to God himself. And
because God is so wonderful and
beyond human comprehension,
no words we have will ever be
good enough to describe God.
The same is then true for this
angel.

What did the name *Samson* mean? (13:24)
The name came from a Hebrew word meaning *sun* or *brightness*. Here it referred to the joy that comes with the birth of a child.

Did God cause Samson to break a commandment? (14:4)
No. God never wants his people to disobey his rules. Samson was responsible for his own actions, even when they violated God's laws. However, God used Samson's failures as well as his successes to accomplish his purposes.

What was wrong with eating honey scooped from a lion's carcass? (14:9)
This was a serious violation of the laws about clean and unclean food outlined in Leviticus 11 (see especially verse 28).

Why did Samson tell a riddle at his wedding celebration? (14:12–14)
The use of riddles at feasts and special celebrations was common in the ancient world. Samson used this riddle to trap his enemies, but when they discovered the answer, they trapped him.

²⁴The woman gave birth to a boy and named him Samson. He grew and the LORD blessed him, ²⁵and the Spirit of the LORD began to stir him while he was in Mahaneh Dan, between Zorah and Eshtaol.

SAMSON'S MARRIAGE

14 Samson went down to Timnah and saw there a young Philistine woman. ²When he returned, he said to his father and mother, "I have seen a Philistine woman in Timnah; now get her for me as my wife."

³His father and mother replied, "Isn't there an acceptable woman among your relatives or among all our people? Must you go to the uncircumcised Philistines to get a wife?"

But Samson said to his father, "Get her for me. She's the right one for me." ⁴(His parents did not know that this was from the LORD, who was seeking an occasion to confront the Philistines; for at that time they were ruling over Israel.)

⁵Samson went down to Timnah together with his father and mother. As they approached the vineyards of Timnah, suddenly a young lion came roaring toward him. ⁶The Spirit of the LORD came powerfully upon him so that he tore the lion apart with his bare hands as he might have torn a young goat. But he told neither his father nor his mother what he had done. ⁷Then he went down and talked with the woman, and he liked her.

⁸Some time later, when he went back to marry her, he turned aside to look at the lion's carcass, and in it he saw a swarm of bees and some honey. ⁹He scooped out the honey with his hands and ate as he went along. When he rejoined his parents, he gave them some, and they too ate it. But he did not tell them that he had taken the honey from the lion's carcass.

¹⁰Now his father went down to see the woman. And there Samson held a feast, as was customary for young men. ¹¹When the people saw him, they chose thirty men to be his companions.

¹²"Let me tell you a riddle," Samson said to them. "If you can tell me the answer within the seven days of the feast, I will give you thirty linen garments and thirty sets of clothes. ¹³If you can't tell me the answer, you must give me thirty linen garments and thirty sets of clothes."

"Tell us your riddle," they said. "Let's hear it."

¹⁴He replied,

"Out of the eater, something to eat;
out of the strong, something sweet."

For three days they could not give the answer.

¹⁵On the fourth[a] day, they said to Samson's wife, "Coax your husband into explaining the riddle for us, or we will burn you and your father's household to death. Did you invite us here to steal our property?"

¹⁶Then Samson's wife threw herself on him, sobbing, "You hate me! You don't really love me. You've given my people a riddle, but you haven't told me the answer."

---

[a] 15 Some Septuagint manuscripts and Syriac; Hebrew *seventh*

"I haven't even explained it to my father or mother," he replied, "so why should I explain it to you?" ¹⁷She cried the whole seven days of the feast. So on the seventh day he finally told her, because she continued to press him. She in turn explained the riddle to her people.

¹⁸Before sunset on the seventh day the men of the town said to him,

"What is sweeter than honey?
   What is stronger than a lion?"

Samson said to them,

"If you had not plowed with my heifer,
   you would not have solved my riddle."

¹⁹Then the Spirit of the LORD came powerfully upon him. He went down to Ashkelon, struck down thirty of their men, stripped them of everything and gave their clothes to those who had explained the riddle. Burning with anger, he returned to his father's home. ²⁰And Samson's wife was given to one of his companions who had attended him at the feast.

SAMSON'S VENGEANCE ON THE PHILISTINES

15 Later on, at the time of wheat harvest, Samson took a young goat and went to visit his wife. He said, "I'm going to my wife's room." But her father would not let him go in.

²"I was so sure you hated her," he said, "that I gave her to your companion. Isn't her younger sister more attractive? Take her instead."

³Samson said to them, "This time I have a right to get even with the Philistines; I will really harm them." ⁴So he went out and caught three hundred foxes and tied them tail to tail in pairs. He then fastened a torch to every pair of tails, ⁵lit the torches and let the foxes loose in the standing grain of the Philistines. He burned up the shocks and standing grain, together with the vineyards and olive groves.

⁶When the Philistines asked, "Who did this?" they were told, "Samson, the Timnite's son-in-law, because his wife was given to his companion."

So the Philistines went up and burned her and her father to death. ⁷Samson said to them, "Since you've acted like this,

Why did the bride's father let her marry someone else? (14:19–20)
They may not have considered the marriage to be official. Since Samson left in such a hurry and so angrily, the bride's father may have thought that Samson had abandoned her and was not going to return.

Why did the Philistines and Samson continue to seek revenge? (15:1–19)
Revenge was common in ancient Middle Eastern culture. If someone wronged another person, that person would seek to harm the person who had done the wrong.

How could Samson catch 300 foxes? (15:4)
Perhaps Samson was not only extremely strong but also extremely fast. It is also possible that he trapped the foxes and waited until he had enough for his revenge on the Philistines.

Can God use sinful people to carry out his purposes?

JUDGES 15

The Bible is filled with stories about people who were sinful but who still were used by God to accomplish his purposes. Samson is just one example. He had been dedicated to God as a Nazirite, but he broke his vows by drinking wine, having contact with dead bodies, eating unclean foods, sleeping with prostitutes, and marrying a Philistine woman.

But God used Samson to keep Israel free from oppression by the Philistines. Because of his strength, Samson killed thousands of Philistines. Before he died, Samson began to regain his commitment to the LORD, and the LORD used him to destroy the temple of the pagan god Dagon and to kill 3,000 Philistines in the process.

God can use righteous, sinful, or evil people to accomplish his purposes, but what he wants is our love and devotion.

Samson and the Philistines
(15:9)

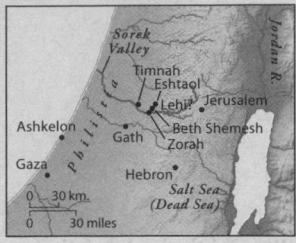

**Why did the Israelites plan
to turn Samson over to the
Philistines? (15:11–12)**
They feared that the cycle of revenge would continue to worsen
and would put the whole nation
at risk.

**Did the fact that God pro-
vided water for Samson
mean that he approved of
his actions? (15:19)**
God provided for Samson's
needs when Samson cried out to
him. But that didn't mean that
God approved of Samson's behavior. Samson had broken many
of God's laws.

I swear that I won't stop until I get my revenge on you." ⁸He
attacked them viciously and slaughtered many of them. Then
he went down and stayed in a cave in the rock of Etam.

⁹The Philistines went up and camped in Judah, spreading
out near Lehi. ¹⁰The people of Judah asked, "Why have you
come to fight us?"

"We have come to take Samson prisoner," they answered,
"to do to him as he did to us."

¹¹Then three thousand men from Judah went down to
the cave in the rock of Etam and said to Samson, "Don't you
realize that the Philistines are rulers over us? What have you
done to us?"

He answered, "I merely did to them what they did to me."

¹²They said to him, "We've come to tie you up and hand
you over to the Philistines."

Samson said, "Swear to me that you won't kill me yourselves."

¹³"Agreed," they answered. "We will only tie you up and
hand you over to them. We will not kill you." So they bound
him with two new ropes and led him up from the rock. ¹⁴As
he approached Lehi, the Philistines came toward him shouting. The Spirit of the LORD came powerfully upon him. The
ropes on his arms became like charred flax, and the bindings
dropped from his hands. ¹⁵Finding a fresh jawbone of a donkey, he grabbed it and struck down a thousand men.

¹⁶Then Samson said,

"With a donkey's jawbone
    I have made donkeys of them.ᵃ
With a donkey's jawbone
    I have killed a thousand men."

¹⁷When he finished speaking, he threw away the jawbone;
and the place was called Ramath Lehi.ᵇ

¹⁸Because he was very thirsty, he cried out to the LORD,
"You have given your servant this great victory. Must I now
die of thirst and fall into the hands of the uncircumcised?"
¹⁹Then God opened up the hollow place in Lehi, and water
came out of it. When Samson drank, his strength returned
and he revived. So the spring was called En Hakkore,ᶜ and
it is still there in Lehi.

²⁰Samson ledᵈ Israel for twenty years in the days of the
Philistines.

SAMSON AND DELILAH

16 One day Samson went to Gaza, where he saw a prostitute. He went in to spend the night with her. ²The
people of Gaza were told, "Samson is here!" So they surrounded the place and lay in wait for him all night at the
city gate. They made no move during the night, saying, "At
dawn we'll kill him."

³But Samson lay there only until the middle of the night.
Then he got up and took hold of the doors of the city gate,

ᵃ 16 Or *made a heap or two*; the Hebrew for *donkey* sounds like the Hebrew
for *heap*.   ᵇ 17 *Ramath Lehi* means *jawbone hill*.   ᶜ 19 *En Hakkore* means
caller's spring.   ᵈ 20 Traditionally *judged*

together with the two posts, and tore them loose, bar and all. He lifted them to his shoulders and carried them to the top of the hill that faces Hebron.

⁴Some time later, he fell in love with a woman in the Valley of Sorek whose name was Delilah. ⁵The rulers of the Philistines went to her and said, "See if you can lure him into showing you the secret of his great strength and how we can overpower him so we may tie him up and subdue him. Each one of us will give you eleven hundred shekels*a* of silver."

⁶So Delilah said to Samson, "Tell me the secret of your great strength and how you can be tied up and subdued."

⁷Samson answered her, "If anyone ties me with seven fresh bowstrings that have not been dried, I'll become as weak as any other man."

⁸Then the rulers of the Philistines brought her seven fresh bowstrings that had not been dried, and she tied him with them. ⁹With men hidden in the room, she called to him, "Samson, the Philistines are upon you!" But he snapped the bowstrings as easily as a piece of string snaps when it comes close to a flame. So the secret of his strength was not discovered.

¹⁰Then Delilah said to Samson, "You have made a fool of me; you lied to me. Come now, tell me how you can be tied."

¹¹He said, "If anyone ties me securely with new ropes that have never been used, I'll become as weak as any other man."

¹²So Delilah took new ropes and tied him with them. Then, with men hidden in the room, she called to him, "Samson, the Philistines are upon you!" But he snapped the ropes off his arms as if they were threads.

¹³Delilah then said to Samson, "All this time you have been making a fool of me and lying to me. Tell me how you can be tied."

He replied, "If you weave the seven braids of my head into the fabric on the loom and tighten it with the pin, I'll become as weak as any other man." So while he was sleeping, Delilah took the seven braids of his head, wove them into the fabric ¹⁴and*b* tightened it with the pin.

Again she called to him, "Samson, the Philistines are upon you!" He awoke from his sleep and pulled up the pin and the loom, with the fabric.

¹⁵Then she said to him, "How can you say, 'I love you,' when you won't confide in me? This is the third time you have made a fool of me and haven't told me the secret of your great strength." ¹⁶With such nagging she prodded him day after day until he was sick to death of it.

¹⁷So he told her everything. "No razor has ever been used on my head," he said, "because I have been a Nazirite dedicated to God from my mother's womb. If my head were shaved, my strength would leave me, and I would become as weak as any other man."

¹⁸When Delilah saw that he had told her everything, she sent word to the rulers of the Philistines, "Come back once

a 5 That is, about 28 pounds or about 13 kilograms   b 13,14 Some Septuagint manuscripts; Hebrew replied, "I can if you weave the seven braids of my head into the fabric on the loom." ¹⁴So she

Why did Samson have seven braids? (16:13)
In ancient Israel, the number seven symbolized completion and perfection. Because Samson was a Nazirite, the seven braids may have symbolized his unique calling from God.

Why did Samson give in to Delilah? (16:17)
Samson was often controlled by his emotions rather than by his commitments. He had insisted on marrying a Philistine bride, he often sought revenge because of his anger, and he fell in love with Delilah, a Philistine woman. He gave in because he was tired of her begging him for the secret of his strength.

Did Samson's hair make him strong? (16:20)
Samson lost his strength not because his hair was short but because he had broken his vows to God as a Nazirite. Even though God had stayed with Samson despite his other sins, this was an open, visible symbol that Samson had turned away from him.

Did the LORD leave Samson permanently? (16:20)
No. God's love for Samson continued even though Samson had broken his vows. During his time as a blind slave to the Philistines, Samson may have recommitted himself to God. His hair began to grow back, and God was able to use him to deliver Israel.

Who was Dagon? (16:23)
Dagon means *grain* in Hebrew, which means the people probably prayed to him for the health of their harvest. This could be why he was one of the most popular of the Philistine gods. The Philistines probably thought that Dagon was furious about the destruction of the fields and vineyards, so Samson's capture was seen as Dagon's revenge.

How could pushing down two pillars cause the building to collapse? (16:29–30)
Archaeologists have found evidence that one type of ancient temple contained two closely spaced central pillars made of wood. These pillars stood on marble bases and supported most of the weight of the roof. Pushing these pillars off their bases would have brought the whole building down.

What future event did Samson's death foreshadow? (16:30)
Through his death, Samson saved his people. That act pointed toward Jesus' death on the cross.

more; he has told me everything." So the rulers of the Philistines returned with the silver in their hands. ¹⁹After putting him to sleep on her lap, she called for someone to shave off the seven braids of his hair, and so began to subdue him.ᵃ And his strength left him.

²⁰Then she called, "Samson, the Philistines are upon you!"

He awoke from his sleep and thought, "I'll go out as before and shake myself free." But he did not know that the LORD had left him.

²¹Then the Philistines seized him, gouged out his eyes and took him down to Gaza. Binding him with bronze shackles, they set him to grinding grain in the prison. ²²But the hair on his head began to grow again after it had been shaved.

THE DEATH OF SAMSON

²³Now the rulers of the Philistines assembled to offer a great sacrifice to Dagon their god and to celebrate, saying, "Our god has delivered Samson, our enemy, into our hands."

²⁴When the people saw him, they praised their god, saying,

"Our god has delivered our enemy
　　into our hands,
the one who laid waste our land
　　and multiplied our slain."

²⁵While they were in high spirits, they shouted, "Bring out Samson to entertain us." So they called Samson out of the prison, and he performed for them.

When they stood him among the pillars, ²⁶Samson said to the servant who held his hand, "Put me where I can feel the pillars that support the temple, so that I may lean against them." ²⁷Now the temple was crowded with men and women; all the rulers of the Philistines were there, and on the roof were about three thousand men and women watching Samson perform. ²⁸Then Samson prayed to the LORD, "Sovereign LORD, remember me. Please, God, strengthen me just once more, and let me with one blow get revenge on the Philistines for my two eyes." ²⁹Then Samson reached toward the two central pillars on which the temple stood. Bracing himself against them, his right hand on the one and his left hand on the other, ³⁰Samson said, "Let me die with the Philistines!" Then he pushed with all his might, and down came the temple on the rulers and all the people in it. Thus he killed many more when he died than while he lived.

³¹Then his brothers and his father's whole family went down to get him. They brought him back and buried him between Zorah and Eshtaol in the tomb of Manoah his father. He had ledᵇ Israel twenty years.

MICAH'S IDOLS

17 Now a man named Micah from the hill country of Ephraim ²said to his mother, "The eleven hundred shekelsᶜ of silver that were taken from you and about

---

ᵃ *19* Hebrew; some Septuagint manuscripts *and he began to weaken*
ᵇ *31* Traditionally *judged*　　ᶜ *2* That is, about 28 pounds or about 13 kilograms

which I heard you utter a curse—I have that silver with me; I took it."

Then his mother said, "The LORD bless you, my son!"

3When he returned the eleven hundred shekels of silver to his mother, she said, "I solemnly consecrate my silver to the LORD for my son to make an image overlaid with silver. I will give it back to you."

4So after he returned the silver to his mother, she took two hundred shekels*a* of silver and gave them to a silversmith, who used them to make the idol. And it was put in Micah's house.

5Now this man Micah had a shrine, and he made an ephod and some household gods and installed one of his sons as his priest. 6In those days Israel had no king; everyone did as they saw fit.

7A young Levite from Bethlehem in Judah, who had been living within the clan of Judah, 8left that town in search of some other place to stay. On his way*b* he came to Micah's house in the hill country of Ephraim.

9Micah asked him, "Where are you from?"

"I'm a Levite from Bethlehem in Judah," he said, "and I'm looking for a place to stay."

10Then Micah said to him, "Live with me and be my father and priest, and I'll give you ten shekels*c* of silver a year, your clothes and your food." 11So the Levite agreed to live with him, and the young man became like one of his sons to him. 12Then Micah installed the Levite, and the young man became his priest and lived in his house. 13And Micah said, "Now I know that the LORD will be good to me, since this Levite has become my priest."

THE DANITES SETTLE IN LAISH

18 In those days Israel had no king.

And in those days the tribe of the Danites was seeking a place of their own where they might settle, because they had not yet come into an inheritance among the tribes of Israel. 2So the Danites sent five of their leading men from Zorah and Eshtaol to spy out the land and explore it. These men represented all the Danites. They told them, "Go, explore the land."

So they entered the hill country of Ephraim and came to the house of Micah, where they spent the night. 3When they were near Micah's house, they recognized the voice of the young Levite; so they turned in there and asked him, "Who brought you here? What are you doing in this place? Why are you here?"

4He told them what Micah had done for him, and said, "He has hired me and I am his priest."

5Then they said to him, "Please inquire of God to learn whether our journey will be successful."

6The priest answered them, "Go in peace. Your journey has the LORD's approval."

7So the five men left and came to Laish, where they saw

a 4 That is, about 5 pounds or about 2.3 kilograms   b 8 Or To carry on his profession   c 10 That is, about 4 ounces or about 115 grams

---

Why did Micah's mother bless him? (17:1–4)
Even though Micah had stolen a large sum from his mother, she blessed him when he admitted and returned it. Then she had the silversmith use part of the silver to make an image and an idol.

Why does the writer keep repeating that Israel had no king? (17:6; 18:1; 19:1; 21:25)
During this time, people did whatever they pleased, rather than obeying God. These verses were written from the perspective of someone looking back who saw how having a king had improved spiritual life in Israel.

Why did the Levite agree to become a personal priest in the house of Micah? (17:12)
Since he later agreed to lead an entire tribe in idol worship, it seems clear that he had turned away from God and was interested only in personal success or fame.

Danites Move North (18:1–2)

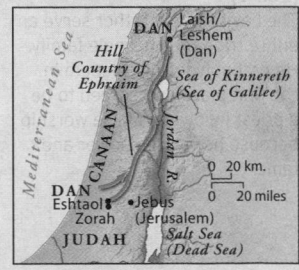

How did the Danite explorers recognize the Levite's voice? (18:3)
It's possible that his southern accent gave him away. It's also possible that they recognized his religious order by the way he chanted the ritual.

that the people were living in safety, like the Sidonians, at peace and secure. And since their land lacked nothing, they were prosperous.[a] Also, they lived a long way from the Sidonians and had no relationship with anyone else.[b]

⁸When they returned to Zorah and Eshtaol, their fellow Danites asked them, "How did you find things?"

⁹They answered, "Come on, let's attack them! We have seen the land, and it is very good. Aren't you going to do something? Don't hesitate to go there and take it over. ¹⁰When you get there, you will find an unsuspecting people and a spacious land that God has put into your hands, a land that lacks nothing whatever."

¹¹Then six hundred men of the Danites, armed for battle, set out from Zorah and Eshtaol. ¹²On their way they set up camp near Kiriath Jearim in Judah. This is why the place west of Kiriath Jearim is called Mahaneh Dan[c] to this day. ¹³From there they went on to the hill country of Ephraim and came to Micah's house.

¹⁴Then the five men who had spied out the land of Laish said to their fellow Danites, "Do you know that one of these houses has an ephod, some household gods and an image overlaid with silver? Now you know what to do." ¹⁵So they turned in there and went to the house of the young Levite at Micah's place and greeted him. ¹⁶The six hundred Danites, armed for battle, stood at the entrance of the gate. ¹⁷The five men who had spied out the land went inside and took the idol, the ephod and the household gods while the priest and the six hundred armed men stood at the entrance of the gate.

¹⁸When the five men went into Micah's house and took the idol, the ephod and the household gods, the priest said to them, "What are you doing?"

¹⁹They answered him, "Be quiet! Don't say a word. Come with us, and be our father and priest. Isn't it better that you serve a tribe and clan in Israel as priest rather than just one man's household?" ²⁰The priest was very pleased. He took the ephod, the household gods and the idol and went along with the people. ²¹Putting their little children, their livestock and their possessions in front of them, they turned away and left.

²²When they had gone some distance from Micah's house, the men who lived near Micah were called together and overtook the Danites. ²³As they shouted after them, the Danites turned and said to Micah, "What's the matter with you that you called out your men to fight?"

²⁴He replied, "You took the gods I made, and my priest, and went away. What else do I have? How can you ask, 'What's the matter with you?'"

²⁵The Danites answered, "Don't argue with us, or some of the men may get angry and attack you, and you and your family will lose your lives." ²⁶So the Danites went their way, and Micah, seeing that they were too strong for him, turned around and went back home.

Why did the Danite men steal the idols? (18:17)
Like Micah, the Danites thought the idols could give them some kind of supernatural power or insight.

Why was the priest glad to go with the Danites? (18:20)
The Levite would rather serve an entire tribe than a single family. He probably left Bethlehem in the first place and agreed to be a priest involved in false worship because he wanted power and fame.

---

[a] 7 The meaning of the Hebrew for this clause is uncertain.   [b] 7 Hebrew; some Septuagint manuscripts *with the Arameans*   [c] 12 *Mahaneh Dan* means *Dan's camp*.

²⁷Then they took what Micah had made, and his priest, and went on to Laish, against a people at peace and secure. They attacked them with the sword and burned down their city. ²⁸There was no one to rescue them because they lived a long way from Sidon and had no relationship with anyone else. The city was in a valley near Beth Rehob.

The Danites rebuilt the city and settled there. ²⁹They named it Dan after their ancestor Dan, who was born to Israel—though the city used to be called Laish. ³⁰There the Danites set up for themselves the idol, and Jonathan son of Gershom, the son of Moses,ᵃ and his sons were priests for the tribe of Dan until the time of the captivity of the land. ³¹They continued to use the idol Micah had made, all the time the house of God was in Shiloh.

A LEVITE AND HIS CONCUBINE

19 In those days Israel had no king.

Now a Levite who lived in a remote area in the hill country of Ephraim took a concubine from Bethlehem in Judah. ²But she was unfaithful to him. She left him and went back to her parents' home in Bethlehem, Judah. After she had been there four months, ³her husband went to her to persuade her to return. He had with him his servant and two donkeys. She took him into her parents' home, and when her father saw him, he gladly welcomed him. ⁴His father-in-law, the woman's father, prevailed on him to stay; so he remained with him three days, eating and drinking, and sleeping there.

⁵On the fourth day they got up early and he prepared to leave, but the woman's father said to his son-in-law, "Refresh yourself with something to eat; then you can go." ⁶So the two of them sat down to eat and drink together. Afterward the woman's father said, "Please stay tonight and enjoy yourself." ⁷And when the man got up to go, his father-in-law persuaded him, so he stayed there that night. ⁸On the morning of the fifth day, when he rose to go, the woman's father said, "Refresh yourself. Wait till afternoon!" So the two of them ate together.

⁹Then when the man, with his concubine and his servant, got up to leave, his father-in-law, the woman's father, said, "Now look, it's almost evening. Spend the night here; the day is nearly over. Stay and enjoy yourself. Early tomorrow morning you can get up and be on your way home." ¹⁰But, unwilling to stay another night, the man left and went toward Jebus (that is, Jerusalem), with his two saddled donkeys and his concubine.

¹¹When they were near Jebus and the day was almost gone, the servant said to his master, "Come, let's stop at this city of the Jebusites and spend the night."

¹²His master replied, "No. We won't go into any city whose people are not Israelites. We will go on to Gibeah." ¹³He added, "Come, let's try to reach Gibeah or Ramah and spend the night in one of those places." ¹⁴So they went on, and the

Was it right for the Danites to destroy Laish (18:27)
No. The Danites lost faith in God. They had been given a territory when Joshua assigned the land of Canaan to the tribes. Their land was located between the territories of Ephraim and Judah. But instead of relying on God to help them drive out the Philistines, they looked for an easier way to find a home.

What was the significance of this new priesthood? (18:30–31)
In their new territory, the descendants of Dan recruited Micah's priest Jonathan, the Levite, as their own. Though he was a grandson of Moses, he led the Danites in idol worship.

Was this woman the Levite's concubine or wife? (19:1, 3–4)
Because her father is called the Levite's father-in-law, the text suggests that she was a second wife, not simply a concubine or slave.

Why did the father show such great hospitality? (19:5–10)
This was the custom in Middle Eastern society. Because his daughter had been unfaithful and had disgraced her husband by returning to her family home, perhaps the father was determined to be an exceptionally gracious host.

ᵃ 30 Many Hebrew manuscripts, some Septuagint manuscripts and Vulgate; many other Hebrew manuscripts and some other Septuagint manuscripts *Manasseh*

sun set as they neared Gibeah in Benjamin. [15]There they stopped to spend the night. They went and sat in the city square, but no one took them in for the night.

[16]That evening an old man from the hill country of Ephraim, who was living in Gibeah (the inhabitants of the place were Benjamites), came in from his work in the fields. [17]When he looked and saw the traveler in the city square, the old man asked, "Where are you going? Where did you come from?"

[18]He answered, "We are on our way from Bethlehem in Judah to a remote area in the hill country of Ephraim where I live. I have been to Bethlehem in Judah and now I am going to the house of the Lord.[a] No one has taken me in for the night. [19]We have both straw and fodder for our donkeys and bread and wine for ourselves your servants—me, the woman and the young man with us. We don't need anything."

[20]"You are welcome at my house," the old man said. "Let me supply whatever you need. Only don't spend the night in the square." [21]So he took him into his house and fed his donkeys. After they had washed their feet, they had something to eat and drink.

[22]While they were enjoying themselves, some of the wicked men of the city surrounded the house. Pounding on the door, they shouted to the old man who owned the house, "Bring out the man who came to your house so we can have sex with him."

[23]The owner of the house went outside and said to them, "No, my friends, don't be so vile. Since this man is my guest, don't do this outrageous thing. [24]Look, here is my virgin daughter, and his concubine. I will bring them out to you now, and you can use them and do to them whatever you wish. But as for this man, don't do such an outrageous thing."

[25]But the men would not listen to him. So the man took his concubine and sent her outside to them, and they raped her and abused her throughout the night, and at dawn they let her go. [26]At daybreak the woman went back to the house where her master was staying, fell down at the door and lay there until daylight.

[27]When her master got up in the morning and opened the door of the house and stepped out to continue on his way, there lay his concubine, fallen in the doorway of the house, with her hands on the threshold. [28]He said to her, "Get up; let's go." But there was no answer. Then the man put her on his donkey and set out for home.

[29]When he reached home, he took a knife and cut up his concubine, limb by limb, into twelve parts and sent them into all the areas of Israel. [30]Everyone who saw it was saying to one another, "Such a thing has never been seen or done, not since the day the Israelites came up out of Egypt. Just imagine! We must do something! So speak up!"

THE ISRAELITES PUNISH THE BENJAMITES

20 Then all Israel from Dan to Beersheba and from the land of Gilead came together as one and assembled

---

[a] 18 Hebrew, Vulgate, Syriac and Targum; Septuagint *going home*

Why would the man sacrifice his daughter in order to protect a stranger? (19:24)
This man had misplaced values. He put the virtue of hospitality above protecting his daughter. This story has similarities to the story of Lot and the visitors (see Genesis 19). In both cases the surrounding culture had become extremely corrupt.

Why did the Levite cut up the dead body of his concubine? (19:29)
The Levite did this horrible deed to prompt the neighboring tribes to seek justice for what had been done to his concubine.

before the Lord in Mizpah. ²The leaders of all the people of the tribes of Israel took their places in the assembly
of God's people, four hundred thousand men armed with
swords. ³(The Benjamites heard that the Israelites had gone
up to Mizpah.) Then the Israelites said, "Tell us how this
awful thing happened."

⁴So the Levite, the husband of the murdered woman, said,
"I and my concubine came to Gibeah in Benjamin to spend
the night. ⁵During the night the men of Gibeah came after
me and surrounded the house, intending to kill me. They
raped my concubine, and she died. ⁶I took my concubine, cut
her into pieces and sent one piece to each region of Israel's
inheritance, because they committed this lewd and outrageous act in Israel. ⁷Now, all you Israelites, speak up and tell
me what you have decided to do."

⁸All the men rose up together as one, saying, "None of us
will go home. No, not one of us will return to his house. ⁹But
now this is what we'll do to Gibeah: We'll go up against it
in the order decided by casting lots. ¹⁰We'll take ten men
out of every hundred from all the tribes of Israel, and a hundred from a thousand, and a thousand from ten thousand, to
get provisions for the army. Then, when the army arrives at
Gibeah*ᵃ* in Benjamin, it can give them what they deserve for
this outrageous act done in Israel." ¹¹So all the Israelites got
together and united as one against the city.

¹²The tribes of Israel sent messengers throughout the tribe
of Benjamin, saying, "What about this awful crime that was
committed among you? ¹³Now turn those wicked men of
Gibeah over to us so that we may put them to death and
purge the evil from Israel."

But the Benjamites would not listen to their fellow Israelites. ¹⁴From their towns they came together at Gibeah to
fight against the Israelites. ¹⁵At once the Benjamites mobilized twenty-six thousand swordsmen from their towns,
in addition to seven hundred able young men from those
living in Gibeah. ¹⁶Among all these soldiers there were seven
hundred select troops who were left-handed, each of whom
could sling a stone at a hair and not miss.

¹⁷Israel, apart from Benjamin, mustered four hundred
thousand swordsmen, all of them fit for battle.

¹⁸The Israelites went up to Bethel*ᵇ* and inquired of God.
They said, "Who of us is to go up first to fight against the
Benjamites?"

The Lord replied, "Judah shall go first."

¹⁹The next morning the Israelites got up and pitched
camp near Gibeah. ²⁰The Israelites went out to fight the
Benjamites and took up battle positions against them at
Gibeah. ²¹The Benjamites came out of Gibeah and cut
down twenty-two thousand Israelites on the battlefield that
day. ²²But the Israelites encouraged one another and again
took up their positions where they had stationed themselves
the first day. ²³The Israelites went up and wept before the
Lord until evening, and they inquired of the Lord. They

**Why did the Benjamites
protect the guilty men?
(20:13–14)**
The Benjamites placed tribal
loyalty above bringing the men
of Gibeah to justice. The Israelites only wanted revenge on
the guilty parties, but when the
Benjamites refused to turn them
over, the battle began.

**How was this war unlike the
other wars the Israelites had
fought? (20:14–17)**
This was a massive war of revenge against fellow Israelites.
The earlier battles had been
fought against pagan tribes.

**How did left-handedness
help these soldiers? (20:16)**
These left-handed warriors had
practiced their skills and become
excellent marksmen with slings.
Stones weighing a pound or
more could be hurled at 90 to
100 miles (144 to 161 kilometers)
per hour.

A Sling (20:16)

*ᵃ 10 One Hebrew manuscript; most Hebrew manuscripts Geba, a variant of
Gibeah   ᵇ 18 Or to the house of God; also in verse 26*

Why did the Israelites lose so many people after receiving guidance from God? (20:18–25)
Before they consulted the LORD, the Israelites had made several vows (20:8; 21:1, 5). This suggests that they did not rely entirely on God but also trusted in their own abilities to give them victory. They should have put their faith in God and God alone.

said, "Shall we go up again to fight against the Benjamites, our fellow Israelites?"

The LORD answered, "Go up against them."

²⁴ Then the Israelites drew near to Benjamin the second day. ²⁵ This time, when the Benjamites came out from Gibeah to oppose them, they cut down another eighteen thousand Israelites, all of them armed with swords.

²⁶ Then all the Israelites, the whole army, went up to Bethel, and there they sat weeping before the LORD. They fasted that day until evening and presented burnt offerings and fellowship offerings to the LORD. ²⁷ And the Israelites inquired of the LORD. (In those days the ark of the covenant of God was there, ²⁸ with Phinehas son of Eleazar, the son of Aaron, ministering before it.) They asked, "Shall we go up again to fight against the Benjamites, our fellow Israelites, or not?"

The LORD responded, "Go, for tomorrow I will give them into your hands."

²⁹ Then Israel set an ambush around Gibeah. ³⁰ They went up against the Benjamites on the third day and took up positions against Gibeah as they had done before. ³¹ The Benjamites came out to meet them and were drawn away from the city. They began to inflict casualties on the Israelites as before, so that about thirty men fell in the open field and on the roads—the one leading to Bethel and the other to Gibeah. ³² While the Benjamites were saying, "We are defeating them as before," the Israelites were saying, "Let's retreat and draw them away from the city to the roads."

³³ All the men of Israel moved from their places and took up positions at Baal Tamar, and the Israelite ambush charged out of its place on the west*ᵃ* of Gibeah.*ᵇ* ³⁴ Then ten thousand of Israel's able young men made a frontal attack on Gibeah. The fighting was so heavy that the Benjamites did not realize how near disaster was. ³⁵ The LORD defeated Benjamin before Israel, and on that day the Israelites struck down 25,100 Benjamites, all armed with swords. ³⁶ Then the Benjamites saw that they were beaten.

Now the men of Israel had given way before Benjamin, because they relied on the ambush they had set near Gibeah. ³⁷ Those who had been in ambush made a sudden dash into Gibeah, spread out and put the whole city to the sword. ³⁸ The Israelites had arranged with the ambush that they should send up a great cloud of smoke from the city, ³⁹ and then the Israelites would counterattack.

The Benjamites had begun to inflict casualties on the Israelites (about thirty), and they said, "We are defeating them as in the first battle." ⁴⁰ But when the column of smoke began to rise from the city, the Benjamites turned and saw the whole city going up in smoke. ⁴¹ Then the Israelites counterattacked, and the Benjamites were terrified, because they realized that disaster had come on them. ⁴² So they fled before the Israelites in the direction of the wilderness, but they could not escape the battle. And the Israelites who came out of the towns cut them down there. ⁴³ They surrounded the

---

ᵃ 33 Some Septuagint manuscripts and Vulgate; the meaning of the Hebrew for this word is uncertain.   *ᵇ 33* Hebrew *Geba*, a variant of *Gibeah*

Benjamites, chased them and easily[a] overran them in the vicinity of Gibeah on the east. ⁴⁴Eighteen thousand Benjamites fell, all of them valiant fighters. ⁴⁵As they turned and fled toward the wilderness to the rock of Rimmon, the Israelites cut down five thousand men along the roads. They kept pressing after the Benjamites as far as Gidom and struck down two thousand more.

⁴⁶On that day twenty-five thousand Benjamite swordsmen fell, all of them valiant fighters. ⁴⁷But six hundred of them turned and fled into the wilderness to the rock of Rimmon, where they stayed four months. ⁴⁸The men of Israel went back to Benjamin and put all the towns to the sword, including the animals and everything else they found. All the towns they came across they set on fire.

WIVES FOR THE BENJAMITES

21 The men of Israel had taken an oath at Mizpah: "Not one of us will give his daughter in marriage to a Benjamite."

²The people went to Bethel,[b] where they sat before God until evening, raising their voices and weeping bitterly. ³"Lord, God of Israel," they cried, "why has this happened to Israel? Why should one tribe be missing from Israel today?"

⁴Early the next day the people built an altar and presented burnt offerings and fellowship offerings.

⁵Then the Israelites asked, "Who from all the tribes of Israel has failed to assemble before the Lord?" For they had taken a solemn oath that anyone who failed to assemble before the Lord at Mizpah was to be put to death.

⁶Now the Israelites grieved for the tribe of Benjamin, their fellow Israelites. "Today one tribe is cut off from Israel," they said. ⁷"How can we provide wives for those who are left, since we have taken an oath by the Lord not to give them any of our daughters in marriage?" ⁸Then they asked, "Which one of the tribes of Israel failed to assemble before the Lord at Mizpah?" They discovered that no one from Jabesh Gilead had come to the camp for the assembly. ⁹For when they counted the people, they found that none of the people of Jabesh Gilead were there.

¹⁰So the assembly sent twelve thousand fighting men with instructions to go to Jabesh Gilead and put to the sword those living there, including the women and children. ¹¹"This is what you are to do," they said. "Kill every male and every woman who is not a virgin." ¹²They found among the people living in Jabesh Gilead four hundred young women who had never slept with a man, and they took them to the camp at Shiloh in Canaan.

¹³Then the whole assembly sent an offer of peace to the Benjamites at the rock of Rimmon. ¹⁴So the Benjamites returned at that time and were given the women of Jabesh Gilead who had been spared. But there were not enough for all of them.

Why did the Israelites try to totally destroy the Benjamites when only a few were guilty? (20:48) The desire for revenge grew out of proportion to the crime. When the Israelites were taking over the land of Canaan, God had told them to completely eliminate the Canaanite tribes. But that was different, because those were pagan tribes who would have a corrupting influence on Israel. In this case, the Israelites fought their own people, and they failed to take into account the laws for limited revenge (see Exodus 21:12 – 36).

Why were the Israelites so concerned about finding wives for the few remaining Benjamite men? (21:1 – 25) They were grieved because one of the tribes of Israel had been almost completely wiped out. In order to help the tribe rebuild, they looked for ways to find wives for the Benjamite men. First, they captured young women from the town of Jabesh Gilead and killed the remaining citizens. Then they suggested that the Benjamites kidnap girls who were dancing in Shiloh.

ᵃ 43 The meaning of the Hebrew for this word is uncertain.   ᵇ 2 Or *to the house of God*

¹⁵The people grieved for Benjamin, because the LORD had made a gap in the tribes of Israel. ¹⁶And the elders of the assembly said, "With the women of Benjamin destroyed, how shall we provide wives for the men who are left? ¹⁷The Benjamite survivors must have heirs," they said, "so that a tribe of Israel will not be wiped out. ¹⁸We can't give them our daughters as wives, since we Israelites have taken this oath: 'Cursed be anyone who gives a wife to a Benjamite.' ¹⁹But look, there is the annual festival of the LORD in Shiloh, which lies north of Bethel, east of the road that goes from Bethel to Shechem, and south of Lebonah."

²⁰So they instructed the Benjamites, saying, "Go and hide in the vineyards ²¹and watch. When the young women of Shiloh come out to join in the dancing, rush from the vineyards and each of you seize one of them to be your wife. Then return to the land of Benjamin. ²²When their fathers or brothers complain to us, we will say to them, 'Do us the favor of helping them, because we did not get wives for them during the war. You will not be guilty of breaking your oath because you did not give your daughters to them.'"

²³So that is what the Benjamites did. While the young women were dancing, each man caught one and carried her off to be his wife. Then they returned to their inheritance and rebuilt the towns and settled in them.

²⁴At that time the Israelites left that place and went home to their tribes and clans, each to his own inheritance.

²⁵In those days Israel had no king; everyone did as they saw fit.

How did the suggestion that the Benjamites kidnap Israelite girls keep the Israelites from breaking a vow? (21:20–22)
The Israelites had foolishly vowed not to give any of their daughters to the Benjamites in marriage. But if the Benjamites kidnapped them, the Israelites would not have been responsible for breaking this vow.

Ruth

INTRODUCTION

Who wrote this book?
The author of Ruth is unknown.

Why was this book written?
The book of Ruth shows that some people trusted God even in the times of the judges.

What happens in this book?
Ruth, a young Moabite widow, travels to Israel with her Jewish mother-in-law and marries a good man there.

What do we learn about God in this book?
God loves people of every nation who put their trust in him.

Who are the key people in this book?
The most important people in this book are Naomi, Ruth, and Boaz.

Where did this happen?
Ruth and Naomi lived in Bethlehem, the city where David and Jesus were later born. (See the map on the next page to see where Bethlehem is.)

What are some of the stories in this book?

Ruth goes with Naomi	Ruth 1
Ruth meets Boaz	Ruth 2
Boaz marries Ruth	Ruth 4

When did these things happen?

1400 BC 1300 1200 1100 1000 900 800 700 600 500 400

ISRAELITES ENTER CANAAN (C. 1406 BC)
JUDGES BEGIN TO RULE (C. 1375 BC)
DEBORAH'S RULE (C. 1209 – 1169 BC)
SAMUEL'S BIRTH (C. 1105 BC)
SAMSON'S RULE (C. 1075 – 1055 BC)
DAVID NAMED KING (C. 1010 BC)
BOOK OF RUTH WRITTEN (C. 1000 BC)
DIVISION OF THE KINGDOM (930 BC)

Setting of Ruth (1:1)

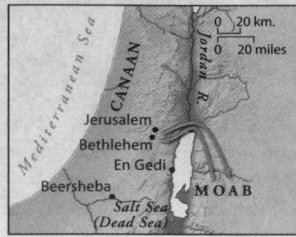

NAOMI LOSES HER HUSBAND AND SONS

1 In the days when the judges ruled,[a] there was a famine in the land. So a man from Bethlehem in Judah, together with his wife and two sons, went to live for a while in the country of Moab. [2]The man's name was Elimelek, his wife's name was Naomi, and the names of his two sons were Mahlon and Kilion. They were Ephrathites from Bethlehem, Judah. And they went to Moab and lived there.

[3]Now Elimelek, Naomi's husband, died, and she was left with her two sons. [4]They married Moabite women, one named Orpah and the other Ruth. After they had lived there about ten years, [5]both Mahlon and Kilion also died, and Naomi was left without her two sons and her husband.

NAOMI AND RUTH RETURN TO BETHLEHEM

[6]When Naomi heard in Moab that the LORD had come to the aid of his people by providing food for them, she and her daughters-in-law prepared to return home from there. [7]With her two daughters-in-law she left the place where she had been living and set out on the road that would take them back to the land of Judah.

[8]Then Naomi said to her two daughters-in-law, "Go back, each of you, to your mother's home. May the LORD show you kindness, as you have shown kindness to your dead husbands and to me. [9]May the LORD grant that each of you will find rest in the home of another husband."

Then she kissed them goodbye and they wept aloud [10]and said to her, "We will go back with you to your people."

[11]But Naomi said, "Return home, my daughters. Why would you come with me? Am I going to have any more sons, who could become your husbands? [12]Return home, my daughters; I am too old to have another husband. Even if I thought there was still hope for me—even if I had a husband tonight and then gave birth to sons— [13]would you wait until they grew up? Would you remain unmarried for them? No, my daughters. It is more bitter for me than for you, because the LORD's hand has turned against me!"

[14]At this they wept aloud again. Then Orpah kissed her mother-in-law goodbye, but Ruth clung to her.

[15]"Look," said Naomi, "your sister-in-law is going back to her people and her gods. Go back with her."

[16]But Ruth replied, "Don't urge me to leave you or to turn back from you. Where you go I will go, and where you stay I will stay. Your people will be my people and your God my God. [17]Where you die I will die, and there I will be buried. May the LORD deal with me, be it ever so severely, if even death separates you and me." [18]When Naomi realized that Ruth was determined to go with her, she stopped urging her.

[19]So the two women went on until they came to Bethlehem. When they arrived in Bethlehem, the whole town was stirred because of them, and the women exclaimed, "Can this be Naomi?"

[20]"Don't call me Naomi,[b]" she told them. "Call me Mara,[c] because the Almighty[d] has made my life very bitter. [21]I went

Why did Naomi urge her daughters-in-law to return home? (1:8–13)
Naomi was a widow and didn't have the ability to support them. She also believed that they would be able to remarry if they went back to their homeland. Naomi would never be able to provide them with husbands herself.

Was Ruth disloyal to her own family and people? (1:16–18)
Ruth's commitment to Naomi, even though the future might not seem promising, was more important to her than family ties. Ruth's decision to leave Moab and go with Naomi showed her strong faith in the God of Israel.

Why did Naomi change her name? (1:20–21)
Naomi means pleasant; Mara means bitter. Naomi said that she went away full and returned empty. These words highlight the theme of the book—how the empty Naomi became full again.

---

[a] 1 Traditionally judged   [b] 20 Naomi means pleasant.   [c] 20 Mara means bitter.   [d] 20 Hebrew Shaddai; also in verse 21

away full, but the LORD has brought me back empty. Why call me Naomi? The LORD has afflicted*a* me; the Almighty has brought misfortune upon me."

²²So Naomi returned from Moab accompanied by Ruth the Moabite, her daughter-in-law, arriving in Bethlehem as the barley harvest was beginning.

RUTH MEETS BOAZ IN THE GRAIN FIELD

2 Now Naomi had a relative on her husband's side, a man of standing from the clan of Elimelek, whose name was Boaz.

²And Ruth the Moabite said to Naomi, "Let me go to the fields and pick up the leftover grain behind anyone in whose eyes I find favor."

Naomi said to her, "Go ahead, my daughter." ³So she went out, entered a field and began to glean behind the harvesters. As it turned out, she was working in a field belonging to Boaz, who was from the clan of Elimelek.

⁴Just then Boaz arrived from Bethlehem and greeted the harvesters, "The LORD be with you!"

"The LORD bless you!" they answered.

⁵Boaz asked the overseer of his harvesters, "Who does that young woman belong to?"

⁶The overseer replied, "She is the Moabite who came back from Moab with Naomi. ⁷She said, 'Please let me glean and gather among the sheaves behind the harvesters.' She came into the field and has remained here from morning till now, except for a short rest in the shelter."

⁸So Boaz said to Ruth, "My daughter, listen to me. Don't go and glean in another field and don't go away from here. Stay here with the women who work for me. ⁹Watch the field where the men are harvesting, and follow along after the women. I have told the men not to lay a hand on you. And whenever you are thirsty, go and get a drink from the water jars the men have filled."

¹⁰At this, she bowed down with her face to the ground. She asked him, "Why have I found such favor in your eyes that you notice me—a foreigner?"

¹¹Boaz replied, "I've been told all about what you have done for your mother-in-law since the death of your husband—how you left your father and mother and your homeland and came to live with a people you did not know before. ¹²May the LORD repay you for what you have done. May you be richly rewarded by the LORD, the God of Israel, under whose wings you have come to take refuge."

¹³"May I continue to find favor in your eyes, my lord," she said. "You have put me at ease by speaking kindly to your servant—though I do not have the standing of one of your servants."

¹⁴At mealtime Boaz said to her, "Come over here. Have some bread and dip it in the wine vinegar."

When she sat down with the harvesters, he offered her some roasted grain. She ate all she wanted and had some left over. ¹⁵As she got up to glean, Boaz gave orders to his men,

Why was Ruth allowed to take grain from other people's fields? (2:2)
The law gave resident foreigners, widows, and orphans the right to take what was left over after a field had been harvested (see Deuteronomy 24:19–20). This was one of God's ways of providing for the poor.

Why was Ruth told to follow behind the servant girls? (2:8–9)
Usually men cut the grain, and servant girls followed behind to bind the grain into sheaves. By following the other women and picking up the grain behind them, she may have been safer from the men who worked in the fields. The fact that Boaz told them to leave her alone suggests that single women were sometimes harassed.

a 21 Or has testified against

What did it mean to thresh barley? (2:17)

To thresh was to separate the kernels of grain from the straw. This was done by laying the cut stalks on a flat rock or packed ground called a threshing floor. Small amounts of grain were beaten with sticks. For large amounts, people used animals to trample the stalks or pushed simple machines over them. This continued until all the grain had been separated from the stalks.

What was a guardian-redeemer? (2:20)

The guardian-redeemer was a close, influential relative to whom members of an extended family could turn for help. The guardian-redeemer had various responsibilities. He could buy back family land that had been sold to pay debts. He could pay the price to redeem relatives who had been enslaved. He could avenge the killing of a relative and could care for relatives during difficult circumstances. He also was responsible for providing an heir when a brother died without children. (This was called levirate marriage.)

Why did Naomi say that the LORD had not stopped showing his kindness? (2:20)

When she realized that Boaz was one of their guardian-redeemers, she realized that they had reason to hope. This is a turning point in the story.

"Let her gather among the sheaves and don't reprimand her. ¹⁶Even pull out some stalks for her from the bundles and leave them for her to pick up, and don't rebuke her."

¹⁷So Ruth gleaned in the field until evening. Then she threshed the barley she had gathered, and it amounted to about an ephah.[a] ¹⁸She carried it back to town, and her mother-in-law saw how much she had gathered. Ruth also brought out and gave her what she had left over after she had eaten enough.

¹⁹Her mother-in-law asked her, "Where did you glean today? Where did you work? Blessed be the man who took notice of you!"

Then Ruth told her mother-in-law about the one at whose place she had been working. "The name of the man I worked with today is Boaz," she said.

²⁰"The LORD bless him!" Naomi said to her daughter-in-law. "He has not stopped showing his kindness to the living and the dead." She added, "That man is our close relative; he is one of our guardian-redeemers.[b]"

²¹Then Ruth the Moabite said, "He even said to me, 'Stay with my workers until they finish harvesting all my grain.'"

²²Naomi said to Ruth her daughter-in-law, "It will be good for you, my daughter, to go with the women who work for him, because in someone else's field you might be harmed."

²³So Ruth stayed close to the women of Boaz to glean until the barley and wheat harvests were finished. And she lived with her mother-in-law.

RUTH AND BOAZ AT THE THRESHING FLOOR

3 One day Ruth's mother-in-law Naomi said to her, "My daughter, I must find a home[c] for you, where you will be well provided for. ²Now Boaz, with whose women you have worked, is a relative of ours. Tonight he will be winnowing barley on the threshing floor. ³Wash, put on perfume, and get dressed in your best clothes. Then go down to the threshing floor, but don't let him know you are there until he has finished eating and drinking. ⁴When he lies down, note the

---

[a] 17 That is, probably about 30 pounds or about 13 kilograms   [b] 20 The Hebrew word for *guardian-redeemer* is a legal term for one who has the obligation to redeem a relative in serious difficulty (see Lev. 25:25-55).
[c] 1 Hebrew *find rest* (see 1:9)

Is it the responsibility of Christians to care for the poor?

RUTH 2

Ruth was able to gather food from the fields because of God's law that governed gleaning. The law gave resident foreigners, widows, and orphans the right to glean what was left over after a field had been harvested. Deuteronomy 24:19–20 says, "When you are harvesting in your field and you overlook a sheaf, do not go back to get it. Leave it for the foreigner, the fatherless and the widow, so that the LORD your God may bless you in all the work of your hands. When you beat the olives from your trees, do not go over the branches a second time. Leave what remains for the foreigner, the fatherless and the widow." This was one of God's ways of providing for the poor.

Throughout the Bible God shows great compassion to those who are poor and who cannot provide for themselves. This emphasizes the need for Christians to be generous to those who are homeless, hungry, or hurting. Jesus said in a parable, "Truly I tell you, whatever you did for one of the least of these brothers and sisters of mine, you did for me" (Matthew 25:40).

place where he is lying. Then go and uncover his feet and lie down. He will tell you what to do."

⁵"I will do whatever you say," Ruth answered. ⁶So she went down to the threshing floor and did everything her mother-in-law told her to do.

⁷When Boaz had finished eating and drinking and was in good spirits, he went over to lie down at the far end of the grain pile. Ruth approached quietly, uncovered his feet and lay down. ⁸In the middle of the night something startled the man; he turned—and there was a woman lying at his feet!

⁹"Who are you?" he asked.

"I am your servant Ruth," she said. "Spread the corner of your garment over me, since you are a guardian-redeemer*ᵃ* of our family."

¹⁰"The LORD bless you, my daughter," he replied. "This kindness is greater than that which you showed earlier: You have not run after the younger men, whether rich or poor. ¹¹And now, my daughter, don't be afraid. I will do for you all you ask. All the people of my town know that you are a woman of noble character. ¹²Although it is true that I am a guardian-redeemer of our family, there is another who is more closely related than I. ¹³Stay here for the night, and in the morning if he wants to do his duty as your guardian-redeemer, good; let him redeem you. But if he is not willing, as surely as the LORD lives I will do it. Lie here until morning."

¹⁴So she lay at his feet until morning, but got up before anyone could be recognized; and he said, "No one must know that a woman came to the threshing floor."

¹⁵He also said, "Bring me the shawl you are wearing and hold it out." When she did so, he poured into it six measures of barley and placed the bundle on her. Then heᵇ went back to town.

¹⁶When Ruth came to her mother-in-law, Naomi asked, "How did it go, my daughter?"

Then she told her everything Boaz had done for her ¹⁷and added, "He gave me these six measures of barley, saying, 'Don't go back to your mother-in-law empty-handed.'"

¹⁸Then Naomi said, "Wait, my daughter, until you find out what happens. For the man will not rest until the matter is settled today."

BOAZ MARRIES RUTH

4 Meanwhile Boaz went up to the town gate and sat down there just as the guardian-redeemerᶜ he had mentioned came along. Boaz said, "Come over here, my friend, and sit down." So he went over and sat down. ²Boaz took ten of the elders of the town and said, "Sit here," and they did so. ³Then he said to the guardian-redeemer, "Naomi, who has come back from Moab, is selling the piece of land that belonged to our relative Elimelek.

Why did Boaz sleep on the threshing floor? (3:7) Robbers would sometimes visit a threshing floor at night to steal grain, so the owner and workers often slept there to protect the crops.

Were Ruth's actions immoral? (3:7–8, 13–14) No. Ruth was making a ceremonial request for a marriage, appealing to Boaz's role as guardian-redeemer.

How had Ruth been kind? (3:10) Ruth had earlier shown her great kindness to Naomi. Now Boaz thanked her for asking him to marry her rather than running after younger men.

ᵃ 9 The Hebrew word for *guardian-redeemer* is a legal term for one who has the obligation to redeem a relative in serious difficulty (see Lev. 25:25-55); also in verses 12 and 13.   *ᵇ* 15 Most Hebrew manuscripts; many Hebrew manuscripts, Vulgate and Syriac *she*   *ᶜ* 1 The Hebrew word for *guardian-redeemer* is a legal term for one who has the obligation to redeem a relative in serious difficulty (see Lev. 25:25-55); also in verses 3, 6, 8 and 14.

[4] I thought I should bring the matter to your attention and suggest that you buy it in the presence of these seated here and in the presence of the elders of my people. If you will redeem it, do so. But if you[a] will not, tell me, so I will know. For no one has the right to do it except you, and I am next in line."

"I will redeem it," he said.

[5] Then Boaz said, "On the day you buy the land from Naomi, you also acquire Ruth the Moabite, the[b] dead man's widow, in order to maintain the name of the dead with his property."

[6] At this, the guardian-redeemer said, "Then I cannot redeem it because I might endanger my own estate. You redeem it yourself. I cannot do it."

[7] (Now in earlier times in Israel, for the redemption and transfer of property to become final, one party took off his sandal and gave it to the other. This was the method of legalizing transactions in Israel.)

[8] So the guardian-redeemer said to Boaz, "Buy it yourself." And he removed his sandal.

[9] Then Boaz announced to the elders and all the people, "Today you are witnesses that I have bought from Naomi all the property of Elimelek, Kilion and Mahlon. [10] I have also acquired Ruth the Moabite, Mahlon's widow, as my wife, in order to maintain the name of the dead with his property, so that his name will not disappear from among his family or from his hometown. Today you are witnesses!"

[11] Then the elders and all the people at the gate said, "We are witnesses. May the LORD make the woman who is coming into your home like Rachel and Leah, who together built up the family of Israel. May you have standing in Ephrathah and be famous in Bethlehem. [12] Through the offspring the LORD gives you by this young woman, may your family be like that of Perez, whom Tamar bore to Judah."

NAOMI GAINS A SON

[13] So Boaz took Ruth and she became his wife. When he made love to her, the LORD enabled her to conceive, and she gave birth to a son. [14] The women said to Naomi: "Praise be to the LORD, who this day has not left you without a guardian-redeemer. May he become famous throughout Israel! [15] He will renew your life and sustain you in your old age. For your daughter-in-law, who loves you and who is better to you than seven sons, has given him birth."

[16] Then Naomi took the child in her arms and cared for him. [17] The women living there said, "Naomi has a son!" And they named him Obed. He was the father of Jesse, the father of David.

THE GENEALOGY OF DAVID

[18] This, then, is the family line of Perez:

Perez was the father of Hezron,

---

[a] 4 Many Hebrew manuscripts, Septuagint, Vulgate and Syriac; most Hebrew manuscripts *he*   [b] 5 Vulgate and Syriac; Hebrew (see also Septuagint) *Naomi and from Ruth the Moabite, you acquire the*

Why was this guardian-redeemer worried about endangering his own estate? (4:6)
He may have been worried that his property would pass to the family of Elimelech. This could happen if he had a son by Ruth who was his only surviving heir. He may also have had a family of his own and been worried about creating a dispute among family members about the inheritance of his property if there was another wife and possible children to divide amongst.

Why was this transaction done in front of the elders? (4:10)
In this day and culture, people did not use written contracts as we do today. Instead, they made oaths in front of people. The people acted as witnesses and held each party to their respective agreements.

Why was a woman from Moab chosen to be the grandmother of David? (4:18–22)
Ruth's faith in the LORD made it possible for her to be an ancestor of David and eventually of Jesus. By choosing her for this role, God showed that his covenant would be for all people.

¹⁹ Hezron the father of Ram,
   Ram the father of Amminadab,
²⁰ Amminadab the father of Nahshon,
   Nahshon the father of Salmon,[a]
²¹ Salmon the father of Boaz,
   Boaz the father of Obed,
²² Obed the father of Jesse,
   and Jesse the father of David.

[a] 20 A few Hebrew manuscripts, some Septuagint manuscripts and Vulgate
(see also verse 21 and Septuagint of 1 Chron. 2:11); most Hebrew
manuscripts *Salma*

1 Samuel

INTRODUCTION

Who wrote this book?	The author of this book is unknown.
Why was this book written?	The book of 1 Samuel shows how the Israelites became a kingdom.
What happens in this book?	Samuel serves as Israel's last judge. Saul becomes Israel's first king. David kills Goliath and joins Saul's army. Saul disobeys God and is killed.
What do we learn about God in this book?	God wants leaders who will obey him.
Who are the key people in this book?	The most important people in this book are Samuel, Saul, and David.
Where did this happen?	The stories in this book happened in the land of Israel. (See the map at the back of this Bible to see where Israel is.)
What are some of the stories in this book?	God calls the boy Samuel — 1 Samuel 3
	The ark is captured and returned — 1 Samuel 4 – 6
	Samuel anoints Saul king — 1 Samuel 9
	Saul disobeys — 1 Samuel 13; 15
	Samuel anoints David king — 1 Samuel 16
	David kills Goliath — 1 Samuel 17
	Saul is jealous of David — 1 Samuel 18
	David and Jonathan — 1 Samuel 20
	David spares Saul's life — 1 Samuel 24
	Abigail faces David — 1 Samuel 25
	David spares Saul again — 1 Samuel 26
	Saul dies in battle — 1 Samuel 31

When did these things happen?

1400 BC 1300 1200 1100 1000 900 800 700 600 500 400

ISRAELITES ENTER CANAAN (C. 1406 BC)

JUDGES BEGIN TO RULE (C. 1375 BC)

SAUL NAMED KING (1050 BC)

DAVID KILLS GOLIATH (C. 1025 BC)

SAUL DIES; DAVID NAMED KING (1010 BC)

SOLOMON'S REIGN (970 – 930 BC)

DIVISION OF THE KINGDOM (930 BC)

BOOK OF 1 SAMUEL WRITTEN (C. 925 BC)

THE BIRTH OF SAMUEL

1 There was a certain man from Ramathaim, a Zuphite[a] from the hill country of Ephraim, whose name was Elkanah son of Jeroham, the son of Elihu, the son of Tohu, the son of Zuph, an Ephraimite. [2] He had two wives; one was called Hannah and the other Peninnah. Peninnah had children, but Hannah had none.

[3] Year after year this man went up from his town to worship and sacrifice to the LORD Almighty at Shiloh, where Hophni and Phinehas, the two sons of Eli, were priests of the LORD. [4] Whenever the day came for Elkanah to sacrifice, he would give portions of the meat to his wife Peninnah and to all her sons and daughters. [5] But to Hannah he gave a double portion because he loved her, and the LORD had closed her womb. [6] Because the LORD had closed Hannah's womb, her rival kept provoking her in order to irritate her. [7] This went on year after year. Whenever Hannah went up to the house of the LORD, her rival provoked her till she wept and would not eat. [8] Her husband Elkanah would say to her, "Hannah, why are you weeping? Why don't you eat? Why are you downhearted? Don't I mean more to you than ten sons?"

[9] Once when they had finished eating and drinking in Shiloh, Hannah stood up. Now Eli the priest was sitting on his chair by the doorpost of the LORD's house. [10] In her deep anguish Hannah prayed to the LORD, weeping bitterly. [11] And she made a vow, saying, "LORD Almighty, if you will only look on your servant's misery and remember me, and not forget your servant but give her a son, then I will give him to the LORD for all the days of his life, and no razor will ever be used on his head."

[12] As she kept on praying to the LORD, Eli observed her mouth. [13] Hannah was praying in her heart, and her lips were moving but her voice was not heard. Eli thought she was drunk [14] and said to her, "How long are you going to stay drunk? Put away your wine."

[15] "Not so, my lord," Hannah replied, "I am a woman who is deeply troubled. I have not been drinking wine or beer; I was pouring out my soul to the LORD. [16] Do not take your servant for a wicked woman; I have been praying here out of my great anguish and grief."

[17] Eli answered, "Go in peace, and may the God of Israel grant you what you have asked of him."

[18] She said, "May your servant find favor in your eyes." Then she went her way and ate something, and her face was no longer downcast.

[19] Early the next morning they arose and worshiped before the LORD and then went back to their home at Ramah. Elkanah made love to his wife Hannah, and the LORD remembered her. [20] So in the course of time Hannah became pregnant and gave birth to a son. She named him Samuel,[b] saying, "Because I asked the LORD for him."

Why did Elkanah have two wives? (1:2)
Even though God had instituted marriage as between one man and one woman, polygamy was not uncommon in the ancient world. Apparently God tolerated the practice.

Did Hannah blame God for not being able to have children? (1:5)
The Israelites saw God as the primary cause behind everything, regardless of the outcome. This was not a matter of blaming God as much as realizing that God was ultimately in control of everything.

Why did Hannah make a vow not to cut her child's hair? (1:11)
This was her promise to devote her child to the LORD's service as a Nazirite (see Judges 13:5). One of the Nazirite vows was not to cut one's hair. Most Nazirite vows were temporary, but Samuel's was for life.

Why did Eli assume that Hannah was drunk? (1:13–14)
Eli was probably used to some worshipers arriving drunk because during the three annual religious festivals, people drank a great deal of wine.

---

[a] 1 See Septuagint and 1 Chron. 6:26-27,33-35; or *from Ramathaim Zuphim.*
[b] 20 *Samuel* sounds like the Hebrew for *heard by God.*

HANNAH DEDICATES SAMUEL

²¹When her husband Elkanah went up with all his family to offer the annual sacrifice to the Lord and to fulfill his vow, ²²Hannah did not go. She said to her husband, "After the boy is weaned, I will take him and present him before the Lord, and he will live there always."ᵃ

²³"Do what seems best to you," her husband Elkanah told her. "Stay here until you have weaned him; only may the Lord make good hisᵇ word." So the woman stayed at home and nursed her son until she had weaned him.

²⁴After he was weaned, she took the boy with her, young as he was, along with a three-year-old bull,ᶜ an ephahᵈ of flour and a skin of wine, and brought him to the house of the Lord at Shiloh. ²⁵When the bull had been sacrificed, they brought the boy to Eli, ²⁶and she said to him, "Pardon me, my lord. As surely as you live, I am the woman who stood here beside you praying to the Lord. ²⁷I prayed for this child, and the Lord has granted me what I asked of him. ²⁸So now I give him to the Lord. For his whole life he will be given over to the Lord." And he worshiped the Lord there.

HANNAH'S PRAYER

2 Then Hannah prayed and said:

"My heart rejoices in the Lord;
    in the Lord my hornᵉ is lifted high.
My mouth boasts over my enemies,
    for I delight in your deliverance.

²"There is no one holy like the Lord;
    there is no one besides you;
    there is no Rock like our God.

³"Do not keep talking so proudly
    or let your mouth speak such arrogance,
for the Lord is a God who knows,
    and by him deeds are weighed.

⁴"The bows of the warriors are broken,
    but those who stumbled are armed with strength.
⁵Those who were full hire themselves out for food,
    but those who were hungry are hungry no more.
She who was barren has borne seven children,
    but she who has had many sons pines away.

⁶"The Lord brings death and makes alive;
    he brings down to the grave and raises up.
⁷The Lord sends poverty and wealth;
    he humbles and he exalts.
⁸He raises the poor from the dust
    and lifts the needy from the ash heap;
he seats them with princes
    and has them inherit a throne of honor.

ᵃ 22 Masoretic Text; Dead Sea Scrolls *always. I have dedicated him as a Nazirite—all the days of his life."*   ᵇ 23 Masoretic Text; Dead Sea Scrolls, Septuagint and Syriac *your*   ᶜ 24 Dead Sea Scrolls, Septuagint and Syriac; Masoretic Text *with three bulls*   ᵈ 24 That is, probably about 36 pounds or about 16 kilograms   ᵉ 1 *Horn* here symbolizes strength; also in verse 10.

Why did Hannah keep Samuel with her until after he was weaned? (1:22)
In the ancient Middle East, children were usually nursed for three or more years. Children did not usually leave their homes for long periods of time until after they had been weaned.

Hannah Dedicates Samuel (1:24)

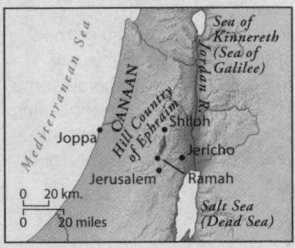

How did Hannah give Samuel to the Lord? (1:28)
After Samuel was weaned, Hannah dedicated him to God for lifelong service in the tabernacle. As a young boy, Samuel did tasks appropriate for his age such as cleaning and running errands.

What was Hannah's horn? (2:1)
In her prayer, she used the term *horn* to symbolize her renewed dignity. Hannah had been honored and lifted high by God's gift of a son. Mothering a child (when she thought she was unable to have children) took away society's disgrace associated with being barren.

Does God make some people poor? (2:7)
As he did for Hannah, God brings some people up, while he sometimes brings others down as punishment for their sins. There is justice in everything God does. This prayer is an example of that.

"For the foundations of the earth are the Lord's;
  on them he has set the world.
[9] He will guard the feet of his faithful servants,
  but the wicked will be silenced in the place of
    darkness.

"It is not by strength that one prevails;
[10] those who oppose the Lord will be broken.
The Most High will thunder from heaven;
  the Lord will judge the ends of the earth.

"He will give strength to his king
  and exalt the horn of his anointed."

[11] Then Elkanah went home to Ramah, but the boy ministered before the Lord under Eli the priest.

ELI'S WICKED SONS

[12] Eli's sons were scoundrels; they had no regard for the Lord. [13] Now it was the practice of the priests that, whenever any of the people offered a sacrifice, the priest's servant would come with a three-pronged fork in his hand while the meat was being boiled [14] and would plunge the fork into the pan or kettle or caldron or pot. Whatever the fork brought up the priest would take for himself. This is how they treated all the Israelites who came to Shiloh. [15] But even before the fat was burned, the priest's servant would come and say to the person who was sacrificing, "Give the priest some meat to roast; he won't accept boiled meat from you, but only raw."

[16] If the person said to him, "Let the fat be burned first, and then take whatever you want," the servant would answer, "No, hand it over now; if you don't, I'll take it by force."

[17] This sin of the young men was very great in the Lord's sight, for they[a] were treating the Lord's offering with contempt.

[18] But Samuel was ministering before the Lord—a boy wearing a linen ephod. [19] Each year his mother made him a little robe and took it to him when she went up with her husband to offer the annual sacrifice. [20] Eli would bless Elkanah and his wife, saying, "May the Lord give you children by this woman to take the place of the one she prayed for and gave to[b] the Lord." Then they would go home. [21] And the Lord was gracious to Hannah; she gave birth to three sons and two daughters. Meanwhile, the boy Samuel grew up in the presence of the Lord.

[22] Now Eli, who was very old, heard about everything his sons were doing to all Israel and how they slept with the women who served at the entrance to the tent of meeting. [23] So he said to them, "Why do you do such things? I hear from all the people about these wicked deeds of yours. [24] No, my sons; the report I hear spreading among the Lord's people is not good. [25] If one person sins against another, God[c] may mediate for the offender; but if anyone sins against the Lord, who will intercede for them?" His sons, however, did

Why was it wrong for the priests to take raw meat? (2:12–15)
The first sin was taking what didn't belong to them. They didn't offer up a portion of the meat to the Lord, and they didn't follow the laws of how to consume the meat.

Who were these women? (2:22)
They probably served at the tabernacle by carrying out domestic tasks like washing or sewing, which would mean they were neither prostitutes nor priestesses.

What other sin did Eli's sons commit? (2:25)
Besides breaking the rules for the offerings and sleeping with women who worked at the tabernacle, Eli's sons failed to respect their father or listen to his advice.

---

[a] 17 Dead Sea Scrolls and Septuagint; Masoretic Text *people*   [b] 20 Dead Sea Scrolls; Masoretic Text *and asked from*   [c] 25 Or *the judges*

not listen to their father's rebuke, for it was the Lord's will to put them to death.

²⁶ And the boy Samuel continued to grow in stature and in favor with the Lord and with people.

PROPHECY AGAINST THE HOUSE OF ELI

²⁷ Now a man of God came to Eli and said to him, "This is what the Lord says: 'Did I not clearly reveal myself to your ancestor's family when they were in Egypt under Pharaoh? ²⁸ I chose your ancestor out of all the tribes of Israel to be my priest, to go up to my altar, to burn incense, and to wear an ephod in my presence. I also gave your ancestor's family all the food offerings presented by the Israelites. ²⁹ Why do you*ᵃ* scorn my sacrifice and offering that I prescribed for my dwelling? Why do you honor your sons more than me by fattening yourselves on the choice parts of every offering made by my people Israel?'

³⁰ "Therefore the Lord, the God of Israel, declares: 'I promised that members of your family would minister before me forever.' But now the Lord declares: 'Far be it from me! Those who honor me I will honor, but those who despise me will be disdained. ³¹ The time is coming when I will cut short your strength and the strength of your priestly house, so that no one in it will reach old age, ³² and you will see distress in my dwelling. Although good will be done to Israel, no one in your family line will ever reach old age. ³³ Every one of you that I do not cut off from serving at my altar I will spare only to destroy your sight and sap your strength, and all your descendants will die in the prime of life.

³⁴ "'And what happens to your two sons, Hophni and Phinehas, will be a sign to you—they will both die on the same day. ³⁵ I will raise up for myself a faithful priest, who will do according to what is in my heart and mind. I will firmly establish his priestly house, and they will minister before my anointed one always. ³⁶ Then everyone left in your family line will come and bow down before him for a piece of silver and a loaf of bread and plead, "Appoint me to some priestly office so I can have food to eat."'"

THE LORD CALLS SAMUEL

3 The boy Samuel ministered before the Lord under Eli. In those days the word of the Lord was rare; there were not many visions.

² One night Eli, whose eyes were becoming so weak that he could barely see, was lying down in his usual place. ³ The lamp of God had not yet gone out, and Samuel was lying down in the house of the Lord, where the ark of God was. ⁴ Then the Lord called Samuel.

Samuel answered, "Here I am." ⁵ And he ran to Eli and said, "Here I am; you called me."

But Eli said, "I did not call; go back and lie down." So he went and lay down.

⁶ Again the Lord called, "Samuel!" And Samuel got up and went to Eli and said, "Here I am; you called me."

Why would Eli's descendants suffer for these sins? (2:31–33)
Sin was not just an individual matter. Those who were guilty had to pay a penalty, but so did family members and the rest of the community.

How could Samuel sleep near the ark of God? (3:3)
Although he was near the ark, Samuel was not in the same room with it. Only the high priest could be that close to the ark. He and Eli slept outside the most holy area of the tent of meeting.

ᵃ 29 The Hebrew is plural.

"My son," Eli said, "I did not call; go back and lie down."

[7] Now Samuel did not yet know the LORD: The word of the LORD had not yet been revealed to him.

[8] A third time the LORD called, "Samuel!" And Samuel got up and went to Eli and said, "Here I am; you called me."

Then Eli realized that the LORD was calling the boy. [9] So Eli told Samuel, "Go and lie down, and if he calls you, say, 'Speak, LORD, for your servant is listening.'" So Samuel went and lay down in his place.

[10] The LORD came and stood there, calling as at the other times, "Samuel! Samuel!"

Then Samuel said, "Speak, for your servant is listening."

[11] And the LORD said to Samuel: "See, I am about to do something in Israel that will make the ears of everyone who hears about it tingle. [12] At that time I will carry out against Eli everything I spoke against his family—from beginning to end. [13] For I told him that I would judge his family forever because of the sin he knew about; his sons blasphemed God,[a] and he failed to restrain them. [14] Therefore I swore to the house of Eli, 'The guilt of Eli's house will never be atoned for by sacrifice or offering.'"

[15] Samuel lay down until morning and then opened the doors of the house of the LORD. He was afraid to tell Eli the vision, [16] but Eli called him and said, "Samuel, my son."

Samuel answered, "Here I am."

[17] "What was it he said to you?" Eli asked. "Do not hide it from me. May God deal with you, be it ever so severely, if you hide from me anything he told you." [18] So Samuel told him everything, hiding nothing from him. Then Eli said, "He is the LORD; let him do what is good in his eyes."

[19] The LORD was with Samuel as he grew up, and he let none of Samuel's words fall to the ground. [20] And all Israel from Dan to Beersheba recognized that Samuel was attested as a prophet of the LORD. [21] The LORD continued to appear at Shiloh, and there he revealed himself to Samuel through his word.

4 And Samuel's word came to all Israel.

THE PHILISTINES CAPTURE THE ARK

Now the Israelites went out to fight against the Philistines. The Israelites camped at Ebenezer, and the Philistines at Aphek. [2] The Philistines deployed their forces to meet Israel, and as the battle spread, Israel was defeated by the Philistines, who killed about four thousand of them on the battlefield. [3] When the soldiers returned to camp, the elders of Israel asked, "Why did the LORD bring defeat on us today before the Philistines? Let us bring the ark of the LORD's covenant from Shiloh, so that he may go with us and save us from the hand of our enemies."

[4] So the people sent men to Shiloh, and they brought back the ark of the covenant of the LORD Almighty, who is enthroned between the cherubim. And Eli's two sons, Hophni and Phinehas, were there with the ark of the covenant of God.

[a] 13 An ancient Hebrew scribal tradition (see also Septuagint); Masoretic Text *sons made themselves contemptible*

Why did Eli threaten Samuel? (3:17)
Breaking an oath resulted in punishment. Eli was highlighting this fact. As the high priest, he made Samuel promise to tell the truth. Eli may have realized that God had bypassed him and spoken directly to Samuel, but he needed verification.

Travels of the Ark (4:3 — 7:1)

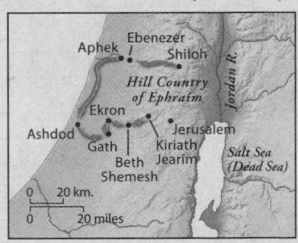

Why did the people send for the ark when they went into battle? (4:4)
The people thought that because the ark was the LORD's dwelling place, he would be with them and help them win the battle. However, the more important issue was whether they were being faithful and true to God. The ark was not a magical box that would guarantee victory.

⁵When the ark of the Lord's covenant came into the camp, all Israel raised such a great shout that the ground shook. ⁶Hearing the uproar, the Philistines asked, "What's all this shouting in the Hebrew camp?"

When they learned that the ark of the Lord had come into the camp, ⁷the Philistines were afraid. "A god has*a* come into the camp," they said. "Oh no! Nothing like this has happened before. ⁸We're doomed! Who will deliver us from the hand of these mighty gods? They are the gods who struck the Egyptians with all kinds of plagues in the wilderness. ⁹Be strong, Philistines! Be men, or you will be subject to the Hebrews, as they have been to you. Be men, and fight!"

¹⁰So the Philistines fought, and the Israelites were defeated and every man fled to his tent. The slaughter was very great; Israel lost thirty thousand foot soldiers. ¹¹The ark of God was captured, and Eli's two sons, Hophni and Phinehas, died.

Why did the Israelites flee to their tents? (4:10)
This does not refer to their army tents but suggests that each soldier tried to run to his hometown. The Israelites scattered when they were defeated by the Philistines.

DEATH OF ELI

¹²That same day a Benjamite ran from the battle line and went to Shiloh with his clothes torn and dust on his head. ¹³When he arrived, there was Eli sitting on his chair by the side of the road, watching, because his heart feared for the ark of God. When the man entered the town and told what had happened, the whole town sent up a cry.

¹⁴Eli heard the outcry and asked, "What is the meaning of this uproar?"

The man hurried over to Eli, ¹⁵who was ninety-eight years old and whose eyes had failed so that he could not see. ¹⁶He told Eli, "I have just come from the battle line; I fled from it this very day."

Eli asked, "What happened, my son?"

¹⁷The man who brought the news replied, "Israel fled before the Philistines, and the army has suffered heavy losses. Also your two sons, Hophni and Phinehas, are dead, and the ark of God has been captured."

¹⁸When he mentioned the ark of God, Eli fell backward off his chair by the side of the gate. His neck was broken and he died, for he was an old man, and he was heavy. He had led*b* Israel forty years.

¹⁹His daughter-in-law, the wife of Phinehas, was pregnant and near the time of delivery. When she heard the news that the ark of God had been captured and that her father-in-law and her husband were dead, she went into labor and gave birth, but was overcome by her labor pains. ²⁰As she was dying, the women attending her said, "Don't despair; you have given birth to a son." But she did not respond or pay any attention.

²¹She named the boy Ichabod,*c* saying, "The Glory has departed from Israel"—because of the capture of the ark of God and the deaths of her father-in-law and her husband. ²²She said, "The Glory has departed from Israel, for the ark of God has been captured."

Why did Phinehas's wife name her son Ichabod? (4:21)
The name *Ichabod* meant "the glory has departed." She was dying, and her husband, brother-in-law, and father-in-law had died. Also, the ark had been captured, so God's presence was no longer with Israel.

---

a 7 Or *"Gods have* (see Septuagint)   *b 18* Traditionally *judged*
c 21 Ichabod means *no glory.*

THE ARK IN ASHDOD AND EKRON

5 After the Philistines had captured the ark of God, they took it from Ebenezer to Ashdod. [2]Then they carried the ark into Dagon's temple and set it beside Dagon. [3]When the people of Ashdod rose early the next day, there was Dagon, fallen on his face on the ground before the ark of the LORD! They took Dagon and put him back in his place. [4]But the following morning when they rose, there was Dagon, fallen on his face on the ground before the ark of the LORD! His head and hands had been broken off and were lying on the threshold; only his body remained. [5]That is why to this day neither the priests of Dagon nor any others who enter Dagon's temple at Ashdod step on the threshold.

[6]The LORD's hand was heavy on the people of Ashdod and its vicinity; he brought devastation on them and afflicted them with tumors.[a] [7]When the people of Ashdod saw what was happening, they said, "The ark of the god of Israel must not stay here with us, because his hand is heavy on us and on Dagon our god." [8]So they called together all the rulers of the Philistines and asked them, "What shall we do with the ark of the god of Israel?"

They answered, "Have the ark of the god of Israel moved to Gath." So they moved the ark of the God of Israel.

[9]But after they had moved it, the LORD's hand was against that city, throwing it into a great panic. He afflicted the people of the city, both young and old, with an outbreak of tumors.[b] [10]So they sent the ark of God to Ekron.

As the ark of God was entering Ekron, the people of Ekron cried out, "They have brought the ark of the god of Israel around to us to kill us and our people." [11]So they called together all the rulers of the Philistines and said, "Send the ark of the god of Israel away; let it go back to its own place, or it[c] will kill us and our people." For death had filled the city with panic; God's hand was very heavy on it. [12]Those who did not die were afflicted with tumors, and the outcry of the city went up to heaven.

THE ARK RETURNED TO ISRAEL

6 When the ark of the LORD had been in Philistine territory seven months, [2]the Philistines called for the priests and the diviners and said, "What shall we do with the ark of the LORD? Tell us how we should send it back to its place."

[3]They answered, "If you return the ark of the god of Israel, do not send it back to him without a gift; by all means send a guilt offering to him. Then you will be healed, and you will know why his hand has not been lifted from you."

[4]The Philistines asked, "What guilt offering should we send to him?"

They replied, "Five gold tumors and five gold rats, according to the number of the Philistine rulers, because the same plague has struck both you and your rulers. [5]Make models of the tumors and of the rats that are destroying the country,

---

Who was Dagon? (5:2)
Dagon was the Philistines' pagan god. Dagon may have been a fish god or a god of grain or weather. Dagon was the son of El and the father of Baal, two other pagan gods.

Why were the Philistines punished? (5:6)
The Philistines had stolen the ark and placed it in the temple of their pagan god Dagon. They wanted to show that their god was superior. But the LORD did not allow such an insult to go unpunished. He knocked over the idol of Dagon, breaking off its head and hands to show his superiority.

Why did the people ask for the ark to be sent back to Israel? (5:11)
After three towns were struck by tumors when the ark arrived, the people realized that the God of Israel was the source of this disease.

How were the rats and tumors connected? (6:4–5)
The rats may have carried the disease that caused the tumors. If that was the case, the disease may have been the bubonic plague, which can be spread by fleas carried by rats.

---

[a] 6 Hebrew; Septuagint and Vulgate *tumors. And rats appeared in their land, and there was death and destruction throughout the city*   [b] 9 Or *with tumors in the groin* (see Septuagint)   [c] 11 Or *he*

How did the Philistines try to find out God's will? (6:7–9)
The Philistines sent the ark back to the Israelites on a cart drawn by two cows that had calves and had never been yoked. If the cows pulled the ark back to the Israelites' territory, then the Philistines would know that the Lord had sent the plague. The cows had not been trained to pull a cart and would not have willingly left their calves.

and give glory to Israel's god. Perhaps he will lift his hand from you and your gods and your land. ⁶Why do you harden your hearts as the Egyptians and Pharaoh did? When Israel's god dealt harshly with them, did they not send the Israelites out so they could go on their way?

⁷"Now then, get a new cart ready, with two cows that have calved and have never been yoked. Hitch the cows to the cart, but take their calves away and pen them up. ⁸Take the ark of the Lord and put it on the cart, and in a chest beside it put the gold objects you are sending back to him as a guilt offering. Send it on its way, ⁹but keep watching it. If it goes up to its own territory, toward Beth Shemesh, then the Lord has brought this great disaster on us. But if it does not, then we will know that it was not his hand that struck us but that it happened to us by chance."

¹⁰So they did this. They took two such cows and hitched them to the cart and penned up their calves. ¹¹They placed the ark of the Lord on the cart and along with it the chest containing the gold rats and the models of the tumors. ¹²Then the cows went straight up toward Beth Shemesh, keeping on the road and lowing all the way; they did not turn to the right or to the left. The rulers of the Philistines followed them as far as the border of Beth Shemesh.

¹³Now the people of Beth Shemesh were harvesting their wheat in the valley, and when they looked up and saw the ark, they rejoiced at the sight. ¹⁴The cart came to the field of Joshua of Beth Shemesh, and there it stopped beside a large rock. The people chopped up the wood of the cart and sacrificed the cows as a burnt offering to the Lord. ¹⁵The Levites took down the ark of the Lord, together with the chest containing the gold objects, and placed them on the large rock. On that day the people of Beth Shemesh offered burnt offerings and made sacrifices to the Lord. ¹⁶The five rulers of the Philistines saw all this and then returned that same day to Ekron.

¹⁷These are the gold tumors the Philistines sent as a guilt offering to the Lord—one each for Ashdod, Gaza, Ashkelon, Gath and Ekron. ¹⁸And the number of the gold rats was according to the number of Philistine towns belonging to the five rulers—the fortified towns with their country villages. The large rock on which the Levites set the ark of the Lord is a witness to this day in the field of Joshua of Beth Shemesh.

¹⁹But God struck down some of the inhabitants of Beth Shemesh, putting seventy[a] of them to death because they looked into the ark of the Lord. The people mourned because of the heavy blow the Lord had dealt them. ²⁰And the people of Beth Shemesh asked, "Who can stand in the presence of the Lord, this holy God? To whom will the ark go up from here?"

²¹Then they sent messengers to the people of Kiriath Jearim, saying, "The Philistines have returned the ark of the Lord. Come down and take it up to your town." ¹So the men of Kiriath Jearim came and took up the ark of the Lord. They brought it to Abinadab's house on the hill and

Why did God kill 70 men from Beth Shemesh? (6:19)
These men had not respected the ark and had disobeyed God's command that no one should touch the ark or look inside it.

---

[a] *19* A few Hebrew manuscripts; most Hebrew manuscripts and Septuagint *50,070*

consecrated Eleazar his son to guard the ark of the LORD. [2]The ark remained at Kiriath Jearim a long time—twenty years in all.

SAMUEL SUBDUES THE PHILISTINES AT MIZPAH

Then all the people of Israel turned back to the LORD. [3]So Samuel said to all the Israelites, "If you are returning to the LORD with all your hearts, then rid yourselves of the foreign gods and the Ashtoreths and commit yourselves to the LORD and serve him only, and he will deliver you out of the hand of the Philistines." [4]So the Israelites put away their Baals and Ashtoreths, and served the LORD only.

[5]Then Samuel said, "Assemble all Israel at Mizpah, and I will intercede with the LORD for you." [6]When they had assembled at Mizpah, they drew water and poured it out before the LORD. On that day they fasted and there they confessed, "We have sinned against the LORD." Now Samuel was serving as leader[a] of Israel at Mizpah.

[7]When the Philistines heard that Israel had assembled at Mizpah, the rulers of the Philistines came up to attack them. When the Israelites heard of it, they were afraid because of the Philistines. [8]They said to Samuel, "Do not stop crying out to the LORD our God for us, that he may rescue us from the hand of the Philistines." [9]Then Samuel took a suckling lamb and sacrificed it as a whole burnt offering to the LORD. He cried out to the LORD on Israel's behalf, and the LORD answered him.

[10]While Samuel was sacrificing the burnt offering, the Philistines drew near to engage Israel in battle. But that day the LORD thundered with loud thunder against the Philistines and threw them into such a panic that they were routed before the Israelites. [11]The men of Israel rushed out of Mizpah and pursued the Philistines, slaughtering them along the way to a point below Beth Kar.

[12]Then Samuel took a stone and set it up between Mizpah and Shen. He named it Ebenezer,[b] saying, "Thus far the LORD has helped us."

[13]So the Philistines were subdued and they stopped invading Israel's territory. Throughout Samuel's lifetime, the hand of the LORD was against the Philistines. [14]The towns from Ekron to Gath that the Philistines had captured from Israel were restored to Israel, and Israel delivered the neighboring territory from the hands of the Philistines. And there was peace between Israel and the Amorites.

[15]Samuel continued as Israel's leader all the days of his life. [16]From year to year he went on a circuit from Bethel to Gilgal to Mizpah, judging Israel in all those places. [17]But he always went back to Ramah, where his home was, and there he also held court for Israel. And he built an altar there to the LORD.

ISRAEL ASKS FOR A KING

8 When Samuel grew old, he appointed his sons as Israel's leaders.[c] [2]The name of his firstborn was Joel and the

---

Why was the ark kept so long at Kiriath Jearim? (7:2)
During this time, the people mourned the way the ark had been disgraced. They may have been waiting for God's instructions about how to move the ark to avoid the fate of those who were killed for looking inside it or died from the rats and tumors associated with the ark.

Who were Ashtoreths? (7:3)
These were female gods such as Ashtoreth and Asherah who, along with Baal the sun god, were the chief gods of Canaan. Ashtoreth was usually considered the goddess of love. She was known by various names: Ishtar in Babylon, Athtart in Aram, Astarte or Aphrodite in Greece, and Venus in Rome. Worship of this goddess often included immoral sexual practices.

Why did they pour out water before the LORD? (7:6)
This ceremony appears to symbolize the act of pouring out their hearts in repentance and humility.

What was the meaning of this stone? (7:12)
Samuel named the stone *Ebenezer*, which means *stone of help*. The Israelites once again turned back to God. They vowed to ask God for help. The stone may have shown how far God had allowed them to push back the Philistines.

---

[a] 6 Traditionally judge; also in verse 15   *[b] 12 Ebenezer means stone of help.*
[c] 1 Traditionally judges

name of his second was Abijah, and they served at Beersheba. ³But his sons did not follow his ways. They turned aside after dishonest gain and accepted bribes and perverted justice.

⁴So all the elders of Israel gathered together and came to Samuel at Ramah. ⁵They said to him, "You are old, and your sons do not follow your ways; now appoint a king to lead*ᵃ* us, such as all the other nations have."

⁶But when they said, "Give us a king to lead us," this displeased Samuel; so he prayed to the LORD. ⁷And the LORD told him: "Listen to all that the people are saying to you; it is not you they have rejected, but they have rejected me as their king. ⁸As they have done from the day I brought them up out of Egypt until this day, forsaking me and serving other gods, so they are doing to you. ⁹Now listen to them; but warn them solemnly and let them know what the king who will reign over them will claim as his rights."

¹⁰Samuel told all the words of the LORD to the people who were asking him for a king. ¹¹He said, "This is what the king who will reign over you will claim as his rights: He will take your sons and make them serve with his chariots and horses, and they will run in front of his chariots. ¹²Some he will assign to be commanders of thousands and commanders of fifties, and others to plow his ground and reap his harvest, and still others to make weapons of war and equipment for his chariots. ¹³He will take your daughters to be perfumers and cooks and bakers. ¹⁴He will take the best of your fields and vineyards and olive groves and give them to his attendants. ¹⁵He will take a tenth of your grain and of your vintage and give it to his officials and attendants. ¹⁶Your male and female servants and the best of your cattle*ᵇ* and donkeys he will take for his own use. ¹⁷He will take a tenth of your flocks, and you yourselves will become his slaves. ¹⁸When that day comes, you will cry out for relief from the king you have chosen, but the LORD will not answer you in that day."

¹⁹But the people refused to listen to Samuel. "No!" they said. "We want a king over us. ²⁰Then we will be like all the other nations, with a king to lead us and to go out before us and fight our battles."

²¹When Samuel heard all that the people said, he repeated it before the LORD. ²²The LORD answered, "Listen to them and give them a king."

Then Samuel said to the Israelites, "Everyone go back to your own town."

SAMUEL ANOINTS SAUL

9 There was a Benjamite, a man of standing, whose name was Kish son of Abiel, the son of Zeror, the son of Bekorath, the son of Aphiah of Benjamin. ²Kish had a son named Saul, as handsome a young man as could be found anywhere in Israel, and he was a head taller than anyone else.

³Now the donkeys belonging to Saul's father Kish were lost, and Kish said to his son Saul, "Take one of the servants with you and go and look for the donkeys." ⁴So he passed

---

Why did the people want a king? (8:5)
The elders said they needed a king because Samuel was getting old and his sons did not follow in their father's footsteps. But the real reason seemed to be that they wanted to be like the other nations. A king would be a symbol of power and would lead them into battle.

What did Samuel say that a king would do? (8:11–18)
Samuel told the people that having a king would not be an easy thing. In essence, they would be slaves to their king's demands.

Samuel Anoints Saul (9:2)

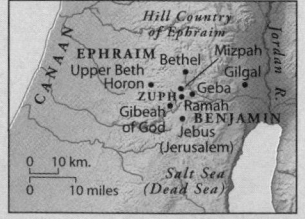

ᵃ 5 Traditionally *judge*; also in verses 6 and 20   *ᵇ 16* Septuagint; Hebrew *young men*

through the hill country of Ephraim and through the area around Shalisha, but they did not find them. They went on into the district of Shaalim, but the donkeys were not there. Then he passed through the territory of Benjamin, but they did not find them.

⁵When they reached the district of Zuph, Saul said to the servant who was with him, "Come, let's go back, or my father will stop thinking about the donkeys and start worrying about us."

⁶But the servant replied, "Look, in this town there is a man of God; he is highly respected, and everything he says comes true. Let's go there now. Perhaps he will tell us what way to take."

⁷Saul said to his servant, "If we go, what can we give the man? The food in our sacks is gone. We have no gift to take to the man of God. What do we have?"

⁸The servant answered him again. "Look," he said, "I have a quarter of a shekel*ᵃ* of silver. I will give it to the man of God so that he will tell us what way to take." ⁹(Formerly in Israel, if someone went to inquire of God, they would say, "Come, let us go to the seer," because the prophet of today used to be called a seer.)

¹⁰"Good," Saul said to his servant. "Come, let's go." So they set out for the town where the man of God was.

¹¹As they were going up the hill to the town, they met some young women coming out to draw water, and they asked them, "Is the seer here?"

¹²"He is," they answered. "He's ahead of you. Hurry now; he has just come to our town today, for the people have a sacrifice at the high place. ¹³As soon as you enter the town, you will find him before he goes up to the high place to eat. The people will not begin eating until he comes, because he must bless the sacrifice; afterward, those who are invited will eat. Go up now; you should find him about this time."

¹⁴They went up to the town, and as they were entering it, there was Samuel, coming toward them on his way up to the high place.

¹⁵Now the day before Saul came, the LORD had revealed this to Samuel: ¹⁶"About this time tomorrow I will send you a man from the land of Benjamin. Anoint him ruler over my people Israel; he will deliver them from the hand of the Philistines. I have looked on my people, for their cry has reached me."

¹⁷When Samuel caught sight of Saul, the LORD said to him, "This is the man I spoke to you about; he will govern my people."

¹⁸Saul approached Samuel in the gateway and asked, "Would you please tell me where the seer's house is?"

¹⁹"I am the seer," Samuel replied. "Go up ahead of me to the high place, for today you are to eat with me, and in the morning I will send you on your way and will tell you all that is in your heart. ²⁰As for the donkeys you lost three days ago, do not worry about them; they have been found. And to whom is all the desire of Israel turned, if not to you and your whole family line?"

ᵃ 8 That is, about 1/10 ounce or about 3 grams

Why did they think it necessary to have a gift for Samuel? (9:7)
It was customary to give a prophet a gift as a sign of respect or as thanks for a sign from God.

Why was worship at a high place allowed here? (9:12)
God had told the Israelites not to be like the Canaanites and to worship at high places. Instead, they were to worship at the central location of the tabernacle. However, since the ark had been removed from the tabernacle in Shiloh, God may have allowed his people to worship here.

What did this anointing mean? (9:16)
Anointing showed that someone was set apart for a special task. It also showed that the LORD had prepared the person for that task.

How had the desire of Israel turned to Saul and his family? (9:20)
Israel desired to have a king, and Samuel identified Saul as the one who would serve as the first king of Israel.

Why did Saul say that he was not worthy to serve? (9:21)
This was a common response from the men God chose to serve in leadership roles. Saul said that he was from the smallest clan (Benjamin), which was true. His tribe had been greatly reduced by this time (see Judges 20:46–48). When God made Saul king, he continued his pattern of selecting leaders who seemed the least qualified.

²¹ Saul answered, "But am I not a Benjamite, from the smallest tribe of Israel, and is not my clan the least of all the clans of the tribe of Benjamin? Why do you say such a thing to me?"

²² Then Samuel brought Saul and his servant into the hall and seated them at the head of those who were invited — about thirty in number. ²³ Samuel said to the cook, "Bring the piece of meat I gave you, the one I told you to lay aside."

²⁴ So the cook took up the thigh with what was on it and set it in front of Saul. Samuel said, "Here is what has been kept for you. Eat, because it was set aside for you for this occasion from the time I said, 'I have invited guests.'" And Saul dined with Samuel that day.

²⁵ After they came down from the high place to the town, Samuel talked with Saul on the roof of his house. ²⁶ They rose about daybreak, and Samuel called to Saul on the roof, "Get ready, and I will send you on your way." When Saul got ready, he and Samuel went outside together. ²⁷ As they were going down to the edge of the town, Samuel said to Saul, "Tell the servant to go on ahead of us" — and the servant did so — "but you stay here for a while, so that I may give you a message from God."

10 Then Samuel took a flask of olive oil and poured it on Saul's head and kissed him, saying, "Has not the LORD anointed you ruler over his inheritance?ᵃ ² When you leave me today, you will meet two men near Rachel's tomb, at Zelzah on the border of Benjamin. They will say to you, 'The donkeys you set out to look for have been found. And now your father has stopped thinking about them and is worried about you. He is asking, "What shall I do about my son?"'

³ "Then you will go on from there until you reach the great tree of Tabor. Three men going up to worship God at Bethel will meet you there. One will be carrying three young goats, another three loaves of bread, and another a skin of wine. ⁴ They will greet you and offer you two loaves of bread, which you will accept from them.

⁵ "After that you will go to Gibeah of God, where there is a Philistine outpost. As you approach the town, you will meet a procession of prophets coming down from the high place with lyres, timbrels, pipes and harps being played before them, and they will be prophesying. ⁶ The Spirit of the LORD will come powerfully upon you, and you will prophesy with them; and you will be changed into a different person. ⁷ Once these signs are fulfilled, do whatever your hand finds to do, for God is with you.

⁸ "Go down ahead of me to Gilgal. I will surely come down to you to sacrifice burnt offerings and fellowship offerings, but you must wait seven days until I come to you and tell you what you are to do."

Who were these prophets? (10:5)
The bands of prophets Samuel was associated with were probably small communities of men who banded together to support one another in their spiritual growth. This group of prophets used musical instruments while praising God.

SAUL MADE KING

⁹ As Saul turned to leave Samuel, God changed Saul's heart, and all these signs were fulfilled that day. ¹⁰ When he and his servant arrived at Gibeah, a procession of prophets

---

ᵃ *1* Hebrew; Septuagint and Vulgate *over his people Israel? You will reign over the LORD's people and save them from the power of their enemies round about. And this will be a sign to you that the LORD has anointed you ruler over his inheritance:*

met him; the Spirit of God came powerfully upon him, and he joined in their prophesying. ¹¹When all those who had formerly known him saw him prophesying with the prophets, they asked each other, "What is this that has happened to the son of Kish? Is Saul also among the prophets?"

¹²A man who lived there answered, "And who is their father?" So it became a saying: "Is Saul also among the prophets?" ¹³After Saul stopped prophesying, he went to the high place.

¹⁴Now Saul's uncle asked him and his servant, "Where have you been?"

"Looking for the donkeys," he said. "But when we saw they were not to be found, we went to Samuel."

¹⁵Saul's uncle said, "Tell me what Samuel said to you."

¹⁶Saul replied, "He assured us that the donkeys had been found." But he did not tell his uncle what Samuel had said about the kingship.

¹⁷Samuel summoned the people of Israel to the LORD at Mizpah ¹⁸and said to them, "This is what the LORD, the God of Israel, says: 'I brought Israel up out of Egypt, and I delivered you from the power of Egypt and all the kingdoms that oppressed you.' ¹⁹But you have now rejected your God, who saves you out of all your disasters and calamities. And you have said, 'No, appoint a king over us.' So now present yourselves before the LORD by your tribes and clans."

²⁰When Samuel had all Israel come forward by tribes, the tribe of Benjamin was taken by lot. ²¹Then he brought forward the tribe of Benjamin, clan by clan, and Matri's clan was taken. Finally Saul son of Kish was taken. But when they looked for him, he was not to be found. ²²So they inquired further of the LORD, "Has the man come here yet?"

And the LORD said, "Yes, he has hidden himself among the supplies."

²³They ran and brought him out, and as he stood among the people he was a head taller than any of the others. ²⁴Samuel said to all the people, "Do you see the man the LORD has chosen? There is no one like him among all the people."

Then the people shouted, "Long live the king!"

²⁵Samuel explained to the people the rights and duties of kingship. He wrote them down on a scroll and deposited it before the LORD. Then Samuel dismissed the people to go to their own homes.

²⁶Saul also went to his home in Gibeah, accompanied by valiant men whose hearts God had touched. ²⁷But some scoundrels said, "How can this fellow save us?" They despised him and brought him no gifts. But Saul kept silent.

SAUL RESCUES THE CITY OF JABESH

11 Nahash[a] the Ammonite went up and besieged Jabesh Gilead. And all the men of Jabesh said to him, "Make a treaty with us, and we will be subject to you."

---

[a] 1 Masoretic Text; Dead Sea Scrolls *gifts. Now Nahash king of the Ammonites oppressed the Gadites and Reubenites severely. He gouged out all their right eyes and struck terror and dread in Israel. Not a man remained among the Israelites beyond the Jordan whose right eye was not gouged out by Nahash king of the Ammonites, except that seven thousand men fled from the Ammonites and entered Jabesh Gilead. About a month later,* ¹*Nahash*

How was Saul changed? (10:9–10)
Through God's intervention, Saul may have gained confidence to lead God's people (see 9:21). The "Spirit of God came powerfully upon him."

How was the tribe of Benjamin chosen? (10:20–21)
The usual way by which God provided specific direction to his people was through casting lots.

What were "the rights and duties of kingship"? (10:25)
These were God's rules for the king, which would serve as safeguards to manage the way they ruled the people. These guidelines would have matched the ones listed in Deuteronomy 17:14–20.

Saul Rescues Jabesh (11:1–11)

Why did Nahash demand that the people have their right eyes gouged out? (11:2) The Ammonites knew that this would demoralize and weaken the people of Jabesh Gilead. Their military force would also become useless if the soldiers and archers couldn't use their right eyes.

Why would the Ammonites give the Israelites a week to mount a defense? (11:3) Nahash knew that if his army attacked the city immediately, many of his soldiers would also die. By waiting seven days, he hoped to avoid unnecessary losses. He probably guessed that the Israelites would surrender because Saul did not have an army yet, Jabesh Gilead was somewhat cut off from the rest of Israel, and Israel didn't have a centralized government.

Why was Saul plowing fields? (11:5) Saul was still making the transition to kingship. He returned to his home and resumed his familiar work until it became clear what was expected of him as king.

Why did Saul have to be confirmed as king? (11:14–15) Even though Saul had been anointed by Samuel and been confirmed as God's choice, some people still didn't accept him as king (see 10:27). But Saul's leadership in the battle unified the nation and established his ability to serve. So Samuel took the

²But Nahash the Ammonite replied, "I will make a treaty with you only on the condition that I gouge out the right eye of every one of you and so bring disgrace on all Israel."

³The elders of Jabesh said to him, "Give us seven days so we can send messengers throughout Israel; if no one comes to rescue us, we will surrender to you."

⁴When the messengers came to Gibeah of Saul and reported these terms to the people, they all wept aloud. ⁵Just then Saul was returning from the fields, behind his oxen, and he asked, "What is wrong with everyone? Why are they weeping?" Then they repeated to him what the men of Jabesh had said.

⁶When Saul heard their words, the Spirit of God came powerfully upon him, and he burned with anger. ⁷He took a pair of oxen, cut them into pieces, and sent the pieces by messengers throughout Israel, proclaiming, "This is what will be done to the oxen of anyone who does not follow Saul and Samuel." Then the terror of the LORD fell on the people, and they came out together as one. ⁸When Saul mustered them at Bezek, the men of Israel numbered three hundred thousand and those of Judah thirty thousand.

⁹They told the messengers who had come, "Say to the men of Jabesh Gilead, 'By the time the sun is hot tomorrow, you will be rescued.'" When the messengers went and reported this to the men of Jabesh, they were elated. ¹⁰They said to the Ammonites, "Tomorrow we will surrender to you, and you can do to us whatever you like."

¹¹The next day Saul separated his men into three divisions; during the last watch of the night they broke into the camp of the Ammonites and slaughtered them until the heat of the day. Those who survived were scattered, so that no two of them were left together.

SAUL CONFIRMED AS KING

¹²The people then said to Samuel, "Who was it that asked, 'Shall Saul reign over us?' Turn these men over to us so that we may put them to death."

¹³But Saul said, "No one will be put to death today, for this day the LORD has rescued Israel."

¹⁴Then Samuel said to the people, "Come, let us go to Gilgal and there renew the kingship." ¹⁵So all the people went to Gilgal and made Saul king in the presence of the LORD. There they sacrificed fellowship offerings before the LORD, and Saul and all the Israelites held a great celebration.

SAMUEL'S FAREWELL SPEECH

12 Samuel said to all Israel, "I have listened to everything you said to me and have set a king over you. ²Now you have a king as your leader. As for me, I am old and gray, and my sons are here with you. I have been your leader from my youth until this day. ³Here I stand. Testify against me in the presence of the LORD and his anointed. Whose ox have I taken? Whose donkey have I taken? Whom have I cheated? Whom have I oppressed? From whose hand have I accepted a bribe to make me shut my eyes? If I have done any of these things, I will make it right."

⁴"You have not cheated or oppressed us," they replied. "You have not taken anything from anyone's hand."

⁵Samuel said to them, "The LORD is witness against you, and also his anointed is witness this day, that you have not found anything in my hand."

"He is witness," they said.

⁶Then Samuel said to the people, "It is the LORD who appointed Moses and Aaron and brought your ancestors up out of Egypt. ⁷Now then, stand here, because I am going to confront you with evidence before the LORD as to all the righteous acts performed by the LORD for you and your ancestors.

⁸"After Jacob entered Egypt, they cried to the LORD for help, and the LORD sent Moses and Aaron, who brought your ancestors out of Egypt and settled them in this place.

⁹"But they forgot the LORD their God; so he sold them into the hand of Sisera, the commander of the army of Hazor, and into the hands of the Philistines and the king of Moab, who fought against them. ¹⁰They cried out to the LORD and said, 'We have sinned; we have forsaken the LORD and served the Baals and the Ashtoreths. But now deliver us from the hands of our enemies, and we will serve you.' ¹¹Then the LORD sent Jerub-Baal,ᵃ Barak,ᵇ Jephthah and Samuel,ᶜ and he delivered you from the hands of your enemies all around you, so that you lived in safety.

¹²"But when you saw that Nahash king of the Ammonites was moving against you, you said to me, 'No, we want a king to rule over us'—even though the LORD your God was your king. ¹³Now here is the king you have chosen, the one you asked for; see, the LORD has set a king over you. ¹⁴If you fear the LORD and serve and obey him and do not rebel against his commands, and if both you and the king who reigns over you follow the LORD your God—good! ¹⁵But if you do not obey the LORD, and if you rebel against his commands, his hand will be against you, as it was against your ancestors.

¹⁶"Now then, stand still and see this great thing the LORD is about to do before your eyes! ¹⁷Is it not wheat harvest now? I will call on the LORD to send thunder and rain. And you will realize what an evil thing you did in the eyes of the LORD when you asked for a king."

¹⁸Then Samuel called on the LORD, and that same day the LORD sent thunder and rain. So all the people stood in awe of the LORD and of Samuel.

¹⁹The people all said to Samuel, "Pray to the LORD your God for your servants so that we will not die, for we have added to all our other sins the evil of asking for a king."

²⁰"Do not be afraid," Samuel replied. "You have done all this evil; yet do not turn away from the LORD, but serve the LORD with all your heart. ²¹Do not turn away after useless idols. They can do you no good, nor can they rescue you, because they are useless. ²²For the sake of his great name the LORD will not reject his people, because the LORD was pleased to make you his own. ²³As for me, far be it from me

Why did Samuel confront the people of Israel? (12:7)
Samuel reminded the people of their sin in desiring a king. God had faithfully cared for his people throughout their history. When they asked for a king, it was as if they were rejecting God's leadership.

Why had the Israelites wanted a king? (12:12)
Perhaps they realized that Nahash was going to attack, and they wanted a strong military leader to be ready to defend Israel. They also wanted to be like the other nations and be ruled by a king rather than by judges.

opportunity to have the people renew their allegiance to the LORD and to confirm Saul as a king who served under God.

ᵃ 11 Also called *Gideon*   ᵇ 11 Some Septuagint manuscripts and Syriac; Hebrew *Bedan*   ᶜ 11 Hebrew; some Septuagint manuscripts and Syriac *Samson*

How would failing to pray
for the Israelites be a sin?
(12:23)
Samuel was a Nazirite, whose
entire life was dedicated to God's
service. Part of that responsibility would have been to offer
prayers on behalf of the people.
If Samuel did not do that, he
would not be living up to his
vows.

How many soldiers were
stationed in an outpost?
(13:3)
It is likely that there were 1,000
soldiers or more.

Why was Samuel late?
(13:11)
Saul was told to wait for Samuel
to give him instructions, but
instead he offered a sacrifice. Being late may have been Samuel's
way of testing Saul's obedience.
Not waiting for Samuel was
wrong because it showed that
Saul trusted in his army more
than God.

Why was Saul's punishment
so severe? (13:14)
Saul was not a religious leader
or a priest. This meant he had no
right to make a sacrifice. Because
he used his position of authority
in a sinful way, God punished him
by not allowing his descendants
to continue to rule Israel.

that I should sin against the LORD by failing to pray for you.
And I will teach you the way that is good and right. [24] But be
sure to fear the LORD and serve him faithfully with all your
heart; consider what great things he has done for you. [25] Yet if
you persist in doing evil, both you and your king will perish."

SAMUEL REBUKES SAUL

13 Saul was thirty[a] years old when he became king, and
he reigned over Israel forty-[b] two years.

[2] Saul chose three thousand men from Israel; two thou-
sand were with him at Mikmash and in the hill country of
Bethel, and a thousand were with Jonathan at Gibeah in
Benjamin. The rest of the men he sent back to their homes.

[3] Jonathan attacked the Philistine outpost at Geba, and the
Philistines heard about it. Then Saul had the trumpet blown
throughout the land and said, "Let the Hebrews hear!" [4] So
all Israel heard the news: "Saul has attacked the Philistine
outpost, and now Israel has become obnoxious to the Philistines." And the people were summoned to join Saul at Gilgal.

[5] The Philistines assembled to fight Israel, with three
thousand[c] chariots, six thousand charioteers, and soldiers as
numerous as the sand on the seashore. They went up and
camped at Mikmash, east of Beth Aven. [6] When the Israelites saw that their situation was critical and that their army
was hard pressed, they hid in caves and thickets, among the
rocks, and in pits and cisterns. [7] Some Hebrews even crossed
the Jordan to the land of Gad and Gilead.

Saul remained at Gilgal, and all the troops with him were
quaking with fear. [8] He waited seven days, the time set by
Samuel; but Samuel did not come to Gilgal, and Saul's men
began to scatter. [9] So he said, "Bring me the burnt offering
and the fellowship offerings." And Saul offered up the burnt
offering. [10] Just as he finished making the offering, Samuel
arrived, and Saul went out to greet him.

[11] "What have you done?" asked Samuel.

Saul replied, "When I saw that the men were scattering,
and that you did not come at the set time, and that the Philistines were assembling at Mikmash, [12] I thought, 'Now the
Philistines will come down against me at Gilgal, and I have
not sought the LORD's favor.' So I felt compelled to offer the
burnt offering."

[13] "You have done a foolish thing," Samuel said. "You have
not kept the command the LORD your God gave you; if you
had, he would have established your kingdom over Israel for
all time. [14] But now your kingdom will not endure; the LORD
has sought out a man after his own heart and appointed him
ruler of his people, because you have not kept the LORD's
command."

[15] Then Samuel left Gilgal[d] and went up to Gibeah in
Benjamin, and Saul counted the men who were with him.
They numbered about six hundred.

---

[a] 1 A few late manuscripts of the Septuagint; Hebrew does not have *thirty*.
[b] 1 Probable reading of the original Hebrew text (see Acts 13:21); Masoretic
Text does not have *forty-*.   [c] 5 Some Septuagint manuscripts and Syriac;
Hebrew *thirty thousand*   [d] 15 Hebrew; Septuagint *Gilgal and went his way;
the rest of the people went after Saul to meet the army, and they went out of Gilgal*

ISRAEL WITHOUT WEAPONS

[16] Saul and his son Jonathan and the men with them were staying in Gibeah[a] in Benjamin, while the Philistines camped at Mikmash. [17] Raiding parties went out from the Philistine camp in three detachments. One turned toward Ophrah in the vicinity of Shual, [18] another toward Beth Horon, and the third toward the borderland overlooking the Valley of Zeboyim facing the wilderness.

[19] Not a blacksmith could be found in the whole land of Israel, because the Philistines had said, "Otherwise the Hebrews will make swords or spears!" [20] So all Israel went down to the Philistines to have their plow points, mattocks, axes and sickles[b] sharpened. [21] The price was two-thirds of a shekel[c] for sharpening plow points and mattocks, and a third of a shekel[d] for sharpening forks and axes and for re-pointing goads.

[22] So on the day of the battle not a soldier with Saul and Jonathan had a sword or spear in his hand; only Saul and his son Jonathan had them.

JONATHAN ATTACKS THE PHILISTINES

[23] Now a detachment of Philistines had gone out to the pass at Mikmash. **14** [1] One day Jonathan son of Saul said to his young armor-bearer, "Come, let's go over to the Philistine outpost on the other side." But he did not tell his father.

[2] Saul was staying on the outskirts of Gibeah under a pomegranate tree in Migron. With him were about six hundred men, [3] among whom was Ahijah, who was wearing an ephod. He was a son of Ichabod's brother Ahitub son of Phinehas, the son of Eli, the LORD's priest in Shiloh. No one was aware that Jonathan had left.

[4] On each side of the pass that Jonathan intended to cross to reach the Philistine outpost was a cliff; one was called Bozez and the other Seneh. [5] One cliff stood to the north toward Mikmash, the other to the south toward Geba.

[6] Jonathan said to his young armor-bearer, "Come, let's go over to the outpost of those uncircumcised men. Perhaps the LORD will act in our behalf. Nothing can hinder the LORD from saving, whether by many or by few."

[7] "Do all that you have in mind," his armor-bearer said. "Go ahead; I am with you heart and soul."

[8] Jonathan said, "Come on, then; we will cross over toward them and let them see us. [9] If they say to us, 'Wait there until we come to you,' we will stay where we are and not go up to them. [10] But if they say, 'Come up to us,' we will climb up, because that will be our sign that the LORD has given them into our hands."

[11] So both of them showed themselves to the Philistine outpost. "Look!" said the Philistines. "The Hebrews are crawling out of the holes they were hiding in." [12] The men of the outpost shouted to Jonathan and his armor-bearer, "Come up to us and we'll teach you a lesson."

---

a 16 Two Hebrew manuscripts; most Hebrew manuscripts *Geba,* a variant of *Gibeah*   *b 20* Septuagint; Hebrew *plow points*   *c 21* That is, about 1/4 ounce or about 8 grams   *d 21* That is, about 1/8 ounce or about 4 grams

---

Why were there no blacksmiths? (13:19–20)
The Philistines closely guarded the secrets of making weapons from iron. Because the Israelites did not have this technology, they were at a disadvantage. With no blacksmiths in Israel, the Israelites had to go to the Philistines to have their tools sharpened.

What weapons did the Israelites use? (13:22)
They may have used tools such as axes, sickles, and goads. They also used slingshots and bows and arrows.

How could Jonathan be sure this sign was from God? (14:10–12)
Jonathan trusted God to show him what to do by testing the enemy's courage. God would give him the sign that he could attack and defeat them if they were too afraid to approach him. Jonathan knew that God would help his people defeat the Philistines, even if they were more powerful.

So Jonathan said to his armor-bearer, "Climb up after me; the LORD has given them into the hand of Israel."

¹³Jonathan climbed up, using his hands and feet, with his armor-bearer right behind him. The Philistines fell before Jonathan, and his armor-bearer followed and killed behind him. ¹⁴In that first attack Jonathan and his armor-bearer killed some twenty men in an area of about half an acre.

ISRAEL ROUTS THE PHILISTINES

¹⁵Then panic struck the whole army—those in the camp and field, and those in the outposts and raiding parties—and the ground shook. It was a panic sent by God.[a]

¹⁶Saul's lookouts at Gibeah in Benjamin saw the army melting away in all directions. ¹⁷Then Saul said to the men who were with him, "Muster the forces and see who has left us." When they did, it was Jonathan and his armor-bearer who were not there.

¹⁸Saul said to Ahijah, "Bring the ark of God." (At that time it was with the Israelites.)[b] ¹⁹While Saul was talking to the priest, the tumult in the Philistine camp increased more and more. So Saul said to the priest, "Withdraw your hand."

²⁰Then Saul and all his men assembled and went to the battle. They found the Philistines in total confusion, striking each other with their swords. ²¹Those Hebrews who had previously been with the Philistines and had gone up with them to their camp went over to the Israelites who were with Saul and Jonathan. ²²When all the Israelites who had hidden in the hill country of Ephraim heard that the Philistines were on the run, they joined the battle in hot pursuit. ²³So on that day the LORD saved Israel, and the battle moved on beyond Beth Aven.

JONATHAN EATS HONEY

²⁴Now the Israelites were in distress that day, because Saul had bound the people under an oath, saying, "Cursed be anyone who eats food before evening comes, before I have avenged myself on my enemies!" So none of the troops tasted food.

²⁵The entire army entered the woods, and there was honey on the ground. ²⁶When they went into the woods, they saw the honey oozing out; yet no one put his hand to his mouth, because they feared the oath. ²⁷But Jonathan had not heard that his father had bound the people with the oath, so he reached out the end of the staff that was in his hand and dipped it into the honeycomb. He raised his hand to his mouth, and his eyes brightened.[c] ²⁸Then one of the soldiers told him, "Your father bound the army under a strict oath, saying, 'Cursed be anyone who eats food today!' That is why the men are faint."

²⁹Jonathan said, "My father has made trouble for the country. See how my eyes brightened when I tasted a little of this honey. ³⁰How much better it would have been if the

How large was the battlefield? (14:14)
The term translated as *acre* refers to the average amount of ground a yoke of oxen could plow in a day. The actual size is not known. A half-acre would have been a relatively small area, so the battle probably ended quickly.

Why did Saul ask for the ark? (14:18)
The Philistines had captured the ark, but now the Israelites had it back. Saul may have wanted to carry the ark into battle. He may have needed God's guidance. He may have been asking for the Urim and Thummim—tools that the prophets used to gain clearer understanding from God—which would have been inside the ark.

Why did Saul tell the priest to withdraw his hand? (14:18–19)
When Saul heard the noise in the Philistine camp, he decided he would attack immediately rather than waiting for God to make his will known.

Why would the Israelites allow traitors and cowards to return? (14:21–22)
Perhaps because he had such a small army, Saul was glad to accept reinforcements, despite their background. These men would have to bear the shame of desertion, but it would have been worse if they had stayed away when it became obvious that Saul would win the battle.

Why did Saul make this oath about not eating? (14:24)
Saul wanted to make sure that all his soldiers kept fighting. But this was a poor strategy because the soldiers grew weak and dissatisfied.

---

[a] 15 Or *a terrible panic*   [b] 18 Hebrew; Septuagint *"Bring the ephod." (At that time he wore the ephod before the Israelites.)*   [c] 27 Or *his strength was renewed*; similarly in verse 29

men had eaten today some of the plunder they took from their enemies. Would not the slaughter of the Philistines have been even greater?"

[31]That day, after the Israelites had struck down the Philistines from Mikmash to Aijalon, they were exhausted. [32]They pounced on the plunder and, taking sheep, cattle and calves, they butchered them on the ground and ate them, together with the blood. [33]Then someone said to Saul, "Look, the men are sinning against the LORD by eating meat that has blood in it."

"You have broken faith," he said. "Roll a large stone over here at once." [34]Then he said, "Go out among the men and tell them, 'Each of you bring me your cattle and sheep, and slaughter them here and eat them. Do not sin against the LORD by eating meat with blood still in it.'"

So everyone brought his ox that night and slaughtered it there. [35]Then Saul built an altar to the LORD; it was the first time he had done this.

[36]Saul said, "Let us go down and pursue the Philistines by night and plunder them till dawn, and let us not leave one of them alive."

"Do whatever seems best to you," they replied.

But the priest said, "Let us inquire of God here."

[37]So Saul asked God, "Shall I go down and pursue the Philistines? Will you give them into Israel's hand?" But God did not answer him that day.

[38]Saul therefore said, "Come here, all you who are leaders of the army, and let us find out what sin has been committed today. [39]As surely as the LORD who rescues Israel lives, even if the guilt lies with my son Jonathan, he must die." But not one of them said a word.

[40]Saul then said to all the Israelites, "You stand over there; I and Jonathan my son will stand over here."

"Do what seems best to you," they replied.

[41]Then Saul prayed to the LORD, the God of Israel, "Why have you not answered your servant today? If the fault is in me or my son Jonathan, respond with Urim, but if the men of Israel are at fault,[a] respond with Thummim." Jonathan and Saul were taken by lot, and the men were cleared. [42]Saul said, "Cast the lot between me and Jonathan my son." And Jonathan was taken.

[43]Then Saul said to Jonathan, "Tell me what you have done."

So Jonathan told him, "I tasted a little honey with the end of my staff. And now I must die!"

[44]Saul said, "May God deal with me, be it ever so severely, if you do not die, Jonathan."

[45]But the men said to Saul, "Should Jonathan die — he who has brought about this great deliverance in Israel? Never! As surely as the LORD lives, not a hair of his head will fall to the ground, for he did this today with God's help." So the men rescued Jonathan, and he was not put to death.

[46]Then Saul stopped pursuing the Philistines, and they withdrew to their own land.

a 41 Septuagint; Hebrew does not have "Why . . . at fault.

Why was it wrong to eat meat with blood still in it? (14:32–33)
God had forbidden his people to eat blood. The blood was used to make atonement on the altar for people's sins (see Leviticus 17:11).

Why didn't God answer Saul's question? (14:37)
God may not have answered because an oath had been broken during the battle, or it may have been because the soldiers had eaten meat with blood still in it.

Why was Saul determined to fulfill his vow? (14:44)
Saul would have been humiliated if he failed to carry out his vow. If he spared Jonathan, it would seem that Saul was admitting he was wrong in making the curse.

⁴⁷After Saul had assumed rule over Israel, he fought against their enemies on every side: Moab, the Ammonites, Edom, the kings*a* of Zobah, and the Philistines. Wherever he turned, he inflicted punishment on them.*b* ⁴⁸He fought valiantly and defeated the Amalekites, delivering Israel from the hands of those who had plundered them.

SAUL'S FAMILY

⁴⁹Saul's sons were Jonathan, Ishvi and Malki-Shua. The name of his older daughter was Merab, and that of the younger was Michal. ⁵⁰His wife's name was Ahinoam daughter of Ahimaaz. The name of the commander of Saul's army was Abner son of Ner, and Ner was Saul's uncle. ⁵¹Saul's father Kish and Abner's father Ner were sons of Abiel.

⁵²All the days of Saul there was bitter war with the Philistines, and whenever Saul saw a mighty or brave man, he took him into his service.

THE LORD REJECTS SAUL AS KING

15 Samuel said to Saul, "I am the one the LORD sent to anoint you king over his people Israel; so listen now to the message from the LORD. ²This is what the LORD Almighty says: 'I will punish the Amalekites for what they did to Israel when they waylaid them as they came up from Egypt. ³Now go, attack the Amalekites and totally destroy*c* all that belongs to them. Do not spare them; put to death men and women, children and infants, cattle and sheep, camels and donkeys.'"

⁴So Saul summoned the men and mustered them at Telaim—two hundred thousand foot soldiers and ten thousand from Judah. ⁵Saul went to the city of Amalek and set an ambush in the ravine. ⁶Then he said to the Kenites, "Go away, leave the Amalekites so that I do not destroy you along with them; for you showed kindness to all the Israelites when they came up out of Egypt." So the Kenites moved away from the Amalekites.

⁷Then Saul attacked the Amalekites all the way from Havilah to Shur, near the eastern border of Egypt. ⁸He took Agag king of the Amalekites alive, and all his people he totally destroyed with the sword. ⁹But Saul and the army spared Agag and the best of the sheep and cattle, the fat calves*d* and lambs—everything that was good. These they were unwilling to destroy completely, but everything that was despised and weak they totally destroyed.

¹⁰Then the word of the LORD came to Samuel: ¹¹"I regret that I have made Saul king, because he has turned away from me and has not carried out my instructions." Samuel was angry, and he cried out to the LORD all that night.

¹²Early in the morning Samuel got up and went to meet Saul, but he was told, "Saul has gone to Carmel. There he

---

Who were the Amalekites? (15:2)
They were a tribe of nomadic people descended from Esau. They usually lived in the Negev and Sinai regions.

Why did God want to wipe out the Amalekites? (15:2–3)
The Amalekites had attacked the weakened Israelites in the desert, and so God had promised to destroy them (see Deuteronomy 25:17–18). He knew they would continue to attack his people if they were not stopped.

Who were the Kenites? (15:6)
The Kenites were descendants of Hobab, Moses' brother-in-law. When the Israelites left Sinai, Moses asked Hobab to serve as their guide (see Numbers 10:29–32). Hobab's descendants were friendly with Israel, so Saul wanted to spare them.

Why didn't Saul kill Agag? (15:8)
Saul probably wanted to humiliate Agag by parading the defeated king before the people of Israel.

---

a 47 Masoretic Text; Dead Sea Scrolls and Septuagint *king*   *b 47* Hebrew; Septuagint *he was victorious*   *c 3* The Hebrew term refers to the irrevocable giving over of things or persons to the LORD, often by totally destroying them; also in verses 8, 9, 15, 18, 20 and 21.   *d 9* Or *the grown bulls*; the meaning of the Hebrew for this phrase is uncertain.

has set up a monument in his own honor and has turned and gone on down to Gilgal."

¹³When Samuel reached him, Saul said, "The LORD bless you! I have carried out the LORD's instructions."

¹⁴But Samuel said, "What then is this bleating of sheep in my ears? What is this lowing of cattle that I hear?"

¹⁵Saul answered, "The soldiers brought them from the Amalekites; they spared the best of the sheep and cattle to sacrifice to the LORD your God, but we totally destroyed the rest."

¹⁶"Enough!" Samuel said to Saul. "Let me tell you what the LORD said to me last night."

"Tell me," Saul replied.

¹⁷Samuel said, "Although you were once small in your own eyes, did you not become the head of the tribes of Israel? The LORD anointed you king over Israel. ¹⁸And he sent you on a mission, saying, 'Go and completely destroy those wicked people, the Amalekites; wage war against them until you have wiped them out.' ¹⁹Why did you not obey the LORD? Why did you pounce on the plunder and do evil in the eyes of the LORD?"

²⁰"But I did obey the LORD," Saul said. "I went on the mission the LORD assigned me. I completely destroyed the Amalekites and brought back Agag their king. ²¹The soldiers took sheep and cattle from the plunder, the best of what was devoted to God, in order to sacrifice them to the LORD your God at Gilgal."

²²But Samuel replied:

"Does the LORD delight in burnt offerings and
  sacrifices
  as much as in obeying the LORD?
To obey is better than sacrifice,
  and to heed is better than the fat of rams.
²³For rebellion is like the sin of divination,
  and arrogance like the evil of idolatry.
Because you have rejected the word of the LORD,
  he has rejected you as king."

²⁴Then Saul said to Samuel, "I have sinned. I violated the LORD's command and your instructions. I was afraid of the men and so I gave in to them. ²⁵Now I beg you, forgive my sin and come back with me, so that I may worship the LORD."

²⁶But Samuel said to him, "I will not go back with you. You have rejected the word of the LORD, and the LORD has rejected you as king over Israel!"

²⁷As Samuel turned to leave, Saul caught hold of the hem of his robe, and it tore. ²⁸Samuel said to him, "The LORD has torn the kingdom of Israel from you today and has given it to one of your neighbors—to one better than you. ²⁹He who is the Glory of Israel does not lie or change his mind; for he is not a human being, that he should change his mind."

³⁰Saul replied, "I have sinned. But please honor me before the elders of my people and before Israel; come back with me, so that I may worship the LORD your God." ³¹So Samuel went back with Saul, and Saul worshiped the LORD.

How did Saul try to excuse what he had done? (15:20–22)
Saul said he had kept the law by killing all of the Amalekites (and bringing back the king) and by killing most of the animals but saving the best as a sacrifice. Samuel told Saul that the LORD is pleased more by obedience than by sacrifices.

Could Saul be forgiven for his sin? (15:25–26)
God punished Saul for his sin. God rejected him as king. This meant that Saul's descendants would not inherit the throne. But that does not mean that God didn't forgive him.

Who was the "Glory of Israel"? (15:29)
Glory means Unchanging One. Samuel was emphasizing that God would not change his mind about replacing Saul with another king. Saul had shown that he was not reliable, but the LORD could be trusted to do what he had said.

32Then Samuel said, "Bring me Agag king of the Amalekites."

Agag came to him in chains.*a* And he thought, "Surely the bitterness of death is past."

33But Samuel said,

"As your sword has made women childless,
so will your mother be childless among women."

And Samuel put Agag to death before the LORD at Gilgal.

34Then Samuel left for Ramah, but Saul went up to his home in Gibeah of Saul. 35Until the day Samuel died, he did not go to see Saul again, though Samuel mourned for him. And the LORD regretted that he had made Saul king over Israel.

SAMUEL ANOINTS DAVID

16 The LORD said to Samuel, "How long will you mourn for Saul, since I have rejected him as king over Israel? Fill your horn with oil and be on your way; I am sending you to Jesse of Bethlehem. I have chosen one of his sons to be king."

2But Samuel said, "How can I go? If Saul hears about it, he will kill me."

The LORD said, "Take a heifer with you and say, 'I have come to sacrifice to the LORD.' 3Invite Jesse to the sacrifice, and I will show you what to do. You are to anoint for me the one I indicate."

4Samuel did what the LORD said. When he arrived at Bethlehem, the elders of the town trembled when they met him. They asked, "Do you come in peace?"

5Samuel replied, "Yes, in peace; I have come to sacrifice to the LORD. Consecrate yourselves and come to the sacrifice with me." Then he consecrated Jesse and his sons and invited them to the sacrifice.

6When they arrived, Samuel saw Eliab and thought, "Surely the LORD's anointed stands here before the LORD."

7But the LORD said to Samuel, "Do not consider his appearance or his height, for I have rejected him. The LORD does not look at the things people look at. People look at the outward appearance, but the LORD looks at the heart."

8Then Jesse called Abinadab and had him pass in front of Samuel. But Samuel said, "The LORD has not chosen this one either." 9Jesse then had Shammah pass by, but Samuel said, "Nor has the LORD chosen this one." 10Jesse had seven of his sons pass before Samuel, but Samuel said to him, "The LORD has not chosen these." 11So he asked Jesse, "Are these all the sons you have?"

"There is still the youngest," Jesse answered. "He is tending the sheep."

Samuel said, "Send for him; we will not sit down until he arrives."

12So he sent for him and had him brought in. He was glowing with health and had a fine appearance and handsome features.

a 32 The meaning of the Hebrew for this phrase is uncertain.

Why did Samuel kill Agag? (15:33)
Samuel killed Agag because Saul had refused to follow the LORD's command to kill all the Amalekites.

Was God encouraging Samuel to be dishonest? (16:1–12)
No. God told Samuel to speak the truth about offering a sacrifice to the LORD, but not to say that he was in Bethlehem to anoint a new king.

Why did God tell Samuel not to consider an outward appearance? (16:7)
The LORD is not concerned with a person's appearance or status. Instead, God looks at a person's heart to see if he or she loves and trusts him. Once again, God chose an unlikely person—the youngest son of someone from a small town—to do an important task.

Then the Lord said, "Rise and anoint him; this is the one."

¹³ So Samuel took the horn of oil and anointed him in the presence of his brothers, and from that day on the Spirit of the Lord came powerfully upon David. Samuel then went to Ramah.

DAVID IN SAUL'S SERVICE

¹⁴ Now the Spirit of the Lord had departed from Saul, and an evil[a] spirit from the Lord tormented him.

¹⁵ Saul's attendants said to him, "See, an evil spirit from God is tormenting you. ¹⁶ Let our lord command his servants here to search for someone who can play the lyre. He will play when the evil spirit from God comes on you, and you will feel better."

¹⁷ So Saul said to his attendants, "Find someone who plays well and bring him to me."

¹⁸ One of the servants answered, "I have seen a son of Jesse of Bethlehem who knows how to play the lyre. He is a brave man and a warrior. He speaks well and is a fine-looking man. And the Lord is with him."

¹⁹ Then Saul sent messengers to Jesse and said, "Send me your son David, who is with the sheep." ²⁰ So Jesse took a donkey loaded with bread, a skin of wine and a young goat and sent them with his son David to Saul.

²¹ David came to Saul and entered his service. Saul liked him very much, and David became one of his armor-bearers. ²² Then Saul sent word to Jesse, saying, "Allow David to remain in my service, for I am pleased with him."

²³ Whenever the spirit from God came on Saul, David would take up his lyre and play. Then relief would come to Saul; he would feel better, and the evil spirit would leave him.

DAVID AND GOLIATH

17 Now the Philistines gathered their forces for war and assembled at Sokoh in Judah. They pitched camp at Ephes Dammim, between Sokoh and Azekah. ² Saul and the Israelites assembled and camped in the Valley of Elah and drew up their battle line to meet the Philistines. ³ The Philistines occupied one hill and the Israelites another, with the valley between them.

⁴ A champion named Goliath, who was from Gath, came out of the Philistine camp. His height was six cubits and a span.[b] ⁵ He had a bronze helmet on his head and wore a coat of scale armor of bronze weighing five thousand shekels[c]; ⁶ on his legs he wore bronze greaves, and a bronze javelin was slung on his back. ⁷ His spear shaft was like a weaver's rod, and its iron point weighed six hundred shekels.[d] His shield bearer went ahead of him.

⁸ Goliath stood and shouted to the ranks of Israel, "Why do you come out and line up for battle? Am I not a Philistine, and are you not the servants of Saul? Choose a man and

---

[a] 14 Or *and a harmful*; similarly in verses 15, 16 and 23   [b] 4 That is, about 9 feet 9 inches or about 3 meters   [c] 5 That is, about 125 pounds or about 58 kilograms   [d] 7 That is, about 15 pounds or about 6.9 kilograms

Did David's family know what Samuel was doing? (16:13)
Probably not. Samuel had good reason to keep it a secret for his own as well as for David's sake. They may have thought the anointing was a special dedication to God's service.

How could an evil spirit be from God? (16:14)
The term *evil spirit* could also mean "a troubling or injurious spirit." Saul may have been overcome with depression because the Spirit of the Lord had left him.

Why did music make Saul feel better? (16:23)
When David played the lyre, it was probably soothing for Saul, who was troubled by the fact that the Lord had left him.

How did armies use champions to fight battles? (17:4)
In ancient times, armies sometimes decided battles by having champions from each side meet to fight as representatives of each army. This was based on the belief that the gods of each army actually fought or decided the outcome of battle.

What were greaves? (17:6)
These were shin guards worn to protect a soldier's legs.

David and Goliath (17:1–53)

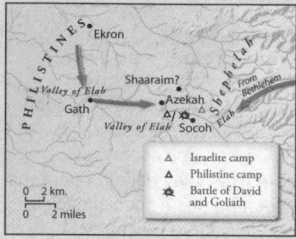

have him come down to me. ⁹If he is able to fight and kill me, we will become your subjects; but if I overcome him and kill him, you will become our subjects and serve us." ¹⁰Then the Philistine said, "This day I defy the armies of Israel! Give me a man and let us fight each other." ¹¹On hearing the Philistine's words, Saul and all the Israelites were dismayed and terrified.

¹²Now David was the son of an Ephrathite named Jesse, who was from Bethlehem in Judah. Jesse had eight sons, and in Saul's time he was very old. ¹³Jesse's three oldest sons had followed Saul to the war: The firstborn was Eliab; the second, Abinadab; and the third, Shammah. ¹⁴David was the youngest. The three oldest followed Saul, ¹⁵but David went back and forth from Saul to tend his father's sheep at Bethlehem.

¹⁶For forty days the Philistine came forward every morning and evening and took his stand.

¹⁷Now Jesse said to his son David, "Take this ephah[a] of roasted grain and these ten loaves of bread for your brothers and hurry to their camp. ¹⁸Take along these ten cheeses to the commander of their unit. See how your brothers are and bring back some assurance[b] from them. ¹⁹They are with Saul and all the men of Israel in the Valley of Elah, fighting against the Philistines."

²⁰Early in the morning David left the flock in the care of a shepherd, loaded up and set out, as Jesse had directed. He reached the camp as the army was going out to its battle positions, shouting the war cry. ²¹Israel and the Philistines were drawing up their lines facing each other. ²²David left his things with the keeper of supplies, ran to the battle lines and asked his brothers how they were. ²³As he was talking with them, Goliath, the Philistine champion from Gath, stepped out from his lines and shouted his usual defiance, and David heard it. ²⁴Whenever the Israelites saw the man, they all fled from him in great fear.

²⁵Now the Israelites had been saying, "Do you see how this man keeps coming out? He comes out to defy Israel. The king will give great wealth to the man who kills him. He will also give him his daughter in marriage and will exempt his family from taxes in Israel."

²⁶David asked the men standing near him, "What will be done for the man who kills this Philistine and removes this disgrace from Israel? Who is this uncircumcised Philistine that he should defy the armies of the living God?"

²⁷They repeated to him what they had been saying and told him, "This is what will be done for the man who kills him."

²⁸When Eliab, David's oldest brother, heard him speaking with the men, he burned with anger at him and asked, "Why have you come down here? And with whom did you leave those few sheep in the wilderness? I know how conceited you are and how wicked your heart is; you came down only to watch the battle."

Why was David's brother so angry with him? (17:28–29) Eliab was probably jealous of David. He had been overlooked when Samuel anointed David. He probably thought he deserved the anointing as the eldest male. He also knew about the honor David had received in Saul's court.

---

[a] 17 That is, probably about 36 pounds or about 16 kilograms
[b] 18 Or *some token;* or *some pledge of spoils*

29"Now what have I done?" said David. "Can't I even speak?" 30 He then turned away to someone else and brought up the same matter, and the men answered him as before. 31 What David said was overheard and reported to Saul, and Saul sent for him.

32 David said to Saul, "Let no one lose heart on account of this Philistine; your servant will go and fight him."

33 Saul replied, "You are not able to go out against this Philistine and fight him; you are only a young man, and he has been a warrior from his youth."

34 But David said to Saul, "Your servant has been keeping his father's sheep. When a lion or a bear came and carried off a sheep from the flock, 35 I went after it, struck it and rescued the sheep from its mouth. When it turned on me, I seized it by its hair, struck it and killed it. 36 Your servant has killed both the lion and the bear; this uncircumcised Philistine will be like one of them, because he has defied the armies of the living God. 37 The LORD who rescued me from the paw of the lion and the paw of the bear will rescue me from the hand of this Philistine."

Saul said to David, "Go, and the LORD be with you."

38 Then Saul dressed David in his own tunic. He put a coat of armor on him and a bronze helmet on his head. 39 David fastened on his sword over the tunic and tried walking around, because he was not used to them.

"I cannot go in these," he said to Saul, "because I am not used to them." So he took them off. 40 Then he took his staff in his hand, chose five smooth stones from the stream, put them in the pouch of his shepherd's bag and, with his sling in his hand, approached the Philistine.

41 Meanwhile, the Philistine, with his shield bearer in front of him, kept coming closer to David. 42 He looked David over and saw that he was little more than a boy, glowing with health and handsome, and he despised him. 43 He said to David, "Am I a dog, that you come at me with sticks?" And the Philistine cursed David by his gods. 44 "Come here," he said, "and I'll give your flesh to the birds and the wild animals!"

45 David said to the Philistine, "You come against me with sword and spear and javelin, but I come against you in the name of the LORD Almighty, the God of the armies of Israel, whom you have defied. 46 This day the LORD will deliver you into my hands, and I'll strike you down and cut off your head. This very day I will give the carcasses of the Philistine army to the birds and the wild animals, and the whole world will know that there is a God in Israel. 47 All those gathered here will know that it is not by sword or spear that the LORD saves; for the battle is the LORD's, and he will give all of you into our hands."

48 As the Philistine moved closer to attack him, David ran quickly toward the battle line to meet him. 49 Reaching into his bag and taking out a stone, he slung it and struck the Philistine on the forehead. The stone sank into his forehead, and he fell facedown on the ground.

50 So David triumphed over the Philistine with a sling and a stone; without a sword in his hand he struck down the Philistine and killed him.

How old was David when he fought Goliath? (17:33)
We don't know for sure. Some think that David may have been 17 or 18 when he fought Goliath.

Was it unusual to use a slingshot as a weapon? (17:40)
No. Many soldiers used slingshots and baseball-sized balls made of flint. Master slingers could probably hurl stones at a speed of almost 100 miles (161 kilometers) per hour.

A Sling (17:40–49)

Why did David keep Goliath's head? (17:54)
God helped his people defeat what seemed like unbeatable enemies. Goliath's head would be a reminder of that victory, as well as a trophy of war. It also would confirm for everyone that Goliath had been killed.

Why didn't Saul recognize David? (17:55)
It has probably been a few years since Saul had last seen David. David grew up in that time, so it's natural to assume that he looked different. Or perhaps Saul wanted to find out the name of David's father so that the family could be rewarded as Saul had promised (v. 25).

What type of friendship did David and Jonathan have? (18:1–3)
They had a strong friendship that expressed itself in the form of a covenant.

What was David's rank in the army? (18:5)
Although his specific rank is not mentioned, he had a position of great authority. Before long he would command 1,000 soldiers.

Did David really kill ten times the number of people that Saul killed? (18:7)
According to the typical patterns of Hebrew poetry, "tens of thousands" is normally used as parallel to "thousands." This may have been a poetic way of saying that Saul and David had together killed thousands. Saul, however, interpreted the song to mean that David was being given much greater credit than he was.

What type of prophesying was this? (18:10)
This was probably more like incoherent babbling or raving caused by an evil spirit.

51 David ran and stood over him. He took hold of the Philistine's sword and drew it from the sheath. After he killed him, he cut off his head with the sword.

When the Philistines saw that their hero was dead, they turned and ran. 52 Then the men of Israel and Judah surged forward with a shout and pursued the Philistines to the entrance of Gath[a] and to the gates of Ekron. Their dead were strewn along the Shaaraim road to Gath and Ekron. 53 When the Israelites returned from chasing the Philistines, they plundered their camp. 54 David took the Philistine's head and brought it to Jerusalem; he put the Philistine's weapons in his own tent.

55 As Saul watched David going out to meet the Philistine, he said to Abner, commander of the army, "Abner, whose son is that young man?"

Abner replied, "As surely as you live, Your Majesty, I don't know."

56 The king said, "Find out whose son this young man is."

57 As soon as David returned from killing the Philistine, Abner took him and brought him before Saul, with David still holding the Philistine's head.

58 "Whose son are you, young man?" Saul asked him.

David said, "I am the son of your servant Jesse of Bethlehem."

SAUL'S GROWING FEAR OF DAVID

18 After David had finished talking with Saul, Jonathan became one in spirit with David, and he loved him as himself. 2 From that day Saul kept David with him and did not let him return home to his family. 3 And Jonathan made a covenant with David because he loved him as himself. 4 Jonathan took off the robe he was wearing and gave it to David, along with his tunic, and even his sword, his bow and his belt.

5 Whatever mission Saul sent him on, David was so successful that Saul gave him a high rank in the army. This pleased all the troops, and Saul's officers as well.

6 When the men were returning home after David had killed the Philistine, the women came out from all the towns of Israel to meet King Saul with singing and dancing, with joyful songs and with timbrels and lyres. 7 As they danced, they sang:

"Saul has slain his thousands,
    and David his tens of thousands."

8 Saul was very angry; this refrain displeased him greatly. "They have credited David with tens of thousands," he thought, "but me with only thousands. What more can he get but the kingdom?" 9 And from that time on Saul kept a close eye on David.

10 The next day an evil[b] spirit from God came forcefully on Saul. He was prophesying in his house, while David was playing the lyre, as he usually did. Saul had a spear in his hand 11 and he hurled it, saying to himself, "I'll pin David to the wall." But David eluded him twice.

a 52 Some Septuagint manuscripts; Hebrew of a valley   b 10 Or a harmful

¹²Saul was afraid of David, because the Lord was with David but had departed from Saul. ¹³So he sent David away from him and gave him command over a thousand men, and David led the troops in their campaigns. ¹⁴In everything he did he had great success, because the Lord was with him. ¹⁵When Saul saw how successful he was, he was afraid of him. ¹⁶But all Israel and Judah loved David, because he led them in their campaigns.

¹⁷Saul said to David, "Here is my older daughter Merab. I will give her to you in marriage; only serve me bravely and fight the battles of the Lord." For Saul said to himself, "I will not raise a hand against him. Let the Philistines do that!"

¹⁸But David said to Saul, "Who am I, and what is my family or my clan in Israel, that I should become the king's son-in-law?" ¹⁹So*ᵃ* when the time came for Merab, Saul's daughter, to be given to David, she was given in marriage to Adriel of Meholah.

²⁰Now Saul's daughter Michal was in love with David, and when they told Saul about it, he was pleased. ²¹"I will give her to him," he thought, "so that she may be a snare to him and so that the hand of the Philistines may be against him." So Saul said to David, "Now you have a second opportunity to become my son-in-law."

²²Then Saul ordered his attendants: "Speak to David privately and say, 'Look, the king likes you, and his attendants all love you; now become his son-in-law.'"

²³They repeated these words to David. But David said, "Do you think it is a small matter to become the king's son-in-law? I'm only a poor man and little known."

²⁴When Saul's servants told him what David had said, ²⁵Saul replied, "Say to David, 'The king wants no other price for the bride than a hundred Philistine foreskins, to take revenge on his enemies.'" Saul's plan was to have David fall by the hands of the Philistines.

²⁶When the attendants told David these things, he was pleased to become the king's son-in-law. So before the allotted time elapsed, ²⁷David took his men with him and went out and killed two hundred Philistines and brought back their foreskins. They counted out the full number to the king so that David might become the king's son-in-law. Then Saul gave him his daughter Michal in marriage.

²⁸When Saul realized that the Lord was with David and that his daughter Michal loved David, ²⁹Saul became still more afraid of him, and he remained his enemy the rest of his days.

³⁰The Philistine commanders continued to go out to battle, and as often as they did, David met with more success than the rest of Saul's officers, and his name became well known.

SAUL TRIES TO KILL DAVID

19 Saul told his son Jonathan and all the attendants to kill David. But Jonathan had taken a great liking to David ²and warned him, "My father Saul is looking for a

How would Michal be a snare for David? (18:21) When Saul learned that his daughter Michal loved David, he promised his daughter's hand to David if he would battle the Philistines. Saul hoped to trap David into fighting so that he would be killed.

Why did Saul want 100 Philistine foreskins? (18:25–28) This would have been proof that David had killed that many Philistines. What Saul actually wanted was for David to be killed by the Philistines, but God did not allow that to happen.

ᵃ *19 Or However,*

chance to kill you. Be on your guard tomorrow morning; go into hiding and stay there. ³I will go out and stand with my father in the field where you are. I'll speak to him about you and will tell you what I find out."

⁴Jonathan spoke well of David to Saul his father and said to him, "Let not the king do wrong to his servant David; he has not wronged you, and what he has done has benefited you greatly. ⁵He took his life in his hands when he killed the Philistine. The LORD won a great victory for all Israel, and you saw it and were glad. Why then would you do wrong to an innocent man like David by killing him for no reason?"

⁶Saul listened to Jonathan and took this oath: "As surely as the LORD lives, David will not be put to death."

⁷So Jonathan called David and told him the whole conversation. He brought him to Saul, and David was with Saul as before.

⁸Once more war broke out, and David went out and fought the Philistines. He struck them with such force that they fled before him.

⁹But an evil*a* spirit from the LORD came on Saul as he was sitting in his house with his spear in his hand. While David was playing the lyre, ¹⁰Saul tried to pin him to the wall with his spear, but David eluded him as Saul drove the spear into the wall. That night David made good his escape.

¹¹Saul sent men to David's house to watch it and to kill him in the morning. But Michal, David's wife, warned him, "If you don't run for your life tonight, tomorrow you'll be killed." ¹²So Michal let David down through a window, and he fled and escaped. ¹³Then Michal took an idol and laid it on the bed, covering it with a garment and putting some goats' hair at the head.

¹⁴When Saul sent the men to capture David, Michal said, "He is ill."

¹⁵Then Saul sent the men back to see David and told them, "Bring him up to me in his bed so that I may kill him." ¹⁶But when the men entered, there was the idol in the bed, and at the head was some goats' hair.

¹⁷Saul said to Michal, "Why did you deceive me like this and send my enemy away so that he escaped?"

Michal told him, "He said to me, 'Let me get away. Why should I kill you?'"

¹⁸When David had fled and made his escape, he went to Samuel at Ramah and told him all that Saul had done to him. Then he and Samuel went to Naioth and stayed there. ¹⁹Word came to Saul: "David is in Naioth at Ramah"; ²⁰so he sent men to capture him. But when they saw a group of prophets prophesying, with Samuel standing there as their leader, the Spirit of God came on Saul's men, and they also prophesied. ²¹Saul was told about it, and he sent more men, and they prophesied too. Saul sent men a third time, and they also prophesied. ²²Finally, he himself left for Ramah and went to the great cistern at Seku. And he asked, "Where are Samuel and David?"

"Over in Naioth at Ramah," they said.

---

a 9 Or *But a harmful*

Why would David have an idol in his house? (19:13)
No one knows for sure. Michal may have kept the idol secretly. Or, it may have been more of a cultural symbol than an actual idol that was worshiped.

Why were Saul's men unable to kill David? (19:19–22)
Each time that Saul sent men to kill David, the Spirit of God came on them and they began to prophesy. God turned Saul's evil intentions to his purposes.

²³So Saul went to Naioth at Ramah. But the Spirit of God came even on him, and he walked along prophesying until he came to Naioth. ²⁴He stripped off his garments, and he too prophesied in Samuel's presence. He lay naked all that day and all that night. This is why people say, "Is Saul also among the prophets?"

DAVID AND JONATHAN

20 Then David fled from Naioth at Ramah and went to Jonathan and asked, "What have I done? What is my crime? How have I wronged your father, that he is trying to kill me?"

²"Never!" Jonathan replied. "You are not going to die! Look, my father doesn't do anything, great or small, without letting me know. Why would he hide this from me? It isn't so!"

³But David took an oath and said, "Your father knows very well that I have found favor in your eyes, and he has said to himself, 'Jonathan must not know this or he will be grieved.' Yet as surely as the LORD lives and as you live, there is only a step between me and death."

⁴Jonathan said to David, "Whatever you want me to do, I'll do for you."

⁵So David said, "Look, tomorrow is the New Moon feast, and I am supposed to dine with the king; but let me go and hide in the field until the evening of the day after tomorrow. ⁶If your father misses me at all, tell him, 'David earnestly asked my permission to hurry to Bethlehem, his hometown, because an annual sacrifice is being made there for his whole clan.' ⁷If he says, 'Very well,' then your servant is safe. But if he loses his temper, you can be sure that he is determined to harm me. ⁸As for you, show kindness to your servant, for you have brought him into a covenant with you before the LORD. If I am guilty, then kill me yourself! Why hand me over to your father?"

⁹"Never!" Jonathan said. "If I had the least inkling that my father was determined to harm you, wouldn't I tell you?"

¹⁰David asked, "Who will tell me if your father answers you harshly?"

¹¹"Come," Jonathan said, "let's go out into the field." So they went there together.

¹²Then Jonathan said to David, "I swear by the LORD, the God of Israel, that I will surely sound out my father by this time the day after tomorrow! If he is favorably disposed toward you, will I not send you word and let you know? ¹³But if my father intends to harm you, may the LORD deal with Jonathan, be it ever so severely, if I do not let you know and send you away in peace. May the LORD be with you as he has been with my father. ¹⁴But show me unfailing kindness like the LORD's kindness as long as I live, so that I may not be killed, ¹⁵and do not ever cut off your kindness from my family—not even when the LORD has cut off every one of David's enemies from the face of the earth."

¹⁶So Jonathan made a covenant with the house of David, saying, "May the LORD call David's enemies to account." ¹⁷And Jonathan had David reaffirm his oath out of love for him, because he loved him as he loved himself.

Why did the Spirit cause Saul to prophesy? (19:23–24)
Since God wanted David to be king, he would not allow anyone—even Saul—to kill him. God most likely caused Saul to prophesy, or to speak his truth, about David's right to the throne.

What was the New Moon feast? (20:5)
The New Moon feast was celebrated at the beginning of each month. On this day, special sacrifices were offered, trumpets were sounded, and normal work activities were stopped.

How could Jonathan not know about his father's plans to kill David? (20:9)
Saul knew that Jonathan was a good friend of David's, so he almost certainly didn't tell Jonathan his plans. In addition, Saul had pledged that he wouldn't kill David (19:6).

Why would Jonathan ask David not to kill him? (20:14)
It was common in the ancient world for the ruler of a new dynasty to kill anyone from the previous dynasty who might make a claim to the throne.

¹⁸Then Jonathan said to David, "Tomorrow is the New Moon feast. You will be missed, because your seat will be empty. ¹⁹The day after tomorrow, toward evening, go to the place where you hid when this trouble began, and wait by the stone Ezel. ²⁰I will shoot three arrows to the side of it, as though I were shooting at a target. ²¹Then I will send a boy and say, 'Go, find the arrows.' If I say to him, 'Look, the arrows are on this side of you; bring them here,' then come, because, as surely as the LORD lives, you are safe; there is no danger. ²²But if I say to the boy, 'Look, the arrows are beyond you,' then you must go, because the LORD has sent you away. ²³And about the matter you and I discussed — remember, the LORD is witness between you and me forever."

²⁴So David hid in the field, and when the New Moon feast came, the king sat down to eat. ²⁵He sat in his customary place by the wall, opposite Jonathan,^a and Abner sat next to Saul, but David's place was empty. ²⁶Saul said nothing that day, for he thought, "Something must have happened to David to make him ceremonially unclean — surely he is unclean." ²⁷But the next day, the second day of the month, David's place was empty again. Then Saul said to his son Jonathan, "Why hasn't the son of Jesse come to the meal, either yesterday or today?"

²⁸Jonathan answered, "David earnestly asked me for permission to go to Bethlehem. ²⁹He said, 'Let me go, because our family is observing a sacrifice in the town and my brother has ordered me to be there. If I have found favor in your eyes, let me get away to see my brothers.' That is why he has not come to the king's table."

³⁰Saul's anger flared up at Jonathan and he said to him, "You son of a perverse and rebellious woman! Don't I know that you have sided with the son of Jesse to your own shame and to the shame of the mother who bore you? ³¹As long as the son of Jesse lives on this earth, neither you nor your kingdom will be established. Now send someone to bring him to me, for he must die!"

³²"Why should he be put to death? What has he done?" Jonathan asked his father. ³³But Saul hurled his spear at him to kill him. Then Jonathan knew that his father intended to kill David.

³⁴Jonathan got up from the table in fierce anger; on that second day of the feast he did not eat, because he was grieved at his father's shameful treatment of David.

³⁵In the morning Jonathan went out to the field for his meeting with David. He had a small boy with him, ³⁶and he said to the boy, "Run and find the arrows I shoot." As the boy ran, he shot an arrow beyond him. ³⁷When the boy came to the place where Jonathan's arrow had fallen, Jonathan called out after him, "Isn't the arrow beyond you?" ³⁸Then he shouted, "Hurry! Go quickly! Don't stop!" The boy picked up the arrow and returned to his master. ³⁹(The boy knew nothing about all this; only Jonathan and David knew.) ⁴⁰Then Jonathan gave his weapons to the boy and said, "Go, carry them back to town."

Why did Jonathan use secret signals? (20:35–40)
Jonathan didn't want anyone to see David because that could endanger him. So he used the signals to communicate with his friend. After Jonathan's servant went back to the city, it was safe for David to come out of hiding.

^a 25 Septuagint; Hebrew *wall. Jonathan arose*

⁴¹After the boy had gone, David got up from the south side of the stone and bowed down before Jonathan three times, with his face to the ground. Then they kissed each other and wept together—but David wept the most.

⁴²Jonathan said to David, "Go in peace, for we have sworn friendship with each other in the name of the Lord, saying, 'The Lord is witness between you and me, and between your descendants and my descendants forever.'" Then David left, and Jonathan went back to the town.ᵃ

DAVID AT NOB

21 ᵇ David went to Nob, to Ahimelek the priest. Ahimelek trembled when he met him, and asked, "Why are you alone? Why is no one with you?"

²David answered Ahimelek the priest, "The king sent me on a mission and said to me, 'No one is to know anything about the mission I am sending you on.' As for my men, I have told them to meet me at a certain place. ³Now then, what do you have on hand? Give me five loaves of bread, or whatever you can find."

⁴But the priest answered David, "I don't have any ordinary bread on hand; however, there is some consecrated bread here—provided the men have kept themselves from women."

⁵David replied, "Indeed women have been kept from us, as usual wheneverᶜ I set out. The men's bodies are holy even on missions that are not holy. How much more so today!" ⁶So the priest gave him the consecrated bread, since there was no bread there except the bread of the Presence that had been removed from before the Lord and replaced by hot bread on the day it was taken away.

⁷Now one of Saul's servants was there that day, detained before the Lord; he was Doeg the Edomite, Saul's chief shepherd.

⁸David asked Ahimelek, "Don't you have a spear or a sword here? I haven't brought my sword or any other weapon, because the king's mission was urgent."

⁹The priest replied, "The sword of Goliath the Philistine, whom you killed in the Valley of Elah, is here; it is wrapped in a cloth behind the ephod. If you want it, take it; there is no sword here but that one."

David said, "There is none like it; give it to me."

DAVID AT GATH

¹⁰That day David fled from Saul and went to Achish king of Gath. ¹¹But the servants of Achish said to him, "Isn't this David, the king of the land? Isn't he the one they sing about in their dances:

"'Saul has slain his thousands,
    and David his tens of thousands'?"

¹²David took these words to heart and was very much afraid of Achish king of Gath. ¹³So he pretended to be insane

---

Why did David bow to Jonathan? (20:41)
In ancient cultures, there were many types of greetings and salutations. David approached Jonathan with the attitude of a servant because his friend had warned him of the danger he was in.

David on the Run (21:1— 23:29)

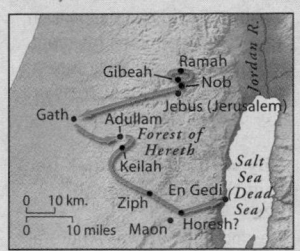

What was consecrated bread? (21:4)
These 12 loaves of bread were made from pure wheat flour and represented the 12 tribes of Israel and their devotion to God. Fresh bread was put before the Lord in the Holy Place of the tabernacle each week, and the old bread was removed and eaten by the priests.

Why would the priest give the consecrated bread to David and his men? (21:4–6)
The priest first made sure that David's men were ceremonially clean, and then he let them eat the bread. In this case, saving the lives of those who were hungry was more important than saving the bread only for the priests.

What did it mean that Doeg was "detained before the Lord"? (21:7)
Doeg may have needed to complete a time of ritual purification.

ᵃ 42 In Hebrew texts this sentence (20:42b) is numbered 21:1.   ᵇ In Hebrew texts 21:1-15 is numbered 21:2-16.   ᶜ 5 Or *from us in the past few days since*

in their presence; and while he was in their hands he acted like a madman, making marks on the doors of the gate and letting saliva run down his beard.

¹⁴ Achish said to his servants, "Look at the man! He is insane! Why bring him to me? ¹⁵ Am I so short of madmen that you have to bring this fellow here to carry on like this in front of me? Must this man come into my house?"

DAVID AT ADULLAM AND MIZPAH

22 David left Gath and escaped to the cave of Adullam. When his brothers and his father's household heard about it, they went down to him there. ² All those who were in distress or in debt or discontented gathered around him, and he became their commander. About four hundred men were with him.

³ From there David went to Mizpah in Moab and said to the king of Moab, "Would you let my father and mother come and stay with you until I learn what God will do for me?" ⁴ So he left them with the king of Moab, and they stayed with him as long as David was in the stronghold.

⁵ But the prophet Gad said to David, "Do not stay in the stronghold. Go into the land of Judah." So David left and went to the forest of Hereth.

SAUL KILLS THE PRIESTS OF NOB

⁶ Now Saul heard that David and his men had been discovered. And Saul was seated, spear in hand, under the tamarisk tree on the hill at Gibeah, with all his officials standing at his side. ⁷ He said to them, "Listen, men of Benjamin! Will the son of Jesse give all of you fields and vineyards? Will he make all of you commanders of thousands and commanders of hundreds? ⁸ Is that why you have all conspired against me? No one tells me when my son makes a covenant with the son of Jesse. None of you is concerned about me or tells me that my son has incited my servant to lie in wait for me, as he does today."

⁹ But Doeg the Edomite, who was standing with Saul's officials, said, "I saw the son of Jesse come to Ahimelek son of Ahitub at Nob. ¹⁰ Ahimelek inquired of the LORD for him; he also gave him provisions and the sword of Goliath the Philistine."

¹¹ Then the king sent for the priest Ahimelek son of Ahitub and all the men of his family, who were the priests at Nob, and they all came to the king. ¹² Saul said, "Listen now, son of Ahitub."

"Yes, my lord," he answered.

¹³ Saul said to him, "Why have you conspired against me, you and the son of Jesse, giving him bread and a sword and inquiring of God for him, so that he has rebelled against me and lies in wait for me, as he does today?"

¹⁴ Ahimelek answered the king, "Who of all your servants is as loyal as David, the king's son-in-law, captain of your bodyguard and highly respected in your household? ¹⁵ Was that day the first time I inquired of God for him? Of course not! Let not the king accuse your servant or any of his father's family, for your servant knows nothing at all about this whole affair."

Who were David's followers? (22:2)
Now that David had become an outlaw, he was joined by about 400 others in similar circumstances, because of distress or debt or discontentment.

Why would David seek help from the king of Moab? (22:3–4)
The king of Moab was a natural ally because Saul had waged war against him (see 14:47), and David's great-grandmother, Ruth, was a Moabitess (see Ruth 4:13, 22).

What was this stronghold? (22:4)
This might have been a fortress, but it was more likely an area where it was easy to hide, such as in caves.

16But the king said, "You will surely die, Ahimelek, you and your whole family."

17Then the king ordered the guards at his side: "Turn and kill the priests of the LORD, because they too have sided with David. They knew he was fleeing, yet they did not tell me."

But the king's officials were unwilling to raise a hand to strike the priests of the LORD.

18The king then ordered Doeg, "You turn and strike down the priests." So Doeg the Edomite turned and struck them down. That day he killed eighty-five men who wore the linen ephod. 19He also put to the sword Nob, the town of the priests, with its men and women, its children and infants, and its cattle, donkeys and sheep.

20But one son of Ahimelek son of Ahitub, named Abiathar, escaped and fled to join David. 21He told David that Saul had killed the priests of the LORD. 22Then David said to Abiathar, "That day, when Doeg the Edomite was there, I knew he would be sure to tell Saul. I am responsible for the death of your whole family. 23Stay with me; don't be afraid. The man who wants to kill you is trying to kill me too. You will be safe with me."

DAVID SAVES KEILAH

23 When David was told, "Look, the Philistines are fighting against Keilah and are looting the threshing floors," 2he inquired of the LORD, saying, "Shall I go and attack these Philistines?"

The LORD answered him, "Go, attack the Philistines and save Keilah."

3But David's men said to him, "Here in Judah we are afraid. How much more, then, if we go to Keilah against the Philistine forces!"

4Once again David inquired of the LORD, and the LORD answered him, "Go down to Keilah, for I am going to give the Philistines into your hand." 5So David and his men went to Keilah, fought the Philistines and carried off their livestock. He inflicted heavy losses on the Philistines and saved the people of Keilah. 6(Now Abiathar son of Ahimelek had brought the ephod down with him when he fled to David at Keilah.)

SAUL PURSUES DAVID

7Saul was told that David had gone to Keilah, and he said, "God has delivered him into my hands, for David has imprisoned himself by entering a town with gates and bars." 8And Saul called up all his forces for battle, to go down to Keilah to besiege David and his men.

9When David learned that Saul was plotting against him, he said to Abiathar the priest, "Bring the ephod." 10David said, "LORD, God of Israel, your servant has heard definitely that Saul plans to come to Keilah and destroy the town on account of me. 11Will the citizens of Keilah surrender me to him? Will Saul come down, as your servant has heard? LORD, God of Israel, tell your servant."

And the LORD said, "He will."

Why did Saul's officials disobey his order? (22:17)
To kill the Lord's priests would have been to declare war on God himself. Even Saul's officials knew that this would be going too far.

Why did David want the ephod? (23:6, 9)
The ephod was a vest-like garment worn by the priest. The breastplate attached to the ephod containing the Urim and Thummim, which were cast as lots to ask the LORD to reveal his will. David wanted to know what God wanted him to do.

Why did David and Jonathan make another covenant? (23:16–18)
This covenant was more serious than their earlier promises. In it, the two friends agreed that after Saul was no longer king, David would take his place and Jonathan would be his second-in-command. This would be a way to unify the people of Israel, bringing together the opposing sides.

[12] Again David asked, "Will the citizens of Keilah surrender me and my men to Saul?"

And the LORD said, "They will."

[13] So David and his men, about six hundred in number, left Keilah and kept moving from place to place. When Saul was told that David had escaped from Keilah, he did not go there.

[14] David stayed in the wilderness strongholds and in the hills of the Desert of Ziph. Day after day Saul searched for him, but God did not give David into his hands.

[15] While David was at Horesh in the Desert of Ziph, he learned that[a] Saul had come out to take his life. [16] And Saul's son Jonathan went to David at Horesh and helped him find strength in God. [17] "Don't be afraid," he said. "My father Saul will not lay a hand on you. You will be king over Israel, and I will be second to you. Even my father Saul knows this." [18] The two of them made a covenant before the LORD. Then Jonathan went home, but David remained at Horesh.

[19] The Ziphites went up to Saul at Gibeah and said, "Is not David hiding among us in the strongholds at Horesh, on the hill of Hakilah, south of Jeshimon? [20] Now, Your Majesty, come down whenever it pleases you to do so, and we will be responsible for giving him into your hands."

[21] Saul replied, "The LORD bless you for your concern for me. [22] Go and get more information. Find out where David usually goes and who has seen him there. They tell me he is very crafty. [23] Find out about all the hiding places he uses and come back to me with definite information. Then I will go with you; if he is in the area, I will track him down among all the clans of Judah."

[24] So they set out and went to Ziph ahead of Saul. Now David and his men were in the Desert of Maon, in the Arabah south of Jeshimon. [25] Saul and his men began the search, and when David was told about it, he went down to the rock and stayed in the Desert of Maon. When Saul heard this, he went into the Desert of Maon in pursuit of David.

[26] Saul was going along one side of the mountain, and David and his men were on the other side, hurrying to get away from Saul. As Saul and his forces were closing in on David and his men to capture them, [27] a messenger came to Saul, saying, "Come quickly! The Philistines are raiding the land." [28] Then Saul broke off his pursuit of David and went to meet the Philistines. That is why they call this place Sela Hammahlekoth.[b] [29] And David went up from there and lived in the strongholds of En Gedi.[c]

DAVID SPARES SAUL'S LIFE

24[d] After Saul returned from pursuing the Philistines, he was told, "David is in the Desert of En Gedi." [2] So Saul took three thousand able young men from all Israel and set out to look for David and his men near the Crags of the Wild Goats.

[3] He came to the sheep pens along the way; a cave was

---

[a] 15 Or *he was afraid because*   [b] 28 *Sela Hammahlekoth* means *rock of parting.*
[c] 29 In Hebrew texts this verse (23:29) is numbered 24:1.   [d] In Hebrew texts 24:1-22 is numbered 24:2-23.

there, and Saul went in to relieve himself. David and his men were far back in the cave. [4]The men said, "This is the day the LORD spoke of when he said[a] to you, 'I will give your enemy into your hands for you to deal with as you wish.'" Then David crept up unnoticed and cut off a corner of Saul's robe.

[5]Afterward, David was conscience-stricken for having cut off a corner of his robe. [6]He said to his men, "The LORD forbid that I should do such a thing to my master, the LORD's anointed, or lay my hand on him; for he is the anointed of the LORD." [7]With these words David sharply rebuked his men and did not allow them to attack Saul. And Saul left the cave and went his way.

[8]Then David went out of the cave and called out to Saul, "My lord the king!" When Saul looked behind him, David bowed down and prostrated himself with his face to the ground. [9]He said to Saul, "Why do you listen when men say, 'David is bent on harming you'? [10]This day you have seen with your own eyes how the LORD delivered you into my hands in the cave. Some urged me to kill you, but I spared you; I said, 'I will not lay my hand on my lord, because he is the LORD's anointed.' [11]See, my father, look at this piece of your robe in my hand! I cut off the corner of your robe but did not kill you. See that there is nothing in my hand to indicate that I am guilty of wrongdoing or rebellion. I have not wronged you, but you are hunting me down to take my life. [12]May the LORD judge between you and me. And may the LORD avenge the wrongs you have done to me, but my hand will not touch you. [13]As the old saying goes, 'From evildoers come evil deeds,' so my hand will not touch you.

[14]"Against whom has the king of Israel come out? Who are you pursuing? A dead dog? A flea? [15]May the LORD be our judge and decide between us. May he consider my cause and uphold it; may he vindicate me by delivering me from your hand."

[16]When David finished saying this, Saul asked, "Is that your voice, David my son?" And he wept aloud. [17]"You are more righteous than I," he said. "You have treated me well, but I have treated you badly. [18]You have just now told me about the good you did to me; the LORD delivered me into your hands, but you did not kill me. [19]When a man finds his enemy, does he let him get away unharmed? May the LORD reward you well for the way you treated me today. [20]I know that you will surely be king and that the kingdom of Israel will be established in your hands. [21]Now swear to me by the LORD that you will not kill off my descendants or wipe out my name from my father's family."

[22]So David gave his oath to Saul. Then Saul returned home, but David and his men went up to the stronghold.

DAVID, NABAL AND ABIGAIL

25 Now Samuel died, and all Israel assembled and mourned for him; and they buried him at his home in Ramah. Then David moved down into the Desert of Paran.[b]

---

[a] 4 Or "Today the LORD is saying   [b] 1 Hebrew and some Septuagint manuscripts; other Septuagint manuscripts Maon

What did it mean to cut off the corner of someone's robe? (24:4)
During that time, cutting off the corner of someone's robe was a symbol of disloyalty and rebellion.

Why did David show Saul the piece of robe? (24:5–6)
David had tried to be loyal to Saul, and he was determined not to take the kingship away but to leave it in God's hands. David regretted cutting the robe because it was a sign of rebellion against Saul's authority as king. He wanted to show Saul his loyalty, so he bowed and showed him the piece of robe.

Was David unfairly demanding protection money from Nabal? (25:7–8)
David's request was common in ancient times when police forces were not available. David was asking for support for his men because they had protected Nabal's shepherds and sheep from wild animals and raids by desert nomads.

How did people extend hospitality during festive times? (25:8)
Sheep-shearing was a harvest festival celebrated by the flock owner. It was the custom to invite neighbors and friends to share in a great feast. The poor and needy were usually among those who attended. David and his men should have been welcomed, especially after protecting Nabal's flocks.

Was it risky for Abigail to make this decision alone? (25:18–19)
Abigail did the responsible thing in an emergency situation in spite of the risk to herself. She thought doing nothing to save her people would be riskier than angering her husband for going against his decision. She told Nabal what she had done after he sobered up.

What was a seah? (25:18)
A seah was a dry measurement of about 7 quarts. Five seahs would probably weigh about 60 pounds (about 27 kilograms).

²A certain man in Maon, who had property there at Carmel, was very wealthy. He had a thousand goats and three thousand sheep, which he was shearing in Carmel. ³His name was Nabal and his wife's name was Abigail. She was an intelligent and beautiful woman, but her husband was surly and mean in his dealings—he was a Calebite.

⁴While David was in the wilderness, he heard that Nabal was shearing sheep. ⁵So he sent ten young men and said to them, "Go up to Nabal at Carmel and greet him in my name. ⁶Say to him: 'Long life to you! Good health to you and your household! And good health to all that is yours!

⁷"'Now I hear that it is sheep-shearing time. When your shepherds were with us, we did not mistreat them, and the whole time they were at Carmel nothing of theirs was missing. ⁸Ask your own servants and they will tell you. Therefore be favorable toward my men, since we come at a festive time. Please give your servants and your son David whatever you can find for them.'"

⁹When David's men arrived, they gave Nabal this message in David's name. Then they waited.

¹⁰Nabal answered David's servants, "Who is this David? Who is this son of Jesse? Many servants are breaking away from their masters these days. ¹¹Why should I take my bread and water, and the meat I have slaughtered for my shearers, and give it to men coming from who knows where?"

¹²David's men turned around and went back. When they arrived, they reported every word. ¹³David said to his men, "Each of you strap on your sword!" So they did, and David strapped his on as well. About four hundred men went up with David, while two hundred stayed with the supplies.

¹⁴One of the servants told Abigail, Nabal's wife, "David sent messengers from the wilderness to give our master his greetings, but he hurled insults at them. ¹⁵Yet these men were very good to us. They did not mistreat us, and the whole time we were out in the fields near them nothing was missing. ¹⁶Night and day they were a wall around us the whole time we were herding our sheep near them. ¹⁷Now think it over and see what you can do, because disaster is hanging over our master and his whole household. He is such a wicked man that no one can talk to him."

¹⁸Abigail acted quickly. She took two hundred loaves of bread, two skins of wine, five dressed sheep, five seahs*a* of roasted grain, a hundred cakes of raisins and two hundred cakes of pressed figs, and loaded them on donkeys. ¹⁹Then she told her servants, "Go on ahead; I'll follow you." But she did not tell her husband Nabal.

²⁰As she came riding her donkey into a mountain ravine, there were David and his men descending toward her, and she met them. ²¹David had just said, "It's been useless—all my watching over this fellow's property in the wilderness so that nothing of his was missing. He has paid me back evil for good. ²²May God deal with David,*b* be it ever so severely, if by morning I leave alive one male of all who belong to him!"

a 18 That is, probably about 60 pounds or about 27 kilograms   b 22 Some Septuagint manuscripts; Hebrew with David's enemies

²³When Abigail saw David, she quickly got off her donkey and bowed down before David with her face to the ground. ²⁴She fell at his feet and said: "Pardon your servant, my lord, and let me speak to you; hear what your servant has to say. ²⁵Please pay no attention, my lord, to that wicked man Nabal. He is just like his name—his name means Fool, and folly goes with him. And as for me, your servant, I did not see the men my lord sent. ²⁶And now, my lord, as surely as the LORD your God lives and as you live, since the LORD has kept you from bloodshed and from avenging yourself with your own hands, may your enemies and all who are intent on harming my lord be like Nabal. ²⁷And let this gift, which your servant has brought to my lord, be given to the men who follow you.

²⁸"Please forgive your servant's presumption. The LORD your God will certainly make a lasting dynasty for my lord, because you fight the LORD's battles, and no wrongdoing will be found in you as long as you live. ²⁹Even though someone is pursuing you to take your life, the life of my lord will be bound securely in the bundle of the living by the LORD your God, but the lives of your enemies he will hurl away as from the pocket of a sling. ³⁰When the LORD has fulfilled for my lord every good thing he promised concerning him and has appointed him ruler over Israel, ³¹my lord will not have on his conscience the staggering burden of needless bloodshed or of having avenged himself. And when the LORD your God has brought my lord success, remember your servant."

³²David said to Abigail, "Praise be to the LORD, the God of Israel, who has sent you today to meet me. ³³May you be blessed for your good judgment and for keeping me from bloodshed this day and from avenging myself with my own hands. ³⁴Otherwise, as surely as the LORD, the God of Israel, lives, who has kept me from harming you, if you had not come quickly to meet me, not one male belonging to Nabal would have been left alive by daybreak."

³⁵Then David accepted from her hand what she had brought him and said, "Go home in peace. I have heard your words and granted your request."

³⁶When Abigail went to Nabal, he was in the house holding a banquet like that of a king. He was in high spirits and very drunk. So she told him nothing at all until daybreak. ³⁷Then in the morning, when Nabal was sober, his wife told him all these things, and his heart failed him and he became like a stone. ³⁸About ten days later, the LORD struck Nabal and he died.

³⁹When David heard that Nabal was dead, he said, "Praise be to the LORD, who has upheld my cause against Nabal for treating me with contempt. He has kept his servant from doing wrong and has brought Nabal's wrongdoing down on his own head."

Then David sent word to Abigail, asking her to become his wife. ⁴⁰His servants went to Carmel and said to Abigail, "David has sent us to you to take you to become his wife."

⁴¹She bowed down with her face to the ground and said, "I am your servant and am ready to serve you and wash the feet of my lord's servants." ⁴²Abigail quickly got on a donkey

Why did Abigail say that her husband's name was Fool? (25:25)
The Hebrew word *nabal* literally means *fool*. This may have been a nickname he acquired at some point in his life because he acted foolishly. He was mean to others and disrespectful to God.

How did Nabal die? (25:37)
When Abigail told him what she had done, he may have had a heart attack or a stroke. He apparently went into a coma ("became like a stone") and died about ten days later.

and, attended by her five female servants, went with David's messengers and became his wife. ⁴³David had also married Ahinoam of Jezreel, and they both were his wives. ⁴⁴But Saul had given his daughter Michal, David's wife, to Paltiel*ᵃ* son of Laish, who was from Gallim.

DAVID AGAIN SPARES SAUL'S LIFE

26 The Ziphites went to Saul at Gibeah and said, "Is not David hiding on the hill of Hakilah, which faces Jeshimon?"

²So Saul went down to the Desert of Ziph, with his three thousand select Israelite troops, to search there for David. ³Saul made his camp beside the road on the hill of Hakilah facing Jeshimon, but David stayed in the wilderness. When he saw that Saul had followed him there, ⁴he sent out scouts and learned that Saul had definitely arrived.

⁵Then David set out and went to the place where Saul had camped. He saw where Saul and Abner son of Ner, the commander of the army, had lain down. Saul was lying inside the camp, with the army encamped around him.

⁶David then asked Ahimelek the Hittite and Abishai son of Zeruiah, Joab's brother, "Who will go down into the camp with me to Saul?"

"I'll go with you," said Abishai.

⁷So David and Abishai went to the army by night, and there was Saul, lying asleep inside the camp with his spear stuck in the ground near his head. Abner and the soldiers were lying around him.

⁸Abishai said to David, "Today God has delivered your enemy into your hands. Now let me pin him to the ground with one thrust of the spear; I won't strike him twice."

⁹But David said to Abishai, "Don't destroy him! Who can lay a hand on the LORD's anointed and be guiltless? ¹⁰As surely as the LORD lives," he said, "the LORD himself will strike him, or his time will come and he will die, or he will go into battle and perish. ¹¹But the LORD forbid that I should lay a hand on the LORD's anointed. Now get the spear and water jug that are near his head, and let's go."

¹²So David took the spear and water jug near Saul's head, and they left. No one saw or knew about it, nor did anyone wake up. They were all sleeping, because the LORD had put them into a deep sleep.

¹³Then David crossed over to the other side and stood on top of the hill some distance away; there was a wide space between them. ¹⁴He called out to the army and to Abner son of Ner, "Aren't you going to answer me, Abner?"

Abner replied, "Who are you who calls to the king?"

¹⁵David said, "You're a man, aren't you? And who is like you in Israel? Why didn't you guard your lord the king? Someone came to destroy your lord the king. ¹⁶What you have done is not good. As surely as the LORD lives, you and your men must die, because you did not guard your master, the LORD's anointed. Look around you. Where are the king's spear and water jug that were near his head?"

Why did David still refer to Saul as "the LORD's anointed"? (26:9)
In the books of Samuel, the term *the Lord's anointed* is substituted for *king* while keeping the same meaning. Saul had been anointed king by Samuel. Even though he repeatedly disobeyed God, he was still king. David had respect for the office in spite of the actions of the person who held it.

ᵃ 44 Hebrew *Palti*, a variant of *Paltiel*

¹⁷Saul recognized David's voice and said, "Is that your voice, David my son?"

David replied, "Yes it is, my lord the king." ¹⁸And he added, "Why is my lord pursuing his servant? What have I done, and what wrong am I guilty of? ¹⁹Now let my lord the king listen to his servant's words. If the LORD has incited you against me, then may he accept an offering. If, however, people have done it, may they be cursed before the LORD! They have driven me today from my share in the LORD's inheritance and have said, 'Go, serve other gods.' ²⁰Now do not let my blood fall to the ground far from the presence of the LORD. The king of Israel has come out to look for a flea—as one hunts a partridge in the mountains."

²¹Then Saul said, "I have sinned. Come back, David my son. Because you considered my life precious today, I will not try to harm you again. Surely I have acted like a fool and have been terribly wrong."

²²"Here is the king's spear," David answered. "Let one of your young men come over and get it. ²³The LORD rewards everyone for their righteousness and faithfulness. The LORD delivered you into my hands today, but I would not lay a hand on the LORD's anointed. ²⁴As surely as I valued your life today, so may the LORD value my life and deliver me from all trouble."

²⁵Then Saul said to David, "May you be blessed, David my son; you will do great things and surely triumph."

So David went on his way, and Saul returned home.

DAVID AMONG THE PHILISTINES

27 But David thought to himself, "One of these days I will be destroyed by the hand of Saul. The best thing I can do is to escape to the land of the Philistines. Then Saul will give up searching for me anywhere in Israel, and I will slip out of his hand."

²So David and the six hundred men with him left and went over to Achish son of Maok king of Gath. ³David and his men settled in Gath with Achish. Each man had his family with him, and David had his two wives: Ahinoam of Jezreel and Abigail of Carmel, the widow of Nabal. ⁴When Saul was told that David had fled to Gath, he no longer searched for him.

⁵Then David said to Achish, "If I have found favor in your eyes, let a place be assigned to me in one of the country towns, that I may live there. Why should your servant live in the royal city with you?"

⁶So on that day Achish gave him Ziklag, and it has belonged to the kings of Judah ever since. ⁷David lived in Philistine territory a year and four months.

⁸Now David and his men went up and raided the Geshurites, the Girzites and the Amalekites. (From ancient times these peoples had lived in the land extending to Shur and Egypt.) ⁹Whenever David attacked an area, he did not leave a man or woman alive, but took sheep and cattle, donkeys and camels, and clothes. Then he returned to Achish.

¹⁰When Achish asked, "Where did you go raiding today?" David would say, "Against the Negev of Judah" or

What was David asking Saul? (26:19)
David wanted to know why Saul was trying to kill him. He asked if it was his fault or if other people had incited Saul to pursue him. He asked if somehow he had offended God. Finally, the real reason was revealed when Saul said he was the one who had sinned.

David Among the Philistines (27:2—30:26)

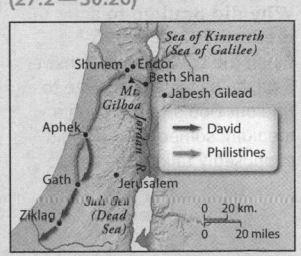

Why did Achish allow David, his men, and their families to live in his territory? (27:2–3)
The king had probably heard about David's military successes against Saul. Also, offering sanctuary meant that David and his men would be obligated to serve Achish in any military actions.

Why did David kill all of the people in any territory he attacked? (27:9)
In one sense he was continuing the job Israel had begun but never finished after taking over the land of Canaan. This was something God had commanded his people to do. From a practical standpoint, he didn't want any survivors to tell Achish what he had done.

"Against the Negev of Jerahmeel" or "Against the Negev of the Kenites." [11]He did not leave a man or woman alive to be brought to Gath, for he thought, "They might inform on us and say, 'This is what David did.'" And such was his practice as long as he lived in Philistine territory. [12]Achish trusted David and said to himself, "He has become so obnoxious to his people, the Israelites, that he will be my servant for life."

28 In those days the Philistines gathered their forces to fight against Israel. Achish said to David, "You must understand that you and your men will accompany me in the army."

[2]David said, "Then you will see for yourself what your servant can do."

Achish replied, "Very well, I will make you my bodyguard for life."

SAUL AND THE MEDIUM AT ENDOR

[3]Now Samuel was dead, and all Israel had mourned for him and buried him in his own town of Ramah. Saul had expelled the mediums and spiritists from the land.

[4]The Philistines assembled and came and set up camp at Shunem, while Saul gathered all Israel and set up camp at Gilboa. [5]When Saul saw the Philistine army, he was afraid; terror filled his heart. [6]He inquired of the Lord, but the Lord did not answer him by dreams or Urim or prophets. [7]Saul then said to his attendants, "Find me a woman who is a medium, so I may go and inquire of her."

"There is one in Endor," they said.

[8]So Saul disguised himself, putting on other clothes, and at night he and two men went to the woman. "Consult a spirit for me," he said, "and bring up for me the one I name."

[9]But the woman said to him, "Surely you know what Saul has done. He has cut off the mediums and spiritists from the land. Why have you set a trap for my life to bring about my death?"

[10]Saul swore to her by the Lord, "As surely as the Lord lives, you will not be punished for this."

[11]Then the woman asked, "Whom shall I bring up for you?"

"Bring up Samuel," he said.

Why did Achish appoint David as his bodyguard when he had earlier thought he was insane? (28:2) Sometime earlier, David had acted insane because he was afraid of Achish (see 21:12–15). In ancient times, people often thought insanity was caused by spirit possession. If David was no longer believed to be possessed, he would be considered sane.

Why did Saul go to a medium? (28:6–7) When the Lord wouldn't answer Saul, he became desperate to find out God's will through a medium, someone who could supposedly talk to the dead.

Can spirits be called from the dead? 1 SAMUEL 28

It isn't clear whether the witch of Endor actually saw the spirit of Samuel or if she had contact with an evil spirit that took the form of Samuel. However, the Bible makes it clear that believers should avoid trying to make contact with the spirit world because it opens a person to the influence of forces that may be evil. Using such seemingly innocent things as Ouija boards can possibly make someone susceptible to the evil influence of a spirit.

Leviticus 19:31 says, "Do not turn to mediums or seek out spiritists, for you will be defiled by them. I am the Lord your God." Deuteronomy 18:10–13 says, "Let no one be found among you who ... practices divination or sorcery, interprets omens, engages in witchcraft, or casts spells, or who is a medium or spiritist or who consults the dead. Anyone who does these things is detestable to the Lord ... You must be blameless before the Lord your God."

Believers should seek God's will through prayer and Scripture reading and should not dabble in the realm of the spirit world.

[12]When the woman saw Samuel, she cried out at the top of her voice and said to Saul, "Why have you deceived me? You are Saul!"

[13]The king said to her, "Don't be afraid. What do you see?"

The woman said, "I see a ghostly figure[a] coming up out of the earth."

[14]"What does he look like?" he asked.

"An old man wearing a robe is coming up," she said.

Then Saul knew it was Samuel, and he bowed down and prostrated himself with his face to the ground.

[15]Samuel said to Saul, "Why have you disturbed me by bringing me up?"

"I am in great distress," Saul said. "The Philistines are fighting against me, and God has departed from me. He no longer answers me, either by prophets or by dreams. So I have called on you to tell me what to do."

[16]Samuel said, "Why do you consult me, now that the LORD has departed from you and become your enemy? [17]The LORD has done what he predicted through me. The LORD has torn the kingdom out of your hands and given it to one of your neighbors—to David. [18]Because you did not obey the LORD or carry out his fierce wrath against the Amalekites, the LORD has done this to you today. [19]The LORD will deliver both Israel and you into the hands of the Philistines, and tomorrow you and your sons will be with me. The LORD will also give the army of Israel into the hands of the Philistines."

[20]Immediately Saul fell full length on the ground, filled with fear because of Samuel's words. His strength was gone, for he had eaten nothing all that day and all that night.

[21]When the woman came to Saul and saw that he was greatly shaken, she said, "Look, your servant has obeyed you. I took my life in my hands and did what you told me to do. [22]Now please listen to your servant and let me give you some food so you may eat and have the strength to go on your way."

[23]He refused and said, "I will not eat."

But his men joined the woman in urging him, and he listened to them. He got up from the ground and sat on the couch.

[24]The woman had a fattened calf at the house, which she butchered at once. She took some flour, kneaded it and baked bread without yeast. [25]Then she set it before Saul and his men, and they ate. That same night they got up and left.

ACHISH SENDS DAVID BACK TO ZIKLAG

29 The Philistines gathered all their forces at Aphek, and Israel camped by the spring in Jezreel. [2]As the Philistine rulers marched with their units of hundreds and thousands, David and his men were marching at the rear with Achish. [3]The commanders of the Philistines asked, "What about these Hebrews?"

Achish replied, "Is this not David, who was an officer of Saul king of Israel? He has already been with me for over a

Why did the medium cry out when Samuel appeared? (28:12)
When she saw Samuel, she realized that she had been deceived and that the man consulting her was really Saul. Because Saul had banished all spirits and mediums, she was frightened that he would kill her.

Was this really Samuel or Samuel's ghost? (28:12)
Several explanations have been given for this appearance: God may have permitted Samuel to appear to the woman; she may have had contact with an evil spirit that took the form of Samuel; or she may have somehow been able to discern Saul's thoughts and conjured up an image of Samuel in her mind. Whatever the explanation, after hearing Samuel's words, Saul realized that both he and the nation of Israel were facing disaster.

[a] 13 Or see spirits; or see gods

year, and from the day he left Saul until now, I have found no fault in him."

⁴But the Philistine commanders were angry with Achish and said, "Send the man back, that he may return to the place you assigned him. He must not go with us into battle, or he will turn against us during the fighting. How better could he regain his master's favor than by taking the heads of our own men? ⁵Isn't this the David they sang about in their dances:

"'Saul has slain his thousands,
    and David his tens of thousands'?"

⁶So Achish called David and said to him, "As surely as the LORD lives, you have been reliable, and I would be pleased to have you serve with me in the army. From the day you came to me until today, I have found no fault in you, but the rulers don't approve of you. ⁷Now turn back and go in peace; do nothing to displease the Philistine rulers."

⁸"But what have I done?" asked David. "What have you found against your servant from the day I came to you until now? Why can't I go and fight against the enemies of my lord the king?"

⁹Achish answered, "I know that you have been as pleasing in my eyes as an angel of God; nevertheless, the Philistine commanders have said, 'He must not go up with us into battle.' ¹⁰Now get up early, along with your master's servants who have come with you, and leave in the morning as soon as it is light."

¹¹So David and his men got up early in the morning to go back to the land of the Philistines, and the Philistines went up to Jezreel.

DAVID DESTROYS THE AMALEKITES

30 David and his men reached Ziklag on the third day. Now the Amalekites had raided the Negev and Ziklag. They had attacked Ziklag and burned it, ²and had taken captive the women and everyone else in it, both young and old. They killed none of them, but carried them off as they went on their way.

³When David and his men reached Ziklag, they found it destroyed by fire and their wives and sons and daughters taken captive. ⁴So David and his men wept aloud until they had no strength left to weep. ⁵David's two wives had been captured—Ahinoam of Jezreel and Abigail, the widow of Nabal of Carmel. ⁶David was greatly distressed because the men were talking of stoning him; each one was bitter in spirit because of his sons and daughters. But David found strength in the LORD his God.

⁷Then David said to Abiathar the priest, the son of Ahimelek, "Bring me the ephod." Abiathar brought it to him, ⁸and David inquired of the LORD, "Shall I pursue this raiding party? Will I overtake them?"

"Pursue them," he answered. "You will certainly overtake them and succeed in the rescue."

⁹David and the six hundred men with him came to the Besor Valley, where some stayed behind. ¹⁰Two hundred of

Why would a Philistine king swear by Israel's God? (29:6)
Achish swore by the God of Israel apparently to prove his sincerity to David. This does not mean that he truly believed in the LORD.

What did the phrase "the enemies of my lord the king" mean? (29:8)
David used a statement that could have several meanings. On the surface, it seemed to refer to the enemies of Achish. But David may have really been thinking of the enemies of King Saul or of the LORD, David's King.

Why did David's men want to stone him? (30:6)
David's men held him responsible for the destruction of Ziklag. David's raids on the Amalekites had led them to seek revenge. Also, when David took all his troops to Aphek (29:1–2), no one was left behind to defend the home base of Ziklag.

them were too exhausted to cross the valley, but David and the other four hundred continued the pursuit.

¹¹ They found an Egyptian in a field and brought him to David. They gave him water to drink and food to eat — ¹² part of a cake of pressed figs and two cakes of raisins. He ate and was revived, for he had not eaten any food or drunk any water for three days and three nights.

¹³ David asked him, "Who do you belong to? Where do you come from?"

He said, "I am an Egyptian, the slave of an Amalekite. My master abandoned me when I became ill three days ago. ¹⁴ We raided the Negev of the Kerethites, some territory belonging to Judah and the Negev of Caleb. And we burned Ziklag."

¹⁵ David asked him, "Can you lead me down to this raiding party?"

He answered, "Swear to me before God that you will not kill me or hand me over to my master, and I will take you down to them."

¹⁶ He led David down, and there they were, scattered over the countryside, eating, drinking and reveling because of the great amount of plunder they had taken from the land of the Philistines and from Judah. ¹⁷ David fought them from dusk until the evening of the next day, and none of them got away, except four hundred young men who rode off on camels and fled. ¹⁸ David recovered everything the Amalekites had taken, including his two wives. ¹⁹ Nothing was missing: young or old, boy or girl, plunder or anything else they had taken. David brought everything back. ²⁰ He took all the flocks and herds, and his men drove them ahead of the other livestock, saying, "This is David's plunder."

²¹ Then David came to the two hundred men who had been too exhausted to follow him and who were left behind at the Besor Valley. They came out to meet David and the men with him. As David and his men approached, he asked them how they were. ²² But all the evil men and troublemakers among David's followers said, "Because they did not go out with us, we will not share with them the plunder we recovered. However, each man may take his wife and children and go."

²³ David replied, "No, my brothers, you must not do that with what the LORD has given us. He has protected us and delivered into our hands the raiding party that came against us. ²⁴ Who will listen to what you say? The share of the man who stayed with the supplies is to be the same as that of him who went down to the battle. All will share alike." ²⁵ David made this a statute and ordinance for Israel from that day to this.

²⁶ When David reached Ziklag, he sent some of the plunder to the elders of Judah, who were his friends, saying, "Here is a gift for you from the plunder of the LORD's enemies."

²⁷ David sent it to those who were in Bethel, Ramoth Negev and Jattir; ²⁸ to those in Aroer, Siphmoth, Eshtemoa ²⁹ and Rakal; to those in the towns of the Jerahmeelites and the Kenites; ³⁰ to those in Hormah, Bor Ashan, Athak ³¹ and Hebron; and to those in all the other places where he and his men had roamed.

SAUL TAKES HIS LIFE

31 Now the Philistines fought against Israel; the Israel-ites fled before them, and many fell dead on Mount Gilboa. ²The Philistines were in hot pursuit of Saul and his sons, and they killed his sons Jonathan, Abinadab and Malki-Shua. ³The fighting grew fierce around Saul, and when the archers overtook him, they wounded him critically.

⁴Saul said to his armor-bearer, "Draw your sword and run me through, or these uncircumcised fellows will come and run me through and abuse me."

But his armor-bearer was terrified and would not do it; so Saul took his own sword and fell on it. ⁵When the armor-bearer saw that Saul was dead, he too fell on his sword and died with him. ⁶So Saul and his three sons and his armor-bearer and all his men died together that same day.

⁷When the Israelites along the valley and those across the Jordan saw that the Israelite army had fled and that Saul and his sons had died, they abandoned their towns and fled. And the Philistines came and occupied them.

⁸The next day, when the Philistines came to strip the dead, they found Saul and his three sons fallen on Mount Gilboa. ⁹They cut off his head and stripped off his armor, and they sent messengers throughout the land of the Philistines to proclaim the news in the temple of their idols and among their people. ¹⁰They put his armor in the temple of the Ashtoreths and fastened his body to the wall of Beth Shan.

¹¹When the people of Jabesh Gilead heard what the Philistines had done to Saul, ¹²all their valiant men marched through the night to Beth Shan. They took down the bodies of Saul and his sons from the wall of Beth Shan and went to Jabesh, where they burned them. ¹³Then they took their bones and buried them under a tamarisk tree at Jabesh, and they fasted seven days.

Why was Saul especially determined not to be captured by the Philistines? (31:4) Sometimes body parts were cut off or mutilated and other types of torture inflicted, especially to leaders or kings who had been taken captive.

Why did the Philistines put Saul's armor in the temple of the Ashtoreths? (31:10) They placed it there as a trophy of the supposed victory of their god over the Israelites' God.

Why did the men of Jabesh Gilead want to recover the bodies of Saul and his sons? (31:11–12) The people of Jabesh Gilead were grateful for the way Saul had come to their defense when they were threatened by the Ammonites. They probably burned the bodies to prevent the Philistines from abusing the bodies any further.

Can a person who commits suicide go to heaven? 1 SAMUEL 31

The Bible mentions six people who committed suicide: Abimelek (*Judges 9:54*), Saul (*1 Samuel 31:4*), Saul's armor-bearer (*1 Samuel 31:4–6*), Ahithophel (*2 Samuel 17:23*), Zimri (*1 Kings 16:18*), and Judas (*Matthew 27:5*). At least five of these were wicked people (we don't know enough about Saul's armor bearer to say.) It's easy to conclude that if an unbeliever commits suicide—just as if he or she dies a natural death—then he or she will not be saved.

But what about a Christian? Nothing in the Bible suggests that a believer who commits suicide will be prevented from going to heaven. In fact, Romans 8:38–39 gives the assurance that "neither death nor life, neither angels nor demons, neither the present nor the future, nor any powers, neither height nor depth, nor anything else in all creation, will be able to separate us from the love of God that is in Christ Jesus our Lord."

2 Samuel

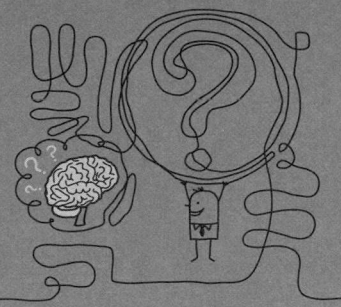

INTRODUCTION

Who wrote this book?	The writer is unknown.
Why was this book written?	The book of 2 Samuel tells the story of David's 40-year reign as Israel's king.
What happens in this book?	David becomes king of Israel. During his reign foreign enemies are defeated and Israel becomes a great nation.
What do we learn about God in this book?	God uses people who love and want to please him, as King David did.
Who is the key person in this book?	The most important person in this book is King David.
Where did this happen?	These events took place in Israel. (See the map at the back of this Bible to see where Israel is.)

What are some of the stories in this book?		
	David conquers Jerusalem	2 Samuel 5
	David brings the ark to Jerusalem	2 Samuel 6
	David helps Mephibosheth	2 Samuel 9
	David sins with Bathsheba	2 Samuel 11
	David confesses his sin	2 Samuel 12
	Absalom leads a rebellion	2 Samuel 15 – 18
	David builds an altar	2 Samuel 24

When did these things happen?

1400 BC 1300 1200 1100 1000 900 800 700 600 500 400

ISRAELITES ENTER CANAAN (C. 1406 BC)

JUDGES BEGIN TO RULE (C. 1375 BC)

SAUL'S REIGN (1050 – 1010 BC)

DAVID'S REIGN (1010 – 970 BC)

DIVISION OF THE KINGDOM (930 BC)

BOOK OF 2 SAMUEL WRITTEN (C. 925 BC)

EXILE OF ISRAEL (722 BC)

FALL OF JERUSALEM (586 BC)

DAVID HEARS OF SAUL'S DEATH

1 After the death of Saul, David returned from striking down the Amalekites and stayed in Ziklag two days. ²On the third day a man arrived from Saul's camp with his clothes torn and dust on his head. When he came to David, he fell to the ground to pay him honor.

³"Where have you come from?" David asked him.

He answered, "I have escaped from the Israelite camp."

⁴"What happened?" David asked. "Tell me."

"The men fled from the battle," he replied. "Many of them fell and died. And Saul and his son Jonathan are dead."

⁵Then David said to the young man who brought him the report, "How do you know that Saul and his son Jonathan are dead?"

⁶"I happened to be on Mount Gilboa," the young man said, "and there was Saul, leaning on his spear, with the chariots and their drivers in hot pursuit. ⁷When he turned around and saw me, he called out to me, and I said, 'What can I do?'

⁸"He asked me, 'Who are you?'

"'An Amalekite,' I answered.

⁹"Then he said to me, 'Stand here by me and kill me! I'm in the throes of death, but I'm still alive.'

¹⁰"So I stood beside him and killed him, because I knew that after he had fallen he could not survive. And I took the crown that was on his head and the band on his arm and have brought them here to my lord."

¹¹Then David and all the men with him took hold of their clothes and tore them. ¹²They mourned and wept and fasted till evening for Saul and his son Jonathan, and for the army of the LORD and for the nation of Israel, because they had fallen by the sword.

¹³David said to the young man who brought him the report, "Where are you from?"

"I am the son of a foreigner, an Amalekite," he answered.

¹⁴David asked him, "Why weren't you afraid to lift your hand to destroy the LORD's anointed?"

¹⁵Then David called one of his men and said, "Go, strike him down!" So he struck him down, and he died. ¹⁶For David had said to him, "Your blood be on your own head. Your own mouth testified against you when you said, 'I killed the LORD's anointed.'"

DAVID'S LAMENT FOR SAUL AND JONATHAN

¹⁷David took up this lament concerning Saul and his son Jonathan, ¹⁸and he ordered that the people of Judah be taught this lament of the bow (it is written in the Book of Jashar):

¹⁹"A gazelle*ᵃ* lies slain on your heights, Israel.
  How the mighty have fallen!

²⁰"Tell it not in Gath,
    proclaim it not in the streets of Ashkelon,
  lest the daughters of the Philistines be glad,
    lest the daughters of the uncircumcised rejoice.

Why did the Amalekite say he had killed Saul? (1:10)
Saul took his own life, so the Amalekite was lying, perhaps to get a reward from David. However, his plan backfired, and he was executed for killing the LORD's anointed one.

Why did David and his men mourn the death of Saul, their enemy? (1:12)
There are probably several reasons they mourned the deaths of Saul and Jonathan. Jonathan was David's close friend, so it makes sense that David would be saddened by his death. Saul was the anointed king of Israel even though he was corrupt and the death of a king would mean difficult times lay ahead for Israel. Also, the death of Saul and others were the result of another defeat by the Philistines.

What was the Book of Jashar? (1:18)
The practice of composing laments for fallen leaders or heroes was common in the ancient Middle East. The Book of Jashar, now lost, was an account of Israel's heroes (perhaps in poetic form).

ᵃ *19 Gazelle* here symbolizes a human dignitary.

²¹"Mountains of Gilboa,
     may you have neither dew nor rain,
     may no showers fall on your terraced fields.*
For there the shield of the mighty was despised,
     the shield of Saul—no longer rubbed with oil.

²²"From the blood of the slain,
     from the flesh of the mighty,
the bow of Jonathan did not turn back,
     the sword of Saul did not return unsatisfied.
²³Saul and Jonathan—
     in life they were loved and admired,
     and in death they were not parted.
They were swifter than eagles,
     they were stronger than lions.

²⁴"Daughters of Israel,
     weep for Saul,
who clothed you in scarlet and finery,
     who adorned your garments with ornaments of gold.

²⁵"How the mighty have fallen in battle!
     Jonathan lies slain on your heights.
²⁶I grieve for you, Jonathan my brother;
     you were very dear to me.
Your love for me was wonderful,
     more wonderful than that of women.

²⁷"How the mighty have fallen!
     The weapons of war have perished!"

DAVID ANOINTED KING OVER JUDAH

2 In the course of time, David inquired of the LORD. "Shall I go up to one of the towns of Judah?" he asked.

The LORD said, "Go up."

David asked, "Where shall I go?"

"To Hebron," the LORD answered.

²So David went up there with his two wives, Ahinoam of Jezreel and Abigail, the widow of Nabal of Carmel. ³David also took the men who were with him, each with his family, and they settled in Hebron and its towns. ⁴Then the men of Judah came to Hebron, and there they anointed David king over the tribe of Judah.

When David was told that it was the men from Jabesh Gilead who had buried Saul, ⁵he sent messengers to them to say to them, "The LORD bless you for showing this kindness to Saul your master by burying him. ⁶May the LORD now show you kindness and faithfulness, and I too will show you the same favor because you have done this. ⁷Now then, be strong and brave, for Saul your master is dead, and the people of Judah have anointed me king over them."

WAR BETWEEN THE HOUSES OF DAVID AND SAUL

⁸Meanwhile, Abner son of Ner, the commander of Saul's army, had taken Ish-Bosheth son of Saul and brought him

---

a 21 Or / nor fields that yield grain for offerings

Why would shields be rubbed with oil? (1:21) Oil protected the shields because they were made of wood or wicker covered with leather. The coat of oil would protect them from rain damage, would help them last longer, and most importantly, the slippery oil would cause the enemies' swords to glance off.

Why did David say that Jonathan's love was more wonderful than that of women? (1:26) Men in that time typically viewed women as inferiors and regarded wives as possessions, so a lot of marriages were not based on trust and commitment, not in the way David and Jonathon's relationship was founded. The two men saw each other as equals and treated each other as such. Even though Jonathan knew that David, and not him, would succeed Saul as king of Israel, he was not resentful. He pledged his loyalty to David.

Why did David thank the men of Jabesh Gilead for burying Saul? (2:5–7) David appreciated the sign of respect they had shown to the LORD's anointed king, Saul. David may also have wanted to thank them for their kindness and bravery in hopes that they would support him as their new king, just as they had supported Saul.

over to Mahanaim. [9] He made him king over Gilead, Ashuri and Jezreel, and also over Ephraim, Benjamin and all Israel.

[10] Ish-Bosheth son of Saul was forty years old when he became king over Israel, and he reigned two years. The tribe of Judah, however, remained loyal to David. [11] The length of time David was king in Hebron over Judah was seven years and six months.

[12] Abner son of Ner, together with the men of Ish-Bosheth son of Saul, left Mahanaim and went to Gibeon. [13] Joab son of Zeruiah and David's men went out and met them at the pool of Gibeon. One group sat down on one side of the pool and one group on the other side.

[14] Then Abner said to Joab, "Let's have some of the young men get up and fight hand to hand in front of us."

"All right, let them do it," Joab said.

[15] So they stood up and were counted off—twelve men for Benjamin and Ish-Bosheth son of Saul, and twelve for David. [16] Then each man grabbed his opponent by the head and thrust his dagger into his opponent's side, and they fell down together. So that place in Gibeon was called Helkath Hazzurim.[a]

[17] The battle that day was very fierce, and Abner and the Israelites were defeated by David's men.

[18] The three sons of Zeruiah were there: Joab, Abishai and Asahel. Now Asahel was as fleet-footed as a wild gazelle. [19] He chased Abner, turning neither to the right nor to the left as he pursued him. [20] Abner looked behind him and asked, "Is that you, Asahel?"

"It is," he answered.

[21] Then Abner said to him, "Turn aside to the right or to the left; take on one of the young men and strip him of his weapons." But Asahel would not stop chasing him.

[22] Again Abner warned Asahel, "Stop chasing me! Why should I strike you down? How could I look your brother Joab in the face?"

[23] But Asahel refused to give up the pursuit; so Abner thrust the butt of his spear into Asahel's stomach, and the spear came out through his back. He fell there and died on the spot. And every man stopped when he came to the place where Asahel had fallen and died.

[24] But Joab and Abishai pursued Abner, and as the sun was setting, they came to the hill of Ammah, near Giah on the way to the wasteland of Gibeon. [25] Then the men of Benjamin rallied behind Abner. They formed themselves into a group and took their stand on top of a hill.

[26] Abner called out to Joab, "Must the sword devour forever? Don't you realize that this will end in bitterness? How long before you order your men to stop pursuing their fellow Israelites?"

[27] Joab answered, "As surely as God lives, if you had not spoken, the men would have continued pursuing them until morning."

[28] So Joab blew the trumpet, and all the troops came to a halt; they no longer pursued Israel, nor did they fight anymore.

Why did the two armies agree to have 12 men from each side fight? (2:14–16)
It's possible that Abner and Joab proposed this type of contest to prevent a larger war. Having a small fight rather than a huge battle would prevent many from being killed. Using champions to fight on behalf of an army was not uncommon. This was the type of contest David and Goliath fought.

Why did a full-scale battle end up taking place? (2:17)
All 24 of the chosen soldiers were killed, so the fight ended in a stalemate. The rest of the soldiers on both sides decided to finish the contest.

Why did every man stop where Asahel died? (2:23)
Asahel died a gruesome death. He was killed when Abner plunged the blunt end of his spear into Asahel's stomach and out through his back. This sight must have stunned the soldiers. Asahel was a good soldier. He was incredibly fast and he was their leader's brother, so it was probably surprising to see such a strong soldier go down in such a tragic way.

---

[a] 16 *Helkath Hazzurim* means *field of daggers* or *field of hostilities*.

²⁹All that night Abner and his men marched through the Arabah. They crossed the Jordan, continued through the morning hours[a] and came to Mahanaim.

³⁰Then Joab stopped pursuing Abner and assembled the whole army. Besides Asahel, nineteen of David's men were found missing. ³¹But David's men had killed three hundred and sixty Benjamites who were with Abner. ³²They took Asahel and buried him in his father's tomb at Bethlehem. Then Joab and his men marched all night and arrived at Hebron by daybreak.

3 The war between the house of Saul and the house of David lasted a long time. David grew stronger and stronger, while the house of Saul grew weaker and weaker.

²Sons were born to David in Hebron:

His firstborn was Amnon the son of Ahinoam of Jezreel;

³his second, Kileab the son of Abigail the widow of Nabal of Carmel;

the third, Absalom the son of Maakah daughter of Talmai king of Geshur;

⁴the fourth, Adonijah the son of Haggith;

the fifth, Shephatiah the son of Abital;

⁵and the sixth, Ithream the son of David's wife Eglah.

These were born to David in Hebron.

ABNER GOES OVER TO DAVID

⁶During the war between the house of Saul and the house of David, Abner had been strengthening his own position in the house of Saul. ⁷Now Saul had had a concubine named Rizpah daughter of Aiah. And Ish-Bosheth said to Abner, "Why did you sleep with my father's concubine?"

⁸Abner was very angry because of what Ish-Bosheth said. So he answered, "Am I a dog's head—on Judah's side? This very day I am loyal to the house of your father Saul and to his family and friends. I haven't handed you over to David. Yet now you accuse me of an offense involving this woman! ⁹May God deal with Abner, be it ever so severely, if I do not do for David what the LORD promised him on oath ¹⁰and transfer the kingdom from the house of Saul and establish David's throne over Israel and Judah from Dan to Beersheba." ¹¹Ish-Bosheth did not dare to say another word to Abner, because he was afraid of him.

¹²Then Abner sent messengers on his behalf to say to David, "Whose land is it? Make an agreement with me, and I will help you bring all Israel over to you."

¹³"Good," said David. "I will make an agreement with you. But I demand one thing of you: Do not come into my presence unless you bring Michal daughter of Saul when you come to see me." ¹⁴Then David sent messengers to Ish-Bosheth son of Saul, demanding, "Give me my wife Michal, whom I betrothed to myself for the price of a hundred Philistine foreskins."

¹⁵So Ish-Bosheth gave orders and had her taken away from her husband Paltiel son of Laish. ¹⁶Her husband, however,

---

Wouldn't referring to yourself as a dog be a compliment? (3:8)
Today a lot of people think of dogs as loyal and dependable. But in the time of the Old Testament, dogs were usually described as wild scavengers. The term *dog* was applied to persons of low character, so this would have been an insult.

Why did David want Michal back? (3:14–15)
David probably wanted her back for political reasons. The reunion of David and Michal would strengthen David's claim to the throne as a son-in-law of Saul. Plus, he had paid the bride-price for Michal and was still married to her when Saul gave her to Paltiel. But it's also possible that David still loved her.

---

[a] 29 See Septuagint; the meaning of the Hebrew for this phrase is uncertain.

went with her, weeping behind her all the way to Bahurim. Then Abner said to him, "Go back home!" So he went back.

[17] Abner conferred with the elders of Israel and said, "For some time you have wanted to make David your king. [18] Now do it! For the LORD promised David, 'By my servant David I will rescue my people Israel from the hand of the Philistines and from the hand of all their enemies.'"

[19] Abner also spoke to the Benjamites in person. Then he went to Hebron to tell David everything that Israel and the whole tribe of Benjamin wanted to do. [20] When Abner, who had twenty men with him, came to David at Hebron, David prepared a feast for him and his men. [21] Then Abner said to David, "Let me go at once and assemble all Israel for my lord the king, so that they may make a covenant with you, and that you may rule over all that your heart desires." So David sent Abner away, and he went in peace.

JOAB MURDERS ABNER

[22] Just then David's men and Joab returned from a raid and brought with them a great deal of plunder. But Abner was no longer with David in Hebron, because David had sent him away, and he had gone in peace. [23] When Joab and all the soldiers with him arrived, he was told that Abner son of Ner had come to the king and that the king had sent him away and that he had gone in peace.

[24] So Joab went to the king and said, "What have you done? Look, Abner came to you. Why did you let him go? Now he is gone! [25] You know Abner son of Ner; he came to deceive you and observe your movements and find out everything you are doing."

[26] Joab then left David and sent messengers after Abner, and they brought him back from the cistern at Sirah. But David did not know it. [27] Now when Abner returned to Hebron, Joab took him aside into an inner chamber, as if to speak with him privately. And there, to avenge the blood of his brother Asahel, Joab stabbed him in the stomach, and he died.

[28] Later, when David heard about this, he said, "I and my kingdom are forever innocent before the LORD concerning the blood of Abner son of Ner. [29] May his blood fall on the head of Joab and on his whole family! May Joab's family never be without someone who has a running sore or leprosy[a] or who leans on a crutch or who falls by the sword or who lacks food."

[30] (Joab and his brother Abishai murdered Abner because he had killed their brother Asahel in the battle at Gibeon.)

[31] Then David said to Joab and all the people with him, "Tear your clothes and put on sackcloth and walk in mourning in front of Abner." King David himself walked behind the bier. [32] They buried Abner in Hebron, and the king wept aloud at Abner's tomb. All the people wept also.

[33] The king sang this lament for Abner:

"Should Abner have died as the lawless die?

Why did David show respect for Abner? (3:31–34)
David wanted to show that he was not responsible for Abner's murder. To do this, David followed Abner's funeral procession and fasted.

What was sackcloth? (3:31)
The English word *sackcloth* comes from the Hebrew word *sak*, which refers to a coarse cloth, dark in color. It was worn by mourners and sometimes by prophets. This uncomfortable garment was often worn next to the skin. Another garment usually covered it.

---

[a] 29 The Hebrew for *leprosy* was used for various diseases affecting the skin.

³⁴ Your hands were not bound,
       your feet were not fettered.
    You fell as one falls before the wicked."

    And all the people wept over him again.

³⁵ Then they all came and urged David to eat something
while it was still day; but David took an oath, saying, "May
God deal with me, be it ever so severely, if I taste bread or
anything else before the sun sets!"

³⁶ All the people took note and were pleased; indeed, everything the king did pleased them. ³⁷ So on that day all the
people there and all Israel knew that the king had no part in
the murder of Abner son of Ner.

³⁸ Then the king said to his men, "Do you not realize that
a commander and a great man has fallen in Israel this day?
³⁹ And today, though I am the anointed king, I am weak, and
these sons of Zeruiah are too strong for me. May the LORD
repay the evildoer according to his evil deeds!"

ISH-BOSHETH MURDERED

4 When Ish-Bosheth son of Saul heard that Abner had
died in Hebron, he lost courage, and all Israel became
alarmed. ² Now Saul's son had two men who were leaders of
raiding bands. One was named Baanah and the other Rekab;
they were sons of Rimmon the Beerothite from the tribe of
Benjamin — Beeroth is considered part of Benjamin, ³ because the people of Beeroth fled to Gittaim and have resided
there as foreigners to this day.

⁴ (Jonathan son of Saul had a son who was lame in both
feet. He was five years old when the news about Saul and
Jonathan came from Jezreel. His nurse picked him up and
fled, but as she hurried to leave, he fell and became disabled.
His name was Mephibosheth.)

⁵ Now Rekab and Baanah, the sons of Rimmon the Beerothite, set out for the house of Ish-Bosheth, and they arrived there in the heat of the day while he was taking his
noonday rest. ⁶ They went into the inner part of the house as
if to get some wheat, and they stabbed him in the stomach.
Then Rekab and his brother Baanah slipped away.

⁷ They had gone into the house while he was lying on the
bed in his bedroom. After they stabbed and killed him, they
cut off his head. Taking it with them, they traveled all night
by way of the Arabah. ⁸ They brought the head of Ish-Bosheth to David at Hebron and said to the king, "Here is the
head of Ish-Bosheth son of Saul, your enemy, who tried to
kill you. This day the LORD has avenged my lord the king
against Saul and his offspring."

⁹ David answered Rekab and his brother Baanah, the sons
of Rimmon the Beerothite, "As surely as the LORD lives, who
has delivered me out of every trouble, ¹⁰ when someone told
me, 'Saul is dead,' and thought he was bringing good news,
I seized him and put him to death in Ziklag. That was the
reward I gave him for his news! ¹¹ How much more — when
wicked men have killed an innocent man in his own house
and on his own bed — should I not now demand his blood
from your hand and rid the earth of you!"

**Why did it matter that
Mephibosheth was crippled?
(4:4)**
Ancient cultures viewed disability
as a sign of either sin or God's
disapproval. So Mephibosheth
would not be a likely choice for
king.

**Why did the murderers take
Ish-Bosheth's head? (4:7–8)**
They took his head as proof that
they had actually killed him. They
expected to be rewarded for
what they had done.

Why were the murderers' hands and feet cut off? (4:12)
The hands that had killed Ish-Bosheth and the feet that had run with the news were cut off. This was typical punishment for those who committed treason, and it served as a warning to others.

What type of pact did the elders make with David? (5:3)
David and Israel entered into a covenant in which they obligated themselves before the LORD to carry out their responsibilities (see 2 Kings 11:17). David was king of Judah because his tribe gave him that position, and later David became king of Jerusalem by conquering the city. But the northern tribes entered into a treaty of submission and anointed David as their king.

Why did David choose Jerusalem as his capital? (5:9–10)
Jerusalem had a central location that could be reached by both the northern and southern tribes. It was a city that was easy to defend because it was on high ground surrounded by three valleys. It did not have a previous attachment to any of the tribes (even though it was in the territory of Benjamin), and it was close to David's hometown of Bethlehem.

¹²So David gave an order to his men, and they killed them. They cut off their hands and feet and hung the bodies by the pool in Hebron. But they took the head of Ish-Bosheth and buried it in Abner's tomb at Hebron.

DAVID BECOMES KING OVER ISRAEL

5 All the tribes of Israel came to David at Hebron and said, "We are your own flesh and blood. ²In the past, while Saul was king over us, you were the one who led Israel on their military campaigns. And the LORD said to you, 'You will shepherd my people Israel, and you will become their ruler.'"

³When all the elders of Israel had come to King David at Hebron, the king made a covenant with them at Hebron before the LORD, and they anointed David king over Israel. ⁴David was thirty years old when he became king, and he reigned forty years. ⁵In Hebron he reigned over Judah seven years and six months, and in Jerusalem he reigned over all Israel and Judah thirty-three years.

DAVID CONQUERS JERUSALEM

⁶The king and his men marched to Jerusalem to attack the Jebusites, who lived there. The Jebusites said to David, "You will not get in here; even the blind and the lame can ward you off." They thought, "David cannot get in here." ⁷Nevertheless, David captured the fortress of Zion—which is the City of David.

⁸On that day David had said, "Anyone who conquers the Jebusites will have to use the water shaft to reach those 'lame and blind' who are David's enemies.ᵃ" That is why they say, "The 'blind and lame' will not enter the palace."

⁹David then took up residence in the fortress and called it the City of David. He built up the area around it, from the terracesᵇ inward. ¹⁰And he became more and more powerful, because the LORD God Almighty was with him.

¹¹Now Hiram king of Tyre sent envoys to David, along with cedar logs and carpenters and stonemasons, and they built a palace for David. ¹²Then David knew that the LORD had established him as king over Israel and had exalted his kingdom for the sake of his people Israel.

¹³After he left Hebron, David took more concubines and wives in Jerusalem, and more sons and daughters were born to him. ¹⁴These are the names of the children born to him there: Shammua, Shobab, Nathan, Solomon, ¹⁵Ibhar, Elishua, Nepheg, Japhia, ¹⁶Elishama, Eliada and Eliphelet.

DAVID DEFEATS THE PHILISTINES

¹⁷When the Philistines heard that David had been anointed king over Israel, they went up in full force to search for him, but David heard about it and went down to the stronghold. ¹⁸Now the Philistines had come and spread out in the Valley of Rephaim; ¹⁹so David inquired of the LORD, "Shall I go and attack the Philistines? Will you deliver them into my hands?"

ᵃ 8 Or *are hated by David*   ᵇ 9 Or *the Millo*

DAVID'S VICTORIES (5:6)

HAMATH

Cun

Gebal

Lebo Hamath

Berothai

Z O B A H

Sidon

Damascus

Abel Beth Maacah

ARAMEANS

B E T H   R E H O B

Tyre

Dan

MAACAH

Hazor

GESHUR

Akko

GALILEE

Geshur

Helam

Sea of Kinnereth (Sea of Galilee)

TOB

Megiddo

Ramoth Gilead

Tob

Jordan R.

Jabesh Gilead

Shechem

Mahanaim

David makes Jerusalem his political and religious capital

Rabbah of the Ammonites

Joppa

AMMON

Gibeon

Jericho

Baal Perazim

Jerusalem

Gath

Medeba

Gaza

Hebron

Joab battles Ammonites and allies from the north

PHILISTINES

Ziklag

Salt Sea (Dead Sea)

Aroer

Arnon Gorge

Beersheba

Kir Moab

MOAB

Brook of Egypt

Valley of Salt

Mediterranean Sea

AMALEKITES

EDOM

→	Israelites
→	Arameans
→	Edomites
→	Ammonites
	Subdued by David

0   40 km.

0   40 miles

The LORD answered him, "Go, for I will surely deliver the Philistines into your hands."

²⁰ So David went to Baal Perazim, and there he defeated them. He said, "As waters break out, the LORD has broken out against my enemies before me." So that place was called Baal Perazim.ᵃ ²¹ The Philistines abandoned their idols there, and David and his men carried them off.

²² Once more the Philistines came up and spread out in the Valley of Rephaim; ²³ so David inquired of the LORD, and he answered, "Do not go straight up, but circle around behind them and attack them in front of the poplar trees. ²⁴ As soon as you hear the sound of marching in the tops of the poplar trees, move quickly, because that will mean the LORD has gone out in front of you to strike the Philistine army." ²⁵ So David did as the LORD commanded him, and he struck down the Philistines all the way from Gibeonᵇ to Gezer.

THE ARK BROUGHT TO JERUSALEM

6 David again brought together all the able young men of Israel—thirty thousand. ²He and all his men went to Baalahᶜ in Judah to bring up from there the ark of God, which is called by the Name,ᵈ the name of the LORD Almighty, who is enthroned between the cherubim on the ark. ³They set the ark of God on a new cart and brought it from the house of Abinadab, which was on the hill. Uzzah and Ahio, sons of Abinadab, were guiding the new cart ⁴with the ark of God on it,ᵉ and Ahio was walking in front of it. ⁵David and all Israel were celebrating with all their might before the LORD, with castanets,ᶠ harps, lyres, timbrels, sistrums and cymbals.

⁶When they came to the threshing floor of Nakon, Uzzah reached out and took hold of the ark of God, because the oxen stumbled. ⁷The LORD's anger burned against Uzzah because of his irreverent act; therefore God struck him down, and he died there beside the ark of God.

⁸Then David was angry because the LORD's wrath had broken out against Uzzah, and to this day that place is called Perez Uzzah.ᵍ

⁹David was afraid of the LORD that day and said, "How can the ark of the LORD ever come to me?" ¹⁰He was not willing to take the ark of the LORD to be with him in the City of David. Instead, he took it to the house of Obed-Edom the Gittite. ¹¹The ark of the LORD remained in the house of Obed-Edom the Gittite for three months, and the LORD blessed him and his entire household.

¹²Now King David was told, "The LORD has blessed the household of Obed-Edom and everything he has, because of the ark of God." So David went to bring up the ark of God from the house of Obed-Edom to the City of David

Why did the Philistines carry idols with them into battle? (5:21)
During this time period, a lot of nations brought religious items into battle with them. For example, the Israelites had brought the ark into battle with them (see 1 Samuel 4:1–9). People thought that idols and religious items would bring luck and good fortune. The Philistines hoped this would guarantee their victory.

ᵃ 20 *Baal Perazim* means *the lord who breaks out.*   ᵇ 25 Septuagint (see also 1 Chron. 14:16); Hebrew *Geba*   ᶜ 2 That is, Kiriath Jearim (see 1 Chron. 13:6)   ᵈ 2 Hebrew; Septuagint and Vulgate do not have *the Name.*
ᵉ 3,4 Dead Sea Scrolls and some Septuagint manuscripts; Masoretic Text *cart* ⁴*and they brought it with the ark of God from the house of Abinadab, which was on the hill*   ᶠ 5 Masoretic Text; Dead Sea Scrolls and Septuagint (see also 1 Chron. 13:8) *songs*   ᵍ 8 *Perez Uzzah* means *outbreak against Uzzah.*

with rejoicing. [13] When those who were carrying the ark of the LORD had taken six steps, he sacrificed a bull and a fattened calf. [14] Wearing a linen ephod, David was dancing before the LORD with all his might, [15] while he and all Israel were bringing up the ark of the LORD with shouts and the sound of trumpets.

[16] As the ark of the LORD was entering the City of David, Michal daughter of Saul watched from a window. And when she saw King David leaping and dancing before the LORD, she despised him in her heart.

[17] They brought the ark of the LORD and set it in its place inside the tent that David had pitched for it, and David sacrificed burnt offerings and fellowship offerings before the LORD. [18] After he had finished sacrificing the burnt offerings and fellowship offerings, he blessed the people in the name of the LORD Almighty. [19] Then he gave a loaf of bread, a cake of dates and a cake of raisins to each person in the whole crowd of Israelites, both men and women. And all the people went to their homes.

[20] When David returned home to bless his household, Michal daughter of Saul came out to meet him and said, "How the king of Israel has distinguished himself today, going around half-naked in full view of the slave girls of his servants as any vulgar fellow would!"

[21] David said to Michal, "It was before the LORD, who chose me rather than your father or anyone from his house when he appointed me ruler over the LORD's people Israel—I will celebrate before the LORD. [22] I will become even more undignified than this, and I will be humiliated in my own eyes. But by these slave girls you spoke of, I will be held in honor."

[23] And Michal daughter of Saul had no children to the day of her death.

GOD'S PROMISE TO DAVID

7 After the king was settled in his palace and the LORD had given him rest from all his enemies around him, [2] he said to Nathan the prophet, "Here I am, living in a house of cedar, while the ark of God remains in a tent."

[3] Nathan replied to the king, "Whatever you have in mind, go ahead and do it, for the LORD is with you."

[4] But that night the word of the LORD came to Nathan, saying:

[5] "Go and tell my servant David, 'This is what the LORD says: Are you the one to build me a house to dwell in? [6] I have not dwelt in a house from the day I brought the Israelites up out of Egypt to this day. I have been moving from place to place with a tent as my dwelling. [7] Wherever I have moved with all the Israelites, did I ever say to any of their rulers whom I commanded to shepherd my people Israel, "Why have you not built me a house of cedar?"'

[8] "Now then, tell my servant David, 'This is what the LORD Almighty says: I took you from the pasture, from tending the flock, and appointed you ruler over my

Why did David dance? (6:14)
Dance was considered an important part of religious ceremonies in ancient Israel. After the temple was built, dancing became far less common and was not usually part of worship at the temple.

Since David wasn't a Levite, how could he sacrifice burnt offerings? (6:17)
It is most likely that the priests actually sacrificed the offerings on behalf of David rather than David sacrificing them himself.

Why was Michal so angry about David's dancing? (6:20)
It wasn't necessarily the dancing that angered Michal. It was what David wore while he was dancing. Most likely to make it easier to dance, he took off his outer royal robe and only left on the shorter robe. Michal thought it was inappropriate to wear a robe that only reached David's mid-thigh and dance in front of his subjects. David rebuked her saying that it was all in celebration of his love for the Lord.

Why did David think a tent was an inappropriate place to house the ark? (7:2)
Now that David himself lived in a royal palace, a symbol of his kingship, a tent did not seem sufficient for the throne of Israel's divine King. He wanted to build Israel's heavenly King a royal house in the capital city of his kingdom.

What was wrong with Nathan's response? (7:3)
In asking a prophet, David sought God's will. Nathan boldly approved of David's plans in the LORD's name before he had received a revelation from the LORD.

people Israel. [9]I have been with you wherever you have gone, and I have cut off all your enemies from before you. Now I will make your name great, like the names of the greatest men on earth. [10]And I will provide a place for my people Israel and will plant them so that they can have a home of their own and no longer be disturbed. Wicked people will not oppress them anymore, as they did at the beginning [11]and have done ever since the time I appointed leaders[a] over my people Israel. I will also give you rest from all your enemies.

"'The LORD declares to you that the LORD himself will establish a house for you: [12]When your days are over and you rest with your ancestors, I will raise up your offspring to succeed you, your own flesh and blood, and I will establish his kingdom. [13]He is the one who will build a house for my Name, and I will establish the throne of his kingdom forever. [14]I will be his father, and he will be my son. When he does wrong, I will punish him with a rod wielded by men, with floggings inflicted by human hands. [15]But my love will never be taken away from him, as I took it away from Saul, whom I removed from before you. [16]Your house and your kingdom will endure forever before me[b]; your throne will be established forever.'"

[17]Nathan reported to David all the words of this entire revelation.

DAVID'S PRAYER

[18]Then King David went in and sat before the LORD, and he said:

"Who am I, Sovereign LORD, and what is my family, that you have brought me this far? [19]And as if this were not enough in your sight, Sovereign LORD, you have also spoken about the future of the house of your servant — and this decree, Sovereign LORD, is for a mere human![c]

[20]"What more can David say to you? For you know your servant, Sovereign LORD. [21]For the sake of your word and according to your will, you have done this great thing and made it known to your servant.

[22]"How great you are, Sovereign LORD! There is no one like you, and there is no God but you, as we have heard with our own ears. [23]And who is like your people Israel — the one nation on earth that God went out to redeem as a people for himself, and to make a name for himself, and to perform great and awesome wonders by driving out nations and their gods from before your people, whom you redeemed from Egypt?[d] [24]You have established your people Israel as your very own forever, and you, LORD, have become their God.

[25]"And now, LORD God, keep forever the promise you

Why didn't God want David to build a temple? (7:13)
David's mission was to fight the LORD's battles by defeating the enemies of Israel until Israel was secure and the kingdom was established. David's son, Solomon, would have the job of building the temple.

How did David's house and kingdom "endure forever"? (7:16)
All the kings who ruled in Jerusalem after David were his descendants. In the end, Christ represented the fulfillment of this promise because it was from this line of kings that the Messiah came.

---

[a] 11 Traditionally *judges*   [b] 16 Some Hebrew manuscripts and Septuagint; most Hebrew manuscripts *you*   [c] 19 Or *for the human race*
[d] 23 See Septuagint and 1 Chron. 17:21; Hebrew *wonders for your land and before your people, whom you redeemed from Egypt, from the nations and their gods*.

have made concerning your servant and his house. Do as you promised, [26] so that your name will be great forever. Then people will say, 'The LORD Almighty is God over Israel!' And the house of your servant David will be established in your sight.

[27] "LORD Almighty, God of Israel, you have revealed this to your servant, saying, 'I will build a house for you.' So your servant has found courage to pray this prayer to you. [28] Sovereign LORD, you are God! Your covenant is trustworthy, and you have promised these good things to your servant. [29] Now be pleased to bless the house of your servant, that it may continue forever in your sight; for you, Sovereign LORD, have spoken, and with your blessing the house of your servant will be blessed forever."

DAVID'S VICTORIES

8 In the course of time, David defeated the Philistines and subdued them, and he took Metheg Ammah from the control of the Philistines.

[2] David also defeated the Moabites. He made them lie down on the ground and measured them off with a length of cord. Every two lengths of them were put to death, and the third length was allowed to live. So the Moabites became subject to David and brought him tribute.

[3] Moreover, David defeated Hadadezer son of Rehob, king of Zobah, when he went to restore his monument at[a] the Euphrates River. [4] David captured a thousand of his chariots, seven thousand charioteers[b] and twenty thousand foot soldiers. He hamstrung all but a hundred of the chariot horses.

[5] When the Arameans of Damascus came to help Hadadezer king of Zobah, David struck down twenty-two thousand of them. [6] He put garrisons in the Aramean kingdom of Damascus, and the Arameans became subject to him and brought tribute. The LORD gave David victory wherever he went.

[7] David took the gold shields that belonged to the officers of Hadadezer and brought them to Jerusalem. [8] From Tebah[c] and Berothai, towns that belonged to Hadadezer, King David took a great quantity of bronze.

[9] When Tou[d] king of Hamath heard that David had defeated the entire army of Hadadezer, [10] he sent his son Joram[e] to King David to greet him and congratulate him on his victory in battle over Hadadezer, who had been at war with Tou. Joram brought with him articles of silver, of gold and of bronze.

[11] King David dedicated these articles to the LORD, as he had done with the silver and gold from all the nations he had subdued: [12] Edom[f] and Moab, the Ammonites and the Philistines, and Amalek. He also dedicated the plunder taken from Hadadezer son of Rehob, king of Zobah.

Was David's treatment of the Moabites brutal? (8:2) Compared with many barbaric customs of ancient warfare, David was actually lenient when he allowed a third of the defeated army to live. Perhaps David let some live because the Moabites were his blood relatives through Ruth.

Why did it mean to hamstring the horses? (8:4) David crippled most of the horses by cutting the muscle on the back of the horses' legs. David's main concern was to keep the horses from being used by his enemies. David was obeying God's decree that the king of Israel should not trust in the strength of chariots and horses but in the strength of the LORD (see Psalm 20:7).

What were garrisons? (8:6, 14) Garrisons were troops stationed in defeated territories. They served as an occupation force to make sure the people obeyed David's rule.

---

[a] 3 Or *his control along*   [b] 4 Septuagint (see also Dead Sea Scrolls and 1 Chron. 18:4); Masoretic Text *captured seventeen hundred of his charioteers*
[c] 8 See some Septuagint manuscripts (see also 1 Chron. 18:8); Hebrew *Betah*.
[d] 9 Hebrew *Toi*, a variant of *Tou*; also in verse 10   [e] 10 A variant of *Hadoram*   [f] 12 Some Hebrew manuscripts, Septuagint and Syriac (see also 1 Chron. 18:11); most Hebrew manuscripts *Aram*

¹³And David became famous after he returned from striking down eighteen thousand Edomites^a in the Valley of Salt.

¹⁴He put garrisons throughout Edom, and all the Edomites became subject to David. The LORD gave David victory wherever he went.

DAVID'S OFFICIALS

¹⁵David reigned over all Israel, doing what was just and right for all his people. ¹⁶Joab son of Zeruiah was over the army; Jehoshaphat son of Ahilud was recorder; ¹⁷Zadok son of Ahitub and Ahimelek son of Abiathar were priests; Seraiah was secretary; ¹⁸Benaiah son of Jehoiada was over the Kerethites and Pelethites; and David's sons were priests.^b

DAVID AND MEPHIBOSHETH

9 David asked, "Is there anyone still left of the house of Saul to whom I can show kindness for Jonathan's sake?"

²Now there was a servant of Saul's household named Ziba. They summoned him to appear before David, and the king said to him, "Are you Ziba?"

"At your service," he replied.

³The king asked, "Is there no one still alive from the house of Saul to whom I can show God's kindness?"

Ziba answered the king, "There is still a son of Jonathan; he is lame in both feet."

⁴"Where is he?" the king asked.

Ziba answered, "He is at the house of Makir son of Ammiel in Lo Debar."

⁵So King David had him brought from Lo Debar, from the house of Makir son of Ammiel.

⁶When Mephibosheth son of Jonathan, the son of Saul, came to David, he bowed down to pay him honor.

David said, "Mephibosheth!"

"At your service," he replied.

⁷"Don't be afraid," David said to him, "for I will surely show you kindness for the sake of your father Jonathan. I will restore to you all the land that belonged to your grandfather Saul, and you will always eat at my table."

⁸Mephibosheth bowed down and said, "What is your servant, that you should notice a dead dog like me?"

⁹Then the king summoned Ziba, Saul's steward, and said to him, "I have given your master's grandson everything that belonged to Saul and his family. ¹⁰You and your sons and your servants are to farm the land for him and bring in the crops, so that your master's grandson may be provided for. And Mephibosheth, grandson of your master, will always eat at my table." (Now Ziba had fifteen sons and twenty servants.)

¹¹Then Ziba said to the king, "Your servant will do whatever my lord the king commands his servant to do." So Mephibosheth ate at David's^c table like one of the king's sons.

How important were these jobs? (8:16–18)
These men were powerful leaders in David's kingdom. Joab led the army, and Jehoshaphat recorded current events. Zadok and Ahimelek were chief priests. And, as secretary, Seraiah wrote and stored official documents and historical records.

Why was Mephibosheth living in Lo Debar? (9:4)
Saul's grandson probably lived far from David's court, in hiding, because he was afraid that David wanted to kill him so he wouldn't pose a threat to the throne—a common occurrence in the ancient world. It's also possible that Mephibosheth, because he was crippled, chose to live an isolated life.

Did Mephibosheth always eat with David? (9:7)
Reserving a spot for Mephibosheth at meals, though not necessarily at the king's table, was David's act of kindness meant for all to see. This great honor was a gesture that fulfilled the covenant he had made with Jonathan (see 1 Samuel 20:14–16).

What kind of servant was Ziba? (9:9–10)
He was the chief steward who oversaw Saul's estate, which had been inherited by Jonathan's son, Mephibosheth. This was a position of management, and Ziba had 20 servants himself. Ziba had earlier served in the household of King Saul.

---

^a 13 A few Hebrew manuscripts, Septuagint and Syriac (see also 1 Chron. 18:12); most Hebrew manuscripts *Aram* (that is, Arameans)   ^b 18 Or *were chief officials* (see Septuagint and Targum; see also 1 Chron. 18:17)   ^c 11 Septuagint; Hebrew *my*

¹²Mephibosheth had a young son named Mika, and all the members of Ziba's household were servants of Mephibosheth. ¹³And Mephibosheth lived in Jerusalem, because he always ate at the king's table; he was lame in both feet.

DAVID DEFEATS THE AMMONITES

10 In the course of time, the king of the Ammonites died, and his son Hanun succeeded him as king. ²David thought, "I will show kindness to Hanun son of Nahash, just as his father showed kindness to me." So David sent a delegation to express his sympathy to Hanun concerning his father.

When David's men came to the land of the Ammonites, ³the Ammonite commanders said to Hanun their lord, "Do you think David is honoring your father by sending envoys to you to express sympathy? Hasn't David sent them to you only to explore the city and spy it out and overthrow it?" ⁴So Hanun seized David's envoys, shaved off half of each man's beard, cut off their garments at the buttocks, and sent them away.

⁵When David was told about this, he sent messengers to meet the men, for they were greatly humiliated. The king said, "Stay at Jericho till your beards have grown, and then come back."

⁶When the Ammonites realized that they had become obnoxious to David, they hired twenty thousand Aramean foot soldiers from Beth Rehob and Zobah, as well as the king of Maakah with a thousand men, and also twelve thousand men from Tob.

⁷On hearing this, David sent Joab out with the entire army of fighting men. ⁸The Ammonites came out and drew up in battle formation at the entrance of their city gate, while the Arameans of Zobah and Rehob and the men of Tob and Maakah were by themselves in the open country.

⁹Joab saw that there were battle lines in front of him and behind him; so he selected some of the best troops in Israel and deployed them against the Arameans. ¹⁰He put the rest of the men under the command of Abishai his brother and deployed them against the Ammonites. ¹¹Joab said, "If the Arameans are too strong for me, then you are to come to my rescue; but if the Ammonites are too strong for you, then I will come to rescue you. ¹²Be strong, and let us fight bravely for our people and the cities of our God. The Lord will do what is good in his sight."

¹³Then Joab and the troops with him advanced to fight the Arameans, and they fled before him. ¹⁴When the Ammonites realized that the Arameans were fleeing, they fled before Abishai and went inside the city. So Joab returned from fighting the Ammonites and came to Jerusalem.

¹⁵After the Arameans saw that they had been routed by Israel, they regrouped. ¹⁶Hadadezer had Arameans brought from beyond the Euphrates River; they went to Helam, with Shobak the commander of Hadadezer's army leading them.

¹⁷When David was told of this, he gathered all Israel, crossed the Jordan and went to Helam. The Arameans

Why did they shave half of each man's beard and cut off their garments? (10:4–6) Both were extremely embarrassing acts in the ancient world. Beards were usually only shaved as a sign of mourning or self-humiliation. And public nakedness was considered shameful, so this was very degrading.

How did they raise these armies? (10:6) Mercenary armies were quite common in Old Testament times. These hired soldiers would be allowed to plunder, meaning to take goods by force from the enemy if they won the battle.

formed their battle lines to meet David and fought against him. [18] But they fled before Israel, and David killed seven hundred of their charioteers and forty thousand of their foot soldiers.[a] He also struck down Shobak the commander of their army, and he died there. [19] When all the kings who were vassals of Hadadezer saw that they had been routed by Israel, they made peace with the Israelites and became subject to them.

So the Arameans were afraid to help the Ammonites anymore.

DAVID AND BATHSHEBA

11 In the spring, at the time when kings go off to war, David sent Joab out with the king's men and the whole Israelite army. They destroyed the Ammonites and besieged Rabbah. But David remained in Jerusalem.

[2] One evening David got up from his bed and walked around on the roof of the palace. From the roof he saw a woman bathing. The woman was very beautiful, [3] and David sent someone to find out about her. The man said, "She is Bathsheba, the daughter of Eliam and the wife of Uriah the Hittite." [4] Then David sent messengers to get her. She came to him, and he slept with her. (Now she was purifying herself from her monthly uncleanness.) Then she went back home. [5] The woman conceived and sent word to David, saying, "I am pregnant."

[6] So David sent this word to Joab: "Send me Uriah the Hittite." And Joab sent him to David. [7] When Uriah came to him, David asked him how Joab was, how the soldiers were and how the war was going. [8] Then David said to Uriah, "Go down to your house and wash your feet." So Uriah left the palace, and a gift from the king was sent after him. [9] But Uriah slept at the entrance to the palace with all his master's servants and did not go down to his house.

[10] David was told, "Uriah did not go home." So he asked Uriah, "Haven't you just come from a military campaign? Why didn't you go home?"

[11] Uriah said to David, "The ark and Israel and Judah are staying in tents,[b] and my commander Joab and my lord's men are camped in the open country. How could I go to my house to eat and drink and make love to my wife? As surely as you live, I will not do such a thing!"

[12] Then David said to him, "Stay here one more day, and tomorrow I will send you back." So Uriah remained in Jerusalem that day and the next. [13] At David's invitation, he ate and drank with him, and David made him drunk. But in the evening Uriah went out to sleep on his mat among his master's servants; he did not go home.

[14] In the morning David wrote a letter to Joab and sent it with Uriah. [15] In it he wrote, "Put Uriah out in front where the fighting is fiercest. Then withdraw from him so he will be struck down and die."

[16] So while Joab had the city under siege, he put Uriah at a

---

Why was there a season for war? (11:1)
David did not have a year-round army. This meant that the men who served as soldiers also worked as farmers. When grain was harvested in the spring and when crops were planted in the fall, the soldiers who had farms had to work, and therefore could not fight. In order to go into battle with his entire army, David had to wait for the farmers' offseason.

Why did people spend time on the roof? (11:2)
Roofs were flat, and David probably went to the roof to enjoy the cool evening air.

Why was Bathsheba bathing? (11:2–4)
She was taking a ritual bath to ceremonially purify herself after her menstrual period. This shows that she was not already pregnant by her husband when David summoned her.

Why did Uriah stay away from his house? (11:11)
During warfare, Israelite soldiers usually abstained from sex. In order to avoid the temptation to break this vow, Uriah stayed away from his own home.

Why did David want Uriah to go home to Bathsheba? (11:12–13)
David wanted Uriah to have sex with his wife so that he would think he was the father when Bathsheba had a child.

---

[a] *18* Some Septuagint manuscripts (see also 1 Chron. 19:18); Hebrew *horsemen*   [b] *11* Or *staying at Sukkoth*

place where he knew the strongest defenders were. [17]When the men of the city came out and fought against Joab, some of the men in David's army fell; moreover, Uriah the Hittite died.

[18]Joab sent David a full account of the battle. [19]He instructed the messenger: "When you have finished giving the king this account of the battle, [20]the king's anger may flare up, and he may ask you, 'Why did you get so close to the city to fight? Didn't you know they would shoot arrows from the wall? [21]Who killed Abimelek son of Jerub-Besheth[a]? Didn't a woman drop an upper millstone on him from the wall, so that he died in Thebez? Why did you get so close to the wall?' If he asks you this, then say to him, 'Moreover, your servant Uriah the Hittite is dead.'"

[22]The messenger set out, and when he arrived he told David everything Joab had sent him to say. [23]The messenger said to David, "The men overpowered us and came out against us in the open, but we drove them back to the entrance of the city gate. [24]Then the archers shot arrows at your servants from the wall, and some of the king's men died. Moreover, your servant Uriah the Hittite is dead."

[25]David told the messenger, "Say this to Joab: 'Don't let this upset you; the sword devours one as well as another. Press the attack against the city and destroy it.' Say this to encourage Joab."

[26]When Uriah's wife heard that her husband was dead, she mourned for him. [27]After the time of mourning was over, David had her brought to his house, and she became his wife and bore him a son. But the thing David had done displeased the LORD.

NATHAN REBUKES DAVID

12 The LORD sent Nathan to David. When he came to him, he said, "There were two men in a certain town, one rich and the other poor. [2]The rich man had a very large number of sheep and cattle, [3]but the poor man had nothing except one little ewe lamb he had bought. He raised it, and it grew up with him and his children. It shared his food, drank from his cup and even slept in his arms. It was like a daughter to him.

[4]"Now a traveler came to the rich man, but the rich man refrained from taking one of his own sheep or cattle to prepare a meal for the traveler who had come to him. Instead, he took the ewe lamb that belonged to the poor man and prepared it for the one who had come to him."

[5]David burned with anger against the man and said to Nathan, "As surely as the LORD lives, the man who did this must die! [6]He must pay for that lamb four times over, because he did such a thing and had no pity."

[7]Then Nathan said to David, "You are the man! This is what the LORD, the God of Israel, says: 'I anointed you king over Israel, and I delivered you from the hand of Saul. [8]I gave your master's house to you, and your master's wives into your arms. I gave you all Israel and Judah. And if all this had been

Why did Joab have the messenger report on the battle this way? (11:18–21)
Joab knew that David might be angry about the army fighting so close to the city walls, because many soldiers were killed. So Joab had the messenger save the news of Uriah's death until the end.

Why did Nathan rebuke David? (12:8)
Nathan chastised David for being so selfish. David stole a number of Saul's wives, even going as far as murdering to cover his tracks. Even though God had given David everything that had been Saul's, it still wasn't enough to fill David's selfish desires.

---

[a] 21 Also known as *Jerub-Baal* (that is, Gideon)

too little, I would have given you even more. [9]Why did you despise the word of the LORD by doing what is evil in his eyes? You struck down Uriah the Hittite with the sword and took his wife to be your own. You killed him with the sword of the Ammonites. [10]Now, therefore, the sword will never depart from your house, because you despised me and took the wife of Uriah the Hittite to be your own.'

[11]"This is what the LORD says: 'Out of your own household I am going to bring calamity on you. Before your very eyes I will take your wives and give them to one who is close to you, and he will sleep with your wives in broad daylight. [12]You did it in secret, but I will do this thing in broad daylight before all Israel.'"

[13]Then David said to Nathan, "I have sinned against the LORD."

Nathan replied, "The LORD has taken away your sin. You are not going to die. [14]But because by doing this you have shown utter contempt for[a] the LORD, the son born to you will die."

[15]After Nathan had gone home, the LORD struck the child that Uriah's wife had borne to David, and he became ill. [16]David pleaded with God for the child. He fasted and spent the nights lying in sackcloth[b] on the ground. [17]The elders of his household stood beside him to get him up from the ground, but he refused, and he would not eat any food with them.

[18]On the seventh day the child died. David's attendants were afraid to tell him that the child was dead, for they thought, "While the child was still living, he wouldn't listen to us when we spoke to him. How can we now tell him the child is dead? He may do something desperate."

[19]David noticed that his attendants were whispering among themselves, and he realized the child was dead. "Is the child dead?" he asked.

"Yes," they replied, "he is dead."

[20]Then David got up from the ground. After he had washed, put on lotions and changed his clothes, he went into the house of the LORD and worshiped. Then he went

---

What did it mean that the sword would never depart from David's house? (12:10)
David's family suffered as a result of his sin. Three of his sons died violent deaths: Amnon (13:28–29), Absalom (18:14), and Adonijah (1 Kings 2:25).

What type of confession did David make? (12:13)
David recognized his guilt and confessed his sin without making any excuses. His confession was sincere, and Nathan told him that the LORD had accepted his confession and forgiven him.

---

[a] 14 An ancient Hebrew scribal tradition; Masoretic Text *for the enemies of*
[b] 16 Dead Sea Scrolls and Septuagint; Masoretic Text does not have *in sackcloth*.

How should we act when someone points out to us that we have sinned?
2 SAMUEL 12

After David sinned by sleeping with another man's wife, getting her pregnant, and then having her husband killed, the prophet Nathan went to David to confront him with his sin. Nathan also told him that God would punish him. David's response was straightforward. He did not deny that he had done wrong, he did not offer any excuses, and he did not try to blame anyone else. Instead, he simply said, "I have sinned against the LORD" (verse 13).

When the LORD punished him by making his child become sick, David prayed and fasted. Psalm 51 is a prayer of David after he admitted his sin. Verses 1–3 say: "Have mercy on me, O God, according to your unfailing love; according to your great compassion blot out my transgressions. Wash away all my iniquity and cleanse me from my sin. For I know my transgressions, and my sin is always before me."

David admitted his sin without any excuses and asked God to forgive him, even though he knew that God would punish him. That is a model of sincere repentance for us to follow.

to his own house, and at his request they served him food, and he ate.

²¹ His attendants asked him, "Why are you acting this way? While the child was alive, you fasted and wept, but now that the child is dead, you get up and eat!"

²² He answered, "While the child was still alive, I fasted and wept. I thought, 'Who knows? The LORD may be gracious to me and let the child live.' ²³ But now that he is dead, why should I go on fasting? Can I bring him back again? I will go to him, but he will not return to me."

²⁴ Then David comforted his wife Bathsheba, and he went to her and made love to her. She gave birth to a son, and they named him Solomon. The LORD loved him; ²⁵ and because the LORD loved him, he sent word through Nathan the prophet to name him Jedidiah.ᵃ

²⁶ Meanwhile Joab fought against Rabbah of the Ammonites and captured the royal citadel. ²⁷ Joab then sent messengers to David, saying, "I have fought against Rabbah and taken its water supply. ²⁸ Now muster the rest of the troops and besiege the city and capture it. Otherwise I will take the city, and it will be named after me."

²⁹ So David mustered the entire army and went to Rabbah, and attacked and captured it. ³⁰ David took the crown from their king'sᵇ head, and it was placed on his own head. It weighed a talentᶜ of gold, and it was set with precious stones. David took a great quantity of plunder from the city ³¹ and brought out the people who were there, consigning them to labor with saws and with iron picks and axes, and he made them work at brickmaking.ᵈ David did this to all the Ammonite towns. Then he and his entire army returned to Jerusalem.

AMNON AND TAMAR

13 In the course of time, Amnon son of David fell in love with Tamar, the beautiful sister of Absalom son of David.

² Amnon became so obsessed with his sister Tamar that he made himself ill. She was a virgin, and it seemed impossible for him to do anything to her.

³ Now Amnon had an adviser named Jonadab son of Shimeah, David's brother. Jonadab was a very shrewd man. ⁴ He asked Amnon, "Why do you, the king's son, look so haggard morning after morning? Won't you tell me?"

Amnon said to him, "I'm in love with Tamar, my brother Absalom's sister."

⁵ "Go to bed and pretend to be ill," Jonadab said. "When your father comes to see you, say to him, 'I would like my sister Tamar to come and give me something to eat. Let her prepare the food in my sight so I may watch her and then eat it from her hand.'"

⁶ So Amnon lay down and pretended to be ill. When the king came to see him, Amnon said to him, "I would like my

What did David mean when he said, "I will go to him"? (12:23)
David knew that his son would never come back to him, but he took comfort knowing that after David died they would be reunited.

What was the new son's name? (12:25)
Apparently the child had two names, even though one was commonly used. *Jedidiah* means *loved by the LORD. Solomon* is a form of the word *shalom*, which means *peace*.

ᵃ *25 Jediiah* means *loved by the LORD.*   ᵇ *30* Or *from Milkom's* (that is, Molek's)   ᶜ *30* That is, about 75 pounds or about 34 kilograms
ᵈ *31* The meaning of the Hebrew for this clause is uncertain.

sister Tamar to come and make some special bread in my sight, so I may eat from her hand."

⁷David sent word to Tamar at the palace: "Go to the house of your brother Amnon and prepare some food for him." ⁸So Tamar went to the house of her brother Amnon, who was lying down. She took some dough, kneaded it, made the bread in his sight and baked it. ⁹Then she took the pan and served him the bread, but he refused to eat.

"Send everyone out of here," Amnon said. So everyone left him. ¹⁰Then Amnon said to Tamar, "Bring the food here into my bedroom so I may eat from your hand." And Tamar took the bread she had prepared and brought it to her brother Amnon in his bedroom. ¹¹But when she took it to him to eat, he grabbed her and said, "Come to bed with me, my sister."

¹²"No, my brother!" she said to him. "Don't force me! Such a thing should not be done in Israel! Don't do this wicked thing. ¹³What about me? Where could I get rid of my disgrace? And what about you? You would be like one of the wicked fools in Israel. Please speak to the king; he will not keep me from being married to you." ¹⁴But he refused to listen to her, and since he was stronger than she, he raped her.

¹⁵Then Amnon hated her with intense hatred. In fact, he hated her more than he had loved her. Amnon said to her, "Get up and get out!"

¹⁶"No!" she said to him. "Sending me away would be a greater wrong than what you have already done to me."

But he refused to listen to her. ¹⁷He called his personal servant and said, "Get this woman out of my sight and bolt the door after her." ¹⁸So his servant put her out and bolted the door after her. She was wearing an ornate*ᵃ* robe, for this was the kind of garment the virgin daughters of the king wore. ¹⁹Tamar put ashes on her head and tore the ornate robe she was wearing. She put her hands on her head and went away, weeping aloud as she went.

²⁰Her brother Absalom said to her, "Has that Amnon, your brother, been with you? Be quiet for now, my sister; he is your brother. Don't take this thing to heart." And Tamar lived in her brother Absalom's house, a desolate woman.

²¹When King David heard all this, he was furious. ²²And Absalom never said a word to Amnon, either good or bad; he hated Amnon because he had disgraced his sister Tamar.

ABSALOM KILLS AMNON

²³Two years later, when Absalom's sheepshearers were at Baal Hazor near the border of Ephraim, he invited all the king's sons to come there. ²⁴Absalom went to the king and said, "Your servant has had shearers come. Will the king and his attendants please join me?"

²⁵"No, my son," the king replied. "All of us should not go; we would only be a burden to you." Although Absalom urged him, he still refused to go but gave him his blessing.

²⁶Then Absalom said, "If not, please let my brother Amnon come with us."

ᵃ 18 The meaning of the Hebrew for this word is uncertain; also in verse 19.

Why did Amnon's love for Tamar so quickly turn to hate? (13:15)
Amnon's love was only lust rather than genuine love.

Why did Tamar want to stay with Amnon? (13:16)
Because Amnon had raped her, it was his responsibility to marry her. In this time and culture, a woman lost her value if she was raped. By Israelite custom no one else would want to marry her, and she would be left humiliated and disgraced (see Deut. 22:28 – 29).

Why did Tamar put ashes on her head and tear her clothing? (13:19)
These were ancient ways of showing grief. Ashes were a sign of death. So putting ashes on one's head was a sign of mourning as if someone had died. Torn clothes showed that a person had great inner pain. Putting a hand on one's head was another sign of grief.

Why didn't David do anything to punish Amnon? (13:21)
Perhaps David recalled his own sin with Bathsheba and felt that he had no right to confront his son. Another possibility is that he was lenient with Amnon because he was his oldest son.

The king asked him, "Why should he go with you?" ²⁷ But Absalom urged him, so he sent with him Amnon and the rest of the king's sons.

²⁸ Absalom ordered his men, "Listen! When Amnon is in high spirits from drinking wine and I say to you, 'Strike Amnon down,' then kill him. Don't be afraid. Haven't I given you this order? Be strong and brave." ²⁹ So Absalom's men did to Amnon what Absalom had ordered. Then all the king's sons got up, mounted their mules and fled.

³⁰ While they were on their way, the report came to David: "Absalom has struck down all the king's sons; not one of them is left." ³¹ The king stood up, tore his clothes and lay down on the ground; and all his attendants stood by with their clothes torn.

³² But Jonadab son of Shimeah, David's brother, said, "My lord should not think that they killed all the princes; only Amnon is dead. This has been Absalom's express intention ever since the day Amnon raped his sister Tamar. ³³ My lord the king should not be concerned about the report that all the king's sons are dead. Only Amnon is dead."

³⁴ Meanwhile, Absalom had fled.

Now the man standing watch looked up and saw many people on the road west of him, coming down the side of the hill. The watchman went and told the king, "I see men in the direction of Horonaim, on the side of the hill."ᵃ

³⁵ Jonadab said to the king, "See, the king's sons have come; it has happened just as your servant said."

³⁶ As he finished speaking, the king's sons came in, wailing loudly. The king, too, and all his attendants wept very bitterly.

³⁷ Absalom fled and went to Talmai son of Ammihud, the king of Geshur. But King David mourned many days for his son.

³⁸ After Absalom fled and went to Geshur, he stayed there three years. ³⁹ And King David longed to go to Absalom, for he was consoled concerning Amnon's death.

ABSALOM RETURNS TO JERUSALEM

14 Joab son of Zeruiah knew that the king's heart longed for Absalom. ² So Joab sent someone to Tekoa and had a wise woman brought from there. He said to her, "Pretend you are in mourning. Dress in mourning clothes, and don't use any cosmetic lotions. Act like a woman who has spent many days grieving for the dead. ³ Then go to the king and speak these words to him." And Joab put the words in her mouth.

⁴ When the woman from Tekoa wentᵇ to the king, she fell with her face to the ground to pay him honor, and she said, "Help me, Your Majesty!"

⁵ The king asked her, "What is troubling you?"

She said, "I am a widow; my husband is dead. ⁶ I your servant had two sons. They got into a fight with each other in the field, and no one was there to separate them. One struck

Why didn't David go to Absalom? (13:39)
With Absalom in exile, David had lost both of his oldest sons. David may have realized that Absalom deserved to be punished but loved him too much to do it himself.

Why did Joab create such an elaborate plot to convince David to send for Absalom? (14:2–3)
Telling a story that was a type of parable was common in ancient cultures. Both Nathan the prophet and Joab probably thought that this type of storytelling would catch David unprepared, and would be the best way to convince him to change his mind.

ᵃ 34 Septuagint; Hebrew does not have this sentence.   ᵇ 4 Many Hebrew manuscripts, Septuagint, Vulgate and Syriac; most Hebrew manuscripts *spoke*

the other and killed him. [7]Now the whole clan has risen up against your servant; they say, 'Hand over the one who struck his brother down, so that we may put him to death for the life of his brother whom he killed; then we will get rid of the heir as well.' They would put out the only burning coal I have left, leaving my husband neither name nor descendant on the face of the earth."

[8]The king said to the woman, "Go home, and I will issue an order in your behalf."

[9]But the woman from Tekoa said to him, "Let my lord the king pardon me and my family, and let the king and his throne be without guilt."

[10]The king replied, "If anyone says anything to you, bring them to me, and they will not bother you again."

[11]She said, "Then let the king invoke the LORD his God to prevent the avenger of blood from adding to the destruction, so that my son will not be destroyed."

"As surely as the LORD lives," he said, "not one hair of your son's head will fall to the ground."

[12]Then the woman said, "Let your servant speak a word to my lord the king."

"Speak," he replied.

[13]The woman said, "Why then have you devised a thing like this against the people of God? When the king says this, does he not convict himself, for the king has not brought back his banished son? [14]Like water spilled on the ground, which cannot be recovered, so we must die. But that is not what God desires; rather, he devises ways so that a banished person does not remain banished from him.

[15]"And now I have come to say this to my lord the king because the people have made me afraid. Your servant thought, 'I will speak to the king; perhaps he will grant his servant's request. [16]Perhaps the king will agree to deliver his servant from the hand of the man who is trying to cut off both me and my son from God's inheritance.'

[17]"And now your servant says, 'May the word of my lord the king secure my inheritance, for my lord the king is like an angel of God in discerning good and evil. May the LORD your God be with you.'"

[18]Then the king said to the woman, "Don't keep from me the answer to what I am going to ask you."

"Let my lord the king speak," the woman said.

[19]The king asked, "Isn't the hand of Joab with you in all this?"

The woman answered, "As surely as you live, my lord the king, no one can turn to the right or to the left from anything my lord the king says. Yes, it was your servant Joab who instructed me to do this and who put all these words into the mouth of your servant. [20]Your servant Joab did this to change the present situation. My lord has wisdom like that of an angel of God—he knows everything that happens in the land."

[21]The king said to Joab, "Very well, I will do it. Go, bring back the young man Absalom."

[22]Joab fell with his face to the ground to pay him honor, and he blessed the king. Joab said, "Today your servant

Why was Joab so eager to have Absalom return? (14:22) Joab was probably concerned about the future because of the unresolved dispute between David and Absalom. As the oldest living son, Absalom was heir to the throne. Joab knew that Absalom needed to stay on good terms with his father in order to avoid potential disputes and a possible war.

knows that he has found favor in your eyes, my lord the king, because the king has granted his servant's request."

²³Then Joab went to Geshur and brought Absalom back to Jerusalem. ²⁴But the king said, "He must go to his own house; he must not see my face." So Absalom went to his own house and did not see the face of the king.

²⁵In all Israel there was not a man so highly praised for his handsome appearance as Absalom. From the top of his head to the sole of his foot there was no blemish in him. ²⁶Whenever he cut the hair of his head—he used to cut his hair once a year because it became too heavy for him—he would weigh it, and its weight was two hundred shekels*ᵃ* by the royal standard.

²⁷Three sons and a daughter were born to Absalom. His daughter's name was Tamar, and she became a beautiful woman.

²⁸Absalom lived two years in Jerusalem without seeing the king's face. ²⁹Then Absalom sent for Joab in order to send him to the king, but Joab refused to come to him. So he sent a second time, but he refused to come. ³⁰Then he said to his servants, "Look, Joab's field is next to mine, and he has barley there. Go and set it on fire." So Absalom's servants set the field on fire.

³¹Then Joab did go to Absalom's house, and he said to him, "Why have your servants set my field on fire?"

³²Absalom said to Joab, "Look, I sent word to you and said, 'Come here so I can send you to the king to ask, "Why have I come from Geshur? It would be better for me if I were still there!"' Now then, I want to see the king's face, and if I am guilty of anything, let him put me to death."

³³So Joab went to the king and told him this. Then the king summoned Absalom, and he came in and bowed down with his face to the ground before the king. And the king kissed Absalom.

ABSALOM'S CONSPIRACY

15 In the course of time, Absalom provided himself with a chariot and horses and with fifty men to run ahead of him. ²He would get up early and stand by the side of the road leading to the city gate. Whenever anyone came with a complaint to be placed before the king for a decision, Absalom would call out to him, "What town are you from?" He would answer, "Your servant is from one of the tribes of Israel." ³Then Absalom would say to him, "Look, your claims are valid and proper, but there is no representative of the king to hear you." ⁴And Absalom would add, "If only I were appointed judge in the land! Then everyone who has a complaint or case could come to me and I would see that they receive justice."

⁵Also, whenever anyone approached him to bow down before him, Absalom would reach out his hand, take hold of him and kiss him. ⁶Absalom behaved in this way toward all the Israelites who came to the king asking for justice, and so he stole the hearts of the people of Israel.

Why did David refuse to see Absalom face to face? (14:24) Apparently David was still unable to forgive Absalom, even though he had allowed Absalom to return to Jerusalem.

Why was Absalom's long hair mentioned? (14:25–26) Absalom's imposing appearance and the absence of blemishes made him an impressive figure who would be seen as kingly. Hair was seen as a sign of vigor. Kings and other heroic figures were usually portrayed with a great deal of hair, while baldness was a sign of disgrace.

Why did David tolerate Absalom's actions? (15:2–6) Even though Absalom was clearly trying to undermine David's authority, David was lenient once again. He may have underestimated the extent to which Absalom would go in order to gain power.

ᵃ 26 That is, about 5 pounds or about 2.3 kilograms

**Why did Absalom choose
Hebron for his uprising?**
(15:8–12)
Absalom may have thought this
would be a good place to begin
his rebellion because there may
have been some resentment in
Hebron. Hebron was where Absalom had been born and where
David had first been proclaimed
king. Absalom hoped there was
a reason David had moved the
capital to Jerusalem.

David's Flight From Absalom
(15:16 — 18:6)

**Who were the Kerethites,
Pelethites, and Gittites?**
(15:18)
The Kerethites and Pelethites
were mercenary soldiers who
formed David's bodyguard. Because they were not Israelites,
they did not care who was in
charge; their loyalty belonged
to whoever hired them. The Gittites were Philistine soldiers from
Gath who had joined David's
military force.

**Why Did David call his son
King Absalom?** (15:19)
By calling Absalom king, David
was acknowledging that Absalom
had succeeded in replacing him
as king. Although David was
surrendering his kingdom, he
was temporarily surrendering
Jerusalem.

[7] At the end of four[a] years, Absalom said to the king, "Let me go to Hebron and fulfill a vow I made to the LORD. [8] While your servant was living at Geshur in Aram, I made this vow: 'If the LORD takes me back to Jerusalem, I will worship the LORD in Hebron.[b]'"

[9] The king said to him, "Go in peace." So he went to Hebron.

[10] Then Absalom sent secret messengers throughout the tribes of Israel to say, "As soon as you hear the sound of the trumpets, then say, 'Absalom is king in Hebron.'" [11] Two hundred men from Jerusalem had accompanied Absalom. They had been invited as guests and went quite innocently, knowing nothing about the matter. [12] While Absalom was offering sacrifices, he also sent for Ahithophel the Gilonite, David's counselor, to come from Giloh, his hometown. And so the conspiracy gained strength, and Absalom's following kept on increasing.

DAVID FLEES

[13] A messenger came and told David, "The hearts of the people of Israel are with Absalom."

[14] Then David said to all his officials who were with him in Jerusalem, "Come! We must flee, or none of us will escape from Absalom. We must leave immediately, or he will move quickly to overtake us and bring ruin on us and put the city to the sword."

[15] The king's officials answered him, "Your servants are ready to do whatever our lord the king chooses."

[16] The king set out, with his entire household following him; but he left ten concubines to take care of the palace. [17] So the king set out, with all the people following him, and they halted at the edge of the city. [18] All his men marched past him, along with all the Kerethites and Pelethites; and all the six hundred Gittites who had accompanied him from Gath marched before the king.

[19] The king said to Ittai the Gittite, "Why should you come along with us? Go back and stay with King Absalom. You are a foreigner, an exile from your homeland. [20] You came only yesterday. And today shall I make you wander about with us, when I do not know where I am going? Go back, and take your people with you. May the LORD show you kindness and faithfulness."[c]

[21] But Ittai replied to the king, "As surely as the LORD lives, and as my lord the king lives, wherever my lord the king may be, whether it means life or death, there will your servant be."

[22] David said to Ittai, "Go ahead, march on." So Ittai the Gittite marched on with all his men and the families that were with him.

[23] The whole countryside wept aloud as all the people passed by. The king also crossed the Kidron Valley, and all the people moved on toward the wilderness.

[24] Zadok was there, too, and all the Levites who were with

---

[a] 7 Some Septuagint manuscripts, Syriac and Josephus; Hebrew *forty*
[b] 8 Some Septuagint manuscripts; Hebrew does not have *in Hebron.*
[c] 20 Septuagint; Hebrew *May kindness and faithfulness be with you*

him were carrying the ark of the covenant of God. They set down the ark of God, and Abiathar offered sacrifices until all the people had finished leaving the city.

²⁵Then the king said to Zadok, "Take the ark of God back into the city. If I find favor in the LORD's eyes, he will bring me back and let me see it and his dwelling place again. ²⁶But if he says, 'I am not pleased with you,' then I am ready; let him do to me whatever seems good to him."

²⁷The king also said to Zadok the priest, "Do you understand? Go back to the city with my blessing. Take your son Ahimaaz with you, and also Abiathar's son Jonathan. You and Abiathar return with your two sons. ²⁸I will wait at the fords in the wilderness until word comes from you to inform me." ²⁹So Zadok and Abiathar took the ark of God back to Jerusalem and stayed there.

³⁰But David continued up the Mount of Olives, weeping as he went; his head was covered and he was barefoot. All the people with him covered their heads too and were weeping as they went up. ³¹Now David had been told, "Ahithophel is among the conspirators with Absalom." So David prayed, "LORD, turn Ahithophel's counsel into foolishness."

³²When David arrived at the summit, where people used to worship God, Hushai the Arkite was there to meet him, his robe torn and dust on his head. ³³David said to him, "If you go with me, you will be a burden to me. ³⁴But if you return to the city and say to Absalom, 'Your Majesty, I will be your servant; I was your father's servant in the past, but now I will be your servant,' then you can help me by frustrating Ahithophel's advice. ³⁵Won't the priests Zadok and Abiathar be there with you? Tell them anything you hear in the king's palace. ³⁶Their two sons, Ahimaaz son of Zadok and Jonathan son of Abiathar, are there with them. Send them to me with anything you hear."

³⁷So Hushai, David's confidant, arrived at Jerusalem as Absalom was entering the city.

DAVID AND ZIBA

16 When David had gone a short distance beyond the summit, there was Ziba, the steward of Mephibosheth, waiting to meet him. He had a string of donkeys saddled and loaded with two hundred loaves of bread, a hundred cakes of raisins, a hundred cakes of figs and a skin of wine.

²The king asked Ziba, "Why have you brought these?"

Ziba answered, "The donkeys are for the king's household to ride on, the bread and fruit are for the men to eat, and the wine is to refresh those who become exhausted in the wilderness."

³The king then asked, "Where is your master's grandson?"

Ziba said to him, "He is staying in Jerusalem, because he thinks, 'Today the Israelites will restore to me my grandfather's kingdom.'"

⁴Then the king said to Ziba, "All that belonged to Mephibosheth is now yours."

"I humbly bow," Ziba said. "May I find favor in your eyes, my lord the king."

Why was covering the head a sign of sorrow? (15:30) Covering the head was an embarrassing show of a loss of freedom because in Israel, an uncovered head was a sign of a man's integrity and freedom before God.

Why did David break his promise to Mephibosheth? (16:4) David believed Ziba's story that Mephibosheth had become a traitor, so David broke his promise.

SHIMEI CURSES DAVID

⁵As King David approached Bahurim, a man from the same clan as Saul's family came out from there. His name was Shimei son of Gera, and he cursed as he came out. ⁶He pelted David and all the king's officials with stones, though all the troops and the special guard were on David's right and left. ⁷As he cursed, Shimei said, "Get out, get out, you murderer, you scoundrel! ⁸The LORD has repaid you for all the blood you shed in the household of Saul, in whose place you have reigned. The LORD has given the kingdom into the hands of your son Absalom. You have come to ruin because you are a murderer!"

⁹Then Abishai son of Zeruiah said to the king, "Why should this dead dog curse my lord the king? Let me go over and cut off his head."

¹⁰But the king said, "What does this have to do with you, you sons of Zeruiah? If he is cursing because the LORD said to him, 'Curse David,' who can ask, 'Why do you do this?'"

¹¹David then said to Abishai and all his officials, "My son, my own flesh and blood, is trying to kill me. How much more, then, this Benjamite! Leave him alone; let him curse, for the LORD has told him to. ¹²It may be that the LORD will look upon my misery and restore to me his covenant blessing instead of his curse today."

¹³So David and his men continued along the road while Shimei was going along the hillside opposite him, cursing as he went and throwing stones at him and showering him with dirt. ¹⁴The king and all the people with him arrived at their destination exhausted. And there he refreshed himself.

THE ADVICE OF AHITHOPHEL AND HUSHAI

¹⁵Meanwhile, Absalom and all the men of Israel came to Jerusalem, and Ahithophel was with him. ¹⁶Then Hushai the Arkite, David's confidant, went to Absalom and said to him, "Long live the king! Long live the king!"

¹⁷Absalom said to Hushai, "So this is the love you show your friend? If he's your friend, why didn't you go with him?"

¹⁸Hushai said to Absalom, "No, the one chosen by the LORD, by these people, and by all the men of Israel—his I will be, and I will remain with him. ¹⁹Furthermore, whom should I serve? Should I not serve the son? Just as I served your father, so I will serve you."

²⁰Absalom said to Ahithophel, "Give us your advice. What should we do?"

²¹Ahithophel answered, "Sleep with your father's concubines whom he left to take care of the palace. Then all Israel will hear that you have made yourself obnoxious to your father, and the hands of everyone with you will be more resolute." ²²So they pitched a tent for Absalom on the roof, and he slept with his father's concubines in the sight of all Israel.

²³Now in those days the advice Ahithophel gave was like that of one who inquires of God. That was how both David and Absalom regarded all of Ahithophel's advice.

Why did David think that Shimei's curses might have come from God? (16:10–11) David realized that Absalom's rebellion was a consequence of his sin against Uriah and Bathsheba. He saw his hardships as God's means of keeping him humble. So he was open to the possibility that Shimei's curses came from the LORD.

Why might David think that God would reward him for being cursed? (16:12) David trusted God to keep the covenant they made. David's previous encounters with God—when God rewarded him for his persecution by Saul—showed him how faithful God is to his people. More importantly, God had made a covenant with David, and he trusted God to remain faithful to his promises.

Why did Absalom sleep with David's concubines? (16:21–22) This demonstrated that Absalom had assumed the kingship. This was a common practice when a king was replaced by a new dynasty. It also fulfilled Nathan's prophecy to David (see 12:11–12).

17 Ahithophel said to Absalom, "I would[a] choose twelve thousand men and set out tonight in pursuit of David. [2] I would attack him while he is weary and weak. I would strike him with terror, and then all the people with him will flee. I would strike down only the king [3] and bring all the people back to you. The death of the man you seek will mean the return of all; all the people will be unharmed." [4] This plan seemed good to Absalom and to all the elders of Israel.

[5] But Absalom said, "Summon also Hushai the Arkite, so we can hear what he has to say as well." [6] When Hushai came to him, Absalom said, "Ahithophel has given this advice. Should we do what he says? If not, give us your opinion."

[7] Hushai replied to Absalom, "The advice Ahithophel has given is not good this time. [8] You know your father and his men; they are fighters, and as fierce as a wild bear robbed of her cubs. Besides, your father is an experienced fighter; he will not spend the night with the troops. [9] Even now, he is hidden in a cave or some other place. If he should attack your troops first,[b] whoever hears about it will say, 'There has been a slaughter among the troops who follow Absalom.' [10] Then even the bravest soldier, whose heart is like the heart of a lion, will melt with fear, for all Israel knows that your father is a fighter and that those with him are brave.

[11] "So I advise you: Let all Israel, from Dan to Beersheba—as numerous as the sand on the seashore—be gathered to you, with you yourself leading them into battle. [12] Then we will attack him wherever he may be found, and we will fall on him as dew settles on the ground. Neither he nor any of his men will be left alive. [13] If he withdraws into a city, then all Israel will bring ropes to that city, and we will drag it down to the valley until not so much as a pebble is left."

[14] Absalom and all the men of Israel said, "The advice of Hushai the Arkite is better than that of Ahithophel." For the LORD had determined to frustrate the good advice of Ahithophel in order to bring disaster on Absalom.

[15] Hushai told Zadok and Abiathar, the priests, "Ahithophel has advised Absalom and the elders of Israel to do such and such, but I have advised them to do so and so. [16] Now send a message at once and tell David, 'Do not spend the night at the fords in the wilderness; cross over without fail, or the king and all the people with him will be swallowed up.'"

[17] Jonathan and Ahimaaz were staying at En Rogel. A female servant was to go and inform them, and they were to go and tell King David, for they could not risk being seen entering the city. [18] But a young man saw them and told Absalom. So the two of them left at once and went to the house of a man in Bahurim. He had a well in his courtyard, and they climbed down into it. [19] His wife took a covering and spread it out over the opening of the well and scattered grain over it. No one knew anything about it.

[20] When Absalom's men came to the woman at the house, they asked, "Where are Ahimaaz and Jonathan?"

Did most houses have wells? (17:18–19)
Most houses at that time would have a cistern (a pit for collecting rainwater). Wells were rare and usually belonged to a clan or a community.

---

[a] 1 Or *Let me*   [b] 9 Or *When some of the men fall at the first attack*

The woman answered them, "They crossed over the brook."[a] The men searched but found no one, so they returned to Jerusalem.

²¹After they had gone, the two climbed out of the well and went to inform King David. They said to him, "Set out and cross the river at once; Ahithophel has advised such and such against you." ²²So David and all the people with him set out and crossed the Jordan. By daybreak, no one was left who had not crossed the Jordan.

²³When Ahithophel saw that his advice had not been followed, he saddled his donkey and set out for his house in his hometown. He put his house in order and then hanged himself. So he died and was buried in his father's tomb.

ABSALOM'S DEATH

²⁴David went to Mahanaim, and Absalom crossed the Jordan with all the men of Israel. ²⁵Absalom had appointed Amasa over the army in place of Joab. Amasa was the son of Jether,[b] an Ishmaelite[c] who had married Abigail,[d] the daughter of Nahash and sister of Zeruiah the mother of Joab. ²⁶The Israelites and Absalom camped in the land of Gilead.

²⁷When David came to Mahanaim, Shobi son of Nahash from Rabbah of the Ammonites, and Makir son of Ammiel from Lo Debar, and Barzillai the Gileadite from Rogelim ²⁸brought bedding and bowls and articles of pottery. They also brought wheat and barley, flour and roasted grain, beans and lentils,[e] ²⁹honey and curds, sheep, and cheese from cows' milk for David and his people to eat. For they said, "The people have become exhausted and hungry and thirsty in the wilderness."

18 David mustered the men who were with him and appointed over them commanders of thousands and commanders of hundreds. ²David sent out his troops, a third under the command of Joab, a third under Joab's brother Abishai son of Zeruiah, and a third under Ittai the Gittite. The king told the troops, "I myself will surely march out with you."

³But the men said, "You must not go out; if we are forced to flee, they won't care about us. Even if half of us die, they won't care; but you are worth ten thousand of us.[f] It would be better now for you to give us support from the city."

⁴The king answered, "I will do whatever seems best to you."

So the king stood beside the gate while all his men marched out in units of hundreds and of thousands. ⁵The king commanded Joab, Abishai and Ittai, "Be gentle with the young man Absalom for my sake." And all the troops heard the king giving orders concerning Absalom to each of the commanders.

⁶David's army marched out of the city to fight Israel, and the battle took place in the forest of Ephraim. ⁷There Israel's

---

Why did Ahithophel hang himself? (17:23)
He may have concluded that Absalom would be defeated. Ahithophel acted cowardly. Instead of facing the punishment for committing treason, he decided to kill himself. Or he may have been upset because no one followed his advice.

Why did David's men say he was worth 10,000 soldiers? (18:3)
As king, David was the commander of the army. If he had been captured or killed, no one would be left to lead the cause. However, even if Absalom captured or destroyed half of David's army, there would still be a chance for them to win because they still had a king who was a strong leader.

---

[a] 20 Or "They passed by the sheep pen toward the water." [b] 25 Hebrew Ithra, a variant of Jether [c] 25 Some Septuagint manuscripts (see also 1 Chron. 2:17); Hebrew and other Septuagint manuscripts Israelite [d] 25 Hebrew Abigal, a variant of Abigail [e] 28 Most Septuagint manuscripts and Syriac; Hebrew lentils, and roasted grain [f] 3 Two Hebrew manuscripts, some Septuagint manuscripts and Vulgate; most Hebrew manuscripts care; for now there are ten thousand like us

troops were routed by David's men, and the casualties that day were great—twenty thousand men. [8]The battle spread out over the whole countryside, and the forest swallowed up more men that day than the sword.

[9]Now Absalom happened to meet David's men. He was riding his mule, and as the mule went under the thick branches of a large oak, Absalom's hair got caught in the tree. He was left hanging in midair, while the mule he was riding kept on going.

[10]When one of the men saw what had happened, he told Joab, "I just saw Absalom hanging in an oak tree."

[11]Joab said to the man who had told him this, "What! You saw him? Why didn't you strike him to the ground right there? Then I would have had to give you ten shekels[a] of silver and a warrior's belt."

[12]But the man replied, "Even if a thousand shekels[b] were weighed out into my hands, I would not lay a hand on the king's son. In our hearing the king commanded you and Abishai and Ittai, 'Protect the young man Absalom for my sake.'[c] [13]And if I had put my life in jeopardy[d]—and nothing is hidden from the king—you would have kept your distance from me."

[14]Joab said, "I'm not going to wait like this for you." So he took three javelins in his hand and plunged them into Absalom's heart while Absalom was still alive in the oak tree. [15]And ten of Joab's armor-bearers surrounded Absalom, struck him and killed him.

[16]Then Joab sounded the trumpet, and the troops stopped pursuing Israel, for Joab halted them. [17]They took Absalom, threw him into a big pit in the forest and piled up a large heap of rocks over him. Meanwhile, all the Israelites fled to their homes.

[18]During his lifetime Absalom had taken a pillar and erected it in the King's Valley as a monument to himself, for he thought, "I have no son to carry on the memory of my name." He named the pillar after himself, and it is called Absalom's Monument to this day.

DAVID MOURNS

[19]Now Ahimaaz son of Zadok said, "Let me run and take the news to the king that the LORD has vindicated him by delivering him from the hand of his enemies."

[20]"You are not the one to take the news today," Joab told him. "You may take the news another time, but you must not do so today, because the king's son is dead."

[21]Then Joab said to a Cushite, "Go, tell the king what you have seen." The Cushite bowed down before Joab and ran off.

[22]Ahimaaz son of Zadok again said to Joab, "Come what may, please let me run behind the Cushite."

But Joab replied, "My son, why do you want to go? You don't have any news that will bring you a reward."

What was symbolic in the way Absalom died? (18:9) Princes and kings usually rode mules, so when Absalom lost his mule, he was also losing his position as king. The fact that he hung in midair left him powerless to defend himself or lead a nation. Most scholars think that his long hair was caught in the tree. This was someone whose hair had been a source of pride, and now it contributed to his death.

Why did Joab disobey orders and kill Absalom? (18:14) David had given the order not to kill his son because he still loved him. However, Joab realized that if Absalom were allowed to live, his followers would have continued to threaten David's kingdom. His concern was for the welfare of the nation, while David's personal concern was for his son.

Didn't Absalom have children? (18:18) Absalom had three sons, who all died young. His daughter was his only living child, which meant he died without an heir (see 14:27).

---

[a] *11 That is, about 4 ounces or about 115 grams*   [b] *12 That is, about 25 pounds or about 12 kilograms*   [c] *12 A few Hebrew manuscripts, Septuagint, Vulgate and Syriac; most Hebrew manuscripts may be translated Absalom, whoever you may be.*   [d] *13 Or Otherwise, if I had acted treacherously toward him*

[23] He said, "Come what may, I want to run."

So Joab said, "Run!" Then Ahimaaz ran by way of the plain[a] and outran the Cushite.

[24] While David was sitting between the inner and outer gates, the watchman went up to the roof of the gateway by the wall. As he looked out, he saw a man running alone. [25] The watchman called out to the king and reported it.

The king said, "If he is alone, he must have good news." And the runner came closer and closer.

[26] Then the watchman saw another runner, and he called down to the gatekeeper, "Look, another man running alone!"

The king said, "He must be bringing good news, too."

[27] The watchman said, "It seems to me that the first one runs like Ahimaaz son of Zadok."

"He's a good man," the king said. "He comes with good news."

[28] Then Ahimaaz called out to the king, "All is well!" He bowed down before the king with his face to the ground and said, "Praise be to the LORD your God! He has delivered up those who lifted their hands against my lord the king."

[29] The king asked, "Is the young man Absalom safe?"

Ahimaaz answered, "I saw great confusion just as Joab was about to send the king's servant and me, your servant, but I don't know what it was."

[30] The king said, "Stand aside and wait here." So he stepped aside and stood there.

[31] Then the Cushite arrived and said, "My lord the king, hear the good news! The LORD has vindicated you today by delivering you from the hand of all who rose up against you."

[32] The king asked the Cushite, "Is the young man Absalom safe?"

The Cushite replied, "May the enemies of my lord the king and all who rise up to harm you be like that young man."

[33] The king was shaken. He went up to the room over the gateway and wept. As he went, he said: "O my son Absalom! My son, my son Absalom! If only I had died instead of you—O Absalom, my son, my son!"[b]

19 [c] Joab was told, "The king is weeping and mourning for Absalom." [2] And for the whole army the victory that day was turned into mourning, because on that day the troops heard it said, "The king is grieving for his son." [3] The men stole into the city that day as men steal in who are ashamed when they flee from battle. [4] The king covered his face and cried aloud, "O my son Absalom! O Absalom, my son, my son!"

[5] Then Joab went into the house to the king and said, "Today you have humiliated all your men, who have just saved your life and the lives of your sons and daughters and the lives of your wives and concubines. [6] You love those who hate you and hate those who love you. You have made it clear today that the commanders and their men mean nothing to you. I see that you would be pleased if Absalom were alive

---

Why did Ahimaaz not answer David's question? (18:29)
Ahimaaz did not want to be killed for bringing bad news, as had been the fate of some messengers in ancient times. Or he may have wanted to be sure that David learned the good news about the victory before hearing the bad news about the death of Absalom.

Why was David so upset about a son he had not seen for many years? (18:33)
David had a very tender heart toward his sons, and he may have been too indulgent toward them. Even though he was angry about their misbehavior, he knew that his sin with Bathsheba was the cause of much of his pain. His wish that he had died in Absalom's place expressed his guilt and sorrow.

How did Joab persuade David to get past his grief and take a leadership role? (19:5–8)
Joab told David that his grief for Absalom's death was almost an insult to the soldiers who had fought to secure David's kingship. He said that if David did not go out and encourage his soldiers, they would desert and turn against him.

---

[a] *23* That is, the plain of the Jordan   [b] *33* In Hebrew texts this verse (18:33) is numbered 19:1.   [c] In Hebrew texts 19:1-43 is numbered 19:2-44.

today and all of us were dead. [7] Now go out and encourage your men. I swear by the LORD that if you don't go out, not a man will be left with you by nightfall. This will be worse for you than all the calamities that have come on you from your youth till now."

[8] So the king got up and took his seat in the gateway. When the men were told, "The king is sitting in the gateway," they all came before him.

Meanwhile, the Israelites had fled to their homes.

DAVID RETURNS TO JERUSALEM

[9] Throughout the tribes of Israel, all the people were arguing among themselves, saying, "The king delivered us from the hand of our enemies; he is the one who rescued us from the hand of the Philistines. But now he has fled the country to escape from Absalom; [10] and Absalom, whom we anointed to rule over us, has died in battle. So why do you say nothing about bringing the king back?"

[11] King David sent this message to Zadok and Abiathar, the priests: "Ask the elders of Judah, 'Why should you be the last to bring the king back to his palace, since what is being said throughout Israel has reached the king at his quarters? [12] You are my relatives, my own flesh and blood. So why should you be the last to bring back the king?' [13] And say to Amasa, 'Are you not my own flesh and blood? May God deal with me, be it ever so severely, if you are not the commander of my army for life in place of Joab.'"

[14] He won over the hearts of the men of Judah so that they were all of one mind. They sent word to the king, "Return, you and all your men." [15] Then the king returned and went as far as the Jordan.

Now the men of Judah had come to Gilgal to go out and meet the king and bring him across the Jordan. [16] Shimei son of Gera, the Benjamite from Bahurim, hurried down with the men of Judah to meet King David. [17] With him were a thousand Benjamites, along with Ziba, the steward of Saul's household, and his fifteen sons and twenty servants. They rushed to the Jordan, where the king was. [18] They crossed at the ford to take the king's household over and to do whatever he wished.

When Shimei son of Gera crossed the Jordan, he fell prostrate before the king [19] and said to him, "May my lord not hold me guilty. Do not remember how your servant did wrong on the day my lord the king left Jerusalem. May the king put it out of his mind. [20] For I your servant know that I have sinned, but today I have come here as the first from the tribes of Joseph to come down and meet my lord the king."

[21] Then Abishai son of Zeruiah said, "Shouldn't Shimei be put to death for this? He cursed the LORD's anointed."

[22] David replied, "What does this have to do with you, you sons of Zeruiah? What right do you have to interfere? Should anyone be put to death in Israel today? Don't I know that today I am king over Israel?" [23] So the king said to Shimei, "You shall not die." And the king promised him on oath.

[24] Mephibosheth, Saul's grandson, also went down to meet

Why did David demote Joab and make Amasa, a rebel leader, commander of the army? (19:13)
David may have suspected that Joab was the one who disobeyed orders and killed Absalom. This would have grieved David, and it would have been seen as a sign of insubordination. Joab chose to disobey a direct order from the king. David may also have thought that appointing Amasa would help gain the support of the Judeans who had followed Absalom.

Why did David refer to some of his supporters as his adversaries? (19:22)
David realized that this was a time for healing rather than for revenge. If David had allowed his soldiers to seek revenge, the chances for peace would be lost.

Why was Mephibosheth in such shabby condition? (19:24)

This was one way he could show his loyalty to David. Because of his disability, Mephibosheth had been unable to leave Jerusalem. And his grief over the recent rebellion against David's kingship was shown by his disheveled appearance.

How did David decide whose story was true? (19:26–29)

Mephibosheth seemed to have been loyal to David consistently, but David may have had doubts about both men. So he decided that the best way to resolve the question would be to split the property.

Why did Barzillai not accept David's offer to provide for him? (19:34–37)

Barzillai was an old man who would not live long enough to benefit from David's generosity, but he wanted to help his family. So he asked David to provide for his son Kimham instead.

the king. He had not taken care of his feet or trimmed his mustache or washed his clothes from the day the king left until the day he returned safely. 25 When he came from Jerusalem to meet the king, the king asked him, "Why didn't you go with me, Mephibosheth?"

26 He said, "My lord the king, since I your servant am lame, I said, 'I will have my donkey saddled and will ride on it, so I can go with the king.' But Ziba my servant betrayed me. 27 And he has slandered your servant to my lord the king. My lord the king is like an angel of God; so do whatever you wish. 28 All my grandfather's descendants deserved nothing but death from my lord the king, but you gave your servant a place among those who eat at your table. So what right do I have to make any more appeals to the king?"

29 The king said to him, "Why say more? I order you and Ziba to divide the land."

30 Mephibosheth said to the king, "Let him take everything, now that my lord the king has returned home safely."

31 Barzillai the Gileadite also came down from Rogelim to cross the Jordan with the king and to send him on his way from there. 32 Now Barzillai was very old, eighty years of age. He had provided for the king during his stay in Mahanaim, for he was a very wealthy man. 33 The king said to Barzillai, "Cross over with me and stay with me in Jerusalem, and I will provide for you."

34 But Barzillai answered the king, "How many more years will I live, that I should go up to Jerusalem with the king? 35 I am now eighty years old. Can I tell the difference between what is enjoyable and what is not? Can your servant taste what he eats and drinks? Can I still hear the voices of male and female singers? Why should your servant be an added burden to my lord the king? 36 Your servant will cross over the Jordan with the king for a short distance, but why should the king reward me in this way? 37 Let your servant return, that I may die in my own town near the tomb of my father and mother. But here is your servant Kimham. Let him cross over with my lord the king. Do for him whatever you wish."

38 The king said, "Kimham shall cross over with me, and I will do for him whatever you wish. And anything you desire from me I will do for you."

39 So all the people crossed the Jordan, and then the king crossed over. The king kissed Barzillai and bid him farewell, and Barzillai returned to his home.

40 When the king crossed over to Gilgal, Kimham crossed with him. All the troops of Judah and half the troops of Israel had taken the king over.

41 Soon all the men of Israel were coming to the king and saying to him, "Why did our brothers, the men of Judah, steal the king away and bring him and his household across the Jordan, together with all his men?"

42 All the men of Judah answered the men of Israel, "We did this because the king is closely related to us. Why are you angry about it? Have we eaten any of the king's provisions? Have we taken anything for ourselves?"

43 Then the men of Israel answered the men of Judah, "We

have ten shares in the king; so we have a greater claim on David than you have. Why then do you treat us with contempt? Weren't we the first to speak of bringing back our king?"

But the men of Judah pressed their claims even more forcefully than the men of Israel.

SHEBA REBELS AGAINST DAVID

20 Now a troublemaker named Sheba son of Bikri, a Benjamite, happened to be there. He sounded the trumpet and shouted,

"We have no share in David,
    no part in Jesse's son!
Every man to his tent, Israel!"

[2] So all the men of Israel deserted David to follow Sheba son of Bikri. But the men of Judah stayed by their king all the way from the Jordan to Jerusalem.

[3] When David returned to his palace in Jerusalem, he took the ten concubines he had left to take care of the palace and put them in a house under guard. He provided for them but had no sexual relations with them. They were kept in confinement till the day of their death, living as widows.

[4] Then the king said to Amasa, "Summon the men of Judah to come to me within three days, and be here yourself." [5] But when Amasa went to summon Judah, he took longer than the time the king had set for him.

[6] David said to Abishai, "Now Sheba son of Bikri will do us more harm than Absalom did. Take your master's men and pursue him, or he will find fortified cities and escape from us."[a] [7] So Joab's men and the Kerethites and Pelethites and all the mighty warriors went out under the command of Abishai. They marched out from Jerusalem to pursue Sheba son of Bikri.

[8] While they were at the great rock in Gibeon, Amasa came to meet them. Joab was wearing his military tunic, and strapped over it at his waist was a belt with a dagger in its sheath. As he stepped forward, it dropped out of its sheath.

[9] Joab said to Amasa, "How are you, my brother?" Then Joab took Amasa by the beard with his right hand to kiss him. [10] Amasa was not on his guard against the dagger in Joab's hand, and Joab plunged it into his belly, and his intestines spilled out on the ground. Without being stabbed again, Amasa died. Then Joab and his brother Abishai pursued Sheba son of Bikri.

[11] One of Joab's men stood beside Amasa and said, "Whoever favors Joab, and whoever is for David, let him follow Joab!" [12] Amasa lay wallowing in his blood in the middle of the road, and the man saw that all the troops came to a halt there. When he realized that everyone who came up to Amasa stopped, he dragged him from the road into a field and threw a garment over him. [13] After Amasa had been removed from the road, everyone went on with Joab to pursue Sheba son of Bikri.

[a] 6 Or *and do us serious injury*

Why were David's concubines kept in confinement? (20:3)
They had been publicly dishonored by Absalom's sexual involvement with them. They were forced to live as widows until they died because they were no longer suitable for David and it was culturally unacceptable for anyone else to marry them.

Why did Joab kill Amasa? (20:10)
After Joab killed David's son Absalom, he was replaced by Amasa as the head of the army. Joab probably killed his rival in order to regain his position. It is possible that Joab suspected Amasa of secretly working against David (see verses 4 – 5).

How did Joab take Amasa by surprise? (20:10)
Being cousins, Amasa may not have suspected that Joab would harm him. Also, Joab extended his right hand in friendship. Typically a person would watch a person's right hand to see if he had a weapon. Instead, Joab tricked Amasa by holding the dagger in his left hand.

¹⁴Sheba passed through all the tribes of Israel to Abel Beth Maakah and through the entire region of the Bikrites,^{*a*} who gathered together and followed him. ¹⁵All the troops with Joab came and besieged Sheba in Abel Beth Maakah. They built a siege ramp up to the city, and it stood against the outer fortifications. While they were battering the wall to bring it down, ¹⁶a wise woman called from the city, "Listen! Listen! Tell Joab to come here so I can speak to him." ¹⁷He went toward her, and she asked, "Are you Joab?"

"I am," he answered.

She said, "Listen to what your servant has to say."

"I'm listening," he said.

¹⁸She continued, "Long ago they used to say, 'Get your answer at Abel,' and that settled it. ¹⁹We are the peaceful and faithful in Israel. You are trying to destroy a city that is a mother in Israel. Why do you want to swallow up the LORD's inheritance?"

²⁰"Far be it from me!" Joab replied, "Far be it from me to swallow up or destroy! ²¹That is not the case. A man named Sheba son of Bikri, from the hill country of Ephraim, has lifted up his hand against the king, against David. Hand over this one man, and I'll withdraw from the city."

The woman said to Joab, "His head will be thrown to you from the wall."

²²Then the woman went to all the people with her wise advice, and they cut off the head of Sheba son of Bikri and threw it to Joab. So he sounded the trumpet, and his men dispersed from the city, each returning to his home. And Joab went back to the king in Jerusalem.

DAVID'S OFFICIALS

²³Joab was over Israel's entire army; Benaiah son of Jehoiada was over the Kerethites and Pelethites; ²⁴Adoniram^{*b*} was in charge of forced labor; Jehoshaphat son of Ahilud was recorder; ²⁵Sheva was secretary; Zadok and Abiathar were priests; ²⁶and Ira the Jairite^{*c*} was David's priest.

THE GIBEONITES AVENGED

21 During the reign of David, there was a famine for three successive years; so David sought the face of the LORD. The LORD said, "It is on account of Saul and his blood-stained house; it is because he put the Gibeonites to death."

²The king summoned the Gibeonites and spoke to them. (Now the Gibeonites were not a part of Israel but were survivors of the Amorites; the Israelites had sworn to spare them, but Saul in his zeal for Israel and Judah had tried to annihilate them.) ³David asked the Gibeonites, "What shall I do for you? How shall I make atonement so that you will bless the LORD's inheritance?"

⁴The Gibeonites answered him, "We have no right to demand silver or gold from Saul or his family, nor do we have the right to put anyone in Israel to death."

"What do you want me to do for you?" David asked.

Who was this wise woman? (20:16–22)
This unnamed woman was responsible for saving her city by giving up the one person, Sheba son of Bicri, who Joab wanted to capture. She was one of many women were looked to as wise counselors in Israel.

What kind of priest was Jairite? (20:26)
Even though he was called a priest, Jairite was not a religious priest or spiritual leader. The term was also used to describe civil leaders such as the king's ministers or advisors.

^{*a*} 14 See Septuagint and Vulgate; Hebrew *Berites*.   ^{*b*} 24 Some Septuagint manuscripts (see also 1 Kings 4:6 and 5:14); Hebrew *Adoram*
^{*c*} 26 Hebrew; some Septuagint manuscripts and Syriac (see also 23:38) *Ithrite*

⁵They answered the king, "As for the man who destroyed us and plotted against us so that we have been decimated and have no place anywhere in Israel, ⁶let seven of his male descendants be given to us to be killed and their bodies exposed before the Lord at Gibeah of Saul—the Lord's chosen one."

So the king said, "I will give them to you."

⁷The king spared Mephibosheth son of Jonathan, the son of Saul, because of the oath before the Lord between David and Jonathan son of Saul. ⁸But the king took Armoni and Mephibosheth, the two sons of Aiah's daughter Rizpah, whom she had borne to Saul, together with the five sons of Saul's daughter Merab,[a] whom she had borne to Adriel son of Barzillai the Meholathite. ⁹He handed them over to the Gibeonites, who killed them and exposed their bodies on a hill before the Lord. All seven of them fell together; they were put to death during the first days of the harvest, just as the barley harvest was beginning.

¹⁰Rizpah daughter of Aiah took sackcloth and spread it out for herself on a rock. From the beginning of the harvest till the rain poured down from the heavens on the bodies, she did not let the birds touch them by day or the wild animals by night. ¹¹When David was told what Aiah's daughter Rizpah, Saul's concubine, had done, ¹²he went and took the bones of Saul and his son Jonathan from the citizens of Jabesh Gilead. (They had stolen their bodies from the public square at Beth Shan, where the Philistines had hung them after they struck Saul down on Gilboa.) ¹³David brought the bones of Saul and his son Jonathan from there, and the bones of those who had been killed and exposed were gathered up.

¹⁴They buried the bones of Saul and his son Jonathan in the tomb of Saul's father Kish, at Zela in Benjamin, and did everything the king commanded. After that, God answered prayer in behalf of the land.

WARS AGAINST THE PHILISTINES

¹⁵Once again there was a battle between the Philistines and Israel. David went down with his men to fight against the Philistines, and he became exhausted. ¹⁶And Ishbi-Benob, one of the descendants of Rapha, whose bronze spearhead weighed three hundred shekels[b] and who was armed with a new sword, said he would kill David. ¹⁷But Abishai son of Zeruiah came to David's rescue; he struck the Philistine down and killed him. Then David's men swore to him, saying, "Never again will you go out with us to battle, so that the lamp of Israel will not be extinguished."

¹⁸In the course of time, there was another battle with the Philistines, at Gob. At that time Sibbekai the Hushathite killed Saph, one of the descendants of Rapha.

¹⁹In another battle with the Philistines at Gob, Elhanan son of Jair[c] the Bethlehemite killed the brother of[d] Goliath the Gittite, who had a spear with a shaft like a weaver's rod.

Who were Rizpah and Merab? (21:8)
Rizpah was one of Saul's concubines (see 3:7). Merab was the daughter of Saul who had been promised to David for killing Goliath (see 1 Samuel 18:19).

How long did Rizpah keep scavengers away from the bodies? (21:10)
If Rizpah watched the bodies from first harvest, sometime in the middle of April, to the rainy season in October and November, it's possible she could have been there for six or seven months. It's also likely that it rained before then making her vigil shorter.

Had David lost his ability as a warrior? (21:15-17)
David was an older man, and he knew when to let others assist him in battle, especially because Ishbi-Benob must have been a huge warrior based on the size and type of weapon he used.

Wasn't Goliath already dead? (21:19)
This was probably a brother of the Goliath who David had killed years earlier.

---

a 8 Two Hebrew manuscripts, some Septuagint manuscripts and Syriac (see also 1 Samuel 18:19); most Hebrew and Septuagint manuscripts *Michal*   b 16 That is, about 7 1/2 pounds or about 3.5 kilograms   c 19 See 1 Chron. 20:5; Hebrew *Jaare-Oregim*.   d 19 See 1 Chron. 20:5; Hebrew does not have *the brother of*.

²⁰In still another battle, which took place at Gath, there was a huge man with six fingers on each hand and six toes on each foot—twenty-four in all. He also was descended from Rapha. ²¹When he taunted Israel, Jonathan son of Shimeah, David's brother, killed him.

²²These four were descendants of Rapha in Gath, and they fell at the hands of David and his men.

DAVID'S SONG OF PRAISE

22 David sang to the LORD the words of this song when the LORD delivered him from the hand of all his enemies and from the hand of Saul. ²He said:

"The LORD is my rock, my fortress and my deliverer;
³   my God is my rock, in whom I take refuge,
     my shield*ᵃ* and the horn*ᵇ* of my salvation.
He is my stronghold, my refuge and my savior—
     from violent people you save me.

⁴"I called to the LORD, who is worthy of praise,
     and have been saved from my enemies.
⁵The waves of death swirled about me;
     the torrents of destruction overwhelmed me.
⁶The cords of the grave coiled around me;
     the snares of death confronted me.

⁷"In my distress I called to the LORD;
     I called out to my God.
From his temple he heard my voice;
     my cry came to his ears.
⁸The earth trembled and quaked,
     the foundations of the heavens*ᶜ* shook;
     they trembled because he was angry.
⁹Smoke rose from his nostrils;
     consuming fire came from his mouth,
     burning coals blazed out of it.
¹⁰He parted the heavens and came down;
     dark clouds were under his feet.
¹¹He mounted the cherubim and flew;
     he soared*ᵈ* on the wings of the wind.
¹²He made darkness his canopy around him—
     the dark*ᵉ* rain clouds of the sky.
¹³Out of the brightness of his presence
     bolts of lightning blazed forth.
¹⁴The LORD thundered from heaven;
     the voice of the Most High resounded.
¹⁵He shot his arrows and scattered the enemy,
     with great bolts of lightning he routed them.
¹⁶The valleys of the sea were exposed
     and the foundations of the earth laid bare
at the rebuke of the LORD,
     at the blast of breath from his nostrils.

From where were these images drawn? (22:14–15)
The image of deities shooting bolts of lightning is similar to images from many of the neighboring regions' stories about gods. David was using a common literary-religious image to describe the power of Israel's God.

ᵃ 3 Or *sovereign*   *ᵇ 3 Horn* here symbolizes strength.   *ᶜ 8* Hebrew; Vulgate and Syriac (see also Psalm 18:7) *mountains*   *ᵈ 11* Many Hebrew manuscripts (see also Psalm 18:10); most Hebrew manuscripts *appeared*
ᵉ 12 Septuagint (see also Psalm 18:11); Hebrew *massed*

17 "He reached down from on high and took hold of me;
   he drew me out of deep waters.
18 He rescued me from my powerful enemy,
   from my foes, who were too strong for me.
19 They confronted me in the day of my disaster,
   but the LORD was my support.
20 He brought me out into a spacious place;
   he rescued me because he delighted in me.

21 "The LORD has dealt with me according to my
      righteousness;
   according to the cleanness of my hands he has
      rewarded me.
22 For I have kept the ways of the LORD;
   I am not guilty of turning from my God.
23 All his laws are before me;
   I have not turned away from his decrees.
24 I have been blameless before him
   and have kept myself from sin.
25 The LORD has rewarded me according to my
      righteousness,
   according to my cleanness*a* in his sight.

26 "To the faithful you show yourself faithful,
   to the blameless you show yourself blameless,
27 to the pure you show yourself pure,
   but to the devious you show yourself shrewd.
28 You save the humble,
   but your eyes are on the haughty to bring them low.
29 You, LORD, are my lamp;
   the LORD turns my darkness into light.
30 With your help I can advance against a troop*b*;
   with my God I can scale a wall.

31 "As for God, his way is perfect:
   The LORD's word is flawless;
   he shields all who take refuge in him.
32 For who is God besides the LORD?
   And who is the Rock except our God?
33 It is God who arms me with strength*c*
   and keeps my way secure.
34 He makes my feet like the feet of a deer;
   he causes me to stand on the heights.
35 He trains my hands for battle;
   my arms can bend a bow of bronze.
36 You make your saving help my shield;
   your help has made*d* me great.
37 You provide a broad path for my feet,
   so that my ankles do not give way.

38 "I pursued my enemies and crushed them;
   I did not turn back till they were destroyed.

How could David say he was "blameless"? (22:24)
This song was written long before David's sin with Bathsheba and murder of Uriah. But even if it had been written afterwards, David could claim to be blameless because God had forgiven him.

---

a 25 Hebrew; Septuagint and Vulgate (see also Psalm 18:24) *to the cleanness of my hands*   *b* 30 Or *can run through a barricade*   *c* 33 Dead Sea Scrolls, some Septuagint manuscripts, Vulgate and Syriac (see also Psalm 18:32); Masoretic Text *who is my strong refuge*   *d* 36 Dead Sea Scrolls; Masoretic Text *shield; / you stoop down to make*

³⁹ I crushed them completely, and they could not rise;
    they fell beneath my feet.
⁴⁰ You armed me with strength for battle;
    you humbled my adversaries before me.
⁴¹ You made my enemies turn their backs in flight,
    and I destroyed my foes.
⁴² They cried for help, but there was no one to save
      them—
    to the Lord, but he did not answer.
⁴³ I beat them as fine as the dust of the earth;
    I pounded and trampled them like mud in the
      streets.

⁴⁴ "You have delivered me from the attacks of the
      peoples;
    you have preserved me as the head of nations.
    People I did not know now serve me,
⁴⁵   foreigners cower before me;
    as soon as they hear of me, they obey me.
⁴⁶ They all lose heart;
    they come trembling*ᵃ* from their strongholds.

⁴⁷ "The Lord lives! Praise be to my Rock!
    Exalted be my God, the Rock, my Savior!
⁴⁸ He is the God who avenges me,
    who puts the nations under me,
⁴⁹   who sets me free from my enemies.
    You exalted me above my foes;
    from a violent man you rescued me.
⁵⁰ Therefore I will praise you, Lord, among the nations;
    I will sing the praises of your name.

⁵¹ "He gives his king great victories;
    he shows unfailing kindness to his anointed,
    to David and his descendants forever."

DAVID'S LAST WORDS

23 These are the last words of David:

    "The inspired utterance of David son of Jesse,
    the utterance of the man exalted by the
      Most High,
the man anointed by the God of Jacob,
    the hero of Israel's songs:

² "The Spirit of the Lord spoke through me;
    his word was on my tongue.
³ The God of Israel spoke,
    the Rock of Israel said to me:
    'When one rules over people in righteousness,
    when he rules in the fear of God,
⁴ he is like the light of morning at sunrise
    on a cloudless morning,
like the brightness after rain
    that brings grass from the earth.'

Why does David call God "my Rock"? (22:47)
David had often taken refuge among the rocks in the desert, but he recognized that true security was found only in the Lord.

ᵃ 46 Some Septuagint manuscripts and Vulgate (see also Psalm 18:45); Masoretic Text *they arm themselves*

[5] "If my house were not right with God,
　　surely he would not have made with me an
　　　　everlasting covenant,
　　arranged and secured in every part;
　　surely he would not bring to fruition
　　　　my salvation
　　and grant me my every desire.
[6] But evil men are all to be cast aside like thorns,
　　which are not gathered with the hand.
[7] Whoever touches thorns
　　uses a tool of iron or the shaft of a spear;
　　they are burned up where they lie."

DAVID'S MIGHTY WARRIORS

[8] These are the names of David's mighty warriors:
Josheb-Basshebeth,[a] a Tahkemonite,[b] was chief of the
Three; he raised his spear against eight hundred men, whom
he killed[c] in one encounter.

[9] Next to him was Eleazar son of Dodai the Ahohite. As
one of the three mighty warriors, he was with David when
they taunted the Philistines gathered at Pas Dammim[d] for
battle. Then the Israelites retreated, [10] but Eleazar stood his
ground and struck down the Philistines till his hand grew
tired and froze to the sword. The LORD brought about a
great victory that day. The troops returned to Eleazar, but
only to strip the dead.

[11] Next to him was Shammah son of Agee the Hararite.
When the Philistines banded together at a place where there
was a field full of lentils, Israel's troops fled from them. [12] But
Shammah took his stand in the middle of the field. He defended it and struck the Philistines down, and the LORD
brought about a great victory.

[13] During harvest time, three of the thirty chief warriors
came down to David at the cave of Adullam, while a band
of Philistines was encamped in the Valley of Rephaim. [14] At
that time David was in the stronghold, and the Philistine
garrison was at Bethlehem. [15] David longed for water and
said, "Oh, that someone would get me a drink of water from
the well near the gate of Bethlehem!" [16] So the three mighty
warriors broke through the Philistine lines, drew water from
the well near the gate of Bethlehem and carried it back to
David. But he refused to drink it; instead, he poured it out
before the LORD. [17] "Far be it from me, LORD, to do this!" he
said. "Is it not the blood of men who went at the risk of their
lives?" And David would not drink it.

Such were the exploits of the three mighty warriors.

[18] Abishai the brother of Joab son of Zeruiah was chief of
the Three.[e] He raised his spear against three hundred men,
whom he killed, and so he became as famous as the Three.

Why do these stories seem out of place? (23:8–39)
These stories of the mighty men are like a flashback in time. This section tells about a much earlier period of David's life when he was a fugitive from Saul or was battling the Philistines.

Why wouldn't David drink the water? (23:16–17)
David poured the water out before the LORD. The three men had risked their lives for the water, and David thought that their loyalty and commitment should be devoted to the LORD rather than to his thirst.

---

[a] 8 Hebrew; some Septuagint manuscripts suggest Ish-Bosheth, that is, Esh-Baal (see also 1 Chron. 11:11 Jashobeam).　　[b] 8 Probably a variant of Hakmonite (see 1 Chron. 11:11)　　[c] 8 Some Septuagint manuscripts (see also 1 Chron. 11:11); Hebrew and other Septuagint manuscripts Three; it was Adino the Eznite who killed eight hundred men　　[d] 9 See 1 Chron. 11:13; Hebrew gathered there.　　[e] 18 Most Hebrew manuscripts (see also 1 Chron. 11:20); two Hebrew manuscripts and Syriac Thirty

¹⁹Was he not held in greater honor than the Three? He became their commander, even though he was not included among them.

²⁰Benaiah son of Jehoiada, a valiant fighter from Kabzeel, performed great exploits. He struck down Moab's two mightiest warriors. He also went down into a pit on a snowy day and killed a lion. ²¹And he struck down a huge Egyptian. Although the Egyptian had a spear in his hand, Benaiah went against him with a club. He snatched the spear from the Egyptian's hand and killed him with his own spear. ²²Such were the exploits of Benaiah son of Jehoiada; he too was as famous as the three mighty warriors. ²³He was held in greater honor than any of the Thirty, but he was not included among the Three. And David put him in charge of his bodyguard.

²⁴Among the Thirty were:
Asahel the brother of Joab,
Elhanan son of Dodo from Bethlehem,
²⁵Shammah the Harodite,
Elika the Harodite,
²⁶Helez the Paltite,
Ira son of Ikkesh from Tekoa,
²⁷Abiezer from Anathoth,
Sibbekai*a* the Hushathite,
²⁸Zalmon the Ahohite,
Maharai the Netophathite,
²⁹Heled*b* son of Baanah the Netophathite,
Ithai son of Ribai from Gibeah in Benjamin,
³⁰Benaiah the Pirathonite,
Hiddai*c* from the ravines of Gaash,
³¹Abi-Albon the Arbathite,
Azmaveth the Barhumite,
³²Eliahba the Shaalbonite,
the sons of Jashen,
Jonathan ³³son of*d* Shammah the Hararite,
Ahiam son of Sharar*e* the Hararite,
³⁴Eliphelet son of Ahasbai the Maakathite,
Eliam son of Ahithophel the Gilonite,
³⁵Hezro the Carmelite,
Paarai the Arbite,
³⁶Igal son of Nathan from Zobah,
the son of Hagri,*f*
³⁷Zelek the Ammonite,
Naharai the Beerothite, the armor-bearer of Joab son of Zeruiah,
³⁸Ira the Ithrite,
Gareb the Ithrite
³⁹and Uriah the Hittite.
There were thirty-seven in all.

---

a 27 Some Septuagint manuscripts (see also 21:18; 1 Chron. 11:29); Hebrew *Mebunnai*   *b 29* Some Hebrew manuscripts and Vulgate (see also 1 Chron. 11:30); most Hebrew; some Septuagint manuscripts *Heleb*   *c 30* Hebrew; some Septuagint manuscripts (see also 1 Chron. 11:32) *Hurai*   *d 33* Some Septuagint manuscripts (see also 1 Chron. 11:34); Hebrew does not have *son of.*
e 33 Hebrew; some Septuagint manuscripts (see also 1 Chron. 11:35) *Sakar*
f 36 Some Septuagint manuscripts (see also 1 Chron. 11:38); Hebrew *Haggadi*

DAVID ENROLLS THE FIGHTING MEN

24 Again the anger of the Lord burned against Israel, and he incited David against them, saying, "Go and take a census of Israel and Judah."

² So the king said to Joab and the army commanders*ᵃ* with him, "Go throughout the tribes of Israel from Dan to Beersheba and enroll the fighting men, so that I may know how many there are."

³ But Joab replied to the king, "May the Lord your God multiply the troops a hundred times over, and may the eyes of my lord the king see it. But why does my lord the king want to do such a thing?"

⁴ The king's word, however, overruled Joab and the army commanders; so they left the presence of the king to enroll the fighting men of Israel.

⁵ After crossing the Jordan, they camped near Aroer, south of the town in the gorge, and then went through Gad and on to Jazer. ⁶ They went to Gilead and the region of Tahtim Hodshi, and on to Dan Jaan and around toward Sidon. ⁷ Then they went toward the fortress of Tyre and all the towns of the Hivites and Canaanites. Finally, they went on to Beersheba in the Negev of Judah.

⁸ After they had gone through the entire land, they came back to Jerusalem at the end of nine months and twenty days.

⁹ Joab reported the number of the fighting men to the king: In Israel there were eight hundred thousand able-bodied men who could handle a sword, and in Judah five hundred thousand.

¹⁰ David was conscience-stricken after he had counted the fighting men, and he said to the Lord, "I have sinned greatly in what I have done. Now, Lord, I beg you, take away the guilt of your servant. I have done a very foolish thing."

¹¹ Before David got up the next morning, the word of the Lord had come to Gad the prophet, David's seer: ¹² "Go and tell David, 'This is what the Lord says: I am giving you three options. Choose one of them for me to carry out against you.'"

¹³ So Gad went to David and said to him, "Shall there come on you three*ᵇ* years of famine in your land? Or three months of fleeing from your enemies while they pursue you? Or three days of plague in your land? Now then, think it over and decide how I should answer the one who sent me."

¹⁴ David said to Gad, "I am in deep distress. Let us fall into the hands of the Lord, for his mercy is great; but do not let me fall into human hands."

¹⁵ So the Lord sent a plague on Israel from that morning until the end of the time designated, and seventy thousand of the people from Dan to Beersheba died. ¹⁶ When the angel stretched out his hand to destroy Jerusalem, the Lord relented concerning the disaster and said to the angel who was afflicting the people, "Enough! Withdraw your hand." The angel of the Lord was then at the threshing floor of Araunah the Jebusite.

What was wrong with taking a census? (24:3, 10)
By counting his soldiers, David started depending on his military strength. This took away from his dependence on God.

Why did David choose plague as a punishment? (24:13–15)
David chose the least severe of the punishments. The plague would last the shortest amount of time, only three days. David begged God for mercy and asked that he be punished rather than the people of Israel.

ᵃ 2 Septuagint (see also verse 4 and 1 Chron. 21:2); Hebrew *Joab the army commander* *ᵇ 13* Septuagint (see also 1 Chron. 21:12); Hebrew *seven*

[17]When David saw the angel who was striking down the people, he said to the Lord, "I have sinned; I, the shepherd,[a] have done wrong. These are but sheep. What have they done? Let your hand fall on me and my family."

DAVID BUILDS AN ALTAR

[18]On that day Gad went to David and said to him, "Go up and build an altar to the Lord on the threshing floor of Araunah the Jebusite." [19]So David went up, as the Lord had commanded through Gad. [20]When Araunah looked and saw the king and his officials coming toward him, he went out and bowed down before the king with his face to the ground.

[21]Araunah said, "Why has my lord the king come to his servant?"

"To buy your threshing floor," David answered, "so I can build an altar to the Lord, that the plague on the people may be stopped."

[22]Araunah said to David, "Let my lord the king take whatever he wishes and offer it up. Here are oxen for the burnt offering, and here are threshing sledges and ox yokes for the wood. [23]Your Majesty, Araunah[b] gives all this to the king." Araunah also said to him, "May the Lord your God accept you."

[24]But the king replied to Araunah, "No, I insist on paying you for it. I will not sacrifice to the Lord my God burnt offerings that cost me nothing."

So David bought the threshing floor and the oxen and paid fifty shekels[c] of silver for them. [25]David built an altar to the Lord there and sacrificed burnt offerings and fellowship offerings. Then the Lord answered his prayer in behalf of the land, and the plague on Israel was stopped.

Why is this site special? (24:18–24)
God eventually chose the threshing floor of Araunah, where David sacrificed for his sin, as the location for the temple David's son, Solomon, would build.

Why did David buy the oxen instead of using his own? (24:24)
David was in a hurry to offer the sacrifice and did not want to wait for his own animals to be brought there.

---

[a] 17 Dead Sea Scrolls and Septuagint; Masoretic Text does not have *the shepherd*.   [b] 23 Some Hebrew manuscripts and Septuagint; most Hebrew manuscripts *King Araunah*   [c] 24 That is, about 1 1/4 pounds or about 575 grams

1 Kings

INTRODUCTION

Who wrote this book?	The author of this book is unknown.
Why was this book written?	The book of 1 Kings shows how the kings of Israel and Judah obeyed or disobeyed God.
What happens in this book?	Solomon rules for 40 years. When he dies his kingdom is divided. The northern ten tribes are called Israel. The southern two tribes are called Judah.
What do we learn about God in this book?	God sends prophets to turn disobedient people back to him.
Who are the key people in this book?	The most important people in this book are Solomon, Elijah, and evil King Ahab of Israel.

What are some of the stories in this book?		
	Solomon asks for wisdom	1 Kings 3
	Solomon builds the temple	1 Kings 6
	Solomon dedicates the temple	1 Kings 8
	A queen visits Solomon	1 Kings 10
	A prophet warns Jeroboam	1 Kings 13
	Elijah is fed by ravens	1 Kings 17
	Elijah on Mount Carmel	1 Kings 18
	Elijah runs away	1 Kings 19
	Ahab steals a vineyard	1 Kings 21
	Ahab dies in battle	1 Kings 22

When did these things happen?

1400 BC 1300 1200 1100 1000 900 800 700 600 500 400

DAVID'S REIGN (1010 – 970 BC)

SOLOMON'S REIGN (970 – 930 BC)

BUILDING OF THE TEMPLE (966 – 959 BC)

DIVISION OF THE KINGDOM (930 BC)

ELIJAH'S MINISTRY IN ISRAEL (C. 875 – 848 BC)

AHAB'S REIGN (874 – 853 BC)

ELISHA'S MINISTRY IN ISRAEL (C. 848 – 797 BC)

BOOK OF 1 KINGS WRITTEN (C. 560 – 550 BC)

Why did the servants look for a virgin to keep David warm? (1:2)
In his old age, David suffered from the chills. There weren't electric blankets back then, so the hope was that with a young woman lying next to him, she would provide body heat to keep him warm.

Why didn't David try to stop Adonijah? (1:5–6)
As a father, David seemed to be consistently too lenient with his sons.

Did an official prophet serve the king? (1:9–10)
Yes. There were two types of prophets in Old Testament times: independent prophets (like Elijah) and official prophets who served in the king's court (like Nathan).

Why would Bathsheba need to be concerned for her life and the life of Solomon? (1:12)
It was common for new kings to kill all others who might claim the throne. If Adonijah had become king, he might have killed Solomon and his mother.

How did Nathan help David decide what to do? (1:22)
Nathan knew how David would react in different situations. He advised Bathsheba about how to approach David, and he came into the king's room to back up her request that Solomon be declared the next king.

ADONIJAH SETS HIMSELF UP AS KING

1 When King David was very old, he could not keep warm even when they put covers over him. ²So his attendants said to him, "Let us look for a young virgin to serve the king and take care of him. She can lie beside him so that our lord the king may keep warm."

³Then they searched throughout Israel for a beautiful young woman and found Abishag, a Shunammite, and brought her to the king. ⁴The woman was very beautiful; she took care of the king and waited on him, but the king had no sexual relations with her.

⁵Now Adonijah, whose mother was Haggith, put himself forward and said, "I will be king." So he got chariots and horses^a ready, with fifty men to run ahead of him. ⁶(His father had never rebuked him by asking, "Why do you behave as you do?" He was also very handsome and was born next after Absalom.)

⁷Adonijah conferred with Joab son of Zeruiah and with Abiathar the priest, and they gave him their support. ⁸But Zadok the priest, Benaiah son of Jehoiada, Nathan the prophet, Shimei and Rei and David's special guard did not join Adonijah.

⁹Adonijah then sacrificed sheep, cattle and fattened calves at the Stone of Zoheleth near En Rogel. He invited all his brothers, the king's sons, and all the royal officials of Judah, ¹⁰but he did not invite Nathan the prophet or Benaiah or the special guard or his brother Solomon.

¹¹Then Nathan asked Bathsheba, Solomon's mother, "Have you not heard that Adonijah, the son of Haggith, has become king, and our lord David knows nothing about it? ¹²Now then, let me advise you how you can save your own life and the life of your son Solomon. ¹³Go in to King David and say to him, 'My lord the king, did you not swear to me your servant: "Surely Solomon your son shall be king after me, and he will sit on my throne"? Why then has Adonijah become king?' ¹⁴While you are still there talking to the king, I will come in and add my word to what you have said."

¹⁵So Bathsheba went to see the aged king in his room, where Abishag the Shunammite was attending him. ¹⁶Bathsheba bowed down, prostrating herself before the king.

"What is it you want?" the king asked.

¹⁷She said to him, "My lord, you yourself swore to me your servant by the LORD your God: 'Solomon your son shall be king after me, and he will sit on my throne.' ¹⁸But now Adonijah has become king, and you, my lord the king, do not know about it. ¹⁹He has sacrificed great numbers of cattle, fattened calves, and sheep, and has invited all the king's sons, Abiathar the priest and Joab the commander of the army, but he has not invited Solomon your servant. ²⁰My lord the king, the eyes of all Israel are on you, to learn from you who will sit on the throne of my lord the king after him. ²¹Otherwise, as soon as my lord the king is laid to rest with his ancestors, I and my son Solomon will be treated as criminals."

²²While she was still speaking with the king, Nathan

^a 5 Or *charioteers*

the prophet arrived. ²³ And the king was told, "Nathan the prophet is here." So he went before the king and bowed with his face to the ground.

²⁴ Nathan said, "Have you, my lord the king, declared that Adonijah shall be king after you, and that he will sit on your throne? ²⁵ Today he has gone down and sacrificed great numbers of cattle, fattened calves, and sheep. He has invited all the king's sons, the commanders of the army and Abiathar the priest. Right now they are eating and drinking with him and saying, 'Long live King Adonijah!' ²⁶ But me your servant, and Zadok the priest, and Benaiah son of Jehoiada, and your servant Solomon he did not invite. ²⁷ Is this something my lord the king has done without letting his servants know who should sit on the throne of my lord the king after him?"

DAVID MAKES SOLOMON KING

²⁸ Then King David said, "Call in Bathsheba." So she came into the king's presence and stood before him.

²⁹ The king then took an oath: "As surely as the LORD lives, who has delivered me out of every trouble, ³⁰ I will surely carry out this very day what I swore to you by the LORD, the God of Israel: Solomon your son shall be king after me, and he will sit on my throne in my place."

³¹ Then Bathsheba bowed down with her face to the ground, prostrating herself before the king, and said, "May my lord King David live forever!"

³² King David said, "Call in Zadok the priest, Nathan the prophet and Benaiah son of Jehoiada." When they came before the king, ³³ he said to them: "Take your lord's servants with you and have Solomon my son mount my own mule and take him down to Gihon. ³⁴ There have Zadok the priest and Nathan the prophet anoint him king over Israel. Blow the trumpet and shout, 'Long live King Solomon!' ³⁵ Then you are to go up with him, and he is to come and sit on my throne and reign in my place. I have appointed him ruler over Israel and Judah."

³⁶ Benaiah son of Jehoiada answered the king, "Amen! May the LORD, the God of my lord the king, so declare it. ³⁷ As the LORD was with my lord the king, so may he be with Solomon to make his throne even greater than the throne of my lord King David!"

³⁸ So Zadok the priest, Nathan the prophet, Benaiah son of Jehoiada, the Kerethites and the Pelethites went down and had Solomon mount King David's mule, and they escorted him to Gihon. ³⁹ Zadok the priest took the horn of oil from the sacred tent and anointed Solomon. Then they sounded the trumpet and all the people shouted, "Long live King Solomon!" ⁴⁰ And all the people went up after him, playing pipes and rejoicing greatly, so that the ground shook with the sound.

⁴¹ Adonijah and all the guests who were with him heard it as they were finishing their feast. On hearing the sound of the trumpet, Joab asked, "What's the meaning of all the noise in the city?"

⁴² Even as he was speaking, Jonathan son of Abiathar the priest arrived. Adonijah said, "Come in. A worthy man like you must be bringing good news."

Why hadn't David already announced that Solomon would succeed him? (1:30) Perhaps David thought that Solomon was still too young to rule the kingdom. Plus, Samuel had anointed both Saul and David. With him gone, David may have been unsure how to proceed.

Why did Solomon ride David's mule? (1:33) During this time, a mule was a royal animal reserved for kings. David wanted others to know that he wanted Solomon to be the next king. Having Solomon ride his mule showed David's desire for passing on the kingship.

Why did a priest anoint Solomon king? (1:39) Kings who were chosen by God but had not inherited the throne were anointed by prophets. But kings who had inherited the kingship from a father were anointed by priests. The priests worked within the established order, while the prophets introduced new initiatives from God.

⁴³"Not at all!" Jonathan answered. "Our lord King David has made Solomon king. ⁴⁴The king has sent with him Zadok the priest, Nathan the prophet, Benaiah son of Jehoiada, the Kerethites and the Pelethites, and they have put him on the king's mule, ⁴⁵and Zadok the priest and Nathan the prophet have anointed him king at Gihon. From there they have gone up cheering, and the city resounds with it. That's the noise you hear. ⁴⁶Moreover, Solomon has taken his seat on the royal throne. ⁴⁷Also, the royal officials have come to congratulate our lord King David, saying, 'May your God make Solomon's name more famous than yours and his throne greater than yours!' And the king bowed in worship on his bed ⁴⁸and said, 'Praise be to the LORD, the God of Israel, who has allowed my eyes to see a successor on my throne today.'"

⁴⁹At this, all Adonijah's guests rose in alarm and dispersed. ⁵⁰But Adonijah, in fear of Solomon, went and took hold of the horns of the altar. ⁵¹Then Solomon was told, "Adonijah is afraid of King Solomon and is clinging to the horns of the altar. He says, 'Let King Solomon swear to me today that he will not put his servant to death with the sword.'"

⁵²Solomon replied, "If he shows himself to be worthy, not a hair of his head will fall to the ground; but if evil is found in him, he will die." ⁵³Then King Solomon sent men, and they brought him down from the altar. And Adonijah came and bowed down to King Solomon, and Solomon said, "Go to your home."

DAVID'S CHARGE TO SOLOMON

2 When the time drew near for David to die, he gave a charge to Solomon his son.

²"I am about to go the way of all the earth," he said. "So be strong, act like a man, ³and observe what the LORD your God requires: Walk in obedience to him, and keep his decrees and commands, his laws and regulations, as written in the Law of Moses. Do this so that you may prosper in all you do and wherever you go ⁴and that the LORD may keep his promise to me: 'If your descendants watch how they live, and if they walk faithfully before me with all their heart and soul, you will never fail to have a successor on the throne of Israel.'

⁵"Now you yourself know what Joab son of Zeruiah did to me—what he did to the two commanders of Israel's armies, Abner son of Ner and Amasa son of Jether. He killed them, shedding their blood in peacetime as if in battle, and with that blood he stained the belt around his waist and the sandals on his feet. ⁶Deal with him according to your wisdom, but do not let his gray head go down to the grave in peace.

⁷"But show kindness to the sons of Barzillai of Gilead and let them be among those who eat at your table. They stood by me when I fled from your brother Absalom.

⁸"And remember, you have with you Shimei son of Gera, the Benjamite from Bahurim, who called down bitter curses on me the day I went to Mahanaim. When he came down to meet me at the Jordan, I swore to him by the LORD: 'I will not put you to death by the sword.' ⁹But now, do not

Why did Adonijah hold onto the horns of the altar? (1:50) Holding the horns of the altar provided protection for an accused person while his case was being reviewed. A person could be completely safe there, but if he was found guilty, he would be removed from the altar to be punished.

What was God's promise to David? (2:4) God had promised David that he would have a dynasty that would rule forever (see 2 Samuel 7:11–16). This promise was without conditions, but God's blessings would be given to David's descendants who followed the Law of Moses. Jesus was the final fulfillment of this promise.

Why did David tell Solomon to deal with Joab? (2:5–6) Joab had been David's commander for many years, and he was the son of David's sister Zeruiah. David wasn't able to bring himself to kill Joab, but because he had shed blood during peacetime, he deserved punishment.

consider him innocent. You are a man of wisdom; you will know what to do to him. Bring his gray head down to the grave in blood."

¹⁰Then David rested with his ancestors and was buried in the City of David. ¹¹He had reigned forty years over Israel—seven years in Hebron and thirty-three in Jerusalem. ¹²So Solomon sat on the throne of his father David, and his rule was firmly established.

SOLOMON'S THRONE ESTABLISHED

¹³Now Adonijah, the son of Haggith, went to Bathsheba, Solomon's mother. Bathsheba asked him, "Do you come peacefully?"

He answered, "Yes, peacefully." ¹⁴Then he added, "I have something to say to you."

"You may say it," she replied.

¹⁵"As you know," he said, "the kingdom was mine. All Israel looked to me as their king. But things changed, and the kingdom has gone to my brother; for it has come to him from the LORD. ¹⁶Now I have one request to make of you. Do not refuse me."

"You may make it," she said.

¹⁷So he continued, "Please ask King Solomon—he will not refuse you—to give me Abishag the Shunammite as my wife."

¹⁸"Very well," Bathsheba replied, "I will speak to the king for you."

¹⁹When Bathsheba went to King Solomon to speak to him for Adonijah, the king stood up to meet her, bowed down to her and sat down on his throne. He had a throne brought for the king's mother, and she sat down at his right hand.

²⁰"I have one small request to make of you," she said. "Do not refuse me."

The king replied, "Make it, my mother; I will not refuse you."

²¹So she said, "Let Abishag the Shunammite be given in marriage to your brother Adonijah."

²²King Solomon answered his mother, "Why do you request Abishag the Shunammite for Adonijah? You might as well request the kingdom for him—after all, he is my older brother—yes, for him and for Abiathar the priest and Joab son of Zeruiah!"

²³Then King Solomon swore by the LORD: "May God deal with me, be it ever so severely, if Adonijah does not pay with his life for this request! ²⁴And now, as surely as the LORD lives—he who has established me securely on the throne of my father David and has founded a dynasty for me as he promised—Adonijah shall be put to death today!" ²⁵So King Solomon gave orders to Benaiah son of Jehoiada, and he struck down Adonijah and he died.

²⁶To Abiathar the priest the king said, "Go back to your fields in Anathoth. You deserve to die, but I will not put you to death now, because you carried the ark of the Sovereign LORD before my father David and shared all my father's hardships." ²⁷So Solomon removed Abiathar from the

Why did Adonijah ask to marry Abishag? (2:17)
Even though Abishag had remained a virgin while she cared for David, her position was the same as a concubine. If Adonijah married her, it would strengthen his claim to the throne.

Why did Solomon refuse Adonijah's request? (2:22–23)
Solomon saw Adonijah's request as an attempt to gain power. The royal harem belonged to the king. Solomon perceived that Adonijah was making a treasonous claim to the throne, and so he ordered his death.

Why did God wait so long to remove the house of Eli from the priesthood? (2:27)
God had told Eli that his family would no longer serve as priests because of his sons' evil behavior (1 Samuel 2:30 – 35). God may have allowed another of Eli's descendants to serve in order to show how contempt for God can be passed from parents to their children. Abiathar's disrespect for Solomon was similar to the disrespect Eli's sons had for God's law.

Why didn't the horns of the altar save Joab? (2:28 – 34)
The right of asylum was only extended to those who had accidentally caused someone's death. Joab had been part of Adonijah's conspiracy and had murdered two innocent men — Abner and Amasa — so Solomon was justified in having him removed from the altar and executed.

Why did Solomon allow Shimei to live in the city? (2:36 – 46)
Even though Shimei deserved to die, David had shown mercy to him. Solomon continued this kindness. But when Shimei disobeyed Solomon's order, Solomon ordered Benaiah to kill him.

priesthood of the LORD, fulfilling the word the LORD had spoken at Shiloh about the house of Eli.

²⁸When the news reached Joab, who had conspired with Adonijah though not with Absalom, he fled to the tent of the LORD and took hold of the horns of the altar. ²⁹King Solomon was told that Joab had fled to the tent of the LORD and was beside the altar. Then Solomon ordered Benaiah son of Jehoiada, "Go, strike him down!"

³⁰So Benaiah entered the tent of the LORD and said to Joab, "The king says, 'Come out!'"

But he answered, "No, I will die here."

Benaiah reported to the king, "This is how Joab answered me."

³¹Then the king commanded Benaiah, "Do as he says. Strike him down and bury him, and so clear me and my whole family of the guilt of the innocent blood that Joab shed. ³²The LORD will repay him for the blood he shed, because without my father David knowing it he attacked two men and killed them with the sword. Both of them — Abner son of Ner, commander of Israel's army, and Amasa son of Jether, commander of Judah's army — were better men and more upright than he. ³³May the guilt of their blood rest on the head of Joab and his descendants forever. But on David and his descendants, his house and his throne, may there be the LORD's peace forever."

³⁴So Benaiah son of Jehoiada went up and struck down Joab and killed him, and he was buried at his home out in the country. ³⁵The king put Benaiah son of Jehoiada over the army in Joab's position and replaced Abiathar with Zadok the priest.

³⁶Then the king sent for Shimei and said to him, "Build yourself a house in Jerusalem and live there, but do not go anywhere else. ³⁷The day you leave and cross the Kidron Valley, you can be sure you will die; your blood will be on your own head."

³⁸Shimei answered the king, "What you say is good. Your servant will do as my lord the king has said." And Shimei stayed in Jerusalem for a long time.

³⁹But three years later, two of Shimei's slaves ran off to Achish son of Maakah, king of Gath, and Shimei was told, "Your slaves are in Gath." ⁴⁰At this, he saddled his donkey and went to Achish at Gath in search of his slaves. So Shimei went away and brought the slaves back from Gath.

⁴¹When Solomon was told that Shimei had gone from Jerusalem to Gath and had returned, ⁴²the king summoned Shimei and said to him, "Did I not make you swear by the LORD and warn you, 'On the day you leave to go anywhere else, you can be sure you will die'? At that time you said to me, 'What you say is good. I will obey.' ⁴³Why then did you not keep your oath to the LORD and obey the command I gave you?"

⁴⁴The king also said to Shimei, "You know in your heart all the wrong you did to my father David. Now the LORD will repay you for your wrongdoing. ⁴⁵But King Solomon will be blessed, and David's throne will remain secure before the LORD forever."

⁴⁶Then the king gave the order to Benaiah son of Jehoiada, and he went out and struck Shimei down and he died.

The kingdom was now established in Solomon's hands.

SOLOMON ASKS FOR WISDOM

3 Solomon made an alliance with Pharaoh king of Egypt and married his daughter. He brought her to the City of David until he finished building his palace and the temple of the LORD, and the wall around Jerusalem. ²The people, however, were still sacrificing at the high places, because a temple had not yet been built for the Name of the LORD. ³Solomon showed his love for the LORD by walking according to the instructions given him by his father David, except that he offered sacrifices and burned incense on the high places.

⁴The king went to Gibeon to offer sacrifices, for that was the most important high place, and Solomon offered a thousand burnt offerings on that altar. ⁵At Gibeon the LORD appeared to Solomon during the night in a dream, and God said, "Ask for whatever you want me to give you."

⁶Solomon answered, "You have shown great kindness to your servant, my father David, because he was faithful to you and righteous and upright in heart. You have continued this great kindness to him and have given him a son to sit on his throne this very day.

⁷"Now, LORD my God, you have made your servant king in place of my father David. But I am only a little child and do not know how to carry out my duties. ⁸Your servant is here among the people you have chosen, a great people, too numerous to count or number. ⁹So give your servant a discerning heart to govern your people and to distinguish between right and wrong. For who is able to govern this great people of yours?"

¹⁰The Lord was pleased that Solomon had asked for this. ¹¹So God said to him, "Since you have asked for this and not for long life or wealth for yourself, nor have asked for the death of your enemies but for discernment in administering justice, ¹²I will do what you have asked. I will give you a wise and discerning heart, so that there will never have been anyone like you, nor will there ever be. ¹³Moreover, I will give you what you have not asked for—both wealth and honor—so that in your lifetime you will have no equal among kings. ¹⁴And if you walk in obedience to me and keep my decrees and commands as David your father did, I will give you a long life." ¹⁵Then Solomon awoke—and he realized it had been a dream.

He returned to Jerusalem, stood before the ark of the Lord's covenant and sacrificed burnt offerings and fellowship offerings. Then he gave a feast for all his court.

A WISE RULING

¹⁶Now two prostitutes came to the king and stood before him. ¹⁷One of them said, "Pardon me, my lord. This woman and I live in the same house, and I had a baby while she was there with me. ¹⁸The third day after my child was born, this woman also had a baby. We were alone; there was no one in the house but the two of us.

Why did Solomon marry a foreigner? (3:1)
Sometimes a king married another king's daughter in order to guarantee peace between the two nations. Solomon probably married most of his 700 wives for political reasons rather than love. This caused his downfall. The Law of Moses warned that a king was not to "take many wives, or his heart will be led astray" (Deuteronomy 17:17).

Why was worshiping at the high places wrong? (3:3)
The high places were open-air shrines that were frequently located on hills. These spots had originally been places where the Canaanites had worshiped their gods. The Israelites often sinned by mixing worship of God with worship of pagan gods.

Why was Gibeon the most important high place? (3:4)
The tent of meeting and the bronze altar were at Gibeon, making it the most significant place to worship.

Why did Solomon call himself a little child? (3:7–9)
Solomon admitted that he did not have much experience or knowledge, and he asked God to give him wisdom. He was only about 20 when he began to reign, a relatively young age for a king.

How did Solomon know which woman was the mother? (3:16–27)
Solomon was able to make the right decision because God had blessed him with wisdom (v. 12). It was clear to him that the woman who was willing to give up the child was the mother.

¹⁹ "During the night this woman's son died because she lay on him. ²⁰ So she got up in the middle of the night and took my son from my side while I your servant was asleep. She put him by her breast and put her dead son by my breast. ²¹ The next morning, I got up to nurse my son—and he was dead! But when I looked at him closely in the morning light, I saw that it wasn't the son I had borne."

²² The other woman said, "No! The living one is my son; the dead one is yours."

But the first one insisted, "No! The dead one is yours; the living one is mine." And so they argued before the king.

²³ The king said, "This one says, 'My son is alive and your son is dead,' while that one says, 'No! Your son is dead and mine is alive.'"

²⁴ Then the king said, "Bring me a sword." So they brought a sword for the king. ²⁵ He then gave an order: "Cut the living child in two and give half to one and half to the other."

²⁶ The woman whose son was alive was deeply moved out of love for her son and said to the king, "Please, my lord, give her the living baby! Don't kill him!"

But the other said, "Neither I nor you shall have him. Cut him in two!"

²⁷ Then the king gave his ruling: "Give the living baby to the first woman. Do not kill him; she is his mother."

²⁸ When all Israel heard the verdict the king had given, they held the king in awe, because they saw that he had wisdom from God to administer justice.

SOLOMON'S OFFICIALS AND GOVERNORS

4 So King Solomon ruled over all Israel. ² And these were his chief officials:

Azariah son of Zadok—the priest;
³ Elihoreph and Ahijah, sons of Shisha—secretaries;
Jehoshaphat son of Ahilud—recorder;
⁴ Benaiah son of Jehoiada—commander in chief;
Zadok and Abiathar—priests;
⁵ Azariah son of Nathan—in charge of the district governors;
Zabud son of Nathan—a priest and adviser to the king;
⁶ Ahishar—palace administrator;
Adoniram son of Abda—in charge of forced labor.

⁷ Solomon had twelve district governors over all Israel, who supplied provisions for the king and the royal household. Each one had to provide supplies for one month in the year. ⁸ These are their names:

Ben-Hur—in the hill country of Ephraim;
⁹ Ben-Deker—in Makaz, Shaalbim, Beth Shemesh and Elon Bethhanan;
¹⁰ Ben-Hesed—in Arubboth (Sokoh and all the land of Hepher were his);
¹¹ Ben-Abinadab—in Naphoth Dor (he was married to Taphath daughter of Solomon);
¹² Baana son of Ahilud—in Taanach and Megiddo, and in

Did Solomon have slaves?
(4:6)
Yes. Solomon had foreign slaves and he also drafted some Israelites into forced manual labor. Samuel had warned that if the people were given a king, their sons and daughters would be required to serve him (see 1 Samuel 8:11–13).

How did the governors provide supplies for the king?
(4:7)
All of the landowners in the district were taxed. Each of the 12 governors was responsible for collecting their people's offerings and presenting them once a year. Samuel had warned about the taxes of produce and livestock the people would be forced to pay.

all of Beth Shan next to Zarethan below Jezreel, from Beth Shan to Abel Meholah across to Jokmeam;

[13] Ben-Geber—in Ramoth Gilead (the settlements of Jair son of Manasseh in Gilead were his, as well as the region of Argob in Bashan and its sixty large walled cities with bronze gate bars);

[14] Ahinadab son of Iddo—in Mahanaim;

[15] Ahimaaz—in Naphtali (he had married Basemath daughter of Solomon);

[16] Baana son of Hushai—in Asher and in Aloth;

[17] Jehoshaphat son of Paruah—in Issachar;

[18] Shimei son of Ela—in Benjamin;

[19] Geber son of Uri—in Gilead (the country of Sihon king of the Amorites and the country of Og king of Bashan). He was the only governor over the district.

SOLOMON'S DAILY PROVISIONS

[20] The people of Judah and Israel were as numerous as the sand on the seashore; they ate, they drank and they were happy. [21] And Solomon ruled over all the kingdoms from the Euphrates River to the land of the Philistines, as far as the border of Egypt. These countries brought tribute and were Solomon's subjects all his life.

[22] Solomon's daily provisions were thirty cors[a] of the finest flour and sixty cors[b] of meal, [23] ten head of stall-fed cattle, twenty of pasture-fed cattle and a hundred sheep and goats, as well as deer, gazelles, roebucks and choice fowl. [24] For he ruled over all the kingdoms west of the Euphrates River, from Tiphsah to Gaza, and had peace on all sides. [25] During Solomon's lifetime Judah and Israel, from Dan to Beersheba, lived in safety, everyone under their own vine and under their own fig tree.

[26] Solomon had four[c] thousand stalls for chariot horses, and twelve thousand horses.[d]

[27] The district governors, each in his month, supplied provisions for King Solomon and all who came to the king's table. They saw to it that nothing was lacking. [28] They also brought to the proper place their quotas of barley and straw for the chariot horses and the other horses.

SOLOMON'S WISDOM

[29] God gave Solomon wisdom and very great insight, and a breadth of understanding as measureless as the sand on the seashore. [30] Solomon's wisdom was greater than the wisdom of all the people of the East, and greater than all the wisdom of Egypt. [31] He was wiser than anyone else, including Ethan the Ezrahite—wiser than Heman, Kalkol and Darda, the sons of Mahol. And his fame spread to all the surrounding nations. [32] He spoke three thousand proverbs and his songs numbered a thousand and five. [33] He spoke about plant life, from the cedar of Lebanon to the hyssop that grows out of walls. He also spoke about animals and birds, reptiles and fish.

[a] 22 That is, probably about 5 1/2 tons or about 5 metric tons   [b] 22 That is, probably about 11 tons or about 10 metric tons   [c] 26 Some Septuagint manuscripts (see also 2 Chron. 9:25); Hebrew *forty*   [d] 26 Or *charioteers*

What was the attitude of the Israelites during this time? (4:20)
The Israelites had grown into a large nation, and during Solomon's reign the nation was at peace and the people had plenty to eat and drink. They were described as being happy, which was not common during their history as a nation.

Solomon's Kingdom (4:21,24)

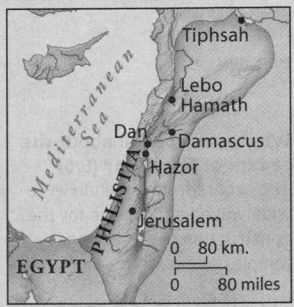

How many people did Solomon have to feed each day? (4:22–23)
Eventually, Solomon had to provide for over a thousand people. He had 700 wives, 300 concubines, and numerous children. This required a huge supply of food.

What did vines and fig trees symbolize? (4:25)
Vines and fig trees symbolized growth and a thriving economy. To say "everyone under their own vine and ... fig tree" meant peace and security.

What type of wisdom did Solomon have? (4:29–34)
Solomon had asked God for discernment so that he could decide between right and wrong and govern fairly. But in addition to having the wisdom to govern a vast kingdom, Solomon had a wide range of scientific and other knowledge. His wisdom extended to music, poetry, and proverbs. Solomon was considered to be the wisest man of his time in the entire Middle East.

[34] From all nations people came to listen to Solomon's wisdom, sent by all the kings of the world, who had heard of his wisdom.[a]

PREPARATIONS FOR BUILDING THE TEMPLE

5 [b] When Hiram king of Tyre heard that Solomon had been anointed king to succeed his father David, he sent his envoys to Solomon, because he had always been on friendly terms with David. [2] Solomon sent back this message to Hiram:

[3] "You know that because of the wars waged against my father David from all sides, he could not build a temple for the Name of the LORD his God until the LORD put his enemies under his feet. [4] But now the LORD my God has given me rest on every side, and there is no adversary or disaster. [5] I intend, therefore, to build a temple for the Name of the LORD my God, as the LORD told my father David, when he said, 'Your son whom I will put on the throne in your place will build the temple for my Name.'

[6] "So give orders that cedars of Lebanon be cut for me. My men will work with yours, and I will pay you for your men whatever wages you set. You know that we have no one so skilled in felling timber as the Sidonians."

[7] When Hiram heard Solomon's message, he was greatly pleased and said, "Praise be to the LORD today, for he has given David a wise son to rule over this great nation."

[8] So Hiram sent word to Solomon:

"I have received the message you sent me and will do all you want in providing the cedar and juniper logs. [9] My men will haul them down from Lebanon to the Mediterranean Sea, and I will float them as rafts by sea to the place you specify. There I will separate them and you can take them away. And you are to grant my wish by providing food for my royal household."

[10] In this way Hiram kept Solomon supplied with all the cedar and juniper logs he wanted, [11] and Solomon gave Hiram twenty thousand cors[c] of wheat as food for his household, in addition to twenty thousand baths[d,e] of pressed olive oil. Solomon continued to do this for Hiram year after year. [12] The LORD gave Solomon wisdom, just as he had promised him. There were peaceful relations between Hiram and Solomon, and the two of them made a treaty.

[13] King Solomon conscripted laborers from all Israel—thirty thousand men. [14] He sent them off to Lebanon in shifts of ten thousand a month, so that they spent one month in Lebanon and two months at home. Adoniram was in charge of the forced labor. [15] Solomon had seventy thousand carriers and eighty thousand stonecutters in the hills,

What was special about the cedars of Lebanon? (5:6)
The cedars from Lebanon were widely used at this time for the construction of palaces and temples.

Did Hiram worship the LORD? (5:7)
It's possible, though it was common for kings at that time to recognize and honor each other's gods. This was another way to cement alliances and trade agreements. Hiram's statement may have been this type of respectful expression, or he may have been an actual believer.

Was Israel permitted to become an ally of pagan nations? (5:12)
Israel was supposed to conquer its pagan neighbors. An exception was made for nations at a distance from Israel. Tyre and Sidon, however, were within the boundaries of the original promised land, so Israel should not have made a treaty with them. But Solomon may have been convinced Hiram's worship of God was sincere, eliminating the reason to destroy them.

Were "conscripted laborers" slaves? (5:13)
Solomon did not make any Israelites into slaves. But he did draft 30,000 Israelite men into forced labor.

---

[a] 34 In Hebrew texts 4:21-34 is numbered 5:1-14.   [b] In Hebrew texts 5:1-18 is numbered 5:15-32.   [c] 11 That is, probably about 3,600 tons or about 3,250 metric tons   [d] 11 Septuagint (see also 2 Chron. 2:10); Hebrew twenty cors   [e] 11 That is, about 120,000 gallons or about 440,000 liters

¹⁶as well as thirty-three hundred^a foremen who supervised the project and directed the workers. ¹⁷At the king's command they removed from the quarry large blocks of high-grade stone to provide a foundation of dressed stone for the temple. ¹⁸The craftsmen of Solomon and Hiram and workers from Byblos cut and prepared the timber and stone for the building of the temple.

SOLOMON BUILDS THE TEMPLE

6 In the four hundred and eightieth^b year after the Israelites came out of Egypt, in the fourth year of Solomon's reign over Israel, in the month of Ziv, the second month, he began to build the temple of the Lord.

²The temple that King Solomon built for the Lord was sixty cubits long, twenty wide and thirty high.^c ³The portico at the front of the main hall of the temple extended the width of the temple, that is twenty cubits,^d and projected ten cubits^e from the front of the temple. ⁴He made narrow windows high up in the temple walls. ⁵Against the walls of the main hall and inner sanctuary he built a structure around the building, in which there were side rooms. ⁶The lowest floor was five cubits^f wide, the middle floor six cubits^g and the third floor seven.^h He made offset ledges around the outside of the temple so that nothing would be inserted into the temple walls.

⁷In building the temple, only blocks dressed at the quarry were used, and no hammer, chisel or any other iron tool was heard at the temple site while it was being built.

⁸The entrance to the lowestⁱ floor was on the south side of the temple; a stairway led up to the middle level and from there to the third. ⁹So he built the temple and completed it, roofing it with beams and cedar planks. ¹⁰And he built the side rooms all along the temple. The height of each was five cubits, and they were attached to the temple by beams of cedar.

¹¹The word of the Lord came to Solomon: ¹²"As for this temple you are building, if you follow my decrees, observe my laws and keep all my commands and obey them, I will fulfill through you the promise I gave to David your father. ¹³And I will live among the Israelites and will not abandon my people Israel."

¹⁴So Solomon built the temple and completed it. ¹⁵He lined its interior walls with cedar boards, paneling them from the floor of the temple to the ceiling, and covered the floor of the temple with planks of juniper. ¹⁶He partitioned off twenty cubits at the rear of the temple with cedar boards from floor to ceiling to form within the temple an inner sanctuary, the Most Holy Place. ¹⁷The main hall in front of this room

Where did Solomon get the plans for the temple? (6:2–9)
The temple's plans were most likely inspired by the tabernacle God had Moses construct (see Exodus 25:9). They had many of the same features. The temple was nearly twice as large as the tabernacle. Canaanite and Phoenician temples from this era were similar in design and construction.

What was the purpose of these high windows? (6:4)
Their purpose was to let sunlight and air into the building.

Why weren't tools allowed at the temple site? (6:7)
During Moses' time, using iron tools to shape rock was considered a pagan practice. God had forbidden him from using "dressed" (shaped) stones to build an altar (see Exodus 20:25).

Solomon's Temple

---

^a 16 Hebrew; some Septuagint manuscripts (see also 2 Chron. 2:2,18) *thirty-six hundred*   ^b 1 Hebrew; Septuagint *four hundred and fortieth*   ^c 2 That is, about 90 feet long, 30 feet wide and 45 feet high or about 27 meters long, 9 meters wide and 14 meters high   ^d 3 That is, about 30 feet or about 9 meters; also in verses 16 and 20   ^e 3 That is, about 15 feet or about 4.5 meters; also in verses 23-26   ^f 6 That is, about 7 1/2 feet or about 2.3 meters; also in verses 10 and 24   ^g 6 That is, about 9 feet or about 2.7 meters   ^h 6 That is, about 11 feet or about 3.2 meters   ⁱ 8 Septuagint; Hebrew *middle*

was forty cubits*ᵃ* long. ¹⁸The inside of the temple was cedar, carved with gourds and open flowers. Everything was cedar; no stone was to be seen.

¹⁹He prepared the inner sanctuary within the temple to set the ark of the covenant of the LORD there. ²⁰The inner sanctuary was twenty cubits long, twenty wide and twenty high. He overlaid the inside with pure gold, and he also overlaid the altar of cedar. ²¹Solomon covered the inside of the temple with pure gold, and he extended gold chains across the front of the inner sanctuary, which was overlaid with gold. ²²So he overlaid the whole interior with gold. He also overlaid with gold the altar that belonged to the inner sanctuary.

²³For the inner sanctuary he made a pair of cherubim out of olive wood, each ten cubits high. ²⁴One wing of the first cherub was five cubits long, and the other wing five cubits—ten cubits from wing tip to wing tip. ²⁵The second cherub also measured ten cubits, for the two cherubim were identical in size and shape. ²⁶The height of each cherub was ten cubits. ²⁷He placed the cherubim inside the innermost room of the temple, with their wings spread out. The wing of one cherub touched one wall, while the wing of the other touched the other wall, and their wings touched each other in the middle of the room. ²⁸He overlaid the cherubim with gold.

²⁹On the walls all around the temple, in both the inner and outer rooms, he carved cherubim, palm trees and open flowers. ³⁰He also covered the floors of both the inner and outer rooms of the temple with gold.

³¹For the entrance to the inner sanctuary he made doors out of olive wood that were one fifth of the width of the sanctuary. ³²And on the two olive-wood doors he carved cherubim, palm trees and open flowers, and overlaid the cherubim and palm trees with hammered gold. ³³In the same way, for the entrance to the main hall he made doorframes out of olive wood that were one fourth of the width of the hall. ³⁴He also made two doors out of juniper wood, each having two leaves that turned in sockets. ³⁵He carved cherubim, palm trees and open flowers on them and overlaid them with gold hammered evenly over the carvings.

³⁶And he built the inner courtyard of three courses of dressed stone and one course of trimmed cedar beams.

³⁷The foundation of the temple of the LORD was laid in the fourth year, in the month of Ziv. ³⁸In the eleventh year in the month of Bul, the eighth month, the temple was finished in all its details according to its specifications. He had spent seven years building it.

SOLOMON BUILDS HIS PALACE

7 It took Solomon thirteen years, however, to complete the construction of his palace. ²He built the Palace of the Forest of Lebanon a hundred cubits long, fifty wide and thirty high,*ᵇ* with four rows of cedar columns supporting

What type of decorative artwork appeared in the temple? (6:29–35)
The temple had carvings of cherubim, palm trees, and flowers. This was reminiscent of the garden of Eden.

Why did Solomon spend more time building his palace than he did the temple? (6:38–7:1)
His priorities were not right. Spending twice as much time building his house showed how his love for material possessions was starting to outweigh his love for the Lord.

Why was Solomon's home named the Palace of the Forest of Lebanon? (7:2)
The four rows of pillars made from the trunks of cedar trees created the impression of a great forest.

ᵃ 17 That is, about 60 feet or about 18 meters   *ᵇ 2* That is, about 150 feet long, 75 feet wide and 45 feet high or about 45 meters long, 23 meters wide and 14 meters high

trimmed cedar beams. ³It was roofed with cedar above the beams that rested on the columns—forty-five beams, fifteen to a row. ⁴Its windows were placed high in sets of three, facing each other. ⁵All the doorways had rectangular frames; they were in the front part in sets of three, facing each other.^a

⁶He made a colonnade fifty cubits long and thirty wide.^b In front of it was a portico, and in front of that were pillars and an overhanging roof.

⁷He built the throne hall, the Hall of Justice, where he was to judge, and he covered it with cedar from floor to ceiling.^c ⁸And the palace in which he was to live, set farther back, was similar in design. Solomon also made a palace like this hall for Pharaoh's daughter, whom he had married.

⁹All these structures, from the outside to the great courtyard and from foundation to eaves, were made of blocks of high-grade stone cut to size and smoothed on their inner and outer faces. ¹⁰The foundations were laid with large stones of good quality, some measuring ten cubits^d and some eight.^e ¹¹Above were high-grade stones, cut to size, and cedar beams. ¹²The great courtyard was surrounded by a wall of three courses of dressed stone and one course of trimmed cedar beams, as was the inner courtyard of the temple of the LORD with its portico.

THE TEMPLE'S FURNISHINGS

¹³King Solomon sent to Tyre and brought Huram,^f ¹⁴whose mother was a widow from the tribe of Naphtali and whose father was from Tyre and a skilled craftsman in bronze. Huram was filled with wisdom, with understanding and with knowledge to do all kinds of bronze work. He came to King Solomon and did all the work assigned to him.

¹⁵He cast two bronze pillars, each eighteen cubits high and twelve cubits in circumference.^g ¹⁶He also made two capitals of cast bronze to set on the tops of the pillars; each capital was five cubits^h high. ¹⁷A network of interwoven chains adorned the capitals on top of the pillars, seven for each capital. ¹⁸He made pomegranates in two rowsⁱ encircling each network to decorate the capitals on top of the pillars.^j He did the same for each capital. ¹⁹The capitals on top of the pillars in the portico were in the shape of lilies, four cubits^k high. ²⁰On the capitals of both pillars, above the bowl-shaped part next to the network, were the two hundred pomegranates in rows all around. ²¹He erected the pillars at the portico of the temple. The pillar to the south he named Jakin^l and the one to the north Boaz.^m ²²The capitals on top

Why did Pharaoh's daughter live in her own palace? (7:8) Solomon wouldn't allow Pharaoh's daughter to live in the holy places where the ark of the Lord had been housed (see 2 Chronicles 8:11).

Why were the pillars given names? (7:21) The freestanding pillars in front of the temple served as monuments or national markers. They did not support any of the temple's structures. The name *Jakin* probably meant *he establishes*. The name *Boaz* probably meant *in him is strength*.

---

^a 5 The meaning of the Hebrew for this verse is uncertain.   ^b 6 That is, about 75 feet long and 45 feet wide or about 23 meters long and 14 meters wide   ^c 7 Vulgate and Syriac; Hebrew *floor*   ^d 10 That is, about 15 feet or about 4.5 meters; also in verse 23   ^e 10 That is, about 12 feet or about 3.6 meters   ^f 13 Hebrew *Hiram*, a variant of *Huram*; also in verses 40 and 45   ^g 15 That is, about 27 feet high and 18 feet in circumference or about 8.1 meters high and 5.4 meters in circumference   ^h 16 That is, about 7 1/2 feet or about 2.3 meters; also in verse 23   ⁱ 18 Two Hebrew manuscripts and Septuagint; most Hebrew manuscripts *made the pillars, and there were two rows*   ^j 18 Many Hebrew manuscripts and Syriac; most Hebrew manuscripts *pomegranates*   ^k 19 That is, about 6 feet or about 1.8 meters; also in verse 38   ^l 21 *Jakin* probably means *he establishes*.   ^m 21 *Boaz* probably means *in him is strength*.

What was the Sea? (7:23)
This was an enormous reservoir or basin that held about 12,000 gallons (44,000 liters) of water.

Why were statues of bulls allowed in the temple? (7:25)
These bulls were not idols, so they were not meant to be worshiped. They were only there to serve as a reminder of God's power. The Canaanite fertility god Baal was represented by a bull, but those in the temple were not in any way associated with the pagan god.

What were these basins used for? (7:38–40)
Ten movable bronze stands were designed to hold water basins that were much smaller than the bronze Sea. The water from these basins was used to wash parts of the animals that were slaughtered for burnt offerings. The bronze basins each held about 240 gallons (880 liters).

were in the shape of lilies. And so the work on the pillars was completed.

²³He made the Sea of cast metal, circular in shape, measuring ten cubits from rim to rim and five cubits high. It took a line of thirty cubits[a] to measure around it. ²⁴Below the rim, gourds encircled it—ten to a cubit. The gourds were cast in two rows in one piece with the Sea.

²⁵The Sea stood on twelve bulls, three facing north, three facing west, three facing south and three facing east. The Sea rested on top of them, and their hindquarters were toward the center. ²⁶It was a handbreadth[b] in thickness, and its rim was like the rim of a cup, like a lily blossom. It held two thousand baths.[c]

²⁷He also made ten movable stands of bronze; each was four cubits long, four wide and three high.[d] ²⁸This is how the stands were made: They had side panels attached to uprights. ²⁹On the panels between the uprights were lions, bulls and cherubim—and on the uprights as well. Above and below the lions and bulls were wreaths of hammered work. ³⁰Each stand had four bronze wheels with bronze axles, and each had a basin resting on four supports, cast with wreaths on each side. ³¹On the inside of the stand there was an opening that had a circular frame one cubit[e] deep. This opening was round, and with its basework it measured a cubit and a half.[f] Around its opening there was engraving. The panels of the stands were square, not round. ³²The four wheels were under the panels, and the axles of the wheels were attached to the stand. The diameter of each wheel was a cubit and a half. ³³The wheels were made like chariot wheels; the axles, rims, spokes and hubs were all of cast metal.

³⁴Each stand had four handles, one on each corner, projecting from the stand. ³⁵At the top of the stand there was a circular band half a cubit[g] deep. The supports and panels were attached to the top of the stand. ³⁶He engraved cherubim, lions and palm trees on the surfaces of the supports and on the panels, in every available space, with wreaths all around. ³⁷This is the way he made the ten stands. They were all cast in the same molds and were identical in size and shape.

³⁸He then made ten bronze basins, each holding forty baths[h] and measuring four cubits across, one basin to go on each of the ten stands. ³⁹He placed five of the stands on the south side of the temple and five on the north. He placed the Sea on the south side, at the southeast corner of the temple. ⁴⁰He also made the pots[i] and shovels and sprinkling bowls.

---

[a] 23 That is, about 45 feet or about 14 meters   [b] 26 That is, about 3 inches or about 7.5 centimeters   [c] 26 That is, about 12,000 gallons or about 44,000 liters; the Septuagint does not have this sentence.   [d] 27 That is, about 6 feet long and wide and about 4 1/2 feet high or about 1.8 meters long and wide and 1.4 meters high   [e] 31 That is, about 18 inches or about 45 centimeters   [f] 31 That is, about 2 1/4 feet or about 68 centimeters; also in verse 32   [g] 35 That is, about 9 inches or about 23 centimeters   [h] 38 That is, about 240 gallons or about 880 liters   [i] 40 Many Hebrew manuscripts, Septuagint, Syriac and Vulgate (see also verse 45 and 2 Chron. 4:11); many other Hebrew manuscripts *basins*

So Huram finished all the work he had undertaken for King Solomon in the temple of the LORD:

⁴¹ the two pillars;

the two bowl-shaped capitals on top of the pillars;

the two sets of network decorating the two bowl-shaped capitals on top of the pillars;

⁴² the four hundred pomegranates for the two sets of network (two rows of pomegranates for each network decorating the bowl-shaped capitals on top of the pillars);

⁴³ the ten stands with their ten basins;

⁴⁴ the Sea and the twelve bulls under it;

⁴⁵ the pots, shovels and sprinkling bowls.

All these objects that Huram made for King Solomon for the temple of the LORD were of burnished bronze. ⁴⁶ The king had them cast in clay molds in the plain of the Jordan between Sukkoth and Zarethan. ⁴⁷ Solomon left all these things unweighed, because there were so many; the weight of the bronze was not determined.

⁴⁸ Solomon also made all the furnishings that were in the LORD's temple:

the golden altar;

the golden table on which was the bread of the Presence;

⁴⁹ the lampstands of pure gold (five on the right and five on the left, in front of the inner sanctuary);

the gold floral work and lamps and tongs;

⁵⁰ the pure gold basins, wick trimmers, sprinkling bowls, dishes and censers;

and the gold sockets for the doors of the innermost room, the Most Holy Place, and also for the doors of the main hall of the temple.

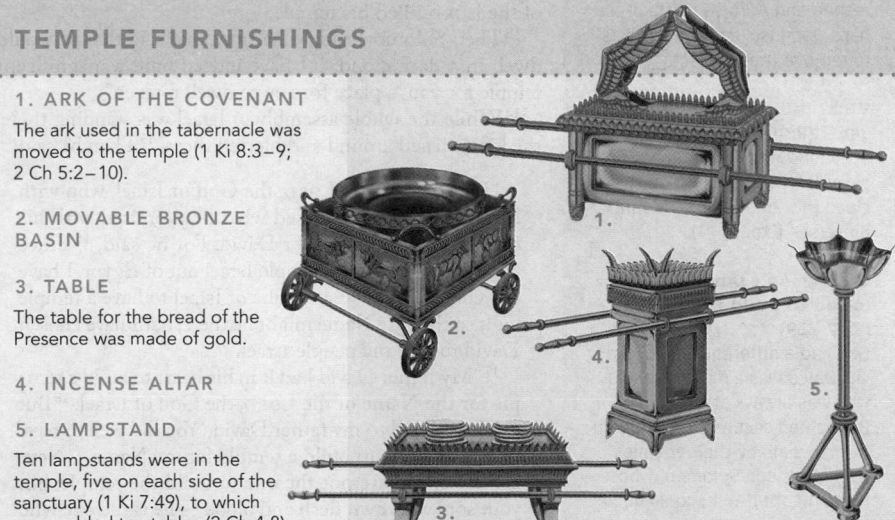

TEMPLE FURNISHINGS

1. ARK OF THE COVENANT

The ark used in the tabernacle was moved to the temple (1 Ki 8:3–9; 2 Ch 5:2–10).

2. MOVABLE BRONZE BASIN

3. TABLE

The table for the bread of the Presence was made of gold.

4. INCENSE ALTAR

5. LAMPSTAND

Ten lampstands were in the temple, five on each side of the sanctuary (1 Ki 7:49), to which were added ten tables (2 Ch 4:8).

What items had David dedicated to the temple? (7:51)
These were valuable objects made of silver or gold that had been plundered during battles or been given to David as tribute by kings seeking his favor.

Where was the ark kept before being placed in the temple? (8:1–6)
The ark's first home in Canaan was Shiloh, where the Philistines captured and held it for seven months. Then it was taken to Beth Shemesh for a short while. It was transferred and stayed 20 years with Abinadab in Kiriath Jearim. It was kept for a short time in the house of Obed-Edom until David took it to a tent in Jerusalem. The ark remained there until it was brought to the temple.

Why were so many sacrifices offered? (8:5)
This is a hyperbole, an extreme exaggeration. The people of Israel offered so much because they were thankful to finally have a permanent place to worship God.

What happened to the objects in the ark? (8:9)
The Bible does not say. Perhaps the Philistines removed the jar of manna and Aaron's staff, or perhaps God instructed the priests to remove these objects.

What did the cloud represent? (8:10–13)
The cloud was a symbol of God's glory. It was a reminder of the cloud that had covered Mount Sinai (see Exodus 19).

Why wasn't David allowed to build the temple? (8:17–19)
God had a different task for David. David was a military leader who was always at war (5:3–5). But he had secured the kingdom from threats by their enemies so that his son Solomon (whose name meant *peace*) could build the temple.

[51]When all the work King Solomon had done for the temple of the LORD was finished, he brought in the things his father David had dedicated — the silver and gold and the furnishings — and he placed them in the treasuries of the LORD's temple.

THE ARK BROUGHT TO THE TEMPLE

8 Then King Solomon summoned into his presence at Jerusalem the elders of Israel, all the heads of the tribes and the chiefs of the Israelite families, to bring up the ark of the LORD's covenant from Zion, the City of David. [2]All the Israelites came together to King Solomon at the time of the festival in the month of Ethanim, the seventh month.

[3]When all the elders of Israel had arrived, the priests took up the ark, [4]and they brought up the ark of the LORD and the tent of meeting and all the sacred furnishings in it. The priests and Levites carried them up, [5]and King Solomon and the entire assembly of Israel that had gathered about him were before the ark, sacrificing so many sheep and cattle that they could not be recorded or counted.

[6]The priests then brought the ark of the LORD's covenant to its place in the inner sanctuary of the temple, the Most Holy Place, and put it beneath the wings of the cherubim. [7]The cherubim spread their wings over the place of the ark and overshadowed the ark and its carrying poles. [8]These poles were so long that their ends could be seen from the Holy Place in front of the inner sanctuary, but not from outside the Holy Place; and they are still there today. [9]There was nothing in the ark except the two stone tablets that Moses had placed in it at Horeb, where the LORD made a covenant with the Israelites after they came out of Egypt.

[10]When the priests withdrew from the Holy Place, the cloud filled the temple of the LORD. [11]And the priests could not perform their service because of the cloud, for the glory of the LORD filled his temple.

[12]Then Solomon said, "The LORD has said that he would dwell in a dark cloud; [13]I have indeed built a magnificent temple for you, a place for you to dwell forever."

[14]While the whole assembly of Israel was standing there, the king turned around and blessed them. [15]Then he said:

"Praise be to the LORD, the God of Israel, who with his own hand has fulfilled what he promised with his own mouth to my father David. For he said, [16]'Since the day I brought my people Israel out of Egypt, I have not chosen a city in any tribe of Israel to have a temple built so that my Name might be there, but I have chosen David to rule my people Israel.'

[17]"My father David had it in his heart to build a temple for the Name of the LORD, the God of Israel. [18]But the LORD said to my father David, 'You did well to have it in your heart to build a temple for my Name. [19]Nevertheless, you are not the one to build the temple, but your son, your own flesh and blood — he is the one who will build the temple for my Name.'

²⁰"The LORD has kept the promise he made: I have succeeded David my father and now I sit on the throne of Israel, just as the LORD promised, and I have built the temple for the Name of the LORD, the God of Israel. ²¹I have provided a place there for the ark, in which is the covenant of the LORD that he made with our ancestors when he brought them out of Egypt."

SOLOMON'S PRAYER OF DEDICATION

²²Then Solomon stood before the altar of the LORD in front of the whole assembly of Israel, spread out his hands toward heaven ²³and said:

"LORD, the God of Israel, there is no God like you in heaven above or on earth below—you who keep your covenant of love with your servants who continue wholeheartedly in your way. ²⁴You have kept your promise to your servant David my father; with your mouth you have promised and with your hand you have fulfilled it—as it is today.

²⁵"Now LORD, the God of Israel, keep for your servant David my father the promises you made to him when you said, 'You shall never fail to have a successor to sit before me on the throne of Israel, if only your descendants are careful in all they do to walk before me faithfully as you have done.' ²⁶And now, God of Israel, let your word that you promised your servant David my father come true.

²⁷"But will God really dwell on earth? The heavens, even the highest heaven, cannot contain you. How much less this temple I have built! ²⁸Yet give attention to your servant's prayer and his plea for mercy, LORD my God. Hear the cry and the prayer that your servant is praying in your presence this day. ²⁹May your eyes be open toward this temple night and day, this place of which you said, 'My Name shall be there,' so that you will hear the prayer your servant prays toward this place. ³⁰Hear the supplication of your servant and of your people Israel when they pray toward this place. Hear from heaven, your dwelling place, and when you hear, forgive.

³¹"When anyone wrongs their neighbor and is required to take an oath and they come and swear the oath before your altar in this temple, ³²then hear from heaven and act. Judge between your servants, condemning the guilty by bringing down on their heads what they have done, and vindicating the innocent by treating them in accordance with their innocence.

³³"When your people Israel have been defeated by an enemy because they have sinned against you, and when they turn back to you and give praise to your name, praying and making supplication to you in this temple, ³⁴then hear from heaven and forgive the sin of your people Israel and bring them back to the land you gave to their ancestors.

³⁵"When the heavens are shut up and there is no rain because your people have sinned against you, and when they pray toward this place and give praise to your name

Was there a difference between a temple for God and a temple for his "Name"? (8:27–29)
Yes. Solomon knew that God's presence is everywhere. Dedicating a temple for God would imply that God was only in the temple. No building can ever contain all of God's glory. So he dedicated the temple to God's name, knowing that God would be present in the temple in a special way.

How were Israelites supposed to pray? (8:30)
When the Israelites were not able to pray in the temple, they were to pray while facing toward the temple. It was the place where God had pledged to be present among his people.

and turn from their sin because you have afflicted them, [36] then hear from heaven and forgive the sin of your servants, your people Israel. Teach them the right way to live, and send rain on the land you gave your people for an inheritance.

[37] "When famine or plague comes to the land, or blight or mildew, locusts or grasshoppers, or when an enemy besieges them in any of their cities, whatever disaster or disease may come, [38] and when a prayer or plea is made by anyone among your people Israel—being aware of the afflictions of their own hearts, and spreading out their hands toward this temple— [39] then hear from heaven, your dwelling place. Forgive and act; deal with everyone according to all they do, since you know their hearts (for you alone know every human heart), [40] so that they will fear you all the time they live in the land you gave our ancestors.

[41] "As for the foreigner who does not belong to your people Israel but has come from a distant land because of your name— [42] for they will hear of your great name and your mighty hand and your outstretched arm— when they come and pray toward this temple, [43] then hear from heaven, your dwelling place. Do whatever the foreigner asks of you, so that all the peoples of the earth may know your name and fear you, as do your own people Israel, and may know that this house I have built bears your Name.

[44] "When your people go to war against their enemies, wherever you send them, and when they pray to the LORD toward the city you have chosen and the temple I have built for your Name, [45] then hear from heaven their prayer and their plea, and uphold their cause.

[46] "When they sin against you—for there is no one who does not sin—and you become angry with them and give them over to their enemies, who take them captive to their own lands, far away or near; [47] and if they have a change of heart in the land where they are held captive, and repent and plead with you in the land of their captors and say, 'We have sinned, we have done wrong, we have acted wickedly'; [48] and if they turn back to you with all their heart and soul in the land of their enemies who took them captive, and pray to you toward the land you gave their ancestors, toward the city you have chosen and the temple I have built for your Name; [49] then from heaven, your dwelling place, hear their prayer and their plea, and uphold their cause. [50] And forgive your people, who have sinned against you; forgive all the offenses they have committed against you, and cause their captors to show them mercy; [51] for they are your people and your inheritance, whom you brought out of Egypt, out of that iron-smelting furnace.

[52] "May your eyes be open to your servant's plea and to the plea of your people Israel, and may you listen to them whenever they cry out to you. [53] For you singled them out from all the nations of the world to be your own inheritance, just as you declared through your

Was Solomon too generous in his prayer for foreigners? (8:41–43)
Solomon's prayer that Gentiles would be drawn to the temple to worship the God of Israel showed that he understood God's promise. This message has appeared in Scripture before. God had told Abraham that all the peoples of the earth would be blessed through him (Gen. 12:33). Israel was called to be a light to the nations that drew people to the one true God.

servant Moses when you, Sovereign Lᴏʀᴅ, brought our ancestors out of Egypt."

⁵⁴When Solomon had finished all these prayers and supplications to the Lᴏʀᴅ, he rose from before the altar of the Lᴏʀᴅ, where he had been kneeling with his hands spread out toward heaven. ⁵⁵He stood and blessed the whole assembly of Israel in a loud voice, saying:

⁵⁶"Praise be to the Lᴏʀᴅ, who has given rest to his people Israel just as he promised. Not one word has failed of all the good promises he gave through his servant Moses. ⁵⁷May the Lᴏʀᴅ our God be with us as he was with our ancestors; may he never leave us nor forsake us. ⁵⁸May he turn our hearts to him, to walk in obedience to him and keep the commands, decrees and laws he gave our ancestors. ⁵⁹And may these words of mine, which I have prayed before the Lᴏʀᴅ, be near to the Lᴏʀᴅ our God day and night, that he may uphold the cause of his servant and the cause of his people Israel according to each day's need, ⁶⁰so that all the peoples of the earth may know that the Lᴏʀᴅ is God and that there is no other. ⁶¹And may your hearts be fully committed to the Lᴏʀᴅ our God, to live by his decrees and obey his commands, as at this time."

THE DEDICATION OF THE TEMPLE

⁶²Then the king and all Israel with him offered sacrifices before the Lᴏʀᴅ. ⁶³Solomon offered a sacrifice of fellowship offerings to the Lᴏʀᴅ: twenty-two thousand cattle and a hundred and twenty thousand sheep and goats. So the king and all the Israelites dedicated the temple of the Lᴏʀᴅ.

⁶⁴On that same day the king consecrated the middle part of the courtyard in front of the temple of the Lᴏʀᴅ, and there he offered burnt offerings, grain offerings and the fat of the fellowship offerings, because the bronze altar that stood before the Lᴏʀᴅ was too small to hold the burnt offerings, the grain offerings and the fat of the fellowship offerings.

⁶⁵So Solomon observed the festival at that time, and all Israel with him—a vast assembly, people from Lebo Hamath to the Wadi of Egypt. They celebrated it before the Lᴏʀᴅ our God for seven days and seven days more, fourteen days in all. ⁶⁶On the following day he sent the people away. They blessed the king and then went home, joyful and glad in heart for all the good things the Lᴏʀᴅ had done for his servant David and his people Israel.

THE LORD APPEARS TO SOLOMON

9 When Solomon had finished building the temple of the Lᴏʀᴅ and the royal palace, and had achieved all he had desired to do, ²the Lᴏʀᴅ appeared to him a second time, as he had appeared to him at Gibeon. ³The Lᴏʀᴅ said to him:

"I have heard the prayer and plea you have made before me; I have consecrated this temple, which you have built, by putting my Name there forever. My eyes and my heart will always be there.

Why is it necessary for God to turn people's hearts toward himself? (8:58) Because of sin, people don't automatically turn toward God. In fact, without his help, we would not believe in him. But we still have to respond to God's prompting. Solomon asked God to give people the ability to follow God and obey his laws.

How did God renew the covenant he had made with David? (9:4–5)
God gave Solomon the same promise he had given David, that his descendants would be the rulers of Israel. But God emphasized the importance of obedience to the covenant in order to experience its blessings rather than its curses.

⁴"As for you, if you walk before me faithfully with integrity of heart and uprightness, as David your father did, and do all I command and observe my decrees and laws, ⁵I will establish your royal throne over Israel forever, as I promised David your father when I said, 'You shall never fail to have a successor on the throne of Israel.'

⁶"But if you[a] or your descendants turn away from me and do not observe the commands and decrees I have given you[a] and go off to serve other gods and worship them, ⁷then I will cut off Israel from the land I have given them and will reject this temple I have consecrated for my Name. Israel will then become a byword and an object of ridicule among all peoples. ⁸This temple will become a heap of rubble. All[b] who pass by will be appalled and will scoff and say, 'Why has the Lord done such a thing to this land and to this temple?' ⁹People will answer, 'Because they have forsaken the Lord their God, who brought their ancestors out of Egypt, and have embraced other gods, worshiping and serving them—that is why the Lord brought all this disaster on them.'"

SOLOMON'S OTHER ACTIVITIES

¹⁰At the end of twenty years, during which Solomon built these two buildings—the temple of the Lord and the royal palace— ¹¹King Solomon gave twenty towns in Galilee to Hiram king of Tyre, because Hiram had supplied him with all the cedar and juniper and gold he wanted. ¹²But when Hiram went from Tyre to see the towns that Solomon had given him, he was not pleased with them. ¹³"What kind of towns are these you have given me, my brother?" he asked. And he called them the Land of Kabul,[c] a name they have to this day. ¹⁴Now Hiram had sent to the king 120 talents[d] of gold.

Why wasn't Hiram pleased with the towns Solomon had given him? (9:12–14)
Apparently Solomon gave Hiram 20 towns along the border as collateral for the repayment of the gold Hiram had given Solomon, which amounted to several tons. Hiram did not think the towns were valuable enough to pay back Israel's debt. Solomon eventually repaid the debt owed to Hiram and rebuilt these towns (2 Chron. 8:1–2).

¹⁵Here is the account of the forced labor King Solomon conscripted to build the Lord's temple, his own palace, the terraces,[e] the wall of Jerusalem, and Hazor, Megiddo and Gezer. ¹⁶(Pharaoh king of Egypt had attacked and captured Gezer. He had set it on fire. He killed its Canaanite inhabitants and then gave it as a wedding gift to his daughter, Solomon's wife. ¹⁷And Solomon rebuilt Gezer.) He built up Lower Beth Horon, ¹⁸Baalath, and Tadmor[f] in the desert, within his land, ¹⁹as well as all his store cities and the towns for his chariots and for his horses[g]—whatever he desired to build in Jerusalem, in Lebanon and throughout all the territory he ruled.

Was it right for Solomon to enslave these people? (9:20–21)
No. He should have destroyed them. As Moses outlined years earlier, the Israelites were to destroy the pagan people who lived in Canaan (Deut. 20:16–18). If these people were not eliminated, the Israelites would be influenced to include their pagan worship practices in their worship of God. Making these people slaves was not an appropriate compromise.

²⁰There were still people left from the Amorites, Hittites, Perizzites, Hivites and Jebusites (these peoples were not Israelites). ²¹Solomon conscripted the descendants of all these peoples remaining in the land—whom the Israelites could not

---

[a] 6 The Hebrew is plural.   [b] 8 See some Septuagint manuscripts, Old Latin, Syriac, Arabic and Targum; Hebrew *And though this temple is now imposing, all*   [c] 13 *Kabul* sounds like the Hebrew for *good-for-nothing.*   [d] 14 That is, about 4 1/2 tons or about 4 metric tons   [e] 15 Or *the Millo*; also in verse 24   [f] 18 The Hebrew may also be read *Tamar.*   [g] 19 Or *charioteers*

exterminate[a]—to serve as slave labor, as it is to this day. [22]But Solomon did not make slaves of any of the Israelites; they were his fighting men, his government officials, his officers, his captains, and the commanders of his chariots and charioteers. [23]They were also the chief officials in charge of Solomon's projects—550 officials supervising those who did the work.

[24]After Pharaoh's daughter had come up from the City of David to the palace Solomon had built for her, he constructed the terraces.

[25]Three times a year Solomon sacrificed burnt offerings and fellowship offerings on the altar he had built for the LORD, burning incense before the LORD along with them, and so fulfilled the temple obligations.

[26]King Solomon also built ships at Ezion Geber, which is near Elath in Edom, on the shore of the Red Sea.[b] [27]And Hiram sent his men—sailors who knew the sea—to serve in the fleet with Solomon's men. [28]They sailed to Ophir and brought back 420 talents[c] of gold, which they delivered to King Solomon.

THE QUEEN OF SHEBA VISITS SOLOMON

10 When the queen of Sheba heard about the fame of Solomon and his relationship to the LORD, she came to test Solomon with hard questions. [2]Arriving at Jerusalem with a very great caravan—with camels carrying spices, large quantities of gold, and precious stones—she came to Solomon and talked with him about all that she had on her mind. [3]Solomon answered all her questions; nothing was too hard for the king to explain to her. [4]When the queen of Sheba saw all the wisdom of Solomon and the palace he had built, [5]the food on his table, the seating of his officials, the attending servants in their robes, his cupbearers, and the burnt offerings he made at[d] the temple of the LORD, she was overwhelmed.

[6]She said to the king, "The report I heard in my own country about your achievements and your wisdom is true. [7]But I did not believe these things until I came and saw with my own eyes. Indeed, not even half was told me; in wisdom and wealth you have far exceeded the report I heard. [8]How happy your people must be! How happy your officials, who continually stand before you and hear your wisdom! [9]Praise be to the LORD your God, who has delighted in you and placed you on the throne of Israel. Because of the LORD's eternal love for Israel, he has made you king to maintain justice and righteousness."

[10]And she gave the king 120 talents[e] of gold, large quantities of spices, and precious stones. Never again were so many spices brought in as those the queen of Sheba gave to King Solomon.

[11](Hiram's ships brought gold from Ophir; and from there they brought great cargoes of almugwood[f] and precious

Why did the queen of Sheba want to test Solomon? (10:1)
The queen had heard about Solomon's God and was curious. She knew there was a connection between Solomon's wisdom and God. She praised the LORD for his love of his people when she saw for herself all the wonderful gifts God had given Solomon (verse 9).

Why did the queen come with such a large caravan? (10:2)
She probably wanted to negotiate trading with the amount of spices, gold, and precious stones she brought with her.

---

[a] 21 The Hebrew term refers to the irrevocable giving over of things or persons to the LORD, often by totally destroying them.   [b] 26 Or *the Sea of Reeds*   [c] 28 That is, about 16 tons or about 14 metric tons   [d] Or *the ascent by which he went up to*   [e] 10 That is, about 4 1/2 tons or about 4 metric tons   [f] 11 Probably a variant of *algumwood*; also in verse 12

Why was almugwood so special? (10:12)
This was a type of wood that was ideal for making certain musical instruments. Since it was from Ophir, some think it was red sandalwood and provided decoration for Solomon's building projects.

How were the golden shields used? (10:16–17)
These gold shields were very valuable. They may have acted as a way of storing Solomon's wealth because these shields were probably for decoration in ceremonies. It's unlikely they were used in active battle.

What was meant by "the whole world"? (10:24)
This referred to the entire known world at the time. During Solomon's time, Israel became a superpower and formed trading relationships with many countries.

stones. [12] The king used the almugwood to make supports[a] for the temple of the LORD and for the royal palace, and to make harps and lyres for the musicians. So much almugwood has never been imported or seen since that day.)

[13] King Solomon gave the queen of Sheba all she desired and asked for, besides what he had given her out of his royal bounty. Then she left and returned with her retinue to her own country.

SOLOMON'S SPLENDOR

[14] The weight of the gold that Solomon received yearly was 666 talents,[b] [15] not including the revenues from merchants and traders and from all the Arabian kings and the governors of the territories.

[16] King Solomon made two hundred large shields of hammered gold; six hundred shekels[c] of gold went into each shield. [17] He also made three hundred small shields of hammered gold, with three minas[d] of gold in each shield. The king put them in the Palace of the Forest of Lebanon.

[18] Then the king made a great throne covered with ivory and overlaid with fine gold. [19] The throne had six steps, and its back had a rounded top. On both sides of the seat were armrests, with a lion standing beside each of them. [20] Twelve lions stood on the six steps, one at either end of each step. Nothing like it had ever been made for any other kingdom. [21] All King Solomon's goblets were gold, and all the household articles in the Palace of the Forest of Lebanon were pure gold. Nothing was made of silver, because silver was considered of little value in Solomon's days. [22] The king had a fleet of trading ships[e] at sea along with the ships of Hiram. Once every three years it returned, carrying gold, silver and ivory, and apes and baboons.

[23] King Solomon was greater in riches and wisdom than all the other kings of the earth. [24] The whole world sought audience with Solomon to hear the wisdom God had put in his heart. [25] Year after year, everyone who came brought a gift—articles of silver and gold, robes, weapons and spices, and horses and mules.

[26] Solomon accumulated chariots and horses; he had fourteen hundred chariots and twelve thousand horses,[f] which he kept in the chariot cities and also with him in Jerusalem. [27] The king made silver as common in Jerusalem as stones, and cedar as plentiful as sycamore-fig trees in the foothills. [28] Solomon's horses were imported from Egypt and from Kue[g]—the royal merchants purchased them from Kue at the current price. [29] They imported a chariot from Egypt for six hundred shekels of silver, and a horse for a hundred and fifty.[h] They also exported them to all the kings of the Hittites and of the Arameans.

---

[a] 12 The meaning of the Hebrew for this word is uncertain.   [b] 14 That is, about 25 tons or about 23 metric tons   [c] 16 That is, about 15 pounds or about 6.9 kilograms; also in verse 29   [d] 17 That is, about 3 3/4 pounds or about 1.7 kilograms; or perhaps reference is to double minas, that is, about 7 1/2 pounds or about 3.5 kilograms.   [e] 22 Hebrew *of ships of Tarshish*   [f] 26 Or *charioteers*   [g] 28 Probably *Cilicia*   [h] 29 That is, about 3 3/4 pounds or about 1.7 kilograms

SOLOMON'S WIVES

11 King Solomon, however, loved many foreign women besides Pharaoh's daughter—Moabites, Ammonites, Edomites, Sidonians and Hittites. ²They were from nations about which the LORD had told the Israelites, "You must not intermarry with them, because they will surely turn your hearts after their gods." Nevertheless, Solomon held fast to them in love. ³He had seven hundred wives of royal birth and three hundred concubines, and his wives led him astray. ⁴As Solomon grew old, his wives turned his heart after other gods, and his heart was not fully devoted to the LORD his God, as the heart of David his father had been. ⁵He followed Ashtoreth the goddess of the Sidonians, and Molek the detestable god of the Ammonites. ⁶So Solomon did evil in the eyes of the LORD; he did not follow the LORD completely, as David his father had done.

⁷On a hill east of Jerusalem, Solomon built a high place for Chemosh the detestable god of Moab, and for Molek the detestable god of the Ammonites. ⁸He did the same for all his foreign wives, who burned incense and offered sacrifices to their gods.

⁹The LORD became angry with Solomon because his heart had turned away from the LORD, the God of Israel, who had appeared to him twice. ¹⁰Although he had forbidden Solomon to follow other gods, Solomon did not keep the LORD's command. ¹¹So the LORD said to Solomon, "Since this is your attitude and you have not kept my covenant and my decrees, which I commanded you, I will most certainly tear the kingdom away from you and give it to one of your subordinates. ¹²Nevertheless, for the sake of David your father, I will not do it during your lifetime. I will tear it out of the hand of your son. ¹³Yet I will not tear the whole kingdom from him, but will give him one tribe for the sake of David my servant and for the sake of Jerusalem, which I have chosen."

SOLOMON'S ADVERSARIES

¹⁴Then the LORD raised up against Solomon an adversary, Hadad the Edomite, from the royal line of Edom. ¹⁵Earlier when David was fighting with Edom, Joab the commander of the army, who had gone up to bury the dead, had struck down all the men in Edom. ¹⁶Joab and all the Israelites stayed there for six months, until they had destroyed all the men in Edom. ¹⁷But Hadad, still only a boy, fled to Egypt with some Edomite officials who had served his father. ¹⁸They set out from Midian and went to Paran. Then taking people from Paran with them, they went to Egypt, to Pharaoh king of Egypt, who gave Hadad a house and land and provided him with food.

¹⁹Pharaoh was so pleased with Hadad that he gave him a sister of his own wife, Queen Tahpenes, in marriage. ²⁰The sister of Tahpenes bore him a son named Genubath, whom Tahpenes brought up in the royal palace. There Genubath lived with Pharaoh's own children.

²¹While he was in Egypt, Hadad heard that David rested with his ancestors and that Joab the commander of the army

---

What was Solomon's mistake? (11:1–4)
Solomon disobeyed God's advice by marrying many wives (Deut. 17:17), and he ignored the commandment not to marry pagan women. Despite his wisdom in many areas, Solomon was foolish in the way he disregarded God's laws.

How was David a man whose heart was "fully devoted to the LORD"? (11:4)
Even though David committed many sins, he seemed to always be truly remorseful when he did wrong. In addition, David never forsook the LORD to worship idols. He did not live a perfect life, but his faith in God was constant.

Did Solomon believe in his wives' gods? (11:5–8)
The fact that Solomon built shrines and offered sacrifices to these false gods showed that his heart had turned away from the LORD.

was also dead. Then Hadad said to Pharaoh, "Let me go, that I may return to my own country."

²²"What have you lacked here that you want to go back to your own country?" Pharaoh asked.

"Nothing," Hadad replied, "but do let me go!"

²³And God raised up against Solomon another adversary, Rezon son of Eliada, who had fled from his master, Hadadezer king of Zobah. ²⁴When David destroyed Zobah's army, Rezon gathered a band of men around him and became their leader; they went to Damascus, where they settled and took control. ²⁵Rezon was Israel's adversary as long as Solomon lived, adding to the trouble caused by Hadad. So Rezon ruled in Aram and was hostile toward Israel.

JEROBOAM REBELS AGAINST SOLOMON

²⁶Also, Jeroboam son of Nebat rebelled against the king. He was one of Solomon's officials, an Ephraimite from Zeredah, and his mother was a widow named Zeruah.

²⁷Here is the account of how he rebelled against the king: Solomon had built the terraces[a] and had filled in the gap in the wall of the city of David his father. ²⁸Now Jeroboam was a man of standing, and when Solomon saw how well the young man did his work, he put him in charge of the whole labor force of the tribes of Joseph.

²⁹About that time Jeroboam was going out of Jerusalem, and Ahijah the prophet of Shiloh met him on the way, wearing a new cloak. The two of them were alone out in the country, ³⁰and Ahijah took hold of the new cloak he was wearing and tore it into twelve pieces. ³¹Then he said to Jeroboam, "Take ten pieces for yourself, for this is what the LORD, the God of Israel, says: 'See, I am going to tear the kingdom out of Solomon's hand and give you ten tribes. ³²But for the sake of my servant David and the city of Jerusalem, which I have chosen out of all the tribes of Israel, he will have one tribe. ³³I will do this because they have[b] forsaken me and worshiped Ashtoreth the goddess of the Sidonians, Chemosh the god of the Moabites, and Molek the god of the Ammonites, and have not walked in obedience to me, nor done what is right in my eyes, nor kept my decrees and laws as David, Solomon's father, did.

³⁴"'But I will not take the whole kingdom out of Solomon's hand; I have made him ruler all the days of his life for the sake of David my servant, whom I chose and who obeyed my commands and decrees. ³⁵I will take the kingdom from his son's hands and give you ten tribes. ³⁶I will give one tribe to his son so that David my servant may always have a lamp before me in Jerusalem, the city where I chose to put my Name. ³⁷However, as for you, I will take you, and you will rule over all that your heart desires; you will be king over Israel. ³⁸If you do whatever I command you and walk in obedience to me and do what is right in my eyes by obeying my decrees and commands, as David my servant did, I will be with you. I will build you a dynasty

Did Jeroboam have the right to become king? (11:26)
Yes. He was one of David's descendants and as long as the rulers obeyed the LORD, God promised that the throne of Israel would stay in their family.

What happened to the twelfth tribe? (11:30–32)
Some people think that because the Levites could not inherit land they were not counted. Other people think that Simeon's tribe combined with Judah's territory. The twelfth tribe could also have been Benjamin's, since that tribe had divided loyalties between Israel and Judah.

What was this lamp? (11:36)
God promised David that kings in Jerusalem would always come from his family. The lamp represented God's living presence. Jesus fulfilled this prophecy, so it was called a Messianic promise.

---

[a] 27 Or the Millo   [b] 33 Hebrew; Septuagint, Vulgate and Syriac because he has

as enduring as the one I built for David and will give Israel to you. ³⁹I will humble David's descendants because of this, but not forever.'"

⁴⁰Solomon tried to kill Jeroboam, but Jeroboam fled to Egypt, to Shishak the king, and stayed there until Solomon's death.

SOLOMON'S DEATH

⁴¹As for the other events of Solomon's reign—all he did and the wisdom he displayed—are they not written in the book of the annals of Solomon? ⁴²Solomon reigned in Jerusalem over all Israel forty years. ⁴³Then he rested with his ancestors and was buried in the city of David his father. And Rehoboam his son succeeded him as king.

ISRAEL REBELS AGAINST REHOBOAM

12 Rehoboam went to Shechem, for all Israel had gone there to make him king. ²When Jeroboam son of Nebat heard this (he was still in Egypt, where he had fled from King Solomon), he returned from*ᵃ* Egypt. ³So they sent for Jeroboam, and he and the whole assembly of Israel went to Rehoboam and said to him: ⁴"Your father put a heavy yoke on us, but now lighten the harsh labor and the heavy yoke he put on us, and we will serve you."

⁵Rehoboam answered, "Go away for three days and then come back to me." So the people went away.

⁶Then King Rehoboam consulted the elders who had served his father Solomon during his lifetime. "How would you advise me to answer these people?" he asked.

⁷They replied, "If today you will be a servant to these people and serve them and give them a favorable answer, they will always be your servants."

⁸But Rehoboam rejected the advice the elders gave him and consulted the young men who had grown up with him and were serving him. ⁹He asked them, "What is your advice? How should we answer these people who say to me, 'Lighten the yoke your father put on us'?"

¹⁰The young men who had grown up with him replied, "These people have said to you, 'Your father put a heavy yoke on us, but make our yoke lighter.' Now tell them, 'My little finger is thicker than my father's waist. ¹¹My father laid on you a heavy yoke; I will make it even heavier. My father scourged you with whips; I will scourge you with scorpions.'"

¹²Three days later Jeroboam and all the people returned to Rehoboam, as the king had said, "Come back to me in three days." ¹³The king answered the people harshly. Rejecting the advice given him by the elders, ¹⁴he followed the advice of the young men and said, "My father made your yoke heavy; I will make it even heavier. My father scourged you with whips; I will scourge you with scorpions." ¹⁵So the king did not listen to the people, for this turn of events was from the LORD, to fulfill the word the LORD had spoken to Jeroboam son of Nebat through Ahijah the Shilonite.

ᵃ 2 Or he remained in

What were the annals of Solomon? (11:41)
The author of 1 and 2 Kings based his account on the historical records or chronicles of Solomon. These records may have been lost when Jerusalem was destroyed.

What was the heavy yoke Solomon put on his people? (12:4)
Solomon made his people support him and his large family. Solomon was not a warrior so he didn't have slave labor from conquered enemies. He did make slaves of foreigners, however, and he made Israelites work one month out of every three (5:13–15). Each of the 12 districts was responsible for providing one month's worth of supplies for his family's consumption.

What were scorpions? (12:11)
These were metal-spiked leather lashes. The burden on the people would increase and so would the penalty for not obeying.

The Divided Kingdom (12:16)

Why did Jeroboam make two golden calves? (12:28)
Bull calves symbolized strength. The problem was that these calves were an example of mixing true worship of the Lord with pagan rituals. They were reminiscent of the golden calf the Israelites had made and wrongly worshiped in the desert (Exodus 32:1–4).

Why did Jeroboam give these gods to Israel? (12:28–33)
Jeroboam's motives were political. He wanted to keep the people from going to Jerusalem to worship. If they went to Jerusalem, they might be persuaded to give their allegiance to David's descendants who ruled there.

Why did Jeroboam make priests of people who were not Levites? (12:31)
The Levites sided with Rehoboam and refused to participate in calf worship. The Levites left their lands and cities throughout Israel and returned to Judah and Jerusalem so they could remain faithful to God.

¹⁶When all Israel saw that the king refused to listen to them, they answered the king:

"What share do we have in David,
    what part in Jesse's son?
To your tents, Israel!
    Look after your own house, David!"

So the Israelites went home. ¹⁷But as for the Israelites who were living in the towns of Judah, Rehoboam still ruled over them.

¹⁸King Rehoboam sent out Adoniram,[a] who was in charge of forced labor, but all Israel stoned him to death. King Rehoboam, however, managed to get into his chariot and escape to Jerusalem. ¹⁹So Israel has been in rebellion against the house of David to this day.

²⁰When all the Israelites heard that Jeroboam had returned, they sent and called him to the assembly and made him king over all Israel. Only the tribe of Judah remained loyal to the house of David.

²¹When Rehoboam arrived in Jerusalem, he mustered all Judah and the tribe of Benjamin—a hundred and eighty thousand able young men—to go to war against Israel and to regain the kingdom for Rehoboam son of Solomon. ²²But this word of God came to Shemaiah the man of God: ²³"Say to Rehoboam son of Solomon king of Judah, to all Judah and Benjamin, and to the rest of the people, ²⁴'This is what the LORD says: Do not go up to fight against your brothers, the Israelites. Go home, every one of you, for this is my doing.'" So they obeyed the word of the LORD and went home again, as the LORD had ordered.

GOLDEN CALVES AT BETHEL AND DAN

²⁵Then Jeroboam fortified Shechem in the hill country of Ephraim and lived there. From there he went out and built up Peniel.[b]

²⁶Jeroboam thought to himself, "The kingdom will now likely revert to the house of David. ²⁷If these people go up to offer sacrifices at the temple of the LORD in Jerusalem, they will again give their allegiance to their lord, Rehoboam king of Judah. They will kill me and return to King Rehoboam."

²⁸After seeking advice, the king made two golden calves. He said to the people, "It is too much for you to go up to Jerusalem. Here are your gods, Israel, who brought you up out of Egypt." ²⁹One he set up in Bethel, and the other in Dan. ³⁰And this thing became a sin; the people came to worship the one at Bethel and went as far as Dan to worship the other.[c]

³¹Jeroboam built shrines on high places and appointed priests from all sorts of people, even though they were not Levites. ³²He instituted a festival on the fifteenth day of the eighth month, like the festival held in Judah, and offered sacrifices on the altar. This he did in Bethel, sacrificing to the

^a 18 Some Septuagint manuscripts and Syriac (see also 4:6 and 5:14); Hebrew *Adoram*   ^b 25 Hebrew *Penuel*, a variant of *Peniel*   ^c 30 Probable reading of the original Hebrew text; Masoretic Text *people went to the one as far as Dan*

calves he had made. And at Bethel he also installed priests at the high places he had made. ³³On the fifteenth day of the eighth month, a month of his own choosing, he offered sacrifices on the altar he had built at Bethel. So he instituted the festival for the Israelites and went up to the altar to make offerings.

THE MAN OF GOD FROM JUDAH

13 By the word of the LORD a man of God came from Judah to Bethel, as Jeroboam was standing by the altar to make an offering. ²By the word of the LORD he cried out against the altar: "Altar, altar! This is what the LORD says: 'A son named Josiah will be born to the house of David. On you he will sacrifice the priests of the high places who make offerings here, and human bones will be burned on you.'" ³That same day the man of God gave a sign: "This is the sign the LORD has declared: The altar will be split apart and the ashes on it will be poured out."

⁴When King Jeroboam heard what the man of God cried out against the altar at Bethel, he stretched out his hand from the altar and said, "Seize him!" But the hand he stretched out toward the man shriveled up, so that he could not pull it back. ⁵Also, the altar was split apart and its ashes poured out according to the sign given by the man of God by the word of the LORD.

⁶Then the king said to the man of God, "Intercede with the LORD your God and pray for me that my hand may be restored." So the man of God interceded with the LORD, and the king's hand was restored and became as it was before.

⁷The king said to the man of God, "Come home with me for a meal, and I will give you a gift."

⁸But the man of God answered the king, "Even if you were to give me half your possessions, I would not go with you, nor would I eat bread or drink water here. ⁹For I was commanded by the word of the LORD: 'You must not eat bread or drink water or return by the way you came.'" ¹⁰So he took another road and did not return by the way he had come to Bethel.

¹¹Now there was a certain old prophet living in Bethel, whose sons came and told him all that the man of God had done there that day. They also told their father what he had said to the king. ¹²Their father asked them, "Which way did he go?" And his sons showed him which road the man of God from Judah had taken. ¹³So he said to his sons, "Saddle the donkey for me." And when they had saddled the donkey for him, he mounted it ¹⁴and rode after the man of God. He found him sitting under an oak tree and asked, "Are you the man of God who came from Judah?"

"I am," he replied.

¹⁵So the prophet said to him, "Come home with me and eat."

¹⁶The man of God said, "I cannot turn back and go with you, nor can I eat bread or drink water with you in this place. ¹⁷I have been told by the word of the LORD: 'You must not eat bread or drink water there or return by the way you came.'"

**Who was this prophet?
(13:1–10)**
The Bible does not give the name of this man of God. God sent him from the southern kingdom to Bethel in the northern kingdom possibly to show that even though the kingdom was divided, God did not want separate places of worship.

**Why did the old prophet lie?
(13:18)**
Perhaps he was testing the man
from Judah to see if his message
really was from God. If the man
from Judah disobeyed God's
orders and returned home safely,
then his message was untrue.
But if he died after breaking
God's command, then his message would be confirmed as true.

**Why did the old prophet
mourn the death he had
caused? (13:29–30)**
The old prophet was seeking
truth. When the man from Judah
was killed after disobeying God,
the old prophet realized that the
other man's words were true. He
was sorry for causing the death
of a true prophet of God, and
he was saddened by what would
happen to Jeroboam and Israel.

**Since God had promised
to send judgment on false
priests, why would anyone
be willing to become one?
(13:33)**
Jeroboam's priests wanted
money and power. They did not
fear the prophecy that had been
given against false priests.

¹⁸The old prophet answered, "I too am a prophet, as you
are. And an angel said to me by the word of the LORD: 'Bring
him back with you to your house so that he may eat bread
and drink water.'" (But he was lying to him.) ¹⁹So the man
of God returned with him and ate and drank in his house.

²⁰While they were sitting at the table, the word of the
LORD came to the old prophet who had brought him back.
²¹He cried out to the man of God who had come from Judah, "This is what the LORD says: 'You have defied the word
of the LORD and have not kept the command the LORD your
God gave you. ²²You came back and ate bread and drank
water in the place where he told you not to eat or drink.
Therefore your body will not be buried in the tomb of your
ancestors.'"

²³When the man of God had finished eating and drinking, the prophet who had brought him back saddled his donkey for him. ²⁴As he went on his way, a lion met him on the
road and killed him, and his body was left lying on the road,
with both the donkey and the lion standing beside it. ²⁵Some
people who passed by saw the body lying there, with the lion
standing beside the body, and they went and reported it in
the city where the old prophet lived.

²⁶When the prophet who had brought him back from his
journey heard of it, he said, "It is the man of God who defied
the word of the LORD. The LORD has given him over to the
lion, which has mauled him and killed him, as the word of
the LORD had warned him."

²⁷The prophet said to his sons, "Saddle the donkey for
me," and they did so. ²⁸Then he went out and found the body
lying on the road, with the donkey and the lion standing beside it. The lion had neither eaten the body nor mauled the
donkey. ²⁹So the prophet picked up the body of the man of
God, laid it on the donkey, and brought it back to his own
city to mourn for him and bury him. ³⁰Then he laid the body
in his own tomb, and they mourned over him and said, "Alas,
my brother!"

³¹After burying him, he said to his sons, "When I die,
bury me in the grave where the man of God is buried; lay my
bones beside his bones. ³²For the message he declared by the
word of the LORD against the altar in Bethel and against all
the shrines on the high places in the towns of Samaria will
certainly come true."

³³Even after this, Jeroboam did not change his evil ways,
but once more appointed priests for the high places from
all sorts of people. Anyone who wanted to become a priest
he consecrated for the high places. ³⁴This was the sin of the
house of Jeroboam that led to its downfall and to its destruction from the face of the earth.

AHIJAH'S PROPHECY AGAINST JEROBOAM

14 At that time Abijah son of Jeroboam became ill, ²and
Jeroboam said to his wife, "Go, disguise yourself, so
you won't be recognized as the wife of Jeroboam. Then go to
Shiloh. Ahijah the prophet is there—the one who told me
I would be king over this people. ³Take ten loaves of bread

with you, some cakes and a jar of honey, and go to him. He will tell you what will happen to the boy." [4]So Jeroboam's wife did what he said and went to Ahijah's house in Shiloh.

Now Ahijah could not see; his sight was gone because of his age. [5]But the LORD had told Ahijah, "Jeroboam's wife is coming to ask you about her son, for he is ill, and you are to give her such and such an answer. When she arrives, she will pretend to be someone else."

[6]So when Ahijah heard the sound of her footsteps at the door, he said, "Come in, wife of Jeroboam. Why this pretense? I have been sent to you with bad news. [7]Go, tell Jeroboam that this is what the LORD, the God of Israel, says: 'I raised you up from among the people and appointed you ruler over my people Israel. [8]I tore the kingdom away from the house of David and gave it to you, but you have not been like my servant David, who kept my commands and followed me with all his heart, doing only what was right in my eyes. [9]You have done more evil than all who lived before you. You have made for yourself other gods, idols made of metal; you have aroused my anger and turned your back on me.

[10]"'Because of this, I am going to bring disaster on the house of Jeroboam. I will cut off from Jeroboam every last male in Israel—slave or free.[a] I will burn up the house of Jeroboam as one burns dung, until it is all gone. [11]Dogs will eat those belonging to Jeroboam who die in the city, and the birds will feed on those who die in the country. The LORD has spoken!'

[12]"As for you, go back home. When you set foot in your city, the boy will die. [13]All Israel will mourn for him and bury him. He is the only one belonging to Jeroboam who will be buried, because he is the only one in the house of Jeroboam in whom the LORD, the God of Israel, has found anything good.

[14]"The LORD will raise up for himself a king over Israel who will cut off the family of Jeroboam. Even now this is beginning to happen.[b] [15]And the LORD will strike Israel, so that it will be like a reed swaying in the water. He will uproot Israel from this good land that he gave to their ancestors and scatter them beyond the Euphrates River, because they aroused the LORD's anger by making Asherah poles.[c] [16]And he will give Israel up because of the sins Jeroboam has committed and has caused Israel to commit."

[17]Then Jeroboam's wife got up and left and went to Tirzah. As soon as she stepped over the threshold of the house, the boy died. [18]They buried him, and all Israel mourned for him, as the LORD had said through his servant the prophet Ahijah.

[19]The other events of Jeroboam's reign, his wars and how he ruled, are written in the book of the annals of the kings of Israel. [20]He reigned for twenty-two years and then rested with his ancestors. And Nadab his son succeeded him as king.

How could Ahijah say that David did "only what was right"? (14:8)
David had sinned, and it was widely known. But David had never turned away from God, and he had been a godly ruler. On the other hand, Jeroboam did not obey the requirements God had given him through Ahijah (11:38).

Why did Jeroboam's wife go home even though it meant that her son would die? (14:12, 17)
Ahijah's prophecy did not cause the boy's death; it merely foretold it. The illness was serious and there was nothing the mother could do to help.

---

[a] 10 Or Israel—every ruler or leader   [b] 14 The meaning of the Hebrew for this sentence is uncertain.   [c] 15 That is, wooden symbols of the goddess Asherah; here and elsewhere in 1 Kings

REHOBOAM KING OF JUDAH

²¹Rehoboam son of Solomon was king in Judah. He was forty-one years old when he became king, and he reigned seventeen years in Jerusalem, the city the LORD had chosen out of all the tribes of Israel in which to put his Name. His mother's name was Naamah; she was an Ammonite.

²²Judah did evil in the eyes of the LORD. By the sins they committed they stirred up his jealous anger more than those who were before them had done. ²³They also set up for themselves high places, sacred stones and Asherah poles on every high hill and under every spreading tree. ²⁴There were even male shrine prostitutes in the land; the people engaged in all the detestable practices of the nations the LORD had driven out before the Israelites.

²⁵In the fifth year of King Rehoboam, Shishak king of Egypt attacked Jerusalem. ²⁶He carried off the treasures of the temple of the LORD and the treasures of the royal palace. He took everything, including all the gold shields Solomon had made. ²⁷So King Rehoboam made bronze shields to replace them and assigned these to the commanders of the guard on duty at the entrance to the royal palace. ²⁸Whenever the king went to the LORD's temple, the guards bore the shields, and afterward they returned them to the guardroom.

²⁹As for the other events of Rehoboam's reign, and all he did, are they not written in the book of the annals of the kings of Judah? ³⁰There was continual warfare between Rehoboam and Jeroboam. ³¹And Rehoboam rested with his ancestors and was buried with them in the City of David. His mother's name was Naamah; she was an Ammonite. And Abijah*ᵃ* his son succeeded him as king.

ABIJAH KING OF JUDAH

15 In the eighteenth year of the reign of Jeroboam son of Nebat, Abijah*ᵇ* became king of Judah, ²and he reigned in Jerusalem three years. His mother's name was Maakah daughter of Abishalom.*ᶜ*

³He committed all the sins his father had done before him; his heart was not fully devoted to the LORD his God, as the heart of David his forefather had been. ⁴Nevertheless, for David's sake the LORD his God gave him a lamp in Jerusalem by raising up a son to succeed him and by making Jerusalem strong. ⁵For David had done what was right in the eyes of the LORD and had not failed to keep any of the LORD's commands all the days of his life — except in the case of Uriah the Hittite.

⁶There was war between Abijah*ᵈ* and Jeroboam throughout Abijah's lifetime. ⁷As for the other events of Abijah's reign, and all he did, are they not written in the book of the annals of the kings of Judah? There was war between Abijah and Jeroboam. ⁸And Abijah rested with his ancestors and

> **What were sacred stones? (14:23)**
> These were stone pillars with religious significance that were placed next to altars. It is likely that the pillars were intended to represent the pagan god being worshiped. The use of such pillars was common among the Canaanites, but the Israelites had been forbidden to use them.

ᵃ 31 Some Hebrew manuscripts and Septuagint (see also 2 Chron. 12:16); most Hebrew manuscripts *Abijam*   *ᵇ 1* Some Hebrew manuscripts and Septuagint (see also 2 Chron. 12:16); most Hebrew manuscripts *Abijam*; also in verses 7 and 8   *ᶜ 2* A variant of *Absalom*; also in verse 10   *ᵈ 6* Some Hebrew manuscripts and Syriac *Abijam* (that is, Abijah); most Hebrew manuscripts *Rehoboam*

was buried in the City of David. And Asa his son succeeded him as king.

ASA KING OF JUDAH

[9] In the twentieth year of Jeroboam king of Israel, Asa became king of Judah, [10] and he reigned in Jerusalem forty-one years. His grandmother's name was Maakah daughter of Abishalom.

[11] Asa did what was right in the eyes of the LORD, as his father David had done. [12] He expelled the male shrine prostitutes from the land and got rid of all the idols his ancestors had made. [13] He even deposed his grandmother Maakah from her position as queen mother, because she had made a repulsive image for the worship of Asherah. Asa cut it down and burned it in the Kidron Valley. [14] Although he did not remove the high places, Asa's heart was fully committed to the LORD all his life. [15] He brought into the temple of the LORD the silver and gold and the articles that he and his father had dedicated.

[16] There was war between Asa and Baasha king of Israel throughout their reigns. [17] Baasha king of Israel went up against Judah and fortified Ramah to prevent anyone from leaving or entering the territory of Asa king of Judah.

[18] Asa then took all the silver and gold that was left in the treasuries of the LORD's temple and of his own palace. He entrusted it to his officials and sent them to Ben-Hadad son of Tabrimmon, the son of Hezion, the king of Aram, who was ruling in Damascus. [19] "Let there be a treaty between me and you," he said, "as there was between my father and your father. See, I am sending you a gift of silver and gold. Now break your treaty with Baasha king of Israel so he will withdraw from me."

[20] Ben-Hadad agreed with King Asa and sent the commanders of his forces against the towns of Israel. He conquered Ijon, Dan, Abel Beth Maakah and all Kinnereth in addition to Naphtali. [21] When Baasha heard this, he stopped building Ramah and withdrew to Tirzah. [22] Then King Asa issued an order to all Judah—no one was exempt—and they carried away from Ramah the stones and timber Baasha had been using there. With them King Asa built up Geba in Benjamin, and also Mizpah.

[23] As for all the other events of Asa's reign, all his achievements, all he did and the cities he built, are they not written in the book of the annals of the kings of Judah? In his old age, however, his feet became diseased. [24] Then Asa rested with his ancestors and was buried with them in the city of his father David. And Jehoshaphat his son succeeded him as king.

NADAB KING OF ISRAEL

[25] Nadab son of Jeroboam became king of Israel in the second year of Asa king of Judah, and he reigned over Israel two years. [26] He did evil in the eyes of the LORD, following the ways of his father and committing the same sin his father had caused Israel to commit.

Why did a good king like Asa send temple treasure to a pagan king? (15:18–19) Asa sent the temple treasure to Ben-Hadad, ruler of Aram in hopes of forming an alliance with Aram. This might stave off an attack by Baasha of Ramah. Baasha threatened to cut off Jerusalem's trade routes and surround the capital. (See 2 Chron. 16:7–10).

Was this Ahijah the same person as the prophet Ahijah who lived in Shiloh? (15:27–29)
Probably not. This is a fairly popular name in the Bible. Three people in the Bible were named Ahijah: the priest under Saul (1 Samuel 14:3), the prophet of Shiloh (11:29), and the father of Baasha, king of Israel (verse 33).

Why would God use an evil man like Baasha to accomplish his purposes? (15:34)
God can do anything, including turning evil intended for selfish gain into a good deed. God used Baasha to punish Jeroboam's family.

Why did God punish Baasha? (16:7)
Baasha's violence accomplished God's purposes, but that action did not excuse him from punishment. God held him accountable for his evil ways. Baasha's intent behind wiping out Jeroboam's clan was to increase his power, not to honor God.

How did Elah fail to live up to his responsibilities? (16:9)
Elah was at someone's house getting drunk while the army was laying siege to Gibbethon (verse 15). He clearly had a poor understanding of his responsibility as king during a battle.

²⁷ Baasha son of Ahijah from the tribe of Issachar plotted against him, and he struck him down at Gibbethon, a Philistine town, while Nadab and all Israel were besieging it. ²⁸ Baasha killed Nadab in the third year of Asa king of Judah and succeeded him as king.

²⁹ As soon as he began to reign, he killed Jeroboam's whole family. He did not leave Jeroboam anyone that breathed, but destroyed them all, according to the word of the LORD given through his servant Ahijah the Shilonite. ³⁰ This happened because of the sins Jeroboam had committed and had caused Israel to commit, and because he aroused the anger of the LORD, the God of Israel.

³¹ As for the other events of Nadab's reign, and all he did, are they not written in the book of the annals of the kings of Israel? ³² There was war between Asa and Baasha king of Israel throughout their reigns.

BAASHA KING OF ISRAEL

³³ In the third year of Asa king of Judah, Baasha son of Ahijah became king of all Israel in Tirzah, and he reigned twenty-four years. ³⁴ He did evil in the eyes of the LORD, following the ways of Jeroboam and committing the same sin Jeroboam had caused Israel to commit.

16 Then the word of the LORD came to Jehu son of Hanani concerning Baasha: ² "I lifted you up from the dust and appointed you ruler over my people Israel, but you followed the ways of Jeroboam and caused my people Israel to sin and to arouse my anger by their sins. ³ So I am about to wipe out Baasha and his house, and I will make your house like that of Jeroboam son of Nebat. ⁴ Dogs will eat those belonging to Baasha who die in the city, and birds will feed on those who die in the country."

⁵ As for the other events of Baasha's reign, what he did and his achievements, are they not written in the book of the annals of the kings of Israel? ⁶ Baasha rested with his ancestors and was buried in Tirzah. And Elah his son succeeded him as king.

⁷ Moreover, the word of the LORD came through the prophet Jehu son of Hanani to Baasha and his house, because of all the evil he had done in the eyes of the LORD, arousing his anger by the things he did, becoming like the house of Jeroboam—and also because he destroyed it.

ELAH KING OF ISRAEL

⁸ In the twenty-sixth year of Asa king of Judah, Elah son of Baasha became king of Israel, and he reigned in Tirzah two years.

⁹ Zimri, one of his officials, who had command of half his chariots, plotted against him. Elah was in Tirzah at the time, getting drunk in the home of Arza, the palace administrator at Tirzah. ¹⁰ Zimri came in, struck him down and killed him in the twenty-seventh year of Asa king of Judah. Then he succeeded him as king.

¹¹ As soon as he began to reign and was seated on the throne, he killed off Baasha's whole family. He did not spare

a single male, whether relative or friend. [12] So Zimri destroyed the whole family of Baasha, in accordance with the word of the LORD spoken against Baasha through the prophet Jehu— [13] because of all the sins Baasha and his son Elah had committed and had caused Israel to commit, so that they aroused the anger of the LORD, the God of Israel, by their worthless idols.

[14] As for the other events of Elah's reign, and all he did, are they not written in the book of the annals of the kings of Israel?

ZIMRI KING OF ISRAEL

[15] In the twenty-seventh year of Asa king of Judah, Zimri reigned in Tirzah seven days. The army was encamped near Gibbethon, a Philistine town. [16] When the Israelites in the camp heard that Zimri had plotted against the king and murdered him, they proclaimed Omri, the commander of the army, king over Israel that very day there in the camp. [17] Then Omri and all the Israelites with him withdrew from Gibbethon and laid siege to Tirzah. [18] When Zimri saw that the city was taken, he went into the citadel of the royal palace and set the palace on fire around him. So he died, [19] because of the sins he had committed, doing evil in the eyes of the LORD and following the ways of Jeroboam and committing the same sin Jeroboam had caused Israel to commit.

[20] As for the other events of Zimri's reign, and the rebellion he carried out, are they not written in the book of the annals of the kings of Israel?

OMRI KING OF ISRAEL

[21] Then the people of Israel were split into two factions; half supported Tibni son of Ginath for king, and the other half supported Omri. [22] But Omri's followers proved stronger than those of Tibni son of Ginath. So Tibni died and Omri became king.

[23] In the thirty-first year of Asa king of Judah, Omri became king of Israel, and he reigned twelve years, six of them in Tirzah. [24] He bought the hill of Samaria from Shemer for two talents[a] of silver and built a city on the hill, calling it Samaria, after Shemer, the name of the former owner of the hill.

[25] But Omri did evil in the eyes of the LORD and sinned more than all those before him. [26] He followed completely the ways of Jeroboam son of Nebat, committing the same sin Jeroboam had caused Israel to commit, so that they aroused the anger of the LORD, the God of Israel, by their worthless idols.

[27] As for the other events of Omri's reign, what he did and the things he achieved, are they not written in the book of the annals of the kings of Israel? [28] Omri rested with his ancestors and was buried in Samaria. And Ahab his son succeeded him as king.

AHAB BECOMES KING OF ISRAEL

[29] In the thirty-eighth year of Asa king of Judah, Ahab son of Omri became king of Israel, and he reigned in Samaria

[a] 24 That is, about 150 pounds or about 68 kilograms

How evil was Ahab? (16:30–33)

Omri sinned more than all the kings before him (verse 25). His son Ahab was even worse, according to verse 30. He married a pagan woman and began to worship Baal. He introduced Baal worship to the northern kingdom by constructing a temple of Baal in Samaria. He also erected an Asherah pole.

What were Jeroboam's sins? (16:31)

Jeroboam had two main sins. He led the people to desert the one prescribed place of worship, the temple in Jerusalem, and he caused them to worship the LORD in the form of idols.

Who was Baal? (16:32)

Baal was the most well known of the Canaanite gods. His name means *master* or *lord*. Baal was a fertility god who was considered responsible for pollinating crops, increasing flocks, and adding children to the community.

Why did Elijah need to hide? (17:3)

God told him to. Prophets were supposed to obey God without asking why. The prophet of God had plenty to eat and drink, while the rest of the people were starving and thirsty. These were the consequences of abandoning God.

Kerith Ravine and Zarephath (17:3,9)

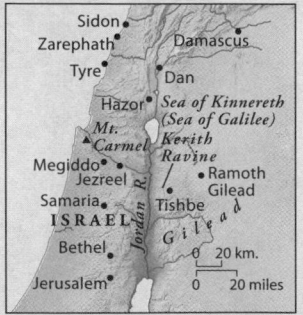

over Israel twenty-two years. ³⁰Ahab son of Omri did more evil in the eyes of the LORD than any of those before him. ³¹He not only considered it trivial to commit the sins of Jeroboam son of Nebat, but he also married Jezebel daughter of Ethbaal king of the Sidonians, and began to serve Baal and worship him. ³²He set up an altar for Baal in the temple of Baal that he built in Samaria. ³³Ahab also made an Asherah pole and did more to arouse the anger of the LORD, the God of Israel, than did all the kings of Israel before him.

³⁴In Ahab's time, Hiel of Bethel rebuilt Jericho. He laid its foundations at the cost of his firstborn son Abiram, and he set up its gates at the cost of his youngest son Segub, in accordance with the word of the LORD spoken by Joshua son of Nun.

ELIJAH ANNOUNCES A GREAT DROUGHT

17 Now Elijah the Tishbite, from Tishbe*ᵃ* in Gilead, said to Ahab, "As the LORD, the God of Israel, lives, whom I serve, there will be neither dew nor rain in the next few years except at my word."

ELIJAH FED BY RAVENS

²Then the word of the LORD came to Elijah: ³"Leave here, turn eastward and hide in the Kerith Ravine, east of the Jordan. ⁴You will drink from the brook, and I have directed the ravens to supply you with food there."

⁵So he did what the LORD had told him. He went to the Kerith Ravine, east of the Jordan, and stayed there. ⁶The ravens brought him bread and meat in the morning and bread and meat in the evening, and he drank from the brook.

ELIJAH AND THE WIDOW AT ZAREPHATH

⁷Some time later the brook dried up because there had been no rain in the land. ⁸Then the word of the LORD came to him: ⁹"Go at once to Zarephath in the region of Sidon and stay there. I have directed a widow there to supply you with food." ¹⁰So he went to Zarephath. When he came to the town gate, a widow was there gathering sticks. He called to her and asked, "Would you bring me a little water in a jar so I may have a drink?" ¹¹As she was going to get it, he called, "And bring me, please, a piece of bread."

¹²"As surely as the LORD your God lives," she replied, "I don't have any bread—only a handful of flour in a jar and a little olive oil in a jug. I am gathering a few sticks to take home and make a meal for myself and my son, that we may eat it—and die."

¹³Elijah said to her, "Don't be afraid. Go home and do as you have said. But first make a small loaf of bread for me from what you have and bring it to me, and then make something for yourself and your son. ¹⁴For this is what the LORD, the God of Israel, says: 'The jar of flour will not be used up and the jug of oil will not run dry until the day the LORD sends rain on the land.'"

¹⁵She went away and did as Elijah had told her. So there

ᵃ 1 Or Tishbite, of the settlers

was food every day for Elijah and for the woman and her family. ¹⁶For the jar of flour was not used up and the jug of oil did not run dry, in keeping with the word of the LORD spoken by Elijah.

¹⁷Some time later the son of the woman who owned the house became ill. He grew worse and worse, and finally stopped breathing. ¹⁸She said to Elijah, "What do you have against me, man of God? Did you come to remind me of my sin and kill my son?"

¹⁹"Give me your son," Elijah replied. He took him from her arms, carried him to the upper room where he was staying, and laid him on his bed. ²⁰Then he cried out to the LORD, "LORD my God, have you brought tragedy even on this widow I am staying with, by causing her son to die?" ²¹Then he stretched himself out on the boy three times and cried out to the LORD, "LORD my God, let this boy's life return to him!"

²²The LORD heard Elijah's cry, and the boy's life returned to him, and he lived. ²³Elijah picked up the child and carried him down from the room into the house. He gave him to his mother and said, "Look, your son is alive!"

²⁴Then the woman said to Elijah, "Now I know that you are a man of God and that the word of the LORD from your mouth is the truth."

ELIJAH AND OBADIAH

18 After a long time, in the third year, the word of the LORD came to Elijah: "Go and present yourself to Ahab, and I will send rain on the land." ²So Elijah went to present himself to Ahab.

Now the famine was severe in Samaria, ³and Ahab had summoned Obadiah, his palace administrator. (Obadiah was a devout believer in the LORD. ⁴While Jezebel was killing off the LORD's prophets, Obadiah had taken a hundred prophets and hidden them in two caves, fifty in each, and had supplied them with food and water.) ⁵Ahab had said to Obadiah, "Go through the land to all the springs and valleys. Maybe we can find some grass to keep the horses and mules alive so we will not have to kill any of our animals." ⁶So they divided the land they were to cover, Ahab going in one direction and Obadiah in another.

⁷As Obadiah was walking along, Elijah met him. Obadiah recognized him, bowed down to the ground, and said, "Is it really you, my lord Elijah?"

⁸"Yes," he replied. "Go tell your master, 'Elijah is here.'"

⁹"What have I done wrong," asked Obadiah, "that you are handing your servant over to Ahab to be put to death? ¹⁰As surely as the LORD your God lives, there is not a nation or kingdom where my master has not sent someone to look for you. And whenever a nation or kingdom claimed you were not there, he made them swear they could not find you. ¹¹But now you tell me to go to my master and say, 'Elijah is here.' ¹²I don't know where the Spirit of the LORD may carry you when I leave you. If I go and tell Ahab and he doesn't find you, he will kill me. Yet I your servant have worshiped the LORD since

Why did God send Elijah to a foreign woman? (17:9)
God blessed this woman because of her faith and because she shared her food with God's prophet. Once again, this was a contrast to the people of Israel who had turned away from God and were starving.

Why did the widow blame Elijah for her son's illness and death? (17:18–20)
She knew that Elijah's presence in her home had brought supernatural power because of the always-full jar of flour and jug of oil. She may have thought that Elijah brought God's punishment for some unnamed sin she had committed. When Elijah brought the boy back to life, the woman expressed faith in God.

How did Obadiah hide and feed 100 prophets during a famine? (18:4)
Obadiah had access to the palace's food and water reserves because of his position as administrator of the palace. He may have taken food from the reserves to give to the prophets. Or God may have taken the food and water they already possessed and multiplied it so they had enough, as he had done for the widow in Zarephath.

Why didn't Obadiah trust Elijah? (18:12)
King Ahab had searched for Elijah for nearly three years without success. Obadiah thought about telling the king he had seen Elijah. But if Elijah disappeared before Ahab could capture him, Ahab might kill Obadiah out of anger.

my youth. [13] Haven't you heard, my lord, what I did while Jezebel was killing the prophets of the LORD? I hid a hundred of the LORD's prophets in two caves, fifty in each, and supplied them with food and water. [14] And now you tell me to go to my master and say, 'Elijah is here.' He will kill me!"

[15] Elijah said, "As the LORD Almighty lives, whom I serve, I will surely present myself to Ahab today."

ELIJAH ON MOUNT CARMEL

[16] So Obadiah went to meet Ahab and told him, and Ahab went to meet Elijah. [17] When he saw Elijah, he said to him, "Is that you, you troubler of Israel?"

[18] "I have not made trouble for Israel," Elijah replied. "But you and your father's family have. You have abandoned the LORD's commands and have followed the Baals. [19] Now summon the people from all over Israel to meet me on Mount Carmel. And bring the four hundred and fifty prophets of Baal and the four hundred prophets of Asherah, who eat at Jezebel's table."

[20] So Ahab sent word throughout all Israel and assembled the prophets on Mount Carmel. [21] Elijah went before the people and said, "How long will you waver between two opinions? If the LORD is God, follow him; but if Baal is God, follow him."

But the people said nothing.

[22] Then Elijah said to them, "I am the only one of the LORD's prophets left, but Baal has four hundred and fifty prophets. [23] Get two bulls for us. Let Baal's prophets choose one for themselves, and let them cut it into pieces and put it on the wood but not set fire to it. I will prepare the other bull and put it on the wood but not set fire to it. [24] Then you call on the name of your god, and I will call on the name of the LORD. The god who answers by fire—he is God."

Then all the people said, "What you say is good."

[25] Elijah said to the prophets of Baal, "Choose one of the bulls and prepare it first, since there are so many of you. Call on the name of your god, but do not light the fire." [26] So they took the bull given them and prepared it.

Then they called on the name of Baal from morning till noon. "Baal, answer us!" they shouted. But there was no response; no one answered. And they danced around the altar they had made.

[27] At noon Elijah began to taunt them. "Shout louder!" he said. "Surely he is a god! Perhaps he is deep in thought, or busy, or traveling. Maybe he is sleeping and must be awakened." [28] So they shouted louder and slashed themselves with swords and spears, as was their custom, until their blood flowed. [29] Midday passed, and they continued their frantic prophesying until the time for the evening sacrifice. But there was no response, no one answered, no one paid attention.

[30] Then Elijah said to all the people, "Come here to me." They came to him, and he repaired the altar of the LORD, which had been torn down. [31] Elijah took twelve stones, one for each of the tribes descended from Jacob, to whom the word of the LORD had come, saying, "Your name shall be Israel."

Why didn't Ahab capture Elijah? (18:17)
Ahab's first interest was solving the problem of the drought. He was desperate for help and would listen to anyone who might be able to help. In addition, God held Ahab's murderous moods in check because God wanted Elijah to call Israel back to him.

Why did the prophets of Baal cut themselves? (18:28)
As Ahab grew impatient, the prophets grew even more frenzied. By cutting themselves, they hoped to convince the gods that they were sincere and deserving of an answer. Although pagans sometimes practiced self-mutilation as part of their rituals, the Israelites were forbidden from cutting themselves (see Leviticus 19:28).

³²With the stones he built an altar in the name of the LORD, and he dug a trench around it large enough to hold two seahs*a* of seed. ³³He arranged the wood, cut the bull into pieces and laid it on the wood. Then he said to them, "Fill four large jars with water and pour it on the offering and on the wood."

³⁴"Do it again," he said, and they did it again.

"Do it a third time," he ordered, and they did it the third time. ³⁵The water ran down around the altar and even filled the trench.

³⁶At the time of sacrifice, the prophet Elijah stepped forward and prayed: "LORD, the God of Abraham, Isaac and Israel, let it be known today that you are God in Israel and that I am your servant and have done all these things at your command. ³⁷Answer me, LORD, answer me, so these people will know that you, LORD, are God, and that you are turning their hearts back again."

³⁸Then the fire of the LORD fell and burned up the sacrifice, the wood, the stones and the soil, and also licked up the water in the trench.

³⁹When all the people saw this, they fell prostrate and cried, "The LORD—he is God! The LORD—he is God!"

⁴⁰Then Elijah commanded them, "Seize the prophets of Baal. Don't let anyone get away!" They seized them, and Elijah had them brought down to the Kishon Valley and slaughtered there.

⁴¹And Elijah said to Ahab, "Go, eat and drink, for there is the sound of a heavy rain." ⁴²So Ahab went off to eat and drink, but Elijah climbed to the top of Carmel, bent down to the ground and put his face between his knees.

⁴³"Go and look toward the sea," he told his servant. And he went up and looked.

"There is nothing there," he said.

Seven times Elijah said, "Go back."

⁴⁴The seventh time the servant reported, "A cloud as small as a man's hand is rising from the sea."

So Elijah said, "Go and tell Ahab, 'Hitch up your chariot and go down before the rain stops you.'"

⁴⁵Meanwhile, the sky grew black with clouds, the wind rose, a heavy rain started falling and Ahab rode off to Jezreel. ⁴⁶The power of the LORD came on Elijah and, tucking his cloak into his belt, he ran ahead of Ahab all the way to Jezreel.

ELIJAH FLEES TO HOREB

19 Now Ahab told Jezebel everything Elijah had done and how he had killed all the prophets with the sword. ²So Jezebel sent a messenger to Elijah to say, "May the gods deal with me, be it ever so severely, if by this time tomorrow I do not make your life like that of one of them."

³Elijah was afraid*b* and ran for his life. When he came to Beersheba in Judah, he left his servant there, ⁴while he himself went a day's journey into the wilderness. He came to a broom bush, sat down under it and prayed that he might die. "I have had enough, LORD," he said. "Take my life; I am

---

Why did Elijah pour so much water on his altar? (18:33–34)
By using water that Baal, the fertility god, had failed to provide during the drought, Elijah was making a point about Baal's lack of power. Also, setting a water-soaked altar on fire would require a miracle, and that would show God's power.

How was it possible for Elijah to outrun a chariot? (18:46)
Elijah was given extraordinary strength by God. The scene of Elijah running, followed by Ahab in his chariot, followed by God's thundercloud would have been a dramatic invitation for the people to turn back to the LORD.

What is a broom bush? (19:4)
The broom bush is a low, bushy desert shrub. Sometimes this shrub grows large enough to offer some shade.

---

a 32 That is, probably about 24 pounds or about 11 kilograms
b 3 Or *Elijah saw*

no better than my ancestors." [5]Then he lay down under the bush and fell asleep.

All at once an angel touched him and said, "Get up and eat." [6]He looked around, and there by his head was some bread baked over hot coals, and a jar of water. He ate and drank and then lay down again.

[7]The angel of the Lord came back a second time and touched him and said, "Get up and eat, for the journey is too much for you." [8]So he got up and ate and drank. Strengthened by that food, he traveled forty days and forty nights until he reached Horeb, the mountain of God. [9]There he went into a cave and spent the night.

THE LORD APPEARS TO ELIJAH

And the word of the Lord came to him: "What are you doing here, Elijah?"

[10]He replied, "I have been very zealous for the Lord God Almighty. The Israelites have rejected your covenant, torn down your altars, and put your prophets to death with the sword. I am the only one left, and now they are trying to kill me too."

[11]The Lord said, "Go out and stand on the mountain in the presence of the Lord, for the Lord is about to pass by."

Then a great and powerful wind tore the mountains apart and shattered the rocks before the Lord, but the Lord was not in the wind. After the wind there was an earthquake, but the Lord was not in the earthquake. [12]After the earthquake came a fire, but the Lord was not in the fire. And after the fire came a gentle whisper. [13]When Elijah heard it, he pulled his cloak over his face and went out and stood at the mouth of the cave.

Then a voice said to him, "What are you doing here, Elijah?"

[14]He replied, "I have been very zealous for the Lord God Almighty. The Israelites have rejected your covenant, torn down your altars, and put your prophets to death with the sword. I am the only one left, and now they are trying to kill me too."

[15]The Lord said to him, "Go back the way you came, and go to the Desert of Damascus. When you get there, anoint Hazael king over Aram. [16]Also, anoint Jehu son of Nimshi

Why wasn't God in the wind, earthquake, or fire? (19:11–13)
Sometimes God showed himself in those ways. But this time he revealed himself in something common and not all that spectacular. In a gentle whisper, God made his will perfectly clear to Elijah.

If I'm depressed, does that mean that I don't have enough faith?
1 KINGS 19

Many of the major figures in the Bible experienced sadness or depression. Elijah, Job, Jonah, David, and many others were at one time or another overwhelmed with the problems that they faced, and they even wondered if God was still present. The Psalms include many examples of believers experiencing great sadness. For example Psalm 42:3 says, "My tears have been my food day and night, while people say to me all day long, 'Where is your God?'"

In life there are many factors that can make us feel overwhelmingly sad or depressed. That is not a sign of spiritual weakness or lack of faith. Often it is a combination of difficult circumstances along with chemical reactions in the brain. Clearly when we feel depressed, we should seek help through prayer, but also by seeking advice from counselors and pastors, and by seeking medical help. Today there are many ways to treat depression, which is a medical condition rather than a lack of faith.

king over Israel, and anoint Elisha son of Shaphat from Abel Meholah to succeed you as prophet. [17] Jehu will put to death any who escape the sword of Hazael, and Elisha will put to death any who escape the sword of Jehu. [18] Yet I reserve seven thousand in Israel—all whose knees have not bowed down to Baal and whose mouths have not kissed him."

THE CALL OF ELISHA

[19] So Elijah went from there and found Elisha son of Shaphat. He was plowing with twelve yoke of oxen, and he himself was driving the twelfth pair. Elijah went up to him and threw his cloak around him. [20] Elisha then left his oxen and ran after Elijah. "Let me kiss my father and mother goodbye," he said, "and then I will come with you."

"Go back," Elijah replied. "What have I done to you?"

[21] So Elisha left him and went back. He took his yoke of oxen and slaughtered them. He burned the plowing equipment to cook the meat and gave it to the people, and they ate. Then he set out to follow Elijah and became his servant.

BEN-HADAD ATTACKS SAMARIA

20 Now Ben-Hadad king of Aram mustered his entire army. Accompanied by thirty-two kings with their horses and chariots, he went up and besieged Samaria and attacked it. [2] He sent messengers into the city to Ahab king of Israel, saying, "This is what Ben-Hadad says: [3] 'Your silver and gold are mine, and the best of your wives and children are mine.'"

[4] The king of Israel answered, "Just as you say, my lord the king. I and all I have are yours."

[5] The messengers came again and said, "This is what Ben-Hadad says: 'I sent to demand your silver and gold, your wives and your children. [6] But about this time tomorrow I am going to send my officials to search your palace and the houses of your officials. They will seize everything you value and carry it away.'"

[7] The king of Israel summoned all the elders of the land and said to them, "See how this man is looking for trouble! When he sent for my wives and my children, my silver and my gold, I did not refuse him."

[8] The elders and the people all answered, "Don't listen to him or agree to his demands."

[9] So he replied to Ben-Hadad's messengers, "Tell my lord the king, 'Your servant will do all you demanded the first time, but this demand I cannot meet.'" They left and took the answer back to Ben-Hadad.

[10] Then Ben-Hadad sent another message to Ahab: "May the gods deal with me, be it ever so severely, if enough dust remains in Samaria to give each of my men a handful."

[11] The king of Israel answered, "Tell him: 'One who puts on his armor should not boast like one who takes it off.'"

[12] Ben-Hadad heard this message while he and the kings were drinking in their tents,[a] and he ordered his men: "Prepare to attack." So they prepared to attack the city.

[a] 12 Or in Sukkoth; also in verse 16

How could Elisha plow with 12 yoke of oxen? (19:19)
Elisha was actually plowing with the last pair of oxen. Farming was often a community activity, and in this case 11 others were helping to plow the field, each with a yoke of oxen.

Why did Elijah throw his cloak on Elisha? (19:19)
A cloak of animal hair was generally recognized as a prophet's clothing. Elisha was given a new identity as one of God's servants when Elijah laid his cloak upon him. This act showed that Elijah chose Elisha to succeed him.

Why was Ahab unwilling to meet Ben-Hadad's second demand? (20:9)
His first demands were accepted by Ahab as a payoff to a stronger army when there was little hope of a military victory. This would result in the end of the siege, spare Ahab's life, and avoid the plundering of the city. In his second demand, Ben-Hadad required the surrender of the city. Ahab knew he could never satisfy the demands, so he resisted.

What did Ahab mean about putting on and taking off armor? (20:11)
This was similar to the saying, "Don't count your chickens before they hatch."

AHAB DEFEATS BEN-HADAD

[13] Meanwhile a prophet came to Ahab king of Israel and announced, "This is what the LORD says: 'Do you see this vast army? I will give it into your hand today, and then you will know that I am the LORD.'"

[14] "But who will do this?" asked Ahab.

The prophet replied, "This is what the LORD says: 'The junior officers under the provincial commanders will do it.'"

"And who will start the battle?" he asked.

The prophet answered, "You will."

[15] So Ahab summoned the 232 junior officers under the provincial commanders. Then he assembled the rest of the Israelites, 7,000 in all. [16] They set out at noon while Ben-Hadad and the 32 kings allied with him were in their tents getting drunk. [17] The junior officers under the provincial commanders went out first.

Now Ben-Hadad had dispatched scouts, who reported, "Men are advancing from Samaria."

[18] He said, "If they have come out for peace, take them alive; if they have come out for war, take them alive."

[19] The junior officers under the provincial commanders marched out of the city with the army behind them [20] and each one struck down his opponent. At that, the Arameans fled, with the Israelites in pursuit. But Ben-Hadad king of Aram escaped on horseback with some of his horsemen. [21] The king of Israel advanced and overpowered the horses and chariots and inflicted heavy losses on the Arameans.

[22] Afterward, the prophet came to the king of Israel and said, "Strengthen your position and see what must be done, because next spring the king of Aram will attack you again."

[23] Meanwhile, the officials of the king of Aram advised him, "Their gods are gods of the hills. That is why they were too strong for us. But if we fight them on the plains, surely we will be stronger than they. [24] Do this: Remove all the kings from their commands and replace them with other officers. [25] You must also raise an army like the one you lost— horse for horse and chariot for chariot—so we can fight Israel on the plains. Then surely we will be stronger than they." He agreed with them and acted accordingly.

[26] The next spring Ben-Hadad mustered the Arameans and went up to Aphek to fight against Israel. [27] When the Israelites were also mustered and given provisions, they marched out to meet them. The Israelites camped opposite them like two small flocks of goats, while the Arameans covered the countryside.

[28] The man of God came up and told the king of Israel, "This is what the LORD says: 'Because the Arameans think the LORD is a god of the hills and not a god of the valleys, I will deliver this vast army into your hands, and you will know that I am the LORD.'"

[29] For seven days they camped opposite each other, and on the seventh day the battle was joined. The Israelites inflicted a hundred thousand casualties on the Aramean foot soldiers in one day. [30] The rest of them escaped to the city of Aphek,

Why did Ben-Hadad command that the enemy be taken alive? (20:18)
He probably wanted to humiliate and torture the Israelites before killing them.

Why did the Arameans fear a god of the hills? (20:23)
Ben-Hadad believed his defeat was due to the strength of Israel's God rather than on the strength of Israel's army. He reasoned that Israel had a hill-god who protected them. He tried to outsmart their hill-god by moving the battle to the plains where his chariots and horsemen could fight more effectively.

where the wall collapsed on twenty-seven thousand of them. And Ben-Hadad fled to the city and hid in an inner room.

³¹ His officials said to him, "Look, we have heard that the kings of Israel are merciful. Let us go to the king of Israel with sackcloth around our waists and ropes around our heads. Perhaps he will spare your life."

³² Wearing sackcloth around their waists and ropes around their heads, they went to the king of Israel and said, "Your servant Ben-Hadad says: 'Please let me live.'"

The king answered, "Is he still alive? He is my brother."

³³ The men took this as a good sign and were quick to pick up his word. "Yes, your brother Ben-Hadad!" they said.

"Go and get him," the king said. When Ben-Hadad came out, Ahab had him come up into his chariot.

³⁴ "I will return the cities my father took from your father," Ben-Hadad offered. "You may set up your own market areas in Damascus, as my father did in Samaria."

Ahab said, "On the basis of a treaty I will set you free." So he made a treaty with him, and let him go.

A PROPHET CONDEMNS AHAB

³⁵ By the word of the LORD one of the company of the prophets said to his companion, "Strike me with your weapon," but he refused.

³⁶ So the prophet said, "Because you have not obeyed the LORD, as soon as you leave me a lion will kill you." And after the man went away, a lion found him and killed him.

³⁷ The prophet found another man and said, "Strike me, please." So the man struck him and wounded him. ³⁸ Then the prophet went and stood by the road waiting for the king. He disguised himself with his headband down over his eyes. ³⁹ As the king passed by, the prophet called out to him, "Your servant went into the thick of the battle, and someone came to me with a captive and said, 'Guard this man. If he is missing, it will be your life for his life, or you must pay a talent[a] of silver.' ⁴⁰ While your servant was busy here and there, the man disappeared."

"That is your sentence," the king of Israel said. "You have pronounced it yourself."

⁴¹ Then the prophet quickly removed the headband from his eyes, and the king of Israel recognized him as one of the prophets. ⁴² He said to the king, "This is what the LORD says: 'You have set free a man I had determined should die.[b] Therefore it is your life for his life, your people for his people.'" ⁴³ Sullen and angry, the king of Israel went to his palace in Samaria.

NABOTH'S VINEYARD

21 Some time later there was an incident involving a vineyard belonging to Naboth the Jezreelite. The vineyard was in Jezreel, close to the palace of Ahab king of Samaria. ² Ahab said to Naboth, "Let me have your vineyard to use for a vegetable garden, since it is close to my palace. In

---

[a] 39 That is, about 75 pounds or about 34 kilograms   [b] 42 The Hebrew term refers to the irrevocable giving over of things or persons to the LORD, often by totally destroying them.

Why did the men come to Ahab wearing sackcloth and ropes? (20:31)
The sackcloth and ropes were symbols of humility and submission.

Why did Ahab set Ben-Hadad free? (20:34)
Ahab called him "brother" and invited him up into his chariot, treating him as an equal. Ahab might have spared Ben-Hadad's life in the selfish hopes of profiting from their trade agreement. However, that mistake would cost Ahab his life (see 22:35).

What was God saying through the prophet? (20:36–42)
The prophet sent a clear message to Ahab that releasing Ben-Hadad without consulting God would result in his own death. Because Ahab sinned in his role as king, the sentence also fell on his people as well.

Why didn't Ahab just take the vineyard? (21:2)
Other kings of that day would not hesitate to use their power to seize personal property, but Ahab's royal power was limited by covenantal law.

exchange I will give you a better vineyard or, if you prefer, I will pay you whatever it is worth."

³But Naboth replied, "The LORD forbid that I should give you the inheritance of my ancestors."

⁴So Ahab went home, sullen and angry because Naboth the Jezreelite had said, "I will not give you the inheritance of my ancestors." He lay on his bed sulking and refused to eat.

⁵His wife Jezebel came in and asked him, "Why are you so sullen? Why won't you eat?"

⁶He answered her, "Because I said to Naboth the Jezreelite, 'Sell me your vineyard; or if you prefer, I will give you another vineyard in its place.' But he said, 'I will not give you my vineyard.'"

⁷Jezebel his wife said, "Is this how you act as king over Israel? Get up and eat! Cheer up. I'll get you the vineyard of Naboth the Jezreelite."

⁸So she wrote letters in Ahab's name, placed his seal on them, and sent them to the elders and nobles who lived in Naboth's city with him. ⁹In those letters she wrote:

> "Proclaim a day of fasting and seat Naboth in a prominent place among the people. ¹⁰But seat two scoundrels opposite him and have them bring charges that he has cursed both God and the king. Then take him out and stone him to death."

¹¹So the elders and nobles who lived in Naboth's city did as Jezebel directed in the letters she had written to them. ¹²They proclaimed a fast and seated Naboth in a prominent place among the people. ¹³Then two scoundrels came and sat opposite him and brought charges against Naboth before the people, saying, "Naboth has cursed both God and the king." So they took him outside the city and stoned him to death. ¹⁴Then they sent word to Jezebel: "Naboth has been stoned to death."

¹⁵As soon as Jezebel heard that Naboth had been stoned to death, she said to Ahab, "Get up and take possession of the vineyard of Naboth the Jezreelite that he refused to sell you. He is no longer alive, but dead." ¹⁶When Ahab heard that Naboth was dead, he got up and went down to take possession of Naboth's vineyard.

¹⁷Then the word of the LORD came to Elijah the Tishbite: ¹⁸"Go down to meet Ahab king of Israel, who rules in Samaria. He is now in Naboth's vineyard, where he has gone to take possession of it. ¹⁹Say to him, 'This is what the LORD says: Have you not murdered a man and seized his property?' Then say to him, 'This is what the LORD says: In the place where dogs licked up Naboth's blood, dogs will lick up your blood—yes, yours!'"

²⁰Ahab said to Elijah, "So you have found me, my enemy!"

"I have found you," he answered, "because you have sold yourself to do evil in the eyes of the LORD. ²¹He says, 'I am going to bring disaster on you. I will wipe out your descendants and cut off from Ahab every last male in Israel—slave or free.ᵃ ²²I will make your house like that of Jeroboam son

Why wouldn't Naboth accept the deal? (21:3)
His refusal was based on his belief that the land was the Lord's and was to be preserved as his family's permanent inheritance in the promised land. To sell it would violate the laws of Leviticus 25.

Why did Jezebel proclaim a day of fasting? (21:9)
She fooled the people into believing that a disaster was approaching. They would need to fast and remove any person whose sin had brought God's judgment on them. The day of fasting was designed to disguise Jezebel's plot.

Was it legal for Ahab to take the vineyard? (21:16)
Naboth's sons were murdered, eliminating any heirs to the land (2 Kings 9:26). The land of a traitor became the property of the king.

ᵃ 21 Or Israel—every ruler or leader

of Nebat and that of Baasha son of Ahijah, because you have aroused my anger and have caused Israel to sin.'

²³"And also concerning Jezebel the LORD says: 'Dogs will devour Jezebel by the wall of*a* Jezreel.'

²⁴"Dogs will eat those belonging to Ahab who die in the city, and the birds will feed on those who die in the country."

²⁵(There was never anyone like Ahab, who sold himself to do evil in the eyes of the LORD, urged on by Jezebel his wife. ²⁶He behaved in the vilest manner by going after idols, like the Amorites the LORD drove out before Israel.)

²⁷When Ahab heard these words, he tore his clothes, put on sackcloth and fasted. He lay in sackcloth and went around meekly.

²⁸Then the word of the LORD came to Elijah the Tishbite: ²⁹"Have you noticed how Ahab has humbled himself before me? Because he has humbled himself, I will not bring this disaster in his day, but I will bring it on his house in the days of his son."

MICAIAH PROPHESIES AGAINST AHAB

22 For three years there was no war between Aram and Israel. ²But in the third year Jehoshaphat king of Judah went down to see the king of Israel. ³The king of Israel had said to his officials, "Don't you know that Ramoth Gilead belongs to us and yet we are doing nothing to retake it from the king of Aram?"

⁴So he asked Jehoshaphat, "Will you go with me to fight against Ramoth Gilead?"

Jehoshaphat replied to the king of Israel, "I am as you are, my people as your people, my horses as your horses." ⁵But Jehoshaphat also said to the king of Israel, "First seek the counsel of the LORD."

⁶So the king of Israel brought together the prophets— about four hundred men—and asked them, "Shall I go to war against Ramoth Gilead, or shall I refrain?"

"Go," they answered, "for the Lord will give it into the king's hand."

⁷But Jehoshaphat asked, "Is there no longer a prophet of the LORD here whom we can inquire of?"

⁸The king of Israel answered Jehoshaphat, "There is still one prophet through whom we can inquire of the LORD, but I hate him because he never prophesies anything good about me, but always bad. He is Micaiah son of Imlah."

"The king should not say such a thing," Jehoshaphat replied.

⁹So the king of Israel called one of his officials and said, "Bring Micaiah son of Imlah at once."

¹⁰Dressed in their royal robes, the king of Israel and Jehoshaphat king of Judah were sitting on their thrones at the threshing floor by the entrance of the gate of Samaria, with all the prophets prophesying before them. ¹¹Now Zedekiah son of Kenaanah had made iron horns and he declared, "This is what the LORD says: 'With these you will gore the Arameans until they are destroyed.'"

---

a 23 Most Hebrew manuscripts; a few Hebrew manuscripts, Vulgate and Syriac (see also 2 Kings 9:26) *the plot of ground at*

Was Ahab's repentance sincere? (21:27–29)
God declared that Ahab's repentance was sincere, so the prophecy was postponed until the time of Ahab's son. Later, Ahab again resisted God's prophet.

Why did Jehoshaphat agree to be Ahab's ally? (22:4)
Jehoshaphat's son married Ahab's daughter (see 2 Chron. 18:1), so they were allied through family ties. Also, if they did not unite, a foreign army could defeat them more easily.

Who were these 400 prophets? (22:6)
These court prophets were false prophets probably associated with pagan worship. They spoke messages designed to please the king in order to stay in his favor. Jehoshaphat recognized that these prophets were not to be trusted, so he consulted with a true prophet of the LORD.

Why did Micaiah agree with the false prophets? (22:15)
Micaiah sarcastically mimicked the false prophets and mocked Ahab. Even Ahab did not believe his words.

Does God approve of lying? (22:20–22)
No, but God allowed the 400 false prophets to speak lies. He used their lies to accomplish his purpose. Micaiah denounced the lies of these prophets. God gave Ahab a choice—believe the lies or believe the truth.

¹²All the other prophets were prophesying the same thing. "Attack Ramoth Gilead and be victorious," they said, "for the LORD will give it into the king's hand."

¹³The messenger who had gone to summon Micaiah said to him, "Look, the other prophets without exception are predicting success for the king. Let your word agree with theirs, and speak favorably."

¹⁴But Micaiah said, "As surely as the LORD lives, I can tell him only what the LORD tells me."

¹⁵When he arrived, the king asked him, "Micaiah, shall we go to war against Ramoth Gilead, or not?"

"Attack and be victorious," he answered, "for the LORD will give it into the king's hand."

¹⁶The king said to him, "How many times must I make you swear to tell me nothing but the truth in the name of the LORD?"

¹⁷Then Micaiah answered, "I saw all Israel scattered on the hills like sheep without a shepherd, and the LORD said, 'These people have no master. Let each one go home in peace.'"

¹⁸The king of Israel said to Jehoshaphat, "Didn't I tell you that he never prophesies anything good about me, but only bad?"

¹⁹Micaiah continued, "Therefore hear the word of the LORD: I saw the LORD sitting on his throne with all the multitudes of heaven standing around him on his right and on his left. ²⁰And the LORD said, 'Who will entice Ahab into attacking Ramoth Gilead and going to his death there?'

"One suggested this, and another that. ²¹Finally, a spirit came forward, stood before the LORD and said, 'I will entice him.'

²²"'By what means?' the LORD asked.

"'I will go out and be a deceiving spirit in the mouths of all his prophets,' he said.

"'You will succeed in enticing him,' said the LORD. 'Go and do it.'

²³"So now the LORD has put a deceiving spirit in the mouths of all these prophets of yours. The LORD has decreed disaster for you."

²⁴Then Zedekiah son of Kenaanah went up and slapped Micaiah in the face. "Which way did the spirit from^a the LORD go when he went from me to speak to you?" he asked.

²⁵Micaiah replied, "You will find out on the day you go to hide in an inner room."

²⁶The king of Israel then ordered, "Take Micaiah and send him back to Amon the ruler of the city and to Joash the king's son ²⁷and say, 'This is what the king says: Put this fellow in prison and give him nothing but bread and water until I return safely.'"

²⁸Micaiah declared, "If you ever return safely, the LORD has not spoken through me." Then he added, "Mark my words, all you people!"

AHAB KILLED AT RAMOTH GILEAD
²⁹So the king of Israel and Jehoshaphat king of Judah

^a 24 Or Spirit of

went up to Ramoth Gilead. ³⁰The king of Israel said to Jehoshaphat, "I will enter the battle in disguise, but you wear
your royal robes." So the king of Israel disguised himself and
went into battle.

³¹Now the king of Aram had ordered his thirty-two chariot commanders, "Do not fight with anyone, small or great,
except the king of Israel." ³²When the chariot commanders
saw Jehoshaphat, they thought, "Surely this is the king of
Israel." So they turned to attack him, but when Jehoshaphat
cried out, ³³the chariot commanders saw that he was not the
king of Israel and stopped pursuing him.

³⁴But someone drew his bow at random and hit the king
of Israel between the sections of his armor. The king told his
chariot driver, "Wheel around and get me out of the fighting. I've been wounded." ³⁵All day long the battle raged, and
the king was propped up in his chariot facing the Arameans.
The blood from his wound ran onto the floor of the chariot, and that evening he died. ³⁶As the sun was setting, a cry
spread through the army: "Every man to his town. Every
man to his land!"

³⁷So the king died and was brought to Samaria, and they
buried him there. ³⁸They washed the chariot at a pool in Samaria (where the prostitutes bathed),ᵃ and the dogs licked up
his blood, as the word of the LORD had declared.

³⁹As for the other events of Ahab's reign, including all he
did, the palace he built and adorned with ivory, and the cities
he fortified, are they not written in the book of the annals
of the kings of Israel? ⁴⁰Ahab rested with his ancestors. And
Ahaziah his son succeeded him as king.

JEHOSHAPHAT KING OF JUDAH

⁴¹Jehoshaphat son of Asa became king of Judah in the
fourth year of Ahab king of Israel. ⁴²Jehoshaphat was thirty five years old when he became king, and he reigned in
Jerusalem twenty-five years. His mother's name was Azubah
daughter of Shilhi. ⁴³In everything he followed the ways of
his father Asa and did not stray from them; he did what was
right in the eyes of the LORD. The high places, however, were
not removed, and the people continued to offer sacrifices and
burn incense there.ᵇ ⁴⁴Jehoshaphat was also at peace with
the king of Israel.

⁴⁵As for the other events of Jehoshaphat's reign, the things
he achieved and his military exploits, are they not written in
the book of the annals of the kings of Judah? ⁴⁶He rid the
land of the rest of the male shrine prostitutes who remained
there even after the reign of his father Asa. ⁴⁷There was then
no king in Edom; a provincial governor ruled.

⁴⁸Now Jehoshaphat built a fleet of trading shipsᶜ to go to
Ophir for gold, but they never set sail—they were wrecked
at Ezion Geber. ⁴⁹At that time Ahaziah son of Ahab said to
Jehoshaphat, "Let my men sail with yours," but Jehoshaphat
refused.

**Why did Ahab disguise him-
self? (22:30)**
He directed attention away from
himself to keep from being targeted. In ancient wars, if a leader
was killed or captured, his army
would fall apart. Also, Ahab tried
to minimize the chance for Micaiah's prediction of his death to
come true.

**Why didn't Ahab get medi-
cal attention? (22:35)**
Ahab probably knew that his
wound was going to kill him.
Perhaps he received enough help
to enable him to still ride in his
chariot and motivate his soldiers
during the daylong battle.

ᵃ 38 Or *Samaria and cleaned the weapons*   ᵇ 43 In Hebrew texts this
sentence (22:43b) is numbered 22:44, and 22:44-53 is numbered 22:45-54.
ᶜ 48 Hebrew *of ships of Tarshish*

⁵⁰Then Jehoshaphat rested with his ancestors and was buried with them in the city of David his father. And Jehoram his son succeeded him as king.

AHAZIAH KING OF ISRAEL

⁵¹Ahaziah son of Ahab became king of Israel in Samaria in the seventeenth year of Jehoshaphat king of Judah, and he reigned over Israel two years. ⁵²He did evil in the eyes of the Lord, because he followed the ways of his father and mother and of Jeroboam son of Nebat, who caused Israel to sin. ⁵³He served and worshiped Baal and aroused the anger of the Lord, the God of Israel, just as his father had done.

What happened to Ahaziah? (22:52–53)

Ahaziah fell and injured himself and was bedridden for the rest of his life. Elijah revealed he was being punished for his idolatry (see 2 Kings 1). Ahaziah left no heir, as Elijah had prophesied (21:21).

2 Kings

INTRODUCTION

Who wrote this book?	The author of this book is unknown.
Why was this book written?	The book of 2 Kings shows why God finally exiled Israel and Judah from the promised land.
What happens in this book?	The stories of many kings of Judah and Israel are told in this book.
What do we learn about God in this book?	God is very patient. But God will punish his people if they keep on disobeying him.
Who are the key people in this book?	The most important people in this book are Elisha, Joash, Hezekiah, and Josiah.
Where did this happen?	These stories happened in Israel and Judah.

What are some of the stories in this book?		
	Elijah goes up to heaven	2 Kings 2
	Naaman is healed of leprosy	2 Kings 5
	Jehu kllls Ahab's family	2 Kings 9 – 10
	Joash repairs the temple	2 Kings 12
	Israel is exiled	2 Kings 17
	Jerusalem is threatened	2 Kings 18
	Jerusalem is saved	2 Kings 19
	Josiah reads God's book	2 Kings 22
	Jerusalem is destroyed	2 Kings 25

When did these things happen?

1400 BC 1300 1200 1100 1000 900 800 700 600 500 400

DIVISION OF THE KINGDOM (930 BC)

ELIJAH'S MINISTRY IN ISRAEL (C. 875 – 848 BC)

ELISHA'S MINISTRY IN ISRAEL (C. 848 – 797 BC)

EXILE OF ISRAEL (722 BC)

HEZEKIAH'S REIGN (715 – 686 BC)

FALL OF JERUSALEM (586 BC)

KING JEHOIACHIN RELEASED FROM PRISON (C. 561 BC)

BOOK OF 2 KINGS WRITTEN (C. 560 – 550 BC)

THE LORD'S JUDGMENT ON AHAZIAH

Who was Baal-Zebub? (1:2)
Baal-Zebub means *lord of the flies.* This was the name the Is-raelites used to mock the pagan god, Baal, whose name translates to *lord* or *master.*

Why did Ahaziah want to capture Elijah? (1:6–15)
Pagan people of that time thought the power of curses could be nullified by forcing the person who pronounced the curse to retract it or by killing him or her, so the curse would go with that person into the world of the dead. Apparently King Ahazi-ah wanted to take Elijah prisoner to counteract his pronouncement that the king would die.

Why did the prophets wear unusual clothing? (1:8)
Elijah's coarse garments were the exact opposite of the fancy clothing (and lifestyles) of the evil kings of his time. To remind himself of the unfaithfulness of the Israelites, Elijah may have worn uncomfortable clothes to express his sorrow for their sins.

1 After Ahab's death, Moab rebelled against Israel. ²Now Ahaziah had fallen through the lattice of his upper room in Samaria and injured himself. So he sent messengers, say-ing to them, "Go and consult Baal-Zebub, the god of Ekron, to see if I will recover from this injury."

³But the angel of the LORD said to Elijah the Tishbite, "Go up and meet the messengers of the king of Samaria and ask them, 'Is it because there is no God in Israel that you are going off to consult Baal-Zebub, the god of Ekron?' ⁴Therefore this is what the LORD says: 'You will not leave the bed you are lying on. You will certainly die!'" So Elijah went.

⁵When the messengers returned to the king, he asked them, "Why have you come back?"

⁶"A man came to meet us," they replied. "And he said to us, 'Go back to the king who sent you and tell him, "This is what the LORD says: Is it because there is no God in Israel that you are sending messengers to consult Baal-Zebub, the god of Ekron? Therefore you will not leave the bed you are lying on. You will certainly die!"'"

⁷The king asked them, "What kind of man was it who came to meet you and told you this?"

⁸They replied, "He had a garment of hair*ᵃ* and had a leather belt around his waist."

The king said, "That was Elijah the Tishbite."

⁹Then he sent to Elijah a captain with his company of fifty men. The captain went up to Elijah, who was sitting on the top of a hill, and said to him, "Man of God, the king says, 'Come down!'"

¹⁰Elijah answered the captain, "If I am a man of God, may fire come down from heaven and consume you and your fifty men!" Then fire fell from heaven and consumed the captain and his men.

¹¹At this the king sent to Elijah another captain with his fifty men. The captain said to him, "Man of God, this is what the king says, 'Come down at once!'"

¹²"If I am a man of God," Elijah replied, "may fire come down from heaven and consume you and your fifty men!" Then the fire of God fell from heaven and consumed him and his fifty men.

¹³So the king sent a third captain with his fifty men. This third captain went up and fell on his knees before Elijah. "Man of God," he begged, "please have respect for my life and the lives of these fifty men, your servants! ¹⁴See, fire has fallen from heaven and consumed the first two captains and all their men. But now have respect for my life!"

¹⁵The angel of the LORD said to Elijah, "Go down with him; do not be afraid of him." So Elijah got up and went down with him to the king.

¹⁶He told the king, "This is what the LORD says: Is it be-cause there is no God in Israel for you to consult that you have sent messengers to consult Baal-Zebub, the god of Ek-ron? Because you have done this, you will never leave the

ᵃ 8 Or He was a hairy man

bed you are lying on. You will certainly die!" [17] So he died, according to the word of the LORD that Elijah had spoken.

Because Ahaziah had no son, Joram[a] succeeded him as king in the second year of Jehoram son of Jehoshaphat king of Judah. [18] As for all the other events of Ahaziah's reign, and what he did, are they not written in the book of the annals of the kings of Israel?

ELIJAH TAKEN UP TO HEAVEN

2 When the LORD was about to take Elijah up to heaven in a whirlwind, Elijah and Elisha were on their way from Gilgal. [2] Elijah said to Elisha, "Stay here; the LORD has sent me to Bethel."

But Elisha said, "As surely as the LORD lives and as you live, I will not leave you." So they went down to Bethel.

[3] The company of the prophets at Bethel came out to Elisha and asked, "Do you know that the LORD is going to take your master from you today?"

"Yes, I know," Elisha replied, "so be quiet."

[4] Then Elijah said to him, "Stay here, Elisha; the LORD has sent me to Jericho."

And he replied, "As surely as the LORD lives and as you live, I will not leave you." So they went to Jericho.

[5] The company of the prophets at Jericho went up to Elisha and asked him, "Do you know that the LORD is going to take your master from you today?"

"Yes, I know," he replied, "so be quiet."

[6] Then Elijah said to him, "Stay here; the LORD has sent me to the Jordan."

And he replied, "As surely as the LORD lives and as you live, I will not leave you." So the two of them walked on.

[7] Fifty men from the company of the prophets went and stood at a distance, facing the place where Elijah and Elisha had stopped at the Jordan. [8] Elijah took his cloak, rolled it up and struck the water with it. The water divided to the right and to the left, and the two of them crossed over on dry ground.

[9] When they had crossed, Elijah said to Elisha, "Tell me, what can I do for you before I am taken from you?"

"Let me inherit a double portion of your spirit," Elisha replied.

[10] "You have asked a difficult thing," Elijah said, "yet if you see me when I am taken from you, it will be yours—otherwise, it will not."

[11] As they were walking along and talking together, suddenly a chariot of fire and horses of fire appeared and separated the two of them, and Elijah went up to heaven in a whirlwind. [12] Elisha saw this and cried out, "My father! My father! The chariots and horsemen of Israel!" And Elisha saw him no more. Then he took hold of his garment and tore it in two.

[13] Elisha then picked up Elijah's cloak that had fallen from him and went back and stood on the bank of the Jordan.

[a] 17 Hebrew *Jehoram*, a variant of *Joram*

What was "the company of prophets"? (2:3–5)
Beginning with the time of Samuel, prophets joined groups that were sometimes known as schools of prophets or sons of prophets. Experienced prophets taught newer prophets about God's will.

What was Elisha asking? (2:9)
Elisha was using terms from inheritance law to show that he wanted to carry on Elijah's ministry. Inheritance law assigned a double portion of a father's possessions to the firstborn son.

What were these chariots and horses of fire? (2:11)
These were probably angels who served God. The term *fire* probably means they glowed, reflecting God's heavenly glory. Whirlwinds and fire were associated with the power and presence of God. Like Enoch, Elijah was taken to heaven without dying (see Genesis 5:24).

[14] He took the cloak that had fallen from Elijah and struck the water with it. "Where now is the LORD, the God of Elijah?" he asked. When he struck the water, it divided to the right and to the left, and he crossed over.

[15] The company of the prophets from Jericho, who were watching, said, "The spirit of Elijah is resting on Elisha." And they went to meet him and bowed to the ground before him. [16] "Look," they said, "we your servants have fifty able men. Let them go and look for your master. Perhaps the Spirit of the LORD has picked him up and set him down on some mountain or in some valley."

"No," Elisha replied, "do not send them."

[17] But they persisted until he was too embarrassed to refuse. So he said, "Send them." And they sent fifty men, who searched for three days but did not find him. [18] When they returned to Elisha, who was staying in Jericho, he said to them, "Didn't I tell you not to go?"

HEALING OF THE WATER

[19] The people of the city said to Elisha, "Look, our lord, this town is well situated, as you can see, but the water is bad and the land is unproductive."

[20] "Bring me a new bowl," he said, "and put salt in it." So they brought it to him.

[21] Then he went out to the spring and threw the salt into it, saying, "This is what the LORD says: 'I have healed this water. Never again will it cause death or make the land unproductive.'" [22] And the water has remained pure to this day, according to the word Elisha had spoken.

ELISHA IS JEERED

[23] From there Elisha went up to Bethel. As he was walking along the road, some boys came out of the town and jeered at him. "Get out of here, baldy!" they said. "Get out of here, baldy!" [24] He turned around, looked at them and called down a curse on them in the name of the LORD. Then two bears came out of the woods and mauled forty-two of the boys. [25] And he went on to Mount Carmel and from there returned to Samaria.

MOAB REVOLTS

3 Joram[a] son of Ahab became king of Israel in Samaria in the eighteenth year of Jehoshaphat king of Judah, and he reigned twelve years. [2] He did evil in the eyes of the LORD, but not as his father and mother had done. He got rid of the sacred stone of Baal that his father had made. [3] Nevertheless he clung to the sins of Jeroboam son of Nebat, which he had caused Israel to commit; he did not turn away from them.

[4] Now Mesha king of Moab raised sheep, and he had to pay the king of Israel a tribute of a hundred thousand lambs and the wool of a hundred thousand rams. [5] But after Ahab died, the king of Moab rebelled against the king of Israel. [6] So at that time King Joram set out from Samaria and mobilized all Israel. [7] He also sent this message to Jehoshaphat

---

[a] 1 Hebrew *Jehoram*, a variant of *Joram*; also in verse 6

Sidebar

Why did Elisha put salt in the spring? (2:21)
As the first act of his ministry, Elisha was used by God to purify the water. The new basin, dedicated to the LORD's use, and the salt were symbols of purification and holiness.

Why did the youths call Elisha a "baldy"? (2:23)
Baldness was uncommon among the ancient Jews, and it was seen as a disgrace. Long, thick hair was thought to be a sign of strength and vigor. By calling Elisha a baldhead, the youths from Bethel expressed that city's disdain for the Lord's representative.

What was the sacred stone of Baal? (3:2)
Joram's father, Ahab, created an engraved image dedicated to Baal (1 Kings 16:32 – 33). Although Joram "got rid of" this stone, it was not completely destroyed until Jehu's men burned it (see 10:26 – 27).

Moab Revolts (3:5)

king of Judah: "The king of Moab has rebelled against me. Will you go with me to fight against Moab?"

"I will go with you," he replied. "I am as you are, my people as your people, my horses as your horses."

⁸"By what route shall we attack?" he asked.

"Through the Desert of Edom," he answered.

⁹So the king of Israel set out with the king of Judah and the king of Edom. After a roundabout march of seven days, the army had no more water for themselves or for the animals with them.

¹⁰"What!" exclaimed the king of Israel. "Has the LORD called us three kings together only to deliver us into the hands of Moab?"

¹¹But Jehoshaphat asked, "Is there no prophet of the LORD here, through whom we may inquire of the LORD?"

An officer of the king of Israel answered, "Elisha son of Shaphat is here. He used to pour water on the hands of Elijah.ᵃ"

¹²Jehoshaphat said, "The word of the LORD is with him." So the king of Israel and Jehoshaphat and the king of Edom went down to him.

¹³Elisha said to the king of Israel, "Why do you want to involve me? Go to the prophets of your father and the prophets of your mother."

"No," the king of Israel answered, "because it was the LORD who called us three kings together to deliver us into the hands of Moab."

¹⁴Elisha said, "As surely as the LORD Almighty lives, whom I serve, if I did not have respect for the presence of Jehoshaphat king of Judah, I would not pay any attention to you. ¹⁵But now bring me a harpist."

While the harpist was playing, the hand of the LORD came on Elisha ¹⁶and he said, "This is what the LORD says: I will fill this valley with pools of water. ¹⁷For this is what the LORD says: You will see neither wind nor rain, yet this valley will be filled with water, and you, your cattle and your other animals will drink. ¹⁸This is an easy thing in the eyes of the LORD; he will also deliver Moab into your hands. ¹⁹You will overthrow every fortified city and every major town. You will cut down every good tree, stop up all the springs, and ruin every good field with stones."

²⁰The next morning, about the time for offering the sacrifice, there it was—water flowing from the direction of Edom! And the land was filled with water.

²¹Now all the Moabites had heard that the kings had come to fight against them; so every man, young and old, who could bear arms was called up and stationed on the border. ²²When they got up early in the morning, the sun was shining on the water. To the Moabites across the way, the water looked red—like blood. ²³"That's blood!" they said. "Those kings must have fought and slaughtered each other. Now to the plunder, Moab!"

²⁴But when the Moabites came to the camp of Israel, the Israelites rose up and fought them until they fled. And the

ᵃ 11 That is, he was Elijah's personal servant.

Why did Joram blame God for his troubles? (3:10)

He tried to shift the blame to God, even though he was the one who had planned the expedition. The three kings did not pray or consult a prophet for advice until after they were in deep trouble.

How did God cause this flow of water? (3:20)

It was common for wadis (dry riverbeds) to become streams after a cloudburst. The storm apparently brought heavy rains to the mountains of Edom, some distance south of Moab, and the water flowed north through the broad, usually dry valley that sloped toward the Dead Sea.

Why did the armies destroy the land of Moab? (3:25)
This was standard practice in ancient warfare. The soldiers wanted to cripple the Moabites' ability to farm successfully, and it would take years for Moab to recover from the loss of crops and food. The LORD used the armies to get rid of the evilness in Moab.

Israelites invaded the land and slaughtered the Moabites. ²⁵They destroyed the towns, and each man threw a stone on every good field until it was covered. They stopped up all the springs and cut down every good tree. Only Kir Hareseth was left with its stones in place, but men armed with slings surrounded it and attacked it.

²⁶When the king of Moab saw that the battle had gone against him, he took with him seven hundred swordsmen to break through to the king of Edom, but they failed. ²⁷Then he took his firstborn son, who was to succeed him as king, and offered him as a sacrifice on the city wall. The fury against Israel was great; they withdrew and returned to their own land.

THE WIDOW'S OLIVE OIL

4 The wife of a man from the company of the prophets cried out to Elisha, "Your servant my husband is dead, and you know that he revered the LORD. But now his creditor is coming to take my two boys as his slaves."

²Elisha replied to her, "How can I help you? Tell me, what do you have in your house?"

"Your servant has nothing there at all," she said, "except a small jar of olive oil."

Why did God use this method to help the widow? (4:1–7)
God performed this miracle to demonstrate his mercy and grace. The widow had faith in God and obeyed the prophet's instructions even though she didn't know what would happen. God rewarded her for her obedience.

³Elisha said, "Go around and ask all your neighbors for empty jars. Don't ask for just a few. ⁴Then go inside and shut the door behind you and your sons. Pour oil into all the jars, and as each is filled, put it to one side."

⁵She left him and shut the door behind her and her sons. They brought the jars to her and she kept pouring. ⁶When all the jars were full, she said to her son, "Bring me another one."

But he replied, "There is not a jar left." Then the oil stopped flowing.

⁷She went and told the man of God, and he said, "Go, sell the oil and pay your debts. You and your sons can live on what is left."

THE SHUNAMMITE'S SON RESTORED TO LIFE

⁸One day Elisha went to Shunem. And a well-to-do woman was there, who urged him to stay for a meal. So whenever he came by, he stopped there to eat. ⁹She said to her husband, "I know that this man who often comes our way is a holy man of God. ¹⁰Let's make a small room on the roof and put in it a bed and a table, a chair and a lamp for him. Then he can stay there whenever he comes to us."

¹¹One day when Elisha came, he went up to his room and lay down there. ¹²He said to his servant Gehazi, "Call the Shunammite." So he called her, and she stood before him. ¹³Elisha said to him, "Tell her, 'You have gone to all this trouble for us. Now what can be done for you? Can we speak on your behalf to the king or the commander of the army?'"

She replied, "I have a home among my own people."

¹⁴"What can be done for her?" Elisha asked.

Gehazi said, "She has no son, and her husband is old."

¹⁵Then Elisha said, "Call her." So he called her, and she stood in the doorway. ¹⁶"About this time next year," Elisha said, "you will hold a son in your arms."

Miracle at Shunem (4:8–37)

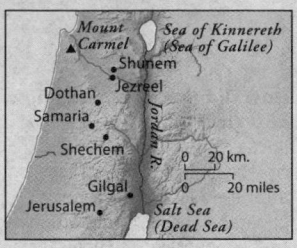

Why did the woman want a son? (4:13–14)
Along with being very disappointing, childlessness meant that the family's name would not continue and their land and possessions would go to others.

"No, my lord!" she objected. "Please, man of God, don't mislead your servant!"

[17] But the woman became pregnant, and the next year about that same time she gave birth to a son, just as Elisha had told her.

[18] The child grew, and one day he went out to his father, who was with the reapers. [19] He said to his father, "My head! My head!"

His father told a servant, "Carry him to his mother." [20] After the servant had lifted him up and carried him to his mother, the boy sat on her lap until noon, and then he died. [21] She went up and laid him on the bed of the man of God, then shut the door and went out.

[22] She called her husband and said, "Please send me one of the servants and a donkey so I can go to the man of God quickly and return."

[23] "Why go to him today?" he asked. "It's not the New Moon or the Sabbath."

"That's all right," she said.

[24] She saddled the donkey and said to her servant, "Lead on; don't slow down for me unless I tell you." [25] So she set out and came to the man of God at Mount Carmel.

When he saw her in the distance, the man of God said to his servant Gehazi, "Look! There's the Shunammite! [26] Run to meet her and ask her, 'Are you all right? Is your husband all right? Is your child all right?'"

"Everything is all right," she said.

[27] When she reached the man of God at the mountain, she took hold of his feet. Gehazi came over to push her away, but the man of God said, "Leave her alone! She is in bitter distress, but the LORD has hidden it from me and has not told me why."

[28] "Did I ask you for a son, my lord?" she said. "Didn't I tell you, 'Don't raise my hopes'?"

[29] Elisha said to Gehazi, "Tuck your cloak into your belt, take my staff in your hand and run. Don't greet anyone you meet, and if anyone greets you, do not answer. Lay my staff on the boy's face."

[30] But the child's mother said, "As surely as the LORD lives and as you live, I will not leave you." So he got up and followed her.

[31] Gehazi went on ahead and laid the staff on the boy's face, but there was no sound or response. So Gehazi went back to meet Elisha and told him, "The boy has not awakened."

[32] When Elisha reached the house, there was the boy lying dead on his couch. [33] He went in, shut the door on the two of them and prayed to the LORD. [34] Then he got on the bed and lay on the boy, mouth to mouth, eyes to eyes, hands to hands. As he stretched himself out on him, the boy's body grew warm. [35] Elisha turned away and walked back and forth in the room and then got on the bed and stretched out on him once more. The boy sneezed seven times and opened his eyes.

[36] Elisha summoned Gehazi and said, "Call the Shunammite." And he did. When she came, he said, "Take your son." [37] She came in, fell at his feet and bowed to the ground. Then she took her son and went out.

Why didn't the woman tell Gehazi that her son had died? (4:26)
She knew that Gehazi could not solve her problem. She needed to speak directly to Elisha. Since Elisha was the one who had promised she would have a son, she went to him when her son died.

Why did Elisha stretch himself out on top of the dead boy? (4:33–35)
Perhaps he remembered that this was what Elijah had done in a similar situation (see 1 Kings 17:20–22).

DEATH IN THE POT

³⁸Elisha returned to Gilgal and there was a famine in that region. While the company of the prophets was meeting with him, he said to his servant, "Put on the large pot and cook some stew for these prophets."

³⁹One of them went out into the fields to gather herbs and found a wild vine and picked as many of its gourds as his garment could hold. When he returned, he cut them up into the pot of stew, though no one knew what they were. ⁴⁰The stew was poured out for the men, but as they began to eat it, they cried out, "Man of God, there is death in the pot!" And they could not eat it.

⁴¹Elisha said, "Get some flour." He put it into the pot and said, "Serve it to the people to eat." And there was nothing harmful in the pot.

FEEDING OF A HUNDRED

⁴²A man came from Baal Shalishah, bringing the man of God twenty loaves of barley bread baked from the first ripe grain, along with some heads of new grain. "Give it to the people to eat," Elisha said.

⁴³"How can I set this before a hundred men?" his servant asked.

But Elisha answered, "Give it to the people to eat. For this is what the LORD says: 'They will eat and have some left over.'" ⁴⁴Then he set it before them, and they ate and had some left over, according to the word of the LORD.

NAAMAN HEALED OF LEPROSY

5 Now Naaman was commander of the army of the king of Aram. He was a great man in the sight of his master and highly regarded, because through him the LORD had given victory to Aram. He was a valiant soldier, but he had leprosy.ᵃ

²Now bands of raiders from Aram had gone out and had taken captive a young girl from Israel, and she served Naaman's wife. ³She said to her mistress, "If only my master would see the prophet who is in Samaria! He would cure him of his leprosy."

⁴Naaman went to his master and told him what the girl from Israel had said. ⁵"By all means, go," the king of Aram replied. "I will send a letter to the king of Israel." So Naaman left, taking with him ten talentsᵇ of silver, six thousand shekelsᶜ of gold and ten sets of clothing. ⁶The letter that he took to the king of Israel read: "With this letter I am sending my servant Naaman to you so that you may cure him of his leprosy."

⁷As soon as the king of Israel read the letter, he tore his robes and said, "Am I God? Can I kill and bring back to life? Why does this fellow send someone to me to be cured of his leprosy? See how he is trying to pick a quarrel with me!"

⁸When Elisha the man of God heard that the king of

What was wrong with the stew? (4:39–40)
Perhaps the gourds from the unknown plant were too bitter to eat or poisonous. But Elisha performed a miracle by throwing some flour in the pot and making the stew edible.

How were 100 men fed by 20 small loaves of bread? (4:42–44)
This was another miracle of God. It's a small-scale version of the miracles Jesus performed to feed 5,000 and 4,000 people (see Matthew 14:15–21 and 15:32–38).

Why would leprosy strike someone God favored? (5:1)
Even when God uses people for good purposes, he doesn't necessarily solve all of their problems, whether those are health related, financial, or emotional. In Naaman's case, his illness showed him how a powerful God can do anything.

ᵃ *1* The Hebrew for *leprosy* was used for various diseases affecting the skin; also in verses 3, 6, 7, 11 and 27.   ᵇ *5* That is, about 750 pounds or about 340 kilograms   ᶜ *5* That is, about 150 pounds or about 69 kilograms

Israel had torn his robes, he sent him this message: "Why have you torn your robes? Have the man come to me and he will know that there is a prophet in Israel." ⁹So Naaman went with his horses and chariots and stopped at the door of Elisha's house. ¹⁰Elisha sent a messenger to say to him, "Go, wash yourself seven times in the Jordan, and your flesh will be restored and you will be cleansed."

¹¹But Naaman went away angry and said, "I thought that he would surely come out to me and stand and call on the name of the LORD his God, wave his hand over the spot and cure me of my leprosy. ¹²Are not Abana and Pharpar, the rivers of Damascus, better than all the waters of Israel? Couldn't I wash in them and be cleansed?" So he turned and went off in a rage.

¹³Naaman's servants went to him and said, "My father, if the prophet had told you to do some great thing, would you not have done it? How much more, then, when he tells you, 'Wash and be cleansed'!" ¹⁴So he went down and dipped himself in the Jordan seven times, as the man of God had told him, and his flesh was restored and became clean like that of a young boy.

¹⁵Then Naaman and all his attendants went back to the man of God. He stood before him and said, "Now I know that there is no God in all the world except in Israel. So please accept a gift from your servant."

¹⁶The prophet answered, "As surely as the LORD lives, whom I serve, I will not accept a thing." And even though Naaman urged him, he refused.

¹⁷"If you will not," said Naaman, "please let me, your servant, be given as much earth as a pair of mules can carry, for your servant will never again make burnt offerings and sacrifices to any other god but the LORD. ¹⁸But may the LORD forgive your servant for this one thing: When my master enters the temple of Rimmon to bow down and he is leaning on my arm and I have to bow there also—when I bow down in the temple of Rimmon, may the LORD forgive your servant for this."

¹⁹"Go in peace," Elisha said.

After Naaman had traveled some distance, ²⁰Gehazi, the servant of Elisha the man of God, said to himself, "My master was too easy on Naaman, this Aramean, by not accepting

Why did Naaman dislike the Jordan River? (5:10–12)
The Jordan was muddy and dirty looking compared to the clear river in Naaman's own nation. God was apparently testing Naaman to see if he would obey even he didn't want to. The LORD knew that Naaman needed healing from leprosy, but he needed faith more.

Why did Naaman want dirt from Israel? (5:17)
In the ancient world, it was commonly thought that a deity could only be worshiped on the soil of the nation where the deity originated. Naaman wanted to take the soil to his homeland so that he could make a place to worship the God of Israel.

Does God punish people by sending diseases like leprosy or AIDS?
2 KINGS 5

There are only three times recorded in the Bible that God punished a person by causing him or her to get leprosy: Miriam (Numbers 12:1–10), Gehazi (2 Kings 5:27), and King Uzziah (2 Chronicles 26:16–21). But in ancient times leprosy, which was a skin disease, was widespread. Even though a person with leprosy was considered ritually unclean and had to remain isolated from other people, this did not mean that the person with leprosy had been cursed by God.

In the modern world, there are many diseases that people can contract, and we should never assume that they are a curse or punishment from God. Clearly, there are some behaviors that can contribute to some illnesses: for example, smoking can cause cancer and unprotected sex can lead to AIDS. So it is important to choose a healthy lifestyle and to avoid dangerous behaviors, but if someone we know becomes ill or contracts a disease, we should not think that God is punishing that person.

from him what he brought. As surely as the LORD lives, I will run after him and get something from him."

²¹ So Gehazi hurried after Naaman. When Naaman saw him running toward him, he got down from the chariot to meet him. "Is everything all right?" he asked.

²² "Everything is all right," Gehazi answered. "My master sent me to say, 'Two young men from the company of the prophets have just come to me from the hill country of Ephraim. Please give them a talent*ᵃ* of silver and two sets of clothing.'"

²³ "By all means, take two talents," said Naaman. He urged Gehazi to accept them, and then tied up the two talents of silver in two bags, with two sets of clothing. He gave them to two of his servants, and they carried them ahead of Gehazi. ²⁴ When Gehazi came to the hill, he took the things from the servants and put them away in the house. He sent the men away and they left.

²⁵ When he went in and stood before his master, Elisha asked him, "Where have you been, Gehazi?"

"Your servant didn't go anywhere," Gehazi answered.

²⁶ But Elisha said to him, "Was not my spirit with you when the man got down from his chariot to meet you? Is this the time to take money or to accept clothes—or olive groves and vineyards, or flocks and herds, or male and female slaves? ²⁷ Naaman's leprosy will cling to you and to your descendants forever." Then Gehazi went from Elisha's presence and his skin was leprous—it had become as white as snow.

AN AXHEAD FLOATS

6 The company of the prophets said to Elisha, "Look, the place where we meet with you is too small for us. ²Let us go to the Jordan, where each of us can get a pole; and let us build a place there for us to meet."

And he said, "Go."

³ Then one of them said, "Won't you please come with your servants?"

"I will," Elisha replied. ⁴ And he went with them.

They went to the Jordan and began to cut down trees. ⁵ As one of them was cutting down a tree, the iron axhead fell into the water. "Oh no, my lord!" he cried out. "It was borrowed!"

⁶ The man of God asked, "Where did it fall?" When he showed him the place, Elisha cut a stick and threw it there, and made the iron float. ⁷ "Lift it out," he said. Then the man reached out his hand and took it.

ELISHA TRAPS BLINDED ARAMEANS

⁸ Now the king of Aram was at war with Israel. After conferring with his officers, he said, "I will set up my camp in such and such a place."

⁹ The man of God sent word to the king of Israel: "Beware of passing that place, because the Arameans are going down there." ¹⁰ So the king of Israel checked on the place indicated by the man of God. Time and again Elisha warned the king, so that he was on his guard in such places.

ᵃ 22 That is, about 75 pounds or about 34 kilograms

How much silver did Naaman give to Gehazi? (5:23)
Silver and gold were measured by weight because coins were not used until the seventh century B.C. Two talents of silver weighed about 150 pounds (about 68 kilograms).

How did Elisha's spirit go with Gehazi? (5:26)
Even though he had not left his home, Elisha's gift of prophesy kept him informed on everything Gehazi had done.

Why was the worker so upset about an axhead? (6:5)
An iron axhead was a costly tool. If the worker could not purchase another or repay the owner, he would have to work as a bond-servant to the owner to pay off the debt.

Why did Elisha throw a stick in the water? (6:6)
This was a sign that just as wood floats, an iron axhead can float when God creates a miracle.

¹¹This enraged the king of Aram. He summoned his officers and demanded of them, "Tell me! Which of us is on the side of the king of Israel?"

¹²"None of us, my lord the king," said one of his officers, "but Elisha, the prophet who is in Israel, tells the king of Israel the very words you speak in your bedroom."

¹³"Go, find out where he is," the king ordered, "so I can send men and capture him." The report came back: "He is in Dothan." ¹⁴Then he sent horses and chariots and a strong force there. They went by night and surrounded the city.

¹⁵When the servant of the man of God got up and went out early the next morning, an army with horses and chariots had surrounded the city. "Oh no, my lord! What shall we do?" the servant asked.

¹⁶"Don't be afraid," the prophet answered. "Those who are with us are more than those who are with them."

¹⁷And Elisha prayed, "Open his eyes, Lord, so that he may see." Then the Lord opened the servant's eyes, and he looked and saw the hills full of horses and chariots of fire all around Elisha.

¹⁸As the enemy came down toward him, Elisha prayed to the Lord, "Strike this army with blindness." So he struck them with blindness, as Elisha had asked.

¹⁹Elisha told them, "This is not the road and this is not the city. Follow me, and I will lead you to the man you are looking for." And he led them to Samaria.

²⁰After they entered the city, Elisha said, "Lord, open the eyes of these men so they can see." Then the Lord opened their eyes and they looked, and there they were, inside Samaria.

²¹When the king of Israel saw them, he asked Elisha, "Shall I kill them, my father? Shall I kill them?"

²²"Do not kill them," he answered. "Would you kill those you have captured with your own sword or bow? Set food and water before them so that they may eat and drink and then go back to their master." ²³So he prepared a great feast for them, and after they had finished eating and drinking, he sent them away, and they returned to their master. So the bands from Aram stopped raiding Israel's territory.

FAMINE IN BESIEGED SAMARIA

²⁴Some time later, Ben-Hadad king of Aram mobilized his entire army and marched up and laid siege to Samaria. ²⁵There was a great famine in the city; the siege lasted so long that a donkey's head sold for eighty shekels*ᵃ* of silver, and a quarter of a cab*ᵇ* of seed pods*ᶜ* for five shekels.*ᵈ*

²⁶As the king of Israel was passing by on the wall, a woman cried to him, "Help me, my lord the king!"

²⁷The king replied, "If the Lord does not help you, where can I get help for you? From the threshing floor? From the winepress?" ²⁸Then he asked her, "What's the matter?"

She answered, "This woman said to me, 'Give up your son

Why did the king call Elisha "my father"? (6:21)
This was a term of honor and respect. The king recognized the prophet's knowledge of God. Similarly, Elisha had called Elijah "my father" (2:12).

ᵃ 25 That is, about 2 pounds or about 920 grams   *ᵇ 25* That is, probably about 1/4 pound or about 100 grams   *ᶜ 25* Or *of doves' dung*   *ᵈ 25* That is, about 2 ounces or about 58 grams

Why did the king wear sackcloth under his clothes? (6:30)

Sackcloth is a rough fabric that would chafe the skin when worn. Wearing it was often a sign of sorrow or repentance. By hiding the sackcloth under his royal robes it's possible the king wanted to maintain a sense of dignity in front of his people.

Why did the king want to kill Elisha? (6:31–32)

He may have blamed Elisha for the Aram's siege on Samaria because it was Elisha's advice to let the army live. Or he may have wanted Elisha to perform a miracle to provide food for the city. The king wanted someone to blame, and he chose Elisha.

Why did the king need to lean on someone's arm? (7:2)

Perhaps he was physically weak, but more likely this officer was someone the king relied on or leaned on.

Why were these lepers camped outside the city gate? (7:3)

According to the Law of Moses, lepers were told to stay outside the community to keep disease and ritual uncleanness away from the rest of the people. During normal times, these lepers would have received food from relatives and friends in the city.

Why did the Arameans leave their horses behind? (7:7)

The Arameans thought it would be easier to just run away. These animals were used for pulling chariots. Although chariots were useful in battle, they were not useful for quick escapes. And because of the panic and very little light, it wouldn't have been easy to hook up the horses to the chariots.

so we may eat him today, and tomorrow we'll eat my son.' ²⁹So we cooked my son and ate him. The next day I said to her, 'Give up your son so we may eat him,' but she had hidden him."

³⁰When the king heard the woman's words, he tore his robes. As he went along the wall, the people looked, and they saw that, under his robes, he had sackcloth on his body. ³¹He said, "May God deal with me, be it ever so severely, if the head of Elisha son of Shaphat remains on his shoulders today!"

³²Now Elisha was sitting in his house, and the elders were sitting with him. The king sent a messenger ahead, but before he arrived, Elisha said to the elders, "Don't you see how this murderer is sending someone to cut off my head? Look, when the messenger comes, shut the door and hold it shut against him. Is not the sound of his master's footsteps behind him?" ³³While he was still talking to them, the messenger came down to him.

The king said, "This disaster is from the LORD. Why should I wait for the LORD any longer?"

7 Elisha replied, "Hear the word of the LORD. This is what the LORD says: About this time tomorrow, a seah^a of the finest flour will sell for a shekel^b and two seahs^c of barley for a shekel at the gate of Samaria."

²The officer on whose arm the king was leaning said to the man of God, "Look, even if the LORD should open the floodgates of the heavens, could this happen?"

"You will see it with your own eyes," answered Elisha, "but you will not eat any of it!"

THE SIEGE LIFTED

³Now there were four men with leprosy^d at the entrance of the city gate. They said to each other, "Why stay here until we die? ⁴If we say, 'We'll go into the city'—the famine is there, and we will die. And if we stay here, we will die. So let's go over to the camp of the Arameans and surrender. If they spare us, we live; if they kill us, then we die."

⁵At dusk they got up and went to the camp of the Arameans. When they reached the edge of the camp, no one was there, ⁶for the Lord had caused the Arameans to hear the sound of chariots and horses and a great army, so that they said to one another, "Look, the king of Israel has hired the Hittite and Egyptian kings to attack us!" ⁷So they got up and fled in the dusk and abandoned their tents and their horses and donkeys. They left the camp as it was and ran for their lives.

⁸The men who had leprosy reached the edge of the camp, entered one of the tents and ate and drank. Then they took silver, gold and clothes, and went off and hid them. They returned and entered another tent and took some things from it and hid them also.

---

^a *1* That is, probably about 12 pounds or about 5.5 kilograms of flour; also in verses 16 and 18   ^b *1* That is, about 2/5 ounce or about 12 grams; also in verses 16 and 18   ^c *1* That is, probably about 20 pounds or about 9 kilograms of barley; also in verses 16 and 18   ^d *3* The Hebrew for *leprosy* was used for various diseases affecting the skin; also in verse 8.

⁹Then they said to each other, "What we're doing is not right. This is a day of good news and we are keeping it to ourselves. If we wait until daylight, punishment will overtake us. Let's go at once and report this to the royal palace."

¹⁰So they went and called out to the city gatekeepers and told them, "We went into the Aramean camp and no one was there—not a sound of anyone—only tethered horses and donkeys, and the tents left just as they were." ¹¹The gatekeepers shouted the news, and it was reported within the palace.

¹²The king got up in the night and said to his officers, "I will tell you what the Arameans have done to us. They know we are starving; so they have left the camp to hide in the countryside, thinking, 'They will surely come out, and then we will take them alive and get into the city.'"

¹³One of his officers answered, "Have some men take five of the horses that are left in the city. Their plight will be like that of all the Israelites left here—yes, they will only be like all these Israelites who are doomed. So let us send them to find out what happened."

¹⁴So they selected two chariots with their horses, and the king sent them after the Aramean army. He commanded the drivers, "Go and find out what has happened." ¹⁵They followed them as far as the Jordan, and they found the whole road strewn with the clothing and equipment the Arameans had thrown away in their headlong flight. So the messengers returned and reported to the king. ¹⁶Then the people went out and plundered the camp of the Arameans. So a seah of the finest flour sold for a shekel, and two seahs of barley sold for a shekel, as the LORD had said.

¹⁷Now the king had put the officer on whose arm he leaned in charge of the gate, and the people trampled him in the gateway, and he died, just as the man of God had foretold when the king came down to his house. ¹⁸It happened as the man of God had said to the king: "About this time tomorrow, a seah of the finest flour will sell for a shekel and two seahs of barley for a shekel at the gate of Samaria."

¹⁹The officer had said to the man of God, "Look, even if the LORD should open the floodgates of the heavens, could this happen?" The man of God had replied, "You will see it with your own eyes, but you will not eat any of it!" ²⁰And that is exactly what happened to him, for the people trampled him in the gateway, and he died.

THE SHUNAMMITE'S LAND RESTORED

8 Now Elisha had said to the woman whose son he had restored to life, "Go away with your family and stay for a while wherever you can, because the LORD has decreed a famine in the land that will last seven years." ²The woman proceeded to do as the man of God said. She and her family went away and stayed in the land of the Philistines seven years.

³At the end of the seven years she came back from the land of the Philistines and went to appeal to the king for her house and land. ⁴The king was talking to Gehazi, the servant

Why do these verses repeat an earlier section of the story? (7:16–20)
The writer wanted to emphasize the way Elisha's prophecy had come true. So he retold key details of the prophecy and showed how the prophecy had been fulfilled.

Who took the woman's land? (8:1–3)
Either someone had illegally occupied her property during her absence, or it had become the king's property because it had been abandoned.

of the man of God, and had said, "Tell me about all the great things Elisha has done." [5] Just as Gehazi was telling the king how Elisha had restored the dead to life, the woman whose son Elisha had brought back to life came to appeal to the king for her house and land.

Gehazi said, "This is the woman, my lord the king, and this is her son whom Elisha restored to life." [6] The king asked the woman about it, and she told him.

Then he assigned an official to her case and said to him, "Give back everything that belonged to her, including all the income from her land from the day she left the country until now."

HAZAEL MURDERS BEN-HADAD

[7] Elisha went to Damascus, and Ben-Hadad king of Aram was ill. When the king was told, "The man of God has come all the way up here," [8] he said to Hazael, "Take a gift with you and go to meet the man of God. Consult the LORD through him; ask him, 'Will I recover from this illness?'"

[9] Hazael went to meet Elisha, taking with him as a gift forty camel-loads of all the finest wares of Damascus. He went in and stood before him, and said, "Your son Ben-Hadad king of Aram has sent me to ask, 'Will I recover from this illness?'"

[10] Elisha answered, "Go and say to him, 'You will certainly recover.' Nevertheless,[a] the LORD has revealed to me that he will in fact die." [11] He stared at him with a fixed gaze until Hazael was embarrassed. Then the man of God began to weep.

[12] "Why is my lord weeping?" asked Hazael.

"Because I know the harm you will do to the Israelites," he answered. "You will set fire to their fortified places, kill their young men with the sword, dash their little children to the ground, and rip open their pregnant women."

[13] Hazael said, "How could your servant, a mere dog, accomplish such a feat?"

"The LORD has shown me that you will become king of Aram," answered Elisha.

[14] Then Hazael left Elisha and returned to his master. When Ben-Hadad asked, "What did Elisha say to you?" Hazael replied, "He told me that you would certainly recover." [15] But the next day he took a thick cloth, soaked it in water and spread it over the king's face, so that he died. Then Hazael succeeded him as king.

JEHORAM KING OF JUDAH

[16] In the fifth year of Joram son of Ahab king of Israel, when Jehoshaphat was king of Judah, Jehoram son of Jehoshaphat began his reign as king of Judah. [17] He was thirty-two years old when he became king, and he reigned in Jerusalem eight years. [18] He followed the ways of the kings of Israel, as the house of Ahab had done, for he married a daughter of Ahab. He did evil in the eyes of the LORD.

[a] 10 The Hebrew may also be read *Go and say, 'You will certainly not recover,' for.*

Who was Hazael? (8:8)
He was the personal assistant of the king of Aram. He became king after killing Ben-Hadad, and he fulfilled Elisha's prediction by inflicting painful defeats on both Israel and Judah.

What were "the ways of the kings of Israel"? (8:18)
Unfortunately, a lot of Israel's kings abandoned God and worshiped pagan gods. Jehoram was no different. Instead of following the righteous path of his father, Jehoshaphat, Jehoram steered the people of Judah into idolatry.

¹⁹Nevertheless, for the sake of his servant David, the LORD was not willing to destroy Judah. He had promised to maintain a lamp for David and his descendants forever.

²⁰In the time of Jehoram, Edom rebelled against Judah and set up its own king. ²¹So Jehoram*ᵃ* went to Zair with all his chariots. The Edomites surrounded him and his chariot commanders, but he rose up and broke through by night; his army, however, fled back home. ²²To this day Edom has been in rebellion against Judah. Libnah revolted at the same time.

²³As for the other events of Jehoram's reign, and all he did, are they not written in the book of the annals of the kings of Judah? ²⁴Jehoram rested with his ancestors and was buried with them in the City of David. And Ahaziah his son succeeded him as king.

AHAZIAH KING OF JUDAH

²⁵In the twelfth year of Joram son of Ahab king of Israel, Ahaziah son of Jehoram king of Judah began to reign. ²⁶Ahaziah was twenty-two years old when he became king, and he reigned in Jerusalem one year. His mother's name was Athaliah, a granddaughter of Omri king of Israel. ²⁷He followed the ways of the house of Ahab and did evil in the eyes of the LORD, as the house of Ahab had done, for he was related by marriage to Ahab's family.

²⁸Ahaziah went with Joram son of Ahab to war against Hazael king of Aram at Ramoth Gilead. The Arameans wounded Joram; ²⁹so King Joram returned to Jezreel to recover from the wounds the Arameans had inflicted on him at Ramoth*ᵇ* in his battle with Hazael king of Aram.

Then Ahaziah son of Jehoram king of Judah went down to Jezreel to see Joram son of Ahab, because he had been wounded.

JEHU ANOINTED KING OF ISRAEL

9 The prophet Elisha summoned a man from the company of the prophets and said to him, "Tuck your cloak into your belt, take this flask of olive oil with you and go to Ramoth Gilead. ²When you get there, look for Jehu son of Jehoshaphat, the son of Nimshi. Go to him, get him away from his companions and take him into an inner room. ³Then take the flask and pour the oil on his head and declare, 'This is what the LORD says: I anoint you king over Israel.' Then open the door and run; don't delay!"

⁴So the young prophet went to Ramoth Gilead. ⁵When he arrived, he found the army officers sitting together. "I have a message for you, commander," he said.

"For which of us?" asked Jehu.

"For you, commander," he replied.

⁶Jehu got up and went into the house. Then the prophet poured the oil on Jehu's head and declared, "This is what the LORD, the God of Israel, says: 'I anoint you king over the LORD's people Israel. ⁷You are to destroy the house of Ahab your master, and I will avenge the blood of my servants the

Why was the young prophet told to run after anointing Jehu? (9:3)
Anointing Jehu would be seen as an act of treason — an attempt to overthrow the current government — by King Joram. Elisha warned the young man to run away to avoid being captured and killed.

ᵃ 21 Hebrew *Joram*, a variant of *Jehoram*; also in verses 23 and 24
ᵇ 29 Hebrew *Ramah*, a variant of *Ramoth*

King Jehu's Mission (9:7–37)

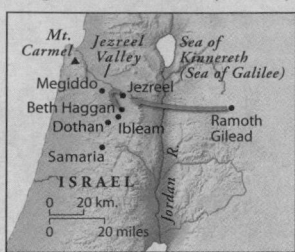

Why did they call the prophet a madman? (9:11)

Prophets often dressed in an unusual way and lived apart from the rest of society. This prophet also acted in an unusual way. He arrived unexpectedly, conducted his business in private, and then ran away.

prophets and the blood of all the LORD's servants shed by Jezebel. [8] The whole house of Ahab will perish. I will cut off from Ahab every last male in Israel—slave or free.[a] [9] I will make the house of Ahab like the house of Jeroboam son of Nebat and like the house of Baasha son of Ahijah. [10] As for Jezebel, dogs will devour her on the plot of ground at Jezreel, and no one will bury her.'" Then he opened the door and ran.

[11] When Jehu went out to his fellow officers, one of them asked him, "Is everything all right? Why did this maniac come to you?"

"You know the man and the sort of things he says," Jehu replied.

[12] "That's not true!" they said. "Tell us."

Jehu said, "Here is what he told me: 'This is what the LORD says: I anoint you king over Israel.'"

[13] They quickly took their cloaks and spread them under him on the bare steps. Then they blew the trumpet and shouted, "Jehu is king!"

JEHU KILLS JORAM AND AHAZIAH

[14] So Jehu son of Jehoshaphat, the son of Nimshi, conspired against Joram. (Now Joram and all Israel had been defending Ramoth Gilead against Hazael king of Aram, [15] but King Joram[b] had returned to Jezreel to recover from the wounds the Arameans had inflicted on him in the battle with Hazael king of Aram.) Jehu said, "If you desire to make me king, don't let anyone slip out of the city to go and tell the news in Jezreel." [16] Then he got into his chariot and rode to Jezreel, because Joram was resting there and Ahaziah king of Judah had gone down to see him.

[17] When the lookout standing on the tower in Jezreel saw Jehu's troops approaching, he called out, "I see some troops coming."

"Get a horseman," Joram ordered. "Send him to meet them and ask, 'Do you come in peace?'"

[18] The horseman rode off to meet Jehu and said, "This is what the king says: 'Do you come in peace?'"

"What do you have to do with peace?" Jehu replied. "Fall in behind me."

The lookout reported, "The messenger has reached them, but he isn't coming back."

[19] So the king sent out a second horseman. When he came to them he said, "This is what the king says: 'Do you come in peace?'"

Jehu replied, "What do you have to do with peace? Fall in behind me."

[20] The lookout reported, "He has reached them, but he isn't coming back either. The driving is like that of Jehu son of Nimshi—he drives like a maniac."

[21] "Hitch up my chariot," Joram ordered. And when it was hitched up, Joram king of Israel and Ahaziah king of Judah rode out, each in his own chariot, to meet Jehu. They met him at the plot of ground that had belonged to Naboth

---

[a] 8 Or *Israel—every ruler or leader*   [b] 15 Hebrew *Jehoram*, a variant of *Joram*; also in verses 17 and 21-24

the Jezreelite. ²²When Joram saw Jehu he asked, "Have you come in peace, Jehu?"

"How can there be peace," Jehu replied, "as long as all the idolatry and witchcraft of your mother Jezebel abound?"

²³Joram turned about and fled, calling out to Ahaziah, "Treachery, Ahaziah!"

²⁴Then Jehu drew his bow and shot Joram between the shoulders. The arrow pierced his heart and he slumped down in his chariot. ²⁵Jehu said to Bidkar, his chariot officer, "Pick him up and throw him on the field that belonged to Naboth the Jezreelite. Remember how you and I were riding together in chariots behind Ahab his father when the LORD spoke this prophecy against him: ²⁶'Yesterday I saw the blood of Naboth and the blood of his sons, declares the LORD, and I will surely make you pay for it on this plot of ground, declares the LORD.'ᵃ Now then, pick him up and throw him on that plot, in accordance with the word of the LORD."

²⁷When Ahaziah king of Judah saw what had happened, he fled up the road to Beth Haggan.ᵇ Jehu chased him, shouting, "Kill him too!" They wounded him in his chariot on the way up to Gur near Ibleam, but he escaped to Megiddo and died there. ²⁸His servants took him by chariot to Jerusalem and buried him with his ancestors in his tomb in the City of David. ²⁹(In the eleventh year of Joram son of Ahab, Ahaziah had become king of Judah.)

JEZEBEL KILLED

³⁰Then Jehu went to Jezreel. When Jezebel heard about it, she put on eye makeup, arranged her hair and looked out of a window. ³¹As Jehu entered the gate, she asked, "Have you come in peace, you Zimri, you murderer of your master?"ᶜ

³²He looked up at the window and called out, "Who is on my side? Who?" Two or three eunuchs looked down at him. ³³"Throw her down!" Jehu said. So they threw her down, and some of her blood spattered the wall and the horses as they trampled her underfoot.

³⁴Jehu went in and ate and drank. "Take care of that cursed woman," he said, "and bury her, for she was a king's daughter." ³⁵But when they went out to bury her, they found nothing except her skull, her feet and her hands. ³⁶They went back and told Jehu, who said, "This is the word of the LORD that he spoke through his servant Elijah the Tishbite: On the plot of ground at Jezreel dogs will devour Jezebel's flesh.ᵈ ³⁷Jezebel's body will be like dung on the ground in the plot at Jezreel, so that no one will be able to say, 'This is Jezebel.'"

AHAB'S FAMILY KILLED

10 Now there were in Samaria seventy sons of the house of Ahab. So Jehu wrote letters and sent them to Samaria: to the officials of Jezreel,ᵉ to the elders and to the guardians of Ahab's children. He said, ²"You have your master's sons

How did Jezebel paint her eyes? (9:30)
At that time women daubed their eyelids with kohl, a sootlike compound, to draw attention to their eyes. This is similar to how woman apply eye shadow today.

Why did Jezebel call Jehu by the name of Zimri? (9:31)
This was a sarcastic reference to an event that had taken place several years earlier. Elah, the king of Israel at that time, was deceived by one of his trusted royal officials, a man named Zimri. Zimri killed Elah so that he could be king (see 1 Kings 16:8 – 20). Jezebel knew that Jehu wanted her dead.

ᵃ 26 See 1 Kings 21:19.   ᵇ 27 Or *fled by way of the garden house*
ᶜ 31 Or *"Was there peace for Zimri, who murdered his master?"*
ᵈ 36 See 1 Kings 21:23.   ᵉ 1 Hebrew; some Septuagint manuscripts and Vulgate *of the city*

with you and you have chariots and horses, a fortified city and weapons. Now as soon as this letter reaches you, ³choose the best and most worthy of your master's sons and set him on his father's throne. Then fight for your master's house."

⁴But they were terrified and said, "If two kings could not resist him, how can we?"

⁵So the palace administrator, the city governor, the elders and the guardians sent this message to Jehu: "We are your servants and we will do anything you say. We will not appoint anyone as king; you do whatever you think best."

⁶Then Jehu wrote them a second letter, saying, "If you are on my side and will obey me, take the heads of your master's sons and come to me in Jezreel by this time tomorrow."

Now the royal princes, seventy of them, were with the leading men of the city, who were rearing them. ⁷When the letter arrived, these men took the princes and slaughtered all seventy of them. They put their heads in baskets and sent them to Jehu in Jezreel. ⁸When the messenger arrived, he told Jehu, "They have brought the heads of the princes."

Then Jehu ordered, "Put them in two piles at the entrance of the city gate until morning."

⁹The next morning Jehu went out. He stood before all the people and said, "You are innocent. It was I who conspired against my master and killed him, but who killed all these? ¹⁰Know, then, that not a word the LORD has spoken against the house of Ahab will fail. The LORD has done what he announced through his servant Elijah." ¹¹So Jehu killed everyone in Jezreel who remained of the house of Ahab, as well as all his chief men, his close friends and his priests, leaving him no survivor.

¹²Jehu then set out and went toward Samaria. At Beth Eked of the Shepherds, ¹³he met some relatives of Ahaziah king of Judah and asked, "Who are you?"

They said, "We are relatives of Ahaziah, and we have come down to greet the families of the king and of the queen mother."

¹⁴"Take them alive!" he ordered. So they took them alive and slaughtered them by the well of Beth Eked—forty-two of them. He left no survivor.

¹⁵After he left there, he came upon Jehonadab son of Rekab, who was on his way to meet him. Jehu greeted him and said, "Are you in accord with me, as I am with you?"

"I am," Jehonadab answered.

"If so," said Jehu, "give me your hand." So he did, and Jehu helped him up into the chariot. ¹⁶Jehu said, "Come with me and see my zeal for the LORD." Then he had him ride along in his chariot.

¹⁷When Jehu came to Samaria, he killed all who were left there of Ahab's family; he destroyed them, according to the word of the LORD spoken to Elijah.

SERVANTS OF BAAL KILLED

¹⁸Then Jehu brought all the people together and said to them, "Ahab served Baal a little; Jehu will serve him much. ¹⁹Now summon all the prophets of Baal, all his servants and all his priests. See that no one is missing, because I am going

Why did Jehu want the heads of the princes? (10:6–8)
Jehu displayed his war trophies—the heads of the men he killed in war—as a testament to how powerful he was, though his method was unusually cruel. He hoped this display would help establish his reputation as a worthy king.

Why did Jehu kill so many people? (10:11, 17)
It was common for kings to eliminate potential rivals for the throne. Jehu killed all those who posed a threat to his claim as king.

Why did Jehu want to impress Jehonadab? (10:16)
Jehu wanted Jehonadab's approval because it would strengthen Jehu's position.

to hold a great sacrifice for Baal. Anyone who fails to come will no longer live." But Jehu was acting deceptively in order to destroy the servants of Baal.

²⁰Jehu said, "Call an assembly in honor of Baal." So they proclaimed it. ²¹Then he sent word throughout Israel, and all the servants of Baal came; not one stayed away. They crowded into the temple of Baal until it was full from one end to the other. ²²And Jehu said to the keeper of the wardrobe, "Bring robes for all the servants of Baal." So he brought out robes for them.

²³Then Jehu and Jehonadab son of Rekab went into the temple of Baal. Jehu said to the servants of Baal, "Look around and see that no one who serves the LORD is here with you— only servants of Baal." ²⁴So they went in to make sacrifices and burnt offerings. Now Jehu had posted eighty men outside with this warning: "If one of you lets any of the men I am placing in your hands escape, it will be your life for his life."

²⁵As soon as Jehu had finished making the burnt offering, he ordered the guards and officers: "Go in and kill them; let no one escape." So they cut them down with the sword. The guards and officers threw the bodies out and then entered the inner shrine of the temple of Baal. ²⁶They brought the sacred stone out of the temple of Baal and burned it. ²⁷They demolished the sacred stone of Baal and tore down the temple of Baal, and people have used it for a latrine to this day.

²⁸So Jehu destroyed Baal worship in Israel. ²⁹However, he did not turn away from the sins of Jeroboam son of Nebat, which he had caused Israel to commit—the worship of the golden calves at Bethel and Dan.

³⁰The LORD said to Jehu, "Because you have done well in accomplishing what is right in my eyes and have done to the house of Ahab all I had in mind to do, your descendants will sit on the throne of Israel to the fourth generation." ³¹Yet Jehu was not careful to keep the law of the LORD, the God of Israel, with all his heart. He did not turn away from the sins of Jeroboam, which he had caused Israel to commit.

³²In those days the LORD began to reduce the size of Israel. Hazael overpowered the Israelites throughout their territory ³³east of the Jordan in all the land of Gilead (the region of Gad, Reuben and Manasseh), from Aroer by the Arnon Gorge through Gilead to Bashan.

³⁴As for the other events of Jehu's reign, all he did, and all his achievements, are they not written in the book of the annals of the kings of Israel?

³⁵Jehu rested with his ancestors and was buried in Samaria. And Jehoahaz his son succeeded him as king. ³⁶The time that Jehu reigned over Israel in Samaria was twenty-eight years.

ATHALIAH AND JOASH

11 When Athaliah the mother of Ahaziah saw that her son was dead, she proceeded to destroy the whole royal family. ²But Jehosheba, the daughter of King Jehoram[a] and sister of Ahaziah, took Joash son of Ahaziah and stole

---

[a] 2 Hebrew *Joram*, a variant of *Jehoram*

Was Jehu justified in lying in order to kill the prophets of Baal? (10:19)
It was right for Jehu to kill the prophets and worshipers of Baal because the punishment for worshiping idols was death. But the way he tricked his victims was not right.

Why did Jehu get rid of Baal but not the golden calves? (10:29)
For Jehu, the political benefits of keeping the calves outweighed his hatred for Baal worship. Keeping the calves would be a way for the northern tribes to set themselves apart from those worshiping the LORD in Jerusalem.

Who was Jehoida? (11:4)
He was the high priest who was a mentor to Joash and who helped David's line keep the throne of Judah in their family.

Why did the soldiers support a rebellion? (11:9)
Athaliah was a woman ruler during a time when men thought themselves superior. They probably would have rather been led by a man. Also, Athaliah was a foreigner from a kingdom north of Israel. Consequently, she did not have that much support from the people of Judah.

What covenant did the young king receive? (11:12)
Israel's rulers were supposed to study the Law (see Deut. 17:18 – 20). Joash may have received a copy of the Ten Commandments, the books of the Law (Genesis through Deuteronomy), or a document dealing with the covenant responsibilities of a king.

him away from among the royal princes, who were about to be murdered. She put him and his nurse in a bedroom to hide him from Athaliah; so he was not killed. ³He remained hidden with his nurse at the temple of the LORD for six years while Athaliah ruled the land.

⁴In the seventh year Jehoiada sent for the commanders of units of a hundred, the Carites and the guards and had them brought to him at the temple of the LORD. He made a covenant with them and put them under oath at the temple of the LORD. Then he showed them the king's son. ⁵He commanded them, saying, "This is what you are to do: You who are in the three companies that are going on duty on the Sabbath—a third of you guarding the royal palace, ⁶a third at the Sur Gate, and a third at the gate behind the guard, who take turns guarding the temple— ⁷and you who are in the other two companies that normally go off Sabbath duty are all to guard the temple for the king. ⁸Station yourselves around the king, each of you with weapon in hand. Anyone who approaches your ranks*a* is to be put to death. Stay close to the king wherever he goes."

⁹The commanders of units of a hundred did just as Jehoiada the priest ordered. Each one took his men—those who were going on duty on the Sabbath and those who were going off duty—and came to Jehoiada the priest. ¹⁰Then he gave the commanders the spears and shields that had belonged to King David and that were in the temple of the LORD. ¹¹The guards, each with weapon in hand, stationed themselves around the king—near the altar and the temple, from the south side to the north side of the temple.

¹²Jehoiada brought out the king's son and put the crown on him; he presented him with a copy of the covenant and proclaimed him king. They anointed him, and the people clapped their hands and shouted, "Long live the king!"

¹³When Athaliah heard the noise made by the guards and the people, she went to the people at the temple of the LORD. ¹⁴She looked and there was the king, standing by the pillar, as the custom was. The officers and the trumpeters were beside the king, and all the people of the land were rejoicing and blowing trumpets. Then Athaliah tore her robes and called out, "Treason! Treason!"

¹⁵Jehoiada the priest ordered the commanders of units of a hundred, who were in charge of the troops: "Bring her out between the ranks*b* and put to the sword anyone who follows her." For the priest had said, "She must not be put to death in the temple of the LORD." ¹⁶So they seized her as she reached the place where the horses enter the palace grounds, and there she was put to death.

¹⁷Jehoiada then made a covenant between the LORD and the king and people that they would be the LORD's people. He also made a covenant between the king and the people. ¹⁸All the people of the land went to the temple of Baal and tore it down. They smashed the altars and idols to pieces and killed Mattan the priest of Baal in front of the altars.

Then Jehoiada the priest posted guards at the temple of

a 8 Or *approaches the precincts*   *b 15* Or *out from the precincts* the LORD. [19]He took with him the commanders of hundreds, the Carites, the guards and all the people of the land, and together they brought the king down from the temple of the LORD and went into the palace, entering by way of the gate of the guards. The king then took his place on the royal throne. [20]All the people of the land rejoiced, and the city was calm, because Athaliah had been slain with the sword at the palace.

[21]Joash[a] was seven years old when he began to reign.[b]

JOASH REPAIRS THE TEMPLE

12[c] In the seventh year of Jehu, Joash[d] became king, and he reigned in Jerusalem forty years. His mother's name was Zibiah; she was from Beersheba. [2]Joash did what was right in the eyes of the LORD all the years Jehoiada the priest instructed him. [3]The high places, however, were not removed; the people continued to offer sacrifices and burn incense there.

[4]Joash said to the priests, "Collect all the money that is brought as sacred offerings to the temple of the LORD—the money collected in the census, the money received from personal vows and the money brought voluntarily to the temple. [5]Let every priest receive the money from one of the treasurers, then use it to repair whatever damage is found in the temple."

[6]But by the twenty-third year of King Joash the priests still had not repaired the temple. [7]Therefore King Joash summoned Jehoiada the priest and the other priests and asked them, "Why aren't you repairing the damage done to the temple? Take no more money from your treasurers, but hand it over for repairing the temple." [8]The priests agreed that they would not collect any more money from the people and that they would not repair the temple themselves.

[9]Jehoiada the priest took a chest and bored a hole in its lid. He placed it beside the altar, on the right side as one enters the temple of the LORD. The priests who guarded the entrance put into the chest all the money that was brought to the temple of the LORD. [10]Whenever they saw that there was a large amount of money in the chest, the royal secretary and the high priest came, counted the money that had been brought into the temple of the LORD and put it into bags. [11]When the amount had been determined, they gave the money to the men appointed to supervise the work on the temple. With it they paid those who worked on the temple of the LORD—the carpenters and builders, [12]the masons and stonecutters. They purchased timber and blocks of dressed stone for the repair of the temple of the LORD, and met all the other expenses of restoring the temple.

[13]The money brought into the temple was not spent for making silver basins, wick trimmers, sprinkling bowls, trumpets or any other articles of gold or silver for the temple of the LORD; [14]it was paid to the workers, who used it to repair

Why did Joash allow the high places to remain? (12:3) Although the people tore down Athaliah's temple of Baal after she died, they did not want to destroy the high places. These shrines to Canaanite gods remained popular because many people considered them necessary to the success of their crops.

Why did the temple need to be repaired? (12:5) The temple was now over a hundred years old. Queen Athaliah and most of the recent kings had not maintained the temple. And over the course of time, enemies had taken or been bribed with riches from the temple (see 1 Kings 14:25 – 26).

---

[a] 21 Hebrew *Jehoash*, a variant of *Joash*   [b] 21 In Hebrew texts this verse (11:21) is numbered 12:1.   [c] In Hebrew texts 12:1-21 is numbered 12:2-22.   [d] 1 Hebrew *Jehoash*, a variant of *Joash*; also in verses 2, 4, 6, 7 and 18

the temple. ¹⁵They did not require an accounting from those to whom they gave the money to pay the workers, because they acted with complete honesty. ¹⁶The money from the guilt offerings and sin offerings*ᵃ* was not brought into the temple of the LORD; it belonged to the priests.

¹⁷About this time Hazael king of Aram went up and attacked Gath and captured it. Then he turned to attack Jerusalem. ¹⁸But Joash king of Judah took all the sacred objects dedicated by his predecessors—Jehoshaphat, Jehoram and Ahaziah, the kings of Judah—and the gifts he himself had dedicated and all the gold found in the treasuries of the temple of the LORD and of the royal palace, and he sent them to Hazael king of Aram, who then withdrew from Jerusalem.

¹⁹As for the other events of the reign of Joash, and all he did, are they not written in the book of the annals of the kings of Judah? ²⁰His officials conspired against him and assassinated him at Beth Millo, on the road down to Silla. ²¹The officials who murdered him were Jozabad son of Shimeath and Jehozabad son of Shomer. He died and was buried with his ancestors in the City of David. And Amaziah his son succeeded him as king.

JEHOAHAZ KING OF ISRAEL

13 In the twenty-third year of Joash son of Ahaziah king of Judah, Jehoahaz son of Jehu became king of Israel in Samaria, and he reigned seventeen years. ²He did evil in the eyes of the LORD by following the sins of Jeroboam son of Nebat, which he had caused Israel to commit, and he did not turn away from them. ³So the LORD's anger burned against Israel, and for a long time he kept them under the power of Hazael king of Aram and Ben-Hadad his son.

⁴Then Jehoahaz sought the LORD's favor, and the LORD listened to him, for he saw how severely the king of Aram was oppressing Israel. ⁵The LORD provided a deliverer for Israel, and they escaped from the power of Aram. So the Israelites lived in their own homes as they had before. ⁶But they did not turn away from the sins of the house of Jeroboam, which he had caused Israel to commit; they continued in them. Also, the Asherah pole*ᵇ* remained standing in Samaria.

⁷Nothing had been left of the army of Jehoahaz except fifty horsemen, ten chariots and ten thousand foot soldiers, for the king of Aram had destroyed the rest and made them like the dust at threshing time.

⁸As for the other events of the reign of Jehoahaz, all he did and his achievements, are they not written in the book of the annals of the kings of Israel? ⁹Jehoahaz rested with his ancestors and was buried in Samaria. And Jehoash*ᶜ* his son succeeded him as king.

JEHOASH KING OF ISRAEL

¹⁰In the thirty-seventh year of Joash king of Judah, Jehoash son of Jehoahaz became king of Israel in Samaria, and he

Why did Joash plunder the newly remodeled temple? (12:18)
Hazael threatened Joash and the city of Jerusalem. Joash had turned away from the LORD after Jehoida died (see 2 Chronicles 24:17–25). Without the LORD's help, Joash concluded that all he could do was to pay Hazael in the hopes that he wouldn't attack Jerusalem.

What were the sins of Jeroboam? (13:2)
Jeroboam set up golden calves at Bethel and Dan for the people to worship (1 Kings 12:28–30). The phrase "the sins of Jeroboam" or "the ways of Jeroboam" became a common way of describing the sins of Israel in general. These phrases appear 17 times in 1 and 2 Kings.

Was Jehoahaz an evil or a good king? (13:2–4)
Jehoahaz never had true faith in God. He prayed to God when he was in trouble, but he also prayed to pagan gods.

ᵃ 16 Or purification offerings ᵇ 6 That is, a wooden symbol of the goddess Asherah; here and elsewhere in 2 Kings ᶜ 9 Hebrew Joash, a variant of Jehoash; also in verses 12-14 and 25 reigned sixteen years. [11] He did evil in the eyes of the LORD and did not turn away from any of the sins of Jeroboam son of Nebat, which he had caused Israel to commit; he continued in them.

[12] As for the other events of the reign of Jehoash, all he did and his achievements, including his war against Amaziah king of Judah, are they not written in the book of the annals of the kings of Israel? [13] Jehoash rested with his ancestors, and Jeroboam succeeded him on the throne. Jehoash was buried in Samaria with the kings of Israel.

[14] Now Elisha had been suffering from the illness from which he died. Jehoash king of Israel went down to see him and wept over him. "My father! My father!" he cried. "The chariots and horsemen of Israel!"

[15] Elisha said, "Get a bow and some arrows," and he did so. [16] "Take the bow in your hands," he said to the king of Israel. When he had taken it, Elisha put his hands on the king's hands.

[17] "Open the east window," he said, and he opened it. "Shoot!" Elisha said, and he shot. "The LORD's arrow of victory, the arrow of victory over Aram!" Elisha declared. "You will completely destroy the Arameans at Aphek."

[18] Then he said, "Take the arrows," and the king took them. Elisha told him, "Strike the ground." He struck it three times and stopped. [19] The man of God was angry with him and said, "You should have struck the ground five or six times; then you would have defeated Aram and completely destroyed it. But now you will defeat it only three times."

[20] Elisha died and was buried.

Now Moabite raiders used to enter the country every spring. [21] Once while some Israelites were burying a man, suddenly they saw a band of raiders; so they threw the man's body into Elisha's tomb. When the body touched Elisha's bones, the man came to life and stood up on his feet.

[22] Hazael king of Aram oppressed Israel throughout the reign of Jehoahaz. [23] But the LORD was gracious to them and had compassion and showed concern for them because of his covenant with Abraham, Isaac and Jacob. To this day he has been unwilling to destroy them or banish them from his presence.

[24] Hazael king of Aram died, and Ben-Hadad his son succeeded him as king. [25] Then Jehoash son of Jehoahaz recaptured from Ben-Hadad son of Hazael the towns he had taken in battle from his father Jehoahaz. Three times Jehoash defeated him, and so he recovered the Israelite towns.

AMAZIAH KING OF JUDAH

14 In the second year of Jehoash[a] son of Jehoahaz king of Israel, Amaziah son of Joash king of Judah began to reign. [2] He was twenty-five years old when he became king, and he reigned in Jerusalem twenty-nine years. His mother's name was Jehoaddan; she was from Jerusalem. [3] He did what was right in the eyes of the LORD, but not as his father David had done. In everything he followed the

---

Why would an evil king honor a prophet of God? (13:14)
Jehoash may not have believed in God, but even an evil king could have respect for God. Elisha had been a strong presence in Israel for a long time. His death would greatly affect the nation.

What was the significance of striking the ground only three times? (13:18–19)
Elisha explained that shooting the arrow out of the window meant that Israel would defeat Aram. Jehoash was criticized for only striking the ground three times because Elisha thought this was a lukewarm response to the omen. Jehoash should have been more enthusiastic about the victory, but the fact that he only struck the ground a few times showed that he lacked faith or courage.

---

[a] 1 Hebrew *Joash*, a variant of *Jehoash*; also in verses 13, 23 and 27

example of his father Joash. [4]The high places, however, were not removed; the people continued to offer sacrifices and burn incense there.

[5]After the kingdom was firmly in his grasp, he executed the officials who had murdered his father the king. [6]Yet he did not put the children of the assassins to death, in accordance with what is written in the Book of the Law of Moses where the LORD commanded: "Parents are not to be put to death for their children, nor children put to death for their parents; each will die for their own sin."[a]

[7]He was the one who defeated ten thousand Edomites in the Valley of Salt and captured Sela in battle, calling it Joktheel, the name it has to this day.

[8]Then Amaziah sent messengers to Jehoash son of Jehoahaz, the son of Jehu, king of Israel, with the challenge: "Come, let us face each other in battle."

[9]But Jehoash king of Israel replied to Amaziah king of Judah: "A thistle in Lebanon sent a message to a cedar in Lebanon, 'Give your daughter to my son in marriage.' Then a wild beast in Lebanon came along and trampled the thistle underfoot. [10]You have indeed defeated Edom and now you are arrogant. Glory in your victory, but stay at home! Why ask for trouble and cause your own downfall and that of Judah also?"

[11]Amaziah, however, would not listen, so Jehoash king of Israel attacked. He and Amaziah king of Judah faced each other at Beth Shemesh in Judah. [12]Judah was routed by Israel, and every man fled to his home. [13]Jehoash king of Israel captured Amaziah king of Judah, the son of Joash, the son of Ahaziah, at Beth Shemesh. Then Jehoash went to Jerusalem and broke down the wall of Jerusalem from the Ephraim Gate to the Corner Gate—a section about four hundred cubits long.[b] [14]He took all the gold and silver and all the articles found in the temple of the LORD and in the treasuries of the royal palace. He also took hostages and returned to Samaria.

[15]As for the other events of the reign of Jehoash, what he did and his achievements, including his war against Amaziah king of Judah, are they not written in the book of the annals of the kings of Israel? [16]Jehoash rested with his ancestors and was buried in Samaria with the kings of Israel. And Jeroboam his son succeeded him as king.

[17]Amaziah son of Joash king of Judah lived for fifteen years after the death of Jehoash son of Jehoahaz king of Israel. [18]As for the other events of Amaziah's reign, are they not written in the book of the annals of the kings of Judah?

[19]They conspired against him in Jerusalem, and he fled to Lachish, but they sent men after him to Lachish and killed him there. [20]He was brought back by horse and was buried in Jerusalem with his ancestors, in the City of David.

[21]Then all the people of Judah took Azariah,[c] who was sixteen years old, and made him king in place of his father Amaziah. [22]He was the one who rebuilt Elath and restored it to Judah after Amaziah rested with his ancestors.

Why did Amaziah challenge Jehoash? (14:8)
In order to defend his honor, Amaziah challenged Jehoash to a fight. Amaziah wanted to get back some of the losses he sustained when a band of mercenaries he hired, then fired, sought revenge and killed thousands of people in Judah (see 2 Chron. 25:5 – 13).

---

[a] 6 Deut. 24:16   [b] 13 That is, about 600 feet or about 180 meters
[c] 21 Also called Uzziah

JEROBOAM II KING OF ISRAEL

²³In the fifteenth year of Amaziah son of Joash king of Judah, Jeroboam son of Jehoash king of Israel became king in Samaria, and he reigned forty-one years. ²⁴He did evil in the eyes of the LORD and did not turn away from any of the sins of Jeroboam son of Nebat, which he had caused Israel to commit. ²⁵He was the one who restored the boundaries of Israel from Lebo Hamath to the Dead Sea,ᵃ in accordance with the word of the LORD, the God of Israel, spoken through his servant Jonah son of Amittai, the prophet from Gath Hepher.

²⁶The LORD had seen how bitterly everyone in Israel, whether slave or free, was suffering;ᵇ there was no one to help them. ²⁷And since the LORD had not said he would blot out the name of Israel from under heaven, he saved them by the hand of Jeroboam son of Jehoash.

²⁸As for the other events of Jeroboam's reign, all he did, and his military achievements, including how he recovered for Israel both Damascus and Hamath, which had belonged to Judah, are they not written in the book of the annals of the kings of Israel? ²⁹Jeroboam rested with his ancestors, the kings of Israel. And Zechariah his son succeeded him as king.

AZARIAH KING OF JUDAH

15 In the twenty-seventh year of Jeroboam king of Israel, Azariahᶜ son of Amaziah king of Judah began to reign. ²He was sixteen years old when he became king, and he reigned in Jerusalem fifty-two years. His mother's name was Jekoliah; she was from Jerusalem. ³He did what was right in the eyes of the LORD, just as his father Amaziah had done. ⁴The high places, however, were not removed; the people continued to offer sacrifices and burn incense there.

⁵The LORD afflicted the king with leprosyᵈ until the day he died, and he lived in a separate house.ᵉ Jotham the king's son had charge of the palace and governed the people of the land.

⁶As for the other events of Azariah's reign, and all he did, are they not written in the book of the annals of the kings of Judah? ⁷Azariah rested with his ancestors and was buried near them in the City of David. And Jotham his son succeeded him as king.

ZECHARIAH KING OF ISRAEL

⁸In the thirty-eighth year of Azariah king of Judah, Zechariah son of Jeroboam became king of Israel in Samaria, and he reigned six months. ⁹He did evil in the eyes of the LORD, as his predecessors had done. He did not turn away from the sins of Jeroboam son of Nebat, which he had caused Israel to commit.

¹⁰Shallum son of Jabesh conspired against Zechariah. He

Is this the same Jonah who was swallowed by the big fish? (14:25)
Yes. This is the same Jonah, son of Amittai, who is the main character in the book of Jonah.

Why were assassins allowed to become kings? (15:10, 14)
There was generally no one to stop an assassin who took the throne by force, especially if the murderer had an army backing him up. The people could do nothing but accept the new ruler.

ᵃ 25 Hebrew *the Sea of the Arabah*   ᵇ 26 Or *Israel was suffering. They were without a ruler or leader, and*   ᶜ 1 Also called *Uzziah*; also in verses 6, 7, 8, 17, 23 and 27   ᵈ 5 The Hebrew for *leprosy* was used for various diseases affecting the skin.   ᵉ 5 Or *in a house where he was relieved of responsibilities*

attacked him in front of the people,[a] assassinated him and succeeded him as king. [11]The other events of Zechariah's reign are written in the book of the annals of the kings of Israel. [12]So the word of the LORD spoken to Jehu was fulfilled: "Your descendants will sit on the throne of Israel to the fourth generation."[b]

SHALLUM KING OF ISRAEL

[13]Shallum son of Jabesh became king in the thirty-ninth year of Uzziah king of Judah, and he reigned in Samaria one month. [14]Then Menahem son of Gadi went from Tirzah up to Samaria. He attacked Shallum son of Jabesh in Samaria, assassinated him and succeeded him as king.

[15]The other events of Shallum's reign, and the conspiracy he led, are written in the book of the annals of the kings of Israel.

[16]At that time Menahem, starting out from Tirzah, attacked Tiphsah and everyone in the city and its vicinity, because they refused to open their gates. He sacked Tiphsah and ripped open all the pregnant women.

MENAHEM KING OF ISRAEL

[17]In the thirty-ninth year of Azariah king of Judah, Menahem son of Gadi became king of Israel, and he reigned in Samaria ten years. [18]He did evil in the eyes of the LORD. During his entire reign he did not turn away from the sins of Jeroboam son of Nebat, which he had caused Israel to commit.

[19]Then Pul[c] king of Assyria invaded the land, and Menahem gave him a thousand talents[d] of silver to gain his support and strengthen his own hold on the kingdom. [20]Menahem exacted this money from Israel. Every wealthy person had to contribute fifty shekels[e] of silver to be given to the king of Assyria. So the king of Assyria withdrew and stayed in the land no longer.

[21]As for the other events of Menahem's reign, and all he did, are they not written in the book of the annals of the kings of Israel? [22]Menahem rested with his ancestors. And Pekahiah his son succeeded him as king.

PEKAHIAH KING OF ISRAEL

[23]In the fiftieth year of Azariah king of Judah, Pekahiah son of Menahem became king of Israel in Samaria, and he reigned two years. [24]Pekahiah did evil in the eyes of the LORD. He did not turn away from the sins of Jeroboam son of Nebat, which he had caused Israel to commit. [25]One of his chief officers, Pekah son of Remaliah, conspired against him. Taking fifty men of Gilead with him, he assassinated Pekahiah, along with Argob and Arieh, in the citadel of the royal palace at Samaria. So Pekah killed Pekahiah and succeeded him as king.

[26]The other events of Pekahiah's reign, and all he did, are written in the book of the annals of the kings of Israel.

Why did the people of Tiphsah refuse to open the city gates? (15:16)

It isn't clear, but perhaps Menahem had done something to make the people not trust him when he was stationed in their region as a commander in Zechariah's army (verse 14). In response, Menahem crushed their objection.

Why would they kill unborn babies? (15:16)

This brutal act was probably meant to keep babies from growing up to be warriors. This was a way to maintain control over conquered people.

---

[a] 10 Hebrew; some Septuagint manuscripts in Ibleam   [b] 12 2 Kings 10:30
[c] 19 Also called Tiglath-Pileser   [d] 19 That is, about 38 tons or about 34 metric tons   [e] 20 That is, about 1 1/4 pounds or about 575 grams

PEKAH KING OF ISRAEL

²⁷ In the fifty-second year of Azariah king of Judah, Pekah son of Remaliah became king of Israel in Samaria, and he reigned twenty years. ²⁸ He did evil in the eyes of the LORD. He did not turn away from the sins of Jeroboam son of Nebat, which he had caused Israel to commit.

²⁹ In the time of Pekah king of Israel, Tiglath-Pileser king of Assyria came and took Ijon, Abel Beth Maakah, Janoah, Kedesh and Hazor. He took Gilead and Galilee, including all the land of Naphtali, and deported the people to Assyria. ³⁰ Then Hoshea son of Elah conspired against Pekah son of Remaliah. He attacked and assassinated him, and then succeeded him as king in the twentieth year of Jotham son of Uzziah.

³¹ As for the other events of Pekah's reign, and all he did, are they not written in the book of the annals of the kings of Israel?

JOTHAM KING OF JUDAH

³² In the second year of Pekah son of Remaliah king of Israel, Jotham son of Uzziah king of Judah began to reign. ³³ He was twenty-five years old when he became king, and he reigned in Jerusalem sixteen years. His mother's name was Jerusha daughter of Zadok. ³⁴ He did what was right in the eyes of the LORD, just as his father Uzziah had done. ³⁵ The high places, however, were not removed; the people continued to offer sacrifices and burn incense there. Jotham rebuilt the Upper Gate of the temple of the LORD.

³⁶ As for the other events of Jotham's reign, and what he did, are they not written in the book of the annals of the kings of Judah? ³⁷ (In those days the LORD began to send Rezin king of Aram and Pekah son of Remaliah against Judah.) ³⁸ Jotham rested with his ancestors and was buried with them in the City of David, the city of his father. And Ahaz his son succeeded him as king.

AHAZ KING OF JUDAH

16 In the seventeenth year of Pekah son of Remaliah, Ahaz son of Jotham king of Judah began to reign. ² Ahaz was twenty years old when he became king, and he reigned in Jerusalem sixteen years. Unlike David his father, he did not do what was right in the eyes of the LORD his God. ³ He followed the ways of the kings of Israel and even sacrificed his son in the fire, engaging in the detestable practices of the nations the LORD had driven out before the Israelites. ⁴ He offered sacrifices and burned incense at the high places, on the hilltops and under every spreading tree.

⁵ Then Rezin king of Aram and Pekah son of Remaliah king of Israel marched up to fight against Jerusalem and besieged Ahaz, but they could not overpower him. ⁶ At that time, Rezin king of Aram recovered Elath for Aram by driving out the people of Judah. Edomites then moved into Elath and have lived there to this day.

⁷ Ahaz sent messengers to say to Tiglath-Pileser king of Assyria, "I am your servant and vassal. Come up and save

Why did the writer refer to Azariah as Uzziah? (15:30)
Perhaps he used two names, his birth name and a name he took when he became king. The writer of this book gathered information from the annals — a record of historical events — of the kings of Israel and the annals of the kings of Judah, and perhaps these sources used different names.

Why did Ahaz sacrifice his son? (16:3)
Ahaz was trying to persuade the nature gods of Canaan to help him. Pagan people thought that if animal sacrifices pleased their gods, human sacrifices would please them even more.

me out of the hand of the king of Aram and of the king of Israel, who are attacking me." [8] And Ahaz took the silver and gold found in the temple of the LORD and in the treasuries of the royal palace and sent it as a gift to the king of Assyria. [9] The king of Assyria complied by attacking Damascus and capturing it. He deported its inhabitants to Kir and put Rezin to death.

[10] Then King Ahaz went to Damascus to meet Tiglath-Pileser king of Assyria. He saw an altar in Damascus and sent to Uriah the priest a sketch of the altar, with detailed plans for its construction. [11] So Uriah the priest built an altar in accordance with all the plans that King Ahaz had sent from Damascus and finished it before King Ahaz returned. [12] When the king came back from Damascus and saw the altar, he approached it and presented offerings[a] on it. [13] He offered up his burnt offering and grain offering, poured out his drink offering, and splashed the blood of his fellowship offerings against the altar. [14] As for the bronze altar that stood before the LORD, he brought it from the front of the temple—from between the new altar and the temple of the LORD—and put it on the north side of the new altar.

[15] King Ahaz then gave these orders to Uriah the priest: "On the large new altar, offer the morning burnt offering and the evening grain offering, the king's burnt offering and his grain offering, and the burnt offering of all the people of the land, and their grain offering and their drink offering. Splash against this altar the blood of all the burnt offerings and sacrifices. But I will use the bronze altar for seeking guidance." [16] And Uriah the priest did just as King Ahaz had ordered.

[17] King Ahaz cut off the side panels and removed the basins from the movable stands. He removed the Sea from the bronze bulls that supported it and set it on a stone base. [18] He took away the Sabbath canopy[b] that had been built at the temple and removed the royal entryway outside the temple of the LORD, in deference to the king of Assyria.

[19] As for the other events of the reign of Ahaz, and what he did, are they not written in the book of the annals of the kings of Judah? [20] Ahaz rested with his ancestors and was buried with them in the City of David. And Hezekiah his son succeeded him as king.

HOSHEA LAST KING OF ISRAEL

17 In the twelfth year of Ahaz king of Judah, Hoshea son of Elah became king of Israel in Samaria, and he reigned nine years. [2] He did evil in the eyes of the LORD, but not like the kings of Israel who preceded him.

[3] Shalmaneser king of Assyria came up to attack Hoshea, who had been Shalmaneser's vassal and had paid him tribute. [4] But the king of Assyria discovered that Hoshea was a traitor, for he had sent envoys to So[c] king of Egypt, and he no longer paid tribute to the king of Assyria, as he had done year by year. Therefore Shalmaneser seized him and put him in prison. [5] The king of Assyria invaded the entire land,

How could Ahaz use the bronze altar to guide him? (16:15)
In ancient times, some people sought guidance from the gods by examining the organs of sacrificed animals. They looked at the shape, color, and markings for a sign about what the future would hold.

What happened during a siege? (17:5)
A siege cut off a city from the outside world. With all traffic stopped, there was no way to get supplies and food inside the city. This was done in the hope that the people in the city would starve or be forced to surrender. A siege of three years was very long and would have produced a great deal of suffering.

[a] 12 Or *and went up*   [b] 18 Or *the dais of his throne* (see Septuagint)
[c] 4 *So* is probably an abbreviation for *Osorkon*.

marched against Samaria and laid siege to it for three years.
[6] In the ninth year of Hoshea, the king of Assyria captured
Samaria and deported the Israelites to Assyria. He settled
them in Halah, in Gozan on the Habor River and in the
towns of the Medes.

ISRAEL EXILED BECAUSE OF SIN

[7] All this took place because the Israelites had sinned
against the LORD their God, who had brought them up out
of Egypt from under the power of Pharaoh king of Egypt.
They worshiped other gods [8] and followed the practices of
the nations the LORD had driven out before them, as well as
the practices that the kings of Israel had introduced. [9] The
Israelites secretly did things against the LORD their God that
were not right. From watchtower to fortified city they built
themselves high places in all their towns. [10] They set up sacred stones and Asherah poles on every high hill and under
every spreading tree. [11] At every high place they burned incense, as the nations whom the LORD had driven out before
them had done. They did wicked things that aroused the
LORD's anger. [12] They worshiped idols, though the LORD had
said, "You shall not do this."[a] [13] The LORD warned Israel and
Judah through all his prophets and seers: "Turn from your
evil ways. Observe my commands and decrees, in accordance
with the entire Law that I commanded your ancestors to
obey and that I delivered to you through my servants the
prophets."

[14] But they would not listen and were as stiff-necked as
their ancestors, who did not trust in the LORD their God.
[15] They rejected his decrees and the covenant he had made
with their ancestors and the statutes he had warned them to
keep. They followed worthless idols and themselves became
worthless. They imitated the nations around them although
the LORD had ordered them, "Do not do as they do."
[16] They forsook all the commands of the LORD their God
and made for themselves two idols cast in the shape of calves,
and an Asherah pole. They bowed down to all the starry
hosts, and they worshiped Baal. [17] They sacrificed their sons
and daughters in the fire. They practiced divination and
sought omens and sold themselves to do evil in the eyes of
the LORD, arousing his anger.

[18] So the LORD was very angry with Israel and removed
them from his presence. Only the tribe of Judah was left,
[19] and even Judah did not keep the commands of the LORD
their God. They followed the practices Israel had introduced.
[20] Therefore the LORD rejected all the people of Israel; he
afflicted them and gave them into the hands of plunderers,
until he thrust them from his presence.

[21] When he tore Israel away from the house of David, they
made Jeroboam son of Nebat their king. Jeroboam enticed
Israel away from following the LORD and caused them to
commit a great sin. [22] The Israelites persisted in all the sins
of Jeroboam and did not turn away from them [23] until the
LORD removed them from his presence, as he had warned

[a] 12 Exodus 20:4,5

Why did Assyria deport the Israelites? (17:6)
The Assyrians often settled con-
quered peoples in other parts of
their kingdom in order to prevent
revolts. The tribes of Israel were
scattered around the Assyrian
kingdom.

Exile of Israel (17:6,23)

**What's the difference be-
tween a prophet and a seer?**
(17:13)
There probably was not much of
a difference. Both were messengers from God to his people.

**What did it mean that the
people were stiff-necked?**
(17:14)
This was how a farmer would
describe an ox or a horse that
would not respond or be led
when its rope was tugged. When
the Israelites were described as
stiff-necked, it meant they were
rebellious and stubborn.

through all his servants the prophets. So the people of Israel were taken from their homeland into exile in Assyria, and they are still there.

SAMARIA RESETTLED

[24]The king of Assyria brought people from Babylon, Kuthah, Avva, Hamath and Sepharvaim and settled them in the towns of Samaria to replace the Israelites. They took over Samaria and lived in its towns. [25]When they first lived there, they did not worship the LORD; so he sent lions among them and they killed some of the people. [26]It was reported to the king of Assyria: "The people you deported and resettled in the towns of Samaria do not know what the god of that country requires. He has sent lions among them, which are killing them off, because the people do not know what he requires."

[27]Then the king of Assyria gave this order: "Have one of the priests you took captive from Samaria go back to live there and teach the people what the god of the land requires." [28]So one of the priests who had been exiled from Samaria came to live in Bethel and taught them how to worship the LORD.

[29]Nevertheless, each national group made its own gods in the several towns where they settled, and set them up in the shrines the people of Samaria had made at the high places. [30]The people from Babylon made Sukkoth Benoth, those from Kuthah made Nergal, and those from Hamath made Ashima; [31]the Avvites made Nibhaz and Tartak, and the Sepharvites burned their children in the fire as sacrifices to Adrammelek and Anammelek, the gods of Sepharvaim. [32]They worshiped the LORD, but they also appointed all sorts of their own people to officiate for them as priests in the shrines at the high places. [33]They worshiped the LORD, but they also served their own gods in accordance with the customs of the nations from which they had been brought.

[34]To this day they persist in their former practices. They neither worship the LORD nor adhere to the decrees and regulations, the laws and commands that the LORD gave the descendants of Jacob, whom he named Israel. [35]When the LORD made a covenant with the Israelites, he commanded them: "Do not worship any other gods or bow down to them, serve them or sacrifice to them. [36]But the LORD, who brought you up out of Egypt with mighty power and outstretched arm, is the one you must worship. To him you shall bow down and to him offer sacrifices. [37]You must always be careful to keep the decrees and regulations, the laws and commands he wrote for you. Do not worship other gods. [38]Do not forget the covenant I have made with you, and do not worship other gods. [39]Rather, worship the LORD your God; it is he who will deliver you from the hand of all your enemies."

[40]They would not listen, however, but persisted in their former practices. [41]Even while these people were worshiping the LORD, they were serving their idols. To this day their children and grandchildren continue to do as their ancestors did.

Why did the Assyrians relocate all these people? (17:24) The Assyrians moved people around to strengthen their hold on them. Moving people to different territories was a way to wipe out their national or ethnic identities, making it less likely that they would rebel.

Did God expect foreigners to worship him? (17:25–26) Perhaps God used the fear of lions to draw these people to him. Or perhaps the writer of this book was simply repeating the people's opinion that the lions were a punishment from God.

What did the priest teach about worship? (17:28) A priest from the northern kingdom would probably have taught people to worship the LORD along with other gods. As a result, the newcomers thought of themselves as Jews while they continued to worship pagan gods. The divide between the Jews and the Samaritans began here.

HEZEKIAH KING OF JUDAH

18 In the third year of Hoshea son of Elah king of Israel, Hezekiah son of Ahaz king of Judah began to reign. ²He was twenty-five years old when he became king, and he reigned in Jerusalem twenty-nine years. His mother's name was Abijah*ᵃ* daughter of Zechariah. ³He did what was right in the eyes of the LORD, just as his father David had done. ⁴He removed the high places, smashed the sacred stones and cut down the Asherah poles. He broke into pieces the bronze snake Moses had made, for up to that time the Israelites had been burning incense to it. (It was called Nehushtan.*ᵇ*)

⁵Hezekiah trusted in the LORD, the God of Israel. There was no one like him among all the kings of Judah, either before him or after him. ⁶He held fast to the LORD and did not stop following him; he kept the commands the LORD had given Moses. ⁷And the LORD was with him; he was successful in whatever he undertook. He rebelled against the king of Assyria and did not serve him. ⁸From watchtower to fortified city, he defeated the Philistines, as far as Gaza and its territory.

⁹In King Hezekiah's fourth year, which was the seventh year of Hoshea son of Elah king of Israel, Shalmaneser king of Assyria marched against Samaria and laid siege to it. ¹⁰At the end of three years the Assyrians took it. So Samaria was captured in Hezekiah's sixth year, which was the ninth year of Hoshea king of Israel. ¹¹The king of Assyria deported Israel to Assyria and settled them in Halah, in Gozan on the Habor River and in towns of the Medes. ¹²This happened because they had not obeyed the LORD their God, but had violated his covenant—all that Moses the servant of the LORD commanded. They neither listened to the commands nor carried them out.

¹³In the fourteenth year of King Hezekiah's reign, Sennacherib king of Assyria attacked all the fortified cities of Judah and captured them. ¹⁴So Hezekiah king of Judah sent this message to the king of Assyria at Lachish: "I have done wrong. Withdraw from me, and I will pay whatever you demand of me." The king of Assyria exacted from Hezekiah king of Judah three hundred talents*ᶜ* of silver and thirty talents*ᵈ* of gold. ¹⁵So Hezekiah gave him all the silver that was found in the temple of the LORD and in the treasuries of the royal palace.

¹⁶At this time Hezekiah king of Judah stripped off the gold with which he had covered the doors and doorposts of the temple of the LORD, and gave it to the king of Assyria.

SENNACHERIB THREATENS JERUSALEM

¹⁷The king of Assyria sent his supreme commander, his chief officer and his field commander with a large army, from Lachish to King Hezekiah at Jerusalem. They came up to Jerusalem and stopped at the aqueduct of the Upper Pool, on the road to the Washerman's Field. ¹⁸They called for the

> **How did the bronze snake become an object of worship? (18:4)**
> It's not likely that the bronze snake was always an object of worship. But over time people may have begun to think of it as something that could help them as it had helped the Israelites in the desert. Gradually it became an idol that was thought to have supernatural powers.

ᵃ 2 Hebrew *Abi*, a variant of *Abijah*   *ᵇ 4 Nehushtan* sounds like the Hebrew for both *bronze* and *snake*.   *ᶜ 14* That is, about 11 tons or about 10 metric tons   *ᵈ 14* That is, about 1 ton or about 1 metric ton

king; and Eliakim son of Hilkiah the palace administrator, Shebna the secretary, and Joah son of Asaph the recorder went out to them.

19 The field commander said to them, "Tell Hezekiah:

"'This is what the great king, the king of Assyria, says: On what are you basing this confidence of yours? 20 You say you have the counsel and the might for war— but you speak only empty words. On whom are you depending, that you rebel against me? 21 Look, I know you are depending on Egypt, that splintered reed of a staff, which pierces the hand of anyone who leans on it! Such is Pharaoh king of Egypt to all who depend on him. 22 But if you say to me, "We are depending on the LORD our God"—isn't he the one whose high places and altars Hezekiah removed, saying to Judah and Jerusalem, "You must worship before this altar in Jerusalem"?

23 "'Come now, make a bargain with my master, the king of Assyria: I will give you two thousand horses— if you can put riders on them! 24 How can you repulse one officer of the least of my master's officials, even though you are depending on Egypt for chariots and horsemen*? 25 Furthermore, have I come to attack and destroy this place without word from the LORD? The LORD himself told me to march against this country and destroy it.'"

26 Then Eliakim son of Hilkiah, and Shebna and Joah said to the field commander, "Please speak to your servants in Aramaic, since we understand it. Don't speak to us in Hebrew in the hearing of the people on the wall."

27 But the commander replied, "Was it only to your master and you that my master sent me to say these things, and not to the people sitting on the wall—who, like you, will have to eat their own excrement and drink their own urine?"

28 Then the commander stood and called out in Hebrew, "Hear the word of the great king, the king of Assyria! 29 This is what the king says: Do not let Hezekiah deceive you. He cannot deliver you from my hand. 30 Do not let Hezekiah persuade you to trust in the LORD when he says, 'The LORD will surely deliver us; this city will not be given into the hand of the king of Assyria.'

31 "Do not listen to Hezekiah. This is what the king of Assyria says: Make peace with me and come out to me. Then each of you will eat fruit from your own vine and fig tree and drink water from your own cistern, 32 until I come and take you to a land like your own—a land of grain and new wine, a land of bread and vineyards, a land of olive trees and honey. Choose life and not death!

"Do not listen to Hezekiah, for he is misleading you when he says, 'The LORD will deliver us.' 33 Has the god of any nation ever delivered his land from the hand of the king of Assyria? 34 Where are the gods of Hamath and Arpad? Where are the gods of Sepharvaim, Hena and Ivvah? Have they rescued Samaria from my hand? 35 Who of all the gods

---

Why did it matter where the people worshiped God? (18:22)
The high places were associated with pagan worship. God did not approve of people worshiping him and pagan gods at the same time. God's people could pray anywhere, but sacrifices could only be offered in Jerusalem.

Why would the king of Assyria have marching orders from God? (18:25)
Sennacherib made this claim in order to intimidate the people. The Assyrian commander claimed that God had sent him and then bragged that God couldn't stop him.

Was the Hebrew language well known? (18:26–28)
Aramaic had become the international language of the Middle East. It was the language used for diplomacy and commerce. It's surprising that the Assyrian official was able to speak the Hebrew dialect of the common people of Judah.

Why did the Assyrians insult the LORD? (18:30, 35)
The Assyrians did not believe that God is the one true God. They thought he was just one of many gods who could be conquered by a more powerful god. But there is no greater god than the LORD.

---

a 24 Or charioteers

of these countries has been able to save his land from me? How then can the LORD deliver Jerusalem from my hand?"

³⁶But the people remained silent and said nothing in reply, because the king had commanded, "Do not answer him."

³⁷Then Eliakim son of Hilkiah the palace administrator, Shebna the secretary, and Joah son of Asaph the recorder went to Hezekiah, with their clothes torn, and told him what the field commander had said.

JERUSALEM'S DELIVERANCE FORETOLD

19 When King Hezekiah heard this, he tore his clothes and put on sackcloth and went into the temple of the LORD. ²He sent Eliakim the palace administrator, Shebna the secretary and the leading priests, all wearing sackcloth, to the prophet Isaiah son of Amoz. ³They told him, "This is what Hezekiah says: This day is a day of distress and rebuke and disgrace, as when children come to the moment of birth and there is no strength to deliver them. ⁴It may be that the LORD your God will hear all the words of the field commander, whom his master, the king of Assyria, has sent to ridicule the living God, and that he will rebuke him for the words the LORD your God has heard. Therefore pray for the remnant that still survives."

⁵When King Hezekiah's officials came to Isaiah, ⁶Isaiah said to them, "Tell your master, 'This is what the LORD says: Do not be afraid of what you have heard—those words with which the underlings of the king of Assyria have blasphemed me. ⁷Listen! When he hears a certain report, I will make him want to return to his own country, and there I will have him cut down with the sword.'"

⁸When the field commander heard that the king of Assyria had left Lachish, he withdrew and found the king fighting against Libnah.

⁹Now Sennacherib received a report that Tirhakah, the king of Cush,ᵃ was marching out to fight against him. So he again sent messengers to Hezekiah with this word: ¹⁰"Say to Hezekiah king of Judah: Do not let the god you depend on deceive you when he says, 'Jerusalem will not be given into the hands of the king of Assyria.' ¹¹Surely you have heard what the kings of Assyria have done to all the countries, destroying them completely. And will you be delivered? ¹²Did the gods of the nations that were destroyed by my predecessors deliver them—the gods of Gozan, Harran, Rezeph and the people of Eden who were in Tel Assar? ¹³Where is the king of Hamath or the king of Arpad? Where are the kings of Lair, Sepharvaim, Hena and Ivvah?"

HEZEKIAH'S PRAYER

¹⁴Hezekiah received the letter from the messengers and read it. Then he went up to the temple of the LORD and spread it out before the LORD. ¹⁵And Hezekiah prayed to the LORD: "LORD, the God of Israel, enthroned between the cherubim, you alone are God over all the kingdoms of the earth. You have made heaven and earth. ¹⁶Give ear, LORD,

What was the remnant? (19:4)
Many Israelites fled the northern kingdom during the Assyrian assaults and settled in Judah. So the nation of Judah was already becoming the "remnant" of Israel.

How did God change the mind of Sennacherib? (19:7)
God probably intended to use Sennacherib's anxiety or other feelings to make him want to return to his own land.

ᵃ 9 That is, the upper Nile region

and hear; open your eyes, LORD, and see; listen to the words Sennacherib has sent to ridicule the living God.

¹⁷"It is true, LORD, that the Assyrian kings have laid waste these nations and their lands. ¹⁸They have thrown their gods into the fire and destroyed them, for they were not gods but only wood and stone, fashioned by human hands. ¹⁹Now, LORD our God, deliver us from his hand, so that all the kingdoms of the earth may know that you alone, LORD, are God."

ISAIAH PROPHESIES SENNACHERIB'S FALL

²⁰Then Isaiah son of Amoz sent a message to Hezekiah: "This is what the LORD, the God of Israel, says: I have heard your prayer concerning Sennacherib king of Assyria. ²¹This is the word that the LORD has spoken against him:

"'Virgin Daughter Zion
　　despises you and mocks you.
Daughter Jerusalem
　　tosses her head as you flee.
²²Who is it you have ridiculed and blasphemed?
　　Against whom have you raised your voice
and lifted your eyes in pride?
　　Against the Holy One of Israel!
²³By your messengers
　　you have ridiculed the Lord.
And you have said,
　　"With my many chariots
I have ascended the heights of the mountains,
　　the utmost heights of Lebanon.
I have cut down its tallest cedars,
　　the choicest of its junipers.
I have reached its remotest parts,
　　the finest of its forests.
²⁴I have dug wells in foreign lands
　　and drunk the water there.
With the soles of my feet
　　I have dried up all the streams of Egypt."

²⁵"'Have you not heard?
　　Long ago I ordained it.
In days of old I planned it;
　　now I have brought it to pass,
that you have turned fortified cities
　　into piles of stone.
²⁶Their people, drained of power,
　　are dismayed and put to shame.
They are like plants in the field,
　　like tender green shoots,
like grass sprouting on the roof,
　　scorched before it grows up.

²⁷"'But I know where you are
　　and when you come and go
　　and how you rage against me.
²⁸Because you rage against me
　　and because your insolence has reached
　　　my ears,

Why did God use Assyria to destroy other nations? (19:25)
God used a variety of means to accomplish his purposes. Sometimes he used natural events. Other times he used people or nations to do his will — even those who did not fear him.

I will put my hook in your nose
and my bit in your mouth,
and I will make you return
by the way you came.'

29 "This will be the sign for you, Hezekiah:

"This year you will eat what grows by itself,
and the second year what springs from that.
But in the third year sow and reap,
plant vineyards and eat their fruit.
30 Once more a remnant of the kingdom of Judah
will take root below and bear fruit above.
31 For out of Jerusalem will come a remnant,
and out of Mount Zion a band of survivors.

"The zeal of the LORD Almighty will accomplish this.

32 "Therefore this is what the LORD says concerning the king of Assyria:

"'He will not enter this city
or shoot an arrow here.
He will not come before it with shield
or build a siege ramp against it.
33 By the way that he came he will return;
he will not enter this city,
declares the LORD.
34 I will defend this city and save it,
for my sake and for the sake of David my servant.'"

35 That night the angel of the LORD went out and put to death a hundred and eighty-five thousand in the Assyrian camp. When the people got up the next morning—there were all the dead bodies! 36 So Sennacherib king of Assyria broke camp and withdrew. He returned to Nineveh and stayed there.

37 One day, while he was worshiping in the temple of his god Nisrok, his sons Adrammelek and Sharezer killed him with the sword, and they escaped to the land of Ararat. And Esarhaddon his son succeeded him as king.

HEZEKIAH'S ILLNESS

20 In those days Hezekiah became ill and was at the point of death. The prophet Isaiah son of Amoz went to him and said, "This is what the LORD says: Put your house in order, because you are going to die; you will not recover."

2 Hezekiah turned his face to the wall and prayed to the LORD, 3 "Remember, LORD, how I have walked before you faithfully and with wholehearted devotion and have done what is good in your eyes." And Hezekiah wept bitterly.

4 Before Isaiah had left the middle court, the word of the LORD came to him: 5 "Go back and tell Hezekiah, the ruler of my people, 'This is what the LORD, the God of your father David, says: I have heard your prayer and seen your tears; I will heal you. On the third day from now you will go up to the temple of the LORD. 6 I will add fifteen years to your life. And I will deliver you and this city from the hand of the king

What did it mean for God to put a hook in Assyria's nose and a bit in its mouth? (19:28)
Nose hooks were used to lead oxen, and bits were used to control horses. The Assyrians often led captives away with a rope fastened to a hook that pierced the nose or lower lip. Here Isaiah predicted that the same thing would happen to Sennacherib.

What kind of plague did God send? (19:35)
One historian claims that the land was overrun with mice and rats. Although we don't know for sure, this may have been a form of the bubonic plague. In any case, 185,000 Assyrians died in a single night.

Why wasn't Hezekiah prepared to face death? (20:2–3)
Israelites considered long life as a sign of God's favor. Dying before one grew old was thought to show God's judgment. Perhaps Hezekiah struggled with the thought of being judged after a life of faithfully serving God.

Did Hezekiah's prayer change God's mind? (20:5–6)
Hezekiah's prayer probably did not actually change God's mind. God was ultimately in control and knew all along what would happen. He may have wanted Hezekiah to express his faith once again.

of Assyria. I will defend this city for my sake and for the sake of my servant David.'"

⁷Then Isaiah said, "Prepare a poultice of figs." They did so and applied it to the boil, and he recovered.

⁸Hezekiah had asked Isaiah, "What will be the sign that the Lord will heal me and that I will go up to the temple of the Lord on the third day from now?"

⁹Isaiah answered, "This is the Lord's sign to you that the Lord will do what he has promised: Shall the shadow go forward ten steps, or shall it go back ten steps?"

¹⁰"It is a simple matter for the shadow to go forward ten steps," said Hezekiah. "Rather, have it go back ten steps."

¹¹Then the prophet Isaiah called on the Lord, and the Lord made the shadow go back the ten steps it had gone down on the stairway of Ahaz.

ENVOYS FROM BABYLON

¹²At that time Marduk-Baladan son of Baladan king of Babylon sent Hezekiah letters and a gift, because he had heard of Hezekiah's illness. ¹³Hezekiah received the envoys and showed them all that was in his storehouses—the silver, the gold, the spices and the fine olive oil—his armory and everything found among his treasures. There was nothing in his palace or in all his kingdom that Hezekiah did not show them.

¹⁴Then Isaiah the prophet went to King Hezekiah and asked, "What did those men say, and where did they come from?"

"From a distant land," Hezekiah replied. "They came from Babylon."

¹⁵The prophet asked, "What did they see in your palace?"

"They saw everything in my palace," Hezekiah said. "There is nothing among my treasures that I did not show them."

¹⁶Then Isaiah said to Hezekiah, "Hear the word of the Lord: ¹⁷The time will surely come when everything in your palace, and all that your predecessors have stored up until this day, will be carried off to Babylon. Nothing will be left, says the Lord. ¹⁸And some of your descendants, your own flesh and blood who will be born to you, will be taken away, and they will become eunuchs in the palace of the king of Babylon."

Why did Hezekiah ask for a sign? (20:8–11)
Hezekiah was confused about what to believe, so he asked for a sign.

Did the earth reverse its rotation? (20:11)
God may have used various methods to cause a shadow to go backward, but all of them would have been miracles. In this way, God showed his faithful servant that he would continue to live.

Why would Hezekiah call this prophecy good? (20:16–19)
Hezekiah may have been relieved that God's judgment would not come immediately. But more importantly, even though he realized that captivity would be difficult for the Israelites, he responded in faith that God's will was good.

Do miracles still happen today?   2 KINGS 20

The word *miracle* literally means a marvelous event or an event that causes wonder. A miracle cannot be explained by normal natural forces; it causes people to look for a supernatural explanation, and it may serve as a sign.

The purpose of miracles in the Bible was to reveal God's power and love and to build up the faith of the people. Many miracles are recorded in both the Old Testament and the New Testament.

God is all-powerful and can do anything, so it is certainly possible that he can do miracles today. Many people have testified to events such as healings that are difficult to explain in normal medical terms. But since New Testament times, God has chosen to reveal himself more often through the miracle of his grace, the strengthening of the Holy Spirit, and the power of his Word in the Bible.

God can do miracles, but Christians have an obligation to seek ordinary means such as maintaining good health and seeking medical care rather than relying on miracles. When prayers are answered and miracles seem to occur, we should give thanks to God.

¹⁹"The word of the LORD you have spoken is good," Hezekiah replied. For he thought, "Will there not be peace and security in my lifetime?"

²⁰As for the other events of Hezekiah's reign, all his achievements and how he made the pool and the tunnel by which he brought water into the city, are they not written in the book of the annals of the kings of Judah? ²¹Hezekiah rested with his ancestors. And Manasseh his son succeeded him as king.

MANASSEH KING OF JUDAH

21 Manasseh was twelve years old when he became king, and he reigned in Jerusalem fifty-five years. His mother's name was Hephzibah. ²He did evil in the eyes of the LORD, following the detestable practices of the nations the LORD had driven out before the Israelites. ³He rebuilt the high places his father Hezekiah had destroyed; he also erected altars to Baal and made an Asherah pole, as Ahab king of Israel had done. He bowed down to all the starry hosts and worshiped them. ⁴He built altars in the temple of the LORD, of which the LORD had said, "In Jerusalem I will put my Name." ⁵In the two courts of the temple of the LORD, he built altars to all the starry hosts. ⁶He sacrificed his own son in the fire, practiced divination, sought omens, and consulted mediums and spiritists. He did much evil in the eyes of the LORD, arousing his anger.

⁷He took the carved Asherah pole he had made and put it in the temple, of which the LORD had said to David and to his son Solomon, "In this temple and in Jerusalem, which I have chosen out of all the tribes of Israel, I will put my Name forever. ⁸I will not again make the feet of the Israelites wander from the land I gave their ancestors, if only they will be careful to do everything I commanded them and will keep the whole Law that my servant Moses gave them." ⁹But the people did not listen. Manasseh led them astray, so that they did more evil than the nations the LORD had destroyed before the Israelites.

¹⁰The LORD said through his servants the prophets: ¹¹"Manasseh king of Judah has committed these detestable sins. He has done more evil than the Amorites who preceded him and has led Judah into sin with his idols. ¹²Therefore this is what the LORD, the God of Israel, says: I am going to bring such disaster on Jerusalem and Judah that the ears of everyone who hears of it will tingle. ¹³I will stretch out over Jerusalem the measuring line used against Samaria and the plumb line used against the house of Ahab. I will wipe out Jerusalem as one wipes a dish, wiping it and turning it upside down. ¹⁴I will forsake the remnant of my inheritance and give them into the hands of enemies. They will be looted and plundered by all their enemies; ¹⁵they have done evil in my eyes and have aroused my anger from the day their ancestors came out of Egypt until this day."

¹⁶Moreover, Manasseh also shed so much innocent blood that he filled Jerusalem from end to end—besides the sin that he had caused Judah to commit, so that they did evil in the eyes of the LORD.

¹⁷As for the other events of Manasseh's reign, and all he did,

In what way were the Israelites more evil than the nations before them? (21:9) The Israelites did the same things the nations before them had done, but they should have known better. They were God's chosen people, yet they rejected the covenant and worshiped idols and not God alone.

Who were Manasseh's innocent victims? (21:16) Manasseh sacrificed his own sons, probably to the god Molek, and may have influenced others to do the same. Manasseh also killed many of God's prophets; according to a Jewish tradition, Isaiah was sawed in two during his reign.

including the sin he committed, are they not written in the book of the annals of the kings of Judah? ¹⁸Manasseh rested with his ancestors and was buried in his palace garden, the garden of Uzza. And Amon his son succeeded him as king.

AMON KING OF JUDAH

¹⁹Amon was twenty-two years old when he became king, and he reigned in Jerusalem two years. His mother's name was Meshullemeth daughter of Haruz; she was from Jotbah. ²⁰He did evil in the eyes of the LORD, as his father Manasseh had done. ²¹He followed completely the ways of his father, worshiping the idols his father had worshiped, and bowing down to them. ²²He forsook the LORD, the God of his ancestors, and did not walk in obedience to him.

²³Amon's officials conspired against him and assassinated the king in his palace. ²⁴Then the people of the land killed all who had plotted against King Amon, and they made Josiah his son king in his place.

²⁵As for the other events of Amon's reign, and what he did, are they not written in the book of the annals of the kings of Judah? ²⁶He was buried in his tomb in the garden of Uzza. And Josiah his son succeeded him as king.

THE BOOK OF THE LAW FOUND

22 Josiah was eight years old when he became king, and he reigned in Jerusalem thirty-one years. His mother's name was Jedidah daughter of Adaiah; she was from Bozkath. ²He did what was right in the eyes of the LORD and followed completely the ways of his father David, not turning aside to the right or to the left.

³In the eighteenth year of his reign, King Josiah sent the secretary, Shaphan son of Azaliah, the son of Meshullam, to the temple of the LORD. He said: ⁴"Go up to Hilkiah the high priest and have him get ready the money that has been brought into the temple of the LORD, which the doorkeepers have collected from the people. ⁵Have them entrust it to the men appointed to supervise the work on the temple. And have these men pay the workers who repair the temple of the LORD— ⁶the carpenters, the builders and the masons. Also have them purchase timber and dressed stone to repair the temple. ⁷But they need not account for the money entrusted to them, because they are honest in their dealings."

⁸Hilkiah the high priest said to Shaphan the secretary, "I have found the Book of the Law in the temple of the LORD." He gave it to Shaphan, who read it. ⁹Then Shaphan the secretary went to the king and reported to him: "Your officials have paid out the money that was in the temple of the LORD and have entrusted it to the workers and supervisors at the temple." ¹⁰Then Shaphan the secretary informed the king, "Hilkiah the priest has given me a book." And Shaphan read from it in the presence of the king.

¹¹When the king heard the words of the Book of the Law, he tore his robes. ¹²He gave these orders to Hilkiah the priest, Ahikam son of Shaphan, Akbor son of Micaiah, Shaphan the secretary and Asaiah the king's attendant: ¹³"Go and inquire

How could Josiah overcome the negative influence of his ancestors? (22:2)
Josiah was only eight years old when he became king, and he was probably raised by God-fearing people. He was the last godly king of David's line prior to the exile.

How could the priests have lost the Book of the Law? (22:8)
Manasseh was devoted to worshiping false gods during his reign. Since God seemed unnecessary to the people, God's law became irrelevant. Only the oldest priests would have remembered God's law; the rest of the people forgot about it entirely.

of the LORD for me and for the people and for all Judah about what is written in this book that has been found. Great is the LORD's anger that burns against us because those who have gone before us have not obeyed the words of this book; they have not acted in accordance with all that is written there concerning us."

[14]Hilkiah the priest, Ahikam, Akbor, Shaphan and Asaiah went to speak to the prophet Huldah, who was the wife of Shallum son of Tikvah, the son of Harhas, keeper of the wardrobe. She lived in Jerusalem, in the New Quarter.

[15]She said to them, "This is what the LORD, the God of Israel, says: Tell the man who sent you to me, [16]'This is what the LORD says: I am going to bring disaster on this place and its people, according to everything written in the book the king of Judah has read. [17]Because they have forsaken me and burned incense to other gods and aroused my anger by all the idols their hands have made,[a] my anger will burn against this place and will not be quenched.' [18]Tell the king of Judah, who sent you to inquire of the LORD, 'This is what the LORD, the God of Israel, says concerning the words you heard: [19]Because your heart was responsive and you humbled yourself before the LORD when you heard what I have spoken against this place and its people — that they would become a curse[b] and be laid waste — and because you tore your robes and wept in my presence, I also have heard you, declares the LORD. [20]Therefore I will gather you to your ancestors, and you will be buried in peace. Your eyes will not see all the disaster I am going to bring on this place.'"

So they took her answer back to the king.

JOSIAH RENEWS THE COVENANT

23 Then the king called together all the elders of Judah and Jerusalem. [2]He went up to the temple of the LORD with the people of Judah, the inhabitants of Jerusalem, the priests and the prophets — all the people from the least to the greatest. He read in their hearing all the words of the Book of the Covenant, which had been found in the temple of the LORD. [3]The king stood by the pillar and renewed the covenant in the presence of the LORD — to follow the LORD and keep his commands, statutes and decrees with all his heart and all his soul, thus confirming the words of the covenant written in this book. Then all the people pledged themselves to the covenant.

[4]The king ordered Hilkiah the high priest, the priests next in rank and the doorkeepers to remove from the temple of the LORD all the articles made for Baal and Asherah and all the starry hosts. He burned them outside Jerusalem in the fields of the Kidron Valley and took the ashes to Bethel. [5]He did away with the idolatrous priests appointed by the kings of Judah to burn incense on the high places of the towns of Judah and on those around Jerusalem — those who burned incense to Baal, to the sun and moon, to the constellations and to all the starry hosts. [6]He took the Asherah pole from

How common were women prophets in Judah? (22:14)
There weren't very many women prophets in Old Testament times. The others mentioned in the Bible are Miriam (Exodus 15:20), Deborah (Judges 4:4), and Isaiah's wife (Isaiah 8:3).

What did it mean that God would gather Josiah to his fathers? (22:20)
This meant that Josiah would die and perhaps meet his ancestors in the afterlife. God assured Josiah that the final judgment on Judah and Jerusalem would not come during his lifetime.

How could Josiah destroy all of these idols and altars without resistance? (23:4–15)
The people generally supported whatever god their leader worshiped. So if a king decided to serve the LORD, the people followed his lead.

---

[a] 17 Or *by everything they have done* [b] 19 That is, their names would be used in cursing (see Jer. 29:22); or, others would see that they are cursed.

What did the women weave
for Asherah? (23:7)
It isn't clear. Perhaps they wove
clothes for the goddess, or they
may have made some kind of
a cloth screen to surround the
images of Asherah.

How were these horses dedicated to the sun? (23:11)
These horses may have been
used to pull chariots that contained images of a sun-god in
religious processions. Worship of
the sun was imported from Egypt
along with horses and chariots.

What was the Hill of Corruption? (23:13)
In ancient Israel, this hill was
called the Mount of Ointment.
But the writer of this book wanted to show that this place where
foreign gods were worshiped was
actually a corrupt place rather
than a place of anointing. In the
New Testament, this hill was
called the Mount of Olives.

Why were human bones
burned on the altars?
(23:19–20)
Josiah wanted to make these
shrines useless, so he killed the
false priests and burned their
bones on the altars, almost as a
sacrifice. Contact with the dead
would desecrate the altar and
its site so that it could never be
used as a place of worship again.

the temple of the LORD to the Kidron Valley outside Jerusalem and burned it there. He ground it to powder and
scattered the dust over the graves of the common people.
⁷He also tore down the quarters of the male shrine prostitutes that were in the temple of the LORD, the quarters where
women did weaving for Asherah.

⁸Josiah brought all the priests from the towns of Judah and
desecrated the high places, from Geba to Beersheba, where
the priests had burned incense. He broke down the gateway
at the entrance of the Gate of Joshua, the city governor, which
was on the left of the city gate. ⁹Although the priests of the
high places did not serve at the altar of the LORD in Jerusalem, they ate unleavened bread with their fellow priests.

¹⁰He desecrated Topheth, which was in the Valley of
Ben Hinnom, so no one could use it to sacrifice their son
or daughter in the fire to Molek. ¹¹He removed from the
entrance to the temple of the LORD the horses that the kings
of Judah had dedicated to the sun. They were in the court*a*
near the room of an official named Nathan-Melek. Josiah
then burned the chariots dedicated to the sun.

¹²He pulled down the altars the kings of Judah had erected on the roof near the upper room of Ahaz, and the altars
Manasseh had built in the two courts of the temple of the
LORD. He removed them from there, smashed them to pieces and threw the rubble into the Kidron Valley. ¹³The king
also desecrated the high places that were east of Jerusalem
on the south of the Hill of Corruption—the ones Solomon
king of Israel had built for Ashtoreth the vile goddess of
the Sidonians, for Chemosh the vile god of Moab, and for
Molek the detestable god of the people of Ammon. ¹⁴Josiah
smashed the sacred stones and cut down the Asherah poles
and covered the sites with human bones.

¹⁵Even the altar at Bethel, the high place made by Jeroboam son of Nebat, who had caused Israel to sin—even
that altar and high place he demolished. He burned the
high place and ground it to powder, and burned the Asherah
pole also. ¹⁶Then Josiah looked around, and when he saw
the tombs that were there on the hillside, he had the bones
removed from them and burned on the altar to defile it, in
accordance with the word of the LORD proclaimed by the
man of God who foretold these things.

¹⁷The king asked, "What is that tombstone I see?"

The people of the city said, "It marks the tomb of the man
of God who came from Judah and pronounced against the
altar of Bethel the very things you have done to it."

¹⁸"Leave it alone," he said. "Don't let anyone disturb his
bones." So they spared his bones and those of the prophet
who had come from Samaria.

¹⁹Just as he had done at Bethel, Josiah removed all the
shrines at the high places that the kings of Israel had built in
the towns of Samaria and that had aroused the LORD's anger.
²⁰Josiah slaughtered all the priests of those high places on
the altars and burned human bones on them. Then he went
back to Jerusalem.

a 11 The meaning of the Hebrew for this word is uncertain.

²¹The king gave this order to all the people: "Celebrate the Passover to the LORD your God, as it is written in this Book of the Covenant." ²²Neither in the days of the judges who led Israel nor in the days of the kings of Israel and the kings of Judah had any such Passover been observed. ²³But in the eighteenth year of King Josiah, this Passover was celebrated to the LORD in Jerusalem.

²⁴Furthermore, Josiah got rid of the mediums and spiritists, the household gods, the idols and all the other detestable things seen in Judah and Jerusalem. This he did to fulfill the requirements of the law written in the book that Hilkiah the priest had discovered in the temple of the LORD. ²⁵Neither before nor after Josiah was there a king like him who turned to the LORD as he did—with all his heart and with all his soul and with all his strength, in accordance with all the Law of Moses.

²⁶Nevertheless, the LORD did not turn away from the heat of his fierce anger, which burned against Judah because of all that Manasseh had done to arouse his anger. ²⁷So the LORD said, "I will remove Judah also from my presence as I removed Israel, and I will reject Jerusalem, the city I chose, and this temple, about which I said, 'My Name shall be there.'ᵃ"

²⁸As for the other events of Josiah's reign, and all he did, are they not written in the book of the annals of the kings of Judah?

²⁹While Josiah was king, Pharaoh Necho king of Egypt went up to the Euphrates River to help the king of Assyria. King Josiah marched out to meet him in battle, but Necho faced him and killed him at Megiddo. ³⁰Josiah's servants brought his body in a chariot from Megiddo to Jerusalem and buried him in his own tomb. And the people of the land took Jehoahaz son of Josiah and anointed him and made him king in place of his father.

JEHOAHAZ KING OF JUDAH

³¹Jehoahaz was twenty-three years old when he became king, and he reigned in Jerusalem three months. His mother's name was Hamutal daughter of Jeremiah; she was from Libnah. ³²He did evil in the eyes of the LORD, just as his predecessors had done. ³³Pharaoh Necho put him in chains at Riblah in the land of Hamath so that he might not reign in Jerusalem, and he imposed on Judah a levy of a hundred talentsᵇ of silver and a talentᶜ of gold. ³⁴Pharaoh Necho made Eliakim son of Josiah king in place of his father Josiah and changed Eliakim's name to Jehoiakim. But he took Jehoahaz and carried him off to Egypt, and there he died. ³⁵Jehoiakim paid Pharaoh Necho the silver and gold he demanded. In order to do so, he taxed the land and exacted the silver and gold from the people of the land according to their assessments.

JEHOIAKIM KING OF JUDAH

³⁶Jehoiakim was twenty-five years old when he became

Why did Pharaoh Necho chain Jehoahaz? (23:33) Pharaoh Necho wanted to show that he was in charge. By replacing Judah's king with the king's brother, he proved that Egypt was in control and not Judah.

ᵃ 27 1 Kings 8:29   ᵇ 33 That is, about 3 3/4 tons or about 3.4 metric tons
ᶜ 33 That is, about 75 pounds or about 34 kilograms

king, and he reigned in Jerusalem eleven years. His mother's name was Zebidah daughter of Pedaiah; she was from Rumah. [37] And he did evil in the eyes of the LORD, just as his predecessors had done.

24 During Jehoiakim's reign, Nebuchadnezzar king of Babylon invaded the land, and Jehoiakim became his vassal for three years. But then he turned against Nebuchadnezzar and rebelled. [2] The LORD sent Babylonian,[a] Aramean, Moabite and Ammonite raiders against him to destroy Judah, in accordance with the word of the LORD proclaimed by his servants the prophets. [3] Surely these things happened to Judah according to the LORD's command, in order to remove them from his presence because of the sins of Manasseh and all he had done, [4] including the shedding of innocent blood. For he had filled Jerusalem with innocent blood, and the LORD was not willing to forgive.

[5] As for the other events of Jehoiakim's reign, and all he did, are they not written in the book of the annals of the kings of Judah? [6] Jehoiakim rested with his ancestors. And Jehoiachin his son succeeded him as king.

[7] The king of Egypt did not march out from his own country again, because the king of Babylon had taken all his territory, from the Wadi of Egypt to the Euphrates River.

JEHOIACHIN KING OF JUDAH

[8] Jehoiachin was eighteen years old when he became king, and he reigned in Jerusalem three months. His mother's name was Nehushta daughter of Elnathan; she was from Jerusalem. [9] He did evil in the eyes of the LORD, just as his father had done.

[10] At that time the officers of Nebuchadnezzar king of Babylon advanced on Jerusalem and laid siege to it, [11] and Nebuchadnezzar himself came up to the city while his officers were besieging it. [12] Jehoiachin king of Judah, his mother, his attendants, his nobles and his officials all surrendered to him.

In the eighth year of the reign of the king of Babylon, he took Jehoiachin prisoner. [13] As the LORD had declared, Nebuchadnezzar removed the treasures from the temple of the LORD and from the royal palace, and cut up the gold articles that Solomon king of Israel had made for the temple of the LORD. [14] He carried all Jerusalem into exile: all the officers and fighting men, and all the skilled workers and artisans—a total of ten thousand. Only the poorest people of the land were left.

[15] Nebuchadnezzar took Jehoiachin captive to Babylon. He also took from Jerusalem to Babylon the king's mother, his wives, his officials and the prominent people of the land. [16] The king of Babylon also deported to Babylon the entire force of seven thousand fighting men, strong and fit for war, and a thousand skilled workers and artisans. [17] He made Mattaniah, Jehoiachin's uncle, king in his place and changed his name to Zedekiah.

[a] 2 Or *Chaldean*

**Who was Nebuchadnezzar?
(24:1)**
His name meant "O (god) Nabu, protect my son!" He was the most powerful king of the Neo-Babylonian empire. Nebuchadnezzar ruled from 605 to 562 B.C.

Did Jehoiakim serve Egypt and Babylon at the same? (24:1)
No. Babylon defeated Egypt, and Judah was part of the spoils. Jehoiakim had been a vassal king under Necho of Egypt, and now he would be a vassal king under Nebuchadnezzar of Babylon. A vassal king had little real power.

Why were the poor left behind? (24:14)
Babylon had made slaves of many people, so they wanted to take only those with skills or talents. The poor, who lacked skills and education, would be a drain on Babylon's economy.

Exile of Judah (24:14)

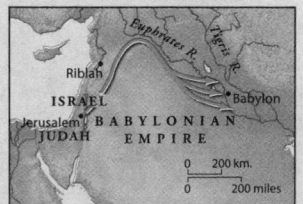

ZEDEKIAH KING OF JUDAH

[18]Zedekiah was twenty-one years old when he became king, and he reigned in Jerusalem eleven years. His mother's name was Hamutal daughter of Jeremiah; she was from Libnah. [19]He did evil in the eyes of the LORD, just as Jehoiakim had done. [20]It was because of the LORD's anger that all this happened to Jerusalem and Judah, and in the end he thrust them from his presence.

THE FALL OF JERUSALEM

Now Zedekiah rebelled against the king of Babylon.

25 So in the ninth year of Zedekiah's reign, on the tenth day of the tenth month, Nebuchadnezzar king of Babylon marched against Jerusalem with his whole army. He encamped outside the city and built siege works all around it. [2]The city was kept under siege until the eleventh year of King Zedekiah.

[3]By the ninth day of the fourth[a] month the famine in the city had become so severe that there was no food for the people to eat. [4]Then the city wall was broken through, and the whole army fled at night through the gate between the two walls near the king's garden, though the Babylonians[b] were surrounding the city. They fled toward the Arabah,[c] [5]but the Babylonian[d] army pursued the king and overtook him in the plains of Jericho. All his soldiers were separated from him and scattered, [6]and he was captured.

He was taken to the king of Babylon at Riblah, where sentence was pronounced on him. [7]They killed the sons of Zedekiah before his eyes. Then they put out his eyes, bound him with bronze shackles and took him to Babylon.

[8]On the seventh day of the fifth month, in the nineteenth year of Nebuchadnezzar king of Babylon, Nebuzaradan commander of the imperial guard, an official of the king of Babylon, came to Jerusalem. [9]He set fire to the temple of the LORD, the royal palace and all the houses of Jerusalem. Every important building he burned down. [10]The whole Babylonian army under the commander of the imperial guard broke down the walls around Jerusalem. [11]Nebuzaradan the commander of the guard carried into exile the people who remained in the city, along with the rest of the populace and those who had deserted to the king of Babylon. [12]But the commander left behind some of the poorest people of the land to work the vineyards and fields.

[13]The Babylonians broke up the bronze pillars, the movable stands and the bronze Sea that were at the temple of the LORD and they carried the bronze to Babylon. [14]They also took away the pots, shovels, wick trimmers, dishes and all the bronze articles used in the temple service. [15]The commander of the imperial guard took away the censers and sprinkling bowls—all that were made of pure gold or silver.

[16]The bronze from the two pillars, the Sea and the movable stands, which Solomon had made for the temple of the

---

[a] 3 Probable reading of the original Hebrew text (see Jer. 52:6); Masoretic Text does not have *fourth*.   [b] 4 Or *Chaldeans*; also in verses 13, 25 and 26   [c] 4 Or *the Jordan Valley*   [d] 5 Or *Chaldean*; also in verses 10 and 24

Why did the king of Babylon spare Zedekiah's life? (25:7) Nebuchadnezzar kept the captive king alive to show what happened to those who rebelled against him. Nebuchadnezzar executed Zedekiah's sons in front of him, blinded him, and chained him as a lesson to others.

Why did the Babylonians wait until later to destroy Jerusalem? (25:8–9) Nebuchadnezzar was more concerned with capturing and punishing the rebel king and using him to terrorize other would-be rebels. He punished him quickly and severely, without mercy. Destroying Jerusalem and the temple could wait.

What was the bronze Sea? (25:13) This was an enormous reservoir of water that held about 11,500 gallons (43,527 liters). It was used by the priests for ritual cleansing.

LORD, was more than could be weighed. [17] Each pillar was eighteen cubits[a] high. The bronze capital on top of one pillar was three cubits[b] high and was decorated with a network and pomegranates of bronze all around. The other pillar, with its network, was similar.

[18] The commander of the guard took as prisoners Seraiah the chief priest, Zephaniah the priest next in rank and the three doorkeepers. [19] Of those still in the city, he took the officer in charge of the fighting men, and five royal advisers. He also took the secretary who was chief officer in charge of conscripting the people of the land and sixty of the conscripts who were found in the city. [20] Nebuzaradan the commander took them all and brought them to the king of Babylon at Riblah. [21] There at Riblah, in the land of Hamath, the king had them executed.

So Judah went into captivity, away from her land.

[22] Nebuchadnezzar king of Babylon appointed Gedaliah son of Ahikam, the son of Shaphan, to be over the people he had left behind in Judah. [23] When all the army officers and their men heard that the king of Babylon had appointed Gedaliah as governor, they came to Gedaliah at Mizpah — Ishmael son of Nethaniah, Johanan son of Kareah, Seraiah son of Tanhumeth the Netophathite, Jaazaniah the son of the Maakathite, and their men. [24] Gedaliah took an oath to reassure them and their men. "Do not be afraid of the Babylonian officials," he said. "Settle down in the land and serve the king of Babylon, and it will go well with you."

[25] In the seventh month, however, Ishmael son of Nethaniah, the son of Elishama, who was of royal blood, came with ten men and assassinated Gedaliah and also the men of Judah and the Babylonians who were with him at Mizpah. [26] At this, all the people from the least to the greatest, together with the army officers, fled to Egypt for fear of the Babylonians.

JEHOIACHIN RELEASED

[27] In the thirty-seventh year of the exile of Jehoiachin king of Judah, in the year Awel-Marduk became king of Babylon, he released Jehoiachin king of Judah from prison. He did this on the twenty-seventh day of the twelfth month. [28] He spoke kindly to him and gave him a seat of honor higher than those of the other kings who were with him in Babylon. [29] So Jehoiachin put aside his prison clothes and for the rest of his life ate regularly at the king's table. [30] Day by day the king gave Jehoiachin a regular allowance as long as he lived.

Why did Ishmael assassinate Gedaliah? (25:25) Gedaliah, the governor of Judah, had urged submission to the Babylonians. Because he was related to the royal family, Ishmael probably thought he could become ruler over what was left of Judah.

---

[a] *17* That is, about 27 feet or about 8.1 meters   [b] *17* That is, about 4 1/2 feet or about 1.4 meters

KINGS OF ISRAEL AND JUDAH

This chart depicts the reigns of the kings of Israel and Judah from Jeroboam of Israel and Rehoboam of Judah until the fall of Jerusalem. As best can be determined, the dates reflect the official reign of each king and not any years of his co-regency with another king. The center column is divided into increments of 20 years; the outside columns give the passages in 1 and 2 Kings and 2 Chronicles where the reign of each king is described. By using this chart, you can see at a glance both the length of each reign and the kings in Israel and Judah who were contemporaries. The final column depicts when the major prophets lived and ministered.

PASSAGES	KINGS OF ISRAEL	DATE BC	KINGS OF JUDAH	PASSAGES		PROPHETS
IKi				IKi	2Ch	
12:25–14:20	JEROBOAM I	930	REHOBOAM	12:1-24; 14:21-31	10:1–12:16	
			ABIJAH	15:1-8	13:1-14:1	
15:25-31	NADAB	910	ASA	15:9-24	14:2–16:14	
15:32–16:7	BAASHA					
		890				
16:8-14	ELAH					
16:15-22	ZIMRI, TIBNI/OMRI					
16:23-28	OMRI					
16:29 –22:40	AHAB					Elijah
		870	JEHOSHAPHAT	22:41-50	17:1–21:3	
2 Kings						
1:1-18	AHAZIAH					
3:1–8:15	JORAM	850				Elisha

KINGS OF ISRAEL AND JUDAH

PASSAGES IKi	KINGS OF ISRAEL	DATE BC	KINGS OF JUDAH	PASSAGES IKi	PASSAGES 2Ch	PROPHETS
		850				Elisha
			JEHORAM	8:16-24	21:4-20	
9:30–10:36	JEHU		AHAZIAH	8:25-29	22:1-9	
			ATHALIAH	11:1-21	22:10–23:21	
			JOASH	12:1-21	24:1-27	
		830				
13:1-9	JEHOAHAZ					
		810				
13:10-25	JEHOASH		AMAZIAH	14:1-22	25:1-28	
		790				Jonah
14:23-29	JEROBOAM II					
		770				
			AZARIAH (UZZIAH)	15:1-7	26:1-23	Amos
						Hosea
15:8-15	ZECHARIAH, SHALLUM					
15:16-22	MENAHEM	750				

KINGS OF ISRAEL AND JUDAH

PASSAGES IKi	KINGS OF ISRAEL	DATE BC	KINGS OF JUDAH	PASSAGES IKi	PASSAGES 2Ch	PROPHETS
		750		IKi	2Ch	Hosea
15:23-26	PEKAHIAH					Micah
15:27-31	PEKAH		JOTHAM	15:32-38	27:1-9	Isaiah
17:1-6	HOSHEA	730	AHAZ	16:1-20	28:1-27	
	FALL OF SAMARIA	722				
			HEZEKIAH	18:1–20:21	29:1–32:33	
		710				
		690				
			MANASSEH	21:1-18	33:1-20	
		670				
						Nahum
		650				

KINGS OF ISRAEL AND JUDAH

PASSAGES	KINGS OF ISRAEL	DATE BC	KINGS OF JUDAH	PASSAGES		PROPHETS
IKi				IKi	2Ch	Nahum
		650				
			AMON	21:19-26	33:21-25	Zephaniah
			JOSIAH	22:1–23:30	34:1–35:27	
		630				Jeremiah
		610	JEHOAHAZ	23:31-33	36:1-4	Habakkuk
			JEHOIAKIM	23:34–24:7	36:5-8	
						Daniel
			JEHOIACHIN	24:8-17	36:9-10	
			ZEDEKIAH	24:18–25:21	36:11-21	Ezekiel
		590				
		586	FALL OF JERUSALEM	25:8-17	36:15-19	
		570				
		550				

1 Chronicles

INTRODUCTION

Who wrote this book?
The author is unknown. Many think the book was written by Ezra.

Why was this book written?
The book of 1 Chronicles gives God's evaluation of David's rule.

What happens in this book?
David becomes king of Israel. He defeats Israel's enemies and works to make Israel a mighty nation.

What do we learn about God in this book?
God gives people who serve him many different abilities.

Who is the key person in this book?
The most important person in this book is David.

Where did this happen?
These events took place in the land of Israel, united by David into a powerful nation. (See the map in the back of this Bible to see where Israel is.)

What are some of the stories in this book?

The ark comes to Jerusalem	1 Chronicles 15
God's promise to David	1 Chronicles 17
David counts his army	1 Chronicles 21
David's plans for the temple	1 Chronicles 28

When did these things happen?

1400 BC 1300 1200 1100 1000 900 800 700 600 500 400

SAUL'S REIGN (1050 – 1010 BC)

DAVID'S REIGN (1010 – 970 BC)

SOLOMON'S REIGN (970 – 930 BC)

BUILDING OF THE TEMPLE (966 – 959 BC)

DIVISION OF THE KINGDOM (930 BC)

EXILE OF ISRAEL (722 BC)

FALL OF JERUSALEM (586 BC)

BOOK OF 1 CHRONICLES WRITTEN (C. 450 – 400 BC)

HISTORICAL RECORDS FROM ADAM TO ABRAHAM

TO NOAH'S SONS

1 Adam, Seth, Enosh, [2] Kenan, Mahalalel, Jared, [3] Enoch, Methuselah, Lamech, Noah.

[4] The sons of Noah:[a]
Shem, Ham and Japheth.

THE JAPHETHITES

[5] The sons[b] of Japheth:
Gomer, Magog, Madai, Javan, Tubal, Meshek and Tiras.
[6] The sons of Gomer:
Ashkenaz, Riphath[c] and Togarmah.
[7] The sons of Javan:
Elishah, Tarshish, the Kittites and the Rodanites.

THE HAMITES

[8] The sons of Ham:
Cush, Egypt, Put and Canaan.
[9] The sons of Cush:
Seba, Havilah, Sabta, Raamah and Sabteka.
The sons of Raamah:
Sheba and Dedan.
[10] Cush was the father[d] of
Nimrod, who became a mighty warrior on earth.
[11] Egypt was the father of
the Ludites, Anamites, Lehabites, Naphtuhites,
[12] Pathrusites, Kasluhites (from whom the Philistines came) and Caphtorites.
[13] Canaan was the father of
Sidon his firstborn,[e] and of the Hittites, [14] Jebusites, Amorites, Girgashites, [15] Hivites, Arkites, Sinites, [16] Arvadites, Zemarites and Hamathites.

THE SEMITES

[17] The sons of Shem:
Elam, Ashur, Arphaxad, Lud and Aram.
The sons of Aram:[f]
Uz, Hul, Gether and Meshek.
[18] Arphaxad was the father of Shelah,
and Shelah the father of Eber.
[19] Two sons were born to Eber:
One was named Peleg,[g] because in his time the earth was divided; his brother was named Joktan.
[20] Joktan was the father of
Almodad, Sheleph, Hazarmaveth, Jerah, [21] Hadoram, Uzal, Diklah, [22] Obal,[h] Abimael, Sheba, [23] Ophir, Havilah and Jobab. All these were sons of Joktan.

---

[a] 4 Septuagint; Hebrew does not have this line.   [b] 5 *Sons* may mean *descendants* or *successors* or *nations*; also in verses 6-9, 17 and 23.   [c] 6 Many Hebrew manuscripts and Vulgate (see also Septuagint and Gen. 10:3); most Hebrew manuscripts *Diphath*   [d] 10 *Father* may mean *ancestor* or *predecessor* or *founder*; also in verses 11, 13, 18 and 20.   [e] 13 Or *of the Sidonians, the foremost*   [f] 17 One Hebrew manuscript and some Septuagint manuscripts (see also Gen. 10:23); most Hebrew manuscripts do not have this line.   [g] 19 *Peleg* means *division*.   [h] 22 Some Hebrew manuscripts and Syriac (see also Gen. 10:28); most Hebrew manuscripts *Ebal*

Why were these genealogies recorded? (1:1–9:44)
The genealogies showed the restored community's connection with the past. They served as a brief history to show that the Israel of the restoration stood at the center of God's plan from the very beginning, starting with Adam.

Why aren't Cain and Abel in the list? (1:1)
The list follows the primary family lines that produced the nations of the Middle East. Cain's children all died in the flood, and Abel did not have children. Their brother Seth was seen as Abel's replacement, so Adam's descendants came from his family.

Why are only sons listed? (1:5)
The Israelites lived in a patriarchal culture where men held the power. The sons received the inheritance, and the family's name was passed on to the next generation through the sons, which helped the Israelites stay connected to their history.

Why did the genealogy include the origin of the Philistines? (1:12)
The genealogy put the nations of the ancient Middle East into the context of their families. Since the Philistines were important to the history of Israel, the author wanted to show how they fit into the family tree.

²⁴ Shem, Arphaxad,ᵃ Shelah,
²⁵ Eber, Peleg, Reu,
²⁶ Serug, Nahor, Terah
²⁷ and Abram (that is, Abraham).

THE FAMILY OF ABRAHAM

²⁸ The sons of Abraham:
    Isaac and Ishmael.

DESCENDANTS OF HAGAR

²⁹ These were their descendants:
    Nebaioth the firstborn of Ishmael, Kedar, Adbeel,
    Mibsam, ³⁰ Mishma, Dumah, Massa, Hadad, Tema,
    ³¹ Jetur, Naphish and Kedemah. These were the sons
    of Ishmael.

DESCENDANTS OF KETURAH

³² The sons born to Keturah, Abraham's concubine:
    Zimran, Jokshan, Medan, Midian, Ishbak and Shuah.
    The sons of Jokshan:
    Sheba and Dedan.
³³ The sons of Midian:
    Ephah, Epher, Hanok, Abida and Eldaah.
    All these were descendants of Keturah.

DESCENDANTS OF SARAH

³⁴ Abraham was the father of Isaac.
    The sons of Isaac:
    Esau and Israel.

ESAU'S SONS

³⁵ The sons of Esau:
    Eliphaz, Reuel, Jeush, Jalam and Korah.
³⁶ The sons of Eliphaz:
    Teman, Omar, Zepho,ᵇ Gatam and Kenaz;
    by Timna: Amalek.ᶜ

ᵃ 24 Hebrew; some Septuagint manuscripts *Arphaxad, Cainan* (see also note
at Gen. 11:10)   ᵇ 36 Many Hebrew manuscripts, some Septuagint
manuscripts and Syriac (see also Gen. 36:11); most Hebrew manuscripts
Zephi   ᶜ 36 Some Septuagint manuscripts (see also Gen. 36:12); Hebrew
Gatam, Kenaz, Timna and Amalek

Why was Abraham's concubine included in the list? (1:32)
Concubines were sometimes included as the entire family could not be listed without mentioning them.

Why was Jacob called Israel here? (1:34)
The author wanted to show God's faithfulness to his people, so he used Jacob's covenant name to remind the Israelites of God's promises.

Why does the Bible include so many lists of names?

1 CHRONICLES 1

There were several reasons that the Bible writers included genealogies. In the first place, they showed the people their background and reminded them of their history. Genealogies also established important facts about inheritances and land ownership, almost as modern records kept by cities and counties do today. Genealogies also helped the people organize themselves according to family groups when they settled in new areas. Perhaps most importantly, genealogies reminded the people of how God had cared for them throughout their history. Many of the genealogies in the Bible trace the roots of God's people back to the patriarchs: Abraham, Isaac, and Jacob. In an indirect way this would remind the people of God's promises to those individuals and the way God had carried out those promises throughout history. This list of names goes back even further to Adam, showing that God had been their God since the very beginning of human history.

37 The sons of Reuel:

Nahath, Zerah, Shammah and Mizzah.

THE PEOPLE OF SEIR IN EDOM

38 The sons of Seir:

Lotan, Shobal, Zibeon, Anah, Dishon, Ezer and Dishan.

39 The sons of Lotan:

Hori and Homam. Timna was Lotan's sister.

40 The sons of Shobal:

Alvan,[a] Manahath, Ebal, Shepho and Onam.

The sons of Zibeon:

Aiah and Anah.

41 The son of Anah:

Dishon.

The sons of Dishon:

Hemdan,[b] Eshban, Ithran and Keran.

42 The sons of Ezer:

Bilhan, Zaavan and Akan.[c]

The sons of Dishan[d]:

Uz and Aran.

THE RULERS OF EDOM

43 These were the kings who reigned in Edom before any Israelite king reigned:

Bela son of Beor, whose city was named Dinhabah.

44 When Bela died, Jobab son of Zerah from Bozrah succeeded him as king.

45 When Jobab died, Husham from the land of the Temanites succeeded him as king.

46 When Husham died, Hadad son of Bedad, who defeated Midian in the country of Moab, succeeded him as king. His city was named Avith.

47 When Hadad died, Samlah from Masrekah succeeded him as king.

48 When Samlah died, Shaul from Rehoboth on the river[e] succeeded him as king.

49 When Shaul died, Baal-Hanan son of Akbor succeeded him as king.

50 When Baal-Hanan died, Hadad succeeded him as king. His city was named Pau,[f] and his wife's name was Mehetabel daughter of Matred, the daughter of Me-Zahab. 51 Hadad also died.

The chiefs of Edom were:

Timna, Alvah, Jetheth, 52 Oholibamah, Elah, Pinon, 53 Kenaz, Teman, Mibzar, 54 Magdiel and Iram. These were the chiefs of Edom.

How were chiefs different from kings? (1:51)
Chiefs worked under the king. There could be one than one chief, but only one king. It's possible a chief was assigned certain regions or districts.

---

[a] 40 Many Hebrew manuscripts and some Septuagint manuscripts (see also Gen. 36:23); most Hebrew manuscripts *Alian*　　[b] 41 Many Hebrew manuscripts and some Septuagint manuscripts (see also Gen. 36:26); most Hebrew manuscripts *Hamran*　　[c] 42 Many Hebrew and Septuagint manuscripts (see also Gen. 36:27); most Hebrew manuscripts *Zaavan, Jaakan*　　[d] 42 See Gen. 36:28; Hebrew *Dishon*, a variant of *Dishan*　　[e] 48 Possibly the Euphrates　　[f] 50 Many Hebrew manuscripts, some Septuagint manuscripts, Vulgate and Syriac (see also Gen. 36:39); most Hebrew manuscripts *Pai*

ISRAEL'S SONS

2 These were the sons of Israel:
Reuben, Simeon, Levi, Judah, Issachar, Zebulun, ²Dan, Joseph, Benjamin, Naphtali, Gad and Asher.

JUDAH
TO HEZRON'S SONS

³The sons of Judah:
Er, Onan and Shelah. These three were born to him by a Canaanite woman, the daughter of Shua. Er, Judah's firstborn, was wicked in the LORD's sight; so the LORD put him to death. ⁴Judah's daughter-in-law Tamar bore Perez and Zerah to Judah. He had five sons in all.

⁵The sons of Perez:
Hezron and Hamul.
⁶The sons of Zerah:
Zimri, Ethan, Heman, Kalkol and Darda*ᵃ*—five in all.
⁷The son of Karmi:
Achar,*ᵇ* who brought trouble on Israel by violating the ban on taking devoted things.*ᶜ*
⁸The son of Ethan:
Azariah.
⁹The sons born to Hezron were:
Jerahmeel, Ram and Caleb.*ᵈ*

FROM RAM SON OF HEZRON

¹⁰Ram was the father of
Amminadab, and Amminadab the father of Nahshon, the leader of the people of Judah. ¹¹Nahshon was the father of Salmon,*ᵉ* Salmon the father of Boaz, ¹²Boaz the father of Obed and Obed the father of Jesse.
¹³Jesse was the father of
Eliab his firstborn; the second son was Abinadab, the third Shimea, ¹⁴the fourth Nethanel, the fifth Raddai, ¹⁵the sixth Ozem and the seventh David. ¹⁶Their sisters were Zeruiah and Abigail. Zeruiah's three sons were Abishai, Joab and Asahel. ¹⁷Abigail was the mother of Amasa, whose father was Jether the Ishmaelite.

CALEB SON OF HEZRON

¹⁸Caleb son of Hezron had children by his wife Azubah (and by Jerioth). These were her sons: Jesher, Shobab and Ardon. ¹⁹When Azubah died, Caleb married Ephrath, who bore him Hur. ²⁰Hur was the father of Uri, and Uri the father of Bezalel.
²¹Later, Hezron, when he was sixty years old, married the daughter of Makir the father of Gilead. He made love to her, and she bore him Segub. ²²Segub was the

Why were David's sisters mentioned? (2:16)
They were probably included because their sons played important roles in Israel's foundation. Abishai, Joab, and Asahel supported David in the battles he fought. Amasa served for a time as commander of David's army.

ᵃ 6 Many Hebrew manuscripts, some Septuagint manuscripts and Syriac (see also 1 Kings 4:31); most Hebrew manuscripts *Dara*   *ᵇ 7 Achar* means *trouble; Achar* is called *Achan* in Joshua.   *ᶜ 7* The Hebrew term refers to the irrevocable giving over of things or persons to the LORD, often by totally destroying them.   *ᵈ 9* Hebrew *Kelubai,* a variant of *Caleb*   *ᵉ 11* Septuagint (see also Ruth 4:21); Hebrew *Salma*

father of Jair, who controlled twenty-three towns in Gilead. ²³(But Geshur and Aram captured Havvoth Jair,^a as well as Kenath with its surrounding settlements—sixty towns.) All these were descendants of Makir the father of Gilead.

²⁴ After Hezron died in Caleb Ephrathah, Abijah the wife of Hezron bore him Ashhur the father^b of Tekoa.

JERAHMEEL SON OF HEZRON

²⁵ The sons of Jerahmeel the firstborn of Hezron:
Ram his firstborn, Bunah, Oren, Ozem and^c Ahijah. ²⁶Jerahmeel had another wife, whose name was Atarah; she was the mother of Onam.
²⁷ The sons of Ram the firstborn of Jerahmeel:
Maaz, Jamin and Eker.
²⁸ The sons of Onam:
Shammai and Jada.
The sons of Shammai:
Nadab and Abishur.
²⁹ Abishur's wife was named Abihail, who bore him Ahban and Molid.
³⁰ The sons of Nadab:
Seled and Appaim. Seled died without children.
³¹ The son of Appaim:
Ishi, who was the father of Sheshan.
Sheshan was the father of Ahlai.
³² The sons of Jada, Shammai's brother:
Jether and Jonathan. Jether died without children.
³³ The sons of Jonathan:
Peleth and Zaza.
These were the descendants of Jerahmeel.
³⁴ Sheshan had no sons—only daughters.
He had an Egyptian servant named Jarha. ³⁵Sheshan gave his daughter in marriage to his servant Jarha, and she bore him Attai.
³⁶ Attai was the father of Nathan,
Nathan the father of Zabad,
³⁷ Zabad the father of Ephlal,
Ephlal the father of Obed,
³⁸ Obed the father of Jehu,
Jehu the father of Azariah,
³⁹ Azariah the father of Helez,
Helez the father of Eleasah,
⁴⁰ Eleasah the father of Sismai,
Sismai the father of Shallum,
⁴¹ Shallum the father of Jekamiah,
and Jekamiah the father of Elishama.

THE CLANS OF CALEB

⁴² The sons of Caleb the brother of Jerahmeel:
Mesha his firstborn, who was the father of Ziph, and his son Mareshah,^d who was the father of Hebron.

Why mention that Jether died without children? (2:32) This detail explained why none of his sons were listed in the genealogy. It was unfortunate not to have children in this culture, so readers were reminded of Jether's bad fortune.

Why marry your daughter to a slave? (2:34–35) Because Sheshan had no sons, his land would be inherited by his daughters, but control of the property would transfer to their husbands. Sheshan decided to adopt his servant as his son, and then he had his servant marry his daughter. In this way, he would be sure that his land would stay in the family.

^a 23 Or *captured the settlements of Jair*   ^b 24 *Father* may mean *civic leader* or *military leader*; also in verses 42, 45, 49-52 and possibly elsewhere.
^c 25 Or *Oren and Ozem, by*   ^d 42 The meaning of the Hebrew for this phrase is uncertain.

⁴³The sons of Hebron:

Korah, Tappuah, Rekem and Shema. ⁴⁴Shema was the father of Raham, and Raham the father of Jorkeam. Rekem was the father of Shammai. ⁴⁵The son of Shammai was Maon, and Maon was the father of Beth Zur.

⁴⁶Caleb's concubine Ephah was the mother of Haran, Moza and Gazez. Haran was the father of Gazez. ⁴⁷The sons of Jahdai:

Regem, Jotham, Geshan, Pelet, Ephah and Shaaph.

⁴⁸Caleb's concubine Maakah was the mother of Sheber and Tirhanah. ⁴⁹She also gave birth to Shaaph the father of Madmannah and to Sheva the father of Makbenah and Gibea. Caleb's daughter was Aksah. ⁵⁰These were the descendants of Caleb.

The sons of Hur the firstborn of Ephrathah:

Shobal the father of Kiriath Jearim, ⁵¹Salma the father of Bethlehem, and Hareph the father of Beth Gader.

⁵²The descendants of Shobal the father of Kiriath Jearim were:

Haroeh, half the Manahathites, ⁵³and the clans of Kiriath Jearim: the Ithrites, Puthites, Shumathites and Mishraites. From these descended the Zorathites and Eshtaolites.

⁵⁴The descendants of Salma:

Bethlehem, the Netophathites, Atroth Beth Joab, half the Manahathites, the Zorites, ⁵⁵and the clans of scribes*ᵃ who lived at Jabez: the Tirathites, Shimeathites and Sucathites. These are the Kenites who came from Hammath, the father of the Rekabites.*ᵇ

THE SONS OF DAVID

3 These were the sons of David born to him in Hebron:

The firstborn was Amnon the son of Ahinoam of Jezreel;

the second, Daniel the son of Abigail of Carmel;

²the third, Absalom the son of Maakah daughter of Talmai king of Geshur;

the fourth, Adonijah the son of Haggith;

³the fifth, Shephatiah the son of Abital;

and the sixth, Ithream, by his wife Eglah.

⁴These six were born to David in Hebron, where he reigned seven years and six months.

David reigned in Jerusalem thirty-three years, ⁵and these were the children born to him there:

Shammua,*ᶜ Shobab, Nathan and Solomon. These four were by Bathsheba*ᵈ daughter of Ammiel. ⁶There were also Ibhar, Elishua,*ᵉ Eliphelet, ⁷Nogah, Nepheg, Japhia, ⁸Elishama, Eliada and Eliphelet—nine in all. ⁹All these were the sons of David, besides his sons by his concubines. And Tamar was their sister.

Why were the sons of concubines included? (2:46)
Concubines and their children were considered members of the family. Even though concubines had a lower status than wives, they still had certain guaranteed rights.

What was the difference between families and clans? (2:52–55)
Though the word *clan* is sometimes used to describe a larger group of relatives than *family*, for the most part, the terms had a similar meaning.

How many wives did David have? (3:1–8)
Only the wives who had children are mentioned here. For example, Michal is not included because she did not have children. David probably had at least nine wives in addition to concubines.

ᵃ 55 Or *of the Sopherites*   ᵇ 55 Or *father of Beth Rekab*   ᶜ 5 Hebrew *Shimea*, a variant of *Shammua*   ᵈ 5 One Hebrew manuscript and Vulgate (see also Septuagint and 2 Samuel 11:3); most Hebrew manuscripts *Bathshua*   ᵉ 6 Two Hebrew manuscripts (see also 2 Samuel 5:15 and 1 Chron. 14:5); most Hebrew manuscripts *Elishama*

THE KINGS OF JUDAH

¹⁰ Solomon's son was Rehoboam,
Abijah his son,
Asa his son,
Jehoshaphat his son,
¹¹ Jehoram*ᵃ* his son,
Ahaziah his son,
Joash his son,
¹² Amaziah his son,
Azariah his son,
Jotham his son,
¹³ Ahaz his son,
Hezekiah his son,
Manasseh his son,
¹⁴ Amon his son,
Josiah his son.
¹⁵ The sons of Josiah:
Johanan the firstborn,
Jehoiakim the second son,
Zedekiah the third,
Shallum the fourth.
¹⁶ The successors of Jehoiakim:
Jehoiachin*ᵇ* his son,
and Zedekiah.

THE ROYAL LINE AFTER THE EXILE

¹⁷ The descendants of Jehoiachin the captive:
Shealtiel his son, ¹⁸ Malkiram, Pedaiah, Shenazzar, Jekamiah, Hoshama and Nedabiah.
¹⁹ The sons of Pedaiah:
Zerubbabel and Shimei.
The sons of Zerubbabel:
Meshullam and Hananiah.
Shelomith was their sister.
²⁰ There were also five others:
Hashubah, Ohel, Berekiah, Hasadiah and Jushab-Hesed.
²¹ The descendants of Hananiah:
Pelatiah and Jeshaiah, and the sons of Rephaiah, of Arnan, of Obadiah and of Shekaniah.
²² The descendants of Shekaniah:
Shemaiah and his sons:
Hattush, Igal, Bariah, Neariah and Shaphat—six in all.
²³ The sons of Neariah:
Elioenai, Hizkiah and Azrikam—three in all.
²⁴ The sons of Elioenai:
Hodaviah, Eliashib, Pelaiah, Akkub, Johanan, Delaiah and Anani—seven in all.

OTHER CLANS OF JUDAH

 The descendants of Judah:
Perez, Hezron, Karmi, Hur and Shobal.

ᵃ 11 Hebrew *Joram,* a variant of *Jehoram*   *ᵇ 16* Hebrew *Jeconiah,* a variant of *Jehoiachin*; also in verse 17

Why was Zedekiah listed as a successor of Jehoiakim? (3:16)
Zedekiah was Jehoiakim's uncle. When the king of Babylon conquered Jerusalem, he took Jehoiakim's son Jehoiachin into captivity and replaced him with Zedekiah, who became the last king of Judah.

²Reaiah son of Shobal was the father of Jahath, and Jahath the father of Ahumai and Lahad. These were the clans of the Zorathites.

³These were the sons*a* of Etam:
Jezreel, Ishma and Idbash. Their sister was named Hazzelelponi. ⁴Penuel was the father of Gedor, and Ezer the father of Hushah.

These were the descendants of Hur, the firstborn of Ephrathah and father*b* of Bethlehem.

⁵Ashhur the father of Tekoa had two wives, Helah and Naarah.

⁶Naarah bore him Ahuzzam, Hepher, Temeni and Haahashtari. These were the descendants of Naarah.

⁷The sons of Helah:
Zereth, Zohar, Ethnan, ⁸and Koz, who was the father of Anub and Hazzobebah and of the clans of Aharhel son of Harum.

⁹Jabez was more honorable than his brothers. His mother had named him Jabez,*c* saying, "I gave birth to him in pain." ¹⁰Jabez cried out to the God of Israel, "Oh, that you would bless me and enlarge my territory! Let your hand be with me, and keep me from harm so that I will be free from pain." And God granted his request.

¹¹Kelub, Shuhah's brother, was the father of Mehir, who was the father of Eshton. ¹²Eshton was the father of Beth Rapha, Paseah and Tehinnah the father of Ir Nahash.*d* These were the men of Rekah.

¹³The sons of Kenaz:
Othniel and Seraiah.
The sons of Othniel:
Hathath and Meonothai.*e* ¹⁴Meonothai was the father of Ophrah.
Seraiah was the father of Joab,
the father of Ge Harashim.*f* It was called this because its people were skilled workers.

¹⁵The sons of Caleb son of Jephunneh:
Iru, Elah and Naam.
The son of Elah:
Kenaz.

¹⁶The sons of Jehallelel:
Ziph, Ziphah, Tiria and Asarel.

¹⁷The sons of Ezrah:
Jether, Mered, Epher and Jalon. One of Mered's wives gave birth to Miriam, Shammai and Ishbah the father of Eshtemoa. ¹⁸(His wife from the tribe of Judah gave birth to Jered the father of Gedor, Heber the father of Soko, and Jekuthiel the father of Zanoah.) These were the children of Pharaoh's daughter Bithiah, whom Mered had married.

Why was Jabez given extra attention in the genealogy? (4:9–10)
It was common practice to insert historical notes into genealogies. Jabez was honored because of his relationship with God.

How could an Israelite marry Pharaoh's daughter? (4:17–18)
Apparently this happened long before Moses' time, when Israel was on good terms with Egypt.

---

a 3 Some Septuagint manuscripts (see also Vulgate); Hebrew *father*
b 4 *Father* may mean *civic leader* or *military leader;* also in verses 12, 14, 17, 18 and possibly elsewhere.   *c 9* Jabez sounds like the Hebrew for *pain.*
d 12 Or *of the city of Nahash*   *e 13* Some Septuagint manuscripts and Vulgate; Hebrew does not have *and Meonothai.*   *f 14* Ge Harashim means *valley of skilled workers.*

[19] The sons of Hodiah's wife, the sister of Naham:
the father of Keilah the Garmite, and Eshtemoa the
Maakathite.
[20] The sons of Shimon:
Amnon, Rinnah, Ben-Hanan and Tilon.
The descendants of Ishi:
Zoheth and Ben-Zoheth.
[21] The sons of Shelah son of Judah:
Er the father of Lekah, Laadah the father of Mareshah and the clans of the linen workers at Beth Ashbea, [22] Jokim, the men of Kozeba, and Joash and Saraph, who ruled in Moab and Jashubi Lehem. (These records are from ancient times.) [23] They were the potters who lived at Netaim and Gederah; they stayed there and worked for the king.

SIMEON

[24] The descendants of Simeon:
Nemuel, Jamin, Jarib, Zerah and Shaul;
[25] Shallum was Shaul's son, Mibsam his son and Mishma his son.
[26] The descendants of Mishma:
Hammuel his son, Zakkur his son and Shimei his son.
[27] Shimei had sixteen sons and six daughters, but his brothers did not have many children; so their entire clan did not become as numerous as the people of Judah. [28] They lived in Beersheba, Moladah, Hazar Shual, [29] Bilhah, Ezem, Tolad, [30] Bethuel, Hormah, Ziklag, [31] Beth Markaboth, Hazar Susim, Beth Biri and Shaaraim. These were their towns until the reign of David. [32] Their surrounding villages were Etam, Ain, Rimmon, Token and Ashan—five towns— [33] and all the villages around these towns as far as Baalath.[a] These were their settlements. And they kept a genealogical record.

[34] Meshobab, Jamlech, Joshah son of Amaziah, [35] Joel, Jehu son of Joshibiah, the son of Seraiah, the son of Asiel, [36] also Elioenai, Jaakobah, Jeshohaiah, Asaiah, Adiel, Jesimiel, Benaiah, [37] and Ziza son of Shiphi, the son of Allon, the son of Jedaiah, the son of Shimri, the son of Shemaiah.

[38] The men listed above by name were leaders of their clans. Their families increased greatly, [39] and they went to the outskirts of Gedor to the east of the valley in search of pasture for their flocks. [40] They found rich, good pasture, and the land was spacious, peaceful and quiet. Some Hamites had lived there formerly.

[41] The men whose names were listed came in the days of Hezekiah king of Judah. They attacked the Hamites in their dwellings and also the Meunites who were there and completely destroyed[b] them, as is evident to this day. Then they settled in their place, because there was pasture for their flocks. [42] And five hundred of these Simeonites, led

---

Why were linen workers and potters mentioned? (4:21–23)
It was common to mention the trade of a clan. It's possible these families created a monopoly on these trades. Mentioning the trade would automatically make a person think of the family.

How were these records kept? (4:33)
Early genealogies were written down and passed down through the generations. The oldest male in the family held on to these records. Because land rights were passed down to future generations, it was important for people to be able to trace their ancestry to a specific family.

---

[a] 33 Some Septuagint manuscripts (see also Joshua 19:8); Hebrew *Baal*
[b] 41 The Hebrew term refers to the irrevocable giving over of things or persons to the Lord, often by totally destroying them.

by Pelatiah, Neariah, Rephaiah and Uzziel, the sons of Ishi,
invaded the hill country of Seir. [43] They killed the remaining Amalekites who had escaped, and they have lived there
to this day.

REUBEN

5 The sons of Reuben the firstborn of Israel (he was the
firstborn, but when he defiled his father's marriage bed,
his rights as firstborn were given to the sons of Joseph son
of Israel; so he could not be listed in the genealogical record
in accordance with his birthright, [2] and though Judah was
the strongest of his brothers and a ruler came from him, the
rights of the firstborn belonged to Joseph)— [3] the sons of
Reuben the firstborn of Israel:

Hanok, Pallu, Hezron and Karmi.
[4] The descendants of Joel:
Shemaiah his son, Gog his son,
Shimei his son, [5] Micah his son,
Reaiah his son, Baal his son,
[6] and Beerah his son, whom Tiglath-Pileser[a] king of
Assyria took into exile. Beerah was a leader of the
Reubenites.
[7] Their relatives by clans, listed according to their genealogical records:
Jeiel the chief, Zechariah, [8] and Bela son of Azaz, the
son of Shema, the son of Joel. They settled in the
area from Aroer to Nebo and Baal Meon. [9] To the
east they occupied the land up to the edge of the desert that extends to the Euphrates River, because their
livestock had increased in Gilead.
[10] During Saul's reign they waged war against the
Hagrites, who were defeated at their hands; they occupied the dwellings of the Hagrites throughout the entire
region east of Gilead.

GAD

[11] The Gadites lived next to them in Bashan, as far as Salekah:
[12] Joel was the chief, Shapham the second, then Janai
and Shaphat, in Bashan.
[13] Their relatives, by families, were:
Michael, Meshullam, Sheba, Jorai, Jakan, Zia and
Eber—seven in all.
[14] These were the sons of Abihail son of Huri, the son
of Jaroah, the son of Gilead, the son of Michael, the
son of Jeshishai, the son of Jahdo, the son of Buz.
[15] Ahi son of Abdiel, the son of Guni, was head of their
family.
[16] The Gadites lived in Gilead, in Bashan and its outlying
villages, and on all the pasturelands of Sharon as far
as they extended.
[17] All these were entered in the genealogical records during the reigns of Jotham king of Judah and Jeroboam king
of Israel.

What were the rights and responsibilities of a firstborn son? (5:1)
The firstborn son typically was assigned clan leadership. He took his father's place as head of the family and he inherited double the amount of land as his brothers. When his father died, he was in charge of his younger siblings, and he was responsible for his mother and unmarried sisters. He also received the covenant blessing.

Who gained Reuben's rights as firstborn? (5:2)
Judah became the clan leader, and Joseph received the covenant blessings because he was firstborn to Rachel, Jacob's favorite wife.

---

[a] 6 Hebrew *Tilgath-Pilneser*, a variant of *Tiglath-Pileser*; also in verse 26

18 The Reubenites, the Gadites and the half-tribe of Manasseh had 44,760 men ready for military service — able-bodied men who could handle shield and sword, who could use a bow, and who were trained for battle. 19 They waged war against the Hagrites, Jetur, Naphish and Nodab. 20 They were helped in fighting them, and God delivered the Hagrites and all their allies into their hands, because they cried out to him during the battle. He answered their prayers, because they trusted in him. 21 They seized the livestock of the Hagrites — fifty thousand camels, two hundred fifty thousand sheep and two thousand donkeys. They also took one hundred thousand people captive, 22 and many others fell slain, because the battle was God's. And they occupied the land until the exile.

THE HALF-TRIBE OF MANASSEH

23 The people of the half-tribe of Manasseh were numerous; they settled in the land from Bashan to Baal Hermon, that is, to Senir (Mount Hermon).

24 These were the heads of their families: Epher, Ishi, Eliel, Azriel, Jeremiah, Hodaviah and Jahdiel. They were brave warriors, famous men, and heads of their families. 25 But they were unfaithful to the God of their ancestors and prostituted themselves to the gods of the peoples of the land, whom God had destroyed before them. 26 So the God of Israel stirred up the spirit of Pul king of Assyria (that is, Tiglath-Pileser king of Assyria), who took the Reubenites, the Gadites and the half-tribe of Manasseh into exile. He took them to Halah, Habor, Hara and the river of Gozan, where they are to this day.

LEVI

6 *a* The sons of Levi:
　　Gershon, Kohath and Merari.
2 The sons of Kohath:
　　Amram, Izhar, Hebron and Uzziel.
3 The children of Amram:
　　Aaron, Moses and Miriam.
　　The sons of Aaron:
　　Nadab, Abihu, Eleazar and Ithamar.
4 Eleazar was the father of Phinehas,
　　Phinehas the father of Abishua,
5 Abishua the father of Bukki,
　　Bukki the father of Uzzi,
6 Uzzi the father of Zerahiah,
　　Zerahiah the father of Meraioth,
7 Meraioth the father of Amariah,
　　Amariah the father of Ahitub,
8 Ahitub the father of Zadok,
　　Zadok the father of Ahimaaz,
9 Ahimaaz the father of Azariah,
　　Azariah the father of Johanan,

Why would these tribes take 100,000 captives? (5:21)
They probably used them as slaves. It was common in the ancient Middle East to force enemy peoples into slavery. Slaves in Israel were treated better than in neighboring nations because of the laws God had given Moses concerning slaves.

Did God use the king of Assyria to accomplish his will? (5:26)
Yes. As the rest of Chronicles shows, one of the themes of this book is that God blesses those who trust him and punishes those who follow other gods. Tiglath-Pileser most likely didn't realize God was using him to punish the Israelites.

---

a In Hebrew texts 6:1-15 is numbered 5:27-41, and 6:16-81 is numbered 6:1-66.

[10] Johanan the father of Azariah (it was he who served
as priest in the temple Solomon built in Jerusalem),
[11] Azariah the father of Amariah,
Amariah the father of Ahitub,
[12] Ahitub the father of Zadok,
Zadok the father of Shallum,
[13] Shallum the father of Hilkiah,
Hilkiah the father of Azariah,
[14] Azariah the father of Seraiah,
and Seraiah the father of Jozadak.[a]

[15] Jozadak was deported when the Lord sent Judah and
Jerusalem into exile by the hand of Nebuchadnezzar.

[16] The sons of Levi:
Gershon,[b] Kohath and Merari.
[17] These are the names of the sons of Gershon:
Libni and Shimei.
[18] The sons of Kohath:
Amram, Izhar, Hebron and Uzziel.
[19] The sons of Merari:
Mahli and Mushi.
These are the clans of the Levites listed according to
their fathers:
[20] Of Gershon:
Libni his son, Jahath his son,
Zimmah his son, [21] Joah his son,
Iddo his son, Zerah his son
and Jeatherai his son.
[22] The descendants of Kohath:
Amminadab his son, Korah his son,
Assir his son, [23] Elkanah his son,
Ebiasaph his son, Assir his son,
[24] Tahath his son, Uriel his son,
Uzziah his son and Shaul his son.
[25] The descendants of Elkanah:
Amasai, Ahimoth,
[26] Elkanah his son,[c] Zophai his son,
Nahath his son, [27] Eliab his son,
Jeroham his son, Elkanah his son
and Samuel his son.[d]
[28] The sons of Samuel:
Joel[e] the firstborn
and Abijah the second son.
[29] The descendants of Merari:
Mahli, Libni his son,
Shimei his son, Uzzah his son,
[30] Shimea his son, Haggiah his son
and Asaiah his son.

What happened to the priesthood during the exile? (6:15)

Without a temple to tend to, the priests' duties naturally ended when the temple was destroyed. However, the priests were assured that their services would still be needed when the time came. God promised the prophets that the Jews would return to the land of Israel and rebuild the temple, so people continued recording genealogies.

[a] 14 Hebrew *Jehozadak*, a variant of *Jozadak*; also in verse 15   [b] 16 Hebrew
Gershom, a variant of *Gershon*; also in verses 17, 20, 43, 62 and 71
[c] 26 Some Hebrew manuscripts, Septuagint and Syriac; most Hebrew
manuscripts *Ahimoth* [26] *and Elkanah. The sons of Elkanah:*   [d] 27 Some
Septuagint manuscripts (see also 1 Samuel 1:19,20 and 1 Chron. 6:33,34);
Hebrew does not have *and Samuel his son.*   [e] 28 Some Septuagint
manuscripts and Syriac (see also 1 Samuel 8:2 and 1 Chron. 6:33); Hebrew
does not have *Joel.*

Why were musicians listed? (6:31)
This genealogy proved that they were descended from the tribe of Levi, so they were legitimate worship leaders. Each of the three clans of Levi provided musicians for the temple.

Who was Asaph? (6:39)
He is sometimes called "the other psalmist" because he wrote several of the psalms included in the Bible. David is referred to as the original psalmist. He was a musician who was assigned the permanent office of sounding cymbals at worship in Jerusalem.

THE TEMPLE MUSICIANS

31 These are the men David put in charge of the music in the house of the LORD after the ark came to rest there. 32 They ministered with music before the tabernacle, the tent of meeting, until Solomon built the temple of the LORD in Jerusalem. They performed their duties according to the regulations laid down for them.

33 Here are the men who served, together with their sons:
From the Kohathites:
  Heman, the musician,
    the son of Joel, the son of Samuel,
34 the son of Elkanah, the son of Jeroham,
    the son of Eliel, the son of Toah,
35 the son of Zuph, the son of Elkanah,
    the son of Mahath, the son of Amasai,
36 the son of Elkanah, the son of Joel,
    the son of Azariah, the son of Zephaniah,
37 the son of Tahath, the son of Assir,
    the son of Ebiasaph, the son of Korah,
38 the son of Izhar, the son of Kohath,
    the son of Levi, the son of Israel;
39 and Heman's associate Asaph, who served at his right hand:
  Asaph son of Berekiah, the son of Shimea,
40 the son of Michael, the son of Baaseiah,[a]
    the son of Malkijah, 41 the son of Ethni,
    the son of Zerah, the son of Adaiah,
42 the son of Ethan, the son of Zimmah,
    the son of Shimei, 43 the son of Jahath,
    the son of Gershon, the son of Levi;
44 and from their associates, the Merarites, at his left hand:
  Ethan son of Kishi, the son of Abdi,
    the son of Malluk, 45 the son of Hashabiah,
    the son of Amaziah, the son of Hilkiah,
46 the son of Amzi, the son of Bani,
    the son of Shemer, 47 the son of Mahli,
    the son of Mushi, the son of Merari,
    the son of Levi.

48 Their fellow Levites were assigned to all the other duties of the tabernacle, the house of God. 49 But Aaron and his descendants were the ones who presented offerings on the altar of burnt offering and on the altar of incense in connection with all that was done in the Most Holy Place, making atonement for Israel, in accordance with all that Moses the servant of God had commanded.

50 These were the descendants of Aaron:
  Eleazar his son, Phinehas his son,
  Abishua his son, 51 Bukki his son,
  Uzzi his son, Zerahiah his son,
52 Meraioth his son, Amariah his son,
  Ahitub his son, 53 Zadok his son
  and Ahimaaz his son.

[a] 40 Most Hebrew manuscripts; some Hebrew manuscripts, one Septuagint manuscript and Syriac *Maaseiah*

⁵⁴These were the locations of their settlements allotted as their territory (they were assigned to the descendants of Aaron who were from the Kohathite clan, because the first lot was for them):

⁵⁵They were given Hebron in Judah with its surrounding pasturelands. ⁵⁶But the fields and villages around the city were given to Caleb son of Jephunneh.

⁵⁷So the descendants of Aaron were given Hebron (a city of refuge), and Libnah,ᵃ Jattir, Eshtemoa, ⁵⁸Hilen, Debir, ⁵⁹Ashan, Juttahᵇ and Beth Shemesh, together with their pasturelands. ⁶⁰And from the tribe of Benjamin they were given Gibeon,ᶜ Geba, Alemeth and Anathoth, together with their pasturelands.

The total number of towns distributed among the Kohathite clans came to thirteen.

⁶¹The rest of Kohath's descendants were allotted ten towns from the clans of half the tribe of Manasseh.

⁶²The descendants of Gershon, clan by clan, were allotted thirteen towns from the tribes of Issachar, Asher and Naphtali, and from the part of the tribe of Manasseh that is in Bashan.

⁶³The descendants of Merari, clan by clan, were allotted twelve towns from the tribes of Reuben, Gad and Zebulun.

⁶⁴So the Israelites gave the Levites these towns and their pasturelands. ⁶⁵From the tribes of Judah, Simeon and Benjamin they allotted the previously named towns.

⁶⁶Some of the Kohathite clans were given as their territory towns from the tribe of Ephraim.

⁶⁷In the hill country of Ephraim they were given Shechem (a city of refuge), and Gezer,ᵈ ⁶⁸Jokmeam, Beth Horon, ⁶⁹Aijalon and Gath Rimmon, together with their pasturelands.

⁷⁰And from half the tribe of Manasseh the Israelites gave Aner and Bileam, together with their pasturelands, to the rest of the Kohathite clans.

⁷¹The Gershonites received the following:
From the clan of the half-tribe of Manasseh
    they received Golan in Bashan and also Ashtaroth, together with their pasturelands;
⁷²from the tribe of Issachar
    they received Kedesh, Daberath, ⁷³Ramoth and Anem, together with their pasturelands;
⁷⁴from the tribe of Asher
    they received Mashal, Abdon, ⁷⁵Hukok and Rehob, together with their pasturelands;
⁷⁶and from the tribe of Naphtali
    they received Kedesh in Galilee, Hammon and Kiriathaim, together with their pasturelands.

⁷⁷The Merarites (the rest of the Levites) received the following:

Why were the towns of the Levites listed? (6:54)
Unlike the other tribes, the Levites were not given their own territory. For this reason, they were spread throughout all of Israel. The towns were listed so that the Israelites could bring their tithes to the Levites as a way of showing that the land belonged to God.

Who defended the Levites' towns in times of war? (6:55–80)
The Levites served God, so they did not have an army. Instead, it was the job of all the other nations to come to the Levites' rescue if they needed help, though the Levites could fight if necessary.

Why were pastures assigned along with towns? (6:76)
The people lived in towns or villages, but they needed the pastures to grow their crops and raise their livestock.

ᵃ 57 See Joshua 21:13; Hebrew *given the cities of refuge: Hebron, Libnah.*
ᵇ 59 Syriac (see also Septuagint and Joshua 21:16); Hebrew does not have *Juttah.*   ᶜ 60 See Joshua 21:17; Hebrew does not have *Gibeon.*
ᵈ 67 See Joshua 21:21; Hebrew *given the cities of refuge: Shechem, Gezer.*

From the tribe of Zebulun
> they received Jokneam, Kartah,[a] Rimmono and Tabor, together with their pasturelands;
[78] from the tribe of Reuben across the Jordan east of Jericho
> they received Bezer in the wilderness, Jahzah, [79] Kedemoth and Mephaath, together with their pasturelands;
[80] and from the tribe of Gad
> they received Ramoth in Gilead, Mahanaim, [81] Heshbon and Jazer, together with their pasturelands.

ISSACHAR

7 The sons of Issachar:
Tola, Puah, Jashub and Shimron—four in all.
[2] The sons of Tola:
> Uzzi, Rephaiah, Jeriel, Jahmai, Ibsam and Samuel—heads of their families. During the reign of David, the descendants of Tola listed as fighting men in their genealogy numbered 22,600.
[3] The son of Uzzi:
> Izrahiah.

The sons of Izrahiah:
> Michael, Obadiah, Joel and Ishiah. All five of them were chiefs. [4] According to their family genealogy, they had 36,000 men ready for battle, for they had many wives and children.
[5] The relatives who were fighting men belonging to all the clans of Issachar, as listed in their genealogy, were 87,000 in all.

BENJAMIN

[6] Three sons of Benjamin:
> Bela, Beker and Jediael.
[7] The sons of Bela:
> Ezbon, Uzzi, Uzziel, Jerimoth and Iri, heads of families—five in all. Their genealogical record listed 22,034 fighting men.
[8] The sons of Beker:
> Zemirah, Joash, Eliezer, Elioenai, Omri, Jeremoth, Abijah, Anathoth and Alemeth. All these were the sons of Beker. [9] Their genealogical record listed the heads of families and 20,200 fighting men.
[10] The son of Jediael:
> Bilhan.

The sons of Bilhan:
> Jeush, Benjamin, Ehud, Kenaanah, Zethan, Tarshish and Ahishahar. [11] All these sons of Jediael were heads of families. There were 17,200 fighting men ready to go out to war.
[12] The Shuppites and Huppites were the descendants of Ir, and the Hushites[b] the descendants of Aher.

---

[a] 77 See Septuagint and Joshua 21:34; Hebrew does not have *Jokneam, Kartah*.   [b] 12 Or *Ir. The sons of Dan: Hushim,* (see Gen. 46:23); Hebrew does not have *The sons of Dan*.

NAPHTALI

¹³ The sons of Naphtali:

Jahziel, Guni, Jezer and Shillem*ᵃ*— the descendants of Bilhah.

MANASSEH

¹⁴ The descendants of Manasseh:

Asriel was his descendant through his Aramean concubine. She gave birth to Makir the father of Gilead. ¹⁵ Makir took a wife from among the Huppites and Shuppites. His sister's name was Maakah.

Another descendant was named Zelophehad, who had only daughters.

¹⁶ Makir's wife Maakah gave birth to a son and named him Peresh. His brother was named Sheresh, and his sons were Ulam and Rakem.

¹⁷ The son of Ulam:

Bedan.

These were the sons of Gilead son of Makir, the son of Manasseh. ¹⁸ His sister Hammoleketh gave birth to Ishhod, Abiezer and Mahlah.

¹⁹ The sons of Shemida were:

Ahian, Shechem, Likhi and Aniam.

EPHRAIM

²⁰ The descendants of Ephraim:

Shuthelah, Bered his son,
Tahath his son, Eleadah his son,
Tahath his son, ²¹ Zabad his son
and Shuthelah his son.

Ezer and Elead were killed by the native-born men of Gath, when they went down to seize their livestock. ²² Their father Ephraim mourned for them many days, and his relatives came to comfort him. ²³ Then he made love to his wife again, and she became pregnant and gave birth to a son. He named him Beriah,*ᵇ* because there had been misfortune in his family. ²⁴ His daughter was Sheerah, who built Lower and Upper Beth Horon as well as Uzzen Sheerah.

²⁵ Rephah was his son, Resheph his son,*ᶜ*
Telah his son, Tahan his son,
²⁶ Ladan his son, Ammihud his son,
Elishama his son, ²⁷ Nun his son
and Joshua his son.

²⁸ Their lands and settlements included Bethel and its surrounding villages, Naaran to the east, Gezer and its villages to the west, and Shechem and its villages all the way to Ayyah and its villages. ²⁹ Along the borders of Manasseh were Beth Shan, Taanach, Megiddo and Dor, together with their villages. The descendants of Joseph son of Israel lived in these towns.

Was it normal for a woman to take charge of a construction project? (7:24)
No. Men were responsible for most construction in this culture. It was remarkable for a woman, Sheerah, to take charge of a project.

ᵃ 13 Some Hebrew and Septuagint manuscripts (see also Gen. 46:24 and Num. 26:49); most Hebrew manuscripts *Shallum*   *ᵇ 23 Beriah* sounds like the Hebrew for *misfortune.*   *ᶜ 25* Some Septuagint manuscripts; Hebrew does not have *his son.*

ASHER

30 The sons of Asher:

Imnah, Ishvah, Ishvi and Beriah. Their sister was
Serah.

31 The sons of Beriah:

Heber and Malkiel, who was the father of Birzaith.

32 Heber was the father of Japhlet, Shomer and Hotham
and of their sister Shua.

33 The sons of Japhlet:

Pasak, Bimhal and Ashvath.
These were Japhlet's sons.

34 The sons of Shomer:

Ahi, Rohgah,*a* Hubbah and Aram.

35 The sons of his brother Helem:

Zophah, Imna, Shelesh and Amal.

36 The sons of Zophah:

Suah, Harnepher, Shual, Beri, Imrah, 37 Bezer, Hod,
Shamma, Shilshah, Ithran*b* and Beera.

38 The sons of Jether:

Jephunneh, Pispah and Ara.

39 The sons of Ulla:

Arah, Hanniel and Rizia.

40 All these were descendants of Asher — heads of families, choice men, brave warriors and outstanding leaders. The
number of men ready for battle, as listed in their genealogy,
was 26,000.

Why did the genealogy list the number of warriors? (7:40)
This was probably a military census which was used to count the number of men who were able to fight in case of a war.

THE GENEALOGY OF SAUL THE BENJAMITE

8 Benjamin was the father of Bela his firstborn,
Ashbel the second son, Aharah the third,
2 Nohah the fourth and Rapha the fifth.

3 The sons of Bela were:

Addar, Gera, Abihud,*c* 4 Abishua, Naaman, Ahoah,
5 Gera, Shephuphan and Huram.

6 These were the descendants of Ehud, who were heads
of families of those living in Geba and were deported
to Manahath:

7 Naaman, Ahijah, and Gera, who deported them and
who was the father of Uzza and Ahihud.

8 Sons were born to Shaharaim in Moab after he had
divorced his wives Hushim and Baara. 9 By his wife
Hodesh he had Jobab, Zibia, Mesha, Malkam, 10 Jeuz,
Sakia and Mirmah. These were his sons, heads of
families. 11 By Hushim he had Abitub and Elpaal.

12 The sons of Elpaal:

Eber, Misham, Shemed (who built Ono and Lod
with its surrounding villages), 13 and Beriah and Shema, who were heads of families of those living in Aijalon and who drove out the inhabitants of Gath.

14 Ahio, Shashak, Jeremoth, 15 Zebadiah, Arad, Eder,
16 Michael, Ishpah and Joha were the sons of Beriah.

17 Zebadiah, Meshullam, Hizki, Heber, 18 Ishmerai, Izliah
and Jobab were the sons of Elpaal.

---

a 34 Or *of his brother Shomer: Rohgah*   *b 37* Possibly a variant of *Jether*
c 3 Or *Gera the father of Ehud*

[19] Jakim, Zikri, Zabdi, [20] Elienai, Zillethai, Eliel, [21] Adaiah,
Beraiah and Shimrath were the sons of Shimei.

[22] Ishpan, Eber, Eliel, [23] Abdon, Zikri, Hanan, [24] Hananiah, Elam, Anthothijah, [25] Iphdeiah and Penuel were
the sons of Shashak.

[26] Shamsherai, Shehariah, Athaliah, [27] Jaareshiah, Elijah
and Zikri were the sons of Jeroham.

[28] All these were heads of families, chiefs as listed in their
genealogy, and they lived in Jerusalem.

[29] Jeiel[a] the father[b] of Gibeon lived in Gibeon.
His wife's name was Maakah, [30] and his firstborn son
was Abdon, followed by Zur, Kish, Baal, Ner,[c] Nadab,
[31] Gedor, Ahio, Zeker [32] and Mikloth, who was the
father of Shimeah. They too lived near their relatives
in Jerusalem.

[33] Ner was the father of Kish, Kish the father of Saul, and
Saul the father of Jonathan, Malki-Shua, Abinadab
and Esh-Baal.[d]

[34] The son of Jonathan:
Merib-Baal,[e] who was the father of Micah.

[35] The sons of Micah:
Pithon, Melek, Tarea and Ahaz.

[36] Ahaz was the father of Jehoaddah, Jehoaddah was the
father of Alemeth, Azmaveth and Zimri, and Zimri
was the father of Moza. [37] Moza was the father of
Binea; Raphah was his son, Eleasah his son and Azel
his son.

[38] Azel had six sons, and these were their names:
Azrikam, Bokeru, Ishmael, Sheariah, Obadiah and
Hanan. All these were the sons of Azel.

[39] The sons of his brother Eshek:
Ulam his firstborn, Jeush the second son and Eliphelet the third. [40] The sons of Ulam were brave warriors
who could handle the bow. They had many sons and
grandsons—150 in all.

All these were the descendants of Benjamin.

9 All Israel was listed in the genealogies recorded in the
book of the kings of Israel and Judah. They were taken
captive to Babylon because of their unfaithfulness.

THE PEOPLE IN JERUSALEM

[2] Now the first to resettle on their own property in their
own towns were some Israelites, priests, Levites and temple
servants.

[3] Those from Judah, from Benjamin, and from Ephraim
and Manasseh who lived in Jerusalem were:

[4] Uthai son of Ammihud, the son of Omri, the son of Imri,
the son of Bani, a descendant of Perez son of Judah.

[5] Of the Shelanites[f]:
Asaiah the firstborn and his sons.

---

[a] 29 Some Septuagint manuscripts (see also 9:35); Hebrew does not have
Jeiel.   [b] 29 *Father* may mean *civic leader* or *military leader.*   [c] 30 Some
Septuagint manuscripts (see also 9:36); Hebrew does not have *Ner.*
[d] 33 Also known as *Ish-Bosheth*   [e] 34 Also known as *Mephibosheth*
[f] 5 See Num. 26:20; Hebrew *Shilonites.*

⁶Of the Zerahites:
    Jeuel.
    The people from Judah numbered 690.
⁷Of the Benjamites:
    Sallu son of Meshullam, the son of Hodaviah, the son
    of Hassenuah;
    ⁸Ibneiah son of Jeroham; Elah son of Uzzi, the son of
    Mikri; and Meshullam son of Shephatiah, the son of
    Reuel, the son of Ibnijah.
    ⁹The people from Benjamin, as listed in their genealo-
    gy, numbered 956. All these men were heads of their
    families.
¹⁰Of the priests:
    Jedaiah; Jehoiarib; Jakin;
    ¹¹Azariah son of Hilkiah, the son of Meshullam, the
    son of Zadok, the son of Meraioth, the son of Ahitub,
    the official in charge of the house of God;
    ¹²Adaiah son of Jeroham, the son of Pashhur, the son of
    Malkijah; and Maasai son of Adiel, the son of Jahze-
    rah, the son of Meshullam, the son of Meshillemith,
    the son of Immer.
    ¹³The priests, who were heads of families, numbered
    1,760. They were able men, responsible for minister-
    ing in the house of God.
¹⁴Of the Levites:
    Shemaiah son of Hasshub, the son of Azrikam, the
    son of Hashabiah, a Merarite; ¹⁵Bakbakkar, Heresh,
    Galal and Mattaniah son of Mika, the son of Zikri,
    the son of Asaph; ¹⁶Obadiah son of Shemaiah, the
    son of Galal, the son of Jeduthun; and Berekiah son
    of Asa, the son of Elkanah, who lived in the villages
    of the Netophathites.
¹⁷The gatekeepers:
    Shallum, Akkub, Talmon, Ahiman and their fellow
    Levites, Shallum their chief ¹⁸being stationed at the
    King's Gate on the east, up to the present time. These
    were the gatekeepers belonging to the camp of the
    Levites. ¹⁹Shallum son of Kore, the son of Ebiasaph,
    the son of Korah, and his fellow gatekeepers from
    his family (the Korahites) were responsible for guard-
    ing the thresholds of the tent just as their ancestors
    had been responsible for guarding the entrance to the
    dwelling of the LORD. ²⁰In earlier times Phinehas son
    of Eleazar was the official in charge of the gatekeep-
    ers, and the LORD was with him. ²¹Zechariah son of
    Meshelemiah was the gatekeeper at the entrance to
    the tent of meeting.
²²Altogether, those chosen to be gatekeepers at the thresholds numbered 212. They were registered by genealogy in
their villages. The gatekeepers had been assigned to their
positions of trust by David and Samuel the seer. ²³They and
their descendants were in charge of guarding the gates of the
house of the LORD—the house called the tent of meeting.
²⁴The gatekeepers were on the four sides: east, west, north
and south. ²⁵Their fellow Levites in their villages had to

come from time to time and share their duties for seven-day periods. ²⁶But the four principal gatekeepers, who were Levites, were entrusted with the responsibility for the rooms and treasuries in the house of God. ²⁷They would spend the night stationed around the house of God, because they had to guard it; and they had charge of the key for opening it each morning.

²⁸Some of them were in charge of the articles used in the temple service; they counted them when they were brought in and when they were taken out. ²⁹Others were assigned to take care of the furnishings and all the other articles of the sanctuary, as well as the special flour and wine, and the olive oil, incense and spices. ³⁰But some of the priests took care of mixing the spices. ³¹A Levite named Mattithiah, the firstborn son of Shallum the Korahite, was entrusted with the responsibility for baking the offering bread. ³²Some of the Kohathites, their fellow Levites, were in charge of preparing for every Sabbath the bread set out on the table.

³³Those who were musicians, heads of Levite families, stayed in the rooms of the temple and were exempt from other duties because they were responsible for the work day and night.

³⁴All these were heads of Levite families, chiefs as listed in their genealogy, and they lived in Jerusalem.

THE GENEALOGY OF SAUL

³⁵Jeiel the father*a* of Gibeon lived in Gibeon.
His wife's name was Maakah, ³⁶and his firstborn son was Abdon, followed by Zur, Kish, Baal, Ner, Nadab, ³⁷Gedor, Ahio, Zechariah and Mikloth. ³⁸Mikloth was the father of Shimeam. They too lived near their relatives in Jerusalem.
³⁹Ner was the father of Kish, Kish the father of Saul, and Saul the father of Jonathan, Malki-Shua, Abinadab and Esh-Baal.*b*
⁴⁰The son of Jonathan:
Merib-Baal,*c* who was the father of Micah.
⁴¹The sons of Micah:
Pithon, Melek, Tahrea and Ahaz.*d*
⁴²Ahaz was the father of Jadah, Jadah*e* was the father of Alemeth, Azmaveth and Zimri, and Zimri was the father of Moza. ⁴³Moza was the father of Binea; Rephaiah was his son, Eleasah his son and Azel his son.
⁴⁴Azel had six sons, and these were their names:
Azrikam, Bokeru, Ishmael, Sheariah, Obadiah and Hanan. These were the sons of Azel.

SAUL TAKES HIS LIFE

10 Now the Philistines fought against Israel; the Israelites fled before them, and many fell dead on Mount Gilboa. ²The Philistines were in hot pursuit of Saul and his

What was the special bread these people prepared? (9:32)
Fresh bread was put before the LORD in the Holy Place of the temple each week. Twelve loaves of bread made from pure wheat flour represented the 12 tribes of Israel and their devotion to God. The old bread was removed and could be eaten by the priests.

Why was Saul's genealogy repeated? (9:35–44)
The author used this genealogy (repeated from 8:29–38) as a transition from Saul's death to the story of David.

---

a 35 Father may mean *civic leader* or *military leader.*   *b 39* Also known as *Ish-Bosheth*   *c 40* Also known as *Mephibosheth*   *d 41* Vulgate and Syriac (see also Septuagint and 8:35); Hebrew does not have *and Ahaz.*
e 42 Some Hebrew manuscripts and Septuagint (see also 8:36); most Hebrew manuscripts *Jarah, Jarah*

sons, and they killed his sons Jonathan, Abinadab and Mal-ki-Shua. ³The fighting grew fierce around Saul, and when the archers overtook him, they wounded him.

⁴Saul said to his armor-bearer, "Draw your sword and run me through, or these uncircumcised fellows will come and abuse me."

But his armor-bearer was terrified and would not do it; so Saul took his own sword and fell on it. ⁵When the armor-bearer saw that Saul was dead, he too fell on his sword and died. ⁶So Saul and his three sons died, and all his house died together.

⁷When all the Israelites in the valley saw that the army had fled and that Saul and his sons had died, they abandoned their towns and fled. And the Philistines came and occupied them.

⁸The next day, when the Philistines came to strip the dead, they found Saul and his sons fallen on Mount Gilboa. ⁹They stripped him and took his head and his armor, and sent messengers throughout the land of the Philistines to proclaim the news among their idols and their people. ¹⁰They put his armor in the temple of their gods and hung up his head in the temple of Dagon.

¹¹When all the inhabitants of Jabesh Gilead heard what the Philistines had done to Saul, ¹²all their valiant men went and took the bodies of Saul and his sons and brought them to Jabesh. Then they buried their bones under the great tree in Jabesh, and they fasted seven days.

¹³Saul died because he was unfaithful to the Lord; he did not keep the word of the Lord and even consulted a medium for guidance, ¹⁴and did not inquire of the Lord. So the Lord put him to death and turned the kingdom over to David son of Jesse.

DAVID BECOMES KING OVER ISRAEL

11 All Israel came together to David at Hebron and said, "We are your own flesh and blood. ²In the past, even while Saul was king, you were the one who led Israel on their military campaigns. And the Lord your God said to you, 'You will shepherd my people Israel, and you will become their ruler.'"

³When all the elders of Israel had come to King David at Hebron, he made a covenant with them at Hebron before the Lord, and they anointed David king over Israel, as the Lord had promised through Samuel.

DAVID CONQUERS JERUSALEM

⁴David and all the Israelites marched to Jerusalem (that is, Jebus). The Jebusites who lived there ⁵said to David, "You will not get in here." Nevertheless, David captured the fortress of Zion—which is the City of David.

⁶David had said, "Whoever leads the attack on the Jebusites will become commander-in-chief." Joab son of Zeruiah went up first, and so he received the command.

⁷David then took up residence in the fortress, and so it was called the City of David. ⁸He built up the city around

How did Saul die? (10:4–6) Saul asked his armor-bearer to kill him, but he would not do it, so Saul committed suicide by falling on his own sword (see 1 Samuel 31:4–6).

How did Saul's unfaithfulness cause his death? (10:13) Saul's sins did not immediately cause him to die, but the many times that he turned away from the Lord, including his meeting with the medium at Endor, led to his death. None of his descendants would inherit the throne because of his disobedience.

it, from the terraces*a* to the surrounding wall, while Joab restored the rest of the city. ⁹And David became more and more powerful, because the LORD Almighty was with him.

DAVID'S MIGHTY WARRIORS

¹⁰These were the chiefs of David's mighty warriors—they, together with all Israel, gave his kingship strong support to extend it over the whole land, as the LORD had promised— ¹¹this is the list of David's mighty warriors:

Jashobeam,*b* a Hakmonite, was chief of the officers*c*; he raised his spear against three hundred men, whom he killed in one encounter.

¹²Next to him was Eleazar son of Dodai the Ahohite, one of the three mighty warriors. ¹³He was with David at Pas Dammim when the Philistines gathered there for battle. At a place where there was a field full of barley, the troops fled from the Philistines. ¹⁴But they took their stand in the middle of the field. They defended it and struck the Philistines down, and the LORD brought about a great victory.

¹⁵Three of the thirty chiefs came down to David to the rock at the cave of Adullam, while a band of Philistines was encamped in the Valley of Rephaim. ¹⁶At that time David was in the stronghold, and the Philistine garrison was at Bethlehem. ¹⁷David longed for water and said, "Oh, that someone would get me a drink of water from the well near the gate of Bethlehem!" ¹⁸So the Three broke through the Philistine lines, drew water from the well near the gate of Bethlehem and carried it back to David. But he refused to drink it; instead, he poured it out to the LORD. ¹⁹"God forbid that I should do this!" he said. "Should I drink the blood of these men who went at the risk of their lives?" Because they risked their lives to bring it back, David would not drink it.

Such were the exploits of the three mighty warriors.

²⁰Abishai the brother of Joab was chief of the Three. He raised his spear against three hundred men, whom he killed, and so he became as famous as the Three. ²¹He was doubly honored above the Three and became their commander, even though he was not included among them.

²²Benaiah son of Jehoiada, a valiant fighter from Kabzeel, performed great exploits. He struck down Moab's two mightiest warriors. He also went down into a pit on a snowy day and killed a lion. ²³And he struck down an Egyptian who was five cubits*d* tall. Although the Egyptian had a spear like a weaver's rod in his hand, Benaiah went against him with a club. He snatched the spear from the Egyptian's hand and killed him with his own spear. ²⁴Such were the exploits of Benaiah son of Jehoiada; he too was as famous as the three mighty warriors. ²⁵He was held in greater honor than any of the Thirty, but he was not included among the Three. And David put him in charge of his bodyguard.

How could one man kill 300 men? (11:11)
It's possible that Jashobeam received the credit on behalf of his men because of his position as chief of the officers. But it's also possible that God gave him the power and strength to defeat his enemies.

Why didn't David drink the water from the well of Bethlehem? (11:18–19)
David poured the water out before the LORD, almost like a sacrifice. The three men had risked their lives for the water, and David thought that their loyalty and commitment should be devoted to the LORD rather than to his thirst.

---

a 8 Or *the Millo*   *b 11* Possibly a variant of *Jashob-Baal*   *c 11* Or *Thirty*; some Septuagint manuscripts *Three* (see also 2 Samuel 23:8)   *d 23* That is, about 7 feet 6 inches or about 2.3 meters

Why were David's recruits listed? (11:26 — 12:40)
These men were listed to show the diversity of the people willing to follow David. Even people associated with Saul followed David. People banded together under David because of his strong faith. This was a sign of what God could do if the people believed.

26 The mighty warriors were:
Asahel the brother of Joab,
Elhanan son of Dodo from Bethlehem,
27 Shammoth the Harorite,
Helez the Pelonite,
28 Ira son of Ikkesh from Tekoa,
Abiezer from Anathoth,
29 Sibbekai the Hushathite,
Ilai the Ahohite,
30 Maharai the Netophathite,
Heled son of Baanah the Netophathite,
31 Ithai son of Ribai from Gibeah in Benjamin,
Benaiah the Pirathonite,
32 Hurai from the ravines of Gaash,
Abiel the Arbathite,
33 Azmaveth the Baharumite,
Eliahba the Shaalbonite,
34 the sons of Hashem the Gizonite,
Jonathan son of Shagee the Hararite,
35 Ahiam son of Sakar the Hararite,
Eliphal son of Ur,
36 Hepher the Mekerathite,
Ahijah the Pelonite,
37 Hezro the Carmelite,
Naarai son of Ezbai,
38 Joel the brother of Nathan,
Mibhar son of Hagri,
39 Zelek the Ammonite,
Naharai the Berothite, the armor-bearer of Joab son of Zeruiah,
40 Ira the Ithrite,
Gareb the Ithrite,
41 Uriah the Hittite,
Zabad son of Ahlai,
42 Adina son of Shiza the Reubenite, who was chief of the Reubenites, and the thirty with him,
43 Hanan son of Maakah,
Joshaphat the Mithnite,
44 Uzzia the Ashterathite,
Shama and Jeiel the sons of Hotham the Aroerite,
45 Jediael son of Shimri,
his brother Joha the Tizite,
46 Eliel the Mahavite,
Jeribai and Joshaviah the sons of Elnaam,
Ithmah the Moabite,
47 Eliel, Obed and Jaasiel the Mezobaite.

Were most warriors ambidextrous? (12:2)
No. The fact that these warriors could fight right-handed or left-handed impressed the writer as another sign of God's blessing.

Why would Saul's kinsmen join David? (12:2)
The writer wanted readers to see how the LORD turned the hearts of all Israel toward his servant David.

WARRIORS JOIN DAVID

12 These were the men who came to David at Ziklag, while he was banished from the presence of Saul son of Kish (they were among the warriors who helped him in battle; 2 they were armed with bows and were able to shoot arrows or to sling stones right-handed or left-handed; they were relatives of Saul from the tribe of Benjamin):

3 Ahiezer their chief and Joash the sons of Shemaah the

Gibeathite; Jeziel and Pelet the sons of Azmaveth; Berakah, Jehu the Anathothite, [4] and Ishmaiah the Gibeonite, a mighty warrior among the Thirty, who was a leader of the Thirty; Jeremiah, Jahaziel, Johanan, Jozabad the Gederathite,[a] [5] Eluzai, Jerimoth, Bealiah, Shemariah and Shephatiah the Haruphite; [6] Elkanah, Ishiah, Azarel, Joezer and Jashobeam the Korahites; [7] and Joelah and Zebadiah the sons of Jeroham from Gedor.

[8] Some Gadites defected to David at his stronghold in the wilderness. They were brave warriors, ready for battle and able to handle the shield and spear. Their faces were the faces of lions, and they were as swift as gazelles in the mountains.

[9] Ezer was the chief,
   Obadiah the second in command, Eliab the third,
[10] Mishmannah the fourth, Jeremiah the fifth,
[11] Attai the sixth, Eliel the seventh,
[12] Johanan the eighth, Elzabad the ninth,
[13] Jeremiah the tenth and Makbannai the eleventh.

[14] These Gadites were army commanders; the least was a match for a hundred, and the greatest for a thousand. [15] It was they who crossed the Jordan in the first month when it was overflowing all its banks, and they put to flight everyone living in the valleys, to the east and to the west.

[16] Other Benjamites and some men from Judah also came to David in his stronghold. [17] David went out to meet them and said to them, "If you have come to me in peace to help me, I am ready for you to join me. But if you have come to betray me to my enemies when my hands are free from violence, may the God of our ancestors see it and judge you."

[18] Then the Spirit came on Amasai, chief of the Thirty, and he said:

"We are yours, David!
   We are with you, son of Jesse!
Success, success to you,
   and success to those who help you,
      for your God will help you."

So David received them and made them leaders of his raiding bands.

[19] Some of the tribe of Manasseh defected to David when he went with the Philistines to fight against Saul. (He and his men did not help the Philistines because, after consultation, their rulers sent him away. They said, "It will cost us our heads if he deserts to his master Saul.") [20] When David went to Ziklag, these were the men of Manasseh who defected to him: Adnah, Jozabad, Jediael, Michael, Jozabad, Elihu and Zillethai, leaders of units of a thousand in Manasseh. [21] They helped David against raiding bands, for all of them were brave warriors, and they were commanders in his army. [22] Day after day men came to help David, until he had a great army, like the army of God.[b]

---

[a] 4 In Hebrew texts the second half of this verse (*Jeremiah . . . Gederathite*) is numbered 12:5, and 12:5-40 is numbered 12:6-41.   [b] 22 Or *a great and mighty army*

How did Amasai convince David to trust the Benjamites? (12:18)
David did not automatically trust Saul's kinsmen, the Benjamites. But Amasai expressed the mood of the people by pledging loyalty to David.

How was David's army like the army of God? (12:22)
This description implies that God gave his blessing to David and his army. It also suggests that the size of the army was very large.

OTHERS JOIN DAVID AT HEBRON

23 These are the numbers of the men armed for battle who came to David at Hebron to turn Saul's kingdom over to him, as the LORD had said:

24 from Judah, carrying shield and spear — 6,800 armed for battle;

25 from Simeon, warriors ready for battle — 7,100;

26 from Levi — 4,600, 27 including Jehoiada, leader of the family of Aaron, with 3,700 men, 28 and Zadok, a brave young warrior, with 22 officers from his family;

29 from Benjamin, Saul's tribe — 3,000, most of whom had remained loyal to Saul's house until then;

30 from Ephraim, brave warriors, famous in their own clans — 20,800;

31 from half the tribe of Manasseh, designated by name to come and make David king — 18,000;

32 from Issachar, men who understood the times and knew what Israel should do — 200 chiefs, with all their relatives under their command;

33 from Zebulun, experienced soldiers prepared for battle with every type of weapon, to help David with undivided loyalty — 50,000;

34 from Naphtali — 1,000 officers, together with 37,000 men carrying shields and spears;

35 from Dan, ready for battle — 28,600;

36 from Asher, experienced soldiers prepared for battle — 40,000;

37 and from east of the Jordan, from Reuben, Gad and the half-tribe of Manasseh, armed with every type of weapon — 120,000.

38 All these were fighting men who volunteered to serve in the ranks. They came to Hebron fully determined to make David king over all Israel. All the rest of the Israelites were also of one mind to make David king. 39 The men spent three days there with David, eating and drinking, for their families had supplied provisions for them. 40 Also, their neighbors from as far away as Issachar, Zebulun and Naphtali came bringing food on donkeys, camels, mules and oxen. There were plentiful supplies of flour, fig cakes, raisin cakes, wine, olive oil, cattle and sheep, for there was joy in Israel.

BRINGING BACK THE ARK

13 David conferred with each of his officers, the commanders of thousands and commanders of hundreds. 2 He then said to the whole assembly of Israel, "If it seems

Why was Manasseh listed twice? (12:31, 37)
The tribe of Manasseh was split in two. The first mention represents the tribe east of the Jordan River, while the second mention represents those people on the west side of the river.

What did it mean to understand the times? (12:32)
This probably means that they were able to see the wisdom in uniting with the other tribes and joining with David.

Did the ark have special powers?   1 CHRONICLES 13

On the one hand, the ark was simply a box covered with gold that had been made by craftsmen. But on the other hand, the ark was an extremely important symbol of God's presence among his people.

The ark was so special that the high priest could only come before it once a year; this symbolized how holy God was. Sometimes God told the people to carry the ark with them into battle. When they achieved victory, it was not the magical power of the ark that caused it, but the fact that God was present. The ark was also a sacred object that could not be treated casually. When Uzzah touched the ark, for example, God struck him down.

good to you and if it is the will of the LORD our God, let us send word far and wide to the rest of our people throughout the territories of Israel, and also to the priests and Levites who are with them in their towns and pasturelands, to come and join us. ³Let us bring the ark of our God back to us, for we did not inquire of*a* it*b* during the reign of Saul." ⁴The whole assembly agreed to do this, because it seemed right to all the people.

⁵So David assembled all Israel, from the Shihor River in Egypt to Lebo Hamath, to bring the ark of God from Kiriath Jearim. ⁶David and all Israel went to Baalah of Judah (Kiriath Jearim) to bring up from there the ark of God the LORD, who is enthroned between the cherubim—the ark that is called by the Name.

⁷They moved the ark of God from Abinadab's house on a new cart, with Uzzah and Ahio guiding it. ⁸David and all the Israelites were celebrating with all their might before God, with songs and with harps, lyres, timbrels, cymbals and trumpets.

⁹When they came to the threshing floor of Kidon, Uzzah reached out his hand to steady the ark, because the oxen stumbled. ¹⁰The LORD's anger burned against Uzzah, and he struck him down because he had put his hand on the ark. So he died there before God.

¹¹Then David was angry because the LORD's wrath had broken out against Uzzah, and to this day that place is called Perez Uzzah.*c*

¹²David was afraid of God that day and asked, "How can I ever bring the ark of God to me?" ¹³He did not take the ark to be with him in the City of David. Instead, he took it to the house of Obed-Edom the Gittite. ¹⁴The ark of God remained with the family of Obed-Edom in his house for three months, and the LORD blessed his household and everything he had.

DAVID'S HOUSE AND FAMILY

14 Now Hiram king of Tyre sent messengers to David, along with cedar logs, stonemasons and carpenters to build a palace for him. ²And David knew that the LORD had established him as king over Israel and that his kingdom had been highly exalted for the sake of his people Israel.

³In Jerusalem David took more wives and became the father of more sons and daughters. ⁴These are the names of the children born to him there: Shammua, Shobab, Nathan, Solomon, ⁵Ibhar, Elishua, Elpelet, ⁶Nogah, Nepheg, Japhia, ⁷Elishama, Beeliada*d* and Eliphelet.

DAVID DEFEATS THE PHILISTINES

⁸When the Philistines heard that David had been anointed king over all Israel, they went up in full force to search for him, but David heard about it and went out to meet them. ⁹Now the Philistines had come and raided the Valley of Rephaim; ¹⁰so David inquired of God: "Shall I go and attack the Philistines? Will you deliver them into my hands?"

How did they plan to inquire of the ark? (13:3)
The high priest probably stood before the ark in the presence of the LORD and used the Urim and Thummim (small stones that were used to receive yes and no answers from the LORD).

With whom was David angry? (13:11)
David was angry that God had killed Uzzah, but he also took some of the blame. David might have thought he was responsible for Uzzah's death in some form, though to some degree, David was mad at Uzzah himself for being so careless.

Who was Obed-Edom? (13:13)
A Gittite was a person from the city of Gath in Philistia. It is possible that Obed-Edom was a Gittite who had immigrated to Israel. It is more likely that Obed-Edom was a Levite. Levites could be called Gittites if they came from the Levite city of Gath Rimmon in Dan or Manasseh.

Why did the king of Tyre support David? (14:1–2)
Hiram knew befriending David would be the most beneficial thing to do. They would both benefit politically if a treaty could be established. David saw this as another example of God's blessings.

---

a 3 Or we neglected   *b 3 Or him*   *c 11 Perez Uzzah means outbreak against Uzzah.*   *d 7 A variant of Eliada*

The Lord answered him, "Go, I will deliver them into your hands."

¹¹ So David and his men went up to Baal Perazim, and there he defeated them. He said, "As waters break out, God has broken out against my enemies by my hand." So that place was called Baal Perazim.ᵃ ¹² The Philistines had abandoned their gods there, and David gave orders to burn them in the fire.

¹³ Once more the Philistines raided the valley; ¹⁴ so David inquired of God again, and God answered him, "Do not go directly after them, but circle around them and attack them in front of the poplar trees. ¹⁵ As soon as you hear the sound of marching in the tops of the poplar trees, move out to battle, because that will mean God has gone out in front of you to strike the Philistine army." ¹⁶ So David did as God commanded him, and they struck down the Philistine army, all the way from Gibeon to Gezer.

¹⁷ So David's fame spread throughout every land, and the Lord made all the nations fear him.

THE ARK BROUGHT TO JERUSALEM

15 After David had constructed buildings for himself in the City of David, he prepared a place for the ark of God and pitched a tent for it. ² Then David said, "No one but the Levites may carry the ark of God, because the Lord chose them to carry the ark of the Lord and to minister before him forever."

³ David assembled all Israel in Jerusalem to bring up the ark of the Lord to the place he had prepared for it. ⁴ He called together the descendants of Aaron and the Levites:

⁵ From the descendants of Kohath,
  Uriel the leader and 120 relatives;
⁶ from the descendants of Merari,
  Asaiah the leader and 220 relatives;
⁷ from the descendants of Gershon,ᵇ
  Joel the leader and 130 relatives;
⁸ from the descendants of Elizaphan,
  Shemaiah the leader and 200 relatives;
⁹ from the descendants of Hebron,
  Eliel the leader and 80 relatives;
¹⁰ from the descendants of Uzziel,
  Amminadab the leader and 112 relatives.

¹¹ Then David summoned Zadok and Abiathar the priests, and Uriel, Asaiah, Joel, Shemaiah, Eliel and Amminadab the Levites. ¹² He said to them, "You are the heads of the Levitical families; you and your fellow Levites are to consecrate yourselves and bring up the ark of the Lord, the God of Israel, to the place I have prepared for it. ¹³ It was because you, the Levites, did not bring it up the first time that the Lord our God broke out in anger against us. We did not inquire of him about how to do it in the prescribed way." ¹⁴ So the priests and Levites consecrated themselves in order to bring up the ark of the Lord, the God of Israel. ¹⁵ And

How did God make the nations fear David? (14:17)
David's army was successful in the battles they fought, so the nations around Israel had good reason to fear. They may have also realized that Israel had the power of God on its side.

How did David discover the proper way to move the ark? (15:2)
The scrolls containing the laws recorded by Moses told how God wanted the ark to be treated and moved.

ᵃ 11 *Baal Perazim* means *the lord who breaks out.*   ᵇ 7 Hebrew *Gershom,* a variant of *Gershon*

the Levites carried the ark of God with the poles on their shoulders, as Moses had commanded in accordance with the word of the LORD.

[16] David told the leaders of the Levites to appoint their fellow Levites as musicians to make a joyful sound with musical instruments: lyres, harps and cymbals.

[17] So the Levites appointed Heman son of Joel; from his relatives, Asaph son of Berekiah; and from their relatives the Merarites, Ethan son of Kushaiah; [18] and with them their relatives next in rank: Zechariah,[a] Jaaziel, Shemiramoth, Jehiel, Unni, Eliab, Benaiah, Maaseiah, Mattithiah, Eliphelehu, Mikneiah, Obed-Edom and Jeiel,[b] the gatekeepers.

[19] The musicians Heman, Asaph and Ethan were to sound the bronze cymbals; [20] Zechariah, Jaaziel,[c] Shemiramoth, Jehiel, Unni, Eliab, Maaseiah and Benaiah were to play the lyres according to *alamoth*,[d] [21] and Mattithiah, Eliphelehu, Mikneiah, Obed-Edom, Jeiel and Azaziah were to play the harps, directing according to *sheminith*.[d] [22] Kenaniah the head Levite was in charge of the singing; that was his responsibility because he was skillful at it.

[23] Berekiah and Elkanah were to be doorkeepers for the ark. [24] Shebaniah, Joshaphat, Nethanel, Amasai, Zechariah, Benaiah and Eliezer the priests were to blow trumpets before the ark of God. Obed-Edom and Jehiah were also to be doorkeepers for the ark.

[25] So David and the elders of Israel and the commanders of units of a thousand went to bring up the ark of the covenant of the LORD from the house of Obed-Edom, with rejoicing. [26] Because God had helped the Levites who were carrying the ark of the covenant of the LORD, seven bulls and seven rams were sacrificed. [27] Now David was clothed in a robe of fine linen, as were all the Levites who were carrying the ark, and as were the musicians, and Kenaniah, who was in charge of the singing of the choirs. David also wore a linen ephod. [28] So all Israel brought up the ark of the covenant of the LORD with shouts, with the sounding of rams' horns and trumpets, and of cymbals, and the playing of lyres and harps.

[29] As the ark of the covenant of the LORD was entering the City of David, Michal daughter of Saul watched from a window. And when she saw King David dancing and celebrating, she despised him in her heart.

MINISTERING BEFORE THE ARK

16 They brought the ark of God and set it inside the tent that David had pitched for it, and they presented burnt offerings and fellowship offerings before God. [2] After David had finished sacrificing the burnt offerings and fellowship offerings, he blessed the people in the name of the LORD. [3] Then he gave a loaf of bread, a cake of dates and a cake of raisins to each Israelite man and woman.

[4] He appointed some of the Levites to minister before the

Why did David tell the Levites to sing and play instruments? (15:16)
David was a talented poet and musician, and he introduced new rituals to the tabernacle worship.

Why was Michal so angry about David's dancing? (15:29)
As the daughter of a king, Michal apparently felt it was undignified for a king to remove his royal robe in order to dance before the ark where his subjects could see him. But David's commitment to the LORD was so strong he was willing to humiliate himself in order to praise God.

Since David was not a Levite, how could he sacrifice burnt offerings? (16:2)
It is most likely that the priests actually sacrificed the offerings on behalf of David rather than David sacrificing them himself.

---

[a] *18* Three Hebrew manuscripts and most Septuagint manuscripts (see also verse 20 and 16:5); most Hebrew manuscripts *Zechariah son and* or *Zechariah, Ben and*   [b] *18* Hebrew; Septuagint (see also verse 21) *Jeiel and Azaziah*   [c] *20* See verse 18; Hebrew *Aziel*, a variant of *Jaaziel*.   [d] *20,21* Probably a musical term

ark of the Lord, to extol,[a] thank, and praise the Lord, the God of Israel: [5] Asaph was the chief, and next to him in rank were Zechariah, then Jaaziel,[b] Shemiramoth, Jehiel, Mattithiah, Eliab, Benaiah, Obed-Edom and Jeiel. They were to play the lyres and harps, Asaph was to sound the cymbals, [6] and Benaiah and Jahaziel the priests were to blow the trumpets regularly before the ark of the covenant of God.

[7] That day David first appointed Asaph and his associates to give praise to the Lord in this manner:

[8] Give praise to the Lord, proclaim his name;
　　make known among the nations what he has done.
[9] Sing to him, sing praise to him;
　　tell of all his wonderful acts.
[10] Glory in his holy name;
　　let the hearts of those who seek the Lord rejoice.
[11] Look to the Lord and his strength;
　　seek his face always.

[12] Remember the wonders he has done,
　　his miracles, and the judgments he pronounced,
[13] you his servants, the descendants of Israel,
　　his chosen ones, the children of Jacob.
[14] He is the Lord our God;
　　his judgments are in all the earth.

[15] He remembers[c] his covenant forever,
　　the promise he made, for a thousand generations,
[16] the covenant he made with Abraham,
　　the oath he swore to Isaac.
[17] He confirmed it to Jacob as a decree,
　　to Israel as an everlasting covenant:
[18] "To you I will give the land of Canaan
　　as the portion you will inherit."

[19] When they were but few in number,
　　few indeed, and strangers in it,
[20] they[d] wandered from nation to nation,
　　from one kingdom to another.
[21] He allowed no one to oppress them;
　　for their sake he rebuked kings:
[22] "Do not touch my anointed ones;
　　do my prophets no harm."

[23] Sing to the Lord, all the earth;
　　proclaim his salvation day after day.
[24] Declare his glory among the nations,
　　his marvelous deeds among all peoples.

[25] For great is the Lord and most worthy of praise;
　　he is to be feared above all gods.
[26] For all the gods of the nations are idols,
　　but the Lord made the heavens.

---

[a] 4 Or *petition*; or *invoke*　[b] 5 See 15:18,20; Hebrew *Jeiel*, possibly another name for *Jaaziel*.　[c] 15 Some Septuagint manuscripts (see also Psalm 105:8); Hebrew *Remember*　[d] 18-20 One Hebrew manuscript, Septuagint and Vulgate (see also Psalm 105:12); most Hebrew manuscripts *inherit, / [19]though you are but few in number, / few indeed, and strangers in it." / [20]They*

²⁷ Splendor and majesty are before him;
  strength and joy are in his dwelling place.

²⁸ Ascribe to the Lᴏʀᴅ, all you families of nations,
  ascribe to the Lᴏʀᴅ glory and strength.
²⁹ Ascribe to the Lᴏʀᴅ the glory due his name;
  bring an offering and come before him.
Worship the Lᴏʀᴅ in the splendor of his*ᵃ holiness.
³⁰   Tremble before him, all the earth!
  The world is firmly established; it cannot be moved.

³¹ Let the heavens rejoice, let the earth be glad;
  let them say among the nations, "The Lᴏʀᴅ reigns!"
³² Let the sea resound, and all that is in it;
  let the fields be jubilant, and everything in them!
³³ Let the trees of the forest sing,
  let them sing for joy before the Lᴏʀᴅ,
  for he comes to judge the earth.

³⁴ Give thanks to the Lᴏʀᴅ, for he is good;
  his love endures forever.
³⁵ Cry out, "Save us, God our Savior;
  gather us and deliver us from the nations,
that we may give thanks to your holy name,
  and glory in your praise."
³⁶ Praise be to the Lᴏʀᴅ, the God of Israel,
  from everlasting to everlasting.

Then all the people said "Amen" and "Praise the Lᴏʀᴅ."

³⁷ David left Asaph and his associates before the ark of the covenant of the Lᴏʀᴅ to minister there regularly, according to each day's requirements. ³⁸ He also left Obed-Edom and his sixty-eight associates to minister with them. Obed-Edom son of Jeduthun, and also Hosah, were gatekeepers.

³⁹ David left Zadok the priest and his fellow priests before the tabernacle of the Lᴏʀᴅ at the high place in Gibeon ⁴⁰ to present burnt offerings to the Lᴏʀᴅ on the altar of burnt offering regularly, morning and evening, in accordance with everything written in the Law of the Lᴏʀᴅ, which he had given Israel. ⁴¹ With them were Heman and Jeduthun and the rest of those chosen and designated by name to give thanks to the Lᴏʀᴅ, "for his love endures forever." ⁴² Heman and Jeduthun were responsible for the sounding of the trumpets and cymbals and for the playing of the other instruments for sacred song. The sons of Jeduthun were stationed at the gate.

⁴³ Then all the people left, each for their own home, and David returned home to bless his family.

GOD'S PROMISE TO DAVID

17 After David was settled in his palace, he said to Nathan the prophet, "Here I am, living in a house of cedar, while the ark of the covenant of the Lᴏʀᴅ is under a tent."

² Nathan replied to David, "Whatever you have in mind, do it, for God is with you."

ᵃ 29 Or Lᴏʀᴅ with the splendor of

How could trees sing for joy? (16:33)
This is a literary technique called personification — giving human traits and emotions to nonliving things. So the trees weren't actually singing. The author says this to highlight how we should rejoice in God for he is good.

How did David bless his family? (16:43)
The father, as head of the family, could pray for God's blessings on each member of his family. Blessings could be prophetic predictions or expressions of good things to come. Blessings could also be the giving of material things such as bread or fruit.

Why did David want to build a temple for God? (17:1–4)
David's desire to build a temple was typical for kings during biblical times. Kings in countries near Israel built great monuments and temples to the gods they considered responsible for establishing them on the throne. Despite his sins, David was devoted to the Lᴏʀᴅ and wanted to honor him for helping to secure the kingdom.

³But that night the word of God came to Nathan, saying:

⁴"Go and tell my servant David, 'This is what the Lord says: You are not the one to build me a house to dwell in. ⁵I have not dwelt in a house from the day I brought Israel up out of Egypt to this day. I have moved from one tent site to another, from one dwelling place to another. ⁶Wherever I have moved with all the Israelites, did I ever say to any of their leaders*ᵃ* whom I commanded to shepherd my people, "Why have you not built me a house of cedar?"'

⁷"Now then, tell my servant David, 'This is what the Lord Almighty says: I took you from the pasture, from tending the flock, and appointed you ruler over my people Israel. ⁸I have been with you wherever you have gone, and I have cut off all your enemies from before you. Now I will make your name like the names of the greatest men on earth. ⁹And I will provide a place for my people Israel and will plant them so that they can have a home of their own and no longer be disturbed. Wicked people will not oppress them anymore, as they did at the beginning ¹⁰and have done ever since the time I appointed leaders over my people Israel. I will also subdue all your enemies.

"'I declare to you that the Lord will build a house for you: ¹¹When your days are over and you go to be with your ancestors, I will raise up your offspring to succeed you, one of your own sons, and I will establish his kingdom. ¹²He is the one who will build a house for me, and I will establish his throne forever. ¹³I will be his father, and he will be my son. I will never take my love away from him, as I took it away from your predecessor. ¹⁴I will set him over my house and my kingdom forever; his throne will be established forever.'"

¹⁵Nathan reported to David all the words of this entire revelation.

DAVID'S PRAYER

¹⁶Then King David went in and sat before the Lord, and he said:

"Who am I, Lord God, and what is my family that you have brought me this far? ¹⁷And as if this were not enough in your sight, my God, you have spoken about the future of the house of your servant. You, Lord God, have looked on me as though I were the most exalted of men.

¹⁸"What more can David say to you for honoring your servant? For you know your servant, ¹⁹Lord. For the sake of your servant and according to your will, you have done this great thing and made known all these great promises.

²⁰"There is no one like you, Lord, and there is no God but you, as we have heard with our own ears. ²¹And who is like your people Israel—the one nation on earth

---

Why did God decide to change his dwelling from the tabernacle to a temple? (17:5–6, 12)
The Israelites were now established in the land of Canaan. The tabernacle had been designed to be portable as the Israelites traveled through the desert and began to settle in the promised land. Now God wanted to establish a permanent, central location for his people to worship him.

What did God mean by saying Israel would "no longer be disturbed"? (17:9)
This promise was about God's kingdom. Even though David's heirs lost the kingdom—the physical nation of Israel—God's kingdom will never be destroyed.

Why did David respond this way? (17:16)
Rather than being angry that he could not build the temple, he was thankful that God had honored him in so many other ways.

ᵃ 6 Traditionally *judges*; also in verse 10

whose God went out to redeem a people for himself, and to make a name for yourself, and to perform great and awesome wonders by driving out nations from before your people, whom you redeemed from Egypt? ²²You made your people Israel your very own forever, and you, LORD, have become their God.

²³"And now, LORD, let the promise you have made concerning your servant and his house be established forever. Do as you promised, ²⁴so that it will be established and that your name will be great forever. Then people will say, 'The LORD Almighty, the God over Israel, is Israel's God!' And the house of your servant David will be established before you.

²⁵"You, my God, have revealed to your servant that you will build a house for him. So your servant has found courage to pray to you. ²⁶You, LORD, are God! You have promised these good things to your servant. ²⁷Now you have been pleased to bless the house of your servant, that it may continue forever in your sight; for you, LORD, have blessed it, and it will be blessed forever."

DAVID'S VICTORIES

18 In the course of time, David defeated the Philistines and subdued them, and he took Gath and its surrounding villages from the control of the Philistines.

²David also defeated the Moabites, and they became subject to him and brought him tribute.

³Moreover, David defeated Hadadezer king of Zobah, in the vicinity of Hamath, when he went to set up his monument at*a* the Euphrates River. ⁴David captured a thousand of his chariots, seven thousand charioteers and twenty thousand foot soldiers. He hamstrung all but a hundred of the chariot horses.

⁵When the Arameans of Damascus came to help Hadadezer king of Zobah, David struck down twenty-two thousand of them. ⁶He put garrisons in the Aramean kingdom of Damascus, and the Arameans became subject to him and brought him tribute. The LORD gave David victory wherever he went.

⁷David took the gold shields carried by the officers of Hadadezer and brought them to Jerusalem. ⁸From Tebah*b* and Kun, towns that belonged to Hadadezer, David took a great quantity of bronze, which Solomon used to make the bronze Sea, the pillars and various bronze articles.

⁹When Tou king of Hamath heard that David had defeated the entire army of Hadadezer king of Zobah, ¹⁰he sent his son Hadoram to King David to greet him and congratulate him on his victory in battle over Hadadezer, who had been at war with Tou. Hadoram brought all kinds of articles of gold, of silver and of bronze.

¹¹King David dedicated these articles to the LORD, as he had done with the silver and gold he had taken from all these nations: Edom and Moab, the Ammonites and the Philistines, and Amalek.

Why did David cripple most of the horses that were captured? (18:4)
God wanted his people to trust him rather than putting their trust in horses and chariots, so he forbid the Israelites from owning too many. David knew this and acted accordingly.

---

a 3 Or *to restore his control over*   *b* 8 Hebrew *Tibhath,* a variant of *Tebah*

Who was Abishai? (18:12)
As the son of Zeruiah, he was the brother of David's top general, Joab. Abishai was one of David's mighty men's commanders (11:20 – 21).

What was the Valley of Salt? (18:12)
This valley was south and southwest of the Dead Sea, toward the land of Edom. The salt marsh there may have slowed down the fleeing Edomites.

What kindness had Nahash shown David? (19:1 – 2)
Nahash probably helped David during his incident with Saul.

Why did Hanun humiliate David's men? (19:3 – 5)
Even though David had sent the delegation as a sincere expression of sympathy, Hanun was suspicious and thought David was trying to trick him.

Why go to war over what Hanun had done to the Israelites? (19:6, 16)
Hamun's humiliation of David's men was extremely insulting. Beards were usually only shaved as a sign of mourning or self-humiliation, and public nakedness was considered shameful. Ironically, by humiliating the prisoners, Hanun started a war rather than avoiding one.

[12] Abishai son of Zeruiah struck down eighteen thousand Edomites in the Valley of Salt. [13] He put garrisons in Edom, and all the Edomites became subject to David. The LORD gave David victory wherever he went.

DAVID'S OFFICIALS

[14] David reigned over all Israel, doing what was just and right for all his people. [15] Joab son of Zeruiah was over the army; Jehoshaphat son of Ahilud was recorder; [16] Zadok son of Ahitub and Ahimelek[a] son of Abiathar were priests; Shavsha was secretary; [17] Benaiah son of Jehoiada was over the Kerethites and Pelethites; and David's sons were chief officials at the king's side.

DAVID DEFEATS THE AMMONITES

19 In the course of time, Nahash king of the Ammonites died, and his son succeeded him as king. [2] David thought, "I will show kindness to Hanun son of Nahash, because his father showed kindness to me." So David sent a delegation to express his sympathy to Hanun concerning his father.

When David's envoys came to Hanun in the land of the Ammonites to express sympathy to him, [3] the Ammonite commanders said to Hanun, "Do you think David is honoring your father by sending envoys to you to express sympathy? Haven't his envoys come to you only to explore and spy out the country and overthrow it?" [4] So Hanun seized David's envoys, shaved them, cut off their garments at the buttocks, and sent them away.

[5] When someone came and told David about the men, he sent messengers to meet them, for they were greatly humiliated. The king said, "Stay at Jericho till your beards have grown, and then come back."

[6] When the Ammonites realized that they had become obnoxious to David, Hanun and the Ammonites sent a thousand talents[b] of silver to hire chariots and charioteers from Aram Naharaim,[c] Aram Maakah and Zobah. [7] They hired thirty-two thousand chariots and charioteers, as well as the king of Maakah with his troops, who came and camped near Medeba, while the Ammonites were mustered from their towns and moved out for battle.

[8] On hearing this, David sent Joab out with the entire army of fighting men. [9] The Ammonites came out and drew up in battle formation at the entrance to their city, while the kings who had come were by themselves in the open country.

[10] Joab saw that there were battle lines in front of him and behind him; so he selected some of the best troops in Israel and deployed them against the Arameans. [11] He put the rest of the men under the command of Abishai his brother, and they were deployed against the Ammonites. [12] Joab said, "If the Arameans are too strong for me, then you are to rescue me; but if the Ammonites are too strong for you, then I will rescue

---

[a] 16 Some Hebrew manuscripts, Vulgate and Syriac (see also 2 Samuel 8:17); most Hebrew manuscripts *Abimelek*   [b] 6 That is, about 38 tons or about 34 metric tons   [c] 6 That is, Northwest Mesopotamia

you. [13] Be strong, and let us fight bravely for our people and the cities of our God. The LORD will do what is good in his sight."

[14] Then Joab and the troops with him advanced to fight the Arameans, and they fled before him. [15] When the Ammonites realized that the Arameans were fleeing, they too fled before his brother Abishai and went inside the city. So Joab went back to Jerusalem.

[16] After the Arameans saw that they had been routed by Israel, they sent messengers and had Arameans brought from beyond the Euphrates River, with Shophak the commander of Hadadezer's army leading them.

[17] When David was told of this, he gathered all Israel and crossed the Jordan; he advanced against them and formed his battle lines opposite them. David formed his lines to meet the Arameans in battle, and they fought against him. [18] But they fled before Israel, and David killed seven thousand of their charioteers and forty thousand of their foot soldiers. He also killed Shophak the commander of their army.

[19] When the vassals of Hadadezer saw that they had been routed by Israel, they made peace with David and became subject to him.

So the Arameans were not willing to help the Ammonites anymore.

THE CAPTURE OF RABBAH

20 In the spring, at the time when kings go off to war, Joab led out the armed forces. He laid waste the land of the Ammonites and went to Rabbah and besieged it, but David remained in Jerusalem. Joab attacked Rabbah and left it in ruins. [2] David took the crown from the head of their king[a]—its weight was found to be a talent[b] of gold, and it was set with precious stones—and it was placed on David's head. He took a great quantity of plunder from the city [3] and brought out the people who were there, consigning them to labor with saws and with iron picks and axes. David did this to all the Ammonite towns. Then David and his entire army returned to Jerusalem.

WAR WITH THE PHILISTINES

[4] In the course of time, war broke out with the Philistines, at Gezer. At that time Sibbekai the Hushathite killed Sippai, one of the descendants of the Rephaites, and the Philistines were subjugated.

[5] In another battle with the Philistines, Elhanan son of Jair killed Lahmi the brother of Goliath the Gittite, who had a spear with a shaft like a weaver's rod.

[6] In still another battle, which took place at Gath, there was a huge man with six fingers on each hand and six toes on each foot—twenty-four in all. He also was descended from Rapha. [7] When he taunted Israel, Jonathan son of Shimea, David's brother, killed him.

[8] These were descendants of Rapha in Gath, and they fell at the hands of David and his men.

---

[a] 2 Or *of Milkom*, that is, Molek　　[b] 2 That is, about 75 pounds or about 34 kilograms

Why was spring a time for war? (20:1)
Battles were often postponed until after the grain harvest in April and May. Farmers served as soldiers when their farming duties permitted. They would need to return to plant crops in September and October.

Why would David wear such a heavy crown? (20:2)
The crown weighed about 75 pounds (34 kilograms). Putting the crown on David's head symbolized his complete victory. David probably only wore the crown for a short period of time and it's likely he had help.

David's Crown

DAVID COUNTS THE FIGHTING MEN

What was wrong with taking a census? (21:1, 6–7)
God did not forbid all census-taking. In fact, he had ordered a census before forming an army to conquer the promised land. But by counting his soldiers now, David exposed his pride. Instead of depending solely on God, he had begun to depend on military strength.

What was a seer? (21:9)
There probably was not much of a difference between a seer and a prophet. Both were messengers from God to his people.

Why would the LORD be grieved by something he had ordered? (21:15)
God realized there would have to be consequences for sin, but he still was troubled when his people suffered.

21 Satan rose up against Israel and incited David to take a census of Israel. ²So David said to Joab and the commanders of the troops, "Go and count the Israelites from Beersheba to Dan. Then report back to me so that I may know how many there are."

³But Joab replied, "May the LORD multiply his troops a hundred times over. My lord the king, are they not all my lord's subjects? Why does my lord want to do this? Why should he bring guilt on Israel?"

⁴The king's word, however, overruled Joab; so Joab left and went throughout Israel and then came back to Jerusalem. ⁵Joab reported the number of the fighting men to David: In all Israel there were one million one hundred thousand men who could handle a sword, including four hundred and seventy thousand in Judah.

⁶But Joab did not include Levi and Benjamin in the numbering, because the king's command was repulsive to him. ⁷This command was also evil in the sight of God; so he punished Israel.

⁸Then David said to God, "I have sinned greatly by doing this. Now, I beg you, take away the guilt of your servant. I have done a very foolish thing."

⁹The LORD said to Gad, David's seer, ¹⁰"Go and tell David, 'This is what the LORD says: I am giving you three options. Choose one of them for me to carry out against you.'"

¹¹So Gad went to David and said to him, "This is what the LORD says: 'Take your choice: ¹²three years of famine, three months of being swept away*a* before your enemies, with their swords overtaking you, or three days of the sword of the LORD—days of plague in the land, with the angel of the LORD ravaging every part of Israel.' Now then, decide how I should answer the one who sent me."

¹³David said to Gad, "I am in deep distress. Let me fall into the hands of the LORD, for his mercy is very great; but do not let me fall into human hands."

¹⁴So the LORD sent a plague on Israel, and seventy thousand men of Israel fell dead. ¹⁵And God sent an angel to destroy Jerusalem. But as the angel was doing so, the LORD saw it and relented concerning the disaster and said to the angel who was destroying the people, "Enough! Withdraw your hand." The angel of the LORD was then standing at the threshing floor of Araunah*b* the Jebusite.

¹⁶David looked up and saw the angel of the LORD standing between heaven and earth, with a drawn sword in his hand extended over Jerusalem. Then David and the elders, clothed in sackcloth, fell facedown.

¹⁷David said to God, "Was it not I who ordered the fighting men to be counted? I, the shepherd,*c* have sinned and done wrong. These are but sheep. What have they done? LORD my God, let your hand fall on me and my family, but do not let this plague remain on your people."

---

a 12 Hebrew; Septuagint and Vulgate (see also 2 Samuel 24:13) *of fleeing*
b 15 Hebrew *Ornan,* a variant of *Araunah*; also in verses 18-28
c 17 Probable reading of the original Hebrew text (see 2 Samuel 24:17 and note); Masoretic Text does not have *the shepherd.*

DAVID BUILDS AN ALTAR

¹⁸Then the angel of the LORD ordered Gad to tell David to go up and build an altar to the LORD on the threshing floor of Araunah the Jebusite. ¹⁹So David went up in obedience to the word that Gad had spoken in the name of the LORD.

²⁰While Araunah was threshing wheat, he turned and saw the angel; his four sons who were with him hid themselves. ²¹Then David approached, and when Araunah looked and saw him, he left the threshing floor and bowed down before David with his face to the ground.

²²David said to him, "Let me have the site of your threshing floor so I can build an altar to the LORD, that the plague on the people may be stopped. Sell it to me at the full price."

²³Araunah said to David, "Take it! Let my lord the king do whatever pleases him. Look, I will give the oxen for the burnt offerings, the threshing sledges for the wood, and the wheat for the grain offering. I will give all this."

²⁴But King David replied to Araunah, "No, I insist on paying the full price. I will not take for the LORD what is yours, or sacrifice a burnt offering that costs me nothing."

²⁵So David paid Araunah six hundred shekels*a* of gold for the site. ²⁶David built an altar to the LORD there and sacrificed burnt offerings and fellowship offerings. He called on the LORD, and the LORD answered him with fire from heaven on the altar of burnt offering.

²⁷Then the LORD spoke to the angel, and he put his sword back into its sheath. ²⁸At that time, when David saw that the LORD had answered him on the threshing floor of Araunah the Jebusite, he offered sacrifices there. ²⁹The tabernacle of the LORD, which Moses had made in the wilderness, and the altar of burnt offering were at that time on the high place at Gibeon. ³⁰But David could not go before it to inquire of God, because he was afraid of the sword of the angel of the LORD.

22 Then David said, "The house of the LORD God is to be here, and also the altar of burnt offering for Israel."

PREPARATIONS FOR THE TEMPLE

²So David gave orders to assemble the foreigners residing in Israel, and from among them he appointed stonecutters to prepare dressed stone for building the house of God. ³He provided a large amount of iron to make nails for the doors of the gateways and for the fittings, and more bronze than could be weighed. ⁴He also provided more cedar logs than could be counted, for the Sidonians and Tyrians had brought large numbers of them to David.

⁵David said, "My son Solomon is young and inexperienced, and the house to be built for the LORD should be of great magnificence and fame and splendor in the sight of all the nations. Therefore I will make preparations for it." So David made extensive preparations before his death.

⁶Then he called for his son Solomon and charged him to

Why did David insist on paying for the threshing floor? (21:24)
David knew that essentially he would get what he paid for in terms of the sacrifice. If he had to pay a high price, it would emphasize his repentance.

How old was Solomon at this time? (22:5)
Solomon was probably between the ages of 14 and 18.

---

a 25 That is, about 15 pounds or about 6.9 kilograms

Why would God not allow David to build the temple? (22:8)
David had been chosen by God to secure the land of Israel and establish a godly monarchy. So Solomon (whose name meant *peace*) was better suited to build the temple than his father.

What were these sacred articles? (22:19)
These were utensils used in the tabernacle. They included the gold-covered altar, a table, and cooking utensils such as dishes, pots, and bowls.

Why was it okay to take a census of the Levites? (23:3)
The motive for the earlier census was to proudly count the number of warriors. This census was a humble act so that the leaders could organize the work of the temple.

Why were the Levites counted in different age groups? (23:3, 27)
The first count included Levites who were 30 years or older. Previously, Levites ages 30 to 50 served in the tabernacle. The second count included those 20 and older. David lowered the age to 20 because more workers were needed for the temple than were previously needed for the tabernacle.

build a house for the LORD, the God of Israel. [7]David said to Solomon: "My son, I had it in my heart to build a house for the Name of the LORD my God. [8]But this word of the LORD came to me: 'You have shed much blood and have fought many wars. You are not to build a house for my Name, because you have shed much blood on the earth in my sight. [9]But you will have a son who will be a man of peace and rest, and I will give him rest from all his enemies on every side. His name will be Solomon,[a] and I will grant Israel peace and quiet during his reign. [10]He is the one who will build a house for my Name. He will be my son, and I will be his father. And I will establish the throne of his kingdom over Israel forever.'

[11]"Now, my son, the LORD be with you, and may you have success and build the house of the LORD your God, as he said you would. [12]May the LORD give you discretion and understanding when he puts you in command over Israel, so that you may keep the law of the LORD your God. [13]Then you will have success if you are careful to observe the decrees and laws that the LORD gave Moses for Israel. Be strong and courageous. Do not be afraid or discouraged.

[14]"I have taken great pains to provide for the temple of the LORD a hundred thousand talents[b] of gold, a million talents[c] of silver, quantities of bronze and iron too great to be weighed, and wood and stone. And you may add to them. [15]You have many workers: stonecutters, masons and carpenters, as well as those skilled in every kind of work [16]in gold and silver, bronze and iron—craftsmen beyond number. Now begin the work, and the LORD be with you."

[17]Then David ordered all the leaders of Israel to help his son Solomon. [18]He said to them, "Is not the LORD your God with you? And has he not granted you rest on every side? For he has given the inhabitants of the land into my hands, and the land is subject to the LORD and to his people. [19]Now devote your heart and soul to seeking the LORD your God. Begin to build the sanctuary of the LORD God, so that you may bring the ark of the covenant of the LORD and the sacred articles belonging to God into the temple that will be built for the Name of the LORD."

THE LEVITES

23 When David was old and full of years, he made his son Solomon king over Israel.

[2]He also gathered together all the leaders of Israel, as well as the priests and Levites. [3]The Levites thirty years old or more were counted, and the total number of men was thirty-eight thousand. [4]David said, "Of these, twenty-four thousand are to be in charge of the work of the temple of the LORD and six thousand are to be officials and judges. [5]Four thousand are to be gatekeepers and four thousand are to praise the LORD with the musical instruments I have provided for that purpose."

---

[a] *9 Solomon* sounds like and may be derived from the Hebrew for *peace*.
[b] *14* That is, about 3,750 tons or about 3,400 metric tons   [c] *14* That is, about 37,500 tons or about 34,000 metric tons

⁶David separated the Levites into divisions corresponding to the sons of Levi: Gershon, Kohath and Merari.

GERSHONITES

⁷Belonging to the Gershonites:
Ladan and Shimei.
⁸The sons of Ladan:
Jehiel the first, Zetham and Joel—three in all.
⁹The sons of Shimei:
Shelomoth, Haziel and Haran—three in all.
These were the heads of the families of Ladan.
¹⁰And the sons of Shimei:
Jahath, Ziza,ᵃ Jeush and Beriah.
These were the sons of Shimei—four in all.
¹¹Jahath was the first and Ziza the second, but Jeush and Beriah did not have many sons; so they were counted as one family with one assignment.

KOHATHITES

¹²The sons of Kohath:
Amram, Izhar, Hebron and Uzziel—four in all.
¹³The sons of Amram:
Aaron and Moses.
Aaron was set apart, he and his descendants forever, to consecrate the most holy things, to offer sacrifices before the LORD, to minister before him and to pronounce blessings in his name forever. ¹⁴The sons of Moses the man of God were counted as part of the tribe of Levi.
¹⁵The sons of Moses:
Gershom and Eliezer.
¹⁶The descendants of Gershom:
Shubael was the first.
¹⁷The descendants of Eliezer:
Rehabiah was the first.
Eliezer had no other sons, but the sons of Rehabiah were very numerous.
¹⁸The sons of Izhar:
Shelomith was the first.
¹⁹The sons of Hebron:
Jeriah the first, Amariah the second, Jahaziel the third and Jekameam the fourth.
²⁰The sons of Uzziel:
Micah the first and Ishiah the second.

MERARITES

²¹The sons of Merari:
Mahli and Mushi.
The sons of Mahli:
Eleazar and Kish.
²²Eleazar died without having sons: he had only daughters. Their cousins, the sons of Kish, married them.
²³The sons of Mushi:
Mahli, Eder and Jerimoth—three in all.

ᵃ 10 One Hebrew manuscript, Septuagint and Vulgate (see also verse 11); most Hebrew manuscripts *Zina*

Why were all these names listed? (23:7–23)
David was creating groups to handle different kinds of work. Each family had an important job, and the list would ensure that everyone knew their responsibilities.

²⁴These were the descendants of Levi by their families—the heads of families as they were registered under their names and counted individually, that is, the workers twenty years old or more who served in the temple of the LORD. ²⁵For David had said, "Since the LORD, the God of Israel, has granted rest to his people and has come to dwell in Jerusalem forever, ²⁶the Levites no longer need to carry the tabernacle or any of the articles used in its service." ²⁷According to the last instructions of David, the Levites were counted from those twenty years old or more.

²⁸The duty of the Levites was to help Aaron's descendants in the service of the temple of the LORD: to be in charge of the courtyards, the side rooms, the purification of all sacred things and the performance of other duties at the house of God. ²⁹They were in charge of the bread set out on the table, the special flour for the grain offerings, the thin loaves made without yeast, the baking and the mixing, and all measurements of quantity and size. ³⁰They were also to stand every morning to thank and praise the LORD. They were to do the same in the evening ³¹and whenever burnt offerings were presented to the LORD on the Sabbaths, at the New Moon feasts and at the appointed festivals. They were to serve before the LORD regularly in the proper number and in the way prescribed for them.

³²And so the Levites carried out their responsibilities for the tent of meeting, for the Holy Place and, under their relatives the descendants of Aaron, for the service of the temple of the LORD.

THE DIVISIONS OF PRIESTS

24 These were the divisions of the descendants of Aaron:
The sons of Aaron were Nadab, Abihu, Eleazar and Ithamar. ²But Nadab and Abihu died before their father did, and they had no sons; so Eleazar and Ithamar served as the priests. ³With the help of Zadok a descendant of Eleazar and Ahimelek a descendant of Ithamar, David separated them into divisions for their appointed order of ministering. ⁴A larger number of leaders were found among Eleazar's descendants than among Ithamar's, and they were divided accordingly: sixteen heads of families from Eleazar's descendants and eight heads of families from Ithamar's descendants. ⁵They divided them impartially by casting lots, for there were officials of the sanctuary and officials of God among the descendants of both Eleazar and Ithamar.

⁶The scribe Shemaiah son of Nethanel, a Levite, recorded their names in the presence of the king and of the officials: Zadok the priest, Ahimelek son of Abiathar and the heads of families of the priests and of the Levites—one family being taken from Eleazar and then one from Ithamar.

⁷The first lot fell to Jehoiarib,
　the second to Jedaiah,
⁸the third to Harim,
　the fourth to Seorim,
⁹the fifth to Malkijah,
　the sixth to Mijamin,

What type of work did the Levites do? (23:26, 28–32)
Levites assisted the priests in many ways. They maintained the equipment in the sanctuary, moved the furnishings, and baked the showbread. They kept the supplies necessary for the offerings. They also played music and helped the priests with sacrifices and ceremonies.

How were the divisions chosen? (24:5)
The divisions were chosen by lot (similar to drawing straws or throwing dice) to discover God's will. This was not a matter of chance; God chose the results.

[10] the seventh to Hakkoz,
the eighth to Abijah,
[11] the ninth to Jeshua,
the tenth to Shekaniah,
[12] the eleventh to Eliashib,
the twelfth to Jakim,
[13] the thirteenth to Huppah,
the fourteenth to Jeshebeab,
[14] the fifteenth to Bilgah,
the sixteenth to Immer,
[15] the seventeenth to Hezir,
the eighteenth to Happizzez,
[16] the nineteenth to Pethahiah,
the twentieth to Jehezkel,
[17] the twenty-first to Jakin,
the twenty-second to Gamul,
[18] the twenty-third to Delaiah
and the twenty-fourth to Maaziah.

[19] This was their appointed order of ministering when they entered the temple of the LORD, according to the regulations prescribed for them by their ancestor Aaron, as the LORD, the God of Israel, had commanded him.

THE REST OF THE LEVITES

[20] As for the rest of the descendants of Levi:
from the sons of Amram: Shubael;
from the sons of Shubael: Jehdeiah.
[21] As for Rehabiah, from his sons:
Ishiah was the first.
[22] From the Izharites: Shelomoth;
from the sons of Shelomoth: Jahath.
[23] The sons of Hebron: Jeriah the first,[a] Amariah the second, Jahaziel the third and Jekameam the fourth.
[24] The son of Uzziel: Micah;
from the sons of Micah: Shamir.
[25] The brother of Micah: Ishiah;
from the sons of Ishiah: Zechariah.
[26] The sons of Merari: Mahli and Mushi.
The son of Jaaziah: Beno.
[27] The sons of Merari:
from Jaaziah: Beno, Shoham, Zakkur and Ibri.
[28] From Mahli: Eleazar, who had no sons.
[29] From Kish: the son of Kish:
Jerahmeel.
[30] And the sons of Mushi: Mahli, Eder and Jerimoth.

These were the Levites, according to their families. [31] They also cast lots, just as their relatives the descendants of Aaron did, in the presence of King David and of Zadok, Ahimelek, and the heads of families of the priests and of the Levites. The families of the oldest brother were treated the same as those of the youngest.

[a] 23 Two Hebrew manuscripts and some Septuagint manuscripts (see also 23:19); most Hebrew manuscripts *The sons of Jeriah:*

Was it unusual to treat the youngest and oldest son the same? (24:31)
Yes. According to the inheritance laws, the firstborn inherited a double portion of his father's possessions. But in serving God, the Levites shared equally.

THE MUSICIANS

25 David, together with the commanders of the army, set apart some of the sons of Asaph, Heman and Jeduthun for the ministry of prophesying, accompanied by harps, lyres and cymbals. Here is the list of the men who performed this service:

²From the sons of Asaph:

Zakkur, Joseph, Nethaniah and Asarelah. The sons of Asaph were under the supervision of Asaph, who prophesied under the king's supervision.

³As for Jeduthun, from his sons:

Gedaliah, Zeri, Jeshaiah, Shimei,[a] Hashabiah and Mattithiah, six in all, under the supervision of their father Jeduthun, who prophesied, using the harp in thanking and praising the LORD.

⁴As for Heman, from his sons:

Bukkiah, Mattaniah, Uzziel, Shubael and Jerimoth; Hananiah, Hanani, Eliathah, Giddalti and Romamti-Ezer; Joshbekashah, Mallothi, Hothir and Mahazioth. ⁵(All these were sons of Heman the king's seer. They were given him through the promises of God to exalt him. God gave Heman fourteen sons and three daughters.)

⁶All these men were under the supervision of their father for the music of the temple of the LORD, with cymbals, lyres and harps, for the ministry at the house of God.

Asaph, Jeduthun and Heman were under the supervision of the king. ⁷Along with their relatives—all of them trained and skilled in music for the LORD—they numbered 288. ⁸Young and old alike, teacher as well as student, cast lots for their duties.

⁹The first lot, which was for Asaph, fell to Joseph,	
his sons and relatives[b]	12[c]
the second to Gedaliah,	
him and his relatives and sons	12
¹⁰the third to Zakkur,	
his sons and relatives	12
¹¹the fourth to Izri,[d]	
his sons and relatives	12
¹²the fifth to Nethaniah,	
his sons and relatives	12
¹³the sixth to Bukkiah,	
his sons and relatives	12
¹⁴the seventh to Jesarelah,[e]	
his sons and relatives	12
¹⁵the eighth to Jeshaiah,	
his sons and relatives	12
¹⁶the ninth to Mattaniah,	
his sons and relatives	12

What did a seer do for David? (25:5)
David consulted Heman, a seer or prophet, who revealed God's will in certain situations. Heman's prophetic ministry sometimes included music.

What kinds of duties were assigned to these musicians? (25:9–31)
Twenty-four groups of twelve musicians led the singing and playing of instruments in the temple. In order to decide when each of the groups would minister, lots were drawn.

---

[a] 3 One Hebrew manuscript and some Septuagint manuscripts (see also verse 17); most Hebrew manuscripts do not have *Shimei*.
[b] 9 See Septuagint; Hebrew does not have *his sons and relatives*.   [c] 9 See the total in verse 7; Hebrew does not have *twelve*.   [d] 11 A variant of *Zeri*
[e] 14 A variant of *Asarelah*

¹⁷ the tenth to Shimei,
    his sons and relatives   12
¹⁸ the eleventh to Azarel,^a
    his sons and relatives   12
¹⁹ the twelfth to Hashabiah,
    his sons and relatives   12
²⁰ the thirteenth to Shubael,
    his sons and relatives   12
²¹ the fourteenth to Mattithiah,
    his sons and relatives   12
²² the fifteenth to Jerimoth,
    his sons and relatives   12
²³ the sixteenth to Hananiah,
    his sons and relatives   12
²⁴ the seventeenth to Joshbekashah,
    his sons and relatives   12
²⁵ the eighteenth to Hanani,
    his sons and relatives   12
²⁶ the nineteenth to Mallothi,
    his sons and relatives   12
²⁷ the twentieth to Eliathah,
    his sons and relatives   12
²⁸ the twenty-first to Hothir,
    his sons and relatives   12
²⁹ the twenty-second to Giddalti,
    his sons and relatives   12
³⁰ the twenty-third to Mahazioth,
    his sons and relatives   12
³¹ the twenty-fourth to Romamti-Ezer,
    his sons and relatives   12.

THE GATEKEEPERS

26 The divisions of the gatekeepers:

From the Korahites: Meshelemiah son of Kore, one of the sons of Asaph.
² Meshelemiah had sons:
    Zechariah the firstborn,
    Jediael the second,
    Zebadiah the third,
    Jathniel the fourth,
  ³ Elam the fifth,
    Jehohanan the sixth
    and Eliehoenai the seventh.
⁴ Obed-Edom also had sons:
    Shemaiah the firstborn,
    Jehozabad the second,
    Joah the third,
    Sakar the fourth,
    Nethanel the fifth,
  ⁵ Ammiel the sixth,
    Issachar the seventh
    and Peullethai the eighth.
    (For God had blessed Obed-Edom.)

What did the gatekeepers do? (26:1)
They collected money from the people and took care of the temple. But their main responsibility was to guard the temple entrances.

^a *18* A variant of *Uzziel*

⁶Obed-Edom's son Shemaiah also had sons, who were leaders in their father's family because they were very capable men. ⁷The sons of Shemaiah: Othni, Rephael, Obed and Elzabad; his relatives Elihu and Semakiah were also able men. ⁸All these were descendants of Obed-Edom; they and their sons and their relatives were capable men with the strength to do the work—descendants of Obed-Edom, 62 in all.

⁹Meshelemiah had sons and relatives, who were able men—18 in all.

¹⁰Hosah the Merarite had sons: Shimri the first (although he was not the firstborn, his father had appointed him the first), ¹¹Hilkiah the second, Tabaliah the third and Zechariah the fourth. The sons and relatives of Hosah were 13 in all.

¹²These divisions of the gatekeepers, through their leaders, had duties for ministering in the temple of the LORD, just as their relatives had. ¹³Lots were cast for each gate, according to their families, young and old alike.

¹⁴The lot for the East Gate fell to Shelemiah.ᵃ Then lots were cast for his son Zechariah, a wise counselor, and the lot for the North Gate fell to him. ¹⁵The lot for the South Gate fell to Obed-Edom, and the lot for the storehouse fell to his sons. ¹⁶The lots for the West Gate and the Shalleketh Gate on the upper road fell to Shuppim and Hosah.

Guard was alongside of guard: ¹⁷There were six Levites a day on the east, four a day on the north, four a day on the south and two at a time at the storehouse. ¹⁸As for the courtᵇ to the west, there were four at the road and two at the courtᵇ itself.

¹⁹These were the divisions of the gatekeepers who were descendants of Korah and Merari.

THE TREASURERS AND OTHER OFFICIALS

²⁰Their fellow Levites wereᶜ in charge of the treasuries of the house of God and the treasuries for the dedicated things.

²¹The descendants of Ladan, who were Gershonites through Ladan and who were heads of families belonging to Ladan the Gershonite, were Jehieli, ²²the sons of Jehieli, Zetham and his brother Joel. They were in charge of the treasuries of the temple of the LORD.

²³From the Amramites, the Izharites, the Hebronites and the Uzzielites:

²⁴Shubael, a descendant of Gershom son of Moses, was the official in charge of the treasuries. ²⁵His relatives through Eliezer: Rehabiah his son, Jeshaiah his son, Joram his son, Zikri his son and Shelomith his son. ²⁶Shelomith and his relatives were in charge of all the treasuries for the things dedicated by King David, by the heads of families who were the commanders of thousands and commanders of hundreds, and by the other army commanders. ²⁷Some of the plunder

---

How could a father transfer the rights of a firstborn? (26:10)
The rights of a firstborn could be given to another son if the older son had shown he was undeserving. For example, Jacob transferred Reuben's rights to Judah and Joseph because of Reuben's misdeeds.

ᵃ 14 A variant of *Meshelemiah*   ᵇ 18 The meaning of the Hebrew for this word is uncertain.   ᶜ 20 Septuagint; Hebrew *As for the Levites, Ahijah was*

taken in battle they dedicated for the repair of the temple of the LORD. [28] And everything dedicated by Samuel the seer and by Saul son of Kish, Abner son of Ner and Joab son of Zeruiah, and all the other dedicated things were in the care of Shelomith and his relatives.

[29] From the Izharites: Kenaniah and his sons were assigned duties away from the temple, as officials and judges over Israel.

[30] From the Hebronites: Hashabiah and his relatives— seventeen hundred able men—were responsible in Israel west of the Jordan for all the work of the LORD and for the king's service. [31] As for the Hebronites, Jeriah was their chief according to the genealogical records of their families. In the fortieth year of David's reign a search was made in the records, and capable men among the Hebronites were found at Jazer in Gilead. [32] Jeriah had twenty-seven hundred relatives, who were able men and heads of families, and King David put them in charge of the Reubenites, the Gadites and the half-tribe of Manasseh for every matter pertaining to God and for the affairs of the king.

ARMY DIVISIONS

27 This is the list of the Israelites—heads of families, commanders of thousands and commanders of hundreds, and their officers, who served the king in all that concerned the army divisions that were on duty month by month throughout the year. Each division consisted of 24,000 men.

[2] In charge of the first division, for the first month, was Jashobeam son of Zabdiel. There were 24,000 men in his division. [3] He was a descendant of Perez and chief of all the army officers for the first month.

[4] In charge of the division for the second month was Dodai the Ahohite; Mikloth was the leader of his division. There were 24,000 men in his division.

[5] The third army commander, for the third month, was Benaiah son of Jehoiada the priest. He was chief and there were 24,000 men in his division. [6] This was the Benaiah who was a mighty warrior among the Thirty and was over the Thirty. His son Ammizabad was in charge of his division.

[7] The fourth, for the fourth month, was Asahel the brother of Joab; his son Zebadiah was his successor. There were 24,000 men in his division.

[8] The fifth, for the fifth month, was the commander Shamhuth the Izrahite. There were 24,000 men in his division.

[9] The sixth, for the sixth month, was Ira the son of Ikkesh the Tekoite. There were 24,000 men in his division.

[10] The seventh, for the seventh month, was Helez the Pelonite, an Ephraimite. There were 24,000 men in his division.

Why did these tribes need someone besides David to be in charge? (26:32) Three of the tribes lived east of the Jordan River and were apparently beyond the reach of the governing Levites. David was getting older, and perhaps he was beginning to hand over more administrative responsibilities.

Who were the Thirty? (27:6) These were David's mighty men. They were strong soldiers who were admired for their courage and loyalty (see 1 Chronicles 11:10 – 47 and 2 Samuel 23:8 – 39).

¹¹ The eighth, for the eighth month, was Sibbekai the Hushathite, a Zerahite. There were 24,000 men in his division.
¹² The ninth, for the ninth month, was Abiezer the Anathothite, a Benjamite. There were 24,000 men in his division.
¹³ The tenth, for the tenth month, was Maharai the Netophathite, a Zerahite. There were 24,000 men in his division.
¹⁴ The eleventh, for the eleventh month, was Benaiah the Pirathonite, an Ephraimite. There were 24,000 men in his division.
¹⁵ The twelfth, for the twelfth month, was Heldai the Netophathite, from the family of Othniel. There were 24,000 men in his division.

LEADERS OF THE TRIBES

¹⁶ The leaders of the tribes of Israel:

over the Reubenites: Eliezer son of Zikri;
over the Simeonites: Shephatiah son of Maakah;
¹⁷ over Levi: Hashabiah son of Kemuel;
over Aaron: Zadok;
¹⁸ over Judah: Elihu, a brother of David;
over Issachar: Omri son of Michael;
¹⁹ over Zebulun: Ishmaiah son of Obadiah;
over Naphtali: Jerimoth son of Azriel;
²⁰ over the Ephraimites: Hoshea son of Azaziah;
over half the tribe of Manasseh: Joel son of Pedaiah;
²¹ over the half-tribe of Manasseh in Gilead: Iddo son of Zechariah;
over Benjamin: Jaasiel son of Abner;
²² over Dan: Azarel son of Jeroham.
These were the leaders of the tribes of Israel.

²³ David did not take the number of the men twenty years old or less, because the LORD had promised to make Israel as numerous as the stars in the sky. ²⁴ Joab son of Zeruiah began to count the men but did not finish. God's wrath came on Israel on account of this numbering, and the number was not entered in the book*ᵃ* of the annals of King David.

THE KING'S OVERSEERS

²⁵ Azmaveth son of Adiel was in charge of the royal storehouses.

Jonathan son of Uzziah was in charge of the storehouses in the outlying districts, in the towns, the villages and the watchtowers.

²⁶ Ezri son of Kelub was in charge of the workers who farmed the land.

²⁷ Shimei the Ramathite was in charge of the vineyards.

Zabdi the Shiphmite was in charge of the produce of the vineyards for the wine vats.

²⁸ Baal-Hanan the Gederite was in charge of the olive and sycamore-fig trees in the western foothills.

Joash was in charge of the supplies of olive oil.

ᵃ 24 Septuagint; Hebrew *number*

²⁹Shitrai the Sharonite was in charge of the herds grazing in Sharon.

Shaphat son of Adlai was in charge of the herds in the valleys.

³⁰Obil the Ishmaelite was in charge of the camels.

Jehdeiah the Meronothite was in charge of the donkeys.

³¹Jaziz the Hagrite was in charge of the flocks.

All these were the officials in charge of King David's property.

³²Jonathan, David's uncle, was a counselor, a man of insight and a scribe. Jehiel son of Hakmoni took care of the king's sons.

³³Ahithophel was the king's counselor.

Hushai the Arkite was the king's confidant. ³⁴Ahithophel was succeeded by Jehoiada son of Benaiah and by Abiathar.

Joab was the commander of the royal army.

DAVID'S PLANS FOR THE TEMPLE

28 David summoned all the officials of Israel to assemble at Jerusalem: the officers over the tribes, the commanders of the divisions in the service of the king, the commanders of thousands and commanders of hundreds, and the officials in charge of all the property and livestock belonging to the king and his sons, together with the palace officials, the warriors and all the brave fighting men.

²King David rose to his feet and said: "Listen to me, my fellow Israelites, my people. I had it in my heart to build a house as a place of rest for the ark of the covenant of the LORD, for the footstool of our God, and I made plans to build it. ³But God said to me, 'You are not to build a house for my Name, because you are a warrior and have shed blood.'

⁴"Yet the LORD, the God of Israel, chose me from my whole family to be king over Israel forever. He chose Judah as leader, and from the tribe of Judah he chose my family, and from my father's sons he was pleased to make me king over all Israel. ⁵Of all my sons—and the LORD has given me many—he has chosen my son Solomon to sit on the throne of the kingdom of the LORD over Israel. ⁶He said to me: 'Solomon your son is the one who will build my house and my courts, for I have chosen him to be my son, and I will be his father. ⁷I will establish his kingdom forever if he is unswerving in carrying out my commands and laws, as is being done at this time.'

⁸"So now I charge you in the sight of all Israel and of the assembly of the LORD, and in the hearing of our God: Be careful to follow all the commands of the LORD your God, that you may possess this good land and pass it on as an inheritance to your descendants forever.

⁹"And you, my son Solomon, acknowledge the God of your father, and serve him with wholehearted devotion and with a willing mind, for the LORD searches every heart and understands every desire and every thought. If you seek him, he will be found by you; but if you forsake him, he will reject you forever. ¹⁰Consider now, for the LORD has chosen you to build a house as the sanctuary. Be strong and do the work."

Why was a friend listed as an official position? (27:33) He may have been a close personal adviser. David might have rewarded Hushai for his part in stopping Absalom's plot (2 Samuel 15:31–37).

¹¹Then David gave his son Solomon the plans for the portico of the temple, its buildings, its storerooms, its upper parts, its inner rooms and the place of atonement. ¹²He gave him the plans of all that the Spirit had put in his mind for the courts of the temple of the Lord and all the surrounding rooms, for the treasuries of the temple of God and for the treasuries for the dedicated things. ¹³He gave him instructions for the divisions of the priests and Levites, and for all the work of serving in the temple of the Lord, as well as for all the articles to be used in its service. ¹⁴He designated the weight of gold for all the gold articles to be used in various kinds of service, and the weight of silver for all the silver articles to be used in various kinds of service: ¹⁵the weight of gold for the gold lampstands and their lamps, with the weight for each lampstand and its lamps; and the weight of silver for each silver lampstand and its lamps, according to the use of each lampstand; ¹⁶the weight of gold for each table for consecrated bread; the weight of silver for the silver tables; ¹⁷the weight of pure gold for the forks, sprinkling bowls and pitchers; the weight of gold for each gold dish; the weight of silver for each silver dish; ¹⁸and the weight of the refined gold for the altar of incense. He also gave him the plan for the chariot, that is, the cherubim of gold that spread their wings and overshadow the ark of the covenant of the Lord.

¹⁹"All this," David said, "I have in writing as a result of the Lord's hand on me, and he enabled me to understand all the details of the plan."

²⁰David also said to Solomon his son, "Be strong and courageous, and do the work. Do not be afraid or discouraged, for the Lord God, my God, is with you. He will not fail you or forsake you until all the work for the service of the temple of the Lord is finished. ²¹The divisions of the priests and Levites are ready for all the work on the temple of God, and every willing person skilled in any craft will help you in all the work. The officials and all the people will obey your every command."

GIFTS FOR BUILDING THE TEMPLE

29 Then King David said to the whole assembly: "My son Solomon, the one whom God has chosen, is young and inexperienced. The task is great, because this palatial structure is not for man but for the Lord God. ²With all my resources I have provided for the temple of my God— gold for the gold work, silver for the silver, bronze for the bronze, iron for the iron and wood for the wood, as well as onyx for the settings, turquoise,ᵃ stones of various colors, and all kinds of fine stone and marble—all of these in large quantities. ³Besides, in my devotion to the temple of my God I now give my personal treasures of gold and silver for the temple of my God, over and above everything I have provided for this holy temple: ⁴three thousand talentsᵇ of gold (gold of Ophir) and seven thousand talentsᶜ of refined silver,

Was this chariot something new? (28:18)
No. This design was also on the cover of the ark. The golden cherubim were thought of as God's chariot.

How was the hand of the Lord on David? (28:19)
David suggested that he received the plans from God in a way similar to how Moses received the law. God inspired David to write these things, just as God inspired other writers of the Bible.

How much was all this gold, silver, bronze, and iron worth? (29:3–7)
Ancient Israel did not have a money-based system, so it is difficult to tell the value. But the weight of the gold alone would be worth millions of dollars today.

ᵃ 2 The meaning of the Hebrew for this word is uncertain.   ᵇ 4 That is, about 110 tons or about 100 metric tons   ᶜ 4 That is, about 260 tons or about 235 metric tons

for the overlaying of the walls of the buildings, [5]for the gold work and the silver work, and for all the work to be done by the craftsmen. Now, who is willing to consecrate themselves to the LORD today?"

[6]Then the leaders of families, the officers of the tribes of Israel, the commanders of thousands and commanders of hundreds, and the officials in charge of the king's work gave willingly. [7]They gave toward the work on the temple of God five thousand talents[a] and ten thousand darics[b] of gold, ten thousand talents[c] of silver, eighteen thousand talents[d] of bronze and a hundred thousand talents[e] of iron. [8]Anyone who had precious stones gave them to the treasury of the temple of the LORD in the custody of Jehiel the Gershonite. [9]The people rejoiced at the willing response of their leaders, for they had given freely and wholeheartedly to the LORD. David the king also rejoiced greatly.

DAVID'S PRAYER

[10]David praised the LORD in the presence of the whole assembly, saying,

"Praise be to you, LORD,
    the God of our father Israel,
    from everlasting to everlasting.
[11]Yours, LORD, is the greatness and the power
    and the glory and the majesty and the splendor,
    for everything in heaven and earth is yours.
Yours, LORD, is the kingdom;
    you are exalted as head over all.
[12]Wealth and honor come from you;
    you are the ruler of all things.
In your hands are strength and power
    to exalt and give strength to all.
[13]Now, our God, we give you thanks,
    and praise your glorious name.

[14]"But who am I, and who are my people, that we should be able to give as generously as this? Everything comes from you, and we have given you only what comes from your hand. [15]We are foreigners and strangers in your sight, as were all our ancestors. Our days on earth are like a shadow, without hope. [16]LORD our God, all this abundance that we have provided for building you a temple for your Holy Name comes from your hand, and all of it belongs to you. [17]I know, my God, that you test the heart and are pleased with integrity. All these things I have given willingly and with honest intent. And now I have seen with joy how willingly your people who are here have given to you. [18]LORD, the God of our fathers Abraham, Isaac and Israel, keep these desires and thoughts in the hearts of your people forever, and keep their hearts loyal to you. [19]And give my son Solomon the wholehearted devotion to keep your commands, statutes and

What was a daric? (29:7)
A daric was a Persian coin, apparently named after Darius I (522 – 486 B.C.)

What did it mean that God tests the heart? (29:17)
David knew that appearances might impress people, but God sees beneath the surface and knows people's motives. God rejoices when his people have a pure heart.

---

[a] 7 That is, about 190 tons or about 170 metric tons   [b] 7 That is, about 185 pounds or about 84 kilograms   [c] 7 That is, about 380 tons or about 340 metric tons   [d] 7 That is, about 675 tons or about 610 metric tons
[e] 7 That is, about 3,800 tons or about 3,400 metric tons

decrees and to do everything to build the palatial structure for which I have provided."

²⁰Then David said to the whole assembly, "Praise the LORD your God." So they all praised the LORD, the God of their fathers; they bowed down, prostrating themselves before the LORD and the king.

SOLOMON ACKNOWLEDGED AS KING

²¹The next day they made sacrifices to the LORD and presented burnt offerings to him: a thousand bulls, a thousand rams and a thousand male lambs, together with their drink offerings, and other sacrifices in abundance for all Israel. ²²They ate and drank with great joy in the presence of the LORD that day.

Then they acknowledged Solomon son of David as king a second time, anointing him before the LORD to be ruler and Zadok to be priest. ²³So Solomon sat on the throne of the LORD as king in place of his father David. He prospered and all Israel obeyed him. ²⁴All the officers and warriors, as well as all of King David's sons, pledged their submission to King Solomon.

²⁵The LORD highly exalted Solomon in the sight of all Israel and bestowed on him royal splendor such as no king over Israel ever had before.

THE DEATH OF DAVID

²⁶David son of Jesse was king over all Israel. ²⁷He ruled over Israel forty years—seven in Hebron and thirty-three in Jerusalem. ²⁸He died at a good old age, having enjoyed long life, wealth and honor. His son Solomon succeeded him as king.

²⁹As for the events of King David's reign, from beginning to end, they are written in the records of Samuel the seer, the records of Nathan the prophet and the records of Gad the seer, ³⁰together with the details of his reign and power, and the circumstances that surrounded him and Israel and the kingdoms of all the other lands.

When was Solomon first anointed? (29:22)
The first anointing is recorded in 1 Kings 1:32–36.

2 Chronicles

INTRODUCTION

Who wrote this book? The author of this book is unknown. Some think he was Ezra.

Why was this book written? The book of 2 Chronicles tells what God thought of the kings of Israel and Judah.

What happens in this book? Solomon is king for 40 years. When he dies, his kingdom is divided into two nations. The people of both Hebrew nations sin, and God punishes them by sending them into exile.

What do we learn about God in this book? God rescues godly leaders who depend on him for help.

Who are the key people in this book? The most important people in this book are Solomon, Ahab, Jehoshaphat, Joash, Hezekiah, and Josiah.

Where did this happen? These things happened in the two kingdoms of Israel and Judah.

What are some of the stories in this book?

Solomon builds the temple	2 Chronicles 3
Solomon dedicates the temple	2 Chronicles 7
Egypt attacks Judah	2 Chronicles 12
Asa worships God	2 Chronicles 15
Ahab is killed	2 Chronicles 18
Jehoshaphat wins a war	2 Chronicles 20
Joash repairs the temple	2 Chronicles 24
Hezekiah trusts God	2 Chronicles 29 – 32
Josiah reforms Judah	2 Chronicles 34 – 35

When did these things happen?

1400 BC 1300 1200 1100 1000 900 800 700 600 500 400

SOLOMON'S REIGN (970 – 930 BC)
BUILDING OF THE TEMPLE (966 – 959 BC)
DIVISION OF THE KINGDOM (930 BC)
EXILE OF ISRAEL (722 BC)
FALL OF JERUSALEM (586 BC)
FIRST RETURN OF EXILES TO JERUSALEM (538 BC)
COMPLETION OF TEMPLE (516 BC)
BOOK OF 2 CHRONICLES WRITTEN (C. 450 – 400 BC)

Why did Solomon worship at a high place? (1:3)
Normally the Israelites were forbidden to worship at hilltop locations because there were often objects of pagan worship in these places. But Gibeon was different because the tent of meeting was there.

Why wasn't the ark in the tent of meeting? (1:4)
The Philistines captured the ark, and from there it made several more stops before David took it to a tent in Jerusalem where it stayed until it was brought to the temple.

What type of wisdom did Solomon have? (1:12)
Solomon had asked God for the discernment to decide between right and wrong and to govern fairly. But in addition to having the wisdom to govern, Solomon had a wide range of knowledge. He was considered the wisest man of his time in the entire Middle East.

Did Solomon's horses and chariots make him a great military leader? (1:14)
The huge number of horses and chariots probably show how extravagant Solomon was rather than how great a military leader he was. By this time, Solomon had no need of chariots and they were more an item of prestige than of tactical value.

SOLOMON ASKS FOR WISDOM

1 Solomon son of David established himself firmly over his kingdom, for the LORD his God was with him and made him exceedingly great.
²Then Solomon spoke to all Israel—to the commanders of thousands and commanders of hundreds, to the judges and to all the leaders in Israel, the heads of families— ³and Solomon and the whole assembly went to the high place at Gibeon, for God's tent of meeting was there, which Moses the LORD's servant had made in the wilderness. ⁴Now David had brought up the ark of God from Kiriath Jearim to the place he had prepared for it, because he had pitched a tent for it in Jerusalem. ⁵But the bronze altar that Bezalel son of Uri, the son of Hur, had made was in Gibeon in front of the tabernacle of the LORD; so Solomon and the assembly inquired of him there. ⁶Solomon went up to the bronze altar before the LORD in the tent of meeting and offered a thousand burnt offerings on it.
⁷That night God appeared to Solomon and said to him, "Ask for whatever you want me to give you."
⁸Solomon answered God, "You have shown great kindness to David my father and have made me king in his place. ⁹Now, LORD God, let your promise to my father David be confirmed, for you have made me king over a people who are as numerous as the dust of the earth. ¹⁰Give me wisdom and knowledge, that I may lead this people, for who is able to govern this great people of yours?"
¹¹God said to Solomon, "Since this is your heart's desire and you have not asked for wealth, possessions or honor, nor for the death of your enemies, and since you have not asked for a long life but for wisdom and knowledge to govern my people over whom I have made you king, ¹²therefore wisdom and knowledge will be given you. And I will also give you wealth, possessions and honor, such as no king who was before you ever had and none after you will have."
¹³Then Solomon went to Jerusalem from the high place at Gibeon, from before the tent of meeting. And he reigned over Israel.
¹⁴Solomon accumulated chariots and horses; he had fourteen hundred chariots and twelve thousand horses,ᵃ which

---

ᵃ *14 Or charioteers*

Can the Bible exaggerate and still be considered true?
2 CHRONICLES 1

When Solomon said that the people were "as numerous as the dust of the earth" (1:9) he wasn't giving a specific or exact number, so it would be wrong to try to estimate the number of people in the kingdom based on this statement. We only know that the number was extremely large. Solomon was using a figure of speech called hyperbole, which is an extreme exaggeration. The Bible has many examples of hyperbole.

God himself used hyperbole when he told Abraham that his descendants would be as plentiful as the grains of sand or the stars in the sky (see Genesis 15:5). Mark said that "all the people of Jerusalem" went out to hear John the Baptist (see Mark 1:5) in order to emphasize how large the crowds were.

It is important to understand the way that the Bible uses many literary devices and figures of speech such as hyperbole, simile, and metaphor. Understanding those techniques will help us to understand the truth that the author is trying to get across in a poetic or figurative way.

he kept in the chariot cities and also with him in Jerusalem. ¹⁵The king made silver and gold as common in Jerusalem as stones, and cedar as plentiful as sycamore-fig trees in the foothills. ¹⁶Solomon's horses were imported from Egypt and from Kue^a—the royal merchants purchased them from Kue at the current price. ¹⁷They imported a chariot from Egypt for six hundred shekels^b of silver, and a horse for a hundred and fifty.^c They also exported them to all the kings of the Hittites and of the Arameans.

PREPARATIONS FOR BUILDING THE TEMPLE

2^d Solomon gave orders to build a temple for the Name of the LORD and a royal palace for himself. ²He conscripted 70,000 men as carriers and 80,000 as stonecutters in the hills and 3,600 as foremen over them.

³Solomon sent this message to Hiram^e king of Tyre:

"Send me cedar logs as you did for my father David when you sent him cedar to build a palace to live in. ⁴Now I am about to build a temple for the Name of the LORD my God and to dedicate it to him for burning fragrant incense before him, for setting out the consecrated bread regularly, and for making burnt offerings every morning and evening and on the Sabbaths, at the New Moons and at the appointed festivals of the LORD our God. This is a lasting ordinance for Israel.

⁵"The temple I am going to build will be great, because our God is greater than all other gods. ⁶But who is able to build a temple for him, since the heavens, even the highest heavens, cannot contain him? Who then am I to build a temple for him, except as a place to burn sacrifices before him?

⁷"Send me, therefore, a man skilled to work in gold and silver, bronze and iron, and in purple, crimson and blue yarn, and experienced in the art of engraving, to work in Judah and Jerusalem with my skilled workers, whom my father David provided.

⁸"Send me also cedar, juniper and algum^f logs from Lebanon, for I know that your servants are skilled in cutting timber there. My servants will work with yours ⁹to provide me with plenty of lumber, because the temple I build must be large and magnificent. ¹⁰I will give your servants, the woodsmen who cut the timber, twenty thousand cors^g of ground wheat, twenty thousand cors^h of barley, twenty thousand bathsⁱ of wine and twenty thousand baths of olive oil."

¹¹Hiram king of Tyre replied by letter to Solomon:

"Because the LORD loves his people, he has made you their king."

Why did Solomon build a temple for God's Name? (2:1) God's name is just as holy as God himself. Solomon wanted to build a temple that would earn respect for God from the people of the surrounding nations.

Why was skill in cutting timber so important? (2:8) Picking out the right trees was an important skill because good trees provide the best wood. The quality of the wood impacted the structure itself, and it made creating the decorative carvings easier.

^a 16 Probably Cilicia   ^b 17 That is, about 15 pounds or about 6.9 kilograms
^c 17 That is, about 3 3/4 pounds or about 1.7 kilograms   ^d In Hebrew texts
2:1 is numbered 1:18, and 2:2-18 is numbered 2:1-17.   ^e 3 Hebrew Huram,
a variant of Hiram; also in verses 11 and 12   ^f 8 Probably a variant of almug
^g 10 That is, probably about 3,600 tons or about 3,200 metric tons of wheat
^h 10 That is, probably about 3,000 tons or about 2,700 metric tons of barley
ⁱ 10 That is, about 120,000 gallons or about 440,000 liters

Did Hiram worship the Lord? (2:12)
It was common for kings at that time to recognize and honor each other's gods. This was another way to cement alliances and trade agreements. Hiram's statement may have been this type of respectful expression.

[12] And Hiram added:

"Praise be to the Lord, the God of Israel, who made heaven and earth! He has given King David a wise son, endowed with intelligence and discernment, who will build a temple for the Lord and a palace for himself.

[13] "I am sending you Huram-Abi, a man of great skill, [14] whose mother was from Dan and whose father was from Tyre. He is trained to work in gold and silver, bronze and iron, stone and wood, and with purple and blue and crimson yarn and fine linen. He is experienced in all kinds of engraving and can execute any design given to him. He will work with your skilled workers and with those of my lord, David your father.

[15] "Now let my lord send his servants the wheat and barley and the olive oil and wine he promised, [16] and we will cut all the logs from Lebanon that you need and will float them as rafts by sea down to Joppa. You can then take them up to Jerusalem."

[17] Solomon took a census of all the foreigners residing in Israel, after the census his father David had taken; and they were found to be 153,600. [18] He assigned 70,000 of them to be carriers and 80,000 to be stonecutters in the hills, with 3,600 foremen over them to keep the people working.

SOLOMON BUILDS THE TEMPLE

Why was the temple built on Mount Moriah? (3:1)
This location had been the site of two significant encounters with God. David built an altar there to stop a plague (2 Samuel 24:18), and it was also the place where Abraham demonstrated his faith by being willing to sacrifice Isaac (Genesis 22).

3 Then Solomon began to build the temple of the Lord in Jerusalem on Mount Moriah, where the Lord had appeared to his father David. It was on the threshing floor of Araunah[a] the Jebusite, the place provided by David. [2] He began building on the second day of the second month in the fourth year of his reign.

[3] The foundation Solomon laid for building the temple of God was sixty cubits long and twenty cubits wide[b] (using the cubit of the old standard). [4] The portico at the front of the temple was twenty cubits[c] long across the width of the building and twenty[d] cubits high.

He overlaid the inside with pure gold. [5] He paneled the main hall with juniper and covered it with fine gold and decorated it with palm tree and chain designs. [6] He adorned the temple with precious stones. And the gold he used was gold of Parvaim. [7] He overlaid the ceiling beams, doorframes, walls and doors of the temple with gold, and he carved cherubim on the walls.

What was gold of Parvaim? (3:6)
The passage suggests that it was more precious than ordinary gold, perhaps because it was of excellent quality or because it was from a foreign land.

[8] He built the Most Holy Place, its length corresponding to the width of the temple—twenty cubits long and twenty cubits wide. He overlaid the inside with six hundred talents[e] of fine gold. [9] The gold nails weighed fifty shekels.[f] He also overlaid the upper parts with gold.

[10] For the Most Holy Place he made a pair of sculptured

---

[a] 1 Hebrew *Ornan*, a variant of *Araunah*   [b] 3 That is, about 90 feet long and 30 feet wide or about 27 meters long and 9 meters wide   [c] 4 That is, about 30 feet or about 9 meters; also in verses 8, 11 and 13   [d] 4 Some Septuagint and Syriac manuscripts; Hebrew *and a hundred and twenty*   [e] 8 That is, about 23 tons or about 21 metric tons   [f] 9 That is, about 1 1/4 pounds or about 575 grams

cherubim and overlaid them with gold. [11] The total wing-
span of the cherubim was twenty cubits. One wing of the
first cherub was five cubits[a] long and touched the temple
wall, while its other wing, also five cubits long, touched the
wing of the other cherub. [12] Similarly one wing of the second cherub was five cubits long and touched the other temple wall, and its other wing, also five cubits long, touched
the wing of the first cherub. [13] The wings of these cherubim
extended twenty cubits. They stood on their feet, facing the
main hall.[b]

[14] He made the curtain of blue, purple and crimson yarn
and fine linen, with cherubim worked into it.

[15] For the front of the temple he made two pillars, which
together were thirty-five cubits[c] long, each with a capital five
cubits high. [16] He made interwoven chains[d] and put them
on top of the pillars. He also made a hundred pomegranates
and attached them to the chains. [17] He erected the pillars
in the front of the temple, one to the south and one to the
north. The one to the south he named Jakin[e] and the one to
the north Boaz.[f]

THE TEMPLE'S FURNISHINGS

4 He made a bronze altar twenty cubits long, twenty cubits wide and ten cubits high.[g] [2] He made the Sea of
cast metal, circular in shape, measuring ten cubits from rim
to rim and five cubits[h] high. It took a line of thirty cubits[i] to
measure around it. [3] Below the rim, figures of bulls encircled
it — ten to a cubit.[j] The bulls were cast in two rows in one
piece with the Sea.

[4] The Sea stood on twelve bulls, three facing north, three
facing west, three facing south and three facing east. The Sea
rested on top of them, and their hindquarters were toward
the center. [5] It was a handbreadth[k] in thickness, and its rim
was like the rim of a cup, like a lily blossom. It held three
thousand baths.[l]

[6] He then made ten basins for washing and placed five on
the south side and five on the north. In them the things to
be used for the burnt offerings were rinsed, but the Sea was
to be used by the priests for washing.

[7] He made ten gold lampstands according to the specifications for them and placed them in the temple, five on the
south side and five on the north.

[8] He made ten tables and placed them in the temple, five
on the south side and five on the north. He also made a hundred gold sprinkling bowls.

[9] He made the courtyard of the priests, and the large court
and the doors for the court, and overlaid the doors with

**Why were the pillars given
names? (3:17)**
These were not ordinary pillars
in the sense that they did not
support any of the building's
weight. They were more similar
to monuments or markers. The
name *Jakin* probably meant *he
establishes*. The name *Boaz* probably meant *in him is strength*.

What was the Sea? (4:2)
This was an enormous bronze
basin that held about 18,000
gallons (66,000 liters) of water.

The Sea of Metal

---

[a] *11 That is, about 7 1/2 feet or about 2.3 meters; also in verse 15*
[b] *13 Or facing inward*   [c] *15 That is, about 53 feet or about 16 meters*
[d] *16 Or possibly made chains in the inner sanctuary; the meaning of the
Hebrew for this phrase is uncertain.*   [e] *17 Jakin probably means he
establishes.*   [f] *17 Boaz probably means in him is strength.*   [g] *1 That is,
about 30 feet long and wide and 15 feet high or about 9 meters long and wide
and 4.5 meters high*   [h] *2 That is, about 7 1/2 feet or about 2.3 meters*
[i] *2 That is, about 45 feet or about 14 meters*   [j] *3 That is, about 18 inches
or about 45 centimeters*   [k] *5 That is, about 3 inches or about 7.5
centimeters*   [l] *5 That is, about 18,000 gallons or about 66,000 liters*

bronze. [10] He placed the Sea on the south side, at the southeast corner.

[11] And Huram also made the pots and shovels and sprinkling bowls.

So Huram finished the work he had undertaken for King Solomon in the temple of God:

[12] the two pillars;

the two bowl-shaped capitals on top of the pillars;

the two sets of network decorating the two bowl-shaped capitals on top of the pillars;

[13] the four hundred pomegranates for the two sets of network (two rows of pomegranates for each network, decorating the bowl-shaped capitals on top of the pillars);

[14] the stands with their basins;

[15] the Sea and the twelve bulls under it;

[16] the pots, shovels, meat forks and all related articles.

All the objects that Huram-Abi made for King Solomon for the temple of the LORD were of polished bronze. [17] The king had them cast in clay molds in the plain of the Jordan between Sukkoth and Zarethan.[a] [18] All these things that Solomon made amounted to so much that the weight of the bronze could not be calculated.

[19] Solomon also made all the furnishings that were in God's temple:

the golden altar;

the tables on which was the bread of the Presence;

[20] the lampstands of pure gold with their lamps, to burn in front of the inner sanctuary as prescribed;

[21] the gold floral work and lamps and tongs (they were solid gold);

[22] the pure gold wick trimmers, sprinkling bowls, dishes and censers; and the gold doors of the temple: the inner doors to the Most Holy Place and the doors of the main hall.

5 When all the work Solomon had done for the temple of the LORD was finished, he brought in the things his father David had dedicated—the silver and gold and all the furnishings—and he placed them in the treasuries of God's temple.

THE ARK BROUGHT TO THE TEMPLE

[2] Then Solomon summoned to Jerusalem the elders of Israel, all the heads of the tribes and the chiefs of the Israelite families, to bring up the ark of the LORD's covenant from Zion, the City of David. [3] And all the Israelites came together to the king at the time of the festival in the seventh month.

[4] When all the elders of Israel had arrived, the Levites took up the ark, [5] and they brought up the ark and the tent of meeting and all the sacred furnishings in it. The Levitical priests carried them up; [6] and King Solomon and the entire

What did pomegranates symbolize? (4:13)
People associated pomegranates with beauty. The purpose of including a large quantity in temple decoration was probably to remind the people of God's beauty during worship.

[a] 17 Hebrew *Zeredatha*, a variant of *Zarethan*

assembly of Israel that had gathered about him were before the ark, sacrificing so many sheep and cattle that they could not be recorded or counted.

⁷The priests then brought the ark of the LORD's covenant to its place in the inner sanctuary of the temple, the Most Holy Place, and put it beneath the wings of the cherubim. ⁸The cherubim spread their wings over the place of the ark and covered the ark and its carrying poles. ⁹These poles were so long that their ends, extending from the ark, could be seen from in front of the inner sanctuary, but not from outside the Holy Place; and they are still there today. ¹⁰There was nothing in the ark except the two tablets that Moses had placed in it at Horeb, where the LORD made a covenant with the Israelites after they came out of Egypt.

¹¹The priests then withdrew from the Holy Place. All the priests who were there had consecrated themselves, regardless of their divisions. ¹²All the Levites who were musicians—Asaph, Heman, Jeduthun and their sons and relatives—stood on the east side of the altar, dressed in fine linen and playing cymbals, harps and lyres. They were accompanied by 120 priests sounding trumpets. ¹³The trumpeters and musicians joined in unison to give praise and thanks to the LORD. Accompanied by trumpets, cymbals and other instruments, the singers raised their voices in praise to the LORD and sang:

"He is good;
    his love endures forever."

Then the temple of the LORD was filled with the cloud, ¹⁴and the priests could not perform their service because of the cloud, for the glory of the LORD filled the temple of God.

6 Then Solomon said, "The LORD has said that he would dwell in a dark cloud; ²I have built a magnificent temple for you, a place for you to dwell forever."

³While the whole assembly of Israel was standing there, the king turned around and blessed them. ⁴Then he said:

"Praise be to the LORD, the God of Israel, who with his hands has fulfilled what he promised with his mouth to my father David. For he said, ⁵'Since the day I brought my people out of Egypt, I have not chosen a city in any tribe of Israel to have a temple built so that my Name might be there, nor have I chosen anyone to be ruler over my people Israel. ⁶But now I have chosen Jerusalem for my Name to be there, and I have chosen David to rule my people Israel.'

⁷"My father David had it in his heart to build a temple for the Name of the LORD, the God of Israel. ⁸But the LORD said to my father David, 'You did well to have it in your heart to build a temple for my Name. ⁹Nevertheless, you are not the one to build the temple, but your son, your own flesh and blood—he is the one who will build the temple for my Name.'

¹⁰"The LORD has kept the promise he made. I have succeeded David my father and now I sit on the throne of Israel, just as the LORD promised, and I have built the

---

Why did they offer so many sacrifices? (5:6)
The people of Israel were so thankful to finally have a permanent place to worship God that they offered more than their usual number of sacrifices to show their dedication to God.

What happened to the other objects in the ark? (5:10)
The Bible does not say. Perhaps the Philistines removed the jar of manna (Exodus 16:32–34) and Aaron's staff that had budded (Numbers 17:10–11).

What did the cloud represent? (5:13–14)
People could not look at God directly, so the cloud was a symbol of God's glory. It was a reminder of the cloud that had covered Mount Sinai (Exodus 19). God had appeared in a cloud that led the people through the desert (Exodus 14:19–20) and had covered the tabernacle when it was dedicated (24:15–18).

temple for the Name of the LORD, the God of Israel. [11] There I have placed the ark, in which is the covenant of the LORD that he made with the people of Israel."

SOLOMON'S PRAYER OF DEDICATION

[12] Then Solomon stood before the altar of the LORD in front of the whole assembly of Israel and spread out his hands. [13] Now he had made a bronze platform, five cubits long, five cubits wide and three cubits high,[a] and had placed it in the center of the outer court. He stood on the platform and then knelt down before the whole assembly of Israel and spread out his hands toward heaven. [14] He said:

"LORD, the God of Israel, there is no God like you in heaven or on earth—you who keep your covenant of love with your servants who continue wholeheartedly in your way. [15] You have kept your promise to your servant David my father; with your mouth you have promised and with your hand you have fulfilled it—as it is today.

[16] "Now, LORD, the God of Israel, keep for your servant David my father the promises you made to him when you said, 'You shall never fail to have a successor to sit before me on the throne of Israel, if only your descendants are careful in all they do to walk before me according to my law, as you have done.' [17] And now, LORD, the God of Israel, let your word that you promised your servant David come true.

[18] "But will God really dwell on earth with humans? The heavens, even the highest heavens, cannot contain you. How much less this temple I have built! [19] Yet, LORD my God, give attention to your servant's prayer and his plea for mercy. Hear the cry and the prayer that your servant is praying in your presence. [20] May your eyes be open toward this temple day and night, this place of which you said you would put your Name there. May you hear the prayer your servant prays toward this place. [21] Hear the supplications of your servant and of your people Israel when they pray toward this place. Hear from heaven, your dwelling place; and when you hear, forgive.

[22] "When anyone wrongs their neighbor and is required to take an oath and they come and swear the oath before your altar in this temple, [23] then hear from heaven and act. Judge between your servants, condemning the guilty and bringing down on their heads what they have done, and vindicating the innocent by treating them in accordance with their innocence.

[24] "When your people Israel have been defeated by an enemy because they have sinned against you and when they turn back and give praise to your name, praying and making supplication before you in this temple, [25] then hear from heaven and forgive the sin of your people Israel and bring them back to the land you gave to them and their ancestors.

Why did Solomon kneel when he prayed? (6:13)
This was an important gesture. As the king, Solomon was in the position of the highest authority; however, when he knelt down, Solomon publicly acknowledged that even he was below God. God is the ultimate authority so even the king was a servant of the LORD.

Why did the Israelites pray toward the temple? (6:21)
When the Israelites were not able to pray in the temple, they were to pray facing that direction. This would remind them of God who had pledged to be present among them.

---

[a] *13* That is, about 7 1/2 feet long and wide and 4 1/2 feet high or about 2.3 meters long and wide and 1.4 meters high

²⁶ "When the heavens are shut up and there is no rain because your people have sinned against you, and when they pray toward this place and give praise to your name and turn from their sin because you have afflicted them, ²⁷ then hear from heaven and forgive the sin of your servants, your people Israel. Teach them the right way to live, and send rain on the land you gave your people for an inheritance.

²⁸ "When famine or plague comes to the land, or blight or mildew, locusts or grasshoppers, or when enemies besiege them in any of their cities, whatever disaster or disease may come, ²⁹ and when a prayer or plea is made by anyone among your people Israel—being aware of their afflictions and pains, and spreading out their hands toward this temple— ³⁰ then hear from heaven, your dwelling place. Forgive, and deal with everyone according to all they do, since you know their hearts (for you alone know the human heart), ³¹ so that they will fear you and walk in obedience to you all the time they live in the land you gave our ancestors.

³² "As for the foreigner who does not belong to your people Israel but has come from a distant land because of your great name and your mighty hand and your outstretched arm—when they come and pray toward this temple, ³³ then hear from heaven, your dwelling place. Do whatever the foreigner asks of you, so that all the peoples of the earth may know your name and fear you, as do your own people Israel, and may know that this house I have built bears your Name.

³⁴ "When your people go to war against their enemies, wherever you send them, and when they pray to you toward this city you have chosen and the temple I have built for your Name, ³⁵ then hear from heaven their prayer and their plea, and uphold their cause.

³⁶ "When they sin against you—for there is no one who does not sin—and you become angry with them and give them over to the enemy, who takes them captive to a land far away or near; ³⁷ and if they have a change of heart in the land where they are held captive, and repent and plead with you in the land of their captivity and say, 'We have sinned, we have done wrong and acted wickedly'; ³⁸ and if they turn back to you with all their heart and soul in the land of their captivity where they were taken, and pray toward the land you gave their ancestors, toward the city you have chosen and toward the temple I have built for your Name; ³⁹ then from heaven, your dwelling place, hear their prayer and their pleas, and uphold their cause. And forgive your people, who have sinned against you.

⁴⁰ "Now, my God, may your eyes be open and your ears attentive to the prayers offered in this place.

⁴¹ "Now arise, LORD God, and come to your resting place,
you and the ark of your might.

Did the Israelites allow foreigners to worship with them? (6:32–33)
Yes. Solomon's prayer that Gentiles would be drawn to the temple to worship the God of Israel showed that he understood God's promise. God had told Abraham that all the peoples of the earth would be blessed through him (Genesis 12:2 – 3. Israel was supposed to be a light that drew people to God.

Why was the temple called God's "resting place"? (6:41)
The temple was where God allowed his people to build a permanent place to worship him. Previously, they worshiped God at the tent of meeting, which had been moved many times.

May your priests, Lord God, be clothed with
  salvation,
may your faithful people rejoice in your
  goodness.
⁴²Lord God, do not reject your anointed one.
  Remember the great love promised to David
  your servant."

THE DEDICATION OF THE TEMPLE

7 When Solomon finished praying, fire came down from heaven and consumed the burnt offering and the sacrifices, and the glory of the Lord filled the temple. ²The priests could not enter the temple of the Lord because the glory of the Lord filled it. ³When all the Israelites saw the fire coming down and the glory of the Lord above the temple, they knelt on the pavement with their faces to the ground, and they worshiped and gave thanks to the Lord, saying,

"He is good;
  his love endures forever."

⁴Then the king and all the people offered sacrifices before the Lord. ⁵And King Solomon offered a sacrifice of twenty-two thousand head of cattle and a hundred and twenty thousand sheep and goats. So the king and all the people dedicated the temple of God. ⁶The priests took their positions, as did the Levites with the Lord's musical instruments, which King David had made for praising the Lord and which were used when he gave thanks, saying, "His love endures forever." Opposite the Levites, the priests blew their trumpets, and all the Israelites were standing.

⁷Solomon consecrated the middle part of the courtyard in front of the temple of the Lord, and there he offered burnt offerings and the fat of the fellowship offerings, because the bronze altar he had made could not hold the burnt offerings, the grain offerings and the fat portions.

⁸So Solomon observed the festival at that time for seven days, and all Israel with him—a vast assembly, people from Lebo Hamath to the Wadi of Egypt. ⁹On the eighth day they held an assembly, for they had celebrated the dedication of the altar for seven days and the festival for seven days more. ¹⁰On the twenty-third day of the seventh month he sent the people to their homes, joyful and glad in heart for the good things the Lord had done for David and Solomon and for his people Israel.

THE LORD APPEARS TO SOLOMON

¹¹When Solomon had finished the temple of the Lord and the royal palace, and had succeeded in carrying out all he had in mind to do in the temple of the Lord and in his own palace, ¹²the Lord appeared to him at night and said:

"I have heard your prayer and have chosen this place for myself as a temple for sacrifices.

¹³"When I shut up the heavens so that there is no rain, or command locusts to devour the land or send a

---

Why were the fire and the glory of the Lord important? (7:1–3)
The fire and glory showed that not only was God pleased with the sacrifice, but that he approved of the temple. His approval meant he would continue to be with his people.

How long would it take to offer 142,000 sacrifices? (7:5)
Probably around two weeks, which was the time the festival lasted.

plague among my people, [14]if my people, who are called by my name, will humble themselves and pray and seek my face and turn from their wicked ways, then I will hear from heaven, and I will forgive their sin and will heal their land. [15]Now my eyes will be open and my ears attentive to the prayers offered in this place. [16]I have chosen and consecrated this temple so that my Name may be there forever. My eyes and my heart will always be there.

[17]"As for you, if you walk before me faithfully as David your father did, and do all I command, and observe my decrees and laws, [18]I will establish your royal throne, as I covenanted with David your father when I said, 'You shall never fail to have a successor to rule over Israel.'

[19]"But if you[a] turn away and forsake the decrees and commands I have given you[a] and go off to serve other gods and worship them, [20]then I will uproot Israel from my land, which I have given them, and will reject this temple I have consecrated for my Name. I will make it a byword and an object of ridicule among all peoples. [21]This temple will become a heap of rubble. All[b] who pass by will be appalled and say, 'Why has the LORD done such a thing to this land and to this temple?' [22]People will answer, 'Because they have forsaken the LORD, the God of their ancestors, who brought them out of Egypt, and have embraced other gods, worshiping and serving them—that is why he brought all this disaster on them.'"

SOLOMON'S OTHER ACTIVITIES

8 At the end of twenty years, during which Solomon built the temple of the LORD and his own palace, [2]Solomon rebuilt the villages that Hiram[c] had given him, and settled Israelites in them. [3]Solomon then went to Hamath Zobah and captured it. [4]He also built up Tadmor in the desert and all the store cities he had built in Hamath. [5]He rebuilt Upper Beth Horon and Lower Beth Horon as fortified cities, with walls and with gates and bars, [6]as well as Baalath and all his store cities, and all the cities for his chariots and for his horses[d]—whatever he desired to build in Jerusalem, in Lebanon and throughout all the territory he ruled.

[7]There were still people left from the Hittites, Amorites, Perizzites, Hivites and Jebusites (these people were not Israelites). [8]Solomon conscripted the descendants of all these people remaining in the land—whom the Israelites had not destroyed—to serve as slave labor, as it is to this day. [9]But Solomon did not make slaves of the Israelites for his work; they were his fighting men, commanders of his captains, and commanders of his chariots and charioteers. [10]They were also King Solomon's chief officials—two hundred and fifty officials supervising the men.

---

[a] 19 The Hebrew is plural.   [b] 21 See some Septuagint manuscripts, Old Latin, Syriac, Arabic and Targum; Hebrew *And though this temple is now so imposing, all*   [c] 2 Hebrew *Huram*, a variant of *Hiram*; also in verse 18   [d] 6 Or *charioteers*

How did God renew the covenant he had made with David? (7:17–22)
God promised Solomon what he had promised David—that his descendants would always rule Israel. But God emphasized the importance of obedience to the covenant in order to experience its blessings rather than its curses.

Was it right for Solomon to enslave these people? (8:8)
No. As Moses pointed out years earlier, God commanded the Israelites to destroy the pagan people who lived in Canaan (Deuteronomy 20:16–18). If these people were not eliminated, their pagan worship practices would contaminate Israel's worship. Making these people slaves was not an appropriate compromise. Too many people were tempted by pagan practices and were led away from God.

Why did Pharaoh's daughter live in her own palace? (8:11) As a foreigner and nonbeliever in God, Pharaoh's daughter was not allowed to live in the holy places where the ark of the LORD had been.

Where was Ophir? (8:18) Its location is not known. It may have been in southern Arabia, East Africa, or northern India. Ophir was known for its fine gold, silver, and ivory, and for its apes and baboons.

Where was Sheba? (9:1) The exact location is unknown. To see Solomon, the queen would probably have traveled around 1,000 miles, though whether she was coming from southern Arabia or Ethiopia is undecided.

Why did the queen of Sheba want to test Solomon? (9:1) The queen knew there was a connection between Solomon's wisdom and the God he served. She tested Solomon with riddles because she wanted to see firsthand the gift God had given Solomon.

¹¹ Solomon brought Pharaoh's daughter up from the City of David to the palace he had built for her, for he said, "My wife must not live in the palace of David king of Israel, because the places the ark of the LORD has entered are holy."

¹² On the altar of the LORD that he had built in front of the portico, Solomon sacrificed burnt offerings to the LORD, ¹³ according to the daily requirement for offerings commanded by Moses for the Sabbaths, the New Moons and the three annual festivals — the Festival of Unleavened Bread, the Festival of Weeks and the Festival of Tabernacles. ¹⁴ In keeping with the ordinance of his father David, he appointed the divisions of the priests for their duties, and the Levites to lead the praise and to assist the priests according to each day's requirement. He also appointed the gatekeepers by divisions for the various gates, because this was what David the man of God had ordered. ¹⁵ They did not deviate from the king's commands to the priests or to the Levites in any matter, including that of the treasuries.

¹⁶ All Solomon's work was carried out, from the day the foundation of the temple of the LORD was laid until its completion. So the temple of the LORD was finished.

¹⁷ Then Solomon went to Ezion Geber and Elath on the coast of Edom. ¹⁸ And Hiram sent him ships commanded by his own men, sailors who knew the sea. These, with Solomon's men, sailed to Ophir and brought back four hundred and fifty talents*a* of gold, which they delivered to King Solomon.

THE QUEEN OF SHEBA VISITS SOLOMON

9 When the queen of Sheba heard of Solomon's fame, she came to Jerusalem to test him with hard questions. Arriving with a very great caravan — with camels carrying spices, large quantities of gold, and precious stones — she came to Solomon and talked with him about all she had on her mind. ² Solomon answered all her questions; nothing was too hard for him to explain to her. ³ When the queen of Sheba saw the wisdom of Solomon, as well as the palace he had built, ⁴ the food on his table, the seating of his officials, the attending servants in their robes, the cupbearers in their robes and the burnt offerings he made at*b* the temple of the LORD, she was overwhelmed.

⁵ She said to the king, "The report I heard in my own country about your achievements and your wisdom is true. ⁶ But I did not believe what they said until I came and saw with my own eyes. Indeed, not even half the greatness of your wisdom was told me; you have far exceeded the report I heard. ⁷ How happy your people must be! How happy your officials, who continually stand before you and hear your wisdom! ⁸ Praise be to the LORD your God, who has delighted in you and placed you on his throne as king to rule for the LORD your God. Because of the love of your God for Israel and his desire to uphold them forever, he has made you king over them, to maintain justice and righteousness."

a 18 That is, about 17 tons or about 15 metric tons　　*b 4* Or *and the ascent by which he went up to*

⁹Then she gave the king 120 talents^a of gold, large quantities of spices, and precious stones. There had never been such spices as those the queen of Sheba gave to King Solomon.

¹⁰(The servants of Hiram and the servants of Solomon brought gold from Ophir; they also brought algumwood^b and precious stones. ¹¹The king used the algumwood to make steps for the temple of the LORD and for the royal palace, and to make harps and lyres for the musicians. Nothing like them had ever been seen in Judah.)

¹²King Solomon gave the queen of Sheba all she desired and asked for; he gave her more than she had brought to him. Then she left and returned with her retinue to her own country.

SOLOMON'S SPLENDOR

¹³The weight of the gold that Solomon received yearly was 666 talents,^c ¹⁴not including the revenues brought in by merchants and traders. Also all the kings of Arabia and the governors of the territories brought gold and silver to Solomon.

¹⁵King Solomon made two hundred large shields of hammered gold; six hundred shekels^d of hammered gold went into each shield. ¹⁶He also made three hundred small shields of hammered gold, with three hundred shekels^e of gold in each shield. The king put them in the Palace of the Forest of Lebanon.

¹⁷Then the king made a great throne covered with ivory and overlaid with pure gold. ¹⁸The throne had six steps, and a footstool of gold was attached to it. On both sides of the seat were armrests, with a lion standing beside each of them. ¹⁹Twelve lions stood on the six steps, one at either end of each step. Nothing like it had ever been made for any other kingdom. ²⁰All King Solomon's goblets were gold, and all the household articles in the Palace of the Forest of Lebanon were pure gold. Nothing was made of silver, because silver was considered of little value in Solomon's day. ²¹The king had a fleet of trading ships^f manned by Hiram's^g servants. Once every three years it returned, carrying gold, silver and ivory, and apes and baboons.

²²King Solomon was greater in riches and wisdom than all the other kings of the earth. ²³All the kings of the earth sought audience with Solomon to hear the wisdom God had put in his heart. ²⁴Year after year, everyone who came brought a gift—articles of silver and gold, and robes, weapons and spices, and horses and mules.

²⁵Solomon had four thousand stalls for horses and chariots, and twelve thousand horses,^b which he kept in the chariot cities and also with him in Jerusalem. ²⁶He ruled over all the kings from the Euphrates River to the land of the Philistines, as far as the border of Egypt. ²⁷The king made silver as common in Jerusalem as stones, and cedar as plentiful as

Why did the queen give Solomon gifts? (9:9)
The gifts probably reflected how impressed she was by Solomon's extensive knowledge. Or she might have brought these items in order to start a profitable trade agreement. It was very common for one ruler to present gifts to another ruler during a visit.

Why was algumwood so special? (9:10–11)
This wood was also called almugwood (1 Kings 10:11). Its origin, Ophir, suggests that it was a type of red sandalwood. Regardless, it was prized for making musical instruments and detailed wood carvings.

Why did Solomon have so many horses? (9:25)
Not all of these horses personally belonged to Solomon. As king, he had ownership of them but they were used by the army. Solomon married Pharaoh's daughter so it is likely that he bought horses and chariots from Egypt, in addition to those purchased from Cilicia.

---

^a 9 That is, about 4 1/2 tons or about 4 metric tons   ^b 10 Probably a variant of *almugwood*   ^c 13 That is, about 25 tons or about 23 metric tons   ^d 15 That is, about 15 pounds or about 6.9 kilograms   ^e 16 That is, about 7 1/2 pounds or about 3.5 kilograms   ^f 21 Hebrew *of ships that could go to Tarshish*   ^g 21 Hebrew *Huram*, a variant of *Hiram*   ^b 25 Or *charioteers*

sycamore-fig trees in the foothills. [28] Solomon's horses were imported from Egypt and from all other countries.

SOLOMON'S DEATH

[29] As for the other events of Solomon's reign, from beginning to end, are they not written in the records of Nathan the prophet, in the prophecy of Ahijah the Shilonite and in the visions of Iddo the seer concerning Jeroboam son of Nebat? [30] Solomon reigned in Jerusalem over all Israel forty years. [31] Then he rested with his ancestors and was buried in the city of David his father. And Rehoboam his son succeeded him as king.

ISRAEL REBELS AGAINST REHOBOAM

10 Rehoboam went to Shechem, for all Israel had gone there to make him king. [2] When Jeroboam son of Nebat heard this (he was in Egypt, where he had fled from King Solomon), he returned from Egypt. [3] So they sent for Jeroboam, and he and all Israel went to Rehoboam and said to him: [4] "Your father put a heavy yoke on us, but now lighten the harsh labor and the heavy yoke he put on us, and we will serve you."

[5] Rehoboam answered, "Come back to me in three days." So the people went away.

[6] Then King Rehoboam consulted the elders who had served his father Solomon during his lifetime. "How would you advise me to answer these people?" he asked.

[7] They replied, "If you will be kind to these people and please them and give them a favorable answer, they will always be your servants."

[8] But Rehoboam rejected the advice the elders gave him and consulted the young men who had grown up with him and were serving him. [9] He asked them, "What is your advice? How should we answer these people who say to me, 'Lighten the yoke your father put on us'?"

[10] The young men who had grown up with him replied, "The people have said to you, 'Your father put a heavy yoke on us, but make our yoke lighter.' Now tell them, 'My little finger is thicker than my father's waist. [11] My father laid on you a heavy yoke; I will make it even heavier. My father scourged you with whips; I will scourge you with scorpions.'"

[12] Three days later Jeroboam and all the people returned to Rehoboam, as the king had said, "Come back to me in three days." [13] The king answered them harshly. Rejecting the advice of the elders, [14] he followed the advice of the young men and said, "My father made your yoke heavy; I will make it even heavier. My father scourged you with whips; I will scourge you with scorpions." [15] So the king did not listen to the people, for this turn of events was from God, to fulfill the word the LORD had spoken to Jeroboam son of Nebat through Ahijah the Shilonite.

[16] When all Israel saw that the king refused to listen to them, they answered the king:

"What share do we have in David,
   what part in Jesse's son?

Why was Rehoboam so unsympathetic to the plight of the people? (10:8–11)
As the son of the king who reigned during prosperous times, Rehoboam, under his father's decree, was provided for by the tax citizens paid. He did not have to earn his food, so he did not understand how difficult it was for everyone else who had to work. He may have been worried that his critics wanted to take his throne away from him.

What were scorpions? (10:11, 14)
These were metal-spiked leather lashes. He was issuing a heavy penalty for disobedience.

To your tents, Israel!
Look after your own house, David!"

So all the Israelites went home. [17]But as for the Israelites
who were living in the towns of Judah, Rehoboam still ruled
over them.

[18]King Rehoboam sent out Adoniram,[a] who was in charge
of forced labor, but the Israelites stoned him to death. King
Rehoboam, however, managed to get into his chariot and
escape to Jerusalem. [19]So Israel has been in rebellion against
the house of David to this day.

11 When Rehoboam arrived in Jerusalem, he mustered
Judah and Benjamin — a hundred and eighty thousand able young men — to go to war against Israel and to
regain the kingdom for Rehoboam.

[2]But this word of the LORD came to Shemaiah the man
of God: [3]"Say to Rehoboam son of Solomon king of Judah
and to all Israel in Judah and Benjamin, [4]"This is what the
LORD says: Do not go up to fight against your fellow Israelites. Go home, every one of you, for this is my doing.'" So
they obeyed the words of the LORD and turned back from
marching against Jeroboam.

REHOBOAM FORTIFIES JUDAH

[5]Rehoboam lived in Jerusalem and built up towns for defense in Judah: [6]Bethlehem, Etam, Tekoa, [7]Beth Zur, Soko,
Adullam, [8]Gath, Mareshah, Ziph, [9]Adoraim, Lachish, Azekah, [10]Zorah, Aijalon and Hebron. These were fortified cities in Judah and Benjamin. [11]He strengthened their defenses
and put commanders in them, with supplies of food, olive oil
and wine. [12]He put shields and spears in all the cities, and
made them very strong. So Judah and Benjamin were his.

[13]The priests and Levites from all their districts throughout Israel sided with him. [14]The Levites even abandoned
their pasturelands and property and came to Judah and Jerusalem, because Jeroboam and his sons had rejected them as
priests of the LORD [15]when he appointed his own priests for
the high places and for the goat and calf idols he had made.
[16]Those from every tribe of Israel who set their hearts on
seeking the LORD, the God of Israel, followed the Levites to
Jerusalem to offer sacrifices to the LORD, the God of their
ancestors. [17]They strengthened the kingdom of Judah and
supported Rehoboam son of Solomon three years, following
the ways of David and Solomon during this time.

REHOBOAM'S FAMILY

[18]Rehoboam married Mahalath, who was the daughter of
David's son Jerimoth and of Abihail, the daughter of Jesse's
son Eliab. [19]She bore him sons: Jeush, Shemariah and Za-
ham. [20]Then he married Maakah daughter of Absalom, who
bore him Abijah, Attai, Ziza and Shelomith. [21]Rehoboam
loved Maakah daughter of Absalom more than any of his
other wives and concubines. In all, he had eighteen wives
and sixty concubines, twenty-eight sons and sixty daughters.

[a] 18 Hebrew *Hadoram*, a variant of *Adoniram*

**Why did the Levites leave
Israel? (11:13 – 15)**
The Levites sided with Rehoboam
and refused to participate in calf
worship. The Levites left their
lands and cities in Israel and
returned to Judah and Jerusalem so they could remain faithful
to God.

**Was the split motivated by
religion or politics? (11:16)**
Both. Jeroboam thought that the
people's loyalty to Jerusalem
would cause problems for him
politically (1 Kings 12:26 – 27). To
lure the people away from Jerusalem, their center of worship,
he built other worship centers.
This separated those faithful to
God and the unfaithful. The faithful moved south to be closer to
their center of worship.

²² Rehoboam appointed Abijah son of Maakah as crown prince among his brothers, in order to make him king. ²³ He acted wisely, dispersing some of his sons throughout the districts of Judah and Benjamin, and to all the fortified cities. He gave them abundant provisions and took many wives for them.

SHISHAK ATTACKS JERUSALEM

12 After Rehoboam's position as king was established and he had become strong, he and all Israel*ᵃ* with him abandoned the law of the LORD. ² Because they had been unfaithful to the LORD, Shishak king of Egypt attacked Jerusalem in the fifth year of King Rehoboam. ³ With twelve hundred chariots and sixty thousand horsemen and the innumerable troops of Libyans, Sukkites and Cushites*ᵇ* that came with him from Egypt, ⁴ he captured the fortified cities of Judah and came as far as Jerusalem.

⁵ Then the prophet Shemaiah came to Rehoboam and to the leaders of Judah who had assembled in Jerusalem for fear of Shishak, and he said to them, "This is what the LORD says, 'You have abandoned me; therefore, I now abandon you to Shishak.'"

⁶ The leaders of Israel and the king humbled themselves and said, "The LORD is just."

⁷ When the LORD saw that they humbled themselves, this word of the LORD came to Shemaiah: "Since they have humbled themselves, I will not destroy them but will soon give them deliverance. My wrath will not be poured out on Jerusalem through Shishak. ⁸ They will, however, become subject to him, so that they may learn the difference between serving me and serving the kings of other lands."

⁹ When Shishak king of Egypt attacked Jerusalem, he carried off the treasures of the temple of the LORD and the treasures of the royal palace. He took everything, including the gold shields Solomon had made. ¹⁰ So King Rehoboam made bronze shields to replace them and assigned these to the commanders of the guard on duty at the entrance to the royal palace. ¹¹ Whenever the king went to the LORD's temple, the guards went with him, bearing the shields, and afterward they returned them to the guardroom.

¹² Because Rehoboam humbled himself, the LORD's anger turned from him, and he was not totally destroyed. Indeed, there was some good in Judah.

¹³ King Rehoboam established himself firmly in Jerusalem and continued as king. He was forty-one years old when he became king, and he reigned seventeen years in Jerusalem, the city the LORD had chosen out of all the tribes of Israel in which to put his Name. His mother's name was Naamah; she was an Ammonite. ¹⁴ He did evil because he had not set his heart on seeking the LORD.

¹⁵ As for the events of Rehoboam's reign, from beginning to end, are they not written in the records of Shemaiah the prophet and of Iddo the seer that deal with genealogies?

Why did Shishak attack Jerusalem? (12:1–2)
This was God's way of punishing the people of Judah for rebelling against him. But because the leaders repented of their sins, God did not allow Shishak to totally destroy the people of Judah (verse 7).

Did bronze take the place of gold? (12:10)
No. Shishak carried off the gold treasures from the temple and the palace, and the people had to settle for a cheap replacement. This humiliation may have helped to lead them back to the LORD.

What kind of evil did Rehoboam do? (12:14)
During Rehoboam's reign, Canaanite idolatry spread throughout Judah. Probably thanks to his pride, he relied on himself instead of putting his trust in God.

ᵃ 1 That is, Judah, as frequently in 2 Chronicles   *ᵇ 3* That is, people from the upper Nile region

There was continual warfare between Rehoboam and Jeroboam. [16] Rehoboam rested with his ancestors and was buried in the City of David. And Abijah his son succeeded him as king.

ABIJAH KING OF JUDAH

13 In the eighteenth year of the reign of Jeroboam, Abijah became king of Judah, [2] and he reigned in Jerusalem three years. His mother's name was Maakah,[a] a daughter[b] of Uriel of Gibeah.

There was war between Abijah and Jeroboam. [3] Abijah went into battle with an army of four hundred thousand able fighting men, and Jeroboam drew up a battle line against him with eight hundred thousand able troops.

[4] Abijah stood on Mount Zemaraim, in the hill country of Ephraim, and said, "Jeroboam and all Israel, listen to me! [5] Don't you know that the LORD, the God of Israel, has given the kingship of Israel to David and his descendants forever by a covenant of salt? [6] Yet Jeroboam son of Nebat, an official of Solomon son of David, rebelled against his master. [7] Some worthless scoundrels gathered around him and opposed Rehoboam son of Solomon when he was young and indecisive and not strong enough to resist them.

[8] "And now you plan to resist the kingdom of the LORD, which is in the hands of David's descendants. You are indeed a vast army and have with you the golden calves that Jeroboam made to be your gods. [9] But didn't you drive out the priests of the LORD, the sons of Aaron, and the Levites, and make priests of your own as the peoples of other lands do? Whoever comes to consecrate himself with a young bull and seven rams may become a priest of what are not gods.

[10] "As for us, the LORD is our God, and we have not forsaken him. The priests who serve the LORD are sons of Aaron, and the Levites assist them. [11] Every morning and evening they present burnt offerings and fragrant incense to the LORD. They set out the bread on the ceremonially clean table and light the lamps on the gold lampstand every evening. We are observing the requirements of the LORD our God. But you have forsaken him. [12] God is with us; he is our leader. His priests with their trumpets will sound the battle cry against you. People of Israel, do not fight against the LORD, the God of your ancestors, for you will not succeed."

[13] Now Jeroboam had sent troops around to the rear, so that while he was in front of Judah the ambush was behind them. [14] Judah turned and saw that they were being attacked at both front and rear. Then they cried out to the LORD. The priests blew their trumpets [15] and the men of Judah raised the battle cry. At the sound of their battle cry, God routed Jeroboam and all Israel before Abijah and Judah. [16] The Israelites fled before Judah, and God delivered them into their hands. [17] Abijah and his troops inflicted heavy losses on them, so that there were five hundred thousand casualties among Israel's able men. [18] The Israelites were subdued

---

[a] 2 Most Septuagint manuscripts and Syriac (see also 11:20 and 1 Kings 15:2); Hebrew *Micaiah*   [b] 2 Or *granddaughter*

What was a covenant of salt? (13:5)
Priests used salt in the sacrificial meal. Salt is a preservative, which means it helps keep food from spoiling. A covenant of salt probably symbolized that the covenant would last forever.

Who were these false priests? (13:9)
After the Levites left the northern kingdom, it appears that a person could pay to become a priest. Jeroboam's priests were probably politically and financially motivated. They did not believe in God or the prophecies that had been given against false priests.

Did 500,000 Israelite soldiers really die? (13:17)
This seems like a very large number, but it apparently was an all-out war. According to the census David took, there were some 630,000 fighting men among the northern tribes.

on that occasion, and the people of Judah were victorious because they relied on the LORD, the God of their ancestors.

¹⁹Abijah pursued Jeroboam and took from him the towns of Bethel, Jeshanah and Ephron, with their surrounding villages. ²⁰Jeroboam did not regain power during the time of Abijah. And the LORD struck him down and he died.

²¹But Abijah grew in strength. He married fourteen wives and had twenty-two sons and sixteen daughters.

²²The other events of Abijah's reign, what he did and what he said, are written in the annotations of the prophet Iddo.

14 *ᵃ* And Abijah rested with his ancestors and was buried in the City of David. Asa his son succeeded him as king, and in his days the country was at peace for ten years.

ASA KING OF JUDAH

²Asa did what was good and right in the eyes of the LORD his God. ³He removed the foreign altars and the high places, smashed the sacred stones and cut down the Asherah poles.*ᵇ* ⁴He commanded Judah to seek the LORD, the God of their ancestors, and to obey his laws and commands. ⁵He removed the high places and incense altars in every town in Judah, and the kingdom was at peace under him. ⁶He built up the fortified cities of Judah, since the land was at peace. No one was at war with him during those years, for the LORD gave him rest.

⁷"Let us build up these towns," he said to Judah, "and put walls around them, with towers, gates and bars. The land is still ours, because we have sought the LORD our God; we sought him and he has given us rest on every side." So they built and prospered.

⁸Asa had an army of three hundred thousand men from Judah, equipped with large shields and with spears, and two hundred and eighty thousand from Benjamin, armed with small shields and with bows. All these were brave fighting men.

⁹Zerah the Cushite marched out against them with an army of thousands upon thousands and three hundred chariots, and came as far as Mareshah. ¹⁰Asa went out to meet him, and they took up battle positions in the Valley of Zephathah near Mareshah.

¹¹Then Asa called to the LORD his God and said, "LORD, there is no one like you to help the powerless against the mighty. Help us, LORD our God, for we rely on you, and in your name we have come against this vast army. LORD, you are our God; do not let mere mortals prevail against you."

¹²The LORD struck down the Cushites before Asa and Judah. The Cushites fled, ¹³and Asa and his army pursued them as far as Gerar. Such a great number of Cushites fell that they could not recover; they were crushed before the LORD and his forces. The men of Judah carried off a large amount of plunder. ¹⁴They destroyed all the villages around Gerar, for the terror of the LORD had fallen on them. They

Asa Defeats the Cushites (14:9–13)

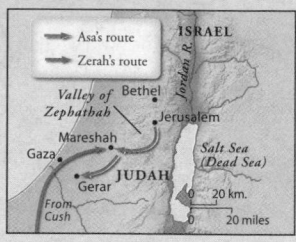

What was "the terror of the LORD"? (14:14–15)

The soldiers were literally too scared to move. They realized that Judah had God on their side and there was no way to defeat the LORD.

ᵃ In Hebrew texts 14:1 is numbered 13:23, and 14:2-15 is numbered 14:1-14.
ᵇ 3 That is, wooden symbols of the goddess Asherah; here and elsewhere in 2 Chronicles

looted all these villages, since there was much plunder there. ¹⁵They also attacked the camps of the herders and carried off droves of sheep and goats and camels. Then they returned to Jerusalem.

ASA'S REFORM

15 The Spirit of God came on Azariah son of Oded. ²He went out to meet Asa and said to him, "Listen to me, Asa and all Judah and Benjamin. The LORD is with you when you are with him. If you seek him, he will be found by you, but if you forsake him, he will forsake you. ³For a long time Israel was without the true God, without a priest to teach and without the law. ⁴But in their distress they turned to the LORD, the God of Israel, and sought him, and he was found by them. ⁵In those days it was not safe to travel about, for all the inhabitants of the lands were in great turmoil. ⁶One nation was being crushed by another and one city by another, because God was troubling them with every kind of distress. ⁷But as for you, be strong and do not give up, for your work will be rewarded."

⁸When Asa heard these words and the prophecy of Azariah son of*ᵃ* Oded the prophet, he took courage. He removed the detestable idols from the whole land of Judah and Benjamin and from the towns he had captured in the hills of Ephraim. He repaired the altar of the LORD that was in front of the portico of the LORD's temple.

⁹Then he assembled all Judah and Benjamin and the people from Ephraim, Manasseh and Simeon who had settled among them, for large numbers had come over to him from Israel when they saw that the LORD his God was with him. ¹⁰They assembled at Jerusalem in the third month of the fifteenth year of Asa's reign. ¹¹At that time they sacrificed to the LORD seven hundred head of cattle and seven thousand sheep and goats from the plunder they had brought back. ¹²They entered into a covenant to seek the LORD, the God of their ancestors, with all their heart and soul. ¹³All who would not seek the LORD, the God of Israel, were to be put to death, whether small or great, man or woman. ¹⁴They took an oath to the LORD with loud acclamation, with shouting and with trumpets and horns. ¹⁵All Judah rejoiced about the oath because they had sworn it wholeheartedly. They sought God eagerly, and he was found by them. So the LORD gave them rest on every side.

¹⁶King Asa also deposed his grandmother Maakah from her position as queen mother, because she had made a repulsive image for the worship of Asherah. Asa cut it down, broke it up and burned it in the Kidron Valley. ¹⁷Although he did not remove the high places from Israel, Asa's heart was fully committed to the LORD all his life. ¹⁸He brought into the temple of God the silver and gold and the articles that he and his father had dedicated.

¹⁹There was no more war until the thirty-fifth year of Asa's reign.

ᵃ *8* Vulgate and Syriac (see also Septuagint and verse 1); Hebrew does not have *Azariah son of.*

Why was a new covenant necessary? (15:12)
The people stopped worshiping God and started worshiping idols. Asa knew that something dramatic had to be done to get the people back to the LORD.

Why did Asa remove his grandmother from power? (15:16)
Queen mothers apparently had considerable power in Judah. After Maacah made an Asherah pole, Asa cut it down and possibly put her under house arrest. This way, she would have had no power and would not have been a threat to Asa's claim to the throne.

Why was the pole taken to the Kidron Valley to be burned? (15:16)
In order to keep from tainting more of the city, it had to be taken away to be burned. Also, Asa carrying the pole out of the city would show the people the king's desire to obey God.

Why did a good king like Asa send temple treasure to a pagan king? (16:1–3)
Asa sent the temple treasure to Ben-Hadad, ruler of Aram in hopes of forming an alliance with Aram. This might stave off an attack by Baasha of Ramah. Baasha threatened to cut off Jerusalem's trade routes and surround the capital. (2 Chron. 16:7–10).

ASA'S LAST YEARS

16 In the thirty-sixth year of Asa's reign Baasha king of Israel went up against Judah and fortified Ramah to prevent anyone from leaving or entering the territory of Asa king of Judah.

² Asa then took the silver and gold out of the treasuries of the LORD's temple and of his own palace and sent it to Ben-Hadad king of Aram, who was ruling in Damascus. ³ "Let there be a treaty between me and you," he said, "as there was between my father and your father. See, I am sending you silver and gold. Now break your treaty with Baasha king of Israel so he will withdraw from me."

⁴ Ben-Hadad agreed with King Asa and sent the commanders of his forces against the towns of Israel. They conquered Ijon, Dan, Abel Maim*ᵃ* and all the store cities of Naphtali. ⁵ When Baasha heard this, he stopped building Ramah and abandoned his work. ⁶ Then King Asa brought all the men of Judah, and they carried away from Ramah the stones and timber Baasha had been using. With them he built up Geba and Mizpah.

⁷ At that time Hanani the seer came to Asa king of Judah and said to him: "Because you relied on the king of Aram and not on the LORD your God, the army of the king of Aram has escaped from your hand. ⁸ Were not the Cushites*ᵇ* and Libyans a mighty army with great numbers of chariots and horsemen*ᶜ*? Yet when you relied on the LORD, he delivered them into your hand. ⁹ For the eyes of the LORD range throughout the earth to strengthen those whose hearts are fully committed to him. You have done a foolish thing, and from now on you will be at war."

¹⁰ Asa was angry with the seer because of this; he was so enraged that he put him in prison. At the same time Asa brutally oppressed some of the people.

¹¹ The events of Asa's reign, from beginning to end, are written in the book of the kings of Judah and Israel. ¹² In the thirty-ninth year of his reign Asa was afflicted with a disease in his feet. Though his disease was severe, even in his illness he did not seek help from the LORD, but only from the physicians. ¹³ Then in the forty-first year of his reign Asa died and rested with his ancestors. ¹⁴ They buried him in the tomb that he had cut out for himself in the City of David. They laid him on a bier covered with spices and various blended perfumes, and they made a huge fire in his honor.

Why was there a bonfire at Asa's funeral? (16:14)
This could have been an act of remembrance, a way to honor the dead. Or it could mean that Asa was cremated, though that is less likely.

JEHOSHAPHAT KING OF JUDAH

17 Jehoshaphat his son succeeded him as king and strengthened himself against Israel. ² He stationed troops in all the fortified cities of Judah and put garrisons in Judah and in the towns of Ephraim that his father Asa had captured.

³ The LORD was with Jehoshaphat because he followed the ways of his father David before him. He did not consult the Baals ⁴ but sought the God of his father and followed his

Why did people consult the Baals? (17:3)
The Baals were thought to give people advice about the future.

ᵃ 4 Also known as *Abel Beth Maakah*   *ᵇ 8* That is, people from the upper Nile region   *ᶜ 8* Or *charioteers*

commands rather than the practices of Israel. ⁵The LORD established the kingdom under his control; and all Judah brought gifts to Jehoshaphat, so that he had great wealth and honor. ⁶His heart was devoted to the ways of the LORD; furthermore, he removed the high places and the Asherah poles from Judah.

⁷In the third year of his reign he sent his officials Ben-Hail, Obadiah, Zechariah, Nethanel and Micaiah to teach in the towns of Judah. ⁸With them were certain Levites—Shemaiah, Nethaniah, Zebadiah, Asahel, Shemiramoth, Jehonathan, Adonijah, Tobijah and Tob-Adonijah—and the priests Elishama and Jehoram. ⁹They taught throughout Judah, taking with them the Book of the Law of the LORD; they went around to all the towns of Judah and taught the people.

¹⁰The fear of the LORD fell on all the kingdoms of the lands surrounding Judah, so that they did not go to war against Jehoshaphat. ¹¹Some Philistines brought Jehoshaphat gifts and silver as tribute, and the Arabs brought him flocks: seven thousand seven hundred rams and seven thousand seven hundred goats.

¹²Jehoshaphat became more and more powerful; he built forts and store cities in Judah ¹³and had large supplies in the towns of Judah. He also kept experienced fighting men in Jerusalem. ¹⁴Their enrollment by families was as follows:

From Judah, commanders of units of 1,000:
   Adnah the commander, with 300,000 fighting men;
¹⁵next, Jehohanan the commander, with 280,000;
¹⁶next, Amasiah son of Zikri, who volunteered himself
   for the service of the LORD, with 200,000.
¹⁷From Benjamin:
   Eliada, a valiant soldier, with 200,000 men armed
   with bows and shields;
¹⁸next, Jehozabad, with 180,000 men armed for battle.

¹⁹These were the men who served the king, besides those he stationed in the fortified cities throughout Judah.

MICAIAH PROPHESIES AGAINST AHAB

18 Now Jehoshaphat had great wealth and honor, and he allied himself with Ahab by marriage. ²Some years later he went down to see Ahab in Samaria. Ahab slaughtered many sheep and cattle for him and the people with him and urged him to attack Ramoth Gilead. ³Ahab king of Israel asked Jehoshaphat king of Judah, "Will you go with me against Ramoth Gilead?"

Jehoshaphat replied, "I am as you are, and my people as your people; we will join you in the war." ⁴But Jehoshaphat also said to the king of Israel, "First seek the counsel of the LORD."

⁵So the king of Israel brought together the prophets—four hundred men—and asked them, "Shall we go to war against Ramoth Gilead, or shall I not?"

"Go," they answered, "for God will give it into the king's hand."

⁶But Jehoshaphat asked, "Is there no longer a prophet of the LORD here whom we can inquire of?"

How did people learn about God before these teachers came? (17:7–9)
Typically people would visit prophets or priests to learn about the government's laws and moral obligations.

Why was an international treaty settled with a wedding? (18:1)
This was common in ancient times. Marriage would mean that breaking the treaty could cause the king personal problems as well as political. The king's family, who now lived with an enemy, would be put in danger.

Ahab Killed (18:3–34)

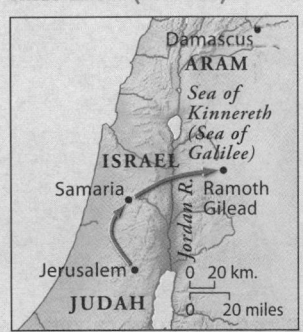

Who were these 400 prophets? (18:5)
These court prophets were false prophets probably associated with pagan worship. They spoke messages designed to please the king in order to stay in his favor. Jehoshaphat recognized that these prophets were not to be trusted.

⁷The king of Israel answered Jehoshaphat, "There is still one prophet through whom we can inquire of the Lord, but I hate him because he never prophesies anything good about me, but always bad. He is Micaiah son of Imlah."

"The king should not say such a thing," Jehoshaphat replied.

⁸So the king of Israel called one of his officials and said, "Bring Micaiah son of Imlah at once."

⁹Dressed in their royal robes, the king of Israel and Jehoshaphat king of Judah were sitting on their thrones at the threshing floor by the entrance of the gate of Samaria, with all the prophets prophesying before them. ¹⁰Now Zedekiah son of Kenaanah had made iron horns, and he declared, "This is what the Lord says: 'With these you will gore the Arameans until they are destroyed.'"

¹¹All the other prophets were prophesying the same thing. "Attack Ramoth Gilead and be victorious," they said, "for the Lord will give it into the king's hand."

¹²The messenger who had gone to summon Micaiah said to him, "Look, the other prophets without exception are predicting success for the king. Let your word agree with theirs, and speak favorably."

¹³But Micaiah said, "As surely as the Lord lives, I can tell him only what my God says."

¹⁴When he arrived, the king asked him, "Micaiah, shall we go to war against Ramoth Gilead, or shall I not?"

"Attack and be victorious," he answered, "for they will be given into your hand."

¹⁵The king said to him, "How many times must I make you swear to tell me nothing but the truth in the name of the Lord?"

¹⁶Then Micaiah answered, "I saw all Israel scattered on the hills like sheep without a shepherd, and the Lord said, 'These people have no master. Let each one go home in peace.'"

¹⁷The king of Israel said to Jehoshaphat, "Didn't I tell you that he never prophesies anything good about me, but only bad?"

¹⁸Micaiah continued, "Therefore hear the word of the Lord: I saw the Lord sitting on his throne with all the multitudes of heaven standing on his right and on his left. ¹⁹And the Lord said, 'Who will entice Ahab king of Israel into attacking Ramoth Gilead and going to his death there?'

"One suggested this, and another that. ²⁰Finally, a spirit came forward, stood before the Lord and said, 'I will entice him.'

"'By what means?' the Lord asked.

²¹"'I will go and be a deceiving spirit in the mouths of all his prophets,' he said.

"'You will succeed in enticing him,' said the Lord. 'Go and do it.'

²²"So now the Lord has put a deceiving spirit in the mouths of these prophets of yours. The Lord has decreed disaster for you."

²³Then Zedekiah son of Kenaanah went up and slapped

Why did Micaiah agree with the false prophets? (18:14) Micaiah sarcastically mimicked the false prophets and mocked Ahab. Even Ahab did not believe his words.

Does God approve of lying? (18:22) No, but God allowed the 400 false prophets to speak lies. He used their lies to accomplish his purpose. Micaiah denounced the lies of these prophets. God gave Ahab a choice — believe the lies or believe the truth. But Ahab already had his mind made up and chose to listen to the false prophets.

Micaiah in the face. "Which way did the spirit from*a* the LORD go when he went from me to speak to you?" he asked.

²⁴Micaiah replied, "You will find out on the day you go to hide in an inner room."

²⁵The king of Israel then ordered, "Take Micaiah and send him back to Amon the ruler of the city and to Joash the king's son, ²⁶and say, 'This is what the king says: Put this fellow in prison and give him nothing but bread and water until I return safely.'"

²⁷Micaiah declared, "If you ever return safely, the LORD has not spoken through me." Then he added, "Mark my words, all you people!"

AHAB KILLED AT RAMOTH GILEAD

²⁸So the king of Israel and Jehoshaphat king of Judah went up to Ramoth Gilead. ²⁹The king of Israel said to Jehoshaphat, "I will enter the battle in disguise, but you wear your royal robes." So the king of Israel disguised himself and went into battle.

³⁰Now the king of Aram had ordered his chariot commanders, "Do not fight with anyone, small or great, except the king of Israel." ³¹When the chariot commanders saw Jehoshaphat, they thought, "This is the king of Israel." So they turned to attack him, but Jehoshaphat cried out, and the LORD helped him. God drew them away from him, ³²for when the chariot commanders saw that he was not the king of Israel, they stopped pursuing him.

³³But someone drew his bow at random and hit the king of Israel between the breastplate and the scale armor. The king told the chariot driver, "Wheel around and get me out of the fighting. I've been wounded." ³⁴All day long the battle raged, and the king of Israel propped himself up in his chariot facing the Arameans until evening. Then at sunset he died.

19 When Jehoshaphat king of Judah returned safely to his palace in Jerusalem, ²Jehu the seer, the son of Hanani, went out to meet him and said to the king, "Should you help the wicked and love*b* those who hate the LORD? Because of this, the wrath of the LORD is on you. ³There is, however, some good in you, for you have rid the land of the Asherah poles and have set your heart on seeking God."

JEHOSHAPHAT APPOINTS JUDGES

⁴Jehoshaphat lived in Jerusalem, and he went out again among the people from Beersheba to the hill country of Ephraim and turned them back to the LORD, the God of their ancestors. ⁵He appointed judges in the land, in each of the fortified cities of Judah. ⁶He told them, "Consider carefully what you do, because you are not judging for mere mortals but for the LORD, who is with you whenever you give a verdict. ⁷Now let the fear of the LORD be on you. Judge carefully, for with the LORD our God there is no injustice or partiality or bribery."

⁸In Jerusalem also, Jehoshaphat appointed some of the

Why did Ahab disguise himself? (18:29)
He directed attention away from himself to keep from being targeted. In ancient wars, if a leader was killed or captured, his army would fall apart. Also, Ahab tried to minimize the chance for Micaiah's prediction of his death to come true.

Why did the soldiers spare Jehoshaphat? (18:30–32)
The soldiers' orders were to fight only Ahab, the king of Israel. God worked through these circumstances to help Jehoshaphat escape.

Why did Jehoshaphat appoint judges? (19:4–5)
People would have had a better understanding of the difference between right and wrong thanks to the spiritual revival. It would be a judge's job to encourage others to act justly.

---

a 23 Or *Spirit of*   *b* 2 Or *and make alliances with*

Levites, priests and heads of Israelite families to administer the law of the LORD and to settle disputes. And they
lived in Jerusalem. ⁹He gave them these orders: "You must
serve faithfully and wholeheartedly in the fear of the LORD.
¹⁰In every case that comes before you from your people who
live in the cities—whether bloodshed or other concerns of
the law, commands, decrees or regulations—you are to warn
them not to sin against the LORD; otherwise his wrath will
come on you and your people. Do this, and you will not sin.
¹¹"Amariah the chief priest will be over you in any matter concerning the LORD, and Zebadiah son of Ishmael, the
leader of the tribe of Judah, will be over you in any matter
concerning the king, and the Levites will serve as officials
before you. Act with courage, and may the LORD be with
those who do well."

JEHOSHAPHAT DEFEATS MOAB AND AMMON

20 After this, the Moabites and Ammonites with some
of the Meunites*ᵃ* came to wage war against Jehoshaphat.
²Some people came and told Jehoshaphat, "A vast army
is coming against you from Edom,*ᵇ* from the other side of
the Dead Sea. It is already in Hazezon Tamar" (that is, En
Gedi). ³Alarmed, Jehoshaphat resolved to inquire of the
LORD, and he proclaimed a fast for all Judah. ⁴The people
of Judah came together to seek help from the LORD; indeed,
they came from every town in Judah to seek him.
⁵Then Jehoshaphat stood up in the assembly of Judah and
Jerusalem at the temple of the LORD in the front of the new
courtyard ⁶and said:

> "LORD, the God of our ancestors, are you not the God
> who is in heaven? You rule over all the kingdoms of the
> nations. Power and might are in your hand, and no one
> can withstand you. ⁷Our God, did you not drive out
> the inhabitants of this land before your people Israel
> and give it forever to the descendants of Abraham your
> friend? ⁸They have lived in it and have built in it a sanc-
> tuary for your Name, saying, ⁹'If calamity comes upon
> us, whether the sword of judgment, or plague or famine,
> we will stand in your presence before this temple that
> bears your Name and will cry out to you in our distress,
> and you will hear us and save us.'
> ¹⁰"But now here are men from Ammon, Moab and
> Mount Seir, whose territory you would not allow Israel
> to invade when they came from Egypt; so they turned
> away from them and did not destroy them. ¹¹See how
> they are repaying us by coming to drive us out of the
> possession you gave us as an inheritance. ¹²Our God,
> will you not judge them? For we have no power to face
> this vast army that is attacking us. We do not know
> what to do, but our eyes are on you."

¹³All the men of Judah, with their wives and children and
little ones, stood there before the LORD.

**Was it common for kings to
pray publicly? (20:5–12)**
The Bible gives other examples
of kings offering public prayers.
David, Solomon, and Josiah all
prayed publicly at special occasions.

ᵃ 1 Some Septuagint manuscripts; Hebrew *Ammonites*   *ᵇ 2* One Hebrew
manuscript; most Hebrew manuscripts, Septuagint and Vulgate *Aram*

¹⁴Then the Spirit of the LORD came on Jahaziel son of Zechariah, the son of Benaiah, the son of Jeiel, the son of Mattaniah, a Levite and descendant of Asaph, as he stood in the assembly.

¹⁵He said: "Listen, King Jehoshaphat and all who live in Judah and Jerusalem! This is what the LORD says to you: 'Do not be afraid or discouraged because of this vast army. For the battle is not yours, but God's. ¹⁶Tomorrow march down against them. They will be climbing up by the Pass of Ziz, and you will find them at the end of the gorge in the Desert of Jeruel. ¹⁷You will not have to fight this battle. Take up your positions; stand firm and see the deliverance the LORD will give you, Judah and Jerusalem. Do not be afraid; do not be discouraged. Go out to face them tomorrow, and the LORD will be with you.'"

¹⁸Jehoshaphat bowed down with his face to the ground, and all the people of Judah and Jerusalem fell down in worship before the LORD. ¹⁹Then some Levites from the Kohathites and Korahites stood up and praised the LORD, the God of Israel, with a very loud voice.

²⁰Early in the morning they left for the Desert of Tekoa. As they set out, Jehoshaphat stood and said, "Listen to me, Judah and people of Jerusalem! Have faith in the LORD your God and you will be upheld; have faith in his prophets and you will be successful." ²¹After consulting the people, Jehoshaphat appointed men to sing to the LORD and to praise him for the splendor of his[a] holiness as they went out at the head of the army, saying:

"Give thanks to the LORD,
    for his love endures forever."

²²As they began to sing and praise, the LORD set ambushes against the men of Ammon and Moab and Mount Seir who were invading Judah, and they were defeated. ²³The Ammonites and Moabites rose up against the men from Mount Seir to destroy and annihilate them. After they finished slaughtering the men from Seir, they helped to destroy one another.

²⁴When the men of Judah came to the place that overlooks the desert and looked toward the vast army, they saw only dead bodies lying on the ground; no one had escaped. ²⁵So Jehoshaphat and his men went to carry off their plunder, and they found among them a great amount of equipment and clothing[b] and also articles of value—more than they could take away. There was so much plunder that it took three days to collect it. ²⁶On the fourth day they assembled in the Valley of Berakah, where they praised the LORD. This is why it is called the Valley of Berakah[c] to this day.

²⁷Then, led by Jehoshaphat, all the men of Judah and Jerusalem returned joyfully to Jerusalem, for the LORD had given them cause to rejoice over their enemies. ²⁸They entered Jerusalem and went to the temple of the LORD with harps and lyres and trumpets.

What does it mean that "the Spirit of the LORD came on Jahaziel"? (20:14)
Before this, Jahaziel was not a prophet. So it was clear that God gave him wisdom when he started preaching with authority. Jahaziel used this gift to spread God's message to others.

Why did Jehoshaphat have a choir lead the army into battle? (20:21)
Chants and songs were used to help keep the soldiers in time with one another. Singing a worship song had two purposes: it banded the soldiers together, and it was a way to ask God for help instead of having the soldiers rely on themselves.

How were their enemies defeated? (20:22–23)
God may have sent angels to ambush them. Regardless, God somehow caused the allied armies to become frightened and confused. In their panic, they began to fight each other.

a 21 Or *him with the splendor of   b 25* Some Hebrew manuscripts and Vulgate; most Hebrew manuscripts *corpses   c 26 Berakah* means *praise.*

²⁹The fear of God came on all the surrounding kingdoms when they heard how the LORD had fought against the enemies of Israel. ³⁰And the kingdom of Jehoshaphat was at peace, for his God had given him rest on every side.

What kind of rest did God give? (20:30)
Throughout Chronicles, rest from enemies is seen as God's blessing for obedience (see 14:5 – 7; 1 Chronicles 22:8 – 9). Righteous kings had victory in war, and wicked rulers experienced defeat.

THE END OF JEHOSHAPHAT'S REIGN

³¹So Jehoshaphat reigned over Judah. He was thirty-five years old when he became king of Judah, and he reigned in Jerusalem twenty-five years. His mother's name was Azubah daughter of Shilhi. ³²He followed the ways of his father Asa and did not stray from them; he did what was right in the eyes of the LORD. ³³The high places, however, were not removed, and the people still had not set their hearts on the God of their ancestors.

³⁴The other events of Jehoshaphat's reign, from beginning to end, are written in the annals of Jehu son of Hanani, which are recorded in the book of the kings of Israel.

³⁵Later, Jehoshaphat king of Judah made an alliance with Ahaziah king of Israel, whose ways were wicked. ³⁶He agreed with him to construct a fleet of trading ships.^a After these were built at Ezion Geber, ³⁷Eliezer son of Dodavahu of Mareshah prophesied against Jehoshaphat, saying, "Because you have made an alliance with Ahaziah, the LORD will destroy what you have made." The ships were wrecked and were not able to set sail to trade.^b

21 Then Jehoshaphat rested with his ancestors and was buried with them in the City of David. And Jehoram his son succeeded him as king. ²Jehoram's brothers, the sons of Jehoshaphat, were Azariah, Jehiel, Zechariah, Azariahu, Michael and Shephatiah. All these were sons of Jehoshaphat king of Israel.^c ³Their father had given them many gifts of silver and gold and articles of value, as well as fortified cities in Judah, but he had given the kingdom to Jehoram because he was his firstborn son.

JEHORAM KING OF JUDAH

⁴When Jehoram established himself firmly over his father's kingdom, he put all his brothers to the sword along with some of the officials of Israel. ⁵Jehoram was thirty-two years old when he became king, and he reigned in Jerusalem eight years. ⁶He followed the ways of the kings of Israel, as the house of Ahab had done, for he married a daughter of Ahab. He did evil in the eyes of the LORD. ⁷Nevertheless, because of the covenant the LORD had made with David, the LORD was not willing to destroy the house of David. He had promised to maintain a lamp for him and his descendants forever.

⁸In the time of Jehoram, Edom rebelled against Judah and set up its own king. ⁹So Jehoram went there with his officers and all his chariots. The Edomites surrounded him and his chariot commanders, but he rose up and broke through by night. ¹⁰To this day Edom has been in rebellion against Judah.

---

^a 36 Hebrew *of ships that could go to Tarshish*   ^b 37 Hebrew *sail for Tarshish*
^c 2 That is, Judah, as frequently in 2 Chronicles

Libnah revolted at the same time, because Jehoram had forsaken the LORD, the God of his ancestors. [11] He had also built high places on the hills of Judah and had caused the people of Jerusalem to prostitute themselves and had led Judah astray.

[12] Jehoram received a letter from Elijah the prophet, which said:

"This is what the LORD, the God of your father David, says: 'You have not followed the ways of your father Jehoshaphat or of Asa king of Judah. [13] But you have followed the ways of the kings of Israel, and you have led Judah and the people of Jerusalem to prostitute themselves, just as the house of Ahab did. You have also murdered your own brothers, members of your own family, men who were better than you. [14] So now the LORD is about to strike your people, your sons, your wives and everything that is yours, with a heavy blow. [15] You yourself will be very ill with a lingering disease of the bowels, until the disease causes your bowels to come out.'"

[16] The LORD aroused against Jehoram the hostility of the Philistines and of the Arabs who lived near the Cushites. [17] They attacked Judah, invaded it and carried off all the goods found in the king's palace, together with his sons and wives. Not a son was left to him except Ahaziah,[a] the youngest.

[18] After all this, the LORD afflicted Jehoram with an incurable disease of the bowels. [19] In the course of time, at the end of the second year, his bowels came out because of the disease, and he died in great pain. His people made no funeral fire in his honor, as they had for his predecessors.

[20] Jehoram was thirty-two years old when he became king, and he reigned in Jerusalem eight years. He passed away, to no one's regret, and was buried in the City of David, but not in the tombs of the kings.

AHAZIAH KING OF JUDAH

22 The people of Jerusalem made Ahaziah, Jehoram's youngest son, king in his place, since the raiders, who came with the Arabs into the camp, had killed all the older sons. So Ahaziah son of Jehoram king of Judah began to reign.

[2] Ahaziah was twenty-two[b] years old when he became king, and he reigned in Jerusalem one year. His mother's name was Athaliah, a granddaughter of Omri.

[3] He too followed the ways of the house of Ahab, for his mother encouraged him to act wickedly. [4] He did evil in the eyes of the LORD, as the house of Ahab had done, for after his father's death they became his advisers, to his undoing. [5] He also followed their counsel when he went with Joram[c] son of Ahab king of Israel to wage war against Hazael king of Aram at Ramoth Gilead. The Arameans wounded Joram;

Why didn't Elijah meet with Jehoram? (21:12)
Prophets often used messengers. And because of Elijah's age, it might have been difficult for him to travel.

Who were Ahaziah's advisers? (22:4)
The royal advisers from the northern court had a great deal of influence over the southern king. His mother, who was Ahab's daughter, also advised him to do wrong.

---

[a] 17 Hebrew *Jehoahaz*, a variant of *Ahaziah*   [b] 2 Some Septuagint manuscripts and Syriac (see also 2 Kings 8:26); Hebrew *forty-two*
[c] 5 Hebrew *Jehoram*, a variant of *Joram*; also in verses 6 and 7

⁶so he returned to Jezreel to recover from the wounds they had inflicted on him at Ramoth*a* in his battle with Hazael king of Aram.

Then Ahaziah*b* son of Jehoram king of Judah went down to Jezreel to see Joram son of Ahab because he had been wounded.

⁷Through Ahaziah's visit to Joram, God brought about Ahaziah's downfall. When Ahaziah arrived, he went out with Joram to meet Jehu son of Nimshi, whom the LORD had anointed to destroy the house of Ahab. ⁸While Jehu was executing judgment on the house of Ahab, he found the officials of Judah and the sons of Ahaziah's relatives, who had been attending Ahaziah, and he killed them. ⁹He then went in search of Ahaziah, and his men captured him while he was hiding in Samaria. He was brought to Jehu and put to death. They buried him, for they said, "He was a son of Jehoshaphat, who sought the LORD with all his heart." So there was no one in the house of Ahaziah powerful enough to retain the kingdom.

ATHALIAH AND JOASH

¹⁰When Athaliah the mother of Ahaziah saw that her son was dead, she proceeded to destroy the whole royal family of the house of Judah. ¹¹But Jehosheba,*c* the daughter of King Jehoram, took Joash son of Ahaziah and stole him away from among the royal princes who were about to be murdered and put him and his nurse in a bedroom. Because Jehosheba,*c* the daughter of King Jehoram and wife of the priest Jehoiada, was Ahaziah's sister, she hid the child from Athaliah so she could not kill him. ¹²He remained hidden with them at the temple of God for six years while Athaliah ruled the land.

23 In the seventh year Jehoiada showed his strength. He made a covenant with the commanders of units of a hundred: Azariah son of Jeroham, Ishmael son of Jehohanan, Azariah son of Obed, Maaseiah son of Adaiah, and Elishaphat son of Zikri. ²They went throughout Judah and gathered the Levites and the heads of Israelite families from all the towns. When they came to Jerusalem, ³the whole assembly made a covenant with the king at the temple of God.

Jehoiada said to them, "The king's son shall reign, as the LORD promised concerning the descendants of David. ⁴Now this is what you are to do: A third of you priests and Levites who are going on duty on the Sabbath are to keep watch at the doors, ⁵a third of you at the royal palace and a third at the Foundation Gate, and all the others are to be in the courtyards of the temple of the LORD. ⁶No one is to enter the temple of the LORD except the priests and Levites on duty; they may enter because they are consecrated, but all the others are to observe the LORD's command not to enter.*d* ⁷The Levites are to station themselves around the king, each with weapon in hand. Anyone who enters the temple is to be put to death. Stay close to the king wherever he goes."

Why would a grandmother murder her own grandchildren? (22:10)
Athaliah killed her grandchildren so she would have a better chance to inherit the throne. If the king had no heirs, she hoped the crown would pass to her.

a 6 Hebrew *Ramah,* a variant of *Ramoth*   *b* 6 Some Hebrew manuscripts, Septuagint, Vulgate and Syriac (see also 2 Kings 8:29); most Hebrew manuscripts *Azariah*   *c* 11 Hebrew *Jehoshabeath,* a variant of *Jehosheba*   *d* 6 Or *are to stand guard where the LORD has assigned them*

⁸The Levites and all the men of Judah did just as Jehoiada the priest ordered. Each one took his men—those who were going on duty on the Sabbath and those who were going off duty—for Jehoiada the priest had not released any of the divisions. ⁹Then he gave the commanders of units of a hundred the spears and the large and small shields that had belonged to King David and that were in the temple of God. ¹⁰He stationed all the men, each with his weapon in his hand, around the king—near the altar and the temple, from the south side to the north side of the temple.

¹¹Jehoiada and his sons brought out the king's son and put the crown on him; they presented him with a copy of the covenant and proclaimed him king. They anointed him and shouted, "Long live the king!"

¹²When Athaliah heard the noise of the people running and cheering the king, she went to them at the temple of the Lord. ¹³She looked, and there was the king, standing by his pillar at the entrance. The officers and the trumpeters were beside the king, and all the people of the land were rejoicing and blowing trumpets, and musicians with their instruments were leading the praises. Then Athaliah tore her robes and shouted, "Treason! Treason!"

¹⁴Jehoiada the priest sent out the commanders of units of a hundred, who were in charge of the troops, and said to them: "Bring her out between the ranksᵃ and put to the sword anyone who follows her." For the priest had said, "Do not put her to death at the temple of the Lord." ¹⁵So they seized her as she reached the entrance of the Horse Gate on the palace grounds, and there they put her to death.

¹⁶Jehoiada then made a covenant that he, the people and the kingᵇ would be the Lord's people. ¹⁷All the people went to the temple of Baal and tore it down. They smashed the altars and idols and killed Mattan the priest of Baal in front of the altars.

¹⁸Then Jehoiada placed the oversight of the temple of the Lord in the hands of the Levitical priests, to whom David had made assignments in the temple, to present the burnt offerings of the Lord as written in the Law of Moses, with rejoicing and singing, as David had ordered. ¹⁹He also stationed gatekeepers at the gates of the Lord's temple so that no one who was in any way unclean might enter.

²⁰He took with him the commanders of hundreds, the nobles, the rulers of the people and all the people of the land and brought the king down from the temple of the Lord. They went into the palace through the Upper Gate and seated the king on the royal throne. ²¹All the people of the land rejoiced, and the city was calm, because Athaliah had been slain with the sword.

JOASH REPAIRS THE TEMPLE

24 Joash was seven years old when he became king, and he reigned in Jerusalem forty years. His mother's name was Zibiah; she was from Beersheba. ²Joash did what

Why were the weapons kept in the temple? (23:9)
Weapons were stored in the temple so people could see and constantly be reminded of how God helped them conquer their enemies.

What type of covenant was this? (23:16–17)
This was both a spiritual and political covenant. By following God's instructions to destroy the altars and idols of Baal, they were keeping the covenant and not worshiping other gods. They kept the political side of the covenant when they declared their loyalty to the king God had chosen for them.

How could the priests tell who was clean and unclean? (23:19)
The doorkeepers probably stopped everyone entering the temple and reminded them that they had to be ceremonially clean in order to enter.

ᵃ 14 Or *out from the precincts*   ᵇ 16 Or *covenant between the Lord and the people and the king that they* (see 2 Kings 11:17)

Why did Jehoiada choose two wives for Joash? (24:3)
Athaliah killed her grandchildren, the heirs to the throne. With no one to inherit the throne, Jehoiada chose two wives to guarantee there was an heir to the throng and to rebuild the royal family.

What was this chest? (24:8)
It was common for temples in ancient times to have a box for people to place their offerings in. Representatives of the king and the temple officials were responsible for collecting and using this money.

Why would a priest be buried with kings? (24:16)
He was not just an ordinary priest. Jehoiada was buried with the kings because of the great impact he had on the nation. He was a highly influential royal advisor who helped the line of David reclaim the kingship.

was right in the eyes of the LORD all the years of Jehoiada the priest. ³Jehoiada chose two wives for him, and he had sons and daughters.

⁴Some time later Joash decided to restore the temple of the LORD. ⁵He called together the priests and Levites and said to them, "Go to the towns of Judah and collect the money due annually from all Israel, to repair the temple of your God. Do it now." But the Levites did not act at once.

⁶Therefore the king summoned Jehoiada the chief priest and said to him, "Why haven't you required the Levites to bring in from Judah and Jerusalem the tax imposed by Moses the servant of the LORD and by the assembly of Israel for the tent of the covenant law?"

⁷Now the sons of that wicked woman Athaliah had broken into the temple of God and had used even its sacred objects for the Baals.

⁸At the king's command, a chest was made and placed outside, at the gate of the temple of the LORD. ⁹A proclamation was then issued in Judah and Jerusalem that they should bring to the LORD the tax that Moses the servant of God had required of Israel in the wilderness. ¹⁰All the officials and all the people brought their contributions gladly, dropping them into the chest until it was full. ¹¹Whenever the chest was brought in by the Levites to the king's officials and they saw that there was a large amount of money, the royal secretary and the officer of the chief priest would come and empty the chest and carry it back to its place. They did this regularly and collected a great amount of money. ¹²The king and Jehoiada gave it to those who carried out the work required for the temple of the LORD. They hired masons and carpenters to restore the LORD's temple, and also workers in iron and bronze to repair the temple.

¹³The men in charge of the work were diligent, and the repairs progressed under them. They rebuilt the temple of God according to its original design and reinforced it. ¹⁴When they had finished, they brought the rest of the money to the king and Jehoiada, and with it were made articles for the LORD's temple: articles for the service and for the burnt offerings, and also dishes and other objects of gold and silver. As long as Jehoiada lived, burnt offerings were presented continually in the temple of the LORD.

¹⁵Now Jehoiada was old and full of years, and he died at the age of a hundred and thirty. ¹⁶He was buried with the kings in the City of David, because of the good he had done in Israel for God and his temple.

THE WICKEDNESS OF JOASH

¹⁷After the death of Jehoiada, the officials of Judah came and paid homage to the king, and he listened to them. ¹⁸They abandoned the temple of the LORD, the God of their ancestors, and worshiped Asherah poles and idols. Because of their guilt, God's anger came on Judah and Jerusalem. ¹⁹Although the LORD sent prophets to the people to bring them back to him, and though they testified against them, they would not listen.

²⁰Then the Spirit of God came on Zechariah son of Jehoiada the priest. He stood before the people and said, "This is what God says: 'Why do you disobey the LORD's commands? You will not prosper. Because you have forsaken the LORD, he has forsaken you.'"

²¹But they plotted against him, and by order of the king they stoned him to death in the courtyard of the LORD's temple. ²²King Joash did not remember the kindness Zechariah's father Jehoiada had shown him but killed his son, who said as he lay dying, "May the LORD see this and call you to account."

²³At the turn of the year,ᵃ the army of Aram marched against Joash; it invaded Judah and Jerusalem and killed all the leaders of the people. They sent all the plunder to their king in Damascus. ²⁴Although the Aramean army had come with only a few men, the LORD delivered into their hands a much larger army. Because Judah had forsaken the LORD, the God of their ancestors, judgment was executed on Joash. ²⁵When the Arameans withdrew, they left Joash severely wounded. His officials conspired against him for murdering the son of Jehoiada the priest, and they killed him in his bed. So he died and was buried in the City of David, but not in the tombs of the kings.

²⁶Those who conspired against him were Zabad,ᵇ son of Shimeath an Ammonite woman, and Jehozabad, son of Shimrithᶜ a Moabite woman. ²⁷The account of his sons, the many prophecies about him, and the record of the restoration of the temple of God are written in the annotations on the book of the kings. And Amaziah his son succeeded him as king.

AMAZIAH KING OF JUDAH

25 Amaziah was twenty-five years old when he became king, and he reigned in Jerusalem twenty-nine years. His mother's name was Jehoaddan; she was from Jerusalem. ²He did what was right in the eyes of the LORD, but not wholeheartedly. ³After the kingdom was firmly in his control, he executed the officials who had murdered his father the king. ⁴Yet he did not put their children to death, but acted in accordance with what is written in the Law, in the Book of Moses, where the LORD commanded: "Parents shall not be put to death for their children, nor children be put to death for their parents; each will die for their own sin."ᵈ

⁵Amaziah called the people of Judah together and assigned them according to their families to commanders of thousands and commanders of hundreds for all Judah and Benjamin. He then mustered those twenty years old or more and found that there were three hundred thousand men fit for military service, able to handle the spear and shield. ⁶He also hired a hundred thousand fighting men from Israel for a hundred talentsᵉ of silver.

⁷But a man of God came to him and said, "Your Majesty, these troops from Israel must not march with you, for

Why wasn't Joash buried in the tombs of the kings? (24:25)
For Joash, being a king was not enough to guarantee burial in the tomb of kings. As with Jehoram, Joash was dishonored and buried elsewhere. The writer of Chronicles saw the burial places of the kings as a commentary on their lives.

How much were soldiers paid? (25:6)
The usual rate was not much — approximately one talent per thousand men, which was about three shekels of silver each (a bit more than an ounce). But food and supplies were also given to them, and they could usually claim the loot they took in battles.

ᵃ 23 Probably in the spring   ᵇ 26 A variant of *Jozabad*   ᶜ 26 A variant of *Shomer*   ᵈ 4 Deut. 24:16   ᵉ 6 That is, about 3 3/4 tons or about 3.4 metric tons; also in verse 9

the LORD is not with Israel—not with any of the people of Ephraim. [8]Even if you go and fight courageously in battle, God will overthrow you before the enemy, for God has the power to help or to overthrow."

[9]Amaziah asked the man of God, "But what about the hundred talents I paid for these Israelite troops?"

The man of God replied, "The LORD can give you much more than that."

[10]So Amaziah dismissed the troops who had come to him from Ephraim and sent them home. They were furious with Judah and left for home in a great rage.

[11]Amaziah then marshaled his strength and led his army to the Valley of Salt, where he killed ten thousand men of Seir. [12]The army of Judah also captured ten thousand men alive, took them to the top of a cliff and threw them down so that all were dashed to pieces.

[13]Meanwhile the troops that Amaziah had sent back and had not allowed to take part in the war raided towns belonging to Judah from Samaria to Beth Horon. They killed three thousand people and carried off great quantities of plunder.

[14]When Amaziah returned from slaughtering the Edomites, he brought back the gods of the people of Seir. He set them up as his own gods, bowed down to them and burned sacrifices to them. [15]The anger of the LORD burned against Amaziah, and he sent a prophet to him, who said, "Why do you consult this people's gods, which could not save their own people from your hand?"

[16]While he was still speaking, the king said to him, "Have we appointed you an adviser to the king? Stop! Why be struck down?"

So the prophet stopped but said, "I know that God has determined to destroy you, because you have done this and have not listened to my counsel."

[17]After Amaziah king of Judah consulted his advisers, he sent this challenge to Jehoash[a] son of Jehoahaz, the son of Jehu, king of Israel: "Come, let us face each other in battle."

[18]But Jehoash king of Israel replied to Amaziah king of Judah: "A thistle in Lebanon sent a message to a cedar in Lebanon, 'Give your daughter to my son in marriage.' Then a wild beast in Lebanon came along and trampled the thistle underfoot. [19]You say to yourself that you have defeated Edom, and now you are arrogant and proud. But stay at home! Why ask for trouble and cause your own downfall and that of Judah also?"

[20]Amaziah, however, would not listen, for God so worked that he might deliver them into the hands of Jehoash, because they sought the gods of Edom. [21]So Jehoash king of Israel attacked. He and Amaziah king of Judah faced each other at Beth Shemesh in Judah. [22]Judah was routed by Israel, and every man fled to his home. [23]Jehoash king of Israel captured Amaziah king of Judah, the son of Joash, the son of Ahaziah,[b] at Beth Shemesh. Then Jehoash brought him to Jerusalem and broke down the wall of Jerusalem from the

Why were these mercenaries so angry? (25:10)
It was normal for soldiers to receive goods in addition to what they were paid. These soldiers were not happy when they were sent away before they could take any loot after winning a battle.

Why did the army of Judah kill prisoners of war? (25:12)
The people of Judah thought the pagan Edomites were a threat to their belief in God. Also, a longstanding rivalry between their ancestors, Jacob and Esau, added to Judah's dislike of the Edomites.

Why did Amaziah worship defeated gods? (25:14)
The people at this time thought the gods were responsible for everything. If you won in a battle, it was because not only did your god help you, but your enemy's god helped you by allowing the enemy to lose. Amaziah thanked the pagan gods for abandoning their people.

Was Amaziah still king of Jerusalem after the battle? (25:23)
Yes, though Amaziah's kingdom was considerably weaker after Jehoash was done with him.

---

[a] 17 Hebrew *Joash*, a variant of *Jehoash*; also in verses 18, 21, 23 and 25
[b] 23 Hebrew *Jehoahaz*, a variant of *Ahaziah*

Ephraim Gate to the Corner Gate—a section about four hundred cubits[a] long. ²⁴He took all the gold and silver and all the articles found in the temple of God that had been in the care of Obed-Edom, together with the palace treasures and the hostages, and returned to Samaria.

²⁵Amaziah son of Joash king of Judah lived for fifteen years after the death of Jehoash son of Jehoahaz king of Israel. ²⁶As for the other events of Amaziah's reign, from beginning to end, are they not written in the book of the kings of Judah and Israel? ²⁷From the time that Amaziah turned away from following the LORD, they conspired against him in Jerusalem and he fled to Lachish, but they sent men after him to Lachish and killed him there. ²⁸He was brought back by horse and was buried with his ancestors in the City of Judah.[b]

UZZIAH KING OF JUDAH

26 Then all the people of Judah took Uzziah,[c] who was sixteen years old, and made him king in place of his father Amaziah. ²He was the one who rebuilt Elath and restored it to Judah after Amaziah rested with his ancestors.

³Uzziah was sixteen years old when he became king, and he reigned in Jerusalem fifty-two years. His mother's name was Jekoliah; she was from Jerusalem. ⁴He did what was right in the eyes of the LORD, just as his father Amaziah had done. ⁵He sought God during the days of Zechariah, who instructed him in the fear[d] of God. As long as he sought the LORD, God gave him success.

⁶He went to war against the Philistines and broke down the walls of Gath, Jabneh and Ashdod. He then rebuilt towns near Ashdod and elsewhere among the Philistines. ⁷God helped him against the Philistines and against the Arabs who lived in Gur Baal and against the Meunites. ⁸The Ammonites brought tribute to Uzziah, and his fame spread as far as the border of Egypt, because he had become very powerful.

⁹Uzziah built towers in Jerusalem at the Corner Gate, at the Valley Gate and at the angle of the wall, and he fortified them. ¹⁰He also built towers in the wilderness and dug many cisterns, because he had much livestock in the foothills and in the plain. He had people working his fields and vineyards in the hills and in the fertile lands, for he loved the soil.

¹¹Uzziah had a well-trained army, ready to go out by divisions according to their numbers as mustered by Jeiel the secretary and Maaseiah the officer under the direction of Hananiah, one of the royal officials. ¹²The total number of family leaders over the fighting men was 2,600. ¹³Under their command was an army of 307,500 men trained for war, a powerful force to support the king against his enemies. ¹⁴Uzziah provided shields, spears, helmets, coats of armor, bows and slingstones for the entire army. ¹⁵In Jerusalem he

What was the fear of God? (26:5)
In this case fear is not the same as being afraid. The fear of God meant Uzziah had extreme respect for God. He was given a better understanding of how God was superior to pagan gods.

Why did Uzziah build towers in the wilderness? (26:10)
Travelers could take refuge from the desert inside the tower. Armies used them as lookout posts and for signaling. And farmers used towers to store crops, water, or farm tools.

---

[a] 23 That is, about 600 feet or about 180 meters   [b] 28 Most Hebrew manuscripts; some Hebrew manuscripts, Septuagint, Vulgate and Syriac (see also 2 Kings 14:20) David   [c] 1 Also called Azariah   [d] 5 Many Hebrew manuscripts, Septuagint and Syriac; other Hebrew manuscripts vision

made devices invented for use on the towers and on the corner defenses so that soldiers could shoot arrows and hurl large stones from the walls. His fame spread far and wide, for he was greatly helped until he became powerful.

[16] But after Uzziah became powerful, his pride led to his downfall. He was unfaithful to the LORD his God, and entered the temple of the LORD to burn incense on the altar of incense. [17] Azariah the priest with eighty other courageous priests of the LORD followed him in. [18] They confronted King Uzziah and said, "It is not right for you, Uzziah, to burn incense to the LORD. That is for the priests, the descendants of Aaron, who have been consecrated to burn incense. Leave the sanctuary, for you have been unfaithful; and you will not be honored by the LORD God."

[19] Uzziah, who had a censer in his hand ready to burn incense, became angry. While he was raging at the priests in their presence before the incense altar in the LORD's temple, leprosy[a] broke out on his forehead. [20] When Azariah the chief priest and all the other priests looked at him, they saw that he had leprosy on his forehead, so they hurried him out. Indeed, he himself was eager to leave, because the LORD had afflicted him.

[21] King Uzziah had leprosy until the day he died. He lived in a separate house[b] — leprous, and banned from the temple of the LORD. Jotham his son had charge of the palace and governed the people of the land.

[22] The other events of Uzziah's reign, from beginning to end, are recorded by the prophet Isaiah son of Amoz. [23] Uzziah rested with his ancestors and was buried near them in a cemetery that belonged to the kings, for people said, "He had leprosy." And Jotham his son succeeded him as king.

JOTHAM KING OF JUDAH

27 Jotham was twenty-five years old when he became king, and he reigned in Jerusalem sixteen years. His mother's name was Jerusha daughter of Zadok. [2] He did what was right in the eyes of the LORD, just as his father Uzziah had done, but unlike him he did not enter the temple of the LORD. The people, however, continued their corrupt practices. [3] Jotham rebuilt the Upper Gate of the temple of the LORD and did extensive work on the wall at the hill of Ophel. [4] He built towns in the hill country of Judah and forts and towers in the wooded areas.

[5] Jotham waged war against the king of the Ammonites and conquered them. That year the Ammonites paid him a hundred talents[c] of silver, ten thousand cors[d] of wheat and ten thousand cors[e] of barley. The Ammonites brought him the same amount also in the second and third years.

[6] Jotham grew powerful because he walked steadfastly before the LORD his God.

[7] The other events in Jotham's reign, including all his wars

---

Why did Uzziah perform the duties of a priest? (26:18)
Uzziah thought he could get away with anything because of his position as king.

How did God punish Uzziah? (26:19)
God caused Uzziah to get leprosy. For the rest of his life, this proud king had to live in separate quarters, and he was reduced from a king to an outcast.

What was wrong with going to the temple? (27:2)
Going to the temple was a good practice. What Uzziah did and why he did it were the problems. He acted as a priest when he wasn't authorized.

What were these corrupt practices? (27:2)
The people continued to worship pagan gods instead of exclusively worshiping the one true God. Jotham should have destroyed all of the pagan altars and idols.

---

[a] 19 The Hebrew for *leprosy* was used for various diseases affecting the skin; also in verses 20, 21 and 23.   [b] 21 Or *in a house where he was relieved of responsibilities*   [c] 5 That is, about 3 3/4 tons or about 3.4 metric tons
[d] 5 That is, probably about 1,800 tons or about 1,600 metric tons of wheat
[e] 5 That is, probably about 1,500 tons or about 1,350 metric tons of barley

and the other things he did, are written in the book of the kings of Israel and Judah. ⁸He was twenty-five years old when he became king, and he reigned in Jerusalem sixteen years. ⁹Jotham rested with his ancestors and was buried in the City of David. And Ahaz his son succeeded him as king.

AHAZ KING OF JUDAH

28 Ahaz was twenty years old when he became king, and he reigned in Jerusalem sixteen years. Unlike David his father, he did not do what was right in the eyes of the LORD. ²He followed the ways of the kings of Israel and also made idols for worshiping the Baals. ³He burned sacrifices in the Valley of Ben Hinnom and sacrificed his children in the fire, engaging in the detestable practices of the nations the LORD had driven out before the Israelites. ⁴He offered sacrifices and burned incense at the high places, on the hilltops and under every spreading tree.

⁵Therefore the LORD his God delivered him into the hands of the king of Aram. The Arameans defeated him and took many of his people as prisoners and brought them to Damascus.

He was also given into the hands of the king of Israel, who inflicted heavy casualties on him. ⁶In one day Pekah son of Remaliah killed a hundred and twenty thousand soldiers in Judah—because Judah had forsaken the LORD, the God of their ancestors. ⁷Zikri, an Ephraimite warrior, killed Maaseiah the king's son, Azrikam the officer in charge of the palace, and Elkanah, second to the king. ⁸The men of Israel took captive from their fellow Israelites who were from Judah two hundred thousand wives, sons and daughters. They also took a great deal of plunder, which they carried back to Samaria.

⁹But a prophet of the LORD named Oded was there, and he went out to meet the army when it returned to Samaria. He said to them, "Because the LORD, the God of your ancestors, was angry with Judah, he gave them into your hand. But you have slaughtered them in a rage that reaches to heaven. ¹⁰And now you intend to make the men and women of Judah and Jerusalem your slaves. But aren't you also guilty of sins against the LORD your God? ¹¹Now listen to me! Send back your fellow Israelites you have taken as prisoners, for the LORD's fierce anger rests on you."

¹²Then some of the leaders in Ephraim—Azariah son of Jehohanan, Berekiah son of Meshillemoth, Jehizkiah son of Shallum, and Amasa son of Hadlai—confronted those who were arriving from the war. ¹³"You must not bring those prisoners here," they said, "or we will be guilty before the LORD. Do you intend to add to our sin and guilt? For our guilt is already great, and his fierce anger rests on Israel."

¹⁴So the soldiers gave up the prisoners and plunder in the presence of the officials and all the assembly. ¹⁵The men designated by name took the prisoners, and from the plunder they clothed all who were naked. They provided them with clothes and sandals, food and drink, and healing balm. All those who were weak they put on donkeys. So they took

What was the Valley of Ben Hinnom? (28:3)
During this time it was a place of idol worship where people often sacrificed their children, among other detestable practices.

Who were the Arameans? (28:5)
They were descendants of Shem (Semites). Saul, David, and Solomon all fought with them.

What was the City of Palms? (28:15)
Jericho earned this nickname because of all of the palm trees that grew there. The climate was perfect for these trees.

Who were the Edomites? (28:17)
The Edomites were descendants of Esau who worshiped pagan gods of fertility.

Why wasn't Ahaz buried in the kings' tombs? (28:27)
The people refused to honor him after his death. Ahaz was the third king whose wickedness resulted in this loss of honor. The others were Jehoram (21:20) and Joash (24:25). Uzziah's sin and leprosy probably brought the same result, even though it is not reported in the same terms (26:23).

them back to their fellow Israelites at Jericho, the City of Palms, and returned to Samaria.

[16] At that time King Ahaz sent to the kings[a] of Assyria for help. [17] The Edomites had again come and attacked Judah and carried away prisoners, [18] while the Philistines had raided towns in the foothills and in the Negev of Judah. They captured and occupied Beth Shemesh, Aijalon and Gederoth, as well as Soko, Timnah and Gimzo, with their surrounding villages. [19] The LORD had humbled Judah because of Ahaz king of Israel,[b] for he had promoted wickedness in Judah and had been most unfaithful to the LORD. [20] Tiglath-Pileser[c] king of Assyria came to him, but he gave him trouble instead of help. [21] Ahaz took some of the things from the temple of the LORD and from the royal palace and from the officials and presented them to the king of Assyria, but that did not help him.

[22] In his time of trouble King Ahaz became even more unfaithful to the LORD. [23] He offered sacrifices to the gods of Damascus, who had defeated him; for he thought, "Since the gods of the kings of Aram have helped them, I will sacrifice to them so they will help me." But they were his downfall and the downfall of all Israel.

[24] Ahaz gathered together the furnishings from the temple of God and cut them in pieces. He shut the doors of the LORD's temple and set up altars at every street corner in Jerusalem. [25] In every town in Judah he built high places to burn sacrifices to other gods and aroused the anger of the LORD, the God of his ancestors.

[26] The other events of his reign and all his ways, from beginning to end, are written in the book of the kings of Judah and Israel. [27] Ahaz rested with his ancestors and was buried in the city of Jerusalem, but he was not placed in the tombs of the kings of Israel. And Hezekiah his son succeeded him as king.

HEZEKIAH PURIFIES THE TEMPLE

29 Hezekiah was twenty-five years old when he became king, and he reigned in Jerusalem twenty-nine years. His mother's name was Abijah daughter of Zechariah. [2] He did what was right in the eyes of the LORD, just as his father David had done.

[3] In the first month of the first year of his reign, he opened the doors of the temple of the LORD and repaired them. [4] He brought in the priests and the Levites, assembled them in the square on the east side [5] and said: "Listen to me, Levites! Consecrate yourselves now and consecrate the temple of the LORD, the God of your ancestors. Remove all defilement from the sanctuary. [6] Our parents were unfaithful; they did evil in the eyes of the LORD our God and forsook him. They turned their faces away from the LORD's dwelling place and turned their backs on him. [7] They also shut the doors of the portico and put out the lamps. They did not burn incense or

---

[a] 16 Most Hebrew manuscripts; one Hebrew manuscript, Septuagint and Vulgate (see also 2 Kings 16:7) king   [b] 19 That is, Judah, as frequently in 2 Chronicles   [c] 20 Hebrew *Tilgath-Pilneser*, a variant of *Tiglath-Pileser*

present any burnt offerings at the sanctuary to the God of Israel. [8] Therefore, the anger of the LORD has fallen on Judah and Jerusalem; he has made them an object of dread and horror and scorn, as you can see with your own eyes. [9] This is why our fathers have fallen by the sword and why our sons and daughters and our wives are in captivity. [10] Now I intend to make a covenant with the LORD, the God of Israel, so that his fierce anger will turn away from us. [11] My sons, do not be negligent now, for the LORD has chosen you to stand before him and serve him, to minister before him and to burn incense."

[12] Then these Levites set to work:

from the Kohathites,
  Mahath son of Amasai and Joel son of Azariah;
from the Merarites,
  Kish son of Abdi and Azariah son of Jehallelel;
from the Gershonites,
  Joah son of Zimmah and Eden son of Joah;
[13] from the descendants of Elizaphan,
  Shimri and Jeiel;
from the descendants of Asaph,
  Zechariah and Mattaniah;
[14] from the descendants of Heman,
  Jehiel and Shimei;
from the descendants of Jeduthun,
  Shemaiah and Uzziel.

[15] When they had assembled their fellow Levites and consecrated themselves, they went in to purify the temple of the LORD, as the king had ordered, following the word of the LORD. [16] The priests went into the sanctuary of the LORD to purify it. They brought out to the courtyard of the LORD's temple everything unclean that they found in the temple of the LORD. The Levites took it and carried it out to the Kidron Valley. [17] They began the consecration on the first day of the first month, and by the eighth day of the month they reached the portico of the LORD. For eight more days they consecrated the temple of the LORD itself, finishing on the sixteenth day of the first month.

[18] Then they went in to King Hezekiah and reported: "We have purified the entire temple of the LORD, the altar of burnt offering with all its utensils, and the table for setting out the consecrated bread, with all its articles. [19] We have prepared and consecrated all the articles that King Ahaz removed in his unfaithfulness while he was king. They are now in front of the LORD's altar."

[20] Early the next morning King Hezekiah gathered the city officials together and went up to the temple of the LORD. [21] They brought seven bulls, seven rams, seven male lambs and seven male goats as a sin offering[a] for the kingdom, for the sanctuary and for Judah. The king commanded the priests, the descendants of Aaron, to offer these on the altar of the LORD. [22] So they slaughtered the bulls, and the priests took the blood and splashed it against the altar; next they slaughtered the rams and splashed their blood against

What was Hezekiah's covenant with the LORD? (29:10)
Hezekiah made a promise to properly worship God, so he merely renewed the covenant currently in place.

How was the temple consecrated again? (29:15–17)
The LORD had not given instructions for purifying the temple because it was never supposed to be defiled. The priests took all the ceremonially unclean objects to the Kidron Valley, where Asa had earlier burned a pagan object (15:16).

What was special about the number seven? (29:21)
Seven represents perfection and rest. It is the number of days God took to create the world.

---

[a] 21 Or *purification offering*; also in verses 23 and 24

the altar; then they slaughtered the lambs and splashed their blood against the altar. ²³The goats for the sin offering were brought before the king and the assembly, and they laid their hands on them. ²⁴The priests then slaughtered the goats and presented their blood on the altar for a sin offering to atone for all Israel, because the king had ordered the burnt offering and the sin offering for all Israel.

²⁵He stationed the Levites in the temple of the Lord with cymbals, harps and lyres in the way prescribed by David and Gad the king's seer and Nathan the prophet; this was commanded by the Lord through his prophets. ²⁶So the Levites stood ready with David's instruments, and the priests with their trumpets.

²⁷Hezekiah gave the order to sacrifice the burnt offering on the altar. As the offering began, singing to the Lord began also, accompanied by trumpets and the instruments of David king of Israel. ²⁸The whole assembly bowed in worship, while the musicians played and the trumpets sounded. All this continued until the sacrifice of the burnt offering was completed.

²⁹When the offerings were finished, the king and everyone present with him knelt down and worshiped. ³⁰King Hezekiah and his officials ordered the Levites to praise the Lord with the words of David and of Asaph the seer. So they sang praises with gladness and bowed down and worshiped.

³¹Then Hezekiah said, "You have now dedicated yourselves to the Lord. Come and bring sacrifices and thank offerings to the temple of the Lord." So the assembly brought sacrifices and thank offerings, and all whose hearts were willing brought burnt offerings.

³²The number of burnt offerings the assembly brought was seventy bulls, a hundred rams and two hundred male lambs—all of them for burnt offerings to the Lord. ³³The animals consecrated as sacrifices amounted to six hundred bulls and three thousand sheep and goats. ³⁴The priests, however, were too few to skin all the burnt offerings; so their relatives the Levites helped them until the task was finished and until other priests had been consecrated, for the Levites had been more conscientious in consecrating themselves than the priests had been. ³⁵There were burnt offerings in abundance, together with the fat of the fellowship offerings and the drink offerings that accompanied the burnt offerings.

So the service of the temple of the Lord was reestablished. ³⁶Hezekiah and all the people rejoiced at what God had brought about for his people, because it was done so quickly.

HEZEKIAH CELEBRATES THE PASSOVER

30 Hezekiah sent word to all Israel and Judah and also wrote letters to Ephraim and Manasseh, inviting them to come to the temple of the Lord in Jerusalem and celebrate the Passover to the Lord, the God of Israel. ²The king and his officials and the whole assembly in Jerusalem decided to celebrate the Passover in the second month. ³They had not been able to celebrate it at the regular

---

How could the king command people to worship God? (29:30)
In ancient cultures, people accepted direction such as this from their leaders. Also, the Levites were glad to worship God, with or without the king's command.

What was the regular time for Passover? (30:3)
The Passover was usually celebrated on the 14th day of Abib. Abib was the first month of their calendar year. It is somewhere between mid-March and mid-April on our calendar.

time because not enough priests had consecrated themselves
and the people had not assembled in Jerusalem. ⁴The plan
seemed right both to the king and to the whole assembly.
⁵They decided to send a proclamation throughout Israel,
from Beersheba to Dan, calling the people to come to Jerusalem and celebrate the Passover to the LORD, the God of
Israel. It had not been celebrated in large numbers according
to what was written.

⁶At the king's command, couriers went throughout Israel
and Judah with letters from the king and from his officials,
which read:

"People of Israel, return to the LORD, the God of
Abraham, Isaac and Israel, that he may return to you
who are left, who have escaped from the hand of the
kings of Assyria. ⁷Do not be like your parents and your
fellow Israelites, who were unfaithful to the LORD, the
God of their ancestors, so that he made them an object
of horror, as you see. ⁸Do not be stiff-necked, as your
ancestors were; submit to the LORD. Come to his sanctuary, which he has consecrated forever. Serve the LORD
your God, so that his fierce anger will turn away from
you. ⁹If you return to the LORD, then your fellow Israelites and your children will be shown compassion by
their captors and will return to this land, for the LORD
your God is gracious and compassionate. He will not
turn his face from you if you return to him."

¹⁰The couriers went from town to town in Ephraim and
Manasseh, as far as Zebulun, but people scorned and ridiculed them. ¹¹Nevertheless, some from Asher, Manasseh and
Zebulun humbled themselves and went to Jerusalem. ¹²Also
in Judah the hand of God was on the people to give them
unity of mind to carry out what the king and his officials had
ordered, following the word of the LORD.

¹³A very large crowd of people assembled in Jerusalem
to celebrate the Festival of Unleavened Bread in the second
month. ¹⁴They removed the altars in Jerusalem and cleared
away the incense altars and threw them into the Kidron
Valley.

¹⁵They slaughtered the Passover lamb on the fourteenth
day of the second month. The priests and the Levites were
ashamed and consecrated themselves and brought burnt offerings to the temple of the LORD. ¹⁶Then they took up their
regular positions as prescribed in the Law of Moses the man
of God. The priests splashed against the altar the blood handed to them by the Levites. ¹⁷Since many in the crowd had
not consecrated themselves, the Levites had to kill the Passover lambs for all those who were not ceremonially clean and
could not consecrate their lambs*a* to the LORD. ¹⁸Although
most of the many people who came from Ephraim, Manasseh, Issachar and Zebulun had not purified themselves, yet
they ate the Passover, contrary to what was written. But Hezekiah prayed for them, saying, "May the LORD, who is good,
pardon everyone ¹⁹who sets their heart on seeking God—

**Why did the people mock
the couriers, the king's messengers? (30:10)**
The people in the northern kingdom had a long history of disobeying God. They hoped mocking the couriers would win them
favor with the Assyrians. They
were probably afraid of possible
political consequences from the
Assyrian masters they served
if they stopped worshiping the
Assyrians' gods.

**What was the Festival of
Unleavened Bread? (30:13)**
This was another name for the
Passover.

a 17 Or consecrate themselves

What were the "instruments
dedicated to the LORD"?
(30:21)
Stringed instruments like the
lyre and harp, wind instruments
like the flute and horn, and per-
cussion instruments like drums
and cymbals were all the LORD's
instruments.

How did the celebration echo
Solomon's dedication of the
temple? (30:23–27)
Both festivals lasted for two
weeks and were extravagant,
and in both cases the prayers of
the people were heard by God in
heaven (see 6:21, 30, 33, 39).

the LORD, the God of their ancestors—even if they are not
clean according to the rules of the sanctuary." [20]And the
LORD heard Hezekiah and healed the people.

[21]The Israelites who were present in Jerusalem celebrated
the Festival of Unleavened Bread for seven days with great
rejoicing, while the Levites and priests praised the LORD every day with resounding instruments dedicated to the LORD.[a]

[22]Hezekiah spoke encouragingly to all the Levites, who
showed good understanding of the service of the LORD. For
the seven days they ate their assigned portion and offered
fellowship offerings and praised[b] the LORD, the God of their
ancestors.

[23]The whole assembly then agreed to celebrate the festival
seven more days; so for another seven days they celebrated joyfully. [24]Hezekiah king of Judah provided a thousand bulls and
seven thousand sheep and goats for the assembly, and the officials provided them with a thousand bulls and ten thousand
sheep and goats. A great number of priests consecrated themselves. [25]The entire assembly of Judah rejoiced, along with the
priests and Levites and all who had assembled from Israel,
including the foreigners who had come from Israel and also
those who resided in Judah. [26]There was great joy in Jerusalem, for since the days of Solomon son of David king of Israel
there had been nothing like this in Jerusalem. [27]The priests
and the Levites stood to bless the people, and God heard
them, for their prayer reached heaven, his holy dwelling place.

31 When all this had ended, the Israelites who were
there went out to the towns of Judah, smashed the
sacred stones and cut down the Asherah poles. They destroyed the high places and the altars throughout Judah and
Benjamin and in Ephraim and Manasseh. After they had
destroyed all of them, the Israelites returned to their own
towns and to their own property.

CONTRIBUTIONS FOR WORSHIP

[2]Hezekiah assigned the priests and Levites to divisions—each of them according to their duties as priests or
Levites—to offer burnt offerings and fellowship offerings,
to minister, to give thanks and to sing praises at the gates of
the LORD's dwelling. [3]The king contributed from his own
possessions for the morning and evening burnt offerings and
for the burnt offerings on the Sabbaths, at the New Moons
and at the appointed festivals as written in the Law of the
LORD. [4]He ordered the people living in Jerusalem to give
the portion due the priests and Levites so they could devote themselves to the Law of the LORD. [5]As soon as the
order went out, the Israelites generously gave the firstfruits
of their grain, new wine, olive oil and honey and all that
the fields produced. They brought a great amount, a tithe
of everything. [6]The people of Israel and Judah who lived in
the towns of Judah also brought a tithe of their herds and
flocks and a tithe of the holy things dedicated to the LORD
their God, and they piled them in heaps. [7]They began doing

What was a tithe? (31:5)
This was ten percent of a person's income. The Israelites were
supposed to give a tithe of whatever they produced or earned to
support the Levites.

Was giving a tithe volun-
tary? (31:6–8)
The tithe was prescribed by the
law Moses had given the people,
and Hezekiah ordered the people
to obey that rule. However, Hezekiah set an example of cheerful
giving, and the people followed
his example. The responsibility to
tithe was not a burden to them.

---

[a] 21 Or priests sang to the LORD every day, accompanied by the LORD's
instruments of praise   [b] 22 Or and confessed their sins to

this in the third month and finished in the seventh month. [8]When Hezekiah and his officials came and saw the heaps, they praised the LORD and blessed his people Israel.

[9]Hezekiah asked the priests and Levites about the heaps; [10]and Azariah the chief priest, from the family of Zadok, answered, "Since the people began to bring their contributions to the temple of the LORD, we have had enough to eat and plenty to spare, because the LORD has blessed his people, and this great amount is left over."

[11]Hezekiah gave orders to prepare storerooms in the temple of the LORD, and this was done. [12]Then they faithfully brought in the contributions, tithes and dedicated gifts. Konaniah, a Levite, was the overseer in charge of these things, and his brother Shimei was next in rank. [13]Jehiel, Azaziah, Nahath, Asahel, Jerimoth, Jozabad, Eliel, Ismakiah, Mahath and Benaiah were assistants of Konaniah and Shimei his brother. All these served by appointment of King Hezekiah and Azariah the official in charge of the temple of God.

[14]Kore son of Imnah the Levite, keeper of the East Gate, was in charge of the freewill offerings given to God, distributing the contributions made to the LORD and also the consecrated gifts. [15]Eden, Miniamin, Jeshua, Shemaiah, Amariah and Shekaniah assisted him faithfully in the towns of the priests, distributing to their fellow priests according to their divisions, old and young alike.

[16]In addition, they distributed to the males three years old or more whose names were in the genealogical records—all who would enter the temple of the LORD to perform the daily duties of their various tasks, according to their responsibilities and their divisions. [17]And they distributed to the priests enrolled by their families in the genealogical records and likewise to the Levites twenty years old or more, according to their responsibilities and their divisions. [18]They included all the little ones, the wives, and the sons and daughters of the whole community listed in these genealogical records. For they were faithful in consecrating themselves.

[19]As for the priests, the descendants of Aaron, who lived on the farmlands around their towns or in any other towns,

Why did children receive tithes even though they were not priests? (31:16) Levites serving in the temple brought their children with them. The tithes the children received helped to provide for their food and care.

What is a tithe, and are Christians supposed to tithe?
2 CHRONICLES 31

Literally, a tithe is a tenth. The Law of Moses said that people were required to give one-tenth of their crops and livestock to the Lord; this tithe was meant to support the Levites in their service as priests and also help those in need.

When Hezekiah restored worship in the temple, the people celebrated with feasts and sacrifices. Hezekiah ordered the people to bring their tithes, and the people gave willingly because they were so happy that the temple was once again being used to worship God.

Today many Christians use the word *tithing* to describe giving gifts and offerings to a church. Some Christians are convinced that God requires them to contribute at least one-tenth of their income to the church and other charitable causes. Other Christians see the idea of a tithe as a symbol of the fact that God has given us everything that we have, and so we should be eager to give a certain amount back to God because of our thankfulness for his blessings. The New Testament does not include a requirement to tithe, but the entire Bible speaks about the need to use our resources in a godly way to support God's work and to help those who are in need.

men were designated by name to distribute portions to every male among them and to all who were recorded in the genealogies of the Levites.

²⁰This is what Hezekiah did throughout Judah, doing what was good and right and faithful before the LORD his God. ²¹In everything that he undertook in the service of God's temple and in obedience to the law and the commands, he sought his God and worked wholeheartedly. And so he prospered.

SENNACHERIB THREATENS JERUSALEM

32 After all that Hezekiah had so faithfully done, Sennacherib king of Assyria came and invaded Judah. He laid siege to the fortified cities, thinking to conquer them for himself. ²When Hezekiah saw that Sennacherib had come and that he intended to wage war against Jerusalem, ³he consulted with his officials and military staff about blocking off the water from the springs outside the city, and they helped him. ⁴They gathered a large group of people who blocked all the springs and the stream that flowed through the land. "Why should the kings*ᵃ* of Assyria come and find plenty of water?" they said. ⁵Then he worked hard repairing all the broken sections of the wall and building towers on it. He built another wall outside that one and reinforced the terraces*ᵇ* of the City of David. He also made large numbers of weapons and shields.

⁶He appointed military officers over the people and assembled them before him in the square at the city gate and encouraged them with these words: ⁷"Be strong and courageous. Do not be afraid or discouraged because of the king of Assyria and the vast army with him, for there is a greater power with us than with him. ⁸With him is only the arm of flesh, but with us is the LORD our God to help us and to fight our battles." And the people gained confidence from what Hezekiah the king of Judah said.

⁹Later, when Sennacherib king of Assyria and all his forces were laying siege to Lachish, he sent his officers to Jerusalem with this message for Hezekiah king of Judah and for all the people of Judah who were there:

¹⁰"This is what Sennacherib king of Assyria says: On what are you basing your confidence, that you remain in Jerusalem under siege? ¹¹When Hezekiah says, 'The LORD our God will save us from the hand of the king of Assyria,' he is misleading you, to let you die of hunger and thirst. ¹²Did not Hezekiah himself remove this god's high places and altars, saying to Judah and Jerusalem, 'You must worship before one altar and burn sacrifices on it'?

¹³"Do you not know what I and my predecessors have done to all the peoples of the other lands? Were the gods of those nations ever able to deliver their land from my hand? ¹⁴Who of all the gods of these nations that my predecessors destroyed has been able to save his people

---

Who was Sennacherib? (32:1)
He was the king of Assyria from 705 to 681 B.C. He attacked Judah in the hopes of bettering his kingdom. He demanded tribute and then surrender from Hezekiah.

What were these terraces? (32:5)
These structures, sometimes called the Millo, were landfill-like mounds to help defend a city.

Had Hezekiah removed altars to the LORD? (32:12)
Yes. These altars were being used to worship both the Lord and other gods. Hezekiah wanted the people to return to worshiping the LORD only at the temple.

ᵃ 4 Hebrew; Septuagint and Syriac *king*   *ᵇ 5* Or *the Millo*

from me? How then can your god deliver you from my hand? ¹⁵Now do not let Hezekiah deceive you and mislead you like this. Do not believe him, for no god of any nation or kingdom has been able to deliver his people from my hand or the hand of my predecessors. How much less will your god deliver you from my hand!"

¹⁶Sennacherib's officers spoke further against the LORD God and against his servant Hezekiah. ¹⁷The king also wrote letters ridiculing the LORD, the God of Israel, and saying this against him: "Just as the gods of the peoples of the other lands did not rescue their people from my hand, so the god of Hezekiah will not rescue his people from my hand." ¹⁸Then they called out in Hebrew to the people of Jerusalem who were on the wall, to terrify them and make them afraid in order to capture the city. ¹⁹They spoke about the God of Jerusalem as they did about the gods of the other peoples of the world—the work of human hands.

²⁰King Hezekiah and the prophet Isaiah son of Amoz cried out in prayer to heaven about this. ²¹And the LORD sent an angel, who annihilated all the fighting men and the commanders and officers in the camp of the Assyrian king. So he withdrew to his own land in disgrace. And when he went into the temple of his god, some of his sons, his own flesh and blood, cut him down with the sword.

²²So the LORD saved Hezekiah and the people of Jerusalem from the hand of Sennacherib king of Assyria and from the hand of all others. He took care of them[a] on every side. ²³Many brought offerings to Jerusalem for the LORD and valuable gifts for Hezekiah king of Judah. From then on he was highly regarded by all the nations.

HEZEKIAH'S PRIDE, SUCCESS AND DEATH

²⁴In those days Hezekiah became ill and was at the point of death. He prayed to the LORD, who answered him and gave him a miraculous sign. ²⁵But Hezekiah's heart was proud and he did not respond to the kindness shown him; therefore the LORD's wrath was on him and on Judah and Jerusalem. ²⁶Then Hezekiah repented of the pride of his heart, as did the people of Jerusalem; therefore the LORD's wrath did not come on them during the days of Hezekiah.

²⁷Hezekiah had very great wealth and honor, and he made treasuries for his silver and gold and for his precious stones, spices, shields and all kinds of valuables. ²⁸He also made buildings to store the harvest of grain, new wine and olive oil; and he made stalls for various kinds of cattle, and pens for the flocks. ²⁹He built villages and acquired great numbers of flocks and herds, for God had given him very great riches.

³⁰It was Hezekiah who blocked the upper outlet of the Gihon spring and channeled the water down to the west side of the City of David. He succeeded in everything he undertook. ³¹But when envoys were sent by the rulers of Babylon to ask him about the miraculous sign that had occurred in the land, God left him to test him and to know everything that was in his heart.

---

[a] 22 Hebrew; Septuagint and Vulgate *He gave them rest*

Why did the Assyrians insult the LORD? (32:16–19)
The Assyrians thought the stronger gods would kill the weaker ones. To them, the LORD was just another god to defeat.

How did God leave Hezekiah? (32:31)
God never truly leaves us. But he does give us the freedom to make our own decisions. God allowed Hezekiah to make his own choices. Hezekiah made a foolish decision. God didn't protect him from the consequences of that decision.

³²The other events of Hezekiah's reign and his acts of devotion are written in the vision of the prophet Isaiah son of Amoz in the book of the kings of Judah and Israel. ³³Hezekiah rested with his ancestors and was buried on the hill where the tombs of David's descendants are. All Judah and the people of Jerusalem honored him when he died. And Manasseh his son succeeded him as king.

MANASSEH KING OF JUDAH

33 Manasseh was twelve years old when he became king, and he reigned in Jerusalem fifty-five years. ²He did evil in the eyes of the LORD, following the detestable practices of the nations the LORD had driven out before the Israelites. ³He rebuilt the high places his father Hezekiah had demolished; he also erected altars to the Baals and made Asherah poles. He bowed down to all the starry hosts and worshiped them. ⁴He built altars in the temple of the LORD, of which the LORD had said, "My Name will remain in Jerusalem forever." ⁵In both courts of the temple of the LORD, he built altars to all the starry hosts. ⁶He sacrificed his children in the fire in the Valley of Ben Hinnom, practiced divination and witchcraft, sought omens, and consulted mediums and spiritists. He did much evil in the eyes of the LORD, arousing his anger.

⁷He took the image he had made and put it in God's temple, of which God had said to David and to his son Solomon, "In this temple and in Jerusalem, which I have chosen out of all the tribes of Israel, I will put my Name forever. ⁸I will not again make the feet of the Israelites leave the land I assigned to your ancestors, if only they will be careful to do everything I commanded them concerning all the laws, decrees and regulations given through Moses." ⁹But Manasseh led Judah and the people of Jerusalem astray, so that they did more evil than the nations the LORD had destroyed before the Israelites.

¹⁰The LORD spoke to Manasseh and his people, but they paid no attention. ¹¹So the LORD brought against them the army commanders of the king of Assyria, who took Manasseh prisoner, put a hook in his nose, bound him with bronze shackles and took him to Babylon. ¹²In his distress he sought the favor of the LORD his God and humbled himself greatly before the God of his ancestors. ¹³And when he prayed to him, the LORD was moved by his entreaty and listened to his plea; so he brought him back to Jerusalem and to his kingdom. Then Manasseh knew that the LORD is God.

¹⁴Afterward he rebuilt the outer wall of the City of David, west of the Gihon spring in the valley, as far as the entrance of the Fish Gate and encircling the hill of Ophel; he also made it much higher. He stationed military commanders in all the fortified cities in Judah.

¹⁵He got rid of the foreign gods and removed the image from the temple of the LORD, as well as all the altars he had built on the temple hill and in Jerusalem; and he threw them out of the city. ¹⁶Then he restored the altar of the LORD and sacrificed fellowship offerings and thank offerings on it, and

Who taught Manasseh to serve pagan gods? (33:3–6) Like the kings before him, Manasseh started serving pagan gods in part because of other pagan nations. He might have wanted to impress the other nations with his respect for their gods, or he might have wanted the same luck he thought the pagan gods were getting for the other nations.

told Judah to serve the LORD, the God of Israel. [17] The people, however, continued to sacrifice at the high places, but only to the LORD their God.

[18] The other events of Manasseh's reign, including his prayer to his God and the words the seers spoke to him in the name of the LORD, the God of Israel, are written in the annals of the kings of Israel.[a] [19] His prayer and how God was moved by his entreaty, as well as all his sins and unfaithfulness, and the sites where he built high places and set up Asherah poles and idols before he humbled himself—all these are written in the records of the seers.[b] [20] Manasseh rested with his ancestors and was buried in his palace. And Amon his son succeeded him as king.

AMON KING OF JUDAH

[21] Amon was twenty-two years old when he became king, and he reigned in Jerusalem two years. [22] He did evil in the eyes of the LORD, as his father Manasseh had done. Amon worshiped and offered sacrifices to all the idols Manasseh had made. [23] But unlike his father Manasseh, he did not humble himself before the LORD; Amon increased his guilt.

[24] Amon's officials conspired against him and assassinated him in his palace. [25] Then the people of the land killed all who had plotted against King Amon, and they made Josiah his son king in his place.

JOSIAH'S REFORMS

34 Josiah was eight years old when he became king, and he reigned in Jerusalem thirty-one years. [2] He did what was right in the eyes of the LORD and followed the ways of his father David, not turning aside to the right or to the left.

[3] In the eighth year of his reign, while he was still young, he began to seek the God of his father David. In his twelfth year he began to purge Judah and Jerusalem of high places, Asherah poles and idols. [4] Under his direction the altars of the Baals were torn down; he cut to pieces the incense altars that were above them, and smashed the Asherah poles and the idols. These he broke to pieces and scattered over the graves of those who had sacrificed to them. [5] He burned the bones of the priests on their altars, and so he purged Judah and Jerusalem. [6] In the towns of Manasseh, Ephraim and Simeon, as far as Naphtali, and in the ruins around them, [7] he tore down the altars and the Asherah poles and crushed the idols to powder and cut to pieces all the incense altars throughout Israel. Then he went back to Jerusalem.

[8] In the eighteenth year of Josiah's reign, to purify the land and the temple, he sent Shaphan son of Azaliah and Maaseiah the ruler of the city, with Joah son of Joahaz, the recorder, to repair the temple of the LORD his God.

[9] They went to Hilkiah the high priest and gave him the money that had been brought into the temple of God, which the Levites who were the gatekeepers had collected from

Why was it wrong to worship the LORD at the high places? (33:17)
Worshiping on a high place like a mountain top was a common pagan practice. God did not want his people to confuse pagan practices and gods with him and how to worship him. Worshiping at a pagan place would make it easier to pick up pagan practices.

What were the annals of the kings of Israel? (33:18)
These were historical records of the kings that have been lost over the years.

How could Josiah overcome the negative influence of his ancestors? (34:2–3)
Josiah was only eight years old when he became king, and he was probably raised by God-fearing people. He was the last godly king of David's line prior to the exile.

How could Josiah destroy these idols and altars without resistance? (34:4–7)
Politics and religion were closely intertwined. If a king honored a particular god, the people quickly followed along. In the same way, if the king decided to serve the LORD, the people followed his lead.

---

[a] *18* That is, Judah, as frequently in 2 Chronicles   [b] *19* One Hebrew manuscript and Septuagint; most Hebrew manuscripts *of Hozai*

the people of Manasseh, Ephraim and the entire remnant of Israel and from all the people of Judah and Benjamin and the inhabitants of Jerusalem. [10]Then they entrusted it to the men appointed to supervise the work on the LORD's temple. These men paid the workers who repaired and restored the temple. [11]They also gave money to the carpenters and builders to purchase dressed stone, and timber for joists and beams for the buildings that the kings of Judah had allowed to fall into ruin.

[12]The workers labored faithfully. Over them to direct them were Jahath and Obadiah, Levites descended from Merari, and Zechariah and Meshullam, descended from Kohath. The Levites—all who were skilled in playing musical instruments— [13]had charge of the laborers and supervised all the workers from job to job. Some of the Levites were secretaries, scribes and gatekeepers.

THE BOOK OF THE LAW FOUND

[14]While they were bringing out the money that had been taken into the temple of the LORD, Hilkiah the priest found the Book of the Law of the LORD that had been given through Moses. [15]Hilkiah said to Shaphan the secretary, "I have found the Book of the Law in the temple of the LORD." He gave it to Shaphan.

[16]Then Shaphan took the book to the king and reported to him: "Your officials are doing everything that has been committed to them. [17]They have paid out the money that was in the temple of the LORD and have entrusted it to the supervisors and workers." [18]Then Shaphan the secretary informed the king, "Hilkiah the priest has given me a book." And Shaphan read from it in the presence of the king.

[19]When the king heard the words of the Law, he tore his robes. [20]He gave these orders to Hilkiah, Ahikam son of Shaphan, Abdon son of Micah,[a] Shaphan the secretary and Asaiah the king's attendant: [21]"Go and inquire of the LORD for me and for the remnant in Israel and Judah about what is written in this book that has been found. Great is the LORD's anger that is poured out on us because those who have gone before us have not kept the word of the LORD; they have not acted in accordance with all that is written in this book."

[22]Hilkiah and those the king had sent with him[b] went to speak to the prophet Huldah, who was the wife of Shallum son of Tokhath,[c] the son of Hasrah,[d] keeper of the wardrobe. She lived in Jerusalem, in the New Quarter.

[23]She said to them, "This is what the LORD, the God of Israel, says: Tell the man who sent you to me, [24]'This is what the LORD says: I am going to bring disaster on this place and its people—all the curses written in the book that has been read in the presence of the king of Judah. [25]Because they have forsaken me and burned incense to other gods and aroused my anger by all that their hands have made,[e]

How could the priests have lost the Book of the Law? (34:14–15)
Manasseh had ruled for 55 years, and he was devoted to worshiping false gods. Since God seemed unnecessary to the people, God's law became irrelevant. Only the oldest priests would have remembered God's law; the rest of the people forgot about it entirely.

How common were female prophets in Judah? (34:22)
Female prophets were rare in Old Testament times. The others mentioned in the Bible are Miriam (Exodus 15:20), Deborah (Judges 4:4), and Isaiah's wife (Isaiah 8:3).

---

[a] 20 Also called *Akbor son of Micaiah*   [b] 22 One Hebrew manuscript, Vulgate and Syriac; most Hebrew manuscripts do not have *had sent with him*.   [c] 22 Also called *Tikvah*   [d] 22 Also called *Harhas*   [e] 25 Or *by everything they have done*

my anger will be poured out on this place and will not be quenched.' ²⁶Tell the king of Judah, who sent you to inquire of the LORD, 'This is what the LORD, the God of Israel, says concerning the words you heard: ²⁷Because your heart was responsive and you humbled yourself before God when you heard what he spoke against this place and its people, and because you humbled yourself before me and tore your robes and wept in my presence, I have heard you, declares the LORD. ²⁸Now I will gather you to your ancestors, and you will be buried in peace. Your eyes will not see all the disaster I am going to bring on this place and on those who live here.'"

So they took her answer back to the king.

²⁹Then the king called together all the elders of Judah and Jerusalem. ³⁰He went up to the temple of the LORD with the people of Judah, the inhabitants of Jerusalem, the priests and the Levites—all the people from the least to the greatest. He read in their hearing all the words of the Book of the Covenant, which had been found in the temple of the LORD. ³¹The king stood by his pillar and renewed the covenant in the presence of the LORD—to follow the LORD and keep his commands, statutes and decrees with all his heart and all his soul, and to obey the words of the covenant written in this book.

³²Then he had everyone in Jerusalem and Benjamin pledge themselves to it; the people of Jerusalem did this in accordance with the covenant of God, the God of their ancestors.

³³Josiah removed all the detestable idols from all the territory belonging to the Israelites, and he had all who were present in Israel serve the LORD their God. As long as he lived, they did not fail to follow the LORD, the God of their ancestors.

JOSIAH CELEBRATES THE PASSOVER

35 Josiah celebrated the Passover to the LORD in Jerusalem, and the Passover lamb was slaughtered on the fourteenth day of the first month. ²He appointed the priests to their duties and encouraged them in the service of the LORD's temple. ³He said to the Levites, who instructed all Israel and who had been consecrated to the LORD: "Put the sacred ark in the temple that Solomon son of David king of Israel built. It is not to be carried about on your shoulders. Now serve the LORD your God and his people Israel. ⁴Prepare yourselves by families in your divisions, according to the instructions written by David king of Israel and by his son Solomon.

⁵"Stand in the holy place with a group of Levites for each subdivision of the families of your fellow Israelites, the lay people. ⁶Slaughter the Passover lambs, consecrate yourselves and prepare the lambs for your fellow Israelites, doing what the LORD commanded through Moses."

⁷Josiah provided for all the lay people who were there a total of thirty thousand lambs and goats for the Passover offerings, and also three thousand cattle—all from the king's own possessions.

What did it mean that God would gather Josiah to his ancestors? (34:27–28)
This meant that Josiah would die and perhaps meet his ancestors in the afterlife. God assured Josiah that the final judgment on Judah and Jerusalem would not come during his lifetime.

What was the king's pillar? (34:31)
The king probably stood next to this pillar, which stood at the entrance to the temple, when he gave public announcements.

Why had the ark been removed from the temple? (35:3)
The ark may have been removed to protect it when the pagans Manasseh or Amon were in power.

[8]His officials also contributed voluntarily to the people and the priests and Levites. Hilkiah, Zechariah and Jehiel, the officials in charge of God's temple, gave the priests twenty-six hundred Passover offerings and three hundred cattle. [9]Also Konaniah along with Shemaiah and Nethanel, his brothers, and Hashabiah, Jeiel and Jozabad, the leaders of the Levites, provided five thousand Passover offerings and five hundred head of cattle for the Levites.

[10]The service was arranged and the priests stood in their places with the Levites in their divisions as the king had ordered. [11]The Passover lambs were slaughtered, and the priests splashed against the altar the blood handed to them, while the Levites skinned the animals. [12]They set aside the burnt offerings to give them to the subdivisions of the families of the people to offer to the LORD, as it is written in the Book of Moses. They did the same with the cattle. [13]They roasted the Passover animals over the fire as prescribed, and boiled the holy offerings in pots, caldrons and pans and served them quickly to all the people. [14]After this, they made preparations for themselves and for the priests, because the priests, the descendants of Aaron, were sacrificing the burnt offerings and the fat portions until nightfall. So the Levites made preparations for themselves and for the Aaronic priests.

[15]The musicians, the descendants of Asaph, were in the places prescribed by David, Asaph, Heman and Jeduthun the king's seer. The gatekeepers at each gate did not need to leave their posts, because their fellow Levites made the preparations for them.

[16]So at that time the entire service of the LORD was carried out for the celebration of the Passover and the offering of burnt offerings on the altar of the LORD, as King Josiah had ordered. [17]The Israelites who were present celebrated the Passover at that time and observed the Festival of Unleavened Bread for seven days. [18]The Passover had not been observed like this in Israel since the days of the prophet Samuel; and none of the kings of Israel had ever celebrated such a Passover as did Josiah, with the priests, the Levites and all Judah and Israel who were there with the people of Jerusalem. [19]This Passover was celebrated in the eighteenth year of Josiah's reign.

THE DEATH OF JOSIAH

[20]After all this, when Josiah had set the temple in order, Necho king of Egypt went up to fight at Carchemish on the Euphrates, and Josiah marched out to meet him in battle. [21]But Necho sent messengers to him, saying, "What quarrel is there, king of Judah, between you and me? It is not you I am attacking at this time, but the house with which I am at war. God has told me to hurry; so stop opposing God, who is with me, or he will destroy you."

[22]Josiah, however, would not turn away from him, but disguised himself to engage him in battle. He would not listen to what Necho had said at God's command but went to fight him on the plain of Megiddo.

When did this celebration of the Passover take place? (35:19)
It was in the eighteenth year of Josiah's reign, the same year the Book of the Law was discovered (see 34:8, 14).

How did the king of Egypt know what God wanted him to do? (35:21–22)
It isn't clear what method God used, but God made Necho understand that he was supposed to help the king of Assyria fight the Babylonians. Josiah ignored the message not to engage Necho in battle.

²³ Archers shot King Josiah, and he told his officers, "Take me away; I am badly wounded." ²⁴ So they took him out of his chariot, put him in his other chariot and brought him to Jerusalem, where he died. He was buried in the tombs of his ancestors, and all Judah and Jerusalem mourned for him.

²⁵ Jeremiah composed laments for Josiah, and to this day all the male and female singers commemorate Josiah in the laments. These became a tradition in Israel and are written in the Laments.

²⁶ The other events of Josiah's reign and his acts of devotion in accordance with what is written in the Law of the LORD— ²⁷ all the events, from beginning to end, are written in the book of the kings of Israel and Judah. ¹ And the people of the land took Jehoahaz son of Josiah and made him king in Jerusalem in place of his father.

JEHOAHAZ KING OF JUDAH

² Jehoahaz*ᵃ* was twenty-three years old when he became king, and he reigned in Jerusalem three months. ³ The king of Egypt dethroned him in Jerusalem and imposed on Judah a levy of a hundred talents*ᵇ* of silver and a talent*ᶜ* of gold. ⁴ The king of Egypt made Eliakim, a brother of Jehoahaz, king over Judah and Jerusalem and changed Eliakim's name to Jehoiakim. But Necho took Eliakim's brother Jehoahaz and carried him off to Egypt.

JEHOIAKIM KING OF JUDAH

⁵ Jehoiakim was twenty-five years old when he became king, and he reigned in Jerusalem eleven years. He did evil in the eyes of the LORD his God. ⁶ Nebuchadnezzar king of Babylon attacked him and bound him with bronze shackles to take him to Babylon. ⁷ Nebuchadnezzar also took to Babylon articles from the temple of the LORD and put them in his temple*ᵈ* there.

⁸ The other events of Jehoiakim's reign, the detestable things he did and all that was found against him, are written in the book of the kings of Israel and Judah. And Jehoiachin his son succeeded him as king.

JEHOIACHIN KING OF JUDAH

⁹ Jehoiachin was eighteen*ᵉ* years old when he became king, and he reigned in Jerusalem three months and ten days. He did evil in the eyes of the LORD. ¹⁰ In the spring, King Nebuchadnezzar sent for him and brought him to Babylon, together with articles of value from the temple of the LORD, and he made Jehoiachin's uncle,*ᶠ* Zedekiah, king over Judah and Jerusalem.

ZEDEKIAH KING OF JUDAH

¹¹ Zedekiah was twenty-one years old when he became king, and he reigned in Jerusalem eleven years. ¹² He did

Why did the king of Egypt change Eliakim's name? (36:4)
Name changes such as this showed that a ruler was under the authority of a more powerful monarch.

ᵃ 2 Hebrew Joahaz, a variant of Jehoahaz; also in verse 4   ᵇ 3 That is, about 3 3/4 tons or about 3.4 metric tons   ᶜ 3 That is, about 75 pounds or about 34 kilograms   ᵈ 7 Or palace   ᵉ 9 One Hebrew manuscript, some Septuagint manuscripts and Syriac (see also 2 Kings 24:8); most Hebrew manuscripts eight   ᶠ 10 Hebrew brother, that is, relative (see 2 Kings 24:17)

What did it mean to be stiff-necked? (36:13)
This expression was one a farmer would use to describe an ox or a horse that would not be led or respond when its rope was tugged. When Zedekiah was described as stiff-necked, it meant he stubbornly refused to turn to the LORD.

evil in the eyes of the LORD his God and did not humble himself before Jeremiah the prophet, who spoke the word of the LORD. [13] He also rebelled against King Nebuchadnezzar, who had made him take an oath in God's name. He became stiff-necked and hardened his heart and would not turn to the LORD, the God of Israel. [14] Furthermore, all the leaders of the priests and the people became more and more unfaithful, following all the detestable practices of the nations and defiling the temple of the LORD, which he had consecrated in Jerusalem.

THE FALL OF JERUSALEM

[15] The LORD, the God of their ancestors, sent word to them through his messengers again and again, because he had pity on his people and on his dwelling place. [16] But they mocked God's messengers, despised his words and scoffed at his prophets until the wrath of the LORD was aroused against his people and there was no remedy. [17] He brought up against them the king of the Babylonians,[a] who killed their young men with the sword in the sanctuary, and did not spare young men or young women, the elderly or the infirm. God gave them all into the hands of Nebuchadnezzar. [18] He carried to Babylon all the articles from the temple of God, both large and small, and the treasures of the LORD's temple and the treasures of the king and his officials. [19] They set fire to God's temple and broke down the wall of Jerusalem; they burned all the palaces and destroyed everything of value there.

Why did the Babylonians destroy Jerusalem? (36:19)
This was God's judgment on the people who had turned away from him. He allowed Nebuchadnezzar to destroy Jerusalem because of the people's disobedience.

[20] He carried into exile to Babylon the remnant, who escaped from the sword, and they became servants to him and his successors until the kingdom of Persia came to power. [21] The land enjoyed its sabbath rests; all the time of its desolation it rested, until the seventy years were completed in fulfillment of the word of the LORD spoken by Jeremiah.

What were sabbath rests? (36:21)
Similar to how people are supposed to rest on the seventh day of the week, they were also to honor God by not farming their land and let it rest every seventh year (Leviticus 25:4). The people failed to follow God's orders, so he claimed all of the sabbath rests at the same time. Crops did not grow for 70 years.

[22] In the first year of Cyrus king of Persia, in order to fulfill the word of the LORD spoken by Jeremiah, the LORD moved the heart of Cyrus king of Persia to make a proclamation throughout his realm and also to put it in writing:

[23] "This is what Cyrus king of Persia says:

"'The LORD, the God of heaven, has given me all the kingdoms of the earth and he has appointed me to build a temple for him at Jerusalem in Judah. Any of his people among you may go up, and may the LORD their God be with them.'"

---

[a] 17 Or *Chaldeans*

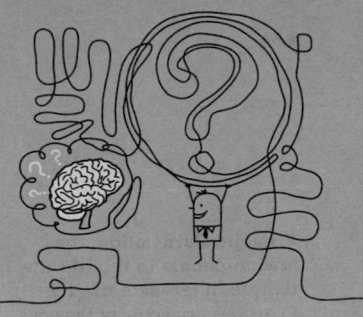

Ezra

INTRODUCTION

Who wrote this book?
The author is unknown. Many people think Ezra wrote much of this book.

Why was this book written?
The book of Ezra shows how God kept his promise and brought the Jews back to their homeland.

What happens in this book?
The Persian ruler Cyrus lets captive people return home. Some of the Jews in Babylon go back to Judah. They rebuild God's temple. Later Ezra comes from Babylon to teach God's law.

What do we learn about God in this book?
God is faithful and keeps his promises.

Who are the key people in this book?
The most important people in this book are King Cyrus and Ezra.

Where did this happen?
The events of this book happened in the land of Judah and the city of Jerusalem. (See the map in the back of this Bible to find these places.)

What are some of the stories in this book?

Exiled Jews return home	Ezra 1–2
Rebuilding the temple	Ezra 3–6
Ezra returns to Jerusalem	Ezra 7–8
Ezra confesses Judah's sins	Ezra 9
The people of Judah confess	Ezra 10

When did these things happen?
1400 BC 1300 1200 1100 1000 900 800 700 600 500 400

FALL OF JERUSALEM (586 BC)

PERSIA'S CONQUEST OF BABYLON (539 BC)

FIRST RETURN OF EXILES TO JERUSALEM (538 BC)

MINISTRIES OF HAGGAI AND ZECHARIAH (C. 520–480 BC)

COMPLETION OF TEMPLE (516 BC)

SECOND RETURN TO JERUSALEM UNDER EZRA (458 BC)

THIRD RETURN TO JERUSALEM UNDER NEHEMIAH (444 BC)

BOOK OF EZRA WRITTEN (C. 440 BC)

CYRUS HELPS THE EXILES TO RETURN

1 In the first year of Cyrus king of Persia, in order to fulfill the word of the LORD spoken by Jeremiah, the LORD moved the heart of Cyrus king of Persia to make a proclamation throughout his realm and also to put it in writing:

² "This is what Cyrus king of Persia says:

" 'The LORD, the God of heaven, has given me all the kingdoms of the earth and he has appointed me to build a temple for him at Jerusalem in Judah. ³ Any of his people among you may go up to Jerusalem in Judah and build the temple of the LORD, the God of Israel, the God who is in Jerusalem, and may their God be with them. ⁴ And in any locality where survivors may now be living, the people are to provide them with silver and gold, with goods and livestock, and with freewill offerings for the temple of God in Jerusalem.' "

⁵ Then the family heads of Judah and Benjamin, and the priests and Levites — everyone whose heart God had moved — prepared to go up and build the house of the LORD in Jerusalem. ⁶ All their neighbors assisted them with articles of silver and gold, with goods and livestock, and with valuable gifts, in addition to all the freewill offerings.

⁷ Moreover, King Cyrus brought out the articles belonging to the temple of the LORD, which Nebuchadnezzar had carried away from Jerusalem and had placed in the temple of his god.ᵃ ⁸ Cyrus king of Persia had them brought by Mithredath the treasurer, who counted them out to Sheshbazzar the prince of Judah.

⁹ This was the inventory:

gold dishes	30
silver dishes	1,000
silver pansᵇ	29
¹⁰ gold bowls	30
matching silver bowls	410
other articles	1,000

¹¹ In all, there were 5,400 articles of gold and of silver. Sheshbazzar brought all these along with the exiles when they came up from Babylon to Jerusalem.

THE LIST OF THE EXILES WHO RETURNED

2 Now these are the people of the province who came up from the captivity of the exiles, whom Nebuchadnezzar king of Babylon had taken captive to Babylon (they returned to Jerusalem and Judah, each to their own town, ² in company with Zerubbabel, Joshua, Nehemiah, Seraiah, Reelaiah, Mordecai, Bilshan, Mispar, Bigvai, Rehum and Baanah):

The list of the men of the people of Israel:

³ the descendants of Parosh	2,172
⁴ of Shephatiah	372
⁵ of Arah	775

ᵃ 7 Or *gods*   ᵇ 9 The meaning of the Hebrew for this word is uncertain.

Why did Cyrus allow the Jewish people to rebuild the temple in Jerusalem? (1:2–3) Cyrus was respectful of the gods of the people who were in captivity. His generosity to the Jews was similar to his generosity to the Babylonians.

Return from Exile (1:3)

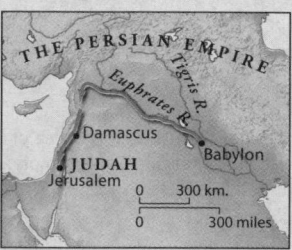

THE PERSIAN EMPIRE

Euphrates R.   Tigris R.

Damascus

JUDAH
Jerusalem   Babylon

0   300 km.

0   300 miles

Why didn't all the Jews want to return? (1:5) Most of them had never been to their native land. They had been in captivity for some 50 to 60 years and were settled into their surroundings. Most of them did not want to leave their homes to try to rebuild.

Why did the Jews who were born in Babylon go to their own towns? (2:1) The rights to land stayed in the family, and the Jews in Judah followed this law. So the people returned to the towns of their ancestors.

Why were all these names listed? (2:2–61) These names represented the thousands of people who were returning to the land of Israel. The detailed list of names and towns shows that God was concerned about all of his people, not just the leaders.

⁶ of Pahath-Moab (through the line
    of Jeshua and Joab)   2,812
⁷ of Elam   1,254
⁸ of Zattu   945
⁹ of Zakkai   760
¹⁰ of Bani   642
¹¹ of Bebai   623
¹² of Azgad   1,222
¹³ of Adonikam   666
¹⁴ of Bigvai   2,056
¹⁵ of Adin   454
¹⁶ of Ater (through Hezekiah)   98
¹⁷ of Bezai   323
¹⁸ of Jorah   112
¹⁹ of Hashum   223
²⁰ of Gibbar   95

²¹ the men of Bethlehem   123
²² of Netophah   56
²³ of Anathoth   128
²⁴ of Azmaveth   42
²⁵ of Kiriath Jearim,^a Kephirah and Beeroth   743
²⁶ of Ramah and Geba   621
²⁷ of Mikmash   122
²⁸ of Bethel and Ai   223
²⁹ of Nebo   52
³⁰ of Magbish   156
³¹ of the other Elam   1,254
³² of Harim   320
³³ of Lod, Hadid and Ono   725
³⁴ of Jericho   345
³⁵ of Senaah   3,630

³⁶ The priests:

the descendants of Jedaiah
    (through the family of Jeshua)   973
³⁷ of Immer   1,052
³⁸ of Pashhur   1,247
³⁹ of Harim   1,017

⁴⁰ The Levites:

the descendants of Jeshua and Kadmiel
    (of the line of Hodaviah)   74

⁴¹ The musicians:

the descendants of Asaph   128

⁴² The gatekeepers of the temple:

the descendants of
    Shallum, Ater, Talmon,
    Akkub, Hatita and Shobai   139

⁴³ The temple servants:

the descendants of
    Ziha, Hasupha, Tabbaoth,

---

^a 25 See Septuagint (see also Neh. 7:29); Hebrew *Kiriath Arim.*

Why was family history so important? (2:59)
Being able to trace one's family history was important for establishing property rights. But it was also important spiritually to show that a family had not been tainted by intermarriage after being in a foreign land.

Why couldn't those without family records serve as priests? (2:62)
Men needed their family records to show that their ancestral line proved them worthy to be a priest. It was very important to maintain the purity of the priesthood. Any priest who attempted to taint the priesthood by serving while unclean would be punished by death (Leviticus 8—10).

What were the Urim and Thummim? (2:63)
The Urim and Thummim may have been small metal objects, stones, or sticks inscribed with symbols. The symbols may have been the 22 letters of the Hebrew alphabet, based on the fact that the first letter of *Urim* (aleph) and the first letter of *Thummim* (tau) are the first and last letters of the Hebrew alphabet. The Urim and Thummim were cast as lots to receive yes or no answers from God.

If 42,360 returned, how many stayed in Babylon? (2:64)
The Bible doesn't say, but the number of Jewish people remaining in Babylon was probably much larger than the number of those who returned to their homeland.

---

⁴⁴ Keros, Siaha, Padon,
⁴⁵ Lebanah, Hagabah, Akkub,
⁴⁶ Hagab, Shalmai, Hanan,
⁴⁷ Giddel, Gahar, Reaiah,
⁴⁸ Rezin, Nekoda, Gazzam,
⁴⁹ Uzza, Paseah, Besai,
⁵⁰ Asnah, Meunim, Nephusim,
⁵¹ Bakbuk, Hakupha, Harhur,
⁵² Bazluth, Mehida, Harsha,
⁵³ Barkos, Sisera, Temah,
⁵⁴ Neziah and Hatipha

⁵⁵ The descendants of the servants of Solomon:

the descendants of
    Sotai, Hassophereth, Peruda,
⁵⁶ Jaala, Darkon, Giddel,
⁵⁷ Shephatiah, Hattil,
    Pokereth-Hazzebaim and Ami

⁵⁸ The temple servants and the descendants
    of the servants of Solomon   392

⁵⁹ The following came up from the towns of Tel Melah, Tel Harsha, Kerub, Addon and Immer, but they could not show that their families were descended from Israel:

⁶⁰ The descendants of
    Delaiah, Tobiah and Nekoda   652

⁶¹ And from among the priests:

The descendants of
    Hobaiah, Hakkoz and Barzillai (a man who had
    married a daughter of Barzillai the Gileadite and
    was called by that name).
⁶² These searched for their family records, but they could not find them and so were excluded from the priesthood as unclean. ⁶³ The governor ordered them not to eat any of the most sacred food until there was a priest ministering with the Urim and Thummim.

⁶⁴ The whole company numbered 42,360, ⁶⁵ besides their 7,337 male and female slaves; and they also had 200 male and female singers. ⁶⁶ They had 736 horses, 245 mules, ⁶⁷ 435 camels and 6,720 donkeys.

⁶⁸ When they arrived at the house of the LORD in Jerusalem, some of the heads of the families gave freewill offerings toward the rebuilding of the house of God on its site. ⁶⁹ According to their ability they gave to the treasury for this work 61,000 darics*ᵃ* of gold, 5,000 minas*ᵇ* of silver and 100 priestly garments.

⁷⁰ The priests, the Levites, the musicians, the gatekeepers and the temple servants settled in their own towns, along with some of the other people, and the rest of the Israelites settled in their towns.

ᵃ 69 That is, about 1,100 pounds or about 500 kilograms   *ᵇ* 69 That is, about 3 tons or about 2.8 metric tons

REBUILDING THE ALTAR

3 When the seventh month came and the Israelites had settled in their towns, the people assembled together as one in Jerusalem. ²Then Joshua son of Jozadak and his fellow priests and Zerubbabel son of Shealtiel and his associates began to build the altar of the God of Israel to sacrifice burnt offerings on it, in accordance with what is written in the Law of Moses the man of God. ³Despite their fear of the peoples around them, they built the altar on its foundation and sacrificed burnt offerings on it to the LORD, both the morning and evening sacrifices. ⁴Then in accordance with what is written, they celebrated the Festival of Tabernacles with the required number of burnt offerings prescribed for each day. ⁵After that, they presented the regular burnt offerings, the New Moon sacrifices and the sacrifices for all the appointed sacred festivals of the LORD, as well as those brought as freewill offerings to the LORD. ⁶On the first day of the seventh month they began to offer burnt offerings to the LORD, though the foundation of the LORD's temple had not yet been laid.

REBUILDING THE TEMPLE

⁷Then they gave money to the masons and carpenters, and gave food and drink and olive oil to the people of Sidon and Tyre, so that they would bring cedar logs by sea from Lebanon to Joppa, as authorized by Cyrus king of Persia.

⁸In the second month of the second year after their arrival at the house of God in Jerusalem, Zerubbabel son of Shealtiel, Joshua son of Jozadak and the rest of the people (the priests and the Levites and all who had returned from the captivity to Jerusalem) began the work. They appointed Levites twenty years old and older to supervise the building of the house of the LORD. ⁹Joshua and his sons and brothers and Kadmiel and his sons (descendants of Hodaviah*a*) and the sons of Henadad and their sons and brothers—all Levites—joined together in supervising those working on the house of God.

¹⁰When the builders laid the foundation of the temple of the LORD, the priests in their vestments and with trumpets, and the Levites (the sons of Asaph) with cymbals, took their places to praise the LORD, as prescribed by David king of Israel. ¹¹With praise and thanksgiving they sang to the LORD:

"He is good;
  his love toward Israel endures forever."

And all the people gave a great shout of praise to the LORD, because the foundation of the house of the LORD was laid. ¹²But many of the older priests and Levites and family heads, who had seen the former temple, wept aloud when they saw the foundation of this temple being laid, while many others shouted for joy. ¹³No one could distinguish the sound of the shouts of joy from the sound of weeping, because the people made so much noise. And the sound was heard far away.

a 9 Hebrew *Yehudah,* a variant of *Hodaviah*

Who was this Joshua? (3:2)
Joshua was the high priest. Because there was no king in Jerusalem after the exile, the office of high priest became an important leadership position.

Why were the people afraid? (3:3)
When the returning exiles built the altar and offered sacrifices, it meant they were going to stay. The land they moved to was probably already claimed by other people. Staying could result in a fight over the land.

Why did the older Israelites weep? (3:12)
This new temple was not as splendid as the one Solomon built. They wept in remembrance.

OPPOSITION TO THE REBUILDING

4 When the enemies of Judah and Benjamin heard that the exiles were building a temple for the LORD, the God of Israel, [2] they came to Zerubbabel and to the heads of the families and said, "Let us help you build because, like you, we seek your God and have been sacrificing to him since the time of Esarhaddon king of Assyria, who brought us here."

[3] But Zerubbabel, Joshua and the rest of the heads of the families of Israel answered, "You have no part with us in building a temple to our God. We alone will build it for the LORD, the God of Israel, as King Cyrus, the king of Persia, commanded us."

[4] Then the peoples around them set out to discourage the people of Judah and make them afraid to go on building.[a] [5] They bribed officials to work against them and frustrate their plans during the entire reign of Cyrus king of Persia and down to the reign of Darius king of Persia.

LATER OPPOSITION UNDER XERXES AND ARTAXERXES

[6] At the beginning of the reign of Xerxes,[b] they lodged an accusation against the people of Judah and Jerusalem.

[7] And in the days of Artaxerxes king of Persia, Bishlam, Mithredath, Tabeel and the rest of his associates wrote a letter to Artaxerxes. The letter was written in Aramaic script and in the Aramaic language.[c,d]

[8] Rehum the commanding officer and Shimshai the secretary wrote a letter against Jerusalem to Artaxerxes the king as follows:

[9] Rehum the commanding officer and Shimshai the secretary, together with the rest of their associates — the judges, officials and administrators over the people from Persia, Uruk and Babylon, the Elamites of Susa, [10] and the other people whom the great and honorable Ashurbanipal deported and settled in the city of Samaria and elsewhere in Trans-Euphrates.

[11] (This is a copy of the letter they sent him.)

To King Artaxerxes,

From your servants in Trans-Euphrates:

[12] The king should know that the people who came up to us from you have gone to Jerusalem and are rebuilding that rebellious and wicked city. They are restoring the walls and repairing the foundations.

[13] Furthermore, the king should know that if this city is built and its walls are restored, no more taxes, tribute or duty will be paid, and eventually the royal revenues will suffer.[e] [14] Now since we are under obligation to the palace and it is not proper for us to see the king dishonored, we are sending this message to inform the king, [15] so that a search may be made in the archives of your

Why did the Jews refuse their enemies help? (4:3) The Jewish people were the only ones who were allowed to build the temple. Other people worshiped pagan gods, so allowing them to help would taint the temple.

---

[a] 4 Or *and troubled them as they built*   [b] 6 Hebrew *Ahasuerus*
[c] 7 Or *written in Aramaic and translated*   [d] 7 The text of 4:8–6:18 is in Aramaic.   [e] 13 The meaning of the Aramaic for this clause is uncertain.

predecessors. In these records you will find that this city is a rebellious city, troublesome to kings and provinces, a place with a long history of sedition. That is why this city was destroyed. [16]We inform the king that if this city is built and its walls are restored, you will be left with nothing in Trans-Euphrates.

[17]The king sent this reply:

To Rehum the commanding officer, Shimshai the secretary and the rest of their associates living in Samaria and elsewhere in Trans-Euphrates:

Greetings.

[18]The letter you sent us has been read and translated in my presence. [19]I issued an order and a search was made, and it was found that this city has a long history of revolt against kings and has been a place of rebellion and sedition. [20]Jerusalem has had powerful kings ruling over the whole of Trans-Euphrates, and taxes, tribute and duty were paid to them. [21]Now issue an order to these men to stop work, so that this city will not be rebuilt until I so order. [22]Be careful not to neglect this matter. Why let this threat grow, to the detriment of the royal interests?

[23]As soon as the copy of the letter of King Artaxerxes was read to Rehum and Shimshai the secretary and their associates, they went immediately to the Jews in Jerusalem and compelled them by force to stop.

[24]Thus the work on the house of God in Jerusalem came to a standstill until the second year of the reign of Darius king of Persia.

TATTENAI'S LETTER TO DARIUS

5 Now Haggai the prophet and Zechariah the prophet, a descendant of Iddo, prophesied to the Jews in Judah and Jerusalem in the name of the God of Israel, who was over them. [2]Then Zerubbabel son of Shealtiel and Joshua son of Jozadak set to work to rebuild the house of God in Jerusalem. And the prophets of God were with them, supporting them.

[3]At that time Tattenai, governor of Trans-Euphrates, and Shethar-Bozenai and their associates went to them and asked, "Who authorized you to rebuild this temple and to finish it?" [4]They[a] also asked, "What are the names of those who are constructing this building?" [5]But the eye of their God was watching over the elders of the Jews, and they were not stopped until a report could go to Darius and his written reply be received.

[6]This is a copy of the letter that Tattenai, governor of Trans-Euphrates, and Shethar-Bozenai and their associates, the officials of Trans-Euphrates, sent to King Darius. [7]The report they sent him read as follows:

[a] 4 See Septuagint; Aramaic *We*.

Why did Artaxerxes order the work stopped? (4:21–22)
The king became worried when the enemies of the Jews claimed they were planning to rebel. He did not override his previous order allowing them to rebuild but ordered them to stop temporarily.

How long did the work stop? (4:24)
The construction stopped for about 16 years.

Were the prophets Haggai and Zechariah the authors of books in the Old Testament? (5:1)
Yes. These two prophets each authored a book in the Bible.

What did it mean that "the eye of their God was watching over" them? (5:5)
This is a metaphor for how the LORD looks after his people. "The king's eyes" was the name given to Persian inspectors. The use of the word eye shows that God's knowledge and power is above that of the king's.

To King Darius:

Cordial greetings.

[8] The king should know that we went to the district of Judah, to the temple of the great God. The people are building it with large stones and placing the timbers in the walls. The work is being carried on with diligence and is making rapid progress under their direction.

[9] We questioned the elders and asked them, "Who authorized you to rebuild this temple and to finish it?" [10] We also asked them their names, so that we could write down the names of their leaders for your information.

[11] This is the answer they gave us:

"We are the servants of the God of heaven and earth, and we are rebuilding the temple that was built many years ago, one that a great king of Israel built and finished. [12] But because our ancestors angered the God of heaven, he gave them into the hands of Nebuchadnezzar the Chaldean, king of Babylon, who destroyed this temple and deported the people to Babylon.

[13] "However, in the first year of Cyrus king of Babylon, King Cyrus issued a decree to rebuild this house of God. [14] He even removed from the temple[a] of Babylon the gold and silver articles of the house of God, which Nebuchadnezzar had taken from the temple in Jerusalem and brought to the temple[a] in Babylon. Then King Cyrus gave them to a man named Sheshbazzar, whom he had appointed governor, [15] and he told him, 'Take these articles and go and deposit them in the temple in Jerusalem. And rebuild the house of God on its site.'

[16] "So this Sheshbazzar came and laid the foundations of the house of God in Jerusalem. From that day to the present it has been under construction but is not yet finished."

[17] Now if it pleases the king, let a search be made in the royal archives of Babylon to see if King Cyrus did in fact issue a decree to rebuild this house of God in Jerusalem. Then let the king send us his decision in this matter.

THE DECREE OF DARIUS

6 King Darius then issued an order, and they searched in the archives stored in the treasury at Babylon. [2] A scroll was found in the citadel of Ecbatana in the province of Media, and this was written on it:

Memorandum:

[3] In the first year of King Cyrus, the king issued a decree concerning the temple of God in Jerusalem:

Let the temple be rebuilt as a place to present sacrifices, and let its foundations be laid. It is to be sixty cubits[b] high and sixty cubits wide, [4] with three courses of large

Why was Cyrus called the king of Babylon? (5:13)
As ruler of the Persian empire, Cyrus could be called the king of all the nations that were part of the empire.

What was the citadel of Ecbatana? (6:2)
Valuables such as metal and important documents were stored in this large fortified city in Media.

---

[a] 14 Or *palace*   [b] 3 That is, about 90 feet or about 27 meters

stones and one of timbers. The costs are to be paid by the royal treasury. ⁵ Also, the gold and silver articles of the house of God, which Nebuchadnezzar took from the temple in Jerusalem and brought to Babylon, are to be returned to their places in the temple in Jerusalem; they are to be deposited in the house of God.

⁶ Now then, Tattenai, governor of Trans-Euphrates, and Shethar-Bozenai and you other officials of that province, stay away from there. ⁷ Do not interfere with the work on this temple of God. Let the governor of the Jews and the Jewish elders rebuild this house of God on its site.

⁸ Moreover, I hereby decree what you are to do for these elders of the Jews in the construction of this house of God:

Their expenses are to be fully paid out of the royal treasury, from the revenues of Trans-Euphrates, so that the work will not stop. ⁹ Whatever is needed—young bulls, rams, male lambs for burnt offerings to the God of heaven, and wheat, salt, wine and olive oil, as requested by the priests in Jerusalem—must be given them daily without fail, ¹⁰ so that they may offer sacrifices pleasing to the God of heaven and pray for the well-being of the king and his sons.

¹¹ Furthermore, I decree that if anyone defies this edict, a beam is to be pulled from their house and they are to be impaled on it. And for this crime their house is to be made a pile of rubble. ¹² May God, who has caused his Name to dwell there, overthrow any king or people who lifts a hand to change this decree or to destroy this temple in Jerusalem.

I Darius have decreed it. Let it be carried out with diligence.

COMPLETION AND DEDICATION OF THE TEMPLE

¹³ Then, because of the decree King Darius had sent, Tattenai, governor of Trans-Euphrates, and Shethar-Bozenai and their associates carried it out with diligence. ¹⁴ So the elders of the Jews continued to build and prosper under the preaching of Haggai the prophet and Zechariah, a descendant of Iddo. They finished building the temple according to the command of the God of Israel and the decrees of Cyrus, Darius and Artaxerxes, kings of Persia. ¹⁵ The temple was completed on the third day of the month Adar, in the sixth year of the reign of King Darius.

¹⁶ Then the people of Israel—the priests, the Levites and the rest of the exiles—celebrated the dedication of the house of God with joy. ¹⁷ For the dedication of this house of God they offered a hundred bulls, two hundred rams, four hundred male lambs and, as a sin offering*a* for all Israel, twelve male goats, one for each of the tribes of Israel. ¹⁸ And they installed the priests in their divisions and the Levites in their groups for the service of God at Jerusalem, according to what is written in the Book of Moses.

a 17 Or purification offering

Why would Darius pay for this project from the royal treasury? (6:4) The money would be provided from taxes (see verse 8). Darius was following the example set by Cyrus.

Why would Darius want the Jews to pray to God for him? (6:10) Darius believed in many gods and would be happy to have anyone pray to any of them for him.

How long did it take to build the temple? (6:15) The project took about 22 years, from 538 to 516 B.C.

THE PASSOVER

¹⁹On the fourteenth day of the first month, the exiles celebrated the Passover. ²⁰The priests and Levites had purified themselves and were all ceremonially clean. The Levites slaughtered the Passover lamb for all the exiles, for their relatives the priests and for themselves. ²¹So the Israelites who had returned from the exile ate it, together with all who had separated themselves from the unclean practices of their Gentile neighbors in order to seek the LORD, the God of Israel. ²²For seven days they celebrated with joy the Festival of Unleavened Bread, because the LORD had filled them with joy by changing the attitude of the king of Assyria so that he assisted them in the work on the house of God, the God of Israel.

EZRA COMES TO JERUSALEM

7 After these things, during the reign of Artaxerxes king of Persia, Ezra son of Seraiah, the son of Azariah, the son of Hilkiah, ²the son of Shallum, the son of Zadok, the son of Ahitub, ³the son of Amariah, the son of Azariah, the son of Meraioth, ⁴the son of Zerahiah, the son of Uzzi, the son of Bukki, ⁵the son of Abishua, the son of Phinehas, the son of Eleazar, the son of Aaron the chief priest— ⁶this Ezra came up from Babylon. He was a teacher well versed in the Law of Moses, which the LORD, the God of Israel, had given. The king had granted him everything he asked, for the hand of the LORD his God was on him. ⁷Some of the Israelites, including priests, Levites, musicians, gatekeepers and temple servants, also came up to Jerusalem in the seventh year of King Artaxerxes.

⁸Ezra arrived in Jerusalem in the fifth month of the seventh year of the king. ⁹He had begun his journey from Babylon on the first day of the first month, and he arrived in Jerusalem on the first day of the fifth month, for the gracious hand of his God was on him. ¹⁰For Ezra had devoted himself to the study and observance of the Law of the LORD, and to teaching its decrees and laws in Israel.

KING ARTAXERXES' LETTER TO EZRA

¹¹This is a copy of the letter King Artaxerxes had given to Ezra the priest, a teacher of the Law, a man learned in matters concerning the commands and decrees of the LORD for Israel:

¹²Artaxerxes, king of kings,

To Ezra the priest, teacher of the Law of the God of heaven:

Greetings.

¹³Now I decree that any of the Israelites in my kingdom, including priests and Levites, who volunteer to go to Jerusalem with you, may go. ¹⁴You are sent by the king and his seven advisers to inquire about Judah and Jerusalem with regard to the Law of your God, which is in your hand. ¹⁵Moreover, you are to take with you the

Why was Ezra's genealogy included? (7:1–6)
Only the direct descendants of Aaron could serve as priests, so Ezra's genealogy was included to prove that he was part of Aaron's family.

silver and gold that the king and his advisers have freely given to the God of Israel, whose dwelling is in Jerusalem, [16] together with all the silver and gold you may obtain from the province of Babylon, as well as the freewill offerings of the people and priests for the temple of their God in Jerusalem. [17] With this money be sure to buy bulls, rams and male lambs, together with their grain offerings and drink offerings, and sacrifice them on the altar of the temple of your God in Jerusalem.

[18] You and your fellow Israelites may then do whatever seems best with the rest of the silver and gold, in accordance with the will of your God. [19] Deliver to the God of Jerusalem all the articles entrusted to you for worship in the temple of your God. [20] And anything else needed for the temple of your God that you are responsible to supply, you may provide from the royal treasury.

[21] Now I, King Artaxerxes, decree that all the treasurers of Trans-Euphrates are to provide with diligence whatever Ezra the priest, the teacher of the Law of the God of heaven, may ask of you— [22] up to a hundred talents[a] of silver, a hundred cors[b] of wheat, a hundred baths[c] of wine, a hundred baths[c] of olive oil, and salt without limit. [23] Whatever the God of heaven has prescribed, let it be done with diligence for the temple of the God of heaven. Why should his wrath fall on the realm of the king and of his sons? [24] You are also to know that you have no authority to impose taxes, tribute or duty on any of the priests, Levites, musicians, gatekeepers, temple servants or other workers at this house of God.

[25] And you, Ezra, in accordance with the wisdom of your God, which you possess, appoint magistrates and judges to administer justice to all the people of Trans-Euphrates—all who know the laws of your God. And you are to teach any who do not know them. [26] Whoever does not obey the law of your God and the law of the king must surely be punished by death, banishment, confiscation of property, or imprisonment.[d]

[27] Praise be to the LORD, the God of our ancestors, who has put it into the king's heart to bring honor to the house of the LORD in Jerusalem in this way [28] and who has extended his good favor to me before the king and his advisers and all the king's powerful officials. Because the hand of the LORD my God was on me, I took courage and gathered leaders from Israel to go up with me.

LIST OF THE FAMILY HEADS RETURNING WITH EZRA

8 These are the family heads and those registered with them who came up with me from Babylon during the reign of King Artaxerxes:

Did Artaxerxes pay for the entire project? (7:15–16)
No. The king made generous gifts of gold and silver to the project, but Ezra also had permission to request contributions from Gentiles in the region and from Jews living in Babylon.

Did Artaxerxes want the whole region to live by the law of God? (7:25–26)
No. He wanted those who believed in Israel's God to live according to his commandments. Artaxerxes wanted to maintain stability in the empire by promoting local laws and customs.

Why does the writing suddenly shift to the first person? (7:28)
The change to first person probably signifies where the author of Ezra started quoting Ezra's own memoir. The rest of the book was written using many different sources.

---

[a] 22 That is, about 3 3/4 tons or about 3.4 metric tons   [b] 22 That is, probably about 18 tons or about 16 metric tons   [c] 22 That is, about 600 gallons or about 2,200 liters   [d] 26 The text of 7:12-26 is in Aramaic.

²of the descendants of Phinehas, Gershom;
of the descendants of Ithamar, Daniel;
of the descendants of David, Hattush ³of the descendants of Shekaniah;

of the descendants of Parosh, Zechariah, and with him
were registered 150 men;

⁴of the descendants of Pahath-Moab, Eliehoenai son of
Zerahiah, and with him 200 men;

⁵of the descendants of Zattu,ᵃ Shekaniah son of Jahaziel,
and with him 300 men;

⁶of the descendants of Adin, Ebed son of Jonathan, and
with him 50 men;

⁷of the descendants of Elam, Jeshaiah son of Athaliah,
and with him 70 men;

⁸of the descendants of Shephatiah, Zebadiah son of Michael, and with him 80 men;

⁹of the descendants of Joab, Obadiah son of Jehiel, and
with him 218 men;

¹⁰of the descendants of Bani,ᵇ Shelomith son of Josiphiah,
and with him 160 men;

¹¹of the descendants of Bebai, Zechariah son of Bebai,
and with him 28 men;

¹²of the descendants of Azgad, Johanan son of Hakkatan,
and with him 110 men;

¹³of the descendants of Adonikam, the last ones, whose
names were Eliphelet, Jeuel and Shemaiah, and with
them 60 men;

¹⁴of the descendants of Bigvai, Uthai and Zakkur, and
with them 70 men.

THE RETURN TO JERUSALEM

¹⁵I assembled them at the canal that flows toward Ahava, and we camped there three days. When I checked among
the people and the priests, I found no Levites there. ¹⁶So I
summoned Eliezer, Ariel, Shemaiah, Elnathan, Jarib, Elnathan, Nathan, Zechariah and Meshullam, who were leaders,
and Joiarib and Elnathan, who were men of learning, ¹⁷and I
ordered them to go to Iddo, the leader in Kasiphia. I told them
what to say to Iddo and his fellow Levites, the temple servants
in Kasiphia, so that they might bring attendants to us for the
house of our God. ¹⁸Because the gracious hand of our God
was on us, they brought us Sherebiah, a capable man, from
the descendants of Mahli son of Levi, the son of Israel, and
Sherebiah's sons and brothers, 18 in all; ¹⁹and Hashabiah, together with Jeshaiah from the descendants of Merari, and his
brothers and nephews, 20 in all. ²⁰They also brought 220 of
the temple servants—a body that David and the officials had
established to assist the Levites. All were registered by name.

²¹There, by the Ahava Canal, I proclaimed a fast, so that
we might humble ourselves before our God and ask him for a
safe journey for us and our children, with all our possessions.
²²I was ashamed to ask the king for soldiers and horsemen

Why was Ezra worried about the lack of Levites? (8:15) With the upcoming celebration, more Levites would be needed because they were the only ones authorized to do temple work.

ᵃ 5 Some Septuagint manuscripts (also 1 Esdras 8:32); Hebrew does not have
Zattu.   ᵇ 10 Some Septuagint manuscripts (also 1 Esdras 8:36); Hebrew
does not have Bani.

to protect us from enemies on the road, because we had told the king, "The gracious hand of our God is on everyone who looks to him, but his great anger is against all who forsake him." ²³ So we fasted and petitioned our God about this, and he answered our prayer.

²⁴ Then I set apart twelve of the leading priests, namely, Sherebiah, Hashabiah and ten of their brothers, ²⁵ and I weighed out to them the offering of silver and gold and the articles that the king, his advisers, his officials and all Israel present there had donated for the house of our God. ²⁶ I weighed out to them 650 talents*ᵃ* of silver, silver articles weighing 100 talents,*ᵇ* 100 talents*ᵇ* of gold, ²⁷ 20 bowls of gold valued at 1,000 darics,*ᶜ* and two fine articles of polished bronze, as precious as gold.

²⁸ I said to them, "You as well as these articles are consecrated to the LORD. The silver and gold are a freewill offering to the LORD, the God of your ancestors. ²⁹ Guard them carefully until you weigh them out in the chambers of the house of the LORD in Jerusalem before the leading priests and the Levites and the family heads of Israel." ³⁰ Then the priests and Levites received the silver and gold and sacred articles that had been weighed out to be taken to the house of our God in Jerusalem.

³¹ On the twelfth day of the first month we set out from the Ahava Canal to go to Jerusalem. The hand of our God was on us, and he protected us from enemies and bandits along the way. ³² So we arrived in Jerusalem, where we rested three days.

³³ On the fourth day, in the house of our God, we weighed out the silver and gold and the sacred articles into the hands of Meremoth son of Uriah, the priest. Eleazar son of Phinehas was with him, and so were the Levites Jozabad son of Jeshua and Noadiah son of Binnui. ³⁴ Everything was accounted for by number and weight, and the entire weight was recorded at that time.

³⁵ Then the exiles who had returned from captivity sacrificed burnt offerings to the God of Israel: twelve bulls for all Israel, ninety-six rams, seventy-seven male lambs and, as a sin offering,*ᵈ* twelve male goats. All this was a burnt offering to the LORD. ³⁶ They also delivered the king's orders to the royal satraps and to the governors of Trans-Euphrates, who then gave assistance to the people and to the house of God.

EZRA'S PRAYER ABOUT INTERMARRIAGE

9 After these things had been done, the leaders came to me and said, "The people of Israel, including the priests and the Levites, have not kept themselves separate from the neighboring peoples with their detestable practices, like those of the Canaanites, Hittites, Perizzites, Jebusites, Ammonites, Moabites, Egyptians and Amorites. ² They have taken some of their daughters as wives for themselves and their sons, and have mingled the holy race with the peoples

What was polished bronze? (8:27)
This may have been orichalc, a bright yellow alloy of copper that looked like gold and was highly prized in ancient times.

Why was the weight recorded in writing? (8:34)
According to Babylonian practice, every transaction, including sales and marriages, had to be recorded in writing.

Who were the royal satraps? (8:36)
In Persia, governors controlled small provinces. The satrap was above the governors. It was his job to rule the greater district that included all of the smaller provinces.

What were the detestable practices of the neighboring peoples? (9:1)
These practices included worshiping pagan gods and may have included sacrifices and prostitution. They represented a turning away from God.

ᵃ 26 That is, about 24 tons or about 22 metric tons   *ᵇ 26* That is, about 3 3/4 tons or about 3.4 metric tons   *ᶜ 27* That is, about 19 pounds or about 8.4 kilograms   *ᵈ 35* Or *purification offering*

around them. And the leaders and officials have led the way in this unfaithfulness."

[3] When I heard this, I tore my tunic and cloak, pulled hair from my head and beard and sat down appalled. [4] Then everyone who trembled at the words of the God of Israel gathered around me because of this unfaithfulness of the exiles. And I sat there appalled until the evening sacrifice.

[5] Then, at the evening sacrifice, I rose from my self-abasement, with my tunic and cloak torn, and fell on my knees with my hands spread out to the LORD my God [6] and prayed:

"I am too ashamed and disgraced, my God, to lift up my face to you, because our sins are higher than our heads and our guilt has reached to the heavens. [7] From the days of our ancestors until now, our guilt has been great. Because of our sins, we and our kings and our priests have been subjected to the sword and captivity, to pillage and humiliation at the hand of foreign kings, as it is today.

[8] "But now, for a brief moment, the LORD our God has been gracious in leaving us a remnant and giving us a firm place[a] in his sanctuary, and so our God gives light to our eyes and a little relief in our bondage. [9] Though we are slaves, our God has not forsaken us in our bondage. He has shown us kindness in the sight of the kings of Persia: He has granted us new life to rebuild the house of our God and repair its ruins, and he has given us a wall of protection in Judah and Jerusalem.

[10] "But now, our God, what can we say after this? For we have forsaken the commands [11] you gave through your servants the prophets when you said: 'The land you are entering to possess is a land polluted by the corruption of its peoples. By their detestable practices they have filled it with their impurity from one end to the other. [12] Therefore, do not give your daughters in marriage to their sons or take their daughters for your sons. Do not seek a treaty of friendship with them at any time, that you may be strong and eat the good things of the land and leave it to your children as an everlasting inheritance.'

[13] "What has happened to us is a result of our evil deeds and our great guilt, and yet, our God, you have punished us less than our sins deserved and have given us a remnant like this. [14] Shall we then break your commands again and intermarry with the peoples who commit such detestable practices? Would you not be angry enough with us to destroy us, leaving us no remnant or survivor? [15] LORD, the God of Israel, you are righteous! We are left this day as a remnant. Here we are before you in our guilt, though because of it not one of us can stand in your presence."

THE PEOPLE'S CONFESSION OF SIN

10 While Ezra was praying and confessing, weeping and throwing himself down before the house of God, a large crowd of Israelites — men, women and children — gathered around him. They too wept bitterly. [2] Then

Why did Ezra confess guilt? (9:6)
As the leader of the community, Ezra offered a prayer of confession on behalf of all the people. Instead of thinking he was better than the people, Ezra identified himself with the community.

Why was intermarriage wrong? (9:14)
Ezra was concerned about religious purity. Marriage to people from other nations often led to idolatry and worship of false gods.

Why did Ezra behave this way? (10:1)
He may have been overcome with grief over the sins of the people. His actions prompted others to repent before the LORD.

[a] 8 Or *a foothold*

Shekaniah son of Jehiel, one of the descendants of Elam, said to Ezra, "We have been unfaithful to our God by marrying foreign women from the peoples around us. But in spite of this, there is still hope for Israel. ³Now let us make a covenant before our God to send away all these women and their children, in accordance with the counsel of my lord and of those who fear the commands of our God. Let it be done according to the Law. ⁴Rise up; this matter is in your hands. We will support you, so take courage and do it."

⁵So Ezra rose up and put the leading priests and Levites and all Israel under oath to do what had been suggested. And they took the oath. ⁶Then Ezra withdrew from before the house of God and went to the room of Jehohanan son of Eliashib. While he was there, he ate no food and drank no water, because he continued to mourn over the unfaithfulness of the exiles.

⁷A proclamation was then issued throughout Judah and Jerusalem for all the exiles to assemble in Jerusalem. ⁸Anyone who failed to appear within three days would forfeit all his property, in accordance with the decision of the officials and elders, and would himself be expelled from the assembly of the exiles.

⁹Within the three days, all the men of Judah and Benjamin had gathered in Jerusalem. And on the twentieth day of the ninth month, all the people were sitting in the square before the house of God, greatly distressed by the occasion and because of the rain. ¹⁰Then Ezra the priest stood up and said to them, "You have been unfaithful; you have married foreign women, adding to Israel's guilt. ¹¹Now honor*a* the LORD, the God of your ancestors, and do his will. Separate yourselves from the peoples around you and from your foreign wives."

¹²The whole assembly responded with a loud voice: "You are right! We must do as you say. ¹³But there are many people here and it is the rainy season; so we cannot stand outside. Besides, this matter cannot be taken care of in a day or two, because we have sinned greatly in this thing. ¹⁴Let our officials act for the whole assembly. Then let everyone in our towns who has married a foreign woman come at a set time, along with the elders and judges of each town, until the fierce anger of our God in this matter is turned away from us." ¹⁵Only Jonathan son of Asahel and Jahzeiah son of Tikvah, supported by Meshullam and Shabbethai the Levite, opposed this.

¹⁶So the exiles did as was proposed. Ezra the priest selected men who were family heads, one from each family division, and all of them designated by name. On the first day of the tenth month they sat down to investigate the cases, ¹⁷and by the first day of the first month they finished dealing with all the men who had married foreign women.

THOSE GUILTY OF INTERMARRIAGE

¹⁸Among the descendants of the priests, the following had married foreign women:

a 11 Or *Now make confession to*

Why were the people unhappy about the rain? (10:9)
Heavy rains could be dangerous in dry regions. The dry ground was not able to absorb the water quickly enough, so floods were likely.

How did God show his fierce anger? (10:14)
He didn't show his anger. The people were afraid that God was about to punish them, so they tried to avoid his anger by changing their ways.

Why did it take so long to decide these cases? (10:17)
This was a serious matter. The council took three months to decide 110 cases because they took the time to investigate each one.

Why was this list included?
(10:18–43)
This list not only pointed toward the guilty; it also allowed those who were not guilty to clear their names because they were not on the list.

From the descendants of Joshua son of Jozadak, and his brothers: Maaseiah, Eliezer, Jarib and Gedaliah. [19] (They all gave their hands in pledge to put away their wives, and for their guilt they each presented a ram from the flock as a guilt offering.)

[20] From the descendants of Immer:
Hanani and Zebadiah.
[21] From the descendants of Harim:
Maaseiah, Elijah, Shemaiah, Jehiel and Uzziah.
[22] From the descendants of Pashhur:
Elioenai, Maaseiah, Ishmael, Nethanel, Jozabad and Elasah.

[23] Among the Levites:

Jozabad, Shimei, Kelaiah (that is, Kelita), Pethahiah, Judah and Eliezer.
[24] From the musicians:
Eliashib.
From the gatekeepers:
Shallum, Telem and Uri.

[25] And among the other Israelites:

From the descendants of Parosh:
Ramiah, Izziah, Malkijah, Mijamin, Eleazar, Malkijah and Benaiah.
[26] From the descendants of Elam:
Mattaniah, Zechariah, Jehiel, Abdi, Jeremoth and Elijah.
[27] From the descendants of Zattu:
Elioenai, Eliashib, Mattaniah, Jeremoth, Zabad and Aziza.
[28] From the descendants of Bebai:
Jehohanan, Hananiah, Zabbai and Athlai.
[29] From the descendants of Bani:
Meshullam, Malluk, Adaiah, Jashub, Sheal and Jeremoth.
[30] From the descendants of Pahath-Moab:
Adna, Kelal, Benaiah, Maaseiah, Mattaniah, Bezalel, Binnui and Manasseh.
[31] From the descendants of Harim:
Eliezer, Ishijah, Malkijah, Shemaiah, Shimeon, [32] Benjamin, Malluk and Shemariah.
[33] From the descendants of Hashum:
Mattenai, Mattattah, Zabad, Eliphelet, Jeremai, Manasseh and Shimei.
[34] From the descendants of Bani:
Maadai, Amram, Uel, [35] Benaiah, Bedeiah, Keluhi, [36] Vaniah, Meremoth, Eliashib, [37] Mattaniah, Mattenai and Jaasu.
[38] From the descendants of Binnui:[a]
Shimei, [39] Shelemiah, Nathan, Adaiah, [40] Maknadebai, Shashai, Sharai, [41] Azarel, Shelemiah, Shemariah, [42] Shallum, Amariah and Joseph.

---

[a] 37,38 See Septuagint (also 1 Esdras 9:34); Hebrew *Jaasu* [38] *and Bani and Binnui.*

⁴³ From the descendants of Nebo:
   Jeiel, Mattithiah, Zabad, Zebina, Jaddai, Joel and Benaiah.

⁴⁴ All these had married foreign women, and some of them
had children by these wives.ᵃ

Nehemiah

INTRODUCTION

Who wrote this book?
The author of Nehemiah is unknown. Many people think the book was written by Ezra.

Why was this book written?
The book of Nehemiah tells how God used Nehemiah to rebuild the walls of Jerusalem.

What happens in this book?
Nehemiah is made governor of Judah. He has the Jews rebuild the city walls. Nehemiah also helps the people of Judah stop living sinful lives.

What do we learn about God in this book?
God wants his people to be courageous and keep on doing his work.

Who is the key person in this book?
The most important person in this book is Nehemiah.

What are some of the stories in this book?

The walls are rebuilt	Nehemiah 3
Nehemiah helps the poor	Nehemiah 5
Opposition to the rebuilding	Nehemiah 6
Ezra reads God's law	Nehemiah 8
The Israelites confess their sins	Nehemiah 9
Nehemiah asks to be remembered	Nehemiah 13

When did these things happen?

1400 BC 1300 1200 1100 1000 900 800 700 600 500 400

FALL OF JERUSALEM (586 BC)

PERSIA'S CONQUEST OF BABYLON (539 BC)

FIRST RETURN OF EXILES TO JERUSALEM (538 BC)

MINISTRIES OF HAGGAI AND ZECHARIAH (C. 520 – 480 BC)

TEMPLE RESTORATION COMPLETED (516 BC)

SECOND RETURN TO JERUSALEM UNDER EZRA (458 BC)

THIRD RETURN TO JERUSALEM UNDER NEHEMIAH (444 BC)

JERUSALEM'S WALL REBUILT (444 BC)

BOOK OF NEHEMIAH WRITTEN (C. 430 BC)

NEHEMIAH'S PRAYER

1 The words of Nehemiah son of Hakaliah:

In the month of Kislev in the twentieth year, while I was in the citadel of Susa, ²Hanani, one of my brothers, came from Judah with some other men, and I questioned them about the Jewish remnant that had survived the exile, and also about Jerusalem.

³They said to me, "Those who survived the exile and are back in the province are in great trouble and disgrace. The wall of Jerusalem is broken down, and its gates have been burned with fire."

⁴When I heard these things, I sat down and wept. For some days I mourned and fasted and prayed before the God of heaven. ⁵Then I said:

"LORD, the God of heaven, the great and awesome God, who keeps his covenant of love with those who love him and keep his commandments, ⁶let your ear be attentive and your eyes open to hear the prayer your servant is praying before you day and night for your servants, the people of Israel. I confess the sins we Israelites, including myself and my father's family, have committed against you. ⁷We have acted very wickedly toward you. We have not obeyed the commands, decrees and laws you gave your servant Moses.

⁸"Remember the instruction you gave your servant Moses, saying, 'If you are unfaithful, I will scatter you among the nations, ⁹but if you return to me and obey my commands, then even if your exiled people are at the farthest horizon, I will gather them from there and bring them to the place I have chosen as a dwelling for my Name.'

¹⁰"They are your servants and your people, whom you redeemed by your great strength and your mighty hand. ¹¹Lord, let your ear be attentive to the prayer of this your servant and to the prayer of your servants who delight in revering your name. Give your servant success today by granting him favor in the presence of this man."

I was cupbearer to the king.

ARTAXERXES SENDS NEHEMIAH TO JERUSALEM

2 In the month of Nisan in the twentieth year of King Artaxerxes, when wine was brought for him, I took the wine and gave it to the king. I had not been sad in his presence before, ²so the king asked me, "Why does your face look so sad when you are not ill? This can be nothing but sadness of heart."

I was very much afraid, ³but I said to the king, "May the king live forever! Why should my face not look sad when the city where my ancestors are buried lies in ruins, and its gates have been destroyed by fire?"

⁴The king said to me, "What is it you want?"

Then I prayed to the God of heaven, ⁵and I answered the

When was the month of Kislev? (1:1)
Kislev was from mid-November to mid-December.

What did a cupbearer do? (1:11)
A cupbearer had to taste the food and drink before it was served to the king to be sure that it was not poisoned. Nehemiah may also have been a confidant and adviser to the king.

Why was Nehemiah afraid? (2:2)
He was probably fearful because he was going to ask to be released from his duties as cupbearer and ask for the king's help to restore a city with a reputation for being difficult.

king, "If it pleases the king and if your servant has found favor in his sight, let him send me to the city in Judah where my ancestors are buried so that I can rebuild it."

[6] Then the king, with the queen sitting beside him, asked me, "How long will your journey take, and when will you get back?" It pleased the king to send me; so I set a time.

[7] I also said to him, "If it pleases the king, may I have letters to the governors of Trans-Euphrates, so that they will provide me safe-conduct until I arrive in Judah? [8] And may I have a letter to Asaph, keeper of the royal park, so he will give me timber to make beams for the gates of the citadel by the temple and for the city wall and for the residence I will occupy?" And because the gracious hand of my God was on me, the king granted my requests. [9] So I went to the governors of Trans-Euphrates and gave them the king's letters. The king had also sent army officers and cavalry with me.

[10] When Sanballat the Horonite and Tobiah the Ammonite official heard about this, they were very much disturbed that someone had come to promote the welfare of the Israelites.

NEHEMIAH INSPECTS JERUSALEM'S WALLS

[11] I went to Jerusalem, and after staying there three days [12] I set out during the night with a few others. I had not told anyone what my God had put in my heart to do for Jerusalem. There were no mounts with me except the one I was riding on. [13] By night I went out through the Valley Gate toward the Jackal[a] Well and the Dung Gate, examining the walls of Jerusalem, which had been broken down, and its gates, which had been destroyed by fire. [14] Then I moved on toward the Fountain Gate and the King's Pool, but there was not enough room for my mount to get through; [15] so I went up the valley by night, examining the wall. Finally, I turned back and reentered through the Valley Gate. [16] The officials did not know where I had gone or what I was doing, because as yet I had said nothing to the Jews or the priests or nobles or officials or any others who would be doing the work.

[17] Then I said to them, "You see the trouble we are in: Jerusalem lies in ruins, and its gates have been burned with fire. Come, let us rebuild the wall of Jerusalem, and we will no longer be in disgrace." [18] I also told them about the gracious hand of my God on me and what the king had said to me.

They replied, "Let us start rebuilding." So they began this good work.

[19] But when Sanballat the Horonite, Tobiah the Ammonite official and Geshem the Arab heard about it, they mocked and ridiculed us. "What is this you are doing?" they asked. "Are you rebelling against the king?"

[20] I answered them by saying, "The God of heaven will give us success. We his servants will start rebuilding, but as for you, you have no share in Jerusalem or any claim or historic right to it."

Why were Sanballat and Tobiah not in favor of rebuilding Jerusalem? (2:10, 19)
These men had become rich and powerful by controlling Jerusalem. They probably wanted to stay in control of this profitable territory.

Why did Nehemiah keep his mission secret? (2:12)
In Jerusalem, there were many non-Jews who would have sold the secret to an enemy of the Jews. Also, without a clear plan for rebuilding the walls, Nehemiah would have had a difficult time persuading people to join his cause.

Why was there only one horse? (2:12)
If there had been more horses, it would have been more difficult to keep their mission secret.

---

[a] 13 Or Serpent or Fig

BUILDERS OF THE WALL

3 Eliashib the high priest and his fellow priests went to work and rebuilt the Sheep Gate. They dedicated it and set its doors in place, building as far as the Tower of the Hundred, which they dedicated, and as far as the Tower of Hananel. ²The men of Jericho built the adjoining section, and Zakkur son of Imri built next to them.

³The Fish Gate was rebuilt by the sons of Hassenaah. They laid its beams and put its doors and bolts and bars in place. ⁴Meremoth son of Uriah, the son of Hakkoz, repaired the next section. Next to him Meshullam son of Berekiah, the son of Meshezabel, made repairs, and next to him Zadok son of Baana also made repairs. ⁵The next section was repaired by the men of Tekoa, but their nobles would not put their shoulders to the work under their supervisors.*a*

⁶The Jeshanah*b* Gate was repaired by Joiada son of Paseah and Meshullam son of Besodeiah. They laid its beams and put its doors with their bolts and bars in place. ⁷Next to them, repairs were made by men from Gibeon and Mizpah—Melatiah of Gibeon and Jadon of Meronoth—places under the authority of the governor of Trans-Euphrates. ⁸Uzziel son of Harhaiah, one of the goldsmiths, repaired the next section; and Hananiah, one of the perfume-makers, made repairs next to that. They restored Jerusalem as far as the Broad Wall. ⁹Rephaiah son of Hur, ruler of a half-district of Jerusalem, repaired the next section. ¹⁰Adjoining this, Jedaiah son of Harumaph made repairs opposite his house, and Hattush son of Hashabneiah made repairs next to him. ¹¹Malkijah son of Harim and Hasshub son of Pahath-Moab repaired another section and the Tower of the Ovens. ¹²Shallum son of Hallohesh, ruler of a half-district of Jerusalem, repaired the next section with the help of his daughters.

¹³The Valley Gate was repaired by Hanun and the residents of Zanoah. They rebuilt it and put its doors with their bolts and bars in place. They also repaired a thousand cubits*c* of the wall as far as the Dung Gate.

¹⁴The Dung Gate was repaired by Malkijah son of Rekab, ruler of the district of Beth Hakkerem. He rebuilt it and put its doors with their bolts and bars in place.

¹⁵The Fountain Gate was repaired by Shallun son of Kol-Hozeh, ruler of the district of Mizpah. He rebuilt it, roofing it over and putting its doors and bolts and bars in place. He also repaired the wall of the Pool of Siloam,*d* by the King's Garden, as far as the steps going down from the City of David. ¹⁶Beyond him, Nehemiah son of Azbuk, ruler of a half-district of Beth Zur, made repairs up to a point opposite the tombs*e* of David, as far as the artificial pool and the House of the Heroes.

ᵇ 5 Or their Lord or the governor   *ᵇ 6 Or Old*   *ᶜ 13 That is, about 1,500 feet or about 450 meters*   *ᵈ 15 Hebrew Shelah, a variant of Shiloah, that is, Siloam*   *ᵉ 16 Hebrew; Septuagint, some Vulgate manuscripts and Syriac tomb*

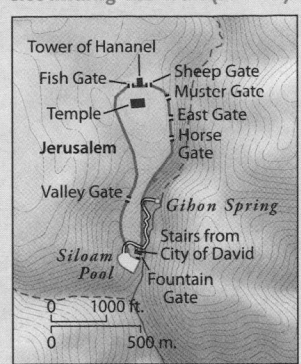

Rebuilding the Wall (3:1–32)

Tower of Hananel
Fish Gate
Sheep Gate
Muster Gate
Temple
East Gate
Horse Gate
Jerusalem
Valley Gate
Gihon Spring
Stairs from City of David
Siloam Pool
Fountain Gate

0   1000 ft.
0   500 m.

Was there a plan for rebuilding the walls? (3:1–32)
The plan was to reconstruct the walls following the pattern of the old walls.

Why did the nobles of Tekoa refuse to work? (3:5)
They may have been people who had never left the region and were jealous of the newcomers.

What kind of perfume did Hananiah make? (3:8)
Perfume makers of that time used ingredients such as aloe, balm, calamus, cassia, and cinnamon. They traded for sap, bark, flowers, and roots from places as far away as India. These things were also used to make perfume.

Why did Shallum's daughters help? (3:12)
Perhaps he had no sons, but it is also possible that Nehemiah wanted to emphasize the widespread support for rebuilding the walls of the city.

¹⁷ Next to him, the repairs were made by the Levites under Rehum son of Bani. Beside him, Hashabiah, ruler of half the district of Keilah, carried out repairs for his district. ¹⁸ Next to him, the repairs were made by their fellow Levites under Binnui*a* son of Henadad, ruler of the other half-district of Keilah. ¹⁹ Next to him, Ezer son of Jeshua, ruler of Mizpah, repaired another section, from a point facing the ascent to the armory as far as the angle of the wall. ²⁰ Next to him, Baruch son of Zabbai zealously repaired another section, from the angle to the entrance of the house of Eliashib the high priest. ²¹ Next to him, Meremoth son of Uriah, the son of Hakkoz, repaired another section, from the entrance of Eliashib's house to the end of it.

²² The repairs next to him were made by the priests from the surrounding region. ²³ Beyond them, Benjamin and Hasshub made repairs in front of their house; and next to them, Azariah son of Maaseiah, the son of Ananiah, made repairs beside his house. ²⁴ Next to him, Binnui son of Henadad repaired another section, from Azariah's house to the angle and the corner, ²⁵ and Palal son of Uzai worked opposite the angle and the tower projecting from the upper palace near the court of the guard. Next to him, Pedaiah son of Parosh ²⁶ and the temple servants living on the hill of Ophel made repairs up to a point opposite the Water Gate toward the east and the projecting tower. ²⁷ Next to them, the men of Tekoa repaired another section, from the great projecting tower to the wall of Ophel.

²⁸ Above the Horse Gate, the priests made repairs, each in front of his own house. ²⁹ Next to them, Zadok son of Immer made repairs opposite his house. Next to him, Shemaiah son of Shekaniah, the guard at the East Gate, made repairs. ³⁰ Next to him, Hananiah son of Shelemiah, and Hanun, the sixth son of Zalaph, repaired another section. Next to them, Meshullam son of Berekiah made repairs opposite his living quarters. ³¹ Next to him, Malkijah, one of the goldsmiths, made repairs as far as the house of the temple servants and the merchants, opposite the Inspection Gate, and as far as the room above the corner; ³² and between the room above the corner and the Sheep Gate the goldsmiths and merchants made repairs.

OPPOSITION TO THE REBUILDING

4 *b* When Sanballat heard that we were rebuilding the wall, he became angry and was greatly incensed. He ridiculed the Jews, ² and in the presence of his associates and the army of Samaria, he said, "What are those feeble Jews doing? Will they restore their wall? Will they offer sacrifices? Will they finish in a day? Can they bring the stones back to life from those heaps of rubble — burned as they are?"

³ Tobiah the Ammonite, who was at his side, said, "What they are building — even a fox climbing up on it would break down their wall of stones!"

---

a 18 Two Hebrew manuscripts and Syriac (see also Septuagint and verse 24); most Hebrew manuscripts *Bavvai*   *b* In Hebrew texts 4:1-6 is numbered 3:33-38, and 4:7-23 is numbered 4:1-17.

What was the condition of the stones? (4:2)
Fire had damaged the stones, which were probably limestone, and had caused many of them to crack and crumble.

⁴Hear us, our God, for we are despised. Turn their insults back on their own heads. Give them over as plunder in a land of captivity. ⁵Do not cover up their guilt or blot out their sins from your sight, for they have thrown insults in the face of*ᵃ the builders.

⁶So we rebuilt the wall till all of it reached half its height, for the people worked with all their heart.

⁷But when Sanballat, Tobiah, the Arabs, the Ammonites and the people of Ashdod heard that the repairs to Jerusalem's walls had gone ahead and that the gaps were being closed, they were very angry. ⁸They all plotted together to come and fight against Jerusalem and stir up trouble against it. ⁹But we prayed to our God and posted a guard day and night to meet this threat.

¹⁰Meanwhile, the people in Judah said, "The strength of the laborers is giving out, and there is so much rubble that we cannot rebuild the wall."

¹¹Also our enemies said, "Before they know it or see us, we will be right there among them and will kill them and put an end to the work."

¹²Then the Jews who lived near them came and told us ten times over, "Wherever you turn, they will attack us."

¹³Therefore I stationed some of the people behind the lowest points of the wall at the exposed places, posting them by families, with their swords, spears and bows. ¹⁴After I looked things over, I stood up and said to the nobles, the officials and the rest of the people, "Don't be afraid of them. Remember the Lord, who is great and awesome, and fight for your families, your sons and your daughters, your wives and your homes."

¹⁵When our enemies heard that we were aware of their plot and that God had frustrated it, we all returned to the wall, each to our own work.

¹⁶From that day on, half of my men did the work, while the other half were equipped with spears, shields, bows and armor. The officers posted themselves behind all the people of Judah ¹⁷who were building the wall. Those who carried materials did their work with one hand and held a weapon in the other, ¹⁸and each of the builders wore his sword at his side as he worked. But the man who sounded the trumpet stayed with me.

¹⁹Then I said to the nobles, the officials and the rest of the people, "The work is extensive and spread out, and we are widely separated from each other along the wall. ²⁰Wherever you hear the sound of the trumpet, join us there. Our God will fight for us!"

²¹So we continued the work with half the men holding spears, from the first light of dawn till the stars came out. ²²At that time I also said to the people, "Have every man and his helper stay inside Jerusalem at night, so they can serve us as guards by night and as workers by day." ²³Neither I nor my brothers nor my men nor the guards with me took off our clothes; each had his weapon, even when he went for water.ᵇ

ᵃ 5 Or *have aroused your anger before*   ᵇ 23 The meaning of the Hebrew for this clause is uncertain.

Why did Nehemiah pray such harsh prayers? (4:4–5)
Nehemiah knew that Sanballat and his supporters were enemies of God who wanted to discourage God's people from doing the work God had told them to do.

Why were the builders losing strength? (4:10)
The work was very difficult, and their self-esteem was weakened by the ridicule and threats of their enemies (see verse 5).

How long did they go without changing their clothes? (4:23)
Nehemiah and his men worked and slept in their clothes so they would be ready at any time for a surprise attack. It took 52 days to complete the walls; they may have stayed in the same clothes this whole time!

NEHEMIAH HELPS THE POOR

5 Now the men and their wives raised a great outcry against their fellow Jews. ²Some were saying, "We and our sons and daughters are numerous; in order for us to eat and stay alive, we must get grain."

³Others were saying, "We are mortgaging our fields, our vineyards and our homes to get grain during the famine."

⁴Still others were saying, "We have had to borrow money to pay the king's tax on our fields and vineyards. ⁵Although we are of the same flesh and blood as our fellow Jews and though our children are as good as theirs, yet we have to subject our sons and daughters to slavery. Some of our daughters have already been enslaved, but we are powerless, because our fields and our vineyards belong to others."

⁶When I heard their outcry and these charges, I was very angry. ⁷I pondered them in my mind and then accused the nobles and officials. I told them, "You are charging your own people interest!" So I called together a large meeting to deal with them ⁸and said: "As far as possible, we have bought back our fellow Jews who were sold to the Gentiles. Now you are selling your own people, only for them to be sold back to us!" They kept quiet, because they could find nothing to say.

⁹So I continued, "What you are doing is not right. Shouldn't you walk in the fear of our God to avoid the reproach of our Gentile enemies? ¹⁰I and my brothers and my men are also lending the people money and grain. But let us stop charging interest! ¹¹Give back to them immediately their fields, vineyards, olive groves and houses, and also the interest you are charging them—one percent of the money, grain, new wine and olive oil."

¹²"We will give it back," they said. "And we will not demand anything more from them. We will do as you say."

Then I summoned the priests and made the nobles and officials take an oath to do what they had promised. ¹³I also shook out the folds of my robe and said, "In this way may God shake out of their house and possessions anyone who does not keep this promise. So may such a person be shaken out and emptied!"

At this the whole assembly said, "Amen," and praised the LORD. And the people did as they had promised.

¹⁴Moreover, from the twentieth year of King Artaxerxes, when I was appointed to be their governor in the land of Judah, until his thirty-second year—twelve years—neither I nor my brothers ate the food allotted to the governor. ¹⁵But the earlier governors—those preceding me—placed a heavy burden on the people and took forty shekels*a* of silver from them in addition to food and wine. Their assistants also lorded it over the people. But out of reverence for God I did not act like that. ¹⁶Instead, I devoted myself to the work on this wall. All my men were assembled there for the work; we*b* did not acquire any land.

¹⁷Furthermore, a hundred and fifty Jews and officials ate

Why did some Jews sell their children into slavery? (5:5)
Sometimes ancient people who had little property would be forced to use family members as collateral for loans. If they weren't able to repay the loan, the person who had loaned the money gained the person or their family member as a slave for a period of time in order to repay the loan.

Where did Nehemiah get his money? (5:14–18)
Nehemiah was probably already rich. He also could have taken money from the government.

Why did Nehemiah feed all these people? (5:17)
It was a Persian custom for the governor to serve a large meal for his government officials and visiting politicians. Nehemiah did this without taxing the people.

---

a 15 That is, about 1 pound or about 460 grams   *b 16* Most Hebrew manuscripts; some Hebrew manuscripts, Septuagint, Vulgate and Syriac *I*

at my table, as well as those who came to us from the surrounding nations. ¹⁸Each day one ox, six choice sheep and
some poultry were prepared for me, and every ten days an
abundant supply of wine of all kinds. In spite of all this, I
never demanded the food allotted to the governor, because
the demands were heavy on these people.

¹⁹Remember me with favor, my God, for all I have done
for these people.

FURTHER OPPOSITION TO THE REBUILDING

6 When word came to Sanballat, Tobiah, Geshem the
Arab and the rest of our enemies that I had rebuilt the
wall and not a gap was left in it — though up to that time I
had not set the doors in the gates — ²Sanballat and Geshem
sent me this message: "Come, let us meet together in one of
the villages*a* on the plain of Ono."

But they were scheming to harm me; ³so I sent messengers to them with this reply: "I am carrying on a great project and cannot go down. Why should the work stop while I
leave it and go down to you?" ⁴Four times they sent me the
same message, and each time I gave them the same answer.

⁵Then, the fifth time, Sanballat sent his aide to me with
the same message, and in his hand was an unsealed letter ⁶in
which was written:

> "It is reported among the nations — and Geshem*b*
> says it is true — that you and the Jews are plotting to re-
> volt, and therefore you are building the wall. Moreover,
> according to these reports you are about to become their
> king ⁷and have even appointed prophets to make this
> proclamation about you in Jerusalem: 'There is a king
> in Judah!' Now this report will get back to the king; so
> come, let us meet together."

⁸I sent him this reply: "Nothing like what you are saying
is happening; you are just making it up out of your head."

⁹They were all trying to frighten us, thinking, "Their
hands will get too weak for the work, and it will not be completed."

But I prayed, "Now strengthen my hands."

¹⁰One day I went to the house of Shemaiah son of Dela-
iah, the son of Mehetabel, who was shut in at his home. He
said, "Let us meet in the house of God, inside the temple,
and let us close the temple doors, because men are coming to
kill you — by night they are coming to kill you."

¹¹But I said, "Should a man like me run away? Or should
someone like me go into the temple to save his life? I will
not go!" ¹²I realized that God had not sent him, but that
he had prophesied against me because Tobiah and Sanballat
had hired him. ¹³He had been hired to intimidate me so that
I would commit a sin by doing this, and then they would give
me a bad name to discredit me.

¹⁴Remember Tobiah and Sanballat, my God, because of
what they have done; remember also the prophet Noadiah

Why was this letter unsealed? (6:5)
During this time, a letter was ordinarily written on a leather or papyrus sheet which was rolled up, tied with a string, and sealed with a clay seal. The seal had to be broken for the letter to be unrolled. A seal still intact ensured that the letter was delivered unread. An unsealed letter meant that Sanballat apparently wanted the contents of this letter to be made known to the public at large.

How would intimidation lead to sin? (6:13)
Shemaiah tried to get Nehemiah to enter the temple, though they both knew that only priests were allowed to enter. This would have been a sin, and it also would have been a sin to give in to threats rather than trusting in God.

---

a 2 Or *in Kephirim*   *b* 6 Hebrew *Gashmu,* a variant of *Geshem*

Why were the surrounding nations afraid? (6:15–16)
It was a miracle that a wall could be built that fast. People in neighboring nations recognized this as a sign that God had a special relationship with the Jews.

Why was Tobiah opposed to the Jews? (6:17–18)
Tobiah did not want the Jews to become powerful because that would have weakened his own power.

Why did Nehemiah wait to have the gates unlocked? (7:3)
Ordinarily the city gates would have been opened each day at dawn, but Nehemiah delayed opening the gates to prevent an enemy attack before the people of Jerusalem were fully awake and alert.

Why did God prompt Nehemiah to register all the people? (7:5)
Registering the people was a way for God to bring them together. Family clans were put in control instead of city heads, impurity in the priesthood was removed, and the people banded together to raise money.

and how she and the rest of the prophets have been trying to intimidate me. [15] So the wall was completed on the twenty-fifth of Elul, in fifty-two days.

OPPOSITION TO THE COMPLETED WALL

[16] When all our enemies heard about this, all the surrounding nations were afraid and lost their self-confidence, because they realized that this work had been done with the help of our God.

[17] Also, in those days the nobles of Judah were sending many letters to Tobiah, and replies from Tobiah kept coming to them. [18] For many in Judah were under oath to him, since he was son-in-law to Shekaniah son of Arah, and his son Jehohanan had married the daughter of Meshullam son of Berekiah. [19] Moreover, they kept reporting to me his good deeds and then telling him what I said. And Tobiah sent letters to intimidate me.

7 After the wall had been rebuilt and I had set the doors in place, the gatekeepers, the musicians and the Levites were appointed. [2] I put in charge of Jerusalem my brother Hanani, along with Hananiah the commander of the citadel, because he was a man of integrity and feared God more than most people do. [3] I said to them, "The gates of Jerusalem are not to be opened until the sun is hot. While the gatekeepers are still on duty, have them shut the doors and bar them. Also appoint residents of Jerusalem as guards, some at their posts and some near their own houses."

THE LIST OF THE EXILES WHO RETURNED

[4] Now the city was large and spacious, but there were few people in it, and the houses had not yet been rebuilt. [5] So my God put it into my heart to assemble the nobles, the officials and the common people for registration by families. I found the genealogical record of those who had been the first to return. This is what I found written there:

[6] These are the people of the province who came up from the captivity of the exiles whom Nebuchadnezzar king of Babylon had taken captive (they returned to Jerusalem and Judah, each to his own town, [7] in company with Zerubbabel, Joshua, Nehemiah, Azariah, Raamiah, Nahamani, Mordecai, Bilshan, Mispereth, Bigvai, Nehum and Baanah):

The list of the men of Israel:

[8] the descendants of Parosh	2,172
[9] of Shephatiah	372
[10] of Arah	652
[11] of Pahath-Moab (through the line of Jeshua and Joab)	2,818
[12] of Elam	1,254
[13] of Zattu	845
[14] of Zakkai	760
[15] of Binnui	648
[16] of Bebai	628

[17] of Azgad	2,322
[18] of Adonikam	667
[19] of Bigvai	2,067
[20] of Adin	655
[21] of Ater (through Hezekiah)	98
[22] of Hashum	328
[23] of Bezai	324
[24] of Hariph	112
[25] of Gibeon	95

[26] the men of Bethlehem and Netophah	188
[27] of Anathoth	128
[28] of Beth Azmaveth	42
[29] of Kiriath Jearim, Kephirah and Beeroth	743
[30] of Ramah and Geba	621
[31] of Mikmash	122
[32] of Bethel and Ai	123
[33] of the other Nebo	52
[34] of the other Elam	1,254
[35] of Harim	320
[36] of Jericho	345
[37] of Lod, Hadid and Ono	721
[38] of Senaah	3,930

[39] The priests:

the descendants of Jedaiah (through the family of Jeshua)	973
[40] of Immer	1,052
[41] of Pashhur	1,247
[42] of Harim	1,017

[43] The Levites:

the descendants of Jeshua (through Kadmiel through the line of Hodaviah)	74

[44] The musicians:

the descendants of Asaph	148

[45] The gatekeepers:

the descendants of Shallum, Ater, Talmon, Akkub, Hatita and Shobai	138

[46] The temple servants:

the descendants of
Ziha, Hasupha, Tabbaoth,
[47] Keros, Sia, Padon,
[48] Lebana, Hagaba, Shalmai,
[49] Hanan, Giddel, Gahar,
[50] Reaiah, Rezin, Nekoda,
[51] Gazzam, Uzza, Paseah,
[52] Besai, Meunim, Nephusim,
[53] Bakbuk, Hakupha, Harhur,
[54] Bazluth, Mehida, Harsha,
[55] Barkos, Sisera, Temah,
[56] Neziah and Hatipha

Who were temple servants and the servants of Solomon? (7:46–60)
Some scholars think that they were captive people who were forced into temple or palace service by Solomon. Others think that Solomon made slaves of the Canaanites.

⁵⁷The descendants of the servants of Solomon:

the descendants of
    Sotai, Sophereth, Perida,
⁵⁸Jaala, Darkon, Giddel,
⁵⁹Shephatiah, Hattil,
    Pokereth-Hazzebaim and Amon

⁶⁰The temple servants and the descendants
    of the servants of Solomon   392

⁶¹The following came up from the towns of Tel Melah, Tel Harsha, Kerub, Addon and Immer, but they could not show that their families were descended from Israel:

⁶²the descendants of
    Delaiah, Tobiah and Nekoda   642

⁶³And from among the priests:

the descendants of
    Hobaiah, Hakkoz and Barzillai (a man who had
    married a daughter of Barzillai the Gileadite and
    was called by that name).
⁶⁴These searched for their family records, but they could not find them and so were excluded from the priesthood as unclean. ⁶⁵The governor, therefore, ordered them not to eat any of the most sacred food until there should be a priest ministering with the Urim and Thummim.

⁶⁶The whole company numbered 42,360, ⁶⁷besides their 7,337 male and female slaves; and they also had 245 male and female singers. ⁶⁸There were 736 horses, 245 mules,ᵃ ⁶⁹435 camels and 6,720 donkeys.

⁷⁰Some of the heads of the families contributed to the work. The governor gave to the treasury 1,000 daricsᵇ of gold, 50 bowls and 530 garments for priests. ⁷¹Some of the heads of the families gave to the treasury for the work 20,000 daricsᶜ of gold and 2,200 minasᵈ of silver. ⁷²The total given by the rest of the people was 20,000 darics of gold, 2,000 minasᵉ of silver and 67 garments for priests.

⁷³The priests, the Levites, the gatekeepers, the musicians and the temple servants, along with certain of the people and the rest of the Israelites, settled in their own towns.

EZRA READS THE LAW

When the seventh month came and the Israelites had
8 settled in their towns, ¹all the people came together as
one in the square before the Water Gate. They told Ezra the teacher of the Law to bring out the Book of the Law of Moses, which the LORD had commanded for Israel.

Why were these priests disqualified? (7:64)
The requirements for serving as a priest were very strict in order to maintain the purity of the priesthood. Anyone who could not prove by family records that he was eligible for priesthood would be considered unclean, and any priest who attempted to serve while being unclean risked death.

ᵃ 68 Some Hebrew manuscripts (see also Ezra 2:66); most Hebrew manuscripts do not have this verse.   ᵇ 70 That is, about 19 pounds or about 8.4 kilograms   ᶜ 71 That is, about 375 pounds or about 170 kilograms; also in verse 72   ᵈ 71 That is, about 1 1/3 tons or about 1.2 metric tons
ᵉ 72 That is, about 1 1/4 tons or about 1.1 metric tons

²So on the first day of the seventh month Ezra the priest brought the Law before the assembly, which was made up of men and women and all who were able to understand. ³He read it aloud from daybreak till noon as he faced the square before the Water Gate in the presence of the men, women and others who could understand. And all the people listened attentively to the Book of the Law.

⁴Ezra the teacher of the Law stood on a high wooden platform built for the occasion. Beside him on his right stood Mattithiah, Shema, Anaiah, Uriah, Hilkiah and Maaseiah; and on his left were Pedaiah, Mishael, Malkijah, Hashum, Hashbaddanah, Zechariah and Meshullam.

⁵Ezra opened the book. All the people could see him because he was standing above them; and as he opened it, the people all stood up. ⁶Ezra praised the LORD, the great God; and all the people lifted their hands and responded, "Amen! Amen!" Then they bowed down and worshiped the LORD with their faces to the ground.

⁷The Levites—Jeshua, Bani, Sherebiah, Jamin, Akkub, Shabbethai, Hodiah, Maaseiah, Kelita, Azariah, Jozabad, Hanan and Pelaiah—instructed the people in the Law while the people were standing there. ⁸They read from the Book of the Law of God, making it clear*a* and giving the meaning so that the people understood what was being read.

⁹Then Nehemiah the governor, Ezra the priest and teacher of the Law, and the Levites who were instructing the people said to them all, "This day is holy to the LORD your God. Do not mourn or weep." For all the people had been weeping as they listened to the words of the Law.

¹⁰Nehemiah said, "Go and enjoy choice food and sweet drinks, and send some to those who have nothing prepared. This day is holy to our Lord. Do not grieve, for the joy of the LORD is your strength."

¹¹The Levites calmed all the people, saying, "Be still, for this is a holy day. Do not grieve."

¹²Then all the people went away to eat and drink, to send portions of food and to celebrate with great joy, because they now understood the words that had been made known to them.

¹³On the second day of the month, the heads of all the families, along with the priests and the Levites, gathered around Ezra the teacher to give attention to the words of the Law. ¹⁴They found written in the Law, which the LORD had commanded through Moses, that the Israelites were to live in temporary shelters during the festival of the seventh month ¹⁵and that they should proclaim this word and spread it throughout their towns and in Jerusalem: "Go out into the hill country and bring back branches from olive and wild olive trees, and from myrtles, palms and shade trees, to make temporary shelters"—as it is written.*b*

¹⁶So the people went out and brought back branches and built themselves temporary shelters on their own roofs, in their courtyards, in the courts of the house of God and in the square by the Water Gate and the one by the Gate of

Did Ezra read the entire Law of Moses? (8:2–3)
Ezra probably read the entire the Law, just not in one night. The festival lasted seven or eight days, which would have been enough time to read the entire Law, the first five books of the Bible.

Why were so many Levites needed to teach the people? (8:7–8)
The Levites may have translated the original Hebrew into Aramaic, which the people would have understood more easily, or Ezra read a section and then the Levites explained it. It is also possible that Ezra would read and then the Levites would repeat the Law together.

a 8 Or God, translating it   b 15 See Lev. 23:37-40.

Why had the Festival of Tabernacles not been celebrated
with such joy for many
years? (8:17)
The festival was a celebration of
God giving the Jews the promise land after wandering in the
desert for years. However, they
couldn't celebrate this festival
when they in captivity. Now the
celebration continued because
they were home.

What was the purpose of
this prayer? (9:5–38)
The Jews recited their people's
history as a reminder of how
their ancestors turned away
from God, and how God always
forgave them. They promised not
to make the same mistakes and
bound themselves to God.

Ephraim. [17] The whole company that had returned from exile built temporary shelters and lived in them. From the days
of Joshua son of Nun until that day, the Israelites had not
celebrated it like this. And their joy was very great.

[18] Day after day, from the first day to the last, Ezra read
from the Book of the Law of God. They celebrated the festival for seven days, and on the eighth day, in accordance with
the regulation, there was an assembly.

THE ISRAELITES CONFESS THEIR SINS

9 On the twenty-fourth day of the same month, the Israelites gathered together, fasting and wearing sackcloth
and putting dust on their heads. [2] Those of Israelite descent
had separated themselves from all foreigners. They stood in
their places and confessed their sins and the sins of their
ancestors. [3] They stood where they were and read from the
Book of the Law of the LORD their God for a quarter of the
day, and spent another quarter in confession and in worshiping the LORD their God. [4] Standing on the stairs of the
Levites were Jeshua, Bani, Kadmiel, Shebaniah, Bunni, Sherebiah, Bani and Kenani. They cried out with loud voices to
the LORD their God. [5] And the Levites—Jeshua, Kadmiel, Bani, Hashabneiah, Sherebiah, Hodiah, Shebaniah and
Pethahiah—said: "Stand up and praise the LORD your God,
who is from everlasting to everlasting.[a]"

"Blessed be your glorious name, and may it be exalted
above all blessing and praise. [6] You alone are the LORD.
You made the heavens, even the highest heavens, and all
their starry host, the earth and all that is on it, the seas
and all that is in them. You give life to everything, and
the multitudes of heaven worship you.

[7] "You are the LORD God, who chose Abram and
brought him out of Ur of the Chaldeans and named
him Abraham. [8] You found his heart faithful to you, and
you made a covenant with him to give to his descendants the land of the Canaanites, Hittites, Amorites,
Perizzites, Jebusites and Girgashites. You have kept your
promise because you are righteous.

[9] "You saw the suffering of our ancestors in Egypt;
you heard their cry at the Red Sea.[b] [10] You sent signs and
wonders against Pharaoh, against all his officials and all
the people of his land, for you knew how arrogantly the
Egyptians treated them. You made a name for yourself,
which remains to this day. [11] You divided the sea before
them, so that they passed through it on dry ground, but
you hurled their pursuers into the depths, like a stone
into mighty waters. [12] By day you led them with a pillar
of cloud, and by night with a pillar of fire to give them
light on the way they were to take.

[13] "You came down on Mount Sinai; you spoke to
them from heaven. You gave them regulations and laws
that are just and right, and decrees and commands that
are good. [14] You made known to them your holy Sabbath

---

[a] 5 Or God for ever and ever　　[b] 9 Or the Sea of Reeds

and gave them commands, decrees and laws through your servant Moses. [15] In their hunger you gave them bread from heaven and in their thirst you brought them water from the rock; you told them to go in and take possession of the land you had sworn with uplifted hand to give them.

[16] "But they, our ancestors, became arrogant and stiff-necked, and they did not obey your commands. [17] They refused to listen and failed to remember the miracles you performed among them. They became stiff-necked and in their rebellion appointed a leader in order to return to their slavery. But you are a forgiving God, gracious and compassionate, slow to anger and abounding in love. Therefore you did not desert them, [18] even when they cast for themselves an image of a calf and said, 'This is your god, who brought you up out of Egypt,' or when they committed awful blasphemies.

[19] "Because of your great compassion you did not abandon them in the wilderness. By day the pillar of cloud did not fail to guide them on their path, nor the pillar of fire by night to shine on the way they were to take. [20] You gave your good Spirit to instruct them. You did not withhold your manna from their mouths, and you gave them water for their thirst. [21] For forty years you sustained them in the wilderness; they lacked nothing, their clothes did not wear out nor did their feet become swollen.

[22] "You gave them kingdoms and nations, allotting to them even the remotest frontiers. They took over the country of Sihon[a] king of Heshbon and the country of Og king of Bashan. [23] You made their children as numerous as the stars in the sky, and you brought them into the land that you told their parents to enter and possess. [24] Their children went in and took possession of the land. You subdued before them the Canaanites, who lived in the land; you gave the Canaanites into their hands, along with their kings and the peoples of the land, to deal with them as they pleased. [25] They captured fortified cities and fertile land; they took possession of houses filled with all kinds of good things, wells already dug, vineyards, olive groves and fruit trees in abundance. They ate to the full and were well-nourished; they reveled in your great goodness.

[26] "But they were disobedient and rebelled against you; they turned their backs on your law. They killed your prophets, who had warned them in order to turn them back to you; they committed awful blasphemies. [27] So you delivered them into the hands of their enemies, who oppressed them. But when they were oppressed they cried out to you. From heaven you heard them, and in your great compassion you gave them deliverers, who rescued them from the hand of their enemies.

[28] "But as soon as they were at rest, they again did

Why was God described as swearing with an uplifted hand? (9:15)
Similar to today's practice of raising a hand and swearing an oath in court, God used this gesture to show that he vowed to keep his promise about the land (Exodus 6:8).

What did it mean to be stiff-necked? (9:16)
This expression was the way a farmer would describe an ox or a horse that would not respond or be led when its rope was tugged. Here it meant that the Israelites stubbornly refused to obey God and rebelled against him.

What were the pillar of cloud and the pillar of fire? (9:19)
When Israel left Egypt, God led them in the desert with a pillar of cloud and a pillar of fire (Exodus 13:21–22). When God wanted the people to move, the pillar would move, and when they were to remain in a place, the pillar would rest over the tabernacle.

Why did they take over existing cities? (9:25)
All the hard work of building homes and walls had been done. They didn't have to worry about water because wells were dug, and they had a food source because the trees there were already fruit bearing.

What did it mean that they turned their backs on God's law? (9:26)
This meant that they ignored it.

---

[a] 22 One Hebrew manuscript and Septuagint; most Hebrew manuscripts *Sihon, that is, the country of the*

what was evil in your sight. Then you abandoned them to the hand of their enemies so that they ruled over them. And when they cried out to you again, you heard from heaven, and in your compassion you delivered them time after time.

²⁹"You warned them in order to turn them back to your law, but they became arrogant and disobeyed your commands. They sinned against your ordinances, of which you said, 'The person who obeys them will live by them.' Stubbornly they turned their backs on you, became stiff-necked and refused to listen. ³⁰For many years you were patient with them. By your Spirit you warned them through your prophets. Yet they paid no attention, so you gave them into the hands of the neighboring peoples. ³¹But in your great mercy you did not put an end to them or abandon them, for you are a gracious and merciful God.

³²"Now therefore, our God, the great God, mighty and awesome, who keeps his covenant of love, do not let all this hardship seem trifling in your eyes—the hardship that has come on us, on our kings and leaders, on our priests and prophets, on our ancestors and all your people, from the days of the kings of Assyria until today. ³³In all that has happened to us, you have remained righteous; you have acted faithfully, while we acted wickedly. ³⁴Our kings, our leaders, our priests and our ancestors did not follow your law; they did not pay attention to your commands or the statutes you warned them to keep. ³⁵Even while they were in their kingdom, enjoying your great goodness to them in the spacious and fertile land you gave them, they did not serve you or turn from their evil ways.

³⁶"But see, we are slaves today, slaves in the land you gave our ancestors so they could eat its fruit and the other good things it produces. ³⁷Because of our sins, its abundant harvest goes to the kings you have placed over us. They rule over our bodies and our cattle as they please. We are in great distress.

THE AGREEMENT OF THE PEOPLE

³⁸"In view of all this, we are making a binding agreement, putting it in writing, and our leaders, our Levites and our priests are affixing their seals to it."*a*

10*b* Those who sealed it were:

Nehemiah the governor, the son of Hakaliah.

Zedekiah, ²Seraiah, Azariah, Jeremiah,
³Pashhur, Amariah, Malkijah,
⁴Hattush, Shebaniah, Malluk,
⁵Harim, Meremoth, Obadiah,
⁶Daniel, Ginnethon, Baruch,
⁷Meshullam, Abijah, Mijamin,

What was this binding agreement? (9:38)
The people agreed to follow the Law of God given through Moses (10:28 – 39).

---

a 38 In Hebrew texts this verse (9:38) is numbered 10:1.   *b* In Hebrew texts 10:1-39 is numbered 10:2-40.

⁸Maaziah, Bilgai and Shemaiah.

These were the priests.

⁹The Levites:

Jeshua son of Azaniah, Binnui of the sons of Henadad, Kadmiel,

¹⁰and their associates: Shebaniah,

Hodiah, Kelita, Pelaiah, Hanan,

¹¹Mika, Rehob, Hashabiah,

¹²Zakkur, Sherebiah, Shebaniah,

¹³Hodiah, Bani and Beninu.

¹⁴The leaders of the people:

Parosh, Pahath-Moab, Elam, Zattu, Bani,

¹⁵Bunni, Azgad, Bebai,

¹⁶Adonijah, Bigvai, Adin,

¹⁷Ater, Hezekiah, Azzur,

¹⁸Hodiah, Hashum, Bezai,

¹⁹Hariph, Anathoth, Nebai,

²⁰Magpiash, Meshullam, Hezir,

²¹Meshezabel, Zadok, Jaddua,

²²Pelatiah, Hanan, Anaiah,

²³Hoshea, Hananiah, Hasshub,

²⁴Hallohesh, Pilha, Shobek,

²⁵Rehum, Hashabnah, Maaseiah,

²⁶Ahiah, Hanan, Anan,

²⁷Malluk, Harim and Baanah.

²⁸"The rest of the people—priests, Levites, gatekeepers, musicians, temple servants and all who separated themselves from the neighboring peoples for the sake of the Law of God, together with their wives and all their sons and daughters who are able to understand— ²⁹all these now join their fellow Israelites the nobles, and bind themselves with a curse and an oath to follow the Law of God given through Moses the servant of God and to obey carefully all the commands, regulations and decrees of the LORD our Lord.

³⁰"We promise not to give our daughters in marriage to the peoples around us or take their daughters for our sons.

³¹"When the neighboring peoples bring merchandise or grain to sell on the Sabbath, we will not buy from them on the Sabbath or on any holy day. Every seventh year we will forgo working the land and will cancel all debts.

³²"We assume the responsibility for carrying out the commands to give a third of a shekel*ᵃ* each year for the service of the house of our God: ³³for the bread set out on the table; for the regular grain offerings and burnt offerings; for the offerings on the Sabbaths, at the New Moon feasts and at the appointed festivals; for the holy offerings; for sin offerings*ᵇ* to make atonement for Israel; and for all the duties of the house of our God.

What did it mean to bind themselves with a curse and an oath? (10:29)
The curse was meant to be a punishment if they failed to keep their promise to God.

What was the New Moon feast? (10:33)
The New Moon was both a religious and civil festival. It was celebrated at the beginning of each month. Special sacrifices were offered, trumpets were sounded, and normal work activities were stopped.

ᵃ 32 That is, about 1/8 ounce or about 4 grams　　*ᵇ 33 Or purification offerings*

What did it mean to cast lots? (10:34)
This was a way to reach decisions. The Israelites believed that God controlled the outcome. No one knows exactly how lots were cast, but it's probable that marked sticks or pebbles were drawn from a container.

Why would they need to bring wood to the temple? (10:34)
Fire was burned continuously on the altar, so there would need to be a constant supply of wood.

Why did they bring their firstborn to the priests? (10:36)
This helped the people remember that everything belonged to God. This law reminded them of the Passover and how God killed the Egyptian's firstborn sons but spared Israel's sons (Exodus 13:14–16). People brought the firstborn animals to sacrifice in place of their firstborn sons.

Why did they have to select people to live in Jerusalem? (11:1–2)
Most of the people probably wanted to stay in their hometowns. But the leaders wanted to make sure that Jerusalem would be populated again, so they selected people to settle there by casting lots.

How many people ended up settling in Jerusalem? (11:4–18)
A total of 3,044 men are mentioned in these verses, so the total population was probably about 5,000 to 8,000.

³⁴ "We—the priests, the Levites and the people—have cast lots to determine when each of our families is to bring to the house of our God at set times each year a contribution of wood to burn on the altar of the LORD our God, as it is written in the Law.

³⁵ "We also assume responsibility for bringing to the house of the LORD each year the firstfruits of our crops and of every fruit tree.

³⁶ "As it is also written in the Law, we will bring the firstborn of our sons and of our cattle, of our herds and of our flocks to the house of our God, to the priests ministering there.

³⁷ "Moreover, we will bring to the storerooms of the house of our God, to the priests, the first of our ground meal, of our grain offerings, of the fruit of all our trees and of our new wine and olive oil. And we will bring a tithe of our crops to the Levites, for it is the Levites who collect the tithes in all the towns where we work. ³⁸ A priest descended from Aaron is to accompany the Levites when they receive the tithes, and the Levites are to bring a tenth of the tithes up to the house of our God, to the storerooms of the treasury. ³⁹ The people of Israel, including the Levites, are to bring their contributions of grain, new wine and olive oil to the storerooms, where the articles for the sanctuary and for the ministering priests, the gatekeepers and the musicians are also kept.

"We will not neglect the house of our God."

THE NEW RESIDENTS OF JERUSALEM

11 Now the leaders of the people settled in Jerusalem. The rest of the people cast lots to bring one out of every ten of them to live in Jerusalem, the holy city, while the remaining nine were to stay in their own towns. ²The people commended all who volunteered to live in Jerusalem.

³These are the provincial leaders who settled in Jerusalem (now some Israelites, priests, Levites, temple servants and descendants of Solomon's servants lived in the towns of Judah, each on their own property in the various towns, ⁴while other people from both Judah and Benjamin lived in Jerusalem):

From the descendants of Judah:

Athaiah son of Uzziah, the son of Zechariah, the son of Amariah, the son of Shephatiah, the son of Mahalalel, a descendant of Perez; ⁵and Maaseiah son of Baruch, the son of Kol-Hozeh, the son of Hazaiah, the son of Adaiah, the son of Joiarib, the son of Zechariah, a descendant of Shelah. ⁶The descendants of Perez who lived in Jerusalem totaled 468 men of standing.

⁷From the descendants of Benjamin:

Sallu son of Meshullam, the son of Joed, the son of Pedaiah, the son of Kolaiah, the son of Maaseiah, the son of Ithiel, the son of Jeshaiah, ⁸and his followers, Gabbai and Sallai—928 men. ⁹Joel son of Zikri was their chief officer, and Judah son of Hassenuah was over the New Quarter of the city.

¹⁰From the priests:

Jedaiah; the son of Joiarib; Jakin; ¹¹Seraiah son of Hilkiah, the son of Meshullam, the son of Zadok, the son of Meraioth, the son of Ahitub, the official in charge of the house of God, ¹²and their associates, who carried on work for the temple—822 men; Adaiah son of Jeroham, the son of Pelaliah, the son of Amzi, the son of Zechariah, the son of Pashhur, the son of Malkijah, ¹³and his associates, who were heads of families—242 men; Amashsai son of Azarel, the son of Ahzai, the son of Meshillemoth, the son of Immer, ¹⁴and his*a* associates, who were men of standing—128. Their chief officer was Zabdiel son of Haggedolim.

¹⁵From the Levites:

Shemaiah son of Hasshub, the son of Azrikam, the son of Hashabiah, the son of Bunni; ¹⁶Shabbethai and Jozabad, two of the heads of the Levites, who had charge of the outside work of the house of God; ¹⁷Mattaniah son of Mika, the son of Zabdi, the son of Asaph, the director who led in thanksgiving and prayer; Bakbukiah, second among his associates; and Abda son of Shammua, the son of Galal, the son of Jeduthun. ¹⁸The Levites in the holy city totaled 284.

¹⁹The gatekeepers:

Akkub, Talmon and their associates, who kept watch at the gates—172 men.

²⁰The rest of the Israelites, with the priests and Levites, were in all the towns of Judah, each on their ancestral property. ²¹The temple servants lived on the hill of Ophel, and Ziha and Gishpa were in charge of them.

²²The chief officer of the Levites in Jerusalem was Uzzi son of Bani, the son of Hashabiah, the son of Mattaniah, the son of Mika. Uzzi was one of Asaph's descendants, who were the musicians responsible for the service of the house of God. ²³The musicians were under the king's orders, which regulated their daily activity.

²⁴Pethahiah son of Meshezabel, one of the descendants of Zerah son of Judah, was the king's agent in all affairs relating to the people.

²⁵As for the villages with their fields, some of the people of Judah lived in Kiriath Arba and its surrounding settlements, in Dibon and its settlements, in Jekabzeel and its villages, ²⁶in Jeshua, in Moladah, in Beth Pelet, ²⁷in Hazar Shual, in Beersheba and its settlements, ²⁸in Ziklag, in Mekonah and its settlements, ²⁹in En Rimmon, in Zorah, in Jarmuth, ³⁰Zanoah, Adullam and their villages, in Lachish and its fields, and in Azekah and its settlements. So they were living all the way from Beersheba to the Valley of Hinnom.

³¹The descendants of the Benjamites from Geba lived in Mikmash, Aija, Bethel and its settlements, ³²in Anathoth, Nob and Ananiah, ³³in Hazor, Ramah and Gittaim, ³⁴in

What was this ancestral property? (11:20)
This was the family land that was passed down from one generation to the next.

Why did the king of Persia regulate the musicians? (11:23)
The king allowed his subjects to follow their own religious practices as a way of keeping peace in the kingdom. He may even have provided funds to support local forms of worship.

---

a 14 Most Septuagint manuscripts; Hebrew *their*

Hadid, Zeboim and Neballat, [35] in Lod and Ono, and in Ge Harashim.

[36] Some of the divisions of the Levites of Judah settled in Benjamin.

PRIESTS AND LEVITES

12 These were the priests and Levites who returned with Zerubbabel son of Shealtiel and with Joshua:
Seraiah, Jeremiah, Ezra,
[2] Amariah, Malluk, Hattush,
[3] Shekaniah, Rehum, Meremoth,
[4] Iddo, Ginnethon,[a] Abijah,
[5] Mijamin,[b] Moadiah, Bilgah,
[6] Shemaiah, Joiarib, Jedaiah,
[7] Sallu, Amok, Hilkiah and Jedaiah.
These were the leaders of the priests and their associates in the days of Joshua.

[8] The Levites were Jeshua, Binnui, Kadmiel, Sherebiah, Judah, and also Mattaniah, who, together with his associates, was in charge of the songs of thanksgiving. [9] Bakbukiah and Unni, their associates, stood opposite them in the services.

[10] Joshua was the father of Joiakim, Joiakim the father of Eliashib, Eliashib the father of Joiada, [11] Joiada the father of Jonathan, and Jonathan the father of Jaddua.

[12] In the days of Joiakim, these were the heads of the priestly families:
of Seraiah's family, Meraiah;
of Jeremiah's, Hananiah;
[13] of Ezra's, Meshullam;
of Amariah's, Jehohanan;
[14] of Malluk's, Jonathan;
of Shekaniah's,[c] Joseph;
[15] of Harim's, Adna;
of Meremoth's,[d] Helkai;
[16] of Iddo's, Zechariah;
of Ginnethon's, Meshullam;
[17] of Abijah's, Zikri;
of Miniamin's and of Moadiah's, Piltai;
[18] of Bilgah's, Shammua;
of Shemaiah's, Jehonathan;
[19] of Joiarib's, Mattenai;
of Jedaiah's, Uzzi;
[20] of Sallu's, Kallai;
of Amok's, Eber;
[21] of Hilkiah's, Hashabiah;
of Jedaiah's, Nethanel.

[22] The family heads of the Levites in the days of Eliashib, Joiada, Johanan and Jaddua, as well as those of the priests, were recorded in the reign of Darius the Persian. [23] The family heads among the descendants of Levi up to the time of Johanan son of Eliashib were recorded in the book of the annals.

Why were these names listed? (12:1)
Nehemiah hoped to lead the people to follow the LORD. The priests and Levites were Israel's direct link to God, and Nehemiah wanted the people to remember that these men were available to teach them about God.

How were the choirs arranged? (12:8–9)
The two groups stood opposite each other. The singing was antiphonal, meaning that one group would sing a line and the other group would answer with the next line.

a 4 Many Hebrew manuscripts and Vulgate (see also verse 16); most Hebrew manuscripts *Ginnethoi*　*b 5* A variant of *Miniamin*　*c 14* Very many Hebrew manuscripts, some Septuagint manuscripts and Syriac (see also verse 3); most Hebrew manuscripts *Shebaniah's*　*d 15* Some Septuagint manuscripts (see also verse 3); Hebrew *Meraioth's*

²⁴And the leaders of the Levites were Hashabiah, Sherebiah, Jeshua son of Kadmiel, and their associates, who stood opposite them to give praise and thanksgiving, one section responding to the other, as prescribed by David the man of God. ²⁵Mattaniah, Bakbukiah, Obadiah, Meshullam, Talmon and Akkub were gatekeepers who guarded the storerooms at the gates. ²⁶They served in the days of Joiakim son of Jeshua, the son of Jozadak, and in the days of Nehemiah the governor and of Ezra the priest, the teacher of the Law.

DEDICATION OF THE WALL OF JERUSALEM

²⁷At the dedication of the wall of Jerusalem, the Levites were sought out from where they lived and were brought to Jerusalem to celebrate joyfully the dedication with songs of thanksgiving and with the music of cymbals, harps and lyres. ²⁸The musicians also were brought together from the region around Jerusalem—from the villages of the Netophathites, ²⁹from Beth Gilgal, and from the area of Geba and Azmaveth, for the musicians had built villages for themselves around Jerusalem. ³⁰When the priests and Levites had purified themselves ceremonially, they purified the people, the gates and the wall.

³¹I had the leaders of Judah go up on top of*ᵃ* the wall. I also assigned two large choirs to give thanks. One was to proceed on top of*ᵇ* the wall to the right, toward the Dung Gate. ³²Hoshaiah and half the leaders of Judah followed them, ³³along with Azariah, Ezra, Meshullam, ³⁴Judah, Benjamin, Shemaiah, Jeremiah, ³⁵as well as some priests with trumpets, and also Zechariah son of Jonathan, the son of Shemaiah, the son of Mattaniah, the son of Micaiah, the son of Zakkur, the son of Asaph, ³⁶and his associates—Shemaiah, Azarel, Milalai, Gilalai, Maai, Nethanel, Judah and Hanani—with musical instruments prescribed by David the man of God. Ezra the teacher of the Law led the procession. ³⁷At the Fountain Gate they continued directly up the steps of the City of David on the ascent to the wall and passed above the site of David's palace to the Water Gate on the east.

³⁸The second choir proceeded in the opposite direction. I followed them on top of*ᶜ* the wall, together with half the people—past the Tower of the Ovens to the Broad Wall, ³⁹over the Gate of Ephraim, the Jeshanah*ᵈ* Gate, the Fish Gate, the Tower of Hananel and the Tower of the Hundred, as far as the Sheep Gate. At the Gate of the Guard they stopped.

⁴⁰The two choirs that gave thanks then took their places in the house of God; so did I, together with half the officials, ⁴¹as well as the priests—Eliakim, Maaseiah, Miniamin, Micaiah, Elioenai, Zechariah and Hananiah with their trumpets— ⁴²and also Maaseiah, Shemaiah, Eleazar, Uzzi, Jehohanan, Malkijah, Elam and Ezer. The choirs sang under the direction of Jezrahiah. ⁴³And on that day they offered great sacrifices, rejoicing because God had given them great joy. The women and children also rejoiced. The sound of rejoicing in Jerusalem could be heard far away.

⁴⁴At that time men were appointed to be in charge of the storerooms for the contributions, firstfruits and tithes.

Why did the singers settle together in villages? (12:29) The singers worked at the temple in Jerusalem, so they would have wanted to live nearby. In addition, they were members of the tribe of Levi, and members of a tribe lived in the same community.

How did the priests and Levites purify themselves? (12:30) Purification rites usually included cleansing the body through fasting, refraining from sex, and washing clothes. It also included spiritual purification which would require the person to examine their conscience, repent of their sins, and then recommit themselves to God.

ᵃ 31 Or *go alongside*   *ᵇ 31* Or *proceed alongside*   *ᶜ 38* Or *them alongside*
ᵈ 39 Or *Old*

From the fields around the towns they were to bring into the storerooms the portions required by the Law for the priests and the Levites, for Judah was pleased with the ministering priests and Levites. [45] They performed the service of their God and the service of purification, as did also the musicians and gatekeepers, according to the commands of David and his son Solomon. [46] For long ago, in the days of David and Asaph, there had been directors for the musicians and for the songs of praise and thanksgiving to God. [47] So in the days of Zerubbabel and of Nehemiah, all Israel contributed the daily portions for the musicians and the gatekeepers. They also set aside the portion for the other Levites, and the Levites set aside the portion for the descendants of Aaron.

NEHEMIAH'S FINAL REFORMS

13 On that day the Book of Moses was read aloud in the hearing of the people and there it was found written that no Ammonite or Moabite should ever be admitted into the assembly of God, [2] because they had not met the Israelites with food and water but had hired Balaam to call a curse down on them. (Our God, however, turned the curse into a blessing.) [3] When the people heard this law, they excluded from Israel all who were of foreign descent.

[4] Before this, Eliashib the priest had been put in charge of the storerooms of the house of our God. He was closely associated with Tobiah, [5] and he had provided him with a large room formerly used to store the grain offerings and incense and temple articles, and also the tithes of grain, new wine and olive oil prescribed for the Levites, musicians and gatekeepers, as well as the contributions for the priests.

[6] But while all this was going on, I was not in Jerusalem, for in the thirty-second year of Artaxerxes king of Babylon I had returned to the king. Some time later I asked his permission [7] and came back to Jerusalem. Here I learned about the evil thing Eliashib had done in providing Tobiah a room in the courts of the house of God. [8] I was greatly displeased and threw all Tobiah's household goods out of the room. [9] I gave orders to purify the rooms, and then I put back into them the equipment of the house of God, with the grain offerings and the incense.

[10] I also learned that the portions assigned to the Levites had not been given to them, and that all the Levites and musicians responsible for the service had gone back to their own fields. [11] So I rebuked the officials and asked them, "Why is the house of God neglected?" Then I called them together and stationed them at their posts.

[12] All Judah brought the tithes of grain, new wine and olive oil into the storerooms. [13] I put Shelemiah the priest, Zadok the scribe, and a Levite named Pedaiah in charge of the storerooms and made Hanan son of Zakkur, the son of Mattaniah, their assistant, because they were considered trustworthy. They were made responsible for distributing the supplies to their fellow Levites.

[14] Remember me for this, my God, and do not blot out what I have so faithfully done for the house of my God and its services.

Why was it wrong to give Tobiah a room in the temple courts? (13:7)
Tobiah had been against rebuilding the walls of Jerusalem. In addition, he was not a priest or Levite in temple service, so he was not supposed to live in the temple.

Why did the people stop caring for the temple? (13:10–11)
The people apparently forgot their promise to take care of the temple (10:32–39). Instead they spent their time improving the lifestyles. No one forced the people to keep their promise when Nehemiah was gone.

Why did Nehemiah ask God to remember him? (13:14, 22)
Nehemiah humbly asked God to show him mercy, reminding God of the way he had faithfully served him.

¹⁵ In those days I saw people in Judah treading winepresses on the Sabbath and bringing in grain and loading it on donkeys, together with wine, grapes, figs and all other kinds of loads. And they were bringing all this into Jerusalem on the Sabbath. Therefore I warned them against selling food on that day. ¹⁶ People from Tyre who lived in Jerusalem were bringing in fish and all kinds of merchandise and selling them in Jerusalem on the Sabbath to the people of Judah. ¹⁷ I rebuked the nobles of Judah and said to them, "What is this wicked thing you are doing—desecrating the Sabbath day? ¹⁸ Didn't your ancestors do the same things, so that our God brought all this calamity on us and on this city? Now you are stirring up more wrath against Israel by desecrating the Sabbath."

¹⁹ When evening shadows fell on the gates of Jerusalem before the Sabbath, I ordered the doors to be shut and not opened until the Sabbath was over. I stationed some of my own men at the gates so that no load could be brought in on the Sabbath day. ²⁰ Once or twice the merchants and sellers of all kinds of goods spent the night outside Jerusalem. ²¹ But I warned them and said, "Why do you spend the night by the wall? If you do this again, I will arrest you." From that time on they no longer came on the Sabbath. ²² Then I commanded the Levites to purify themselves and go and guard the gates in order to keep the Sabbath day holy.

Remember me for this also, my God, and show mercy to me according to your great love.

²³ Moreover, in those days I saw men of Judah who had married women from Ashdod, Ammon and Moab. ²⁴ Half of their children spoke the language of Ashdod or the language of one of the other peoples, and did not know how to speak the language of Judah. ²⁵ I rebuked them and called curses down on them. I beat some of the men and pulled out their hair. I made them take an oath in God's name and said: "You are not to give your daughters in marriage to their sons, nor are you to take their daughters in marriage for your sons or for yourselves. ²⁶ Was it not because of marriages like these that Solomon king of Israel sinned? Among the many nations there was no king like him. He was loved by his God, and God made him king over all Israel, but even he was led into sin by foreign women. ²⁷ Must we hear now that you too are doing all this terrible wickedness and are being unfaithful to our God by marrying foreign women?"

²⁸ One of the sons of Joiada son of Eliashib the high priest was son-in-law to Sanballat the Horonite. And I drove him away from me.

²⁹ Remember them, my God, because they defiled the priestly office and the covenant of the priesthood and of the Levites.

³⁰ So I purified the priests and the Levites of everything foreign, and assigned them duties, each to his own task. ³¹ I also made provision for contributions of wood at designated times, and for the firstfruits.

Remember me with favor, my God.

How did foreign women cause Solomon to sin? (13:26)
Solomon married many foreign women who led him to worship foreign gods when they asked him to build altars and idols so they could worship their pagan gods.

Why did Nehemiah drive away the high priest's grandson? (13:28)
Jews were not allowed to marry outsiders, especially priests who were supposed to be the leaders of the spiritual community. This man was removed because he could eventually inherit his father's position as high priest.

Esther

INTRODUCTION

Who wrote this book?
The author of this book is unknown.

Why was this book written?
The book of Esther reveals how God takes care of his people.

What happens in this book?
A Jewish girl, Esther, becomes queen of Persia. An evil man named Haman plots to kill all Jews everywhere. Esther saves her people.

What do we learn about God in this book?
God does not need to do miracles to rescue his people. He is able to work through ordinary events and ordinary people.

Who are the key people in this book?
The most important people in this book are King Xerxes, Haman, Esther, and Mordecai.

Where did this happen?
These events happened in Persia's capital, Susa, a royal city built by the king.

What are some of the stories in this book?

Xerxes divorces Vashti	Esther 1
Esther becomes queen	Esther 2
Haman's plot	Esther 3
Esther's courage	Esther 4 – 5
Xerxes honors Mordecai	Esther 6
Haman is hanged	Esther 7
The Jews are saved	Esther 8 – 9

When did these things happen?
1400 BC 1300 1200 1100 1000 900 800 700 600 500 400

FALL OF JERUSALEM (586 BC)

PERSIA'S CONQUEST OF BABYLON (539 BC)

FIRST RETURN OF EXILES TO JERUSALEM (538 BC)

XERXES' REIGN IN PERSIA (486 – 465 BC)

ESTHER BECOMES QUEEN OF PERSIA (479 BC)

SECOND RETURN TO JERUSALEM UNDER EZRA (458 BC)

THIRD RETURN TO JERUSALEM UNDER NEHEMIAH (444 BC)

JERUSALEM'S WALL REBUILT (444 BC)

BOOK OF ESTHER WRITTEN (C. 460 – 350 BC)

QUEEN VASHTI DEPOSED

1 This is what happened during the time of Xerxes,[a] the Xerxes who ruled over 127 provinces stretching from India to Cush[b]: ²At that time King Xerxes reigned from his royal throne in the citadel of Susa, ³and in the third year of his reign he gave a banquet for all his nobles and officials. The military leaders of Persia and Media, the princes, and the nobles of the provinces were present.

⁴For a full 180 days he displayed the vast wealth of his kingdom and the splendor and glory of his majesty. ⁵When these days were over, the king gave a banquet, lasting seven days, in the enclosed garden of the king's palace, for all the people from the least to the greatest who were in the citadel of Susa. ⁶The garden had hangings of white and blue linen, fastened with cords of white linen and purple material to silver rings on marble pillars. There were couches of gold and silver on a mosaic pavement of porphyry, marble, mother-of-pearl and other costly stones. ⁷Wine was served in goblets of gold, each one different from the other, and the royal wine was abundant, in keeping with the king's liberality. ⁸By the king's command each guest was allowed to drink with no restrictions, for the king instructed all the wine stewards to serve each man what he wished.

⁹Queen Vashti also gave a banquet for the women in the royal palace of King Xerxes.

¹⁰On the seventh day, when King Xerxes was in high spirits from wine, he commanded the seven eunuchs who served him—Mehuman, Biztha, Harbona, Bigtha, Abagtha, Zethar and Karkas— ¹¹to bring before him Queen Vashti, wearing her royal crown, in order to display her beauty to the people and nobles, for she was lovely to look at. ¹²But when the attendants delivered the king's command, Queen Vashti refused to come. Then the king became furious and burned with anger.

¹³Since it was customary for the king to consult experts in matters of law and justice, he spoke with the wise men who understood the times ¹⁴and were closest to the king—Karshena, Shethar, Admatha, Tarshish, Meres, Marsena and Memukan, the seven nobles of Persia and Media who had special access to the king and were highest in the kingdom.

¹⁵"According to law, what must be done to Queen Vashti?" he asked. "She has not obeyed the command of King Xerxes that the eunuchs have taken to her."

¹⁶Then Memukan replied in the presence of the king and the nobles, "Queen Vashti has done wrong, not only against the king but also against all the nobles and the peoples of all the provinces of King Xerxes. ¹⁷For the queen's conduct will become known to all the women, and so they will despise their husbands and say, 'King Xerxes commanded Queen Vashti to be brought before him, but she would not come.' ¹⁸This very day the Persian and Median women of the nobility who have heard about the queen's conduct will respond to all the king's nobles in the same way. There will be no end of disrespect and discord.

---

[a] *1* Hebrew *Ahasuerus*; here and throughout Esther   [b] *1* That is, the upper Nile region

---

Who was Xerxes? (1:1)
Xerxes was the son of Darius and ruler of the Persian Empire from 485 to 465 B.C.

Setting of Esther (1:1)

What kind of display would last 180 days? (1:4–5)
The 180 days were used as a time for Xerxes to show off the wealth gained during the revolts in Egypt and Babylon. The six months also served as a time for Xerxes and his men to celebrate their victory and to start planning their next campaign. The final seven days marked the end of the celebration.

What did it mean that each guest could drink with no restrictions? (1:8)
Instead of only drinking when the king drank, as Persian law usually dictated, Xerxes threw away this rule and let his guests drink as much as they wanted, when they wanted.

Why was there a separate banquet for women? (1:9)
That was probably not the usual custom in Persia, but perhaps because of all the drinking, the king's banquet would be considered too vulgar for women to attend.

Why did Queen Vashti refuse the king's order to come to the banquet? (1:12)
The Bible doesn't explain her refusal. Some historians believe the king wanted her to appear wearing nothing but her crown. After Vashti refused to appear, the king banished her from his sight.

¹⁹"Therefore, if it pleases the king, let him issue a royal decree and let it be written in the laws of Persia and Media, which cannot be repealed, that Vashti is never again to enter the presence of King Xerxes. Also let the king give her royal position to someone else who is better than she. ²⁰Then when the king's edict is proclaimed throughout all his vast realm, all the women will respect their husbands, from the least to the greatest."

²¹The king and his nobles were pleased with this advice, so the king did as Memukan proposed. ²²He sent dispatches to all parts of the kingdom, to each province in its own script and to each people in their own language, proclaiming that every man should be ruler over his own household, using his native tongue.

ESTHER MADE QUEEN

2 Later when King Xerxes' fury had subsided, he remembered Vashti and what she had done and what he had decreed about her. ²Then the king's personal attendants proposed, "Let a search be made for beautiful young virgins for the king. ³Let the king appoint commissioners in every province of his realm to bring all these beautiful young women into the harem at the citadel of Susa. Let them be placed under the care of Hegai, the king's eunuch, who is in charge of the women; and let beauty treatments be given to them. ⁴Then let the young woman who pleases the king be queen instead of Vashti." This advice appealed to the king, and he followed it.

⁵Now there was in the citadel of Susa a Jew of the tribe of Benjamin, named Mordecai son of Jair, the son of Shimei, the son of Kish, ⁶who had been carried into exile from Jerusalem by Nebuchadnezzar king of Babylon, among those taken captive with Jehoiachin*ᵃ* king of Judah. ⁷Mordecai had a cousin named Hadassah, whom he had brought up because she had neither father nor mother. This young woman, who was also known as Esther, had a lovely figure and was beautiful. Mordecai had taken her as his own daughter when her father and mother died.

⁸When the king's order and edict had been proclaimed, many young women were brought to the citadel of Susa and put under the care of Hegai. Esther also was taken to the king's palace and entrusted to Hegai, who had charge of the harem. ⁹She pleased him and won his favor. Immediately he provided her with her beauty treatments and special food. He assigned to her seven female attendants selected from the king's palace and moved her and her attendants into the best place in the harem.

¹⁰Esther had not revealed her nationality and family background, because Mordecai had forbidden her to do so. ¹¹Every day he walked back and forth near the courtyard of the harem to find out how Esther was and what was happening to her.

¹²Before a young woman's turn came to go in to King Xerxes, she had to complete twelve months of beauty treatments

---

ᵃ 6 Hebrew *Jeconiah,* a variant of *Jehoiachin*

Why did Esther have two names? (2:7)
In order to keep her nationality a secret, Esther was called by her Persian name throughout most of the story. Hadassah was her Hebrew name.

Did the girls who were selected for the harem have any choice in the matter? (2:8)
Probably not. The king ordered beautiful young women to be brought to him, and in this culture, women had little power to refuse him.

Why did Mordecai tell Esther not to reveal her nationality? (2:10)
Many members of the king's court disliked Jews, so Mordecai wanted to protect Esther from any mistreatment.

prescribed for the women, six months with oil of myrrh and six with perfumes and cosmetics. ¹³And this is how she would go to the king: Anything she wanted was given her to take with her from the harem to the king's palace. ¹⁴In the evening she would go there and in the morning return to another part of the harem to the care of Shaashgaz, the king's eunuch who was in charge of the concubines. She would not return to the king unless he was pleased with her and summoned her by name.

¹⁵When the turn came for Esther (the young woman Mordecai had adopted, the daughter of his uncle Abihail) to go to the king, she asked for nothing other than what Hegai, the king's eunuch who was in charge of the harem, suggested. And Esther won the favor of everyone who saw her. ¹⁶She was taken to King Xerxes in the royal residence in the tenth month, the month of Tebeth, in the seventh year of his reign.

¹⁷Now the king was attracted to Esther more than to any of the other women, and she won his favor and approval more than any of the other virgins. So he set a royal crown on her head and made her queen instead of Vashti. ¹⁸And the king gave a great banquet, Esther's banquet, for all his nobles and officials. He proclaimed a holiday throughout the provinces and distributed gifts with royal liberality.

MORDECAI UNCOVERS A CONSPIRACY

¹⁹When the virgins were assembled a second time, Mordecai was sitting at the king's gate. ²⁰But Esther had kept secret her family background and nationality just as Mordecai had told her to do, for she continued to follow Mordecai's instructions as she had done when he was bringing her up.

²¹During the time Mordecai was sitting at the king's gate, Bigthana[a] and Teresh, two of the king's officers who guarded the doorway, became angry and conspired to assassinate King Xerxes. ²²But Mordecai found out about the plot and told Queen Esther, who in turn reported it to the king, giving credit to Mordecai. ²³And when the report was investigated and found to be true, the two officials were impaled on poles. All this was recorded in the book of the annals in the presence of the king.

HAMAN'S PLOT TO DESTROY THE JEWS

3 After these events, King Xerxes honored Haman son of Hammedatha, the Agagite, elevating him and giving him a seat of honor higher than that of all the other nobles. ²All the royal officials at the king's gate knelt down and paid honor to Haman, for the king had commanded this concerning him. But Mordecai would not kneel down or pay him honor.

³Then the royal officials at the king's gate asked Mordecai, "Why do you disobey the king's command?" ⁴Day after day they spoke to him but he refused to comply. Therefore they told Haman about it to see whether Mordecai's behavior would be tolerated, for he had told them he was a Jew.

[a] *21 Hebrew Bigthan, a variant of Bigthana*

Why did no one check Esther's background before she became queen? (2:17) The king, his eunuch, and many other officials in his court were so impressed with Esther and her beauty that it's likely no one thought it necessary.

Why did Mordecai sit at the king's gate? (2:19) Mordecai became one of the king's officials. As part of his job, Mordecai sat at the gates because this was the place where many legal and business transactions took place.

Why did Mordecai disobey the king's command? (3:2–5) Haman was a wicked man who wanted to kill all of the Jews in the city. Mordecai realized this, and therefore refused to honor Haman.

⁵When Haman saw that Mordecai would not kneel down or pay him honor, he was enraged. ⁶Yet having learned who Mordecai's people were, he scorned the idea of killing only Mordecai. Instead Haman looked for a way to destroy all Mordecai's people, the Jews, throughout the whole kingdom of Xerxes.

⁷In the twelfth year of King Xerxes, in the first month, the month of Nisan, the *pur* (that is, the lot) was cast in the presence of Haman to select a day and month. And the lot fell on*a* the twelfth month, the month of Adar.

⁸Then Haman said to King Xerxes, "There is a certain people dispersed among the peoples in all the provinces of your kingdom who keep themselves separate. Their customs are different from those of all other people, and they do not obey the king's laws; it is not in the king's best interest to tolerate them. ⁹If it pleases the king, let a decree be issued to destroy them, and I will give ten thousand talents*b* of silver to the king's administrators for the royal treasury."

¹⁰So the king took his signet ring from his finger and gave it to Haman son of Hammedatha, the Agagite, the enemy of the Jews. ¹¹"Keep the money," the king said to Haman, "and do with the people as you please."

¹²Then on the thirteenth day of the first month the royal secretaries were summoned. They wrote out in the script of each province and in the language of each people all Haman's orders to the king's satraps, the governors of the various provinces and the nobles of the various peoples. These were written in the name of King Xerxes himself and sealed with his own ring. ¹³Dispatches were sent by couriers to all the king's provinces with the order to destroy, kill and annihilate all the Jews—young and old, women and children—on a single day, the thirteenth day of the twelfth month, the month of Adar, and to plunder their goods. ¹⁴A copy of the text of the edict was to be issued as law in every province and made known to the people of every nationality so they would be ready for that day.

¹⁵The couriers went out, spurred on by the king's command, and the edict was issued in the citadel of Susa. The king and Haman sat down to drink, but the city of Susa was bewildered.

MORDECAI PERSUADES ESTHER TO HELP

4 When Mordecai learned of all that had been done, he tore his clothes, put on sackcloth and ashes, and went out into the city, wailing loudly and bitterly. ²But he went only as far as the king's gate, because no one clothed in sackcloth was allowed to enter it. ³In every province to which the edict and order of the king came, there was great mourning among the Jews, with fasting, weeping and wailing. Many lay in sackcloth and ashes.

⁴When Esther's eunuchs and female attendants came and told her about Mordecai, she was in great distress. She sent clothes for him to put on instead of his sackcloth, but he

What was a signet ring? (3:10)
In the way signatures are used today to authenticate something or make documents legitimate, a signet ring had the same job. Melted wax or soft clay was put on important documents, and then the ring wearer would press his ring onto it like a stamp. Each ring had a different symbol on it, so every person's "signature" was different. By giving his ring to Haman, Xerxes gave him a lot of power.

Why was the city of Susa bewildered? (3:15)
There didn't seem to be any reason for the king to wipe out an entire ethnic group. The Jews were hard-working people, good citizens, and peaceful. Most people in the kingdom had no hostility toward the Jews.

Why did Mordecai tear his clothes? (4:1–2)
People living during this time tore their clothes and wore sackcloth and ashes as a way to show their grief.

---

a 7 Septuagint; Hebrew does not have *And the lot fell on.*   *b* 9 That is, about 375 tons or about 340 metric tons

would not accept them. ⁵Then Esther summoned Hathak, one of the king's eunuchs assigned to attend her, and ordered him to find out what was troubling Mordecai and why.

⁶So Hathak went out to Mordecai in the open square of the city in front of the king's gate. ⁷Mordecai told him everything that had happened to him, including the exact amount of money Haman had promised to pay into the royal treasury for the destruction of the Jews. ⁸He also gave him a copy of the text of the edict for their annihilation, which had been published in Susa, to show to Esther and explain it to her, and he told him to instruct her to go into the king's presence to beg for mercy and plead with him for her people.

⁹Hathak went back and reported to Esther what Mordecai had said. ¹⁰Then she instructed him to say to Mordecai, ¹¹"All the king's officials and the people of the royal provinces know that for any man or woman who approaches the king in the inner court without being summoned the king has but one law: that they be put to death unless the king extends the gold scepter to them and spares their lives. But thirty days have passed since I was called to go to the king."

¹²When Esther's words were reported to Mordecai, ¹³he sent back this answer: "Do not think that because you are in the king's house you alone of all the Jews will escape. ¹⁴For if you remain silent at this time, relief and deliverance for the Jews will arise from another place, but you and your father's family will perish. And who knows but that you have come to your royal position for such a time as this?"

¹⁵Then Esther sent this reply to Mordecai: ¹⁶"Go, gather together all the Jews who are in Susa, and fast for me. Do not eat or drink for three days, night or day. I and my attendants will fast as you do. When this is done, I will go to the king, even though it is against the law. And if I perish, I perish."

¹⁷So Mordecai went away and carried out all of Esther's instructions.

ESTHER'S REQUEST TO THE KING

5 On the third day Esther put on her royal robes and stood in the inner court of the palace, in front of the king's hall. The king was sitting on his royal throne in the hall, facing the entrance. ²When he saw Queen Esther standing in the court, he was pleased with her and held out to her the gold scepter that was in his hand. So Esther approached and touched the tip of the scepter.

³Then the king asked, "What is it, Queen Esther? What is your request? Even up to half the kingdom, it will be given you."

⁴"If it pleases the king," replied Esther, "let the king, together with Haman, come today to a banquet I have prepared for him."

⁵"Bring Haman at once," the king said, "so that we may do what Esther asks."

So the king and Haman went to the banquet Esther had prepared. ⁶As they were drinking wine, the king again asked Esther, "Now what is your petition? It will be given you. And what is your request? Even up to half the kingdom, it will be granted."

Couldn't the queen escape the king's edict? (4:11–14) No. In ancient Persia, once an edict had been issued by the king, it could not be canceled. If it was discovered that she was a Jew, she would be killed.

Why did Esther wait until the second banquet to make her request? (5:8)
She may have wanted to please the king enough that he would grant her request, or she may have been too fearful at the first banquet. It's also possible that God led her to wait.

Why would Haman build such a high gallows? (5:14)
The gallows may have been on top of a wall or another structure, making it 75 feet above the ground. The gallows may actually have been a stake on which Mordecai would be impaled (pierced). This type of execution was common in Persia.

Why was wearing the king's clothing so special? (6:8)
In ancient times, the king's garments had great significance, representing his power and glory. To wear a king's robe was to share in the king's honor, and it showed the king's special favor to the person.

[7] Esther replied, "My petition and my request is this: [8] If the king regards me with favor and if it pleases the king to grant my petition and fulfill my request, let the king and Haman come tomorrow to the banquet I will prepare for them. Then I will answer the king's question."

HAMAN'S RAGE AGAINST MORDECAI

[9] Haman went out that day happy and in high spirits. But when he saw Mordecai at the king's gate and observed that he neither rose nor showed fear in his presence, he was filled with rage against Mordecai. [10] Nevertheless, Haman restrained himself and went home.

Calling together his friends and Zeresh, his wife, [11] Haman boasted to them about his vast wealth, his many sons, and all the ways the king had honored him and how he had elevated him above the other nobles and officials. [12] "And that's not all," Haman added. "I'm the only person Queen Esther invited to accompany the king to the banquet she gave. And she has invited me along with the king tomorrow. [13] But all this gives me no satisfaction as long as I see that Jew Mordecai sitting at the king's gate."

[14] His wife Zeresh and all his friends said to him, "Have a pole set up, reaching to a height of fifty cubits,[a] and ask the king in the morning to have Mordecai impaled on it. Then go with the king to the banquet and enjoy yourself." This suggestion delighted Haman, and he had the pole set up.

MORDECAI HONORED

6 That night the king could not sleep; so he ordered the book of the chronicles, the record of his reign, to be brought in and read to him. [2] It was found recorded there that Mordecai had exposed Bigthana and Teresh, two of the king's officers who guarded the doorway, who had conspired to assassinate King Xerxes.

[3] "What honor and recognition has Mordecai received for this?" the king asked.

"Nothing has been done for him," his attendants answered.

[4] The king said, "Who is in the court?" Now Haman had just entered the outer court of the palace to speak to the king about impaling Mordecai on the pole he had set up for him.

[5] His attendants answered, "Haman is standing in the court."

"Bring him in," the king ordered.

[6] When Haman entered, the king asked him, "What should be done for the man the king delights to honor?"

Now Haman thought to himself, "Who is there that the king would rather honor than me?" [7] So he answered the king, "For the man the king delights to honor, [8] have them bring a royal robe the king has worn and a horse the king has ridden, one with a royal crest placed on its head. [9] Then let the robe and horse be entrusted to one of the king's most noble princes. Let them robe the man the king delights to honor, and lead him on the horse through the city streets, proclaiming before him, 'This is what is done for the man the king delights to honor!'"

[a] 14 That is, about 75 feet or about 23 meters

¹⁰ "Go at once," the king commanded Haman. "Get the robe and the horse and do just as you have suggested for Mordecai the Jew, who sits at the king's gate. Do not neglect anything you have recommended."

¹¹ So Haman got the robe and the horse. He robed Mordecai, and led him on horseback through the city streets, proclaiming before him, "This is what is done for the man the king delights to honor!"

¹² Afterward Mordecai returned to the king's gate. But Haman rushed home, with his head covered in grief, ¹³ and told Zeresh his wife and all his friends everything that had happened to him.

His advisers and his wife Zeresh said to him, "Since Mordecai, before whom your downfall has started, is of Jewish origin, you cannot stand against him — you will surely come to ruin!" ¹⁴ While they were still talking with him, the king's eunuchs arrived and hurried Haman away to the banquet Esther had prepared.

HAMAN IMPALED

7 So the king and Haman went to Queen Esther's banquet, ² and as they were drinking wine on the second day, the king again asked, "Queen Esther, what is your petition? It will be given you. What is your request? Even up to half the kingdom, it will be granted."

³ Then Queen Esther answered, "If I have found favor with you, Your Majesty, and if it pleases you, grant me my life — this is my petition. And spare my people — this is my request. ⁴ For I and my people have been sold to be destroyed, killed and annihilated. If we had merely been sold as male and female slaves, I would have kept quiet, because no such distress would justify disturbing the king.ᵃ"

⁵ King Xerxes asked Queen Esther, "Who is he? Where is he — the man who has dared to do such a thing?"

⁶ Esther said, "An adversary and enemy! This vile Haman!"

Then Haman was terrified before the king and queen. ⁷ The king got up in a rage, left his wine and went out into the palace garden. But Haman, realizing that the king had already decided his fate, stayed behind to beg Queen Esther for his life.

⁸ Just as the king returned from the palace garden to the banquet hall, Haman was falling on the couch where Esther was reclining.

The king exclaimed, "Will he even molest the queen while she is with me in the house?"

As soon as the word left the king's mouth, they covered Haman's face. ⁹ Then Harbona, one of the eunuchs attending the king, said, "A pole reaching to a height of fifty cubitsᵇ stands by Haman's house. He had it set up for Mordecai, who spoke up to help the king."

The king said, "Impale him on it!" ¹⁰ So they impaled Haman on the pole he had set up for Mordecai. Then the king's fury subsided.

ᵃ 4 Or quiet, but the compensation our adversary offers cannot be compared with the loss the king would suffer   ᵇ 9 That is, about 75 feet or about 23 meters

Why did Haman cover his head? (6:12)
This was a typical expression of grief. Haman was both sad and angry because he could not kill Mordecai and because he had been humiliated by having to honor Mordecai.

Why did the king's servants lead Haman to Esther's banquet? (6:14)
Guests were usually escorted to feasts such as this.

Why didn't Xerxes remember that he had signed the order to destroy the Jews? (7:5)
Haman never specifically said that it was the Jews who were going to be destroyed. He only told him that a certain group of people with differing customs was being disobedient (see 3:8–9). Neither Haman nor the king knew that Esther was a Jew.

Why was the king so angry when he returned? (7:8)
Only the king was allowed to be alone with a woman from the royal harem. When the king left, Haman stayed behind, probably realizing that his fate was already sealed. When the king returned and saw him alone with the queen on her couch, he was furious.

THE KING'S EDICT IN BEHALF OF THE JEWS

8 That same day King Xerxes gave Queen Esther the estate of Haman, the enemy of the Jews. And Mordecai came into the presence of the king, for Esther had told how he was related to her. ²The king took off his signet ring, which he had reclaimed from Haman, and presented it to Mordecai. And Esther appointed him over Haman's estate.

³Esther again pleaded with the king, falling at his feet and weeping. She begged him to put an end to the evil plan of Haman the Agagite, which he had devised against the Jews. ⁴Then the king extended the gold scepter to Esther and she arose and stood before him.

⁵"If it pleases the king," she said, "and if he regards me with favor and thinks it the right thing to do, and if he is pleased with me, let an order be written overruling the dispatches that Haman son of Hammedatha, the Agagite, devised and wrote to destroy the Jews in all the king's provinces. ⁶For how can I bear to see disaster fall on my people? How can I bear to see the destruction of my family?"

⁷King Xerxes replied to Queen Esther and to Mordecai the Jew, "Because Haman attacked the Jews, I have given his estate to Esther, and they have impaled him on the pole he set up. ⁸Now write another decree in the king's name in behalf of the Jews as seems best to you, and seal it with the king's signet ring—for no document written in the king's name and sealed with his ring can be revoked."

⁹At once the royal secretaries were summoned—on the twenty-third day of the third month, the month of Sivan. They wrote out all Mordecai's orders to the Jews, and to the satraps, governors and nobles of the 127 provinces stretching from India to Cush.ᵃ These orders were written in the script of each province and the language of each people and also to the Jews in their own script and language. ¹⁰Mordecai wrote in the name of King Xerxes, sealed the dispatches with the king's signet ring, and sent them by mounted couriers, who rode fast horses especially bred for the king.

¹¹The king's edict granted the Jews in every city the right to assemble and protect themselves; to destroy, kill and annihilate the armed men of any nationality or province who might attack them and their women and children,ᵇ and to plunder the property of their enemies. ¹²The day appointed for the Jews to do this in all the provinces of King Xerxes was the thirteenth day of the twelfth month, the month of Adar. ¹³A copy of the text of the edict was to be issued as law in every province and made known to the people of every nationality so that the Jews would be ready on that day to avenge themselves on their enemies.

¹⁴The couriers, riding the royal horses, went out, spurred on by the king's command, and the edict was issued in the citadel of Susa.

THE TRIUMPH OF THE JEWS

¹⁵When Mordecai left the king's presence, he was wearing royal garments of blue and white, a large crown of gold and a

The King's Signet Ring (8:2)

Why couldn't the king change his own decrees? (8:8)
A royal decree that had been written in the king's name and sealed with his ring could not be stopped, even by the king. The most that could be done was to write another decree that would override it, which is what Xerxes allowed Mordecai and Esther to do.

Why was this date chosen for Jews to protect themselves from their enemies? (8:12–13)
This was the date Haman had chosen for the Jews to be slaughtered. So Mordecai chose that date as the one when the Jews would be granted the right to defend themselves against their enemies.

ᵃ 9 That is, the upper Nile region   ᵇ 11 Or *province, together with their women and children, who might attack them;*

purple robe of fine linen. And the city of Susa held a joyous celebration. ¹⁶For the Jews it was a time of happiness and joy, gladness and honor. ¹⁷In every province and in every city to which the edict of the king came, there was joy and gladness among the Jews, with feasting and celebrating. And many people of other nationalities became Jews because fear of the Jews had seized them.

9 On the thirteenth day of the twelfth month, the month of Adar, the edict commanded by the king was to be carried out. On this day the enemies of the Jews had hoped to overpower them, but now the tables were turned and the Jews got the upper hand over those who hated them. ²The Jews assembled in their cities in all the provinces of King Xerxes to attack those determined to destroy them. No one could stand against them, because the people of all the other nationalities were afraid of them. ³And all the nobles of the provinces, the satraps, the governors and the king's administrators helped the Jews, because fear of Mordecai had seized them. ⁴Mordecai was prominent in the palace; his reputation spread throughout the provinces, and he became more and more powerful.

⁵The Jews struck down all their enemies with the sword, killing and destroying them, and they did what they pleased to those who hated them. ⁶In the citadel of Susa, the Jews killed and destroyed five hundred men. ⁷They also killed Parshandatha, Dalphon, Aspatha, ⁸Poratha, Adalia, Aridatha, ⁹Parmashta, Arisai, Aridai and Vaizatha, ¹⁰the ten sons of Haman son of Hammedatha, the enemy of the Jews. But they did not lay their hands on the plunder.

¹¹The number of those killed in the citadel of Susa was reported to the king that same day. ¹²The king said to Queen Esther, "The Jews have killed and destroyed five hundred men and the ten sons of Haman in the citadel of Susa. What have they done in the rest of the king's provinces? Now what is your petition? It will be given you. What is your request? It will also be granted."

¹³"If it pleases the king," Esther answered, "give the Jews in Susa permission to carry out this day's edict tomorrow also, and let Haman's ten sons be impaled on poles."

¹⁴So the king commanded that this be done. An edict was issued in Susa, and they impaled the ten sons of Haman. ¹⁵The Jews in Susa came together on the fourteenth day of the month of Adar, and they put to death in Susa three hundred men, but they did not lay their hands on the plunder.

¹⁶Meanwhile, the remainder of the Jews who were in the king's provinces also assembled to protect themselves and get relief from their enemies. They killed seventy-five thousand of them but did not lay their hands on the plunder. ¹⁷This happened on the thirteenth day of the month of Adar, and on the fourteenth they rested and made it a day of feasting and joy.

¹⁸The Jews in Susa, however, had assembled on the thirteenth and fourteenth, and then on the fifteenth they rested and made it a day of feasting and joy. ¹⁹That is why rural Jews—those living in villages—observe the fourteenth of the month of Adar as a day of joy and feasting, a day for giving presents to each other.

How could someone who wasn't a Jew become a Jew? (8:17)
To become a Jew meant to accept and obey Jewish law. While they were in exile, some of the laws (such as laws about the temple) did not apply. But many of the laws still had to be followed including circumcision, observance of holy days, and dietary laws.

Why were they afraid of Mordecai? (9:3–4)
The rulers of the provinces probably recognized the power Mordecai had been given.

Why didn't the Jews take any plunder? (9:10, 15)
This was a holy war. Financial gain through plunder would have taken away from the reason of a holy war—to remove evil as commanded by the LORD.

Why were Haman's sons hung on the gallows? (9:13)
Even though they were already dead, their dead bodies were hung on the gallows to serve as an example to those who might want to attack the Jews in the future. The Jews would see this as evidence that God's curse against those who cursed them was still in force (Genesis 12:3; 27:29; Numbers 9:24).

PURIM ESTABLISHED

20 Mordecai recorded these events, and he sent letters to all the Jews throughout the provinces of King Xerxes, near and far, 21 to have them celebrate annually the fourteenth and fifteenth days of the month of Adar 22 as the time when the Jews got relief from their enemies, and as the month when their sorrow was turned into joy and their mourning into a day of celebration. He wrote them to observe the days as days of feasting and joy and giving presents of food to one another and gifts to the poor.

23 So the Jews agreed to continue the celebration they had begun, doing what Mordecai had written to them. 24 For Haman son of Hammedatha, the Agagite, the enemy of all the Jews, had plotted against the Jews to destroy them and had cast the *pur* (that is, the lot) for their ruin and destruction. 25 But when the plot came to the king's attention,[a] he issued written orders that the evil scheme Haman had devised against the Jews should come back onto his own head, and that he and his sons should be impaled on poles. 26 (Therefore these days were called Purim, from the word *pur*.) Because of everything written in this letter and because of what they had seen and what had happened to them, 27 the Jews took it on themselves to establish the custom that they and their descendants and all who join them should without fail observe these two days every year, in the way prescribed and at the time appointed. 28 These days should be remembered and observed in every generation by every family, and in every province and in every city. And these days of Purim should never fail to be celebrated by the Jews—nor should the memory of these days die out among their descendants.

29 So Queen Esther, daughter of Abihail, along with Mordecai the Jew, wrote with full authority to confirm this second letter concerning Purim. 30 And Mordecai sent letters to all the Jews in the 127 provinces of Xerxes' kingdom—words of goodwill and assurance— 31 to establish these days of Purim at their designated times, as Mordecai the Jew and Queen Esther had decreed for them, and as they had established for themselves and their descendants in regard to their times of fasting and lamentation. 32 Esther's decree confirmed these regulations about Purim, and it was written down in the records.

THE GREATNESS OF MORDECAI

10 King Xerxes imposed tribute throughout the empire, to its distant shores. 2 And all his acts of power and might, together with a full account of the greatness of Mordecai, whom the king had promoted, are they not written in the book of the annals of the kings of Media and Persia? 3 Mordecai the Jew was second in rank to King Xerxes, preeminent among the Jews, and held in high esteem by his many fellow Jews, because he worked for the good of his people and spoke up for the welfare of all the Jews.

What does Purim mean? (9:26)
Purim is a combination of the Persian word for *lot* (*pur*) with the Hebrew plural ending (-*im*). The day was originally chosen by lot as the day the Jews would be attacked. Instead, in a dramatic turn of events, it became a time for the Jews to celebrate their victory over those who would have destroyed them.

How much power did Mordecai have as second in rank to the king? (10:3)
He had the trust and confidence of the king, and he would have been able to help shape the policies of the empire. Mordecai's high position guaranteed the welfare of the Jews while they lived in a foreign land. God used Mordecai in the same way he used Joseph and Daniel to provide for and protect his people.

---

[a] 25 Or *when Esther came before the king*

Job

INTRODUCTION

Who wrote this book?	The writer of Job is unknown.
Why was this book written?	The book of Job was written to help people learn that suffering is not always punishment from God.
What happens in this book?	Terrible things happen to Job. Job and his three friends discuss why God has let these things happen. God tells Job and his friends to just trust him. God then heals Job and makes him wealthy again.
What do we learn about God in this book?	God does let bad things happen to good people. When bad things happen, it does not mean that God is punishing them for some sin.
Who is important in this book?	Job is the most important person in this book.
Where did this happen?	The story of Job took place in a land called Uz, probably located east of Canaan.
What are some of the stories in this book?	Satan destroys Job's wealth and family — Job 1 Satan makes Job very ill — Job 2 Job says God isn't fair — Job 9; 12 God shows his greatness to Job — Job 40 – 41 God makes Job well and wealthy — Job 42

When did these things happen?

	2200 BC	2100	2000	1900	1800	1700	1600	1500	1400

CREATION, FALL, FLOOD

ABRAHAM'S LIFE (C. 2166 – 1991 BC)

ISAAC'S LIFE (C. 2066 – 1886 BC)

JACOB'S LIFE (C. 2006 – 1859 BC)

JOSEPH'S LIFE (C. 1915 – 1805 BC)

HISTORICAL SETTING OF JOB (C. 1900 – 1700 BC)

MOSES' LIFE (C. 1526 – 1406 BC)

Was Job perfect? (1:1)
Only God is perfect. Job was not
without sin, but he feared God
and tried to follow God's law. He
even offered sacrifices in case
his children had sinned.

Location of Uz (1:1)

**How wealthy was Job?
(1:2–3)**
Job was considered the wealthi-
est man of the region. His wealth
was in livestock rather than in
land.

**Did God want Satan to test
Job? (1:8–12)**
When talking with Satan, God
called attention to Job as an
example of someone who faithfully served him. When Satan
said it was easy for Job to fear
God because of his wealth, God
allowed Satan to test Job. Satan
was really attacking God rather
than Job.

PROLOGUE

1 In the land of Uz there lived a man whose name was Job.
This man was blameless and upright; he feared God and
shunned evil. ²He had seven sons and three daughters, ³and
he owned seven thousand sheep, three thousand camels, five
hundred yoke of oxen and five hundred donkeys, and had a
large number of servants. He was the greatest man among all
the people of the East.

⁴His sons used to hold feasts in their homes on their
birthdays, and they would invite their three sisters to eat
and drink with them. ⁵When a period of feasting had run
its course, Job would make arrangements for them to be
purified. Early in the morning he would sacrifice a burnt
offering for each of them, thinking, "Perhaps my children
have sinned and cursed God in their hearts." This was Job's
regular custom.

⁶One day the angels*ᵃ* came to present themselves before
the LORD, and Satan*ᵇ* also came with them. ⁷The LORD said
to Satan, "Where have you come from?"

Satan answered the LORD, "From roaming throughout the
earth, going back and forth on it."

⁸Then the LORD said to Satan, "Have you considered my
servant Job? There is no one on earth like him; he is blameless and upright, a man who fears God and shuns evil."

⁹"Does Job fear God for nothing?" Satan replied. ¹⁰"Have
you not put a hedge around him and his household and everything he has? You have blessed the work of his hands, so
that his flocks and herds are spread throughout the land.
¹¹But now stretch out your hand and strike everything he
has, and he will surely curse you to your face."

¹²The LORD said to Satan, "Very well, then, everything
he has is in your power, but on the man himself do not lay
a finger."

Then Satan went out from the presence of the LORD.

¹³One day when Job's sons and daughters were feasting
and drinking wine at the oldest brother's house, ¹⁴a messenger came to Job and said, "The oxen were plowing and
the donkeys were grazing nearby, ¹⁵and the Sabeans attacked

ᵃ 6 Hebrew *the sons of God*   *ᵇ* 6 Hebrew *satan* means *adversary.*

Why does God allow his people to suffer?   JOB 1

God was the one who first mentioned Job as someone who was God's servant and who tried to serve
the LORD. God held Job up to Satan as an example of someone who faithfully served him. When Satan
said that it was easy for Job to fear God because of all his wealth, God allowed Satan to test Job. Satan
was really attacking God rather than Job.

Job's friends thought they had the answers to why Job was suffering. They said that God was testing
him or punishing him for sins that he had committed; they could not imagine that a good God would
ever allow someone to suffer except as a punishment for sin. But it was Satan who was tormenting Job,
not God.

The simple answer is that we don't know why people — even good people — suffer. Because we live
in a fallen world there is hardship and pain. Some of that we bring on ourselves through bad choices or
poor lifestyles. But often there is no clear explanation. What we do know is that when we live with God
forever in the new heaven and earth, all tears will be removed from our eyes. There will be no more
suffering for believers.

and made off with them. They put the servants to the sword, and I am the only one who has escaped to tell you!"

¹⁶While he was still speaking, another messenger came and said, "The fire of God fell from the heavens and burned up the sheep and the servants, and I am the only one who has escaped to tell you!"

¹⁷While he was still speaking, another messenger came and said, "The Chaldeans formed three raiding parties and swept down on your camels and made off with them. They put the servants to the sword, and I am the only one who has escaped to tell you!"

¹⁸While he was still speaking, yet another messenger came and said, "Your sons and daughters were feasting and drinking wine at the oldest brother's house, ¹⁹when suddenly a mighty wind swept in from the desert and struck the four corners of the house. It collapsed on them and they are dead, and I am the only one who has escaped to tell you!"

²⁰At this, Job got up and tore his robe and shaved his head. Then he fell to the ground in worship ²¹and said:

"Naked I came from my mother's womb,
    and naked I will depart.ᵃ
The Lᴏʀᴅ gave and the Lᴏʀᴅ has taken away;
    may the name of the Lᴏʀᴅ be praised."

²²In all this, Job did not sin by charging God with wrongdoing.

2 On another day the angelsᵇ came to present themselves before the Lᴏʀᴅ, and Satan also came with them to present himself before him. ²And the Lᴏʀᴅ said to Satan, "Where have you come from?"

Satan answered the Lᴏʀᴅ, "From roaming throughout the earth, going back and forth on it."

³Then the Lᴏʀᴅ said to Satan, "Have you considered my servant Job? There is no one on earth like him; he is blameless and upright, a man who fears God and shuns evil. And he still maintains his integrity, though you incited me against him to ruin him without any reason."

⁴"Skin for skin!" Satan replied. "A man will give all he has for his own life. ⁵But now stretch out your hand and strike his flesh and bones, and he will surely curse you to your face."

⁶The Lᴏʀᴅ said to Satan, "Very well, then, he is in your hands; but you must spare his life."

⁷So Satan went out from the presence of the Lᴏʀᴅ and afflicted Job with painful sores from the soles of his feet to the crown of his head. ⁸Then Job took a piece of broken pottery and scraped himself with it as he sat among the ashes.

⁹His wife said to him, "Are you still maintaining your integrity? Curse God and die!"

¹⁰He replied, "You are talking like a foolishᶜ woman. Shall we accept good from God, and not trouble?"

In all this, Job did not sin in what he said.

¹¹When Job's three friends, Eliphaz the Temanite, Bildad the Shuhite and Zophar the Naamathite, heard about

---

ᵃ 21 Or *will return there*   ᵇ 1 Hebrew *the sons of God*   ᶜ 10 The Hebrew word rendered *foolish* denotes moral deficiency.

How did Job show his grief? (1:20)
People often showed their grief during ancient times by tearing their clothes and shaving their heads. Despite his sorrow, Job did not give up his faith in God.

What type of sickness did Job have? (2:7)
It isn't clear what his illness was, but the symptoms included sores over his whole body (2:7), scabs (30:30), bad breath (19:17), fever (30:30), and constant pain (30:17).

How did Job's wife react to his pain? (2:9)
Since Job had lost so much and was in such pain, she suggested that the only thing left for him to do would be to curse God. Because those who cursed God could be put to death (Leviticus 24:10–16), Job's misery would then be over.

all the troubles that had come upon him, they set out from their homes and met together by agreement to go and sympathize with him and comfort him. [12]When they saw him from a distance, they could hardly recognize him; they began to weep aloud, and they tore their robes and sprinkled dust on their heads. [13]Then they sat on the ground with him for seven days and seven nights. No one said a word to him, because they saw how great his suffering was.

JOB SPEAKS

3 After this, Job opened his mouth and cursed the day of his birth. [2]He said:

[3]"May the day of my birth perish,
   and the night that said, 'A boy is conceived!'
[4]That day—may it turn to darkness;
   may God above not care about it;
   may no light shine on it.
[5]May gloom and utter darkness claim it once more;
   may a cloud settle over it;
   may blackness overwhelm it.
[6]That night—may thick darkness seize it;
   may it not be included among the days of the year
   nor be entered in any of the months.
[7]May that night be barren;
   may no shout of joy be heard in it.
[8]May those who curse days[a] curse that day,
   those who are ready to rouse Leviathan.
[9]May its morning stars become dark;
   may it wait for daylight in vain
   and not see the first rays of dawn,
[10]for it did not shut the doors of the womb on me
   to hide trouble from my eyes.

[11]"Why did I not perish at birth,
   and die as I came from the womb?
[12]Why were there knees to receive me
   and breasts that I might be nursed?
[13]For now I would be lying down in peace;
   I would be asleep and at rest
[14]with kings and rulers of the earth,
   who built for themselves places now lying in ruins,
[15]with princes who had gold,
   who filled their houses with silver.
[16]Or why was I not hidden away in the ground like a
      stillborn child,
   like an infant who never saw the light of day?
[17]There the wicked cease from turmoil,
   and there the weary are at rest.
[18]Captives also enjoy their ease;
   they no longer hear the slave driver's shout.
[19]The small and the great are there,
   and the slaves are freed from their owners.

[20]"Why is light given to those in misery,
   and life to the bitter of soul,

When Job cursed the day of his birth, was he cursing God for allowing him to be born? (3:3)
Job's life had been wonderful, and now it was terrible. Job expressed his thought that it might have been better if he had never been born. But even in his great suffering, Job did not curse God.

What was Leviathan? (3:8)
This may be a reference to a dragon-like creature or sea monster from Canaanite mythology. Later in the book of Job, Leviathan appears to be a crocodile (see chapter 41).

What was Job wishing for in these verses? (3:16–19)
Job thought that if he had died while he was being born or soon after, he would have had the peace and rest he wanted so badly (see verse 26).

---

[a] 8 Or *curse the sea*

²¹ to those who long for death that does not come,
 who search for it more than for hidden treasure,
²² who are filled with gladness
 and rejoice when they reach the grave?
²³ Why is life given to a man
 whose way is hidden,
 whom God has hedged in?
²⁴ For sighing has become my daily food;
 my groans pour out like water.
²⁵ What I feared has come upon me;
 what I dreaded has happened to me.
²⁶ I have no peace, no quietness;
 I have no rest, but only turmoil."

ELIPHAZ

4 Then Eliphaz the Temanite replied:

² "If someone ventures a word with you, will you be
 impatient?
 But who can keep from speaking?
³ Think how you have instructed many,
 how you have strengthened feeble hands.
⁴ Your words have supported those who stumbled;
 you have strengthened faltering knees.
⁵ But now trouble comes to you, and you are
 discouraged;
 it strikes you, and you are dismayed.
⁶ Should not your piety be your confidence
 and your blameless ways your hope?

⁷ "Consider now: Who, being innocent, has ever
 perished?
 Where were the upright ever destroyed?
⁸ As I have observed, those who plow evil
 and those who sow trouble reap it.
⁹ At the breath of God they perish;
 at the blast of his anger they are no more.
¹⁰ The lions may roar and growl,
 yet the teeth of the great lions are broken.
¹¹ The lion perishes for lack of prey,
 and the cubs of the lioness are scattered.

¹² "A word was secretly brought to me,
 my ears caught a whisper of it.
¹³ Amid disquieting dreams in the night,
 when deep sleep falls on people,
¹⁴ fear and trembling seized me
 and made all my bones shake.
¹⁵ A spirit glided past my face,
 and the hair on my body stood on end.
¹⁶ It stopped,
 but I could not tell what it was.
 A form stood before my eyes,
 and I heard a hushed voice:
¹⁷ 'Can a mortal be more righteous than God?
 Can even a strong man be more pure than his Maker?

What kind of vision did Eliphaz have? (4:12–16)
Eliphaz said that during the night a spirit appeared to him in a dream and provided him with an insight from God.

How did Eliphaz compare angels and human beings? (4:18–19)
He said that if spiritual beings like angels could be guilty in God's sight, human beings who were created from the dust of the ground were even more likely to be sinful.

¹⁸ If God places no trust in his servants,
    if he charges his angels with error,
¹⁹ how much more those who live in houses of clay,
    whose foundations are in the dust,
    who are crushed more readily than a moth!
²⁰ Between dawn and dusk they are broken to pieces;
    unnoticed, they perish forever.
²¹ Are not the cords of their tent pulled up,
    so that they die without wisdom?'

5 "Call if you will, but who will answer you?
    To which of the holy ones will you turn?
² Resentment kills a fool,
    and envy slays the simple.
³ I myself have seen a fool taking root,
    but suddenly his house was cursed.
⁴ His children are far from safety,
    crushed in court without a defender.
⁵ The hungry consume his harvest,
    taking it even from among thorns,
    and the thirsty pant after his wealth.
⁶ For hardship does not spring from the soil,
    nor does trouble sprout from the ground.
⁷ Yet man is born to trouble
    as surely as sparks fly upward.

What was the main advice Eliphaz gave Job? (5:8–16)
Job should humble himself and make his case to God.

⁸ "But if I were you, I would appeal to God;
    I would lay my cause before him.
⁹ He performs wonders that cannot be fathomed,
    miracles that cannot be counted.
¹⁰ He provides rain for the earth;
    he sends water on the countryside.
¹¹ The lowly he sets on high,
    and those who mourn are lifted to safety.
¹² He thwarts the plans of the crafty,
    so that their hands achieve no success.
¹³ He catches the wise in their craftiness,
    and the schemes of the wily are swept away.
¹⁴ Darkness comes upon them in the daytime;
    at noon they grope as in the night.
¹⁵ He saves the needy from the sword in their mouth;
    he saves them from the clutches of the powerful.
¹⁶ So the poor have hope,
    and injustice shuts its mouth.

How did Eliphaz explain Job's suffering? (5:17)
Eliphaz apparently thought that God was disciplining Job for his sin and that all he needed to do was to repent. He believed that God's discipline was temporary and that good people would be rewarded.

¹⁷ "Blessed is the one whom God corrects;
    so do not despise the discipline of the Almighty.ᵃ
¹⁸ For he wounds, but he also binds up;
    he injures, but his hands also heal.
¹⁹ From six calamities he will rescue you;
    in seven no harm will touch you.
²⁰ In famine he will deliver you from death,
    and in battle from the stroke of the sword.
²¹ You will be protected from the lash of the tongue,
    and need not fear when destruction comes.

ᵃ 17 Hebrew *Shaddai*; here and throughout Job

²²You will laugh at destruction and famine,
and need not fear the wild animals.
²³For you will have a covenant with the stones of the field,
and the wild animals will be at peace with you.
²⁴You will know that your tent is secure;
you will take stock of your property and find
nothing missing.
²⁵You will know that your children will be many,
and your descendants like the grass of the earth.
²⁶You will come to the grave in full vigor,
like sheaves gathered in season.

²⁷"We have examined this, and it is true.
So hear it and apply it to yourself."

JOB

6 Then Job replied:

²"If only my anguish could be weighed
and all my misery be placed on the scales!
³It would surely outweigh the sand of the seas—
no wonder my words have been impetuous.
⁴The arrows of the Almighty are in me,
my spirit drinks in their poison;
God's terrors are marshaled against me.
⁵Does a wild donkey bray when it has grass,
or an ox bellow when it has fodder?
⁶Is tasteless food eaten without salt,
or is there flavor in the sap of the mallow*ᵃ*?
⁷I refuse to touch it;
such food makes me ill.

⁸"Oh, that I might have my request,
that God would grant what I hope for,
⁹that God would be willing to crush me,
to let loose his hand and cut off my life!
¹⁰Then I would still have this consolation—
my joy in unrelenting pain—
that I had not denied the words of the Holy One.

¹¹"What strength do I have, that I should still hope?
What prospects, that I should be patient?
¹²Do I have the strength of stone?
Is my flesh bronze?
¹³Do I have any power to help myself,
now that success has been driven from me?

¹⁴"Anyone who withholds kindness from a friend
forsakes the fear of the Almighty.
¹⁵But my brothers are as undependable as intermittent
streams,
as the streams that overflow
¹⁶when darkened by thawing ice
and swollen with melting snow,
¹⁷but that stop flowing in the dry season,
and in the heat vanish from their channels.

ᵃ 6 The meaning of the Hebrew for this phrase is uncertain.

Why did Job mention a braying donkey and a bellowing ox? (6:5)
Job used these word pictures to explain why he had the right to bray and bellow in his suffering. He went on to describe the advice given by Eliphaz as tasteless food (verse 6).

What was Job's desire? (6:8–10)
Job wanted to die in order to escape his pain and suffering. Even more importantly, he wanted to stay true to God by not denying or turning away from him.

Why did Job think his friends were undependable? (6:14–17)
Their advice wasn't useful, because they did not seem to understand his situation. They implied that Job had brought his suffering on himself by being disobedient to God. Job knew that was not true.

¹⁸ Caravans turn aside from their routes;
   they go off into the wasteland and perish.
¹⁹ The caravans of Tema look for water,
   the traveling merchants of Sheba look in hope.
²⁰ They are distressed, because they had been confident;
   they arrive there, only to be disappointed.
²¹ Now you too have proved to be of no help;
   you see something dreadful and are afraid.
²² Have I ever said, 'Give something on my behalf,
   pay a ransom for me from your wealth,
²³ deliver me from the hand of the enemy,
   rescue me from the clutches of the ruthless'?

²⁴ "Teach me, and I will be quiet;
   show me where I have been wrong.
²⁵ How painful are honest words!
   But what do your arguments prove?
²⁶ Do you mean to correct what I say,
   and treat my desperate words as wind?
²⁷ You would even cast lots for the fatherless
   and barter away your friend.

²⁸ "But now be so kind as to look at me.
   Would I lie to your face?
²⁹ Relent, do not be unjust;
   reconsider, for my integrity is at stake.ᵃ
³⁰ Is there any wickedness on my lips?
   Can my mouth not discern malice?

7 "Do not mortals have hard service on earth?
   Are not their days like those of hired laborers?
² Like a slave longing for the evening shadows,
   or a hired laborer waiting to be paid,
³ so I have been allotted months of futility,
   and nights of misery have been assigned to me.
⁴ When I lie down I think, 'How long before I get up?'
   The night drags on, and I toss and turn until dawn.
⁵ My body is clothed with worms and scabs,
   my skin is broken and festering.

⁶ "My days are swifter than a weaver's shuttle,
   and they come to an end without hope.
⁷ Remember, O God, that my life is but a breath;
   my eyes will never see happiness again.
⁸ The eye that now sees me will see me no longer;
   you will look for me, but I will be no more.
⁹ As a cloud vanishes and is gone,
   so one who goes down to the grave does not return.
¹⁰ He will never come to his house again;
   his place will know him no more.

¹¹ "Therefore I will not keep silent;
   I will speak out in the anguish of my spirit,
   I will complain in the bitterness of my soul.
¹² Am I the sea, or the monster of the deep,
   that you put me under guard?
¹³ When I think my bed will comfort me

ᵃ 29 Or *my righteousness still stands*

What shift happened at the beginning of this chapter? (7:1)
Job stopped answering Eliphaz and began to speak directly to God.

What was Job's point? (7:6–9)
Job used several word pictures to describe the shortness of life: a weaver's shuttle speeding back and forth on a loom, a puff of breath, and a passing cloud. And in verse 9 he referred to the Mesopotamian netherworld, the place where people were thought to go after they die called the land of no return. Job saw death as his only hope.

and my couch will ease my complaint,
¹⁴ even then you frighten me with dreams
and terrify me with visions,
¹⁵ so that I prefer strangling and death,
rather than this body of mine.
¹⁶ I despise my life; I would not live forever.
Let me alone; my days have no meaning.

¹⁷ "What is mankind that you make so much of them,
that you give them so much attention,
¹⁸ that you examine them every morning
and test them every moment?
¹⁹ Will you never look away from me,
or let me alone even for an instant?
²⁰ If I have sinned, what have I done to you,
you who see everything we do?
Why have you made me your target?
Have I become a burden to you?^a
²¹ Why do you not pardon my offenses
and forgive my sins?
For I will soon lie down in the dust;
you will search for me, but I will be no more."

BILDAD

8 Then Bildad the Shuhite replied:

² "How long will you say such things?
Your words are a blustering wind.
³ Does God pervert justice?
Does the Almighty pervert what is right?
⁴ When your children sinned against him,
he gave them over to the penalty of their sin.
⁵ But if you will seek God earnestly
and plead with the Almighty,
⁶ if you are pure and upright,
even now he will rouse himself on your behalf
and restore you to your prosperous state.
⁷ Your beginnings will seem humble,
so prosperous will your future be.

⁸ "Ask the former generation
and find out what their ancestors learned,
⁹ for we were born only yesterday and know nothing,
and our days on earth are but a shadow.
¹⁰ Will they not instruct you and tell you?
Will they not bring forth words from their
understanding?
¹¹ Can papyrus grow tall where there is no marsh?
Can reeds thrive without water?
¹² While still growing and uncut,
they wither more quickly than grass.
¹³ Such is the destiny of all who forget God;
so perishes the hope of the godless.

---

^a 20 A few manuscripts of the Masoretic Text, an ancient Hebrew scribal
tradition and Septuagint; most manuscripts of the Masoretic Text *I have
become a burden to myself.*

**Did Job admit he was a
sinner? (7:20–21)**
Job did not claim to be perfect,
but he asked God why he would
not forgive his sins and take
away his suffering.

**In Bildad's opinion, what
was the cause of Job's
suffering? (8:4–6)**
Bildad thought Job's children
had died because of their sins
and that Job was suffering because of his sin. He told Job to
ask God for mercy.

¹⁴What they trust in is fragile*;
  what they rely on is a spider's web.
¹⁵They lean on the web, but it gives way;
  they cling to it, but it does not hold.
¹⁶They are like a well-watered plant in the sunshine,
  spreading its shoots over the garden;
¹⁷it entwines its roots around a pile of rocks
  and looks for a place among the stones.
¹⁸But when it is torn from its spot,
  that place disowns it and says, 'I never saw you.'
¹⁹Surely its life withers away,
  and* from the soil other plants grow.

²⁰"Surely God does not reject one who is blameless
  or strengthen the hands of evildoers.
²¹He will yet fill your mouth with laughter
  and your lips with shouts of joy.
²²Your enemies will be clothed in shame,
  and the tents of the wicked will be no more."

JOB

9 Then Job replied:

²"Indeed, I know that this is true.
  But how can mere mortals prove their innocence
    before God?
³Though they wished to dispute with him,
  they could not answer him one time out of a
    thousand.
⁴His wisdom is profound, his power is vast.
  Who has resisted him and come out unscathed?
⁵He moves mountains without their knowing it
  and overturns them in his anger.
⁶He shakes the earth from its place
  and makes its pillars tremble.
⁷He speaks to the sun and it does not shine;
  he seals off the light of the stars.
⁸He alone stretches out the heavens
  and treads on the waves of the sea.
⁹He is the Maker of the Bear* and Orion,
  the Pleiades and the constellations of the south.
¹⁰He performs wonders that cannot be fathomed,
  miracles that cannot be counted.
¹¹When he passes me, I cannot see him;
  when he goes by, I cannot perceive him.
¹²If he snatches away, who can stop him?
  Who can say to him, 'What are you doing?'
¹³God does not restrain his anger;
  even the cohorts of Rahab cowered at his feet.

¹⁴"How then can I dispute with him?
  How can I find words to argue with him?
¹⁵Though I were innocent, I could not answer him;
  I could only plead with my Judge for mercy.

How did Bildad sum up his speech? (8:20–21)
Bildad stated his belief that God would not allow a righteous person to suffer or an evil person to be successful.

How did Job answer Bildad's argument? (9:1–2)
Job agreed with Bildad that God is both just and holy. But he wanted to know how any person could ever be righteous before God.

Who was Rahab? (9:13)
This was not the Rahab who protected the spies (Joshua 2). This Rahab was a mythical sea monster.

---

a 14 The meaning of the Hebrew for this word is uncertain.   *b 19* Or *Surely all the joy it has / is that*   *c 9* Or *of Leo*

¹⁶ Even if I summoned him and he responded,
   I do not believe he would give me a hearing.
¹⁷ He would crush me with a storm
   and multiply my wounds for no reason.
¹⁸ He would not let me catch my breath
   but would overwhelm me with misery.
¹⁹ If it is a matter of strength, he is mighty!
   And if it is a matter of justice, who can challenge
      him*?
²⁰ Even if I were innocent, my mouth would condemn me;
   if I were blameless, it would pronounce me guilty.

²¹ "Although I am blameless,
   I have no concern for myself;
   I despise my own life.
²² It is all the same; that is why I say,
   'He destroys both the blameless and the wicked.'
²³ When a scourge brings sudden death,
   he mocks the despair of the innocent.
²⁴ When a land falls into the hands of the wicked,
   he blindfolds its judges.
   If it is not he, then who is it?

²⁵ "My days are swifter than a runner;
   they fly away without a glimpse of joy.
²⁶ They skim past like boats of papyrus,
   like eagles swooping down on their prey.
²⁷ If I say, 'I will forget my complaint,
   I will change my expression, and smile,'
²⁸ I still dread all my sufferings,
   for I know you will not hold me innocent.
²⁹ Since I am already found guilty,
   why should I struggle in vain?
³⁰ Even if I washed myself with soap
   and my hands with cleansing powder,
³¹ you would plunge me into a slime pit
   so that even my clothes would detest me.

³² "He is not a mere mortal like me that I might answer
      him,
   that we might confront each other in court.
³³ If only there were someone to mediate between us,
   someone to bring us together,
³⁴ someone to remove God's rod from me,
   so that his terror would frighten me no more.
³⁵ Then I would speak up without fear of him,
   but as it now stands with me, I cannot.

10 "I loathe my very life;
   therefore I will give free rein to my complaint
   and speak out in the bitterness of my soul.
² I say to God: Do not declare me guilty,
   but tell me what charges you have against me.
³ Does it please you to oppress me,
   to spurn the work of your hands,
   while you smile on the plans of the wicked?

ᵃ 19 See Septuagint; Hebrew *me.*

Was it wrong for Job to ask God why he was suffering? (10:2)
No. Job wasn't being rebellious or challenging God's authority. He was using the wording of a court hearing. He wanted to know the charges against him so he could understand why he was suffering and possibly defend himself.

⁴ Do you have eyes of flesh?
     Do you see as a mortal sees?
⁵ Are your days like those of a mortal
     or your years like those of a strong man,
⁶ that you must search out my faults
     and probe after my sin—
⁷ though you know that I am not guilty
     and that no one can rescue me from your hand?

⁸ "Your hands shaped me and made me.
     Will you now turn and destroy me?
⁹ Remember that you molded me like clay.
     Will you now turn me to dust again?
¹⁰ Did you not pour me out like milk
     and curdle me like cheese,
¹¹ clothe me with skin and flesh
     and knit me together with bones and sinews?
¹² You gave me life and showed me kindness,
     and in your providence watched over my spirit.

¹³ "But this is what you concealed in your heart,
     and I know that this was in your mind:
¹⁴ If I sinned, you would be watching me
     and would not let my offense go unpunished.
¹⁵ If I am guilty—woe to me!
     Even if I am innocent, I cannot lift my head,
for I am full of shame
     and drowned in*ᵃ* my affliction.
¹⁶ If I hold my head high, you stalk me like a lion
     and again display your awesome power against me.
¹⁷ You bring new witnesses against me
     and increase your anger toward me;
     your forces come against me wave upon wave.

¹⁸ "Why then did you bring me out of the womb?
     I wish I had died before any eye saw me.
¹⁹ If only I had never come into being,
     or had been carried straight from the womb to the grave!
²⁰ Are not my few days almost over?
     Turn away from me so I can have a moment's joy
²¹ before I go to the place of no return,
     to the land of gloom and utter darkness,
²² to the land of deepest night,
     of utter darkness and disorder,
     where even the light is like darkness."

ZOPHAR

11 Then Zophar the Naamathite replied:

² "Are all these words to go unanswered?
     Is this talker to be vindicated?
³ Will your idle talk reduce others to silence?
     Will no one rebuke you when you mock?
⁴ You say to God, 'My beliefs are flawless
     and I am pure in your sight.'

ᵃ 15 Or and aware of

Why did Job ask God why he had been born? (10:18)
Job believed he could never satisfy the requirements of a righteous God and that God would always find some reason to punish him. Job reasoned that since God knew all this before he was born, it would have been better if he had not been allowed to live.

⁵ Oh, how I wish that God would speak,
  that he would open his lips against you
⁶ and disclose to you the secrets of wisdom,
  for true wisdom has two sides.
  Know this: God has even forgotten some of your
  sin.

⁷ "Can you fathom the mysteries of God?
  Can you probe the limits of the Almighty?
⁸ They are higher than the heavens above—what can
  you do?
  They are deeper than the depths below—what can
  you know?
⁹ Their measure is longer than the earth
  and wider than the sea.

¹⁰ "If he comes along and confines you in prison
  and convenes a court, who can oppose him?
¹¹ Surely he recognizes deceivers;
  and when he sees evil, does he not take note?
¹² But the witless can no more become wise
  than a wild donkey's colt can be born human.ᵃ

¹³ "Yet if you devote your heart to him
  and stretch out your hands to him,
¹⁴ if you put away the sin that is in your hand
  and allow no evil to dwell in your tent,
¹⁵ then, free of fault, you will lift up your face;
  you will stand firm and without fear.
¹⁶ You will surely forget your trouble,
  recalling it only as waters gone by.
¹⁷ Life will be brighter than noonday,
  and darkness will become like morning.
¹⁸ You will be secure, because there is hope;
  you will look about you and take your rest in safety.
¹⁹ You will lie down, with no one to make you afraid,
  and many will court your favor.
²⁰ But the eyes of the wicked will fail,
  and escape will elude them;
  their hope will become a dying gasp."

JOB

12

Then Job replied:

² "Doubtless you are the only people who matter,
  and wisdom will die with you!
³ But I have a mind as well as you;
  I am not inferior to you.
  Who does not know all these things?

⁴ "I have become a laughingstock to my friends,
  though I called on God and he answered—
  a mere laughingstock, though righteous and
  blameless!
⁵ Those who are at ease have contempt for misfortune
  as the fate of those whose feet are slipping.

How did Zophar criticize Job? (11:7)
Zophar accused Job of saying he understood the mysteries of God, which are beyond human understanding. But Job was simply seeking an answer to the question of why he was suffering.

What was Zophar saying about Job? (11:10–12)
Zophar was suggesting that because God knows everything, no one should question him. He also suggested that it would take a miracle for Job to change.

How did Job react to Zophar's speech? (12:2–3)
Job was sarcastic about the wisdom his friends claimed to have and their criticisms of him. Job said he had a mind as good as theirs and that their advice was common and obvious.

ᵃ 12 Or *wild donkey can be born tame*

⁶The tents of marauders are undisturbed,
and those who provoke God are secure—
those God has in his hand.^a

⁷"But ask the animals, and they will teach you,
or the birds in the sky, and they will tell you;
⁸or speak to the earth, and it will teach you,
or let the fish in the sea inform you.
⁹Which of all these does not know
that the hand of the LORD has done this?
¹⁰In his hand is the life of every creature
and the breath of all mankind.
¹¹Does not the ear test words
as the tongue tastes food?
¹²Is not wisdom found among the aged?
Does not long life bring understanding?

¹³"To God belong wisdom and power;
counsel and understanding are his.
¹⁴What he tears down cannot be rebuilt;
those he imprisons cannot be released.
¹⁵If he holds back the waters, there is drought;
if he lets them loose, they devastate the land.
¹⁶To him belong strength and insight;
both deceived and deceiver are his.
¹⁷He leads rulers away stripped
and makes fools of judges.
¹⁸He takes off the shackles put on by kings
and ties a loincloth^b around their waist.
¹⁹He leads priests away stripped
and overthrows officials long established.
²⁰He silences the lips of trusted advisers
and takes away the discernment of elders.
²¹He pours contempt on nobles
and disarms the mighty.
²²He reveals the deep things of darkness
and brings utter darkness into the light.
²³He makes nations great, and destroys them;
he enlarges nations, and disperses them.
²⁴He deprives the leaders of the earth of their reason;
he makes them wander in a trackless waste.
²⁵They grope in darkness with no light;
he makes them stagger like drunkards.

13 "My eyes have seen all this,
my ears have heard and understood it.
²What you know, I also know;
I am not inferior to you.
³But I desire to speak to the Almighty
and to argue my case with God.
⁴You, however, smear me with lies;
you are worthless physicians, all of you!
⁵If only you would be altogether silent!
For you, that would be wisdom.

How did Job use creation to make his case? (12:7–12)
Job pointed toward creation to prove that God is free to do what he pleases with his creation, even if it means righteous people suffer and evil people are secure.

Did Job believe God is in control? (12:13)
Job believed that God is in control of the created world. The rest of this section focuses on the negative things God controls or allows to happen.

What did Job want his friends to do? (13:3–5)
Job wanted to make his case to God as if in a court of law, and his friends had become false witnesses by giving dishonest testimony about him. Job wanted them to remain silent rather than offering explanations for his suffering.

---

^a 6 Or *those whose god is in their own hand*   ^b 18 Or *shackles of kings / and ties a belt*

⁶ Hear now my argument;
   listen to the pleas of my lips.
⁷ Will you speak wickedly on God's behalf?
   Will you speak deceitfully for him?
⁸ Will you show him partiality?
   Will you argue the case for God?
⁹ Would it turn out well if he examined you?
   Could you deceive him as you might deceive a
      mortal?
¹⁰ He would surely call you to account
   if you secretly showed partiality.
¹¹ Would not his splendor terrify you?
   Would not the dread of him fall on you?
¹² Your maxims are proverbs of ashes;
   your defenses are defenses of clay.

¹³ "Keep silent and let me speak;
   then let come to me what may.
¹⁴ Why do I put myself in jeopardy
   and take my life in my hands?
¹⁵ Though he slay me, yet will I hope in him;^a
   I will surely^a defend my ways to his face.
¹⁶ Indeed, this will turn out for my deliverance,
   for no godless person would dare come before him!
¹⁷ Listen carefully to what I say;
   let my words ring in your ears.
¹⁸ Now that I have prepared my case,
   I know I will be vindicated.
¹⁹ Can anyone bring charges against me?
   If so, I will be silent and die.

²⁰ "Only grant me these two things, God,
   and then I will not hide from you:
²¹ Withdraw your hand far from me,
   and stop frightening me with your terrors.
²² Then summon me and I will answer,
   or let me speak, and you reply to me.
²³ How many wrongs and sins have I committed?
   Show me my offense and my sin.
²⁴ Why do you hide your face
   and consider me your enemy?
²⁵ Will you torment a windblown leaf?
   Will you chase after dry chaff?
²⁶ For you write down bitter things against me
   and make me reap the sins of my youth.
²⁷ You fasten my feet in shackles;
   you keep close watch on all my paths
   by putting marks on the soles of my feet.

²⁸ "So man wastes away like something rotten,
   like a garment eaten by moths.

14 "Mortals, born of woman,
   are of few days and full of trouble.
² They spring up like flowers and wither away;
   like fleeting shadows, they do not endure.

^a 15 Or *He will surely slay me; I have no hope — / yet I will*

What risk was Job willing to take? (13:14–15)
Job wanted to make his case directly to God, even though he knew God could punish him with death. Job believed that only a righteous person would dare to approach God in this way.

What did Job want from God? (13:20–22)
Job wanted God to withdraw his hand of punishment and to start communicating with him.

What argument did Job make to God about human beings? (14:1–6)
Job said human beings are insignificant, their lives are short, and they lack purity. Job asked why God would therefore take human beings so seriously, and he asked God to leave them alone.

³ Do you fix your eye on them?
    Will you bring them[a] before you for judgment?
⁴ Who can bring what is pure from the impure?
    No one!
⁵ A person's days are determined;
    you have decreed the number of his months
    and have set limits he cannot exceed.
⁶ So look away from him and let him alone,
    till he has put in his time like a hired laborer.

⁷ "At least there is hope for a tree:
    If it is cut down, it will sprout again,
    and its new shoots will not fail.
⁸ Its roots may grow old in the ground
    and its stump die in the soil,
⁹ yet at the scent of water it will bud
    and put forth shoots like a plant.
¹⁰ But a man dies and is laid low;
    he breathes his last and is no more.
¹¹ As the water of a lake dries up
    or a riverbed becomes parched and dry,
¹² so he lies down and does not rise;
    till the heavens are no more, people will
        not awake
    or be roused from their sleep.

To what type of renewal was Job referring? (14:13–17)
In this section, Job said God could allow a person to die and then bring that person back to life when he was no longer angry with him or her.

¹³ "If only you would hide me in the grave
    and conceal me till your anger has passed!
    If only you would set me a time
    and then remember me!
¹⁴ If someone dies, will they live again?
    All the days of my hard service
    I will wait for my renewal[b] to come.
¹⁵ You will call and I will answer you;
    you will long for the creature your hands
        have made.
¹⁶ Surely then you will count my steps
    but not keep track of my sin.
¹⁷ My offenses will be sealed up in a bag;
    you will cover over my sin.

¹⁸ "But as a mountain erodes and crumbles
    and as a rock is moved from its place,
¹⁹ as water wears away stones
    and torrents wash away the soil,
    so you destroy a person's hope.
²⁰ You overpower them once for all, and they
        are gone;
    you change their countenance and send
        them away.
²¹ If their children are honored, they do not know it;
    if their offspring are brought low, they do
        not see it.
²² They feel but the pain of their own bodies
    and mourn only for themselves."

---

a 3 Septuagint, Vulgate and Syriac; Hebrew *me*   *b 14* Or *release*

ELIPHAZ

15 Then Eliphaz the Temanite replied:

2 "Would a wise person answer with empty notions
   or fill their belly with the hot east wind?
3 Would they argue with useless words,
   with speeches that have no value?
4 But you even undermine piety
   and hinder devotion to God.
5 Your sin prompts your mouth;
   you adopt the tongue of the crafty.
6 Your own mouth condemns you, not mine;
   your own lips testify against you.

7 "Are you the first man ever born?
   Were you brought forth before the hills?
8 Do you listen in on God's council?
   Do you have a monopoly on wisdom?
9 What do you know that we do not know?
   What insights do you have that we do not have?
10 The gray-haired and the aged are on our side,
   men even older than your father.
11 Are God's consolations not enough for you,
   words spoken gently to you?
12 Why has your heart carried you away,
   and why do your eyes flash,
13 so that you vent your rage against God
   and pour out such words from your mouth?

14 "What are mortals, that they could be pure,
   or those born of woman, that they could be
      righteous?
15 If God places no trust in his holy ones,
   if even the heavens are not pure in his eyes,
16 how much less mortals, who are vile and corrupt,
   who drink up evil like water!

17 "Listen to me and I will explain to you;
   let me tell you what I have seen,
18 what the wise have declared,
   hiding nothing received from their ancestors
19 (to whom alone the land was given
   when no foreigners moved among them):

How did Eliphaz criticize Job? (15:7–13)
Eliphaz said Job claimed to be wise enough to sit in God's heavenly council even though he was not as wise as his friends, who spoke with the authority of the aged. He also criticized Job for being angry with his friends who were trying to comfort him with words from God.

According to Eliphaz, what happens to the wicked? (15:17–26)
Eliphaz described the fate of the wicked as being characterized by inner turmoil.

Is it wrong to be angry with God?   JOB 15

Job was angry because of his suffering, and he wanted to know why God had permitted it when Job had lived a righteous life. But God refused to answer him. It is natural to feel angry sometimes about life's hardships and even to blame God for allowing bad things to happen.

The Bible describes all sorts of ways that people related to God. For example, Abraham bargained with God to spare Sodom and Gomorrah. Moses begged God to care for the people in the wilderness. Many of the prophets asked God to punish unbelievers. Even Jesus asked the Father to take away his suffering. Thomas expressed doubts about Jesus' resurrection.

Because we are made in God's image, God knows about our feelings and emotions, and he wants us to be honest with him about our feelings. But at the same time, we need to be willing to accept God's will, even if it sometimes is difficult to understand. We should never become so angry with God that we insult him or lose our faith.

²⁰All his days the wicked man suffers torment,
the ruthless man through all the years stored up for
him.
²¹Terrifying sounds fill his ears;
when all seems well, marauders attack him.
²²He despairs of escaping the realm of darkness;
he is marked for the sword.
²³He wanders about for food like a vulture;
he knows the day of darkness is at hand.
²⁴Distress and anguish fill him with terror;
troubles overwhelm him, like a king poised to
attack,
²⁵because he shakes his fist at God
and vaunts himself against the Almighty,
²⁶defiantly charging against him
with a thick, strong shield.

²⁷"Though his face is covered with fat
and his waist bulges with flesh,
²⁸he will inhabit ruined towns
and houses where no one lives,
houses crumbling to rubble.
²⁹He will no longer be rich and his wealth will not
endure,
nor will his possessions spread over the land.
³⁰He will not escape the darkness;
a flame will wither his shoots,
and the breath of God's mouth will carry him away.
³¹Let him not deceive himself by trusting what is
worthless,
for he will get nothing in return.
³²Before his time he will wither,
and his branches will not flourish.
³³He will be like a vine stripped of its unripe grapes,
like an olive tree shedding its blossoms.
³⁴For the company of the godless will be barren,
and fire will consume the tents of those who love
bribes.
³⁵They conceive trouble and give birth to evil;
their womb fashions deceit."

JOB

16

Then Job replied:

²"I have heard many things like these;
you are miserable comforters, all of you!
³Will your long-winded speeches never end?
What ails you that you keep on arguing?
⁴I also could speak like you,
if you were in my place;
I could make fine speeches against you
and shake my head at you.
⁵But my mouth would encourage you;
comfort from my lips would bring you relief.

⁶"Yet if I speak, my pain is not relieved;
and if I refrain, it does not go away.

Why were fat people singled out? (15:27)
In ancient times, wealthy people were often described as being fat. Because the wealthy did not have to work for a living and could afford plenty of food, obesity was often seen as a sign of blessing. But in this case, a wealthy person who turned away from God would be punished.

Were Job's friends good comforters? (16:2–5)
Job called his friends "miserable comforters" because they made long speeches that were very critical of him. He said that had he been in their place, he would have offered encouragement and comfort.

⁷ Surely, God, you have worn me out;
    you have devastated my entire household.
⁸ You have shriveled me up — and it has become a
        witness;
    my gauntness rises up and testifies against me.
⁹ God assails me and tears me in his anger
    and gnashes his teeth at me;
    my opponent fastens on me his piercing eyes.
¹⁰ People open their mouths to jeer at me;
    they strike my cheek in scorn
    and unite together against me.
¹¹ God has turned me over to the ungodly
    and thrown me into the clutches of the wicked.
¹² All was well with me, but he shattered me;
    he seized me by the neck and crushed me.
    He has made me his target;
¹³   his archers surround me.
    Without pity, he pierces my kidneys
    and spills my gall on the ground.
¹⁴ Again and again he bursts upon me;
    he rushes at me like a warrior.

¹⁵ "I have sewed sackcloth over my skin
    and buried my brow in the dust.
¹⁶ My face is red with weeping,
    dark shadows ring my eyes;
¹⁷ yet my hands have been free of violence
    and my prayer is pure.

¹⁸ "Earth, do not cover my blood;
    may my cry never be laid to rest!
¹⁹ Even now my witness is in heaven;
    my advocate is on high.
²⁰ My intercessor is my friend*ª*
    as my eyes pour out tears to God;
²¹ on behalf of a man he pleads with God
    as one pleads for a friend.

²² "Only a few years will pass
    before I take the path of no return.

17 ¹ My spirit is broken,
    my days are cut short,
    the grave awaits me.
² Surely mockers surround me;
    my eyes must dwell on their hostility.

³ "Give me, O God, the pledge you demand.
    Who else will put up security for me?
⁴ You have closed their minds to understanding;
    therefore you will not let them triumph.
⁵ If anyone denounces their friends for reward,
    the eyes of their children will fail.

⁶ "God has made me a byword to everyone,
    a man in whose face people spit.
⁷ My eyes have grown dim with grief;
    my whole frame is but a shadow.

ª 20 Or My friends treat me with scorn

What was sackcloth? (16:15)
The English word *sackcloth* comes from the Hebrew word *sak*, which refers to a coarse cloth. This garment was worn by mourners and often by prophets. It usually was worn next to the skin with another garment over it.

What did Job mean when he said he had become a byword? (17:6)
Job's name had become an object of hatred and ridicule.

⁸The upright are appalled at this;
   the innocent are aroused against the ungodly.
⁹Nevertheless, the righteous will hold to their ways,
   and those with clean hands will grow stronger.

¹⁰"But come on, all of you, try again!
   I will not find a wise man among you.
¹¹My days have passed, my plans are shattered.
   Yet the desires of my heart
¹²turn night into day;
   in the face of the darkness light is near.
¹³If the only home I hope for is the grave,
   if I spread out my bed in the realm of darkness,
¹⁴if I say to corruption, 'You are my father,'
   and to the worm, 'My mother' or 'My sister,'
¹⁵where then is my hope—
   who can see any hope for me?
¹⁶Will it go down to the gates of death?
   Will we descend together into the dust?"

BILDAD

18 Then Bildad the Shuhite replied:

²"When will you end these speeches?
   Be sensible, and then we can talk.
³Why are we regarded as cattle
   and considered stupid in your sight?
⁴You who tear yourself to pieces in your anger,
   is the earth to be abandoned for your sake?
   Or must the rocks be moved from their place?

⁵"The lamp of a wicked man is snuffed out;
   the flame of his fire stops burning.
⁶The light in his tent becomes dark;
   the lamp beside him goes out.
⁷The vigor of his step is weakened;
   his own schemes throw him down.
⁸His feet thrust him into a net;
   he wanders into its mesh.
⁹A trap seizes him by the heel;
   a snare holds him fast.
¹⁰A noose is hidden for him on the ground;
   a trap lies in his path.
¹¹Terrors startle him on every side
   and dog his every step.
¹²Calamity is hungry for him;
   disaster is ready for him when he falls.
¹³It eats away parts of his skin;
   death's firstborn devours his limbs.
¹⁴He is torn from the security of his tent
   and marched off to the king of terrors.
¹⁵Fire resides*a* in his tent;
   burning sulfur is scattered over his dwelling.
¹⁶His roots dry up below
   and his branches wither above.

What were the gates of death? (17:16)
In Mesopotamian literature, everyone who entered the netherworld after death passed through a series of seven gates.

What was Bildad's attitude toward Job? (18:2–4)
Bildad wanted Job to stop arguing and accept the fact that the wicked suffered for their sins. Instead of sympathizing with Job, Bildad and the others wanted to win what they considered a theological debate.

---

a 15 Or *Nothing he had remains*

¹⁷The memory of him perishes from the earth;
  he has no name in the land.
¹⁸He is driven from light into the realm of darkness
  and is banished from the world.
¹⁹He has no offspring or descendants among his people,
  no survivor where once he lived.
²⁰People of the west are appalled at his fate;
  those of the east are seized with horror.
²¹Surely such is the dwelling of an evil man;
  such is the place of one who does not know God."

JOB

19

Then Job replied:

²"How long will you torment me
  and crush me with words?
³Ten times now you have reproached me;
  shamelessly you attack me.
⁴If it is true that I have gone astray,
  my error remains my concern alone.
⁵If indeed you would exalt yourselves above me
  and use my humiliation against me,
⁶then know that God has wronged me
  and drawn his net around me.

⁷"Though I cry, 'Violence!' I get no response;
  though I call for help, there is no justice.
⁸He has blocked my way so I cannot pass;
  he has shrouded my paths in darkness.
⁹He has stripped me of my honor
  and removed the crown from my head.
¹⁰He tears me down on every side till I am gone;
  he uproots my hope like a tree.
¹¹His anger burns against me;
  he counts me among his enemies.
¹²His troops advance in force;
  they build a siege ramp against me
  and encamp around my tent.

¹³"He has alienated my family from me;
  my acquaintances are completely estranged from me.
¹⁴My relatives have gone away;
  my closest friends have forgotten me.

Who were the "people of the west" and "those of the east"? (18:20)
This was a poetic way of saying that people everywhere would be horrified by the way a wicked person was punished.

Why was Job alone? (19:13–19)
Job's children were dead, and his wife, brothers, friends, and servants found him repulsive.

If God is all-powerful, why does he allow Satan to do evil things and to harm people?

JOB 19

God is both all-powerful and all-good. So God is not responsible for the harm and pain that Satan causes. It is not correct to blame God for the sickness, sadness, or suffering that people experience.

God the Father sent Jesus to earth to redeem the world and to defeat the power of Satan. Jesus accomplished that work by living a perfect life, dying on the cross for the sins of humanity, rising after three days in the grave, and ascending to rule with God in heaven. However, Satan is still a force in the world. Although Satan's power has been destroyed for eternity, in our current world, Satan still has some power. It is only when Christ returns that Satan's influence will no longer exist.

Even though God permits Satan to have some power, God can never be blamed for any evil. As Psalm 5:4–5 says, "You are not a God who is pleased with wickedness; with you, evil people are not welcome. The arrogant cannot stand in your presence. You hate all who do wrong."

¹⁵My guests and my female servants count me a
　　foreigner;
　　they look on me as on a stranger.
¹⁶I summon my servant, but he does not answer,
　　though I beg him with my own mouth.
¹⁷My breath is offensive to my wife;
　　I am loathsome to my own family.
¹⁸Even the little boys scorn me;
　　when I appear, they ridicule me.
¹⁹All my intimate friends detest me;
　　those I love have turned against me.
²⁰I am nothing but skin and bones;
　　I have escaped only by the skin of my teeth.ᵃ

²¹"Have pity on me, my friends, have pity,
　　for the hand of God has struck me.
²²Why do you pursue me as God does?
　　Will you never get enough of my flesh?

²³"Oh, that my words were recorded,
　　that they were written on a scroll,
²⁴that they were inscribed with an iron tool onᵇ lead,
　　or engraved in rock forever!
²⁵I know that my redeemerᶜ lives,
　　and that in the end he will stand on the earth.ᵈ
²⁶And after my skin has been destroyed,
　　yetᵉ inᶠ my flesh I will see God;
²⁷I myself will see him
　　with my own eyes—I, and not another.
　　How my heart yearns within me!

²⁸"If you say, 'How we will hound him,
　　since the root of the trouble lies in him,ᵍ'
²⁹you should fear the sword yourselves;
　　for wrath will bring punishment by the sword,
　　and then you will know that there is judgment.ʰ"

ZOPHAR

20 Then Zophar the Naamathite replied:

²"My troubled thoughts prompt me to answer
　　because I am greatly disturbed.
³I hear a rebuke that dishonors me,
　　and my understanding inspires me to reply.

⁴"Surely you know how it has been from of old,
　　ever since mankindⁱ was placed on the earth,
⁵that the mirth of the wicked is brief,
　　the joy of the godless lasts but a moment.
⁶Though the pride of the godless person reaches
　　to the heavens
　　and his head touches the clouds,
⁷he will perish forever, like his own dung;
　　those who have seen him will say, 'Where is he?'

**Who was Job's redeemer?
(19:25)**
Here the redeemer seems to
be God himself. Job seems to
be saying that God would stand
and vindicate his faithful servant
against all false accusations.

**Did Job believe in heaven?
(19:26–27)**
Job sensed that his disease
would eventually kill him, but he
also believed that someday he
would stand in the presence of
God and see him with his own
eyes.

**What was the rebuke Zophar
heard? (20:2–3)**
Job had said that his friends,
who wanted to blame him for
his suffering, should be afraid
of being punished themselves
(19:28–29).

ᵃ 20 Or *only by my gums*　　ᵇ 24 Or *and*　　ᶜ 25 Or *vindicator*　　ᵈ 25 Or *on
my grave*　　ᵉ 26 Or *And after I awake, / though this body has been destroyed, /
then*　　ᶠ 26 Or *destroyed, / apart from*　　ᵍ 28 Many Hebrew manuscripts,
Septuagint and Vulgate; most Hebrew manuscripts *me*　　ʰ 29 Or *sword, /
that you may come to know the Almighty*　　ⁱ 4 Or *Adam*

⁸ Like a dream he flies away, no more to be found,
　banished like a vision of the night.
⁹ The eye that saw him will not see him again;
　his place will look on him no more.
¹⁰ His children must make amends to the poor;
　his own hands must give back his wealth.
¹¹ The youthful vigor that fills his bones
　will lie with him in the dust.

¹² "Though evil is sweet in his mouth
　and he hides it under his tongue,
¹³ though he cannot bear to let it go
　and lets it linger in his mouth,
¹⁴ yet his food will turn sour in his stomach;
　it will become the venom of serpents within him.
¹⁵ He will spit out the riches he swallowed;
　God will make his stomach vomit them up.
¹⁶ He will suck the poison of serpents;
　the fangs of an adder will kill him.
¹⁷ He will not enjoy the streams,
　the rivers flowing with honey and cream.
¹⁸ What he toiled for he must give back uneaten;
　he will not enjoy the profit from his trading.
¹⁹ For he has oppressed the poor and left them destitute;
　he has seized houses he did not build.

²⁰ "Surely he will have no respite from his craving;
　he cannot save himself by his treasure.
²¹ Nothing is left for him to devour;
　his prosperity will not endure.
²² In the midst of his plenty, distress will overtake him;
　the full force of misery will come upon him.
²³ When he has filled his belly,
　God will vent his burning anger against him
　and rain down his blows on him.
²⁴ Though he flees from an iron weapon,
　a bronze-tipped arrow pierces him.
²⁵ He pulls it out of his back,
　the gleaming point out of his liver.
　Terrors will come over him;
²⁶ 　total darkness lies in wait for his treasures.
　A fire unfanned will consume him
　and devour what is left in his tent.
²⁷ The heavens will expose his guilt;
　the earth will rise up against him.
²⁸ A flood will carry off his house,
　rushing waters*a* on the day of God's wrath.
²⁹ Such is the fate God allots the wicked,
　the heritage appointed for them by God."

JOB

21 Then Job replied:

² "Listen carefully to my words;
　let this be the consolation you give me.

---

a 28 Or *The possessions in his house will be carried off, / washed away*

What was Zophar's argument? (20:4–29)
Zophar said that the wicked might be happy for a short time, but that they would be punished by God. He tried to prove that God rewarded good people and punished bad people.

How could rivers flow with honey and cream? (20:17)
This was a poetic way of describing the good life, in which people had plenty to eat and drink. In a similar way, Canaan was described as a land flowing with milk and honey (Exodus 13:5).

Why did these friends continue to argue? (21:3)
Arguing about Scripture or the events of life was an accepted part of Hebrew culture. People believed truth could be discovered by challenging one another's ideas and arguments.

How did Job answer the arguments of his counselors? (21:7–15)
Job's counselors claimed that the wicked were punished by God, but Job said just the opposite was true: The wicked seemed to be successful in everything.

Was Job bitter about the way God treated the wicked? (21:17)
Job was not accusing God of being unjust. He was countering the arguments made by his friends and pointing out that God often allowed the wicked to go unpunished.

What point was Job making about death? (21:23–26)
All people die, both those who fear God and those who don't.

³ Bear with me while I speak,
and after I have spoken, mock on.

⁴ "Is my complaint directed to a human being?
Why should I not be impatient?
⁵ Look at me and be appalled;
clap your hand over your mouth.
⁶ When I think about this, I am terrified;
trembling seizes my body.
⁷ Why do the wicked live on,
growing old and increasing in power?
⁸ They see their children established around them,
their offspring before their eyes.
⁹ Their homes are safe and free from fear;
the rod of God is not on them.
¹⁰ Their bulls never fail to breed;
their cows calve and do not miscarry.
¹¹ They send forth their children as a flock;
their little ones dance about.
¹² They sing to the music of timbrel and lyre;
they make merry to the sound of the pipe.
¹³ They spend their years in prosperity
and go down to the grave in peace.ᵃ
¹⁴ Yet they say to God, 'Leave us alone!
We have no desire to know your ways.
¹⁵ Who is the Almighty, that we should serve him?
What would we gain by praying to him?'
¹⁶ But their prosperity is not in their own hands,
so I stand aloof from the plans of the wicked.

¹⁷ "Yet how often is the lamp of the wicked snuffed out?
How often does calamity come upon them,
the fate God allots in his anger?
¹⁸ How often are they like straw before the wind,
like chaff swept away by a gale?
¹⁹ It is said, 'God stores up the punishment of the wicked
for their children.'
Let him repay the wicked, so that they themselves
will experience it!
²⁰ Let their own eyes see their destruction;
let them drink the cup of the wrath of the Almighty.
²¹ For what do they care about the families they leave
behind
when their allotted months come to an end?

²² "Can anyone teach knowledge to God,
since he judges even the highest?
²³ One person dies in full vigor,
completely secure and at ease,
²⁴ well nourished in body,ᵇ
bones rich with marrow.
²⁵ Another dies in bitterness of soul,
never having enjoyed anything good.
²⁶ Side by side they lie in the dust,
and worms cover them both.

ᵃ 13 Or *in an instant*   ᵇ 24 The meaning of the Hebrew for this word is uncertain.

²⁷ "I know full well what you are thinking,
   the schemes by which you would wrong me.
²⁸ You say, 'Where now is the house of the great,
   the tents where the wicked lived?'
²⁹ Have you never questioned those who travel?
   Have you paid no regard to their accounts—
³⁰ that the wicked are spared from the day of calamity,
   that they are delivered from^a the day of wrath?
³¹ Who denounces their conduct to their face?
   Who repays them for what they have done?
³² They are carried to the grave,
   and watch is kept over their tombs.
³³ The soil in the valley is sweet to them;
   everyone follows after them,
   and a countless throng goes^b before them.

³⁴ "So how can you console me with your nonsense?
   Nothing is left of your answers but falsehood!"

ELIPHAZ

22 Then Eliphaz the Temanite replied:

² "Can a man be of benefit to God?
   Can even a wise person benefit him?
³ What pleasure would it give the Almighty if you were
     righteous?
   What would he gain if your ways were blameless?

⁴ "Is it for your piety that he rebukes you
   and brings charges against you?
⁵ Is not your wickedness great?
   Are not your sins endless?
⁶ You demanded security from your relatives for
     no reason;
   you stripped people of their clothing, leaving
     them naked.
⁷ You gave no water to the weary
   and you withheld food from the hungry,
⁸ though you were a powerful man, owning land—
   an honored man, living on it.
⁹ And you sent widows away empty-handed
   and broke the strength of the fatherless.
¹⁰ That is why snares are all around you,
   why sudden peril terrifies you,
¹¹ why it is so dark you cannot see,
   and why a flood of water covers you.

¹² "Is not God in the heights of heaven?
   And see how lofty are the highest stars!
¹³ Yet you say, 'What does God know?
   Does he judge through such darkness?
¹⁴ Thick clouds veil him, so he does not see us
   as he goes about in the vaulted heavens.'
¹⁵ Will you keep to the old path
   that the wicked have trod?

Did Job actually behave in this evil way? (22:6–9) Eliphaz accused Job of serious wrongdoing, but he offered no proof. Job emphatically denied these charges (see chapter 29).

^a 30 Or *wicked are reserved for the day of calamity, / that they are brought forth to*
^b 33 Or *them, / as a countless throng went*

¹⁶ They were carried off before their time,
    their foundations washed away by a flood.
¹⁷ They said to God, 'Leave us alone!
    What can the Almighty do to us?'
¹⁸ Yet it was he who filled their houses with
      good things,
    so I stand aloof from the plans of the wicked.
¹⁹ The righteous see their ruin and rejoice;
    the innocent mock them, saying,
²⁰ 'Surely our foes are destroyed,
    and fire devours their wealth.'

²¹ "Submit to God and be at peace with him;
    in this way prosperity will come to you.
²² Accept instruction from his mouth
    and lay up his words in your heart.
²³ If you return to the Almighty, you will be restored:
    If you remove wickedness far from your tent
²⁴ and assign your nuggets to the dust,
    your gold of Ophir to the rocks in the ravines,
²⁵ then the Almighty will be your gold,
    the choicest silver for you.
²⁶ Surely then you will find delight in the Almighty
    and will lift up your face to God.
²⁷ You will pray to him, and he will hear you,
    and you will fulfill your vows.
²⁸ What you decide on will be done,
    and light will shine on your ways.
²⁹ When people are brought low and you say,
     'Lift them up!'
    then he will save the downcast.
³⁰ He will deliver even one who is not innocent,
    who will be delivered through the cleanness
      of your hands."

JOB

23

Then Job replied:

² "Even today my complaint is bitter;
    his hand^a is heavy in spite of^b my groaning.
³ If only I knew where to find him;
    if only I could go to his dwelling!
⁴ I would state my case before him
    and fill my mouth with arguments.
⁵ I would find out what he would answer me,
    and consider what he would say to me.
⁶ Would he vigorously oppose me?
    No, he would not press charges against me.
⁷ There the upright can establish their innocence
     before him,
    and there I would be delivered forever from
     my judge.
⁸ "But if I go to the east, he is not there;
    if I go to the west, I do not find him.

What did Eliphaz assume about Job? (22:21)
He assumed that Job had committed serious sins. Then he tried to persuade Job to repent, assuming that he wanted to return to prosperity.

Where was Ophir? (22:24)
Its exact location is unknown. Sites in southern Arabia, East Africa, and northern India are possibilities. Ophir was known for fine gold, silver, and ivory.

Did Job claim to be without sin? (23:7, 11–12)
No, but he did claim to be an honest man. He believed that he was innocent, and if he could present his case to God as if in a court of law, God would agree.

---

^a 2 Septuagint and Syriac; Hebrew / *the hand on me*   ^b 2 Or *heavy on me in*

⁹When he is at work in the north, I do not see him;
    when he turns to the south, I catch no glimpse of him.
¹⁰But he knows the way that I take;
    when he has tested me, I will come forth as gold.
¹¹My feet have closely followed his steps;
    I have kept to his way without turning aside.
¹²I have not departed from the commands of his lips;
    I have treasured the words of his mouth more than
       my daily bread.

¹³"But he stands alone, and who can oppose him?
    He does whatever he pleases.
¹⁴He carries out his decree against me,
    and many such plans he still has in store.
¹⁵That is why I am terrified before him;
    when I think of all this, I fear him.
¹⁶God has made my heart faint;
    the Almighty has terrified me.
¹⁷Yet I am not silenced by the darkness,
    by the thick darkness that covers my face.

24 "Why does the Almighty not set times for
      judgment?
  Why must those who know him look in vain for
      such days?
²There are those who move boundary stones;
    they pasture flocks they have stolen.
³They drive away the orphan's donkey
    and take the widow's ox in pledge.
⁴They thrust the needy from the path
    and force all the poor of the land into hiding.
⁵Like wild donkeys in the desert,
    the poor go about their labor of foraging food;
    the wasteland provides food for their children.
⁶They gather fodder in the fields
    and glean in the vineyards of the wicked.
⁷Lacking clothes, they spend the night naked;
    they have nothing to cover themselves in the cold.
⁸They are drenched by mountain rains
    and hug the rocks for lack of shelter.
⁹The fatherless child is snatched from the breast;
    the infant of the poor is seized for a debt.
¹⁰Lacking clothes, they go about naked;
    they carry the sheaves, but still go hungry.
¹¹They crush olives among the terraces*ᵃ*;
    they tread the winepresses, yet suffer thirst.
¹²The groans of the dying rise from the city,
    and the souls of the wounded cry out for help.
    But God charges no one with wrongdoing.

¹³"There are those who rebel against the light,
    who do not know its ways
    or stay in its paths.
¹⁴When daylight is gone, the murderer rises up,
    kills the poor and needy,
    and in the night steals forth like a thief.

ᵃ 11 The meaning of the Hebrew for this word is uncertain.

Did Job have a correct opinion about God? (23:13–17)
Even though Job was not an Israelite, he worshiped the one true God. Job didn't know what God had in store for him, and he was afraid. But he never claimed that God was not holy or just. The book of Job was most likely written before God established the nation of Israel.

How did Job describe the injustice in the world? (24:2–12)
Job gave several examples of ways the poor and powerless were mistreated by others. Job could not explain why God allowed such mistreatment and misery, but the fact that God permitted it disproved his counselors' theory of suffering.

¹⁵ The eye of the adulterer watches for dusk;
    he thinks, 'No eye will see me,'
    and he keeps his face concealed.
¹⁶ In the dark, thieves break into houses,
    but by day they shut themselves in;
    they want nothing to do with the light.
¹⁷ For all of them, midnight is their morning;
    they make friends with the terrors of darkness.

¹⁸ "Yet they are foam on the surface of the water;
    their portion of the land is cursed,
    so that no one goes to the vineyards.
¹⁹ As heat and drought snatch away the melted snow,
    so the grave snatches away those who have sinned.
²⁰ The womb forgets them,
    the worm feasts on them;
  the wicked are no longer remembered
    but are broken like a tree.
²¹ They prey on the barren and childless woman,
    and to the widow they show no kindness.
²² But God drags away the mighty by his power;
    though they become established, they have no
        assurance of life.
²³ He may let them rest in a feeling of security,
    but his eyes are on their ways.
²⁴ For a little while they are exalted, and then they are
        gone;
    they are brought low and gathered up like all others;
    they are cut off like heads of grain.

²⁵ "If this is not so, who can prove me false
    and reduce my words to nothing?"

BILDAD

25 Then Bildad the Shuhite replied:

² "Dominion and awe belong to God;
    he establishes order in the heights of heaven.
³ Can his forces be numbered?
    On whom does his light not rise?
⁴ How then can a mortal be righteous before God?
    How can one born of woman be pure?
⁵ If even the moon is not bright
    and the stars are not pure in his eyes,
⁶ how much less a mortal, who is but a maggot—
    a human being, who is only a worm!"

JOB

26 Then Job replied:

² "How you have helped the powerless!
    How you have saved the arm that is feeble!
³ What advice you have offered to one without wisdom!
    And what great insight you have displayed!
⁴ Who has helped you utter these words?
    And whose spirit spoke from your mouth?

Did Job think God would judge the wicked? (24:22–24)
Job believed God would judge the wicked in his own time, but he wished that God would give righteous people the satisfaction of seeing it happen (see verse 1).

Did Job agree that God punished wicked people? (24:24)
Job's friends had argued that suffering was God's punishment for wickedness. Since Job was suffering, they thought he must have been wicked. Job agreed that evil people would be punished at some point, but he wasn't willing to say that his own suffering was the result of sin he had committed.

What was Bildad's point? (25:2–6)
Bildad did not add anything new to the discussion. He simply said that human beings, because they were so inferior to God, could not be righteous.

⁵"The dead are in deep anguish,
  those beneath the waters and all that live in them.
⁶The realm of the dead is naked before God;
  Destruction*ᵃ* lies uncovered.
⁷He spreads out the northern skies over empty space;
  he suspends the earth over nothing.
⁸He wraps up the waters in his clouds,
  yet the clouds do not burst under their weight.
⁹He covers the face of the full moon,
  spreading his clouds over it.
¹⁰He marks out the horizon on the face of the waters
  for a boundary between light and darkness.
¹¹The pillars of the heavens quake,
  aghast at his rebuke.
¹²By his power he churned up the sea;
  by his wisdom he cut Rahab to pieces.
¹³By his breath the skies became fair;
  his hand pierced the gliding serpent.
¹⁴And these are but the outer fringe of his works;
  how faint the whisper we hear of him!
  Who then can understand the thunder of his power?"

JOB'S FINAL WORD TO HIS FRIENDS

27 And Job continued his discourse:

²"As surely as God lives, who has denied me justice,
  the Almighty, who has made my life bitter,
³as long as I have life within me,
  the breath of God in my nostrils,
⁴my lips will not say anything wicked,
  and my tongue will not utter lies.
⁵I will never admit you are in the right;
  till I die, I will not deny my integrity.
⁶I will maintain my innocence and never let go of it;
  my conscience will not reproach me as long as I live.

⁷"May my enemy be like the wicked,
  my adversary like the unjust!
⁸For what hope have the godless when they are cut off,
  when God takes away their life?
⁹Does God listen to their cry
  when distress comes upon them?
¹⁰Will they find delight in the Almighty?
  Will they call on God at all times?

¹¹"I will teach you about the power of God;
  the ways of the Almighty I will not conceal.
¹²You have all seen this yourselves.
  Why then this meaningless talk?

¹³"Here is the fate God allots to the wicked,
  the heritage a ruthless man receives from the
    Almighty:
¹⁴However many his children, their fate is the sword;
  his offspring will never have enough to eat.

ᵃ 6 Hebrew *Abaddon*

What was a gliding serpent? (26:13)
The gliding serpent was a mythological beast in some ancient Middle Eastern stories. It was an enormous, destructive monster that symbolized the damage nature could inflict.

What did Job say about God's power? (26:14)
God has great power over natural and supernatural forces, but this is just a whisper of God's power. Human beings are able to comprehend only a small part of his power.

What is the breath of God? (27:3)
The breath of God is life itself. When God created Adam, he breathed into him "the breath of life" (Genesis 2:7).

¹⁵The plague will bury those who survive him,
   and their widows will not weep for them.
¹⁶Though he heaps up silver like dust
   and clothes like piles of clay,
¹⁷what he lays up the righteous will wear,
   and the innocent will divide his silver.
¹⁸The house he builds is like a moth's cocoon,
   like a hut made by a watchman.
¹⁹He lies down wealthy, but will do so no more;
   when he opens his eyes, all is gone.
²⁰Terrors overtake him like a flood;
   a tempest snatches him away in the night.
²¹The east wind carries him off, and he is gone;
   it sweeps him out of his place.
²²It hurls itself against him without mercy
   as he flees headlong from its power.
²³It claps its hands in derision
   and hisses him out of his place."

INTERLUDE: WHERE WISDOM IS FOUND

28 There is a mine for silver
   and a place where gold is refined.
²Iron is taken from the earth,
   and copper is smelted from ore.
³Mortals put an end to the darkness;
   they search out the farthest recesses
   for ore in the blackest darkness.
⁴Far from human dwellings they cut a shaft,
   in places untouched by human feet;
   far from other people they dangle and sway.
⁵The earth, from which food comes,
   is transformed below as by fire;
⁶lapis lazuli comes from its rocks,
   and its dust contains nuggets of gold.
⁷No bird of prey knows that hidden path,
   no falcon's eye has seen it.
⁸Proud beasts do not set foot on it,
   and no lion prowls there.
⁹People assault the flinty rock with their hands
   and lay bare the roots of the mountains.
¹⁰They tunnel through the rock;
   their eyes see all its treasures.
¹¹They search^a the sources of the rivers
   and bring hidden things to light.

¹²But where can wisdom be found?
   Where does understanding dwell?
¹³No mortal comprehends its worth;
   it cannot be found in the land of the living.
¹⁴The deep says, "It is not in me";
   the sea says, "It is not with me."
¹⁵It cannot be bought with the finest gold,
   nor can its price be weighed out in silver.
¹⁶It cannot be bought with the gold of Ophir,
   with precious onyx or lapis lazuli.

What was the east wind? (27:21)
The east wind, also called a sirocco, was an extremely hot wind that blew in from the desert.

What is the theme of this chapter? (28:1–28)
This chapter asks where wisdom can be found. Its three sections convey: Precious stones and metals are found in the deepest mines (verses 1–11), wisdom is not found in mines and cannot be bought with precious stones or metals (verses 12–19), and wisdom can only be found in God (verses 20–28).

^a 11 Septuagint, Aquila and Vulgate; Hebrew They dam up

¹⁷ Neither gold nor crystal can compare with it,
    nor can it be had for jewels of gold.
¹⁸ Coral and jasper are not worthy of mention;
    the price of wisdom is beyond rubies.
¹⁹ The topaz of Cush cannot compare with it;
    it cannot be bought with pure gold.

²⁰ Where then does wisdom come from?
    Where does understanding dwell?
²¹ It is hidden from the eyes of every living thing,
    concealed even from the birds in the sky.
²² Destruction*ᵃ* and Death say,
    "Only a rumor of it has reached our ears."
²³ God understands the way to it
    and he alone knows where it dwells,
²⁴ for he views the ends of the earth
    and sees everything under the heavens.
²⁵ When he established the force of the wind
    and measured out the waters,
²⁶ when he made a decree for the rain
    and a path for the thunderstorm,
²⁷ then he looked at wisdom and appraised it;
    he confirmed it and tested it.
²⁸ And he said to the human race,
    "The fear of the Lord—that is wisdom,
    and to shun evil is understanding."

JOB'S FINAL DEFENSE

29 Job continued his discourse:

² "How I long for the months gone by,
    for the days when God watched over me,
³ when his lamp shone on my head
    and by his light I walked through darkness!
⁴ Oh, for the days when I was in my prime,
    when God's intimate friendship blessed my house,
⁵ when the Almighty was still with me
    and my children were around me,
⁶ when my path was drenched with cream
    and the rock poured out for me streams of olive oil.

⁷ "When I went to the gate of the city
    and took my seat in the public square,
⁸ the young men saw me and stepped aside
    and the old men rose to their feet;
⁹ the chief men refrained from speaking
    and covered their mouths with their hands;
¹⁰ the voices of the nobles were hushed,
    and their tongues stuck to the roof of their mouths.
¹¹ Whoever heard me spoke well of me,
    and those who saw me commended me,
¹² because I rescued the poor who cried for help,
    and the fatherless who had none to assist them.
¹³ The one who was dying blessed me;
    I made the widow's heart sing.

ᵃ *22* Hebrew *Abaddon*

Where was Cush? (28:19)
Cush was located in the upper Nile region, south of Egypt.

Cush

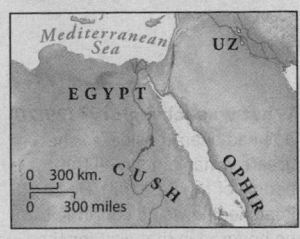

Why were cream and olive oil mentioned as signs of God's blessing? (29:6)
Both cream and olive oil were symbols of richness and luxury.

Why would Job have gone to the gate of the city? (29:7)
The gate of the city was where people conducted business and where legal matters were settled. Job was obviously respected as a city elder but also as someone who helped the poor and needy.

¹⁴ I put on righteousness as my clothing;
　　justice was my robe and my turban.
¹⁵ I was eyes to the blind
　　and feet to the lame.
¹⁶ I was a father to the needy;
　　I took up the case of the stranger.
¹⁷ I broke the fangs of the wicked
　　and snatched the victims from their teeth.

¹⁸ "I thought, 'I will die in my own house,
　　my days as numerous as the grains of sand.
¹⁹ My roots will reach to the water,
　　and the dew will lie all night on my branches.
²⁰ My glory will not fade;
　　the bow will be ever new in my hand.'

²¹ "People listened to me expectantly,
　　waiting in silence for my counsel.
²² After I had spoken, they spoke no more;
　　my words fell gently on their ears.
²³ They waited for me as for showers
　　and drank in my words as the spring rain.
²⁴ When I smiled at them, they scarcely believed it;
　　the light of my face was precious to them.[a]
²⁵ I chose the way for them and sat as their chief;
　　I dwelt as a king among his troops;
　　I was like one who comforts mourners.

30 "But now they mock me,
　　men younger than I,
whose fathers I would have disdained
　　to put with my sheep dogs.
² Of what use was the strength of their hands to me,
　　since their vigor had gone from them?
³ Haggard from want and hunger,
　　they roamed[b] the parched land
　　in desolate wastelands at night.
⁴ In the brush they gathered salt herbs,
　　and their food[c] was the root of the broom bush.
⁵ They were banished from human society,
　　shouted at as if they were thieves.
⁶ They were forced to live in the dry stream beds,
　　among the rocks and in holes in the ground.
⁷ They brayed among the bushes
　　and huddled in the undergrowth.
⁸ A base and nameless brood,
　　they were driven out of the land.

⁹ "And now those young men mock me in song;
　　I have become a byword among them.
¹⁰ They detest me and keep their distance;
　　they do not hesitate to spit in my face.
¹¹ Now that God has unstrung my bow and
　　afflicted me,
　　they throw off restraint in my presence.

What was Job's glory? (29:20)
Job had been considered the greatest man among all the people of the East (1:3). He had imagined he would continue to be honored in that way for the rest of his life.

Who was mocking Job? (30:1–9)
In contrast to Job's earlier status, Job now was mocked by the lowest class of people and the social outcasts.

What did it mean that God had unstrung Job's bow? (30:11)
In ancient times, a bow was used as a weapon and for hunting and was a sign of strength. Job used a word picture to show how he had been humbled. In his earlier life, Job had believed his bow would remain strong (29:20). But now that his bow did not have a bowstring, it was useless.

---

[a] 24 The meaning of the Hebrew for this clause is uncertain.
[b] 3 Or gnawed   [c] 4 Or fuel

¹²On my right the tribe*ᵃ* attacks;
    they lay snares for my feet,
    they build their siege ramps against me.
¹³They break up my road;
    they succeed in destroying me.
    'No one can help him,' they say.
¹⁴They advance as through a gaping breach;
    amid the ruins they come rolling in.
¹⁵Terrors overwhelm me;
    my dignity is driven away as by the wind,
    my safety vanishes like a cloud.

¹⁶"And now my life ebbs away;
    days of suffering grip me.
¹⁷Night pierces my bones;
    my gnawing pains never rest.
¹⁸In his great power God becomes like clothing to me*ᵇ*;
    he binds me like the neck of my garment.
¹⁹He throws me into the mud,
    and I am reduced to dust and ashes.

²⁰"I cry out to you, God, but you do not answer;
    I stand up, but you merely look at me.
²¹You turn on me ruthlessly;
    with the might of your hand you attack me.
²²You snatch me up and drive me before the wind;
    you toss me about in the storm.
²³I know you will bring me down to death,
    to the place appointed for all the living.

²⁴"Surely no one lays a hand on a broken man
    when he cries for help in his distress.
²⁵Have I not wept for those in trouble?
    Has not my soul grieved for the poor?
²⁶Yet when I hoped for good, evil came;
    when I looked for light, then came darkness.
²⁷The churning inside me never stops;
    days of suffering confront me.
²⁸I go about blackened, but not by the sun;
    I stand up in the assembly and cry for help.
²⁹I have become a brother of jackals,
    a companion of owls.
³⁰My skin grows black and peels;
    my body burns with fever.
³¹My lyre is tuned to mourning,
    and my pipe to the sound of wailing.

31

"I made a covenant with my eyes
    not to look lustfully at a young woman.
²For what is our lot from God above,
    our heritage from the Almighty on high?
³Is it not ruin for the wicked,
    disaster for those who do wrong?
⁴Does he not see my ways
    and count my every step?

What did dust and ashes symbolize? (30:19)
Dust and ashes symbolized humiliation and insignificance. Later Job used dust and ashes to symbolize repentance.

What covenant did Job make with his eyes? (31:1)
Job had made a promise not to look lustfully at a woman. In this section, Job focused on sins of the heart: lust (1–4), cheating in business (5–8), and unfaithfulness (9–12).

ᵃ 12 The meaning of the Hebrew for this word is uncertain.   *ᵇ 18* Hebrew;
Septuagint *power he grasps my clothing*

Why did Job invite judgment and curses on himself? (31:1–40)
Job continued to testify about his behavior as if he were in court. He described several sins and said that if he had committed them, he was willing to endure extremely harsh punishments. Job continued to declare that he was not guilty of sins that deserved the kind of suffering he experienced.

5 "If I have walked with falsehood
    or my foot has hurried after deceit—
6 let God weigh me in honest scales
    and he will know that I am blameless—
7 if my steps have turned from the path,
    if my heart has been led by my eyes,
    or if my hands have been defiled,
8 then may others eat what I have sown,
    and may my crops be uprooted.

9 "If my heart has been enticed by a woman,
    or if I have lurked at my neighbor's door,
10 then may my wife grind another man's grain,
    and may other men sleep with her.
11 For that would have been wicked,
    a sin to be judged.
12 It is a fire that burns to Destruction*;
    it would have uprooted my harvest.

13 "If I have denied justice to any of my servants,
    whether male or female,
    when they had a grievance against me,
14 what will I do when God confronts me?
    What will I answer when called to account?
15 Did not he who made me in the womb make them?
    Did not the same one form us both within our
        mothers?

16 "If I have denied the desires of the poor
    or let the eyes of the widow grow weary,
17 if I have kept my bread to myself,
    not sharing it with the fatherless—
18 but from my youth I reared them as a father would,
    and from my birth I guided the widow—
19 if I have seen anyone perishing for lack of clothing,
    or the needy without garments,
20 and their hearts did not bless me
    for warming them with the fleece from my sheep,
21 if I have raised my hand against the fatherless,
    knowing that I had influence in court,
22 then let my arm fall from the shoulder,
    let it be broken off at the joint.
23 For I dreaded destruction from God,
    and for fear of his splendor I could not do such things.

24 "If I have put my trust in gold
    or said to pure gold, 'You are my security,'
25 if I have rejoiced over my great wealth,
    the fortune my hands had gained,
26 if I have regarded the sun in its radiance
    or the moon moving in splendor,
27 so that my heart was secretly enticed
    and my hand offered them a kiss of homage,
28 then these also would be sins to be judged,
    for I would have been unfaithful to God on high.

29 "If I have rejoiced at my enemy's misfortune
    or gloated over the trouble that came to him—

What was a kiss of homage? (31:27)
In ancient times, a kiss made with the hand was often a gesture of worship for the sun or moon.

---
a 12 Hebrew *Abaddon*

³⁰ I have not allowed my mouth to sin
    by invoking a curse against their life—
³¹ if those of my household have never said,
    'Who has not been filled with Job's meat?'—
³² but no stranger had to spend the night in the street,
    for my door was always open to the traveler—
³³ if I have concealed my sin as people do,^a
    by hiding my guilt in my heart
³⁴ because I so feared the crowd
    and so dreaded the contempt of the clans
    that I kept silent and would not go outside—

³⁵ ("Oh, that I had someone to hear me!
    I sign now my defense—let the Almighty answer me;
    let my accuser put his indictment in writing.
³⁶ Surely I would wear it on my shoulder,
    I would put it on like a crown.
³⁷ I would give him an account of my every step;
    I would present it to him as to a ruler.)—

³⁸ "if my land cries out against me
    and all its furrows are wet with tears,
³⁹ if I have devoured its yield without payment
    or broken the spirit of its tenants,
⁴⁰ then let briers come up instead of wheat
    and stinkweed instead of barley."

The words of Job are ended.

ELIHU

32 So these three men stopped answering Job, because he was righteous in his own eyes. ² But Elihu son of Barakel the Buzite, of the family of Ram, became very angry with Job for justifying himself rather than God. ³ He was also angry with the three friends, because they had found no way to refute Job, and yet had condemned him.^b ⁴ Now Elihu had waited before speaking to Job because they were older than he. ⁵ But when he saw that the three men had nothing more to say, his anger was aroused.

⁶ So Elihu son of Barakel the Buzite said:

"I am young in years,
    and you are old;
that is why I was fearful,
    not daring to tell you what I know.
⁷ I thought, 'Age should speak;
    advanced years should teach wisdom.'
⁸ But it is the spirit^c in a person,
    the breath of the Almighty, that gives them
        understanding.
⁹ It is not only the old^d who are wise,
    not only the aged who understand what is right.

¹⁰ "Therefore I say: Listen to me;
    I too will tell you what I know.

What did Job mean by saying he would wear the written charges on his shoulder? (31:35–36)
Job was still using the metaphor of a lawsuit in which he was the defendant. If there were charges against him, he wanted them to be in writing.

Who was Elihu? (32:1–5)
He was a man from Buz, a desert region in the east. He had been listening to the speeches of the others but had respectfully remained silent because he was younger. He was angry because Job still claimed to be innocent and because the others had not been able to win the argument.

---

^a 33 Or *as Adam did*   ^b 3 Masoretic Text; an ancient Hebrew scribal tradition *Job, and so had condemned God*   ^c 8 Or *Spirit*; also in verse 18 ^d 9 Or *many*; or *great*

¹¹ I waited while you spoke,
  I listened to your reasoning;
while you were searching for words,
¹² I gave you my full attention.
But not one of you has proved Job wrong;
  none of you has answered his arguments.
¹³ Do not say, 'We have found wisdom;
  let God, not a man, refute him.'
¹⁴ But Job has not marshaled his words against me,
  and I will not answer him with your arguments.

¹⁵ "They are dismayed and have no more to say;
  words have failed them.
¹⁶ Must I wait, now that they are silent,
  now that they stand there with no reply?
¹⁷ I too will have my say;
  I too will tell what I know.
¹⁸ For I am full of words,
  and the spirit within me compels me;
¹⁹ inside I am like bottled-up wine,
  like new wineskins ready to burst.
²⁰ I must speak and find relief;
  I must open my lips and reply.
²¹ I will show no partiality,
  nor will I flatter anyone;
²² for if I were skilled in flattery,
  my Maker would soon take me away.

33 "But now, Job, listen to my words;
  pay attention to everything I say.
² I am about to open my mouth;
  my words are on the tip of my tongue.
³ My words come from an upright heart;
  my lips sincerely speak what I know.
⁴ The Spirit of God has made me;
  the breath of the Almighty gives me life.
⁵ Answer me then, if you can;
  stand up and argue your case before me.
⁶ I am the same as you in God's sight;
  I too am a piece of clay.
⁷ No fear of me should alarm you,
  nor should my hand be heavy on you.

⁸ "But you have said in my hearing—
  I heard the very words—
⁹ 'I am pure, I have done no wrong;
  I am clean and free from sin.
¹⁰ Yet God has found fault with me;
  he considers me his enemy.
¹¹ He fastens my feet in shackles;
  he keeps close watch on all my paths.'

¹² "But I tell you, in this you are not right,
  for God is greater than any mortal.
¹³ Why do you complain to him
  that he responds to no one's words*a*?

---

a 13 Or *that he does not answer for any of his actions*

How was Elihu like bottled-up wine? (32:19)
When wine ferments, it releases gases that can break open a container. Elihu had been waiting to speak, and he was ready to explode.

Why did Elihu think Job was wrong? (33:12)
Elihu thought Job was claiming to be perfect. He also took Job's complaint about God's silence in his present circumstances to mean that Job thought God never spoke to people.

¹⁴ For God does speak—now one way, now another—
    though no one perceives it.
¹⁵ In a dream, in a vision of the night,
    when deep sleep falls on people
    as they slumber in their beds,
¹⁶ he may speak in their ears
    and terrify them with warnings,
¹⁷ to turn them from wrongdoing
    and keep them from pride,
¹⁸ to preserve them from the pit,
    their lives from perishing by the sword.ᵃ

¹⁹ "Or someone may be chastened on a bed of pain
    with constant distress in their bones,
²⁰ so that their body finds food repulsive
    and their soul loathes the choicest meal.
²¹ Their flesh wastes away to nothing,
    and their bones, once hidden, now stick out.
²² They draw near to the pit,
    and their life to the messengers of death.ᵇ
²³ Yet if there is an angel at their side,
    a messenger, one out of a thousand,
    sent to tell them how to be upright,
²⁴ and he is gracious to that person and says to God,
    'Spare them from going down to the pit;
    I have found a ransom for them—
²⁵ let their flesh be renewed like a child's;
    let them be restored as in the days of their youth'—
²⁶ then that person can pray to God and find favor
      with him,
    they will see God's face and shout for joy;
    he will restore them to full well-being.
²⁷ And they will go to others and say,
    'I have sinned, I have perverted what is right,
    but I did not get what I deserved.
²⁸ God has delivered me from going down to the pit,
    and I shall live to enjoy the light of life.'

²⁹ "God does all these things to a person—
    twice, even three times—
³⁰ to turn them back from the pit,
    that the light of life may shine on them.

³¹ "Pay attention, Job, and listen to me;
    be silent, and I will speak.
³² If you have anything to say, answer me;
    speak up, for I want to vindicate you.
³³ But if not, then listen to me;
    be silent, and I will teach you wisdom."

34 Then Elihu said:

² "Hear my words, you wise men;
    listen to me, you men of learning.
³ For the ear tests words
    as the tongue tastes food.

What was the pit? (33:18)
This was a metaphor for the grave, or death.

What did Elihu think Job needed to do? (33:23–28)
Elihu thought Job needed to repent, and then an angel or other mediator could argue his case before God.

ᵃ *18 Or from crossing the river*   ᵇ *22 Or to the place of the dead*

⁴ Let us discern for ourselves what is right;
  let us learn together what is good.

⁵ "Job says, 'I am innocent,
  but God denies me justice.
⁶ Although I am right,
  I am considered a liar;
  although I am guiltless,
  his arrow inflicts an incurable wound.'
⁷ Is there anyone like Job,
  who drinks scorn like water?
⁸ He keeps company with evildoers;
  he associates with the wicked.
⁹ For he says, 'There is no profit
  in trying to please God.'

Why did Elihu defend God? (34:10)
Elihu thought Job was calling God the author of evil. In fact, Job had come close to claiming that God had acted wrongfully.

¹⁰ "So listen to me, you men of understanding.
  Far be it from God to do evil,
  from the Almighty to do wrong.
¹¹ He repays everyone for what they have done;
  he brings on them what their conduct deserves.
¹² It is unthinkable that God would do wrong,
  that the Almighty would pervert justice.
¹³ Who appointed him over the earth?
  Who put him in charge of the whole world?
¹⁴ If it were his intention
  and he withdrew his spirit ᵃ and breath,
¹⁵ all humanity would perish together
  and mankind would return to the dust.

¹⁶ "If you have understanding, hear this;
  listen to what I say.
¹⁷ Can someone who hates justice govern?
  Will you condemn the just and mighty One?
¹⁸ Is he not the One who says to kings, 'You are worthless,'
  and to nobles, 'You are wicked,'
¹⁹ who shows no partiality to princes
  and does not favor the rich over the poor,
  for they are all the work of his hands?
²⁰ They die in an instant, in the middle of the night;
  the people are shaken and they pass away;
  the mighty are removed without human hand.

²¹ "His eyes are on the ways of mortals;
  he sees their every step.
²² There is no deep shadow, no utter darkness,
  where evildoers can hide.
²³ God has no need to examine people further,
  that they should come before him for judgment.
²⁴ Without inquiry he shatters the mighty
  and sets up others in their place.
²⁵ Because he takes note of their deeds,
  he overthrows them in the night and they are crushed.
²⁶ He punishes them for their wickedness
  where everyone can see them,
²⁷ because they turned from following him
  and had no regard for any of his ways.

ᵃ 14 Or *Spirit*

28 They caused the cry of the poor to come before him,
so that he heard the cry of the needy.
29 But if he remains silent, who can condemn him?
If he hides his face, who can see him?
Yet he is over individual and nation alike,
30 to keep the godless from ruling,
from laying snares for the people.

31 "Suppose someone says to God,
'I am guilty but will offend no more.
32 Teach me what I cannot see;
if I have done wrong, I will not do so again.'
33 Should God then reward you on your terms,
when you refuse to repent?
You must decide, not I;
so tell me what you know.

34 "Men of understanding declare,
wise men who hear me say to me,
35 'Job speaks without knowledge;
his words lack insight.'
36 Oh, that Job might be tested to the utmost
for answering like a wicked man!
37 To his sin he adds rebellion;
scornfully he claps his hands among us
and multiplies his words against God."

35 Then Elihu said:

2 "Do you think this is just?
You say, 'I am in the right, not God.'
3 Yet you ask him, 'What profit is it to me,[a]
and what do I gain by not sinning?'

4 "I would like to reply to you
and to your friends with you.
5 Look up at the heavens and see;
gaze at the clouds so high above you.
6 If you sin, how does that affect him?
If your sins are many, what does that do to him?
7 If you are righteous, what do you give to him,
or what does he receive from your hand?
8 Your wickedness only affects humans like yourself,
and your righteousness only other people.

9 "People cry out under a load of oppression;
they plead for relief from the arm of the powerful.
10 But no one says, 'Where is God my Maker,
who gives songs in the night,
11 who teaches us more than he teaches[b] the beasts
of the earth
and makes us wiser than[c] the birds in the sky?'
12 He does not answer when people cry out
because of the arrogance of the wicked.
13 Indeed, God does not listen to their empty plea;
the Almighty pays no attention to it.

[a] 3 Or you   [b] 10,11 Or night, / [11] who teaches us by   [c] 11 Or us wise by

How did Elihu explain God's silence? (34:29–30)
Elihu said that God watches over people and nations to make sure right is done.

What was Job's mistake according to Elihu? (34:31–33)
He thought Job should repent of his sin rather than acting as if he were innocent and asking God to show him how he had sinned.

Was Job rebelling against God? (34:37)
No. Job was not rebelling against God. He was revolting against the injustice in his life. He was complaining because God allowed the injustice to remain unanswered.

Did Elihu think people could influence God by their actions? (35:5–8)
Elihu said God is so far above human beings that whatever they do—whether good or bad—will not affect him.

Was Job arrogant? (35:12–13)
Elihu defended God by saying he did not answer people who called on him when they were unrepentant. He suggested that Job was guilty and therefore God did not need to answer him.

¹⁴ How much less, then, will he listen
    when you say that you do not see him,
that your case is before him
    and you must wait for him,
¹⁵ and further, that his anger never punishes
    and he does not take the least notice of wickedness.ᵃ
¹⁶ So Job opens his mouth with empty talk;
    without knowledge he multiplies words."

36 Elihu continued:

² "Bear with me a little longer and I will show you
    that there is more to be said in God's behalf.
³ I get my knowledge from afar;
    I will ascribe justice to my Maker.
⁴ Be assured that my words are not false;
    one who has perfect knowledge is with you.

⁵ "God is mighty, but despises no one;
    he is mighty, and firm in his purpose.
⁶ He does not keep the wicked alive
    but gives the afflicted their rights.
⁷ He does not take his eyes off the righteous;
    he enthrones them with kings
    and exalts them forever.
⁸ But if people are bound in chains,
    held fast by cords of affliction,
⁹ he tells them what they have done—
    that they have sinned arrogantly.
¹⁰ He makes them listen to correction
    and commands them to repent of their evil.
¹¹ If they obey and serve him,
    they will spend the rest of their days in prosperity
    and their years in contentment.
¹² But if they do not listen,
    they will perish by the swordᵇ
    and die without knowledge.

¹³ "The godless in heart harbor resentment;
    even when he fetters them, they do not cry for help.
¹⁴ They die in their youth,
    among male prostitutes of the shrines.
¹⁵ But those who suffer he delivers in their suffering;
    he speaks to them in their affliction.

¹⁶ "He is wooing you from the jaws of distress
    to a spacious place free from restriction,
    to the comfort of your table laden with choice food.
¹⁷ But now you are laden with the judgment due the wicked;
    judgment and justice have taken hold of you.
¹⁸ Be careful that no one entices you by riches;
    do not let a large bribe turn you aside.
¹⁹ Would your wealth or even all your mighty efforts
    sustain you so you would not be in distress?

What were "male prostitutes of the shrines"? (36:14)
Pagan worshipers thought that by taking on the role of the gods, prostitutes could force the gods to do certain things. Prostitution became a way of "praying" for outcomes such as a good harvest.

Did Job trust in his wealth or drag people from their homes? (36:19-21)
There is no evidence that Job did either of these things. Elihu may have simply been trying to come up with an explanation for Job's suffering.

ᵃ 15 Symmachus, Theodotion and Vulgate; the meaning of the Hebrew for this word is uncertain.   ᵇ 12 Or *will cross the river*

²⁰ Do not long for the night,
　　to drag people away from their homes.ᵃ
²¹ Beware of turning to evil,
　　which you seem to prefer to affliction.

²² "God is exalted in his power.
　　Who is a teacher like him?
²³ Who has prescribed his ways for him,
　　or said to him, 'You have done wrong'?
²⁴ Remember to extol his work,
　　which people have praised in song.
²⁵ All humanity has seen it;
　　mortals gaze on it from afar.
²⁶ How great is God—beyond our understanding!
　　The number of his years is past finding out.

²⁷ "He draws up the drops of water,
　　which distill as rain to the streamsᵇ;
²⁸ the clouds pour down their moisture
　　and abundant showers fall on mankind.
²⁹ Who can understand how he spreads out the clouds,
　　how he thunders from his pavilion?
³⁰ See how he scatters his lightning about him,
　　bathing the depths of the sea.
³¹ This is the way he governsᶜ the nations
　　and provides food in abundance.
³² He fills his hands with lightning
　　and commands it to strike its mark.
³³ His thunder announces the coming storm;
　　even the cattle make known its approach.ᵈ

37 "At this my heart pounds
　　and leaps from its place.
² Listen! Listen to the roar of his voice,
　　to the rumbling that comes from his mouth.
³ He unleashes his lightning beneath the whole heaven
　　and sends it to the ends of the earth.
⁴ After that comes the sound of his roar;
　　he thunders with his majestic voice.
　When his voice resounds,
　　he holds nothing back.
⁵ God's voice thunders in marvelous ways;
　　he does great things beyond our understanding.
⁶ He says to the snow, 'Fall on the earth,'
　　and to the rain shower, 'Be a mighty downpour.'
⁷ So that everyone he has made may know his work,
　　he stops all people from their labor.ᵉ
⁸ The animals take cover;
　　they remain in their dens.
⁹ The tempest comes out from its chamber,
　　the cold from the driving winds.
¹⁰ The breath of God produces ice,
　　and the broad waters become frozen.

Is God beyond human understanding? (36:26)
Yes. God is so magnificent that human beings cannot comprehend him. The Bible uses human terms to try to describe him, but they only hint at what God is truly like.

Is God in charge of nature? (37:1–13)
Yes. Elihu describes the awesome power God displays in nature. His description is a sophisticated observation of atmospheric conditions.

ᵃ 20 The meaning of the Hebrew for verses 18-20 is uncertain.
ᵇ 27 Or *distill from the mist as rain*　ᶜ 31 Or *nourishes*　ᵈ 33 Or *announces his coming — / the One zealous against evil*　ᵉ 7 Or *work, / he fills all people with fear by his power*

¹¹ He loads the clouds with moisture;
  he scatters his lightning through them.
¹² At his direction they swirl around
    over the face of the whole earth
    to do whatever he commands them.
¹³ He brings the clouds to punish people,
    or to water his earth and show his love.

¹⁴ "Listen to this, Job;
    stop and consider God's wonders.
¹⁵ Do you know how God controls the clouds
    and makes his lightning flash?
¹⁶ Do you know how the clouds hang poised,
    those wonders of him who has perfect knowledge?
¹⁷ You who swelter in your clothes
    when the land lies hushed under the south wind,
¹⁸ can you join him in spreading out the skies,
    hard as a mirror of cast bronze?

¹⁹ "Tell us what we should say to him;
    we cannot draw up our case because of our darkness.
²⁰ Should he be told that I want to speak?
    Would anyone ask to be swallowed up?
²¹ Now no one can look at the sun,
    bright as it is in the skies
    after the wind has swept them clean.
²² Out of the north he comes in golden splendor;
    God comes in awesome majesty.
²³ The Almighty is beyond our reach and exalted in
        power;
    in his justice and great righteousness, he does not
        oppress.
²⁴ Therefore, people revere him,
    for does he not have regard for all the wise in heart?ᵃ"

THE LORD SPEAKS

38 Then the LORD spoke to Job out of the storm. He
said:

² "Who is this that obscures my plans
    with words without knowledge?
³ Brace yourself like a man;
    I will question you,
    and you shall answer me.

⁴ "Where were you when I laid the earth's foundation?
    Tell me, if you understand.
⁵ Who marked off its dimensions? Surely you know!
    Who stretched a measuring line across it?
⁶ On what were its footings set,
    or who laid its cornerstone—
⁷ while the morning stars sang together
    and all the angelsᵇ shouted for joy?

⁸ "Who shut up the sea behind doors
    when it burst forth from the womb,

How is God like the sun?
(37:21–22)
In the Bible, God's glory is often compared to the sun. People cannot look directly at God, just as they cannot look directly at the sun. Like the sun, God is powerful and glorious.

Who are the wise in heart?
(37:24)
In the book of Job, wisdom is defined as accepting whatever God sends, whether it is good or bad. According to Elihu, those who are wise in heart believe that God never allows trouble to come to those who are righteous.

How did God appear to Job?
(38:1)
In the Old Testament, God appeared to people in various ways. Here he appeared to Job in a storm.

How did God answer Job's charges? (38:1–41)
God did not make any reference to Job's suffering. Instead, God reminded Job that he is an all-powerful and all-loving God. Even though evil and suffering take place, God is still in control.

ᵃ 24 Or *for he does not have regard for any who think they are wise.*
ᵇ 7 Hebrew *the sons of God*

⁹when I made the clouds its garment
  and wrapped it in thick darkness,
¹⁰when I fixed limits for it
  and set its doors and bars in place,
¹¹when I said, 'This far you may come and no farther;
  here is where your proud waves halt'?

¹²"Have you ever given orders to the morning,
  or shown the dawn its place,
¹³that it might take the earth by the edges
  and shake the wicked out of it?
¹⁴The earth takes shape like clay under a seal;
  its features stand out like those of a garment.
¹⁵The wicked are denied their light,
  and their upraised arm is broken.

¹⁶"Have you journeyed to the springs of the sea
  or walked in the recesses of the deep?
¹⁷Have the gates of death been shown to you?
  Have you seen the gates of the deepest darkness?
¹⁸Have you comprehended the vast expanses of the
  earth?
  Tell me, if you know all this.

¹⁹"What is the way to the abode of light?
  And where does darkness reside?
²⁰Can you take them to their places?
  Do you know the paths to their dwellings?
²¹Surely you know, for you were already born!
  You have lived so many years!

²²"Have you entered the storehouses of the snow
  or seen the storehouses of the hail,
²³which I reserve for times of trouble,
  for days of war and battle?
²⁴What is the way to the place where the lightning is
  dispersed,
  or the place where the east winds are scattered over
  the earth?
²⁵Who cuts a channel for the torrents of rain,
  and a path for the thunderstorm,
²⁶to water a land where no one lives,
  an uninhabited desert,
²⁷to satisfy a desolate wasteland
  and make it sprout with grass?
²⁸Does the rain have a father?
  Who fathers the drops of dew?
²⁹From whose womb comes the ice?
  Who gives birth to the frost from the heavens
³⁰when the waters become hard as stone,
  when the surface of the deep is frozen?

³¹"Can you bind the chains*a* of the Pleiades?
  Can you loosen Orion's belt?
³²Can you bring forth the constellations in their seasons*b*
  or lead out the Bear*c* with its cubs?

a 31 Septuagint; Hebrew beauty   *b 32 Or* the morning star in its season
c 32 Or out Leo

What was clay under a seal? (38:14)
This refers to the way documents were sealed. People used a small cylinder seal or a stamp seal pressed in soft wax or clay to close documents and to show that the documents were legal.

33 Do you know the laws of the heavens?
Can you set up God's[a] dominion over the earth?

34 "Can you raise your voice to the clouds
and cover yourself with a flood of water?
35 Do you send the lightning bolts on their way?
Do they report to you, 'Here we are'?
36 Who gives the ibis wisdom[b]
or gives the rooster understanding?[c]
37 Who has the wisdom to count the clouds?
Who can tip over the water jars of the heavens
38 when the dust becomes hard
and the clods of earth stick together?

39 "Do you hunt the prey for the lioness
and satisfy the hunger of the lions
40 when they crouch in their dens
or lie in wait in a thicket?
41 Who provides food for the raven
when its young cry out to God
and wander about for lack of food?

39 "Do you know when the mountain goats
give birth?
Do you watch when the doe bears her fawn?
2 Do you count the months till they bear?
Do you know the time they give birth?
3 They crouch down and bring forth their young;
their labor pains are ended.
4 Their young thrive and grow strong in the wilds;
they leave and do not return.

5 "Who let the wild donkey go free?
Who untied its ropes?
6 I gave it the wasteland as its home,
the salt flats as its habitat.
7 It laughs at the commotion in the town;
it does not hear a driver's shout.
8 It ranges the hills for its pasture
and searches for any green thing.

9 "Will the wild ox consent to serve you?
Will it stay by your manger at night?
10 Can you hold it to the furrow with a harness?
Will it till the valleys behind you?
11 Will you rely on it for its great strength?
Will you leave your heavy work to it?
12 Can you trust it to haul in your grain
and bring it to your threshing floor?

13 "The wings of the ostrich flap joyfully,
though they cannot compare
with the wings and feathers of the stork.
14 She lays her eggs on the ground
and lets them warm in the sand,

What can the animal kingdom teach us about God?
(39:1–30)
The animal kingdom shows that God is pleased with variety. It also shows God's loving control over all creation. In his providence, God cares for all of his creatures.

What was the wild ox?
(39:9–11)
In the Old Testament, the wild ox (also called the aurochs or urus) often symbolized strength. The animal is now extinct.

---

a 33 Or *their* b 36 That is, wisdom about the flooding of the Nile
c 36 That is, understanding of when to crow; the meaning of the Hebrew for
this verse is uncertain.

¹⁵unmindful that a foot may crush them,
　　that some wild animal may trample them.
¹⁶She treats her young harshly, as if they were not hers;
　　she cares not that her labor was in vain,
¹⁷for God did not endow her with wisdom
　　or give her a share of good sense.
¹⁸Yet when she spreads her feathers to run,
　　she laughs at horse and rider.”

¹⁹“Do you give the horse its strength
　　or clothe its neck with a flowing mane?
²⁰Do you make it leap like a locust,
　　striking terror with its proud snorting?
²¹It paws fiercely, rejoicing in its strength,
　　and charges into the fray.
²²It laughs at fear, afraid of nothing;
　　it does not shy away from the sword.
²³The quiver rattles against its side,
　　along with the flashing spear and lance.
²⁴In frenzied excitement it eats up the ground;
　　it cannot stand still when the trumpet sounds.
²⁵At the blast of the trumpet it snorts, ‘Aha!’
　　It catches the scent of battle from afar,
　　the shout of commanders and the battle cry.

²⁶“Does the hawk take flight by your wisdom
　　and spread its wings toward the south?
²⁷Does the eagle soar at your command
　　and build its nest on high?
²⁸It dwells on a cliff and stays there at night;
　　a rocky crag is its stronghold.
²⁹From there it looks for food;
　　its eyes detect it from afar.
³⁰Its young ones feast on blood,
　　and where the slain are, there it is.”

40 The Lord said to Job:

²“Will the one who contends with the Almighty
　　　correct him?
　　Let him who accuses God answer him!”

³Then Job answered the Lord:

⁴“I am unworthy—how can I reply to you?
　　I put my hand over my mouth.
⁵I spoke once, but I have no answer—
　　twice, but I will say no more.”

⁶Then the Lord spoke to Job out of the storm:

⁷“Brace yourself like a man;
　　I will question you,
　　and you shall answer me.

⁸“Would you discredit my justice?
　　Would you condemn me to justify yourself?
⁹Do you have an arm like God’s,
　　and can your voice thunder like his?

How did Job respond to the Lord? (40:4–5)
Job did not offer any further complaints and put his hand over his mouth, a traditional sign of respect and submission to a powerful ruler.

Had Job condemned God to justify himself? (40:8)
In a way, he had. Job had said, “God has wronged me” (19:6).

¹⁰ Then adorn yourself with glory and splendor,
    and clothe yourself in honor and majesty.
¹¹ Unleash the fury of your wrath,
    look at all who are proud and bring them low,
¹² look at all who are proud and humble them,
    crush the wicked where they stand.
¹³ Bury them all in the dust together;
    shroud their faces in the grave.
¹⁴ Then I myself will admit to you
    that your own right hand can save you.

¹⁵ "Look at Behemoth,
    which I made along with you
    and which feeds on grass like an ox.
¹⁶ What strength it has in its loins,
    what power in the muscles of its belly!
¹⁷ Its tail sways like a cedar;
    the sinews of its thighs are close-knit.
¹⁸ Its bones are tubes of bronze,
    its limbs like rods of iron.
¹⁹ It ranks first among the works of God,
    yet its Maker can approach it with
        his sword.
²⁰ The hills bring it their produce,
    and all the wild animals play nearby.
²¹ Under the lotus plants it lies,
    hidden among the reeds in the marsh.
²² The lotuses conceal it in their shadow;
    the poplars by the stream surround it.
²³ A raging river does not alarm it;
    it is secure, though the Jordan should surge
        against its mouth.
²⁴ Can anyone capture it by the eyes,
    or trap it and pierce its nose?

41 ᵃ "Can you pull in Leviathan with a fishhook
    or tie down its tongue with a rope?
² Can you put a cord through its nose
    or pierce its jaw with a hook?
³ Will it keep begging you for mercy?
    Will it speak to you with gentle words?

ᵃ In Hebrew texts 41:1-8 is numbered 40:25-32, and 41:9-34 is numbered 41:1-26.

What was a Behemoth?
(40:15)
The Hebrew word *Behemoth* means *beast par excellence* and describes a large land animal, possibly a hippopotamus, elephant, or what we now call a dinosaur. This was a real animal rather than a mythological creature.

What was this Leviathan?
(41:1–34)
Literally, the Leviathan may have been a crocodile. But symbolically, the leviathan may have represented evil political powers. A human being could not stand up to a leviathan, yet God was even more powerful than this creature.

Did God create dinosaurs?

JOB 40

Yes. Scientists continue to uncover dinosaur bones and to learn more about their appearance, habitat, and behavior. Science and the Bible do not have to be seen as being in conflict. In fact, there are some passages in Scripture that seem to describe dinosaur-like creatures. For example, Job 40:15–18 says: "Look at Behemoth which I made along with you and which feeds on grass like an ox. What strength it has in his loins, what power in the muscles of its belly! Its tail sways like a cedar; the sinews of its thighs are close-knit. Its bones are tubes of bronze, its limbs like rods of iron." Although this passage might describe an elephant or a hippopotamus, it might more accurately describe a dinosaur like a Diplodocus or Apatosaurus. Although we don't know all the details about when dinosaurs lived or how they became extinct, it does seem clear that they were creatures that once inhabited the earth, and — like all other creatures — they were created by God.

⁴ Will it make an agreement with you
     for you to take it as your slave for life?
⁵ Can you make a pet of it like a bird
     or put it on a leash for the young women in your
        house?
⁶ Will traders barter for it?
     Will they divide it up among the merchants?
⁷ Can you fill its hide with harpoons
     or its head with fishing spears?
⁸ If you lay a hand on it,
     you will remember the struggle and never
        do it again!
⁹ Any hope of subduing it is false;
     the mere sight of it is overpowering.
¹⁰ No one is fierce enough to rouse it.
     Who then is able to stand against me?
¹¹ Who has a claim against me that I must pay?
     Everything under heaven belongs to me.

¹² "I will not fail to speak of Leviathan's limbs,
     its strength and its graceful form.
¹³ Who can strip off its outer coat?
     Who can penetrate its double coat of armor^a?
¹⁴ Who dares open the doors of its mouth,
     ringed about with fearsome teeth?
¹⁵ Its back has^b rows of shields
     tightly sealed together;
¹⁶ each is so close to the next
     that no air can pass between.
¹⁷ They are joined fast to one another;
     they cling together and cannot be parted.
¹⁸ Its snorting throws out flashes of light;
     its eyes are like the rays of dawn.
¹⁹ Flames stream from its mouth;
     sparks of fire shoot out.
²⁰ Smoke pours from its nostrils
     as from a boiling pot over burning reeds.
²¹ Its breath sets coals ablaze,
     and flames dart from its mouth.
²² Strength resides in its neck;
     dismay goes before it.
²³ The folds of its flesh are tightly joined;
     they are firm and immovable.
²⁴ Its chest is hard as rock,
     hard as a lower millstone.
²⁵ When it rises up, the mighty are terrified;
     they retreat before its thrashing.
²⁶ The sword that reaches it has no effect,
     nor does the spear or the dart or the javelin.
²⁷ Iron it treats like straw
     and bronze like rotten wood.
²⁸ Arrows do not make it flee;
     slingstones are like chaff to it.
²⁹ A club seems to it but a piece of straw;
     it laughs at the rattling of the lance.

What had Job claimed that God owed him? (41:11)
Job demanded God give him an explanation. He wanted to know what he was guilty of (7:20), and he wanted those charges put in writing (31:35).

---

^a 13 Septuagint; Hebrew *double bridle*   ^b 15 Or *Its pride is its*

³⁰ Its undersides are jagged potsherds,
    leaving a trail in the mud like a threshing sledge.
³¹ It makes the depths churn like a boiling caldron
    and stirs up the sea like a pot of ointment.
³² It leaves a glistening wake behind it;
    one would think the deep had white hair.
³³ Nothing on earth is its equal—
    a creature without fear.
³⁴ It looks down on all that are haughty;
    it is king over all that are proud."

JOB

42

Then Job replied to the LORD:

² "I know that you can do all things;
    no purpose of yours can be thwarted.
³ You asked, 'Who is this that obscures my plans
      without knowledge?'
Surely I spoke of things I did not understand,
    things too wonderful for me to know.

⁴ "You said, 'Listen now, and I will speak;
    I will question you,
    and you shall answer me.'
⁵ My ears had heard of you
    but now my eyes have seen you.
⁶ Therefore I despise myself
    and repent in dust and ashes."

EPILOGUE

⁷ After the LORD had said these things to Job, he said to Eliphaz the Temanite, "I am angry with you and your two friends, because you have not spoken the truth about me, as my servant Job has. ⁸ So now take seven bulls and seven rams and go to my servant Job and sacrifice a burnt offering for yourselves. My servant Job will pray for you, and I will accept his prayer and not deal with you according to your folly. You have not spoken the truth about me, as my servant Job has." ⁹ So Eliphaz the Temanite, Bildad the Shuhite and Zophar the Naamathite did what the LORD told them; and the LORD accepted Job's prayer.

¹⁰ After Job had prayed for his friends, the LORD restored his fortunes and gave him twice as much as he had before. ¹¹ All his brothers and sisters and everyone who had known him before came and ate with him in his house. They comforted and consoled him over all the trouble the LORD had brought on him, and each one gave him a piece of silver^a and a gold ring.

¹² The LORD blessed the latter part of Job's life more than the former part. He had fourteen thousand sheep, six thousand camels, a thousand yoke of oxen and a thousand donkeys. ¹³ And he also had seven sons and three daughters. ¹⁴ The first daughter he named Jemimah, the second Keziah

---

How did Job humble himself before God? (42:6)
Job repented with dust and ashes to show that he had been wrong to question God's decisions.

In what way had Job's counselors not spoken what was right? (42:8)
They had claimed that wicked people always suffer and that righteous people always prosper.

How did God bless Job? (42:12–17)
He received twice as many animals as he had owned before. He also had seven sons and three daughters and lived a long and full life.

---

^a 11 Hebrew *him a kesitah*; a kesitah was a unit of money of unknown weight and value.

and the third Keren-Happuch. ¹⁵Nowhere in all the land were there found women as beautiful as Job's daughters, and their father granted them an inheritance along with their brothers.

¹⁶After this, Job lived a hundred and forty years; he saw his children and their children to the fourth generation. ¹⁷And so Job died, an old man and full of years.

Psalms

INTRODUCTION

Who wrote this book?	David wrote 73 of the 150 psalms. Several different people wrote the others.
Why was this book written?	The psalms show God's people how to talk to him and to worship him.
What kinds of psalms are there?	There are seven kinds of psalms: 1. *Praise psalms* like Psalms 33 and 103 show us how to thank God for who he is. 2. *History psalms* like Psalms 68 and 106 tell what God has done for his people. 3. *Friendship psalms* like Psalms 8 and 23 remind us that God loves us and tell us how we can show our love to him. 4. *Anger psalms* like Psalms 35 and 137 ask God to punish the evil. 5. *Confession psalms* like Psalms 32 and 51 show how to talk to God about our sins. 6. *Messiah psalms* like Psalms 22 and 89 tell us about Jesus. 7. *Worship psalms* like Psalms 30 and 122 were used on special religious holidays to worship God with other people.
What kind of poetry is used in this book?	The psalms do not rhyme. Hebrew poetry repeats ideas instead of repeating sounds.
What are some favorite psalms?	God's creation and Word — Psalm 19 God is our shepherd — Psalm 23 Confessing sin to God — Psalm 32 Trusting God — Psalm 37 God's great love — Psalm 89 How great God is — Psalm 104 Loving God's Word — Psalm 119

When did these things happen?

1400 BC 1300 1200 1100 1000 900 800 700 600 500 400

PSALMS WRITTEN (C. 1410 – 430 BC)

ISRAELITES ENTER CANAAN (C. 1406 BC)

JUDGES BEGIN TO RULE (C. 1375 BC)

SAUL'S REIGN (1050 – 1010 BC)

DAVID'S REIGN (1010 – 970 BC)

SOLOMON'S REIGN (970 – 930 BC)

DIVISION OF THE KINGDOM (930 BC)

FALL OF JERUSALEM (586 BC)

FIRST RETURN OF EXILES TO JERUSALEM (538 BC)

BOOK I

PSALMS 1 – 41

PSALM 1

[1] Blessed is the one
    who does not walk in step with the wicked
or stand in the way that sinners take
    or sit in the company of mockers,
[2] but whose delight is in the law of the Lord,
    and who meditates on his law day and night.
[3] That person is like a tree planted by streams of water,
    which yields its fruit in season
and whose leaf does not wither—
    whatever they do prospers.

[4] Not so the wicked!
    They are like chaff
    that the wind blows away.
[5] Therefore the wicked will not stand in the judgment,
    nor sinners in the assembly of the righteous.

[6] For the Lord watches over the way of the righteous,
    but the way of the wicked leads to destruction.

PSALM 2

[1] Why do the nations conspire[a]
    and the peoples plot in vain?
[2] The kings of the earth rise up
    and the rulers band together
    against the Lord and against his anointed, saying,
[3] "Let us break their chains
    and throw off their shackles."

[4] The One enthroned in heaven laughs;
    the Lord scoffs at them.
[5] He rebukes them in his anger
    and terrifies them in his wrath, saying,
[6] "I have installed my king
    on Zion, my holy mountain."

[7] I will proclaim the Lord's decree:

He said to me, "You are my son;
    today I have become your father.
[8] Ask me,
    and I will make the nations your inheritance,
    the ends of the earth your possession.
[9] You will break them with a rod of iron[b];
    you will dash them to pieces like pottery."

[10] Therefore, you kings, be wise;
    be warned, you rulers of the earth.

[a] *1* Hebrew; Septuagint *rage*   [b] *9* Or *will rule them with an iron scepter* (see Septuagint and Syriac)

What does this verse say about how sin grows? (1:1)
The verse shows a progression from walking, to standing, to finally sitting. A person will be blessed by avoiding the advice of those who do not love the Lord, which leads to ungodly behavior.

What does it mean to be blessed? (1:1)
It means to be filled with the joy that comes from serving God and having a strong relationship with him.

Who was the Lord's Anointed? (2:2)
The psalm originally referred to the king of the Israelites, but it also pointed toward Jesus. *Messiah* comes from the Hebrew word for anointed.

Why did God describe the king as his son? (2:7)
It was common for kings to refer to the lesser kings who ruled under them as sons. In this way King David was God's son, who ruled under him.

¹¹ Serve the LORD with fear
  and celebrate his rule with trembling.
¹² Kiss his son, or he will be angry
  and your way will lead to your destruction,
for his wrath can flare up in a moment.
  Blessed are all who take refuge in him.

PSALM 3[a]

A psalm of David. When he fled from his son Absalom.

¹ LORD, how many are my foes!
  How many rise up against me!
² Many are saying of me,
  "God will not deliver him."[b]

³ But you, LORD, are a shield around me,
  my glory, the One who lifts my head high.
⁴ I call out to the LORD,
  and he answers me from his holy mountain.

⁵ I lie down and sleep;
  I wake again, because the LORD sustains me.
⁶ I will not fear though tens of thousands
  assail me on every side.

⁷ Arise, LORD!
  Deliver me, my God!
Strike all my enemies on the jaw;
  break the teeth of the wicked.

⁸ From the LORD comes deliverance.
  May your blessing be on your people.

PSALM 4[c]

For the director of music. With stringed instruments. A psalm of David.

¹ Answer me when I call to you,
  my righteous God.
Give me relief from my distress;
  have mercy on me and hear my prayer.

² How long will you people turn my glory into shame?
  How long will you love delusions and seek false
    gods[d]?[e]
³ Know that the LORD has set apart his faithful servant
    for himself;
  the LORD hears when I call to him.

⁴ Tremble and[f] do not sin;
  when you are on your beds,
  search your hearts and be silent.
⁵ Offer the sacrifices of the righteous
  and trust in the LORD.

What was the background to this psalm? (3:1)
Absalom led a rebellion against his father, King David, and as a result David had to leave Jerusalem (see 2 Samuel 15 – 18).

Why was the LORD described as a shield? (3:3)
In ancient Israel, it was common for a king to be thought of as a shield or protector for his people.

What was the setting of this psalm? (4:1)
This psalm was probably written as a prayer for relief during a natural disaster such as a drought. An event like that often led the Israelites to question God's power and to turn toward pagan fertility gods.

Who was the LORD's faithful servant? (4:3)
The Hebrew word *hasid* is usually translated as "the godly" or "saints." The word refers to God's people who are or should be devoted to God and faithful to him.

---

[a] In Hebrew texts 3:1-8 is numbered 3:2-9.   [b] 2 The Hebrew has *Selah* (a word of uncertain meaning) here and at the end of verses 4 and 8.   [c] In Hebrew texts 4:1-8 is numbered 4:2-9.   [d] 2 Or *seek lies*   [e] 2 The Hebrew has *Selah* (a word of uncertain meaning) here and at the end of verse 4.   [f] 4 Or *In your anger* (see Septuagint)

⁶Many, LORD, are asking, "Who will bring us prosperity?"
　Let the light of your face shine on us.
⁷Fill my heart with joy
　when their grain and new wine abound.

⁸In peace I will lie down and sleep,
　for you alone, LORD,
　make me dwell in safety.

PSALM 5ᵃ

For the director of music. For pipes. A psalm of David.

¹Listen to my words, LORD,
　consider my lament.
²Hear my cry for help,
　my King and my God,
　for to you I pray.

³In the morning, LORD, you hear my voice;
　in the morning I lay my requests before you
　and wait expectantly.
⁴For you are not a God who is pleased with
　　wickedness;
　with you, evil people are not welcome.
⁵The arrogant cannot stand
　in your presence.
You hate all who do wrong;
⁶　you destroy those who tell lies.
The bloodthirsty and deceitful
　you, LORD, detest.
⁷But I, by your great love,
　can come into your house;
in reverence I bow down
　toward your holy temple.

⁸Lead me, LORD, in your righteousness
　because of my enemies—
　make your way straight before me.
⁹Not a word from their mouth can be trusted;
　their heart is filled with malice.
Their throat is an open grave;
　with their tongues they tell lies.
¹⁰Declare them guilty, O God!
　Let their intrigues be their downfall.
Banish them for their many sins,
　for they have rebelled against you.
¹¹But let all who take refuge in you be glad;
　let them ever sing for joy.
Spread your protection over them,
　that those who love your name may
　　rejoice in you.

¹²Surely, LORD, you bless the righteous;
　you surround them with your favor as
　　with a shield.

ᵃ In Hebrew texts 5:1-12 is numbered 5:2-13.

Why was this prayer offered in the morning? (5:3)
There were set times during the day when people prayed. These requests were probably included in morning prayers because they were so urgent.

Why do many of the psalms ask God to punish wicked people? (5:10)
These prayers or curses were appeals for God to punish people who had done wrong. Instead of trying to seek revenge themselves, the writers of the psalms asked God to administer justice.

PSALM 6[a]

For the director of music. With stringed instruments.
According to sheminith.[b] *A psalm of David.*

[1] LORD, do not rebuke me in your anger
　　or discipline me in your wrath.
[2] Have mercy on me, LORD, for I am faint;
　　heal me, LORD, for my bones are in agony.
[3] My soul is in deep anguish.
　　How long, LORD, how long?

[4] Turn, LORD, and deliver me;
　　save me because of your unfailing love.
[5] Among the dead no one proclaims your name.
　　Who praises you from the grave?

[6] I am worn out from my groaning.

All night long I flood my bed with weeping
　　and drench my couch with tears.
[7] My eyes grow weak with sorrow;
　　they fail because of all my foes.

[8] Away from me, all you who do evil,
　　for the LORD has heard my weeping.
[9] The LORD has heard my cry for mercy;
　　the LORD accepts my prayer.
[10] All my enemies will be overwhelmed with
　　　　shame and anguish;
　　they will turn back and suddenly be put
　　　　to shame.

PSALM 7[c]

A shiggaion[d] *of David, which he sang to*
the LORD *concerning Cush, a Benjamite.*

[1] LORD my God, I take refuge in you;
　　save and deliver me from all who pursue me,
[2] or they will tear me apart like a lion
　　and rip me to pieces with no one to rescue me.

[3] LORD my God, if I have done this
　　and there is guilt on my hands—
[4] if I have repaid my ally with evil
　　or without cause have robbed my foe—
[5] then let my enemy pursue and overtake me;
　　let him trample my life to the ground
　　and make me sleep in the dust.[e]

[6] Arise, LORD, in your anger;
　　rise up against the rage of my enemies.
　　Awake, my God; decree justice.
[7] Let the assembled peoples gather around you,
　　while you sit enthroned over them on high.

Was David physically sick?
(6:2–7)
David groaned, wept, and grew
faint because of his strong feelings of sorrow. He may have
been experiencing a severe case
of depression.

Why did David say that "no
one proclaims your name"?
(6:5)
David was saying that God's
praise was at stake. It was the
living, not the dead, who would
remember God's mercy and celebrate his acts of salvation.

Did David have confidence
in God? (6:8–10)
Yes. Despite his great sadness,
David was sure that the LORD had
heard his prayer. He believed his
enemies would be ashamed when
God restored him.

Who was Cush? (7: title)
Cush is not mentioned anywhere
else in the Bible. Because he
was a Benjamite, he was likely
a supporter of Saul. The psalm
probably was written during the
time when Saul was trying to kill
David.

Why did David ask God to
wake up? (7:6)
David did not think God actually
slept, but he was impatient for
God to take some action to save
him.

---

[a] In Hebrew texts 6:1-10 is numbered 6:2-11.　[b] Title: Probably a musical
term　[c] In Hebrew texts 7:1-17 is numbered 7:2-18.　[d] Title: Probably a
literary or musical term　[e] 5 The Hebrew has *Selah* (a word of uncertain
meaning) here.

8   Let the LORD judge the peoples.
   Vindicate me, LORD, according to my righteousness,
     according to my integrity, O Most High.
9 Bring to an end the violence of the wicked
   and make the righteous secure—
  you, the righteous God
   who probes minds and hearts.

10 My shield*a* is God Most High,
   who saves the upright in heart.
11 God is a righteous judge,
   a God who displays his wrath every day.
12 If he does not relent,
   he*b* will sharpen his sword;
   he will bend and string his bow.
13 He has prepared his deadly weapons;
   he makes ready his flaming arrows.

14 Whoever is pregnant with evil
   conceives trouble and gives birth to disillusionment.
15 Whoever digs a hole and scoops it out
   falls into the pit they have made.
16 The trouble they cause recoils on them;
   their violence comes down on their own heads.

17 I will give thanks to the LORD because of his
    righteousness;
   I will sing the praises of the name of the LORD
    Most High.

PSALM 8*c*

For the director of music. According to gittith.*d A psalm of David.*

1 LORD, our Lord,
   how majestic is your name in all the earth!

  You have set your glory
   in the heavens.
2 Through the praise of children and infants
   you have established a stronghold against your
    enemies,
  to silence the foe and the avenger.
3 When I consider your heavens,
   the work of your fingers,
  the moon and the stars,
   which you have set in place,
4 what is mankind that you are mindful of them,
   human beings that you care for them?*e*

5 You have made them*f* a little lower than the angels*g*
   and crowned them*f* with glory and honor.
6 You made them rulers over the works of your hands;
   you put everything under their*h* feet:

a 10 Or sovereign   *b 12 Or* If anyone does not repent, / God   *c* In Hebrew
texts 8:1-9 is numbered 8:2-10.   *d* Title: Probably a musical term
e 4 Or what is a human being that you are mindful of him, / a son of man that you
care for him?   *f 5 Or* him   *g 5 Or* than God   *h 6 Or* made him ruler . . . ;
/ . . . his

Did David think wicked people would be punished? (7:14–16)
David believed that God would make sure justice was carried out for those who were God's enemies.

How is it possible for babies to praise God? (8:2)
All of God's creation can express praise to God. Mountains, trees, and hills can praise him (Isaiah 55:12), and so can children and infants. Their cries and peals of laughter are both sounds that give glory to God.

How important are human beings? (8:4–5)
In comparison to the entire universe God created, human beings are quite insignificant. Yet God honored human beings by putting them in charge of his creation.

⁷all flocks and herds,
  and the animals of the wild,
⁸the birds in the sky,
  and the fish in the sea,
  all that swim the paths of the seas.

⁹Lord, our Lord,
  how majestic is your name in all the earth!

PSALM 9ᵃ,ᵇ

For the director of music.
To the tune of "The Death of the Son." A psalm of David.

¹I will give thanks to you, Lord, with all my heart;
  I will tell of all your wonderful deeds.
²I will be glad and rejoice in you;
  I will sing the praises of your name,
    O Most High.

³My enemies turn back;
  they stumble and perish before you.
⁴For you have upheld my right and my cause,
  sitting enthroned as the righteous judge.
⁵You have rebuked the nations and destroyed
    the wicked;
  you have blotted out their name for ever and ever.
⁶Endless ruin has overtaken my enemies,
  you have uprooted their cities;
  even the memory of them has perished.

⁷The Lord reigns forever;
  he has established his throne for judgment.
⁸He rules the world in righteousness
  and judges the peoples with equity.
⁹The Lord is a refuge for the oppressed,
  a stronghold in times of trouble.
¹⁰Those who know your name trust in you,
  for you, Lord, have never forsaken those
    who seek you.

¹¹Sing the praises of the Lord, enthroned in Zion;
  proclaim among the nations what he has done.
¹²For he who avenges blood remembers;
  he does not ignore the cries of the afflicted.

¹³Lord, see how my enemies persecute me!
  Have mercy and lift me up from the gates
    of death,
¹⁴that I may declare your praises
  in the gates of Daughter Zion,
  and there rejoice in your salvation.

¹⁵The nations have fallen into the pit they have dug;
  their feet are caught in the net they have hidden.

What were the gates of death? (9:13)
This was a poetic way of saying someone was close to death.

What were these pits and nets? (9:15)
Hunters in ancient times used these types of traps to catch animals. A pit was a hole in the ground camouflaged in the hopes an animal would fall into it. A net was hung from a tree that would snatch the animal up when it walked on the net. David used these terms to describe how his enemies had fallen into their own traps.

ᵃ Psalms 9 and 10 may originally have been a single acrostic poem in which alternating lines began with the successive letters of the Hebrew alphabet. In the Septuagint they constitute one psalm.   ᵇ In Hebrew texts 9:1-20 is numbered 9:2-21.

16 The Lord is known by his acts of justice;
  the wicked are ensnared by the work of their hands. *a*
17 The wicked go down to the realm of the dead,
  all the nations that forget God.
18 But God will never forget the needy;
  the hope of the afflicted will never perish.

19 Arise, Lord, do not let mortals triumph;
  let the nations be judged in your presence.
20 Strike them with terror, Lord;
  let the nations know they are only mortal.

How does this verse offer hope? (9:18)
It gives assurance that God will not forget those who are needy and afflicted.

PSALM 10 *b*

1 Why, Lord, do you stand far off?
  Why do you hide yourself in times of trouble?

2 In his arrogance the wicked man hunts down the
    weak,
  who are caught in the schemes he devises.
3 He boasts about the cravings of his heart;
  he blesses the greedy and reviles the Lord.
4 In his pride the wicked man does not seek him;
  in all his thoughts there is no room for God.
5 His ways are always prosperous;
  your laws are rejected by *c* him;
  he sneers at all his enemies.
6 He says to himself, "Nothing will ever shake me."
  He swears, "No one will ever do me harm."

7 His mouth is full of lies and threats;
  trouble and evil are under his tongue.
8 He lies in wait near the villages;
  from ambush he murders the innocent.
  His eyes watch in secret for his victims;
9   like a lion in cover he lies in wait.
  He lies in wait to catch the helpless;
  he catches the helpless and drags them off in his net.
10 His victims are crushed, they collapse;
  they fall under his strength.
11 He says to himself, "God will never notice;
  he covers his face and never sees."

Why did the wicked person speak lies and threats? (10:7)
These were considered weapons that could be spoken. Lies could destroy a person's reputation. Threats represented something to be feared.

12 Arise, Lord! Lift up your hand, O God.
  Do not forget the helpless.
13 Why does the wicked man revile God?
  Why does he say to himself,
  "He won't call me to account"?
14 But you, God, see the trouble of the afflicted;
  you consider their grief and take it in hand.
  The victims commit themselves to you;
  you are the helper of the fatherless.

a 16 The Hebrew has *Higgaion* and *Selah* (words of uncertain meaning) here; *Selah* occurs also at the end of verse 20.   *b* Psalms 9 and 10 may originally have been a single acrostic poem in which alternating lines began with the successive letters of the Hebrew alphabet. In the Septuagint they constitute one psalm.   *c 5* See Septuagint; Hebrew / *they are haughty, and your laws are far from*

Why ask God to break the arm of a wicked person? (10:15)
This would make a person helpless and keep him from doing harm.

¹⁵Break the arm of the wicked man;
　　call the evildoer to account for his wickedness
　　that would not otherwise be found out.

¹⁶The Lord is King for ever and ever;
　　the nations will perish from his land.
¹⁷You, Lord, hear the desire of the afflicted;
　　you encourage them, and you listen to
　　　their cry,
¹⁸defending the fatherless and the oppressed,
　　so that mere earthly mortals
　　will never again strike terror.

PSALM 11

For the director of music. Of David.

¹In the Lord I take refuge.
　　How then can you say to me:
　　"Flee like a bird to your mountain.
²For look, the wicked bend their bows;
　　they set their arrows against the strings
to shoot from the shadows
　　at the upright in heart.
³When the foundations are being destroyed,
　　what can the righteous do?"

⁴The Lord is in his holy temple;
　　the Lord is on his heavenly throne.
He observes everyone on earth;
　　his eyes examine them.
⁵The Lord examines the righteous,
　　but the wicked, those who love violence,
　　he hates with a passion.
⁶On the wicked he will rain
　　fiery coals and burning sulfur;
　　a scorching wind will be their lot.

⁷For the Lord is righteous,
　　he loves justice;
　　the upright will see his face.

What did it mean to see the Lord's face? (11:7)
The Hebrew phrase for "seeing the king's face" meant having access to the king. This would be a special privilege for any person.

PSALM 12 *^a*

*For the director of music.
According to* sheminith.*^b A psalm of David.*

¹Help, Lord, for no one is faithful anymore;
　　those who are loyal have vanished from
　　　the human race.
²Everyone lies to their neighbor;
　　they flatter with their lips
　　but harbor deception in their hearts.

³May the Lord silence all flattering lips
　　and every boastful tongue—

Where had all the faithful people gone? (12:1)
David was exaggerating to make the point that many people had turned away from the Lord.

---

^a In Hebrew texts 12:1-8 is numbered 12:2-9.　　*^b* Title: Probably a musical term

4 those who say,
"By our tongues we will prevail;
our own lips will defend us—who is lord over us?"

5 "Because the poor are plundered and the needy groan,
I will now arise," says the LORD.
"I will protect them from those who malign them."
6 And the words of the LORD are flawless,
like silver purified in a crucible,
like gold*a* refined seven times.

7 You, LORD, will keep the needy safe
and will protect us forever from the wicked,
8 who freely strut about
when what is vile is honored by the human race.

PSALM 13*b*

For the director of music. A psalm of David.

1 How long, LORD? Will you forget me forever?
How long will you hide your face from me?
2 How long must I wrestle with my thoughts
and day after day have sorrow in my heart?
How long will my enemy triumph over me?

3 Look on me and answer, LORD my God.
Give light to my eyes, or I will sleep in death,
4 and my enemy will say, "I have overcome him,"
and my foes will rejoice when I fall.

5 But I trust in your unfailing love;
my heart rejoices in your salvation.
6 I will sing the LORD's praise,
for he has been good to me.

PSALM 14

For the director of music. Of David.

1 The fool*c* says in his heart,
"There is no God."

a 6 Probable reading of the original Hebrew text; Masoretic Text *earth*   *b* In Hebrew texts 13:1-6 is numbered 13:2-6.   *c* 1 The Hebrew words rendered *fool* in Psalms denote one who is morally deficient.

Why would gold be refined seven times? (12:6)
The number seven was a symbol of completeness and perfection.

How could the psalmist go from despair to such optimism? (13:5 – 6)
This was a typical pattern in the psalms. The writer often began by expressing great sadness or despair. But by the end of the psalm, he often expressed strong faith and trust in God, expecting that God would answer his prayer.

What psalm does Psalm 14 closely resemble?
Psalm 53 is a slightly revised version of this psalm.

Did the author use overly strong language to describe unbelievers? (14:1)
Because this is poetry, the author used vivid language. He called them fools who are corrupt and vile and who do nothing good. The author said that the LORD would judge the wicked, and he hoped for the day when he would restore Israel from its enemies.

May Christians question God?

PSALM 13

In this psalm David accuses God of hiding from him and forgetting him. He speaks of having troubling thoughts and sorrow that overcomes him every day. He says that if God does not answer him, he may even die and his enemies would gloat about his death.

Many of the psalms express strong emotions like these. In many cases, the psalmist feels as if God has abandoned him or does not care about him. Psalms like these let us know that God is willing to listen to us even when we are depressed or angry, and God is willing to allow us to ask him why bad things are happening to us.

The final verses of this psalm seem to shift completely to confidence, trust, and praise. Even when David felt completely alone in the world, he did not lose his faith in God, and he did not forget what God had done for him in the past. In the same way, even when we feel terrible, we can express those feelings to God without giving up our faith.

They are corrupt, their deeds are vile;
    there is no one who does good.

² The Lord looks down from heaven
    on all mankind
to see if there are any who understand,
    any who seek God.
³ All have turned away, all have become corrupt;
    there is no one who does good,
    not even one.

⁴ Do all these evildoers know nothing?

They devour my people as though eating bread;
    they never call on the Lord.
⁵ But there they are, overwhelmed with dread,
    for God is present in the company of the righteous.
⁶ You evildoers frustrate the plans of the poor,
    but the Lord is their refuge.

⁷ Oh, that salvation for Israel would come out of Zion!
    When the Lord restores his people,
    let Jacob rejoice and Israel be glad!

PSALM 15

A psalm of David.

¹ Lord, who may dwell in your sacred tent?
    Who may live on your holy mountain?

² The one whose walk is blameless,
    who does what is righteous,
    who speaks the truth from their heart;
³ whose tongue utters no slander,
    who does no wrong to a neighbor,
    and casts no slur on others;
⁴ who despises a vile person
    but honors those who fear the Lord;
who keeps an oath even when it hurts,
    and does not change their mind;
⁵ who lends money to the poor without interest;
    who does not accept a bribe against the innocent.

Whoever does these things
    will never be shaken.

PSALM 16

A miktam^a of David.

¹ Keep me safe, my God,
    for in you I take refuge.

² I say to the Lord, "You are my Lord;
    apart from you I have no good thing."
³ I say of the holy people who are in the land,
    "They are the noble ones in whom is all
      my delight."

^a Title: Probably a literary or musical term

What was the sacred tent? (15:1)
This was the tabernacle, the place where God was present so that his people could come to worship him. The temple was not built until after David's death.

⁴Those who run after other gods will suffer more
      and more.
    I will not pour out libations of blood to such gods
      or take up their names on my lips.

⁵LORD, you alone are my portion and my cup;
    you make my lot secure.
⁶The boundary lines have fallen for me in pleasant places;
    surely I have a delightful inheritance.
⁷I will praise the LORD, who counsels me;
    even at night my heart instructs me.
⁸I keep my eyes always on the LORD.
    With him at my right hand, I will not be shaken.

⁹Therefore my heart is glad and my tongue rejoices;
    my body also will rest secure,
¹⁰because you will not abandon me to the realm
      of the dead,
    nor will you let your faithful*a* one see decay.
¹¹You make known to me the path of life;
    you will fill me with joy in your presence,
    with eternal pleasures at your right hand.

PSALM 17

A prayer of David.

¹Hear me, LORD, my plea is just;
    listen to my cry.
  Hear my prayer—
    it does not rise from deceitful lips.
²Let my vindication come from you;
    may your eyes see what is right.

³Though you probe my heart,
    though you examine me at night and test me,
  you will find that I have planned no evil;
    my mouth has not transgressed.
⁴Though people tried to bribe me,
    I have kept myself from the ways of the violent
    through what your lips have commanded.
⁵My steps have held to your paths;
    my feet have not stumbled.

⁶I call on you, my God, for you will answer me;
    turn your ear to me and hear my prayer.
⁷Show me the wonders of your great love,
    you who save by your right hand
    those who take refuge in you from their foes.
⁸Keep me as the apple of your eye;
    hide me in the shadow of your wings
⁹from the wicked who are out to destroy me,
    from my mortal enemies who surround me.

¹⁰They close up their callous hearts,
    and their mouths speak with arrogance.
¹¹They have tracked me down, they now surround me,
    with eyes alert, to throw me to the ground.

a 10 Or holy

What were libations of blood? (16:4)
This refers to the blood of sacrifices poured out on altars.

What does the cup represent? (16:5)
The cup is a symbol of what a host would offer his guests to drink. The LORD offers his people a cup of blessing or salvation, but he makes the wicked drink a cup of wrath.

How could David claim to be sinless? (17:3–5)
David was not perfect, but he may have been comparing himself with people who did not believe in God.

What is the apple of the eye? (17:8)
This image refers to the pupil of the eye, something that is protected and carefully watched over.

¹² They are like a lion hungry for prey,
    like a fierce lion crouching in cover.

¹³ Rise up, LORD, confront them, bring them down;
    with your sword rescue me from the wicked.
¹⁴ By your hand save me from such people, LORD,
    from those of this world whose reward is in this life.
  May what you have stored up for the wicked fill
        their bellies;
    may their children gorge themselves on it,
    and may there be leftovers for their little ones.

¹⁵ As for me, I will be vindicated and will see your face;
    when I awake, I will be satisfied with seeing
        your likeness.

Where else in the Bible does Psalm 18 appear?
This psalm, with some variations, also appears in 2 Samuel 22.

Why did David call God a rock? (18:2)
David had often taken refuge among the rocks in the desert, but he recognized that true security was found only in the LORD.

PSALM 18*ᵃ*

*For the director of music. Of David the servant of the LORD. He sang
to the LORD the words of this song when the LORD delivered him from
the hand of all his enemies and from the hand of Saul. He said:*

¹ I love you, LORD, my strength.

² The LORD is my rock, my fortress and my deliverer;
    my God is my rock, in whom I take refuge,
    my shield*ᵇ* and the horn*ᶜ* of my salvation, my
        stronghold.

³ I called to the LORD, who is worthy of praise,
    and I have been saved from my enemies.
⁴ The cords of death entangled me;
    the torrents of destruction overwhelmed me.
⁵ The cords of the grave coiled around me;
    the snares of death confronted me.

⁶ In my distress I called to the LORD;
    I cried to my God for help.
  From his temple he heard my voice;
    my cry came before him, into his ears.
⁷ The earth trembled and quaked,
    and the foundations of the mountains shook;
    they trembled because he was angry.
⁸ Smoke rose from his nostrils;
    consuming fire came from his mouth,
    burning coals blazed out of it.
⁹ He parted the heavens and came down;
    dark clouds were under his feet.
¹⁰ He mounted the cherubim and flew;
    he soared on the wings of the wind.
¹¹ He made darkness his covering, his canopy around
        him—
    the dark rain clouds of the sky.
¹² Out of the brightness of his presence
        clouds advanced,
    with hailstones and bolts of lightning.

*ᵃ In Hebrew texts 18:1-50 is numbered 18:2-51.   ᵇ 2 Or sovereign
ᶜ 2 Horn here symbolizes strength.*

¹³The Lord thundered from heaven;
  the voice of the Most High resounded.^a
¹⁴He shot his arrows and scattered the enemy,
  with great bolts of lightning he routed them.
¹⁵The valleys of the sea were exposed
  and the foundations of the earth laid bare
at your rebuke, Lord,
  at the blast of breath from your nostrils.

¹⁶He reached down from on high and took hold of me;
  he drew me out of deep waters.
¹⁷He rescued me from my powerful enemy,
  from my foes, who were too strong for me.
¹⁸They confronted me in the day of my disaster,
  but the Lord was my support.
¹⁹He brought me out into a spacious place;
  he rescued me because he delighted in me.

²⁰The Lord has dealt with me according to
    my righteousness;
  according to the cleanness of my hands he has
    rewarded me.
²¹For I have kept the ways of the Lord;
  I am not guilty of turning from my God.
²²All his laws are before me;
  I have not turned away from his decrees.
²³I have been blameless before him
  and have kept myself from sin.
²⁴The Lord has rewarded me according to my
    righteousness,
  according to the cleanness of my hands in
    his sight.

²⁵To the faithful you show yourself faithful,
  to the blameless you show yourself blameless,
²⁶to the pure you show yourself pure,
  but to the devious you show yourself shrewd.
²⁷You save the humble
  but bring low those whose eyes are haughty.
²⁸You, Lord, keep my lamp burning;
  my God turns my darkness into light.
²⁹With your help I can advance against a troop^b;
  with my God I can scale a wall.

³⁰As for God, his way is perfect:
  The Lord's word is flawless;
  he shields all who take refuge in him.
³¹For who is God besides the Lord?
  And who is the Rock except our God?
³²It is God who arms me with strength
  and keeps my way secure.
³³He makes my feet like the feet of a deer;
  he causes me to stand on the heights.
³⁴He trains my hands for battle;
  my arms can bend a bow of bronze.

When were the valleys of the sea exposed? (18:15)
This may refer to the way God saved the Israelites by parting the Red Sea when they were leaving Egypt.

Why was a spacious place such a good thing? (18:19)
An open space provided freedom from the threats and dangers that had hemmed him in.

How could David claim to be blameless? (18:20–24)
This psalm was written before David had stolen another man's wife. But even if it had been written afterwards, David could claim to be blameless because God had forgiven him.

---

^a 13 Some Hebrew manuscripts and Septuagint (see also 2 Samuel 22:14);
most Hebrew manuscripts *resounded, / amid hailstones and bolts of lightning*
^b 29 Or *can run through a barricade*

³⁵ You make your saving help my shield,
    and your right hand sustains me;
    your help has made me great.
³⁶ You provide a broad path for my feet,
    so that my ankles do not give way.

³⁷ I pursued my enemies and overtook them;
    I did not turn back till they were destroyed.
³⁸ I crushed them so that they could not rise;
    they fell beneath my feet.
³⁹ You armed me with strength for battle;
    you humbled my adversaries before me.
⁴⁰ You made my enemies turn their backs in flight,
    and I destroyed my foes.
⁴¹ They cried for help, but there was no one to
        save them—
    to the LORD, but he did not answer.
⁴² I beat them as fine as windblown dust;
    I trampled them[a] like mud in the streets.
⁴³ You have delivered me from the attacks of the people;
    you have made me the head of nations.
    People I did not know now serve me,
⁴⁴   foreigners cower before me;
    as soon as they hear of me, they obey me.
⁴⁵ They all lose heart;
    they come trembling from their strongholds.

⁴⁶ The LORD lives! Praise be to my Rock!
    Exalted be God my Savior!
⁴⁷ He is the God who avenges me,
    who subdues nations under me,
⁴⁸   who saves me from my enemies.
    You exalted me above my foes;
    from a violent man you rescued me.
⁴⁹ Therefore I will praise you, LORD, among the nations;
    I will sing the praises of your name.

⁵⁰ He gives his king great victories;
    he shows unfailing love to his anointed,
    to David and to his descendants forever.

PSALM 19[b]

For the director of music. A psalm of David.

¹ The heavens declare the glory of God;
    the skies proclaim the work of his hands.
² Day after day they pour forth speech;
    night after night they reveal knowledge.
³ They have no speech, they use no words;
    no sound is heard from them.
⁴ Yet their voice[c] goes out into all the earth,
    their words to the ends of the world.
    In the heavens God has pitched a tent for the sun.

What does David's victory suggest? (18:37–42)
This suggests that one of the ways God blessed David was by allowing him to crush all of his enemies.

What does the sun symbolize in this psalm? (19:4–6)
The sun is a sign of God's awesome creative power, his glory, and his love. God loved us so much that he created the sun to warm us and give us light. The sun also symbolizes Jesus, the light of the world.

---

[a] 42 Many Hebrew manuscripts, Septuagint, Syriac and Targum (see also 2 Samuel 22:43); Masoretic Text *I poured them out*   [b] In Hebrew texts 19:1-14 is numbered 19:2-15.   [c] 4 Septuagint, Jerome and Syriac; Hebrew *measuring line*

⁵ It is like a bridegroom coming out of his chamber,
   like a champion rejoicing to run his course.
⁶ It rises at one end of the heavens
   and makes its circuit to the other;
   nothing is deprived of its warmth.

⁷ The law of the LORD is perfect,
   refreshing the soul.
  The statutes of the LORD are trustworthy,
   making wise the simple.
⁸ The precepts of the LORD are right,
   giving joy to the heart.
  The commands of the LORD are radiant,
   giving light to the eyes.
⁹ The fear of the LORD is pure,
   enduring forever.
  The decrees of the LORD are firm,
   and all of them are righteous.

¹⁰ They are more precious than gold,
    than much pure gold;
   they are sweeter than honey,
    than honey from the honeycomb.
¹¹ By them your servant is warned;
    in keeping them there is great reward.
¹² But who can discern their own errors?
    Forgive my hidden faults.
¹³ Keep your servant also from willful sins;
    may they not rule over me.
   Then I will be blameless,
    innocent of great transgression.

¹⁴ May these words of my mouth and this meditation
     of my heart
   be pleasing in your sight,
   LORD, my Rock and my Redeemer.

PSALM 20ᵃ

For the director of music. A psalm of David.

¹ May the LORD answer you when you are in distress;
   may the name of the God of Jacob protect you.

ᵃ In Hebrew texts 20:1-9 is numbered 20:2-10.

Did David need to be forgiven of sins he didn't even realize he had committed? (19:12–13)
Yes. As with everyone, David's conscience was not a perfect guide to good behavior. People need forgiveness for all of their sins, but the sins that are committed deliberately are a form of rebellion against God. That is why David asked God to keep him from willful sin.

How can I know that God really exists?

PSALM 19

The existence of God cannot be proved, so belief in God is a matter of faith (and that faith is given by God). The Bible talks about God and his workings in the lives of his people, but unbelievers can reject that. For example, Psalm 14 says that "The fool says in his heart, 'There is no God.'"

There have been many arguments that people have put forth to try to show that God is real. There is the argument from nature: "The heavens declare the glory of God; the skies proclaim the work of his hands" (Psalm 19:1). Since the universe has such an amazing design, there must have been a Designer. Another argument claims that because all people share a basic understanding of good and evil, this understanding must have come from a holy God.

No matter how convincing the arguments are, it is faith that allows us to believe in God, and faith is a gift of God through the Holy Spirit.

**What was the sanctuary?
(20:2)**
The sanctuary was the holy place
in the tent in Jerusalem that held
the ark of the covenant, the sign
that God was present. Later the
ark would be kept in the temple
built on the holy mountain of
Zion.

**Who is the anointed one
that the LORD gives victory
to? (20:6)**
The man God chose to be king
of Israel was anointed with oil by
one of God's prophets to show
that he was meant to be appointed.

2 May he send you help from the sanctuary
    and grant you support from Zion.
3 May he remember all your sacrifices
    and accept your burnt offerings. *a*
4 May he give you the desire of your heart
    and make all your plans succeed.
5 May we shout for joy over your victory
    and lift up our banners in the name of our God.

May the LORD grant all your requests.

6 Now this I know:
    The LORD gives victory to his anointed.
He answers him from his heavenly sanctuary
    with the victorious power of his right hand.
7 Some trust in chariots and some in horses,
    but we trust in the name of the LORD our God.
8 They are brought to their knees and fall,
    but we rise up and stand firm.
9 LORD, give victory to the king!
    Answer us when we call!

PSALM 21 *b*

For the director of music. A psalm of David.

1 The king rejoices in your strength, LORD.
    How great is his joy in the victories you give!

2 You have granted him his heart's desire
    and have not withheld the request of his lips. *a*
3 You came to greet him with rich blessings
    and placed a crown of pure gold on his head.
4 He asked you for life, and you gave it to him —
    length of days, for ever and ever.
5 Through the victories you gave, his glory is great;
    you have bestowed on him splendor and majesty.
6 Surely you have granted him unending blessings
    and made him glad with the joy of your presence.
7 For the king trusts in the LORD;
    through the unfailing love of the Most High
    he will not be shaken.

8 Your hand will lay hold on all your enemies;
    your right hand will seize your foes.
9 When you appear for battle,
    you will burn them up as in a blazing furnace.
The LORD will swallow them up in his wrath,
    and his fire will consume them.
10 You will destroy their descendants from the earth,
    their posterity from mankind.
11 Though they plot evil against you
    and devise wicked schemes, they cannot succeed.
12 You will make them turn their backs
    when you aim at them with drawn bow.

13 Be exalted in your strength, LORD;
    we will sing and praise your might.

**What victories was the
psalmist thankful for? (21:1, 5)**
The victories could refer to the
battle prayed for in Psalm 20 or
other battles David fought.

**What does a blazing furnace
refer to? (21:9)**
The furnace is a word picture of
God's judgment of the wicked.

**Why would the enemies'
descendants be destroyed?
(21:10 – 11)**
The descendants of a defeated
king would want to seek revenge.
They would be destroyed so that
they could not one day wage war
against the king.

a 3,2 The Hebrew has *Selah* (a word of uncertain meaning) here.   *b* In
Hebrew texts 21:1-13 is numbered 21:2-14.

PSALM 22[a]

For the director of music.
To the tune of "The Doe of the Morning." A psalm of David.

[1] My God, my God, why have you forsaken me?
 Why are you so far from saving me,
  so far from my cries of anguish?
[2] My God, I cry out by day, but you do not answer,
  by night, but I find no rest.[b]

[3] Yet you are enthroned as the Holy One;
  you are the one Israel praises.[c]
[4] In you our ancestors put their trust;
  they trusted and you delivered them.
[5] To you they cried out and were saved;
  in you they trusted and were not put to shame.

[6] But I am a worm and not a man,
  scorned by everyone, despised by the people.
[7] All who see me mock me;
  they hurl insults, shaking their heads.
[8] "He trusts in the LORD," they say,
  "let the LORD rescue him.
 Let him deliver him,
  since he delights in him."

[9] Yet you brought me out of the womb;
  you made me trust in you, even at my mother's
   breast.
[10] From birth I was cast on you;
  from my mother's womb you have been my God.

[11] Do not be far from me,
  for trouble is near
  and there is no one to help.

[12] Many bulls surround me;
  strong bulls of Bashan encircle me.
[13] Roaring lions that tear their prey
  open their mouths wide against me.
[14] I am poured out like water,
  and all my bones are out of joint.
 My heart has turned to wax;
  it has melted within me.
[15] My mouth[d] is dried up like a potsherd,
  and my tongue sticks to the roof of my mouth;
  you lay me in the dust of death.

[16] Dogs surround me,
  a pack of villains encircles me;
  they pierce[e] my hands and my feet.
[17] All my bones are on display;
  people stare and gloat over me.
[18] They divide my clothes among them
  and cast lots for my garment.

Who were the ancestors who trusted God? (22:4)
David called to mind his ancestors who had trusted and been helped by God — men such as Abraham, Isaac, Jacob, and Joseph.

Why did David say that bulls, lions, and dogs were attacking him? (22:12–13, 16)
The psalms often refer to attacks by wild animals to symbolize attacks by enemies.

What was a potsherd? (22:15)
A potsherd was a piece or fragment of a broken clay pot.

---

[a] In Hebrew texts 22:1-31 is numbered 22:2-32.   [b] 2 Or *night, and am not silent*   [c] 3 Or *Yet you are holy, / enthroned on the praises of Israel*
[d] 15 Probable reading of the original Hebrew text; Masoretic Text *strength*   [e] 16 Dead Sea Scrolls and some manuscripts of the Masoretic Text, Septuagint and Syriac; most manuscripts of the Masoretic Text *me, / like a lion*

¹⁹ But you, Lord, do not be far from me.
  You are my strength; come quickly to help me.
²⁰ Deliver me from the sword,
  my precious life from the power of the dogs.
²¹ Rescue me from the mouth of the lions;
  save me from the horns of the wild oxen.

²² I will declare your name to my people;
  in the assembly I will praise you.
²³ You who fear the Lord, praise him!
  All you descendants of Jacob, honor him!
  Revere him, all you descendants of Israel!
²⁴ For he has not despised or scorned
  the suffering of the afflicted one;
  he has not hidden his face from him
  but has listened to his cry for help.

²⁵ From you comes the theme of my praise in the
    great assembly;
  before those who fear you[a] I will fulfill
    my vows.
²⁶ The poor will eat and be satisfied;
  those who seek the Lord will praise him—
  may your hearts live forever!

²⁷ All the ends of the earth
  will remember and turn to the Lord,
  and all the families of the nations
  will bow down before him,
²⁸ for dominion belongs to the Lord
  and he rules over the nations.

²⁹ All the rich of the earth will feast and worship;
  all who go down to the dust will kneel
    before him—
  those who cannot keep themselves alive.
³⁰ Posterity will serve him;
  future generations will be told about the Lord.
³¹ They will proclaim his righteousness,
  declaring to a people yet unborn:
  He has done it!

[a] 25 Hebrew *him*

What was the great assembly? (22:25)
This was the congregation gathered to praise and worship God. Perhaps it hints at a future gathering of all those around the world who serve the Lord (see verses 27 – 31).

What vows had David made? (22:25)
He had probably promised to worship and honor God with offerings for saving him and wanted to lead others to do the same.

Why is God compared to a shepherd?   PSALM 23

During ancient times, a shepherd was a metaphor that was widely used to describe kings in Israel and elsewhere in the Middle East. The Bible often refers to the Lord as the shepherd of Israel.

Sheep were an important resource, and shepherds knew their sheep and called them by their names. Because sheep were likely to wander off on their own and could be attacked by wild animals, the shepherd was a person who protected his sheep. In the same way, God knows his people by name and protects them from harm.

Isaiah 40:11 uses the metaphor of a shepherd to describe how deeply God loves his people: "He tends his flock like a shepherd: He gathers the lambs in his arms and carries them close to his heart; he gently leads those that have young."

In the New Testament, Jesus calls himself the Good Shepherd who is willing to lay down his life for his sheep (John 10:11). This image of sacrifice in order to protect the flock reflects the great care that shepherds in ancient times had for their sheep.

PSALM 23

A psalm of David.

¹The LORD is my shepherd, I lack nothing.
² He makes me lie down in green pastures,
he leads me beside quiet waters,
³ he refreshes my soul.
He guides me along the right paths
for his name's sake.
⁴Even though I walk
through the darkest valley,ᵃ
I will fear no evil,
for you are with me;
your rod and your staff,
they comfort me.

⁵You prepare a table before me
in the presence of my enemies.
You anoint my head with oil;
my cup overflows.
⁶Surely your goodness and love will follow me
all the days of my life,
and I will dwell in the house of the LORD
forever.

PSALM 24

Of David. A psalm.

¹The earth is the LORD's, and everything in it,
the world, and all who live in it;
²for he founded it on the seas
and established it on the waters.

³Who may ascend the mountain of the LORD?
Who may stand in his holy place?
⁴The one who has clean hands and a pure heart,
who does not trust in an idol
or swear by a false god.ᵇ

⁵They will receive blessing from the LORD
and vindication from God their Savior.
⁶Such is the generation of those who seek him,
who seek your face, God of Jacob.ᶜ,ᵈ

⁷Lift up your heads, you gates;
be lifted up, you ancient doors,
that the King of glory may come in.
⁸Who is this King of glory?
The LORD strong and mighty,
the LORD mighty in battle.
⁹Lift up your heads, you gates;
lift them up, you ancient doors,
that the King of glory may come in.

What did a shepherd symbolize? (23:1)
This was a metaphor used for kings. The Bible often refers to the LORD as the shepherd of Israel. Here David acknowledged God as his Shepherd-King.

The Shepherd's Staff (23:4)

Why was there a meal at the end of the psalm? (23:5)
In biblical times, after people made covenants they often shared a meal together to symbolize their friendship.

Why was Psalm 24 written?
This was a song celebrating the LORD's entrance into Zion. It was composed for the occasion when David brought the ark into Jerusalem or for a festival remembering that event.

What were the doors and gates? (24:7–9)
These terms both refer to either the gates of the city or the sanctuary. This is a picture of a victorious king returning to Jerusalem and receiving the praise of his subjects.

ᵃ 4 Or *the valley of the shadow of death*   ᵇ 4 Or *swear falsely*
ᶜ 6 Two Hebrew manuscripts and Syriac (see also Septuagint); most Hebrew
manuscripts *face, Jacob*   ᵈ 6 The Hebrew has *Selah* (a word of uncertain
meaning) here and at the end of verse 10.

¹⁰Who is he, this King of glory?
    The LORD Almighty—
    he is the King of glory.

PSALM 25ᵃ

Of David.

¹In you, LORD my God,
    I put my trust.

²I trust in you;
    do not let me be put to shame,
    nor let my enemies triumph over me.
³No one who hopes in you
    will ever be put to shame,
but shame will come on those
    who are treacherous without cause.

⁴Show me your ways, LORD,
    teach me your paths.
⁵Guide me in your truth and teach me,
    for you are God my Savior,
    and my hope is in you all day long.
⁶Remember, LORD, your great mercy and love,
    for they are from of old.
⁷Do not remember the sins of my youth
    and my rebellious ways;
according to your love remember me,
    for you, LORD, are good.

⁸Good and upright is the LORD;
    therefore he instructs sinners in his ways.
⁹He guides the humble in what is right
    and teaches them his way.
¹⁰All the ways of the LORD are loving and faithful
    toward those who keep the demands of his
      covenant.
¹¹For the sake of your name, LORD,
    forgive my iniquity, though it is great.

¹²Who, then, are those who fear the LORD?
    He will instruct them in the ways they should
      choose.ᵇ
¹³They will spend their days in prosperity,
    and their descendants will inherit the land.
¹⁴The LORD confides in those who fear him;
    he makes his covenant known to them.
¹⁵My eyes are ever on the LORD,
    for only he will release my feet from
      the snare.

¹⁶Turn to me and be gracious to me,
    for I am lonely and afflicted.
¹⁷Relieve the troubles of my heart
    and free me from my anguish.

Does God ever forget things? (25:6–7)
God is not forgetful and always keeps his promises. Here the psalmist is reminding God of his mercy and love and asking him to hurry to carry out his promises.

Why would the psalmist ask God to act on the basis of his name? (25:11)
God's name is an expression of his character and reputation. Because God's character is merciful, he will forgive his people. And to preserve his reputation, he will act on their behalf.

ᵃ This psalm is an acrostic poem, the verses of which begin with the successive letters of the Hebrew alphabet.   ᵇ *12* Or *ways he chooses*

¹⁸ Look on my affliction and my distress
    and take away all my sins.
¹⁹ See how numerous are my enemies
    and how fiercely they hate me!

²⁰ Guard my life and rescue me;
    do not let me be put to shame,
    for I take refuge in you.
²¹ May integrity and uprightness protect me,
    because my hope, Lord,ᵃ is in you.

²² Deliver Israel, O God,
    from all their troubles!

PSALM 26

Of David.

¹ Vindicate me, Lord,
    for I have led a blameless life;
I have trusted in the Lord
    and have not faltered.
² Test me, Lord, and try me,
    examine my heart and my mind;
³ for I have always been mindful of your unfailing love
    and have lived in reliance on your faithfulness.

⁴ I do not sit with the deceitful,
    nor do I associate with hypocrites.
⁵ I abhor the assembly of evildoers
    and refuse to sit with the wicked.
⁶ I wash my hands in innocence,
    and go about your altar, Lord,
⁷ proclaiming aloud your praise
    and telling of all your wonderful deeds.

⁸ Lord, I love the house where you live,
    the place where your glory dwells.
⁹ Do not take away my soul along with sinners,
    my life with those who are bloodthirsty,
¹⁰ in whose hands are wicked schemes,
    whose right hands are full of bribes.
¹¹ I lead a blameless life;
    deliver me and be merciful to me.

¹² My feet stand on level ground;
    in the great congregation I will praise
      the Lord.

PSALM 27

Of David.

¹ The Lord is my light and my salvation—
    whom shall I fear?
The Lord is the stronghold of my life—
    of whom shall I be afraid?

ᵃ 21 Septuagint; Hebrew does not have *Lord*.

Why did David ask God to deliver Israel? (25:22)
David turned from his personal requests and asked God to redeem the nation of Israel. As king, David had a responsibility for the welfare of the nation, so he asked his King to keep the nation safe.

Had David led a blameless life? (26:1)
David was not claiming he had never sinned, but he consistently trusted in God and repented when he broke God's law.

Why did David refuse to associate with sinful people? (26:4–5)
David did not want to be influenced by their evil (see Psalm 1:1).

² When the wicked advance against me
   to devour*ᵃ* me,
it is my enemies and my foes
   who will stumble and fall.
³ Though an army besiege me,
   my heart will not fear;
though war break out against me,
   even then I will be confident.

Why did David want to live
in the house of the LORD?
(27:4–6)
The tabernacle, or house of the
LORD, was the place where God's
presence was, and it was a place
of safety. David was saying he
wanted to be close to God and
wanted his protection.

⁴ One thing I ask from the LORD,
   this only do I seek:
that I may dwell in the house of the LORD
   all the days of my life,
to gaze on the beauty of the LORD
   and to seek him in his temple.
⁵ For in the day of trouble
   he will keep me safe in his dwelling;
he will hide me in the shelter of his sacred tent
   and set me high upon a rock.

⁶ Then my head will be exalted
   above the enemies who surround me;
at his sacred tent I will sacrifice with shouts of joy;
   I will sing and make music to the LORD.

⁷ Hear my voice when I call, LORD;
   be merciful to me and answer me.
⁸ My heart says of you, "Seek his face!"
   Your face, LORD, I will seek.
⁹ Do not hide your face from me,
   do not turn your servant away in anger;
   you have been my helper.
Do not reject me or forsake me,
   God my Savior.
¹⁰ Though my father and mother forsake me,
   the LORD will receive me.
¹¹ Teach me your way, LORD;
   lead me in a straight path
   because of my oppressors.
¹² Do not turn me over to the desire of my foes,
   for false witnesses rise up against me,
   spouting malicious accusations.

¹³ I remain confident of this:
   I will see the goodness of the LORD
   in the land of the living.
¹⁴ Wait for the LORD;
   be strong and take heart
   and wait for the LORD.

What does "wait for the
LORD" mean? (27:14)
This means trusting that God
hears and answers prayer.
Sometimes the answers do not
come immediately or the way we
expect, so it also means having
patience and confidence that
God will do what is best.

PSALM 28

Of David.

¹ To you, LORD, I call;
   you are my Rock,
   do not turn a deaf ear to me.

ᵃ 2 Or slander

For if you remain silent,
  I will be like those who go down to the pit.
[2] Hear my cry for mercy
  as I call to you for help,
  as I lift up my hands
  toward your Most Holy Place.

[3] Do not drag me away with the wicked,
  with those who do evil,
  who speak cordially with their neighbors
  but harbor malice in their hearts.
[4] Repay them for their deeds
  and for their evil work;
  repay them for what their hands have done
  and bring back on them what they deserve.

[5] Because they have no regard for the deeds
    of the LORD
  and what his hands have done,
  he will tear them down
  and never build them up again.

[6] Praise be to the LORD,
  for he has heard my cry for mercy.
[7] The LORD is my strength and my shield;
  my heart trusts in him, and he helps me.
My heart leaps for joy,
  and with my song I praise him.

[8] The LORD is the strength of his people,
  a fortress of salvation for his anointed one.
[9] Save your people and bless your inheritance;
  be their shepherd and carry them forever.

PSALM 29

A psalm of David.

[1] Ascribe to the LORD, you heavenly beings,
  ascribe to the LORD glory and strength.
[2] Ascribe to the LORD the glory due his name;
  worship the LORD in the splendor of his[a] holiness.

[3] The voice of the LORD is over the waters;
  the God of glory thunders,
  the LORD thunders over the mighty waters.
[4] The voice of the LORD is powerful;
  the voice of the LORD is majestic.
[5] The voice of the LORD breaks the cedars;
  the LORD breaks in pieces the cedars of Lebanon.
[6] He makes Lebanon leap like a calf,
  Sirion[b] like a young wild ox.
[7] The voice of the LORD strikes
  with flashes of lightning.
[8] The voice of the LORD shakes the desert;
  the LORD shakes the Desert of Kadesh.

---

[a] 2 Or LORD *with the splendor of*   [b] 6 That is, Mount Hermon

What was the pit? (28:1)
This was a metaphor for the grave.

What was the Most Holy Place? (28:2)
This was the inner sanctuary of the tabernacle where the ark was placed. It was God's throne room on earth.

What type of psalm was this? (29)
This was a hymn of praise to the King of creation, whose power and majesty can be seen in the thunderstorm. It was also a rejection of the worship of Baal, who was thought to be the god of thunderstorms.

What were the cedars of Lebanon? (29:5)
They were the largest, most spectacular trees in the region. They were considered sacred by the local people. Solomon used them to build his palace and the temple. Yet with his voice alone God could break these strong trees (verse 9).

⁹The voice of the LORD twists the oaks^a
and strips the forests bare.
And in his temple all cry, "Glory!"

¹⁰The LORD sits enthroned over the flood;
the LORD is enthroned as King forever.
¹¹The LORD gives strength to his people;
the LORD blesses his people with peace.

PSALM 30^b

A psalm. A song. For the dedication of the temple.^c Of David.

¹I will exalt you, LORD,
for you lifted me out of the depths
and did not let my enemies gloat over me.
²LORD my God, I called to you for help,
and you healed me.
³You, LORD, brought me up from the realm of the dead;
you spared me from going down to the pit.

⁴Sing the praises of the LORD, you his faithful people;
praise his holy name.
⁵For his anger lasts only a moment,
but his favor lasts a lifetime;
weeping may stay for the night,
but rejoicing comes in the morning.

⁶When I felt secure, I said,
"I will never be shaken."
⁷LORD, when you favored me,
you made my royal mountain^d stand firm;
but when you hid your face,
I was dismayed.

⁸To you, LORD, I called;
to the Lord I cried for mercy:
⁹"What is gained if I am silenced,
if I go down to the pit?
Will the dust praise you?
Will it proclaim your faithfulness?
¹⁰Hear, LORD, and be merciful to me;
LORD, be my help."

¹¹You turned my wailing into dancing;
you removed my sackcloth and clothed me with joy,
¹²that my heart may sing your praises and not be silent.
LORD my God, I will praise you forever.

PSALM 31^e

For the director of music. A psalm of David.

¹In you, LORD, I have taken refuge;
let me never be put to shame;
deliver me in your righteousness.

What were the depths? (30:1)
David may have been referring to death and the various things associated with it in the Bible: silence, darkness, destruction, corruption, and mire. This psalm was possibly written for the dedication of David's palace, and David may have been thanking God for healing or saving him.

Why did weeping last only for a night? (30:5)
The Hebrew literally means "come in at evening to lodge." The description creates the picture of a guest who only stays overnight.

---

^a 9 Or *LORD makes the deer give birth*   ^b In Hebrew texts 30:1-12 is numbered 30:2-13.   ^c Title: Or *palace*   ^d 7 That is, Mount Zion
^e In Hebrew texts 31:1-24 is numbered 31:2-25.

2 Turn your ear to me,
   come quickly to my rescue;
be my rock of refuge,
   a strong fortress to save me.
3 Since you are my rock and my fortress,
   for the sake of your name lead and guide me.
4 Keep me free from the trap that is set for me,
   for you are my refuge.
5 Into your hands I commit my spirit;
   deliver me, Lord, my faithful God.

6 I hate those who cling to worthless idols;
   as for me, I trust in the Lord.
7 I will be glad and rejoice in your love,
   for you saw my affliction
   and knew the anguish of my soul.
8 You have not given me into the hands of the enemy
   but have set my feet in a spacious place.

9 Be merciful to me, Lord, for I am in distress;
   my eyes grow weak with sorrow,
   my soul and body with grief.
10 My life is consumed by anguish
   and my years by groaning;
   my strength fails because of my affliction,*a*
   and my bones grow weak.
11 Because of all my enemies,
   I am the utter contempt of my neighbors
   and an object of dread to my closest friends—
   those who see me on the street flee from me.
12 I am forgotten as though I were dead;
   I have become like broken pottery.
13 For I hear many whispering,
   "Terror on every side!"
   They conspire against me
   and plot to take my life.

14 But I trust in you, Lord;
   I say, "You are my God."
15 My times are in your hands;
   deliver me from the hands of my enemies,
   from those who pursue me.
16 Let your face shine on your servant;
   save me in your unfailing love.
17 Let me not be put to shame, Lord,
   for I have cried out to you;
   but let the wicked be put to shame
   and be silent in the realm of the dead.
18 Let their lying lips be silenced,
   for with pride and contempt
   they speak arrogantly against the righteous.

19 How abundant are the good things
   that you have stored up for those who fear you,
   that you bestow in the sight of all,
   on those who take refuge in you.

Who quoted the words "into your hands I commit my spirit"? (31:5)
When Jesus was on the cross, he spoke these words right before he died (Luke 23:46). Here David was willing to trust God with his life or spirit.

Why did David compare himself to broken pottery? (31:12)
Broken pieces of pottery were pretty much worthless. David said people had abandoned him as if he were worthless.

---

a 10 Or guilt

²⁰ In the shelter of your presence you hide them
    from all human intrigues;
you keep them safe in your dwelling
    from accusing tongues.

²¹ Praise be to the LORD,
    for he showed me the wonders of his love
    when I was in a city under siege.
²² In my alarm I said,
    "I am cut off from your sight!"
Yet you heard my cry for mercy
    when I called to you for help.

²³ Love the LORD, all his faithful people!
    The LORD preserves those who are true to him,
    but the proud he pays back in full.
²⁴ Be strong and take heart,
    all you who hope in the LORD.

PSALM 32

Of David. A maskil.ᵃ

¹ Blessed is the one
    whose transgressions are forgiven,
    whose sins are covered.
² Blessed is the one
    whose sin the LORD does not count against them
    and in whose spirit is no deceit.

³ When I kept silent,
    my bones wasted away
    through my groaning all day long.
⁴ For day and night
    your hand was heavy on me;
my strength was sapped
    as in the heat of summer.ᵇ

⁵ Then I acknowledged my sin to you
    and did not cover up my iniquity.
I said, "I will confess
    my transgressions to the LORD."
And you forgave
    the guilt of my sin.

⁶ Therefore let all the faithful pray to you
    while you may be found;
surely the rising of the mighty waters
    will not reach them.
⁷ You are my hiding place;
    you will protect me from trouble
    and surround me with songs of deliverance.

⁸ I will instruct you and teach you in the way
        you should go;
    I will counsel you with my loving eye on you.

What does "when I was in a city under siege" refer to? (31:21–22)
David used a word picture to describe how he felt cut off from God, just as someone in a besieged city would feel cut off from the outside world.

Why was silence such a bad thing? (32:3–5)
David had not admitted or confessed his sins to God. Until he did, he suffered greatly. When he finally asked God for forgiveness, he experienced a tremendous sense of relief.

What were the *mighty waters*? (32:6)
This is an image of dangerous or threatening forces. In many ancient Middle Eastern creation stories, a god had to overcome the powerful surging waters before being able to create the world. The mighty waters were also associated with the seas that threatened to overtake the dry ground.

ᵃ Title: Probably a literary or musical term   ᵇ 4 The Hebrew has *Selah* (a word of uncertain meaning) here and at the end of verses 5 and 7.

⁹ Do not be like the horse or the mule,
  which have no understanding
but must be controlled by bit and bridle
  or they will not come to you.
¹⁰ Many are the woes of the wicked,
  but the LORD's unfailing love
  surrounds the one who trusts in him.

¹¹ Rejoice in the LORD and be glad, you righteous;
  sing, all you who are upright in heart!

PSALM 33

¹ Sing joyfully to the LORD, you righteous;
  it is fitting for the upright to praise him.
² Praise the LORD with the harp;
  make music to him on the ten-stringed lyre.
³ Sing to him a new song;
  play skillfully, and shout for joy.

⁴ For the word of the LORD is right and true;
  he is faithful in all he does.
⁵ The LORD loves righteousness and justice;
  the earth is full of his unfailing love.

⁶ By the word of the LORD the heavens were made,
  their starry host by the breath of his mouth.
⁷ He gathers the waters of the sea into jarsᵃ;
  he puts the deep into storehouses.
⁸ Let all the earth fear the LORD;
  let all the people of the world revere him.
⁹ For he spoke, and it came to be;
  he commanded, and it stood firm.

¹⁰ The LORD foils the plans of the nations;
  he thwarts the purposes of the peoples.
¹¹ But the plans of the LORD stand firm forever,
  the purposes of his heart through all generations.

¹² Blessed is the nation whose God is the LORD,
  the people he chose for his inheritance.
¹³ From heaven the LORD looks down
  and sees all mankind;
¹⁴ from his dwelling place he watches
  all who live on earth—
¹⁵ he who forms the hearts of all,
  who considers everything they do.

¹⁶ No king is saved by the size of his army;
  no warrior escapes by his great strength.
¹⁷ A horse is a vain hope for deliverance;
  despite all its great strength it cannot save.
¹⁸ But the eyes of the LORD are on those who fear him,
  on those whose hope is in his unfailing love,
¹⁹ to deliver them from death
  and keep them alive in famine.

ᵃ 7 Or *sea as into a heap*

How was this psalm spoken or sung? (33)
This was a liturgy of praise to God. It is possible that the leader spoke verses 1–3, the choir of Levites responded with verses 4–19, and the congregation answered with verses 20–22. The structure of the psalm is a call to praise, the praise itself, and the response.

To what nation does this verse refer? (33:12)
This was the nation of Israel, God's chosen people.

²⁰We wait in hope for the LORD;
    he is our help and our shield.
²¹In him our hearts rejoice,
    for we trust in his holy name.
²²May your unfailing love be with us, LORD,
    even as we put our hope in you.

PSALM 34^{a,b}

*Of David. When he pretended to be insane before Abimelek,
who drove him away, and he left.*

¹I will extol the LORD at all times;
    his praise will always be on my lips.
²I will glory in the LORD;
    let the afflicted hear and rejoice.
³Glorify the LORD with me;
    let us exalt his name together.

⁴I sought the LORD, and he answered me;
    he delivered me from all my fears.
⁵Those who look to him are radiant;
    their faces are never covered with shame.
⁶This poor man called, and the LORD heard him;
    he saved him out of all his troubles.
⁷The angel of the LORD encamps around those who
        fear him,
    and he delivers them.

⁸Taste and see that the LORD is good;
    blessed is the one who takes refuge in him.
⁹Fear the LORD, you his holy people,
    for those who fear him lack nothing.
¹⁰The lions may grow weak and hungry,
    but those who seek the LORD lack no good thing.
¹¹Come, my children, listen to me;
    I will teach you the fear of the LORD.
¹²Whoever of you loves life
    and desires to see many good days,
¹³keep your tongue from evil
    and your lips from telling lies.
¹⁴Turn from evil and do good;
    seek peace and pursue it.

¹⁵The eyes of the LORD are on the righteous,
    and his ears are attentive to their cry;
¹⁶but the face of the LORD is against those who do evil,
    to blot out their name from the earth.

¹⁷The righteous cry out, and the LORD hears them;
    he delivers them from all their troubles.
¹⁸The LORD is close to the brokenhearted
    and saves those who are crushed in spirit.

¹⁹The righteous person may have many troubles,
    but the LORD delivers him from them all;

Who protected David?
(34:6 – 7)
The angel of the LORD (who might have been the LORD himself) protected him.

What righteous man died a terrible death but did not have his bones broken?
(34:19 – 20)
The sinless Son of God, Jesus, was crucified, but none of his bones were broken, which was a fulfillment of this prophecy (see John 19:36).

---

^a This psalm is an acrostic poem, the verses of which begin with the successive letters of the Hebrew alphabet.   ^b In Hebrew texts 34:1-22 is numbered 34:2-23.

²⁰ he protects all his bones,
   not one of them will be broken.

²¹ Evil will slay the wicked;
   the foes of the righteous will be condemned.

²² The LORD will rescue his servants;
   no one who takes refuge in him will be condemned.

PSALM 35

Of David.

¹ Contend, LORD, with those who contend with me;
   fight against those who fight against me.

² Take up shield and armor;
   arise and come to my aid.

³ Brandish spear and javelin*ᵃ*
   against those who pursue me.
 Say to me,
   "I am your salvation."

⁴ May those who seek my life
   be disgraced and put to shame;
 may those who plot my ruin
   be turned back in dismay.

⁵ May they be like chaff before the wind,
   with the angel of the LORD driving them away;

⁶ may their path be dark and slippery,
   with the angel of the LORD pursuing them.

⁷ Since they hid their net for me without cause
   and without cause dug a pit for me,

⁸ may ruin overtake them by surprise—
   may the net they hid entangle them,
   may they fall into the pit, to their ruin.

⁹ Then my soul will rejoice in the LORD
   and delight in his salvation.

¹⁰ My whole being will exclaim,
   "Who is like you, LORD?
 You rescue the poor from those too strong for them,
   the poor and needy from those who rob them."

¹¹ Ruthless witnesses come forward;
   they question me on things I know nothing about.

¹² They repay me evil for good
   and leave me like one bereaved.

¹³ Yet when they were ill, I put on sackcloth
   and humbled myself with fasting.
 When my prayers returned to me unanswered,

¹⁴   I went about mourning
   as though for my friend or brother.
 I bowed my head in grief
   as though weeping for my mother.

¹⁵ But when I stumbled, they gathered in glee;
   assailants gathered against me without my knowledge.
 They slandered me without ceasing.

ᵃ 3 Or and block the way

What was a shield and armor? (35:2)
The first shield was a small round or oblong type that could be carried easily. Armor protected the entire body. This was David's way of saying that God protects us completely.

Shield and armor

What were nets and pits? (35:7)
Pits and nets and other types of traps were used to capture enemies in warfare.

What did it mean to gnash one's teeth? (35:16)
In the Old Testament, this expression represented rage or hatred. In the New Testament, the phrase represented disappointment or agony of spirit.

What were these lions? (35:17)
As a young shepherd, David had been attacked by lions (1 Samuel 17:34 – 35). Throughout the psalms, the attack of enemies is described as being similar to the attack of ferocious animals, especially lions.

[16] Like the ungodly they maliciously mocked;[a]
     they gnashed their teeth at me.

[17] How long, Lord, will you look on?
     Rescue me from their ravages,
       my precious life from these lions.
[18] I will give you thanks in the great assembly;
       among the throngs I will praise you.
[19] Do not let those gloat over me
       who are my enemies without cause;
     do not let those who hate me without reason
       maliciously wink the eye.
[20] They do not speak peaceably,
       but devise false accusations
     against those who live quietly in the land.
[21] They sneer at me and say, "Aha! Aha!
       With our own eyes we have seen it."

[22] Lord, you have seen this; do not be silent.
       Do not be far from me, Lord.
[23] Awake, and rise to my defense!
       Contend for me, my God and Lord.
[24] Vindicate me in your righteousness, Lord my God;
       do not let them gloat over me.
[25] Do not let them think, "Aha, just what we wanted!"
       or say, "We have swallowed him up."

[26] May all who gloat over my distress
       be put to shame and confusion;
     may all who exalt themselves over me
       be clothed with shame and disgrace.
[27] May those who delight in my vindication
       shout for joy and gladness;
     may they always say, "The Lord be exalted,
       who delights in the well-being of his servant."

[28] My tongue will proclaim your righteousness,
       your praises all day long.

PSALM 36[b]

For the director of music. Of David the servant of the Lord.

[1] I have a message from God in my heart
       concerning the sinfulness of the wicked:[c]
     There is no fear of God
       before their eyes.

[2] In their own eyes they flatter themselves
       too much to detect or hate their sin.
[3] The words of their mouths are wicked and deceitful;
       they fail to act wisely or do good.
[4] Even on their beds they plot evil;
       they commit themselves to a sinful course
     and do not reject what is wrong.

What kind of "message" was this? (36:1)
This was a revelation from God, such as a word spoken by a prophet.

---

[a] 16 Septuagint; Hebrew may mean *Like an ungodly circle of mockers,*   [b] In Hebrew texts 36:1-12 is numbered 36:2-13.   [c] 1 Or *A message from God: The transgression of the wicked / resides in their hearts.*

⁵ Your love, Lord, reaches to the heavens,
  your faithfulness to the skies.
⁶ Your righteousness is like the highest mountains,
  your justice like the great deep.
  You, Lord, preserve both people and animals.
⁷ How priceless is your unfailing love, O God!
  People take refuge in the shadow of your wings.
⁸ They feast on the abundance of your house;
  you give them drink from your river of delights.
⁹ For with you is the fountain of life;
  in your light we see light.

¹⁰ Continue your love to those who know you,
  your righteousness to the upright in heart.
¹¹ May the foot of the proud not come against me,
  nor the hand of the wicked drive me away.
¹² See how the evildoers lie fallen—
  thrown down, not able to rise!

How could a shadow offer protection? (36:7)
This was poetic language that showed David's desire for God to protect him as a bird protects its young.

PSALM 37ᵃ

Of David.

¹ Do not fret because of those who are evil
  or be envious of those who do wrong;
² for like the grass they will soon wither,
  like green plants they will soon die away.

³ Trust in the Lord and do good;
  dwell in the land and enjoy safe pasture.
⁴ Take delight in the Lord,
  and he will give you the desires of your heart.

⁵ Commit your way to the Lord;
  trust in him and he will do this:
⁶ He will make your righteous reward shine like the
    dawn,
  your vindication like the noonday sun.

⁷ Be still before the Lord
  and wait patiently for him;
 do not fret when people succeed in their ways,
  when they carry out their wicked schemes.

⁸ Refrain from anger and turn from wrath;
  do not fret—it leads only to evil.
⁹ For those who are evil will be destroyed,
  but those who hope in the Lord will inherit the
    land.

¹⁰ A little while, and the wicked will be no more;
  though you look for them, they will not be found.
¹¹ But the meek will inherit the land
  and enjoy peace and prosperity.

¹² The wicked plot against the righteous
  and gnash their teeth at them;

Why did David think God's people should be patient? (37:7–9)
David knew that in the future God would punish the wicked and the righteous would inherit the land.

Why was inheriting land considered so important? (37:9)
Land represented more than just a place to live or an area to grow crops. Owning land was a symbol that God's blessing and presence were with that person.

ᵃ This psalm is an acrostic poem, the stanzas of which begin with the successive letters of the Hebrew alphabet.

¹³ but the Lord laughs at the wicked,
for he knows their day is coming.

¹⁴ The wicked draw the sword
and bend the bow
to bring down the poor and needy,
to slay those whose ways are upright.
¹⁵ But their swords will pierce their own hearts,
and their bows will be broken.

¹⁶ Better the little that the righteous have
than the wealth of many wicked;
¹⁷ for the power of the wicked will be broken,
but the Lord upholds the righteous.

¹⁸ The blameless spend their days under the Lord's care,
and their inheritance will endure forever.
¹⁹ In times of disaster they will not wither;
in days of famine they will enjoy plenty.

²⁰ But the wicked will perish:
Though the Lord's enemies are like the flowers
of the field,
they will be consumed, they will go up in smoke.

²¹ The wicked borrow and do not repay,
but the righteous give generously;
²² those the Lord blesses will inherit the land,
but those he curses will be destroyed.

²³ The Lord makes firm the steps
of the one who delights in him;
²⁴ though he may stumble, he will not fall,
for the Lord upholds him with his hand.

²⁵ I was young and now I am old,
yet I have never seen the righteous forsaken
or their children begging bread.
²⁶ They are always generous and lend freely;
their children will be a blessing.ᵃ

²⁷ Turn from evil and do good;
then you will dwell in the land forever.
²⁸ For the Lord loves the just
and will not forsake his faithful ones.

Wrongdoers will be completely destroyedᵇ;
the offspring of the wicked will perish.
²⁹ The righteous will inherit the land
and dwell in it forever.

³⁰ The mouths of the righteous utter wisdom,
and their tongues speak what is just.
³¹ The law of their God is in their hearts;
their feet do not slip.

³² The wicked lie in wait for the righteous,
intent on putting them to death;

ᵃ 26 Or *freely; / the names of their children will be used in blessings* (see Gen.
48:20); or *freely; / others will see that their children are blessed*   ᵇ 28 See
Septuagint; Hebrew *They will be protected forever*

³³ but the LORD will not leave them in the power
        of the wicked
   or let them be condemned when brought to trial.

³⁴ Hope in the LORD
     and keep his way.
 He will exalt you to inherit the land;
   when the wicked are destroyed, you will see it.

³⁵ I have seen a wicked and ruthless man
   flourishing like a luxuriant native tree,
³⁶ but he soon passed away and was no more;
   though I looked for him, he could not be found.

³⁷ Consider the blameless, observe the upright;
   a future awaits those who seek peace.^a
³⁸ But all sinners will be destroyed;
   there will be no future^b for the wicked.

³⁹ The salvation of the righteous comes from the LORD;
   he is their stronghold in time of trouble.
⁴⁰ The LORD helps them and delivers them;
   he delivers them from the wicked and saves them,
   because they take refuge in him.

PSALM 38^c

A psalm of David. A petition.

¹ LORD, do not rebuke me in your anger
   or discipline me in your wrath.
² Your arrows have pierced me,
   and your hand has come down on me.
³ Because of your wrath there is no health in my body;
   there is no soundness in my bones because of my sin.
⁴ My guilt has overwhelmed me
   like a burden too heavy to bear.

⁵ My wounds fester and are loathsome
   because of my sinful folly.
⁶ I am bowed down and brought very low;
   all day long I go about mourning.
⁷ My back is filled with searing pain;
   there is no health in my body.
⁸ I am feeble and utterly crushed;
   I groan in anguish of heart.

⁹ All my longings lie open before you, Lord;
   my sighing is not hidden from you.
¹⁰ My heart pounds, my strength fails me;
   even the light has gone from my eyes.
¹¹ My friends and companions avoid me because
       of my wounds;
   my neighbors stay far away.
¹² Those who want to kill me set their traps,
   those who would harm me talk of my ruin;
   all day long they scheme and lie.

**Who were the blameless?
(37:37)**
These were not people who were
without sin. They were those who
continued to put their trust and
confidence in God.

**What was the source of
David's misery? (38:4)**
David was afflicted with physical
illness, but he also was burdened
with guilt.

**What was David's illness?
(38:5 – 8)**
It isn't clear what illness he had,
but it was very painful. It also
caused people to stay away from
him, so he was lonely.

---

^a 37 Or *upright; / those who seek peace will have posterity*   ^b 38 Or *posterity*
^c In Hebrew texts 38:1-22 is numbered 38:2-23.

¹³ I am like the deaf, who cannot hear,
    like the mute, who cannot speak;
¹⁴ I have become like one who does not hear,
    whose mouth can offer no reply.
¹⁵ Lord, I wait for you;
    you will answer, Lord my God.
¹⁶ For I said, "Do not let them gloat
    or exalt themselves over me when my feet slip."

¹⁷ For I am about to fall,
    and my pain is ever with me.
¹⁸ I confess my iniquity;
    I am troubled by my sin.
¹⁹ Many have become my enemies without cause^a;
    those who hate me without reason are numerous.
²⁰ Those who repay my good with evil
    lodge accusations against me,
    though I seek only to do what is good.

²¹ Lord, do not forsake me;
    do not be far from me, my God.
²² Come quickly to help me,
    my Lord and my Savior.

Did David trust God to deliver him? (38:21–22)
David trusted in God despite his pain and suffering. He believed God would not leave him, but he asked to be delivered quickly.

PSALM 39^b

For the director of music. For Jeduthun. A psalm of David.

¹ I said, "I will watch my ways
    and keep my tongue from sin;
I will put a muzzle on my mouth
    while in the presence of the wicked."
² So I remained utterly silent,
    not even saying anything good.
But my anguish increased;
³   my heart grew hot within me.
While I meditated, the fire burned;
    then I spoke with my tongue:

⁴ "Show me, Lord, my life's end
    and the number of my days;
    let me know how fleeting my life is.
⁵ You have made my days a mere handbreadth;
    the span of my years is as nothing before you.
Everyone is but a breath,
    even those who seem secure.^c

⁶ "Surely everyone goes around like a mere phantom;
    in vain they rush about, heaping up wealth
    without knowing whose it will finally be.

⁷ "But now, Lord, what do I look for?
    My hope is in you.
⁸ Save me from all my transgressions;
    do not make me the scorn of fools.

Why did David want to know when he would die? (39:4–5)
David wanted to be reminded that he was not going to live forever. That reminder would encourage him to make good use of the time he had left.

---

^a 19 One Dead Sea Scrolls manuscript; Masoretic Text *my vigorous enemies*
^b In Hebrew texts 39:1-13 is numbered 39:2-14.   ^c 5 The Hebrew has *Selah* (a word of uncertain meaning) here and at the end of verse 11.

⁹I was silent; I would not open my mouth,
  for you are the one who has done this.
¹⁰Remove your scourge from me;
  I am overcome by the blow of your hand.
¹¹When you rebuke and discipline anyone for
      their sin,
  you consume their wealth like a moth—
  surely everyone is but a breath.

¹²"Hear my prayer, LORD,
  listen to my cry for help;
  do not be deaf to my weeping.
  I dwell with you as a foreigner,
  a stranger, as all my ancestors were.
¹³Look away from me, that I may enjoy life again
  before I depart and am no more."

PSALM 40ᵃ

For the director of music. Of David. A psalm.

¹I waited patiently for the LORD;
  he turned to me and heard my cry.
²He lifted me out of the slimy pit,
  out of the mud and mire;
  he set my feet on a rock
  and gave me a firm place to stand.
³He put a new song in my mouth,
  a hymn of praise to our God.
  Many will see and fear the LORD
  and put their trust in him.

⁴Blessed is the one
  who trusts in the LORD,
  who does not look to the proud,
  to those who turn aside to false gods.ᵇ
⁵Many, LORD my God,
  are the wonders you have done,
  the things you planned for us.
  None can compare with you;
  were I to speak and tell of your deeds,
  they would be too many to declare.

⁶Sacrifice and offering you did not desire—
  but my ears you have openedᶜ—
  burnt offerings and sin offeringsᵈ you did not
      require.
⁷Then I said, "Here I am, I have come—
  it is written about me in the scroll.ᵉ
⁸I desire to do your will, my God;
  your law is within my heart."

⁹I proclaim your saving acts in the great assembly;
  I do not seal my lips, LORD,
  as you know.

Who were the foreigners and strangers? (39:12)
These were people who lived among the Israelites and could not inherit land because they were not Israelites. They had few rights. David used this as a word picture of the way he felt alienated from God.

What type of pit was David in? (40:2)
This may have been a pit dug for water, a dungeon, or even a reference to the grave. In any case, David was in a very bad situation, and God rescued him.

How were David's ears opened? (40:6)
David may have been saying that his ears were opened and ready to hear God's words.

ᵃ In Hebrew texts 40:1-17 is numbered 40:2-18.   ᵇ 4 Or *to lies*
ᶜ 6 Hebrew; some Septuagint manuscripts *but a body you have prepared for me*
ᵈ 6 Or *purification offerings*   ᵉ 7 Or *come / with the scroll written for me*

¹⁰ I do not hide your righteousness in my heart;
    I speak of your faithfulness and your saving help.
I do not conceal your love and your faithfulness
    from the great assembly.

¹¹ Do not withhold your mercy from me, LORD;
    may your love and faithfulness always protect me.
¹² For troubles without number surround me;
    my sins have overtaken me, and I cannot see.
They are more than the hairs of my head,
    and my heart fails within me.
¹³ Be pleased to save me, LORD;
    come quickly, LORD, to help me.

¹⁴ May all who want to take my life
    be put to shame and confusion;
may all who desire my ruin
    be turned back in disgrace.
¹⁵ May those who say to me, "Aha! Aha!"
    be appalled at their own shame.
¹⁶ But may all who seek you
    rejoice and be glad in you;
may those who long for your saving help
        always say,
    "The LORD is great!"

Why did wealthy King David describe himself as poor and needy? (40:17)
With this phrase David expressed his physical or spiritual need for God's help.

¹⁷ But as for me, I am poor and needy;
    may the Lord think of me.
You are my help and my deliverer;
    you are my God, do not delay.

PSALM 41ᵃ

For the director of music. A psalm of David.

¹ Blessed are those who have regard for the weak;
    the LORD delivers them in times of trouble.
² The LORD protects and preserves them—
    they are counted among the blessed in the land—
he does not give them over to the desire of their
        foes.
³ The LORD sustains them on their sickbed
    and restores them from their bed of illness.

What type of healing did David need? (41:4)
This was probably healing for David's soul because of his sin.

⁴ I said, "Have mercy on me, LORD;
    heal me, for I have sinned against you."
⁵ My enemies say of me in malice,
    "When will he die and his name perish?"
⁶ When one of them comes to see me,
    he speaks falsely, while his heart gathers slander;
    then he goes out and spreads it around.

⁷ All my enemies whisper together against me;
    they imagine the worst for me, saying,
⁸ "A vile disease has afflicted him;
    he will never get up from the place
        where he lies."

ᵃ In Hebrew texts 41:1-13 is numbered 41:2-14.

⁹ Even my close friend,
    someone I trusted,
one who shared my bread,
    has turned^a against me.

¹⁰ But may you have mercy on me, LORD;
    raise me up, that I may repay them.
¹¹ I know that you are pleased with me,
    for my enemy does not triumph over me.
¹² Because of my integrity you uphold me
    and set me in your presence forever.

¹³ Praise be to the LORD, the God of Israel,
    from everlasting to everlasting.
        Amen and Amen.

BOOK II

PSALMS 42 – 72

PSALM 42^{b,c}

For the director of music. A maskil^d of the Sons of Korah.

¹ As the deer pants for streams of water,
    so my soul pants for you, my God.
² My soul thirsts for God, for the living God.
    When can I go and meet with God?
³ My tears have been my food
    day and night,
while people say to me all day long,
    "Where is your God?"
⁴ These things I remember
    as I pour out my soul:
how I used to go to the house of God
    under the protection of the Mighty One^e
with shouts of joy and praise
    among the festive throng.

⁵ Why, my soul, are you downcast?
    Why so disturbed within me?
Put your hope in God,
    for I will yet praise him,
        my Savior and my God.

⁶ My soul is downcast within me;
    therefore I will remember you
from the land of the Jordan,
    the heights of Hermon—from Mount Mizar.
⁷ Deep calls to deep
    in the roar of your waterfalls;
all your waves and breakers
    have swept over me.

---

^a 9 Hebrew *has lifted up his heel*   ^b In many Hebrew manuscripts Psalms 42 and 43 constitute one psalm.   ^c In Hebrew texts 42:1-11 is numbered 42:2-12.   ^d Title: Probably a literary or musical term   ^e 4 See Septuagint and Syriac; the meaning of the Hebrew for this line is uncertain.

What did it mean to "turn against" someone? (41:9)
This meant to betray someone, possibly by saying false things about that person.

What is this verse saying? (42:4)
This verse suggests that the author of the psalm had once had a leading role in the liturgy of the temple.

What is the meaning of the phrase "deep calls to deep"? (42:7)
This may be a reference to God's storehouse of water above the earth that fills the rivers and streams that empty into the seas.

⁸ By day the LORD directs his love,
    at night his song is with me—
    a prayer to the God of my life.

⁹ I say to God my Rock,
    "Why have you forgotten me?
Why must I go about mourning,
    oppressed by the enemy?"
¹⁰ My bones suffer mortal agony
    as my foes taunt me,
saying to me all day long,
    "Where is your God?"

¹¹ Why, my soul, are you downcast?
    Why so disturbed within me?
Put your hope in God,
    for I will yet praise him,
    my Savior and my God.

PSALM 43ᵃ

¹ Vindicate me, my God,
    and plead my cause
    against an unfaithful nation.
Rescue me from those who are
    deceitful and wicked.
² You are God my stronghold.
    Why have you rejected me?
Why must I go about mourning,
    oppressed by the enemy?
³ Send me your light and your faithful care,
    let them lead me;
let them bring me to your holy mountain,
    to the place where you dwell.
⁴ Then I will go to the altar of God,
    to God, my joy and my delight.
I will praise you with the lyre,
    O God, my God.

⁵ Why, my soul, are you downcast?
    Why so disturbed within me?
Put your hope in God,
    for I will yet praise him,
    my Savior and my God.

PSALM 44ᵇ

For the director of music. Of the Sons of Korah. A maskil.ᶜ

¹ We have heard it with our ears, O God;
    our ancestors have told us
what you did in their days,
    in days long ago.
² With your hand you drove out the nations
    and planted our ancestors;

What was God's light? (43:3)
The psalmist was describing God's messengers who carry out God's plans and guide his people.

What was God's holy mountain? (43:3)
This was the site of the temple in Jerusalem, Mount Zion.

ᵃ In many Hebrew manuscripts Psalms 42 and 43 constitute one psalm.
ᵇ In Hebrew texts 44:1-26 is numbered 44:2-27.   ᶜ Title: Probably a literary or musical term

you crushed the peoples
　　and made our ancestors flourish.
³It was not by their sword that they won the land,
　　nor did their arm bring them victory;
it was your right hand, your arm,
　　and the light of your face, for you loved them.

⁴You are my King and my God,
　　who decrees*ᵃ* victories for Jacob.
⁵Through you we push back our enemies;
　　through your name we trample our foes.
⁶I put no trust in my bow,
　　my sword does not bring me victory;
⁷but you give us victory over our enemies,
　　you put our adversaries to shame.
⁸In God we make our boast all day long,
　　and we will praise your name forever.*ᵇ*

⁹But now you have rejected and humbled us;
　　you no longer go out with our armies.
¹⁰You made us retreat before the enemy,
　　and our adversaries have plundered us.
¹¹You gave us up to be devoured like sheep
　　and have scattered us among the nations.
¹²You sold your people for a pittance,
　　gaining nothing from their sale.

¹³You have made us a reproach to our neighbors,
　　the scorn and derision of those around us.
¹⁴You have made us a byword among the nations;
　　the peoples shake their heads at us.
¹⁵I live in disgrace all day long,
　　and my face is covered with shame
¹⁶at the taunts of those who reproach and revile me,
　　because of the enemy, who is bent on revenge.

¹⁷All this came upon us,
　　though we had not forgotten you;
　　we had not been false to your covenant.
¹⁸Our hearts had not turned back;
　　our feet had not strayed from your path.
¹⁹But you crushed us and made us a haunt
　　　　for jackals;
　　you covered us over with deep darkness.

²⁰If we had forgotten the name of our God
　　or spread out our hands to a foreign god,
²¹would not God have discovered it,
　　since he knows the secrets of the heart?
²²Yet for your sake we face death all day long;
　　we are considered as sheep to be slaughtered.

²³Awake, Lord! Why do you sleep?
　　Rouse yourself! Do not reject us forever.
²⁴Why do you hide your face
　　and forget our misery and oppression?

How had God forsaken the people? (44:9–16)
God caused them to suffer defeat (vv. 9–12), and he shamed them before their enemies (vv. 13–16).

What did it mean that Israel had been made a haunt for jackals? (44:19)
Since jackals were scavengers that avoided populated areas, the psalmist implied that Israel was scarcely inhabited. Perhaps this was a warning of what could happen.

ᵃ 4 Septuagint, Aquila and Syriac; Hebrew *King, O God; / command*
ᵇ 8 The Hebrew has *Selah* (a word of uncertain meaning) here.

²⁵ We are brought down to the dust;
     our bodies cling to the ground.
²⁶ Rise up and help us;
     rescue us because of your unfailing love.

PSALM 45^a

For the director of music. To the tune of "Lilies."
Of the Sons of Korah. A maskil.^b A wedding song.

¹ My heart is stirred by a noble theme
     as I recite my verses for the king;
     my tongue is the pen of a skillful writer.

² You are the most excellent of men
     and your lips have been anointed with grace,
     since God has blessed you forever.

³ Gird your sword on your side, you mighty one;
     clothe yourself with splendor and majesty.
⁴ In your majesty ride forth victoriously
     in the cause of truth, humility and justice;
     let your right hand achieve awesome deeds.
⁵ Let your sharp arrows pierce the hearts of the
         king's enemies;
     let the nations fall beneath your feet.
⁶ Your throne, O God,^c will last for ever and ever;
     a scepter of justice will be the scepter of
         your kingdom.
⁷ You love righteousness and hate wickedness;
     therefore God, your God, has set you above your
         companions
     by anointing you with the oil of joy.
⁸ All your robes are fragrant with myrrh and aloes
         and cassia;
     from palaces adorned with ivory
     the music of the strings makes you glad.
⁹ Daughters of kings are among your honored women;
     at your right hand is the royal bride in gold
         of Ophir.

¹⁰ Listen, daughter, and pay careful attention:
     Forget your people and your father's house.
¹¹ Let the king be enthralled by your beauty;
     honor him, for he is your lord.
¹² The city of Tyre will come with a gift,^d
     people of wealth will seek your favor.
¹³ All glorious is the princess within her chamber;
     her gown is interwoven with gold.
¹⁴ In embroidered garments she is led to the king;
     her virgin companions follow her—
     those brought to be with her.
¹⁵ Led in with joy and gladness,
     they enter the palace of the king.

Why was this psalm written? (45:1–17)
This psalm was probably written as a wedding song in praise of the king on his wedding day. The king was from the line of David, and the bride was a foreign princess. The first part (vv. 2–9) is addressed to the king, and the second part (vv. 10–17) is addressed to the bride. This psalm also points to the coming of Jesus.

What was God's throne? (45:6)
The king's throne may have been called God's throne because the king was God's anointed one.

What was gold of Ophir? (45:9)
This was very rare gold of the highest purity that was imported into Israel.

---

^a In Hebrew texts 45:1-17 is numbered 45:2-18.   ^b Title: Probably a literary or musical term   ^c 6 Here the king is addressed as God's representative.   ^d 12 Or *A Tyrian robe is among the gifts*

¹⁶ Your sons will take the place of your fathers;
   you will make them princes throughout the land.

¹⁷ I will perpetuate your memory through all generations;
   therefore the nations will praise you for ever and ever.

PSALM 46^a

*For the director of music. Of the Sons of Korah.
According to* alamoth.^b *A song.*

¹ God is our refuge and strength,
   an ever-present help in trouble.
² Therefore we will not fear, though the earth give way
   and the mountains fall into the heart of the sea,
³ though its waters roar and foam
   and the mountains quake with their surging.^c

⁴ There is a river whose streams make glad the city
      of God,
   the holy place where the Most High dwells.
⁵ God is within her, she will not fall;
   God will help her at break of day.
⁶ Nations are in uproar, kingdoms fall;
   he lifts his voice, the earth melts.

⁷ The LORD Almighty is with us;
   the God of Jacob is our fortress.

⁸ Come and see what the LORD has done,
   the desolations he has brought on the earth.
⁹ He makes wars cease
   to the ends of the earth.
   He breaks the bow and shatters the spear;
   he burns the shields^d with fire.
¹⁰ He says, "Be still, and know that I am God;
   I will be exalted among the nations,
   I will be exalted in the earth."

¹¹ The LORD Almighty is with us;
   the God of Jacob is our fortress.

PSALM 47^e

For the director of music. Of the Sons of Korah. A psalm.

¹ Clap your hands, all you nations;
   shout to God with cries of joy.

² For the LORD Most High is awesome,
   the great King over all the earth.
³ He subdued nations under us,
   peoples under our feet.
⁴ He chose our inheritance for us,
   the pride of Jacob, whom he loved.^f

What river was this? (46:4)
Unlike many capital cities, Jerusalem did not have a river that ran through it. This "river" is a metaphor for the continual blessings of God, which made the city of God like the Garden of Eden.

What type of safety would God provide for his people? (46:8–10)
The psalmist wrote about God preserving the nation of Israel from its enemies, but he also described a time when peace would cover the entire earth.

What was this inheritance? (47:4)
The inheritance of Jacob refers to the promised land and specifically to Jerusalem, the city where God's presence was with his people.

---

^a In Hebrew texts 46:1-11 is numbered 46:2-12.   ^b Title: Probably a musical term   ^c 3 The Hebrew has *Selah* (a word of uncertain meaning) here and at the end of verses 7 and 11.   ^d 9 Or *chariots*   ^e In Hebrew texts 47:1-9 is numbered 47:2-10.   ^f 4 The Hebrew has *Selah* (a word of uncertain meaning) here.

What type of trumpets were these? (47:5)
These were ram's horn trumpets that announced the presence of God the King.

Where was God's holy throne? (47:8)
This was the Most Holy Place of the temple, the place from which God ruled.

Why was Mount Zion so remarkable? (48:2–3)
Mount Zion was not the highest mountain in the area, but God had chosen it as his home, which made it the highest in importance. God himself defended the city of Jerusalem.

What type of ships were these? (48:7)
These were the great merchant ships of the Mediterranean Sea.

Why were the people told to look at Zion? (48:12–13)
The people were supposed to think about how God had protected and preserved them so they could tell the next generation about God's great salvation.

⁵ God has ascended amid shouts of joy,
     the LORD amid the sounding of trumpets.
⁶ Sing praises to God, sing praises;
     sing praises to our King, sing praises.
⁷ For God is the King of all the earth;
     sing to him a psalm of praise.

⁸ God reigns over the nations;
     God is seated on his holy throne.
⁹ The nobles of the nations assemble
     as the people of the God of Abraham,
for the kings*a* of the earth belong to God;
     he is greatly exalted.

PSALM 48*b*

A song. A psalm of the Sons of Korah.

¹ Great is the LORD, and most worthy of praise,
     in the city of our God, his holy mountain.

² Beautiful in its loftiness,
     the joy of the whole earth,
like the heights of Zaphon*c* is Mount Zion,
     the city of the Great King.
³ God is in her citadels;
     he has shown himself to be her fortress.

⁴ When the kings joined forces,
     when they advanced together,
⁵ they saw her and were astounded;
     they fled in terror.
⁶ Trembling seized them there,
     pain like that of a woman in labor.
⁷ You destroyed them like ships of Tarshish
     shattered by an east wind.

⁸ As we have heard,
     so we have seen
in the city of the LORD Almighty,
     in the city of our God:
God makes her secure
     forever.*d*

⁹ Within your temple, O God,
     we meditate on your unfailing love.
¹⁰ Like your name, O God,
     your praise reaches to the ends of the earth;
     your right hand is filled with
        righteousness.
¹¹ Mount Zion rejoices,
     the villages of Judah are glad
     because of your judgments.

¹² Walk about Zion, go around her,
     count her towers,

---

a 9 Or *shields*   *b* In Hebrew texts 48:1-14 is numbered 48:2-15.
c 2 Zaphon was the most sacred mountain of the Canaanites.   *d 8* The Hebrew has *Selah* (a word of uncertain meaning) here.

¹³ consider well her ramparts,
  view her citadels,
that you may tell of them
  to the next generation.

¹⁴ For this God is our God for ever and ever;
  he will be our guide even to the end.

PSALM 49ᵃ

For the director of music. Of the Sons of Korah. A psalm.

¹ Hear this, all you peoples;
  listen, all who live in this world,
² both low and high,
  rich and poor alike:
³ My mouth will speak words of wisdom;
  the meditation of my heart will give you
    understanding.
⁴ I will turn my ear to a proverb;
  with the harp I will expound my riddle:

⁵ Why should I fear when evil days come,
  when wicked deceivers surround me—
⁶ those who trust in their wealth
  and boast of their great riches?
⁷ No one can redeem the life of another
  or give to God a ransom for them—
⁸ the ransom for a life is costly,
  no payment is ever enough—
⁹ so that they should live on forever
  and not see decay.
¹⁰ For all can see that the wise die,
  that the foolish and the senseless also perish,
  leaving their wealth to others.
¹¹ Their tombs will remain their housesᵇ forever,
  their dwellings for endless generations,
  though they hadᶜ named lands after themselves.

¹² People, despite their wealth, do not endure;
  they are like the beasts that perish.

¹³ This is the fate of those who trust in themselves,
  and of their followers, who approve their sayings.ᵈ
¹⁴ They are like sheep and are destined to die;
  death will be their shepherd
  (but the upright will prevail over them in the
    morning).
  Their forms will decay in the grave,
  far from their princely mansions.
¹⁵ But God will redeem me from the realm of the dead;
  he will surely take me to himself.
¹⁶ Do not be overawed when others grow rich,
  when the splendor of their houses increases;

What will always happen to people, whether they are rich or poor? (49:5–9)
Everyone will eventually die, and no amount of money can prevent death.

Did people in Old Testament times believe in heaven? (49:15)
There is not much said about life after death in the Old Testament. However, this verse hints at it. The psalmist suggests that even though he will die, he will live with God after his death.

What does this psalm teach about being rich? (49:16–20)
Having riches without wisdom is worthless, because when a person dies he leaves it all behind.

ᵃ In Hebrew texts 49:1-20 is numbered 49:2-21.   ᵇ 11 Septuagint and Syriac; Hebrew *In their thoughts their houses will remain*
ᶜ 11 Or *generations, / for they have*   ᵈ 13 The Hebrew has *Selah* (a word of uncertain meaning) here and at the end of verse 15.

¹⁷ for they will take nothing with them when
     they die,
     their splendor will not descend with them.
¹⁸ Though while they live they count themselves
     blessed—
     and people praise you when you prosper—
¹⁹ they will join those who have gone before them,
     who will never again see the light of life.

²⁰ People who have wealth but lack understanding
     are like the beasts that perish.

PSALM 50

A psalm of Asaph.

¹ The Mighty One, God, the LORD,
     speaks and summons the earth
     from the rising of the sun to where it sets.
² From Zion, perfect in beauty,
     God shines forth.
³ Our God comes
     and will not be silent;
    a fire devours before him,
     and around him a tempest rages.
⁴ He summons the heavens above,
     and the earth, that he may judge his people:
⁵ "Gather to me this consecrated people,
     who made a covenant with me by sacrifice."
⁶ And the heavens proclaim his righteousness,
     for he is a God of justice.^{a,b}

⁷ "Listen, my people, and I will speak;
     I will testify against you, Israel:
     I am God, your God.
⁸ I bring no charges against you concerning
     your sacrifices
     or concerning your burnt offerings, which are
     ever before me.
⁹ I have no need of a bull from your stall
     or of goats from your pens,
¹⁰ for every animal of the forest is mine,
     and the cattle on a thousand hills.
¹¹ I know every bird in the mountains,
     and the insects in the fields are mine.
¹² If I were hungry I would not tell you,
     for the world is mine, and all that is in it.
¹³ Do I eat the flesh of bulls
     or drink the blood of goats?

¹⁴ "Sacrifice thank offerings to God,
     fulfill your vows to the Most High,
¹⁵ and call on me in the day of trouble;
     I will deliver you, and you will honor me."

Why was God's name repeated? (50:1)
It is a common literary technique to repeat words or phrases in poetry. Repeating God's name emphasized his power and glory.

Why had sacrifices been offered? (50:5)
Sacrifices were part of the ritual that sealed the covenant. In this psalm, God rebuked the people who thought sacrifices alone were enough to satisfy him.

---

^a 6 With a different word division of the Hebrew; Masoretic Text *for God himself is judge*   ^b 6 The Hebrew has *Selah* (a word of uncertain meaning) here.

[16] But to the wicked person, God says:

"What right have you to recite my laws
    or take my covenant on your lips?
[17] You hate my instruction
    and cast my words behind you.
[18] When you see a thief, you join with him;
    you throw in your lot with adulterers.
[19] You use your mouth for evil
    and harness your tongue to deceit.
[20] You sit and testify against your brother
    and slander your own mother's son.
[21] When you did these things and I kept silent,
    you thought I was exactly[a] like you.
But I now arraign you
    and set my accusations before you.

[22] "Consider this, you who forget God,
    or I will tear you to pieces, with no one to rescue
      you:
[23] Those who sacrifice thank offerings honor me,
    and to the blameless[b] I will show my salvation."

PSALM 51[c]

*For the director of music. A psalm of David. When the prophet Nathan
came to him after David had committed adultery with Bathsheba.*

[1] Have mercy on me, O God,
    according to your unfailing love;
according to your great compassion
    blot out my transgressions.
[2] Wash away all my iniquity
    and cleanse me from my sin.

[3] For I know my transgressions,
    and my sin is always before me.
[4] Against you, you only, have I sinned
    and done what is evil in your sight;
so you are right in your verdict
    and justified when you judge.
[5] Surely I was sinful at birth,
    sinful from the time my mother conceived me.
[6] Yet you desired faithfulness even in the womb;
    you taught me wisdom in that secret place.

[7] Cleanse me with hyssop, and I will be clean;
    wash me, and I will be whiter than snow.
[8] Let me hear joy and gladness;
    let the bones you have crushed rejoice.
[9] Hide your face from my sins
    and blot out all my iniquity.

[10] Create in me a pure heart, O God,
    and renew a steadfast spirit within me.

---

[a] 21 Or *thought the 'I AM' was*   [b] 23 Probable reading of the original
Hebrew text; the meaning of the Masoretic Text for this phrase is uncertain.
[c] In Hebrew texts 51:1-19 is numbered 51:3-21.

**What was necessary besides
sacrifices? (50:23)**
The people couldn't bribe God by
offering sacrifices. They needed
to offer sacrifices to express
their thanks to God and to repent
of their sins so they could have a
good relationship with God.

**How did God blot out sins?
(51:1)**
This is a word picture describing
how God removes the sins from
our lives in a way that someone
erases ink from a page. In the
time this psalm was written, ink
was typically a mixture of soot or
charcoal and water, which could
be easily removed by dabbing a
damp cloth on the paper.

What is hyssop? (51:7)
Hyssop is a plant from the mint
family with a straight stalk and
white flowers. The hairy surface
of the leaves and branches
held liquids well. It was dipped
in sacrificial blood, which was
then brushed or sprinkled on the
object or person being ritually
cleansed.

¹¹ Do not cast me from your presence
　　or take your Holy Spirit from me.
¹² Restore to me the joy of your salvation
　　and grant me a willing spirit, to sustain me.

¹³ Then I will teach transgressors your ways,
　　so that sinners will turn back to you.
¹⁴ Deliver me from the guilt of bloodshed, O God,
　　you who are God my Savior,
　　and my tongue will sing of your righteousness.
¹⁵ Open my lips, Lord,
　　and my mouth will declare your praise.
¹⁶ You do not delight in sacrifice, or I would bring it;
　　you do not take pleasure in burnt offerings.
¹⁷ My sacrifice, O God, is*a* a broken spirit;
　　a broken and contrite heart
　　you, God, will not despise.

¹⁸ May it please you to prosper Zion,
　　to build up the walls of Jerusalem.
¹⁹ Then you will delight in the sacrifices of the righteous,
　　in burnt offerings offered whole;
　　then bulls will be offered on your altar.

What did God want more than sacrifices? (51:16–17)
God takes delight in a person who has a humble heart and who turns to him to ask forgiveness.

PSALM 52*b*

*For the director of music. A maskil*c *of David.*
When Doeg the Edomite had gone to Saul and told him:
"David has gone to the house of Ahimelek."

¹ Why do you boast of evil, you mighty hero?
　　Why do you boast all day long,
　　you who are a disgrace in the eyes of God?
² You who practice deceit,
　　your tongue plots destruction;
　　it is like a sharpened razor.
³ You love evil rather than good,
　　falsehood rather than speaking the truth.*d*
⁴ You love every harmful word,
　　you deceitful tongue!

⁵ Surely God will bring you down to everlasting ruin:
　　He will snatch you up and pluck you from your tent;
　　he will uproot you from the land of the living.
⁶ The righteous will see and fear;
　　they will laugh at you, saying,
⁷ "Here now is the man
　　who did not make God his stronghold
　but trusted in his great wealth
　　and grew strong by destroying others!"

⁸ But I am like an olive tree
　　flourishing in the house of God;
　I trust in God's unfailing love
　　for ever and ever.

What will happen to an evil person? (52:5)
God will bring him down, snatch him up, and uproot him. In each of these examples, the person would not be able to remain upright.

In what ways was David like an olive tree? (52:8)
An olive tree lives for hundreds of years. The ancient Hebrews considered the olive tree to be a symbol of beauty, strength, prosperity, and blessing.

a 17 Or *The sacrifices of God are*　*b* In Hebrew texts 52:1-9 is numbered 52:3-11.　*c* Title: Probably a literary or musical term　*d 3* The Hebrew has *Selah* (a word of uncertain meaning) here and at the end of verse 5.

⁹ For what you have done I will always praise you
in the presence of your faithful people.
And I will hope in your name,
for your name is good.

PSALM 53 *ᵃ*

For the director of music. According to mahalath.*ᵇ A* maskil*ᶜ of David.*

¹ The fool says in his heart,
"There is no God."
They are corrupt, and their ways are vile;
there is no one who does good.

² God looks down from heaven
on all mankind
to see if there are any who understand,
any who seek God.
³ Everyone has turned away, all have become corrupt;
there is no one who does good,
not even one.

⁴ Do all these evildoers know nothing?

They devour my people as though eating bread;
they never call on God.
⁵ But there they are, overwhelmed with dread,
where there was nothing to dread.
God scattered the bones of those who attacked you;
you put them to shame, for God despised them.

⁶ Oh, that salvation for Israel would come out
of Zion!
When God restores his people,
let Jacob rejoice and Israel be glad!

Why is this psalm repeated? (53:1–6)
This psalm is almost the same as Psalm 14. David may have slightly revised that psalm for a different occasion.

PSALM 54 *ᵈ*

For the director of music. With stringed instruments. A maskil*ᶜ
of David. When the Ziphites had gone to Saul and said,
"Is not David hiding among us?"*

¹ Save me, O God, by your name;
vindicate me by your might.
² Hear my prayer, O God;
listen to the words of my mouth.

³ Arrogant foes are attacking me;
ruthless people are trying to kill me—
people without regard for God.*ᵉ*

⁴ Surely God is my help;
the Lord is the one who sustains me.

⁵ Let evil recoil on those who slander me;
in your faithfulness destroy them.

Why was this psalm written? (54)
It is a prayer for deliverance from enemies who wanted to kill David. This psalm is symmetrical: The beginning asks for God's salvation, and the end praises God for deliverance. The central verse (4) is a confident statement about God's help.

ᵃ In Hebrew texts 53:1-6 is numbered 53:2-7.   *ᵇ* Title: Probably a musical term   *ᶜ* Title: Probably a literary or musical term   *ᵈ* In Hebrew texts 54:1-7 is numbered 54:3-9.   *ᵉ 3* The Hebrew has *Selah* (a word of uncertain meaning) here.

⁶ I will sacrifice a freewill offering to you;
    I will praise your name, LORD, for it is good.
⁷ You have delivered me from all my troubles,
    and my eyes have looked in triumph on my foes.

PSALM 55ᵃ

*For the director of music. With stringed instruments.
A maskilᵇ of David.*

¹ Listen to my prayer, O God,
    do not ignore my plea;
²   hear me and answer me.
My thoughts trouble me and I am distraught
³   because of what my enemy is saying,
    because of the threats of the wicked;
for they bring down suffering on me
    and assail me in their anger.

⁴ My heart is in anguish within me;
    the terrors of death have fallen on me.
⁵ Fear and trembling have beset me;
    horror has overwhelmed me.
⁶ I said, "Oh, that I had the wings of a dove!
    I would fly away and be at rest.
⁷ I would flee far away
    and stay in the desert;ᶜ
⁸ I would hurry to my place of shelter,
    far from the tempest and storm."

⁹ Lord, confuse the wicked, confound their words,
    for I see violence and strife in the city.
¹⁰ Day and night they prowl about on its walls;
    malice and abuse are within it.
¹¹ Destructive forces are at work in the city;
    threats and lies never leave its streets.

¹² If an enemy were insulting me,
    I could endure it;
if a foe were rising against me,
    I could hide.
¹³ But it is you, a man like myself,
    my companion, my close friend,
¹⁴ with whom I once enjoyed sweet fellowship
    at the house of God,
as we walked about
    among the worshipers.

¹⁵ Let death take my enemies by surprise;
    let them go down alive to the realm
        of the dead,
    for evil finds lodging among them.

¹⁶ As for me, I call to God,
    and the LORD saves me.

What was the situation when this psalm was written? (55)
This psalm was a prayer for help when David was faced with a conspiracy against him in Jerusalem.

How did David want God to deal with his enemies? (55:9)
David wanted God to confuse their speech as he had done at the tower of Babel, so they would not be able to communicate with each other.

Is it right to want our enemies dead? (55:15)
We are not supposed to hate our enemies, but in this case, David's enemies were also enemies of God.

ᵃ In Hebrew texts 55:1-23 is numbered 55:2-24.   ᵇ Title: Probably a literary or musical term   ᶜ 7 The Hebrew has *Selah* (a word of uncertain meaning) here and in the middle of verse 19.

¹⁷Evening, morning and noon
 I cry out in distress,
 and he hears my voice.
¹⁸He rescues me unharmed
 from the battle waged against me,
 even though many oppose me.
¹⁹God, who is enthroned from of old,
 who does not change—
he will hear them and humble them,
 because they have no fear of God.

²⁰My companion attacks his friends;
 he violates his covenant.
²¹His talk is smooth as butter,
 yet war is in his heart;
his words are more soothing than oil,
 yet they are drawn swords.

²²Cast your cares on the LORD
 and he will sustain you;
he will never let
 the righteous be shaken.
²³But you, God, will bring down the wicked
 into the pit of decay;
the bloodthirsty and deceitful
 will not live out half their days.

But as for me, I trust in you.

PSALM 56^a

For the director of music. To the tune of "A Dove on Distant Oaks."
Of David. A miktam.^b *When the Philistines had seized him in Gath.*

¹Be merciful to me, my God,
 for my enemies are in hot pursuit;
 all day long they press their attack.
²My adversaries pursue me all day long;
 in their pride many are attacking me.

³When I am afraid, I put my trust in you.
⁴ In God, whose word I praise—
 in God I trust and am not afraid.
 What can mere mortals do to me?

⁵All day long they twist my words;
 all their schemes are for my ruin.
⁶They conspire, they lurk,
 they watch my steps,
 hoping to take my life.
⁷Because of their wickedness do not^c let them escape;
 in your anger, God, bring the nations down.

⁸Record my misery;
 list my tears on your scroll^d—
 are they not in your record?

What were David's enemies saying about him? (56:2–5)
They were saying false things about him and plotting to harm him.

What kind of record did David want God to keep? (56:8)
David wanted God to take special note of his troubles as if writing them on a scroll.

^a In Hebrew texts 56:1-13 is numbered 56:2-14.   ^b Title: Probably a
literary or musical term   ^c 7 Probable reading of the original Hebrew text;
Masoretic Text does not have *do not.*   ^d 8 Or *misery; / put my tears in your*
wineskin

⁹ Then my enemies will turn back
    when I call for help.
  By this I will know that God is for me.

¹⁰ In God, whose word I praise,
     in the LORD, whose word I praise—
¹¹ in God I trust and am not afraid.
     What can man do to me?

¹² I am under vows to you, my God;
     I will present my thank offerings to you.
¹³ For you have delivered me from death
     and my feet from stumbling,
   that I may walk before God
     in the light of life.

PSALM 57[a]

For the director of music. To the tune of "Do Not Destroy." Of David.
A miktam.[b] When he had fled from Saul into the cave.

¹ Have mercy on me, my God, have mercy on me,
    for in you I take refuge.
  I will take refuge in the shadow of your wings
    until the disaster has passed.

² I cry out to God Most High,
    to God, who vindicates me.
³ He sends from heaven and saves me,
    rebuking those who hotly pursue me—[c]
  God sends forth his love and his faithfulness.

⁴ I am in the midst of lions;
    I am forced to dwell among ravenous beasts—
  men whose teeth are spears and arrows,
    whose tongues are sharp swords.

⁵ Be exalted, O God, above the heavens;
    let your glory be over all the earth.

⁶ They spread a net for my feet—
    I was bowed down in distress.
  They dug a pit in my path—
    but they have fallen into it themselves.

⁷ My heart, O God, is steadfast,
    my heart is steadfast;
  I will sing and make music.
⁸ Awake, my soul!
    Awake, harp and lyre!
  I will awaken the dawn.

⁹ I will praise you, Lord, among the nations;
    I will sing of you among the peoples.
¹⁰ For great is your love, reaching to the heavens;
     your faithfulness reaches to the skies.

¹¹ Be exalted, O God, above the heavens;
     let your glory be over all the earth.

How can a shadow offer protection? (57:1)
This is an image of being sheltered, as young birds are sheltered under the wings of their mother and as someone is protected from the sun in the shadow of a tree.

Why were the harp and lyre called to wake up? (57:8)
The harp and lyre were instruments used to praise God at the temple. Here they were personified (given human characteristics) in order to give praise to God.

---

[a] In Hebrew texts 57:1-11 is numbered 57:2-12.   [b] Title: Probably a
literary or musical term   [c] 3 The Hebrew has *Selah* (a word of uncertain
meaning) here and at the end of verse 6.

PSALM 58[a]

For the director of music. To the tune of "Do Not Destroy."
Of David. A miktam.[b]

[1] Do you rulers indeed speak justly?
  Do you judge people with equity?
[2] No, in your heart you devise injustice,
  and your hands mete out violence on the earth.

[3] Even from birth the wicked go astray;
  from the womb they are wayward, spreading lies.
[4] Their venom is like the venom of a snake,
  like that of a cobra that has stopped its ears,
[5] that will not heed the tune of the charmer,
  however skillful the enchanter may be.

[6] Break the teeth in their mouths, O God;
  LORD, tear out the fangs of those lions!
[7] Let them vanish like water that flows away;
  when they draw the bow, let their arrows fall short.
[8] May they be like a slug that melts away as it moves
    along,
  like a stillborn child that never sees the sun.

[9] Before your pots can feel the heat of the thorns—
  whether they be green or dry—the wicked will be
    swept away.[c]
[10] The righteous will be glad when they are avenged,
  when they dip their feet in the blood of the wicked.
[11] Then people will say,
  "Surely the righteous still are rewarded;
  surely there is a God who judges the earth."

PSALM 59[d]

For the director of music. To the tune of "Do Not Destroy."
Of David. A miktam.[b] *When Saul had sent men to*
watch David's house in order to kill him.

[1] Deliver me from my enemies, O God;
  be my fortress against those who are attacking me.
[2] Deliver me from evildoers
  and save me from those who are after my blood.

[3] See how they lie in wait for me!
  Fierce men conspire against me
  for no offense or sin of mine, LORD.
[4] I have done no wrong, yet they are ready to
    attack me.
  Arise to help me; look on my plight!
[5] You, LORD God Almighty,
  you who are the God of Israel,
  rouse yourself to punish all the nations;
  show no mercy to wicked traitors.[e]

Why did the psalmist accuse the judges of being unjust? (58:1)
Throughout the Old Testament, there is a theme of God administering justice through his appointed representatives. When those people were corrupt, justice was not being served.

Why would people dip their feet in blood? (58:10)
The image of splashing in the blood of an enemy was a common image in ancient literature. Here it may express how great the joy will be when God brings justice.

Why was David afraid? (59:2)
David feared for his life when Saul was trying to kill him (1 Samuel 19:11–13). The psalm may have been revised when Jerusalem was under siege from an enemy nation.

---

[a] In Hebrew texts 58:1-11 is numbered 58:2-12.   [b] Title: Probably a
literary or musical term   [c] 9 The meaning of the Hebrew for this verse is
uncertain.   [d] In Hebrew texts 59:1-17 is numbered 59:2-18.   [e] 5 The
Hebrew has *Selah* (a word of uncertain meaning) here and at the end of
verse 13.

⁶They return at evening,
　　snarling like dogs,
　　and prowl about the city.
⁷See what they spew from their mouths—
　　the words from their lips are sharp as swords,
　　and they think, "Who can hear us?"
⁸But you laugh at them, LORD;
　　you scoff at all those nations.

⁹You are my strength, I watch for you;
　　you, God, are my fortress,
¹⁰　　my God on whom I can rely.

God will go before me
　　and will let me gloat over those who slander me.
¹¹But do not kill them, Lord our shield,ᵃ
　　or my people will forget.
In your might uproot them
　　and bring them down.
¹²For the sins of their mouths,
　　for the words of their lips,
　　let them be caught in their pride.
For the curses and lies they utter,
¹³　　consume them in your wrath,
　　consume them till they are no more.
Then it will be known to the ends of the earth
　　that God rules over Jacob.

¹⁴They return at evening,
　　snarling like dogs,
　　and prowl about the city.
¹⁵They wander about for food
　　and howl if not satisfied.
¹⁶But I will sing of your strength,
　　in the morning I will sing of your love;
for you are my fortress,
　　my refuge in times of trouble.

¹⁷You are my strength, I sing praise to you;
　　you, God, are my fortress,
　　my God on whom I can rely.

PSALM 60ᵇ

*For the director of music. To the tune of "The Lily of the Covenant."
A miktamᶜ of David. For teaching. When he fought Aram Naharaimᵈ
and Aram Zobah,ᵉ and when Joab returned and struck down twelve
thousand Edomites in the Valley of Salt.*

¹You have rejected us, God, and burst upon us;
　　you have been angry—now restore us!
²You have shaken the land and torn it open;
　　mend its fractures, for it is quaking.
³You have shown your people desperate times;
　　you have given us wine that makes us stagger.

Why didn't David want God to kill his enemies? (59:11)
David wanted God to make his enemies suffer in order to make a public example of them.

How had God rejected Israel? (60:1)
David was asking for God's help after a military defeat, probably from Edom.

ᵃ *11* Or *sovereign*　　ᵇ In Hebrew texts 60:1-12 is numbered 60:3-14.
ᶜ Title: Probably a literary or musical term　　ᵈ Title: That is, Arameans of Northwest Mesopotamia　　ᵉ Title: That is, Arameans of central Syria

⁴But for those who fear you, you have raised a banner
to be unfurled against the bow.*

⁵Save us and help us with your right hand,
that those you love may be delivered.
⁶God has spoken from his sanctuary:
"In triumph I will parcel out Shechem
and measure off the Valley of Sukkoth.
⁷Gilead is mine, and Manasseh is mine;
Ephraim is my helmet,
Judah is my scepter.
⁸Moab is my washbasin,
on Edom I toss my sandal;
over Philistia I shout in triumph."

⁹Who will bring me to the fortified city?
Who will lead me to Edom?
¹⁰Is it not you, God, you who have now rejected us
and no longer go out with our armies?
¹¹Give us aid against the enemy,
for human help is worthless.
¹²With God we will gain the victory,
and he will trample down our enemies.

PSALM 61ᵇ

For the director of music. With stringed instruments. Of David.

¹Hear my cry, O God;
listen to my prayer.

²From the ends of the earth I call to you,
I call as my heart grows faint;
lead me to the rock that is higher than I.
³For you have been my refuge,
a strong tower against the foe.

⁴I long to dwell in your tent forever
and take refuge in the shelter of your wings.*
⁵For you, God, have heard my vows;
you have given me the heritage of those who fear
your name.

⁶Increase the days of the king's life,
his years for many generations.
⁷May he be enthroned in God's presence forever;
appoint your love and faithfulness to protect him.

⁸Then I will ever sing in praise of your name
and fulfill my vows day after day.

PSALM 62ᶜ

For the director of music. For Jeduthun. A psalm of David.

¹Truly my soul finds rest in God;
my salvation comes from him.

What did it mean to raise a banner? (60:4)
Flags and banners were used to bring together troops and lead them into battle. This word picture describes how God would inspire confidence in his people like a banner unfolded against "the bow" (the enemy).

Who was praying for the king's life? (61:6)
It may have been David himself, who spoke of himself in the third person. Or this may have been the prayer offered by the people.

ᵃ 4 The Hebrew has *Selah* (a word of uncertain meaning) here.   *ᵇ In* Hebrew texts 61:1-8 is numbered 61:2-9.   *ᶜ In* Hebrew texts 62:1-12 is numbered 62:2-13.

Why did David describe himself as a leaning wall and tottering fence? (62:3)
This was a word picture for David's fragile condition. He may have been saying that he had no strength in himself, that he was in a weakened condition, or that this was how his enemies saw him.

What types of lies did David hear? (62:4)
He probably heard lies and rumors about his enemies as well as lies from those who seemed to support him but who were actually his opponents.

2 Truly he is my rock and my salvation;
    he is my fortress, I will never be shaken.

3 How long will you assault me?
    Would all of you throw me down—
    this leaning wall, this tottering fence?
4 Surely they intend to topple me
    from my lofty place;
    they take delight in lies.
With their mouths they bless,
    but in their hearts they curse.*a*

5 Yes, my soul, find rest in God;
    my hope comes from him.
6 Truly he is my rock and my salvation;
    he is my fortress, I will not be shaken.
7 My salvation and my honor depend on God*b*;
    he is my mighty rock, my refuge.
8 Trust in him at all times, you people;
    pour out your hearts to him,
    for God is our refuge.

9 Surely the lowborn are but a breath,
    the highborn are but a lie.
If weighed on a balance, they are nothing;
    together they are only a breath.
10 Do not trust in extortion
    or put vain hope in stolen goods;
though your riches increase,
    do not set your heart on them.

11 One thing God has spoken,
    two things I have heard:
"Power belongs to you, God,
12   and with you, Lord, is unfailing love";
and, "You reward everyone
    according to what they have done."

PSALM 63*c*

A psalm of David. When he was in the Desert of Judah.

1 You, God, are my God,
    earnestly I seek you;
I thirst for you,
    my whole being longs for you,
in a dry and parched land
    where there is no water.

2 I have seen you in the sanctuary
    and beheld your power and your glory.
3 Because your love is better than life,
    my lips will glorify you.
4 I will praise you as long as I live,
    and in your name I will lift up my hands.

Why did David lift up his hands? (63:4)
Since ancient times, people have raised their hands to express praise and petition. The Israelites lifted their hands in dependence on God, trusting that he would give them blessings.

a 4 The Hebrew has *Selah* (a word of uncertain meaning) here and at the end of verse 8.   *b* 7 Or / *God Most High is my salvation and my honor*   *c* In Hebrew texts 63:1-11 is numbered 63:2-12.

⁵ I will be fully satisfied as with the richest
        of foods;
    with singing lips my mouth will praise you.

⁶ On my bed I remember you;
    I think of you through the watches of
        the night.
⁷ Because you are my help,
    I sing in the shadow of your wings.
⁸ I cling to you;
    your right hand upholds me.

⁹ Those who want to kill me will be destroyed;
    they will go down to the depths of
        the earth.
¹⁰ They will be given over to the sword
    and become food for jackals.

¹¹ But the king will rejoice in God;
    all who swear by God will glory in him,
    while the mouths of liars will be silenced.

PSALM 64*a*

For the director of music. A psalm of David.

¹ Hear me, my God, as I voice my complaint;
    protect my life from the threat of the enemy.

² Hide me from the conspiracy of the wicked,
    from the plots of evildoers.
³ They sharpen their tongues like swords
    and aim cruel words like deadly arrows.
⁴ They shoot from ambush at the innocent;
    they shoot suddenly, without fear.

⁵ They encourage each other in evil plans,
    they talk about hiding their snares;
    they say, "Who will see it*b*?"
⁶ They plot injustice and say,
    "We have devised a perfect plan!"
    Surely the human mind and heart
        are cunning.

⁷ But God will shoot them with his arrows;
    they will suddenly be struck down.
⁸ He will turn their own tongues against them
    and bring them to ruin;
    all who see them will shake their heads
        in scorn.
⁹ All people will fear;
    they will proclaim the works of God
    and ponder what he has done.

¹⁰ The righteous will rejoice in the Lord
    and take refuge in him;
    all the upright in heart will glory in him!

---

a In Hebrew texts 64:1-10 is numbered 64:2-11.   *b* 5 Or *us*

What were the watches of the night? (63:6)
These were the divisions into which the 12 hours of darkness were divided. The Israelites divided night into three watches, from 6:00 until 10:00 P.M., from 10:00 until 2:00 A.M., and from 2:00 until 6:00 A.M.

What weapons did David's enemies use? (64:3 – 6)
The main weapons were their tongues. They told lies about him, spoke against his kingship, or plotted his downfall.

What hope did David have? (64:7 – 8)
David was confident that God would trip up his enemies so that their lies would condemn them.

PSALM 65[a]

For the director of music. A psalm of David. A song.

[1] Praise awaits[b] you, our God, in Zion;
    to you our vows will be fulfilled.
[2] You who answer prayer,
    to you all people will come.
[3] When we were overwhelmed by sins,
    you forgave[c] our transgressions.
[4] Blessed are those you choose
    and bring near to live in your courts!
We are filled with the good things of your house,
    of your holy temple.

[5] You answer us with awesome and
       righteous deeds,
    God our Savior,
the hope of all the ends of the earth
    and of the farthest seas,
[6] who formed the mountains by your power,
    having armed yourself with strength,
[7] who stilled the roaring of the seas,
    the roaring of their waves,
    and the turmoil of the nations.
[8] The whole earth is filled with awe at
       your wonders;
    where morning dawns, where evening fades,
    you call forth songs of joy.

[9] You care for the land and water it;
    you enrich it abundantly.
The streams of God are filled with water
    to provide the people with grain,
    for so you have ordained it.[d]
[10] You drench its furrows and level its ridges;
    you soften it with showers and bless its crops.
[11] You crown the year with your bounty,
    and your carts overflow with abundance.
[12] The grasslands of the wilderness overflow;
    the hills are clothed with gladness.
[13] The meadows are covered with flocks
    and the valleys are mantled with grain;
    they shout for joy and sing.

PSALM 66

For the director of music. A song. A psalm.

[1] Shout for joy to God, all the earth!
[2]   Sing the glory of his name;
    make his praise glorious.
[3] Say to God, "How awesome are your deeds!
    So great is your power
    that your enemies cringe before you.

Who were the blessed people? (65:4)

The Levites were the ones who cared for the temple, but these blessings were for all of God's chosen people who worshiped him and were accepted at the temple.

What were God's awesome deeds? (65:5–7)

God created the world and brought the people of Israel out of Egypt and into the promised land. One day God will bring peace to Israel.

---

[a] In Hebrew texts 65:1-13 is numbered 65:2-14.   [b] *1* Or *befits*; the meaning of the Hebrew for this word is uncertain.   [c] *3* Or *made atonement for*   [d] *9* Or *for that is how you prepare the land*

4 All the earth bows down to you;
　　they sing praise to you,
　　they sing the praises of your name.”[a]

5 Come and see what God has done,
　　his awesome deeds for mankind!
6 He turned the sea into dry land,
　　they passed through the waters on foot—
　　come, let us rejoice in him.
7 He rules forever by his power,
　　his eyes watch the nations—
　　let not the rebellious rise up against him.

8 Praise our God, all peoples,
　　let the sound of his praise be heard;
9 he has preserved our lives
　　and kept our feet from slipping.
10 For you, God, tested us;
　　you refined us like silver.
11 You brought us into prison
　　and laid burdens on our backs.
12 You let people ride over our heads;
　　we went through fire and water,
　　but you brought us to a place of abundance.

13 I will come to your temple with burnt offerings
　　and fulfill my vows to you—
14 vows my lips promised and my mouth spoke
　　when I was in trouble.
15 I will sacrifice fat animals to you
　　and an offering of rams;
　　I will offer bulls and goats.

16 Come and hear, all you who fear God;
　　let me tell you what he has done for me.
17 I cried out to him with my mouth;
　　his praise was on my tongue.
18 If I had cherished sin in my heart,
　　the Lord would not have listened;
19 but God has surely listened
　　and has heard my prayer.
20 Praise be to God,
　　who has not rejected my prayer
　　or withheld his love from me!

PSALM 67[b]

For the director of music. With stringed instruments.
A psalm. A song.

1 May God be gracious to us and bless us
　　and make his face shine on us—[c]
2 so that your ways may be known on earth,
　　your salvation among all nations.

When did God part the waters? (66:6)
God parted the waters so the Israelites could cross into the promised land, and he parted the Red Sea so they could escape from Egypt.

What did it mean that God tested his people? (66:10)
Just as silver is heated to determine if there are any impurities in it, the Israelites were tested to reveal their shortcomings. The goal was that they grow stronger through difficulty. This is also how God sometimes tests us today.

---

[a] 4 The Hebrew has *Selah* (a word of uncertain meaning) here and at the end of verses 7 and 15.　　[b] In Hebrew texts 67:1-7 is numbered 67:2-8.
[c] 1 The Hebrew has *Selah* (a word of uncertain meaning) here and at the end of verse 4.

What was the psalmist asking God to do? (67:3–5)
The psalmist was asking God to bless his people so that they would praise him. The nations around Israel would be so impressed by this that they would also praise God.

³ May the peoples praise you, God;
    may all the peoples praise you.
⁴ May the nations be glad and sing for joy,
    for you rule the peoples with equity
    and guide the nations of the earth.
⁵ May the peoples praise you, God;
    may all the peoples praise you.

⁶ The land yields its harvest;
    God, our God, blesses us.
⁷ May God bless us still,
    so that all the ends of the earth will fear him.

PSALM 68ᵃ

For the director of music. Of David. A psalm. A song.

¹ May God arise, may his enemies be scattered;
    may his foes flee before him.
² May you blow them away like smoke—
    as wax melts before the fire,
    may the wicked perish before God.
³ But may the righteous be glad
    and rejoice before God;
    may they be happy and joyful.

What did it mean for God to ride on the clouds? (68:4)
This was an image the Canaanites used to describe their god Baal. But here the author used that image to describe the power of God.

⁴ Sing to God, sing in praise of his name,
    extol him who rides on the cloudsᵇ;
    rejoice before him—his name is the LORD.
⁵ A father to the fatherless, a defender of widows,
    is God in his holy dwelling.
⁶ God sets the lonely in families,ᶜ
    he leads out the prisoners with singing;
    but the rebellious live in a sun-scorched land.

What did it mean for God to make people part of families? (68:5–6)
In Old Testament times, being childless was very unfortunate. David talks about everyone being a part of God's family.

⁷ When you, God, went out before your people,
    when you marched through the wilderness,ᵈ
⁸ the earth shook, the heavens poured down rain,
    before God, the One of Sinai,
    before God, the God of Israel.
⁹ You gave abundant showers, O God;
    you refreshed your weary inheritance.

What does the One of Sinai mean? (68:8)
Mount Sinai was where God gave the law to Moses. It's possible that a volcano also erupted at this time to show God's power.

¹⁰ Your people settled in it,
    and from your bounty, God, you provided for the poor.

¹¹ The Lord announces the word,
    and the women who proclaim it are a mighty throng:
¹² "Kings and armies flee in haste;
    the women at home divide the plunder.
¹³ Even while you sleep among the sheep pens,ᵉ
    the wings of my dove are sheathed with silver,
    its feathers with shining gold."

What did it mean for the dove's wings to be sheathed in silver and gold? (68:13)
This is a word picture of the way the nation of Israel had been blessed by God by receiving plunder from the nations of Canaan.

ᵃ In Hebrew texts 68:1-35 is numbered 68:2-36.   ᵇ 4 Or *name, / prepare the way for him who rides through the deserts*   ᶜ 6 Or *the desolate in a homeland*
ᵈ 7 The Hebrew has *Selah* (a word of uncertain meaning) here and at the end of verses 19 and 32.   ᵉ 13 Or *the campfires; or the saddlebags*

¹⁴ When the Almighty*ᵃ* scattered the kings in the land,
　　it was like snow fallen on Mount Zalmon.

¹⁵ Mount Bashan, majestic mountain,
　　Mount Bashan, rugged mountain,
¹⁶ why gaze in envy, you rugged mountain,
　　at the mountain where God chooses to reign,
　　where the Lᴏʀᴅ himself will dwell forever?
¹⁷ The chariots of God are tens of thousands
　　and thousands of thousands;
　　the Lord has come from Sinai into his sanctuary.*ᵇ*
¹⁸ When you ascended on high,
　　you took many captives;
　　you received gifts from people,
　　even from*ᶜ* the rebellious—
　　that you,*ᵈ* Lᴏʀᴅ God, might dwell there.

¹⁹ Praise be to the Lord, to God our Savior,
　　who daily bears our burdens.
²⁰ Our God is a God who saves;
　　from the Sovereign Lᴏʀᴅ comes escape from death.
²¹ Surely God will crush the heads of his enemies,
　　the hairy crowns of those who go on in their sins.
²² The Lord says, "I will bring them from Bashan;
　　I will bring them from the depths of the sea,
²³ that your feet may wade in the blood of your foes,
　　while the tongues of your dogs have their share."

²⁴ Your procession, God, has come into view,
　　the procession of my God and King into the
　　　　sanctuary.
²⁵ In front are the singers, after them the musicians;
　　with them are the young women playing the timbrels.
²⁶ Praise God in the great congregation;
　　praise the Lᴏʀᴅ in the assembly of Israel.
²⁷ There is the little tribe of Benjamin, leading them,
　　there the great throng of Judah's princes,
　　and there the princes of Zebulun and of Naphtali.

²⁸ Summon your power, God*ᵉ*;
　　show us your strength, our God, as you have done
　　　　before.
²⁹ Because of your temple at Jerusalem
　　kings will bring you gifts.
³⁰ Rebuke the beast among the reeds,
　　the herd of bulls among the calves of the nations.
　　Humbled, may the beast bring bars of silver.
　　Scatter the nations who delight in war.
³¹ Envoys will come from Egypt;
　　Cush*ᶠ* will submit herself to God.

³² Sing to God, you kingdoms of the earth,
　　sing praise to the Lord,

What was this joyful procession? (68:24–25)
This procession was similar to a parade for a victorious warrior. This also may have described the procession of people going to the temple to worship God.

ᵃ 14 Hebrew *Shaddai*　　*ᵇ 17* Probable reading of the original Hebrew text;
Masoretic Text *Lord is among them at Sinai in holiness*　　*ᶜ 18* Or *gifts for
people, / even*　　*ᵈ 18* Or *they*　　*ᵉ 28* Many Hebrew manuscripts, Septuagint
and Syriac; most Hebrew manuscripts *Your God has summoned power for you*
ᶠ 31 That is, the upper Nile region

³³ to him who rides across the highest heavens,
　　the ancient heavens,
　who thunders with mighty voice.
³⁴ Proclaim the power of God,
　　whose majesty is over Israel,
　　whose power is in the heavens.
³⁵ You, God, are awesome in your sanctuary;
　　the God of Israel gives power and strength
　　　to his people.

Praise be to God!

PSALM 69 [a]

For the director of music. To the tune of "Lilies." Of David.

Why was David so unhappy? (69:1–3)
The specific reason David felt so overwhelmed is not known, but even in his deepest depression he called out to God for relief.

¹ Save me, O God,
　for the waters have come up to my neck.
² I sink in the miry depths,
　where there is no foothold.
I have come into the deep waters;
　the floods engulf me.
³ I am worn out calling for help;
　my throat is parched.
My eyes fail,
　looking for my God.
⁴ Those who hate me without reason
　outnumber the hairs of my head;
many are my enemies without cause,
　those who seek to destroy me.
I am forced to restore
　what I did not steal.

Why did David not want to be disgraced? (69:5–6)
David did not want his trouble to cause others to turn away from God.

⁵ You, God, know my folly;
　my guilt is not hidden from you.

⁶ Lord, the LORD Almighty,
　may those who hope in you
　not be disgraced because of me;
God of Israel,
　may those who seek you
　not be put to shame because of me.
⁷ For I endure scorn for your sake,
　and shame covers my face.
⁸ I am a foreigner to my own family,
　a stranger to my own mother's children;

What did it mean to have zeal for God's house? (69:9)
David was devoted to God and would do whatever he could to bring honor to God's name, even if it meant humiliating himself.

⁹ for zeal for your house consumes me,
　and the insults of those who insult you fall
　　on me.
¹⁰ When I weep and fast,
　I must endure scorn;
¹¹ when I put on sackcloth,
　people make sport of me.
¹² Those who sit at the gate mock me,
　and I am the song of the drunkards.

---

[a] In Hebrew texts 69:1-36 is numbered 69:2-37.

¹³ But I pray to you, Lord,
    in the time of your favor;
  in your great love, O God,
    answer me with your sure salvation.
¹⁴ Rescue me from the mire,
    do not let me sink;
  deliver me from those who hate me,
    from the deep waters.
¹⁵ Do not let the floodwaters engulf me
    or the depths swallow me up
    or the pit close its mouth over me.

¹⁶ Answer me, Lord, out of the goodness of your love;
    in your great mercy turn to me.
¹⁷ Do not hide your face from your servant;
    answer me quickly, for I am in trouble.
¹⁸ Come near and rescue me;
    deliver me because of my foes.

¹⁹ You know how I am scorned, disgraced and shamed;
    all my enemies are before you.
²⁰ Scorn has broken my heart
    and has left me helpless;
  I looked for sympathy, but there was none,
    for comforters, but I found none.
²¹ They put gall in my food
    and gave me vinegar for my thirst.

²² May the table set before them become a snare;
    may it become retribution and*ᵃ* a trap.
²³ May their eyes be darkened so they cannot see,
    and their backs be bent forever.
²⁴ Pour out your wrath on them;
    let your fierce anger overtake them.
²⁵ May their place be deserted;
    let there be no one to dwell in their tents.
²⁶ For they persecute those you wound
    and talk about the pain of those you hurt.
²⁷ Charge them with crime upon crime;
    do not let them share in your salvation.
²⁸ May they be blotted out of the book of life
    and not be listed with the righteous.

²⁹ But as for me, afflicted and in pain—
    may your salvation, God, protect me.

³⁰ I will praise God's name in song
    and glorify him with thanksgiving.
³¹ This will please the Lord more than an ox,
    more than a bull with its horns and hooves.
³² The poor will see and be glad—
    you who seek God, may your hearts live!
³³ The Lord hears the needy
    and does not despise his captive people.

³⁴ Let heaven and earth praise him,
    the seas and all that move in them,

What was gall? (69:21)
This was a semi-poisonous wine given to prisoners who were thirsty. It left a very bitter aftertaste.

ᵃ *22 Or snare / and their fellowship become*

³⁵ for God will save Zion
and rebuild the cities of Judah.
Then people will settle there and possess it;
³⁶ the children of his servants will inherit it,
and those who love his name will dwell there.

PSALM 70 ^a

For the director of music. Of David. A petition.

¹ Hasten, O God, to save me;
come quickly, Lord, to help me.

² May those who want to take my life
be put to shame and confusion;
may all who desire my ruin
be turned back in disgrace.
³ May those who say to me, "Aha! Aha!"
turn back because of their shame.
⁴ But may all who seek you
rejoice and be glad in you;
may those who long for your saving help always say,
"The Lord is great!"

⁵ But as for me, I am poor and needy;
come quickly to me, O God.
You are my help and my deliverer;
Lord, do not delay.

PSALM 71

¹ In you, Lord, I have taken refuge;
let me never be put to shame.
² In your righteousness, rescue me and deliver me;
turn your ear to me and save me.
³ Be my rock of refuge,
to which I can always go;
give the command to save me,
for you are my rock and my fortress.
⁴ Deliver me, my God, from the hand of the wicked,
from the grasp of those who are evil and cruel.

⁵ For you have been my hope, Sovereign Lord,
my confidence since my youth.
⁶ From birth I have relied on you;
you brought me forth from my mother's womb.
I will ever praise you.
⁷ I have become a sign to many;
you are my strong refuge.
⁸ My mouth is filled with your praise,
declaring your splendor all day long.

⁹ Do not cast me away when I am old;
do not forsake me when my strength is gone.
¹⁰ For my enemies speak against me;
those who wait to kill me conspire together.

---

^a In Hebrew texts 70:1-5 is numbered 70:2-6.

Where else did this psalm appear? (70)
This is a somewhat revised version of Psalm 40:13–17.

Why was David poor and needy? (70:5)
Although David was a wealthy king, he realized he was spiritually wanting and needed God's help.

How was God a rock of refuge? (71:3)
A rock was a conventional symbol of security and safety. Huge rocks provided protection for fortified cities. Like this type of rock, God was seen as a protector of his people.

Why did the psalmist fear that God would reject him? (71:9)
The author may have feared that if he lost strength or power God would turn away from him and choose another king to replace him.

¹¹ They say, "God has forsaken him;
    pursue him and seize him,
    for no one will rescue him."
¹² Do not be far from me, my God;
    come quickly, God, to help me.
¹³ May my accusers perish in shame;
    may those who want to harm me
    be covered with scorn and disgrace.

¹⁴ As for me, I will always have hope;
    I will praise you more and more.
¹⁵ My mouth will tell of your righteous deeds,
    of your saving acts all day long—
    though I know not how to relate them all.
¹⁶ I will come and proclaim your mighty acts,
        Sovereign Lord;
    I will proclaim your righteous deeds,
        yours alone.
¹⁷ Since my youth, God, you have taught me,
    and to this day I declare your marvelous deeds.
¹⁸ Even when I am old and gray,
    do not forsake me, my God,
    till I declare your power to the next generation,
    your mighty acts to all who are to come.

¹⁹ Your righteousness, God, reaches to
        the heavens,
    you who have done great things.
    Who is like you, God?
²⁰ Though you have made me see troubles,
    many and bitter,
    you will restore my life again;
    from the depths of the earth
    you will again bring me up.
²¹ You will increase my honor
    and comfort me once more.

²² I will praise you with the harp
    for your faithfulness, my God;
    I will sing praise to you with the lyre,
    Holy One of Israel.
²³ My lips will shout for joy
    when I sing praise to you—
    I whom you have delivered.
²⁴ My tongue will tell of your righteous acts
    all day long,
    for those who wanted to harm me
    have been put to shame and confusion.

PSALM 72

Of Solomon.

¹ Endow the king with your justice, O God,
    the royal son with your righteousness.
² May he judge your people in righteousness,
    your afflicted ones with justice.

What was the author's hope? (71:19–21)
The author said that even though he had experienced troubles, he believed God would restore him, increase his honor, and comfort him. In exchange, he would praise God for his goodness.

Who wrote this psalm? (72)
Solomon may have been either the author or the inspiration of this psalm. It is possible that he was both.

³ May the mountains bring prosperity to
    the people,
  the hills the fruit of righteousness.
⁴ May he defend the afflicted among the people
  and save the children of the needy;
  may he crush the oppressor.
⁵ May he endure^a as long as the sun,
  as long as the moon, through all generations.
⁶ May he be like rain falling on a mown field,
  like showers watering the earth.
⁷ In his days may the righteous flourish
  and prosperity abound till the moon
    is no more.

⁸ May he rule from sea to sea
  and from the River^b to the ends of the earth.
⁹ May the desert tribes bow before him
  and his enemies lick the dust.
¹⁰ May the kings of Tarshish and of distant shores
  bring tribute to him.
  May the kings of Sheba and Seba
  present him gifts.
¹¹ May all kings bow down to him
  and all nations serve him.

¹² For he will deliver the needy who cry out,
  the afflicted who have no one to help.
¹³ He will take pity on the weak and the needy
  and save the needy from death.
¹⁴ He will rescue them from oppression
    and violence,
  for precious is their blood in his sight.

¹⁵ Long may he live!
  May gold from Sheba be given him.
  May people ever pray for him
  and bless him all day long.
¹⁶ May grain abound throughout the land;
  on the tops of the hills may it sway.
  May the crops flourish like Lebanon
  and thrive^c like the grass of the field.
¹⁷ May his name endure forever;
  may it continue as long as the sun.

  Then all nations will be blessed through him,^d
  and they will call him blessed.

¹⁸ Praise be to the LORD God, the God of Israel,
  who alone does marvelous deeds.
¹⁹ Praise be to his glorious name forever;
  may the whole earth be filled with his glory.
      Amen and Amen.

²⁰ This concludes the prayers of David son of Jesse.

---

^a 5 Septuagint; Hebrew *You will be feared*   ^b 8 That is, the Euphrates
^c 16 Probable reading of the original Hebrew text; Masoretic Text *Lebanon, /
from the city*   ^d 17 Or *will use his name in blessings* (see Gen. 48:20)

What were the desert tribes?
(72:9)
These were the tribes living in
the Arabian Desert to the east.

How wealthy was Sheba?
(72:15)
Sheba was located in a region
containing many minerals and
spices, and it was very wealthy. It
was a regular stop for Solomon's
trading fleet.

BOOK III

PSALMS 73 – 89

PSALM 73

A psalm of Asaph.

¹ Surely God is good to Israel,
   to those who are pure in heart.

² But as for me, my feet had almost slipped;
   I had nearly lost my foothold.
³ For I envied the arrogant
   when I saw the prosperity of the wicked.

⁴ They have no struggles;
   their bodies are healthy and strong.ᵃ
⁵ They are free from common human burdens;
   they are not plagued by human ills.
⁶ Therefore pride is their necklace;
   they clothe themselves with violence.
⁷ From their callous hearts comes iniquityᵇ;
   their evil imaginations have no limits.
⁸ They scoff, and speak with malice;
   with arrogance they threaten oppression.
⁹ Their mouths lay claim to heaven,
   and their tongues take possession of the earth.
¹⁰ Therefore their people turn to them
   and drink up waters in abundance.ᶜ
¹¹ They say, "How would God know?
   Does the Most High know anything?"

¹² This is what the wicked are like—
   always free of care, they go on amassing wealth.

¹³ Surely in vain I have kept my heart pure
   and have washed my hands in innocence.
¹⁴ All day long I have been afflicted,
   and every morning brings new punishments.

¹⁵ If I had spoken out like that,
   I would have betrayed your children.
¹⁶ When I tried to understand all this,
   it troubled me deeply
¹⁷ till I entered the sanctuary of God;
   then I understood their final destiny.

¹⁸ Surely you place them on slippery ground;
   you cast them down to ruin.
¹⁹ How suddenly are they destroyed,
   completely swept away by terrors!
²⁰ They are like a dream when one awakes;
   when you arise, Lord,
   you will despise them as fantasies.

ᵃ *4* With a different word division of the Hebrew; Masoretic Text *struggles at their death; / their bodies are healthy*   ᵇ *7* Syriac (see also Septuagint); Hebrew *Their eyes bulge with fat*   ᶜ *10* The meaning of the Hebrew for this verse is uncertain.

Who was Asaph? (73: title)
Asaph, a Levite, was a worship leader appointed by David (1 Chronicles 16:4 – 6). Twelve psalms have his name attached to them (50; 73 – 83).

Why were the wicked people free from burdens? (73:4 – 5)
The author felt that wicked people had an easy life and didn't seem to suffer for their sins.

What was the author's complaint? (73:13 – 14)
Even though he served God, he faced hardships, while those who didn't fear God seemed to thrive.

21 When my heart was grieved
　　and my spirit embittered,
22 I was senseless and ignorant;
　　I was a brute beast before you.

23 Yet I am always with you;
　　you hold me by my right hand.
24 You guide me with your counsel,
　　and afterward you will take me into glory.
25 Whom have I in heaven but you?
　　And earth has nothing I desire besides you.
26 My flesh and my heart may fail,
　　but God is the strength of my heart
　　and my portion forever.

27 Those who are far from you will perish;
　　you destroy all who are unfaithful to you.
28 But as for me, it is good to be near God.
　　I have made the Sovereign LORD my refuge;
　　I will tell of all your deeds.

PSALM 74

A maskil[a] of Asaph.

1 O God, why have you rejected us forever?
　　Why does your anger smolder against the sheep of
　　　　your pasture?
2 Remember the nation you purchased long ago,
　　the people of your inheritance, whom you
　　　　redeemed—
　　Mount Zion, where you dwelt.
3 Turn your steps toward these everlasting ruins,
　　all this destruction the enemy has brought on the
　　　　sanctuary.

4 Your foes roared in the place where you met with us;
　　they set up their standards as signs.
5 They behaved like men wielding axes
　　to cut through a thicket of trees.
6 They smashed all the carved paneling
　　with their axes and hatchets.
7 They burned your sanctuary to the ground;
　　they defiled the dwelling place of your Name.
8 They said in their hearts, "We will crush them
　　　　completely!"
　　They burned every place where God was worshiped
　　　　in the land.

9 We are given no signs from God;
　　no prophets are left,
　　and none of us knows how long this will be.
10 How long will the enemy mock you, God?
　　Will the foe revile your name forever?
11 Why do you hold back your hand, your right hand?
　　Take it from the folds of your garment and destroy
　　　　them!

---

a Title: Probably a literary or musical term

What did the author conclude about God? (73:27–28)
He realized that God would eventually reward his followers and punish the wicked.

When was this psalm written? (74:1–3)
The psalm was written when Israel was in exile and facing mockery from its enemies.

Weren't the people supposed to worship God in Jerusalem? (74:8)
Jerusalem was where the main religious festivals took place, but people also offered sacrifices and worshiped in their local communities.

¹²But God is my King from long ago;
  he brings salvation on the earth.

¹³It was you who split open the sea by your power;
  you broke the heads of the monster in the waters.

¹⁴It was you who crushed the heads of Leviathan
  and gave it as food to the creatures of the desert.

¹⁵It was you who opened up springs and streams;
  you dried up the ever-flowing rivers.

¹⁶The day is yours, and yours also the night;
  you established the sun and moon.

¹⁷It was you who set all the boundaries of the earth;
  you made both summer and winter.

¹⁸Remember how the enemy has mocked you, Lord,
  how foolish people have reviled your name.

¹⁹Do not hand over the life of your dove to wild beasts;
  do not forget the lives of your afflicted people
    forever.

²⁰Have regard for your covenant,
  because haunts of violence fill the dark places of the
    land.

²¹Do not let the oppressed retreat in disgrace;
  may the poor and needy praise your name.

²²Rise up, O God, and defend your cause;
  remember how fools mock you all day long.

²³Do not ignore the clamor of your adversaries,
  the uproar of your enemies, which rises continually.

PSALM 75 ᵃ

For the director of music. To the tune of "Do Not Destroy."
A psalm of Asaph. A song.

¹We praise you, God,
  we praise you, for your Name is near;
  people tell of your wonderful deeds.

²You say, "I choose the appointed time;
  it is I who judge with equity.
³When the earth and all its people quake,
  it is I who hold its pillars firm.ᵇ
⁴To the arrogant I say, 'Boast no more,'
  and to the wicked, 'Do not lift up your horns.ᶜ
⁵Do not lift your horns against heaven;
  do not speak so defiantly.'"

⁶No one from the east or the west
  or from the desert can exalt themselves.
⁷It is God who judges:
  He brings one down, he exalts another.
⁸In the hand of the Lord is a cup
  full of foaming wine mixed with spices;
  he pours it out, and all the wicked of the earth
  drink it down to its very dregs.

ᵃ In Hebrew texts 75:1-10 is numbered 75:2-11.   ᵇ *3* The Hebrew has
Selah (a word of uncertain meaning) here.   ᶜ *4 Horns* here symbolize
strength; also in verses 5 and 10.

Why did God break the head of the sea monsters? (74:13 – 14)
Ancient mythology often included stories of how the gods had defeated the sea and tamed it by dividing it into the heavens and the earth. The author used these stories to make a statement about the one true God.

What were the haunts of violence? (74:20)
There are many caves in the land of Israel. Robbers and criminals would hide in these caves and use them as a base for their criminal activities.

What was foaming wine? (75:8)
A very strong alcoholic drink, it might have tasted pleasant at first, but drinking too much of it would make the person drunk.

⁹As for me, I will declare this forever;
    I will sing praise to the God of Jacob,
¹⁰who says, "I will cut off the horns of all the wicked,
    but the horns of the righteous will be lifted up."

PSALM 76 *ᵃ*

For the director of music. With stringed instruments.
A psalm of Asaph. A song.

¹God is renowned in Judah;
    in Israel his name is great.
²His tent is in Salem,
    his dwelling place in Zion.
³There he broke the flashing arrows,
    the shields and the swords, the weapons of war.*ᵇ*

⁴You are radiant with light,
    more majestic than mountains rich with game.
⁵The valiant lie plundered,
    they sleep their last sleep;
not one of the warriors
    can lift his hands.
⁶At your rebuke, God of Jacob,
    both horse and chariot lie still.

⁷It is you alone who are to be feared.
    Who can stand before you when you are angry?
⁸From heaven you pronounced judgment,
    and the land feared and was quiet—
⁹when you, God, rose up to judge,
    to save all the afflicted of the land.
¹⁰Surely your wrath against mankind brings you praise,
    and the survivors of your wrath are restrained.*ᶜ*

¹¹Make vows to the Lᴏʀᴅ your God and fulfill them;
    let all the neighboring lands
    bring gifts to the One to be feared.
¹²He breaks the spirit of rulers;
    he is feared by the kings of the earth.

PSALM 77 *ᵈ*

For the director of music. For Jeduthun. Of Asaph. A psalm.

¹I cried out to God for help;
    I cried out to God to hear me.
²When I was in distress, I sought the Lord;
    at night I stretched out untiring hands,
    and I would not be comforted.

³I remembered you, God, and I groaned;
    I meditated, and my spirit grew faint.*ᵉ*

Where was Salem? (76:2)
Salem was a shortened form (and the original name) of Jerusalem. It is referred to in Genesis 14:18. The verse in this psalm speaks of God's presence with his people in the temple in Jerusalem.

How did God's wrath bring praise? (76:10)
When God punished the Israelites' enemies, his people were delivered and praised him.

ᵃ In Hebrew texts 76:1-12 is numbered 76:2-13.   *ᵇ 3* The Hebrew has *Selah* (a word of uncertain meaning) here and at the end of verse 9.
ᶜ 10 Or *Surely the wrath of mankind brings you praise, / and with the remainder of wrath you arm yourself*   *ᵈ* In Hebrew texts 77:1-20 is numbered 77:2-21.
ᵉ 3 The Hebrew has *Selah* (a word of uncertain meaning) here and at the end of verses 9 and 15.

⁴You kept my eyes from closing;
  I was too troubled to speak.
⁵I thought about the former days,
  the years of long ago;
⁶I remembered my songs in the night.
  My heart meditated and my spirit asked:

⁷"Will the Lord reject forever?
  Will he never show his favor again?
⁸Has his unfailing love vanished forever?
  Has his promise failed for all time?
⁹Has God forgotten to be merciful?
  Has he in anger withheld his compassion?"

¹⁰Then I thought, "To this I will appeal:
  the years when the Most High stretched out
    his right hand.
¹¹I will remember the deeds of the LORD;
  yes, I will remember your miracles of
    long ago.
¹²I will consider all your works
  and meditate on all your mighty deeds."

¹³Your ways, God, are holy.
  What god is as great as our God?
¹⁴You are the God who performs miracles;
  you display your power among the peoples.
¹⁵With your mighty arm you redeemed
      your people,
  the descendants of Jacob and Joseph.

¹⁶The waters saw you, God,
  the waters saw you and writhed;
  the very depths were convulsed.
¹⁷The clouds poured down water,
  the heavens resounded with thunder;
  your arrows flashed back and forth.
¹⁸Your thunder was heard in the whirlwind,
  your lightning lit up the world;
  the earth trembled and quaked.
¹⁹Your path led through the sea,
  your way through the mighty waters,
  though your footprints were not seen.
²⁰You led your people like a flock
  by the hand of Moses and Aaron.

PSALM 78

A maskil[a] of Asaph.

¹My people, hear my teaching;
  listen to the words of my mouth.
²I will open my mouth with a parable;
  I will utter hidden things, things from of old—
³things we have heard and known,
  things our ancestors have told us.

---

[a] Title: Probably a literary or musical term

Who were the descendants of Jacob and Joseph? (77:15)
This was a description of the whole nation of Israel.

What event do these verses describe? (77:16–19)
This is a description of God's mighty power in leading the Israelites out of Egypt by parting the Red Sea.

What is a parable? (78:2)
In this case, the word *parable* refers to a teaching from history.

What did the people promise to tell the next generation? (78:3–4)
They promised to tell their children about the great works of the LORD, their deliverer.

⁴We will not hide them from their descendants;
   we will tell the next generation
the praiseworthy deeds of the Lord,
   his power, and the wonders he has done.
⁵He decreed statutes for Jacob
   and established the law in Israel,
which he commanded our ancestors
   to teach their children,
⁶so the next generation would know them,
   even the children yet to be born,
   and they in turn would tell their children.
⁷Then they would put their trust in God
   and would not forget his deeds
   but would keep his commands.
⁸They would not be like their ancestors —
   a stubborn and rebellious generation,
whose hearts were not loyal to God,
   whose spirits were not faithful to him.

⁹The men of Ephraim, though armed with bows,
   turned back on the day of battle;
¹⁰they did not keep God's covenant
   and refused to live by his law.
¹¹They forgot what he had done,
   the wonders he had shown them.
¹²He did miracles in the sight of their ancestors
   in the land of Egypt, in the region of Zoan.
¹³He divided the sea and led them through;
   he made the water stand up like a wall.
¹⁴He guided them with the cloud by day
   and with light from the fire all night.
¹⁵He split the rocks in the wilderness
   and gave them water as abundant as the seas;
¹⁶he brought streams out of a rocky crag
   and made water flow down like rivers.

¹⁷But they continued to sin against him,
   rebelling in the wilderness against the
      Most High.
¹⁸They willfully put God to the test
   by demanding the food they craved.
¹⁹They spoke against God;
   they said, "Can God really
   spread a table in the wilderness?
²⁰True, he struck the rock,
   and water gushed out,
   streams flowed abundantly,
but can he also give us bread?
   Can he supply meat for his people?"
²¹When the Lord heard them, he was furious;
   his fire broke out against Jacob,
   and his wrath rose against Israel,
²²for they did not believe in God
   or trust in his deliverance.
²³Yet he gave a command to the skies above
   and opened the doors of the heavens;

Where was Zoan? (78:12)
Zoan was a city in Egypt where God miraculously released the Israelites from slavery.

What did it mean to put God to the test? (78:18)
While in the desert, the Israelites did this by demanding God meet their needs. They were willing to believe in God's power only if he gave them what they wanted.

²⁴ he rained down manna for the people to eat,
   he gave them the grain of heaven.
²⁵ Human beings ate the bread of angels;
   he sent them all the food they could eat.
²⁶ He let loose the east wind from the heavens
   and by his power made the south wind blow.
²⁷ He rained meat down on them like dust,
   birds like sand on the seashore.
²⁸ He made them come down inside their camp,
   all around their tents.
²⁹ They ate till they were gorged—
   he had given them what they craved.
³⁰ But before they turned from what they craved,
   even while the food was still in their mouths,
³¹ God's anger rose against them;
   he put to death the sturdiest among them,
   cutting down the young men of Israel.

³² In spite of all this, they kept on sinning;
   in spite of his wonders, they did not believe.
³³ So he ended their days in futility
   and their years in terror.
³⁴ Whenever God slew them, they would seek him;
   they eagerly turned to him again.
³⁵ They remembered that God was their Rock,
   that God Most High was their Redeemer.
³⁶ But then they would flatter him with their mouths,
   lying to him with their tongues;
³⁷ their hearts were not loyal to him,
   they were not faithful to his covenant.
³⁸ Yet he was merciful;
   he forgave their iniquities
   and did not destroy them.
   Time after time he restrained his anger
   and did not stir up his full wrath.
³⁹ He remembered that they were but flesh,
   a passing breeze that does not return.

⁴⁰ How often they rebelled against him in the wilderness
   and grieved him in the wasteland!
⁴¹ Again and again they put God to the test;
   they vexed the Holy One of Israel.
⁴² They did not remember his power—
   the day he redeemed them from the oppressor,
⁴³ the day he displayed his signs in Egypt,
   his wonders in the region of Zoan.
⁴⁴ He turned their river into blood;
   they could not drink from their streams.
⁴⁵ He sent swarms of flies that devoured them,
   and frogs that devastated them.
⁴⁶ He gave their crops to the grasshopper,
   their produce to the locust.
⁴⁷ He destroyed their vines with hail
   and their sycamore-figs with sleet.
⁴⁸ He gave over their cattle to the hail,
   their livestock to bolts of lightning.

What was the bread of angels? (78:25)
This was the manna God provided the Israelites when they were in the desert. It was called bread of angels because it came down from heaven.

What did it mean that they were flesh? (78:39)
They were human beings who were not able to obey God perfectly.

What events do these verses describe? (78:44–51)
These were the plagues God sent to Egypt to free the Israelites.

49 He unleashed against them his hot anger,
   his wrath, indignation and hostility—
   a band of destroying angels.
50 He prepared a path for his anger;
   he did not spare them from death
   but gave them over to the plague.
51 He struck down all the firstborn of Egypt,
   the firstfruits of manhood in the tents of Ham.
52 But he brought his people out like a flock;
   he led them like sheep through the wilderness.
53 He guided them safely, so they were unafraid;
   but the sea engulfed their enemies.
54 And so he brought them to the border of his
        holy land,
   to the hill country his right hand had taken.
55 He drove out nations before them
   and allotted their lands to them as an inheritance;
   he settled the tribes of Israel in their homes.

56 But they put God to the test
   and rebelled against the Most High;
   they did not keep his statutes.
57 Like their ancestors they were disloyal and faithless,
   as unreliable as a faulty bow.
58 They angered him with their high places;
   they aroused his jealousy with their idols.
59 When God heard them, he was furious;
   he rejected Israel completely.
60 He abandoned the tabernacle of Shiloh,
   the tent he had set up among humans.
61 He sent the ark of his might into captivity,
   his splendor into the hands of the enemy.
62 He gave his people over to the sword;
   he was furious with his inheritance.
63 Fire consumed their young men,
   and their young women had no wedding songs;
64 their priests were put to the sword,
   and their widows could not weep.

65 Then the Lord awoke as from sleep,
   as a warrior wakes from the stupor of wine.
66 He beat back his enemies;
   he put them to everlasting shame.
67 Then he rejected the tents of Joseph,
   he did not choose the tribe of Ephraim;
68 but he chose the tribe of Judah,
   Mount Zion, which he loved.
69 He built his sanctuary like the heights,
   like the earth that he established forever.
70 He chose David his servant
   and took him from the sheep pens;
71 from tending the sheep he brought him
   to be the shepherd of his people Jacob,
   of Israel his inheritance.
72 And David shepherded them with integrity of heart;
   with skillful hands he led them.

What was a faulty bow?
(78:57)
This was a bow that was too loose or slack to reliably shoot an arrow. In the same way, Israel was not reliable or faithful to God even though he had brought them from Egypt into the promised land.

PSALM 79

A psalm of Asaph.

[1] O God, the nations have invaded your inheritance;
  they have defiled your holy temple,
  they have reduced Jerusalem to rubble.
[2] They have left the dead bodies of your servants
  as food for the birds of the sky,
  the flesh of your own people for the animals
    of the wild.
[3] They have poured out blood like water
  all around Jerusalem,
  and there is no one to bury the dead.
[4] We are objects of contempt to our neighbors,
  of scorn and derision to those around us.

[5] How long, Lord? Will you be angry forever?
  How long will your jealousy burn like fire?
[6] Pour out your wrath on the nations
  that do not acknowledge you,
 on the kingdoms
  that do not call on your name;
[7] for they have devoured Jacob
  and devastated his homeland.

[8] Do not hold against us the sins of past generations;
  may your mercy come quickly to meet us,
  for we are in desperate need.
[9] Help us, God our Savior,
  for the glory of your name;
 deliver us and forgive our sins
  for your name's sake.
[10] Why should the nations say,
  "Where is their God?"

Before our eyes, make known among the nations
  that you avenge the outpoured blood of your servants.
[11] May the groans of the prisoners come before you;
  with your strong arm preserve those condemned
    to die.
[12] Pay back into the laps of our neighbors seven times
  the contempt they have hurled at you, Lord.
[13] Then we your people, the sheep of your pasture,
  will praise you forever;
 from generation to generation
  we will proclaim your praise.

Why was God angry? (79:5)
God was angry because his people had rebelled and failed to serve him.

Who were these prisoners? (79:11)
They were the Israelites who were exiled in Babylon.

PSALM 80[a]

For the director of music.
To the tune of "The Lilies of the Covenant." Of Asaph. A psalm.

[1] Hear us, Shepherd of Israel,
  you who lead Joseph like a flock.
 You who sit enthroned between the cherubim,
  shine forth [2] before Ephraim, Benjamin and
    Manasseh.

[a] In Hebrew texts 80:1-19 is numbered 80:2-20.

Awaken your might;
    come and save us.

³ Restore us, O God;
    make your face shine on us,
    that we may be saved.

⁴ How long, LORD God Almighty,
    will your anger smolder
    against the prayers of your people?
⁵ You have fed them with the bread of tears;
    you have made them drink tears by the bowlful.
⁶ You have made us an object of derision*
    to our neighbors,
    and our enemies mock us.

⁷ Restore us, God Almighty;
    make your face shine on us,
    that we may be saved.

⁸ You transplanted a vine from Egypt;
    you drove out the nations and planted it.
⁹ You cleared the ground for it,
    and it took root and filled the land.
¹⁰ The mountains were covered with its shade,
    the mighty cedars with its branches.
¹¹ Its branches reached as far as the Sea,ᵇ
    its shoots as far as the River.ᶜ
¹² Why have you broken down its walls
    so that all who pass by pick its grapes?
¹³ Boars from the forest ravage it,
    and insects from the fields feed on it.
¹⁴ Return to us, God Almighty!
    Look down from heaven and see!
    Watch over this vine,
¹⁵   the root your right hand has planted,
    the sonᵈ you have raised up for yourself.

¹⁶ Your vine is cut down, it is burned with fire;
    at your rebuke your people perish.
¹⁷ Let your hand rest on the man at your right hand,
    the son of man you have raised up for yourself.
¹⁸ Then we will not turn away from you;
    revive us, and we will call on your name.

¹⁹ Restore us, LORD God Almighty;
    make your face shine on us,
    that we may be saved.

PSALM 81ᵉ

For the director of music. According to gittith.ᶠ Of Asaph.

¹ Sing for joy to God our strength;
    shout aloud to the God of Jacob!

How was Israel like a grapevine? (80:8–16)
This is a word picture describing how Israel had been transplanted from Egypt to Canaan. When Israel was obedient to God, it flourished like a healthy vine; but when Israel turned away from God, other nations destroyed parts of the vine.

Who was the son of man? (80:17)
This could refer to Israel, the son of God (verse 15). It could also point toward the coming Messiah. Jesus called himself the Son of Man (Matthew 12:40).

ᵃ 6 Probable reading of the original Hebrew text; Masoretic Text *contention*
ᵇ 11 Probably the Mediterranean   *ᶜ 11* That is, the Euphrates
ᵈ 15 Or *branch*   *ᵉ* In Hebrew texts 81:1-16 is numbered 81:2-17.   *ᶠ* Title: Probably a musical term

2 Begin the music, strike the timbrel,
　　play the melodious harp and lyre.

3 Sound the ram's horn at the New Moon,
　　and when the moon is full, on the day of our festival;
4 this is a decree for Israel,
　　an ordinance of the God of Jacob.
5 When God went out against Egypt,
　　he established it as a statute for Joseph.

　I heard an unknown voice say:

6 "I removed the burden from their shoulders;
　　their hands were set free from the basket.
7 In your distress you called and I rescued you,
　　I answered you out of a thundercloud;
　　I tested you at the waters of Meribah.[a]
8 Hear me, my people, and I will warn you—
　　if you would only listen to me, Israel!
9 You shall have no foreign god among you;
　　you shall not worship any god other than me.
10 I am the LORD your God,
　　who brought you up out of Egypt.
　Open wide your mouth and I will fill it.

11 "But my people would not listen to me;
　　Israel would not submit to me.
12 So I gave them over to their stubborn hearts
　　to follow their own devices.

13 "If my people would only listen to me,
　　if Israel would only follow my ways,
14 how quickly I would subdue their enemies
　　and turn my hand against their foes!
15 Those who hate the LORD would cringe before him,
　　and their punishment would last forever.
16 But you would be fed with the finest of wheat;
　　with honey from the rock I would satisfy you."

PSALM 82

A psalm of Asaph.

1 God presides in the great assembly;
　　he renders judgment among the "gods":

2 "How long will you[b] defend the unjust
　　and show partiality to the wicked?[c]
3 Defend the weak and the fatherless;
　　uphold the cause of the poor and the oppressed.
4 Rescue the weak and the needy;
　　deliver them from the hand of the wicked.

5 "The 'gods' know nothing, they understand nothing.
　　They walk about in darkness;
　　all the foundations of the earth are shaken.

---

a 7 The Hebrew has *Selah* (a word of uncertain meaning) here.
b 2 The Hebrew is plural.　　*c 2* The Hebrew has *Selah* (a word of uncertain meaning) here.

What was the New Moon festival? (81:3)
The New Moon was both a religious and civil festival that was celebrated at the beginning of each month. Special sacrifices were offered, trumpets were sounded, and normal work activities were stopped.

What were the waters of Meribah? (81:7)
When the Israelites were in the desert near Meribah and complained about not having water, God told Moses to use his staff to strike a rock. When he did, water gushed out (Exodus 17:1–7).

How could honey come from a rock? (81:16)
In Canaan, bees sometimes built their hives in rocky cliffs. Travelers would eat the honey and gain strength for their journey.

Who were these gods? (82:1)
In the ancient world, kings and rulers were sometimes called gods or sons of God. The term may also refer to the false gods of the surrounding nations. In either case, here God is judging them for their unjust behavior.

⁶ "I said, 'You are "gods";
　　you are all sons of the Most High.'
⁷ But you will die like mere mortals;
　　you will fall like every other ruler."

⁸ Rise up, O God, judge the earth,
　　for all the nations are your inheritance.

PSALM 83[a]

A song. A psalm of Asaph.

¹ O God, do not remain silent;
　　do not turn a deaf ear,
　　do not stand aloof, O God.
² See how your enemies growl,
　　how your foes rear their heads.
³ With cunning they conspire against your people;
　　they plot against those you cherish.
⁴ "Come," they say, "let us destroy them as a nation,
　　so that Israel's name is remembered no more."

⁵ With one mind they plot together;
　　they form an alliance against you—
⁶ the tents of Edom and the Ishmaelites,
　　of Moab and the Hagrites,
⁷ Byblos, Ammon and Amalek,
　　Philistia, with the people of Tyre.
⁸ Even Assyria has joined them
　　to reinforce Lot's descendants.[b]

⁹ Do to them as you did to Midian,
　　as you did to Sisera and Jabin at the
　　　　river Kishon,
¹⁰ who perished at Endor
　　and became like dung on the ground.
¹¹ Make their nobles like Oreb and Zeeb,
　　all their princes like Zebah and Zalmunna,
¹² who said, "Let us take possession
　　of the pasturelands of God."

¹³ Make them like tumbleweed, my God,
　　like chaff before the wind.
¹⁴ As fire consumes the forest
　　or a flame sets the mountains ablaze,
¹⁵ so pursue them with your tempest
　　and terrify them with your storm.
¹⁶ Cover their faces with shame, LORD,
　　so that they will seek your name.

¹⁷ May they ever be ashamed and dismayed;
　　may they perish in disgrace.
¹⁸ Let them know that you, whose name is
　　　　the LORD—
　　that you alone are the Most High over
　　　　all the earth.

Who were these enemies? (83:5–8)
These were countries that sought to forcibly gain territory from Israel. Because they fought against God's people, they were God's enemies also.

What was the psalmist asking God to do? (83:9–12)
The psalmist was asking God to defeat Israel's enemies just as he had during the time of the judges.

---

[a] In Hebrew texts 83:1-18 is numbered 83:2-19.　[b] *8* The Hebrew has *Selah* (a word of uncertain meaning) here.

PSALM 84[a]

For the director of music. According to gittith.[b]
Of the Sons of Korah. A psalm.

¹ How lovely is your dwelling place,
  LORD Almighty!
² My soul yearns, even faints,
  for the courts of the LORD;
  my heart and my flesh cry out
  for the living God.
³ Even the sparrow has found a home,
  and the swallow a nest for herself,
  where she may have her young—
  a place near your altar,
  LORD Almighty, my King and my God.
⁴ Blessed are those who dwell in your house;
  they are ever praising you.[c]

⁵ Blessed are those whose strength is in you,
  whose hearts are set on pilgrimage.
⁶ As they pass through the Valley of Baka,
  they make it a place of springs;
  the autumn rains also cover it with pools.[d]
⁷ They go from strength to strength,
  till each appears before God in Zion.

⁸ Hear my prayer, LORD God Almighty;
  listen to me, God of Jacob.
⁹ Look on our shield,[e] O God;
  look with favor on your anointed one.

¹⁰ Better is one day in your courts
  than a thousand elsewhere;
  I would rather be a doorkeeper in the house of my God
  than dwell in the tents of the wicked.
¹¹ For the LORD God is a sun and shield;
  the LORD bestows favor and honor;
  no good thing does he withhold
  from those whose walk is blameless.

¹² LORD Almighty,
  blessed is the one who trusts in you.

PSALM 85[f]

For the director of music. Of the Sons of Korah. A psalm.

¹ You, LORD, showed favor to your land;
  you restored the fortunes of Jacob.
² You forgave the iniquity of your people
  and covered all their sins.[g]
³ You set aside all your wrath
  and turned from your fierce anger.

Why did the psalmist long for the temple? (84:1–2)
The author was probably a temple worker who was unable to serve because Israel was under attack, possibly by Sennacherib (2 Kings 18:13–16).

Who was the shield? (84:9)
This was the king of Israel, God's anointed one, who was supposed to protect his people. In verse 11, the psalmist refers to God as the people's shield or protector.

---

[a] In Hebrew texts 84:1-12 is numbered 84:2-13.   [b] Title: Probably a musical term   [c] 4 The Hebrew has *Selah* (a word of uncertain meaning) here and at the end of verse 8.   [d] 6 Or *blessings*   [e] 9 Or *sovereign*   [f] In Hebrew texts 85:1-13 is numbered 85:2-14.   [g] 2 The Hebrew has *Selah* (a word of uncertain meaning) here.

Why was God angry with his people? (85:4)
The people of Israel had repeatedly turned away from God and failed to live according to his laws. This may have been a time of drought when the people believed God was punishing them.

What literary technique did the psalmist use in these verses? (85:10–11)
This is called personification, which means to give human characteristics to something. Jesus is the perfect picture of love and faithfulness, righteousness and peace.

Why did David describe himself as poor and needy? (86:1)
David needed God's support because he was spiritually needy, not because he lacked money.

Why did David compare God to other gods? (86:8)
David knew there was only one true God, as verse 10 makes clear. He was contrasting God's greatness with the false gods of the neighboring countries.

⁴Restore us again, God our Savior,
  and put away your displeasure toward us.
⁵Will you be angry with us forever?
  Will you prolong your anger through all
    generations?
⁶Will you not revive us again,
  that your people may rejoice in you?
⁷Show us your unfailing love, Lord,
  and grant us your salvation.

⁸I will listen to what God the Lord says;
  he promises peace to his people, his faithful
    servants—
  but let them not turn to folly.
⁹Surely his salvation is near those who fear him,
  that his glory may dwell in our land.

¹⁰Love and faithfulness meet together;
  righteousness and peace kiss each other.
¹¹Faithfulness springs forth from the earth,
  and righteousness looks down from heaven.
¹²The Lord will indeed give what is good,
  and our land will yield its harvest.
¹³Righteousness goes before him
  and prepares the way for his steps.

PSALM 86

A prayer of David.

¹Hear me, Lord, and answer me,
  for I am poor and needy.
²Guard my life, for I am faithful to you;
  save your servant who trusts in you.
  You are my God; ³have mercy on me, Lord,
  for I call to you all day long.
⁴Bring joy to your servant, Lord,
  for I put my trust in you.

⁵You, Lord, are forgiving and good,
  abounding in love to all who call to you.
⁶Hear my prayer, Lord;
  listen to my cry for mercy.
⁷When I am in distress, I call to you,
  because you answer me.

⁸Among the gods there is none like you, Lord;
  no deeds can compare with yours.
⁹All the nations you have made
  will come and worship before you, Lord;
  they will bring glory to your name.
¹⁰For you are great and do marvelous deeds;
  you alone are God.

¹¹Teach me your way, Lord,
  that I may rely on your faithfulness;
  give me an undivided heart,
  that I may fear your name.

12 I will praise you, Lord my God, with all my heart;
    I will glorify your name forever.
13 For great is your love toward me;
    you have delivered me from the depths,
    from the realm of the dead.

14 Arrogant foes are attacking me, O God;
    ruthless people are trying to kill me—
    they have no regard for you.
15 But you, Lord, are a compassionate and gracious God,
    slow to anger, abounding in love and faithfulness.
16 Turn to me and have mercy on me;
    show your strength in behalf of your servant;
save me, because I serve you
    just as my mother did.
17 Give me a sign of your goodness,
    that my enemies may see it and be put to shame,
    for you, Lord, have helped me and comforted me.

PSALM 87

Of the Sons of Korah. A psalm. A song.

1 He has founded his city on the holy mountain.
2 The Lord loves the gates of Zion
    more than all the other dwellings of Jacob.

3 Glorious things are said of you,
    city of God:*a*
4 "I will record Rahab*b* and Babylon
    among those who acknowledge me—
Philistia too, and Tyre, along with Cush*c*—
    and will say, 'This one was born in Zion.'"*d*
5 Indeed, of Zion it will be said,
    "This one and that one were born in her,
    and the Most High himself will establish her."
6 The Lord will write in the register of the peoples:
    "This one was born in Zion."

7 As they make music they will sing,
    "All my fountains are in you."

PSALM 88*e*

A song. A psalm of the Sons of Korah. For the director of music.
According to mahalath leannoth.*f A* maskil*g of Heman the Ezrahite.*

1 Lord, you are the God who saves me;
    day and night I cry out to you.
2 May my prayer come before you;
    turn your ear to my cry.

---

a 3 The Hebrew has *Selah* (a word of uncertain meaning) here and at the end
of verse 6.   *b 4* A poetic name for Egypt   *c 4* That is, the upper Nile
region   *d 4* Or *'I will record concerning those who acknowledge me: / 'This one*
was born in Zion.' / Hear this, Rahab and Babylon, / and you too, Philistia, Tyre
and Cush."   e In Hebrew texts 88:1-18 is numbered 88:2-19.   *f* Title:
Possibly a tune, "The Suffering of Affliction"   *g* Title: Probably a literary or
musical term

What type of sign did David want? (86:17)
David had already expressed his faith in God's goodness and love. Now he wanted God to show his goodness so that David's enemies would see it.

What was God's holy mountain? (87:1–2)
This was Mount Zion in Jerusalem, the site of the temple where God was present with his people.

What was this Rahab? (87:4)
This was a reference to Egypt.

What is the mood of this psalm? (88:1–3)
This psalm expresses the misery of someone who is close to death and has lost his closest friends and loved ones. But even in this great sorrow, he calls out to God.

³I am overwhelmed with troubles
　　and my life draws near to death.
⁴I am counted among those who go down to the pit;
　　I am like one without strength.
⁵I am set apart with the dead,
　　like the slain who lie in the grave,
　whom you remember no more,
　　who are cut off from your care.

⁶You have put me in the lowest pit,
　　in the darkest depths.
⁷Your wrath lies heavily on me;
　　you have overwhelmed me with all your waves.ᵃ
⁸You have taken from me my closest friends
　　and have made me repulsive to them.
　I am confined and cannot escape;
⁹　my eyes are dim with grief.

　I call to you, LORD, every day;
　　I spread out my hands to you.
¹⁰Do you show your wonders to the dead?
　　Do their spirits rise up and praise you?
¹¹Is your love declared in the grave,
　　your faithfulness in Destructionᵇ?
¹²Are your wonders known in the place of darkness,
　　or your righteous deeds in the land of oblivion?

¹³But I cry to you for help, LORD;
　　in the morning my prayer comes before you.
¹⁴Why, LORD, do you reject me
　　and hide your face from me?

¹⁵From my youth I have suffered and been close to
　　death;
　　I have borne your terrors and am in despair.
¹⁶Your wrath has swept over me;
　　your terrors have destroyed me.
¹⁷All day long they surround me like a flood;
　　they have completely engulfed me.
¹⁸You have taken from me friend and neighbor—
　　darkness is my closest friend.

PSALM 89ᶜ

A maskilᵈ of Ethan the Ezrahite.

¹I will sing of the LORD's great love forever;
　　with my mouth I will make your faithfulness known
　　through all generations.
²I will declare that your love stands firm forever,
　　that you have established your faithfulness in
　　heaven itself.
³You said, "I have made a covenant with my
　　chosen one,
　　I have sworn to David my servant,

Why was the psalmist being punished? (88:6)
The author did not explain why God would punish him, but he believed he was suffering because God was angry with him.

What was this covenant? (89:3)
God had made a covenant with David and promised to establish his kingdom forever (2 Samuel 7:8–16).

ᵃ 7 The Hebrew has *Selah* (a word of uncertain meaning) here and at the end of verse 10.   ᵇ 11 Hebrew *Abaddon*   ᶜ In Hebrew texts 89:1-52 is numbered 89:2-53.   ᵈ Title: Probably a literary or musical term

⁴'I will establish your line forever
   and make your throne firm through all
      generations.'"ᵃ

⁵The heavens praise your wonders, LORD,
   your faithfulness too, in the assembly of the
      holy ones.
⁶For who in the skies above can compare with
      the LORD?
   Who is like the LORD among the heavenly beings?
⁷In the council of the holy ones God is greatly feared;
   he is more awesome than all who surround him.
⁸Who is like you, LORD God Almighty?
   You, LORD, are mighty, and your faithfulness
      surrounds you.

⁹You rule over the surging sea;
   when its waves mount up, you still them.
¹⁰You crushed Rahab like one of the slain;
   with your strong arm you scattered your enemies.
¹¹The heavens are yours, and yours also the earth;
   you founded the world and all that is in it.
¹²You created the north and the south;
   Tabor and Hermon sing for joy at your name.
¹³Your arm is endowed with power;
   your hand is strong, your right hand exalted.

¹⁴Righteousness and justice are the foundation of
      your throne;
   love and faithfulness go before you.
¹⁵Blessed are those who have learned to acclaim you,
   who walk in the light of your presence, LORD.
¹⁶They rejoice in your name all day long;
   they celebrate your righteousness.
¹⁷For you are their glory and strength,
   and by your favor you exalt our horn.ᵇ
¹⁸Indeed, our shieldᶜ belongs to the LORD,
   our king to the Holy One of Israel.

¹⁹Once you spoke in a vision,
   to your faithful people you said:
  "I have bestowed strength on a warrior;
   I have raised up a young man from among
      the people.
²⁰I have found David my servant;
   with my sacred oil I have anointed him.
²¹My hand will sustain him;
   surely my arm will strengthen him.
²²The enemy will not get the better of him;
   the wicked will not oppress him.
²³I will crush his foes before him
   and strike down his adversaries.
²⁴My faithful love will be with him,
   and through my name his hornᵈ will be exalted.

What was this Rahab? (89:10)
This Rahab refers to the sea or a mythical sea monster. It symbolized opposition to God and his people.

ᵃ *4* The Hebrew has *Selah* (a word of uncertain meaning) here and at the end of verses 37, 45 and 48.   ᵇ *17 Horn* here symbolizes strong one.
ᶜ *18* Or *sovereign*   ᵈ *24 Horn* here symbolizes strength.

What were the sea and the rivers? (89:25)
This refers to David's kingdom extending from the Mediterranean Sea on the west to the Euphrates River on the east.

Who was the firstborn? (89:27)
Even though David was not the firstborn son in his family, God gave him the blessings that would normally be given the firstborn.

Why did the psalmist accuse God of breaking the covenant? (89:39)
This psalm was probably written after David's family line had ended. So it would have seemed impossible for God to keep his promise to give David an everlasting kingdom.

---

^{25} I will set his hand over the sea,
     his right hand over the rivers.
^{26} He will call out to me, 'You are my Father,
     my God, the Rock my Savior.'
^{27} And I will appoint him to be my firstborn,
     the most exalted of the kings of the earth.
^{28} I will maintain my love to him forever,
     and my covenant with him will never fail.
^{29} I will establish his line forever,
     his throne as long as the heavens endure.

^{30} "If his sons forsake my law
     and do not follow my statutes,
^{31} if they violate my decrees
     and fail to keep my commands,
^{32} I will punish their sin with the rod,
     their iniquity with flogging;
^{33} but I will not take my love from him,
     nor will I ever betray my faithfulness.
^{34} I will not violate my covenant
     or alter what my lips have uttered.
^{35} Once for all, I have sworn by my holiness—
     and I will not lie to David—
^{36} that his line will continue forever
     and his throne endure before me like the sun;
^{37} it will be established forever like the moon,
     the faithful witness in the sky."

^{38} But you have rejected, you have spurned,
     you have been very angry with your
         anointed one.
^{39} You have renounced the covenant with
         your servant
     and have defiled his crown in the dust.
^{40} You have broken through all his walls
     and reduced his strongholds to ruins.
^{41} All who pass by have plundered him;
     he has become the scorn of his neighbors.
^{42} You have exalted the right hand of his foes;
     you have made all his enemies rejoice.
^{43} Indeed, you have turned back the edge of
         his sword
     and have not supported him in battle.
^{44} You have put an end to his splendor
     and cast his throne to the ground.
^{45} You have cut short the days of his youth;
     you have covered him with a mantle of shame.

^{46} How long, Lord? Will you hide yourself forever?
     How long will your wrath burn like fire?
^{47} Remember how fleeting is my life.
     For what futility you have created all humanity!
^{48} Who can live and not see death,
     or who can escape the power of the grave?
^{49} Lord, where is your former great love,
     which in your faithfulness you swore
         to David?

⁵⁰ Remember, Lord, how your servant has*
       been mocked,
    how I bear in my heart the taunts of all
       the nations,
⁵¹ the taunts with which your enemics, Lᴏʀᴅ, have
       mocked,
    with which they have mocked every step of your
       anointed one.

⁵² Praise be to the Lᴏʀᴅ forever!
              Amen and Amen.

BOOK IV

PSALMS 90 – 106

PSALM 90

A prayer of Moses the man of God.

¹ Lord, you have been our dwelling place
       throughout all generations.
² Before the mountains were born
       or you brought forth the whole world,
       from everlasting to everlasting you are God.

³ You turn people back to dust,
       saying, "Return to dust, you mortals."
⁴ A thousand years in your sight
       are like a day that has just gone by,
       or like a watch in the night.
⁵ Yet you sweep people away in the sleep of death—
       they are like the new grass of the morning:
⁶ In the morning it springs up new,
       but by evening it is dry and withered.

⁷ We are consumed by your anger
       and terrified by your indignation.
⁸ You have set our iniquities before you,
       our secret sins in the light of your presence.
⁹ All our days pass away under your wrath;
       we finish our years with a moan.
¹⁰ Our days may come to seventy years,
       or eighty, if our strength endures;
    yet the best of them are but trouble and sorrow,
       for they quickly pass, and we fly away.
¹¹ If only we knew the power of your anger!
       Your wrath is as great as the fear that
       is your due.
¹² Teach us to number our days,
       that we may gain a heart of wisdom.

¹³ Relent, Lᴏʀᴅ! How long will it be?
       Have compassion on your servants.

ª 50 Or *your servants have*

After complaining about God's actions, why does the psalm end on a note of praise? (89:52)
The last verse serves as the conclusion to the end of Book III of the psalms, not just Psalm 89.

How does the psalm say human beings compare to God? (90:3–6)
From God's eternal perspective, human life is short, almost like grass that grows and dies within a day.

What were the watches of the night? (90:4)
These were the divisions into which the 12 hours of darkness were divided. The Israelites divided night into three watches, from 6:00 until 10:00 ᴘ.ᴍ., from 10:00 until 2:00 ᴀ.ᴍ., and from 2:00 until 6:00 ᴀ.ᴍ.

¹⁴Satisfy us in the morning with your unfailing love,
    that we may sing for joy and be glad all our days.
¹⁵Make us glad for as many days as you have afflicted us,
    for as many years as we have seen trouble.
¹⁶May your deeds be shown to your servants,
    your splendor to their children.

¹⁷May the favor[a] of the Lord our God rest on us;
    establish the work of our hands for us—
    yes, establish the work of our hands.

What was the psalmist asking? (90:17)
Even though human lives are insignificant compared to eternity, the psalmist prayed that God would bless what he had done during his lifetime.

PSALM 91

¹Whoever dwells in the shelter of the Most High
    will rest in the shadow of the Almighty.[b]
²I will say of the LORD, "He is my refuge and my
        fortress,
    my God, in whom I trust."

What was a fowler? (91:3)
This was a person who hunted or trapped birds.

³Surely he will save you
    from the fowler's snare
    and from the deadly pestilence.
⁴He will cover you with his feathers,
    and under his wings you will find refuge;
    his faithfulness will be your shield and rampart.

How is God like a bird? (91:4)
This word picture describes God as being like a mother bird that protects her young under her wings. This is an image of safety and comfort.

⁵You will not fear the terror of night,
    nor the arrow that flies by day,
⁶nor the pestilence that stalks in the darkness,
    nor the plague that destroys at midday.
⁷A thousand may fall at your side,
    ten thousand at your right hand,
    but it will not come near you.
⁸You will only observe with your eyes
    and see the punishment of the wicked.

⁹If you say, "The LORD is my refuge,"
    and you make the Most High your dwelling,
¹⁰no harm will overtake you,
    no disaster will come near your tent.

---

a 17 Or beauty   b 1 Hebrew Shaddai

Do people have guardian angels to protect them?   PSALM 91

There are many passages in the Bible that speak about angels, but there is still a great deal of mystery that surrounds them. Angels are spiritual beings that sometimes can take on a physical form in order to bring God's messages to people such as Zechariah and Mary. They serve God, and they praise and worship him. They sometimes are instruments of God's judgment or rescue. For example, an angel helped Peter escape from prison in Acts 12.

They also can encourage, protect, and care for God's people. For example, the author of the Hebrews describes angels as "ministering spirits sent to serve those who will inherit salvation" (1:14). And in Matthew 18:10, Jesus says, "See that you do not look down on one of these little ones. For I tell you that their angels in heaven always see the face of my Father in heaven." (Here the little ones could be little children or Jesus' followers.)

The Bible does not answer the question of whether each person has a specific angel that is assigned to him or her. This was an idea that developed among the Jewish people during the time between the Old and New Testaments. However, the Bible is clear that angels exist and that they do God's will. Part of that task is caring for God's people in a variety of ways.

¹¹ For he will command his angels concerning you
    to guard you in all your ways;
¹² they will lift you up in their hands,
    so that you will not strike your foot against a stone.
¹³ You will tread on the lion and the cobra;
    you will trample the great lion and the serpent.

¹⁴ "Because he^a loves me," says the LORD, "I will rescue
    him;
  I will protect him, for he acknowledges my name.
¹⁵ He will call on me, and I will answer him;
    I will be with him in trouble,
    I will deliver him and honor him.
¹⁶ With long life I will satisfy him
    and show him my salvation."

PSALM 92^b

A psalm. A song. For the Sabbath day.

¹ It is good to praise the LORD
    and make music to your name, O Most High,
² proclaiming your love in the morning
    and your faithfulness at night,
³ to the music of the ten-stringed lyre
    and the melody of the harp.

⁴ For you make me glad by your deeds, LORD;
    I sing for joy at what your hands have done.
⁵ How great are your works, LORD,
    how profound your thoughts!
⁶ Senseless people do not know,
    fools do not understand,
⁷ that though the wicked spring up like grass
    and all evildoers flourish,
    they will be destroyed forever.

⁸ But you, LORD, are forever exalted.

⁹ For surely your enemies, LORD,
    surely your enemies will perish;
    all evildoers will be scattered.
¹⁰ You have exalted my horn^c like that of a wild ox;
    fine oils have been poured on me.
¹¹ My eyes have seen the defeat of my adversaries;
    my ears have heard the rout of my wicked foes.

¹² The righteous will flourish like a palm tree,
    they will grow like a cedar of Lebanon;
¹³ planted in the house of the LORD,
    they will flourish in the courts of our God.
¹⁴ They will still bear fruit in old age,
    they will stay fresh and green,
¹⁵ proclaiming, "The LORD is upright;
    he is my Rock, and there is no wickedness
    in him."

^a 14 That is, probably the king   ^b In Hebrew texts 92:1-15 is numbered 92:2-16.   ^c 10 Horn here symbolizes strength.

An Angel

What did it mean for fine oils to be poured on someone? (92:10)
This symbolized that someone was anointed by God.

What was special about the cedars of Lebanon? (92:12)
The cedars in Lebanon were tall, stately trees. They were widely used throughout the Middle East for the construction of royal palaces.

PSALM 93

¹ The LORD reigns, he is robed in majesty;
  the LORD is robed in majesty and armed with
    strength;
  indeed, the world is established, firm and secure.
² Your throne was established long ago;
  you are from all eternity.

³ The seas have lifted up, LORD,
  the seas have lifted up their voice;
  the seas have lifted up their pounding waves.
⁴ Mightier than the thunder of the great waters,
  mightier than the breakers of the sea —
  the LORD on high is mighty.

⁵ Your statutes, LORD, stand firm;
  holiness adorns your house
  for endless days.

PSALM 94

¹ The LORD is a God who avenges.
  O God who avenges, shine forth.
² Rise up, Judge of the earth;
  pay back to the proud what they deserve.
³ How long, LORD, will the wicked,
  how long will the wicked be jubilant?

⁴ They pour out arrogant words;
  all the evildoers are full of boasting.
⁵ They crush your people, LORD;
  they oppress your inheritance.
⁶ They slay the widow and the foreigner;
  they murder the fatherless.
⁷ They say, "The LORD does not see;
  the God of Jacob takes no notice."

⁸ Take notice, you senseless ones among
      the people;
  you fools, when will you become wise?
⁹ Does he who fashioned the ear not hear?
  Does he who formed the eye not see?
¹⁰ Does he who disciplines nations not punish?
  Does he who teaches mankind lack knowledge?
¹¹ The LORD knows all human plans;
  he knows that they are futile.

¹² Blessed is the one you discipline, LORD,
  the one you teach from your law;
¹³ you grant them relief from days of trouble,
  till a pit is dug for the wicked.
¹⁴ For the LORD will not reject his people;
  he will never forsake his inheritance.
¹⁵ Judgment will again be founded on righteousness,
  and all the upright in heart will follow it.

¹⁶ Who will rise up for me against the wicked?
  Who will take a stand for me against evildoers?

What does this reference to seas say about God? (93:3 – 4)
In ancient times, the raging oceans represented chaos. But the psalmist declared that God was much more powerful than the oceans and was able to tame them.

Why is God called the God of Jacob? (94:7)
Jacob was also called Israel. Here God's name refers to his chosen people.

How can discipline be a blessing? (94:12 – 13)
Discipline is not just punishment. It involves direction and instruction in how to serve God. People who live according to God's law find happiness and peace.

17 Unless the LORD had given me help,
   I would soon have dwelt in the silence of death.
18 When I said, "My foot is slipping,"
   your unfailing love, LORD, supported me.
19 When anxiety was great within me,
   your consolation brought me joy.

20 Can a corrupt throne be allied with you—
   a throne that brings on misery by its decrees?
21 The wicked band together against the righteous
   and condemn the innocent to death.
22 But the LORD has become my fortress,
   and my God the rock in whom I take refuge.
23 He will repay them for their sins
   and destroy them for their wickedness;
   the LORD our God will destroy them.

PSALM 95

1 Come, let us sing for joy to the LORD;
   let us shout aloud to the Rock of our salvation.
2 Let us come before him with thanksgiving
   and extol him with music and song.

3 For the LORD is the great God,
   the great King above all gods.
4 In his hand are the depths of the earth,
   and the mountain peaks belong to him.
5 The sea is his, for he made it,
   and his hands formed the dry land.

6 Come, let us bow down in worship,
   let us kneel before the LORD our Maker;
7 for he is our God
   and we are the people of his pasture,
   the flock under his care.

   Today, if only you would hear his voice,
8 "Do not harden your hearts as you did at Meribah,[a]
   as you did that day at Massah[b] in the wilderness,
9 where your ancestors tested me;
   they tried me, though they had seen what I did.
10 For forty years I was angry with that generation;
   I said, 'They are a people whose hearts go astray,
   and they have not known my ways.'
11 So I declared on oath in my anger,
   'They shall never enter my rest.'"

PSALM 96

1 Sing to the LORD a new song;
   sing to the LORD, all the earth.
2 Sing to the LORD, praise his name;
   proclaim his salvation day after day.
3 Declare his glory among the nations,
   his marvelous deeds among all peoples.

What was Meribah and Massah? (95:8–9)
This was the place where God enabled Moses to provide water from a rock when the Israelites were complaining of thirst in the desert.

What punishment did God impose on the Israelites? (95:10–11)
Because the Israelites complained and failed to trust God, he kept them from entering the promised land (Numbers 14:34).

---

a 8 Meribah means quarreling.   *b 8 Massah means testing.*

⁴For great is the Lᴏʀᴅ and most worthy of praise;
  he is to be feared above all gods.
⁵For all the gods of the nations are idols,
  but the Lᴏʀᴅ made the heavens.
⁶Splendor and majesty are before him;
  strength and glory are in his sanctuary.

⁷Ascribe to the Lᴏʀᴅ, all you families of nations,
  ascribe to the Lᴏʀᴅ glory and strength.
⁸Ascribe to the Lᴏʀᴅ the glory due his name;
  bring an offering and come into his courts.
⁹Worship the Lᴏʀᴅ in the splendor of his*ᵃ holiness;
  tremble before him, all the earth.
¹⁰Say among the nations, "The Lᴏʀᴅ reigns."
  The world is firmly established, it cannot
    be moved;
  he will judge the peoples with equity.

¹¹Let the heavens rejoice, let the earth be glad;
  let the sea resound, and all that is in it.
¹²Let the fields be jubilant, and everything in them;
  let all the trees of the forest sing for joy.
¹³Let all creation rejoice before the Lᴏʀᴅ, for he comes,
  he comes to judge the earth.
He will judge the world in righteousness
  and the peoples in his faithfulness.

PSALM 97

¹The Lᴏʀᴅ reigns, let the earth be glad;
  let the distant shores rejoice.
²Clouds and thick darkness surround him;
  righteousness and justice are the foundation
    of his throne.
³Fire goes before him
  and consumes his foes on every side.
⁴His lightning lights up the world;
  the earth sees and trembles.
⁵The mountains melt like wax before the Lᴏʀᴅ,
  before the Lord of all the earth.
⁶The heavens proclaim his righteousness,
  and all peoples see his glory.

⁷All who worship images are put to shame,
  those who boast in idols—
  worship him, all you gods!

⁸Zion hears and rejoices
  and the villages of Judah are glad
  because of your judgments, Lᴏʀᴅ.
⁹For you, Lᴏʀᴅ, are the Most High over all
    the earth;
  you are exalted far above all gods.
¹⁰Let those who love the Lᴏʀᴅ hate evil,
  for he guards the lives of his faithful ones
  and delivers them from the hand of the wicked.

What does *ascribe* mean?
(96:7–8)
It means to give praise or credit.

Why would all creation rejoice if God came to judge the earth? (96:11–13)
This imagery pictured how the people of Israel looked forward both to the coming of the Messiah and to the time when God would judge wickedness and establish righteousness on the earth.

What do these word pictures tell about God? (97:2–6)
The psalmist used powerful images from nature to describe God's greatness. God is so great that the only way human beings can understand him is through comparisons such as these.

What were God's judgments? (97:8)
These were God's righteous actions in human affairs, especially his saving acts on behalf of Israel.

ᵃ 9 Or Lᴏʀᴅ with the splendor of

¹¹ Light shines*ᵃ* on the righteous
    and joy on the upright in heart.
¹² Rejoice in the LORD, you who are righteous,
    and praise his holy name.

PSALM 98

A psalm.

¹ Sing to the LORD a new song,
    for he has done marvelous things;
  his right hand and his holy arm
    have worked salvation for him.
² The LORD has made his salvation known
    and revealed his righteousness to the nations.
³ He has remembered his love
    and his faithfulness to Israel;
  all the ends of the earth have seen
    the salvation of our God.

⁴ Shout for joy to the LORD, all the earth,
    burst into jubilant song with music;
⁵ make music to the LORD with the harp,
    with the harp and the sound of singing,
⁶ with trumpets and the blast of the ram's horn—
    shout for joy before the LORD, the King.

⁷ Let the sea resound, and everything in it,
    the world, and all who live in it.
⁸ Let the rivers clap their hands,
    let the mountains sing together for joy;
⁹ let them sing before the LORD,
    for he comes to judge the earth.
  He will judge the world in righteousness
    and the peoples with equity.

PSALM 99

¹ The LORD reigns,
    let the nations tremble;
  he sits enthroned between the cherubim,
    let the earth shake.
² Great is the LORD in Zion;
    he is exalted over all the nations.
³ Let them praise your great and awesome name—
    he is holy.

⁴ The King is mighty, he loves justice—
    you have established equity;
  in Jacob you have done
    what is just and right.
⁵ Exalt the LORD our God
    and worship at his footstool;
  he is holy.

ᵃ 11 One Hebrew manuscript and ancient versions (see also 112:4); most
Hebrew manuscripts *Light is sown*

Why did the psalmist talk about God's right hand? (98:1)
In ancient times, the right hand was a symbol of strength, authority, and honor.

What type of trumpets were these? (98:6)
These were the long, straight, silver trumpets used in the temple (Numbers 10:1–10).

What was God's footstool? (99:5)
If God is pictured as sitting on his throne in heaven, the earth can be imagined as his footstool.

842

PSALM 99:6

6 Moses and Aaron were among his priests,
  Samuel was among those who called on his name;
  they called on the Lord
    and he answered them.
7 He spoke to them from the pillar of cloud;
  they kept his statutes and the decrees he gave them.

8 Lord our God,
  you answered them;
  you were to Israel a forgiving God,
    though you punished their misdeeds.ᵃ
9 Exalt the Lord our God
  and worship at his holy mountain,
  for the Lord our God is holy.

PSALM 100

A psalm. For giving grateful praise.

1 Shout for joy to the Lord, all the earth.
2   Worship the Lord with gladness;
    come before him with joyful songs.
3 Know that the Lord is God.
    It is he who made us, and we are hisᵇ;
    we are his people, the sheep of his pasture.

4 Enter his gates with thanksgiving
    and his courts with praise;
    give thanks to him and praise his name.
5 For the Lord is good and his love endures forever;
    his faithfulness continues through all generations.

PSALM 101

Of David. A psalm.

1 I will sing of your love and justice;
    to you, Lord, I will sing praise.
2 I will be careful to lead a blameless life—
    when will you come to me?

  I will conduct the affairs of my house
    with a blameless heart.

ᵃ 8 Or *God, / an avenger of the wrongs done to them*   ᵇ 3 Or *and not we ourselves*

Why were people described as sheep? (100:3)
In ancient times, kings were often described as shepherds of their people. Sheep depend on the shepherd to care for them and protect them in the same way that God's people depend on God.

Who wrote this psalm? (101)
It was written by one of the kings of Israel, either David or one of his descendants. The psalm is similar to a treaty in which the king promised to administer justice and to live up to God's requirements for rulers.

How can we be joyful when we're sad or things are not going our way?
PSALM 100

When the Bible urges believers to be joyful it does not mean that they necessarily forget their problems or their pain. What it does mean is that regardless of what happens in life, we understand that God is always in control, and his will controls the course of human events.

Jesus himself asked God to take away his suffering when he prayed in the Garden of Gethsemane, but he also said, "not my will, but yours be done" (Luke 22:42).

Having joy in the Lord means having confidence that God is the source of our salvation, that he loves us, and that we will live with him forever. Even if we are unhappy or depressed about life's difficulties, we can have this confidence that God cares for us no matter how painful our circumstances may be.

³ I will not look with approval
  on anything that is vile.

I hate what faithless people do;
  I will have no part in it.
⁴ The perverse of heart shall be far from me;
  I will have nothing to do with what is evil.

⁵ Whoever slanders their neighbor in secret,
  I will put to silence;
whoever has haughty eyes and a proud heart,
  I will not tolerate.

⁶ My eyes will be on the faithful in the land,
  that they may dwell with me;
the one whose walk is blameless
  will minister to me.

⁷ No one who practices deceit
  will dwell in my house;
no one who speaks falsely
  will stand in my presence.

⁸ Every morning I will put to silence
  all the wicked in the land;
I will cut off every evildoer
  from the city of the LORD.

PSALM 102[a]

*A prayer of an afflicted person who has grown weak
and pours out a lament before the LORD.*

¹ Hear my prayer, LORD;
  let my cry for help come to you.
² Do not hide your face from me
  when I am in distress.
Turn your ear to me;
  when I call, answer me quickly.

³ For my days vanish like smoke;
  my bones burn like glowing embers.
⁴ My heart is blighted and withered like grass;
  I forget to eat my food.
⁵ In my distress I groan aloud
  and am reduced to skin and bones.
⁶ I am like a desert owl,
  like an owl among the ruins.
⁷ I lie awake; I have become
  like a bird alone on a roof.
⁸ All day long my enemies taunt me;
  those who rail against me use my name as a curse.
⁹ For I eat ashes as my food
  and mingle my drink with tears
¹⁰ because of your great wrath,
  for you have taken me up and thrown me aside.
¹¹ My days are like the evening shadow;
  I wither away like grass.

---

[a] In Hebrew texts 102:1-28 is numbered 102:2-29.

What type of distress did the author experience? (102:3–11)
The author felt abandoned by God, which caused him physical and emotional pain.

¹²But you, LORD, sit enthroned forever;
   your renown endures through all generations.
¹³You will arise and have compassion on Zion,
   for it is time to show favor to her;
   the appointed time has come.
¹⁴For her stones are dear to your servants;
   her very dust moves them to pity.
¹⁵The nations will fear the name of the LORD,
   all the kings of the earth will revere your glory.
¹⁶For the LORD will rebuild Zion
   and appear in his glory.
¹⁷He will respond to the prayer of the destitute;
   he will not despise their plea.

¹⁸Let this be written for a future generation,
   that a people not yet created may praise the LORD:
¹⁹"The LORD looked down from his sanctuary on high,
   from heaven he viewed the earth,
²⁰to hear the groans of the prisoners
   and release those condemned to death."
²¹So the name of the LORD will be declared in Zion
   and his praise in Jerusalem
²²when the peoples and the kingdoms
   assemble to worship the LORD.

²³In the course of my life*a* he broke my strength;
   he cut short my days.
²⁴So I said:
   "Do not take me away, my God, in the midst of my
      days;
   your years go on through all generations.
²⁵In the beginning you laid the foundations of the earth,
   and the heavens are the work of your hands.
²⁶They will perish, but you remain;
   they will all wear out like a garment.
  Like clothing you will change them
   and they will be discarded.
²⁷But you remain the same,
   and your years will never end.
²⁸The children of your servants will live in your
      presence;
   their descendants will be established before you."

PSALM 103

Of David.

¹Praise the LORD, my soul;
   all my inmost being, praise his holy name.
²Praise the LORD, my soul,
   and forget not all his benefits—
³who forgives all your sins
   and heals all your diseases,
⁴who redeems your life from the pit
   and crowns you with love and compassion,

When was this psalm written? (102:16–22)
The psalm was probably written when Israel was in exile in Babylon, because the author asked God to rebuild Jerusalem.

Why did the psalmist have confidence in God? (102:25–28)
The psalmist declared that even though the things God created would change or end, God himself would never change. Because of that, he was confident that Israel's future was secure.

Why did the psalmist say, "my soul"? (103:1–2)
This was a conventional Hebrew way of speaking to oneself.

---

a 23 Or By his power

⁵who satisfies your desires with good things
   so that your youth is renewed like the eagle's.

⁶The LORD works righteousness
   and justice for all the oppressed.

⁷He made known his ways to Moses,
   his deeds to the people of Israel:
⁸The LORD is compassionate and gracious,
   slow to anger, abounding in love.
⁹He will not always accuse,
   nor will he harbor his anger forever;
¹⁰he does not treat us as our sins deserve
   or repay us according to our iniquities.
¹¹For as high as the heavens are above the earth,
   so great is his love for those who fear him;
¹²as far as the east is from the west,
   so far has he removed our transgressions from us.

¹³As a father has compassion on his children,
   so the LORD has compassion on those who fear him;
¹⁴for he knows how we are formed,
   he remembers that we are dust.
¹⁵The life of mortals is like grass,
   they flourish like a flower of the field;
¹⁶the wind blows over it and it is gone,
   and its place remembers it no more.
¹⁷But from everlasting to everlasting
   the LORD's love is with those who fear him,
   and his righteousness with their children's
      children—
¹⁸with those who keep his covenant
   and remember to obey his precepts.

¹⁹The LORD has established his throne in heaven,
   and his kingdom rules over all.

²⁰Praise the LORD, you his angels,
   you mighty ones who do his bidding,
   who obey his word.
²¹Praise the LORD, all his heavenly hosts,
   you his servants who do his will.
²²Praise the LORD, all his works
   everywhere in his dominion.

   Praise the LORD, my soul.

PSALM 104

¹Praise the LORD, my soul.

LORD my God, you are very great;
   you are clothed with splendor and majesty.

²The LORD wraps himself in light as with a garment;
   he stretches out the heavens like a tent
³   and lays the beams of his upper chambers on
      their waters.
He makes the clouds his chariot
   and rides on the wings of the wind.

How did the psalmist describe God's love? (103:11–12)
The author used a word picture to describe God's love as enormous, beyond measure, which was shown by his forgiveness of Israel's sins.

How are God's blessings transferred from one generation to the next? (103:17–18)
Because God is faithful to his covenant, he continues to care for his people. Those who love God train their children in righteousness and thus pass along the blessings.

⁴He makes winds his messengers,ᵃ
    flames of fire his servants.

⁵He set the earth on its foundations;
    it can never be moved.
⁶You covered it with the watery depths as with
        a garment;
    the waters stood above the mountains.
⁷But at your rebuke the waters fled,
    at the sound of your thunder they took to flight;
⁸they flowed over the mountains,
    they went down into the valleys,
    to the place you assigned for them.
⁹You set a boundary they cannot cross;
    never again will they cover the earth.

¹⁰He makes springs pour water into the ravines;
    it flows between the mountains.
¹¹They give water to all the beasts of the field;
    the wild donkeys quench their thirst.
¹²The birds of the sky nest by the waters;
    they sing among the branches.
¹³He waters the mountains from his upper chambers;
    the land is satisfied by the fruit of his work.
¹⁴He makes grass grow for the cattle,
    and plants for people to cultivate—
    bringing forth food from the earth:
¹⁵wine that gladdens human hearts,
    oil to make their faces shine,
    and bread that sustains their hearts.
¹⁶The trees of the LORD are well watered,
    the cedars of Lebanon that he planted.
¹⁷There the birds make their nests;
    the stork has its home in the junipers.
¹⁸The high mountains belong to the wild goats;
    the crags are a refuge for the hyrax.

¹⁹He made the moon to mark the seasons,
    and the sun knows when to go down.
²⁰You bring darkness, it becomes night,
    and all the beasts of the forest prowl.
²¹The lions roar for their prey
    and seek their food from God.
²²The sun rises, and they steal away;
    they return and lie down in their dens.
²³Then people go out to their work,
    to their labor until evening.

²⁴How many are your works, LORD!
    In wisdom you made them all;
    the earth is full of your creatures.
²⁵There is the sea, vast and spacious,
    teeming with creatures beyond number—
    living things both large and small.
²⁶There the ships go to and fro,
    and Leviathan, which you formed to frolic there.

ᵃ 4 Or *angels*

How does the psalmist describe God's creation? (104:10–18)
This is a picture of a beautiful garden, almost like the Garden of Eden. In this garden, all God's creatures are provided for.

What was a hyrax? (104:18)
This animal is about the size of a rabbit, and it lives in rocky areas.

What is *Leviathan*? (104:26)
This was probably either a whale or a mythological sea monster. Here the psalmist describes the frightening creature as God's harmless pet.

²⁷ All creatures look to you
    to give them their food at the proper time.
²⁸ When you give it to them,
    they gather it up;
  when you open your hand,
    they are satisfied with good things.
²⁹ When you hide your face,
    they are terrified;
  when you take away their breath,
    they die and return to the dust.
³⁰ When you send your Spirit,
    they are created,
  and you renew the face of the ground.

³¹ May the glory of the LORD endure forever;
    may the LORD rejoice in his works—
³² he who looks at the earth, and it trembles,
    who touches the mountains, and they smoke.

³³ I will sing to the LORD all my life;
    I will sing praise to my God as long as I live.
³⁴ May my meditation be pleasing to him,
    as I rejoice in the LORD.
³⁵ But may sinners vanish from the earth
    and the wicked be no more.

Praise the LORD, my soul.

Praise the LORD.ᵃ

When was a mountain covered with smoke? (104:32)
When God gave the law to Moses, Mount Sinai was covered with smoke (Exodus 19:18).

PSALM 105

¹ Give praise to the LORD, proclaim his name;
    make known among the nations what he has done.
² Sing to him, sing praise to him;
    tell of all his wonderful acts.
³ Glory in his holy name;
    let the hearts of those who seek the LORD rejoice.
⁴ Look to the LORD and his strength;
    seek his face always.

⁵ Remember the wonders he has done,
    his miracles, and the judgments he pronounced,
⁶ you his servants, the descendants of Abraham,
    his chosen ones, the children of Jacob.
⁷ He is the LORD our God;
    his judgments are in all the earth.

⁸ He remembers his covenant forever,
    the promise he made, for a thousand generations,
⁹ the covenant he made with Abraham,
    the oath he swore to Isaac.
¹⁰ He confirmed it to Jacob as a decree,
    to Israel as an everlasting covenant:
¹¹ "To you I will give the land of Canaan
    as the portion you will inherit."

What were the people supposed to remember? (105:5 – 11)
The psalm reminded the people of how God had remembered and been faithful to his covenant promises to Abraham by caring for them.

ᵃ 35 Hebrew *Hallelu Yah*; in the Septuagint this line stands at the beginning of Psalm 105.

¹² When they were but few in number,
　　few indeed, and strangers in it,
¹³ they wandered from nation to nation,
　　from one kingdom to another.
¹⁴ He allowed no one to oppress them;
　　for their sake he rebuked kings:
¹⁵ "Do not touch my anointed ones;
　　do my prophets no harm."

¹⁶ He called down famine on the land
　　and destroyed all their supplies of food;
¹⁷ and he sent a man before them—
　　Joseph, sold as a slave.
¹⁸ They bruised his feet with shackles,
　　his neck was put in irons,
¹⁹ till what he foretold came to pass,
　　till the word of the LORD proved him true.
²⁰ The king sent and released him,
　　the ruler of peoples set him free.
²¹ He made him master of his household,
　　ruler over all he possessed,
²² to instruct his princes as he pleased
　　and teach his elders wisdom.

²³ Then Israel entered Egypt;
　　Jacob resided as a foreigner in the land of Ham.
²⁴ The LORD made his people very fruitful;
　　he made them too numerous for their foes,
²⁵ whose hearts he turned to hate his people,
　　to conspire against his servants.
²⁶ He sent Moses his servant,
　　and Aaron, whom he had chosen.
²⁷ They performed his signs among them,
　　his wonders in the land of Ham.
²⁸ He sent darkness and made the land dark—
　　for had they not rebelled against his words?
²⁹ He turned their waters into blood,
　　causing their fish to die.
³⁰ Their land teemed with frogs,
　　which went up into the bedrooms of their rulers.
³¹ He spoke, and there came swarms of flies,
　　and gnats throughout their country.
³² He turned their rain into hail,
　　with lightning throughout their land;
³³ he struck down their vines and fig trees
　　and shattered the trees of their country.
³⁴ He spoke, and the locusts came,
　　grasshoppers without number;
³⁵ they ate up every green thing in their land,
　　ate up the produce of their soil.
³⁶ Then he struck down all the firstborn in their land,
　　the firstfruits of all their manhood.
³⁷ He brought out Israel, laden with silver and gold,
　　and from among their tribes no one faltered.
³⁸ Egypt was glad when they left,
　　because dread of Israel had fallen on them.

Who were God's anointed ones? (105:15)
These were people such as priests and kings who were set apart to do God's work. In this verse, the psalmist spoke of prophets.

Why call Egypt "the land of Ham"? (105:23)
Ham was one of Noah's sons. The descendents of Ham's three sons lived in Egypt.

³⁹ He spread out a cloud as a covering,
  and a fire to give light at night.
⁴⁰ They asked, and he brought them quail;
  he fed them well with the bread of heaven.
⁴¹ He opened the rock, and water gushed out;
  it flowed like a river in the desert.

⁴² For he remembered his holy promise
  given to his servant Abraham.
⁴³ He brought out his people with rejoicing,
  his chosen ones with shouts of joy;
⁴⁴ he gave them the lands of the nations,
  and they fell heir to what others had toiled for—
⁴⁵ that they might keep his precepts
  and observe his laws.

  Praise the LORD.^a

PSALM 106

¹ Praise the LORD.^b

  Give thanks to the LORD, for he is good;
  his love endures forever.

² Who can proclaim the mighty acts of the LORD
  or fully declare his praise?
³ Blessed are those who act justly,
  who always do what is right.

⁴ Remember me, LORD, when you show favor to
      your people,
  come to my aid when you save them,
⁵ that I may enjoy the prosperity of your chosen ones,
  that I may share in the joy of your nation
  and join your inheritance in giving praise.

⁶ We have sinned, even as our ancestors did;
  we have done wrong and acted wickedly.
⁷ When our ancestors were in Egypt,
  they gave no thought to your miracles;
  they did not remember your many kindnesses,
  and they rebelled by the sea, the Red Sea.^c
⁸ Yet he saved them for his name's sake,
  to make his mighty power known.
⁹ He rebuked the Red Sea, and it dried up;
  he led them through the depths as through a desert.
¹⁰ He saved them from the hand of the foe;
  from the hand of the enemy he redeemed them.
¹¹ The waters covered their adversaries;
  not one of them survived.
¹² Then they believed his promises
  and sang his praise.

¹³ But they soon forgot what he had done
  and did not wait for his plan to unfold.

How did God want his people to respond to his faithfulness? (105:44–45)
God had kept his covenant promises, and he expected his chosen people to obey him and keep his commandments.

How are Psalms 105 and 106 related? (106)
Both psalms tell about God saving and caring for his people, but Psalm 106 focuses on the way Israel continually rebelled against God.

---

^a 45 Hebrew *Hallelu Yah*   ^b 1 Hebrew *Hallelu Yah*; also in verse 48
^c 7 Or *the Sea of Reeds*; also in verses 9 and 22

¹⁴ In the desert they gave in to their craving;
in the wilderness they put God to the test.
¹⁵ So he gave them what they asked for,
but sent a wasting disease among them.

¹⁶ In the camp they grew envious of Moses
and of Aaron, who was consecrated to
the Lord.
¹⁷ The earth opened up and swallowed Dathan;
it buried the company of Abiram.
¹⁸ Fire blazed among their followers;
a flame consumed the wicked.
¹⁹ At Horeb they made a calf
and worshiped an idol cast from metal.
²⁰ They exchanged their glorious God
for an image of a bull, which eats grass.
²¹ They forgot the God who saved them,
who had done great things in Egypt,
²² miracles in the land of Ham
and awesome deeds by the Red Sea.
²³ So he said he would destroy them—
had not Moses, his chosen one,
stood in the breach before him
to keep his wrath from destroying them.

²⁴ Then they despised the pleasant land;
they did not believe his promise.
²⁵ They grumbled in their tents
and did not obey the Lord.
²⁶ So he swore to them with uplifted hand
that he would make them fall in the wilderness,
²⁷ make their descendants fall among the nations
and scatter them throughout the lands.

²⁸ They yoked themselves to the Baal of Peor
and ate sacrifices offered to lifeless gods;
²⁹ they aroused the Lord's anger by their
wicked deeds,
and a plague broke out among them.
³⁰ But Phinehas stood up and intervened,
and the plague was checked.
³¹ This was credited to him as righteousness
for endless generations to come.
³² By the waters of Meribah they angered the Lord,
and trouble came to Moses because of them;
³³ for they rebelled against the Spirit of God,
and rash words came from Moses' lips.^a

³⁴ They did not destroy the peoples
as the Lord had commanded them,
³⁵ but they mingled with the nations
and adopted their customs.
³⁶ They worshiped their idols,
which became a snare to them.
³⁷ They sacrificed their sons
and their daughters to false gods.

^a 33 Or against his spirit, / and rash words came from his lips

How did Phinehas intervene? (106:30)
Phinehas was a priest who obeyed God's command by killing a man and woman who were worshiping Baal with immoral sexual activities. Because of his action, God stopped the plague he had sent to Israel (see Numbers 25:7–11).

Why were they told to destroy the Canaanites? (106:34)
God wanted them to eliminate all of the pagan people from the promised land so they would not influence the Israelites to worship other gods (see Exodus 23:32–33).

³⁸ They shed innocent blood,
  the blood of their sons and daughters,
  whom they sacrificed to the idols of Canaan,
  and the land was desecrated by their blood.
³⁹ They defiled themselves by what they did;
  by their deeds they prostituted themselves.

⁴⁰ Therefore the LORD was angry with his people
  and abhorred his inheritance.
⁴¹ He gave them into the hands of the nations,
  and their foes ruled over them.
⁴² Their enemies oppressed them
  and subjected them to their power.
⁴³ Many times he delivered them,
  but they were bent on rebellion
  and they wasted away in their sin.
⁴⁴ Yet he took note of their distress
  when he heard their cry;
⁴⁵ for their sake he remembered his covenant
  and out of his great love he relented.
⁴⁶ He caused all who held them captive
  to show them mercy.

⁴⁷ Save us, LORD our God,
  and gather us from the nations,
  that we may give thanks to your holy name
  and glory in your praise.

⁴⁸ Praise be to the LORD, the God of Israel,
  from everlasting to everlasting.

Let all the people say, "Amen!"

Praise the LORD.

BOOK V

PSALMS 107 – 150

PSALM 107

¹ Give thanks to the LORD, for he is good;
  his love endures forever.

² Let the redeemed of the LORD tell their story—
  those he redeemed from the hand of the foe,
³ those he gathered from the lands,
  from east and west, from north and south.ᵃ

⁴ Some wandered in desert wastelands,
  finding no way to a city where they could settle.
⁵ They were hungry and thirsty,
  and their lives ebbed away.
⁶ Then they cried out to the LORD in their trouble,
  and he delivered them from their distress.
⁷ He led them by a straight way
  to a city where they could settle.

Where had the people been scattered? (106:47)
This psalm was probably written after Judah had been conquered by Babylon. In order to reduce the chance of rebellion, Babylon relocated the national groups they conquered. The Israelites were mainly placed in the eastern provinces of Babylon.

What is the theme of this psalm? (107)
The psalmist urges the people to praise God because he hears the prayers of people in need and saves them.

ᵃ 3 Hebrew *north and the sea*

⁸ Let them give thanks to the LORD for his unfailing love
　　and his wonderful deeds for mankind,
⁹ for he satisfies the thirsty
　　and fills the hungry with good things.

¹⁰ Some sat in darkness, in utter darkness,
　　prisoners suffering in iron chains,
¹¹ because they rebelled against God's commands
　　and despised the plans of the Most High.
¹² So he subjected them to bitter labor;
　　they stumbled, and there was no one to help.
¹³ Then they cried to the LORD in their trouble,
　　and he saved them from their distress.
¹⁴ He brought them out of darkness, the utter darkness,
　　and broke away their chains.
¹⁵ Let them give thanks to the LORD for his unfailing love
　　and his wonderful deeds for mankind,
¹⁶ for he breaks down gates of bronze
　　and cuts through bars of iron.

¹⁷ Some became fools through their rebellious ways
　　and suffered affliction because of their iniquities.
¹⁸ They loathed all food
　　and drew near the gates of death.
¹⁹ Then they cried to the LORD in their trouble,
　　and he saved them from their distress.
²⁰ He sent out his word and healed them;
　　he rescued them from the grave.
²¹ Let them give thanks to the LORD for his unfailing
　　love
　　and his wonderful deeds for mankind.
²² Let them sacrifice thank offerings
　　and tell of his works with songs of joy.

²³ Some went out on the sea in ships;
　　they were merchants on the mighty waters.
²⁴ They saw the works of the LORD,
　　his wonderful deeds in the deep.
²⁵ For he spoke and stirred up a tempest
　　that lifted high the waves.
²⁶ They mounted up to the heavens and went down to
　　the depths;
　　in their peril their courage melted away.
²⁷ They reeled and staggered like drunkards;
　　they were at their wits' end.
²⁸ Then they cried out to the LORD in their trouble,
　　and he brought them out of their distress.
²⁹ He stilled the storm to a whisper;
　　the waves of the sea*ᵃ* were hushed.
³⁰ They were glad when it grew calm,
　　and he guided them to their desired haven.
³¹ Let them give thanks to the LORD for his unfailing love
　　and his wonderful deeds for mankind.
³² Let them exalt him in the assembly of the people
　　and praise him in the council of the elders.

What were the gates of bronze and bars of iron? (107:16)
City gates and the bars that secured them were usually made of wood. But the strongest gates and bars were made of bronze.

What were the gates of death? (107:18)
The realm of the dead was sometimes depicted as a city with seven concentric walls and gates to keep people from returning to the land of the living.

What were the mighty waters? (107:23–24)
People who lived on the eastern coast of the Mediterranean Sea thought of the huge waves of the sea as being like the chaotic waters before the earth was created. But God was able to tame the storms and protect his people.

ᵃ *29* Dead Sea Scrolls; Masoretic Text / *their waves*

33 He turned rivers into a desert,
   flowing springs into thirsty ground,
34 and fruitful land into a salt waste,
   because of the wickedness of those who lived there.
35 He turned the desert into pools of water
   and the parched ground into flowing springs;
36 there he brought the hungry to live,
   and they founded a city where they could settle.
37 They sowed fields and planted vineyards
   that yielded a fruitful harvest;
38 he blessed them, and their numbers greatly increased,
   and he did not let their herds diminish.

39 Then their numbers decreased, and they were humbled
   by oppression, calamity and sorrow;
40 he who pours contempt on nobles
   made them wander in a trackless waste.
41 But he lifted the needy out of their affliction
   and increased their families like flocks.
42 The upright see and rejoice,
   but all the wicked shut their mouths.

43 Let the one who is wise heed these things
   and ponder the loving deeds of the LORD.

PSALM 108 [a]

A song. A psalm of David.

1 My heart, O God, is steadfast;
   I will sing and make music with all my soul.
2 Awake, harp and lyre!
   I will awaken the dawn.
3 I will praise you, LORD, among the nations;
   I will sing of you among the peoples.
4 For great is your love, higher than the heavens;
   your faithfulness reaches to the skies.
5 Be exalted, O God, above the heavens;
   let your glory be over all the earth.

6 Save us and help us with your right hand,
   that those you love may be delivered.
7 God has spoken from his sanctuary:
   "In triumph I will parcel out Shechem
   and measure off the Valley of Sukkoth.
8 Gilead is mine, Manasseh is mine;
   Ephraim is my helmet,
   Judah is my scepter.
9 Moab is my washbasin,
   on Edom I toss my sandal;
   over Philistia I shout in triumph."

10 Who will bring me to the fortified city?
   Who will lead me to Edom?
11 Is it not you, God, you who have rejected us
   and no longer go out with our armies?

a In Hebrew texts 108:1-13 is numbered 108:2-14.

Why would God destroy the environment? (107:33–34)
God punished the wicked by turning the land into a desert, but he blessed those who were obedient by giving them rich land for crops and herds (verses 35–38).

Why were the harp and lyre called to wake up? (108:2)
The harp and lyre were instruments used to praise God at the temple, and here they were personified (given human characteristics) in order to give praise to God.

What does it mean to toss one's sandal? (108:9)
Since sandals were normally given to slaves upon entering a home, it could mean to treat as slaves. Tossing a sandal on a piece of land also may have indicated a claim of ownership.

¹² Give us aid against the enemy,
     for human help is worthless.
¹³ With God we will gain the victory,
     and he will trample down our enemies.

PSALM 109

For the director of music. Of David. A psalm.

¹ My God, whom I praise,
     do not remain silent,
² for people who are wicked and deceitful
     have opened their mouths against me;
     they have spoken against me with lying tongues.
³ With words of hatred they surround me;
     they attack me without cause.
⁴ In return for my friendship they accuse me,
     but I am a man of prayer.
⁵ They repay me evil for good,
     and hatred for my friendship.

⁶ Appoint someone evil to oppose my enemy;
     let an accuser stand at his right hand.
⁷ When he is tried, let him be found guilty,
     and may his prayers condemn him.
⁸ May his days be few;
     may another take his place of leadership.
⁹ May his children be fatherless
     and his wife a widow.
¹⁰ May his children be wandering beggars;
     may they be driven[a] from their ruined homes.
¹¹ May a creditor seize all he has;
     may strangers plunder the fruits of his labor.
¹² May no one extend kindness to him
     or take pity on his fatherless children.
¹³ May his descendants be cut off,
     their names blotted out from the next generation.
¹⁴ May the iniquity of his fathers be remembered before
     the Lord;
     may the sin of his mother never be blotted out.
¹⁵ May their sins always remain before the Lord,
     that he may blot out their name from the earth.

¹⁶ For he never thought of doing a kindness,
     but hounded to death the poor
     and the needy and the brokenhearted.
¹⁷ He loved to pronounce a curse—
     may it come back on him.
He found no pleasure in blessing—
     may it be far from him.
¹⁸ He wore cursing as his garment;
     it entered into his body like water,
     into his bones like oil.
¹⁹ May it be like a cloak wrapped about him,
     like a belt tied forever around him.

What did David's enemies say about him? (109:2–5) We don't know the specifics, but David was betrayed by people who told lies about him.

[a] *10* Septuagint; Hebrew *sought*

²⁰ May this be the LORD's payment to my accusers,
    to those who speak evil of me.

²¹ But you, Sovereign LORD,
    help me for your name's sake;
    out of the goodness of your love, deliver me.
²² For I am poor and needy,
    and my heart is wounded within me.
²³ I fade away like an evening shadow;
    I am shaken off like a locust.
²⁴ My knees give way from fasting;
    my body is thin and gaunt.
²⁵ I am an object of scorn to my accusers;
    when they see me, they shake their heads.

²⁶ Help me, LORD my God;
    save me according to your unfailing love.
²⁷ Let them know that it is your hand,
    that you, LORD, have done it.
²⁸ While they curse, may you bless;
    may those who attack me be put to shame,
    but may your servant rejoice.
²⁹ May my accusers be clothed with disgrace
    and wrapped in shame as in a cloak.

³⁰ With my mouth I will greatly extol the LORD;
    in the great throng of worshipers I will praise him.
³¹ For he stands at the right hand of the needy,
    to save their lives from those who would condemn
    them.

PSALM 110

Of David. A psalm.

¹ The LORD says to my lord:*ᵃ*

"Sit at my right hand
    until I make your enemies
    a footstool for your feet."

² The LORD will extend your mighty scepter from Zion,
        saying,
    "Rule in the midst of your enemies!"
³ Your troops will be willing
    on your day of battle.
Arrayed in holy splendor,
    your young men will come to you
    like dew from the morning's womb.*ᵇ*

⁴ The LORD has sworn
    and will not change his mind:
"You are a priest forever,
    in the order of Melchizedek."

⁵ The Lord is at your right hand*ᶜ*;
    he will crush kings on the day of his wrath.

ᵃ 1 Or Lord   ᵇ 3 The meaning of the Hebrew for this sentence is uncertain.
ᶜ 5 Or My lord is at your right hand, LORD

How did David appeal to God's reputation? (109:21–29)
David said that if God saved him from his enemies, God would receive the credit. But if David suffered, God's reputation would be damaged because David trusted in him.

What future event does this psalm point toward? (110)
The psalm was written to be sung when future kings were crowned. But the psalm also points toward the coming of the Messiah.

Who was Melchizedek? (110:4)
Melchizedek had been a king and priest of Salem (later called Jerusalem). Abraham brought offerings to him to thank God for giving him a victory (see Genesis 14:18–20).

⁶He will judge the nations, heaping up the dead
    and crushing the rulers of the whole earth.
⁷He will drink from a brook along the way,ᵃ
    and so he will lift his head high.

PSALM 111ᵇ

¹Praise the LORD.ᶜ

I will extol the LORD with all my heart
    in the council of the upright and in the assembly.

²Great are the works of the LORD;
    they are pondered by all who delight in them.
³Glorious and majestic are his deeds,
    and his righteousness endures forever.
⁴He has caused his wonders to be remembered;
    the LORD is gracious and compassionate.
⁵He provides food for those who fear him;
    he remembers his covenant forever.

⁶He has shown his people the power of his works,
    giving them the lands of other nations.
⁷The works of his hands are faithful and just;
    all his precepts are trustworthy.
⁸They are established for ever and ever,
    enacted in faithfulness and uprightness.
⁹He provided redemption for his people;
    he ordained his covenant forever—
    holy and awesome is his name.

¹⁰The fear of the LORD is the beginning of wisdom;
    all who follow his precepts have good
        understanding.
    To him belongs eternal praise.

Which covenant is being described? (111:5–9)
This section refers to the covenant God made with Abram to multiply his descendants and give them the land of Canaan (see Genesis 17:4–8).

PSALM 112ᵇ

¹Praise the LORD.ᶜ

Blessed are those who fear the LORD,
    who find great delight in his commands.

²Their children will be mighty in the land;
    the generation of the upright will be blessed.
³Wealth and riches are in their houses,
    and their righteousness endures forever.
⁴Even in darkness light dawns for the upright,
    for those who are gracious and compassionate
        and righteous.
⁵Good will come to those who are generous and
        lend freely,
    who conduct their affairs with justice.

⁶Surely the righteous will never be shaken;
    they will be remembered forever.

ᵃ 7 The meaning of the Hebrew for this clause is uncertain.   ᵇ This psalm is an acrostic poem, the lines of which begin with the successive letters of the Hebrew alphabet.   ᶜ 1 Hebrew *Hallelu Yah*

⁷They will have no fear of bad news;
  their hearts are steadfast, trusting in the LORD.
⁸Their hearts are secure, they will have no fear;
  in the end they will look in triumph on their foes.
⁹They have freely scattered their gifts to the poor,
  their righteousness endures forever;
  their horn*ᵃ* will be lifted high in honor.

¹⁰The wicked will see and be vexed,
  they will gnash their teeth and waste away;
  the longings of the wicked will come
    to nothing.

PSALM 113

¹Praise the LORD.*ᵇ*

Praise the LORD, you his servants;
  praise the name of the LORD.
²Let the name of the LORD be praised,
  both now and forevermore.
³From the rising of the sun to the place
    where it sets,
  the name of the LORD is to be praised.

⁴The LORD is exalted over all the nations,
  his glory above the heavens.
⁵Who is like the LORD our God,
  the One who sits enthroned on high,
⁶who stoops down to look
  on the heavens and the earth?

⁷He raises the poor from the dust
  and lifts the needy from the ash heap;
⁸he seats them with princes,
  with the princes of his people.
⁹He settles the childless woman in her home
  as a happy mother of children.

Praise the LORD.

PSALM 114

¹When Israel came out of Egypt,
  Jacob from a people of foreign tongue,
²Judah became God's sanctuary,
  Israel his dominion.

³The sea looked and fled,
  the Jordan turned back;
⁴the mountains leaped like rams,
  the hills like lambs.

⁵Why was it, sea, that you fled?
  Why, Jordan, did you turn back?
⁶Why, mountains, did you leap like rams,
  you hills, like lambs?

What did it mean to gnash one's teeth? (112:10)
This is the same as grinding one's teeth. In the Old Testament, this expression represented rage, anger, or hatred. In the New Testament, the phrase represented disappointment or agony of spirit.

How does God show concern for the poor? (113:7)
God cares for ordinary people, such as the poor and the childless, and raises them "from the dust." The Bible is filled with illustrations of childless women who were given children (Sarah, Rachel, Hannah) and poor and lowly who became great (David).

ᵃ 9 Horn here symbolizes dignity.   *ᵇ 1* Hebrew Hallelu Yah; also in verse 9

When did God turn a rock into a pool? (114:8)
When the people of Israel were in the desert, they grumbled about not having water. Twice God caused water to gush out of a rock (Exodus 17:6; Numbers 20:11).

Why did the nations taunt Israel? (115:2)
Israel experienced many hardships throughout its history. Because Israel was known to worship God, the foreign nations mocked them for believing in a God who allowed these events to happen.

How would idolaters become like the idols they worshiped? (115:4–8)
Those who worshiped idols would end up being like them: helpless, powerless, and lifeless.

[7] Tremble, earth, at the presence of the Lord,
    at the presence of the God of Jacob,
[8] who turned the rock into a pool,
    the hard rock into springs of water.

PSALM 115

[1] Not to us, LORD, not to us
    but to your name be the glory,
    because of your love and faithfulness.

[2] Why do the nations say,
    "Where is their God?"
[3] Our God is in heaven;
    he does whatever pleases him.
[4] But their idols are silver and gold,
    made by human hands.
[5] They have mouths, but cannot speak,
    eyes, but cannot see.
[6] They have ears, but cannot hear,
    noses, but cannot smell.
[7] They have hands, but cannot feel,
    feet, but cannot walk,
    nor can they utter a sound with their throats.
[8] Those who make them will be like them,
    and so will all who trust in them.

[9] All you Israelites, trust in the LORD—
    he is their help and shield.
[10] House of Aaron, trust in the LORD—
    he is their help and shield.
[11] You who fear him, trust in the LORD—
    he is their help and shield.

[12] The LORD remembers us and will bless us:
    He will bless his people Israel,
    he will bless the house of Aaron,
[13] he will bless those who fear the LORD—
    small and great alike.

[14] May the LORD cause you to flourish,
    both you and your children.
[15] May you be blessed by the LORD,
    the Maker of heaven and earth.

[16] The highest heavens belong to the LORD,
    but the earth he has given to mankind.
[17] It is not the dead who praise the LORD,
    those who go down to the place of silence;
[18] it is we who extol the LORD,
    both now and forevermore.

Praise the LORD.[a]

PSALM 116

[1] I love the LORD, for he heard my voice;
    he heard my cry for mercy.

[a] 18 Hebrew *Hallelu Yah*

² Because he turned his ear to me,
   I will call on him as long as I live.

³ The cords of death entangled me,
   the anguish of the grave came over me;
   I was overcome by distress and sorrow.
⁴ Then I called on the name of the LORD:
   "LORD, save me!"

⁵ The LORD is gracious and righteous;
   our God is full of compassion.
⁶ The LORD protects the unwary;
   when I was brought low, he saved me.

⁷ Return to your rest, my soul,
   for the LORD has been good to you.

⁸ For you, LORD, have delivered me from death,
   my eyes from tears,
   my feet from stumbling,
⁹ that I may walk before the LORD
   in the land of the living.

¹⁰ I trusted in the LORD when I said,
   "I am greatly afflicted";
¹¹ in my alarm I said,
   "Everyone is a liar."

¹² What shall I return to the LORD
   for all his goodness to me?

¹³ I will lift up the cup of salvation
   and call on the name of the LORD.
¹⁴ I will fulfill my vows to the LORD
   in the presence of all his people.

¹⁵ Precious in the sight of the LORD
   is the death of his faithful servants.
¹⁶ Truly I am your servant, LORD;
   I serve you just as my mother did;
   you have freed me from my chains.

¹⁷ I will sacrifice a thank offering to you
   and call on the name of the LORD.
¹⁸ I will fulfill my vows to the LORD
   in the presence of all his people,
¹⁹ in the courts of the house of the LORD—
   in your midst, Jerusalem.

Praise the LORD.[a]

PSALM 117

¹ Praise the LORD, all you nations;
   extol him, all you peoples.
² For great is his love toward us,
   and the faithfulness of the LORD endures forever.

Praise the LORD.[a]

[a] 19,2 Hebrew *Hallelu Yah*

What was the cup of salvation? (116:13)
This probably refers to the cup of wine drunk at the meal after a thank offering. It was called the cup of salvation because the thank offering and its meal celebrated the LORD's deliverance.

Why is death precious to God? (116:15)
The verse does not mean that God is glad when his people die. Instead, it means that he cares deeply or pays special attention because he loves those who follow him.

PSALM 118

¹ Give thanks to the LORD, for he is good;
  his love endures forever.

² Let Israel say:
  "His love endures forever."
³ Let the house of Aaron say:
  "His love endures forever."
⁴ Let those who fear the LORD say:
  "His love endures forever."

⁵ When hard pressed, I cried to the LORD;
  he brought me into a spacious place.
⁶ The LORD is with me; I will not be afraid.
  What can mere mortals do to me?
⁷ The LORD is with me; he is my helper.
  I look in triumph on my enemies.

⁸ It is better to take refuge in the LORD
  than to trust in humans.
⁹ It is better to take refuge in the LORD
  than to trust in princes.
¹⁰ All the nations surrounded me,
  but in the name of the LORD I cut them down.
¹¹ They surrounded me on every side,
  but in the name of the LORD I cut them down.
¹² They swarmed around me like bees,
  but they were consumed as quickly as burning
    thorns;
  in the name of the LORD I cut them down.
¹³ I was pushed back and about to fall,
  but the LORD helped me.
¹⁴ The LORD is my strength and my defense[a];
  he has become my salvation.

¹⁵ Shouts of joy and victory
  resound in the tents of the righteous:
  "The LORD's right hand has done mighty things!
¹⁶   The LORD's right hand is lifted high;
  the LORD's right hand has done
    mighty things!"
¹⁷ I will not die but live,
  and will proclaim what the LORD has done.
¹⁸ The LORD has chastened me severely,
  but he has not given me over to death.
¹⁹ Open for me the gates of the righteous;
  I will enter and give thanks to the LORD.
²⁰ This is the gate of the LORD
  through which the righteous may enter.
²¹ I will give you thanks, for you answered me;
  you have become my salvation.

²² The stone the builders rejected
  has become the cornerstone;
²³ the LORD has done this,
  and it is marvelous in our eyes.

What were the gates of righteousness? (118:19–20)
This probably refers to gates leading to the inner temple court through which the righteous entered to worship God.

What was a cornerstone? (118:22)
This was a large stone over a doorway, a rock used to anchor and align a wall, or the keystone of an arch. Here the stone is a metaphor for either the king, who was scorned by invaders, or the nation of Israel.

Gate with cornerstone

---

a 14 Or song

²⁴The Lord has done it this very day;
　　let us rejoice today and be glad.

²⁵Lord, save us!
　　Lord, grant us success!

²⁶Blessed is he who comes in the name of
　　the Lord.
　　From the house of the Lord we bless you.ᵃ
²⁷The Lord is God,
　　and he has made his light shine on us.
　　With boughs in hand, join in the festal procession
　　upᵇ to the horns of the altar.

²⁸You are my God, and I will praise you;
　　you are my God, and I will exalt you.

²⁹Give thanks to the Lord, for he is good;
　　his love endures forever.

PSALM 119ᶜ

א Aleph

¹Blessed are those whose ways are blameless,
　　who walk according to the law of the Lord.
²Blessed are those who keep his statutes
　　and seek him with all their heart—
³they do no wrong
　　but follow his ways.
⁴You have laid down precepts
　　that are to be fully obeyed.
⁵Oh, that my ways were steadfast
　　in obeying your decrees!
⁶Then I would not be put to shame
　　when I consider all your commands.
⁷I will praise you with an upright heart
　　as I learn your righteous laws.
⁸I will obey your decrees;
　　do not utterly forsake me.

ᵃ 26 The Hebrew is plural.　ᵇ 27 Or *Bind the festal sacrifice with ropes / and take it*　ᶜ This psalm is an acrostic poem, the stanzas of which begin with successive letters of the Hebrew alphabet; moreover, the verses of each stanza begin with the same letter of the Hebrew alphabet.

Can people keep God's law perfectly? (119:1–3)
No. But those who love God try to live according to his commandments. For example, David committed sins during his lifetime, but he never lost faith in God; and when he sinned, he asked God for forgiveness.

How can Christians meditate on God's Word?　PSALM 119

Meditation is a process of reflecting, reviewing, thinking, evaluating, feeling, and applying. Meditating on God's Word involves all of these elements, but each person will probably do it somewhat differently. Verse 11 says, "I have hidden your word in my heart." This suggests that it is important to memorize Scripture. Knowing God's Word "by heart" means that it is something you hold dear and that cannot be taken away from you.

In addition to memorizing Scripture, we should read the Bible frequently and carefully, listening to what God is saying to us about our lives and our decisions. Praying about what we have read is another good suggestion, while inviting the Holy Spirit to apply the truths of the Bible to our hearts. Thinking about a passage and how it relates to other passages in Scripture can help us get a sense of the "big picture" of what God wants for us. Allowing the Bible to influence our emotions and our behavior is the next step, where we begin to apply the Bible directly to our lives.

ב Beth

9 How can a young person stay on the path
of purity?
By living according to your word.
10 I seek you with all my heart;
do not let me stray from your commands.
11 I have hidden your word in my heart
that I might not sin against you.
12 Praise be to you, LORD;
teach me your decrees.
13 With my lips I recount
all the laws that come from your mouth.
14 I rejoice in following your statutes
as one rejoices in great riches.
15 I meditate on your precepts
and consider your ways.
16 I delight in your decrees;
I will not neglect your word.

ג Gimel

17 Be good to your servant while I live,
that I may obey your word.
18 Open my eyes that I may see
wonderful things in your law.
19 I am a stranger on earth;
do not hide your commands from me.
20 My soul is consumed with longing
for your laws at all times.
21 You rebuke the arrogant, who are accursed,
those who stray from your commands.
22 Remove from me their scorn and contempt,
for I keep your statutes.
23 Though rulers sit together and slander me,
your servant will meditate on your decrees.
24 Your statutes are my delight;
they are my counselors.

ד Daleth

25 I am laid low in the dust;
preserve my life according to your word.
26 I gave an account of my ways and you answered me;
teach me your decrees.
27 Cause me to understand the way of your precepts,
that I may meditate on your wonderful deeds.
28 My soul is weary with sorrow;
strengthen me according to your word.
29 Keep me from deceitful ways;
be gracious to me and teach me your law.
30 I have chosen the way of faithfulness;
I have set my heart on your laws.
31 I hold fast to your statutes, LORD;
do not let me be put to shame.
32 I run in the path of your commands,
for you have broadened my understanding.

How can people hide God's Word in their hearts? (119:11)
Studying, memorizing, and reflecting on Scripture can help us to understand how God wants us to live.

Why was the psalmist a stranger on earth? (119:19)
As a follower of God, his primary citizenship was as a member of God's kingdom. But this does not mean that believers should think their lives on earth are unimportant.

How was the psalmist laid low? (119:25)
The author was probably ridiculed or even persecuted for trying to follow God's laws.

ה He

³³ Teach me, LORD, the way of your decrees,
 that I may follow it to the end.ᵃ
³⁴ Give me understanding, so that I may keep your law
 and obey it with all my heart.
³⁵ Direct me in the path of your commands,
 for there I find delight.
³⁶ Turn my heart toward your statutes
 and not toward selfish gain.
³⁷ Turn my eyes away from worthless things;
 preserve my life according to your word.ᵇ
³⁸ Fulfill your promise to your servant,
 so that you may be feared.
³⁹ Take away the disgrace I dread,
 for your laws are good.
⁴⁰ How I long for your precepts!
 In your righteousness preserve my life.

ו Waw

⁴¹ May your unfailing love come to me, LORD,
 your salvation, according to your promise;
⁴² then I can answer anyone who taunts me,
 for I trust in your word.
⁴³ Never take your word of truth from my mouth,
 for I have put my hope in your laws.
⁴⁴ I will always obey your law,
 for ever and ever.
⁴⁵ I will walk about in freedom,
 for I have sought out your precepts.
⁴⁶ I will speak of your statutes before kings
 and will not be put to shame,
⁴⁷ for I delight in your commands
 because I love them.
⁴⁸ I reach out for your commands, which I love,
 that I may meditate on your decrees.

ז Zayin

⁴⁹ Remember your word to your servant,
 for you have given me hope.
⁵⁰ My comfort in my suffering is this:
 Your promise preserves my life.
⁵¹ The arrogant mock me unmercifully,
 but I do not turn from your law.
⁵² I remember, LORD, your ancient laws,
 and I find comfort in them.
⁵³ Indignation grips me because of the wicked,
 who have forsaken your law.
⁵⁴ Your decrees are the theme of my song
 wherever I lodge.
⁵⁵ In the night, LORD, I remember your name,
 that I may keep your law.
⁵⁶ This has been my practice:
 I obey your precepts.

Do ancient laws still apply to people today? (119:52)
Since God's law is based on his unchanging truth, it is still relevant for us today.

ᵃ 33 Or *follow it for its reward*   ᵇ 37 Two manuscripts of the Masoretic Text and Dead Sea Scrolls; most manuscripts of the Masoretic Text *life in your way*

ח Heth

⁵⁷ You are my portion, LORD;
    I have promised to obey your words.
⁵⁸ I have sought your face with all my heart;
    be gracious to me according to your promise.
⁵⁹ I have considered my ways
    and have turned my steps to your statutes.
⁶⁰ I will hasten and not delay
    to obey your commands.
⁶¹ Though the wicked bind me with ropes,
    I will not forget your law.
⁶² At midnight I rise to give you thanks
    for your righteous laws.
⁶³ I am a friend to all who fear you,
    to all who follow your precepts.
⁶⁴ The earth is filled with your love, LORD;
    teach me your decrees.

ט Teth

⁶⁵ Do good to your servant
    according to your word, LORD.
⁶⁶ Teach me knowledge and good judgment,
    for I trust your commands.
⁶⁷ Before I was afflicted I went astray,
    but now I obey your word.
⁶⁸ You are good, and what you do is good;
    teach me your decrees.
⁶⁹ Though the arrogant have smeared me with lies,
    I keep your precepts with all my heart.
⁷⁰ Their hearts are callous and unfeeling,
    but I delight in your law.
⁷¹ It was good for me to be afflicted
    so that I might learn your decrees.
⁷² The law from your mouth is more precious to me
    than thousands of pieces of silver and gold.

י Yodh

⁷³ Your hands made me and formed me;
    give me understanding to learn your commands.
⁷⁴ May those who fear you rejoice when they see me,
    for I have put my hope in your word.
⁷⁵ I know, LORD, that your laws are righteous,
    and that in faithfulness you have afflicted me.
⁷⁶ May your unfailing love be my comfort,
    according to your promise to your servant.
⁷⁷ Let your compassion come to me that I may live,
    for your law is my delight.
⁷⁸ May the arrogant be put to shame for wronging me
        without cause;
    but I will meditate on your precepts.
⁷⁹ May those who fear you turn to me,
    those who understand your statutes.
⁸⁰ May I wholeheartedly follow your decrees,
    that I may not be put to shame.

How does affliction serve as a positive influence? (119:67) Before the psalmist faced difficulties, he went his own way rather than following God's law. After experiencing suffering and abuse, he understood how important it was to obey God's Word.

כ Kaph

⁸¹My soul faints with longing for your salvation,
  but I have put my hope in your word.
⁸²My eyes fail, looking for your promise;
  I say, "When will you comfort me?"
⁸³Though I am like a wineskin in the smoke,
  I do not forget your decrees.
⁸⁴How long must your servant wait?
  When will you punish my persecutors?
⁸⁵The arrogant dig pits to trap me,
  contrary to your law.
⁸⁶All your commands are trustworthy;
  help me, for I am being persecuted without cause.
⁸⁷They almost wiped me from the earth,
  but I have not forsaken your precepts.
⁸⁸In your unfailing love preserve my life,
  that I may obey the statutes of your mouth.

ל Lamedh

⁸⁹Your word, Lord, is eternal;
  it stands firm in the heavens.
⁹⁰Your faithfulness continues through
    all generations;
  you established the earth, and it endures.
⁹¹Your laws endure to this day,
  for all things serve you.
⁹²If your law had not been my delight,
  I would have perished in my affliction.
⁹³I will never forget your precepts,
  for by them you have preserved my life.
⁹⁴Save me, for I am yours;
  I have sought out your precepts.
⁹⁵The wicked are waiting to destroy me,
  but I will ponder your statutes.
⁹⁶To all perfection I see a limit,
  but your commands are boundless.

מ Mem

⁹⁷Oh, how I love your law!
  I meditate on it all day long.
⁹⁸Your commands are always with me
  and make me wiser than my enemies.
⁹⁹I have more insight than all my teachers,
  for I meditate on your statutes.
¹⁰⁰I have more understanding than the elders,
  for I obey your precepts.
¹⁰¹I have kept my feet from every evil path
  so that I might obey your word.
¹⁰²I have not departed from your laws,
  for you yourself have taught me.
¹⁰³How sweet are your words to my taste,
  sweeter than honey to my mouth!
¹⁰⁴I gain understanding from your precepts;
  therefore I hate every wrong path.

How was the psalmist like a wineskin in smoke? (119:83) A wineskin hung in the smoke and heat above a fire would become dirty and shriveled. This word picture illustrated that the author was being persecuted. Yet he refused to turn away from God and his laws.

How did God's law keep the psalmist going? (119:92) Because of his trust in God and commitment to keeping God's law, the psalmist was able to endure the affliction he suffered.

Was the psalmist being proud? (119:98–99) The author was not boasting about his own wisdom. He was saying the truth of God's law contains abundant wisdom.

נ Nun

105 Your word is a lamp for my feet,
    a light on my path.
106 I have taken an oath and confirmed it,
    that I will follow your righteous laws.
107 I have suffered much;
    preserve my life, LORD, according to
        your word.
108 Accept, LORD, the willing praise of my mouth,
    and teach me your laws.
109 Though I constantly take my life in my hands,
    I will not forget your law.
110 The wicked have set a snare for me,
    but I have not strayed from your precepts.
111 Your statutes are my heritage forever;
    they are the joy of my heart.
112 My heart is set on keeping your decrees
    to the very end.ᵃ

ס Samekh

113 I hate double-minded people,
    but I love your law.
114 You are my refuge and my shield;
    I have put my hope in your word.
115 Away from me, you evildoers,
    that I may keep the commands of my God!
116 Sustain me, my God, according to your promise,
        and I will live;
    do not let my hopes be dashed.
117 Uphold me, and I will be delivered;
    I will always have regard for your decrees.
118 You reject all who stray from your decrees,
    for their delusions come to nothing.
119 All the wicked of the earth you discard
        like dross;
    therefore I love your statutes.
120 My flesh trembles in fear of you;
    I stand in awe of your laws.

ע Ayin

121 I have done what is righteous and just;
    do not leave me to my oppressors.
122 Ensure your servant's well-being;
    do not let the arrogant oppress me.
123 My eyes fail, looking for your salvation,
    looking for your righteous promise.
124 Deal with your servant according to your love
    and teach me your decrees.
125 I am your servant; give me discernment
    that I may understand your statutes.
126 It is time for you to act, LORD;
    your law is being broken.

What does it mean to be double-minded? (119:113)
It means not making a commitment to one point of view or opinion.

What is dross? (119:119)
This is the worthless scum removed from precious metals like gold and silver when they are melted.

ᵃ 112 Or *decrees / for their enduring reward*

127 Because I love your commands
more than gold, more than pure gold,
128 and because I consider all your precepts right,
I hate every wrong path.

⊃ Pe

129 Your statutes are wonderful;
therefore I obey them.
130 The unfolding of your words gives light;
it gives understanding to the simple.
131 I open my mouth and pant,
longing for your commands.
132 Turn to me and have mercy on me,
as you always do to those who love your name.
133 Direct my footsteps according to your word;
let no sin rule over me.
134 Redeem me from human oppression,
that I may obey your precepts.
135 Make your face shine on your servant
and teach me your decrees.
136 Streams of tears flow from my eyes,
for your law is not obeyed.

צ Tsadhe

137 You are righteous, LORD,
and your laws are right.
138 The statutes you have laid down are righteous;
they are fully trustworthy.
139 My zeal wears me out,
for my enemies ignore your words.
140 Your promises have been thoroughly tested,
and your servant loves them.
141 Though I am lowly and despised,
I do not forget your precepts.
142 Your righteousness is everlasting
and your law is true.
143 Trouble and distress have come upon me,
but your commands give me delight.
144 Your statutes are always righteous;
give me understanding that I may live.

ק Qoph

145 I call with all my heart; answer me, LORD,
and I will obey your decrees.
146 I call out to you; save me
and I will keep your statutes.
147 I rise before dawn and cry for help;
I have put my hope in your word.
148 My eyes stay open through the watches of the night,
that I may meditate on your promises.
149 Hear my voice in accordance with your love;
preserve my life, LORD, according to your laws.
150 Those who devise wicked schemes are near,
but they are far from your law.

What were the watches of the night? (119:148)
These were the divisions into which the 12 hours of darkness were divided. The Israelites divided night into three watches, from 6:00 until 10:00 P.M., from 10:00 until 2:00 A.M., and from 2:00 until 6:00 A.M.

¹⁵¹ Yet you are near, Lord,
     and all your commands are true.
¹⁵² Long ago I learned from your statutes
     that you established them to last forever.

ר Resh

¹⁵³ Look on my suffering and deliver me,
     for I have not forgotten your law.
¹⁵⁴ Defend my cause and redeem me;
     preserve my life according to your promise.
¹⁵⁵ Salvation is far from the wicked,
     for they do not seek out your decrees.
¹⁵⁶ Your compassion, Lord, is great;
     preserve my life according to your laws.
¹⁵⁷ Many are the foes who persecute me,
     but I have not turned from your statutes.
¹⁵⁸ I look on the faithless with loathing,
     for they do not obey your word.
¹⁵⁹ See how I love your precepts;
     preserve my life, Lord, in accordance with your love.
¹⁶⁰ All your words are true;
     all your righteous laws are eternal.

ש Sin and Shin

¹⁶¹ Rulers persecute me without cause,
     but my heart trembles at your word.
¹⁶² I rejoice in your promise
     like one who finds great spoil.
¹⁶³ I hate and detest falsehood
     but I love your law.
¹⁶⁴ Seven times a day I praise you
     for your righteous laws.
¹⁶⁵ Great peace have those who love your law,
     and nothing can make them stumble.
¹⁶⁶ I wait for your salvation, Lord,
     and I follow your commands.
¹⁶⁷ I obey your statutes,
     for I love them greatly.
¹⁶⁸ I obey your precepts and your statutes,
     for all my ways are known to you.

ת Taw

¹⁶⁹ May my cry come before you, Lord;
     give me understanding according to your word.
¹⁷⁰ May my supplication come before you;
     deliver me according to your promise.
¹⁷¹ May my lips overflow with praise,
     for you teach me your decrees.
¹⁷² May my tongue sing of your word,
     for all your commands are righteous.
¹⁷³ May your hand be ready to help me,
     for I have chosen your precepts.
¹⁷⁴ I long for your salvation, Lord,
     and your law gives me delight.

How was God's Word like great spoil? (119:162)
The psalmist used the word picture of a soldier who won a battle and was able to carry away the treasure or spoils. To him, God's Word was a great treasure.

Why did the psalmist praise God seven times each day? (119:164)
The number seven represented completeness or perfection. The author implied that he praised God throughout the entire day.

¹⁷⁵ Let me live that I may praise you,
    and may your laws sustain me.
¹⁷⁶ I have strayed like a lost sheep.
    Seek your servant,
    for I have not forgotten your commands.

PSALM 120

A song of ascents.

¹ I call on the LORD in my distress,
    and he answers me.
² Save me, LORD,
    from lying lips
    and from deceitful tongues.

³ What will he do to you,
    and what more besides,
    you deceitful tongue?
⁴ He will punish you with a warrior's sharp arrows,
    with burning coals of the broom bush.

⁵ Woe to me that I dwell in Meshek,
    that I live among the tents of Kedar!
⁶ Too long have I lived
    among those who hate peace.
⁷ I am for peace;
    but when I speak, they are for war.

PSALM 121

A song of ascents.

¹ I lift up my eyes to the mountains—
    where does my help come from?
² My help comes from the LORD,
    the Maker of heaven and earth.

³ He will not let your foot slip—
    he who watches over you will not slumber;
⁴ indeed, he who watches over Israel
    will neither slumber nor sleep.

⁵ The LORD watches over you—
    the LORD is your shade at your right hand;
⁶ the sun will not harm you by day,
    nor the moon by night.

⁷ The LORD will keep you from all harm—
    he will watch over your life;
⁸ the LORD will watch over your coming and going
    both now and forevermore.

PSALM 122

A song of ascents. Of David.

¹ I rejoiced with those who said to me,
    "Let us go to the house of the LORD."
² Our feet are standing
    in your gates, Jerusalem.

How could someone who loved God's law stray like a lost sheep? (119:176)
The author was honest about the fact that he could not keep God's law perfectly. That is why he asked God to help him obey his commandments.

What was a song of ascents? (120)
Most scholars think this refers to a song the pilgrims sang as they made their way each year to the temple to offer sacrifices.

Why did the people lift their eyes to the mountains? (121:1)
Pagans used hilltops as a place to build their shrines and altars. As the pilgrims traveled to Jerusalem, they could see the hills around the city. The psalmist was reminded that his help came from God, not from idols.

³Jerusalem is built like a city
  that is closely compacted together.
⁴That is where the tribes go up—
  the tribes of the LORD—
to praise the name of the LORD
  according to the statute given to Israel.
⁵There stand the thrones for judgment,
  the thrones of the house of David.

⁶Pray for the peace of Jerusalem:
  "May those who love you be secure.
⁷May there be peace within your walls
  and security within your citadels."
⁸For the sake of my family and friends,
  I will say, "Peace be within you."
⁹For the sake of the house of the LORD our God,
  I will seek your prosperity.

What were the thrones for judgment? (122:5)
Jerusalem was the city where people went to worship. Pilgrimages were made three times annually, during the Festivals of Passover, Firstfruits, and Tabernacles. But Jerusalem was also the royal city of David, from which he governed the people and administered justice.

PSALM 123

A song of ascents.

¹I lift up my eyes to you,
  to you who sit enthroned in heaven.
²As the eyes of slaves look to the hand of their master,
  as the eyes of a female slave look to the hand of
    her mistress,
so our eyes look to the LORD our God,
  till he shows us his mercy.

³Have mercy on us, LORD, have mercy on us,
  for we have endured no end of contempt.
⁴We have endured no end
  of ridicule from the arrogant,
  of contempt from the proud.

Are we God's slaves? (123:2)
This is a comparison that emphasizes how people are humbly dependent on God. It does not imply that God is a harsh master; rather, he is loving and kind.

PSALM 124

A song of ascents. Of David.

¹If the LORD had not been on our side—
  let Israel say—
²if the LORD had not been on our side
  when people attacked us,
³they would have swallowed us alive
  when their anger flared against us;
⁴the flood would have engulfed us,
  the torrent would have swept over us,
⁵the raging waters
  would have swept us away.

⁶Praise be to the LORD,
  who has not let us be torn by their teeth.
⁷We have escaped like a bird
  from the fowler's snare;
the snare has been broken,
  and we have escaped.
⁸Our help is in the name of the LORD,
  the Maker of heaven and earth.

What was a fowler's snare? (124:7)
A fowler was a bird hunter, who used a snare to trap birds. This word picture showed how the Israelites escaped from captivity in Babylon.

PSALM 125

A song of ascents.

¹Those who trust in the LORD are like Mount Zion,
  which cannot be shaken but endures forever.
²As the mountains surround Jerusalem,
  so the LORD surrounds his people
  both now and forevermore.

³The scepter of the wicked will not remain
  over the land allotted to the righteous,
for then the righteous might use
  their hands to do evil.

⁴LORD, do good to those who are good,
  to those who are upright in heart.
⁵But those who turn to crooked ways
  the LORD will banish with the evildoers.

Peace be on Israel.

PSALM 126

A song of ascents.

¹When the LORD restored the fortunes of*ª* Zion,
  we were like those who dreamed.*ᵇ*
²Our mouths were filled with laughter,
  our tongues with songs of joy.
Then it was said among the nations,
  "The LORD has done great things for them."
³The LORD has done great things for us,
  and we are filled with joy.

⁴Restore our fortunes,*ᶜ* LORD,
  like streams in the Negev.
⁵Those who sow with tears
  will reap with songs of joy.
⁶Those who go out weeping,
  carrying seed to sow,
will return with songs of joy,
  carrying sheaves with them.

PSALM 127

A song of ascents. Of Solomon.

¹Unless the LORD builds the house,
  the builders labor in vain.
Unless the LORD watches over the city,
  the guards stand watch in vain.
²In vain you rise early
  and stay up late,
toiling for food to eat—
  for he grants sleep to*ᵈ* those he loves.

³Children are a heritage from the LORD,
  offspring a reward from him.

Is Jerusalem surrounded by mountains? (125:2)
Jerusalem is not completely surrounded by a ring of mountains, but it is in a mountainous region that protected the city in the same way God protects his people.

Why would people weep while planting seeds? (126:5–6)
When there was no rain, people were worried because they had no idea if the seeds would grow or produce a harvest. But the psalm reminded people that God provided blessings even when it didn't seem likely to happen.

ª 1 Or LORD brought back the captives to   *ᵇ 1 Or those restored to health*
ᶜ 4 Or Bring back our captives   *ᵈ 2 Or eat— / for while they sleep he provides for*

Why were children seen as a blessing? (127:3–5)
Having many children meant that parents would be cared for when they were old. Also, the ability to provide for a large family meant a family had been blessed by God. And children would be able to inherit their parents' land to keep it in the family.

What did the vine and olive shoots symbolize? (128:3)
These were symbols of long life and productivity. The grapevines and olive shoots produced the wine and oil that played such an important role in the people's meals. Having a wife and children was seen as a similar blessing.

Why did grass wither on a roof? (129:6)
Grass that grew on flat roofs in the hot sun would wither and die. This verse asked that the same fate would happen to the enemies of Israel.

⁴Like arrows in the hands of a warrior
  are children born in one's youth.
⁵Blessed is the man
  whose quiver is full of them.
 They will not be put to shame
  when they contend with their opponents in court.

PSALM 128

A song of ascents.

¹Blessed are all who fear the Lord,
  who walk in obedience to him.
²You will eat the fruit of your labor;
  blessings and prosperity will be yours.
³Your wife will be like a fruitful vine
  within your house;
 your children will be like olive shoots
  around your table.
⁴Yes, this will be the blessing
  for the man who fears the Lord.

⁵May the Lord bless you from Zion;
  may you see the prosperity of Jerusalem
  all the days of your life.
⁶May you live to see your children's children—
  peace be on Israel.

PSALM 129

A song of ascents.

¹"They have greatly oppressed me from my youth,"
  let Israel say;
²"they have greatly oppressed me from my youth,
  but they have not gained the victory over me.
³Plowmen have plowed my back
  and made their furrows long.
⁴But the Lord is righteous;
  he has cut me free from the cords of the wicked."

⁵May all who hate Zion
  be turned back in shame.
⁶May they be like grass on the roof,
  which withers before it can grow;
⁷a reaper cannot fill his hands with it,
  nor one who gathers fill his arms.
⁸May those who pass by not say to them,
  "The blessing of the Lord be on you;
  we bless you in the name of the Lord."

PSALM 130

A song of ascents.

¹Out of the depths I cry to you, Lord;
² Lord, hear my voice.

Let your ears be attentive
  to my cry for mercy.
[3] If you, LORD, kept a record of sins,
  Lord, who could stand?
[4] But with you there is forgiveness,
  so that we can, with reverence, serve you.

[5] I wait for the LORD, my whole being waits,
  and in his word I put my hope.
[6] I wait for the Lord
  more than watchmen wait for the morning,
  more than watchmen wait for the morning.

[7] Israel, put your hope in the LORD,
  for with the LORD is unfailing love
  and with him is full redemption.
[8] He himself will redeem Israel
  from all their sins.

PSALM 131

A song of ascents. Of David.

[1] My heart is not proud, LORD,
  my eyes are not haughty;
  I do not concern myself with great matters
  or things too wonderful for me.
[2] But I have calmed and quieted myself,
  I am like a weaned child with its mother;
  like a weaned child I am content.

[3] Israel, put your hope in the LORD
  both now and forevermore.

PSALM 132

A song of ascents.

[1] LORD, remember David
  and all his self-denial.

[2] He swore an oath to the LORD,
  he made a vow to the Mighty One of Jacob:
[3] "I will not enter my house
  or go to my bed,
[4] I will allow no sleep to my eyes
  or slumber to my eyelids,
[5] till I find a place for the LORD,
  a dwelling for the Mighty One of Jacob."

[6] We heard it in Ephrathah,
  we came upon it in the fields of Jaar:[a]
[7] "Let us go to his dwelling place,
  let us worship at his footstool, saying,
[8] 'Arise, LORD, and come to your resting place,
  you and the ark of your might.

---

*a 6 Or heard of it in Ephrathah, / we found it in the fields of Jearim. (See
1 Chron. 13:5,6) (And no quotation marks around verses 7-9)*

**Why didn't God keep a
record of sins? (130:3–4)**
God does keep a record, but he
was quick to forgive people's
sins if they repented and offered
sacrifices.

**How was David calmed like
a weaned child? (131:2)**
A weaned child was mature
enough to speak and ask for food
or drink, so he or she wouldn't
have to cry to obtain food. David
learned that he could depend on
God and not always have to cry
out for help.

**Where were Ephrathah and
Jaar? (132:6)**
Ephrathah was a region around
Bethlehem, David's hometown.
Jaar was another name for
Kiriath Jearim, where the ark
was kept after the Philistines
returned it (see 1 Samuel 7:1).

⁹May your priests be clothed with your righteousness;
  may your faithful people sing for joy.'"

¹⁰For the sake of your servant David,
  do not reject your anointed one.

¹¹The LORD swore an oath to David,
  a sure oath he will not revoke:
"One of your own descendants
  I will place on your throne.
¹²If your sons keep my covenant
  and the statutes I teach them,
then their sons will sit
  on your throne for ever and ever."

¹³For the LORD has chosen Zion,
  he has desired it for his dwelling, saying,
¹⁴"This is my resting place for ever and ever;
  here I will sit enthroned, for I have desired it.
¹⁵I will bless her with abundant provisions;
  her poor I will satisfy with food.
¹⁶I will clothe her priests with salvation,
  and her faithful people will ever sing for joy.

¹⁷"Here I will make a horn*ᵃ* grow for David
  and set up a lamp for my anointed one.
¹⁸I will clothe his enemies with shame,
  but his head will be adorned with a
    radiant crown."

PSALM 133

A song of ascents. Of David.

¹How good and pleasant it is
  when God's people live together in unity!

²It is like precious oil poured on the head,
  running down on the beard,
running down on Aaron's beard,
  down on the collar of his robe.
³It is as if the dew of Hermon
  were falling on Mount Zion.
For there the LORD bestows his blessing,
  even life forevermore.

PSALM 134

A song of ascents.

¹Praise the LORD, all you servants of the LORD
  who minister by night in the house of
    the LORD.
²Lift up your hands in the sanctuary
  and praise the LORD.

³May the LORD bless you from Zion,
  he who is the Maker of heaven and earth.

ᵃ *17 Horn* here symbolizes strong one, that is, king.

What was this horn? (132:17)
The horn symbolized the strong king, God's anointed one.

What was precious oil? (133:2)
This was the oil poured on Aaron's head when he was anointed as priest (Exodus 29:7; Leviticus 21:10). The oil completely covered his beard and clothing. This symbolized a joyous occasion.

What servants of the LORD worked at night? (134:1)
Some of the Levites served God in the temple day and night keeping the altar fire and lampstands burning.

PSALM 135

[1] Praise the LORD.[a]

Praise the name of the LORD;
  praise him, you servants of the LORD,
[2] you who minister in the house of the LORD,
  in the courts of the house of our God.

[3] Praise the LORD, for the LORD is good;
  sing praise to his name, for that is pleasant.
[4] For the LORD has chosen Jacob to be his own,
  Israel to be his treasured possession.

[5] I know that the LORD is great,
  that our Lord is greater than all gods.
[6] The LORD does whatever pleases him,
  in the heavens and on the earth,
  in the seas and all their depths.
[7] He makes clouds rise from the ends of the earth;
  he sends lightning with the rain
  and brings out the wind from his storehouses.

[8] He struck down the firstborn of Egypt,
  the firstborn of people and animals.
[9] He sent his signs and wonders into your
    midst, Egypt,
  against Pharaoh and all his servants.
[10] He struck down many nations
  and killed mighty kings—
[11] Sihon king of the Amorites,
  Og king of Bashan,
  and all the kings of Canaan—
[12] and he gave their land as an inheritance,
  an inheritance to his people Israel.

[13] Your name, LORD, endures forever,
  your renown, LORD, through all generations.
[14] For the LORD will vindicate his people
  and have compassion on his servants.

[15] The idols of the nations are silver and gold,
  made by human hands.
[16] They have mouths, but cannot speak,
  eyes, but cannot see.
[17] They have ears, but cannot hear,
  nor is there breath in their mouths.
[18] Those who make them will be like them,
  and so will all who trust in them.

[19] All you Israelites, praise the LORD;
  house of Aaron, praise the LORD;
[20] house of Levi, praise the LORD;
  you who fear him, praise the LORD.
[21] Praise be to the LORD from Zion,
  to him who dwells in Jerusalem.

Praise the LORD.

---

[a] 1 Hebrew *Hallelu Yah*; also in verses 3 and 21

Why were the heavens, earth, and seas mentioned? (135:6)
Ancient people saw these as the three visible domains of creation.

What type of psalm was this? (136)
This was a liturgy of praise to the LORD as the Creator and as Israel's Redeemer. It is likely that a Levitical song leader led the recital, and the Levitical choir or worshipers answered with the refrain.

What mighty deeds does the psalm record? (136)
The psalm begins with God's creation of the universe and then moves to Israel's release from Egypt and the people's conquer of the promised land.

PSALM 136

¹ Give thanks to the LORD, for he is good.
His love endures forever.
² Give thanks to the God of gods.
His love endures forever.
³ Give thanks to the Lord of lords:
His love endures forever.

⁴ to him who alone does great wonders,
His love endures forever.
⁵ who by his understanding made the heavens,
His love endures forever.
⁶ who spread out the earth upon the waters,
His love endures forever.
⁷ who made the great lights—
His love endures forever.
⁸ the sun to govern the day,
His love endures forever.
⁹ the moon and stars to govern the night;
His love endures forever.

¹⁰ to him who struck down the firstborn of Egypt
His love endures forever.
¹¹ and brought Israel out from among them
His love endures forever.
¹² with a mighty hand and outstretched arm;
His love endures forever.

¹³ to him who divided the Red Sea*a* asunder
His love endures forever.
¹⁴ and brought Israel through the midst of it,
His love endures forever.
¹⁵ but swept Pharaoh and his army into the
Red Sea;
His love endures forever.

¹⁶ to him who led his people through the wilderness;
His love endures forever.

¹⁷ to him who struck down great kings,
His love endures forever.
¹⁸ and killed mighty kings—
His love endures forever.
¹⁹ Sihon king of the Amorites
His love endures forever.
²⁰ and Og king of Bashan—
His love endures forever.
²¹ and gave their land as an inheritance,
His love endures forever.
²² an inheritance to his servant Israel.
His love endures forever.

²³ He remembered us in our low estate
His love endures forever.
²⁴ and freed us from our enemies.
His love endures forever.

a 13 Or the Sea of Reeds; also in verse 15

²⁵ He gives food to every creature.
His love endures forever.

²⁶ Give thanks to the God of heaven.
His love endures forever.

PSALM 137

¹ By the rivers of Babylon we sat and wept
when we remembered Zion.
² There on the poplars
we hung our harps,
³ for there our captors asked us for songs,
our tormentors demanded songs of joy;
they said, "Sing us one of the songs of Zion!"

⁴ How can we sing the songs of the LORD
while in a foreign land?
⁵ If I forget you, Jerusalem,
may my right hand forget its skill.
⁶ May my tongue cling to the roof of my mouth
if I do not remember you,
if I do not consider Jerusalem
my highest joy.

⁷ Remember, LORD, what the Edomites did
on the day Jerusalem fell.
"Tear it down," they cried,
"tear it down to its foundations!"
⁸ Daughter Babylon, doomed to destruction,
happy is the one who repays you
according to what you have done to us.
⁹ Happy is the one who seizes your infants
and dashes them against the rocks.

PSALM 138

Of David.

¹ I will praise you, LORD, with all my heart;
before the "gods" I will sing your praise.
² I will bow down toward your holy temple
and will praise your name
for your unfailing love and your faithfulness,
for you have so exalted your solemn decree
that it surpasses your fame.
³ When I called, you answered me;
you greatly emboldened me.

⁴ May all the kings of the earth praise you, LORD,
when they hear what you have decreed.
⁵ May they sing of the ways of the LORD,
for the glory of the LORD is great.

⁶ Though the LORD is exalted, he looks kindly
on the lowly;
though lofty, he sees them from afar.

What rivers were these? (137:1)
These were the Tigris and Euphrates Rivers and the waterways that fed into them in Babylon.

Why did they hang up their harps? (137:2–4)
The Babylonians wanted them to sing joyful songs of Zion, but the captives were so unhappy about being in a foreign land that they did not want to provide entertainment for their captors.

How had God exalted his solemn decree? (138:2)
God's answers to prayer made his name and promises more valuable than anything else a king might possess.

⁷Though I walk in the midst of trouble,
  you preserve my life.
You stretch out your hand against the anger
    of my foes;
  with your right hand you save me.
⁸The Lord will vindicate me;
  your love, Lord, endures forever—
  do not abandon the works of your hands.

PSALM 139

For the director of music. Of David. A psalm.

¹You have searched me, Lord,
  and you know me.
²You know when I sit and when I rise;
  you perceive my thoughts from afar.
³You discern my going out and my lying down;
  you are familiar with all my ways.
⁴Before a word is on my tongue
  you, Lord, know it completely.
⁵You hem me in behind and before,
  and you lay your hand upon me.
⁶Such knowledge is too wonderful for me,
  too lofty for me to attain.

⁷Where can I go from your Spirit?
  Where can I flee from your presence?
⁸If I go up to the heavens, you are there;
  if I make my bed in the depths, you are there.
⁹If I rise on the wings of the dawn,
  if I settle on the far side of the sea,
¹⁰even there your hand will guide me,
  your right hand will hold me fast.
¹¹If I say, "Surely the darkness will hide me
  and the light become night around me,"
¹²even the darkness will not be dark to you;
  the night will shine like the day,
  for darkness is as light to you.

¹³For you created my inmost being;
  you knit me together in my mother's womb.

What were the wings of the dawn and the far side of the sea? (139:9)
These were poetic ways to express the east (the sunrise) and the west (the Mediterranean Sea) and the great distance between them.

Does God create each unborn child?   PSALM 139

God is the Creator of life, but today there are more options available to people than ever before. For example, couples who have difficulty conceiving children can opt for adoption, surrogacy, artificial insemination, or in vitro fertilization. Are these methods appropriate, or are people taking over God's role?

Other people want to avoid or postpone having children, so they use various birth control methods. Are all of these methods appropriate for Christians?

These ethical questions are debated by Christians and non-Christians, but the important principle to remember is that God is the one who gives life. This psalm talks about the fact that God knows everything about us right from the moment that we are conceived. It also praises God for how wonderful and amazing his creation of human beings is. Even though believers may have different opinions about methods of becoming pregnant or preventing pregnancy, they can agree that God is the one who gives life, and his gift of life should be respected.

¹⁴ I praise you because I am fearfully and wonderfully
        made;
    your works are wonderful,
    I know that full well.
¹⁵ My frame was not hidden from you
    when I was made in the secret place,
    when I was woven together in the depths of the earth.
¹⁶ Your eyes saw my unformed body;
    all the days ordained for me were written in your
        book
    before one of them came to be.
¹⁷ How precious to me are your thoughts,ᵃ God!
    How vast is the sum of them!
¹⁸ Were I to count them,
    they would outnumber the grains of sand—
    when I awake, I am still with you.

¹⁹ If only you, God, would slay the wicked!
    Away from me, you who are bloodthirsty!
²⁰ They speak of you with evil intent;
    your adversaries misuse your name.
²¹ Do I not hate those who hate you, Lord,
    and abhor those who are in rebellion against you?
²² I have nothing but hatred for them;
    I count them my enemies.
²³ Search me, God, and know my heart;
    test me and know my anxious thoughts.
²⁴ See if there is any offensive way in me,
    and lead me in the way everlasting.

PSALM 140ᵇ

For the director of music. A psalm of David.

¹ Rescue me, Lord, from evildoers;
    protect me from the violent,
² who devise evil plans in their hearts
    and stir up war every day.
³ They make their tongues as sharp as a serpent's;
    the poison of vipers is on their lips.ᶜ

⁴ Keep me safe, Lord, from the hands of the wicked;
    protect me from the violent,
    who devise ways to trip my feet.
⁵ The arrogant have hidden a snare for me;
    they have spread out the cords of their net
    and have set traps for me along my path.

⁶ I say to the Lord, "You are my God."
    Hear, Lord, my cry for mercy.
⁷ Sovereign Lord, my strong deliverer,
    you shield my head in the day of battle.
⁸ Do not grant the wicked their desires, Lord;
    do not let their plans succeed.

What was the secret place? (139:15)
This is a description of the womb. It is like the depths of the earth because it is a dark place absent of light.

What type of pledge was this? (139:21–22)
These verses echo a pledge of loyalty ancient kings required of their vassals. For example, one such pledge said, "With my friend you shall be friend, and with my enemy you shall be enemy."

Why was this psalm written? (140)
This was a prayer that God would rescue the psalmist from the plots and slanders of unscrupulous people. The psalm includes many references to body parts: head, heart, tongue, lips, hands, feet, ears, and teeth.

ᵃ 17 Or *How amazing are your thoughts concerning me*   ᵇ In Hebrew texts
140:1-13 is numbered 140:2-14.   ᶜ 3 The Hebrew has *Selah* (a word of
uncertain meaning) here and at the end of verses 5 and 8.

⁹Those who surround me proudly rear their heads;
  may the mischief of their lips engulf them.
¹⁰May burning coals fall on them;
  may they be thrown into the fire,
  into miry pits, never to rise.
¹¹May slanderers not be established in the land;
  may disaster hunt down the violent.

¹²I know that the LORD secures justice for the poor
  and upholds the cause of the needy.
¹³Surely the righteous will praise your name,
  and the upright will live in your presence.

PSALM 141

A psalm of David.

¹I call to you, LORD, come quickly to me;
  hear me when I call to you.
²May my prayer be set before you like incense;
  may the lifting up of my hands be like the
    evening sacrifice.

³Set a guard over my mouth, LORD;
  keep watch over the door of my lips.
⁴Do not let my heart be drawn to what is evil
  so that I take part in wicked deeds
along with those who are evildoers;
  do not let me eat their delicacies.

⁵Let a righteous man strike me—that is a kindness;
  let him rebuke me—that is oil on my head.
My head will not refuse it,
  for my prayer will still be against the deeds
    of evildoers.

⁶Their rulers will be thrown down from the cliffs,
  and the wicked will learn that my words were
    well spoken.
⁷They will say, "As one plows and breaks up the earth,
  so our bones have been scattered at the mouth
    of the grave."

⁸But my eyes are fixed on you, Sovereign LORD;
  in you I take refuge—do not give me over to death.
⁹Keep me safe from the traps set by evildoers,
  from the snares they have laid for me.
¹⁰Let the wicked fall into their own nets,
  while I pass by in safety.

PSALM 142[a]

A maskil[b] of David. When he was in the cave. A prayer.

¹I cry aloud to the LORD;
  I lift up my voice to the LORD for mercy.

How did David want to be protected from evil? (141:3–4)
He asked God to keep him from speaking, desiring, or doing what was evil.

Why would it be a kindness for a righteous man to strike David? (141:5)
If a righteous person corrected or disciplined him so that he would avoid evil, it would be a great kindness.

Why was David in a cave? (142: title)
David may have written this psalm while he was hiding in a cave from Saul (see 1 Samuel 22:1).

---

[a] In Hebrew texts 142:1-7 is numbered 142:2-8. [b] Title: Probably a literary or musical term

² I pour out before him my complaint;
  before him I tell my trouble.

³ When my spirit grows faint within me,
  it is you who watch over my way.
In the path where I walk
  people have hidden a snare for me.
⁴ Look and see, there is no one at my right hand;
  no one is concerned for me.
I have no refuge;
  no one cares for my life.

⁵ I cry to you, LORD;
  I say, "You are my refuge,
  my portion in the land of the living."

⁶ Listen to my cry,
  for I am in desperate need;
rescue me from those who pursue me,
  for they are too strong for me.
⁷ Set me free from my prison,
  that I may praise your name.
Then the righteous will gather about me
  because of your goodness to me.

PSALM 143

A psalm of David.

¹ LORD, hear my prayer,
  listen to my cry for mercy;
in your faithfulness and righteousness
  come to my relief.
² Do not bring your servant into judgment,
  for no one living is righteous before you.
³ The enemy pursues me,
  he crushes me to the ground;
he makes me dwell in the darkness
  like those long dead.
⁴ So my spirit grows faint within me;
  my heart within me is dismayed.

How can I know God's will for my life? How does God speak to people today?
PSALM 143

Psalm 143:10 says, "Teach me to do your will, for you are my God; may your good Spirit lead me on level ground." In Bible times God often spoke directly to people or sent messengers such as angels to communicate with people. But today that is not God's typical way of communicating with his people.

Instead, God has given us the Bible, which records his dealings with people throughout history. But the Bible doesn't answer all of our specific questions, like what career should I choose? Or whom should I marry? The Bible sets out general principles for believers, but it doesn't give advice for our specific situations. God wants us to pray about our questions, and his Holy Spirit will help us discover answers. God also wants us to seek advice from mature Christians, who can often see our situation from a more objective perspective.

Some Christians say, "God told me that he wants me to do this thing or that thing." We should be very careful about making statements like that. Rather, we should be humble and admit that we are not always completely sure of what God wants us to do, even though we may have a strong sense of leading from the Bible, the Holy Spirit, and mature Christian mentors.

How did remembering the past encourage him? (143:5–6)
When David remembered the many ways God had delivered him in the past, he was encouraged to ask for help in his present situation.

When would morning come? (143:8)
Morning symbolized salvation from the psalmist's present darkness (verse 3).

⁵I remember the days of long ago;
    I meditate on all your works
    and consider what your hands have done.
⁶I spread out my hands to you;
    I thirst for you like a parched land.ᵃ

⁷Answer me quickly, LORD;
    my spirit fails.
Do not hide your face from me
    or I will be like those who go down to the pit.
⁸Let the morning bring me word of your unfailing love,
    for I have put my trust in you.
Show me the way I should go,
    for to you I entrust my life.
⁹Rescue me from my enemies, LORD,
    for I hide myself in you.
¹⁰Teach me to do your will,
    for you are my God;
may your good Spirit
    lead me on level ground.

¹¹For your name's sake, LORD, preserve my life;
    in your righteousness, bring me out of trouble.
¹²In your unfailing love, silence my enemies;
    destroy all my foes,
    for I am your servant.

PSALM 144

Of David.

¹Praise be to the LORD my Rock,
    who trains my hands for war,
    my fingers for battle.
²He is my loving God and my fortress,
    my stronghold and my deliverer,
my shield, in whom I take refuge,
    who subdues peoplesᵇ under me.

How did David describe human beings? (144:3–4)
He described them as being insignificant, like a puff of air or a shadow that lasts only briefly.

What was a ten-stringed lyre? (144:9)
This was an instrument made of wood. It may have looked something like a guitar and been played like a harp.

Musical Instruments

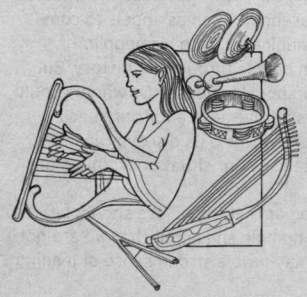

³LORD, what are human beings that you care for them,
    mere mortals that you think of them?
⁴They are like a breath;
    their days are like a fleeting shadow.

⁵Part your heavens, LORD, and come down;
    touch the mountains, so that they smoke.
⁶Send forth lightning and scatter the enemy;
    shoot your arrows and rout them.
⁷Reach down your hand from on high;
    deliver me and rescue me
from the mighty waters,
    from the hands of foreigners
⁸whose mouths are full of lies,
    whose right hands are deceitful.

⁹I will sing a new song to you, my God;
    on the ten-stringed lyre I will make music to you,

ᵃ 6 The Hebrew has *Selah* (a word of uncertain meaning) here.   ᵇ 2 Many manuscripts of the Masoretic Text, Dead Sea Scrolls, Aquila, Jerome and Syriac; most manuscripts of the Masoretic Text *subdues my people*

¹⁰ to the One who gives victory to kings,
    who delivers his servant David.

From the deadly sword ¹¹ deliver me;
    rescue me from the hands of foreigners
whose mouths are full of lies,
    whose right hands are deceitful.

¹² Then our sons in their youth
    will be like well-nurtured plants,
and our daughters will be like pillars
    carved to adorn a palace.
¹³ Our barns will be filled
    with every kind of provision.
Our sheep will increase by thousands,
    by tens of thousands in our fields;
¹⁴ our oxen will draw heavy loads.ᵃ
There will be no breaching of walls,
    no going into captivity,
    no cry of distress in our streets.
¹⁵ Blessed is the people of whom this is true;
    blessed is the people whose God is the LORD.

PSALM 145ᵇ

A psalm of praise. Of David.

¹ I will exalt you, my God the King;
    I will praise your name for ever and ever.
² Every day I will praise you
    and extol your name for ever and ever.
³ Great is the LORD and most worthy of praise;
    his greatness no one can fathom.
⁴ One generation commends your works to another;
    they tell of your mighty acts.
⁵ They speak of the glorious splendor of your majesty—
    and I will meditate on your wonderful works.ᶜ
⁶ They tell of the power of your awesome works—
    and I will proclaim your great deeds.
⁷ They celebrate your abundant goodness
    and joyfully sing of your righteousness.

⁸ The LORD is gracious and compassionate,
    slow to anger and rich in love.

⁹ The LORD is good to all;
    he has compassion on all he has made.
¹⁰ All your works praise you, LORD;
    your faithful people extol you.
¹¹ They tell of the glory of your kingdom
    and speak of your might,
¹² so that all people may know of your mighty acts
    and the glorious splendor of your kingdom.

How were daughters like pillars? (144:12)
In the ancient world, it was not uncommon for temple columns to be carved in the shape of women.

ᵃ 14 Or *our chieftains will be firmly established*   ᵇ This psalm is an acrostic poem, the verses of which (including verse 13b) begin with the successive letters of the Hebrew alphabet.   ᶜ 5 Dead Sea Scrolls and Syriac (see also Septuagint); Masoretic Text *On the glorious splendor of your majesty / and on your wonderful works I will meditate*

How was God's kingdom an everlasting kingdom? (145:13)
David realized that God was king above all human kings. Even though human kings would die, God would continue to rule the earth.

Does God provide everyone with what they need at all times? (145:14–16)
No. Many people experience sorrow, illness, or hunger. The psalmist was painting a picture of God's marvelous goodness, but he was not saying that people never experience hardships. We can understand these statements about God to be true in spiritual and eternal ways if not always in physical ways.

Why should people not put trust in human beings? (146:3–4)
People should not place their ultimate trust in human beings who are unable to save. Instead, they should trust in God, who is able to grant salvation.

Why were these categories of people mentioned? (146:7–9)
The psalmist wanted to emphasize that God does not only help the rich and powerful. Rather, he takes special care of those who are weak, poor, or on the fringes of society.

13 Your kingdom is an everlasting kingdom,
and your dominion endures through all generations.

The Lord is trustworthy in all he promises
and faithful in all he does. [a]
14 The Lord upholds all who fall
and lifts up all who are bowed down.
15 The eyes of all look to you,
and you give them their food at the proper time.
16 You open your hand
and satisfy the desires of every living thing.

17 The Lord is righteous in all his ways
and faithful in all he does.
18 The Lord is near to all who call on him,
to all who call on him in truth.
19 He fulfills the desires of those who fear him;
he hears their cry and saves them.
20 The Lord watches over all who love him,
but all the wicked he will destroy.

21 My mouth will speak in praise of the Lord.
Let every creature praise his holy name
for ever and ever.

PSALM 146

1 Praise the Lord. [b]

Praise the Lord, my soul.

2 I will praise the Lord all my life;
I will sing praise to my God as long as I live.
3 Do not put your trust in princes,
in human beings, who cannot save.
4 When their spirit departs, they return to the ground;
on that very day their plans come to nothing.
5 Blessed are those whose help is the God of Jacob,
whose hope is in the Lord their God.

6 He is the Maker of heaven and earth,
the sea, and everything in them—
he remains faithful forever.
7 He upholds the cause of the oppressed
and gives food to the hungry.
The Lord sets prisoners free,
8 the Lord gives sight to the blind,
the Lord lifts up those who are bowed down,
the Lord loves the righteous.
9 The Lord watches over the foreigner
and sustains the fatherless and the widow,
but he frustrates the ways of the wicked.

10 The Lord reigns forever,
your God, O Zion, for all generations.

Praise the Lord.

a 13 One manuscript of the Masoretic Text, Dead Sea Scrolls and Syriac (see also Septuagint); most manuscripts of the Masoretic Text do not have the last two lines of verse 13.   b 1 Hebrew Hallelu Yah; also in verse 10

PSALM 147

[1] Praise the LORD.[a]

How good it is to sing praises to our God,
how pleasant and fitting to praise him!

[2] The LORD builds up Jerusalem;
he gathers the exiles of Israel.
[3] He heals the brokenhearted
and binds up their wounds.
[4] He determines the number of the stars
and calls them each by name.
[5] Great is our Lord and mighty in power;
his understanding has no limit.
[6] The LORD sustains the humble
but casts the wicked to the ground.

[7] Sing to the LORD with grateful praise;
make music to our God on the harp.

[8] He covers the sky with clouds;
he supplies the earth with rain
and makes grass grow on the hills.
[9] He provides food for the cattle
and for the young ravens when they call.

[10] His pleasure is not in the strength of
the horse,
nor his delight in the legs of the warrior;
[11] the LORD delights in those who fear him,
who put their hope in his unfailing love.

[12] Extol the LORD, Jerusalem;
praise your God, Zion.

[13] He strengthens the bars of your gates
and blesses your people within you.
[14] He grants peace to your borders
and satisfies you with the finest
of wheat.

[15] He sends his command to the earth;
his word runs swiftly.
[16] He spreads the snow like wool
and scatters the frost like ashes.
[17] He hurls down his hail like pebbles.
Who can withstand his icy blast?
[18] He sends his word and melts them;
he stirs up his breezes, and the
waters flow.

[19] He has revealed his word to Jacob,
his laws and decrees to Israel.
[20] He has done this for no other nation;
they do not know his laws.[b]

Praise the LORD.

[a] 1 Hebrew *Hallelu Yah*; also in verse 20   [b] 20 Masoretic Text; Dead Sea
Scrolls and Septuagint *nation; / he has not made his laws known to them*

How did God build up Jerusalem and gather the exiles? (147:2)
This refers to the restoration of Israel and Jerusalem after the exile in Babylon.

Why doesn't God take pleasure in the strength of a horse or the legs of a warrior? (147:10–11)
God takes pleasure in his creation, but that pleasure isn't based on how strong or fast his creatures are. God takes pleasure in those who follow and serve him.

What was God's special blessing to the people of Israel? (147:19–20)
God revealed his Word only to Israel. This was his redemptive Word, explaining his plan of salvation and holy will.

PSALM 148

Who is called to praise the Lord? (148:1–12)
All of creation — everything that God made — is called to give praise to God because he is the awesome Creator of it all.

¹ Praise the Lord.^{*a*}

Praise the Lord from the heavens;
  praise him in the heights above.
² Praise him, all his angels;
  praise him, all his heavenly hosts.
³ Praise him, sun and moon;
  praise him, all you shining stars.
⁴ Praise him, you highest heavens
  and you waters above the skies.

⁵ Let them praise the name of the Lord,
  for at his command they were created,
⁶ and he established them for ever and ever —
  he issued a decree that will never pass away.

⁷ Praise the Lord from the earth,
  you great sea creatures and all ocean depths,
⁸ lightning and hail, snow and clouds,
  stormy winds that do his bidding,
⁹ you mountains and all hills,
  fruit trees and all cedars,
¹⁰ wild animals and all cattle,
  small creatures and flying birds,
¹¹ kings of the earth and all nations,
  you princes and all rulers on earth,
¹² young men and women,
  old men and children.

¹³ Let them praise the name of the Lord,
  for his name alone is exalted;
  his splendor is above the earth and the heavens.
¹⁴ And he has raised up for his people a horn,^{*b*}
  the praise of all his faithful servants,
  of Israel, the people close to his heart.

Praise the Lord.

What is the horn? (148:14)
The horn symbolizes strength and specifically refers to the king.

PSALM 149

¹ Praise the Lord.^{*c*}

Sing to the Lord a new song,
  his praise in the assembly of his faithful people.

² Let Israel rejoice in their Maker;
  let the people of Zion be glad in their King.
³ Let them praise his name with dancing
  and make music to him with timbrel and harp.
⁴ For the Lord takes delight in his people;
  he crowns the humble with victory.
⁵ Let his faithful people rejoice in this honor
  and sing for joy on their beds.

⁶ May the praise of God be in their mouths
  and a double-edged sword in their hands,

^{*a*} 1 Hebrew *Hallelu Yah*; also in verse 14   ^{*b*} 14 *Horn* here symbolizes strength.   ^{*c*} 1 Hebrew *Hallelu Yah*; also in verse 9

[7] to inflict vengeance on the nations
and punishment on the peoples,
[8] to bind their kings with fetters,
their nobles with shackles of iron,
[9] to carry out the sentence written against them—
this is the glory of all his faithful people.

Praise the Lord.

PSALM 150

[1] Praise the Lord.[a]

Praise God in his sanctuary;
praise him in his mighty heavens.
[2] Praise him for his acts of power;
praise him for his surpassing greatness.
[3] Praise him with the sounding of the trumpet,
praise him with the harp and lyre,
[4] praise him with timbrel and dancing,
praise him with the strings and pipe,
[5] praise him with the clash of cymbals,
praise him with resounding cymbals.

[6] Let everything that has breath praise the Lord.

Praise the Lord.

Why would Israel praise God while carrying out vengeance? (149:6–9)
God had equipped Israel to do battle against evil. God's people were to praise him as they carried out this responsibility.

How should God be praised? (150:3–6)
God should be praised by everyone and everything, in a variety of ways with music and dance and expressions of thankfulness.

[a] 1 Hebrew *Hallelu Yah*; also in verse 6

Proverbs

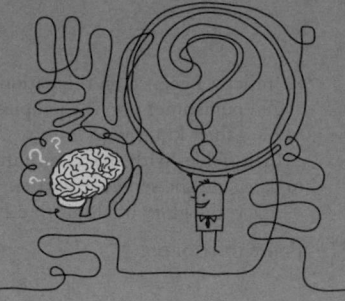

INTRODUCTION

Who wrote this book?
Solomon wrote many of the proverbs. Other wise men added others.

Why was this book written?
The book of Proverbs was written to help people make wise choices.

For whom was this book written?
This book was written for everyone. Even people who do not believe in God can use its good advice.

What kind of advice is found in Proverbs?
This book gives advice on making friends, living in a family, handling money, doing right, caring about poor people, and many other important things.

What are some proverbs for children in this book?

Advice about trusting God	Proverbs 3:5 – 6
Advice about working hard	Proverbs 6:6 – 11
Advice about insults	Proverbs 12:16
Advice about gossip	Proverbs 17:9
Advice about revenge	Proverbs 20:22
Advice about discipline	Proverbs 22:15

When did these things happen?
1400 BC 1300 1200 1100 1000 900 800 700 600 500 400

DAVID'S REIGN (1010 – 970 BC)
SOLOMON'S REIGN (970 – 930 BC)
MANY PROVERBS WRITTEN (C. 970 – 930 BC)
DIVISION OF THE KINGDOM (930 BC)
EXILE OF ISRAEL (722 BC)
HEZEKIAH'S REIGN (715 – 686 BC)
PROVERBS COMPILED AND EDITED (715 – 686 BC)
FALL OF JERUSALEM (586 BC)

PURPOSE AND THEME

1 The proverbs of Solomon son of David, king of Israel:

² for gaining wisdom and instruction;
    for understanding words of insight;
³ for receiving instruction in prudent behavior,
    doing what is right and just and fair;
⁴ for giving prudence to those who are simple,ᵃ
    knowledge and discretion to the young—
⁵ let the wise listen and add to their learning,
    and let the discerning get guidance—
⁶ for understanding proverbs and parables,
    the sayings and riddles of the wise.ᵇ

⁷ The fear of the LORD is the beginning of knowledge,
    but foolsᶜ despise wisdom and instruction.

PROLOGUE: EXHORTATIONS
TO EMBRACE WISDOM

WARNING AGAINST THE INVITATION
OF SINFUL MEN

⁸ Listen, my son, to your father's instruction
    and do not forsake your mother's teaching.
⁹ They are a garland to grace your head
    and a chain to adorn your neck.

¹⁰ My son, if sinful men entice you,
    do not give in to them.
¹¹ If they say, "Come along with us;
    let's lie in wait for innocent blood,
    let's ambush some harmless soul;
¹² let's swallow them alive, like the grave,
    and whole, like those who go down to the pit;
¹³ we will get all sorts of valuable things
    and fill our houses with plunder;
¹⁴ cast lots with us;
    we will all share the loot"—
¹⁵ my son, do not go along with them,
    do not set foot on their paths;
¹⁶ for their feet rush into evil,
    they are swift to shed blood.
¹⁷ How useless to spread a net
    where every bird can see it!
¹⁸ These men lie in wait for their own blood;
    they ambush only themselves!
¹⁹ Such are the paths of all who go after ill-gotten gain;
    it takes away the life of those who get it.

WISDOM'S REBUKE

²⁰ Out in the open wisdom calls aloud,
    she raises her voice in the public square;

ᵃ 4 The Hebrew word rendered *simple* in Proverbs denotes a person who is gullible, without moral direction and inclined to evil.   ᵇ 6 Or *understanding a proverb, namely, a parable, / and the sayings of the wise, their riddles*   ᶜ 7 The Hebrew words rendered *fool* in Proverbs, and often elsewhere in the Old Testament, denote a person who is morally deficient.

What is a proverb? (1:1)
The Hebrew word translated as *proverb* can also be translated as *oracle* or *parable*, so it has a broader meaning than the English word. Most proverbs are short, compact statements that express truths about human behavior.

What was the purpose of these proverbs? (1:2–7)
The proverbs were meant to give a description of wisdom. Proverbs also give practical advice about living in a godly way.

Who is the son in this verse? (1:8)
Proverbs were written to give guidance and instruction to the young so that by fearing God they would gain wisdom and live holy lives. It was common in ancient wisdom literature to present the ideas in the form of a father teaching a child. In this verse and in Proverbs 6:20, the mother is also depicted as the teacher.

Why was wisdom portrayed as a woman? (1:20)
This is an example of personification, a literary technique of giving human characteristics to an abstract idea. Both wisdom and folly are portrayed as women in the book of Proverbs. Each one tries to persuade the young to follow her.

²¹on top of the wall*ᵃ* she cries out,
    at the city gate she makes her speech:

²²"How long will you who are simple love your simple
        ways?
  How long will mockers delight in mockery
    and fools hate knowledge?
²³Repent at my rebuke!
  Then I will pour out my thoughts to you,
    I will make known to you my teachings.
²⁴But since you refuse to listen when I call
  and no one pays attention when I stretch out my
        hand,
²⁵since you disregard all my advice
  and do not accept my rebuke,
²⁶I in turn will laugh when disaster strikes you;
  I will mock when calamity overtakes you—
²⁷when calamity overtakes you like a storm,
  when disaster sweeps over you like a whirlwind,
  when distress and trouble overwhelm you.

²⁸"Then they will call to me but I will not answer;
  they will look for me but will not find me,
²⁹since they hated knowledge
  and did not choose to fear the LORD.
³⁰Since they would not accept my advice
  and spurned my rebuke,
³¹they will eat the fruit of their ways
  and be filled with the fruit of their schemes.
³²For the waywardness of the simple will kill them,
  and the complacency of fools will destroy them;
³³but whoever listens to me will live in safety
  and be at ease, without fear of harm."

MORAL BENEFITS OF WISDOM

2 My son, if you accept my words
   and store up my commands within you,
  ²turning your ear to wisdom
    and applying your heart to understanding—
  ³indeed, if you call out for insight
    and cry aloud for understanding,
  ⁴and if you look for it as for silver
    and search for it as for hidden treasure,

ᵃ 21 Septuagint; Hebrew / at noisy street corners

What did it mean for someone to eat the fruit of their ways? (1:31)
Those who reject wisdom would get what they deserved.

How did ancient people search for silver? (2:4)
Job 28:1–12 describes ancient mining techniques and compares them to looking for wisdom.

What does it mean to fear God?

The word *fear* can also mean reverence or worship. Fearing God does not mean being afraid of God, but it may mean being careful to avoid offending or dishonoring him. Proverbs 1:7 says "the fear of the LORD is the beginning of knowledge." Because the book of Proverbs is about wisdom, it goes on to describe how we can fear God in our daily lives through our speech, our finances, and our relationships.

Fearing God means obeying his laws and seeking to honor him with our behavior. Believers do not have to be afraid of God, but they may be in awe of his power and majesty. But they also know that God's love is constant. Romans 8:38–39 says, "For I am convinced that neither death nor life, neither angels nor demons, neither the present nor the future, nor any powers, neither height nor depth, nor anything else in all creation, will be able to separate us from the love of God that is in Christ Jesus our Lord."

5 then you will understand the fear of the LORD
    and find the knowledge of God.
6 For the LORD gives wisdom;
    from his mouth come knowledge and
        understanding.
7 He holds success in store for the upright,
    he is a shield to those whose walk is blameless,
8 for he guards the course of the just
    and protects the way of his faithful ones.

9 Then you will understand what is right and just
    and fair—every good path.
10 For wisdom will enter your heart,
    and knowledge will be pleasant to your soul.
11 Discretion will protect you,
    and understanding will guard you.

12 Wisdom will save you from the ways of wicked men,
    from men whose words are perverse,
13 who have left the straight paths
    to walk in dark ways,
14 who delight in doing wrong
    and rejoice in the perverseness of evil,
15 whose paths are crooked
    and who are devious in their ways.

16 Wisdom will save you also from the adulterous
        woman,
    from the wayward woman with her seductive words,
17 who has left the partner of her youth
    and ignored the covenant she made before God.*a*
18 Surely her house leads down to death
    and her paths to the spirits of the dead.
19 None who go to her return
    or attain the paths of life.

20 Thus you will walk in the ways of the good
    and keep to the paths of the righteous.
21 For the upright will live in the land,
    and the blameless will remain in it;
22 but the wicked will be cut off from the land,
    and the unfaithful will be torn from it.

WISDOM BESTOWS WELL-BEING

3 My son, do not forget my teaching,
    but keep my commands in your heart,
2 for they will prolong your life many years
    and bring you peace and prosperity.

3 Let love and faithfulness never leave you;
    bind them around your neck,
    write them on the tablet of your heart.
4 Then you will win favor and a good name
    in the sight of God and man.

5 Trust in the LORD with all your heart
    and lean not on your own understanding;

---

a 17 Or covenant of her God

How can wisdom save and protect people? (2:11–17)
Having wisdom can save a person from giving into the temptations offered by evil people.

How would the wicked be cut off from the land? (2:22)
This could refer to death, or being cut off from the land of the living. It could also refer to losing the opportunity to enjoy the benefits of being among the righteous.

⁶ in all your ways submit to him,
  and he will make your paths straight.^a

⁷ Do not be wise in your own eyes;
  fear the LORD and shun evil.
⁸ This will bring health to your body
  and nourishment to your bones.

⁹ Honor the LORD with your wealth,
  with the firstfruits of all your crops;
¹⁰ then your barns will be filled to overflowing,
  and your vats will brim over with new wine.

¹¹ My son, do not despise the LORD's discipline,
  and do not resent his rebuke,
¹² because the LORD disciplines those he loves,
  as a father the son he delights in.^b

¹³ Blessed are those who find wisdom,
  those who gain understanding,
¹⁴ for she is more profitable than silver
  and yields better returns than gold.
¹⁵ She is more precious than rubies;
  nothing you desire can compare with her.
¹⁶ Long life is in her right hand;
  in her left hand are riches and honor.
¹⁷ Her ways are pleasant ways,
  and all her paths are peace.
¹⁸ She is a tree of life to those who take hold of her;
  those who hold her fast will be blessed.

¹⁹ By wisdom the LORD laid the earth's foundations,
  by understanding he set the heavens in place;
²⁰ by his knowledge the watery depths were divided,
  and the clouds let drop the dew.

²¹ My son, do not let wisdom and understanding out of
    your sight,
  preserve sound judgment and discretion;
²² they will be life for you,
  an ornament to grace your neck.

---

^a 6 Or *will direct your paths*   ^b 12 Hebrew; Septuagint *loves, / and he chastens everyone he accepts as his child*

What were the firstfruits? (3:9)
The Israelites were required to give the priests the first part of the olive oil, wine, and grain produced each year (Leviticus 23:10; Number 18:12–13).

What is the LORD's discipline? (3:11–12)
God teaches his children about himself, about how they should live, and about how to become stronger in faith through correction and consequences.

What is the ultimate source of wisdom? (3:19–20)
God, who guided the creation of the universe, is the source of all wisdom. Living by wisdom means to imitate the Lord and to conform to his plan for creation.

Do righteous people always prosper and live long lives?
PROVERBS 3

No. As a general principle God blesses those who serve him, but God's people can certainly experience suffering, and unrighteous people sometimes seem to thrive. When the Bible describes the promises that God makes to people who follow his laws, it is in the context of God's covenant with his people. God promises to love and protect his children, and in turn he expects them to honor and serve him by obeying his laws and serving him with their lives.

God's promises about prosperity and long life do not mean that we can automatically become rich and live to an old age by following God's laws. Many Christians are poor, and many believers die young. God loves all of his people, and his promises about prosperity do not necessarily refer to material wealth. Instead, they refer to *shalom* — the feeling of peace and fulfillment — that comes from obeying God's laws. The promise about long lives should be understood as a promise that Christians will live at peace with God both in this life and for eternity.

²³ Then you will go on your way in safety,
   and your foot will not stumble.
²⁴ When you lie down, you will not be afraid;
   when you lie down, your sleep will be sweet.
²⁵ Have no fear of sudden disaster
   or of the ruin that overtakes the wicked,
²⁶ for the LORD will be at your side
   and will keep your foot from being snared.

²⁷ Do not withhold good from those to whom it is due,
   when it is in your power to act.
²⁸ Do not say to your neighbor,
   "Come back tomorrow and I'll give it to you"—
   when you already have it with you.
²⁹ Do not plot harm against your neighbor,
   who lives trustfully near you.
³⁰ Do not accuse anyone for no reason—
   when they have done you no harm.

³¹ Do not envy the violent
   or choose any of their ways.

³² For the LORD detests the perverse
   but takes the upright into his confidence.
³³ The LORD's curse is on the house of the wicked,
   but he blesses the home of the righteous.
³⁴ He mocks proud mockers
   but shows favor to the humble and oppressed.
³⁵ The wise inherit honor,
   but fools get only shame.

GET WISDOM AT ANY COST

4 Listen, my sons, to a father's instruction;
   pay attention and gain understanding.
² I give you sound learning,
   so do not forsake my teaching.
³ For I too was a son to my father,
   still tender, and cherished by my mother.
⁴ Then he taught me, and he said to me,
   "Take hold of my words with all your heart;
   keep my commands, and you will live.
⁵ Get wisdom, get understanding;
   do not forget my words or turn away from them.
⁶ Do not forsake wisdom, and she will protect you;
   love her, and she will watch over you.
⁷ The beginning of wisdom is this: Get^a wisdom.
   Though it cost all you have,^b get understanding.
⁸ Cherish her, and she will exalt you;
   embrace her, and she will honor you.
⁹ She will give you a garland to grace your head
   and present you with a glorious crown."

¹⁰ Listen, my son, accept what I say,
   and the years of your life will be many.
¹¹ I instruct you in the way of wisdom
   and lead you along straight paths.

---

^a 7 Or *Wisdom is supreme; therefore get*   ^b 7 Or *wisdom. / Whatever else you get*

How should God's followers treat those who need help? (3:27–28)
Throughout Scripture, God urges his people to care for those who are poor and needy. Instead of sending someone away empty handed, a wise or righteous person meets the other's immediate need.

Is this a reference to King David? (4:3–4)
Yes. This type of autobiographical statement was common in wisdom literature. It probably refers to David instructing Solomon when he was young.

Is wisdom the most important thing in life? (4:7)
Yes. True wisdom begins with deep respect for God, which blossoms into a sense of sin and the need for salvation. Then wisdom leads people to seek God's will and to live godly lives.

When were garlands and crowns worn? (4:9)
They were worn on joyous occasions such as weddings and feasts.

¹²When you walk, your steps will not be hampered;
    when you run, you will not stumble.
¹³Hold on to instruction, do not let it go;
    guard it well, for it is your life.
¹⁴Do not set foot on the path of the wicked
    or walk in the way of evildoers.
¹⁵Avoid it, do not travel on it;
    turn from it and go on your way.
¹⁶For they cannot rest until they do evil;
    they are robbed of sleep till they make
      someone stumble.
¹⁷They eat the bread of wickedness
    and drink the wine of violence.

¹⁸The path of the righteous is like the morning sun,
    shining ever brighter till the full light of day.
¹⁹But the way of the wicked is like deep darkness;
    they do not know what makes them stumble.

²⁰My son, pay attention to what I say;
    turn your ear to my words.
²¹Do not let them out of your sight,
    keep them within your heart;
²²for they are life to those who find them
    and health to one's whole body.
²³Above all else, guard your heart,
    for everything you do flows from it.
²⁴Keep your mouth free of perversity;
    keep corrupt talk far from your lips.
²⁵Let your eyes look straight ahead;
    fix your gaze directly before you.
²⁶Give careful thought to the*ᵃ* paths for your feet
    and be steadfast in all your ways.
²⁷Do not turn to the right or the left;
    keep your foot from evil.

WARNING AGAINST ADULTERY

5 My son, pay attention to my wisdom,
    turn your ear to my words of insight,
²that you may maintain discretion
    and your lips may preserve knowledge.
³For the lips of the adulterous woman drip honey,
    and her speech is smoother than oil;
⁴but in the end she is bitter as gall,
    sharp as a double-edged sword.
⁵Her feet go down to death;
    her steps lead straight to the grave.
⁶She gives no thought to the way of life;
    her paths wander aimlessly, but she does not know it.

⁷Now then, my sons, listen to me;
    do not turn aside from what I say.
⁸Keep to a path far from her,
    do not go near the door of her house,
⁹lest you lose your honor to others
    and your dignityᵇ to one who is cruel,

How was the heart the well-spring of life? (4:23)
Ancient people believed the heart was the source of intelligence and decision making. Staying away from evil would help to keep the heart wise and pure.

Why were the consequences of adultery so severe? (5:7 – 14)
Adultery usually led to shame, regret, and ruin.

ᵃ 26 Or *Make level*   ᵇ 9 Or *years*

¹⁰lest strangers feast on your wealth
　　and your toil enrich the house of another.
¹¹At the end of your life you will groan,
　　when your flesh and body are spent.
¹²You will say, "How I hated discipline!
　　How my heart spurned correction!
¹³I would not obey my teachers
　　or turn my ear to my instructors.
¹⁴And I was soon in serious trouble
　　in the assembly of God's people."

¹⁵Drink water from your own cistern,
　　running water from your own well.
¹⁶Should your springs overflow in the streets,
　　your streams of water in the public squares?
¹⁷Let them be yours alone,
　　never to be shared with strangers.
¹⁸May your fountain be blessed,
　　and may you rejoice in the wife of your youth.
¹⁹A loving doe, a graceful deer—
　　may her breasts satisfy you always,
　　may you ever be intoxicated with her love.
²⁰Why, my son, be intoxicated with another man's wife?
　　Why embrace the bosom of a wayward woman?

²¹For your ways are in full view of the LORD,
　　and he examines all your paths.
²²The evil deeds of the wicked ensnare them;
　　the cords of their sins hold them fast.
²³For lack of discipline they will die,
　　led astray by their own great folly.

WARNINGS AGAINST FOLLY

6 My son, if you have put up security for your neighbor,
　　if you have shaken hands in pledge for a stranger,
²you have been trapped by what you said,
　　ensnared by the words of your mouth.
³So do this, my son, to free yourself,
　　since you have fallen into your neighbor's hands:
　Go—to the point of exhaustion—ᵃ
　　and give your neighbor no rest!
⁴Allow no sleep to your eyes,
　　no slumber to your eyelids.
⁵Free yourself, like a gazelle from the hand of the
　　　hunter,
　　like a bird from the snare of the fowler.

⁶Go to the ant, you sluggard;
　　consider its ways and be wise!
⁷It has no commander,
　　no overseer or ruler,
⁸yet it stores its provisions in summer
　　and gathers its food at harvest.

⁹How long will you lie there, you sluggard?
　　When will you get up from your sleep?

ᵃ 3 Or *Go and humble yourself,*

Why is this advice about drinking water included? (5:15–18)
Here the author used a metaphor to compare water to marital intimacy. Water was rare in the Middle East, so when a man had his own cistern or fountain, he was grateful. In the same way, a man should find pleasure in his wife alone.

Why was it risky to guarantee someone else's loan? (6:1–5)
Taking responsibility for someone else's debt could lead to poverty or even slavery. It's important to be cautious when making these kinds of big financial decisions.

What's a sluggard? (6:6)
A sluggard is a lazy person who refuses to work. In contrast, the ant is industrious and stores food during the summer.

¹⁰ A little sleep, a little slumber,
  a little folding of the hands to rest—
¹¹ and poverty will come on you like a thief
  and scarcity like an armed man.

¹² A troublemaker and a villain,
  who goes about with a corrupt mouth,
¹³   who winks maliciously with his eye,
  signals with his feet
  and motions with his fingers,
¹⁴   who plots evil with deceit in his heart—
  he always stirs up conflict.
¹⁵ Therefore disaster will overtake him in an instant;
  he will suddenly be destroyed—
  without remedy.

¹⁶ There are six things the LORD hates,
  seven that are detestable to him:
¹⁷   haughty eyes,
  a lying tongue,
  hands that shed innocent blood,
¹⁸   a heart that devises wicked schemes,
  feet that are quick to rush into evil,
¹⁹   a false witness who pours out lies
  and a person who stirs up conflict in the
    community.

WARNING AGAINST ADULTERY

²⁰ My son, keep your father's command
  and do not forsake your mother's teaching.
²¹ Bind them always on your heart;
  fasten them around your neck.
²² When you walk, they will guide you;
  when you sleep, they will watch over you;
  when you awake, they will speak to you.
²³ For this command is a lamp,
  this teaching is a light,
  and correction and instruction
  are the way to life,
²⁴ keeping you from your neighbor's wife,
  from the smooth talk of a wayward woman.

²⁵ Do not lust in your heart after her beauty
  or let her captivate you with her eyes.

²⁶ For a prostitute can be had for a loaf of bread,
  but another man's wife preys on your very life.
²⁷ Can a man scoop fire into his lap
  without his clothes being burned?
²⁸ Can a man walk on hot coals
  without his feet being scorched?
²⁹ So is he who sleeps with another man's wife;
  no one who touches her will go unpunished.

³⁰ People do not despise a thief if he steals
  to satisfy his hunger when he is starving.
³¹ Yet if he is caught, he must pay sevenfold,
  though it costs him all the wealth of his house.

What are haughty eyes?
(6:17)
Haughty eyes reflect a proud heart rather than a humble spirit, which God wants.

How was the son to fasten his parents' advice around his neck? (6:20–21)
This was a reminder to remember his parents' words and keep them close to his heart. If he did that, he would walk in the path of wisdom.

What do these verses warn against? (6:27–29)
Like all other sins, people should avoid adultery altogether. It is foolish to think one can sin just once or only a little without consequences. This resembles the modern saying that a person who plays with fire will get burned.

³²But a man who commits adultery has no sense;
   whoever does so destroys himself.
³³Blows and disgrace are his lot,
   and his shame will never be wiped away.

³⁴For jealousy arouses a husband's fury,
   and he will show no mercy when he takes revenge.
³⁵He will not accept any compensation;
   he will refuse a bribe, however great it is.

WARNING AGAINST THE ADULTEROUS WOMAN

7 My son, keep my words
   and store up my commands within you.
²Keep my commands and you will live;
   guard my teachings as the apple of your eye.
³Bind them on your fingers;
   write them on the tablet of your heart.
⁴Say to wisdom, "You are my sister,"
   and to insight, "You are my relative."
⁵They will keep you from the adulterous woman,
   from the wayward woman with her seductive words.

⁶At the window of my house
   I looked down through the lattice.
⁷I saw among the simple,
   I noticed among the young men,
   a youth who had no sense.
⁸He was going down the street near her corner,
   walking along in the direction of her house
⁹at twilight, as the day was fading,
   as the dark of night set in.

¹⁰Then out came a woman to meet him,
   dressed like a prostitute and with crafty intent.
¹¹(She is unruly and defiant,
   her feet never stay at home;
¹²now in the street, now in the squares,
   at every corner she lurks.)
¹³She took hold of him and kissed him
   and with a brazen face she said:

¹⁴"Today I fulfilled my vows,
   and I have food from my fellowship offering at home.
¹⁵So I came out to meet you;
   I looked for you and have found you!
¹⁶I have covered my bed
   with colored linens from Egypt.
¹⁷I have perfumed my bed
   with myrrh, aloes and cinnamon.
¹⁸Come, let's drink deeply of love till morning;
   let's enjoy ourselves with love!
¹⁹My husband is not at home;
   he has gone on a long journey.
²⁰He took his purse filled with money
   and will not be home till full moon."

²¹With persuasive words she led him astray;
   she seduced him with her smooth talk.

What is the apple of the eye? (7:2)
This refers to the pupil of the eye. The pupil is necessary for sight and therefore must be protected at all costs.

How would this woman be dressed? (7:10)
She may have been dressed in gaudy clothing and heavily veiled.

²² All at once he followed her
     like an ox going to the slaughter,
   like a deer^a stepping into a noose^b
²³   till an arrow pierces his liver,
   like a bird darting into a snare,
     little knowing it will cost him his life.

²⁴ Now then, my sons, listen to me;
     pay attention to what I say.
²⁵ Do not let your heart turn to her ways
     or stray into her paths.
²⁶ Many are the victims she has brought down;
     her slain are a mighty throng.
²⁷ Her house is a highway to the grave,
     leading down to the chambers of death.

WISDOM'S CALL

8 Does not wisdom call out?
     Does not understanding raise her voice?
² At the highest point along the way,
     where the paths meet, she takes her stand;
³ beside the gate leading into the city,
     at the entrance, she cries aloud:
⁴ "To you, O people, I call out;
     I raise my voice to all mankind.
⁵ You who are simple, gain prudence;
     you who are foolish, set your hearts on it.^c
⁶ Listen, for I have trustworthy things to say;
     I open my lips to speak what is right.
⁷ My mouth speaks what is true,
     for my lips detest wickedness.
⁸ All the words of my mouth are just;
     none of them is crooked or perverse.
⁹ To the discerning all of them are right;
     they are upright to those who have found
          knowledge.
¹⁰ Choose my instruction instead of silver,
     knowledge rather than choice gold,
¹¹ for wisdom is more precious than rubies,
     and nothing you desire can compare with her.

¹² "I, wisdom, dwell together with prudence;
     I possess knowledge and discretion.
¹³ To fear the LORD is to hate evil;
     I hate pride and arrogance,
     evil behavior and perverse speech.
¹⁴ Counsel and sound judgment are mine;
     I have insight, I have power.
¹⁵ By me kings reign
     and rulers issue decrees that are just;
¹⁶ by me princes govern,
     and nobles—all who rule on earth.^d

Why is wisdom more valuable than silver, gold, or rubies? (8:10–11)
Precious stones and metals cannot buy wisdom or the fruits of wisdom, which include a godly character and a close relationship with God.

---

^a 22 Syriac (see also Septuagint); Hebrew *fool*   ^b 22 The meaning of the Hebrew for this line is uncertain.   ^c 5 Septuagint; Hebrew *foolish, instruct your minds*   ^d 16 Some Hebrew manuscripts and Septuagint; other Hebrew manuscripts *all righteous rulers*

17 I love those who love me,
and those who seek me find me.
18 With me are riches and honor,
enduring wealth and prosperity.
19 My fruit is better than fine gold;
what I yield surpasses choice silver.
20 I walk in the way of righteousness,
along the paths of justice,
21 bestowing a rich inheritance on those who love me
and making their treasuries full.

22 "The LORD brought me forth as the first of
his works,*a,b*
before his deeds of old;
23 I was formed long ages ago,
at the very beginning, when the world came to be.
24 When there were no watery depths, I was given birth,
when there were no springs overflowing with water;
25 before the mountains were settled in place,
before the hills, I was given birth,
26 before he made the world or its fields
or any of the dust of the earth.
27 I was there when he set the heavens in place,
when he marked out the horizon on the face
of the deep,
28 when he established the clouds above
and fixed securely the fountains of the deep,
29 when he gave the sea its boundary
so the waters would not overstep his command,
and when he marked out the foundations of the earth.
30 Then I was constantly*c* at his side.
I was filled with delight day after day,
rejoicing always in his presence,
31 rejoicing in his whole world
and delighting in mankind.

32 "Now then, my children, listen to me;
blessed are those who keep my ways.
33 Listen to my instruction and be wise;
do not disregard it.
34 Blessed are those who listen to me,
watching daily at my doors,
waiting at my doorway.
35 For those who find me find life
and receive favor from the LORD.
36 But those who fail to find me harm themselves;
all who hate me love death."

INVITATIONS OF WISDOM AND FOLLY

9 Wisdom has built her house;
she has set up*d* its seven pillars.
2 She has prepared her meat and mixed her wine;
she has also set her table.

How did wisdom play a role in the creation of the universe? (8:22–31)
It was because of his wisdom that God could call into being his marvelous creation.

---

a 22 Or *way*; or *dominion*   *b* 22 Or *The LORD possessed me at the beginning of his work*; or *The LORD brought me forth at the beginning of his work*
c 30 Or *was the artisan*; or *was a little child*   *d* 1 Septuagint, Syriac and Targum; Hebrew *has hewn out*

³ She has sent out her servants, and she calls
    from the highest point of the city,
⁴ "Let all who are simple come to my house!"
  To those who have no sense she says,
⁵ "Come, eat my food
    and drink the wine I have mixed.
⁶ Leave your simple ways and you will live;
    walk in the way of insight."

⁷ Whoever corrects a mocker invites insults;
    whoever rebukes the wicked incurs abuse.
⁸ Do not rebuke mockers or they will hate you;
    rebuke the wise and they will love you.
⁹ Instruct the wise and they will be wiser still;
    teach the righteous and they will add to their
    learning.

¹⁰ The fear of the LORD is the beginning of wisdom,
    and knowledge of the Holy One is understanding.
¹¹ For through wisdom^a your days will be many,
    and years will be added to your life.
¹² If you are wise, your wisdom will reward you;
    if you are a mocker, you alone will suffer.

¹³ Folly is an unruly woman;
    she is simple and knows nothing.
¹⁴ She sits at the door of her house,
    on a seat at the highest point of the city,
¹⁵ calling out to those who pass by,
    who go straight on their way,
¹⁶ "Let all who are simple come to my house!"
  To those who have no sense she says,
¹⁷ "Stolen water is sweet;
    food eaten in secret is delicious!"
¹⁸ But little do they know that the dead are there,
    that her guests are deep in the realm of the dead.

PROVERBS OF SOLOMON

10 The proverbs of Solomon:

A wise son brings joy to his father,
    but a foolish son brings grief to his mother.

² Ill-gotten treasures have no lasting value,
    but righteousness delivers from death.

³ The LORD does not let the righteous go hungry,
    but he thwarts the craving of the wicked.

⁴ Lazy hands make for poverty,
    but diligent hands bring wealth.

⁵ He who gathers crops in summer is a prudent son,
    but he who sleeps during harvest is a disgraceful son.

⁶ Blessings crown the head of the righteous,
    but violence overwhelms the mouth of the wicked.^{b}

Why did folly sit at the highest point of the city? (9:14)
Both wisdom and folly called to people from the highest point in the city in order to be heard and to attract attention. Just as people did then, we still must choose between wisdom and foolishness.

What type of meal was this? (9:17–18)
This was the stolen pleasures of sex outside marriage. But the sweetness couldn't cover up the nasty aftertaste that accompanied the meal. Though it might seem thrilling at the time, this type of intimacy always has devastating consequences.

How does the book of Proverbs shift at this point? (10:1)
The first nine chapters include descriptions of wisdom and how it is better than folly. Now the book moves into more practical suggestions and advice for virtuous, successful living.

Why is hard work praised? (10:4)
Many proverbs criticize laziness as a cause of poverty and praise diligence and the rewards it brings.

^{a} 11 Septuagint, Syriac and Targum; Hebrew *me* ^{b} 6 Or *righteous, / but the mouth of the wicked conceals violence*

⁷The name of the righteous is used in blessings,ᵃ
    but the name of the wicked will rot.

⁸The wise in heart accept commands,
    but a chattering fool comes to ruin.

⁹Whoever walks in integrity walks securely,
    but whoever takes crooked paths will be found out.

¹⁰Whoever winks maliciously causes grief,
    and a chattering fool comes to ruin.

¹¹The mouth of the righteous is a fountain of life,
    but the mouth of the wicked conceals violence.

¹²Hatred stirs up conflict,
    but love covers over all wrongs.

¹³Wisdom is found on the lips of the discerning,
    but a rod is for the back of one who has no sense.

¹⁴The wise store up knowledge,
    but the mouth of a fool invites ruin.

¹⁵The wealth of the rich is their fortified city,
    but poverty is the ruin of the poor.

¹⁶The wages of the righteous is life,
    but the earnings of the wicked are sin and death.

¹⁷Whoever heeds discipline shows the way to life,
    but whoever ignores correction leads others astray.

¹⁸Whoever conceals hatred with lying lips
    and spreads slander is a fool.

¹⁹Sin is not ended by multiplying words,
    but the prudent hold their tongues.

²⁰The tongue of the righteous is choice silver,
    but the heart of the wicked is of little value.

²¹The lips of the righteous nourish many,
    but fools die for lack of sense.

²²The blessing of the Lord brings wealth,
    without painful toil for it.

²³A fool finds pleasure in wicked schemes,
    but a person of understanding delights in wisdom.

²⁴What the wicked dread will overtake them;
    what the righteous desire will be granted.

²⁵When the storm has swept by, the wicked are gone,
    but the righteous stand firm forever.

²⁶As vinegar to the teeth and smoke to the eyes,
    so are sluggards to those who send them.

²⁷The fear of the Lord adds length to life,
    but the years of the wicked are cut short.

²⁸The prospect of the righteous is joy,
    but the hopes of the wicked come to nothing.

ᵃ 7 See Gen. 48:20.

What does Solomon say about love in this verse? (10:12)
Love is able to cover over all wrongs because it promotes forgiveness. This verse is quoted in James 5:20 and 1 Peter 4:8.

Does God promise his people a life without trouble? (10:22)
No. This verse says that those who trust in God will be blessed by him. If a person is wealthy, it often is a gift from God rather than human achievement.

²⁹ The way of the LORD is a refuge for the blameless,
     but it is the ruin of those who do evil.

³⁰ The righteous will never be uprooted,
     but the wicked will not remain in the land.

³¹ From the mouth of the righteous comes the fruit
         of wisdom,
     but a perverse tongue will be silenced.

³² The lips of the righteous know what finds favor,
     but the mouth of the wicked only what is perverse.

11 The LORD detests dishonest scales,
     but accurate weights find favor with him.

² When pride comes, then comes disgrace,
     but with humility comes wisdom.

³ The integrity of the upright guides them,
     but the unfaithful are destroyed by their duplicity.

⁴ Wealth is worthless in the day of wrath,
     but righteousness delivers from death.

⁵ The righteousness of the blameless makes their
         paths straight,
     but the wicked are brought down by their
         own wickedness.

⁶ The righteousness of the upright delivers them,
     but the unfaithful are trapped by evil desires.

⁷ Hopes placed in mortals die with them;
     all the promise of*ᵃ* their power comes to nothing.

⁸ The righteous person is rescued from trouble,
     and it falls on the wicked instead.

⁹ With their mouths the godless destroy their neighbors,
     but through knowledge the righteous escape.

¹⁰ When the righteous prosper, the city rejoices;
     when the wicked perish, there are shouts of joy.

¹¹ Through the blessing of the upright a city is exalted,
     but by the mouth of the wicked it is destroyed.

¹² Whoever derides their neighbor has no sense,
     but the one who has understanding holds
         their tongue.

¹³ A gossip betrays a confidence,
     but a trustworthy person keeps a secret.

¹⁴ For lack of guidance a nation falls,
     but victory is won through many advisers.

¹⁵ Whoever puts up security for a stranger will
         surely suffer,
     but whoever refuses to shake hands in pledge is safe.

¹⁶ A kindhearted woman gains honor,
     but ruthless men gain only wealth.

What is the day of wrath? (11:4)
This is the day of judgment when everyone will be called to account for what he or she has done. A person's wealth will be useless on that day.

How do the upright bring blessing to a city? (11:11)
People who live honest and virtuous lives and who seek justice for their neighbors make life in a community safe and pleasant.

ᵃ 7 Two Hebrew manuscripts; most Hebrew manuscripts, Vulgate, Syriac and Targum *When the wicked die, their hope perishes; / all they expected from*

17 Those who are kind benefit themselves,
but the cruel bring ruin on themselves.

18 A wicked person earns deceptive wages,
but the one who sows righteousness reaps
a sure reward.

19 Truly the righteous attain life,
but whoever pursues evil finds death.

20 The LORD detests those whose hearts are perverse,
but he delights in those whose ways are blameless.

21 Be sure of this: The wicked will not go unpunished,
but those who are righteous will go free.

22 Like a gold ring in a pig's snout
is a beautiful woman who shows no discretion.

23 The desire of the righteous ends only in good,
but the hope of the wicked only in wrath.

24 One person gives freely, yet gains even more;
another withholds unduly, but comes to poverty.

25 A generous person will prosper;
whoever refreshes others will be refreshed.

26 People curse the one who hoards grain,
but they pray God's blessing on the one who is
willing to sell.

27 Whoever seeks good finds favor,
but evil comes to one who searches for it.

28 Those who trust in their riches will fall,
but the righteous will thrive like a green leaf.

29 Whoever brings ruin on their family will inherit
only wind,
and the fool will be servant to the wise.

30 The fruit of the righteous is a tree of life,
and the one who is wise saves lives.

31 If the righteous receive their due on earth,
how much more the ungodly and the sinner!

12 Whoever loves discipline loves knowledge,
but whoever hates correction is stupid.

2 Good people obtain favor from the LORD,
but he condemns those who devise
wicked schemes.

3 No one can be established through wickedness,
but the righteous cannot be uprooted.

4 A wife of noble character is her husband's crown,
but a disgraceful wife is like decay in his bones.

5 The plans of the righteous are just,
but the advice of the wicked is deceitful.

6 The words of the wicked lie in wait for blood,
but the speech of the upright rescues them.

Can any person be truly blameless? (11:20)
This does not mean that a person is perfect or without sin. Instead, it refers to someone with spiritual and moral integrity.

What does the image of a pig with a ring in its snout mean? (11:22)
This example of overstatement shows how indiscretion can't be covered up by beauty. The Israelites considered pigs ceremonially unclean animals that could not be eaten or even touched. So even if a pig had a beautiful ring in its snout, it would still be unclean.

Will a generous person always prosper? (11:25)
A generous person receives God's blessing even if he or she does not become wealthy.

What did this proverb mean? (12:9)
Even people with moderate means had servants during this time, so it was better to be a person of average wealth with a servant than someone who spent all his money trying to act important and ending up with nothing.

Whose advice does a foolish person follow? (12:15)
A foolish person relies on his or her own instincts and ignores the advice of other people who have wisdom and insight.

When is it a good idea to remain quiet? (12:23)
Wise people keep quiet so they don't share secrets or offer advice to people who won't take it. Foolish people speak without thinking of the consequences. Their words can be hurtful. Therefore, the wise know when to speak and when to remain silent.

How can friends be helpful or harmful? (12:26)
A righteous person chooses friends wisely, but a foolish person is often led down the wrong path by poorly chosen friends.

⁷The wicked are overthrown and are no more,
  but the house of the righteous stands firm.

⁸A person is praised according to their prudence,
  and one with a warped mind is despised.

⁹Better to be a nobody and yet have a servant
  than pretend to be somebody and have no food.

¹⁰The righteous care for the needs of their animals,
  but the kindest acts of the wicked are cruel.

¹¹Those who work their land will have abundant food,
  but those who chase fantasies have no sense.

¹²The wicked desire the stronghold of evildoers,
  but the root of the righteous endures.

¹³Evildoers are trapped by their sinful talk,
  and so the innocent escape trouble.

¹⁴From the fruit of their lips people are filled with
    good things,
  and the work of their hands brings them reward.

¹⁵The way of fools seems right to them,
  but the wise listen to advice.

¹⁶Fools show their annoyance at once,
  but the prudent overlook an insult.

¹⁷An honest witness tells the truth,
  but a false witness tells lies.

¹⁸The words of the reckless pierce like swords,
  but the tongue of the wise brings healing.

¹⁹Truthful lips endure forever,
  but a lying tongue lasts only a moment.

²⁰Deceit is in the hearts of those who plot evil,
  but those who promote peace have joy.

²¹No harm overtakes the righteous,
  but the wicked have their fill of trouble.

²²The LORD detests lying lips,
  but he delights in people who are trustworthy.

²³The prudent keep their knowledge to themselves,
  but a fool's heart blurts out folly.

²⁴Diligent hands will rule,
  but laziness ends in forced labor.

²⁵Anxiety weighs down the heart,
  but a kind word cheers it up.

²⁶The righteous choose their friends carefully,
  but the way of the wicked leads them astray.

²⁷The lazy do not roast*a* any game,
  but the diligent feed on the riches of the hunt.

²⁸In the way of righteousness there is life;
  along that path is immortality.

a 27 The meaning of the Hebrew for this word is uncertain.

13 A wise son heeds his father's instruction,
   but a mocker does not respond to rebukes.

2 From the fruit of their lips people enjoy good things,
   but the unfaithful have an appetite for violence.

3 Those who guard their lips preserve their lives,
   but those who speak rashly will come to ruin.

4 A sluggard's appetite is never filled,
   but the desires of the diligent are fully satisfied.

5 The righteous hate what is false,
   but the wicked make themselves a stench
   and bring shame on themselves.

6 Righteousness guards the person of integrity,
   but wickedness overthrows the sinner.

7 One person pretends to be rich, yet has nothing;
   another pretends to be poor, yet has great wealth.

8 A person's riches may ransom their life,
   but the poor cannot respond to threatening rebukes.

9 The light of the righteous shines brightly,
   but the lamp of the wicked is snuffed out.

10 Where there is strife, there is pride,
   but wisdom is found in those who take advice.

11 Dishonest money dwindles away,
   but whoever gathers money little by little
      makes it grow.

12 Hope deferred makes the heart sick,
   but a longing fulfilled is a tree of life.

13 Whoever scorns instruction will pay for it,
   but whoever respects a command is rewarded.

14 The teaching of the wise is a fountain of life,
   turning a person from the snares of death.

15 Good judgment wins favor,
   but the way of the unfaithful leads to
      their destruction. *a*

16 All who are prudent act with *b* knowledge,
   but fools expose their folly.

17 A wicked messenger falls into trouble,
   but a trustworthy envoy brings healing.

18 Whoever disregards discipline comes to poverty
      and shame,
   but whoever heeds correction is honored.

19 A longing fulfilled is sweet to the soul,
   but fools detest turning from evil.

20 Walk with the wise and become wise,
   for a companion of fools suffers harm.

Why is it wrong to pretend to be rich or poor? (13:7)
Both of these are dishonest and deceptive. Both lead to folly.

Why is discipline praised? (13:18)
Discipline and correction are necessary to help keep a person on the path of wisdom.

---

a 15 Septuagint and Syriac; the meaning of the Hebrew for this phrase is uncertain.   *b 16* Or *prudent protect themselves through*

²¹ Trouble pursues the sinner,
  but the righteous are rewarded with good things.

²² A good person leaves an inheritance for their children's
    children,
  but a sinner's wealth is stored up for the righteous.

²³ An unplowed field produces food for the poor,
  but injustice sweeps it away.

²⁴ Whoever spares the rod hates their children,
  but the one who loves their children is careful to
    discipline them.

²⁵ The righteous eat to their hearts' content,
  but the stomach of the wicked goes hungry.

14 The wise woman builds her house,
  but with her own hands the foolish one tears
    hers down.

² Whoever fears the LORD walks uprightly,
  but those who despise him are devious in their ways.

³ A fool's mouth lashes out with pride,
  but the lips of the wise protect them.

⁴ Where there are no oxen, the manger is empty,
  but from the strength of an ox come abundant
    harvests.

⁵ An honest witness does not deceive,
  but a false witness pours out lies.

⁶ The mocker seeks wisdom and finds none,
  but knowledge comes easily to the discerning.

⁷ Stay away from a fool,
  for you will not find knowledge on their lips.

⁸ The wisdom of the prudent is to give thought to
    their ways,
  but the folly of fools is deception.

⁹ Fools mock at making amends for sin,
  but goodwill is found among the upright.

¹⁰ Each heart knows its own bitterness,
  and no one else can share its joy.

¹¹ The house of the wicked will be destroyed,
  but the tent of the upright will flourish.

¹² There is a way that appears to be right,
  but in the end it leads to death.

¹³ Even in laughter the heart may ache,
  and rejoicing may end in grief.

¹⁴ The faithless will be fully repaid for their ways,
  and the good rewarded for theirs.

¹⁵ The simple believe anything,
  but the prudent give thought to their steps.

¹⁶ The wise fear the LORD and shun evil,
  but a fool is hotheaded and yet feels secure.

What is the meaning of this well-known proverb? (13:24)
Some people have used this verse to justify spanking children. Others believe it speaks metaphorically about disciplining and correcting children. The key is in the second half of the proverb: Parents who love their children discipline them so that they will learn to follow God's commandments.

What is the point of this proverb? (14:4)
In a farming culture, it was important to take care of one's oxen in order to be able to work the fields and reap a good harvest.

Is joy only temporary? (14:13)
The proverbs are realistic about the lives of human beings. The wise person knows that even when times are good, a person may be carrying sadness inside. Joyful times do not always end in grief, but sometimes they do. We should be prepared to deal with both joy and sorrow.

¹⁷ A quick-tempered person does foolish things,
　　and the one who devises evil schemes is hated.

¹⁸ The simple inherit folly,
　　but the prudent are crowned with knowledge.

¹⁹ Evildoers will bow down in the presence of the good,
　　and the wicked at the gates of the righteous.

²⁰ The poor are shunned even by their neighbors,
　　but the rich have many friends.

²¹ It is a sin to despise one's neighbor,
　　but blessed is the one who is kind to the needy.

²² Do not those who plot evil go astray?
　　But those who plan what is good find[a] love
　　and faithfulness.

²³ All hard work brings a profit,
　　but mere talk leads only to poverty.

²⁴ The wealth of the wise is their crown,
　　but the folly of fools yields folly.

²⁵ A truthful witness saves lives,
　　but a false witness is deceitful.

²⁶ Whoever fears the Lord has a secure fortress,
　　and for their children it will be a refuge.

²⁷ The fear of the Lord is a fountain of life,
　　turning a person from the snares of death.

²⁸ A large population is a king's glory,
　　but without subjects a prince is ruined.

²⁹ Whoever is patient has great understanding,
　　but one who is quick-tempered displays folly.

³⁰ A heart at peace gives life to the body,
　　but envy rots the bones.

³¹ Whoever oppresses the poor shows contempt for
　　their Maker,
　　but whoever is kind to the needy honors God.

³² When calamity comes, the wicked are brought down,
　　but even in death the righteous seek refuge in God.

³³ Wisdom reposes in the heart of the discerning
　　and even among fools she lets herself be known.[b]

³⁴ Righteousness exalts a nation,
　　but sin condemns any people.

³⁵ A king delights in a wise servant,
　　but a shameful servant arouses his fury.

15 A gentle answer turns away wrath,
　　but a harsh word stirs up anger.

² The tongue of the wise adorns knowledge,
　　but the mouth of the fool gushes folly.

---

a 22 Or *show*　　*b 33* Hebrew; Septuagint and Syriac *discerning / but in the heart of fools she is not known*

What commandment does this proverb echo? (14:21)
It reflects the same idea as "love your neighbor as yourself" (in Leviticus 19:18 and quoted later by Jesus as the second great commandment). It also reflects God's continuing concern that the poor be taken care of (see 14:31).

How do the righteous have a refuge even in death? (14:32)
The faith of the righteous gives them hope beyond the grave.

³ The eyes of the LORD are everywhere,
  keeping watch on the wicked and the good.

⁴ The soothing tongue is a tree of life,
  but a perverse tongue crushes the spirit.

⁵ A fool spurns a parent's discipline,
  but whoever heeds correction shows prudence.

⁶ The house of the righteous contains great treasure,
  but the income of the wicked brings ruin.

⁷ The lips of the wise spread knowledge,
  but the hearts of fools are not upright.

⁸ The LORD detests the sacrifice of the wicked,
  but the prayer of the upright pleases him.

⁹ The LORD detests the way of the wicked,
  but he loves those who pursue righteousness.

¹⁰ Stern discipline awaits anyone who leaves the path;
   the one who hates correction will die.

¹¹ Death and Destruction*ª* lie open before
       the LORD—
   how much more do human hearts!

¹² Mockers resent correction,
   so they avoid the wise.

¹³ A happy heart makes the face cheerful,
   but heartache crushes the spirit.

¹⁴ The discerning heart seeks knowledge,
   but the mouth of a fool feeds on folly.

¹⁵ All the days of the oppressed are wretched,
   but the cheerful heart has a continual feast.

¹⁶ Better a little with the fear of the LORD
   than great wealth with turmoil.

¹⁷ Better a small serving of vegetables with love
   than a fattened calf with hatred.

¹⁸ A hot-tempered person stirs up conflict,
   but the one who is patient calms a quarrel.

¹⁹ The way of the sluggard is blocked with thorns,
   but the path of the upright is a highway.

²⁰ A wise son brings joy to his father,
   but a foolish man despises his mother.

²¹ Folly brings joy to one who has no sense,
   but whoever has understanding keeps a straight
       course.

²² Plans fail for lack of counsel,
   but with many advisers they succeed.

²³ A person finds joy in giving an apt reply—
   and how good is a timely word!

What type of treasure do the righteous gain? (15:6)
This may refer to material wealth, but more importantly it speaks of the spiritual treasure of being blessed with godly character through doing God's will.

When are the poor better off than the rich? (15:16–17)
Love and peace within a family are far superior to riches when there is tension or anger.

What is the advantage of patience? (15:18)
Many of the proverbs talk about the wisdom of being patient. Impatience leads to impulsive words and actions that often lead to serious problems.

ª *11* Hebrew *Abaddon*

²⁴ The path of life leads upward for the prudent
   to keep them from going down to the realm
      of the dead.

²⁵ The LORD tears down the house of the proud,
   but he sets the widow's boundary stones in place.

²⁶ The LORD detests the thoughts of the wicked,
   but gracious words are pure in his sight.

²⁷ The greedy bring ruin to their households,
   but the one who hates bribes will live.

²⁸ The heart of the righteous weighs its answers,
   but the mouth of the wicked gushes evil.

²⁹ The LORD is far from the wicked,
   but he hears the prayer of the righteous.

³⁰ Light in a messenger's eyes brings joy to the heart,
   and good news gives health to the bones.

³¹ Whoever heeds life-giving correction
   will be at home among the wise.

³² Those who disregard discipline despise themselves,
   but the one who heeds correction gains
      understanding.

³³ Wisdom's instruction is to fear the LORD,
   and humility comes before honor.

16 To humans belong the plans of the heart,
   but from the LORD comes the proper answer
      of the tongue.

² All a person's ways seem pure to them,
   but motives are weighed by the LORD.

³ Commit to the LORD whatever you do,
   and he will establish your plans.

⁴ The LORD works out everything to its
      proper end—
   even the wicked for a day of disaster.

⁵ The LORD detests all the proud of heart.
   Be sure of this: They will not go unpunished.

⁶ Through love and faithfulness sin is atoned for;
   through the fear of the LORD evil is avoided.

⁷ When the LORD takes pleasure in anyone's way,
   he causes their enemies to make peace with them.

⁸ Better a little with righteousness
   than much gain with injustice.

⁹ In their hearts humans plan their course,
   but the LORD establishes their steps.

¹⁰ The lips of a king speak as an oracle,
   and his mouth does not betray justice.

¹¹ Honest scales and balances belong to the LORD;
   all the weights in the bag are of his making.

What were the "boundary stones" mentioned here? (15:25)
In ancient times, boundary stones marked the corners of a person's property. Anyone who moved a boundary stone was, in effect, stealing land from that person. God again shows his care for those, like widows, who needed help and protection.

What did it mean for a king to "speak as an oracle"? (16:10)
In judging cases brought before him, a king acted as God's representative. Therefore, he needed wisdom to discern right from wrong in order to give judgment as God's spokesman.

How were items weighed in ancient times? (16:11)
Merchants carried stones of different sizes to weigh and measure quantities of silver for payment. Weights labeled incorrectly allowed for cheating, which God condemned.

¹²Kings detest wrongdoing,
for a throne is established through righteousness.

¹³Kings take pleasure in honest lips;
they value the one who speaks what is right.

¹⁴A king's wrath is a messenger of death,
but the wise will appease it.

Why was spring rain a good sign? (16:15)
Spring rain usually meant there would be abundant wheat and barley harvests.

¹⁵When a king's face brightens, it means life;
his favor is like a rain cloud in spring.

¹⁶How much better to get wisdom than gold,
to get insight rather than silver!

¹⁷The highway of the upright avoids evil;
those who guard their ways preserve their lives.

¹⁸Pride goes before destruction,
a haughty spirit before a fall.

¹⁹Better to be lowly in spirit along with the oppressed
than to share plunder with the proud.

²⁰Whoever gives heed to instruction prospers,ᵃ
and blessed is the one who trusts in the LORD.

²¹The wise in heart are called discerning,
and gracious words promote instruction.ᵇ

²²Prudence is a fountain of life to the prudent,
but folly brings punishment to fools.

²³The hearts of the wise make their mouths prudent,
and their lips promote instruction.ᶜ

²⁴Gracious words are a honeycomb,
sweet to the soul and healing to the bones.

²⁵There is a way that appears to be right,
but in the end it leads to death.

²⁶The appetite of laborers works for them;
their hunger drives them on.

²⁷A scoundrel plots evil,
and on their lips it is like a scorching fire.

²⁸A perverse person stirs up conflict,
and a gossip separates close friends.

²⁹A violent person entices their neighbor
and leads them down a path that is not good.

³⁰Whoever winks with their eye is plotting perversity;
whoever purses their lips is bent on evil.

Why was gray hair a sign of honor? (16:31)
In ancient times, elderly people were treated with great respect.

³¹Gray hair is a crown of splendor;
it is attained in the way of righteousness.

³²Better a patient person than a warrior,
one with self-control than one who takes a city.

³³The lot is cast into the lap,
but its every decision is from the LORD.

ᵃ 20 Or *whoever speaks prudently finds what is good*   ᵇ 21 Or *words make a person persuasive*   ᶜ 23 Or *prudent / and make their lips persuasive*

17 Better a dry crust with peace and quiet
than a house full of feasting, with strife.

² A prudent servant will rule over a disgraceful son
and will share the inheritance as one of the family.

³ The crucible for silver and the furnace for gold,
but the LORD tests the heart.

⁴ A wicked person listens to deceitful lips;
a liar pays attention to a destructive tongue.

⁵ Whoever mocks the poor shows contempt for
their Maker;
whoever gloats over disaster will not go unpunished.

⁶ Children's children are a crown to the aged,
and parents are the pride of their children.

⁷ Eloquent lips are unsuited to a godless fool —
how much worse lying lips to a ruler!

⁸ A bribe is seen as a charm by the one who gives it;
they think success will come at every turn.

⁹ Whoever would foster love covers over an offense,
but whoever repeats the matter separates
close friends.

¹⁰ A rebuke impresses a discerning person
more than a hundred lashes a fool.

¹¹ Evildoers foster rebellion against God;
the messenger of death will be sent against them.

¹² Better to meet a bear robbed of her cubs
than a fool bent on folly.

¹³ Evil will never leave the house
of one who pays back evil for good.

¹⁴ Starting a quarrel is like breaching a dam;
so drop the matter before a dispute breaks out.

¹⁵ Acquitting the guilty and condemning the innocent —
the LORD detests them both.

¹⁶ Why should fools have money in hand to buy wisdom,
when they are not able to understand it?

¹⁷ A friend loves at all times,
and a brother is born for a time of adversity.

¹⁸ One who has no sense shakes hands in pledge
and puts up security for a neighbor.

¹⁹ Whoever loves a quarrel loves sin;
whoever builds a high gate invites destruction.

²⁰ One whose heart is corrupt does not prosper;
one whose tongue is perverse falls into trouble.

²¹ To have a fool for a child brings grief;
there is no joy for the parent of a godless fool.

²² A cheerful heart is good medicine,
but a crushed spirit dries up the bones.

How were silver and gold refined? (17:3)
Silver and gold were melted in high heat in order to remove their impurities.

Why were children's children a crown to the aged? (17:6)
Living long enough to see one's grandchildren was considered to be a great blessing.

²³ The wicked accept bribes in secret
    to pervert the course of justice.

²⁴ A discerning person keeps wisdom in view,
    but a fool's eyes wander to the ends of the earth.

²⁵ A foolish son brings grief to his father
    and bitterness to the mother who bore him.

²⁶ If imposing a fine on the innocent is not good,
    surely to flog honest officials is not right.

²⁷ The one who has knowledge uses words with restraint,
    and whoever has understanding is even-tempered.

²⁸ Even fools are thought wise if they keep silent,
    and discerning if they hold their tongues.

18 An unfriendly person pursues selfish ends
    and against all sound judgment starts quarrels.

² Fools find no pleasure in understanding
    but delight in airing their own opinions.

³ When wickedness comes, so does contempt,
    and with shame comes reproach.

⁴ The words of the mouth are deep waters,
    but the fountain of wisdom is a rushing stream.

⁵ It is not good to be partial to the wicked
    and so deprive the innocent of justice.

⁶ The lips of fools bring them strife,
    and their mouths invite a beating.

⁷ The mouths of fools are their undoing,
    and their lips are a snare to their very lives.

⁸ The words of a gossip are like choice morsels;
    they go down to the inmost parts.

⁹ One who is slack in his work
    is brother to one who destroys.

¹⁰ The name of the LORD is a fortified tower;
    the righteous run to it and are safe.

¹¹ The wealth of the rich is their fortified city;
    they imagine it a wall too high to scale.

¹² Before a downfall the heart is haughty,
    but humility comes before honor.

¹³ To answer before listening—
    that is folly and shame.

¹⁴ The human spirit can endure in sickness,
    but a crushed spirit who can bear?

¹⁵ The heart of the discerning acquires knowledge,
    for the ears of the wise seek it out.

¹⁶ A gift opens the way
    and ushers the giver into the presence of the great.

¹⁷ In a lawsuit the first to speak seems right,
    until someone comes forward and cross-examines.

What does this proverb mean? (17:28)
Even a foolish person can appear to be wise if he or she does not say anything that would let people know otherwise. There is wisdom in knowing when to be silent.

Why was it wrong to be partial to the wicked? (18:5)
Favoritism of any kind in legal matters was condemned in the law (see Leviticus 19:15; Deuteronomy 1:17; 16:19).

How are a gossip's words like choice morsels? (18:8)
People love to hear juicy bits of gossip about others. But gossip has a life of its own. Once someone develops a taste for gossip, it's hard to stop.

Why is it important to hear both sides in a dispute? (18:17)
The proverb correctly states that the person who first presents his case usually seems right, but there is always another side.

¹⁸ Casting the lot settles disputes
and keeps strong opponents apart.

¹⁹ A brother wronged is more unyielding than
a fortified city;
disputes are like the barred gates of a citadel.

²⁰ From the fruit of their mouth a person's stomach
is filled;
with the harvest of their lips they are satisfied.

²¹ The tongue has the power of life and death,
and those who love it will eat its fruit.

²² He who finds a wife finds what is good
and receives favor from the LORD.

²³ The poor plead for mercy,
but the rich answer harshly.

²⁴ One who has unreliable friends soon comes
to ruin,
but there is a friend who sticks closer than
a brother.

19 Better the poor whose walk is blameless
than a fool whose lips are perverse.

² Desire without knowledge is not good—
how much more will hasty feet miss the way!

³ A person's own folly leads to their ruin,
yet their heart rages against the LORD.

⁴ Wealth attracts many friends,
but even the closest friend of the poor person
deserts them.

⁵ A false witness will not go unpunished,
and whoever pours out lies will not go free.

⁶ Many curry favor with a ruler,
and everyone is the friend of one who gives gifts.

⁷ The poor are shunned by all their relatives—
how much more do their friends avoid them!
Though the poor pursue them with pleading,
they are nowhere to be found.ᵃ

⁸ The one who gets wisdom loves life;
the one who cherishes understanding will
soon prosper.

⁹ A false witness will not go unpunished,
and whoever pours out lies will perish.

¹⁰ It is not fitting for a fool to live in luxury—
how much worse for a slave to rule over princes!

¹¹ A person's wisdom yields patience;
it is to one's glory to overlook an offense.

¹² A king's rage is like the roar of a lion,
but his favor is like dew on the grass.

Why do rulers seem to have many friends? (19:6)
People want to become friends with those who are in power because by doing so they believe it will give them certain advantages.

ᵃ 7 The meaning of the Hebrew for this sentence is uncertain.

¹³ A foolish child is a father's ruin,
　　and a quarrelsome wife is like
　　the constant dripping of a leaky roof.

¹⁴ Houses and wealth are inherited from parents,
　　but a prudent wife is from the LORD.

¹⁵ Laziness brings on deep sleep,
　　and the shiftless go hungry.

¹⁶ Whoever keeps commandments keeps their life,
　　but whoever shows contempt for their ways will die.

¹⁷ Whoever is kind to the poor lends to the LORD,
　　and he will reward them for what they have done.

¹⁸ Discipline your children, for in that there is hope;
　　do not be a willing party to their death.

¹⁹ A hot-tempered person must pay the penalty;
　　rescue them, and you will have to do it again.

²⁰ Listen to advice and accept discipline,
　　and at the end you will be counted among the wise.

²¹ Many are the plans in a person's heart,
　　but it is the LORD's purpose that prevails.

²² What a person desires is unfailing love*;
　　better to be poor than a liar.

²³ The fear of the LORD leads to life;
　　then one rests content, untouched by trouble.

²⁴ A sluggard buries his hand in the dish;
　　he will not even bring it back to his mouth!

²⁵ Flog a mocker, and the simple will learn prudence;
　　rebuke the discerning, and they will gain knowledge.

²⁶ Whoever robs their father and drives out their mother
　　is a child who brings shame and disgrace.

²⁷ Stop listening to instruction, my son,
　　and you will stray from the words of knowledge.

²⁸ A corrupt witness mocks at justice,
　　and the mouth of the wicked gulps down evil.

²⁹ Penalties are prepared for mockers,
　　and beatings for the backs of fools.

20 Wine is a mocker and beer a brawler;
　　whoever is led astray by them is not wise.

² A king's wrath strikes terror like the roar of a lion;
　　those who anger him forfeit their lives.

³ It is to one's honor to avoid strife,
　　but every fool is quick to quarrel.

⁴ Sluggards do not plow in season;
　　so at harvest time they look but find nothing.

⁵ The purposes of a person's heart are deep waters,
　　but one who has insight draws them out.

a 22 Or *Greed is a person's shame*

How can helping the poor be a loan to God? (19:17)
God has great love and concern for the poor and needy. Those who help the poor are in effect giving to God.

What does this proverb say about people's lives? (19:21)
People may make all the plans they want, but ultimately it is God who decides how things will turn out.

Why were these behaviors singled out? (19:26)
Children were expected to take care of their parents when they were sick or old. Robbing or attacking one's parents were serious crimes.

⁶ Many claim to have unfailing love,
　　but a faithful person who can find?

⁷ The righteous lead blameless lives;
　　blessed are their children after them.

⁸ When a king sits on his throne to judge,
　　he winnows out all evil with his eyes.

⁹ Who can say, "I have kept my heart pure;
　　I am clean and without sin"?

¹⁰ Differing weights and differing measures—
　　the LORD detests them both.

¹¹ Even small children are known by their actions,
　　so is their conduct really pure and upright?

¹² Ears that hear and eyes that see—
　　the LORD has made them both.

¹³ Do not love sleep or you will grow poor;
　　stay awake and you will have food to spare.

¹⁴ "It's no good, it's no good!" says the buyer—
　　then goes off and boasts about the purchase.

¹⁵ Gold there is, and rubies in abundance,
　　but lips that speak knowledge are a rare jewel.

¹⁶ Take the garment of one who puts up security
　　　for a stranger;
　　hold it in pledge if it is done for an outsider.

¹⁷ Food gained by fraud tastes sweet,
　　but one ends up with a mouth full of gravel.

¹⁸ Plans are established by seeking advice;
　　so if you wage war, obtain guidance.

¹⁹ A gossip betrays a confidence;
　　so avoid anyone who talks too much.

²⁰ If someone curses their father or mother,
　　their lamp will be snuffed out in pitch darkness.

²¹ An inheritance claimed too soon
　　will not be blessed at the end.

²² Do not say, "I'll pay you back for this wrong!"
　　Wait for the LORD, and he will avenge you.

²³ The LORD detests differing weights,
　　and dishonest scales do not please him.

²⁴ A person's steps are directed by the LORD.
　　How then can anyone understand their own way?

²⁵ It is a trap to dedicate something rashly
　　and only later to consider one's vows.

²⁶ A wise king winnows out the wicked;
　　he drives the threshing wheel over them.

²⁷ The human spirit is*ᵃ* the lamp of the LORD
　　that sheds light on one's inmost being.

ᵃ 27 Or *A person's words are*

What type of fraud was being practiced here? (20:14)
Prices were often agreed upon by bargaining, so the buyer was questioning the value of the product in order to pay less than it was worth.

What is this proverb about? (20:16)
A garment could be taken as security for a debt. But assuming the debt of someone whose reliability was unknown or questionable was foolish.

What happened to a person who cursed his father or mother? (20:20)
This was a sin punishable by death (Leviticus 20:9).

²⁸ Love and faithfulness keep a king safe;
    through love his throne is made secure.

²⁹ The glory of young men is their strength,
    gray hair the splendor of the old.

³⁰ Blows and wounds scrub away evil,
    and beatings purge the inmost being.

21 In the LORD's hand the king's heart is
    a stream of water
    that he channels toward all who please him.

² A person may think their own ways are right,
    but the LORD weighs the heart.

³ To do what is right and just
    is more acceptable to the LORD than sacrifice.

⁴ Haughty eyes and a proud heart—
    the unplowed field of the wicked—produce sin.

⁵ The plans of the diligent lead to profit
    as surely as haste leads to poverty.

⁶ A fortune made by a lying tongue
    is a fleeting vapor and a deadly snare.^a

⁷ The violence of the wicked will drag them away,
    for they refuse to do what is right.

⁸ The way of the guilty is devious,
    but the conduct of the innocent is upright.

⁹ Better to live on a corner of the roof
    than share a house with a quarrelsome wife.

¹⁰ The wicked crave evil;
    their neighbors get no mercy from them.

¹¹ When a mocker is punished, the simple gain wisdom;
    by paying attention to the wise they get knowledge.

¹² The Righteous One^b takes note of the house
        of the wicked
    and brings the wicked to ruin.

¹³ Whoever shuts their ears to the cry of the poor
    will also cry out and not be answered.

¹⁴ A gift given in secret soothes anger,
    and a bribe concealed in the cloak pacifies great
        wrath.

¹⁵ When justice is done, it brings joy to the righteous
    but terror to evildoers.

¹⁶ Whoever strays from the path of prudence
    comes to rest in the company of the dead.

¹⁷ Whoever loves pleasure will become poor;
    whoever loves wine and olive oil will never
        be rich.

How could someone live on the roof? (21:9)
At that time, houses had flat roofs on which produce could be spread out to dry. Small rooms could also be built there.

The Roof of a House

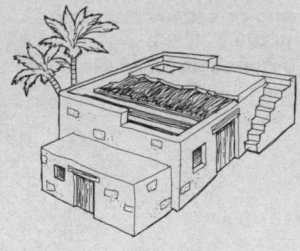

How would wine and oil keep someone from becoming rich? (21:17)
Wine and oil were common parts of a lavish lifestyle. Oil was often used in perfumes and lotions that were very expensive. Buying too much oil would be a way for a person to spend all of their money and end up broke.

^a 6 Some Hebrew manuscripts, Septuagint and Vulgate; most Hebrew manuscripts *vapor for those who seek death*   ^b 12 Or *The righteous person*

¹⁸ The wicked become a ransom for the righteous,
   and the unfaithful for the upright.

¹⁹ Better to live in a desert
   than with a quarrelsome and nagging wife.

²⁰ The wise store up choice food and olive oil,
   but fools gulp theirs down.

²¹ Whoever pursues righteousness and love
   finds life, prosperity*a* and honor.

²² One who is wise can go up against the city
        of the mighty
   and pull down the stronghold in which they trust.

²³ Those who guard their mouths and their tongues
   keep themselves from calamity.

²⁴ The proud and arrogant person—"Mocker" is
        his name—
   behaves with insolent fury.

²⁵ The craving of a sluggard will be the death of him,
   because his hands refuse to work.

²⁶ All day long he craves for more,
   but the righteous give without sparing.

²⁷ The sacrifice of the wicked is detestable—
   how much more so when brought with evil intent!

²⁸ A false witness will perish,
   but a careful listener will testify successfully.

²⁹ The wicked put up a bold front,
   but the upright give thought to their ways.

³⁰ There is no wisdom, no insight, no plan
   that can succeed against the LORD.

³¹ The horse is made ready for the day of battle,
   but victory rests with the LORD.

22 A good name is more desirable than great riches;
        to be esteemed is better than silver or gold.

² Rich and poor have this in common:
   The LORD is the Maker of them all.

³ The prudent see danger and take refuge,
   but the simple keep going and pay the penalty.

⁴ Humility is the fear of the LORD;
   its wages are riches and honor and life.

⁵ In the paths of the wicked are snares and pitfalls,
   but those who would preserve their life stay
        far from them.

⁶ Start children off on the way they should go,
   and even when they are old they will not turn from it.

⁷ The rich rule over the poor,
   and the borrower is slave to the lender.

a 21 Or righteousness

Why would a wise man attack a city? (21:22)
This was another way of saying that wisdom is better than strength and the righteous can overcome the wicked.

What is the meaning of this proverb? (21:31)
God often warned against placing trust in horses and chariots. It isn't military might or human strength that wins wars; rather, it is God who gives the victory.

How are rich and poor people alike? (22:2)
Both must answer to God, their Creator.

How did parents in ancient times train their children? (22:6)
Much of the training took place through stories of the family and the nation's history. Parents also modeled proper worship and moral behavior.

⁸ Whoever sows injustice reaps calamity,
     and the rod they wield in fury will be broken.

⁹ The generous will themselves be blessed,
     for they share their food with the poor.

¹⁰ Drive out the mocker, and out goes strife;
     quarrels and insults are ended.

¹¹ One who loves a pure heart and who speaks with grace
     will have the king for a friend.

¹² The eyes of the Lord keep watch over knowledge,
     but he frustrates the words of the unfaithful.

¹³ The sluggard says, "There's a lion outside!
     I'll be killed in the public square!"

¹⁴ The mouth of an adulterous woman is a deep pit;
     a man who is under the Lord's wrath falls into it.

¹⁵ Folly is bound up in the heart of a child,
     but the rod of discipline will drive it far away.

¹⁶ One who oppresses the poor to increase his wealth
     and one who gives gifts to the rich—both come
     to poverty.

THIRTY SAYINGS OF THE WISE

SAYING 1

¹⁷ Pay attention and turn your ear to the sayings
     of the wise;
     apply your heart to what I teach,
¹⁸ for it is pleasing when you keep them in your heart
     and have all of them ready on your lips.
¹⁹ So that your trust may be in the Lord,
     I teach you today, even you.
²⁰ Have I not written thirty sayings for you,
     sayings of counsel and knowledge,
²¹ teaching you to be honest and to speak the truth,
     so that you bring back truthful reports
     to those you serve?

SAYING 2

²² Do not exploit the poor because they are poor
     and do not crush the needy in court,
²³ for the Lord will take up their case
     and will exact life for life.

SAYING 3

²⁴ Do not make friends with a hot-tempered person,
     do not associate with one easily angered,
²⁵ or you may learn their ways
     and get yourself ensnared.

SAYING 4

²⁶ Do not be one who shakes hands in pledge
     or puts up security for debts;
²⁷ if you lack the means to pay,
     your very bed will be snatched from under you.

How can friends influence attitudes and behavior? (22:24–25)
A person with a negative trait such as a bad temper can influence his or her friends, and they may begin to act the same way.

SAYING 5

²⁸ Do not move an ancient boundary stone
    set up by your ancestors.

SAYING 6

²⁹ Do you see someone skilled in their work?
    They will serve before kings;
    they will not serve before officials
        of low rank.

SAYING 7

23 When you sit to dine with a ruler,
    note well what*ᵃ* is before you,
² and put a knife to your throat
    if you are given to gluttony.
³ Do not crave his delicacies,
    for that food is deceptive.

SAYING 8

⁴ Do not wear yourself out to get rich;
    do not trust your own cleverness.
⁵ Cast but a glance at riches, and they are gone,
    for they will surely sprout wings
    and fly off to the sky like an eagle.

SAYING 9

⁶ Do not eat the food of a begrudging host,
    do not crave his delicacies;
⁷ for he is the kind of person
    who is always thinking about the cost.*ᵇ*
"Eat and drink," he says to you,
    but his heart is not with you.
⁸ You will vomit up the little you have eaten
    and will have wasted your compliments.

SAYING 10

⁹ Do not speak to fools,
    for they will scorn your prudent words.

SAYING 11

¹⁰ Do not move an ancient boundary stone
    or encroach on the fields of the fatherless,
¹¹ for their Defender is strong;
    he will take up their case against you.

SAYING 12

¹² Apply your heart to instruction
    and your ears to words of knowledge.

SAYING 13

¹³ Do not withhold discipline from a child;
    if you punish them with the rod,
        they will not die.
¹⁴ Punish them with the rod
    and save them from death.

What is the author's advice about seeking riches? (23:4–5)
The desire to get rich can ruin a person physically and spiritually. In addition, riches are often only temporary.

Who was the Defender? (23:11)
This was the kinsman-redeemer, someone who helped close relatives regain their land (see Leviticus 25:25).

ᵃ 1 Or *who*   *ᵇ 7* Or *for as he thinks within himself, / so he is*; or *for as he puts on a feast, / so he is*

SAYING 14

¹⁵ My son, if your heart is wise,
    then my heart will be glad indeed;
¹⁶ my inmost being will rejoice
    when your lips speak what is right.

SAYING 15

¹⁷ Do not let your heart envy sinners,
    but always be zealous for the fear of the LORD.
¹⁸ There is surely a future hope for you,
    and your hope will not be cut off.

SAYING 16

¹⁹ Listen, my son, and be wise,
    and set your heart on the right path:
²⁰ Do not join those who drink too much wine
    or gorge themselves on meat,
²¹ for drunkards and gluttons become poor,
    and drowsiness clothes them in rags.

SAYING 17

²² Listen to your father, who gave you life,
    and do not despise your mother when she is old.
²³ Buy the truth and do not sell it—
    wisdom, instruction and insight as well.
²⁴ The father of a righteous child has great joy;
    a man who fathers a wise son rejoices in him.
²⁵ May your father and mother rejoice;
    may she who gave you birth be joyful!

SAYING 18

²⁶ My son, give me your heart
    and let your eyes delight in my ways,
²⁷ for an adulterous woman is a deep pit,
    and a wayward wife is a narrow well.
²⁸ Like a bandit she lies in wait
    and multiplies the unfaithful among men.

SAYING 19

²⁹ Who has woe? Who has sorrow?
    Who has strife? Who has complaints?
    Who has needless bruises? Who has bloodshot eyes?

What are the risks of alcoholism? (23:29–35)
This extended section describes with vivid word pictures several consequences of drinking too much. These include feeling unnecessarily sad, being angry, hurting yourself and others, and having bloodshot eyes.

How can we develop wise hearts?   PROVERBS 23

The book of Proverbs focuses on the theme of wisdom. The writer often contrasts wisdom with foolishness to make the point clear. Most proverbs are short, compact statements about human behavior. The author talks about issues that face people in their daily lives. He warns against sexual immorality, violence, dishonesty, laziness, overeating, and pride, along with other kinds of foolish behavior. All of the proverbs express a general truth, but they should not be understood as commandments or promises.

For example, Proverbs 22:6 says, "Start children off on the way they should go, and even when they are old they will not turn from it." This expresses the general principle that parents are responsible to bring up their children well and to teach them how they should behave. Children who are raised this way are more likely to have good morals and beliefs. The proverb does not mean that every child from a Christian family will *always* grow up to be a believer or a good person. It also doesn't mean that if someone grows up to be a bad person, then his or her parents are responsible.

Wisdom in the book of Proverbs is always based on loving God and honoring him by seeking to follow his will.

30 Those who linger over wine,
 who go to sample bowls of mixed wine.
31 Do not gaze at wine when it is red,
 when it sparkles in the cup,
 when it goes down smoothly!
32 In the end it bites like a snake
 and poisons like a viper.
33 Your eyes will see strange sights,
 and your mind will imagine confusing things.
34 You will be like one sleeping on the high seas,
 lying on top of the rigging.
35 "They hit me," you will say, "but I'm not hurt!
 They beat me, but I don't feel it!
 When will I wake up
  so I can find another drink?"

SAYING 20

24 Do not envy the wicked,
 do not desire their company;
2 for their hearts plot violence,
 and their lips talk about making trouble.

SAYING 21

3 By wisdom a house is built,
 and through understanding it is established;
4 through knowledge its rooms are filled
 with rare and beautiful treasures.

SAYING 22

5 The wise prevail through great power,
 and those who have knowledge muster their
  strength.
6 Surely you need guidance to wage war,
 and victory is won through many advisers.

SAYING 23

7 Wisdom is too high for fools;
 in the assembly at the gate they must not
  open their mouths.

SAYING 24

8 Whoever plots evil
 will be known as a schemer.
9 The schemes of folly are sin,
 and people detest a mocker.

SAYING 25

10 If you falter in a time of trouble,
 how small is your strength!
11 Rescue those being led away to death;
 hold back those staggering toward slaughter.
12 If you say, "But we knew nothing about this,"
 does not he who weighs the heart perceive it?
Does not he who guards your life know it?
 Will he not repay everyone according to what
  they have done?

What was the assembly at the gate? (24:7)
The city gate was where the leaders of the city met to hold court, where the marketplace was located, and where official business took place.

Why should someone eat honey? (24:13)
This is a word picture comparing wisdom to honey. Both provide nourishment and are sweet.

SAYING 26

¹³ Eat honey, my son, for it is good;
  honey from the comb is sweet to your taste.
¹⁴ Know also that wisdom is like honey for you:
  If you find it, there is a future hope for you,
  and your hope will not be cut off.

SAYING 27

¹⁵ Do not lurk like a thief near the house of the righteous,
  do not plunder their dwelling place;
¹⁶ for though the righteous fall seven times, they rise again,
  but the wicked stumble when calamity strikes.

SAYING 28

¹⁷ Do not gloat when your enemy falls;
  when they stumble, do not let your heart rejoice,
¹⁸ or the LORD will see and disapprove
  and turn his wrath away from them.

SAYING 29

¹⁹ Do not fret because of evildoers
  or be envious of the wicked,
²⁰ for the evildoer has no future hope,
  and the lamp of the wicked will be snuffed out.

SAYING 30

Whom would wise people obey? (24:21)
They would obey the LORD and the LORD's representative, the king.

²¹ Fear the LORD and the king, my son,
  and do not join with rebellious officials,
²² for those two will send sudden destruction on them,
  and who knows what calamities they can bring?

FURTHER SAYINGS OF THE WISE

²³ These also are sayings of the wise:

To show partiality in judging is not good:
²⁴ Whoever says to the guilty, "You are innocent,"
  will be cursed by peoples and denounced by nations.
²⁵ But it will go well with those who convict the guilty,
  and rich blessing will come on them.

²⁶ An honest answer
  is like a kiss on the lips.

²⁷ Put your outdoor work in order
  and get your fields ready;
  after that, build your house.

What does this proverb mean? (24:27)
The idea here is that a person should plan carefully and have income before building a house. Preparation and planning are important.

²⁸ Do not testify against your neighbor without cause—
  would you use your lips to mislead?
²⁹ Do not say, "I'll do to them as they have done to me;
  I'll pay them back for what they did."

³⁰ I went past the field of a sluggard,
  past the vineyard of someone who has no sense;
³¹ thorns had come up everywhere,
  the ground was covered with weeds,
  and the stone wall was in ruins.

³²I applied my heart to what I observed
  and learned a lesson from what I saw:
³³A little sleep, a little slumber,
  a little folding of the hands to rest—
³⁴and poverty will come on you like a thief
  and scarcity like an armed man.

MORE PROVERBS OF SOLOMON

25 These are more proverbs of Solomon, compiled by
  the men of Hezekiah king of Judah:

²It is the glory of God to conceal a matter;
  to search out a matter is the glory of kings.
³As the heavens are high and the earth is deep,
  so the hearts of kings are unsearchable.

⁴Remove the dross from the silver,
  and a silversmith can produce a vessel;
⁵remove wicked officials from the king's presence,
  and his throne will be established through
    righteousness.

⁶Do not exalt yourself in the king's presence,
  and do not claim a place among his great men;
⁷it is better for him to say to you, "Come up here,"
  than for him to humiliate you before his nobles.

What you have seen with your eyes
⁸ do not bring[a] hastily to court,
for what will you do in the end
  if your neighbor puts you to shame?
⁹If you take your neighbor to court,
  do not betray another's confidence,
¹⁰or the one who hears it may shame you
  and the charge against you will stand.

¹¹Like apples[b] of gold in settings of silver
  is a ruling rightly given.
¹²Like an earring of gold or an ornament of fine gold
  is the rebuke of a wise judge to a listening ear.

¹³Like a snow-cooled drink at harvest time
  is a trustworthy messenger to the one who sends him;
  he refreshes the spirit of his master.
¹⁴Like clouds and wind without rain
  is one who boasts of gifts never given.

¹⁵Through patience a ruler can be persuaded,
  and a gentle tongue can break a bone.

¹⁶If you find honey, eat just enough—
  too much of it, and you will vomit.
¹⁷Seldom set foot in your neighbor's house—
  too much of you, and they will hate you.

¹⁸Like a club or a sword or a sharp arrow
  is one who gives false testimony against a neighbor.

How valuable is wise speech? (25:11–12)
The author compares wise speech and careful correction to fine jewelry.

---

a 7,8 Or nobles / on whom you had set your eyes. /⁸Do not go   *b 11 Or possibly apricots*

Why would someone heap burning coals on a person's head? (25:21–22)
Treating an enemy with kindness could cause that person to repent. In this case, the hot coals represent the regret or shame the guilty person feels after these kind acts. Another possible explanation is that it refers to an Egyptian practice of having a guilty person carry a basin of hot coals on his head as a sign of repentance.

What was the condition of a city with broken walls? (25:28)
A city with broken-down walls was considered defenseless and disgraced.

What good was a sling with a stone tied into it? (26:8)
A sling with a stone tied into it was useless as a weapon. In the same way, it is useless to honor a foolish person.

¹⁹ Like a broken tooth or a lame foot
     is reliance on the unfaithful in a time of trouble.
²⁰ Like one who takes away a garment on a cold day,
     or like vinegar poured on a wound,
     is one who sings songs to a heavy heart.

²¹ If your enemy is hungry, give him food to eat;
     if he is thirsty, give him water to drink.
²² In doing this, you will heap burning coals on his head,
     and the LORD will reward you.

²³ Like a north wind that brings unexpected rain
     is a sly tongue—which provokes a horrified look.

²⁴ Better to live on a corner of the roof
     than share a house with a quarrelsome wife.

²⁵ Like cold water to a weary soul
     is good news from a distant land.
²⁶ Like a muddied spring or a polluted well
     are the righteous who give way to the wicked.

²⁷ It is not good to eat too much honey,
     nor is it honorable to search out matters that
        are too deep.

²⁸ Like a city whose walls are broken through
     is a person who lacks self-control.

26 Like snow in summer or rain in harvest,
     honor is not fitting for a fool.
² Like a fluttering sparrow or a darting swallow,
     an undeserved curse does not come to rest.
³ A whip for the horse, a bridle for the donkey,
     and a rod for the backs of fools!
⁴ Do not answer a fool according to his folly,
     or you yourself will be just like him.
⁵ Answer a fool according to his folly,
     or he will be wise in his own eyes.
⁶ Sending a message by the hands of a fool
     is like cutting off one's feet or drinking poison.
⁷ Like the useless legs of one who is lame
     is a proverb in the mouth of a fool.
⁸ Like tying a stone in a sling
     is the giving of honor to a fool.
⁹ Like a thornbush in a drunkard's hand
     is a proverb in the mouth of a fool.
¹⁰ Like an archer who wounds at random
     is one who hires a fool or any passer-by.
¹¹ As a dog returns to its vomit,
     so fools repeat their folly.
¹² Do you see a person wise in their own eyes?
     There is more hope for a fool than for them.

¹³ A sluggard says, "There's a lion in the road,
     a fierce lion roaming the streets!"
¹⁴ As a door turns on its hinges,
     so a sluggard turns on his bed.
¹⁵ A sluggard buries his hand in the dish;
     he is too lazy to bring it back to his mouth.

16 A sluggard is wiser in his own eyes
    than seven people who answer discreetly.

17 Like one who grabs a stray dog by the ears
    is someone who rushes into a quarrel not their own.

18 Like a maniac shooting
    flaming arrows of death
19 is one who deceives their neighbor
    and says, "I was only joking!"

20 Without wood a fire goes out;
    without a gossip a quarrel dies down.
21 As charcoal to embers and as wood to fire,
    so is a quarrelsome person for kindling strife.
22 The words of a gossip are like choice morsels;
    they go down to the inmost parts.

23 Like a coating of silver dross on earthenware
    are fervent*a* lips with an evil heart.
24 Enemies disguise themselves with their lips,
    but in their hearts they harbor deceit.
25 Though their speech is charming, do not
        believe them,
    for seven abominations fill their hearts.
26 Their malice may be concealed by deception,
    but their wickedness will be exposed in
        the assembly.
27 Whoever digs a pit will fall into it;
    if someone rolls a stone, it will roll back on them.
28 A lying tongue hates those it hurts,
    and a flattering mouth works ruin.

27 Do not boast about tomorrow,
        for you do not know what a day may bring.

2 Let someone else praise you, and not your
        own mouth;
    an outsider, and not your own lips.

3 Stone is heavy and sand a burden,
    but a fool's provocation is heavier than both.

4 Anger is cruel and fury overwhelming,
    but who can stand before jealousy?

5 Better is open rebuke
    than hidden love.

6 Wounds from a friend can be trusted,
    but an enemy multiplies kisses.

7 One who is full loathes honey from the comb,
    but to the hungry even what is bitter tastes sweet.

8 Like a bird that flees its nest
    is anyone who flees from home.

9 Perfume and incense bring joy to the heart,
    and the pleasantness of a friend
        springs from their heartfelt advice.

a 23 Hebrew; Septuagint *smooth*

What would happen if a person shot flaming arrows? (26:18–19)
These could easily ignite sheaves of grain or cause other disastrous fires. In the same way, if a person lies and then claims to be only joking, it may be too late to undo the damage.

What is the point of this proverb? (26:27)
If a person tries to harm someone else by digging a pit or rolling a stone, he may fall into his own trap. In other words, his evil intentions may harm him rather than his intended victim.

Why is it better for someone else to praise you? (27:2)
Someone else will notice and offer praise if you deserve it. Their praise will be more convincing than any boastful comments you make about yourself.

¹⁰ Do not forsake your friend or a friend of your family,
   and do not go to your relative's house when disaster
      strikes you—
better a neighbor nearby than a relative far away.

¹¹ Be wise, my son, and bring joy to my heart;
   then I can answer anyone who treats me with
      contempt.

¹² The prudent see danger and take refuge,
   but the simple keep going and pay the penalty.

¹³ Take the garment of one who puts up security
      for a stranger;
   hold it in pledge if it is done for an outsider.

¹⁴ If anyone loudly blesses their neighbor early
      in the morning,
   it will be taken as a curse.

¹⁵ A quarrelsome wife is like the dripping
      of a leaky roof in a rainstorm;
¹⁶ restraining her is like restraining the wind
   or grasping oil with the hand.

¹⁷ As iron sharpens iron,
   so one person sharpens another.

¹⁸ The one who guards a fig tree will eat its fruit,
   and whoever protects their master will be honored.

¹⁹ As water reflects the face,
   so one's life reflects the heart.ᵃ

²⁰ Death and Destructionᵇ are never satisfied,
   and neither are human eyes.

²¹ The crucible for silver and the furnace for gold,
   but people are tested by their praise.

²² Though you grind a fool in a mortar,
   grinding them like grain with a pestle,
   you will not remove their folly from them.

²³ Be sure you know the condition of your flocks,
   give careful attention to your herds;
²⁴ for riches do not endure forever,
   and a crown is not secure for all generations.
²⁵ When the hay is removed and new growth appears
   and the grass from the hills is gathered in,
²⁶ the lambs will provide you with clothing,
   and the goats with the price of a field.
²⁷ You will have plenty of goats' milk to feed your family
   and to nourish your female servants.

28 The wicked flee though no one pursues,
      but the righteous are as bold as a lion.

² When a country is rebellious, it has many rulers,
   but a ruler with discernment and knowledge
      maintains order.

How do people sharpen each other? (27:17)
Because people have different opinions and ideas, when they exchange those ideas or even argue about them, they both sharpen their ideas and their thinking.

What were a mortar and pestle? (27:22)
A mortar was a bowl, and a pestle was a blunt tool used for grinding or pounding grain or herbs.

ᵃ 19 Or *so others reflect your heart back to you*   ᵇ 20 Hebrew *Abaddon*

³A ruler*a* who oppresses the poor
  is like a driving rain that leaves no crops.

⁴Those who forsake instruction praise the wicked,
  but those who heed it resist them.

⁵Evildoers do not understand what is right,
  but those who seek the LORD understand it fully.

⁶Better the poor whose walk is blameless
  than the rich whose ways are perverse.

⁷A discerning son heeds instruction,
  but a companion of gluttons disgraces his father.

⁸Whoever increases wealth by taking interest or profit
      from the poor
  amasses it for another, who will be kind to the poor.

⁹If anyone turns a deaf ear to my instruction,
  even their prayers are detestable.

¹⁰Whoever leads the upright along an evil path
  will fall into their own trap,
  but the blameless will receive a good inheritance.

¹¹The rich are wise in their own eyes;
  one who is poor and discerning sees how deluded
      they are.

¹²When the righteous triumph, there is great elation;
  but when the wicked rise to power, people go
      into hiding.

¹³Whoever conceals their sins does not prosper,
  but the one who confesses and renounces them
      finds mercy.

¹⁴Blessed is the one who always trembles before God,
  but whoever hardens their heart falls into trouble.

What does it mean to harden one's heart? (28:14)
Similar to oxen that stubbornly resist the yoke around their necks, when people harden their hearts, they stubbornly resist God's commands.

¹⁵Like a roaring lion or a charging bear
  is a wicked ruler over a helpless people.

¹⁶A tyrannical ruler practices extortion,
  but one who hates ill-gotten gain will enjoy
      a long reign.

¹⁷Anyone tormented by the guilt of murder
  will seek refuge in the grave;
  let no one hold them back.

¹⁸The one whose walk is blameless is kept safe,
  but the one whose ways are perverse will fall into
      the pit.*b*

¹⁹Those who work their land will have abundant food,
  but those who chase fantasies will have their
      fill of poverty.

What does it mean to chase fantasies? (28:19)
A farmer and others who work hard will gather a good crop, but someone who has get-rich-quick schemes will be unsuccessful.

²⁰A faithful person will be richly blessed,
  but one eager to get rich will not go unpunished.

²¹To show partiality is not good—
  yet a person will do wrong for a piece of bread.

---

a 3 Or *A poor person*   *b 18* Syriac (see Septuagint); Hebrew *into one*

²² The stingy are eager to get rich
and are unaware that poverty awaits them.

²³ Whoever rebukes a person will in the end gain favor
rather than one who has a flattering tongue.

²⁴ Whoever robs their father or mother
and says, "It's not wrong,"
is partner to one who destroys.

²⁵ The greedy stir up conflict,
but those who trust in the LORD will prosper.

²⁶ Those who trust in themselves are fools,
but those who walk in wisdom are kept safe.

²⁷ Those who give to the poor will lack nothing,
but those who close their eyes to them receive
many curses.

²⁸ When the wicked rise to power, people go into hiding;
but when the wicked perish, the righteous thrive.

29

Whoever remains stiff-necked after many rebukes
will suddenly be destroyed—without remedy.

² When the righteous thrive, the people rejoice;
when the wicked rule, the people groan.

³ A man who loves wisdom brings joy to his father,
but a companion of prostitutes squanders
his wealth.

⁴ By justice a king gives a country stability,
but those who are greedy for^a bribes tear it down.

⁵ Those who flatter their neighbors
are spreading nets for their feet.

⁶ Evildoers are snared by their own sin,
but the righteous shout for joy and are glad.

⁷ The righteous care about justice for the poor,
but the wicked have no such concern.

⁸ Mockers stir up a city,
but the wise turn away anger.

⁹ If a wise person goes to court with a fool,
the fool rages and scoffs, and there is no peace.

¹⁰ The bloodthirsty hate a person of integrity
and seek to kill the upright.

¹¹ Fools give full vent to their rage,
but the wise bring calm in the end.

¹² If a ruler listens to lies,
all his officials become wicked.

¹³ The poor and the oppressor have this in common:
The LORD gives sight to the eyes of both.

¹⁴ If a king judges the poor with fairness,
his throne will be established forever.

Why is self-confidence foolish? (28:26)
Those who rely only on their own abilities and opinions are likely to be misguided, but those who seek wise counsel and try to follow God's commandments will be blessed.

What did it mean to be stiff-necked? (29:1)
This was how a farmer would describe an ox or a horse that would not be led or respond when its rope was tugged. Here it referred to a stubborn person who would not accept correction.

---

^a 4 Or who give

¹⁵ A rod and a reprimand impart wisdom,
    but a child left undisciplined disgraces its mother.

¹⁶ When the wicked thrive, so does sin,
    but the righteous will see their downfall.

¹⁷ Discipline your children, and they will give
      you peace;
    they will bring you the delights you desire.

¹⁸ Where there is no revelation, people cast off restraint;
    but blessed is the one who heeds wisdom's
      instruction.

¹⁹ Servants cannot be corrected by mere words;
    though they understand, they will not respond.

²⁰ Do you see someone who speaks in haste?
    There is more hope for a fool than for them.

²¹ A servant pampered from youth
    will turn out to be insolent.

²² An angry person stirs up conflict,
    and a hot-tempered person commits many sins.

²³ Pride brings a person low,
    but the lowly in spirit gain honor.

²⁴ The accomplices of thieves are their own enemies;
    they are put under oath and dare not testify.

²⁵ Fear of man will prove to be a snare,
    but whoever trusts in the LORD is kept safe.

²⁶ Many seek an audience with a ruler,
    but it is from the LORD that one gets justice.

²⁷ The righteous detest the dishonest;
    the wicked detest the upright.

SAYINGS OF AGUR

30 The sayings of Agur son of Jakeh — an inspired utterance.

This man's utterance to Ithiel:

"I am weary, God,
    but I can prevail.ᵃ
² Surely I am only a brute, not a man;
    I do not have human understanding.
³ I have not learned wisdom,
    nor have I attained to the knowledge of the
      Holy One.
⁴ Who has gone up to heaven and come down?
    Whose hands have gathered up the wind?
Who has wrapped up the waters in a cloak?
    Who has established all the ends of the earth?
What is his name, and what is the name of his son?
    Surely you know!

ᵃ *1* With a different word division of the Hebrew; Masoretic Text *utterance to Ithiel, / to Ithiel and Ukal:*

What is the purpose of the rod of correction? (29:15)
This points to how discipline is seen as a way to help children gain wisdom.

What does this proverb mean? (29:24)
A person becomes his own enemy when he is an accomplice to a crime. Because he is unwilling to testify at the trial, he is declaring himself guilty.

Why would the Bible include the proverbs of an ignorant man? (30:2-3)
Agur's expression of ignorance is actually a sign of his humility. Agur claimed that human beings cannot know anything apart from God's Word.

⁵ "Every word of God is flawless;
    he is a shield to those who take refuge in him.
⁶ Do not add to his words,
    or he will rebuke you and prove you a liar.

⁷ "Two things I ask of you, LORD;
    do not refuse me before I die:
⁸ Keep falsehood and lies far from me;
    give me neither poverty nor riches,
    but give me only my daily bread.
⁹ Otherwise, I may have too much and disown you
    and say, 'Who is the LORD?'
Or I may become poor and steal,
    and so dishonor the name of my God.

¹⁰ "Do not slander a servant to their master,
    or they will curse you, and you will pay for it.

¹¹ "There are those who curse their fathers
    and do not bless their mothers;
¹² those who are pure in their own eyes
    and yet are not cleansed of their filth;
¹³ those whose eyes are ever so haughty,
    whose glances are so disdainful;
¹⁴ those whose teeth are swords
    and whose jaws are set with knives
to devour the poor from the earth
    and the needy from among mankind.

¹⁵ "The leech has two daughters.
    'Give! Give!' they cry.

"There are three things that are never satisfied,
    four that never say, 'Enough!':
¹⁶ the grave, the barren womb,
    land, which is never satisfied with water,
    and fire, which never says, 'Enough!'

¹⁷ "The eye that mocks a father,
    that scorns an aged mother,
will be pecked out by the ravens of the valley,
    will be eaten by the vultures.

¹⁸ "There are three things that are too amazing for me,
    four that I do not understand:
¹⁹ the way of an eagle in the sky,
    the way of a snake on a rock,
the way of a ship on the high seas,
    and the way of a man with a young woman.

²⁰ "This is the way of an adulterous woman:
    She eats and wipes her mouth
    and says, 'I've done nothing wrong.'

²¹ "Under three things the earth trembles,
    under four it cannot bear up:
²² a servant who becomes king,
    a godless fool who gets plenty to eat,
²³ a contemptible woman who gets married,
    and a servant who displaces her mistress.

What does a barren womb represent? (30:16)
In ancient Israel, a wife without children was a reason for extreme sadness and a sign of disgrace.

24 "Four things on earth are small,
    yet they are extremely wise:
25 Ants are creatures of little strength,
    yet they store up their food in the summer;
26 hyraxes are creatures of little power,
    yet they make their home in the crags;
27 locusts have no king,
    yet they advance together in ranks;
28 a lizard can be caught with the hand,
    yet it is found in kings' palaces.

29 "There are three things that are stately in their stride,
    four that move with stately bearing:
30 a lion, mighty among beasts,
    who retreats before nothing;
31 a strutting rooster, a he-goat,
    and a king secure against revolt.[a]

32 "If you play the fool and exalt yourself,
    or if you plan evil,
    clap your hand over your mouth!
33 For as churning cream produces butter,
    and as twisting the nose produces blood,
    so stirring up anger produces strife."

SAYINGS OF KING LEMUEL

31 The sayings of King Lemuel—an inspired utterance
his mother taught him.

2 Listen, my son! Listen, son of my womb!
    Listen, my son, the answer to my prayers!
3 Do not spend your strength[b] on women,
    your vigor on those who ruin kings.

4 It is not for kings, Lemuel—
    it is not for kings to drink wine,
    not for rulers to crave beer,
5 lest they drink and forget what has been decreed,
    and deprive all the oppressed of their rights.
6 Let beer be for those who are perishing,
    wine for those who are in anguish!
7 Let them drink and forget their poverty
    and remember their misery no more.

8 Speak up for those who cannot speak for themselves,
    for the rights of all who are destitute.
9 Speak up and judge fairly;
    defend the rights of the poor and needy.

EPILOGUE: THE WIFE
OF NOBLE CHARACTER

10 [c]A wife of noble character who can find?
    She is worth far more than rubies.
11 Her husband has full confidence in her
    and lacks nothing of value.

---

[a] 31 The meaning of the Hebrew for this phrase is uncertain.   [b] 3 Or *wealth*
[c] 10 Verses 10-31 are an acrostic poem, the verses of which begin with the
successive letters of the Hebrew alphabet.

What is a hyrax? (30:26)
This is another name for a Syrian rock coney, an animal about the size of a rabbit that lives in rocky areas of the Holy Land.

A Locust (30:27)

Who was King Lemuel? (31:1)
He was a non-Israelite, but nothing else is known about him. Tradition, however, associates the name with Solomon.

Why was the king supposed to offer wine? (31:4–7)
Kings were supposed to stay sober so that they could rule wisely. But they were to offer wine to comfort those who were hurting in the kingdom.

How competent was the wife of noble character? (31:10–31)
These verses showed that a godly woman can succeed in any aspect of her life, including her personal life in the home, her professional life in a career, or as an individual in the community.

¹² She brings him good, not harm,
all the days of her life.
¹³ She selects wool and flax
and works with eager hands.
¹⁴ She is like the merchant ships,
bringing her food from afar.
¹⁵ She gets up while it is still night;
she provides food for her family
and portions for her female servants.
¹⁶ She considers a field and buys it;
out of her earnings she plants a vineyard.
¹⁷ She sets about her work vigorously;
her arms are strong for her tasks.
¹⁸ She sees that her trading is profitable,
and her lamp does not go out at night.
¹⁹ In her hand she holds the distaff
and grasps the spindle with her fingers.
²⁰ She opens her arms to the poor
and extends her hands to the needy.
²¹ When it snows, she has no fear for her household;
for all of them are clothed in scarlet.
²² She makes coverings for her bed;
she is clothed in fine linen and purple.
²³ Her husband is respected at the city gate,
where he takes his seat among the elders of the land.
²⁴ She makes linen garments and sells them,
and supplies the merchants with sashes.
²⁵ She is clothed with strength and dignity;
she can laugh at the days to come.
²⁶ She speaks with wisdom,
and faithful instruction is on her tongue.
²⁷ She watches over the affairs of her household
and does not eat the bread of idleness.
²⁸ Her children arise and call her blessed;
her husband also, and he praises her:
²⁹ "Many women do noble things,
but you surpass them all."
³⁰ Charm is deceptive, and beauty is fleeting;
but a woman who fears the LORD is to be praised.
³¹ Honor her for all that her hands have done,
and let her works bring her praise at the city gate.

Ecclesiastes

INTRODUCTION

Who wrote this book?

Solomon.

Why was this book written?

The book of Ecclesiastes shows that no one can have a happy life without God.

For whom was this book written?

Ecclesiastes was written for anyone who thinks that God is not important.

What do we learn about God in this book?

God is more important than money, pleasure, work, or anything else in life.

What are some important passages in this book?

Pleasure can't make people happy	Ecclesiastes 2:1–11
Success can't make people happy	Ecclesiastes 2:17–26
Riches can't make people happy	Ecclesiastes 5:8–6:2

With all the problems in the world, does life sometimes seem meaningless?

When did these things happen?

1400 BC 1300 1200 1100 1000 900 800 700 600 500 400

SAUL'S REIGN (1050 – 1010 BC)

DAVID'S REIGN (1010 – 970 BC)

SOLOMON'S REIGN (970 – 930 BC)

BOOK OF ECCLESIASTES WRITTEN (C. 970 – 930 BC)

BUILDING OF THE TEMPLE (966 – 959 BC)

DIVISION OF THE KINGDOM (930 BC)

EXILE OF ISRAEL (722 BC)

FALL OF JERUSALEM (586 BC)

EVERYTHING IS MEANINGLESS

1 The words of the Teacher,[a] son of David, king in Jerusalem:

2 "Meaningless! Meaningless!"
   says the Teacher.
"Utterly meaningless!
   Everything is meaningless."

3 What do people gain from all their labors
   at which they toil under the sun?
4 Generations come and generations go,
   but the earth remains forever.
5 The sun rises and the sun sets,
   and hurries back to where it rises.
6 The wind blows to the south
   and turns to the north;
round and round it goes,
   ever returning on its course.
7 All streams flow into the sea,
   yet the sea is never full.
To the place the streams come from,
   there they return again.
8 All things are wearisome,
   more than one can say.
The eye never has enough of seeing,
   nor the ear its fill of hearing.
9 What has been will be again,
   what has been done will be done again;
   there is nothing new under the sun.
10 Is there anything of which one can say,
   "Look! This is something new"?
It was here already, long ago;
   it was here before our time.
11 No one remembers the former
     generations,
   and even those yet to come
will not be remembered
   by those who follow them.

---

[a] 1 Or *the leader of the assembly*; also in verses 2 and 12

Why did the Teacher say everything is meaningless? (1:2)
The word *meaningless* appears about 35 times in this book. The point of the book may be that everything is meaningless unless it is related to God.

With all the problems in the world, does life sometimes seem meaningless?
ECCLESIASTES 1

The author of the book of Ecclesiastes is writing as an old man who has lived most of his life and had found that much of it is meaningless. The author talks about the meaninglessness of life apart from God. Among the things that he finds meaningless are wisdom, pleasures, work, advancement or status, and riches. The author has looked for meaning and happiness in all of these materialistic areas of life, but he has concluded that they don't give meaning or happiness.

After searching for meaning and failing to find it, the author finally concludes that human beings should accept the fact that God has arranged everything according to his purposes. Human beings must be patient and accept life as God gives it rather than chasing after pleasure. He concludes in 12:13 – 14 by saying that meaning is only found in serving God and keeping his commandments: "Now all has been heard; here is the conclusion of the matter: Fear God and keep his commandments, for this is the duty of all mankind. For God will bring every deed into judgment, including every hidden thing, whether it is good or evil."

WISDOM IS MEANINGLESS

¹²I, the Teacher, was king over Israel in Jerusalem. ¹³I applied my mind to study and to explore by wisdom all that is done under the heavens. What a heavy burden God has laid on mankind! ¹⁴I have seen all the things that are done under the sun; all of them are meaningless, a chasing after the wind.

¹⁵What is crooked cannot be straightened;
   what is lacking cannot be counted.

¹⁶I said to myself, "Look, I have increased in wisdom more than anyone who has ruled over Jerusalem before me; I have experienced much of wisdom and knowledge." ¹⁷Then I applied myself to the understanding of wisdom, and also of madness and folly, but I learned that this, too, is a chasing after the wind.

¹⁸For with much wisdom comes much sorrow;
   the more knowledge, the more grief.

PLEASURES ARE MEANINGLESS

2 I said to myself, "Come now, I will test you with pleasure to find out what is good." But that also proved to be meaningless. ²"Laughter," I said, "is madness. And what does pleasure accomplish?" ³I tried cheering myself with wine, and embracing folly—my mind still guiding me with wisdom. I wanted to see what was good for people to do under the heavens during the few days of their lives.

⁴I undertook great projects: I built houses for myself and planted vineyards. ⁵I made gardens and parks and planted all kinds of fruit trees in them. ⁶I made reservoirs to water groves of flourishing trees. ⁷I bought male and female slaves and had other slaves who were born in my house. I also owned more herds and flocks than anyone in Jerusalem before me. ⁸I amassed silver and gold for myself, and the treasure of kings and provinces. I acquired male and female singers, and a harem*a* as well—the delights of a man's heart. ⁹I became greater by far than anyone in Jerusalem before me. In all this my wisdom stayed with me.

¹⁰I denied myself nothing my eyes desired;
   I refused my heart no pleasure.
My heart took delight in all my labor,
   and this was the reward for all my toil.
¹¹Yet when I surveyed all that my hands had done
   and what I had toiled to achieve,
everything was meaningless, a chasing after the wind;
   nothing was gained under the sun.

WISDOM AND FOLLY ARE MEANINGLESS

¹²Then I turned my thoughts to consider wisdom,
   and also madness and folly.
What more can the king's successor do
   than what has already been done?
¹³I saw that wisdom is better than folly,
   just as light is better than darkness.

a 8 The meaning of the Hebrew for this phrase is uncertain.

How can wisdom cause sorrow? (1:18)
Human wisdom—wisdom without God—has no real value. Wisdom can, however, bring sadness.

Why is pleasure meaningless? (2:1)
Pleasure is something God gives to human beings, but pleasure for the sake of pleasure does not give meaning to life.

How are wisdom and foolishness similar? (2:14)
Even though wisdom is better than foolishness, both wise and foolish people die.

¹⁴The wise have eyes in their heads,
  while the fool walks in the darkness;
but I came to realize
  that the same fate overtakes them both.

¹⁵Then I said to myself,

"The fate of the fool will overtake me also.
  What then do I gain by being wise?"
I said to myself,
  "This too is meaningless."
¹⁶For the wise, like the fool, will not be long
    remembered;
  the days have already come when both have
    been forgotten.
Like the fool, the wise too must die!

TOIL IS MEANINGLESS

Why is work meaningless? (2:17–23)
Whatever a person is able to accomplish in life through hard work will be left behind when that person dies.

¹⁷So I hated life, because the work that is done under the sun was grievous to me. All of it is meaningless, a chasing after the wind. ¹⁸I hated all the things I had toiled for under the sun, because I must leave them to the one who comes after me. ¹⁹And who knows whether that person will be wise or foolish? Yet they will have control over all the fruit of my toil into which I have poured my effort and skill under the sun. This too is meaningless. ²⁰So my heart began to despair over all my toilsome labor under the sun. ²¹For a person may labor with wisdom, knowledge and skill, and then they must leave all they own to another who has not toiled for it. This too is meaningless and a great misfortune. ²²What do people get for all the toil and anxious striving with which they labor under the sun? ²³All their days their work is grief and pain; even at night their minds do not rest. This too is meaningless.

How does God make life meaningful? (2:24–25)
Life only has meaning and pleasure in God. Without God, nothing gives lasting satisfaction or enjoyment.

²⁴A person can do nothing better than to eat and drink and find satisfaction in their own toil. This too, I see, is from the hand of God, ²⁵for without him, who can eat or find enjoyment? ²⁶To the person who pleases him, God gives wisdom, knowledge and happiness, but to the sinner he gives the task of gathering and storing up wealth to hand it over to the one who pleases God. This too is meaningless, a chasing after the wind.

A TIME FOR EVERYTHING

3 There is a time for everything,
  and a season for every activity under the heavens:

² a time to be born and a time to die,
    a time to plant and a time to uproot,
³ a time to kill and a time to heal,
    a time to tear down and a time to build,
⁴ a time to weep and a time to laugh,
    a time to mourn and a time to dance,
⁵ a time to scatter stones and a time to gather them,
    a time to embrace and a time to refrain
      from embracing,
⁶ a time to search and a time to give up,
    a time to keep and a time to throw away,

7   a time to tear and a time to mend,
    a time to be silent and a time to speak,
8   a time to love and a time to hate,
    a time for war and a time for peace.

⁹What do workers gain from their toil? ¹⁰I have seen the burden God has laid on the human race. ¹¹He has made everything beautiful in its time. He has also set eternity in the human heart; yet*ᵃ* no one can fathom what God has done from beginning to end. ¹²I know that there is nothing better for people than to be happy and to do good while they live. ¹³That each of them may eat and drink, and find satisfaction in all their toil—this is the gift of God. ¹⁴I know that everything God does will endure forever; nothing can be added to it and nothing taken from it. God does it so that people will fear him.

¹⁵Whatever is has already been,
    and what will be has been before;
    and God will call the past to account.ᵇ

¹⁶And I saw something else under the sun:

In the place of judgment—wickedness was there,
    in the place of justice—wickedness was there.

¹⁷I said to myself,

"God will bring into judgment
    both the righteous and the wicked,
for there will be a time for every activity,
    a time to judge every deed."

¹⁸I also said to myself, "As for humans, God tests them so that they may see that they are like the animals. ¹⁹Surely the fate of human beings is like that of the animals; the same fate awaits them both: As one dies, so dies the other. All have the same breathᶜ; humans have no advantage over animals. Everything is meaningless. ²⁰All go to the same place; all come from dust, and to dust all return. ²¹Who knows if the human spirit rises upward and if the spirit of the animal goes down into the earth?"

²²So I saw that there is nothing better for a person than to enjoy their work, because that is their lot. For who can bring them to see what will happen after them?

OPPRESSION, TOIL, FRIENDLESSNESS

4 Again I looked and saw all the oppression that was taking place under the sun:

I saw the tears of the oppressed—
    and they have no comforter;
power was on the side of their oppressors—
    and they have no comforter.
²And I declared that the dead,
    who had already died,
are happier than the living,
    who are still alive.

Who established the various times and seasons? (3:11)
God established everything human beings experience in this life. But his greatness in eternity is too huge for human beings to understand.

How are human beings like animals? (3:18–21)
Both animals and humans were created by God, and both will die. The author was not sure that there was any difference after death for animals and humans.

If everything is meaningless, what should people do? (3:22)
The author said people should enjoy their work because it isn't known what will happen after death.

Why did the author think it was better not to have been born? (4:1–3)
Since the poor and the powerless were abused by those in power, he felt it would be better never to have been born and experienced such hardships.

ᵃ 11 Or *also placed ignorance in the human heart, so that*   ᵇ 15 Or *God calls back the past*   ᶜ 19 Or *spirit*

What did the author think about work and achievement? (4:4–6)
The author thought that human beings only worked hard because of envy or in order to get ahead of their neighbors.

In a meaningless world, is there anything that can help? (4:9–12)
If a person is all alone, he or she has nobody to rely on. Having a friend or companion can help someone cope with the meaninglessness of life.

What was a sacrifice of fools? (5:1)
This was a sacrifice offered because of tradition or custom, not out of a sincere faith.

³ But better than both
    is the one who has never been born,
who has not seen the evil
    that is done under the sun.

⁴ And I saw that all toil and all achievement spring from one person's envy of another. This too is meaningless, a chasing after the wind.

⁵ Fools fold their hands
    and ruin themselves.
⁶ Better one handful with tranquillity
    than two handfuls with toil
    and chasing after the wind.

⁷ Again I saw something meaningless under the sun:

⁸ There was a man all alone;
    he had neither son nor brother.
There was no end to his toil,
    yet his eyes were not content with his wealth.
"For whom am I toiling," he asked,
    "and why am I depriving myself of enjoyment?"
This too is meaningless—
    a miserable business!

⁹ Two are better than one,
    because they have a good return for their labor:
¹⁰ If either of them falls down,
    one can help the other up.
But pity anyone who falls
    and has no one to help them up.
¹¹ Also, if two lie down together, they will keep warm.
    But how can one keep warm alone?
¹² Though one may be overpowered,
    two can defend themselves.
A cord of three strands is not quickly broken.

ADVANCEMENT IS MEANINGLESS

¹³ Better a poor but wise youth than an old but foolish king who no longer knows how to heed a warning. ¹⁴ The youth may have come from prison to the kingship, or he may have been born in poverty within his kingdom. ¹⁵ I saw that all who lived and walked under the sun followed the youth, the king's successor. ¹⁶ There was no end to all the people who were before them. But those who came later were not pleased with the successor. This too is meaningless, a chasing after the wind.

FULFILL YOUR VOW TO GOD

5ᵃ Guard your steps when you go to the house of God. Go near to listen rather than to offer the sacrifice of fools, who do not know that they do wrong.

² Do not be quick with your mouth,
    do not be hasty in your heart
    to utter anything before God.

ᵃ In Hebrew texts 5:1 is numbered 4:17, and 5:2-20 is numbered 5:1-19.

God is in heaven
and you are on earth,
so let your words be few.
³A dream comes when there are many cares,
and many words mark the speech of a fool.

⁴When you make a vow to God, do not delay to fulfill
it. He has no pleasure in fools; fulfill your vow. ⁵It is better
not to make a vow than to make one and not fulfill it. ⁶Do
not let your mouth lead you into sin. And do not protest to
the temple messenger, "My vow was a mistake." Why should
God be angry at what you say and destroy the work of your
hands? ⁷Much dreaming and many words are meaningless.
Therefore fear God.

RICHES ARE MEANINGLESS

⁸If you see the poor oppressed in a district, and justice and
rights denied, do not be surprised at such things; for one official is eyed by a higher one, and over them both are others
higher still. ⁹The increase from the land is taken by all; the
king himself profits from the fields.

¹⁰Whoever loves money never has enough;
whoever loves wealth is never satisfied with their
income.
This too is meaningless.

¹¹As goods increase,
so do those who consume them.
And what benefit are they to the owners
except to feast their eyes on them?

¹²The sleep of a laborer is sweet,
whether they eat little or much,
but as for the rich, their abundance
permits them no sleep.

¹³I have seen a grievous evil under the sun:

wealth hoarded to the harm of its owners,
¹⁴   or wealth lost through some misfortune,
so that when they have children
there is nothing left for them to inherit.
¹⁵Everyone comes naked from their mother's womb,
and as everyone comes, so they depart.
They take nothing from their toil
that they can carry in their hands.

¹⁶This too is a grievous evil:

As everyone comes, so they depart,
and what do they gain,
since they toil for the wind?
¹⁷All their days they eat in darkness,
with great frustration, affliction and anger.

¹⁸This is what I have observed to be good: that it is appropriate for a person to eat, to drink and to find satisfaction
in their toilsome labor under the sun during the few days of
life God has given them—for this is their lot. ¹⁹Moreover,

**What was the author's view
of human society? (5:8–9)**
The author believed that oppression reached up to the highest
levels of government or leadership.

**Why did the rich person get
no sleep? (5:12)**
A rich man was unable to sleep
because he was worried about
losing his money or thinking
about acquiring more.

when God gives someone wealth and possessions, and the ability to enjoy them, to accept their lot and be happy in their toil—this is a gift of God. ²⁰They seldom reflect on the days of their life, because God keeps them occupied with gladness of heart.

6 I have seen another evil under the sun, and it weighs heavily on mankind: ²God gives some people wealth, possessions and honor, so that they lack nothing their hearts desire, but God does not grant them the ability to enjoy them, and strangers enjoy them instead. This is meaningless, a grievous evil.

³A man may have a hundred children and live many years; yet no matter how long he lives, if he cannot enjoy his prosperity and does not receive proper burial, I say that a stillborn child is better off than he. ⁴It comes without meaning, it departs in darkness, and in darkness its name is shrouded. ⁵Though it never saw the sun or knew anything, it has more rest than does that man— ⁶even if he lives a thousand years twice over but fails to enjoy his prosperity. Do not all go to the same place?

⁷Everyone's toil is for their mouth,
    yet their appetite is never satisfied.
⁸What advantage have the wise over fools?
What do the poor gain
    by knowing how to conduct themselves before others?
⁹Better what the eye sees
    than the roving of the appetite.
This too is meaningless,
    a chasing after the wind.

¹⁰Whatever exists has already been named,
    and what humanity is has been known;
no one can contend
    with someone who is stronger.
¹¹The more the words,
    the less the meaning,
    and how does that profit anyone?

¹²For who knows what is good for a person in life, during the few and meaningless days they pass through like a shadow? Who can tell them what will happen under the sun after they are gone?

WISDOM

7 A good name is better than fine perfume,
    and the day of death better than the day of birth.
²It is better to go to a house of mourning
    than to go to a house of feasting,
for death is the destiny of everyone;
    the living should take this to heart.
³Frustration is better than laughter,
    because a sad face is good for the heart.
⁴The heart of the wise is in the house of mourning,
    but the heart of fools is in the house of pleasure.
⁵It is better to heed the rebuke of a wise person
    than to listen to the song of fools.

How could a stillborn child be better off than a person who did not receive a proper burial? (6:3)
If a person died without anyone caring enough to give him a proper burial, that person's life had been meaningless. It would have been better to die while being born than to live such a life.

Why did many words mean less meaning? (6:11)
The author claimed that a person couldn't make his or her words more important by talking a lot or by repetition.

Why is frustration better than laughter? (7:3)
A person who experiences frustration understands the reality of life—its pain as well as its joy.

⁶ Like the crackling of thorns under the pot,
   so is the laughter of fools.
   This too is meaningless.

⁷ Extortion turns a wise person into a fool,
   and a bribe corrupts the heart.

⁸ The end of a matter is better than its beginning,
   and patience is better than pride.
⁹ Do not be quickly provoked in your spirit,
   for anger resides in the lap of fools.

¹⁰ Do not say, "Why were the old days better than these?"
   For it is not wise to ask such questions.

¹¹ Wisdom, like an inheritance, is a good thing
   and benefits those who see the sun.
¹² Wisdom is a shelter
   as money is a shelter,
   but the advantage of knowledge is this:
   Wisdom preserves those who have it.

¹³ Consider what God has done:

   Who can straighten
   what he has made crooked?
¹⁴ When times are good, be happy;
   but when times are bad, consider this:
   God has made the one
   as well as the other.
   Therefore, no one can discover
   anything about their future.

¹⁵ In this meaningless life of mine I have seen both of these:

   the righteous perishing in their righteousness,
   and the wicked living long in their wickedness.
¹⁶ Do not be overrighteous,
   neither be overwise—
   why destroy yourself?
¹⁷ Do not be overwicked,
   and do not be a fool—
   why die before your time?
¹⁸ It is good to grasp the one
   and not let go of the other.
   Whoever fears God will avoid all extremes.ᵃ

¹⁹ Wisdom makes one wise person more powerful
   than ten rulers in a city.

²⁰ Indeed, there is no one on earth who is righteous,
   no one who does what is right and never sins.

²¹ Do not pay attention to every word people say,
   or you may hear your servant cursing you—
²² for you know in your heart
   that many times you yourself have cursed others.

²³ All this I tested by wisdom and I said,

   "I am determined to be wise"—
   but this was beyond me.

ᵃ 18 Or *will follow them both*

What is the Teacher saying here? (7:13)
God is all-powerful, and human beings cannot change what he has done or established.

Can any person keep God's law perfectly? (7:20)
No one is able to perfectly obey God's law or to live a life without sin. That is why we need a Savior.

²⁴Whatever exists is far off and most profound—
    who can discover it?
²⁵So I turned my mind to understand,
    to investigate and to search out wisdom and the
        scheme of things
and to understand the stupidity of wickedness
    and the madness of folly.

²⁶I find more bitter than death
    the woman who is a snare,
whose heart is a trap
    and whose hands are chains.
The man who pleases God will escape her,
    but the sinner she will ensnare.

²⁷"Look," says the Teacher,[a] "this is what I have discovered:

"Adding one thing to another to discover the scheme
      of things—
²⁸ while I was still searching
    but not finding—
I found one upright man among a thousand,
    but not one upright woman among them all.
²⁹This only have I found:
    God created mankind upright,
    but they have gone in search of many schemes."

8 Who is like the wise?
    Who knows the explanation of things?
A person's wisdom brightens their face
    and changes its hard appearance.

OBEY THE KING

²Obey the king's command, I say, because you took an oath before God. ³Do not be in a hurry to leave the king's presence. Do not stand up for a bad cause, for he will do whatever he pleases. ⁴Since a king's word is supreme, who can say to him, "What are you doing?"

⁵Whoever obeys his command will come to no harm,
    and the wise heart will know the proper time and
        procedure.
⁶For there is a proper time and procedure for every
      matter,
    though a person may be weighed down by misery.

⁷Since no one knows the future,
    who can tell someone else what is to come?
⁸As no one has power over the wind to contain it,
    so[b] no one has power over the time of their death.
As no one is discharged in time of war,
    so wickedness will not release those who practice it.

⁹All this I saw, as I applied my mind to everything done under the sun. There is a time when a man lords it over others to his own[c] hurt. ¹⁰Then too, I saw the wicked buried—those

---

Why are human beings sinful? (7:29)
When God created human beings, they were perfect. But because Adam and Eve sinned in the garden, all human beings have been affected by sin and its negative results.

Why should people obey their rulers? (8:2–6)
As responsible citizens, people should obey their rulers. Disobedience will get them into trouble.

ᵃ 27 Or *the leader of the assembly*   ᵇ 8 Or *over the human spirit to retain it, / and so*   ᶜ 9 Or *to their*

who used to come and go from the holy place and receive praise*a* in the city where they did this. This too is meaningless.

[11]When the sentence for a crime is not quickly carried out, people's hearts are filled with schemes to do wrong. [12]Although a wicked person who commits a hundred crimes may live a long time, I know that it will go better with those who fear God, who are reverent before him. [13]Yet because the wicked do not fear God, it will not go well with them, and their days will not lengthen like a shadow.

[14]There is something else meaningless that occurs on earth: the righteous who get what the wicked deserve, and the wicked who get what the righteous deserve. This too, I say, is meaningless. [15]So I commend the enjoyment of life, because there is nothing better for a person under the sun than to eat and drink and be glad. Then joy will accompany them in their toil all the days of the life God has given them under the sun.

[16]When I applied my mind to know wisdom and to observe the labor that is done on earth—people getting no sleep day or night— [17]then I saw all that God has done. No one can comprehend what goes on under the sun. Despite all their efforts to search it out, no one can discover its meaning. Even if the wise claim they know, they cannot really comprehend it.

A COMMON DESTINY FOR ALL

9 So I reflected on all this and concluded that the righteous and the wise and what they do are in God's hands, but no one knows whether love or hate awaits them. [2]All share a common destiny—the righteous and the wicked, the good and the bad,*b* the clean and the unclean, those who offer sacrifices and those who do not.

> As it is with the good,
>   so with the sinful;
> as it is with those who take oaths,
>   so with those who are afraid to take them.

[3]This is the evil in everything that happens under the sun: The same destiny overtakes all. The hearts of people, moreover, are full of evil and there is madness in their hearts while they live, and afterward they join the dead. [4]Anyone who is among the living has hope*c*—even a live dog is better off than a dead lion!

> [5]For the living know that they will die,
>   but the dead know nothing;
> they have no further reward,
>   and even their name is forgotten.
> [6]Their love, their hate
>   and their jealousy have long since vanished;
> never again will they have a part
>   in anything that happens under the sun.

---

a 10 Some Hebrew manuscripts and Septuagint (Aquila); most Hebrew manuscripts *and are forgotten*   *b 2* Septuagint (Aquila), Vulgate and Syriac; Hebrew does not have *and the bad.*   *c 4* Or *What then is to be chosen? With all who live, there is hope*

Is injustice part of the meaninglessness of life? (8:14)
Sometimes the wicked succeed and the righteous suffer. To the author, this was another example of how life was meaningless.

Is it impossible for human beings to understand reality? (8:17)
Human beings cannot completely comprehend the meaning of everything that happens because they cannot completely understand God or his plan.

What is the destiny of all people? (9:1–3)
The author said all people will eventually die.

Since everything is meaningless, what should people do? (9:7-10)
The author advised everyone to enjoy life on this earth because they would soon be dead.

[7]Go, eat your food with gladness, and drink your wine with a joyful heart, for God has already approved what you do. [8]Always be clothed in white, and always anoint your head with oil. [9]Enjoy life with your wife, whom you love, all the days of this meaningless life that God has given you under the sun—all your meaningless days. For this is your lot in life and in your toilsome labor under the sun. [10]Whatever your hand finds to do, do it with all your might, for in the realm of the dead, where you are going, there is neither working nor planning nor knowledge nor wisdom.

[11]I have seen something else under the sun:

The race is not to the swift
	or the battle to the strong,
nor does food come to the wise
	or wealth to the brilliant
	or favor to the learned;
but time and chance happen to them all.

[12]Moreover, no one knows when their hour will come:

As fish are caught in a cruel net,
	or birds are taken in a snare,
so people are trapped by evil times
	that fall unexpectedly upon them.

WISDOM BETTER THAN FOLLY

What did the Teacher say about a wise person's advice? (9:13-16)
In this example, a wise person saved an entire city but did not receive thanks or credit for his advice. It is better to be wise than strong.

[13]I also saw under the sun this example of wisdom that greatly impressed me: [14]There was once a small city with only a few people in it. And a powerful king came against it, surrounded it and built huge siege works against it. [15]Now there lived in that city a man poor but wise, and he saved the city by his wisdom. But nobody remembered that poor man. [16]So I said, "Wisdom is better than strength." But the poor man's wisdom is despised, and his words are no longer heeded.

[17]The quiet words of the wise are more to be heeded
	than the shouts of a ruler of fools.
[18]Wisdom is better than weapons of war,
	but one sinner destroys much good.

10 As dead flies give perfume a bad smell,
	so a little folly outweighs wisdom and honor.
[2]The heart of the wise inclines to the right,
	but the heart of the fool to the left.
[3]Even as fools walk along the road,
	they lack sense
	and show everyone how stupid they are.
[4]If a ruler's anger rises against you,
	do not leave your post;
	calmness can lay great offenses to rest.

What were some things in life the author did not consider fair or just? (10:6-7)
People often do not seem to get what they deserve. For example, foolish people are given positions of responsibility, and slaves are given honor and respect.

[5]There is an evil I have seen under the sun,
	the sort of error that arises from a ruler:
[6]Fools are put in many high positions,
	while the rich occupy the low ones.
[7]I have seen slaves on horseback,
	while princes go on foot like slaves.

⁸Whoever digs a pit may fall into it;
    whoever breaks through a wall may be bitten
        by a snake.
⁹Whoever quarries stones may be injured by them;
    whoever splits logs may be endangered by them.

¹⁰If the ax is dull
    and its edge unsharpened,
more strength is needed,
    but skill will bring success.

¹¹If a snake bites before it is charmed,
    the charmer receives no fee.

¹²Words from the mouth of the wise are gracious,
    but fools are consumed by their own lips.
¹³At the beginning their words are folly;
    at the end they are wicked madness—
¹⁴   and fools multiply words.

No one knows what is coming—
    who can tell someone else what will happen
        after them?

¹⁵The toil of fools wearies them;
    they do not know the way to town.

¹⁶Woe to the land whose king was a servant*ᵃ*
    and whose princes feast in the morning.
¹⁷Blessed is the land whose king is of noble birth
    and whose princes eat at a proper time—
        for strength and not for drunkenness.

¹⁸Through laziness, the rafters sag;
    because of idle hands, the house leaks.

¹⁹A feast is made for laughter,
    wine makes life merry,
    and money is the answer for everything.

²⁰Do not revile the king even in your thoughts,
    or curse the rich in your bedroom,
because a bird in the sky may carry your words,
    and a bird on the wing may report what
        you say.

INVEST IN MANY VENTURES

11 Ship your grain across the sea;
    after many days you may receive a return.
²Invest in seven ventures, yes, in eight;
    you do not know what disaster may come upon
        the land.

³If clouds are full of water,
    they pour rain on the earth.
Whether a tree falls to the south or to the north,
    in the place where it falls, there it will lie.
⁴Whoever watches the wind will not plant;
    whoever looks at the clouds will not reap.

Can people avoid risks?
(10:8–9)
Any type of work carried risks.
This could also be another example of life's unfairness, since
people who were doing hard
work could end up being injured.

Did the Teacher really think
money was the answer for
everything? (10:19)
He may have been using sarcasm
or irony when he wrote this. But
he also may have been implying
that if everything is meaningless,
at least money can buy things
that bring pleasure.

What did it mean to "ship
your grain across the sea"?
(11:1)
This verse seems to advise
people to be adventurous, like
those who accept the risks and
reap the benefits of sea trading.

ᵃ 16 Or king is a child

[5] As you do not know the path of the wind,
    or how the body is formed[a] in a mother's womb,
so you cannot understand the work of God,
    the Maker of all things.

[6] Sow your seed in the morning,
    and at evening let your hands not be idle,
for you do not know which will succeed,
    whether this or that,
    or whether both will do equally well.

REMEMBER YOUR CREATOR WHILE YOUNG

[7] Light is sweet,
    and it pleases the eyes to see the sun.
[8] However many years anyone may live,
    let them enjoy them all.
But let them remember the days of darkness,
    for there will be many.
    Everything to come is meaningless.

[9] You who are young, be happy while you
      are young,
    and let your heart give you joy in the days of
      your youth.
Follow the ways of your heart
    and whatever your eyes see,
but know that for all these things
    God will bring you into judgment.
[10] So then, banish anxiety from your heart
    and cast off the troubles of your body,
for youth and vigor are meaningless.

12 Remember your Creator
    in the days of your youth,
before the days of trouble come
    and the years approach when you will say,
    "I find no pleasure in them"—
[2] before the sun and the light
    and the moon and the stars grow dark,
    and the clouds return after the rain;
[3] when the keepers of the house tremble,
    and the strong men stoop,
when the grinders cease because they are few,
    and those looking through the windows
      grow dim;
[4] when the doors to the street are closed
    and the sound of grinding fades;
when people rise up at the sound of birds,
    but all their songs grow faint;
[5] when people are afraid of heights
    and of dangers in the streets;
when the almond tree blossoms
    and the grasshopper drags itself along
    and desire no longer is stirred.
Then people go to their eternal home
    and mourners go about the streets.

---

[a] 5 Or *know how life* (or *the spirit*) / *enters the body being formed*

Why should people remember the bad times? (11:8)
This helps to keep things in perspective because people are not able to stay happy and well forever.

Why is it important to remember the Creator when we are young? (12:1–5)
The Teacher speaks about the infirmities and limitations of old age, so he suggests that young people remember God when their lives are still relatively free from pain and worries.

⁶Remember him—before the silver cord is severed,
    and the golden bowl is broken;
before the pitcher is shattered at the spring,
    and the wheel broken at the well,
⁷and the dust returns to the ground it came from,
    and the spirit returns to God who gave it.

⁸"Meaningless! Meaningless!" says the Teacher.ᵃ
    "Everything is meaningless!"

THE CONCLUSION OF THE MATTER

⁹Not only was the Teacher wise, but he also imparted knowledge to the people. He pondered and searched out and set in order many proverbs. ¹⁰The Teacher searched to find just the right words, and what he wrote was upright and true.

¹¹The words of the wise are like goads, their collected sayings like firmly embedded nails—given by one shepherd.ᵇ ¹²Be warned, my son, of anything in addition to them.

Of making many books there is no end, and much study wearies the body.

¹³Now all has been heard;
    here is the conclusion of the matter:
Fear God and keep his commandments,
    for this is the duty of all mankind.
¹⁴For God will bring every deed into judgment,
    including every hidden thing,
    whether it is good or evil.

What was meant by the silver cord, golden bowl, pitcher, and wheel? (12:6)
The breaking of all these objects symbolized death.

If life is meaningless, what should people do? (12:13–14)
Even if life is unpleasant and seems meaningless, happiness or contentment is not the highest goal. What is important is to fear God and serve him, and God will take care of the rest.

ᵃ 8 Or *the leader of the assembly*; also in verses 9 and 10   ᵇ 11 Or *Shepherd*

Song of Songs

INTRODUCTION

Who wrote this book? This book was probably written by Solomon.

What is this book about? The book of Song of Songs is a collection of poems about grown-up love between a man and a woman.

For whom was this book written? The book was written for adults to help them understand love and marriage.

1 Solomon's Song of Songs.

SHE [a]

² Let him kiss me with the kisses of his mouth—
    for your love is more delightful than wine.
³ Pleasing is the fragrance of your perfumes;
    your name is like perfume poured out.
    No wonder the young women love you!
⁴ Take me away with you—let us hurry!
    Let the king bring me into his chambers.

FRIENDS

We rejoice and delight in you [b];
    we will praise your love more than wine.

SHE

How right they are to adore you!

⁵ Dark am I, yet lovely,
    daughters of Jerusalem,
dark like the tents of Kedar,
    like the tent curtains of Solomon. [c]
⁶ Do not stare at me because I am dark,
    because I am darkened by the sun.
My mother's sons were angry with me
    and made me take care of the vineyards;
    my own vineyard I had to neglect.
⁷ Tell me, you whom I love,
    where you graze your flock
    and where you rest your sheep at midday.
Why should I be like a veiled woman
    beside the flocks of your friends?

FRIENDS

⁸ If you do not know, most beautiful of women,
    follow the tracks of the sheep
and graze your young goats
    by the tents of the shepherds.

a The main male and female speakers (identified primarily on the basis of the gender of the relevant Hebrew forms) are indicated by the captions *He* and *She* respectively. The words of others are marked *Friends*. In some instances the divisions and their captions are debatable.   *b 4* The Hebrew is masculine singular.   *c 5* Or *Salma*

Why does the Bible include a poem about romance and sex? (1:2–40)

God created human beings as sexual beings, and sex is a part of life. Before sin, there was no shame in sex. Now conversation about sex is usually avoided, but within the context of a loving marriage relationship, sex is a gift from God.

Why did the woman speak of her dark complexion? (1:5)

Even though she realized she was lovely, she was self-conscious about her dark skin, which was not considered attractive by upper class women at the time. She had a tan complexion from working in the vineyards.

Why does the Bible include this poem about sensual love?

SONG OF SONGS

For a long time people have tried to decide what the book is supposed to mean. In some older interpretations, scholars thought that the book was an allegory or metaphor for the love of God for Israel or the love of Jesus for the Christian church. Some other scholars thought that the book described Solomon's efforts to win the love of a woman who was in love with a shepherd. Nowadays, many scholars think that the book should be thought of as a poetic expression of the beauty and power of strong, pure love. All the emotions of love come into play: passion, separation, longing, pain, joy, fear, and peace.

As you read the book, notice that there are three voices speaking: the woman, the man, and the friends (sometimes called "daughters of Jerusalem"). Don't be embarrassed by the language. God created the gift of sexuality and gave it to human beings for their joy and pleasure. But God also wants people to be sexually pure and to experience sex only within the committed bonds of marriage. That's what this poem shows us.

HE

⁹ I liken you, my darling, to a mare
   among Pharaoh's chariot horses.
¹⁰ Your cheeks are beautiful with earrings,
   your neck with strings of jewels.
¹¹ We will make you earrings of gold,
   studded with silver.

SHE

¹² While the king was at his table,
   my perfume spread its fragrance.
¹³ My beloved is to me a sachet of myrrh
   resting between my breasts.
¹⁴ My beloved is to me a cluster of henna blossoms
   from the vineyards of En Gedi.

HE

¹⁵ How beautiful you are, my darling!
   Oh, how beautiful!
   Your eyes are doves.

SHE

¹⁶ How handsome you are, my beloved!
   Oh, how charming!
   And our bed is verdant.

HE

¹⁷ The beams of our house are cedars;
   our rafters are firs.

SHE *ᵃ*

2 I am a rose*ᵇ* of Sharon,
   a lily of the valleys.

HE

² Like a lily among thorns
   is my darling among the young women.

SHE

³ Like an apple*ᶜ* tree among the trees of the forest
   is my beloved among the young men.
 I delight to sit in his shade,
   and his fruit is sweet to my taste.
⁴ Let him lead me to the banquet hall,
   and let his banner over me be love.
⁵ Strengthen me with raisins,
   refresh me with apples,
   for I am faint with love.
⁶ His left arm is under my head,
   and his right arm embraces me.
⁷ Daughters of Jerusalem, I charge you
   by the gazelles and by the does of the field:
 Do not arouse or awaken love
   until it so desires.

What was myrrh? (1:13)
This was an aromatic resin from the bark of the balsam tree that grows in Arabia, Ethiopia, and India. It was commonly used as perfume for women, but it was also used to perfume royal wedding robes.

Why mention the beams and rafters? (1:17)
Wood was scarce in Israel, and cedar and fir were expensive to import. Their use in a house suggested that the owner was wealthy.

How large was the husband's love? (2:4)
His love was displayed for everyone to see like a large military banner.

What were the raisins and apples? (2:5)
These were probably metaphors for love's caresses and embraces.

ᵃ Or *He*   *ᵇ 1* Probably a member of the crocus family   *ᶜ 3* Or possibly *apricot*; here and elsewhere in Song of Songs

⁸ Listen! My beloved!
    Look! Here he comes,
  leaping across the mountains,
    bounding over the hills.
⁹ My beloved is like a gazelle or a young stag.
    Look! There he stands behind our wall,
  gazing through the windows,
    peering through the lattice.
¹⁰ My beloved spoke and said to me,
    "Arise, my darling,
    my beautiful one, come with me.
¹¹ See! The winter is past;
    the rains are over and gone.
¹² Flowers appear on the earth;
    the season of singing has come,
  the cooing of doves
    is heard in our land.
¹³ The fig tree forms its early fruit;
    the blossoming vines spread their
        fragrance.
  Arise, come, my darling;
    my beautiful one, come with me."

HE

¹⁴ My dove in the clefts of the rock,
    in the hiding places on the mountainside,
  show me your face,
    let me hear your voice;
  for your voice is sweet,
    and your face is lovely.
¹⁵ Catch for us the foxes,
    the little foxes
  that ruin the vineyards,
    our vineyards that are in bloom.

SHE

¹⁶ My beloved is mine and I am his;
    he browses among the lilies.
¹⁷ Until the day breaks
    and the shadows flee,
  turn, my beloved,
    and be like a gazelle
  or like a young stag
    on the rugged hills.ᵃ

3 All night long on my bed
    I looked for the one my heart loves;
    I looked for him but did not find him.
² I will get up now and go about the city,
    through its streets and squares;
  I will search for the one my heart loves.
    So I looked for him but did not find him.
³ The watchmen found me
    as they made their rounds in the city.
    "Have you seen the one my heart loves?"

ᵃ 17 Or *the hills of Bether*

**What were the little foxes?
(2:15)**
Foxes were a nuisance to the
owners of vineyards because
they dug up the vines. Here the
foxes represented threats to the
love between the couple.

Why would the couple go to her mother's house? (3:4)
This may have shown that their love was pure. Later they returned to the mother's house, perhaps showing that the wedding festivities were over and their life together had begun (see 8:5–9)

⁴ Scarcely had I passed them
      when I found the one my heart loves.
   I held him and would not let him go
      till I had brought him to my mother's house,
      to the room of the one who conceived me.
⁵ Daughters of Jerusalem, I charge you
      by the gazelles and by the does of the field:
   Do not arouse or awaken love
      until it so desires.

⁶ Who is this coming up from the wilderness
      like a column of smoke,
   perfumed with myrrh and incense
      made from all the spices of the merchant?
⁷ Look! It is Solomon's carriage,
      escorted by sixty warriors,
      the noblest of Israel,
⁸ all of them wearing the sword,
      all experienced in battle,
   each with his sword at his side,
      prepared for the terrors of the night.
⁹ King Solomon made for himself the carriage;
      he made it of wood from Lebanon.
¹⁰ Its posts he made of silver,
      its base of gold.
   Its seat was upholstered with purple,
      its interior inlaid with love.
   Daughters of Jerusalem, ¹¹ come out,
      and look, you daughters of Zion.
   Look*a* on King Solomon wearing a crown,
      the crown with which his mother
            crowned him
   on the day of his wedding,
      the day his heart rejoiced.

Was King Solomon the lover? (3:11)
He may have been, but this could also be the the woman's exaggerated description of her lover, who seemed as splendid as Solomon to her on her wedding day.

HE

4 How beautiful you are, my darling!
      Oh, how beautiful!
      Your eyes behind your veil are doves.
   Your hair is like a flock of goats
      descending from the hills of Gilead.
² Your teeth are like a flock of sheep just shorn,
      coming up from the washing.
   Each has its twin;
      not one of them is alone.
³ Your lips are like a scarlet ribbon;
      your mouth is lovely.
   Your temples behind your veil
      are like the halves of a pomegranate.
⁴ Your neck is like the tower of David,
      built with courses of stone*b*;
   on it hang a thousand shields,
      all of them shields of warriors.

How was the woman's hair like goats? (4:1)
Goats in Canaan were usually black. The woman's long, black hair reminded the lover of a herd of goats heading down from the hills. The man's hair was also black (see 5:11).

---

a 10,11 Or *interior lovingly inlaid / by the daughters of Jerusalem. / ¹¹ Come out, you daughters of Zion, / and look*   *b* 4 The meaning of the Hebrew for this phrase is uncertain.

⁵ Your breasts are like two fawns,
    like twin fawns of a gazelle
    that browse among the lilies.
⁶ Until the day breaks
    and the shadows flee,
  I will go to the mountain of myrrh
    and to the hill of incense.
⁷ You are altogether beautiful, my darling;
    there is no flaw in you.

⁸ Come with me from Lebanon, my bride,
    come with me from Lebanon.
  Descend from the crest of Amana,
    from the top of Senir, the summit of Hermon,
  from the lions' dens
    and the mountain haunts of leopards.
⁹ You have stolen my heart, my sister, my bride;
    you have stolen my heart
  with one glance of your eyes,
    with one jewel of your necklace.
¹⁰ How delightful is your love, my sister, my bride!
    How much more pleasing is your love than wine,
  and the fragrance of your perfume
    more than any spice!
¹¹ Your lips drop sweetness as the honeycomb, my bride;
    milk and honey are under your tongue.
  The fragrance of your garments
    is like the fragrance of Lebanon.
¹² You are a garden locked up, my sister, my bride;
    you are a spring enclosed, a sealed fountain.
¹³ Your plants are an orchard of pomegranates
    with choice fruits,
    with henna and nard,
¹⁴   nard and saffron,
    calamus and cinnamon,
    with every kind of incense tree,
    with myrrh and aloes
    and all the finest spices.
¹⁵ You areᵃ a garden fountain,
    a well of flowing water
    streaming down from Lebanon.

SHE

¹⁶ Awake, north wind,
    and come, south wind!
  Blow on my garden,
    that its fragrance may spread everywhere.
  Let my beloved come into his garden
    and taste its choice fruits.

HE

5 I have come into my garden, my sister, my bride;
    I have gathered my myrrh with my spice.
  I have eaten my honeycomb and my honey;
    I have drunk my wine and my milk.

ᵃ *15 Or I am* (spoken by *She*)

Why call the woman "my sister"? (4:9)
Lovers would often address each other as brother or sister, especially in love poetry in the ancient Middle East.

How was the bride like a locked garden? (4:12)
The garden was a place for sensual delights. The fact that she was locked up, enclosed, and sealed may mean she was a virgin or that she saved herself exclusively for her husband.

FRIENDS

Eat, friends, and drink;
  drink your fill of love.

SHE

[2] I slept but my heart was awake.
  Listen! My beloved is knocking:
"Open to me, my sister, my darling,
  my dove, my flawless one.
My head is drenched with dew,
  my hair with the dampness of the night."
[3] I have taken off my robe—
  must I put it on again?
I have washed my feet—
  must I soil them again?
[4] My beloved thrust his hand through the
      latch-opening;
  my heart began to pound for him.
[5] I arose to open for my beloved,
  and my hands dripped with myrrh,
my fingers with flowing myrrh,
  on the handles of the bolt.
[6] I opened for my beloved,
  but my beloved had left; he was gone.
  My heart sank at his departure. [a]
I looked for him but did not find him.
  I called him but he did not answer.
[7] The watchmen found me
  as they made their rounds in the city.
They beat me, they bruised me;
  they took away my cloak,
  those watchmen of the walls!
[8] Daughters of Jerusalem, I charge you—
  if you find my beloved,
what will you tell him?
  Tell him I am faint with love.

FRIENDS

[9] How is your beloved better than others,
  most beautiful of women?
How is your beloved better than others,
  that you so charge us?

SHE

[10] My beloved is radiant and ruddy,
  outstanding among ten thousand.
[11] His head is purest gold;
  his hair is wavy
  and black as a raven.
[12] His eyes are like doves
  by the water streams,
washed in milk,
  mounted like jewels.
[13] His cheeks are like beds of spice
  yielding perfume.

What happened to separate the lovers? (5:2–8)
This may have been a dream, or it may have been a real event. In any case, the bride and groom were separated. When he returned, she was too drowsy to respond to him, so he went away again. Then she went looking for him.

What is unusual about this poem? (5:10–16)
This is one of the few poems from ancient times in which a woman gives a detailed description of a man's physical features.

---

[a] 6 Or *heart had gone out to him when he spoke*

His lips are like lilies
    dripping with myrrh.
14 His arms are rods of gold
    set with topaz.
His body is like polished ivory
    decorated with lapis lazuli.
15 His legs are pillars of marble
    set on bases of pure gold.
His appearance is like Lebanon,
    choice as its cedars.
16 His mouth is sweetness itself;
    he is altogether lovely.
This is my beloved, this is my friend,
    daughters of Jerusalem.

FRIENDS

6 Where has your beloved gone,
    most beautiful of women?
Which way did your beloved turn,
    that we may look for him with you?

SHE

2 My beloved has gone down to his garden,
    to the beds of spices,
to browse in the gardens
    and to gather lilies.
3 I am my beloved's and my beloved is mine;
    he browses among the lilies.

HE

4 You are as beautiful as Tirzah, my darling,
    as lovely as Jerusalem,
    as majestic as troops with banners.
5 Turn your eyes from me;
    they overwhelm me.
Your hair is like a flock of goats
    descending from Gilead.
6 Your teeth are like a flock of sheep
    coming up from the washing.
Each has its twin,
    not one of them is missing.
7 Your temples behind your veil
    are like the halves of a pomegranate.
8 Sixty queens there may be,
    and eighty concubines,
    and virgins beyond number;
9 but my dove, my perfect one, is unique,
    the only daughter of her mother,
    the favorite of the one who bore her.
The young women saw her and called her blessed;
    the queens and concubines praised her.

FRIENDS

10 Who is this that appears like the dawn,
    fair as the moon, bright as the sun,
    majestic as the stars in procession?

**What was the garden?
(6:2 – 3)**
This section metaphorically describes the lover's enjoyment of his beloved's sensual delights.

HE

¹¹ I went down to the grove of nut trees
    to look at the new growth in the valley,
to see if the vines had budded
    or the pomegranates were in bloom.
¹² Before I realized it,
    my desire set me among the royal chariots of my
        people.*a*

FRIENDS

¹³ Come back, come back, O Shulammite;
    come back, come back, that we may gaze on you!

HE

Why would you gaze on the Shulammite
    as on the dance of Mahanaim?*b*

7*c* How beautiful your sandaled feet,
    O prince's daughter!
Your graceful legs are like jewels,
    the work of an artist's hands.
² Your navel is a rounded goblet
    that never lacks blended wine.
Your waist is a mound of wheat
    encircled by lilies.
³ Your breasts are like two fawns,
    like twin fawns of a gazelle.
⁴ Your neck is like an ivory tower.
Your eyes are the pools of Heshbon
    by the gate of Bath Rabbim.
Your nose is like the tower of Lebanon
    looking toward Damascus.
⁵ Your head crowns you like Mount Carmel.
    Your hair is like royal tapestry;
    the king is held captive by its tresses.
⁶ How beautiful you are and how pleasing,
    my love, with your delights!
⁷ Your stature is like that of the palm,
    and your breasts like clusters of fruit.
⁸ I said, "I will climb the palm tree;
    I will take hold of its fruit."
May your breasts be like clusters of grapes
    on the vine,
    the fragrance of your breath like apples,
⁹   and your mouth like the best wine.

SHE

May the wine go straight to my beloved,
    flowing gently over lips and teeth.*d*
¹⁰ I belong to my beloved,
    and his desire is for me.
¹¹ Come, my beloved, let us go to the countryside,
    let us spend the night in the villages.*e*

---

*a 12 Or among the chariots of Amminadab; or among the chariots of the people of
the prince   b 13 In Hebrew texts this verse (6:13) is numbered 7:1.   c In
Hebrew texts 7:1-13 is numbered 7:2-14.   d 9 Septuagint, Aquila, Vulgate
and Syriac; Hebrew lips of sleepers   e 11 Or the henna bushes*

**What was a Shulammite?
(6:13)**
This could be a feminine form of
the word "Solomon," meaning
Solomon's girl; or it could be a
different form of the word "Shunammite," a young woman from
Shunem.

**Setting of Song of Songs
(6:13)**

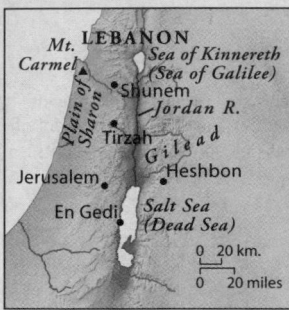

**Why was the lover so en-
tranced? (7:1–9)**
The lover could hardly find words
to describe the beauty of his
beloved. In verse 8, he said he
would climb the palm tree, in
other words, become physically
intimate with her.

¹² Let us go early to the vineyards
    to see if the vines have budded,
if their blossoms have opened,
    and if the pomegranates are in bloom—
there I will give you my love.
¹³ The mandrakes send out their fragrance,
    and at our door is every delicacy,
both new and old,
    that I have stored up for you, my beloved.

8 If only you were to me like a brother,
    who was nursed at my mother's breasts!
Then, if I found you outside,
    I would kiss you,
    and no one would despise me.
² I would lead you
    and bring you to my mother's house—
    she who has taught me.
I would give you spiced wine to drink,
    the nectar of my pomegranates.
³ His left arm is under my head
    and his right arm embraces me.
⁴ Daughters of Jerusalem, I charge you:
    Do not arouse or awaken love
    until it so desires.

FRIENDS

⁵ Who is this coming up from the wilderness
    leaning on her beloved?

SHE

Under the apple tree I roused you;
    there your mother conceived you,
    there she who was in labor gave you birth.
⁶ Place me like a seal over your heart,
    like a seal on your arm;
for love is as strong as death,
    its jealousy[a] unyielding as the grave.
It burns like blazing fire,
    like a mighty flame.[b]
⁷ Many waters cannot quench love;
    rivers cannot sweep it away.
If one were to give
    all the wealth of one's house for love,
    it[c] would be utterly scorned.

FRIENDS

⁸ We have a little sister,
    and her breasts are not yet grown.
What shall we do for our sister
    on the day she is spoken for?
⁹ If she is a wall,
    we will build towers of silver on her.
If she is a door,
    we will enclose her with panels of cedar.

What are mandrakes? (7:13)
Mandrake plants have pungent blossoms and their forked roots resemble the lower part of the human body. They were supposed to arouse desire and increase fertility.

Why couldn't the lovers kiss in public? (8:1)
Cultural norms allowed immediate family members to show affection publicly but not married couples.

Why was a seal important? (8:6)
Seals were valuable to their owners and were as precious as their names. A seal over the heart would show how permanent their love was.

How strong was their love? (8:6–7)
Their love was stronger than death, fire, or floods. There were no natural forces that could extinguish it.

---

[a] 6 Or *ardor*   [b] 6 Or *fire, / like the very flame of the* LORD   [c] 7 Or *he*

SHE

¹⁰ I am a wall,
  and my breasts are like towers.
Thus I have become in his eyes
  like one bringing contentment.
¹¹ Solomon had a vineyard in Baal Hamon;
  he let out his vineyard to tenants.
Each was to bring for its fruit
  a thousand shekels^{*a*} of silver.
¹² But my own vineyard is mine to give;
  the thousand shekels are for you, Solomon,
  and two hundred^{*b*} are for those who tend its fruit.

HE

¹³ You who dwell in the gardens
  with friends in attendance,
  let me hear your voice!

SHE

¹⁴ Come away, my beloved,
  and be like a gazelle
or like a young stag
  on the spice-laden mountains.

---

^{*a*} *11* That is, about 25 pounds or about 12 kilograms; also in verse 12
^{*b*} *12* That is, about 5 pounds or about 2.3 kilograms

Isaiah

INTRODUCTION

Who wrote this book?

The prophet Isaiah.

Why was this book written?

The book of Isaiah warns the people of Judah that God will punish them just as he is punishing Israel, if they keep on doing wicked things. Isaiah also promises that God will comfort his people after punishing them and that he will make their nation strong again.

What do we learn about God in this book?

Isaiah uses many special names for God. These names show that God is holy, God is our judge, and God is our salvation.

What is special about this book?

Isaiah gives many wonderful prophecies about Jesus, the coming Savior.

What are some important chapters in this book?

The wickedness of Judah	Isaiah 1
God's holiness	Isaiah 6
Who Jesus is	Isaiah 9:1–7
What Jesus will do	Isaiah 11
God is better than idols	Isaiah 44
Jesus' death on the cross	Isaiah 53
A new heaven and earth	Isaiah 65

When did these things happen?

1300 BC 1200 1100 1000 900 800 700 600 500 400

DIVISION OF THE KINGDOM (930 BC)

MINISTRIES OF ELIJAH AND ELISHA IN ISRAEL (C. 875 – 797 BC)

MINISTRIES OF AMOS AND HOSEA IN ISRAEL (C. 760 – 715 BC)

ISAIAH'S MINISTRY IN JUDAH (C. 740 – 681 BC)

MICAH'S MINISTRY IN JUDAH (C. 735 – 700 BC)

EXILE OF ISRAEL (722 BC)

BOOK OF ISAIAH WRITTEN (C. 700 – 681 BC)

FALL OF JERUSALEM (586 BC)

What was this vision? (1:1)
This was a revelation or prophecy based on what God revealed to Isaiah.

1 The vision concerning Judah and Jerusalem that Isaiah son of Amoz saw during the reigns of Uzziah, Jotham, Ahaz and Hezekiah, kings of Judah.

A REBELLIOUS NATION

2 Hear me, you heavens! Listen, earth!
    For the Lord has spoken:
"I reared children and brought them up,
    but they have rebelled against me.
3 The ox knows its master,
    the donkey its owner's manger,
but Israel does not know,
    my people do not understand."

4 Woe to the sinful nation,
    a people whose guilt is great,
a brood of evildoers,
    children given to corruption!
They have forsaken the Lord;
    they have spurned the Holy One of Israel
    and turned their backs on him.

5 Why should you be beaten anymore?
    Why do you persist in rebellion?
Your whole head is injured,
    your whole heart afflicted.
6 From the sole of your foot to the top of your head
    there is no soundness—
only wounds and welts
    and open sores,
not cleansed or bandaged
    or soothed with olive oil.

Why was the land of Judah desolate? (1:7–9)
It was the result of invasions by foreign nations, especially Assyria.

7 Your country is desolate,
    your cities burned with fire;
your fields are being stripped by foreigners
    right before you,
    laid waste as when overthrown by strangers.
8 Daughter Zion is left
    like a shelter in a vineyard,
like a hut in a cucumber field,
    like a city under siege.
9 Unless the Lord Almighty
    had left us some survivors,
we would have become like Sodom,
    we would have been like Gomorrah.

Who was "Daughter of Zion"? (1:8)
This is a personification of Jerusalem and its people.

Why did Isaiah speak to the people of Sodom and Gomorrah, who had been destroyed? (1:10)
He was making a comparison between the people of Jerusalem and the people of Sodom and Gomorrah to show how sinful they were.

10 Hear the word of the Lord,
    you rulers of Sodom;
listen to the instruction of our God,
    you people of Gomorrah!
11 "The multitude of your sacrifices—
    what are they to me?" says the Lord.
"I have more than enough of burnt offerings,
    of rams and the fat of fattened animals;
I have no pleasure
    in the blood of bulls and lambs and goats.

¹²When you come to appear before me,
　who has asked this of you,
　　this trampling of my courts?
¹³Stop bringing meaningless offerings!
　Your incense is detestable to me.
New Moons, Sabbaths and convocations—
　I cannot bear your worthless assemblies.
¹⁴Your New Moon feasts and your appointed festivals
　I hate with all my being.
They have become a burden to me;
　I am weary of bearing them.
¹⁵When you spread out your hands in prayer,
　I hide my eyes from you;
even when you offer many prayers,
　I am not listening.

Your hands are full of blood!

¹⁶Wash and make yourselves clean.
　Take your evil deeds out of my sight;
　　stop doing wrong.
¹⁷Learn to do right; seek justice.
　Defend the oppressed.^a
Take up the cause of the fatherless;
　plead the case of the widow.

¹⁸"Come now, let us settle the matter,"
　says the LORD.
"Though your sins are like scarlet,
　they shall be as white as snow;
though they are red as crimson,
　they shall be like wool.
¹⁹If you are willing and obedient,
　you will eat the good things of the land;
²⁰but if you resist and rebel,
　you will be devoured by the sword."
　　　　　For the mouth of the LORD has spoken.

²¹See how the faithful city
　has become a prostitute!
She once was full of justice;
　righteousness used to dwell in her—
　　but now murderers!
²²Your silver has become dross,
　your choice wine is diluted with water.
²³Your rulers are rebels,
　partners with thieves;
they all love bribes
　and chase after gifts.
They do not defend the cause of the fatherless;
　the widow's case does not come before them.

²⁴Therefore the Lord, the LORD Almighty,
　the Mighty One of Israel, declares:
"Ah! I will vent my wrath on my foes
　and avenge myself on my enemies.

^a 17 Or justice. / Correct the oppressor

What was the New Moon festival? (1:13)
The New Moon was both a religious and civil festival. It was celebrated at the beginning of each month. Special sacrifices were offered, trumpets were sounded, and normal work activities were stopped.

What does this image suggest? (1:18)
This is a powerful image of blood that stained the hands of murderers. Because of God's forgiveness, our sins will be completely washed clean when we repent (turn away from) our sin.

How had Jerusalem become a prostitute? (1:21)
Jerusalem, representing all of Judah, was like an unfaithful wife to God.

²⁵I will turn my hand against you;ᵃ
    I will thoroughly purge away your dross
    and remove all your impurities.
²⁶I will restore your leaders as in days of old,
    your rulers as at the beginning.
Afterward you will be called
    the City of Righteousness,
    the Faithful City."

²⁷Zion will be delivered with justice,
    her penitent ones with righteousness.
²⁸But rebels and sinners will both be broken,
    and those who forsake the Lord will perish.

²⁹"You will be ashamed because of the sacred oaks
    in which you have delighted;
you will be disgraced because of the gardens
    that you have chosen.
³⁰You will be like an oak with fading leaves,
    like a garden without water.
³¹The mighty man will become tinder
    and his work a spark;
both will burn together,
    with no one to quench the fire."

THE MOUNTAIN OF THE LORD

2 This is what Isaiah son of Amoz saw concerning Judah and Jerusalem:

²In the last days

the mountain of the Lord's temple will be established
    as the highest of the mountains;
it will be exalted above the hills,
    and all nations will stream to it.

³Many peoples will come and say,

"Come, let us go up to the mountain of the Lord,
    to the temple of the God of Jacob.
He will teach us his ways,
    so that we may walk in his paths."
The law will go out from Zion,
    the word of the Lord from Jerusalem.
⁴He will judge between the nations
    and will settle disputes for many peoples.
They will beat their swords into plowshares
    and their spears into pruning hooks.
Nation will not take up sword against nation,
    nor will they train for war anymore.

⁵Come, descendants of Jacob,
    let us walk in the light of the Lord.

THE DAY OF THE LORD

⁶You, Lord, have abandoned your people,
    the descendants of Jacob.

What are the last days? (2:2)
This could refer to the future in general or a future time of judgment, but usually it refers to the Messianic age. This view holds that the last days began with the coming of Christ and will be fulfilled when Christ comes again.

ᵃ 25 That is, against Jerusalem

They are full of superstitions from the East;
    they practice divination like the Philistines
    and embrace pagan customs.
⁷Their land is full of silver and gold;
    there is no end to their treasures.
Their land is full of horses;
    there is no end to their chariots.
⁸Their land is full of idols;
    they bow down to the work of their hands,
    to what their fingers have made.
⁹So people will be brought low
    and everyone humbled—
    do not forgive them.ᵃ

¹⁰Go into the rocks, hide in the ground
    from the fearful presence of the LORD
    and the splendor of his majesty!
¹¹The eyes of the arrogant will be humbled
    and human pride brought low;
    the LORD alone will be exalted in that day.

¹²The LORD Almighty has a day in store
    for all the proud and lofty,
    for all that is exalted
    (and they will be humbled),
¹³for all the cedars of Lebanon, tall and lofty,
    and all the oaks of Bashan,
¹⁴for all the towering mountains
    and all the high hills,
¹⁵for every lofty tower
    and every fortified wall,
¹⁶for every trading shipᵇ
    and every stately vessel.
¹⁷The arrogance of man will be brought low
    and human pride humbled;
    the LORD alone will be exalted in that day,
¹⁸ and the idols will totally disappear.

¹⁹People will flee to caves in the rocks
    and to holes in the ground
    from the fearful presence of the LORD
    and the splendor of his majesty,
    when he rises to shake the earth.
²⁰In that day people will throw away
    to the moles and bats
    their idols of silver and idols of gold,
    which they made to worship.
²¹They will flee to caverns in the rocks
    and to the overhanging crags
    from the fearful presence of the LORD
    and the splendor of his majesty,
    when he rises to shake the earth.

²²Stop trusting in mere humans,
    who have but a breath in their nostrils.
    Why hold them in esteem?

ᵃ 9 Or *not raise them up*   ᵇ 16 Hebrew *every ship of Tarshish*

Why were large quantities of silver, gold, and horses a bad thing? (2:7)
The king was forbidden from accumulating large quantities of these things (see Deuteronomy 17:16–17).

What were these trading ships? (2:16)
These ships were large vessels used by Solomon and the Phoenicians to travel the seas in commercial ventures.

JUDGMENT ON JERUSALEM AND JUDAH

3 See now, the Lord,
  the Lord Almighty,
is about to take from Jerusalem and Judah
    both supply and support:
all supplies of food and all supplies of water,
  ² the hero and the warrior,
the judge and the prophet,
    the diviner and the elder,
³ the captain of fifty and the man of rank,
    the counselor, skilled craftsman and clever enchanter.

⁴ "I will make mere youths their officials;
    children will rule over them."

⁵ People will oppress each other—
    man against man, neighbor against neighbor.
The young will rise up against the old,
    the nobody against the honored.

⁶ A man will seize one of his brothers
    in his father's house, and say,
"You have a cloak, you be our leader;
    take charge of this heap of ruins!"
⁷ But in that day he will cry out,
    "I have no remedy.
I have no food or clothing in my house;
    do not make me the leader of the people."

⁸ Jerusalem staggers,
    Judah is falling;
their words and deeds are against the Lord,
    defying his glorious presence.
⁹ The look on their faces testifies against them;
    they parade their sin like Sodom;
    they do not hide it.
Woe to them!
    They have brought disaster upon themselves.

¹⁰ Tell the righteous it will be well with them,
    for they will enjoy the fruit of their deeds.
¹¹ Woe to the wicked!
    Disaster is upon them!
They will be paid back
    for what their hands have done.

¹² Youths oppress my people,
    women rule over them.
My people, your guides lead you astray;
    they turn you from the path.

¹³ The Lord takes his place in court;
    he rises to judge the people.
¹⁴ The Lord enters into judgment
    against the elders and leaders of his people:
"It is you who have ruined my vineyard;
    the plunder from the poor is in your houses.
¹⁵ What do you mean by crushing my people
    and grinding the faces of the poor?"
        declares the Lord, the Lord Almighty.

Who were diviners and enchanters? (3:2–3)
These were people who performed occult practices and snake charming. Their activities were forbidden (see Deuteronomy 18:10–11).

Why would young people and women be considered poor leaders? (3:12)
In the ancient world, neither young people nor women were thought fit to be rulers.

[16] The LORD says,
 "The women of Zion are haughty,
walking along with outstretched necks,
 flirting with their eyes,
strutting along with swaying hips,
 with ornaments jingling on their ankles.
[17] Therefore the Lord will bring sores on the heads of
    the women of Zion;
 the LORD will make their scalps bald."

[18] In that day the Lord will snatch away their finery: the
bangles and headbands and crescent necklaces, [19] the earrings
and bracelets and veils, [20] the headdresses and anklets and
sashes, the perfume bottles and charms, [21] the signet rings
and nose rings, [22] the fine robes and the capes and cloaks,
the purses [23] and mirrors, and the linen garments and tiaras
and shawls.

[24] Instead of fragrance there will be a stench;
    instead of a sash, a rope;
instead of well-dressed hair, baldness;
    instead of fine clothing, sackcloth;
    instead of beauty, branding.
[25] Your men will fall by the sword,
    your warriors in battle.
[26] The gates of Zion will lament and mourn;
    destitute, she will sit on the ground.

4 [1] In that day seven women
    will take hold of one man
and say, "We will eat our own food
    and provide our own clothes;
only let us be called by your name.
    Take away our disgrace!"

THE BRANCH OF THE LORD

[2] In that day the Branch of the LORD will be beautiful and
glorious, and the fruit of the land will be the pride and glory
of the survivors in Israel. [3] Those who are left in Zion, who
remain in Jerusalem, will be called holy, all who are recorded
among the living in Jerusalem. [4] The Lord will wash away
the filth of the women of Zion; he will cleanse the blood-
stains from Jerusalem by a spirit[a] of judgment and a spirit[a]
of fire. [5] Then the LORD will create over all of Mount Zion
and over those who assemble there a cloud of smoke by day
and a glow of flaming fire by night; over everything the glory[b] will be a canopy. [6] It will be a shelter and shade from
the heat of the day, and a refuge and hiding place from the
storm and rain.

THE SONG OF THE VINEYARD

5 I will sing for the one I love
    a song about his vineyard:
My loved one had a vineyard
    on a fertile hillside.

**Why would there be so
many women in the land?
(4:1)**
War would wipe out the male
population, leaving many women
with the double disgrace of being
widows and childless.

---

[a] 4 Or *the Spirit*   [b] 5 Or *over all the glory there*

A Winepress (5:2)

Why was the absence of rain a curse? (5:6)
In an area where farmers depended on rain to water their crops, the lack of rain would be seen as a curse.

How large was an acre? (5:10)
The word translated as *acre* refers to the average amount of land that could be plowed by one yoke of oxen within a day.

² He dug it up and cleared it of stones
    and planted it with the choicest vines.
He built a watchtower in it
    and cut out a winepress as well.
Then he looked for a crop of good grapes,
    but it yielded only bad fruit.

³ "Now you dwellers in Jerusalem and people of Judah,
    judge between me and my vineyard.
⁴ What more could have been done for my vineyard
    than I have done for it?
When I looked for good grapes,
    why did it yield only bad?
⁵ Now I will tell you
    what I am going to do to my vineyard:
I will take away its hedge,
    and it will be destroyed;
I will break down its wall,
    and it will be trampled.
⁶ I will make it a wasteland,
    neither pruned nor cultivated,
    and briers and thorns will grow there.
I will command the clouds
    not to rain on it."

⁷ The vineyard of the LORD Almighty
    is the nation of Israel,
and the people of Judah
    are the vines he delighted in.
And he looked for justice, but saw bloodshed;
    for righteousness, but heard cries of distress.

WOES AND JUDGMENTS

⁸ Woe to you who add house to house
    and join field to field
till no space is left
    and you live alone in the land.

⁹ The LORD Almighty has declared in my hearing:

"Surely the great houses will become desolate,
    the fine mansions left without occupants.
¹⁰ A ten-acre vineyard will produce only a bath*a* of wine;
    a homer*b* of seed will yield only an ephah*c* of grain."

¹¹ Woe to those who rise early in the morning
    to run after their drinks,
who stay up late at night
    till they are inflamed with wine.
¹² They have harps and lyres at their banquets,
    pipes and timbrels and wine,
but they have no regard for the deeds of the LORD,
    no respect for the work of his hands.
¹³ Therefore my people will go into exile
    for lack of understanding;

---

a 10 That is, about 6 gallons or about 22 liters   *b 10* That is, probably about 360 pounds or about 160 kilograms   *c 10* That is, probably about 36 pounds or about 16 kilograms

those of high rank will die of hunger
   and the common people will be parched with thirst.
¹⁴Therefore Death expands its jaws,
   opening wide its mouth;
into it will descend their nobles and masses
   with all their brawlers and revelers.
¹⁵So people will be brought low
   and everyone humbled,
   the eyes of the arrogant humbled.
¹⁶But the LORD Almighty will be exalted by his justice,
   and the holy God will be proved holy by his
      righteous acts.
¹⁷Then sheep will graze as in their own pasture;
   lambs will feed*a* among the ruins of the rich.

¹⁸Woe to those who draw sin along with cords
      of deceit,
   and wickedness as with cart ropes,
¹⁹to those who say, "Let God hurry;
   let him hasten his work
   so we may see it.
The plan of the Holy One of Israel—
   let it approach, let it come into view,
   so we may know it."

²⁰Woe to those who call evil good
   and good evil,
who put darkness for light
   and light for darkness,
who put bitter for sweet
   and sweet for bitter.

²¹Woe to those who are wise in their own eyes
   and clever in their own sight.

²²Woe to those who are heroes at drinking wine
   and champions at mixing drinks,
²³who acquit the guilty for a bribe,
   but deny justice to the innocent.
²⁴Therefore, as tongues of fire lick up straw
   and as dry grass sinks down in the flames,
so their roots will decay
   and their flowers blow away like dust;
for they have rejected the law of the LORD Almighty
   and spurned the word of the Holy One of Israel.
²⁵Therefore the LORD's anger burns against his people;
   his hand is raised and he strikes them down.
The mountains shake,
   and the dead bodies are like refuse in the streets.

Yet for all this, his anger is not turned away,
   his hand is still upraised.

²⁶He lifts up a banner for the distant nations,
   he whistles for those at the ends of the earth.
Here they come,
   swiftly and speedily!

a 17 Septuagint; Hebrew / *strangers will eat*

How would God be exalted by Jerusalem's judgment? (5:15–16)
Jerusalem deserved to be punished. This judgment honored God because it was the right thing to do.

What were mixed drinks? (5:22)
Spices were often added to beer and wine to make these drinks tastier or stronger.

What type of banner was this? (5:26)
A banner attached to a pole was often placed on a hilltop to gather troops. In the book of Isaiah, this was frequently used as a symbol for bringing Israel back home.

²⁷ Not one of them grows tired or stumbles,
　　 not one slumbers or sleeps;
　 not a belt is loosened at the waist,
　　 not a sandal strap is broken.
²⁸ Their arrows are sharp,
　　 all their bows are strung;
　 their horses' hooves seem like flint,
　　 their chariot wheels like a whirlwind.
²⁹ Their roar is like that of the lion,
　　 they roar like young lions;
　 they growl as they seize their prey
　　 and carry it off with no one to rescue.
³⁰ In that day they will roar over it
　　 like the roaring of the sea.
　 And if one looks at the land,
　　 there is only darkness and distress;
　　 even the sun will be darkened by clouds.

ISAIAH'S COMMISSION

6 In the year that King Uzziah died, I saw the Lord, high and exalted, seated on a throne; and the train of his robe filled the temple. ² Above him were seraphim, each with six wings: With two wings they covered their faces, with two they covered their feet, and with two they were flying. ³ And they were calling to one another:

"Holy, holy, holy is the Lord Almighty;
　 the whole earth is full of his glory."

⁴ At the sound of their voices the doorposts and thresholds shook and the temple was filled with smoke.

⁵ "Woe to me!" I cried. "I am ruined! For I am a man of unclean lips, and I live among a people of unclean lips, and my eyes have seen the King, the Lord Almighty."

⁶ Then one of the seraphim flew to me with a live coal in his hand, which he had taken with tongs from the altar. ⁷ With it he touched my mouth and said, "See, this has touched your lips; your guilt is taken away and your sin atoned for."

⁸ Then I heard the voice of the Lord saying, "Whom shall I send? And who will go for us?"

And I said, "Here am I. Send me!"

⁹ He said, "Go and tell this people:

"'Be ever hearing, but never understanding;
　 be ever seeing, but never perceiving.'
¹⁰ Make the heart of this people calloused;
　 make their ears dull
　 and close their eyes.ᵃ
Otherwise they might see with their eyes,
　 hear with their ears,
　 understand with their hearts,
and turn and be healed."

¹¹ Then I said, "For how long, Lord?"

And he answered:

What were seraphim? (6:2)
These were angelic creatures. The Hebrew word means "burning ones," possibly referring to their purity.

What is the significance of a live coal? (6:6–7)
Coals of fire were taken by the priest into the Most Holy Place on the Day of Atonement to atone for his sin and the sins of the people. The hot coal symbolized both God's anger at sin and purification.

ᵃ 9,10 Hebrew; Septuagint 'You will be ever hearing, but never understanding; / you will be ever seeing, but never perceiving.' / ¹⁰ This people's heart has become calloused; / they hardly hear with their ears, / and they have closed their eyes

"Until the cities lie ruined
  and without inhabitant,
until the houses are left deserted
  and the fields ruined and ravaged,
¹²until the Lord has sent everyone far away
  and the land is utterly forsaken.
¹³And though a tenth remains in the land,
  it will again be laid waste.
But as the terebinth and oak
  leave stumps when they are cut down,
  so the holy seed will be the stump in the land."

THE SIGN OF IMMANUEL

7 When Ahaz son of Jotham, the son of Uzziah, was king of Judah, King Rezin of Aram and Pekah son of Remaliah king of Israel marched up to fight against Jerusalem, but they could not overpower it.

²Now the house of David was told, "Aram has allied itself with*a* Ephraim"; so the hearts of Ahaz and his people were shaken, as the trees of the forest are shaken by the wind.

³Then the Lord said to Isaiah, "Go out, you and your son Shear-Jashub,*b* to meet Ahaz at the end of the aqueduct of the Upper Pool, on the road to the Launderer's Field. ⁴Say to him, 'Be careful, keep calm and don't be afraid. Do not lose heart because of these two smoldering stubs of firewood — because of the fierce anger of Rezin and Aram and of the son of Remaliah. ⁵Aram, Ephraim and Remaliah's son have plotted your ruin, saying, ⁶"Let us invade Judah; let us tear it apart and divide it among ourselves, and make the son of Tabeel king over it." ⁷Yet this is what the Sovereign Lord says:

"'It will not take place,
  it will not happen,
⁸for the head of Aram is Damascus,
  and the head of Damascus is only Rezin.
Within sixty-five years
  Ephraim will be too shattered to be a people.
⁹The head of Ephraim is Samaria,
  and the head of Samaria is only Remaliah's son.
If you do not stand firm in your faith,
  you will not stand at all.'"

¹⁰Again the Lord spoke to Ahaz, ¹¹"Ask the Lord your God for a sign, whether in the deepest depths or in the highest heights."

¹²But Ahaz said, "I will not ask; I will not put the Lord to the test."

¹³Then Isaiah said, "Hear now, you house of David! Is it not enough to try the patience of humans? Will you try the patience of my God also? ¹⁴Therefore the Lord himself will give you*c* a sign: The virgin*d* will conceive and give birth to a son, and*e* will call him Immanuel.*f* ¹⁵He will be eating curds and honey when he knows enough to reject the wrong and

How were clothes washed in ancient times? (7:3)
Clothes were washed by trampling on them in cold water and using soap (soda) or bleach.

Why would their diet be curds and honey? (7:15)
Curds (a kind of yogurt) and honey meant a return to the simple diet of those who lived off the land. The Assyrian invasion would devastate the country and make farming impossible.

---

a 2 Or *has set up camp in*   *b* 3 *Shear-Jashub* means *a remnant will return.*
c 14 The Hebrew is plural.   *d* 14 Or *young woman*   *e* 14 Masoretic Text;
Dead Sea Scrolls *son, and he* or *son, and they*   *f* 14 *Immanuel* means *God with us.*

choose the right, [16] for before the boy knows enough to reject the wrong and choose the right, the land of the two kings you dread will be laid waste. [17] The LORD will bring on you and on your people and on the house of your father a time unlike any since Ephraim broke away from Judah—he will bring the king of Assyria."

ASSYRIA, THE LORD'S INSTRUMENT

[18] In that day the LORD will whistle for flies from the Nile delta in Egypt and for bees from the land of Assyria. [19] They will all come and settle in the steep ravines and in the crevices in the rocks, on all the thornbushes and at all the water holes. [20] In that day the Lord will use a razor hired from beyond the Euphrates River—the king of Assyria—to shave your head and private parts, and to cut off your beard also. [21] In that day, a person will keep alive a young cow and two goats. [22] And because of the abundance of the milk they give, there will be curds to eat. All who remain in the land will eat curds and honey. [23] In that day, in every place where there were a thousand vines worth a thousand silver shekels,[a] there will be only briers and thorns. [24] Hunters will go there with bow and arrow, for the land will be covered with briers and thorns. [25] As for all the hills once cultivated by the hoe, you will no longer go there for fear of the briers and thorns; they will become places where cattle are turned loose and where sheep run.

ISAIAH AND HIS CHILDREN AS SIGNS

8 The LORD said to me, "Take a large scroll and write on it with an ordinary pen: Maher-Shalal-Hash-Baz."[b] [2] So I called in Uriah the priest and Zechariah son of Jeberekiah as reliable witnesses for me. [3] Then I made love to the prophetess, and she conceived and gave birth to a son. And the LORD said to me, "Name him Maher-Shalal-Hash-Baz. [4] For before the boy knows how to say 'My father' or 'My mother,' the wealth of Damascus and the plunder of Samaria will be carried off by the king of Assyria."

[5] The LORD spoke to me again:

[6] "Because this people has rejected
 the gently flowing waters of Shiloah
and rejoices over Rezin
 and the son of Remaliah,
[7] therefore the Lord is about to bring against them
 the mighty floodwaters of the Euphrates—
 the king of Assyria with all his pomp.
It will overflow all its channels,
 run over all its banks
[8] and sweep on into Judah, swirling over it,
 passing through it and reaching up to the neck.
Its outspread wings will cover the breadth of your land,
 Immanuel[c]!"

What were the flies and bees? (7:18)
This refers to the invasions of the Egyptians and Assyrians, which were compared to annoying and painful swarms of insects.

Why would the Israelites' hair be shaved? (7:20)
For an Israelite man to be shaved against his will was an extreme insult causing great shame.

What were the waters of Shiloah? (8:6)
This was a peaceful stream that flowed from the spring of Gihon to the pool of Siloam. Here the stream symbolized the peace and sustaining power of the Lord.

What were these floodwaters? (8:7–8)
The image of floodwaters was often used to symbolize a powerful invading army.

---

[a] 23 That is, about 25 pounds or about 12 kilograms   [b] 1 Maher-Shalal-Hash-Baz means quick to the plunder, swift to the spoil; also in verse 3.
[c] 8 Immanuel means God with us.

⁹ Raise the war cry,ᵃ you nations, and be shattered!
　 Listen, all you distant lands.
　 Prepare for battle, and be shattered!
　 Prepare for battle, and be shattered!
¹⁰ Devise your strategy, but it will be thwarted;
　 propose your plan, but it will not stand,
　 for God is with us.ᵇ

¹¹ This is what the LORD says to me with his strong hand
upon me, warning me not to follow the way of this people:

¹² "Do not call conspiracy
　 everything this people calls a conspiracy;
　 do not fear what they fear,
　 and do not dread it.
¹³ The LORD Almighty is the one you are to regard as
　 holy,
　 he is the one you are to fear,
　 he is the one you are to dread.
¹⁴ He will be a holy place;
　 for both Israel and Judah he will be
　 a stone that causes people to stumble
　 and a rock that makes them fall.
　 And for the people of Jerusalem he will be
　 a trap and a snare.
¹⁵ Many of them will stumble;
　 they will fall and be broken,
　 they will be snared and captured."

¹⁶ Bind up this testimony of warning
　 and seal up God's instruction among my disciples.
¹⁷ I will wait for the LORD,
　 who is hiding his face from the descendants of
　 Jacob.
　 I will put my trust in him.

¹⁸ Here am I, and the children the LORD has given me. We
are signs and symbols in Israel from the LORD Almighty,
who dwells on Mount Zion.

THE DARKNESS TURNS TO LIGHT

¹⁹ When someone tells you to consult mediums and spiritists, who whisper and mutter, should not a people inquire
of their God? Why consult the dead on behalf of the living?
²⁰ Consult God's instruction and the testimony of warning.
If anyone does not speak according to this word, they have
no light of dawn. ²¹ Distressed and hungry, they will roam
through the land; when they are famished, they will become
enraged and, looking upward, will curse their king and their
God. ²² Then they will look toward the earth and see only
distress and darkness and fearful gloom, and they will be
thrust into utter darkness.

9 ᶜ Nevertheless, there will be no more gloom for those
　 who were in distress. In the past he humbled the land
of Zebulun and the land of Naphtali, but in the future he will

**How could God's instruction
be sealed? (8:16)**
This may refer to the scroll in
verse 1 that would be sealed until
the events happened as God had
predicted.

ᵃ 9 Or *Do your worst*　ᵇ 10 Hebrew *Immanuel*　ᶜ In Hebrew texts 9:1 is
numbered 8:23, and 9:2-21 is numbered 9:1-20.

honor Galilee of the nations, by the Way of the Sea, beyond
the Jordan—

**What was this great light?
(9:2)**
Some believe this pointed to
future kings of Israel such as
Josiah and Hezekiah who tried
to turn Israel back to God. But it
also pointed to Jesus, who would
be a light to the Gentiles (see
42:6 and 49:6).

² The people walking in darkness
    have seen a great light;
on those living in the land of deep darkness
    a light has dawned.
³ You have enlarged the nation
    and increased their joy;
they rejoice before you
    as people rejoice at the harvest,
as warriors rejoice
    when dividing the plunder.
⁴ For as in the day of Midian's defeat,
    you have shattered
the yoke that burdens them,
    the bar across their shoulders,
    the rod of their oppressor.
⁵ Every warrior's boot used in battle
    and every garment rolled in blood
will be destined for burning,
    will be fuel for the fire.

Who was this child? (9:6–7)
This prophecy points to the coming Messiah, who was a descendant of David.

⁶ For to us a child is born,
    to us a son is given,
    and the government will be on his shoulders.
And he will be called
    Wonderful Counselor, Mighty God,
    Everlasting Father, Prince of Peace.
⁷ Of the greatness of his government and peace
    there will be no end.
He will reign on David's throne
    and over his kingdom,
establishing and upholding it
    with justice and righteousness
    from that time on and forever.
The zeal of the LORD Almighty
    will accomplish this.

THE LORD'S ANGER AGAINST ISRAEL

⁸ The Lord has sent a message against Jacob;
    it will fall on Israel.
⁹ All the people will know it—
    Ephraim and the inhabitants of Samaria—
who say with pride
    and arrogance of heart,

**Why would the bricks have
fallen down? (9:10)**
Bricks made of clay and dried
in the sun crumbled easily. God
had instructed his people to build
altars from uncut stones (see
Exodus 20:25).

¹⁰ "The bricks have fallen down,
    but we will rebuild with dressed stone;
the fig trees have been felled,
    but we will replace them with cedars."
¹¹ But the LORD has strengthened Rezin's foes
    against them
    and has spurred their enemies on.
¹² Arameans from the east and Philistines from the west
    have devoured Israel with open mouth.

Yet for all this, his anger is not turned away,
    his hand is still upraised.

¹³ But the people have not returned to him who
   struck them,
   nor have they sought the Lᴏʀᴅ Almighty.
¹⁴ So the Lᴏʀᴅ will cut off from Israel both head
   and tail,
   both palm branch and reed in a single day;
¹⁵ the elders and dignitaries are the head,
   the prophets who teach lies are the tail.
¹⁶ Those who guide this people mislead them,
   and those who are guided are led astray.
¹⁷ Therefore the Lord will take no pleasure in the
   young men,
   nor will he pity the fatherless and widows,
   for everyone is ungodly and wicked,
   every mouth speaks folly.

Yet for all this, his anger is not turned away,
   his hand is still upraised.

¹⁸ Surely wickedness burns like a fire;
   it consumes briers and thorns,
   it sets the forest thickets ablaze,
   so that it rolls upward in a column of smoke.
¹⁹ By the wrath of the Lᴏʀᴅ Almighty
   the land will be scorched
   and the people will be fuel for the fire;
   they will not spare one another.
²⁰ On the right they will devour,
   but still be hungry;
   on the left they will eat,
   but not be satisfied.
   Each will feed on the flesh of their own offspringᵃ:
²¹   Manasseh will feed on Ephraim, and Ephraim on
     Manasseh;
     together they will turn against Judah.

Yet for all this, his anger is not turned away,
   his hand is still upraised.

10 Woe to those who make unjust laws,
     to those who issue oppressive decrees,
² to deprive the poor of their rights
   and withhold justice from the oppressed of my
   people,
   making widows their prey
   and robbing the fatherless.
³ What will you do on the day of reckoning,
   when disaster comes from afar?
   To whom will you run for help?
   Where will you leave your riches?
⁴ Nothing will remain but to cringe among
   the captives
   or fall among the slain.

Yet for all this, his anger is not turned away,
   his hand is still upraised.

How would God cut off Israel's head and tail? (9:14–16)
This meant God would cut off the leaders and the ordinary people because all were ungodly.

Why would Manasseh and Ephraim be at odds? (9:21)
These were the two most prominent tribes of the northern kingdom. Both were Joseph's sons. The brothers' conflict continued down through the generations, so that their descendants fought as well.

What rights did the poor have? (10:2)
The law gave the poor many rights. The weekly Sabbath, Sabbatical Year, and Year of Jubilee were designed to restore property to the poor and relieve their debts.

ᵃ 20 Or *arm*

GOD'S JUDGMENT ON ASSYRIA

Why would God use a wicked nation to punish Israel? (10:5–6)
God was totally in control and could use whatever means he wished to punish Israel, including using evil nations.

⁵ "Woe to the Assyrian, the rod of my anger,
    in whose hand is the club of my wrath!
⁶ I send him against a godless nation,
    I dispatch him against a people who anger me,
to seize loot and snatch plunder,
    and to trample them down like mud in the streets.
⁷ But this is not what he intends,
    this is not what he has in mind;
his purpose is to destroy,
    to put an end to many nations.
⁸ 'Are not my commanders all kings?' he says.
⁹ 'Has not Kalno fared like Carchemish?
Is not Hamath like Arpad,
    and Samaria like Damascus?
¹⁰ As my hand seized the kingdoms of the idols,
    kingdoms whose images excelled those of Jerusalem
        and Samaria—
¹¹ shall I not deal with Jerusalem and her images
    as I dealt with Samaria and her idols?'"

¹² When the Lord has finished all his work against Mount Zion and Jerusalem, he will say, "I will punish the king of Assyria for the willful pride of his heart and the haughty look in his eyes. ¹³ For he says:

"'By the strength of my hand I have done this,
    and by my wisdom, because I have understanding.
I removed the boundaries of nations,
    I plundered their treasures;
    like a mighty one I subdued*ᵃ* their kings.
¹⁴ As one reaches into a nest,
    so my hand reached for the wealth of the nations;
as people gather abandoned eggs,
    so I gathered all the countries;
not one flapped a wing,
    or opened its mouth to chirp.'"

¹⁵ Does the ax raise itself above the person who swings it,
    or the saw boast against the one who uses it?
As if a rod were to wield the person who lifts it up,
    or a club brandish the one who is not wood!

What was this wasting disease? (10:16)
The angel may have used a severe and contagious plague to put to death 185,000 of Sennacherib's soldiers (see Isaiah 37:36–37).

¹⁶ Therefore, the Lord, the LORD Almighty,
    will send a wasting disease upon his sturdy warriors;
under his pomp a fire will be kindled
    like a blazing flame.
¹⁷ The Light of Israel will become a fire,
    their Holy One a flame;
in a single day it will burn and consume
    his thorns and his briers.
¹⁸ The splendor of his forests and fertile fields
    it will completely destroy,
    as when a sick person wastes away.
¹⁹ And the remaining trees of his forests will be so few
    that a child could write them down.

ᵃ 13 Or *treasures; / I subdued the mighty,*

THE REMNANT OF ISRAEL

[20] In that day the remnant of Israel,
  the survivors of Jacob,
will no longer rely on him
  who struck them down
but will truly rely on the LORD,
  the Holy One of Israel.
[21] A remnant will return,[a] a remnant of Jacob
  will return to the Mighty God.
[22] Though your people be like the sand by the sea, Israel,
  only a remnant will return.
Destruction has been decreed,
  overwhelming and righteous.
[23] The Lord, the LORD Almighty, will carry out
  the destruction decreed upon the whole land.

[24] Therefore this is what the Lord, the LORD Almighty, says:

"My people who live in Zion,
  do not be afraid of the Assyrians,
who beat you with a rod
  and lift up a club against you, as Egypt did.
[25] Very soon my anger against you will end
  and my wrath will be directed to their destruction."

[26] The LORD Almighty will lash them with a whip,
  as when he struck down Midian at the rock of Oreb;
and he will raise his staff over the waters,
  as he did in Egypt.
[27] In that day their burden will be lifted from
      your shoulders,
  their yoke from your neck;
the yoke will be broken
  because you have grown so fat.[b]

[28] They enter Aiath;
  they pass through Migron;
  they store supplies at Mikmash.
[29] They go over the pass, and say,
  "We will camp overnight at Geba."
Ramah trembles;
  Gibeah of Saul flees.
[30] Cry out, Daughter Gallim!
  Listen, Laishah!
  Poor Anathoth!
[31] Madmenah is in flight;
  the people of Gebim take cover.
[32] This day they will halt at Nob;
  they will shake their fist
at the mount of Daughter Zion,
  at the hill of Jerusalem.

[33] See, the Lord, the LORD Almighty,
  will lop off the boughs with great power.
The lofty trees will be felled,
  the tall ones will be brought low.

**Who was the remnant?
(10:20–22)**
The remnant — meaning the
remaining people — might refer
to the group of people who survived Nebuchadnezzar's invasion
and destruction of Jerusalem.
It also might refer to the people
left after the fall of the northern
kingdom. But it could also be
referencing a time in the future
where the people would turn
back to God and place their
complete trust in him. (See also
Romans 9:27 – 29.)

**What did it mean that the
oxen would be fat enough to
break a yoke? (10:27)**
God was predicting that the
people would become powerful
enough to rid themselves of
Assyrian oppression.

---

a 21 Hebrew *shear-jashub* (see 7:3 and note); also in verse 22   *b 27* Hebrew;
Septuagint *broken / from your shoulders*

34 He will cut down the forest thickets with an ax;
    Lebanon will fall before the Mighty One.

THE BRANCH FROM JESSE

11 A shoot will come up from the stump of Jesse;
    from his roots a Branch will bear fruit.
2 The Spirit of the LORD will rest on him—
    the Spirit of wisdom and of understanding,
    the Spirit of counsel and of might,
    the Spirit of the knowledge and fear of
      the LORD—
3 and he will delight in the fear of the LORD.

He will not judge by what he sees with his eyes,
    or decide by what he hears with his ears;
4 but with righteousness he will judge the needy,
    with justice he will give decisions for the poor of
      the earth.
He will strike the earth with the rod of his mouth;
    with the breath of his lips he will slay the wicked.
5 Righteousness will be his belt
    and faithfulness the sash around his waist.

6 The wolf will live with the lamb,
    the leopard will lie down with the goat,
the calf and the lion and the yearling*a* together;
    and a little child will lead them.
7 The cow will feed with the bear,
    their young will lie down together,
    and the lion will eat straw like the ox.
8 The infant will play near the cobra's den,
    and the young child will put its hand into the
      viper's nest.
9 They will neither harm nor destroy
    on all my holy mountain,
for the earth will be filled with the knowledge of
      the LORD
    as the waters cover the sea.

10 In that day the Root of Jesse will stand as a banner for the peoples; the nations will rally to him, and his resting place will be glorious. 11 In that day the Lord will reach out his hand a second time to reclaim the surviving remnant of his people from Assyria, from Lower Egypt, from Upper Egypt, from Cush,*b* from Elam, from Babylonia,*c* from Hamath and from the islands of the Mediterranean.

12 He will raise a banner for the nations
    and gather the exiles of Israel;
he will assemble the scattered people of Judah
    from the four quarters of the earth.
13 Ephraim's jealousy will vanish,
    and Judah's enemies*d* will be destroyed;
Ephraim will not be jealous of Judah,
    nor Judah hostile toward Ephraim.

a 6 Hebrew; Septuagint *lion will feed*   *b* 11 That is, the upper Nile region   *c* 11 Hebrew *Shinar*   *d* 13 Or *hostility*

What was the stump of Jesse? (11:1)
Judah had been destroyed like a tree that was chopped down. But God would keep his promise that David's dynasty would continue. The Messiah would grow like a branch from the family tree of Jesse, David's father.

When will this prophecy of a peaceable kingdom be fulfilled? (11:6–9)
This time of perfect peace will take place when Christ returns to establish his kingdom in the new heaven and new earth.

Why did Ephraim and Judah not get along? (11:13)
Before the exile, Ephraim in the north and Judah in the south were often rivals that fought each other. This rivalry led to war when Judah's king Ahaz refused to join with Ephraim and Syria to fight the Assyrians.

14 They will swoop down on the slopes of Philistia
    to the west;
together they will plunder the people to
    the east.
They will subdue Edom and Moab,
    and the Ammonites will be subject to them.
15 The Lord will dry up
    the gulf of the Egyptian sea;
with a scorching wind he will sweep his hand
    over the Euphrates River.
He will break it up into seven streams
    so that anyone can cross over in sandals.
16 There will be a highway for the remnant of
    his people
    that is left from Assyria,
as there was for Israel
    when they came up from Egypt.

SONGS OF PRAISE

12 In that day you will say:

"I will praise you, Lord.
    Although you were angry with me,
your anger has turned away
    and you have comforted me.
2 Surely God is my salvation;
    I will trust and not be afraid.
The Lord, the Lord himself, is my strength and
    my defense[a];
    he has become my salvation."
3 With joy you will draw water
    from the wells of salvation.

4 In that day you will say:

"Give praise to the Lord, proclaim his name;
    make known among the nations what he has done,
    and proclaim that his name is exalted.
5 Sing to the Lord, for he has done glorious things;
    let this be known to all the world.
6 Shout aloud and sing for joy, people of Zion,
    for great is the Holy One of Israel among you."

A PROPHECY AGAINST BABYLON

13 A prophecy against Babylon that Isaiah son of Amoz
saw:

2 Raise a banner on a bare hilltop,
    shout to them;
beckon to them
    to enter the gates of the nobles.
3 I have commanded those I prepared for battle;
    I have summoned my warriors to carry out my
        wrath —
    those who rejoice in my triumph.

What were the wells of salvation? (12:3)
This may be a reminder of the way God provided water for the Israelites in the desert. But here God's future salvation is itself the "well" from which Israel would drink life-giving water.

What was a prophecy? (13:1)
This was a message from God, often a message of doom.

[a] 2 Or *song*

⁴Listen, a noise on the mountains,
　like that of a great multitude!
Listen, an uproar among the kingdoms,
　like nations massing together!
The Lᴏʀᴅ Almighty is mustering
　an army for war.
⁵They come from faraway lands,
　from the ends of the heavens—
the Lᴏʀᴅ and the weapons of his wrath—
　to destroy the whole country.

⁶Wail, for the day of the Lᴏʀᴅ is near;
　it will come like destruction from the Almighty.ᵃ
⁷Because of this, all hands will go limp,
　every heart will melt with fear.
⁸Terror will seize them,
　pain and anguish will grip them;
　they will writhe like a woman in labor.
They will look aghast at each other,
　their faces aflame.

⁹See, the day of the Lᴏʀᴅ is coming
　—a cruel day, with wrath and fierce anger—
to make the land desolate
　and destroy the sinners within it.
¹⁰The stars of heaven and their constellations
　will not show their light.
The rising sun will be darkened
　and the moon will not give its light.
¹¹I will punish the world for its evil,
　the wicked for their sins.
I will put an end to the arrogance of the haughty
　and will humble the pride of the ruthless.
¹²I will make people scarcer than pure gold,
　more rare than the gold of Ophir.
¹³Therefore I will make the heavens tremble;
　and the earth will shake from its place
at the wrath of the Lᴏʀᴅ Almighty,
　in the day of his burning anger.

¹⁴Like a hunted gazelle,
　like sheep without a shepherd,
they will all return to their own people,
　they will flee to their native land.
¹⁵Whoever is captured will be thrust through;
　all who are caught will fall by the sword.
¹⁶Their infants will be dashed to pieces before
　　their eyes;
　their houses will be looted and their wives violated.

¹⁷See, I will stir up against them the Medes,
　who do not care for silver
　and have no delight in gold.
¹⁸Their bows will strike down the young men;
　they will have no mercy on infants,
　nor will they look with compassion on children.

ᵃ 6 Hebrew *Shaddai*

What were some visible signs of the "day of the Lᴏʀᴅ"? (13:10–13)
Darkness, thunderstorms, and earthquakes are all mentioned as signs of God's anger and judgment.

Why would God permit this violence toward women and children? (13:16)
This continues the imagery of God's wrath on the day of the Lord. Invading armies often slaughtered women and children, so the enemy would not be able to raise another generation of warriors. In order to eliminate their evil influence, God sometimes allowed this type of cruelty toward the enemies of his people.

¹⁹ Babylon, the jewel of kingdoms,
    the pride and glory of the Babylonians,ᵃ
will be overthrown by God
    like Sodom and Gomorrah.
²⁰ She will never be inhabited
    or lived in through all generations;
there no nomads will pitch their tents,
    there no shepherds will rest their flocks.
²¹ But desert creatures will lie there,
    jackals will fill her houses;
there the owls will dwell,
    and there the wild goats will leap about.
²² Hyenas will inhabit her strongholds,
    jackals her luxurious palaces.
Her time is at hand,
    and her days will not be prolonged.

14 The LORD will have compassion on Jacob;
    once again he will choose Israel
and will settle them in their own land.
Foreigners will join them
    and unite with the descendants of Jacob.
² Nations will take them
    and bring them to their own place.
And Israel will take possession of the nations
    and make them male and female servants in the
        LORD's land.
They will make captives of their captors
    and rule over their oppressors.

³ On the day the LORD gives you relief from your suffering and turmoil and from the harsh labor forced on you, ⁴ you will take up this taunt against the king of Babylon:

How the oppressor has come to an end!
    How his furyᵇ has ended!
⁵ The LORD has broken the rod of the wicked,
    the scepter of the rulers,
⁶ which in anger struck down peoples
    with unceasing blows,
and in fury subdued nations
    with relentless aggression.
⁷ All the lands are at rest and at peace;
    they break into singing.
⁸ Even the junipers and the cedars of Lebanon
    gloat over you and say,
"Now that you have been laid low,
    no one comes to cut us down."
⁹ The realm of the dead below is all astir
    to meet you at your coming;
it rouses the spirits of the departed to greet you—
    all those who were leaders in the world;
it makes them rise from their thrones—
    all those who were kings over the nations.

ᵃ 19 Or *Chaldeans*   ᵇ 4 Dead Sea Scrolls, Septuagint and Syriac; the meaning of the word in the Masoretic Text is uncertain.

Why was Babylon the jewel of the kingdoms? (13:19)
With its temples and palaces, Babylon was a very beautiful city. The hanging gardens of Nebuchadnezzar were one of the seven wonders of the ancient world.

When would this event take place? (14:1)
This "second exodus" occurred when King Cyrus allowed the Jews to return to Jerusalem to rebuild the temple (see Ezra 1:1–4).

Why would the trees gloat? (14:8)
The highly prized cedars of Lebanon had been hauled away for centuries by the kings of Assyria and Babylon. With Babylon's defeat, this would no longer happen.

¹⁰ They will all respond,
    they will say to you,
"You also have become weak, as we are;
    you have become like us."
¹¹ All your pomp has been brought down to the grave,
    along with the noise of your harps;
maggots are spread out beneath you
    and worms cover you.

¹² How you have fallen from heaven,
    morning star, son of the dawn!
You have been cast down to the earth,
    you who once laid low the nations!
¹³ You said in your heart,
    "I will ascend to the heavens;
I will raise my throne
    above the stars of God;
I will sit enthroned on the mount of assembly,
    on the utmost heights of Mount Zaphon.ᵃ
¹⁴ I will ascend above the tops of the clouds;
    I will make myself like the Most High."
¹⁵ But you are brought down to the realm of the dead,
    to the depths of the pit.

¹⁶ Those who see you stare at you,
    they ponder your fate:
"Is this the man who shook the earth
    and made kingdoms tremble,
¹⁷ the man who made the world a wilderness,
    who overthrew its cities
    and would not let his captives go home?"

¹⁸ All the kings of the nations lie in state,
    each in his own tomb.
¹⁹ But you are cast out of your tomb
    like a rejected branch;
you are covered with the slain,
    with those pierced by the sword,
    those who descend to the stones of the pit.
Like a corpse trampled underfoot,
²⁰   you will not join them in burial,
for you have destroyed your land
    and killed your people.

Let the offspring of the wicked
    never be mentioned again.
²¹ Prepare a place to slaughter his children
    for the sins of their ancestors;
they are not to rise to inherit the land
    and cover the earth with their cities.

²² "I will rise up against them,"
    declares the LORD Almighty.
"I will wipe out Babylon's name and survivors,
    her offspring and descendants,"
                   declares the LORD.

ᵃ 13 Or *of the north*; Zaphon was the most sacred mountain of the Canaanites.

What was the sacred mountain? (14:13)
Mount Zaphon, also called Mount Casius, was about 25 miles (40 kilometers) northeast of Ugarit in Syria. The Canaanites considered it the home and meeting place of the gods, like Mount Olympus for the Greeks.

Why would being cast out of a tomb be a disgrace? (14:19)
A proper burial was considered very important, especially for a king. To have one's body simply discarded was a humiliating fate.

23 "I will turn her into a place for owls
and into swampland;
I will sweep her with the broom of destruction,"
declares the LORD Almighty.

24 The LORD Almighty has sworn,

"Surely, as I have planned, so it will be,
and as I have purposed, so it will happen.
25 I will crush the Assyrian in my land;
on my mountains I will trample him down.
His yoke will be taken from my people,
and his burden removed from their shoulders."

26 This is the plan determined for the whole world;
this is the hand stretched out over all nations.
27 For the LORD Almighty has purposed, and who can
thwart him?
His hand is stretched out, and who can turn
it back?

A PROPHECY AGAINST THE PHILISTINES

28 This prophecy came in the year King Ahaz died:

29 Do not rejoice, all you Philistines,
that the rod that struck you is broken;
from the root of that snake will spring up a viper,
its fruit will be a darting, venomous serpent.
30 The poorest of the poor will find pasture,
and the needy will lie down in safety.
But your root I will destroy by famine;
it will slay your survivors.

31 Wail, you gate! Howl, you city!
Melt away, all you Philistines!
A cloud of smoke comes from the north,
and there is not a straggler in its ranks.
32 What answer shall be given
to the envoys of that nation?
"The LORD has established Zion,
and in her his afflicted people will find refuge."

A PROPHECY AGAINST MOAB

15 A prophecy against Moab:

Ar in Moab is ruined,
destroyed in a night!
Kir in Moab is ruined,
destroyed in a night!
2 Dibon goes up to its temple,
to its high places to weep;
Moab wails over Nebo and Medeba.
Every head is shaved
and every beard cut off.
3 In the streets they wear sackcloth;
on the roofs and in the public squares
they all wail,
prostrate with weeping.

How certain were these prophecies? (14:24–27)
The Lord declared that his sovereign purposes regarding Assyria and Babylon would be carried out.

Why did the Philistines want to rejoice? (14:29)
God rejoiced because the cruel Sargon of Assyria had died. But the prophecy stated that Sargon's successors would continue to attack the Philistines.

Why would Moab be destroyed? (15:1–4)
Moab, located east of the Dead Sea, was a constant enemy of Israel.

Why would heads be shaved, beards be cut off, and sackcloth be worn? (15:2–3)
These were symbols of extreme grief and mourning.

⁴Heshbon and Elealeh cry out,
　　their voices are heard all the way to Jahaz.
Therefore the armed men of Moab cry out,
　　and their hearts are faint.

⁵My heart cries out over Moab;
　　her fugitives flee as far as Zoar,
　　as far as Eglath Shelishiyah.
They go up the hill to Luhith,
　　weeping as they go;
on the road to Horonaim
　　they lament their destruction.
⁶The waters of Nimrim are dried up
　　and the grass is withered;
the vegetation is gone
　　and nothing green is left.
⁷So the wealth they have acquired and stored up
　　they carry away over the Ravine of the Poplars.
⁸Their outcry echoes along the border of Moab;
　　their wailing reaches as far as Eglaim,
　　their lamentation as far as Beer Elim.
⁹The waters of Dimon*ᵃ* are full of blood,
　　but I will bring still more upon Dimon*ᵃ*—
a lion upon the fugitives of Moab
　　and upon those who remain in the land.

16 Send lambs as tribute
　　to the ruler of the land,
from Sela, across the desert,
　　to the mount of Daughter Zion.
²Like fluttering birds
　　pushed from the nest,
so are the women of Moab
　　at the fords of the Arnon.

³"Make up your mind," Moab says.
　　"Render a decision.
Make your shadow like night—
　　at high noon.
Hide the fugitives,
　　do not betray the refugees.
⁴Let the Moabite fugitives stay with you;
　　be their shelter from the destroyer."

The oppressor will come to an end,
　　and destruction will cease;
　　the aggressor will vanish from the land.
⁵In love a throne will be established;
　　in faithfulness a man will sit on it—
　　one from the house*ᵇ* of David—
one who in judging seeks justice
　　and speeds the cause of righteousness.

⁶We have heard of Moab's pride—
　　how great is her arrogance!—

Why would Moab send lambs as tribute? (16:1) During King Ahab's reign, the Moabite king Mesha sent Israel 100,000 lambs each year (2 Kings 3:4–5). Now Moab, which had often oppressed Israel, was advised to submit to Jerusalem once more.

Why was Moab proud? (16:6) Moab did not have much to boast about. It was only a small nation, especially when compared with Assyria. Its pride was out of proportion to its importance and power.

ᵃ 9 Dimon, a wordplay on Dibon (see verse 2), sounds like the Hebrew for blood.   ᵇ 5 Hebrew tent

of her conceit, her pride and her insolence;
   but her boasts are empty.
⁷Therefore the Moabites wail,
   they wail together for Moab.
Lament and grieve
   for the raisin cakes of Kir Hareseth.
⁸The fields of Heshbon wither,
   the vines of Sibmah also.
The rulers of the nations
   have trampled down the choicest vines,
which once reached Jazer
   and spread toward the desert.
Their shoots spread out
   and went as far as the sea.ᵃ
⁹So I weep, as Jazer weeps,
   for the vines of Sibmah.
Heshbon and Elealeh,
   I drench you with tears!
The shouts of joy over your ripened fruit
   and over your harvests have been stilled.
¹⁰Joy and gladness are taken away from the orchards;
   no one sings or shouts in the vineyards;
no one treads out wine at the presses,
   for I have put an end to the shouting.
¹¹My heart laments for Moab like a harp,
   my inmost being for Kir Hareseth.
¹²When Moab appears at her high place,
   she only wears herself out;
when she goes to her shrine to pray,
   it is to no avail.

¹³This is the word the Lord has already spoken concerning Moab. ¹⁴But now the Lord says: "Within three years, as a servant bound by contract would count them, Moab's splendor and all her many people will be despised, and her survivors will be very few and feeble."

A PROPHECY AGAINST DAMASCUS

17 A prophecy against Damascus:

"See, Damascus will no longer be a city
   but will become a heap of ruins.
²The cities of Aroer will be deserted
   and left to flocks, which will lie down,
   with no one to make them afraid.
³The fortified city will disappear from Ephraim,
   and royal power from Damascus;
the remnant of Aram will be
   like the glory of the Israelites,"
           declares the Lord Almighty.

⁴"In that day the glory of Jacob will fade;
   the fat of his body will waste away.
⁵It will be as when reapers harvest the standing grain,
   gathering the grain in their arms—

How did Moab wear itself out at the high place? (16:12) Moab's god, Chemosh, was a mere idol, so worshiping that god was simply a waste of time.

How was Damascus reduced to ruins? (17:1) In 732 B.C., Assyrian king Tiglath-Pileser III destroyed Damascus.

ᵃ 8 Probably the Dead Sea

as when someone gleans heads of grain
  in the Valley of Rephaim.
⁶Yet some gleanings will remain,
  as when an olive tree is beaten,
leaving two or three olives on the topmost branches,
  four or five on the fruitful boughs,"
                    declares the Lord, the God of Israel.

⁷In that day people will look to their Maker
  and turn their eyes to the Holy One of Israel.
⁸They will not look to the altars,
  the work of their hands,
and they will have no regard for the Asherah poles*ᵃ*
  and the incense altars their fingers have made.

⁹In that day their strong cities, which they left because of
the Israelites, will be like places abandoned to thickets and
undergrowth. And all will be desolation.

¹⁰You have forgotten God your Savior;
  you have not remembered the Rock, your fortress.
Therefore, though you set out the finest plants
  and plant imported vines,
¹¹though on the day you set them out, you make
      them grow,
  and on the morning when you plant them, you bring
      them to bud,
yet the harvest will be as nothing
  in the day of disease and incurable pain.

¹²Woe to the many nations that rage—
  they rage like the raging sea!
Woe to the peoples who roar—
  they roar like the roaring of great waters!
¹³Although the peoples roar like the roar of surging
      waters,
  when he rebukes them they flee far away,
driven before the wind like chaff on the hills,
  like tumbleweed before a gale.
¹⁴In the evening, sudden terror!
  Before the morning, they are gone!
This is the portion of those who loot us,
  the lot of those who plunder us.

A PROPHECY AGAINST CUSH

18 Woe to the land of whirring wings*ᵇ*
    along the rivers of Cush,*ᶜ*
²which sends envoys by sea
  in papyrus boats over the water.

Go, swift messengers,
to a people tall and smooth-skinned,
  to a people feared far and wide,
an aggressive nation of strange speech,
  whose land is divided by rivers.

What were these altars and Asherah poles? (17:8)
These were altars to Baal on the high places and poles or sacred trees dedicated to the worship of the fertility goddess Asherah.

Why were the people of Damascus described as being like chaff and tumbleweed? (17:13)
These were symbols of the enemy who would be blown away by God's power.

What were the whirring wings? (18:1)
This may be a reference to insects (locusts) or a description of the sound made by the canvas sails of ships.

ᵃ 8 That is, wooden symbols of the goddess Asherah   ᵇ 1 Or of locusts
ᶜ 1 That is, the upper Nile region

³ All you people of the world,
    you who live on the earth,
when a banner is raised on the mountains,
    you will see it,
and when a trumpet sounds,
    you will hear it.
⁴ This is what the LORD says to me:
    "I will remain quiet and will look on from my
        dwelling place,
like shimmering heat in the sunshine,
    like a cloud of dew in the heat of harvest."
⁵ For, before the harvest, when the blossom is gone
    and the flower becomes a ripening grape,
he will cut off the shoots with pruning knives,
    and cut down and take away the spreading branches.
⁶ They will all be left to the mountain birds of prey
    and to the wild animals;
the birds will feed on them all summer,
    the wild animals all winter.

⁷ At that time gifts will be brought to the LORD Almighty

from a people tall and smooth-skinned,
    from a people feared far and wide,
an aggressive nation of strange speech,
    whose land is divided by rivers—

the gifts will be brought to Mount Zion, the place of the
Name of the LORD Almighty.

A PROPHECY AGAINST EGYPT

19 A prophecy against Egypt:

See, the LORD rides on a swift cloud
    and is coming to Egypt.
The idols of Egypt tremble before him,
    and the hearts of the Egyptians melt with fear.

² "I will stir up Egyptian against Egyptian—
    brother will fight against brother,
    neighbor against neighbor,
    city against city,
    kingdom against kingdom.
³ The Egyptians will lose heart,
    and I will bring their plans to nothing;
they will consult the idols and the spirits of the dead,
    the mediums and the spiritists.
⁴ I will hand the Egyptians over
    to the power of a cruel master,
and a fierce king will rule over them,"
    declares the Lord, the LORD Almighty.

⁵ The waters of the river will dry up,
    and the riverbed will be parched and dry.
⁶ The canals will stink;
    the streams of Egypt will dwindle and dry up.
The reeds and rushes will wither,
⁷   also the plants along the Nile,
    at the mouth of the river.

Why would non-Israelites give gifts to the Lord? (18:7) These were gifts of tribute. They were given to show that a nation acknowledged their defeat. After Sennacherib's death, gifts were brought to Hezekiah. And in Isaiah 16:1, the Moabites were asked to send tribute to Mount Zion.

Why would the drying up of the Nile produce so much hardship? (19:5–10) The Nile was the lifeline of Egypt. The annual flooding produced fertile soil and provided irrigation. Without their main source of water, life was very hard for the people.

What other hardships would this cause? (19:8–9)
Fish would no longer be available, and the people who processed flax would not have the water necessary to do the work.

Every sown field along the Nile
　will become parched, will blow away and be no more.
⁸The fishermen will groan and lament,
　all who cast hooks into the Nile;
　those who throw nets on the water
　　will pine away.
⁹Those who work with combed flax will despair,
　the weavers of fine linen will lose hope.
¹⁰The workers in cloth will be dejected,
　and all the wage earners will be sick at heart.

¹¹The officials of Zoan are nothing but fools;
　the wise counselors of Pharaoh give senseless advice.
How can you say to Pharaoh,
　"I am one of the wise men,
　a disciple of the ancient kings"?

¹²Where are your wise men now?
　Let them show you and make known
　what the LORD Almighty
　　has planned against Egypt.
¹³The officials of Zoan have become fools,
　the leaders of Memphis are deceived;
　the cornerstones of her peoples
　have led Egypt astray.
¹⁴The LORD has poured into them
　a spirit of dizziness;
　they make Egypt stagger in all that she does,
　as a drunkard staggers around in his vomit.
¹⁵There is nothing Egypt can do—
　head or tail, palm branch or reed.

Where was Memphis? (19:13)
This was an important city 15 miles (24 kilometers) south of the Nile delta which served as the capital of Egypt during the Old Kingdom.

¹⁶In that day the Egyptians will become weaklings. They will shudder with fear at the uplifted hand that the LORD Almighty raises against them. ¹⁷And the land of Judah will bring terror to the Egyptians; everyone to whom Judah is mentioned will be terrified, because of what the LORD Almighty is planning against them.

¹⁸In that day five cities in Egypt will speak the language of Canaan and swear allegiance to the LORD Almighty. One of them will be called the City of the Sun.ᵃ

¹⁹In that day there will be an altar to the LORD in the heart of Egypt, and a monument to the LORD at its border. ²⁰It will be a sign and witness to the LORD Almighty in the land of Egypt. When they cry out to the LORD because of their oppressors, he will send them a savior and defender, and he will rescue them. ²¹So the LORD will make himself known to the Egyptians, and in that day they will acknowledge the LORD. They will worship with sacrifices and grain offerings; they will make vows to the LORD and keep them. ²²The LORD will strike Egypt with a plague; he will strike them and heal them. They will turn to the LORD, and he will respond to their pleas and heal them.

²³In that day there will be a highway from Egypt to Assyria. The Assyrians will go to Egypt and the Egyptians to

Why would this highway be important? (19:23–24)
It would represent the peaceful relations between Egypt, Assyria, and Israel as they together worshiped the Lord.

ᵃ *18* Some manuscripts of the Masoretic Text, Dead Sea Scrolls, Symmachus and Vulgate; most manuscripts of the Masoretic Text *City of Destruction*

Assyria. The Egyptians and Assyrians will worship together. ²⁴In that day Israel will be the third, along with Egypt and Assyria, a blessing*ᵃ* on the earth. ²⁵The LORD Almighty will bless them, saying, "Blessed be Egypt my people, Assyria my handiwork, and Israel my inheritance."

A PROPHECY AGAINST EGYPT AND CUSH

20 In the year that the supreme commander, sent by Sargon king of Assyria, came to Ashdod and attacked and captured it— ²at that time the LORD spoke through Isaiah son of Amoz. He said to him, "Take off the sackcloth from your body and the sandals from your feet." And he did so, going around stripped and barefoot.

³Then the LORD said, "Just as my servant Isaiah has gone stripped and barefoot for three years, as a sign and portent against Egypt and Cush,*ᵇ* ⁴so the king of Assyria will lead away stripped and barefoot the Egyptian captives and Cushite exiles, young and old, with buttocks bared—to Egypt's shame. ⁵Those who trusted in Cush and boasted in Egypt will be dismayed and put to shame. ⁶In that day the people who live on this coast will say, 'See what has happened to those we relied on, those we fled to for help and deliverance from the king of Assyria! How then can we escape?'"

A PROPHECY AGAINST BABYLON

21 A prophecy against the Desert by the Sea:

Like whirlwinds sweeping through the southland,
    an invader comes from the desert,
    from a land of terror.

²A dire vision has been shown to me:
    The traitor betrays, the looter takes loot.
Elam, attack! Media, lay siege!
    I will bring to an end all the groaning she caused.

³At this my body is racked with pain,
    pangs seize me, like those of a woman in labor;
I am staggered by what I hear,
    I am bewildered by what I see.
⁴My heart falters,
    fear makes me tremble;
the twilight I longed for
    has become a horror to me.

⁵They set the tables,
    they spread the rugs,
    they eat, they drink!
Get up, you officers,
    oil the shields!

⁶This is what the Lord says to me:

"Go, post a lookout
    and have him report what he sees.

> **Why was Isaiah told to take off his clothes? (20:2)**
> This was a dramatic sign to warn the king and the people about what could happen if they were taken captive.

> **What was the Desert by the Sea? (21:1)**
> Verse 9 makes it clear that this refers to Babylon.

ᵃ 24 Or *Assyria, whose names will be used in blessings* (see Gen. 48:20); or *Assyria, who will be seen by others as blessed*   *ᵇ* 3 That is, the upper Nile region; also in verse 5

⁷When he sees chariots
    with teams of horses,
riders on donkeys
    or riders on camels,
let him be alert,
    fully alert."

⁸And the lookout*ᵃ* shouted,

"Day after day, my lord, I stand on the watchtower;
    every night I stay at my post.
⁹Look, here comes a man in a chariot
    with a team of horses.
And he gives back the answer:
    'Babylon has fallen, has fallen!
All the images of its gods
    lie shattered on the ground!'"

¹⁰My people who are crushed on the threshing floor,
    I tell you what I have heard
from the LORD Almighty,
    from the God of Israel.

A PROPHECY AGAINST EDOM

¹¹A prophecy against Dumah*ᵇ*:

Someone calls to me from Seir,
    "Watchman, what is left of the night?
    Watchman, what is left of the night?"
¹²The watchman replies,
    "Morning is coming, but also the night.
If you would ask, then ask;
    and come back yet again."

A PROPHECY AGAINST ARABIA

¹³A prophecy against Arabia:

You caravans of Dedanites,
    who camp in the thickets of Arabia,
¹⁴   bring water for the thirsty;
you who live in Tema,
    bring food for the fugitives.
¹⁵They flee from the sword,
    from the drawn sword,
from the bent bow
    and from the heat of battle.

¹⁶This is what the Lord says to me: "Within one year, as a servant bound by contract would count it, all the splendor of Kedar will come to an end. ¹⁷The survivors of the archers, the warriors of Kedar, will be few." The LORD, the God of Israel, has spoken.

A PROPHECY ABOUT JERUSALEM

22 A prophecy against the Valley of Vision:

What troubles you now,
    that you have all gone up on the roofs,

ᵃ 8 Dead Sea Scrolls and Syriac; Masoretic Text *A lion*   *ᵇ 11 Dumah*, a wordplay on *Edom*, means *silence* or *stillness*.

What was the significance of the threshing floor? (21:10)
Threshing was a common metaphor for judgment or destruction from war.

What did the watchman's reply mean? (21:12)
It may have meant that the "night" of Assyrian oppression was almost over, but there would only be a short "morning" before Babylon conquered the people.

Who were the Dedanites? (21:13)
This was an Arabian merchant tribe. They were attacked first by the Assyrians and then the Babylonians.

What was the Valley of Vision? (22:1)
This was probably a valley near Jerusalem where God revealed himself to Isaiah in this vision.

Why did the people go to their roofs? (22:1)
The people's flat roofs were used as gathering places, especially in the cool evening air. The people may have gone up to fearfully watch the enemy advancing, or perhaps they went up to celebrate the enemy's retreat.

² you town so full of commotion,
　　you city of tumult and revelry?
Your slain were not killed by the sword,
　　nor did they die in battle.
³ All your leaders have fled together;
　　they have been captured without using the bow.
All you who were caught were taken prisoner together,
　　having fled while the enemy was still far away.
⁴ Therefore I said, "Turn away from me;
　　let me weep bitterly.
Do not try to console me
　　over the destruction of my people."

⁵ The Lord, the LORD Almighty, has a day
　　of tumult and trampling and terror
　　in the Valley of Vision,
a day of battering down walls
　　and of crying out to the mountains.
⁶ Elam takes up the quiver,
　　with her charioteers and horses;
　　Kir uncovers the shield.
⁷ Your choicest valleys are full of chariots,
　　and horsemen are posted at the city gates.

⁸ The Lord stripped away the defenses of Judah,
　　and you looked in that day
　　to the weapons in the Palace of the Forest.
⁹ You saw that the walls of the City of David
　　were broken through in many places;
you stored up water
　　in the Lower Pool.
¹⁰ You counted the buildings in Jerusalem
　　and tore down houses to strengthen the wall.
¹¹ You built a reservoir between the two walls
　　for the water of the Old Pool,
but you did not look to the One who made it,
　　or have regard for the One who planned it long ago.

¹² The Lord, the LORD Almighty,
　　called you on that day
to weep and to wail,
　　to tear out your hair and put on sackcloth.
¹³ But see, there is joy and revelry,
　　slaughtering of cattle and killing of sheep,
　　eating of meat and drinking of wine!
"Let us eat and drink," you say,
　　"for tomorrow we die!"

¹⁴ The LORD Almighty has revealed this in my hearing: "Till your dying day this sin will not be atoned for," says the Lord, the LORD Almighty.

¹⁵ This is what the Lord, the LORD Almighty, says:

"Go, say to this steward,
　　to Shebna the palace administrator:
¹⁶ What are you doing here and who gave you
　　　permission
　　to cut out a grave for yourself here,

What was the Palace of the Forest? (22:8)
This was the palace built by King Solomon. The four rows of pillars made from the trunks of cedar trees created the impression of a great forest (see 1 Kings 7:2).

Who was Shebna? (22:15–22)
Shebna was once a high-ranking government official. His position put him at the top, answering only to the king. However, he was later stripped of his title and demoted. Eliakim replaced him (2 Kings 18:18).

Why would someone create his own grave? (22:16)
The place of a person's burial was considered very important, and Shebna wanted to have a tomb that was as good as a king's.

hewing your grave on the height
and chiseling your resting place in the rock?

[17] "Beware, the LORD is about to take firm hold of you
and hurl you away, you mighty man.
[18] He will roll you up tightly like a ball
and throw you into a large country.
There you will die
and there the chariots you were so proud of
will become a disgrace to your master's house.
[19] I will depose you from your office,
and you will be ousted from your position.

[20] "In that day I will summon my servant, Eliakim son of Hilkiah. [21] I will clothe him with your robe and fasten your sash around him and hand your authority over to him. He will be a father to those who live in Jerusalem and to the people of Judah. [22] I will place on his shoulder the key to the house of David; what he opens no one can shut, and what he shuts no one can open. [23] I will drive him like a peg into a firm place; he will become a seat[a] of honor for the house of his father. [24] All the glory of his family will hang on him: its offspring and offshoots — all its lesser vessels, from the bowls to all the jars.

[25] "In that day," declares the LORD Almighty, "the peg driven into the firm place will give way; it will be sheared off and will fall, and the load hanging on it will be cut down." The LORD has spoken.

A PROPHECY AGAINST TYRE

23 A prophecy against Tyre:

Wail, you ships of Tarshish!
For Tyre is destroyed
and left without house or harbor.
From the land of Cyprus
word has come to them.

[2] Be silent, you people of the island
and you merchants of Sidon,
whom the seafarers have enriched.
[3] On the great waters
came the grain of the Shihor;
the harvest of the Nile[b] was the revenue of Tyre,
and she became the marketplace of the nations.

[4] Be ashamed, Sidon, and you fortress of the sea,
for the sea has spoken:
"I have neither been in labor nor given birth;
I have neither reared sons nor brought up daughters."
[5] When word comes to Egypt,
they will be in anguish at the report from Tyre.

[6] Cross over to Tarshish;
wail, you people of the island.

How was Tyre destroyed?
(23:1–5)
Part of the city sat on two rocky islands about half a mile from shore. Nebuchadnezzar captured the mainland city in 572 B.C. The island fortress was not taken until Alexander the Great destroyed it in 332.

---

[a] 23 Or *throne*   [b] 2,3 Masoretic Text; Dead Sea Scrolls *Sidon, / who cross over the sea; / your envoys* [3] *are on the great waters. / The grain of the Shihor, / the harvest of the Nile,*

⁷ Is this your city of revelry,
    the old, old city,
  whose feet have taken her
    to settle in far-off lands?
⁸ Who planned this against Tyre,
    the bestower of crowns,
  whose merchants are princes,
    whose traders are renowned in the earth?
⁹ The LORD Almighty planned it,
    to bring down her pride in all her splendor
    and to humble all who are renowned on the earth.

¹⁰ Till*ᵃ* your land as they do along the Nile,
    Daughter Tarshish,
  for you no longer have a harbor.
¹¹ The LORD has stretched out his hand over the sea
    and made its kingdoms tremble.
  He has given an order concerning Phoenicia
    that her fortresses be destroyed.
¹² He said, "No more of your reveling,
    Virgin Daughter Sidon, now crushed!

  "Up, cross over to Cyprus;
    even there you will find no rest."
¹³ Look at the land of the Babylonians,*ᵇ*
    this people that is now of no account!
  The Assyrians have made it
    a place for desert creatures;
  they raised up their siege towers,
    they stripped its fortresses bare
    and turned it into a ruin.

¹⁴ Wail, you ships of Tarshish;
    your fortress is destroyed!

¹⁵ At that time Tyre will be forgotten for seventy years, the span of a king's life. But at the end of these seventy years, it will happen to Tyre as in the song of the prostitute:

¹⁶ "Take up a harp, walk through the city,
    you forgotten prostitute;
  play the harp well, sing many a song,
    so that you will be remembered."

¹⁷ At the end of seventy years, the LORD will deal with Tyre. She will return to her lucrative prostitution and will ply her trade with all the kingdoms on the face of the earth. ¹⁸ Yet her profit and her earnings will be set apart for the LORD; they will not be stored up or hoarded. Her profits will go to those who live before the LORD, for abundant food and fine clothes.

THE LORD'S DEVASTATION OF THE EARTH

24 See, the LORD is going to lay waste the earth
    and devastate it;
  he will ruin its face
    and scatter its inhabitants —

How was Tyre a prostitute nation? (23:17)
Tyre was like a prostitute because it tried to make the most money possible regardless of the means. Tyre also used temple prostitutes to worship Baal.

ᵃ 10 Dead Sea Scrolls and some Septuagint manuscripts; Masoretic Text *Go through*   *ᵇ 13* Or *Chaldeans*

Would the judgment affect everyone? (24:2)
There would be no distinction between people when the Lord came to deliver judgment; all would be judged.

² it will be the same
　　for priest as for people,
　　for the master as for his servant,
　　for the mistress as for her servant,
　　for seller as for buyer,
　　for borrower as for lender,
　　for debtor as for creditor.
³ The earth will be completely laid waste
　　and totally plundered.
　　　　　　The LORD has spoken this word.

⁴ The earth dries up and withers,
　　the world languishes and withers,
　　the heavens languish with the earth.
⁵ The earth is defiled by its people;
　　they have disobeyed the laws,
　violated the statutes
　　and broken the everlasting covenant.

Would God's punishment be universal? (24:6)
Because there was so much evil in the world, God's punishment would be widespread.

⁶ Therefore a curse consumes the earth;
　　its people must bear their guilt.
　Therefore earth's inhabitants are burned up,
　　and very few are left.
⁷ The new wine dries up and the vine withers;
　　all the merrymakers groan.
⁸ The joyful timbrels are stilled,
　　the noise of the revelers has stopped,
　　the joyful harp is silent.
⁹ No longer do they drink wine with a song;
　　the beer is bitter to its drinkers.

What was the ruined city? (24:10)
This may have been Jerusalem or it could refer to all the cities that were opposed to God, such as Babylon, Tyre, and Rome.

¹⁰ The ruined city lies desolate;
　　the entrance to every house is barred.
¹¹ In the streets they cry out for wine;
　　all joy turns to gloom,
　　all joyful sounds are banished from the earth.
¹² The city is left in ruins,
　　its gate is battered to pieces.
¹³ So will it be on the earth
　　and among the nations,
　as when an olive tree is beaten,
　　or as when gleanings are left after the grape harvest.

¹⁴ They raise their voices, they shout for joy;
　　from the west they acclaim the LORD's majesty.
¹⁵ Therefore in the east give glory to the LORD;
　　exalt the name of the LORD, the God of Israel,
　　in the islands of the sea.

What were the islands of the sea? (24:15)
This is probably a reference to Mediterranean coastlands and islands.

¹⁶ From the ends of the earth we hear singing:
　　"Glory to the Righteous One."

　But I said, "I waste away, I waste away!
　　Woe to me!
　The treacherous betray!
　　With treachery the treacherous betray!"
¹⁷ Terror and pit and snare await you,
　　people of the earth.
¹⁸ Whoever flees at the sound of terror
　　will fall into a pit;

whoever climbs out of the pit
  will be caught in a snare.

The floodgates of the heavens are opened,
  the foundations of the earth shake.
¹⁹ The earth is broken up,
  the earth is split asunder,
  the earth is violently shaken.
²⁰ The earth reels like a drunkard,
  it sways like a hut in the wind;
so heavy upon it is the guilt of its rebellion
  that it falls—never to rise again.

²¹ In that day the LORD will punish
  the powers in the heavens above
  and the kings on the earth below.
²² They will be herded together
  like prisoners bound in a dungeon;
they will be shut up in prison
  and be punished^a after many days.
²³ The moon will be dismayed,
  the sun ashamed;
for the LORD Almighty will reign
  on Mount Zion and in Jerusalem,
  and before its elders—with great glory.

PRAISE TO THE LORD

25 LORD, you are my God;
  I will exalt you and praise your name,
for in perfect faithfulness
  you have done wonderful things,
  things planned long ago.
² You have made the city a heap of rubble,
  the fortified town a ruin,
the foreigners' stronghold a city no more;
  it will never be rebuilt.
³ Therefore strong peoples will honor you;
  cities of ruthless nations will revere you.
⁴ You have been a refuge for the poor,
  a refuge for the needy in their distress,
a shelter from the storm
  and a shade from the heat.
For the breath of the ruthless
  is like a storm driving against a wall
⁵ and like the heat of the desert.
You silence the uproar of foreigners;
  as heat is reduced by the shadow of a cloud,
  so the song of the ruthless is stilled.

⁶ On this mountain the LORD Almighty will prepare
  a feast of rich food for all peoples,
a banquet of aged wine—
  the best of meats and the finest of wines.
⁷ On this mountain he will destroy
  the shroud that enfolds all peoples,
the sheet that covers all nations;

Why would God be praised for destroying cities and people? (25:1–3)
The righteous would praise God for imposing his judgment on evil people.

What will happen on Mount Zion? (25:6–8)
The Lord will prepare a feast similar to that given for a coronation or banquet.

^a 22 Or *released*

8 he will swallow up death forever.
 The Sovereign Lord will wipe away the tears
     from all faces;
 he will remove his people's disgrace
     from all the earth.

                    The Lord has spoken.

9 In that day they will say,

"Surely this is our God;
   we trusted in him, and he saved us.
 This is the Lord, we trusted in him;
   let us rejoice and be glad in his salvation."

10 The hand of the Lord will rest on this mountain;
     but Moab will be trampled in their land
     as straw is trampled down in the manure.
11 They will stretch out their hands in it,
     as swimmers stretch out their hands to swim.
 God will bring down their pride
     despite the cleverness[a] of their hands.
12 He will bring down your high fortified walls
     and lay them low;
 he will bring them down to the ground,
     to the very dust.

A SONG OF PRAISE

26 In that day this song will be sung in the land of Judah:

We have a strong city;
   God makes salvation
   its walls and ramparts.
2 Open the gates
   that the righteous nation may enter,
   the nation that keeps faith.
3 You will keep in perfect peace
   those whose minds are steadfast,
   because they trust in you.
4 Trust in the Lord forever,
   for the Lord, the Lord himself, is the Rock eternal.
5 He humbles those who dwell on high,
   he lays the lofty city low;
 he levels it to the ground
   and casts it down to the dust.
6 Feet trample it down—
   the feet of the oppressed,
   the footsteps of the poor.

7 The path of the righteous is level;
   you, the Upright One, make the way of the
       righteous smooth.
8 Yes, Lord, walking in the way of your laws,[b]
   we wait for you;
 your name and renown
   are the desire of our hearts.

What will happen on that "day"? (25:9)
The people will praise the Lord because they trusted in him for their salvation.

What were ramparts? (26:1)
These were sloping fortifications of earth or stone used as protective barriers against invaders.

What is the level path? (26:7)
The Bible frequently speaks of God making paths level for his people. He makes the way to follow him plain or easy.

[a] 11 The meaning of the Hebrew for this word is uncertain.
[b] 8 Or judgments

⁹ My soul yearns for you in the night;
 in the morning my spirit longs for you.
When your judgments come upon the earth,
 the people of the world learn righteousness.
¹⁰ But when grace is shown to the wicked,
 they do not learn righteousness;
even in a land of uprightness they go on doing evil
 and do not regard the majesty of the Lord.
¹¹ Lord, your hand is lifted high,
 but they do not see it.
Let them see your zeal for your people and be put to
 shame;
 let the fire reserved for your enemies consume them.

¹² Lord, you establish peace for us;
 all that we have accomplished you have done
  for us.
¹³ Lord our God, other lords besides you have ruled
  over us,
 but your name alone do we honor.
¹⁴ They are now dead, they live no more;
 their spirits do not rise.
You punished them and brought them to ruin;
 you wiped out all memory of them.
¹⁵ You have enlarged the nation, Lord;
 you have enlarged the nation.
You have gained glory for yourself;
 you have extended all the borders of the land.

¹⁶ Lord, they came to you in their distress;
 when you disciplined them,
 they could barely whisper a prayer.ᵃ
¹⁷ As a pregnant woman about to give birth
 writhes and cries out in her pain,
so were we in your presence, Lord.
¹⁸ We were with child, we writhed in labor,
 but we gave birth to wind.
We have not brought salvation to the earth,
 and the people of the world have not come
  to life.

¹⁹ But your dead will live, Lord;
 their bodies will rise—
let those who dwell in the dust
 wake up and shout for joy—
your dew is like the dew of the morning;
 the earth will give birth to her dead.

²⁰ Go, my people, enter your rooms
 and shut the doors behind you;
hide yourselves for a little while
 until his wrath has passed by.
²¹ See, the Lord is coming out of his dwelling
 to punish the people of the earth for their sins.
The earth will disclose the blood shed on it;
 the earth will conceal its slain no longer.

ᵃ 16 The meaning of the Hebrew for this clause is uncertain.

Does judgment teach righteousness? (26:9–10)
God can use judgment to get people's attention and prompt them to turn to him.

Why would the Lord lift his hand high? (26:11)
A king lifted his hand high as a symbol of power.

What was Leviathan? (27:1)
This was a mythological sea monster. Here it is a symbol of wicked nations such as Egypt.

DELIVERANCE OF ISRAEL

27 In that day,

the LORD will punish with his sword —
　　his fierce, great and powerful sword —
Leviathan the gliding serpent,
　　Leviathan the coiling serpent;
he will slay the monster of the sea.

²In that day —

"Sing about a fruitful vineyard:
³ 　I, the LORD, watch over it;
　　I water it continually.
I guard it day and night
　　so that no one may harm it.
⁴ 　I am not angry.
If only there were briers and thorns confronting me!
　　I would march against them in battle;
　　I would set them all on fire.
⁵ Or else let them come to me for refuge;
　　let them make peace with me,
　　yes, let them make peace with me."

⁶ In days to come Jacob will take root,
　　Israel will bud and blossom
　　and fill all the world with fruit.

⁷ Has the LORD struck her
　　as he struck down those who struck her?
Has she been killed
　　as those were killed who killed her?
⁸ By warfare[a] and exile you contend with her —
　　with his fierce blast he drives her out,
　　as on a day the east wind blows.
⁹ By this, then, will Jacob's guilt be atoned for,
　　and this will be the full fruit of the removal of his
　　　　sin:
When he makes all the altar stones
　　to be like limestone crushed to pieces,
no Asherah poles[b] or incense altars
　　will be left standing.
¹⁰ The fortified city stands desolate,
　　an abandoned settlement, forsaken like the
　　　　wilderness;
there the calves graze,
　　there they lie down;
　　they strip its branches bare.
¹¹ When its twigs are dry, they are broken off
　　and women come and make fires with them.
For this is a people without understanding;
　　so their Maker has no compassion on them,
　　and their Creator shows them no favor.

What was this threshing? (27:12)
This represents judgment on the nations where the people of Israel had been scattered. The threshing would separate the Israelites from the Gentiles.

¹²In that day the LORD will thresh from the flowing Euphrates to the Wadi of Egypt, and you, Israel, will be gathered

---

[a] 8 See Septuagint; the meaning of the Hebrew for this word is uncertain.
[b] 9 That is, wooden symbols of the goddess Asherah

up one by one. ¹³And in that day a great trumpet will sound. Those who were perishing in Assyria and those who were exiled in Egypt will come and worship the LORD on the holy mountain in Jerusalem.

WOE TO THE LEADERS OF EPHRAIM AND JUDAH

28 Woe to that wreath, the pride of Ephraim's drunkards,
  to the fading flower, his glorious beauty,
set on the head of a fertile valley—
  to that city, the pride of those laid low by wine!
²See, the Lord has one who is powerful and strong.
  Like a hailstorm and a destructive wind,
like a driving rain and a flooding downpour,
  he will throw it forcefully to the ground.
³That wreath, the pride of Ephraim's drunkards,
  will be trampled underfoot.
⁴That fading flower, his glorious beauty,
  set on the head of a fertile valley,
will be like figs ripe before harvest—
  as soon as people see them and take them
    in hand,
  they swallow them.

⁵In that day the LORD Almighty
  will be a glorious crown,
a beautiful wreath
  for the remnant of his people.
⁶He will be a spirit of justice
  to the one who sits in judgment,
a source of strength
  to those who turn back the battle at the gate.

⁷And these also stagger from wine
  and reel from beer:
Priests and prophets stagger from beer
  and are befuddled with wine;
they reel from beer,
  they stagger when seeing visions,
  they stumble when rendering decisions.
⁸All the tables are covered with vomit
  and there is not a spot without filth.

⁹"Who is it he is trying to teach?
  To whom is he explaining his message?
To children weaned from their milk,
  to those just taken from the breast?
¹⁰For it is:
  Do this, do that,
  a rule for this, a rule for that*;
  a little here, a little there."

¹¹Very well then, with foreign lips and strange tongues
  God will speak to this people,

---

a 10 Hebrew / *sav lasav sav lasav / kav lakav kav lakav* (probably meaningless sounds mimicking the prophet's words); also in verse 13

Why was Samaria called a wreath? (28:1)
Samaria, the capital of the northern kingdom, was a beautiful city on a hill. This word picture compared the city to a crown or wreath that ancient people sometimes wore at parties.

Who is speaking in these verses? (28:9–10)
These are the words of the drunken priests who mocked and criticized Isaiah. They claimed that Isaiah's teachings were overly simple.

¹²to whom he said,
  "This is the resting place, let the weary rest";
and, "This is the place of repose"—
  but they would not listen.
¹³So then, the word of the LORD to them will become:
  Do this, do that,
  a rule for this, a rule for that;
  a little here, a little there—
so that as they go they will fall backward;
  they will be injured and snared and captured.

¹⁴Therefore hear the word of the LORD, you scoffers
  who rule this people in Jerusalem.
¹⁵You boast, "We have entered into a covenant
    with death,
  with the realm of the dead we have made
    an agreement.
When an overwhelming scourge sweeps by,
  it cannot touch us,
for we have made a lie our refuge
  and falsehood*ᵃ* our hiding place."

¹⁶So this is what the Sovereign LORD says:

"See, I lay a stone in Zion, a tested stone,
  a precious cornerstone for a sure foundation;
the one who relies on it
  will never be stricken with panic.
¹⁷I will make justice the measuring line
  and righteousness the plumb line;
hail will sweep away your refuge, the lie,
  and water will overflow your hiding place.
¹⁸Your covenant with death will be annulled;
  your agreement with the realm of the dead will
    not stand.
When the overwhelming scourge sweeps by,
  you will be beaten down by it.
¹⁹As often as it comes it will carry you away;
  morning after morning, by day and by night,
  it will sweep through."

The understanding of this message
  will bring sheer terror.
²⁰The bed is too short to stretch out on,
  the blanket too narrow to wrap around you.
²¹The LORD will rise up as he did at Mount Perazim,
  he will rouse himself as in the Valley of Gibeon—
to do his work, his strange work,
  and perform his task, his alien task.
²²Now stop your mocking,
  or your chains will become heavier;
the Lord, the LORD Almighty, has told me
  of the destruction decreed against the whole land.

²³Listen and hear my voice;
  pay attention and hear what I say.

What was the covenant with death? (28:15)
This may have been a reference to pagan practices of summoning the spirits of dead people. The priests believed they had made a type of bargain that protected the nation from danger.

How would God judge the people? (28:17)
The standards the Lord would use were his justice and righteousness.

What did a short bed and narrow blanket mean? (28:19–20)
Isaiah was making use of a proverb of the time to say that the covenant with death would not provide Israel with comfort or protection.

ᵃ 15 Or false gods

²⁴When a farmer plows for planting, does he plow
      continually?
  Does he keep on breaking up and working the soil?
²⁵When he has leveled the surface,
    does he not sow caraway and scatter cumin?
Does he not plant wheat in its place,^{*a*}
  barley in its plot,^{*a*}
  and spelt in its field?
²⁶His God instructs him
  and teaches him the right way.

²⁷Caraway is not threshed with a sledge,
    nor is the wheel of a cart rolled over cumin;
caraway is beaten out with a rod,
  and cumin with a stick.
²⁸Grain must be ground to make bread;
    so one does not go on threshing it forever.
The wheels of a threshing cart may be rolled over it,
  but one does not use horses to grind grain.
²⁹All this also comes from the LORD Almighty,
  whose plan is wonderful,
  whose wisdom is magnificent.

WOE TO DAVID'S CITY

29 Woe to you, Ariel, Ariel,
  the city where David settled!
Add year to year
  and let your cycle of festivals go on.
²Yet I will besiege Ariel;
  she will mourn and lament,
  she will be to me like an altar hearth.^{*b*}
³I will encamp against you on all sides;
  I will encircle you with towers
  and set up my siege works against you.
⁴Brought low, you will speak from the ground;
  your speech will mumble out of the dust.
Your voice will come ghostlike from the earth;
  out of the dust your speech will whisper.

⁵But your many enemies will become like fine dust,
  the ruthless hordes like blown chaff.
Suddenly, in an instant,
⁶ the LORD Almighty will come
with thunder and earthquake and great noise,
  with windstorm and tempest and flames of a
      devouring fire.
⁷Then the hordes of all the nations that fight against
    Ariel,
  that attack her and her fortress and besiege her,
will be as it is with a dream,
  with a vision in the night—
⁸as when a hungry person dreams of eating,
  but awakens hungry still;
as when a thirsty person dreams of drinking,
  but awakens faint and thirsty still.

**What do these verses mean?
(28:27–29)**
This is a poetic way of saying
that even though God would punish Israel, he would not completely destroy his chosen people.

**Why was Jerusalem called
Ariel? (29:1–2)**
Ariel literally meant *altar hearth*.
This may have been a nickname
for the city because people came
to worship at the temple altar
in Jerusalem. Here it could also
mean that fighting and bloodshed would turn the city into a
place where many people would
die as if they had been sacrificed
on an altar.

**How were towers used in
battle? (29:3)**
In ancient times, armies would
push wheeled towers up to the
wall of a city they were attacking
so they could fight the people
defending the city from the top
of the wall.

---

^{*a*} *25* The meaning of the Hebrew for this word is uncertain.   ^{*b*} *2* The
Hebrew for *altar hearth* sounds like the Hebrew for *Ariel*.

So will it be with the hordes of all the nations
     that fight against Mount Zion.

**Why were the leaders
unable to understand the
prophecies? (29:9–12)**
They had rebelled against the
Lord for such a long time that
they were unable to understand
the meaning of his message.

⁹ Be stunned and amazed,
     blind yourselves and be sightless;
be drunk, but not from wine,
     stagger, but not from beer.
¹⁰ The LORD has brought over you a deep sleep:
     He has sealed your eyes (the prophets);
     he has covered your heads (the seers).

¹¹ For you this whole vision is nothing but words sealed in a scroll. And if you give the scroll to someone who can read, and say, "Read this, please," they will answer, "I can't; it is sealed." ¹² Or if you give the scroll to someone who cannot read, and say, "Read this, please," they will answer, "I don't know how to read."

¹³ The Lord says:

"These people come near to me with their mouth
     and honor me with their lips,
     but their hearts are far from me.
Their worship of me
     is based on merely human rules they have
          been taught.ᵃ
¹⁴ Therefore once more I will astound these people
     with wonder upon wonder;
the wisdom of the wise will perish,
     the intelligence of the intelligent will vanish."
¹⁵ Woe to those who go to great depths
     to hide their plans from the LORD,
who do their work in darkness and think,
     "Who sees us? Who will know?"
¹⁶ You turn things upside down,
     as if the potter were thought to be like the clay!
Shall what is formed say to the one who formed it,
     "You did not make me"?
Can the pot say to the potter,
     "You know nothing"?

**What does the reference to
Lebanon mean? (29:17)**
This may be a symbolic reference
to Assyria. The forests of Lebanon were magnificent, so being
turned into a fertile field would
mean a reduced status.

¹⁷ In a very short time, will not Lebanon be turned into
          a fertile field
     and the fertile field seem like a forest?
¹⁸ In that day the deaf will hear the words of the scroll,
     and out of gloom and darkness
     the eyes of the blind will see.
¹⁹ Once more the humble will rejoice in the LORD;
     the needy will rejoice in the Holy One of Israel.
²⁰ The ruthless will vanish,
     the mockers will disappear,
     and all who have an eye for evil will be cut down—
²¹ those who with a word make someone out to be guilty,
     who ensnare the defender in court
     and with false testimony deprive the innocent of
          justice.

ᵃ 13 Hebrew; Septuagint *They worship me in vain; / their teachings are merely
human rules*

²²Therefore this is what the LORD, who redeemed Abraham, says to the descendants of Jacob:

"No longer will Jacob be ashamed;
    no longer will their faces grow pale.
²³When they see among them their children,
    the work of my hands,
they will keep my name holy;
    they will acknowledge the holiness of the Holy One
        of Jacob,
    and will stand in awe of the God of Israel.
²⁴Those who are wayward in spirit will gain
        understanding;
    those who complain will accept instruction."

WOE TO THE OBSTINATE NATION

30 "Woe to the obstinate children,"
        declares the LORD,
"to those who carry out plans that are not mine,
    forming an alliance, but not by my Spirit,
    heaping sin upon sin;
²who go down to Egypt
    without consulting me;
who look for help to Pharaoh's protection,
    to Egypt's shade for refuge.
³But Pharaoh's protection will be to your shame,
    Egypt's shade will bring you disgrace.
⁴Though they have officials in Zoan
    and their envoys have arrived in Hanes,
⁵everyone will be put to shame
    because of a people useless to them,
who bring neither help nor advantage,
    but only shame and disgrace."

⁶A prophecy concerning the animals of the Negev:

Through a land of hardship and distress,
    of lions and lionesses,
    of adders and darting snakes,
the envoys carry their riches on donkeys' backs,
    their treasures on the humps of camels,
to that unprofitable nation,
⁷   to Egypt, whose help is utterly useless.
Therefore I call her
    Rahab the Do-Nothing.

⁸Go now, write it on a tablet for them,
    inscribe it on a scroll,
that for the days to come
    it may be an everlasting witness.
⁹For these are rebellious people, deceitful children,
    children unwilling to listen to the LORD's instruction.
¹⁰They say to the seers,
    "See no more visions!"
and to the prophets,
    "Give us no more visions of what is right!
Tell us pleasant things,
    prophesy illusions.

What improper alliance had Judah made? (30:1–2) Judah had joined with some other nations in the region in asking for help from Egypt in their struggle with Assyria. God's people should have trusted God to provide for their safety.

What is the Negev? (30:6) This is a dry region in the southern part of the Holy Land.

What was Rahab? (30:7) This was a mythical sea monster, whose name literally meant *storm* or *arrogance*. Here the name is used to symbolize Egypt.

¹¹ Leave this way,
　　get off this path,
and stop confronting us
　　with the Holy One of Israel!"

¹² Therefore this is what the Holy One of Israel says:

"Because you have rejected this message,
　　relied on oppression
　　and depended on deceit,
¹³ this sin will become for you
　　like a high wall, cracked and bulging,
　　that collapses suddenly, in an instant.
¹⁴ It will break in pieces like pottery,
　　shattered so mercilessly
that among its pieces not a fragment will be found
　　for taking coals from a hearth
　　or scooping water out of a cistern."

¹⁵ This is what the Sovereign Lord, the Holy One of Israel, says:

"In repentance and rest is your salvation,
　　in quietness and trust is your strength,
　　but you would have none of it.
¹⁶ You said, 'No, we will flee on horses.'
　　Therefore you will flee!
You said, 'We will ride off on swift horses.'
　　Therefore your pursuers will be swift!
¹⁷ A thousand will flee
　　at the threat of one;
at the threat of five
　　you will all flee away,
till you are left
　　like a flagstaff on a mountaintop,
　　like a banner on a hill."

¹⁸ Yet the Lord longs to be gracious to you;
　　therefore he will rise up to show you compassion.
For the Lord is a God of justice.
　　Blessed are all who wait for him!

¹⁹ People of Zion, who live in Jerusalem, you will weep no more. How gracious he will be when you cry for help! As soon as he hears, he will answer you. ²⁰ Although the Lord gives you the bread of adversity and the water of affliction, your teachers will be hidden no more; with your own eyes you will see them. ²¹ Whether you turn to the right or to the left, your ears will hear a voice behind you, saying, "This is the way; walk in it." ²² Then you will desecrate your idols overlaid with silver and your images covered with gold; you will throw them away like a menstrual cloth and say to them, "Away with you!"

²³ He will also send you rain for the seed you sow in the ground, and the food that comes from the land will be rich and plentiful. In that day your cattle will graze in broad meadows. ²⁴ The oxen and donkeys that work the soil will eat fodder and mash, spread out with fork and shovel. ²⁵ In the day of great slaughter, when the towers fall, streams of

What should the people have done? (30:15)
The people should have repented and had confidence that God would protect them.

How had the Lord tried to turn his people back to him? (30:20)
He had caused hardships to come to them.

water will flow on every high mountain and every lofty hill.
²⁶The moon will shine like the sun, and the sunlight will be
seven times brighter, like the light of seven full days, when
the LORD binds up the bruises of his people and heals the
wounds he inflicted.

²⁷ See, the Name of the LORD comes from afar,
    with burning anger and dense clouds of smoke;
his lips are full of wrath,
    and his tongue is a consuming fire.
²⁸ His breath is like a rushing torrent,
    rising up to the neck.
He shakes the nations in the sieve of destruction;
    he places in the jaws of the peoples
    a bit that leads them astray.
²⁹ And you will sing
    as on the night you celebrate a holy festival;
your hearts will rejoice
    as when people playing pipes go up
to the mountain of the LORD,
    to the Rock of Israel.
³⁰ The LORD will cause people to hear his majestic voice
    and will make them see his arm coming down
with raging anger and consuming fire,
    with cloudburst, thunderstorm and hail.
³¹ The voice of the LORD will shatter Assyria;
    with his rod he will strike them down.
³² Every stroke the LORD lays on them
    with his punishing club
will be to the music of timbrels and harps,
    as he fights them in battle with the blows of his arm.
³³ Topheth has long been prepared;
    it has been made ready for the king.
Its fire pit has been made deep and wide,
    with an abundance of fire and wood;
the breath of the LORD,
    like a stream of burning sulfur,
    sets it ablaze.

WOE TO THOSE WHO RELY ON EGYPT

31 Woe to those who go down to Egypt for help,
    who rely on horses,
who trust in the multitude of their chariots
    and in the great strength of their horsemen,
but do not look to the Holy One of Israel,
    or seek help from the LORD.
² Yet he too is wise and can bring disaster;
    he does not take back his words.
He will rise up against that wicked nation,
    against those who help evildoers.
³ But the Egyptians are mere mortals and not God;
    their horses are flesh and not spirit.
When the LORD stretches out his hand,
    those who help will stumble,
    those who are helped will fall;
    all will perish together.

What was Topheth? (30:33)
This was an area outside Jerusalem where garbage was burned.
Human sacrifices had sometimes
been performed there, so it was
considered an evil and shameful
place.

⁴This is what the LORD says to me:

"As a lion growls,
  a great lion over its prey—
and though a whole band of shepherds
  is called together against it,
it is not frightened by their shouts
  or disturbed by their clamor—
so the LORD Almighty will come down
  to do battle on Mount Zion and on its heights.
⁵ Like birds hovering overhead,
  the LORD Almighty will shield Jerusalem;
he will shield it and deliver it,
  he will 'pass over' it and will rescue it."

⁶Return, you Israelites, to the One you have so greatly revolted against. ⁷For in that day every one of you will reject the idols of silver and gold your sinful hands have made.

⁸ "Assyria will fall by no human sword;
  a sword, not of mortals, will devour them.
They will flee before the sword
  and their young men will be put to forced labor.
⁹ Their stronghold will fall because of terror;
  at the sight of the battle standard their commanders
    will panic,"
declares the LORD,
  whose fire is in Zion,
  whose furnace is in Jerusalem.

THE KINGDOM OF RIGHTEOUSNESS

32 See, a king will reign in righteousness
  and rulers will rule with justice.
² Each one will be like a shelter from the wind
  and a refuge from the storm,
like streams of water in the desert
  and the shadow of a great rock in a thirsty land.

³ Then the eyes of those who see will no longer
    be closed,
  and the ears of those who hear will listen.
⁴ The fearful heart will know and understand,
  and the stammering tongue will be fluent and clear.
⁵ No longer will the fool be called noble
  nor the scoundrel be highly respected.
⁶ For fools speak folly,
  their hearts are bent on evil:
They practice ungodliness
  and spread error concerning the LORD;
the hungry they leave empty
  and from the thirsty they withhold water.
⁷ Scoundrels use wicked methods,
  they make up evil schemes
to destroy the poor with lies,
  even when the plea of the needy is just.
⁸ But the noble make noble plans,
  and by noble deeds they stand.

How would this prophecy remind the people of their history? (31:5)
The word translated as *pass over* is the same word used in Exodus when the angel "passed over" every house in Egypt with blood painted on its doorposts.

How was this prophecy fulfilled? (31:9)
Nineveh, Assyria's stronghold, was destroyed by the Medes and Babylonians in about 612 B.C.

Who was the king who would reign in righteousness? (32:1)
This was a prophecy about the coming Messiah, who would rule righteously, as would the rulers who served him.

THE WOMEN OF JERUSALEM

⁹You women who are so complacent,
   rise up and listen to me;
you daughters who feel secure,
   hear what I have to say!
¹⁰In little more than a year
   you who feel secure will tremble;
the grape harvest will fail,
   and the harvest of fruit will not come.
¹¹Tremble, you complacent women;
   shudder, you daughters who feel secure!
Strip off your fine clothes
   and wrap yourselves in rags.
¹²Beat your breasts for the pleasant fields,
   for the fruitful vines
¹³and for the land of my people,
   a land overgrown with thorns and briers—
yes, mourn for all houses of merriment
   and for this city of revelry.
¹⁴The fortress will be abandoned,
   the noisy city deserted;
citadel and watchtower will become a wasteland
      forever,
   the delight of donkeys, a pasture for flocks,
¹⁵till the Spirit is poured on us from on high,
   and the desert becomes a fertile field,
   and the fertile field seems like a forest.
¹⁶The LORD's justice will dwell in the desert,
   his righteousness live in the fertile field.
¹⁷The fruit of that righteousness will be peace;
   its effect will be quietness and confidence forever.
¹⁸My people will live in peaceful dwelling places,
   in secure homes,
   in undisturbed places of rest.
¹⁹Though hail flattens the forest
   and the city is leveled completely,
²⁰how blessed you will be,
   sowing your seed by every stream,
   and letting your cattle and donkeys range free.

DISTRESS AND HELP

33 Woe to you, destroyer,
   you who have not been destroyed!
Woe to you, betrayer,
   you who have not been betrayed!
When you stop destroying,
   you will be destroyed;
when you stop betraying,
   you will be betrayed.

²LORD, be gracious to us;
   we long for you.
Be our strength every morning,
   our salvation in time of distress.
³At the uproar of your army, the peoples flee;
   when you rise up, the nations scatter.

What year was this? (32:10)
This may have been a reference to the invasion of Sennacherib in 701 B.C.

What would happen when the Spirit was poured out on God's people? (32:15)
They would be blessed abundantly and live in peace.

Who was the destroyer and betrayer? (33:1)
This was probably Assyria.

⁴Your plunder, O nations, is harvested as by young locusts;
    like a swarm of locusts people pounce on it.

⁵The LORD is exalted, for he dwells on high;
    he will fill Zion with his justice and righteousness.
⁶He will be the sure foundation for your times,
    a rich store of salvation and wisdom and knowledge;
    the fear of the LORD is the key to this treasure.ᵃ

⁷Look, their brave men cry aloud in the streets;
    the envoys of peace weep bitterly.
⁸The highways are deserted,
    no travelers are on the roads.
The treaty is broken,
    its witnessesᵇ are despised,
    no one is respected.
⁹The land dries up and wastes away,
    Lebanon is ashamed and withers;
Sharon is like the Arabah,
    and Bashan and Carmel drop their leaves.

¹⁰"Now will I arise," says the LORD.
    "Now will I be exalted;
    now will I be lifted up.
¹¹You conceive chaff,
    you give birth to straw;
    your breath is a fire that consumes you.
¹²The peoples will be burned to ashes;
    like cut thornbushes they will be set ablaze."

¹³You who are far away, hear what I have done;
    you who are near, acknowledge my power!
¹⁴The sinners in Zion are terrified;
    trembling grips the godless:
"Who of us can dwell with the consuming fire?
    Who of us can dwell with everlasting burning?"
¹⁵Those who walk righteously
    and speak what is right,
who reject gain from extortion
    and keep their hands from accepting bribes,
who stop their ears against plots of murder
    and shut their eyes against contemplating evil—
¹⁶they are the ones who will dwell on the heights,
    whose refuge will be the mountain fortress.
Their bread will be supplied,
    and water will not fail them.

¹⁷Your eyes will see the king in his beauty
    and view a land that stretches afar.
¹⁸In your thoughts you will ponder the former terror:
    "Where is that chief officer?
Where is the one who took the revenue?
    Where is the officer in charge of the towers?"
¹⁹You will see those arrogant people no more,
    people whose speech is obscure,
    whose language is strange and incomprehensible.

Why would the roads be deserted? (33:8)
The treaties had been broken, and it was not safe to use the roads for travel or for purposes of trade. This created great economic hardship.

What was the consuming fire? (33:14–16)
This was the presence of the God of judgment. The sinners would live in fear, but the righteous would have safety, along with food and drink.

ᵃ 6 Or *is a treasure from him*   ᵇ 8 Dead Sea Scrolls; Masoretic Text / *the cities*

²⁰ Look on Zion, the city of our festivals;
      your eyes will see Jerusalem,
      a peaceful abode, a tent that will not be moved;
   its stakes will never be pulled up,
      nor any of its ropes broken.
²¹ There the LORD will be our Mighty One.
      It will be like a place of broad rivers and streams.
   No galley with oars will ride them,
      no mighty ship will sail them.
²² For the LORD is our judge,
      the LORD is our lawgiver,
   the LORD is our king;
      it is he who will save us.

²³ Your rigging hangs loose:
      The mast is not held secure,
      the sail is not spread.
   Then an abundance of spoils will be divided
      and even the lame will carry off plunder.
²⁴ No one living in Zion will say, "I am ill";
      and the sins of those who dwell there will be
         forgiven.

JUDGMENT AGAINST THE NATIONS

34 Come near, you nations, and listen;
      pay attention, you peoples!
   Let the earth hear, and all that is in it,
      the world, and all that comes out of it!
² The LORD is angry with all nations;
      his wrath is on all their armies.
   He will totally destroy^a them,
      he will give them over to slaughter.
³ Their slain will be thrown out,
      their dead bodies will stink;
      the mountains will be soaked with their blood.
⁴ All the stars in the sky will be dissolved
      and the heavens rolled up like a scroll;
   all the starry host will fall
      like withered leaves from the vine,
      like shriveled figs from the fig tree.

⁵ My sword has drunk its fill in the heavens;
      see, it descends in judgment on Edom,
      the people I have totally destroyed.
⁶ The sword of the LORD is bathed in blood,
      it is covered with fat—
   the blood of lambs and goats,
      fat from the kidneys of rams.
   For the LORD has a sacrifice in Bozrah
      and a great slaughter in the land of Edom.
⁷ And the wild oxen will fall with them,
      the bull calves and the great bulls.
   Their land will be drenched with blood,
      and the dust will be soaked with fat.

Why was Jerusalem described as a ship? (33:23)
This word picture was used to show that Jerusalem was like a ship unprepared to sail into battle against Assyria.

What was Edom? (34:5)
Edom symbolized everyone who posed a threat to God and his followers.

^a 2 The Hebrew term refers to the irrevocable giving over of things or persons to the LORD, often by totally destroying them; also in verse 5.

Why were these birds and animals mentioned? (34:11–15)
These were unclean creatures that lived in ruined places. The cities that had once been filled with people would become like a desert or a wilderness.

What did it mean that God would allot their portions? (34:17)
God would give the desert creatures ownership of the land of Edom forever.

What literary technique did Isaiah use here? (35:1)
This is personification, describing something that is not human (the desert) as having human emotions.

⁸ For the LORD has a day of vengeance,
a year of retribution, to uphold Zion's cause.
⁹ Edom's streams will be turned into pitch,
her dust into burning sulfur;
her land will become blazing pitch!
¹⁰ It will not be quenched night or day;
its smoke will rise forever.
From generation to generation it will lie desolate;
no one will ever pass through it again.
¹¹ The desert owl^a and screech owl^a will possess it;
the great owl^a and the raven will nest there.
God will stretch out over Edom
the measuring line of chaos
and the plumb line of desolation.
¹² Her nobles will have nothing there to be called
a kingdom,
all her princes will vanish away.
¹³ Thorns will overrun her citadels,
nettles and brambles her strongholds.
She will become a haunt for jackals,
a home for owls.
¹⁴ Desert creatures will meet with hyenas,
and wild goats will bleat to each other;
there the night creatures will also lie down
and find for themselves places of rest.
¹⁵ The owl will nest there and lay eggs,
she will hatch them, and care for her young
under the shadow of her wings;
there also the falcons will gather,
each with its mate.

¹⁶ Look in the scroll of the LORD and read:

None of these will be missing,
not one will lack her mate.
For it is his mouth that has given the order,
and his Spirit will gather them together.
¹⁷ He allots their portions;
his hand distributes them by measure.
They will possess it forever
and dwell there from generation to generation.

JOY OF THE REDEEMED

35 The desert and the parched land will be glad;
the wilderness will rejoice and blossom.
Like the crocus, ² it will burst into bloom;
it will rejoice greatly and shout for joy.
The glory of Lebanon will be given to it,
the splendor of Carmel and Sharon;
they will see the glory of the LORD,
the splendor of our God.

³ Strengthen the feeble hands,
steady the knees that give way;
⁴ say to those with fearful hearts,
"Be strong, do not fear;

^a 11 The precise identification of these birds is uncertain.

your God will come,
he will come with vengeance;
with divine retribution
he will come to save you."

⁵ Then will the eyes of the blind be opened
and the ears of the deaf unstopped.
⁶ Then will the lame leap like a deer,
and the mute tongue shout for joy.
Water will gush forth in the wilderness
and streams in the desert.
⁷ The burning sand will become a pool,
the thirsty ground bubbling springs.
In the haunts where jackals once lay,
grass and reeds and papyrus will grow.

⁸ And a highway will be there;
it will be called the Way of Holiness;
it will be for those who walk on that Way.
The unclean will not journey on it;
wicked fools will not go about on it.
⁹ No lion will be there,
nor any ravenous beast;
they will not be found there.
But only the redeemed will walk there,
10   and those the LORD has rescued will return.
They will enter Zion with singing;
everlasting joy will crown their heads.
Gladness and joy will overtake them,
and sorrow and sighing will flee away.

SENNACHERIB THREATENS JERUSALEM

36 In the fourteenth year of King Hezekiah's reign, Sennacherib king of Assyria attacked all the fortified cities of Judah and captured them. ² Then the king of Assyria sent his field commander with a large army from Lachish to King Hezekiah at Jerusalem. When the commander stopped at the aqueduct of the Upper Pool, on the road to the Launderer's Field, ³ Eliakim son of Hilkiah the palace administrator, Shebna the secretary, and Joah son of Asaph the recorder went out to him.

⁴ The field commander said to them, "Tell Hezekiah:

"'This is what the great king, the king of Assyria, says: On what are you basing this confidence of yours? ⁵ You say you have counsel and might for war—but you speak only empty words. On whom are you depending, that you rebel against me? ⁶ Look, I know you are depending on Egypt, that splintered reed of a staff, which pierces the hand of anyone who leans on it! Such is Pharaoh king of Egypt to all who depend on him. ⁷ But if you say to me, "We are depending on the LORD our God"—isn't he the one whose high places and altars Hezekiah removed, saying to Judah and Jerusalem, "You must worship before this altar"?

⁸ "'Come now, make a bargain with my master, the king of Assyria: I will give you two thousand horses—if you

Who were the rescued people who would return to Zion? (35:10)
These were the Israelites when they returned from exile in Babylon. The prophecy also hints at a future time when God's redeemed people would receive his blessings and everlasting joy.

Assyria Threatens Jerusalem (36:1)

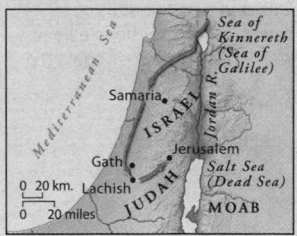

Why would the king of Assyria have marching orders from God? (36:10)
This was Sennacherib's claim, not God's. In order to intimidate the people, the Assyrian commander claimed that God had sent him to destroy Judah.

Was the Hebrew language well known? (36:11)
Aramaic had become the international language of the Middle East; it was the language used for diplomacy and commerce. It is surprising that the Assyrian officials were able to speak the Hebrew dialect of the common people of Judah.

Why did the Assyrians insult the Lord? (36:18–20)
The Assyrians believed the supernatural world included gods who ruled over limited territories. They thought that weaker gods could be conquered by more-powerful gods. The Assyrians said that the gods of other countries had not been able to stop them, so neither could the Lord.

can put riders on them! ⁹How then can you repulse one officer of the least of my master's officials, even though you are depending on Egypt for chariots and horsemen*?* ¹⁰Furthermore, have I come to attack and destroy this land without the Lᴏʀᴅ? The Lᴏʀᴅ himself told me to march against this country and destroy it.'"

¹¹Then Eliakim, Shebna and Joah said to the field commander, "Please speak to your servants in Aramaic, since we understand it. Don't speak to us in Hebrew in the hearing of the people on the wall."

¹²But the commander replied, "Was it only to your master and you that my master sent me to say these things, and not to the people sitting on the wall—who, like you, will have to eat their own excrement and drink their own urine?"

¹³Then the commander stood and called out in Hebrew, "Hear the words of the great king, the king of Assyria! ¹⁴This is what the king says: Do not let Hezekiah deceive you. He cannot deliver you! ¹⁵Do not let Hezekiah persuade you to trust in the Lᴏʀᴅ when he says, 'The Lᴏʀᴅ will surely deliver us; this city will not be given into the hand of the king of Assyria.'

¹⁶"Do not listen to Hezekiah. This is what the king of Assyria says: Make peace with me and come out to me. Then each of you will eat fruit from your own vine and fig tree and drink water from your own cistern, ¹⁷until I come and take you to a land like your own—a land of grain and new wine, a land of bread and vineyards.

¹⁸"Do not let Hezekiah mislead you when he says, 'The Lᴏʀᴅ will deliver us.' Have the gods of any nations ever delivered their lands from the hand of the king of Assyria? ¹⁹Where are the gods of Hamath and Arpad? Where are the gods of Sepharvaim? Have they rescued Samaria from my hand? ²⁰Who of all the gods of these countries have been able to save their lands from me? How then can the Lᴏʀᴅ deliver Jerusalem from my hand?"

²¹But the people remained silent and said nothing in reply, because the king had commanded, "Do not answer him."

²²Then Eliakim son of Hilkiah the palace administrator, Shebna the secretary and Joah son of Asaph the recorder went to Hezekiah, with their clothes torn, and told him what the field commander had said.

JERUSALEM'S DELIVERANCE FORETOLD

37 When King Hezekiah heard this, he tore his clothes and put on sackcloth and went into the temple of the Lᴏʀᴅ. ²He sent Eliakim the palace administrator, Shebna the secretary, and the leading priests, all wearing sackcloth, to the prophet Isaiah son of Amoz. ³They told him, "This is what Hezekiah says: This day is a day of distress and rebuke and disgrace, as when children come to the moment of birth and there is no strength to deliver them. ⁴It may be that the Lᴏʀᴅ your God will hear the words of the field commander, whom his master, the king of Assyria, has sent to ridicule the

ᵃ 9 Or charioteers

living God, and that he will rebuke him for the words the
LORD your God has heard. Therefore pray for the remnant
that still survives."

[5] When King Hezekiah's officials came to Isaiah, [6] Isaiah
said to them, "Tell your master, 'This is what the LORD says:
Do not be afraid of what you have heard—those words with
which the underlings of the king of Assyria have blasphemed
me. [7] Listen! When he hears a certain report, I will make him
want to return to his own country, and there I will have him
cut down with the sword.'"

[8] When the field commander heard that the king of Assyria had left Lachish, he withdrew and found the king fighting
against Libnah.

[9] Now Sennacherib received a report that Tirhakah, the
king of Cush,[a] was marching out to fight against him. When
he heard it, he sent messengers to Hezekiah with this word:
[10] "Say to Hezekiah king of Judah: Do not let the god you
depend on deceive you when he says, 'Jerusalem will not be
given into the hands of the king of Assyria.' [11] Surely you
have heard what the kings of Assyria have done to all the
countries, destroying them completely. And will you be delivered? [12] Did the gods of the nations that were destroyed
by my predecessors deliver them—the gods of Gozan, Harran, Rezeph and the people of Eden who were in Tel Assar? [13] Where is the king of Hamath or the king of Arpad?
Where are the kings of Lair, Sepharvaim, Hena and Ivvah?"

HEZEKIAH'S PRAYER

[14] Hezekiah received the letter from the messengers and
read it. Then he went up to the temple of the LORD and
spread it out before the LORD. [15] And Hezekiah prayed to
the LORD: [16] "LORD Almighty, the God of Israel, enthroned
between the cherubim, you alone are God over all the kingdoms of the earth. You have made heaven and earth. [17] Give
ear, LORD, and hear; open your eyes, LORD, and see; listen to
all the words Sennacherib has sent to ridicule the living God.

[18] "It is true, LORD, that the Assyrian kings have laid waste
all these peoples and their lands. [19] They have thrown their
gods into the fire and destroyed them, for they were not gods
but only wood and stone, fashioned by human hands. [20] Now,
LORD our God, deliver us from his hand, so that all the kingdoms of the earth may know that you, LORD, are the only
God.[b]"

SENNACHERIB'S FALL

[21] Then Isaiah son of Amoz sent a message to Hezekiah:
"This is what the LORD, the God of Israel, says: Because you
have prayed to me concerning Sennacherib king of Assyria,
[22] this is the word the LORD has spoken against him:

"Virgin Daughter Zion
  despises and mocks you.
Daughter Jerusalem
  tosses her head as you flee.

---

[a] 9 That is, the upper Nile region   [b] 20 Dead Sea Scrolls (see also 2 Kings
19:19); Masoretic Text *you alone are the LORD*

**How did God cause
Sennacherib to want to
return? (37:7)**
God's Spirit must have convinced
him to return to his own country.

What were cherubim? (37:16)
They were winged creatures who
existed primarily to glorify God.
The ark of the covenant included
two sculptures of cherubim.

**Did Hezekiah's prayer
change God's mind? (37:21)**
Hezekiah's prayer probably did
not change God's mind, but this
was a way to describe the turn
of events. God was ultimately in
control and knew all along what
would happen. He may have
wanted Hezekiah to express his
faith once again.

**Who was Virgin Daughter
Zion? (37:22)**
This was a symbolic description
of Jerusalem and its inhabitants.

²³Who is it you have ridiculed and blasphemed?
  Against whom have you raised your voice
and lifted your eyes in pride?
  Against the Holy One of Israel!
²⁴By your messengers
  you have ridiculed the Lord.
And you have said,
  'With my many chariots
I have ascended the heights of the mountains,
  the utmost heights of Lebanon.
I have cut down its tallest cedars,
  the choicest of its junipers.
I have reached its remotest heights,
  the finest of its forests.
²⁵I have dug wells in foreign lands^a
  and drunk the water there.
With the soles of my feet
  I have dried up all the streams of Egypt.'

²⁶"Have you not heard?
  Long ago I ordained it.
In days of old I planned it;
  now I have brought it to pass,
that you have turned fortified cities
  into piles of stone.
²⁷Their people, drained of power,
  are dismayed and put to shame.
They are like plants in the field,
  like tender green shoots,
like grass sprouting on the roof,
  scorched^b before it grows up.

²⁸"But I know where you are
  and when you come and go
  and how you rage against me.
²⁹Because you rage against me
  and because your insolence has reached my ears,
I will put my hook in your nose
  and my bit in your mouth,
and I will make you return
  by the way you came.

³⁰"This will be the sign for you, Hezekiah:

"This year you will eat what grows by itself,
  and the second year what springs from that.
But in the third year sow and reap,
  plant vineyards and eat their fruit.
³¹Once more a remnant of the kingdom of Judah
  will take root below and bear fruit above.
³²For out of Jerusalem will come a remnant,
  and out of Mount Zion a band of survivors.
The zeal of the LORD Almighty
  will accomplish this.

Why was grass growing on the roof? (37:27)
Houses in this region were made of clay, and roofs were flat. The wind blew seeds onto the roofs, or they were dropped there by birds. But the soil wasn't deep enough for the plants to thrive, so they would wither and die.

What did it mean for God to put a hook in Assyria's nose and a bit in its mouth? (37:29)
Nose hooks were used to lead oxen, and bits were used to control horses. In addition, the Assyrians often led captives away with a rope fastened to a hook that pierced the nose or lower lip. Here Isaiah predicted that this would happen to Sennacherib.

---

^a 25 Dead Sea Scrolls (see also 2 Kings 19:24); Masoretic Text does not have *in foreign lands.*   ^b 27 Some manuscripts of the Masoretic Text, Dead Sea Scrolls and some Septuagint manuscripts (see also 2 Kings 19:26); most manuscripts of the Masoretic Text *roof / and terraced fields*

33 "Therefore this is what the LORD says concerning the king of Assyria:

"He will not enter this city
or shoot an arrow here.
He will not come before it with shield
or build a siege ramp against it.
34 By the way that he came he will return;
he will not enter this city,"

declares the LORD.

35 "I will defend this city and save it,
for my sake and for the sake of David my servant!'"

36 Then the angel of the LORD went out and put to death a hundred and eighty-five thousand in the Assyrian camp. When the people got up the next morning—there were all the dead bodies! 37 So Sennacherib king of Assyria broke camp and withdrew. He returned to Nineveh and stayed there.

38 One day, while he was worshiping in the temple of his god Nisrok, his sons Adrammelek and Sharezer killed him with the sword, and they escaped to the land of Ararat. And Esarhaddon his son succeeded him as king.

HEZEKIAH'S ILLNESS

38 In those days Hezekiah became ill and was at the point of death. The prophet Isaiah son of Amoz went to him and said, "This is what the LORD says: Put your house in order, because you are going to die; you will not recover."

2 Hezekiah turned his face to the wall and prayed to the LORD, 3 "Remember, LORD, how I have walked before you faithfully and with wholehearted devotion and have done what is good in your eyes." And Hezekiah wept bitterly.

4 Then the word of the LORD came to Isaiah: 5 "Go and tell Hezekiah, 'This is what the LORD, the God of your father David, says: I have heard your prayer and seen your tears; I will add fifteen years to your life. 6 And I will deliver you and this city from the hand of the king of Assyria. I will defend this city.

7 "'This is the LORD's sign to you that the LORD will do what he has promised: 8 I will make the shadow cast by the sun go back the ten steps it has gone down on the stairway of Ahaz.'" So the sunlight went back the ten steps it had gone down.

9 A writing of Hezekiah king of Judah after his illness and recovery:

10 I said, "In the prime of my life
must I go through the gates of death
and be robbed of the rest of my years?"
11 I said, "I will not again see the LORD himself
in the land of the living;
no longer will I look on my fellow man,
or be with those who now dwell in this world.
12 Like a shepherd's tent my house
has been pulled down and taken from me.

What kind of plague did God send? (37:36)
Josephus, an ancient historian, wrote that this incident was accompanied by an infestation of mice and rats. Although we don't know for sure, perhaps this was a form of the bubonic plague. In any case, God caused 185,000 Assyrians to die in a single night.

Did the earth reverse its rotation? (38:7–8)
God may have used a variety of methods to cause a shadow to go backward, but all of them would have been miracles. In this way, God showed his faithful servant that he would continue to live.

What word pictures did Hezekiah use to describe his condition? (38:12–13)
He described himself as a tent that was pulled down, as a piece of cloth cut from the loom, and as someone whose bones had been broken by a lion. These poetic word pictures all symbolized someone near death.

Like a weaver I have rolled up my life,
    and he has cut me off from the loom;
    day and night you made an end of me.
¹³ I waited patiently till dawn,
    but like a lion he broke all my bones;
    day and night you made an end of me.
¹⁴ I cried like a swift or thrush,
    I moaned like a mourning dove.
My eyes grew weak as I looked to the heavens.
    I am being threatened; Lord, come to my aid!"

¹⁵ But what can I say?
    He has spoken to me, and he himself has
        done this.
I will walk humbly all my years
    because of this anguish of my soul.
¹⁶ Lord, by such things people live;
    and my spirit finds life in them too.
You restored me to health
    and let me live.
¹⁷ Surely it was for my benefit
    that I suffered such anguish.
In your love you kept me
    from the pit of destruction;
you have put all my sins
    behind your back.
¹⁸ For the grave cannot praise you,
    death cannot sing your praise;
those who go down to the pit
    cannot hope for your faithfulness.
¹⁹ The living, the living—they praise you,
    as I am doing today;
parents tell their children
    about your faithfulness.

²⁰ The Lord will save me,
    and we will sing with stringed instruments
all the days of our lives
    in the temple of the Lord.

²¹ Isaiah had said, "Prepare a poultice of figs and apply it to the boil, and he will recover."
²² Hezekiah had asked, "What will be the sign that I will go up to the temple of the Lord?"

ENVOYS FROM BABYLON

39 At that time Marduk-Baladan son of Baladan king of Babylon sent Hezekiah letters and a gift, because he had heard of his illness and recovery. ² Hezekiah received the envoys gladly and showed them what was in his storehouses—the silver, the gold, the spices, the fine olive oil—his entire armory and everything found among his treasures. There was nothing in his palace or in all his kingdom that Hezekiah did not show them.

³ Then Isaiah the prophet went to King Hezekiah and asked, "What did those men say, and where did they come from?"

Why had Hezekiah asked for a sign? (38:22)
Confused about which message he should believe—that he would die or that he would live—Hezekiah asked for a sign, and God showed that he would live.

"From a distant land," Hezekiah replied. "They came to me from Babylon."

⁴The prophet asked, "What did they see in your palace?"

"They saw everything in my palace," Hezekiah said. "There is nothing among my treasures that I did not show them."

⁵Then Isaiah said to Hezekiah, "Hear the word of the LORD Almighty: ⁶The time will surely come when everything in your palace, and all that your predecessors have stored up until this day, will be carried off to Babylon. Nothing will be left, says the LORD. ⁷And some of your descendants, your own flesh and blood who will be born to you, will be taken away, and they will become eunuchs in the palace of the king of Babylon."

⁸"The word of the LORD you have spoken is good," Hezekiah replied. For he thought, "There will be peace and security in my lifetime."

COMFORT FOR GOD'S PEOPLE

40 Comfort, comfort my people,
    says your God.
²Speak tenderly to Jerusalem,
    and proclaim to her
that her hard service has been completed,
    that her sin has been paid for,
that she has received from the LORD's hand
    double for all her sins.

³A voice of one calling:
"In the wilderness prepare
    the way for the LORD*ᵃ*;
make straight in the desert
    a highway for our God.*ᵇ*
⁴Every valley shall be raised up,
    every mountain and hill made low;
the rough ground shall become level,
    the rugged places a plain.
⁵And the glory of the LORD will be revealed,
    and all people will see it together.
                For the mouth of the LORD has spoken."

⁶A voice says, "Cry out."
    And I said, "What shall I cry?"

"All people are like grass,
    and all their faithfulness is like the flowers of the
        field.
⁷The grass withers and the flowers fall,
    because the breath of the LORD blows on them.
    Surely the people are grass.
⁸The grass withers and the flowers fall,
    but the word of our God endures forever."

⁹You who bring good news to Zion,
    go up on a high mountain.

ᵃ 3 Or A voice of one calling in the wilderness: / "Prepare the way for the LORD
ᵇ 3 Hebrew; Septuagint make straight the paths of our God

Why would Hezekiah call this prophecy good? (39:8)
Hezekiah may have been relieved that God's judgment would not come immediately. But more importantly, even though he realized that captivity would be difficult for the Israelites, Hezekiah responded in faith that God's will was good.

What New Testament figure do these verses describe? (40:3–5)
All four Gospels link this passage to John the Baptist, who prepared the way for Jesus. The image is of representatives going ahead of a monarch to prepare the processional highway for the visit of a king.

What was the good news? (40:9)
This was the news that God would lead his people back to Judah. In the New Testament, this "good news" is the salvation that Christ brings to the world.

You who bring good news to Jerusalem,[a]
  lift up your voice with a shout,
lift it up, do not be afraid;
  say to the towns of Judah,
  "Here is your God!"
10 See, the Sovereign LORD comes with power,
  and he rules with a mighty arm.
See, his reward is with him,
  and his recompense accompanies him.
11 He tends his flock like a shepherd:
  He gathers the lambs in his arms
and carries them close to his heart;
  he gently leads those that have young.

What are the two images of God presented here? (40:10–11)
God is presented as the powerful king or ruler of all people but also as a gentle shepherd who cares tenderly for his people.

12 Who has measured the waters in the hollow of his hand,
  or with the breadth of his hand marked off
    the heavens?
Who has held the dust of the earth in a basket,
  or weighed the mountains on the scales
    and the hills in a balance?
13 Who can fathom the Spirit[b] of the LORD,
  or instruct the LORD as his counselor?
14 Whom did the LORD consult to enlighten him,
  and who taught him the right way?
Who was it that taught him knowledge,
  or showed him the path of understanding?

15 Surely the nations are like a drop in a bucket;
  they are regarded as dust on the scales;
he weighs the islands as though they were fine dust.
16 Lebanon is not sufficient for altar fires,
  nor its animals enough for burnt offerings.
17 Before him all the nations are as nothing;
  they are regarded by him as worthless
  and less than nothing.

Why were the nations seen as insignificant? (40:15–17)
This was an exaggerated way of saying that in comparison to God's power and splendor, the nations of the earth amount to nothing.

18 With whom, then, will you compare God?
  To what image will you liken him?
19 As for an idol, a metalworker casts it,
  and a goldsmith overlays it with gold
  and fashions silver chains for it.
20 A person too poor to present such an offering
  selects wood that will not rot;
they look for a skilled worker
  to set up an idol that will not topple.

21 Do you not know?
  Have you not heard?
Has it not been told you from the beginning?
  Have you not understood since the earth was
    founded?
22 He sits enthroned above the circle of the earth,
  and its people are like grasshoppers.
He stretches out the heavens like a canopy,
  and spreads them out like a tent to live in.

What is the circle of the earth? (40:22)
It refers to the horizon. This is the only occurrence of the phrase in the Bible.

[a] 9 Or Zion, bringer of good news, / go up on a high mountain. / Jerusalem, bringer of good news   [b] 13 Or mind

²³ He brings princes to naught
and reduces the rulers of this world to nothing.
²⁴ No sooner are they planted,
no sooner are they sown,
no sooner do they take root in the ground,
than he blows on them and they wither,
and a whirlwind sweeps them away like chaff.

²⁵ "To whom will you compare me?
Or who is my equal?" says the Holy One.
²⁶ Lift up your eyes and look to the heavens:
Who created all these?
He who brings out the starry host one by one
and calls forth each of them by name.
Because of his great power and mighty strength,
not one of them is missing.

²⁷ Why do you complain, Jacob?
Why do you say, Israel,
"My way is hidden from the LORD;
my cause is disregarded by my God"?
²⁸ Do you not know?
Have you not heard?
The LORD is the everlasting God,
the Creator of the ends of the earth.
He will not grow tired or weary,
and his understanding no one can fathom.
²⁹ He gives strength to the weary
and increases the power of the weak.
³⁰ Even youths grow tired and weary,
and young men stumble and fall;
³¹ but those who hope in the LORD
will renew their strength.
They will soar on wings like eagles;
they will run and not grow weary,
they will walk and not be faint.

THE HELPER OF ISRAEL

41 "Be silent before me, you islands!
Let the nations renew their strength!
Let them come forward and speak;
let us meet together at the place of judgment.

² "Who has stirred up one from the east,
calling him in righteousness to his service*?
He hands nations over to him
and subdues kings before him.
He turns them to dust with his sword,
to windblown chaff with his bow.
³ He pursues them and moves on unscathed,
by a path his feet have not traveled before.
⁴ Who has done this and carried it through,
calling forth the generations from the beginning?
I, the LORD — with the first of them
and with the last — I am he."

a 2 Or east, / whom victory meets at every step

In what way does this passage present a more tender image of God? (40:28–31)
After Isaiah describes God's power and majesty, he stresses God's goodness to his people. God would restore his people and deliver them if they placed their trust in him.

Who was the one from the east? (41:2)
This was Cyrus the Great, king of Persia, who conquered Babylon in 539 B.C. and later allowed the Israelites to return to Jerusalem.

1018

ISAIAH 41:5

What were the ends of the earth? (41:5)
By 546 B.C., Cyrus had fought his way to the west coast of Asia Minor. The ends of the earth were the boundaries of the lands he had conquered.

Why call God's people a "worm"? (41:14)
This refers to their weakened and pitiful condition in exile.

Who was the Redeemer? (41:14)
This was a description of the Lord, who delivered his people from exile. The Lord is described as a kinsman-redeemer who would redeem his people's property, guarantee their freedom, avenge them against their enemies, and make their future safe.

How would God transform the desert? (41:17–20)
He would turn the desert from a dry and barren place into a land overflowing with water and filled with beautiful trees.

⁵The islands have seen it and fear;
   the ends of the earth tremble.
They approach and come forward;
⁶   they help each other
   and say to their companions, "Be strong!"
⁷The metalworker encourages the goldsmith,
   and the one who smooths with the hammer
   spurs on the one who strikes the anvil.
One says of the welding, "It is good."
   The other nails down the idol so it will not topple.

⁸"But you, Israel, my servant,
   Jacob, whom I have chosen,
   you descendants of Abraham my friend,
⁹I took you from the ends of the earth,
   from its farthest corners I called you.
I said, 'You are my servant';
   I have chosen you and have not rejected you.
¹⁰So do not fear, for I am with you;
   do not be dismayed, for I am your God.
I will strengthen you and help you;
   I will uphold you with my righteous right hand.

¹¹"All who rage against you
   will surely be ashamed and disgraced;
those who oppose you
   will be as nothing and perish.
¹²Though you search for your enemies,
   you will not find them.
Those who wage war against you
   will be as nothing at all.
¹³For I am the LORD your God
   who takes hold of your right hand
and says to you, Do not fear;
   I will help you.
¹⁴Do not be afraid, you worm Jacob,
   little Israel, do not fear,
for I myself will help you," declares the LORD,
   your Redeemer, the Holy One of Israel.
¹⁵"See, I will make you into a threshing sledge,
   new and sharp, with many teeth.
You will thresh the mountains and crush them,
   and reduce the hills to chaff.
¹⁶You will winnow them, the wind will pick them up,
   and a gale will blow them away.
But you will rejoice in the LORD
   and glory in the Holy One of Israel.

¹⁷"The poor and needy search for water,
   but there is none;
   their tongues are parched with thirst.
But I the LORD will answer them;
   I, the God of Israel, will not forsake them.
¹⁸I will make rivers flow on barren heights,
   and springs within the valleys.
I will turn the desert into pools of water,
   and the parched ground into springs.

¹⁹I will put in the desert
    the cedar and the acacia, the myrtle and the olive.
I will set junipers in the wasteland,
    the fir and the cypress together,
²⁰so that people may see and know,
    may consider and understand,
that the hand of the LORD has done this,
    that the Holy One of Israel has created it.

²¹"Present your case," says the LORD.
    "Set forth your arguments," says Jacob's King.
²²"Tell us, you idols,
    what is going to happen.
Tell us what the former things were,
    so that we may consider them
    and know their final outcome.
Or declare to us the things to come,
²³   tell us what the future holds,
    so we may know that you are gods.
Do something, whether good or bad,
    so that we will be dismayed and filled with fear.
²⁴But you are less than nothing
    and your works are utterly worthless;
    whoever chooses you is detestable.

²⁵"I have stirred up one from the north, and he comes—
    one from the rising sun who calls on my name.
He treads on rulers as if they were mortar,
    as if he were a potter treading the clay.
²⁶Who told of this from the beginning, so we
        could know,
    or beforehand, so we could say, 'He was right'?
No one told of this,
    no one foretold it,
    no one heard any words from you.
²⁷I was the first to tell Zion, 'Look, here they are!'
    I gave to Jerusalem a messenger of good news.
²⁸I look but there is no one—
    no one among the gods to give counsel,
    no one to give answer when I ask them.
²⁹See, they are all false!
    Their deeds amount to nothing;
    their images are but wind and confusion.

THE SERVANT OF THE LORD

42 "Here is my servant, whom I uphold,
    my chosen one in whom I delight;
I will put my Spirit on him,
    and he will bring justice to the nations.
²He will not shout or cry out,
    or raise his voice in the streets.
³A bruised reed he will not break,
    and a smoldering wick he will not snuff out.
In faithfulness he will bring forth justice;
⁴   he will not falter or be discouraged
till he establishes justice on earth.
    In his teaching the islands will put their hope."

Who was the one from the north? (41:25)
This was Cyrus. Even though he was earlier described as coming from the east, he had conquered a number of kingdoms north of Babylon early in his reign. From the perspective of a writer in Jerusalem, invasions came mainly from the north.

Who was the chosen servant? (42:1–4)
This points to the Messiah and is quoted in part in Matthew 12:18–21 with reference to Christ. In the book of Isaiah, there are four "servant songs" about the Messiah, who will deliver the world from sin (42:1–9; 49:1–7; 50:4–11; 52:13—53:12).

⁵This is what God the Lord says—
  the Creator of the heavens, who stretches them out,
    who spreads out the earth with all that springs
        from it,
    who gives breath to its people,
    and life to those who walk on it:
⁶"I, the Lord, have called you in righteousness;
    I will take hold of your hand.
  I will keep you and will make you
    to be a covenant for the people
    and a light for the Gentiles,
⁷to open eyes that are blind,
    to free captives from prison
    and to release from the dungeon those who
        sit in darkness.

⁸"I am the Lord; that is my name!
    I will not yield my glory to another
    or my praise to idols.
⁹See, the former things have taken place,
    and new things I declare;
  before they spring into being
    I announce them to you."

SONG OF PRAISE TO THE LORD

¹⁰Sing to the Lord a new song,
    his praise from the ends of the earth,
  you who go down to the sea, and all that is in it,
    you islands, and all who live in them.
¹¹Let the wilderness and its towns raise their voices;
    let the settlements where Kedar lives rejoice.
  Let the people of Sela sing for joy;
    let them shout from the mountaintops.
¹²Let them give glory to the Lord
    and proclaim his praise in the islands.
¹³The Lord will march out like a champion,
    like a warrior he will stir up his zeal;
  with a shout he will raise the battle cry
    and will triumph over his enemies.

¹⁴"For a long time I have kept silent,
    I have been quiet and held myself back.
  But now, like a woman in childbirth,
    I cry out, I gasp and pant.
¹⁵I will lay waste the mountains and hills
    and dry up all their vegetation;
  I will turn rivers into islands
    and dry up the pools.
¹⁶I will lead the blind by ways they have not known,
    along unfamiliar paths I will guide them;
  I will turn the darkness into light before them
    and make the rough places smooth.
  These are the things I will do;
    I will not forsake them.
¹⁷But those who trust in idols,
    who say to images, 'You are our gods,'
    will be turned back in utter shame.

How would the servant be a light for the Gentiles? (42:6)
The Messiah would welcome Gentiles along with Jews into his presence.

When was God silent? (42:14)
In a way, God was silent when he allowed his people to be taken into captivity. He was waiting until the right time to bring judgment on Babylon and restore his people.

ISRAEL BLIND AND DEAF

18 "Hear, you deaf;
    look, you blind, and see!
19 Who is blind but my servant,
    and deaf like the messenger I send?
Who is blind like the one in covenant with me,
    blind like the servant of the LORD?
20 You have seen many things, but you pay no attention;
    your ears are open, but you do not listen."
21 It pleased the LORD
    for the sake of his righteousness
    to make his law great and glorious.
22 But this is a people plundered and looted,
    all of them trapped in pits
    or hidden away in prisons.
They have become plunder,
    with no one to rescue them;
they have been made loot,
    with no one to say, "Send them back."

23 Which of you will listen to this
    or pay close attention in time to come?
24 Who handed Jacob over to become loot,
    and Israel to the plunderers?
Was it not the LORD,
    against whom we have sinned?
For they would not follow his ways;
    they did not obey his law.
25 So he poured out on them his burning anger,
    the violence of war.
It enveloped them in flames, yet they did
        not understand;
    it consumed them, but they did not take it to heart.

ISRAEL'S ONLY SAVIOR

43 But now, this is what the LORD says—
    he who created you, Jacob,
    he who formed you, Israel:
"Do not fear, for I have redeemed you;
    I have summoned you by name; you are mine.
2 When you pass through the waters,
    I will be with you;
and when you pass through the rivers,
    they will not sweep over you.
When you walk through the fire,
    you will not be burned;
    the flames will not set you ablaze.
3 For I am the LORD your God,
    the Holy One of Israel, your Savior;
I give Egypt for your ransom,
    Cush[a] and Seba in your stead.
4 Since you are precious and honored in my sight,
    and because I love you,
I will give people in exchange for you,
    nations in exchange for your life.

---

[a] 3 That is, the upper Nile region

How was it possible for Israel to be taken captive? (42:24–25)
Babylon did not conquer Israel because its gods were stronger than the Lord but because the Lord allowed his people to be punished for their disobedience.

How were Egypt, Cush, and Seba given as ransom? (43:3)
God may have been rewarding the Persians for their kindness to Israel by allowing them to conquer these countries.

What did the east, west, north, and south refer to? (43:5–6)
The east referred to the area including Assyria and Babylon, the west to the islands of the Mediterranean, the north to locations such as Hamath, and the south specifically to Egypt. One day God will gather his people from all corners of the world.

⁵Do not be afraid, for I am with you;
    I will bring your children from the east
    and gather you from the west.
⁶I will say to the north, 'Give them up!'
    and to the south, 'Do not hold them back.'
Bring my sons from afar
    and my daughters from the ends of the earth—
⁷everyone who is called by my name,
    whom I created for my glory,
    whom I formed and made."

⁸Lead out those who have eyes but are blind,
    who have ears but are deaf.
⁹All the nations gather together
    and the peoples assemble.
Which of their gods foretold this
    and proclaimed to us the former things?
Let them bring in their witnesses to prove they
        were right,
    so that others may hear and say, "It is true."
¹⁰"You are my witnesses," declares the LORD,
    "and my servant whom I have chosen,
so that you may know and believe me
    and understand that I am he.
Before me no god was formed,
    nor will there be one after me.
¹¹I, even I, am the LORD,
    and apart from me there is no savior.
¹²I have revealed and saved and proclaimed—
    I, and not some foreign god among you.
You are my witnesses," declares the LORD, "that I
        am God.
¹³   Yes, and from ancient days I am he.
No one can deliver out of my hand.
    When I act, who can reverse it?"

Who were the Lord's witnesses? (43:10–13)
Israel would testify that the Lord was more powerful than any god or idol.

GOD'S MERCY AND ISRAEL'S UNFAITHFULNESS

¹⁴This is what the LORD says—
    your Redeemer, the Holy One of Israel:
"For your sake I will send to Babylon
    and bring down as fugitives all the
        Babylonians,ᵃ
    in the ships in which they took pride.
¹⁵I am the LORD, your Holy One,
    Israel's Creator, your King."

¹⁶This is what the LORD says—
    he who made a way through the sea,
    a path through the mighty waters,
¹⁷who drew out the chariots and horses,
    the army and reinforcements together,
and they lay there, never to rise again,
    extinguished, snuffed out like a wick:
¹⁸"Forget the former things;
    do not dwell on the past.

What event is recalled in these verses? (43:16–17)
This was a reference to the crossing of the Red Sea. When the Israelites left Egypt, the waters parted and they crossed on dry ground. But Pharaoh's chariots and horsemen were destroyed when the waters covered them.

ᵃ 14 Or Chaldeans

¹⁹ See, I am doing a new thing!
    Now it springs up; do you not perceive it?
I am making a way in the wilderness
    and streams in the wasteland.
²⁰ The wild animals honor me,
    the jackals and the owls,
because I provide water in the wilderness
    and streams in the wasteland,
to give drink to my people, my chosen,
²¹   the people I formed for myself
    that they may proclaim my praise.

²² "Yet you have not called on me, Jacob,
    you have not wearied yourselves for^a me, Israel.
²³ You have not brought me sheep for burnt offerings,
    nor honored me with your sacrifices.
I have not burdened you with grain offerings
    nor wearied you with demands for incense.
²⁴ You have not bought any fragrant calamus for me,
    or lavished on me the fat of your sacrifices.
But you have burdened me with your sins
    and wearied me with your offenses.

²⁵ "I, even I, am he who blots out
    your transgressions, for my own sake,
    and remembers your sins no more.
²⁶ Review the past for me,
    let us argue the matter together;
    state the case for your innocence.
²⁷ Your first father sinned;
    those I sent to teach you rebelled against me.
²⁸ So I disgraced the dignitaries of your temple;
    I consigned Jacob to destruction^b
    and Israel to scorn.

ISRAEL THE CHOSEN

44 "But now listen, Jacob, my servant,
    Israel, whom I have chosen.
² This is what the LORD says—
    he who made you, who formed you in the womb,
    and who will help you:
Do not be afraid, Jacob, my servant,
    Jeshurun,^c whom I have chosen.
³ For I will pour water on the thirsty land,
    and streams on the dry ground;
I will pour out my Spirit on your offspring,
    and my blessing on your descendants.
⁴ They will spring up like grass in a meadow,
    like poplar trees by flowing streams.
⁵ Some will say, 'I belong to the LORD';
    others will call themselves by the name of Jacob;
still others will write on their hand, 'The LORD's,'
    and will take the name Israel.

What was calamus? (43:24)
Calamus was a reed-like plant said to have grown in the valley of Lebanon. The sweet-smelling oil obtained from crushing its stalk was used in incense offerings and for anointing.

Who was the first father? (43:27)
This could refer to Adam. It might also refer to Abraham or to Jacob (Israel), all of whom had sinned.

Who was Jeshurun? (44:2)
This was another name for Israel, found elsewhere only in Deuteronomy (32:15; 33:5, 26).

^a 22 Or *Jacob; / surely you have grown weary of*   ^b 28 The Hebrew term refers to the irrevocable giving over of things or persons to the LORD, often by totally destroying them.   ^c 2 *Jeshurun* means *the upright one*, that is, Israel.

THE LORD, NOT IDOLS

6 "This is what the LORD says—
   Israel's King and Redeemer, the LORD Almighty:
I am the first and I am the last;
   apart from me there is no God.
7 Who then is like me? Let him proclaim it.
   Let him declare and lay out before me
what has happened since I established my
      ancient people,
   and what is yet to come—
   yes, let them foretell what will come.
8 Do not tremble, do not be afraid.
   Did I not proclaim this and foretell it long ago?
You are my witnesses. Is there any God besides me?
   No, there is no other Rock; I know not one."

9 All who make idols are nothing,
   and the things they treasure are worthless.
Those who would speak up for them are blind;
   they are ignorant, to their own shame.
10 Who shapes a god and casts an idol,
   which can profit nothing?
11 People who do that will be put to shame;
   such craftsmen are only human beings.
Let them all come together and take their stand;
   they will be brought down to terror and shame.

12 The blacksmith takes a tool
   and works with it in the coals;
he shapes an idol with hammers,
   he forges it with the might of his arm.
He gets hungry and loses his strength;
   he drinks no water and grows faint.
13 The carpenter measures with a line
   and makes an outline with a marker;
he roughs it out with chisels
   and marks it with compasses.
He shapes it in human form,
   human form in all its glory,
   that it may dwell in a shrine.
14 He cut down cedars,
   or perhaps took a cypress or oak.
He let it grow among the trees of the forest,
   or planted a pine, and the rain made it grow.
15 It is used as fuel for burning;
   some of it he takes and warms himself,
   he kindles a fire and bakes bread.
But he also fashions a god and worships it;
   he makes an idol and bows down to it.
16 Half of the wood he burns in the fire;
   over it he prepares his meal,
   he roasts his meat and eats his fill.
He also warms himself and says,
   "Ah! I am warm; I see the fire."
17 From the rest he makes a god, his idol;
   he bows down to it and worships.

What was significant about cedars, cypress, and oak? (44:14)
These were the most valuable types of wood during this time period.

How did Isaiah criticize idols made of wood? (44:14–20)
He described someone cutting down a tree and then using some of the wood to make a fire and the rest to carve an idol. He pointed out that in both cases the wood was simply wood, nothing more.

He prays to it and says,
    "Save me! You are my god!"
¹⁸They know nothing, they understand nothing;
    their eyes are plastered over so they cannot see,
    and their minds closed so they cannot understand.
¹⁹No one stops to think,
    no one has the knowledge or understanding to say,
"Half of it I used for fuel;
    I even baked bread over its coals,
    I roasted meat and I ate.
Shall I make a detestable thing from what is left?
    Shall I bow down to a block of wood?"
²⁰Such a person feeds on ashes; a deluded heart
      misleads him;
    he cannot save himself, or say,
    "Is not this thing in my right hand a lie?"

²¹"Remember these things, Jacob,
    for you, Israel, are my servant.
I have made you, you are my servant;
    Israel, I will not forget you.
²²I have swept away your offenses like a cloud,
    your sins like the morning mist.
Return to me,
    for I have redeemed you."

²³Sing for joy, you heavens, for the LORD has done this;
    shout aloud, you earth beneath.
Burst into song, you mountains,
    you forests and all your trees,
for the LORD has redeemed Jacob,
    he displays his glory in Israel.

JERUSALEM TO BE INHABITED

²⁴"This is what the LORD says—
    your Redeemer, who formed you in the womb:

I am the LORD,
    the Maker of all things,
    who stretches out the heavens,
    who spreads out the earth by myself,
²⁵who foils the signs of false prophets
    and makes fools of diviners,
who overthrows the learning of the wise
    and turns it into nonsense,
²⁶who carries out the words of his servants
    and fulfills the predictions of his messengers,

who says of Jerusalem, 'It shall be inhabited,'
    of the towns of Judah, 'They shall be rebuilt,'
    and of their ruins, 'I will restore them,'
²⁷who says to the watery deep, 'Be dry,
    and I will dry up your streams,'
²⁸who says of Cyrus, 'He is my shepherd
    and will accomplish all that I please;
he will say of Jerusalem, "Let it be rebuilt,"
    and of the temple, "Let its foundations be laid."'

How great was the joy for the Lord's redemption of Israel? (44:23)
All of nature was invited to give praise to God: the heavens, the earth, the mountains, and the forests.

Why was Cyrus described as a shepherd? (44:28)
In ancient times, rulers were often referred to as shepherds to their subjects. It was the leaders' job to protect and care for their flock, the people. Cyrus's decree to rebuild the temple eventually led to a restored Jerusalem.

Why was Cyrus called the Lord's anointed? (45:1)
Even though Cyrus did not worship the Lord (verse 4), he was appointed by God to carry out the important task of returning the Jews to their homeland.

45 "This is what the LORD says to his anointed,
to Cyrus, whose right hand I take hold of
to subdue nations before him
and to strip kings of their armor,
to open doors before him
so that gates will not be shut:
² I will go before you
and will level the mountains*;*
I will break down gates of bronze
and cut through bars of iron.
³ I will give you hidden treasures,
riches stored in secret places,
so that you may know that I am the LORD,
the God of Israel, who summons you by name.
⁴ For the sake of Jacob my servant,
of Israel my chosen,
I summon you by name
and bestow on you a title of honor,
though you do not acknowledge me.
⁵ I am the LORD, and there is no other;
apart from me there is no God.
I will strengthen you,
though you have not acknowledged me,
⁶ so that from the rising of the sun
to the place of its setting
people may know there is none besides me.
I am the LORD, and there is no other.
⁷ I form the light and create darkness,
I bring prosperity and create disaster;
I, the LORD, do all these things.

⁸ "You heavens above, rain down my righteousness;
let the clouds shower it down.
Let the earth open wide,
let salvation spring up,
let righteousness flourish with it;
I, the LORD, have created it.

What was a potsherd? (45:9)
This was a broken piece of pottery. Here it is a word picture showing the insignificance of people who quarrel with God.

⁹ "Woe to those who quarrel with their Maker,
those who are nothing but potsherds
among the potsherds on the ground.
Does the clay say to the potter,
'What are you making?'
Does your work say,
'The potter has no hands'?
¹⁰ Woe to the one who says to a father,
'What have you begotten?'
or to a mother,
'What have you brought to birth?'

¹¹ "This is what the LORD says—
the Holy One of Israel, and its Maker:
Concerning things to come,
do you question me about my children,
or give me orders about the work of my hands?

ᵃ 2 Dead Sea Scrolls and Septuagint; the meaning of the word in the Masoretic Text is uncertain.

¹² It is I who made the earth
    and created mankind on it.
My own hands stretched out the heavens;
    I marshaled their starry hosts.
¹³ I will raise up Cyrus^{*a*} in my righteousness:
    I will make all his ways straight.
He will rebuild my city
    and set my exiles free,
but not for a price or reward,
    says the LORD Almighty."

¹⁴ This is what the LORD says:

"The products of Egypt and the merchandise of
    Cush,^{*b*}
  and those tall Sabeans—
they will come over to you
    and will be yours;
they will trudge behind you,
    coming over to you in chains.
They will bow down before you
    and plead with you, saying,
'Surely God is with you, and there is no other;
    there is no other god.'"

¹⁵ Truly you are a God who has been hiding himself,
    the God and Savior of Israel.
¹⁶ All the makers of idols will be put to shame and
    disgraced;
    they will go off into disgrace together.
¹⁷ But Israel will be saved by the LORD
    with an everlasting salvation;
you will never be put to shame or disgraced,
    to ages everlasting.

¹⁸ For this is what the LORD says—
he who created the heavens,
    he is God;
he who fashioned and made the earth,
    he founded it;
he did not create it to be empty,
    but formed it to be inhabited—
he says:
"I am the LORD,
    and there is no other.
¹⁹ I have not spoken in secret,
    from somewhere in a land of darkness;
I have not said to Jacob's descendants,
    'Seek me in vain.'
I, the LORD, speak the truth;
    I declare what is right.

²⁰ "Gather together and come;
    assemble, you fugitives from the nations.
Ignorant are those who carry about idols of wood,
    who pray to gods that cannot save.

Why would the Lord be called a God who hides himself? (45:15)
This may be saying that the Lord's ways sometimes seem mysterious to human beings. It may also mean that God was unlike the visible, man-made gods or idols of surrounding nations.

What did it mean that God did not speak in secret from a land of darkness? (45:19)
This is meant to contrast with the methods of mediums and spirit worshipers. God displayed himself openly in the mighty works of creation.

---

^{*a*} *13* Hebrew *him*   ^{*b*} *14* That is, the upper Nile region

²¹ Declare what is to be, present it—
    let them take counsel together.
Who foretold this long ago,
    who declared it from the distant past?
Was it not I, the LORD?
    And there is no God apart from me,
a righteous God and a Savior;
    there is none but me.

²² "Turn to me and be saved,
    all you ends of the earth;
    for I am God, and there is no other.
²³ By myself I have sworn,
    my mouth has uttered in all integrity
    a word that will not be revoked:
Before me every knee will bow;
    by me every tongue will swear.
²⁴ They will say of me, 'In the LORD alone
    are deliverance and strength.'"
All who have raged against him
    will come to him and be put to shame.
²⁵ But all the descendants of Israel
    will find deliverance in the LORD
    and will make their boast in him.

GODS OF BABYLON

46 Bel bows down, Nebo stoops low;
    their idols are borne by beasts of burden.ᵃ
The images that are carried about are burdensome,
    a burden for the weary.
² They stoop and bow down together;
    unable to rescue the burden,
    they themselves go off into captivity.

³ "Listen to me, you descendants of Jacob,
    all the remnant of the people of Israel,
you whom I have upheld since your birth,
    and have carried since you were born.
⁴ Even to your old age and gray hairs
    I am he, I am he who will sustain you.
I have made you and I will carry you;
    I will sustain you and I will rescue you.

⁵ "With whom will you compare me or count me equal?
    To whom will you liken me that we may be
        compared?
⁶ Some pour out gold from their bags
    and weigh out silver on the scales;
they hire a goldsmith to make it into a god,
    and they bow down and worship it.
⁷ They lift it to their shoulders and carry it;
    they set it up in its place, and there it stands.
    From that spot it cannot move.
Even though someone cries out to it, it cannot answer;
    it cannot save them from their troubles.

ᵃ 1 Or *are but beasts and cattle*

Who were Bel and Nebo?
(46:1)
These were Babylonian gods.
Bel means *lord* and refers to the
chief god, Marduk. Nebo (also
called Nabu) was Marduk's son.

**How were the pagan gods
limited in their power? (46:2)**
The pagan gods were taken into
captivity along with those who
worshiped them. They were unable to save themselves or their
followers.

8 "Remember this, keep it in mind,
   take it to heart, you rebels.
9 Remember the former things, those of long ago;
   I am God, and there is no other;
   I am God, and there is none like me.
10 I make known the end from the beginning,
   from ancient times, what is still to come.
I say, 'My purpose will stand,
   and I will do all that I please.'
11 From the east I summon a bird of prey;
   from a far-off land, a man to fulfill my purpose.
What I have said, that I will bring about;
   what I have planned, that I will do.
12 Listen to me, you stubborn-hearted,
   you who are now far from my righteousness.
13 I am bringing my righteousness near,
   it is not far away;
   and my salvation will not be delayed.
I will grant salvation to Zion,
   my splendor to Israel.

THE FALL OF BABYLON

47 "Go down, sit in the dust,
   Virgin Daughter Babylon;
sit on the ground without a throne,
   queen city of the Babylonians.[a]
No more will you be called
   tender or delicate.
2 Take millstones and grind flour;
   take off your veil.
Lift up your skirts, bare your legs,
   and wade through the streams.
3 Your nakedness will be exposed
   and your shame uncovered.
I will take vengeance;
   I will spare no one."

4 Our Redeemer—the LORD Almighty is
   his name—
is the Holy One of Israel.

5 "Sit in silence, go into darkness,
   queen city of the Babylonians;
no more will you be called
   queen of kingdoms.
6 I was angry with my people
   and desecrated my inheritance;
I gave them into your hand,
   and you showed them no mercy.
Even on the aged
   you laid a very heavy yoke.
7 You said, 'I am forever—
   the eternal queen!'
But you did not consider these things
   or reflect on what might happen.

[a] 1 Or *Chaldeans*; also in verse 5

Who was this bird of prey? (46:11)
This refers to Cyrus, the king of Persia, who conquered Babylon. One ancient historian said that Cyrus's royal banner included the symbol of an eagle.

Why would Babylon sit in the dust? (47:1–3)
This was a sign of mourning. Here Babylon was personified as a royal princess. Rather than being a pampered princess, she would be reduced to the status of a menial worker and would be humiliated by having her bare legs exposed.

Why was the claim "I am, and there is none beside me" so wrong? (47:8)
This was a truth only God had a right to claim for himself (see 43:11; 45:5 – 6).

8 "Now then, listen, you lover of pleasure,
   lounging in your security
and saying to yourself,
   'I am, and there is none besides me.
I will never be a widow
   or suffer the loss of children.'
9 Both of these will overtake you
   in a moment, on a single day:
   loss of children and widowhood.
They will come upon you in full measure,
   in spite of your many sorceries
   and all your potent spells.
10 You have trusted in your wickedness
   and have said, 'No one sees me.'
Your wisdom and knowledge mislead you
   when you say to yourself,
   'I am, and there is none besides me.'
11 Disaster will come upon you,
   and you will not know how to conjure it away.
A calamity will fall upon you
   that you cannot ward off with a ransom;
a catastrophe you cannot foresee
   will suddenly come upon you.

What were these sorceries and spells? (47:12)
These were magical practices which were thought helpful to avoid danger and inflict harm on an enemy.

12 "Keep on, then, with your magic spells
   and with your many sorceries,
   which you have labored at since childhood.
Perhaps you will succeed,
   perhaps you will cause terror.
13 All the counsel you have received has only worn
        you out!
   Let your astrologers come forward,
those stargazers who make predictions month by month,
   let them save you from what is coming upon you.
14 Surely they are like stubble;
   the fire will burn them up.
They cannot even save themselves
   from the power of the flame.
These are not coals for warmth;
   this is not a fire to sit by.
15 That is all they are to you —
   these you have dealt with
   and labored with since childhood.
All of them go on in their error;
   there is not one that can save you.

STUBBORN ISRAEL

48 "Listen to this, you descendants of Jacob,
   you who are called by the name of Israel
   and come from the line of Judah,
you who take oaths in the name of the LORD
   and invoke the God of Israel —
   but not in truth or righteousness —
2 you who call yourselves citizens of the holy city
   and claim to rely on the God of Israel —
   the LORD Almighty is his name:

³I foretold the former things long ago,
  my mouth announced them and I made
    them known;
  then suddenly I acted, and they came
    to pass.
⁴For I knew how stubborn you were;
  your neck muscles were iron,
  your forehead was bronze.
⁵Therefore I told you these things long ago;
  before they happened I announced them to you
so that you could not say,
  'My images brought them about;
  my wooden image and metal god ordained them.'
⁶You have heard these things; look at them all.
  Will you not admit them?

"From now on I will tell you of new things,
  of hidden things unknown to you.
⁷They are created now, and not long ago;
  you have not heard of them before today.
So you cannot say,
  'Yes, I knew of them.'
⁸You have neither heard nor understood;
  from of old your ears have not been open.
Well do I know how treacherous you are;
  you were called a rebel from birth.
⁹For my own name's sake I delay my wrath;
  for the sake of my praise I hold it back
    from you,
  so as not to destroy you completely.
¹⁰See, I have refined you, though not as silver;
  I have tested you in the furnace of affliction.
¹¹For my own sake, for my own sake, I do this.
  How can I let myself be defamed?
  I will not yield my glory to another.

ISRAEL FREED

¹²"Listen to me, Jacob,
  Israel, whom I have called:
I am he;
  I am the first and I am the last.
¹³My own hand laid the foundations of the earth,
  and my right hand spread out the heavens;
when I summon them,
  they all stand up together.

¹⁴"Come together, all of you, and listen:
  Which of the idols has foretold these things?
The LORD's chosen ally
  will carry out his purpose against Babylon;
  his arm will be against the Babylonians.ᵃ
¹⁵I, even I, have spoken;
  yes, I have called him.
I will bring him,
  and he will succeed in his mission.

ᵃ 14 Or Chaldeans; also in verse 20

What new things did God reveal to his people? (48:6)
God revealed that they would be freed and would be allowed to return to Judah.

Who was the "LORD's ally"? (48:14)
This was Cyrus, who allowed the Jews to return to their homeland and rebuild the temple.

¹⁶"Come near me and listen to this:

"From the first announcement I have not spoken
        in secret;
    at the time it happens, I am there."

And now the Sovereign LORD has sent me,
    endowed with his Spirit.

¹⁷This is what the LORD says—
    your Redeemer, the Holy One of Israel:
"I am the LORD your God,
    who teaches you what is best for you,
    who directs you in the way you should go.
¹⁸If only you had paid attention to my commands,
    your peace would have been like a river,
    your well-being like the waves of the sea.
¹⁹Your descendants would have been like the sand,
    your children like its numberless grains;
    their name would never be blotted out
    nor destroyed from before me."

²⁰Leave Babylon,
    flee from the Babylonians!
Announce this with shouts of joy
    and proclaim it.
Send it out to the ends of the earth;
    say, "The LORD has redeemed his servant Jacob."
²¹They did not thirst when he led them through
        the deserts;
    he made water flow for them from the rock;
he split the rock
    and water gushed out.

²²"There is no peace," says the LORD, "for the wicked."

THE SERVANT OF THE LORD

49 Listen to me, you islands;
        hear this, you distant nations:
Before I was born the LORD called me;
    from my mother's womb he has spoken my name.
²He made my mouth like a sharpened sword,
    in the shadow of his hand he hid me;
he made me into a polished arrow
    and concealed me in his quiver.
³He said to me, "You are my servant,
    Israel, in whom I will display my splendor."
⁴But I said, "I have labored in vain;
    I have spent my strength for nothing at all.
Yet what is due me is in the LORD's hand,
    and my reward is with my God."

⁵And now the LORD says—
    he who formed me in the womb to be his servant
to bring Jacob back to him
    and gather Israel to himself,
for I am^a honored in the eyes of the LORD
    and my God has been my strength—

How had God's people failed to live up to their responsibilities? (48:18–19)
The people had rebelled against God and his commandments and had been punished for their rebellion.

---

^a 5 Or *him, / but Israel would not be gathered; / yet I will be*

6 he says:

"It is too small a thing for you to be my servant
    to restore the tribes of Jacob
    and bring back those of Israel I have kept.
I will also make you a light for the Gentiles,
    that my salvation may reach to the ends of the
        earth."

7 This is what the LORD says—
    the Redeemer and Holy One of Israel—
to him who was despised and abhorred by the nation,
    to the servant of rulers:
"Kings will see you and stand up,
    princes will see and bow down,
because of the LORD, who is faithful,
    the Holy One of Israel, who has chosen you."

RESTORATION OF ISRAEL

8 This is what the LORD says:

"In the time of my favor I will answer you,
    and in the day of salvation I will help you;
I will keep you and will make you
    to be a covenant for the people,
to restore the land
    and to reassign its desolate inheritances,
9 to say to the captives, 'Come out,'
    and to those in darkness, 'Be free!'

"They will feed beside the roads
    and find pasture on every barren hill.
10 They will neither hunger nor thirst,
    nor will the desert heat or the sun beat down on
        them.
He who has compassion on them will guide them
    and lead them beside springs of water.
11 I will turn all my mountains into roads,
    and my highways will be raised up.
12 See, they will come from afar—
    some from the north, some from the west,
    some from the region of Aswan.ᵃ"

13 Shout for joy, you heavens;
    rejoice, you earth;
    burst into song, you mountains!
For the LORD comforts his people
    and will have compassion on his afflicted ones.

14 But Zion said, "The LORD has forsaken me,
    the Lord has forgotten me."

15 "Can a mother forget the baby at her breast
    and have no compassion on the child she has borne?
Though she may forget,
    I will not forget you!
16 See, I have engraved you on the palms of my hands;
    your walls are ever before me.

ᵃ 12 Dead Sea Scrolls; Masoretic Text *Sinim*

What was Israel's role in God's plan? (49:6)
Israel would become a light for the Gentiles, drawing people from all ends of the earth to God.

What was the time of God's favor? (49:8–9)
The background of this verse is probably the Year of Jubilee, when slaves were freed and land was returned to its original owners (Leviticus 25:10). The return from exile would restore the land to the people just as the Year of Jubilee did.

How were their names engraved on God's hands? (49:16)
The names of the tribes of Israel were engraved on stones and fastened to the ephod of the high priest as a memorial to the Lord (Exodus 28:9–12). In a similar way, the Lord would write or tattoo their names on his hands symbolizing how he remembered them.

¹⁷ Your children hasten back,
and those who laid you waste depart from you.
¹⁸ Lift up your eyes and look around;
all your children gather and come to you.
As surely as I live," declares the LORD,
"you will wear them all as ornaments;
you will put them on, like a bride.

¹⁹ "Though you were ruined and made desolate
and your land laid waste,
now you will be too small for your people,
and those who devoured you will be far away.
²⁰ The children born during your bereavement
will yet say in your hearing,
'This place is too small for us;
give us more space to live in.'
²¹ Then you will say in your heart,
'Who bore me these?
I was bereaved and barren;
I was exiled and rejected.
Who brought these up?
I was left all alone,
but these—where have they come from?'"

²² This is what the Sovereign LORD says:

"See, I will beckon to the nations,
I will lift up my banner to the peoples;
they will bring your sons in their arms
and carry your daughters on their hips.
²³ Kings will be your foster fathers,
and their queens your nursing mothers.
They will bow down before you with their faces
to the ground;
they will lick the dust at your feet.
Then you will know that I am the LORD;
those who hope in me will not be disappointed."

²⁴ Can plunder be taken from warriors,
or captives be rescued from the fierce^a?

²⁵ But this is what the LORD says:

"Yes, captives will be taken from warriors,
and plunder retrieved from the fierce;
I will contend with those who contend with you,
and your children I will save.
²⁶ I will make your oppressors eat their own flesh;
they will be drunk on their own blood, as with wine.
Then all mankind will know
that I, the LORD, am your Savior,
your Redeemer, the Mighty One of Jacob."

ISRAEL'S SIN AND THE SERVANT'S OBEDIENCE

50 This is what the LORD says:

"Where is your mother's certificate of divorce

^a 24 Dead Sea Scrolls, Vulgate and Syriac (see also Septuagint and verse 25);
Masoretic Text *righteous*

Why was Israel depicted as a barren woman? (49:21)
Barrenness was a disgrace and tragedy for a woman in ancient times. Israel's barrenness paved the way for God to adopt children from among the Gentiles.

What did this prophecy refer to? (49:26)
During the siege of Jerusalem, the people living there were reduced to cannibalism.

What was a certificate of divorce? (50:1)
A husband was required to give this certificate to his wife if he wanted to divorce her (see Deuteronomy 24:1–3). Even though Judah broke its relationship with God, the Lord had not given them a certificate and would take them back.

with which I sent her away?
Or to which of my creditors
    did I sell you?
Because of your sins you were sold;
    because of your transgressions your mother was
        sent away.
2 When I came, why was there no one?
    When I called, why was there no one
        to answer?
Was my arm too short to deliver you?
    Do I lack the strength to rescue you?
By a mere rebuke I dry up the sea,
    I turn rivers into a desert;
their fish rot for lack of water
    and die of thirst.
3 I clothe the heavens with darkness
    and make sackcloth its covering."

4 The Sovereign LORD has given me a well-instructed
        tongue,
    to know the word that sustains the weary.
He wakens me morning by morning,
    wakens my ear to listen like one being
        instructed.
5 The Sovereign LORD has opened my ears;
    I have not been rebellious,
    I have not turned away.
6 I offered my back to those who beat me,
    my cheeks to those who pulled out my beard;
I did not hide my face
    from mocking and spitting.
7 Because the Sovereign LORD helps me,
    I will not be disgraced.
Therefore have I set my face like flint,
    and I know I will not be put to shame.
8 He who vindicates me is near.
    Who then will bring charges against me?
    Let us face each other!
Who is my accuser?
    Let him confront me!
9 It is the Sovereign LORD who helps me.
    Who will condemn me?
They will all wear out like a garment;
    the moths will eat them up.

10 Who among you fears the LORD
    and obeys the word of his servant?
Let the one who walks in the dark,
    who has no light,
trust in the name of the LORD
    and rely on their God.
11 But now, all you who light fires
    and provide yourselves with flaming torches,
go, walk in the light of your fires
    and of the torches you have set ablaze.
This is what you shall receive from my hand:
    You will lie down in torment.

How were these punishments a form of humiliation? (50:6)
Beatings were for criminals or fools; pulling out the beard was a sign of disrespect and contempt; and mocking and spitting showed hatred. These were humiliations that Jesus suffered before his death.

What did this word picture describe? (50:9)
Those who made false accusations against the righteous would be destroyed in the same way that moths eat a piece of clothing.

EVERLASTING SALVATION FOR ZION

51 "Listen to me, you who pursue righteousness
and who seek the Lord:
Look to the rock from which you were cut
and to the quarry from which you were hewn;
² look to Abraham, your father,
and to Sarah, who gave you birth.
When I called him he was only one man,
and I blessed him and made him many.
³ The Lord will surely comfort Zion
and will look with compassion on all her ruins;
he will make her deserts like Eden,
her wastelands like the garden of the Lord.
Joy and gladness will be found in her,
thanksgiving and the sound of singing.

⁴ "Listen to me, my people;
hear me, my nation:
Instruction will go out from me;
my justice will become a light to the nations.
⁵ My righteousness draws near speedily,
my salvation is on the way,
and my arm will bring justice to the nations.
The islands will look to me
and wait in hope for my arm.
⁶ Lift up your eyes to the heavens,
look at the earth beneath;
the heavens will vanish like smoke,
the earth will wear out like a garment
and its inhabitants die like flies.
But my salvation will last forever,
my righteousness will never fail.

⁷ "Hear me, you who know what is right,
you people who have taken my instruction to heart:
Do not fear the reproach of mere mortals
or be terrified by their insults.
⁸ For the moth will eat them up like a garment;
the worm will devour them like wool.
But my righteousness will last forever,
my salvation through all generations."

⁹ Awake, awake, arm of the Lord,
clothe yourself with strength!
Awake, as in days gone by,
as in generations of old.
Was it not you who cut Rahab to pieces,
who pierced that monster through?
¹⁰ Was it not you who dried up the sea,
the waters of the great deep,
who made a road in the depths of the sea
so that the redeemed might cross over?
¹¹ Those the Lord has rescued will return.
They will enter Zion with singing;
everlasting joy will crown their heads.
Gladness and joy will overtake them,
and sorrow and sighing will flee away.

What was Rahab? (51:9)
This was a mythical sea monster.
The name came to symbolize
Egypt.

What sea was this? (51:10)
This was the Red Sea. The Israelites crossed this sea when they
fled Egypt.

12 "I, even I, am he who comforts you.
    Who are you that you fear mere mortals,
    human beings who are but grass,
13 that you forget the LORD your Maker,
    who stretches out the heavens
    and who lays the foundations of the earth,
  that you live in constant terror every day
    because of the wrath of the oppressor,
    who is bent on destruction?
  For where is the wrath of the oppressor?
14   The cowering prisoners will soon be set free;
    they will not die in their dungeon,
    nor will they lack bread.
15 For I am the LORD your God,
    who stirs up the sea so that its waves roar—
    the LORD Almighty is his name.
16 I have put my words in your mouth
    and covered you with the shadow of my hand—
  I who set the heavens in place,
    who laid the foundations of the earth,
    and who say to Zion, 'You are my people.'"

THE CUP OF THE LORD'S WRATH

17 Awake, awake!
    Rise up, Jerusalem,
  you who have drunk from the hand of the LORD
    the cup of his wrath,
  you who have drained to its dregs
    the goblet that makes people stagger.
18 Among all the children she bore
    there was none to guide her;
  among all the children she reared
    there was none to take her by the hand.
19 These double calamities have come upon you—
    who can comfort you?—
  ruin and destruction, famine and sword—
    who can[a] console you?
20 Your children have fainted;
    they lie at every street corner,
    like antelope caught in a net.
  They are filled with the wrath of the LORD,
    with the rebuke of your God.

21 Therefore hear this, you afflicted one,
    made drunk, but not with wine.
22 This is what your Sovereign LORD says,
    your God, who defends his people:
  "See, I have taken out of your hand
    the cup that made you stagger;
  from that cup, the goblet of my wrath,
    you will never drink again.
23 I will put it into the hands of your tormentors,
    who said to you,
    'Fall prostrate that we may walk on you.'

---

[a] 19 Dead Sea Scrolls, Septuagint, Vulgate and Syriac; Masoretic Text / how can I

What did it mean to drink the cup of the Lord's wrath? (51:17)
Experiencing God's judgment was often compared to becoming drunk on strong wine. It made people stagger.

Why was the lack of sons a problem for Jerusalem? (51:18)
Grown children were expected to take care of their parents when they were sick or old.

And you made your back like the ground,
    like a street to be walked on."

52 Awake, awake, Zion,
    clothe yourself with strength!
Put on your garments of splendor,
    Jerusalem, the holy city.
The uncircumcised and defiled
    will not enter you again.
² Shake off your dust;
    rise up, sit enthroned, Jerusalem.
Free yourself from the chains on your neck,
    Daughter Zion, now a captive.

³ For this is what the LORD says:

"You were sold for nothing,
    and without money you will be redeemed."

⁴ For this is what the Sovereign LORD says:

"At first my people went down to Egypt to live;
    lately, Assyria has oppressed them.

⁵ "And now what do I have here?" declares the LORD.

"For my people have been taken away for nothing,
    and those who rule them mock,ᵃ"
                  declares the LORD.
"And all day long
    my name is constantly blasphemed.
⁶ Therefore my people will know my name;
    therefore in that day they will know
that it is I who foretold it.
    Yes, it is I."

⁷ How beautiful on the mountains
    are the feet of those who bring good news,
who proclaim peace,
    who bring good tidings,
    who proclaim salvation,
who say to Zion,
    "Your God reigns!"
⁸ Listen! Your watchmen lift up their voices;
    together they shout for joy.
When the LORD returns to Zion,
    they will see it with their own eyes.
⁹ Burst into songs of joy together,
    you ruins of Jerusalem,
for the LORD has comforted his people,
    he has redeemed Jerusalem.
¹⁰ The LORD will lay bare his holy arm
    in the sight of all the nations,
and all the ends of the earth will see
    the salvation of our God.

¹¹ Depart, depart, go out from there!
    Touch no unclean thing!

ᵃ 5 Dead Sea Scrolls and Vulgate; Masoretic Text *wail*

Who were the people who brought good news? (52:7)
These were messengers who ran from the scene of a battle to bring the news of the outcome to the waiting king and people. Here the news was the return from exile.

What did God's holy arm symbolize? (52:10)
God's arm often symbolized his power as well as the redemption and salvation he gave to his people.

Come out from it and be pure,
    you who carry the articles of the LORD's house.
¹²But you will not leave in haste
    or go in flight;
for the LORD will go before you,
    the God of Israel will be your rear guard.

THE SUFFERING AND GLORY OF THE SERVANT

¹³See, my servant will act wisely*ᵃ*;
    he will be raised and lifted up and highly exalted.
¹⁴Just as there were many who were appalled at him*ᵇ*—
    his appearance was so disfigured beyond that of any
        human being
    and his form marred beyond human likeness—
¹⁵so he will sprinkle many nations,*ᶜ*
    and kings will shut their mouths because of him.
For what they were not told, they will see,
    and what they have not heard, they will understand.

53 Who has believed our message
    and to whom has the arm of the LORD
        been revealed?
²He grew up before him like a tender shoot,
    and like a root out of dry ground.
He had no beauty or majesty to attract us to him,
    nothing in his appearance that we should desire him.
³He was despised and rejected by mankind,
    a man of suffering, and familiar with pain.
Like one from whom people hide their faces
    he was despised, and we held him in low esteem.

⁴Surely he took up our pain
    and bore our suffering,
yet we considered him punished by God,
    stricken by him, and afflicted.
⁵But he was pierced for our transgressions,
    he was crushed for our iniquities;
the punishment that brought us peace was on him,
    and by his wounds we are healed.

ᵃ 13 Or *will prosper*   *ᵇ 14* Hebrew *you*   *ᶜ 15* Or *so will many nations be amazed at him* (see also Septuagint)

How did this prophecy point toward the Messiah? (52:14)
The treatment Jesus suffered before and during his death on the cross was terrible. Many of those who witnessed it were appalled by how horrible it was.

Who was Isaiah describing? (53:2–3)
This was a picture of the coming Messiah who would come from the line of Jesse (see 11:1). He would endure great suffering and be despised by many.

What does the prophecy of the suffering servant foretell about the coming Messiah?

ISAIAH 53

This is one of the most extensive and well-known Old Testament prophecies about the coming Messiah. Perhaps one reason that this chapter is so well known is that several sections of Handel's *Messiah* use parts of the chapter as the words for musical selections.

Isaiah emphasizes that the Messiah would suffer greatly. Some of the New Testament writers referred to this text when they wrote about Jesus. For example, Matthew described Jesus' healing ministry and quoted this passage: "This was to fulfill what was spoken through the prophet Isaiah: 'He took up our infirmities and bore our diseases'" (Matthew 8:17). And Peter described Jesus' death on the cross as his way of taking on our sins: "'He himself bore our sins' in his body on the cross, so that we might die to sins and live for righteousness; 'by his wounds you have been healed'" (1 Peter 2:24).

This memorable chapter speaks of the Messiah's need to suffer in order to pay the price for human sin. Like an animal that was sacrificed, he took on himself the guilt of sinners.

How are people like sheep? (53:6)

Sheep are helpless and ignorant animals that often stray and get into dangerous situations. The same is true for human beings who wander away from God.

⁶We all, like sheep, have gone astray,
    each of us has turned to our own way;
and the LORD has laid on him
    the iniquity of us all.

⁷He was oppressed and afflicted,
    yet he did not open his mouth;
he was led like a lamb to the slaughter,
    and as a sheep before its shearers is silent,
    so he did not open his mouth.
⁸By oppression^a and judgment he was taken away.
    Yet who of his generation protested?
For he was cut off from the land of the living;
    for the transgression of my people he
        was punished.^b
⁹He was assigned a grave with the wicked,
    and with the rich in his death,
though he had done no violence,
    nor was any deceit in his mouth.

What was an offering for sin? (53:10)

In the Israelite sacrificial system, an offering was made for a person who committed both unintentional sins and sins the person might not be aware he or she committed. The person brought a ram to the priest for sacrifice, made amends for their sins, and paid a fine (see Leviticus 5:14 – 19). Jesus became an offering for the sin of his people.

¹⁰Yet it was the LORD's will to crush him and cause him
    to suffer,
    and though the LORD makes^c his life an offering
        for sin,
he will see his offspring and prolong his days,
    and the will of the LORD will prosper in his hand.
¹¹After he has suffered,
    he will see the light of life^d and be satisfied^e;
by his knowledge^f my righteous servant will
        justify many,
    and he will bear their iniquities.
¹²Therefore I will give him a portion among the great,^g
    and he will divide the spoils with the strong,^h
because he poured out his life unto death,
    and was numbered with the transgressors.
For he bore the sin of many,
    and made intercession for the transgressors.

THE FUTURE GLORY OF ZION

54 "Sing, barren woman,
    you who never bore a child;
burst into song, shout for joy,
    you who were never in labor;
because more are the children of the desolate woman
    than of her who has a husband,"
                        says the LORD.

Who was the barren woman? (54:1)

This was a picture of Jerusalem (representing Israel), especially during the time of exile. Infertility and widowhood were considered disgraceful.

Why would tents need to be enlarged? (54:2)

This may refer to the growth of Jerusalem after the exile, but it may also include the idea of making room for Gentiles in the family of God.

²"Enlarge the place of your tent,
    stretch your tent curtains wide,
    do not hold back;
lengthen your cords,
    strengthen your stakes.

---

^a 8 Or *From arrest*   ^b 8 Or *generation considered / that he was cut off from the land of the living, / that he was punished for the transgression of my people?*   ^c 10 Hebrew *though you make*   ^d 11 Dead Sea Scrolls (see also Septuagint); Masoretic Text does not have *the light of life.*   ^e 11 Or (with Masoretic Text) *11 He will see the fruit of his suffering / and will be satisfied*   ^f 11 Or *by knowledge of him*   ^g 12 Or *many*   ^h 12 Or *numerous*

³ For you will spread out to the right and to the left;
   your descendants will dispossess nations
   and settle in their desolate cities.

⁴ "Do not be afraid; you will not be put to shame.
   Do not fear disgrace; you will not be humiliated.
You will forget the shame of your youth
   and remember no more the reproach of your
      widowhood.
⁵ For your Maker is your husband—
   the LORD Almighty is his name—
the Holy One of Israel is your Redeemer;
   he is called the God of all the earth.
⁶ The LORD will call you back
   as if you were a wife deserted and distressed in
      spirit—
a wife who married young,
   only to be rejected," says your God.
⁷ "For a brief moment I abandoned you,
   but with deep compassion I will bring you back.
⁸ In a surge of anger
   I hid my face from you for a moment,
but with everlasting kindness
   I will have compassion on you,"
says the LORD your Redeemer.

⁹ "To me this is like the days of Noah,
   when I swore that the waters of Noah would never
      again cover the earth.
So now I have sworn not to be angry with you,
   never to rebuke you again.
¹⁰ Though the mountains be shaken
   and the hills be removed,
yet my unfailing love for you will not be shaken
   nor my covenant of peace be removed,"
   says the LORD, who has compassion on you.

¹¹ "Afflicted city, lashed by storms and not comforted,
   I will rebuild you with stones of turquoise,ᵃ
   your foundations with lapis lazuli.
¹² I will make your battlements of rubies,
   your gates of sparkling jewels,
   and all your walls of precious stones.
¹³ All your children will be taught by the LORD,
   and great will be their peace.
¹⁴ In righteousness you will be established:
Tyranny will be far from you;
   you will have nothing to fear.
Terror will be far removed;
   it will not come near you.
¹⁵ If anyone does attack you, it will not be my doing;
   whoever attacks you will surrender to you.

¹⁶ "See, it is I who created the blacksmith
   who fans the coals into flame
   and forges a weapon fit for its work.

ᵃ 11 The meaning of the Hebrew for this word is uncertain.

What covenant did God make? (54:9–10)
This was like the covenant God made with Noah to never again destroy the world with a flood. God promised his unfailing love to Israel.

What were battlements? (54:11–12)
These were low walls on the top of towers for the concealment and protection of soldiers. The description of the various parts of the city as being made with precious stones is a picture of the New Jerusalem.

And it is I who have created the destroyer to
    wreak havoc;
17 no weapon forged against you will prevail,
    and you will refute every tongue that accuses you.
This is the heritage of the servants of the LORD,
    and this is their vindication from me,"

declares the LORD.

INVITATION TO THE THIRSTY

55 "Come, all you who are thirsty,
    come to the waters;
and you who have no money,
    come, buy and eat!
Come, buy wine and milk
    without money and without cost.
2 Why spend money on what is not bread,
    and your labor on what does not satisfy?
Listen, listen to me, and eat what is good,
    and you will delight in the richest of fare.
3 Give ear and come to me;
    listen, that you may live.
I will make an everlasting covenant with you,
    my faithful love promised to David.
4 See, I have made him a witness to the peoples,
    a ruler and commander of the peoples.
5 Surely you will summon nations you know not,
    and nations you do not know will come running
      to you,
because of the LORD your God,
    the Holy One of Israel,
for he has endowed you with splendor."

6 Seek the LORD while he may be found;
    call on him while he is near.
7 Let the wicked forsake their ways
    and the unrighteous their thoughts.
Let them turn to the LORD, and he will have mercy
    on them,
    and to our God, for he will freely pardon.

8 "For my thoughts are not your thoughts,
    neither are your ways my ways,"

declares the LORD.

9 "As the heavens are higher than the earth,
    so are my ways higher than your ways
    and my thoughts than your thoughts.
10 As the rain and the snow
    come down from heaven,
and do not return to it
    without watering the earth
and making it bud and flourish,
    so that it yields seed for the sower and bread for
      the eater,
11 so is my word that goes out from my mouth:
    It will not return to me empty,
but will accomplish what I desire
    and achieve the purpose for which I sent it.

How could hungry and thirsty people with no money buy wine, bread, and milk? (55:1)
In the same way God makes his gifts available to his people, the seller could make his goods available to poor buyers if he priced everything at zero. People who are spiritually thirsty can have their needs met because the price has already been paid by Jesus' death (53:5 – 9).

What is the "everlasting covenant"? (55:3)
God made many covenants with his people. The covenant with David was that his descendant would rule forever. Jesus, a descendant of David, fulfilled this promise and became the everlasting covenant. Those who believe in him are able to become part of God's family.

What is this "word"? (55:11)
This refers to God's promises. During Isaiah's time, people heard God's words mainly through the prophets. Later, they relied more on the written word in the Scriptures. Like a decree issued by a king, God's Word accomplishes his purposes.

¹²You will go out in joy
     and be led forth in peace;
the mountains and hills
     will burst into song before you,
and all the trees of the field
     will clap their hands.
¹³Instead of the thornbush will grow the juniper,
     and instead of briers the myrtle will grow.
This will be for the LORD's renown,
     for an everlasting sign,
     that will endure forever."

SALVATION FOR OTHERS

56 This is what the LORD says:

"Maintain justice
     and do what is right,
for my salvation is close at hand
     and my righteousness will soon be revealed.
²Blessed is the one who does this—
     the person who holds it fast,
who keeps the Sabbath without desecrating it,
     and keeps their hands from doing any evil."

³Let no foreigner who is bound to the LORD say,
     "The LORD will surely exclude me from
          his people."
And let no eunuch complain,
     "I am only a dry tree."

⁴For this is what the LORD says:

"To the eunuchs who keep my Sabbaths,
     who choose what pleases me
     and hold fast to my covenant—
⁵to them I will give within my temple and
          its walls
     a memorial and a name
     better than sons and daughters;
I will give them an everlasting name
     that will endure forever.
⁶And foreigners who bind themselves to the LORD
     to minister to him,
to love the name of the LORD,
     and to be his servants,
all who keep the Sabbath without desecrating it
     and who hold fast to my covenant—
⁷these I will bring to my holy mountain
     and give them joy in my house of prayer.
Their burnt offerings and sacrifices
     will be accepted on my altar;
for my house will be called
     a house of prayer for all nations."
⁸The Sovereign LORD declares—
     he who gathers the exiles of Israel:
"I will gather still others to them
     besides those already gathered."

How does creation praise God? (55:12–13)
Isaiah uses poetic language to emphasize that all of creation, including mountains and trees, will praise the Creator. This is a picture of renewal. The curse of sin represented by thorns and briers will be lifted, and beautiful trees will take their place.

Why is keeping the Sabbath included in this passage? (56:1–2)
God expects his people to obey all of his laws, including maintaining justice (love of neighbors) and keeping the Sabbath (honoring God).

Why were foreigners and eunuchs mentioned? (56:3–8)
Foreigners and eunuchs who lived with the Israelites were not allowed to worship with God's people (see Deuteronomy 23:1–2). Yet here the prophet said that even those who had been outcasts would have a place in the renewed kingdom of God.

GOD'S ACCUSATION AGAINST THE WICKED

⁹ Come, all you beasts of the field,
　come and devour, all you beasts of the forest!
¹⁰ Israel's watchmen are blind,
　they all lack knowledge;
they are all mute dogs,
　they cannot bark;
they lie around and dream,
　they love to sleep.
¹¹ They are dogs with mighty appetites;
　they never have enough.
They are shepherds who lack understanding;
　they all turn to their own way,
　they seek their own gain.
¹² "Come," each one cries, "let me get wine!
　Let us drink our fill of beer!
And tomorrow will be like today,
　or even far better."

57 The righteous perish,
　　and no one takes it to heart;
the devout are taken away,
　and no one understands
that the righteous are taken away
　to be spared from evil.
² Those who walk uprightly
　enter into peace;
　they find rest as they lie in death.

³ "But you—come here, you children of
　　a sorceress,
　you offspring of adulterers and prostitutes!
⁴ Who are you mocking?
　At whom do you sneer
　and stick out your tongue?
Are you not a brood of rebels,
　the offspring of liars?
⁵ You burn with lust among the oaks
　and under every spreading tree;
you sacrifice your children in the ravines
　and under the overhanging crags.
⁶ The idols among the smooth stones of the ravines
　　are your portion;
　indeed, they are your lot.
Yes, to them you have poured out drink offerings
　and offered grain offerings.
　In view of all this, should I relent?
⁷ You have made your bed on a high and lofty hill;
　there you went up to offer your sacrifices.
⁸ Behind your doors and your doorposts
　you have put your pagan symbols.
Forsaking me, you uncovered your bed,
　you climbed into it and opened it wide;
you made a pact with those whose beds you love,
　and you looked with lust on their
　　naked bodies.

Who were watchmen?
(56:10)
Similar to how soldiers protected the city from military attacks, it was the watchmen's job to protect the city from spiritual attacks. However, they failed to do their job properly because they were either blind or asleep.

What took place among the oaks? (57:5)
These were pagan rituals involving sexual immorality. Worship of Molek or Baal sometimes included sacrifices of children.

What were pagan symbols?
(57:8)
God's people were supposed to place God's commands on their doorposts to remind themselves of the Lord. Instead, the people put pagan symbols of idolatry on their doors.

⁹You went to Molek^a with olive oil
     and increased your perfumes.
You sent your ambassadors^b far away;
     you descended to the very realm of the dead!
¹⁰You wearied yourself by such going about,
     but you would not say, 'It is hopeless.'
You found renewal of your strength,
     and so you did not faint.

¹¹"Whom have you so dreaded and feared
     that you have not been true to me,
and have neither remembered me
     nor taken this to heart?
Is it not because I have long been silent
     that you do not fear me?
¹²I will expose your righteousness and your works,
     and they will not benefit you.
¹³When you cry out for help,
     let your collection of idols save you!
The wind will carry all of them off,
     a mere breath will blow them away.
But whoever takes refuge in me
     will inherit the land
     and possess my holy mountain."

COMFORT FOR THE CONTRITE
¹⁴And it will be said:

"Build up, build up, prepare the road!
     Remove the obstacles out of the way of
          my people."
¹⁵For this is what the high and exalted One says—
     he who lives forever, whose name is holy:
"I live in a high and holy place,
     but also with the one who is contrite and lowly
          in spirit,
to revive the spirit of the lowly
     and to revive the heart of the contrite.
¹⁶I will not accuse them forever,
     nor will I always be angry,
for then they would faint away because of me—
     the very people I have created.
¹⁷I was enraged by their sinful greed;
     I punished them, and hid my face in anger,
     yet they kept on in their willful ways.
¹⁸I have seen their ways, but I will heal them;
     I will guide them and restore comfort to Israel's
          mourners,
¹⁹   creating praise on their lips.
Peace, peace, to those far and near,"
     says the LORD. "And I will heal them."
²⁰But the wicked are like the tossing sea,
     which cannot rest,
     whose waves cast up mire and mud.
²¹"There is no peace," says my God, "for the wicked."

^a 9 Or *to the king*   ^b 9 Or *idols*

Where does God live? (57:15)
God, the high and lofty One, lives in a high and holy place—heaven. But he also lives within the hearts of the humble.

Would God always be angry with Israel? (57:16–21)
No. God was angry at those who rebelled against him, but he would forgive and restore his people.

TRUE FASTING

58 "Shout it aloud, do not hold back.
Raise your voice like a trumpet.
Declare to my people their rebellion
and to the descendants of Jacob their sins.
² For day after day they seek me out;
they seem eager to know my ways,
as if they were a nation that does what is right
and has not forsaken the commands of its God.
They ask me for just decisions
and seem eager for God to come near them.
³ 'Why have we fasted,' they say,
'and you have not seen it?
Why have we humbled ourselves,
and you have not noticed?'

"Yet on the day of your fasting, you do as you please
and exploit all your workers.
⁴ Your fasting ends in quarreling and strife,
and in striking each other with wicked fists.
You cannot fast as you do today
and expect your voice to be heard on high.
⁵ Is this the kind of fast I have chosen,
only a day for people to humble themselves?
Is it only for bowing one's head like a reed
and for lying in sackcloth and ashes?
Is that what you call a fast,
a day acceptable to the LORD?

⁶ "Is not this the kind of fasting I have chosen:
to loose the chains of injustice
and untie the cords of the yoke,
to set the oppressed free
and break every yoke?
⁷ Is it not to share your food with the hungry
and to provide the poor wanderer with shelter—
when you see the naked, to clothe them,
and not to turn away from your own flesh
and blood?
⁸ Then your light will break forth like the dawn,
and your healing will quickly appear;
then your righteousness*ᵃ* will go before you,
and the glory of the LORD will be your rear guard.
⁹ Then you will call, and the LORD will answer;
you will cry for help, and he will say: Here am I.

"If you do away with the yoke of oppression,
with the pointing finger and malicious talk,
¹⁰ and if you spend yourselves in behalf of the hungry
and satisfy the needs of the oppressed,
then your light will rise in the darkness,
and your night will become like the noonday.
¹¹ The LORD will guide you always;
he will satisfy your needs in a sun-scorched land
and will strengthen your frame.

Why was their fasting not acceptable? (58:3–5)
Though they fasted, they did it in order to get God's blessing and then were disappointed when he did not reward them. And they continued to behave in ways that dishonored God, such as quarreling and exploiting their workers. In other words, their fasting was hypocritical because their hearts and attitudes did not change.

What did God expect from his people? (58:6–9)
God expected that they would seek justice, free the captives, share with the poor, and provide clothing and safe haven for those without clothing or places to stay.

ᵃ 8 Or your righteous One

You will be like a well-watered garden,
    like a spring whose waters never fail.
¹²Your people will rebuild the ancient ruins
    and will raise up the age-old foundations;
you will be called Repairer of Broken Walls,
    Restorer of Streets with Dwellings.

¹³"If you keep your feet from breaking the Sabbath
    and from doing as you please on my holy day,
if you call the Sabbath a delight
    and the LORD's holy day honorable,
and if you honor it by not going your own way
    and not doing as you please or speaking idle words,
¹⁴then you will find your joy in the LORD,
    and I will cause you to ride in triumph on the
        heights of the land
    and to feast on the inheritance of your father Jacob."
        For the mouth of the LORD has spoken.

What ruins would be rebuilt? (58:12)
The people would rebuild the ruins of Jerusalem as a sign that God was with them once again.

SIN, CONFESSION AND REDEMPTION

59 Surely the arm of the LORD is not too short
        to save,
    nor his ear too dull to hear.
²But your iniquities have separated
    you from your God;
your sins have hidden his face from you,
    so that he will not hear.
³For your hands are stained with blood,
    your fingers with guilt.
Your lips have spoken falsely,
    and your tongue mutters wicked things.
⁴No one calls for justice;
    no one pleads a case with integrity.
They rely on empty arguments, they utter lies;
    they conceive trouble and give birth to evil.
⁵They hatch the eggs of vipers
    and spin a spider's web.
Whoever eats their eggs will die,
    and when one is broken, an adder is hatched.
⁶Their cobwebs are useless for clothing;
    they cannot cover themselves with what they make.
Their deeds are evil deeds,
    and acts of violence are in their hands.
⁷Their feet rush into sin;
    they are swift to shed innocent blood.
They pursue evil schemes;
    acts of violence mark their ways.
⁸The way of peace they do not know;
    there is no justice in their paths.
They have turned them into crooked roads;
    no one who walks along them will know peace.

⁹So justice is far from us,
    and righteousness does not reach us.
We look for light, but all is darkness;
    for brightness, but we walk in deep shadows.

What were some of the sins of the people? (59:3–4)
They were guilty of violence, lying, injustice, and troublemaking.

¹⁰ Like the blind we grope along the wall,
feeling our way like people without eyes.
At midday we stumble as if it were twilight;
among the strong, we are like the dead.
¹¹ We all growl like bears;
we moan mournfully like doves.
We look for justice, but find none;
for deliverance, but it is far away.

¹² For our offenses are many in your sight,
and our sins testify against us.
Our offenses are ever with us,
and we acknowledge our iniquities:
¹³ rebellion and treachery against the LORD,
turning our backs on our God,
inciting revolt and oppression,
uttering lies our hearts have conceived.
¹⁴ So justice is driven back,
and righteousness stands at a distance;
truth has stumbled in the streets,
honesty cannot enter.
¹⁵ Truth is nowhere to be found,
and whoever shuns evil becomes a prey.

The LORD looked and was displeased
that there was no justice.
¹⁶ He saw that there was no one,
he was appalled that there was no one to intervene;
so his own arm achieved salvation for him,
and his own righteousness sustained him.
¹⁷ He put on righteousness as his breastplate,
and the helmet of salvation on his head;
he put on the garments of vengeance
and wrapped himself in zeal as in a cloak.
¹⁸ According to what they have done,
so will he repay
wrath to his enemies
and retribution to his foes;
he will repay the islands their due.
¹⁹ From the west, people will fear the name of the LORD,
and from the rising of the sun, they will revere his
glory.
For he will come like a pent-up flood
that the breath of the LORD drives along.^a

²⁰ "The Redeemer will come to Zion,
to those in Jacob who repent of their sins,"
declares the LORD.

²¹ "As for me, this is my covenant with them," says the
LORD. "My Spirit, who is on you, will not depart from you,
and my words that I have put in your mouth will always be
on your lips, on the lips of your children and on the lips of
their descendants—from this time on and forever," says the
LORD.

---

*^a 19 Or When enemies come in like a flood, / the Spirit of the LORD will put them
to flight*

Why did Isaiah confess on behalf of the people? (59:12)
Isaiah was a representative of the entire community. Because of the communal attitude of the society, if someone in the community sinned, all were guilty of that sin.

Who would be drawn into the kingdom of God? (59:19)
All nations from the east to the west would see God's saving work on behalf of his people and would honor him.

What covenant did God make with his people? (59:21)
God promised that his Spirit would not leave his people.

THE GLORY OF ZION

60 "Arise, shine, for your light has come,
and the glory of the LORD rises upon you.
² See, darkness covers the earth
and thick darkness is over the peoples,
but the LORD rises upon you
and his glory appears over you.
³ Nations will come to your light,
and kings to the brightness of your dawn.

⁴ "Lift up your eyes and look about you:
All assemble and come to you;
your sons come from afar,
and your daughters are carried on the hip.
⁵ Then you will look and be radiant,
your heart will throb and swell with joy;
the wealth on the seas will be brought to you,
to you the riches of the nations will come.
⁶ Herds of camels will cover your land,
young camels of Midian and Ephah.
And all from Sheba will come,
bearing gold and incense
and proclaiming the praise of the LORD.
⁷ All Kedar's flocks will be gathered to you,
the rams of Nebaioth will serve you;
they will be accepted as offerings on my altar,
and I will adorn my glorious temple.

⁸ "Who are these that fly along like clouds,
like doves to their nests?
⁹ Surely the islands look to me;
in the lead are the ships of Tarshish,ᵃ
bringing your children from afar,
with their silver and gold,
to the honor of the LORD your God,
the Holy One of Israel,
for he has endowed you with splendor.

¹⁰ "Foreigners will rebuild your walls,
and their kings will serve you.
Though in anger I struck you,
in favor I will show you compassion.
¹¹ Your gates will always stand open,
they will never be shut, day or night,
so that people may bring you the wealth of the
nations—
their kings led in triumphal procession.
¹² For the nation or kingdom that will not serve you will
perish;
it will be utterly ruined.

¹³ "The glory of Lebanon will come to you,
the juniper, the fir and the cypress together,
to adorn my sanctuary;
and I will glorify the place for my feet.

ᵃ 9 Or the trading ships

What does this image of light in the midst of darkness picture? (60:1–3) Though the world seems to be covered in darkness, God's people reflect the light of God's love in their lives. Jesus brought light to the darkness of the world.

What did the riches, gold, and camels represent? (60:5–7) They represented God's blessings on his people. These miraculous blessings showed how God would bring them back to Jerusalem.

What were Midian, Ephah, Sheba, Kedar, and Nebaioth? (60:6–7) These were wealthy tribes that lived in Arabia.

When would the Israelites be allowed to rebuild the walls? (60:10) In 444 B.C., Artaxerxes issued the decree that allowed Nehemiah to rebuild the walls of Jerusalem.

¹⁴The children of your oppressors will come bowing
>   before you;
>   all who despise you will bow down at your feet
> and will call you the City of the Lord,
>   Zion of the Holy One of Israel.

¹⁵"Although you have been forsaken and hated,
>   with no one traveling through,
>   I will make you the everlasting pride
>   and the joy of all generations.
¹⁶You will drink the milk of nations
>   and be nursed at royal breasts.
>   Then you will know that I, the Lord, am your Savior,
>   your Redeemer, the Mighty One of Jacob.
¹⁷Instead of bronze I will bring you gold,
>   and silver in place of iron.
>   Instead of wood I will bring you bronze,
>   and iron in place of stones.
>   I will make peace your governor
>   and well-being your ruler.
¹⁸No longer will violence be heard in your land,
>   nor ruin or destruction within your borders,
>   but you will call your walls Salvation
>   and your gates Praise.
¹⁹The sun will no more be your light by day,
>   nor will the brightness of the moon shine on you,
>   for the Lord will be your everlasting light,
>   and your God will be your glory.
²⁰Your sun will never set again,
>   and your moon will wane no more;
>   the Lord will be your everlasting light,
>   and your days of sorrow will end.
²¹Then all your people will be righteous
>   and they will possess the land forever.
>   They are the shoot I have planted,
>   the work of my hands,
>   for the display of my splendor.
²²The least of you will become a thousand,
>   the smallest a mighty nation.
>   I am the Lord;
>   in its time I will do this swiftly."

THE YEAR OF THE LORD'S FAVOR

61 The Spirit of the Sovereign Lord is on me,
>   because the Lord has anointed me
>   to proclaim good news to the poor.
>   He has sent me to bind up the brokenhearted,
>   to proclaim freedom for the captives
>   and release from darkness for the prisoners,^a
> ²to proclaim the year of the Lord's favor
>   and the day of vengeance of our God,
>   to comfort all who mourn,
> ³   and provide for those who grieve in Zion—
>   to bestow on them a crown of beauty
>   instead of ashes,

What was the milk of nations? (60:16)
This was the salvation the Lord gave to his people.

^a 1 Hebrew; Septuagint *the blind*

the oil of joy
  instead of mourning,
and a garment of praise
  instead of a spirit of despair.
They will be called oaks of righteousness,
  a planting of the LORD
  for the display of his splendor.

⁴They will rebuild the ancient ruins
  and restore the places long devastated;
they will renew the ruined cities
  that have been devastated for generations.
⁵Strangers will shepherd your flocks;
  foreigners will work your fields and vineyards.
⁶And you will be called priests of the LORD,
  you will be named ministers of our God.
You will feed on the wealth of nations,
  and in their riches you will boast.

⁷Instead of your shame
  you will receive a double portion,
and instead of disgrace
  you will rejoice in your inheritance.
And so you will inherit a double portion in your land,
  and everlasting joy will be yours.

⁸"For I, the LORD, love justice;
  I hate robbery and wrongdoing.
In my faithfulness I will reward my people
  and make an everlasting covenant with them.
⁹Their descendants will be known among the nations
  and their offspring among the peoples.
All who see them will acknowledge
  that they are a people the LORD has blessed."

¹⁰I delight greatly in the LORD;
  my soul rejoices in my God.
For he has clothed me with garments of salvation
  and arrayed me in a robe of his righteousness,
as a bridegroom adorns his head like a priest,
  and as a bride adorns herself with her jewels.
¹¹For as the soil makes the sprout come up
  and a garden causes seeds to grow,
so the Sovereign LORD will make righteousness
  and praise spring up before all nations.

ZION'S NEW NAME

62 For Zion's sake I will not keep silent,
  for Jerusalem's sake I will not remain quiet,
till her vindication shines out like the dawn,
  her salvation like a blazing torch.
²The nations will see your vindication,
  and all kings your glory;
you will be called by a new name
  that the mouth of the LORD will bestow.
³You will be a crown of splendor in the LORD's hand,
  a royal diadem in the hand of your God.

How would oil replace ashes? (61:3)
Ashes were a sign of mourning. But olive oil represented joyous occasions, such as when kings were anointed. Their sadness would be turned to joy.

How did a bridegroom and a priest dress in similar ways? (61:10)
A bridegroom, like a priest, often wore a turban.

Why would their names be changed? (62:4)
The new names expressed happiness rather than sadness. Changing names was an excellent way of expressing a change in circumstances.

Who were these watchmen? (62:6)
These were probably the ones who were waiting for the messenger with good news (see 52:8). They would be praying that God would not be silent but would restore Jerusalem.

What were Edom and Bozrah? (63:1)
Edom was a region southeast of Israel. Bozrah was its capital. Here Edom symbolized a world that hated God's people.

What was a winepress? (63:2)
A winepress is used to make wine. People stand inside a large tub filled with grapes. They stomp on the grapes to squeeze out the juice. Feet and clothes were often stained from the juice.

⁴No longer will they call you Deserted,
  or name your land Desolate.
But you will be called Hephzibah,ᵃ
  and your land Beulahᵇ;
for the LORD will take delight in you,
  and your land will be married.
⁵As a young man marries a young woman,
  so will your Builder marry you;
as a bridegroom rejoices over his bride,
  so will your God rejoice over you.

⁶I have posted watchmen on your walls, Jerusalem;
  they will never be silent day or night.
You who call on the LORD,
  give yourselves no rest,
⁷and give him no rest till he establishes Jerusalem
  and makes her the praise of the earth.

⁸The LORD has sworn by his right hand
  and by his mighty arm:
"Never again will I give your grain
  as food for your enemies,
and never again will foreigners drink the new wine
  for which you have toiled;
⁹but those who harvest it will eat it
  and praise the LORD,
and those who gather the grapes will drink it
  in the courts of my sanctuary."

¹⁰Pass through, pass through the gates!
  Prepare the way for the people.
Build up, build up the highway!
  Remove the stones.
Raise a banner for the nations.

¹¹The LORD has made proclamation
  to the ends of the earth:
"Say to Daughter Zion,
  'See, your Savior comes!
See, his reward is with him,
  and his recompense accompanies him.'"
¹²They will be called the Holy People,
  the Redeemed of the LORD;
and you will be called Sought After,
  the City No Longer Deserted.

GOD'S DAY OF VENGEANCE AND REDEMPTION

63 Who is this coming from Edom,
  from Bozrah, with his garments stained crimson?
Who is this, robed in splendor,
  striding forward in the greatness of his strength?

"It is I, proclaiming victory,
  mighty to save."

²Why are your garments red,
  like those of one treading the winepress?

ᵃ 4 Hephzibah means *my delight is in her.*   ᵇ 4 Beulah means *married.*

³"I have trodden the winepress alone;
  from the nations no one was with me.
I trampled them in my anger
  and trod them down in my wrath;
their blood spattered my garments,
  and I stained all my clothing.
⁴It was for me the day of vengeance;
  the year for me to redeem had come.
⁵I looked, but there was no one to help,
  I was appalled that no one gave support;
so my own arm achieved salvation for me,
  and my own wrath sustained me.
⁶I trampled the nations in my anger;
  in my wrath I made them drunk
  and poured their blood on the ground."

PRAISE AND PRAYER

⁷I will tell of the kindnesses of the LORD,
  the deeds for which he is to be praised,
  according to all the LORD has done for us—
yes, the many good things
  he has done for Israel,
  according to his compassion and many kindnesses.
⁸He said, "Surely they are my people,
  children who will be true to me";
  and so he became their Savior.
⁹In all their distress he too was distressed,
  and the angel of his presence saved them.^a
In his love and mercy he redeemed them;
  he lifted them up and carried them
  all the days of old.
¹⁰Yet they rebelled
  and grieved his Holy Spirit.
So he turned and became their enemy
  and he himself fought against them.

¹¹Then his people recalled^b the days of old,
  the days of Moses and his people—
where is he who brought them through the sea,
  with the shepherd of his flock?
Where is he who set
  his Holy Spirit among them,
¹²who sent his glorious arm of power
  to be at Moses' right hand,
who divided the waters before them,
  to gain for himself everlasting renown,
¹³who led them through the depths?
Like a horse in open country,
  they did not stumble;
¹⁴like cattle that go down to the plain,
  they were given rest by the Spirit of the LORD.
This is how you guided your people
  to make for yourself a glorious name.

---

^a 9 Or Savior ⁹in their distress. / It was no envoy or angel / but his own presence
that saved them   ^b 11 Or But may he recall

A Winepress (63:3)

What does this passage refer to? (63:11–13)
This is a description of the Lord leading the Israelites out of Egypt through the Red Sea on dry ground.

¹⁵ Look down from heaven and see,
    from your lofty throne, holy and glorious.
  Where are your zeal and your might?
      Your tenderness and compassion are withheld
        from us.
¹⁶ But you are our Father,
      though Abraham does not know us
      or Israel acknowledge us;
    you, LORD, are our Father,
      our Redeemer from of old is your name.
¹⁷ Why, LORD, do you make us wander from
        your ways
      and harden our hearts so we do not revere you?
    Return for the sake of your servants,
      the tribes that are your inheritance.
¹⁸ For a little while your people possessed your
        holy place,
      but now our enemies have trampled down
        your sanctuary.
¹⁹ We are yours from of old;
      but you have not ruled over them,
      they have not been called*ᵃ* by your name.

64 ᵇ Oh, that you would rend the heavens and
        come down,
      that the mountains would tremble before you!
² As when fire sets twigs ablaze
      and causes water to boil,
    come down to make your name known to your
        enemies
      and cause the nations to quake before you!
³ For when you did awesome things that we did
        not expect,
      you came down, and the mountains trembled
        before you.
⁴ Since ancient times no one has heard,
      no ear has perceived,
    no eye has seen any God besides you,
      who acts on behalf of those who wait for him.
⁵ You come to the help of those who gladly do right,
      who remember your ways.
    But when we continued to sin against them,
      you were angry.
      How then can we be saved?
⁶ All of us have become like one who is unclean,
      and all our righteous acts are like filthy rags;
    we all shrivel up like a leaf,
      and like the wind our sins sweep us away.
⁷ No one calls on your name
      or strives to lay hold of you;
    for you have hidden your face from us
      and have given us over toᶜ our sins.

Did God make his people wander from him? (63:17)
God allowed his people the freedom to wander from him, but he certainly did not force them away from him. God never wants us to sin.

What does it mean to wait for the Lord? (64:4)
Waiting for God means to trust him and promise to serve him even when things are going badly. It means to have patient trust in God.

ᵃ 19 Or *We are like those you have never ruled, / like those never called*   *ᵇ* In Hebrew texts 64:1 is numbered 63:19b, and 64:2-12 is numbered 64:1-11.
ᶜ 7 Septuagint, Syriac and Targum; Hebrew *have made us melt because of*

⁸ Yet you, LORD, are our Father.
    We are the clay, you are the potter;
    we are all the work of your hand.
⁹ Do not be angry beyond measure, LORD;
    do not remember our sins forever.
  Oh, look on us, we pray,
    for we are all your people.
¹⁰ Your sacred cities have become a wasteland;
    even Zion is a wasteland, Jerusalem a desolation.
¹¹ Our holy and glorious temple, where our ancestors
        praised you,
    has been burned with fire,
    and all that we treasured lies in ruins.
¹² After all this, LORD, will you hold yourself back?
    Will you keep silent and punish us beyond
        measure?

JUDGMENT AND SALVATION

65 "I revealed myself to those who did not ask
        for me;
    I was found by those who did not seek me.
  To a nation that did not call on my name,
    I said, 'Here am I, here am I.'
² All day long I have held out my hands
    to an obstinate people,
  who walk in ways not good,
    pursuing their own imaginations—
³ a people who continually provoke me
    to my very face,
  offering sacrifices in gardens
    and burning incense on altars of brick;
⁴ who sit among the graves
    and spend their nights keeping secret vigil;
  who eat the flesh of pigs,
    and whose pots hold broth of impure meat;
⁵ who say, 'Keep away; don't come near me,
    for I am too sacred for you!'
  Such people are smoke in my nostrils,
    a fire that keeps burning all day.

⁶ "See, it stands written before me:
    I will not keep silent but will pay back in full;
    I will pay it back into their laps—
⁷ both your sins and the sins of your ancestors,"
    says the LORD.
  "Because they burned sacrifices on the mountains
    and defied me on the hills,
  I will measure into their laps
    the full payment for their former deeds."

⁸ This is what the LORD says:

  "As when juice is still found in a cluster of grapes
    and people say, 'Don't destroy it,
    there is still a blessing in it,'
  so will I do in behalf of my servants;
    I will not destroy them all.

What does the image of the potter suggest? (64:8)
The Bible often describes God as the potter who created his people. He is the artist, and we are his creation.

Why would people sit among graves? (65:4)
They may have sat among the graves in an attempt to contact the dead.

What were Sharon and the Valley of Achor? (65:10)
They were places on the extreme west and east of the land of Israel, so together they probably represented the whole country.

9 I will bring forth descendants from Jacob,
   and from Judah those who will possess
      my mountains;
my chosen people will inherit them,
   and there will my servants live.
10 Sharon will become a pasture for flocks,
   and the Valley of Achor a resting place for herds,
      for my people who seek me.

11 "But as for you who forsake the LORD
   and forget my holy mountain,
who spread a table for Fortune
   and fill bowls of mixed wine for Destiny,
12 I will destine you for the sword,
   and all of you will fall in the slaughter;
for I called but you did not answer,
   I spoke but you did not listen.
You did evil in my sight
   and chose what displeases me."

13 Therefore this is what the Sovereign LORD says:

"My servants will eat,
   but you will go hungry;
my servants will drink,
   but you will go thirsty;
my servants will rejoice,
   but you will be put to shame.
14 My servants will sing
   out of the joy of their hearts,
but you will cry out
   from anguish of heart
   and wail in brokenness of spirit.
15 You will leave your name
   for my chosen ones to use in their curses;
the Sovereign LORD will put you to death,
   but to his servants he will give another name.
16 Whoever invokes a blessing in the land
   will do so by the one true God;
whoever takes an oath in the land
   will swear by the one true God.
For the past troubles will be forgotten
   and hidden from my eyes.

NEW HEAVENS AND A NEW EARTH

17 "See, I will create
   new heavens and a new earth.
The former things will not be remembered,
   nor will they come to mind.
18 But be glad and rejoice forever
   in what I will create,
for I will create Jerusalem to be a delight
   and its people a joy.
19 I will rejoice over Jerusalem
   and take delight in my people;
the sound of weeping and of crying
   will be heard in it no more.

What were the new heavens and the new earth? (65:17)
This is talking about a time in the future when God grants his people salvation and everything will be transformed.

20 "Never again will there be in it
     an infant who lives but a few days,
     or an old man who does not live out his years;
   the one who dies at a hundred
     will be thought a mere child;
   the one who fails to reach^a a hundred
     will be considered accursed.
21 They will build houses and dwell in them;
     they will plant vineyards and eat their fruit.
22 No longer will they build houses and others live
         in them,
     or plant and others eat.
   For as the days of a tree,
     so will be the days of my people;
   my chosen ones will long enjoy
     the work of their hands.
23 They will not labor in vain,
     nor will they bear children doomed
         to misfortune;
   for they will be a people blessed by the Lord,
     they and their descendants with them.
24 Before they call I will answer;
     while they are still speaking I will hear.
25 The wolf and the lamb will feed together,
     and the lion will eat straw like the ox,
     and dust will be the serpent's food.
   They will neither harm nor destroy
     on all my holy mountain,"
                                          says the Lord.

JUDGMENT AND HOPE

66 This is what the Lord says:

   "Heaven is my throne,
     and the earth is my footstool.
   Where is the house you will build for me?
     Where will my resting place be?
2 Has not my hand made all these things,
     and so they came into being?"
                                      declares the Lord.

   "These are the ones I look on with favor:
     those who are humble and contrite in spirit,
     and who tremble at my word.
3 But whoever sacrifices a bull
     is like one who kills a person,
   and whoever offers a lamb
     is like one who breaks a dog's neck;
   whoever makes a grain offering
     is like one who presents pig's blood,
   and whoever burns memorial incense
     is like one who worships an idol.
   They have chosen their own ways,
     and they delight in their abominations;

---

^a 20 Or *the sinner who reaches*

What will life be like in the new kingdom? (65:20–25)
People will enjoy long life, their work will be blessed by the Lord, the Lord will hear their prayers, and there will be peace in the land.

Why were sacrifices criticized? (66:3)
Sacrifices were only acceptable to God if they were offered sincerely and with a pure heart. Sacrifices that were not sincere were as bad as offering unclean sacrifices.

⁴ so I also will choose harsh treatment for them
  and will bring on them what they dread.
For when I called, no one answered,
  when I spoke, no one listened.
They did evil in my sight
  and chose what displeases me."

⁵ Hear the word of the Lord,
  you who tremble at his word:
"Your own people who hate you,
  and exclude you because of my name,
    have said,
'Let the Lord be glorified,
  that we may see your joy!'
  Yet they will be put to shame.
⁶ Hear that uproar from the city,
  hear that noise from the temple!
It is the sound of the Lord
  repaying his enemies all they deserve.

⁷ "Before she goes into labor,
  she gives birth;
before the pains come upon her,
  she delivers a son.
⁸ Who has ever heard of such things?
  Who has ever seen things like this?
Can a country be born in a day
  or a nation be brought forth in a moment?
Yet no sooner is Zion in labor
  than she gives birth to her children.
⁹ Do I bring to the moment of birth
  and not give delivery?" says the Lord.
"Do I close up the womb
  when I bring to delivery?" says your God.
¹⁰ "Rejoice with Jerusalem and be glad for her,
  all you who love her;
rejoice greatly with her,
  all you who mourn over her.
¹¹ For you will nurse and be satisfied
  at her comforting breasts;
you will drink deeply
  and delight in her overflowing abundance."

¹² For this is what the Lord says:

"I will extend peace to her like a river,
  and the wealth of nations like a flooding stream;
you will nurse and be carried on her arm
  and dandled on her knees.
¹³ As a mother comforts her child,
  so will I comfort you;
and you will be comforted over Jerusalem."

¹⁴ When you see this, your heart will rejoice
  and you will flourish like grass;
the hand of the Lord will be made known to
    his servants,
  but his fury will be shown to his foes.

¹⁵ See, the LORD is coming with fire,
    and his chariots are like a whirlwind;
he will bring down his anger with fury,
    and his rebuke with flames of fire.
¹⁶ For with fire and with his sword
    the LORD will execute judgment on all people,
    and many will be those slain by the LORD.

¹⁷ "Those who consecrate and purify themselves to go into the gardens, following one who is among those who eat the flesh of pigs, rats and other unclean things—they will meet their end together with the one they follow," declares the LORD.

¹⁸ "And I, because of what they have planned and done, am about to come[a] and gather the people of all nations and languages, and they will come and see my glory.

¹⁹ "I will set a sign among them, and I will send some of those who survive to the nations—to Tarshish, to the Libyans[b] and Lydians (famous as archers), to Tubal and Greece, and to the distant islands that have not heard of my fame or seen my glory. They will proclaim my glory among the nations. ²⁰ And they will bring all your people, from all the nations, to my holy mountain in Jerusalem as an offering to the LORD—on horses, in chariots and wagons, and on mules and camels," says the LORD. "They will bring them, as the Israelites bring their grain offerings, to the temple of the LORD in ceremonially clean vessels. ²¹ And I will select some of them also to be priests and Levites," says the LORD.

²² "As the new heavens and the new earth that I make will endure before me," declares the LORD, "so will your name and descendants endure. ²³ From one New Moon to another and from one Sabbath to another, all mankind will come and bow down before me," says the LORD. ²⁴ "And they will go out and look on the dead bodies of those who rebelled against me; the worms that eat them will not die, the fire that burns them will not be quenched, and they will be loathsome to all mankind."

What do the images of whirlwind and fire suggest? (66:15–16)
These are images of God's judgment.

What were Tarshish, Libya, Lydia, Tubal, and Greece? (66:19)
These various locations taken together represented the entire world. God would send the news of his glory to all the earth.

What did it mean that the worms would not die and the fire would not be quenched? (66:24)
There would be eternal torment for those who did not follow God. Worms and fire usually consumed corpses rather quickly, but in this case the decay and destruction would last forever.

---

[a] 18 The meaning of the Hebrew for this clause is uncertain.   [b] 19 Some Septuagint manuscripts Put (Libyans); Hebrew Pul

Jeremiah

INTRODUCTION

Who wrote this book?	The prophet Jeremiah.
Why was this book written?	God intended to use Babylon to punish Judah's sin. Jeremiah urged the king and people to surrender to Babylon.
What is special about this book?	Jeremiah is faithful to God even though the people of Judah mock and hate him. Jeremiah prophesies that one day God will forgive and restore his people.

What chapters tell about Jeremiah's experiences?		
	God calls Jeremiah	Jeremiah 1
	Jeremiah is beaten	Jeremiah 20
	Jeremiah is threatened	Jeremiah 26
	Jeremiah and a false prophet	Jeremiah 28
	Jeremiah buys a field	Jeremiah 32
	Jeremiah in a cistern	Jeremiah 38
	Jeremiah is set free	Jeremiah 40

What are some important chapters in this book?		
	The wickedness of Judah	Jeremiah 5
	God and idols	Jeremiah 10
	False prophets	Jeremiah 23
	God's lasting love	Jeremiah 31
	A family that obeyed God	Jeremiah 35
	God's future punishment	Jeremiah 51

When did these things happen?

1300 BC 1200 1100 1000 900 800 700 600 500 400

DIVISION OF THE KINGDOM (930 BC)	
MINISTRIES OF ELIJAH AND ELISHA IN ISRAEL (C. 875 – 797 BC)	
MINISTRIES OF AMOS AND HOSEA IN ISRAEL (C. 760 – 715 BC)	
MINISTRIES OF MICAH AND ISAIAH IN JUDAH (C. 740 – 681 BC)	
EXILE OF ISRAEL (722 BC)	
JEREMIAH'S MINISTRY IN JUDAH (C. 626 – 585 BC)	
FALL OF JERUSALEM (586 BC)	
BOOK OF JEREMIAH WRITTEN (C. 585 – 580 BC)	

1 The words of Jeremiah son of Hilkiah, one of the priests at Anathoth in the territory of Benjamin. ²The word of the LORD came to him in the thirteenth year of the reign of Josiah son of Amon king of Judah, ³and through the reign of Jehoiakim son of Josiah king of Judah, down to the fifth month of the eleventh year of Zedekiah son of Josiah king of Judah, when the people of Jerusalem went into exile.

THE CALL OF JEREMIAH

⁴The word of the LORD came to me, saying,

⁵"Before I formed you in the womb I knew*a* you,
    before you were born I set you apart;
    I appointed you as a prophet to the nations."

⁶"Alas, Sovereign LORD," I said, "I do not know how to speak; I am too young."

⁷But the LORD said to me, "Do not say, 'I am too young.' You must go to everyone I send you to and say whatever I command you. ⁸Do not be afraid of them, for I am with you and will rescue you," declares the LORD.

⁹Then the LORD reached out his hand and touched my mouth and said to me, "I have put my words in your mouth. ¹⁰See, today I appoint you over nations and kingdoms to uproot and tear down, to destroy and overthrow, to build and to plant."

¹¹The word of the LORD came to me: "What do you see, Jeremiah?"

"I see the branch of an almond tree," I replied.

¹²The LORD said to me, "You have seen correctly, for I am watching*b* to see that my word is fulfilled."

¹³The word of the LORD came to me again: "What do you see?"

"I see a pot that is boiling," I answered. "It is tilting toward us from the north."

¹⁴The LORD said to me, "From the north disaster will be poured out on all who live in the land. ¹⁵I am about to summon all the peoples of the northern kingdoms," declares the LORD.

"Their kings will come and set up their thrones
    in the entrance of the gates of Jerusalem;
they will come against all her surrounding walls
    and against all the towns of Judah.
¹⁶I will pronounce my judgments on my people
    because of their wickedness in forsaking me,
in burning incense to other gods
    and in worshiping what their hands have made.

¹⁷"Get yourself ready! Stand up and say to them whatever I command you. Do not be terrified by them, or I will terrify you before them. ¹⁸Today I have made you a fortified city, an iron pillar and a bronze wall to stand against the whole land—against the kings of Judah, its officials, its priests and the people of the land. ¹⁹They will fight against you but will not overcome you, for I am with you and will rescue you," declares the LORD.

---

a 5 Or *chose*   *b* 12 The Hebrew for *watching* sounds like the Hebrew for *almond tree.*

How did Jeremiah respond when God called him to be a prophet? (1:6)
He claimed to be too young to be qualified to speak for the Lord. God rejected his excuse.

What were the northern kingdoms? (1:15)
This is probably a reference to Babylon and its allies.

What do the images of a fortified city, an iron pillar, and a bronze wall represent? (1:18)
These are word pictures that suggest strength and security. God would give Jeremiah the ability to withstand abuse and persecution.

ISRAEL FORSAKES GOD

2 The word of the Lord came to me: [2]"Go and proclaim in the hearing of Jerusalem:

"This is what the Lord says:

"'I remember the devotion of your youth,
    how as a bride you loved me
and followed me through the wilderness,
    through a land not sown.
[3] Israel was holy to the Lord,
    the firstfruits of his harvest;
all who devoured her were held guilty,
    and disaster overtook them,'"

declares the Lord.

[4] Hear the word of the Lord, you descendants
        of Jacob,
    all you clans of Israel.

[5] This is what the Lord says:

"What fault did your ancestors find in me,
    that they strayed so far from me?
They followed worthless idols
    and became worthless themselves.
[6] They did not ask, 'Where is the Lord,
    who brought us up out of Egypt
and led us through the barren wilderness,
    through a land of deserts and ravines,
a land of drought and utter darkness,
    a land where no one travels and no one lives?'
[7] I brought you into a fertile land
    to eat its fruit and rich produce.
But you came and defiled my land
    and made my inheritance detestable.
[8] The priests did not ask,
    'Where is the Lord?'
Those who deal with the law did not know me;
    the leaders rebelled against me.
The prophets prophesied by Baal,
    following worthless idols.

[9] "Therefore I bring charges against you again,"

declares the Lord.

    "And I will bring charges against your children's
        children.
[10] Cross over to the coasts of Cyprus and look,
    send to Kedar[a] and observe closely;
    see if there has ever been anything like this:
[11] Has a nation ever changed its gods?
    (Yet they are not gods at all.)
But my people have exchanged their glorious God
    for worthless idols.
[12] Be appalled at this, you heavens,
    and shudder with great horror,"

declares the Lord.

How was Israel holy? (2:3)
Israel was set apart by God for a special purpose — to be the nation through which other nations would be blessed. Like the firstfruits for an offering, Israel would be first in line to receive God's blessings.

Why were the people drawn to worshiping idols? (2:8, 27)
They may have believed that a different god lived inside each idol. But they also may have worshiped Assyrian gods to stay on good terms with the Assyrians.

---

a 10 In the Syro-Arabian desert

¹³ "My people have committed two sins:
　They have forsaken me,
　　the spring of living water,
　and have dug their own cisterns,
　　broken cisterns that cannot hold water.
¹⁴ Is Israel a servant, a slave by birth?
　Why then has he become plunder?
¹⁵ Lions have roared;
　they have growled at him.
　They have laid waste his land;
　　his towns are burned and deserted.
¹⁶ Also, the men of Memphis and Tahpanhes
　have cracked your skull.
¹⁷ Have you not brought this on yourselves
　　by forsaking the LORD your God
　　when he led you in the way?
¹⁸ Now why go to Egypt
　　to drink water from the Nile*?
　And why go to Assyria
　　to drink water from the Euphrates?
¹⁹ Your wickedness will punish you;
　your backsliding will rebuke you.
　Consider then and realize
　　how evil and bitter it is for you
　when you forsake the LORD your God
　　and have no awe of me,"
　　　　　　　　declares the Lord, the LORD Almighty.

²⁰ "Long ago you broke off your yoke
　　and tore off your bonds;
　　you said, 'I will not serve you!'
　Indeed, on every high hill
　　and under every spreading tree
　　you lay down as a prostitute.
²¹ I had planted you like a choice vine
　　of sound and reliable stock.
　How then did you turn against me
　　into a corrupt, wild vine?
²² Although you wash yourself with soap
　　and use an abundance of cleansing powder,
　　the stain of your guilt is still before me,"
　　　　　　　　declares the Sovereign LORD.
²³ "How can you say, 'I am not defiled;
　I have not run after the Baals'?
　See how you behaved in the valley;
　　consider what you have done.
　You are a swift she-camel
　　running here and there,
²⁴ a wild donkey accustomed to the desert,
　　sniffing the wind in her craving—
　　in her heat who can restrain her?
　Any males that pursue her need not tire
　　　　themselves;
　　at mating time they will find her.

ᵃ *18* Hebrew *Shihor*; that is, a branch of the Nile

**What was the significance
of high hills and spreading
trees? (2:20)**
These were the locations of
pagan worship.

**What were cleansing
powder and soap? (2:22)**
These were mineral alkali and
vegetable alkali (a salt found
in the ashes of plants) used for
washing. This verse says that
sins can be removed only when
the sinner repents.

²⁵ Do not run until your feet are bare
　　　and your throat is dry.
　　But you said, 'It's no use!
　　　I love foreign gods,
　　　and I must go after them.'

²⁶ "As a thief is disgraced when he is caught,
　　　so the people of Israel are disgraced—
　　they, their kings and their officials,
　　　their priests and their prophets.
²⁷ They say to wood, 'You are my father,'
　　　and to stone, 'You gave me birth.'
　　They have turned their backs to me
　　　and not their faces;
　　yet when they are in trouble, they say,
　　　'Come and save us!'

²⁸ Where then are the gods you made for yourselves?
　　　Let them come if they can save you
　　　when you are in trouble!
　　For you, Judah, have as many gods
　　　as you have towns.

²⁹ "Why do you bring charges against me?
　　　You have all rebelled against me,"
　　　　　　　　　　declares the Lord.

³⁰ "In vain I punished your people;
　　　they did not respond to correction.
　　Your sword has devoured your prophets
　　　like a ravenous lion.

³¹ "You of this generation, consider the word of the Lord:

　　"Have I been a desert to Israel
　　　or a land of great darkness?
　　Why do my people say, 'We are free to roam;
　　　we will come to you no more'?
³² Does a young woman forget her jewelry,
　　　a bride her wedding ornaments?
　　Yet my people have forgotten me,
　　　days without number.
³³ How skilled you are at pursuing love!
　　　Even the worst of women can learn from your ways.
³⁴ On your clothes is found
　　　the lifeblood of the innocent poor,
　　　though you did not catch them breaking in.
　　Yet in spite of all this
³⁵ 　you say, 'I am innocent;
　　　he is not angry with me.'
　　But I will pass judgment on you
　　　because you say, 'I have not sinned.'
³⁶ Why do you go about so much,
　　　changing your ways?
　　You will be disappointed by Egypt
　　　as you were by Assyria.
³⁷ You will also leave that place
　　　with your hands on your head,
　　for the Lord has rejected those you trust;
　　　you will not be helped by them.

What did it mean that they had as many gods as they had towns? (2:28)
Every ancient town of any importance had its own patron deity, and many towns were named after their gods.

3 "If a man divorces his wife
and she leaves him and marries another man,
should he return to her again?
        Would not the land be completely defiled?
But you have lived as a prostitute with many lovers—
        would you now return to me?"

declares the Lord.

² "Look up to the barren heights and see.
        Is there any place where you have not been ravished?
By the roadside you sat waiting for lovers,
        sat like a nomad in the desert.
You have defiled the land
        with your prostitution and wickedness.
³ Therefore the showers have been withheld,
        and no spring rains have fallen.
Yet you have the brazen look of a prostitute;
        you refuse to blush with shame.
⁴ Have you not just called to me:
        'My Father, my friend from my youth,
⁵ will you always be angry?
        Will your wrath continue forever?'
This is how you talk,
        but you do all the evil you can."

UNFAITHFUL ISRAEL

⁶ During the reign of King Josiah, the Lord said to me, "Have you seen what faithless Israel has done? She has gone up on every high hill and under every spreading tree and has committed adultery there. ⁷ I thought that after she had done all this she would return to me but she did not, and her unfaithful sister Judah saw it. ⁸ I gave faithless Israel her certificate of divorce and sent her away because of all her adulteries. Yet I saw that her unfaithful sister Judah had no fear; she also went out and committed adultery. ⁹ Because Israel's immorality mattered so little to her, she defiled the land and committed adultery with stone and wood. ¹⁰ In spite of all this, her unfaithful sister Judah did not return to me with all her heart, but only in pretense," declares the Lord.

¹¹ The Lord said to me, "Faithless Israel is more righteous than unfaithful Judah. ¹² Go, proclaim this message toward the north:

"'Return, faithless Israel,' declares the Lord,
        'I will frown on you no longer,
for I am faithful,' declares the Lord,
        'I will not be angry forever.
¹³ Only acknowledge your guilt—
        you have rebelled against the Lord your God,
you have scattered your favors to foreign gods
        under every spreading tree,
        and have not obeyed me,'"

declares the Lord.

¹⁴ "Return, faithless people," declares the Lord, "for I am your husband. I will choose you—one from a town and two from a clan—and bring you to Zion. ¹⁵ Then I will give you shepherds after my own heart, who will lead you with

How was Judah like an unfaithful wife? (3:1)
Judah had turned away from God in order to worship other gods, almost like a wife who runs away from her husband with another man.

Why was Israel more righteous than Judah? (3:11)
Both Israel and Judah had rejected the Lord, but Judah's sin was worse. Judah should have looked to Israel as an example of what could happen if they were to turn away from God; however they chose to ignore Israel's example and the prophets God sent to preach to them.

Who were these shepherds? (3:15)
Throughout the ancient world, rulers were often referred to as shepherds.

What did God mean when he said people will no longer remember "the ark of the covenant of the LORD"? (3:16)
God was prophesying by telling of a time when Jesus would die for the sins of his people. Then the gap between God and his believers will no longer exist. The ark will no longer be important because God will live with his people.

knowledge and understanding. ¹⁶In those days, when your numbers have increased greatly in the land," declares the LORD, "people will no longer say, 'The ark of the covenant of the LORD.' It will never enter their minds or be remembered; it will not be missed, nor will another one be made. ¹⁷At that time they will call Jerusalem The Throne of the LORD, and all nations will gather in Jerusalem to honor the name of the LORD. No longer will they follow the stubbornness of their evil hearts. ¹⁸In those days the people of Judah will join the people of Israel, and together they will come from a northern land to the land I gave your ancestors as an inheritance.

¹⁹"I myself said,

"'How gladly would I treat you like my children
    and give you a pleasant land,
    the most beautiful inheritance of any nation.'
I thought you would call me 'Father'
    and not turn away from following me.
²⁰But like a woman unfaithful to her husband,
    so you, Israel, have been unfaithful to me,"
                                        declares the LORD.

²¹A cry is heard on the barren heights,
    the weeping and pleading of the people of Israel,
because they have perverted their ways
    and have forgotten the LORD their God.

Was God willing to accept his people if they returned to him? (3:22)
Yes. God urged his people to repent and turn back to him, and he promised them blessings if they did.

²²"Return, faithless people;
    I will cure you of backsliding."

"Yes, we will come to you,
    for you are the LORD our God.
²³Surely the idolatrous commotion on the hills
    and mountains is a deception;
surely in the LORD our God
    is the salvation of Israel.
²⁴From our youth shameful gods have consumed
    the fruits of our ancestors' labor—
their flocks and herds,
    their sons and daughters.
²⁵Let us lie down in our shame,
    and let our disgrace cover us.
We have sinned against the LORD our God,
    both we and our ancestors;
from our youth till this day
    we have not obeyed the LORD our God."

4 "If you, Israel, will return,
    then return to me,"
                                        declares the LORD.
"If you put your detestable idols out of my sight
    and no longer go astray,
²and if in a truthful, just and righteous way
    you swear, 'As surely as the LORD lives,'
then the nations will invoke blessings by him
    and in him they will boast."

³This is what the LORD says to the people of Judah and to Jerusalem:

"Break up your unplowed ground
    and do not sow among thorns.
⁴Circumcise yourselves to the LORD,
    circumcise your hearts,
    you people of Judah and inhabitants of Jerusalem,
or my wrath will flare up and burn like fire
    because of the evil you have done—
    burn with no one to quench it.

DISASTER FROM THE NORTH

⁵"Announce in Judah and proclaim in Jerusalem and say:
    'Sound the trumpet throughout the land!'
Cry aloud and say:
    'Gather together!
    Let us flee to the fortified cities!'
⁶Raise the signal to go to Zion!
    Flee for safety without delay!
For I am bringing disaster from the north,
    even terrible destruction."

⁷A lion has come out of his lair;
    a destroyer of nations has set out.
He has left his place
    to lay waste your land.
Your towns will lie in ruins
    without inhabitant.
⁸So put on sackcloth,
    lament and wail,
for the fierce anger of the LORD
    has not turned away from us.

⁹"In that day," declares the LORD,
    "the king and the officials will lose heart,
the priests will be horrified,
    and the prophets will be appalled."

¹⁰Then I said, "Alas, Sovereign LORD! How completely you have deceived this people and Jerusalem by saying, 'You will have peace,' when the sword is at our throats!"

¹¹At that time this people and Jerusalem will be told, "A scorching wind from the barren heights in the desert blows toward my people, but not to winnow or cleanse; ¹²a wind too strong for that comes from me. Now I pronounce my judgments against them."

¹³Look! He advances like the clouds,
    his chariots come like a whirlwind,
his horses are swifter than eagles.
    Woe to us! We are ruined!
¹⁴Jerusalem, wash the evil from your heart and be saved.
    How long will you harbor wicked thoughts?
¹⁵A voice is announcing from Dan,
    proclaiming disaster from the hills of Ephraim.
¹⁶"Tell this to the nations,
    proclaim concerning Jerusalem:
'A besieging army is coming from a distant land,
    raising a war cry against the cities of Judah.

What did it mean to "circumcise your hearts"? (4:4)
This was a way of saying that the people needed to cut the sinful behaviors from their lives that negatively affected their spiritual growth.

What did the trumpet announce? (4:5)
The trumpet was usually made of a ram's or bull's horn. When it was sounded, people would take refuge in the nearest walled town in order to avoid capture by the enemy.

What was the invasion from the north? (4:6–7)
This pointed to the invasion by Babylon. The lion was a symbol of Babylon, referred to here as a destroyer.

What was sackcloth? (4:8)
This was coarse fabric that was worn when people were mourning to serve as a constant reminder of their sadness.

What was this scorching wind? (4:11)
This refers to the sirocco or khamsin, a hot, dry wind that carried with it a great deal of sand and dust. God's judgment would be like a destructive wind that would sweep away everything in its path.

¹⁷They surround her like men guarding a field,
   because she has rebelled against me,'"
                              declares the LORD.

¹⁸"Your own conduct and actions
      have brought this on you.
   This is your punishment.
      How bitter it is!
      How it pierces to the heart!"

¹⁹Oh, my anguish, my anguish!
      I writhe in pain.
   Oh, the agony of my heart!
      My heart pounds within me,
      I cannot keep silent.
   For I have heard the sound of the trumpet;
      I have heard the battle cry.
²⁰Disaster follows disaster;
      the whole land lies in ruins.
   In an instant my tents are destroyed,
      my shelter in a moment.
²¹How long must I see the battle standard
      and hear the sound of the trumpet?

²²"My people are fools;
      they do not know me.
   They are senseless children;
      they have no understanding.
   They are skilled in doing evil;
      they know not how to do good."

²³I looked at the earth,
      and it was formless and empty;
   and at the heavens,
      and their light was gone.
²⁴I looked at the mountains,
      and they were quaking;
   all the hills were swaying.
²⁵I looked, and there were no people;
      every bird in the sky had flown away.
²⁶I looked, and the fruitful land was a desert;
      all its towns lay in ruins
   before the LORD, before his fierce anger.

²⁷This is what the LORD says:

   "The whole land will be ruined,
      though I will not destroy it completely.
²⁸Therefore the earth will mourn
      and the heavens above grow dark,
   because I have spoken and will not relent,
      I have decided and will not turn back."

²⁹At the sound of horsemen and archers
      every town takes to flight.
   Some go into the thickets;
      some climb up among the rocks.
   All the towns are deserted;
      no one lives in them.

Why was the prophet in anguish? (4:19)
Jeremiah loved the people of Judah, and it was painful for him to have to tell them that they were going to suffer.

30 What are you doing, you devastated one?
    Why dress yourself in scarlet
    and put on jewels of gold?
Why highlight your eyes with makeup?
    You adorn yourself in vain.
Your lovers despise you;
    they want to kill you.

31 I hear a cry as of a woman in labor,
    a groan as of one bearing her first child—
the cry of Daughter Zion gasping for breath,
    stretching out her hands and saying,
"Alas! I am fainting;
    my life is given over to murderers."

NOT ONE IS UPRIGHT

5 "Go up and down the streets of Jerusalem,
    look around and consider,
    search through her squares.
If you can find but one person
    who deals honestly and seeks the truth,
    I will forgive this city.
2 Although they say, 'As surely as the Lord lives,'
    still they are swearing falsely."

3 Lord, do not your eyes look for truth?
    You struck them, but they felt no pain;
    you crushed them, but they refused correction.
They made their faces harder than stone
    and refused to repent.
4 I thought, "These are only the poor;
    they are foolish,
for they do not know the way of the Lord,
    the requirements of their God.
5 So I will go to the leaders
    and speak to them;
surely they know the way of the Lord,
    the requirements of their God."
But with one accord they too had broken off
    the yoke
    and torn off the bonds.
6 Therefore a lion from the forest will
    attack them,
    a wolf from the desert will ravage them,
a leopard will lie in wait near their towns
    to tear to pieces any who venture out,
for their rebellion is great
    and their backslidings many.

7 "Why should I forgive you?
    Your children have forsaken me
    and sworn by gods that are not gods.
I supplied all their needs,
    yet they committed adultery
    and thronged to the houses of prostitutes.
8 They are well-fed, lusty stallions,
    each neighing for another man's wife.

What did God's challenge represent? (5:1)
It was similar to Abraham bargaining with God to spare Sodom and Gomorrah. There were some righteous people in Jerusalem, but God was making the point that there were very few of them.

Why would the lion, wolf, and leopard attack the people? (5:6)
This attack by wild animals was symbolic of the punishment the people would receive for turning away from God.

How were the people compared to unfaithful spouses? (5:7–8)
Instead of keeping their vows to God, they turned away from him. They were like a husband who leaves his wife to take up with a prostitute. In effect, they had committed adultery with other gods.

⁹ Should I not punish them for this?"
       declares the LORD.
"Should I not avenge myself
       on such a nation as this?

¹⁰ "Go through her vineyards and ravage them,
       but do not destroy them completely.
Strip off her branches,
       for these people do not belong to the LORD.
¹¹ The people of Israel and the people of Judah
       have been utterly unfaithful to me,"
                                   declares the LORD.

¹² They have lied about the LORD;
       they said, "He will do nothing!
No harm will come to us;
       we will never see sword or famine.
¹³ The prophets are but wind
       and the word is not in them;
       so let what they say be done to them."

¹⁴ Therefore this is what the LORD God Almighty says:

"Because the people have spoken these words,
       I will make my words in your mouth a fire
       and these people the wood it consumes.
¹⁵ People of Israel," declares the LORD,
       "I am bringing a distant nation against you—
an ancient and enduring nation,
       a people whose language you do not know,
       whose speech you do not understand.
¹⁶ Their quivers are like an open grave;
       all of them are mighty warriors.
¹⁷ They will devour your harvests and food,
       devour your sons and daughters;
they will devour your flocks and herds,
       devour your vines and fig trees.
With the sword they will destroy
       the fortified cities in which you trust.

¹⁸ "Yet even in those days," declares the LORD, "I will not destroy you completely. ¹⁹ And when the people ask, 'Why has the LORD our God done all this to us?' you will tell them, 'As you have forsaken me and served foreign gods in your own land, so now you will serve foreigners in a land not your own.'

²⁰ "Announce this to the descendants of Jacob
       and proclaim it in Judah:
²¹ Hear this, you foolish and senseless people,
       who have eyes but do not see,
       who have ears but do not hear:
²² Should you not fear me?" declares the LORD.
       "Should you not tremble in my presence?
I made the sand a boundary for the sea,
       an everlasting barrier it cannot cross.
The waves may roll, but they cannot prevail;
       they may roar, but they cannot cross it.

In what other ways did the people turn from God? (5:12–13)
They ignored the warnings of the prophets and didn't take them seriously.

What distant nation would punish Judah? (5:15)
This was the nation of Babylon, which had a history of more than 2,000 years.

23 But these people have stubborn and rebellious hearts;
  they have turned aside and gone away.
24 They do not say to themselves,
  'Let us fear the LORD our God,
who gives autumn and spring rains in season,
  who assures us of the regular weeks of harvest.'
25 Your wrongdoings have kept these away;
  your sins have deprived you of good.

26 "Among my people are the wicked
  who lie in wait like men who snare birds
  and like those who set traps to catch people.
27 Like cages full of birds,
  their houses are full of deceit;
they have become rich and powerful
28   and have grown fat and sleek.
Their evil deeds have no limit;
  they do not seek justice.
They do not promote the case of the fatherless;
  they do not defend the just cause of the poor.
29 Should I not punish them for this?"
  declares the LORD.
"Should I not avenge myself
  on such a nation as this?

30 "A horrible and shocking thing
  has happened in the land:
31 The prophets prophesy lies,
  the priests rule by their own authority,
and my people love it this way.
  But what will you do in the end?

JERUSALEM UNDER SIEGE

6 "Flee for safety, people of Benjamin!
  Flee from Jerusalem!
Sound the trumpet in Tekoa!
  Raise the signal over Beth Hakkerem!
For disaster looms out of the north,
  even terrible destruction.
2 I will destroy Daughter Zion,
  so beautiful and delicate.
3 Shepherds with their flocks will come against her;
  they will pitch their tents around her,
  each tending his own portion."

4 "Prepare for battle against her!
  Arise, let us attack at noon!
But, alas, the daylight is fading,
  and the shadows of evening grow long.
5 So arise, let us attack at night
  and destroy her fortresses!"

6 This is what the LORD Almighty says:

"Cut down the trees
  and build siege ramps against Jerusalem.
This city must be punished;
  it is filled with oppression.

How did the image of trapping birds paint a picture of the rich? (5:26–29)
In ancient times, people would lure wild birds into a trap by placing tame birds inside a cage. In a way, the rich did this by setting traps for the poor to snare even more wealth for themselves.

Why would the army attack at noon? (6:4)
This would create an element of surprise, because the usual time to attack was early in the morning.

What were siege ramps? (6:6)
These were wheeled ramps that helped an invading army bring battering rams into position and scale the walls of the city.

⁷As a well pours out its water,
  so she pours out her wickedness.
Violence and destruction resound in her;
  her sickness and wounds are ever before me.
⁸Take warning, Jerusalem,
  or I will turn away from you
and make your land desolate
  so no one can live in it."

⁹This is what the LORD Almighty says:

"Let them glean the remnant of Israel
  as thoroughly as a vine;
pass your hand over the branches again,
  like one gathering grapes."

¹⁰To whom can I speak and give warning?
  Who will listen to me?
Their ears are closed[a]
  so they cannot hear.
The word of the LORD is offensive to them;
  they find no pleasure in it.
¹¹But I am full of the wrath of the LORD,
  and I cannot hold it in.

"Pour it out on the children in the street
  and on the young men gathered together;
both husband and wife will be caught in it,
  and the old, those weighed down with years.
¹²Their houses will be turned over to others,
  together with their fields and their wives,
when I stretch out my hand
  against those who live in the land,"
                    declares the LORD.
¹³"From the least to the greatest,
  all are greedy for gain;
prophets and priests alike,
  all practice deceit.
¹⁴They dress the wound of my people
  as though it were not serious.
'Peace, peace,' they say,
  when there is no peace.
¹⁵Are they ashamed of their detestable conduct?
  No, they have no shame at all;
  they do not even know how to blush.
So they will fall among the fallen;
  they will be brought down when
    I punish them,"
                    says the LORD.

¹⁶This is what the LORD says:

"Stand at the crossroads and look;
  ask for the ancient paths,
ask where the good way is, and walk in it,
  and you will find rest for your souls.
But you said, 'We will not walk in it.'

What was the message of these prophets? (6:14)
These false religious leaders ignored the sins of the people and promised a peaceful future even though God was about to punish them for their sins.

What were the ancient paths? (6:16)
Judah's ancestors had followed the Lord's commands and walked in his ways. If the people had followed this path, they would have found rest for their souls.

---

a 10 Hebrew *uncircumcised*

¹⁷ I appointed watchmen over you and said,
  'Listen to the sound of the trumpet!'
  But you said, 'We will not listen.'
¹⁸ Therefore hear, you nations;
  you who are witnesses,
  observe what will happen to them.
¹⁹ Hear, you earth:
  I am bringing disaster on this people,
  the fruit of their schemes,
  because they have not listened to my words
  and have rejected my law.
²⁰ What do I care about incense from Sheba
  or sweet calamus from a distant land?
  Your burnt offerings are not acceptable;
  your sacrifices do not please me."

²¹ Therefore this is what the LORD says:

  "I will put obstacles before this people.
  Parents and children alike will stumble over them;
  neighbors and friends will perish."

²² This is what the LORD says:

  "Look, an army is coming
  from the land of the north;
  a great nation is being stirred up
  from the ends of the earth.
²³ They are armed with bow and spear;
  they are cruel and show no mercy.
  They sound like the roaring sea
  as they ride on their horses;
  they come like men in battle formation
  to attack you, Daughter Zion."

²⁴ We have heard reports about them,
  and our hands hang limp.
  Anguish has gripped us,
  pain like that of a woman in labor.
²⁵ Do not go out to the fields
  or walk on the roads,
  for the enemy has a sword,
  and there is terror on every side.
²⁶ Put on sackcloth, my people,
  and roll in ashes;
  mourn with bitter wailing
  as for an only son,
  for suddenly the destroyer
  will come upon us.

²⁷ "I have made you a tester of metals
  and my people the ore,
  that you may observe
  and test their ways.
²⁸ They are all hardened rebels,
  going about to slander.
  They are bronze and iron;
  they all act corruptly.

What was calamus? (6:20)
Calamus was a reed-like plant said to have grown in the valley of Lebanon. The sweet-smelling oil obtained from crushing its stalk was used in incense offerings and for anointing.

²⁹The bellows blow fiercely
　　to burn away the lead with fire,
but the refining goes on in vain;
　　the wicked are not purged out.
³⁰They are called rejected silver,
　　because the LORD has rejected them."

FALSE RELIGION WORTHLESS

7 This is the word that came to Jeremiah from the LORD:
² "Stand at the gate of the LORD's house and there proclaim this message:

"'Hear the word of the LORD, all you people of Judah who come through these gates to worship the LORD. ³This is what the LORD Almighty, the God of Israel, says: Reform your ways and your actions, and I will let you live in this place. ⁴Do not trust in deceptive words and say, "This is the temple of the LORD, the temple of the LORD, the temple of the LORD!" ⁵If you really change your ways and your actions and deal with each other justly, ⁶if you do not oppress the foreigner, the fatherless or the widow and do not shed innocent blood in this place, and if you do not follow other gods to your own harm, ⁷then I will let you live in this place, in the land I gave your ancestors for ever and ever. ⁸But look, you are trusting in deceptive words that are worthless.

⁹"'Will you steal and murder, commit adultery and perjury,[a] burn incense to Baal and follow other gods you have not known, ¹⁰and then come and stand before me in this house, which bears my Name, and say, "We are safe"—safe to do all these detestable things? ¹¹Has this house, which bears my Name, become a den of robbers to you? But I have been watching! declares the LORD.

¹²"'Go now to the place in Shiloh where I first made a dwelling for my Name, and see what I did to it because of the wickedness of my people Israel. ¹³While you were doing all these things, declares the LORD, I spoke to you again and again, but you did not listen; I called you, but you did not answer. ¹⁴Therefore, what I did to Shiloh I will now do to the house that bears my Name, the temple you trust in, the place I gave to you and your ancestors. ¹⁵I will thrust you from my presence, just as I did all your fellow Israelites, the people of Ephraim.'

¹⁶"So do not pray for this people nor offer any plea or petition for them; do not plead with me, for I will not listen to you. ¹⁷Do you not see what they are doing in the towns of Judah and in the streets of Jerusalem? ¹⁸The children gather wood, the fathers light the fire, and the women knead the dough and make cakes to offer to the Queen of Heaven. They pour out drink offerings to other gods to arouse my anger. ¹⁹But am I the one they are provoking? declares the LORD. Are they not rather harming themselves, to their own shame?

²⁰"'Therefore this is what the Sovereign LORD says: My anger and my wrath will be poured out on this place—on man and beast, on the trees of the field and on the crops of your land—and it will burn and not be quenched.

Why preach at the temple gate? (7:1–2)
Worshipers had to go through the gate to get to the activities in the temple court. This would be a good place to capture people's attention and remind them of their need for repentance.

What were the deceptive words that some prophets spoke? (7:4)
They claimed that God would not allow Jerusalem to be destroyed because it was the site of God's holy temple.

What had happened in Shiloh? (7:12)
This was the place where Samuel served in the temple (1 Samuel 1:24–28), and it was the location of the tabernacle after the conquest of Canaan. It had probably been destroyed by the Assyrian army about 100 years earlier.

Who was the Queen of Heaven? (7:18)
This describes Ishtar, the Babylonian goddess of love, sex, and fertility.

---

a 9 Or and swear by false gods

²¹"'This is what the LORD Almighty, the God of Israel, says: Go ahead, add your burnt offerings to your other sacrifices and eat the meat yourselves! ²²For when I brought your ancestors out of Egypt and spoke to them, I did not just give them commands about burnt offerings and sacrifices, ²³but I gave them this command: Obey me, and I will be your God and you will be my people. Walk in obedience to all I command you, that it may go well with you. ²⁴But they did not listen or pay attention; instead, they followed the stubborn inclinations of their evil hearts. They went backward and not forward. ²⁵From the time your ancestors left Egypt until now, day after day, again and again I sent you my servants the prophets. ²⁶But they did not listen to me or pay attention. They were stiff-necked and did more evil than their ancestors.'

²⁷"When you tell them all this, they will not listen to you; when you call to them, they will not answer. ²⁸Therefore say to them, 'This is the nation that has not obeyed the LORD its God or responded to correction. Truth has perished; it has vanished from their lips.

²⁹"'Cut off your hair and throw it away; take up a lament on the barren heights, for the LORD has rejected and abandoned this generation that is under his wrath.

THE VALLEY OF SLAUGHTER

³⁰"'The people of Judah have done evil in my eyes, declares the LORD. They have set up their detestable idols in the house that bears my Name and have defiled it. ³¹They have built the high places of Topheth in the Valley of Ben Hinnom to burn their sons and daughters in the fire—something I did not command, nor did it enter my mind. ³²So beware, the days are coming, declares the LORD, when people will no longer call it Topheth or the Valley of Ben Hinnom, but the Valley of Slaughter, for they will bury the dead in Topheth until there is no more room. ³³Then the carcasses of this people will become food for the birds and the wild animals, and there will be no one to frighten them away. ³⁴I will bring an end to the sounds of joy and gladness and to the voices of bride and bridegroom in the towns of Judah and the streets of Jerusalem, for the land will become desolate.

8 "'At that time, declares the LORD, the bones of the kings and officials of Judah, the bones of the priests and prophets, and the bones of the people of Jerusalem will be removed from their graves. ²They will be exposed to the sun and the moon and all the stars of the heavens, which they have loved and served and which they have followed and consulted and worshiped. They will not be gathered up or buried, but will be like dung lying on the ground. ³Wherever I banish them, all the survivors of this evil nation will prefer death to life, declares the LORD Almighty.'

SIN AND PUNISHMENT

⁴"Say to them, 'This is the LORD says:

"'When people fall down, do they not get up?
When someone turns away, do they not return?

What was Topeth? (7:31)
This was a valley near Jerusalem where human sacrifices had sometimes been made to the pagan god Molek. It had become a garbage dump where fires burned constantly, and it grew to be a symbol of eternal punishment.

Why would bones be removed from graves? (8:1)
This would have been a serious insult and sacrilege. Perhaps the Babylonians looted the graves to get the valuables that were buried with the kings and officials.

5 Why then have these people turned away?
    Why does Jerusalem always turn away?
They cling to deceit;
    they refuse to return.
6 I have listened attentively,
    but they do not say what is right.
None of them repent of their wickedness,
    saying, "What have I done?"
Each pursues their own course
    like a horse charging into battle.
7 Even the stork in the sky
    knows her appointed seasons,
and the dove, the swift and the thrush
    observe the time of their migration.
But my people do not know
    the requirements of the LORD.

8 "How can you say, "We are wise,
    for we have the law of the LORD,"
when actually the lying pen of the scribes
    has handled it falsely?
9 The wise will be put to shame;
    they will be dismayed and trapped.
Since they have rejected the word of the LORD,
    what kind of wisdom do they have?
10 Therefore I will give their wives to other men
    and their fields to new owners.
From the least to the greatest,
    all are greedy for gain;
prophets and priests alike,
    all practice deceit.
11 They dress the wound of my people
    as though it were not serious.
"Peace, peace," they say,
    when there is no peace.
12 Are they ashamed of their detestable conduct?
    No, they have no shame at all;
    they do not even know how to blush.
So they will fall among the fallen;
    they will be brought down when they
        are punished,
                              says the LORD.

13 "I will take away their harvest,
                              declares the LORD.
    There will be no grapes on the vine.
There will be no figs on the tree,
    and their leaves will wither.
What I have given them
    will be taken from them.ᵃ"

14 Why are we sitting here?
    Gather together!
Let us flee to the fortified cities
    and perish there!

Why were the people compared to birds? (8:7)
Birds instinctively know when it is time to migrate, but God's rebellious people foolishly refused to obey his laws.

What wrong had the scribes committed? (8:8)
They permitted the people to worship other gods in order to keep the peace, rather than insisting that they worship God alone.

ᵃ 13 The meaning of the Hebrew for this sentence is uncertain.

For the Lord our God has doomed us to perish
  and given us poisoned water to drink,
    because we have sinned against him.
¹⁵ We hoped for peace
    but no good has come,
  for a time of healing
    but there is only terror.
¹⁶ The snorting of the enemy's horses
    is heard from Dan;
  at the neighing of their stallions
    the whole land trembles.
  They have come to devour
    the land and everything in it,
    the city and all who live there.

¹⁷ "See, I will send venomous snakes among you,
    vipers that cannot be charmed,
  and they will bite you,"

                    declares the Lord.

¹⁸ You who are my Comforter*ᵃ in sorrow,
    my heart is faint within me.
¹⁹ Listen to the cry of my people
    from a land far away:
  "Is the Lord not in Zion?
    Is her King no longer there?"

  "Why have they aroused my anger with their images,
    with their worthless foreign idols?"

²⁰ "The harvest is past,
    the summer has ended,
  and we are not saved."

²¹ Since my people are crushed, I am crushed;
    I mourn, and horror grips me.
²² Is there no balm in Gilead?
    Is there no physician there?
  Why then is there no healing
    for the wound of my people?

9 ᵇ ¹ Oh, that my head were a spring of water
    and my eyes a fountain of tears!
  I would weep day and night
    for the slain of my people.
² Oh, that I had in the desert
    a lodging place for travelers,
  so that I might leave my people
    and go away from them;
  for they are all adulterers,
    a crowd of unfaithful people.

³ "They make ready their tongue
    like a bow, to shoot lies;
  it is not by truth
    that they triumphᶜ in the land.

Who is speaking in this verse? (8:19)
First, Jeremiah speaks, and then the Lord's words follow. The people wondered how God could have permitted the land and the temple to be destroyed, but God was clearly angry because his people had turned away from him to worship idols.

Why did Jeremiah want to leave? (9:2)
Jeremiah was saddened by the suffering of his people, but he also wished he could get away from their lies, hypocrisy, and idolatry.

ᵃ 18 The meaning of the Hebrew for this word is uncertain.   ᵇ In Hebrew
texts 9:1 is numbered 8:23, and 9:2-26 is numbered 9:1-25.   ᶜ 3 Or lies; /
they are not valiant for truth

They go from one sin to another;
  they do not acknowledge me,"
                    declares the LORD.
⁴ "Beware of your friends;
  do not trust anyone in your clan.
For every one of them is a deceiver,*ª*
  and every friend a slanderer.
⁵ Friend deceives friend,
  and no one speaks the truth.
They have taught their tongues to lie;
  they weary themselves with sinning.
⁶ You*ᵇ* live in the midst of deception;
  in their deceit they refuse to acknowledge me,"
                    declares the LORD.

⁷ Therefore this is what the LORD Almighty says:

"See, I will refine and test them,
  for what else can I do
  because of the sin of my people?
⁸ Their tongue is a deadly arrow;
  it speaks deceitfully.
With their mouths they all speak cordially to their
    neighbors,
  but in their hearts they set traps for them.
⁹ Should I not punish them for this?"
  declares the LORD.
"Should I not avenge myself
  on such a nation as this?"

¹⁰ I will weep and wail for the mountains
  and take up a lament concerning the wilderness
    grasslands.
They are desolate and untraveled,
  and the lowing of cattle is not heard.
The birds have all fled
  and the animals are gone.

¹¹ "I will make Jerusalem a heap of ruins,
  a haunt of jackals;
and I will lay waste the towns of Judah
  so no one can live there."

¹² Who is wise enough to understand this? Who has been instructed by the LORD and can explain it? Why has the land been ruined and laid waste like a desert that no one can cross?

¹³ The LORD said, "It is because they have forsaken my law, which I set before them; they have not obeyed me or followed my law. ¹⁴ Instead, they have followed the stubbornness of their hearts; they have followed the Baals, as their ancestors taught them." ¹⁵ Therefore this is what the LORD Almighty, the God of Israel, says: "See, I will make this people eat bitter food and drink poisoned water. ¹⁶ I will scatter them among nations that neither they nor their ancestors have known, and I will pursue them with the sword until I have made an end of them."

How did God destroy Israel? (9:16)
God scattered his people, so the nation was destroyed, but only for a generation. The new Israel would include Gentiles as well as Jews.

ª 4 Or a deceiving Jacob   *ᵇ 6 That is, Jeremiah (the Hebrew is singular)*

¹⁷This is what the LORD Almighty says:

"Consider now! Call for the wailing women to come;
    send for the most skillful of them.
¹⁸Let them come quickly
    and wail over us
till our eyes overflow with tears
    and water streams from our eyelids.
¹⁹The sound of wailing is heard from Zion:
    'How ruined we are!
    How great is our shame!
We must leave our land
    because our houses are in ruins.'"

²⁰Now, you women, hear the word of the LORD;
    open your ears to the words of his mouth.
Teach your daughters how to wail;
    teach one another a lament.
²¹Death has climbed in through our windows
    and has entered our fortresses;
it has removed the children from the streets
    and the young men from the public squares.

²²Say, "This is what the LORD declares:

"'Dead bodies will lie
    like dung on the open field,
like cut grain behind the reaper,
    with no one to gather them.'"

²³This is what the LORD says:

"Let not the wise boast of their wisdom
    or the strong boast of their strength
    or the rich boast of their riches,
²⁴but let the one who boasts boast about this:
    that they have the understanding to know me,
that I am the LORD, who exercises kindness,
    justice and righteousness on earth,
    for in these I delight,"

                                        declares the LORD.

²⁵"The days are coming," declares the LORD, "when I will punish all who are circumcised only in the flesh— ²⁶Egypt, Judah, Edom, Ammon, Moab and all who live in the wilderness in distant places.ᵃ For all these nations are really uncircumcised, and even the whole house of Israel is uncircumcised in heart."

GOD AND IDOLS

10 Hear what the LORD says to you, people of Israel. ²This is what the LORD says:

"Do not learn the ways of the nations
    or be terrified by signs in the heavens,
    though the nations are terrified by them.
³For the practices of the peoples are worthless;
    they cut a tree out of the forest,
    and a craftsman shapes it with his chisel.

ᵃ 26 Or *wilderness and who clip the hair by their foreheads*

Who were the wailing women? (9:17)
These were professional mourners who were paid to mourn at funerals and other sorrowful occasions.

Why did other nations practice circumcision? (9:25–26)
This may simply have been a superstitious practice designed to ward off evil. There is no evidence that they understood or appreciated the religious aspect of circumcision as practiced by the nation of Israel.

How were idols made? (10:3–4)
Idols were carved out of wood and then were plated with precious metals.

Smelting Metal (10:9)

Why was this verse originally written in Aramaic? (10:11)
This verse was aimed at the people who worshiped pagan idols. They probably would have understood Aramaic better than Hebrew.

⁴They adorn it with silver and gold;
  they fasten it with hammer and nails
  so it will not totter.
⁵Like a scarecrow in a cucumber field,
  their idols cannot speak;
they must be carried
  because they cannot walk.
Do not fear them;
  they can do no harm
  nor can they do any good."

⁶No one is like you, Lord;
  you are great,
  and your name is mighty in power.
⁷Who should not fear you,
  King of the nations?
  This is your due.
Among all the wise leaders of the nations
  and in all their kingdoms,
  there is no one like you.

⁸They are all senseless and foolish;
  they are taught by worthless wooden idols.
⁹Hammered silver is brought from Tarshish
  and gold from Uphaz.
What the craftsman and goldsmith have made
  is then dressed in blue and purple—
  all made by skilled workers.
¹⁰But the Lord is the true God;
  he is the living God, the eternal King.
When he is angry, the earth trembles;
  the nations cannot endure his wrath.

¹¹"Tell them this: 'These gods, who did not make the heavens and the earth, will perish from the earth and from under the heavens.'"ᵃ

¹²But God made the earth by his power;
  he founded the world by his wisdom
  and stretched out the heavens by
      his understanding.
¹³When he thunders, the waters in the heavens roar;
  he makes clouds rise from the ends of the earth.
He sends lightning with the rain
  and brings out the wind from his storehouses.

¹⁴Everyone is senseless and without knowledge;
  every goldsmith is shamed by his idols.
The images he makes are a fraud;
  they have no breath in them.
¹⁵They are worthless, the objects of mockery;
  when their judgment comes, they will perish.
¹⁶He who is the Portion of Jacob is not like these,
  for he is the Maker of all things,
including Israel, the people of his inheritance—
  the Lord Almighty is his name.

ᵃ *11* The text of this verse is in Aramaic.

COMING DESTRUCTION

[17] Gather up your belongings to leave the land,
    you who live under siege.
[18] For this is what the LORD says:
    "At this time I will hurl out
    those who live in this land;
    I will bring distress on them
    so that they may be captured."

[19] Woe to me because of my injury!
    My wound is incurable!
    Yet I said to myself,
    "This is my sickness, and I must endure it."
[20] My tent is destroyed;
    all its ropes are snapped.
    My children are gone from me and are no more;
    no one is left now to pitch my tent
    or to set up my shelter.
[21] The shepherds are senseless
    and do not inquire of the LORD;
    so they do not prosper
    and all their flock is scattered.
[22] Listen! The report is coming—
    a great commotion from the land of the north!
    It will make the towns of Judah desolate,
    a haunt of jackals.

JEREMIAH'S PRAYER

[23] LORD, I know that people's lives are not their own;
    it is not for them to direct their steps.
[24] Discipline me, LORD, but only in due measure—
    not in your anger,
    or you will reduce me to nothing.
[25] Pour out your wrath on the nations
    that do not acknowledge you,
    on the peoples who do not call on your name.
    For they have devoured Jacob;
    they have devoured him completely
    and destroyed his homeland.

THE COVENANT IS BROKEN

11 This is the word that came to Jeremiah from the LORD: [2] "Listen to the terms of this covenant and tell them to the people of Judah and to those who live in Jerusalem. [3] Tell them that this is what the LORD, the God of Israel, says: 'Cursed is the one who does not obey the terms of this covenant— [4] the terms I commanded your ancestors when I brought them out of Egypt, out of the iron-smelting furnace.' I said, 'Obey me and do everything I command you, and you will be my people, and I will be your God. [5] Then I will fulfill the oath I swore to your ancestors, to give them a land flowing with milk and honey'—the land you possess today."

I answered, "Amen, LORD."

[6] The LORD said to me, "Proclaim all these words in the towns of Judah and in the streets of Jerusalem: 'Listen to the terms of this covenant and follow them. [7] From the time I

How was Jeremiah injured? (10:19)
This is a word picture describing how upset he was about the sin of the people and how they were going to be punished because of it.

What was the commotion from the north? (10:22)
This was the sound of the invaders who were coming from Babylon.

Which covenant was this? (11:2)
This was the covenant God had made with his people when Moses was on Mount Sinai: God would bless his people if they obeyed him, but he would punish them if they disobeyed.

brought your ancestors up from Egypt until today, I warned them again and again, saying, "Obey me." [8] But they did not listen or pay attention; instead, they followed the stubbornness of their evil hearts. So I brought on them all the curses of the covenant I had commanded them to follow but that they did not keep.'"

[9] Then the LORD said to me, "There is a conspiracy among the people of Judah and those who live in Jerusalem. [10] They have returned to the sins of their ancestors, who refused to listen to my words. They have followed other gods to serve them. Both Israel and Judah have broken the covenant I made with their ancestors. [11] Therefore this is what the LORD says: 'I will bring on them a disaster they cannot escape. Although they cry out to me, I will not listen to them. [12] The towns of Judah and the people of Jerusalem will go and cry out to the gods to whom they burn incense, but they will not help them at all when disaster strikes. [13] You, Judah, have as many gods as you have towns; and the altars you have set up to burn incense to that shameful god Baal are as many as the streets of Jerusalem.'

[14] "Do not pray for this people or offer any plea or petition for them, because I will not listen when they call to me in the time of their distress.

[15] "What is my beloved doing in my temple
   as she, with many others, works out her evil schemes?
   Can consecrated meat avert your punishment?
When you engage in your wickedness,
   then you rejoice.[a]"

[16] The LORD called you a thriving olive tree
   with fruit beautiful in form.
But with the roar of a mighty storm
   he will set it on fire,
   and its branches will be broken.

[17] The LORD Almighty, who planted you, has decreed disaster for you, because the people of both Israel and Judah have done evil and aroused my anger by burning incense to Baal.

PLOT AGAINST JEREMIAH

[18] Because the LORD revealed their plot to me, I knew it, for at that time he showed me what they were doing. [19] I had been like a gentle lamb led to the slaughter; I did not realize that they had plotted against me, saying,

"Let us destroy the tree and its fruit;
   let us cut him off from the land of the living,
   that his name be remembered no more."

[20] But you, LORD Almighty, who judge righteously
   and test the heart and mind,
let me see your vengeance on them,
   for to you I have committed my cause.

[21] Therefore this is what the LORD says about the people of Anathoth who are threatening to kill you, saying, "Do not prophesy in the name of the LORD or you will die by our hands"— [22] therefore this is what the LORD Almighty says:

How many gods did the people worship? (11:13)
The exact number isn't known, but their Canaanite neighbors had an estimated 2,000 to 3,000 gods. The pagan nations believed that each town had its own god to protect it, and Israel may have accepted this idea.

Why had the Lord called his people an olive tree? (11:16)
An olive tree could live for hundreds of years, so it was a symbol of long life and productivity.

What plot was this? (11:18)
Men from Jeremiah's hometown were planning to kill him because he was undermining their influence. Jeremiah supported the king's reforms, including destroying the altars of the local idol.

---

[a] 15 Or *Could consecrated meat avert your punishment? / Then you would rejoice*

"I will punish them. Their young men will die by the sword, their sons and daughters by famine. [23] Not even a remnant will be left to them, because I will bring disaster on the people of Anathoth in the year of their punishment."

JEREMIAH'S COMPLAINT

12
You are always righteous, LORD,
    when I bring a case before you.
Yet I would speak with you about your justice:
    Why does the way of the wicked prosper?
    Why do all the faithless live at ease?
[2] You have planted them, and they have taken root;
    they grow and bear fruit.
You are always on their lips
    but far from their hearts.
[3] Yet you know me, LORD;
    you see me and test my thoughts about you.
Drag them off like sheep to be butchered!
    Set them apart for the day of slaughter!
[4] How long will the land lie parched
    and the grass in every field be withered?
Because those who live in it are wicked,
    the animals and birds have perished.
Moreover, the people are saying,
    "He will not see what happens to us."

GOD'S ANSWER

[5] "If you have raced with men on foot
    and they have worn you out,
    how can you compete with horses?
If you stumble[a] in safe country,
    how will you manage in the thickets by[b] the Jordan?
[6] Your relatives, members of your own family—
    even they have betrayed you;
    they have raised a loud cry against you.
Do not trust them,
    though they speak well of you.

[7] "I will forsake my house,
    abandon my inheritance;
I will give the one I love
    into the hands of her enemies.
[8] My inheritance has become to me
    like a lion in the forest.
She roars at me;
    therefore I hate her.
[9] Has not my inheritance become to me
    like a speckled bird of prey
    that other birds of prey surround and attack?
Go and gather all the wild beasts;
    bring them to devour.
[10] Many shepherds will ruin my vineyard
    and trample down my field;
they will turn my pleasant field
    into a desolate wasteland.

---

[a] 5 Or *you feel secure only*   [b] 5 Or *the flooding of*

How was God always on the people's lips? (12:2)
They spoke about God reverently, but they also worshiped other gods. Jesus quoted part of this verse in Matthew 15:8 – 9.

What did God tell Jeremiah? (12:5 – 6)
God used word pictures to explain that Jeremiah would face even more serious trouble in the future.

What were these birds of prey and wild beasts? (12:9)
These were the enemies of Judah.

¹¹ It will be made a wasteland,
  parched and desolate before me;
the whole land will be laid waste
  because there is no one who cares.
¹² Over all the barren heights in the desert
  destroyers will swarm,
for the sword of the LORD will devour
  from one end of the land to the other;
  no one will be safe.
¹³ They will sow wheat but reap thorns;
  they will wear themselves out but gain nothing.
They will bear the shame of their harvest
  because of the LORD's fierce anger."

¹⁴This is what the LORD says: "As for all my wicked neighbors who seize the inheritance I gave my people Israel, I will uproot them from their lands and I will uproot the people of Judah from among them. ¹⁵But after I uproot them, I will again have compassion and will bring each of them back to their own inheritance and their own country. ¹⁶And if they learn well the ways of my people and swear by my name, saying, 'As surely as the LORD lives'—even as they once taught my people to swear by Baal—then they will be established among my people. ¹⁷But if any nation does not listen, I will completely uproot and destroy it," declares the LORD.

A LINEN BELT

13 This is what the LORD said to me: "Go and buy a linen belt and put it around your waist, but do not let it touch water." ²So I bought a belt, as the LORD directed, and put it around my waist.

³Then the word of the LORD came to me a second time: ⁴"Take the belt you bought and are wearing around your waist, and go now to Perath^a and hide it there in a crevice in the rocks." ⁵So I went and hid it at Perath, as the LORD told me.

⁶Many days later the LORD said to me, "Go now to Perath and get the belt I told you to hide there." ⁷So I went to Perath and dug up the belt and took it from the place where I had hidden it, but now it was ruined and completely useless.

⁸Then the word of the LORD came to me: ⁹"This is what the LORD says: 'In the same way I will ruin the pride of Judah and the great pride of Jerusalem. ¹⁰These wicked people, who refuse to listen to my words, who follow the stubbornness of their hearts and go after other gods to serve and worship them, will be like this belt—completely useless! ¹¹For as a belt is bound around the waist, so I bound all the people of Israel and all the people of Judah to me,' declares the LORD, 'to be my people for my renown and praise and honor. But they have not listened.'

WINESKINS

¹²"Say to them: 'This is what the LORD, the God of Israel, says: Every wineskin should be filled with wine.' And if they

---

How would God restore his people? (12:15)
Eventually they would be brought back from exile to their own land.

What did the linen belt illustrate? (13:1–11)
The priests' garments were made from linen, which symbolized holiness and God's special relationship with his people. But after this belt was buried, it rotted and became useless. God told Jeremiah that Israel was like this belt: It had once been special, but it had become spoiled by sin.

---

^a 4 Or possibly *to the Euphrates*; similarly in verses 5-7

say to you, 'Don't we know that every wineskin should be filled with wine?' ¹³ then tell them, 'This is what the LORD says: I am going to fill with drunkenness all who live in this land, including the kings who sit on David's throne, the priests, the prophets and all those living in Jerusalem. ¹⁴ I will smash them one against the other, parents and children alike, declares the LORD. I will allow no pity or mercy or compassion to keep me from destroying them.'"

THREAT OF CAPTIVITY

¹⁵ Hear and pay attention,
   do not be arrogant,
   for the LORD has spoken.
¹⁶ Give glory to the LORD your God
   before he brings the darkness,
before your feet stumble
   on the darkening hills.
You hope for light,
   but he will turn it to utter darkness
   and change it to deep gloom.
¹⁷ If you do not listen,
   I will weep in secret
   because of your pride;
my eyes will weep bitterly,
   overflowing with tears,
   because the LORD's flock will be taken captive.

¹⁸ Say to the king and to the queen mother,
   "Come down from your thrones,
for your glorious crowns
   will fall from your heads."
¹⁹ The cities in the Negev will be shut up,
   and there will be no one to open them.
All Judah will be carried into exile,
   carried completely away.

²⁰ Look up and see
   those who are coming from the north.
Where is the flock that was entrusted to you,
   the sheep of which you boasted?
²¹ What will you say when the LORD sets over you
   those you cultivated as your special allies?
Will not pain grip you
   like that of a woman in labor?
²² And if you ask yourself,
   "Why has this happened to me?"—
it is because of your many sins
   that your skirts have been torn off
   and your body mistreated.
²³ Can an Ethiopian*ᵃ* change his skin
   or a leopard its spots?
Neither can you do good
   who are accustomed to doing evil.

²⁴ "I will scatter you like chaff
   driven by the desert wind.

ᵃ 23 Hebrew *Cushite* (probably a person from the upper Nile region)

Who were the king and his mother? (13:18)
This was probably Jehoiachin and Nehushta, who were taken into captivity in 597 B.C.

What was the meaning of these questions? (13:23)
These were rhetorical questions. The point was that the people had become so sinful they were not able to change their ways on their own. Only God could change them.

²⁵ This is your lot,
    the portion I have decreed for you,"

                        declares the LORD,
"because you have forgotten me
    and trusted in false gods.
²⁶ I will pull up your skirts over your face
    that your shame may be seen —
²⁷ your adulteries and lustful neighings,
    your shameless prostitution!
I have seen your detestable acts
    on the hills and in the fields.
Woe to you, Jerusalem!
    How long will you be unclean?"

DROUGHT, FAMINE, SWORD

14 This is the word of the LORD that came to Jeremiah concerning the drought:

² "Judah mourns,
    her cities languish;
they wail for the land,
    and a cry goes up from Jerusalem.
³ The nobles send their servants for water;
    they go to the cisterns
    but find no water.
They return with their jars unfilled;
    dismayed and despairing,
    they cover their heads.
⁴ The ground is cracked
    because there is no rain in the land;
the farmers are dismayed
    and cover their heads.
⁵ Even the doe in the field
    deserts her newborn fawn
    because there is no grass.
⁶ Wild donkeys stand on the barren heights
    and pant like jackals;
their eyes fail
    for lack of food."

⁷ Although our sins testify against us,
    do something, LORD, for the sake of your name.
For we have often rebelled;
    we have sinned against you.
⁸ You who are the hope of Israel,
    its Savior in times of distress,
why are you like a stranger in the land,
    like a traveler who stays only a night?
⁹ Why are you like a man taken by surprise,
    like a warrior powerless to save?
You are among us, LORD,
    and we bear your name;
    do not forsake us!

¹⁰ This is what the LORD says about this people:

"They greatly love to wander;
    they do not restrain their feet.

What did it mean that God would pull up their skirts? (13:26)
This was a way of comparing Israel to a prostitute or a woman who was unfaithful to her husband. Promiscuous women were publicly shamed by being stripped or having their skirts pulled over their heads.

Why would they cover their heads? (14:3)
This was a common symbol of mourning.

Why did God seem like a stranger? (14:8–9)
God seemed like a stranger to the people because they had separated themselves from him by following false gods.

So the Lord does not accept them;
   he will now remember their wickedness
   and punish them for their sins."

¹¹Then the Lord said to me, "Do not pray for the well-being of this people. ¹²Although they fast, I will not listen to their cry; though they offer burnt offerings and grain offerings, I will not accept them. Instead, I will destroy them with the sword, famine and plague."

¹³But I said, "Alas, Sovereign Lord! The prophets keep telling them, 'You will not see the sword or suffer famine. Indeed, I will give you lasting peace in this place.'"

¹⁴Then the Lord said to me, "The prophets are prophesying lies in my name. I have not sent them or appointed them or spoken to them. They are prophesying to you false visions, divinations, idolatries *a* and the delusions of their own minds. ¹⁵Therefore this is what the Lord says about the prophets who are prophesying in my name: I did not send them, yet they are saying, 'No sword or famine will touch this land.' Those same prophets will perish by sword and famine. ¹⁶And the people they are prophesying to will be thrown out into the streets of Jerusalem because of the famine and sword. There will be no one to bury them, their wives, their sons and their daughters. I will pour out on them the calamity they deserve.

¹⁷"Speak this word to them:

"'Let my eyes overflow with tears
   night and day without ceasing;
for the Virgin Daughter, my people,
   has suffered a grievous wound,
   a crushing blow.
¹⁸If I go into the country,
   I see those slain by the sword;
if I go into the city,
   I see the ravages of famine.
Both prophet and priest
   have gone to a land they know not.'"

¹⁹Have you rejected Judah completely?
   Do you despise Zion?
Why have you afflicted us
   so that we cannot be healed?
We hoped for peace
   but no good has come,
for a time of healing
   but there is only terror.
²⁰We acknowledge our wickedness, Lord,
   and the guilt of our ancestors;
   we have indeed sinned against you.
²¹For the sake of your name do not despise us;
   do not dishonor your glorious throne.
Remember your covenant with us
   and do not break it.
²²Do any of the worthless idols of the nations bring rain?
   Do the skies themselves send down showers?

a 14 Or visions, worthless divinations

Why did God tell Jeremiah not to pray for the people of Israel? (14:11)
It was too late for prayers or sacrifices to make a difference because the people had rebelled against God for such a long time that he had already judged them.

Who were these false prophets? (14:13–14)
These were probably prophets of Baal, who were from Anathoth, Jeremiah's hometown. They told the people they would not be invaded or suffer a famine.

What was God's glorious throne? (14:21)
This was the temple in Jerusalem. Jeremiah asked God to preserve his good name by showing mercy on the people even though they didn't deserve it.

No, it is you, LORD our God.
    Therefore our hope is in you,
    for you are the one who does all this.

15 Then the LORD said to me: "Even if Moses and Samuel were to stand before me, my heart would not go out to this people. Send them away from my presence! Let them go! ²And if they ask you, 'Where shall we go?' tell them, 'This is what the LORD says:

"'Those destined for death, to death;
    those for the sword, to the sword;
    those for starvation, to starvation;
    those for captivity, to captivity.'

³"I will send four kinds of destroyers against them," declares the LORD, "the sword to kill and the dogs to drag away and the birds and the wild animals to devour and destroy. ⁴I will make them abhorrent to all the kingdoms of the earth because of what Manasseh son of Hezekiah king of Judah did in Jerusalem.

⁵"Who will have pity on you, Jerusalem?
    Who will mourn for you?
    Who will stop to ask how you are?
⁶You have rejected me," declares the LORD.
    "You keep on backsliding.
So I will reach out and destroy you;
    I am tired of holding back.
⁷I will winnow them with a winnowing fork
    at the city gates of the land.
I will bring bereavement and destruction on my
        people,
    for they have not changed their ways.
⁸I will make their widows more numerous
    than the sand of the sea.
At midday I will bring a destroyer
    against the mothers of their young men;
suddenly I will bring down on them
    anguish and terror.
⁹The mother of seven will grow faint
    and breathe her last.
Her sun will set while it is still day;
    she will be disgraced and humiliated.
I will put the survivors to the sword
    before their enemies,"
                            declares the LORD.

¹⁰Alas, my mother, that you gave me birth,
    a man with whom the whole land strives and
            contends!
I have neither lent nor borrowed,
    yet everyone curses me.

¹¹The LORD said,

"Surely I will deliver you for a good purpose;
    surely I will make your enemies plead with you
    in times of disaster and times of distress.

Why were Moses and Samuel mentioned? (15:1)
Moses and Samuel had often prayed to God for the people of Israel. God was saying that even their prayers would not have an impact because the people had become so wicked.

Why would there be four kinds of destroyers? (15:3)
This corresponds to various curses from the ancient world. The point is that the destruction would be harsh and complete.

How would the people be winnowed? (15:7)
After grain was harvested, it was loosened from the straw (threshed). Then it was tossed in the air with a large winnowing fork, so that the wind would blow away the lighter straw and chaff and leave the grain behind. This is a picture of how God would judge the people.

¹²"Can a man break iron—
    iron from the north—or bronze?

¹³"Your wealth and your treasures
    I will give as plunder, without charge,
because of all your sins
    throughout your country.
¹⁴I will enslave you to your enemies
    in*ª* a land you do not know,
for my anger will kindle a fire
    that will burn against you."

¹⁵LORD, you understand;
    remember me and care for me.
Avenge me on my persecutors.
You are long-suffering—do not take me away;
    think of how I suffer reproach for your sake.
¹⁶When your words came, I ate them;
    they were my joy and my heart's delight,
for I bear your name,
    LORD God Almighty.
¹⁷I never sat in the company of revelers,
    never made merry with them;
I sat alone because your hand was on me
    and you had filled me with indignation.
¹⁸Why is my pain unending
    and my wound grievous and incurable?
You are to me like a deceptive brook,
    like a spring that fails.

¹⁹Therefore this is what the LORD says:

"If you repent, I will restore you
    that you may serve me;
if you utter worthy, not worthless, words,
    you will be my spokesman.
Let this people turn to you,
    but you must not turn to them.
²⁰I will make you a wall to this people,
    a fortified wall of bronze;
they will fight against you
    but will not overcome you,
for I am with you
    to rescue and save you,"
                                        declares the LORD.
²¹"I will save you from the hands of the wicked
    and deliver you from the grasp of the cruel."

DAY OF DISASTER

16 Then the word of the LORD came to me: ²"You must not marry and have sons or daughters in this place." ³For this is what the LORD says about the sons and daughters born in this land and about the women who are their mothers and the men who are their fathers: ⁴"They will die of deadly diseases. They will not be mourned or buried but will be like dung lying on the ground. They will perish by sword

---

ª 14 Some Hebrew manuscripts, Septuagint and Syriac (see also 17:4); most Hebrew manuscripts *I will cause your enemies to bring you / into*

How would Jeremiah become a wall? (15:20)
God told Jeremiah to repent and to deliver God's message to his people. If he did, God would make him like a strong bronze wall that could not be shattered.

Why did God tell Jeremiah not to get married? (16:1–4)
It may have been so that Jeremiah would stay focused only on his ministry. It may also have been because God wanted to spare Jeremiah from the pain the next generation would experience.

and famine, and their dead bodies will become food for the birds and the wild animals."

⁵For this is what the LORD says: "Do not enter a house where there is a funeral meal; do not go to mourn or show sympathy, because I have withdrawn my blessing, my love and my pity from this people," declares the LORD. ⁶"Both high and low will die in this land. They will not be buried or mourned, and no one will cut themselves or shave their head for the dead. ⁷No one will offer food to comfort those who mourn for the dead—not even for a father or a mother— nor will anyone give them a drink to console them.

⁸"And do not enter a house where there is feasting and sit down to eat and drink. ⁹For this is what the LORD Almighty, the God of Israel, says: Before your eyes and in your days I will bring an end to the sounds of joy and gladness and to the voices of bride and bridegroom in this place.

¹⁰"When you tell these people all this and they ask you, 'Why has the LORD decreed such a great disaster against us? What wrong have we done? What sin have we committed against the LORD our God?' ¹¹then say to them, 'It is because your ancestors forsook me,' declares the LORD, 'and followed other gods and served and worshiped them. They forsook me and did not keep my law. ¹²But you have behaved more wickedly than your ancestors. See how all of you are following the stubbornness of your evil hearts instead of obeying me. ¹³So I will throw you out of this land into a land neither you nor your ancestors have known, and there you will serve other gods day and night, for I will show you no favor.'

¹⁴"However, the days are coming," declares the LORD, "when it will no longer be said, 'As surely as the LORD lives, who brought the Israelites up out of Egypt,' ¹⁵but it will be said, 'As surely as the LORD lives, who brought the Israelites up out of the land of the north and out of all the countries where he had banished them.' For I will restore them to the land I gave their ancestors.

¹⁶"But now I will send for many fishermen," declares the LORD, "and they will catch them. After that I will send for many hunters, and they will hunt them down on every mountain and hill and from the crevices of the rocks. ¹⁷My eyes are on all their ways; they are not hidden from me, nor is their sin concealed from my eyes. ¹⁸I will repay them double for their wickedness and their sin, because they have defiled my land with the lifeless forms of their vile images and have filled my inheritance with their detestable idols."

¹⁹LORD, my strength and my fortress,
    my refuge in time of distress,
to you the nations will come
    from the ends of the earth and say,
"Our ancestors possessed nothing but false gods,
    worthless idols that did them no good.
²⁰Do people make their own gods?
    Yes, but they are not gods!"

²¹"Therefore I will teach them—
    this time I will teach them
    my power and might.

Who were these fishermen and hunters? (16:16)
These were symbolic descriptions of the people who would conquer Israel.

Then they will know
　　that my name is the Lord.

17 "Judah's sin is engraved with an iron tool,
　　　　inscribed with a flint point,
on the tablets of their hearts
　　and on the horns of their altars.
² Even their children remember
　　their altars and Asherah poles[a]
beside the spreading trees
　　and on the high hills.
³ My mountain in the land
　　and your[b] wealth and all your treasures
I will give away as plunder,
　　together with your high places,
　　because of sin throughout your country.
⁴ Through your own fault you will lose
　　the inheritance I gave you.
I will enslave you to your enemies
　　in a land you do not know,
for you have kindled my anger,
　　and it will burn forever."

⁵ This is what the Lord says:

"Cursed is the one who trusts in man,
　　who draws strength from mere flesh
　　and whose heart turns away from the Lord.
⁶ That person will be like a bush in the wastelands;
　　they will not see prosperity when it comes.
They will dwell in the parched places of
　　　　the desert,
　　in a salt land where no one lives.

⁷ "But blessed is the one who trusts in the Lord,
　　whose confidence is in him.
⁸ They will be like a tree planted by the water
　　that sends out its roots by the stream.
It does not fear when heat comes;
　　its leaves are always green.
It has no worries in a year of drought
　　and never fails to bear fruit."

⁹ The heart is deceitful above all things
　　and beyond cure.
　　Who can understand it?

¹⁰ "I the Lord search the heart
　　and examine the mind,
to reward each person according to their conduct,
　　according to what their deeds deserve."

¹¹ Like a partridge that hatches eggs it did not lay
　　are those who gain riches by unjust means.
When their lives are half gone, their riches will
　　　　desert them,
　　and in the end they will prove to be fools.

a 2 That is, wooden symbols of the goddess Asherah　　*b 2,3 Or hills / ³and
the mountains of the land. / Your*

**Why was their sin engraved
with an iron tool? (17:1)**
Iron tools were used to chisel
words in stone. These were the
most permanent form of records,
and this shows how pervasive
their sin had become.

**What would God give away?
(17:3)**
He would give away his holy
mountain (Zion) along with all of
the high places the people had
used for worshiping foreign gods.

**Which psalm do these
verses resemble? (17:7–8)**
These verses sound like Psalm
1:3 — Jeremiah is quoting or
paraphrasing here.

¹² A glorious throne, exalted from the beginning,
    is the place of our sanctuary.
¹³ LORD, you are the hope of Israel;
    all who forsake you will be put to shame.
Those who turn away from you will be written
       in the dust
    because they have forsaken the LORD,
    the spring of living water.

¹⁴ Heal me, LORD, and I will be healed;
    save me and I will be saved,
    for you are the one I praise.
¹⁵ They keep saying to me,
    "Where is the word of the LORD?
    Let it now be fulfilled!"
¹⁶ I have not run away from being your shepherd;
    you know I have not desired the day of despair.
What passes my lips is open before you.
¹⁷ Do not be a terror to me;
    you are my refuge in the day of disaster.
¹⁸ Let my persecutors be put to shame,
    but keep me from shame;
let them be terrified,
    but keep me from terror.
Bring on them the day of disaster;
    destroy them with double destruction.

KEEPING THE SABBATH DAY HOLY

¹⁹ This is what the LORD said to me: "Go and stand at the Gate of the People,[a] through which the kings of Judah go in and out; stand also at all the other gates of Jerusalem. ²⁰ Say to them, 'Hear the word of the LORD, you kings of Judah and all people of Judah and everyone living in Jerusalem who come through these gates. ²¹ This is what the LORD says: Be careful not to carry a load on the Sabbath day or bring it through the gates of Jerusalem. ²² Do not bring a load out of your houses or do any work on the Sabbath, but keep the Sabbath day holy, as I commanded your ancestors. ²³ Yet they did not listen or pay attention; they were stiff-necked and would not listen or respond to discipline. ²⁴ But if you are careful to obey me, declares the LORD, and bring no load through the gates of this city on the Sabbath, but keep the Sabbath day holy by not doing any work on it, ²⁵ then kings who sit on David's throne will come through the gates of this city with their officials. They and their officials will come riding in chariots and on horses, accompanied by the men of Judah and those living in Jerusalem, and this city will be inhabited forever. ²⁶ People will come from the towns of Judah and the villages around Jerusalem, from the territory of Benjamin and the western foothills, from the hill country and the Negev, bringing burnt offerings and sacrifices, grain offerings and incense, and bringing thank offerings to the house of the LORD. ²⁷ But if you do not obey me to keep the Sabbath day holy by not carrying any load as you come

---

How did Jeremiah's enemies attack him? (17:15)
They accused him of being a false prophet because his prophecies had not yet come to pass.

What was the Gate of the People? (17:19)
This probably refers to the east gate of the temple, where large numbers of people gathered and where kings frequently entered.

ᵃ 19 Or *Army*

through the gates of Jerusalem on the Sabbath day, then I will kindle an unquenchable fire in the gates of Jerusalem that will consume her fortresses.'"

AT THE POTTER'S HOUSE

18 This is the word that came to Jeremiah from the LORD: ²"Go down to the potter's house, and there I will give you my message." ³So I went down to the potter's house, and I saw him working at the wheel. ⁴But the pot he was shaping from the clay was marred in his hands; so the potter formed it into another pot, shaping it as seemed best to him.

⁵Then the word of the LORD came to me. ⁶He said, "Can I not do with you, Israel, as this potter does?" declares the LORD. "Like clay in the hand of the potter, so are you in my hand, Israel. ⁷If at any time I announce that a nation or kingdom is to be uprooted, torn down and destroyed, ⁸and if that nation I warned repents of its evil, then I will relent and not inflict on it the disaster I had planned. ⁹And if at another time I announce that a nation or kingdom is to be built up and planted, ¹⁰and if it does evil in my sight and does not obey me, then I will reconsider the good I had intended to do for it.

¹¹"Now therefore say to the people of Judah and those living in Jerusalem, 'This is what the LORD says: Look! I am preparing a disaster for you and devising a plan against you. So turn from your evil ways, each one of you, and reform your ways and your actions.' ¹²But they will reply, 'It's no use. We will continue with our own plans; we will all follow the stubbornness of our evil hearts.'"

¹³Therefore this is what the LORD says:

"Inquire among the nations:
    Who has ever heard anything like this?
A most horrible thing has been done
    by Virgin Israel.
¹⁴Does the snow of Lebanon
    ever vanish from its rocky slopes?
Do its cool waters from distant sources
    ever stop flowing?ᵃ
¹⁵Yet my people have forgotten me;
    they burn incense to worthless idols,
which made them stumble in their ways,
    in the ancient paths.
They made them walk in byways,
    on roads not built up.
¹⁶Their land will be an object of horror
    and of lasting scorn;
all who pass by will be appalled
    and will shake their heads.
¹⁷Like a wind from the east,
    I will scatter them before their enemies;
I will show them my back and not my face
    in the day of their disaster."

ᵃ 14 The meaning of the Hebrew for this sentence is uncertain.

What sort of wheel was this? (18:3)
This was a potter's wheel, which included two stone or wood discs attached to an upright shaft. One end of the shaft was stuck in the ground. The potter would spin the lower wheel with his foot and shape the clay on the smaller, upper wheel.

Why was Israel called a virgin? (18:13)
This emphasized the people's earlier purity and commitment to God. But Israel had become like an unfaithful wife by pursuing pagan gods.

What was the wind from the east? (18:17)
This refers to the sirocco or khamsin, a hot, dry wind that carried a great deal of sand and dust (see 4:11).

¹⁸They said, "Come, let's make plans against Jeremiah; for the teaching of the law by the priest will not cease, nor will counsel from the wise, nor the word from the prophets. So come, let's attack him with our tongues and pay no attention to anything he says."

¹⁹ Listen to me, LORD;
    hear what my accusers are saying!
²⁰ Should good be repaid with evil?
    Yet they have dug a pit for me.
Remember that I stood before you
    and spoke in their behalf
    to turn your wrath away from them.
²¹ So give their children over to famine;
    hand them over to the power of the sword.
Let their wives be made childless and widows;
    let their men be put to death,
    their young men slain by the sword in battle.
²² Let a cry be heard from their houses
    when you suddenly bring invaders
        against them,
for they have dug a pit to capture me
    and have hidden snares for my feet.
²³ But you, LORD, know
    all their plots to kill me.
Do not forgive their crimes
    or blot out their sins from your sight.
Let them be overthrown before you;
    deal with them in the time of your anger.

What type of jar was this? (19:1)
This was probably a jar with a narrow neck, perhaps a water decanter.

19 This is what the LORD says: "Go and buy a clay jar from a potter. Take along some of the elders of the people and of the priests ²and go out to the Valley of Ben Hinnom, near the entrance of the Potsherd Gate. There proclaim the words I tell you, ³and say, 'Hear the word of the LORD, you kings of Judah and people of Jerusalem. This is what the LORD Almighty, the God of Israel, says: Listen! I am going to bring a disaster on this place that will make the ears of everyone who hears of it tingle. ⁴For they have forsaken me and made this a place of foreign gods; they have burned incense in it to gods that neither they nor their ancestors nor the kings of Judah ever knew, and they have filled this place with the blood of the innocent. ⁵They have built the high places of Baal to burn their children in the fire as offerings to Baal—something I did not command or mention, nor did it enter my mind. ⁶So beware, the days are coming, declares the LORD, when people will no longer call this place Topheth or the Valley of Ben Hinnom, but the Valley of Slaughter.

⁷"'In this place I will ruin*ᵃ* the plans of Judah and Jerusalem. I will make them fall by the sword before their enemies, at the hands of those who want to kill them, and I will give their carcasses as food to the birds and the wild animals. ⁸I will devastate this city and make it an object of horror and

ᵃ 7 The Hebrew for ruin sounds like the Hebrew for jar (see verses 1 and 10).

scorn; all who pass by will be appalled and will scoff because of all its wounds. ⁹I will make them eat the flesh of their sons and daughters, and they will eat one another's flesh because their enemies will press the siege so hard against them to destroy them.'

¹⁰"Then break the jar while those who go with you are watching, ¹¹and say to them, 'This is what the LORD Almighty says: I will smash this nation and this city just as this potter's jar is smashed and cannot be repaired. They will bury the dead in Topheth until there is no more room. ¹²This is what I will do to this place and to those who live here, declares the LORD. I will make this city like Topheth. ¹³The houses in Jerusalem and those of the kings of Judah will be defiled like this place, Topheth—all the houses where they burned incense on the roofs to all the starry hosts and poured out drink offerings to other gods.'"

¹⁴Jeremiah then returned from Topheth, where the LORD had sent him to prophesy, and stood in the court of the LORD's temple and said to all the people, ¹⁵"This is what the LORD Almighty, the God of Israel, says: 'Listen! I am going to bring on this city and all the villages around it every disaster I pronounced against them, because they were stiff-necked and would not listen to my words.'"

JEREMIAH AND PASHHUR

20 When the priest Pashhur son of Immer, the official in charge of the temple of the LORD, heard Jeremiah prophesying these things, ²he had Jeremiah the prophet beaten and put in the stocks at the Upper Gate of Benjamin at the LORD's temple. ³The next day, when Pashhur released him from the stocks, Jeremiah said to him, "The LORD's name for you is not Pashhur, but Terror on Every Side. ⁴For this is what the LORD says: 'I will make you a terror to yourself and to all your friends; with your own eyes you will see them fall by the sword of their enemies. I will give all Judah into the hands of the king of Babylon, who will carry them away to Babylon or put them to the sword. ⁵I will deliver all the wealth of this city into the hands of their enemies—all its products, all its valuables and all the treasures of the kings of Judah. They will take it away as plunder and carry it off to Babylon. ⁶And you, Pashhur, and all who live in your house will go into exile to Babylon. There you will die and be buried, you and all your friends to whom you have prophesied lies.'"

JEREMIAH'S COMPLAINT

⁷You deceived*ᵃ* me, LORD, and I was deceived*ᵃ*;
    you overpowered me and prevailed.
I am ridiculed all day long;
    everyone mocks me.
⁸Whenever I speak, I cry out
    proclaiming violence and destruction.
So the word of the LORD has brought me
    insult and reproach all day long.

ᵃ 7 Or persuaded

Did this prophecy come true? (19:9)
Yes. When the Babylonians laid siege to Jerusalem and the food ran out, the people did resort to cannibalism.

How was a broken jar like the nation of Israel? (19:11)
This was a dramatic way of showing what God would do to Israel. In ancient times, Egyptians etched the names of enemies on pottery bowls and then smashed them, hoping to break their power.

Who was the king of Babylon? (20:4)
This was Nebuchadnezzar, who became ruler of Babylon in 605 B.C.

What tension did Jeremiah feel? (20:8–9)
When he prophesied, he was persecuted. But when he tried to stay silent, he was unable to keep God's word bottled up inside him.

⁹But if I say, "I will not mention his word
    or speak anymore in his name,"
his word is in my heart like a fire,
    a fire shut up in my bones.
I am weary of holding it in;
    indeed, I cannot.
¹⁰I hear many whispering,
    "Terror on every side!
    Denounce him! Let's denounce him!"
All my friends
    are waiting for me to slip, saying,
"Perhaps he will be deceived;
    then we will prevail over him
    and take our revenge on him."

¹¹But the Lord is with me like a mighty warrior;
    so my persecutors will stumble and not prevail.
They will fail and be thoroughly disgraced;
    their dishonor will never be forgotten.
¹²Lord Almighty, you who examine the righteous
    and probe the heart and mind,
let me see your vengeance on them,
    for to you I have committed my cause.

¹³Sing to the Lord!
    Give praise to the Lord!
He rescues the life of the needy
    from the hands of the wicked.

¹⁴Cursed be the day I was born!
    May the day my mother bore me not be blessed!
¹⁵Cursed be the man who brought my father the news,
    who made him very glad, saying,
    "A child is born to you—a son!"
¹⁶May that man be like the towns
    the Lord overthrew without pity.
May he hear wailing in the morning,
    a battle cry at noon.
¹⁷For he did not kill me in the womb,
    with my mother as my grave,
    her womb enlarged forever.
¹⁸Why did I ever come out of the womb
    to see trouble and sorrow
    and to end my days in shame?

GOD REJECTS ZEDEKIAH'S REQUEST

21 The word came to Jeremiah from the Lord when King Zedekiah sent to him Pashhur son of Malkijah and the priest Zephaniah son of Maaseiah. They said: ²"Inquire now of the Lord for us because Nebuchadnezzar*ᵃ* king of Babylon is attacking us. Perhaps the Lord will perform wonders for us as in times past so that he will withdraw from us."

³But Jeremiah answered them, "Tell Zedekiah, ⁴'This is what the Lord, the God of Israel, says: I am about to turn

---

ᵃ 2 Hebrew *Nebuchadrezzar*, of which *Nebuchadnezzar* is a variant; here and often in Jeremiah and Ezekiel

---

What were the towns God overthrew? (20:16)
Sodom and Gomorrah (see Genesis 19:24–25).

Why was Jeremiah so bitter? (20:17–18)
Because Jeremiah proclaimed the Lord's message, he was criticized, attacked, and ignored. People plotted against his life and tried to undercut his ministry. It grieved him that the work God called him to do made his life so hard.

What did it mean to "inquire of the Lord"? (21:2)
This meant to ask for knowledge or information, not necessarily to ask for help.

against you the weapons of war that are in your hands, which you are using to fight the king of Babylon and the Babylonians*a* who are outside the wall besieging you. And I will gather them inside this city. [5]I myself will fight against you with an outstretched hand and a mighty arm in furious anger and in great wrath. [6]I will strike down those who live in this city—both man and beast—and they will die of a terrible plague. [7]After that, declares the LORD, I will give Zedekiah king of Judah, his officials and the people in this city who survive the plague, sword and famine, into the hands of Nebuchadnezzar king of Babylon and to their enemies who want to kill them. He will put them to the sword; he will show them no mercy or pity or compassion.'

[8]"Furthermore, tell the people, 'This is what the LORD says: See, I am setting before you the way of life and the way of death. [9]Whoever stays in this city will die by the sword, famine or plague. But whoever goes out and surrenders to the Babylonians who are besieging you will live; they will escape with their lives. [10]I have determined to do this city harm and not good, declares the LORD. It will be given into the hands of the king of Babylon, and he will destroy it with fire.'

[11]"Moreover, say to the royal house of Judah, 'Hear the word of the LORD. [12]This is what the LORD says to you, house of David:

"'Administer justice every morning;
    rescue from the hand of the oppressor
    the one who has been robbed,
or my wrath will break out and burn like fire
    because of the evil you have done—
    burn with no one to quench it.
[13]I am against you, Jerusalem,
    you who live above this valley
    on the rocky plateau, declares the LORD—
you who say, "Who can come against us?
    Who can enter our refuge?"
[14]I will punish you as your deeds deserve,
    declares the LORD.
I will kindle a fire in your forests
    that will consume everything around you.'"

JUDGMENT AGAINST WICKED KINGS

22 This is what the LORD says: "Go down to the palace of the king of Judah and proclaim this message there: [2]'Hear the word of the LORD to you, king of Judah, you who sit on David's throne—you, your officials and your people who come through these gates. [3]This is what the LORD says: Do what is just and right. Rescue from the hand of the oppressor the one who has been robbed. Do no wrong or violence to the foreigner, the fatherless or the widow, and do not shed innocent blood in this place. [4]For if you are careful to carry out these commands, then kings who sit on David's throne will come through the gates of this palace, riding in chariots and on horses, accompanied

---

a 4 Or Chaldeans; also in verse 9

Who were the Babylonians? (21:4)
They were the Chaldeans, a Bedouin people until about 1000 B.C. when they settled in southern Mesopotamia.

What is the geography of Jerusalem? (21:13)
Jerusalem sits on a hill surrounded on three sides by valleys.

Why did God swear by himself? (22:5)
God did not need to take an oath because he always spoke the truth, but he did this for emphasis. He swore by himself because there was nothing or no one greater to swear by.

Who was the dead king? (22:10)
This was Josiah, who died in a battle with Pharaoh Necho of Egypt. Jeremiah said not to weep for him but for his son, who would be sent into exile and never see his homeland again.

Who was Jeremiah talking about here? (22:13–14)
He was probably talking about King Jehoiakim, who did not pay the workers who built his extravagant palace.

by their officials and their people. ⁵But if you do not obey these commands, declares the LORD, I swear by myself that this palace will become a ruin.'"

⁶For this is what the LORD says about the palace of the king of Judah:

"Though you are like Gilead to me,
  like the summit of Lebanon,
I will surely make you like a wasteland,
  like towns not inhabited.
⁷I will send destroyers against you,
  each man with his weapons,
and they will cut up your fine cedar beams
  and throw them into the fire.

⁸"People from many nations will pass by this city and will ask one another, 'Why has the LORD done such a thing to this great city?' ⁹And the answer will be: 'Because they have forsaken the covenant of the LORD their God and have worshiped and served other gods.'"

¹⁰Do not weep for the dead king or mourn his loss;
  rather, weep bitterly for him who is exiled,
because he will never return
  nor see his native land again.

¹¹For this is what the LORD says about Shallumᵃ son of Josiah, who succeeded his father as king of Judah but has gone from this place: "He will never return. ¹²He will die in the place where they have led him captive; he will not see this land again."

¹³"Woe to him who builds his palace by unrighteousness,
  his upper rooms by injustice,
making his own people work for nothing,
  not paying them for their labor.
¹⁴He says, 'I will build myself a great palace
  with spacious upper rooms.'
So he makes large windows in it,
  panels it with cedar
  and decorates it in red.

¹⁵"Does it make you a king
  to have more and more cedar?
Did not your father have food and drink?
  He did what was right and just,
  so all went well with him.
¹⁶He defended the cause of the poor and needy,
  and so all went well.
Is that not what it means to know me?"
  declares the LORD.
¹⁷"But your eyes and your heart
  are set only on dishonest gain,
on shedding innocent blood
  and on oppression and extortion."

¹⁸Therefore this is what the LORD says about Jehoiakim son of Josiah king of Judah:

ᵃ 11 Also called Jehoahaz

"They will not mourn for him:
    'Alas, my brother! Alas, my sister!'
They will not mourn for him:
    'Alas, my master! Alas, his splendor!'
¹⁹ He will have the burial of a donkey—
    dragged away and thrown
    outside the gates of Jerusalem."

²⁰ "Go up to Lebanon and cry out,
    let your voice be heard in Bashan,
cry out from Abarim,
    for all your allies are crushed.
²¹ I warned you when you felt secure,
    but you said, 'I will not listen!'
This has been your way from your youth;
    you have not obeyed me.
²² The wind will drive all your shepherds away,
    and your allies will go into exile.
Then you will be ashamed and disgraced
    because of all your wickedness.
²³ You who live in 'Lebanon,^a'
    who are nestled in cedar buildings,
how you will groan when pangs come upon you,
    pain like that of a woman in labor!

²⁴ "As surely as I live," declares the LORD, "even if you, Je-
hoiachin^b son of Jehoiakim king of Judah, were a signet ring
on my right hand, I would still pull you off. ²⁵ I will deliver
you into the hands of those who want to kill you, those you
fear—Nebuchadnezzar king of Babylon and the Babyloni-
ans.^c ²⁶ I will hurl you and the mother who gave you birth
into another country, where neither of you was born, and
there you both will die. ²⁷ You will never come back to the
land you long to return to."

²⁸ Is this man Jehoiachin a despised, broken pot,
    an object no one wants?
Why will he and his children be hurled out,
    cast into a land they do not know?
²⁹ O land, land, land,
    hear the word of the LORD!
³⁰ This is what the LORD says:
    "Record this man as if childless,
    a man who will not prosper in his lifetime,
for none of his offspring will prosper,
    none will sit on the throne of David
    or rule anymore in Judah."

THE RIGHTEOUS BRANCH

23 "Woe to the shepherds who are destroying and scattering the sheep of my pasture!" declares the LORD.
² Therefore this is what the LORD, the God of Israel, says to
the shepherds who tend my people: "Because you have scattered my flock and driven them away and have not bestowed
care on them, I will bestow punishment on you for the evil

**What were Lebanon, Bashan,
and Abarim? (22:20)**
These were locations in different
parts of Israel that together represented the entire nation.

**What was a signet ring?
(22:24)**
A signet ring had the king or
other official's symbol on it and
was a sign of his authority. It
was pressed into soft wax to seal
important documents.

**Who were these bad shep-
herds? (23:1)**
These were the leaders of the
people—the priests, false prophets, and king—who were leading
the people down the wrong path.

^a 23 That is, the palace in Jerusalem (see 1 Kings 7:2)   ^b 24 Hebrew
Koniah, a variant of *Jehoiachin*; also in verse 28   ^c 25 Or *Chaldeans*

you have done," declares the LORD. ³"I myself will gather the remnant of my flock out of all the countries where I have driven them and will bring them back to their pasture, where they will be fruitful and increase in number. ⁴I will place shepherds over them who will tend them, and they will no longer be afraid or terrified, nor will any be missing," declares the LORD.

⁵"The days are coming," declares the LORD,
    "when I will raise up for David*ᵃ* a righteous Branch,
  a King who will reign wisely
    and do what is just and right in the land.
⁶In his days Judah will be saved
    and Israel will live in safety.
This is the name by which he will be called:
    The LORD Our Righteous Savior.

⁷"So then, the days are coming," declares the LORD, "when people will no longer say, 'As surely as the LORD lives, who brought the Israelites up out of Egypt,' ⁸but they will say, 'As surely as the LORD lives, who brought the descendants of Israel up out of the land of the north and out of all the countries where he had banished them.' Then they will live in their own land."

LYING PROPHETS

⁹Concerning the prophets:

My heart is broken within me;
    all my bones tremble.
I am like a drunken man,
    like a strong man overcome by wine,
because of the LORD
    and his holy words.
¹⁰The land is full of adulterers;
    because of the curse*ᵇ* the land lies parched
    and the pastures in the wilderness are withered.
The prophets follow an evil course
    and use their power unjustly.

¹¹"Both prophet and priest are godless;
    even in my temple I find their wickedness,"
                          declares the LORD.
¹²"Therefore their path will become slippery;
    they will be banished to darkness
    and there they will fall.
I will bring disaster on them
    in the year they are punished,"
                          declares the LORD.

¹³"Among the prophets of Samaria
    I saw this repulsive thing:
They prophesied by Baal
    and led my people Israel astray.
¹⁴And among the prophets of Jerusalem
    I have seen something horrible:
They commit adultery and live a lie.

What had these false prophets done? (23:9–10)
They worshiped idols and lead the people away from God by setting immoral examples for others to follow.

ᵃ 5 Or *up from David's line*   *ᵇ 10* Or *because of these things*

They strengthen the hands of evildoers,
　　so that not one of them turns from their wickedness.
They are all like Sodom to me;
　　the people of Jerusalem are like Gomorrah."

¹⁵ Therefore this is what the LORD Almighty says concerning the prophets:

"I will make them eat bitter food
　　and drink poisoned water,
because from the prophets of Jerusalem
　　ungodliness has spread throughout the land."

¹⁶ This is what the LORD Almighty says:

"Do not listen to what the prophets are prophesying to
　　you;
　　they fill you with false hopes.
They speak visions from their own minds,
　　not from the mouth of the LORD.
¹⁷ They keep saying to those who despise me,
　　'The LORD says: You will have peace.'
And to all who follow the stubbornness of their hearts
　　they say, 'No harm will come to you.'
¹⁸ But which of them has stood in the council
　　of the LORD
to see or to hear his word?
　　Who has listened and heard his word?
¹⁹ See, the storm of the LORD
　　will burst out in wrath,
a whirlwind swirling down
　　on the heads of the wicked.
²⁰ The anger of the LORD will not turn back
　　until he fully accomplishes
　　the purposes of his heart.
In days to come
　　you will understand it clearly.
²¹ I did not send these prophets,
　　yet they have run with their message;
I did not speak to them,
　　yet they have prophesied.
²² But if they had stood in my council,
　　they would have proclaimed my words to my people
and would have turned them from their evil ways
　　and from their evil deeds.

²³ "Am I only a God nearby,"
　　　　　　　　　　　　declares the LORD,
　　"and not a God far away?
²⁴ Who can hide in secret places
　　so that I cannot see them?"
　　　　　　　　　　　　declares the LORD.
　　"Do not I fill heaven and earth?"
　　　　　　　　　　　　declares the LORD.

²⁵ "I have heard what the prophets say who prophesy lies in my name. They say, 'I had a dream! I had a dream!' ²⁶ How long will this continue in the hearts of these lying prophets, who prophesy the delusions of their own minds? ²⁷ They

What was the council of the Lord? (23:18)
This referred to those with whom the Lord shared his plans, like a king who had a group of royal officials.

Is it possible for people to hide from God? (23:23–24)
Since God is everywhere, there is no place where people can hide and not be seen by him.

How is the true word of God described? (23:28–29)
It is described as grain (that can feed people), like fire (that can purify or destroy), and like a hammer (that can break something in its path).

think the dreams they tell one another will make my people forget my name, just as their ancestors forgot my name through Baal worship. [28] Let the prophet who has a dream recount the dream, but let the one who has my word speak it faithfully. For what has straw to do with grain?" declares the LORD. [29] "Is not my word like fire," declares the LORD, "and like a hammer that breaks a rock in pieces?

[30] "Therefore," declares the LORD, "I am against the prophets who steal from one another words supposedly from me. [31] Yes," declares the LORD, "I am against the prophets who wag their own tongues and yet declare, 'The LORD declares.' [32] Indeed, I am against those who prophesy false dreams," declares the LORD. "They tell them and lead my people astray with their reckless lies, yet I did not send or appoint them. They do not benefit these people in the least," declares the LORD.

FALSE PROPHECY

[33] "When these people, or a prophet or a priest, ask you, 'What is the message from the LORD?' say to them, 'What message? I will forsake you, declares the LORD.' [34] If a prophet or a priest or anyone else claims, 'This is a message from the LORD,' I will punish them and their household. [35] This is what each of you keeps saying to your friends and other Israelites: 'What is the LORD's answer?' or 'What has the LORD spoken?' [36] But you must not mention 'a message from the LORD' again, because each one's word becomes their own message. So you distort the words of the living God, the LORD Almighty, our God. [37] This is what you keep saying to a prophet: 'What is the LORD's answer to you?' or 'What has the LORD spoken?' [38] Although you claim, 'This is a message from the LORD,' this is what the LORD says: You used the words, 'This is a message from the LORD,' even though I told you that you must not claim, 'This is a message from the LORD.' [39] Therefore, I will surely forget you and cast you out of my presence along with the city I gave to you and your ancestors. [40] I will bring on you everlasting disgrace — everlasting shame that will not be forgotten."

TWO BASKETS OF FIGS

24 After Jehoiachin[a] son of Jehoiakim king of Judah and the officials, the skilled workers and the artisans of Judah were carried into exile from Jerusalem to Babylon by Nebuchadnezzar king of Babylon, the LORD showed me two baskets of figs placed in front of the temple of the LORD. [2] One basket had very good figs, like those that ripen early; the other basket had very bad figs, so bad they could not be eaten.

[3] Then the LORD asked me, "What do you see, Jeremiah?"

"Figs," I answered. "The good ones are very good, but the bad ones are so bad they cannot be eaten."

[4] Then the word of the LORD came to me: [5] "This is what the LORD, the God of Israel, says: 'Like these good figs, I regard as good the exiles from Judah, whom I sent away from this place to the land of the Babylonians.[b] [6] My eyes will watch over them for their good, and I will bring them back to this

What were good figs? (24:2)
The first figs to ripen in June were especially juicy and sweet. They were a symbol of the first group of exiles who had been taken to Babylon. This group included officials, priests, and craftsmen, and only the poor and weak were left behind.

---

a 1 Hebrew *Jeconiah,* a variant of *Jehoiachin   b 5* Or *Chaldeans*

land. I will build them up and not tear them down; I will plant them and not uproot them. ⁷I will give them a heart to know me, that I am the LORD. They will be my people, and I will be their God, for they will return to me with all their heart.

⁸"'But like the bad figs, which are so bad they cannot be eaten,' says the LORD, 'so will I deal with Zedekiah king of Judah, his officials and the survivors from Jerusalem, whether they remain in this land or live in Egypt. ⁹I will make them abhorrent and an offense to all the kingdoms of the earth, a reproach and a byword, a curse*a* and an object of ridicule, wherever I banish them. ¹⁰I will send the sword, famine and plague against them until they are destroyed from the land I gave to them and their ancestors.'"

SEVENTY YEARS OF CAPTIVITY

25 The word came to Jeremiah concerning all the people of Judah in the fourth year of Jehoiakim son of Josiah king of Judah, which was the first year of Nebuchadnezzar king of Babylon. ²So Jeremiah the prophet said to all the people of Judah and to all those living in Jerusalem: ³For twenty-three years—from the thirteenth year of Josiah son of Amon king of Judah until this very day—the word of the LORD has come to me and I have spoken to you again and again, but you have not listened.

⁴And though the LORD has sent all his servants the prophets to you again and again, you have not listened or paid any attention. ⁵They said, "Turn now, each of you, from your evil ways and your evil practices, and you can stay in the land the LORD gave to you and your ancestors for ever and ever. ⁶Do not follow other gods to serve and worship them; do not arouse my anger with what your hands have made. Then I will not harm you."

⁷"But you did not listen to me," declares the LORD, "and you have aroused my anger with what your hands have made, and you have brought harm to yourselves."

⁸Therefore the LORD Almighty says this: "Because you have not listened to my words, ⁹I will summon all the peoples of the north and my servant Nebuchadnezzar king of Babylon," declares the LORD, "and I will bring them against this land and its inhabitants and against all the surrounding nations. I will completely destroy*b* them and make them an object of horror and scorn, and an everlasting ruin. ¹⁰I will banish from them the sounds of joy and gladness, the voices of bride and bridegroom, the sound of millstones and the light of the lamp. ¹¹This whole country will become a desolate wasteland, and these nations will serve the king of Babylon seventy years.

¹²"But when the seventy years are fulfilled, I will punish the king of Babylon and his nation, the land of the Babylonians,*c* for their guilt," declares the LORD, "and will make it desolate forever. ¹³I will bring on that land all the things

How would the exiles return? (24:7)
God would work in their hearts so that they would return to him, and then they would be able to return to their land.

Who were the peoples of the north? (25:9)
They were Babylon and its allies.

Why would Nebuchadnezzar be called God's servant? (25:9)
This was not because he worshiped the Lord, but because God used him to carry out his purposes.

---

a 9 That is, their names will be used in cursing (see 29:22); or, others will see that they are cursed.   *b 9* The Hebrew term refers to the irrevocable giving over of things or persons to the LORD, often by totally destroying them.
c 12 Or *Chaldeans*

I have spoken against it, all that are written in this book and prophesied by Jeremiah against all the nations. [14]They themselves will be enslaved by many nations and great kings; I will repay them according to their deeds and the work of their hands."

THE CUP OF GOD'S WRATH

[15]This is what the LORD, the God of Israel, said to me: "Take from my hand this cup filled with the wine of my wrath and make all the nations to whom I send you drink it. [16]When they drink it, they will stagger and go mad because of the sword I will send among them."

[17]So I took the cup from the LORD's hand and made all the nations to whom he sent me drink it: [18]Jerusalem and the towns of Judah, its kings and officials, to make them a ruin and an object of horror and scorn, a curse[a] — as they are today; [19]Pharaoh king of Egypt, his attendants, his officials and all his people, [20]and all the foreign people there; all the kings of Uz; all the kings of the Philistines (those of Ashkelon, Gaza, Ekron, and the people left at Ashdod); [21]Edom, Moab and Ammon; [22]all the kings of Tyre and Sidon; the kings of the coastlands across the sea; [23]Dedan, Tema, Buz and all who are in distant places[b]; [24]all the kings of Arabia and all the kings of the foreign people who live in the wilderness; [25]all the kings of Zimri, Elam and Media; [26]and all the kings of the north, near and far, one after the other—all the kingdoms on the face of the earth. And after all of them, the king of Sheshak[c] will drink it too.

[27]"Then tell them, 'This is what the LORD Almighty, the God of Israel, says: Drink, get drunk and vomit, and fall to rise no more because of the sword I will send among you.' [28]But if they refuse to take the cup from your hand and drink, tell them, 'This is what the LORD Almighty says: You must drink it! [29]See, I am beginning to bring disaster on the city that bears my Name, and will you indeed go unpunished? You will not go unpunished, for I am calling down a sword on all who live on the earth, declares the LORD Almighty.'

[30]"Now prophesy all these words against them and say to them:

> "'The LORD will roar from on high;
>   he will thunder from his holy dwelling
>   and roar mightily against his land.
> He will shout like those who tread the grapes,
>   shout against all who live on the earth.
> [31]The tumult will resound to the ends of the earth,
>   for the LORD will bring charges against
>   the nations;
> he will bring judgment on all mankind
>   and put the wicked to the sword,'"
>   declares the LORD.

[32]This is what the LORD Almighty says:

What was the wine of God's wrath? (25:15)
This was a metaphor describing God's anger as like a cup of strong wine that would make the people stagger and fall. They would stagger because God would allow them to be killed by the sword.

What was Sheshak? (25:26)
This was a cryptogram, or code name, for Babylon. It isn't clear why Jeremiah used a code name to describe Babylon.

What was the city that bore God's Name? (25:29)
This was the city of Jerusalem.

Why would grape treaders shout? (25:30)
People who were trampling grapes were usually in a happy mood because of the harvest, so they made lots of noise.

---

[a] 18 That is, their names to be used in cursing (see 29:22); or, to be seen by others as cursed   [b] 23 Or *who clip the hair by their foreheads*   [c] 26 Sheshak is a cryptogram for Babylon.

"Look! Disaster is spreading
  from nation to nation;
a mighty storm is rising
  from the ends of the earth."

³³ At that time those slain by the LORD will be everywhere —
from one end of the earth to the other. They will not be
mourned or gathered up or buried, but will be like dung lying
on the ground.

³⁴ Weep and wail, you shepherds;
  roll in the dust, you leaders of the flock.
For your time to be slaughtered has come;
  you will fall like the best of the rams.ᵃ
³⁵ The shepherds will have nowhere to flee,
  the leaders of the flock no place to escape.
³⁶ Hear the cry of the shepherds,
  the wailing of the leaders of the flock,
  for the LORD is destroying their pasture.
³⁷ The peaceful meadows will be laid waste
  because of the fierce anger of the LORD.
³⁸ Like a lion he will leave his lair,
  and their land will become desolate
because of the swordᵇ of the oppressor
  and because of the LORD's fierce anger.

JEREMIAH THREATENED WITH DEATH

26 Early in the reign of Jehoiakim son of Josiah king
of Judah, this word came from the LORD: ² "This is
what the LORD says: Stand in the courtyard of the LORD's
house and speak to all the people of the towns of Judah who
come to worship in the house of the LORD. Tell them everything I command you; do not omit a word. ³ Perhaps they
will listen and each will turn from their evil ways. Then I will
relent and not inflict on them the disaster I was planning because of the evil they have done. ⁴ Say to them, 'This is what
the LORD says: If you do not listen to me and follow my law,
which I have set before you, ⁵ and if you do not listen to the
words of my servants the prophets, whom I have sent to you
again and again (though you have not listened), ⁶ then I will
make this house like Shiloh and this city a curseᶜ among all
the nations of the earth.'"

⁷ The priests, the prophets and all the people heard Jeremiah speak these words in the house of the LORD. ⁸ But as soon
as Jeremiah finished telling all the people everything the
LORD had commanded him to say, the priests, the prophets
and all the people seized him and said, "You must die! ⁹ Why
do you prophesy in the LORD's name that this house will
be like Shiloh and this city will be desolate and deserted?"
And all the people crowded around Jeremiah in the house
of the LORD.

¹⁰ When the officials of Judah heard about these things,
they went up from the royal palace to the house of the LORD

**What happened to Shiloh?
(26:6)**
Shiloh was destroyed around
1050 B.C. It was the city where
the ark was first placed in the
promised land, and it had been
the center of worship. But now it
was empty and ruined.

ᵃ 34 Septuagint; Hebrew *fall and be shattered like fine pottery*   ᵇ 38 Some
Hebrew manuscripts and Septuagint (see also 46:16 and 50:16); most
Hebrew manuscripts *anger*   ᶜ 6 That is, its name will be used in cursing
(see 29:22); or, others will see that it is cursed.

How was Jeremiah saved from being killed? (26:10–19)
The people finally recognized that he was speaking God's truth, and they recalled other prophets who had brought a similar message.

and took their places at the entrance of the New Gate of the LORD's house. [11] Then the priests and the prophets said to the officials and all the people, "This man should be sentenced to death because he has prophesied against this city. You have heard it with your own ears!"

[12] Then Jeremiah said to all the officials and all the people: "The LORD sent me to prophesy against this house and this city all the things you have heard. [13] Now reform your ways and your actions and obey the LORD your God. Then the LORD will relent and not bring the disaster he has pronounced against you. [14] As for me, I am in your hands; do with me whatever you think is good and right. [15] Be assured, however, that if you put me to death, you will bring the guilt of innocent blood on yourselves and on this city and on those who live in it, for in truth the LORD has sent me to you to speak all these words in your hearing."

[16] Then the officials and all the people said to the priests and the prophets, "This man should not be sentenced to death! He has spoken to us in the name of the LORD our God."

[17] Some of the elders of the land stepped forward and said to the entire assembly of people, [18] "Micah of Moresheth prophesied in the days of Hezekiah king of Judah. He told all the people of Judah, 'This is what the LORD Almighty says:

"'Zion will be plowed like a field,
　　Jerusalem will become a heap of rubble,
　　the temple hill a mound overgrown with thickets.'[a]

[19] "Did Hezekiah king of Judah or anyone else in Judah put him to death? Did not Hezekiah fear the LORD and seek his favor? And did not the LORD relent, so that he did not bring the disaster he pronounced against them? We are about to bring a terrible disaster on ourselves!"

[20] (Now Uriah son of Shemaiah from Kiriath Jearim was another man who prophesied in the name of the LORD; he prophesied the same things against this city and this land as Jeremiah did. [21] When King Jehoiakim and all his officers and officials heard his words, the king was determined to put him to death. But Uriah heard of it and fled in fear to Egypt. [22] King Jehoiakim, however, sent Elnathan son of Akbor to Egypt, along with some other men. [23] They brought Uriah out of Egypt and took him to King Jehoiakim, who had him struck down with a sword and his body thrown into the burial place of the common people.)

[24] Furthermore, Ahikam son of Shaphan supported Jeremiah, and so he was not handed over to the people to be put to death.

Why did Ahikam have such influence? (26:24)
Ahikam had been an official in the court of King Josiah, and he continued to have a strong reputation and influence after Josiah's death.

Why did Jeremiah wear a yoke? (27:2)
This yoke, which was like that worn by oxen, was here a symbol of political submission.

JUDAH TO SERVE NEBUCHADNEZZAR

27 Early in the reign of Zedekiah[b] son of Josiah king of Judah, this word came to Jeremiah from the LORD: [2] This is what the LORD said to me: "Make a yoke out of

---

[a] 18 Micah 3:12　　[b] 1 A few Hebrew manuscripts and Syriac (see also 27:3,12 and 28:1); most Hebrew manuscripts *Jehoiakim* (Most Septuagint manuscripts do not have this verse.)

straps and crossbars and put it on your neck. ³Then send word to the kings of Edom, Moab, Ammon, Tyre and Sidon through the envoys who have come to Jerusalem to Zedekiah king of Judah. ⁴Give them a message for their masters and say, 'This is what the LORD Almighty, the God of Israel, says: "Tell this to your masters: ⁵With my great power and outstretched arm I made the earth and its people and the animals that are on it, and I give it to anyone I please. ⁶Now I will give all your countries into the hands of my servant Nebuchadnezzar king of Babylon; I will make even the wild animals subject to him. ⁷All nations will serve him and his son and his grandson until the time for his land comes; then many nations and great kings will subjugate him.

⁸"'If, however, any nation or kingdom will not serve Nebuchadnezzar king of Babylon or bow its neck under his yoke, I will punish that nation with the sword, famine and plague, declares the LORD, until I destroy it by his hand. ⁹So do not listen to your prophets, your diviners, your interpreters of dreams, your mediums or your sorcerers who tell you, 'You will not serve the king of Babylon.' ¹⁰They prophesy lies to you that will only serve to remove you far from your lands; I will banish you and you will perish. ¹¹But if any nation will bow its neck under the yoke of the king of Babylon and serve him, I will let that nation remain in its own land to till it and to live there, declares the LORD.'"'

¹²I gave the same message to Zedekiah king of Judah. I said, "Bow your neck under the yoke of the king of Babylon; serve him and his people, and you will live. ¹³Why will you and your people die by the sword, famine and plague with which the LORD has threatened any nation that will not serve the king of Babylon? ¹⁴Do not listen to the words of the prophets who say to you, 'You will not serve the king of Babylon,' for they are prophesying lies to you. ¹⁵'I have not sent them,' declares the LORD. 'They are prophesying lies in my name. Therefore, I will banish you and you will perish, both you and the prophets who prophesy to you.'"

¹⁶Then I said to the priests and all these people, "This is what the LORD says: Do not listen to the prophets who say, 'Very soon now the articles from the LORD's house will be brought back from Babylon.' They are prophesying lies to you. ¹⁷Do not listen to them. Serve the king of Babylon, and you will live. Why should this city become a ruin? ¹⁸If they are prophets and have the word of the LORD, let them plead with the LORD Almighty that the articles remaining in the house of the LORD and in the palace of the king of Judah and in Jerusalem not be taken to Babylon. ¹⁹For this is what the LORD Almighty says about the pillars, the bronze Sea, the movable stands and the other articles that are left in this city, ²⁰which Nebuchadnezzar king of Babylon did not take away when he carried Jehoiachinᵃ son of Jehoiakim king of Judah into exile from Jerusalem to Babylon, along with all the nobles of Judah and Jerusalem— ²¹yes, this is what the LORD Almighty, the God of Israel, says about the things that are left in the house of the LORD and in the palace of the king

Who were the diviners, interpreters of dreams, mediums, and sorcerers? (27:9) In the ancient Middle East, people placed great significance on dreams and their meaning. God told the people to ignore what these so-called experts said and to listen to his message instead.

What was God's message to the people? (27:16–22) God told them not to resist Babylon, but to accept the fact that they were going to be taken into captivity.

ᵃ 20 Hebrew *Jeconiah,* a variant of *Jehoiachin*

of Judah and in Jerusalem: ²²'They will be taken to Babylon and there they will remain until the day I come for them,' declares the LORD. 'Then I will bring them back and restore them to this place.'"

THE FALSE PROPHET HANANIAH

28 In the fifth month of that same year, the fourth year, early in the reign of Zedekiah king of Judah, the prophet Hananiah son of Azzur, who was from Gibeon, said to me in the house of the LORD in the presence of the priests and all the people: ²"This is what the LORD Almighty, the God of Israel, says: 'I will break the yoke of the king of Babylon. ³Within two years I will bring back to this place all the articles of the LORD's house that Nebuchadnezzar king of Babylon removed from here and took to Babylon. ⁴I will also bring back to this place Jehoiachin^a son of Jehoiakim king of Judah and all the other exiles from Judah who went to Babylon,' declares the LORD, 'for I will break the yoke of the king of Babylon.'"

⁵Then the prophet Jeremiah replied to the prophet Hananiah before the priests and all the people who were standing in the house of the LORD. ⁶He said, "Amen! May the LORD do so! May the LORD fulfill the words you have prophesied by bringing the articles of the LORD's house and all the exiles back to this place from Babylon. ⁷Nevertheless, listen to what I have to say in your hearing and in the hearing of all the people: ⁸From early times the prophets who preceded you and me have prophesied war, disaster and plague against many countries and great kingdoms. ⁹But the prophet who prophesies peace will be recognized as one truly sent by the LORD only if his prediction comes true."

¹⁰Then the prophet Hananiah took the yoke off the neck of the prophet Jeremiah and broke it, ¹¹and he said before all the people, "This is what the LORD says: 'In the same way I will break the yoke of Nebuchadnezzar king of Babylon off the neck of all the nations within two years.'" At this, the prophet Jeremiah went on his way.

¹²After the prophet Hananiah had broken the yoke off the neck of the prophet Jeremiah, the word of the LORD came to Jeremiah: ¹³"Go and tell Hananiah, 'This is what the LORD says: You have broken a wooden yoke, but in its place you will get a yoke of iron. ¹⁴This is what the LORD Almighty, the God of Israel, says: I will put an iron yoke on the necks of all these nations to make them serve Nebuchadnezzar king of Babylon, and they will serve him. I will even give him control over the wild animals.'"

¹⁵Then the prophet Jeremiah said to Hananiah the prophet, "Listen, Hananiah! The LORD has not sent you, yet you have persuaded this nation to trust in lies. ¹⁶Therefore this is what the LORD says: 'I am about to remove you from the face of the earth. This very year you are going to die, because you have preached rebellion against the LORD.'"

¹⁷In the seventh month of that same year, Hananiah the prophet died.

---

^a 4 Hebrew *Jeconiah*, a variant of *Jehoiachin*

Did Jeremiah continually wear the yoke? (28:10)
Apparently he did in order to remind the people in a vivid way of the Lord's prophecy.

After Hananiah broke the wooden yoke, what did Jeremiah tell him? (28:14)
Jeremiah told him that the Lord would place an unbreakable iron yoke on the necks of the nations to make them serve Nebuchadnezzar.

How did Nebuchadnezzar have control over wild animals? (28:14)
This was an exaggeration meant to show that Nebuchadnezzar would have absolute rule over all the nations.

A LETTER TO THE EXILES

29 This is the text of the letter that the prophet Jeremiah sent from Jerusalem to the surviving elders among the exiles and to the priests, the prophets and all the other people Nebuchadnezzar had carried into exile from Jerusalem to Babylon. ² (This was after King Jehoiachin*a* and the queen mother, the court officials and the leaders of Judah and Jerusalem, the skilled workers and the artisans had gone into exile from Jerusalem.) ³ He entrusted the letter to Elasah son of Shaphan and to Gemariah son of Hilkiah, whom Zedekiah king of Judah sent to King Nebuchadnezzar in Babylon. It said:

⁴ This is what the LORD Almighty, the God of Israel, says to all those I carried into exile from Jerusalem to Babylon: ⁵ "Build houses and settle down; plant gardens and eat what they produce. ⁶ Marry and have sons and daughters; find wives for your sons and give your daughters in marriage, so that they too may have sons and daughters. Increase in number there; do not decrease. ⁷ Also, seek the peace and prosperity of the city to which I have carried you into exile. Pray to the LORD for it, because if it prospers, you too will prosper." ⁸ Yes, this is what the LORD Almighty, the God of Israel, says: "Do not let the prophets and diviners among you deceive you. Do not listen to the dreams you encourage them to have. ⁹ They are prophesying lies to you in my name. I have not sent them," declares the LORD.

¹⁰ This is what the LORD says: "When seventy years are completed for Babylon, I will come to you and fulfill my good promise to bring you back to this place. ¹¹ For I know the plans I have for you," declares the LORD, "plans to prosper you and not to harm you, plans to give you hope and a future. ¹² Then you will call on me and come and pray to me, and I will listen to you. ¹³ You will seek me and find me when you seek me with all your heart. ¹⁴ I will be found by you," declares the LORD, "and will bring you back from captivity.*b* I will gather you from all the nations and places where I have banished you," declares the LORD, "and will bring you back to the place from which I carried you into exile."

a 2 Hebrew *Jeconiah,* a variant of *Jehoiachin*   *b 14* Or *will restore your fortunes*

How did Jeremiah make sure the letter would arrive safely? (29:3)
He placed it in the ancient equivalent of a diplomatic pouch and sent it with two trusted messengers.

What was unusual about this instruction? (29:7)
Praying for one's captors and working toward their prosperity was unheard of in the ancient world.

Why was it a comfort to the exiles that the Lord had plans for them? (29:10–11)
They realized that the Lord had not forgotten them and that he would eventually restore them.

Does God have a plan for each of us?   JEREMIAH 29

Yes. In this passage, Jeremiah was speaking God's words to the Jewish people who were in exile in Babylon. The letter that he wrote offered the promise that God would restore his people after 70 years. God assured them in Jeremiah's letter that he would carry out his plan for them and would bless them.

The fact that God took care of his people and loved them even when they turned away from him and were being punished is encouraging. This is just one of the many places in the Bible where God revealed that he has plans for his people, and he will bring them about. Another example of this is the story of Joseph, who was sold into slavery but eventually saved the people of Egypt from famine. Throughout the Bible, God had plans for his people even when they were in difficult situations.

We know that God loves his people and will care for us today as he has cared for his people in the past. We can try to discover God's plan for our lives by reading the Bible, praying, and seeking advice from parents and mentors.

¹⁵You may say, "The LORD has raised up prophets for us in Babylon," ¹⁶but this is what the LORD says about the king who sits on David's throne and all the people who remain in this city, your fellow citizens who did not go with you into exile— ¹⁷yes, this is what the LORD Almighty says: "I will send the sword, famine and plague against them and I will make them like figs that are so bad they cannot be eaten. ¹⁸I will pursue them with the sword, famine and plague and will make them abhorrent to all the kingdoms of the earth, a curse*ᵃ* and an object of horror, of scorn and reproach, among all the nations where I drive them. ¹⁹For they have not listened to my words," declares the LORD, "words that I sent to them again and again by my servants the prophets. And you exiles have not listened either," declares the LORD.

²⁰Therefore, hear the word of the LORD, all you exiles whom I have sent away from Jerusalem to Babylon. ²¹This is what the LORD Almighty, the God of Israel, says about Ahab son of Kolaiah and Zedekiah son of Maaseiah, who are prophesying lies to you in my name: "I will deliver them into the hands of Nebuchadnezzar king of Babylon, and he will put them to death before your very eyes. ²²Because of them, all the exiles from Judah who are in Babylon will use this curse: 'May the LORD treat you like Zedekiah and Ahab, whom the king of Babylon burned in the fire.' ²³For they have done outrageous things in Israel; they have committed adultery with their neighbors' wives, and in my name they have uttered lies—which I did not authorize. I know it and am a witness to it," declares the LORD.

MESSAGE TO SHEMAIAH

²⁴Tell Shemaiah the Nehelamite, ²⁵"This is what the LORD Almighty, the God of Israel, says: You sent letters in your own name to all the people in Jerusalem, to the priest Zephaniah son of Maaseiah, and to all the other priests. You said to Zephaniah, ²⁶'The LORD has appointed you priest in place of Jehoiada to be in charge of the house of the LORD; you should put any maniac who acts like a prophet into the stocks and neck-irons. ²⁷So why have you not reprimanded Jeremiah from Anathoth, who poses as a prophet among you? ²⁸He has sent this message to us in Babylon: It will be a long time. Therefore build houses and settle down; plant gardens and eat what they produce.'"

²⁹Zephaniah the priest, however, read the letter to Jeremiah the prophet. ³⁰Then the word of the LORD came to Jeremiah: ³¹"Send this message to all the exiles: 'This is what the LORD says about Shemaiah the Nehelamite: Because Shemaiah has prophesied to you, even though I did not send him, and has persuaded you to trust in lies, ³²this is what the LORD says: I will surely punish Shemaiah the Nehelamite and his descendants. He will have no one left among this people, nor will he see the good things I will do for my people, declares the LORD, because he has preached rebellion against me.'"

ᵃ 18 That is, their names will be used in cursing (see verse 22); or, others will see that they are cursed.

Why would the king burn these false prophets? (29:22)
The Babylonians used fire as a method of execution.

Why would prophets sometimes be considered insane? (29:26)
Prophets often had very strange appearances and behaviors. For example, Jeremiah went around with a yoke on his neck. The test of whether a person was a prophet or simply insane was if the prophecies came true.

RESTORATION OF ISRAEL

30 This is the word that came to Jeremiah from the LORD: ²"This is what the LORD, the God of Israel, says: 'Write in a book all the words I have spoken to you. ³The days are coming,' declares the LORD, 'when I will bring my people Israel and Judah back from captivity*ᵃ* and restore them to the land I gave their ancestors to possess,' says the LORD."

⁴These are the words the LORD spoke concerning Israel and Judah: ⁵"This is what the LORD says:

"'Cries of fear are heard—
    terror, not peace.
⁶ Ask and see:
    Can a man bear children?
Then why do I see every strong man
    with his hands on his stomach like a woman
        in labor,
    every face turned deathly pale?
⁷ How awful that day will be!
    No other will be like it.
It will be a time of trouble for Jacob,
    but he will be saved out of it.

⁸ "'In that day,' declares the LORD Almighty,
    'I will break the yoke off their necks
and will tear off their bonds;
    no longer will foreigners enslave them.
⁹ Instead, they will serve the LORD their God
    and David their king,
    whom I will raise up for them.

¹⁰ "'So do not be afraid, Jacob my servant;
    do not be dismayed, Israel,'

                            declares the LORD.
'I will surely save you out of a distant place,
    your descendants from the land of their exile.
Jacob will again have peace and security,
    and no one will make him afraid.
¹¹ I am with you and will save you,'
    declares the LORD.
'Though I completely destroy all the nations
    among which I scatter you,
    I will not completely destroy you.
I will discipline you but only in due measure;
    I will not let you go entirely unpunished.'

¹² "This is what the LORD says:

"'Your wound is incurable,
    your injury beyond healing.
¹³ There is no one to plead your cause,
    no remedy for your sore,
    no healing for you.
¹⁴ All your allies have forgotten you;
    they care nothing for you.

ᵃ 3 Or will restore the fortunes of my people Israel and Judah

What was this time of trouble? (30:7)
This is a description of the day of the Lord. This prophecy would be fulfilled in the near future when the nation experienced severe discipline before being restored, but it also pointed to the future Messianic age.

How would they serve King David? (30:9)
Here David is a metaphor for the Messiah.

I have struck you as an enemy would
   and punished you as would the cruel,
because your guilt is so great
   and your sins so many.
¹⁵ Why do you cry out over your wound,
   your pain that has no cure?
Because of your great guilt and many sins
   I have done these things to you.

¹⁶ "But all who devour you will be devoured;
   all your enemies will go into exile.
Those who plunder you will be plundered;
   all who make spoil of you I will despoil.
¹⁷ But I will restore you to health
   and heal your wounds,'
                                            declares the LORD,
'because you are called an outcast,
   Zion for whom no one cares.'

¹⁸ "This is what the LORD says:

"'I will restore the fortunes of Jacob's tents
   and have compassion on his dwellings;
the city will be rebuilt on her ruins,
   and the palace will stand in its proper place.
¹⁹ From them will come songs of thanksgiving
   and the sound of rejoicing.
I will add to their numbers,
   and they will not be decreased;
I will bring them honor,
   and they will not be disdained.
²⁰ Their children will be as in days of old,
   and their community will be established
      before me;
I will punish all who oppress them.
²¹ Their leader will be one of their own;
   their ruler will arise from among them.
I will bring him near and he will come close
      to me—
for who is he who will devote himself
   to be close to me?'
                                            declares the LORD.
²² "'So you will be my people,
   and I will be your God.'"

²³ See, the storm of the LORD
   will burst out in wrath,
a driving wind swirling down
   on the heads of the wicked.
²⁴ The fierce anger of the LORD will not turn back
   until he fully accomplishes
      the purposes of his heart.
In days to come
   you will understand this.

31 "At that time," declares the LORD, "I will be the God of all the families of Israel, and they will be my people."
²This is what the LORD says:

What were these ruins? (30:18)
The Hebrew word for this is *tel* (tell), which refers to a mound of ruins from a previous time. Over the years, towns and villages were often built on the ruins of earlier towns.

What were the days of old? (30:20)
This probably referred to the time when David was king and the kingdom was united.

Who fulfilled this promise? (30:21)
This probably referred to the rulers of Judah immediately after the exile, but it also pointed forward to Jesus, the Messiah.

"The people who survive the sword
    will find favor in the wilderness;
    I will come to give rest to Israel."

³The Lord appeared to us in the past,ᵃ saying:

"I have loved you with an everlasting love;
    I have drawn you with unfailing kindness.
⁴I will build you up again,
    and you, Virgin Israel, will be rebuilt.
Again you will take up your timbrels
    and go out to dance with the joyful.
⁵Again you will plant vineyards
    on the hills of Samaria;
the farmers will plant them
    and enjoy their fruit.
⁶There will be a day when watchmen cry out
    on the hills of Ephraim,
'Come, let us go up to Zion,
    to the Lord our God.'"

⁷This is what the Lord says:

"Sing with joy for Jacob;
    shout for the foremost of the nations.
Make your praises heard, and say,
    'Lord, save your people,
    the remnant of Israel.'
⁸See, I will bring them from the land of the north
    and gather them from the ends of the earth.
Among them will be the blind and the lame,
    expectant mothers and women in labor;
    a great throng will return.
⁹They will come with weeping;
    they will pray as I bring them back.
I will lead them beside streams of water
    on a level path where they will not stumble,
because I am Israel's father,
    and Ephraim is my firstborn son.

¹⁰"Hear the word of the Lord, you nations;
    proclaim it in distant coastlands:
'He who scattered Israel will gather them
    and will watch over his flock like a shepherd.'
¹¹For the Lord will deliver Jacob
    and redeem them from the hand of those stronger
        than they.
¹²They will come and shout for joy on the heights of Zion;
    they will rejoice in the bounty of the Lord—
the grain, the new wine and the olive oil,
    the young of the flocks and herds.
They will be like a well-watered garden,
    and they will sorrow no more.
¹³Then young women will dance and be glad,
    young men and old as well.
I will turn their mourning into gladness;
    I will give them comfort and joy instead of sorrow.

ᵃ 3 Or Lord *has appeared to us from afar*

When did people play timbrels? (31:4)
Timbrels were usually played on joyful occasions, especially after a military victory. Dancing was often part of religious ceremonies.

What did watchmen do? (31:6)
Watchmen were stationed at the city gates and on the city walls. They patrolled the streets at night and were supposed to warn of danger. They also kept track of the phases of the moon so that feasts could be held at the correct times.

Why would people "go up" to Jerusalem? (31:6)
Because Jerusalem (Zion) sat on ground that was higher than the surrounding area and because it was the royal city and the center of Israel's religious life, people usually spoke of going up to Jerusalem.

¹⁴ I will satisfy the priests with abundance,
  and my people will be filled with my bounty,"
                              declares the LORD.

¹⁵ This is what the LORD says:

"A voice is heard in Ramah,
  mourning and great weeping,
Rachel weeping for her children
  and refusing to be comforted,
  because they are no more."

¹⁶ This is what the LORD says:

"Restrain your voice from weeping
  and your eyes from tears,
for your work will be rewarded,"
                              declares the LORD.
  "They will return from the land of the enemy.
¹⁷ So there is hope for your descendants,"
                              declares the LORD.
  "Your children will return to their own land.

¹⁸ "I have surely heard Ephraim's moaning:
  'You disciplined me like an unruly calf,
  and I have been disciplined.
Restore me, and I will return,
  because you are the LORD my God.
¹⁹ After I strayed,
  I repented;
after I came to understand,
  I beat my breast.
I was ashamed and humiliated
  because I bore the disgrace of my youth.'
²⁰ Is not Ephraim my dear son,
  the child in whom I delight?
Though I often speak against him,
  I still remember him.
Therefore my heart yearns for him;
  I have great compassion for him,"
                              declares the LORD.

²¹ "Set up road signs;
  put up guideposts.
Take note of the highway,
  the road that you take.
Return, Virgin Israel,
  return to your towns.
²² How long will you wander,
  unfaithful Daughter Israel?
The LORD will create a new thing on earth—
  the woman will return to^a the man."

²³ This is what the LORD Almighty, the God of Israel, says: "When I bring them back from captivity,^b the people in the land of Judah and in its towns will once again use these words: 'The LORD bless you, you prosperous city, you sacred mountain.' ²⁴ People will live together in Judah and all

What was meant by this reference to Rachel? (31:15)
Rachel was the grandmother of Ephraim and Manasseh, and the two tribes by those names had become the most powerful in the northern kingdom. Here Rachel is a personification of the northern kingdom.

Why were the exiles supposed to set up road signs as they left? (31:21)
The signs would help them find their way back when they returned from exile. In the ancient world, road signs were tombstone-shaped markers.

^a 22 Or *will protect*   ^b 23 Or *I restore their fortunes*

its towns—farmers and those who move about with their flocks. 25 I will refresh the weary and satisfy the faint."

26 At this I awoke and looked around. My sleep had been pleasant to me.

27 "The days are coming," declares the LORD, "when I will plant the kingdoms of Israel and Judah with the offspring of people and of animals. 28 Just as I watched over them to uproot and tear down, and to overthrow, destroy and bring disaster, so I will watch over them to build and to plant," declares the LORD. 29 "In those days people will no longer say,

'The parents have eaten sour grapes,
    and the children's teeth are set on edge.'

30 Instead, everyone will die for their own sin; whoever eats sour grapes—their own teeth will be set on edge.

31 "The days are coming," declares the LORD,
    "when I will make a new covenant
with the people of Israel
    and with the people of Judah.
32 It will not be like the covenant
    I made with their ancestors
when I took them by the hand
    to lead them out of Egypt,
because they broke my covenant,
    though I was a husband to[a] them,[b]"
            declares the LORD.
33 "This is the covenant I will make with the people
        of Israel
    after that time," declares the LORD.
"I will put my law in their minds
    and write it on their hearts.
I will be their God,
    and they will be my people.
34 No longer will they teach their neighbor,
    or say to one another, 'Know the LORD,'
because they will all know me,
    from the least of them to the greatest,"
            declares the LORD.
"For I will forgive their wickedness
    and will remember their sins no more."

35 This is what the LORD says,

he who appoints the sun
    to shine by day,
who decrees the moon and stars
    to shine by night,
who stirs up the sea
    so that its waves roar—
    the LORD Almighty is his name:
36 "Only if these decrees vanish from my sight,"
            declares the LORD,
    "will Israel ever cease
        being a nation before me."

What did this proverb mean? (31:29)
This was a popular proverb based on a misunderstanding of passages like Exodus 20:5 and Numbers 14:18. This proverb taught that a person's sins could have a negative effect on his or her descendants. In Jeremiah's time, many people thought they were being punished for the sins of their ancestors.

What was the significance of the new covenant? (31:31–34)
Because the people had broken the original covenant, God gave them a new one. Through it God would turn his people to him, and they would be his people. These verses are quoted in Hebrews 8:8–12.

---

a 32 Hebrew; Septuagint and Syriac / *and I turned away from*   *b 32* Or *was their master*

³⁷This is what the LORD says:

"Only if the heavens above can be measured
   and the foundations of the earth below be searched
      out
will I reject all the descendants of Israel
   because of all they have done,"
                    declares the LORD.

³⁸"The days are coming," declares the LORD, "when this city will be rebuilt for me from the Tower of Hananel to the Corner Gate. ³⁹The measuring line will stretch from there straight to the hill of Gareb and then turn to Goah. ⁴⁰The whole valley where dead bodies and ashes are thrown, and all the terraces out to the Kidron Valley on the east as far as the corner of the Horse Gate, will be holy to the LORD. The city will never again be uprooted or demolished."

JEREMIAH BUYS A FIELD

32 This is the word that came to Jeremiah from the LORD in the tenth year of Zedekiah king of Judah, which was the eighteenth year of Nebuchadnezzar. ²The army of the king of Babylon was then besieging Jerusalem, and Jeremiah the prophet was confined in the courtyard of the guard in the royal palace of Judah.

³Now Zedekiah king of Judah had imprisoned him there, saying, "Why do you prophesy as you do? You say, 'This is what the LORD says: I am about to give this city into the hands of the king of Babylon, and he will capture it. ⁴Zedekiah king of Judah will not escape the Babylonians*ᵃ* but will certainly be given into the hands of the king of Babylon, and will speak with him face to face and see him with his own eyes. ⁵He will take Zedekiah to Babylon, where he will remain until I deal with him, declares the LORD. If you fight against the Babylonians, you will not succeed.'"

⁶Jeremiah said, "The word of the LORD came to me: ⁷Hanamel son of Shallum your uncle is going to come to you and say, 'Buy my field at Anathoth, because as nearest relative it is your right and duty to buy it.'

⁸"Then, just as the LORD had said, my cousin Hanamel came to me in the courtyard of the guard and said, 'Buy my field at Anathoth in the territory of Benjamin. Since it is your right to redeem it and possess it, buy it for yourself.'

"I knew that this was the word of the LORD; ⁹so I bought the field at Anathoth from my cousin Hanamel and weighed out for him seventeen shekels*ᵇ* of silver. ¹⁰I signed and sealed the deed, had it witnessed, and weighed out the silver on the scales. ¹¹I took the deed of purchase—the sealed copy containing the terms and conditions, as well as the unsealed copy— ¹²and I gave this deed to Baruch son of Neriah, the son of Mahseiah, in the presence of my cousin Hanamel and of the witnesses who had signed the deed and of all the Jews sitting in the courtyard of the guard.

¹³"In their presence I gave Baruch these instructions:

Why was Jeremiah imprisoned? (32:1–2)
Zedekiah, the king of Judah, imprisoned Jeremiah for telling the people there was nothing to be gained by fighting the Babylonians. They would still be taken into captivity.

Why did Jeremiah buy the field at Anathoth? (32:6–15)
Jeremiah obeyed the Lord's command to buy it. It was a visible sign that God would restore his people to their land.

Why was the deed sealed? (32:10–11)
This was to keep the contents from being changed or tampered with. The unsealed copy was kept for purposes of comparison.

ᵃ 4 Or *Chaldeans;* also in verses 5, 24, 25, 28, 29 and 43   *ᵇ 9* That is, about 7 ounces or about 200 grams

¹⁴'This is what the LORD Almighty, the God of Israel, says: Take these documents, both the sealed and unsealed copies of the deed of purchase, and put them in a clay jar so they will last a long time. ¹⁵For this is what the LORD Almighty, the God of Israel, says: Houses, fields and vineyards will again be bought in this land.'

¹⁶"After I had given the deed of purchase to Baruch son of Neriah, I prayed to the LORD:

¹⁷"Ah, Sovereign LORD, you have made the heavens and the earth by your great power and outstretched arm. Nothing is too hard for you. ¹⁸You show love to thousands but bring the punishment for the parents' sins into the laps of their children after them. Great and mighty God, whose name is the LORD Almighty, ¹⁹great are your purposes and mighty are your deeds. Your eyes are open to the ways of all mankind; you reward each person according to their conduct and as their deeds deserve. ²⁰You performed signs and wonders in Egypt and have continued them to this day, in Israel and among all mankind, and have gained the renown that is still yours. ²¹You brought your people Israel out of Egypt with signs and wonders, by a mighty hand and an outstretched arm and with great terror. ²²You gave them this land you had sworn to give their ancestors, a land flowing with milk and honey. ²³They came in and took possession of it, but they did not obey you or follow your law; they did not do what you commanded them to do. So you brought all this disaster on them.

²⁴"See how the siege ramps are built up to take the city. Because of the sword, famine and plague, the city will be given into the hands of the Babylonians who are attacking it. What you said has happened, as you now see. ²⁵And though the city will be given into the hands of the Babylonians, you, Sovereign LORD, say to me, 'Buy the field with silver and have the transaction witnessed.'"

²⁶Then the word of the LORD came to Jeremiah: ²⁷"I am the LORD, the God of all mankind. Is anything too hard for me? ²⁸Therefore this is what the LORD says: I am about to give this city into the hands of the Babylonians and to Nebuchadnezzar king of Babylon, who will capture it. ²⁹The Babylonians who are attacking this city will come in and set it on fire; they will burn it down, along with the houses where the people aroused my anger by burning incense on the roofs to Baal and by pouring out drink offerings to other gods.

³⁰"The people of Israel and Judah have done nothing but evil in my sight from their youth; indeed, the people of Israel have done nothing but arouse my anger with what their hands have made, declares the LORD. ³¹From the day it was built until now, this city has so aroused my anger and wrath that I must remove it from my sight. ³²The people of Israel and Judah have provoked me by all the evil they have done — they, their kings and officials, their priests and prophets, the people of Judah and those living in Jerusalem. ³³They turned

What were these miraculous signs and wonders? (32:20–23)
Jeremiah mentions the plagues that God sent to Egypt, the way God brought his people out of slavery, and the fact that the people were able to conquer Canaan.

their backs to me and not their faces; though I taught them again and again, they would not listen or respond to discipline. [34]They set up their vile images in the house that bears my Name and defiled it. [35]They built high places for Baal in the Valley of Ben Hinnom to sacrifice their sons and daughters to Molek, though I never commanded—nor did it enter my mind—that they should do such a detestable thing and so make Judah sin.

[36]"You are saying about this city, 'By the sword, famine and plague it will be given into the hands of the king of Babylon'; but this is what the LORD, the God of Israel, says: [37]I will surely gather them from all the lands where I banish them in my furious anger and great wrath; I will bring them back to this place and let them live in safety. [38]They will be my people, and I will be their God. [39]I will give them singleness of heart and action, so that they will always fear me and that all will then go well for them and for their children after them. [40]I will make an everlasting covenant with them: I will never stop doing good to them, and I will inspire them to fear me, so that they will never turn away from me. [41]I will rejoice in doing them good and will assuredly plant them in this land with all my heart and soul.

[42]"This is what the LORD says: As I have brought all this great calamity on this people, so I will give them all the prosperity I have promised them. [43]Once more fields will be bought in this land of which you say, 'It is a desolate waste, without people or animals, for it has been given into the hands of the Babylonians.' [44]Fields will be bought for silver, and deeds will be signed, sealed and witnessed in the territory of Benjamin, in the villages around Jerusalem, in the towns of Judah and in the towns of the hill country, of the western foothills and of the Negev, because I will restore their fortunes,[a] declares the LORD."

PROMISE OF RESTORATION

33 While Jeremiah was still confined in the courtyard of the guard, the word of the LORD came to him a second time: [2]"This is what the LORD says, he who made the earth, the LORD who formed it and established it—the LORD is his name: [3]'Call to me and I will answer you and tell you great and unsearchable things you do not know.' [4]For this is what the LORD, the God of Israel, says about the houses in this city and the royal palaces of Judah that have been torn down to be used against the siege ramps and the sword [5]in the fight with the Babylonians[b]: 'They will be filled with the dead bodies of the people I will slay in my anger and wrath. I will hide my face from this city because of all its wickedness.

[6]"'Nevertheless, I will bring health and healing to it; I will heal my people and will let them enjoy abundant peace and security. [7]I will bring Judah and Israel back from captivity[c] and will rebuild them as they were before. [8]I will cleanse them from all the sin they have committed against me and

Why were the houses torn down? (33:4)
Jerusalem's houses were torn down so the stones could be used to repair the city walls.

[a] 44 Or *will bring them back from captivity*   [b] 5 Or *Chaldeans*   [c] 7 Or *will restore the fortunes of Judah and Israel*

will forgive all their sins of rebellion against me. ⁹Then this city will bring me renown, joy, praise and honor before all nations on earth that hear of all the good things I do for it; and they will be in awe and will tremble at the abundant prosperity and peace I provide for it.'

¹⁰"This is what the LORD says: 'You say about this place, "It is a desolate waste, without people or animals." Yet in the towns of Judah and the streets of Jerusalem that are deserted, inhabited by neither people nor animals, there will be heard once more ¹¹the sounds of joy and gladness, the voices of bride and bridegroom, and the voices of those who bring thank offerings to the house of the LORD, saying,

"Give thanks to the LORD Almighty,
    for the LORD is good;
    his love endures forever."

For I will restore the fortunes of the land as they were before,' says the LORD.

¹²"This is what the LORD Almighty says: 'In this place, desolate and without people or animals—in all its towns there will again be pastures for shepherds to rest their flocks. ¹³In the towns of the hill country, of the western foothills and of the Negev, in the territory of Benjamin, in the villages around Jerusalem and in the towns of Judah, flocks will again pass under the hand of the one who counts them,' says the LORD.

¹⁴"'The days are coming,' declares the LORD, 'when I will fulfill the good promise I made to the people of Israel and Judah.

¹⁵"'In those days and at that time
    I will make a righteous Branch sprout from David's
        line;
    he will do what is just and right in the land.
¹⁶In those days Judah will be saved
    and Jerusalem will live in safety.
    This is the name by which it*a* will be called:
    The LORD Our Righteous Savior.'

¹⁷For this is what the LORD says: 'David will never fail to have a man to sit on the throne of Israel, ¹⁸nor will the Levitical priests ever fail to have a man to stand before me continually to offer burnt offerings, to burn grain offerings and to present sacrifices.'"

¹⁹The word of the LORD came to Jeremiah: ²⁰"This is what the LORD says: 'If you can break my covenant with the day and my covenant with the night, so that day and night no longer come at their appointed time, ²¹then my covenant with David my servant—and my covenant with the Levites who are priests ministering before me—can be broken and David will no longer have a descendant to reign on his throne. ²²I will make the descendants of David my servant and the Levites who minister before me as countless as the stars in the sky and as measureless as the sand on the seashore.'"

a 16 Or he

How did shepherds count their sheep? (33:12–13)
It was difficult to count large flocks of sheep. When the sheep were gathered around a watering hole, they would be much easier to count.

How would David be able to have an heir on the throne of Israel? (33:17)
This prophecy was fulfilled by Jesus, who was a descendant of David.

How could there be so many Levites? (33:22)
Levites, or priests, prayed and offered sacrifices to God for the people. Today all believers in Christ are called to be priests. Believers do not need a priest to stand between them and God but can go directly to God.

²³The word of the LORD came to Jeremiah: ²⁴"Have you not noticed that these people are saying, 'The LORD has rejected the two kingdoms*ᵃ* he chose'? So they despise my people and no longer regard them as a nation. ²⁵This is what the LORD says: 'If I have not made my covenant with day and night and established the laws of heaven and earth, ²⁶then I will reject the descendants of Jacob and David my servant and will not choose one of his sons to rule over the descendants of Abraham, Isaac and Jacob. For I will restore their fortunes*ᵇ* and have compassion on them.'"

WARNING TO ZEDEKIAH

34 While Nebuchadnezzar king of Babylon and all his army and all the kingdoms and peoples in the empire he ruled were fighting against Jerusalem and all its surrounding towns, this word came to Jeremiah from the LORD: ²"This is what the LORD, the God of Israel, says: Go to Zedekiah king of Judah and tell him, 'This is what the LORD says: I am about to give this city into the hands of the king of Babylon, and he will burn it down. ³You will not escape from his grasp but will surely be captured and given into his hands. You will see the king of Babylon with your own eyes, and he will speak with you face to face. And you will go to Babylon.

⁴"'Yet hear the LORD's promise to you, Zedekiah king of Judah. This is what the LORD says concerning you: You will not die by the sword; ⁵you will die peacefully. As people made a funeral fire in honor of your predecessors, the kings who ruled before you, so they will make a fire in your honor and lament, "Alas, master!" I myself make this promise, declares the LORD.'"

⁶Then Jeremiah the prophet told all this to Zedekiah king of Judah, in Jerusalem, ⁷while the army of the king of Babylon was fighting against Jerusalem and the other cities of Judah that were still holding out—Lachish and Azekah. These were the only fortified cities left in Judah.

FREEDOM FOR SLAVES

⁸The word came to Jeremiah from the LORD after King Zedekiah had made a covenant with all the people in Jerusalem to proclaim freedom for the slaves. ⁹Everyone was to free their Hebrew slaves, both male and female; no one was to hold a fellow Hebrew in bondage. ¹⁰So all the officials and people who entered into this covenant agreed that they would free their male and female slaves and no longer hold them in bondage. They agreed, and set them free. ¹¹But afterward they changed their minds and took back the slaves they had freed and enslaved them again.

¹²Then the word of the LORD came to Jeremiah: ¹³"This is what the LORD, the God of Israel, says: I made a covenant with your ancestors when I brought them out of Egypt, out of the land of slavery. I said, ¹⁴'Every seventh year each of you must free any fellow Hebrews who have sold themselves to you. After they have served you six years, you must let

What was a funeral fire? (34:5)
This was not cremation but a memorial fire honoring the king who had died.

ᵃ 24 Or *families*   *ᵇ* 26 Or *will bring them back from captivity*

them go free.'[a] Your ancestors, however, did not listen to me or pay attention to me. [15]Recently you repented and did what is right in my sight: Each of you proclaimed freedom to your own people. You even made a covenant before me in the house that bears my Name. [16]But now you have turned around and profaned my name; each of you has taken back the male and female slaves you had set free to go where they wished. You have forced them to become your slaves again.

[17]"Therefore this is what the LORD says: You have not obeyed me; you have not proclaimed freedom to your own people. So I now proclaim 'freedom' for you, declares the LORD—'freedom' to fall by the sword, plague and famine. I will make you abhorrent to all the kingdoms of the earth. [18]Those who have violated my covenant and have not fulfilled the terms of the covenant they made before me, I will treat like the calf they cut in two and then walked between its pieces. [19]The leaders of Judah and Jerusalem, the court officials, the priests and all the people of the land who walked between the pieces of the calf, [20]I will deliver into the hands of their enemies who want to kill them. Their dead bodies will become food for the birds and the wild animals.

[21]"I will deliver Zedekiah king of Judah and his officials into the hands of their enemies who want to kill them, to the army of the king of Babylon, which has withdrawn from you. [22]I am going to give the order, declares the LORD, and I will bring them back to this city. They will fight against it, take it and burn it down. And I will lay waste the towns of Judah so no one can live there."

THE REKABITES

35 This is the word that came to Jeremiah from the LORD during the reign of Jehoiakim son of Josiah king of Judah: [2]"Go to the Rekabite family and invite them to come to one of the side rooms of the house of the LORD and give them wine to drink."

[3]So I went to get Jaazaniah son of Jeremiah, the son of Habazziniah, and his brothers and all his sons—the whole family of the Rekabites. [4]I brought them into the house of the LORD, into the room of the sons of Hanan son of Igdaliah the man of God. It was next to the room of the officials, which was over that of Maaseiah son of Shallum the doorkeeper. [5]Then I set bowls full of wine and some cups before the Rekabites and said to them, "Drink some wine."

[6]But they replied, "We do not drink wine, because our forefather Jehonadab[b] son of Rekab gave us this command: 'Neither you nor your descendants must ever drink wine. [7]Also you must never build houses, sow seed or plant vineyards; you must never have any of these things, but must always live in tents. Then you will live a long time in the land where you are nomads.' [8]We have obeyed everything our forefather Jehonadab son of Rekab commanded us. Neither we nor our wives nor our sons and daughters have ever drunk wine [9]or built houses to live in or had vineyards, fields or

What was the ceremony of walking between two halves of a calf? (34:18)
This was an ancient custom used when covenants or promises were made. The people making the oath would walk between the animal halves to show that they would die, just as the animals had died, if they broke the agreement.

Why was it a curse for the dead bodies to be food for birds and animals? (34:20)
It was a great dishonor in ancient times for a dead person not to be buried.

Is this section a flashback? (chapters 35 and 36)
These two chapters tell about events during the reign of Jehoiakim, who was king before Zedekiah. The writers of the Bible were more concerned about their message than about strict chronology.

Who were the Rekabites? (35:2)
This was a tribe of nomadic people who were related to the Kenites (see 1 Chronicles 2:55). They lived among or near the Israelites and were on good terms with them.

---

[a] 14 Deut. 15:12   [b] 6 Hebrew *Jonadab*, a variant of *Jehonadab*; here and often in this chapter

crops. [10]We have lived in tents and have fully obeyed everything our forefather Jehonadab commanded us. [11]But when Nebuchadnezzar king of Babylon invaded this land, we said, 'Come, we must go to Jerusalem to escape the Babylonian[a] and Aramean armies.' So we have remained in Jerusalem."

[12]Then the word of the LORD came to Jeremiah, saying: [13]"This is what the LORD Almighty, the God of Israel, says: Go and tell the people of Judah and those living in Jerusalem, 'Will you not learn a lesson and obey my words?' declares the LORD. [14]'Jehonadab son of Rekab ordered his descendants not to drink wine and this command has been kept. To this day they do not drink wine, because they obey their forefather's command. But I have spoken to you again and again, yet you have not obeyed me. [15]Again and again I sent all my servants the prophets to you. They said, "Each of you must turn from your wicked ways and reform your actions; do not follow other gods to serve them. Then you will live in the land I have given to you and your ancestors." But you have not paid attention or listened to me. [16]The descendants of Jehonadab son of Rekab have carried out the command their forefather gave them, but these people have not obeyed me.'

[17]"Therefore this is what the LORD God Almighty, the God of Israel, says: 'Listen! I am going to bring on Judah and on everyone living in Jerusalem every disaster I pronounced against them. I spoke to them, but they did not listen; I called to them, but they did not answer.'"

[18]Then Jeremiah said to the family of the Rekabites, "This is what the LORD Almighty, the God of Israel, says: 'You have obeyed the command of your forefather Jehonadab and have followed all his instructions and have done everything he ordered.' [19]Therefore this is what the LORD Almighty, the God of Israel, says: 'Jehonadab son of Rekab will never fail to have a descendant to serve me.'"

JEHOIAKIM BURNS JEREMIAH'S SCROLL

36 In the fourth year of Jehoiakim son of Josiah king of Judah, this word came to Jeremiah from the LORD: [2]"Take a scroll and write on it all the words I have spoken to you concerning Israel, Judah and all the other nations from the time I began speaking to you in the reign of Josiah till now. [3]Perhaps when the people of Judah hear about every disaster I plan to inflict on them, they will each turn from their wicked ways; then I will forgive their wickedness and their sin."

[4]So Jeremiah called Baruch son of Neriah, and while Jeremiah dictated all the words the LORD had spoken to him, Baruch wrote them on the scroll. [5]Then Jeremiah told Baruch, "I am restricted; I am not allowed to go to the LORD's temple. [6]So you go to the house of the LORD on a day of fasting and read to the people from the scroll the words of the LORD that you wrote as I dictated. Read them to all the people of Judah who come in from their towns. [7]Perhaps they will bring their petition before the LORD and will each

How did the Lord use the Rekabites as an example to the people of Judah? (35:14–15)
The Rekabites had kept the commandments their ancestor had given, but the people of Judah continually failed to obey God.

Why couldn't Jeremiah go to the temple? (36:5)
Perhaps he was not allowed to preach publicly because his message was unpopular. He also may have been in prison.

Why was there a special day of fasting? (36:6)
A day of fasting was often proclaimed when there was a national emergency, in this case possibly the Babylonian attack.

[a] 11 Or *Chaldean*

turn from their wicked ways, for the anger and wrath pronounced against this people by the LORD are great."

⁸Baruch son of Neriah did everything Jeremiah the prophet told him to do; at the LORD's temple he read the words of the LORD from the scroll. ⁹In the ninth month of the fifth year of Jehoiakim son of Josiah king of Judah, a time of fasting before the LORD was proclaimed for all the people in Jerusalem and those who had come from the towns of Judah. ¹⁰From the room of Gemariah son of Shaphan the secretary, which was in the upper courtyard at the entrance of the New Gate of the temple, Baruch read to all the people at the LORD's temple the words of Jeremiah from the scroll.

¹¹When Micaiah son of Gemariah, the son of Shaphan, heard all the words of the LORD from the scroll, ¹²he went down to the secretary's room in the royal palace, where all the officials were sitting: Elishama the secretary, Delaiah son of Shemaiah, Elnathan son of Akbor, Gemariah son of Shaphan, Zedekiah son of Hananiah, and all the other officials. ¹³After Micaiah told them everything he had heard Baruch read to the people from the scroll, ¹⁴all the officials sent Jehudi son of Nethaniah, the son of Shelemiah, the son of Cushi, to say to Baruch, "Bring the scroll from which you have read to the people and come." So Baruch son of Neriah went to them with the scroll in his hand. ¹⁵They said to him, "Sit down, please, and read it to us."

So Baruch read it to them. ¹⁶When they heard all these words, they looked at each other in fear and said to Baruch, "We must report all these words to the king." ¹⁷Then they asked Baruch, "Tell us, how did you come to write all this? Did Jeremiah dictate it?"

¹⁸"Yes," Baruch replied, "he dictated all these words to me, and I wrote them in ink on the scroll."

¹⁹Then the officials said to Baruch, "You and Jeremiah, go and hide. Don't let anyone know where you are."

²⁰After they put the scroll in the room of Elishama the secretary, they went to the king in the courtyard and reported everything to him. ²¹The king sent Jehudi to get the scroll, and Jehudi brought it from the room of Elishama the secretary and read it to the king and all the officials standing beside him. ²²It was the ninth month and the king was sitting in the winter apartment, with a fire burning in the firepot in front of him. ²³Whenever Jehudi had read three or four columns of the scroll, the king cut them off with a scribe's knife and threw them into the firepot, until the entire scroll was burned in the fire. ²⁴The king and all his attendants who heard all these words showed no fear, nor did they tear their clothes. ²⁵Even though Elnathan, Delaiah and Gemariah urged the king not to burn the scroll, he would not listen to them. ²⁶Instead, the king commanded Jerahmeel, a son of the king, Seraiah son of Azriel and Shelemiah son of Abdeel to arrest Baruch the scribe and Jeremiah the prophet. But the LORD had hidden them.

²⁷After the king burned the scroll containing the words that Baruch had written at Jeremiah's dictation, the word of the LORD came to Jeremiah: ²⁸"Take another scroll and write

What was ink made from? **(36:18)**
In ancient times, ink was made from fine, black soot (lampblack) mixed with gum arabic, oil, or a metallic substance. This is the only time ink is mentioned in the Old Testament.

What was a winter apartment? (36:22)
This was probably a large room in the king's palace with a firepot, a depression in the floor, or a container where coals were kept burning.

How was this prophecy fulfilled? (36:30)
Jehoiakim's son, Jehoiachin, ruled for only three months and then was taken into exile in Babylon, where he eventually died.

on it all the words that were on the first scroll, which Jehoiakim king of Judah burned up. [29] Also tell Jehoiakim king of Judah, 'This is what the LORD says: You burned that scroll and said, "Why did you write on it that the king of Babylon would certainly come and destroy this land and wipe from it both man and beast?" [30] Therefore this is what the LORD says about Jehoiakim king of Judah: He will have no one to sit on the throne of David; his body will be thrown out and exposed to the heat by day and the frost by night. [31] I will punish him and his children and his attendants for their wickedness; I will bring on them and those living in Jerusalem and the people of Judah every disaster I pronounced against them, because they have not listened.'"

[32] So Jeremiah took another scroll and gave it to the scribe Baruch son of Neriah, and as Jeremiah dictated, Baruch wrote on it all the words of the scroll that Jehoiakim king of Judah had burned in the fire. And many similar words were added to them.

JEREMIAH IN PRISON

How did Zedekiah become king? (37:1)
Nebuchadnezzar made him king in place of Jehoiachin in 597 B.C.

37 Zedekiah son of Josiah was made king of Judah by Nebuchadnezzar king of Babylon; he reigned in place of Jehoiachin[a] son of Jehoiakim. [2] Neither he nor his attendants nor the people of the land paid any attention to the words the LORD had spoken through Jeremiah the prophet.

[3] King Zedekiah, however, sent Jehukal son of Shelemiah with the priest Zephaniah son of Maaseiah to Jeremiah the prophet with this message: "Please pray to the LORD our God for us."

[4] Now Jeremiah was free to come and go among the people, for he had not yet been put in prison. [5] Pharaoh's army had marched out of Egypt, and when the Babylonians[b] who were besieging Jerusalem heard the report about them, they withdrew from Jerusalem.

[6] Then the word of the LORD came to Jeremiah the prophet: [7] "This is what the LORD, the God of Israel, says: Tell the king of Judah, who sent you to inquire of me, 'Pharaoh's army, which has marched out to support you, will go back to its own land, to Egypt. [8] Then the Babylonians will return and attack this city; they will capture it and burn it down.'

[9] "This is what the LORD says: Do not deceive yourselves, thinking, 'The Babylonians will surely leave us.' They will not! [10] Even if you were to defeat the entire Babylonian[c] army that is attacking you and only wounded men were left in their tents, they would come out and burn this city down."

[11] After the Babylonian army had withdrawn from Jerusalem because of Pharaoh's army, [12] Jeremiah started to leave the city to go to the territory of Benjamin to get his share of the property among the people there. [13] But when he reached the Benjamin Gate, the captain of the guard, whose name was Irijah son of Shelemiah, the son of Hananiah, arrested him and said, "You are deserting to the Babylonians!"

Why did Jeremiah want to go to the territory of Benjamin? (37:12)
While there was a brief lull in the Babylonian invasion, Jeremiah wanted to settle property matters with his family. He also may have wanted to demonstrate his belief that the Lord would allow his people to return to their land after exile.

[a] 1 Hebrew *Koniah*, a variant of *Jehoiachin*   [b] 5 Or *Chaldeans*; also in verses 8, 9, 13 and 14   [c] 10 Or *Chaldean*; also in verse 11

¹⁴"That's not true!" Jeremiah said. "I am not deserting to the Babylonians." But Irijah would not listen to him; instead, he arrested Jeremiah and brought him to the officials. ¹⁵They were angry with Jeremiah and had him beaten and imprisoned in the house of Jonathan the secretary, which they had made into a prison.

¹⁶Jeremiah was put into a vaulted cell in a dungeon, where he remained a long time. ¹⁷Then King Zedekiah sent for him and had him brought to the palace, where he asked him privately, "Is there any word from the LORD?"

"Yes," Jeremiah replied, "you will be delivered into the hands of the king of Babylon."

¹⁸Then Jeremiah said to King Zedekiah, "What crime have I committed against you or your attendants or this people, that you have put me in prison? ¹⁹Where are your prophets who prophesied to you, 'The king of Babylon will not attack you or this land'? ²⁰But now, my lord the king, please listen. Let me bring my petition before you: Do not send me back to the house of Jonathan the secretary, or I will die there."

²¹King Zedekiah then gave orders for Jeremiah to be placed in the courtyard of the guard and given a loaf of bread from the street of the bakers each day until all the bread in the city was gone. So Jeremiah remained in the courtyard of the guard.

JEREMIAH THROWN INTO A CISTERN

38 Shephatiah son of Mattan, Gedaliah son of Pashhur, Jehukal*ᵃ* son of Shelemiah, and Pashhur son of Malkijah heard what Jeremiah was telling all the people when he said, ²"This is what the LORD says: 'Whoever stays in this city will die by the sword, famine or plague, but whoever goes over to the Babylonians*ᵇ* will live. They will escape with their lives; they will live.' ³And this is what the LORD says: 'This city will certainly be given into the hands of the army of the king of Babylon, who will capture it.'"

⁴Then the officials said to the king, "This man should be put to death. He is discouraging the soldiers who are left in this city, as well as all the people, by the things he is saying to them. This man is not seeking the good of these people but their ruin."

⁵"He is in your hands," King Zedekiah answered. "The king can do nothing to oppose you."

⁶So they took Jeremiah and put him into the cistern of Malkijah, the king's son, which was in the courtyard of the guard. They lowered Jeremiah by ropes into the cistern; it had no water in it, only mud, and Jeremiah sank down into the mud.

⁷But Ebed-Melek, a Cushite,*ᶜ* an official*ᵈ* in the royal palace, heard that they had put Jeremiah into the cistern. While the king was sitting in the Benjamin Gate, ⁸Ebed-Melek went out of the palace and said to him, ⁹"My lord the king, these men have acted wickedly in all they have done to Jeremiah the

What type of dungeon was this? (37:16)
This was probably an underground room or cistern.

What was the courtyard of the guard? (37:21)
This was a less objectionable prison than the dungeon. Jeremiah was given food, and he could receive visitors.

What was this cistern like? (38:6)
It was a bell-shaped pit with a narrow opening at the top.

ᵃ 1 Hebrew *Jukal,* a variant of *Jehukal*   *ᵇ 2* Or *Chaldeans*; also in verses 18, 19 and 23   *ᶜ 7* Probably from the upper Nile region   *ᵈ 7* Or *a eunuch*

prophet. They have thrown him into a cistern, where he will starve to death when there is no longer any bread in the city."

¹⁰Then the king commanded Ebed-Melek the Cushite, "Take thirty men from here with you and lift Jeremiah the prophet out of the cistern before he dies."

¹¹So Ebed-Melek took the men with him and went to a room under the treasury in the palace. He took some old rags and worn-out clothes from there and let them down with ropes to Jeremiah in the cistern. ¹²Ebed-Melek the Cushite said to Jeremiah, "Put these old rags and worn-out clothes under your arms to pad the ropes." Jeremiah did so, ¹³and they pulled him up with the ropes and lifted him out of the cistern. And Jeremiah remained in the courtyard of the guard.

ZEDEKIAH QUESTIONS JEREMIAH AGAIN

¹⁴Then King Zedekiah sent for Jeremiah the prophet and had him brought to the third entrance to the temple of the Lord. "I am going to ask you something," the king said to Jeremiah. "Do not hide anything from me."

¹⁵Jeremiah said to Zedekiah, "If I give you an answer, will you not kill me? Even if I did give you counsel, you would not listen to me."

¹⁶But King Zedekiah swore this oath secretly to Jeremiah: "As surely as the Lord lives, who has given us breath, I will neither kill you nor hand you over to those who want to kill you."

¹⁷Then Jeremiah said to Zedekiah, "This is what the Lord God Almighty, the God of Israel, says: 'If you surrender to the officers of the king of Babylon, your life will be spared and this city will not be burned down; you and your family will live. ¹⁸But if you will not surrender to the officers of the king of Babylon, this city will be given into the hands of the Babylonians and they will burn it down; you yourself will not escape from them.'"

¹⁹King Zedekiah said to Jeremiah, "I am afraid of the Jews who have gone over to the Babylonians, for the Babylonians may hand me over to them and they will mistreat me."

²⁰"They will not hand you over," Jeremiah replied. "Obey the Lord by doing what I tell you. Then it will go well with you, and your life will be spared. ²¹But if you refuse to surrender, this is what the Lord has revealed to me: ²²All the women left in the palace of the king of Judah will be brought out to the officials of the king of Babylon. Those women will say to you:

"'They misled you and overcame you —
   those trusted friends of yours.
Your feet are sunk in the mud;
   your friends have deserted you.'

²³"All your wives and children will be brought out to the Babylonians. You yourself will not escape from their hands but will be captured by the king of Babylon; and this city will*ᵃ* be burned down."

ᵃ 23 Or *and you will cause this city to*

What was this room under the treasury? (38:11)
This may have been a wardrobe storeroom.

Who were the officers of the king of Babylon? (38:17–18)
These were the men in charge of the siege of Jerusalem.

What would happen to the women if the Babylonians conquered the city? (38:22–23)
In ancient times, the women in a conquered king's harem would become the property of the conquerors.

²⁴Then Zedekiah said to Jeremiah, "Do not let anyone know about this conversation, or you may die. ²⁵If the officials hear that I talked with you, and they come to you and say, 'Tell us what you said to the king and what the king said to you; do not hide it from us or we will kill you,' ²⁶then tell them, 'I was pleading with the king not to send me back to Jonathan's house to die there.'"

²⁷All the officials did come to Jeremiah and question him, and he told them everything the king had ordered him to say. So they said no more to him, for no one had heard his conversation with the king.

²⁸And Jeremiah remained in the courtyard of the guard until the day Jerusalem was captured.

THE FALL OF JERUSALEM

39 This is how Jerusalem was taken: ¹In the ninth year of Zedekiah king of Judah, in the tenth month, Nebuchadnezzar king of Babylon marched against Jerusalem with his whole army and laid siege to it. ²And on the ninth day of the fourth month of Zedekiah's eleventh year, the city wall was broken through. ³Then all the officials of the king of Babylon came and took seats in the Middle Gate: Nergal-Sharezer of Samgar, Nebo-Sarsekim a chief officer, Nergal-Sharezer a high official and all the other officials of the king of Babylon. ⁴When Zedekiah king of Judah and all the soldiers saw them, they fled; they left the city at night by way of the king's garden, through the gate between the two walls, and headed toward the Arabah.ᵃ

⁵But the Babylonianᵇ army pursued them and overtook Zedekiah in the plains of Jericho. They captured him and took him to Nebuchadnezzar king of Babylon at Riblah in the land of Hamath, where he pronounced sentence on him. ⁶There at Riblah the king of Babylon slaughtered the sons of Zedekiah before his eyes and also killed all the nobles of Judah. ⁷Then he put out Zedekiah's eyes and bound him with bronze shackles to take him to Babylon.

⁸The Babyloniansᶜ set fire to the royal palace and the houses of the people and broke down the walls of Jerusalem. ⁹Nebuzaradan commander of the imperial guard carried into exile to Babylon the people who remained in the city, along with those who had gone over to him, and the rest of the people. ¹⁰But Nebuzaradan the commander of the guard left behind in the land of Judah some of the poor people, who owned nothing; and at that time he gave them vineyards and fields.

¹¹Now Nebuchadnezzar king of Babylon had given these orders about Jeremiah through Nebuzaradan commander of the imperial guard: ¹²"Take him and look after him; don't harm him but do for him whatever he asks." ¹³So Nebuzaradan the commander of the guard, Nebushazban a chief officer, Nergal-Sharezer a high official and all the other officers of the king of Babylon ¹⁴sent and had Jeremiah taken out of the courtyard of the guard. They turned him over to Gedaliah son of Ahikam, the son of Shaphan, to take him back to his home. So he remained among his own people.

Why did Nebuchadnezzar kill the nobles and blind the king? (39:6–7)
He probably wanted to intimidate other nations that might have considered resisting the Babylonians.

Why did Nebuchadnezzar treat Jeremiah so well? (39:11–14)
He probably heard about Jeremiah's efforts to persuade his people to surrender.

ᵃ 4 Or *the Jordan Valley*   ᵇ 5 Or *Chaldean*   ᶜ 5 Or *Chaldeans*

[15]While Jeremiah had been confined in the courtyard of the guard, the word of the Lord came to him: [16]"Go and tell Ebed-Melek the Cushite, 'This is what the Lord Almighty, the God of Israel, says: I am about to fulfill my words against this city—words concerning disaster, not prosperity. At that time they will be fulfilled before your eyes. [17]But I will rescue you on that day, declares the Lord; you will not be given into the hands of those you fear. [18]I will save you; you will not fall by the sword but will escape with your life, because you trust in me, declares the Lord.'"

JEREMIAH FREED

40 The word came to Jeremiah from the Lord after Nebuzaradan commander of the imperial guard had released him at Ramah. He had found Jeremiah bound in chains among all the captives from Jerusalem and Judah who were being carried into exile to Babylon. [2]When the commander of the guard found Jeremiah, he said to him, "The Lord your God decreed this disaster for this place. [3]And now the Lord has brought it about; he has done just as he said he would. All this happened because you people sinned against the Lord and did not obey him. [4]But today I am freeing you from the chains on your wrists. Come with me to Babylon, if you like, and I will look after you; but if you do not want to, then don't come. Look, the whole country lies before you; go wherever you please." [5]However, before Jeremiah turned to go,[a] Nebuzaradan added, "Go back to Gedaliah son of Ahikam, the son of Shaphan, whom the king of Babylon has appointed over the towns of Judah, and live with him among the people, or go anywhere else you please."

Then the commander gave him provisions and a present and let him go. [6]So Jeremiah went to Gedaliah son of Ahikam at Mizpah and stayed with him among the people who were left behind in the land.

GEDALIAH ASSASSINATED

[7]When all the army officers and their men who were still in the open country heard that the king of Babylon had appointed Gedaliah son of Ahikam as governor over the land and had put him in charge of the men, women and children who were the poorest in the land and who had not been carried into exile to Babylon, [8]they came to Gedaliah at Mizpah—Ishmael son of Nethaniah, Johanan and Jonathan the sons of Kareah, Seraiah son of Tanhumeth, the sons of Ephai the Netophathite, and Jaazaniah[b] the son of the Maakathite, and their men. [9]Gedaliah son of Ahikam, the son of Shaphan, took an oath to reassure them and their men. "Do not be afraid to serve the Babylonians,[c]" he said. "Settle down in the land and serve the king of Babylon, and it will go well with you. [10]I myself will stay at Mizpah to represent you before the Babylonians who come to us, but you are to harvest the wine, summer fruit and olive oil, and put them in your storage jars, and live in the towns you have taken over."

How did Nebuzaradan know that God had allowed Jerusalem to be conquered? (40:2) Other prisoners might have told him about Jeremiah's prophecies. Within the region, Israel's God was well known, and the Babylonians probably believed that God had permitted them to succeed.

---

[a] 5 Or *Jeremiah answered*   [b] 8 Hebrew *Jezaniah*, a variant of *Jaazaniah*
[c] 9 Or *Chaldeans*; also in verse 10

¹¹When all the Jews in Moab, Ammon, Edom and all the other countries heard that the king of Babylon had left a remnant in Judah and had appointed Gedaliah son of Ahikam, the son of Shaphan, as governor over them, ¹²they all came back to the land of Judah, to Gedaliah at Mizpah, from all the countries where they had been scattered. And they harvested an abundance of wine and summer fruit.

¹³Johanan son of Kareah and all the army officers still in the open country came to Gedaliah at Mizpah ¹⁴and said to him, "Don't you know that Baalis king of the Ammonites has sent Ishmael son of Nethaniah to take your life?" But Gedaliah son of Ahikam did not believe them.

¹⁵Then Johanan son of Kareah said privately to Gedaliah in Mizpah, "Let me go and kill Ishmael son of Nethaniah, and no one will know it. Why should he take your life and cause all the Jews who are gathered around you to be scattered and the remnant of Judah to perish?"

¹⁶But Gedaliah son of Ahikam said to Johanan son of Kareah, "Don't do such a thing! What you are saying about Ishmael is not true."

41 In the seventh month Ishmael son of Nethaniah, the son of Elishama, who was of royal blood and had been one of the king's officers, came with ten men to Gedaliah son of Ahikam at Mizpah. While they were eating together there, ²Ishmael son of Nethaniah and the ten men who were with him got up and struck down Gedaliah son of Ahikam, the son of Shaphan, with the sword, killing the one whom the king of Babylon had appointed as governor over the land. ³Ishmael also killed all the men of Judah who were with Gedaliah at Mizpah, as well as the Babylonian*a* soldiers who were there.

⁴The day after Gedaliah's assassination, before anyone knew about it, ⁵eighty men who had shaved off their beards, torn their clothes and cut themselves came from Shechem, Shiloh and Samaria, bringing grain offerings and incense with them to the house of the LORD. ⁶Ishmael son of Nethaniah went out from Mizpah to meet them, weeping as he went. When he met them, he said, "Come to Gedaliah son of Ahikam." ⁷When they went into the city, Ishmael son of Nethaniah and the men who were with him slaughtered them and threw them into a cistern. ⁸But ten of them said to Ishmael, "Don't kill us! We have wheat and barley, olive oil and honey, hidden in a field." So he let them alone and did not kill them with the others. ⁹Now the cistern where he threw all the bodies of the men he had killed along with Gedaliah was the one King Asa had made as part of his defense against Baasha king of Israel. Ishmael son of Nethaniah filled it with the dead.

¹⁰Ishmael made captives of all the rest of the people who were in Mizpah—the king's daughters along with all the others who were left there, over whom Nebuzaradan commander of the imperial guard had appointed Gedaliah son of Ahikam. Ishmael son of Nethaniah took them captive and set out to cross over to the Ammonites.

¹¹When Johanan son of Kareah and all the army officers

How many people had fled Jerusalem? (40:11)
The number isn't known, but those who fled were probably rich and influential. The poor were unable to flee the city.

Where was Mizpah located? (40:12)
Several places had the name *Mizpah*, which meant *watchtower* or *lookout point*. This one was probably in the territory of Benjamin (see Joshua 18:26).

Why did the men shave their beards, tear their clothes, and cut themselves? (41:5)
These were all signs of mourning. They were probably mourning the destruction of Jerusalem.

Who were the king's daughters? (41:10)
They were women who had been members of Zedekiah's court. They were not necessarily daughters of the king himself.

a 3 Or Chaldean

who were with him heard about all the crimes Ishmael son of Nethaniah had committed, [12] they took all their men and went to fight Ishmael son of Nethaniah. They caught up with him near the great pool in Gibeon. [13] When all the people Ishmael had with him saw Johanan son of Kareah and the army officers who were with him, they were glad. [14] All the people Ishmael had taken captive at Mizpah turned and went over to Johanan son of Kareah. [15] But Ishmael son of Nethaniah and eight of his men escaped from Johanan and fled to the Ammonites.

FLIGHT TO EGYPT

[16] Then Johanan son of Kareah and all the army officers who were with him led away all the people of Mizpah who had survived, whom Johanan had recovered from Ishmael son of Nethaniah after Ishmael had assassinated Gedaliah son of Ahikam — the soldiers, women, children and court officials he had recovered from Gibeon. [17] And they went on, stopping at Geruth Kimham near Bethlehem on their way to Egypt [18] to escape the Babylonians.[a] They were afraid of them because Ishmael son of Nethaniah had killed Gedaliah son of Ahikam, whom the king of Babylon had appointed as governor over the land.

42 Then all the army officers, including Johanan son of Kareah and Jezaniah[b] son of Hoshaiah, and all the people from the least to the greatest approached [2] Jeremiah the prophet and said to him, "Please hear our petition and pray to the LORD your God for this entire remnant. For as you now see, though we were once many, now only a few are left. [3] Pray that the LORD your God will tell us where we should go and what we should do."

[4] "I have heard you," replied Jeremiah the prophet. "I will certainly pray to the LORD your God as you have requested; I will tell you everything the LORD says and will keep nothing back from you."

[5] Then they said to Jeremiah, "May the LORD be a true and faithful witness against us if we do not act in accordance with everything the LORD your God sends you to tell us. [6] Whether it is favorable or unfavorable, we will obey the LORD our God, to whom we are sending you, so that it will go well with us, for we will obey the LORD our God."

[7] Ten days later the word of the LORD came to Jeremiah. [8] So he called together Johanan son of Kareah and all the army officers who were with him and all the people from the least to the greatest. [9] He said to them, "This is what the LORD, the God of Israel, to whom you sent me to present your petition, says: [10] 'If you stay in this land, I will build you up and not tear you down; I will plant you and not uproot you, for I have relented concerning the disaster I have inflicted on you. [11] Do not be afraid of the king of Babylon, whom you now fear. Do not be afraid of him, declares the LORD, for I am with you and will save you and deliver you from his hands. [12] I will show you compassion so that he will have compassion on you and restore you to your land.'

Why did they plan to travel to Egypt? (41:17)
Egypt probably seemed safer than staying in Judah. They were afraid that the Babylonians would seek revenge for the murder of Gedaliah.

Why did they ask Jeremiah to pray for God's guidance when they already knew what they wanted to do? (42:3)
Perhaps they simply wanted God's blessing or specific guidance on how best to make the journey.

---

[a] 18 Or *Chaldeans*   [b] 1 Hebrew; Septuagint (see also 43:2) *Azariah*

¹³"However, if you say, 'We will not stay in this land,' and so disobey the Lᴏʀᴅ your God, ¹⁴and if you say, 'No, we will go and live in Egypt, where we will not see war or hear the trumpet or be hungry for bread,' ¹⁵then hear the word of the Lᴏʀᴅ, you remnant of Judah. This is what the Lᴏʀᴅ Almighty, the God of Israel, says: 'If you are determined to go to Egypt and you do go to settle there, ¹⁶then the sword you fear will overtake you there, and the famine you dread will follow you into Egypt, and there you will die. ¹⁷Indeed, all who are determined to go to Egypt to settle there will die by the sword, famine and plague; not one of them will survive or escape the disaster I will bring on them.' ¹⁸This is what the Lᴏʀᴅ Almighty, the God of Israel, says: 'As my anger and wrath have been poured out on those who lived in Jerusalem, so will my wrath be poured out on you when you go to Egypt. You will be a curse*a* and an object of horror, a curse*a* and an object of reproach; you will never see this place again.'

¹⁹"Remnant of Judah, the Lᴏʀᴅ has told you, 'Do not go to Egypt.' Be sure of this: I warn you today ²⁰that you made a fatal mistake when you sent me to the Lᴏʀᴅ your God and said, 'Pray to the Lᴏʀᴅ our God for us; tell us everything he says and we will do it.' ²¹I have told you today, but you still have not obeyed the Lᴏʀᴅ your God in all he sent me to tell you. ²²So now, be sure of this: You will die by the sword, famine and plague in the place where you want to go to settle."

43 When Jeremiah had finished telling the people all the words of the Lᴏʀᴅ their God—everything the Lᴏʀᴅ had sent him to tell them— ²Azariah son of Hoshaiah and Johanan son of Kareah and all the arrogant men said to Jeremiah, "You are lying! The Lᴏʀᴅ our God has not sent you to say, 'You must not go to Egypt to settle there.' ³But Baruch son of Neriah is inciting you against us to hand us over to the Babylonians,*b* so they may kill us or carry us into exile to Babylon."

⁴So Johanan son of Kareah and all the army officers and all the people disobeyed the Lᴏʀᴅ's command to stay in the land of Judah. ⁵Instead, Johanan son of Kareah and all the army officers led away all the remnant of Judah who had come back to live in the land of Judah from all the nations where they had been scattered. ⁶They also led away all those whom Nebuzaradan commander of the imperial guard had left with Gedaliah son of Ahikam, the son of Shaphan—the men, the women, the children and the king's daughters. And they took Jeremiah the prophet and Baruch son of Neriah along with them. ⁷So they entered Egypt in disobedience to the Lᴏʀᴅ and went as far as Tahpanhes.

⁸In Tahpanhes the word of the Lᴏʀᴅ came to Jeremiah: ⁹"While the Jews are watching, take some large stones with you and bury them in clay in the brick pavement at the entrance to Pharaoh's palace in Tahpanhes. ¹⁰Then say to them, 'This is what the Lᴏʀᴅ Almighty, the God of Israel, says: I will send for my servant Nebuchadnezzar king of Babylon, and I will set his throne over these stones I have buried here; he will spread his royal canopy above them. ¹¹He will come

---

a 18 That is, your name will be used in cursing (see 29:22); or, others will see that you are cursed.   *b 3* Or *Chaldeans*

How did Jeremiah know that they were not going to obey God's instructions? (42:21) When the Lord spoke to Jeremiah, he may have told him how the people would respond.

What path did they follow to Egypt? (43:5) See the map below.

Flight to Egypt (43:5)

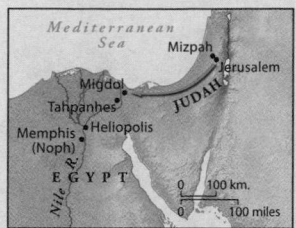

Flight to Egypt map: Mediterranean Sea, Mizpah, Jerusalem, Migdol, Tahpanhes, Memphis (Noph), Heliopolis, JUDAH, EGYPT, Nile, 0 100 km., 0 100 miles

Did Baruch and Jeremiah go to Egypt willingly? (43:6) It's not likely that they went willingly because they knew the Lord's will. They had seen that the Lord always did what he said he would do.

and attack Egypt, bringing death to those destined for death, captivity to those destined for captivity, and the sword to those destined for the sword. [12] He will set fire to the temples of the gods of Egypt; he will burn their temples and take their gods captive. As a shepherd picks his garment clean of lice, so he will pick Egypt clean and depart. [13] There in the temple of the sun[a] in Egypt he will demolish the sacred pillars and will burn down the temples of the gods of Egypt.'"

DISASTER BECAUSE OF IDOLATRY

44 This word came to Jeremiah concerning all the Jews living in Lower Egypt—in Migdol, Tahpanhes and Memphis—and in Upper Egypt: [2] "This is what the LORD Almighty, the God of Israel, says: You saw the great disaster I brought on Jerusalem and on all the towns of Judah. Today they lie deserted and in ruins [3] because of the evil they have done. They aroused my anger by burning incense to and worshiping other gods that neither they nor you nor your ancestors ever knew. [4] Again and again I sent my servants the prophets, who said, 'Do not do this detestable thing that I hate!' [5] But they did not listen or pay attention; they did not turn from their wickedness or stop burning incense to other gods. [6] Therefore, my fierce anger was poured out; it raged against the towns of Judah and the streets of Jerusalem and made them the desolate ruins they are today.

[7] "Now this is what the LORD God Almighty, the God of Israel, says: Why bring such great disaster on yourselves by cutting off from Judah the men and women, the children and infants, and so leave yourselves without a remnant? [8] Why arouse my anger with what your hands have made, burning incense to other gods in Egypt, where you have come to live? You will destroy yourselves and make yourselves a curse[b] and an object of reproach among all the nations on earth. [9] Have you forgotten the wickedness committed by your ancestors and by the kings and queens of Judah and the wickedness committed by you and your wives in the land of Judah and the streets of Jerusalem? [10] To this day they have not humbled themselves or shown reverence, nor have they followed my law and the decrees I set before you and your ancestors.

[11] "Therefore this is what the LORD Almighty, the God of Israel, says: I am determined to bring disaster on you and to destroy all Judah. [12] I will take away the remnant of Judah who were determined to go to Egypt to settle there. They will all perish in Egypt; they will fall by the sword or die from famine. From the least to the greatest, they will die by sword or famine. They will become a curse and an object of horror, a curse and an object of reproach. [13] I will punish those who live in Egypt with the sword, famine and plague, as I punished Jerusalem. [14] None of the remnant of Judah who have gone to live in Egypt will escape or survive to return to the land of Judah, to which they long to return and live; none will return except a few fugitives."

Why did the Israelites worship the gods of Egypt? (44:8)
They worshiped local pagan gods in Judah, and they continued this practice in Egypt. They may have believed that worshiping local gods would provide safety or security in the region where that god ruled.

---

[a] 13 Or *in Heliopolis*   [b] 8 That is, your name will be used in cursing (see 29:22); or, others will see that you are cursed; also in verse 12; similarly in verse 22.

¹⁵Then all the men who knew that their wives were burning incense to other gods, along with all the women who were present—a large assembly—and all the people living in Lower and Upper Egypt, said to Jeremiah, ¹⁶"We will not listen to the message you have spoken to us in the name of the Lord! ¹⁷We will certainly do everything we said we would: We will burn incense to the Queen of Heaven and will pour out drink offerings to her just as we and our ancestors, our kings and our officials did in the towns of Judah and in the streets of Jerusalem. At that time we had plenty of food and were well off and suffered no harm. ¹⁸But ever since we stopped burning incense to the Queen of Heaven and pouring out drink offerings to her, we have had nothing and have been perishing by sword and famine."

¹⁹The women added, "When we burned incense to the Queen of Heaven and poured out drink offerings to her, did not our husbands know that we were making cakes impressed with her image and pouring out drink offerings to her?"

²⁰Then Jeremiah said to all the people, both men and women, who were answering him, ²¹"Did not the Lord remember and call to mind the incense burned in the towns of Judah and the streets of Jerusalem by you and your ancestors, your kings and your officials and the people of the land? ²²When the Lord could no longer endure your wicked actions and the detestable things you did, your land became a curse and a desolate waste without inhabitants, as it is today. ²³Because you have burned incense and have sinned against the Lord and have not obeyed him or followed his law or his decrees or his stipulations, this disaster has come upon you, as you now see."

²⁴Then Jeremiah said to all the people, including the women, "Hear the word of the Lord, all you people of Judah in Egypt. ²⁵This is what the Lord Almighty, the God of Israel, says: You and your wives have done what you said you would do when you promised, 'We will certainly carry out the vows we made to burn incense and pour out drink offerings to the Queen of Heaven.'

"Go ahead then, do what you promised! Keep your vows! ²⁶But hear the word of the Lord, all you Jews living in Egypt: 'I swear by my great name,' says the Lord, 'that no one from Judah living anywhere in Egypt will ever again invoke my name or swear, "As surely as the Sovereign Lord lives." ²⁷For I am watching over them for harm, not for good; the Jews in Egypt will perish by sword and famine until they are all destroyed. ²⁸Those who escape the sword and return to the land of Judah from Egypt will be very few. Then the whole remnant of Judah who came to live in Egypt will know whose word will stand—mine or theirs.

²⁹"'This will be the sign to you that I will punish you in this place,' declares the Lord, 'so that you will know that my threats of harm against you will surely stand.' ³⁰This is what the Lord says: 'I am going to deliver Pharaoh Hophra king of Egypt into the hands of his enemies who want to kill him, just as I gave Zedekiah king of Judah into the hands of Nebuchadnezzar king of Babylon, the enemy who wanted to kill him.'"

Who was the Queen of Heaven? (44:17)
This was Ishtar, an important goddess in the ranks of Babylonian gods.

Why did they think that failing to worship Ishtar had brought them trouble? (44:18)
King Josiah had led a reform movement to end the worship of pagan gods. After Josiah died, there had been invasions and exile. Now the people foolishly thought these misfortunes had happened because they stopped worshiping Ishtar.

Why did the women blame their husbands? (44:19)
In Jewish society, men could give their wives orders. So these women said they weren't responsible for the idol worship because their husbands could have stopped them.

Who was Pharaoh Hophra? (44:30)
He ruled Egypt around 588 to 569 B.C. He was killed by his rivals during a power struggle.

A MESSAGE TO BARUCH

45 When Baruch son of Neriah wrote on a scroll the words Jeremiah the prophet dictated in the fourth year of Jehoiakim son of Josiah king of Judah, Jeremiah said this to Baruch: ²"This is what the LORD, the God of Israel, says to you, Baruch: ³You said, 'Woe to me! The LORD has added sorrow to my pain; I am worn out with groaning and find no rest.' ⁴But the LORD has told me to say to you, 'This is what the LORD says: I will overthrow what I have built and uproot what I have planted, throughout the earth. ⁵Should you then seek great things for yourself? Do not seek them. For I will bring disaster on all people, declares the LORD, but wherever you go I will let you escape with your life.'"

What great things did Baruch want? (45:5)
It isn't clear, but the Lord told him not to seek great things, and he promised to spare Baruch's life.

A MESSAGE ABOUT EGYPT

46 This is the word of the LORD that came to Jeremiah the prophet concerning the nations:

²Concerning Egypt:

This is the message against the army of Pharaoh Necho king of Egypt, which was defeated at Carchemish on the Euphrates River by Nebuchadnezzar king of Babylon in the fourth year of Jehoiakim son of Josiah king of Judah:

³"Prepare your shields, both large and small,
　　and march out for battle!
⁴Harness the horses,
　　mount the steeds!
Take your positions
　　with helmets on!
Polish your spears,
　　put on your armor!
⁵What do I see?
　　They are terrified,
they are retreating,
　　their warriors are defeated.
They flee in haste
　　without looking back,
　　and there is terror on every side,"
　　　　　　　　　　　　declares the LORD.
⁶"The swift cannot flee
　　nor the strong escape.
In the north by the River Euphrates
　　they stumble and fall.

⁷"Who is this that rises like the Nile,
　　like rivers of surging waters?
⁸Egypt rises like the Nile,
　　like rivers of surging waters.
She says, 'I will rise and cover the earth;
　　I will destroy cities and their people.'
⁹Charge, you horses!
　　Drive furiously, you charioteers!
March on, you warriors—men of Cush*ᵃ* and Put who
　　carry shields,
　　men of Lydia who draw the bow.

ᵃ 9 That is, the upper Nile region

¹⁰But that day belongs to the Lord, the LORD
        Almighty—
    a day of vengeance, for vengeance on his foes.
The sword will devour till it is satisfied,
    till it has quenched its thirst with blood.
For the Lord, the LORD Almighty, will offer sacrifice
    in the land of the north by the River Euphrates.

¹¹"Go up to Gilead and get balm,
    Virgin Daughter Egypt.
But you try many medicines in vain;
    there is no healing for you.
¹²The nations will hear of your shame;
    your cries will fill the earth.
One warrior will stumble over another;
    both will fall down together."

¹³This is the message the LORD spoke to Jeremiah the
prophet about the coming of Nebuchadnezzar king of Babylon to attack Egypt:

¹⁴"Announce this in Egypt, and proclaim it in Migdol;
    proclaim it also in Memphis and Tahpanhes:
'Take your positions and get ready,
    for the sword devours those around you.'
¹⁵Why will your warriors be laid low?
    They cannot stand, for the LORD will push
        them down.
¹⁶They will stumble repeatedly;
    they will fall over each other.
They will say, 'Get up, let us go back
    to our own people and our native lands,
    away from the sword of the oppressor.'
¹⁷There they will exclaim,
    'Pharaoh king of Egypt is only a loud noise;
    he has missed his opportunity.'

¹⁸"As surely as I live," declares the King,
    whose name is the LORD Almighty,
"one will come who is like Tabor among the mountains,
    like Carmel by the sea.
¹⁹Pack your belongings for exile,
    you who live in Egypt,
for Memphis will be laid waste
    and lie in ruins without inhabitant.

²⁰"Egypt is a beautiful heifer,
    but a gadfly is coming
        against her from the north.
²¹The mercenaries in her ranks
    are like fattened calves.
They too will turn and flee together,
    they will not stand their ground,
for the day of disaster is coming upon them,
    the time for them to be punished.
²²Egypt will hiss like a fleeing serpent
    as the enemy advances in force;
they will come against her with axes,
    like men who cut down trees.

Why travel to Gilead for balm? (46:11)
The territory of Gilead was an important source of spices and medicinal herbs.

What did God tell Jeremiah to announce? (46:14)
The Lord told him to prophesy about the coming destruction of Egypt by Nebuchadnezzar.

Why would Egypt be called a heifer? (46:20)
This might have been an ironic reference to the fact that the Egyptians worshiped Apis, a bull-god.

What is a gadfly? (46:20)
This was a biting or stinging insect. Insects were often used to symbolize attacking armies (see verse 23, where an invading army is compared to locusts). Here the reference is to Nebuchadnezzar.

²³ They will chop down her forest,"
                                    declares the LORD,
    "dense though it be.
They are more numerous than locusts,
    they cannot be counted.
²⁴ Daughter Egypt will be put to shame,
    given into the hands of the people of the north."

²⁵ The LORD Almighty, the God of Israel, says: "I am about to bring punishment on Amon god of Thebes, on Pharaoh, on Egypt and her gods and her kings, and on those who rely on Pharaoh. ²⁶ I will give them into the hands of those who want to kill them — Nebuchadnezzar king of Babylon and his officers. Later, however, Egypt will be inhabited as in times past," declares the LORD.

²⁷ "Do not be afraid, Jacob my servant;
    do not be dismayed, Israel.
I will surely save you out of a distant place,
    your descendants from the land of their exile.
Jacob will again have peace and security,
    and no one will make him afraid.
²⁸ Do not be afraid, Jacob my servant,
    for I am with you," declares the LORD.
"Though I completely destroy all the nations
    among which I scatter you,
    I will not completely destroy you.
I will discipline you but only in due measure;
    I will not let you go entirely unpunished."

Why do these verses sound familiar? (46:27–28)
They are repeated almost word-for-word from Jeremiah 30:10–11.

A MESSAGE ABOUT THE PHILISTINES

47 This is the word of the LORD that came to Jeremiah the prophet concerning the Philistines before Pharaoh attacked Gaza:

² This is what the LORD says:

"See how the waters are rising in the north;
    they will become an overflowing torrent.
They will overflow the land and everything in it,
    the towns and those who live in them.
The people will cry out;
    all who dwell in the land will wail
³ at the sound of the hooves of galloping steeds,
    at the noise of enemy chariots
    and the rumble of their wheels.
Parents will not turn to help their children;
    their hands will hang limp.
⁴ For the day has come
    to destroy all the Philistines
and to remove all survivors
    who could help Tyre and Sidon.
The LORD is about to destroy the Philistines,
    the remnant from the coasts of Caphtor.ᵃ
⁵ Gaza will shave her head in mourning;
    Ashkelon will be silenced.

When did this prophecy come to pass? (47:4)
The immediate fulfillment took place under Nebuchadnezzar in 604 B.C.

ᵃ 4 That is, Crete

You remnant on the plain,
how long will you cut yourselves?

6 "'Alas, sword of the LORD,
how long till you rest?
Return to your sheath;
cease and be still.'
7 But how can it rest
when the LORD has commanded it,
when he has ordered it
to attack Ashkelon and the coast?"

A MESSAGE ABOUT MOAB

48 Concerning Moab:

This is what the LORD Almighty, the God of Israel, says:

"Woe to Nebo, for it will be ruined.
Kiriathaim will be disgraced and captured;
the stronghold*a* will be disgraced and shattered.
2 Moab will be praised no more;
in Heshbon*b* people will plot her downfall:
'Come, let us put an end to that nation.'
You, the people of Madmen,*c* will also be silenced;
the sword will pursue you.
3 Cries of anguish arise from Horonaim,
cries of great havoc and destruction.
4 Moab will be broken;
her little ones will cry out.*d*
5 They go up the hill to Luhith,
weeping bitterly as they go;
on the road down to Horonaim
anguished cries over the destruction are heard.
6 Flee! Run for your lives;
become like a bush*e* in the desert.
7 Since you trust in your deeds and riches,
you too will be taken captive,
and Chemosh will go into exile,
together with his priests and officials.
8 The destroyer will come against every town,
and not a town will escape.
The valley will be ruined
and the plateau destroyed,
because the LORD has spoken.
9 Put salt on Moab,
for she will be laid waste*f*;
her towns will become desolate,
with no one to live in them.
10 "A curse on anyone who is lax in doing the LORD's
work!
A curse on anyone who keeps their sword from
bloodshed!

Who was Chemosh? (48:7)
This was the national god of
Moab. Images of pagan gods
were often carried around from
place to place.

**Why did conquering armies
often spread salt on the
earth of defeated territories?
(48:9)**
They did this to make the land
barren and unfit for farming.

a 1 Or *captured; / Misgab*   *b 2* The Hebrew for *Heshbon* sounds like the
Hebrew for *plot.*   *c 2* The name of the Moabite town Madmen sounds like
the Hebrew for *be silenced.*   *d 4* Hebrew; Septuagint */ proclaim it to Zoar*
e 6 Or *like Aroer*   *f 9* Or *Give wings to Moab, / for she will fly away*

11 "Moab has been at rest from youth,
     like wine left on its dregs,
not poured from one jar to another—
     she has not gone into exile.
So she tastes as she did,
     and her aroma is unchanged.
12 But days are coming,"
     declares the LORD,
"when I will send men who pour from pitchers,
     and they will pour her out;
they will empty her pitchers
     and smash her jars.
13 Then Moab will be ashamed of Chemosh,
     as Israel was ashamed
     when they trusted in Bethel.

14 "How can you say, 'We are warriors,
     men valiant in battle'?
15 Moab will be destroyed and her towns invaded;
     her finest young men will go down in the slaughter,"
     declares the King, whose name is the LORD
         Almighty.
16 "The fall of Moab is at hand;
     her calamity will come quickly.
17 Mourn for her, all who live around her,
     all who know her fame;
say, 'How broken is the mighty scepter,
     how broken the glorious staff!'

18 "Come down from your glory
     and sit on the parched ground,
     you inhabitants of Daughter Dibon,
for the one who destroys Moab
     will come up against you
     and ruin your fortified cities.
19 Stand by the road and watch,
     you who live in Aroer.
Ask the man fleeing and the woman escaping,
     ask them, 'What has happened?'
20 Moab is disgraced, for she is shattered.
     Wail and cry out!
Announce by the Arnon
     that Moab is destroyed.
21 Judgment has come to the plateau—
     to Holon, Jahzah and Mephaath,
22   to Dibon, Nebo and Beth Diblathaim,
23   to Kiriathaim, Beth Gamul and Beth Meon,
24   to Kerioth and Bozrah—
to all the towns of Moab, far and near.
25 Moab's horn[a] is cut off;
     her arm is broken,"
                            declares the LORD.

26 "Make her drunk,
     for she has defied the LORD.

What did broken scepters and staffs symbolize? (48:17)
This is a symbol for the loss of power and ruling authority.

---

[a] 25 *Horn* here symbolizes strength.

Let Moab wallow in her vomit;
    let her be an object of ridicule.
27 Was not Israel the object of your ridicule?
    Was she caught among thieves,
that you shake your head in scorn
    whenever you speak of her?
28 Abandon your towns and dwell among the rocks,
    you who live in Moab.
Be like a dove that makes its nest
    at the mouth of a cave.

29 "We have heard of Moab's pride—
    how great is her arrogance!—
of her insolence, her pride, her conceit
    and the haughtiness of her heart.
30 I know her insolence but it is futile,"
                    declares the LORD,
    "and her boasts accomplish nothing.
31 Therefore I wail over Moab,
    for all Moab I cry out,
    I moan for the people of Kir Hareseth.
32 I weep for you, as Jazer weeps,
    you vines of Sibmah.
Your branches spread as far as the sea[a];
    they reached as far as[b] Jazer.
The destroyer has fallen
    on your ripened fruit and grapes.
33 Joy and gladness are gone
    from the orchards and fields of Moab.
I have stopped the flow of wine from the presses;
    no one treads them with shouts of joy.
Although there are shouts,
    they are not shouts of joy.

34 "The sound of their cry rises
    from Heshbon to Elealeh and Jahaz,
from Zoar as far as Horonaim and Eglath Shelishiyah,
    for even the waters of Nimrim are dried up.
35 In Moab I will put an end
    to those who make offerings on the high places
    and burn incense to their gods,"
                    declares the LORD.
36 "So my heart laments for Moab like the music of a pipe;
    it laments like a pipe for the people of Kir Hareseth.
    The wealth they acquired is gone.
37 Every head is shaved
    and every beard cut off;
every hand is slashed
    and every waist is covered with sackcloth.
38 On all the roofs in Moab
    and in the public squares
there is nothing but mourning,
    for I have broken Moab
    like a jar that no one wants,"
                    declares the LORD.

---

[a] 32 Probably the Dead Sea   [b] 32 Two Hebrew manuscripts and
Septuagint; most Hebrew manuscripts *as far as the Sea of*

Why did Jeremiah use the image of a pipe? (48:36)
Jeremiah was lamenting the destruction of Moab. A flute-like instrument made from a pipe was traditionally played by mourners at funerals.

³⁹ "How shattered she is! How they wail!
    How Moab turns her back in shame!
Moab has become an object of ridicule,
    an object of horror to all those around her."

⁴⁰ This is what the LORD says:

"Look! An eagle is swooping down,
    spreading its wings over Moab.
⁴¹ Kerioth^a will be captured
    and the strongholds taken.
In that day the hearts of Moab's warriors
    will be like the heart of a woman in labor.
⁴² Moab will be destroyed as a nation
    because she defied the LORD.
⁴³ Terror and pit and snare await you,
    you people of Moab,"

           declares the LORD.

⁴⁴ "Whoever flees from the terror
    will fall into a pit,
whoever climbs out of the pit
    will be caught in a snare;
for I will bring on Moab
    the year of her punishment,"

           declares the LORD.

⁴⁵ "In the shadow of Heshbon
    the fugitives stand helpless,
for a fire has gone out from Heshbon,
    a blaze from the midst of Sihon;
it burns the foreheads of Moab,
    the skulls of the noisy boasters.
⁴⁶ Woe to you, Moab!
    The people of Chemosh are destroyed;
your sons are taken into exile
    and your daughters into captivity.

⁴⁷ "Yet I will restore the fortunes of Moab
    in days to come,"

           declares the LORD.

Here ends the judgment on Moab.

A MESSAGE ABOUT AMMON

49 Concerning the Ammonites:

This is what the LORD says:

"Has Israel no sons?
    Has Israel no heir?
Why then has Molek^b taken possession of Gad?
    Why do his people live in its towns?
² But the days are coming,"
    declares the LORD,
"when I will sound the battle cry
    against Rabbah of the Ammonites;
it will become a mound of ruins,
    and its surrounding villages will be set on fire.

Who was symbolized by the eagle? (48:40)
This was a symbol for Nebuchadnezzar.

Why did the Lord say the people would not be able to flee? (48:44)
The Lord's judgment was unavoidable.

Who was Molek? (49:1)
Molek, also known as Milcom, was the chief god of the Ammonites. This was a god to whom child sacrifices were sometimes offered.

---

^a 41 Or *The cities*   ^b 1 Or *their king*; also in verse 3

Then Israel will drive out
    those who drove her out,"

says the LORD.

³ "Wail, Heshbon, for Ai is destroyed!
    Cry out, you inhabitants of Rabbah!
Put on sackcloth and mourn;
    rush here and there inside the walls,
for Molek will go into exile,
    together with his priests and officials.
⁴ Why do you boast of your valleys,
    boast of your valleys so fruitful?
Unfaithful Daughter Ammon,
    you trust in your riches and say,
    'Who will attack me?'
⁵ I will bring terror on you
    from all those around you,"

declares the Lord, the LORD Almighty.

"Every one of you will be driven away,
    and no one will gather the fugitives.

⁶ "Yet afterward, I will restore the fortunes of the
    Ammonites,"

declares the LORD.

A MESSAGE ABOUT EDOM

⁷ Concerning Edom:

This is what the LORD Almighty says:

"Is there no longer wisdom in Teman?
    Has counsel perished from the prudent?
    Has their wisdom decayed?
⁸ Turn and flee, hide in deep caves,
    you who live in Dedan,
for I will bring disaster on Esau
    at the time when I punish him.
⁹ If grape pickers came to you,
    would they not leave a few grapes?
If thieves came during the night,
    would they not steal only as much as they wanted?
¹⁰ But I will strip Esau bare;
    I will uncover his hiding places,
    so that he cannot conceal himself.
His armed men are destroyed,
    also his allies and neighbors,
    so there is no one to say,
¹¹ 'Leave your fatherless children; I will keep them alive.
    Your widows too can depend on me.'"

¹² This is what the LORD says: "If those who do not deserve to drink the cup must drink it, why should you go unpunished? You will not go unpunished, but must drink it. ¹³ I swear by myself," declares the LORD, "that Bozrah will become a ruin and a curse,ᵃ an object of horror and reproach; and all its towns will be in ruins forever."

ᵃ 13 That is, its name will be used in cursing (see 29:22); or, others will see that it is cursed.

¹⁴ I have heard a message from the LORD;
　　an envoy was sent to the nations to say,
　"Assemble yourselves to attack it!
　　Rise up for battle!"

¹⁵ "Now I will make you small among the nations,
　　despised by mankind.
¹⁶ The terror you inspire
　　and the pride of your heart have deceived you,
　you who live in the clefts of the rocks,
　　who occupy the heights of the hill.
　Though you build your nest as high as the eagle's,
　　from there I will bring you down,"
　　　　　　　　　　　　　　　declares the LORD.
¹⁷ "Edom will become an object of horror;
　　all who pass by will be appalled and
　　　　will scoff
　because of all its wounds.
¹⁸ As Sodom and Gomorrah were overthrown,
　　along with their neighboring towns,"
　　　　　　　　　　　　　　　says the LORD,
　"so no one will live there;
　　no people will dwell in it.

¹⁹ "Like a lion coming up from Jordan's thickets
　　to a rich pastureland,
　I will chase Edom from its land in an instant.
　　Who is the chosen one I will appoint for this?
　Who is like me and who can challenge me?
　　And what shepherd can stand against me?"

²⁰ Therefore, hear what the LORD has planned against
　　　　Edom,
　　what he has purposed against those who live in
　　　　Teman:
　The young of the flock will be dragged away;
　　their pasture will be appalled at their fate.
²¹ At the sound of their fall the earth will tremble;
　　their cry will resound to the Red Sea.ᵃ
²² Look! An eagle will soar and swoop down,
　　spreading its wings over Bozrah.
　In that day the hearts of Edom's warriors
　　will be like the heart of a woman in labor.

A MESSAGE ABOUT DAMASCUS

²³ Concerning Damascus:

　"Hamath and Arpad are dismayed,
　　for they have heard bad news.
　They are disheartened,
　　troubled likeᵇ the restless sea.
²⁴ Damascus has become feeble,
　　she has turned to flee
　　and panic has gripped her;
　anguish and pain have seized her,
　　pain like that of a woman in labor.

Where were these rocks?
(49:16)
This may be a reference to Petra, a city in Edom in which all the structures had been carved into cliffs.

What were these thickets?
(49:19)
This was dense brush that grew along the banks of the Jordan River. Lions and other predatory animals lived in the thickets and raided nearby flocks.

ᵃ 21 Or *the Sea of Reeds*　　ᵇ 23 Hebrew *on* or *by*

²⁵ Why has the city of renown not been abandoned,
    the town in which I delight?
²⁶ Surely, her young men will fall in the streets;
    all her soldiers will be silenced in that day,"
declares the LORD Almighty.

²⁷ "I will set fire to the walls of Damascus;
    it will consume the fortresses of Ben-Hadad."

A MESSAGE ABOUT KEDAR AND HAZOR

²⁸ Concerning Kedar and the kingdoms of Hazor, which
Nebuchadnezzar king of Babylon attacked:

This is what the LORD says:

"Arise, and attack Kedar
    and destroy the people of the East.
²⁹ Their tents and their flocks will be taken;
    their shelters will be carried off
    with all their goods and camels.
People will shout to them,
    'Terror on every side!'

³⁰ "Flee quickly away!
    Stay in deep caves, you who live in Hazor,"
declares the LORD.

"Nebuchadnezzar king of Babylon has plotted
    against you;
    he has devised a plan against you.

³¹ "Arise and attack a nation at ease,
    which lives in confidence,"
declares the LORD,

    "a nation that has neither gates nor bars;
    its people live far from danger.
³² Their camels will become plunder,
    and their large herds will be spoils of war.
I will scatter to the winds those who are in
        distant places*ᵃ*
    and will bring disaster on them from
        every side,"
declares the LORD.

³³ "Hazor will become a haunt of jackals,
    a desolate place forever.
No one will live there;
    no people will dwell in it."

A MESSAGE ABOUT ELAM

³⁴ This is the word of the LORD that came to Jeremiah
the prophet concerning Elam, early in the reign of Zedekiah
king of Judah:

³⁵ This is what the LORD Almighty says:

"See, I will break the bow of Elam,
    the mainstay of their might.
³⁶ I will bring against Elam the four winds
    from the four quarters of heaven;

ᵃ 32 Or who clip the hair by their foreheads

**What was a nation that had
no gates or bars? (49:31)**
This refers to people, perhaps
nomads, who lived in villages
without walls.

**Why did the Lord say he
would break the bow of
Elam? (49:35)**
The Elamites were skilled archers, so symbolically this would
be a fitting punishment.

I will scatter them to the four winds,
    and there will not be a nation
    where Elam's exiles do not go.
³⁷ I will shatter Elam before their foes,
    before those who want to kill them;
I will bring disaster on them,
    even my fierce anger,"

declares the LORD.

"I will pursue them with the sword
    until I have made an end of them.
³⁸ I will set my throne in Elam
    and destroy her king and officials,"

declares the LORD.

³⁹ "Yet I will restore the fortunes of Elam
    in days to come,"

declares the LORD.

A MESSAGE ABOUT BABYLON

50 This is the word the LORD spoke through Jeremiah the prophet concerning Babylon and the land of the Babylonians*:

² "Announce and proclaim among the nations,
    lift up a banner and proclaim it;
    keep nothing back, but say,
'Babylon will be captured;
    Bel will be put to shame,
    Marduk filled with terror.
Her images will be put to shame
    and her idols filled with terror.'
³ A nation from the north will attack her
    and lay waste her land.
No one will live in it;
    both people and animals will flee away.

⁴ "In those days, at that time,"
    declares the LORD,
"the people of Israel and the people of Judah together
    will go in tears to seek the LORD their God.
⁵ They will ask the way to Zion
    and turn their faces toward it.
They will come and bind themselves to the LORD
    in an everlasting covenant
    that will not be forgotten.

⁶ "My people have been lost sheep;
    their shepherds have led them astray
    and caused them to roam on the mountains.
They wandered over mountain and hill
    and forgot their own resting place.
⁷ Whoever found them devoured them;
    their enemies said, 'We are not guilty,
for they sinned against the LORD, their verdant
      pasture,
    the LORD, the hope of their ancestors.'

Who were Bel and Marduk? (50:2)
These were names for one of the chief Babylonian gods.

What was this everlasting covenant? (50:5)
This was called the new covenant in Jeremiah 31:31. God would again turn his people to him, and they would be his people.

---

a 1 Or *Chaldeans*; also in verses 8, 25, 35 and 45

⁸ "Flee out of Babylon;
   leave the land of the Babylonians,
   and be like the goats that lead the flock.
⁹ For I will stir up and bring against Babylon
   an alliance of great nations from the land of the
      north.
They will take up their positions against her,
   and from the north she will be captured.
Their arrows will be like skilled warriors
   who do not return empty-handed.
¹⁰ So Babylonia*ᵃ* will be plundered;
   all who plunder her will have their fill,"
                              declares the LORD.

¹¹ "Because you rejoice and are glad,
   you who pillage my inheritance,
because you frolic like a heifer threshing grain
   and neigh like stallions,
¹² your mother will be greatly ashamed;
   she who gave you birth will be disgraced.
She will be the least of the nations—
   a wilderness, a dry land, a desert.
¹³ Because of the LORD's anger she will not be inhabited
   but will be completely desolate.
All who pass Babylon will be appalled;
   they will scoff because of all her wounds.

¹⁴ "Take up your positions around Babylon,
   all you who draw the bow.
Shoot at her! Spare no arrows,
   for she has sinned against the LORD.
¹⁵ Shout against her on every side!
   She surrenders, her towers fall,
   her walls are torn down.
Since this is the vengeance of the LORD,
   take vengeance on her;
   do to her as she has done to others.
¹⁶ Cut off from Babylon the sower,
   and the reaper with his sickle at harvest.
Because of the sword of the oppressor
   let everyone return to their own people,
   let everyone flee to their own land.

¹⁷ "Israel is a scattered flock
   that lions have chased away.
The first to devour them
   was the king of Assyria;
the last to crush their bones
   was Nebuchadnezzar king of Babylon."

¹⁸ Therefore this is what the LORD Almighty, the God of
Israel, says:

"I will punish the king of Babylon and his land
   as I punished the king of Assyria.
¹⁹ But I will bring Israel back to their own pasture,
   and they will graze on Carmel and Bashan;

What did the lions symbolize? (50:17)
The lions represented Assyria and Babylon.

ᵃ 10 Or *Chaldea*

their appetite will be satisfied
    on the hills of Ephraim and Gilead.
²⁰ In those days, at that time,"
    declares the LORD,
"search will be made for Israel's guilt,
    but there will be none,
and for the sins of Judah,
    but none will be found,
    for I will forgive the remnant I spare.

²¹ "Attack the land of Merathaim
    and those who live in Pekod.
Pursue, kill and completely destroy*a* them,"
                    declares the LORD.
"Do everything I have commanded you.
²² The noise of battle is in the land,
    the noise of great destruction!
²³ How broken and shattered
    is the hammer of the whole earth!
How desolate is Babylon
    among the nations!
²⁴ I set a trap for you, Babylon,
    and you were caught before you knew it;
you were found and captured
    because you opposed the LORD.
²⁵ The LORD has opened his arsenal
    and brought out the weapons of his wrath,
for the Sovereign LORD Almighty has work to do
    in the land of the Babylonians.
²⁶ Come against her from afar.
    Break open her granaries;
    pile her up like heaps of grain.
Completely destroy her
    and leave her no remnant.
²⁷ Kill all her young bulls;
    let them go down to the slaughter!
Woe to them! For their day has come,
    the time for them to be punished.
²⁸ Listen to the fugitives and refugees from Babylon
    declaring in Zion
how the LORD our God has taken vengeance,
    vengeance for his temple.

²⁹ "Summon archers against Babylon,
    all those who draw the bow.
Encamp all around her;
    let no one escape.
Repay her for her deeds;
    do to her as she has done.
For she has defied the LORD,
    the Holy One of Israel.
³⁰ Therefore, her young men will fall in the streets;
    all her soldiers will be silenced in that day,"
                    declares the LORD.

---

a 21 The Hebrew term refers to the irrevocable giving over of things or persons to the LORD, often by totally destroying them; also in verse 26.

Why would the young bulls be killed? (50:27)
This was figurative language for the people of Babylon, especially the fighting men.

³¹"See, I am against you, you arrogant one,"
    declares the Lord, the LORD Almighty,
  "for your day has come,
    the time for you to be punished.
³²The arrogant one will stumble and fall
    and no one will help her up;
  I will kindle a fire in her towns
    that will consume all who are around her."

³³This is what the LORD Almighty says:

  "The people of Israel are oppressed,
    and the people of Judah as well.
  All their captors hold them fast,
    refusing to let them go.
³⁴Yet their Redeemer is strong;
    the LORD Almighty is his name.
  He will vigorously defend their cause
    so that he may bring rest to their land,
    but unrest to those who live in Babylon.

³⁵"A sword against the Babylonians!"
    declares the LORD—
  "against those who live in Babylon
    and against her officials and wise men!
³⁶A sword against her false prophets!
    They will become fools.
  A sword against her warriors!
    They will be filled with terror.
³⁷A sword against her horses and chariots
    and all the foreigners in her ranks!
    They will become weaklings.
  A sword against her treasures!
    They will be plundered.
³⁸A drought on ª her waters!
    They will dry up.
  For it is a land of idols,
    idols that will go mad with terror.

³⁹"So desert creatures and hyenas will live there,
    and there the owl will dwell.
  It will never again be inhabited
    or lived in from generation to generation.
⁴⁰As I overthrew Sodom and Gomorrah
    along with their neighboring towns,"
                          declares the LORD,
  "so no one will live there;
    no people will dwell in it.

⁴¹"Look! An army is coming from the north;
    a great nation and many kings
    are being stirred up from the ends of the earth.
⁴²They are armed with bows and spears;
    they are cruel and without mercy.
  They sound like the roaring sea
    as they ride on their horses;
  they come like men in battle formation
    to attack you, Daughter Babylon.

ª 38 Or *A sword against*

Where did these words appear earlier? (50:41–43)
These verses are repeated almost word-for-word from Jeremiah 6:22–24, which described what would happen to Jerusalem. Here these verses tell about what would happen to Babylon.

⁴³ The king of Babylon has heard reports about them,
    and his hands hang limp.
Anguish has gripped him,
    pain like that of a woman in labor.
⁴⁴ Like a lion coming up from Jordan's thickets
    to a rich pastureland,
I will chase Babylon from its land in an instant.
    Who is the chosen one I will appoint for this?
Who is like me and who can challenge me?
    And what shepherd can stand against me?"

⁴⁵ Therefore, hear what the LORD has planned against
        Babylon,
    what he has purposed against the land of the
        Babylonians:
The young of the flock will be dragged away;
    their pasture will be appalled at their fate.
⁴⁶ At the sound of Babylon's capture the earth will
        tremble;
    its cry will resound among the nations.

51 This is what the LORD says:

"See, I will stir up the spirit of a destroyer
    against Babylon and the people of Leb Kamai.ᵃ
² I will send foreigners to Babylon
    to winnow her and to devastate her land;
they will oppose her on every side
    in the day of her disaster.
³ Let not the archer string his bow,
    nor let him put on his armor.
Do not spare her young men;
    completely destroyᵇ her army.
⁴ They will fall down slain in Babylon,ᶜ
    fatally wounded in her streets.
⁵ For Israel and Judah have not been forsaken
    by their God, the LORD Almighty,
though their landᵈ is full of guilt
    before the Holy One of Israel.

⁶ "Flee from Babylon!
    Run for your lives!
    Do not be destroyed because of her sins.
It is time for the LORD's vengeance;
    he will repay her what she deserves.
⁷ Babylon was a gold cup in the LORD's hand;
    she made the whole earth drunk.
The nations drank her wine;
    therefore they have now gone mad.
⁸ Babylon will suddenly fall and be broken.
    Wail over her!
Get balm for her pain;
    perhaps she can be healed.

ᵃ 1 *Leb Kamai* is a cryptogram for Chaldea, that is, Babylonia.
ᵇ 3 The Hebrew term refers to the irrevocable giving over of things or persons
to the LORD, often by totally destroying them.   ᶜ 4 Or *Chaldea*
ᵈ 5 Or *Almighty, / and the land of the Babylonians*

9 "'We would have healed Babylon,
  but she cannot be healed;
let us leave her and each go to our own land,
  for her judgment reaches to the skies,
  it rises as high as the heavens.'

10 "'The LORD has vindicated us;
  come, let us tell in Zion
  what the LORD our God has done.'

11 "Sharpen the arrows,
  take up the shields!
The LORD has stirred up the kings of the Medes,
  because his purpose is to destroy Babylon.
The LORD will take vengeance,
  vengeance for his temple.

12 Lift up a banner against the walls of Babylon!
  Reinforce the guard,
station the watchmen,
  prepare an ambush!
The LORD will carry out his purpose,
  his decree against the people of Babylon.

13 You who live by many waters
  and are rich in treasures,
your end has come,
  the time for you to be destroyed.

14 The LORD Almighty has sworn by himself:
  I will surely fill you with troops, as with a swarm
    of locusts,
  and they will shout in triumph over you.

15 "He made the earth by his power;
  he founded the world by his wisdom
  and stretched out the heavens by his understanding.

16 When he thunders, the waters in the heavens roar;
  he makes clouds rise from the ends of the earth.
He sends lightning with the rain
  and brings out the wind from his storehouses.

17 "Everyone is senseless and without knowledge;
  every goldsmith is shamed by his idols.
The images he makes are a fraud;
  they have no breath in them.

18 They are worthless, the objects of mockery;
  when their judgment comes, they will perish.

19 He who is the Portion of Jacob is not like these,
  for he is the Maker of all things,
including the people of his inheritance —
  the LORD Almighty is his name.

20 "You are my war club,
  my weapon for battle —
with you I shatter nations,
  with you I destroy kingdoms,

21 with you I shatter horse and rider,
  with you I shatter chariot and driver,

22 with you I shatter man and woman,
  with you I shatter old man and youth,
  with you I shatter young man and young woman,

What were the "many waters"? (51:13)
These were the rivers of Babylon, including the Euphrates River and an elaborate system of irrigation canals.

Who was the "Portion of Jacob"? (51:19)
This refers to the Lord, who was the God of Jacob.

Who was God's "war club"? (51:20)
This could refer to Cyrus of Persia, who would soon conquer Babylon, or Babylon itself, the destroyer of nations.

²³ with you I shatter shepherd and flock,
    with you I shatter farmer and oxen,
    with you I shatter governors and officials.

²⁴ "Before your eyes I will repay Babylon and all who live in Babylonia*a* for all the wrong they have done in Zion," declares the LORD.

²⁵ "I am against you, you destroying mountain,
    you who destroy the whole earth,"
                                        declares the LORD.
"I will stretch out my hand against you,
    roll you off the cliffs,
    and make you a burned-out mountain.
²⁶ No rock will be taken from you for a cornerstone,
    nor any stone for a foundation,
    for you will be desolate forever,"
                                        declares the LORD.

²⁷ "Lift up a banner in the land!
    Blow the trumpet among the nations!
Prepare the nations for battle against her;
    summon against her these kingdoms:
    Ararat, Minni and Ashkenaz.
Appoint a commander against her;
    send up horses like a swarm of locusts.
²⁸ Prepare the nations for battle against her—
    the kings of the Medes,
their governors and all their officials,
    and all the countries they rule.
²⁹ The land trembles and writhes,
    for the LORD's purposes against Babylon stand—
to lay waste the land of Babylon
    so that no one will live there.
³⁰ Babylon's warriors have stopped fighting;
    they remain in their strongholds.
Their strength is exhausted;
    they have become weaklings.
Her dwellings are set on fire;
    the bars of her gates are broken.
³¹ One courier follows another
    and messenger follows messenger
to announce to the king of Babylon
    that his entire city is captured,
³² the river crossings seized,
    the marshes set on fire,
    and the soldiers terrified."

³³ This is what the LORD Almighty, the God of Israel, says:

"Daughter Babylon is like a threshing floor
    at the time it is trampled;
    the time to harvest her will soon come."

³⁴ "Nebuchadnezzar king of Babylon has devoured us,
    he has thrown us into confusion,
    he has made us an empty jar.

Why would the marshes be set on fire? (51:32)
The fires would be set to destroy the reeds so that fugitives could not hide there.

---

a 24 Or *Chaldea*; also in verse 35

Like a serpent he has swallowed us
    and filled his stomach with our delicacies,
    and then has spewed us out.
35 May the violence done to our flesh*a* be
        on Babylon,"
    say the inhabitants of Zion.
"May our blood be on those who live
        in Babylonia,"
    says Jerusalem.

36 Therefore this is what the LORD says:

"See, I will defend your cause
    and avenge you;
I will dry up her sea
    and make her springs dry.
37 Babylon will be a heap of ruins,
    a haunt of jackals,
an object of horror and scorn,
    a place where no one lives.
38 Her people all roar like young lions,
    they growl like lion cubs.
39 But while they are aroused,
    I will set out a feast for them
    and make them drunk,
so that they shout with laughter—
    then sleep forever and not awake,"
                        declares the LORD.
40 "I will bring them down
    like lambs to the slaughter,
    like rams and goats.

41 "How Sheshak*b* will be captured,
    the boast of the whole earth seized!
How desolate Babylon will be
    among the nations!
42 The sea will rise over Babylon;
    its roaring waves will cover her.
43 Her towns will be desolate,
    a dry and desert land,
a land where no one lives,
    through which no one travels.
44 I will punish Bel in Babylon
    and make him spew out what he has swallowed.
The nations will no longer stream to him.
    And the wall of Babylon will fall.

45 "Come out of her, my people!
    Run for your lives!
    Run from the fierce anger of the LORD.
46 Do not lose heart or be afraid
    when rumors are heard in the land;
one rumor comes this year, another the next,
    rumors of violence in the land
    and of ruler against ruler.

How would the sea rise over Babylon? (51:42)
This was a word picture describing how Babylon would be flooded by foreign invaders and swept away.

---

a 35 Or *done to us and to our children*   *b* 41 *Sheshak* is a cryptogram for
Babylon.

⁴⁷For the time will surely come
    when I will punish the idols of Babylon;
her whole land will be disgraced
    and her slain will all lie fallen within her.
⁴⁸Then heaven and earth and all that is in them
    will shout for joy over Babylon,
for out of the north
    destroyers will attack her,"

declares the LORD.

⁴⁹"Babylon must fall because of Israel's slain,
    just as the slain in all the earth
    have fallen because of Babylon.
⁵⁰You who have escaped the sword,
    leave and do not linger!
Remember the LORD in a distant land,
    and call to mind Jerusalem."

⁵¹"We are disgraced,
    for we have been insulted
    and shame covers our faces,
because foreigners have entered
    the holy places of the LORD's house."

⁵²"But days are coming," declares the LORD,
    "when I will punish her idols,
and throughout her land
    the wounded will groan.
⁵³Even if Babylon ascends to the heavens
    and fortifies her lofty stronghold,
I will send destroyers against her,"

declares the LORD.

⁵⁴"The sound of a cry comes from Babylon,
    the sound of great destruction
    from the land of the Babylonians.ᵃ
⁵⁵The LORD will destroy Babylon;
    he will silence her noisy din.
Waves of enemies will rage like great waters;
    the roar of their voices will resound.
⁵⁶A destroyer will come against Babylon;
    her warriors will be captured,
    and their bows will be broken.
For the LORD is a God of retribution;
    he will repay in full.
⁵⁷I will make her officials and wise men drunk,
    her governors, officers and warriors as well;
they will sleep forever and not awake,"
    declares the King, whose name is the LORD
        Almighty.

⁵⁸This is what the LORD Almighty says:

"Babylon's thick wall will be leveled
    and her high gates set on fire;
the peoples exhaust themselves for nothing,
    the nations' labor is only fuel for the flames."

ᵃ 54 Or *Chaldeans*

What foreigners entered the holy places of the temple? (51:51)
Nebuchadnezzar defiled the temple in 586 B.C. The same thing later happened under Antiochus Epiphanes in 168 B.C. and under the Romans in A.D. 70.

What were the thick wall and high gates? (51:58)
Babylon was famous for its walls and for the Ishtar Gate, which was almost 40 feet (12 meters) high.

⁵⁹This is the message Jeremiah the prophet gave to the staff officer Seraiah son of Neriah, the son of Mahseiah, when he went to Babylon with Zedekiah king of Judah in the fourth year of his reign. ⁶⁰Jeremiah had written on a scroll about all the disasters that would come upon Babylon—all that had been recorded concerning Babylon. ⁶¹He said to Seraiah, "When you get to Babylon, see that you read all these words aloud. ⁶²Then say, 'LORD, you have said you will destroy this place, so that neither people nor animals will live in it; it will be desolate forever.' ⁶³When you finish reading this scroll, tie a stone to it and throw it into the Euphrates. ⁶⁴Then say, 'So will Babylon sink to rise no more because of the disaster I will bring on her. And her people will fall.'"

The words of Jeremiah end here.

THE FALL OF JERUSALEM

52 Zedekiah was twenty-one years old when he became king, and he reigned in Jerusalem eleven years. His mother's name was Hamutal daughter of Jeremiah; she was from Libnah. ²He did evil in the eyes of the LORD, just as Jehoiakim had done. ³It was because of the LORD's anger that all this happened to Jerusalem and Judah, and in the end he thrust them from his presence.

Now Zedekiah rebelled against the king of Babylon.

⁴So in the ninth year of Zedekiah's reign, on the tenth day of the tenth month, Nebuchadnezzar king of Babylon marched against Jerusalem with his whole army. They encamped outside the city and built siege works all around it. ⁵The city was kept under siege until the eleventh year of King Zedekiah.

⁶By the ninth day of the fourth month the famine in the city had become so severe that there was no food for the people to eat. ⁷Then the city wall was broken through, and the whole army fled. They left the city at night through the gate between the two walls near the king's garden, though the Babylonians* were surrounding the city. They fled toward the Arabah,ᵇ ⁸but the Babylonianᶜ army pursued King Zedekiah and overtook him in the plains of Jericho. All his soldiers were separated from him and scattered, ⁹and he was captured.

He was taken to the king of Babylon at Riblah in the land of Hamath, where he pronounced sentence on him. ¹⁰There at Riblah the king of Babylon killed the sons of Zedekiah before his eyes; he also killed all the officials of Judah. ¹¹Then he put out Zedekiah's eyes, bound him with bronze shackles and took him to Babylon, where he put him in prison till the day of his death.

¹²On the tenth day of the fifth month, in the nineteenth year of Nebuchadnezzar king of Babylon, Nebuzaradan commander of the imperial guard, who served the king of Babylon, came to Jerusalem. ¹³He set fire to the temple of the LORD, the royal palace and all the houses of Jerusalem. Every important building he burned down. ¹⁴The whole

Who was Seraiah? (51:59)
He was a brother of Jeremiah's secretary, Baruch. As staff officer, he was in charge of making arrangements for food and lodging for the royal party when they traveled.

What is the purpose of this chapter? (chapter 52)
This is an appendix to the book, written by someone other than Jeremiah—possibly Baruch. It is a close parallel to the conclusion of 2 Kings.

ᵃ 7 Or *Chaldeans*; also in verse 17   ᵇ 7 Or *the Jordan Valley*
ᶜ 8 Or *Chaldean*; also in verse 14

Babylonian army, under the commander of the imperial guard, broke down all the walls around Jerusalem. [15]Nebuzaradan the commander of the guard carried into exile some of the poorest people and those who remained in the city, along with the rest of the craftsmen[a] and those who had deserted to the king of Babylon. [16]But Nebuzaradan left behind the rest of the poorest people of the land to work the vineyards and fields.

[17]The Babylonians broke up the bronze pillars, the movable stands and the bronze Sea that were at the temple of the LORD and they carried all the bronze to Babylon. [18]They also took away the pots, shovels, wick trimmers, sprinkling bowls, dishes and all the bronze articles used in the temple service. [19]The commander of the imperial guard took away the basins, censers, sprinkling bowls, pots, lampstands, dishes and bowls used for drink offerings—all that were made of pure gold or silver.

[20]The bronze from the two pillars, the Sea and the twelve bronze bulls under it, and the movable stands, which King Solomon had made for the temple of the LORD, was more than could be weighed. [21]Each pillar was eighteen cubits high and twelve cubits in circumference[b]; each was four fingers thick, and hollow. [22]The bronze capital on top of one pillar was five cubits[c] high and was decorated with a network and pomegranates of bronze all around. The other pillar, with its pomegranates, was similar. [23]There were ninety-six pomegranates on the sides; the total number of pomegranates above the surrounding network was a hundred.

[24]The commander of the guard took as prisoners Seraiah the chief priest, Zephaniah the priest next in rank and the three doorkeepers. [25]Of those still in the city, he took the officer in charge of the fighting men, and seven royal advisers. He also took the secretary who was chief officer in charge of conscripting the people of the land, sixty of whom were found in the city. [26]Nebuzaradan the commander took them all and brought them to the king of Babylon at Riblah. [27]There at Riblah, in the land of Hamath, the king had them executed.

So Judah went into captivity, away from her land. [28]This is the number of the people Nebuchadnezzar carried into exile:

in the seventh year, 3,023 Jews;
[29]in Nebuchadnezzar's eighteenth year,
  832 people from Jerusalem;
[30]in his twenty-third year,
  745 Jews taken into exile by Nebuzaradan the commander of the imperial guard.
There were 4,600 people in all.

JEHOIACHIN RELEASED

[31]In the thirty-seventh year of the exile of Jehoiachin king of Judah, in the year Awel-Marduk became king of Babylon, on the twenty-fifth day of the twelfth month, he released

When were these three deportations? (52:28–30) The first one was in 597 B.C. The second one was when Jerusalem fell in 586 B.C. The third one took place in 581 B.C., possibly in retaliation for Gedaliah's assassination. The numbers here are not the same as in 2 Kings 24, which leads some to think that these totals included only adult men.

---

[a] 15 Or *the populace*　　[b] 21 That is, about 27 feet high and 18 feet in circumference or about 8.1 meters high and 5.4 meters in circumference
[c] 22 That is, about 7 1/2 feet or about 2.3 meters

Jehoiachin king of Judah and freed him from prison. ³²He spoke kindly to him and gave him a seat of honor higher than those of the other kings who were with him in Babylon. ³³So Jehoiachin put aside his prison clothes and for the rest of his life ate regularly at the king's table. ³⁴Day by day the king of Babylon gave Jehoiachin a regular allowance as long as he lived, till the day of his death.

Lamentations

INTRODUCTION

Who wrote this book? The writer is unknown. Many people think Jeremiah is the author.

Why was this book written? The book of Lamentations shows how sad the captives in Babylon were, and it shows that they finally realized that they were being punished because of their sin.

What is special about this book? Lamentations is "dirge poetry." This is very sad poetry, like sadness over a person's death.

Where was this book written? Lamentations was written in Babylon, where the Jewish people were taken as captives. (See the map at the back of this Bible to find Babylon.)

When did these things happen?   1300 BC 1200   1100   1000   900   800   700   600   500   400

DIVISION OF THE KINGDOM (930 BC)

MINISTRIES OF ELIJAH AND ELISHA IN ISRAEL (C. 875 – 797 BC)

MINISTRIES OF AMOS AND HOSEA IN ISRAEL (C. 760 – 715 BC)

MINISTRIES OF MICAH AND ISAIAH IN JUDAH (C. 740 – 681 BC)

EXILE OF ISRAEL (722 BC)

JEREMIAH'S MINISTRY IN JUDAH (C. 626 – 585 BC)

FALL OF JERUSALEM (586 BC)

BOOK OF LAMENTATIONS WRITTEN (C. 586 – 580 BC)

1 *a* How deserted lies the city,
   once so full of people!
   How like a widow is she,
      who once was great among the nations!
   She who was queen among the provinces
      has now become a slave.

2 Bitterly she weeps at night,
   tears are on her cheeks.
   Among all her lovers
      there is no one to comfort her.
   All her friends have betrayed her;
      they have become her enemies.

3 After affliction and harsh labor,
   Judah has gone into exile.
   She dwells among the nations;
      she finds no resting place.
   All who pursue her have overtaken her
      in the midst of her distress.

4 The roads to Zion mourn,
   for no one comes to her appointed festivals.
   All her gateways are desolate,
      her priests groan,
   her young women grieve,
      and she is in bitter anguish.

5 Her foes have become her masters;
   her enemies are at ease.
   The LORD has brought her grief
      because of her many sins.
   Her children have gone into exile,
      captive before the foe.

6 All the splendor has departed
      from Daughter Zion.
   Her princes are like deer
      that find no pasture;
   in weakness they have fled
      before the pursuer.

7 In the days of her affliction and wandering
      Jerusalem remembers all the treasures
      that were hers in days of old.
   When her people fell into enemy hands,
      there was no one to help her.
   Her enemies looked at her
      and laughed at her destruction.

8 Jerusalem has sinned greatly
      and so has become unclean.
   All who honored her despise her,
      for they have all seen her naked;
   she herself groans
      and turns away.

---

a This chapter is an acrostic poem, the verses of which begin with the successive letters of the Hebrew alphabet.

Who were these lovers and friends? (1:2)
These were the allies who the people of Jerusalem and Judah looked to for security. All of them had betrayed the people of Judah.

Who was "Daughter Zion"? (1:6)
This was a personification of Jerusalem and the people who lived there.

How was Jerusalem unclean? (1:8)
Jerusalem had become unclean because of her sin of idolatry. "Unclean" is a way of describing something unacceptable to the Lord.

⁹ Her filthiness clung to her skirts;
     she did not consider her future.
Her fall was astounding;
     there was none to comfort her.
"Look, Lord, on my affliction,
     for the enemy has triumphed."

¹⁰ The enemy laid hands
     on all her treasures;
she saw pagan nations
     enter her sanctuary—
those you had forbidden
     to enter your assembly.

Why would the people be searching for bread? (1:11) Food shortages were a continuing problem during and after the siege of Jerusalem.

¹¹ All her people groan
     as they search for bread;
they barter their treasures for food
     to keep themselves alive.
"Look, Lord, and consider,
     for I am despised."

¹² "Is it nothing to you, all you who pass by?
     Look around and see.
Is any suffering like my suffering
     that was inflicted on me,
that the Lord brought on me
     in the day of his fierce anger?

¹³ "From on high he sent fire,
     sent it down into my bones.
He spread a net for my feet
     and turned me back.
He made me desolate,
     faint all the day long.

¹⁴ "My sins have been bound into a yoke[a];
     by his hands they were woven together.
They have been hung on my neck,
     and the Lord has sapped my strength.
He has given me into the hands
     of those I cannot withstand.

In what way would Jerusalem be trampled in a winepress? (1:15) This was a common metaphor for divine judgment.

¹⁵ "The Lord has rejected
     all the warriors in my midst;
he has summoned an army against me
     to[b] crush my young men.
In his winepress the Lord has trampled
     Virgin Daughter Judah.

¹⁶ "This is why I weep
     and my eyes overflow with tears.
No one is near to comfort me,
     no one to restore my spirit.
My children are destitute
     because the enemy has prevailed."

¹⁷ Zion stretches out her hands,
     but there is no one to comfort her.

---

[a] 14 Most Hebrew manuscripts; many Hebrew manuscripts and Septuagint *He kept watch over my sins*   [b] 15 Or *has set a time for me / when he will*

The Lord has decreed for Jacob
   that his neighbors become his foes;
Jerusalem has become
   an unclean thing among them.

18 "The Lord is righteous,
   yet I rebelled against his command.
Listen, all you peoples;
   look on my suffering.
My young men and young women
   have gone into exile.

19 "I called to my allies
   but they betrayed me.
My priests and my elders
   perished in the city
while they searched for food
   to keep themselves alive.

20 "See, Lord, how distressed I am!
   I am in torment within,
and in my heart I am disturbed,
   for I have been most rebellious.
Outside, the sword bereaves;
   inside, there is only death.

21 "People have heard my groaning,
   but there is no one to comfort me.
All my enemies have heard of my distress;
   they rejoice at what you have done.
May you bring the day you have announced
   so they may become like me.

22 "Let all their wickedness come before you;
   deal with them
as you have dealt with me
   because of all my sins.
My groans are many
   and my heart is faint."

2 ^a How the Lord has covered Daughter Zion
   with the cloud of his anger^b!
He has hurled down the splendor of Israel
   from heaven to earth;
he has not remembered his footstool
   in the day of his anger.

2 Without pity the Lord has swallowed up
   all the dwellings of Jacob;
in his wrath he has torn down
   the strongholds of Daughter Judah.
He has brought her kingdom and its princes
   down to the ground in dishonor.

3 In fierce anger he has cut off
   every horn^{c,d} of Israel.

What was the day that had been announced? (1:21)
This was the day of God's judgment on the nations.

What was God's footstool? (2:1)
This could refer either to the ark of the covenant or to Mount Zion.

What does it mean for a horn to be cut off? (2:3)
Here the horn symbolizes strength, so God had weakened Israel.

---

^a This chapter is an acrostic poem, the verses of which begin with the successive letters of the Hebrew alphabet.   ^b 1 Or *How the Lord in his anger / has treated Daughter Zion with contempt*   ^c 3 Or *off / all the strength*; or *every king*   ^d 3 *Horn* here symbolizes strength.

He has withdrawn his right hand
    at the approach of the enemy.
He has burned in Jacob like a flaming fire
    that consumes everything around it.

How was God like an enemy? (2:4–5)
God was not really Judah's enemy. However, he had to punish Judah for its wickedness.

4 Like an enemy he has strung his bow;
    his right hand is ready.
Like a foe he has slain
    all who were pleasing to the eye;
he has poured out his wrath like fire
    on the tent of Daughter Zion.

5 The Lord is like an enemy;
    he has swallowed up Israel.
He has swallowed up all her palaces
    and destroyed her strongholds.
He has multiplied mourning and lamentation
    for Daughter Judah.

6 He has laid waste his dwelling like a garden;
    he has destroyed his place of meeting.
The Lord has made Zion forget
    her appointed festivals and her Sabbaths;
in his fierce anger he has spurned
    both king and priest.

7 The Lord has rejected his altar
    and abandoned his sanctuary.
He has given the walls of her palaces
    into the hands of the enemy;
they have raised a shout in the house of the Lord
    as on the day of an appointed festival.

What were ramparts? (2:8)
Ramparts were sloping, wall-like fortifications of earth or stone that were used to strengthen a city's walls and protect it from invaders.

8 The Lord determined to tear down
    the wall around Daughter Zion.
He stretched out a measuring line
    and did not withhold his hand from destroying.
He made ramparts and walls lament;
    together they wasted away.

9 Her gates have sunk into the ground;
    their bars he has broken and destroyed.
Her king and her princes are exiled among the nations,
    the law is no more,

Why would God allow innocent children to suffer?
LAMENTATIONS 2

The question of human suffering is always a difficult one, but it is even more difficult when those who are suffering are seemingly innocent children. The first thing to note is that God does not punish children with illness and starvation because of their disobedience or the disobedience of their parents. However, sometimes the actions of parents can contribute to their children's suffering. For example, if the parents are abusive, are addicts, or are homeless, children will probably experience the consequences.

It is true that all people since the time of Adam and Even have been born into sin, and this sin has affected every generation. So it is not completely accurate to say that these children — or any people — are innocent of sin.

God's plan for his people is that they will be happy and will serve him. That reality won't come about fully until the new heaven and the new earth.

and her prophets no longer find
   visions from the Lord.

10 The elders of Daughter Zion
   sit on the ground in silence;
they have sprinkled dust on their heads
   and put on sackcloth.
The young women of Jerusalem
   have bowed their heads to
     the ground.

11 My eyes fail from weeping,
   I am in torment within;
my heart is poured out on the ground
   because my people are destroyed,
because children and infants faint
   in the streets of the city.

12 They say to their mothers,
   "Where is bread and wine?"
as they faint like the wounded
   in the streets of the city,
as their lives ebb away
   in their mothers' arms.

13 What can I say for you?
   With what can I compare you,
   Daughter Jerusalem?
To what can I liken you,
   that I may comfort you,
   Virgin Daughter Zion?
Your wound is as deep as the sea.
   Who can heal you?

14 The visions of your prophets
   were false and worthless;
they did not expose your sin
   to ward off your captivity.
The prophecies they gave you
   were false and misleading.

15 All who pass your way
   clap their hands at you;
they scoff and shake their heads
   at Daughter Jerusalem:
"Is this the city that was called
   the perfection of beauty,
   the joy of the whole earth?"

16 All your enemies open their mouths
   wide against you;
they scoff and gnash their teeth
   and say, "We have swallowed her up.
This is the day we have waited for;
   we have lived to see it."

17 The Lord has done what he planned;
   he has fulfilled his word,
   which he decreed long ago.

He has overthrown you without pity,
　　he has let the enemy gloat over you,
　　he has exalted the horn*a* of your foes.

18 The hearts of the people
　　cry out to the Lord.
You walls of Daughter Zion,
　　let your tears flow like a river
　　day and night;
give yourself no relief,
　　your eyes no rest.

What were the watches of the night? (2:19)
These were the divisions into which the hours of darkness were divided. The Israelites divided night into three watches, from sunset until 10:00 P.M., from 10:00 P.M. until 2:00 A.M., and from 2:00 A.M. until sunrise.

19 Arise, cry out in the night,
　　as the watches of the night begin;
pour out your heart like water
　　in the presence of the Lord.
Lift up your hands to him
　　for the lives of your children,
who faint from hunger
　　at every street corner.

20 "Look, Lord, and consider:
　　Whom have you ever treated like this?
Should women eat their offspring,
　　the children they have cared for?
Should priest and prophet be killed
　　in the sanctuary of the Lord?

21 "Young and old lie together
　　in the dust of the streets;
my young men and young women
　　have fallen by the sword.
You have slain them in the day of your anger;
　　you have slaughtered them without pity.

22 "As you summon to a feast day,
　　so you summoned against me terrors on every side.
In the day of the Lord's anger
　　no one escaped or survived;
those I cared for and reared
　　my enemy has destroyed."

3 *b* I am the man who has seen affliction
　　by the rod of the Lord's wrath.
2 He has driven me away and made me walk
　　in darkness rather than light;
3 indeed, he has turned his hand against me
　　again and again, all day long.

4 He has made my skin and my flesh grow old
　　and has broken my bones.
5 He has besieged me and surrounded me
　　with bitterness and hardship.
6 He has made me dwell in darkness
　　like those long dead.

How had God turned his hand against the writer? (3:3)
God was punishing the entire nation, not just the author, Jeremiah. He may have felt like God abandoned him, but deep down Jeremiah knew God would never leave him.

a 17 *Horn* here symbolizes strength.　　*b* This chapter is an acrostic poem; the verses of each stanza begin with the successive letters of the Hebrew alphabet, and the verses within each stanza begin with the same letter.

⁷He has walled me in so I cannot escape;
  he has weighed me down with chains.
⁸Even when I call out or cry for help,
  he shuts out my prayer.
⁹He has barred my way with blocks of stone;
  he has made my paths crooked.

¹⁰Like a bear lying in wait,
  like a lion in hiding,
¹¹he dragged me from the path and mangled me
  and left me without help.
¹²He drew his bow
  and made me the target for his arrows.

¹³He pierced my heart
  with arrows from his quiver.
¹⁴I became the laughingstock of all my people;
  they mock me in song all day long.
¹⁵He has filled me with bitter herbs
  and given me gall to drink.

¹⁶He has broken my teeth with gravel;
  he has trampled me in the dust.
¹⁷I have been deprived of peace;
  I have forgotten what prosperity is.
¹⁸So I say, "My splendor is gone
  and all that I had hoped from the Lord."

¹⁹I remember my affliction and my wandering,
  the bitterness and the gall.
²⁰I well remember them,
  and my soul is downcast within me.
²¹Yet this I call to mind
  and therefore I have hope:

²²Because of the Lord's great love we are not consumed,
  for his compassions never fail.
²³They are new every morning;
  great is your faithfulness.
²⁴I say to myself, "The Lord is my portion;
  therefore I will wait for him."

²⁵The Lord is good to those whose hope is in him,
  to the one who seeks him;
²⁶it is good to wait quietly
  for the salvation of the Lord.
²⁷It is good for a man to bear the yoke
  while he is young.

²⁸Let him sit alone in silence,
  for the Lord has laid it on him.
²⁹Let him bury his face in the dust—
  there may yet be hope.
³⁰Let him offer his cheek to one who would strike him,
  and let him be filled with disgrace.

³¹For no one is cast off
  by the Lord forever.
³²Though he brings grief, he will show compassion,
  so great is his unfailing love.

What did it mean to bury one's face in the dust? (3:29)
This was a symbol of humble submission to God.

How does this verse reveal God's character? (3:32)
Even though God judges sin and punishes wickedness, he is also a God of compassion and love.

³³ For he does not willingly bring affliction
    or grief to anyone.

³⁴ To crush underfoot
    all prisoners in the land,
³⁵ to deny people their rights
    before the Most High,
³⁶ to deprive them of justice—
    would not the Lord see such things?

³⁷ Who can speak and have it happen
    if the Lord has not decreed it?
³⁸ Is it not from the mouth of the Most High
    that both calamities and good things come?
³⁹ Why should the living complain
    when punished for their sins?

⁴⁰ Let us examine our ways and test them,
    and let us return to the Lord.
⁴¹ Let us lift up our hearts and our hands
    to God in heaven, and say:
⁴² "We have sinned and rebelled
    and you have not forgiven.

⁴³ "You have covered yourself with anger and pursued us;
    you have slain without pity.
⁴⁴ You have covered yourself with a cloud
    so that no prayer can get through.
⁴⁵ You have made us scum and refuse
    among the nations.

⁴⁶ "All our enemies have opened their mouths
    wide against us.
⁴⁷ We have suffered terror and pitfalls,
    ruin and destruction."
⁴⁸ Streams of tears flow from my eyes
    because my people are destroyed.

⁴⁹ My eyes will flow unceasingly,
    without relief,
⁵⁰ until the Lord looks down
    from heaven and sees.
⁵¹ What I see brings grief to my soul
    because of all the women of my city.

⁵² Those who were my enemies without cause
    hunted me like a bird.
⁵³ They tried to end my life in a pit
    and threw stones at me;
⁵⁴ the waters closed over my head,
    and I thought I was about to perish.

⁵⁵ I called on your name, Lord,
    from the depths of the pit.
⁵⁶ You heard my plea: "Do not close your ears
    to my cry for relief."
⁵⁷ You came near when I called you,
    and you said, "Do not fear."

⁵⁸ You, Lord, took up my case;
    you redeemed my life.

How did the enemies of Judah open their mouths wide? (3:46)
This is an image of Judah being swallowed up by Babylon.

Who was thrown into a pit? (3:53)
Jeremiah was probably the author of the book of Lamentations, so this may be a reference to when he was thrown into a cistern.

⁵⁹ LORD, you have seen the wrong done to me.
　　Uphold my cause!
⁶⁰ You have seen the depth of their vengeance,
　　all their plots against me.

⁶¹ LORD, you have heard their insults,
　　all their plots against me—
⁶² what my enemies whisper and mutter
　　against me all day long.
⁶³ Look at them! Sitting or standing,
　　they mock me in their songs.

⁶⁴ Pay them back what they deserve, LORD,
　　for what their hands have done.
⁶⁵ Put a veil over their hearts,
　　and may your curse be on them!
⁶⁶ Pursue them in anger and destroy them
　　from under the heavens of the LORD.

4 ᵃ How the gold has lost its luster,
　　the fine gold become dull!
The sacred gems are scattered
　　at every street corner.

² How the precious children of Zion,
　　once worth their weight in gold,
are now considered as pots of clay,
　　the work of a potter's hands!

³ Even jackals offer their breasts
　　to nurse their young,
but my people have become heartless
　　like ostriches in the desert.

⁴ Because of thirst the infant's tongue
　　sticks to the roof of its mouth;
the children beg for bread,
　　but no one gives it to them.

⁵ Those who once ate delicacies
　　are destitute in the streets.
Those brought up in royal purple
　　now lie on ash heaps.

⁶ The punishment of my people
　　is greater than that of Sodom,
which was overthrown in a moment
　　without a hand turned to help her.

⁷ Their princes were brighter than snow
　　and whiter than milk,
their bodies more ruddy than rubies,
　　their appearance like lapis lazuli.

⁸ But now they are blacker than soot;
　　they are not recognized in the streets.
Their skin has shriveled on their bones;
　　it has become as dry as a stick.

ᵃ This chapter is an acrostic poem, the verses of which begin with the
successive letters of the Hebrew alphabet.

What were the gold and gems? (4:1)
These were symbols of God's chosen people.

Who were "those brought up in royal purple"? (4:5)
Purple was the color of royalty, so these would be members of the royal court.

Did the people resort to cannibalism? (4:9–10)
During the siege of Jerusalem, some mothers actually cooked and ate their own children. The author says it would be better to be killed quickly rather than to die of famine or resort to cannibalism.

⁹ Those killed by the sword are better off
     than those who die of famine;
racked with hunger, they waste away
     for lack of food from the field.

¹⁰ With their own hands compassionate women
     have cooked their own children,
who became their food
     when my people were destroyed.

¹¹ The LORD has given full vent to his wrath;
     he has poured out his fierce anger.
He kindled a fire in Zion
     that consumed her foundations.

¹² The kings of the earth did not believe,
     nor did any of the peoples of the world,
that enemies and foes could enter
     the gates of Jerusalem.

¹³ But it happened because of the sins of
        her prophets
     and the iniquities of her priests,
who shed within her
     the blood of the righteous.

¹⁴ Now they grope through the streets
     as if they were blind.
They are so defiled with blood
     that no one dares to touch their garments.

Why would people cry out, "Unclean!"? (4:15)
People who had skin diseases were required to call out, "Unclean!" when someone approached.

¹⁵ "Go away! You are unclean!" people cry to them.
     "Away! Away! Don't touch us!"
When they flee and wander about,
     people among the nations say,
     "They can stay here no longer."

¹⁶ The LORD himself has scattered them;
     he no longer watches over them.
The priests are shown no honor,
     the elders no favor.

¹⁷ Moreover, our eyes failed,
     looking in vain for help;
from our towers we watched
     for a nation that could not save us.

¹⁸ People stalked us at every step,
     so we could not walk in our streets.
Our end was near, our days were numbered,
     for our end had come.

¹⁹ Our pursuers were swifter
     than eagles in the sky;
they chased us over the mountains
     and lay in wait for us in the desert.

Who was the Lord's anointed? (4:20)
This refers to King Zedekiah, who was from the dynasty of David.

²⁰ The LORD's anointed, our very life breath,
     was caught in their traps.
We thought that under his shadow
     we would live among the nations.

²¹ Rejoice and be glad, Daughter Edom,
    you who live in the land of Uz.
But to you also the cup will be passed;
    you will be drunk and stripped naked.

²² Your punishment will end, Daughter Zion;
    he will not prolong your exile.
But he will punish your sin, Daughter Edom,
    and expose your wickedness.

5 Remember, Lord, what has happened to us;
    look, and see our disgrace.
² Our inheritance has been turned over to strangers,
    our homes to foreigners.
³ We have become fatherless,
    our mothers are widows.
⁴ We must buy the water we drink;
    our wood can be had only at a price.
⁵ Those who pursue us are at our heels;
    we are weary and find no rest.
⁶ We submitted to Egypt and Assyria
    to get enough bread.
⁷ Our ancestors sinned and are no more,
    and we bear their punishment.
⁸ Slaves rule over us,
    and there is no one to free us from their hands.
⁹ We get our bread at the risk of our lives
    because of the sword in the desert.
¹⁰ Our skin is hot as an oven,
    feverish from hunger.
¹¹ Women have been violated in Zion,
    and virgins in the towns of Judah.
¹² Princes have been hung up by their hands;
    elders are shown no respect.
¹³ Young men toil at the millstones;
    boys stagger under loads of wood.
¹⁴ The elders are gone from the city gate;
    the young men have stopped their music.
¹⁵ Joy is gone from our hearts;
    our dancing has turned to mourning.
¹⁶ The crown has fallen from our head.
    Woe to us, for we have sinned!
¹⁷ Because of this our hearts are faint,
    because of these things our eyes grow dim
¹⁸ for Mount Zion, which lies desolate,
    with jackals prowling over it.

¹⁹ You, Lord, reign forever;
    your throne endures from generation to generation.
²⁰ Why do you always forget us?
    Why do you forsake us so long?
²¹ Restore us to yourself, Lord, that we may return;
    renew our days as of old
²² unless you have utterly rejected us
    and are angry with us beyond measure.

What was meant by "our inheritance"? (5:2)
This referred to the land of Judah.

What did it mean that jackals were prowling on Mount Zion? (5:18)
Because the temple and the city of Jerusalem were destroyed, the place had become like a wilderness where wild animals lived.

Ezekiel

INTRODUCTION

Who wrote this book?
The prophet Ezekiel.

Why was this book written?
The first part of the book of Ezekiel shows why God must punish the wicked people still in Judah. The second part shows that God will bring his people back to their land and that their faith and position before God will be restored.

What do we learn about God in this book?
God is holy. He will not live among a wicked people.

What is special about this book?
Ezekiel acts out many of his prophecies. Ezekiel vividly pictures both Judah's punishment and restoration.

Where was this book written?
Ezekiel was a captive in Babylon when he wrote this book. (See the map at the back of this Bible to find Babylon.)

What chapters tell about Ezekiel's experiences?

Ezekiel's vision	Ezekiel 1; 10
Ezekiel acts out the attack on Jerusalem	Ezekiel 4
Ezekiel, God's watchman	Ezekiel 33

When did these things happen?

1300 BC 1200 1100 1000 900 800 700 600 500 400

DIVISION OF THE KINGDOM (930 BC)

MINISTRIES OF MICAH AND ISAIAH IN JUDAH (C. 740 – 681 BC)

JEREMIAH'S MINISTRY IN JUDAH (C. 626 – 585 BC)

DANIEL'S EXILE IN BABYLON (C. 605 – 536 BC)

EZEKIEL'S MINISTRY (C. 593 – 571 BC)

FALL OF JERUSALEM (586 BC)

BOOK OF EZEKIEL WRITTEN (C. 571 BC)

FIRST RETURN OF EXILES TO JERUSALEM (538 BC)

EZEKIEL'S INAUGURAL VISION

1 In my thirtieth year, in the fourth month on the fifth day, while I was among the exiles by the Kebar River, the heavens were opened and I saw visions of God.

² On the fifth of the month—it was the fifth year of the exile of King Jehoiachin— ³ the word of the LORD came to Ezekiel the priest, the son of Buzi, by the Kebar River in the land of the Babylonians.*ᵃ* There the hand of the LORD was on him.

⁴ I looked, and I saw a windstorm coming out of the north—an immense cloud with flashing lightning and surrounded by brilliant light. The center of the fire looked like glowing metal, ⁵ and in the fire was what looked like four living creatures. In appearance their form was human, ⁶ but each of them had four faces and four wings. ⁷ Their legs were straight; their feet were like those of a calf and gleamed like burnished bronze. ⁸ Under their wings on their four sides they had human hands. All four of them had faces and wings, ⁹ and the wings of one touched the wings of another. Each one went straight ahead; they did not turn as they moved.

¹⁰ Their faces looked like this: Each of the four had the face of a human being, and on the right side each had the face of a lion, and on the left the face of an ox; each also had the face of an eagle. ¹¹ Such were their faces. They each had two wings spreading out upward, each wing touching that of the creature on either side; and each had two other wings covering its body. ¹² Each one went straight ahead. Wherever the spirit would go, they would go, without turning as they went. ¹³ The appearance of the living creatures was like burning coals of fire or like torches. Fire moved back and forth among the creatures; it was bright, and lightning flashed out of it. ¹⁴ The creatures sped back and forth like flashes of lightning.

¹⁵ As I looked at the living creatures, I saw a wheel on the ground beside each creature with its four faces. ¹⁶ This was the appearance and structure of the wheels: They sparkled like topaz, and all four looked alike. Each appeared to be made like a wheel intersecting a wheel. ¹⁷ As they moved, they would go in any one of the four directions the creatures faced; the wheels did not change direction as the creatures went. ¹⁸ Their rims were high and awesome, and all four rims were full of eyes all around.

¹⁹ When the living creatures moved, the wheels beside them moved; and when the living creatures rose from the ground, the wheels also rose. ²⁰ Wherever the spirit would go, they would go, and the wheels would rise along with them, because the spirit of the living creatures was in the wheels. ²¹ When the creatures moved, they also moved; when the creatures stood still, they also stood still; and when the creatures rose from the ground, the wheels rose along with them, because the spirit of the living creatures was in the wheels.

²² Spread out above the heads of the living creatures was what looked something like a vault, sparkling like crystal, and awesome. ²³ Under the vault their wings were stretched

ᵃ *3 Or Chaldeans*

What was the thirtieth year? (1:1)
This was probably Ezekiel's age. According to Numbers 4:3, a man entered the Levitical priesthood in his 30ᵗʰ year. Because of the exile, Ezekiel could not become a priest. But he was called by God to be a prophet.

Ezekiel in Babylon (1:1)

How was the hand of God on him? (1:3)
This expression indicates an overpowering experience in which God revealed his divine message to the prophet.

What were these four creatures? (1:5–10)
These were cherubim who represented God's creation. The man represented God's ruler of creation; the lion represented the strongest wild beast; the ox represented the most powerful domesticated animal; the eagle represented the mightiest bird.

What were these intersecting wheels? (1:16–18)
The two wheels probably intersected at right angles, so they could move in all four directions. This symbolized God's omnipresence (his presence everywhere). The eyes represented God's ability to see and know all things.

out one toward the other, and each had two wings covering its body. [24]When the creatures moved, I heard the sound of their wings, like the roar of rushing waters, like the voice of the Almighty,[a] like the tumult of an army. When they stood still, they lowered their wings.

[25]Then there came a voice from above the vault over their heads as they stood with lowered wings. [26]Above the vault over their heads was what looked like a throne of lapis lazuli, and high above on the throne was a figure like that of a man. [27]I saw that from what appeared to be his waist up he looked like glowing metal, as if full of fire, and that from there down he looked like fire; and brilliant light surrounded him. [28]Like the appearance of a rainbow in the clouds on a rainy day, so was the radiance around him.

This was the appearance of the likeness of the glory of the Lord. When I saw it, I fell facedown, and I heard the voice of one speaking.

EZEKIEL'S CALL TO BE A PROPHET

2 He said to me, "Son of man,[b] stand up on your feet and I will speak to you." [2]As he spoke, the Spirit came into me and raised me to my feet, and I heard him speaking to me.

[3]He said: "Son of man, I am sending you to the Israelites, to a rebellious nation that has rebelled against me; they and their ancestors have been in revolt against me to this very day. [4]The people to whom I am sending you are obstinate and stubborn. Say to them, 'This is what the Sovereign Lord says.' [5]And whether they listen or fail to listen—for they are a rebellious people—they will know that a prophet has been among them. [6]And you, son of man, do not be afraid of them or their words. Do not be afraid, though briers and thorns are all around you and you live among scorpions. Do not be afraid of what they say or be terrified by them, though they are a rebellious people. [7]You must speak my words to them, whether they listen or fail to listen, for they are rebellious. [8]But you, son of man, listen to what I say to you. Do not rebel like that rebellious people; open your mouth and eat what I give you."

[9]Then I looked, and I saw a hand stretched out to me. In it was a scroll, [10]which he unrolled before me. On both sides of it were written words of lament and mourning and woe.

3 And he said to me, "Son of man, eat what is before you, eat this scroll; then go and speak to the people of Israel." [2]So I opened my mouth, and he gave me the scroll to eat.

[3]Then he said to me, "Son of man, eat this scroll I am giving you and fill your stomach with it." So I ate it, and it tasted as sweet as honey in my mouth.

[4]He then said to me: "Son of man, go now to the people of Israel and speak my words to them. [5]You are not being sent to a people of obscure speech and strange language, but to the people of Israel— [6]not to many peoples of obscure

Why was Ezekiel called "son of man"? (2:1)
This phrase appears 93 times in the book of Ezekiel. It emphasizes the fact that he was a human being who was being addressed by an almighty God.

Why did he eat the scroll? (3:1–3)
This action symbolized that he was to preach only the message God gave him. He experienced the sweetness of God's words even though the message was a bitter one.

---

[a] 24 Hebrew *Shaddai*   [b] 1 The Hebrew phrase *ben adam* means *human being*. The phrase *son of man* is retained as a form of address here and throughout Ezekiel because of its possible association with "Son of Man" in the New Testament.

speech and strange language, whose words you cannot understand. Surely if I had sent you to them, they would have listened to you. ⁷But the people of Israel are not willing to listen to you because they are not willing to listen to me, for all the Israelites are hardened and obstinate. ⁸But I will make you as unyielding and hardened as they are. ⁹I will make your forehead like the hardest stone, harder than flint. Do not be afraid of them or terrified by them, though they are a rebellious people."

¹⁰And he said to me, "Son of man, listen carefully and take to heart all the words I speak to you. ¹¹Go now to your people in exile and speak to them. Say to them, 'This is what the Sovereign LORD says,' whether they listen or fail to listen."

¹²Then the Spirit lifted me up, and I heard behind me a loud rumbling sound as the glory of the LORD rose from the place where it was standing.^a ¹³It was the sound of the wings of the living creatures brushing against each other and the sound of the wheels beside them, a loud rumbling sound. ¹⁴The Spirit then lifted me up and took me away, and I went in bitterness and in the anger of my spirit, with the strong hand of the LORD on me. ¹⁵I came to the exiles who lived at Tel Aviv near the Kebar River. And there, where they were living, I sat among them for seven days—deeply distressed.

EZEKIEL'S TASK AS WATCHMAN

¹⁶At the end of seven days the word of the LORD came to me: ¹⁷"Son of man, I have made you a watchman for the people of Israel; so hear the word I speak and give them warning from me. ¹⁸When I say to a wicked person, 'You will surely die,' and you do not warn them or speak out to dissuade them from their evil ways in order to save their life, that wicked person will die for^b their sin, and I will hold you accountable for their blood. ¹⁹But if you do warn the wicked person and they do not turn from their wickedness or from their evil ways, they will die for their sin; but you will have saved yourself.

²⁰"Again, when a righteous person turns from their righteousness and does evil, and I put a stumbling block before them, they will die. Since you did not warn them, they will die for their sin. The righteous things that person did will

Why would God make Ezekiel's forehead like a hard stone? (3:9)
Ezekiel would need a great deal of strength and courage when he preached God's judgment. Jeremiah was also strengthened by God for his prophetic role (see Jeremiah 1:18).

Why did God call Ezekiel a watchman? (3:17)
In ancient times, watchmen were stationed on the highest sections of a city wall and at the city gates to tell the people of the city about the progress of a battle or to announce the arrival of a messenger. The prophets were spiritual watchmen who relayed God's Word to his people.

---

^a *12 Probable reading of the original Hebrew text; Masoretic Text* sound— *may the glory of the LORD be praised from his place*   ^b *18 Or in; also in verses 19 and 20*

Why did Ezekiel act in such unusual ways in order to communicate his prophecy?
EZEKIEL 3

The prophets often were very unconventional in the way they ate, dressed, or behaved. Ezekiel followed God's instructions to lie on his side facing a model of the city of Jerusalem as if he were bearing the sins of the people. The people of Israel thought that exile would be their only punishment. They did not believe that Jerusalem would be attacked and that there would be great suffering. Ezekiel's approach was designed to get the people's attention. Even though they didn't accept his message, he did act out an important truth: that God demands holiness and is offended by sin. Sinful behavior on our part will be punished.

not be remembered, and I will hold you accountable for their blood. ²¹But if you do warn the righteous person not to sin and they do not sin, they will surely live because they took warning, and you will have saved yourself."

²²The hand of the LORD was on me there, and he said to me, "Get up and go out to the plain, and there I will speak to you." ²³So I got up and went out to the plain. And the glory of the LORD was standing there, like the glory I had seen by the Kebar River, and I fell facedown. ²⁴Then the Spirit came into me and raised me to my feet. He spoke to me and said: "Go, shut yourself inside your house. ²⁵And you, son of man, they will tie with ropes; you will be bound so that you cannot go out among the people. ²⁶I will make your tongue stick to the roof of your mouth so that you will be silent and unable to rebuke them, for they are a rebellious people. ²⁷But when I speak to you, I will open your mouth and you shall say to them, 'This is what the Sovereign LORD says.' Whoever will listen let them listen, and whoever will refuse let them refuse; for they are a rebellious people.

SIEGE OF JERUSALEM SYMBOLIZED

4 "Now, son of man, take a block of clay, put it in front of you and draw the city of Jerusalem on it. ²Then lay siege to it: Erect siege works against it, build a ramp up to it, set up camps against it and put battering rams around it. ³Then take an iron pan, place it as an iron wall between you and the city and turn your face toward it. It will be under siege, and you shall besiege it. This will be a sign to the people of Israel.

⁴"Then lie on your left side and put the sin of the people of Israel upon yourself.ᵃ You are to bear their sin for the number of days you lie on your side. ⁵I have assigned you the same number of days as the years of their sin. So for 390 days you will bear the sin of the people of Israel.

⁶"After you have finished this, lie down again, this time on your right side, and bear the sin of the people of Judah. I have assigned you 40 days, a day for each year. ⁷Turn your face toward the siege of Jerusalem and with bared arm prophesy against her. ⁸I will tie you up with ropes so that you cannot turn from one side to the other until you have finished the days of your siege.

⁹"Take wheat and barley, beans and lentils, millet and spelt; put them in a storage jar and use them to make bread for yourself. You are to eat it during the 390 days you lie on your side. ¹⁰Weigh out twenty shekelsᵇ of food to eat each day and eat it at set times. ¹¹Also measure out a sixth of a hinᶜ of water and drink it at set times. ¹²Eat the food as you would a loaf of barley bread; bake it in the sight of the people, using human excrement for fuel." ¹³The LORD said, "In this way the people of Israel will eat defiled food among the nations where I will drive them."

¹⁴Then I said, "Not so, Sovereign LORD! I have never

Why did God make him silent? (3:26–27)
Just as the people would not be able to speak in the face of God's judgment, the prophet would be unable to speak except when he had a direct word from God.

Why did God assign these activities to Ezekiel? (4:1–13)
The Lord told the prophet to carry out several symbolic actions in order to show the people that he was going to judge them for their sins.

Did Ezekiel bear the sin of the people? (4:5)
Ezekiel symbolically carried the sins of Israel, but this was a representative activity only.

ᵃ 4 Or *upon your side*   ᵇ 10 That is, about 8 ounces or about 230 grams
ᶜ 11 That is, about 2/3 quart or about 0.6 liter

defiled myself. From my youth until now I have never eaten anything found dead or torn by wild animals. No impure meat has ever entered my mouth."

¹⁵ "Very well," he said, "I will let you bake your bread over cow dung instead of human excrement."

¹⁶ He then said to me: "Son of man, I am about to cut off the food supply in Jerusalem. The people will eat rationed food in anxiety and drink rationed water in despair, ¹⁷ for food and water will be scarce. They will be appalled at the sight of each other and will waste away because of[a] their sin.

GOD'S RAZOR OF JUDGMENT

5 "Now, son of man, take a sharp sword and use it as a barber's razor to shave your head and your beard. Then take a set of scales and divide up the hair. ² When the days of your siege come to an end, burn a third of the hair inside the city. Take a third and strike it with the sword all around the city. And scatter a third to the wind. For I will pursue them with drawn sword. ³ But take a few hairs and tuck them away in the folds of your garment. ⁴ Again, take a few of these and throw them into the fire and burn them up. A fire will spread from there to all Israel.

⁵ "This is what the Sovereign LORD says: This is Jerusalem, which I have set in the center of the nations, with countries all around her. ⁶ Yet in her wickedness she has rebelled against my laws and decrees more than the nations and countries around her. She has rejected my laws and has not followed my decrees.

⁷ "Therefore this is what the Sovereign LORD says: You have been more unruly than the nations around you and have not followed my decrees or kept my laws. You have not even[b] conformed to the standards of the nations around you.

⁸ "Therefore this is what the Sovereign LORD says: I myself am against you, Jerusalem, and I will inflict punishment on you in the sight of the nations. ⁹ Because of all your detestable idols, I will do to you what I have never done before and will never do again. ¹⁰ Therefore in your midst parents will eat their children, and children will eat their parents. I will inflict punishment on you and will scatter all your survivors to the winds. ¹¹ Therefore as surely as I live, declares the Sovereign LORD, because you have defiled my sanctuary with all your vile images and detestable practices, I myself will shave you; I will not look on you with pity or spare you. ¹² A third of your people will die of the plague or perish by famine inside you; a third will fall by the sword outside your walls; and a third I will scatter to the winds and pursue with drawn sword.

¹³ "Then my anger will cease and my wrath against them will subside, and I will be avenged. And when I have spent my wrath on them, they will know that I the LORD have spoken in my zeal.

¹⁴ "I will make you a ruin and a reproach among the nations

Why did Ezekiel shave his head with a sword? (5:1) Shaving one's head was a sign of shame, and using a sword to do it symbolized the fact that God was going to allow Jerusalem to be destroyed by a military attack.

Would the people resort to cannibalism? (5:10) Food was so scarce in Jerusalem during the long siege that some parents did eat their children in order to survive (see Jeremiah 19:9 and Lamentations 2:20).

How would the people know that the Lord had spoken? (5:12–13) Since the people would not repent when God implored them to, he would show by his actions that he would not allow their sin to go unpunished.

---

[a] 17 Or *away in*   [b] 7 Most Hebrew manuscripts; some Hebrew manuscripts and Syriac *You have*

around you, in the sight of all who pass by. [15]You will be a reproach and a taunt, a warning and an object of horror to the nations around you when I inflict punishment on you in anger and in wrath and with stinging rebuke. I the LORD have spoken. [16]When I shoot at you with my deadly and destructive arrows of famine, I will shoot to destroy you. I will bring more and more famine upon you and cut off your supply of food. [17]I will send famine and wild beasts against you, and they will leave you childless. Plague and bloodshed will sweep through you, and I will bring the sword against you. I the LORD have spoken.'"

DOOM FOR THE MOUNTAINS OF ISRAEL

6 The word of the LORD came to me: [2]"Son of man, set your face against the mountains of Israel; prophesy against them [3]and say: 'You mountains of Israel, hear the word of the Sovereign LORD. This is what the Sovereign LORD says to the mountains and hills, to the ravines and valleys: I am about to bring a sword against you, and I will destroy your high places. [4]Your altars will be demolished and your incense altars will be smashed; and I will slay your people in front of your idols. [5]I will lay the dead bodies of the Israelites in front of their idols, and I will scatter your bones around your altars. [6]Wherever you live, the towns will be laid waste and the high places demolished, so that your altars will be laid waste and devastated, your idols smashed and ruined, your incense altars broken down, and what you have made wiped out. [7]Your people will fall slain among you, and you will know that I am the LORD.

[8]"'But I will spare some, for some of you will escape the sword when you are scattered among the lands and nations. [9]Then in the nations where they have been carried captive, those who escape will remember me—how I have been grieved by their adulterous hearts, which have turned away from me, and by their eyes, which have lusted after their idols. They will loathe themselves for the evil they have done and for all their detestable practices. [10]And they will know that I am the LORD; I did not threaten in vain to bring this calamity on them.

[11]"'This is what the Sovereign LORD says: Strike your hands together and stamp your feet and cry out "Alas!" because of all the wicked and detestable practices of the people of Israel, for they will fall by the sword, famine and plague. [12]One who is far away will die of the plague, and one who is near will fall by the sword, and anyone who survives and is spared will die of famine. So will I pour out my wrath on them. [13]And they will know that I am the LORD, when their people lie slain among their idols around their altars, on every high hill and on all the mountaintops, under every spreading tree and every leafy oak—places where they offered fragrant incense to all their idols. [14]And I will stretch out my hand against them and make the land a desolate waste from the desert to Diblah[a]—wherever they live. Then they will know that I am the LORD.'"

Why would the mountains and hills be prophesied against? (6:1–3)
The shrines for pagan gods were generally on hills or other high places. So this was a public expression of disproval concerning Israel's practice of idolatry.

Why were the people described as adulterous? (6:9)
They had broken their vows to remain faithful to God and had worshiped other gods. They were like an unfaithful spouse.

---

[a] 14 Most Hebrew manuscripts; a few Hebrew manuscripts *Riblah*

THE END HAS COME

7 The word of the LORD came to me: ²"Son of man, this is what the Sovereign LORD says to the land of Israel:

"'The end! The end has come
  upon the four corners of the land!
³ The end is now upon you,
  and I will unleash my anger against you.
I will judge you according to your conduct
  and repay you for all your detestable practices.
⁴ I will not look on you with pity;
  I will not spare you.
I will surely repay you for your conduct
  and for the detestable practices among you.

"'Then you will know that I am the LORD.'

⁵ "This is what the Sovereign LORD says:

"'Disaster! Unheard-of*ᵃ* disaster!
  See, it comes!
⁶ The end has come!
  The end has come!
It has roused itself against you.
  See, it comes!
⁷ Doom has come upon you,
  upon you who dwell in the land.
The time has come! The day is near!
  There is panic, not joy, on the mountains.
⁸ I am about to pour out my wrath on you
  and spend my anger against you.
I will judge you according to your conduct
  and repay you for all your detestable practices.
⁹ I will not look on you with pity;
  I will not spare you.
I will repay you for your conduct
  and for the detestable practices among you.

"'Then you will know that it is I the LORD who strikes you.

¹⁰ "'See, the day!
  See, it comes!
Doom has burst forth,
  the rod has budded,
  arrogance has blossomed!
¹¹ Violence has arisen,*ᵇ*
  a rod to punish the wicked.
None of the people will be left,
  none of that crowd—
none of their wealth,
  nothing of value.
¹² The time has come!
  The day has arrived!
Let not the buyer rejoice
  nor the seller grieve,
  for my wrath is on the whole crowd.

What did the four corners of the land represent? (7:2)
This represented the entire world which would be affected by God's judgment on the land of Israel. At the time of Ezekiel's writing, the prophet and everyone in his culture thought of the earth as a flat square or rectangle. The four corners were taken literally.

What day was this? (7:7)
This was the day of the Lord, which would be a time of great judgment. That judgment would sweep away all of the enemies threatening God's people.

ᵃ 5 Most Hebrew manuscripts; some Hebrew manuscripts and Syriac *Disaster after*   *ᵇ 11* Or *The violent one has become*

¹³The seller will not recover
　　the property that was sold—
　　as long as both buyer and seller live.
For the vision concerning the whole crowd
　　will not be reversed.
Because of their sins, not one of them
　　will preserve their life.

¹⁴"They have blown the trumpet,
　　they have made all things ready,
but no one will go into battle,
　　for my wrath is on the whole crowd.
¹⁵Outside is the sword;
　　inside are plague and famine.
Those in the country
　　will die by the sword;
those in the city
　　will be devoured by famine and plague.
¹⁶The fugitives who escape
　　will flee to the mountains.
Like doves of the valleys,
　　they will all moan,
　　each for their own sins.
¹⁷Every hand will go limp;
　　every leg will be wet with urine.
¹⁸They will put on sackcloth
　　and be clothed with terror.
Every face will be covered with shame,
　　and every head will be shaved.

¹⁹"They will throw their silver into the streets,
　　and their gold will be treated as a thing unclean.
Their silver and gold
　　will not be able to deliver them
　　in the day of the Lord's wrath.
It will not satisfy their hunger
　　or fill their stomachs,
　　for it has caused them to stumble into sin.
²⁰They took pride in their beautiful jewelry
　　and used it to make their detestable idols.
They made it into vile images;
　　therefore I will make it a thing unclean for them.
²¹I will give their wealth as plunder to foreigners
　　and as loot to the wicked of the earth,
　　who will defile it.
²²I will turn my face away from the people,
　　and robbers will desecrate the place I treasure.
They will enter it
　　and will defile it.

²³"Prepare chains!
　　For the land is full of bloodshed,
　　and the city is full of violence.
²⁴I will bring the most wicked of nations
　　to take possession of their houses.
I will put an end to the pride of the mighty,
　　and their sanctuaries will be desecrated.

What was God's treasured place? (7:22)
This was the temple in Jerusalem.

²⁵ When terror comes,
　　 they will seek peace in vain.
²⁶ Calamity upon calamity will come,
　　 and rumor upon rumor.
　 They will go searching for a vision from
　　　　 the prophet,
　　 priestly instruction in the law will cease,
　　 the counsel of the elders will come to an end.
²⁷ The king will mourn,
　　 the prince will be clothed with despair,
　　 and the hands of the people of the land
　　　　 will tremble.
　 I will deal with them according to their conduct,
　　 and by their own standards I will judge them.

"'Then they will know that I am the Lord.'"

IDOLATRY IN THE TEMPLE

8 In the sixth year, in the sixth month on the fifth day, while I was sitting in my house and the elders of Judah were sitting before me, the hand of the Sovereign Lord came on me there. ² I looked, and I saw a figure like that of a man.^a From what appeared to be his waist down he was like fire, and from there up his appearance was as bright as glowing metal. ³ He stretched out what looked like a hand and took me by the hair of my head. The Spirit lifted me up between earth and heaven and in visions of God he took me to Jerusalem, to the entrance of the north gate of the inner court, where the idol that provokes to jealousy stood. ⁴ And there before me was the glory of the God of Israel, as in the vision I had seen in the plain.

⁵ Then he said to me, "Son of man, look toward the north." So I looked, and in the entrance north of the gate of the altar I saw this idol of jealousy.

⁶ And he said to me, "Son of man, do you see what they are doing—the utterly detestable things the Israelites are doing here, things that will drive me far from my sanctuary? But you will see things that are even more detestable."

⁷ Then he brought me to the entrance to the court. I looked, and I saw a hole in the wall. ⁸ He said to me, "Son of man, now dig into the wall." So I dug into the wall and saw a doorway there.

⁹ And he said to me, "Go in and see the wicked and detestable things they are doing here." ¹⁰ So I went in and looked, and I saw portrayed all over the walls all kinds of crawling things and unclean animals and all the idols of Israel. ¹¹ In front of them stood seventy elders of Israel, and Jaazaniah son of Shaphan was standing among them. Each had a censer in his hand, and a fragrant cloud of incense was rising.

¹² He said to me, "Son of man, have you seen what the elders of Israel are doing in the darkness, each at the shrine of his own idol? They say, 'The Lord does not see us; the Lord has forsaken the land.'" ¹³ Again, he said, "You will see them doing things that are even more detestable."

Why would the prophets, priests, and elders be unable to help? (7:26)
There would be no guidance from God because he had withdrawn his presence due to their continual sins.

What was this idol? (8:3)
This may have been a statue of Asherah, the Canaanite goddess of fertility, which Josiah had removed 30 years earlier.

What detestable things had been done in the temple? (8:6–11)
The priests had begun to secretly practice animal and idol worship.

^a 2 Or *saw a fiery figure*

Why were the men's backs toward the temple? (8:16)
Because almost all ancient temples faced east, these men who were worshiping the sun had their backs to the temple. This symbolized that they had turned their backs to the Lord.

Who were these guardians of the city and a man clothed in linen? (9:2)
These were the six guardian angels of the city along with a seventh angel carrying a writing kit.

What was this mark? (9:4)
Similar in look to the letter "x," this was a *taw*, the last letter of the Hebrew alphabet.

¹⁴Then he brought me to the entrance of the north gate of the house of the Lord, and I saw women sitting there, mourning the god Tammuz. ¹⁵He said to me, "Do you see this, son of man? You will see things that are even more detestable than this."

¹⁶He then brought me into the inner court of the house of the Lord, and there at the entrance to the temple, between the portico and the altar, were about twenty-five men. With their backs toward the temple of the Lord and their faces toward the east, they were bowing down to the sun in the east.

¹⁷He said to me, "Have you seen this, son of man? Is it a trivial matter for the people of Judah to do the detestable things they are doing here? Must they also fill the land with violence and continually arouse my anger? Look at them putting the branch to their nose! ¹⁸Therefore I will deal with them in anger; I will not look on them with pity or spare them. Although they shout in my ears, I will not listen to them."

JUDGMENT ON THE IDOLATERS

9 Then I heard him call out in a loud voice, "Bring near those who are appointed to execute judgment on the city, each with a weapon in his hand." ²And I saw six men coming from the direction of the upper gate, which faces north, each with a deadly weapon in his hand. With them was a man clothed in linen who had a writing kit at his side. They came in and stood beside the bronze altar.

³Now the glory of the God of Israel went up from above the cherubim, where it had been, and moved to the threshold of the temple. Then the Lord called to the man clothed in linen who had the writing kit at his side ⁴and said to him, "Go throughout the city of Jerusalem and put a mark on the foreheads of those who grieve and lament over all the detestable things that are done in it."

⁵As I listened, he said to the others, "Follow him through the city and kill, without showing pity or compassion. ⁶Slaughter the old men, the young men and women, the mothers and children, but do not touch anyone who has the mark. Begin at my sanctuary." So they began with the old men who were in front of the temple.

⁷Then he said to them, "Defile the temple and fill the courts with the slain. Go!" So they went out and began killing throughout the city. ⁸While they were killing and I was left alone, I fell facedown, crying out, "Alas, Sovereign Lord! Are you going to destroy the entire remnant of Israel in this outpouring of your wrath on Jerusalem?"

⁹He answered me, "The sin of the people of Israel and Judah is exceedingly great; the land is full of bloodshed and the city is full of injustice. They say, 'The Lord has forsaken the land; the Lord does not see.' ¹⁰So I will not look on them with pity or spare them, but I will bring down on their own heads what they have done."

¹¹Then the man in linen with the writing kit at his side brought back word, saying, "I have done as you commanded."

GOD'S GLORY DEPARTS FROM THE TEMPLE

10 I looked, and I saw the likeness of a throne of lapis lazuli above the vault that was over the heads of the cherubim. ²The LORD said to the man clothed in linen, "Go in among the wheels beneath the cherubim. Fill your hands with burning coals from among the cherubim and scatter them over the city." And as I watched, he went in.

³Now the cherubim were standing on the south side of the temple when the man went in, and a cloud filled the inner court. ⁴Then the glory of the LORD rose from above the cherubim and moved to the threshold of the temple. The cloud filled the temple, and the court was full of the radiance of the glory of the LORD. ⁵The sound of the wings of the cherubim could be heard as far away as the outer court, like the voice of God Almighty*a* when he speaks.

⁶When the LORD commanded the man in linen, "Take fire from among the wheels, from among the cherubim," the man went in and stood beside a wheel. ⁷Then one of the cherubim reached out his hand to the fire that was among them. He took up some of it and put it into the hands of the man in linen, who took it and went out. ⁸(Under the wings of the cherubim could be seen what looked like human hands.)

⁹I looked, and I saw beside the cherubim four wheels, one beside each of the cherubim; the wheels sparkled like topaz. ¹⁰As for their appearance, the four of them looked alike; each was like a wheel intersecting a wheel. ¹¹As they moved, they would go in any one of the four directions the cherubim faced; the wheels did not turn about*b* as the cherubim went. The cherubim went in whatever direction the head faced, without turning as they went. ¹²Their entire bodies, including their backs, their hands and their wings, were completely full of eyes, as were their four wheels. ¹³I heard the wheels being called "the whirling wheels." ¹⁴Each of the cherubim had four faces: One face was that of a cherub, the second the face of a human being, the third the face of a lion, and the fourth the face of an eagle.

¹⁵Then the cherubim rose upward. These were the living creatures I had seen by the Kebar River. ¹⁶When the cherubim moved, the wheels beside them moved; and when the cherubim spread their wings to rise from the ground, the wheels did not leave their side. ¹⁷When the cherubim stood still, they also stood still; and when the cherubim rose, they rose with them, because the spirit of the living creatures was in them.

¹⁸Then the glory of the LORD departed from over the threshold of the temple and stopped above the cherubim. ¹⁹While I watched, the cherubim spread their wings and rose from the ground, and as they went, the wheels went with them. They stopped at the entrance of the east gate of the LORD's house, and the glory of the God of Israel was above them.

²⁰These were the living creatures I had seen beneath the God of Israel by the Kebar River, and I realized that they were cherubim. ²¹Each had four faces and four wings,

---

a 5 Hebrew *El-Shaddai*   *b* 11 Or *aside*

Why did God want burning coals scattered over the city? (10:2)
This represented his judgment by fire.

Why were the cherubim covered with eyes? (10:12)
This symbolized God's ability to see and know all things.

Why did the glory of the Lord depart? (10:18)
The glory of the Lord left the temple because it had become defiled by the worship of other gods.

and under their wings was what looked like human hands. [22]Their faces had the same appearance as those I had seen by the Kebar River. Each one went straight ahead.

GOD'S SURE JUDGMENT ON JERUSALEM

11 Then the Spirit lifted me up and brought me to the gate of the house of the LORD that faces east. There at the entrance of the gate were twenty-five men, and I saw among them Jaazaniah son of Azzur and Pelatiah son of Benaiah, leaders of the people. [2]The LORD said to me, "Son of man, these are the men who are plotting evil and giving wicked advice in this city. [3]They say, 'Haven't our houses been recently rebuilt? This city is a pot, and we are the meat in it.' [4]Therefore prophesy against them; prophesy, son of man."

[5]Then the Spirit of the LORD came on me, and he told me to say: "This is what the LORD says: That is what you are saying, you leaders in Israel, but I know what is going through your mind. [6]You have killed many people in this city and filled its streets with the dead.

[7]"Therefore this is what the Sovereign LORD says: The bodies you have thrown there are the meat and this city is the pot, but I will drive you out of it. [8]You fear the sword, and the sword is what I will bring against you, declares the Sovereign LORD. [9]I will drive you out of the city and deliver you into the hands of foreigners and inflict punishment on you. [10]You will fall by the sword, and I will execute judgment on you at the borders of Israel. Then you will know that I am the LORD. [11]This city will not be a pot for you, nor will you be the meat in it; I will execute judgment on you at the borders of Israel. [12]And you will know that I am the LORD, for you have not followed my decrees or kept my laws but have conformed to the standards of the nations around you."

[13]Now as I was prophesying, Pelatiah son of Benaiah died. Then I fell facedown and cried out in a loud voice, "Alas, Sovereign LORD! Will you completely destroy the remnant of Israel?"

THE PROMISE OF ISRAEL'S RETURN

[14]The word of the LORD came to me: [15]"Son of man, the people of Jerusalem have said of your fellow exiles and all the other Israelites, 'They are far away from the LORD; this land was given to us as our possession.'

[16]"Therefore say: 'This is what the Sovereign LORD says: Although I sent them far away among the nations and scattered them among the countries, yet for a little while I have been a sanctuary for them in the countries where they have gone.'

[17]"Therefore say: 'This is what the Sovereign LORD says: I will gather you from the nations and bring you back from the countries where you have been scattered, and I will give you back the land of Israel again.'

[18]"They will return to it and remove all its vile images and detestable idols. [19]I will give them an undivided heart and put a new spirit in them; I will remove from them their heart of stone and give them a heart of flesh. [20]Then they

---

What did the leaders mean when they called themselves the meat? (11:3)
If Jerusalem was a cooking pot, these leaders considered themselves to be the choice portions of meat left in the city, while the exiles were just the discarded scraps and bones.

What did it mean that God was their sanctuary? (11:16)
Even though the exiles had been driven away from Jerusalem, God himself had become their sanctuary. In other words, he was present among them.

How did God take away their heart of stone and give them a heart of flesh? (11:19)
God gave the exiles new hearts that were open to him rather than to the idols they had worshiped in the past.

will follow my decrees and be careful to keep my laws. They will be my people, and I will be their God. [21]But as for those whose hearts are devoted to their vile images and detestable idols, I will bring down on their own heads what they have done, declares the Sovereign LORD."

[22]Then the cherubim, with the wheels beside them, spread their wings, and the glory of the God of Israel was above them. [23]The glory of the LORD went up from within the city and stopped above the mountain east of it. [24]The Spirit lifted me up and brought me to the exiles in Babylonia[a] in the vision given by the Spirit of God.

Then the vision I had seen went up from me, [25]and I told the exiles everything the LORD had shown me.

THE EXILE SYMBOLIZED

12 The word of the LORD came to me: [2]"Son of man, you are living among a rebellious people. They have eyes to see but do not see and ears to hear but do not hear, for they are a rebellious people.

[3]"Therefore, son of man, pack your belongings for exile and in the daytime, as they watch, set out and go from where you are to another place. Perhaps they will understand, though they are a rebellious people. [4]During the daytime, while they watch, bring out your belongings packed for exile. Then in the evening, while they are watching, go out like those who go into exile. [5]While they watch, dig through the wall and take your belongings out through it. [6]Put them on your shoulder as they are watching and carry them out at dusk. Cover your face so that you cannot see the land, for I have made you a sign to the Israelites."

[7]So I did as I was commanded. During the day I brought out my things packed for exile. Then in the evening I dug through the wall with my hands. I took my belongings out at dusk, carrying them on my shoulders while they watched.

[8]In the morning the word of the LORD came to me: [9]"Son of man, did not the Israelites, that rebellious people, ask you, 'What are you doing?'

[10]"Say to them, 'This is what the Sovereign LORD says: This prophecy concerns the prince in Jerusalem and all the Israelites who are there.' [11]Say to them, 'I am a sign to you.'

"As I have done, so it will be done to them. They will go into exile as captives.

[12]"The prince among them will put his things on his shoulder at dusk and leave, and a hole will be dug in the wall for him to go through. He will cover his face so that he cannot see the land. [13]I will spread my net for him, and he will be caught in my snare; I will bring him to Babylonia, the land of the Chaldeans, but he will not see it, and there he will die. [14]I will scatter to the winds all those around him—his staff and all his troops—and I will pursue them with drawn sword.

[15]"They will know that I am the LORD, when I disperse them among the nations and scatter them through the countries. [16]But I will spare a few of them from the sword,

Where was God's glory going? (11:23)
This was the final eastward movement of the glory of God as the Lord left his temple. The glory of the Lord stopped above the Mount of Olives.

What wall was Ezekiel supposed to dig through? (12:5)
This was not the city wall, which was made of stone and was several feet thick, but the brick wall of his house.

Who was the prince in Jerusalem? (12:12)
This was King Zedekiah, who was captured by the Babylonians when he tried to escape.

[a] 24 Or *Chaldea*

famine and plague, so that in the nations where they go they may acknowledge all their detestable practices. Then they will know that I am the LORD."

¹⁷The word of the LORD came to me: ¹⁸"Son of man, tremble as you eat your food, and shudder in fear as you drink your water. ¹⁹Say to the people of the land: 'This is what the Sovereign LORD says about those living in Jerusalem and in the land of Israel: They will eat their food in anxiety and drink their water in despair, for their land will be stripped of everything in it because of the violence of all who live there. ²⁰The inhabited towns will be laid waste and the land will be desolate. Then you will know that I am the LORD.'"

THERE WILL BE NO DELAY

²¹The word of the LORD came to me: ²²"Son of man, what is this proverb you have in the land of Israel: 'The days go by and every vision comes to nothing'? ²³Say to them, 'This is what the Sovereign LORD says: I am going to put an end to this proverb, and they will no longer quote it in Israel.' Say to them, 'The days are near when every vision will be fulfilled. ²⁴For there will be no more false visions or flattering divinations among the people of Israel. ²⁵But I the LORD will speak what I will, and it shall be fulfilled without delay. For in your days, you rebellious people, I will fulfill whatever I say, declares the Sovereign LORD.'"

²⁶The word of the LORD came to me: ²⁷"Son of man, the Israelites are saying, 'The vision he sees is for many years from now, and he prophesies about the distant future.'

²⁸"Therefore say to them, 'This is what the Sovereign LORD says: None of my words will be delayed any longer; whatever I say will be fulfilled, declares the Sovereign LORD.'"

FALSE PROPHETS CONDEMNED

13 The word of the LORD came to me: ²"Son of man, prophesy against the prophets of Israel who are now prophesying. Say to those who prophesy out of their own imagination: 'Hear the word of the LORD! ³This is what the Sovereign LORD says: Woe to the foolish^a prophets who follow their own spirit and have seen nothing! ⁴Your prophets, Israel, are like jackals among ruins. ⁵You have not gone up to the breaches in the wall to repair it for the people of Israel so that it will stand firm in the battle on the day of the LORD. ⁶Their visions are false and their divinations a lie. Even though the LORD has not sent them, they say, "The LORD declares," and expect him to fulfill their words. ⁷Have you not seen false visions and uttered lying divinations when you say, "The LORD declares," though I have not spoken?

⁸"Therefore this is what the Sovereign LORD says: Because of your false words and lying visions, I am against you, declares the Sovereign LORD. ⁹My hand will be against the prophets who see false visions and utter lying divinations. They will not belong to the council of my people or be listed

Why was Ezekiel supposed to tremble when he ate and drank? (12:17–18)
This was to symbolize the fear and anxiety the people would experience.

What was this proverb? (12:21–23)
The proverb implied that the prophecies of God's judgment never came about, but the Lord said that the time was near when all those prophecies would be fulfilled.

^a 3 Or *wicked*

in the records of Israel, nor will they enter the land of Israel. Then you will know that I am the Sovereign LORD.

¹⁰ "'Because they lead my people astray, saying, "Peace," when there is no peace, and because, when a flimsy wall is built, they cover it with whitewash, ¹¹ therefore tell those who cover it with whitewash that it is going to fall. Rain will come in torrents, and I will send hailstones hurtling down, and violent winds will burst forth. ¹² When the wall collapses, will people not ask you, "Where is the whitewash you covered it with?"

¹³ "'Therefore this is what the Sovereign LORD says: In my wrath I will unleash a violent wind, and in my anger hailstones and torrents of rain will fall with destructive fury. ¹⁴ I will tear down the wall you have covered with whitewash and will level it to the ground so that its foundation will be laid bare. When it*ᵃ* falls, you will be destroyed in it; and you will know that I am the LORD. ¹⁵ So I will pour out my wrath against the wall and against those who covered it with whitewash. I will say to you, "The wall is gone and so are those who whitewashed it, ¹⁶ those prophets of Israel who prophesied to Jerusalem and saw visions of peace for her when there was no peace, declares the Sovereign LORD."'

¹⁷ "Now, son of man, set your face against the daughters of your people who prophesy out of their own imagination. Prophesy against them ¹⁸ and say, 'This is what the Sovereign LORD says: Woe to the women who sew magic charms on all their wrists and make veils of various lengths for their heads in order to ensnare people. Will you ensnare the lives of my people but preserve your own? ¹⁹ You have profaned me among my people for a few handfuls of barley and scraps of bread. By lying to my people, who listen to lies, you have killed those who should not have died and have spared those who should not live.

²⁰ "'Therefore this is what the Sovereign LORD says: I am against your magic charms with which you ensnare people like birds and I will tear them from your arms; I will set free the people that you ensnare like birds. ²¹ I will tear off your veils and save my people from your hands, and they will no longer fall prey to your power. Then you will know that I am the LORD. ²² Because you disheartened the righteous with your lies, when I had brought them no grief, and because you encouraged the wicked not to turn from their evil ways and so save their lives, ²³ therefore you will no longer see false visions or practice divination. I will save my people from your hands. And then you will know that I am the LORD.'"

IDOLATERS CONDEMNED

14 Some of the elders of Israel came to me and sat down in front of me. ² Then the word of the LORD came to me: ³ "Son of man, these men have set up idols in their hearts and put wicked stumbling blocks before their faces. Should I let them inquire of me at all? ⁴ Therefore speak to them and tell them, 'This is what the Sovereign LORD says: When any of the Israelites set up idols in their hearts and put a wicked

What was whitewash? (13:10–16)
This was a covering applied to a poorly constructed wall to hide its weakness. The message of the false prophets was also flimsy; even though they tried to make it look good, their message would fail.

What sort of magic charms were these? (13:18)
It is not known exactly what type of magic or sorcery these women were practicing, but it is clear that it was not of God and was a type of black magic or voodoo. The writers of the Bible never described occult practices in detail.

ᵃ *14* Or *the city*

stumbling block before their faces and then go to a prophet,
I the LORD will answer them myself in keeping with their
great idolatry. [5]I will do this to recapture the hearts of the
people of Israel, who have all deserted me for their idols.'

[6]"Therefore say to the people of Israel, 'This is what the
Sovereign LORD says: Repent! Turn from your idols and renounce all your detestable practices!

[7]"When any of the Israelites or any foreigner residing in
Israel separate themselves from me and set up idols in their
hearts and put a wicked stumbling block before their faces
and then go to a prophet to inquire of me, I the LORD will
answer them myself. [8]I will set my face against them and
make them an example and a byword. I will remove them
from my people. Then you will know that I am the LORD.

[9]"And if the prophet is enticed to utter a prophecy, I the
LORD have enticed that prophet, and I will stretch out my
hand against him and destroy him from among my people
Israel. [10]They will bear their guilt—the prophet will be as
guilty as the one who consults him. [11]Then the people of
Israel will no longer stray from me, nor will they defile themselves anymore with all their sins. They will be my people,
and I will be their God, declares the Sovereign LORD.'"

JERUSALEM'S JUDGMENT INESCAPABLE

[12]The word of the LORD came to me: [13]"Son of man, if
a country sins against me by being unfaithful and I stretch
out my hand against it to cut off its food supply and send
famine upon it and kill its people and their animals, [14]even if
these three men—Noah, Daniel[a] and Job—were in it, they
could save only themselves by their righteousness, declares
the Sovereign LORD.

[15]"Or if I send wild beasts through that country and they
leave it childless and it becomes desolate so that no one can
pass through it because of the beasts, [16]as surely as I live, declares the Sovereign LORD, even if these three men were in it,
they could not save their own sons or daughters. They alone
would be saved, but the land would be desolate.

[17]"Or if I bring a sword against that country and say, 'Let
the sword pass throughout the land,' and I kill its people
and their animals, [18]as surely as I live, declares the Sovereign
LORD, even if these three men were in it, they could not save
their own sons or daughters. They alone would be saved.

[19]"Or if I send a plague into that land and pour out my
wrath on it through bloodshed, killing its people and their
animals, [20]as surely as I live, declares the Sovereign LORD,
even if Noah, Daniel and Job were in it, they could save neither son nor daughter. They would save only themselves by
their righteousness.

[21]"For this is what the Sovereign LORD says: How much
worse will it be when I send against Jerusalem my four
dreadful judgments—sword and famine and wild beasts and
plague—to kill its men and their animals! [22]Yet there will
be some survivors—sons and daughters who will be brought
out of it. They will come to you, and when you see their

What were these detestable practices? (14:6)
These practices involved idolatry and pagan rituals including child sacrifice and animal worship.

Why were Noah, Daniel, and Job singled out? (14:14, 20)
They were examples of righteous men who faithfully served God. But the Lord said that even they would not be able to persuade him to spare the wicked people of Ezekiel's generation.

What were the four dreadful judgments? (14:21)
These were the sword (blood-shed), famine, wild beasts, and the plague God would send as punishment on the people.

---

[a] 14 Or Danel, a man of renown in ancient literature; also in verse 20

conduct and their actions, you will be consoled regarding the disaster I have brought on Jerusalem—every disaster I have brought on it. [23] You will be consoled when you see their conduct and their actions, for you will know that I have done nothing in it without cause, declares the Sovereign LORD."

JERUSALEM AS A USELESS VINE

15 The word of the LORD came to me: [2] "Son of man, how is the wood of a vine different from that of a branch from any of the trees in the forest? [3] Is wood ever taken from it to make anything useful? Do they make pegs from it to hang things on? [4] And after it is thrown on the fire as fuel and the fire burns both ends and chars the middle, is it then useful for anything? [5] If it was not useful for anything when it was whole, how much less can it be made into something useful when the fire has burned it and it is charred?

[6] "Therefore this is what the Sovereign LORD says: As I have given the wood of the vine among the trees of the forest as fuel for the fire, so will I treat the people living in Jerusalem. [7] I will set my face against them. Although they have come out of the fire, the fire will yet consume them. And when I set my face against them, you will know that I am the LORD. [8] I will make the land desolate because they have been unfaithful, declares the Sovereign LORD."

JERUSALEM AS AN ADULTEROUS WIFE

16 The word of the LORD came to me: [2] "Son of man, confront Jerusalem with her detestable practices [3] and say, 'This is what the Sovereign LORD says to Jerusalem: Your ancestry and birth were in the land of the Canaanites; your father was an Amorite and your mother a Hittite. [4] On the day you were born your cord was not cut, nor were you washed with water to make you clean, nor were you rubbed with salt or wrapped in cloths. [5] No one looked on you with pity or had compassion enough to do any of these things for you. Rather, you were thrown out into the open field, for on the day you were born you were despised.

[6] "Then I passed by and saw you kicking about in your blood, and as you lay there in your blood I said to you, "Live!"[a] [7] I made you grow like a plant of the field. You grew and developed and entered puberty. Your breasts had formed and your hair had grown, yet you were stark naked.

[8] "Later I passed by, and when I looked at you and saw that you were old enough for love, I spread the corner of my garment over you and covered your naked body. I gave you my solemn oath and entered into a covenant with you, declares the Sovereign LORD, and you became mine.

[9] "I bathed you with water and washed the blood from you and put ointments on you. [10] I clothed you with an embroidered dress and put sandals of fine leather on you. I dressed you in fine linen and covered you with costly garments. [11] I adorned you with jewelry: I put bracelets on your arms and a necklace around your neck, [12] and I put a ring on your nose,

---

[a] 6 A few Hebrew manuscripts, Septuagint and Syriac; most Hebrew manuscripts repeat *and as you lay there in your blood I said to you, "Live!"*

How had Israel come out of the fire? (15:7)
Jerusalem was not destroyed in 597 B.C. when Nebuchadnezzar plundered the city and carried away thousands of people. But there would be another siege when the Babylonians would break down the walls of Jerusalem and set fire to the city.

What did it mean that Jerusalem's father was an Amorite and its mother a Hittite? (16:3)
Jerusalem had been a Canaanite city that was home to pagan people, and it only became a completely Israelite city after David's conquest (see 2 Samuel 5:6–9).

What did it mean that Jerusalem was thrown into an open field on the day it was born? (16:5)
In some ancient pagan societies, parents would abandon unwanted newborn babies in a field to die of exposure. The Israelites considered this practice extremely wicked.

What did it mean that God spread a garment over Jerusalem? (16:8)
This was symbolic of entering into a marriage relationship (see Ruth 3:9).

How did God treat Jerusalem? (16:9–14)
Continuing this personification of Jerusalem as a young woman, God speaks of clothing her in the finest garments, giving her costly jewelry, providing the finest food and drink, and making her a queen. All of this showed God's love for Jerusalem.

How did Jerusalem repay God for his great love? (16:15–22)
Instead of thanking God for his gifts and serving him with love, the people turned away from God, worshiped idols, and offered human sacrifices to pagan gods.

earrings on your ears and a beautiful crown on your head. [13] So you were adorned with gold and silver; your clothes were of fine linen and costly fabric and embroidered cloth. Your food was honey, olive oil and the finest flour. You became very beautiful and rose to be a queen. [14] And your fame spread among the nations on account of your beauty, because the splendor I had given you made your beauty perfect, declares the Sovereign LORD.

[15] "'But you trusted in your beauty and used your fame to become a prostitute. You lavished your favors on anyone who passed by and your beauty became his. [16] You took some of your garments to make gaudy high places, where you carried on your prostitution. You went to him, and he possessed your beauty.[a] [17] You also took the fine jewelry I gave you, the jewelry made of my gold and silver, and you made for yourself male idols and engaged in prostitution with them. [18] And you took your embroidered clothes to put on them, and you offered my oil and incense before them. [19] Also the food I provided for you—the flour, olive oil and honey I gave you to eat—you offered as fragrant incense before them. That is what happened, declares the Sovereign LORD.

[20] "'And you took your sons and daughters whom you bore to me and sacrificed them as food to the idols. Was your prostitution not enough? [21] You slaughtered my children and sacrificed them to the idols. [22] In all your detestable practices and your prostitution you did not remember the days of your youth, when you were naked and bare, kicking about in your blood.

[23] "'Woe! Woe to you, declares the Sovereign LORD. In addition to all your other wickedness, [24] you built a mound for yourself and made a lofty shrine in every public square. [25] At every street corner you built your lofty shrines and degraded your beauty, spreading your legs with increasing promiscuity to anyone who passed by. [26] You engaged in prostitution with the Egyptians, your neighbors with large genitals, and aroused my anger with your increasing promiscuity. [27] So I stretched out my hand against you and reduced your territory; I gave you over to the greed of your enemies, the daughters of the Philistines, who were shocked by your lewd conduct. [28] You engaged in prostitution with the Assyrians too, because you were insatiable; and even after that, you still were not satisfied. [29] Then you increased your promiscuity to include Babylonia,[b] a land of merchants, but even with this you were not satisfied.

[30] "'I am filled with fury against you,[c] declares the Sovereign LORD, when you do all these things, acting like a brazen prostitute! [31] When you built your mounds at every street corner and made your lofty shrines in every public square, you were unlike a prostitute, because you scorned payment.

[32] "'You adulterous wife! You prefer strangers to your own husband! [33] All prostitutes receive gifts, but you give gifts to all your lovers, bribing them to come to you from everywhere for your illicit favors. [34] So in your prostitution you are the

How was Jerusalem worse than an unfaithful wife or a prostitute? (16:33)
Symbolically, Jerusalem went so far as to seek out other lovers and bribed or paid them to join in her unfaithfulness.

[a] 16 The meaning of the Hebrew for this sentence is uncertain.
[b] 29 Or Chaldea   [c] 30 Or How feverish is your heart,

opposite of others; no one runs after you for your favors. You are the very opposite, for you give payment and none is given to you.

35"'Therefore, you prostitute, hear the word of the LORD! 36 This is what the Sovereign LORD says: Because you poured out your lust and exposed your naked body in your promiscuity with your lovers, and because of all your detestable idols, and because you gave them your children's blood, 37 therefore I am going to gather all your lovers, with whom you found pleasure, those you loved as well as those you hated. I will gather them against you from all around and will strip you in front of them, and they will see you stark naked. 38 I will sentence you to the punishment of women who commit adultery and who shed blood; I will bring on you the blood vengeance of my wrath and jealous anger. 39 Then I will deliver you into the hands of your lovers, and they will tear down your mounds and destroy your lofty shrines. They will strip you of your clothes and take your fine jewelry and leave you stark naked. 40 They will bring a mob against you, who will stone you and hack you to pieces with their swords. 41 They will burn down your houses and inflict punishment on you in the sight of many women. I will put a stop to your prostitution, and you will no longer pay your lovers. 42 Then my wrath against you will subside and my jealous anger will turn away from you; I will be calm and no longer angry.

43"'Because you did not remember the days of your youth but enraged me with all these things, I will surely bring down on your head what you have done, declares the Sovereign LORD. Did you not add lewdness to all your other detestable practices?

44"'Everyone who quotes proverbs will quote this proverb about you: "Like mother, like daughter." 45 You are a true daughter of your mother, who despised her husband and her children; and you are a true sister of your sisters, who despised their husbands and their children. Your mother was a Hittite and your father an Amorite. 46 Your older sister was Samaria, who lived to the north of you with her daughters; and your younger sister, who lived to the south of you with her daughters, was Sodom. 47 You not only followed their ways and copied their detestable practices, but in all your ways you soon became more depraved than they. 48 As surely as I live, declares the Sovereign LORD, your sister Sodom and her daughters never did what you and your daughters have done.

49"'Now this was the sin of your sister Sodom: She and her daughters were arrogant, overfed and unconcerned; they did not help the poor and needy. 50 They were haughty and did detestable things before me. Therefore I did away with them as you have seen. 51 Samaria did not commit half the sins you did. You have done more detestable things than they, and have made your sisters seem righteous by all these things you have done. 52 Bear your disgrace, for you have furnished some justification for your sisters. Because your sins were more vile than theirs, they appear more righteous than you. So then, be ashamed and bear your disgrace, for you have made your sisters appear righteous.

⁵³"'However, I will restore the fortunes of Sodom and her daughters and of Samaria and her daughters, and your fortunes along with them, ⁵⁴so that you may bear your disgrace and be ashamed of all you have done in giving them comfort. ⁵⁵And your sisters, Sodom with her daughters and Samaria with her daughters, will return to what they were before; and you and your daughters will return to what you were before. ⁵⁶You would not even mention your sister Sodom in the day of your pride, ⁵⁷before your wickedness was uncovered. Even so, you are now scorned by the daughters of Edom^a and all her neighbors and the daughters of the Philistines—all those around you who despise you. ⁵⁸You will bear the consequences of your lewdness and your detestable practices, declares the LORD.

⁵⁹"'This is what the Sovereign LORD says: I will deal with you as you deserve, because you have despised my oath by breaking the covenant. ⁶⁰Yet I will remember the covenant I made with you in the days of your youth, and I will establish an everlasting covenant with you. ⁶¹Then you will remember your ways and be ashamed when you receive your sisters, both those who are older than you and those who are younger. I will give them to you as daughters, but not on the basis of my covenant with you. ⁶²So I will establish my covenant with you, and you will know that I am the LORD. ⁶³Then, when I make atonement for you for all you have done, you will remember and be ashamed and never again open your mouth because of your humiliation, declares the Sovereign LORD.'"

TWO EAGLES AND A VINE

17 The word of the LORD came to me: ²"Son of man, set forth an allegory and tell it to the Israelites as a parable. ³Say to them, 'This is what the Sovereign LORD says: A great eagle with powerful wings, long feathers and full plumage of varied colors came to Lebanon. Taking hold of the top of a cedar, ⁴he broke off its topmost shoot and carried it away to a land of merchants, where he planted it in a city of traders.

⁵"'He took one of the seedlings of the land and put it in fertile soil. He planted it like a willow by abundant water, ⁶and it sprouted and became a low, spreading vine. Its branches turned toward him, but its roots remained under it. So it became a vine and produced branches and put out leafy boughs.

⁷"'But there was another great eagle with powerful wings and full plumage. The vine now sent out its roots toward him from the plot where it was planted and stretched out its branches to him for water. ⁸It had been planted in good soil by abundant water so that it would produce branches, bear fruit and become a splendid vine.'

⁹"Say to them, 'This is what the Sovereign LORD says: Will it thrive? Will it not be uprooted and stripped of its fruit so that it withers? All its new growth will wither. It will not take a strong arm or many people to pull it up by the roots. ¹⁰It has been planted, but will it thrive? Will it not wither

What everlasting covenant would God make with Jerusalem? (16:60)
God would forgive Jerusalem and renew his marriage relationship with her by turning the hearts of the people to him.

Who was this "great eagle"? (17:3–4)
This eagle was Nebuchadnezzar, who forced Judah's king Jehoiachin out of the country. The second eagle was one of the pharaohs of Egypt who offered to help Jerusalem.

^a 57 Many Hebrew manuscripts and Syriac; most Hebrew manuscripts, Septuagint and Vulgate *Aram*

completely when the east wind strikes it—wither away in the plot where it grew?'"

¹¹Then the word of the LORD came to me: ¹²"Say to this rebellious people, 'Do you not know what these things mean?' Say to them: 'The king of Babylon went to Jerusalem and carried off her king and her nobles, bringing them back with him to Babylon. ¹³Then he took a member of the royal family and made a treaty with him, putting him under oath. He also carried away the leading men of the land, ¹⁴so that the kingdom would be brought low, unable to rise again, surviving only by keeping his treaty. ¹⁵But the king rebelled against him by sending his envoys to Egypt to get horses and a large army. Will he succeed? Will he who does such things escape? Will he break the treaty and yet escape?

¹⁶"'As surely as I live, declares the Sovereign LORD, he shall die in Babylon, in the land of the king who put him on the throne, whose oath he despised and whose treaty he broke. ¹⁷Pharaoh with his mighty army and great horde will be of no help to him in war, when ramps are built and siege works erected to destroy many lives. ¹⁸He despised the oath by breaking the covenant. Because he had given his hand in pledge and yet did all these things, he shall not escape.

¹⁹"'Therefore this is what the Sovereign LORD says: As surely as I live, I will repay him for despising my oath and breaking my covenant. ²⁰I will spread my net for him, and he will be caught in my snare. I will bring him to Babylon and execute judgment on him there because he was unfaithful to me. ²¹All his choice troops will fall by the sword, and the survivors will be scattered to the winds. Then you will know that I the LORD have spoken.

²²"This is what the Sovereign LORD says: I myself will take a shoot from the very top of a cedar and plant it; I will break off a tender sprig from its topmost shoots and plant it on a high and lofty mountain. ²³On the mountain heights of Israel I will plant it; it will produce branches and bear fruit and become a splendid cedar. Birds of every kind will nest in it; they will find shelter in the shade of its branches. ²⁴All the trees of the forest will know that I the LORD bring down the tall tree and make the low tree grow tall. I dry up the green tree and make the dry tree flourish.

"'I the LORD have spoken, and I will do it.'"

THE ONE WHO SINS WILL DIE

18 The word of the LORD came to me: ²"What do you people mean by quoting this proverb about the land of Israel:

"'The parents eat sour grapes,
　　and the children's teeth are set on edge'?

³"As surely as I live, declares the Sovereign LORD, you will no longer quote this proverb in Israel. ⁴For everyone belongs to me, the parent as well as the child—both alike belong to me. The one who sins is the one who will die.

⁵"Suppose there is a righteous man
　　who does what is just and right.

What were ramps and siege works? (17:17)
These were wheeled ramps that helped an invading army bring battering rams into position and scale the walls of a city.

What was the new shoot the Lord would plant? (17:22–24)
The Lord would take a shoot from David's family tree and use it to restore the dynasty of David. This was a prophecy of the coming Messiah.

What did "the one who sins is the one who will die" mean? (18:4)
Ezekiel was speaking out against the idea that people suffered unjustly for the sins of previous generations. He went on to give an extended example to show that those who follow God's law are blessed and that those who disobey God are punished.

What did it mean to eat at the mountain shrines? (18:6)
This referred to eating meat sacrificed to idols on the high places.

What did it mean to lend "at interest"? (18:8)
God's people were forbidden to charge interest on loans to needy fellow Israelites. But during Israel's time in Babylon, many abuses arose in connection with the lending of money.

⁶ He does not eat at the mountain shrines
   or look to the idols of Israel.
He does not defile his neighbor's wife
   or have sexual relations with a woman during
     her period.
⁷ He does not oppress anyone,
   but returns what he took in pledge for a loan.
He does not commit robbery
   but gives his food to the hungry
   and provides clothing for the naked.
⁸ He does not lend to them at interest
   or take a profit from them.
He withholds his hand from doing wrong
   and judges fairly between two parties.
⁹ He follows my decrees
   and faithfully keeps my laws.
That man is righteous;
   he will surely live,
               declares the Sovereign LORD.

¹⁰"Suppose he has a violent son, who sheds blood or does any of these other things^a ¹¹(though the father has done none of them):

"He eats at the mountain shrines.
He defiles his neighbor's wife.
¹² He oppresses the poor and needy.
He commits robbery.
He does not return what he took in pledge.
He looks to the idols.
He does detestable things.
¹³ He lends at interest and takes a profit.

Will such a man live? He will not! Because he has done all these detestable things, he is to be put to death; his blood will be on his own head.

¹⁴"But suppose this son has a son who sees all the sins his father commits, and though he sees them, he does not do such things:

¹⁵"He does not eat at the mountain shrines
   or look to the idols of Israel.
He does not defile his neighbor's wife.
¹⁶ He does not oppress anyone
   or require a pledge for a loan.
He does not commit robbery
   but gives his food to the hungry
   and provides clothing for the naked.
¹⁷ He withholds his hand from mistreating the poor
   and takes no interest or profit from them.
He keeps my laws and follows my decrees.

He will not die for his father's sin; he will surely live. ¹⁸But his father will die for his own sin, because he practiced extortion, robbed his brother and did what was wrong among his people.

¹⁹"Yet you ask, 'Why does the son not share the guilt of his father?' Since the son has done what is just and right and

^a 10 Or things to a brother

has been careful to keep all my decrees, he will surely live. ²⁰The one who sins is the one who will die. The child will not share the guilt of the parent, nor will the parent share the guilt of the child. The righteousness of the righteous will be credited to them, and the wickedness of the wicked will be charged against them.

²¹"But if a wicked person turns away from all the sins they have committed and keeps all my decrees and does what is just and right, that person will surely live; they will not die. ²²None of the offenses they have committed will be remembered against them. Because of the righteous things they have done, they will live. ²³Do I take any pleasure in the death of the wicked? declares the Sovereign LORD. Rather, am I not pleased when they turn from their ways and live?

²⁴"But if a righteous person turns from their righteousness and commits sin and does the same detestable things the wicked person does, will they live? None of the righteous things that person has done will be remembered. Because of the unfaithfulness they are guilty of and because of the sins they have committed, they will die.

²⁵"Yet you say, 'The way of the Lord is not just.' Hear, you Israelites: Is my way unjust? Is it not your ways that are unjust? ²⁶If a righteous person turns from their righteousness and commits sin, they will die for it; because of the sin they have committed they will die. ²⁷But if a wicked person turns away from the wickedness they have committed and does what is just and right, they will save their life. ²⁸Because they consider all the offenses they have committed and turn away from them, that person will surely live; they will not die. ²⁹Yet the Israelites say, 'The way of the Lord is not just.' Are my ways unjust, people of Israel? Is it not your ways that are unjust?

³⁰"Therefore, you Israelites, I will judge each of you according to your own ways, declares the Sovereign LORD. Repent! Turn away from all your offenses; then sin will not be your downfall. ³¹Rid yourselves of all the offenses you have committed, and get a new heart and a new spirit. Why will you die, people of Israel? ³²For I take no pleasure in the death of anyone, declares the Sovereign LORD. Repent and live!

A LAMENT OVER ISRAEL'S PRINCES

19 "Take up a lament concerning the princes of Israel ²and say:

"'What a lioness was your mother
among the lions!
She lay down among them
and reared her cubs.
³She brought up one of her cubs,
and he became a strong lion.
He learned to tear the prey
and he became a man-eater.
⁴The nations heard about him,
and he was trapped in their pit.
They led him with hooks
to the land of Egypt.

Does this verse provide a way to avoid physical death? (18:21)
No, if a person repents and turns away from sin, God will forgive him.

What was the meaning of this verse? (18:24)
If a person turns away from God and gives in to sin, he or she will be punished.

What was a lament? (19:1)
A lament was a chant usually composed for the funeral of a fallen leader. Here the lament is for the fallen nation of Israel.

Who or what was the lioness? (19:2)
The lioness may be a personification of Israel, Judah, or Jerusalem, all of which could be thought of as being the mother of kings.

⁵ "'When she saw her hope unfulfilled,
     her expectation gone,
she took another of her cubs
     and made him a strong lion.
⁶ He prowled among the lions,
     for he was now a strong lion.
He learned to tear the prey
     and he became a man-eater.
⁷ He broke down*ᵃ* their strongholds
     and devastated their towns.
The land and all who were in it
     were terrified by his roaring.
⁸ Then the nations came against him,
     those from regions round about.
They spread their net for him,
     and he was trapped in their pit.
⁹ With hooks they pulled him into a cage
     and brought him to the king of Babylon.
They put him in prison,
     so his roar was heard no longer
     on the mountains of Israel.

¹⁰ "'Your mother was like a vine in your vineyardᵇ
     planted by the water;
it was fruitful and full of branches
     because of abundant water.
¹¹ Its branches were strong,
     fit for a ruler's scepter.
It towered high
     above the thick foliage,
conspicuous for its height
     and for its many branches.
¹² But it was uprooted in fury
     and thrown to the ground.
The east wind made it shrivel,
     it was stripped of its fruit;
its strong branches withered
     and fire consumed them.
¹³ Now it is planted in the desert,
     in a dry and thirsty land.
¹⁴ Fire spread from one of its mainᶜ branches
     and consumed its fruit.
No strong branch is left on it
     fit for a ruler's scepter.'

"This is a lament and is to be used as a lament."

REBELLIOUS ISRAEL PURGED

20 In the seventh year, in the fifth month on the tenth day, some of the elders of Israel came to inquire of the LORD, and they sat down in front of me.

² Then the word of the LORD came to me: ³ "Son of man, speak to the elders of Israel and say to them, 'This is what the Sovereign LORD says: Have you come to inquire of me?

ᵃ *7* Targum (see Septuagint); Hebrew *He knew*   ᵇ *10* Two Hebrew manuscripts; most Hebrew manuscripts *your blood*   ᶜ *14* Or *from under its*

As surely as I live, I will not let you inquire of me, declares the Sovereign LORD.'

⁴"Will you judge them? Will you judge them, son of man? Then confront them with the detestable practices of their ancestors ⁵and say to them: 'This is what the Sovereign LORD says: On the day I chose Israel, I swore with uplifted hand to the descendants of Jacob and revealed myself to them in Egypt. With uplifted hand I said to them, "I am the LORD your God." ⁶On that day I swore to them that I would bring them out of Egypt into a land I had searched out for them, a land flowing with milk and honey, the most beautiful of all lands. ⁷And I said to them, "Each of you, get rid of the vile images you have set your eyes on, and do not defile yourselves with the idols of Egypt. I am the LORD your God."

⁸"But they rebelled against me and would not listen to me; they did not get rid of the vile images they had set their eyes on, nor did they forsake the idols of Egypt. So I said I would pour out my wrath on them and spend my anger against them in Egypt. ⁹But for the sake of my name, I brought them out of Egypt. I did it to keep my name from being profaned in the eyes of the nations among whom they lived and in whose sight I had revealed myself to the Israelites. ¹⁰Therefore I led them out of Egypt and brought them into the wilderness. ¹¹I gave them my decrees and made known to them my laws, by which the person who obeys them will live. ¹²Also I gave them my Sabbaths as a sign between us, so they would know that I the LORD made them holy.

¹³"Yet the people of Israel rebelled against me in the wilderness. They did not follow my decrees but rejected my laws—by which the person who obeys them will live—and they utterly desecrated my Sabbaths. So I said I would pour out my wrath on them and destroy them in the wilderness. ¹⁴But for the sake of my name I did what would keep it from being profaned in the eyes of the nations in whose sight I had brought them out. ¹⁵Also with uplifted hand I swore to them in the wilderness that I would not bring them into the land I had given them—a land flowing with milk and honey, the most beautiful of all lands— ¹⁶because they rejected my laws and did not follow my decrees and desecrated my Sabbaths. For their hearts were devoted to their idols. ¹⁷Yet I looked on them with pity and did not destroy them or put an end to them in the wilderness. ¹⁸I said to their children in the wilderness, "Do not follow the statutes of your parents or keep their laws or defile yourselves with their idols. ¹⁹I am the LORD your God; follow my decrees and be careful to keep my laws. ²⁰Keep my Sabbaths holy, that they may be a sign between us. Then you will know that I am the LORD your God."

²¹"But the children rebelled against me: They did not follow my decrees, they were not careful to keep my laws, of which I said, "The person who obeys them will live by them," and they desecrated my Sabbaths. So I said I would pour out my wrath on them and spend my anger against them in the wilderness. ²²But I withheld my hand, and for the

What was the meaning of an uplifted hand? (20:5)
Raising one's hand was a standard practice when taking an oath.

Why was God concerned about his reputation? (20:9)
In ancient times, a person's identity and reputation were closely connected. God wanted people to have a correct understanding of who he was and how he was in control of the history of his people.

How were Sabbaths a sign to God's people? (20:12)
Israel's observance of the Sabbath was to serve as a sign that they were God's holy people.

sake of my name I did what would keep it from being profaned in the eyes of the nations in whose sight I had brought them out. ²³ Also with uplifted hand I swore to them in the wilderness that I would disperse them among the nations and scatter them through the countries, ²⁴ because they had not obeyed my laws but had rejected my decrees and desecrated my Sabbaths, and their eyes lusted after their parents' idols. ²⁵ So I gave them other statutes that were not good and laws through which they could not live; ²⁶ I defiled them through their gifts—the sacrifice of every firstborn—that I might fill them with horror so they would know that I am the Lord.'

²⁷ "Therefore, son of man, speak to the people of Israel and say to them, 'This is what the Sovereign Lord says: In this also your ancestors blasphemed me by being unfaithful to me: ²⁸ When I brought them into the land I had sworn to give them and they saw any high hill or any leafy tree, there they offered their sacrifices, made offerings that aroused my anger, presented their fragrant incense and poured out their drink offerings. ²⁹ Then I said to them: What is this high place you go to?'" (It is called Bamah^a to this day.)

REBELLIOUS ISRAEL RENEWED

³⁰ "Therefore say to the Israelites: 'This is what the Sovereign Lord says: Will you defile yourselves the way your ancestors did and lust after their vile images? ³¹ When you offer your gifts—the sacrifice of your children in the fire—you continue to defile yourselves with all your idols to this day. Am I to let you inquire of me, you Israelites? As surely as I live, declares the Sovereign Lord, I will not let you inquire of me.

³² "'You say, "We want to be like the nations, like the peoples of the world, who serve wood and stone." But what you have in mind will never happen. ³³ As surely as I live, declares the Sovereign Lord, I will reign over you with a mighty hand and an outstretched arm and with outpoured wrath. ³⁴ I will bring you from the nations and gather you from the countries where you have been scattered—with a mighty hand and an outstretched arm and with outpoured wrath. ³⁵ I will bring you into the wilderness of the nations and there, face to face, I will execute judgment upon you. ³⁶ As I judged your ancestors in the wilderness of the land of Egypt, so I will judge you, declares the Sovereign Lord. ³⁷ I will take note of you as you pass under my rod, and I will bring you into the bond of the covenant. ³⁸ I will purge you of those who revolt and rebel against me. Although I will bring them out of the land where they are living, yet they will not enter the land of Israel. Then you will know that I am the Lord.

³⁹ "'As for you, people of Israel, this is what the Sovereign Lord says: Go and serve your idols, every one of you! But afterward you will surely listen to me and no longer profane my holy name with your gifts and idols. ⁴⁰ For on my holy mountain, the high mountain of Israel, declares the Sovereign Lord, there in the land all the people of Israel will serve

Why did the people offer sacrifices at high hills and near leafy trees? (20:28)
The Israelites were influenced by the pagan beliefs of the Canaanites, and they began to worship Baal, the god of fertility, because they thought it ensured a good harvest for their crops.

Why would they pass under his rod? (20:37)
This was how a shepherd counted and kept track of his sheep. It was also the way a shepherd would divide his flock into separate parts.

^a 29 Bamah means high place.

me, and there I will accept them. There I will require your offerings and your choice gifts,[a] along with all your holy sacrifices. [41] I will accept you as fragrant incense when I bring you out from the nations and gather you from the countries where you have been scattered, and I will be proved holy through you in the sight of the nations. [42] Then you will know that I am the LORD, when I bring you into the land of Israel, the land I had sworn with uplifted hand to give to your ancestors. [43] There you will remember your conduct and all the actions by which you have defiled yourselves, and you will loathe yourselves for all the evil you have done. [44] You will know that I am the LORD, when I deal with you for my name's sake and not according to your evil ways and your corrupt practices, you people of Israel, declares the Sovereign LORD.'"

PROPHECY AGAINST THE SOUTH

[45] The word of the LORD came to me: [46] "Son of man, set your face toward the south; preach against the south and prophesy against the forest of the southland. [47] Say to the southern forest: 'Hear the word of the LORD. This is what the Sovereign LORD says: I am about to set fire to you, and it will consume all your trees, both green and dry. The blazing flame will not be quenched, and every face from south to north will be scorched by it. [48] Everyone will see that I the LORD have kindled it; it will not be quenched.'"

[49] Then I said, "Sovereign LORD, they are saying of me, 'Isn't he just telling parables?'"[b]

BABYLON AS GOD'S SWORD OF JUDGMENT

21[c] The word of the LORD came to me: [2] "Son of man, set your face against Jerusalem and preach against the sanctuary. Prophesy against the land of Israel [3] and say to her: 'This is what the LORD says: I am against you. I will draw my sword from its sheath and cut off from you both the righteous and the wicked. [4] Because I am going to cut off the righteous and the wicked, my sword will be unsheathed against everyone from south to north. [5] Then all people will know that I the LORD have drawn my sword from its sheath; it will not return again.'

[6] "Therefore groan, son of man! Groan before them with broken heart and bitter grief. [7] And when they ask you, 'Why are you groaning?' you shall say, 'Because of the news that is coming. Every heart will melt with fear and every hand go limp; every spirit will become faint and every leg will be wet with urine.' It is coming! It will surely take place, declares the Sovereign LORD."

[8] The word of the LORD came to me: [9] "Son of man, prophesy and say, 'This is what the Lord says:

"'A sword, a sword,
    sharpened and polished—
[10] sharpened for the slaughter,
    polished to flash like lightning!

---

[a] 40 Or *and the gifts of your firstfruits*   [b] 49 In Hebrew texts 20:45-49 is numbered 21:1-5.   [c] In Hebrew texts 21:1-32 is numbered 21:6-37.

Who was Ezekiel prophesying against here? (20:46)
He was prophesying against Judah and Jerusalem as if he were standing on the northern border of Judah.

What was this sword? (21:3)
Here the sword refers to Babylon and Nebuchadnezzar. No one would escape, not even the righteous.

What is this sword song? (21:9–10)
This song may have been accompanied by dancing or symbolic actions. It is the type of song sung by warriors who were going into battle.

"'Shall we rejoice in the scepter of my royal son? The sword despises every such stick.

¹¹ "'The sword is appointed to be polished,
　　to be grasped with the hand;
　it is sharpened and polished,
　　made ready for the hand of the slayer.
¹² Cry out and wail, son of man,
　　for it is against my people;
　　it is against all the princes of Israel.
　They are thrown to the sword
　　along with my people.
　Therefore beat your breast.

¹³ "'Testing will surely come. And what if even the scepter, which the sword despises, does not continue? declares the Sovereign Lord.'

¹⁴ "So then, son of man, prophesy
　　and strike your hands together.
　Let the sword strike twice,
　　even three times.
　It is a sword for slaughter—
　　a sword for great slaughter,
　　closing in on them from every side.
¹⁵ So that hearts may melt with fear
　　and the fallen be many,
　I have stationed the sword for slaughter^a
　　at all their gates.
　Look! It is forged to strike like lightning,
　　it is grasped for slaughter.
¹⁶ Slash to the right, you sword,
　　then to the left,
　　wherever your blade is turned.
¹⁷ I too will strike my hands together,
　　and my wrath will subside.
　I the Lord have spoken."

¹⁸ The word of the Lord came to me: ¹⁹ "Son of man, mark out two roads for the sword of the king of Babylon to take, both starting from the same country. Make a signpost where the road branches off to the city. ²⁰ Mark out one road for the sword to come against Rabbah of the Ammonites and another against Judah and fortified Jerusalem. ²¹ For the king of Babylon will stop at the fork in the road, at the junction of the two roads, to seek an omen: He will cast lots with arrows, he will consult his idols, he will examine the liver. ²² Into his right hand will come the lot for Jerusalem, where he is to set up battering rams, to give the command to slaughter, to sound the battle cry, to set battering rams against the gates, to build a ramp and to erect siege works. ²³ It will seem like a false omen to those who have sworn allegiance to him, but he will remind them of their guilt and take them captive.

²⁴ "Therefore this is what the Sovereign Lord says: 'Because you people have brought to mind your guilt by your open rebellion, revealing your sins in all that you do—because you have done this, you will be taken captive.

How would examining a liver be an omen? (21:21) Looking at the color and shape of sheep livers to predict the future was common in ancient Babylon and Rome.

---

^a *15* Septuagint; the meaning of the Hebrew for this word is uncertain.

25 "'You profane and wicked prince of Israel, whose day has come, whose time of punishment has reached its climax, 26 this is what the Sovereign LORD says: Take off the turban, remove the crown. It will not be as it was: The lowly will be exalted and the exalted will be brought low. 27 A ruin! A ruin! I will make it a ruin! The crown will not be restored until he to whom it rightfully belongs shall come; to him I will give it.'

28 "And you, son of man, prophesy and say, 'This is what the Sovereign LORD says about the Ammonites and their insults:

"'A sword, a sword,
    drawn for the slaughter,
polished to consume
    and to flash like lightning!
29 Despite false visions concerning you
    and lying divinations about you,
it will be laid on the necks
    of the wicked who are to be slain,
whose day has come,
    whose time of punishment has reached its climax.

30 "'Let the sword return to its sheath.
    In the place where you were created,
in the land of your ancestry,
    I will judge you.
31 I will pour out my wrath on you
    and breathe out my fiery anger against you;
I will deliver you into the hands of brutal men,
    men skilled in destruction.
32 You will be fuel for the fire,
    your blood will be shed in your land,
you will be remembered no more;
    for I the LORD have spoken.'"

JUDGMENT ON JERUSALEM'S SINS

22 The word of the LORD came to me:

2 "Son of man, will you judge her? Will you judge this city of bloodshed? Then confront her with all her detestable practices 3 and say: 'This is what the Sovereign LORD says: You city that brings on herself doom by shedding blood in her midst and defiles herself by making idols, 4 you have become guilty because of the blood you have shed and have become defiled by the idols you have made. You have brought your days to a close, and the end of your years has come. Therefore I will make you an object of scorn to the nations and a laughingstock to all the countries. 5 Those who are near and those who are far away will mock you, you infamous city, full of turmoil.

6 "'See how each of the princes of Israel who are in you uses his power to shed blood. 7 In you they have treated father and mother with contempt; in you they have oppressed the foreigner and mistreated the fatherless and the widow. 8 You have despised my holy things and desecrated my Sabbaths.

Who was the wicked prince of Israel? (21:25)
This was Judah's last king, Zedekiah.

Who wore turbans? (21:26)
Turbans, made of fine linen, were worn by priests. Turbans were also a setting for the crown, and in this verse the turban is worn by a king.

What city was this? (22:2)
This was the city of Jerusalem, the main focus of Ezekiel's prophecy.

What did it mean that they ate at mountain shrines? (22:9)
This referred to pagan worship practices. Sacrifices were offered to pagan gods at altars on high places, and then people would eat the meat of the animal that had been sacrificed.

What is dross? (22:18)
Dross is the mixture of undesirable metals that remains behind when silver is melted to purify it. Here it refers to the Lord's destruction of the wicked.

Who were the wicked people in Jerusalem? (22:25–29)
All of Jerusalem's leaders and people were included: princes, priests, officials, prophets, and people.

⁹In you are slanderers who are bent on shedding blood; in you are those who eat at the mountain shrines and commit lewd acts. ¹⁰In you are those who dishonor their father's bed; in you are those who violate women during their period, when they are ceremonially unclean. ¹¹In you one man commits a detestable offense with his neighbor's wife, another shamefully defiles his daughter-in-law, and another violates his sister, his own father's daughter. ¹²In you are people who accept bribes to shed blood; you take interest and make a profit from the poor. You extort unjust gain from your neighbors. And you have forgotten me, declares the Sovereign LORD.

¹³"'I will surely strike my hands together at the unjust gain you have made and at the blood you have shed in your midst. ¹⁴Will your courage endure or your hands be strong in the day I deal with you? I the LORD have spoken, and I will do it. ¹⁵I will disperse you among the nations and scatter you through the countries; and I will put an end to your uncleanness. ¹⁶When you have been defiled*ᵃ* in the eyes of the nations, you will know that I am the LORD.'"

¹⁷Then the word of the LORD came to me: ¹⁸"Son of man, the people of Israel have become dross to me; all of them are the copper, tin, iron and lead left inside a furnace. They are but the dross of silver. ¹⁹Therefore this is what the Sovereign LORD says: 'Because you have all become dross, I will gather you into Jerusalem. ²⁰As silver, copper, iron, lead and tin are gathered into a furnace to be melted with a fiery blast, so will I gather you in my anger and my wrath and put you inside the city and melt you. ²¹I will gather you and I will blow on you with my fiery wrath, and you will be melted inside her. ²²As silver is melted in a furnace, so you will be melted inside her, and you will know that I the LORD have poured out my wrath on you.'"

²³Again the word of the LORD came to me: ²⁴"Son of man, say to the land, 'You are a land that has not been cleansed or rained on in the day of wrath.' ²⁵There is a conspiracy of her princes*ᵇ* within her like a roaring lion tearing its prey; they devour people, take treasures and precious things and make many widows within her. ²⁶Her priests do violence to my law and profane my holy things; they do not distinguish between the holy and the common; they teach that there is no difference between the unclean and the clean; and they shut their eyes to the keeping of my Sabbaths, so that I am profaned among them. ²⁷Her officials within her are like wolves tearing their prey; they shed blood and kill people to make unjust gain. ²⁸Her prophets whitewash these deeds for them by false visions and lying divinations. They say, 'This is what the Sovereign LORD says'—when the LORD has not spoken. ²⁹The people of the land practice extortion and commit robbery; they oppress the poor and needy and mistreat the foreigner, denying them justice.

³⁰"I looked for someone among them who would build up the wall and stand before me in the gap on behalf of the land so I would not have to destroy it, but I found no one. ³¹So I

ᵃ 16 Or *When I have allotted you your inheritance* *ᵇ 25* Septuagint; Hebrew *prophets*

will pour out my wrath on them and consume them with my
fiery anger, bringing down on their own heads all they have
done, declares the Sovereign Lord."

TWO ADULTEROUS SISTERS

23 The word of the Lord came to me: ² "Son of man,
there were two women, daughters of the same mother. ³ They became prostitutes in Egypt, engaging in prostitution from their youth. In that land their breasts were fondled and their virgin bosoms caressed. ⁴ The older was named
Oholah, and her sister was Oholibah. They were mine and
gave birth to sons and daughters. Oholah is Samaria, and
Oholibah is Jerusalem.

⁵ "Oholah engaged in prostitution while she was still mine;
and she lusted after her lovers, the Assyrians — warriors
⁶ clothed in blue, governors and commanders, all of them
handsome young men, and mounted horsemen. ⁷ She gave
herself as a prostitute to all the elite of the Assyrians and
defiled herself with all the idols of everyone she lusted after.
⁸ She did not give up the prostitution she began in Egypt,
when during her youth men slept with her, caressed her virgin bosom and poured out their lust on her.

⁹ "Therefore I delivered her into the hands of her lovers,
the Assyrians, for whom she lusted. ¹⁰ They stripped her naked, took away her sons and daughters and killed her with
the sword. She became a byword among women, and punishment was inflicted on her.

¹¹ "Her sister Oholibah saw this, yet in her lust and prostitution she was more depraved than her sister. ¹² She too lusted after the Assyrians — governors and commanders, warriors in full dress, mounted horsemen, all handsome young
men. ¹³ I saw that she too defiled herself; both of them went
the same way.

¹⁴ "But she carried her prostitution still further. She saw
men portrayed on a wall, figures of Chaldeans*ᵃ* portrayed
in red, ¹⁵ with belts around their waists and flowing turbans
on their heads; all of them looked like Babylonian chariot
officers, natives of Chaldea.*ᵇ* ¹⁶ As soon as she saw them, she
lusted after them and sent messengers to them in Chaldea.
¹⁷ Then the Babylonians came to her, to the bed of love, and
in their lust they defiled her. After she had been defiled by
them, she turned away from them in disgust. ¹⁸ When she
carried on her prostitution openly and exposed her naked
body, I turned away from her in disgust, just as I had turned
away from her sister. ¹⁹ Yet she became more and more promiscuous as she recalled the days of her youth, when she was
a prostitute in Egypt. ²⁰ There she lusted after her lovers,
whose genitals were like those of donkeys and whose emission was like that of horses. ²¹ So you longed for the lewdness
of your youth, when in Egypt your bosom was caressed and
your young breasts fondled.*ᶜ*

²² "Therefore, Oholibah, this is what the Sovereign Lord
says: I will stir up your lovers against you, those you turned

**What type of prostitution
was this? (23:5)**
This refers to political alliances
with pagan nations, not to idolatry as in chapter 16.

**What did it mean that they
stripped her naked? (23:10)**
This refers to the fall of Samaria
to the Assyrians in 722 – 721 B.C.

ᵃ 14 Or *Babylonians*   *ᵇ 15* Or *Babylonia*; also in verse 16   *ᶜ 21* Syriac (see
also verse 3); Hebrew *caressed because of your young breasts*

What cup was this?
(23:31–34)
This was a symbolic cup filled with God's anger that would destroy Jerusalem.

away from in disgust, and I will bring them against you from every side— ²³the Babylonians and all the Chaldeans, the men of Pekod and Shoa and Koa, and all the Assyrians with them, handsome young men, all of them governors and commanders, chariot officers and men of high rank, all mounted on horses. ²⁴They will come against you with weapons,ᵃ chariots and wagons and with a throng of people; they will take up positions against you on every side with large and small shields and with helmets. I will turn you over to them for punishment, and they will punish you according to their standards. ²⁵I will direct my jealous anger against you, and they will deal with you in fury. They will cut off your noses and your ears, and those of you who are left will fall by the sword. They will take away your sons and daughters, and those of you who are left will be consumed by fire. ²⁶They will also strip you of your clothes and take your fine jewelry. ²⁷So I will put a stop to the lewdness and prostitution you began in Egypt. You will not look on these things with longing or remember Egypt anymore.

²⁸"For this is what the Sovereign LORD says: I am about to deliver you into the hands of those you hate, to those you turned away from in disgust. ²⁹They will deal with you in hatred and take away everything you have worked for. They will leave you stark naked, and the shame of your prostitution will be exposed. Your lewdness and promiscuity ³⁰have brought this on you, because you lusted after the nations and defiled yourself with their idols. ³¹You have gone the way of your sister; so I will put her cup into your hand.

³²"This is what the Sovereign LORD says:

"You will drink your sister's cup,
    a cup large and deep;
it will bring scorn and derision,
    for it holds so much.
³³You will be filled with drunkenness and sorrow,
    the cup of ruin and desolation,
    the cup of your sister Samaria.
³⁴You will drink it and drain it dry
    and chew on its pieces—
    and you will tear your breasts.

I have spoken, declares the Sovereign LORD.

³⁵"Therefore this is what the Sovereign LORD says: Since you have forgotten me and turned your back on me, you must bear the consequences of your lewdness and prostitution."

³⁶The LORD said to me: "Son of man, will you judge Oholah and Oholibah? Then confront them with their detestable practices, ³⁷for they have committed adultery and blood is on their hands. They committed adultery with their idols; they even sacrificed their children, whom they bore to me, as food for them. ³⁸They have also done this to me: At that same time they defiled my sanctuary and desecrated my Sabbaths. ³⁹On the very day they sacrificed their children to their idols, they entered my sanctuary and desecrated it. That is what they did in my house.

ᵃ 24 The meaning of the Hebrew for this word is uncertain.

40 "They even sent messengers for men who came from far away, and when they arrived you bathed yourself for them, applied eye makeup and put on your jewelry. 41 You sat on an elegant couch, with a table spread before it on which you had placed the incense and olive oil that belonged to me.

42 "The noise of a carefree crowd was around her; drunkards were brought from the desert along with men from the rabble, and they put bracelets on the wrists of the woman and her sister and beautiful crowns on their heads. 43 Then I said about the one worn out by adultery, 'Now let them use her as a prostitute, for that is all she is.' 44 And they slept with her. As men sleep with a prostitute, so they slept with those lewd women, Oholah and Oholibah. 45 But righteous judges will sentence them to the punishment of women who commit adultery and shed blood, because they are adulterous and blood is on their hands.

46 "This is what the Sovereign Lord says: Bring a mob against them and give them over to terror and plunder. 47 The mob will stone them and cut them down with their swords; they will kill their sons and daughters and burn down their houses.

48 "So I will put an end to lewdness in the land, that all women may take warning and not imitate you. 49 You will suffer the penalty for your lewdness and bear the consequences of your sins of idolatry. Then you will know that I am the Sovereign Lord."

JERUSALEM AS A COOKING POT

24 In the ninth year, in the tenth month on the tenth day, the word of the Lord came to me: 2 "Son of man, record this date, this very date, because the king of Babylon has laid siege to Jerusalem this very day. 3 Tell this rebellious people a parable and say to them: 'This is what the Sovereign Lord says:

"'Put on the cooking pot; put it on
    and pour water into it.
4 Put into it the pieces of meat,
    all the choice pieces—the leg and the shoulder.
Fill it with the best of these bones;
5   take the pick of the flock.
Pile wood beneath it for the bones;
    bring it to a boil
    and cook the bones in it.

6 "'For this is what the Sovereign Lord says:

"'Woe to the city of bloodshed,
    to the pot now encrusted,
    whose deposit will not go away!
Take the meat out piece by piece
    in whatever order it comes.

7 "'For the blood she shed is in her midst:
    She poured it on the bare rock;
she did not pour it on the ground,
    where the dust would cover it.

How did women in ancient times paint their eyes? (23:40)
Women drew attention to their eyes by painting their eyelids with kohl, a soot-like compound.

What did the choice pieces of meat represent? (24:4)
This referred to the people of Jerusalem who thought they had been spared from exile in 597 B.C. because of their goodness (see Ezekiel 11:3).

What wood was this? (24:5)
This represented Nebuchadnezzar's siege equipment.

⁸To stir up wrath and take revenge
   I put her blood on the bare rock,
     so that it would not be covered.

⁹"'Therefore this is what the Sovereign LORD says:

"'Woe to the city of bloodshed!
   I, too, will pile the wood high.
¹⁰So heap on the wood
   and kindle the fire.
Cook the meat well,
   mixing in the spices;
   and let the bones be charred.
¹¹Then set the empty pot on the coals
   till it becomes hot and its copper glows,
so that its impurities may be melted
   and its deposit burned away.
¹²It has frustrated all efforts;
   its heavy deposit has not been removed,
     not even by fire.

¹³"'Now your impurity is lewdness. Because I tried to cleanse you but you would not be cleansed from your impurity, you will not be clean again until my wrath against you has subsided.

¹⁴"'I the LORD have spoken. The time has come for me to act. I will not hold back; I will not have pity, nor will I relent. You will be judged according to your conduct and your actions, declares the Sovereign LORD.'"

EZEKIEL'S WIFE DIES

¹⁵The word of the LORD came to me: ¹⁶"Son of man, with one blow I am about to take away from you the delight of your eyes. Yet do not lament or weep or shed any tears. ¹⁷Groan quietly; do not mourn for the dead. Keep your turban fastened and your sandals on your feet; do not cover your mustache and beard or eat the customary food of mourners."

¹⁸So I spoke to the people in the morning, and in the evening my wife died. The next morning I did as I had been commanded.

¹⁹Then the people asked me, "Won't you tell us what these things have to do with us? Why are you acting like this?"

²⁰So I said to them, "The word of the LORD came to me: ²¹Say to the people of Israel, 'This is what the Sovereign LORD says: I am about to desecrate my sanctuary—the stronghold in which you take pride, the delight of your eyes, the object of your affection. The sons and daughters you left behind will fall by the sword. ²²And you will do as I have done. You will not cover your mustache and beard or eat the customary food of mourners. ²³You will keep your turbans on your heads and your sandals on your feet. You will not mourn or weep but will waste away because of*ᵃ* your sins and groan among yourselves. ²⁴Ezekiel will be a sign to you; you will do just as he has done. When this happens, you will know that I am the Sovereign LORD.'

ᵃ 23 Or *away in*

What would happen to Jerusalem? (24:11)
After all the people of Jerusalem had been taken away, the city would be set on fire.

Why was Ezekiel supposed to keep his turban fastened? (24:17)
Mourners typically removed their turbans and put dust on their heads as a sign of mourning. Ezekiel was also supposed to keep his sandals on; mourners removed them to show their grief.

How would God desecrate his sanctuary? (24:21)
God would allow Nebuchadnezzar to burn the temple.

²⁵"And you, son of man, on the day I take away their stronghold, their joy and glory, the delight of their eyes, their heart's desire, and their sons and daughters as well— ²⁶on that day a fugitive will come to tell you the news. ²⁷At that time your mouth will be opened; you will speak with him and will no longer be silent. So you will be a sign to them, and they will know that I am the LORD."

A PROPHECY AGAINST AMMON

25 The word of the LORD came to me: ²"Son of man, set your face against the Ammonites and prophesy against them. ³Say to them, 'Hear the word of the Sovereign LORD. This is what the Sovereign LORD says: Because you said "Aha!" over my sanctuary when it was desecrated and over the land of Israel when it was laid waste and over the people of Judah when they went into exile, ⁴therefore I am going to give you to the people of the East as a possession. They will set up their camps and pitch their tents among you; they will eat your fruit and drink your milk. ⁵I will turn Rabbah into a pasture for camels and Ammon into a resting place for sheep. Then you will know that I am the LORD. ⁶For this is what the Sovereign LORD says: Because you have clapped your hands and stamped your feet, rejoicing with all the malice of your heart against the land of Israel, ⁷therefore I will stretch out my hand against you and give you as plunder to the nations. I will wipe you out from among the nations and exterminate you from the countries. I will destroy you, and you will know that I am the LORD.'"

A PROPHECY AGAINST MOAB

⁸"This is what the Sovereign LORD says: 'Because Moab and Seir said, "Look, Judah has become like all the other nations," ⁹therefore I will expose the flank of Moab, beginning at its frontier towns—Beth Jeshimoth, Baal Meon and Kiriathaim—the glory of that land. ¹⁰I will give Moab along with the Ammonites to the people of the East as a possession, so that the Ammonites will not be remembered among the nations; ¹¹and I will inflict punishment on Moab. Then they will know that I am the LORD.'"

A PROPHECY AGAINST EDOM

¹²"This is what the Sovereign LORD says: 'Because Edom took revenge on Judah and became very guilty by doing so, ¹³therefore this is what the Sovereign LORD says: I will stretch out my hand against Edom and kill both man and beast. I will lay it waste, and from Teman to Dedan they will fall by the sword. ¹⁴I will take vengeance on Edom by the hand of my people Israel, and they will deal with Edom in accordance with my anger and my wrath; they will know my vengeance, declares the Sovereign LORD.'"

A PROPHECY AGAINST PHILISTIA

¹⁵"This is what the Sovereign LORD says: 'Because the Philistines acted in vengeance and took revenge with malice in their hearts, and with ancient hostility sought to destroy

Judah's Enemies (25:2,8,12,15)

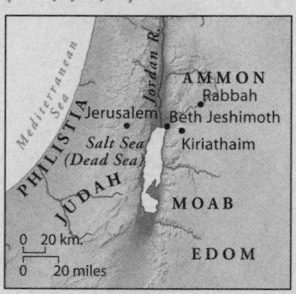

Who were the people of the East? (25:4)
These were probably the nomadic tribes of the desert east of Ammon, though this could be a reference to Nebuchadnezzar and his army.

What was the point of the punishments of these nations? (25:7,11,14,17)
God wanted people to recognize that he was the Lord and that he would not tolerate sin.

Judah, [16] therefore this is what the Sovereign LORD says: I am about to stretch out my hand against the Philistines, and I will wipe out the Kerethites and destroy those remaining along the coast. [17] I will carry out great vengeance on them and punish them in my wrath. Then they will know that I am the LORD, when I take vengeance on them.'"

A PROPHECY AGAINST TYRE

26 In the eleventh month of the twelfth[a] year, on the first day of the month, the word of the LORD came to me: [2] "Son of man, because Tyre has said of Jerusalem, 'Aha! The gate to the nations is broken, and its doors have swung open to me; now that she lies in ruins I will prosper,' [3] therefore this is what the Sovereign LORD says: I am against you, Tyre, and I will bring many nations against you, like the sea casting up its waves. [4] They will destroy the walls of Tyre and pull down her towers; I will scrape away her rubble and make her a bare rock. [5] Out in the sea she will become a place to spread fishnets, for I have spoken, declares the Sovereign LORD. She will become plunder for the nations, [6] and her settlements on the mainland will be ravaged by the sword. Then they will know that I am the LORD.

[7] "For this is what the Sovereign LORD says: From the north I am going to bring against Tyre Nebuchadnezzar[b] king of Babylon, king of kings, with horses and chariots, with horsemen and a great army. [8] He will ravage your settlements on the mainland with the sword; he will set up siege works against you, build a ramp up to your walls and raise his shields against you. [9] He will direct the blows of his battering rams against your walls and demolish your towers with his weapons. [10] His horses will be so many that they will cover you with dust. Your walls will tremble at the noise of the warhorses, wagons and chariots when he enters your gates as men enter a city whose walls have been broken through. [11] The hooves of his horses will trample all your streets; he will kill your people with the sword, and your strong pillars will fall to the ground. [12] They will plunder your wealth and loot your merchandise; they will break down your walls and demolish your fine houses and throw your stones, timber and rubble into the sea. [13] I will put an end to your noisy songs, and the music of your harps will be heard no more. [14] I will make you a bare rock, and you will become a place to spread fishnets. You will never be rebuilt, for I the LORD have spoken, declares the Sovereign LORD.

[15] "This is what the Sovereign LORD says to Tyre: Will not the coastlands tremble at the sound of your fall, when the wounded groan and the slaughter takes place in you? [16] Then all the princes of the coast will step down from their thrones and lay aside their robes and take off their embroidered garments. Clothed with terror, they will sit on the ground, trembling every moment, appalled at you. [17] Then they will take up a lament concerning you and say to you:

Why would Nebuchadnezzar enter Tyre from the north? (26:7)
Nebuchadnezzar would march his army up the Euphrates River Valley rather than crossing the Arabian Desert.

Who were the princes of the coast? (26:16)
They were probably trading partners with Tyre.

---

[a] 1 Probable reading of the original Hebrew text; Masoretic Text does not have *month of the twelfth*.   [b] 7 Hebrew *Nebuchadrezzar*, of which *Nebuchadnezzar* is a variant; here and often in Ezekiel and Jeremiah

"'How you are destroyed, city of renown,
  peopled by men of the sea!
You were a power on the seas,
  you and your citizens;
you put your terror
  on all who lived there.
¹⁸ Now the coastlands tremble
  on the day of your fall;
the islands in the sea
  are terrified at your collapse.'

¹⁹ "This is what the Sovereign Lord says: When I make you a desolate city, like cities no longer inhabited, and when I bring the ocean depths over you and its vast waters cover you, ²⁰ then I will bring you down with those who go down to the pit, to the people of long ago. I will make you dwell in the earth below, as in ancient ruins, with those who go down to the pit, and you will not return or take your place^a in the land of the living. ²¹ I will bring you to a horrible end and you will be no more. You will be sought, but you will never again be found, declares the Sovereign Lord."

A LAMENT OVER TYRE

27 The word of the Lord came to me: ²"Son of man, take up a lament concerning Tyre. ³ Say to Tyre, situated at the gateway to the sea, merchant of peoples on many coasts, 'This is what the Sovereign Lord says:

"'You say, Tyre,
  "I am perfect in beauty."
⁴ Your domain was on the high seas;
  your builders brought your beauty to perfection.
⁵ They made all your timbers
  of juniper from Senir^b;
they took a cedar from Lebanon
  to make a mast for you.
⁶ Of oaks from Bashan
  they made your oars;
of cypress wood^c from the coasts of Cyprus
  they made your deck, adorned with ivory.
⁷ Fine embroidered linen from Egypt was your sail
  and served as your banner;
your awnings were of blue and purple
  from the coasts of Elishah.
⁸ Men of Sidon and Arvad were your oarsmen;
  your skilled men, Tyre, were aboard as your sailors.
⁹ Veteran craftsmen of Byblos were on board
  as shipwrights to caulk your seams.
All the ships of the sea and their sailors
  came alongside to trade for your wares.
¹⁰ "'Men of Persia, Lydia and Put
  served as soldiers in your army.
They hung their shields and helmets on your walls,
  bringing you splendor.

What were the ocean depths? (26:19)
This refers to the primeval, chaotic mass — the deep of Genesis 1:2.

Why was Tyre a merchant on many coasts? (27:2)
Since their territory was a narrow strip of land on the coast of the Mediterranean Sea, they became the sailors and navigators of the ancient world.

---

^a 20 Septuagint; Hebrew *return, and I will give glory*   ^b 5 That is, Mount Hermon   ^c 6 Targum; the Masoretic Text has a different division of the consonants.

^{11}Men of Arvad and Helek
  guarded your walls on every side;
men of Gammad
  were in your towers.
They hung their shields around your walls;
  they brought your beauty to perfection.

Why are all of Tyre's trading partners mentioned?
(27:12–24)
It was important to understand
the extent of Tyre's wealth and
influence in order to understand
how far the city fell.

^{12}"'Tarshish did business with you because of your great wealth of goods; they exchanged silver, iron, tin and lead for your merchandise.

^{13}"'Greece, Tubal and Meshek did business with you; they traded human beings and articles of bronze for your wares.

^{14}"'Men of Beth Togarmah exchanged chariot horses, cavalry horses and mules for your merchandise.

^{15}"'The men of Rhodes^a traded with you, and many coastlands were your customers; they paid you with ivory tusks and ebony.

^{16}"'Aram^b did business with you because of your many products; they exchanged turquoise, purple fabric, embroidered work, fine linen, coral and rubies for your merchandise.

^{17}"'Judah and Israel traded with you; they exchanged wheat from Minnith and confections,^{c} honey, olive oil and balm for your wares.

^{18}"'Damascus did business with you because of your many products and great wealth of goods. They offered wine from Helbon, wool from Zahar ^{19}and casks of wine from Izal in exchange for your wares: wrought iron, cassia and calamus.

^{20}"'Dedan traded in saddle blankets with you.

^{21}"'Arabia and all the princes of Kedar were your customers; they did business with you in lambs, rams and goats.

^{22}"'The merchants of Sheba and Raamah traded with you; for your merchandise they exchanged the finest of all kinds of spices and precious stones, and gold.

^{23}"'Harran, Kanneh and Eden and merchants of Sheba, Ashur and Kilmad traded with you. ^{24}In your marketplace they traded with you beautiful garments, blue fabric, embroidered work and multicolored rugs with cords twisted and tightly knotted.

^{25}"'The ships of Tarshish serve
  as carriers for your wares.
You are filled with heavy cargo
  as you sail the sea.
^{26}Your oarsmen take you
  out to the high seas.
But the east wind will break you to pieces
  far out at sea.
^{27}Your wealth, merchandise and wares,
  your mariners, sailors and shipwrights,
your merchants and all your soldiers,
  and everyone else on board
will sink into the heart of the sea
  on the day of your shipwreck.

Why was the east wind so
dangerous? (27:26)
An east wind could be disastrous
at sea and on land. Here it may
have been a symbol for Nebuchadnezzar.

^{a} 15 Septuagint; Hebrew *Dedan* ^{b} 16 Most Hebrew manuscripts; some
Hebrew manuscripts and Syriac *Edom* ^{c} 17 The meaning of the Hebrew
for this word is uncertain.

²⁸ The shorelands will quake
    when your sailors cry out.
²⁹ All who handle the oars
    will abandon their ships;
  the mariners and all the sailors
    will stand on the shore.
³⁰ They will raise their voice
    and cry bitterly over you;
  they will sprinkle dust on their heads
    and roll in ashes.
³¹ They will shave their heads because of you
    and will put on sackcloth.
  They will weep over you with anguish of soul
    and with bitter mourning.
³² As they wail and mourn over you,
    they will take up a lament concerning you:
  "Who was ever silenced like Tyre,
    surrounded by the sea?"
³³ When your merchandise went out on the seas,
    you satisfied many nations;
  with your great wealth and your wares
    you enriched the kings of the earth.
³⁴ Now you are shattered by the sea
    in the depths of the waters;
  your wares and all your company
    have gone down with you.
³⁵ All who live in the coastlands
    are appalled at you;
  their kings shudder with horror
    and their faces are distorted with fear.
³⁶ The merchants among the nations scoff at you;
    you have come to a horrible end
    and will be no more.'"

A PROPHECY AGAINST THE KING OF TYRE

28 The word of the LORD came to me: ²"Son of man, say to the ruler of Tyre, 'This is what the Sovereign LORD says:

  "'In the pride of your heart
    you say, "I am a god;
  I sit on the throne of a god
    in the heart of the seas."
  But you are a mere mortal and not a god,
    though you think you are as wise as a god.
³ Are you wiser than Daniel*?
    Is no secret hidden from you?
⁴ By your wisdom and understanding
    you have gained wealth for yourself
  and amassed gold and silver
    in your treasuries.
⁵ By your great skill in trading
    you have increased your wealth,
  and because of your wealth
    your heart has grown proud.

---

a 3 Or Danel, a man of renown in ancient literature

Why would other nations mourn Tyre's downfall? (27:28–32)
Tyre had made many nations wealthy, so they lost a source of income and probably felt vulnerable.

Why would they sprinkle dust on their heads and roll in ashes? (27:30)
These were symbols of mourning.

Why were the kings afraid? (27:35)
They feared that just as Babylon had destroyed Tyre, they might also destroy them.

Who were these foreigners? (28:7)
This refers to the Babylonians.

What was the pit? (28:8)
This was a metaphor for the grave.

What does the term uncircumcised mean here? (28:10)
Here it does not refer to the act of physical circumcision. Instead, it carries the sense of one who is a barbarian.

What did it mean for Ezekiel to say that the king of Tyre was in Eden? (28:13)
Ezekiel used images of the creation and the fall to describe the career of the king of Tyre and the depths to which he fell.

⁶"'Therefore this is what the Sovereign LORD says:

"'Because you think you are wise,
    as wise as a god,
⁷I am going to bring foreigners against you,
    the most ruthless of nations;
they will draw their swords against your beauty
    and wisdom
    and pierce your shining splendor.
⁸They will bring you down to the pit,
    and you will die a violent death
    in the heart of the seas.
⁹Will you then say, "I am a god,"
    in the presence of those who kill you?
You will be but a mortal, not a god,
    in the hands of those who slay you.
¹⁰You will die the death of the uncircumcised
    at the hands of foreigners.

I have spoken, declares the Sovereign LORD.'"

¹¹The word of the LORD came to me: ¹²"Son of man, take up a lament concerning the king of Tyre and say to him: 'This is what the Sovereign LORD says:

"'You were the seal of perfection,
    full of wisdom and perfect in beauty.
¹³You were in Eden,
    the garden of God;
every precious stone adorned you:
    carnelian, chrysolite and emerald,
    topaz, onyx and jasper,
    lapis lazuli, turquoise and beryl.ᵃ
Your settings and mountingsᵇ were made of gold;
    on the day you were created they were prepared.
¹⁴You were anointed as a guardian cherub,
    for so I ordained you.
You were on the holy mount of God;
    you walked among the fiery stones.
¹⁵You were blameless in your ways
    from the day you were created
    till wickedness was found in you.
¹⁶Through your widespread trade
    you were filled with violence,
    and you sinned.
So I drove you in disgrace from the mount
    of God,
and I expelled you, guardian cherub,
    from among the fiery stones.
¹⁷Your heart became proud
    on account of your beauty,
and you corrupted your wisdom
    because of your splendor.
So I threw you to the earth;
    I made a spectacle of you before kings.

ᵃ 13 The precise identification of some of these precious stones is uncertain.
ᵇ 13 The meaning of the Hebrew for this phrase is uncertain.

¹⁸ By your many sins and dishonest trade
    you have desecrated your sanctuaries.
So I made a fire come out from you,
    and it consumed you,
and I reduced you to ashes on the ground
    in the sight of all who were watching.
¹⁹ All the nations who knew you
    are appalled at you;
you have come to a horrible end
    and will be no more.'"

A PROPHECY AGAINST SIDON

²⁰ The word of the LORD came to me: ²¹ "Son of man, set your face against Sidon; prophesy against her ²² and say: 'This is what the Sovereign LORD says:

"'I am against you, Sidon,
    and among you I will display my glory.
You will know that I am the LORD,
    when I inflict punishment on you
    and within you am proved to be holy.
²³ I will send a plague upon you
    and make blood flow in your streets.
The slain will fall within you,
    with the sword against you on every side.
Then you will know that I am the LORD.

²⁴ "'No longer will the people of Israel have malicious neighbors who are painful briers and sharp thorns. Then they will know that I am the Sovereign LORD.

²⁵ "'This is what the Sovereign LORD says: When I gather the people of Israel from the nations where they have been scattered, I will be proved holy through them in the sight of the nations. Then they will live in their own land, which I gave to my servant Jacob. ²⁶ They will live there in safety and will build houses and plant vineyards; they will live in safety when I inflict punishment on all their neighbors who maligned them. Then they will know that I am the LORD their God.'"

A PROPHECY AGAINST EGYPT
JUDGMENT ON PHARAOH

29 In the tenth year, in the tenth month on the twelfth day, the word of the LORD came to me: ² "Son of man, set your face against Pharaoh king of Egypt and prophesy against him and against all Egypt. ³ Speak to him and say: 'This is what the Sovereign LORD says:

"'I am against you, Pharaoh king of Egypt,
    you great monster lying among your streams.
You say, "The Nile belongs to me;
    I made it for myself."
⁴ But I will put hooks in your jaws
    and make the fish of your streams stick to your
        scales.
I will pull you out from among your streams,
    with all the fish sticking to your scales.

What would life be like for the returning exiles? (28:26)
They would live in peace and safety. They would have houses and vineyards — aspects of a good life.

What was this great monster? (29:3)
This was probably a crocodile.

Why would this be a disgrace for the pharaoh? (29:5)
The Egyptians believed in an afterlife and made great preparations for it, such as building pyramids.

⁵I will leave you in the desert,
　　you and all the fish of your streams.
You will fall on the open field
　　and not be gathered or picked up.
I will give you as food
　　to the beasts of the earth and the birds of the sky.

⁶Then all who live in Egypt will know that I am the LORD.

⁷"'You have been a staff of reed for the people of Israel. ⁷When they grasped you with their hands, you splintered and you tore open their shoulders; when they leaned on you, you broke and their backs were wrenched.*ᵃ*

⁸"'Therefore this is what the Sovereign LORD says: I will bring a sword against you and kill both man and beast. ⁹Egypt will become a desolate wasteland. Then they will know that I am the LORD.

"'Because you said, "The Nile is mine; I made it," ¹⁰therefore I am against you and against your streams, and I will make the land of Egypt a ruin and a desolate waste from Migdol to Aswan, as far as the border of Cush.*ᵇ* ¹¹The foot of neither man nor beast will pass through it; no one will live there for forty years. ¹²I will make the land of Egypt desolate among devastated lands, and her cities will lie desolate forty years among ruined cities. And I will disperse the Egyptians among the nations and scatter them through the countries.

¹³"'Yet this is what the Sovereign LORD says: At the end of forty years I will gather the Egyptians from the nations where they were scattered. ¹⁴I will bring them back from captivity and return them to Upper Egypt, the land of their ancestry. There they will be a lowly kingdom. ¹⁵It will be the lowliest of kingdoms and will never again exalt itself above the other nations. I will make it so weak that it will never again rule over the nations. ¹⁶Egypt will no longer be a source of confidence for the people of Israel but will be a reminder of their sin in turning to her for help. Then they will know that I am the Sovereign LORD.'"

What was the significance of 40 years? (29:13)
Forty years was sometimes used to symbolize a long and difficult period of time. It is a significant number that occurs throughout the Bible.

NEBUCHADNEZZAR'S REWARD

¹⁷In the twenty-seventh year, in the first month on the first day, the word of the LORD came to me: ¹⁸"Son of man, Nebuchadnezzar king of Babylon drove his army in a hard campaign against Tyre; every head was rubbed bare and every shoulder made raw. Yet he and his army got no reward from the campaign he led against Tyre. ¹⁹Therefore this is what the Sovereign LORD says: I am going to give Egypt to Nebuchadnezzar king of Babylon, and he will carry off its wealth. He will loot and plunder the land as pay for his army. ²⁰I have given him Egypt as a reward for his efforts because he and his army did it for me, declares the Sovereign LORD.

²¹"On that day I will make a horn*ᶜ* grow for the Israelites, and I will open your mouth among them. Then they will know that I am the LORD."

ᵃ 7 Syriac (see also Septuagint and Vulgate); Hebrew *and you caused their backs to stand*　　*ᵇ* 10 That is, the upper Nile region　　*ᶜ* 21 *Horn* here symbolizes strength.

A LAMENT OVER EGYPT

30

The word of the LORD came to me: [2]"Son of man, prophesy and say: 'This is what the Sovereign LORD says:

"'Wail and say,
    "Alas for that day!"
[3]For the day is near,
    the day of the LORD is near—
a day of clouds,
    a time of doom for the nations.
[4]A sword will come against Egypt,
    and anguish will come upon Cush.[a]
When the slain fall in Egypt,
    her wealth will be carried away
    and her foundations torn down.

[5]Cush and Libya, Lydia and all Arabia, Kub and the people of the covenant land will fall by the sword along with Egypt.

[6]"'This is what the LORD says:

"'The allies of Egypt will fall
    and her proud strength will fail.
From Migdol to Aswan
    they will fall by the sword within her,
                declares the Sovereign LORD.
[7]"'They will be desolate
    among desolate lands,
and their cities will lie
    among ruined cities.
[8]Then they will know that I am the LORD,
    when I set fire to Egypt
    and all her helpers are crushed.

[9]"'On that day messengers will go out from me in ships to frighten Cush out of her complacency. Anguish will take hold of them on the day of Egypt's doom, for it is sure to come.

[10]"'This is what the Sovereign LORD says:

"'I will put an end to the hordes of Egypt
    by the hand of Nebuchadnezzar king of Babylon.
[11]He and his army—the most ruthless of nations—
    will be brought in to destroy the land.
They will draw their swords against Egypt
    and fill the land with the slain.
[12]I will dry up the waters of the Nile
    and sell the land to an evil nation;
by the hand of foreigners
    I will lay waste the land and everything in it.

I the LORD have spoken.

[13]"'This is what the Sovereign LORD says:

"'I will destroy the idols
    and put an end to the images in Memphis.
No longer will there be a prince in Egypt,
    and I will spread fear throughout the land.

[a] *4 That is, the upper Nile region; also in verses 5 and 9*

Who was the "sword"? (30:4)
The sword referred to Nebuchadnezzar.

What was "the most ruthless of nations"? (30:11)
This was a common description for the Babylonians, who were known for their cruelty.

¹⁴ I will lay waste Upper Egypt,
    set fire to Zoan
    and inflict punishment on Thebes.
¹⁵ I will pour out my wrath on Pelusium,
    the stronghold of Egypt,
    and wipe out the hordes of Thebes.
¹⁶ I will set fire to Egypt;
    Pelusium will writhe in agony.
Thebes will be taken by storm;
    Memphis will be in constant distress.
¹⁷ The young men of Heliopolis and Bubastis
    will fall by the sword,
    and the cities themselves will go into captivity.
¹⁸ Dark will be the day at Tahpanhes
    when I break the yoke of Egypt;
    there her proud strength will come to an end.
She will be covered with clouds,
    and her villages will go into captivity.
¹⁹ So I will inflict punishment on Egypt,
    and they will know that I am the Lord.'"

PHARAOH'S ARMS ARE BROKEN

²⁰ In the eleventh year, in the first month on the seventh day, the word of the Lord came to me: ²¹ "Son of man, I have broken the arm of Pharaoh king of Egypt. It has not been bound up to be healed or put in a splint so that it may become strong enough to hold a sword. ²² Therefore this is what the Sovereign Lord says: I am against Pharaoh king of Egypt. I will break both his arms, the good arm as well as the broken one, and make the sword fall from his hand. ²³ I will disperse the Egyptians among the nations and scatter them through the countries. ²⁴ I will strengthen the arms of the king of Babylon and put my sword in his hand, but I will break the arms of Pharaoh, and he will groan before him like a mortally wounded man. ²⁵ I will strengthen the arms of the king of Babylon, but the arms of Pharaoh will fall limp. Then they will know that I am the Lord, when I put my sword into the hand of the king of Babylon and he brandishes it against Egypt. ²⁶ I will disperse the Egyptians among the nations and scatter them through the countries. Then they will know that I am the Lord."

PHARAOH AS A FELLED CEDAR OF LEBANON

31 In the eleventh year, in the third month on the first day, the word of the Lord came to me: ² "Son of man, say to Pharaoh king of Egypt and to his hordes:

"'Who can be compared with you in majesty?
³ Consider Assyria, once a cedar in Lebanon,
    with beautiful branches overshadowing the forest;
it towered on high,
    its top above the thick foliage.
⁴ The waters nourished it,
    deep springs made it grow tall;
their streams flowed
    all around its base
and sent their channels
    to all the trees of the field.

How were Pharaoh's arms broken? (30:24)
The language is symbolic. It refers to Pharaoh's defeat by Nebuchadnezzar.

Why was Assyria compared to a cedar? (31:3)
Assyria had once been a great empire, mighty and strong like a cedar tree. However, after being destroyed by the Babylonians, Assyria passed from history.

What were these waters? (31:4)
These were the Tigris and Euphrates Rivers.

⁵ So it towered higher
    than all the trees of the field;
its boughs increased
    and its branches grew long,
    spreading because of abundant waters.
⁶ All the birds of the sky
    nested in its boughs,
all the animals of the wild
    gave birth under its branches;
all the great nations
    lived in its shade.
⁷ It was majestic in beauty,
    with its spreading boughs,
for its roots went down
    to abundant waters.
⁸ The cedars in the garden of God
    could not rival it,
nor could the junipers
    equal its boughs,
nor could the plane trees
    compare with its branches—
no tree in the garden of God
    could match its beauty.
⁹ I made it beautiful
    with abundant branches,
the envy of all the trees of Eden
    in the garden of God.

¹⁰ "'Therefore this is what the Sovereign LORD says: Because the great cedar towered over the thick foliage, and because it was proud of its height, ¹¹ I gave it into the hands of the ruler of the nations, for him to deal with according to its wickedness. I cast it aside, ¹² and the most ruthless of foreign nations cut it down and left it. Its boughs fell on the mountains and in all the valleys; its branches lay broken in all the ravines of the land. All the nations of the earth came out from under its shade and left it. ¹³ All the birds settled on the fallen tree, and all the wild animals lived among its branches. ¹⁴ Therefore no other trees by the waters are ever to tower proudly on high, lifting their tops above the thick foliage. No other trees so well-watered are ever to reach such a height; they are all destined for death, for the earth below, among mortals who go down to the realm of the dead.

¹⁵ "'This is what the Sovereign LORD says: On the day it was brought down to the realm of the dead I covered the deep springs with mourning for it; I held back its streams, and its abundant waters were restrained. Because of it I clothed Lebanon with gloom, and all the trees of the field withered away. ¹⁶ I made the nations tremble at the sound of its fall when I brought it down to the realm of the dead to be with those who go down to the pit. Then all the trees of Eden, the choicest and best of Lebanon, the well-watered trees, were consoled in the earth below. ¹⁷ They too, like the great cedar, had gone down to the realm of the dead, to those killed by the sword, along with the armed men who lived in its shade among the nations.

What was Ezekiel's warning to the pharaoh? (31:18)
God would bring judgment to Egypt, just as he had judged Assyria.

What metaphors did Ezekiel use to describe Egypt? (32:2)
He compared it to a lion and a monster. The lion was a symbol of royalty and grandeur. The monster was a crocodile, which lived in the Nile River.

18 "'Which of the trees of Eden can be compared with you in splendor and majesty? Yet you, too, will be brought down with the trees of Eden to the earth below; you will lie among the uncircumcised, with those killed by the sword.

"'This is Pharaoh and all his hordes, declares the Sovereign LORD.'"

A LAMENT OVER PHARAOH

32 In the twelfth year, in the twelfth month on the first day, the word of the LORD came to me: ² "Son of man, take up a lament concerning Pharaoh king of Egypt and say to him:

"'You are like a lion among the nations;
   you are like a monster in the seas
thrashing about in your streams,
   churning the water with your feet
   and muddying the streams.

³ "'This is what the Sovereign LORD says:

"'With a great throng of people
   I will cast my net over you,
   and they will haul you up in my net.
⁴ I will throw you on the land
   and hurl you on the open field.
I will let all the birds of the sky settle on you
   and all the animals of the wild gorge themselves
      on you.
⁵ I will spread your flesh on the mountains
   and fill the valleys with your remains.
⁶ I will drench the land with your flowing blood
   all the way to the mountains,
   and the ravines will be filled with your flesh.
⁷ When I snuff you out, I will cover the heavens
   and darken their stars;
I will cover the sun with a cloud,
   and the moon will not give its light.
⁸ All the shining lights in the heavens
   I will darken over you;
I will bring darkness over your land,
                     declares the Sovereign LORD.
⁹ I will trouble the hearts of many peoples
   when I bring about your destruction among
      the nations,
   among*ᵃ* lands you have not known.
¹⁰ I will cause many peoples to be appalled at you,
   and their kings will shudder with horror because
      of you
   when I brandish my sword before them.
On the day of your downfall
   each of them will tremble
   every moment for his life.

¹¹ "'For this is what the Sovereign LORD says:

"'The sword of the king of Babylon
   will come against you.

ᵃ 9 Hebrew; Septuagint bring you into captivity among the nations, / to

¹²I will cause your hordes to fall
  by the swords of mighty men—
  the most ruthless of all nations.
They will shatter the pride of Egypt,
  and all her hordes will be overthrown.
¹³I will destroy all her cattle
  from beside abundant waters
no longer to be stirred by the foot of man
  or muddied by the hooves of cattle.
¹⁴Then I will let her waters settle
  and make her streams flow like oil,
                    declares the Sovereign LORD.
¹⁵When I make Egypt desolate
  and strip the land of everything in it,
when I strike down all who live there,
  then they will know that I am the LORD.'

¹⁶"This is the lament they will chant for her. The daughters of the nations will chant it; for Egypt and all her hordes they will chant it, declares the Sovereign LORD."

EGYPT'S DESCENT INTO THE REALM OF THE DEAD

¹⁷In the twelfth year, on the fifteenth day of the month, the word of the LORD came to me: ¹⁸"Son of man, wail for the hordes of Egypt and consign to the earth below both her and the daughters of mighty nations, along with those who go down to the pit. ¹⁹Say to them, 'Are you more favored than others? Go down and be laid among the uncircumcised.' ²⁰They will fall among those killed by the sword. The sword is drawn; let her be dragged off with all her hordes. ²¹From within the realm of the dead the mighty leaders will say of Egypt and her allies, 'They have come down and they lie with the uncircumcised, with those killed by the sword.'

²²"Assyria is there with her whole army; she is surrounded by the graves of all her slain, all who have fallen by the sword. ²³Their graves are in the depths of the pit and her army lies around her grave. All who had spread terror in the land of the living are slain, fallen by the sword.

²⁴"Elam is there, with all her hordes around her grave. All of them are slain, fallen by the sword. All who had spread terror in the land of the living went down uncircumcised to the earth below. They bear their shame with those who go down to the pit. ²⁵A bed is made for her among the slain, with all her hordes around her grave. All of them are uncircumcised, killed by the sword. Because their terror had spread in the land of the living, they bear their shame with those who go down to the pit; they are laid among the slain.

²⁶"Meshek and Tubal are there, with all their hordes around their graves. All of them are uncircumcised, killed by the sword because they spread their terror in the land of the living. ²⁷But they do not lie with the fallen warriors of old,ᵃ who went down to the realm of the dead with their weapons of war—their swords placed under their heads and their

What was the pride of Egypt? (32:12)
This referred to the Egyptian army.

How would leaders speak from the grave? (32:21)
The bodies of the leaders killed by the Babylonians would be a symbolic message that no nation could withstand them.

ᵃ 27 Septuagint; Hebrew *warriors who were uncircumcised*

shields[a] resting on their bones—though these warriors also had terrorized the land of the living.

²⁸"You too, Pharaoh, will be broken and will lie among the uncircumcised, with those killed by the sword.

²⁹"Edom is there, her kings and all her princes; despite their power, they are laid with those killed by the sword. They lie with the uncircumcised, with those who go down to the pit.

³⁰"All the princes of the north and all the Sidonians are there; they went down with the slain in disgrace despite the terror caused by their power. They lie uncircumcised with those killed by the sword and bear their shame with those who go down to the pit.

³¹"Pharaoh—he and all his army—will see them and he will be consoled for all his hordes that were killed by the sword, declares the Sovereign Lord. ³²Although I had him spread terror in the land of the living, Pharaoh and all his hordes will be laid among the uncircumcised, with those killed by the sword, declares the Sovereign Lord."

RENEWAL OF EZEKIEL'S CALL AS WATCHMAN

33 The word of the Lord came to me: ²"Son of man, speak to your people and say to them: 'When I bring the sword against a land, and the people of the land choose one of their men and make him their watchman, ³and he sees the sword coming against the land and blows the trumpet to warn the people, ⁴then if anyone hears the trumpet but does not heed the warning and the sword comes and takes their life, their blood will be on their own head. ⁵Since they heard the sound of the trumpet but did not heed the warning, their blood will be on their own head. If they had heeded the warning, they would have saved themselves. ⁶But if the watchman sees the sword coming and does not blow the trumpet to warn the people and the sword comes and takes someone's life, that person's life will be taken because of their sin, but I will hold the watchman accountable for their blood.'

⁷"Son of man, I have made you a watchman for the people of Israel; so hear the word I speak and give them warning from me. ⁸When I say to the wicked, 'You wicked person, you will surely die,' and you do not speak out to dissuade them from their ways, that wicked person will die for[b] their sin, and I will hold you accountable for their blood. ⁹But if you do warn the wicked person to turn from their ways and they do not do so, they will die for their sin, though you yourself will be saved.

¹⁰"Son of man, say to the Israelites, 'This is what you are saying: "Our offenses and sins weigh us down, and we are wasting away because of[c] them. How then can we live?"' ¹¹Say to them, 'As surely as I live, declares the Sovereign Lord, I take no pleasure in the death of the wicked, but rather that they turn from their ways and live. Turn! Turn from your evil ways! Why will you die, people of Israel?'

What kind of trumpet was this? (33:3)
This was an instrument often used to signal danger. It was made from a ram's horn.

What type of warning was this? (33:6–9)
God warned Ezekiel that he would be held accountable if he was like a poor watchman and failed to warn the people to repent.

---

^a 27 Probable reading of the original Hebrew text; Masoretic Text *punishment*   ^b 8 Or *in*; also in verse 9   ^c 10 Or *away in*

¹²"Therefore, son of man, say to your people, 'If someone who is righteous disobeys, that person's former righteousness will count for nothing. And if someone who is wicked repents, that person's former wickedness will not bring condemnation. The righteous person who sins will not be allowed to live even though they were formerly righteous.' ¹³If I tell a righteous person that they will surely live, but then they trust in their righteousness and do evil, none of the righteous things that person has done will be remembered; they will die for the evil they have done. ¹⁴And if I say to a wicked person, 'You will surely die,' but they then turn away from their sin and do what is just and right— ¹⁵if they give back what they took in pledge for a loan, return what they have stolen, follow the decrees that give life, and do no evil—that person will surely live; they will not die. ¹⁶None of the sins that person has committed will be remembered against them. They have done what is just and right; they will surely live.

¹⁷"Yet your people say, 'The way of the Lord is not just.' But it is their way that is not just. ¹⁸If a righteous person turns from their righteousness and does evil, they will die for it. ¹⁹And if a wicked person turns away from their wickedness and does what is just and right, they will live by doing so. ²⁰Yet you Israelites say, 'The way of the Lord is not just.' But I will judge each of you according to your own ways."

JERUSALEM'S FALL EXPLAINED

²¹In the twelfth year of our exile, in the tenth month on the fifth day, a man who had escaped from Jerusalem came to me and said, "The city has fallen!" ²²Now the evening before the man arrived, the hand of the LORD was on me, and he opened my mouth before the man came to me in the morning. So my mouth was opened and I was no longer silent.

²³Then the word of the LORD came to me: ²⁴"Son of man, the people living in those ruins in the land of Israel are saying, 'Abraham was only one man, yet he possessed the land. But we are many; surely the land has been given to us as our possession.' ²⁵Therefore say to them, 'This is what the Sovereign LORD says: Since you eat meat with the blood still in it and look to your idols and shed blood, should you then possess the land? ²⁶You rely on your sword, you do detestable things, and each of you defiles his neighbor's wife. Should you then possess the land?'

²⁷"Say this to them: 'This is what the Sovereign LORD says: As surely as I live, those who are left in the ruins will fall by the sword, those out in the country I will give to the wild animals to be devoured, and those in strongholds and caves will die of a plague. ²⁸I will make the land a desolate waste, and her proud strength will come to an end, and the mountains of Israel will become desolate so that no one will cross them. ²⁹Then they will know that I am the LORD, when I have made the land a desolate waste because of all the detestable things they have done.'

³⁰"As for you, son of man, your people are talking together about you by the walls and at the doors of the houses, saying to each other, 'Come and hear the message that has come

How did God explain that he was just? (33:17–20)
God said that he would punish those who turned away from him and spare those who repented and turned back to him.

Who were the people living in the ruins? (33:24)
These were the people living in Jerusalem who were not exiled in 586 B.C.

How did God assure Ezekiel?
(33:30–33)
God told him that although the people listened to his words, they did not put them into practice. But God also said that when they experienced the fulfillment of the prophecies, they would know that Ezekiel had been a true prophet.

Who were the shepherds of Israel? (34:2)
These were the people responsible for providing leadership, especially the kings and their officials but also the prophets and priests.

How were the people of Israel scattered like sheep? (34:5–6)
Ezekiel frequently used this metaphor to describe how the people had been exiled and scattered among the nations.

How would God become the people's shepherd? (34:11–16)
The Lord would search for his scattered people and bring them back from captivity. He would rule them directly, using leaders he appointed, rather than allowing kings to rule the people.

from the Lord.' ³¹My people come to you, as they usually do, and sit before you to hear your words, but they do not put them into practice. Their mouths speak of love, but their hearts are greedy for unjust gain. ³²Indeed, to them you are nothing more than one who sings love songs with a beautiful voice and plays an instrument well, for they hear your words but do not put them into practice.

³³"When all this comes true—and it surely will—then they will know that a prophet has been among them."

THE LORD WILL BE ISRAEL'S SHEPHERD

34 The word of the Lord came to me: ²"Son of man, prophesy against the shepherds of Israel; prophesy and say to them: 'This is what the Sovereign Lord says: Woe to you shepherds of Israel who only take care of yourselves! Should not shepherds take care of the flock? ³You eat the curds, clothe yourselves with the wool and slaughter the choice animals, but you do not take care of the flock. ⁴You have not strengthened the weak or healed the sick or bound up the injured. You have not brought back the strays or searched for the lost. You have ruled them harshly and brutally. ⁵So they were scattered because there was no shepherd, and when they were scattered they became food for all the wild animals. ⁶My sheep wandered over all the mountains and on every high hill. They were scattered over the whole earth, and no one searched or looked for them.

⁷"'Therefore, you shepherds, hear the word of the Lord: ⁸As surely as I live, declares the Sovereign Lord, because my flock lacks a shepherd and so has been plundered and has become food for all the wild animals, and because my shepherds did not search for my flock but cared for themselves rather than for my flock, ⁹therefore, you shepherds, hear the word of the Lord: ¹⁰This is what the Sovereign Lord says: I am against the shepherds and will hold them accountable for my flock. I will remove them from tending the flock so that the shepherds can no longer feed themselves. I will rescue my flock from their mouths, and it will no longer be food for them.

¹¹"'For this is what the Sovereign Lord says: I myself will search for my sheep and look after them. ¹²As a shepherd looks after his scattered flock when he is with them, so will I look after my sheep. I will rescue them from all the places where they were scattered on a day of clouds and darkness. ¹³I will bring them out from the nations and gather them from the countries, and I will bring them into their own land. I will pasture them on the mountains of Israel, in the ravines and in all the settlements in the land. ¹⁴I will tend them in a good pasture, and the mountain heights of Israel will be their grazing land. There they will lie down in good grazing land, and there they will feed in a rich pasture on the mountains of Israel. ¹⁵I myself will tend my sheep and have them lie down, declares the Sovereign Lord. ¹⁶I will search for the lost and bring back the strays. I will bind up the injured and strengthen the weak, but the sleek and the strong I will destroy. I will shepherd the flock with justice.

¹⁷"'As for you, my flock, this is what the Sovereign LORD says: I will judge between one sheep and another, and between rams and goats. ¹⁸Is it not enough for you to feed on the good pasture? Must you also trample the rest of your pasture with your feet? Is it not enough for you to drink clear water? Must you also muddy the rest with your feet? ¹⁹Must my flock feed on what you have trampled and drink what you have muddied with your feet?

²⁰"'Therefore this is what the Sovereign LORD says to them: See, I myself will judge between the fat sheep and the lean sheep. ²¹Because you shove with flank and shoulder, butting all the weak sheep with your horns until you have driven them away, ²²I will save my flock, and they will no longer be plundered. I will judge between one sheep and another. ²³I will place over them one shepherd, my servant David, and he will tend them; he will tend them and be their shepherd. ²⁴I the LORD will be their God, and my servant David will be prince among them. I the LORD have spoken.

²⁵"'I will make a covenant of peace with them and rid the land of savage beasts so that they may live in the wilderness and sleep in the forests in safety. ²⁶I will make them and the places surrounding my hill a blessing.ᵃ I will send down showers in season; there will be showers of blessing. ²⁷The trees will yield their fruit and the ground will yield its crops; the people will be secure in their land. They will know that I am the LORD, when I break the bars of their yoke and rescue them from the hands of those who enslaved them. ²⁸They will no longer be plundered by the nations, nor will wild animals devour them. They will live in safety, and no one will make them afraid. ²⁹I will provide for them a land renowned for its crops, and they will no longer be victims of famine in the land or bear the scorn of the nations. ³⁰Then they will know that I, the LORD their God, am with them and that they, the Israelites, are my people, declares the Sovereign LORD. ³¹You are my sheep, the sheep of my pasture, and I am your God, declares the Sovereign LORD.'"

A PROPHECY AGAINST EDOM

35 The word of the LORD came to me: ²"Son of man, set your face against Mount Seir; prophesy against it ³and say: 'This is what the Sovereign LORD says: I am against you, Mount Seir, and I will stretch out my hand against you and make you a desolate waste. ⁴I will turn your towns into ruins and you will be desolate. Then you will know that I am the LORD.

⁵"'Because you harbored an ancient hostility and delivered the Israelites over to the sword at the time of their calamity, the time their punishment reached its climax, ⁶therefore as surely as I live, declares the Sovereign LORD, I will give you over to bloodshed and it will pursue you. Since you did not hate bloodshed, bloodshed will pursue you. ⁷I will make Mount Seir a desolate waste and cut off from it all who come

ᵃ 26 Or *I will cause them and the places surrounding my hill to be named in blessings* (see Gen. 48:20); or *I will cause them and the places surrounding my hill to be seen as blessed*

What was the season for showers? (34:26)
The rainy season in Israel begins with autumn rains and ends with spring rains.

What was Mount Seir? (35:2)
This was the country of Edom.

What was this ancient hostility? (35:5)
The Edomites were descendants of Esau, and the Israelites were descendants of Jacob. The rivalry began when Jacob cheated Esau out of his birthright and continued throughout history, including when Edom looted Jerusalem in 586 B.C.

and go. [8] I will fill your mountains with the slain; those killed by the sword will fall on your hills and in your valleys and in all your ravines. [9] I will make you desolate forever; your towns will not be inhabited. Then you will know that I am the LORD.

[10] "'Because you have said, "These two nations and countries will be ours and we will take possession of them," even though I the LORD was there, [11] therefore as surely as I live, declares the Sovereign LORD, I will treat you in accordance with the anger and jealousy you showed in your hatred of them and I will make myself known among them when I judge you. [12] Then you will know that I the LORD have heard all the contemptible things you have said against the mountains of Israel. You said, "They have been laid waste and have been given over to us to devour." [13] You boasted against me and spoke against me without restraint, and I heard it. [14] This is what the Sovereign LORD says: While the whole earth rejoices, I will make you desolate. [15] Because you rejoiced when the inheritance of Israel became desolate, that is how I will treat you. You will be desolate, Mount Seir, you and all of Edom. Then they will know that I am the LORD.'"

HOPE FOR THE MOUNTAINS OF ISRAEL

36 "Son of man, prophesy to the mountains of Israel and say, 'Mountains of Israel, hear the word of the LORD. [2] This is what the Sovereign LORD says: The enemy said of you, "Aha! The ancient heights have become our possession."' [3] Therefore prophesy and say, 'This is what the Sovereign LORD says: Because they ravaged and crushed you from every side so that you became the possession of the rest of the nations and the object of people's malicious talk and slander, [4] therefore, mountains of Israel, hear the word of the Sovereign LORD: This is what the Sovereign LORD says to the mountains and hills, to the ravines and valleys, to the desolate ruins and the deserted towns that have been plundered and ridiculed by the rest of the nations around you— [5] this is what the Sovereign LORD says: In my burning zeal I have spoken against the rest of the nations, and against all Edom, for with glee and with malice in their hearts they made my land their own possession so that they might plunder its pastureland.' [6] Therefore prophesy concerning the land of Israel and say to the mountains and hills, to the ravines and valleys: 'This is what the Sovereign LORD says: I speak in my jealous wrath because you have suffered the scorn of the nations. [7] Therefore this is what the Sovereign LORD says: I swear with uplifted hand that the nations around you will also suffer scorn.

[8] "'But you, mountains of Israel, will produce branches and fruit for my people Israel, for they will soon come home. [9] I am concerned for you and will look on you with favor; you will be plowed and sown, [10] and I will cause many people to live on you—yes, all of Israel. The towns will be inhabited and the ruins rebuilt. [11] I will increase the number of people and animals living on you, and they will be fruitful and become numerous. I will settle people on you as in the past and

What were the ancient heights? (36:2)
This was the promised land, or more specifically, the heights of Zion.

Why was the Lord so angry? (36:6)
The Lord was offended by the ridicule of the nations because they were mocking and plundering his special land.

What were the branches and fruit? (36:8)
They were signs that the land would become productive again because the Lord was planning to have the exiles return.

What did this language echo? (36:11)
The blessing of increasing the number of people and making them fruitful is similar to the terminology at the time of creation (see Genesis 1:22, 28).

will make you prosper more than before. Then you will know that I am the Lord. ¹²I will cause people, my people Israel, to live on you. They will possess you, and you will be their inheritance; you will never again deprive them of their children.

¹³"'This is what the Sovereign Lord says: Because some say to you, "You devour people and deprive your nation of its children," ¹⁴therefore you will no longer devour people or make your nation childless, declares the Sovereign Lord. ¹⁵No longer will I make you hear the taunts of the nations, and no longer will you suffer the scorn of the peoples or cause your nation to fall, declares the Sovereign Lord.'"

ISRAEL'S RESTORATION ASSURED

¹⁶Again the word of the Lord came to me: ¹⁷"Son of man, when the people of Israel were living in their own land, they defiled it by their conduct and their actions. Their conduct was like a woman's monthly uncleanness in my sight. ¹⁸So I poured out my wrath on them because they had shed blood in the land and because they had defiled it with their idols. ¹⁹I dispersed them among the nations, and they were scattered through the countries; I judged them according to their conduct and their actions. ²⁰And wherever they went among the nations they profaned my holy name, for it was said of them, 'These are the Lord's people, and yet they had to leave his land.' ²¹I had concern for my holy name, which the people of Israel profaned among the nations where they had gone.

²²"Therefore say to the Israelites, 'This is what the Sovereign Lord says: It is not for your sake, people of Israel, that I am going to do these things, but for the sake of my holy name, which you have profaned among the nations where you have gone. ²³I will show the holiness of my great name, which has been profaned among the nations, the name you have profaned among them. Then the nations will know that I am the Lord, declares the Sovereign Lord, when I am proved holy through you before their eyes.

²⁴"'For I will take you out of the nations; I will gather you from all the countries and bring you back into your own land. ²⁵I will sprinkle clean water on you, and you will be clean; I will cleanse you from all your impurities and from all your idols. ²⁶I will give you a new heart and put a new spirit in you; I will remove from you your heart of stone and give you a heart of flesh. ²⁷And I will put my Spirit in you and move you to follow my decrees and be careful to keep my laws. ²⁸Then you will live in the land I gave your ancestors; you will be my people, and I will be your God. ²⁹I will save you from all your uncleanness. I will call for the grain and make it plentiful and will not bring famine upon you. ³⁰I will increase the fruit of the trees and the crops of the field, so that you will no longer suffer disgrace among the nations because of famine. ³¹Then you will remember your evil ways and wicked deeds, and you will loathe yourselves for your sins and detestable practices. ³²I want you to know that I am not doing this for your sake, declares the Sovereign Lord. Be ashamed and disgraced for your conduct, people of Israel!

How had the people of Israel profaned God's holy name? (36:20)
Because Israel had been removed from her land, it seemed to the surrounding nations that God was unable to protect and save her.

What were the new heart and the new spirit? (36:26)
God promised that he would transform his people's minds and hearts.

³³"'This is what the Sovereign LORD says: On the day I cleanse you from all your sins, I will resettle your towns, and the ruins will be rebuilt. ³⁴The desolate land will be cultivated instead of lying desolate in the sight of all who pass through it. ³⁵They will say, "This land that was laid waste has become like the garden of Eden; the cities that were lying in ruins, desolate and destroyed, are now fortified and inhabited." ³⁶Then the nations around you that remain will know that I the LORD have rebuilt what was destroyed and have replanted what was desolate. I the LORD have spoken, and I will do it.'

³⁷"This is what the Sovereign LORD says: Once again I will yield to Israel's plea and do this for them: I will make their people as numerous as sheep, ³⁸as numerous as the flocks for offerings at Jerusalem during her appointed festivals. So will the ruined cities be filled with flocks of people. Then they will know that I am the LORD."

THE VALLEY OF DRY BONES

37 The hand of the LORD was on me, and he brought me out by the Spirit of the LORD and set me in the middle of a valley; it was full of bones. ²He led me back and forth among them, and I saw a great many bones on the floor of the valley, bones that were very dry. ³He asked me, "Son of man, can these bones live?"

I said, "Sovereign LORD, you alone know."

⁴Then he said to me, "Prophesy to these bones and say to them, 'Dry bones, hear the word of the LORD! ⁵This is what the Sovereign LORD says to these bones: I will make breath*ᵃ* enter you, and you will come to life. ⁶I will attach tendons to you and make flesh come upon you and cover you with skin; I will put breath in you, and you will come to life. Then you will know that I am the LORD.'"

⁷So I prophesied as I was commanded. And as I was prophesying, there was a noise, a rattling sound, and the bones came together, bone to bone. ⁸I looked, and tendons and flesh appeared on them and skin covered them, but there was no breath in them.

⁹Then he said to me, "Prophesy to the breath; prophesy, son of man, and say to it, 'This is what the Sovereign LORD says: Come, breath, from the four winds and breathe into these slain, that they may live.'" ¹⁰So I prophesied as he commanded me, and breath entered them; they came to life and stood up on their feet—a vast army.

¹¹Then he said to me: "Son of man, these bones are the people of Israel. They say, 'Our bones are dried up and our hope is gone; we are cut off.' ¹²Therefore prophesy and say to them: 'This is what the Sovereign LORD says: My people, I am going to open your graves and bring you up from them; I will bring you back to the land of Israel. ¹³Then you, my people, will know that I am the LORD, when I open your graves and bring you up from them. ¹⁴I will put my Spirit in you and you will live, and I will settle you in your own land. Then you will know that I the LORD have spoken, and I have done it, declares the LORD.'"

What did these bones represent? (37:2)
All these "very dry" bones symbolized the community of exiles.

Why did these bones come to life? (37:10)
This is the spiritual resurrection God would give to the exiles. God would bring life to the spiritually dead nation.

ᵃ 5 The Hebrew for this word can also mean *wind* or *spirit* (see verses 6-14).

ONE NATION UNDER ONE KING

[15] The word of the LORD came to me: [16] "Son of man, take a stick of wood and write on it, 'Belonging to Judah and the Israelites associated with him.' Then take another stick of wood, and write on it, 'Belonging to Joseph (that is, to Ephraim) and all the Israelites associated with him.' [17] Join them together into one stick so that they will become one in your hand.

[18] "When your people ask you, 'Won't you tell us what you mean by this?' [19] say to them, 'This is what the Sovereign LORD says: I am going to take the stick of Joseph—which is in Ephraim's hand—and of the Israelite tribes associated with him, and join it to Judah's stick. I will make them into a single stick of wood, and they will become one in my hand.' [20] Hold before their eyes the sticks you have written on [21] and say to them, 'This is what the Sovereign LORD says: I will take the Israelites out of the nations where they have gone. I will gather them from all around and bring them back into their own land. [22] I will make them one nation in the land, on the mountains of Israel. There will be one king over all of them and they will never again be two nations or be divided into two kingdoms. [23] They will no longer defile themselves with their idols and vile images or with any of their offenses, for I will save them from all their sinful backsliding,[a] and I will cleanse them. They will be my people, and I will be their God.

[24] "'My servant David will be king over them, and they will all have one shepherd. They will follow my laws and be careful to keep my decrees. [25] They will live in the land I gave to my servant Jacob, the land where your ancestors lived. They and their children and their children's children will live there forever, and David my servant will be their prince forever. [26] I will make a covenant of peace with them; it will be an everlasting covenant. I will establish them and increase their numbers, and I will put my sanctuary among them forever. [27] My dwelling place will be with them; I will be their God, and they will be my people. [28] Then the nations will know that I the LORD make Israel holy, when my sanctuary is among them forever.'"

THE LORD'S GREAT VICTORY OVER THE NATIONS

38 The word of the LORD came to me: [2] "Son of man, set your face against Gog, of the land of Magog, the chief prince of[b] Meshek and Tubal; prophesy against him [3] and say: 'This is what the Sovereign LORD says: I am against you, Gog, chief prince of[c] Meshek and Tubal. [4] I will turn you around, put hooks in your jaws and bring you out with your whole army—your horses, your horsemen fully armed, and a great horde with large and small shields, all of them brandishing their swords. [5] Persia, Cush[d] and Put will be with them, all with shields and helmets, [6] also Gomer with

How would David rule Israel again? (37:24)
The coming ruler was referred to as David because he was a descendant of David. This was a reference to the coming Messiah, Jesus.

Who was Gog? (38:2)
This was apparently a leader or king who was an enemy of God's people.

---

[a] 23 Many Hebrew manuscripts (see also Septuagint); most Hebrew manuscripts *all their dwelling places where they sinned*   [b] 2 Or *the prince of Rosh,*   [c] 3 Or *Gog, prince of Rosh,*   [d] 5 That is, the upper Nile region

all its troops, and Beth Togarmah from the far north with all its troops—the many nations with you.

⁷"'Get ready; be prepared, you and all the hordes gathered about you, and take command of them. ⁸After many days you will be called to arms. In future years you will invade a land that has recovered from war, whose people were gathered from many nations to the mountains of Israel, which had long been desolate. They had been brought out from the nations, and now all of them live in safety. ⁹You and all your troops and the many nations with you will go up, advancing like a storm; you will be like a cloud covering the land.

¹⁰"'This is what the Sovereign Lord says: On that day thoughts will come into your mind and you will devise an evil scheme. ¹¹You will say, "I will invade a land of unwalled villages; I will attack a peaceful and unsuspecting people— all of them living without walls and without gates and bars. ¹²I will plunder and loot and turn my hand against the resettled ruins and the people gathered from the nations, rich in livestock and goods, living at the center of the land.ᵃ" ¹³Sheba and Dedan and the merchants of Tarshish and all her villagesᵇ will say to you, "Have you come to plunder? Have you gathered your hordes to loot, to carry off silver and gold, to take away livestock and goods and to seize much plunder?"'

¹⁴"Therefore, son of man, prophesy and say to Gog: 'This is what the Sovereign Lord says: In that day, when my people Israel are living in safety, will you not take notice of it? ¹⁵You will come from your place in the far north, you and many nations with you, all of them riding on horses, a great horde, a mighty army. ¹⁶You will advance against my people Israel like a cloud that covers the land. In days to come, Gog, I will bring you against my land, so that the nations may know me when I am proved holy through you before their eyes.

¹⁷"'This is what the Sovereign Lord says: You are the one I spoke of in former days by my servants the prophets of Israel. At that time they prophesied for years that I would bring you against them. ¹⁸This is what will happen in that day: When Gog attacks the land of Israel, my hot anger will be aroused, declares the Sovereign Lord. ¹⁹In my zeal and fiery wrath I declare that at that time there shall be a great earthquake in the land of Israel. ²⁰The fish in the sea, the birds in the sky, the beasts of the field, every creature that moves along the ground, and all the people on the face of the earth will tremble at my presence. The mountains will be overturned, the cliffs will crumble and every wall will fall to the ground. ²¹I will summon a sword against Gog on all my mountains, declares the Sovereign Lord. Every man's sword will be against his brother. ²²I will execute judgment on him with plague and bloodshed; I will pour down torrents of rain, hailstones and burning sulfur on him and on his troops and on the many nations with him. ²³And so I will show my greatness and my holiness, and I will make myself known in the sight of many nations. Then they will know that I am the Lord.'

What was a "land of unwalled villages"? (38:11)
This was a place of peace where walls or fortifications were not necessary.

What was "the center of the land"? (38:12)
The Hebrew word for *center* also means *navel*, which symbolizes the fact that Israel was a vital link between God and the world.

ᵃ *12* The Hebrew for this phrase means *the navel of the earth.*　　ᵇ *13* Or *her strong lions*

39 "Son of man, prophesy against Gog and say: 'This is what the Sovereign LORD says: I am against you, Gog, chief prince of[a] Meshek and Tubal. ²I will turn you around and drag you along. I will bring you from the far north and send you against the mountains of Israel. ³Then I will strike your bow from your left hand and make your arrows drop from your right hand. ⁴On the mountains of Israel you will fall, you and all your troops and the nations with you. I will give you as food to all kinds of carrion birds and to the wild animals. ⁵You will fall in the open field, for I have spoken, declares the Sovereign LORD. ⁶I will send fire on Magog and on those who live in safety in the coastlands, and they will know that I am the LORD.

⁷"I will make known my holy name among my people Israel. I will no longer let my holy name be profaned, and the nations will know that I the LORD am the Holy One in Israel. ⁸It is coming! It will surely take place, declares the Sovereign LORD. This is the day I have spoken of.

⁹"Then those who live in the towns of Israel will go out and use the weapons for fuel and burn them up—the small and large shields, the bows and arrows, the war clubs and spears. For seven years they will use them for fuel. ¹⁰They will not need to gather wood from the fields or cut it from the forests, because they will use the weapons for fuel. And they will plunder those who plundered them and loot those who looted them, declares the Sovereign LORD.

¹¹"On that day I will give Gog a burial place in Israel, in the valley of those who travel east of the Sea. It will block the way of travelers, because Gog and all his hordes will be buried there. So it will be called the Valley of Hamon Gog.[b]

¹²"For seven months the Israelites will be burying them in order to cleanse the land. ¹³All the people of the land will bury them, and the day I display my glory will be a memorable day for them, declares the Sovereign LORD. ¹⁴People will be continually employed in cleansing the land. They will spread out across the land and, along with others, they will bury any bodies that are lying on the ground.

"'After the seven months they will carry out a more detailed search. ¹⁵As they go through the land, anyone who sees a human bone will leave a marker beside it until the gravediggers bury it in the Valley of Hamon Gog, ¹⁶near a town called Hamonah.[c] And so they will cleanse the land.'

¹⁷"Son of man, this is what the Sovereign LORD says: Call out to every kind of bird and all the wild animals: 'Assemble and come together from all around to the sacrifice I am preparing for you, the great sacrifice on the mountains of Israel. There you will eat flesh and drink blood. ¹⁸You will eat the flesh of mighty men and drink the blood of the princes of the earth as if they were rams and lambs, goats and bulls—all of them fattened animals from Bashan. ¹⁹At the sacrifice I am preparing for you, you will eat fat till you are glutted and drink blood till you are drunk. ²⁰At my table you will eat your fill of horses and riders, mighty men and soldiers of every kind,' declares the Sovereign LORD.

---

[a] 1 Or Gog, prince of Rosh,   [b] 11 Hamon Gog means hordes of Gog.
[c] 16 Hamonah means horde.

How would the land be purified? (39:14)
After the seven-month burial period, special squads would be employed to ensure that the land was totally cleansed by making sure that any bones they found would be buried.

What was Bashan? (39:18)
This was rich pastureland east of the Sea of Galilee, known for its sleek cattle and oak trees.

How would the people know
that God was in charge?
(39:21–23)
The people of Israel and the
other nations would realize
that the God who had saved
and protected his people was
now judging them for their sins.
Eventually, they would also see
how God restored his people (see
verses 27–28).

[21] "I will display my glory among the nations, and all the nations will see the punishment I inflict and the hand I lay on them. [22] From that day forward the people of Israel will know that I am the LORD their God. [23] And the nations will know that the people of Israel went into exile for their sin, because they were unfaithful to me. So I hid my face from them and handed them over to their enemies, and they all fell by the sword. [24] I dealt with them according to their uncleanness and their offenses, and I hid my face from them.

[25] "Therefore this is what the Sovereign LORD says: I will now restore the fortunes of Jacob[a] and will have compassion on all the people of Israel, and I will be zealous for my holy name. [26] They will forget their shame and all the unfaithfulness they showed toward me when they lived in safety in their land with no one to make them afraid. [27] When I have brought them back from the nations and have gathered them from the countries of their enemies, I will be proved holy through them in the sight of many nations. [28] Then they will know that I am the LORD their God, for though I sent them into exile among the nations, I will gather them to their own land, not leaving any behind. [29] I will no longer hide my face from them, for I will pour out my Spirit on the people of Israel, declares the Sovereign LORD."

THE TEMPLE AREA RESTORED

40 In the twenty-fifth year of our exile, at the beginning of the year, on the tenth of the month, in the fourteenth year after the fall of the city—on that very day the hand of the LORD was on me and he took me there. [2] In visions of God he took me to the land of Israel and set me on a very high mountain, on whose south side were some buildings that looked like a city. [3] He took me there, and I saw a man whose appearance was like bronze; he was standing in the gateway with a linen cord and a measuring rod in his hand. [4] The man said to me, "Son of man, look carefully and listen closely and pay attention to everything I am going to show you, for that is why you have been brought here. Tell the people of Israel everything you see."

THE EAST GATE TO THE OUTER COURT

[5] I saw a wall completely surrounding the temple area. The length of the measuring rod in the man's hand was six long cubits,[b] each of which was a cubit and a handbreadth. He measured the wall; it was one measuring rod thick and one rod high.

What was the very high
mountain? (40:2)
This was Mount Zion. The height
of the mountain indicates its
importance as the place where
God lived on earth.

What was the importance of
this wall? (40:5)
The wall separated the temple
from the surrounding area. It
represented the separation of
the holy from the secular, not
relating to religion.

[6] Then he went to the east gate. He climbed its steps and measured the threshold of the gate; it was one rod deep. [7] The alcoves for the guards were one rod long and one rod wide, and the projecting walls between the alcoves were five cubits[c] thick. And the threshold of the gate next to the portico facing the temple was one rod deep.

---

[a] 25 Or *now bring Jacob back from captivity*   [b] 5 That is, about 11 feet or about 3.2 meters; also in verse 12. The long cubit of about 21 inches or about 53 centimeters is the basic unit of measurement of length throughout chapters 40–48.   [c] 7 That is, about 8 3/4 feet or about 2.7 meters; also in verse 48

[8]Then he measured the portico of the gateway; [9]it[a] was eight cubits[b] deep and its jambs were two cubits[c] thick. The portico of the gateway faced the temple.

[10]Inside the east gate were three alcoves on each side; the three had the same measurements, and the faces of the projecting walls on each side had the same measurements. [11]Then he measured the width of the entrance of the gateway; it was ten cubits and its length was thirteen cubits.[d] [12]In front of each alcove was a wall one cubit high, and the alcoves were six cubits square. [13]Then he measured the gateway from the top of the rear wall of one alcove to the top of the opposite one; the distance was twenty-five cubits[e] from one parapet opening to the opposite one. [14]He measured along the faces of the projecting walls all around the inside of the gateway—sixty cubits.[f] The measurement was up to the portico[g] facing the courtyard.[h] [15]The distance from the entrance of the gateway to the far end of its portico was fifty cubits.[i] [16]The alcoves and the projecting walls inside the gateway were surmounted by narrow parapet openings all around, as was the portico; the openings all around faced inward. The faces of the projecting walls were decorated with palm trees.

THE OUTER COURT

[17]Then he brought me into the outer court. There I saw some rooms and a pavement that had been constructed all around the court; there were thirty rooms along the pavement. [18]It abutted the sides of the gateways and was as wide as they were long; this was the lower pavement. [19]Then he measured the distance from the inside of the lower gateway to the outside of the inner court; it was a hundred cubits[j] on the east side as well as on the north.

THE NORTH GATE

[20]Then he measured the length and width of the north gate, leading into the outer court. [21]Its alcoves—three on each side—its projecting walls and its portico had the same measurements as those of the first gateway. It was fifty cubits long and twenty-five cubits wide. [22]Its openings, its portico and its palm tree decorations had the same measurements as those of the gate facing east. Seven steps led up to it, with its portico opposite them. [23]There was a gate to the inner court facing the north gate, just as there was on the east. He measured from one gate to the opposite one; it was a hundred cubits.

---

[a] *8,9* Many Hebrew manuscripts, Septuagint, Vulgate and Syriac; most Hebrew manuscripts *gateway facing the temple; it was one rod deep.* [9]*Then he measured the portico of the gateway; it*   [b] *9* That is, about 14 feet or about 4.2 meters   [c] *9* That is, about 3 1/2 feet or about 1 meter   [d] *11* That is, about 18 feet wide and 23 feet long or about 5.3 meters wide and 6.9 meters long   [e] *13* That is, about 44 feet or about 13 meters; also in verses 21, 25, 29, 30, 33 and 36   [f] *14* That is, about 105 feet or about 32 meters   [g] *14* Septuagint; Hebrew *projecting wall*   [h] *14* The meaning of the Hebrew for this verse is uncertain.   [i] *15* That is, about 88 feet or about 27 meters; also in verses 21, 25, 29, 33 and 36   [j] *19* That is, about 175 feet or about 53 meters; also in verses 23, 27 and 47

THE SOUTH GATE

²⁴Then he led me to the south side and I saw the south gate. He measured its jambs and its portico, and they had the same measurements as the others. ²⁵The gateway and its portico had narrow openings all around, like the openings of the others. It was fifty cubits long and twenty-five cubits wide. ²⁶Seven steps led up to it, with its portico opposite them; it had palm tree decorations on the faces of the projecting walls on each side. ²⁷The inner court also had a gate facing south, and he measured from this gate to the outer gate on the south side; it was a hundred cubits.

THE GATES TO THE INNER COURT

²⁸Then he brought me into the inner court through the south gate, and he measured the south gate; it had the same measurements as the others. ²⁹Its alcoves, its projecting walls and its portico had the same measurements as the others. The gateway and its portico had openings all around. It was fifty cubits long and twenty-five cubits wide. ³⁰(The porticoes of the gateways around the inner court were twenty-five cubits wide and five cubits deep.) ³¹Its portico faced the outer court; palm trees decorated its jambs, and eight steps led up to it.

³²Then he brought me to the inner court on the east side, and he measured the gateway; it had the same measurements as the others. ³³Its alcoves, its projecting walls and its portico had the same measurements as the others. The gateway and its portico had openings all around. It was fifty cubits long and twenty-five cubits wide. ³⁴Its portico faced the outer court; palm trees decorated the jambs on either side, and eight steps led up to it.

³⁵Then he brought me to the north gate and measured it. It had the same measurements as the others, ³⁶as did its alcoves, its projecting walls and its portico, and it had openings all around. It was fifty cubits long and twenty-five cubits wide. ³⁷Its portico[a] faced the outer court; palm trees decorated the jambs on either side, and eight steps led up to it.

THE ROOMS FOR PREPARING SACRIFICES

³⁸A room with a doorway was by the portico in each of the inner gateways, where the burnt offerings were washed. ³⁹In the portico of the gateway were two tables on each side, on which the burnt offerings, sin offerings[b] and guilt offerings were slaughtered. ⁴⁰By the outside wall of the portico of the gateway, near the steps at the entrance of the north gateway were two tables, and on the other side of the steps were two tables. ⁴¹So there were four tables on one side of the gateway and four on the other—eight tables in all—on which the sacrifices were slaughtered. ⁴²There were also four tables of dressed stone for the burnt offerings, each a cubit and a half long, a cubit and a half wide and a cubit high.[c] On them were placed the utensils for slaughtering the burnt offerings

---

[a] 37 Septuagint (see also verses 31 and 34); Hebrew *jambs*
[b] 39 Or *purification offerings*   [c] 42 That is, about 2 2/3 feet long and wide and 21 inches high or about 80 centimeters long and wide and 53 centimeters high

and the other sacrifices. ⁴³ And double-pronged hooks, each a handbreadth^{*a*} long, were attached to the wall all around. The tables were for the flesh of the offerings.

THE ROOMS FOR THE PRIESTS

⁴⁴ Outside the inner gate, within the inner court, were two rooms, one^{*b*} at the side of the north gate and facing south, and another at the side of the south^{*c*} gate and facing north. ⁴⁵ He said to me, "The room facing south is for the priests who guard the temple, ⁴⁶ and the room facing north is for the priests who guard the altar. These are the sons of Zadok, who are the only Levites who may draw near to the LORD to minister before him."

⁴⁷ Then he measured the court: It was square — a hundred cubits long and a hundred cubits wide. And the altar was in front of the temple.

THE NEW TEMPLE

⁴⁸ He brought me to the portico of the temple and measured the jambs of the portico; they were five cubits wide on either side. The width of the entrance was fourteen cubits^{*d*} and its projecting walls were^{*e*} three cubits^{*f*} wide on either side. ⁴⁹ The portico was twenty cubits^{*g*} wide, and twelve^{*h*} cubits^{*i*} from front to back. It was reached by a flight of stairs,^{*j*} and there were pillars on each side of the jambs.

41 Then the man brought me to the main hall and measured the jambs; the width of the jambs was six cubits^{*k*} on each side.^{*l*} ² The entrance was ten cubits^{*m*} wide, and the projecting walls on each side of it were five cubits^{*n*} wide. He also measured the main hall; it was forty cubits long and twenty cubits wide.^{*o*}

³ Then he went into the inner sanctuary and measured the jambs of the entrance; each was two cubits^{*p*} wide. The entrance was six cubits wide, and the projecting walls on each side of it were seven cubits^{*q*} wide. ⁴ And he measured the length of the inner sanctuary; it was twenty cubits, and its width was twenty cubits across the end of the main hall. He said to me, "This is the Most Holy Place."

⁵ Then he measured the wall of the temple; it was six cubits thick, and each side room around the temple was four cubits^{*r*} wide. ⁶ The side rooms were on three levels, one above another, thirty on each level. There were ledges all around the wall of the temple to serve as supports for the side rooms, so that the supports were not inserted into the wall of the

What was the outer sanctuary like? (41:1)
This was the largest of the three rooms of the temple. This outer sanctuary was the same size as it had been in Solomon's temple.

What was the "Most Holy Place"? (41:3 – 4)
This inner sanctuary of the temple contained the ark of the covenant. Only the high priest could enter the Most Holy Place once each year.

---

^{*a*} *43* That is, about 3 1/2 inches or about 9 centimeters   ^{*b*} *44* Septuagint; Hebrew *were rooms for singers, which were*   ^{*c*} *44* Septuagint; Hebrew *east*   ^{*d*} *48* That is, about 25 feet or about 7.4 meters   ^{*e*} *48* Septuagint; Hebrew *entrance was*   ^{*f*} *48* That is, about 5 1/4 feet or about 1.6 meters   ^{*g*} *49* That is, about 35 feet or about 11 meters   ^{*h*} *49* Septuagint; Hebrew *eleven*   ^{*i*} *49* That is, about 21 feet or about 6.4 meters   ^{*j*} *49* Hebrew; Septuagint *Ten steps led up to it*   ^{*k*} *1* That is, about 11 feet or about 3.2 meters; also in verses 3, 5 and 8   ^{*l*} *1* One Hebrew manuscript *side, the width of the tent*   ^{*m*} *2* That is, about 18 feet or about 5.3 meters; also in verses 9, 11 and 12   ^{*n*} *2* That is, about 8 3/4 feet or about 2.7 meters; also in verses 9, 11 and 12   ^{*o*} *2* That is, about 70 feet long and 35 feet wide or about 21 meters long and 11 meters wide   ^{*p*} *3* That is, about 3 1/2 feet or about 1.1 meters; also in verse 22   ^{*q*} *3* That is, about 12 feet or about 3.7 meters   ^{*r*} *5* That is, about 7 feet or about 2.1 meters

temple. [7]The side rooms all around the temple were wider at each successive level. The structure surrounding the temple was built in ascending stages, so that the rooms widened as one went upward. A stairway went up from the lowest floor to the top floor through the middle floor.

[8]I saw that the temple had a raised base all around it, forming the foundation of the side rooms. It was the length of the rod, six long cubits. [9]The outer wall of the side rooms was five cubits thick. The open area between the side rooms of the temple [10]and the priests' rooms was twenty cubits wide all around the temple. [11]There were entrances to the side rooms from the open area, one on the north and another on the south; and the base adjoining the open area was five cubits wide all around.

[12]The building facing the temple courtyard on the west side was seventy cubits[a] wide. The wall of the building was five cubits thick all around, and its length was ninety cubits.[b]

[13]Then he measured the temple; it was a hundred cubits[c] long, and the temple courtyard and the building with its walls were also a hundred cubits long. [14]The width of the temple courtyard on the east, including the front of the temple, was a hundred cubits.

[15]Then he measured the length of the building facing the courtyard at the rear of the temple, including its galleries on each side; it was a hundred cubits.

The main hall, the inner sanctuary and the portico facing the court, [16]as well as the thresholds and the narrow windows and galleries around the three of them—everything beyond and including the threshold was covered with wood. The floor, the wall up to the windows, and the windows were covered. [17]In the space above the outside of the entrance to the inner sanctuary and on the walls at regular intervals all around the inner and outer sanctuary [18]were carved cherubim and palm trees. Palm trees alternated with cherubim. Each cherub had two faces: [19]the face of a human being toward the palm tree on one side and the face of a lion toward the palm tree on the other. They were carved all around the whole temple. [20]From the floor to the area above the entrance, cherubim and palm trees were carved on the wall of the main hall.

[21]The main hall had a rectangular doorframe, and the one at the front of the Most Holy Place was similar. [22]There was a wooden altar three cubits[d] high and two cubits square[e]; its corners, its base[f] and its sides were of wood. The man said to me, "This is the table that is before the LORD." [23]Both the main hall and the Most Holy Place had double doors. [24]Each door had two leaves—two hinged leaves for each door. [25]And on the doors of the main hall were carved cherubim and palm trees like those carved on the walls, and there was a wooden overhang on the front of the portico. [26]On the sidewalls of the portico were narrow windows with palm trees carved on each side. The side rooms of the temple also had overhangs.

What were cherubim? (41:18)
The word *cherubim* is the plural form of cherub, a type of angel. These carvings of cherubim probably resembled the winged figures that stood guard at the entrances to palaces and temples in this part of the ancient world.

---

[a] *12* That is, about 123 feet or about 37 meters   [b] *12* That is, about 158 feet or about 48 meters   [c] *13* That is, about 175 feet or about 53 meters; also in verses 14 and 15   [d] *22* That is, about 5 1/4 feet or about 1.5 meters   [e] *22* Septuagint; Hebrew *long*   [f] *22* Septuagint; Hebrew *length*

THE ROOMS FOR THE PRIESTS

42 Then the man led me northward into the outer court and brought me to the rooms opposite the temple courtyard and opposite the outer wall on the north side. ²The building whose door faced north was a hundred cubits long and fifty cubits wide.*ᵃ* ³Both in the section twenty cubits*ᵇ* from the inner court and in the section opposite the pavement of the outer court, gallery faced gallery at the three levels. ⁴In front of the rooms was an inner passageway ten cubits wide and a hundred cubits*ᶜ* long.*ᵈ* Their doors were on the north. ⁵Now the upper rooms were narrower, for the galleries took more space from them than from the rooms on the lower and middle floors of the building. ⁶The rooms on the top floor had no pillars, as the courts had; so they were smaller in floor space than those on the lower and middle floors. ⁷There was an outer wall parallel to the rooms and the outer court; it extended in front of the rooms for fifty cubits. ⁸While the row of rooms on the side next to the outer court was fifty cubits long, the row on the side nearest the sanctuary was a hundred cubits long. ⁹The lower rooms had an entrance on the east side as one enters them from the outer court.

¹⁰On the south side*ᵉ* along the length of the wall of the outer court, adjoining the temple courtyard and opposite the outer wall, were rooms ¹¹with a passageway in front of them. These were like the rooms on the north; they had the same length and width, with similar exits and dimensions. Similar to the doorways on the north ¹²were the doorways of the rooms on the south. There was a doorway at the beginning of the passageway that was parallel to the corresponding wall extending eastward, by which one enters the rooms.

¹³Then he said to me, "The north and south rooms facing the temple courtyard are the priests' rooms, where the priests who approach the LORD will eat the most holy offerings. There they will put the most holy offerings—the grain offerings, the sin offerings*ᶠ* and the guilt offerings—for the place is holy. ¹⁴Once the priests enter the holy precincts, they are not to go into the outer court until they leave behind the garments in which they minister, for these are holy. They are to put on other clothes before they go near the places that are for the people."

¹⁵When he had finished measuring what was inside the temple area, he led me out by the east gate and measured the area all around: ¹⁶He measured the east side with the measuring rod; it was five hundred cubits.*ᵍ,ʰ* ¹⁷He measured the north side; it was five hundred cubits*ⁱ* by the measuring rod. ¹⁸He measured the south side; it was five hundred cubits by the measuring rod. ¹⁹Then he turned to the west side and

Why would the priests eat some of the sacrifices? (42:13)
According to the laws God set forth in Leviticus, the priests were allowed to eat certain sacrifices.

Was the temple symmetrical? (42:16–20)
The temple was exactly as long as it was wide. It was a perfect square, which symbolized perfection.

ᵃ 2 That is, about 175 feet long and 88 feet wide or about 53 meters long and 27 meters wide   *ᵇ 3* That is, about 35 feet or about 11 meters
ᶜ 4 Septuagint and Syriac; Hebrew *and one cubit*   *ᵈ 4* That is, about 18 feet wide and 175 feet long or about 5.3 meters wide and 53 meters long
ᵉ 10 Septuagint; Hebrew *Eastward*   *ᶠ 13* Or *purification offerings*
ᵍ 16 See Septuagint of verse 17; Hebrew *rods*; also in verses 18 and 19.
ʰ 16 Five hundred cubits equal about 875 feet or about 265 meters; also in verses 17, 18 and 19.   *ⁱ 17* Septuagint; Hebrew *rods*

measured; it was five hundred cubits by the measuring rod. ²⁰ So he measured the area on all four sides. It had a wall around it, five hundred cubits long and five hundred cubits wide, to separate the holy from the common.

GOD'S GLORY RETURNS TO THE TEMPLE

43 Then the man brought me to the gate facing east, ² and I saw the glory of the God of Israel coming from the east. His voice was like the roar of rushing waters, and the land was radiant with his glory. ³ The vision I saw was like the vision I had seen when he*ᵃ* came to destroy the city and like the visions I had seen by the Kebar River, and I fell facedown. ⁴ The glory of the LORD entered the temple through the gate facing east. ⁵ Then the Spirit lifted me up and brought me into the inner court, and the glory of the LORD filled the temple.

⁶ While the man was standing beside me, I heard someone speaking to me from inside the temple. ⁷ He said: "Son of man, this is the place of my throne and the place for the soles of my feet. This is where I will live among the Israelites forever. The people of Israel will never again defile my holy name—neither they nor their kings—by their prostitution and the funeral offerings*ᵇ* for their kings at their death.*ᶜ* ⁸ When they placed their threshold next to my threshold and their doorposts beside my doorposts, with only a wall between me and them, they defiled my holy name by their detestable practices. So I destroyed them in my anger. ⁹ Now let them put away from me their prostitution and the funeral offerings for their kings, and I will live among them forever.

¹⁰ "Son of man, describe the temple to the people of Israel, that they may be ashamed of their sins. Let them consider its perfection, ¹¹ and if they are ashamed of all they have done, make known to them the design of the temple—its arrangement, its exits and entrances—its whole design and all its regulations*ᵈ* and laws. Write these down before them so that they may be faithful to its design and follow all its regulations.

¹² "This is the law of the temple: All the surrounding area on top of the mountain will be most holy. Such is the law of the temple.

THE GREAT ALTAR RESTORED

¹³ "These are the measurements of the altar in long cubits,*ᵉ* that cubit being a cubit and a handbreadth: Its gutter is a cubit deep and a cubit wide, with a rim of one span*ᶠ* around the edge. And this is the height of the altar: ¹⁴ From the gutter on the ground up to the lower ledge that goes around the altar it is two cubits high, and the ledge is a cubit wide.*ᵍ* From

What was the "glory of the LORD"? (43:4–5)
This was a physical display of God's presence and power among his people.

What were the funeral offerings for their kings? (43:7)
This is a reference either to idols or to the monuments or graves of past kings. They were worthless because God alone is worthy of worship.

What was Ezekiel's altar like? (43:13–17)
Ezekiel's altar was much larger than Solomon's. It was more than 20 feet tall and was made of three slabs of decreasing size, like a pyramid.

ᵃ 3 Some Hebrew manuscripts and Vulgate; most Hebrew manuscripts *I*
ᵇ 7 Or *the memorial monuments*; also in verse 9   *ᶜ 7* Or *their high places*
ᵈ 11 Some Hebrew manuscripts and Septuagint; most Hebrew manuscripts *regulations and its whole design*   *ᵉ 13* That is, about 21 inches or about 53 centimeters; also in verses 14 and 17. The long cubit is the basic unit for linear measurement throughout Ezekiel 40–48.   *ᶠ 13* That is, about 11 inches or about 27 centimeters   *ᵍ 14* That is, about 3 1/2 feet high and 1 3/4 feet wide or about 105 centimeters high and 53 centimeters wide

this lower ledge to the upper ledge that goes around the altar it is four cubits high, and that ledge is also a cubit wide.[a] [15]Above that, the altar hearth is four cubits high, and four horns project upward from the hearth. [16]The altar hearth is square, twelve cubits[b] long and twelve cubits wide. [17]The upper ledge also is square, fourteen cubits[c] long and fourteen cubits wide. All around the altar is a gutter of one cubit with a rim of half a cubit.[d] The steps of the altar face east."

[18]Then he said to me, "Son of man, this is what the Sovereign LORD says: These will be the regulations for sacrificing burnt offerings and splashing blood against the altar when it is built: [19]You are to give a young bull as a sin offering[e] to the Levitical priests of the family of Zadok, who come near to minister before me, declares the Sovereign LORD. [20]You are to take some of its blood and put it on the four horns of the altar and on the four corners of the upper ledge and all around the rim, and so purify the altar and make atonement for it. [21]You are to take the bull for the sin offering and burn it in the designated part of the temple area outside the sanctuary.

[22]"On the second day you are to offer a male goat without defect for a sin offering, and the altar is to be purified as it was purified with the bull. [23]When you have finished purifying it, you are to offer a young bull and a ram from the flock, both without defect. [24]You are to offer them before the LORD, and the priests are to sprinkle salt on them and sacrifice them as a burnt offering to the LORD.

[25]"For seven days you are to provide a male goat daily for a sin offering; you are also to provide a young bull and a ram from the flock, both without defect. [26]For seven days they are to make atonement for the altar and cleanse it; thus they will dedicate it. [27]At the end of these days, from the eighth day on, the priests are to present your burnt offerings and fellowship offerings on the altar. Then I will accept you, declares the Sovereign LORD."

THE PRIESTHOOD RESTORED

44 Then the man brought me back to the outer gate of the sanctuary, the one facing east, and it was shut. [2]The LORD said to me, "This gate is to remain shut. It must not be opened; no one may enter through it. It is to remain shut because the LORD, the God of Israel, has entered through it. [3]The prince himself is the only one who may sit inside the gateway to eat in the presence of the LORD. He is to enter by way of the portico of the gateway and go out the same way."

[4]Then the man brought me by way of the north gate to the front of the temple. I looked and saw the glory of the LORD filling the temple of the LORD, and I fell facedown.

[5]The LORD said to me, "Son of man, look carefully, listen closely and give attention to everything I tell you concerning all the regulations and instructions regarding the temple of

Why would the eastern gate remain shut? (44:2)
The eastern gate would remain shut because God had entered through it and thus had made it holy.

---

[a] *14* That is, about 7 feet high and 1 3/4 feet wide or about 2.1 meters high and 53 centimeters wide   [b] *16* That is, about 21 feet or about 6.4 meters   [c] *17* That is, about 25 feet or about 7.4 meters   [d] *17* That is, about 11 inches or about 27 centimeters   [e] *19* Or *purification offering*; also in verses 21, 22 and 25

the LORD. Give attention to the entrance to the temple and all the exits of the sanctuary. ⁶Say to rebellious Israel, 'This is what the Sovereign LORD says: Enough of your detestable practices, people of Israel! ⁷In addition to all your other detestable practices, you brought foreigners uncircumcised in heart and flesh into my sanctuary, desecrating my temple while you offered me food, fat and blood, and you broke my covenant. ⁸Instead of carrying out your duty in regard to my holy things, you put others in charge of my sanctuary. ⁹This is what the Sovereign LORD says: No foreigner uncircumcised in heart and flesh is to enter my sanctuary, not even the foreigners who live among the Israelites.

Were foreigners forbidden to enter the sanctuary? (44:9) Foreigners could become part of Israel, but they were still not allowed to enter the sanctuary. Nehemiah enforced this restriction.

¹⁰"'The Levites who went far from me when Israel went astray and who wandered from me after their idols must bear the consequences of their sin. ¹¹They may serve in my sanctuary, having charge of the gates of the temple and serving in it; they may slaughter the burnt offerings and sacrifices for the people and stand before the people and serve them. ¹²But because they served them in the presence of their idols and made the people of Israel fall into sin, therefore I have sworn with uplifted hand that they must bear the consequences of their sin, declares the Sovereign LORD. ¹³They are not to come near to serve me as priests or come near any of my holy things or my most holy offerings; they must bear the shame of their detestable practices. ¹⁴And I will appoint them to guard the temple for all the work that is to be done in it.

¹⁵"'But the Levitical priests, who are descendants of Zadok and who guarded my sanctuary when the Israelites went astray from me, are to come near to minister before me; they are to stand before me to offer sacrifices of fat and blood, declares the Sovereign LORD. ¹⁶They alone are to enter my sanctuary; they alone are to come near my table to minister before me and serve me as guards.

¹⁷"'When they enter the gates of the inner court, they are to wear linen clothes; they must not wear any woolen garment while ministering at the gates of the inner court or inside the temple. ¹⁸They are to wear linen turbans on their heads and linen undergarments around their waists. They must not wear anything that makes them perspire. ¹⁹When they go out into the outer court where the people are, they are to take off the clothes they have been ministering in and are to leave them in the sacred rooms, and put on other clothes, so that the people are not consecrated through contact with their garments.

Why were the priests not supposed to perspire? (44:18) Sweat would make the priests ceremonially unclean.

²⁰"'They must not shave their heads or let their hair grow long, but they are to keep the hair of their heads trimmed. ²¹No priest is to drink wine when he enters the inner court. ²²They must not marry widows or divorced women; they may marry only virgins of Israelite descent or widows of priests. ²³They are to teach my people the difference between the holy and the common and show them how to distinguish between the unclean and the clean.

²⁴"'In any dispute, the priests are to serve as judges and decide it according to my ordinances. They are to keep my laws and my decrees for all my appointed festivals, and they are to keep my Sabbaths holy.

²⁵"'A priest must not defile himself by going near a dead person; however, if the dead person was his father or mother, son or daughter, brother or unmarried sister, then he may defile himself. ²⁶After he is cleansed, he must wait seven days. ²⁷On the day he goes into the inner court of the sanctuary to minister in the sanctuary, he is to offer a sin offering^a for himself, declares the Sovereign LORD.

²⁸"'I am to be the only inheritance the priests have. You are to give them no possession in Israel; I will be their possession. ²⁹They will eat the grain offerings, the sin offerings and the guilt offerings; and everything in Israel devoted^b to the LORD will belong to them. ³⁰The best of all the firstfruits and of all your special gifts will belong to the priests. You are to give them the first portion of your ground meal so that a blessing may rest on your household. ³¹The priests must not eat anything, whether bird or animal, found dead or torn by wild animals.

ISRAEL FULLY RESTORED

45 "'When you allot the land as an inheritance, you are to present to the LORD a portion of the land as a sacred district, 25,000 cubits^c long and 20,000^d cubits^e wide; the entire area will be holy. ²Of this, a section 500 cubits^f square is to be for the sanctuary, with 50 cubits^g around it for open land. ³In the sacred district, measure off a section 25,000 cubits long and 10,000 cubits ^h wide. In it will be the sanctuary, the Most Holy Place. ⁴It will be the sacred portion of the land for the priests, who minister in the sanctuary and who draw near to minister before the LORD. It will be a place for their houses as well as a holy place for the sanctuary. ⁵An area 25,000 cubits long and 10,000 cubits wide will belong to the Levites, who serve in the temple, as their possession for towns to live in.ⁱ

⁶"'You are to give the city as its property an area 5,000 cubits^j wide and 25,000 cubits long, adjoining the sacred portion; it will belong to all Israel.

⁷"'The prince will have the land bordering each side of the area formed by the sacred district and the property of the city. It will extend westward from the west side and eastward from the east side, running lengthwise from the western to the eastern border parallel to one of the tribal portions. ⁸This land will be his possession in Israel. And my princes will no longer oppress my people but will allow the people of Israel to possess the land according to their tribes.

⁹"'This is what the Sovereign LORD says: You have gone far enough, princes of Israel! Give up your violence and oppression and do what is just and right. Stop dispossessing my people, declares the Sovereign LORD. ¹⁰You are to use accurate

Why was contact with a dead person forbidden? (44:25)
Contact with a dead body made someone ceremonially unclean (see Leviticus 21:1–3).

Why were the priests not supposed to own possessions? (44:28)
Because they had been set apart for special service to God, he wanted them to depend on him only.

What was the open land? (45:2)
This was a buffer of unoccupied land around the holy area where the sanctuary would be built.

---

^a 27 Or *purification offering*; also in verse 29   ^b 29 The Hebrew term refers to the irrevocable giving over of things or persons to the LORD.   ^c 1 That is, about 8 miles or about 13 kilometers; also in verses 3, 5 and 6
^d 1 Septuagint (see also verses 3 and 5 and 48:9); Hebrew *10,000*   ^e 1 That is, about 6 1/2 miles or about 11 kilometers   ^f 2 That is, about 875 feet or about 265 meters   ^g 2 That is, about 88 feet or about 27 meters   ^h 3 That is, about 3 1/3 miles or about 5.3 kilometers; also in verse 5   ⁱ 5 Septuagint; Hebrew *temple; they will have as their possession 20 rooms*   ^j 6 That is, about 1 2/3 miles or about 2.7 kilometers

What practices were being
criticized here? (45:10–11)
Cheating with weights and measures was a common practice,
and the prophets consistently
condemned it.

What was this special gift?
(45:13)
This was a gift given to a prince
rather than to the priests. The
prince was supposed to use
these gifts in part for offerings to
the Lord.

scales, an accurate ephah*a* and an accurate bath.*b* **11**The ephah
and the bath are to be the same size, the bath containing a
tenth of a homer and the ephah a tenth of a homer; the homer is to be the standard measure for both. **12**The shekel*c* is
to consist of twenty gerahs. Twenty shekels plus twenty-five
shekels plus fifteen shekels equal one mina.*d*

13"'This is the special gift you are to offer: a sixth of an
ephah*e* from each homer of wheat and a sixth of an ephah*f*
from each homer of barley. **14**The prescribed portion of olive
oil, measured by the bath, is a tenth of a bath*g* from each cor
(which consists of ten baths or one homer, for ten baths are
equivalent to a homer). **15**Also one sheep is to be taken from
every flock of two hundred from the well-watered pastures
of Israel. These will be used for the grain offerings, burnt
offerings and fellowship offerings to make atonement for
the people, declares the Sovereign LORD. **16**All the people of
the land will be required to give this special offering to the
prince in Israel. **17**It will be the duty of the prince to provide
the burnt offerings, grain offerings and drink offerings at the
festivals, the New Moons and the Sabbaths—at all the appointed festivals of Israel. He will provide the sin offerings,*b*
grain offerings, burnt offerings and fellowship offerings to
make atonement for the Israelites.

18"'This is what the Sovereign LORD says: In the first
month on the first day you are to take a young bull without
defect and purify the sanctuary. **19**The priest is to take some
of the blood of the sin offering and put it on the doorposts of
the temple, on the four corners of the upper ledge of the altar
and on the gateposts of the inner court. **20**You are to do the
same on the seventh day of the month for anyone who sins
unintentionally or through ignorance; so you are to make
atonement for the temple.

21"'In the first month on the fourteenth day you are to observe the Passover, a festival lasting seven days, during which
you shall eat bread made without yeast. **22**On that day the
prince is to provide a bull as a sin offering for himself and for
all the people of the land. **23**Every day during the seven days
of the festival he is to provide seven bulls and seven rams
without defect as a burnt offering to the LORD, and a male
goat for a sin offering. **24**He is to provide as a grain offering
an ephah for each bull and an ephah for each ram, along with
a hin*i* of olive oil for each ephah.

25"'During the seven days of the festival, which begins
in the seventh month on the fifteenth day, he is to make
the same provision for sin offerings, burnt offerings, grain
offerings and oil.

46 "'This is what the Sovereign LORD says: The gate
of the inner court facing east is to be shut on the six

What festival was this?
(45:25)
This was the Festival (or feast) of
the Ingathering, which was also
called the Festival of the Tabernacles.

Why was the eastern gate
unique? (46:1–3)
This was the gate where the
glory of the Lord had entered. No
one would be allowed to contaminate that gate by entering it.

a 10 An ephah was a dry measure having the capacity of about 3/5 bushel or
about 22 liters.   *b 10* A bath was a liquid measure equaling about 6 gallons
or about 22 liters.   *c 12* A shekel weighed about 2/5 ounce or about 12
grams.   *d 12* That is, 60 shekels; the common mina was 50 shekels. Sixty
shekels were about 1 1/2 pounds or about 690 grams.   *e 13* That is, probably
about 6 pounds or about 2.7 kilograms   *f 13* That is, probably about
5 pounds or about 2.3 kilograms   *g 14* That is, about 2 1/2 quarts or about
2.2 liters   *b 17* Or *purification offerings*; also in verses 19, 22, 23 and 25
i 24 That is, about 1 gallon or about 3.8 liters

working days, but on the Sabbath day and on the day of the New Moon it is to be opened. [2]The prince is to enter from the outside through the portico of the gateway and stand by the gatepost. The priests are to sacrifice his burnt offering and his fellowship offerings. He is to bow down in worship at the threshold of the gateway and then go out, but the gate will not be shut until evening. [3]On the Sabbaths and New Moons the people of the land are to worship in the presence of the LORD at the entrance of that gateway. [4]The burnt offering the prince brings to the LORD on the Sabbath day is to be six male lambs and a ram, all without defect. [5]The grain offering given with the ram is to be an ephah,[a] and the grain offering with the lambs is to be as much as he pleases, along with a hin[b] of olive oil for each ephah. [6]On the day of the New Moon he is to offer a young bull, six lambs and a ram, all without defect. [7]He is to provide as a grain offering one ephah with the bull, one ephah with the ram, and with the lambs as much as he wants to give, along with a hin of oil for each ephah. [8]When the prince enters, he is to go in through the portico of the gateway, and he is to come out the same way.

[9]"When the people of the land come before the LORD at the appointed festivals, whoever enters by the north gate to worship is to go out the south gate; and whoever enters by the south gate is to go out the north gate. No one is to return through the gate by which they entered, but each is to go out the opposite gate. [10]The prince is to be among them, going in when they go in and going out when they go out. [11]At the feasts and the appointed festivals, the grain offering is to be an ephah with a bull, an ephah with a ram, and with the lambs as much as he pleases, along with a hin of oil for each ephah.

[12]"When the prince provides a freewill offering to the LORD—whether a burnt offering or fellowship offerings—the gate facing east is to be opened for him. He shall offer his burnt offering or his fellowship offerings as he does on the Sabbath day. Then he shall go out, and after he has gone out, the gate will be shut.

[13]"Every day you are to provide a year-old lamb without defect for a burnt offering to the LORD; morning by morning you shall provide it. [14]You are also to provide with it morning by morning a grain offering, consisting of a sixth of an ephah[c] with a third of a hin[d] of oil to moisten the flour. The presenting of this grain offering to the LORD is a lasting ordinance. [15]So the lamb and the grain offering and the oil shall be provided morning by morning for a regular burnt offering.

[16]"This is what the Sovereign LORD says: If the prince makes a gift from his inheritance to one of his sons, it will also belong to his descendants; it is to be their property by inheritance. [17]If, however, he makes a gift from his inheritance to one of his servants, the servant may keep it until the

Why did people have to leave through a different gate? (46:9)
This was probably a way to avoid congestion because so many people came to worship at the temple.

---

[a] *5* That is, probably about 35 pounds or about 16 kilograms; also in verses 7 and 11   [b] *5* That is, about 1 gallon or about 3.8 liters; also in verses 7 and 11   [c] *14* That is, probably about 6 pounds or about 2.7 kilograms   [d] *14* That is, about 1 1/2 quarts or about 1.3 liters

What was the year of freedom? (46:17)
This was the Year of Jubilee, held theoretically every 50th year.

year of freedom; then it will revert to the prince. His inheritance belongs to his sons only; it is theirs. ¹⁸The prince must not take any of the inheritance of the people, driving them off their property. He is to give his sons their inheritance out of his own property, so that not one of my people will be separated from their property.'"

¹⁹Then the man brought me through the entrance at the side of the gate to the sacred rooms facing north, which belonged to the priests, and showed me a place at the western end. ²⁰He said to me, "This is the place where the priests are to cook the guilt offering and the sin offering*ᵃ* and bake the grain offering, to avoid bringing them into the outer court and consecrating the people."

²¹He then brought me to the outer court and led me around to its four corners, and I saw in each corner another court. ²²In the four corners of the outer court were enclosed*ᵇ* courts, forty cubits long and thirty cubits wide;*ᶜ* each of the courts in the four corners was the same size. ²³Around the inside of each of the four courts was a ledge of stone, with places for fire built all around under the ledge. ²⁴He said to me, "These are the kitchens where those who minister at the temple are to cook the sacrifices of the people."

THE RIVER FROM THE TEMPLE

47 The man brought me back to the entrance to the temple, and I saw water coming out from under the threshold of the temple toward the east (for the temple faced east). The water was coming down from under the south side of the temple, south of the altar. ²He then brought me out through the north gate and led me around the outside to the outer gate facing east, and the water was trickling from the south side.

³As the man went eastward with a measuring line in his hand, he measured off a thousand cubits*ᵈ* and then led me through water that was ankle-deep. ⁴He measured off another thousand cubits and led me through water that was knee-deep. He measured off another thousand and led me through water that was up to the waist. ⁵He measured off another thousand, but now it was a river that I could not cross, because the water had risen and was deep enough to swim in—a river that no one could cross. ⁶He asked me, "Son of man, do you see this?"

Then he led me back to the bank of the river. ⁷When I arrived there, I saw a great number of trees on each side of

Who was this man? (47:1)
This was Ezekiel's angelic guide, who took him on the final tour of the temple.

What was the Arabah? (47:8)
This was the Jordan Valley, a waterless region between Jerusalem and the Dead Sea.

the river. ⁸He said to me, "This water flows toward the eastern region and goes down into the Arabah,*ᵉ* where it enters the Dead Sea. When it empties into the sea, the salty water there becomes fresh. ⁹Swarms of living creatures will live wherever the river flows. There will be large numbers of fish, because this water flows there and makes the salt water fresh; so where the river flows everything will live. ¹⁰Fishermen will stand along the shore; from En Gedi to En Eglaim there

ᵃ 20 Or *purification offering*   *ᵇ 22* The meaning of the Hebrew for this word is uncertain.   *ᶜ 22* That is, about 70 feet long and 53 feet wide or about 21 meters long and 16 meters wide   *ᵈ 3* That is, about 1,700 feet or about 530 meters   *ᵉ 8* Or *the Jordan Valley*

will be places for spreading nets. The fish will be of many kinds—like the fish of the Mediterranean Sea. [11]But the swamps and marshes will not become fresh; they will be left for salt. [12]Fruit trees of all kinds will grow on both banks of the river. Their leaves will not wither, nor will their fruit fail. Every month they will bear fruit, because the water from the sanctuary flows to them. Their fruit will serve for food and their leaves for healing."

THE BOUNDARIES OF THE LAND

[13]This is what the Sovereign Lord says: "These are the boundaries of the land that you will divide among the twelve tribes of Israel as their inheritance, with two portions for Joseph. [14]You are to divide it equally among them. Because I swore with uplifted hand to give it to your ancestors, this land will become your inheritance.

[15]"This is to be the boundary of the land:

"On the north side it will run from the Mediterranean Sea by the Hethlon road past Lebo Hamath to Zedad, [16]Berothah[a] and Sibraim (which lies on the border between Damascus and Hamath), as far as Hazer Hattikon, which is on the border of Hauran. [17]The boundary will extend from the sea to Hazar Enan,[b] along the northern border of Damascus, with the border of Hamath to the north. This will be the northern boundary.
[18]"On the east side the boundary will run between Hauran and Damascus, along the Jordan between Gilead and the land of Israel, to the Dead Sea and as far as Tamar.[c] This will be the eastern boundary.
[19]"On the south side it will run from Tamar as far as the waters of Meribah Kadesh, then along the Wadi of Egypt to the Mediterranean Sea. This will be the southern boundary.
[20]"On the west side, the Mediterranean Sea will be the boundary to a point opposite Lebo Hamath. This will be the western boundary.

[21]"You are to distribute this land among yourselves according to the tribes of Israel. [22]You are to allot it as an inheritance for yourselves and for the foreigners residing among you and who have children. You are to consider them as native-born Israelites; along with you they are to be allotted an inheritance among the tribes of Israel. [23]In whatever tribe a foreigner resides, there you are to give them their inheritance," declares the Sovereign Lord.

THE DIVISION OF THE LAND

48 "These are the tribes, listed by name: At the northern frontier, Dan will have one portion; it will follow the Hethlon road to Lebo Hamath; Hazar Enan and the northern border of Damascus next to Hamath will be part of its border from the east side to the west side.

---

[a] 15,16 See Septuagint and 48:1; Hebrew *road to go into Zedad,* [16]*Hamath, Berothah.*   [b] 17 Hebrew *Enon,* a variant of *Enan*   [c] 18 See Syriac; Hebrew *Israel. You will measure to the Dead Sea.*

Were these boundaries the same as for the 12 tribes? (47:13–20)
These boundaries were similar to what God had originally promised to Moses in Numbers 34:1–12. The land east of the Jordan River is not included.

How could foreigners become citizens of Israel? (47:22)
God allowed foreigners to join with his people if the men agreed to the covenant of circumcision. God's kingdom was expanding and would eventually include people from all over the world who believed in Christ.

How was the land divided? (48:1–29)
The tribes were assigned equal portions of land running in strips from east to west.

²"Asher will have one portion; it will border the territory of Dan from east to west.

³"Naphtali will have one portion; it will border the territory of Asher from east to west.

⁴"Manasseh will have one portion; it will border the territory of Naphtali from east to west.

⁵"Ephraim will have one portion; it will border the territory of Manasseh from east to west.

⁶"Reuben will have one portion; it will border the territory of Ephraim from east to west.

⁷"Judah will have one portion; it will border the territory of Reuben from east to west.

⁸"Bordering the territory of Judah from east to west will be the portion you are to present as a special gift. It will be 25,000 cubits^a wide, and its length from east to west will equal one of the tribal portions; the sanctuary will be in the center of it.

⁹"The special portion you are to offer to the LORD will be 25,000 cubits long and 10,000 cubits^b wide. ¹⁰This will be the sacred portion for the priests. It will be 25,000 cubits long on the north side, 10,000 cubits wide on the west side, 10,000 cubits wide on the east side and 25,000 cubits long on the south side. In the center of it will be the sanctuary of the LORD. ¹¹This will be for the consecrated priests, the Zadokites, who were faithful in serving me and did not go astray as the Levites did when the Israelites went astray. ¹²It will be a special gift to them from the sacred portion of the land, a most holy portion, bordering the territory of the Levites.

¹³"Alongside the territory of the priests, the Levites will have an allotment 25,000 cubits long and 10,000 cubits wide. Its total length will be 25,000 cubits and its width 10,000 cubits. ¹⁴They must not sell or exchange any of it. This is the best of the land and must not pass into other hands, because it is holy to the LORD.

¹⁵"The remaining area, 5,000 cubits^c wide and 25,000 cubits long, will be for the common use of the city, for houses and for pastureland. The city will be in the center of it ¹⁶and will have these measurements: the north side 4,500 cubits,^{d} the south side 4,500 cubits, the east side 4,500 cubits, and the west side 4,500 cubits. ¹⁷The pastureland for the city will be 250 cubits^e on the north, 250 cubits on the south, 250 cubits on the east, and 250 cubits on the west. ¹⁸What remains of the area, bordering on the sacred portion and running the length of it, will be 10,000 cubits on the east side and 10,000 cubits on the west side. Its produce will supply food for the workers of the city. ¹⁹The workers from the city who farm it will come from all the tribes of Israel. ²⁰The entire portion will be a square, 25,000 cubits on each side. As a special gift you will set aside the sacred portion, along with the property of the city.

---

^{a} 8 That is, about 8 miles or about 13 kilometers; also in verses 9, 10, 13, 15, 20 and 21 ^{b} 9 That is, about 3 1/3 miles or about 5.3 kilometers; also in verses 10, 13 and 18 ^{c} 15 That is, about 1 2/3 miles or about 2.7 kilometers ^{d} 16 That is, about 1 1/2 miles or about 2.4 kilometers; also in verses 30, 32, 33 and 34 ^{e} 17 That is, about 440 feet or about 135 meters

[21] "What remains on both sides of the area formed by the sacred portion and the property of the city will belong to the prince. It will extend eastward from the 25,000 cubits of the sacred portion to the eastern border, and westward from the 25,000 cubits to the western border. Both these areas running the length of the tribal portions will belong to the prince, and the sacred portion with the temple sanctuary will be in the center of them. [22] So the property of the Levites and the property of the city will lie in the center of the area that belongs to the prince. The area belonging to the prince will lie between the border of Judah and the border of Benjamin.

[23] "As for the rest of the tribes: Benjamin will have one portion; it will extend from the east side to the west side.

[24] "Simeon will have one portion; it will border the territory of Benjamin from east to west.

[25] "Issachar will have one portion; it will border the territory of Simeon from east to west.

[26] "Zebulun will have one portion; it will border the territory of Issachar from east to west.

[27] "Gad will have one portion; it will border the territory of Zebulun from east to west.

[28] "The southern boundary of Gad will run south from Tamar to the waters of Meribah Kadesh, then along the Wadi of Egypt to the Mediterranean Sea.

[29] "This is the land you are to allot as an inheritance to the tribes of Israel, and these will be their portions," declares the Sovereign LORD.

THE GATES OF THE NEW CITY

[30] "These will be the exits of the city: Beginning on the north side, which is 4,500 cubits long, [31] the gates of the city will be named after the tribes of Israel. The three gates on the north side will be the gate of Reuben, the gate of Judah and the gate of Levi.

[32] "On the east side, which is 4,500 cubits long, will be three gates: the gate of Joseph, the gate of Benjamin and the gate of Dan.

[33] "On the south side, which measures 4,500 cubits, will be three gates: the gate of Simeon, the gate of Issachar and the gate of Zebulun.

[34] "On the west side, which is 4,500 cubits long, will be three gates: the gate of Gad, the gate of Asher and the gate of Naphtali.

[35] "The distance all around will be 18,000 cubits.[a]

"And the name of the city from that time on will be:

THE LORD IS THERE."

How would the new city be symmetrical? (48:30–35)
The new city, like the temple, would be a perfect square. The 12 gates of the city would be named for the 12 tribes of Israel. Since Levi was included, Joseph represented Manasseh and Ephraim.

Was this city Jerusalem? (48:35)
Yes, but its name was changed to show that God once again lived there.

---

[a] 35 That is, about 6 miles or about 9.5 kilometers

Daniel

INTRODUCTION

Who wrote this book?	The book of Daniel, a Jew who became an important government official in Babylon and Persia, wrote this book.
Why was this book written?	The book of Daniel shows the Jewish people that foreign nations will have power over their homeland until God sends the promised Savior.
What do we learn about God in this book?	God is in charge of history. He knows ahead of time what will happen in our world.
What is special about this book?	The first part of the book tells stories of Daniel's life. The second part of the book tells about future governments that will have power over the Holy Land.

When did these things happen?

1400 BC 1300 1200 1100 1000 900 800 700 600 500 400

DANIEL'S TRAINING IN BABYLON

1 In the third year of the reign of Jehoiakim king of Judah, Nebuchadnezzar king of Babylon came to Jerusalem and besieged it. ²And the Lord delivered Jehoiakim king of Judah into his hand, along with some of the articles from the temple of God. These he carried off to the temple of his god in Babylonia*ᵃ* and put in the treasure house of his god.

³Then the king ordered Ashpenaz, chief of his court officials, to bring into the king's service some of the Israelites from the royal family and the nobility— ⁴young men without any physical defect, handsome, showing aptitude for every kind of learning, well informed, quick to understand, and qualified to serve in the king's palace. He was to teach them the language and literature of the Babylonians.*ᵇ* ⁵The king assigned them a daily amount of food and wine from the king's table. They were to be trained for three years, and after that they were to enter the king's service.

⁶Among those who were chosen were some from Judah: Daniel, Hananiah, Mishael and Azariah. ⁷The chief official gave them new names: to Daniel, the name Belteshazzar; to Hananiah, Shadrach; to Mishael, Meshach; and to Azariah, Abednego.

⁸But Daniel resolved not to defile himself with the royal food and wine, and he asked the chief official for permission not to defile himself this way. ⁹Now God had caused the official to show favor and compassion to Daniel, ¹⁰but the official told Daniel, "I am afraid of my lord the king, who has assigned your*ᶜ* food and drink. Why should he see you looking worse than the other young men your age? The king would then have my head because of you."

¹¹Daniel then said to the guard whom the chief official had appointed over Daniel, Hananiah, Mishael and Azariah, ¹²"Please test your servants for ten days: Give us nothing but vegetables to eat and water to drink. ¹³Then compare our appearance with that of the young men who eat the royal food, and treat your servants in accordance with what you see." ¹⁴So he agreed to this and tested them for ten days.

¹⁵At the end of the ten days they looked healthier and better nourished than any of the young men who ate the royal

ᵃ 2 Hebrew Shinar   ᵇ 4 Or Chaldeans   ᶜ 10 The Hebrew for your and you in this verse is plural.

What was the name of the god Nebuchadnezzar served? (1:2)
He worshiped the god Bel, also called Marduk, the Babylonians' chief god.

What is the meaning of these men's names? (1:6)
Daniel means "God is my judge," *Hananiah* means "the Lord shows grace," *Mishael* means "who is what God is?" and *Azariah* means "the Lord helps."

Daniel in Babylon (1:6)

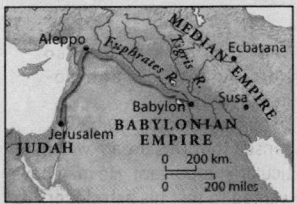

Why would Daniel not eat or drink the food or wine from the king's table? (1:8)
The Israelites considered the food from the king's table to be contaminated because a portion of it was offered to idols.

Does God use dreams to speak to people today?   DANIEL 1

Throughout the Bible there are many times that God spoke to people in dreams to show people what would happen in the future or to show people what they were supposed to do. So it is possible for God to use dreams to communicate. However, one of the reasons that God may have used dreams during ancient times was because the Bible had not yet been written. Now that we have God's Word in written form, it should be our guide for how to live.

Dreams are often confusing or not clear. They often incorporate events that we have recently experienced or people that we have recently had contact with. They often seem to deal with issues that are troubling or confusing. For these reasons, Christians should be careful not to base decisions only on dreams. God has given us the Bible as his authoritative Word and guide for living. He has also provided pastors, parents, and counselors who can give good advice. Along with the Holy Spirit working in our heart, these are the typical ways that God communicates with his people today.

food. ¹⁶So the guard took away their choice food and the wine they were to drink and gave them vegetables instead.

¹⁷To these four young men God gave knowledge and understanding of all kinds of literature and learning. And Daniel could understand visions and dreams of all kinds.

¹⁸At the end of the time set by the king to bring them into his service, the chief official presented them to Nebuchadnezzar. ¹⁹The king talked with them, and he found none equal to Daniel, Hananiah, Mishael and Azariah; so they entered the king's service. ²⁰In every matter of wisdom and understanding about which the king questioned them, he found them ten times better than all the magicians and enchanters in his whole kingdom.

²¹And Daniel remained there until the first year of King Cyrus.

NEBUCHADNEZZAR'S DREAM

2 In the second year of his reign, Nebuchadnezzar had dreams; his mind was troubled and he could not sleep. ²So the king summoned the magicians, enchanters, sorcerers and astrologers*ᵃ* to tell him what he had dreamed. When they came in and stood before the king, ³he said to them, "I have had a dream that troubles me and I want to know what it means.*ᵇ*"

⁴Then the astrologers answered the king,*ᶜ* "May the king live forever! Tell your servants the dream, and we will interpret it."

⁵The king replied to the astrologers, "This is what I have firmly decided: If you do not tell me what my dream was and interpret it, I will have you cut into pieces and your houses turned into piles of rubble. ⁶But if you tell me the dream and explain it, you will receive from me gifts and rewards and great honor. So tell me the dream and interpret it for me."

⁷Once more they replied, "Let the king tell his servants the dream, and we will interpret it."

⁸Then the king answered, "I am certain that you are trying to gain time, because you realize that this is what I have firmly decided: ⁹If you do not tell me the dream, there is only one penalty for you. You have conspired to tell me misleading and wicked things, hoping the situation will change. So then, tell me the dream, and I will know that you can interpret it for me."

¹⁰The astrologers answered the king, "There is no one on earth who can do what the king asks! No king, however great and mighty, has ever asked such a thing of any magician or enchanter or astrologer. ¹¹What the king asks is too difficult. No one can reveal it to the king except the gods, and they do not live among humans."

¹²This made the king so angry and furious that he ordered the execution of all the wise men of Babylon. ¹³So the decree was issued to put the wise men to death, and men were sent to look for Daniel and his friends to put them to death.

Why did the king deal so harshly with the astrologers? (2:5)
Nebuchadnezzar may have sensed that this dream was particularly important. He may have wanted to test his astrologers to see if they actually had the ability to see into the future.

ᵃ 2 Or Chaldeans; also in verses 4, 5 and 10   ᵇ 3 Or was   ᶜ 4 At this point the Hebrew text has in Aramaic, indicating that the text from here through the end of chapter 7 is in Aramaic.

¹⁴When Arioch, the commander of the king's guard, had gone out to put to death the wise men of Babylon, Daniel spoke to him with wisdom and tact. ¹⁵He asked the king's officer, "Why did the king issue such a harsh decree?" Arioch then explained the matter to Daniel. ¹⁶At this, Daniel went in to the king and asked for time, so that he might interpret the dream for him.

¹⁷Then Daniel returned to his house and explained the matter to his friends Hananiah, Mishael and Azariah. ¹⁸He urged them to plead for mercy from the God of heaven concerning this mystery, so that he and his friends might not be executed with the rest of the wise men of Babylon. ¹⁹During the night the mystery was revealed to Daniel in a vision. Then Daniel praised the God of heaven ²⁰and said:

"Praise be to the name of God for ever and ever;
    wisdom and power are his.
²¹He changes times and seasons;
    he deposes kings and raises up others.
He gives wisdom to the wise
    and knowledge to the discerning.
²²He reveals deep and hidden things;
    he knows what lies in darkness,
    and light dwells with him.
²³I thank and praise you, God of my ancestors:
    You have given me wisdom and power,
you have made known to me what we asked of you,
    you have made known to us the dream of the king."

DANIEL INTERPRETS THE DREAM

²⁴Then Daniel went to Arioch, whom the king had appointed to execute the wise men of Babylon, and said to him, "Do not execute the wise men of Babylon. Take me to the king, and I will interpret his dream for him."

²⁵Arioch took Daniel to the king at once and said, "I have found a man among the exiles from Judah who can tell the king what his dream means."

²⁶The king asked Daniel (also called Belteshazzar), "Are you able to tell me what I saw in my dream and interpret it?"

²⁷Daniel replied, "No wise man, enchanter, magician or diviner can explain to the king the mystery he has asked about, ²⁸but there is a God in heaven who reveals mysteries. He has shown King Nebuchadnezzar what will happen in days to come. Your dream and the visions that passed through your mind as you were lying in bed are these:

²⁹"As Your Majesty was lying there, your mind turned to things to come, and the revealer of mysteries showed you what is going to happen. ³⁰As for me, this mystery has been revealed to me, not because I have greater wisdom than anyone else alive, but so that Your Majesty may know the interpretation and that you may understand what went through your mind.

³¹"Your Majesty looked, and there before you stood a large statue—an enormous, dazzling statue, awesome in appearance. ³²The head of the statue was made of pure gold, its chest and arms of silver, its belly and thighs of bronze, ³³its legs of iron, its feet partly of iron and partly of baked clay.

³⁴While you were watching, a rock was cut out, but not by human hands. It struck the statue on its feet of iron and clay and smashed them. ³⁵Then the iron, the clay, the bronze, the silver and the gold were all broken to pieces and became like chaff on a threshing floor in the summer. The wind swept them away without leaving a trace. But the rock that struck the statue became a huge mountain and filled the whole earth.

³⁶"This was the dream, and now we will interpret it to the king. ³⁷Your Majesty, you are the king of kings. The God of heaven has given you dominion and power and might and glory; ³⁸in your hands he has placed all mankind and the beasts of the field and the birds in the sky. Wherever they live, he has made you ruler over them all. You are that head of gold.

³⁹"After you, another kingdom will arise, inferior to yours. Next, a third kingdom, one of bronze, will rule over the whole earth. ⁴⁰Finally, there will be a fourth kingdom, strong as iron—for iron breaks and smashes everything—and as iron breaks things to pieces, so it will crush and break all the others. ⁴¹Just as you saw that the feet and toes were partly of baked clay and partly of iron, so this will be a divided kingdom; yet it will have some of the strength of iron in it, even as you saw iron mixed with clay. ⁴²As the toes were partly iron and partly clay, so this kingdom will be partly strong and partly brittle. ⁴³And just as you saw the iron mixed with baked clay, so the people will be a mixture and will not remain united, any more than iron mixes with clay.

⁴⁴"In the time of those kings, the God of heaven will set up a kingdom that will never be destroyed, nor will it be left to another people. It will crush all those kingdoms and bring them to an end, but it will itself endure forever. ⁴⁵This is the meaning of the vision of the rock cut out of a mountain, but not by human hands—a rock that broke the iron, the bronze, the clay, the silver and the gold to pieces.

"The great God has shown the king what will take place in the future. The dream is true and its interpretation is trustworthy."

⁴⁶Then King Nebuchadnezzar fell prostrate before Daniel and paid him honor and ordered that an offering and incense be presented to him. ⁴⁷The king said to Daniel, "Surely your God is the God of gods and the Lord of kings and a revealer of mysteries, for you were able to reveal this mystery."

⁴⁸Then the king placed Daniel in a high position and lavished many gifts on him. He made him ruler over the entire province of Babylon and placed him in charge of all its wise men. ⁴⁹Moreover, at Daniel's request the king appointed Shadrach, Meshach and Abednego administrators over the province of Babylon, while Daniel himself remained at the royal court.

THE IMAGE OF GOLD AND THE BLAZING FURNACE

3 King Nebuchadnezzar made an image of gold, sixty cubits high and six cubits wide,^a and set it up on the plain

^a *1* That is, about 90 feet high and 9 feet wide or about 27 meters high and 2.7 meters wide

---

What was the meaning of the dream? (2:36–43)
The statue represented kingdoms that would control Israel throughout history. All of these kingdoms would be destroyed.

What was the fifth kingdom? (2:44)
This was the eternal kingdom of God, who would rule over the entire earth.

Why wasn't Nebuchadnezzar angry about Daniel's prophecy? (2:46)
He could tell that Daniel had not only seen the dream but could interpret it. The king could prepare for what would happen. He also was assured that his own reign would continue.

Why would a captive be placed in a position of authority? (2:48)
Daniel had proven he was able to interpret dreams and had dared to tell the king the truth. Nebuchadnezzar realized he could trust Daniel and rely on him for solid information.

What was this statue like? (3:1)
This statue was 90 feet tall (27.4 meters). It was probably not solid gold but was made of wood plated with gold. It probably represented the god Nabu, whose name was the first part of Nebuchadnezzar's name.

of Dura in the province of Babylon. ²He then summoned the satraps, prefects, governors, advisers, treasurers, judges, magistrates and all the other provincial officials to come to the dedication of the image he had set up. ³So the satraps, prefects, governors, advisers, treasurers, judges, magistrates and all the other provincial officials assembled for the dedication of the image that King Nebuchadnezzar had set up, and they stood before it.

⁴Then the herald loudly proclaimed, "Nations and peoples of every language, this is what you are commanded to do: ⁵As soon as you hear the sound of the horn, flute, zither, lyre, harp, pipe and all kinds of music, you must fall down and worship the image of gold that King Nebuchadnezzar has set up. ⁶Whoever does not fall down and worship will immediately be thrown into a blazing furnace."

⁷Therefore, as soon as they heard the sound of the horn, flute, zither, lyre, harp and all kinds of music, all the nations and peoples of every language fell down and worshiped the image of gold that King Nebuchadnezzar had set up.

⁸At this time some astrologers*a* came forward and denounced the Jews. ⁹They said to King Nebuchadnezzar, "May the king live forever! ¹⁰Your Majesty has issued a decree that everyone who hears the sound of the horn, flute, zither, lyre, harp, pipe and all kinds of music must fall down and worship the image of gold, ¹¹and that whoever does not fall down and worship will be thrown into a blazing furnace. ¹²But there are some Jews whom you have set over the affairs of the province of Babylon—Shadrach, Meshach and Abednego—who pay no attention to you, Your Majesty. They neither serve your gods nor worship the image of gold you have set up."

¹³Furious with rage, Nebuchadnezzar summoned Shadrach, Meshach and Abednego. So these men were brought before the king, ¹⁴and Nebuchadnezzar said to them, "Is it true, Shadrach, Meshach and Abednego, that you do not serve my gods or worship the image of gold I have set up? ¹⁵Now when you hear the sound of the horn, flute, zither, lyre, harp, pipe and all kinds of music, if you are ready to fall down and worship the image I made, very good. But if

a 8 Or Chaldeans

Who were satraps and prefects? (3:2)
Satraps were the king's chief representatives, and prefects were his military commanders.

What did the term *Jew* represent? (3:8)
The term was a shortened form of *Judahite*.

Why did these men not worship Nebuchadnezzar's god? (3:12)
Instead of obeying the king, they obeyed the word of God.

What does the story of the blazing furnace teach about worshiping God alone?

DANIEL 3

Shadrach, Meshach, and Abednego refused the king's command to worship the image that the king had created. They believed in the true God and would not compromise their faith by bowing down to an idol. This would have been blasphemy and would have broken God's laws about not worshiping pagan idols.

When they were thrown into the blazing furnace as punishment for disobeying the king's order, a fourth figure appeared, possibly an angel, and protected them from being burned. God created this miracle to show that he was the only true God.

God does not always do miracles to save his people. Even today in many parts of the world Christians are persecuted for their faith and are sometimes thrown into prison, physically punished, or even killed. As people who have the freedom to worship God, we give thanks for that liberty and we should pray for and seek to help those who suffer for their faith.

How confident were these men that they were doing the right thing? (3:17–18)
They said that God could save them but that even if he didn't they would continue to place their trust in him.

you do not worship it, you will be thrown immediately into a blazing furnace. Then what god will be able to rescue you from my hand?"

[16] Shadrach, Meshach and Abednego replied to him, "King Nebuchadnezzar, we do not need to defend ourselves before you in this matter. [17] If we are thrown into the blazing furnace, the God we serve is able to deliver us from it, and he will deliver us[a] from Your Majesty's hand. [18] But even if he does not, we want you to know, Your Majesty, that we will not serve your gods or worship the image of gold you have set up."

[19] Then Nebuchadnezzar was furious with Shadrach, Meshach and Abednego, and his attitude toward them changed. He ordered the furnace heated seven times hotter than usual [20] and commanded some of the strongest soldiers in his army to tie up Shadrach, Meshach and Abednego and throw them into the blazing furnace. [21] So these men, wearing their robes, trousers, turbans and other clothes, were bound and thrown into the blazing furnace. [22] The king's command was so urgent and the furnace so hot that the flames of the fire killed the soldiers who took up Shadrach, Meshach and Abednego, [23] and these three men, firmly tied, fell into the blazing furnace.

[24] Then King Nebuchadnezzar leaped to his feet in amazement and asked his advisers, "Weren't there three men that we tied up and threw into the fire?"

They replied, "Certainly, Your Majesty."

[25] He said, "Look! I see four men walking around in the fire, unbound and unharmed, and the fourth looks like a son of the gods."

Who was the fourth man in the furnace? (3:25)
Nebuchadnezzar thought the fourth figure was a supernatural being or angel. Some commentators believe this was an early appearance of the Son of God.

[26] Nebuchadnezzar then approached the opening of the blazing furnace and shouted, "Shadrach, Meshach and Abednego, servants of the Most High God, come out! Come here!"

So Shadrach, Meshach and Abednego came out of the fire, [27] and the satraps, prefects, governors and royal advisers crowded around them. They saw that the fire had not harmed their bodies, nor was a hair of their heads singed; their robes were not scorched, and there was no smell of fire on them.

[28] Then Nebuchadnezzar said, "Praise be to the God of Shadrach, Meshach and Abednego, who has sent his angel and rescued his servants! They trusted in him and defied the king's command and were willing to give up their lives rather than serve or worship any god except their own God. [29] Therefore I decree that the people of any nation or language who say anything against the God of Shadrach, Meshach and Abednego be cut into pieces and their houses be turned into piles of rubble, for no other god can save in this way."

Why did Nebuchadnezzar issue this order? (3:29)
He didn't want to appear indecisive. He would have contradicted his earlier decree if he allowed the Jews to worship their God. So promising to kill anyone who opposed the Lord allowed him to remain authoritative.

[30] Then the king promoted Shadrach, Meshach and Abednego in the province of Babylon.

[a] 17 Or *If the God we serve is able to deliver us, then he will deliver us from the blazing furnace and*

NEBUCHADNEZZAR'S DREAM OF A TREE

 ^a King Nebuchadnezzar,

To the nations and peoples of every language, who live in all the earth:

May you prosper greatly!

²It is my pleasure to tell you about the miraculous signs and wonders that the Most High God has performed for me.

³How great are his signs,
   how mighty his wonders!
His kingdom is an eternal kingdom;
   his dominion endures from generation to
      generation.

⁴I, Nebuchadnezzar, was at home in my palace, contented and prosperous. ⁵I had a dream that made me afraid. As I was lying in bed, the images and visions that passed through my mind terrified me. ⁶So I commanded that all the wise men of Babylon be brought before me to interpret the dream for me. ⁷When the magicians, enchanters, astrologers^b and diviners came, I told them the dream, but they could not interpret it for me. ⁸Finally, Daniel came into my presence and I told him the dream. (He is called Belteshazzar, after the name of my god, and the spirit of the holy gods is in him.)

⁹I said, "Belteshazzar, chief of the magicians, I know that the spirit of the holy gods is in you, and no mystery is too difficult for you. Here is my dream; interpret it for me. ¹⁰These are the visions I saw while lying in bed: I looked, and there before me stood a tree in the middle of the land. Its height was enormous. ¹¹The tree grew large and strong and its top touched the sky; it was visible to the ends of the earth. ¹²Its leaves were beautiful, its fruit abundant, and on it was food for all. Under it the wild animals found shelter, and the birds lived in its branches; from it every creature was fed.

¹³"In the visions I saw while lying in bed, I looked, and there before me was a holy one, a messenger,^c coming down from heaven. ¹⁴He called in a loud voice: 'Cut down the tree and trim off its branches; strip off its leaves and scatter its fruit. Let the animals flee from under it and the birds from its branches. ¹⁵But let the stump and its roots, bound with iron and bronze, remain in the ground, in the grass of the field.

"'Let him be drenched with the dew of heaven, and let him live with the animals among the plants of the earth. ¹⁶Let his mind be changed from that of a man and let him be given the mind of an animal, till seven times^d pass by for him.

¹⁷"'The decision is announced by messengers, the

What did Daniel's Babylonian name mean? (4:8)
Daniel's Babylonian name, Belteshazzar, was formed from *Bel*, a title of the Babylonian God Marduk.

Who was this messenger? (4:13)
This was most likely an angel.

---

^a In Aramaic texts 4:1-3 is numbered 3:31-33, and 4:4-37 is numbered 4:1-34.
^b 7 Or *Chaldeans*   ^c 13 Or *watchman*; also in verses 17 and 23
^d 16 Or *years*; also in verses 23, 25 and 32

holy ones declare the verdict, so that the living may know that the Most High is sovereign over all kingdoms on earth and gives them to anyone he wishes and sets over them the lowliest of people.'

¹⁸ "This is the dream that I, King Nebuchadnezzar, had. Now, Belteshazzar, tell me what it means, for none of the wise men in my kingdom can interpret it for me. But you can, because the spirit of the holy gods is in you."

DANIEL INTERPRETS THE DREAM

¹⁹ Then Daniel (also called Belteshazzar) was greatly perplexed for a time, and his thoughts terrified him. So the king said, "Belteshazzar, do not let the dream or its meaning alarm you."

Belteshazzar answered, "My lord, if only the dream applied to your enemies and its meaning to your adversaries! ²⁰ The tree you saw, which grew large and strong, with its top touching the sky, visible to the whole earth, ²¹ with beautiful leaves and abundant fruit, providing food for all, giving shelter to the wild animals, and having nesting places in its branches for the birds— ²² Your Majesty, you are that tree! You have become great and strong; your greatness has grown until it reaches the sky, and your dominion extends to distant parts of the earth.

²³ "Your Majesty saw a holy one, a messenger, coming down from heaven and saying, 'Cut down the tree and destroy it, but leave the stump, bound with iron and bronze, in the grass of the field, while its roots remain in the ground. Let him be drenched with the dew of heaven; let him live with the wild animals, until seven times pass by for him.'

²⁴ "This is the interpretation, Your Majesty, and this is the decree the Most High has issued against my lord the king: ²⁵ You will be driven away from people and will live with the wild animals; you will eat grass like the ox and be drenched with the dew of heaven. Seven times will pass by for you until you acknowledge that the Most High is sovereign over all kingdoms on earth and gives them to anyone he wishes. ²⁶ The command to leave the stump of the tree with its roots means that your kingdom will be restored to you when you acknowledge that Heaven rules. ²⁷ Therefore, Your Majesty, be pleased to accept my advice: Renounce your sins by doing what is right, and your wickedness by being kind to the oppressed. It may be that then your prosperity will continue."

THE DREAM IS FULFILLED

²⁸ All this happened to King Nebuchadnezzar. ²⁹ Twelve months later, as the king was walking on the roof of the royal palace of Babylon, ³⁰ he said, "Is not this the great Babylon I have built as the royal residence, by my mighty power and for the glory of my majesty?"

³¹ Even as the words were on his lips, a voice came from heaven, "This is what is decreed for you, King Nebuchadnezzar: Your royal authority has been taken

What would happen to Nebuchadnezzar? (4:25) Nebuchadnezzar would become so insane that he wouldn't be able to be around people. He would be driven out of the palace and would live with the animals in the fields.

from you. ³²You will be driven away from people and will live with the wild animals; you will eat grass like the ox. Seven times will pass by for you until you acknowledge that the Most High is sovereign over all kingdoms on earth and gives them to anyone he wishes."

³³Immediately what had been said about Nebuchadnezzar was fulfilled. He was driven away from people and ate grass like the ox. His body was drenched with the dew of heaven until his hair grew like the feathers of an eagle and his nails like the claws of a bird.

³⁴At the end of that time, I, Nebuchadnezzar, raised my eyes toward heaven, and my sanity was restored. Then I praised the Most High; I honored and glorified him who lives forever.

His dominion is an eternal dominion;
    his kingdom endures from generation to generation.
³⁵All the peoples of the earth
    are regarded as nothing.
He does as he pleases
    with the powers of heaven
    and the peoples of the earth.
No one can hold back his hand
    or say to him: "What have you done?"

³⁶At the same time that my sanity was restored, my honor and splendor were returned to me for the glory of my kingdom. My advisers and nobles sought me out, and I was restored to my throne and became even greater than before. ³⁷Now I, Nebuchadnezzar, praise and exalt and glorify the King of heaven, because everything he does is right and all his ways are just. And those who walk in pride he is able to humble.

THE WRITING ON THE WALL

5 King Belshazzar gave a great banquet for a thousand of his nobles and drank wine with them. ²While Belshazzar was drinking his wine, he gave orders to bring in the gold and silver goblets that Nebuchadnezzar his father*ᵃ* had taken from the temple in Jerusalem, so that the king and his nobles, his wives and his concubines might drink from them. ³So they brought in the gold goblets that had been taken from the temple of God in Jerusalem, and the king and his nobles, his wives and his concubines drank from them. ⁴As they drank the wine, they praised the gods of gold and silver, of bronze, iron, wood and stone.

⁵Suddenly the fingers of a human hand appeared and wrote on the plaster of the wall, near the lampstand in the royal palace. The king watched the hand as it wrote. ⁶His face turned pale and he was so frightened that his legs became weak and his knees were knocking.

⁷The king summoned the enchanters, astrologers*ᵇ* and diviners. Then he said to these wise men of Babylon, "Whoever reads this writing and tells me what it means will be clothed

---

ᵃ 2 Or *ancestor*; or *predecessor*; also in verses 11, 13 and 18
ᵇ 7 Or *Chaldeans*; also in verse 11

How was the king driven away from the palace? (4:33)
His mental condition was such that he did not put up any resistance. There may have been large parks on the palace ground where the king could dwell among the animals.

Did Nebuchadnezzar become a true believer? (4:37)
Nebuchadnezzar saw that God rules over all, but this didn't mean that he abandoned the Babylonian gods.

Who were these gods? (5:4)
The people of the region worshiped hundreds of gods. These particular gods weren't identified.

in purple and have a gold chain placed around his neck, and he will be made the third highest ruler in the kingdom."

⁸Then all the king's wise men came in, but they could not read the writing or tell the king what it meant. ⁹So King Belshazzar became even more terrified and his face grew more pale. His nobles were baffled.

¹⁰The queen,ᵃ hearing the voices of the king and his nobles, came into the banquet hall. "May the king live forever!" she said. "Don't be alarmed! Don't look so pale! ¹¹There is a man in your kingdom who has the spirit of the holy gods in him. In the time of your father he was found to have insight and intelligence and wisdom like that of the gods. Your father, King Nebuchadnezzar, appointed him chief of the magicians, enchanters, astrologers and diviners. ¹²He did this because Daniel, whom the king called Belteshazzar, was found to have a keen mind and knowledge and understanding, and also the ability to interpret dreams, explain riddles and solve difficult problems. Call for Daniel, and he will tell you what the writing means."

¹³So Daniel was brought before the king, and the king said to him, "Are you Daniel, one of the exiles my father the king brought from Judah? ¹⁴I have heard that the spirit of the gods is in you and that you have insight, intelligence and outstanding wisdom. ¹⁵The wise men and enchanters were brought before me to read this writing and tell me what it means, but they could not explain it. ¹⁶Now I have heard that you are able to give interpretations and to solve difficult problems. If you can read this writing and tell me what it means, you will be clothed in purple and have a gold chain placed around your neck, and you will be made the third highest ruler in the kingdom."

¹⁷Then Daniel answered the king, "You may keep your gifts for yourself and give your rewards to someone else. Nevertheless, I will read the writing for the king and tell him what it means.

¹⁸"Your Majesty, the Most High God gave your father Nebuchadnezzar sovereignty and greatness and glory and splendor. ¹⁹Because of the high position he gave him, all the nations and peoples of every language dreaded and feared him. Those the king wanted to put to death, he put to death; those he wanted to spare, he spared; those he wanted to promote, he promoted; and those he wanted to humble, he humbled. ²⁰But when his heart became arrogant and hardened with pride, he was deposed from his royal throne and stripped of his glory. ²¹He was driven away from people and given the mind of an animal; he lived with the wild donkeys and ate grass like the ox; and his body was drenched with the dew of heaven, until he acknowledged that the Most High God is sovereign over all kingdoms on earth and sets over them anyone he wishes.

²²"But you, Belshazzar, his son,ᵇ have not humbled yourself, though you knew all this. ²³Instead, you have set yourself up against the Lord of heaven. You had the goblets from his temple brought to you, and you and your nobles, your wives and your concubines drank wine from them. You praised the gods of silver and gold, of bronze, iron, wood and stone,

How could Daniel be in charge of things that God condemned? (5:11) His position as chief of the magicians and astrologers may have meant that he was not their supervisor but was higher in rank than them because of his ability to predict the future.

Was it dangerous to speak to the king in this way? (5:17) Daniel had a reputation for speaking the truth to the king and for being able to accurately interpret dreams, so it was not dangerous for him to speak in this direct way to the king.

ᵃ 10 Or queen mother ᵇ 22 Or descendant; or successor

which cannot see or hear or understand. But you did not
honor the God who holds in his hand your life and all your
ways. [24]Therefore he sent the hand that wrote the inscription.
[25]"This is the inscription that was written:

MENE, MENE, TEKEL, PARSIN

[26]"Here is what these words mean:

Mene[a]: God has numbered the days of your reign
and brought it to an end.
[27] Tekel[b]: You have been weighed on the scales and
found wanting.
[28] Peres[c]: Your kingdom is divided and given to the
Medes and Persians."

[29]Then at Belshazzar's command, Daniel was clothed in
purple, a gold chain was placed around his neck, and he was
proclaimed the third highest ruler in the kingdom.
[30]That very night Belshazzar, king of the Babylonians,[d]
was slain, [31]and Darius the Mede took over the kingdom, at
the age of sixty-two.[e]

DANIEL IN THE DEN OF LIONS

6[f] It pleased Darius to appoint 120 satraps to rule
throughout the kingdom, [2]with three administrators
over them, one of whom was Daniel. The satraps were made
accountable to them so that the king might not suffer loss.
[3]Now Daniel so distinguished himself among the administrators and the satraps by his exceptional qualities that the
king planned to set him over the whole kingdom. [4]At this,
the administrators and the satraps tried to find grounds for
charges against Daniel in his conduct of government affairs,
but they were unable to do so. They could find no corruption
in him, because he was trustworthy and neither corrupt nor
negligent. [5]Finally these men said, "We will never find any
basis for charges against this man Daniel unless it has something to do with the law of his God."
[6]So these administrators and satraps went as a group to the
king and said: "May King Darius live forever! [7]The royal administrators, prefects, satraps, advisers and governors have all
agreed that the king should issue an edict and enforce the
decree that anyone who prays to any god or human being during the next thirty days, except to you, Your Majesty, shall be
thrown into the lions' den. [8]Now, Your Majesty, issue the decree and put it in writing so that it cannot be altered—in accordance with the law of the Medes and Persians, which cannot be repealed." [9]So King Darius put the decree in writing.
[10]Now when Daniel learned that the decree had been
published, he went home to his upstairs room where the
windows opened toward Jerusalem. Three times a day he got
down on his knees and prayed, giving thanks to his God, just

---

[a] 26 Mene can mean numbered or mina (a unit of money).   [b] 27 Tekel can
mean weighed or shekel.   [c] 28 Peres (the singular of Parsin) can mean
divided or Persia or a half mina or a half shekel.   [d] 30 Or Chaldeans
[e] 31 In Aramaic texts this verse (5:31) is numbered 6:1.   [f] In Aramaic texts
6:1-28 is numbered 6:2-29.

**Why did Belshazzar reward
David for interpreting these
words? (5:29)**
Even though the words spelled
out his destruction, Belshazzar kept his word to reward the
person who interpreted the
message.

**How could someone who
had served the previous
leader continue under the
new ruler? (6:2)**
The new ruler was usually a relative or son of the former king,
so many of the officials from the
previous regime would continue
in their positions.

**What was a lions' den like?
(6:7)**
It was a pit with a relatively small
opening at the top, making it impossible for a prisoner to escape.

**Why couldn't the laws of the
Medes and the Persians be
repealed? (6:8)**
In that culture, it was impossible for a king to revoke a law.
So a ruler would have to find
a way around the situation if
he changed his mind about a
decree.

**Why did Daniel face Jerusa-
lem to pray? (6:10)**
It was customary for Jews who
were away from Jerusalem to
pray in the direction of the holy
city and God's temple.

as he had done before. ¹¹ Then these men went as a group and found Daniel praying and asking God for help. ¹² So they went to the king and spoke to him about his royal decree: "Did you not publish a decree that during the next thirty days anyone who prays to any god or human being except to you, Your Majesty, would be thrown into the lions' den?"

The king answered, "The decree stands — in accordance with the law of the Medes and Persians, which cannot be repealed."

¹³ Then they said to the king, "Daniel, who is one of the exiles from Judah, pays no attention to you, Your Majesty, or to the decree you put in writing. He still prays three times a day." ¹⁴ When the king heard this, he was greatly distressed; he was determined to rescue Daniel and made every effort until sundown to save him.

¹⁵ Then the men went as a group to King Darius and said to him, "Remember, Your Majesty, that according to the law of the Medes and Persians no decree or edict that the king issues can be changed."

¹⁶ So the king gave the order, and they brought Daniel and threw him into the lions' den. The king said to Daniel, "May your God, whom you serve continually, rescue you!"

¹⁷ A stone was brought and placed over the mouth of the den, and the king sealed it with his own signet ring and with the rings of his nobles, so that Daniel's situation might not be changed. ¹⁸ Then the king returned to his palace and spent the night without eating and without any entertainment being brought to him. And he could not sleep.

¹⁹ At the first light of dawn, the king got up and hurried to the lions' den. ²⁰ When he came near the den, he called to Daniel in an anguished voice, "Daniel, servant of the living God, has your God, whom you serve continually, been able to rescue you from the lions?"

²¹ Daniel answered, "May the king live forever! ²² My God sent his angel, and he shut the mouths of the lions. They have not hurt me, because I was found innocent in his sight. Nor have I ever done any wrong before you, Your Majesty."

²³ The king was overjoyed and gave orders to lift Daniel out of the den. And when Daniel was lifted from the den, no wound was found on him, because he had trusted in his God.

²⁴ At the king's command, the men who had falsely accused Daniel were brought in and thrown into the lions' den, along with their wives and children. And before they reached the floor of the den, the lions overpowered them and crushed all their bones.

²⁵ Then King Darius wrote to all the nations and peoples of every language in all the earth:

"May you prosper greatly!

²⁶ "I issue a decree that in every part of my kingdom people must fear and reverence the God of Daniel.

"For he is the living God
and he endures forever;
his kingdom will not be destroyed,
his dominion will never end.

Did the king want Daniel to be destroyed by the lions? (6:16)
No, the king expressed the hope that Daniel's God would save him.

How were Daniel's accusers punished? (6:24)
They were thrown into the lions' den and were killed before they even reached the floor.

²⁷ He rescues and he saves;
  he performs signs and wonders
  in the heavens and on the earth.
He has rescued Daniel
  from the power of the lions.”

²⁸ So Daniel prospered during the reign of Darius and the
reign of Cyrus^a the Persian.

DANIEL'S DREAM OF FOUR BEASTS

7 In the first year of Belshazzar king of Babylon, Daniel
had a dream, and visions passed through his mind as he
was lying in bed. He wrote down the substance of his dream.
² Daniel said: “In my vision at night I looked, and there
before me were the four winds of heaven churning up the
great sea. ³ Four great beasts, each different from the others,
came up out of the sea.

⁴ “The first was like a lion, and it had the wings of an eagle.
I watched until its wings were torn off and it was lifted from
the ground so that it stood on two feet like a human being,
and the mind of a human was given to it.

⁵ “And there before me was a second beast, which looked
like a bear. It was raised up on one of its sides, and it had
three ribs in its mouth between its teeth. It was told, ‘Get up
and eat your fill of flesh!’

⁶ “After that, I looked, and there before me was another
beast, one that looked like a leopard. And on its back it had
four wings like those of a bird. This beast had four heads, and
it was given authority to rule.

⁷ “After that, in my vision at night I looked, and there
before me was a fourth beast—terrifying and frightening
and very powerful. It had large iron teeth; it crushed and
devoured its victims and trampled underfoot whatever was
left. It was different from all the former beasts, and it had
ten horns.

⁸ “While I was thinking about the horns, there before me
was another horn, a little one, which came up among them;
and three of the first horns were uprooted before it. This
horn had eyes like the eyes of a human being and a mouth
that spoke boastfully.

⁹ “As I looked,

“thrones were set in place,
  and the Ancient of Days took his seat.
His clothing was as white as snow;
  the hair of his head was white like wool.
His throne was flaming with fire,
  and its wheels were all ablaze.
¹⁰ A river of fire was flowing,
  coming out from before him.
Thousands upon thousands attended him;
  ten thousand times ten thousand stood before him.
The court was seated,
  and the books were opened.

---

^a 28 Or *Darius, that is, the reign of Cyrus*

What was this lion with eagles' wings? (7:4)
This was a cherub symbolizing the Neo-Babylonian Empire.

Why did this beast have ten horns? (7:7)
This showed how widespread the beast's authority was.

Who was the Ancient of Days? (7:9)
This was a reference to God.

What sort of court was this? (7:10)
This appears to be God's judging of the nations and individuals. The books contained the evidence of the deeds the people had done.

Who was this son of man?
(7:13)
This is the first reference to
the Messiah as the son of man,
a term Jesus used to describe
himself.

¹¹ "Then I continued to watch because of the boastful words the horn was speaking. I kept looking until the beast was slain and its body destroyed and thrown into the blazing fire. ¹² (The other beasts had been stripped of their authority, but were allowed to live for a period of time.)

¹³ "In my vision at night I looked, and there before me was one like a son of man,ᵃ coming with the clouds of heaven. He approached the Ancient of Days and was led into his presence. ¹⁴ He was given authority, glory and sovereign power; all nations and peoples of every language worshiped him. His dominion is an everlasting dominion that will not pass away, and his kingdom is one that will never be destroyed.

THE INTERPRETATION OF THE DREAM

¹⁵ "I, Daniel, was troubled in spirit, and the visions that passed through my mind disturbed me. ¹⁶ I approached one of those standing there and asked him the meaning of all this.

"So he told me and gave me the interpretation of these things: ¹⁷ 'The four great beasts are four kings that will rise from the earth. ¹⁸ But the holy people of the Most High will receive the kingdom and will possess it forever — yes, for ever and ever.'

¹⁹ "Then I wanted to know the meaning of the fourth beast, which was different from all the others and most terrifying, with its iron teeth and bronze claws — the beast that crushed and devoured its victims and trampled underfoot whatever was left. ²⁰ I also wanted to know about the ten horns on its head and about the other horn that came up, before which three of them fell — the horn that looked more imposing than the others and that had eyes and a mouth that spoke boastfully. ²¹ As I watched, this horn was waging war against the holy people and defeating them, ²² until the Ancient of Days came and pronounced judgment in favor of the holy people of the Most High, and the time came when they possessed the kingdom.

²³ "He gave me this explanation: 'The fourth beast is a fourth kingdom that will appear on earth. It will be different from all the other kingdoms and will devour the whole earth, trampling it down and crushing it. ²⁴ The ten horns are ten kings who will come from this kingdom. After them another king will arise, different from the earlier ones; he will subdue three kings. ²⁵ He will speak against the Most High and oppress his holy people and try to change the set times and the laws. The holy people will be delivered into his hands for a time, times and half a time.ᵇ

²⁶ "'But the court will sit, and his power will be taken away and completely destroyed forever. ²⁷ Then the sovereignty, power and greatness of all the kingdoms under heaven will be handed over to the holy people of the Most High. His kingdom will be an everlasting kingdom, and all rulers will worship and obey him.'

ᵃ 13 The Aramaic phrase *bar enash* means *human being.* The phrase *son of man* is retained here because of its use in the New Testament as a title of Jesus, probably based largely on this verse.　　ᵇ 25 Or *for a year, two years and half a year*

²⁸ "This is the end of the matter. I, Daniel, was deeply troubled by my thoughts, and my face turned pale, but I kept the matter to myself."

DANIEL'S VISION OF A RAM AND A GOAT

8 In the third year of King Belshazzar's reign, I, Daniel, had a vision, after the one that had already appeared to me. ²In my vision I saw myself in the citadel of Susa in the province of Elam; in the vision I was beside the Ulai Canal. ³I looked up, and there before me was a ram with two horns, standing beside the canal, and the horns were long. One of the horns was longer than the other but grew up later. ⁴I watched the ram as it charged toward the west and the north and the south. No animal could stand against it, and none could rescue from its power. It did as it pleased and became great.

⁵As I was thinking about this, suddenly a goat with a prominent horn between its eyes came from the west, crossing the whole earth without touching the ground. ⁶It came toward the two-horned ram I had seen standing beside the canal and charged at it in great rage. ⁷I saw it attack the ram furiously, striking the ram and shattering its two horns. The ram was powerless to stand against it; the goat knocked it to the ground and trampled on it, and none could rescue the ram from its power. ⁸The goat became very great, but at the height of its power the large horn was broken off, and in its place four prominent horns grew up toward the four winds of heaven.

⁹Out of one of them came another horn, which started small but grew in power to the south and to the east and toward the Beautiful Land. ¹⁰It grew until it reached the host of the heavens, and it threw some of the starry host down to the earth and trampled on them. ¹¹It set itself up to be as great as the commander of the army of the Lord; it took

What did the ram represent? (8:3)
The ram represented the Medo-Persian Empire. The longer horn reflected the prominence of Persia.

Who was the goat? (8:5-6)
The goat represented Greece, and the prominent horn was Alexander the Great.

What was the "Beautiful Land"? (8:9)
This was the land of Israel.

IDENTIFICATION OF THE FOUR KINGDOMS

VISION IN CH. 2	VISION IN CH. 7	VISION IN CH. 8	EMPIRE	PERIOD OF DOMINATION
Head of gold	Lion		BABYLONIAN 2:37-38	626 BC–539 BC
Chest and arms of silver	Bear	Ram	MEDO-PERSIAN 8:20	539 BC–330 BC
Belly and thighs of bronze	Leopard	Goat	GRECIAN 8:21	330 BC–146 BC
Legs of iron	Terrifying and frightening beast		ROMAN	146 BC–AD 476
Feet of clay with iron mixed				

away the daily sacrifice from the LORD, and his sanctuary was thrown down. [12] Because of rebellion, the LORD's people[a] and the daily sacrifice were given over to it. It prospered in everything it did, and truth was thrown to the ground.

[13] Then I heard a holy one speaking, and another holy one said to him, "How long will it take for the vision to be fulfilled—the vision concerning the daily sacrifice, the rebellion that causes desolation, the surrender of the sanctuary and the trampling underfoot of the LORD's people?"

[14] He said to me, "It will take 2,300 evenings and mornings; then the sanctuary will be reconsecrated."

THE INTERPRETATION OF THE VISION

[15] While I, Daniel, was watching the vision and trying to understand it, there before me stood one who looked like a man. [16] And I heard a man's voice from the Ulai calling, "Gabriel, tell this man the meaning of the vision."

[17] As he came near the place where I was standing, I was terrified and fell prostrate. "Son of man,"[b] he said to me, "understand that the vision concerns the time of the end."

[18] While he was speaking to me, I was in a deep sleep, with my face to the ground. Then he touched me and raised me to my feet.

[19] He said: "I am going to tell you what will happen later in the time of wrath, because the vision concerns the appointed time of the end.[c] [20] The two-horned ram that you saw represents the kings of Media and Persia. [21] The shaggy goat is the king of Greece, and the large horn between its eyes is the first king. [22] The four horns that replaced the one that was broken off represent four kingdoms that will emerge from his nation but will not have the same power.

[23] "In the latter part of their reign, when rebels have become completely wicked, a fierce-looking king, a master of intrigue, will arise. [24] He will become very strong, but not by his own power. He will cause astounding devastation and will succeed in whatever he does. He will destroy those who are mighty, the holy people. [25] He will cause deceit to prosper, and he will consider himself superior. When they feel secure, he will destroy many and take his stand against the Prince of princes. Yet he will be destroyed, but not by human power.

[26] "The vision of the evenings and mornings that has been given you is true, but seal up the vision, for it concerns the distant future."

[27] I, Daniel, was worn out. I lay exhausted for several days. Then I got up and went about the king's business. I was appalled by the vision; it was beyond understanding.

DANIEL'S PRAYER

9 In the first year of Darius son of Xerxes[d] (a Mede by descent), who was made ruler over the Babylonian[e] kingdom— [2] in the first year of his reign, I, Daniel, understood

Who do these verses describe? (8:23–25)
These verses describe Antiochus IV and his rise to power through intrigue and deceit.

---

[a] 12 Or rebellion, the armies   [b] 17 The Hebrew phrase ben adam means human being. The phrase son of man is retained as a form of address here because of its possible association with "Son of Man" in the New Testament.
[c] 19 Or because the end will be at the appointed time   [d] 1 Hebrew Ahasuerus
[e] 1 Or Chaldean

from the Scriptures, according to the word of the LORD giv-
en to Jeremiah the prophet, that the desolation of Jerusalem
would last seventy years. ³So I turned to the Lord God and
pleaded with him in prayer and petition, in fasting, and in
sackcloth and ashes.

⁴I prayed to the LORD my God and confessed:

"Lord, the great and awesome God, who keeps his
covenant of love with those who love him and keep his
commandments, ⁵we have sinned and done wrong. We
have been wicked and have rebelled; we have turned
away from your commands and laws. ⁶We have not listened to your servants the prophets, who spoke in your
name to our kings, our princes and our ancestors, and to
all the people of the land.

⁷"Lord, you are righteous, but this day we are covered
with shame—the people of Judah and the inhabitants
of Jerusalem and all Israel, both near and far, in all the
countries where you have scattered us because of our
unfaithfulness to you. ⁸We and our kings, our princes
and our ancestors are covered with shame, LORD, because we have sinned against you. ⁹The Lord our God
is merciful and forgiving, even though we have rebelled
against him; ¹⁰we have not obeyed the LORD our God
or kept the laws he gave us through his servants the
prophets. ¹¹All Israel has transgressed your law and
turned away, refusing to obey you.

"Therefore the curses and sworn judgments written
in the Law of Moses, the servant of God, have been
poured out on us, because we have sinned against you.
¹²You have fulfilled the words spoken against us and
against our rulers by bringing on us great disaster. Under the whole heaven nothing has ever been done like
what has been done to Jerusalem. ¹³Just as it is written
in the Law of Moses, all this disaster has come on us,
yet we have not sought the favor of the LORD our God
by turning from our sins and giving attention to your
truth. ¹⁴The LORD did not hesitate to bring the disaster
on us, for the LORD our God is righteous in everything
he does; yet we have not obeyed him.

¹⁵"Now, Lord our God, who brought your people out
of Egypt with a mighty hand and who made for yourself
a name that endures to this day, we have sinned, we have
done wrong. ¹⁶Lord, in keeping with all your righteous
acts, turn away your anger and your wrath from Jerusalem, your city, your holy hill. Our sins and the iniquities
of our ancestors have made Jerusalem and your people
an object of scorn to all those around us.

¹⁷"Now, our God, hear the prayers and petitions of
your servant. For your sake, Lord, look with favor on
your desolate sanctuary. ¹⁸Give ear, our God, and hear;
open your eyes and see the desolation of the city that
bears your Name. We do not make requests of you because we are righteous, but because of your great mercy.
¹⁹Lord, listen! Lord, forgive! Lord, hear and act! For
your sake, my God, do not delay, because your city and
your people bear your Name."

**What did sackcloth and
ashes symbolize? (9:3)**
These were traditional signs of
mourning.

**What was the city that bore
God's Name? (9:18)**
This was the city of Jerusalem.

THE SEVENTY "SEVENS"

²⁰While I was speaking and praying, confessing my sin and the sin of my people Israel and making my request to the Lᴏʀᴅ my God for his holy hill— ²¹while I was still in prayer, Gabriel, the man I had seen in the earlier vision, came to me in swift flight about the time of the evening sacrifice. ²²He instructed me and said to me, "Daniel, I have now come to give you insight and understanding. ²³As soon as you began to pray, a word went out, which I have come to tell you, for you are highly esteemed. Therefore, consider the word and understand the vision:

²⁴"Seventy 'sevens'ᵃ are decreed for your people and your holy city to finishᵇ transgression, to put an end to sin, to atone for wickedness, to bring in everlasting righteousness, to seal up vision and prophecy and to anoint the Most Holy Place.ᶜ

²⁵"Know and understand this: From the time the word goes out to restore and rebuild Jerusalem until the Anointed One,ᵈ the ruler, comes, there will be seven 'sevens,' and sixty-two 'sevens.' It will be rebuilt with streets and a trench, but in times of trouble. ²⁶After the sixty-two 'sevens,' the Anointed One will be put to death and will have nothing.ᵉ The people of the ruler who will come will destroy the city and the sanctuary. The end will come like a flood: War will continue until the end, and desolations have been decreed. ²⁷He will confirm a covenant with many for one 'seven.'ᶠ In the middle of the 'seven'ᶠ he will put an end to sacrifice and offering. And at the templeᵍ he will set up an abomination that causes desolation, until the end that is decreed is poured out on him.ᵇ"ⁱ

DANIEL'S VISION OF A MAN

10 In the third year of Cyrus king of Persia, a revelation was given to Daniel (who was called Belteshazzar). Its message was true and it concerned a great war.ʲ The understanding of the message came to him in a vision.

²At that time I, Daniel, mourned for three weeks. ³I ate no choice food; no meat or wine touched my lips; and I used no lotions at all until the three weeks were over.

⁴On the twenty-fourth day of the first month, as I was standing on the bank of the great river, the Tigris, ⁵I looked up and there before me was a man dressed in linen, with a belt of fine gold from Uphaz around his waist. ⁶His body was like topaz, his face like lightning, his eyes like flaming torches, his arms and legs like the gleam of burnished bronze, and his voice like the sound of a multitude.

⁷I, Daniel, was the only one who saw the vision; those who were with me did not see it, but such terror overwhelmed them that they fled and hid themselves. ⁸So I was left alone, gazing at this great vision; I had no strength left, my face

Who was this man? (10:5)
This was probably an angel, perhaps Gabriel (see 8:16).

ᵃ 24 Or 'weeks'; also in verses 25 and 26   ᵇ 24 Or restrain   ᶜ 24 Or the most holy One   ᵈ 25 Or an anointed one; also in verse 26   ᵉ 26 Or death and will have no one; or death, but not for himself   ᶠ 27 Or 'week'   ᵍ 27 Septuagint and Theodotion; Hebrew wing   ᵇ 27 Or it   ⁱ 27 Or And one who causes desolation will come upon the wing of the abominable temple, until the end that is decreed is poured out on the desolated city   ʲ 1 Or true and burdensome

turned deathly pale and I was helpless. ⁹Then I heard him speaking, and as I listened to him, I fell into a deep sleep, my face to the ground.

¹⁰A hand touched me and set me trembling on my hands and knees. ¹¹He said, "Daniel, you who are highly esteemed, consider carefully the words I am about to speak to you, and stand up, for I have now been sent to you." And when he said this to me, I stood up trembling.

¹²Then he continued, "Do not be afraid, Daniel. Since the first day that you set your mind to gain understanding and to humble yourself before your God, your words were heard, and I have come in response to them. ¹³But the prince of the Persian kingdom resisted me twenty-one days. Then Michael, one of the chief princes, came to help me, because I was detained there with the king of Persia. ¹⁴Now I have come to explain to you what will happen to your people in the future, for the vision concerns a time yet to come."

¹⁵While he was saying this to me, I bowed with my face toward the ground and was speechless. ¹⁶Then one who looked like a man*a* touched my lips, and I opened my mouth and began to speak. I said to the one standing before me, "I am overcome with anguish because of the vision, my lord, and I feel very weak. ¹⁷How can I, your servant, talk with you, my lord? My strength is gone and I can hardly breathe."

¹⁸Again the one who looked like a man touched me and gave me strength. ¹⁹"Do not be afraid, you who are highly esteemed," he said. "Peace! Be strong now; be strong."

When he spoke to me, I was strengthened and said, "Speak, my lord, since you have given me strength."

²⁰So he said, "Do you know why I have come to you? Soon I will return to fight against the prince of Persia, and when I go, the prince of Greece will come; ²¹but first I will tell you what is written in the Book of Truth. (No one supports me **11** against them except Michael, your prince. ¹And in the first year of Darius the Mede, I took my stand to support and protect him.)

THE KINGS OF THE SOUTH AND THE NORTH

²"Now then, I tell you the truth: Three more kings will arise in Persia, and then a fourth, who will be far richer than all the others. When he has gained power by his wealth, he will stir up everyone against the kingdom of Greece. ³Then a mighty king will arise, who will rule with great power and do as he pleases. ⁴After he has arisen, his empire will be broken up and parceled out toward the four winds of heaven. It will not go to his descendants, nor will it have the power he exercised, because his empire will be uprooted and given to others.

⁵"The king of the South will become strong, but one of his commanders will become even stronger than he and will rule his own kingdom with great power. ⁶After some years, they will become allies. The daughter of the king of the South will

Who was this prince of the Persian kingdom? (10:13) This may have been a demon who was exercising influence over the Persian realm.

What was the "Book of Truth"? (10:21) This was perhaps a reference to the divine record of the destinies of all human beings.

Who was the king of the South? (11:5) This was probably Ptolemy I of Egypt.

Who was the daughter of the king of the South? (11:6) This probably referred to Berenice, daughter of Ptolemy II.

---

a 16 Most manuscripts of the Masoretic Text; one manuscript of the Masoretic Text, Dead Sea Scrolls and Septuagint *Then something that looked like a human hand*

go to the king of the North to make an alliance, but she will not retain her power, and he and his power*a* will not last. In those days she will be betrayed, together with her royal escort and her father*b* and the one who supported her.

7 "One from her family line will arise to take her place. He will attack the forces of the king of the North and enter his fortress; he will fight against them and be victorious. 8 He will also seize their gods, their metal images and their valuable articles of silver and gold and carry them off to Egypt. For some years he will leave the king of the North alone. 9 Then the king of the North will invade the realm of the king of the South but will retreat to his own country. 10 His sons will prepare for war and assemble a great army, which will sweep on like an irresistible flood and carry the battle as far as his fortress.

11 "Then the king of the South will march out in a rage and fight against the king of the North, who will raise a large army, but it will be defeated. 12 When the army is carried off, the king of the South will be filled with pride and will slaughter many thousands, yet he will not remain triumphant. 13 For the king of the North will muster another army, larger than the first; and after several years, he will advance with a huge army fully equipped.

14 "In those times many will rise against the king of the South. Those who are violent among your own people will rebel in fulfillment of the vision, but without success. 15 Then the king of the North will come and build up siege ramps and will capture a fortified city. The forces of the South will be powerless to resist; even their best troops will not have the strength to stand. 16 The invader will do as he pleases; no one will be able to stand against him. He will establish himself in the Beautiful Land and will have the power to destroy it. 17 He will determine to come with the might of his entire kingdom and will make an alliance with the king of the South. And he will give him a daughter in marriage in order to overthrow the kingdom, but his plans*c* will not succeed or help him. 18 Then he will turn his attention to the coastlands and will take many of them, but a commander will put an end to his insolence and will turn his insolence back on him. 19 After this, he will turn back toward the fortresses of his own country but will stumble and fall, to be seen no more.

20 "His successor will send out a tax collector to maintain the royal splendor. In a few years, however, he will be destroyed, yet not in anger or in battle.

21 "He will be succeeded by a contemptible person who has not been given the honor of royalty. He will invade the kingdom when its people feel secure, and he will seize it through intrigue. 22 Then an overwhelming army will be swept away before him; both it and a prince of the covenant will be destroyed. 23 After coming to an agreement with him, he will act deceitfully, and with only a few people he will rise to power. 24 When the richest provinces feel secure, he will invade them and will achieve what neither his fathers nor his forefathers did. He will distribute plunder, loot and wealth

---

a 6 Or *offspring*   *b* 6 Or *child* (see Vulgate and Syriac)   *c* 17 Or *but she*

among his followers. He will plot the overthrow of fortresses—but only for a time.

25 "With a large army he will stir up his strength and courage against the king of the South. The king of the South will wage war with a large and very powerful army, but he will not be able to stand because of the plots devised against him. 26 Those who eat from the king's provisions will try to destroy him; his army will be swept away, and many will fall in battle. 27 The two kings, with their hearts bent on evil, will sit at the same table and lie to each other, but to no avail, because an end will still come at the appointed time. 28 The king of the North will return to his own country with great wealth, but his heart will be set against the holy covenant. He will take action against it and then return to his own country.

29 "At the appointed time he will invade the South again, but this time the outcome will be different from what it was before. 30 Ships of the western coastlands will oppose him, and he will lose heart. Then he will turn back and vent his fury against the holy covenant. He will return and show favor to those who forsake the holy covenant.

31 "His armed forces will rise up to desecrate the temple fortress and will abolish the daily sacrifice. Then they will set up the abomination that causes desolation. 32 With flattery he will corrupt those who have violated the covenant, but the people who know their God will firmly resist him.

33 "Those who are wise will instruct many, though for a time they will fall by the sword or be burned or captured or plundered. 34 When they fall, they will receive a little help, and many who are not sincere will join them. 35 Some of the wise will stumble, so that they may be refined, purified and made spotless until the time of the end, for it will still come at the appointed time.

THE KING WHO EXALTS HIMSELF

36 "The king will do as he pleases. He will exalt and magnify himself above every god and will say unheard-of things against the God of gods. He will be successful until the time of wrath is completed, for what has been determined must take place. 37 He will show no regard for the gods of his ancestors or for the one desired by women, nor will he regard any god, but will exalt himself above them all. 38 Instead of them, he will honor a god of fortresses; a god unknown to his ancestors he will honor with gold and silver, with precious stones and costly gifts. 39 He will attack the mightiest fortresses with the help of a foreign god and will greatly honor those who acknowledge him. He will make them rulers over many people and will distribute the land at a price.*

40 "At the time of the end the king of the South will engage him in battle, and the king of the North will storm out against him with chariots and cavalry and a great fleet of ships. He will invade many countries and sweep through them like a flood. 41 He will also invade the Beautiful Land. Many countries will fall, but Edom, Moab and the leaders

---

What was the holy covenant? (11:28)
When the Jews returned to Israel, God would enter into a new covenant with them. He would reestablish his gracious relationship with them, restore his Law, and reinstate sacrificial worship.

How was the temple a fortress? (11:31)
Although the temple was not the type of fortress that would hold back an army, it was an earthly headquarters for the Lord, a source of strength for the Jewish people, and a central focus for their faith.

Who was this king? (11:36)
This description seems to fit the Caesars of the Roman Empire.

---

a 39 Or land for a reward

of Ammon will be delivered from his hand. ⁴²He will extend his power over many countries; Egypt will not escape. ⁴³He will gain control of the treasures of gold and silver and all the riches of Egypt, with the Libyans and Cushites[a] in submission. ⁴⁴But reports from the east and the north will alarm him, and he will set out in a great rage to destroy and annihilate many. ⁴⁵He will pitch his royal tents between the seas at[b] the beautiful holy mountain. Yet he will come to his end, and no one will help him.

THE END TIMES

12 "At that time Michael, the great prince who protects your people, will arise. There will be a time of distress such as has not happened from the beginning of nations until then. But at that time your people—everyone whose name is found written in the book—will be delivered. ²Multitudes who sleep in the dust of the earth will awake: some to everlasting life, others to shame and everlasting contempt. ³Those who are wise[c] will shine like the brightness of the heavens, and those who lead many to righteousness, like the stars for ever and ever. ⁴But you, Daniel, roll up and seal the words of the scroll until the time of the end. Many will go here and there to increase knowledge."

⁵Then I, Daniel, looked, and there before me stood two others, one on this bank of the river and one on the opposite bank. ⁶One of them said to the man clothed in linen, who was above the waters of the river, "How long will it be before these astonishing things are fulfilled?"

⁷The man clothed in linen, who was above the waters of the river, lifted his right hand and his left hand toward heaven, and I heard him swear by him who lives forever, saying, "It will be for a time, times and half a time.[d] When the power of the holy people has been finally broken, all these things will be completed."

⁸I heard, but I did not understand. So I asked, "My lord, what will the outcome of all this be?"

⁹He replied, "Go your way, Daniel, because the words are rolled up and sealed until the time of the end. ¹⁰Many will be purified, made spotless and refined, but the wicked will continue to be wicked. None of the wicked will understand, but those who are wise will understand.

¹¹"From the time that the daily sacrifice is abolished and the abomination that causes desolation is set up, there will be 1,290 days. ¹²Blessed is the one who waits for and reaches the end of the 1,335 days.

¹³"As for you, go your way till the end. You will rest, and then at the end of the days you will rise to receive your allotted inheritance."

Who is this "great prince"? (12:1)
This was Michael, the archangel who defends God's people against the power of Satan.

Is this a reference to the resurrection? (12:2)
Yes. This is the first clear reference to the resurrection of both the righteous and the wicked.

Hosea

INTRODUCTION

Who wrote this book?
The prophet Hosea.

Why was this book written?
The book of Hosea warns the people of Israel about their unfaithfulness to God.

What do we learn about God in this book?
God keeps on loving us even if we are unfaithful. Punishment does not mean that God has stopped loving us.

What is special about this book?
Hosea's wife is not faithful to him, but Hosea keeps on loving her. Even though the people of Israel are unfaithful to God, God keeps on loving them.

What are some important chapters in this book?

Israel's unfaithfulness	Hosea 4
God's love for Israel	Hosea 11

When did these things happen? 1300 BC 1200 1100 1000 900 800 700 600 500 400

DIVISION OF THE KINGDOM (930 BC)

MINISTRIES OF ELIJAH AND ELISHA IN ISRAEL (C. 875 – 797 BC)

AMOS'S MINISTRY IN ISRAEL (C. 760 – 750 BC)

HOSEA'S MINISTRY IN ISRAEL (C. 753 – 715 BC)

MINISTRIES OF MICAH AND ISAIAH IN JUDAH (C. 740 – 681 BC)

EXILE OF ISRAEL (722 BC)

BOOK OF HOSEA WRITTEN (C. 715 BC)

FALL OF JERUSALEM (586 BC)

1 The word of the LORD that came to Hosea son of Beeri during the reigns of Uzziah, Jotham, Ahaz and Hezekiah, kings of Judah, and during the reign of Jeroboam son of Jehoash[a] king of Israel:

HOSEA'S WIFE AND CHILDREN

²When the LORD began to speak through Hosea, the LORD said to him, "Go, marry a promiscuous woman and have children with her, for like an adulterous wife this land is guilty of unfaithfulness to the LORD." ³So he married Gomer daughter of Diblaim, and she conceived and bore him a son.

⁴Then the LORD said to Hosea, "Call him Jezreel, because I will soon punish the house of Jehu for the massacre at Jezreel, and I will put an end to the kingdom of Israel. ⁵In that day I will break Israel's bow in the Valley of Jezreel."

⁶Gomer conceived again and gave birth to a daughter. Then the LORD said to Hosea, "Call her Lo-Ruhamah (which means "not loved"), for I will no longer show love to Israel, that I should at all forgive them. ⁷Yet I will show love to Judah; and I will save them—not by bow, sword or battle, or by horses and horsemen, but I, the LORD their God, will save them."

⁸After she had weaned Lo-Ruhamah, Gomer had another son. ⁹Then the LORD said, "Call him Lo-Ammi (which means "not my people"), for you are not my people, and I am not your God.[b]

¹⁰"Yet the Israelites will be like the sand on the seashore, which cannot be measured or counted. In the place where it was said to them, 'You are not my people,' they will be called 'children of the living God.' ¹¹The people of Judah and the people of Israel will come together; they will appoint one leader and will come up out of the land, for great will be the day of Jezreel.[c]

2[d] "Say of your brothers, 'My people,' and of your sisters, 'My loved one.'

ISRAEL PUNISHED AND RESTORED

²"Rebuke your mother, rebuke her,
    for she is not my wife,
    and I am not her husband.
Let her remove the adulterous look from her face
    and the unfaithfulness from between her breasts.
³Otherwise I will strip her naked
    and make her as bare as on the day she was born;
I will make her like a desert,
    turn her into a parched land,
    and slay her with thirst.
⁴I will not show my love to her children,
    because they are the children of adultery.
⁵Their mother has been unfaithful
    and has conceived them in disgrace.
She said, 'I will go after my lovers,
    who give me my food and my water,
    my wool and my linen, my olive oil and my drink.'

Why did God tell Hosea to marry an adulteress? (1:2)
God often told the prophets to bring his message to his people through their actions. In this case, God was showing the people of Israel how God loved them even though they had behaved as an unfaithful spouse.

What did the name *Jezreel* mean? (1:4)
The word meant "God scatters." This was a warning for how God would punish the dynasty of Jehu and the Israelites because of the massacre carried out at Jezreel (1 Kings 21:21; 2 Kings 10:1–11).

---

[a] *1* Hebrew *Joash,* a variant of *Jehoash*   [b] *9* Or *your I AM*   [c] *11* In Hebrew texts 1:10,11 is numbered 2:1,2.   [d] In Hebrew texts 2:1-23 is numbered 2:3-25.

⁶Therefore I will block her path with thornbushes;
    I will wall her in so that she cannot find her way.
⁷She will chase after her lovers but not catch them;
    she will look for them but not find them.
Then she will say,
    'I will go back to my husband as at first,
    for then I was better off than now.'
⁸She has not acknowledged that I was the one
    who gave her the grain, the new wine and oil,
who lavished on her the silver and gold—
    which they used for Baal.

⁹"Therefore I will take away my grain when it ripens,
    and my new wine when it is ready.
I will take back my wool and my linen,
    intended to cover her naked body.
¹⁰So now I will expose her lewdness
    before the eyes of her lovers;
    no one will take her out of my hands.
¹¹I will stop all her celebrations:
    her yearly festivals, her New Moons,
    her Sabbath days—all her appointed festivals.
¹²I will ruin her vines and her fig trees,
    which she said were her pay from her lovers;
I will make them a thicket,
    and wild animals will devour them.
¹³I will punish her for the days
    she burned incense to the Baals;
she decked herself with rings and jewelry,
    and went after her lovers,
    but me she forgot,"
                                        declares the LORD.

¹⁴"Therefore I am now going to allure her;
    I will lead her into the wilderness
    and speak tenderly to her.
¹⁵There I will give her back her vineyards,
    and will make the Valley of Achorᵃ a door of hope.
There she will respondᵇ as in the days of her youth,
    as in the day she came up out of Egypt.

¹⁶"In that day," declares the LORD,
    "you will call me 'my husband';
    you will no longer call me 'my master.'ᶜ
¹⁷I will remove the names of the Baals from her lips;
    no longer will their names be invoked.
¹⁸In that day I will make a covenant for them
    with the beasts of the field, the birds in the sky
    and the creatures that move along the ground.
Bow and sword and battle
    I will abolish from the land,
    so that all may lie down in safety.
¹⁹I will betroth you to me forever;
    I will betroth you inᵈ righteousness and justice,
    inᵈ love and compassion.

ᵃ 15 Achor means trouble.   ᵇ 15 Or sing   ᶜ 16 Hebrew baal
ᵈ 19 Or with

Why was Hosea supposed to take back his unfaithful wife? (2:6–7)
This symbolized the way the Lord would forgive Israel's sin and unfaithfulness to him.

Why did the Israelites think that Baal had provided their food and drink? (2:8)
The Israelites adopted the Canaanites' belief that Baal provided grain, wine, and oil because Baal was the god who supposedly controlled fertility and weather.

Why would God lead Israel into the wilderness? (2:14)
This refers to the time when Israel wandered in the wilderness before entering the promised land and before the people were tempted to worship pagan gods in Canaan.

What would take the place of the bride-price? (2:19–20)
Rather than money, these five traits would make up the bride-price: righteousness, justice, love, compassion, and faithfulness.

²⁰ I will betroth you in*a* faithfulness,
    and you will acknowledge the LORD.

²¹ "In that day I will respond,"
    declares the LORD—
"I will respond to the skies,
    and they will respond to the earth;
²² and the earth will respond to the grain,
    the new wine and the olive oil,
    and they will respond to Jezreel.*b*
²³ I will plant her for myself in the land;
    I will show my love to the one I called 'Not my
        loved one.'*c*
I will say to those called 'Not my people,'*d* 'You are
        my people';
    and they will say, 'You are my God.'"

HOSEA'S RECONCILIATION WITH HIS WIFE

3 The LORD said to me, "Go, show your love to your wife again, though she is loved by another man and is an adulteress. Love her as the LORD loves the Israelites, though they turn to other gods and love the sacred raisin cakes."

² So I bought her for fifteen shekels*e* of silver and about a homer and a lethek*f* of barley. ³ Then I told her, "You are to live with me many days; you must not be a prostitute or be intimate with any man, and I will behave the same way toward you."

⁴ For the Israelites will live many days without king or prince, without sacrifice or sacred stones, without ephod or household gods. ⁵ Afterward the Israelites will return and seek the LORD their God and David their king. They will come trembling to the LORD and to his blessings in the last days.

THE CHARGE AGAINST ISRAEL

4 Hear the word of the LORD, you Israelites,
    because the LORD has a charge to bring
    against you who live in the land:
"There is no faithfulness, no love,
    no acknowledgment of God in the land.
² There is only cursing,*g* lying and murder,
    stealing and adultery;
they break all bounds,
    and bloodshed follows bloodshed.
³ Because of this the land dries up,
    and all who live in it waste away;
the beasts of the field, the birds in the sky
    and the fish in the sea are swept away.

⁴ "But let no one bring a charge,
    let no one accuse another,
for your people are like those
    who bring charges against a priest.

What did Hosea have to do to reunite with Gomer? (3:2)
Apparently she had sold herself into slavery as a prostitute, and Hosea had to buy her back so she again would be his wife.

Was Hosea exaggerating? (4:1–2)
Probably. A lot of the people of Israel had turned away from the Lord, but there were probably some, like Hosea, who still were faithful to God. However, in general, the people had abandoned God.

How were the priests responsible for the situation that Israel was in? (4:4–9)
The priests were supposed to be the guardians of God's law and were to give the people religious instruction. Hosea warned the priests not to accuse the people for bringing God's judgment on the nation because they were guilty as well.

---

a 20 Or *with*   *b 22 Jezreel* means *God plants.*   *c 23* Hebrew *Lo-Ruhamah* (see 1:6)   *d 23* Hebrew *Lo-Ammi* (see 1:9)   *e 2* That is, about 6 ounces or about 170 grams   *f 2* A homer and a lethek possibly weighed about 430 pounds or about 195 kilograms.   *g 2* That is, to pronounce a curse on

⁵ You stumble day and night,
and the prophets stumble with you.
So I will destroy your mother—
⁶   my people are destroyed from lack of knowledge.

"Because you have rejected knowledge,
I also reject you as my priests;
because you have ignored the law of your God,
I also will ignore your children.
⁷ The more priests there were,
the more they sinned against me;
they exchanged their glorious God^a for something
disgraceful.
⁸ They feed on the sins of my people
and relish their wickedness.
⁹ And it will be: Like people, like priests.
I will punish both of them for their ways
and repay them for their deeds.

¹⁰ "They will eat but not have enough;
they will engage in prostitution but not flourish,
because they have deserted the LORD
to give themselves ¹¹ to prostitution;
old wine and new wine
take away their understanding.
¹² My people consult a wooden idol,
and a diviner's rod speaks to them.
A spirit of prostitution leads them astray;
they are unfaithful to their God.
¹³ They sacrifice on the mountaintops
and burn offerings on the hills,
under oak, poplar and terebinth,
where the shade is pleasant.
Therefore your daughters turn to prostitution
and your daughters-in-law to adultery.

¹⁴ "I will not punish your daughters
when they turn to prostitution,
nor your daughters-in-law
when they commit adultery,
because the men themselves consort with harlots
and sacrifice with shrine prostitutes—
a people without understanding will come to ruin!

¹⁵ "Though you, Israel, commit adultery,
do not let Judah become guilty.

"Do not go to Gilgal;
do not go up to Beth Aven.^b
And do not swear, 'As surely as the LORD lives!'
¹⁶ The Israelites are stubborn,
like a stubborn heifer.
How then can the LORD pasture them
like lambs in a meadow?
¹⁷ Ephraim is joined to idols;
leave him alone!

^a 7 Syriac (see also an ancient Hebrew scribal tradition); Masoretic Text *me; /
I will exchange their glory*   ^b 15 *Beth Aven* means *house of wickedness* (a
derogatory name for Bethel, which means *house of God*).

**Why would the people be
"destroyed from lack of
knowledge"? (4:6)**
The people would be destroyed
because they failed to know and
to follow God's law.

**How were the men of Israel
hypocritical? (4:14)**
The men would punish women for
immorality while they themselves
had relations with prostitutes.

¹⁸ Even when their drinks are gone,
    they continue their prostitution;
    their rulers dearly love shameful ways.
¹⁹ A whirlwind will sweep them away,
    and their sacrifices will bring them shame.

JUDGMENT AGAINST ISRAEL

5 "Hear this, you priests!
    Pay attention, you Israelites!
Listen, royal house!
    This judgment is against you:
You have been a snare at Mizpah,
    a net spread out on Tabor.
² The rebels are knee-deep in slaughter.
    I will discipline all of them.
³ I know all about Ephraim;
    Israel is not hidden from me.
Ephraim, you have now turned to prostitution;
    Israel is corrupt.

⁴ "Their deeds do not permit them
    to return to their God.
A spirit of prostitution is in their heart;
    they do not acknowledge the LORD.
⁵ Israel's arrogance testifies against them;
    the Israelites, even Ephraim, stumble in their sin;
    Judah also stumbles with them.
⁶ When they go with their flocks and herds
    to seek the LORD,
they will not find him;
    he has withdrawn himself from them.
⁷ They are unfaithful to the LORD;
    they give birth to illegitimate children.
When they celebrate their New Moon feasts,
    he will devour^a their fields.

⁸ "Sound the trumpet in Gibeah,
    the horn in Ramah.
Raise the battle cry in Beth Aven^b;
    lead on, Benjamin.
⁹ Ephraim will be laid waste
    on the day of reckoning.
Among the tribes of Israel
    I proclaim what is certain.
¹⁰ Judah's leaders are like those
    who move boundary stones.
I will pour out my wrath on them
    like a flood of water.
¹¹ Ephraim is oppressed,
    trampled in judgment,
    intent on pursuing idols.^c
¹² I am like a moth to Ephraim,
    like rot to the people of Judah.

Why did Hosea single out Ephraim? (5:3)
Hosea frequently used Ephraim as a symbol for all of Israel. Ephraim was the largest tribe of the northern kingdom and had come to be associated with the whole nation.

The Trumpet/Shofar (5:8)

What was wrong with moving boundary stones? (5:10)
A boundary stone was a marker that established the boundary of a person's property. The stone may have had engravings on it stating the rights of ownership or even blessings and curses. Moving a stone was forbidden because it amounted to stealing land.

---

^a 7 Or *Now their New Moon feasts / will devour them* and   ^b 8 *Beth Aven* means *house of wickedness* (a derogatory name for Bethel, which means *house of God*).   ^c 11 The meaning of the Hebrew for this word is uncertain.

¹³ "When Ephraim saw his sickness,
    and Judah his sores,
  then Ephraim turned to Assyria,
    and sent to the great king for help.
  But he is not able to cure you,
    not able to heal your sores.
¹⁴ For I will be like a lion to Ephraim,
    like a great lion to Judah.
  I will tear them to pieces and go away;
    I will carry them off, with no one to
      rescue them.
¹⁵ Then I will return to my lair
    until they have borne their guilt
  and seek my face—
  in their misery
    they will earnestly seek me."

ISRAEL UNREPENTANT

6 "Come, let us return to the LORD.
    He has torn us to pieces
      but he will heal us;
  he has injured us
    but he will bind up our wounds.
² After two days he will revive us;
    on the third day he will restore us,
    that we may live in his presence.
³ Let us acknowledge the LORD;
    let us press on to acknowledge him.
  As surely as the sun rises,
    he will appear;
  he will come to us like the winter rains,
    like the spring rains that water the earth."

⁴ "What can I do with you, Ephraim?
    What can I do with you, Judah?
  Your love is like the morning mist,
    like the early dew that disappears.
⁵ Therefore I cut you in pieces with my prophets,
    I killed you with the words of my mouth—
    then my judgments go forth like the sun.ᵃ
⁶ For I desire mercy, not sacrifice,
    and acknowledgment of God rather than burnt
      offerings.
⁷ As at Adam,ᵇ they have broken the covenant;
    they were unfaithful to me there.
⁸ Gilead is a city of evildoers,
    stained with footprints of blood.
⁹ As marauders lie in ambush for a victim,
    so do bands of priests;
  they murder on the road to Shechem,
    carrying out their wicked schemes.
¹⁰ I have seen a horrible thing in Israel:
    There Ephraim is given to prostitution,
    Israel is defiled.

ᵃ 5 The meaning of the Hebrew for this line is uncertain.   ᵇ 7 Or *Like
Adam*; or *Like human beings*

**What were these sicknesses
and sores? (5:13)**
These were metaphors for
wounds the nations had received
from their enemies.

**Was this genuine repen-
tance? (6:1–2)**
The repentance seemed half-
hearted. If it was genuine, it did
not last long. Israel supposed
that God would be angry only for
a brief time.

**Why didn't God want
sacrifices? (6:6)**
God wanted his people to live a
repentant lifestyle and to turn
away from sin. Sacrifices had
become empty religious rituals
for many, and God wanted true
repentance.

What did this harvest symbolize? (6:11)
This was a symbol of God's judgments.

What were Ephraim and Samaria? (7:1)
These were both names for the northern kingdom.

What was the festival of the king? (7:5)
This was probably a coronation or birthday celebration that turned into a drunken party.

What did this image mean? (7:8)
Bread was baked on stones. If it was not turned over, it would be burned on the bottom and raw on the top. In other words, it would be worthless.

11 "Also for you, Judah,
     a harvest is appointed.

"Whenever I would restore the fortunes of my people,
7 ¹whenever I would heal Israel,
     the sins of Ephraim are exposed
     and the crimes of Samaria revealed.
They practice deceit,
     thieves break into houses,
     bandits rob in the streets;
²but they do not realize
     that I remember all their evil deeds.
Their sins engulf them;
     they are always before me.

³"They delight the king with their wickedness,
     the princes with their lies.
⁴They are all adulterers,
     burning like an oven
whose fire the baker need not stir
     from the kneading of the dough till it rises.
⁵On the day of the festival of our king
     the princes become inflamed with wine,
     and he joins hands with the mockers.
⁶Their hearts are like an oven;
     they approach him with intrigue.
Their passion smolders all night;
     in the morning it blazes like a flaming fire.
⁷All of them are hot as an oven;
     they devour their rulers.
All their kings fall,
     and none of them calls on me.

⁸"Ephraim mixes with the nations;
     Ephraim is a flat loaf not turned over.
⁹Foreigners sap his strength,
     but he does not realize it.
His hair is sprinkled with gray,
     but he does not notice.
¹⁰Israel's arrogance testifies against him,
     but despite all this
he does not return to the LORD his God
     or search for him.

¹¹"Ephraim is like a dove,
     easily deceived and senseless—
now calling to Egypt,
     now turning to Assyria.
¹²When they go, I will throw my net over them;
     I will pull them down like the birds in the sky.
When I hear them flocking together,
     I will catch them.
¹³Woe to them,
     because they have strayed from me!
Destruction to them,
     because they have rebelled against me!
I long to redeem them
     but they speak about me falsely.

¹⁴They do not cry out to me from their hearts
   but wail on their beds.
They slash themselves,ᵃ appealing to their gods
   for grain and new wine,
   but they turn away from me.
¹⁵I trained them and strengthened their arms,
   but they plot evil against me.
¹⁶They do not turn to the Most High;
   they are like a faulty bow.
Their leaders will fall by the sword
   because of their insolent words.
For this they will be ridiculed
   in the land of Egypt.

ISRAEL TO REAP THE WHIRLWIND

8 "Put the trumpet to your lips!
   An eagle is over the house of the LORD
because the people have broken my covenant
   and rebelled against my law.
²Israel cries out to me,
   'Our God, we acknowledge you!'
³But Israel has rejected what is good;
   an enemy will pursue him.
⁴They set up kings without my consent;
   they choose princes without my approval.
With their silver and gold
   they make idols for themselves
   to their own destruction.
⁵Samaria, throw out your calf-idol!
   My anger burns against them.
How long will they be incapable of purity?
⁶ They are from Israel!
This calf—a metalworker has made it;
   it is not God.
It will be broken in pieces,
   that calf of Samaria.

⁷"They sow the wind
   and reap the whirlwind.
The stalk has no head;
   it will produce no flour.
Were it to yield grain,
   foreigners would swallow it up.
⁸Israel is swallowed up;
   now she is among the nations
   like something no one wants.
⁹For they have gone up to Assyria
   like a wild donkey wandering alone.
Ephraim has sold herself to lovers.
¹⁰Although they have sold themselves among the
       nations,
   I will now gather them together.
They will begin to waste away
   under the oppression of the mighty king.

ᵃ *14* Some Hebrew manuscripts and Septuagint; most Hebrew manuscripts
They gather together

What was this eagle? (8:1)
This may have been a description of a vulture. It referred to Assyria, which would arrive and devour Israel.

What did it mean to sow the wind and reap the whirlwind? (8:7)
This was a common proverb about the results of doing evil. Israel sowed the wind of idolatry and reaped the whirlwind of Assyria's destruction.

How had Israel become worthless? (8:8)
By worshiping pagan gods, Israel had turned itself into just another pagan nation and ignored its special relationship with the Lord.

11 "Though Ephraim built many altars for sin
        offerings,
    these have become altars for sinning.
12 I wrote for them the many things of my law,
    but they regarded them as something foreign.
13 Though they offer sacrifices as gifts to me,
    and though they eat the meat,
    the LORD is not pleased with them.
  Now he will remember their wickedness
    and punish their sins:
    They will return to Egypt.
14 Israel has forgotten their Maker
    and built palaces;
  Judah has fortified many towns.
  But I will send fire on their cities
    that will consume their fortresses."

PUNISHMENT FOR ISRAEL

9 Do not rejoice, Israel;
    do not be jubilant like the other nations.
  For you have been unfaithful to your God;
    you love the wages of a prostitute
    at every threshing floor.
2 Threshing floors and winepresses will not feed
        the people;
    the new wine will fail them.
3 They will not remain in the LORD's land;
    Ephraim will return to Egypt
    and eat unclean food in Assyria.
4 They will not pour out wine offerings to the LORD,
    nor will their sacrifices please him.
  Such sacrifices will be to them like the bread of
        mourners;
    all who eat them will be unclean.
  This food will be for themselves;
    it will not come into the temple of the LORD.

5 What will you do on the day of your appointed
        festivals,
    on the feast days of the LORD?
6 Even if they escape from destruction,
    Egypt will gather them,
    and Memphis will bury them.
  Their treasures of silver will be taken over by briers,
    and thorns will overrun their tents.
7 The days of punishment are coming,
    the days of reckoning are at hand.
    Let Israel know this.
  Because your sins are so many
    and your hostility so great,
  the prophet is considered a fool,
    the inspired person a maniac.
8 The prophet, along with my God,
    is the watchman over Ephraim,[a]

What was the "bread of mourners"? (9:4)
This symbolized something that was unclean, like bread in a house where there had been a death. All who touched it became ceremonially unclean.

Why did they think Hosea was a fool or a maniac? (9:7)
He remained faithful to his adulterous wife, and he continued to bring prophecies of judgment that the people didn't believe.

---

a 8 Or The prophet is the watchman over Ephraim, / the people of my God

yet snares await him on all his paths,
　　and hostility in the house of his God.
⁹They have sunk deep into corruption,
　　as in the days of Gibeah.
God will remember their wickedness
　　and punish them for their sins.

¹⁰"When I found Israel,
　　it was like finding grapes in the desert;
when I saw your ancestors,
　　it was like seeing the early fruit on the fig tree.
But when they came to Baal Peor,
　　they consecrated themselves to that shameful
　　　idol
　　and became as vile as the thing they loved.
¹¹Ephraim's glory will fly away like a bird—
　　no birth, no pregnancy, no conception.
¹²Even if they rear children,
　　I will bereave them of every one.
Woe to them
　　when I turn away from them!
¹³I have seen Ephraim, like Tyre,
　　planted in a pleasant place.
But Ephraim will bring out
　　their children to the slayer."

¹⁴Give them, Lord—
　　what will you give them?
Give them wombs that miscarry
　　and breasts that are dry.

¹⁵"Because of all their wickedness in Gilgal,
　　I hated them there.
Because of their sinful deeds,
　　I will drive them out of my house.
I will no longer love them;
　　all their leaders are rebellious.
¹⁶Ephraim is blighted,
　　their root is withered,
　　they yield no fruit.
Even if they bear children,
　　I will slay their cherished offspring."

¹⁷My God will reject them
　　because they have not obeyed him;
　　they will be wanderers among the nations.

10 Israel was a spreading vine;
　　he brought forth fruit for himself.
As his fruit increased,
　　he built more altars;
as his land prospered,
　　he adorned his sacred stones.
²Their heart is deceitful,
　　and now they must bear their guilt.
The Lord will demolish their altars
　　and destroy their sacred stones.

How had Israel once seemed to God? (9:10)
Israel had been like a special delicacy, like grapes in the desert or sweet, early figs, when the nation committed itself to obey God. But when they turned away from God, they became vile.

³Then they will say, "We have no king
  because we did not revere the LORD.
But even if we had a king,
  what could he do for us?"
⁴They make many promises,
  take false oaths
  and make agreements;
therefore lawsuits spring up
  like poisonous weeds in a plowed field.
⁵The people who live in Samaria fear
  for the calf-idol of Beth Aven.ᵃ
Its people will mourn over it,
  and so will its idolatrous priests,
those who had rejoiced over its splendor,
  because it is taken from them into exile.
⁶It will be carried to Assyria
  as tribute for the great king.
Ephraim will be disgraced;
  Israel will be ashamed of its foreign alliances.
⁷Samaria's king will be destroyed,
  swept away like a twig on the surface of
    the waters.
⁸The high places of wickednessᵇ will be destroyed—
  it is the sin of Israel.
Thorns and thistles will grow up
  and cover their altars.
Then they will say to the mountains, "Cover us!"
  and to the hills, "Fall on us!"

⁹"Since the days of Gibeah, you have sinned, Israel,
  and there you have remained.ᶜ
Will not war again overtake
  the evildoers in Gibeah?
¹⁰When I please, I will punish them;
  nations will be gathered against them
to put them in bonds for their double sin.
¹¹Ephraim is a trained heifer
  that loves to thresh;
so I will put a yoke
  on her fair neck.
I will drive Ephraim,
  Judah must plow,
  and Jacob must break up the ground.
¹²Sow righteousness for yourselves,
  reap the fruit of unfailing love,
and break up your unplowed ground;
  for it is time to seek the LORD,
until he comes
  and showers his righteousness on you.
¹³But you have planted wickedness,
  you have reaped evil,
  you have eaten the fruit of deception.

What was this calf-idol?
(10:5)
This was the idol Jeroboam set
up at Bethel (1 Kings 12:32–33).

What did this image mean?
(10:11)
Up until now, Ephraim (Israel)
had been as contented as a
young cow that ate while threshing.
Now God would make Israel
(called both Ephraim and Jacob)
do the heavy work of plowing
under a yoke, a picture of the
coming captivity.

How could Israel reap the
fruit of unfailing love?
(10:12)
If Israel would repent and do
what was right, she would be
blessed by God.

ᵃ 5 *Beth Aven* means *house of wickedness* (a derogatory name for Bethel, which
means *house of God*).   ᵇ 8 Hebrew *aven*, a reference to Beth Aven (a
derogatory name for Bethel); see verse 5.   ᶜ 9 Or *there a stand was taken*

Because you have depended on your own
            strength
    and on your many warriors,
¹⁴ the roar of battle will rise against your people,
    so that all your fortresses will be devastated —
as Shalman devastated Beth Arbel on the day of
            battle,
    when mothers were dashed to the ground with
            their children.
¹⁵ So will it happen to you, Bethel,
    because your wickedness is great.
When that day dawns,
    the king of Israel will be completely destroyed.

GOD'S LOVE FOR ISRAEL

11 "When Israel was a child, I loved him,
    and out of Egypt I called my son.
² But the more they were called,
    the more they went away from me.*
They sacrificed to the Baals
    and they burned incense to images.
³ It was I who taught Ephraim to walk,
    taking them by the arms;
but they did not realize
    it was I who healed them.
⁴ I led them with cords of human kindness,
    with ties of love.
To them I was like one who lifts
    a little child to the cheek,
    and I bent down to feed them.

⁵ "Will they not return to Egypt
    and will not Assyria rule over them
    because they refuse to repent?
⁶ A sword will flash in their cities;
    it will devour their false prophets
    and put an end to their plans.
⁷ My people are determined to turn from me.
    Even though they call me God Most High,
    I will by no means exalt them.

⁸ "How can I give you up, Ephraim?
    How can I hand you over, Israel?
How can I treat you like Admah?
    How can I make you like Zeboyim?
My heart is changed within me;
    all my compassion is aroused.
⁹ I will not carry out my fierce anger,
    nor will I devastate Ephraim again.
For I am God, and not a man —
    the Holy One among you.
    I will not come against their cities.
¹⁰ They will follow the LORD;
    he will roar like a lion.

---

a 2 Septuagint; Hebrew them

How did the metaphor change here? (11:1)
Instead of using the husband-wife analogy, Hosea pictured Israel as God's children. They were taught by God to walk, but they wandered away from him.

How would God continue to love his people? (11:9)
God would punish the people of Israel but would not destroy them.

What would this roaring mean? (11:10)
This would be God's signal for his people to return from exile.

When he roars,
    his children will come trembling from
        the west.
11 They will come from Egypt,
    trembling like sparrows,
    from Assyria, fluttering like doves.
I will settle them in their homes,"
    declares the Lord.

ISRAEL'S SIN

12 Ephraim has surrounded me with lies,
    Israel with deceit.
And Judah is unruly against God,
    even against the faithful Holy One.*a*

12 *b* 1 Ephraim feeds on the wind;
    he pursues the east wind all day
    and multiplies lies and violence.
He makes a treaty with Assyria
    and sends olive oil to Egypt.
2 The Lord has a charge to bring against Judah;
    he will punish Jacob*c* according to his ways
    and repay him according to his deeds.
3 In the womb he grasped his brother's heel;
    as a man he struggled with God.
4 He struggled with the angel and overcame him;
    he wept and begged for his favor.
He found him at Bethel
    and talked with him there—
5 the Lord God Almighty,
    the Lord is his name!
6 But you must return to your God;
    maintain love and justice,
    and wait for your God always.

7 The merchant uses dishonest scales
    and loves to defraud.
8 Ephraim boasts,
    "I am very rich; I have become wealthy.
With all my wealth they will not find in me
    any iniquity or sin."

9 "I have been the Lord your God
    ever since you came out of Egypt;
I will make you live in tents again,
    as in the days of your appointed festivals.
10 I spoke to the prophets,
    gave them many visions
    and told parables through them."

11 Is Gilead wicked?
    Its people are worthless!
Do they sacrifice bulls in Gilgal?
    Their altars will be like piles of stones
    on a plowed field.

What did it mean to chase the east wind? (12:1)
Pursuing the wind referred to Israel's foreign policy of going back and forth between Egypt and Assyria.

---

a 12 In Hebrew texts this verse (11:12) is numbered 12:1.   *b* In Hebrew texts 12:1-14 is numbered 12:2-15.   *c* 2 *Jacob* means *he grasps the heel*, a Hebrew idiom for *he takes advantage of* or *he deceives*.

¹²Jacob fled to the country of Aram*ᵃ*;
    Israel served to get a wife,
    and to pay for her he tended sheep.
¹³The LORD used a prophet to bring Israel up from
        Egypt,
    by a prophet he cared for him.
¹⁴But Ephraim has aroused his bitter anger;
    his Lord will leave on him the guilt of his bloodshed
    and will repay him for his contempt.

THE LORD'S ANGER AGAINST ISRAEL

13 When Ephraim spoke, people trembled;
        he was exalted in Israel.
    But he became guilty of Baal worship and died.
²Now they sin more and more;
    they make idols for themselves from their silver,
    cleverly fashioned images,
        all of them the work of craftsmen.
    It is said of these people,
        "They offer human sacrifices!
        They kiss*ᵇ* calf-idols!"
³Therefore they will be like the morning mist,
    like the early dew that disappears,
    like chaff swirling from a threshing floor,
    like smoke escaping through a window.

⁴"But I have been the LORD your God
    ever since you came out of Egypt.
    You shall acknowledge no God but me,
        no Savior except me.
⁵I cared for you in the wilderness,
    in the land of burning heat.
⁶When I fed them, they were satisfied;
    when they were satisfied, they became proud;
        then they forgot me.
⁷So I will be like a lion to them,
    like a leopard I will lurk by the path.
⁸Like a bear robbed of her cubs,
    I will attack them and rip them open;
    like a lion I will devour them—
        a wild animal will tear them apart.

⁹"You are destroyed, Israel,
    because you are against me, against your helper.
¹⁰Where is your king, that he may save you?
    Where are your rulers in all your towns,
    of whom you said,
        'Give me a king and princes'?
¹¹So in my anger I gave you a king,
    and in my wrath I took him away.
¹²The guilt of Ephraim is stored up,
    his sins are kept on record.
¹³Pains as of a woman in childbirth come to him,
    but he is a child without wisdom;

Why was God angry with Ephraim? (12:14)
Ephraim had practiced the same kind of idolatry as the other tribes.

What do these word pictures say about the condition of Ephraim? (13:3)
It would soon vanish.

ᵃ 12 That is, Northwest Mesopotamia   *ᵇ 2* Or *"Men who sacrifice / kiss*

What did God promise?
(13:14)
Even though he would punish
them, he would restore them.

**What was the east wind
like? (13:15)**
The east wind was a hot, dry
wind that often destroyed crops.
Here it is a symbol for Assyria.

**Why did they have to take
words? (14:2)**
Sacrifices alone would not be
enough. They had to express true
repentance with their words.

**What did the dew
symbolize? (14:5)**
Here the dew symbolized God's
blessing.

when the time arrives,
he doesn't have the sense to come out of the womb.

¹⁴"I will deliver this people from the power of
the grave;
I will redeem them from death.
Where, O death, are your plagues?
Where, O grave, is your destruction?

"I will have no compassion,
¹⁵   even though he thrives among his brothers.
An east wind from the LORD will come,
blowing in from the desert;
his spring will fail
and his well dry up.
His storehouse will be plundered
of all its treasures.
¹⁶The people of Samaria must bear their guilt,
because they have rebelled against their God.
They will fall by the sword;
their little ones will be dashed to the ground,
their pregnant women ripped open."ᵃ

REPENTANCE TO BRING BLESSING

14 ᵇ Return, Israel, to the LORD your God.
Your sins have been your downfall!
²Take words with you
and return to the LORD.
Say to him:
"Forgive all our sins
and receive us graciously,
that we may offer the fruit of our lips.ᶜ
³Assyria cannot save us;
we will not mount warhorses.
We will never again say 'Our gods'
to what our own hands have made,
for in you the fatherless find compassion."

⁴"I will heal their waywardness
and love them freely,
for my anger has turned away from them.
⁵I will be like the dew to Israel;
he will blossom like a lily.
Like a cedar of Lebanon
he will send down his roots;
⁶   his young shoots will grow.
His splendor will be like an olive tree,
his fragrance like a cedar of Lebanon.
⁷People will dwell again in his shade;
they will flourish like the grain,
they will blossom like the vine—
Israel's fame will be like the wine of Lebanon.
⁸Ephraim, what more have Iᵈ to do with idols?
I will answer him and care for him.

ᵃ 16 In Hebrew texts this verse (13:16) is numbered 14:1.   ᵇ In Hebrew
texts 14:1-9 is numbered 14:2-10.   ᶜ 2 Or offer our lips as sacrifices of bulls
ᵈ 8 Or Hebrew; Septuagint What more has Ephraim

I am like a flourishing juniper;
  your fruitfulness comes from me."

[9] Who is wise? Let them realize these things.
  Who is discerning? Let them understand.
The ways of the Lord are right;
  the righteous walk in them,
  but the rebellious stumble in them.

Joel

INTRODUCTION

Who wrote this book?
The prophet Joel.

Why was this book written?
Joel wants the people of Judah to repent and stop sinning.

What do we learn about God in this book?
God is judge. He will punish people who sin.

What is special about this book?
Joel realizes that the swarm of locusts is like the great enemy army God will use someday to punish his people for their sins. Joel promises that God will save and bless his people after he punishes them.

What are some important passages in this book?

How to repent	Joel 2:12 – 14
How God will bless	Joel 2:18 – 27

When did these things happen?

1300 BC 1200   1100   1000   900   800   700   600   500   400

DIVISION OF THE KINGDOM (930 BC)

MINISTRIES OF ELIJAH AND ELISHA IN ISRAEL (C. 875 – 797 BC)

JOEL'S MINISTRY IN JUDAH (C. 835 – 796 BC?)

JONAH'S MINISTRY IN NINEVEH (C. 800 – 750 BC)

AMOS'S MINISTRY IN ISRAEL (C. 760 – 750 BC)

HOSEA'S MINISTRY IN ISRAEL (C. 753 – 715 BC)

EXILE OF ISRAEL (722 BC)

FALL OF JERUSALEM (586 BC)

1
The word of the LORD that came to Joel son of Pethuel.

AN INVASION OF LOCUSTS

² Hear this, you elders;
     listen, all who live in the land.
Has anything like this ever happened in
          your days
     or in the days of your ancestors?
³ Tell it to your children,
     and let your children tell it to their children,
     and their children to the next generation.
⁴ What the locust swarm has left
     the great locusts have eaten;
what the great locusts have left
     the young locusts have eaten;
what the young locusts have left
     other locusts*ᵃ* have eaten.

⁵ Wake up, you drunkards, and weep!
     Wail, all you drinkers of wine;
wail because of the new wine,
     for it has been snatched from your lips.
⁶ A nation has invaded my land,
     a mighty army without number;
it has the teeth of a lion,
     the fangs of a lioness.
⁷ It has laid waste my vines
     and ruined my fig trees.
It has stripped off their bark
     and thrown it away,
     leaving their branches white.

⁸ Mourn like a virgin in sackcloth
     grieving for the betrothed of her youth.
⁹ Grain offerings and drink offerings
     are cut off from the house of the LORD.
The priests are in mourning,
     those who minister before the LORD.
¹⁰ The fields are ruined,
     the ground is dried up;
the grain is destroyed,
     the new wine is dried up,
     the olive oil fails.

¹¹ Despair, you farmers,
     wail, you vine growers;
grieve for the wheat and the barley,
     because the harvest of the field is destroyed.
¹² The vine is dried up
     and the fig tree is withered;
the pomegranate, the palm and the apple*ᵇ* tree—
     all the trees of the field—are dried up.
Surely the people's joy
     is withered away.

Who were the elders? (1:2)
They were either the older men of the community or the community's officials.

What nation was this? (1:6)
Here Joel referred to the locusts as a nation and later in the book as the Lord's army.

How could a virgin grieve a husband? (1:8)
In Israel when a woman was promised to be married to a man, he was called her husband and she was called his wife, even before the marriage. This husband died before their wedding.

ᵃ 4 The precise meaning of the four Hebrew words used here for locusts is uncertain.   *ᵇ 12* Or possibly *apricot*

A CALL TO LAMENTATION

¹³ Put on sackcloth, you priests, and mourn;
  wail, you who minister before the altar.
Come, spend the night in sackcloth,
  you who minister before my God;
for the grain offerings and drink offerings
  are withheld from the house of your God.
¹⁴ Declare a holy fast;
  call a sacred assembly.
Summon the elders
  and all who live in the land
to the house of the Lord your God,
  and cry out to the Lord.

¹⁵ Alas for that day!
  For the day of the Lord is near;
  it will come like destruction from the Almighty.^a

¹⁶ Has not the food been cut off
  before our very eyes—
joy and gladness
  from the house of our God?
¹⁷ The seeds are shriveled
  beneath the clods.^b
The storehouses are in ruins,
  the granaries have been broken down,
  for the grain has dried up.
¹⁸ How the cattle moan!
  The herds mill about
because they have no pasture;
  even the flocks of sheep are suffering.

¹⁹ To you, Lord, I call,
  for fire has devoured the pastures in the wilderness
  and flames have burned up all the trees of the field.
²⁰ Even the wild animals pant for you;
  the streams of water have dried up
  and fire has devoured the pastures in
    the wilderness.

AN ARMY OF LOCUSTS

2 Blow the trumpet in Zion;
  sound the alarm on my holy hill.

Let all who live in the land tremble,
  for the day of the Lord is coming.
It is close at hand—
²   a day of darkness and gloom,
  a day of clouds and blackness.
Like dawn spreading across the mountains
  a large and mighty army comes,
such as never was in ancient times
  nor ever will be in ages to come.

³ Before them fire devours,
  behind them a flame blazes.

---

^a 15 Hebrew *Shaddai*   ^b 17 The meaning of the Hebrew for this word is uncertain.

Why did Joel urge the priests to call a sacred assembly? (1:13–14)
Times of national prayer and fasting were called when there was an extraordinary event or disaster.

Why would the trumpet be blown? (2:1)
The shofar (a trumpet made of a ram's horn) was sounded to warn of coming danger.

The Trumpet/Shofar (2:1)

Before them the land is like the garden of Eden,
   behind them, a desert waste—
   nothing escapes them.
[4] They have the appearance of horses;
   they gallop along like cavalry.
[5] With a noise like that of chariots
   they leap over the mountaintops,
like a crackling fire consuming stubble,
   like a mighty army drawn up for battle.

[6] At the sight of them, nations are in anguish;
   every face turns pale.
[7] They charge like warriors;
   they scale walls like soldiers.
They all march in line,
   not swerving from their course.
[8] They do not jostle each other;
   each marches straight ahead.
They plunge through defenses
   without breaking ranks.
[9] They rush upon the city;
   they run along the wall.
They climb into the houses;
   like thieves they enter through the windows.

[10] Before them the earth shakes,
   the heavens tremble,
the sun and moon are darkened,
   and the stars no longer shine.
[11] The LORD thunders
   at the head of his army;
his forces are beyond number,
   and mighty is the army that obeys his command.
The day of the LORD is great;
   it is dreadful.
   Who can endure it?

REND YOUR HEART

[12] "Even now," declares the LORD,
   "return to me with all your heart,
   with fasting and weeping and mourning."

[13] Rend your heart
   and not your garments.
Return to the LORD your God,
   for he is gracious and compassionate,
slow to anger and abounding in love,
   and he relents from sending calamity.
[14] Who knows? He may turn and relent
   and leave behind a blessing—
grain offerings and drink offerings
   for the LORD your God.

[15] Blow the trumpet in Zion,
   declare a holy fast,
   call a sacred assembly.
[16] Gather the people,
   consecrate the assembly;

Why would the Lord be at the head of the army of locusts? (2:11)
The Lord used the locusts as his instruments of judgment.

What was the prophet's message of hope? (2:12–14)
He told the people to repent and turn back to the Lord because he is a compassionate and loving God.

bring together the elders,
> gather the children,
> those nursing at the breast.
Let the bridegroom leave his room
> and the bride her chamber.

17 Let the priests, who minister before the Lord,
> weep between the portico and the altar.
Let them say, "Spare your people, Lord.
> Do not make your inheritance an object of scorn,
> a byword among the nations.
Why should they say among the peoples,
> 'Where is their God?'"

THE LORD'S ANSWER

18 Then the Lord was jealous for his land
> and took pity on his people.

19 The Lord replied*a* to them:

"I am sending you grain, new wine and olive oil,
> enough to satisfy you fully;
never again will I make you
> an object of scorn to the nations.

20 "I will drive the northern horde far from you,
> pushing it into a parched and barren land;
its eastern ranks will drown in the Dead Sea
> and its western ranks in the Mediterranean Sea.
And its stench will go up;
> its smell will rise."

Surely he has done great things!
21   Do not be afraid, land of Judah;
> be glad and rejoice.
Surely the Lord has done great things!
22   Do not be afraid, you wild animals,
> for the pastures in the wilderness are becoming green.
The trees are bearing their fruit;
> the fig tree and the vine yield their riches.

23 Be glad, people of Zion,
> rejoice in the Lord your God,
for he has given you the autumn rains
> because he is faithful.
He sends you abundant showers,
> both autumn and spring rains, as before.

24 The threshing floors will be filled with grain;
> the vats will overflow with new wine and oil.

25 "I will repay you for the years the locusts have eaten—
> the great locust and the young locust,
> the other locusts and the locust swarm*b*—
my great army that I sent among you.

26 You will have plenty to eat, until you are full,
> and you will praise the name of the Lord your God,
> who has worked wonders for you;
never again will my people be shamed.

What did it mean that God was jealous for his land? (2:18)
God had great love for his people. He is described as jealous because he wanted them to remain faithful only to him.

How could the locusts eat so much? (2:25)
Each new wave of locusts ate what the previous wave had left behind.

---

a 18,19 Or *Lord will be jealous . . . / and take pity . . . / ¹⁹The Lord will reply*
b 25 The precise meaning of the four Hebrew words used here for locusts is uncertain.

27 Then you will know that I am in Israel,
    that I am the LORD your God,
    and that there is no other;
    never again will my people be shamed.

THE DAY OF THE LORD

28 "And afterward,
    I will pour out my Spirit on all people.
Your sons and daughters will prophesy,
    your old men will dream dreams,
    your young men will see visions.
29 Even on my servants, both men and women,
    I will pour out my Spirit in those days.
30 I will show wonders in the heavens
    and on the earth,
    blood and fire and billows of smoke.
31 The sun will be turned to darkness
    and the moon to blood
    before the coming of the great and dreadful day of
      the LORD.
32 And everyone who calls
    on the name of the LORD will be saved;
for on Mount Zion and in Jerusalem
    there will be deliverance,
    as the LORD has said,
even among the survivors
    whom the LORD calls.ᵃ

> **How would the sun be turned to darkness and the moon turned to blood? (2:31)** These are vivid descriptions of a total eclipse of the sun and moon.

THE NATIONS JUDGED

3 ᵇ "In those days and at that time,
    when I restore the fortunes of Judah and Jerusalem,
2 I will gather all nations
    and bring them down to the Valley of Jehoshaphat.ᶜ
There I will put them on trial
    for what they did to my inheritance, my people Israel,
because they scattered my people among the nations
    and divided up my land.
3 They cast lots for my people
    and traded boys for prostitutes;
    they sold girls for wine to drink.

4 "Now what have you against me, Tyre and Sidon and all you regions of Philistia? Are you repaying me for something I have done? If you are paying me back, I will swiftly and speedily return on your own heads what you have done. 5 For you took my silver and my gold and carried off my finest treasures to your temples.ᵈ 6 You sold the people of Judah and Jerusalem to the Greeks, that you might send them far from their homeland.

7 "See, I am going to rouse them out of the places to which you sold them, and I will return on your own heads what you have done. 8 I will sell your sons and daughters to the people of Judah, and they will sell them to the Sabeans, a nation far away." The LORD has spoken.

> **The Nations Judged (3:2)**
>
>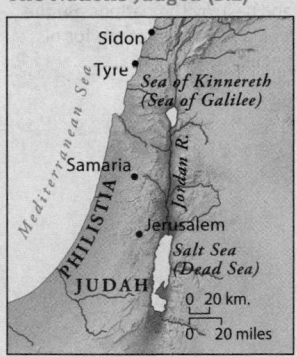
>
> **When did these events take place? (3:3)** This happened to Judah at the time of the captivity (586 B.C.) and is also mentioned in Obadiah 11.

ᵃ 32 In Hebrew texts 2:28-32 is numbered 3:1-5.   ᵇ In Hebrew texts 3:1-21 is numbered 4:1-21.   ᶜ 2 *Jehoshaphat* means *the LORD judges*; also in verse 12.   ᵈ 5 Or *palaces*

What was a pruning hook?
(3:10)
This was an agricultural tool
used for cultivating grapevines.
It had a sharp, knifelike end for
pruning.

9 Proclaim this among the nations:
    Prepare for war!
Rouse the warriors!
    Let all the fighting men draw near and attack.
10 Beat your plowshares into swords
    and your pruning hooks into spears.
Let the weakling say,
    "I am strong!"
11 Come quickly, all you nations from every side,
    and assemble there.

Bring down your warriors, LORD!

12 "Let the nations be roused;
    let them advance into the Valley of Jehoshaphat,
for there I will sit
    to judge all the nations on every side.
13 Swing the sickle,
    for the harvest is ripe.
Come, trample the grapes,
    for the winepress is full
    and the vats overflow—
so great is their wickedness!"

14 Multitudes, multitudes
    in the valley of decision!
For the day of the LORD is near
    in the valley of decision.
15 The sun and moon will be darkened,
    and the stars no longer shine.
16 The LORD will roar from Zion
    and thunder from Jerusalem;
    the earth and the heavens will tremble.
But the LORD will be a refuge for his people,
    a stronghold for the people of Israel.

**What metaphor is being
used for God? (3:16)**
The Lord would roar like a lion
and destroy the nations. But he
would provide a refuge for his
people.

BLESSINGS FOR GOD'S PEOPLE

17 "Then you will know that I, the LORD your God,
    dwell in Zion, my holy hill.
Jerusalem will be holy;
    never again will foreigners invade her.

18 "In that day the mountains will drip new wine,
    and the hills will flow with milk;
    all the ravines of Judah will run with water.
A fountain will flow out of the LORD's house
    and will water the valley of acacias.ᵃ
19 But Egypt will be desolate,
    Edom a desert waste,
because of violence done to the people of Judah,
    in whose land they shed innocent blood.
20 Judah will be inhabited forever
    and Jerusalem through all generations.
21 Shall I leave their innocent blood unavenged?
    No, I will not."

**Why would Egypt and Edom
be turned into wasteland?**
(3:19)
They stood for all of Israel's enemies who were hostile to God.
The Lord would bring judgment
to them.

The LORD dwells in Zion!

ᵃ 18 Or *Valley of Shittim*

Amos

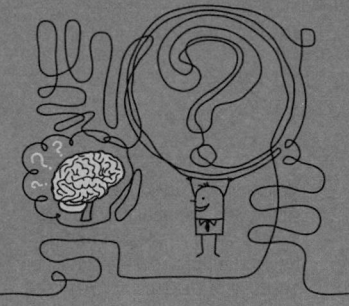

INTRODUCTION

Who wrote this book?
Amos wrote this book. He was a shepherd whom God sent from Judah to preach to the people of Israel.

Why was this book written?
Amos preaches against rich people who are cruel to the poor. He warns the Israelites that God is angry and tells them that they must begin doing right.

What do we learn about God in this book?
God cares very much about people who are poor and helpless. He wants fair treatment for everyone.

What is special about this book?
Amos shows us that sins bring a nation under God's judgment. He also shows us how important it is to see that everyone in a nation is treated fairly.

What are some important passages in this book?

Doing justice	Amos 5:7 – 15
Rich people who don't care about the poor	Amos 6:1 – 7
What God will do to people who oppress the poor	Amos 8:4 – 14

When did these things happen?

1300 BC 1200 · 1100 · 1000 · 900 · 800 · 700 · 600 · 500 · 400

DIVISION OF THE KINGDOM (930 BC) _____

MINISTRIES OF ELIJAH AND ELISHA IN ISRAEL (C. 875 – 797 BC) _____

AMOS'S MINISTRY IN ISRAEL (C. 760 – 750 BC) _____

BOOK OF AMOS WRITTEN (C. 760 – 750 BC) _____

HOSEA'S MINISTRY IN ISRAEL (C. 753 – 715 BC) _____

MINISTRIES OF MICAH AND ISAIAH IN JUDAH (C. 740 – 681 BC) _____

EXILE OF ISRAEL (722 BC) _____

FALL OF JERUSALEM (586 BC) _____

1 The words of Amos, one of the shepherds of Tekoa—
the vision he saw concerning Israel two years before the
earthquake, when Uzziah was king of Judah and Jeroboam
son of Jehoash[a] was king of Israel. ²He said:

> "The LORD roars from Zion
>   and thunders from Jerusalem;
> the pastures of the shepherds dry up,
>   and the top of Carmel withers."

JUDGMENT ON ISRAEL'S NEIGHBORS

³This is what the LORD says:

> "For three sins of Damascus,
>   even for four, I will not relent.
> Because she threshed Gilead
>   with sledges having iron teeth,
> ⁴I will send fire on the house of Hazael
>   that will consume the fortresses of Ben-Hadad.
> ⁵I will break down the gate of Damascus;
>   I will destroy the king who is in[b] the Valley of Aven[c]
> and the one who holds the scepter in Beth Eden.
>   The people of Aram will go into exile to Kir,"
>   says the LORD.

⁶This is what the LORD says:

> "For three sins of Gaza,
>   even for four, I will not relent.
> Because she took captive whole communities
>   and sold them to Edom,
> ⁷I will send fire on the walls of Gaza
>   that will consume her fortresses.
> ⁸I will destroy the king[d] of Ashdod
>   and the one who holds the scepter in Ashkelon.
> I will turn my hand against Ekron,
>   till the last of the Philistines are dead,"
>   says the Sovereign LORD.

⁹This is what the LORD says:

> "For three sins of Tyre,
>   even for four, I will not relent.
> Because she sold whole communities of captives
>   to Edom,
>   disregarding a treaty of brotherhood,
> ¹⁰I will send fire on the walls of Tyre
>   that will consume her fortresses."

¹¹This is what the LORD says:

> "For three sins of Edom,
>   even for four, I will not relent.
> Because he pursued his brother with a sword
>   and slaughtered the women of the land,
> because his anger raged continually
>   and his fury flamed unchecked,

Who was Amos? (1:2)
Amos was a shepherd who was
sent to warn Israel that he had
heard the Lord roaring like a lion
because of the sins of the people.

**What did the expression "for
three sins ... even for four"
mean? (1:3)**
This phrase was meant to stand
for a large number of sins, including the one mentioned for
each nation.

**Judgment on Israel's Neigh-
bors (1:3—2:5)**

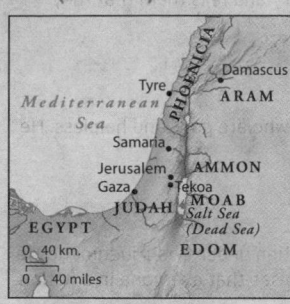

---

a 1 Hebrew *Joash,* a variant of *Jehoash*   *b 5* Or *the inhabitants of*   *c 5 Aven*
means *wickedness.*   *d 8* Or *inhabitants*

¹² I will send fire on Teman
    that will consume the fortresses of Bozrah."

¹³ This is what the LORD says:

"For three sins of Ammon,
    even for four, I will not relent.
Because he ripped open the pregnant women of Gilead
    in order to extend his borders,
¹⁴ I will set fire to the walls of Rabbah
    that will consume her fortresses
amid war cries on the day of battle,
    amid violent winds on a stormy day.
¹⁵ Her king*ᵃ* will go into exile,
    he and his officials together,"

                              says the LORD.

2 This is what the LORD says:

"For three sins of Moab,
    even for four, I will not relent.
Because he burned to ashes
    the bones of Edom's king,
² I will send fire on Moab
    that will consume the fortresses of Kerioth.*ᵇ*
Moab will go down in great tumult
    amid war cries and the blast of the trumpet.
³ I will destroy her ruler
    and kill all her officials with him,"

                              says the LORD.

⁴ This is what the LORD says:

"For three sins of Judah,
    even for four, I will not relent.
Because they have rejected the law of the LORD
    and have not kept his decrees,
because they have been led astray by false gods,*ᶜ*
    the gods*ᵈ* their ancestors followed,
⁵ I will send fire on Judah
    that will consume the fortresses of Jerusalem."

JUDGMENT ON ISRAEL

⁶ This is what the LORD says:

"For three sins of Israel,
    even for four, I will not relent.
They sell the innocent for silver,
    and the needy for a pair of sandals.
⁷ They trample on the heads of the poor
    as on the dust of the ground
    and deny justice to the oppressed.
Father and son use the same girl
    and so profane my holy name.
⁸ They lie down beside every altar
    on garments taken in pledge.
In the house of their god
    they drink wine taken as fines.

Why would burning the king's bones be wrong? (2:1)
In the ancient world, this was thought to deprive the dead person's spirit of the rest that a decent burial would provide.

How were Judah's sins different from the sins of the other nations? (2:4)
The other nations sinned against widely recognized laws of humanity, but Judah disobeyed the law given to them by God.

What were Israel's sins? (2:6–7)
They oppressed the poor and committed sexual sins.

ᵃ 15 Or / Molek   *ᵇ 2 Or of her cities*   *ᶜ 4 Or by lies*   *ᵈ 4 Or lies*

How had they insulted the Lord? (2:11–12)
They ordered the prophets not to tell them the Lord's message, and they made the Nazirites break their vows to not drink wine.

⁹ "Yet I destroyed the Amorites before them,
  though they were tall as the cedars
  and strong as the oaks.
I destroyed their fruit above
  and their roots below.
¹⁰ I brought you up out of Egypt
  and led you forty years in the wilderness
  to give you the land of the Amorites.

¹¹ "I also raised up prophets from among your children
  and Nazirites from among your youths.
Is this not true, people of Israel?"

                                        declares the LORD.

¹² "But you made the Nazirites drink wine
  and commanded the prophets not to prophesy.

¹³ "Now then, I will crush you
  as a cart crushes when loaded with grain.
¹⁴ The swift will not escape,
  the strong will not muster their strength,
  and the warrior will not save his life.
¹⁵ The archer will not stand his ground,
  the fleet-footed soldier will not get away,
  and the horseman will not save his life.
¹⁶ Even the bravest warriors
  will flee naked on that day,"

                                        declares the LORD.

WITNESSES SUMMONED AGAINST ISRAEL

3 Hear this word, people of Israel, the word the LORD has spoken against you — against the whole family I brought up out of Egypt:

² "You only have I chosen
  of all the families of the earth;
therefore I will punish you
  for all your sins."

³ Do two walk together
  unless they have agreed to do so?
⁴ Does a lion roar in the thicket
  when it has no prey?
Does it growl in its den
  when it has caught nothing?
⁵ Does a bird swoop down to a trap on the ground
  when no bait is there?
Does a trap spring up from the ground
  if it has not caught anything?
⁶ When a trumpet sounds in a city,
  do not the people tremble?
When disaster comes to a city,
  has not the LORD caused it?

⁷ Surely the Sovereign LORD does nothing
  without revealing his plan
  to his servants the prophets.

⁸ The lion has roared —
  who will not fear?

Why did Amos ask these questions? (3:3–6)
In each case, there was a cause and effect example drawn from everyday life. He built up to the final question to show that if a city came to disaster it was because of the Lord's judgment. Amos was warning the Israelites that the signs all pointed to their destruction.

The Sovereign Lord has spoken—
who can but prophesy?

9 Proclaim to the fortresses of Ashdod
and to the fortresses of Egypt:
"Assemble yourselves on the mountains of Samaria;
see the great unrest within her
and the oppression among her people."

10 "They do not know how to do right," declares the
Lord,
"who store up in their fortresses
what they have plundered and looted."

11 Therefore this is what the Sovereign Lord says:

"An enemy will overrun your land,
pull down your strongholds
and plunder your fortresses."

12 This is what the Lord says:

"As a shepherd rescues from the lion's mouth
only two leg bones or a piece of an ear,
so will the Israelites living in Samaria be rescued,
with only the head of a bed
and a piece of fabric*a* from a couch.*b*"

13 "Hear this and testify against the descendants of Jacob,"
declares the Lord, the Lord God Almighty.

14 "On the day I punish Israel for her sins,
I will destroy the altars of Bethel;
the horns of the altar will be cut off
and fall to the ground.
15 I will tear down the winter house
along with the summer house;
the houses adorned with ivory will be destroyed
and the mansions will be demolished,"
declares the Lord.

ISRAEL HAS NOT RETURNED TO GOD

4 Hear this word, you cows of Bashan on Mount
Samaria,
you women who oppress the poor and crush the
needy
and say to your husbands, "Bring us some drinks!"
2 The Sovereign Lord has sworn by his holiness:
"The time will surely come
when you will be taken away with hooks,
the last of you with fishhooks.*c*
3 You will each go straight out
through breaches in the wall,
and you will be cast out toward Harmon,*d*"
declares the Lord.

Why would a shepherd save part of the sheep? (3:12)
This would prove to the owner that a wild animal had eaten the sheep and that it had not been stolen by the shepherd. This word picture showed that only a wounded remnant of God's people would survive.

---

a 12 The meaning of the Hebrew for this phrase is uncertain.
b 12 Or *Israelites be rescued, / those who sit in Samaria / on the edge of their beds / and in Damascus on their couches.*   *c 2* Or *away in baskets, / the last of you in fish baskets*   *d 3* Masoretic Text; with a different word division of the Hebrew (see Septuagint) *out, you mountain of oppression*

⁴"Go to Bethel and sin;
    go to Gilgal and sin yet more.
Bring your sacrifices every morning,
    your tithes every three years.ᵃ
⁵Burn leavened bread as a thank offering
    and brag about your freewill offerings—
boast about them, you Israelites,
    for this is what you love to do,"

        declares the Sovereign LORD.

⁶"I gave you empty stomachs in every city
    and lack of bread in every town,
yet you have not returned to me,"

        declares the LORD.

⁷"I also withheld rain from you
    when the harvest was still three months away.
I sent rain on one town,
    but withheld it from another.
One field had rain;
    another had none and dried up.
⁸People staggered from town to town for water
    but did not get enough to drink,
yet you have not returned to me,"

        declares the LORD.

⁹"Many times I struck your gardens and vineyards,
    destroying them with blight and mildew.
Locusts devoured your fig and olive trees,
    yet you have not returned to me,"

        declares the LORD.

¹⁰"I sent plagues among you
    as I did to Egypt.
I killed your young men with the sword,
    along with your captured horses.
I filled your nostrils with the stench of
        your camps,
    yet you have not returned to me,"

        declares the LORD.

¹¹"I overthrew some of you
    as I overthrew Sodom and Gomorrah.
You were like a burning stick snatched from the fire,
    yet you have not returned to me,"

        declares the LORD.

¹²"Therefore this is what I will do to you, Israel,
    and because I will do this to you, Israel,
    prepare to meet your God."

¹³He who forms the mountains,
    who creates the wind,
    and who reveals his thoughts to mankind,
who turns dawn to darkness,
    and treads on the heights of the earth—
    the LORD God Almighty is his name.

ᵃ 4 Or *days*

How had the Lord tried to turn his people back to him? (4:6–11)
The Lord had sent famine, drought, blight and mildew, locusts, plagues, and destruction to get the people's attention, but the people had not returned to God.

Why did the people need to prepare to meet their God? (4:12)
They were going to come face-to-face with God's judgment.

A LAMENT AND CALL TO REPENTANCE

5 Hear this word, Israel, this lament I take up concerning you:

2 "Fallen is Virgin Israel,
    never to rise again,
deserted in her own land,
    with no one to lift her up."

3 This is what the Sovereign Lord says to Israel:

"Your city that marches out a thousand strong
    will have only a hundred left;
your town that marches out a hundred strong
    will have only ten left."

4 This is what the Lord says to Israel:

"Seek me and live;
5   do not seek Bethel,
do not go to Gilgal,
    do not journey to Beersheba.
For Gilgal will surely go into exile,
    and Bethel will be reduced to nothing.*"
6 Seek the Lord and live,
    or he will sweep through the tribes of Joseph like
        a fire;
it will devour them,
    and Bethel will have no one to quench it.

7 There are those who turn justice into bitterness
    and cast righteousness to the ground.

8 He who made the Pleiades and Orion,
    who turns midnight into dawn
    and darkens day into night,
who calls for the waters of the sea
    and pours them out over the face of the land—
    the Lord is his name.
9 With a blinding flash he destroys the stronghold
    and brings the fortified city to ruin.

10 There are those who hate the one who upholds justice
        in court
    and detest the one who tells the truth.

11 You levy a straw tax on the poor
    and impose a tax on their grain.
Therefore, though you have built stone mansions,
    you will not live in them;
though you have planted lush vineyards,
    you will not drink their wine.
12 For I know how many are your offenses
    and how great your sins.

There are those who oppress the innocent and
        take bribes
    and deprive the poor of justice in the courts.

What was the house of Joseph? (5:6)
This referred to the northern kingdom of Israel. It was dominated by the tribe of Ephraim, which had descended from Joseph.

How did the people turn justice into bitterness? (5:7–13)
This section described how the people had corrupted the process of justice in the courts with slander, bribery, and by intimidating witnesses. They also showed injustice to the poor and oppressed the righteous.

---

*a 5 Hebrew aven, a reference to Beth Aven (a derogatory name for Bethel);
see Hosea 4:15.

¹³ Therefore the prudent keep quiet in such times,
for the times are evil.

¹⁴ Seek good, not evil,
that you may live.
Then the Lord God Almighty will be with you,
just as you say he is.
¹⁵ Hate evil, love good;
maintain justice in the courts.
Perhaps the Lord God Almighty will have mercy
on the remnant of Joseph.

¹⁶ Therefore this is what the Lord, the Lord God Almighty, says:

"There will be wailing in all the streets
and cries of anguish in every public square.
The farmers will be summoned to weep
and the mourners to wail.
¹⁷ There will be wailing in all the vineyards,
for I will pass through your midst,"

says the Lord.

THE DAY OF THE LORD

¹⁸ Woe to you who long
for the day of the Lord!
Why do you long for the day of the Lord?
That day will be darkness, not light.
¹⁹ It will be as though a man fled from a lion
only to meet a bear,
as though he entered his house
and rested his hand on the wall
only to have a snake bite him.
²⁰ Will not the day of the Lord be darkness, not light—
pitch-dark, without a ray of brightness?

²¹ "I hate, I despise your religious festivals;
your assemblies are a stench to me.
²² Even though you bring me burnt offerings and
grain offerings,
I will not accept them.
Though you bring choice fellowship offerings,
I will have no regard for them.
²³ Away with the noise of your songs!
I will not listen to the music of your harps.
²⁴ But let justice roll on like a river,
righteousness like a never-failing stream!

²⁵ "Did you bring me sacrifices and offerings
forty years in the wilderness, people of Israel?
²⁶ You have lifted up the shrine of your king,
the pedestal of your idols,
the star of your god^a—
which you made for yourselves.
²⁷ Therefore I will send you into exile beyond Damascus,"
says the Lord, whose name is God Almighty.

^a 26 Or *lifted up Sakkuth your king / and Kaiwan your idols, / your star-gods;* Septuagint *lifted up the shrine of Molek / and the star of your god Rephan, / their idols*

What were ancient funeral processions like? (5:16)
Wailing relatives, often accompanied by paid mourners and musicians, walked ahead of the body that was being carried to the grave.

Why did Israel long for the day of the Lord? (5:18)
Israel expected to receive God's blessings when he came to judge the nations. But Amos warned that it would be a day of darkness, not light, because Israel had been unfaithful to God.

Why did God hate their religious festivals and offerings? (5:21–24)
The people continued to observe the outward forms of worship, but they failed to promote justice and righteousness.

WOE TO THE COMPLACENT

6 Woe to you who are complacent in Zion,
and to you who feel secure on Mount Samaria,
you notable men of the foremost nation,
to whom the people of Israel come!

² Go to Kalneh and look at it;
go from there to great Hamath,
and then go down to Gath in Philistia.
Are they better off than your two kingdoms?
Is their land larger than yours?

³ You put off the day of disaster
and bring near a reign of terror.

⁴ You lie on beds adorned with ivory
and lounge on your couches.
You dine on choice lambs
and fattened calves.

⁵ You strum away on your harps like David
and improvise on musical instruments.

⁶ You drink wine by the bowlful
and use the finest lotions,
but you do not grieve over the ruin of Joseph.

⁷ Therefore you will be among the first to go into exile;
your feasting and lounging will end.

THE LORD ABHORS THE PRIDE OF ISRAEL

⁸ The Sovereign Lord has sworn by himself—the Lord
God Almighty declares:

"I abhor the pride of Jacob
and detest his fortresses;
I will deliver up the city
and everything in it."

⁹ If ten people are left in one house, they too will die. ¹⁰ And
if the relative who comes to carry the bodies out of the house
to burn them^a asks anyone who might be hiding there, "Is
anyone else with you?" and he says, "No," then he will go on
to say, "Hush! We must not mention the name of the Lord."

¹¹ For the Lord has given the command,
and he will smash the great house into pieces
and the small house into bits.

¹² Do horses run on the rocky crags?
Does one plow the sea^b with oxen?
But you have turned justice into poison
and the fruit of righteousness into bitterness—

¹³ you who rejoice in the conquest of Lo Debar^c
and say, "Did we not take Karnaim^d by our
own strength?"

¹⁴ For the Lord God Almighty declares,
"I will stir up a nation against you, Israel,
that will oppress you all the way
from Lebo Hamath to the valley of the Arabah."

What was lotion used for in the ancient world? (6:6)
Lotion or perfume, in the form of ointment or scented oil, was probably originally used in the Middle East for ceremonial purposes, first religious and then secular. Perfume was widely used as a form of deodorant; and it was used so commonly that not applying it was a sign of mourning.

What were these fortresses? (6:8)
This may refer to the palace-fortresses built by wealthy people, and it could also refer to the citadels that were symbols of Israel's past military successes.

Was cremation widespread? (6:10)
Cremation was not generally practiced, so this might refer to burning a memorial fire in honor of the dead.

---

^a 10 Or *to make a funeral fire in honor of the dead*   ^b 12 With a different
word division of the Hebrew; Masoretic Text *plow there*   ^c 13 *Lo Debar*
means *nothing.*   ^d 13 *Karnaim* means *horns*; horn here symbolizes strength.

What was the "king's share"? (7:1)
This was apparently the first crop from which the royal taxes were taken. The second crop was what grew in the fields after the grains and early hay were harvested.

What did the plumb line show? (7:7–8)
A plumb line was a cord with a weight on the end that was used to determine if a wall was straight. Israel was like a crooked wall. Their ungodly behavior did not meet God's standards.

Why did Amos say that he was not a prophet or a prophet's son? (7:14)
Amaziah implied that Amos made his living by being a prophet, but Amos explained that he had not been hired to preach about the judgment that was coming.

LOCUSTS, FIRE AND A PLUMB LINE

7 This is what the Sovereign LORD showed me: He was preparing swarms of locusts after the king's share had been harvested and just as the late crops were coming up. ²When they had stripped the land clean, I cried out, "Sovereign LORD, forgive! How can Jacob survive? He is so small!"

³So the LORD relented.

"This will not happen," the LORD said.

⁴This is what the Sovereign LORD showed me: The Sovereign LORD was calling for judgment by fire; it dried up the great deep and devoured the land. ⁵Then I cried out, "Sovereign LORD, I beg you, stop! How can Jacob survive? He is so small!"

⁶So the LORD relented.

"This will not happen either," the Sovereign LORD said.

⁷This is what he showed me: The Lord was standing by a wall that had been built true to plumb,ᵃ with a plumb lineᵇ in his hand. ⁸And the LORD asked me, "What do you see, Amos?"

"A plumb line," I replied.

Then the Lord said, "Look, I am setting a plumb line among my people Israel; I will spare them no longer.

⁹ "The high places of Isaac will be destroyed
    and the sanctuaries of Israel will be ruined;
  with my sword I will rise against the house of
    Jeroboam."

AMOS AND AMAZIAH

¹⁰Then Amaziah the priest of Bethel sent a message to Jeroboam king of Israel: "Amos is raising a conspiracy against you in the very heart of Israel. The land cannot bear all his words. ¹¹For this is what Amos is saying:

"'Jeroboam will die by the sword,
    and Israel will surely go into exile,
  away from their native land.'"

¹²Then Amaziah said to Amos, "Get out, you seer! Go back to the land of Judah. Earn your bread there and do your prophesying there. ¹³Don't prophesy anymore at Bethel, because this is the king's sanctuary and the temple of the kingdom."

¹⁴Amos answered Amaziah, "I was neither a prophet nor the son of a prophet, but I was a shepherd, and I also took care of sycamore-fig trees. ¹⁵But the LORD took me from tending the flock and said to me, 'Go, prophesy to my people Israel.' ¹⁶Now then, hear the word of the LORD. You say,

"'Do not prophesy against Israel,
    and stop preaching against the descendants of Isaac.'

¹⁷"Therefore this is what the LORD says:

"'Your wife will become a prostitute in the city,
    and your sons and daughters will fall by the sword.

ᵃ 7 The meaning of the Hebrew for this phrase is uncertain.   ᵇ 7 The meaning of the Hebrew for this phrase is uncertain; also in verse 8.

Your land will be measured and divided up,
   and you yourself will die in a pagan^a country.
And Israel will surely go into exile,
   away from their native land.'"

A BASKET OF RIPE FRUIT

8 This is what the Sovereign LORD showed me: a basket of ripe fruit. ² "What do you see, Amos?" he asked.

"A basket of ripe fruit," I answered.

Then the LORD said to me, "The time is ripe for my people Israel; I will spare them no longer.

³ "In that day," declares the Sovereign LORD, "the songs in the temple will turn to wailing.^b Many, many bodies — flung everywhere! Silence!"

⁴ Hear this, you who trample the needy
   and do away with the poor of the land,

⁵ saying,

"When will the New Moon be over
   that we may sell grain,
and the Sabbath be ended
   that we may market wheat?" —
skimping on the measure,
   boosting the price
   and cheating with dishonest scales,
⁶ buying the poor with silver
   and the needy for a pair of sandals,
   selling even the sweepings with the wheat.

⁷ The LORD has sworn by himself, the Pride of Jacob: "I will never forget anything they have done.

⁸ "Will not the land tremble for this,
   and all who live in it mourn?
The whole land will rise like the Nile;
   it will be stirred up and then sink
   like the river of Egypt.

⁹ "In that day," declares the Sovereign LORD,

"I will make the sun go down at noon
   and darken the earth in broad daylight.
¹⁰ I will turn your religious festivals into mourning
   and all your singing into weeping.
I will make all of you wear sackcloth
   and shave your heads.
I will make that time like mourning for an only son
   and the end of it like a bitter day.

¹¹ "The days are coming," declares the Sovereign LORD,
   "when I will send a famine through the land —
not a famine of food or a thirst for water,
   but a famine of hearing the words of the LORD.
¹² People will stagger from sea to sea
   and wander from north to east,
searching for the word of the LORD,
   but they will not find it.

How did the people mistreat the poor? (8:6)
They treated the poor unjustly and made slaves of them.

How did the Nile rise? (8:8)
Because of the heavy rains, each year the Nile River rose by as much as 25 feet, flooding the whole valley. The water carried a large amount of rich soil that was left behind when the water receded.

---

^a 17 Hebrew an unclean   ^b 3 Or "the temple singers will wail

13 "In that day

"the lovely young women and strong young men
    will faint because of thirst.
14 Those who swear by the sin of Samaria—
    who say, 'As surely as your god lives, Dan,'
    or, 'As surely as the god*a* of Beersheba lives'—
    they will fall, never to rise again."

ISRAEL TO BE DESTROYED

9 I saw the Lord standing by the altar, and he said:

"Strike the tops of the pillars
    so that the thresholds shake.
Bring them down on the heads of all the people;
    those who are left I will kill with the sword.
Not one will get away,
    none will escape.
2 Though they dig down to the depths below,
    from there my hand will take them.
Though they climb up to the heavens above,
    from there I will bring them down.
3 Though they hide themselves on the top of Carmel,
    there I will hunt them down and seize them.
Though they hide from my eyes at the bottom of the
        sea,
    there I will command the serpent to bite them.
4 Though they are driven into exile by their enemies,
    there I will command the sword to slay them.

"I will keep my eye on them
    for harm and not for good."

5 The Lord, the LORD Almighty—
    he touches the earth and it melts,
    and all who live in it mourn;
the whole land rises like the Nile,
    then sinks like the river of Egypt;
6 he builds his lofty palace*b* in the heavens
    and sets its foundation*c* on the earth;
he calls for the waters of the sea
    and pours them out over the face of the land—
    the LORD is his name.

7 "Are not you Israelites
    the same to me as the Cushites*d*?"
                                    declares the LORD.
"Did I not bring Israel up from Egypt,
    the Philistines from Caphtor*e*
    and the Arameans from Kir?

8 "Surely the eyes of the Sovereign LORD
    are on the sinful kingdom.
I will destroy it
    from the face of the earth.

What was the significance of Dan and Beersheba? (8:14) These cities marked the northern and southern boundaries of Israel. They also were places where pagan shrines had been built.

Why were the Israelites compared to the Cushites? (9:7) The Cushites were a pagan people who lived south of Egypt. The only difference between Israel and the pagan nations was that God had made a covenant with Israel, but Israel had broken the covenant repeatedly.

---

a 14 Hebrew *the way*   *b* 6 The meaning of the Hebrew for this phrase is uncertain.   *c* 6 The meaning of the Hebrew for this word is uncertain.
d 7 That is, people from the upper Nile region   *e* 7 That is, Crete

Yet I will not totally destroy
   the descendants of Jacob,"

                    declares the LORD.

[9] "For I will give the command,
   and I will shake the people of Israel
   among all the nations
as grain is shaken in a sieve,
   and not a pebble will reach the ground.
[10] All the sinners among my people
   will die by the sword,
all those who say,
   'Disaster will not overtake or meet us.'

ISRAEL'S RESTORATION

[11] "In that day

"I will restore David's fallen shelter—
   I will repair its broken walls
   and restore its ruins—
   and will rebuild it as it used to be,
[12] so that they may possess the remnant of Edom
   and all the nations that bear my name,[a]"
        declares the LORD, who will do these things.

[13] "The days are coming," declares the LORD,

"when the reaper will be overtaken by the plowman
   and the planter by the one treading grapes.
New wine will drip from the mountains
   and flow from all the hills,
[14]   and I will bring my people Israel back from exile.[b]

"They will rebuild the ruined cities and live in them.
   They will plant vineyards and drink their wine;
   they will make gardens and eat their fruit.
[15] I will plant Israel in their own land,
   never again to be uprooted
   from the land I have given them,"

                says the LORD your God.

Why was grain shaken in a sieve? (9:9)
When grain was gathered from the ground, it was sifted in a sieve in order to remove objects such as small stones. Only the grain dropped through, and the stones would be discarded.

How would God restore David's tent? (9:11)
This could mean that David's dynasty would be restored when the Messiah came, or it could refer to David's kingdom being reunited.

---

[a] 12 Hebrew; Septuagint *so that the remnant of people / and all the nations that bear my name may seek me*   [b] 14 Or *will restore the fortunes of my people Israel*

Obadiah

INTRODUCTION

Who wrote this book?
Obadiah wrote this book. Nothing more is known about this prophet.

Why was this book written?
Obadiah speaks of the punishment God will bring on the Edomites. They invaded Judah and plundered Jerusalem.

What do we learn about God in this book?
God is faithful. He will keep his promise to Abraham: "Whoever curses you I will curse" (Genesis 12:3).

When did these things happen?

1300 BC 1200   1100   1000   900   800   700   600   500   400

DIVISION OF THE KINGDOM (930 BC)

MINISTRIES OF ELIJAH AND ELISHA IN ISRAEL (C. 875 – 797 BC)

JOEL'S MINISTRY IN JUDAH (C. 835 – 796 BC?)

JONAH'S MINISTRY IN NINEVEH (C. 800 – 750 BC)

AMOS'S MINISTRY IN ISRAEL (C. 760 – 750 BC)

HOSEA'S MINISTRY IN ISRAEL (C. 753 – 715 BC)

EXILE OF ISRAEL (722 BC)

OBADIAH'S MINISTRY (C. 605 – 585 BC?)

FALL OF JERUSALEM (586 BC)

OBADIAH'S VISION

¹The vision of Obadiah.

This is what the Sovereign LORD says about Edom—

We have heard a message from the LORD:
　An envoy was sent to the nations to say,
　"Rise, let us go against her for battle"—

²"See, I will make you small among the nations;
　you will be utterly despised.
³The pride of your heart has deceived you,
　you who live in the clefts of the rocks*a*
　and make your home on the heights,
you who say to yourself,
　'Who can bring me down to the ground?'
⁴Though you soar like the eagle
　and make your nest among the stars,
　from there I will bring you down,"
　　　　　　　　　　　　　declares the LORD.
⁵"If thieves came to you,
　if robbers in the night—
oh, what a disaster awaits you!—
　would they not steal only as much as
　　　they wanted?
If grape pickers came to you,
　would they not leave a few grapes?
⁶But how Esau will be ransacked,
　his hidden treasures pillaged!
⁷All your allies will force you to the border;
　your friends will deceive and overpower you;
those who eat your bread will set a trap for you,*b*
　but you will not detect it.

⁸"In that day," declares the LORD,
　"will I not destroy the wise men of Edom,
　those of understanding in the mountains
　　of Esau?
⁹Your warriors, Teman, will be terrified,
　and everyone in Esau's mountains
　will be cut down in the slaughter.
¹⁰Because of the violence against your brother Jacob,
　you will be covered with shame;
　you will be destroyed forever.
¹¹On the day you stood aloof
　while strangers carried off his wealth
and foreigners entered his gates
　and cast lots for Jerusalem,
　you were like one of them.
¹²You should not gloat over your brother
　in the day of his misfortune,
nor rejoice over the people of Judah
　in the day of their destruction,
nor boast so much
　in the day of their trouble.

Where did Esau keep his hidden treasures? (v. 6)
This refers to the Edomites, the descendants of Esau. The ancient Greek historian Diodorus Siculus said that the Edomites put their wealth in vaults in the rocks.

Why were Edom's crimes condemned? (v. 10)
Edom had treated Israel with cruelty by standing by while Jerusalem was conquered and had even participated in the looting. This was made worse by the fact that they both were descended from Isaac.

a 3 Or *of Sela*　　*b 7* The meaning of the Hebrew for this clause is uncertain.

¹³ You should not march through the gates of
　　　my people
　　　　in the day of their disaster,
　　　nor gloat over them in their calamity
　　　　in the day of their disaster,
　　　nor seize their wealth
　　　　in the day of their disaster.
¹⁴ You should not wait at the crossroads
　　　　to cut down their fugitives,
　　　nor hand over their survivors
　　　　in the day of their trouble.

¹⁵ "The day of the LORD is near
　　　　for all nations.
　　As you have done, it will be done to you;
　　　　your deeds will return upon your own head.
¹⁶ Just as you drank on my holy hill,
　　　　so all the nations will drink continually;
　　they will drink and drink
　　　　and be as if they had never been.
¹⁷ But on Mount Zion will be deliverance;
　　　　it will be holy,
　　　and Jacob will possess his inheritance.
¹⁸ Jacob will be a fire
　　　　and Joseph a flame;
　　Esau will be stubble,
　　　　and they will set him on fire and destroy him.
　　There will be no survivors
　　　　from Esau."

　　　　　　　　　　The LORD has spoken.

¹⁹ People from the Negev will occupy
　　　　the mountains of Esau,
　　and people from the foothills will possess
　　　　the land of the Philistines.
　　They will occupy the fields of Ephraim and Samaria,
　　　　and Benjamin will possess Gilead.
²⁰ This company of Israelite exiles who are in Canaan
　　　　will possess the land as far as Zarephath;
　　the exiles from Jerusalem who are in Sepharad
　　　　will possess the towns of the Negev.
²¹ Deliverers will go up on^a Mount Zion
　　　　to govern the mountains of Esau.
　　And the kingdom will be the LORD's.

Who would occupy Edom after it was destroyed? (v. 19) The land would probably be occupied by the remnant of Israel.

^a 21 Or from

Jonah

INTRODUCTION

Who wrote this book?
The prophet Jonah.

Why was this book written?
The book of Jonah shows Israel that God does not punish if people repent and are sorry for their sins.

What do we learn about God in this book?
God forgives his disobedient prophet and gives Jonah a second chance. God also forgives the people of Nineveh. God does not punish people who repent.

What is special about this book?
God shows love for the foreign people in Nineveh as well as for his own Hebrew people.

What are some of the stories of this book?

Jonah is swallowed by a fish	Jonah 1
The people of Nineveh repent	Jonah 3
God teaches Jonah to care about all people	Jonah 4

When did these things happen?

1300 BC 1200 1100 1000 900 800 700 600 500 400

DIVISION OF THE KINGDOM (930 BC)

MINISTRIES OF ELIJAH AND ELISHA IN ISRAEL (C. 875 – 797 BC)

JONAH'S MINISTRY IN NINEVEH (C. 800 – 750 BC)

BOOK OF JONAH WRITTEN (C. 785 – 750 BC)

MINISTRIES OF AMOS AND HOSEA IN ISRAEL (C. 760 – 715 BC)

MICAH'S MINISTRY IN JUDAH (C. 735 – 700 BC)

ISAIAH'S MINISTRY IN JUDAH (C. 740 – 681 BC)

EXILE OF ISRAEL (722 BC)

FALL OF JERUSALEM (586 BC)

How did someone receive "the word of the LORD"? (1:1)
This was a common phrase used to describe how a prophet received a divine revelation from God. It may have been in the form of a vision, a dream, a sign in nature, or a direct word.

Where was Tarshish? (1:3)
Tarshish was a city in Spain in the opposite direction of Nineveh.

Jonah on the Run (1:3)

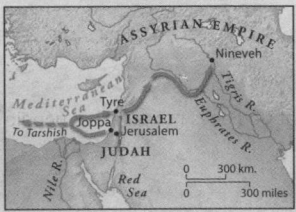

How did the sailors cast lots? (1:7)
Casting lots was a common practice in the ancient world. The exact method isn't known, but the sailors probably drew pebbles or sticks from a container to determine who was responsible for the storm.

How did the sailors try to get back to land? (1:13)
The Hebrew word for *row* literally meant *to dig*. This shows how much effort they put into rowing to try to get back to shore. The ship may have been powered by oars, sails, or both.

JONAH FLEES FROM THE LORD

1 The word of the LORD came to Jonah son of Amittai: ² "Go to the great city of Nineveh and preach against it, because its wickedness has come up before me."

³ But Jonah ran away from the LORD and headed for Tarshish. He went down to Joppa, where he found a ship bound for that port. After paying the fare, he went aboard and sailed for Tarshish to flee from the LORD.

⁴ Then the LORD sent a great wind on the sea, and such a violent storm arose that the ship threatened to break up. ⁵ All the sailors were afraid and each cried out to his own god. And they threw the cargo into the sea to lighten the ship.

But Jonah had gone below deck, where he lay down and fell into a deep sleep. ⁶ The captain went to him and said, "How can you sleep? Get up and call on your god! Maybe he will take notice of us so that we will not perish."

⁷ Then the sailors said to each other, "Come, let us cast lots to find out who is responsible for this calamity." They cast lots and the lot fell on Jonah. ⁸ So they asked him, "Tell us, who is responsible for making all this trouble for us? What kind of work do you do? Where do you come from? What is your country? From what people are you?"

⁹ He answered, "I am a Hebrew and I worship the LORD, the God of heaven, who made the sea and the dry land."

¹⁰ This terrified them and they asked, "What have you done?" (They knew he was running away from the LORD, because he had already told them so.)

¹¹ The sea was getting rougher and rougher. So they asked him, "What should we do to you to make the sea calm down for us?"

¹² "Pick me up and throw me into the sea," he replied, "and it will become calm. I know that it is my fault that this great storm has come upon you."

¹³ Instead, the men did their best to row back to land. But they could not, for the sea grew even wilder than before. ¹⁴ Then they cried out to the LORD, "Please, LORD, do not let us die for taking this man's life. Do not hold us accountable for killing an innocent man, for you, LORD, have done as you pleased." ¹⁵ Then they took Jonah and threw him overboard, and the raging sea grew calm. ¹⁶ At this the men greatly

Was it really possible for Jonah to survive inside a huge fish for three days?
JONAH 1

Bible scholars and scientists have discussed this question for many years. There are some who claim that a particular type of whale, not normally found in this part of the Mediterranean Sea, would have been able to trap Jonah in its mouth. Because whales are mammals and have to surface occasionally to get air, it may have been possible for Jonah to survive in this way. Other experts claim that there is no species of fish or whale that could swallow a person whole and have that person survive for three days.

In any case, if a huge fish swallowed Jonah and spit him out after three days, it would have been a miracle. The point of the story is not what type of fish this may have been, but how God worked in Jonah's life to convince him to follow God's will. Jonah was not willing to go to Nineveh, but God persuaded Jonah to go to Nineveh to deliver God's message. The theme of the book is that God is in control of everything, that God has compassion and mercy for people, and that God wants people to turn toward him and believe in him.

feared the LORD, and they offered a sacrifice to the LORD and made vows to him.

JONAH'S PRAYER

¹⁷Now the LORD provided a huge fish to swallow Jonah, and Jonah was in the belly of the fish three days and three nights. ¹From inside the fish Jonah prayed to the LORD his God. ²He said:

> "In my distress I called to the LORD,
>   and he answered me.
> From deep in the realm of the dead I called for help,
>   and you listened to my cry.
> ³You hurled me into the depths,
>   into the very heart of the seas,
>   and the currents swirled about me;
> all your waves and breakers
>   swept over me.
> ⁴I said, 'I have been banished
>   from your sight;
> yet I will look again
>   toward your holy temple.'
> ⁵The engulfing waters threatened me,^b
>   the deep surrounded me;
>   seaweed was wrapped around my head.
> ⁶To the roots of the mountains I sank down;
>   the earth beneath barred me in forever.
> But you, LORD my God,
>   brought my life up from the pit.
>
> ⁷"When my life was ebbing away,
>   I remembered you, LORD,
> and my prayer rose to you,
>   to your holy temple.
>
> ⁸"Those who cling to worthless idols
>   turn away from God's love for them.
> ⁹But I, with shouts of grateful praise,
>   will sacrifice to you.
> What I have vowed I will make good.
>   I will say, 'Salvation comes from the LORD.'"

¹⁰And the LORD commanded the fish, and it vomited Jonah onto dry land.

JONAH GOES TO NINEVEH

Then the word of the LORD came to Jonah a second time: ²"Go to the great city of Nineveh and proclaim to it the message I give you."

³Jonah obeyed the word of the LORD and went to Nineveh. Now Nineveh was a very large city; it took three days to go through it. ⁴Jonah began by going a day's journey into the city, proclaiming, "Forty more days and Nineveh will be overthrown." ⁵The Ninevites believed God. A fast was proclaimed, and all of them, from the greatest to the least, put on sackcloth.

^a In Hebrew texts 2:1 is numbered 1:17, and 2:1-10 is numbered 2:2-11.
^b 5 Or *waters were at my throat*

What type of prayer did Jonah pray? (2:2)
Jonah's prayer was one of thanksgiving for being delivered from death in the sea. He realized that although he deserved to die, God had shown mercy to him.

What was the pit? (2:6)
This was a term that referred to the grave or death.

Why was Jonah told to proclaim God's message? (3:2)
Prophets primarily bore messages from God rather than foretell future events.

Why would a visit to Nineveh require three days? (3:3)
According to Jonah 4:11, the city had 120,000 citizens. Archaeological excavations show that the imperial city of Nineveh was about 8 miles around. It is possible that "Nineveh" referred to both the city itself and its surrounding suburbs, which was an area of about 60 miles.

⁶When Jonah's warning reached the king of Nineveh, he rose from his throne, took off his royal robes, covered himself with sackcloth and sat down in the dust. ⁷This is the proclamation he issued in Nineveh:

"By the decree of the king and his nobles:

Do not let people or animals, herds or flocks, taste anything; do not let them eat or drink. ⁸But let people and animals be covered with sackcloth. Let everyone call urgently on God. Let them give up their evil ways and their violence. ⁹Who knows? God may yet relent and with compassion turn from his fierce anger so that we will not perish."

¹⁰When God saw what they did and how they turned from their evil ways, he relented and did not bring on them the destruction he had threatened.

JONAH'S ANGER AT THE LORD'S COMPASSION

4 But to Jonah this seemed very wrong, and he became angry. ²He prayed to the LORD, "Isn't this what I said, LORD, when I was still at home? That is what I tried to forestall by fleeing to Tarshish. I knew that you are a gracious and compassionate God, slow to anger and abounding in love, a God who relents from sending calamity. ³Now, LORD, take away my life, for it is better for me to die than to live."

⁴But the LORD replied, "Is it right for you to be angry?"

⁵Jonah had gone out and sat down at a place east of the city. There he made himself a shelter, sat in its shade and waited to see what would happen to the city. ⁶Then the LORD God provided a leafy plant*a* and made it grow up over Jonah to give shade for his head to ease his discomfort, and Jonah was very happy about the plant. ⁷But at dawn the next day God provided a worm, which chewed the plant so that it withered. ⁸When the sun rose, God provided a scorching east wind, and the sun blazed on Jonah's head so that he grew faint. He wanted to die, and said, "It would be better for me to die than to live."

⁹But God said to Jonah, "Is it right for you to be angry about the plant?"

"It is," he said. "And I'm so angry I wish I were dead."

¹⁰But the LORD said, "You have been concerned about this plant, though you did not tend it or make it grow. It sprang up overnight and died overnight. ¹¹And should I not have concern for the great city of Nineveh, in which there are more than a hundred and twenty thousand people who cannot tell their right hand from their left—and also many animals?"

What type of plant was this? (4:6)
This was probably a castor oil plant, a shrub that grew over 12 feet high with large, shade-producing leaves.

What did it mean that they could not tell their right hand from the left? (4:11)
They were unable to understand spiritual truths without God's help.

---

a 6 The precise identification of this plant is uncertain; also in verses 7, 9 and 10.

Micah

INTRODUCTION

Who wrote this book?	The prophet Micah.
Why was this book written?	The book of Micah reveals God's concern for justice in Judah as well as in Israel.
What do we learn about God in this book?	God cares for the poor and helpless. God will judge the rich who mistreat them.
What is special about this book?	Micah tells people to turn to God. Only love for God will move people to do what is right, and so save Judah from judgment.
What are some important passages in this book?	Punishment for the wicked Micah 2:1 – 5 A ruler from Bethlehem Micah 5:1 – 5 Our forgiving God Micah 7:18 – 20

When did these things happen?

1 The word of the LORD that came to Micah of Moresheth during the reigns of Jotham, Ahaz and Hezekiah, kings of Judah — the vision he saw concerning Samaria and Jerusalem.

² Hear, you peoples, all of you,
　listen, earth and all who live in it,
that the Sovereign LORD may bear witness against you,
　the Lord from his holy temple.

JUDGMENT AGAINST SAMARIA AND JERUSALEM

³ Look! The LORD is coming from his dwelling place;
　he comes down and treads on the heights of the earth.
⁴ The mountains melt beneath him
　and the valleys split apart,
like wax before the fire,
　like water rushing down a slope.
⁵ All this is because of Jacob's transgression,
　because of the sins of the people of Israel.
What is Jacob's transgression?
　Is it not Samaria?
What is Judah's high place?
　Is it not Jerusalem?

⁶ "Therefore I will make Samaria a heap of rubble,
　a place for planting vineyards.
I will pour her stones into the valley
　and lay bare her foundations.
⁷ All her idols will be broken to pieces;
　all her temple gifts will be burned with fire;
　I will destroy all her images.
Since she gathered her gifts from the wages of
　　prostitutes,
　as the wages of prostitutes they will again be used."

WEEPING AND MOURNING

⁸ Because of this I will weep and wail;
　I will go about barefoot and naked.
I will howl like a jackal
　and moan like an owl.
⁹ For Samaria's plague is incurable;
　it has spread to Judah.
It has reached the very gate of my people,
　even to Jerusalem itself.
¹⁰ Tell it not in Gath*ᵃ*;
　weep not at all.
In Beth Ophrah*ᵇ*
　roll in the dust.
¹¹ Pass by naked and in shame,
　you who live in Shaphir.*ᶜ*
Those who live in Zaanan*ᵈ*
　will not come out.
Beth Ezel is in mourning;
　it no longer protects you.

ᵃ *10 Gath sounds like the Hebrew for tell.*   ᵇ *10 Beth Ophrah means house of dust.*   ᶜ *11 Shaphir means pleasant.*   ᵈ *11 Zaanan sounds like the Hebrew for come out.*

Judgment on Samaria and Jerusalem (1:5)

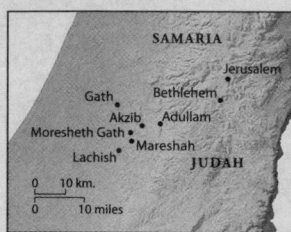

Why would the prophet go barefoot? (1:8)
Going barefoot was a sign of mourning. It is possible that Micah actually walked barefoot through Jerusalem wearing only a loincloth of sackcloth (in effect "naked").

Why was the city gate so important? (1:9)
The city gate was where the people of the city met to hold court, where the marketplace was located, and where official business took place.

Why would someone "roll in the dust"? (1:10)
This was another sign of mourning, in this case because of the coming catastrophe.

¹² Those who live in Maroth^a writhe in pain,
    waiting for relief,
because disaster has come from the LORD,
    even to the gate of Jerusalem.
¹³ You who live in Lachish,
    harness fast horses to the chariot.
You are where the sin of Daughter Zion
      began,
    for the transgressions of Israel were found
      in you.
¹⁴ Therefore you will give parting gifts
    to Moresheth Gath.
The town of Akzib^b will prove deceptive
    to the kings of Israel.
¹⁵ I will bring a conqueror against you
    who live in Mareshah.^c
The nobles of Israel
    will flee to Adullam.
¹⁶ Shave your head in mourning
    for the children in whom you delight;
make yourself as bald as the vulture,
    for they will go from you into exile.

HUMAN PLANS AND GOD'S PLANS

2 Woe to those who plan iniquity,
    to those who plot evil on their beds!
At morning's light they carry it out
    because it is in their power to do it.
² They covet fields and seize them,
    and houses, and take them.
They defraud people of their homes,
    they rob them of their inheritance.

³ Therefore, the LORD says:

"I am planning disaster against this people,
    from which you cannot save yourselves.
You will no longer walk proudly,
    for it will be a time of calamity.
⁴ In that day people will ridicule you;
    they will taunt you with this mournful song:
'We are utterly ruined;
    my people's possession is divided up.
He takes it from me!
    He assigns our fields to traitors.'"

⁵ Therefore you will have no one in the assembly
      of the LORD
    to divide the land by lot.

FALSE PROPHETS

⁶ "Do not prophesy," their prophets say.
    "Do not prophesy about these things;
    disgrace will not overtake us."

---

^a *12 Maroth* sounds like the Hebrew for *bitter.*   ^b *14 Akzib* means *deception.*
^c *15 Mareshah* sounds like the Hebrew for *conqueror.*

Who was "Daughter Zion"? (1:13)
This was a personification of Jerusalem and the people who lived there.

How would God reward the traitors? (2:4)
The traitors — the Assyrians — would take away the property of the rich when they invaded the land. This would be a punishment on the wealthy who had abused their poor neighbors.

⁷You descendants of Jacob, should it be said,
  "Does the LORD become*a* impatient?
  Does he do such things?"

 "Do not my words do good
  to the one whose ways are upright?
⁸Lately my people have risen up
  like an enemy.
 You strip off the rich robe
  from those who pass by without a care,
  like men returning from battle.
⁹You drive the women of my people
  from their pleasant homes.
 You take away my blessing
  from their children forever.
¹⁰Get up, go away!
  For this is not your resting place,
 because it is defiled,
  it is ruined, beyond all remedy.
¹¹If a liar and deceiver comes and says,
  'I will prophesy for you plenty of wine and beer,'
  that would be just the prophet for this people!

DELIVERANCE PROMISED

¹²"I will surely gather all of you, Jacob;
  I will surely bring together the remnant of Israel.
 I will bring them together like sheep in a pen,
  like a flock in its pasture;
  the place will throng with people.
¹³The One who breaks open the way will go up
  before them;
  they will break through the gate and go out.
 Their King will pass through before them,
  the LORD at their head."

LEADERS AND PROPHETS REBUKED

3 Then I said,

 "Listen, you leaders of Jacob,
  you rulers of Israel.
 Should you not embrace justice,
² you who hate good and love evil;
 who tear the skin from my people
  and the flesh from their bones;
³who eat my people's flesh,
  strip off their skin
  and break their bones in pieces;
 who chop them up like meat for the pan,
  like flesh for the pot?"

⁴Then they will cry out to the LORD,
  but he will not answer them.
 At that time he will hide his face from them
  because of the evil they have done.

Why would a lying prophet be right for these people? (2:11)
The people would be glad to reward someone for positive prophecies. They didn't want to hear the truth.

How would the Lord restore Israel? (2:12)
Even though they would be brought into captivity, a group of people would return.

What do these images suggest? (3:2–3)
These word pictures describe in figurative language the cruelty of the leaders.

---

a 7 Or *Is the Spirit of the LORD*

⁵This is what the LORD says:

"As for the prophets
who lead my people astray,
they proclaim 'peace'
if they have something to eat,
but prepare to wage war against anyone
who refuses to feed them.
⁶Therefore night will come over you, without visions,
and darkness, without divination.
The sun will set for the prophets,
and the day will go dark for them.
⁷The seers will be ashamed
and the diviners disgraced.
They will all cover their faces
because there is no answer from God."
⁸But as for me, I am filled with power,
with the Spirit of the LORD,
and with justice and might,
to declare to Jacob his transgression,
to Israel his sin.

⁹Hear this, you leaders of Jacob,
you rulers of Israel,
who despise justice
and distort all that is right;
¹⁰who build Zion with bloodshed,
and Jerusalem with wickedness.
¹¹Her leaders judge for a bribe,
her priests teach for a price,
and her prophets tell fortunes for money.
Yet they look for the LORD's support and say,
"Is not the LORD among us?
No disaster will come upon us."
¹²Therefore because of you,
Zion will be plowed like a field,
Jerusalem will become a heap of rubble,
the temple hill a mound overgrown with thickets.

THE MOUNTAIN OF THE LORD

4 In the last days

the mountain of the LORD's temple will be established
as the highest of the mountains;
it will be exalted above the hills,
and peoples will stream to it.

²Many nations will come and say,

"Come, let us go up to the mountain of the LORD,
to the temple of the God of Jacob.
He will teach us his ways,
so that we may walk in his paths."
The law will go out from Zion,
the word of the LORD from Jerusalem.
³He will judge between many peoples
and will settle disputes for strong nations far
and wide.

What was the difference between true and false prophets? (3:5)
The false prophets predicted peace for Judah, but Micah predicted destruction and captivity.

What were seers? (3:7)
This was an older term for prophets.

What was a plowshare? (4:3)
A plowshare was an iron point mounted on a wooden beam that was used to dig furrows for planting seeds.

What did it mean to sit under one's own vine and fig tree? (4:4)
This was a picture of peace, security, and contentment.

They will beat their swords into plowshares
and their spears into pruning hooks.
Nation will not take up sword against nation,
nor will they train for war anymore.
⁴Everyone will sit under their own vine
and under their own fig tree,
and no one will make them afraid,
for the LORD Almighty has spoken.
⁵All the nations may walk
in the name of their gods,
but we will walk in the name of the LORD
our God for ever and ever.

THE LORD'S PLAN

⁶"In that day," declares the LORD,

"I will gather the lame;
I will assemble the exiles
and those I have brought to grief.
⁷I will make the lame my remnant,
those driven away a strong nation.
The LORD will rule over them in Mount Zion
from that day and forever.
⁸As for you, watchtower of the flock,
stronghold[a] of Daughter Zion,
the former dominion will be restored to you;
kingship will come to Daughter Jerusalem."

⁹Why do you now cry aloud—
have you no king[b]?
Has your ruler[c] perished,
that pain seizes you like that of a woman in labor?
¹⁰Writhe in agony, Daughter Zion,
like a woman in labor,
for now you must leave the city
to camp in the open field.
You will go to Babylon;
there you will be rescued.
There the LORD will redeem you
out of the hand of your enemies.

¹¹But now many nations
are gathered against you.
They say, "Let her be defiled,
let our eyes gloat over Zion!"
¹²But they do not know
the thoughts of the LORD;
they do not understand his plan,
that he has gathered them like sheaves to the
threshing floor.
¹³"Rise and thresh, Daughter Zion,
for I will give you horns of iron;
I will give you hooves of bronze,
and you will break to pieces many nations."
You will devote their ill-gotten gains to the LORD,
their wealth to the Lord of all the earth.

What was the "watchtower of the flock"? (4:8)
The watchtower of the flock refers to Jerusalem, the city of David, the shepherd-king.

ᵃ 8 Or hill   ᵇ 9 Or King   ᶜ 9 Or Ruler

A PROMISED RULER FROM BETHLEHEM

5[a] Marshal your troops now, city of troops,
   for a siege is laid against us.
They will strike Israel's ruler
   on the cheek with a rod.

² "But you, Bethlehem Ephrathah,
   though you are small among the clans[b]
      of Judah,
out of you will come for me
   one who will be ruler over Israel,
whose origins are from of old,
   from ancient times."

³ Therefore Israel will be abandoned
   until the time when she who is in labor
      bears a son,
and the rest of his brothers return
   to join the Israelites.

⁴ He will stand and shepherd his flock
   in the strength of the LORD,
   in the majesty of the name of the LORD his God.
And they will live securely, for then his greatness
   will reach to the ends of the earth.

⁵ And he will be our peace
   when the Assyrians invade our land
   and march through our fortresses.
We will raise against them seven shepherds,
   even eight commanders,
⁶ who will rule[c] the land of Assyria with the sword,
   the land of Nimrod with drawn sword.[d]
He will deliver us from the Assyrians
   when they invade our land
   and march across our borders.

⁷ The remnant of Jacob will be
   in the midst of many peoples
like dew from the LORD,
   like showers on the grass,
which do not wait for anyone
   or depend on man.
⁸ The remnant of Jacob will be among the nations,
   in the midst of many peoples,
like a lion among the beasts of the forest,
   like a young lion among flocks of sheep,
which mauls and mangles as it goes,
   and no one can rescue.
⁹ Your hand will be lifted up in triumph over your
      enemies,
   and all your foes will be destroyed.

¹⁰ "In that day," declares the LORD,

"I will destroy your horses from among you
   and demolish your chariots.

---

[a] In Hebrew texts 5:1 is numbered 4:14, and 5:2-15 is numbered 5:1-14.
[b] 2 Or *rulers*   [c] 6 Or *crush*   [d] 6 Or *Nimrod in its gates*

When was this prophecy fulfilled? (5:2)
This prophecy was fulfilled when Jesus was born in Bethlehem (see Matthew 2:6).

Who were these Assyrians? (5:5)
Here "the Assyrians" stood for all of the enemies of Israel.

What did "seven ... even eight" mean? (5:5)
This was a figurative way of saying "many."

¹¹ I will destroy the cities of your land
     and tear down all your strongholds.
¹² I will destroy your witchcraft
     and you will no longer cast spells.
¹³ I will destroy your idols
     and your sacred stones from among you;
you will no longer bow down
     to the work of your hands.
¹⁴ I will uproot from among you your Asherah poles[a]
     when I demolish your cities.
¹⁵ I will take vengeance in anger and wrath
     on the nations that have not obeyed me."

THE LORD'S CASE AGAINST ISRAEL

6 Listen to what the LORD says:

"Stand up, plead my case before the mountains;
     let the hills hear what you have to say.

² "Hear, you mountains, the LORD's accusation;
     listen, you everlasting foundations of the earth.
For the LORD has a case against his people;
     he is lodging a charge against Israel.

³ "My people, what have I done to you?
     How have I burdened you? Answer me.
⁴ I brought you up out of Egypt
     and redeemed you from the land of slavery.
I sent Moses to lead you,
     also Aaron and Miriam.
⁵ My people, remember
     what Balak king of Moab plotted
     and what Balaam son of Beor answered.
Remember your journey from Shittim to Gilgal,
     that you may know the righteous acts of the LORD."

⁶ With what shall I come before the LORD
     and bow down before the exalted God?
Shall I come before him with burnt offerings,
     with calves a year old?
⁷ Will the LORD be pleased with thousands of rams,
     with ten thousand rivers of olive oil?

[a] 14 That is, wooden symbols of the goddess Asherah

Why were the mountains and foundations of the earth called to be witnesses? (6:1–2)
If they were alive, they would be able to tell if someone's claims were true or not because they had been in existence for a very long time.

What does God require from his people?   MICAH 6:8

People cannot earn their salvation; ever since Adam and Eve first sinned, no one has been able to obey God's laws perfectly. God saves his people through grace because of Jesus' death and resurrection. But God wants his people to live lives that honor him and that serve their fellow human beings. Believers respect God's laws and do their best to keep them as a form of thankfulness for their salvation.

During Micah's time many people failed to live up to God's standards. They exploited the poor, rebelled against God's authority, and rejected his prophets. However, many still observed the rituals of worship by offering sacrifices. God did not want people to worship him with sacrifices unless they also loved him with their hearts and followed him with their lives. The words of Micah 6:8 sum up what God wanted from his people then and what he wants from us today: "to act justly and to love mercy and to walk humbly with your God."

Shall I offer my firstborn for my transgression,
  the fruit of my body for the sin of my soul?
[8] He has shown you, O mortal, what is good.
  And what does the LORD require of you?
To act justly and to love mercy
  and to walk humbly[a] with your God.

ISRAEL'S GUILT AND PUNISHMENT

[9] Listen! The LORD is calling to the city—
  and to fear your name is wisdom—
  "Heed the rod and the One who appointed it.[b]
[10] Am I still to forget your ill-gotten treasures, you
    wicked house,
  and the short ephah,[c] which is accursed?
[11] Shall I acquit someone with dishonest scales,
  with a bag of false weights?
[12] Your rich people are violent;
  your inhabitants are liars
  and their tongues speak deceitfully.
[13] Therefore, I have begun to destroy you,
  to ruin[d] you because of your sins.
[14] You will eat but not be satisfied;
  your stomach will still be empty.[e]
You will store up but save nothing,
  because what you save[f] I will give to the sword.
[15] You will plant but not harvest;
  you will press olives but not use the oil,
  you will crush grapes but not drink the wine.
[16] You have observed the statutes of Omri
  and all the practices of Ahab's house;
  you have followed their traditions.
Therefore I will give you over to ruin
  and your people to derision;
  you will bear the scorn of the nations.[g]"

ISRAEL'S MISERY

7 What misery is mine!
  I am like one who gathers summer fruit
  at the gleaning of the vineyard;
there is no cluster of grapes to eat,
  none of the early figs that I crave.
[2] The faithful have been swept from the land;
  not one upright person remains.
Everyone lies in wait to shed blood;
  they hunt each other with nets.
[3] Both hands are skilled in doing evil;
  the ruler demands gifts,
the judge accepts bribes,
  the powerful dictate what they desire—
  they all conspire together.

How much was an ephah?
(6:10)
An ephah was a unit of measurement that equaled half a bushel.

What were these scales like?
(6:11)
The balance consisted of a horizontal bar, suspended from a cord held in the hand or balanced on a perpendicular rod. Pans were hung from both ends of the bar, one for the weight and the other for the object to be weighed. It was possible to cheat when weighing items using this type of scale.

What type of curse was this?
(6:14–15)
This was a curse for disobedience (see Deuteronomy 28:38–39).

What did this image mean?
(7:1–2)
Looking for the godly was like looking for fruit when the harvest ended, because they were so scarce.

---

[a] 8 Or *prudently*   [b] 9 The meaning of the Hebrew for this line is uncertain.
[c] 10 An ephah was a dry measure.   [d] 13 Or *Therefore, I will make you ill and destroy you; I will ruin*   [e] 14 The meaning of the Hebrew for this word is uncertain.   [f] 14 Or *You will press toward birth but not give birth, / and what you bring to birth*   [g] 16 Septuagint; Hebrew *scorn due my people*

What was this day the "watchmen sound the alarm"? (7:4)
This was the day of judgment the prophets had warned about.

⁴The best of them is like a brier,
　　the most upright worse than a thorn hedge.
The day God visits you has come,
　　the day your watchmen sound the alarm.
Now is the time of your confusion.
⁵Do not trust a neighbor;
　　put no confidence in a friend.
Even with the woman who lies in your embrace
　　guard the words of your lips.
⁶For a son dishonors his father,
　　a daughter rises up against her mother,
a daughter-in-law against her mother-in-law—
　　a man's enemies are the members of his
　　　　own household.

⁷But as for me, I watch in hope for the LORD,
　　I wait for God my Savior;
　　my God will hear me.

ISRAEL WILL RISE

⁸Do not gloat over me, my enemy!
　　Though I have fallen, I will rise.
Though I sit in darkness,
　　the LORD will be my light.
⁹Because I have sinned against him,
　　I will bear the LORD's wrath,
until he pleads my case
　　and upholds my cause.
He will bring me out into the light;
　　I will see his righteousness.
¹⁰Then my enemy will see it
　　and will be covered with shame,
she who said to me,
　　"Where is the LORD your God?"
My eyes will see her downfall;
　　even now she will be trampled underfoot
　　like mire in the streets.

¹¹The day for building your walls will come,
　　the day for extending your boundaries.
¹²In that day people will come to you
　　from Assyria and the cities of Egypt,
even from Egypt to the Euphrates
　　and from sea to sea
　　and from mountain to mountain.
¹³The earth will become desolate because of
　　　　its inhabitants,
　　as the result of their deeds.

PRAYER AND PRAISE

Who was this shepherd? (7:14)
Throughout the ancient world, leaders were often referred to as the shepherds of their people.

¹⁴Shepherd your people with your staff,
　　the flock of your inheritance,
which lives by itself in a forest,
　　in fertile pasturelands.ᵃ
Let them feed in Bashan and Gilead
　　as in days long ago.

ᵃ 14 Or in the middle of Carmel

15 "As in the days when you came out of Egypt,
    I will show them my wonders."

16 Nations will see and be ashamed,
      deprived of all their power.
  They will put their hands over their mouths
      and their ears will become deaf.
17 They will lick dust like a snake,
      like creatures that crawl on the ground.
  They will come trembling out of their dens;
      they will turn in fear to the Lord our God
      and will be afraid of you.
18 Who is a God like you,
      who pardons sin and forgives the transgression
      of the remnant of his inheritance?
  You do not stay angry forever
      but delight to show mercy.
19 You will again have compassion on us;
      you will tread our sins underfoot
      and hurl all our iniquities into the depths of the sea.
20 You will be faithful to Jacob,
      and show love to Abraham,
  as you pledged on oath to our ancestors
      in days long ago.

How would nations react
when they saw God's power
at the Messiah's coming?
(7:16)
They would be ashamed and
frightened.

Nahum

INTRODUCTION

Who wrote this book?
The prophet Nahum.

Why was this book written?
The book of Nahum assures the people of Judah that God will destroy Nineveh, the capital city of their great enemy, Assyria.

What do we learn about God in this book?
God will punish the enemies of the people he loves.

What is special about this book?
The city of Nineveh is captured, just as Nahum says, by using a river (Nahum 2:5 – 10).

When did these things happen? 1300 BC 1200   1100   1000   900   800   700   600   500   400

MINISTRIES OF MICAH AND ISAIAH IN JUDAH (C. 740 – 681 BC)_____

EXILE OF ISRAEL (722 BC)_____

NAHUM'S MINISTRY (C. 645 – 620 BC) _____

BOOK OF NAHUM WRITTEN (C. 645 – 620 BC) _____

ZEPHANIAH'S MINISTRY IN JUDAH (C. 640 – 627 BC)_____

JEREMIAH'S MINISTRY IN JUDAH (C. 626 – 585 BC) _____

HABAKKUK'S MINISTRY IN JUDAH (C. 605 – 588 BC) _____

FALL OF JERUSALEM (586 BC) _____

MINISTRIES OF HAGGAI AND ZECHARIAH (C. 520 – 480 BC) _____

1 A prophecy concerning Nineveh. The book of the vision of Nahum the Elkoshite.

THE LORD'S ANGER AGAINST NINEVEH

² The LORD is a jealous and avenging God;
   the LORD takes vengeance and is filled with wrath.
The LORD takes vengeance on his foes
   and vents his wrath against his enemies.
³ The LORD is slow to anger but great in power;
   the LORD will not leave the guilty unpunished.
His way is in the whirlwind and the storm,
   and clouds are the dust of his feet.
⁴ He rebukes the sea and dries it up;
   he makes all the rivers run dry.
Bashan and Carmel wither
   and the blossoms of Lebanon fade.
⁵ The mountains quake before him
   and the hills melt away.
The earth trembles at his presence,
   the world and all who live in it.
⁶ Who can withstand his indignation?
   Who can endure his fierce anger?
His wrath is poured out like fire;
   the rocks are shattered before him.

⁷ The LORD is good,
   a refuge in times of trouble.
He cares for those who trust in him,
⁸   but with an overwhelming flood
he will make an end of Nineveh;
   he will pursue his foes into the realm of darkness.

⁹ Whatever they plot against the LORD
   he will bring[a] to an end;
   trouble will not come a second time.
¹⁰ They will be entangled among thorns
   and drunk from their wine;
   they will be consumed like dry stubble.[b]
¹¹ From you, Nineveh, has one come forth
   who plots evil against the LORD
   and devises wicked plans.

¹² This is what the LORD says:

"Although they have allies and are numerous,
   they will be destroyed and pass away.
Although I have afflicted you, Judah,
   I will afflict you no more.
¹³ Now I will break their yoke from your neck
   and tear your shackles away."

¹⁴ The LORD has given a command concerning you,
      Nineveh:
   "You will have no descendants to bear your name.
I will destroy the images and idols
   that are in the temple of your gods.

---

[a] 9 Or *What do you foes plot against the LORD? / He will bring it*
[b] 10 The meaning of the Hebrew for this verse is uncertain.

When did God dry up the sea and make the rivers run dry? (1:4)
God parted the waters of the Red Sea when the Israelites escaped from Egypt (Exodus 14), and he parted the waters of the Jordan River when the Israelites crossed into Canaan (Joshua 3).

How would Bashan, Carmel, and Lebanon be singled out? (1:4)
These three places were noted for their fertility, vineyards, and trees, but the Lord would cause them to wither.

What did the yoke symbolize? (1:13)
The yoke was a common symbol of political submission. Here it symbolized Judah's submission as Assyria's vassal or servant.

> I will prepare your grave,
>   for you are vile.”

¹⁵ Look, there on the mountains,
>   the feet of one who brings good news,
>   who proclaims peace!
> Celebrate your festivals, Judah,
>   and fulfill your vows.
> No more will the wicked invade you;
>   they will be completely destroyed.^a

NINEVEH TO FALL

2^b An attacker advances against you, Nineveh.
>   Guard the fortress,
> watch the road,
> brace yourselves,
> marshal all your strength!

² The Lord will restore the splendor of Jacob
>   like the splendor of Israel,
> though destroyers have laid them waste
>   and have ruined their vines.

³ The shields of the soldiers are red;
>   the warriors are clad in scarlet.
> The metal on the chariots flashes
>   on the day they are made ready;
> the spears of juniper are brandished.^c

⁴ The chariots storm through the streets,
>   rushing back and forth through the squares.
> They look like flaming torches;
>   they dart about like lightning.

⁵ Nineveh summons her picked troops,
>   yet they stumble on their way.
> They dash to the city wall;
>   the protective shield is put in place.

⁶ The river gates are thrown open
>   and the palace collapses.

⁷ It is decreed^d that Nineveh
>   be exiled and carried away.
> Her female slaves moan like doves
>   and beat on their breasts.

⁸ Nineveh is like a pool
>   whose water is draining away.
> “Stop! Stop!” they cry,
>   but no one turns back.

⁹ Plunder the silver!
>   Plunder the gold!
> The supply is endless,
>   the wealth from all its treasures!

¹⁰ She is pillaged, plundered, stripped!
>   Hearts melt, knees give way,
> bodies tremble, every face grows pale.

Who was the attacker? (2:1)
This probably referred to the alliance of the Babylonians, Medes, and Scythians who joined forces to destroy Nineveh.

What were the river gates? (2:6)
These were probably the dams on the Khosr River, which ran through Nineveh to the Tigris River. The dams were already in place or were built quickly and then released so that the flood would damage the city walls.

---

^a 15 In Hebrew texts this verse (1:15) is numbered 2:1.   ^b In Hebrew texts 2:1-13 is numbered 2:2-14.   ^c 3 Hebrew; Septuagint and Syriac *ready; / the horsemen rush to and fro.*   ^d 7 The meaning of the Hebrew for this word is uncertain.

11 Where now is the lions' den,
the place where they fed their young,
where the lion and lioness went,
and the cubs, with nothing to fear?
12 The lion killed enough for his cubs
and strangled the prey for his mate,
filling his lairs with the kill
and his dens with the prey.

13 "I am against you,"
declares the LORD Almighty.
"I will burn up your chariots in smoke,
and the sword will devour your young lions.
I will leave you no prey on the earth.
The voices of your messengers
will no longer be heard."

WOE TO NINEVEH

3 Woe to the city of blood,
full of lies,
full of plunder,
never without victims!
2 The crack of whips,
the clatter of wheels,
galloping horses
and jolting chariots!
3 Charging cavalry,
flashing swords
and glittering spears!
Many casualties,
piles of dead,
bodies without number,
people stumbling over the corpses—
4 all because of the wanton lust of a prostitute,
alluring, the mistress of sorceries,
who enslaved nations by her prostitution
and peoples by her witchcraft.

5 "I am against you," declares the LORD
Almighty.
"I will lift your skirts over your face.
I will show the nations your nakedness
and the kingdoms your shame.
6 I will pelt you with filth,
I will treat you with contempt
and make you a spectacle.

What did the lion symbolize? (2:11)
The lion was a symbol for Assyria because its people and policies were very vicious. The city of Nineveh in Assyria contained many lion sculptures.

Why was Nineveh called a "city of blood"? (3:1)
The Assyrians were known for their ruthlessness and brutality. Many of their victims were beheaded, impaled, or burned.

Why would God say he would lift Nineveh's skirts over her head? (3:5)
Nineveh was being compared to a prostitute, and this type of public disgrace was a common punishment for prostitutes.

Can people pass the point of being forgiven by God?   NAHUM 3

God invites people to turn away from sin, to seek forgiveness, and to do God's will. However, sometimes those who rebel against God become so numb to the working of the Holy Spirit that they cut themselves off from God completely. When this happens, God gives consequences for their sin and rebellion. When God sends his judgment in a situation like this, it is too late for someone to beg for mercy.

However, for God's children nothing can separate them from God's love. God will forgive his people who are truly sorry for their sins and who wish to dedicate their lives to him. It is only those who persistently reject God and defy him that will be cut off from his mercy.

⁷ All who see you will flee from you and say,
'Nineveh is in ruins—who will mourn for her?'
Where can I find anyone to comfort you?"

⁸ Are you better than Thebes,
situated on the Nile,
with water around her?
The river was her defense,
the waters her wall.
⁹ Cush*a* and Egypt were her boundless strength;
Put and Libya were among her allies.
¹⁰ Yet she was taken captive
and went into exile.
Her infants were dashed to pieces
at every street corner.
Lots were cast for her nobles,
and all her great men were put in chains.
¹¹ You too will become drunk;
you will go into hiding
and seek refuge from the enemy.

¹² All your fortresses are like fig trees
with their first ripe fruit;
when they are shaken,
the figs fall into the mouth of the eater.
¹³ Look at your troops—
they are all weaklings.
The gates of your land
are wide open to your enemies;
fire has consumed the bars of your gates.

¹⁴ Draw water for the siege,
strengthen your defenses!
Work the clay,
tread the mortar,
repair the brickwork!
¹⁵ There the fire will consume you;
the sword will cut you down—
they will devour you like a swarm of locusts.
Multiply like grasshoppers,
multiply like locusts!
¹⁶ You have increased the number of your merchants
till they are more numerous than the stars in the sky,
but like locusts they strip the land
and then fly away.
¹⁷ Your guards are like locusts,
your officials like swarms of locusts
that settle in the walls on a cold day—
but when the sun appears they fly away,
and no one knows where.

¹⁸ King of Assyria, your shepherds*b* slumber;
your nobles lie down to rest.
Your people are scattered on the mountains
with no one to gather them.

Why were locusts feared?
(3:17)
Farmers feared locusts because
they came in huge swarms and
devoured everything in their
path.

a 9 That is, the upper Nile region   *b 18* That is, rulers

19 Nothing can heal you;
  your wound is fatal.
All who hear the news about you
  clap their hands at your fall,
for who has not felt
  your endless cruelty?

Habakkuk

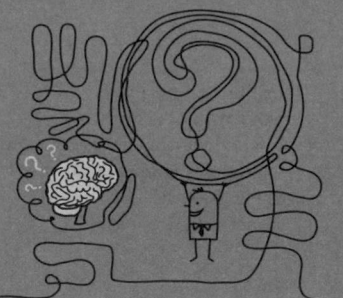

INTRODUCTION

Who wrote this book? The prophet Habakkuk.

Why was this book written? The book of Habakkuk shows that people never get away with being wicked and that God will punish the wicked.

What do we learn about God in this book? God is too holy to let people get away with sin. He punishes everyone who sins, even people like the Babylonians, who seemed to get rich by being wicked.

What is special about this book? Habakkuk is afraid when he learns that God will send the Babylonians against Judah. But in the end Habakkuk decides to trust God anyway.

When did these things happen?   1300 BC 1200   1100   1000   900   800   700   600   500   400

MINISTRIES OF MICAH AND ISAIAH IN JUDAH (C. 740 – 681 BC)

EXILE OF ISRAEL (722 BC)

NAHUM'S MINISTRY (C. 645 – 620 BC)

ZEPHANIAH'S MINISTRY IN JUDAH (C. 640 – 627 BC)

JEREMIAH'S MINISTRY IN JUDAH (C. 626 – 585 BC)

HABAKKUK'S MINISTRY IN JUDAH (C. 605 – 588 BC)

BOOK OF HABAKKUK WRITTEN (C. 605 BC)

FALL OF JERUSALEM (586 BC)

1

The prophecy that Habakkuk the prophet received.

HABAKKUK'S COMPLAINT

²How long, Lord, must I call for help,
   but you do not listen?
Or cry out to you, "Violence!"
   but you do not save?
³Why do you make me look at injustice?
   Why do you tolerate wrongdoing?
Destruction and violence are before me;
   there is strife, and conflict abounds.
⁴Therefore the law is paralyzed,
   and justice never prevails.
The wicked hem in the righteous,
   so that justice is perverted.

THE LORD'S ANSWER

⁵"Look at the nations and watch—
   and be utterly amazed.
For I am going to do something in your days
   that you would not believe,
   even if you were told.
⁶I am raising up the Babylonians,ᵃ
   that ruthless and impetuous people,
who sweep across the whole earth
   to seize dwellings not their own.
⁷They are a feared and dreaded people;
   they are a law to themselves
   and promote their own honor.
⁸Their horses are swifter than leopards,
   fiercer than wolves at dusk.
Their cavalry gallops headlong;
   their horsemen come from afar.
They fly like an eagle swooping to devour;
⁹   they all come intent on violence.
Their hordesᵇ advance like a desert wind
   and gather prisoners like sand.
¹⁰They mock kings
   and scoff at rulers.
They laugh at all fortified cities;
   by building earthen ramps they capture them.
¹¹Then they sweep past like the wind and go on—
   guilty people, whose own strength is
      their god."

HABAKKUK'S SECOND COMPLAINT

¹²Lord, are you not from everlasting?
   My God, my Holy One, youᶜ will never die.
You, Lord, have appointed them to
      execute judgment;
   you, my Rock, have ordained them to punish.
¹³Your eyes are too pure to look on evil;
   you cannot tolerate wrongdoing.

What was a prophecy? (1:1)
A prophecy was an announcement from God. It frequently referred to revelations about impending doom, but it could also refer to messages containing hope for the future.

The Babylonian Empire (1:6)

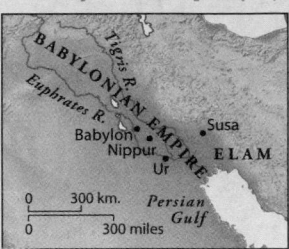

Why were the Babylonians so greatly feared? (1:8–9)
They attacked swiftly, and they were cruel. They deported the people they conquered as a matter of national policy.

ᵃ 6 Or *Chaldeans*   ᵇ 9 The meaning of the Hebrew for this word is
uncertain.   ᶜ 12 An ancient Hebrew scribal tradition; Masoretic Text *we*

Why did the prophet use this image of a net? (1:15–16)
The victims of Babylon were as helpless as fish caught in a net. Some ancient Babylonian artwork shows the Babylonians capturing their enemies in nets.

What did it mean to stand at one's watch? (2:1)
This was an image of a guard looking out from a tower and expecting an answer to his challenge to anyone approaching the city.

Why was the grave called "greedy"? (2:5)
The grave never seems to be satisfied and always claims more people as everyone eventually dies.

Why then do you tolerate the treacherous?
Why are you silent while the wicked
swallow up those more righteous than themselves?
[14] You have made people like the fish in the sea,
like the sea creatures that have no ruler.
[15] The wicked foe pulls all of them up with hooks,
he catches them in his net,
he gathers them up in his dragnet;
and so he rejoices and is glad.
[16] Therefore he sacrifices to his net
and burns incense to his dragnet,
for by his net he lives in luxury
and enjoys the choicest food.
[17] Is he to keep on emptying his net,
destroying nations without mercy?

2 I will stand at my watch
and station myself on the ramparts;
I will look to see what he will say to me,
and what answer I am to give to this complaint.[a]

THE LORD'S ANSWER

[2] Then the LORD replied:

"Write down the revelation
and make it plain on tablets
so that a herald[b] may run with it.
[3] For the revelation awaits an appointed time;
it speaks of the end
and will not prove false.
Though it linger, wait for it;
it[c] will certainly come
and will not delay.

[4] "See, the enemy is puffed up;
his desires are not upright—
but the righteous person will live by his
faithfulness[d]—
[5] indeed, wine betrays him;
he is arrogant and never at rest.
Because he is as greedy as the grave
and like death is never satisfied,
he gathers to himself all the nations
and takes captive all the peoples.

[6] "Will not all of them taunt him with ridicule and scorn, saying,

"'Woe to him who piles up stolen goods
and makes himself wealthy by extortion!
How long must this go on?'
[7] Will not your creditors suddenly arise?
Will they not wake up and make you tremble?
Then you will become their prey.
[8] Because you have plundered many nations,
the peoples who are left will plunder you.

[a] 1 Or *and what to answer when I am rebuked*   [b] 2 Or *so that whoever reads it*
[c] 3 Or *Though he linger, wait for him; / he*   [d] 4 Or *faith*

For you have shed human blood;
 you have destroyed lands and cities and everyone in
  them.

⁹ "Woe to him who builds his house by unjust gain,
 setting his nest on high
 to escape the clutches of ruin!
¹⁰ You have plotted the ruin of many peoples,
 shaming your own house and forfeiting your life.
¹¹ The stones of the wall will cry out,
 and the beams of the woodwork will echo it.

¹² "Woe to him who builds a city with bloodshed
 and establishes a town by injustice!
¹³ Has not the LORD Almighty determined
 that the people's labor is only fuel for the fire,
 that the nations exhaust themselves for nothing?
¹⁴ For the earth will be filled with the knowledge of the
  glory of the LORD
 as the waters cover the sea.

¹⁵ "Woe to him who gives drink to his neighbors,
 pouring it from the wineskin till they are drunk,
 so that he can gaze on their naked bodies!
¹⁶ You will be filled with shame instead of glory.
 Now it is your turn! Drink and let your nakedness
  be exposed*!
 The cup from the LORD's right hand is coming around
  to you,
 and disgrace will cover your glory.
¹⁷ The violence you have done to Lebanon will
  overwhelm you,
 and your destruction of animals will terrify you.
 For you have shed human blood;
 you have destroyed lands and cities and everyone
  in them.

¹⁸ "Of what value is an idol carved by a craftsman?
 Or an image that teaches lies?
 For the one who makes it trusts in his own creation;
 he makes idols that cannot speak.
¹⁹ Woe to him who says to wood, 'Come to life!'
 Or to lifeless stone, 'Wake up!'
 Can it give guidance?
 It is covered with gold and silver;
 there is no breath in it."

²⁰ The LORD is in his holy temple;
 let all the earth be silent before him.

HABAKKUK'S PRAYER

3 A prayer of Habakkuk the prophet. On *shigionoth*.ᵇ

² LORD, I have heard of your fame;
 I stand in awe of your deeds, LORD.

---

*16 Masoretic Text; Dead Sea Scrolls, Aquila, Vulgate and Syriac (see also
Septuagint) *and stagger*   ᵇ 1 Probably a literary or musical term

How would the stones and the beams cry out? (2:11)
The stones and beams in Babylon had been purchased with plunder, so in effect they testified against the people who lived in those houses.

What would become fuel for the fire? (2:12–13)
The cities built by the Babylonians would be burned.

How had the Babylonians done violence to Lebanon? (2:17)
Apparently the Babylonians and Assyrians for many years had destroyed the cedar forests of Lebanon to obtain wood for their temples and palaces.

What was a shigionoth? (3:1)
This was probably a literary or musical term. This chapter may have been a hymn that was added later.

Repeat them in our day,
  in our time make them known;
  in wrath remember mercy.

³ God came from Teman,
  the Holy One from Mount Paran.ᵃ
His glory covered the heavens
  and his praise filled the earth.
⁴ His splendor was like the sunrise;
  rays flashed from his hand,
  where his power was hidden.
⁵ Plague went before him;
  pestilence followed his steps.
⁶ He stood, and shook the earth;
  he looked, and made the nations tremble.
The ancient mountains crumbled
  and the age-old hills collapsed—
  but he marches on forever.
⁷ I saw the tents of Cushan in distress,
  the dwellings of Midian in anguish.

⁸ Were you angry with the rivers, LORD?
  Was your wrath against the streams?
Did you rage against the sea
  when you rode your horses
  and your chariots to victory?
⁹ You uncovered your bow,
  you called for many arrows.
You split the earth with rivers;
10   the mountains saw you and writhed.
Torrents of water swept by;
  the deep roared
  and lifted its waves on high.

¹¹ Sun and moon stood still in the heavens
  at the glint of your flying arrows,
  at the lightning of your flashing spear.
¹² In wrath you strode through the earth
  and in anger you threshed the nations.
¹³ You came out to deliver your people,
  to save your anointed one.
You crushed the leader of the land of wickedness,
  you stripped him from head to foot.
¹⁴ With his own spear you pierced his head
  when his warriors stormed out to scatter us,
  gloating as though about to devour
  the wretched who were in hiding.
¹⁵ You trampled the sea with your horses,
  churning the great waters.

¹⁶ I heard and my heart pounded,
  my lips quivered at the sound;
decay crept into my bones,
  and my legs trembled.
Yet I will wait patiently for the day of calamity
  to come on the nation invading us.

Why were plagues and pestilence mentioned? (3:5)
These widespread diseases were forms of divine punishment.

When did the sun and moon stand still? (3:11)
This was probably an allusion to the victory at Gibeon (see Joshua 10:12–13). This was to show that God's victory over his enemies would be just as complete as on that occasion.

ᵃ 3 The Hebrew has *Selah* (a word of uncertain meaning) here and at the middle of verse 9 and at the end of verse 13.

¹⁷Though the fig tree does not bud
 and there are no grapes on the vines,
though the olive crop fails
 and the fields produce no food,
though there are no sheep in the pen
 and no cattle in the stalls,
¹⁸yet I will rejoice in the LORD,
 I will be joyful in God my Savior.

¹⁹The Sovereign LORD is my strength;
 he makes my feet like the feet of a deer,
 he enables me to tread on the heights.

For the director of music. On my stringed instruments.

How would Habakkuk respond to disastrous events? (3:17–18)
Even if there were a great disaster and no food, Habakkuk would still trust in God and rejoice in his Savior. This is one of the strongest affirmations of faith in the Bible.

Zephaniah

INTRODUCTION

Who wrote this book?
The prophet Zephaniah, a descendant of good King Hezekiah, wrote this book.

Why was this book written?
The book of Zephaniah prepares Judah for Josiah's revival of 621 B.C. Zephaniah warns Judah that God will judge a sinful people.

What do we learn about God in this book?
God is a God of judgment. He will punish sin when history comes to an end. But God does not wait. He also punishes sinful nations now.

What is special about this book?
Zephaniah's preaching may have helped to turn people to God during Josiah's revival.

When did these things happen?

	1300 BC	1200	1100	1000	900	800	700	600	500	400

MINISTRIES OF MICAH AND ISAIAH IN JUDAH (C. 740 – 681 BC)

EXILE OF ISRAEL (722 BC)

NAHUM'S MINISTRY (C. 645 – 620 BC)

ZEPHANIAH'S MINISTRY IN JUDAH (C. 640 – 627 BC)

BOOK OF ZEPHANIAH WRITTEN (C. 640 – 612 BC)

JEREMIAH'S MINISTRY IN JUDAH (C. 626 – 585 BC)

HABAKKUK'S MINISTRY IN JUDAH (C. 605 – 588 BC)

FALL OF JERUSALEM (586 BC)

1 The word of the LORD that came to Zephaniah son of Cushi, the son of Gedaliah, the son of Amariah, the son of Hezekiah, during the reign of Josiah son of Amon king of Judah:

JUDGMENT ON THE WHOLE EARTH IN THE DAY OF THE LORD

2 "I will sweep away everything
  from the face of the earth,"
                    declares the LORD.
3 "I will sweep away both man and beast;
  I will sweep away the birds in the sky
    and the fish in the sea—
  and the idols that cause the wicked to stumble." [a]

  "When I destroy all mankind
    on the face of the earth,"
                    declares the LORD,
4 "I will stretch out my hand against Judah
    and against all who live in Jerusalem.
  I will destroy every remnant of Baal worship in
        this place,
    the very names of the idolatrous priests—
5 those who bow down on the roofs
    to worship the starry host,
  those who bow down and swear by the LORD
    and who also swear by Molek, [b]
6 those who turn back from following the LORD
    and neither seek the LORD nor inquire of him."

7 Be silent before the Sovereign LORD,
    for the day of the LORD is near.
  The LORD has prepared a sacrifice;
    he has consecrated those he has invited.

8 "On the day of the LORD's sacrifice
    I will punish the officials
    and the king's sons
  and all those clad
    in foreign clothes.
9 On that day I will punish
    all who avoid stepping on the threshold, [c]
  who fill the temple of their gods
    with violence and deceit.

10 "On that day,"
    declares the LORD,
  "a cry will go up from the Fish Gate,
    wailing from the New Quarter,
    and a loud crash from the hills.
11 Wail, you who live in the market district [d];
    all your merchants will be wiped out,
    all who trade with [e] silver will be destroyed.
12 At that time I will search Jerusalem with lamps
    and punish those who are complacent,
    who are like wine left on its dregs,

Why would people worship on roofs? (1:5)
Incense was often burned to pagan gods on rooftops, and the kings of Judah had erected pagan altars on the roof of the palace in Jerusalem.

Why did people avoid stepping on the threshold? (1:9)
Apparently there was a widespread belief that the threshold was where spirits lived. This was a superstitious belief that began during the time of Samuel when the idol of Dagon was broken on the threshold (see 1 Samuel 5:1–5).

Where was the Fish Gate? (1:10)
The Fish Gate was located in the northern wall of Jerusalem in the northwestern corner. Jerusalem was vulnerable to attacks from the north.

[a] 3 The meaning of the Hebrew for this line is uncertain.   [b] 5 Hebrew *Malkam*   [c] 9 See 1 Samuel 5:5.   [d] 11 Or *the Mortar*   [e] 11 Or *in*

who think, 'The Lord will do nothing,
    either good or bad.'
¹³ Their wealth will be plundered,
    their houses demolished.
Though they build houses,
    they will not live in them;
though they plant vineyards,
    they will not drink the wine."

¹⁴ The great day of the Lord is near—
    near and coming quickly.
The cry on the day of the Lord is bitter;
    the Mighty Warrior shouts his battle cry.
¹⁵ That day will be a day of wrath—
    a day of distress and anguish,
      a day of trouble and ruin,
    a day of darkness and gloom,
      a day of clouds and blackness—
¹⁶   a day of trumpet and battle cry
against the fortified cities
    and against the corner towers.

¹⁷ "I will bring such distress on all people
    that they will grope about like those who are blind,
    because they have sinned against the Lord.
Their blood will be poured out like dust
    and their entrails like dung.
¹⁸ Neither their silver nor their gold
    will be able to save them
    on the day of the Lord's wrath."

In the fire of his jealousy
    the whole earth will be consumed,
for he will make a sudden end
    of all who live on the earth.

JUDAH AND JERUSALEM JUDGED ALONG WITH THE NATIONS
JUDAH SUMMONED TO REPENT

2 Gather together, gather yourselves together,
    you shameful nation,
² before the decree takes effect
    and that day passes like windblown chaff,
before the Lord's fierce anger
    comes upon you,
before the day of the Lord's wrath
    comes upon you.
³ Seek the Lord, all you humble of the land,
    you who do what he commands.
Seek righteousness, seek humility;
    perhaps you will be sheltered
    on the day of the Lord's anger.

PHILISTIA

⁴ Gaza will be abandoned
    and Ashkelon left in ruins.
At midday Ashdod will be emptied
    and Ekron uprooted.

Why did the prophet urge the people to seek the Lord? (2:3)
Even though the destruction was about to take place, there was still time for the people to repent.

⁵Woe to you who live by the sea,
  you Kerethite people;
the word of the LORD is against you,
  Canaan, land of the Philistines.
He says, "I will destroy you,
  and none will be left."
⁶The land by the sea will become pastures
  having wells for shepherds
  and pens for flocks.
⁷That land will belong
  to the remnant of the people of Judah;
  there they will find pasture.
In the evening they will lie down
  in the houses of Ashkelon.
The LORD their God will care for them;
  he will restore their fortunes.ᵃ

MOAB AND AMMON

⁸"I have heard the insults of Moab
  and the taunts of the Ammonites,
who insulted my people
  and made threats against their land.
⁹Therefore, as surely as I live,"
  declares the LORD Almighty,
  the God of Israel,
"surely Moab will become like Sodom,
  the Ammonites like Gomorrah—
a place of weeds and salt pits,
  a wasteland forever.
The remnant of my people will plunder them;
  the survivors of my nation will inherit their land."

¹⁰This is what they will get in return for
      their pride,
  for insulting and mocking
  the people of the LORD Almighty.
¹¹The LORD will be awesome to them
  when he destroys all the gods of the earth.
Distant nations will bow down to him,
  all of them in their own lands.

CUSH

¹²"You Cushites,ᵇ too,
  will be slain by my sword."

ASSYRIA

¹³He will stretch out his hand against the north
  and destroy Assyria,
leaving Nineveh utterly desolate
  and dry as the desert.
¹⁴Flocks and herds will lie down there,
  creatures of every kind.
The desert owl and the screech owl
  will roost on her columns.

ᵃ 7 Or *will bring back their captives*   ᵇ 12 That is, people from the upper
Nile region

Why were Sodom and Gomorrah used as comparisons? (2:9)
Sodom and Gomorrah had become a symbol of wickedness and God's judgment.

The Assyrian Empire (2:13)

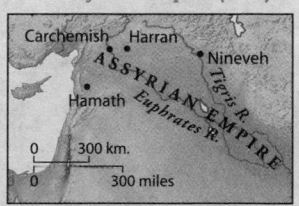

Their hooting will echo through the windows,
      rubble will fill the doorways,
      the beams of cedar will be exposed.
[15] This is the city of revelry
      that lived in safety.
She said to herself,
      "I am the one! And there is none besides me."
What a ruin she has become,
      a lair for wild beasts!
All who pass by her scoff
      and shake their fists.

JERUSALEM

3 Woe to the city of oppressors,
      rebellious and defiled!
[2] She obeys no one,
      she accepts no correction.
She does not trust in the LORD,
      she does not draw near to her God.
[3] Her officials within her
      are roaring lions;
her rulers are evening wolves,
      who leave nothing for the morning.
[4] Her prophets are unprincipled;
      they are treacherous people.
Her priests profane the sanctuary
      and do violence to the law.
[5] The LORD within her is righteous;
      he does no wrong.
Morning by morning he dispenses his justice,
      and every new day he does not fail,
      yet the unrighteous know no shame.

JERUSALEM REMAINS UNREPENTANT

[6] "I have destroyed nations;
      their strongholds are demolished.
I have left their streets deserted,
      with no one passing through.
Their cities are laid waste;
      they are deserted and empty.
[7] Of Jerusalem I thought,
      'Surely you will fear me
      and accept correction!'
Then her place of refuge[a] would not be destroyed,
      nor all my punishments come upon[b] her.
But they were still eager
      to act corruptly in all they did.
[8] Therefore wait for me,"
      declares the LORD,
      "for the day I will stand up to testify.[c]
I have decided to assemble the nations,
      to gather the kingdoms
and to pour out my wrath on them —
      all my fierce anger.

What was this evil city?
(3:1 – 5)
This was Jerusalem. The officials, rulers, prophets, and priests — all classes of Judah's leaders — were criticized for violating their calling and responsibilities as leaders of the people.

---

[a] 7 Or *her sanctuary*   [b] 7 Or *all those I appointed over*   [c] 8 Septuagint and Syriac; Hebrew *will rise up to plunder*

The whole world will be consumed
    by the fire of my jealous anger.

RESTORATION OF ISRAEL'S REMNANT

9 "Then I will purify the lips of the peoples,
    that all of them may call on the name of the Lord
    and serve him shoulder to shoulder.
10 From beyond the rivers of Cush*a*
    my worshipers, my scattered people,
    will bring me offerings.
11 On that day you, Jerusalem, will not be put to shame
    for all the wrongs you have done to me,
because I will remove from you
    your arrogant boasters.
Never again will you be haughty
    on my holy hill.
12 But I will leave within you
    the meek and humble.
The remnant of Israel
    will trust in the name of the Lord.
13 They will do no wrong;
    they will tell no lies.
A deceitful tongue
    will not be found in their mouths.
They will eat and lie down
    and no one will make them afraid."

14 Sing, Daughter Zion;
    shout aloud, Israel!
Be glad and rejoice with all your heart,
    Daughter Jerusalem!
15 The Lord has taken away your punishment,
    he has turned back your enemy.
The Lord, the King of Israel, is with you;
    never again will you fear any harm.
16 On that day
    they will say to Jerusalem,
"Do not fear, Zion;
    do not let your hands hang limp.
17 The Lord your God is with you,
    the Mighty Warrior who saves.

a 10 That is, the upper Nile region

What was the holy hill? (3:11)
This was Mount Zion.

What did it mean for their hands to hang limp? (3:16)
This was a sign of discouragement. In this verse, the people are told to be encouraged.

Is this book of prophecy meant to be a warning or an encouragement?
ZEPHANIAH 3

Like most Old Testament prophetic books, Zephaniah is both a warning and an encouragement. The prophets were addressing a wide audience including some who faithfully served God and others who had turned their backs to him.

The prophets directed their criticisms especially at the leaders of the people who had broken God's laws and put the nation at risk of judgment. The harsh words of judgment were meant to bring people back to the Lord, but they often refused to do so.

Most of the prophecies balance the words of judgment with words of hope and restoration, telling how God will eventually save his people. These promises would help God's faithful followers get through the difficult times of judgment or punishment.

He will take great delight in you;
in his love he will no longer rebuke you,
but will rejoice over you with singing."

¹⁸ "I will remove from you
all who mourn over the loss of your appointed
festivals,
which is a burden and reproach for you.
¹⁹ At that time I will deal
with all who oppressed you.
I will rescue the lame;
I will gather the exiles.
I will give them praise and honor
in every land where they have suffered shame.
²⁰ At that time I will gather you;
at that time I will bring you home.
I will give you honor and praise
among all the peoples of the earth
when I restore your fortunes*a*
before your very eyes,"

says the LORD.

a 20 Or I bring back your captives

Haggai

INTRODUCTION

Who wrote this book?
The prophet Haggai.

Why was this book written?
The people had stopped rebuilding God's temple. Haggai tells them the temple must be rebuilt—now.

What do we learn about God in this book?
God will bless people when they put him first.

What is special about this book?
The people listen to Haggai's preaching. They go to work and finish rebuilding the temple.

What are some important passages in this book?

The people are poor because they have not put God first	Haggai 1:2 – 11
The people have obeyed and from now on God will bless them	Haggai 2:15 – 19

When did these things happen?

1300 BC 1200 1100 1000 900 800 700 600 500 400

A CALL TO BUILD THE HOUSE OF THE LORD

1 In the second year of King Darius, on the first day of the sixth month, the word of the LORD came through the prophet Haggai to Zerubbabel son of Shealtiel, governor of Judah, and to Joshua son of Jozadak,*a* the high priest:

² This is what the LORD Almighty says: "These people say, 'The time has not yet come to rebuild the LORD's house.'"

³ Then the word of the LORD came through the prophet Haggai: ⁴ "Is it a time for you yourselves to be living in your paneled houses, while this house remains a ruin?"

⁵ Now this is what the LORD Almighty says: "Give careful thought to your ways. ⁶ You have planted much, but harvested little. You eat, but never have enough. You drink, but never have your fill. You put on clothes, but are not warm. You earn wages, only to put them in a purse with holes in it."

⁷ This is what the LORD Almighty says: "Give careful thought to your ways. ⁸ Go up into the mountains and bring down timber and build my house, so that I may take pleasure in it and be honored," says the LORD. ⁹ "You expected much, but see, it turned out to be little. What you brought home, I blew away. Why?" declares the LORD Almighty. "Because of my house, which remains a ruin, while each of you is busy with your own house. ¹⁰ Therefore, because of you the heavens have withheld their dew and the earth its crops. ¹¹ I called for a drought on the fields and the mountains, on the grain, the new wine, the olive oil and everything else the ground produces, on people and livestock, and on all the labor of your hands."

¹² Then Zerubbabel son of Shealtiel, Joshua son of Jozadak, the high priest, and the whole remnant of the people obeyed the voice of the LORD their God and the message of the prophet Haggai, because the LORD their God had sent him. And the people feared the LORD.

¹³ Then Haggai, the LORD's messenger, gave this message of the LORD to the people: "I am with you," declares the LORD. ¹⁴ So the LORD stirred up the spirit of Zerubbabel son of Shealtiel, governor of Judah, and the spirit of Joshua son of Jozadak, the high priest, and the spirit of the whole remnant of the people. They came and began to work on the house of the LORD Almighty, their God, ¹⁵ on the twenty-fourth day of the sixth month.

THE PROMISED GLORY OF THE NEW HOUSE

2 In the second year of King Darius, ¹ on the twenty-first day of the seventh month, the word of the LORD came through the prophet Haggai: ² "Speak to Zerubbabel son of Shealtiel, governor of Judah, to Joshua son of Jozadak,*b* the high priest, and to the remnant of the people. Ask them, ³ 'Who of you is left who saw this house in its former glory? How does it look to you now? Does it not seem to you like nothing? ⁴ But now be strong, Zerubbabel,' declares the LORD. 'Be strong, Joshua son of Jozadak, the high priest. Be strong, all you people of the land,' declares the LORD,

What were paneled houses? (1:4)
This usually referred to royal dwellings, which often had cedar paneling.

Why were grain, wine, and oil mentioned? (1:11)
These were the three main crops of the land, and they were often mentioned in connection with blessings and curses.

What did the term *messenger* mean? (1:13)
This was another title for the prophets or priests of God.

How many people had seen the former temple? (2:3)
Since the temple had been destroyed 66 years earlier, only a few people could recall its glory.

---

a 1 Hebrew *Jehozadak*, a variant of *Jozadak*; also in verses 12 and 14
b 2 Hebrew *Jehozadak*, a variant of *Jozadak*; also in verse 4

'and work. For I am with you,' declares the LORD Almighty.
⁵"This is what I covenanted with you when you came out
of Egypt. And my Spirit remains among you. Do not fear.'

⁶"This is what the LORD Almighty says: 'In a little while
I will once more shake the heavens and the earth, the sea
and the dry land. ⁷I will shake all nations, and what is desired by all nations will come, and I will fill this house with
glory,' says the LORD Almighty. ⁸'The silver is mine and the
gold is mine,' declares the LORD Almighty. ⁹'The glory of
this present house will be greater than the glory of the former house,' says the LORD Almighty. 'And in this place I will
grant peace,' declares the LORD Almighty."

BLESSINGS FOR A DEFILED PEOPLE

¹⁰On the twenty-fourth day of the ninth month, in the
second year of Darius, the word of the LORD came to the
prophet Haggai: ¹¹"This is what the LORD Almighty says:
'Ask the priests what the law says: ¹²If someone carries consecrated meat in the fold of their garment, and that fold
touches some bread or stew, some wine, olive oil or other
food, does it become consecrated?'"

The priests answered, "No."

¹³Then Haggai said, "If a person defiled by contact with a
dead body touches one of these things, does it become defiled?"

"Yes," the priests replied, "it becomes defiled."

¹⁴Then Haggai said, "'So it is with this people and this
nation in my sight,' declares the LORD. 'Whatever they do
and whatever they offer there is defiled.

¹⁵"'Now give careful thought to this from this day on[a] —
consider how things were before one stone was laid on another in the LORD's temple. ¹⁶When anyone came to a heap
of twenty measures, there were only ten. When anyone went
to a wine vat to draw fifty measures, there were only twenty.
¹⁷I struck all the work of your hands with blight, mildew and
hail, yet you did not return to me,' declares the LORD. ¹⁸'From
this day on, from this twenty-fourth day of the ninth month,
give careful thought to the day when the foundation of the
LORD's temple was laid. Give careful thought: ¹⁹Is there yet
any seed left in the barn? Until now, the vine and the fig
tree, the pomegranate and the olive tree have not borne fruit.

"'From this day on I will bless you.'"

ZERUBBABEL THE LORD'S SIGNET RING

²⁰The word of the LORD came to Haggai a second time
on the twenty-fourth day of the month: ²¹"Tell Zerubbabel governor of Judah that I am going to shake the heavens
and the earth. ²²I will overturn royal thrones and shatter the
power of the foreign kingdoms. I will overthrow chariots and
their drivers; horses and their riders will fall, each by the
sword of his brother.

²³"'On that day,' declares the LORD Almighty, 'I will take
you, my servant Zerubbabel son of Shealtiel,' declares the
LORD, 'and I will make you like my signet ring, for I have
chosen you,' declares the LORD Almighty."

[a] 15 Or *to the days past*

**How did consecrated meat
make a garment holy? (2:12)**
Consecrated meat made a garment holy because it was in
direct contact with the garment,
but the garment could not pass
that holiness on to a third object.

**What caused the blight?
(2:17)**
This was probably caused by the
scorching east wind (sirocco) that
blew in from the desert in late
spring and early fall.

**What was a signet ring?
(2:23)**
A signet ring had the owner's
symbol on it. It was pressed into
soft wax to seal or guarantee
important documents.

Zechariah

INTRODUCTION

Who wrote this book? The prophet Zechariah.

Why was this book written? The book of Zechariah encourages the people of Judah to finish rebuilding the temple.

What do we learn about God in this book? God will cleanse the sin of his people. God will come and rule the earth.

What is special about this book? Zechariah uses many symbols that are hard to understand, like a flying scroll and a woman in a basket.

What are some important chapters in this book?

God wants his people to love justice and mercy	Zechariah 7 – 8
God will come to earth and rule as King	Zechariah 14

When did these things happen?

1300 BC 1200 1100 1000 900 800 700 600 500 400

FALL OF JERUSALEM (586 BC)

FIRST RETURN OF EXILES TO JERUSALEM (538 BC)

MINISTRIES OF HAGGAI AND ZECHARIAH (C. 520 – 480 BC)

BOOK OF ZECHARIAH WRITTEN (C. 520 – 480 BC)

COMPLETION OF TEMPLE (516 BC)

SECOND RETURN TO JERUSALEM UNDER EZRA (458 BC)

THIRD RETURN TO JERUSALEM UNDER NEHEMIAH (444 BC)

MALACHI'S MINISTRY (C. 440 – 430 BC)

A CALL TO RETURN TO THE LORD

1 In the eighth month of the second year of Darius, the word of the LORD came to the prophet Zechariah son of Berekiah, the son of Iddo:

² "The LORD was very angry with your ancestors. ³ Therefore tell the people: This is what the LORD Almighty says: 'Return to me,' declares the LORD Almighty, 'and I will return to you,' says the LORD Almighty. ⁴ Do not be like your ancestors, to whom the earlier prophets proclaimed: This is what the LORD Almighty says: 'Turn from your evil ways and your evil practices.' But they would not listen or pay attention to me, declares the LORD. ⁵ Where are your ancestors now? And the prophets, do they live forever? ⁶ But did not my words and my decrees, which I commanded my servants the prophets, overtake your ancestors?

"Then they repented and said, 'The LORD Almighty has done to us what our ways and practices deserve, just as he determined to do.'"

THE MAN AMONG THE MYRTLE TREES

⁷ On the twenty-fourth day of the eleventh month, the month of Shebat, in the second year of Darius, the word of the LORD came to the prophet Zechariah son of Berekiah, the son of Iddo.

⁸ During the night I had a vision, and there before me was a man mounted on a red horse. He was standing among the myrtle trees in a ravine. Behind him were red, brown and white horses.

⁹ I asked, "What are these, my lord?"

The angel who was talking with me answered, "I will show you what they are."

¹⁰ Then the man standing among the myrtle trees explained, "They are the ones the LORD has sent to go throughout the earth."

¹¹ And they reported to the angel of the LORD who was standing among the myrtle trees, "We have gone throughout the earth and found the whole world at rest and in peace."

¹² Then the angel of the LORD said, "LORD Almighty, how long will you withhold mercy from Jerusalem and from the towns of Judah, which you have been angry with these seventy years?" ¹³ So the LORD spoke kind and comforting words to the angel who talked with me.

¹⁴ Then the angel who was speaking to me said, "Proclaim this word: This is what the LORD Almighty says: 'I am very jealous for Jerusalem and Zion, ¹⁵ and I am very angry with the nations that feel secure. I was only a little angry, but they went too far with the punishment.'

¹⁶ "Therefore this is what the LORD says: 'I will return to Jerusalem with mercy, and there my house will be rebuilt. And the measuring line will be stretched out over Jerusalem,' declares the LORD Almighty.

¹⁷ "Proclaim further: This is what the LORD Almighty says: 'My towns will again overflow with prosperity, and the LORD will again comfort Zion and choose Jerusalem.'"

Why was God angry with the people's forefathers? (1:2)
God was angry because they had broken the covenant, turned away from him, and disobeyed his laws.

Who were the earlier prophets? (1:4)
They included Isaiah, Jeremiah, and Ezekiel.

What type of vision did Zechariah have? (1:8)
Zechariah had eight visions in a single night (1:7 – 6:8). The visions were not dreams but were experienced while he was awake. The first vision was to assure the Israelites of God's special care for and interest in them.

FOUR HORNS AND FOUR CRAFTSMEN

What was the meaning of the second vision? (1:18–21)
This was a vivid picture of the destruction of the nations that had devastated Israel.

FOUR HORNS AND FOUR CRAFTSMEN

[18]Then I looked up, and there before me were four horns. [19]I asked the angel who was speaking to me, "What are these?"

He answered me, "These are the horns that scattered Judah, Israel and Jerusalem."

[20]Then the LORD showed me four craftsmen. [21]I asked, "What are these coming to do?"

He answered, "These are the horns that scattered Judah so that no one could raise their head, but the craftsmen have come to terrify them and throw down these horns of the nations who lifted up their horns against the land of Judah to scatter its people."[a]

A Man with a Measuring Line (2:1)

A MAN WITH A MEASURING LINE

2[b] Then I looked up, and there before me was a man with a measuring line in his hand. [2]I asked, "Where are you going?"

He answered me, "To measure Jerusalem, to find out how wide and how long it is."

[3]While the angel who was speaking to me was leaving, another angel came to meet him [4]and said to him: "Run, tell that young man, 'Jerusalem will be a city without walls because of the great number of people and animals in it. [5]And I myself will be a wall of fire around it,' declares the LORD, 'and I will be its glory within.'

What did it mean that Jerusalem would be a city without walls? (2:4–5)
The population of Jerusalem would grow so large that it would overflow, as if the city had no walls. And walls would not be needed since God would keep them safe.

[6]"Come! Come! Flee from the land of the north," declares the LORD, "for I have scattered you to the four winds of heaven," declares the LORD.

[7]"Come, Zion! Escape, you who live in Daughter Babylon!" [8]For this is what the LORD Almighty says: "After the Glorious One has sent me against the nations that have plundered you—for whoever touches you touches the apple of his eye— [9]I will surely raise my hand against them so that their slaves will plunder them.[c] Then you will know that the LORD Almighty has sent me.

[10]"Shout and be glad, Daughter Zion. For I am coming, and I will live among you," declares the LORD. [11]"Many nations will be joined with the LORD in that day and will become my people. I will live among you and you will know that the LORD Almighty has sent me to you. [12]The LORD will inherit Judah as his portion in the holy land and will again choose Jerusalem. [13]Be still before the LORD, all mankind, because he has roused himself from his holy dwelling."

Why was the land holy? (2:12)
The land was holy because it was where God's sanctuary was located.

CLEAN GARMENTS FOR THE HIGH PRIEST

3 Then he showed me Joshua the high priest standing before the angel of the LORD, and Satan[d] standing at his right side to accuse him. [2]The LORD said to Satan, "The LORD rebuke you, Satan! The LORD, who has chosen Jerusalem, rebuke you! Is not this man a burning stick snatched from the fire?"

How was Israel like a burning stick? (3:2)
The Jews were like a stick pulled out of the fire. God was bringing them back from exile in Babylon to carry out his purposes.

[a] 21 In Hebrew texts 1:18-21 is numbered 2:1-4.   [b] In Hebrew texts 2:1-13 is numbered 2:5-17.   [c] 8,9 Or says after . . . eye: [9]"I . . . plunder them."
[d] 1 Hebrew satan means adversary.

³Now Joshua was dressed in filthy clothes as he stood before the angel. ⁴The angel said to those who were standing before him, "Take off his filthy clothes."

Then he said to Joshua, "See, I have taken away your sin, and I will put fine garments on you."

⁵Then I said, "Put a clean turban on his head." So they put a clean turban on his head and clothed him, while the angel of the LORD stood by.

⁶The angel of the LORD gave this charge to Joshua: ⁷"This is what the LORD Almighty says: 'If you will walk in obedience to me and keep my requirements, then you will govern my house and have charge of my courts, and I will give you a place among these standing here.

⁸"'Listen, High Priest Joshua, you and your associates seated before you, who are men symbolic of things to come: I am going to bring my servant, the Branch. ⁹See, the stone I have set in front of Joshua! There are seven eyes*a* on that one stone, and I will engrave an inscription on it,' says the LORD Almighty, 'and I will remove the sin of this land in a single day.

¹⁰"'In that day each of you will invite your neighbor to sit under your vine and fig tree,' declares the LORD Almighty."

THE GOLD LAMPSTAND AND THE TWO OLIVE TREES

4 Then the angel who talked with me returned and woke me up, like someone awakened from sleep. ²He asked me, "What do you see?"

I answered, "I see a solid gold lampstand with a bowl at the top and seven lamps on it, with seven channels to the lamps. ³Also there are two olive trees by it, one on the right of the bowl and the other on its left."

⁴I asked the angel who talked with me, "What are these, my lord?"

⁵He answered, "Do you not know what these are?"

"No, my lord," I replied.

⁶So he said to me, "This is the word of the LORD to Zerubbabel: 'Not by might nor by power, but by my Spirit,' says the LORD Almighty.

⁷"What are you, mighty mountain? Before Zerubbabel you will become level ground. Then he will bring out the capstone to shouts of 'God bless it! God bless it!'"

⁸Then the word of the LORD came to me: ⁹"The hands of Zerubbabel have laid the foundation of this temple; his hands will also complete it. Then you will know that the LORD Almighty has sent me to you.

¹⁰"Who dares despise the day of small things, since the seven eyes of the LORD that range throughout the earth will rejoice when they see the chosen capstone*b* in the hand of Zerubbabel?"

¹¹Then I asked the angel, "What are these two olive trees on the right and the left of the lampstand?"

¹²Again I asked him, "What are these two olive branches beside the two gold pipes that pour out golden oil?"

What did the bowl of the lampstand symbolize? (4:2)
The bowl represented an abundant supply of oil, symbolizing God's power through his Spirit.

What did the olive trees represent? (4:3)
The olive trees represented the two men God had chosen to serve him: Joshua, the priest, and Zerubbabel, the governor.

a 9 Or facets   b 10 Or the plumb line

¹³ He replied, "Do you not know what these are?"

"No, my lord," I said.

¹⁴ So he said, "These are the two who are anointed to^a serve the Lord of all the earth."

THE FLYING SCROLL

5 I looked again, and there before me was a flying scroll. ² He asked me, "What do you see?"

I answered, "I see a flying scroll, twenty cubits long and ten cubits wide.^b"

³ And he said to me, "This is the curse that is going out over the whole land; for according to what it says on one side, every thief will be banished, and according to what it says on the other, everyone who swears falsely will be banished. ⁴ The LORD Almighty declares, 'I will send it out, and it will enter the house of the thief and the house of anyone who swears falsely by my name. It will remain in that house and destroy it completely, both its timbers and its stones.'"

THE WOMAN IN A BASKET

⁵ Then the angel who was speaking to me came forward and said to me, "Look up and see what is appearing."

⁶ I asked, "What is it?"

He replied, "It is a basket." And he added, "This is the iniquity^c of the people throughout the land."

⁷ Then the cover of lead was raised, and there in the basket sat a woman! ⁸ He said, "This is wickedness," and he pushed her back into the basket and pushed its lead cover down on it.

⁹ Then I looked up — and there before me were two women, with the wind in their wings! They had wings like those of a stork, and they lifted up the basket between heaven and earth.

¹⁰ "Where are they taking the basket?" I asked the angel who was speaking to me.

¹¹ He replied, "To the country of Babylonia^d to build a house for it. When the house is ready, the basket will be set there in its place."

FOUR CHARIOTS

6 I looked up again, and there before me were four chariots coming out from between two mountains — mountains of bronze. ² The first chariot had red horses, the second black, ³ the third white, and the fourth dappled — all of them powerful. ⁴ I asked the angel who was speaking to me, "What are these, my lord?"

⁵ The angel answered me, "These are the four spirits^e of heaven, going out from standing in the presence of the Lord of the whole world. ⁶ The one with the black horses is going toward the north country, the one with the white horses toward the west,^f and the one with the dappled horses toward the south."

What was the meaning of the flying scroll in this sixth vision? (5:1–2)
The scroll was like a large banner in the sky that was meant for all people to see. The vision proclaimed that the land would be purified from wickedness when the temple was built and God's law was taught.

What did this vision mean? (5:5–11)
The wickedness of the people would be carried off to a distant place. This implied that with sin gone, holiness could take its place.

What happened in the final vision? (6:1–8)
In this vision, four war chariots went out to protect God's people, which confirmed God's protective providence.

---

^a 14 Or *two who bring oil and*   ^b 2 That is, about 30 feet long and 15 feet wide or about 9 meters long and 4.5 meters wide   ^c 6 Or *appearance*
^d 11 Hebrew *Shinar*   ^e 5 Or *winds*   ^f 6 Or *horses after them*

[7]When the powerful horses went out, they were straining to go throughout the earth. And he said, "Go throughout the earth!" So they went throughout the earth.

[8]Then he called to me, "Look, those going toward the north country have given my Spirit[a] rest in the land of the north."

A CROWN FOR JOSHUA

[9]The word of the LORD came to me: [10]"Take silver and gold from the exiles Heldai, Tobijah and Jedaiah, who have arrived from Babylon. Go the same day to the house of Josiah son of Zephaniah. [11]Take the silver and gold and make a crown, and set it on the head of the high priest, Joshua son of Jozadak.[b] [12]Tell him this is what the LORD Almighty says: 'Here is the man whose name is the Branch, and he will branch out from his place and build the temple of the LORD. [13]It is he who will build the temple of the LORD, and he will be clothed with majesty and will sit and rule on his throne. And he[c] will be a priest on his throne. And there will be harmony between the two.' [14]The crown will be given to Heldai,[d] Tobijah, Jedaiah and Hen[e] son of Zephaniah as a memorial in the temple of the LORD. [15]Those who are far away will come and help to build the temple of the LORD, and you will know that the LORD Almighty has sent me to you. This will happen if you diligently obey the LORD your God."

JUSTICE AND MERCY, NOT FASTING

7 In the fourth year of King Darius, the word of the LORD came to Zechariah on the fourth day of the ninth month, the month of Kislev. [2]The people of Bethel had sent Sharezer and Regem-Melek, together with their men, to entreat the LORD [3]by asking the priests of the house of the LORD Almighty and the prophets, "Should I mourn and fast in the fifth month, as I have done for so many years?"

[4]Then the word of the LORD Almighty came to me: [5]"Ask all the people of the land and the priests, 'When you fasted and mourned in the fifth and seventh months for the past seventy years, was it really for me that you fasted? [6]And when you were eating and drinking, were you not just feasting for yourselves? [7]Are these not the words the LORD proclaimed through the earlier prophets when Jerusalem and its surrounding towns were at rest and prosperous, and the Negev and the western foothills were settled?'"

[8]And the word of the LORD came again to Zechariah: [9]"This is what the LORD Almighty said: 'Administer true justice; show mercy and compassion to one another. [10]Do not oppress the widow or the fatherless, the foreigner or the poor. Do not plot evil against each other.'

[11]"But they refused to pay attention; stubbornly they turned their backs and covered their ears. [12]They made their hearts as hard as flint and would not listen to the law or to the words that the LORD Almighty had sent by his Spirit through the earlier prophets. So the LORD Almighty was very angry.

What did the crowning of Joshua represent? (6:11–13) In Israel, a priest could not hold also the office of king. This symbolic ceremony pointed to the Branch (the coming Messiah), who would hold both offices.

Why did the Lord instruct Zechariah to tell the people to show mercy and compassion? (7:8–10) Throughout Scripture, God often told his people to not oppress others but to show mercy to those who needed it most — widows, orphans, foreigners, and the poor.

---

[a] 8 Or *spirit*   [b] 11 Hebrew *Jehozadak*, a variant of *Jozadak*   [c] 13 Or *there*
[d] 14 Syriac; Hebrew *Helem*   [e] 14 Or *and the gracious one, the*

Why would the people be scattered? (7:14)
This was a punishment for disobeying God over and over again.

[13] "'When I called, they did not listen; so when they called, I would not listen,' says the Lord Almighty. [14] 'I scattered them with a whirlwind among all the nations, where they were strangers. The land they left behind them was so desolate that no one traveled through it. This is how they made the pleasant land desolate.'"

THE LORD PROMISES TO BLESS JERUSALEM

8 The word of the Lord Almighty came to me. [2] This is what the Lord Almighty says: "I am very jealous for Zion; I am burning with jealousy for her."

[3] This is what the Lord says: "I will return to Zion and dwell in Jerusalem. Then Jerusalem will be called the Faithful City, and the mountain of the Lord Almighty will be called the Holy Mountain."

[4] This is what the Lord Almighty says: "Once again men and women of ripe old age will sit in the streets of Jerusalem, each of them with cane in hand because of their age. [5] The city streets will be filled with boys and girls playing there."

[6] This is what the Lord Almighty says: "It may seem marvelous to the remnant of this people at that time, but will it seem marvelous to me?" declares the Lord Almighty.

[7] This is what the Lord Almighty says: "I will save my people from the countries of the east and the west. [8] I will bring them back to live in Jerusalem; they will be my people, and I will be faithful and righteous to them as their God."

What promise is contained in these words? (8:8)
When God said that "they will be my people, and I will be ... their God," he was reaffirming his covenant relationship with his people.

[9] This is what the Lord Almighty says: "Now hear these words, 'Let your hands be strong so that the temple may be built.' This is also what the prophets said who were present when the foundation was laid for the house of the Lord Almighty. [10] Before that time there were no wages for people or hire for animals. No one could go about their business safely because of their enemies, since I had turned everyone against their neighbor. [11] But now I will not deal with the remnant of this people as I did in the past," declares the Lord Almighty.

[12] "The seed will grow well, the vine will yield its fruit, the ground will produce its crops, and the heavens will drop their dew. I will give all these things as an inheritance to the remnant of this people. [13] Just as you, Judah and Israel, have been a curse[a] among the nations, so I will save you, and you will be a blessing.[b] Do not be afraid, but let your hands be strong."

[14] This is what the Lord Almighty says: "Just as I had determined to bring disaster on you and showed no pity when your ancestors angered me," says the Lord Almighty, [15] "so now I have determined to do good again to Jerusalem and Judah. Do not be afraid. [16] These are the things you are to do: Speak the truth to each other, and render true and sound judgment in your courts; [17] do not plot evil against each other, and do not love to swear falsely. I hate all this," declares the Lord.

Where were the courts located? (8:16)
This literally refers to the city gates, where legal matters were handled.

[18] The word of the Lord Almighty came to me. [19] This is what the Lord Almighty says: "The fasts of the fourth, fifth, seventh and tenth months will become joyful

Why were so many fasts observed? (8:19)
The fasts were times of mourning. Since Israel had many experiences to mourn, several days of fasting were observed.

---

[a] 13 That is, your name has been used in cursing (see Jer. 29:22); or, you have been regarded as under a curse.   [b] 13 Or *and your name will be used in blessings* (see Gen. 48:20); or *and you will be seen as blessed*

and glad occasions and happy festivals for Judah. Therefore love truth and peace."

²⁰ This is what the LORD Almighty says: "Many peoples and the inhabitants of many cities will yet come, ²¹ and the inhabitants of one city will go to another and say, 'Let us go at once to entreat the LORD and seek the LORD Almighty. I myself am going.' ²² And many peoples and powerful nations will come to Jerusalem to seek the LORD Almighty and to entreat him."

²³ This is what the LORD Almighty says: "In those days ten people from all languages and nations will take firm hold of one Jew by the hem of his robe and say, 'Let us go with you, because we have heard that God is with you.'"

JUDGMENT ON ISRAEL'S ENEMIES

9 A prophecy:

The word of the LORD is against the land of Hadrak
    and will come to rest on Damascus—
for the eyes of all people and all the tribes of Israel
    are on the LORD—ᵃ
² and on Hamath too, which borders on it,
    and on Tyre and Sidon, though they are very skillful.
³ Tyre has built herself a stronghold;
    she has heaped up silver like dust,
    and gold like the dirt of the streets.
⁴ But the Lord will take away her possessions
    and destroy her power on the sea,
    and she will be consumed by fire.
⁵ Ashkelon will see it and fear;
    Gaza will writhe in agony,
    and Ekron too, for her hope will wither.
Gaza will lose her king
    and Ashkelon will be deserted.
⁶ A mongrel people will occupy Ashdod,
    and I will put an end to the pride of the Philistines.
⁷ I will take the blood from their mouths,
    the forbidden food from between their teeth.
Those who are left will belong to our God
    and become a clan in Judah,
    and Ekron will be like the Jebusites.
⁸ But I will encamp at my temple
    to guard it against marauding forces.
Never again will an oppressor overrun my people,
    for now I am keeping watch.

THE COMING OF ZION'S KING

⁹ Rejoice greatly, Daughter Zion!
    Shout, Daughter Jerusalem!
See, your king comes to you,
    righteous and victorious,
lowly and riding on a donkey,
    on a colt, the foal of a donkey.

ᵃ 1 Or *Damascus. / For the eye of the LORD is on all people, / as well as on the tribes of Israel,*

To what did this prophecy refer? (9:9)
This prophecy pointed toward Jesus' triumphal entry into Jerusalem (see Matthew 21:5 and John 12:15).

Why would the king ride a donkey? (9:9)
The donkey was an animal of peace, not war, and was a mount used by princes. (David and his sons rode mules.)

What was a waterless pit? (9:11)
This referred to an empty cistern that would sometimes be used as a place to detain prisoners.

¹⁰ I will take away the chariots from Ephraim
and the warhorses from Jerusalem,
and the battle bow will be broken.
He will proclaim peace to the nations.
His rule will extend from sea to sea
and from the River[a] to the ends of the earth.
¹¹ As for you, because of the blood of my covenant
with you,
I will free your prisoners from the waterless pit.
¹² Return to your fortress, you prisoners of hope;
even now I announce that I will restore twice as
much to you.
¹³ I will bend Judah as I bend my bow
and fill it with Ephraim.
I will rouse your sons, Zion,
against your sons, Greece,
and make you like a warrior's sword.

THE LORD WILL APPEAR

¹⁴ Then the Lord will appear over them;
his arrow will flash like lightning.
The Sovereign Lord will sound the trumpet;
he will march in the storms of the south,
¹⁵ and the Lord Almighty will shield them.
They will destroy
and overcome with slingstones.
They will drink and roar as with wine;
they will be full like a bowl
used for sprinkling[b] the corners of the altar.
¹⁶ The Lord their God will save his people on that day
as a shepherd saves his flock.
They will sparkle in his land
like jewels in a crown.
¹⁷ How attractive and beautiful they will be!
Grain will make the young men thrive,
and new wine the young women.

THE LORD WILL CARE FOR JUDAH

Why would the people need to be told that God controls the weather? (10:1)
Many of the people worshiped pagan gods and thought that the fertility god Baal controlled the weather. God wanted the people to know that he was in charge of the weather and the crops.

10 Ask the Lord for rain in the springtime;
it is the Lord who sends the thunderstorms.
He gives showers of rain to all people,
and plants of the field to everyone.
² The idols speak deceitfully,
diviners see visions that lie;
they tell dreams that are false,
they give comfort in vain.
Therefore the people wander like sheep
oppressed for lack of a shepherd.

³ "My anger burns against the shepherds,
and I will punish the leaders;
for the Lord Almighty will care
for his flock, the people of Judah,
and make them like a proud horse in battle.

[a] 10 That is, the Euphrates   [b] 15 Or bowl, / like

⁴From Judah will come the cornerstone,
    from him the tent peg,
from him the battle bow,
    from him every ruler.
⁵Together they*ᵃ* will be like warriors in battle
    trampling their enemy into the mud of
        the streets.
They will fight because the LORD is with them,
    and they will put the enemy horsemen
        to shame.

⁶"I will strengthen Judah
    and save the tribes of Joseph.
I will restore them
    because I have compassion on them.
They will be as though
    I had not rejected them,
for I am the LORD their God
    and I will answer them.
⁷The Ephraimites will become like warriors,
    and their hearts will be glad as with wine.
Their children will see it and be joyful;
    their hearts will rejoice in the LORD.
⁸I will signal for them
    and gather them in.
Surely I will redeem them;
    they will be as numerous as before.
⁹Though I scatter them among the peoples,
    yet in distant lands they will remember me.
They and their children will survive,
    and they will return.
¹⁰I will bring them back from Egypt
    and gather them from Assyria.
I will bring them to Gilead and Lebanon,
    and there will not be room enough for them.
¹¹They will pass through the sea of trouble;
    the surging sea will be subdued
    and all the depths of the Nile will dry up.
Assyria's pride will be brought down
    and Egypt's scepter will pass away.
¹²I will strengthen them in the LORD
    and in his name they will live securely,"
                            declares the LORD.

ᵃ 4,5 Or ruler, all of them together. / ⁵They

What did it mean that God would signal for them? (10:8)
This literally meant to whistle to gather them. This continued the metaphor of God as shepherd (see verse 2).

What did Egypt and Assyria represent? (10:10)
They probably represented all of the countries where the Israelites had been dispersed.

What does God want us to pray for?   ZECHARIAH 10

Zechariah told the people to pray for rain because he wanted the people to realize that they depended on God for everything in their lives. The people in the surrounding lands relied on pagan gods for their daily needs. But the Israelites depended on God to provide for all that they needed; they acknowledged that he was the source of all things.

Since the people had just returned from the exile in Babylon, Zechariah wanted to teach the people to trust in God to provide everything that they would require. Even though God sends rain on the just and the unjust (see Matthew 5:45), acknowledging God as Provider by praying to him about everyday needs reinforces our faith in God's love and providence. God wants us to talk with him about the big things and the little things of life.

11 Open your doors, Lebanon,
so that fire may devour your cedars!
² Wail, you juniper, for the cedar has fallen;
the stately trees are ruined!
Wail, oaks of Bashan;
the dense forest has been cut down!
³ Listen to the wail of the shepherds;
their rich pastures are destroyed!
Listen to the roar of the lions;
the lush thicket of the Jordan is ruined!

TWO SHEPHERDS

⁴ This is what the Lord my God says: "Shepherd the flock marked for slaughter. ⁵ Their buyers slaughter them and go unpunished. Those who sell them say, 'Praise the Lord, I am rich!' Their own shepherds do not spare them. ⁶ For I will no longer have pity on the people of the land," declares the Lord. "I will give everyone into the hands of their neighbors and their king. They will devastate the land, and I will not rescue anyone from their hands."

⁷ So I shepherded the flock marked for slaughter, particularly the oppressed of the flock. Then I took two staffs and called one Favor and the other Union, and I shepherded the flock. ⁸ In one month I got rid of the three shepherds.

The flock detested me, and I grew weary of them ⁹ and said, "I will not be your shepherd. Let the dying die, and the perishing perish. Let those who are left eat one another's flesh."

¹⁰ Then I took my staff called Favor and broke it, revoking the covenant I had made with all the nations. ¹¹ It was revoked on that day, and so the oppressed of the flock who were watching me knew it was the word of the Lord.

¹² I told them, "If you think it best, give me my pay; but if not, keep it." So they paid me thirty pieces of silver.

¹³ And the Lord said to me, "Throw it to the potter"—the handsome price at which they valued me! So I took the thirty pieces of silver and threw them to the potter at the house of the Lord.

¹⁴ Then I broke my second staff called Union, breaking the family bond between Judah and Israel.

¹⁵ Then the Lord said to me, "Take again the equipment of a foolish shepherd. ¹⁶ For I am going to raise up a shepherd over the land who will not care for the lost, or seek the young, or heal the injured, or feed the healthy, but will eat the meat of the choice sheep, tearing off their hooves.

¹⁷ "Woe to the worthless shepherd,
who deserts the flock!
May the sword strike his arm and his right eye!
May his arm be completely withered,
his right eye totally blinded!"

JERUSALEM'S ENEMIES TO BE DESTROYED

12 A prophecy: The word of the Lord concerning Israel.

The Lord, who stretches out the heavens, who lays the

Did this prophecy come true? (11:9)
According to the historian Josephus, cannibalism did occur during the Roman siege of Jerusalem in A.D. 70.

How was the brotherhood between Judah and Israel broken? (11:14)
After Solomon's death, the kingdom of Israel was divided into the northern and southern kingdoms, each with its own ruler.

foundation of the earth, and who forms the human spirit within a person, declares: ²"I am going to make Jerusalem a cup that sends all the surrounding peoples reeling. Judah will be besieged as well as Jerusalem. ³On that day, when all the nations of the earth are gathered against her, I will make Jerusalem an immovable rock for all the nations. All who try to move it will injure themselves. ⁴On that day I will strike every horse with panic and its rider with madness," declares the LORD. "I will keep a watchful eye over Judah, but I will blind all the horses of the nations. ⁵Then the clans of Judah will say in their hearts, 'The people of Jerusalem are strong, because the LORD Almighty is their God.'

⁶"On that day I will make the clans of Judah like a firepot in a woodpile, like a flaming torch among sheaves. They will consume all the surrounding peoples right and left, but Jerusalem will remain intact in her place.

⁷"The LORD will save the dwellings of Judah first, so that the honor of the house of David and of Jerusalem's inhabitants may not be greater than that of Judah. ⁸On that day the LORD will shield those who live in Jerusalem, so that the feeblest among them will be like David, and the house of David will be like God, like the angel of the LORD going before them. ⁹On that day I will set out to destroy all the nations that attack Jerusalem.

MOURNING FOR THE ONE THEY PIERCED

¹⁰"And I will pour out on the house of David and the inhabitants of Jerusalem a spirit*a* of grace and supplication. They will look on*b* me, the one they have pierced, and they will mourn for him as one mourns for an only child, and grieve bitterly for him as one grieves for a firstborn son. ¹¹On that day the weeping in Jerusalem will be as great as the weeping of Hadad Rimmon in the plain of Megiddo. ¹²The land will mourn, each clan by itself, with their wives by themselves: the clan of the house of David and their wives, the clan of the house of Nathan and their wives, ¹³the clan of the house of Levi and their wives, the clan of Shimei and their wives, ¹⁴and all the rest of the clans and their wives.

CLEANSING FROM SIN

13 "On that day a fountain will be opened to the house of David and the inhabitants of Jerusalem, to cleanse them from sin and impurity.

²"On that day, I will banish the names of the idols from the land, and they will be remembered no more," declares the LORD Almighty. "I will remove both the prophets and the spirit of impurity from the land. ³And if anyone still prophesies, their father and mother, to whom they were born, will say to them, 'You must die, because you have told lies in the LORD's name.' Then their own parents will stab the one who prophesies.

⁴"On that day every prophet will be ashamed of their prophetic vision. They will not put on a prophet's garment of hair in order to deceive. ⁵Each will say, 'I am not a prophet.

How would Jerusalem be like a cup that sent others reeling? (12:2)
This was a metaphor describing the terrible consequences that would come to those who had to drink the cup of God's judgment.

Who was the one who was pierced? (12:10)
This was a prophecy predicting the coming Messiah. He suffered without deserving it (see John 19:37 and Revelation 1:7).

Which prophets are referred to here? (13:2)
These were false prophets. Even after the exile, false prophets tried to lead the people to believe messages that were not from God.

---

a 10 Or *the Spirit*   *b* 10 Or *to*

I am a farmer; the land has been my livelihood since my youth.'[a] [6]If someone asks, 'What are these wounds on your body[b]?' they will answer, 'The wounds I was given at the house of my friends.'

THE SHEPHERD STRUCK, THE SHEEP SCATTERED

[7]"Awake, sword, against my shepherd,
  against the man who is close to me!"
  declares the LORD Almighty.
"Strike the shepherd,
  and the sheep will be scattered,
  and I will turn my hand against the little ones.
[8]In the whole land," declares the LORD,
  "two-thirds will be struck down and perish;
  yet one-third will be left in it.
[9]This third I will put into the fire;
  I will refine them like silver
  and test them like gold.
They will call on my name
  and I will answer them;
I will say, 'They are my people,'
  and they will say, 'The LORD is our God.'"

THE LORD COMES AND REIGNS

14 A day of the LORD is coming, Jerusalem, when your possessions will be plundered and divided up within your very walls.

[2]I will gather all the nations to Jerusalem to fight against it; the city will be captured, the houses ransacked, and the women raped. Half of the city will go into exile, but the rest of the people will not be taken from the city. [3]Then the LORD will go out and fight against those nations, as he fights on a day of battle. [4]On that day his feet will stand on the Mount of Olives, east of Jerusalem, and the Mount of Olives will be split in two from east to west, forming a great valley, with half of the mountain moving north and half moving south. [5]You will flee by my mountain valley, for it will extend to Azel. You will flee as you fled from the earthquake[c] in the days of Uzziah king of Judah. Then the LORD my God will come, and all the holy ones with him.

[6]On that day there will be neither sunlight nor cold, frosty darkness. [7]It will be a unique day—a day known only to the LORD—with no distinction between day and night. When evening comes, there will be light.

[8]On that day living water will flow out from Jerusalem, half of it east to the Dead Sea and half of it west to the Mediterranean Sea, in summer and in winter.

[9]The LORD will be king over the whole earth. On that day there will be one LORD, and his name the only name.

[10]The whole land, from Geba to Rimmon, south of Jerusalem, will become like the Arabah. But Jerusalem will be

Who is the shepherd? (13:7)
This was a prophecy about the Messiah, the Good Shepherd. Jesus quoted from these verses to describe himself, and he talked about the scattering of the sheep in connection with the dispersal of the apostles.

What is the Dea Sea like? (14:8)
The Dead Sea has the earth's lowest surface—1,300 feet (400 meters) below sea level. It measures about 47 by 10 miles (76 x 16 km). This sea is almost 6 times more salty than the ocean.

---

[a] 5 Or *farmer; a man sold me in my youth*   [b] 6 Or *wounds between your hands*
[c] 5 Or *My mountain valley will be blocked and will extend to Azel. It will be blocked as it was blocked because of the earthquake*

raised up high from the Benjamin Gate to the site of the First Gate, to the Corner Gate, and from the Tower of Hananel to the royal winepresses, and will remain in its place. ¹¹ It will be inhabited; never again will it be destroyed. Jerusalem will be secure.

¹² This is the plague with which the LORD will strike all the nations that fought against Jerusalem: Their flesh will rot while they are still standing on their feet, their eyes will rot in their sockets, and their tongues will rot in their mouths. ¹³ On that day people will be stricken by the LORD with great panic. They will seize each other by the hand and attack one another. ¹⁴ Judah too will fight at Jerusalem. The wealth of all the surrounding nations will be collected—great quantities of gold and silver and clothing. ¹⁵ A similar plague will strike the horses and mules, the camels and donkeys, and all the animals in those camps.

¹⁶ Then the survivors from all the nations that have attacked Jerusalem will go up year after year to worship the King, the LORD Almighty, and to celebrate the Festival of Tabernacles. ¹⁷ If any of the peoples of the earth do not go up to Jerusalem to worship the King, the LORD Almighty, they will have no rain. ¹⁸ If the Egyptian people do not go up and take part, they will have no rain. The LORD*a* will bring on them the plague he inflicts on the nations that do not go up to celebrate the Festival of Tabernacles. ¹⁹ This will be the punishment of Egypt and the punishment of all the nations that do not go up to celebrate the Festival of Tabernacles.

²⁰ On that day HOLY TO THE LORD will be inscribed on the bells of the horses, and the cooking pots in the LORD's house will be like the sacred bowls in front of the altar. ²¹ Every pot in Jerusalem and Judah will be holy to the LORD Almighty, and all who come to sacrifice will take some of the pots and cook in them. And on that day there will no longer be a Canaanite*b* in the house of the LORD Almighty.

How would drought affect Egypt? (14:18)
Rain was necessary to swell the Nile River so that it would flood its banks and deposit rich soil for crops.

Where was the phrase "HOLY TO THE LORD" also inscribed? (14:20)
This phrase was also engraved on the gold plate worn on the high priest's turban (Exodus 28:36 – 38) as a reminder of his dedication to the Lord's service.

---

a 18 Or *part, then the* LORD   *b* 21 Or *merchant*

Malachi

INTRODUCTION

Who wrote this book? The prophet Malachi.

Why was this book written? The book of Malachi shows how the children of the people who returned to Judah from Babylon have wandered away from God.

What do we learn about God in this book? God deserves our best. God will remember those who love him and talk about him.

What is special about this book? The prophet answers foolish questions the people ask. His answers teach us how to show love for God.

What are some important passages in this book?

Honoring God	Malachi 1:6 – 11
Robbing God	Malachi 3:6 – 12
God's treasured possession	Malachi 3:16 – 18

When did these things happen?

1300 BC 1200 1100 1000 900 800 700 600 500 400

FALL OF JERUSALEM (586 BC)

FIRST RETURN OF EXILES TO JERUSALEM (538 BC)

MINISTRIES OF HAGGAI AND ZECHARIAH (C. 520 – 480 BC)

COMPLETION OF TEMPLE (516 BC)

SECOND RETURN TO JERUSALEM UNDER EZRA (458 BC)

THIRD RETURN TO JERUSALEM UNDER NEHEMIAH (444 BC)

MALACHI'S MINISTRY (C. 440 – 430 BC)

BOOK OF MALACHI WRITTEN (C. 430 BC)

1

A prophecy: The word of the LORD to Israel through Malachi.[a]

ISRAEL DOUBTS GOD'S LOVE

[2] "I have loved you," says the LORD.

"But you ask, 'How have you loved us?'

"Was not Esau Jacob's brother?" declares the LORD. "Yet I have loved Jacob, [3] but Esau I have hated, and I have turned his hill country into a wasteland and left his inheritance to the desert jackals."

[4] Edom may say, "Though we have been crushed, we will rebuild the ruins."

But this is what the LORD Almighty says: "They may build, but I will demolish. They will be called the Wicked Land, a people always under the wrath of the LORD. [5] You will see it with your own eyes and say, 'Great is the LORD— even beyond the borders of Israel!'

BREAKING COVENANT THROUGH BLEMISHED SACRIFICES

[6] "A son honors his father, and a slave his master. If I am a father, where is the honor due me? If I am a master, where is the respect due me?" says the LORD Almighty.

"It is you priests who show contempt for my name.

"But you ask, 'How have we shown contempt for your name?'

[7] "By offering defiled food on my altar.

"But you ask, 'How have we defiled you?'

"By saying that the LORD's table is contemptible. [8] When you offer blind animals for sacrifice, is that not wrong? When you sacrifice lame or diseased animals, is that not wrong? Try offering them to your governor! Would he be pleased with you? Would he accept you?" says the LORD Almighty.

[9] "Now plead with God to be gracious to us. With such offerings from your hands, will he accept you?"— says the LORD Almighty.

[10] "Oh, that one of you would shut the temple doors, so that you would not light useless fires on my altar! I am not pleased with you," says the LORD Almighty, "and I will accept no offering from your hands. [11] My name will be great among the nations, from where the sun rises to where it sets. In every place incense and pure offerings will be brought to me, because my name will be great among the nations," says the LORD Almighty.

[12] "But you profane it by saying, 'The Lord's table is defiled,' and, 'Its food is contemptible.' [13] And you say, 'What a burden!' and you sniff at it contemptuously," says the LORD Almighty.

"When you bring injured, lame or diseased animals and offer them as sacrifices, should I accept them from your hands?" says the LORD. [14] "Cursed is the cheat who has an acceptable male in his flock and vows to give it, but then sacrifices a blemished animal to the Lord. For I am a great king," says the LORD Almighty, "and my name is to be feared among the nations.

[a] 1 *Malachi* means *my messenger.*

Why did God love Jacob and hate Esau? (1:2–3)
God made a covenant with Jacob. He loved Jacob because of this covenant relationship. He did not hate Esau but regarded him in a different way.

How did the priests defile God's altar? (1:7–8)
The priests offered animals that weren't perfect. In this way they disobeyed God's law for sacrifices and insulted him.

What type of animals could be sacrificed? (1:14)
An animal sacrificed in fulfillment of a vow was supposed to be a male without defect or blemish (see Leviticus 22:18–21).

What would happen if God cursed the priests? (2:2)
The priests' job was to pronounce God's blessings to the people. If they were cursed, their blessings would become curses, and their priestly role would be worthless.

What was the role of priests? (2:6–7)
In addition to offering sacrifices, priests were supposed to teach the law of Moses.

ADDITIONAL WARNING TO THE PRIESTS

2 "And now, you priests, this warning is for you. ²If you do not listen, and if you do not resolve to honor my name," says the Lord Almighty, "I will send a curse on you, and I will curse your blessings. Yes, I have already cursed them, because you have not resolved to honor me.

³"Because of you I will rebuke your descendants*ᵃ*; I will smear on your faces the dung from your festival sacrifices, and you will be carried off with it. ⁴And you will know that I have sent you this warning so that my covenant with Levi may continue," says the Lord Almighty. ⁵"My covenant was with him, a covenant of life and peace, and I gave them to him; this called for reverence and he revered me and stood in awe of my name. ⁶True instruction was in his mouth and nothing false was found on his lips. He walked with me in peace and uprightness, and turned many from sin.

⁷"For the lips of a priest ought to preserve knowledge, because he is the messenger of the Lord Almighty and people seek instruction from his mouth. ⁸But you have turned from the way and by your teaching have caused many to stumble; you have violated the covenant with Levi," says the Lord Almighty. ⁹"So I have caused you to be despised and humiliated before all the people, because you have not followed my ways but have shown partiality in matters of the law."

BREAKING COVENANT THROUGH DIVORCE

¹⁰Do we not all have one Father*ᵇ*? Did not one God create us? Why do we profane the covenant of our ancestors by being unfaithful to one another?

¹¹Judah has been unfaithful. A detestable thing has been committed in Israel and in Jerusalem: Judah has desecrated the sanctuary the Lord loves by marrying women who worship a foreign god. ¹²As for the man who does this, whoever he may be, may the Lord remove him from the tents of Jacob*ᶜ*—even though he brings an offering to the Lord Almighty.

¹³Another thing you do: You flood the Lord's altar with tears. You weep and wail because he no longer looks with favor on your offerings or accepts them with pleasure from your hands. ¹⁴You ask, "Why?" It is because the Lord is the witness between you and the wife of your youth. You have been unfaithful to her, though she is your partner, the wife of your marriage covenant.

¹⁵Has not the one God made you? You belong to him in body and spirit. And what does the one God seek? Godly offspring.*ᵈ* So be on your guard, and do not be unfaithful to the wife of your youth.

¹⁶"The man who hates and divorces his wife," says the Lord, the God of Israel, "does violence to the one he should protect,"*ᵉ* says the Lord Almighty.

So be on your guard, and do not be unfaithful.

ᵃ 3 Or *will blight your grain*   ᵇ 10 Or *father*   ᶜ 12 Or *¹²May the Lord remove from the tents of Jacob anyone who gives testimony in behalf of the man who does this*   ᵈ 15 The meaning of the Hebrew for the first part of this verse is uncertain.   ᵉ 16 Or *"I hate divorce," says the Lord, the God of Israel, "because the man who divorces his wife covers his garment with violence,"*

BREAKING COVENANT THROUGH INJUSTICE

¹⁷You have wearied the LORD with your words.

"How have we wearied him?" you ask.

By saying, "All who do evil are good in the eyes of the LORD, and he is pleased with them" or "Where is the God of justice?"

3 "I will send my messenger, who will prepare the way before me. Then suddenly the Lord you are seeking will come to his temple; the messenger of the covenant, whom you desire, will come," says the LORD Almighty.

²But who can endure the day of his coming? Who can stand when he appears? For he will be like a refiner's fire or a launderer's soap. ³He will sit as a refiner and purifier of silver; he will purify the Levites and refine them like gold and silver. Then the LORD will have men who will bring offerings in righteousness, ⁴and the offerings of Judah and Jerusalem will be acceptable to the LORD, as in days gone by, as in former years.

⁵"So I will come to put you on trial. I will be quick to testify against sorcerers, adulterers and perjurers, against those who defraud laborers of their wages, who oppress the widows and the fatherless, and deprive the foreigners among you of justice, but do not fear me," says the LORD Almighty.

BREAKING COVENANT BY WITHHOLDING TITHES

⁶"I the LORD do not change. So you, the descendants of Jacob, are not destroyed. ⁷Ever since the time of your ancestors you have turned away from my decrees and have not kept them. Return to me, and I will return to you," says the LORD Almighty.

"But you ask, 'How are we to return?'

⁸"Will a mere mortal rob God? Yet you rob me.

"But you ask, 'How are we robbing you?'

"In tithes and offerings. ⁹You are under a curse—your whole nation—because you are robbing me. ¹⁰Bring the whole tithe into the storehouse, that there may be food in my house. Test me in this," says the LORD Almighty, "and see if I will not throw open the floodgates of heaven and pour out so much blessing that there will not be room enough to store it. ¹¹I will prevent pests from devouring your crops, and the vines in your fields will not drop their fruit before it is ripe," says the LORD Almighty. ¹²"Then all the nations will call you blessed, for yours will be a delightful land," says the LORD Almighty.

ISRAEL SPEAKS ARROGANTLY AGAINST GOD

¹³"You have spoken arrogantly against me," says the LORD.

"Yet you ask, 'What have we said against you?'

¹⁴"You have said, 'It is futile to serve God. What do we gain by carrying out his requirements and going about like mourners before the LORD Almighty? ¹⁵But now we call the arrogant blessed. Certainly evildoers prosper, and even when they put God to the test, they get away with it.'"

Who was this messenger? (3:1)
This was John the Baptist, who would prepare the way for the Lord.

What was the day of his coming? (3:2)
This referred to the day of the Lord, when God would complete his work in history. On this day, God's promises would be fulfilled by the Messiah, who would come to purify the people.

What was the storehouse? (3:10)
These were the treasury rooms of the temple that were used to store provisions and valuable objects.

THE FAITHFUL REMNANT

¹⁶Then those who feared the Lord talked with each other, and the Lord listened and heard. A scroll of remembrance was written in his presence concerning those who feared the Lord and honored his name.

¹⁷"On the day when I act," says the Lord Almighty, "they will be my treasured possession. I will spare them, just as a father has compassion and spares his son who serves him. ¹⁸And you will again see the distinction between the righteous and the wicked, between those who serve God and those who do not.

JUDGMENT AND COVENANT RENEWAL

4 ᵃ "Surely the day is coming; it will burn like a furnace. All the arrogant and every evildoer will be stubble, and the day that is coming will set them on fire," says the Lord Almighty. "Not a root or a branch will be left to them. ²But for you who revere my name, the sun of righteousness will rise with healing in its rays. And you will go out and frolic like well-fed calves. ³Then you will trample on the wicked; they will be ashes under the soles of your feet on the day when I act," says the Lord Almighty.

⁴"Remember the law of my servant Moses, the decrees and laws I gave him at Horeb for all Israel.

⁵"See, I will send the prophet Elijah to you before that great and dreadful day of the Lord comes. ⁶He will turn the hearts of the parents to their children, and the hearts of the children to their parents; or else I will come and strike the land with total destruction."

ᵃ In Hebrew texts 4:1-6 is numbered 3:19-24.

What was the sun of righteousness? (4:2)
God and his glory are compared to the sun in Isaiah 60 verses 1 and 19. Jesus, the Messiah, would be the sun rising from heaven (see Luke 1:78–79).

What was the day of the Lord that the prophets spoke about?
MALACHI 4

The day of the Lord refers to a time when God acts in a powerful way in human history to carry out his plan for his people.

In the Old Testament the prophets often talked about the day of the Lord as a time when God would bring judgment on his people for their disobedience or lack of faith. The event would be violent and harsh, and it was fulfilled in various ways, including the fall of Israel and Judah and the destruction of Jerusalem.

Both the Old and New Testaments also describe the day of the Lord as the time when Christ will return to judge the nations. In addition, the day of the Lord can refer to the purification of the current creation by fire as preparation for the new creation (see 2 Peter 3:10–13).

FROM MALACHI TO CHRIST

	450 BC
	440
	430
THE PERSIAN PERIOD	420
450–330 BC	410
	400
For about 200 years after Nehemiah's time the	390
Persians controlled Judah, but the Jews were allowed	380
to carry on their religious observances and were not	370
interfered with. During this time Judah was ruled by	360
high priests, who answered to the Persian authorities.	350
	340
	330

ALEXANDER THE GREAT — 320

	310
THE HELLENISTIC PERIOD	300
330–166 BC	290
	280
In the late fourth century BC, Alexander the Great	270
defeated the Persians repeatedly in battle and	
quickly conquered the eastern Mediterranean	RULE OF THE PTOLEMIES · 260
region, including Syria, Egypt, Persia and Babylonia.	OF EGYPT · 250
Alexander believed in the superiority of Greek culture	240
and was convinced that it was the one force that could	230
unify the world. Alexander permitted the Jews to	220
observe their laws and even granted them exemption	210
from tribute or tax during their sabbath years. When	200
he built Alexandria in Egypt, he encouraged Jews	190
to live there. The Greek conquest prepared the way	RULE OF THE SELEUCIDS · 180
for the translation of the Hebrew Old Testament into	OF SYRIA · 170
Greek (Septuagint version), beginning c. 250 BC.	160

	150
THE HASMONEAN PERIOD	140
166–63 BC	130
	120
When this historical period began, the Jews were	110
being greatly oppressed. The Ptolemies of Egypt had	HASMONEAN DYNASTY · 110
been tolerant of the Jews and their religious practices,	100
but the Seleucid rulers of Syria were determined to	90
force Hellenism on them. Copies of the Scriptures	80
were ordered destroyed, and laws were enforced	70
banning circumcision and other Jewish practices. The	60
oppressed Jews revolted, led by Judas Maccabeus.	

	50
THE ROMAN PERIOD	40
BEGINS IN 63 BC	30
	HEROD THE GREAT · 20
In the year 63 BC, Pompey, the Roman general,	RULES AS KING;
captured Jerusalem, and the provinces in the Holy	SUBJECT TO ROME · 10
Land became subject to Rome. The Romans ruled at	1
times through local vassal kings and at other times	10
through Roman governors who were appointed by	20
the emperors. Herod the Great was ruler of that whole	
region at the time of Jesus' birth.	AD 30

New Testament

Matthew

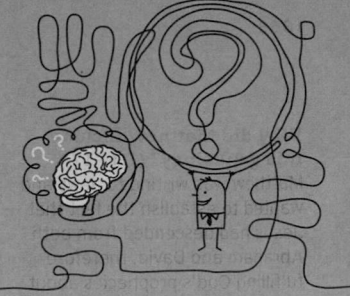

INTRODUCTION

Who wrote this book? Matthew, one of Jesus' 12 disciples, wrote this book.

Why was this book written? The Gospel of Matthew shows the Jews that Jesus is the Messiah promised in the Old Testament.

For whom was this book written? Matthew was written for the Jewish people.

What happens in this book? This book tells about Jesus' birth, his life as an adult, his teaching, death, and resurrection.

Who is the key person in this book? Jesus is the most important person in this book.

Where did this happen? Most events took place in towns in Galilee. (Turn the page to see a map of the region.)

What are some of the stories in this book?

Magi visit Jesus	Matthew 2:1 – 23
How to be blessed	Matthew 5:1 – 12
The Lord's Prayer	Matthew 6:9 – 13
Jesus feeds 5,000 people	Matthew 14:13 – 21
Jesus walks on water	Matthew 14:22 – 33
Lost sheep	Matthew 18:10 – 14
Jesus enters Jerusalem	Matthew 21:1 – 11
Jesus is crucified	Matthew 27:32 – 56
Jesus returns to life	Matthew 28:1 – 10
Jesus' Great Commission	Matthew 28:16 – 20

When did these things happen?

40 BC 30 20 10 AD 1 10 20 30 40 50 60 70

HEROD THE GREAT'S REIGN (C. 37 - 4 BC)	
JESUS' BIRTH (C. 6/5 BC)	
JESUS' FLIGHT TO EGYPT (C. 5/4 BC)	
BEGINNING OF JOHN THE BAPTIST'S MINISTRY (C. AD 26)	
BEGINNING OF JESUS' MINISTRY (C. AD 26)	
JESUS' DEATH, RESURRECTION AND ASCENSION (C. AD 30)	
PAUL'S CONVERSION (C. AD 35)	
BOOK OF MATTHEW WRITTEN (C. AD 60 - 70)	

THE GENEALOGY OF JESUS THE MESSIAH

Why did Matthew include this genealogy? (1:1–17)
Matthew was writing to Jews and wanted to establish the fact that Jesus had descended from both Abraham and David, therefore fulfilling God's prophecies about the Messiah.

Why did Matthew include women in the genealogy? (1:3, 5, 6)
Matthew included four women in the genealogy: Tamar, Rahab, Ruth, and Bathsheba (by description, not by name). The first three of these women were Gentiles. Matthew may have been showing that God's kingdom is not limited to men or to the people of Israel.

1 This is the genealogy*a* of Jesus the Messiah*b* the son of David, the son of Abraham:

2 Abraham was the father of Isaac,
  Isaac the father of Jacob,
  Jacob the father of Judah and his brothers,
3 Judah the father of Perez and Zerah, whose mother was Tamar,
  Perez the father of Hezron,
  Hezron the father of Ram,
4 Ram the father of Amminadab,
  Amminadab the father of Nahshon,
  Nahshon the father of Salmon,
5 Salmon the father of Boaz, whose mother was Rahab,
  Boaz the father of Obed, whose mother was Ruth,
  Obed the father of Jesse,
6 and Jesse the father of King David.

David was the father of Solomon, whose mother had been Uriah's wife,
7 Solomon the father of Rehoboam,
  Rehoboam the father of Abijah,
  Abijah the father of Asa,
8 Asa the father of Jehoshaphat,
  Jehoshaphat the father of Jehoram,
  Jehoram the father of Uzziah,
9 Uzziah the father of Jotham,
  Jotham the father of Ahaz,
  Ahaz the father of Hezekiah,
10 Hezekiah the father of Manasseh,
  Manasseh the father of Amon,
  Amon the father of Josiah,
11 and Josiah the father of Jeconiah*c* and his brothers at the time of the exile to Babylon.

a 1 Or *is an account of the origin*   *b 1* Or *Jesus Christ. Messiah* (Hebrew) and *Christ* (Greek) both mean *Anointed One*; also in verse 18.   *c 11* That is, Jehoiachin; also in verse 12

Why are there four different books in the Bible that tell about Jesus' life on earth?
MATTHEW 1

During Jesus' life, many people heard what he said and saw what he did. The first four books of the New Testament were written by people who had knowledge of Jesus' ministry. The authors of these books were writing to different groups of people and had different purposes in mind when they were writing.

Matthew was one of Jesus' disciples. He wrote his book to prove to Jewish people that Jesus was the Messiah. He did this by showing how Jesus fulfilled the prophecies about the Messiah in the Old Testament. Mark wrote his book for Gentile readers, possibly those who were facing persecution in Rome. He explained some of the Jewish customs for his readers so they could understand how Jesus fit into his Jewish background. Luke wrote to strengthen the faith of believers and to convince unbelievers that Jesus was the Savior for both Jews and Gentiles. John was one of Jesus' disciples. He wrote his account of Jesus in order to convince his readers that Jesus was truly the Son of God.

There are many sections of these four books that overlap, but there are also differences. Together, they give us a description of Jesus that allows us to understand why he came to earth and to believe in him.

SETTING OF THE GOSPELS

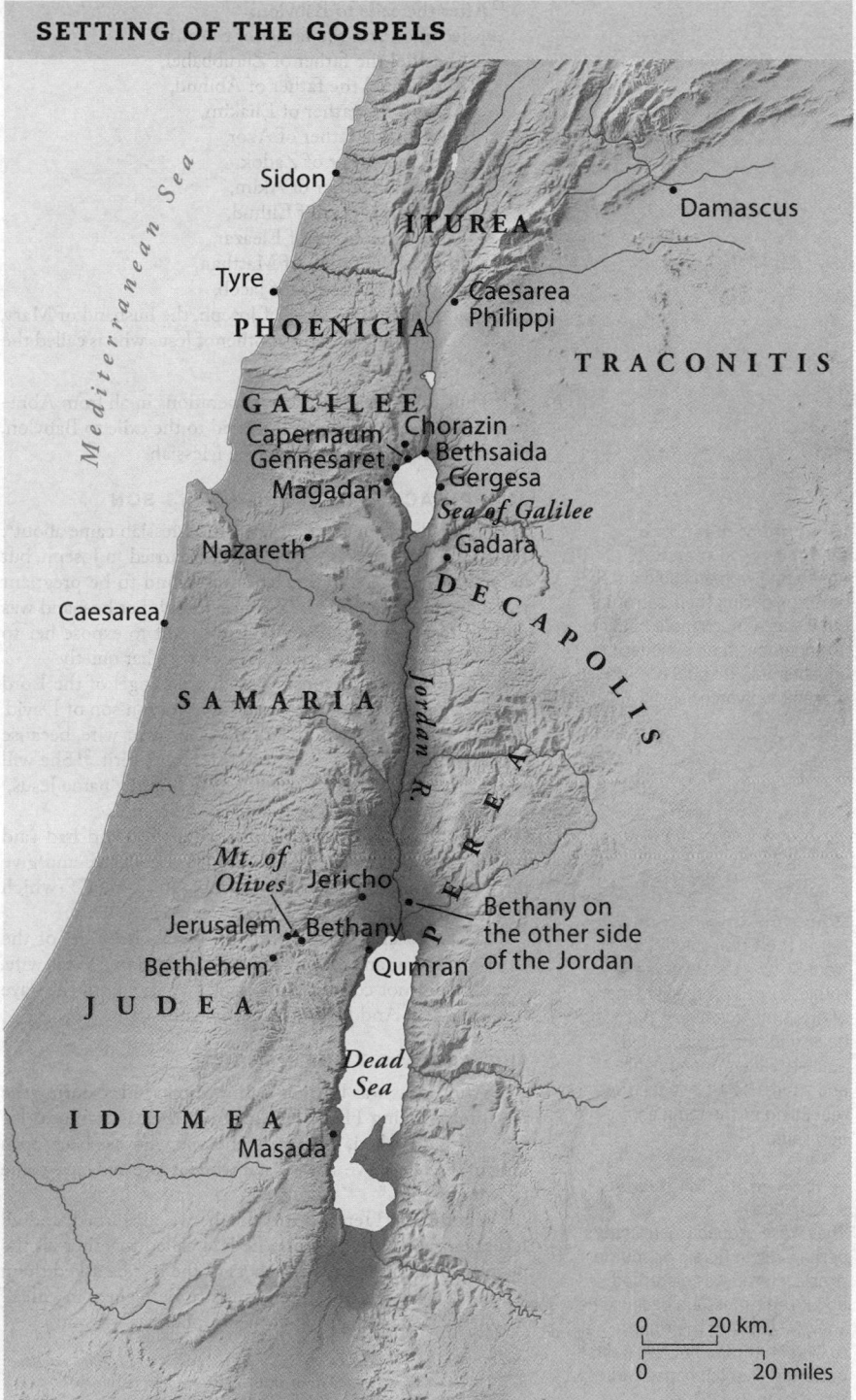

Mediterranean Sea

Sidon

Damascus

ITUREA

Tyre

Caesarea
Philippi

PHOENICIA

TRACONITIS

GALILEE

Capernaum   Chorazin
Gennesaret   • Bethsaida
Magadan   Gergesa
                        Sea of Galilee

Nazareth   Gadara

Caesarea   DECAPOLIS

SAMARIA

Jordan R.

P E R E A

*Mt. of
Olives*   Jericho

Jerusalem   Bethany   Bethany on
                                the other side
Bethlehem   Qumran   of the Jordan

JUDEA

*Dead
Sea*

IDUMEA

Masada

0   20 km.

0   20 miles

¹² After the exile to Babylon:
Jeconiah was the father of Shealtiel,
Shealtiel the father of Zerubbabel,
¹³ Zerubbabel the father of Abihud,
Abihud the father of Eliakim,
Eliakim the father of Azor,
¹⁴ Azor the father of Zadok,
Zadok the father of Akim,
Akim the father of Elihud,
¹⁵ Elihud the father of Eleazar,
Eleazar the father of Matthan,
Matthan the father of Jacob,
¹⁶ and Jacob the father of Joseph, the husband of Mary,
and Mary was the mother of Jesus who is called the
Messiah.

¹⁷ Thus there were fourteen generations in all from Abraham to David, fourteen from David to the exile to Babylon, and fourteen from the exile to the Messiah.

JOSEPH ACCEPTS JESUS AS HIS SON

¹⁸ This is how the birth of Jesus the Messiah came about*: His mother Mary was pledged to be married to Joseph, but before they came together, she was found to be pregnant through the Holy Spirit. ¹⁹ Because Joseph her husband was faithful to the law, and yet*ᵇ did not want to expose her to public disgrace, he had in mind to divorce her quietly.

²⁰ But after he had considered this, an angel of the Lord appeared to him in a dream and said, "Joseph son of David, do not be afraid to take Mary home as your wife, because what is conceived in her is from the Holy Spirit. ²¹ She will give birth to a son, and you are to give him the name Jesus,ᶜ because he will save his people from their sins."

²² All this took place to fulfill what the Lord had said through the prophet: ²³ "The virgin will conceive and give birth to a son, and they will call him Immanuel"ᵈ (which means "God with us").

²⁴ When Joseph woke up, he did what the angel of the Lord had commanded him and took Mary home as his wife. ²⁵ But he did not consummate their marriage until she gave birth to a son. And he gave him the name Jesus.

THE MAGI VISIT THE MESSIAH

2 After Jesus was born in Bethlehem in Judea, during the time of King Herod, Magiᵉ from the east came to Jerusalem ²and asked, "Where is the one who has been born king of the Jews? We saw his star when it rose and have come to worship him."

³When King Herod heard this he was disturbed, and all Jerusalem with him. ⁴When he had called together all the people's chief priests and teachers of the law, he asked them where the Messiah was to be born. ⁵"In Bethlehem in Judea," they replied, "for this is what the prophet has written:

What did it mean to be pledged to be married? (1:18) A man and woman could not have sex during their betrothal, but it was a much more binding arrangement than a modern engagement. It could only be broken by divorce.

Who was King Herod? (2:1) Herod the Great ruled Judea from 37 to 4 B.C. He was a ruthless tyrant who killed many of his family members. But he also built many splendid amphitheaters, monuments, and altars. He also began the rebuilding of the temple in Jerusalem.

Who were the Magi (wise men)? (2:1) They were probably astrologers, perhaps from Persia or southern Arabia. Herod was disturbed about their message because he knew he was not the rightful heir to Israel's throne but had gained power by aligning himself with the Romans.

ᵃ 18 Or *The origin of Jesus the Messiah was like this   ᵇ 19* Or *was a righteous man and   ᶜ 21 Jesus* is the Greek form of *Joshua,* which means *the LORD saves.   ᵈ 23* Isaiah 7:14   *ᵉ 1* Traditionally *wise men*

⁶"'But you, Bethlehem, in the land of Judah,
    are by no means least among the rulers of Judah;
for out of you will come a ruler
    who will shepherd my people Israel.'ᵃ"

⁷Then Herod called the Magi secretly and found out from them the exact time the star had appeared. ⁸He sent them to Bethlehem and said, "Go and search carefully for the child. As soon as you find him, report to me, so that I too may go and worship him."

⁹After they had heard the king, they went on their way, and the star they had seen when it rose went ahead of them until it stopped over the place where the child was. ¹⁰When they saw the star, they were overjoyed. ¹¹On coming to the house, they saw the child with his mother Mary, and they bowed down and worshiped him. Then they opened their treasures and presented him with gifts of gold, frankincense and myrrh. ¹²And having been warned in a dream not to go back to Herod, they returned to their country by another route.

THE ESCAPE TO EGYPT

¹³When they had gone, an angel of the Lord appeared to Joseph in a dream. "Get up," he said, "take the child and his mother and escape to Egypt. Stay there until I tell you, for Herod is going to search for the child to kill him."

¹⁴So he got up, took the child and his mother during the night and left for Egypt, ¹⁵where he stayed until the death of Herod. And so was fulfilled what the Lord had said through the prophet: "Out of Egypt I called my son."ᵇ

¹⁶When Herod realized that he had been outwitted by the Magi, he was furious, and he gave orders to kill all the boys in Bethlehem and its vicinity who were two years old and under, in accordance with the time he had learned from the Magi. ¹⁷Then what was said through the prophet Jeremiah was fulfilled:

¹⁸"A voice is heard in Ramah,
    weeping and great mourning,
Rachel weeping for her children
    and refusing to be comforted,
    because they are no more."ᶜ

THE RETURN TO NAZARETH

¹⁹After Herod died, an angel of the Lord appeared in a dream to Joseph in Egypt ²⁰and said, "Get up, take the child and his mother and go to the land of Israel, for those who were trying to take the child's life are dead."

²¹So he got up, took the child and his mother and went to the land of Israel. ²²But when he heard that Archelaus was reigning in Judea in place of his father Herod, he was afraid to go there. Having been warned in a dream, he withdrew to the district of Galilee, ²³and he went and lived in a town called Nazareth. So was fulfilled what was said through the prophets, that he would be called a Nazarene.

ᵃ 6 Micah 5:2,4   ᵇ 15 Hosea 11:1   ᶜ 18 Jer. 31:15

Where did the Magi visit Jesus? (2:11)
They did not visit him when he was in the manger, but in a house some months later.

How many Magi (wise men) visited Jesus? (2:11)
The Bible doesn't say, but some people guess that there were three because three gifts were presented.

Escape to Egypt (2:13)

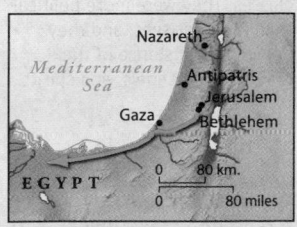

How many baby boys were killed? (2:16)
The number was probably not large because Bethlehem was a small village. However, the act was still brutal.

What was a Nazarene? (2:23)
A Nazarene was a person who lived in Nazareth. Calling a person a Nazarene was often considered an insult. People who lived in Nazareth or anywhere else in Galilee were considered to be part of the lower class.

JOHN THE BAPTIST PREPARES THE WAY

3 In those days John the Baptist came, preaching in the wilderness of Judea ²and saying, "Repent, for the kingdom of heaven has come near." ³This is he who was spoken of through the prophet Isaiah:

"A voice of one calling in the wilderness,
'Prepare the way for the Lord,
    make straight paths for him.'"ᵃ

⁴John's clothes were made of camel's hair, and he had a leather belt around his waist. His food was locusts and wild honey. ⁵People went out to him from Jerusalem and all Judea and the whole region of the Jordan. ⁶Confessing their sins, they were baptized by him in the Jordan River.

⁷But when he saw many of the Pharisees and Sadducees coming to where he was baptizing, he said to them: "You brood of vipers! Who warned you to flee from the coming wrath? ⁸Produce fruit in keeping with repentance. ⁹And do not think you can say to yourselves, 'We have Abraham as our father.' I tell you that out of these stones God can raise up children for Abraham. ¹⁰The ax is already at the root of the trees, and every tree that does not produce good fruit will be cut down and thrown into the fire.

¹¹"I baptize you withᵇ water for repentance. But after me comes one who is more powerful than I, whose sandals I am not worthy to carry. He will baptize you withᵇ the Holy Spirit and fire. ¹²His winnowing fork is in his hand, and he will clear his threshing floor, gathering his wheat into the barn and burning up the chaff with unquenchable fire."

THE BAPTISM OF JESUS

¹³Then Jesus came from Galilee to the Jordan to be baptized by John. ¹⁴But John tried to deter him, saying, "I need to be baptized by you, and do you come to me?"

¹⁵Jesus replied, "Let it be so now; it is proper for us to do this to fulfill all righteousness." Then John consented.

¹⁶As soon as Jesus was baptized, he went up out of the water. At that moment heaven was opened, and he saw the Spirit of God descending like a dove and alighting on him. ¹⁷And a voice from heaven said, "This is my Son, whom I love; with him I am well pleased."

JESUS IS TESTED IN THE WILDERNESS

4 Then Jesus was led by the Spirit into the wilderness to be temptedᶜ by the devil. ²After fasting forty days and forty nights, he was hungry. ³The tempter came to him and said, "If you are the Son of God, tell these stones to become bread."

⁴Jesus answered, "It is written: 'Man shall not live on bread alone, but on every word that comes from the mouth of God.'ᵈ"

⁵Then the devil took him to the holy city and had him stand on the highest point of the temple. ⁶"If you are the Son of God," he said, "throw yourself down. For it is written:

ᵃ 3 Isaiah 40:3   ᵇ 11 Or in   ᶜ 1 The Greek for *tempted* can also mean *tested*.   ᵈ 4 Deut. 8:3

What is "the kingdom of heaven"? (3:2)
Matthew uses this term 33 times. It refers to God's rule in our hearts in the present reality and to his future kingdom here on earth. The idea of God's kingdom was a central part of Matthew's message.

Who were the Pharisees and Sadducees? (3:7)
The Pharisees were a legalistic and separatist group who strictly obeyed the laws of Moses and the other traditional laws that had been passed down. They were not a large group, but they enjoyed the support of the people. The Sadducees were a Jewish party that represented the wealthy and sophisticated classes. They were more political than the Pharisees, and they denied the existence of the resurrection, angels, and spirits.

Where did Jesus' temptations take place? (4:1)
They took place in a wilderness region in the lower Jordan Valley, on a high mountain (possibly one of the tall cliffs near Jericho), and on the highest point of the temple, where the priests sounded the trumpet to announce important events.

Temptation of Jesus (4:1)

"'He will command his angels concerning you,
  and they will lift you up in their hands,
  so that you will not strike your foot against a
    stone.'ᵃ"

⁷Jesus answered him, "It is also written: 'Do not put the Lord your God to the test.'ᵇ"

⁸Again, the devil took him to a very high mountain and showed him all the kingdoms of the world and their splendor. ⁹"All this I will give you," he said, "if you will bow down and worship me."

¹⁰Jesus said to him, "Away from me, Satan! For it is written: 'Worship the Lord your God, and serve him only.'ᶜ"

¹¹Then the devil left him, and angels came and attended him.

JESUS BEGINS TO PREACH

¹²When Jesus heard that John had been put in prison, he withdrew to Galilee. ¹³Leaving Nazareth, he went and lived in Capernaum, which was by the lake in the area of Zebulun and Naphtali— ¹⁴to fulfill what was said through the prophet Isaiah:

¹⁵"Land of Zebulun and land of Naphtali,
  the Way of the Sea, beyond the Jordan,
  Galilee of the Gentiles—
¹⁶the people living in darkness
  have seen a great light;
on those living in the land of the shadow of death
  a light has dawned."ᵈ

¹⁷From that time on Jesus began to preach, "Repent, for the kingdom of heaven has come near."

JESUS CALLS HIS FIRST DISCIPLES

¹⁸As Jesus was walking beside the Sea of Galilee, he saw two brothers, Simon called Peter and his brother Andrew. They were casting a net into the lake, for they were fishermen. ¹⁹"Come, follow me," Jesus said, "and I will send you out to fish for people." ²⁰At once they left their nets and followed him.

²¹Going on from there, he saw two other brothers, James son of Zebedee and his brother John. They were in a boat with their father Zebedee, preparing their nets. Jesus called them, ²²and immediately they left the boat and their father and followed him.

JESUS HEALS THE SICK

²³Jesus went throughout Galilee, teaching in their synagogues, proclaiming the good news of the kingdom, and healing every disease and sickness among the people. ²⁴News about him spread all over Syria, and people brought to him all who were ill with various diseases, those suffering severe pain, the demon-possessed, those having seizures, and the paralyzed; and he healed them. ²⁵Large crowds from Galilee,

---

ᵃ 6 Psalm 91:11,12   ᵇ 7 Deut. 6:16   ᶜ 10 Deut. 6:13   ᵈ 16 Isaiah 9:1,2

Why did the Spirit lead Jesus to be tempted by the devil? (4:1)
At the beginning of his ministry, Jesus was tested in a way that was similar to the Israelites being tested in the desert. Jesus' mission was to remain faithful to God and to conquer Satan. He showed that he was able to carry out the task.

Where was this prophecy first spoken? (4:15–16)
This was from Isaiah 9:1–2. Matthew wanted to establish for his readers that Jesus was indeed the promised Messiah. In fact, he included more quotations from and allusions to the Old Testament than any other New Testament writer.

In what three types of ministry did Jesus engage? (4:23)
The three main areas were teaching, preaching, and healing. The synagogues provided a place for him to teach on the Sabbath. During the week, he preached to larger crowds in the open.

the Decapolis,[a] Jerusalem, Judea and the region across the Jordan followed him.

INTRODUCTION TO THE SERMON ON THE MOUNT

5 Now when Jesus saw the crowds, he went up on a mountainside and sat down. His disciples came to him, [2]and he began to teach them.

THE BEATITUDES

He said:

[3]"Blessed are the poor in spirit,
    for theirs is the kingdom of heaven.
[4]Blessed are those who mourn,
    for they will be comforted.
[5]Blessed are the meek,
    for they will inherit the earth.
[6]Blessed are those who hunger and thirst for
        righteousness,
    for they will be filled.
[7]Blessed are the merciful,
    for they will be shown mercy.
[8]Blessed are the pure in heart,
    for they will see God.
[9]Blessed are the peacemakers,
    for they will be called children of God.
[10]Blessed are those who are persecuted because of
        righteousness,
    for theirs is the kingdom of heaven.

[11]"Blessed are you when people insult you, persecute you and falsely say all kinds of evil against you because of me. [12]Rejoice and be glad, because great is your reward in heaven, for in the same way they persecuted the prophets who were before you.

SALT AND LIGHT

[13]"You are the salt of the earth. But if the salt loses its saltiness, how can it be made salty again? It is no longer good for anything, except to be thrown out and trampled underfoot.

[14]"You are the light of the world. A town built on a hill cannot be hidden. [15]Neither do people light a lamp and put it under a bowl. Instead they put it on its stand, and it gives light to everyone in the house. [16]In the same way, let your light shine before others, that they may see your good deeds and glorify your Father in heaven.

THE FULFILLMENT OF THE LAW

[17]"Do not think that I have come to abolish the Law or the Prophets; I have not come to abolish them but to fulfill them. [18]For truly I tell you, until heaven and earth disappear, not the smallest letter, not the least stroke of a pen, will by any means disappear from the Law until everything is accomplished. [19]Therefore anyone who sets aside one of

[a] 25 That is, the Ten Cities

What does the word beatitude mean? (5:2-12)
The word means either the joys of heaven or a declaration of blessedness, especially by Christ. *Blessed* means much more than *happy*. It refers to the ultimate well-being and joy of those who share in the salvation of the kingdom of God.

What was salt used for? (5:13)
Salt was used for flavoring and preserving. Most of the salt used in Israel came from the Dead Sea and was filled with impurities. This caused it to lose some of its flavor.

What was Jesus' attitude toward the Law? (5:18)
Jesus did not come to get rid of the Law. However, he warned against trying to keep every commandment simply in order to win favor with God. Jesus contradicted the teaching of the Pharisees that salvation can come through keeping the Law. Instead, righteousness comes through faith in Jesus and his work.

the least of these commands and teaches others accordingly will be called least in the kingdom of heaven, but whoever practices and teaches these commands will be called great in the kingdom of heaven. [20] For I tell you that unless your righteousness surpasses that of the Pharisees and the teachers of the law, you will certainly not enter the kingdom of heaven.

MURDER

[21] "You have heard that it was said to the people long ago, 'You shall not murder,[a] and anyone who murders will be subject to judgment.' [22] But I tell you that anyone who is angry with a brother or sister[b,c] will be subject to judgment. Again, anyone who says to a brother or sister, 'Raca,'[d] is answerable to the court. And anyone who says, 'You fool!' will be in danger of the fire of hell.

[23] "Therefore, if you are offering your gift at the altar and there remember that your brother or sister has something against you, [24] leave your gift there in front of the altar. First go and be reconciled to them; then come and offer your gift.

[25] "Settle matters quickly with your adversary who is taking you to court. Do it while you are still together on the way, or your adversary may hand you over to the judge, and the judge may hand you over to the officer, and you may be thrown into prison. [26] Truly I tell you, you will not get out until you have paid the last penny.

ADULTERY

[27] "You have heard that it was said, 'You shall not commit adultery.'[e] [28] But I tell you that anyone who looks at a woman lustfully has already committed adultery with her in his heart. [29] If your right eye causes you to stumble, gouge it out and throw it away. It is better for you to lose one part of your body than for your whole body to be thrown into hell. [30] And if your right hand causes you to stumble, cut it off and throw it away. It is better for you to lose one part of your body than for your whole body to go into hell.

DIVORCE

[31] "It has been said, 'Anyone who divorces his wife must give her a certificate of divorce.'[f] [32] But I tell you that anyone who divorces his wife, except for sexual immorality, makes her the victim of adultery, and anyone who marries a divorced woman commits adultery.

OATHS

[33] "Again, you have heard that it was said to the people long ago, 'Do not break your oath, but fulfill to the Lord the vows you have made.' [34] But I tell you, do not swear an oath at all: either by heaven, for it is God's throne; [35] or by the earth, for it is his footstool; or by Jerusalem, for it is the city of the Great King. [36] And do not swear by your head, for you

[a] 21 Exodus 20:13   [b] 22 The Greek word for *brother or sister* (*adelphos*) refers here to a fellow disciple, whether man or woman; also in verse 23. [c] 22 Some manuscripts *brother or sister without cause*   [d] 22 An Aramaic term of contempt   [e] 27 Exodus 20:14   [f] 31 Deut. 24:1

How did Jesus extend the meaning of the commandment against murder? (5:21–22)
Jesus said that the commandment meant more than not killing another person, because if that were all it took to keep the commandment, most people would be able to obey it perfectly. Instead, he said it also meant not having a hateful attitude toward another person.

What did Jesus teach about adultery? (5:27–30)
Again Jesus emphasized that a person's heart (thoughts and intentions) could be sinful even if his or her actions were not.

Is divorce always wrong? (5:31–32)
Jesus was not creating a new law about marriage or divorce but was referring to the Old Testament law in Deuteronomy 24:1-4. At this time, women had little legal protection. Jesus stressed the value of marriage and criticized a casual attitude toward divorce. Divorce is permissible in the case of unfaithfulness or adultery. Paul also suggests in 1 Corinthians 7:15 that when an unbelieving spouse deserts a believer, the believer is "not bound."

cannot make even one hair white or black. [37] All you need to say is simply 'Yes' or 'No'; anything beyond this comes from the evil one.[a]

EYE FOR EYE

[38] "You have heard that it was said, 'Eye for eye, and tooth for tooth.'[b] [39] But I tell you, do not resist an evil person. If anyone slaps you on the right cheek, turn to them the other cheek also. [40] And if anyone wants to sue you and take your shirt, hand over your coat as well. [41] If anyone forces you to go one mile, go with them two miles. [42] Give to the one who asks you, and do not turn away from the one who wants to borrow from you.

LOVE FOR ENEMIES

[43] "You have heard that it was said, 'Love your neighbor[c] and hate your enemy.' [44] But I tell you, love your enemies and pray for those who persecute you, [45] that you may be children of your Father in heaven. He causes his sun to rise on the evil and the good, and sends rain on the righteous and the unrighteous. [46] If you love those who love you, what reward will you get? Are not even the tax collectors doing that? [47] And if you greet only your own people, what are you doing more than others? Do not even pagans do that? [48] Be perfect, therefore, as your heavenly Father is perfect.

GIVING TO THE NEEDY

6 "Be careful not to practice your righteousness in front of others to be seen by them. If you do, you will have no reward from your Father in heaven.

[2] "So when you give to the needy, do not announce it with trumpets, as the hypocrites do in the synagogues and on the streets, to be honored by others. Truly I tell you, they have received their reward in full. [3] But when you give to the needy, do not let your left hand know what your right hand is doing, [4] so that your giving may be in secret. Then your Father, who sees what is done in secret, will reward you.

PRAYER

[5] "And when you pray, do not be like the hypocrites, for they love to pray standing in the synagogues and on the street corners to be seen by others. Truly I tell you, they have received their reward in full. [6] But when you pray, go into your room, close the door and pray to your Father, who is unseen. Then your Father, who sees what is done in secret, will reward you. [7] And when you pray, do not keep on babbling like pagans, for they think they will be heard because of their many words. [8] Do not be like them, for your Father knows what you need before you ask him.

[9] "This, then, is how you should pray:

"'Our Father in heaven,
hallowed be your name,

Did the Law anywhere command hatred for one's enemy? (5:43)
No, but hatred of one's enemies was an accepted part of the Jewish value system at that time. Jesus taught his followers that we are to hate the sin, not the sinner.

What did it mean to not let your left hand know what your right hand is doing? (6:3)
Jesus was emphasizing that people should not call attention to themselves when they give.

How often did pious Jews pray? (6:5)
Pious Jews prayed publicly at set times, usually morning, afternoon, and evening.

How did the pagans babble? (6:7)
They had long lists of gods that they would mention in their prayers, hoping that the correct god would hear and help them. Jesus wanted people to pray only to the one true God.

---

[a] 37 Or *from evil*　　[b] 38 Exodus 21:24; Lev. 24:20; Deut. 19:21
[c] 43 Lev. 19:18

¹⁰your kingdom come,
   your will be done,
      on earth as it is in heaven.
¹¹Give us today our daily bread.
¹²And forgive us our debts,
   as we also have forgiven our debtors.
¹³And lead us not into temptation,ᵃ
   but deliver us from the evil one.ᵇ

¹⁴For if you forgive other people when they sin against you, your heavenly Father will also forgive you. ¹⁵But if you do not forgive others their sins, your Father will not forgive your sins.

FASTING

¹⁶"When you fast, do not look somber as the hypocrites do, for they disfigure their faces to show others they are fasting. Truly I tell you, they have received their reward in full. ¹⁷But when you fast, put oil on your head and wash your face, ¹⁸so that it will not be obvious to others that you are fasting, but only to your Father, who is unseen; and your Father, who sees what is done in secret, will reward you.

TREASURES IN HEAVEN

¹⁹"Do not store up for yourselves treasures on earth, where moths and vermin destroy, and where thieves break in and steal. ²⁰But store up for yourselves treasures in heaven, where moths and vermin do not destroy, and where thieves do not break in and steal. ²¹For where your treasure is, there your heart will be also.

²²"The eye is the lamp of the body. If your eyes are healthy,ᶜ your whole body will be full of light. ²³But if your eyes are unhealthy,ᵈ your whole body will be full of darkness. If then the light within you is darkness, how great is that darkness!

²⁴"No one can serve two masters. Either you will hate the one and love the other, or you will be devoted to the one and despise the other. You cannot serve both God and money.

ᵃ *13* The Greek for *temptation* can also mean *testing.* ᵇ *13* Or *from evil*; some late manuscripts *one,* / *for yours is the kingdom and the power and the glory forever. Amen.* ᶜ *22* The Greek for *healthy* here implies *generous.* ᵈ *23* The Greek for *unhealthy* here implies *stingy.*

Where is the "ending" to the Lord's Prayer? (6:13)
Some late manuscripts add "for yours is the kingdom and the power and the glory forever. Amen." It is included in the footnote below.

How does the Lord's Prayer help us pray?   MATTHEW 6

Most Christians pray the Lord's Prayer (which also appears in Luke 11:2 – 4) because it is the prayer that Jesus taught his followers. The prayer gives Christians a model to follow when they pray to God. "Our Father in heaven" shows that God is our Father and we are his children; we may speak to him directly without going through anyone else. "Hallowed be your name" reminds us that God is holy and that we should give him our praise and honor. "Your kingdom come, your will be done" is a reminder that we should not just ask for what we want but that we should seek God's will for our lives and should be willing to accept his plan. "Give us today our daily bread" asks God to take care of all our needs and reminds us that he is the one we should trust. "Forgive us our debts" is a way of asking God to forgive our sins through Jesus Christ. "Lead us not into temptation, but deliver us from the evil one" reminds us that by ourselves we are not strong enough to keep from sinning, but God can give us strength to avoid temptation.

Is it wrong to worry? (6:25)
This is not a commandment but a promise that God loves his people and will take care of them. Jesus reminds us that worrying does not help us; instead we should rely on God because he knows all our needs.

DO NOT WORRY

25 "Therefore I tell you, do not worry about your life, what you will eat or drink; or about your body, what you will wear. Is not life more than food, and the body more than clothes? 26 Look at the birds of the air; they do not sow or reap or store away in barns, and yet your heavenly Father feeds them. Are you not much more valuable than they? 27 Can any one of you by worrying add a single hour to your life*?

28 "And why do you worry about clothes? See how the flowers of the field grow. They do not labor or spin. 29 Yet I tell you that not even Solomon in all his splendor was dressed like one of these. 30 If that is how God clothes the grass of the field, which is here today and tomorrow is thrown into the fire, will he not much more clothe you— you of little faith? 31 So do not worry, saying, 'What shall we eat?' or 'What shall we drink?' or 'What shall we wear?' 32 For the pagans run after all these things, and your heavenly Father knows that you need them. 33 But seek first his kingdom and his righteousness, and all these things will be given to you as well. 34 Therefore do not worry about tomorrow, for tomorrow will worry about itself. Each day has enough trouble of its own.

JUDGING OTHERS

7 "Do not judge, or you too will be judged. 2 For in the same way you judge others, you will be judged, and with the measure you use, it will be measured to you.

3 "Why do you look at the speck of sawdust in your brother's eye and pay no attention to the plank in your own eye? 4 How can you say to your brother, 'Let me take the speck out of your eye,' when all the time there is a plank in your own eye? 5 You hypocrite, first take the plank out of your own eye, and then you will see clearly to remove the speck from your brother's eye.

What did Jesus mean by a plank in one's eye? (7:3)
This was an example of exaggeration (sometimes called hyperbole) to make a point dramatically so that people listening to the message would remember it.

6 "Do not give dogs what is sacred; do not throw your pearls to pigs. If you do, they may trample them under their feet, and turn and tear you to pieces.

ASK, SEEK, KNOCK

7 "Ask and it will be given to you; seek and you will find; knock and the door will be opened to you. 8 For everyone who asks receives; the one who seeks finds; and to the one who knocks, the door will be opened.

9 "Which of you, if your son asks for bread, will give him a stone? 10 Or if he asks for a fish, will give him a snake? 11 If you, then, though you are evil, know how to give good gifts to your children, how much more will your Father in heaven give good gifts to those who ask him! 12 So in everything, do to others what you would have them do to you, for this sums up the Law and the Prophets.

Did Jesus promise that we would get everything we pray for? (7:7–8)
No. Jesus promised that the Holy Spirit will help guide us so that we will receive what we need, not necessarily what we want.

THE NARROW AND WIDE GATES

13 "Enter through the narrow gate. For wide is the gate and broad is the road that leads to destruction, and many enter

a 27 Or single cubit to your height

through it. [14]But small is the gate and narrow the road that leads to life, and only a few find it.

TRUE AND FALSE PROPHETS

[15]"Watch out for false prophets. They come to you in sheep's clothing, but inwardly they are ferocious wolves. [16]By their fruit you will recognize them. Do people pick grapes from thornbushes, or figs from thistles? [17]Likewise, every good tree bears good fruit, but a bad tree bears bad fruit. [18]A good tree cannot bear bad fruit, and a bad tree cannot bear good fruit. [19]Every tree that does not bear good fruit is cut down and thrown into the fire. [20]Thus, by their fruit you will recognize them.

TRUE AND FALSE DISCIPLES

[21]"Not everyone who says to me, 'Lord, Lord,' will enter the kingdom of heaven, but only the one who does the will of my Father who is in heaven. [22]Many will say to me on that day, 'Lord, Lord, did we not prophesy in your name and in your name drive out demons and in your name perform many miracles?' [23]Then I will tell them plainly, 'I never knew you. Away from me, you evildoers!'

THE WISE AND FOOLISH BUILDERS

[24]"Therefore everyone who hears these words of mine and puts them into practice is like a wise man who built his house on the rock. [25]The rain came down, the streams rose, and the winds blew and beat against that house; yet it did not fall, because it had its foundation on the rock. [26]But everyone who hears these words of mine and does not put them into practice is like a foolish man who built his house on sand. [27]The rain came down, the streams rose, and the winds blew and beat against that house, and it fell with a great crash."

[28]When Jesus had finished saying these things, the crowds were amazed at his teaching, [29]because he taught as one who had authority, and not as their teachers of the law.

JESUS HEALS A MAN WITH LEPROSY

8 When Jesus came down from the mountainside, large crowds followed him. [2]A man with leprosy[a] came and knelt before him and said, "Lord, if you are willing, you can make me clean."

[3]Jesus reached out his hand and touched the man. "I am willing," he said. "Be clean!" Immediately he was cleansed of his leprosy. [4]Then Jesus said to him, "See that you don't tell anyone. But go, show yourself to the priest and offer the gift Moses commanded, as a testimony to them."

THE FAITH OF THE CENTURION

[5]When Jesus had entered Capernaum, a centurion came to him, asking for help. [6]"Lord," he said, "my servant lies at home paralyzed, suffering terribly."

[a] 2 The Greek word traditionally translated *leprosy* was used for various diseases affecting the skin.

What did it mean that people could recognize false prophets based on their fruit? (7:20)
In order to decide whether or not someone is speaking God's truth, it is important to look at how they live their lives and whether their behavior is godly.

How did the geography around the Sea of Galilee influence this parable? (7:24–27)
The sand around the Sea of Galilee was rock hard during the summer. But a wise builder would dig down 10 feet (3 meters) to bedrock to ensure that the foundations of a house could withstand the winter rains, which caused much flooding.

What was a centurion? (8:5)
A centurion was a Roman military officer in charge of a group of soldiers that could range in number from 60 to 160 but was typically 80.

[7]Jesus said to him, "Shall I come and heal him?"

[8]The centurion replied, "Lord, I do not deserve to have you come under my roof. But just say the word, and my servant will be healed. [9]For I myself am a man under authority, with soldiers under me. I tell this one, 'Go,' and he goes; and that one, 'Come,' and he comes. I say to my servant, 'Do this,' and he does it."

[10]When Jesus heard this, he was amazed and said to those following him, "Truly I tell you, I have not found anyone in Israel with such great faith. [11]I say to you that many will come from the east and the west, and will take their places at the feast with Abraham, Isaac and Jacob in the kingdom of heaven. [12]But the subjects of the kingdom will be thrown outside, into the darkness, where there will be weeping and gnashing of teeth."

[13]Then Jesus said to the centurion, "Go! Let it be done just as you believed it would." And his servant was healed at that moment.

JESUS HEALS MANY

[14]When Jesus came into Peter's house, he saw Peter's mother-in-law lying in bed with a fever. [15]He touched her hand and the fever left her, and she got up and began to wait on him.

[16]When evening came, many who were demon-possessed were brought to him, and he drove out the spirits with a word and healed all the sick. [17]This was to fulfill what was spoken through the prophet Isaiah:

"He took up our infirmities
    and bore our diseases."[a]

THE COST OF FOLLOWING JESUS

[18]When Jesus saw the crowd around him, he gave orders to cross to the other side of the lake. [19]Then a teacher of the law came to him and said, "Teacher, I will follow you wherever you go."

[20]Jesus replied, "Foxes have dens and birds have nests, but the Son of Man has no place to lay his head."

[21]Another disciple said to him, "Lord, first let me go and bury my father."

[22]But Jesus told him, "Follow me, and let the dead bury their own dead."

JESUS CALMS THE STORM

[23]Then he got into the boat and his disciples followed him. [24]Suddenly a furious storm came up on the lake, so that the waves swept over the boat. But Jesus was sleeping. [25]The disciples went and woke him, saying, "Lord, save us! We're going to drown!"

[26]He replied, "You of little faith, why are you so afraid?" Then he got up and rebuked the winds and the waves, and it was completely calm.

[27]The men were amazed and asked, "What kind of man is this? Even the winds and the waves obey him!"

[a] 17 Isaiah 53:4 (see Septuagint)

What did it mean to gnash one's teeth? (8:12)
In the Old Testament, this expression represented rage, anger, or hatred. In the New Testament, the phrase represented disappointment or agony of spirit.

What did Jesus mean by saying, "let the dead bury their own dead"? (8:22)
In effect, Jesus was saying that those who were spiritually dead could bury the physically dead. Even though the Jews placed great importance on the obligation of children to bury their parents, Jesus said that those who followed him would have to make sacrifices.

JESUS RESTORES TWO DEMON-POSSESSED MEN

[28] When he arrived at the other side in the region of the Gadarenes,[a] two demon-possessed men coming from the tombs met him. They were so violent that no one could pass that way. [29] "What do you want with us, Son of God?" they shouted. "Have you come here to torture us before the appointed time?"

[30] Some distance from them a large herd of pigs was feeding. [31] The demons begged Jesus, "If you drive us out, send us into the herd of pigs."

[32] He said to them, "Go!" So they came out and went into the pigs, and the whole herd rushed down the steep bank into the lake and died in the water. [33] Those tending the pigs ran off, went into the town and reported all this, including what had happened to the demon-possessed men. [34] Then the whole town went out to meet Jesus. And when they saw him, they pleaded with him to leave their region.

Did Jews raise pigs? (8:30)
Normally Jews did not raise pigs because they were considered the most "unclean" of all animals. But large numbers of Gentiles lived in Galilee, so these pigs probably were the property of a Gentile.

JESUS FORGIVES AND HEALS A PARALYZED MAN

9 Jesus stepped into a boat, crossed over and came to his own town. [2] Some men brought to him a paralyzed man, lying on a mat. When Jesus saw their faith, he said to the man, "Take heart, son; your sins are forgiven."

[3] At this, some of the teachers of the law said to themselves, "This fellow is blaspheming!"

[4] Knowing their thoughts, Jesus said, "Why do you entertain evil thoughts in your hearts? [5] Which is easier: to say, 'Your sins are forgiven,' or to say, 'Get up and walk'? [6] But I want you to know that the Son of Man has authority on earth to forgive sins." So he said to the paralyzed man, "Get up, take your mat and go home." [7] Then the man got up and went home. [8] When the crowd saw this, they were filled with awe; and they praised God, who had given such authority to man.

What was his "own town"? (9:1)
This was Capernaum, which had become a sizable town by this time. Peter's house in that town was a base of operations for Jesus' ministry in Galilee.

THE CALLING OF MATTHEW

[9] As Jesus went on from there, he saw a man named Matthew sitting at the tax collector's booth. "Follow me," he told him, and Matthew got up and followed him.

[10] While Jesus was having dinner at Matthew's house, many tax collectors and sinners came and ate with him and his disciples. [11] When the Pharisees saw this, they asked his disciples, "Why does your teacher eat with tax collectors and sinners?"

[12] On hearing this, Jesus said, "It is not the healthy who need a doctor, but the sick. [13] But go and learn what this means: 'I desire mercy, not sacrifice.'[b] For I have not come to call the righteous, but sinners."

JESUS QUESTIONED ABOUT FASTING

[14] Then John's disciples came and asked him, "How is it that we and the Pharisees fast often, but your disciples do not fast?"

---

[a] 28 Some manuscripts *Gergesenes*; other manuscripts *Gerasenes*
[b] 13 Hosea 6:6

What were wineskins like? (9:17)
In ancient times, goatskins were used to hold wine. As the fresh grape juice fermented, the wine would expand and stretch a new wineskin. But old wineskins that were already stretched would burst.

What was wrong with the woman who had been hemorrhaging for 12 years? (9:20)
Her precise medical condition isn't known, but she would have been considered ritually unclean and so would have been excluded from social and religious activities.

Who were these pipe players? (9:23)
At ancient Middle Eastern funerals, musicians were often hired to play music. Professional mourners were also hired to add their voices to the expressions of grief.

What did Jesus mean by saying that she was only asleep? (9:24)
He meant that she was not permanently dead.

¹⁵Jesus answered, "How can the guests of the bridegroom mourn while he is with them? The time will come when the bridegroom will be taken from them; then they will fast.

¹⁶"No one sews a patch of unshrunk cloth on an old garment, for the patch will pull away from the garment, making the tear worse. ¹⁷Neither do people pour new wine into old wineskins. If they do, the skins will burst; the wine will run out and the wineskins will be ruined. No, they pour new wine into new wineskins, and both are preserved."

JESUS RAISES A DEAD GIRL AND HEALS A SICK WOMAN

¹⁸While he was saying this, a synagogue leader came and knelt before him and said, "My daughter has just died. But come and put your hand on her, and she will live." ¹⁹Jesus got up and went with him, and so did his disciples.

²⁰Just then a woman who had been subject to bleeding for twelve years came up behind him and touched the edge of his cloak. ²¹She said to herself, "If I only touch his cloak, I will be healed."

²²Jesus turned and saw her. "Take heart, daughter," he said, "your faith has healed you." And the woman was healed at that moment.

²³When Jesus entered the synagogue leader's house and saw the noisy crowd and people playing pipes, ²⁴he said, "Go away. The girl is not dead but asleep." But they laughed at him. ²⁵After the crowd had been put outside, he went in and took the girl by the hand, and she got up. ²⁶News of this spread through all that region.

JESUS HEALS THE BLIND AND THE MUTE

²⁷As Jesus went on from there, two blind men followed him, calling out, "Have mercy on us, Son of David!"

²⁸When he had gone indoors, the blind men came to him, and he asked them, "Do you believe that I am able to do this?"

"Yes, Lord," they replied.

²⁹Then he touched their eyes and said, "According to your faith let it be done to you"; ³⁰and their sight was restored. Jesus warned them sternly, "See that no one knows about this." ³¹But they went out and spread the news about him all over that region.

³²While they were going out, a man who was demon-possessed and could not talk was brought to Jesus. ³³And when the demon was driven out, the man who had been mute spoke. The crowd was amazed and said, "Nothing like this has ever been seen in Israel."

³⁴But the Pharisees said, "It is by the prince of demons that he drives out demons."

THE WORKERS ARE FEW

³⁵Jesus went through all the towns and villages, teaching in their synagogues, proclaiming the good news of the kingdom and healing every disease and sickness. ³⁶When he saw the crowds, he had compassion on them, because they

were harassed and helpless, like sheep without a shepherd. [37] Then he said to his disciples, "The harvest is plentiful but the workers are few. [38] Ask the Lord of the harvest, therefore, to send out workers into his harvest field."

JESUS SENDS OUT THE TWELVE

10 Jesus called his twelve disciples to him and gave them authority to drive out impure spirits and to heal every disease and sickness.

[2] These are the names of the twelve apostles: first, Simon (who is called Peter) and his brother Andrew; James son of Zebedee, and his brother John; [3] Philip and Bartholomew; Thomas and Matthew the tax collector; James son of Alphaeus, and Thaddaeus; [4] Simon the Zealot and Judas Iscariot, who betrayed him.

[5] These twelve Jesus sent out with the following instructions: "Do not go among the Gentiles or enter any town of the Samaritans. [6] Go rather to the lost sheep of Israel. [7] As you go, proclaim this message: 'The kingdom of heaven has come near.' [8] Heal the sick, raise the dead, cleanse those who have leprosy,[a] drive out demons. Freely you have received; freely give.

[9] "Do not get any gold or silver or copper to take with you in your belts— [10] no bag for the journey or extra shirt or sandals or a staff, for the worker is worth his keep. [11] Whatever town or village you enter, search there for some worthy person and stay at their house until you leave. [12] As you enter the home, give it your greeting. [13] If the home is deserving, let your peace rest on it; if it is not, let your peace return to you. [14] If anyone will not welcome you or listen to your words, leave that home or town and shake the dust off your feet. [15] Truly I tell you, it will be more bearable for Sodom and Gomorrah on the day of judgment than for that town.

[16] "I am sending you out like sheep among wolves. Therefore be as shrewd as snakes and as innocent as doves. [17] Be on your guard; you will be handed over to the local councils and be flogged in the synagogues. [18] On my account you will be brought before governors and kings as witnesses to them and to the Gentiles. [19] But when they arrest you, do not worry about what to say or how to say it. At that time you will be given what to say, [20] for it will not be you speaking, but the Spirit of your Father speaking through you.

[21] "Brother will betray brother to death, and a father his child; children will rebel against their parents and have them put to death. [22] You will be hated by everyone because of me, but the one who stands firm to the end will be saved. [23] When you are persecuted in one place, flee to another. Truly I tell you, you will not finish going through the towns of Israel before the Son of Man comes.

[24] "The student is not above the teacher, nor a servant above his master. [25] It is enough for students to be like their teachers, and servants like their masters. If the head of the house has been called Beelzebul, how much more the members of his household!

---

[a] 8 The Greek word traditionally translated *leprosy* was used for various diseases affecting the skin.

Why was Simon called "the Zealot"? (10:4)
The term referred either to his religious zeal or to his membership in the party of the Zealots, a Jewish revolutionary group that was violently opposed to Roman rule in Israel.

Why did Jesus tell his disciples not to go to the Gentiles or Samaritans? (10:5)
The good news about the kingdom was to be preached at first to the Jews only. Then the Jews were to spread the good news to everyone else.

Who were the Samaritans? (10:5)
This was a race of people resulting from the intermarriage of Israelites, who were left behind when the people of the northern kingdom were exiled, and Gentiles who were brought into the land by the Assyrians. In Jesus' day, there was bitter hostility between the Jews and the Samaritans.

What did it mean for the disciples to shake the dust off their feet? (10:14)
This was the symbolic act the Pharisees did when they left a ceremonially unclean Gentile area. Here it represented a solemn warning to those who rejected God's message.

Who was Beelzebul? (10:25)
This name refers to Satan (see 12:24).

²⁶"So do not be afraid of them, for there is nothing concealed that will not be disclosed, or hidden that will not be made known. ²⁷What I tell you in the dark, speak in the daylight; what is whispered in your ear, proclaim from the roofs. ²⁸Do not be afraid of those who kill the body but cannot kill the soul. Rather, be afraid of the One who can destroy both soul and body in hell. ²⁹Are not two sparrows sold for a penny? Yet not one of them will fall to the ground outside your Father's care.^a ³⁰And even the very hairs of your head are all numbered. ³¹So don't be afraid; you are worth more than many sparrows.

³²"Whoever acknowledges me before others, I will also acknowledge before my Father in heaven. ³³But whoever disowns me before others, I will disown before my Father in heaven.

³⁴"Do not suppose that I have come to bring peace to the earth. I did not come to bring peace, but a sword. ³⁵For I have come to turn

> "'a man against his father,
>   a daughter against her mother,
>   a daughter-in-law against her mother-in-law—
> ³⁶   a man's enemies will be the members of his own
>   household.'^b

³⁷"Anyone who loves their father or mother more than me is not worthy of me; anyone who loves their son or daughter more than me is not worthy of me. ³⁸Whoever does not take up their cross and follow me is not worthy of me. ³⁹Whoever finds their life will lose it, and whoever loses their life for my sake will find it.

⁴⁰"Anyone who welcomes you welcomes me, and anyone who welcomes me welcomes the one who sent me. ⁴¹Whoever welcomes a prophet as a prophet will receive a prophet's reward, and whoever welcomes a righteous person as a righteous person will receive a righteous person's reward. ⁴²And if anyone gives even a cup of cold water to one of these little ones who is my disciple, truly I tell you, that person will certainly not lose their reward."

JESUS AND JOHN THE BAPTIST

11 After Jesus had finished instructing his twelve disciples, he went on from there to teach and preach in the towns of Galilee.^c

²When John, who was in prison, heard about the deeds of the Messiah, he sent his disciples ³to ask him, "Are you the one who is to come, or should we expect someone else?"

⁴Jesus replied, "Go back and report to John what you hear and see: ⁵The blind receive sight, the lame walk, those who have leprosy^d are cleansed, the deaf hear, the dead are raised, and the good news is proclaimed to the poor. ⁶Blessed is anyone who does not stumble on account of me."

⁷As John's disciples were leaving, Jesus began to speak to

---

^a 29 Or *will*; or *knowledge*   ^b 36 Micah 7:6   ^c 1 Greek *in their towns*
^d 5 The Greek word traditionally translated *leprosy* was used for various diseases affecting the skin.

the crowd about John: "What did you go out into the wilderness to see? A reed swayed by the wind? [8]If not, what did you go out to see? A man dressed in fine clothes? No, those who wear fine clothes are in kings' palaces. [9]Then what did you go out to see? A prophet? Yes, I tell you, and more than a prophet. [10]This is the one about whom it is written:

> "'I will send my messenger ahead of you,
>   who will prepare your way before you.'[a]

[11]Truly I tell you, among those born of women there has not risen anyone greater than John the Baptist; yet whoever is least in the kingdom of heaven is greater than he. [12]From the days of John the Baptist until now, the kingdom of heaven has been subjected to violence,[b] and violent people have been raiding it. [13]For all the Prophets and the Law prophesied until John. [14]And if you are willing to accept it, he is the Elijah who was to come. [15]Whoever has ears, let them hear.

[16]"To what can I compare this generation? They are like children sitting in the marketplaces and calling out to others:

> [17]"'We played the pipe for you,
>   and you did not dance;
> we sang a dirge,
>   and you did not mourn.'

[18]For John came neither eating nor drinking, and they say, 'He has a demon.' [19]The Son of Man came eating and drinking, and they say, 'Here is a glutton and a drunkard, a friend of tax collectors and sinners.' But wisdom is proved right by her deeds."

WOE ON UNREPENTANT TOWNS

[20]Then Jesus began to denounce the towns in which most of his miracles had been performed, because they did not repent. [21]"Woe to you, Chorazin! Woe to you, Bethsaida! For if the miracles that were performed in you had been performed in Tyre and Sidon, they would have repented long ago in sackcloth and ashes. [22]But I tell you, it will be more bearable for Tyre and Sidon on the day of judgment than for you. [23]And you, Capernaum, will you be lifted to the heavens? No, you will go down to Hades.[c] For if the miracles that were performed in you had been performed in Sodom, it would have remained to this day. [24]But I tell you that it will be more bearable for Sodom on the day of judgment than for you."

THE FATHER REVEALED IN THE SON

[25]At that time Jesus said, "I praise you, Father, Lord of heaven and earth, because you have hidden these things from the wise and learned, and revealed them to little children. [26]Yes, Father, for this is what you were pleased to do.

[27]"All things have been committed to me by my Father. No one knows the Son except the Father, and no one knows the Father except the Son and those to whom the Son chooses to reveal him.

Why did Jesus refer to John the Baptist as Elijah? (11:14)
This was a reference to Malachi 4:5, which prophesied the reappearance of Elijah before the day of the Lord. John was not literally Elijah, but he did fulfill the role of the prophet. John fulfilled the prophecy.

How did Jesus criticize the people? (11:18–19)
He said that they refused to accept the messages brought by John the Baptist and by himself. Even though they ministered in different ways, both were criticized by the people.

[a] 10 Mal. 3:1   [b] 12 Or been forcefully advancing   [c] 23 That is, the realm of the dead

What burden had been placed on the people? (11:28)
The Pharisees had placed a burden on the people by insisting on a strict obedience to the Law, which no one could achieve perfectly.

A Yoke (11:29)

What was unlawful on the Sabbath? (12:2)
According to Jewish tradition, harvesting was unlawful on the Sabbath, and that is what the disciples technically were doing.

How did Jesus justify the disciples' actions? (12:3–8)
Jesus described some times when the Sabbath rules had been broken to accomplish a greater good. The rules for the Sabbath had become so specific and numerous that people had lost sight of the original purpose of the Sabbath, which was for humans to experience physical, mental, and spiritual restoration.

Why didn't Jesus want people to tell others who he was? (12:16)
There may have been several reasons: He did not want to be thought of as just a miracle worker; he may not have wanted his teaching ministry to be overshadowed by the healing miracles; he didn't want the authorities to arrest him before his ministry was accomplished; or possibly he didn't want the crowds to grow even larger and make it more difficult for him and the disciples to move from place to place.

28 "Come to me, all you who are weary and burdened, and I will give you rest. 29 Take my yoke upon you and learn from me, for I am gentle and humble in heart, and you will find rest for your souls. 30 For my yoke is easy and my burden is light."

JESUS IS LORD OF THE SABBATH

12 At that time Jesus went through the grainfields on the Sabbath. His disciples were hungry and began to pick some heads of grain and eat them. 2 When the Pharisees saw this, they said to him, "Look! Your disciples are doing what is unlawful on the Sabbath."

3 He answered, "Haven't you read what David did when he and his companions were hungry? 4 He entered the house of God, and he and his companions ate the consecrated bread—which was not lawful for them to do, but only for the priests. 5 Or haven't you read in the Law that the priests on Sabbath duty in the temple desecrate the Sabbath and yet are innocent? 6 I tell you that something greater than the temple is here. 7 If you had known what these words mean, 'I desire mercy, not sacrifice,'[a] you would not have condemned the innocent. 8 For the Son of Man is Lord of the Sabbath."

9 Going on from that place, he went into their synagogue, 10 and a man with a shriveled hand was there. Looking for a reason to bring charges against Jesus, they asked him, "Is it lawful to heal on the Sabbath?"

11 He said to them, "If any of you has a sheep and it falls into a pit on the Sabbath, will you not take hold of it and lift it out? 12 How much more valuable is a person than a sheep! Therefore it is lawful to do good on the Sabbath."

13 Then he said to the man, "Stretch out your hand." So he stretched it out and it was completely restored, just as sound as the other. 14 But the Pharisees went out and plotted how they might kill Jesus.

GOD'S CHOSEN SERVANT

15 Aware of this, Jesus withdrew from that place. A large crowd followed him, and he healed all who were ill. 16 He warned them not to tell others about him. 17 This was to fulfill what was spoken through the prophet Isaiah:

18 "Here is my servant whom I have chosen,
    the one I love, in whom I delight;
I will put my Spirit on him,
    and he will proclaim justice to the nations.
19 He will not quarrel or cry out;
    no one will hear his voice in the streets.
20 A bruised reed he will not break,
    and a smoldering wick he will not snuff out,
    till he has brought justice through to victory.
21   In his name the nations will put their hope."[b]

JESUS AND BEELZEBUL

22 Then they brought him a demon-possessed man who was blind and mute, and Jesus healed him, so that he could

---

[a] 7 Hosea 6:6   [b] 21 Isaiah 42:1-4

both talk and see. ²³All the people were astonished and said, "Could this be the Son of David?"

²⁴But when the Pharisees heard this, they said, "It is only by Beelzebul, the prince of demons, that this fellow drives out demons."

²⁵Jesus knew their thoughts and said to them, "Every kingdom divided against itself will be ruined, and every city or household divided against itself will not stand. ²⁶If Satan drives out Satan, he is divided against himself. How then can his kingdom stand? ²⁷And if I drive out demons by Beelzebul, by whom do your people drive them out? So then, they will be your judges. ²⁸But if it is by the Spirit of God that I drive out demons, then the kingdom of God has come upon you.

²⁹"Or again, how can anyone enter a strong man's house and carry off his possessions unless he first ties up the strong man? Then he can plunder his house.

³⁰"Whoever is not with me is against me, and whoever does not gather with me scatters. ³¹And so I tell you, every kind of sin and slander can be forgiven, but blasphemy against the Spirit will not be forgiven. ³²Anyone who speaks a word against the Son of Man will be forgiven, but anyone who speaks against the Holy Spirit will not be forgiven, either in this age or in the age to come.

³³"Make a tree good and its fruit will be good, or make a tree bad and its fruit will be bad, for a tree is recognized by its fruit. ³⁴You brood of vipers, how can you who are evil say anything good? For the mouth speaks what the heart is full of. ³⁵A good man brings good things out of the good stored up in him, and an evil man brings evil things out of the evil stored up in him. ³⁶But I tell you that everyone will have to give account on the day of judgment for every empty word they have spoken. ³⁷For by your words you will be acquitted, and by your words you will be condemned."

THE SIGN OF JONAH

³⁸Then some of the Pharisees and teachers of the law said to him, "Teacher, we want to see a sign from you."

³⁹He answered, "A wicked and adulterous generation asks for a sign! But none will be given it except the sign of the prophet Jonah. ⁴⁰For as Jonah was three days and three nights in the belly of a huge fish, so the Son of Man will be three days and three nights in the heart of the earth. ⁴¹The men of Nineveh will stand up at the judgment with this generation and condemn it; for they repented at the preaching of Jonah, and now something greater than Jonah is here. ⁴²The Queen of the South will rise at the judgment with this generation and condemn it; for she came from the ends of the earth to listen to Solomon's wisdom, and now something greater than Solomon is here.

⁴³"When an impure spirit comes out of a person, it goes through arid places seeking rest and does not find it. ⁴⁴Then it says, 'I will return to the house I left.' When it arrives, it finds the house unoccupied, swept clean and put in order. ⁴⁵Then it goes and takes with it seven other spirits more

What was the unpardonable sin? (12:31)
The context suggests that the sin that would not be forgiven was claiming that Jesus' miracles done in the power of the Holy Spirit were really caused by Satan. In other words, rejecting Jesus as Savior and Lord and denying the divine role of the Holy Spirit is the unpardonable sin. This is not a one-time sin but instead is an ongoing attitude of rejection and rebellion.

How was the experience of Jonah a sign? (12:39–42)
Just as Jonah had spent three days and nights in the fish and then had been spit out onto dry ground, Jesus would spend three days and nights in the grave before his resurrection.

wicked than itself, and they go in and live there. And the final condition of that person is worse than the first. That is how it will be with this wicked generation."

JESUS' MOTHER AND BROTHERS

[46] While Jesus was still talking to the crowd, his mother and brothers stood outside, wanting to speak to him. [47] Someone told him, "Your mother and brothers are standing outside, wanting to speak to you."

[48] He replied to him, "Who is my mother, and who are my brothers?" [49] Pointing to his disciples, he said, "Here are my mother and my brothers. [50] For whoever does the will of my Father in heaven is my brother and sister and mother."

THE PARABLE OF THE SOWER

13 That same day Jesus went out of the house and sat by the lake. [2] Such large crowds gathered around him that he got into a boat and sat in it, while all the people stood on the shore. [3] Then he told them many things in parables, saying: "A farmer went out to sow his seed. [4] As he was scattering the seed, some fell along the path, and the birds came and ate it up. [5] Some fell on rocky places, where it did not have much soil. It sprang up quickly, because the soil was shallow. [6] But when the sun came up, the plants were scorched, and they withered because they had no root. [7] Other seed fell among thorns, which grew up and choked the plants. [8] Still other seed fell on good soil, where it produced a crop — a hundred, sixty or thirty times what was sown. [9] Whoever has ears, let them hear."

[10] The disciples came to him and asked, "Why do you speak to the people in parables?"

[11] He replied, "Because the knowledge of the secrets of the kingdom of heaven has been given to you, but not to them. [12] Whoever has will be given more, and they will have an abundance. Whoever does not have, even what they have will be taken from them. [13] This is why I speak to them in parables:

"Though seeing, they do not see;
though hearing, they do not hear or understand.

[14] In them is fulfilled the prophecy of Isaiah:

"'You will be ever hearing but never understanding;
you will be ever seeing but never perceiving.

Why did Jesus sit in the boat? (13:2)
Rabbis usually taught from a sitting position rather than standing up.

What were parables? (13:3)
Our word "parable" comes from a Greek word that means "a placing beside." Its most common use in the New Testament is the illustrative stories that Jesus drew from nature and everyday life where he compares one thing to another. Another definition of a parable is "an earthly story with a heavenly meaning."

What were "rocky places"? (13:5)
This was not ground covered with small stones, but areas that had only a shallow amount of soil on top of solid rock.

Why did Jesus use parables when he was preaching to the people?
MATTHEW 13

The word *parable* comes from a Greek word that means "a placing beside." In other words, it is an illustration or comparison. It was common for Jewish teachers to use parables to explain religious ideas to their followers. An older definition of a parable is "an earthly story with a heavenly meaning."

Jesus used parables because people could easily remember the stories that he used because they were from everyday life. He also used parables because some of the ideas that he was trying to get across to his followers were not always easy to understand. Jesus' parables are not like puzzles that have a simple solution. Instead, they give a hint of an important truth about God and his kingdom, but they do not tell the whole story. Jesus' parables were meant to make people then and now think about their meaning rather than spell everything out.

[15] For this people's heart has become calloused;
     they hardly hear with their ears,
     and they have closed their eyes.
   Otherwise they might see with their eyes,
     hear with their ears,
     understand with their hearts
   and turn, and I would heal them.'[a]

[16] But blessed are your eyes because they see, and your ears because they hear. [17] For truly I tell you, many prophets and righteous people longed to see what you see but did not see it, and to hear what you hear but did not hear it.

[18] "Listen then to what the parable of the sower means: [19] When anyone hears the message about the kingdom and does not understand it, the evil one comes and snatches away what was sown in their heart. This is the seed sown along the path. [20] The seed falling on rocky ground refers to someone who hears the word and at once receives it with joy. [21] But since they have no root, they last only a short time. When trouble or persecution comes because of the word, they quickly fall away. [22] The seed falling among the thorns refers to someone who hears the word, but the worries of this life and the deceitfulness of wealth choke the word, making it unfruitful. [23] But the seed falling on good soil refers to someone who hears the word and understands it. This is the one who produces a crop, yielding a hundred, sixty or thirty times what was sown."

THE PARABLE OF THE WEEDS

[24] Jesus told them another parable: "The kingdom of heaven is like a man who sowed good seed in his field. [25] But while everyone was sleeping, his enemy came and sowed weeds among the wheat, and went away. [26] When the wheat sprouted and formed heads, then the weeds also appeared.

[27] "The owner's servants came to him and said, 'Sir, didn't you sow good seed in your field? Where then did the weeds come from?'

[28] "'An enemy did this,' he replied.

"The servants asked him, 'Do you want us to go and pull them up?'

[29] "'No,' he answered, 'because while you are pulling the weeds, you may uproot the wheat with them. [30] Let both grow together until the harvest. At that time I will tell the harvesters: First collect the weeds and tie them in bundles to be burned; then gather the wheat and bring it into my barn.'"

THE PARABLES OF THE MUSTARD SEED
AND THE YEAST

[31] He told them another parable: "The kingdom of heaven is like a mustard seed, which a man took and planted in his field. [32] Though it is the smallest of all seeds, yet when it grows, it is the largest of garden plants and becomes a tree, so that the birds come and perch in its branches."

[33] He told them still another parable: "The kingdom of

[a] 15 Isaiah 6:9,10 (see Septuagint)

What is a mustard seed like? (13:32)
The mustard seed is not the smallest seed known today, but it was the smallest seed used by farmers and gardeners in the Holy Land. Under favorable conditions, it could grow to ten feet (three meters) tall.

What did yeast symbolize?
(13:33)
In the Bible, yeast usually
symbolized something evil that
spreads. But in this instance it is
a positive symbol of growth.

heaven is like yeast that a woman took and mixed into about
sixty pounds[a] of flour until it worked all through the dough."

³⁴Jesus spoke all these things to the crowd in parables; he
did not say anything to them without using a parable. ³⁵So
was fulfilled what was spoken through the prophet:

"I will open my mouth in parables,
     I will utter things hidden since the creation of the
          world."[b]

THE PARABLE OF THE WEEDS
EXPLAINED

³⁶Then he left the crowd and went into the house. His
disciples came to him and said, "Explain to us the parable of
the weeds in the field."

³⁷He answered, "The one who sowed the good seed is the
Son of Man. ³⁸The field is the world, and the good seed
stands for the people of the kingdom. The weeds are the
people of the evil one, ³⁹and the enemy who sows them is
the devil. The harvest is the end of the age, and the harvesters are angels.

⁴⁰"As the weeds are pulled up and burned in the fire, so
it will be at the end of the age. ⁴¹The Son of Man will send
out his angels, and they will weed out of his kingdom everything that causes sin and all who do evil. ⁴²They will throw
them into the blazing furnace, where there will be weeping
and gnashing of teeth. ⁴³Then the righteous will shine like
the sun in the kingdom of their Father. Whoever has ears,
let them hear.

THE PARABLES OF THE HIDDEN TREASURE
AND THE PEARL

What do these two parables
mean? (13:44–46)
These parables indicate that the
kingdom of heaven is so valuable
that people should be willing to
give up everything else in order
to gain it.

⁴⁴"The kingdom of heaven is like treasure hidden in a
field. When a man found it, he hid it again, and then in his
joy went and sold all he had and bought that field.

⁴⁵"Again, the kingdom of heaven is like a merchant looking for fine pearls. ⁴⁶When he found one of great value, he
went away and sold everything he had and bought it.

THE PARABLE OF THE NET

What does the parable of the
net teach? (13:47–51)
This parable teaches that there
will be a final separation of the
righteous and the wicked. The
wicked will be sent to a fiery
punishment.

⁴⁷"Once again, the kingdom of heaven is like a net that
was let down into the lake and caught all kinds of fish.
⁴⁸When it was full, the fishermen pulled it up on the shore.
Then they sat down and collected the good fish in baskets,
but threw the bad away. ⁴⁹This is how it will be at the end of
the age. The angels will come and separate the wicked from
the righteous ⁵⁰and throw them into the blazing furnace,
where there will be weeping and gnashing of teeth.

⁵¹"Have you understood all these things?" Jesus asked.

"Yes," they replied.

⁵²He said to them, "Therefore every teacher of the law
who has become a disciple in the kingdom of heaven is like
the owner of a house who brings out of his storeroom new
treasures as well as old."

---

[a] 33 Or about 27 kilograms   [b] 35 Psalm 78:2

A PROPHET WITHOUT HONOR

⁵³When Jesus had finished these parables, he moved on from there. ⁵⁴Coming to his hometown, he began teaching the people in their synagogue, and they were amazed. "Where did this man get this wisdom and these miraculous powers?" they asked. ⁵⁵"Isn't this the carpenter's son? Isn't his mother's name Mary, and aren't his brothers James, Joseph, Simon and Judas? ⁵⁶Aren't all his sisters with us? Where then did this man get all these things?" ⁵⁷And they took offense at him.

But Jesus said to them, "A prophet is not without honor except in his own town and in his own home."

⁵⁸And he did not do many miracles there because of their lack of faith.

JOHN THE BAPTIST BEHEADED

14 At that time Herod the tetrarch heard the reports about Jesus, ²and he said to his attendants, "This is John the Baptist; he has risen from the dead! That is why miraculous powers are at work in him."

³Now Herod had arrested John and bound him and put him in prison because of Herodias, his brother Philip's wife, ⁴for John had been saying to him: "It is not lawful for you to have her." ⁵Herod wanted to kill John, but he was afraid of the people, because they considered John a prophet.

⁶On Herod's birthday the daughter of Herodias danced for the guests and pleased Herod so much ⁷that he promised with an oath to give her whatever she asked. ⁸Prompted by her mother, she said, "Give me here on a platter the head of John the Baptist." ⁹The king was distressed, but because of his oaths and his dinner guests, he ordered that her request be granted ¹⁰and had John beheaded in the prison. ¹¹His head was brought in on a platter and given to the girl, who carried it to her mother. ¹²John's disciples came and took his body and buried it. Then they went and told Jesus.

JESUS FEEDS THE FIVE THOUSAND

¹³When Jesus heard what had happened, he withdrew by boat privately to a solitary place. Hearing of this, the crowds followed him on foot from the towns. ¹⁴When Jesus landed and saw a large crowd, he had compassion on them and healed their sick.

¹⁵As evening approached, the disciples came to him and said, "This is a remote place, and it's already getting late. Send the crowds away, so they can go to the villages and buy themselves some food."

¹⁶Jesus replied, "They do not need to go away. You give them something to eat."

¹⁷"We have here only five loaves of bread and two fish," they answered.

¹⁸"Bring them here to me," he said. ¹⁹And he directed the people to sit down on the grass. Taking the five loaves and the two fish and looking up to heaven, he gave thanks and broke the loaves. Then he gave them to the disciples, and the disciples gave them to the people. ²⁰They all ate and were

Who was Herod the tetrarch? (14:1)
A tetrarch was the ruler of one-fourth of a region. Herod the tetrarch (Herod Antipas) was one of several sons of Herod the Great. He ruled over Galilee and Perea from 4 B.C. to A.D. 39.

What was the size of these baskets? (14:20)
The New Testament makes reference to two kinds of baskets. The 12 baskets that were used here were relatively small and could be carried on a person's back. The larger kind of basket was big enough to hold a person. Seven of these were used to gather the leftovers from the feeding of the 4,000 (see Matthew 16:9 – 10).

satisfied, and the disciples picked up twelve basketfuls of broken pieces that were left over. ²¹The number of those who ate was about five thousand men, besides women and children.

JESUS WALKS ON THE WATER

²²Immediately Jesus made the disciples get into the boat and go on ahead of him to the other side, while he dismissed the crowd. ²³After he had dismissed them, he went up on a mountainside by himself to pray. Later that night, he was there alone, ²⁴and the boat was already a considerable distance from land, buffeted by the waves because the wind was against it.

²⁵Shortly before dawn Jesus went out to them, walking on the lake. ²⁶When the disciples saw him walking on the lake, they were terrified. "It's a ghost," they said, and cried out in fear.

²⁷But Jesus immediately said to them: "Take courage! It is I. Don't be afraid."

²⁸"Lord, if it's you," Peter replied, "tell me to come to you on the water."

²⁹"Come," he said.

Then Peter got down out of the boat, walked on the water and came toward Jesus. ³⁰But when he saw the wind, he was afraid and, beginning to sink, cried out, "Lord, save me!"

³¹Immediately Jesus reached out his hand and caught him. "You of little faith," he said, "why did you doubt?"

³²And when they climbed into the boat, the wind died down. ³³Then those who were in the boat worshiped him, saying, "Truly you are the Son of God."

³⁴When they had crossed over, they landed at Gennesaret. ³⁵And when the men of that place recognized Jesus, they sent word to all the surrounding country. People brought all their sick to him ³⁶and begged him to let the sick just touch the edge of his cloak, and all who touched it were healed.

THAT WHICH DEFILES

15 Then some Pharisees and teachers of the law came to Jesus from Jerusalem and asked, ²"Why do your disciples break the tradition of the elders? They don't wash their hands before they eat!"

³Jesus replied, "And why do you break the command of God for the sake of your tradition? ⁴For God said, 'Honor your father and mother'ᵃ and 'Anyone who curses their father or mother is to be put to death.'ᵇ ⁵But you say that if anyone declares that what might have been used to help their father or mother is 'devoted to God,' ⁶they are not to 'honor their father or mother' with it. Thus you nullify the word of God for the sake of your tradition. ⁷You hypocrites! Isaiah was right when he prophesied about you:

⁸"'These people honor me with their lips,
    but their hearts are far from me.
⁹They worship me in vain;
    their teachings are merely human rules.'ᶜ"

ᵃ 4 Exodus 20:12; Deut. 5:16   ᵇ 4 Exodus 21:17; Lev. 20:9   ᶜ 9 Isaiah 29:13

Why did Jesus have to pray? (14:23) Jesus used prayer as a way to communicate with God the Father and the Holy Spirit. He asked God for help and guidance and thanked him for his love, the same way we pray. This also provided the disciples a good example of how to pray.

What was the tradition of the elders? (15:2) After the exile, the Jewish rabbis began to make very specific rules and regulations about the daily lives of the people. These were interpretations and applications of the law of Moses handed down from generation to generation by oral tradition.

[10]Jesus called the crowd to him and said, "Listen and understand. [11]What goes into someone's mouth does not defile them, but what comes out of their mouth, that is what defiles them."

[12]Then the disciples came to him and asked, "Do you know that the Pharisees were offended when they heard this?"

[13]He replied, "Every plant that my heavenly Father has not planted will be pulled up by the roots. [14]Leave them; they are blind guides.*a* If the blind lead the blind, both will fall into a pit."

[15]Peter said, "Explain the parable to us."

[16]"Are you still so dull?" Jesus asked them. [17]"Don't you see that whatever enters the mouth goes into the stomach and then out of the body? [18]But the things that come out of a person's mouth come from the heart, and these defile them. [19]For out of the heart come evil thoughts — murder, adultery, sexual immorality, theft, false testimony, slander. [20]These are what defile a person; but eating with unwashed hands does not defile them."

THE FAITH OF A CANAANITE WOMAN

[21]Leaving that place, Jesus withdrew to the region of Tyre and Sidon. [22]A Canaanite woman from that vicinity came to him, crying out, "Lord, Son of David, have mercy on me! My daughter is demon-possessed and suffering terribly."

[23]Jesus did not answer a word. So his disciples came to him and urged him, "Send her away, for she keeps crying out after us."

[24]He answered, "I was sent only to the lost sheep of Israel."

[25]The woman came and knelt before him. "Lord, help me!" she said.

[26]He replied, "It is not right to take the children's bread and toss it to the dogs."

[27]"Yes it is, Lord," she said. "Even the dogs eat the crumbs that fall from their master's table."

[28]Then Jesus said to her, "Woman, you have great faith! Your request is granted." And her daughter was healed at that moment.

JESUS FEEDS THE FOUR THOUSAND

[29]Jesus left there and went along the Sea of Galilee. Then he went up on a mountainside and sat down. [30]Great crowds came to him, bringing the lame, the blind, the crippled, the mute and many others, and laid them at his feet; and he healed them. [31]The people were amazed when they saw the mute speaking, the crippled made well, the lame walking and the blind seeing. And they praised the God of Israel.

[32]Jesus called his disciples to him and said, "I have compassion for these people; they have already been with me three days and have nothing to eat. I do not want to send them away hungry, or they may collapse on the way."

[33]His disciples answered, "Where could we get enough bread in this remote place to feed such a crowd?"

a 14 Some manuscripts blind guides of the blind

Who were the Canaanites? (15:22)
There are many references to Canaanites in the Old Testament, but this is the only one in the New Testament. The country of Canaan no longer existed at this time, so some think this referred to the people of Phoenicia.

What did Jesus mean about not giving the children's bread to dogs? (15:26–28)
Jesus' point was that the gospel was given first to the Jews. The woman understood Jesus' reply and said that she would be willing to settle for crumbs. Jesus rewarded her for her faith.

³⁴"How many loaves do you have?" Jesus asked.

"Seven," they replied, "and a few small fish."

³⁵He told the crowd to sit down on the ground. ³⁶Then he took the seven loaves and the fish, and when he had given thanks, he broke them and gave them to the disciples, and they in turn to the people. ³⁷They all ate and were satisfied. Afterward the disciples picked up seven basketfuls of broken pieces that were left over. ³⁸The number of those who ate was four thousand men, besides women and children. ³⁹After Jesus had sent the crowd away, he got into the boat and went to the vicinity of Magadan.

THE DEMAND FOR A SIGN

16 The Pharisees and Sadducees came to Jesus and tested him by asking him to show them a sign from heaven.

²He replied, "When evening comes, you say, 'It will be fair weather, for the sky is red,' ³and in the morning, 'Today it will be stormy, for the sky is red and overcast.' You know how to interpret the appearance of the sky, but you cannot interpret the signs of the times.ᵃ ⁴A wicked and adulterous generation looks for a sign, but none will be given it except the sign of Jonah." Jesus then left them and went away.

THE YEAST OF THE PHARISEES AND SADDUCEES

⁵When they went across the lake, the disciples forgot to take bread. ⁶"Be careful," Jesus said to them. "Be on your guard against the yeast of the Pharisees and Sadducees."

⁷They discussed this among themselves and said, "It is because we didn't bring any bread."

⁸Aware of their discussion, Jesus asked, "You of little faith, why are you talking among yourselves about having no bread? ⁹Do you still not understand? Don't you remember the five loaves for the five thousand, and how many basketfuls you gathered? ¹⁰Or the seven loaves for the four thousand, and how many basketfuls you gathered? ¹¹How is it you don't understand that I was not talking to you about bread? But be on your guard against the yeast of the Pharisees and Sadducees." ¹²Then they understood that he was not telling them to guard against the yeast used in bread, but against the teaching of the Pharisees and Sadducees.

PETER DECLARES THAT JESUS IS THE MESSIAH

¹³When Jesus came to the region of Caesarea Philippi, he asked his disciples, "Who do people say the Son of Man is?"

¹⁴They replied, "Some say John the Baptist; others say Elijah; and still others, Jeremiah or one of the prophets."

¹⁵"But what about you?" he asked. "Who do you say I am?"

¹⁶Simon Peter answered, "You are the Messiah, the Son of the living God."

¹⁷Jesus replied, "Blessed are you, Simon son of Jonah, for this was not revealed to you by flesh and blood, but by my

Jesus Visits Caesarea Philippi (16:13)

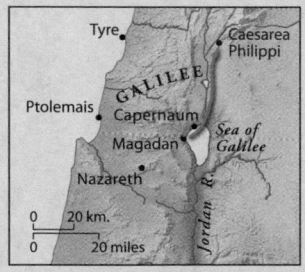

ᵃ 2,3 Some early manuscripts do not have *When evening comes . . . of the times.*

Father in heaven. ¹⁸And I tell you that you are Peter,^{*a*} and on this rock I will build my church, and the gates of Hades^{*b*} will not overcome it. ¹⁹I will give you the keys of the kingdom of heaven; whatever you bind on earth will be^{*c*} bound in heaven, and whatever you loose on earth will be^{*c*} loosed in heaven." ²⁰Then he ordered his disciples not to tell anyone that he was the Messiah.

JESUS PREDICTS HIS DEATH

²¹From that time on Jesus began to explain to his disciples that he must go to Jerusalem and suffer many things at the hands of the elders, the chief priests and the teachers of the law, and that he must be killed and on the third day be raised to life.

²²Peter took him aside and began to rebuke him. "Never, Lord!" he said. "This shall never happen to you!"

²³Jesus turned and said to Peter, "Get behind me, Satan! You are a stumbling block to me; you do not have in mind the concerns of God, but merely human concerns."

²⁴Then Jesus said to his disciples, "Whoever wants to be my disciple must deny themselves and take up their cross and follow me. ²⁵For whoever wants to save their life^{*d*} will lose it, but whoever loses their life for me will find it. ²⁶What good will it be for someone to gain the whole world, yet forfeit their soul? Or what can anyone give in exchange for their soul? ²⁷For the Son of Man is going to come in his Father's glory with his angels, and then he will reward each person according to what they have done.

²⁸"Truly I tell you, some who are standing here will not taste death before they see the Son of Man coming in his kingdom."

THE TRANSFIGURATION

17 After six days Jesus took with him Peter, James and John the brother of James, and led them up a high mountain by themselves. ²There he was transfigured before them. His face shone like the sun, and his clothes became as white as the light. ³Just then there appeared before them Moses and Elijah, talking with Jesus.

⁴Peter said to Jesus, "Lord, it is good for us to be here. If you wish, I will put up three shelters—one for you, one for Moses and one for Elijah."

⁵While he was still speaking, a bright cloud covered them, and a voice from the cloud said, "This is my Son, whom I love; with him I am well pleased. Listen to him!"

⁶When the disciples heard this, they fell facedown to the ground, terrified. ⁷But Jesus came and touched them. "Get up," he said. "Don't be afraid." ⁸When they looked up, they saw no one except Jesus.

⁹As they were coming down the mountain, Jesus instructed them, "Don't tell anyone what you have seen, until the Son of Man has been raised from the dead."

What were the "gates of Hades"? (16:18)
Hades was the Greek name for the place where spirits went to reside after death, generally equivalent to the Hebrew *Sheol*. The gates of Hades may mean the powers of death or the forces that oppose Christ and his kingdom.

What were the "keys of the kingdom"? (16:19)
These were symbolic keys that represented power and authority given from God. Peter may have used these "keys" on Pentecost when he announced that the door of the kingdom was open to all believers.

What do the words "from that time on" indicate? (16:21)
This was the beginning of a new emphasis in Jesus' ministry. Instead of teaching the crowds in parables, he concentrated on preparing his disciples for his coming suffering and death.

What does this verse mean? (16:28)
There are two main interpretations. First, it may have been a prediction of the transfiguration that would happen one week later. Second, it could refer to Jesus' resurrection.

What did it mean that Jesus was transfigured? (17:2)
His appearance changed, and his disciples saw him as he would appear in heaven.

What was significant about God's words? (17:5)
These were the same words from heaven that were spoken at Jesus' baptism. Again God confirmed that Jesus was his Son and that he approved Jesus' actions.

---

^{*a*} 18 The Greek word for *Peter* means *rock*.   ^{*b*} 18 That is, the realm of the dead   ^{*c*} 19 Or *will have been*   ^{*d*} 25 The Greek word means either *life* or *soul*; also in verse 26.

[10] The disciples asked him, "Why then do the teachers of the law say that Elijah must come first?"

[11] Jesus replied, "To be sure, Elijah comes and will restore all things. [12] But I tell you, Elijah has already come, and they did not recognize him, but have done to him everything they wished. In the same way the Son of Man is going to suffer at their hands." [13] Then the disciples understood that he was talking to them about John the Baptist.

JESUS HEALS A DEMON-POSSESSED BOY

[14] When they came to the crowd, a man approached Jesus and knelt before him. [15] "Lord, have mercy on my son," he said. "He has seizures and is suffering greatly. He often falls into the fire or into the water. [16] I brought him to your disciples, but they could not heal him."

[17] "You unbelieving and perverse generation," Jesus replied, "how long shall I stay with you? How long shall I put up with you? Bring the boy here to me." [18] Jesus rebuked the demon, and it came out of the boy, and he was healed at that moment.

[19] Then the disciples came to Jesus in private and asked, "Why couldn't we drive it out?"

[20] He replied, "Because you have so little faith. Truly I tell you, if you have faith as small as a mustard seed, you can say to this mountain, 'Move from here to there,' and it will move. Nothing will be impossible for you." [21] a

JESUS PREDICTS HIS DEATH A SECOND TIME

[22] When they came together in Galilee, he said to them, "The Son of Man is going to be delivered into the hands of men. [23] They will kill him, and on the third day he will be raised to life." And the disciples were filled with grief.

THE TEMPLE TAX

[24] After Jesus and his disciples arrived in Capernaum, the collectors of the two-drachma temple tax came to Peter and asked, "Doesn't your teacher pay the temple tax?"

[25] "Yes, he does," he replied.

When Peter came into the house, Jesus was the first to speak. "What do you think, Simon?" he asked. "From whom do the kings of the earth collect duty and taxes—from their own children or from others?"

[26] "From others," Peter answered.

"Then the children are exempt," Jesus said to him. [27] "But so that we may not cause offense, go to the lake and throw out your line. Take the first fish you catch; open its mouth and you will find a four-drachma coin. Take it and give it to them for my tax and yours."

THE GREATEST IN THE KINGDOM OF HEAVEN

18 At that time the disciples came to Jesus and asked, "Who, then, is the greatest in the kingdom of heaven?"

[2] He called a little child to him, and placed the child among them. [3] And he said: "Truly I tell you, unless you change and

---

What caused the boy's seizures? (17:15–18)
Though not all seizures were the result of demon possession, this boy's seizures were.

What was the two-drachma tax? (17:24)
This was the annual temple tax required of every male 20 years of age or older (see Exodus 30:13–15; 2 Chronicles 24:9). It was worth half a shekel (about two days' wages) and was used for the upkeep of the temple.

Did Jesus want everyone to act like little children? (18:3–4)
Jesus wanted his followers to be humble like a child who depends on and trusts his parents to provide all that he needs. Jesus wanted them to depend on and trust him in this way.

---

a 21 Some manuscripts include here words similar to Mark 9:29.

become like little children, you will never enter the kingdom of heaven. ⁴Therefore, whoever takes the lowly position of this child is the greatest in the kingdom of heaven. ⁵And whoever welcomes one such child in my name welcomes me.

CAUSING TO STUMBLE

⁶"If anyone causes one of these little ones—those who believe in me—to stumble, it would be better for them to have a large millstone hung around their neck and to be drowned in the depths of the sea. ⁷Woe to the world because of the things that cause people to stumble! Such things must come, but woe to the person through whom they come! ⁸If your hand or your foot causes you to stumble, cut it off and throw it away. It is better for you to enter life maimed or crippled than to have two hands or two feet and be thrown into eternal fire. ⁹And if your eye causes you to stumble, gouge it out and throw it away. It is better for you to enter life with one eye than to have two eyes and be thrown into the fire of hell.

THE PARABLE OF THE WANDERING SHEEP

¹⁰"See that you do not despise one of these little ones. For I tell you that their angels in heaven always see the face of my Father in heaven. [11]ᵃ

¹²"What do you think? If a man owns a hundred sheep, and one of them wanders away, will he not leave the ninety-nine on the hills and go to look for the one that wandered off? ¹³And if he finds it, truly I tell you, he is happier about that one sheep than about the ninety-nine that did not wander off. ¹⁴In the same way your Father in heaven is not willing that any of these little ones should perish.

DEALING WITH SIN IN THE CHURCH

¹⁵"If your brother or sisterᵇ sins,ᶜ go and point out their fault, just between the two of you. If they listen to you, you have won them over. ¹⁶But if they will not listen, take one or two others along, so that 'every matter may be established

ᵃ 11 Some manuscripts include here the words of Luke 19:10.   ᵇ 15 The Greek word for *brother or sister* (*adelphos*) refers here to a fellow disciple, whether man or woman; also in verses 21 and 35.   ᶜ 15 Some manuscripts *sins against you*

What was a millstone? (18:6)
It was one of a pair of large, round stones used for grinding grain. A millstone was turned by a donkey and was much larger and heavier than the small stones women used to grind grain.

A Millstone

Do we have guardian angels? (18:10)
There may be angels who look after specific people, but Jesus was emphasizing here that every person is important to God. Even children are important enough to be looked after by angels.

Why was the shepherd so concerned about one lost sheep that he left the others behind? (18:12–13)
This is a metaphor for how God seeks those who are lost. A flock of sheep this large would need more than one shepherd. If one sheep was lost, the head shepherd would go looking for it. The other sheep would have another shepherd to look after them until the head shepherd returned.

What did Jesus teach about forgiveness?   MATTHEW 18

It is clear from the Bible that ever since the time of Adam and Eve all people have sinned, and all people need to be forgiven. Throughout history God has shown mercy to his people and has forgiven them when they have turned to him after they have sinned. God's love is so great that he even sent his Son, Jesus, to the world to redeem people from their sins.

God expects his people to extend the same kind of love and forgiveness to other people. When Peter asked Jesus how many times he should forgive someone who had done something wrong to him, Jesus said, "Seventy-seven times." This was a way of saying that Christians should not keep count of the times that they forgive others but should continue to forgive because they have been forgiven in an even greater way by God.

Jesus said in Matthew 6:15, "If you do not forgive others their sins, your Father will not forgive your sins." What he meant was that Christians who have been saved by God will reflect that in the way they live their lives. If they do not show God's love to others, that may be a sign that they may not be true followers of Christ.

by the testimony of two or three witnesses.'[a] [17]If they still refuse to listen, tell it to the church; and if they refuse to listen even to the church, treat them as you would a pagan or a tax collector.

[18]"Truly I tell you, whatever you bind on earth will be[b] bound in heaven, and whatever you loose on earth will be[b] loosed in heaven.

[19]"Again, truly I tell you that if two of you on earth agree about anything they ask for, it will be done for them by my Father in heaven. [20]For where two or three gather in my name, there am I with them."

THE PARABLE OF THE UNMERCIFUL SERVANT

[21]Then Peter came to Jesus and asked, "Lord, how many times shall I forgive my brother or sister who sins against me? Up to seven times?"

[22]Jesus answered, "I tell you, not seven times, but seventy-seven times.[c]

[23]"Therefore, the kingdom of heaven is like a king who wanted to settle accounts with his servants. [24]As he began the settlement, a man who owed him ten thousand bags of gold[d] was brought to him. [25]Since he was not able to pay, the master ordered that he and his wife and his children and all that he had be sold to repay the debt.

[26]"At this the servant fell on his knees before him. 'Be patient with me,' he begged, 'and I will pay back everything.' [27]The servant's master took pity on him, canceled the debt and let him go.

[28]"But when that servant went out, he found one of his fellow servants who owed him a hundred silver coins.[e] He grabbed him and began to choke him. 'Pay back what you owe me!' he demanded.

[29]"His fellow servant fell to his knees and begged him, 'Be patient with me, and I will pay it back.'

[30]"But he refused. Instead, he went off and had the man thrown into prison until he could pay the debt. [31]When the other servants saw what had happened, they were outraged and went and told their master everything that had happened.

[32]"Then the master called the servant in. 'You wicked servant,' he said, 'I canceled all that debt of yours because you begged me to. [33]Shouldn't you have had mercy on your fellow servant just as I had on you?' [34]In anger his master handed him over to the jailers to be tortured, until he should pay back all he owed.

[35]"This is how my heavenly Father will treat each of you unless you forgive your brother or sister from your heart."

DIVORCE

19 When Jesus had finished saying these things, he left Galilee and went into the region of Judea to the other side of the Jordan. [2]Large crowds followed him, and he healed them there.

What did Jesus mean when he said we should forgive 77 times? (18:22)
Jesus used a large number to emphasize the importance of forgiveness. His point was not about an exact number but instead that his followers should be more willing to show mercy than to seek justice. Showing mercy, however, does not exclude the possibility of seeking justice.

How large were these debts? (18:24, 28)
The first debt was probably equal to several million dollars — a sum impossible to repay. The second debt equaled about a few months' wages, a debt that was much more possible to repay.

---

[a] 16 Deut. 19:15   [b] 18 Or will have been   [c] 22 Or seventy times seven
[d] 24 Greek ten thousand talents; a talent was worth about 20 years of a day laborer's wages.   [e] 28 Greek a hundred denarii; a denarius was the usual daily wage of a day laborer (see 20:2).

³Some Pharisees came to him to test him. They asked, "Is it lawful for a man to divorce his wife for any and every reason?"

⁴"Haven't you read," he replied, "that at the beginning the Creator 'made them male and female,'ᵃ ⁵and said, 'For this reason a man will leave his father and mother and be united to his wife, and the two will become one flesh'ᵇ? ⁶So they are no longer two, but one flesh. Therefore what God has joined together, let no one separate."

⁷"Why then," they asked, "did Moses command that a man give his wife a certificate of divorce and send her away?"

⁸Jesus replied, "Moses permitted you to divorce your wives because your hearts were hard. But it was not this way from the beginning. ⁹I tell you that anyone who divorces his wife, except for sexual immorality, and marries another woman commits adultery."

¹⁰The disciples said to him, "If this is the situation between a husband and wife, it is better not to marry."

¹¹Jesus replied, "Not everyone can accept this word, but only those to whom it has been given. ¹²For there are eunuchs who were born that way, and there are eunuchs who have been made eunuchs by others—and there are those who choose to live like eunuchs for the sake of the kingdom of heaven. The one who can accept this should accept it."

THE LITTLE CHILDREN AND JESUS

¹³Then people brought little children to Jesus for him to place his hands on them and pray for them. But the disciples rebuked them.

¹⁴Jesus said, "Let the little children come to me, and do not hinder them, for the kingdom of heaven belongs to such as these." ¹⁵When he had placed his hands on them, he went on from there.

THE RICH AND THE KINGDOM OF GOD

¹⁶Just then a man came up to Jesus and asked, "Teacher, what good thing must I do to get eternal life?"

¹⁷"Why do you ask me about what is good?" Jesus replied. "There is only One who is good. If you want to enter life, keep the commandments."

ᵃ 4 Gen. 1:27   ᵇ 5 Gen. 2:24

Is divorce always wrong?

From the time of Adam and Eve, God created the institution of marriage and said that "a man leaves his father and mother and is united to his wife, and they become one flesh" (Genesis 2:24). However, in biblical times women had few legal rights; they could be divorced just for displeasing their husbands. Jesus emphasized that God wants people to keep their marriage vows.

Jesus said that if one spouse is unfaithful, then divorce is an option. Later on Paul said that divorce is permitted when a believer is deserted by an unbelieving spouse (1 Corinthians 7:15). It is clear that God wants marriage to be a permanent relationship that is not broken just because people have fallen out of love or found someone else that they are attracted to. God wants each husband and wife to do all that they can to preserve their marriage, but God still loves people who are divorced even if they made mistakes in their marriages.

¹⁸"Which ones?" he inquired.

Jesus replied, "'You shall not murder, you shall not commit adultery, you shall not steal, you shall not give false testimony, ¹⁹honor your father and mother,'^a and 'love your neighbor as yourself.'^b

²⁰"All these I have kept," the young man said. "What do I still lack?"

²¹Jesus answered, "If you want to be perfect, go, sell your possessions and give to the poor, and you will have treasure in heaven. Then come, follow me."

²²When the young man heard this, he went away sad, because he had great wealth.

²³Then Jesus said to his disciples, "Truly I tell you, it is hard for someone who is rich to enter the kingdom of heaven. ²⁴Again I tell you, it is easier for a camel to go through the eye of a needle than for someone who is rich to enter the kingdom of God."

²⁵When the disciples heard this, they were greatly astonished and asked, "Who then can be saved?"

²⁶Jesus looked at them and said, "With man this is impossible, but with God all things are possible."

²⁷Peter answered him, "We have left everything to follow you! What then will there be for us?"

²⁸Jesus said to them, "Truly I tell you, at the renewal of all things, when the Son of Man sits on his glorious throne, you who have followed me will also sit on twelve thrones, judging the twelve tribes of Israel. ²⁹And everyone who has left houses or brothers or sisters or father or mother or wife^c or children or fields for my sake will receive a hundred times as much and will inherit eternal life. ³⁰But many who are first will be last, and many who are last will be first.

THE PARABLE OF THE WORKERS IN THE VINEYARD

20 "For the kingdom of heaven is like a landowner who went out early in the morning to hire workers for his vineyard. ²He agreed to pay them a denarius^d for the day and sent them into his vineyard.

³"About nine in the morning he went out and saw others standing in the marketplace doing nothing. ⁴He told them, 'You also go and work in my vineyard, and I will pay you whatever is right.' ⁵So they went.

"He went out again about noon and about three in the afternoon and did the same thing. ⁶About five in the afternoon he went out and found still others standing around. He asked them, 'Why have you been standing here all day long doing nothing?'

⁷"'Because no one has hired us,' they answered.

"He said to them, 'You also go and work in my vineyard.'

⁸"When evening came, the owner of the vineyard said to his foreman, 'Call the workers and pay them their wages, beginning with the last ones hired and going on to the first.'

Do believers need to sell everything they own to get to heaven? (19:21)
No, Jesus was saying that his followers need to give up whatever they love more than him. The young man loved his possessions more than he loved God, so Jesus told him to sell them all. The young man couldn't bring himself to do that, so he went away sad.

Is it possible for a camel to fit through a needle's eye? (19:24)
Here Jesus used an exaggerated example to help his disciples understand that people's love of money or things can hurt their spiritual life.

What did Jesus mean by "the first will be last"? (19:30)
In God's kingdom, the things that matter are the things that seem weak or less valuable to the rest of the world. Money, power, and appearance do not matter to God; instead, God values people's love for him and for their neighbors.

The Denarius (20:2)

---

^a 19 Exodus 20:12-16; Deut. 5:16-20   ^b 19 Lev. 19:18   ^c 29 Some manuscripts do not have *or wife*.   ^d 2 A denarius was the usual daily wage of a day laborer.

⁹"The workers who were hired about five in the afternoon came and each received a denarius. ¹⁰So when those came who were hired first, they expected to receive more. But each one of them also received a denarius. ¹¹When they received it, they began to grumble against the landowner. ¹²'These who were hired last worked only one hour,' they said, 'and you have made them equal to us who have borne the burden of the work and the heat of the day.'

¹³"But he answered one of them, 'I am not being unfair to you, friend. Didn't you agree to work for a denarius? ¹⁴Take your pay and go. I want to give the one who was hired last the same as I gave you. ¹⁵Don't I have the right to do what I want with my own money? Or are you envious because I am generous?'

¹⁶"So the last will be first, and the first will be last."

JESUS PREDICTS HIS DEATH A THIRD TIME

¹⁷Now Jesus was going up to Jerusalem. On the way, he took the Twelve aside and said to them, ¹⁸"We are going up to Jerusalem, and the Son of Man will be delivered over to the chief priests and the teachers of the law. They will condemn him to death ¹⁹and will hand him over to the Gentiles to be mocked and flogged and crucified. On the third day he will be raised to life!"

A MOTHER'S REQUEST

²⁰Then the mother of Zebedee's sons came to Jesus with her sons and, kneeling down, asked a favor of him.

²¹"What is it you want?" he asked.

She said, "Grant that one of these two sons of mine may sit at your right and the other at your left in your kingdom."

²²"You don't know what you are asking," Jesus said to them. "Can you drink the cup I am going to drink?"

"We can," they answered.

²³Jesus said to them, "You will indeed drink from my cup, but to sit at my right or left is not for me to grant. These places belong to those for whom they have been prepared by my Father."

²⁴When the ten heard about this, they were indignant with the two brothers. ²⁵Jesus called them together and said, "You know that the rulers of the Gentiles lord it over them, and their high officials exercise authority over them. ²⁶Not so with you. Instead, whoever wants to become great among you must be your servant, ²⁷and whoever wants to be first must be your slave— ²⁸just as the Son of Man did not come to be served, but to serve, and to give his life as a ransom for many."

TWO BLIND MEN RECEIVE SIGHT

²⁹As Jesus and his disciples were leaving Jericho, a large crowd followed him. ³⁰Two blind men were sitting by the roadside, and when they heard that Jesus was going by, they shouted, "Lord, Son of David, have mercy on us!"

³¹The crowd rebuked them and told them to be quiet,

What did this parable mean? (20:9–16)
This parable is about God's grace to "latecomers" into his kingdom. It was addressed to those who could not accept or understand God's grace, especially the religious leaders.

Who was the Son of Man, and how would he be "delivered over"? (20:18–19)
Jesus was the Son of Man, and here he was predicting his betrayal by Judas, as well as his death and resurrection.

What did the mother's request mean? (20:21)
She asked that her sons sit on Jesus' right and left, which meant that the two disciples would have places of power and honor in Jesus' kingdom.

What did "drink the cup" mean? (20:22)
This is a figure of speech that means to "experience." Here Jesus is referring to his suffering.

Why did the blind men call Jesus the Son of David? (20:30)
They accepted Jesus as the Messiah, who the prophets had said would be a descendant of King David.

but they shouted all the louder, "Lord, Son of David, have mercy on us!"

32 Jesus stopped and called them. "What do you want me to do for you?" he asked.

33 "Lord," they answered, "we want our sight."

34 Jesus had compassion on them and touched their eyes. Immediately they received their sight and followed him.

JESUS COMES TO JERUSALEM AS KING

21 As they approached Jerusalem and came to Bethphage on the Mount of Olives, Jesus sent two disciples, ² saying to them, "Go to the village ahead of you, and at once you will find a donkey tied there, with her colt by her. Untie them and bring them to me. ³ If anyone says anything to you, say that the Lord needs them, and he will send them right away."

⁴ This took place to fulfill what was spoken through the prophet:

⁵ "Say to Daughter Zion,
　'See, your king comes to you,
　gentle and riding on a donkey,
　and on a colt, the foal of a donkey.'"ᵃ

⁶ The disciples went and did as Jesus had instructed them. ⁷ They brought the donkey and the colt and placed their cloaks on them for Jesus to sit on. ⁸ A very large crowd spread their cloaks on the road, while others cut branches from the trees and spread them on the road. ⁹ The crowds that went ahead of him and those that followed shouted,

"Hosannaᵇ to the Son of David!"

"Blessed is he who comes in the name of the Lord!"ᶜ

"Hosannaᵇ in the highest heaven!"

10 When Jesus entered Jerusalem, the whole city was stirred and asked, "Who is this?"

11 The crowds answered, "This is Jesus, the prophet from Nazareth in Galilee."

JESUS AT THE TEMPLE

12 Jesus entered the temple courts and drove out all who were buying and selling there. He overturned the tables of the money changers and the benches of those selling doves. 13 "It is written," he said to them, "'My house will be called a house of prayer,'ᵈ but you are making it 'a den of robbers.'ᵉ"

14 The blind and the lame came to him at the temple, and he healed them. 15 But when the chief priests and the teachers of the law saw the wonderful things he did and the children shouting in the temple courts, "Hosanna to the Son of David," they were indignant.

16 "Do you hear what these children are saying?" they asked him.

The Triumphal Entry (21:1)

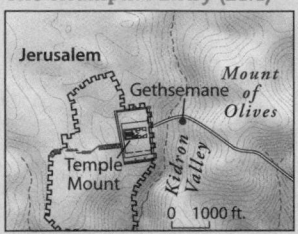

Jerusalem — Mount of Olives — Gethsemane — Temple Mount — Kidron Valley
0   1000 ft.

Why would Jesus ride on a donkey? (21:7)
A donkey symbolized humility and peace but also royalty. Zechariah had prophesied that the Messiah would ride on a donkey (Zechariah 9:9).

Why did the people spread their cloaks on the roads? (21:8)
This was a way of honoring a king.

What did "Hosanna" mean? (21:9)
The word originally meant "save now, pray," but by New Testament times it had lost its primary meaning and had become an exclamation of praise.

Where did the buying and selling of animals take place? (21:12)
This buying and selling of animals (at sometimes exorbitant prices) took place in the large outer court of the Gentiles, which covered several acres.

Why was it unusual that Jesus healed handicapped people at the temple? (21:14)
The Jewish authorities typically restricted the lame, blind, mute, and deaf from entering the temple in order to symbolize the purity that was required.

ᵃ 5 Zech. 9:9   ᵇ 9 A Hebrew expression meaning "Save!" which became an exclamation of praise; also in verse 15   ᶜ 9 Psalm 118:25,26
ᵈ 13 Isaiah 56:7   ᵉ 13 Jer. 7:11

"Yes," replied Jesus, "have you never read,

"'From the lips of children and infants
　　you, Lord, have called forth your praise'[a]?"

17 And he left them and went out of the city to Bethany, where he spent the night.

JESUS CURSES A FIG TREE

18 Early in the morning, as Jesus was on his way back to the city, he was hungry. 19 Seeing a fig tree by the road, he went up to it but found nothing on it except leaves. Then he said to it, "May you never bear fruit again!" Immediately the tree withered.

20 When the disciples saw this, they were amazed. "How did the fig tree wither so quickly?" they asked.

21 Jesus replied, "Truly I tell you, if you have faith and do not doubt, not only can you do what was done to the fig tree, but also you can say to this mountain, 'Go, throw yourself into the ~~sea,~~ ~~22 If~~ you believe, you will receive whatever you ask for in prayer."

~~AUTHO~~RITY OF JESUS QUESTIONED

~~23~~ Jesus entered the temple courts, and, while he was teaching, the chief priests and the elders of the people came to him. "By what authority are you doing these things?" they asked. "And who gave you this authority?"

24 Jesus replied, "I will also ask you one question. If you answer me, I will tell you by what authority I am doing these things. 25 John's baptism—where did it come from? Was it from heaven, or of human origin?"

They discussed it among themselves and said, "If we say, 'From heaven,' he will ask, 'Then why didn't you believe him?' 26 But if we say, 'Of human origin'—we are afraid of the people, for they all hold that John was a prophet."

27 So they answered Jesus, "We don't know."

Then he said, "Neither will I tell you by what authority I am doing these things.

THE PARABLE OF THE TWO SONS

28 "What do you think? There was a man who had two sons. He went to the first and said, 'Son, go and work today in the vineyard.'

29 "'I will not,' he answered, but later he changed his mind and went.

30 "Then the father went to the other son and said the same thing. He answered, 'I will, sir,' but he did not go.

31 "Which of the two did what his father wanted?"

"The first," they answered.

Jesus said to them, "Truly I tell you, the tax collectors and the prostitutes are entering the kingdom of God ahead of you. 32 For John came to you to show you the way of righteousness, and you did not believe him, but the tax collectors and the prostitutes did. And even after you saw this, you did not repent and believe him.

[a] 16 Psalm 8:2 (see Septuagint)

Where was Bethany? (21:17)
Bethany was a village on the eastern slope of the Mount of Olives about 2 miles (3.2 kilometers) from Jerusalem. It was the home of Mary, Martha, and Lazarus. See map on page 1336.

THE PARABLE OF THE TENANTS

What was the purpose of a watchtower? (21:33)
The watchtower was designed for guarding the vineyard, especially when the grapes ripened.

33 "Listen to another parable: There was a landowner who planted a vineyard. He put a wall around it, dug a winepress in it and built a watchtower. Then he rented the vineyard to some farmers and moved to another place. 34 When the harvest time approached, he sent his servants to the tenants to collect his fruit.

35 "The tenants seized his servants; they beat one, killed another, and stoned a third. 36 Then he sent other servants to them, more than the first time, and the tenants treated them the same way. 37 Last of all, he sent his son to them. 'They will respect my son,' he said.

Who did the characters represent in the parable? (21:35–37)
The tenants stood for the Jews and their leaders. The servants represented the Old Testament prophets, many of whom were killed. The son represented Jesus, who was condemned to death by religious leaders.

38 "But when the tenants saw the son, they said to each other, 'This is the heir. Come, let's kill him and take his inheritance.' 39 So they took him and threw him out of the vineyard and killed him.

40 "Therefore, when the owner of the vineyard comes, what will he do to those tenants?"

41 "He will bring those wretches to a wretched end," they replied, "and he will rent the vineyard to other tenants, who will give him his share of the crop at harvest time."

42 Jesus said to them, "Have you never read in the Scriptures:

"'The stone the builders rejected
    has become the cornerstone;
the Lord has done this,
    and it is marvelous in our eyes'[a]?

43 "Therefore I tell you that the kingdom of God will be taken away from you and given to a people who will produce its fruit. 44 Anyone who falls on this stone will be broken to pieces; anyone on whom it falls will be crushed."[b]

45 When the chief priests and the Pharisees heard Jesus' parables, they knew he was talking about them. 46 They looked for a way to arrest him, but they were afraid of the crowd because the people held that he was a prophet.

THE PARABLE OF THE WEDDING BANQUET

22 Jesus spoke to them again in parables, saying: 2 "The kingdom of heaven is like a king who prepared a wedding banquet for his son. 3 He sent his servants to those who had been invited to the banquet to tell them to come, but they refused to come.

4 "Then he sent some more servants and said, 'Tell those who have been invited that I have prepared my dinner: My oxen and fattened cattle have been butchered, and everything is ready. Come to the wedding banquet.'

5 "But they paid no attention and went off—one to his field, another to his business. 6 The rest seized his servants, mistreated them and killed them. 7 The king was enraged. He sent his army and destroyed those murderers and burned their city.

Why would the king burn the city? (22:7)
This was a common military practice. Here it might be an allusion to the destruction of Jerusalem.

8 "Then he said to his servants, 'The wedding banquet is ready, but those I invited did not deserve to come. 9 So go to the street corners and invite to the banquet anyone you find.'

[a] 42 Psalm 118:22,23   [b] 44 Some manuscripts do not have verse 44.

¹⁰So the servants went out into the streets and gathered all the people they could find, the bad as well as the good, and the wedding hall was filled with guests.

¹¹"But when the king came in to see the guests, he noticed a man there who was not wearing wedding clothes. ¹²He asked, 'How did you get in here without wedding clothes, friend?' The man was speechless.

¹³"Then the king told the attendants, 'Tie him hand and foot, and throw him outside, into the darkness, where there will be weeping and gnashing of teeth.'

¹⁴"For many are invited, but few are chosen."

PAYING THE IMPERIAL TAX TO CAESAR

¹⁵Then the Pharisees went out and laid plans to trap him in his words. ¹⁶They sent their disciples to him along with the Herodians. "Teacher," they said, "we know that you are a man of integrity and that you teach the way of God in accordance with the truth. You aren't swayed by others, because you pay no attention to who they are. ¹⁷Tell us then, what is your opinion? Is it right to pay the imperial tax*a* to Caesar or not?"

¹⁸But Jesus, knowing their evil intent, said, "You hypocrites, why are you trying to trap me? ¹⁹Show me the coin used for paying the tax." They brought him a denarius, ²⁰and he asked them, "Whose image is this? And whose inscription?"

²¹"Caesar's," they replied.

Then he said to them, "So give back to Caesar what is Caesar's, and to God what is God's."

²²When they heard this, they were amazed. So they left him and went away.

MARRIAGE AT THE RESURRECTION

²³That same day the Sadducees, who say there is no resurrection, came to him with a question. ²⁴"Teacher," they said, "Moses told us that if a man dies without having children, his brother must marry the widow and raise up offspring for him. ²⁵Now there were seven brothers among us. The first one married and died, and since he had no children, he left his wife to his brother. ²⁶The same thing happened to the second and third brother, right on down to the seventh. ²⁷Finally, the woman died. ²⁸Now then, at the resurrection, whose wife will she be of the seven, since all of them were married to her?"

²⁹Jesus replied, "You are in error because you do not know the Scriptures or the power of God. ³⁰At the resurrection people will neither marry nor be given in marriage; they will be like the angels in heaven. ³¹But about the resurrection of the dead—have you not read what God said to you, ³²'I am the God of Abraham, the God of Isaac, and the God of Jacob'*b*? He is not the God of the dead but of the living."

³³When the crowds heard this, they were astonished at his teaching.

a 17 A special tax levied on subject peoples, not on Roman citizens   *b 32* Exodus 3:6

Why was the man without wedding clothes thrown out? (22:11)
It was a custom for the host to provide wedding garments for the guests, and that would have been especially necessary in this case. Because the guest did not take a wedding garment, it would be an insult to the host, who had made the garments available. This symbolized what happens to those who reject Christ's gift of salvation.

How did this verse sum up the parable? (22:14)
The parable suggests that God, the King, invites many to be part of his kingdom, but only a few accept his invitation through faith and are thus allowed in.

How did these groups try to trap Jesus? (22:15–17)
The Pharisees were nationalists who hated Roman rule, while the Herodians supported the Roman rule of Herod. Depending on how Jesus answered the question, one group or the other would have reason to criticize him.

THE GREATEST COMMANDMENT

³⁴ Hearing that Jesus had silenced the Sadducees, the Pharisees got together. ³⁵ One of them, an expert in the law, tested him with this question: ³⁶ "Teacher, which is the greatest commandment in the Law?"

³⁷ Jesus replied: "'Love the Lord your God with all your heart and with all your soul and with all your mind.'ᵃ ³⁸ This is the first and greatest commandment. ³⁹ And the second is like it: 'Love your neighbor as yourself.'ᵇ ⁴⁰ All the Law and the Prophets hang on these two commandments."

WHOSE SON IS THE MESSIAH?

⁴¹ While the Pharisees were gathered together, Jesus asked them, ⁴² "What do you think about the Messiah? Whose son is he?"

"The son of David," they replied.

⁴³ He said to them, "How is it then that David, speaking by the Spirit, calls him 'Lord'? For he says,

⁴⁴ "'The Lord said to my Lord:
    "Sit at my right hand
until I put your enemies
    under your feet."'ᶜ

⁴⁵ If then David calls him 'Lord,' how can he be his son?" ⁴⁶ No one could say a word in reply, and from that day on no one dared to ask him any more questions.

A WARNING AGAINST HYPOCRISY

23 Then Jesus said to the crowds and to his disciples: ² "The teachers of the law and the Pharisees sit in Moses' seat. ³ So you must be careful to do everything they tell you. But do not do what they do, for they do not practice what they preach. ⁴ They tie up heavy, cumbersome loads and put them on other people's shoulders, but they themselves are not willing to lift a finger to move them.

⁵ "Everything they do is done for people to see: They make their phylacteriesᵈ wide and the tassels on their garments long; ⁶ they love the place of honor at banquets and the most important seats in the synagogues; ⁷ they love to be greeted with respect in the marketplaces and to be called 'Rabbi' by others.

⁸ "But you are not to be called 'Rabbi,' for you have one Teacher, and you are all brothers. ⁹ And do not call anyone on earth 'father,' for you have one Father, and he is in heaven. ¹⁰ Nor are you to be called instructors, for you have one Instructor, the Messiah. ¹¹ The greatest among you will be your servant. ¹² For those who exalt themselves will be humbled, and those who humble themselves will be exalted.

SEVEN WOES ON THE TEACHERS OF THE LAW AND THE PHARISEES

¹³ "Woe to you, teachers of the law and Pharisees, you hypocrites! You shut the door of the kingdom of heaven in peo-

How did Jesus challenge the Pharisees? (22:41–45)
The Jews generally did not believe that the Messiah would be divine. Jesus quoted a passage from the Old Testament (Psalm 110:1) to show that their concept of the Messiah was too limited.

What were these heavy loads? (23:4)
These were the regulations the Pharisees tried to impose on the people. These oral traditions were far more extensive and burdensome than the Law.

What are phylacteries? (23:5)
These were little boxes strapped to the arm or the forehead that contained parchment strips with passages of Scripture written on them. The boxes contained four passages: Exodus 13:1–10; 13:11–16; Deuteronomy 6:4–9; and 11:13–21.

Phylacteries

ᵃ 37 Deut. 6:5   ᵇ 39 Lev. 19:18   ᶜ 44 Psalm 110:1   ᵈ 5 That is, boxes containing Scripture verses, worn on forehead and arm

ple's faces. You yourselves do not enter, nor will you let those enter who are trying to. [14]*a*

¹⁵ "Woe to you, teachers of the law and Pharisees, you hypocrites! You travel over land and sea to win a single convert, and when you have succeeded, you make them twice as much a child of hell as you are.

¹⁶ "Woe to you, blind guides! You say, 'If anyone swears by the temple, it means nothing; but anyone who swears by the gold of the temple is bound by that oath.' ¹⁷ You blind fools! Which is greater: the gold, or the temple that makes the gold sacred? ¹⁸ You also say, 'If anyone swears by the altar, it means nothing; but anyone who swears by the gift on the altar is bound by that oath.' ¹⁹ You blind men! Which is greater: the gift, or the altar that makes the gift sacred? ²⁰ Therefore, anyone who swears by the altar swears by it and by everything on it. ²¹ And anyone who swears by the temple swears by it and by the one who dwells in it. ²² And anyone who swears by heaven swears by God's throne and by the one who sits on it.

²³ "Woe to you, teachers of the law and Pharisees, you hypocrites! You give a tenth of your spices — mint, dill and cumin. But you have neglected the more important matters of the law — justice, mercy and faithfulness. You should have practiced the latter, without neglecting the former. ²⁴ You blind guides! You strain out a gnat but swallow a camel.

²⁵ "Woe to you, teachers of the law and Pharisees, you hypocrites! You clean the outside of the cup and dish, but inside they are full of greed and self-indulgence. ²⁶ Blind Pharisee! First clean the inside of the cup and dish, and then the outside also will be clean.

²⁷ "Woe to you, teachers of the law and Pharisees, you hypocrites! You are like whitewashed tombs, which look beautiful on the outside but on the inside are full of the bones of the dead and everything unclean. ²⁸ In the same way, on the outside you appear to people as righteous but on the inside you are full of hypocrisy and wickedness.

²⁹ "Woe to you, teachers of the law and Pharisees, you hypocrites! You build tombs for the prophets and decorate the graves of the righteous. ³⁰ And you say, 'If we had lived in the days of our ancestors, we would not have taken part with them in shedding the blood of the prophets.' ³¹ So you testify against yourselves that you are the descendants of those who murdered the prophets. ³² Go ahead, then, and complete what your ancestors started!

³³ "You snakes! You brood of vipers! How will you escape being condemned to hell? ³⁴ Therefore I am sending you prophets and sages and teachers. Some of them you will kill and crucify; others you will flog in your synagogues and pursue from town to town. ³⁵ And so upon you will come all the righteous blood that has been shed on earth, from the blood of righteous Abel to the blood of Zechariah son of Berekiah, whom you murdered between the temple and the altar. ³⁶ Truly I tell you, all this will come on this generation.

³⁷ "Jerusalem, Jerusalem, you who kill the prophets and

---

a 14 Some manuscripts include here words similar to Mark 12:40 and Luke 20:47.

What did this saying mean? (23:24)
Strict Pharisees would carefully strain their drinking water through a cloth to avoid swallowing a tiny gnat, an unclean animal. But figuratively they would swallow a camel, one of the largest unclean animals, because they ignored the important aspects of the law — justice, mercy, and faithfulness.

What were whitewashed tombs? (23:27)
A Jew who stepped on a grave became ceremonially unclean, so graves were whitewashed to make them visible, especially at night. They appeared clean and beautiful on the outside but were dirty and rotten inside. This was a metaphor that Jesus applied to the hypocritical Pharisees.

Why did Jesus mention the killing of Abel and Zechariah? (23:35)
Abel was killed during the early years of the Old Testament and Zechariah near the end. Jesus was summing up the history of martyrdom in the Old Testament.

stone those sent to you, how often I have longed to gather your children together, as a hen gathers her chicks under her wings, and you were not willing. ³⁸ Look, your house is left to you desolate. ³⁹ For I tell you, you will not see me again until you say, 'Blessed is he who comes in the name of the Lord.'ᵃ"

THE DESTRUCTION OF THE TEMPLE
AND SIGNS OF THE END TIMES

24 Jesus left the temple and was walking away when his disciples came up to him to call his attention to its buildings. ² "Do you see all these things?" he asked. "Truly I tell you, not one stone here will be left on another; every one will be thrown down."

³ As Jesus was sitting on the Mount of Olives, the disciples came to him privately. "Tell us," they said, "when will this happen, and what will be the sign of your coming and of the end of the age?"

⁴ Jesus answered: "Watch out that no one deceives you. ⁵ For many will come in my name, claiming, 'I am the Messiah,' and will deceive many. ⁶ You will hear of wars and rumors of wars, but see to it that you are not alarmed. Such things must happen, but the end is still to come. ⁷ Nation will rise against nation, and kingdom against kingdom. There will be famines and earthquakes in various places. ⁸ All these are the beginning of birth pains.

⁹ "Then you will be handed over to be persecuted and put to death, and you will be hated by all nations because of me. ¹⁰ At that time many will turn away from the faith and will betray and hate each other, ¹¹ and many false prophets will appear and deceive many people. ¹² Because of the increase of wickedness, the love of most will grow cold, ¹³ but the one who stands firm to the end will be saved. ¹⁴ And this gospel of the kingdom will be preached in the whole world as a testimony to all nations, and then the end will come.

¹⁵ "So when you see standing in the holy place 'the abomination that causes desolation,'ᵇ spoken of through the prophet Daniel—let the reader understand— ¹⁶ then let those who are in Judea flee to the mountains. ¹⁷ Let no one on the housetop go down to take anything out of the house. ¹⁸ Let no one in the field go back to get their cloak. ¹⁹ How dreadful it will be in those days for pregnant women and nursing mothers! ²⁰ Pray that your flight will not take place in winter or on the Sabbath. ²¹ For then there will be great distress, unequaled from the beginning of the world until now—and never to be equaled again.

²² "If those days had not been cut short, no one would survive, but for the sake of the elect those days will be shortened. ²³ At that time if anyone says to you, 'Look, here is the Messiah!' or, 'There he is!' do not believe it. ²⁴ For false messiahs and false prophets will appear and perform great signs and wonders to deceive, if possible, even the elect. ²⁵ See, I have told you ahead of time.

²⁶ "So if anyone tells you, 'There he is, out in the wilderness,' do not go out; or, 'Here he is, in the inner rooms,' do

When was this prophecy fulfilled? (24:2)
It was fulfilled literally in A.D. 70, when the Romans completely destroyed Jerusalem and the temple.

Where is the Mount of Olives? (24:3)
This is a ridge a little more than a mile long beyond the Kidron Valley east of Jerusalem and rising about 200 feet above the city.

The Mount of Olives

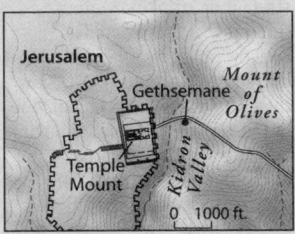

What was this abomination? (24:15)
In 168 B.C., Antiochus Epiphanes erected a pagan altar to Zeus on the holy altar in Jerusalem.

ᵃ *39* Psalm 118:26   ᵇ *15* Daniel 9:27; 11:31; 12:11

not believe it. [27] For as lightning that comes from the east is visible even in the west, so will be the coming of the Son of Man. [28] Wherever there is a carcass, there the vultures will gather.

[29] "Immediately after the distress of those days

"'the sun will be darkened,
   and the moon will not give its light;
the stars will fall from the sky,
   and the heavenly bodies will be shaken.'[a]

[30] "Then will appear the sign of the Son of Man in heaven. And then all the peoples of the earth[b] will mourn when they see the Son of Man coming on the clouds of heaven, with power and great glory.[c] [31] And he will send his angels with a loud trumpet call, and they will gather his elect from the four winds, from one end of the heavens to the other.

[32] "Now learn this lesson from the fig tree: As soon as its twigs get tender and its leaves come out, you know that summer is near. [33] Even so, when you see all these things, you know that it[d] is near, right at the door. [34] Truly I tell you, this generation will certainly not pass away until all these things have happened. [35] Heaven and earth will pass away, but my words will never pass away.

THE DAY AND HOUR UNKNOWN

[36] "But about that day or hour no one knows, not even the angels in heaven, nor the Son,[e] but only the Father. [37] As it was in the days of Noah, so it will be at the coming of the Son of Man. [38] For in the days before the flood, people were eating and drinking, marrying and giving in marriage, up to the day Noah entered the ark; [39] and they knew nothing about what would happen until the flood came and took them all away. That is how it will be at the coming of the Son of Man. [40] Two men will be in the field; one will be taken and the other left. [41] Two women will be grinding with a hand mill; one will be taken and the other left.

[42] "Therefore keep watch, because you do not know on what day your Lord will come. [43] But understand this: If the owner of the house had known at what time of night the thief was coming, he would have kept watch and would not have let his house be broken into. [44] So you also must be ready, because the Son of Man will come at an hour when you do not expect him.

[45] "Who then is the faithful and wise servant, whom the master has put in charge of the servants in his household to give them their food at the proper time? [46] It will be good for that servant whose master finds him doing so when he returns. [47] Truly I tell you, he will put him in charge of all his possessions. [48] But suppose that servant is wicked and says to himself, 'My master is staying away a long time,' [49] and he then begins to beat his fellow servants and to eat and drink with drunkards. [50] The master of that servant will come on a day when he does not expect him and at an hour he is not

Will the arrival of the Messiah be a secret? (24:27–28)
Jesus said that his second coming would be as obvious as lightning or the circling of vultures.

How was a hand mill operated? (24:41)
The grinding of grain between two heavy stones, a job usually done by women, required two people working together.

A Hand Mill

---

[a] 29 Isaiah 13:10; 34:4   [b] 30 Or *the tribes of the land*   [c] 30 See Daniel 7:13-14.   [d] 33 Or *he*   [e] 36 Some manuscripts do not have *nor the Son*.

aware of. ⁵¹He will cut him to pieces and assign him a place with the hypocrites, where there will be weeping and gnashing of teeth.

THE PARABLE OF THE TEN VIRGINS

25 "At that time the kingdom of heaven will be like ten virgins who took their lamps and went out to meet the bridegroom. ²Five of them were foolish and five were wise. ³The foolish ones took their lamps but did not take any oil with them. ⁴The wise ones, however, took oil in jars along with their lamps. ⁵The bridegroom was a long time in coming, and they all became drowsy and fell asleep.

⁶"At midnight the cry rang out: 'Here's the bridegroom! Come out to meet him!'

⁷"Then all the virgins woke up and trimmed their lamps. ⁸The foolish ones said to the wise, 'Give us some of your oil; our lamps are going out.'

⁹"'No,' they replied, 'there may not be enough for both us and you. Instead, go to those who sell oil and buy some for yourselves.'

¹⁰"But while they were on their way to buy the oil, the bridegroom arrived. The virgins who were ready went in with him to the wedding banquet. And the door was shut.

¹¹"Later the others also came. 'Lord, Lord,' they said, 'open the door for us!'

¹²"But he replied, 'Truly I tell you, I don't know you.'

¹³"Therefore keep watch, because you do not know the day or the hour.

THE PARABLE OF THE BAGS OF GOLD

¹⁴"Again, it will be like a man going on a journey, who called his servants and entrusted his wealth to them. ¹⁵To one he gave five bags of gold, to another two bags, and to another one bag,^a each according to his ability. Then he went on his journey. ¹⁶The man who had received five bags of gold went at once and put his money to work and gained five bags more. ¹⁷So also, the one with two bags of gold gained two more. ¹⁸But the man who had received one bag went off, dug a hole in the ground and hid his master's money.

¹⁹"After a long time the master of those servants returned and settled accounts with them. ²⁰The man who had received five bags of gold brought the other five. 'Master,' he said, 'you entrusted me with five bags of gold. See, I have gained five more.'

²¹"His master replied, 'Well done, good and faithful servant! You have been faithful with a few things; I will put you in charge of many things. Come and share your master's happiness!'

²²"The man with two bags of gold also came. 'Master,' he said, 'you entrusted me with two bags of gold; see, I have gained two more.'

²³"His master replied, 'Well done, good and faithful servant! You have been faithful with a few things; I will put

---

Who were the ten virgins? (25:1)
In this story that Jesus told, they were bridesmaids who were waiting to join the bride and bridegroom as they went into the banquet. Their lamps were probably torches that consisted of a long pole with oil-drenched rags at the top.

What did it mean to keep the lamps trimmed? (25:7)
The charred ends of the rags had to be cut off, and oil needed to be added about every 15 minutes in order to keep the torches burning.

How much was entrusted? (25:15)
Each bag (or talent) was worth about 20 years of a day laborer's wage. The current meaning of *talent* as an ability or gift is drawn from this parable.

---

^a 15 Greek *five talents . . . two talents . . . one talent*; also throughout this parable; a talent was worth about 20 years of a day laborer's wage.

you in charge of many things. Come and share your master's happiness!'

²⁴ "Then the man who had received one bag of gold came. 'Master,' he said, 'I knew that you are a hard man, harvesting where you have not sown and gathering where you have not scattered seed. ²⁵ So I was afraid and went out and hid your gold in the ground. See, here is what belongs to you.'

²⁶ "His master replied, 'You wicked, lazy servant! So you knew that I harvest where I have not sown and gather where I have not scattered seed? ²⁷ Well then, you should have put my money on deposit with the bankers, so that when I returned I would have received it back with interest.

²⁸ "'So take the bag of gold from him and give it to the one who has ten bags. ²⁹ For whoever has will be given more, and they will have an abundance. Whoever does not have, even what they have will be taken from them. ³⁰ And throw that worthless servant outside, into the darkness, where there will be weeping and gnashing of teeth.'

THE SHEEP AND THE GOATS

³¹ "When the Son of Man comes in his glory, and all the angels with him, he will sit on his glorious throne. ³² All the nations will be gathered before him, and he will separate the people one from another as a shepherd separates the sheep from the goats. ³³ He will put the sheep on his right and the goats on his left.

³⁴ "Then the King will say to those on his right, 'Come, you who are blessed by my Father; take your inheritance, the kingdom prepared for you since the creation of the world. ³⁵ For I was hungry and you gave me something to eat, I was thirsty and you gave me something to drink, I was a stranger and you invited me in, ³⁶ I needed clothes and you clothed me, I was sick and you looked after me, I was in prison and you came to visit me.'

³⁷ "Then the righteous will answer him, 'Lord, when did we see you hungry and feed you, or thirsty and give you something to drink? ³⁸ When did we see you a stranger and invite you in, or needing clothes and clothe you? ³⁹ When did we see you sick or in prison and go to visit you?'

⁴⁰ "The King will reply, 'Truly I tell you, whatever you did for one of the least of these brothers and sisters of mine, you did for me.'

⁴¹ "Then he will say to those on his left, 'Depart from me, you who are cursed, into the eternal fire prepared for the devil and his angels. ⁴² For I was hungry and you gave me nothing to eat, I was thirsty and you gave me nothing to drink, ⁴³ I was a stranger and you did not invite me in, I needed clothes and you did not clothe me, I was sick and in prison and you did not look after me.'

⁴⁴ "They also will answer, 'Lord, when did we see you hungry or thirsty or a stranger or needing clothes or sick or in prison, and did not help you?'

⁴⁵ "He will reply, 'Truly I tell you, whatever you did not do for one of the least of these, you did not do for me.'

⁴⁶ "Then they will go away to eternal punishment, but the righteous to eternal life."

How are people rewarded for what they do to serve others? (25:34–40) Rewards in the kingdom of heaven are given to those who serve without thought of a reward. God gives rewards because of his grace, not because of human merit.

THE PLOT AGAINST JESUS

26 When Jesus had finished saying all these things, he said to his disciples, [2]"As you know, the Passover is two days away—and the Son of Man will be handed over to be crucified."

[3]Then the chief priests and the elders of the people assembled in the palace of the high priest, whose name was Caiaphas, [4]and they schemed to arrest Jesus secretly and kill him. [5]"But not during the festival," they said, "or there may be a riot among the people."

JESUS ANOINTED AT BETHANY

[6]While Jesus was in Bethany in the home of Simon the Leper, [7]a woman came to him with an alabaster jar of very expensive perfume, which she poured on his head as he was reclining at the table.

[8]When the disciples saw this, they were indignant. "Why this waste?" they asked. [9]"This perfume could have been sold at a high price and the money given to the poor."

[10]Aware of this, Jesus said to them, "Why are you bothering this woman? She has done a beautiful thing to me. [11]The poor you will always have with you,[a] but you will not always have me. [12]When she poured this perfume on my body, she did it to prepare me for burial. [13]Truly I tell you, wherever this gospel is preached throughout the world, what she has done will also be told, in memory of her."

JUDAS AGREES TO BETRAY JESUS

[14]Then one of the Twelve—the one called Judas Iscariot—went to the chief priests [15]and asked, "What are you willing to give me if I deliver him over to you?" So they counted out for him thirty pieces of silver. [16]From then on Judas watched for an opportunity to hand him over.

THE LAST SUPPER

[17]On the first day of the Festival of Unleavened Bread, the disciples came to Jesus and asked, "Where do you want us to make preparations for you to eat the Passover?"

[18]He replied, "Go into the city to a certain man and tell him, 'The Teacher says: My appointed time is near. I am going to celebrate the Passover with my disciples at your house.'" [19]So the disciples did as Jesus had directed them and prepared the Passover.

[20]When evening came, Jesus was reclining at the table with the Twelve. [21]And while they were eating, he said, "Truly I tell you, one of you will betray me."

[22]They were very sad and began to say to him one after the other, "Surely you don't mean me, Lord?"

[23]Jesus replied, "The one who has dipped his hand into the bowl with me will betray me. [24]The Son of Man will go just as it is written about him. But woe to that man who betrays the Son of Man! It would be better for him if he had not been born."

[25]Then Judas, the one who would betray him, said, "Surely you don't mean me, Rabbi?"

[a] 11 See Deut. 15:11.

Who was Caiaphas? (26:3)
He was the high priest from A.D. 18 to 36. He was the son-in-law of Annas, a former high priest, who served from A.D. 6 to 15.

Why were the chief priests and elders afraid of a riot? (26:5)
Hundreds of thousands of Jewish pilgrims had come to Jerusalem for the Passover. Many of them admired Jesus and would probably start to riot if something happened to him.

What was alabaster? (26:7)
Most alabaster stone in ancient times was actually marble.

What was the value of thirty pieces of silver? (26:15)
Thirty silver coins were equivalent to 120 denarii. Laborers usually received one denarius for a day's work.

What did it mean to dip one's hand in the bowl? (26:23)
It was the custom to take a piece of bread or a piece of meat wrapped in bread and dip it into a bowl of sauce on the table. To eat a meal with a person in the culture of that day was in effect saying, "I am your friend, and I will not hurt you."

Jesus answered, "You have said so."

²⁶While they were eating, Jesus took bread, and when he had given thanks, he broke it and gave it to his disciples, saying, "Take and eat; this is my body."

²⁷Then he took a cup, and when he had given thanks, he gave it to them, saying, "Drink from it, all of you. ²⁸This is my blood of the*ᵃ* covenant, which is poured out for many for the forgiveness of sins. ²⁹I tell you, I will not drink from this fruit of the vine from now on until that day when I drink it new with you in my Father's kingdom."

³⁰When they had sung a hymn, they went out to the Mount of Olives.

JESUS PREDICTS PETER'S DENIAL

³¹Then Jesus told them, "This very night you will all fall away on account of me, for it is written:

"'I will strike the shepherd,
    and the sheep of the flock will be scattered.'ᵇ

³²But after I have risen, I will go ahead of you into Galilee."

³³Peter replied, "Even if all fall away on account of you, I never will."

³⁴"Truly I tell you," Jesus answered, "this very night, before the rooster crows, you will disown me three times."

³⁵But Peter declared, "Even if I have to die with you, I will never disown you." And all the other disciples said the same.

GETHSEMANE

³⁶Then Jesus went with his disciples to a place called Gethsemane, and he said to them, "Sit here while I go over there and pray." ³⁷He took Peter and the two sons of Zebedee along with him, and he began to be sorrowful and troubled. ³⁸Then he said to them, "My soul is overwhelmed with sorrow to the point of death. Stay here and keep watch with me."

³⁹Going a little farther, he fell with his face to the ground and prayed, "My Father, if it is possible, may this cup be taken from me. Yet not as I will, but as you will."

⁴⁰Then he returned to his disciples and found them sleeping. "Couldn't you men keep watch with me for one hour?" he asked Peter. ⁴¹"Watch and pray so that you will not fall into temptation. The spirit is willing, but the flesh is weak."

⁴²He went away a second time and prayed, "My Father, if it is not possible for this cup to be taken away unless I drink it, may your will be done."

⁴³When he came back, he again found them sleeping, because their eyes were heavy. ⁴⁴So he left them and went away once more and prayed the third time, saying the same thing.

⁴⁵Then he returned to the disciples and said to them, "Are you still sleeping and resting? Look, the hour has come, and the Son of Man is delivered into the hands of sinners. ⁴⁶Rise! Let us go! Here comes my betrayer!"

JESUS ARRESTED

⁴⁷While he was still speaking, Judas, one of the Twelve, arrived. With him was a large crowd armed with swords and

ᵃ 28 Some manuscripts *the new*   *ᵇ 31* Zech. 13:7

What was the cup? (26:27)
This was either the first or the third cup of the four that were shared during the Passover meal.

What hymns were sung? (26:30)
Traditionally, Psalms 113 – 114 were sung before the meal, and Psalms 115 – 118 were sung following the meal.

Who were the two sons of Zebedee? (26:37)
They were James and John, who, along with Peter, were especially close to Jesus.

What cup was this? (26:39)
This was a symbol of deep sorrow and suffering. Jesus was willing to accept what the Father had in store for him even though he knew it would be extremely difficult.

clubs, sent from the chief priests and the elders of the people. [48]Now the betrayer had arranged a signal with them: "The one I kiss is the man; arrest him." [49]Going at once to Jesus, Judas said, "Greetings, Rabbi!" and kissed him.

[50]Jesus replied, "Do what you came for, friend."[a]

Then the men stepped forward, seized Jesus and arrested him. [51]With that, one of Jesus' companions reached for his sword, drew it out and struck the servant of the high priest, cutting off his ear.

[52]"Put your sword back in its place," Jesus said to him, "for all who draw the sword will die by the sword. [53]Do you think I cannot call on my Father, and he will at once put at my disposal more than twelve legions of angels? [54]But how then would the Scriptures be fulfilled that say it must happen in this way?"

[55]In that hour Jesus said to the crowd, "Am I leading a rebellion, that you have come out with swords and clubs to capture me? Every day I sat in the temple courts teaching, and you did not arrest me. [56]But this has all taken place that the writings of the prophets might be fulfilled." Then all the disciples deserted him and fled.

JESUS BEFORE THE SANHEDRIN

[57]Those who had arrested Jesus took him to Caiaphas the high priest, where the teachers of the law and the elders had assembled. [58]But Peter followed him at a distance, right up to the courtyard of the high priest. He entered and sat down with the guards to see the outcome.

[59]The chief priests and the whole Sanhedrin were looking for false evidence against Jesus so that they could put him to death. [60]But they did not find any, though many false witnesses came forward.

Finally two came forward [61]and declared, "This fellow said, 'I am able to destroy the temple of God and rebuild it in three days.'"

[62]Then the high priest stood up and said to Jesus, "Are you not going to answer? What is this testimony that these men are bringing against you?" [63]But Jesus remained silent.

The high priest said to him, "I charge you under oath by the living God: Tell us if you are the Messiah, the Son of God."

[64]"You have said so," Jesus replied. "But I say to all of you: From now on you will see the Son of Man sitting at the right hand of the Mighty One and coming on the clouds of heaven."[b]

[65]Then the high priest tore his clothes and said, "He has spoken blasphemy! Why do we need any more witnesses? Look, now you have heard the blasphemy. [66]What do you think?"

"He is worthy of death," they answered.

[67]Then they spit in his face and struck him with their fists. Others slapped him [68]and said, "Prophesy to us, Messiah. Who hit you?"

Why did the high priest tear his clothes? (26:65)
Tearing one's clothing was an expression of grief. Ordinarily the high priest was forbidden from doing this, but this was an unusual situation. The high priest interpreted Jesus' answer as an expression of blasphemy.

---

[a] 50 Or "Why have you come, friend?"   [b] 64 See Psalm 110:1; Daniel 7:13.

PETER DISOWNS JESUS

[69] Now Peter was sitting out in the courtyard, and a servant girl came to him. "You also were with Jesus of Galilee," she said.

[70] But he denied it before them all. "I don't know what you're talking about," he said.

[71] Then he went out to the gateway, where another servant girl saw him and said to the people there, "This fellow was with Jesus of Nazareth."

[72] He denied it again, with an oath: "I don't know the man!"

[73] After a little while, those standing there went up to Peter and said, "Surely you are one of them; your accent gives you away."

[74] Then he began to call down curses, and he swore to them, "I don't know the man!"

Immediately a rooster crowed. [75] Then Peter remembered the word Jesus had spoken: "Before the rooster crows, you will disown me three times." And he went outside and wept bitterly.

JUDAS HANGS HIMSELF

27 Early in the morning, all the chief priests and the elders of the people made their plans how to have Jesus executed. [2] So they bound him, led him away and handed him over to Pilate the governor.

[3] When Judas, who had betrayed him, saw that Jesus was condemned, he was seized with remorse and returned the thirty pieces of silver to the chief priests and the elders. [4] "I have sinned," he said, "for I have betrayed innocent blood."

"What is that to us?" they replied. "That's your responsibility."

[5] So Judas threw the money into the temple and left. Then he went away and hanged himself.

[6] The chief priests picked up the coins and said, "It is against the law to put this into the treasury, since it is blood money." [7] So they decided to use the money to buy the potter's field as a burial place for foreigners. [8] That is why it has been called the Field of Blood to this day. [9] Then what was spoken by Jeremiah the prophet was fulfilled: "They took the thirty pieces of silver, the price set on him by the people of Israel, [10] and they used them to buy the potter's field, as the Lord commanded me."[a]

JESUS BEFORE PILATE

[11] Meanwhile Jesus stood before the governor, and the governor asked him, "Are you the king of the Jews?"

"You have said so," Jesus replied.

[12] When he was accused by the chief priests and the elders, he gave no answer. [13] Then Pilate asked him, "Don't you hear the testimony they are bringing against you?" [14] But Jesus made no reply, not even to a single charge — to the great amazement of the governor.

[15] Now it was the governor's custom at the festival to release a prisoner chosen by the crowd. [16] At that time they

Why did the Sanhedrin meet in the morning? (27:1)
The Sanhedrin could not have a legal session at night, so they met at daybreak to make the death sentence official.

Why did the Sanhedrin turn Jesus over to Pilate? (27:2)
The Roman government had taken away the right of the Sanhedrin to carry out capital punishment except in the case of a foreigner who entered the temple. So they turned Jesus over to Pilate for execution.

Who was the governor? (27:11)
This was Pontius Pilate.

[a] 10 See Zech. 11:12,13; Jer. 19:1-13; 32:6-9.

**What was Barabbas's crime?
(27:16)**
He had taken part in a rebellion,
presumably against the Romans,
so he may have been a sort of
folk hero to some of the Jews.
Matthew referred to him as a
notorious prisoner, and the other
Gospel writers stated that he
had been arrested for robbery,
sedition, and murder.

had a well-known prisoner whose name was Jesus[a] Barabbas. [17]So when the crowd had gathered, Pilate asked them,
"Which one do you want me to release to you: Jesus Barabbas, or Jesus who is called the Messiah?" [18]For he knew it was
out of self-interest that they had handed Jesus over to him.

[19]While Pilate was sitting on the judge's seat, his wife sent
him this message: "Don't have anything to do with that innocent man, for I have suffered a great deal today in a dream
because of him."

[20]But the chief priests and the elders persuaded the crowd
to ask for Barabbas and to have Jesus executed.

[21]"Which of the two do you want me to release to you?"
asked the governor.

"Barabbas," they answered.

[22]"What shall I do, then, with Jesus who is called the Messiah?" Pilate asked.

They all answered, "Crucify him!"

[23]"Why? What crime has he committed?" asked Pilate.

But they shouted all the louder, "Crucify him!"

[24]When Pilate saw that he was getting nowhere, but that
instead an uproar was starting, he took water and washed
his hands in front of the crowd. "I am innocent of this man's
blood," he said. "It is your responsibility!"

[25]All the people answered, "His blood is on us and on our
children!"

[26]Then he released Barabbas to them. But he had Jesus
flogged, and handed him over to be crucified.

**How severe was the
punishment of flogging?
(27:26)**
Roman floggings were so harsh
that sometimes the victim died
before being crucified.

THE SOLDIERS MOCK JESUS

[27]Then the governor's soldiers took Jesus into the Praetorium and gathered the whole company of soldiers around
him. [28]They stripped him and put a scarlet robe on him,
[29]and then twisted together a crown of thorns and set it on
his head. They put a staff in his right hand. Then they knelt
in front of him and mocked him. "Hail, king of the Jews!"
they said. [30]They spit on him, and took the staff and struck
him on the head again and again. [31]After they had mocked
him, they took off the robe and put his own clothes on him.
Then they led him away to crucify him.

**What was the Praetorium?
(27:27)**
This was the governor's official
residence in Jerusalem.

THE CRUCIFIXION OF JESUS

[32]As they were going out, they met a man from Cyrene,
named Simon, and they forced him to carry the cross. [33]They
came to a place called Golgotha (which means "the place of
the skull"). [34]There they offered Jesus wine to drink, mixed
with gall; but after tasting it, he refused to drink it. [35]When
they had crucified him, they divided up his clothes by casting lots. [36]And sitting down, they kept watch over him there.
[37]Above his head they placed the written charge against him:
THIS IS JESUS, THE KING OF THE JEWS.

[38]Two rebels were crucified with him, one on his right
and one on his left. [39]Those who passed by hurled insults at
him, shaking their heads [40]and saying, "You who are going
to destroy the temple and build it in three days, save yourself!

**Why was wine mixed with
gall? (27:34)**
According to tradition, the
women of Jerusalem often
gave this pain-killing narcotic to
prisoners who were crucified.

---

[a] 16 Many manuscripts do not have *Jesus*; also in verse 17.

Come down from the cross, if you are the Son of God!" [41] In the same way the chief priests, the teachers of the law and the elders mocked him. [42] "He saved others," they said, "but he can't save himself! He's the king of Israel! Let him come down now from the cross, and we will believe in him. [43] He trusts in God. Let God rescue him now if he wants him, for he said, 'I am the Son of God.'" [44] In the same way the rebels who were crucified with him also heaped insults on him.

THE DEATH OF JESUS

[45] From noon until three in the afternoon darkness came over all the land. [46] About three in the afternoon Jesus cried out in a loud voice, *"Eli, Eli,[a] lema sabachthani?"* (which means "My God, my God, why have you forsaken me?").[b]

[47] When some of those standing there heard this, they said, "He's calling Elijah."

[48] Immediately one of them ran and got a sponge. He filled it with wine vinegar, put it on a staff, and offered it to Jesus to drink. [49] The rest said, "Now leave him alone. Let's see if Elijah comes to save him."

[50] And when Jesus had cried out again in a loud voice, he gave up his spirit.

[51] At that moment the curtain of the temple was torn in two from top to bottom. The earth shook, the rocks split [52] and the tombs broke open. The bodies of many holy people who had died were raised to life. [53] They came out of the tombs after Jesus' resurrection and[c] went into the holy city and appeared to many people.

[54] When the centurion and those with him who were guarding Jesus saw the earthquake and all that had happened, they were terrified, and exclaimed, "Surely he was the Son of God!"

[55] Many women were there, watching from a distance. They had followed Jesus from Galilee to care for his needs. [56] Among them were Mary Magdalene, Mary the mother of James and Joseph,[d] and the mother of Zebedee's sons.

THE BURIAL OF JESUS

[57] As evening approached, there came a rich man from Arimathea, named Joseph, who had himself become a disciple of Jesus. [58] Going to Pilate, he asked for Jesus' body, and Pilate ordered that it be given to him. [59] Joseph took the body, wrapped it in a clean linen cloth, [60] and placed it in his own new tomb that he had cut out of the rock. He rolled a big stone in front of the entrance to the tomb and went away. [61] Mary Magdalene and the other Mary were sitting there opposite the tomb.

THE GUARD AT THE TOMB

[62] The next day, the one after Preparation Day, the chief priests and the Pharisees went to Pilate. [63] "Sir," they said, "we remember that while he was still alive that deceiver said, 'After three days I will rise again.' [64] So give the order for the

---

What curtain was torn? (27:51)
This was the inner curtain that separated the Holy Place from the Most Holy Place. The torn curtain symbolized tearing down the barrier that previously separated believers from God. The direction of the tear (top to bottom) shows that God caused this to happen. When Jesus died, he became the bridge that allows believers to go directly into God's presence.

Typical Cave Tomb (27:60)

What was the next day? (27:62)
The next day was Saturday, the Sabbath. Friday was the Preparation Day for the Sabbath (which went from sunset Friday to sunset Saturday).

---

[a] 46 Some manuscripts *Eloi, Eloi*   [b] 46 Psalm 22:1   [c] 53 Or *tombs, and after Jesus' resurrection they*   [d] 56 Greek *Joses,* a variant of *Joseph*

tomb to be made secure until the third day. Otherwise, his disciples may come and steal the body and tell the people that he has been raised from the dead. This last deception will be worse than the first."

[65]"Take a guard," Pilate answered. "Go, make the tomb as secure as you know how." [66]So they went and made the tomb secure by putting a seal on the stone and posting the guard.

JESUS HAS RISEN

28 After the Sabbath, at dawn on the first day of the week, Mary Magdalene and the other Mary went to look at the tomb.

[2]There was a violent earthquake, for an angel of the Lord came down from heaven and, going to the tomb, rolled back the stone and sat on it. [3]His appearance was like lightning, and his clothes were white as snow. [4]The guards were so afraid of him that they shook and became like dead men.

[5]The angel said to the women, "Do not be afraid, for I know that you are looking for Jesus, who was crucified. [6]He is not here; he has risen, just as he said. Come and see the place where he lay. [7]Then go quickly and tell his disciples: 'He has risen from the dead and is going ahead of you into Galilee. There you will see him.' Now I have told you."

[8]So the women hurried away from the tomb, afraid yet filled with joy, and ran to tell his disciples. [9]Suddenly Jesus met them. "Greetings," he said. They came to him, clasped his feet and worshiped him. [10]Then Jesus said to them, "Do not be afraid. Go and tell my brothers to go to Galilee; there they will see me."

THE GUARDS' REPORT

[11]While the women were on their way, some of the guards went into the city and reported to the chief priests everything that had happened. [12]When the chief priests had met with the elders and devised a plan, they gave the soldiers a large sum of money, [13]telling them, "You are to say, 'His disciples came during the night and stole him away while we were asleep.' [14]If this report gets to the governor, we will satisfy him and keep you out of trouble." [15]So the soldiers took the money and did as they were instructed. And this story has been widely circulated among the Jews to this very day.

THE GREAT COMMISSION

[16]Then the eleven disciples went to Galilee, to the mountain where Jesus had told them to go. [17]When they saw him, they worshiped him; but some doubted. [18]Then Jesus came to them and said, "All authority in heaven and on earth has been given to me. [19]Therefore go and make disciples of all nations, baptizing them in the name of the Father and of the Son and of the Holy Spirit, [20]and teaching them to obey everything I have commanded you. And surely I am with you always, to the very end of the age."

When did the earthquake take place? (28:2–4)
It is clear from the accounts in Mark, Luke, and John that the earthquake had taken place before the women arrived at the tomb. Only Matthew mentions this earthquake and the one at Jesus' death.

Why were there only eleven disciples? (28:16)
Judas had committed suicide (27:5).

How did the Great Commission extend the reach of the gospel? (28:19–20)
The gospel was now to be preached to all nations rather than being limited to the people of Israel.

Mark

INTRODUCTION

Who wrote this book?	A young man named John Mark wrote down stories Peter told about Jesus.
Why was this book written?	The book of Mark shows people who Jesus is by telling what Jesus did.
For whom was this book written?	Mark wrote this book for Gentiles (people who were not Jews).
What happens in this book?	Jesus shows his power by performing miracles that help people, and he teaches his disciples.
Who is the key person in this book?	Jesus is the most important person in this book.
Where did this happen?	Most events in Mark 1 – 9 happened in Galilee. Most events in Mark 10 – 16 took place in or near Jerusalem.
What are some of the stories in this book?	Jesus heals a paralyzed man — Mark 2:1 – 12 Jesus calms a storm — Mark 4:35 – 41 Jesus raises a dead girl — Mark 5:21 – 43 Jesus walks on water — Mark 6:45 – 56 Jesus feeds 4,000 people — Mark 8:1 – 10 Jesus heals a young boy — Mark 9:14 – 32 Jesus holds the Last Supper — Mark 14:12 – 26 Jesus dies and is buried — Mark 15:21 – 47 Jesus is raised again — Mark 16:1 – 8

When did these things happen?

40 BC 30 20 10 AD 1 10 20 30 40 50 60 70

HEROD THE GREAT'S REIGN (C. 37 - 4 BC)	
JESUS' BIRTH (C. 6/5 BC)	
JESUS' FLIGHT TO EGYPT (C. 5/4 BC)	
BEGINNING OF JOHN THE BAPTIST'S MINISTRY (C. AD 26)	
BEGINNING OF JESUS' MINISTRY (C. AD 26)	
JESUS' DEATH, RESURRECTION AND ASCENSION (C. AD 30)	
PAUL'S CONVERSION (C. AD 35)	
BOOK OF MARK WRITTEN (C. AD 55 - 65)	

JOHN THE BAPTIST PREPARES THE WAY

1 The beginning of the good news about Jesus the Messiah,[a] the Son of God,[b] [2] as it is written in Isaiah the prophet:

"I will send my messenger ahead of you,
who will prepare your way"[c]—
[3] "a voice of one calling in the wilderness,
'Prepare the way for the Lord,
make straight paths for him.'"[d]

[4] And so John the Baptist appeared in the wilderness, preaching a baptism of repentance for the forgiveness of sins. [5] The whole Judean countryside and all the people of Jerusalem went out to him. Confessing their sins, they were baptized by him in the Jordan River. [6] John wore clothing made of camel's hair, with a leather belt around his waist, and he ate locusts and wild honey. [7] And this was his message: "After me comes the one more powerful than I, the straps of whose sandals I am not worthy to stoop down and untie. [8] I baptize you with[e] water, but he will baptize you with[e] the Holy Spirit."

THE BAPTISM AND TESTING OF JESUS

[9] At that time Jesus came from Nazareth in Galilee and was baptized by John in the Jordan. [10] Just as Jesus was coming up out of the water, he saw heaven being torn open and the Spirit descending on him like a dove. [11] And a voice came from heaven: "You are my Son, whom I love; with you I am well pleased."

[12] At once the Spirit sent him out into the wilderness, [13] and he was in the wilderness forty days, being tempted[f] by Satan. He was with the wild animals, and angels attended him.

JESUS ANNOUNCES THE GOOD NEWS

[14] After John was put in prison, Jesus went into Galilee, proclaiming the good news of God. [15] "The time has come," he said. "The kingdom of God has come near. Repent and believe the good news!"

JESUS CALLS HIS FIRST DISCIPLES

[16] As Jesus walked beside the Sea of Galilee, he saw Simon and his brother Andrew casting a net into the lake, for they were fishermen. [17] "Come, follow me," Jesus said, "and I will send you out to fish for people." [18] At once they left their nets and followed him.

[19] When he had gone a little farther, he saw James son of Zebedee and his brother John in a boat, preparing their nets. [20] Without delay he called them, and they left their father Zebedee in the boat with the hired men and followed him.

JESUS DRIVES OUT AN IMPURE SPIRIT

[21] They went to Capernaum, and when the Sabbath came, Jesus went into the synagogue and began to teach. [22] The

---

What kind of clothing was this? (1:6)
Elijah and other prophets wore clothing made of camel's hair and a leather belt (see 2 Kings 1:8 and Zechariah 13:4).

Why did he eat this type of food? (1:6)
No one who lived in the desert would hesitate to eat insects, and locusts were among the ceremonially clean foods that the Jews could eat. John's simple clothing, diet, and lifestyle showed his focus on his ministry and were a symbolic criticism of self-indulgence.

How was the Trinity revealed at Jesus' baptism? (1:10–11)
All three persons of the Trinity were involved: the Father spoke, the Son was baptized, and the Spirit descended like a dove.

Was the wilderness a dangerous place? (1:13)
In Jesus' time, there were many more wild animals in Israel than there are today. Mark mentions the wild animals (which included lions), emphasizing that God kept Jesus safe in the wilderness.

---

[a] 1 Or *Jesus Christ. Messiah* (Hebrew) and *Christ* (Greek) both mean *Anointed One.*   [b] 1 Some manuscripts do not have *the Son of God.*   [c] 2 Mal. 3:1   [d] 3 Isaiah 40:3   [e] 8 Or *in*   [f] 13 The Greek for *tempted* can also mean *tested.*

people were amazed at his teaching, because he taught them as one who had authority, not as the teachers of the law. [23]Just then a man in their synagogue who was possessed by an impure spirit cried out, [24]"What do you want with us, Jesus of Nazareth? Have you come to destroy us? I know who you are—the Holy One of God!"

[25]"Be quiet!" said Jesus sternly. "Come out of him!" [26]The impure spirit shook the man violently and came out of him with a shriek.

[27]The people were all so amazed that they asked each other, "What is this? A new teaching—and with authority! He even gives orders to impure spirits and they obey him." [28]News about him spread quickly over the whole region of Galilee.

JESUS HEALS MANY

[29]As soon as they left the synagogue, they went with James and John to the home of Simon and Andrew. [30]Simon's mother-in-law was in bed with a fever, and they immediately told Jesus about her. [31]So he went to her, took her hand and helped her up. The fever left her and she began to wait on them.

[32]That evening after sunset the people brought to Jesus all the sick and demon-possessed. [33]The whole town gathered at the door, [34]and Jesus healed many who had various diseases. He also drove out many demons, but he would not let the demons speak because they knew who he was.

JESUS PRAYS IN A SOLITARY PLACE

[35]Very early in the morning, while it was still dark, Jesus got up, left the house and went off to a solitary place, where he prayed. [36]Simon and his companions went to look for him, [37]and when they found him, they exclaimed: "Everyone is looking for you!"

[38]Jesus replied, "Let us go somewhere else—to the nearby villages—so I can preach there also. That is why I have come." [39]So he traveled throughout Galilee, preaching in their synagogues and driving out demons.

JESUS HEALS A MAN WITH LEPROSY

[40]A man with leprosy[a] came to him and begged him on his knees, "If you are willing, you can make me clean."

[41]Jesus was indignant.[b] He reached out his hand and touched the man. "I am willing," he said. "Be clean!" [42]Immediately the leprosy left him and he was cleansed.

[43]Jesus sent him away at once with a strong warning: [44]"See that you don't tell this to anyone. But go, show yourself to the priest and offer the sacrifices that Moses commanded for your cleansing, as a testimony to them." [45]Instead he went out and began to talk freely, spreading the news. As a result, Jesus could no longer enter a town openly but stayed outside in lonely places. Yet the people still came to him from everywhere.

[a] 40 The Greek word traditionally translated *leprosy* was used for various diseases affecting the skin.   [b] 41 Many manuscripts *Jesus was filled with compassion*

Why did the demon call Jesus the "Holy One of God"? (1:24) This pointed to Jesus' divine nature rather than to his role as Messiah or Savior. The name may have been used by the demons out of fear or out of an attempt to exercise control over him. The occult belief at the time was that the precise use of a person's name gave the speaker control over that person.

Why did the people wait until after sunset to bring sick people to Jesus? (1:32) The Jewish people were not supposed to carry anything on the Sabbath, which ended at sunset.

Where did Jesus stay? (2:1)
When he was in Capernaum, Jesus probably stayed at Peter's house.

How could the men get their paralyzed friend to Jesus through the roof? (2:4)
A typical house in Israel had a flat roof with a staircase that led to it. The roof was often made of a thick layer of clay, supported by mats of branches across wooden beams. The men created an opening in the roof and lowered their friend down with ropes.

What did the Jewish people think about tax collectors? (2:14)
Because tax collectors were Jews who collected tolls for Rome, they were considered traitors. They also were considered extremely dishonest. They could not serve as witnesses or judges, and they were expelled from the synagogue. Their disgrace extended to their families.

What did Jesus mean when he spoke about the guests fasting? (2:19)
Jesus compared his disciples with the guests at a wedding and compared himself to a bridegroom. Jewish weddings were joyful affairs that often lasted for a week. Fasting would have been out of the question at a celebration like this.

JESUS FORGIVES AND HEALS A PARALYZED MAN

2 A few days later, when Jesus again entered Capernaum, the people heard that he had come home. ²They gathered in such large numbers that there was no room left, not even outside the door, and he preached the word to them. ³Some men came, bringing to him a paralyzed man, carried by four of them. ⁴Since they could not get him to Jesus because of the crowd, they made an opening in the roof above Jesus by digging through it and then lowered the mat the man was lying on. ⁵When Jesus saw their faith, he said to the paralyzed man, "Son, your sins are forgiven."

⁶Now some teachers of the law were sitting there, thinking to themselves, ⁷"Why does this fellow talk like that? He's blaspheming! Who can forgive sins but God alone?"

⁸Immediately Jesus knew in his spirit that this was what they were thinking in their hearts, and he said to them, "Why are you thinking these things? ⁹Which is easier: to say to this paralyzed man, 'Your sins are forgiven,' or to say, 'Get up, take your mat and walk'? ¹⁰But I want you to know that the Son of Man has authority on earth to forgive sins." So he said to the man, ¹¹"I tell you, get up, take your mat and go home." ¹²He got up, took his mat and walked out in full view of them all. This amazed everyone and they praised God, saying, "We have never seen anything like this!"

JESUS CALLS LEVI AND EATS WITH SINNERS

¹³Once again Jesus went out beside the lake. A large crowd came to him, and he began to teach them. ¹⁴As he walked along, he saw Levi son of Alphaeus sitting at the tax collector's booth. "Follow me," Jesus told him, and Levi got up and followed him.

¹⁵While Jesus was having dinner at Levi's house, many tax collectors and sinners were eating with him and his disciples, for there were many who followed him. ¹⁶When the teachers of the law who were Pharisees saw him eating with the sinners and tax collectors, they asked his disciples: "Why does he eat with tax collectors and sinners?"

¹⁷On hearing this, Jesus said to them, "It is not the healthy who need a doctor, but the sick. I have not come to call the righteous, but sinners."

JESUS QUESTIONED ABOUT FASTING

¹⁸Now John's disciples and the Pharisees were fasting. Some people came and asked Jesus, "How is it that John's disciples and the disciples of the Pharisees are fasting, but yours are not?"

¹⁹Jesus answered, "How can the guests of the bridegroom fast while he is with them? They cannot, so long as they have him with them. ²⁰But the time will come when the bridegroom will be taken from them, and on that day they will fast.

²¹"No one sews a patch of unshrunk cloth on an old garment. Otherwise, the new piece will pull away from the old, making the tear worse. ²²And no one pours new wine into

old wineskins. Otherwise, the wine will burst the skins, and both the wine and the wineskins will be ruined. No, they pour new wine into new wineskins."

JESUS IS LORD OF THE SABBATH

23 One Sabbath Jesus was going through the grainfields, and as his disciples walked along, they began to pick some heads of grain. 24 The Pharisees said to him, "Look, why are they doing what is unlawful on the Sabbath?"

25 He answered, "Have you never read what David did when he and his companions were hungry and in need? 26 In the days of Abiathar the high priest, he entered the house of God and ate the consecrated bread, which is lawful only for priests to eat. And he also gave some to his companions."

27 Then he said to them, "The Sabbath was made for man, not man for the Sabbath. 28 So the Son of Man is Lord even of the Sabbath."

JESUS HEALS ON THE SABBATH

3 Another time Jesus went into the synagogue, and a man with a shriveled hand was there. 2 Some of them were looking for a reason to accuse Jesus, so they watched him closely to see if he would heal him on the Sabbath. 3 Jesus said to the man with the shriveled hand, "Stand up in front of everyone."

4 Then Jesus asked them, "Which is lawful on the Sabbath: to do good or to do evil, to save life or to kill?" But they remained silent.

5 He looked around at them in anger and, deeply distressed at their stubborn hearts, said to the man, "Stretch out your hand." He stretched it out, and his hand was completely restored. 6 Then the Pharisees went out and began to plot with the Herodians how they might kill Jesus.

CROWDS FOLLOW JESUS

7 Jesus withdrew with his disciples to the lake, and a large crowd from Galilee followed. 8 When they heard about all he was doing, many people came to him from Judea, Jerusalem, Idumea, and the regions across the Jordan and around Tyre and Sidon. 9 Because of the crowd he told his disciples to have a small boat ready for him, to keep the people from crowding him. 10 For he had healed many, so that those with

What did Jesus mean that the Sabbath was made for man? (2:27)
Jewish traditions had built up so many requirements for the Sabbath that the burden had become enormous. Jesus emphasized that God had instituted the Sabbath as a day of spiritual, mental, and physical restoration.

Who were the Herodians? (3:6)
They were influential Jews who favored the Herodian dynasty, which meant that they were supporters of Rome. They joined with the Pharisees because they thought Jesus might upset the political system.

How far did people travel to see Jesus? (3:8)
As Jesus' popularity grew, people traveled great distances from all parts of Israel and the surrounding countries to see him.

Is there a sin that God won't forgive?

MARK 3:29

When some of the Pharisees saw Jesus performing miracles, they said that Jesus was possessed by the devil and was driving out demons because of Satan's power. This was an example of very serious blasphemy, because they denied that Jesus was the Son of God and denied that Jesus did miracles with the power of the Holy Spirit.

Throughout the Bible it is clear that God is willing to forgive sins if people repent and ask for forgiveness. The Bible says, "If we confess our sins, he is faithful and just and will forgive us our sins and purify us from all unrighteousness" (1 John 1:9). God does not say that if a person commits a single sin he or she can never be forgiven. But if a person continues to deny that Jesus is God's Son and refuses to accept the Holy Spirit's work, that person has chosen to separate himself or herself from God, and God will not allow or forgive that.

diseases were pushing forward to touch him. ¹¹Whenever the impure spirits saw him, they fell down before him and cried out, "You are the Son of God." ¹²But he gave them strict orders not to tell others about him.

JESUS APPOINTS THE TWELVE

¹³Jesus went up on a mountainside and called to him those he wanted, and they came to him. ¹⁴He appointed twelve*ᵃ* that they might be with him and that he might send them out to preach ¹⁵and to have authority to drive out demons. ¹⁶These are the twelve he appointed: Simon (to whom he gave the name Peter), ¹⁷James son of Zebedee and his brother John (to them he gave the name Boanerges, which means "sons of thunder"), ¹⁸Andrew, Philip, Bartholomew, Matthew, Thomas, James son of Alphaeus, Thaddaeus, Simon the Zealot ¹⁹and Judas Iscariot, who betrayed him.

JESUS ACCUSED BY HIS FAMILY AND BY TEACHERS OF THE LAW

²⁰Then Jesus entered a house, and again a crowd gathered, so that he and his disciples were not even able to eat. ²¹When his family*ᵇ* heard about this, they went to take charge of him, for they said, "He is out of his mind."

²²And the teachers of the law who came down from Jerusalem said, "He is possessed by Beelzebul! By the prince of demons he is driving out demons."

²³So Jesus called them over to him and began to speak to them in parables: "How can Satan drive out Satan? ²⁴If a kingdom is divided against itself, that kingdom cannot stand. ²⁵If a house is divided against itself, that house cannot stand. ²⁶And if Satan opposes himself and is divided, he cannot stand; his end has come. ²⁷In fact, no one can enter a strong man's house without first tying him up. Then he can plunder the strong man's house. ²⁸Truly I tell you, people can be forgiven all their sins and every slander they utter, ²⁹but whoever blasphemes against the Holy Spirit will never be forgiven; they are guilty of an eternal sin."

³⁰He said this because they were saying, "He has an impure spirit."

³¹Then Jesus' mother and brothers arrived. Standing outside, they sent someone in to call him. ³²A crowd was sitting around him, and they told him, "Your mother and brothers are outside looking for you."

³³"Who are my mother and my brothers?" he asked.

³⁴Then he looked at those seated in a circle around him and said, "Here are my mother and my brothers! ³⁵Whoever does God's will is my brother and sister and mother."

THE PARABLE OF THE SOWER

4 Again Jesus began to teach by the lake. The crowd that gathered around him was so large that he got into a boat and sat in it out on the lake, while all the people were along the shore at the water's edge. ²He taught them many

What sin did Jesus call unforgivable? (3:29–30) Stubbornly saying that the work of the Holy Spirit was the work of Satan was blasphemy of the worst kind. This was a denial of God and his power.

What were parables? (4:2) These were stories drawn from ordinary life that were used to illustrate spiritual or moral truths. They often took the form of similes, comparisons, analogies, or proverbial sayings. They usually had one main point.

ᵃ 14 Some manuscripts twelve—designating them apostles—   *ᵇ 21 Or his associates*

things by parables, and in his teaching said: ³"Listen! A farmer went out to sow his seed. ⁴As he was scattering the seed, some fell along the path, and the birds came and ate it up. ⁵Some fell on rocky places, where it did not have much soil. It sprang up quickly, because the soil was shallow. ⁶But when the sun came up, the plants were scorched, and they withered because they had no root. ⁷Other seed fell among thorns, which grew up and choked the plants, so that they did not bear grain. ⁸Still other seed fell on good soil. It came up, grew and produced a crop, some multiplying thirty, some sixty, some a hundred times."

⁹Then Jesus said, "Whoever has ears to hear, let them hear."

¹⁰When he was alone, the Twelve and the others around him asked him about the parables. ¹¹He told them, "The secret of the kingdom of God has been given to you. But to those on the outside everything is said in parables ¹²so that,

> "'they may be ever seeing but never perceiving,
>   and ever hearing but never understanding;
> otherwise they might turn and be forgiven!'ᵃ"

¹³Then Jesus said to them, "Don't you understand this parable? How then will you understand any parable? ¹⁴The farmer sows the word. ¹⁵Some people are like seed along the path, where the word is sown. As soon as they hear it, Satan comes and takes away the word that was sown in them. ¹⁶Others, like seed sown on rocky places, hear the word and at once receive it with joy. ¹⁷But since they have no root, they last only a short time. When trouble or persecution comes because of the word, they quickly fall away. ¹⁸Still others, like seed sown among thorns, hear the word; ¹⁹but the worries of this life, the deceitfulness of wealth and the desires for other things come in and choke the word, making it unfruitful. ²⁰Others, like seed sown on good soil, hear the word, accept it, and produce a crop—some thirty, some sixty, some a hundred times what was sown."

A LAMP ON A STAND

²¹He said to them, "Do you bring in a lamp to put it under a bowl or a bed? Instead, don't you put it on its stand? ²²For whatever is hidden is meant to be disclosed, and whatever is concealed is meant to be brought out into the open. ²³If anyone has ears to hear, let them hear."

²⁴"Consider carefully what you hear," he continued. "With the measure you use, it will be measured to you—and even more. ²⁵Whoever has will be given more; whoever does not have, even what they have will be taken from them."

THE PARABLE OF THE GROWING SEED

²⁶He also said, "This is what the kingdom of God is like. A man scatters seed on the ground. ²⁷Night and day, whether he sleeps or gets up, the seed sprouts and grows, though he does not know how. ²⁸All by itself the soil produces grain— first the stalk, then the head, then the full kernel in the head.

Why did Jesus say that parables would keep some people from understanding? (4:11–12)
Jesus compared his preaching to the ministry of Isaiah, who gained some followers but who also exposed the resistance of many people to God's warnings and calls for repentance. Those who desired to hear would understand, but those who were rebellious would not.

ᵃ *12* Isaiah 6:9,10

²⁹As soon as the grain is ripe, he puts the sickle to it, because the harvest has come."

THE PARABLE OF THE MUSTARD SEED

³⁰Again he said, "What shall we say the kingdom of God is like, or what parable shall we use to describe it? ³¹It is like a mustard seed, which is the smallest of all seeds on earth. ³²Yet when planted, it grows and becomes the largest of all garden plants, with such big branches that the birds can perch in its shade."

³³With many similar parables Jesus spoke the word to them, as much as they could understand. ³⁴He did not say anything to them without using a parable. But when he was alone with his own disciples, he explained everything.

JESUS CALMS THE STORM

³⁵That day when evening came, he said to his disciples, "Let us go over to the other side." ³⁶Leaving the crowd behind, they took him along, just as he was, in the boat. There were also other boats with him. ³⁷A furious squall came up, and the waves broke over the boat, so that it was nearly swamped. ³⁸Jesus was in the stern, sleeping on a cushion. The disciples woke him and said to him, "Teacher, don't you care if we drown?"

³⁹He got up, rebuked the wind and said to the waves, "Quiet! Be still!" Then the wind died down and it was completely calm.

⁴⁰He said to his disciples, "Why are you so afraid? Do you still have no faith?"

⁴¹They were terrified and asked each other, "Who is this? Even the wind and the waves obey him!"

JESUS RESTORES A DEMON-POSSESSED MAN

5 They went across the lake to the region of the Gerasenes.ᵃ ²When Jesus got out of the boat, a man with an impure spirit came from the tombs to meet him. ³This man lived in the tombs, and no one could bind him anymore, not even with a chain. ⁴For he had often been chained hand and foot, but he tore the chains apart and broke the irons on his feet. No one was strong enough to subdue him. ⁵Night and day among the tombs and in the hills he would cry out and cut himself with stones.

⁶When he saw Jesus from a distance, he ran and fell on his knees in front of him. ⁷He shouted at the top of his voice, "What do you want with me, Jesus, Son of the Most High God? In God's name don't torture me!" ⁸For Jesus had said to him, "Come out of this man, you impure spirit!"

⁹Then Jesus asked him, "What is your name?"

"My name is Legion," he replied, "for we are many." ¹⁰And he begged Jesus again and again not to send them out of the area.

¹¹A large herd of pigs was feeding on the nearby hillside. ¹²The demons begged Jesus, "Send us among the pigs; allow us to go into them." ¹³He gave them permission, and the

ᵃ 1 Some manuscripts *Gadarenes*; other manuscripts *Gergesenes*

What did the parable of the mustard seed mean? (4:30–34)
The main point is that the kingdom of God had seemingly insignificant beginnings. But a day would come when the whole world would recognize the greatness and power of God's kingdom.

Why did the disciples ask, "Who is this?" (4:41)
When they saw Jesus miraculously calm the storm, they were amazed and asked rhetorically who Jesus was. He was and is the Son of God (see Mark 1:1).

Jesus Heals a Demon-Possessed Man (5:1–2)

Why would someone live in a tomb? (5:3)
It was not unusual for the same cave (tomb) to be a burial spot for the dead and to provide shelter for the living. Very poor people often lived in such caves.

What did the name *Legion* mean? (5:9)
A Roman legion was made up of 6,000 soldiers. Here the term suggests that the man was possessed by numerous demons.

impure spirits came out and went into the pigs. The herd, about two thousand in number, rushed down the steep bank into the lake and were drowned.

¹⁴Those tending the pigs ran off and reported this in the town and countryside, and the people went out to see what had happened. ¹⁵When they came to Jesus, they saw the man who had been possessed by the legion of demons, sitting there, dressed and in his right mind; and they were afraid. ¹⁶Those who had seen it told the people what had happened to the demon-possessed man—and told about the pigs as well. ¹⁷Then the people began to plead with Jesus to leave their region.

¹⁸As Jesus was getting into the boat, the man who had been demon-possessed begged to go with him. ¹⁹Jesus did not let him, but said, "Go home to your own people and tell them how much the Lord has done for you, and how he has had mercy on you." ²⁰So the man went away and began to tell in the Decapolis*a* how much Jesus had done for him. And all the people were amazed.

JESUS RAISES A DEAD GIRL AND HEALS A SICK WOMAN

²¹When Jesus had again crossed over by boat to the other side of the lake, a large crowd gathered around him while he was by the lake. ²²Then one of the synagogue leaders, named Jairus, came, and when he saw Jesus, he fell at his feet. ²³He pleaded earnestly with him, "My little daughter is dying. Please come and put your hands on her so that she will be healed and live." ²⁴So Jesus went with him.

A large crowd followed and pressed around him. ²⁵And a woman was there who had been subject to bleeding for twelve years. ²⁶She had suffered a great deal under the care of many doctors and had spent all she had, yet instead of getting better she grew worse. ²⁷When she heard about Jesus, she came up behind him in the crowd and touched his cloak, ²⁸because she thought, "If I just touch his clothes, I will be healed." ²⁹Immediately her bleeding stopped and she felt in her body that she was freed from her suffering.

³⁰At once Jesus realized that power had gone out from him. He turned around in the crowd and asked, "Who touched my clothes?"

³¹"You see the people crowding against you," his disciples answered, "and yet you can ask, 'Who touched me?'"

³²But Jesus kept looking around to see who had done it. ³³Then the woman, knowing what had happened to her, came and fell at his feet and, trembling with fear, told him the whole truth. ³⁴He said to her, "Daughter, your faith has healed you. Go in peace and be freed from your suffering."

³⁵While Jesus was still speaking, some people came from the house of Jairus, the synagogue leader. "Your daughter is dead," they said. "Why bother the teacher anymore?"

³⁶Overhearing*b* what they said, Jesus told him, "Don't be afraid; just believe."

What type of illness did the woman have? (5:25)
The exact nature of her problem is not known. Her life would have been miserable because she was shunned by people. Any contact with her would have made someone ceremonially unclean.

a 20 That is, the Ten Cities   b 36 Or Ignoring

³⁷He did not let anyone follow him except Peter, James and John the brother of James. ³⁸When they came to the home of the synagogue leader, Jesus saw a commotion, with people crying and wailing loudly. ³⁹He went in and said to them, "Why all this commotion and wailing? The child is not dead but asleep." ⁴⁰But they laughed at him.

After he put them all out, he took the child's father and mother and the disciples who were with him, and went in where the child was. ⁴¹He took her by the hand and said to her, "*Talitha koum!*" (which means "Little girl, I say to you, get up!"). ⁴²Immediately the girl stood up and began to walk around (she was twelve years old). At this they were completely astonished. ⁴³He gave strict orders not to let anyone know about this, and told them to give her something to eat.

A PROPHET WITHOUT HONOR

6 Jesus left there and went to his hometown, accompanied by his disciples. ²When the Sabbath came, he began to teach in the synagogue, and many who heard him were amazed.

"Where did this man get these things?" they asked. "What's this wisdom that has been given him? What are these remarkable miracles he is performing? ³Isn't this the carpenter? Isn't this Mary's son and the brother of James, Joseph,ᵃ Judas and Simon? Aren't his sisters here with us?" And they took offense at him.

⁴Jesus said to them, "A prophet is not without honor except in his own town, among his relatives and in his own home." ⁵He could not do any miracles there, except lay his hands on a few sick people and heal them. ⁶He was amazed at their lack of faith.

JESUS SENDS OUT THE TWELVE

Then Jesus went around teaching from village to village. ⁷Calling the Twelve to him, he began to send them out two by two and gave them authority over impure spirits.

⁸These were his instructions: "Take nothing for the journey except a staff—no bread, no bag, no money in your belts. ⁹Wear sandals but not an extra shirt. ¹⁰Whenever you enter a house, stay there until you leave that town. ¹¹And if any place will not welcome you or listen to you, leave that place and shake the dust off your feet as a testimony against them."

¹²They went out and preached that people should repent. ¹³They drove out many demons and anointed many sick people with oil and healed them.

JOHN THE BAPTIST BEHEADED

¹⁴King Herod heard about this, for Jesus' name had become well known. Some were saying,ᵇ "John the Baptist has been raised from the dead, and that is why miraculous powers are at work in him."

¹⁵Others said, "He is Elijah."

And still others claimed, "He is a prophet, like one of the prophets of long ago."

Why did Jesus tell people not to spread the word about his miracles? (5:43)
In Galilee, Jesus often told people not to tell others about the healings he performed. His popularity along with the opposition from the religious leaders could have created a crisis before he was finished with his ministry.

Was Jesus a carpenter? (6:3)
Matthew reports that Jesus was a carpenter's son (see Matthew 13:55). Only Mark refers to Jesus as a carpenter. The Greek word could also refer to a mason, a smith, or a builder, but here it probably has the usual meaning of carpenter. The question in this verse was a negative one, implying that Jesus was just a common laborer.

Why were the disciples not supposed to take any bread, a bag, or money? (6:8)
They were supposed to depend on the hospitality of the people they visited. They also were instructed not to take an extra shirt but were to rely on God to provide them with lodging at night.

ᵃ 3 Greek *Joses,* a variant of *Joseph*   ᵇ 14 Some early manuscripts *He was saying*

¹⁶But when Herod heard this, he said, "John, whom I beheaded, has been raised from the dead!"

¹⁷For Herod himself had given orders to have John arrested, and he had him bound and put in prison. He did this because of Herodias, his brother Philip's wife, whom he had married. ¹⁸For John had been saying to Herod, "It is not lawful for you to have your brother's wife." ¹⁹So Herodias nursed a grudge against John and wanted to kill him. But she was not able to, ²⁰because Herod feared John and protected him, knowing him to be a righteous and holy man. When Herod heard John, he was greatly puzzled*ᵃ*; yet he liked to listen to him.

²¹Finally the opportune time came. On his birthday Herod gave a banquet for his high officials and military commanders and the leading men of Galilee. ²²When the daughter of *ᵇ* Herodias came in and danced, she pleased Herod and his dinner guests.

The king said to the girl, "Ask me for anything you want, and I'll give it to you." ²³And he promised her with an oath, "Whatever you ask I will give you, up to half my kingdom."

²⁴She went out and said to her mother, "What shall I ask for?"

"The head of John the Baptist," she answered.

²⁵At once the girl hurried in to the king with the request: "I want you to give me right now the head of John the Baptist on a platter."

²⁶The king was greatly distressed, but because of his oaths and his dinner guests, he did not want to refuse her. ²⁷So he immediately sent an executioner with orders to bring John's head. The man went, beheaded John in the prison, ²⁸and brought back his head on a platter. He presented it to the girl, and she gave it to her mother. ²⁹On hearing of this, John's disciples came and took his body and laid it in a tomb.

JESUS FEEDS THE FIVE THOUSAND

³⁰The apostles gathered around Jesus and reported to him all they had done and taught. ³¹Then, because so many people were coming and going that they did not even have a chance to eat, he said to them, "Come with me by yourselves to a quiet place and get some rest."

³²So they went away by themselves in a boat to a solitary place. ³³But many who saw them leaving recognized them and ran on foot from all the towns and got there ahead of them. ³⁴When Jesus landed and saw a large crowd, he had compassion on them, because they were like sheep without a shepherd. So he began teaching them many things.

³⁵By this time it was late in the day, so his disciples came to him. "This is a remote place," they said, "and it's already very late. ³⁶Send the people away so that they can go to the surrounding countryside and villages and buy themselves something to eat."

³⁷But he answered, "You give them something to eat."

They said to him, "That would take more than half a year's

ᵃ 20 Some early manuscripts *he did many things*   *ᵇ 22* Some early manuscripts *When his daughter*

wages*! Are we to go and spend that much on bread and give it to them to eat?"

38 "How many loaves do you have?" he asked. "Go and see." When they found out, they said, "Five — and two fish."

39 Then Jesus directed them to have all the people sit down in groups on the green grass. 40 So they sat down in groups of hundreds and fifties. 41 Taking the five loaves and the two fish and looking up to heaven, he gave thanks and broke the loaves. Then he gave them to his disciples to distribute to the people. He also divided the two fish among them all. 42 They all ate and were satisfied, 43 and the disciples picked up twelve basketfuls of broken pieces of bread and fish. 44 The number of the men who had eaten was five thousand.

JESUS WALKS ON THE WATER

45 Immediately Jesus made his disciples get into the boat and go on ahead of him to Bethsaida, while he dismissed the crowd. 46 After leaving them, he went up on a mountainside to pray.

47 Later that night, the boat was in the middle of the lake, and he was alone on land. 48 He saw the disciples straining at the oars, because the wind was against them. Shortly before dawn he went out to them, walking on the lake. He was about to pass by them, 49 but when they saw him walking on the lake, they thought he was a ghost. They cried out, 50 because they all saw him and were terrified.

Immediately he spoke to them and said, "Take courage! It is I. Don't be afraid." 51 Then he climbed into the boat with them, and the wind died down. They were completely amazed, 52 for they had not understood about the loaves; their hearts were hardened.

53 When they had crossed over, they landed at Gennesaret and anchored there. 54 As soon as they got out of the boat, people recognized Jesus. 55 They ran throughout that whole region and carried the sick on mats to wherever they heard he was. 56 And wherever he went — into villages, towns or countryside — they placed the sick in the marketplaces. They begged him to let them touch even the edge of his cloak, and all who touched it were healed.

THAT WHICH DEFILES

7 The Pharisees and some of the teachers of the law who had come from Jerusalem gathered around Jesus 2 and saw some of his disciples eating food with hands that were defiled, that is, unwashed. 3 (The Pharisees and all the Jews do not eat unless they give their hands a ceremonial washing, holding to the tradition of the elders. 4 When they come from the marketplace they do not eat unless they wash. And they observe many other traditions, such as the washing of cups, pitchers and kettles.*)

5 So the Pharisees and teachers of the law asked Jesus, "Why don't your disciples live according to the tradition of the elders instead of eating their food with defiled hands?"

Why was the leftover bread gathered up? (6:43)
Bread was regarded by the Jews as a gift from God, and it was required that the scraps that fell on the ground during a meal be picked up. Each disciple returned with a basket full of bread.

What did it mean that the disciples' hearts were hardened? (6:52)
They hadn't understood the significance of the miracle of feeding the 5,000. The miracle showed that Jesus was the Son of God. If they had understood and believed that, they would know that he would be able to protect them from the storm.

---

a 37 Greek *take two hundred denarii* *b* 4 Some early manuscripts *pitchers, kettles and dining couches*

⁶He replied, "Isaiah was right when he prophesied about you hypocrites; as it is written:

"'These people honor me with their lips,
  but their hearts are far from me.
⁷They worship me in vain;
  their teachings are merely human rules.'ᵃ

⁸You have let go of the commands of God and are holding on to human traditions."

⁹And he continued, "You have a fine way of setting aside the commands of God in order to observeᵇ your own traditions! ¹⁰For Moses said, 'Honor your father and mother,'ᶜ and, 'Anyone who curses their father or mother is to be put to death.'ᵈ ¹¹But you say that if anyone declares that what might have been used to help their father or mother is Corban (that is, devoted to God)— ¹²then you no longer let them do anything for their father or mother. ¹³Thus you nullify the word of God by your tradition that you have handed down. And you do many things like that."

¹⁴Again Jesus called the crowd to him and said, "Listen to me, everyone, and understand this. ¹⁵Nothing outside a person can defile them by going into them. Rather, it is what comes out of a person that defiles them." [16]ᵉ

¹⁷After he had left the crowd and entered the house, his disciples asked him about this parable. ¹⁸"Are you so dull?" he asked. "Don't you see that nothing that enters a person from the outside can defile them? ¹⁹For it doesn't go into their heart but into their stomach, and then out of the body." (In saying this, Jesus declared all foods clean.)

²⁰He went on: "What comes out of a person is what defiles them. ²¹For it is from within, out of a person's heart, that evil thoughts come—sexual immorality, theft, murder, ²²adultery, greed, malice, deceit, lewdness, envy, slander, arrogance and folly. ²³All these evils come from inside and defile a person."

JESUS HONORS A SYROPHOENICIAN WOMAN'S FAITH

²⁴Jesus left that place and went to the vicinity of Tyre.ᶠ He entered a house and did not want anyone to know it; yet he could not keep his presence secret. ²⁵In fact, as soon as she heard about him, a woman whose little daughter was possessed by an impure spirit came and fell at his feet. ²⁶The woman was a Greek, born in Syrian Phoenicia. She begged Jesus to drive the demon out of her daughter.

²⁷"First let the children eat all they want," he told her, "for it is not right to take the children's bread and toss it to the dogs."

²⁸"Lord," she replied, "even the dogs under the table eat the children's crumbs."

²⁹Then he told her, "For such a reply, you may go; the demon has left your daughter."

ᵃ 6,7 Isaiah 29:13   ᵇ 9 Some manuscripts set up   ᶜ 10 Exodus 20:12;
Deut. 5:16   ᵈ 10 Exodus 21:17; Lev. 20:9   ᵉ 16 Some manuscripts
include here the words of 4:23.   ᶠ 24 Many early manuscripts Tyre and Sidon

Why did Jesus criticize the Pharisees and teachers of the law? (7:6–8)
Jesus called them hypocrites for following the traditions of the elders. They washed their hands faithfully but did not love God with their hearts.

What did it mean for someone to declare "Corban"? (7:11)
By saying that word, which was a vow, people could declare that their money was "dedicated to God." This was often a way for children to avoid caring for their parents and to hang on to their money. This was another way that people observed the letter of the law but not the spirit of it.

What was Jesus' radical message? (7:19–20)
Mark points out that Jesus in effect declared all foods clean. Uncleanness came from an impure heart, not from eating certain foods.

Jesus Visits Phoenicia (7:24)

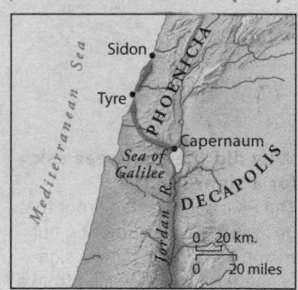

What did Jesus mean about not giving the children's bread to the dogs? (7:27–29)
Jesus' point was that the gospel was given first to the Jews. The woman understood Jesus' reply and said that she would be willing to settle for crumbs. Jesus rewarded her for her faith.

³⁰ She went home and found her child lying on the bed, and the demon gone.

JESUS HEALS A DEAF AND MUTE MAN

³¹ Then Jesus left the vicinity of Tyre and went through Sidon, down to the Sea of Galilee and into the region of the Decapolis.ᵃ ³² There some people brought to him a man who was deaf and could hardly talk, and they begged Jesus to place his hand on him.

³³ After he took him aside, away from the crowd, Jesus put his fingers into the man's ears. Then he spit and touched the man's tongue. ³⁴ He looked up to heaven and with a deep sigh said to him, *"Ephphatha!"* (which means "Be opened!"). ³⁵ At this, the man's ears were opened, his tongue was loosened and he began to speak plainly.

³⁶ Jesus commanded them not to tell anyone. But the more he did so, the more they kept talking about it. ³⁷ People were overwhelmed with amazement. "He has done everything well," they said. "He even makes the deaf hear and the mute speak."

JESUS FEEDS THE FOUR THOUSAND

8 During those days another large crowd gathered. Since they had nothing to eat, Jesus called his disciples to him and said, ² "I have compassion for these people; they have already been with me three days and have nothing to eat. ³ If I send them home hungry, they will collapse on the way, because some of them have come a long distance."

⁴ His disciples answered, "But where in this remote place can anyone get enough bread to feed them?"

⁵ "How many loaves do you have?" Jesus asked.

"Seven," they replied.

⁶ He told the crowd to sit down on the ground. When he had taken the seven loaves and given thanks, he broke them and gave them to his disciples to distribute to the people, and they did so. ⁷ They had a few small fish as well; he gave thanks for them also and told the disciples to distribute them. ⁸ The people ate and were satisfied. Afterward the disciples picked up seven basketfuls of broken pieces that were left over. ⁹ About four thousand were present. After he had sent them away, ¹⁰ he got into the boat with his disciples and went to the region of Dalmanutha.

¹¹ The Pharisees came and began to question Jesus. To test him, they asked him for a sign from heaven. ¹² He sighed deeply and said, "Why does this generation ask for a sign? Truly I tell you, no sign will be given to it." ¹³ Then he left them, got back into the boat and crossed to the other side.

THE YEAST OF THE PHARISEES AND HEROD

¹⁴ The disciples had forgotten to bring bread, except for one loaf they had with them in the boat. ¹⁵ "Be careful," Jesus warned them. "Watch out for the yeast of the Pharisees and that of Herod."

Why did the Pharisees ask for a sign? (8:11)
The Pharisees wanted proof that Jesus had divine authority, but he refused to give them a sign because they were asking from a position of unbelief.

What was the yeast of the Pharisees and Herod? (8:15)
Yeast was often a symbol of evil or corruption. A tiny amount of yeast could ferment a large amount of dough. In this case, it referred to the evil influence of the Pharisees and Herod Antipas.

ᵃ *31* That is, the Ten Cities

¹⁶They discussed this with one another and said, "It is because we have no bread."

¹⁷Aware of their discussion, Jesus asked them: "Why are you talking about having no bread? Do you still not see or understand? Are your hearts hardened? ¹⁸Do you have eyes but fail to see, and ears but fail to hear? And don't you remember? ¹⁹When I broke the five loaves for the five thousand, how many basketfuls of pieces did you pick up?"

"Twelve," they replied.

²⁰"And when I broke the seven loaves for the four thousand, how many basketfuls of pieces did you pick up?"

They answered, "Seven."

²¹He said to them, "Do you still not understand?"

JESUS HEALS A BLIND MAN AT BETHSAIDA

²²They came to Bethsaida, and some people brought a blind man and begged Jesus to touch him. ²³He took the blind man by the hand and led him outside the village. When he had spit on the man's eyes and put his hands on him, Jesus asked, "Do you see anything?"

²⁴He looked up and said, "I see people; they look like trees walking around."

²⁵Once more Jesus put his hands on the man's eyes. Then his eyes were opened, his sight was restored, and he saw everything clearly. ²⁶Jesus sent him home, saying, "Don't even go into*ᵃ* the village."

PETER DECLARES THAT JESUS IS THE MESSIAH

²⁷Jesus and his disciples went on to the villages around Caesarea Philippi. On the way he asked them, "Who do people say I am?"

²⁸They replied, "Some say John the Baptist; others say Elijah; and still others, one of the prophets."

²⁹"But what about you?" he asked. "Who do you say I am?"

Peter answered, "You are the Messiah."

³⁰Jesus warned them not to tell anyone about him.

JESUS PREDICTS HIS DEATH

³¹He then began to teach them that the Son of Man must suffer many things and be rejected by the elders, the chief priests and the teachers of the law, and that he must be killed and after three days rise again. ³²He spoke plainly about this, and Peter took him aside and began to rebuke him.

³³But when Jesus turned and looked at his disciples, he rebuked Peter. "Get behind me, Satan!" he said. "You do not have in mind the concerns of God, but merely human concerns."

THE WAY OF THE CROSS

³⁴Then he called the crowd to him along with his disciples and said: "Whoever wants to be my disciple must deny themselves and take up their cross and follow me. ³⁵For whoever wants to save their life*ᵇ* will lose it, but whoever

Why did the blind man now see people like trees walking? (8:24)
The blind man had probably bumped into trees when he was blind, so he had some idea of what trees were like. Now he dimly saw people who seemed to him like tree trunks that were walking.

Why did Jesus avoid the term *the Messiah*? (8:29)
Jewish people associated the term *Messiah* with political and national ideals, so Jesus generally avoided using the term to describe himself.

ᵃ 26 Some manuscripts *go and tell anyone in*   *ᵇ 35* The Greek word means either *life* or *soul*; also in verses 36 and 37.

loses their life for me and for the gospel will save it. ³⁶What good is it for someone to gain the whole world, yet forfeit their soul? ³⁷Or what can anyone give in exchange for their soul? ³⁸If anyone is ashamed of me and my words in this adulterous and sinful generation, the Son of Man will be ashamed of them when he comes in his Father's glory with the holy angels."

9 And he said to them, "Truly I tell you, some who are standing here will not taste death before they see that the kingdom of God has come with power."

THE TRANSFIGURATION

²After six days Jesus took Peter, James and John with him and led them up a high mountain, where they were all alone. There he was transfigured before them. ³His clothes became dazzling white, whiter than anyone in the world could bleach them. ⁴And there appeared before them Elijah and Moses, who were talking with Jesus.

⁵Peter said to Jesus, "Rabbi, it is good for us to be here. Let us put up three shelters—one for you, one for Moses and one for Elijah." ⁶(He did not know what to say, they were so frightened.)

⁷Then a cloud appeared and covered them, and a voice came from the cloud: "This is my Son, whom I love. Listen to him!"

⁸Suddenly, when they looked around, they no longer saw anyone with them except Jesus.

⁹As they were coming down the mountain, Jesus gave them orders not to tell anyone what they had seen until the Son of Man had risen from the dead. ¹⁰They kept the matter to themselves, discussing what "rising from the dead" meant.

¹¹And they asked him, "Why do the teachers of the law say that Elijah must come first?"

¹²Jesus replied, "To be sure, Elijah does come first, and restores all things. Why then is it written that the Son of Man must suffer much and be rejected? ¹³But I tell you, Elijah has come, and they have done to him everything they wished, just as it is written about him."

JESUS HEALS A BOY POSSESSED BY AN IMPURE SPIRIT

¹⁴When they came to the other disciples, they saw a large crowd around them and the teachers of the law arguing with them. ¹⁵As soon as all the people saw Jesus, they were overwhelmed with wonder and ran to greet him.

¹⁶"What are you arguing with them about?" he asked.

¹⁷A man in the crowd answered, "Teacher, I brought you my son, who is possessed by a spirit that has robbed him of speech. ¹⁸Whenever it seizes him, it throws him to the ground. He foams at the mouth, gnashes his teeth and becomes rigid. I asked your disciples to drive out the spirit, but they could not."

¹⁹"You unbelieving generation," Jesus replied, "how long shall I stay with you? How long shall I put up with you? Bring the boy to me."

What shelters did Peter want to construct? (9:5)
He may have wanted to erect new tents of meeting where God could communicate with his people, or he may have been thinking of the booths used in the Festival of the Tabernacles (see Leviticus 23:42).

Why were the disciples not to tell what they had seen until after the resurrection? (9:9)
Jesus wanted the disciples to be able to communicate his finished or completed work, which would demonstrate his full identity as the Messiah.

What caused the boy's seizures? (9:18)
Not all seizures were the result of demon possession, but this boy's seizures were.

²⁰ So they brought him. When the spirit saw Jesus, it immediately threw the boy into a convulsion. He fell to the ground and rolled around, foaming at the mouth.

²¹ Jesus asked the boy's father, "How long has he been like this?"

"From childhood," he answered. ²² "It has often thrown him into fire or water to kill him. But if you can do anything, take pity on us and help us."

²³ " 'If you can'?" said Jesus. "Everything is possible for one who believes."

²⁴ Immediately the boy's father exclaimed, "I do believe; help me overcome my unbelief!"

²⁵ When Jesus saw that a crowd was running to the scene, he rebuked the impure spirit. "You deaf and mute spirit," he said, "I command you, come out of him and never enter him again."

²⁶ The spirit shrieked, convulsed him violently and came out. The boy looked so much like a corpse that many said, "He's dead." ²⁷ But Jesus took him by the hand and lifted him to his feet, and he stood up.

²⁸ After Jesus had gone indoors, his disciples asked him privately, "Why couldn't we drive it out?"

²⁹ He replied, "This kind can come out only by prayer.ᵃ"

JESUS PREDICTS HIS DEATH A SECOND TIME

³⁰ They left that place and passed through Galilee. Jesus did not want anyone to know where they were, ³¹ because he was teaching his disciples. He said to them, "The Son of Man is going to be delivered into the hands of men. They will kill him, and after three days he will rise." ³² But they did not understand what he meant and were afraid to ask him about it.

³³ They came to Capernaum. When he was in the house, he asked them, "What were you arguing about on the road?" ³⁴ But they kept quiet because on the way they had argued about who was the greatest.

³⁵ Sitting down, Jesus called the Twelve and said, "Anyone who wants to be first must be the very last, and the servant of all."

ᵃ 29 Some manuscripts *prayer and fasting*

What did the boy's father mean when he said, "I do believe; help me overcome my unbelief"? (9:24)
Faith is never perfect, so faith and doubt, belief and unbelief, are often mixed.

Why would the disciples argue about who was the greatest? (9:34)
Questions of rank and status were very important to Jewish people at this time. However, Jesus did not place importance on rank or status.

What are demons?

MARK 9

Demons are evil spiritual beings that are opposed to God and human beings. They do the work of Satan, and many people believe that they are angels who were thrown from heaven along with Satan when he rebelled against God. For example, Revelation 12:9 says, "The great dragon was hurled down — that ancient serpent called the devil, or Satan, who leads the whole world astray. He was hurled to the earth, and his angels with him."

In the Bible demons have various powers. They could take over a person and control a person's speech and actions. They often caused people to become physically and mentally ill. They knew who Jesus was. When Jesus met someone who was possessed by demons, he commanded the demons to leave the person and cured the person of his or her suffering.

Some people believe that demons are still able to possess people today. The practice of casting demons out of a person in Jesus' name is called exorcism. However, there is no evidence that Christians who love the Lord and have the Holy Spirit in their hearts can be taken over by demons.

36 He took a little child whom he placed among them. Taking the child in his arms, he said to them, 37 "Whoever welcomes one of these little children in my name welcomes me; and whoever welcomes me does not welcome me but the one who sent me."

WHOEVER IS NOT AGAINST US IS FOR US

38 "Teacher," said John, "we saw someone driving out demons in your name and we told him to stop, because he was not one of us."

39 "Do not stop him," Jesus said. "For no one who does a miracle in my name can in the next moment say anything bad about me, 40 for whoever is not against us is for us. 41 Truly I tell you, anyone who gives you a cup of water in my name because you belong to the Messiah will certainly not lose their reward.

CAUSING TO STUMBLE

42 "If anyone causes one of these little ones — those who believe in me — to stumble, it would be better for them if a large millstone were hung around their neck and they were thrown into the sea. 43 If your hand causes you to stumble, cut it off. It is better for you to enter life maimed than with two hands to go into hell, where the fire never goes out. [44] a 45 And if your foot causes you to stumble, cut it off. It is better for you to enter life crippled than to have two feet and be thrown into hell. [46] a 47 And if your eye causes you to stumble, pluck it out. It is better for you to enter the kingdom of God with one eye than to have two eyes and be thrown into hell, 48 where

"'the worms that eat them do not die,
and the fire is not quenched.'b

49 Everyone will be salted with fire.

50 "Salt is good, but if it loses its saltiness, how can you make it salty again? Have salt among yourselves, and be at peace with each other."

DIVORCE

10 Jesus then left that place and went into the region of Judea and across the Jordan. Again crowds of people came to him, and as was his custom, he taught them.

2 Some Pharisees came and tested him by asking, "Is it lawful for a man to divorce his wife?"

3 "What did Moses command you?" he replied.

4 They said, "Moses permitted a man to write a certificate of divorce and send her away."

5 "It was because your hearts were hard that Moses wrote you this law," Jesus replied. 6 "But at the beginning of creation God 'made them male and female.'c 7 'For this reason a man will leave his father and mother and be united to his wife,d 8 and the two will become one flesh.'e So they are no longer

What did Jesus mean about cutting off a hand or a foot? (9:43)
This was exaggeration or hyperbole, where Jesus was saying that anything that got in the way of God's kingdom should be eliminated.

How did Jesus emphasize the importance of marriage? (10:6–9)
Jesus went back to the time before human sin to show God's original intention for marriage.

---

a 44,46 Some manuscripts include here the words of verse 48.　　b 48 Isaiah 66:24　　c 6 Gen. 1:27　　d 7 Some early manuscripts do not have *and be united to his wife.*　　e 8 Gen. 2:24

two, but one flesh. [9] Therefore what God has joined together, let no one separate."

[10] When they were in the house again, the disciples asked Jesus about this. [11] He answered, "Anyone who divorces his wife and marries another woman commits adultery against her. [12] And if she divorces her husband and marries another man, she commits adultery."

THE LITTLE CHILDREN AND JESUS

[13] People were bringing little children to Jesus for him to place his hands on them, but the disciples rebuked them. [14] When Jesus saw this, he was indignant. He said to them, "Let the little children come to me, and do not hinder them, for the kingdom of God belongs to such as these. [15] Truly I tell you, anyone who will not receive the kingdom of God like a little child will never enter it." [16] And he took the children in his arms, placed his hands on them and blessed them.

THE RICH AND THE KINGDOM OF GOD

[17] As Jesus started on his way, a man ran up to him and fell on his knees before him. "Good teacher," he asked, "what must I do to inherit eternal life?"

[18] "Why do you call me good?" Jesus answered. "No one is good—except God alone. [19] You know the commandments: 'You shall not murder, you shall not commit adultery, you shall not steal, you shall not give false testimony, you shall not defraud, honor your father and mother.'[a]"

[20] "Teacher," he declared, "all these I have kept since I was a boy."

[21] Jesus looked at him and loved him. "One thing you lack," he said. "Go, sell everything you have and give to the poor, and you will have treasure in heaven. Then come, follow me."

[22] At this the man's face fell. He went away sad, because he had great wealth.

[23] Jesus looked around and said to his disciples, "How hard it is for the rich to enter the kingdom of God!"

[24] The disciples were amazed at his words. But Jesus said again, "Children, how hard it is[b] to enter the kingdom of God! [25] It is easier for a camel to go through the eye of a needle than for someone who is rich to enter the kingdom of God."

[26] The disciples were even more amazed, and said to each other, "Who then can be saved?"

[27] Jesus looked at them and said, "With man this is impossible, but not with God; all things are possible with God."

[28] Then Peter spoke up, "We have left everything to follow you!"

[29] "Truly I tell you," Jesus replied, "no one who has left home or brothers or sisters or mother or father or children or fields for me and the gospel [30] will fail to receive a hundred times as much in this present age: homes, brothers, sisters, mothers, children and fields—along with persecutions—and in the age to come eternal life. [31] But many who are first will be last, and the last first."

[a] 19 Exodus 20:12 16; Deut. 5:16-20　　[b] 24 Some manuscripts *is for those who trust in riches*

What was Jesus' position on divorce? (10:9–12)
In Jewish practice, divorce was initiated by the husband. Jesus emphasized that marriage was meant to be permanent.

What did Jesus mean that the kingdom of God belonged to children? (10:14)
The kingdom of God belongs to those who, like children, can receive it as a gift.

Why did Jesus tell him to sell all that he had? (10:21)
The young man's problem was his wealth. The fact that he was rich kept him from relying on God for everything. By giving away his wealth, the young man would have removed the obstacle that kept him from trusting In Jesus.

JESUS PREDICTS HIS DEATH
A THIRD TIME

³²They were on their way up to Jerusalem, with Jesus leading the way, and the disciples were astonished, while those who followed were afraid. Again he took the Twelve aside and told them what was going to happen to him. ³³"We are going up to Jerusalem," he said, "and the Son of Man will be delivered over to the chief priests and the teachers of the law. They will condemn him to death and will hand him over to the Gentiles, ³⁴who will mock him and spit on him, flog him and kill him. Three days later he will rise."

THE REQUEST OF JAMES AND JOHN

What were James and John asking from Jesus? (10:35–37)
They were requesting positions of prestige and power.

³⁵Then James and John, the sons of Zebedee, came to him. "Teacher," they said, "we want you to do for us whatever we ask."

³⁶"What do you want me to do for you?" he asked.

³⁷They replied, "Let one of us sit at your right and the other at your left in your glory."

³⁸"You don't know what you are asking," Jesus said. "Can you drink the cup I drink or be baptized with the baptism I am baptized with?"

What did Jesus ask? (10:38)
He asked if they would be able to drink the cup he was about to drink; in other words, if they could share in his suffering.

³⁹"We can," they answered.

Jesus said to them, "You will drink the cup I drink and be baptized with the baptism I am baptized with, ⁴⁰but to sit at my right or left is not for me to grant. These places belong to those for whom they have been prepared."

⁴¹When the ten heard about this, they became indignant with James and John. ⁴²Jesus called them together and said, "You know that those who are regarded as rulers of the Gentiles lord it over them, and their high officials exercise authority over them. ⁴³Not so with you. Instead, whoever wants to become great among you must be your servant, ⁴⁴and whoever wants to be first must be slave of all. ⁴⁵For even the Son of Man did not come to be served, but to serve, and to give his life as a ransom for many."

What was Jesus' role? (10:45)
Jesus came to earth as a servant who would suffer and die to redeem people from their sin. Jesus gave his life to redeem people from the bondage to sin and death.

BLIND BARTIMAEUS RECEIVES
HIS SIGHT

⁴⁶Then they came to Jericho. As Jesus and his disciples, together with a large crowd, were leaving the city, a blind man, Bartimaeus (which means "son of Timaeus"), was sitting by the roadside begging. ⁴⁷When he heard that it was Jesus of Nazareth, he began to shout, "Jesus, Son of David, have mercy on me!"

⁴⁸Many rebuked him and told him to be quiet, but he shouted all the more, "Son of David, have mercy on me!"

⁴⁹Jesus stopped and said, "Call him."

So they called to the blind man, "Cheer up! On your feet! He's calling you." ⁵⁰Throwing his cloak aside, he jumped to his feet and came to Jesus.

⁵¹"What do you want me to do for you?" Jesus asked him. The blind man said, "Rabbi, I want to see."

⁵²"Go," said Jesus, "your faith has healed you." Immediately he received his sight and followed Jesus along the road.

JESUS COMES TO JERUSALEM AS KING

11 As they approached Jerusalem and came to Bethphage and Bethany at the Mount of Olives, Jesus sent two of his disciples, [2]saying to them, "Go to the village ahead of you, and just as you enter it, you will find a colt tied there, which no one has ever ridden. Untie it and bring it here. [3]If anyone asks you, 'Why are you doing this?' say, 'The Lord needs it and will send it back here shortly.'"

[4]They went and found a colt outside in the street, tied at a doorway. As they untied it, [5]some people standing there asked, "What are you doing, untying that colt?" [6]They answered as Jesus had told them to, and the people let them go. [7]When they brought the colt to Jesus and threw their cloaks over it, he sat on it. [8]Many people spread their cloaks on the road, while others spread branches they had cut in the fields. [9]Those who went ahead and those who followed shouted,

"Hosanna![a]"

"Blessed is he who comes in the name of the Lord!"[b]

[10]"Blessed is the coming kingdom of our father David!"

"Hosanna in the highest heaven!"

[11]Jesus entered Jerusalem and went into the temple courts. He looked around at everything, but since it was already late, he went out to Bethany with the Twelve.

JESUS CURSES A FIG TREE AND CLEARS THE TEMPLE COURTS

[12]The next day as they were leaving Bethany, Jesus was hungry. [13]Seeing in the distance a fig tree in leaf, he went to find out if it had any fruit. When he reached it, he found nothing but leaves, because it was not the season for figs. [14]Then he said to the tree, "May no one ever eat fruit from you again." And his disciples heard him say it.

[15]On reaching Jerusalem, Jesus entered the temple courts and began driving out those who were buying and selling there. He overturned the tables of the money changers and the benches of those selling doves, [16]and would not allow anyone to carry merchandise through the temple courts. [17]And as he taught them, he said, "Is it not written: 'My house will be called a house of prayer for all nations'[c]? But you have made it 'a den of robbers.'[d]"

[18]The chief priests and the teachers of the law heard this and began looking for a way to kill him, for they feared him, because the whole crowd was amazed at his teaching.

[19]When evening came, Jesus and his disciples[e] went out of the city.

[20]In the morning, as they went along, they saw the fig tree withered from the roots. [21]Peter remembered and said to Jesus, "Rabbi, look! The fig tree you cursed has withered!"

[22]"Have faith in God," Jesus answered. [23]"Truly[f] I tell

What did "Hosanna" mean? (11:9–10)
The word originally meant "save now, pray," but by New Testament times it had lost its primary meaning and had become an exclamation of praise.

When did fig trees produce fruit? (11:13)
Fig trees around Jerusalem normally began to bud in March or April but did not produce figs until June when their leaves were all out. This tree was an exception because it was full of leaves by the time of Passover. A fully leafed tree would normally have fruit, but this one did not.

What was this temple court? (11:15)
This was the court of the Gentiles, the only part of the temple where Gentiles could worship God and gather for prayer.

---

[a] *9* A Hebrew expression meaning "Save!" which became an exclamation of praise; also in verse 10   [b] *9* Psalm 118:25,26   [c] *17* Isaiah 56:7   [d] *17* Jer. 7:11   [e] *19* Some early manuscripts *came, Jesus*   [f] *22,23* Some early manuscripts *"If you have faith in God," Jesus answered, [23]"truly*

you, if anyone says to this mountain, 'Go, throw yourself into the sea,' and does not doubt in their heart but believes that what they say will happen, it will be done for them. [24] Therefore I tell you, whatever you ask for in prayer, believe that you have received it, and it will be yours. [25] And when you stand praying, if you hold anything against anyone, forgive them, so that your Father in heaven may forgive you your sins." [26] a

THE AUTHORITY OF JESUS QUESTIONED

[27] They arrived again in Jerusalem, and while Jesus was walking in the temple courts, the chief priests, the teachers of the law and the elders came to him. [28] "By what authority are you doing these things?" they asked. "And who gave you authority to do this?"

[29] Jesus replied, "I will ask you one question. Answer me, and I will tell you by what authority I am doing these things. [30] John's baptism—was it from heaven, or of human origin? Tell me!"

[31] They discussed it among themselves and said, "If we say, 'From heaven,' he will ask, 'Then why didn't you believe him?' [32] But if we say, 'Of human origin' . . ." (They feared the people, for everyone held that John really was a prophet.)

[33] So they answered Jesus, "We don't know."

Jesus said, "Neither will I tell you by what authority I am doing these things."

THE PARABLE OF THE TENANTS

12 Jesus then began to speak to them in parables: "A man planted a vineyard. He put a wall around it, dug a pit for the winepress and built a watchtower. Then he rented the vineyard to some farmers and moved to another place. [2] At harvest time he sent a servant to the tenants to collect from them some of the fruit of the vineyard. [3] But they seized him, beat him and sent him away empty-handed. [4] Then he sent another servant to them; they struck this man on the head and treated him shamefully. [5] He sent still another, and that one they killed. He sent many others; some of them they beat, others they killed.

[6] "He had one left to send, a son, whom he loved. He sent him last of all, saying, 'They will respect my son.'

[7] "But the tenants said to one another, 'This is the heir. Come, let's kill him, and the inheritance will be ours.' [8] So they took him and killed him, and threw him out of the vineyard.

[9] "What then will the owner of the vineyard do? He will come and kill those tenants and give the vineyard to others. [10] Haven't you read this passage of Scripture:

" 'The stone the builders rejected
    has become the cornerstone;
[11] the Lord has done this,
    and it is marvelous in our eyes' b?"

What did Jesus mean when he asked if John's authority was from heaven or of human origin? (11:30)
"Heaven" was a common Jewish term for God, and it was often substituted for his name to avoid misusing it. Jesus' question implied that his authority came from God.

How were large estates farmed in Jesus' time? (12:1–12)
Large estates, owned by absent landlords, were put in the hands of local peasants who cultivated the land as tenant farmers. This parable exposed the planned attempt on Jesus' life and God's judgment on those who had made the plans.

---

a 26 Some manuscripts include here words similar to Matt. 6:15.
b 11 Psalm 118:22,23

¹²Then the chief priests, the teachers of the law and the elders looked for a way to arrest him because they knew he had spoken the parable against them. But they were afraid of the crowd; so they left him and went away.

PAYING THE IMPERIAL TAX TO CAESAR

¹³Later they sent some of the Pharisees and Herodians to Jesus to catch him in his words. ¹⁴They came to him and said, "Teacher, we know that you are a man of integrity. You aren't swayed by others, because you pay no attention to who they are; but you teach the way of God in accordance with the truth. Is it right to pay the imperial tax*a* to Caesar or not? ¹⁵Should we pay or shouldn't we?"

But Jesus knew their hypocrisy. "Why are you trying to trap me?" he asked. "Bring me a denarius and let me look at it." ¹⁶They brought the coin, and he asked them, "Whose image is this? And whose inscription?"

"Caesar's," they replied.

¹⁷Then Jesus said to them, "Give back to Caesar what is Caesar's and to God what is God's."

And they were amazed at him.

MARRIAGE AT THE RESURRECTION

¹⁸Then the Sadducees, who say there is no resurrection, came to him with a question. ¹⁹"Teacher," they said, "Moses wrote for us that if a man's brother dies and leaves a wife but no children, the man must marry the widow and raise up offspring for his brother. ²⁰Now there were seven brothers. The first one married and died without leaving any children. ²¹The second one married the widow, but he also died, leaving no child. It was the same with the third. ²²In fact, none of the seven left any children. Last of all, the woman died too. ²³At the resurrection*b* whose wife will she be, since the seven were married to her?"

²⁴Jesus replied, "Are you not in error because you do not know the Scriptures or the power of God? ²⁵When the dead rise, they will neither marry nor be given in marriage; they will be like the angels in heaven. ²⁶Now about the dead rising—have you not read in the Book of Moses, in the account of the burning bush, how God said to him, 'I am the God of Abraham, the God of Isaac, and the God of Jacob'*c*? ²⁷He is not the God of the dead, but of the living. You are badly mistaken!"

THE GREATEST COMMANDMENT

²⁸One of the teachers of the law came and heard them debating. Noticing that Jesus had given them a good answer, he asked him, "Of all the commandments, which is the most important?"

²⁹"The most important one," answered Jesus, "is this: 'Hear, O Israel: The Lord our God, the Lord is one.*d* ³⁰Love the Lord your God with all your heart and with all your soul

---

a 14 A special tax levied on subject peoples, not on Roman citizens
b 23 Some manuscripts resurrection, when people rise from the dead,
c 26 Exodus 3:6   d 29 Or The Lord our God is one Lord

What was this tax? (12:14)
Jews in Judea were required to pay tribute money to the emperor. The tax was highly unpopular, and some Jews refused to pay it because they thought it would be an admission of the Roman right to rule.

The Denarius (12:15)

What did it mean to give back to Caesar what was Caesar's? (12:17)
Jesus meant that there are obligations to the state that do not infringe on our obligations to God.

What was the most important law? (12:29 – 31)
The first quotation came from Deuteronomy 6:4 – 5 and was known as the Shema, which in Hebrew means "hear." To the Shema, Jesus added the commandment from Leviticus 19:18 to love one's neighbor.

and with all your mind and with all your strength.'* 31 The second is this: 'Love your neighbor as yourself.'* There is no commandment greater than these."

32 "Well said, teacher," the man replied. "You are right in saying that God is one and there is no other but him. 33 To love him with all your heart, with all your understanding and with all your strength, and to love your neighbor as yourself is more important than all burnt offerings and sacrifices."

34 When Jesus saw that he had answered wisely, he said to him, "You are not far from the kingdom of God." And from then on no one dared ask him any more questions.

WHOSE SON IS THE MESSIAH?

35 While Jesus was teaching in the temple courts, he asked, "Why do the teachers of the law say that the Messiah is the son of David? 36 David himself, speaking by the Holy Spirit, declared:

"'The Lord said to my Lord:
    "Sit at my right hand
until I put your enemies
    under your feet."'*

37 David himself calls him 'Lord.' How then can he be his son?" The large crowd listened to him with delight.

WARNING AGAINST THE TEACHERS OF THE LAW

38 As he taught, Jesus said, "Watch out for the teachers of the law. They like to walk around in flowing robes and be greeted with respect in the marketplaces, 39 and have the most important seats in the synagogues and the places of honor at banquets. 40 They devour widows' houses and for a show make lengthy prayers. These men will be punished most severely."

THE WIDOW'S OFFERING

41 Jesus sat down opposite the place where the offerings were put and watched the crowd putting their money into the temple treasury. Many rich people threw in large amounts. 42 But a poor widow came and put in two very small copper coins, worth only a few cents.

43 Calling his disciples to him, Jesus said, "Truly I tell you, this poor widow has put more into the treasury than all the others. 44 They all gave out of their wealth; but she, out of her poverty, put in everything—all she had to live on."

THE DESTRUCTION OF THE TEMPLE AND SIGNS OF THE END TIMES

13 As Jesus was leaving the temple, one of his disciples said to him, "Look, Teacher! What massive stones! What magnificent buildings!"

2 "Do you see all these great buildings?" replied Jesus. "Not one stone here will be left on another; every one will be thrown down."

What were the teachers of the law like? (12:38–40)
They wore long, flowing linen robes that were fringed and almost reached to the ground. They took the most prominent seats in the synagogue, and they depended on the generosity of patrons for their livelihood, so they sometimes exploited widows and others.

How large were these massive stones? (13:1)
According to Josephus, some of these stones were 37 feet long, 12 feet high, and 18 feet wide.

30 Deut. 6:4,5   *31* Lev. 19:18   *36* Psalm 110:1

³As Jesus was sitting on the Mount of Olives opposite the temple, Peter, James, John and Andrew asked him privately, ⁴"Tell us, when will these things happen? And what will be the sign that they are all about to be fulfilled?"

⁵Jesus said to them: "Watch out that no one deceives you. ⁶Many will come in my name, claiming, 'I am he,' and will deceive many. ⁷When you hear of wars and rumors of wars, do not be alarmed. Such things must happen, but the end is still to come. ⁸Nation will rise against nation, and kingdom against kingdom. There will be earthquakes in various places, and famines. These are the beginning of birth pains.

⁹"You must be on your guard. You will be handed over to the local councils and flogged in the synagogues. On account of me you will stand before governors and kings as witnesses to them. ¹⁰And the gospel must first be preached to all nations. ¹¹Whenever you are arrested and brought to trial, do not worry beforehand about what to say. Just say whatever is given you at the time, for it is not you speaking, but the Holy Spirit.

¹²"Brother will betray brother to death, and a father his child. Children will rebel against their parents and have them put to death. ¹³Everyone will hate you because of me, but the one who stands firm to the end will be saved.

¹⁴"When you see 'the abomination that causes desolation'ᵃ standing where itᵇ does not belong—let the reader understand—then let those who are in Judea flee to the mountains. ¹⁵Let no one on the housetop go down or enter the house to take anything out. ¹⁶Let no one in the field go back to get their cloak. ¹⁷How dreadful it will be in those days for pregnant women and nursing mothers! ¹⁸Pray that this will not take place in winter, ¹⁹because those will be days of distress unequaled from the beginning, when God created the world, until now—and never to be equaled again.

²⁰"If the Lord had not cut short those days, no one would survive. But for the sake of the elect, whom he has chosen, he has shortened them. ²¹At that time if anyone says to you, 'Look, here is the Messiah!' or, 'Look, there he is!' do not believe it. ²²For false messiahs and false prophets will appear and perform signs and wonders to deceive, if possible, even the elect. ²³So be on your guard; I have told you everything ahead of time.

²⁴"But in those days, following that distress,

"'the sun will be darkened,
　　and the moon will not give its light;
²⁵the stars will fall from the sky,
　　and the heavenly bodies will be shaken.'ᶜ

²⁶"At that time people will see the Son of Man coming in clouds with great power and glory. ²⁷And he will send his angels and gather his elect from the four winds, from the ends of the earth to the ends of the heavens.

²⁸"Now learn this lesson from the fig tree: As soon as its twigs get tender and its leaves come out, you know that summer is near. ²⁹Even so, when you see these things happening,

Why did Jesus tell his disciples to watch out? (13:5)
In this verse and in several others, Jesus warned his disciples to be careful not to be deceived.

What was the penalty for breaking Jewish regulations? (13:9)
The local councils administered justice. Offenses were punishable by flogging, and the maximum penalty was 39 lashes with a whip.

What was winter like in Israel? (13:18)
This was the time when the heavy rains caused streams to become swollen and impossible to cross, preventing many from reaching a place of refuge.

ᵃ 14 Daniel 9:27; 11:31; 12:11　　ᵇ 14 Or he　　ᶜ 25 Isaiah 13:10; 34:4

you know that it[a] is near, right at the door. [30]Truly I tell you, this generation will certainly not pass away until all these things have happened. [31]Heaven and earth will pass away, but my words will never pass away.

THE DAY AND HOUR UNKNOWN

[32]"But about that day or hour no one knows, not even the angels in heaven, nor the Son, but only the Father. [33]Be on guard! Be alert[b]! You do not know when that time will come. [34]It's like a man going away: He leaves his house and puts his servants in charge, each with their assigned task, and tells the one at the door to keep watch.

[35]"Therefore keep watch because you do not know when the owner of the house will come back—whether in the evening, or at midnight, or when the rooster crows, or at dawn. [36]If he comes suddenly, do not let him find you sleeping. [37]What I say to you, I say to everyone: 'Watch!'"

JESUS ANOINTED AT BETHANY

14 Now the Passover and the Festival of Unleavened Bread were only two days away, and the chief priests and the teachers of the law were scheming to arrest Jesus secretly and kill him. [2]"But not during the festival," they said, "or the people may riot."

[3]While he was in Bethany, reclining at the table in the home of Simon the Leper, a woman came with an alabaster jar of very expensive perfume, made of pure nard. She broke the jar and poured the perfume on his head.

[4]Some of those present were saying indignantly to one another, "Why this waste of perfume? [5]It could have been sold for more than a year's wages[c] and the money given to the poor." And they rebuked her harshly.

[6]"Leave her alone," said Jesus. "Why are you bothering her? She has done a beautiful thing to me. [7]The poor you will always have with you,[d] and you can help them any time you want. But you will not always have me. [8]She did what she could. She poured perfume on my body beforehand to prepare for my burial. [9]Truly I tell you, wherever the gospel is preached throughout the world, what she has done will also be told, in memory of her."

[10]Then Judas Iscariot, one of the Twelve, went to the chief priests to betray Jesus to them. [11]They were delighted to hear this and promised to give him money. So he watched for an opportunity to hand him over.

THE LAST SUPPER

[12]On the first day of the Festival of Unleavened Bread, when it was customary to sacrifice the Passover lamb, Jesus' disciples asked him, "Where do you want us to go and make preparations for you to eat the Passover?"

[13]So he sent two of his disciples, telling them, "Go into the city, and a man carrying a jar of water will meet you. Follow him. [14]Say to the owner of the house he enters, 'The Teacher

---

What is significant about the four time periods in this verse? (13:35)
This verse includes all four watches of the night used by the Romans. In other words, Jesus could come back at any time.

Why were the priests worried about rioting during the Passover? (14:1–2)
During the Festival of Unleavened Bread and the Passover, the population of Jerusalem increased from about 50,000 to several hundred thousand. This would be a disastrous time to arrest and kill Jesus.

Who was this woman? (14:3)
We know from John's Gospel (12:3) that this was Mary, the sister of Martha and Lazarus.

What was the custom of giving to the poor? (14:5)
It was the custom of the Jews to give gifts to the poor on the evening of the Passover.

How did this prepare Jesus' body for burial? (14:8)
It was a normal Jewish custom to anoint a body with aromatic oils when preparing the body for burial.

Which two disciples did Jesus send? (14:13)
They were Peter and John (see Luke 22:8).

---

[a] 29 Or *he*   [b] 33 Some manuscripts *alert and pray*   [c] 5 Greek *than three hundred denarii*   [d] 7 See Deut. 15:11.

asks: Where is my guest room, where I may eat the Passover with my disciples?' ¹⁵He will show you a large room upstairs, furnished and ready. Make preparations for us there."

¹⁶The disciples left, went into the city and found things just as Jesus had told them. So they prepared the Passover.

¹⁷When evening came, Jesus arrived with the Twelve. ¹⁸While they were reclining at the table eating, he said, "Truly I tell you, one of you will betray me—one who is eating with me."

¹⁹They were saddened, and one by one they said to him, "Surely you don't mean me?"

²⁰"It is one of the Twelve," he replied, "one who dips bread into the bowl with me. ²¹The Son of Man will go just as it is written about him. But woe to that man who betrays the Son of Man! It would be better for him if he had not been born."

²²While they were eating, Jesus took bread, and when he had given thanks, he broke it and gave it to his disciples, saying, "Take it; this is my body."

²³Then he took a cup, and when he had given thanks, he gave it to them, and they all drank from it.

²⁴"This is my blood of theᵃ covenant, which is poured out for many," he said to them. ²⁵"Truly I tell you, I will not drink again from the fruit of the vine until that day when I drink it new in the kingdom of God."

²⁶When they had sung a hymn, they went out to the Mount of Olives.

JESUS PREDICTS PETER'S DENIAL

²⁷"You will all fall away," Jesus told them, "for it is written:

"'I will strike the shepherd,
    and the sheep will be scattered.'ᵇ

²⁸But after I have risen, I will go ahead of you into Galilee."

²⁹Peter declared, "Even if all fall away, I will not."

³⁰"Truly I tell you," Jesus answered, "today—yes, tonight—before the rooster crows twiceᶜ you yourself will disown me three times."

³¹But Peter insisted emphatically, "Even if I have to die with you, I will never disown you." And all the others said the same.

GETHSEMANE

³²They went to a place called Gethsemane, and Jesus said to his disciples, "Sit here while I pray." ³³He took Peter, James and John along with him, and he began to be deeply distressed and troubled. ³⁴"My soul is overwhelmed with sorrow to the point of death," he said to them. "Stay here and keep watch."

³⁵Going a little farther, he fell to the ground and prayed that if possible the hour might pass from him. ³⁶"Abba,ᵈ Father," he said, "everything is possible for you. Take this cup from me. Yet not what I will, but what you will."

³⁷Then he returned to his disciples and found them sleep-

ᵃ 24 Some manuscripts the new manuscripts do not have twice.   ᵇ 27 Zech. 13:7   ᶜ 30 Some early   ᵈ 36 Aramaic for father

What do the bread and the wine represent? (14:22–24)
Jesus gave a new meaning to the Passover celebration by saying that the bread represented his body and the wine represented his blood. Jesus was showing the disciples that his death was the way by which believers would be saved.

Where did the term Eucharist come from? (14:23)
The term Eucharist, another name for Communion or the Lord's Supper, came from the Greek word translated as "giving thanks" in this verse.

What does Abba mean? (14:36)
This is an Aramaic word that was a small child's way of saying "Daddy." It represented Jesus' close and intimate relationship with God the Father.

ing. "Simon," he said to Peter, "are you asleep? Couldn't you keep watch for one hour? ³⁸Watch and pray so that you will not fall into temptation. The spirit is willing, but the flesh is weak."

³⁹Once more he went away and prayed the same thing. ⁴⁰When he came back, he again found them sleeping, because their eyes were heavy. They did not know what to say to him.

⁴¹Returning the third time, he said to them, "Are you still sleeping and resting? Enough! The hour has come. Look, the Son of Man is delivered into the hands of sinners. ⁴²Rise! Let us go! Here comes my betrayer!"

JESUS ARRESTED

⁴³Just as he was speaking, Judas, one of the Twelve, appeared. With him was a crowd armed with swords and clubs, sent from the chief priests, the teachers of the law, and the elders.

⁴⁴Now the betrayer had arranged a signal with them: "The one I kiss is the man; arrest him and lead him away under guard." ⁴⁵Going at once to Jesus, Judas said, "Rabbi!" and kissed him. ⁴⁶The men seized Jesus and arrested him. ⁴⁷Then one of those standing near drew his sword and struck the servant of the high priest, cutting off his ear.

⁴⁸"Am I leading a rebellion," said Jesus, "that you have come out with swords and clubs to capture me? ⁴⁹Every day I was with you, teaching in the temple courts, and you did not arrest me. But the Scriptures must be fulfilled." ⁵⁰Then everyone deserted him and fled.

⁵¹A young man, wearing nothing but a linen garment, was following Jesus. When they seized him, ⁵²he fled naked, leaving his garment behind.

JESUS BEFORE THE SANHEDRIN

⁵³They took Jesus to the high priest, and all the chief priests, the elders and the teachers of the law came together. ⁵⁴Peter followed him at a distance, right into the courtyard of the high priest. There he sat with the guards and warmed himself at the fire.

⁵⁵The chief priests and the whole Sanhedrin were looking for evidence against Jesus so that they could put him to death, but they did not find any. ⁵⁶Many testified falsely against him, but their statements did not agree.

⁵⁷Then some stood up and gave this false testimony against him: ⁵⁸"We heard him say, 'I will destroy this temple made with human hands and in three days will build another, not made with hands.'" ⁵⁹Yet even then their testimony did not agree.

⁶⁰Then the high priest stood up before them and asked Jesus, "Are you not going to answer? What is this testimony that these men are bringing against you?" ⁶¹But Jesus remained silent and gave no answer.

Again the high priest asked him, "Are you the Messiah, the Son of the Blessed One?"

⁶²"I am," said Jesus. "And you will see the Son of Man

Why would Judas kiss Jesus? (14:45)
This was a common greeting of respect with which disciples greeted their master. But Judas used this greeting as a signal to those who were going to arrest Jesus.

Who was the high priest? (14:53)
The high priest was Caiaphas, son-in-law of Annas, the former high priest.

What was the Sanhedrin? (14:55)
This was the high court of the Jews. It consisted of 71 members: chief priests, elders, teachers of the law, and the high priest. The Roman government gave the Sanhedrin a great deal of authority, but it could not impose capital punishment.

sitting at the right hand of the Mighty One and coming on the clouds of heaven."

⁶³The high priest tore his clothes. "Why do we need any more witnesses?" he asked. ⁶⁴"You have heard the blasphemy. What do you think?"

They all condemned him as worthy of death. ⁶⁵Then some began to spit at him; they blindfolded him, struck him with their fists, and said, "Prophesy!" And the guards took him and beat him.

PETER DISOWNS JESUS

⁶⁶While Peter was below in the courtyard, one of the servant girls of the high priest came by. ⁶⁷When she saw Peter warming himself, she looked closely at him.

"You also were with that Nazarene, Jesus," she said.

⁶⁸But he denied it. "I don't know or understand what you're talking about," he said, and went out into the entry-way.ᵃ

⁶⁹When the servant girl saw him there, she said again to those standing around, "This fellow is one of them." ⁷⁰Again he denied it.

After a little while, those standing near said to Peter, "Surely you are one of them, for you are a Galilean."

⁷¹He began to call down curses, and he swore to them, "I don't know this man you're talking about."

⁷²Immediately the rooster crowed the second time.ᵇ Then Peter remembered the word Jesus had spoken to him: "Before the rooster crows twiceᶜ you will disown me three times." And he broke down and wept.

JESUS BEFORE PILATE

15 Very early in the morning, the chief priests, with the elders, the teachers of the law and the whole Sanhedrin, made their plans. So they bound Jesus, led him away and handed him over to Pilate.

²"Are you the king of the Jews?" asked Pilate.

"You have said so," Jesus replied.

³The chief priests accused him of many things. ⁴So again Pilate asked him, "Aren't you going to answer? See how many things they are accusing you of."

⁵But Jesus still made no reply, and Pilate was amazed.

ᵃ 68 Some early manuscripts *entryway and the rooster crowed*   ᵇ 72 Some early manuscripts do not have *the second time*.   ᶜ 72 Some early manuscripts do not have *twice*.

Why was Jesus accused of blasphemy? (14:64)
Blasphemy included an insult to God or any challenge to his authority or majesty. Since Jesus claimed to be the Messiah, God's Son, this was considered blasphemy.

Why did Jesus have to suffer and die?

In the beginning God created Adam and Eve as perfect creatures. However, they disobeyed God and sinned by eating fruit from the tree that God had told them not to. Because of that sin there were consequences; pain and death came into the world. And human beings from that time on were unable to keep God's law perfectly.

Because God is just, he required that his law be kept. Because God is merciful, he sent his Son down from heaven to redeem the world. Even though Jesus was innocent, he suffered and died in order to become a sacrifice for human sin. By paying the price for sin, he set believers free from eternal punishment and gained for his people God's grace, righteousness, and eternal life.

How did they flog Jesus?
(15:15)
The Romans used a whip made of several pieces of leather that included sharp stones and shards of bone attached.

A Roman Whip

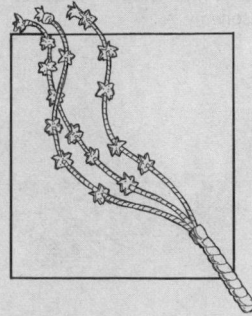

What was the Praetorium?
(15:16)
The word was originally used to describe a general's tent or the headquarters in a military camp. It came to refer to the governor's official residence in Jerusalem.

What was this crown of thorns? (15:17)
Made from a prickly plant, the mock crown and the purple robe were part of the mocking attire that Jesus was made to wear.

What did it mean to be crucified? (15:24)
This was a Roman means of execution in which a victim was nailed to a cross. Heavy nails were driven through the wrists and heel bones. Then the cross was raised. As the victim hung there, it was difficult for them to breathe. At a certain point, if the person was still alive, his legs were broken to hasten their death by suffocation. Only slaves, the worst criminals, and people who weren't Roman citizens were executed in this way. It was the right of the executioner's squad to divide up the victim's clothing.

[6] Now it was the custom at the festival to release a prisoner whom the people requested. [7] A man called Barabbas was in prison with the insurrectionists who had committed murder in the uprising. [8] The crowd came up and asked Pilate to do for them what he usually did.

[9] "Do you want me to release to you the king of the Jews?" asked Pilate, [10] knowing it was out of self-interest that the chief priests had handed Jesus over to him. [11] But the chief priests stirred up the crowd to have Pilate release Barabbas instead.

[12] "What shall I do, then, with the one you call the king of the Jews?" Pilate asked them.

[13] "Crucify him!" they shouted.

[14] "Why? What crime has he committed?" asked Pilate.

But they shouted all the louder, "Crucify him!"

[15] Wanting to satisfy the crowd, Pilate released Barabbas to them. He had Jesus flogged, and handed him over to be crucified.

THE SOLDIERS MOCK JESUS

[16] The soldiers led Jesus away into the palace (that is, the Praetorium) and called together the whole company of soldiers. [17] They put a purple robe on him, then twisted together a crown of thorns and set it on him. [18] And they began to call out to him, "Hail, king of the Jews!" [19] Again and again they struck him on the head with a staff and spit on him. Falling on their knees, they paid homage to him. [20] And when they had mocked him, they took off the purple robe and put his own clothes on him. Then they led him out to crucify him.

THE CRUCIFIXION OF JESUS

[21] A certain man from Cyrene, Simon, the father of Alexander and Rufus, was passing by on his way in from the country, and they forced him to carry the cross. [22] They brought Jesus to the place called Golgotha (which means "the place of the skull"). [23] Then they offered him wine mixed with myrrh, but he did not take it. [24] And they crucified him. Dividing up his clothes, they cast lots to see what each would get.

[25] It was nine in the morning when they crucified him. [26] The written notice of the charge against him read: THE KING OF THE JEWS.

[27] They crucified two rebels with him, one on his right and one on his left. [28]a [29] Those who passed by hurled insults at him, shaking their heads and saying, "So! You who are going to destroy the temple and build it in three days, [30] come down from the cross and save yourself!" [31] In the same way the chief priests and the teachers of the law mocked him among themselves. "He saved others," they said, "but he can't save himself! [32] Let this Messiah, this king of Israel, come down now from the cross, that we may see and believe." Those crucified with him also heaped insults on him.

---

a 28 Some manuscripts include here words similar to Luke 22:37.

THE DEATH OF JESUS

³³ At noon, darkness came over the whole land until three in the afternoon. ³⁴ And at three in the afternoon Jesus cried out in a loud voice, *"Eloi, Eloi, lema sabachthani?"* (which means "My God, my God, why have you forsaken me?").ᵃ

³⁵ When some of those standing near heard this, they said, "Listen, he's calling Elijah."

³⁶ Someone ran, filled a sponge with wine vinegar, put it on a staff, and offered it to Jesus to drink. "Now leave him alone. Let's see if Elijah comes to take him down," he said.

³⁷ With a loud cry, Jesus breathed his last.

³⁸ The curtain of the temple was torn in two from top to bottom. ³⁹ And when the centurion, who stood there in front of Jesus, saw how he died,ᵇ he said, "Surely this man was the Son of God!"

⁴⁰ Some women were watching from a distance. Among them were Mary Magdalene, Mary the mother of James the younger and of Joseph,ᶜ and Salome. ⁴¹ In Galilee these women had followed him and cared for his needs. Many other women who had come up with him to Jerusalem were also there.

Why was the curtain of the temple torn? (15:38)
This symbolized that Christ had torn down the barrier that separated people from God. Through his death, people now had direct access to God. The direction of the tear (top to bottom) shows that God caused this to happen.

THE BURIAL OF JESUS

⁴² It was Preparation Day (that is, the day before the Sabbath). So as evening approached, ⁴³ Joseph of Arimathea, a prominent member of the Council, who was himself waiting for the kingdom of God, went boldly to Pilate and asked for Jesus' body. ⁴⁴ Pilate was surprised to hear that he was already dead. Summoning the centurion, he asked him if Jesus had already died. ⁴⁵ When he learned from the centurion that it was so, he gave the body to Joseph. ⁴⁶ So Joseph bought some linen cloth, took down the body, wrapped it in the linen, and placed it in a tomb cut out of rock. Then he rolled a stone against the entrance of the tomb. ⁴⁷ Mary Magdalene and Mary the mother of Joseph saw where he was laid.

JESUS HAS RISEN

16 When the Sabbath was over, Mary Magdalene, Mary the mother of James, and Salome bought spices so that they might go to anoint Jesus' body. ² Very early on the first day of the week, just after sunrise, they were on their way to the tomb ³ and they asked each other, "Who will roll the stone away from the entrance of the tomb?"

⁴ But when they looked up, they saw that the stone, which was very large, had been rolled away. ⁵ As they entered the tomb, they saw a young man dressed in a white robe sitting on the right side, and they were alarmed.

⁶ "Don't be alarmed," he said. "You are looking for Jesus the Nazarene, who was crucified. He has risen! He is not here. See the place where they laid him. ⁷ But go, tell his disciples and Peter, 'He is going ahead of you into Galilee. There you will see him, just as he told you.'"

Why was removing the stone difficult? (16:3)
Setting the large stone in place was a relatively easy task, but once it had slipped into the groove in the bedrock in front of the entrance, it would be very difficult to remove.

Who was the young man dressed in white? (16:5)
Matthew identifies the man as an angel (Matthew 28:2).

ᵃ *34* Psalm 22:1   ᵇ *39* Some manuscripts *saw that he died with such a cry*
ᶜ *40* Greek *Joses,* a variant of *Joseph*; also in verse 47

⁸Trembling and bewildered, the women went out and fled from the tomb. They said nothing to anyone, because they were afraid.[a]

[The earliest manuscripts and some other ancient witnesses do not have verses 9–20.]

⁹When Jesus rose early on the first day of the week, he appeared first to Mary Magdalene, out of whom he had driven seven demons. ¹⁰She went and told those who had been with him and who were mourning and weeping. ¹¹When they heard that Jesus was alive and that she had seen him, they did not believe it.

¹²Afterward Jesus appeared in a different form to two of them while they were walking in the country. ¹³These returned and reported it to the rest; but they did not believe them either.

¹⁴Later Jesus appeared to the Eleven as they were eating; he rebuked them for their lack of faith and their stubborn refusal to believe those who had seen him after he had risen.

¹⁵He said to them, "Go into all the world and preach the gospel to all creation. ¹⁶Whoever believes and is baptized will be saved, but whoever does not believe will be condemned. ¹⁷And these signs will accompany those who believe: In my name they will drive out demons; they will speak in new tongues; ¹⁸they will pick up snakes with their hands; and when they drink deadly poison, it will not hurt them at all; they will place their hands on sick people, and they will get well."

¹⁹After the Lord Jesus had spoken to them, he was taken up into heaven and he sat at the right hand of God. ²⁰Then the disciples went out and preached everywhere, and the Lord worked with them and confirmed his word by the signs that accompanied it.

---

[a] 8 Some manuscripts have the following ending between verses 8 and 9, and one manuscript has it after verse 8 (omitting verses 9-20): *Then they quickly reported all these instructions to those around Peter. After this, Jesus himself also sent out through them from east to west the sacred and imperishable proclamation of eternal salvation. Amen.*

THE MINISTRY OF JESUS

EVENT	PLACE	MATTHEW	MARK	LUKE	JOHN
Jesus baptized	Jordan River	3:13–17	1:9–11	3:21–22	1:29–34
Jesus tempted by Satan	Desert	4:1–11	1:12–13	4:1–13	
Jesus' first miracle	Cana				2:1–11
Jesus and Nicodemus	Judea				3:1–21
Jesus talks to a Samaritan woman	Samaria				4:5–42
Jesus heals an official's son	Cana				4:46–54
The people of Nazareth try to kill Jesus	Nazareth			4:16–30	
Jesus calls four fishermen	Sea of Galilee	4:18–22	1:16–20	5:1–11	
Jesus heals Peter's mother-in-law	Capernaum	8:14–15	1:29–31	4:38–39	
Jesus begins preaching in Galilee	Galilee	4:23–25	1:35–39	4:42–44	
Matthew decides to follow Jesus	Capernaum	9:9–13	2:13–17	5:27–32	
Jesus chooses twelve disciples	Galilee	10:2–4	3:13–19	6:12–15	
Jesus preaches the Sermon on the Mount	Galilee	5:1—7:29		6:20–49	
A sinful woman anoints Jesus	Capernaum			7:36–50	
Jesus travels again through Galilee	Galilee			8:1–3	
Jesus tells kingdom parables	Galilee	13:1–52	4:1–34	8:4–18	
Jesus quiets the storm	Sea of Galilee	8:23–27	4:35–41	8:22–25	
Jairus's daughter raised to life	Capernaum	9:18–26	5:21–43	8:40–56	
Jesus sends out the Twelve	Galilee	9:35—11:1	6:6–13	9:1–6	
John the Baptist killed by Herod	Machaerus in Judea	14:1–12	6:14–29	9:7–9	
Jesus feeds the 5,000	Bethsaida	14:13–21	6:30–44	9:10–17	6:1–14
Jesus walks on water	Sea of Galilee	14:22–32	6:47–52		6:16–21
Jesus feeds the 4,000	Sea of Galilee	15:32–39	8:1–10		
Peter confesses Jesus as the Son of God	Caesarea Philippi	16:13–20	8:27–30	9:18–21	
Jesus predicts his death	Caesarea Philippi	16:21–26	8:31–37	9:22–25	
Jesus is transfigured	Mount Hermon	17:1–13	9:2–13	9:28–36	
Jesus pays his temple taxes	Capernaum	17:24–27			
Jesus attends the Festival of Tabernacles	Jerusalem				7:10–52
Jesus heals a man born blind	Jerusalem				9:1–41
Jesus visits Mary and Martha	Bethany			10:38–42	
Jesus raises Lazarus from the dead	Bethany				11:1–44
Jesus begins his last trip to Jerusalem	Border road			17:11	
Jesus blesses the little children	Transjordan	19:13–15	10:13–16	18:15–17	
Jesus talks to the rich young man	Transjordan	19:16–30	10:17–31	18:18–30	
Jesus again predicts his death	Near the Jordan	20:17–19	10:32–34	18:31–34	
Jesus heals blind Bartimaeus	Jericho	20:29–34	10:46–52	18:35–43	
Jesus talks to Zacchaeus	Jericho			19:1–10	
Jesus visits Mary and Martha again	Bethany				12:1–11

THE LAST WEEK

EVENT	PLACE	DAY OF THE WEEK	MATTHEW	MARK	LUKE	JOHN
Jesus comes to Jerusalem as King	Jerusalem	Sunday	21:1–11	11:1–11	19:29–44	12:12–19
Jesus curses the fig tree	Jerusalem	Monday	21:18–22	11:12–14		
Jesus clears the temple	Jerusalem	Monday	21:12–13	11:15–18	19:45–48	
The authority of Jesus questioned	Jerusalem	Tuesday	21:23–27	11:27–33	20:1–8	
Jesus teaches in the temple	Jerusalem	Tuesday	21:28—23:39	12:1–44	20:9—21:4	
Jesus' feet anointed	Bethany	Tuesday	26:6–13	14:3–9		12:2–11
The plot against Jesus	Jerusalem	Wednesday	26:14–16	14:10–11	22:3–6	
The Last Supper	Jerusalem	Thursday	26:17–29	14:12–25	22:7–38	13:1–38
Jesus comforts his disciples	Jerusalem	Thursday				14:1—16:33
Jesus' high priestly prayer	Jerusalem	Thursday				17:1–26
Gethsemane	Jerusalem	Thursday	26:36–46	14:32–42	22:40–46	
Jesus' arrest and trial	Jerusalem	Friday	26:47—27:26	14:43—15:15	22:47—23:25	18:2—19:16
Jesus' crucifixion and death	Golgotha	Friday	27:27–56	15:16–41	23:26–49	19:17–37
The burial of Jesus	Garden tomb	Friday	27:57–66	15:42–47	23:50–56	19:38–42

RESURRECTION APPEARANCES

APPEARANCE	PLACE	TIME	MATTHEW	MARK	LUKE	JOHN	ACTS	1CO
The empty tomb	Jerusalem	Resurrection Sunday	28:1–8	16:1–8	24:1–12	20:1–10]		
To Mary Magdalene in the garden	Jerusalem	Resurrection Sunday		16:9–11		20:11–18		
To other women	Jerusalem	Resurrection Sunday	28:9–10					
To two people going to Emmaus	Road to Emmaus	Resurrection Sunday		16:12–13	24:13–32			
To Peter	Jerusalem	Resurrection Sunday			24:34			15:5
To the 10 disciples in the upper room	Jerusalem	Resurrection Sunday			24:36–43	20:19–25		
To the 11 disciples in the upper room	Jerusalem	Following Sunday		16:14		20:26–31		15:5
To 7 disciples fishing	Sea of Galilee	Some time later				21:1–23		
To the 11 disciples on a mountain	Galilee	Some time later	28:16–20	16:15–18				
To more than 500 hundred	Unknown	Some time later						15:6
To James	Unknown	Some time later						15:7
To his disciples at his ascension	Mount of Olives	40 days after Jesus' resurrection			24:36–51		1:3–9	
To Paul	Damascus	Several years later					9:1–19 22:3–16 26:9–18	9:1

Luke

INTRODUCTION

Who wrote this book?	Luke, a physician who often traveled with Paul, wrote this book.
Why was this book written?	The book of Luke tells what many people who knew Jesus remembered of his life and teaching.
For whom was this book written?	Luke wrote for people who wanted to know the kind of person Jesus was.
What happens in this book?	Jesus meets, teaches, and helps many different kinds of people.
Who is the key person in this book?	Jesus is the most important person in this book.
Where did this happen?	Most of the events in this book happened in Galilee and Judea. (See the map at the back of this Bible to find these places.)

What are some stories found in this book?	
The birth of John the Baptist	Luke 1:57 – 80
The shepherds and the angels	Luke 2:8 – 20
Jesus raises a widow's son	Luke 7:11 – 17
The good Samaritan	Luke 10:25 – 37
The rich fool	Luke 12:13 – 21
The lost son	Luke 15:11 – 32
The rich man and Lazarus	Luke 16:19 – 31
Jesus heals ten lepers	Luke 17:11 – 19
The Pharisee and the tax collector	Luke 18:9 – 14
Zacchaeus	Luke 19:1 – 10

When did these things happen?

40 BC 30 20 10 AD 1 10 20 30 40 50 60 70

HEROD THE GREAT'S REIGN (C. 37 - 4 BC)

JESUS' BIRTH (C. 6/5 BC)

JESUS' FLIGHT TO EGYPT (C. 5/4 BC)

JESUS' VISIT TO THE TEMPLE (C. AD 7/8)

BEGINNING OF JOHN THE BAPTIST'S MINISTRY (C. AD 26)

BEGINNING OF JESUS' MINISTRY (C. AD 26)

JESUS' DEATH, RESURRECTION AND ASCENSION (C. AD 30)

PAUL'S CONVERSION (C. AD 35)

BOOK OF LUKE WRITTEN (C. AD 59 - 63)

INTRODUCTION

1 Many have undertaken to draw up an account of the things that have been fulfilled*a* among us, ²just as they were handed down to us by those who from the first were eyewitnesses and servants of the word. ³With this in mind, since I myself have carefully investigated everything from the beginning, I too decided to write an orderly account for you, most excellent Theophilus, ⁴so that you may know the certainty of the things you have been taught.

THE BIRTH OF JOHN THE BAPTIST FORETOLD

⁵In the time of Herod king of Judea there was a priest named Zechariah, who belonged to the priestly division of Abijah; his wife Elizabeth was also a descendant of Aaron. ⁶Both of them were righteous in the sight of God, observing all the Lord's commands and decrees blamelessly. ⁷But they were childless because Elizabeth was not able to conceive, and they were both very old.

⁸Once when Zechariah's division was on duty and he was serving as priest before God, ⁹he was chosen by lot, according to the custom of the priesthood, to go into the temple of the Lord and burn incense. ¹⁰And when the time for the burning of incense came, all the assembled worshipers were praying outside.

¹¹Then an angel of the Lord appeared to him, standing at the right side of the altar of incense. ¹²When Zechariah saw him, he was startled and was gripped with fear. ¹³But the angel said to him: "Do not be afraid, Zechariah; your prayer has been heard. Your wife Elizabeth will bear you a son, and you are to call him John. ¹⁴He will be a joy and delight to you, and many will rejoice because of his birth, ¹⁵for he will be great in the sight of the Lord. He is never to take wine or other fermented drink, and he will be filled with the Holy Spirit even before he is born. ¹⁶He will bring back many of the people of Israel to the Lord their God. ¹⁷And he will go on before the Lord, in the spirit and power of Elijah, to turn the hearts of the parents to their children and the disobedient to the wisdom of the righteous—to make ready a people prepared for the Lord."

¹⁸Zechariah asked the angel, "How can I be sure of this? I am an old man and my wife is well along in years."

¹⁹The angel said to him, "I am Gabriel. I stand in the presence of God, and I have been sent to speak to you and to tell you this good news. ²⁰And now you will be silent and not able to speak until the day this happens, because you did not believe my words, which will come true at their appointed time."

²¹Meanwhile, the people were waiting for Zechariah and wondering why he stayed so long in the temple. ²²When he came out, he could not speak to them. They realized he had seen a vision in the temple, for he kept making signs to them but remained unable to speak.

²³When his time of service was completed, he returned

Who was Herod? (1:5)
Herod the Great ruled Judea from 37 to 4 B.C. His reputation was one of a vicious and cruel ruler who even killed some of his own family members.

Were Elizabeth and Zechariah sinless? (1:6)
They were not sinless, but they were faithful and sincere in keeping the Lord's commandments.

What responsibility did the priest have for the incense? (1:9)
The priest was responsible for keeping the incense burning on the altar in front of the Most Holy Place. He added fresh incense before the morning sacrifice and after the evening sacrifice.

---

a 1 Or *been surely believed*

home. [24]After this his wife Elizabeth became pregnant and for five months remained in seclusion. [25]"The Lord has done this for me," she said. "In these days he has shown his favor and taken away my disgrace among the people."

THE BIRTH OF JESUS FORETOLD

[26]In the sixth month of Elizabeth's pregnancy, God sent the angel Gabriel to Nazareth, a town in Galilee, [27]to a virgin pledged to be married to a man named Joseph, a descendant of David. The virgin's name was Mary. [28]The angel went to her and said, "Greetings, you who are highly favored! The Lord is with you."

[29]Mary was greatly troubled at his words and wondered what kind of greeting this might be. [30]But the angel said to her, "Do not be afraid, Mary; you have found favor with God. [31]You will conceive and give birth to a son, and you are to call him Jesus. [32]He will be great and will be called the Son of the Most High. The Lord God will give him the throne of his father David, [33]and he will reign over Jacob's descendants forever; his kingdom will never end."

[34]"How will this be," Mary asked the angel, "since I am a virgin?"

[35]The angel answered, "The Holy Spirit will come on you, and the power of the Most High will overshadow you. So the holy one to be born will be called[a] the Son of God. [36]Even Elizabeth your relative is going to have a child in her old age, and she who was said to be unable to conceive is in her sixth month. [37]For no word from God will ever fail."

[38]"I am the Lord's servant," Mary answered. "May your word to me be fulfilled." Then the angel left her.

MARY VISITS ELIZABETH

[39]At that time Mary got ready and hurried to a town in the hill country of Judea, [40]where she entered Zechariah's home and greeted Elizabeth. [41]When Elizabeth heard Mary's greeting, the baby leaped in her womb, and Elizabeth was filled with the Holy Spirit. [42]In a loud voice she exclaimed: "Blessed are you among women, and blessed is the child you will bear! [43]But why am I so favored, that the mother of my Lord should come to me? [44]As soon as the sound of your greeting reached my ears, the baby in my womb leaped for joy. [45]Blessed is she who has believed that the Lord would fulfill his promises to her!"

MARY'S SONG

[46]And Mary said:

"My soul glorifies the Lord
[47]   and my spirit rejoices in God my Savior,
[48]for he has been mindful
     of the humble state of his servant.
   From now on all generations will call me blessed,
[49]   for the Mighty One has done great things for me—
     holy is his name.

[a] 35 Or *So the child to be born will be called holy,*

How did God remove Elizabeth's disgrace? (1:25)
Not having children meant that a family had no heirs who could inherit the family's possessions. It also was seen as a sign of God's disfavor.

What did it mean to be pledged to be married? (1:26)
A man and woman could not have sex during their betrothal, but it was a much more binding arrangement than a modern engagement. It could only be broken by divorce. Jesus did not have a biological father, but he had an earthly mother. He was both fully God and fully human.

Why is Mary's song known as the Magnificat? (1:46-55)
In the Latin translation of the Bible, the first word of her song is *magnificat*, which means *glorifies*. This song is like a psalm and can be compared to the song of Hannah (see 1 Samuel 2:1-10).

⁵⁰ His mercy extends to those who fear him,
  from generation to generation.
⁵¹ He has performed mighty deeds with his arm;
  he has scattered those who are proud in their inmost
    thoughts.
⁵² He has brought down rulers from their thrones
  but has lifted up the humble.
⁵³ He has filled the hungry with good things
  but has sent the rich away empty.
⁵⁴ He has helped his servant Israel,
  remembering to be merciful
⁵⁵ to Abraham and his descendants forever,
  just as he promised our ancestors."

⁵⁶ Mary stayed with Elizabeth for about three months and then returned home.

THE BIRTH OF JOHN THE BAPTIST

⁵⁷ When it was time for Elizabeth to have her baby, she gave birth to a son. ⁵⁸ Her neighbors and relatives heard that the Lord had shown her great mercy, and they shared her joy.

⁵⁹ On the eighth day they came to circumcise the child, and they were going to name him after his father Zechariah, ⁶⁰ but his mother spoke up and said, "No! He is to be called John."

⁶¹ They said to her, "There is no one among your relatives who has that name."

⁶² Then they made signs to his father, to find out what he would like to name the child. ⁶³ He asked for a writing tablet, and to everyone's astonishment he wrote, "His name is John." ⁶⁴ Immediately his mouth was opened and his tongue set free, and he began to speak, praising God. ⁶⁵ All the neighbors were filled with awe, and throughout the hill country of Judea people were talking about all these things. ⁶⁶ Everyone who heard this wondered about it, asking, "What then is this child going to be?" For the Lord's hand was with him.

ZECHARIAH'S SONG

⁶⁷ His father Zechariah was filled with the Holy Spirit and prophesied:

⁶⁸ "Praise be to the Lord, the God of Israel,
  because he has come to his people and redeemed
    them.
⁶⁹ He has raised up a horn^a of salvation for us
  in the house of his servant David
⁷⁰ (as he said through his holy prophets of long ago),
⁷¹ salvation from our enemies
  and from the hand of all who hate us—
⁷² to show mercy to our ancestors
  and to remember his holy covenant,
⁷³   the oath he swore to our father Abraham:
⁷⁴ to rescue us from the hand of our enemies,
  and to enable us to serve him without fear
⁷⁵   in holiness and righteousness before him all our days.

What was the horn of salvation? (1:69)
A horn, such as the horn of an animal, was a symbol of strength. Jesus, the Messiah, would have the strength or power to save his people.

^a 69 *Horn* here symbolizes a strong king.

76 And you, my child, will be called a prophet of the
    Most High;
    for you will go on before the Lord to prepare the
        way for him,
77 to give his people the knowledge of salvation
    through the forgiveness of their sins,
78 because of the tender mercy of our God,
    by which the rising sun will come to us from heaven
79 to shine on those living in darkness
    and in the shadow of death,
    to guide our feet into the path of peace."

80 And the child grew and became strong in spirit*a*; and he lived in the wilderness until he appeared publicly to Israel.

THE BIRTH OF JESUS

2 In those days Caesar Augustus issued a decree that a census should be taken of the entire Roman world. 2 (This was the first census that took place while*b* Quirinius was governor of Syria.) 3 And everyone went to their own town to register.

4 So Joseph also went up from the town of Nazareth in Galilee to Judea, to Bethlehem the town of David, because he belonged to the house and line of David. 5 He went there to register with Mary, who was pledged to be married to him and was expecting a child. 6 While they were there, the time came for the baby to be born, 7 and she gave birth to her firstborn, a son. She wrapped him in cloths and placed him in a manger, because there was no guest room available for them.

8 And there were shepherds living out in the fields nearby, keeping watch over their flocks at night. 9 An angel of the Lord appeared to them, and the glory of the Lord shone around them, and they were terrified. 10 But the angel said to them, "Do not be afraid. I bring you good news that will cause great joy for all the people. 11 Today in the town of David a Savior has been born to you; he is the Messiah, the Lord. 12 This will be a sign to you: You will find a baby wrapped in cloths and lying in a manger."

13 Suddenly a great company of the heavenly host appeared with the angel, praising God and saying,

a 80 Or in the Spirit   *b 2 Or This census took place before*

Jesus Is Born (2:4)

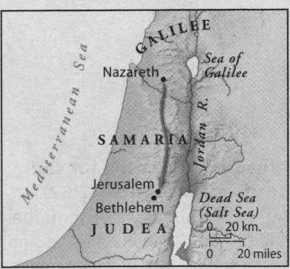

What is a *manger*? (2:7)
This was a feeding trough for animals. This is the only clue that Jesus was born in a stable; early tradition suggests that it was a cave used as a stable.

What was the town of David? (2:11)
This was Bethlehem.

Did Jesus really live on the earth?   LUKE 2

Yes. Even though Jesus is God, he took on human form and became a living human being. He was born in Bethlehem to a young woman named Mary, who was a virgin. Jesus' family tree shows that he was a descendant of King David. Like all Jewish boys, Jesus was taken to the temple to be circumcised when he was eight days old. When Jesus was about two, Mary and Joseph fled to Egypt because Herod was about to kill young boys since he did not want any rivals to his throne. A few years later, the family moved back to Nazareth in Galilee. The only story that the Bible tells about Jesus' childhood is when he went with his family to the temple (verses 41 – 52).

    The Bible begins telling the story of Jesus again when he was about 30 years old as he began his ministry. Jesus was a living human being in every way, except for the fact that he was without sin. Jesus was, and is, completely God. Because Jesus lived on earth as a human being, he understands our human situation, our pains, and our hurts.

14 "Glory to God in the highest heaven,
　　and on earth peace to those on whom his favor rests."

15 When the angels had left them and gone into heaven, the shepherds said to one another, "Let's go to Bethlehem and see this thing that has happened, which the Lord has told us about."

16 So they hurried off and found Mary and Joseph, and the baby, who was lying in the manger. 17 When they had seen him, they spread the word concerning what had been told them about this child, 18 and all who heard it were amazed at what the shepherds said to them. 19 But Mary treasured up all these things and pondered them in her heart. 20 The shepherds returned, glorifying and praising God for all the things they had heard and seen, which were just as they had been told.

21 On the eighth day, when it was time to circumcise the child, he was named Jesus, the name the angel had given him before he was conceived.

JESUS PRESENTED IN THE TEMPLE

22 When the time came for the purification rites required by the Law of Moses, Joseph and Mary took him to Jerusalem to present him to the Lord 23 (as it is written in the Law of the Lord, "Every firstborn male is to be consecrated to the Lord"[a]), 24 and to offer a sacrifice in keeping with what is said in the Law of the Lord: "a pair of doves or two young pigeons."[b]

25 Now there was a man in Jerusalem called Simeon, who was righteous and devout. He was waiting for the consolation of Israel, and the Holy Spirit was on him. 26 It had been revealed to him by the Holy Spirit that he would not die before he had seen the Lord's Messiah. 27 Moved by the Spirit, he went into the temple courts. When the parents brought in the child Jesus to do for him what the custom of the Law required, 28 Simeon took him in his arms and praised God, saying:

29 "Sovereign Lord, as you have promised,
　　you may now dismiss[c] your servant in peace.
30 For my eyes have seen your salvation,
31 　which you have prepared in the sight of all nations:
32 a light for revelation to the Gentiles,
　　and the glory of your people Israel."

33 The child's father and mother marveled at what was said about him. 34 Then Simeon blessed them and said to Mary, his mother: "This child is destined to cause the falling and rising of many in Israel, and to be a sign that will be spoken against, 35 so that the thoughts of many hearts will be revealed. And a sword will pierce your own soul too."

36 There was also a prophet, Anna, the daughter of Penuel, of the tribe of Asher. She was very old; she had lived with her husband seven years after her marriage, 37 and then was a widow until she was eighty-four.[d] She never left the temple

What was the time for the purification rights? (2:22)
After the birth of a son, a mother had to wait 40 days before going to the temple to offer sacrifices for her purification. If she could not afford a lamb and a pigeon as a sacrifice, then two pigeons (or doves) would be acceptable. Bethlehem was only about 6 miles (9.7 kilometers) from Jerusalem.

Did Anna live in the temple? (2:37)
Herod's temple was quite large and included rooms for various uses, so Anna may have been allowed to live in one of them. But the statement probably means that she spent all of her daytime hours worshiping in the temple.

---

[a] 23 Exodus 13:2,12 　 [b] 24 Lev. 12:8 　 [c] 29 Or promised, / now dismiss
[d] 37 Or then had been a widow for eighty-four years.

but worshiped night and day, fasting and praying. [38]Coming up to them at that very moment, she gave thanks to God and spoke about the child to all who were looking forward to the redemption of Jerusalem.

[39]When Joseph and Mary had done everything required by the Law of the Lord, they returned to Galilee to their own town of Nazareth. [40]And the child grew and became strong; he was filled with wisdom, and the grace of God was on him.

THE BOY JESUS AT THE TEMPLE

[41]Every year Jesus' parents went to Jerusalem for the Festival of the Passover. [42]When he was twelve years old, they went up to the festival, according to the custom. [43]After the festival was over, while his parents were returning home, the boy Jesus stayed behind in Jerusalem, but they were unaware of it. [44]Thinking he was in their company, they traveled on for a day. Then they began looking for him among their relatives and friends. [45]When they did not find him, they went back to Jerusalem to look for him. [46]After three days they found him in the temple courts, sitting among the teachers, listening to them and asking them questions. [47]Everyone who heard him was amazed at his understanding and his answers. [48]When his parents saw him, they were astonished. His mother said to him, "Son, why have you treated us like this? Your father and I have been anxiously searching for you."

[49]"Why were you searching for me?" he asked. "Didn't you know I had to be in my Father's house?"[a] [50]But they did not understand what he was saying to them.

[51]Then he went down to Nazareth with them and was obedient to them. But his mother treasured all these things in her heart. [52]And Jesus grew in wisdom and stature, and in favor with God and man.

JOHN THE BAPTIST PREPARES THE WAY

3 In the fifteenth year of the reign of Tiberius Caesar— when Pontius Pilate was governor of Judea, Herod tetrarch of Galilee, his brother Philip tetrarch of Iturea and Traconitis, and Lysanias tetrarch of Abilene— [2]during the high-priesthood of Annas and Caiaphas, the word of God came to John son of Zechariah in the wilderness. [3]He went into all the country around the Jordan, preaching a baptism of repentance for the forgiveness of sins. [4]As it is written in the book of the words of Isaiah the prophet:

"A voice of one calling in the wilderness,
  'Prepare the way for the Lord,
    make straight paths for him.
[5] Every valley shall be filled in,
    every mountain and hill made low.
  The crooked roads shall become straight,
    the rough ways smooth.
[6] And all people will see God's salvation.'"[b]

[7]John said to the crowds coming out to be baptized by him, "You brood of vipers! Who warned you to flee from the

[a] 49 Or be about my Father's business   [b] 6 Isaiah 40:3-5

What did Jewish boys begin to do at age 12? (2:42)
At age 12, boys began preparing to take their places in the religious community the next year.

What types of preparations would be made for a king? (3:4)
Before a king made a journey to a distant country, the roads he would travel on were improved. John the Baptist prepared the way for Jesus' ministry by focusing on repentance and the need for a Savior.

What did it mean that "all people will see God's salvation"? (3:6)
A major theme of Luke's gospel is that God's salvation would be made available to both Jews and Gentiles.

coming wrath? [8]Produce fruit in keeping with repentance. And do not begin to say to yourselves, 'We have Abraham as our father.' For I tell you that out of these stones God can raise up children for Abraham. [9]The ax is already at the root of the trees, and every tree that does not produce good fruit will be cut down and thrown into the fire."

[10]"What should we do then?" the crowd asked.

[11]John answered, "Anyone who has two shirts should share with the one who has none, and anyone who has food should do the same."

[12]Even tax collectors came to be baptized. "Teacher," they asked, "what should we do?"

[13]"Don't collect any more than you are required to," he told them.

[14]Then some soldiers asked him, "And what should we do?"

He replied, "Don't extort money and don't accuse people falsely—be content with your pay."

[15]The people were waiting expectantly and were all wondering in their hearts if John might possibly be the Messiah. [16]John answered them all, "I baptize you with[a] water. But one who is more powerful than I will come, the straps of whose sandals I am not worthy to untie. He will baptize you with[a] the Holy Spirit and fire. [17]His winnowing fork is in his hand to clear his threshing floor and to gather the wheat into his barn, but he will burn up the chaff with unquenchable fire." [18]And with many other words John exhorted the people and proclaimed the good news to them.

[19]But when John rebuked Herod the tetrarch because of his marriage to Herodias, his brother's wife, and all the other evil things he had done, [20]Herod added this to them all: He locked John up in prison.

THE BAPTISM AND GENEALOGY OF JESUS

[21]When all the people were being baptized, Jesus was baptized too. And as he was praying, heaven was opened [22]and the Holy Spirit descended on him in bodily form like a dove. And a voice came from heaven: "You are my Son, whom I love; with you I am well pleased."

[23]Now Jesus himself was about thirty years old when he began his ministry. He was the son, so it was thought, of Joseph,

the son of Heli, [24]the son of Matthat,
the son of Levi, the son of Melki,
the son of Jannai, the son of Joseph,
[25]the son of Mattathias, the son of Amos,
the son of Nahum, the son of Esli,
the son of Naggai, [26]the son of Maath,
the son of Mattathias, the son of Semein,
the son of Josek, the son of Joda,
[27]the son of Joanan, the son of Rhesa,
the son of Zerubbabel, the son of Shealtiel,
the son of Neri, [28]the son of Melki,

[a] 16 Or in

What were these shirts like? (3:11)
This shirt was like a long undershirt. Since a person did not need two of these, John said the second one should be given to a person who needs one.

When did God speak from heaven during Jesus' lifetime? (3:22)
The Gospel writers record two other times when God spoke from heaven: on the Mount of Transfiguration (Luke 9:35) and in the temple area during Jesus' final week (John 12:28).

Was this genealogy identical to the one in the Gospel of Matthew? (3:23–38)
There are several differences. Matthew's begins with Abraham, while Luke goes in reverse order back to Adam, showing Jesus' connection to the whole human race. Matthew follows the line of Joseph, but Luke follows the line of Mary. Even though tracing a genealogy through the mother's side of a family was unusual, the virgin birth made it necessary.

the son of Addi, the son of Cosam,
the son of Elmadam, the son of Er,
29 the son of Joshua, the son of Eliezer,
the son of Jorim, the son of Matthat,
the son of Levi, 30 the son of Simeon,
the son of Judah, the son of Joseph,
the son of Jonam, the son of Eliakim,
31 the son of Melea, the son of Menna,
the son of Mattatha, the son of Nathan,
the son of David, 32 the son of Jesse,
the son of Obed, the son of Boaz,
the son of Salmon,*a* the son of Nahshon,
33 the son of Amminadab, the son of Ram,*b*
the son of Hezron, the son of Perez,
the son of Judah, 34 the son of Jacob,
the son of Isaac, the son of Abraham,
the son of Terah, the son of Nahor,
35 the son of Serug, the son of Reu,
the son of Peleg, the son of Eber,
the son of Shelah, 36 the son of Cainan,
the son of Arphaxad, the son of Shem,
the son of Noah, the son of Lamech,
37 the son of Methuselah, the son of Enoch,
the son of Jared, the son of Mahalalel,
the son of Kenan, 38 the son of Enosh,
the son of Seth, the son of Adam,
the son of God.

JESUS IS TESTED IN THE WILDERNESS

4 Jesus, full of the Holy Spirit, left the Jordan and was led by the Spirit into the wilderness, 2 where for forty days he was tempted*c* by the devil. He ate nothing during those days, and at the end of them he was hungry.

3 The devil said to him, "If you are the Son of God, tell this stone to become bread."

4 Jesus answered, "It is written: 'Man shall not live on bread alone.'*d*"

5 The devil led him up to a high place and showed him in an instant all the kingdoms of the world. 6 And he said to

---

a 32 Some early manuscripts *Sala* *b* 33 Some manuscripts *Amminadab, the son of Admin, the son of Arni*; other manuscripts vary widely. *c* 2 The Greek for *tempted* can also mean *tested*. *d* 4 Deut. 8:3

Where did Jesus' temptations take place? (4:1–12)
They took place in a wilderness region in the lower Jordan Valley, on a high mountain (possibly one of the tall cliffs near Jericho), and on the highest point of the temple, where the priests sounded the trumpet to announce important events.

How did Jesus answer Satan? (4:4, 8, 12)
In each case, Jesus quoted Scripture to Satan (Deuteronomy 8:3; 6:13; and 6:16).

What should we do when we are tempted to sin? LUKE 4

Everyone is tempted to sin. We might read something, see something on television, hear some words in a song, or have a friend suggest something that makes us want to do something that we know is wrong. Being tempted is not bad—even Jesus was tempted—but giving in to temptation is wrong.

When Jesus was tempted in the wilderness, he had gone without food for 40 days, so he was in a weakened condition. The devil tempted him with food, with the possibility of gaining power and avoiding death, and with the idea of testing God. In each case, Jesus resisted the temptation and quoted a Bible passage to the devil. Jesus gave us this model to follow when we are tempted. We should think about what we might be tempted to do, and we should ask whether it is what God would want us to do. We should also pray to ask God for the strength to resist the temptation. But if we give in and do something that is wrong, we should ask God to forgive us and help us not do it again.

What was Satan tempting Jesus to do? (4:7)
Satan promised Jesus that he could rule the entire world and avoid the sufferings of the cross if he worshiped him.

him, "I will give you all their authority and splendor; it has been given to me, and I can give it to anyone I want to. [7] If you worship me, it will all be yours."

[8] Jesus answered, "It is written: 'Worship the Lord your God and serve him only.'[a]"

[9] The devil led him to Jerusalem and had him stand on the highest point of the temple. "If you are the Son of God," he said, "throw yourself down from here. [10] For it is written:

"'He will command his angels concerning you
　　to guard you carefully;
[11] they will lift you up in their hands,
　　so that you will not strike your foot against a
　　　stone.'[b]"

[12] Jesus answered, "It is said: 'Do not put the Lord your God to the test.'[c]"

[13] When the devil had finished all this tempting, he left him until an opportune time.

JESUS REJECTED AT NAZARETH

[14] Jesus returned to Galilee in the power of the Spirit, and news about him spread through the whole countryside. [15] He was teaching in their synagogues, and everyone praised him.

[16] He went to Nazareth, where he had been brought up, and on the Sabbath day he went into the synagogue, as was his custom. He stood up to read, [17] and the scroll of the prophet Isaiah was handed to him. Unrolling it, he found the place where it is written:

What was the scroll of Isaiah? (4:17)
The books of the Old Testament were written on scrolls which were kept in a special place in the synagogue and handed to the reader by an attendant. The passage Jesus read about the Messiah (Isaiah 61:1 – 2) may have been the assigned passage for the day or a passage he chose to read.

[18] "The Spirit of the Lord is on me,
　　because he has anointed me
　　to proclaim good news to the poor.
He has sent me to proclaim freedom for the prisoners
　　and recovery of sight for the blind,
　　to set the oppressed free,
[19]　　to proclaim the year of the Lord's favor."[d]

[20] Then he rolled up the scroll, gave it back to the attendant and sat down. The eyes of everyone in the synagogue were fastened on him. [21] He began by saying to them, "Today this scripture is fulfilled in your hearing."

[22] All spoke well of him and were amazed at the gracious words that came from his lips. "Isn't this Joseph's son?" they asked.

[23] Jesus said to them, "Surely you will quote this proverb to me: 'Physician, heal yourself!' And you will tell me, 'Do here in your hometown what we have heard that you did in Capernaum.'"

[24] "Truly I tell you," he continued, "no prophet is accepted in his hometown. [25] I assure you that there were many widows in Israel in Elijah's time, when the sky was shut for three and a half years and there was a severe famine throughout the land. [26] Yet Elijah was not sent to any of them, but to a widow in Zarephath in the region of Sidon. [27] And there

---

[a] 8 Deut. 6:13　　[b] 11 Psalm 91:11,12　　[c] 12 Deut. 6:16
[d] 19 Isaiah 61:1,2 (see Septuagint); Isaiah 58:6

were many in Israel with leprosy[a] in the time of Elisha the prophet, yet not one of them was cleansed—only Naaman the Syrian."

[28] All the people in the synagogue were furious when they heard this. [29] They got up, drove him out of the town, and took him to the brow of the hill on which the town was built, in order to throw him off the cliff. [30] But he walked right through the crowd and went on his way.

JESUS DRIVES OUT AN IMPURE SPIRIT

[31] Then he went down to Capernaum, a town in Galilee, and on the Sabbath he taught the people. [32] They were amazed at his teaching, because his words had authority.

[33] In the synagogue there was a man possessed by a demon, an impure spirit. He cried out at the top of his voice, [34] "Go away! What do you want with us, Jesus of Nazareth? Have you come to destroy us? I know who you are—the Holy One of God!"

[35] "Be quiet!" Jesus said sternly. "Come out of him!" Then the demon threw the man down before them all and came out without injuring him.

[36] All the people were amazed and said to each other, "What words these are! With authority and power he gives orders to impure spirits and they come out!" [37] And the news about him spread throughout the surrounding area.

JESUS HEALS MANY

[38] Jesus left the synagogue and went to the home of Simon. Now Simon's mother-in-law was suffering from a high fever, and they asked Jesus to help her. [39] So he bent over her and rebuked the fever, and it left her. She got up at once and began to wait on them.

[40] At sunset, the people brought to Jesus all who had various kinds of sickness, and laying his hands on each one, he healed them. [41] Moreover, demons came out of many people, shouting, "You are the Son of God!" But he rebuked them and would not allow them to speak, because they knew he was the Messiah.

[42] At daybreak, Jesus went out to a solitary place. The people were looking for him and when they came to where he was, they tried to keep him from leaving them. [43] But he said, "I must proclaim the good news of the kingdom of God to the other towns also, because that is why I was sent." [44] And he kept on preaching in the synagogues of Judea.

JESUS CALLS HIS FIRST DISCIPLES

5 One day as Jesus was standing by the Lake of Gennesaret,[b] the people were crowding around him and listening to the word of God. [2] He saw at the water's edge two boats, left there by the fishermen, who were washing their nets. [3] He got into one of the boats, the one belonging to Simon, and asked him to put out a little from shore. Then he sat down and taught the people from the boat.

[a] 27 The Greek word traditionally translated *leprosy* was used for various diseases affecting the skin.   [b] 1 That is, the Sea of Galilee

---

Why did people bring their sick friends to Jesus at sunset? (4:40)
The Sabbath was over at sunset. Until then, Jews could not travel more than two-thirds of a mile (one kilometer) or carry a burden. Only after sunset could they carry these sick people to Jesus to be healed.

Why were the fishermen washing their nets? (5:2)
After each time they fished, fishermen washed, stretched, and repaired their nets in preparation for the next day.

Why did Jesus sit in the boat? (5:3)
Rabbis usually taught from a sitting position rather than standing up. The boat was far enough away so that the crowd would not press in on Jesus, but it was close enough that he could be seen and heard.

[4] When he had finished speaking, he said to Simon, "Put out into deep water, and let down the nets for a catch."

[5] Simon answered, "Master, we've worked hard all night and haven't caught anything. But because you say so, I will let down the nets."

[6] When they had done so, they caught such a large number of fish that their nets began to break. [7] So they signaled their partners in the other boat to come and help them, and they came and filled both boats so full that they began to sink.

[8] When Simon Peter saw this, he fell at Jesus' knees and said, "Go away from me, Lord; I am a sinful man!" [9] For he and all his companions were astonished at the catch of fish they had taken, [10] and so were James and John, the sons of Zebedee, Simon's partners.

Then Jesus said to Simon, "Don't be afraid; from now on you will fish for people." [11] So they pulled their boats up on shore, left everything and followed him.

JESUS HEALS A MAN WITH LEPROSY

[12] While Jesus was in one of the towns, a man came along who was covered with leprosy.[a] When he saw Jesus, he fell with his face to the ground and begged him, "Lord, if you are willing, you can make me clean."

[13] Jesus reached out his hand and touched the man. "I am willing," he said. "Be clean!" And immediately the leprosy left him.

[14] Then Jesus ordered him, "Don't tell anyone, but go, show yourself to the priest and offer the sacrifices that Moses commanded for your cleansing, as a testimony to them."

[15] Yet the news about him spread all the more, so that crowds of people came to hear him and to be healed of their sicknesses. [16] But Jesus often withdrew to lonely places and prayed.

JESUS FORGIVES AND HEALS A PARALYZED MAN

[17] One day Jesus was teaching, and Pharisees and teachers of the law were sitting there. They had come from every village of Galilee and from Judea and Jerusalem. And the power of the Lord was with Jesus to heal the sick. [18] Some men came carrying a paralyzed man on a mat and tried to take him into the house to lay him before Jesus. [19] When they could not find a way to do this because of the crowd, they went up on the roof and lowered him on his mat through the tiles into the middle of the crowd, right in front of Jesus.

[20] When Jesus saw their faith, he said, "Friend, your sins are forgiven."

[21] The Pharisees and the teachers of the law began thinking to themselves, "Who is this fellow who speaks blasphemy? Who can forgive sins but God alone?"

[22] Jesus knew what they were thinking and asked, "Why are you thinking these things in your hearts? [23] Which is easier: to say, 'Your sins are forgiven,' or to say, 'Get up and

Who were the Pharisees and teachers of the law? (5:17) The Pharisees were a legalistic and separatist group who strictly obeyed the laws of Moses and the other traditional laws of the elders that had been passed down. They were not a large group, but they enjoyed the support of the people. The teachers of the law were scribes who studied, interpreted, and taught the law.

---

[a] 12 The Greek word traditionally translated *leprosy* was used for various diseases affecting the skin.

walk'? ²⁴But I want you to know that the Son of Man has authority on earth to forgive sins." So he said to the paralyzed man, "I tell you, get up, take your mat and go home." ²⁵Immediately he stood up in front of them, took what he had been lying on and went home praising God. ²⁶Everyone was amazed and gave praise to God. They were filled with awe and said, "We have seen remarkable things today."

JESUS CALLS LEVI AND EATS WITH SINNERS

²⁷After this, Jesus went out and saw a tax collector by the name of Levi sitting at his tax booth. "Follow me," Jesus said to him, ²⁸and Levi got up, left everything and followed him.

²⁹Then Levi held a great banquet for Jesus at his house, and a large crowd of tax collectors and others were eating with them. ³⁰But the Pharisees and the teachers of the law who belonged to their sect complained to his disciples, "Why do you eat and drink with tax collectors and sinners?"

³¹Jesus answered them, "It is not the healthy who need a doctor, but the sick. ³²I have not come to call the righteous, but sinners to repentance."

JESUS QUESTIONED ABOUT FASTING

³³They said to him, "John's disciples often fast and pray, and so do the disciples of the Pharisees, but yours go on eating and drinking."

³⁴Jesus answered, "Can you make the friends of the bridegroom fast while he is with them? ³⁵But the time will come when the bridegroom will be taken from them; in those days they will fast."

³⁶He told them this parable: "No one tears a piece out of a new garment to patch an old one. Otherwise, they will have torn the new garment, and the patch from the new will not match the old. ³⁷And no one pours new wine into old wineskins. Otherwise, the new wine will burst the skins; the wine will run out and the wineskins will be ruined. ³⁸No, new wine must be poured into new wineskins. ³⁹And no one after drinking old wine wants the new, for they say, 'The old is better.'"

JESUS IS LORD OF THE SABBATH

6 One Sabbath Jesus was going through the grainfields, and his disciples began to pick some heads of grain, rub them in their hands and eat the kernels. ²Some of the Pharisees asked, "Why are you doing what is unlawful on the Sabbath?"

³Jesus answered them, "Have you never read what David did when he and his companions were hungry? ⁴He entered the house of God, and taking the consecrated bread, he ate what is lawful only for priests to eat. And he also gave some to his companions." ⁵Then Jesus said to them, "The Son of Man is Lord of the Sabbath."

⁶On another Sabbath he went into the synagogue and was teaching, and a man was there whose right hand was shriveled. ⁷The Pharisees and the teachers of the law were looking for a reason to accuse Jesus, so they watched him closely

What did the Jews think about tax collectors? (5:27)
Because Jewish tax collectors collected tolls for Rome, they were considered traitors. They also were considered extremely dishonest. They could not serve as witnesses or judges, and they were expelled from the synagogue. Their disgrace extended to members of their families.

What were wineskins? (5:37 – 38)
In ancient times, goatskins were used to hold wine. As the fresh grape juice fermented, the wine would expand and stretch a new wineskin. But old wineskins that were already stretched would burst. Jesus compared the Jewish system to old wineskins that could not accommodate the new wine of the kingdom of God.

What did they do that was unlawful on the Sabbath? (6:2)
According to Jewish tradition, harvesting was unlawful on the Sabbath, and that is what the disciples technically were doing.

How did Jesus justify their actions? (6:3 – 5)
Jesus described a time when the Sabbath rules had been broken to accomplish a greater good. The rules for the Sabbath had become so detailed and burdensome that people had lost sight of the original purpose of the Sabbath, which was for humans to experience physical, mental, and spiritual restoration.

to see if he would heal on the Sabbath. [8] But Jesus knew what they were thinking and said to the man with the shriveled hand, "Get up and stand in front of everyone." So he got up and stood there.

[9] Then Jesus said to them, "I ask you, which is lawful on the Sabbath: to do good or to do evil, to save life or to destroy it?"

[10] He looked around at them all, and then said to the man, "Stretch out your hand." He did so, and his hand was completely restored. [11] But the Pharisees and the teachers of the law were furious and began to discuss with one another what they might do to Jesus.

THE TWELVE APOSTLES

[12] One of those days Jesus went out to a mountainside to pray, and spent the night praying to God. [13] When morning came, he called his disciples to him and chose twelve of them, whom he also designated apostles: [14] Simon (whom he named Peter), his brother Andrew, James, John, Philip, Bartholomew, [15] Matthew, Thomas, James son of Alphaeus, Simon who was called the Zealot, [16] Judas son of James, and Judas Iscariot, who became a traitor.

BLESSINGS AND WOES

[17] He went down with them and stood on a level place. A large crowd of his disciples was there and a great number of people from all over Judea, from Jerusalem, and from the coastal region around Tyre and Sidon, [18] who had come to hear him and to be healed of their diseases. Those troubled by impure spirits were cured, [19] and the people all tried to touch him, because power was coming from him and healing them all.

[20] Looking at his disciples, he said:

"Blessed are you who are poor,
    for yours is the kingdom of God.
[21] Blessed are you who hunger now,
    for you will be satisfied.
Blessed are you who weep now,
    for you will laugh.
[22] Blessed are you when people hate you,
    when they exclude you and insult you
    and reject your name as evil,
        because of the Son of Man.

[23] "Rejoice in that day and leap for joy, because great is your reward in heaven. For that is how their ancestors treated the prophets.

[24] "But woe to you who are rich,
    for you have already received your comfort.
[25] Woe to you who are well fed now,
    for you will go hungry.
Woe to you who laugh now,
    for you will mourn and weep.
[26] Woe to you when everyone speaks well of you,
    for that is how their ancestors treated the false
        prophets.

How is this sermon similar to the Sermon on the Mount in Matthew 5–7? (6:20–49) This sermon is shorter, but like the sermon in Matthew it begins with the Beatitudes and ends with the lesson of the builders.

LOVE FOR ENEMIES

[27] "But to you who are listening I say: Love your enemies, do good to those who hate you, [28] bless those who curse you, pray for those who mistreat you. [29] If someone slaps you on one cheek, turn to them the other also. If someone takes your coat, do not withhold your shirt from them. [30] Give to everyone who asks you, and if anyone takes what belongs to you, do not demand it back. [31] Do to others as you would have them do to you.

[32] "If you love those who love you, what credit is that to you? Even sinners love those who love them. [33] And if you do good to those who are good to you, what credit is that to you? Even sinners do that. [34] And if you lend to those from whom you expect repayment, what credit is that to you? Even sinners lend to sinners, expecting to be repaid in full. [35] But love your enemies, do good to them, and lend to them without expecting to get anything back. Then your reward will be great, and you will be children of the Most High, because he is kind to the ungrateful and wicked. [36] Be merciful, just as your Father is merciful.

JUDGING OTHERS

[37] "Do not judge, and you will not be judged. Do not condemn, and you will not be condemned. Forgive, and you will be forgiven. [38] Give, and it will be given to you. A good measure, pressed down, shaken together and running over, will be poured into your lap. For with the measure you use, it will be measured to you."

[39] He also told them this parable: "Can the blind lead the blind? Will they not both fall into a pit? [40] The student is not above the teacher, but everyone who is fully trained will be like their teacher.

[41] "Why do you look at the speck of sawdust in your brother's eye and pay no attention to the plank in your own eye? [42] How can you say to your brother, 'Brother, let me take the speck out of your eye,' when you yourself fail to see the plank in your own eye? You hypocrite, first take the plank out of your eye, and then you will see clearly to remove the speck from your brother's eye.

A TREE AND ITS FRUIT

[43] "No good tree bears bad fruit, nor does a bad tree bear good fruit. [44] Each tree is recognized by its own fruit. People do not pick figs from thornbushes, or grapes from briers. [45] A good man brings good things out of the good stored up in his heart, and an evil man brings evil things out of the evil stored up in his heart. For the mouth speaks what the heart is full of.

THE WISE AND FOOLISH BUILDERS

[46] "Why do you call me, 'Lord, Lord,' and do not do what I say? [47] As for everyone who comes to me and hears my words and puts them into practice, I will show you what they are like. [48] They are like a man building a house, who dug down deep and laid the foundation on rock. When a flood

What was the heart of Jesus' teaching? (6:27)
The heart of Jesus' teaching was love, even love for one's enemies.

What did it mean for grain to be poured into one's lap? (6:38)
This probably referred to the way an outer garment was worn so that it could be folded over the belt and used as a large pocket to hold a measure of wheat.

came, the torrent struck that house but could not shake it, because it was well built. ⁴⁹But the one who hears my words and does not put them into practice is like a man who built a house on the ground without a foundation. The moment the torrent struck that house, it collapsed and its destruction was complete."

THE FAITH OF THE CENTURION

7 When Jesus had finished saying all this to the people who were listening, he entered Capernaum. ²There a centurion's servant, whom his master valued highly, was sick and about to die. ³The centurion heard of Jesus and sent some elders of the Jews to him, asking him to come and heal his servant. ⁴When they came to Jesus, they pleaded earnestly with him, "This man deserves to have you do this, ⁵because he loves our nation and has built our synagogue." ⁶So Jesus went with them.

He was not far from the house when the centurion sent friends to say to him: "Lord, don't trouble yourself, for I do not deserve to have you come under my roof. ⁷That is why I did not even consider myself worthy to come to you. But say the word, and my servant will be healed. ⁸For I myself am a man under authority, with soldiers under me. I tell this one, 'Go,' and he goes; and that one, 'Come,' and he comes. I say to my servant, 'Do this,' and he does it."

⁹When Jesus heard this, he was amazed at him, and turning to the crowd following him, he said, "I tell you, I have not found such great faith even in Israel." ¹⁰Then the men who had been sent returned to the house and found the servant well.

JESUS RAISES A WIDOW'S SON

¹¹Soon afterward, Jesus went to a town called Nain, and his disciples and a large crowd went along with him. ¹²As he approached the town gate, a dead person was being carried out—the only son of his mother, and she was a widow. And a large crowd from the town was with her. ¹³When the Lord saw her, his heart went out to her and he said, "Don't cry."

¹⁴Then he went up and touched the bier they were carrying him on, and the bearers stood still. He said, "Young man, I say to you, get up!" ¹⁵The dead man sat up and began to talk, and Jesus gave him back to his mother.

¹⁶They were all filled with awe and praised God. "A great prophet has appeared among us," they said. "God has come to help his people." ¹⁷This news about Jesus spread throughout Judea and the surrounding country.

JESUS AND JOHN THE BAPTIST

¹⁸John's disciples told him about all these things. Calling two of them, ¹⁹he sent them to the Lord to ask, "Are you the one who is to come, or should we expect someone else?"

²⁰When the men came to Jesus, they said, "John the Baptist sent us to you to ask, 'Are you the one who is to come, or should we expect someone else?'"

²¹At that very time Jesus cured many who had diseases,

Who were the elders of the Jews? (7:3)
These were respected leaders in the community. In Matthew's account of this story (8:5 – 13), the centurion spoke to Jesus himself, but in Luke's account he asked friends to present his request.

Jesus Visits Nain (7:11)

What is a bier? (7:14)
This was probably an open coffin, which was in keeping with Jewish custom and the fact that he sat up when Jesus commanded him to.

sicknesses and evil spirits, and gave sight to many who were blind. [22] So he replied to the messengers, "Go back and report to John what you have seen and heard: The blind receive sight, the lame walk, those who have leprosy[a] are cleansed, the deaf hear, the dead are raised, and the good news is proclaimed to the poor. [23] Blessed is anyone who does not stumble on account of me."

[24] After John's messengers left, Jesus began to speak to the crowd about John: "What did you go out into the wilderness to see? A reed swayed by the wind? [25] If not, what did you go out to see? A man dressed in fine clothes? No, those who wear expensive clothes and indulge in luxury are in palaces. [26] But what did you go out to see? A prophet? Yes, I tell you, and more than a prophet. [27] This is the one about whom it is written:

> "'I will send my messenger ahead of you,
>   who will prepare your way before you.'[b]

[28] I tell you, among those born of women there is no one greater than John; yet the one who is least in the kingdom of God is greater than he."

[29] (All the people, even the tax collectors, when they heard Jesus' words, acknowledged that God's way was right, because they had been baptized by John. [30] But the Pharisees and the experts in the law rejected God's purpose for themselves, because they had not been baptized by John.)

[31] Jesus went on to say, "To what, then, can I compare the people of this generation? What are they like? [32] They are like children sitting in the marketplace and calling out to each other:

> "'We played the pipe for you,
>   and you did not dance;
> we sang a dirge,
>   and you did not cry.'

[33] For John the Baptist came neither eating bread nor drinking wine, and you say, 'He has a demon.' [34] The Son of Man came eating and drinking, and you say, 'Here is a glutton and a drunkard, a friend of tax collectors and sinners.' [35] But wisdom is proved right by all her children."

JESUS ANOINTED BY A SINFUL WOMAN

[36] When one of the Pharisees invited Jesus to have dinner with him, he went to the Pharisee's house and reclined at the table. [37] A woman in that town who lived a sinful life learned that Jesus was eating at the Pharisee's house, so she came there with an alabaster jar of perfume. [38] As she stood behind him at his feet weeping, she began to wet his feet with her tears. Then she wiped them with her hair, kissed them and poured perfume on them.

[39] When the Pharisee who had invited him saw this, he said to himself, "If this man were a prophet, he would know

What did Jesus mean by comparing the people to children in the marketplace? (7:32) People rejected both John the Baptist and Jesus but for different reasons — almost like children who refused to play either a mournful game or a joyful one. They thought John was too strict and Jesus was too free.

---

[a] 22 The Greek word traditionally translated *leprosy* was used for various diseases affecting the skin.   [b] 27 Mal. 3:1

who is touching him and what kind of woman she is — that she is a sinner."

⁴⁰Jesus answered him, "Simon, I have something to tell you."

"Tell me, teacher," he said.

⁴¹"Two people owed money to a certain moneylender. One owed him five hundred denarii,ᵃ and the other fifty. ⁴²Neither of them had the money to pay him back, so he forgave the debts of both. Now which of them will love him more?"

⁴³Simon replied, "I suppose the one who had the bigger debt forgiven."

"You have judged correctly," Jesus said.

⁴⁴Then he turned toward the woman and said to Simon, "Do you see this woman? I came into your house. You did not give me any water for my feet, but she wet my feet with her tears and wiped them with her hair. ⁴⁵You did not give me a kiss, but this woman, from the time I entered, has not stopped kissing my feet. ⁴⁶You did not put oil on my head, but she has poured perfume on my feet. ⁴⁷Therefore, I tell you, her many sins have been forgiven — as her great love has shown. But whoever has been forgiven little loves little."

⁴⁸Then Jesus said to her, "Your sins are forgiven."

⁴⁹The other guests began to say among themselves, "Who is this who even forgives sins?"

⁵⁰Jesus said to the woman, "Your faith has saved you; go in peace."

THE PARABLE OF THE SOWER

8 After this, Jesus traveled about from one town and village to another, proclaiming the good news of the kingdom of God. The Twelve were with him, ²and also some women who had been cured of evil spirits and diseases: Mary (called Magdalene) from whom seven demons had come out; ³Joanna the wife of Chuza, the manager of Herod's household; Susanna; and many others. These women were helping to support them out of their own means.

⁴While a large crowd was gathering and people were coming to Jesus from town after town, he told this parable: ⁵"A farmer went out to sow his seed. As he was scattering the seed, some fell along the path; it was trampled on, and the birds ate it up. ⁶Some fell on rocky ground, and when it came up, the plants withered because they had no moisture. ⁷Other seed fell among thorns, which grew up with it and choked the plants. ⁸Still other seed fell on good soil. It came up and yielded a crop, a hundred times more than was sown."

When he said this, he called out, "Whoever has ears to hear, let them hear."

⁹His disciples asked him what this parable meant. ¹⁰He said, "The knowledge of the secrets of the kingdom of God has been given to you, but to others I speak in parables, so that,

"'though seeing, they may not see;
　　though hearing, they may not understand.'ᵇ

Why did Jesus point out that the host had not given Jesus water for his feet? (7:44) Providing water to wash one's feet was considered a gesture of hospitality.

How was seed typically sown? (8:5) The practice was to sow (scatter) the seed and then plow the field afterward. Roads and pathways often went through fields, and the traffic made much of the surface too hard for seed to take root.

What were the "secrets of the kingdom of God"? (8:10) These were truths that could only be known if God revealed them. The quotation from Isaiah 6:9 states that those who were unwilling to receive Jesus' message would find the truth hidden from them.

ᵃ *41 A denarius was the usual daily wage of a day laborer (see Matt. 20:2).*
ᵇ *10 Isaiah 6:9*

MIRACLES OF JESUS

HEALING MIRACLES	MATTHEW	MARK	LUKE	JOHN
Man with leprosy	8:2–4	1:40–42	5:12–13	
Roman centurion's servant	8:5–13		7:1–10	
Peter's mother-in-law	8:14–15	1:30–31	4:38–39	
Two demon-possessed men	8:28–34	5:1–15	8:27–35	
Paralyzed man	9:2–7	2:3–12	5:18–25	
Woman with bleeding	9:20–22	5:25–29	8:43–48	
Two blind men	9:27–31			
Mute, demon-possessed man	9:32–33			
Man with a shriveled hand	12:10–13	3:1–5	6:6–10	
Blind, mute, demon-possessed man	12:22		11:14	
Canaanite woman's daughter	15:21–28	7:24–30		
Demon-possessed boy	17:14–18	9:17–29	9:38–43	
Two blind men (including Bartimaeus)	20:29–34	10:46–52	18:35–43	
Deaf and mute man		7:31–37		
Possessed man in synagogue		1:23–26	4:33–35	
Blind man at Bethsaida		8:22–26		
Crippled woman			13:11–13	
Man with abnormal swelling			14:1–4	
Ten men with leprosy			17:11–19	
The high priest's servant			22:50–51	
Official's son at Capernaum				4:46–54
Sick man at pool of Bethesda				5:1–9
Man born blind				9:1–7
MIRACLES SHOWING POWER OVER NATURE				
Calming the storm	8:23–27	4:37–41	8:22–25	
Walking on water	14:25	6:48–51		6:19–21
Feeding of the 5,000	14:15–21	6:35–44	9:12–17	6:6–13
Feeding of the 4,000	15:32–38	8:1–9		
Coin in fish's mouth	17:24–27			
Fig tree withered	21:18–22	11:12–14, 20–25		
Large catch of fish			5:4–11	
Water turned into wine				2:1–11
Another large catch of fish				21:1–11
MIRACLES OF RAISING THE DEAD				
Jairus's daughter	9:18–19, 23–25	5:22–24, 38–42	8:41–42, 49–56	
Widow's son at Nain			7:11–15	
Lazarus				11:1–44

¹¹"This is the meaning of the parable: The seed is the word of God. ¹²Those along the path are the ones who hear, and then the devil comes and takes away the word from their hearts, so that they may not believe and be saved. ¹³Those on the rocky ground are the ones who receive the word with joy when they hear it, but they have no root. They believe for a while, but in the time of testing they fall away. ¹⁴The seed that fell among thorns stands for those who hear, but as they go on their way they are choked by life's worries, riches and pleasures, and they do not mature. ¹⁵But the seed on good soil stands for those with a noble and good heart, who hear the word, retain it, and by persevering produce a crop.

A LAMP ON A STAND

¹⁶"No one lights a lamp and hides it in a clay jar or puts it under a bed. Instead, they put it on a stand, so that those who come in can see the light. ¹⁷For there is nothing hidden that will not be disclosed, and nothing concealed that will not be known or brought out into the open. ¹⁸Therefore consider carefully how you listen. Whoever has will be given more; whoever does not have, even what they think they have will be taken from them."

JESUS' MOTHER AND BROTHERS

¹⁹Now Jesus' mother and brothers came to see him, but they were not able to get near him because of the crowd. ²⁰Someone told him, "Your mother and brothers are standing outside, wanting to see you."

²¹He replied, "My mother and brothers are those who hear God's word and put it into practice."

JESUS CALMS THE STORM

²²One day Jesus said to his disciples, "Let us go over to the other side of the lake." So they got into a boat and set out. ²³As they sailed, he fell asleep. A squall came down on the lake, so that the boat was being swamped, and they were in great danger.

²⁴The disciples went and woke him, saying, "Master, Master, we're going to drown!"

He got up and rebuked the wind and the raging waters; the storm subsided, and all was calm. ²⁵"Where is your faith?" he asked his disciples.

In fear and amazement they asked one another, "Who is this? He commands even the winds and the water, and they obey him."

JESUS RESTORES A DEMON-POSSESSED MAN

²⁶They sailed to the region of the Gerasenes,^a which is across the lake from Galilee. ²⁷When Jesus stepped ashore, he was met by a demon-possessed man from the town. For a long time this man had not worn clothes or lived in a house, but had lived in the tombs. ²⁸When he saw Jesus, he cried out and fell at his feet, shouting at the top of his voice, "What

Why would a lamp be put on a stand? (8:16)
In Jesus' day, people used small clay lamps that burned olive oil drawn up by a wick. Because they gave off only a small amount of light, they were often placed on a stand to given maximum light.

Why would someone live in a tomb? (8:27)
In that day, caves served as tombs. It was not unusual for the same cave to be a burial spot for the dead and to provide shelter for the living. Very poor people often lived in such caves.

^a 26 Some manuscripts *Gadarenes*; other manuscripts *Gergesenes*; also in verse 37

do you want with me, Jesus, Son of the Most High God? I beg you, don't torture me!" ²⁹For Jesus had commanded the impure spirit to come out of the man. Many times it had seized him, and though he was chained hand and foot and kept under guard, he had broken his chains and had been driven by the demon into solitary places.

³⁰Jesus asked him, "What is your name?"

"Legion," he replied, because many demons had gone into him. ³¹And they begged Jesus repeatedly not to order them to go into the Abyss.

³²A large herd of pigs was feeding there on the hillside. The demons begged Jesus to let them go into the pigs, and he gave them permission. ³³When the demons came out of the man, they went into the pigs, and the herd rushed down the steep bank into the lake and was drowned.

³⁴When those tending the pigs saw what had happened, they ran off and reported this in the town and countryside, ³⁵and the people went out to see what had happened. When they came to Jesus, they found the man from whom the demons had gone out, sitting at Jesus' feet, dressed and in his right mind; and they were afraid. ³⁶Those who had seen it told the people how the demon-possessed man had been cured. ³⁷Then all the people of the region of the Gerasenes asked Jesus to leave them, because they were overcome with fear. So he got into the boat and left.

³⁸The man from whom the demons had gone out begged to go with him, but Jesus sent him away, saying, ³⁹"Return home and tell how much God has done for you." So the man went away and told all over town how much Jesus had done for him.

JESUS RAISES A DEAD GIRL AND HEALS A SICK WOMAN

⁴⁰Now when Jesus returned, a crowd welcomed him, for they were all expecting him. ⁴¹Then a man named Jairus, a synagogue leader, came and fell at Jesus' feet, pleading with him to come to his house ⁴²because his only daughter, a girl of about twelve, was dying.

As Jesus was on his way, the crowds almost crushed him. ⁴³And a woman was there who had been subject to bleeding for twelve years,[a] but no one could heal her. ⁴⁴She came up behind him and touched the edge of his cloak, and immediately her bleeding stopped.

⁴⁵"Who touched me?" Jesus asked.

When they all denied it, Peter said, "Master, the people are crowding and pressing against you."

⁴⁶But Jesus said, "Someone touched me; I know that power has gone out from me."

⁴⁷Then the woman, seeing that she could not go unnoticed, came trembling and fell at his feet. In the presence of all the people, she told why she had touched him and how she had been instantly healed. ⁴⁸Then he said to her, "Daughter, your faith has healed you. Go in peace."

What did the name Legion mean? (8:30)
A Roman legion was made up of 6,000 soldiers. Here the term suggests that the man was possessed by numerous demons.

What type of illness did the woman have? (8:43)
The exact nature of her problem is unknown. Her life would have been miserable because she was shunned. Any contact with her would have made someone ceremonially unclean.

---

[a] 43 Many manuscripts *years, and she had spent all she had on doctors*

⁴⁹While Jesus was still speaking, someone came from the house of Jairus, the synagogue leader. "Your daughter is dead," he said. "Don't bother the teacher anymore."

⁵⁰Hearing this, Jesus said to Jairus, "Don't be afraid; just believe, and she will be healed."

⁵¹When he arrived at the house of Jairus, he did not let anyone go in with him except Peter, John and James, and the child's father and mother. ⁵²Meanwhile, all the people were wailing and mourning for her. "Stop wailing," Jesus said. "She is not dead but asleep."

⁵³They laughed at him, knowing that she was dead. ⁵⁴But he took her by the hand and said, "My child, get up!" ⁵⁵Her spirit returned, and at once she stood up. Then Jesus told them to give her something to eat. ⁵⁶Her parents were astonished, but he ordered them not to tell anyone what had happened.

JESUS SENDS OUT THE TWELVE

9 When Jesus had called the Twelve together, he gave them power and authority to drive out all demons and to cure diseases, ²and he sent them out to proclaim the kingdom of God and to heal the sick. ³He told them: "Take nothing for the journey—no staff, no bag, no bread, no money, no extra shirt. ⁴Whatever house you enter, stay there until you leave that town. ⁵If people do not welcome you, leave their town and shake the dust off your feet as a testimony against them." ⁶So they set out and went from village to village, proclaiming the good news and healing people everywhere.

⁷Now Herod the tetrarch heard about all that was going on. And he was perplexed because some were saying that John had been raised from the dead, ⁸others that Elijah had appeared, and still others that one of the prophets of long ago had come back to life. ⁹But Herod said, "I beheaded John. Who, then, is this I hear such things about?" And he tried to see him.

JESUS FEEDS THE FIVE THOUSAND

¹⁰When the apostles returned, they reported to Jesus what they had done. Then he took them with him and they withdrew by themselves to a town called Bethsaida, ¹¹but the crowds learned about it and followed him. He welcomed them and spoke to them about the kingdom of God, and healed those who needed healing.

¹²Late in the afternoon the Twelve came to him and said, "Send the crowd away so they can go to the surrounding villages and countryside and find food and lodging, because we are in a remote place here."

¹³He replied, "You give them something to eat."

They answered, "We have only five loaves of bread and two fish—unless we go and buy food for all this crowd." ¹⁴(About five thousand men were there.)

But he said to his disciples, "Have them sit down in groups of about fifty each." ¹⁵The disciples did so, and everyone sat down. ¹⁶Taking the five loaves and the two fish and looking up to heaven, he gave thanks and broke them. Then he gave

Why did Jesus tell people not to spread the word about his miracles? (8:56)
In Galilee, Jesus often told people not to tell about the healings he performed. His popularity along with the opposition from the religious leaders could have caused an early end to his ministry.

Why were the disciples not supposed to take anything with them? (9:3)
They were supposed to depend on the hospitality of the townspeople. They also were to rely on God to provide them with what they needed.

What did it mean to shake the dust from their feet? (9:5)
If the people of a town rejected God's message, the disciples did this to show separation from everything associated with the place. It was also a warning of judgment.

them to the disciples to distribute to the people. [17]They all ate and were satisfied, and the disciples picked up twelve basketfuls of broken pieces that were left over.

PETER DECLARES THAT JESUS IS THE MESSIAH

[18]Once when Jesus was praying in private and his disciples were with him, he asked them, "Who do the crowds say I am?"

[19]They replied, "Some say John the Baptist; others say Elijah; and still others, that one of the prophets of long ago has come back to life."

[20]"But what about you?" he asked. "Who do you say I am?" Peter answered, "God's Messiah."

JESUS PREDICTS HIS DEATH

[21]Jesus strictly warned them not to tell this to anyone. [22]And he said, "The Son of Man must suffer many things and be rejected by the elders, the chief priests and the teachers of the law, and he must be killed and on the third day be raised to life."

[23]Then he said to them all: "Whoever wants to be my disciple must deny themselves and take up their cross daily and follow me. [24]For whoever wants to save their life will lose it, but whoever loses their life for me will save it. [25]What good is it for someone to gain the whole world, and yet lose or forfeit their very self? [26]Whoever is ashamed of me and my words, the Son of Man will be ashamed of them when he comes in his glory and in the glory of the Father and of the holy angels.

[27]"Truly I tell you, some who are standing here will not taste death before they see the kingdom of God."

THE TRANSFIGURATION

[28]About eight days after Jesus said this, he took Peter, John and James with him and went up onto a mountain to pray. [29]As he was praying, the appearance of his face changed, and his clothes became as bright as a flash of lightning. [30]Two men, Moses and Elijah, appeared in glorious splendor, talking with Jesus. [31]They spoke about his departure,[a] which he was about to bring to fulfillment at Jerusalem. [32]Peter and his companions were very sleepy, but when they became fully awake, they saw his glory and the two men standing with him. [33]As the men were leaving Jesus, Peter said to him, "Master, it is good for us to be here. Let us put up three shelters—one for you, one for Moses and one for Elijah." (He did not know what he was saying.)

[34]While he was speaking, a cloud appeared and covered them, and they were afraid as they entered the cloud. [35]A voice came from the cloud, saying, "This is my Son, whom I have chosen; listen to him." [36]When the voice had spoken, they found that Jesus was alone. The disciples kept this to themselves and did not tell anyone at that time what they had seen.

[a] 31 Greek exodos

What did it mean that they collected 12 basketfuls of leftovers? (9:17)
This was a demonstration that everyone had been more than adequately fed.

Why did Peter answer the question? (9:20)
Peter seems to have been the most outspoken disciple, and he became the spokesperson on the day of Pentecost.

What did Jesus require from his followers? (9:23)
Jesus said that those who followed him would have to deny themselves and obediently follow him.

Why did Moses and Elijah appear? (9:30–31)
Moses was the deliverer and lawgiver, and Elijah was the representative of the prophets. Together they represented the way God had led his people throughout their history.

What types of shelters did Peter want to construct? (9:33)
He may have wanted to erect new tents of meeting where God could communicate with his people, or he may have been thinking of the booths used in the Festival of the Tabernacles (see Leviticus 23:42).

JESUS HEALS A DEMON-POSSESSED BOY

37 The next day, when they came down from the mountain, a large crowd met him. 38 A man in the crowd called out, "Teacher, I beg you to look at my son, for he is my only child. 39 A spirit seizes him and he suddenly screams; it throws him into convulsions so that he foams at the mouth. It scarcely ever leaves him and is destroying him. 40 I begged your disciples to drive it out, but they could not."

41 "You unbelieving and perverse generation," Jesus replied, "how long shall I stay with you and put up with you? Bring your son here."

42 Even while the boy was coming, the demon threw him to the ground in a convulsion. But Jesus rebuked the impure spirit, healed the boy and gave him back to his father. 43 And they were all amazed at the greatness of God.

JESUS PREDICTS HIS DEATH A SECOND TIME

While everyone was marveling at all that Jesus did, he said to his disciples, 44 "Listen carefully to what I am about to tell you: The Son of Man is going to be delivered into the hands of men." 45 But they did not understand what this meant. It was hidden from them, so that they did not grasp it, and they were afraid to ask him about it.

46 An argument started among the disciples as to which of them would be the greatest. 47 Jesus, knowing their thoughts, took a little child and had him stand beside him. 48 Then he said to them, "Whoever welcomes this little child in my name welcomes me; and whoever welcomes me welcomes the one who sent me. For it is the one who is least among you all who is the greatest."

49 "Master," said John, "we saw someone driving out demons in your name and we tried to stop him, because he is not one of us."

50 "Do not stop him," Jesus said, "for whoever is not against you is for you."

SAMARITAN OPPOSITION

51 As the time approached for him to be taken up to heaven, Jesus resolutely set out for Jerusalem. 52 And he sent messengers on ahead, who went into a Samaritan village to get things ready for him; 53 but the people there did not welcome him, because he was heading for Jerusalem. 54 When the disciples James and John saw this, they asked, "Lord, do you want us to call fire down from heaven to destroy them*a*?" 55 But Jesus turned and rebuked them. 56 Then he and his disciples went to another village.

THE COST OF FOLLOWING JESUS

57 As they were walking along the road, a man said to him, "I will follow you wherever you go."

58 Jesus replied, "Foxes have dens and birds have nests, but the Son of Man has no place to lay his head."

59 He said to another man, "Follow me."

Why didn't the Samaritans welcome them? (9:52–53) Samaritans were hostile to the Jews, especially when they were on their way to observe religious festivals in Jerusalem. It was at least a three-day journey from Galilee to Jerusalem through Samaria, and the Samaritans would not provide overnight lodging. Because of that, the Jews frequently bypassed Samaria.

---

a 54 Some manuscripts *them, just as Elijah did*

But he replied, "Lord, first let me go and bury my father."

⁶⁰Jesus said to him, "Let the dead bury their own dead, but you go and proclaim the kingdom of God."

⁶¹Still another said, "I will follow you, Lord; but first let me go back and say goodbye to my family."

⁶²Jesus replied, "No one who puts a hand to the plow and looks back is fit for service in the kingdom of God."

JESUS SENDS OUT THE SEVENTY-TWO

10 After this the Lord appointed seventy-two*ᵃ* others and sent them two by two ahead of him to every town and place where he was about to go. ²He told them, "The harvest is plentiful, but the workers are few. Ask the Lord of the harvest, therefore, to send out workers into his harvest field. ³Go! I am sending you out like lambs among wolves. ⁴Do not take a purse or bag or sandals; and do not greet anyone on the road.

⁵"When you enter a house, first say, 'Peace to this house.' ⁶If someone who promotes peace is there, your peace will rest on them; if not, it will return to you. ⁷Stay there, eating and drinking whatever they give you, for the worker deserves his wages. Do not move around from house to house.

⁸"When you enter a town and are welcomed, eat what is offered to you. ⁹Heal the sick who are there and tell them, 'The kingdom of God has come near to you.' ¹⁰But when you enter a town and are not welcomed, go into its streets and say, ¹¹'Even the dust of your town we wipe from our feet as a warning to you. Yet be sure of this: The kingdom of God has come near.' ¹²I tell you, it will be more bearable on that day for Sodom than for that town.

¹³"Woe to you, Chorazin! Woe to you, Bethsaida! For if the miracles that were performed in you had been performed in Tyre and Sidon, they would have repented long ago, sitting in sackcloth and ashes. ¹⁴But it will be more bearable for Tyre and Sidon at the judgment than for you. ¹⁵And you, Capernaum, will you be lifted to the heavens? No, you will go down to Hades.*ᵇ*

¹⁶"Whoever listens to you listens to me; whoever rejects you rejects me; but whoever rejects me rejects him who sent me."

¹⁷The seventy-two returned with joy and said, "Lord, even the demons submit to us in your name."

¹⁸He replied, "I saw Satan fall like lightning from heaven. ¹⁹I have given you authority to trample on snakes and scorpions and to overcome all the power of the enemy; nothing will harm you. ²⁰However, do not rejoice that the spirits submit to you, but rejoice that your names are written in heaven."

²¹At that time Jesus, full of joy through the Holy Spirit, said, "I praise you, Father, Lord of heaven and earth, because you have hidden these things from the wise and learned, and revealed them to little children. Yes, Father, for this is what you were pleased to do.

²²"All things have been committed to me by my Father.

Why did Jesus send so many people to spread his message? (10:1)
Jesus wanted to cover Judea with his message as thoroughly as he had covered Galilee.

What were the snakes and scorpions? (10:19)
They represented evil. The enemy refers to Satan.

ᵃ 1 Some manuscripts *seventy*; also in verse 17   *ᵇ 15* That is, the realm of the dead

No one knows who the Son is except the Father, and no one knows who the Father is except the Son and those to whom the Son chooses to reveal him.'"

²³Then he turned to his disciples and said privately, "Blessed are the eyes that see what you see. ²⁴For I tell you that many prophets and kings wanted to see what you see but did not see it, and to hear what you hear but did not hear it."

THE PARABLE OF THE GOOD SAMARITAN

²⁵On one occasion an expert in the law stood up to test Jesus. "Teacher," he asked, "what must I do to inherit eternal life?"

²⁶"What is written in the Law?" he replied. "How do you read it?"

²⁷He answered, "'Love the Lord your God with all your heart and with all your soul and with all your strength and with all your mind'ᵃ; and, 'Love your neighbor as yourself.'ᵇ"

²⁸"You have answered correctly," Jesus replied. "Do this and you will live."

²⁹But he wanted to justify himself, so he asked Jesus, "And who is my neighbor?"

³⁰In reply Jesus said: "A man was going down from Jerusalem to Jericho, when he was attacked by robbers. They stripped him of his clothes, beat him and went away, leaving him half dead. ³¹A priest happened to be going down the same road, and when he saw the man, he passed by on the other side. ³²So too, a Levite, when he came to the place and saw him, passed by on the other side. ³³But a Samaritan, as he traveled, came where the man was; and when he saw him, he took pity on him. ³⁴He went to him and bandaged his wounds, pouring on oil and wine. Then he put the man on his own donkey, brought him to an inn and took care of him. ³⁵The next day he took out two denariiᶜ and gave them to the innkeeper. 'Look after him,' he said, 'and when I return, I will reimburse you for any extra expense you may have.'

³⁶"Which of these three do you think was a neighbor to the man who fell into the hands of robbers?"

³⁷The expert in the law replied, "The one who had mercy on him."

Jesus told him, "Go and do likewise."

AT THE HOME OF MARTHA AND MARY

³⁸As Jesus and his disciples were on their way, he came to a village where a woman named Martha opened her home to him. ³⁹She had a sister called Mary, who sat at the Lord's feet listening to what he said. ⁴⁰But Martha was distracted by all the preparations that had to be made. She came to him and asked, "Lord, don't you care that my sister has left me to do the work by myself? Tell her to help me!"

⁴¹"Martha, Martha," the Lord answered, "you are worried and upset about many things, ⁴²but few things are needed— or indeed only one.ᵈ Mary has chosen what is better, and it will not be taken away from her."

How far was Jerusalem from Jericho? (10:30)
The distance from Jerusalem to Jericho was 17 miles (27 kilometers) with a descent from about 25,000 feet above sea level to 800 feet below sea level. The road ran through rocky terrain that provided hiding places for robbers.

Who were the Samaritans? (10:33)
This was a race of people resulting from the intermarriage of Israelites who were left behind when the people of the northern kingdom were exiled and Gentiles who were brought into the land by the Assyrians. In Jesus' day, there was bitter hostility between the Jews and the Samaritans.

What was the value of two denarii? (10:35)
This would be equal to about two days' wages and would be enough to pay for about two months' lodging in an inn.

ᵃ 27 Deut. 6:5   ᵇ 27 Lev. 19:18   ᶜ 35 A denarius was the usual daily wage of a day laborer (see Matt. 20:2).   ᵈ 42 Some manuscripts *but only one thing is needed*

JESUS' TEACHING ON PRAYER

11 One day Jesus was praying in a certain place. When he finished, one of his disciples said to him, "Lord, teach us to pray, just as John taught his disciples."

[2] He said to them, "When you pray, say:

"'Father,[a]
hallowed be your name,
your kingdom come.[b]
[3] Give us each day our daily bread.
[4] Forgive us our sins,
    for we also forgive everyone who sins against us.[c]
And lead us not into temptation.[d]'"

[5] Then Jesus said to them, "Suppose you have a friend, and you go to him at midnight and say, 'Friend, lend me three loaves of bread; [6] a friend of mine on a journey has come to me, and I have no food to offer him.' [7] And suppose the one inside answers, 'Don't bother me. The door is already locked, and my children and I are in bed. I can't get up and give you anything.' [8] I tell you, even though he will not get up and give you the bread because of friendship, yet because of your shameless audacity[e] he will surely get up and give you as much as you need.

[9] "So I say to you: Ask and it will be given to you; seek and you will find; knock and the door will be opened to you. [10] For everyone who asks receives; the one who seeks finds; and to the one who knocks, the door will be opened.

[11] "Which of you fathers, if your son asks for[f] a fish, will give him a snake instead? [12] Or if he asks for an egg, will give him a scorpion? [13] If you then, though you are evil, know how to give good gifts to your children, how much more will your Father in heaven give the Holy Spirit to those who ask him!"

JESUS AND BEELZEBUL

[14] Jesus was driving out a demon that was mute. When the demon left, the man who had been mute spoke, and the crowd was amazed. [15] But some of them said, "By Beelzebul, the prince of demons, he is driving out demons." [16] Others tested him by asking for a sign from heaven.

[17] Jesus knew their thoughts and said to them: "Any kingdom divided against itself will be ruined, and a house divided against itself will fall. [18] If Satan is divided against himself, how can his kingdom stand? I say this because you claim that I drive out demons by Beelzebul. [19] Now if I drive out demons by Beelzebul, by whom do your followers drive them out? So then, they will be your judges. [20] But if I drive out demons by the finger of God, then the kingdom of God has come upon you.

[21] "When a strong man, fully armed, guards his own house, his possessions are safe. [22] But when someone stronger attacks

Where else does the Lord's Prayer appear? (11:2-4)
It also appears in Matthew 6:9–13.

What did it mean to forgive sins? (11:4)
In Matthew 6:12, the term is "debts," but the meaning is the same as "sins." The Lord's Prayer provides a pattern for believers, who have already been forgiven. Jesus speaks of daily forgiveness, which is necessary to restore communion with God.

Who was Beelzebul? (11:15)
This was a name for the prince of demons or Satan (see verse 18). It was a Greek form of the name Baal-Zebub, a sarcastic name for the god Baal (see 2 Kings 1:2).

What did it mean that the kingdom of God had come? (11:20)
This meant that the King was present in the person of Jesus, and the powers of evil were being overthrown.

---

a 2 Some manuscripts *Our Father in heaven*   *b 2* Some manuscripts *come. May your will be done on earth as it is in heaven.*   *c 4* Greek *everyone who is indebted to us*   *d 4* Some manuscripts *temptation, but deliver us from the evil one*   *e 8* Or *yet to preserve his good name*   *f 11* Some manuscripts *for bread, will give him a stone? Or if he asks for*

and overpowers him, he takes away the armor in which the man trusted and divides up his plunder.

23 "Whoever is not with me is against me, and whoever does not gather with me scatters.

24 "When an impure spirit comes out of a person, it goes through arid places seeking rest and does not find it. Then it says, 'I will return to the house I left.' 25 When it arrives, it finds the house swept clean and put in order. 26 Then it goes and takes seven other spirits more wicked than itself, and they go in and live there. And the final condition of that person is worse than the first."

27 As Jesus was saying these things, a woman in the crowd called out, "Blessed is the mother who gave you birth and nursed you."

28 He replied, "Blessed rather are those who hear the word of God and obey it."

THE SIGN OF JONAH

29 As the crowds increased, Jesus said, "This is a wicked generation. It asks for a sign, but none will be given it except the sign of Jonah. 30 For as Jonah was a sign to the Ninevites, so also will the Son of Man be to this generation. 31 The Queen of the South will rise at the judgment with the people of this generation and condemn them, for she came from the ends of the earth to listen to Solomon's wisdom; and now something greater than Solomon is here. 32 The men of Nineveh will stand up at the judgment with this generation and condemn it, for they repented at the preaching of Jonah; and now something greater than Jonah is here.

THE LAMP OF THE BODY

33 "No one lights a lamp and puts it in a place where it will be hidden, or under a bowl. Instead they put it on its stand, so that those who come in may see the light. 34 Your eye is the lamp of your body. When your eyes are healthy,*a* your whole body also is full of light. But when they are unhealthy,*b* your body also is full of darkness. 35 See to it, then, that the light within you is not darkness. 36 Therefore, if your whole body is full of light, and no part of it dark, it will be just as full of light as when a lamp shines its light on you."

WOES ON THE PHARISEES AND THE EXPERTS IN THE LAW

37 When Jesus had finished speaking, a Pharisee invited him to eat with him; so he went in and reclined at the table. 38 But the Pharisee was surprised when he noticed that Jesus did not first wash before the meal.

39 Then the Lord said to him, "Now then, you Pharisees clean the outside of the cup and dish, but inside you are full of greed and wickedness. 40 You foolish people! Did not the one who made the outside make the inside also? 41 But now as for what is inside you — be generous to the poor, and everything will be clean for you.

What did Jesus mean about putting a light where it could be seen? (11:33) Jesus had publicly exhibited the light of the gospel, but the people had wanted more spectacular signs. The problem was not with Jesus' part in giving light but with the people who refused to see him for who he really was.

---

a 34 The Greek for *healthy* here implies *generous*.　*b* 34 The Greek for *unhealthy* here implies *stingy*.

⁴²"Woe to you Pharisees, because you give God a tenth of your mint, rue and all other kinds of garden herbs, but you neglect justice and the love of God. You should have practiced the latter without leaving the former undone.

⁴³"Woe to you Pharisees, because you love the most important seats in the synagogues and respectful greetings in the marketplaces.

⁴⁴"Woe to you, because you are like unmarked graves, which people walk over without knowing it."

⁴⁵One of the experts in the law answered him, "Teacher, when you say these things, you insult us also."

⁴⁶Jesus replied, "And you experts in the law, woe to you, because you load people down with burdens they can hardly carry, and you yourselves will not lift one finger to help them.

⁴⁷"Woe to you, because you build tombs for the prophets, and it was your ancestors who killed them. ⁴⁸So you testify that you approve of what your ancestors did; they killed the prophets, and you build their tombs. ⁴⁹Because of this, God in his wisdom said, 'I will send them prophets and apostles, some of whom they will kill and others they will persecute.' ⁵⁰Therefore this generation will be held responsible for the blood of all the prophets that has been shed since the beginning of the world, ⁵¹from the blood of Abel to the blood of Zechariah, who was killed between the altar and the sanctuary. Yes, I tell you, this generation will be held responsible for it all.

⁵²"Woe to you experts in the law, because you have taken away the key to knowledge. You yourselves have not entered, and you have hindered those who were entering."

⁵³When Jesus went outside, the Pharisees and the teachers of the law began to oppose him fiercely and to besiege him with questions, ⁵⁴waiting to catch him in something he might say.

WARNINGS AND ENCOURAGEMENTS

12 Meanwhile, when a crowd of many thousands had gathered, so that they were trampling on one another, Jesus began to speak first to his disciples, saying: "Be*ᵃ* on your guard against the yeast of the Pharisees, which is hypocrisy. ²There is nothing concealed that will not be disclosed, or hidden that will not be made known. ³What you have said in the dark will be heard in the daylight, and what you have whispered in the ear in the inner rooms will be proclaimed from the roofs.

⁴"I tell you, my friends, do not be afraid of those who kill the body and after that can do no more. ⁵But I will show you whom you should fear: Fear him who, after your body has been killed, has authority to throw you into hell. Yes, I tell you, fear him. ⁶Are not five sparrows sold for two pennies? Yet not one of them is forgotten by God. ⁷Indeed, the very hairs of your head are all numbered. Don't be afraid; you are worth more than many sparrows.

⁸"I tell you, whoever publicly acknowledges me before others, the Son of Man will also acknowledge before the

What were the most important seats in the synagogue? (11:43)
This referred to the bench in front of the ark that contained the sacred scrolls. People who sat there could be seen by everyone in the synagogue.

What did it mean that they built tombs for the prophets? (11:47)
The people appeared to honor the prophets by building memorials, but their ancestors had rejected and killed the prophets just as they rejected the Messiah the prophets had announced.

What were the inner rooms? (12:3)
This probably refers to storerooms that were surrounded by other rooms so that no one could dig in from the outside to steal the contents. Here, too, was where one could talk in apparent privacy.

ᵃ 1 Or speak to his disciples, saying: "First of all, be

angels of God. [9]But whoever disowns me before others will be disowned before the angels of God. [10]And everyone who speaks a word against the Son of Man will be forgiven, but anyone who blasphemes against the Holy Spirit will not be forgiven.

[11]"When you are brought before synagogues, rulers and authorities, do not worry about how you will defend yourselves or what you will say, [12]for the Holy Spirit will teach you at that time what you should say."

THE PARABLE OF THE RICH FOOL

[13]Someone in the crowd said to him, "Teacher, tell my brother to divide the inheritance with me."

[14]Jesus replied, "Man, who appointed me a judge or an arbiter between you?" [15]Then he said to them, "Watch out! Be on your guard against all kinds of greed; life does not consist in an abundance of possessions."

[16]And he told them this parable: "The ground of a certain rich man yielded an abundant harvest. [17]He thought to himself, 'What shall I do? I have no place to store my crops.'

[18]"Then he said, 'This is what I'll do. I will tear down my barns and build bigger ones, and there I will store my surplus grain. [19]And I'll say to myself, "You have plenty of grain laid up for many years. Take life easy; eat, drink and be merry."'

[20]"But God said to him, 'You fool! This very night your life will be demanded from you. Then who will get what you have prepared for yourself?'

[21]"This is how it will be with whoever stores up things for themselves but is not rich toward God."

DO NOT WORRY

[22]Then Jesus said to his disciples: "Therefore I tell you, do not worry about your life, what you will eat; or about your body, what you will wear. [23]For life is more than food, and the body more than clothes. [24]Consider the ravens: They do not sow or reap, they have no storeroom or barn; yet God feeds them. And how much more valuable you are than birds! [25]Who of you by worrying can add a single hour to your life[a]? [26]Since you cannot do this very little thing, why do you worry about the rest?

[27]"Consider how the wild flowers grow. They do not labor or spin. Yet I tell you, not even Solomon in all his splendor was dressed like one of these. [28]If that is how God clothes the grass of the field, which is here today, and tomorrow is thrown into the fire, how much more will he clothe you — you of little faith! [29]And do not set your heart on what you will eat or drink; do not worry about it. [30]For the pagan world runs after all such things, and your Father knows that you need them. [31]But seek his kingdom, and these things will be given to you as well.

[32]"Do not be afraid, little flock, for your Father has been pleased to give you the kingdom. [33]Sell your possessions and give to the poor. Provide purses for yourselves that will not wear out, a treasure in heaven that will never fail, where no

[a] 25 Or *single cubit to your height*

What were the rules of inheritance? (12:13)
According to Deuteronomy 21:17, the elder son usually received double the amount of the younger son's portion. This man's request of Jesus was selfish and materialistic.

What does it mean to seek God's kingdom? (12:31)
This does not mean that God's kingdom is difficult to find. Since Jesus was speaking to his disciples, who were believers, he probably meant that they should seek the spiritual benefits of God's kingdom rather than material things.

thief comes near and no moth destroys. ³⁴ For where your treasure is, there your heart will be also.

WATCHFULNESS

³⁵ "Be dressed ready for service and keep your lamps burning, ³⁶ like servants waiting for their master to return from a wedding banquet, so that when he comes and knocks they can immediately open the door for him. ³⁷ It will be good for those servants whose master finds them watching when he comes. Truly I tell you, he will dress himself to serve, will have them recline at the table and will come and wait on them. ³⁸ It will be good for those servants whose master finds them ready, even if he comes in the middle of the night or toward daybreak. ³⁹ But understand this: If the owner of the house had known at what hour the thief was coming, he would not have let his house be broken into. ⁴⁰ You also must be ready, because the Son of Man will come at an hour when you do not expect him."

⁴¹ Peter asked, "Lord, are you telling this parable to us, or to everyone?"

⁴² The Lord answered, "Who then is the faithful and wise manager, whom the master puts in charge of his servants to give them their food allowance at the proper time? ⁴³ It will be good for that servant whom the master finds doing so when he returns. ⁴⁴ Truly I tell you, he will put him in charge of all his possessions. ⁴⁵ But suppose the servant says to himself, 'My master is taking a long time in coming,' and he then begins to beat the other servants, both men and women, and to eat and drink and get drunk. ⁴⁶ The master of that servant will come on a day when he does not expect him and at an hour he is not aware of. He will cut him to pieces and assign him a place with the unbelievers.

⁴⁷ "The servant who knows the master's will and does not get ready or does not do what the master wants will be beaten with many blows. ⁴⁸ But the one who does not know and does things deserving punishment will be beaten with few blows. From everyone who has been given much, much will be demanded; and from the one who has been entrusted with much, much more will be asked.

NOT PEACE BUT DIVISION

⁴⁹ "I have come to bring fire on the earth, and how I wish it were already kindled! ⁵⁰ But I have a baptism to undergo, and what constraint I am under until it is completed! ⁵¹ Do you think I came to bring peace on earth? No, I tell you, but division. ⁵² From now on there will be five in one family divided against each other, three against two and two against three. ⁵³ They will be divided, father against son and son against father, mother against daughter and daughter against mother, mother-in-law against daughter-in-law and daughter-in-law against mother-in-law."

INTERPRETING THE TIMES

⁵⁴ He said to the crowd: "When you see a cloud rising in the west, immediately you say, 'It's going to rain,' and it does. ⁵⁵ And when the south wind blows, you say, 'It's going to be

---

Who was the wise manager? (12:42)
This was a trustworthy slave who had been put in charge of the estate.

What did fire symbolize? (12:49)
In this verse, it is associated with judgment and in verse 51 with division. The wicked will be judged and separated from the righteous.

How did the Jewish people predict the weather? (12:54–55)
Wind from the west was from the Mediterranean Sea and brought rain; wind from the south was from the desert and was hot and dry.

hot,' and it is. [56] Hypocrites! You know how to interpret the appearance of the earth and the sky. How is it that you don't know how to interpret this present time?

[57] "Why don't you judge for yourselves what is right? [58] As you are going with your adversary to the magistrate, try hard to be reconciled on the way, or your adversary may drag you off to the judge, and the judge turn you over to the officer, and the officer throw you into prison. [59] I tell you, you will not get out until you have paid the last penny."

REPENT OR PERISH

13 Now there were some present at that time who told Jesus about the Galileans whose blood Pilate had mixed with their sacrifices. [2] Jesus answered, "Do you think that these Galileans were worse sinners than all the other Galileans because they suffered this way? [3] I tell you, no! But unless you repent, you too will all perish. [4] Or those eighteen who died when the tower in Siloam fell on them—do you think they were more guilty than all the others living in Jerusalem? [5] I tell you, no! But unless you repent, you too will all perish."

[6] Then he told this parable: "A man had a fig tree growing in his vineyard, and he went to look for fruit on it but did not find any. [7] So he said to the man who took care of the vineyard, 'For three years now I've been coming to look for fruit on this fig tree and haven't found any. Cut it down! Why should it use up the soil?'

[8] "'Sir,' the man replied, 'leave it alone for one more year, and I'll dig around it and fertilize it. [9] If it bears fruit next year, fine! If not, then cut it down.'"

JESUS HEALS A CRIPPLED WOMAN ON THE SABBATH

[10] On a Sabbath Jesus was teaching in one of the synagogues, [11] and a woman was there who had been crippled by a spirit for eighteen years. She was bent over and could not straighten up at all. [12] When Jesus saw her, he called her forward and said to her, "Woman, you are set free from your infirmity." [13] Then he put his hands on her, and immediately she straightened up and praised God.

[14] Indignant because Jesus had healed on the Sabbath, the synagogue leader said to the people, "There are six days for work. So come and be healed on those days, not on the Sabbath."

[15] The Lord answered him, "You hypocrites! Doesn't each of you on the Sabbath untie your ox or donkey from the stall and lead it out to give it water? [16] Then should not this woman, a daughter of Abraham, whom Satan has kept bound for eighteen long years, be set free on the Sabbath day from what bound her?"

[17] When he said this, all his opponents were humiliated, but the people were delighted with all the wonderful things he was doing.

THE PARABLES OF THE MUSTARD SEED AND THE YEAST

[18] Then Jesus asked, "What is the kingdom of God like? What shall I compare it to? [19] It is like a mustard seed, which

---

Why were these Galileans killed? (13:1–5)
The specific details aren't known, but the harsh punishment fits with Pilate's reputation. In ancient times, people often assumed that only very sinful people would experience a calamity. Jesus said that everyone is a sinner and needs to repent.

What did it mean that this woman was crippled by a spirit? (13:11)
Various disorders were caused by evil spirits. The description suggests that the bones of this woman's spine were fused so that she could not stand upright.

Why did Jesus call the synagogue rulers "hypocrites"? (13:15–16)
They claimed to be concerned for the law, but they were only interested in attacking Jesus. He pointed out that on the Sabbath they led their animals to a watering trough, yet they criticized Jesus for healing a woman who had been suffering for 18 years.

a man took and planted in his garden. It grew and became a tree, and the birds perched in its branches."

²⁰Again he asked, "What shall I compare the kingdom of God to? ²¹It is like yeast that a woman took and mixed into about sixty pounds*a* of flour until it worked all through the dough."

THE NARROW DOOR

²²Then Jesus went through the towns and villages, teaching as he made his way to Jerusalem. ²³Someone asked him, "Lord, are only a few people going to be saved?"

He said to them, ²⁴"Make every effort to enter through the narrow door, because many, I tell you, will try to enter and will not be able to. ²⁵Once the owner of the house gets up and closes the door, you will stand outside knocking and pleading, 'Sir, open the door for us.'

"But he will answer, 'I don't know you or where you come from.'

²⁶"Then you will say, 'We ate and drank with you, and you taught in our streets.'

²⁷"But he will reply, 'I don't know you or where you come from. Away from me, all you evildoers!'

²⁸"There will be weeping there, and gnashing of teeth, when you see Abraham, Isaac and Jacob and all the prophets in the kingdom of God, but you yourselves thrown out. ²⁹People will come from east and west and north and south, and will take their places at the feast in the kingdom of God. ³⁰Indeed there are those who are last who will be first, and first who will be last."

JESUS' SORROW FOR JERUSALEM

³¹At that time some Pharisees came to Jesus and said to him, "Leave this place and go somewhere else. Herod wants to kill you."

³²He replied, "Go tell that fox, 'I will keep on driving out demons and healing people today and tomorrow, and on the third day I will reach my goal.' ³³In any case, I must press on today and tomorrow and the next day—for surely no prophet can die outside Jerusalem!

³⁴"Jerusalem, Jerusalem, you who kill the prophets and stone those sent to you, how often I have longed to gather your children together, as a hen gathers her chicks under her wings, and you were not willing. ³⁵Look, your house is left to you desolate. I tell you, you will not see me again until you say, 'Blessed is he who comes in the name of the Lord.'*b*"

JESUS AT A PHARISEE'S HOUSE

14 One Sabbath, when Jesus went to eat in the house of a prominent Pharisee, he was being carefully watched. ²There in front of him was a man suffering from abnormal swelling of his body. ³Jesus asked the Pharisees and experts in the law, "Is it lawful to heal on the Sabbath or not?" ⁴But they remained silent. So taking hold of the man, he healed him and sent him on his way.

a 21 Or about 27 kilograms   *b 35* Psalm 118:26

What is a mustard seed like? (13:19)
The mustard seed is not the smallest seed known today, but it was the smallest seed used by farmers and gardeners in the area now known as the Holy Land. Under favorable conditions, it could grow to ten feet (three meters) tall.

Who will be included in the kingdom of God? (13:29)
Believers from all across the world and from among all people, including Gentiles, will be part of God's kingdom.

What was this abnormal swelling? (14:2)
This refers to an excessive amount of fluid in the body, probably caused by some other illness.

⁵Then he asked them, "If one of you has a child*a* or an ox that falls into a well on the Sabbath day, will you not immediately pull it out?" ⁶And they had nothing to say.

⁷When he noticed how the guests picked the places of honor at the table, he told them this parable: ⁸"When someone invites you to a wedding feast, do not take the place of honor, for a person more distinguished than you may have been invited. ⁹If so, the host who invited both of you will come and say to you, 'Give this person your seat.' Then, humiliated, you will have to take the least important place. ¹⁰But when you are invited, take the lowest place, so that when your host comes, he will say to you, 'Friend, move up to a better place.' Then you will be honored in the presence of all the other guests. ¹¹For all those who exalt themselves will be humbled, and those who humble themselves will be exalted."

¹²Then Jesus said to his host, "When you give a luncheon or dinner, do not invite your friends, your brothers or sisters, your relatives, or your rich neighbors; if you do, they may invite you back and so you will be repaid. ¹³But when you give a banquet, invite the poor, the crippled, the lame, the blind, ¹⁴and you will be blessed. Although they cannot repay you, you will be repaid at the resurrection of the righteous."

THE PARABLE OF THE GREAT BANQUET

¹⁵When one of those at the table with him heard this, he said to Jesus, "Blessed is the one who will eat at the feast in the kingdom of God."

¹⁶Jesus replied: "A certain man was preparing a great banquet and invited many guests. ¹⁷At the time of the banquet he sent his servant to tell those who had been invited, 'Come, for everything is now ready.'

¹⁸"But they all alike began to make excuses. The first said, 'I have just bought a field, and I must go and see it. Please excuse me.'

¹⁹"Another said, 'I have just bought five yoke of oxen, and I'm on my way to try them out. Please excuse me.'

²⁰"Still another said, 'I just got married, so I can't come.'

²¹"The servant came back and reported this to his master. Then the owner of the house became angry and ordered his servant, 'Go out quickly into the streets and alleys of the town and bring in the poor, the crippled, the blind and the lame.'

²²"'Sir,' the servant said, 'what you ordered has been done, but there is still room.'

²³"Then the master told his servant, 'Go out to the roads and country lanes and compel them to come in, so that my house will be full. ²⁴I tell you, not one of those who were invited will get a taste of my banquet.'"

THE COST OF BEING A DISCIPLE

²⁵Large crowds were traveling with Jesus, and turning to them he said: ²⁶"If anyone comes to me and does not hate father and mother, wife and children, brothers and sisters—yes, even their own life—such a person cannot be my disciple.

a 5 Some manuscripts donkey

Why were people invited twice? (14:16–17)
It was Jewish custom to send two invitations: an advance notice and then a follow-up announcement when the feast was ready.

What were the excuses for not attending the feast? (14:18–20)
All of them were insults and probably lies. A person would not buy a piece of land or a team of oxen without examining them first. A wedding celebration would have been scheduled in advance, so the person would not have another event at the same time.

Did Jesus really mean that his followers had to hate their parents and other family members? (14:26)
Certainly not. This was an example of exaggeration (hyperbole) that Jesus used to show that a believer had to love Jesus even more than his or her family.

²⁷And whoever does not carry their cross and follow me cannot be my disciple.

²⁸"Suppose one of you wants to build a tower. Won't you first sit down and estimate the cost to see if you have enough money to complete it? ²⁹For if you lay the foundation and are not able to finish it, everyone who sees it will ridicule you, ³⁰saying, 'This person began to build and wasn't able to finish.'

³¹"Or suppose a king is about to go to war against another king. Won't he first sit down and consider whether he is able with ten thousand men to oppose the one coming against him with twenty thousand? ³²If he is not able, he will send a delegation while the other is still a long way off and will ask for terms of peace. ³³In the same way, those of you who do not give up everything you have cannot be my disciples.

³⁴"Salt is good, but if it loses its saltiness, how can it be made salty again? ³⁵It is fit neither for the soil nor for the manure pile; it is thrown out.

"Whoever has ears to hear, let them hear."

THE PARABLE OF THE LOST SHEEP

15 Now the tax collectors and sinners were all gathering around to hear Jesus. ²But the Pharisees and the teachers of the law muttered, "This man welcomes sinners and eats with them."

³Then Jesus told them this parable: ⁴"Suppose one of you has a hundred sheep and loses one of them. Doesn't he leave the ninety-nine in the open country and go after the lost sheep until he finds it? ⁵And when he finds it, he joyfully puts it on his shoulders ⁶and goes home. Then he calls his friends and neighbors together and says, 'Rejoice with me; I have found my lost sheep.' ⁷I tell you that in the same way there will be more rejoicing in heaven over one sinner who repents than over ninety-nine righteous persons who do not need to repent.

THE PARABLE OF THE LOST COIN

⁸"Or suppose a woman has ten silver coins*ᵃ* and loses one. Doesn't she light a lamp, sweep the house and search carefully until she finds it? ⁹And when she finds it, she calls her friends and neighbors together and says, 'Rejoice with me; I have found my lost coin.' ¹⁰In the same way, I tell you, there is rejoicing in the presence of the angels of God over one sinner who repents."

THE PARABLE OF THE LOST SON

¹¹Jesus continued: "There was a man who had two sons. ¹²The younger one said to his father, 'Father, give me my share of the estate.' So he divided his property between them.

¹³"Not long after that, the younger son got together all he had, set off for a distant country and there squandered his wealth in wild living. ¹⁴After he had spent everything, there was a severe famine in that whole country, and he began to be in need. ¹⁵So he went and hired himself out to a citizen

---

ᵃ 8 Greek ten drachmas, each worth about a day's wages

What was salt used for? (14:34)
Salt was used for flavoring and preserving. Most of the salt used in Israel came from the Dead Sea and was filled with impurities. This caused it to lose some of its flavor. Jesus' followers were supposed to purify, preserve, and penetrate society.

What did people think about tax collectors? (15:1)
Because tax collectors collected tolls for Rome, they were considered traitors. They also were considered extremely dishonest. They could not serve as witnesses or judges, and they were expelled from the synagogue. Their disgrace extended to other members of their families.

What were these silver coins? (15:8)
The silver coins were drachmas. A drachma was a Greek coin that was approximately equivalent to a Roman denarius, worth about a day's wage.

How did the younger son insult his father? (15:12)
An estate usually was not divided until the owner died. By asking for his inheritance, the son implied that he wished that his father were already dead.

How did Jews regard feeding pigs? (15:15)
This was the ultimate indignity for a Jew. The work was filthy, and pigs were "unclean" animals.

of that country, who sent him to his fields to feed pigs. ¹⁶ He longed to fill his stomach with the pods that the pigs were eating, but no one gave him anything.

¹⁷ "When he came to his senses, he said, 'How many of my father's hired servants have food to spare, and here I am starving to death! ¹⁸ I will set out and go back to my father and say to him: Father, I have sinned against heaven and against you. ¹⁹ I am no longer worthy to be called your son; make me like one of your hired servants.' ²⁰ So he got up and went to his father.

"But while he was still a long way off, his father saw him and was filled with compassion for him; he ran to his son, threw his arms around him and kissed him.

²¹ "The son said to him, 'Father, I have sinned against heaven and against you. I am no longer worthy to be called your son.'

²² "But the father said to his servants, 'Quick! Bring the best robe and put it on him. Put a ring on his finger and sandals on his feet. ²³ Bring the fattened calf and kill it. Let's have a feast and celebrate. ²⁴ For this son of mine was dead and is alive again; he was lost and is found.' So they began to celebrate.

²⁵ "Meanwhile, the older son was in the field. When he came near the house, he heard music and dancing. ²⁶ So he called one of the servants and asked him what was going on. ²⁷ 'Your brother has come,' he replied, 'and your father has killed the fattened calf because he has him back safe and sound.'

²⁸ "The older brother became angry and refused to go in. So his father went out and pleaded with him. ²⁹ But he answered his father, 'Look! All these years I've been slaving for you and never disobeyed your orders. Yet you never gave me even a young goat so I could celebrate with my friends. ³⁰ But when this son of yours who has squandered your property with prostitutes comes home, you kill the fattened calf for him!'

³¹ "'My son,' the father said, 'you are always with me, and everything I have is yours. ³² But we had to celebrate and be glad, because this brother of yours was dead and is alive again; he was lost and is found.'"

THE PARABLE OF THE SHREWD MANAGER

16 Jesus told his disciples: "There was a rich man whose manager was accused of wasting his possessions. ² So he called him in and asked him, 'What is this I hear about you? Give an account of your management, because you cannot be manager any longer.'

³ "The manager said to himself, 'What shall I do now? My master is taking away my job. I'm not strong enough to dig, and I'm ashamed to beg— ⁴ I know what I'll do so that, when I lose my job here, people will welcome me into their houses.'

⁵ "So he called in each one of his master's debtors. He asked the first, 'How much do you owe my master?'

How did the manager try to solve his problem? (16:3 – 7)
He discounted the amounts that debtors owed to his master. In this way, he was endearing himself to people who would feel compelled to help him if he lost his job.

6 " 'Nine hundred gallons*a* of olive oil,' he replied.

"The manager told him, 'Take your bill, sit down quickly, and make it four hundred and fifty.'

7 "Then he asked the second, 'And how much do you owe?'

" 'A thousand bushels*b* of wheat,' he replied.

"He told him, 'Take your bill and make it eight hundred.'

8 "The master commended the dishonest manager because he had acted shrewdly. For the people of this world are more shrewd in dealing with their own kind than are the people of the light. 9 I tell you, use worldly wealth to gain friends for yourselves, so that when it is gone, you will be welcomed into eternal dwellings.

10 "Whoever can be trusted with very little can also be trusted with much, and whoever is dishonest with very little will also be dishonest with much. 11 So if you have not been trustworthy in handling worldly wealth, who will trust you with true riches? 12 And if you have not been trustworthy with someone else's property, who will give you property of your own?

13 "No one can serve two masters. Either you will hate the one and love the other, or you will be devoted to the one and despise the other. You cannot serve both God and money."

14 The Pharisees, who loved money, heard all this and were sneering at Jesus. 15 He said to them, "You are the ones who justify yourselves in the eyes of others, but God knows your hearts. What people value highly is detestable in God's sight.

ADDITIONAL TEACHINGS

16 "The Law and the Prophets were proclaimed until John. Since that time, the good news of the kingdom of God is being preached, and everyone is forcing their way into it. 17 It is easier for heaven and earth to disappear than for the least stroke of a pen to drop out of the Law.

18 "Anyone who divorces his wife and marries another woman commits adultery, and the man who marries a divorced woman commits adultery.

THE RICH MAN AND LAZARUS

19 "There was a rich man who was dressed in purple and fine linen and lived in luxury every day. 20 At his gate was laid a beggar named Lazarus, covered with sores 21 and longing to eat what fell from the rich man's table. Even the dogs came and licked his sores.

---

a 6 Or about 3,000 liters   *b* 7 Or about 30 tons

What did this parable mean? (16:8–9)
This is a difficult parable because the manager is dishonest. The point that Jesus seems to be making is that people should use their money shrewdly, ultimately for God's kingdom.

What did garments of purple and fine linen symbolize? (16:19)
These were symbols of wealth.

What is hell like?

Hell is the place of eternal punishment for those who have rejected God. All human beings will continue to exist after they die. Those who are God's children will live with him in heaven forever, and those who are not his children will suffer in hell forever.

The Bible gives various word pictures to describe both heaven and hell, but those word pictures give only a general idea about heaven and hell because human beings are not capable of completely understanding how wonderful heaven is or how terrible hell is.

When the Bible speaks of hell, it often refers to it as a place of fire. We do not know if the fire is literal or if it is a symbol for the pain that people suffer when they are separated from God for all of eternity.

What did it mean to be at Abraham's side? (16:22)
Abraham's side was a blessed place (heaven) where the righteous would go after death. It represented a place of honor and peace.

What did Moses and the Prophets represent? (16:29)
This was a way of describing the entire Old Testament.

What was a millstone? (17:2)
It was one of a pair of large rounded stones used for grinding grain. A large millstone was turned by a donkey and was much larger and heavier than the stones women used to grind grain.

Does this mean we should limit the number of times we forgive others? (17:4)
No. Jesus used the number seven—which symbolized perfection—to emphasize the importance of forgiveness. His point was that his followers should be more willing to show mercy than to seek justice.

Why wouldn't a master be expected to appreciate the service his servant performed? (17:7–10)
The servant was simply carrying out his duties. Jesus wanted his followers to know that they should not expect special treatment for serving their Master.

[22]"The time came when the beggar died and the angels carried him to Abraham's side. The rich man also died and was buried. [23]In Hades, where he was in torment, he looked up and saw Abraham far away, with Lazarus by his side. [24]So he called to him, 'Father Abraham, have pity on me and send Lazarus to dip the tip of his finger in water and cool my tongue, because I am in agony in this fire.'

[25]"But Abraham replied, 'Son, remember that in your lifetime you received your good things, while Lazarus received bad things, but now he is comforted here and you are in agony. [26]And besides all this, between us and you a great chasm has been set in place, so that those who want to go from here to you cannot, nor can anyone cross over from there to us.'

[27]"He answered, 'Then I beg you, father, send Lazarus to my family, [28]for I have five brothers. Let him warn them, so that they will not also come to this place of torment.'

[29]"Abraham replied, 'They have Moses and the Prophets; let them listen to them.'

[30]"'No, father Abraham,' he said, 'but if someone from the dead goes to them, they will repent.'

[31]"He said to him, 'If they do not listen to Moses and the Prophets, they will not be convinced even if someone rises from the dead.'"

SIN, FAITH, DUTY

17 Jesus said to his disciples: "Things that cause people to stumble are bound to come, but woe to anyone through whom they come. [2]It would be better for them to be thrown into the sea with a millstone tied around their neck than to cause one of these little ones to stumble. [3]So watch yourselves.

"If your brother or sister[a] sins against you, rebuke them; and if they repent, forgive them. [4]Even if they sin against you seven times in a day and seven times come back to you saying 'I repent,' you must forgive them."

[5]The apostles said to the Lord, "Increase our faith!"

[6]He replied, "If you have faith as small as a mustard seed, you can say to this mulberry tree, 'Be uprooted and planted in the sea,' and it will obey you.

[7]"Suppose one of you has a servant plowing or looking after the sheep. Will he say to the servant when he comes in from the field, 'Come along now and sit down to eat'? [8]Won't he rather say, 'Prepare my supper, get yourself ready and wait on me while I eat and drink; after that you may eat and drink'? [9]Will he thank the servant because he did what he was told to do? [10]So you also, when you have done everything you were told to do, should say, 'We are unworthy servants; we have only done our duty.'"

JESUS HEALS TEN MEN WITH LEPROSY

[11]Now on his way to Jerusalem, Jesus traveled along the border between Samaria and Galilee. [12]As he was going into a village, ten men who had leprosy[b] met him. They stood at

---

[a] 3 The Greek word for *brother or sister* (*adelphos*) refers here to a fellow disciple, whether man or woman.   [b] 12 The Greek word traditionally translated *leprosy* was used for various diseases affecting the skin.

PARABLES OF JESUS

PARABLE	MATTHEW	MARK	LUKE
Lamp under a bowl	5:14–15	4:21–22	8:16; 11:33
Wise and foolish builders	7:24–27		6:47–49
New cloth on an old coat	9:16	2:21	5:36
New wine in old wineskins	9:17	2:22	5:37–38
Sower and the soils	13:3–8,18–23	4:3–8,14–20	8:5–8,11–15
Weeds	13:24–30,36–43		
Mustard seed	13:31–32	4:30–32	13:18–19
Yeast	13:33		13:20–21
Hidden treasure	13:44		
Valuable pearl	13:45–46		
Net	13:47–50		
Owner of a house	13:52		
Lost sheep	18:12–14		15:4–7
Unmerciful servant	18:23–34		
Workers in the vineyard	20:1–16		
Two sons	21:28–32		
Tenants	21:33–44	12:1–11	2:9–18
Wedding banquet	22:2–14		
Fig tree	24:32–35	13:28–29	21:29–31
Faithful and wise servant	24:45–51		12:42–48
Ten virgins	25:1–13		
Bags of gold (talents)	25:14–30		19:12–27
Sheep and goats	25:31–46		
Growing seed		4:26–29	
Watchful servants		13:35–37	12:35–40
Moneylender			7:41–43
Good Samaritan			10:30–37
Friend in need			11:5–8
Rich fool			12:16–21
Unfruitful fig tree			13:6–9
Lowest seat at the feast			14:7–14
Great banquet			14:16–24
Cost of discipleship			14:28–33
Lost sheep			15:1–7
Lost coin			15:8–10
Lost (prodigal) son			15:11–32
Shrewd manager			16:1–8
Rich man and Lazarus			16:19–31
Master and his servant			17:7–10
Persistent widow			18:2–8
Pharisee and tax collector			18:10–14

a distance [13] and called out in a loud voice, "Jesus, Master, have pity on us!"

[14] When he saw them, he said, "Go, show yourselves to the priests." And as they went, they were cleansed.

[15] One of them, when he saw he was healed, came back, praising God in a loud voice. [16] He threw himself at Jesus' feet and thanked him—and he was a Samaritan.

[17] Jesus asked, "Were not all ten cleansed? Where are the other nine? [18] Has no one returned to give praise to God except this foreigner?" [19] Then he said to him, "Rise and go; your faith has made you well."

THE COMING OF THE KINGDOM OF GOD

[20] Once, on being asked by the Pharisees when the kingdom of God would come, Jesus replied, "The coming of the kingdom of God is not something that can be observed, [21] nor will people say, 'Here it is,' or 'There it is,' because the kingdom of God is in your midst."[a]

[22] Then he said to his disciples, "The time is coming when you will long to see one of the days of the Son of Man, but you will not see it. [23] People will tell you, 'There he is!' or 'Here he is!' Do not go running off after them. [24] For the Son of Man in his day[b] will be like the lightning, which flashes and lights up the sky from one end to the other. [25] But first he must suffer many things and be rejected by this generation.

[26] "Just as it was in the days of Noah, so also will it be in the days of the Son of Man. [27] People were eating, drinking, marrying and being given in marriage up to the day Noah entered the ark. Then the flood came and destroyed them all.

[28] "It was the same in the days of Lot. People were eating and drinking, buying and selling, planting and building. [29] But the day Lot left Sodom, fire and sulfur rained down from heaven and destroyed them all.

[30] "It will be just like this on the day the Son of Man is revealed. [31] On that day no one who is on the housetop, with possessions inside, should go down to get them. Likewise, no one in the field should go back for anything. [32] Remember Lot's wife! [33] Whoever tries to keep their life will lose it, and whoever loses their life will preserve it. [34] I tell you, on that night two people will be in one bed; one will be taken and the other left. [35] Two women will be grinding grain together; one will be taken and the other left." [36][c]

[37] "Where, Lord?" they asked.

He replied, "Where there is a dead body, there the vultures will gather."

THE PARABLE OF THE PERSISTENT WIDOW

18 Then Jesus told his disciples a parable to show them that they should always pray and not give up. [2] He said: "In a certain town there was a judge who neither feared God nor cared what people thought. [3] And there was a widow in that town who kept coming to him with the plea, 'Grant me justice against my adversary.'

Why would people be on the roof of their house? (17:31)
It was customary for people to relax on their rooftops, which were flat. Jesus was saying that when he returns, people should not think of going into their house to retrieve material possessions, which will be of no use.

What will happen at the final judgment? (17:35)
People will be taken to destruction or taken into the kingdom. This verse points out that no matter how close people may be in life, their eternal destiny may differ.

Why was this widow so helpless? (18:3)
A widow with no husband or male relative had no one to uphold her cause, so she could only rely on the willingness of others to act with justice.

[a] 21 Or is within you   [b] 24 Some manuscripts do not have in his day.
[c] 36 Some manuscripts include here words similar to Matt. 24:40.

4 "For some time he refused. But finally he said to himself, 'Even though I don't fear God or care what people think, 5 yet because this widow keeps bothering me, I will see that she gets justice, so that she won't eventually come and attack me!'"

6 And the Lord said, "Listen to what the unjust judge says. 7 And will not God bring about justice for his chosen ones, who cry out to him day and night? Will he keep putting them off? 8 I tell you, he will see that they get justice, and quickly. However, when the Son of Man comes, will he find faith on the earth?"

THE PARABLE OF THE PHARISEE AND THE TAX COLLECTOR

9 To some who were confident of their own righteousness and looked down on everyone else, Jesus told this parable: 10 "Two men went up to the temple to pray, one a Pharisee and the other a tax collector. 11 The Pharisee stood by himself and prayed: 'God, I thank you that I am not like other people — robbers, evildoers, adulterers — or even like this tax collector. 12 I fast twice a week and give a tenth of all I get.'

13 "But the tax collector stood at a distance. He would not even look up to heaven, but beat his breast and said, 'God, have mercy on me, a sinner.'

14 "I tell you that this man, rather than the other, went home justified before God. For all those who exalt themselves will be humbled, and those who humble themselves will be exalted."

THE LITTLE CHILDREN AND JESUS

15 People were also bringing babies to Jesus for him to place his hands on them. When the disciples saw this, they rebuked them. 16 But Jesus called the children to him and said, "Let the little children come to me, and do not hinder them, for the kingdom of God belongs to such as these. 17 Truly I tell you, anyone who will not receive the kingdom of God like a little child will never enter it."

THE RICH AND THE KINGDOM OF GOD

18 A certain ruler asked him, "Good teacher, what must I do to inherit eternal life?"

19 "Why do you call me good?" Jesus answered. "No one is

Why did the Pharisee fast twice a week? (18:12) Fasting was only required in the law of Moses on the Day of Atonement. However, the Pharisees traditionally fasted on Mondays and Thursdays.

Are Christians supposed to give up all of their belongings in order to follow Jesus?
LUKE 18

In this story, the rich young man wanted to know how he could earn eternal life. When Jesus told him to keep God's commandments, the man said that he had kept them all since he was a boy. But no one is able to keep God's law perfectly. Everyone is a sinner, and because of this no one can be saved by following the law. That is why Jesus came to earth — to save people from their sins.

Jesus told the wealthy man to sell his belongings and to follow Jesus, because it is only through Jesus that people can be saved. But the man was not willing to do that. He loved his money and his possessions too much to give them up in order to trust Jesus for his salvation. The story is a reminder that Christians should not let their money or the things they own get in the way of trusting Jesus and serving him.

good — except God alone. 20You know the commandments: 'You shall not commit adultery, you shall not murder, you shall not steal, you shall not give false testimony, honor your father and mother.'*"

21"All these I have kept since I was a boy," he said.

22When Jesus heard this, he said to him, "You still lack one thing. Sell everything you have and give to the poor, and you will have treasure in heaven. Then come, follow me."

23When he heard this, he became very sad, because he was very wealthy. 24Jesus looked at him and said, "How hard it is for the rich to enter the kingdom of God! 25Indeed, it is easier for a camel to go through the eye of a needle than for someone who is rich to enter the kingdom of God."

26Those who heard this asked, "Who then can be saved?"

27Jesus replied, "What is impossible with man is possible with God."

28Peter said to him, "We have left all we had to follow you!"

29"Truly I tell you," Jesus said to them, "no one who has left home or wife or brothers or sisters or parents or children for the sake of the kingdom of God 30will fail to receive many times as much in this age, and in the age to come eternal life."

JESUS PREDICTS HIS DEATH A THIRD TIME

31Jesus took the Twelve aside and told them, "We are going up to Jerusalem, and everything that is written by the prophets about the Son of Man will be fulfilled. 32He will be delivered over to the Gentiles. They will mock him, insult him and spit on him; 33they will flog him and kill him. On the third day he will rise again."

34The disciples did not understand any of this. Its meaning was hidden from them, and they did not know what he was talking about.

A BLIND BEGGAR RECEIVES HIS SIGHT

35As Jesus approached Jericho, a blind man was sitting by the roadside begging. 36When he heard the crowd going by, he asked what was happening. 37They told him, "Jesus of Nazareth is passing by."

38He called out, "Jesus, Son of David, have mercy on me!"

39Those who led the way rebuked him and told him to be quiet, but he shouted all the more, "Son of David, have mercy on me!"

40Jesus stopped and ordered the man to be brought to him. When he came near, Jesus asked him, 41"What do you want me to do for you?"

"Lord, I want to see," he replied.

42Jesus said to him, "Receive your sight; your faith has healed you." 43Immediately he received his sight and followed Jesus, praising God. When all the people saw it, they also praised God.

20 Exodus 20:12-16; Deut. 5:16-20

Why did Jesus tell him to sell all he had? (18:22)
The young man's problem was his love of wealth. The fact that he was rich kept him from relying on God for everything. By giving away his wealth, the young man would have removed the obstacle that kept him from trusting in Jesus.

Why did the blind man call Jesus the "Son of David"? (18:38–39)
This was a Messianic title — meaning a title that referred to Jesus the Messiah — that acknowledged that Jesus was the heir of David's throne.

ZACCHAEUS THE TAX COLLECTOR

19 Jesus entered Jericho and was passing through. [2] A man was there by the name of Zacchaeus; he was a chief tax collector and was wealthy. [3] He wanted to see who Jesus was, but because he was short he could not see over the crowd. [4] So he ran ahead and climbed a sycamore-fig tree to see him, since Jesus was coming that way.

[5] When Jesus reached the spot, he looked up and said to him, "Zacchaeus, come down immediately. I must stay at your house today." [6] So he came down at once and welcomed him gladly.

[7] All the people saw this and began to mutter, "He has gone to be the guest of a sinner."

[8] But Zacchaeus stood up and said to the Lord, "Look, Lord! Here and now I give half of my possessions to the poor, and if I have cheated anybody out of anything, I will pay back four times the amount."

[9] Jesus said to him, "Today salvation has come to this house, because this man, too, is a son of Abraham. [10] For the Son of Man came to seek and to save the lost."

THE PARABLE OF THE TEN MINAS

[11] While they were listening to this, he went on to tell them a parable, because he was near Jerusalem and the people thought that the kingdom of God was going to appear at once. [12] He said: "A man of noble birth went to a distant country to have himself appointed king and then to return. [13] So he called ten of his servants and gave them ten minas.[a] 'Put this money to work,' he said, 'until I come back.'

[14] "But his subjects hated him and sent a delegation after him to say, 'We don't want this man to be our king.'

[15] "He was made king, however, and returned home. Then he sent for the servants to whom he had given the money, in order to find out what they had gained with it.

[16] "The first one came and said, 'Sir, your mina has earned ten more.'

[17] "'Well done, my good servant!' his master replied. 'Because you have been trustworthy in a very small matter, take charge of ten cities.'

[18] "The second came and said, 'Sir, your mina has earned five more.'

[19] "His master answered, 'You take charge of five cities.'

[20] "Then another servant came and said, 'Sir, here is your mina; I have kept it laid away in a piece of cloth. [21] I was afraid of you, because you are a hard man. You take out what you did not put in and reap what you did not sow.'

[22] "His master replied, 'I will judge you by your own words, you wicked servant! You knew, did you, that I am a hard man, taking out what I did not put in, and reaping what I did not sow? [23] Why then didn't you put my money on deposit, so that when I came back, I could have collected it with interest?'

[24] "Then he said to those standing by, 'Take his mina away from him and give it to the one who has ten minas.'

[a] *13 A mina was about three months' wages.*

What is a sycamore-fig tree like? (19:4)
It is a sturdy tree that reaches about 30 to 40 feet tall with a short trunk and spreading branches. It can hold the weight of a grown man.

Why did Jesus call Zacchaeus a son of Abraham? (19:9)
Jesus was acknowledging that he was a true Jew, someone who was a descendant of Abraham and who shared his faith.

How much was a mina worth? (19:13)
A mina was worth about three months' wages. So, 10 minas would be worth between two and three years' average wages.

25 "'Sir,' they said, 'he already has ten!'

26 "He replied, 'I tell you that to everyone who has, more will be given, but as for the one who has nothing, even what they have will be taken away. 27 But those enemies of mine who did not want me to be king over them—bring them here and kill them in front of me.'"

JESUS COMES TO JERUSALEM AS KING

28 After Jesus had said this, he went on ahead, going up to Jerusalem. 29 As he approached Bethphage and Bethany at the hill called the Mount of Olives, he sent two of his disciples, saying to them, 30 "Go to the village ahead of you, and as you enter it, you will find a colt tied there, which no one has ever ridden. Untie it and bring it here. 31 If anyone asks you, 'Why are you untying it?' say, 'The Lord needs it.'"

32 Those who were sent ahead went and found it just as he had told them. 33 As they were untying the colt, its owners asked them, "Why are you untying the colt?"

34 They replied, "The Lord needs it."

35 They brought it to Jesus, threw their cloaks on the colt and put Jesus on it. 36 As he went along, people spread their cloaks on the road.

37 When he came near the place where the road goes down the Mount of Olives, the whole crowd of disciples began joyfully to praise God in loud voices for all the miracles they had seen:

38 "Blessed is the king who comes in the name of the
    Lord!"*a*

"Peace in heaven and glory in the highest!"

39 Some of the Pharisees in the crowd said to Jesus, "Teacher, rebuke your disciples!"

40 "I tell you," he replied, "if they keep quiet, the stones will cry out."

41 As he approached Jerusalem and saw the city, he wept over it 42 and said, "If you, even you, had only known on this day what would bring you peace—but now it is hidden from your eyes. 43 The days will come upon you when your enemies will build an embankment against you and encircle you and hem you in on every side. 44 They will dash you to the ground, you and the children within your walls. They will not leave one stone on another, because you did not recognize the time of God's coming to you."

JESUS AT THE TEMPLE

45 When Jesus entered the temple courts, he began to drive out those who were selling. 46 "It is written," he said to them, "'My house will be a house of prayer'*b*; but you have made it 'a den of robbers.'*c*"

47 Every day he was teaching at the temple. But the chief priests, the teachers of the law and the leaders among the people were trying to kill him. 48 Yet they could not find any way to do it, because all the people hung on his words.

Why would Jesus ride on a colt? (19:30)
A king rode on a donkey (or colt). Jesus did this to show that he was the chosen Son to sit on David's throne.

When did Jesus' prophecy come true? (19:43)
This was fulfilled when the Romans took Jerusalem in A.D. 70, using an embankment to attack the city.

---

a 38 Psalm 118:26   *b 46* Isaiah 56:7   *c 46* Jer. 7:11

THE AUTHORITY OF JESUS QUESTIONED

20 One day as Jesus was teaching the people in the temple courts and proclaiming the good news, the chief priests and the teachers of the law, together with the elders, came up to him. ²"Tell us by what authority you are doing these things," they said. "Who gave you this authority?"

³He replied, "I will also ask you a question. Tell me: ⁴John's baptism—was it from heaven, or of human origin?"

⁵They discussed it among themselves and said, "If we say, 'From heaven,' he will ask, 'Why didn't you believe him?' ⁶But if we say, 'Of human origin,' all the people will stone us, because they are persuaded that John was a prophet."

⁷So they answered, "We don't know where it was from."

⁸Jesus said, "Neither will I tell you by what authority I am doing these things."

THE PARABLE OF THE TENANTS

⁹He went on to tell the people this parable: "A man planted a vineyard, rented it to some farmers and went away for a long time. ¹⁰At harvest time he sent a servant to the tenants so they would give him some of the fruit of the vineyard. But the tenants beat him and sent him away empty-handed. ¹¹He sent another servant, but that one also they beat and treated shamefully and sent away empty-handed. ¹²He sent still a third, and they wounded him and threw him out.

¹³"Then the owner of the vineyard said, 'What shall I do? I will send my son, whom I love; perhaps they will respect him.'

¹⁴"But when the tenants saw him, they talked the matter over. 'This is the heir,' they said. 'Let's kill him, and the inheritance will be ours.' ¹⁵So they threw him out of the vineyard and killed him.

"What then will the owner of the vineyard do to them? ¹⁶He will come and kill those tenants and give the vineyard to others."

When the people heard this, they said, "God forbid!"

¹⁷Jesus looked directly at them and asked, "Then what is the meaning of that which is written:

"'The stone the builders rejected
 has become the cornerstone'ᵃ?

¹⁸Everyone who falls on that stone will be broken to pieces; anyone on whom it falls will be crushed."

¹⁹The teachers of the law and the chief priests looked for a way to arrest him immediately, because they knew he had spoken this parable against them. But they were afraid of the people.

PAYING TAXES TO CAESAR

²⁰Keeping a close watch on him, they sent spies, who pretended to be sincere. They hoped to catch Jesus in something he said, so that they might hand him over to the power and authority of the governor. ²¹So the spies questioned him:

How were large estates farmed in Jesus' time? (20:10–13)
Large estates owned by absentee landlords were put in the hands of local peasants who cultivated the land as tenant farmers. This parable exposed the planned attempt on Jesus' life and God's judgment on those who had made the plans.

What will happen to those who reject Jesus? (20:17–18)
They will be like a pot that is smashed against a stone or like someone who has a stone fall on him or her and is crushed.

ᵃ 17 Psalm 118:22

1496

LUKE 20:22

"Teacher, we know that you speak and teach what is right, and that you do not show partiality but teach the way of God in accordance with the truth. ²²Is it right for us to pay taxes to Caesar or not?"

²³He saw through their duplicity and said to them, ²⁴"Show me a denarius. Whose image and inscription are on it?"

"Caesar's," they replied.

²⁵He said to them, "Then give back to Caesar what is Caesar's, and to God what is God's."

²⁶They were unable to trap him in what he had said there in public. And astonished by his answer, they became silent.

THE RESURRECTION AND MARRIAGE

²⁷Some of the Sadducees, who say there is no resurrection, came to Jesus with a question. ²⁸"Teacher," they said, "Moses wrote for us that if a man's brother dies and leaves a wife but no children, the man must marry the widow and raise up offspring for his brother. ²⁹Now there were seven brothers. The first one married a woman and died childless. ³⁰The second ³¹and then the third married her, and in the same way the seven died, leaving no children. ³²Finally, the woman died too. ³³Now then, at the resurrection whose wife will she be, since the seven were married to her?"

³⁴Jesus replied, "The people of this age marry and are given in marriage. ³⁵But those who are considered worthy of taking part in the age to come and in the resurrection from the dead will neither marry nor be given in marriage, ³⁶and they can no longer die; for they are like the angels. They are God's children, since they are children of the resurrection. ³⁷But in the account of the burning bush, even Moses showed that the dead rise, for he calls the Lord 'the God of Abraham, and the God of Isaac, and the God of Jacob.'^a ³⁸He is not the God of the dead, but of the living, for to him all are alive."

³⁹Some of the teachers of the law responded, "Well said, teacher!" ⁴⁰And no one dared to ask him any more questions.

WHOSE SON IS THE MESSIAH?

⁴¹Then Jesus said to them, "Why is it said that the Messiah is the son of David? ⁴²David himself declares in the Book of Psalms:

"'The Lord said to my Lord:
  "Sit at my right hand
⁴³until I make your enemies
    a footstool for your feet."'^b

⁴⁴David calls him 'Lord.' How then can he be his son?"

WARNING AGAINST THE TEACHERS OF THE LAW

⁴⁵While all the people were listening, Jesus said to his disciples, ⁴⁶"Beware of the teachers of the law. They like to walk around in flowing robes and love to be greeted with respect

^a 37 Exodus 3:6   ^b 43 Psalm 110:1

A Denarius (20:24)

What did Jesus teach about the Messiah? (20:41–44)
The Pharisees thought that the Messiah would be a human, political leader. Jesus wanted them to see that the Son of David was also the Son of God.

What were the teachers of the law like? (20:46–47)
They wore long, flowing linen robes that were fringed. They took the most prominent seats in the synagogue, and they depended on the generosity of patrons for their livelihood. They pretended to be holy yet sometimes exploited widows and others.

in the marketplaces and have the most important seats in the synagogues and the places of honor at banquets. ⁴⁷They devour widows' houses and for a show make lengthy prayers. These men will be punished most severely."

THE WIDOW'S OFFERING

21 As Jesus looked up, he saw the rich putting their gifts into the temple treasury. ²He also saw a poor widow put in two very small copper coins. ³"Truly I tell you," he said, "this poor widow has put in more than all the others. ⁴All these people gave their gifts out of their wealth; but she out of her poverty put in all she had to live on."

THE DESTRUCTION OF THE TEMPLE AND SIGNS OF THE END TIMES

⁵Some of his disciples were remarking about how the temple was adorned with beautiful stones and with gifts dedicated to God. But Jesus said, ⁶"As for what you see here, the time will come when not one stone will be left on another; every one of them will be thrown down."

⁷"Teacher," they asked, "when will these things happen? And what will be the sign that they are about to take place?"

⁸He replied: "Watch out that you are not deceived. For many will come in my name, claiming, 'I am he,' and, 'The time is near.' Do not follow them. ⁹When you hear of wars and uprisings, do not be frightened. These things must happen first, but the end will not come right away."

¹⁰Then he said to them: "Nation will rise against nation, and kingdom against kingdom. ¹¹There will be great earthquakes, famines and pestilences in various places, and fearful events and great signs from heaven.

¹²"But before all this, they will seize you and persecute you. They will hand you over to synagogues and put you in prison, and you will be brought before kings and governors, and all on account of my name. ¹³And so you will bear testimony to me. ¹⁴But make up your mind not to worry beforehand how you will defend yourselves. ¹⁵For I will give you words and wisdom that none of your adversaries will be able to resist or contradict. ¹⁶You will be betrayed even by parents, brothers and sisters, relatives and friends, and they will put some of you to death. ¹⁷Everyone will hate you because of me. ¹⁸But not a hair of your head will perish. ¹⁹Stand firm, and you will win life.

²⁰"When you see Jerusalem being surrounded by armies, you will know that its desolation is near. ²¹Then let those who are in Judea flee to the mountains, let those in the city get out, and let those in the country not enter the city. ²²For this is the time of punishment in fulfillment of all that has been written. ²³How dreadful it will be in those days for pregnant women and nursing mothers! There will be great distress in the land and wrath against this people. ²⁴They will fall by the sword and will be taken as prisoners to all the nations. Jerusalem will be trampled on by the Gentiles until the times of the Gentiles are fulfilled.

²⁵"There will be signs in the sun, moon and stars. On the

How were people able to make contributions to the temple? (21:1)
In the court of the women, there were 13 boxes into which worshipers could place their offerings.

When was this prophecy fulfilled? (21:6)
This was fulfilled in A.D. 70 when the Romans took over Jerusalem and destroyed the temple.

What were synagogues used for? (21:12)
They were used not only for worship and school but also for community administration and confinement while awaiting trial.

earth, nations will be in anguish and perplexity at the roaring and tossing of the sea. ²⁶People will faint from terror, apprehensive of what is coming on the world, for the heavenly bodies will be shaken. ²⁷At that time they will see the Son of Man coming in a cloud with power and great glory. ²⁸When these things begin to take place, stand up and lift up your heads, because your redemption is drawing near."

²⁹He told them this parable: "Look at the fig tree and all the trees. ³⁰When they sprout leaves, you can see for yourselves and know that summer is near. ³¹Even so, when you see these things happening, you know that the kingdom of God is near.

³²"Truly I tell you, this generation will certainly not pass away until all these things have happened. ³³Heaven and earth will pass away, but my words will never pass away.

³⁴"Be careful, or your hearts will be weighed down with carousing, drunkenness and the anxieties of life, and that day will close on you suddenly like a trap. ³⁵For it will come on all those who live on the face of the whole earth. ³⁶Be always on the watch, and pray that you may be able to escape all that is about to happen, and that you may be able to stand before the Son of Man."

³⁷Each day Jesus was teaching at the temple, and each evening he went out to spend the night on the hill called the Mount of Olives, ³⁸and all the people came early in the morning to hear him at the temple.

JUDAS AGREES TO BETRAY JESUS

22 Now the Festival of Unleavened Bread, called the Passover, was approaching, ²and the chief priests and the teachers of the law were looking for some way to get rid of Jesus, for they were afraid of the people. ³Then Satan entered Judas, called Iscariot, one of the Twelve. ⁴And Judas went to the chief priests and the officers of the temple guard and discussed with them how he might betray Jesus. ⁵They were delighted and agreed to give him money. ⁶He consented, and watched for an opportunity to hand Jesus over to them when no crowd was present.

THE LAST SUPPER

⁷Then came the day of Unleavened Bread on which the Passover lamb had to be sacrificed. ⁸Jesus sent Peter and John, saying, "Go and make preparations for us to eat the Passover."

⁹"Where do you want us to prepare for it?" they asked.

¹⁰He replied, "As you enter the city, a man carrying a jar of water will meet you. Follow him to the house that he enters, ¹¹and say to the owner of the house, 'The Teacher asks: Where is the guest room, where I may eat the Passover with my disciples?' ¹²He will show you a large room upstairs, all furnished. Make preparations there."

¹³They left and found things just as Jesus had told them. So they prepared the Passover.

¹⁴When the hour came, Jesus and his apostles reclined at the table. ¹⁵And he said to them, "I have eagerly desired to

---

Why did Jesus tell his listeners to "look at the fig tree"? (21:29–30)
The coming of spring is announced by the growth of leaves. In a similar way, one can anticipate the coming of God's kingdom by certain signs.

Who were the officers of the temple guard? (22:4)
These were Jews selected mostly from the Levites.

Why did Jesus tell them to follow a man carrying a jar? (22:10)
It was very rare to see a man carrying a jar of water because this was considered a woman's task.

Why did Jesus want to celebrate this Passover with his disciples? (22:14–16)
This would be the last time Jesus could share a meal with them before he himself became the "Passover lamb" and sacrificed his life to redeem the world.

eat this Passover with you before I suffer. ¹⁶For I tell you, I will not eat it again until it finds fulfillment in the kingdom of God."

¹⁷After taking the cup, he gave thanks and said, "Take this and divide it among you. ¹⁸For I tell you I will not drink again from the fruit of the vine until the kingdom of God comes."

¹⁹And he took bread, gave thanks and broke it, and gave it to them, saying, "This is my body given for you; do this in remembrance of me."

²⁰In the same way, after the supper he took the cup, saying, "This cup is the new covenant in my blood, which is poured out for you.ᵃ ²¹But the hand of him who is going to betray me is with mine on the table. ²²The Son of Man will go as it has been decreed. But woe to that man who betrays him!" ²³They began to question among themselves which of them it might be who would do this.

²⁴A dispute also arose among them as to which of them was considered to be greatest. ²⁵Jesus said to them, "The kings of the Gentiles lord it over them; and those who exercise authority over them call themselves Benefactors. ²⁶But you are not to be like that. Instead, the greatest among you should be like the youngest, and the one who rules like the one who serves. ²⁷For who is greater, the one who is at the table or the one who serves? Is it not the one who is at the table? But I am among you as one who serves. ²⁸You are those who have stood by me in my trials. ²⁹And I confer on you a kingdom, just as my Father conferred one on me, ³⁰so that you may eat and drink at my table in my kingdom and sit on thrones, judging the twelve tribes of Israel.

³¹"Simon, Simon, Satan has asked to sift all of you as wheat. ³²But I have prayed for you, Simon, that your faith may not fail. And when you have turned back, strengthen your brothers."

³³But he replied, "Lord, I am ready to go with you to prison and to death."

³⁴Jesus answered, "I tell you, Peter, before the rooster crows today, you will deny three times that you know me."

³⁵Then Jesus asked them, "When I sent you without purse, bag or sandals, did you lack anything?"

"Nothing," they answered.

³⁶He said to them, "But now if you have a purse, take it, and also a bag; and if you don't have a sword, sell your cloak and buy one. ³⁷It is written: 'And he was numbered with the transgressors'ᵇ; and I tell you that this must be fulfilled in me. Yes, what is written about me is reaching its fulfillment."

³⁸The disciples said, "See, Lord, here are two swords."

"That's enough!" he replied.

JESUS PRAYS ON THE MOUNT OF OLIVES

³⁹Jesus went out as usual to the Mount of Olives, and his disciples followed him. ⁴⁰On reaching the place, he said to them, "Pray that you will not fall into temptation." ⁴¹He

---

ᵃ *19,20* Some manuscripts do not have *given for you . . . poured out for you.*
ᵇ *37* Isaiah 53:12

What did Jesus say about his disciples' desire for greatness? (22:25–27)
People should not seek greatness in the kingdom of God but instead should achieve great things by being willing to serve others, just as Jesus did.

Where did Jesus go to pray? (22:39)
Matthew called the place Gethsemane (Matthew 26:26), and John referred to it as an olive grove (John 18:1). The place was apparently on the lower slopes of the Mount of Olives.

withdrew about a stone's throw beyond them, knelt down and prayed, [42]"Father, if you are willing, take this cup from me; yet not my will, but yours be done." [43]An angel from heaven appeared to him and strengthened him. [44]And being in anguish, he prayed more earnestly, and his sweat was like drops of blood falling to the ground.[a]

[45]When he rose from prayer and went back to the disciples, he found them asleep, exhausted from sorrow. [46]"Why are you sleeping?" he asked them. "Get up and pray so that you will not fall into temptation."

JESUS ARRESTED

[47]While he was still speaking a crowd came up, and the man who was called Judas, one of the Twelve, was leading them. He approached Jesus to kiss him, [48]but Jesus asked him, "Judas, are you betraying the Son of Man with a kiss?"

[49]When Jesus' followers saw what was going to happen, they said, "Lord, should we strike with our swords?" [50]And one of them struck the servant of the high priest, cutting off his right ear.

[51]But Jesus answered, "No more of this!" And he touched the man's ear and healed him.

[52]Then Jesus said to the chief priests, the officers of the temple guard, and the elders, who had come for him, "Am I leading a rebellion, that you have come with swords and clubs? [53]Every day I was with you in the temple courts, and you did not lay a hand on me. But this is your hour—when darkness reigns."

PETER DISOWNS JESUS

[54]Then seizing him, they led him away and took him into the house of the high priest. Peter followed at a distance. [55]And when some there had kindled a fire in the middle of the courtyard and had sat down together, Peter sat down with them. [56]A servant girl saw him seated there in the firelight. She looked closely at him and said, "This man was with him."

[57]But he denied it. "Woman, I don't know him," he said.

[58]A little later someone else saw him and said, "You also are one of them."

"Man, I am not!" Peter replied.

[59]About an hour later another asserted, "Certainly this fellow was with him, for he is a Galilean."

[60]Peter replied, "Man, I don't know what you're talking about!" Just as he was speaking, the rooster crowed. [61]The Lord turned and looked straight at Peter. Then Peter remembered the word the Lord had spoken to him: "Before the rooster crows today, you will disown me three times." [62]And he went outside and wept bitterly.

THE GUARDS MOCK JESUS

[63]The men who were guarding Jesus began mocking and beating him. [64]They blindfolded him and demanded,

Who was the high priest?
(22:54)
This was Caiaphas, who was the high priest from A.D. 18 to 36. He was the son-in-law of Annas, a former high priest, who served from A.D. 6 to 15.

[a] *43,44* Many early manuscripts do not have verses 43 and 44.

"Prophesy! Who hit you?" [65] And they said many other insulting things to him.

JESUS BEFORE PILATE AND HEROD

[66] At daybreak the council of the elders of the people, both the chief priests and the teachers of the law, met together, and Jesus was led before them. [67] "If you are the Messiah," they said, "tell us."

Jesus answered, "If I tell you, you will not believe me, [68] and if I asked you, you would not answer. [69] But from now on, the Son of Man will be seated at the right hand of the mighty God."

[70] They all asked, "Are you then the Son of God?"

He replied, "You say that I am."

[71] Then they said, "Why do we need any more testimony? We have heard it from his own lips."

23 Then the whole assembly rose and led him off to Pilate. [2] And they began to accuse him, saying, "We have found this man subverting our nation. He opposes payment of taxes to Caesar and claims to be Messiah, a king."

[3] So Pilate asked Jesus, "Are you the king of the Jews?"

"You have said so," Jesus replied.

[4] Then Pilate announced to the chief priests and the crowd, "I find no basis for a charge against this man."

[5] But they insisted, "He stirs up the people all over Judea by his teaching. He started in Galilee and has come all the way here."

[6] On hearing this, Pilate asked if the man was a Galilean. [7] When he learned that Jesus was under Herod's jurisdiction, he sent him to Herod, who was also in Jerusalem at that time.

[8] When Herod saw Jesus, he was greatly pleased, because for a long time he had been wanting to see him. From what he had heard about him, he hoped to see him perform a sign of some sort. [9] He plied him with many questions, but Jesus gave him no answer. [10] The chief priests and the teachers of the law were standing there, vehemently accusing him. [11] Then Herod and his soldiers ridiculed and mocked him. Dressing him in an elegant robe, they sent him back to Pilate. [12] That day Herod and Pilate became friends—before this they had been enemies.

[13] Pilate called together the chief priests, the rulers and the people, [14] and said to them, "You brought me this man as one who was inciting the people to rebellion. I have examined him in your presence and have found no basis for your charges against him. [15] Neither has Herod, for he sent him back to us; as you can see, he has done nothing to deserve death. [16] Therefore, I will punish him and then release him." [17] [a]

[18] But the whole crowd shouted, "Away with this man! Release Barabbas to us!" [19] (Barabbas had been thrown into prison for an insurrection in the city, and for murder.)

[20] Wanting to release Jesus, Pilate appealed to them again. [21] But they kept shouting, "Crucify him! Crucify him!"

a 17 Some manuscripts include here words similar to Matt. 27:15 and Mark 15:6.

Why did they wait to decide on a verdict until daybreak? (22:66)
Only then could a legal trial take place for the whole council (the Sanhedrin) to impose the death sentence.

Why was Pilate willing to punish Jesus? (23:16)
Although Pilate found Jesus not guilty, he was willing to have him beaten in order to satisfy the chief priests and the people.

²²For the third time he spoke to them: "Why? What crime has this man committed? I have found in him no grounds for the death penalty. Therefore I will have him punished and then release him."

²³But with loud shouts they insistently demanded that he be crucified, and their shouts prevailed. ²⁴So Pilate decided to grant their demand. ²⁵He released the man who had been thrown into prison for insurrection and murder, the one they asked for, and surrendered Jesus to their will.

THE CRUCIFIXION OF JESUS

²⁶As the soldiers led him away, they seized Simon from Cyrene, who was on his way in from the country, and put the cross on him and made him carry it behind Jesus. ²⁷A large number of people followed him, including women who mourned and wailed for him. ²⁸Jesus turned and said to them, "Daughters of Jerusalem, do not weep for me; weep for yourselves and for your children. ²⁹For the time will come when you will say, 'Blessed are the childless women, the wombs that never bore and the breasts that never nursed!' ³⁰Then

> "'they will say to the mountains, "Fall on us!"
> and to the hills, "Cover us!"'ᵃ

³¹For if people do these things when the tree is green, what will happen when it is dry?"

³²Two other men, both criminals, were also led out with him to be executed. ³³When they came to the place called the Skull, they crucified him there, along with the criminals—one on his right, the other on his left. ³⁴Jesus said, "Father, forgive them, for they do not know what they are doing."ᵇ And they divided up his clothes by casting lots.

³⁵The people stood watching, and the rulers even sneered at him. They said, "He saved others; let him save himself if he is God's Messiah, the Chosen One."

³⁶The soldiers also came up and mocked him. They offered him wine vinegar ³⁷and said, "If you are the king of the Jews, save yourself."

³⁸There was a written notice above him, which read: THIS IS THE KING OF THE JEWS.

³⁹One of the criminals who hung there hurled insults at him: "Aren't you the Messiah? Save yourself and us!"

ᵃ 30 Hosea 10:8   ᵇ 34 Some early manuscripts do not have this sentence.

Why did Simon have to carry the cross? (23:26)
Men who were to be crucified were usually forced to carry a beam of their cross weighing 30 to 40 pounds (14 – 18 kilograms) to the place of crucifixion. Jesus began by carrying the cross (see John 19:17), but he was not able to carry it the whole way, probably because he had been weakened by the beating.

Why did the soldiers divide up Jesus' clothes? (23:34)
Any possessions an executed person had with him were taken by the executioners. The soldiers were fulfilling the prophecy made in Psalm 22:18.

Did Jesus really die and come back to life?   LUKE 23 – 24

Yes. Just as Jesus truly was born, he truly died. He hung on the cross for several hours, and many witnesses were there to observe it, including his disciples and other followers as well as Jewish leaders, bystanders, and Roman soldiers. John reports that after Jesus died, one of the soldiers stuck a spear in his side, and blood mixed with fluids gushed out. By dying, Jesus became the sacrifice for the sins of the world.

Jesus also rose from the dead. The Roman soldiers were careful to make sure that Jesus' disciples could not remove his body from the tomb. But Jesus arose and appeared after his resurrection to many witnesses. By rising from the dead Jesus overcame death and guaranteed that believers would also overcome death and live with him forever.

⁴⁰But the other criminal rebuked him. "Don't you fear God," he said, "since you are under the same sentence? ⁴¹We are punished justly, for we are getting what our deeds deserve. But this man has done nothing wrong."

⁴²Then he said, "Jesus, remember me when you come into your kingdom.ᵃ"

⁴³Jesus answered him, "Truly I tell you, today you will be with me in paradise."

THE DEATH OF JESUS

⁴⁴It was now about noon, and darkness came over the whole land until three in the afternoon, ⁴⁵for the sun stopped shining. And the curtain of the temple was torn in two. ⁴⁶Jesus called out with a loud voice, "Father, into your hands I commit my spirit."ᵇ When he had said this, he breathed his last.

⁴⁷The centurion, seeing what had happened, praised God and said, "Surely this was a righteous man." ⁴⁸When all the people who had gathered to witness this sight saw what took place, they beat their breasts and went away. ⁴⁹But all those who knew him, including the women who had followed him from Galilee, stood at a distance, watching these things.

THE BURIAL OF JESUS

⁵⁰Now there was a man named Joseph, a member of the Council, a good and upright man, ⁵¹who had not consented to their decision and action. He came from the Judean town of Arimathea, and he himself was waiting for the kingdom of God. ⁵²Going to Pilate, he asked for Jesus' body. ⁵³Then he took it down, wrapped it in linen cloth and placed it in a tomb cut in the rock, one in which no one had yet been laid. ⁵⁴It was Preparation Day, and the Sabbath was about to begin.

⁵⁵The women who had come with Jesus from Galilee followed Joseph and saw the tomb and how his body was laid in it. ⁵⁶Then they went home and prepared spices and perfumes. But they rested on the Sabbath in obedience to the commandment.

JESUS HAS RISEN

24 On the first day of the week, very early in the morning, the women took the spices they had prepared and went to the tomb. ²They found the stone rolled away from the tomb, ³but when they entered, they did not find the body of the Lord Jesus. ⁴While they were wondering about this, suddenly two men in clothes that gleamed like lightning stood beside them. ⁵In their fright the women bowed down with their faces to the ground, but the men said to them, "Why do you look for the living among the dead? ⁶He is not here; he has risen! Remember how he told you, while he was still with you in Galilee: ⁷'The Son of Man must be delivered over to the hands of sinners, be crucified and on the third day be raised again.'" ⁸Then they remembered his words.

Jesus on the Cross

Why was the curtain of the temple torn? (23:45)
When the curtain between the Holy Place and the Most Holy Place was torn, it symbolized that through Jesus' death on the cross people now had access to God.

How were bodies prepared for burial? (23:55–56)
Yards of cloth and large quantities of spices were used in preparing a body for burial. Seventy-five pounds of myrrh and aloe were used on the first evening (see John 19:39).

Were tombs usually sealed with stones? (24:2)
A tomb's entrance was normally closed to keep vandals and animals from disturbing the bodies. This stone had been sealed by the Roman authorities because they didn't want Jesus' disciples to take the body and claim that he had risen from the dead.

ᵃ 42 Some manuscripts *come with your kingly power*   ᵇ 46 Psalm 31:5

[9]When they came back from the tomb, they told all these things to the Eleven and to all the others. [10]It was Mary Magdalene, Joanna, Mary the mother of James, and the others with them who told this to the apostles. [11]But they did not believe the women, because their words seemed to them like nonsense. [12]Peter, however, got up and ran to the tomb. Bending over, he saw the strips of linen lying by themselves, and he went away, wondering to himself what had happened.

ON THE ROAD TO EMMAUS

[13]Now that same day two of them were going to a village called Emmaus, about seven miles[a] from Jerusalem. [14]They were talking with each other about everything that had happened. [15]As they talked and discussed these things with each other, Jesus himself came up and walked along with them; [16]but they were kept from recognizing him.

[17]He asked them, "What are you discussing together as you walk along?"

They stood still, their faces downcast. [18]One of them, named Cleopas, asked him, "Are you the only one visiting Jerusalem who does not know the things that have happened there in these days?"

[19]"What things?" he asked.

"About Jesus of Nazareth," they replied. "He was a prophet, powerful in word and deed before God and all the people. [20]The chief priests and our rulers handed him over to be sentenced to death, and they crucified him; [21]but we had hoped that he was the one who was going to redeem Israel. And what is more, it is the third day since all this took place. [22]In addition, some of our women amazed us. They went to the tomb early this morning [23]but didn't find his body. They came and told us that they had seen a vision of angels, who said he was alive. [24]Then some of our companions went to the tomb and found it just as the women had said, but they did not see Jesus."

[25]He said to them, "How foolish you are, and how slow to believe all that the prophets have spoken! [26]Did not the Messiah have to suffer these things and then enter his glory?" [27]And beginning with Moses and all the Prophets, he explained to them what was said in all the Scriptures concerning himself.

[28]As they approached the village to which they were going, Jesus continued on as if he were going farther. [29]But they urged him strongly, "Stay with us, for it is nearly evening; the day is almost over." So he went in to stay with them.

[30]When he was at the table with them, he took bread, gave thanks, broke it and began to give it to them. [31]Then their eyes were opened and they recognized him, and he disappeared from their sight. [32]They asked each other, "Were not our hearts burning within us while he talked with us on the road and opened the Scriptures to us?"

[33]They got up and returned at once to Jerusalem. There they found the Eleven and those with them, assembled together [34]and saying, "It is true! The Lord has risen and has

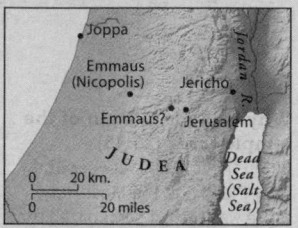

On the Road to Emmaus
(24:13)

Joppa
Emmaus
(Nicopolis)   Jericho
Emmaus?   Jerusalem
JUDEA
Jordan R.
Dead Sea (Salt Sea)
0   20 km.
0   20 miles

---

[a] 13 Or about 11 kilometers

appeared to Simon." [35] Then the two told what had happened on the way, and how Jesus was recognized by them when he broke the bread.

JESUS APPEARS TO THE DISCIPLES

[36] While they were still talking about this, Jesus himself stood among them and said to them, "Peace be with you."

[37] They were startled and frightened, thinking they saw a ghost. [38] He said to them, "Why are you troubled, and why do doubts rise in your minds? [39] Look at my hands and my feet. It is I myself! Touch me and see; a ghost does not have flesh and bones, as you see I have."

[40] When he had said this, he showed them his hands and feet. [41] And while they still did not believe it because of joy and amazement, he asked them, "Do you have anything here to eat?" [42] They gave him a piece of broiled fish, [43] and he took it and ate it in their presence.

[44] He said to them, "This is what I told you while I was still with you: Everything must be fulfilled that is written about me in the Law of Moses, the Prophets and the Psalms."

[45] Then he opened their minds so they could understand the Scriptures. [46] He told them, "This is what is written: The Messiah will suffer and rise from the dead on the third day, [47] and repentance for the forgiveness of sins will be preached in his name to all nations, beginning at Jerusalem. [48] You are witnesses of these things. [49] I am going to send you what my Father has promised; but stay in the city until you have been clothed with power from on high."

THE ASCENSION OF JESUS

[50] When he had led them out to the vicinity of Bethany, he lifted up his hands and blessed them. [51] While he was blessing them, he left them and was taken up into heaven. [52] Then they worshiped him and returned to Jerusalem with great joy. [53] And they stayed continually at the temple, praising God.

Why did Jesus show them his hands and feet? (24:40) Jesus' hands and feet had been nailed to the cross and still showed the marks of the crucifixion.

John

INTRODUCTION

Who wrote this book?	John, the disciple of Jesus, wrote this book.
Why was this book written?	The Gospel of John shows that Jesus is the Son of God and helps people believe in him.
For whom was this book written?	John was written for everyone who wants to understand who Jesus really is.
What happens in this book?	John reports miracles and teachings that show that Jesus is the Son of God.
Who is the key person in this book?	Jesus is the most important person in this book.
Where did this happen?	Most of the events in this book happened in Judea.

When did these things happen?

10 BC AD 1 10 20 30 40 50 60 70 80 90 100

HEROD THE GREAT'S REIGN (C. 37 – 4 BC)

JESUS' BIRTH (C. 6/5 BC)

JESUS' FLIGHT TO EGYPT (C. 5/4 BC)

BEGINNING OF JOHN THE BAPTIST'S MINISTRY (C. AD 26)

BEGINNING OF JESUS' MINISTRY (C. AD 26)

JESUS' DEATH, RESURRECTION AND ASCENSION (C. AD 30)

PAUL'S CONVERSION (C. AD 35)

BOOK OF JOHN WRITTEN (C. AD 60 – 95)

JOHN'S EXILE ON PATMOS (C. AD 90 – 95)

THE WORD BECAME FLESH

1 In the beginning was the Word, and the Word was with God, and the Word was God. [2]He was with God in the beginning. [3]Through him all things were made; without him nothing was made that has been made. [4]In him was life, and that life was the light of all mankind. [5]The light shines in the darkness, and the darkness has not overcome[a] it.

[6]There was a man sent from God whose name was John. [7]He came as a witness to testify concerning that light, so that through him all might believe. [8]He himself was not the light; he came only as a witness to the light.

[9]The true light that gives light to everyone was coming into the world. [10]He was in the world, and though the world was made through him, the world did not recognize him. [11]He came to that which was his own, but his own did not receive him. [12]Yet to all who did receive him, to those who believed in his name, he gave the right to become children of God— [13]children born not of natural descent, nor of human decision or a husband's will, but born of God.

[14]The Word became flesh and made his dwelling among us. We have seen his glory, the glory of the one and only Son, who came from the Father, full of grace and truth.

[15](John testified concerning him. He cried out, saying, "This is the one I spoke about when I said, 'He who comes after me has surpassed me because he was before me.'") [16]Out of his fullness we have all received grace in place of grace already given. [17]For the law was given through Moses; grace and truth came through Jesus Christ. [18]No one has ever seen God, but the one and only Son, who is himself God and[b] is in closest relationship with the Father, has made him known.

JOHN THE BAPTIST DENIES BEING THE MESSIAH

[19]Now this was John's testimony when the Jewish leaders[c] in Jerusalem sent priests and Levites to ask him who he was. [20]He did not fail to confess, but confessed freely, "I am not the Messiah."

[a] 5 Or *understood*   [b] 18 Some manuscripts *but the only Son, who*
[c] 19 The Greek term traditionally translated *the Jews* (*hoi Ioudaioi*) refers here and elsewhere in John's Gospel to those Jewish leaders who opposed Jesus; also in 5:10, 15, 16; 7:1, 11, 13; 9:22; 18:14, 28, 36; 19:7, 12, 31, 38; 20:19.

Why are light and life important images for this book? (1:4)
John used the term *life* in reference to Jesus 36 times in this book. He also linked Christ with the image of light, particularly the "light of the world," who offers hope to humankind.

Why did John the Baptist need to say that Jesus was greater than he (John) was? (1:15)
In ancient times, an older person was given more respect than a younger person, so ordinarily John would have been more highly regarded that Jesus. But John pointed out that Jesus actually came before him, because Jesus existed before he was born on earth.

Who created God, and where does he live?   JOHN 1

When John wrote "in the beginning," he did not mean that there was a specific point in time when God started to exist. God is beyond the human idea of time. He has always existed and will always exist; he is eternal. Psalm 90:2 says, "Before the mountains were born or you brought forth the whole world, from everlasting to everlasting you are God."

God is a spirit rather than a physical being. He is present everywhere. God also is all-powerful; he is in control of all things. In addition, God is all-knowing. He knows the past, present, and future.

As human beings, we have a sense of who God is and what God's qualities are. He has revealed himself to us through the universe that he created, through the Bible, through his Son, Jesus, and through the Holy Spirit who works in our hearts. But we will know God much more completely in the new heaven and new earth, when we as believers live with him forever.

Why did the people ask John the Baptist if he was Elijah? (1:21)
They remembered that Elijah had not died, and they expected that he would return to earth to announce the end time.

Why did John say that he was not worthy to untie Jesus' sandal straps? (1:27)
Disciples performed all sorts of service for their rabbis (teachers), but untying the straps of a sandal was considered the job of a slave.

Why was Jesus called the "Lamb of God"? (1:29)
In the entire Bible, this term is found only in this verse and in verse 36. The term refers to Jesus as the sacrificial Lamb who would atone for the sins of the world through his death.

[21] They asked him, "Then who are you? Are you Elijah?" He said, "I am not."

"Are you the Prophet?"

He answered, "No."

[22] Finally they said, "Who are you? Give us an answer to take back to those who sent us. What do you say about yourself?"

[23] John replied in the words of Isaiah the prophet, "I am the voice of one calling in the wilderness, 'Make straight the way for the Lord.'"[a]

[24] Now the Pharisees who had been sent [25] questioned him, "Why then do you baptize if you are not the Messiah, nor Elijah, nor the Prophet?"

[26] "I baptize with[b] water," John replied, "but among you stands one you do not know. [27] He is the one who comes after me, the straps of whose sandals I am not worthy to untie."

[28] This all happened at Bethany on the other side of the Jordan, where John was baptizing.

JOHN TESTIFIES ABOUT JESUS

[29] The next day John saw Jesus coming toward him and said, "Look, the Lamb of God, who takes away the sin of the world! [30] This is the one I meant when I said, 'A man who comes after me has surpassed me because he was before me.' [31] I myself did not know him, but the reason I came baptizing with water was that he might be revealed to Israel."

[32] Then John gave this testimony: "I saw the Spirit come down from heaven as a dove and remain on him. [33] And I myself did not know him, but the one who sent me to baptize with water told me, 'The man on whom you see the Spirit come down and remain is the one who will baptize with the Holy Spirit.' [34] I have seen and I testify that this is God's Chosen One."[c]

JOHN'S DISCIPLES FOLLOW JESUS

[35] The next day John was there again with two of his disciples. [36] When he saw Jesus passing by, he said, "Look, the Lamb of God!"

[37] When the two disciples heard him say this, they followed Jesus. [38] Turning around, Jesus saw them following and asked, "What do you want?"

They said, "Rabbi" (which means "Teacher"), "where are you staying?"

[39] "Come," he replied, "and you will see."

So they went and saw where he was staying, and they spent that day with him. It was about four in the afternoon.

[40] Andrew, Simon Peter's brother, was one of the two who heard what John had said and who had followed Jesus. [41] The first thing Andrew did was to find his brother Simon and tell him, "We have found the Messiah" (that is, the Christ). [42] And he brought him to Jesus.

Jesus looked at him and said, "You are Simon son of John. You will be called Cephas" (which, when translated, is Peter[d]).

---

[a] 23 Isaiah 40:3   [b] 26 Or in; also in verses 31 and 33 (twice)   [c] 34 See Isaiah 42:1; many manuscripts is the Son of God.   [d] 42 Cephas (Aramaic) and Peter (Greek) both mean rock.

JESUS CALLS PHILIP AND NATHANAEL

⁴³The next day Jesus decided to leave for Galilee. Finding Philip, he said to him, "Follow me."

⁴⁴Philip, like Andrew and Peter, was from the town of Bethsaida. ⁴⁵Philip found Nathanael and told him, "We have found the one Moses wrote about in the Law, and about whom the prophets also wrote—Jesus of Nazareth, the son of Joseph."

⁴⁶"Nazareth! Can anything good come from there?" Nathanael asked.

"Come and see," said Philip.

⁴⁷When Jesus saw Nathanael approaching, he said of him, "Here truly is an Israelite in whom there is no deceit."

⁴⁸"How do you know me?" Nathanael asked.

Jesus answered, "I saw you while you were still under the fig tree before Philip called you."

⁴⁹Then Nathanael declared, "Rabbi, you are the Son of God; you are the king of Israel."

⁵⁰Jesus said, "You believe*ᵃ* because I told you I saw you under the fig tree. You will see greater things than that." ⁵¹He then added, "Very truly I tell you,*ᵇ* you*ᵇ* will see 'heaven open, and the angels of God ascending and descending on'*ᶜ* the Son of Man."

JESUS CHANGES WATER INTO WINE

2 On the third day a wedding took place at Cana in Galilee. Jesus' mother was there, ²and Jesus and his disciples had also been invited to the wedding. ³When the wine was gone, Jesus' mother said to him, "They have no more wine."

⁴"Woman,*ᵈ* why do you involve me?" Jesus replied. "My hour has not yet come."

⁵His mother said to the servants, "Do whatever he tells you."

⁶Nearby stood six stone water jars, the kind used by the Jews for ceremonial washing, each holding from twenty to thirty gallons.*ᵉ*

⁷Jesus said to the servants, "Fill the jars with water"; so they filled them to the brim.

⁸Then he told them, "Now draw some out and take it to the master of the banquet."

They did so, ⁹and the master of the banquet tasted the water that had been turned into wine. He did not realize where it had come from, though the servants who had drawn the water knew. Then he called the bridegroom aside ¹⁰and said, "Everyone brings out the choice wine first and then the cheaper wine after the guests have had too much to drink; but you have saved the best till now."

¹¹What Jesus did here in Cana of Galilee was the first of the signs through which he revealed his glory; and his disciples believed in him.

¹²After this he went down to Capernaum with his mother and brothers and his disciples. There they stayed for a few days.

*ᵃ 50 Or Do you believe . . . ?   ᵇ 51 The Greek is plural.   ᶜ 51 Gen. 28:12
ᵈ 4 The Greek for Woman does not denote any disrespect.   ᵉ 6 Or from about 75 to about 115 liters*

Why did Nathanael ask if anything good could come from Nazareth? (1:46)
People who lived in Nazareth or anywhere else in Galilee were often viewed as second-class citizens. It was a little, insignificant town, and Roman soldiers were stationed there.

Jesus Visits Cana (2:1)

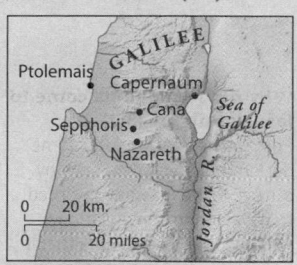

Why was running out of wine such a major problem? (2:3)
During a wedding feast, the family had an obligation to provide enough wine, the main beverage, to last the entire celebration. If the wine ran out, people would regard the hosts as not living up to their responsibility.

What were these signs? (2:11)
John referred to Jesus' miracles as signs in order to emphasize the significance of the action rather than the miracle itself. These signs revealed Jesus' glory.

JESUS CLEARS THE TEMPLE COURTS

¹³When it was almost time for the Jewish Passover, Jesus went up to Jerusalem. ¹⁴In the temple courts he found people selling cattle, sheep and doves, and others sitting at tables exchanging money. ¹⁵So he made a whip out of cords, and drove all from the temple courts, both sheep and cattle; he scattered the coins of the money changers and overturned their tables. ¹⁶To those who sold doves he said, "Get these out of here! Stop turning my Father's house into a market!" ¹⁷His disciples remembered that it is written: "Zeal for your house will consume me."ᵃ

¹⁸The Jews then responded to him, "What sign can you show us to prove your authority to do all this?"

¹⁹Jesus answered them, "Destroy this temple, and I will raise it again in three days."

²⁰They replied, "It has taken forty-six years to build this temple, and you are going to raise it in three days?" ²¹But the temple he had spoken of was his body. ²²After he was raised from the dead, his disciples recalled what he had said. Then they believed the scripture and the words that Jesus had spoken.

²³Now while he was in Jerusalem at the Passover Festival, many people saw the signs he was performing and believed in his name.ᵇ ²⁴But Jesus would not entrust himself to them, for he knew all people. ²⁵He did not need any testimony about mankind, for he knew what was in each person.

JESUS TEACHES NICODEMUS

3 Now there was a Pharisee, a man named Nicodemus who was a member of the Jewish ruling council. ²He came to Jesus at night and said, "Rabbi, we know that you are a teacher who has come from God. For no one could perform the signs you are doing if God were not with him."

³Jesus replied, "Very truly I tell you, no one can see the kingdom of God unless they are born again.ᶜ"

⁴"How can someone be born when they are old?" Nicodemus asked. "Surely they cannot enter a second time into their mother's womb to be born!"

⁵Jesus answered, "Very truly I tell you, no one can enter the kingdom of God unless they are born of water and the Spirit. ⁶Flesh gives birth to flesh, but the Spiritᵈ gives birth to spirit. ⁷You should not be surprised at my saying, 'Youᵉ must be born again.' ⁸The wind blows wherever it pleases. You hear its sound, but you cannot tell where it comes from or where it is going. So it is with everyone born of the Spirit."ᶠ

⁹"How can this be?" Nicodemus asked.

¹⁰"You are Israel's teacher," said Jesus, "and do you not understand these things? ¹¹Very truly I tell you, we speak of what we know, and we testify to what we have seen, but still you people do not accept our testimony. ¹²I have spoken to you of earthly things and you do not believe; how then will you believe if I speak of heavenly things? ¹³No one has ever

When did this take place? (2:20)
The temple was not finally completed until A.D. 64. Since the work began in 20 B.C., the year recorded here was A.D. 27.

Why did Nicodemus come to Jesus at night? (3:2)
Perhaps he was afraid to come during the day and be seen by others. Or he may have wanted to have a long conversation, which would have been difficult during the daytime because of the crowds.

ᵃ 17 Psalm 69:9   ᵇ 23 Or *in him*   ᶜ 3 The Greek for *again* also means *from above*; also in verse 7.   ᵈ 6 Or *but spirit*   ᵉ 7 The Greek is plural.   ᶠ 8 The Greek for *Spirit* is the same as that for *wind*.

gone into heaven except the one who came from heaven—the Son of Man.[a] [14]Just as Moses lifted up the snake in the wilderness, so the Son of Man must be lifted up,[b] [15]that everyone who believes may have eternal life in him."[c]

[16]For God so loved the world that he gave his one and only Son, that whoever believes in him shall not perish but have eternal life. [17]For God did not send his Son into the world to condemn the world, but to save the world through him. [18]Whoever believes in him is not condemned, but whoever does not believe stands condemned already because they have not believed in the name of God's one and only Son. [19]This is the verdict: Light has come into the world, but people loved darkness instead of light because their deeds were evil. [20]Everyone who does evil hates the light, and will not come into the light for fear that their deeds will be exposed. [21]But whoever lives by the truth comes into the light, so that it may be seen plainly that what they have done has been done in the sight of God.

JOHN TESTIFIES AGAIN ABOUT JESUS

[22]After this, Jesus and his disciples went out into the Judean countryside, where he spent some time with them, and baptized. [23]Now John also was baptizing at Aenon near Salim, because there was plenty of water, and people were coming and being baptized. [24](This was before John was put in prison.) [25]An argument developed between some of John's disciples and a certain Jew over the matter of ceremonial washing. [26]They came to John and said to him, "Rabbi, that man who was with you on the other side of the Jordan—the one you testified about—look, he is baptizing, and everyone is going to him."

[27]To this John replied, "A person can receive only what is given them from heaven. [28]You yourselves can testify that I said, 'I am not the Messiah but am sent ahead of him.' [29]The bride belongs to the bridegroom. The friend who attends the bridegroom waits and listens for him, and is full of joy when he hears the bridegroom's voice. That joy is mine, and it is now complete. [30]He must become greater; I must become less."[d]

[31]The one who comes from above is above all; the one who is from the earth belongs to the earth, and speaks as one from the earth. The one who comes from heaven is above all. [32]He testifies to what he has seen and heard, but no one accepts his testimony. [33]Whoever has accepted it has certified that God is truthful. [34]For the one whom God has sent speaks the words of God, for God[e] gives the Spirit without limit. [35]The Father loves the Son and has placed everything in his hands. [36]Whoever believes in the Son has eternal life, but whoever rejects the Son will not see life, for God's wrath remains on them.

JESUS TALKS WITH A SAMARITAN WOMAN

4 Now Jesus learned that the Pharisees had heard that he was gaining and baptizing more disciples than John— [2]although in fact it was not Jesus who baptized, but his disciples. [3]So he left Judea and went back once more to Galilee.

Why did John the Baptist compare himself to a best man at a wedding? (3:29) The most important man at the wedding was the groom. The friend (best man) was there to help the bridegroom. This was the role John saw for himself.

[a] 13 Some manuscripts *Man, who is in heaven*   [b] 14 The Greek for *lifted up* also means *exalted*.   [c] 15 Some interpreters end the quotation with verse 21.   [d] 30 Some interpreters end the quotation with verse 36.   [e] 34 Greek *he*

What did Samaria refer to here? (4:4)
This was the whole region rather than just the city of Samaria.

What was a well? (4:6)
At its most basic, a well was a pit or hole dug into the earth down to the water table. Some wells were very elaborate, and others were quite basic. They were generally surrounded by walls of stone.

Why was it significant that the woman had five husbands? (4:18)
Divorced women were considered shameful. Therefore the Samaritan woman, who had been married five times and was now living with a man who was not her husband, would have been shunned and ridiculed by her neighbors.

Why were the disciples surprised that Jesus was talking with a woman? (4:27)
Jewish religious leaders rarely spoke with women in public, and Jews typically did not associate with Samaritans.

⁴Now he had to go through Samaria. ⁵So he came to a town in Samaria called Sychar, near the plot of ground Jacob had given to his son Joseph. ⁶Jacob's well was there, and Jesus, tired as he was from the journey, sat down by the well. It was about noon.

⁷When a Samaritan woman came to draw water, Jesus said to her, "Will you give me a drink?" ⁸(His disciples had gone into the town to buy food.)

⁹The Samaritan woman said to him, "You are a Jew and I am a Samaritan woman. How can you ask me for a drink?" (For Jews do not associate with Samaritans.ᵃ)

¹⁰Jesus answered her, "If you knew the gift of God and who it is that asks you for a drink, you would have asked him and he would have given you living water."

¹¹"Sir," the woman said, "you have nothing to draw with and the well is deep. Where can you get this living water? ¹²Are you greater than our father Jacob, who gave us the well and drank from it himself, as did also his sons and his livestock?"

¹³Jesus answered, "Everyone who drinks this water will be thirsty again, ¹⁴but whoever drinks the water I give them will never thirst. Indeed, the water I give them will become in them a spring of water welling up to eternal life."

¹⁵The woman said to him, "Sir, give me this water so that I won't get thirsty and have to keep coming here to draw water."

¹⁶He told her, "Go, call your husband and come back."

¹⁷"I have no husband," she replied.

Jesus said to her, "You are right when you say you have no husband. ¹⁸The fact is, you have had five husbands, and the man you now have is not your husband. What you have just said is quite true."

¹⁹"Sir," the woman said, "I can see that you are a prophet. ²⁰Our ancestors worshiped on this mountain, but you Jews claim that the place where we must worship is in Jerusalem."

²¹"Woman," Jesus replied, "believe me, a time is coming when you will worship the Father neither on this mountain nor in Jerusalem. ²²You Samaritans worship what you do not know; we worship what we do know, for salvation is from the Jews. ²³Yet a time is coming and has now come when the true worshipers will worship the Father in the Spirit and in truth, for they are the kind of worshipers the Father seeks. ²⁴God is spirit, and his worshipers must worship in the Spirit and in truth."

²⁵The woman said, "I know that Messiah" (called Christ) "is coming. When he comes, he will explain everything to us."

²⁶Then Jesus declared, "I, the one speaking to you—I am he."

THE DISCIPLES REJOIN JESUS

²⁷Just then his disciples returned and were surprised to find him talking with a woman. But no one asked, "What do you want?" or "Why are you talking with her?"

²⁸Then, leaving her water jar, the woman went back to the

ᵃ 9 Or *do not use dishes Samaritans have used*

town and said to the people, ²⁹"Come, see a man who told me everything I ever did. Could this be the Messiah?" ³⁰They came out of the town and made their way toward him.

³¹Meanwhile his disciples urged him, "Rabbi, eat something."

³²But he said to them, "I have food to eat that you know nothing about."

³³Then his disciples said to each other, "Could someone have brought him food?"

³⁴"My food," said Jesus, "is to do the will of him who sent me and to finish his work. ³⁵Don't you have a saying, 'It's still four months until harvest'? I tell you, open your eyes and look at the fields! They are ripe for harvest. ³⁶Even now the one who reaps draws a wage and harvests a crop for eternal life, so that the sower and the reaper may be glad together. ³⁷Thus the saying 'One sows and another reaps' is true. ³⁸I sent you to reap what you have not worked for. Others have done the hard work, and you have reaped the benefits of their labor."

MANY SAMARITANS BELIEVE

³⁹Many of the Samaritans from that town believed in him because of the woman's testimony, "He told me everything I ever did." ⁴⁰So when the Samaritans came to him, they urged him to stay with them, and he stayed two days. ⁴¹And because of his words many more became believers.

⁴²They said to the woman, "We no longer believe just because of what you said; now we have heard for ourselves, and we know that this man really is the Savior of the world."

JESUS HEALS AN OFFICIAL'S SON

⁴³After the two days he left for Galilee. ⁴⁴(Now Jesus himself had pointed out that a prophet has no honor in his own country.) ⁴⁵When he arrived in Galilee, the Galileans welcomed him. They had seen all that he had done in Jerusalem at the Passover Festival, for they also had been there.

⁴⁶Once more he visited Cana in Galilee, where he had turned the water into wine. And there was a certain royal official whose son lay sick at Capernaum. ⁴⁷When this man heard that Jesus had arrived in Galilee from Judea, he went to him and begged him to come and heal his son, who was close to death.

⁴⁸"Unless you people see signs and wonders," Jesus told him, "you will never believe."

⁴⁹The royal official said, "Sir, come down before my child dies."

⁵⁰"Go," Jesus replied, "your son will live."

The man took Jesus at his word and departed. ⁵¹While he was still on the way, his servants met him with the news that his boy was living. ⁵²When he inquired as to the time when his son got better, they said to him, "Yesterday, at one in the afternoon, the fever left him."

⁵³Then the father realized that this was the exact time at which Jesus had said to him, "Your son will live." So he and his whole household believed.

What did it mean that Jesus was the Savior of the world? (4:42)
This pointed to the fact that Jesus' salvation extended to the entire world, to all who believed.

⁵⁴This was the second sign Jesus performed after coming from Judea to Galilee.

THE HEALING AT THE POOL

5 Some time later, Jesus went up to Jerusalem for one of the Jewish festivals. ²Now there is in Jerusalem near the Sheep Gate a pool, which in Aramaic is called Bethesda[a] and which is surrounded by five covered colonnades. ³Here a great number of disabled people used to lie—the blind, the lame, the paralyzed. [4][b] ⁵One who was there had been an invalid for thirty-eight years. ⁶When Jesus saw him lying there and learned that he had been in this condition for a long time, he asked him, "Do you want to get well?"

⁷"Sir," the invalid replied, "I have no one to help me into the pool when the water is stirred. While I am trying to get in, someone else goes down ahead of me."

⁸Then Jesus said to him, "Get up! Pick up your mat and walk." ⁹At once the man was cured; he picked up his mat and walked.

The day on which this took place was a Sabbath, ¹⁰and so the Jewish leaders said to the man who had been healed, "It is the Sabbath; the law forbids you to carry your mat."

¹¹But he replied, "The man who made me well said to me, 'Pick up your mat and walk.'"

¹²So they asked him, "Who is this fellow who told you to pick it up and walk?"

¹³The man who was healed had no idea who it was, for Jesus had slipped away into the crowd that was there.

¹⁴Later Jesus found him at the temple and said to him, "See, you are well again. Stop sinning or something worse may happen to you." ¹⁵The man went away and told the Jewish leaders that it was Jesus who had made him well.

THE AUTHORITY OF THE SON

¹⁶So, because Jesus was doing these things on the Sabbath, the Jewish leaders began to persecute him. ¹⁷In his defense Jesus said to them, "My Father is always at his work to this very day, and I too am working." ¹⁸For this reason they tried all the more to kill him; not only was he breaking the Sabbath, but he was even calling God his own Father, making himself equal with God.

¹⁹Jesus gave them this answer: "Very truly I tell you, the Son can do nothing by himself; he can do only what he sees his Father doing, because whatever the Father does the Son also does. ²⁰For the Father loves the Son and shows him all he does. Yes, and he will show him even greater works than these, so that you will be amazed. ²¹For just as the Father raises the dead and gives them life, even so the Son gives life to whom he is pleased to give it. ²²Moreover, the Father judges no one, but has entrusted all judgment to the Son, ²³that all may honor the Son just as they honor the Father.

Why was the man forbidden to carry his mat on the Sabbath? (5:10)
This was not a violation of the law of Moses but a traditional interpretation of it that prohibited carrying loads of any kind on the Sabbath.

Why did the Jews want to kill Jesus? (5:18)
They considered Jesus' claim—that he had a special relationship to the Father that made him equal to God—as blasphemous.

Why did they object to Jesus raising the dead? (5:21)
The Jews (except for the Sadducees) believed that God could raise the dead. However, they did not think that God gave this privilege to anyone else.

---

a 2 Some manuscripts Bethzatha; other manuscripts Bethsaida   b 3,4 Some manuscripts include here, wholly or in part, paralyzed—and they waited for the moving of the waters. 4From time to time an angel of the Lord would come down and stir up the waters. The first one into the pool after each such disturbance would be cured of whatever disease they had.

Whoever does not honor the Son does not honor the Father, who sent him.

²⁴"Very truly I tell you, whoever hears my word and believes him who sent me has eternal life and will not be judged but has crossed over from death to life. ²⁵Very truly I tell you, a time is coming and has now come when the dead will hear the voice of the Son of God and those who hear will live. ²⁶For as the Father has life in himself, so he has granted the Son also to have life in himself. ²⁷And he has given him authority to judge because he is the Son of Man.

²⁸"Do not be amazed at this, for a time is coming when all who are in their graves will hear his voice ²⁹and come out—those who have done what is good will rise to live, and those who have done what is evil will rise to be condemned. ³⁰By myself I can do nothing; I judge only as I hear, and my judgment is just, for I seek not to please myself but him who sent me.

TESTIMONIES ABOUT JESUS

³¹"If I testify about myself, my testimony is not true. ³²There is another who testifies in my favor, and I know that his testimony about me is true.

³³"You have sent to John and he has testified to the truth. ³⁴Not that I accept human testimony; but I mention it that you may be saved. ³⁵John was a lamp that burned and gave light, and you chose for a time to enjoy his light.

³⁶"I have testimony weightier than that of John. For the works that the Father has given me to finish—the very works that I am doing—testify that the Father has sent me. ³⁷And the Father who sent me has himself testified concerning me. You have never heard his voice nor seen his form, ³⁸nor does his word dwell in you, for you do not believe the one he sent. ³⁹You study*ᵃ* the Scriptures diligently because you think that in them you have eternal life. These are the very Scriptures that testify about me, ⁴⁰yet you refuse to come to me to have life.

⁴¹"I do not accept glory from human beings, ⁴²but I know you. I know that you do not have the love of God in your hearts. ⁴³I have come in my Father's name, and you do not accept me; but if someone else comes in his own name, you will accept him. ⁴⁴How can you believe since you accept glory from one another but do not seek the glory that comes from the only God*ᵇ*?

⁴⁵"But do not think I will accuse you before the Father. Your accuser is Moses, on whom your hopes are set. ⁴⁶If you believed Moses, you would believe me, for he wrote about me. ⁴⁷But since you do not believe what he wrote, how are you going to believe what I say?"

JESUS FEEDS THE FIVE THOUSAND

6 Some time after this, Jesus crossed to the far shore of the Sea of Galilee (that is, the Sea of Tiberias), ²and a great crowd of people followed him because they saw the signs he had performed by healing the sick. ³Then Jesus went up on

ᵃ 39 Or ³⁹Study   ᵇ 44 Some early manuscripts the Only One

What testimonies are stressed here? (5:31–47)
This section stresses the testimonies of John the Baptist (verse 33), the works of Jesus (verse 36), the works of God the Father (verse 37), the Scriptures (verse 39), and Moses (verse 46).

How was Moses their accuser? (5:45)
Even though Jesus' listeners prided themselves on following the law of Moses, they overlooked the fact that Jesus was the fulfillment of Moses' law.

What did this miracle show? (6:1–15)
The feeding of the 5,000 is the one miracle, apart from the resurrection, that appears in all four Gospels. It showed that Jesus is the supplier of human need, and it set the stage for his testimony that he is the bread of life.

a mountainside and sat down with his disciples. ⁴The Jewish Passover Festival was near.

⁵When Jesus looked up and saw a great crowd coming toward him, he said to Philip, "Where shall we buy bread for these people to eat?" ⁶He asked this only to test him, for he already had in mind what he was going to do.

⁷Philip answered him, "It would take more than half a year's wages*a* to buy enough bread for each one to have a bite!"

⁸Another of his disciples, Andrew, Simon Peter's brother, spoke up, ⁹"Here is a boy with five small barley loaves and two small fish, but how far will they go among so many?"

¹⁰Jesus said, "Have the people sit down." There was plenty of grass in that place, and they sat down (about five thousand men were there). ¹¹Jesus then took the loaves, gave thanks, and distributed to those who were seated as much as they wanted. He did the same with the fish.

¹²When they had all had enough to eat, he said to his disciples, "Gather the pieces that are left over. Let nothing be wasted." ¹³So they gathered them and filled twelve baskets with the pieces of the five barley loaves left over by those who had eaten.

¹⁴After the people saw the sign Jesus performed, they began to say, "Surely this is the Prophet who is to come into the world." ¹⁵Jesus, knowing that they intended to come and make him king by force, withdrew again to a mountain by himself.

JESUS WALKS ON THE WATER

¹⁶When evening came, his disciples went down to the lake, ¹⁷where they got into a boat and set off across the lake for Capernaum. By now it was dark, and Jesus had not yet joined them. ¹⁸A strong wind was blowing and the waters grew rough. ¹⁹When they had rowed about three or four miles,*b* they saw Jesus approaching the boat, walking on the water; and they were frightened. ²⁰But he said to them, "It is I; don't be afraid." ²¹Then they were willing to take him into the boat, and immediately the boat reached the shore where they were heading.

²²The next day the crowd that had stayed on the opposite shore of the lake realized that only one boat had been there, and that Jesus had not entered it with his disciples, but that they had gone away alone. ²³Then some boats from Tiberias landed near the place where the people had eaten the bread after the Lord had given thanks. ²⁴Once the crowd realized that neither Jesus nor his disciples were there, they got into the boats and went to Capernaum in search of Jesus.

JESUS THE BREAD OF LIFE

²⁵When they found him on the other side of the lake, they asked him, "Rabbi, when did you get here?"

²⁶Jesus answered, "Very truly I tell you, you are looking for me, not because you saw the signs I performed but because you ate the loaves and had your fill. ²⁷Do not work for food that spoils, but for food that endures to eternal life, which the

What were barley loaves? (6:9)
This was inexpensive bread which poor people typically ate.

How many people were present? (6:10)
There were 5,000 men. The women and children were not counted.

Why did Jesus withdraw? (6:15)
He knew that the people wanted to make him king, but he was not the type of king they were looking for.

---

a 7 Greek *take two hundred denarii*   *b 19* Or about 5 or 6 kilometers

Son of Man will give you. For on him God the Father has placed his seal of approval."

²⁸Then they asked him, "What must we do to do the works God requires?"

²⁹Jesus answered, "The work of God is this: to believe in the one he has sent."

³⁰So they asked him, "What sign then will you give that we may see it and believe you? What will you do? ³¹Our ancestors ate the manna in the wilderness; as it is written: 'He gave them bread from heaven to eat.'ᵃ"

³²Jesus said to them, "Very truly I tell you, it is not Moses who has given you the bread from heaven, but it is my Father who gives you the true bread from heaven. ³³For the bread of God is the bread that comes down from heaven and gives life to the world."

³⁴"Sir," they said, "always give us this bread."

³⁵Then Jesus declared, "I am the bread of life. Whoever comes to me will never go hungry, and whoever believes in me will never be thirsty. ³⁶But as I told you, you have seen me and still you do not believe. ³⁷All those the Father gives me will come to me, and whoever comes to me I will never drive away. ³⁸For I have come down from heaven not to do my will but to do the will of him who sent me. ³⁹And this is the will of him who sent me, that I shall lose none of all those he has given me, but raise them up at the last day. ⁴⁰For my Father's will is that everyone who looks to the Son and believes in him shall have eternal life, and I will raise them up at the last day."

⁴¹At this the Jews there began to grumble about him because he said, "I am the bread that came down from heaven." ⁴²They said, "Is this not Jesus, the son of Joseph, whose father and mother we know? How can he now say, 'I came down from heaven'?"

⁴³"Stop grumbling among yourselves," Jesus answered. ⁴⁴"No one can come to me unless the Father who sent me draws them, and I will raise them up at the last day. ⁴⁵It is written in the Prophets: 'They will all be taught by God.'ᵇ Everyone who has heard the Father and learned from him comes to me. ⁴⁶No one has seen the Father except the one who is from God; only he has seen the Father. ⁴⁷Very truly I tell you, the one who believes has eternal life. ⁴⁸I am the bread of life. ⁴⁹Your ancestors ate the manna in the wilderness, yet they died. ⁵⁰But here is the bread that comes down from heaven, which anyone may eat and not die. ⁵¹I am the living bread that came down from heaven. Whoever eats this bread will live forever. This bread is my flesh, which I will give for the life of the world."

⁵²Then the Jews began to argue sharply among themselves, "How can this man give us his flesh to eat?"

⁵³Jesus said to them, "Very truly I tell you, unless you eat the flesh of the Son of Man and drink his blood, you have no life in you. ⁵⁴Whoever eats my flesh and drinks my blood has eternal life, and I will raise them up at the last day. ⁵⁵For my flesh is real food and my blood is real drink. ⁵⁶Whoever

ᵃ 31 Exodus 16:4; Neh. 9:15; Psalm 78:24,25   ᵇ 45 Isaiah 54:13

What was wrong with their question? (6:28–29)
They thought they had to do something to earn eternal life, but it is a gift of God.

What did Jesus call himself in the book of John? (6:35)
Jesus said he was the bread of life (6:35); the light of the world (8:12); the gate for the sheep (10:7); the good shepherd (10:11, 14); the resurrection and the life (11:25); the way, the truth, and the life (14:6); and the true vine (15:1).

Why was this a hard teaching? (6:53–60)
The thought of eating Jesus' flesh and drinking his blood was probably shocking to most of his listeners. Jesus meant that he would be the sacrifice for the sins of the world.

eats my flesh and drinks my blood remains in me, and I in them. [57] Just as the living Father sent me and I live because of the Father, so the one who feeds on me will live because of me. [58] This is the bread that came down from heaven. Your ancestors ate manna and died, but whoever feeds on this bread will live forever." [59] He said this while teaching in the synagogue in Capernaum.

MANY DISCIPLES DESERT JESUS

[60] On hearing it, many of his disciples said, "This is a hard teaching. Who can accept it?"

[61] Aware that his disciples were grumbling about this, Jesus said to them, "Does this offend you? [62] Then what if you see the Son of Man ascend to where he was before! [63] The Spirit gives life; the flesh counts for nothing. The words I have spoken to you—they are full of the Spirit[a] and life. [64] Yet there are some of you who do not believe." For Jesus had known from the beginning which of them did not believe and who would betray him. [65] He went on to say, "This is why I told you that no one can come to me unless the Father has enabled them."

[66] From this time many of his disciples turned back and no longer followed him.

[67] "You do not want to leave too, do you?" Jesus asked the Twelve.

[68] Simon Peter answered him, "Lord, to whom shall we go? You have the words of eternal life. [69] We have come to believe and to know that you are the Holy One of God."

[70] Then Jesus replied, "Have I not chosen you, the Twelve? Yet one of you is a devil!" [71] (He meant Judas, the son of Simon Iscariot, who, though one of the Twelve, was later to betray him.)

JESUS GOES TO THE FESTIVAL OF TABERNACLES

7 After this, Jesus went around in Galilee. He did not want[b] to go about in Judea because the Jewish leaders there were looking for a way to kill him. [2] But when the Jewish Festival of Tabernacles was near, [3] Jesus' brothers said to him, "Leave Galilee and go to Judea, so that your disciples there may see the works you do. [4] No one who wants to become a public figure acts in secret. Since you are doing these things, show yourself to the world." [5] For even his own brothers did not believe in him.

[6] Therefore Jesus told them, "My time is not yet here; for you any time will do. [7] The world cannot hate you, but it hates me because I testify that its works are evil. [8] You go to the festival. I am not[c] going up to this festival, because my time has not yet fully come." [9] After he had said this, he stayed in Galilee.

[10] However, after his brothers had left for the festival, he went also, not publicly, but in secret. [11] Now at the festival the Jewish leaders were watching for Jesus and asking, "Where is he?"

What did the Festival of Tabernacles celebrate? (7:2) The Festival of Tabernacles celebrated the completion of the harvest and commemorated God's care for his people when they wandered in the wilderness.

[a] 63 Or *are Spirit*; or *are spirit*   [b] 1 Some manuscripts *not have authority*
[c] 8 Some manuscripts *not yet*

¹²Among the crowds there was widespread whispering about him. Some said, "He is a good man."

Others replied, "No, he deceives the people." ¹³But no one would say anything publicly about him for fear of the leaders.

JESUS TEACHES AT THE FESTIVAL

¹⁴Not until halfway through the festival did Jesus go up to the temple courts and begin to teach. ¹⁵The Jews there were amazed and asked, "How did this man get such learning without having been taught?"

¹⁶Jesus answered, "My teaching is not my own. It comes from the one who sent me. ¹⁷Anyone who chooses to do the will of God will find out whether my teaching comes from God or whether I speak on my own. ¹⁸Whoever speaks on their own does so to gain personal glory, but he who seeks the glory of the one who sent him is a man of truth; there is nothing false about him. ¹⁹Has not Moses given you the law? Yet not one of you keeps the law. Why are you trying to kill me?"

²⁰"You are demon-possessed," the crowd answered. "Who is trying to kill you?"

²¹Jesus said to them, "I did one miracle, and you are all amazed. ²²Yet, because Moses gave you circumcision (though actually it did not come from Moses, but from the patriarchs), you circumcise a boy on the Sabbath. ²³Now if a boy can be circumcised on the Sabbath so that the law of Moses may not be broken, why are you angry with me for healing a man's whole body on the Sabbath? ²⁴Stop judging by mere appearances, but instead judge correctly."

DIVISION OVER WHO JESUS IS

²⁵At that point some of the people of Jerusalem began to ask, "Isn't this the man they are trying to kill? ²⁶Here he is, speaking publicly, and they are not saying a word to him. Have the authorities really concluded that he is the Messiah? ²⁷But we know where this man is from; when the Messiah comes, no one will know where he is from."

²⁸Then Jesus, still teaching in the temple courts, cried out, "Yes, you know me, and you know where I am from. I am not here on my own authority, but he who sent me is true. You do not know him, ²⁹but I know him because I am from him and he sent me."

³⁰At this they tried to seize him, but no one laid a hand on him, because his hour had not yet come. ³¹Still, many in the crowd believed in him. They said, "When the Messiah comes, will he perform more signs than this man?"

³²The Pharisees heard the crowd whispering such things about him. Then the chief priests and the Pharisees sent temple guards to arrest him.

³³Jesus said, "I am with you for only a short time, and then I am going to the one who sent me. ³⁴You will look for me, but you will not find me; and where I am, you cannot come."

³⁵The Jews said to one another, "Where does this man intend to go that we cannot find him? Will he go where our people live scattered among the Greeks, and teach the

---

Why did Jesus wait until halfway through the festival to go to the temple? (7:14) At that time the crowds would have been at their largest, so he could reach a large audience.

Why did they say that Jesus had not been taught? (7:15–16) Jesus had never studied under a rabbi. He explained that his teachings came directly from God.

What did Jesus mean by this statement? (7:28–29) Jesus pointed out that they knew where he was from — Nazareth — but in a deeper sense they did not know that he was the Son of God, sent by the Father to redeem the world.

Greeks? ³⁶What did he mean when he said, 'You will look for me, but you will not find me,' and 'Where I am, you cannot come'?"

³⁷On the last and greatest day of the festival, Jesus stood and said in a loud voice, "Let anyone who is thirsty come to me and drink. ³⁸Whoever believes in me, as Scripture has said, rivers of living water will flow from within them."*a* ³⁹By this he meant the Spirit, whom those who believed in him were later to receive. Up to that time the Spirit had not been given, since Jesus had not yet been glorified.

⁴⁰On hearing his words, some of the people said, "Surely this man is the Prophet."

⁴¹Others said, "He is the Messiah."

Still others asked, "How can the Messiah come from Galilee? ⁴²Does not Scripture say that the Messiah will come from David's descendants and from Bethlehem, the town where David lived?" ⁴³Thus the people were divided because of Jesus. ⁴⁴Some wanted to seize him, but no one laid a hand on him.

UNBELIEF OF THE JEWISH LEADERS

⁴⁵Finally the temple guards went back to the chief priests and the Pharisees, who asked them, "Why didn't you bring him in?"

⁴⁶"No one ever spoke the way this man does," the guards replied.

⁴⁷"You mean he has deceived you also?" the Pharisees retorted. ⁴⁸"Have any of the rulers or of the Pharisees believed in him? ⁴⁹No! But this mob that knows nothing of the law—there is a curse on them."

⁵⁰Nicodemus, who had gone to Jesus earlier and who was one of their own number, asked, ⁵¹"Does our law condemn a man without first hearing him to find out what he has been doing?"

⁵²They replied, "Are you from Galilee, too? Look into it, and you will find that a prophet does not come out of Galilee."

[The earliest manuscripts and many other ancient witnesses do not have John 7:53—8:11. A few manuscripts include these verses, wholly or in part, after John 7:36, John 21:25, Luke 21:38 or Luke 24:53.]

8 ⁵³*Then they all went home,* ¹*but Jesus went to the Mount of Olives.* ²*At dawn he appeared again in the temple courts, where all the people gathered around him, and he sat down to teach them.* ³*The teachers of the law and the Pharisees brought in a woman caught in adultery. They made her stand before the group* ⁴*and said to Jesus, "Teacher, this woman was caught in the act of adultery.* ⁵*In the Law Moses commanded us to stone such women. Now what do you say?"* ⁶*They were using this question as a trap, in order to have a basis for accusing him.*

But Jesus bent down and started to write on the ground with his finger. ⁷*When they kept on questioning him, he straightened up and said to them,*

---

a 37,38 Or *me. And let anyone drink* ³⁸*who believes in me." As Scripture has said, "Out of him* (or *them*) *will flow rivers of living water."*

Why did Jesus stand? (7:37)
Teachers usually sat, so Jesus would have drawn special attention by standing.

Were the chief priests right in saying that no prophet came from Galilee? (7:52)
They were wrong. Jonah had come from Galilee, and perhaps other prophets had come from there as well.

Why was it necessary for her to have been caught in the act? (8:3–4)
Compromising circumstances were not strong enough evidence. Jewish law required witnesses who had seen the act.

"Let any one of you who is without sin be the first to throw a stone at her."
⁸Again he stooped down and wrote on the ground.

⁹At this, those who heard began to go away one at a time, the older ones first, until only Jesus was left, with the woman still standing there. ¹⁰Jesus straightened up and asked her, "Woman, where are they? Has no one condemned you?"

¹¹"No one, sir," she said.

"Then neither do I condemn you," Jesus declared. "Go now and leave your life of sin."

Why did the older ones leave first? (8:9)
They were probably the first to realize that they were not without sin. But all the accusers were either conscience stricken or afraid, and finally only Jesus and the woman were left.

DISPUTE OVER JESUS' TESTIMONY

¹²When Jesus spoke again to the people, he said, "I am the light of the world. Whoever follows me will never walk in darkness, but will have the light of life."

¹³The Pharisees challenged him, "Here you are, appearing as your own witness; your testimony is not valid."

¹⁴Jesus answered, "Even if I testify on my own behalf, my testimony is valid, for I know where I came from and where I am going. But you have no idea where I come from or where I am going. ¹⁵You judge by human standards; I pass judgment on no one. ¹⁶But if I do judge, my decisions are true, because I am not alone. I stand with the Father, who sent me. ¹⁷In your own Law it is written that the testimony of two witnesses is true. ¹⁸I am one who testifies for myself; my other witness is the Father, who sent me."

¹⁹Then they asked him, "Where is your father?"

"You do not know me or my Father," Jesus replied. "If you knew me, you would know my Father also." ²⁰He spoke these words while teaching in the temple courts near the place where the offerings were put. Yet no one seized him, because his hour had not yet come.

What did Jesus mean by these words? (8:19)
Jesus said that the Father is known through the Son and that to know one is to know the other.

DISPUTE OVER WHO JESUS IS

²¹Once more Jesus said to them, "I am going away, and you will look for me, and you will die in your sin. Where I go, you cannot come."

²²This made the Jews ask, "Will he kill himself? Is that why he says, 'Where I go, you cannot come'?"

²³But he continued, "You are from below; I am from above. You are of this world; I am not of this world. ²⁴I told you that you would die in your sins; if you do not believe that I am he, you will indeed die in your sins."

²⁵"Who are you?" they asked.

"Just what I have been telling you from the beginning," Jesus replied. ²⁶"I have much to say in judgment of you. But he who sent me is trustworthy, and what I have heard from him I tell the world."

²⁷They did not understand that he was telling them about his Father. ²⁸So Jesus said, "When you have lifted up*ᵃ* the Son of Man, then you will know that I am he and that I do nothing on my own but speak just what the Father has taught me. ²⁹The one who sent me is with me; he has not

What did it mean to be lifted up? (8:28)
In the Old Testament, this usually meant to be exalted, but here Jesus was referring to his crucifixion.

ᵃ 28 The Greek for lifted up also means exalted.

left me alone, for I always do what pleases him." [30] Even as he spoke, many believed in him.

DISPUTE OVER WHOSE CHILDREN JESUS' OPPONENTS ARE

[31] To the Jews who had believed him, Jesus said, "If you hold to my teaching, you are really my disciples. [32] Then you will know the truth, and the truth will set you free."

[33] They answered him, "We are Abraham's descendants and have never been slaves of anyone. How can you say that we shall be set free?"

[34] Jesus replied, "Very truly I tell you, everyone who sins is a slave to sin. [35] Now a slave has no permanent place in the family, but a son belongs to it forever. [36] So if the Son sets you free, you will be free indeed. [37] I know that you are Abraham's descendants. Yet you are looking for a way to kill me, because you have no room for my word. [38] I am telling you what I have seen in the Father's presence, and you are doing what you have heard from your father.[a]"

[39] "Abraham is our father," they answered.

"If you were Abraham's children," said Jesus, "then you would[b] do what Abraham did. [40] As it is, you are looking for a way to kill me, a man who has told you the truth that I heard from God. Abraham did not do such things. [41] You are doing the works of your own father."

"We are not illegitimate children," they protested. "The only Father we have is God himself."

[42] Jesus said to them, "If God were your Father, you would love me, for I have come here from God. I have not come on my own; God sent me. [43] Why is my language not clear to you? Because you are unable to hear what I say. [44] You belong to your father, the devil, and you want to carry out your father's desires. He was a murderer from the beginning, not holding to the truth, for there is no truth in him. When he lies, he speaks his native language, for he is a liar and the father of lies. [45] Yet because I tell the truth, you do not believe me! [46] Can any of you prove me guilty of sin? If I am telling the truth, why don't you believe me? [47] Whoever belongs to God hears what God says. The reason you do not hear is that you do not belong to God."

JESUS' CLAIMS ABOUT HIMSELF

[48] The Jews answered him, "Aren't we right in saying that you are a Samaritan and demon-possessed?"

[49] "I am not possessed by a demon," said Jesus, "but I honor my Father and you dishonor me. [50] I am not seeking glory for myself; but there is one who seeks it, and he is the judge. [51] Very truly I tell you, whoever obeys my word will never see death."

[52] At this they exclaimed, "Now we know that you are demon-possessed! Abraham died and so did the prophets, yet you say that whoever obeys your word will never taste death. [53] Are you greater than our father Abraham? He died, and so did the prophets. Who do you think you are?"

Had the Israelites never been slaves? (8:33)
They had been slaves to the Romans, Assyrians, Babylonians, Persians, Syrians, and Egyptians. Perhaps they meant that they had never accepted slavery as their proper role because they were descendants of Abraham.

What did Jesus mean that their father was Satan? (8:44)
These words were directed to those who wanted to kill him. They were carrying out Satan's work of murder and falsehood.

---

[a] 38 Or *presence. Therefore do what you have heard from the Father.*
[b] 39 Some early manuscripts *"If you are Abraham's children," said Jesus, "then*

[54] Jesus replied, "If I glorify myself, my glory means nothing. My Father, whom you claim as your God, is the one who glorifies me. [55] Though you do not know him, I know him. If I said I did not, I would be a liar like you, but I do know him and obey his word. [56] Your father Abraham rejoiced at the thought of seeing my day; he saw it and was glad."

[57] "You are not yet fifty years old," they said to him, "and you have seen Abraham!"

[58] "Very truly I tell you," Jesus answered, "before Abraham was born, I am!" [59] At this, they picked up stones to stone him, but Jesus hid himself, slipping away from the temple grounds.

JESUS HEALS A MAN BORN BLIND

9 As he went along, he saw a man blind from birth. [2] His disciples asked him, "Rabbi, who sinned, this man or his parents, that he was born blind?"

[3] "Neither this man nor his parents sinned," said Jesus, "but this happened so that the works of God might be displayed in him. [4] As long as it is day, we must do the works of him who sent me. Night is coming, when no one can work. [5] While I am in the world, I am the light of the world."

[6] After saying this, he spit on the ground, made some mud with the saliva, and put it on the man's eyes. [7] "Go," he told him, "wash in the Pool of Siloam" (this word means "Sent"). So the man went and washed, and came home seeing.

[8] His neighbors and those who had formerly seen him begging asked, "Isn't this the same man who used to sit and beg?" [9] Some claimed that he was.

Others said, "No, he only looks like him."

But he himself insisted, "I am the man."

[10] "How then were your eyes opened?" they asked.

[11] He replied, "The man they call Jesus made some mud and put it on my eyes. He told me to go to Siloam and wash. So I went and washed, and then I could see."

[12] "Where is this man?" they asked him.

"I don't know," he said.

THE PHARISEES INVESTIGATE THE HEALING

[13] They brought to the Pharisees the man who had been blind. [14] Now the day on which Jesus had made the mud and opened the man's eyes was a Sabbath. [15] Therefore the Pharisees also asked him how he had received his sight. "He put mud on my eyes," the man replied, "and I washed, and now I see."

[16] Some of the Pharisees said, "This man is not from God, for he does not keep the Sabbath."

But others asked, "How can a sinner perform such signs?" So they were divided.

[17] Then they turned again to the blind man, "What have you to say about him? It was your eyes he opened."

The man replied, "He is a prophet."

[18] They still did not believe that he had been blind and had received his sight until they sent for the man's parents. [19] "Is

Is Jesus eternal? (8:58)
Yes. When he said "I am," he echoed God's words in Exodus 3:14. This expressed his eternal existence and his oneness with the Father.

Why did the disciples ask who had sinned? (9:2)
The rabbis taught that if someone suffered from a physical ailment, then the person or his parents or grandparents had sinned. They even believed that a person could sin before birth.

Where was the Pool of Siloam? (9:7)
This was a pool cut into the rock on the southern edge of the main ridge on which Jerusalem was built. It served as part of the water system developed by King Hezekiah.

this your son?" they asked. "Is this the one you say was born blind? How is it that now he can see?"

²⁰"We know he is our son," the parents answered, "and we know he was born blind. ²¹But how he can see now, or who opened his eyes, we don't know. Ask him. He is of age; he will speak for himself." ²²His parents said this because they were afraid of the Jewish leaders, who already had decided that anyone who acknowledged that Jesus was the Messiah would be put out of the synagogue. ²³That was why his parents said, "He is of age; ask him."

²⁴A second time they summoned the man who had been blind. "Give glory to God by telling the truth," they said. "We know this man is a sinner."

²⁵He replied, "Whether he is a sinner or not, I don't know. One thing I do know. I was blind but now I see!"

²⁶Then they asked him, "What did he do to you? How did he open your eyes?"

²⁷He answered, "I have told you already and you did not listen. Why do you want to hear it again? Do you want to become his disciples too?"

²⁸Then they hurled insults at him and said, "You are this fellow's disciple! We are disciples of Moses! ²⁹We know that God spoke to Moses, but as for this fellow, we don't even know where he comes from."

³⁰The man answered, "Now that is remarkable! You don't know where he comes from, yet he opened my eyes. ³¹We know that God does not listen to sinners. He listens to the godly person who does his will. ³²Nobody has ever heard of opening the eyes of a man born blind. ³³If this man were not from God, he could do nothing."

³⁴To this they replied, "You were steeped in sin at birth; how dare you lecture us!" And they threw him out.

SPIRITUAL BLINDNESS

³⁵Jesus heard that they had thrown him out, and when he found him, he said, "Do you believe in the Son of Man?"

³⁶"Who is he, sir?" the man asked. "Tell me so that I may believe in him."

³⁷Jesus said, "You have now seen him; in fact, he is the one speaking with you."

³⁸Then the man said, "Lord, I believe," and he worshiped him.

³⁹Jesus said,ᵃ "For judgment I have come into this world, so that the blind will see and those who see will become blind."

⁴⁰Some Pharisees who were with him heard him say this and asked, "What? Are we blind too?"

⁴¹Jesus said, "If you were blind, you would not be guilty of sin; but now that you claim you can see, your guilt remains.

THE GOOD SHEPHERD AND HIS SHEEP

10 "Very truly I tell you Pharisees, anyone who does not enter the sheep pen by the gate, but climbs in by some other way, is a thief and a robber. ²The one who enters by

ᵃ 38,39 Some early manuscripts do not have *Then the man said . . . ³⁹Jesus said.*

Why were the man's parents frightened by the Pharisees? (9:22)
The Pharisees had decided that anyone who believed that Jesus was the Christ would not be permitted to enter the synagogue, the center of Jewish religious and social life.

What was the Pharisees' problem? (9:40–41)
They claimed that they were not spiritually blind. Jesus said that because they could see but still denied that he was the Messiah, they were guilty.

How was a sheep pen constructed? (10:1)
It was a closed space with stone walls that had only one entrance. Its walls kept the sheep from wandering away.

the gate is the shepherd of the sheep. [3] The gatekeeper opens the gate for him, and the sheep listen to his voice. He calls his own sheep by name and leads them out. [4] When he has brought out all his own, he goes on ahead of them, and his sheep follow him because they know his voice. [5] But they will never follow a stranger; in fact, they will run away from him because they do not recognize a stranger's voice." [6] Jesus used this figure of speech, but the Pharisees did not understand what he was telling them.

[7] Therefore Jesus said again, "Very truly I tell you, I am the gate for the sheep. [8] All who have come before me are thieves and robbers, but the sheep have not listened to them. [9] I am the gate; whoever enters through me will be saved.[a] They will come in and go out, and find pasture. [10] The thief comes only to steal and kill and destroy; I have come that they may have life, and have it to the full.

[11] "I am the good shepherd. The good shepherd lays down his life for the sheep. [12] The hired hand is not the shepherd and does not own the sheep. So when he sees the wolf coming, he abandons the sheep and runs away. Then the wolf attacks the flock and scatters it. [13] The man runs away because he is a hired hand and cares nothing for the sheep.

[14] "I am the good shepherd; I know my sheep and my sheep know me— [15] just as the Father knows me and I know the Father—and I lay down my life for the sheep. [16] I have other sheep that are not of this sheep pen. I must bring them also. They too will listen to my voice, and there shall be one flock and one shepherd. [17] The reason my Father loves me is that I lay down my life—only to take it up again. [18] No one takes it from me, but I lay it down of my own accord. I have authority to lay it down and authority to take it up again. This command I received from my Father."

[19] The Jews who heard these words were again divided. [20] Many of them said, "He is demon-possessed and raving mad. Why listen to him?"

[21] But others said, "These are not the sayings of a man possessed by a demon. Can a demon open the eyes of the blind?"

FURTHER CONFLICT OVER JESUS' CLAIMS

[22] Then came the Festival of Dedication[b] at Jerusalem. It was winter, [23] and Jesus was in the temple courts walking in Solomon's Colonnade. [24] The Jews who were there gathered around him, saying, "How long will you keep us in suspense? If you are the Messiah, tell us plainly."

[25] Jesus answered, "I did tell you, but you do not believe. The works I do in my Father's name testify about me, [26] but you do not believe because you are not my sheep. [27] My sheep listen to my voice; I know them, and they follow me. [28] I give them eternal life, and they shall never perish; no one will snatch them out of my hand. [29] My Father, who has given them to me, is greater than all[c]; no one can snatch them out of my Father's hand. [30] I and the Father are one."

a 9 Or *kept safe*   *b 22* That is, Hanukkah   *c 29* Many early manuscripts *What my Father has given me is greater than all*

A Sheep Pen (10:1–3)

Who was the gate keeper? (10:3)
Apparently he was in charge of a large fold, or enclosure, where several flocks were kept. The sheep recognized the voice of their own shepherd and responded only to him.

Why did Jesus refer to himself as the shepherd? (10:11–18)
In the ancient Middle East, the ruler was considered a shepherd to his people. Jesus is the Good Shepherd who died to make a way for his sheep to be with him forever.

Why did the Jews want to stone Jesus? (10:30–33)
When Jesus said that he and the Father were one, he was clearly claiming to be God. The Jews considered this to be blasphemy.

³¹ Again his Jewish opponents picked up stones to stone him, ³² but Jesus said to them, "I have shown you many good works from the Father. For which of these do you stone me?"

³³ "We are not stoning you for any good work," they replied, "but for blasphemy, because you, a mere man, claim to be God."

³⁴ Jesus answered them, "Is it not written in your Law, 'I have said you are "gods"'ᵃ? ³⁵ If he called them 'gods,' to whom the word of God came—and Scripture cannot be set aside— ³⁶ what about the one whom the Father set apart as his very own and sent into the world? Why then do you accuse me of blasphemy because I said, 'I am God's Son'? ³⁷ Do not believe me unless I do the works of my Father. ³⁸ But if I do them, even though you do not believe me, believe the works, that you may know and understand that the Father is in me, and I in the Father." ³⁹ Again they tried to seize him, but he escaped their grasp.

⁴⁰ Then Jesus went back across the Jordan to the place where John had been baptizing in the early days. There he stayed, ⁴¹ and many people came to him. They said, "Though John never performed a sign, all that John said about this man was true." ⁴² And in that place many believed in Jesus.

THE DEATH OF LAZARUS

11 Now a man named Lazarus was sick. He was from Bethany, the village of Mary and her sister Martha. ² (This Mary, whose brother Lazarus now lay sick, was the same one who poured perfume on the Lord and wiped his feet with her hair.) ³ So the sisters sent word to Jesus, "Lord, the one you love is sick."

⁴ When he heard this, Jesus said, "This sickness will not end in death. No, it is for God's glory so that God's Son may be glorified through it." ⁵ Now Jesus loved Martha and her sister and Lazarus. ⁶ So when he heard that Lazarus was sick, he stayed where he was two more days, ⁷ and then he said to his disciples, "Let us go back to Judea."

⁸ "But Rabbi," they said, "a short while ago the Jews there tried to stone you, and yet you are going back?"

⁹ Jesus answered, "Are there not twelve hours of daylight? Anyone who walks in the daytime will not stumble, for they see by this world's light. ¹⁰ It is when a person walks at night that they stumble, for they have no light."

¹¹ After he had said this, he went on to tell them, "Our friend Lazarus has fallen asleep; but I am going there to wake him up."

¹² His disciples replied, "Lord, if he sleeps, he will get better." ¹³ Jesus had been speaking of his death, but his disciples thought he meant natural sleep.

¹⁴ So then he told them plainly, "Lazarus is dead, ¹⁵ and for your sake I am glad I was not there, so that you may believe. But let us go to him."

¹⁶ Then Thomas (also known as Didymusᵇ) said to the rest of the disciples, "Let us also go, that we may die with him."

Jesus Raises Lazarus (11:1)

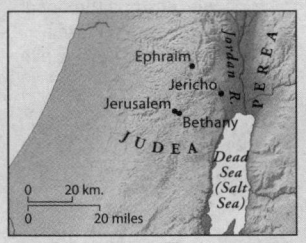

ᵃ 34 Psalm 82:6   ᵇ 16 *Thomas* (Aramaic) and *Didymus* (Greek) both mean *twin*.

JESUS COMFORTS THE SISTERS OF LAZARUS

[17] On his arrival, Jesus found that Lazarus had already been in the tomb for four days. [18] Now Bethany was less than two miles[a] from Jerusalem, [19] and many Jews had come to Martha and Mary to comfort them in the loss of their brother. [20] When Martha heard that Jesus was coming, she went out to meet him, but Mary stayed at home.

[21] "Lord," Martha said to Jesus, "if you had been here, my brother would not have died. [22] But I know that even now God will give you whatever you ask."

[23] Jesus said to her, "Your brother will rise again."

[24] Martha answered, "I know he will rise again in the resurrection at the last day."

[25] Jesus said to her, "I am the resurrection and the life. The one who believes in me will live, even though they die; [26] and whoever lives by believing in me will never die. Do you believe this?"

[27] "Yes, Lord," she replied, "I believe that you are the Messiah, the Son of God, who is to come into the world."

[28] After she had said this, she went back and called her sister Mary aside. "The Teacher is here," she said, "and is asking for you." [29] When Mary heard this, she got up quickly and went to him. [30] Now Jesus had not yet entered the village, but was still at the place where Martha had met him. [31] When the Jews who had been with Mary in the house, comforting her, noticed how quickly she got up and went out, they followed her, supposing she was going to the tomb to mourn there.

[32] When Mary reached the place where Jesus was and saw him, she fell at his feet and said, "Lord, if you had been here, my brother would not have died."

[33] When Jesus saw her weeping, and the Jews who had come along with her also weeping, he was deeply moved in spirit and troubled. [34] "Where have you laid him?" he asked.

"Come and see, Lord," they replied.

[35] Jesus wept.

[36] Then the Jews said, "See how he loved him!"

[37] But some of them said, "Could not he who opened the eyes of the blind man have kept this man from dying?"

JESUS RAISES LAZARUS FROM THE DEAD

[38] Jesus, once more deeply moved, came to the tomb. It was a cave with a stone laid across the entrance. [39] "Take away the stone," he said.

"But, Lord," said Martha, the sister of the dead man, "by this time there is a bad odor, for he has been there four days."

[40] Then Jesus said, "Did I not tell you that if you believe, you will see the glory of God?"

[41] So they took away the stone. Then Jesus looked up and said, "Father, I thank you that you have heard me. [42] I knew that you always hear me, but I said this for the benefit of the people standing here, that they may believe that you sent me."

[a] 18 Or about 3 kilometers

Why was the fact that Lazarus had been dead for four days so final? (11:17)
Many Jews believed that the soul remained near the body for three days after death in hope of returning to it. But four days had passed, so Lazarus was considered by all to be dead.

When Jesus promised that Lazarus would rise, what did Martha think he meant? (11:23–24)
Martha thought that Jesus was referring to the resurrection at the end of time (see Job 19:25–27).

Why did Jesus weep? (11:35)
Commentators have offered a variety of interpretations. Some say that this reinforces the genuine humanity of Jesus — he shed real tears, probably because of his empathy with their grief. Others suggest that he was sad that Lazarus had died; in fact, this was what the bystanders thought.

Was this a typical burial place? (11:38)
A cave with a stone covering the entrance was a common burial place in the Middle East at this time.

Typical Cave Tomb (11:38)

[43] When he had said this, Jesus called in a loud voice, "Lazarus, come out!" [44] The dead man came out, his hands and feet wrapped with strips of linen, and a cloth around his face. Jesus said to them, "Take off the grave clothes and let him go."

THE PLOT TO KILL JESUS

[45] Therefore many of the Jews who had come to visit Mary, and had seen what Jesus did, believed in him. [46] But some of them went to the Pharisees and told them what Jesus had done. [47] Then the chief priests and the Pharisees called a meeting of the Sanhedrin.

"What are we accomplishing?" they asked. "Here is this man performing many signs. [48] If we let him go on like this, everyone will believe in him, and then the Romans will come and take away both our temple and our nation."

[49] Then one of them, named Caiaphas, who was high priest that year, spoke up, "You know nothing at all! [50] You do not realize that it is better for you that one man die for the people than that the whole nation perish."

[51] He did not say this on his own, but as high priest that year he prophesied that Jesus would die for the Jewish nation, [52] and not only for that nation but also for the scattered children of God, to bring them together and make them one. [53] So from that day on they plotted to take his life.

[54] Therefore Jesus no longer moved about publicly among the people of Judea. Instead he withdrew to a region near the wilderness, to a village called Ephraim, where he stayed with his disciples.

[55] When it was almost time for the Jewish Passover, many went up from the country to Jerusalem for their ceremonial cleansing before the Passover. [56] They kept looking for Jesus, and as they stood in the temple courts they asked one another, "What do you think? Isn't he coming to the festival at all?" [57] But the chief priests and the Pharisees had given orders that anyone who found out where Jesus was should report it so that they might arrest him.

JESUS ANOINTED AT BETHANY

12 Six days before the Passover, Jesus came to Bethany, where Lazarus lived, whom Jesus had raised from the dead. [2] Here a dinner was given in Jesus' honor. Martha served, while Lazarus was among those reclining at the table with him. [3] Then Mary took about a pint[a] of pure nard, an expensive perfume; she poured it on Jesus' feet and wiped his feet with her hair. And the house was filled with the fragrance of the perfume.

[4] But one of his disciples, Judas Iscariot, who was later to betray him, objected, [5] "Why wasn't this perfume sold and the money given to the poor? It was worth a year's wages.[b]" [6] He did not say this because he cared about the poor but because he was a thief; as keeper of the money bag, he used to help himself to what was put into it.

[7] "Leave her alone," Jesus replied. "It was intended that she

[a] 3 Or about 0.5 liter   [b] 5 Greek *three hundred denarii*

Who had the power to stop Jesus? (11:47)
The Pharisees seemed to be Jesus' principal opponents during his ministry, but it was the chief priests who were prominent in the events leading to his crucifixion. Ultimately, no one could stop Jesus. It was Jesus' plan from the beginning to die for our sins.

Who was the high priest? (11:49–53)
This was Caiaphas, high priest from A.D. 18 to 36. He believed that if Jesus' followers continued to increase in number, this would cause a rebellion which would lead to harsh treatment from their Roman rulers and an end to the religious leaders' power. Caiaphas said it would be better for one person (Jesus) to die than to put the whole Jewish community at risk.

What was unusual about Mary's actions? (12:3)
Nard was the name of a plant and the oil it yielded. It was very expensive (a pint would have cost about one year's wages for a laborer). Her actions were unusual because she poured the oil on Jesus' feet, while normally it would have been poured on someone's head. And she used her hair to wipe Jesus' feet. Respectable women did not unbind their hair in public.

should save this perfume for the day of my burial. [8]You will always have the poor among you,[a] but you will not always have me."

[9]Meanwhile a large crowd of Jews found out that Jesus was there and came, not only because of him but also to see Lazarus, whom he had raised from the dead. [10]So the chief priests made plans to kill Lazarus as well, [11]for on account of him many of the Jews were going over to Jesus and believing in him.

JESUS COMES TO JERUSALEM AS KING

[12]The next day the great crowd that had come for the festival heard that Jesus was on his way to Jerusalem. [13]They took palm branches and went out to meet him, shouting,

"Hosanna![b]"

"Blessed is he who comes in the name of the Lord!"[c]

"Blessed is the king of Israel!"

[14]Jesus found a young donkey and sat on it, as it is written:

[15]"Do not be afraid, Daughter Zion;
    see, your king is coming,
    seated on a donkey's colt."[d]

[16]At first his disciples did not understand all this. Only after Jesus was glorified did they realize that these things had been written about him and that these things had been done to him.

[17]Now the crowd that was with him when he called Lazarus from the tomb and raised him from the dead continued to spread the word. [18]Many people, because they had heard that he had performed this sign, went out to meet him. [19]So the Pharisees said to one another, "See, this is getting us nowhere. Look how the whole world has gone after him!"

JESUS PREDICTS HIS DEATH

[20]Now there were some Greeks among those who went up to worship at the festival. [21]They came to Philip, who was from Bethsaida in Galilee, with a request. "Sir," they said, "we would like to see Jesus." [22]Philip went to tell Andrew; Andrew and Philip in turn told Jesus.

[23]Jesus replied, "The hour has come for the Son of Man to be glorified. [24]Very truly I tell you, unless a kernel of wheat falls to the ground and dies, it remains only a single seed. But if it dies, it produces many seeds. [25]Anyone who loves their life will lose it, while anyone who hates their life in this world will keep it for eternal life. [26]Whoever serves me must follow me; and where I am, my servant also will be. My Father will honor the one who serves me.

[27]"Now my soul is troubled, and what shall I say? 'Father, save me from this hour'? No, it was for this very reason I came to this hour. [28]Father, glorify your name!"

Then a voice came from heaven, "I have glorified it, and

Why did the chief priests want to kill Lazarus? (12:9–11)
They were concerned that too many people were putting their faith in Jesus because he had raised Lazarus from the dead.

What did "Hosanna" mean? (12:13)
The word originally meant "save now, pray," but by New Testament times it had lost its primary meaning and had become an exclamation of praise.

Why would Jesus ride on a donkey? (12:14)
A donkey symbolized humility and peace but also royalty. Zechariah had prophesied that the Messiah would ride on a donkey (see Zechariah 9:9).

What did Jesus mean? (12:23–24)
Jesus meant that the time had come for him to die and that through his death and through his resurrection would come new life for all who believed in him as their Savior.

---

[a] 8 See Deut. 15:11.   [b] 13 A Hebrew expression meaning "Save!" which became an exclamation of praise   [c] 13 Psalm 118:25,26   [d] 15 Zech. 9:9

How did the voice from heaven confirm what Jesus was about to do? (12:28–33) Jesus did not pray to be delivered but prayed that the Father would be glorified. The voice from heaven affirmed that the Father had been glorified by Jesus' willingness to make himself a sacrifice.

will glorify it again." ²⁹ The crowd that was there and heard it said it had thundered; others said an angel had spoken to him.

³⁰ Jesus said, "This voice was for your benefit, not mine. ³¹ Now is the time for judgment on this world; now the prince of this world will be driven out. ³² And I, when I am lifted up[a] from the earth, will draw all people to myself." ³³ He said this to show the kind of death he was going to die.

³⁴ The crowd spoke up, "We have heard from the Law that the Messiah will remain forever, so how can you say, 'The Son of Man must be lifted up'? Who is this 'Son of Man'?"

³⁵ Then Jesus told them, "You are going to have the light just a little while longer. Walk while you have the light, before darkness overtakes you. Whoever walks in the dark does not know where they are going. ³⁶ Believe in the light while you have the light, so that you may become children of light." When he had finished speaking, Jesus left and hid himself from them.

BELIEF AND UNBELIEF AMONG THE JEWS

³⁷ Even after Jesus had performed so many signs in their presence, they still would not believe in him. ³⁸ This was to fulfill the word of Isaiah the prophet:

"Lord, who has believed our message
    and to whom has the arm of the Lord been
        revealed?"[b]

³⁹ For this reason they could not believe, because, as Isaiah says elsewhere:

⁴⁰ "He has blinded their eyes
    and hardened their hearts,
so they can neither see with their eyes,
    nor understand with their hearts,
        nor turn—and I would heal them."[c]

⁴¹ Isaiah said this because he saw Jesus' glory and spoke about him.

⁴² Yet at the same time many even among the leaders believed in him. But because of the Pharisees they would not openly acknowledge their faith for fear they would be put out of the synagogue; ⁴³ for they loved human praise more than praise from God.

⁴⁴ Then Jesus cried out, "Whoever believes in me does not believe in me only, but in the one who sent me. ⁴⁵ The one who looks at me is seeing the one who sent me. ⁴⁶ I have come into the world as a light, so that no one who believes in me should stay in darkness.

⁴⁷ "If anyone hears my words but does not keep them, I do not judge that person. For I did not come to judge the world, but to save the world. ⁴⁸ There is a judge for the one who rejects me and does not accept my words; the very words I have spoken will condemn them at the last day. ⁴⁹ For I did not speak on my own, but the Father who sent me commanded

[a] 32 The Greek for lifted up also means exalted.   [b] 38 Isaiah 53:1
[c] 40 Isaiah 6:10

me to say all that I have spoken. ⁵⁰I know that his command leads to eternal life. So whatever I say is just what the Father has told me to say."

JESUS WASHES HIS DISCIPLES' FEET

13 It was just before the Passover Festival. Jesus knew that the hour had come for him to leave this world and go to the Father. Having loved his own who were in the world, he loved them to the end.

²The evening meal was in progress, and the devil had already prompted Judas, the son of Simon Iscariot, to betray Jesus. ³Jesus knew that the Father had put all things under his power, and that he had come from God and was returning to God; ⁴so he got up from the meal, took off his outer clothing, and wrapped a towel around his waist. ⁵After that, he poured water into a basin and began to wash his disciples' feet, drying them with the towel that was wrapped around him.

⁶He came to Simon Peter, who said to him, "Lord, are you going to wash my feet?"

⁷Jesus replied, "You do not realize now what I am doing, but later you will understand."

⁸"No," said Peter, "you shall never wash my feet."

Jesus answered, "Unless I wash you, you have no part with me."

⁹"Then, Lord," Simon Peter replied, "not just my feet but my hands and my head as well!"

¹⁰Jesus answered, "Those who have had a bath need only to wash their feet; their whole body is clean. And you are clean, though not every one of you." ¹¹For he knew who was going to betray him, and that was why he said not every one was clean.

¹²When he had finished washing their feet, he put on his clothes and returned to his place. "Do you understand what I have done for you?" he asked them. ¹³"You call me 'Teacher' and 'Lord,' and rightly so, for that is what I am. ¹⁴Now that I, your Lord and Teacher, have washed your feet, you also should wash one another's feet. ¹⁵I have set you an example that you should do as I have done for you. ¹⁶Very truly I tell you, no servant is greater than his master, nor is a messenger greater than the one who sent him. ¹⁷Now that you know these things, you will be blessed if you do them.

JESUS PREDICTS HIS BETRAYAL

¹⁸"I am not referring to all of you; I know those I have chosen. But this is to fulfill this passage of Scripture: 'He who shared my bread has turned[a] against me.'[b]

¹⁹"I am telling you now before it happens, so that when it does happen you will believe that I am who I am. ²⁰Very truly I tell you, whoever accepts anyone I send accepts me; and whoever accepts me accepts the one who sent me."

²¹After he had said this, Jesus was troubled in spirit and testified, "Very truly I tell you, one of you is going to betray me."

²²His disciples stared at one another, at a loss to know

---

a 18 Greek *has lifted up his heel*   *b 18* Psalm 41:9

Why did Jesus wash his disciples' feet? (13:5)
The people walked on dusty roads in sandals, so their feet became encrusted with dirt. Etiquette demanded that a host make sure that his guests' feet were washed. This was usually done by the lowest servant in the household. Jesus wanted to teach his disciples a lesson about servanthood.

Why did Peter tell Jesus not to wash his feet? (13:8)
He misunderstood Jesus' actions. Peter may have felt humbled by the prospect, while at the same time feeling that Jesus was demeaning himself. But Jesus said that Peter had to be washed spiritually. The external washing was a symbol of the washing away of sin.

Why was eating bread together an important activity? (13:18)
It was a sign of close friendship.

Why was Jesus troubled? (13:21)
Even though Jesus knew what was about to happen, he was grieved by the fact that Judas would betray him.

which of them he meant. ²³ One of them, the disciple whom Jesus loved, was reclining next to him. ²⁴ Simon Peter motioned to this disciple and said, "Ask him which one he means."

²⁵ Leaning back against Jesus, he asked him, "Lord, who is it?"

²⁶ Jesus answered, "It is the one to whom I will give this piece of bread when I have dipped it in the dish." Then, dipping the piece of bread, he gave it to Judas, the son of Simon Iscariot. ²⁷ As soon as Judas took the bread, Satan entered into him.

So Jesus told him, "What you are about to do, do quickly." ²⁸ But no one at the meal understood why Jesus said this to him. ²⁹ Since Judas had charge of the money, some thought Jesus was telling him to buy what was needed for the festival, or to give something to the poor. ³⁰ As soon as Judas had taken the bread, he went out. And it was night.

JESUS PREDICTS PETER'S DENIAL

³¹ When he was gone, Jesus said, "Now the Son of Man is glorified and God is glorified in him. ³² If God is glorified in him,ᵃ God will glorify the Son in himself, and will glorify him at once.

³³ "My children, I will be with you only a little longer. You will look for me, and just as I told the Jews, so I tell you now: Where I am going, you cannot come.

³⁴ "A new command I give you: Love one another. As I have loved you, so you must love one another. ³⁵ By this everyone will know that you are my disciples, if you love one another."

³⁶ Simon Peter asked him, "Lord, where are you going?"

Jesus replied, "Where I am going, you cannot follow now, but you will follow later."

³⁷ Peter asked, "Lord, why can't I follow you now? I will lay down my life for you."

³⁸ Then Jesus answered, "Will you really lay down your life for me? Very truly I tell you, before the rooster crows, you will disown me three times!

JESUS COMFORTS HIS DISCIPLES

14 "Do not let your hearts be troubled. You believe in Godᵇ; believe also in me. ² My Father's house has many rooms; if that were not so, would I have told you that I am going there to prepare a place for you? ³ And if I go and prepare a place for you, I will come back and take you to be with me that you also may be where I am. ⁴ You know the way to the place where I am going."

JESUS THE WAY TO THE FATHER

⁵ Thomas said to him, "Lord, we don't know where you are going, so how can we know the way?"

⁶ Jesus answered, "I am the way and the truth and the life. No one comes to the Father except through me. ⁷ If you really

Was this a new commandment? (13:34)
In a sense it was an old command (see Leviticus 19:18), but for the disciples it was new because it was a mark of their brotherhood created by Christ's great love for them.

Is Jesus the only way to God? (14:6)
Jesus said that he was not just one of many ways but was, in fact, the only way to the Father. Only through belief in Jesus as our Savior are we assured a place in heaven with the Father.

ᵃ 32 Many early manuscripts do not have *If God is glorified in him.*
ᵇ 1 Or *Believe in God*

know me, you will know*a* my Father as well. From now on, you do know him and have seen him."

[8] Philip said, "Lord, show us the Father and that will be enough for us."

[9] Jesus answered: "Don't you know me, Philip, even after I have been among you such a long time? Anyone who has seen me has seen the Father. How can you say, 'Show us the Father'? [10] Don't you believe that I am in the Father, and that the Father is in me? The words I say to you I do not speak on my own authority. Rather, it is the Father, living in me, who is doing his work. [11] Believe me when I say that I am in the Father and the Father is in me; or at least believe on the evidence of the works themselves. [12] Very truly I tell you, whoever believes in me will do the works I have been doing, and they will do even greater things than these, because I am going to the Father. [13] And I will do whatever you ask in my name, so that the Father may be glorified in the Son. [14] You may ask me for anything in my name, and I will do it.

JESUS PROMISES THE HOLY SPIRIT

[15] "If you love me, keep my commands. [16] And I will ask the Father, and he will give you another advocate to help you and be with you forever— [17] the Spirit of truth. The world cannot accept him, because it neither sees him nor knows him. But you know him, for he lives with you and will be*b* in you. [18] I will not leave you as orphans; I will come to you. [19] Before long, the world will not see me anymore, but you will see me. Because I live, you also will live. [20] On that day you will realize that I am in my Father, and you are in me, and I am in you. [21] Whoever has my commands and keeps them is the one who loves me. The one who loves me will be loved by my Father, and I too will love them and show myself to them."

[22] Then Judas (not Judas Iscariot) said, "But, Lord, why do you intend to show yourself to us and not to the world?"

a 7 Some manuscripts *If you really knew me, you would know*   *b* 17 Some early manuscripts *and is*

Why was the Holy Spirit referred to as an advocate? (14:16)
An advocate was someone who helped a person in trouble with the law. Here it refers to the Holy Spirit's role as the one who convicts us of sin but who is also our guide and comforter.

Does obedience or love come first? (14:21, 23)
Neither. Love and obedience compliment each another. Loving God and obeying him are part of a single act.

With so many religions in the world, is Jesus really the only path to salvation?
JOHN 14

When Jesus was on earth, he taught that he was the Son of God and that salvation is only available to people who have faith in him. But many other religions also claim that they are the way to God, and many people nowadays think that all religions have an element of truth and that the important thing is for people to be on a path that is looking for God.

When Jesus said that he was the only way to God, he was making an exclusive claim. He said that faith in him was necessary for salvation. The Bible supports Jesus' claim by telling the story of God and his people. God created a perfect universe and perfect people. People disobeyed God and brought sin into the world. God loved people enough to send his Son to redeem the world. God will come again to judge people and create a new earth and heaven.

The Holy Spirit creates faith in people and draws them to God. But people must also accept God's invitation to become part of his family. Christianity is either true or false. If belief in Christ is not necessary for salvation, then Jesus was not telling the truth. But if Jesus was telling the truth—and he was—then it is important to put our faith in him. We cannot earn salvation by ourselves or through anyone or anything else.

²³Jesus replied, "Anyone who loves me will obey my teaching. My Father will love them, and we will come to them and make our home with them. ²⁴Anyone who does not love me will not obey my teaching. These words you hear are not my own; they belong to the Father who sent me.

²⁵"All this I have spoken while still with you. ²⁶But the Advocate, the Holy Spirit, whom the Father will send in my name, will teach you all things and will remind you of everything I have said to you. ²⁷Peace I leave with you; my peace I give you. I do not give to you as the world gives. Do not let your hearts be troubled and do not be afraid.

²⁸"You heard me say, 'I am going away and I am coming back to you.' If you loved me, you would be glad that I am going to the Father, for the Father is greater than I. ²⁹I have told you now before it happens, so that when it does happen you will believe. ³⁰I will not say much more to you, for the prince of this world is coming. He has no hold over me, ³¹but he comes so that the world may learn that I love the Father and do exactly what my Father has commanded me.

"Come now; let us leave."

THE VINE AND THE BRANCHES

15 "I am the true vine, and my Father is the gardener. ²He cuts off every branch in me that bears no fruit, while every branch that does bear fruit he prunes[a] so that it will be even more fruitful. ³You are already clean because of the word I have spoken to you. ⁴Remain in me, as I also remain in you. No branch can bear fruit by itself; it must remain in the vine. Neither can you bear fruit unless you remain in me.

⁵"I am the vine; you are the branches. If you remain in me and I in you, you will bear much fruit; apart from me you can do nothing. ⁶If you do not remain in me, you are like a branch that is thrown away and withers; such branches are picked up, thrown into the fire and burned. ⁷If you remain in me and my words remain in you, ask whatever you wish, and it will be done for you. ⁸This is to my Father's glory, that you bear much fruit, showing yourselves to be my disciples.

⁹"As the Father has loved me, so have I loved you. Now

What did the image of the vine represent? (15:1)
In the Old Testament, the vine often was used as a symbol of Israel, who was God's vine taken from Egypt and transplanted in the promised land. But often Israel, because of her sin, was like a wild or unruly vine that needed to be punished or cut off. Jesus is "the true vine."

Why would branches without fruit be cut off? (15:2)
This type of pruning would result in more fruit. In the New Testament, the image of good fruit represents the product of a godly life or virtues of character.

---

[a] 2 The Greek for *he prunes* also means *he cleans*.

How can God be three persons in one?

JOHN 15

God is beyond human understanding, so we cannot explain in human terms exactly how there can be one God with three persons. We do know from many passages in the Bible that there is only one God. Deuteronomy 6:4 says, "Hear, O Israel: The LORD our God, the LORD is one." But the Bible also teaches that there are three persons in the Trinity: the Father, the Son, and the Holy Spirit. Each of the persons is fully God, but each of the persons is also distinct.

The persons of the Trinity have different tasks. In basic terms, God the Father created the world and cares for it through his love. The Son was sent by the Father to bring salvation to the world through his death and resurrection. The Holy Spirit creates faith in people's hearts and prompts them to live lives that are pleasing to God. This is similar to how H_2O can take on three forms: water, ice, and steam.

Like many of the truths in the Bible, the idea of the Trinity is one that is difficult to understand in human terms. But all will be made clear when we live with God in heaven.

remain in my love. [10] If you keep my commands, you will remain in my love, just as I have kept my Father's commands and remain in his love. [11] I have told you this so that my joy may be in you and that your joy may be complete. [12] My command is this: Love each other as I have loved you. [13] Greater love has no one than this: to lay down one's life for one's friends. [14] You are my friends if you do what I command. [15] I no longer call you servants, because a servant does not know his master's business. Instead, I have called you friends, for everything that I learned from my Father I have made known to you. [16] You did not choose me, but I chose you and appointed you so that you might go and bear fruit—fruit that will last—and so that whatever you ask in my name the Father will give you. [17] This is my command: Love each other.

THE WORLD HATES THE DISCIPLES

[18] "If the world hates you, keep in mind that it hated me first. [19] If you belonged to the world, it would love you as its own. As it is, you do not belong to the world, but I have chosen you out of the world. That is why the world hates you. [20] Remember what I told you: 'A servant is not greater than his master.'[a] If they persecuted me, they will persecute you also. If they obeyed my teaching, they will obey yours also. [21] They will treat you this way because of my name, for they do not know the one who sent me. [22] If I had not come and spoken to them, they would not be guilty of sin; but now they have no excuse for their sin. [23] Whoever hates me hates my Father as well. [24] If I had not done among them the works no one else did, they would not be guilty of sin. As it is, they have seen, and yet they have hated both me and my Father. [25] But this is to fulfill what is written in their Law: 'They hated me without reason.'[b]

THE WORK OF THE HOLY SPIRIT

[26] "When the Advocate comes, whom I will send to you from the Father—the Spirit of truth who goes out from the Father—he will testify about me. [27] And you also must testify, for you have been with me from the beginning.

16 "All this I have told you so that you will not fall away. [2] They will put you out of the synagogue; in fact, the time is coming when anyone who kills you will think they are offering a service to God. [3] They will do such things because they have not known the Father or me. [4] I have told you this, so that when their time comes you will remember that I warned you about them. I did not tell you this from the beginning because I was with you, [5] but now I am going to him who sent me. None of you asks me, 'Where are you going?' [6] Rather, you are filled with grief because I have said these things. [7] But very truly I tell you, it is for your good that I am going away. Unless I go away, the Advocate will not come to you; but if I go, I will send him to you. [8] When he comes, he will prove the world to be in the wrong about sin and righteousness and judgment: [9] about sin, because people do not believe in me; [10] about righteousness, because I am

[a] 20 John 13:16   [b] 25 Psalms 35:19; 69:4

Why did Jesus say that he chose his disciples? (15:16) Normally disciples chose the rabbi they would follow, but Jesus had chosen his disciples with the purpose of having them bear fruit.

Why did the people Jesus spoke to have no excuse for not believing in him? (15:22) He had appeared to the Jewish people directly, and they had the benefit of having access to God's words in the Old Testament. When they rejected Jesus, they were guilty and had no excuse.

Why would the Holy Spirit not come until Jesus had gone away? (16:7) Jesus taught that his saving work on the cross was necessary before the Spirit would be sent. We had no need of the Spirit while Jesus was on the earth.

going to the Father, where you can see me no longer; [11] and about judgment, because the prince of this world now stands condemned.

[12] "I have much more to say to you, more than you can now bear. [13] But when he, the Spirit of truth, comes, he will guide you into all the truth. He will not speak on his own; he will speak only what he hears, and he will tell you what is yet to come. [14] He will glorify me because it is from me that he will receive what he will make known to you. [15] All that belongs to the Father is mine. That is why I said the Spirit will receive from me what he will make known to you."

THE DISCIPLES' GRIEF WILL TURN TO JOY

[16] Jesus went on to say, "In a little while you will see me no more, and then after a little while you will see me."

[17] At this, some of his disciples said to one another, "What does he mean by saying, 'In a little while you will see me no more, and then after a little while you will see me,' and 'Because I am going to the Father'?" [18] They kept asking, "What does he mean by 'a little while'? We don't understand what he is saying."

[19] Jesus saw that they wanted to ask him about this, so he said to them, "Are you asking one another what I meant when I said, 'In a little while you will see me no more, and then after a little while you will see me'? [20] Very truly I tell you, you will weep and mourn while the world rejoices. You will grieve, but your grief will turn to joy. [21] A woman giving birth to a child has pain because her time has come; but when her baby is born she forgets the anguish because of her joy that a child is born into the world. [22] So with you: Now is your time of grief, but I will see you again and you will rejoice, and no one will take away your joy. [23] In that day you will no longer ask me anything. Very truly I tell you, my Father will give you whatever you ask in my name. [24] Until now you have not asked for anything in my name. Ask and you will receive, and your joy will be complete.

[25] "Though I have been speaking figuratively, a time is coming when I will no longer use this kind of language but will tell you plainly about my Father. [26] In that day you will ask in my name. I am not saying that I will ask the Father on your behalf. [27] No, the Father himself loves you because you have loved me and have believed that I came from God. [28] I came from the Father and entered the world; now I am leaving the world and going back to the Father."

[29] Then Jesus' disciples said, "Now you are speaking clearly and without figures of speech. [30] Now we can see that you know all things and that you do not even need to have anyone ask you questions. This makes us believe that you came from God."

[31] "Do you now believe?" Jesus replied. [32] "A time is coming and in fact has come when you will be scattered, each to your own home. You will leave me all alone. Yet I am not alone, for my Father is with me.

[33] "I have told you these things, so that in me you may have peace. In this world you will have trouble. But take heart! I have overcome the world."

Why did Jesus compare the disciples' grief to a woman giving birth? (16:21–22)
A woman who gives birth experiences great pain but then joy at seeing her child. In the same way, the disciples would be sad to lose Jesus, but they would see him after his resurrection and their joy would be complete.

What did Jesus mean that his disciples would be scattered? (16:32)
Jesus knew that his disciples would desert him after he was arrested. Though the disciples had faith, they did not have enough to stand firm in the face of disaster. Jesus also knew that God's kingdom relies on his ability to use people even after they have failed.

JESUS PRAYS TO BE GLORIFIED

17 After Jesus said this, he looked toward heaven and prayed:

"Father, the hour has come. Glorify your Son, that your Son may glorify you. ²For you granted him authority over all people that he might give eternal life to all those you have given him. ³Now this is eternal life: that they know you, the only true God, and Jesus Christ, whom you have sent. ⁴I have brought you glory on earth by finishing the work you gave me to do. ⁵And now, Father, glorify me in your presence with the glory I had with you before the world began.

JESUS PRAYS FOR HIS DISCIPLES

⁶"I have revealed you*ᵃ* to those whom you gave me out of the world. They were yours; you gave them to me and they have obeyed your word. ⁷Now they know that everything you have given me comes from you. ⁸For I gave them the words you gave me and they accepted them. They knew with certainty that I came from you, and they believed that you sent me. ⁹I pray for them. I am not praying for the world, but for those you have given me, for they are yours. ¹⁰All I have is yours, and all you have is mine. And glory has come to me through them. ¹¹I will remain in the world no longer, but they are still in the world, and I am coming to you. Holy Father, protect them by the power of*ᵇ* your name, the name you gave me, so that they may be one as we are one. ¹²While I was with them, I protected them and kept them safe by*ᶜ* that name you gave me. None has been lost except the one doomed to destruction so that Scripture would be fulfilled.

¹³"I am coming to you now, but I say these things while I am still in the world, so that they may have the full measure of my joy within them. ¹⁴I have given them your word and the world has hated them, for they are not of the world any more than I am of the world. ¹⁵My prayer is not that you take them out of the world but that you protect them from the evil one. ¹⁶They are not of the world, even as I am not of it. ¹⁷Sanctify them by*ᵈ* the truth; your word is truth. ¹⁸As you sent me into the world, I have sent them into the world. ¹⁹For them I sanctify myself, that they too may be truly sanctified.

JESUS PRAYS FOR ALL BELIEVERS

²⁰"My prayer is not for them alone. I pray also for those who will believe in me through their message, ²¹that all of them may be one, Father, just as you are in me and I am in you. May they also be in us so that the world may believe that you have sent me. ²²I have given them the glory that you gave me, that they may be one as we are one— ²³I in them and you in me—so that

---

Why did Jesus look upward when praying? (17:1)
This was the customary posture for prayer, but Jesus sometimes lay face down when praying.

Prayer

Why did Jesus ask to be glorified? (17:5)
Jesus asked the Father to return him to his previous position of glory to show that he had fulfilled the work he set out to do. This would also demonstrate God's love and power. This took place at Christ's resurrection and ascension.

Why were the disciples to be commended? (17:8)
They accepted Jesus' teaching, they knew his origin, and they believed.

Why did Jesus pray for the unity of believers? (17:21–22)
When believers are unified, it helps to convince unbelievers of the truth of the gospel, and it reflects the unity of God the Father, Son, and Holy Spirit.

ᵃ 6 Greek *your name*   *ᵇ 11* Or *Father, keep them faithful to*   *ᶜ 12* Or *kept them faithful to*   *ᵈ 17* Or *them to live in accordance with*

they may be brought to complete unity. Then the world will know that you sent me and have loved them even as you have loved me.

²⁴"Father, I want those you have given me to be with me where I am, and to see my glory, the glory you have given me because you loved me before the creation of the world.

²⁵"Righteous Father, though the world does not know you, I know you, and they know that you have sent me. ²⁶I have made you*ᵃ* known to them, and will continue to make you known in order that the love you have for me may be in them and that I myself may be in them."

JESUS ARRESTED

18 When he had finished praying, Jesus left with his disciples and crossed the Kidron Valley. On the other side there was a garden, and he and his disciples went into it.

²Now Judas, who betrayed him, knew the place, because Jesus had often met there with his disciples. ³So Judas came to the garden, guiding a detachment of soldiers and some officials from the chief priests and the Pharisees. They were carrying torches, lanterns and weapons.

⁴Jesus, knowing all that was going to happen to him, went out and asked them, "Who is it you want?"

⁵"Jesus of Nazareth," they replied.

"I am he," Jesus said. (And Judas the traitor was standing there with them.) ⁶When Jesus said, "I am he," they drew back and fell to the ground.

⁷Again he asked them, "Who is it you want?"

"Jesus of Nazareth," they said.

⁸Jesus answered, "I told you that I am he. If you are looking for me, then let these men go." ⁹This happened so that the words he had spoken would be fulfilled: "I have not lost one of those you gave me."*ᵇ*

¹⁰Then Simon Peter, who had a sword, drew it and struck the high priest's servant, cutting off his right ear. (The servant's name was Malchus.)

¹¹Jesus commanded Peter, "Put your sword away! Shall I not drink the cup the Father has given me?"

¹²Then the detachment of soldiers with its commander and the Jewish officials arrested Jesus. They bound him ¹³and brought him first to Annas, who was the father-in-law of Caiaphas, the high priest that year. ¹⁴Caiaphas was the one who had advised the Jewish leaders that it would be good if one man died for the people.

PETER'S FIRST DENIAL

¹⁵Simon Peter and another disciple were following Jesus. Because this disciple was known to the high priest, he went with Jesus into the high priest's courtyard, ¹⁶but Peter had to wait outside at the door. The other disciple, who was known to the high priest, came back, spoke to the servant girl on duty there and brought Peter in.

Where was the Kidron Valley? (18:1)
The valley was east of Jerusalem and was dry except during the rainy season.

Kidron Valley

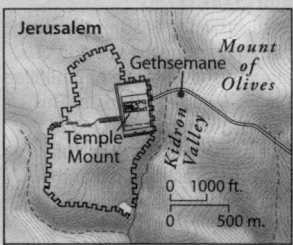

Jerusalem
Mount of Olives
Gethsemane
Temple Mount
Kidron Valley

0 1000 ft.
0 500 m.

What did Jewish law require for sentencing? (18:13)
In Jewish law, a person could not be sentenced on the day his trial was held. The two examinations — this one and the one before Caiaphas — may have been conducted to create a sense of legitimacy.

ᵃ 26 Greek *your name*   ᵇ 9 John 6:39

17 "You aren't one of this man's disciples too, are you?" she asked Peter.

He replied, "I am not."

18 It was cold, and the servants and officials stood around a fire they had made to keep warm. Peter also was standing with them, warming himself.

THE HIGH PRIEST QUESTIONS JESUS

19 Meanwhile, the high priest questioned Jesus about his disciples and his teaching.

20 "I have spoken openly to the world," Jesus replied. "I always taught in synagogues or at the temple, where all the Jews come together. I said nothing in secret. 21 Why question me? Ask those who heard me. Surely they know what I said."

22 When Jesus said this, one of the officials nearby slapped him in the face. "Is this the way you answer the high priest?" he demanded.

23 "If I said something wrong," Jesus replied, "testify as to what is wrong. But if I spoke the truth, why did you strike me?" 24 Then Annas sent him bound to Caiaphas the high priest.

PETER'S SECOND AND THIRD DENIALS

25 Meanwhile, Simon Peter was still standing there warming himself. So they asked him, "You aren't one of his disciples too, are you?"

He denied it, saying, "I am not."

26 One of the high priest's servants, a relative of the man whose ear Peter had cut off, challenged him, "Didn't I see you with him in the garden?" 27 Again Peter denied it, and at that moment a rooster began to crow.

JESUS BEFORE PILATE

28 Then the Jewish leaders took Jesus from Caiaphas to the palace of the Roman governor. By now it was early morning, and to avoid ceremonial uncleanness they did not enter the palace, because they wanted to be able to eat the Passover. 29 So Pilate came out to them and asked, "What charges are you bringing against this man?"

30 "If he were not a criminal," they replied, "we would not have handed him over to you."

31 Pilate said, "Take him yourselves and judge him by your own law."

"But we have no right to execute anyone," they objected. 32 This took place to fulfill what Jesus had said about the kind of death he was going to die.

33 Pilate then went back inside the palace, summoned Jesus and asked him, "Are you the king of the Jews?"

34 "Is that your own idea," Jesus asked, "or did others talk to you about me?"

35 "Am I a Jew?" Pilate replied. "Your own people and chief priests handed you over to me. What is it you have done?"

36 Jesus said, "My kingdom is not of this world. If it were, my servants would fight to prevent my arrest by the Jewish leaders. But now my kingdom is from another place."

During Peter's denial of Christ, who asked Peter the first question? (18:17)
All four Gospels say that the first question was asked by a slave girl, which made her the most unimportant person imaginable.

How did Jewish trials proceed? (18:19–21)
In a formal Jewish trial, the judge did not ask questions of the person who was accused. Instead, witnesses were called to give testimony. If two or more of them agreed, the verdict was sealed.

Who was the Roman governor? (18:28–31)
The Roman governor at this time was Pontius Pilate. He concluded that because there had been no violation of Roman law, the Jews should try Jesus themselves.

³⁷"You are a king, then!" said Pilate.

Jesus answered, "You say that I am a king. In fact, the reason I was born and came into the world is to testify to the truth. Everyone on the side of truth listens to me."

³⁸"What is truth?" retorted Pilate. With this he went out again to the Jews gathered there and said, "I find no basis for a charge against him. ³⁹But it is your custom for me to release to you one prisoner at the time of the Passover. Do you want me to release 'the king of the Jews'?"

⁴⁰They shouted back, "No, not him! Give us Barabbas!" Now Barabbas had taken part in an uprising.

JESUS SENTENCED TO BE CRUCIFIED

19 Then Pilate took Jesus and had him flogged. ²The soldiers twisted together a crown of thorns and put it on his head. They clothed him in a purple robe ³and went up to him again and again, saying, "Hail, king of the Jews!" And they slapped him in the face.

⁴Once more Pilate came out and said to the Jews gathered there, "Look, I am bringing him out to you to let you know that I find no basis for a charge against him." ⁵When Jesus came out wearing the crown of thorns and the purple robe, Pilate said to them, "Here is the man!"

⁶As soon as the chief priests and their officials saw him, they shouted, "Crucify! Crucify!"

But Pilate answered, "You take him and crucify him. As for me, I find no basis for a charge against him."

⁷The Jewish leaders insisted, "We have a law, and according to that law he must die, because he claimed to be the Son of God."

⁸When Pilate heard this, he was even more afraid, ⁹and he went back inside the palace. "Where do you come from?" he asked Jesus, but Jesus gave him no answer. ¹⁰"Do you refuse to speak to me?" Pilate said. "Don't you realize I have power either to free you or to crucify you?"

¹¹Jesus answered, "You would have no power over me if it were not given to you from above. Therefore the one who handed me over to you is guilty of a greater sin."

¹²From then on, Pilate tried to set Jesus free, but the Jewish leaders kept shouting, "If you let this man go, you are no friend of Caesar. Anyone who claims to be a king opposes Caesar."

¹³When Pilate heard this, he brought Jesus out and sat down on the judge's seat at a place known as the Stone Pavement (which in Aramaic is Gabbatha). ¹⁴It was the day of Preparation of the Passover; it was about noon.

"Here is your king," Pilate said to the Jews.

¹⁵But they shouted, "Take him away! Take him away! Crucify him!"

"Shall I crucify your king?" Pilate asked.

"We have no king but Caesar," the chief priests answered. ¹⁶Finally Pilate handed him over to them to be crucified.

THE CRUCIFIXION OF JESUS

So the soldiers took charge of Jesus. ¹⁷Carrying his own cross, he went out to the place of the Skull (which in Arama-

---

What did Pilate mean when he said he could find no basis for a charge against Jesus? (19:6)
This was the third time Pilate said he could not find Jesus guilty of any wrongdoing.

Why would Jesus carry his own cross? (19:17)
To further humiliate him, the condemned person would normally carry a beam of the cross to the place of execution.

ic is called Golgotha). [18]There they crucified him, and with him two others—one on each side and Jesus in the middle.

[19]Pilate had a notice prepared and fastened to the cross. It read: JESUS OF NAZARETH, THE KING OF THE JEWS. [20]Many of the Jews read this sign, for the place where Jesus was crucified was near the city, and the sign was written in Aramaic, Latin and Greek. [21]The chief priests of the Jews protested to Pilate, "Do not write 'The King of the Jews,' but that this man claimed to be king of the Jews."

[22]Pilate answered, "What I have written, I have written."

[23]When the soldiers crucified Jesus, they took his clothes, dividing them into four shares, one for each of them, with the undergarment remaining. This garment was seamless, woven in one piece from top to bottom.

[24]"Let's not tear it," they said to one another. "Let's decide by lot who will get it."

This happened that the scripture might be fulfilled that said,

"They divided my clothes among them
    and cast lots for my garment."[a]

So this is what the soldiers did.

[25]Near the cross of Jesus stood his mother, his mother's sister, Mary the wife of Clopas, and Mary Magdalene. [26]When Jesus saw his mother there, and the disciple whom he loved standing nearby, he said to her, "Woman,[b] here is your son," [27]and to the disciple, "Here is your mother." From that time on, this disciple took her into his home.

THE DEATH OF JESUS

[28]Later, knowing that everything had now been finished, and so that Scripture would be fulfilled, Jesus said, "I am thirsty." [29]A jar of wine vinegar was there, so they soaked a sponge in it, put the sponge on a stalk of the hyssop plant, and lifted it to Jesus' lips. [30]When he had received the drink, Jesus said, "It is finished." With that, he bowed his head and gave up his spirit.

[31]Now it was the day of Preparation, and the next day was to be a special Sabbath. Because the Jewish leaders did not want the bodies left on the crosses during the Sabbath, they asked Pilate to have the legs broken and the bodies taken down. [32]The soldiers therefore came and broke the legs of the first man who had been crucified with Jesus, and then those of the other. [33]But when they came to Jesus and found that he was already dead, they did not break his legs. [34]Instead, one of the soldiers pierced Jesus' side with a spear, bringing a sudden flow of blood and water. [35]The man who saw it has given testimony, and his testimony is true. He knows that he tells the truth, and he testifies so that you also may believe. [36]These things happened so that the scripture would be fulfilled: "Not one of his bones will be broken,"[c] [37]and, as another scripture says, "They will look on the one they have pierced."[d]

[a] 24 Psalm 22:18   [b] 26 The Greek for Woman does not denote any disrespect.   [c] 36 Exodus 12:46; Num. 9:12; Psalm 34:20   [d] 37 Zech. 12:10

Why would a notice be attached to the cross? (19:19)
Often a placard would be attached to a cross stating the crime the person was being executed for. In this case, it stated that Jesus was the king of the Jews.

What was wine vinegar? (19:29)
This may have been cheap wine, the drink of ordinary people. A sponge was a useful way of giving it to a person hanging on a cross.

Why would the soldiers break the legs of those who were being crucified? (19:31)
This would make death come faster because the victim could not push himself up with his legs in order to get a full breath. Death came by suffocation.

Who was Joseph of
Arimathea? (19:38)
He was a rich man, a member
of the Sanhedrin, and a secret
follower of Jesus. He acted
secretly because he feared what
the other Jewish leaders might
do to him.

THE BURIAL OF JESUS

³⁸ Later, Joseph of Arimathea asked Pilate for the body of
Jesus. Now Joseph was a disciple of Jesus, but secretly because he feared the Jewish leaders. With Pilate's permission,
he came and took the body away. ³⁹ He was accompanied by
Nicodemus, the man who earlier had visited Jesus at night.
Nicodemus brought a mixture of myrrh and aloes, about
seventy-five pounds.ᵃ ⁴⁰ Taking Jesus' body, the two of them
wrapped it, with the spices, in strips of linen. This was in
accordance with Jewish burial customs. ⁴¹ At the place where
Jesus was crucified, there was a garden, and in the garden a
new tomb, in which no one had ever been laid. ⁴² Because it
was the Jewish day of Preparation and since the tomb was
nearby, they laid Jesus there.

THE EMPTY TOMB

20 Early on the first day of the week, while it was still
dark, Mary Magdalene went to the tomb and saw
that the stone had been removed from the entrance. ² So she
came running to Simon Peter and the other disciple, the one
Jesus loved, and said, "They have taken the Lord out of the
tomb, and we don't know where they have put him!"

³ So Peter and the other disciple started for the tomb.
⁴ Both were running, but the other disciple outran Peter and
reached the tomb first. ⁵ He bent over and looked in at the
strips of linen lying there but did not go in. ⁶ Then Simon
Peter came along behind him and went straight into the
tomb. He saw the strips of linen lying there, ⁷ as well as the
cloth that had been wrapped around Jesus' head. The cloth
was still lying in its place, separate from the linen. ⁸ Finally
the other disciple, who had reached the tomb first, also went
inside. He saw and believed. ⁹ (They still did not understand
from Scripture that Jesus had to rise from the dead.) ¹⁰ Then
the disciples went back to where they were staying.

JESUS APPEARS TO MARY MAGDALENE

¹¹ Now Mary stood outside the tomb crying. As she wept,
she bent over to look into the tomb ¹² and saw two angels in
white, seated where Jesus' body had been, one at the head and
the other at the foot.

Why did John mention the
burial cloths? (20:7)
If the grave had been robbed,
the cloths would not have been
there.

ᵃ *39* Or about 34 kilograms

Can a person have doubts and still be a Christian?   JOHN 20

Every Christian probably has times of wondering whether the Bible is true and whether God is real.
Often these doubts enter people's minds when bad things happen to them. A sickness, an accident,
a death of someone close, or other troubles in life often cause people to wonder whether what they
believe is real.

Thomas was someone who wanted proof that Jesus had risen from the dead. The other disciples
had seen Jesus, but he had not, so he said that he wanted to see Jesus and touch him before he could
be positive that Jesus was alive again. When Jesus appeared to the disciples a week later, he did not
criticize Thomas. Instead, he told Thomas to touch him and to believe.

Having doubts about faith is not the same as saying that our faith isn't true. But when we wonder
about the reality of God, we should pray, read the Bible, and talk to other believers. The Holy Spirit can
use these things to help strengthen our faith.

¹³They asked her, "Woman, why are you crying?"

"They have taken my Lord away," she said, "and I don't know where they have put him." ¹⁴At this, she turned around and saw Jesus standing there, but she did not realize that it was Jesus.

¹⁵He asked her, "Woman, why are you crying? Who is it you are looking for?"

Thinking he was the gardener, she said, "Sir, if you have carried him away, tell me where you have put him, and I will get him."

¹⁶Jesus said to her, "Mary."

She turned toward him and cried out in Aramaic, "Rabboni!" (which means "Teacher").

¹⁷Jesus said, "Do not hold on to me, for I have not yet ascended to the Father. Go instead to my brothers and tell them, 'I am ascending to my Father and your Father, to my God and your God.'"

¹⁸Mary Magdalene went to the disciples with the news: "I have seen the Lord!" And she told them that he had said these things to her.

JESUS APPEARS TO HIS DISCIPLES

¹⁹On the evening of that first day of the week, when the disciples were together, with the doors locked for fear of the Jewish leaders, Jesus came and stood among them and said, "Peace be with you!" ²⁰After he said this, he showed them his hands and side. The disciples were overjoyed when they saw the Lord.

²¹Again Jesus said, "Peace be with you! As the Father has sent me, I am sending you." ²²And with that he breathed on them and said, "Receive the Holy Spirit. ²³If you forgive anyone's sins, their sins are forgiven; if you do not forgive them, they are not forgiven."

Why did Jesus say, "Peace be with you"? (20:21)
This was a typical Hebrew greeting.

JESUS APPEARS TO THOMAS

²⁴Now Thomas (also known as Didymus*), one of the Twelve, was not with the disciples when Jesus came. ²⁵So the other disciples told him, "We have seen the Lord!"

But he said to them, "Unless I see the nail marks in his hands and put my finger where the nails were, and put my hand into his side, I will not believe."

²⁶A week later his disciples were in the house again, and Thomas was with them. Though the doors were locked, Jesus came and stood among them and said, "Peace be with you!" ²⁷Then he said to Thomas, "Put your finger here; see my hands. Reach out your hand and put it into my side. Stop doubting and believe."

²⁸Thomas said to him, "My Lord and my God!"

²⁹Then Jesus told him, "Because you have seen me, you have believed; blessed are those who have not seen and yet have believed."

Why was Thomas skeptical about Jesus' resurrection? (20:25)
He wanted to see for himself that Jesus had actually risen from the grave.

Did Thomas believe? (20:28)
By calling Jesus his Lord and his God, he showed that he had faith that Jesus was the risen Lord.

THE PURPOSE OF JOHN'S GOSPEL

³⁰Jesus performed many other signs in the presence of his disciples, which are not recorded in this book. ³¹But these

---

ᵃ 24 Thomas (Aramaic) and *Didymus* (Greek) both mean *twin*.

are written that you may believe[a] that Jesus is the Messiah, the Son of God, and that by believing you may have life in his name.

JESUS AND THE MIRACULOUS CATCH OF FISH

21 Afterward Jesus appeared again to his disciples, by the Sea of Galilee.[b] It happened this way: [2]Simon Peter, Thomas (also known as Didymus[c]), Nathanael from Cana in Galilee, the sons of Zebedee, and two other disciples were together. [3]"I'm going out to fish," Simon Peter told them, and they said, "We'll go with you." So they went out and got into the boat, but that night they caught nothing.

[4]Early in the morning, Jesus stood on the shore, but the disciples did not realize that it was Jesus.

[5]He called out to them, "Friends, haven't you any fish?"

"No," they answered.

[6]He said, "Throw your net on the right side of the boat and you will find some." When they did, they were unable to haul the net in because of the large number of fish.

[7]Then the disciple whom Jesus loved said to Peter, "It is the Lord!" As soon as Simon Peter heard him say, "It is the Lord," he wrapped his outer garment around him (for he had taken it off) and jumped into the water. [8]The other disciples followed in the boat, towing the net full of fish, for they were not far from shore, about a hundred yards.[d] [9]When they landed, they saw a fire of burning coals there with fish on it, and some bread.

[10]Jesus said to them, "Bring some of the fish you have just caught." [11]So Simon Peter climbed back into the boat and dragged the net ashore. It was full of large fish, 153, but even with so many the net was not torn. [12]Jesus said to them, "Come and have breakfast." None of the disciples dared ask him, "Who are you?" They knew it was the Lord. [13]Jesus came, took the bread and gave it to them, and did the same with the fish. [14]This was now the third time Jesus appeared to his disciples after he was raised from the dead.

JESUS REINSTATES PETER

[15]When they had finished eating, Jesus said to Simon Peter, "Simon son of John, do you love me more than these?"

"Yes, Lord," he said, "you know that I love you."

Jesus said, "Feed my lambs."

[16]Again Jesus said, "Simon son of John, do you love me?"

He answered, "Yes, Lord, you know that I love you."

Jesus said, "Take care of my sheep."

[17]The third time he said to him, "Simon son of John, do you love me?"

Peter was hurt because Jesus asked him the third time, "Do you love me?" He said, "Lord, you know all things; you know that I love you."

Jesus said, "Feed my sheep. [18]Very truly I tell you, when you were younger you dressed yourself and went where you wanted; but when you are old you will stretch out your hands,

---

How did the men know this was Jesus? (21:11–14)
They knew because of the full catch of fish and because of the way Jesus spoke to them. This was the third time he had appeared to them after the resurrection.

Why did Jesus ask Peter if he loved him three times? (21:15–19)
It is possible that because Peter had denied Jesus three times, Jesus wanted him to affirm his love for Jesus three times. Jesus did this for Peter's benefit.

---

[a] 31 Or *may continue to believe*   [b] 1 Greek *Tiberias*   [c] 2 *Thomas* (Aramaic) and *Didymus* (Greek) both mean *twin.*   [d] 8 Or about 90 meters

and someone else will dress you and lead you where you do not want to go." ¹⁹Jesus said this to indicate the kind of death by which Peter would glorify God. Then he said to him, "Follow me!"

²⁰Peter turned and saw that the disciple whom Jesus loved was following them. (This was the one who had leaned back against Jesus at the supper and had said, "Lord, who is going to betray you?") ²¹When Peter saw him, he asked, "Lord, what about him?"

²²Jesus answered, "If I want him to remain alive until I return, what is that to you? You must follow me." ²³Because of this, the rumor spread among the believers that this disciple would not die. But Jesus did not say that he would not die; he only said, "If I want him to remain alive until I return, what is that to you?"

²⁴This is the disciple who testifies to these things and who wrote them down. We know that his testimony is true.

²⁵Jesus did many other things as well. If every one of them were written down, I suppose that even the whole world would not have room for the books that would be written.

Why did John write that Jesus did "many other things"? (21:25)
John wanted people to know that his written record was only a partial account of the many things that Jesus did both before and after his resurrection.

Acts

INTRODUCTION

Who wrote this book?	Luke, the physician who traveled as a missionary with Paul, wrote this book.
Why was this book written?	The book of Acts tells how the Christian faith spread to the whole world.
For whom was this book written?	Acts was written for everyone who wants to know what happened after Jesus returned to heaven.
Who are the key people in this book?	The most important people in this book are Peter and Paul.
Where did this happen?	The events in this book happened in many important cities in the Roman Empire.

What are some of the stories in this book?	Jesus goes to heaven	Acts 1:1 – 11
	The Holy Spirit comes	Acts 2:1 – 13
	Peter heals a beggar	Acts 3:1 – 10
	Peter and John are arrested	Acts 4:1 – 31
	Ananias and Sapphira lie	Acts 5:1 – 11
	Stephen, the first martyr	Acts 6:8 – 7:60
	Saul is converted	Acts 9:1 – 31
	Peter has a vision	Acts 10:1 – 48
	Peter escapes from prison	Acts 12:1 – 19
	Prisoners are freed	Acts 16:16 – 40
	A riot in Ephesus	Acts 19:23 – 41
	Paul goes on trial	Acts 24:1 – 27
	Paul is shipwrecked	Acts 27:1 – 44
	Paul goes to Rome	Acts 28:1 – 31

When did these things happen?

10 BC AD 1   10   20   30   40   50   60   70   80   90   100

JESUS' LIFE (C. 6/5 BC – AD 30) _____

PAUL'S CONVERSION (C. AD 35) _____

PAUL'S FIRST MISSIONARY JOURNEY (C. AD 46 – 48) _____

COUNCIL AT JERUSALEM (C. AD 49/50) _____

PAUL'S SECOND MISSIONARY JOURNEY (C. AD 50 – 52) _____

PAUL'S THIRD MISSIONARY JOURNEY (C. AD 53 – 57) _____

BOOK OF ACTS WRITTEN (C. AD 62) _____

PAUL'S FOURTH MISSIONARY JOURNEY (C. AD 62 – 67) _____

PAUL'S IMPRISONMENT AND DEATH IN ROME (C. AD 67 – 68) _____

JESUS TAKEN UP INTO HEAVEN

1 In my former book, Theophilus, I wrote about all that Jesus began to do and to teach ²until the day he was taken up to heaven, after giving instructions through the Holy Spirit to the apostles he had chosen. ³After his suffering, he presented himself to them and gave many convincing proofs that he was alive. He appeared to them over a period of forty days and spoke about the kingdom of God. ⁴On one occasion, while he was eating with them, he gave them this command: "Do not leave Jerusalem, but wait for the gift my Father promised, which you have heard me speak about. ⁵For John baptized with*a* water, but in a few days you will be baptized with*a* the Holy Spirit."

⁶Then they gathered around him and asked him, "Lord, are you at this time going to restore the kingdom to Israel?"

⁷He said to them: "It is not for you to know the times or dates the Father has set by his own authority. ⁸But you will receive power when the Holy Spirit comes on you; and you

a 5 Or in

What was the former book? (1:1–2)
The former book was the Gospel of Luke, which was also addressed to Theophilus. The book of Acts continues to describe Jesus' work through the ministry of the Holy Spirit.

SETTING OF ACTS

will be my witnesses in Jerusalem, and in all Judea and Samaria, and to the ends of the earth."

[9] After he said this, he was taken up before their very eyes, and a cloud hid him from their sight.

[10] They were looking intently up into the sky as he was going, when suddenly two men dressed in white stood beside them. [11] "Men of Galilee," they said, "why do you stand here looking into the sky? This same Jesus, who has been taken from you into heaven, will come back in the same way you have seen him go into heaven."

MATTHIAS CHOSEN TO REPLACE JUDAS

[12] Then the apostles returned to Jerusalem from the hill called the Mount of Olives, a Sabbath day's walk[a] from the city. [13] When they arrived, they went upstairs to the room where they were staying. Those present were Peter, John, James and Andrew; Philip and Thomas, Bartholomew and Matthew; James son of Alphaeus and Simon the Zealot, and Judas son of James. [14] They all joined together constantly in prayer, along with the women and Mary the mother of Jesus, and with his brothers.

[15] In those days Peter stood up among the believers (a group numbering about a hundred and twenty) [16] and said, "Brothers and sisters,[b] the Scripture had to be fulfilled in which the Holy Spirit spoke long ago through David concerning Judas, who served as guide for those who arrested Jesus. [17] He was one of our number and shared in our ministry."

[18] (With the payment he received for his wickedness, Judas bought a field; there he fell headlong, his body burst open and all his intestines spilled out. [19] Everyone in Jerusalem heard about this, so they called that field in their language Akeldama, that is, Field of Blood.)

[20] "For," said Peter, "it is written in the Book of Psalms:

"'May his place be deserted;
    let there be no one to dwell in it,'[c]

and,

"'May another take his place of leadership.'[d]

[21] Therefore it is necessary to choose one of the men who have been with us the whole time the Lord Jesus was living among us, [22] beginning from John's baptism to the time when Jesus was taken up from us. For one of these must become a witness with us of his resurrection."

[23] So they nominated two men: Joseph called Barsabbas (also known as Justus) and Matthias. [24] Then they prayed, "Lord, you know everyone's heart. Show us which of these two you have chosen [25] to take over this apostolic ministry, which Judas left to go where he belongs." [26] Then they cast lots, and the lot fell to Matthias; so he was added to the eleven apostles.

Why were Jesus' disciples called "men of Galilee"? (1:11)
All of his 12 disciples, except for Judas who had hung himself, were from Galilee.

Where did the ascension take place? (1:12)
The ascension took place on the eastern slope of the Mount of Olives between Jerusalem and Bethany.

Why did they cast lots? (1:26)
They cast lots in order to allow the Lord to decide who should take the place of Judas.

---

[a] *12* That is, about 5/8 mile or about 1 kilometer   [b] *16* The Greek word for *brothers and sisters* (*adelphoi*) refers here to believers, both men and women, as part of God's family; also in 6:3; 11:29; 12:17; 16:40; 18:18, 27; 21:7, 17; 28:14, 15.   [c] *20* Psalm 69:25   [d] *20* Psalm 109:8

THE HOLY SPIRIT COMES AT PENTECOST

2 When the day of Pentecost came, they were all together in one place. ²Suddenly a sound like the blowing of a violent wind came from heaven and filled the whole house where they were sitting. ³They saw what seemed to be tongues of fire that separated and came to rest on each of them. ⁴All of them were filled with the Holy Spirit and began to speak in other tongues*a* as the Spirit enabled them.

⁵Now there were staying in Jerusalem God-fearing Jews from every nation under heaven. ⁶When they heard this sound, a crowd came together in bewilderment, because each one heard their own language being spoken. ⁷Utterly amazed, they asked: "Aren't all these who are speaking Galileans? ⁸Then how is it that each of us hears them in our native language? ⁹Parthians, Medes and Elamites; residents of Mesopotamia, Judea and Cappadocia, Pontus and Asia,*b* ¹⁰Phrygia and Pamphylia, Egypt and the parts of Libya near Cyrene; visitors from Rome ¹¹(both Jews and converts to Judaism); Cretans and Arabs—we hear them declaring the wonders of God in our own tongues!" ¹²Amazed and perplexed, they asked one another, "What does this mean?"

¹³Some, however, made fun of them and said, "They have had too much wine."

a 4 Or languages; also in verse 11   b 9 That is, the Roman province by that name

What did the wind symbolize? (2:2)
Breath or wind was a symbol of the Spirit of God.

Who were these God-fearing Jews? (2:5)
These were devout Jews from around the world who gathered in Jerusalem either as residents or as pilgrims to celebrate Pentecost.

Who were these converts to Judaism? (2:11)
These were Gentiles who followed the law of Moses and were received into fellowship with the Jews.

JEWS FROM EVERY NATION (2:5)

PETER ADDRESSES THE CROWD

¹⁴Then Peter stood up with the Eleven, raised his voice and addressed the crowd: "Fellow Jews and all of you who live in Jerusalem, let me explain this to you; listen carefully to what I say. ¹⁵These people are not drunk, as you suppose. It's only nine in the morning! ¹⁶No, this is what was spoken by the prophet Joel:

¹⁷"'In the last days, God says,
    I will pour out my Spirit on all people.
  Your sons and daughters will prophesy,
    your young men will see visions,
    your old men will dream dreams.
¹⁸Even on my servants, both men and women,
    I will pour out my Spirit in those days,
    and they will prophesy.
¹⁹I will show wonders in the heavens above
    and signs on the earth below,
    blood and fire and billows of smoke.
²⁰The sun will be turned to darkness
    and the moon to blood
    before the coming of the great and glorious day of
        the Lord.
²¹And everyone who calls
    on the name of the Lord will be saved.'ᵃ

²²"Fellow Israelites, listen to this: Jesus of Nazareth was a man accredited by God to you by miracles, wonders and signs, which God did among you through him, as you yourselves know. ²³This man was handed over to you by God's deliberate plan and foreknowledge; and you, with the help of wicked men,ᵇ put him to death by nailing him to the cross. ²⁴But God raised him from the dead, freeing him from the agony of death, because it was impossible for death to keep its hold on him. ²⁵David said about him:

"'I saw the Lord always before me.
    Because he is at my right hand,
    I will not be shaken.
²⁶Therefore my heart is glad and my tongue rejoices;
    my body also will rest in hope,

ᵃ 21 Joel 2:28-32   ᵇ 23 Or *of those not having the law* (that is, Gentiles)

Why would it have been unlikely that they were drunk? (2:15)
On a festival day such as Pentecost, a Jew would not break his fast until at least 10:00 A.M. So it was extremely unlikely that a group would be drunk at such an early hour.

Why is Pentecost important in the history of the church?

ACTS 2

Pentecost is said to be the beginning of the church. This was the time when God sent his Holy Spirit to the apostles so that they would begin preaching the good news of Jesus to people from all different backgrounds.

Of course the Holy Spirit had been present forever. When Jesus was born in Bethlehem, it was a special beginning to his work. Pentecost was a special beginning to the work of the Holy Spirit. When the apostles were filled with the Holy Spirit, they were able to preach to people in their own languages and were able to persuade them to believe in Jesus. In this way they were able to carry out Jesus' commandment in the Great Commission: "Therefore go and make disciples of all nations, baptizing them in the name of the Father and of the Son and of the Holy Spirit, and teaching them to obey everything I have commanded you" (Matthew 28:19 – 20).

²⁷because you will not abandon me to the realm of
the dead,
you will not let your holy one see decay.
²⁸You have made known to me the paths of life;
you will fill me with joy in your presence.'^a

²⁹"Fellow Israelites, I can tell you confidently that the patriarch David died and was buried, and his tomb is here to this day. ³⁰But he was a prophet and knew that God had promised him on oath that he would place one of his descendants on his throne. ³¹Seeing what was to come, he spoke of the resurrection of the Messiah, that he was not abandoned to the realm of the dead, nor did his body see decay. ³²God has raised this Jesus to life, and we are all witnesses of it. ³³Exalted to the right hand of God, he has received from the Father the promised Holy Spirit and has poured out what you now see and hear. ³⁴For David did not ascend to heaven, and yet he said,

"'The Lord said to my Lord:
"Sit at my right hand
³⁵until I make your enemies
a footstool for your feet."'^b

³⁶"Therefore let all Israel be assured of this: God has made this Jesus, whom you crucified, both Lord and Messiah."

³⁷When the people heard this, they were cut to the heart and said to Peter and the other apostles, "Brothers, what shall we do?"

³⁸Peter replied, "Repent and be baptized, every one of you, in the name of Jesus Christ for the forgiveness of your sins. And you will receive the gift of the Holy Spirit. ³⁹The promise is for you and your children and for all who are far off—for all whom the Lord our God will call."

⁴⁰With many other words he warned them; and he pleaded with them, "Save yourselves from this corrupt generation." ⁴¹Those who accepted his message were baptized, and about three thousand were added to their number that day.

THE FELLOWSHIP OF THE BELIEVERS

⁴²They devoted themselves to the apostles' teaching and to fellowship, to the breaking of bread and to prayer. ⁴³Everyone was filled with awe at the many wonders and signs performed by the apostles. ⁴⁴All the believers were together and had everything in common. ⁴⁵They sold property and

^a 28 Psalm 16:8-11 (see Septuagint)   ^b 35 Psalm 110:1

Where was the tomb of David? (2:29)
The tomb of David was in Jerusalem and still contained the remains of David's body.

Why were repentance and baptism stressed? (2:38)
Repentance and baptism were important parts of the message of both John the Baptist and Jesus.

What did the apostles teach? (2:42)
The apostles taught what Jesus had taught. Their teaching came from God and had his authority.

What is the meaning of baptism?   ACTS 2

Baptism is a sign of the washing away of sin. Just as water washes dirt from a person's body, baptism is a sign that a person's sins are washed away. Because Christ died on the cross, our sins have been forgiven, and the Holy Spirit renews us to live a life that is pleasing to God.

Some churches practice infant baptism as a sign that the children of believing parents are part of God's family. Other churches wait to baptize people until they are old enough to make a commitment to God and to accept his promises. It is a sign of God's great love and the fact that the person being baptized has been saved by grace and belongs to God's family.

possessions to give to anyone who had need. ⁴⁶Every day they continued to meet together in the temple courts. They broke bread in their homes and ate together with glad and sincere hearts, ⁴⁷praising God and enjoying the favor of all the people. And the Lord added to their number daily those who were being saved.

PETER HEALS A LAME BEGGAR

3 One day Peter and John were going up to the temple at the time of prayer—at three in the afternoon. ²Now a man who was lame from birth was being carried to the temple gate called Beautiful, where he was put every day to beg from those going into the temple courts. ³When he saw Peter and John about to enter, he asked them for money. ⁴Peter looked straight at him, as did John. Then Peter said, "Look at us!" ⁵So the man gave them his attention, expecting to get something from them.

⁶Then Peter said, "Silver or gold I do not have, but what I do have I give you. In the name of Jesus Christ of Nazareth, walk." ⁷Taking him by the right hand, he helped him up, and instantly the man's feet and ankles became strong. ⁸He jumped to his feet and began to walk. Then he went with them into the temple courts, walking and jumping, and praising God. ⁹When all the people saw him walking and praising God, ¹⁰they recognized him as the same man who used to sit begging at the temple gate called Beautiful, and they were filled with wonder and amazement at what had happened to him.

PETER SPEAKS TO THE ONLOOKERS

¹¹While the man held on to Peter and John, all the people were astonished and came running to them in the place called Solomon's Colonnade. ¹²When Peter saw this, he said to them: "Fellow Israelites, why does this surprise you? Why do you stare at us as if by our own power or godliness we had made this man walk? ¹³The God of Abraham, Isaac and Jacob, the God of our fathers, has glorified his servant Jesus. You handed him over to be killed, and you disowned him before Pilate, though he had decided to let him go. ¹⁴You disowned the Holy and Righteous One and asked that a murderer be released to you. ¹⁵You killed the author of life, but God raised him from the dead. We are witnesses of this. ¹⁶By faith in the name of Jesus, this man whom you see and know was made strong. It is Jesus' name and the faith that comes through him that has completely healed him, as you can all see.

¹⁷"Now, fellow Israelites, I know that you acted in ignorance, as did your leaders. ¹⁸But this is how God fulfilled what he had foretold through all the prophets, saying that his Messiah would suffer. ¹⁹Repent, then, and turn to God, so that your sins may be wiped out, that times of refreshing may come from the Lord, ²⁰and that he may send the Messiah, who has been appointed for you—even Jesus. ²¹Heaven must receive him until the time comes for God to restore everything, as he promised long ago through his holy prophets. ²²For Moses said, 'The Lord your God will raise up for you a

What was the "gate called Beautiful"? (3:2)
This was a favorite entrance to the temple court. It was probably the bronze-covered gate that was also called the Nicanor Gate.

What was Solomon's Colonnade? (3:11)
This was a porch along the inner side of the wall enclosing the outer court, with rows of tall stone columns and a roof made of cedar.

Why was repentance necessary? (3:19)
Repentance is a change of will and mind that arises from sorrow for sin and leads to a changed life. This allows a person to be in a right relationship with God.

prophet like me from among your own people; you must listen to everything he tells you. [23] Anyone who does not listen to him will be completely cut off from their people.'[a]

[24] "Indeed, beginning with Samuel, all the prophets who have spoken have foretold these days. [25] And you are heirs of the prophets and of the covenant God made with your fathers. He said to Abraham, 'Through your offspring all peoples on earth will be blessed.'[b] [26] When God raised up his servant, he sent him first to you to bless you by turning each of you from your wicked ways."

PETER AND JOHN BEFORE THE SANHEDRIN

4 The priests and the captain of the temple guard and the Sadducees came up to Peter and John while they were speaking to the people. [2] They were greatly disturbed because the apostles were teaching the people, proclaiming in Jesus the resurrection of the dead. [3] They seized Peter and John and, because it was evening, they put them in jail until the next day. [4] But many who heard the message believed; so the number of men who believed grew to about five thousand.

[5] The next day the rulers, the elders and the teachers of the law met in Jerusalem. [6] Annas the high priest was there, and so were Caiaphas, John, Alexander and others of the high priest's family. [7] They had Peter and John brought before them and began to question them: "By what power or what name did you do this?"

[8] Then Peter, filled with the Holy Spirit, said to them: "Rulers and elders of the people! [9] If we are being called to account today for an act of kindness shown to a man who was lame and are being asked how he was healed, [10] then know this, you and all the people of Israel: It is by the name of Jesus Christ of Nazareth, whom you crucified but whom God raised from the dead, that this man stands before you healed. [11] Jesus is

"'the stone you builders rejected,
    which has become the cornerstone.'[c]

[12] Salvation is found in no one else, for there is no other name under heaven given to mankind by which we must be saved."

[13] When they saw the courage of Peter and John and realized that they were unschooled, ordinary men, they were astonished and they took note that these men had been with Jesus. [14] But since they could see the man who had been healed standing there with them, there was nothing they could say. [15] So they ordered them to withdraw from the Sanhedrin and then conferred together. [16] "What are we going to do with these men?" they asked. "Everyone living in Jerusalem knows they have performed a notable sign, and we cannot deny it. [17] But to stop this thing from spreading any further among the people, we must warn them to speak no longer to anyone in this name."

[18] Then they called them in again and commanded them not to speak or teach at all in the name of Jesus. [19] But Peter

Who was the captain of the temple guard? (4:1)
The captain was a member of one of the leading priestly families and was next in rank to the high priest.

Why did the trial have to wait until the next day? (4:3)
The evening sacrifices ended around 4:00 P.M., and the temple gates would then be closed. All judgments involving a death sentence had to begin and end during daylight hours.

What did it mean that Peter and John were unschooled? (4:13)
They had not been trained in a rabbinic school, and they did not hold official positions in any established religious group.

---

[a] 23 Deut. 18:15,18,19   [b] 25 Gen. 22:18; 26:4   [c] 11 Psalm 118:22

and John replied, "Which is right in God's eyes: to listen to you, or to him? You be the judges! 20 As for us, we cannot help speaking about what we have seen and heard."

21 After further threats they let them go. They could not decide how to punish them, because all the people were praising God for what had happened. 22 For the man who was miraculously healed was over forty years old.

THE BELIEVERS PRAY

23 On their release, Peter and John went back to their own people and reported all that the chief priests and the elders had said to them. 24 When they heard this, they raised their voices together in prayer to God. "Sovereign Lord," they said, "you made the heavens and the earth and the sea, and everything in them. 25 You spoke by the Holy Spirit through the mouth of your servant, our father David:

"'Why do the nations rage
  and the peoples plot in vain?
26 The kings of the earth rise up
  and the rulers band together
against the Lord
  and against his anointed one.'*a b*

27 Indeed Herod and Pontius Pilate met together with the Gentiles and the people of Israel in this city to conspire against your holy servant Jesus, whom you anointed. 28 They did what your power and will had decided beforehand should happen. 29 Now, Lord, consider their threats and enable your servants to speak your word with great boldness. 30 Stretch out your hand to heal and perform signs and wonders through the name of your holy servant Jesus."

31 After they prayed, the place where they were meeting was shaken. And they were all filled with the Holy Spirit and spoke the word of God boldly.

THE BELIEVERS SHARE THEIR POSSESSIONS

32 All the believers were one in heart and mind. No one claimed that any of their possessions was their own, but they shared everything they had. 33 With great power the apostles continued to testify to the resurrection of the Lord Jesus. And God's grace was so powerfully at work in them all 34 that there were no needy persons among them. For from time to time those who owned land or houses sold them, brought the money from the sales 35 and put it at the apostles' feet, and it was distributed to anyone who had need.

36 Joseph, a Levite from Cyprus, whom the apostles called Barnabas (which means "son of encouragement"), 37 sold a field he owned and brought the money and put it at the apostles' feet.

ANANIAS AND SAPPHIRA

5 Now a man named Ananias, together with his wife Sapphira, also sold a piece of property. 2 With his wife's full knowledge he kept back part of the money for himself, but brought the rest and put it at the apostles' feet.

Why was the man's age important? (4:22)
Apparently he had been lame for so long that there was no hope that his condition would improve on its own.

Why was the room shaken? (4:31)
This was a sign from God that their prayers had been heard.

Was it wrong for Ananias and Sapphira to keep some of the money? (5:2)
They were free to keep some or all of the money. Their sin was in pretending that they were giving all of it to the apostles.

a 26 That is, Messiah or Christ   b 26 Psalm 2:1,2

³Then Peter said, "Ananias, how is it that Satan has so filled your heart that you have lied to the Holy Spirit and have kept for yourself some of the money you received for the land? ⁴Didn't it belong to you before it was sold? And after it was sold, wasn't the money at your disposal? What made you think of doing such a thing? You have not lied just to human beings but to God."

⁵When Ananias heard this, he fell down and died. And great fear seized all who heard what had happened. ⁶Then some young men came forward, wrapped up his body, and carried him out and buried him.

⁷About three hours later his wife came in, not knowing what had happened. ⁸Peter asked her, "Tell me, is this the price you and Ananias got for the land?"

"Yes," she said, "that is the price."

⁹Peter said to her, "How could you conspire to test the Spirit of the Lord? Listen! The feet of the men who buried your husband are at the door, and they will carry you out also."

¹⁰At that moment she fell down at his feet and died. Then the young men came in and, finding her dead, carried her out and buried her beside her husband. ¹¹Great fear seized the whole church and all who heard about these events.

THE APOSTLES HEAL MANY

¹²The apostles performed many signs and wonders among the people. And all the believers used to meet together in Solomon's Colonnade. ¹³No one else dared join them, even though they were highly regarded by the people. ¹⁴Nevertheless, more and more men and women believed in the Lord and were added to their number. ¹⁵As a result, people brought the sick into the streets and laid them on beds and mats so that at least Peter's shadow might fall on some of them as he passed by. ¹⁶Crowds gathered also from the towns around Jerusalem, bringing their sick and those tormented by impure spirits, and all of them were healed.

THE APOSTLES PERSECUTED

¹⁷Then the high priest and all his associates, who were members of the party of the Sadducees, were filled with jealousy. ¹⁸They arrested the apostles and put them in the public jail. ¹⁹But during the night an angel of the Lord opened the doors of the jail and brought them out. ²⁰"Go, stand in the temple courts," he said, "and tell the people all about this new life."

²¹At daybreak they entered the temple courts, as they had been told, and began to teach the people.

When the high priest and his associates arrived, they called together the Sanhedrin—the full assembly of the elders of Israel—and sent to the jail for the apostles. ²²But on arriving at the jail, the officers did not find them there. So they went back and reported, ²³"We found the jail securely locked, with the guards standing at the doors; but when we opened them, we found no one inside." ²⁴On hearing this report, the captain of the temple guard and the chief priests were at a loss, wondering what this might lead to.

What did the term *church* refer to? (5:11)
This is the first use of the term in Acts. It could refer to the local congregation or to the universal church.

Who was the high priest? (5:17)
The official high priest recognized by Rome was Caiaphas, but the Jews considered Annas (Caiaphas's father-in-law) to be the high priest because the position was meant to be a lifetime appointment.

What did it mean that they were making the Sanhedrin guilty of Jesus' blood? (5:28)
The apostles preached that some of the Jews and their leaders were guilty of killing Jesus.

Who was Gamaliel? (5:34)
He was the most famous Jewish teacher of his time and was traditionally listed among the "heads of the schools." He was Paul's teacher.

How were the apostles flogged? (5:40)
They were whipped 39 times, or "forty lashes minus one" (2 Corinthians 11:24).

[Sidebar notes, left column:]

What did it mean that they were making the Sanhedrin guilty of Jesus' blood? (5:28)
The apostles preached that some of the Jews and their leaders were guilty of killing Jesus.

Who was Gamaliel? (5:34)
He was the most famous Jewish teacher of his time and was traditionally listed among the "heads of the schools." He was Paul's teacher.

How were the apostles flogged? (5:40)
They were whipped 39 times, or "forty lashes minus one" (2 Corinthians 11:24).

[Main column:]

²⁵Then someone came and said, "Look! The men you put in jail are standing in the temple courts teaching the people." ²⁶At that, the captain went with his officers and brought the apostles. They did not use force, because they feared that the people would stone them.

²⁷The apostles were brought in and made to appear before the Sanhedrin to be questioned by the high priest. ²⁸"We gave you strict orders not to teach in this name," he said. "Yet you have filled Jerusalem with your teaching and are determined to make us guilty of this man's blood."

²⁹Peter and the other apostles replied: "We must obey God rather than human beings! ³⁰The God of our ancestors raised Jesus from the dead—whom you killed by hanging him on a cross. ³¹God exalted him to his own right hand as Prince and Savior that he might bring Israel to repentance and forgive their sins. ³²We are witnesses of these things, and so is the Holy Spirit, whom God has given to those who obey him."

³³When they heard this, they were furious and wanted to put them to death. ³⁴But a Pharisee named Gamaliel, a teacher of the law, who was honored by all the people, stood up in the Sanhedrin and ordered that the men be put outside for a little while. ³⁵Then he addressed the Sanhedrin: "Men of Israel, consider carefully what you intend to do to these men. ³⁶Some time ago Theudas appeared, claiming to be somebody, and about four hundred men rallied to him. He was killed, all his followers were dispersed, and it all came to nothing. ³⁷After him, Judas the Galilean appeared in the days of the census and led a band of people in revolt. He too was killed, and all his followers were scattered. ³⁸Therefore, in the present case I advise you: Leave these men alone! Let them go! For if their purpose or activity is of human origin, it will fail. ³⁹But if it is from God, you will not be able to stop these men; you will only find yourselves fighting against God."

⁴⁰His speech persuaded them. They called the apostles in and had them flogged. Then they ordered them not to speak in the name of Jesus, and let them go.

⁴¹The apostles left the Sanhedrin, rejoicing because they had been counted worthy of suffering disgrace for the Name. ⁴²Day after day, in the temple courts and from house to house, they never stopped teaching and proclaiming the good news that Jesus is the Messiah.

THE CHOOSING OF THE SEVEN

6 In those days when the number of disciples was increasing, the Hellenistic Jews*ᵃ* among them complained against the Hebraic Jews because their widows were being overlooked in the daily distribution of food. ²So the Twelve gathered all the disciples together and said, "It would not be right for us to neglect the ministry of the word of God in order to wait on tables. ³Brothers and sisters, choose seven men from among you who are known to be full of the Spirit and wisdom. We will turn this responsibility over to them ⁴and will give our attention to prayer and the ministry of the word."

ᵃ 1 That is, Jews who had adopted the Greek language and culture

⁵This proposal pleased the whole group. They chose Stephen, a man full of faith and of the Holy Spirit; also Philip, Procorus, Nicanor, Timon, Parmenas, and Nicolas from Antioch, a convert to Judaism. ⁶They presented these men to the apostles, who prayed and laid their hands on them.

⁷So the word of God spread. The number of disciples in Jerusalem increased rapidly, and a large number of priests became obedient to the faith.

STEPHEN SEIZED

⁸Now Stephen, a man full of God's grace and power, performed great wonders and signs among the people. ⁹Opposition arose, however, from members of the Synagogue of the Freedmen (as it was called)—Jews of Cyrene and Alexandria as well as the provinces of Cilicia and Asia—who began to argue with Stephen. ¹⁰But they could not stand up against the wisdom the Spirit gave him as he spoke.

¹¹Then they secretly persuaded some men to say, "We have heard Stephen speak blasphemous words against Moses and against God."

¹²So they stirred up the people and the elders and the teachers of the law. They seized Stephen and brought him before the Sanhedrin. ¹³They produced false witnesses, who testified, "This fellow never stops speaking against this holy place and against the law. ¹⁴For we have heard him say that this Jesus of Nazareth will destroy this place and change the customs Moses handed down to us."

¹⁵All who were sitting in the Sanhedrin looked intently at Stephen, and they saw that his face was like the face of an angel.

STEPHEN'S SPEECH TO THE SANHEDRIN

7 Then the high priest asked Stephen, "Are these charges true?"

²To this he replied: "Brothers and fathers, listen to me! The God of glory appeared to our father Abraham while he was still in Mesopotamia, before he lived in Harran. ³'Leave your country and your people,' God said, 'and go to the land I will show you.'ᵃ

⁴"So he left the land of the Chaldeans and settled in Harran. After the death of his father, God sent him to this land where you are now living. ⁵He gave him no inheritance here, not even enough ground to set his foot on. But God promised him that he and his descendants after him would possess the land, even though at that time Abraham had no child. ⁶God spoke to him in this way: 'For four hundred years your descendants will be strangers in a country not their own, and they will be enslaved and mistreated. ⁷But I will punish the nation they serve as slaves,' God said, 'and afterward they will come out of that country and worship me in this place.'ᵇ ⁸Then he gave Abraham the covenant of circumcision. And Abraham became the father of Isaac and circumcised him eight days after his birth. Later Isaac became the father of Jacob, and Jacob became the father of the twelve patriarchs.

What did the laying on of hands represent? (6:6)
In the New Testament period, the laying on of hands was used for healing, blessing, ordaining or commissioning, and imparting spiritual gifts.

Why is it surprising that a large number of priests became converts? (6:7)
The priests may have been among the religious leaders who persecuted Jesus and looked for a way to kill him. Moreover, because of his sacrifice, Jesus had made their former responsibilities of sacrifice no longer necessary.

ᵃ 3 Gen. 12:1   ᵇ 7 Gen. 15:13,14

⁹"Because the patriarchs were jealous of Joseph, they sold him as a slave into Egypt. But God was with him ¹⁰and rescued him from all his troubles. He gave Joseph wisdom and enabled him to gain the goodwill of Pharaoh king of Egypt. So Pharaoh made him ruler over Egypt and all his palace.

¹¹"Then a famine struck all Egypt and Canaan, bringing great suffering, and our ancestors could not find food. ¹²When Jacob heard that there was grain in Egypt, he sent our forefathers on their first visit. ¹³On their second visit, Joseph told his brothers who he was, and Pharaoh learned about Joseph's family. ¹⁴After this, Joseph sent for his father Jacob and his whole family, seventy-five in all. ¹⁵Then Jacob went down to Egypt, where he and our ancestors died. ¹⁶Their bodies were brought back to Shechem and placed in the tomb that Abraham had bought from the sons of Hamor at Shechem for a certain sum of money.

¹⁷"As the time drew near for God to fulfill his promise to Abraham, the number of our people in Egypt had greatly increased. ¹⁸Then 'a new king, to whom Joseph meant nothing, came to power in Egypt.'ᵃ ¹⁹He dealt treacherously with our people and oppressed our ancestors by forcing them to throw out their newborn babies so that they would die.

²⁰"At that time Moses was born, and he was no ordinary child.ᵇ For three months he was cared for by his family. ²¹When he was placed outside, Pharaoh's daughter took him and brought him up as her own son. ²²Moses was educated in all the wisdom of the Egyptians and was powerful in speech and action.

²³"When Moses was forty years old, he decided to visit his own people, the Israelites. ²⁴He saw one of them being mistreated by an Egyptian, so he went to his defense and avenged him by killing the Egyptian. ²⁵Moses thought that his own people would realize that God was using him to rescue them, but they did not. ²⁶The next day Moses came upon two Israelites who were fighting. He tried to reconcile them by saying, 'Men, you are brothers; why do you want to hurt each other?'

²⁷"But the man who was mistreating the other pushed Moses aside and said, 'Who made you ruler and judge over us? ²⁸Are you thinking of killing me as you killed the Egyptian yesterday?'ᶜ ²⁹When Moses heard this, he fled to Midian, where he settled as a foreigner and had two sons.

³⁰"After forty years had passed, an angel appeared to Moses in the flames of a burning bush in the desert near Mount Sinai. ³¹When he saw this, he was amazed at the sight. As he went over to get a closer look, he heard the Lord say: ³²'I am the God of your fathers, the God of Abraham, Isaac and Jacob.'ᵈ Moses trembled with fear and did not dare to look.

³³"Then the Lord said to him, 'Take off your sandals, for the place where you are standing is holy ground. ³⁴I have indeed seen the oppression of my people in Egypt. I have heard their groaning and have come down to set them free. Now come, I will send you back to Egypt.'ᵉ

ᵃ 18 Exodus 1:8   ᵇ 20 Or was fair in the sight of God   ᶜ 28 Exodus 2:14
ᵈ 32 Exodus 3:6   ᵉ 34 Exodus 3:5,7,8,10

[35] "This is the same Moses they had rejected with the words, 'Who made you ruler and judge?' He was sent to be their ruler and deliverer by God himself, through the angel who appeared to him in the bush. [36] He led them out of Egypt and performed wonders and signs in Egypt, at the Red Sea and for forty years in the wilderness.

[37] "This is the Moses who told the Israelites, 'God will raise up for you a prophet like me from your own people.'[a] [38] He was in the assembly in the wilderness, with the angel who spoke to him on Mount Sinai, and with our ancestors; and he received living words to pass on to us.

[39] "But our ancestors refused to obey him. Instead, they rejected him and in their hearts turned back to Egypt. [40] They told Aaron, 'Make us gods who will go before us. As for this fellow Moses who led us out of Egypt—we don't know what has happened to him!'[b] [41] That was the time they made an idol in the form of a calf. They brought sacrifices to it and reveled in what their own hands had made. [42] But God turned away from them and gave them over to the worship of the sun, moon and stars. This agrees with what is written in the book of the prophets:

"'Did you bring me sacrifices and offerings
forty years in the wilderness, people of Israel?
[43] You have taken up the tabernacle of Molek
and the star of your god Rephan,
the idols you made to worship.
Therefore I will send you into exile'[c] beyond Babylon.

[44] "Our ancestors had the tabernacle of the covenant law with them in the wilderness. It had been made as God directed Moses, according to the pattern he had seen. [45] After receiving the tabernacle, our ancestors under Joshua brought it with them when they took the land from the nations God drove out before them. It remained in the land until the time of David, [46] who enjoyed God's favor and asked that he might provide a dwelling place for the God of Jacob.[d] [47] But it was Solomon who built a house for him.

[48] "However, the Most High does not live in houses made by human hands. As the prophet says:

[49] "'Heaven is my throne,
and the earth is my footstool.
What kind of house will you build for me?
says the Lord.
Or where will my resting place be?
[50] Has not my hand made all these things?'[e]

[51] "You stiff-necked people! Your hearts and ears are still uncircumcised. You are just like your ancestors: You always resist the Holy Spirit! [52] Was there ever a prophet your ancestors did not persecute? They even killed those who predicted the coming of the Righteous One. And now you have betrayed and murdered him— [53] you who have received the law that was given through angels but have not obeyed it."

[a] 37 Deut. 18:15   [b] 40 Exodus 32:1   [c] 43 Amos 5:25-27 (see Septuagint)   [d] 46 Some early manuscripts the house of Jacob
[e] 50 Isaiah 66:1,2

Why did Stephen review the history of the tabernacle and the temple? (7:44–50)
In his speech, Stephen took the opportunity to give a summary of the Old Testament and proclaim the truth of the gospel. He closed by reminding his listeners that worship of God was no longer restricted to the temple.

Why did Stephen say that the people had uncircumcised hearts and ears? (7:51)
Even though they were physically circumcised, they were not truly consecrated, or dedicated, to the Lord. Throughout their history, the Israelites had rejected and even persecuted prophets who had been sent to them.

THE STONING OF STEPHEN

⁵⁴When the members of the Sanhedrin heard this, they were furious and gnashed their teeth at him. ⁵⁵But Stephen, full of the Holy Spirit, looked up to heaven and saw the glory of God, and Jesus standing at the right hand of God. ⁵⁶"Look," he said, "I see heaven open and the Son of Man standing at the right hand of God."

⁵⁷At this they covered their ears and, yelling at the top of their voices, they all rushed at him, ⁵⁸dragged him out of the city and began to stone him. Meanwhile, the witnesses laid their coats at the feet of a young man named Saul.

⁵⁹While they were stoning him, Stephen prayed, "Lord Jesus, receive my spirit." ⁶⁰Then he fell on his knees and cried out, "Lord, do not hold this sin against them." When he had said this, he fell asleep.

8 And Saul approved of their killing him.

THE CHURCH PERSECUTED AND SCATTERED

On that day a great persecution broke out against the church in Jerusalem, and all except the apostles were scattered throughout Judea and Samaria. ²Godly men buried Stephen and mourned deeply for him. ³But Saul began to destroy the church. Going from house to house, he dragged off both men and women and put them in prison.

PHILIP IN SAMARIA

⁴Those who had been scattered preached the word wherever they went. ⁵Philip went down to a city in Samaria and proclaimed the Messiah there. ⁶When the crowds heard Philip and saw the signs he performed, they all paid close attention to what he said. ⁷For with shrieks, impure spirits came out of many, and many who were paralyzed or lame were healed. ⁸So there was great joy in that city.

SIMON THE SORCERER

⁹Now for some time a man named Simon had practiced sorcery in the city and amazed all the people of Samaria. He boasted that he was someone great, ¹⁰and all the people, both high and low, gave him their attention and exclaimed, "This man is rightly called the Great Power of God." ¹¹They followed him because he had amazed them for a long time with his sorcery. ¹²But when they believed Philip as he proclaimed the good news of the kingdom of God and the name of Jesus Christ, they were baptized, both men and women. ¹³Simon himself believed and was baptized. And he followed Philip everywhere, astonished by the great signs and miracles he saw.

¹⁴When the apostles in Jerusalem heard that Samaria had accepted the word of God, they sent Peter and John to Samaria. ¹⁵When they arrived, they prayed for the new believers there that they might receive the Holy Spirit, ¹⁶because the Holy Spirit had not yet come on any of them; they had simply been baptized in the name of the Lord Jesus. ¹⁷Then Peter and John placed their hands on them, and they received the Holy Spirit.

How was Saul involved? (7:58)
Some people believe that because they laid their clothes at the feet of Saul, he was in charge of the execution.

How did Stephen echo Jesus' words when he was dying? (7:60)
Like Jesus who asked the Father to forgive his executioners (Luke 23:34), Stephen asked God not to hold this sin against them.

How did persecution help spread the gospel? (8:1)
Because persecution broke out in Jerusalem, many of the believers scattered throughout Judea and Samaria, preaching the gospel wherever they went.

Philip's Journeys (8:15)

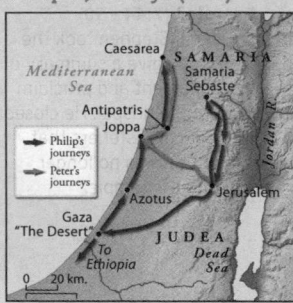

Who was Simon? (8:9)
He was a sorcerer who claimed to be either God or God's chief representative.

[18] When Simon saw that the Spirit was given at the laying on of the apostles' hands, he offered them money [19] and said, "Give me also this ability so that everyone on whom I lay my hands may receive the Holy Spirit."

[20] Peter answered: "May your money perish with you, because you thought you could buy the gift of God with money! [21] You have no part or share in this ministry, because your heart is not right before God. [22] Repent of this wickedness and pray to the Lord in the hope that he may forgive you for having such a thought in your heart. [23] For I see that you are full of bitterness and captive to sin."

[24] Then Simon answered, "Pray to the Lord for me so that nothing you have said may happen to me."

[25] After they had further proclaimed the word of the Lord and testified about Jesus, Peter and John returned to Jerusalem, preaching the gospel in many Samaritan villages.

PHILIP AND THE ETHIOPIAN

[26] Now an angel of the Lord said to Philip, "Go south to the road—the desert road—that goes down from Jerusalem to Gaza." [27] So he started out, and on his way he met an Ethiopian[a] eunuch, an important official in charge of all the treasury of the Kandake (which means "queen of the Ethiopians"). This man had gone to Jerusalem to worship, [28] and on his way home was sitting in his chariot reading the Book of Isaiah the prophet. [29] The Spirit told Philip, "Go to that chariot and stay near it."

[30] Then Philip ran up to the chariot and heard the man reading Isaiah the prophet. "Do you understand what you are reading?" Philip asked.

[31] "How can I," he said, "unless someone explains it to me?" So he invited Philip to come up and sit with him.

[32] This is the passage of Scripture the eunuch was reading:

"He was led like a sheep to the slaughter,
    and as a lamb before its shearer is silent,
    so he did not open his mouth.
[33] In his humiliation he was deprived of justice.
    Who can speak of his descendants?
    For his life was taken from the earth."[b]

[34] The eunuch asked Philip, "Tell me, please, who is the prophet talking about, himself or someone else?" [35] Then Philip began with that very passage of Scripture and told him the good news about Jesus.

[36] As they traveled along the road, they came to some water and the eunuch said, "Look, here is water. What can stand in the way of my being baptized?" [37][c] [38] And he gave orders to stop the chariot. Then both Philip and the eunuch went down into the water and Philip baptized him. [39] When they came up out of the water, the Spirit of the Lord suddenly took Philip away, and the eunuch did not see him again,

What was Simon's sin? (8:18–19)
Simon, who had boasted of his great powers, wanted to buy the magical power he thought the apostles had. He hoped to gain more power and praise for himself.

Why was the Ethiopian reading aloud? (8:30)
In ancient times, this was the usual custom.

---

[a] 27 That is, from the southern Nile region   [b] 33 Isaiah 53:7,8 (see Septuagint)   [c] 37 Some manuscripts include here Philip said, "If you believe with all your heart, you may." The eunuch answered, "I believe that Jesus Christ is the Son of God."

but went on his way rejoicing. [40]Philip, however, appeared at Azotus and traveled about, preaching the gospel in all the towns until he reached Caesarea.

SAUL'S CONVERSION

9 Meanwhile, Saul was still breathing out murderous threats against the Lord's disciples. He went to the high priest [2]and asked him for letters to the synagogues in Damascus, so that if he found any there who belonged to the Way, whether men or women, he might take them as prisoners to Jerusalem. [3]As he neared Damascus on his journey, suddenly a light from heaven flashed around him. [4]He fell to the ground and heard a voice say to him, "Saul, Saul, why do you persecute me?"

[5]"Who are you, Lord?" Saul asked.

"I am Jesus, whom you are persecuting," he replied. [6]"Now get up and go into the city, and you will be told what you must do."

[7]The men traveling with Saul stood there speechless; they heard the sound but did not see anyone. [8]Saul got up from the ground, but when he opened his eyes he could see nothing. So they led him by the hand into Damascus. [9]For three days he was blind, and did not eat or drink anything.

[10]In Damascus there was a disciple named Ananias. The Lord called to him in a vision, "Ananias!"

"Yes, Lord," he answered.

[11]The Lord told him, "Go to the house of Judas on Straight Street and ask for a man from Tarsus named Saul, for he is praying. [12]In a vision he has seen a man named Ananias come and place his hands on him to restore his sight."

[13]"Lord," Ananias answered, "I have heard many reports about this man and all the harm he has done to your holy people in Jerusalem. [14]And he has come here with authority from the chief priests to arrest all who call on your name."

[15]But the Lord said to Ananias, "Go! This man is my chosen instrument to proclaim my name to the Gentiles and their kings and to the people of Israel. [16]I will show him how much he must suffer for my name."

[17]Then Ananias went to the house and entered it. Placing his hands on Saul, he said, "Brother Saul, the Lord—Jesus, who appeared to you on the road as you were coming here—has sent me so that you may see again and be filled with the Holy Spirit." [18]Immediately, something like scales fell from Saul's eyes, and he could see again. He got up and was baptized, [19]and after taking some food, he regained his strength.

SAUL IN DAMASCUS AND JERUSALEM

Saul spent several days with the disciples in Damascus. [20]At once he began to preach in the synagogues that Jesus is the Son of God. [21]All those who heard him were astonished and asked, "Isn't he the man who raised havoc in Jerusalem among those who call on this name? And hasn't he come here to take them as prisoners to the chief priests?" [22]Yet Saul grew more and more powerful and baffled the Jews living in Damascus by proving that Jesus is the Messiah.

What was the Way? (9:2)
This term for Christianity appears several times in Acts.

Saul in Damascus (9:3)

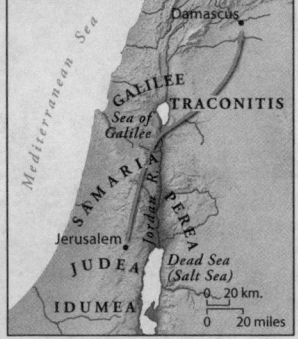

How would a Jewish person interpret a voice from heaven? (9:4–5)
In the rabbinic tradition, this would have been understood as being the voice of God himself.

Where did Saul focus his preaching? (9:20)
Saul's regular practice was to preach at every opportunity in the synagogues.

²³After many days had gone by, there was a conspiracy among the Jews to kill him, ²⁴but Saul learned of their plan. Day and night they kept close watch on the city gates in order to kill him. ²⁵But his followers took him by night and lowered him in a basket through an opening in the wall.

²⁶When he came to Jerusalem, he tried to join the disciples, but they were all afraid of him, not believing that he really was a disciple. ²⁷But Barnabas took him and brought him to the apostles. He told them how Saul on his journey had seen the Lord and that the Lord had spoken to him, and how in Damascus he had preached fearlessly in the name of Jesus. ²⁸So Saul stayed with them and moved about freely in Jerusalem, speaking boldly in the name of the Lord. ²⁹He talked and debated with the Hellenistic Jews,ᵃ but they tried to kill him. ³⁰When the believers learned of this, they took him down to Caesarea and sent him off to Tarsus.

³¹Then the church throughout Judea, Galilee and Samaria enjoyed a time of peace and was strengthened. Living in the fear of the Lord and encouraged by the Holy Spirit, it increased in numbers.

AENEAS AND DORCAS

³²As Peter traveled about the country, he went to visit the Lord's people who lived in Lydda. ³³There he found a man named Aeneas, who was paralyzed and had been bedridden for eight years. ³⁴"Aeneas," Peter said to him, "Jesus Christ heals you. Get up and roll up your mat." Immediately Aeneas got up. ³⁵All those who lived in Lydda and Sharon saw him and turned to the Lord.

³⁶In Joppa there was a disciple named Tabitha (in Greek her name is Dorcas); she was always doing good and helping the poor. ³⁷About that time she became sick and died, and her body was washed and placed in an upstairs room. ³⁸Lydda was near Joppa; so when the disciples heard that Peter was in Lydda, they sent two men to him and urged him, "Please come at once!"

³⁹Peter went with them, and when he arrived he was taken upstairs to the room. All the widows stood around him, crying and showing him the robes and other clothing that Dorcas had made while she was still with them.

⁴⁰Peter sent them all out of the room; then he got down on his knees and prayed. Turning toward the dead woman, he said, "Tabitha, get up." She opened her eyes, and seeing Peter she sat up. ⁴¹He took her by the hand and helped her to her feet. Then he called for the believers, especially the widows, and presented her to them alive. ⁴²This became known all over Joppa, and many people believed in the Lord. ⁴³Peter stayed in Joppa for some time with a tanner named Simon.

CORNELIUS CALLS FOR PETER

10 At Caesarea there was a man named Cornelius, a centurion in what was known as the Italian Regiment. ²He and all his family were devout and God-fearing; he gave generously to those in need and prayed to God regularly.

ᵃ 29 That is, Jews who had adopted the Greek language and culture

Saul in Tarsus (9:30)

What does the term church refer to here? (9:31)
This does not refer to individual congregations but to the whole body of believers throughout the region.

What were the burial customs? (9:37)
The body was washed in preparation for burial, a custom followed by both Jews and Greeks. If burial was delayed, the body was usually laid in an upper room. In Jerusalem, the body had to be buried the day the person died, but outside Jerusalem up to three days were allowed for burial.

Why would Peter stay with a tanner? (9:43)
Tanners treated the skins of dead animals. Since the Jews considered contact with dead animals as unclean, Peter's decision to stay with Simon shows that he was willing to put aside Jewish prejudice and reach out in his ministry to the Gentiles.

What was a centurion? (10:1)
This was a Roman soldier who commanded a military unit that included at least 100 soldiers.

Who were God-fearers? (10:2)
They were non-Jews who believed in God, attended the synagogue, and respected Jewish teachings. However, they did not practice all the Jewish customs such as circumcision.

³One day at about three in the afternoon he had a vision. He distinctly saw an angel of God, who came to him and said, "Cornelius!"

⁴Cornelius stared at him in fear. "What is it, Lord?" he asked.

The angel answered, "Your prayers and gifts to the poor have come up as a memorial offering before God. ⁵Now send men to Joppa to bring back a man named Simon who is called Peter. ⁶He is staying with Simon the tanner, whose house is by the sea."

⁷When the angel who spoke to him had gone, Cornelius called two of his servants and a devout soldier who was one of his attendants. ⁸He told them everything that had happened and sent them to Joppa.

PETER'S VISION

⁹About noon the following day as they were on their journey and approaching the city, Peter went up on the roof to pray. ¹⁰He became hungry and wanted something to eat, and while the meal was being prepared, he fell into a trance. ¹¹He saw heaven opened and something like a large sheet being let down to earth by its four corners. ¹²It contained all kinds of four-footed animals, as well as reptiles and birds. ¹³Then a voice told him, "Get up, Peter. Kill and eat."

¹⁴"Surely not, Lord!" Peter replied. "I have never eaten anything impure or unclean."

¹⁵The voice spoke to him a second time, "Do not call anything impure that God has made clean."

¹⁶This happened three times, and immediately the sheet was taken back to heaven.

¹⁷While Peter was wondering about the meaning of the vision, the men sent by Cornelius found out where Simon's house was and stopped at the gate. ¹⁸They called out, asking if Simon who was known as Peter was staying there.

¹⁹While Peter was still thinking about the vision, the Spirit said to him, "Simon, three*ᵃ* men are looking for you. ²⁰So get up and go downstairs. Do not hesitate to go with them, for I have sent them."

²¹Peter went down and said to the men, "I'm the one you're looking for. Why have you come?"

²²The men replied, "We have come from Cornelius the centurion. He is a righteous and God-fearing man, who is respected by all the Jewish people. A holy angel told him to ask you to come to his house so that he could hear what you have to say." ²³Then Peter invited the men into the house to be his guests.

PETER AT CORNELIUS'S HOUSE

The next day Peter started out with them, and some of the believers from Joppa went along. ²⁴The following day he arrived in Caesarea. Cornelius was expecting them and had called together his relatives and close friends. ²⁵As Peter entered the house, Cornelius met him and fell at his feet in reverence. ²⁶But Peter made him get up. "Stand up," he said, "I am only a man myself."

Why was it significant that Peter provided lodging for these men? (10:23)
Peter was already taking the first step toward accepting Gentiles. Such a close relationship with Gentiles was contrary to Jewish practice.

Peter in Caesarea (10:24)

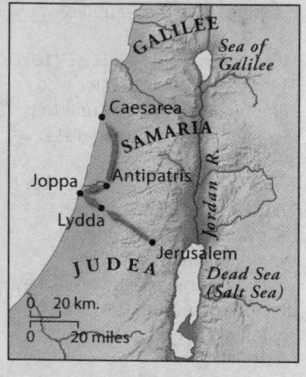

ᵃ 19 One early manuscript two; other manuscripts do not have the number.

²⁷While talking with him, Peter went inside and found a large gathering of people. ²⁸He said to them: "You are well aware that it is against our law for a Jew to associate with or visit a Gentile. But God has shown me that I should not call anyone impure or unclean. ²⁹So when I was sent for, I came without raising any objection. May I ask why you sent for me?"

³⁰Cornelius answered: "Three days ago I was in my house praying at this hour, at three in the afternoon. Suddenly a man in shining clothes stood before me ³¹and said, 'Cornelius, God has heard your prayer and remembered your gifts to the poor. ³²Send to Joppa for Simon who is called Peter. He is a guest in the home of Simon the tanner, who lives by the sea.' ³³So I sent for you immediately, and it was good of you to come. Now we are all here in the presence of God to listen to everything the Lord has commanded you to tell us."

³⁴Then Peter began to speak: "I now realize how true it is that God does not show favoritism ³⁵but accepts from every nation the one who fears him and does what is right. ³⁶You know the message God sent to the people of Israel, announcing the good news of peace through Jesus Christ, who is Lord of all. ³⁷You know what has happened throughout the province of Judea, beginning in Galilee after the baptism that John preached— ³⁸how God anointed Jesus of Nazareth with the Holy Spirit and power, and how he went around doing good and healing all who were under the power of the devil, because God was with him.

³⁹"We are witnesses of everything he did in the country of the Jews and in Jerusalem. They killed him by hanging him on a cross, ⁴⁰but God raised him from the dead on the third day and caused him to be seen. ⁴¹He was not seen by all the people, but by witnesses whom God had already chosen—by us who ate and drank with him after he rose from the dead. ⁴²He commanded us to preach to the people and to testify that he is the one whom God appointed as judge of the living and the dead. ⁴³All the prophets testify about him that everyone who believes in him receives forgiveness of sins through his name."

⁴⁴While Peter was still speaking these words, the Holy Spirit came on all who heard the message. ⁴⁵The circumcised believers who had come with Peter were astonished that the gift of the Holy Spirit had been poured out even on Gentiles. ⁴⁶For they heard them speaking in tongues*a* and praising God.

Then Peter said, ⁴⁷"Surely no one can stand in the way of their being baptized with water. They have received the Holy Spirit just as we have." ⁴⁸So he ordered that they be baptized in the name of Jesus Christ. Then they asked Peter to stay with them for a few days.

PETER EXPLAINS HIS ACTIONS

11 The apostles and the believers throughout Judea heard that the Gentiles also had received the word of God. ²So when Peter went up to Jerusalem, the circumcised believers criticized him ³and said, "You went into the house of uncircumcised men and ate with them."

a 46 Or other languages

What had God revealed to Peter? (10:28)
By way of the vision, God showed Peter that the barrier between Jews and Gentiles had been removed.

What was the sign that the Gentiles had received the Holy Spirit? (10:46)
They began speaking in tongues just as the apostles had on Pentecost.

[4] Starting from the beginning, Peter told them the whole story: [5] "I was in the city of Joppa praying, and in a trance I saw a vision. I saw something like a large sheet being let down from heaven by its four corners, and it came down to where I was. [6] I looked into it and saw four-footed animals of the earth, wild beasts, reptiles and birds. [7] Then I heard a voice telling me, 'Get up, Peter. Kill and eat.'

[8] "I replied, 'Surely not, Lord! Nothing impure or unclean has ever entered my mouth.'

[9] "The voice spoke from heaven a second time, 'Do not call anything impure that God has made clean.' [10] This happened three times, and then it was all pulled up to heaven again.

[11] "Right then three men who had been sent to me from Caesarea stopped at the house where I was staying. [12] The Spirit told me to have no hesitation about going with them. These six brothers also went with me, and we entered the man's house. [13] He told us how he had seen an angel appear in his house and say, 'Send to Joppa for Simon who is called Peter. [14] He will bring you a message through which you and all your household will be saved.'

[15] "As I began to speak, the Holy Spirit came on them as he had come on us at the beginning. [16] Then I remembered what the Lord had said: 'John baptized with[a] water, but you will be baptized with[a] the Holy Spirit.' [17] So if God gave them the same gift he gave us who believed in the Lord Jesus Christ, who was I to think that I could stand in God's way?"

[18] When they heard this, they had no further objections and praised God, saying, "So then, even to Gentiles God has granted repentance that leads to life."

THE CHURCH IN ANTIOCH

[19] Now those who had been scattered by the persecution that broke out when Stephen was killed traveled as far as Phoenicia, Cyprus and Antioch, spreading the word only among Jews. [20] Some of them, however, men from Cyprus and Cyrene, went to Antioch and began to speak to Greeks also, telling them the good news about the Lord Jesus. [21] The Lord's hand was with them, and a great number of people believed and turned to the Lord.

[22] News of this reached the church in Jerusalem, and they sent Barnabas to Antioch. [23] When he arrived and saw what the grace of God had done, he was glad and encouraged them all to remain true to the Lord with all their hearts. [24] He was a good man, full of the Holy Spirit and faith, and a great number of people were brought to the Lord.

[25] Then Barnabas went to Tarsus to look for Saul, [26] and when he found him, he brought him to Antioch. So for a whole year Barnabas and Saul met with the church and taught great numbers of people. The disciples were called Christians first at Antioch.

[27] During this time some prophets came down from Jerusalem to Antioch. [28] One of them, named Agabus, stood up and through the Spirit predicted that a severe famine would spread over the entire Roman world. (This happened during

Why did Peter say he could not stand in God's way? (11:17) Since God had given the Gentiles the gift of the Holy Spirit, he could not deny their request to be baptized.

Where did the term *Christian* come from? (11:26) It isn't clear whether the term was first used by believers or was used in a negative way by nonbelievers. Literally, the word means *little messiahs* or *belonging to Christ*.

[a] *16* Or *in*

the reign of Claudius.) ²⁹The disciples, as each one was able, decided to provide help for the brothers and sisters living in Judea. ³⁰This they did, sending their gift to the elders by Barnabas and Saul.

PETER'S MIRACULOUS ESCAPE FROM PRISON

12 It was about this time that King Herod arrested some who belonged to the church, intending to persecute them. ²He had James, the brother of John, put to death with the sword. ³When he saw that this met with approval among the Jews, he proceeded to seize Peter also. This happened during the Festival of Unleavened Bread. ⁴After arresting him, he put him in prison, handing him over to be guarded by four squads of four soldiers each. Herod intended to bring him out for public trial after the Passover.

⁵So Peter was kept in prison, but the church was earnestly praying to God for him.

⁶The night before Herod was to bring him to trial, Peter was sleeping between two soldiers, bound with two chains, and sentries stood guard at the entrance. ⁷Suddenly an angel of the Lord appeared and a light shone in the cell. He struck Peter on the side and woke him up. "Quick, get up!" he said, and the chains fell off Peter's wrists.

⁸Then the angel said to him, "Put on your clothes and sandals." And Peter did so. "Wrap your cloak around you and follow me," the angel told him. ⁹Peter followed him out of the prison, but he had no idea that what the angel was doing was really happening; he thought he was seeing a vision. ¹⁰They passed the first and second guards and came to the iron gate leading to the city. It opened for them by itself, and they went through it. When they had walked the length of one street, suddenly the angel left him.

¹¹Then Peter came to himself and said, "Now I know without a doubt that the Lord has sent his angel and rescued me from Herod's clutches and from everything the Jewish people were hoping would happen."

¹²When this had dawned on him, he went to the house of Mary the mother of John, also called Mark, where many people had gathered and were praying. ¹³Peter knocked at the outer entrance, and a servant named Rhoda came to answer the door. ¹⁴When she recognized Peter's voice, she was so overjoyed she ran back without opening it and exclaimed, "Peter is at the door!"

¹⁵"You're out of your mind," they told her. When she kept insisting that it was so, they said, "It must be his angel."

¹⁶But Peter kept on knocking, and when they opened the door and saw him, they were astonished. ¹⁷Peter motioned with his hand for them to be quiet and described how the Lord had brought him out of prison. "Tell James and the other brothers and sisters about this," he said, and then he left for another place.

¹⁸In the morning, there was no small commotion among the soldiers as to what had become of Peter. ¹⁹After Herod had a thorough search made for him and did not find him, he cross-examined the guards and ordered that they be executed.

Who were the elders? (11:30) This is the first reference to elders in Acts. Since the apostles are not mentioned, they may have been absent from Jerusalem at this time.

Who was James? (12:2) James was the brother of John and the son of Zebedee (see Matthew 4:21).

What were the four squads? (12:4) This was one company, or group, of four soldiers for each of the four watches of the night.

What was this light? (12:7) This was the glory of the Lord (see Luke 2:9).

HEROD'S DEATH

Then Herod went from Judea to Caesarea and stayed there. ²⁰He had been quarreling with the people of Tyre and Sidon; they now joined together and sought an audience with him. After securing the support of Blastus, a trusted personal servant of the king, they asked for peace, because they depended on the king's country for their food supply.

²¹On the appointed day Herod, wearing his royal robes, sat on his throne and delivered a public address to the people. ²²They shouted, "This is the voice of a god, not of a man." ²³Immediately, because Herod did not give praise to God, an angel of the Lord struck him down, and he was eaten by worms and died.

²⁴But the word of God continued to spread and flourish.

BARNABAS AND SAUL SENT OFF

²⁵When Barnabas and Saul had finished their mission, they returned from*a* Jerusalem, taking with them John, also **13** called Mark. ¹Now in the church at Antioch there were prophets and teachers: Barnabas, Simeon called Niger, Lucius of Cyrene, Manaen (who had been brought up

a 25 Some manuscripts to

Why did God kill Herod? (12:21–23)
When the crowd referred to him as a god, he did not deny it, so God struck him dead.

PAUL'S FIRST MISSIONARY JOURNEY (13:4 – 14:28)

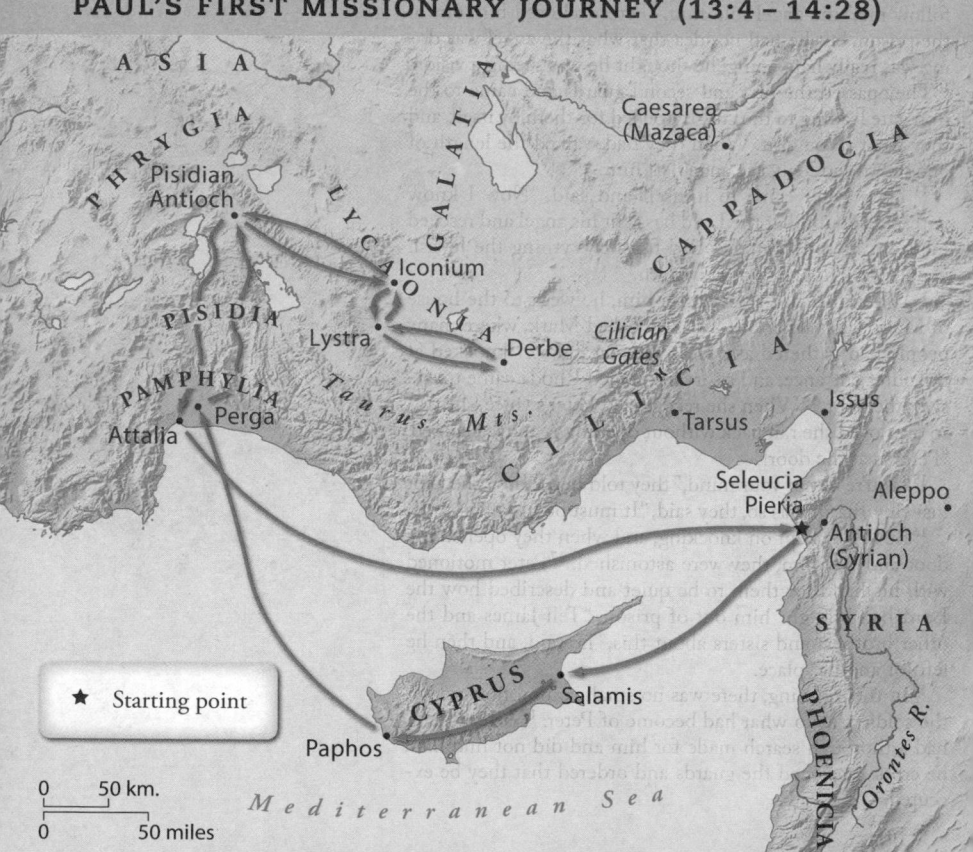

with Herod the tetrarch) and Saul. ²While they were worshiping the Lord and fasting, the Holy Spirit said, "Set apart for me Barnabas and Saul for the work to which I have called them." ³So after they had fasted and prayed, they placed their hands on them and sent them off.

ON CYPRUS

⁴The two of them, sent on their way by the Holy Spirit, went down to Seleucia and sailed from there to Cyprus. ⁵When they arrived at Salamis, they proclaimed the word of God in the Jewish synagogues. John was with them as their helper.

⁶They traveled through the whole island until they came to Paphos. There they met a Jewish sorcerer and false prophet named Bar-Jesus, ⁷who was an attendant of the proconsul, Sergius Paulus. The proconsul, an intelligent man, sent for Barnabas and Saul because he wanted to hear the word of God. ⁸But Elymas the sorcerer (for that is what his name means) opposed them and tried to turn the proconsul from the faith. ⁹Then Saul, who was also called Paul, filled with the Holy Spirit, looked straight at Elymas and said, ¹⁰"You are a child of the devil and an enemy of everything that is right! You are full of all kinds of deceit and trickery. Will you never stop perverting the right ways of the Lord? ¹¹Now the hand of the Lord is against you. You are going to be blind for a time, not even able to see the light of the sun."

Immediately mist and darkness came over him, and he groped about, seeking someone to lead him by the hand. ¹²When the proconsul saw what had happened, he believed, for he was amazed at the teaching about the Lord.

IN PISIDIAN ANTIOCH

¹³From Paphos, Paul and his companions sailed to Perga in Pamphylia, where John left them to return to Jerusalem. ¹⁴From Perga they went on to Pisidian Antioch. On the Sabbath they entered the synagogue and sat down. ¹⁵After the reading from the Law and the Prophets, the leaders of the synagogue sent word to them, saying, "Brothers, if you have a word of exhortation for the people, please speak."

¹⁶Standing up, Paul motioned with his hand and said: "Fellow Israelites and you Gentiles who worship God, listen to me! ¹⁷The God of the people of Israel chose our ancestors; he made the people prosper during their stay in Egypt; with mighty power he led them out of that country; ¹⁸for about forty years he endured their conduct* in the wilderness; ¹⁹and he overthrew seven nations in Canaan, giving their land to his people as their inheritance. ²⁰All this took about 450 years.

"After this, God gave them judges until the time of Samuel the prophet. ²¹Then the people asked for a king, and he gave them Saul son of Kish, of the tribe of Benjamin, who ruled forty years. ²²After removing Saul, he made David their king. God testified concerning him: 'I have found

---

ᵃ 18 Some manuscripts he cared for them

Why was Saul's name changed? (13:9)
Jews at this time often had two names: a Hebrew name (in this case Saul) and a Greek-Roman name (Paul). Paul began to refer to himself as Paul from this point on, perhaps because of his mission to reach Gentiles.

Why did Paul begin his preaching in the synagogue? (13:14)
He was attempting to reach both Jews and Gentiles with the gospel message. The synagogues were a good place to preach because regular meetings were held there, and they attracted people who knew the Old Testament. It was customary to invite visiting rabbis like Paul to speak in the synagogues.

What was a typical synagogue service like? (13:15)
Sections of the Old Testament were read, and then people offered explanations and encouragement.

David son of Jesse, a man after my own heart; he will do everything I want him to do.'

²³ "From this man's descendants God has brought to Israel the Savior Jesus, as he promised. ²⁴ Before the coming of Jesus, John preached repentance and baptism to all the people of Israel. ²⁵ As John was completing his work, he said: 'Who do you suppose I am? I am not the one you are looking for. But there is one coming after me whose sandals I am not worthy to untie.'

²⁶ "Fellow children of Abraham and you God-fearing Gentiles, it is to us that this message of salvation has been sent. ²⁷ The people of Jerusalem and their rulers did not recognize Jesus, yet in condemning him they fulfilled the words of the prophets that are read every Sabbath. ²⁸ Though they found no proper ground for a death sentence, they asked Pilate to have him executed. ²⁹ When they had carried out all that was written about him, they took him down from the cross and laid him in a tomb. ³⁰ But God raised him from the dead, ³¹ and for many days he was seen by those who had traveled with him from Galilee to Jerusalem. They are now his witnesses to our people.

³² "We tell you the good news: What God promised our ancestors ³³ he has fulfilled for us, their children, by raising up Jesus. As it is written in the second Psalm:

"'You are my son;
      today I have become your father.'ᵃ

³⁴ God raised him from the dead so that he will never be subject to decay. As God has said,

"'I will give you the holy and sure blessings promised
      to David.'ᵇ

³⁵ So it is also stated elsewhere:

"'You will not let your holy one see decay.'ᶜ

³⁶ "Now when David had served God's purpose in his own generation, he fell asleep; he was buried with his ancestors and his body decayed. ³⁷ But the one whom God raised from the dead did not see decay.

³⁸ "Therefore, my friends, I want you to know that through Jesus the forgiveness of sins is proclaimed to you. ³⁹ Through him everyone who believes is set free from every sin, a justification you were not able to obtain under the law of Moses. ⁴⁰ Take care that what the prophets have said does not happen to you:

⁴¹ "'Look, you scoffers,
      wonder and perish,
for I am going to do something in your days
      that you would never believe,
      even if someone told you.'ᵈ"

⁴² As Paul and Barnabas were leaving the synagogue, the people invited them to speak further about these things on the next Sabbath. ⁴³ When the congregation was dismissed,

What is justification? (13:39)
A person who believes in Jesus and asks for forgiveness is justified, or declared sinless, through Christ's death on the cross for our sins.

ᵃ 33 Psalm 2:7   ᵇ 34 Isaiah 55:3   ᶜ 35 Psalm 16:10 (see Septuagint)
ᵈ 41 Hab. 1:5

many of the Jews and devout converts to Judaism followed Paul and Barnabas, who talked with them and urged them to continue in the grace of God.

⁴⁴On the next Sabbath almost the whole city gathered to hear the word of the Lord. ⁴⁵When the Jews saw the crowds, they were filled with jealousy. They began to contradict what Paul was saying and heaped abuse on him.

⁴⁶Then Paul and Barnabas answered them boldly: "We had to speak the word of God to you first. Since you reject it and do not consider yourselves worthy of eternal life, we now turn to the Gentiles. ⁴⁷For this is what the Lord has commanded us:

"'I have made you*a* a light for the Gentiles,
    that you*a* may bring salvation to the ends of the
        earth.'*b*"

⁴⁸When the Gentiles heard this, they were glad and honored the word of the Lord; and all who were appointed for eternal life believed.

⁴⁹The word of the Lord spread through the whole region. ⁵⁰But the Jewish leaders incited the God-fearing women of high standing and the leading men of the city. They stirred up persecution against Paul and Barnabas, and expelled them from their region. ⁵¹So they shook the dust off their feet as a warning to them and went to Iconium. ⁵²And the disciples were filled with joy and with the Holy Spirit.

IN ICONIUM

14 At Iconium Paul and Barnabas went as usual into the Jewish synagogue. There they spoke so effectively that a great number of Jews and Greeks believed. ²But the Jews who refused to believe stirred up the other Gentiles and poisoned their minds against the brothers. ³So Paul and Barnabas spent considerable time there, speaking boldly for the Lord, who confirmed the message of his grace by enabling them to perform signs and wonders. ⁴The people of the city were divided; some sided with the Jews, others with the apostles. ⁵There was a plot afoot among both Gentiles and Jews, together with their leaders, to mistreat them and stone them. ⁶But they found out about it and fled to the Lycaonian cities of Lystra and Derbe and to the surrounding country, ⁷where they continued to preach the gospel.

IN LYSTRA AND DERBE

⁸In Lystra there sat a man who was lame. He had been that way from birth and had never walked. ⁹He listened to Paul as he was speaking. Paul looked directly at him, saw that he had faith to be healed ¹⁰and called out, "Stand up on your feet!" At that, the man jumped up and began to walk.

¹¹When the crowd saw what Paul had done, they shouted in the Lycaonian language, "The gods have come down to us in human form!" ¹²Barnabas they called Zeus, and Paul they called Hermes because he was the chief speaker. ¹³The priest of Zeus, whose temple was just outside the city, brought bulls

---

a 47 The Greek is singular.   *b 47* Isaiah 49:6

What did it mean for them to shake the dust off their feet? (13:51)
This was a symbolic act to show that they were not responsible for the community that had persecuted them. Here it also represented a solemn warning to those who rejected God's message.

Who were Zeus and Hermes? (14:12)
Zeus was the patron god of the city, and Hermes was the Greek name for the Roman god Mercury.

and wreaths to the city gates because he and the crowd wanted to offer sacrifices to them.

[14] But when the apostles Barnabas and Paul heard of this, they tore their clothes and rushed out into the crowd, shouting: [15] "Friends, why are you doing this? We too are only human, like you. We are bringing you good news, telling you to turn from these worthless things to the living God, who made the heavens and the earth and the sea and everything in them. [16] In the past, he let all nations go their own way. [17] Yet he has not left himself without testimony: He has shown kindness by giving you rain from heaven and crops in their seasons; he provides you with plenty of food and fills your hearts with joy." [18] Even with these words, they had difficulty keeping the crowd from sacrificing to them.

[19] Then some Jews came from Antioch and Iconium and won the crowd over. They stoned Paul and dragged him outside the city, thinking he was dead. [20] But after the disciples had gathered around him, he got up and went back into the city. The next day he and Barnabas left for Derbe.

THE RETURN TO ANTIOCH IN SYRIA

[21] They preached the gospel in that city and won a large number of disciples. Then they returned to Lystra, Iconium and Antioch, [22] strengthening the disciples and encouraging them to remain true to the faith. "We must go through many hardships to enter the kingdom of God," they said. [23] Paul and Barnabas appointed elders[a] for them in each church and, with prayer and fasting, committed them to the Lord, in whom they had put their trust. [24] After going through Pisidia, they came into Pamphylia, [25] and when they had preached the word in Perga, they went down to Attalia.

[26] From Attalia they sailed back to Antioch, where they had been committed to the grace of God for the work they had now completed. [27] On arriving there, they gathered the church together and reported all that God had done through them and how he had opened a door of faith to the Gentiles. [28] And they stayed there a long time with the disciples.

THE COUNCIL AT JERUSALEM

15 Certain people came down from Judea to Antioch and were teaching the believers: "Unless you are circumcised, according to the custom taught by Moses, you cannot be saved." [2] This brought Paul and Barnabas into sharp dispute and debate with them. So Paul and Barnabas were appointed, along with some other believers, to go up to Jerusalem to see the apostles and elders about this question. [3] The church sent them on their way, and as they traveled through Phoenicia and Samaria, they told how the Gentiles had been converted. This news made all the believers very glad. [4] When they came to Jerusalem, they were welcomed by the church and the apostles and elders, to whom they reported everything God had done through them.

[5] Then some of the believers who belonged to the party of

How long did they stay in Antioch? (14:28)
They probably stayed there more than a year.

---

[a] 23 Or *Barnabas ordained elders*; or *Barnabas had elders elected*

the Pharisees stood up and said, "The Gentiles must be circumcised and required to keep the law of Moses."

⁶The apostles and elders met to consider this question. ⁷After much discussion, Peter got up and addressed them: "Brothers, you know that some time ago God made a choice among you that the Gentiles might hear from my lips the message of the gospel and believe. ⁸God, who knows the heart, showed that he accepted them by giving the Holy Spirit to them, just as he did to us. ⁹He did not discriminate between us and them, for he purified their hearts by faith. ¹⁰Now then, why do you try to test God by putting on the necks of Gentiles a yoke that neither we nor our ancestors have been able to bear? ¹¹No! We believe it is through the grace of our Lord Jesus that we are saved, just as they are."

¹²The whole assembly became silent as they listened to Barnabas and Paul telling about the signs and wonders God had done among the Gentiles through them. ¹³When they finished, James spoke up. "Brothers," he said, "listen to me. ¹⁴Simon*ᵃ* has described to us how God first intervened to choose a people for his name from the Gentiles. ¹⁵The words of the prophets are in agreement with this, as it is written:

¹⁶"'After this I will return
    and rebuild David's fallen tent.
  Its ruins I will rebuild,
    and I will restore it,
¹⁷that the rest of mankind may seek the Lord,
    even all the Gentiles who bear my name,
  says the Lord, who does these things'ᵇ—
¹⁸   things known from long ago.'ᶜ

¹⁹"It is my judgment, therefore, that we should not make it difficult for the Gentiles who are turning to God. ²⁰Instead we should write to them, telling them to abstain from food polluted by idols, from sexual immorality, from the meat of strangled animals and from blood. ²¹For the law of Moses has been preached in every city from the earliest times and is read in the synagogues on every Sabbath."

THE COUNCIL'S LETTER TO GENTILE BELIEVERS

²²Then the apostles and elders, with the whole church, decided to choose some of their own men and send them to Antioch with Paul and Barnabas. They chose Judas (called Barsabbas) and Silas, men who were leaders among the believers. ²³With them they sent the following letter:

The apostles and elders, your brothers,

To the Gentile believers in Antioch, Syria and Cilicia:

Greetings.

²⁴We have heard that some went out from us without our authorization and disturbed you, troubling your

What was this yoke? (15:10)
This yoke was the law, which put an unnecessary burden on the people.

How did Peter say that salvation was accomplished? (15:11)
Peter explained that salvation came not through the law but by grace.

ᵃ *14* Greek *Simeon*, a variant of *Simon*; that is, Peter   ᵇ *17* Amos 9:11,12 (see Septuagint)   ᶜ *17,18* Some manuscripts *things'—* / *¹⁸the Lord's work is known to him from long ago*

minds by what they said. ²⁵So we all agreed to choose some men and send them to you with our dear friends Barnabas and Paul— ²⁶men who have risked their lives for the name of our Lord Jesus Christ. ²⁷Therefore we are sending Judas and Silas to confirm by word of mouth what we are writing. ²⁸It seemed good to the Holy Spirit and to us not to burden you with anything beyond the following requirements: ²⁹You are to abstain from food sacrificed to idols, from blood, from the meat of strangled animals and from sexual immorality. You will do well to avoid these things.

Farewell.

³⁰So the men were sent off and went down to Antioch, where they gathered the church together and delivered the letter. ³¹The people read it and were glad for its encouraging message. ³²Judas and Silas, who themselves were prophets, said much to encourage and strengthen the believers. ³³After spending some time there, they were sent off by the believers with the blessing of peace to return to those who had sent them. [³⁴]ᵃ ³⁵But Paul and Barnabas remained in Antioch, where they and many others taught and preached the word of the Lord.

DISAGREEMENT BETWEEN PAUL AND BARNABAS

³⁶Some time later Paul said to Barnabas, "Let us go back and visit the believers in all the towns where we preached the word of the Lord and see how they are doing." ³⁷Barnabas wanted to take John, also called Mark, with them, ³⁸but Paul did not think it wise to take him, because he had deserted them in Pamphylia and had not continued with them in the work. ³⁹They had such a sharp disagreement that they parted company. Barnabas took Mark and sailed for Cyprus, ⁴⁰but Paul chose Silas and left, commended by the believers to the grace of the Lord. ⁴¹He went through Syria and Cilicia, strengthening the churches.

TIMOTHY JOINS PAUL AND SILAS

16 Paul came to Derbe and then to Lystra, where a disciple named Timothy lived, whose mother was Jewish and a believer but whose father was a Greek. ²The believers

---

ᵃ *34 Some manuscripts include here* But Silas decided to remain there.

What must a person do to be saved?

This was the question that the jailer asked Paul and Silas. Their answer was simple: Believe in Jesus. This is like the truth of the gospel that is contained in John 3:16: "For God so loved the world that he gave his one and only Son, that whoever believes in him shall not perish but have eternal life." The only requirement for salvation is faith in Jesus. The Holy Spirit works in a person's heart before a person is able to believe in Jesus, but a person must also accept the grace that God has given.

The Holy Spirit continues to work in the hearts of those who are children of God, helping them to become more godly in the way they live their lives. Christians need to try to follow God's law, not in order to earn salvation, but as a way of showing how thankful they are for God's love. Christians also need to show God's love to others as a way of witnessing to others that God is gracious.

at Lystra and Iconium spoke well of him. ³Paul wanted to take him along on the journey, so he circumcised him because of the Jews who lived in that area, for they all knew that his father was a Greek. ⁴As they traveled from town to town, they delivered the decisions reached by the apostles and elders in Jerusalem for the people to obey. ⁵So the churches were strengthened in the faith and grew daily in numbers.

PAUL'S VISION OF THE MAN OF MACEDONIA

⁶Paul and his companions traveled throughout the region of Phrygia and Galatia, having been kept by the Holy Spirit from preaching the word in the province of Asia. ⁷When they came to the border of Mysia, they tried to enter Bithynia, but the Spirit of Jesus would not allow them to. ⁸So they passed by Mysia and went down to Troas. ⁹During the night Paul had a vision of a man of Macedonia standing and begging him, "Come over to Macedonia and help us." ¹⁰After Paul had seen the vision, we got ready at once to leave for Macedonia, concluding that God had called us to preach the gospel to them.

LYDIA'S CONVERSION IN PHILIPPI

¹¹From Troas we put out to sea and sailed straight for Samothrace, and the next day we went on to Neapolis. ¹²From there we traveled to Philippi, a Roman colony and the leading city of that district*a* of Macedonia. And we stayed there several days.

a 12 The text and meaning of the Greek for *the leading city of that district* are uncertain.

Why was Timothy circumcised? (16:3)
Paul had Timothy circumcised so that he would be more readily accepted by the Jews he ministered to. Timothy was half Jewish, on his mother's side. In the eyes of Jewish people, Timothy would have been considered a Gentile because he was the uncircumcised son of a Greek.

PAUL'S SECOND MISSIONARY JOURNEY (15:36 – 18:22)

What was this place of prayer? (16:13)
There were so few Jews in Philippi that there was no synagogue, so these women met outside for prayer at the banks of a river.

What was the marketplace? (16:19)
The marketplace (or agora) was the center for social, political, and administrative matters. This was a place where people discussed ideas, bought and sold goods, and conducted official city business.

Was it legal for Paul and Silas to be stripped, beaten, and sent to jail without a trial? (16:22–23)
It was not legal because Paul and Silas were Roman citizens, as Paul pointed out in verse 37.

Why was the jailer going to kill himself? (16:27)
If a prisoner escaped, the jailer would be held responsible and would be killed. It would be quicker and less shameful for the jailer to commit suicide.

¹³On the Sabbath we went outside the city gate to the river, where we expected to find a place of prayer. We sat down and began to speak to the women who had gathered there. ¹⁴One of those listening was a woman from the city of Thyatira named Lydia, a dealer in purple cloth. She was a worshiper of God. The Lord opened her heart to respond to Paul's message. ¹⁵When she and the members of her household were baptized, she invited us to her home. "If you consider me a believer in the Lord," she said, "come and stay at my house." And she persuaded us.

PAUL AND SILAS IN PRISON

¹⁶Once when we were going to the place of prayer, we were met by a female slave who had a spirit by which she predicted the future. She earned a great deal of money for her owners by fortune-telling. ¹⁷She followed Paul and the rest of us, shouting, "These men are servants of the Most High God, who are telling you the way to be saved." ¹⁸She kept this up for many days. Finally Paul became so annoyed that he turned around and said to the spirit, "In the name of Jesus Christ I command you to come out of her!" At that moment the spirit left her.

¹⁹When her owners realized that their hope of making money was gone, they seized Paul and Silas and dragged them into the marketplace to face the authorities. ²⁰They brought them before the magistrates and said, "These men are Jews, and are throwing our city into an uproar ²¹by advocating customs unlawful for us Romans to accept or practice."

²²The crowd joined in the attack against Paul and Silas, and the magistrates ordered them to be stripped and beaten with rods. ²³After they had been severely flogged, they were thrown into prison, and the jailer was commanded to guard them carefully. ²⁴When he received these orders, he put them in the inner cell and fastened their feet in the stocks.

²⁵About midnight Paul and Silas were praying and singing hymns to God, and the other prisoners were listening to them. ²⁶Suddenly there was such a violent earthquake that the foundations of the prison were shaken. At once all the prison doors flew open, and everyone's chains came loose. ²⁷The jailer woke up, and when he saw the prison doors open, he drew his sword and was about to kill himself because he thought the prisoners had escaped. ²⁸But Paul shouted, "Don't harm yourself! We are all here!"

²⁹The jailer called for lights, rushed in and fell trembling before Paul and Silas. ³⁰He then brought them out and asked, "Sirs, what must I do to be saved?"

³¹They replied, "Believe in the Lord Jesus, and you will be saved—you and your household." ³²Then they spoke the word of the Lord to him and to all the others in his house. ³³At that hour of the night the jailer took them and washed their wounds; then immediately he and all his household were baptized. ³⁴The jailer brought them into his house and set a meal before them; he was filled with joy because he had come to believe in God—he and his whole household.

³⁵When it was daylight, the magistrates sent their officers to the jailer with the order: "Release those men." ³⁶The jailer

told Paul, "The magistrates have ordered that you and Silas be released. Now you can leave. Go in peace."

³⁷But Paul said to the officers: "They beat us publicly without a trial, even though we are Roman citizens, and threw us into prison. And now do they want to get rid of us quietly? No! Let them come themselves and escort us out."

³⁸The officers reported this to the magistrates, and when they heard that Paul and Silas were Roman citizens, they were alarmed. ³⁹They came to appease them and escorted them from the prison, requesting them to leave the city. ⁴⁰After Paul and Silas came out of the prison, they went to Lydia's house, where they met with the brothers and sisters and encouraged them. Then they left.

IN THESSALONICA

17 When Paul and his companions had passed through Amphipolis and Apollonia, they came to Thessalonica, where there was a Jewish synagogue. ²As was his custom, Paul went into the synagogue, and on three Sabbath days he reasoned with them from the Scriptures, ³explaining and proving that the Messiah had to suffer and rise from the dead. "This Jesus I am proclaiming to you is the Messiah," he said. ⁴Some of the Jews were persuaded and joined Paul and Silas, as did a large number of God-fearing Greeks and quite a few prominent women.

⁵But other Jews were jealous; so they rounded up some bad characters from the marketplace, formed a mob and started a riot in the city. They rushed to Jason's house in search of Paul and Silas in order to bring them out to the crowd.^a ⁶But when they did not find them, they dragged Jason and some other believers before the city officials, shouting: "These men who have caused trouble all over the world have now come here, ⁷and Jason has welcomed them into his house. They are all defying Caesar's decrees, saying that there is another king, one called Jesus." ⁸When they heard this, the crowd and the city officials were thrown into turmoil. ⁹Then they made Jason and the others post bond and let them go.

IN BEREA

¹⁰As soon as it was night, the believers sent Paul and Silas away to Berea. On arriving there, they went to the Jewish synagogue. ¹¹Now the Berean Jews were of more noble character than those in Thessalonica, for they received the message with great eagerness and examined the Scriptures every day to see if what Paul said was true. ¹²As a result, many of them believed, as did also a number of prominent Greek women and many Greek men.

¹³But when the Jews in Thessalonica learned that Paul was preaching the word of God at Berea, some of them went there too, agitating the crowds and stirring them up. ¹⁴The believers immediately sent Paul to the coast, but Silas and Timothy stayed at Berea. ¹⁵Those who escorted Paul brought him to Athens and then left with instructions for Silas and Timothy to join him as soon as possible.

What crime were they accused of? (17:6–7) The crime was treason — supporting or promoting a king other than Caesar. This was the worst crime a Roman citizen could commit.

^a 5 Or *the assembly of the people*

IN ATHENS

¹⁶While Paul was waiting for them in Athens, he was greatly distressed to see that the city was full of idols. ¹⁷So he reasoned in the synagogue with both Jews and God-fearing Greeks, as well as in the marketplace day by day with those who happened to be there. ¹⁸A group of Epicurean and Stoic philosophers began to debate with him. Some of them asked, "What is this babbler trying to say?" Others remarked, "He seems to be advocating foreign gods." They said this because Paul was preaching the good news about Jesus and the resurrection. ¹⁹Then they took him and brought him to a meeting of the Areopagus, where they said to him, "May we know what this new teaching is that you are presenting? ²⁰You are bringing some strange ideas to our ears, and we would like to know what they mean." ²¹(All the Athenians and the foreigners who lived there spent their time doing nothing but talking about and listening to the latest ideas.)

²²Paul then stood up in the meeting of the Areopagus and said: "People of Athens! I see that in every way you are very religious. ²³For as I walked around and looked carefully at your objects of worship, I even found an altar with this inscription: TO AN UNKNOWN GOD. So you are ignorant of the very thing you worship—and this is what I am going to proclaim to you.

²⁴"The God who made the world and everything in it is the Lord of heaven and earth and does not live in temples built by human hands. ²⁵And he is not served by human hands, as if he needed anything. Rather, he himself gives everyone life and breath and everything else. ²⁶From one man he made all the nations, that they should inhabit the whole earth; and he marked out their appointed times in history and the boundaries of their lands. ²⁷God did this so that they would seek him and perhaps reach out for him and find him, though he is not far from any one of us. ²⁸'For in him we live and move and have our being.'ᵃ As some of your own poets have said, 'We are his offspring.'ᵇ

²⁹"Therefore since we are God's offspring, we should not think that the divine being is like gold or silver or stone—an image made by human design and skill. ³⁰In the past God overlooked such ignorance, but now he commands all people everywhere to repent. ³¹For he has set a day when he will judge the world with justice by the man he has appointed. He has given proof of this to everyone by raising him from the dead."

³²When they heard about the resurrection of the dead, some of them sneered, but others said, "We want to hear you again on this subject." ³³At that, Paul left the Council. ³⁴Some of the people became followers of Paul and believed. Among them was Dionysius, a member of the Areopagus, also a woman named Damaris, and a number of others.

IN CORINTH

18 After this, Paul left Athens and went to Corinth. ²There he met a Jew named Aquila, a native of Pontus, who had recently come from Italy with his wife Priscilla, be-

ᵃ 28 From the Cretan philosopher Epimenides   ᵇ 28 From the Cilician Stoic philosopher Aratus

---

What did Epicurean philosophers teach? (17:18)
Originally, Epicureans taught that the chief goal for human beings was to achieve happiness. By Paul's time, the philosophy had degenerated into a view that sensual pleasure was all that mattered in life.

What did the Stoics teach? (17:18)
Originally, they taught that people should live in harmony with nature and suppress their own desires, but by Paul's time this view had become a matter of pride.

Why would the Greeks build an altar to an unknown god? (17:23)
They were fearful of offending any god by not acknowledging him, so they tried to prevent offense by making an altar for unknown gods.

cause Claudius had ordered all Jews to leave Rome. Paul went to see them, [3] and because he was a tentmaker as they were, he stayed and worked with them. [4] Every Sabbath he reasoned in the synagogue, trying to persuade Jews and Greeks.

[5] When Silas and Timothy came from Macedonia, Paul devoted himself exclusively to preaching, testifying to the Jews that Jesus was the Messiah. [6] But when they opposed Paul and became abusive, he shook out his clothes in protest and said to them, "Your blood be on your own heads! I am innocent of it. From now on I will go to the Gentiles."

[7] Then Paul left the synagogue and went next door to the house of Titius Justus, a worshiper of God. [8] Crispus, the synagogue leader, and his entire household believed in the Lord; and many of the Corinthians who heard Paul believed and were baptized.

[9] One night the Lord spoke to Paul in a vision: "Do not be afraid; keep on speaking, do not be silent. [10] For I am with you, and no one is going to attack and harm you, because I have many people in this city." [11] So Paul stayed in Corinth for a year and a half, teaching them the word of God.

[12] While Gallio was proconsul of Achaia, the Jews of Corinth made a united attack on Paul and brought him to the place of judgment. [13] "This man," they charged, "is persuading the people to worship God in ways contrary to the law."

[14] Just as Paul was about to speak, Gallio said to them, "If you Jews were making a complaint about some misdemeanor or serious crime, it would be reasonable for me to listen to you. [15] But since it involves questions about words and names and your own law—settle the matter yourselves. I will not be a judge of such things." [16] So he drove them off. [17] Then the crowd there turned on Sosthenes the synagogue leader and beat him in front of the proconsul; and Gallio showed no concern whatever.

PRISCILLA, AQUILA AND APOLLOS

[18] Paul stayed on in Corinth for some time. Then he left the brothers and sisters and sailed for Syria, accompanied by Priscilla and Aquila. Before he sailed, he had his hair cut off at Cenchreae because of a vow he had taken. [19] They arrived at Ephesus, where Paul left Priscilla and Aquila. He himself went into the synagogue and reasoned with the Jews. [20] When they asked him to spend more time with them, he declined. [21] But as he left, he promised, "I will come back if it is God's will." Then he set sail from Ephesus. [22] When he landed at Caesarea, he went up to Jerusalem and greeted the church and then went down to Antioch.

[23] After spending some time in Antioch, Paul set out from there and traveled from place to place throughout the region of Galatia and Phrygia, strengthening all the disciples.

[24] Meanwhile a Jew named Apollos, a native of Alexandria, came to Ephesus. He was a learned man, with a thorough knowledge of the Scriptures. [25] He had been instructed in the way of the Lord, and he spoke with great fervor[a] and taught about Jesus accurately, though he knew only the baptism of

[a] 25 Or with fervor in the Spirit

Why did Paul shake out his clothes? (18:6)
This was like shaking the dust off one's shoes. He was showing that he would not take any further responsibility for these people.

What charge did the Jews make against Paul? (18:13)
They claimed that he was promoting a religion that was not recognized by Roman law as Judaism was.

Why did Paul cut his hair? (18:18)
Men of that time typically cut or shaved their hair after fulfilling a vow. Paul may have cut his hair as an expression of thanks for his safety in Corinth and the positive response to his preaching.

What did it mean that Apollos "knew only the baptism of John"? (18:25)
He was still looking forward to the coming of the Messiah. After Priscilla and Aquila taught him about Jesus, he became an effective preacher for Jesus.

John. ²⁶He began to speak boldly in the synagogue. When Priscilla and Aquila heard him, they invited him to their home and explained to him the way of God more adequately.

²⁷When Apollos wanted to go to Achaia, the brothers and sisters encouraged him and wrote to the disciples there to welcome him. When he arrived, he was a great help to those who by grace had believed. ²⁸For he vigorously refuted his Jewish opponents in public debate, proving from the Scriptures that Jesus was the Messiah.

PAUL IN EPHESUS

19 While Apollos was at Corinth, Paul took the road through the interior and arrived at Ephesus. There he found some disciples ²and asked them, "Did you receive the Holy Spirit when[a] you believed?"

They answered, "No, we have not even heard that there is a Holy Spirit."

³So Paul asked, "Then what baptism did you receive?"

"John's baptism," they replied.

⁴Paul said, "John's baptism was a baptism of repentance. He told the people to believe in the one coming after him, that is, in Jesus." ⁵On hearing this, they were baptized in the name of the Lord Jesus. ⁶When Paul placed his hands on them, the Holy Spirit came on them, and they spoke in tongues[b] and prophesied. ⁷There were about twelve men in all.

[a] 2 Or *after*   [b] 6 Or *other languages*

PAUL'S THIRD MISSIONARY JOURNEY (18:23 – 21:14)

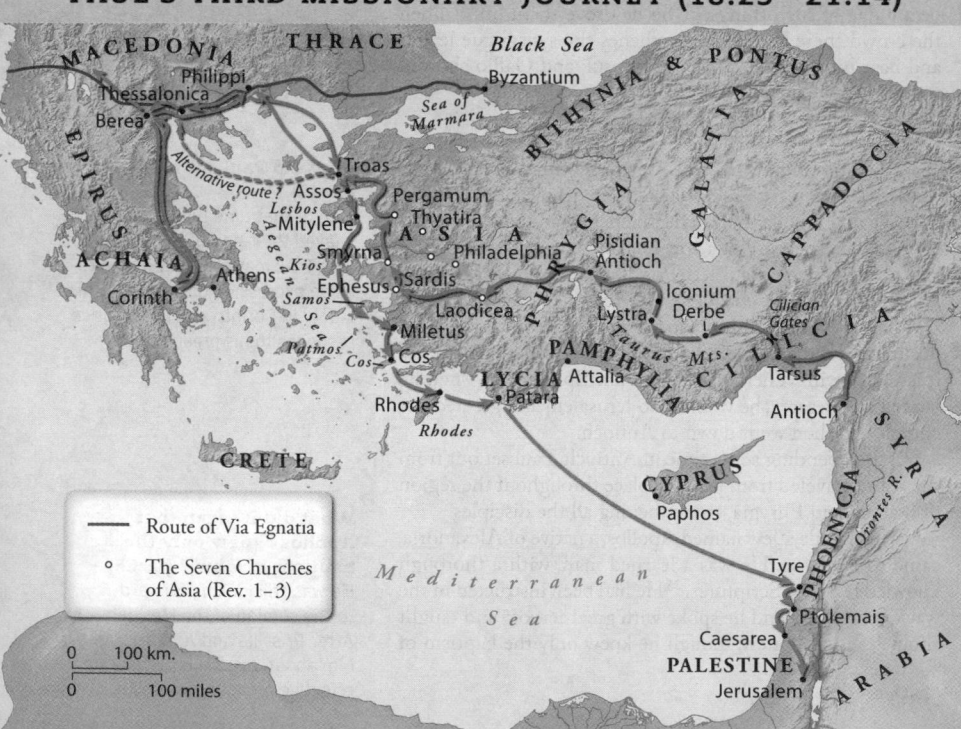

⁸Paul entered the synagogue and spoke boldly there for three months, arguing persuasively about the kingdom of God. ⁹But some of them became obstinate; they refused to believe and publicly maligned the Way. So Paul left them. He took the disciples with him and had discussions daily in the lecture hall of Tyrannus. ¹⁰This went on for two years, so that all the Jews and Greeks who lived in the province of Asia heard the word of the Lord.

¹¹God did extraordinary miracles through Paul, ¹²so that even handkerchiefs and aprons that had touched him were taken to the sick, and their illnesses were cured and the evil spirits left them.

¹³Some Jews who went around driving out evil spirits tried to invoke the name of the Lord Jesus over those who were demon-possessed. They would say, "In the name of the Jesus whom Paul preaches, I command you to come out." ¹⁴Seven sons of Sceva, a Jewish chief priest, were doing this. ¹⁵One day the evil spirit answered them, "Jesus I know, and Paul I know about, but who are you?" ¹⁶Then the man who had the evil spirit jumped on them and overpowered them all. He gave them such a beating that they ran out of the house naked and bleeding.

¹⁷When this became known to the Jews and Greeks living in Ephesus, they were all seized with fear, and the name of the Lord Jesus was held in high honor. ¹⁸Many of those who believed now came and openly confessed what they had done. ¹⁹A number who had practiced sorcery brought their scrolls together and burned them publicly. When they calculated the value of the scrolls, the total came to fifty thousand drachmas.ᵃ ²⁰In this way the word of the Lord spread widely and grew in power.

²¹After all this had happened, Paul decidedᵇ to go to Jerusalem, passing through Macedonia and Achaia. "After I have been there," he said, "I must visit Rome also." ²²He sent two of his helpers, Timothy and Erastus, to Macedonia, while he stayed in the province of Asia a little longer.

THE RIOT IN EPHESUS

²³About that time there arose a great disturbance about the Way. ²⁴A silversmith named Demetrius, who made silver shrines of Artemis, brought in a lot of business for the craftsmen there. ²⁵He called them together, along with the workers in related trades, and said: "You know, my friends, that we receive a good income from this business. ²⁶And you see and hear how this fellow Paul has convinced and led astray large numbers of people here in Ephesus and in practically the whole province of Asia. He says that gods made by human hands are no gods at all. ²⁷There is danger not only that our trade will lose its good name, but also that the temple of the great goddess Artemis will be discredited; and the goddess herself, who is worshiped throughout the province of Asia and the world, will be robbed of her divine majesty."

²⁸When they heard this, they were furious and began

ᵃ 19 A drachma was a silver coin worth about a day's wages.
ᵇ 21 Or decided in the Spirit

How could someone be healed through Paul's handkerchief or apron? (19:12)
Verse 11 makes it clear that these miracles were the work of God meant to show his awesome power. This is the only incident in the New Testament of healing taking place this way. It is similar, however, to those who were healed when they touched the hem of Jesus' robe (Mark 5:27 and 6:56).

What were these scrolls? (19:19)
These scrolls contained magical formulas and secret information. These were very valuable items because of the supposed power of the words and formulas they contained.

Who was Demetrius? (19:24–25)
Each trade, or occupation, had its guild (group with members of the same occupation), and Demetrius was probably a leader of the guild for the making of silver shrines and images.

What was the temple of Artemis like? (19:27)
It was considered one of the seven wonders of the ancient world. It was 425 feet (130 meters) long and 220 feet (67 meters) wide. It had 127 white marble columns that were 62 feet (19 meters) tall. In the inner sanctuary was the many-breasted image that supposedly had been dropped there from heaven.

shouting: "Great is Artemis of the Ephesians!" ²⁹Soon the whole city was in an uproar. The people seized Gaius and Aristarchus, Paul's traveling companions from Macedonia, and all of them rushed into the theater together. ³⁰Paul wanted to appear before the crowd, but the disciples would not let him. ³¹Even some of the officials of the province, friends of Paul, sent him a message begging him not to venture into the theater.

³²The assembly was in confusion: Some were shouting one thing, some another. Most of the people did not even know why they were there. ³³The Jews in the crowd pushed Alexander to the front, and they shouted instructions to him. He motioned for silence in order to make a defense before the people. ³⁴But when they realized he was a Jew, they all shouted in unison for about two hours: "Great is Artemis of the Ephesians!"

³⁵The city clerk quieted the crowd and said: "Fellow Ephesians, doesn't all the world know that the city of Ephesus is the guardian of the temple of the great Artemis and of her image, which fell from heaven? ³⁶Therefore, since these facts are undeniable, you ought to calm down and not do anything rash. ³⁷You have brought these men here, though they have neither robbed temples nor blasphemed our goddess. ³⁸If, then, Demetrius and his fellow craftsmen have a grievance against anybody, the courts are open and there are proconsuls. They can press charges. ³⁹If there is anything further you want to bring up, it must be settled in a legal assembly. ⁴⁰As it is, we are in danger of being charged with rioting because of what happened today. In that case we would not be able to account for this commotion, since there is no reason for it." ⁴¹After he had said this, he dismissed the assembly.

THROUGH MACEDONIA AND GREECE

20 When the uproar had ended, Paul sent for the disciples and, after encouraging them, said goodbye and set out for Macedonia. ²He traveled through that area, speaking many words of encouragement to the people, and finally arrived in Greece, ³where he stayed three months. Because some Jews had plotted against him just as he was about to sail for Syria, he decided to go back through Macedonia. ⁴He was accompanied by Sopater son of Pyrrhus from Berea, Aristarchus and Secundus from Thessalonica, Gaius from Derbe, Timothy also, and Tychicus and Trophimus from the province of Asia. ⁵These men went on ahead and waited for us at Troas. ⁶But we sailed from Philippi after the Festival of Unleavened Bread, and five days later joined the others at Troas, where we stayed seven days.

EUTYCHUS RAISED FROM THE DEAD AT TROAS

⁷On the first day of the week we came together to break bread. Paul spoke to the people and, because he intended to leave the next day, kept on talking until midnight. ⁸There were many lamps in the upstairs room where we were meeting. ⁹Seated in a window was a young man named Eutychus,

What was the legal assembly? (19:39)
This was the regular civil meeting that was usually held three times per month.

Through Macedonia and Greece (20:1)

What did it mean to break bread? (20:7)
This meant to eat a meal with others. Here it referred to the celebration of the Lord's Supper.

who was sinking into a deep sleep as Paul talked on and on. When he was sound asleep, he fell to the ground from the third story and was picked up dead. [10] Paul went down, threw himself on the young man and put his arms around him. "Don't be alarmed," he said. "He's alive!" [11] Then he went upstairs again and broke bread and ate. After talking until daylight, he left. [12] The people took the young man home alive and were greatly comforted.

PAUL'S FAREWELL TO THE EPHESIAN ELDERS

[13] We went on ahead to the ship and sailed for Assos, where we were going to take Paul aboard. He had made this arrangement because he was going there on foot. [14] When he met us at Assos, we took him aboard and went on to Mitylene. [15] The next day we set sail from there and arrived off Chios. The day after that we crossed over to Samos, and on the following day arrived at Miletus. [16] Paul had decided to sail past Ephesus to avoid spending time in the province of Asia, for he was in a hurry to reach Jerusalem, if possible, by the day of Pentecost.

[17] From Miletus, Paul sent to Ephesus for the elders of the church. [18] When they arrived, he said to them: "You know how I lived the whole time I was with you, from the first day I came into the province of Asia. [19] I served the Lord with great humility and with tears and in the midst of severe testing by the plots of my Jewish opponents. [20] You know that I have not hesitated to preach anything that would be helpful to you but have taught you publicly and from house to house. [21] I have declared to both Jews and Greeks that they must turn to God in repentance and have faith in our Lord Jesus.

[22] "And now, compelled by the Spirit, I am going to Jerusalem, not knowing what will happen to me there. [23] I only know that in every city the Holy Spirit warns me that prison and hardships are facing me. [24] However, I consider my life worth nothing to me; my only aim is to finish the race and complete the task the Lord Jesus has given me—the task of testifying to the good news of God's grace.

[25] "Now I know that none of you among whom I have gone about preaching the kingdom will ever see me again. [26] Therefore, I declare to you today that I am innocent of the blood of any of you. [27] For I have not hesitated to proclaim to you the whole will of God. [28] Keep watch over yourselves and all the flock of which the Holy Spirit has made you overseers. Be shepherds of the church of God,*a* which he bought with his own blood.*b* [29] I know that after I leave, savage wolves will come in among you and will not spare the flock. [30] Even from your own number men will arise and distort the truth in order to draw away disciples after them. [31] So be on your guard! Remember that for three years I never stopped warning each of you night and day with tears.

[32] "Now I commit you to God and to the word of his grace, which can build you up and give you an inheritance among all those who are sanctified. [33] I have not coveted anyone's

Who were the elders of the church? (20:17)
These were respected believers whom Paul had appointed to lead the church.

Who were the overseers? (20:28)
These were the elders of the church, also called shepherds.

a 28 Many manuscripts *of the Lord*   *b 28* Or *with the blood of his own Son.*

When did Jesus make this statement? (20:35)
Paul quotes Jesus, but the statement does not appear in the Gospels. That doesn't mean that Jesus did not say these words, simply that they were not recorded by the Gospel writers.

silver or gold or clothing. ³⁴You yourselves know that these hands of mine have supplied my own needs and the needs of my companions. ³⁵In everything I did, I showed you that by this kind of hard work we must help the weak, remembering the words the Lord Jesus himself said: 'It is more blessed to give than to receive.'"

³⁶When Paul had finished speaking, he knelt down with all of them and prayed. ³⁷They all wept as they embraced him and kissed him. ³⁸What grieved them most was his statement that they would never see his face again. Then they accompanied him to the ship.

ON TO JERUSALEM

21 After we had torn ourselves away from them, we put out to sea and sailed straight to Kos. The next day we went to Rhodes and from there to Patara. ²We found a ship crossing over to Phoenicia, went on board and set sail. ³After sighting Cyprus and passing to the south of it, we sailed on to Syria. We landed at Tyre, where our ship was to unload its cargo. ⁴We sought out the disciples there and stayed with them seven days. Through the Spirit they urged Paul not to go on to Jerusalem. ⁵When it was time to leave, we left and continued on our way. All of them, including wives and children, accompanied us out of the city, and there on the beach we knelt to pray. ⁶After saying goodbye to each other, we went aboard the ship, and they returned home.

⁷We continued our voyage from Tyre and landed at Ptolemais, where we greeted the brothers and sisters and stayed with them for a day. ⁸Leaving the next day, we reached Caesarea and stayed at the house of Philip the evangelist, one of the Seven. ⁹He had four unmarried daughters who prophesied.

Who were these daughters of Philip? (21:9)
These unmarried daughters may have been dedicated in a special way to serving the Lord because of their gift of prophecy.

Who was Agabus? (21:10)
Evidently he held the office of prophet, as Philip held the office of evangelist (see verse 8). Many years earlier he had prophesied the coming famine in Jerusalem (see 11:27 – 28).

¹⁰After we had been there a number of days, a prophet named Agabus came down from Judea. ¹¹Coming over to us, he took Paul's belt, tied his own hands and feet with it and said, "The Holy Spirit says, 'In this way the Jewish leaders in Jerusalem will bind the owner of this belt and will hand him over to the Gentiles.'"

¹²When we heard this, we and the people there pleaded with Paul not to go up to Jerusalem. ¹³Then Paul answered, "Why are you weeping and breaking my heart? I am ready not only to be bound, but also to die in Jerusalem for the name of the Lord Jesus." ¹⁴When he would not be dissuaded, we gave up and said, "The Lord's will be done."

¹⁵After this, we started on our way up to Jerusalem. ¹⁶Some of the disciples from Caesarea accompanied us and brought us to the home of Mnason, where we were to stay. He was a man from Cyprus and one of the early disciples.

PAUL'S ARRIVAL AT JERUSALEM

Who was James? (21:18)
He was the brother of Jesus and a leader in the Jerusalem church. He is believed to be the author of the book of James.

¹⁷When we arrived at Jerusalem, the brothers and sisters received us warmly. ¹⁸The next day Paul and the rest of us went to see James, and all the elders were present. ¹⁹Paul greeted them and reported in detail what God had done among the Gentiles through his ministry.

[20]When they heard this, they praised God. Then they said to Paul: "You see, brother, how many thousands of Jews have believed, and all of them are zealous for the law. [21]They have been informed that you teach all the Jews who live among the Gentiles to turn away from Moses, telling them not to circumcise their children or live according to our customs. [22]What shall we do? They will certainly hear that you have come, [23]so do what we tell you. There are four men with us who have made a vow. [24]Take these men, join in their purification rites and pay their expenses, so that they can have their heads shaved. Then everyone will know there is no truth in these reports about you, but that you yourself are living in obedience to the law. [25]As for the Gentile believers, we have written to them our decision that they should abstain from food sacrificed to idols, from blood, from the meat of strangled animals and from sexual immorality."

[26]The next day Paul took the men and purified himself along with them. Then he went to the temple to give notice of the date when the days of purification would end and the offering would be made for each of them.

PAUL ARRESTED

[27]When the seven days were nearly over, some Jews from the province of Asia saw Paul at the temple. They stirred up the whole crowd and seized him, [28]shouting, "Fellow Israelites, help us! This is the man who teaches everyone everywhere against our people and our law and this place. And besides, he has brought Greeks into the temple and defiled this holy place." [29](They had previously seen Trophimus the Ephesian in the city with Paul and assumed that Paul had brought him into the temple.)

[30]The whole city was aroused, and the people came running from all directions. Seizing Paul, they dragged him from the temple, and immediately the gates were shut. [31]While they were trying to kill him, news reached the commander of the Roman troops that the whole city of Jerusalem was in an uproar. [32]He at once took some officers and soldiers and ran down to the crowd. When the rioters saw the commander and his soldiers, they stopped beating Paul.

[33]The commander came up and arrested him and ordered him to be bound with two chains. Then he asked who he was and what he had done. [34]Some in the crowd shouted one thing and some another, and since the commander could not get at the truth because of the uproar, he ordered that Paul be taken into the barracks. [35]When Paul reached the steps, the violence of the mob was so great he had to be carried by the soldiers. [36]The crowd that followed kept shouting, "Get rid of him!"

PAUL SPEAKS TO THE CROWD

[37]As the soldiers were about to take Paul into the barracks, he asked the commander, "May I say something to you?"

"Do you speak Greek?" he replied. [38]"Aren't you the Egyptian who started a revolt and led four thousand terrorists out into the wilderness some time ago?"

How was Paul bound? (21:33)
Paul's hands were probably chained to a soldier on either side of him.

Where was Paul taken? (21:37)
He was taken to the Fortress of Antonia, which was connected to the northern end of the temple area by two flights of stairs.

³⁹Paul answered, "I am a Jew, from Tarsus in Cilicia, a citizen of no ordinary city. Please let me speak to the people."

⁴⁰After receiving the commander's permission, Paul stood on the steps and motioned to the crowd. When they were all **22** silent, he said to them in Aramaic*a*: ¹"Brothers and fathers, listen now to my defense."

²When they heard him speak to them in Aramaic, they became very quiet.

Then Paul said: ³"I am a Jew, born in Tarsus of Cilicia, but brought up in this city. I studied under Gamaliel and was thoroughly trained in the law of our ancestors. I was just as zealous for God as any of you are today. ⁴I persecuted the followers of this Way to their death, arresting both men and women and throwing them into prison, ⁵as the high priest and all the Council can themselves testify. I even obtained letters from them to their associates in Damascus, and went there to bring these people as prisoners to Jerusalem to be punished.

⁶"About noon as I came near Damascus, suddenly a bright light from heaven flashed around me. ⁷I fell to the ground and heard a voice say to me, 'Saul! Saul! Why do you persecute me?'

⁸"'Who are you, Lord?' I asked.

"'I am Jesus of Nazareth, whom you are persecuting,' he replied. ⁹My companions saw the light, but they did not understand the voice of him who was speaking to me.

¹⁰"'What shall I do, Lord?' I asked.

"'Get up,' the Lord said, 'and go into Damascus. There you will be told all that you have been assigned to do.' ¹¹My companions led me by the hand into Damascus, because the brilliance of the light had blinded me.

¹²"A man named Ananias came to see me. He was a devout observer of the law and highly respected by all the Jews living there. ¹³He stood beside me and said, 'Brother Saul, receive your sight!' And at that very moment I was able to see him.

¹⁴"Then he said: 'The God of our ancestors has chosen you to know his will and to see the Righteous One and to hear words from his mouth. ¹⁵You will be his witness to all people of what you have seen and heard. ¹⁶And now what are you waiting for? Get up, be baptized and wash your sins away, calling on his name.'

¹⁷"When I returned to Jerusalem and was praying at the temple, I fell into a trance ¹⁸and saw the Lord speaking to me. 'Quick!' he said. 'Leave Jerusalem immediately, because the people here will not accept your testimony about me.'

¹⁹"'Lord,' I replied, 'these people know that I went from one synagogue to another to imprison and beat those who believe in you. ²⁰And when the blood of your martyr*b* Stephen was shed, I stood there giving my approval and guarding the clothes of those who were killing him.'

²¹"Then the Lord said to me, 'Go; I will send you far away to the Gentiles.'"

What convinced Paul of the truth of the gospel? (22:14)
Seeing the risen Jesus, the Righteous One, was central to his faith and theology.

What does baptism symbolize? (22:16)
Baptism symbolizes the washing away of sins. It is the outward symbol of an inward work of grace.

---

a 40 Or possibly *Hebrew*; also in 22:2   *b* 20 Or *witness*

PAUL THE ROMAN CITIZEN

²²The crowd listened to Paul until he said this. Then they raised their voices and shouted, "Rid the earth of him! He's not fit to live!"

²³As they were shouting and throwing off their cloaks and flinging dust into the air, ²⁴the commander ordered that Paul be taken into the barracks. He directed that he be flogged and interrogated in order to find out why the people were shouting at him like this. ²⁵As they stretched him out to flog him, Paul said to the centurion standing there, "Is it legal for you to flog a Roman citizen who hasn't even been found guilty?"

²⁶When the centurion heard this, he went to the commander and reported it. "What are you going to do?" he asked. "This man is a Roman citizen."

²⁷The commander went to Paul and asked, "Tell me, are you a Roman citizen?"

"Yes, I am," he answered.

²⁸Then the commander said, "I had to pay a lot of money for my citizenship."

"But I was born a citizen," Paul replied.

²⁹Those who were about to interrogate him withdrew immediately. The commander himself was alarmed when he realized that he had put Paul, a Roman citizen, in chains.

PAUL BEFORE THE SANHEDRIN

³⁰The commander wanted to find out exactly why Paul was being accused by the Jews. So the next day he released him and ordered the chief priests and all the members of the Sanhedrin to assemble. Then he brought Paul and had him stand before them.

23 Paul looked straight at the Sanhedrin and said, "My brothers, I have fulfilled my duty to God in all good conscience to this day." ²At this the high priest Ananias ordered those standing near Paul to strike him on the mouth. ³Then Paul said to him, "God will strike you, you whitewashed wall! You sit there to judge me according to the law, yet you yourself violate the law by commanding that I be struck!"

⁴Those who were standing near Paul said, "How dare you insult God's high priest!"

⁵Paul replied, "Brothers, I did not realize that he was the high priest; for it is written: 'Do not speak evil about the ruler of your people.'ᵃ"

⁶Then Paul, knowing that some of them were Sadducees and the others Pharisees, called out in the Sanhedrin, "My brothers, I am a Pharisee, descended from Pharisees. I stand on trial because of the hope of the resurrection of the dead." ⁷When he said this, a dispute broke out between the Pharisees and the Sadducees, and the assembly was divided. ⁸(The Sadducees say that there is no resurrection, and that there are neither angels nor spirits, but the Pharisees believe all these things.)

How could a person become a Roman citizen? (22:28)
There were three ways to gain citizenship: receive it as a reward for outstanding service to Rome, buy it for a high price, or be born into a family of Roman citizens.

What did Paul mean by a whitewashed wall? (23:3)
This was a metaphor for a hypocrite. It meant to have an attractive exterior but to be unclean inside, like a tomb that was painted white.

ᵃ 5 Exodus 22:28

⁹There was a great uproar, and some of the teachers of the law who were Pharisees stood up and argued vigorously. "We find nothing wrong with this man," they said. "What if a spirit or an angel has spoken to him?" ¹⁰The dispute became so violent that the commander was afraid Paul would be torn to pieces by them. He ordered the troops to go down and take him away from them by force and bring him into the barracks.

¹¹The following night the Lord stood near Paul and said, "Take courage! As you have testified about me in Jerusalem, so you must also testify in Rome."

THE PLOT TO KILL PAUL

¹²The next morning some Jews formed a conspiracy and bound themselves with an oath not to eat or drink until they had killed Paul. ¹³More than forty men were involved in this plot. ¹⁴They went to the chief priests and the elders and said, "We have taken a solemn oath not to eat anything until we have killed Paul. ¹⁵Now then, you and the Sanhedrin petition the commander to bring him before you on the pretext of wanting more accurate information about his case. We are ready to kill him before he gets here."

¹⁶But when the son of Paul's sister heard of this plot, he went into the barracks and told Paul.

¹⁷Then Paul called one of the centurions and said, "Take this young man to the commander; he has something to tell him." ¹⁸So he took him to the commander.

The centurion said, "Paul, the prisoner, sent for me and asked me to bring this young man to you because he has something to tell you."

¹⁹The commander took the young man by the hand, drew him aside and asked, "What is it you want to tell me?"

²⁰He said: "Some Jews have agreed to ask you to bring Paul before the Sanhedrin tomorrow on the pretext of wanting more accurate information about him. ²¹Don't give in to them, because more than forty of them are waiting in ambush for him. They have taken an oath not to eat or drink until they have killed him. They are ready now, waiting for your consent to their request."

²²The commander dismissed the young man with this warning: "Don't tell anyone that you have reported this to me."

PAUL TRANSFERRED TO CAESAREA

²³Then he called two of his centurions and ordered them, "Get ready a detachment of two hundred soldiers, seventy horsemen and two hundred spearmen[a] to go to Caesarea at nine tonight. ²⁴Provide horses for Paul so that he may be taken safely to Governor Felix."

²⁵He wrote a letter as follows:

²⁶Claudius Lysias,

To His Excellency, Governor Felix:

Greetings.

²⁷This man was seized by the Jews and they were about to kill him, but I came with my troops and res-

Is Paul's family mentioned elsewhere in the Bible? (23:16)
This is the only mention of Paul's family. His nephew came to warn Paul about the plot on his life.

Why did the commander assign so many troops to transport Paul? (23:23–24)
He did not want anything to happen to Paul, who was a Roman citizen.

ᵃ 23 The meaning of the Greek for this word is uncertain.

cued him, for I had learned that he is a Roman citizen.
²⁸I wanted to know why they were accusing him, so I
brought him to their Sanhedrin. ²⁹I found that the accusation had to do with questions about their law, but
there was no charge against him that deserved death or
imprisonment. ³⁰When I was informed of a plot to be
carried out against the man, I sent him to you at once.
I also ordered his accusers to present to you their case
against him.

³¹So the soldiers, carrying out their orders, took Paul with
them during the night and brought him as far as Antipatris.
³²The next day they let the cavalry go on with him, while
they returned to the barracks. ³³When the cavalry arrived
in Caesarea, they delivered the letter to the governor and
handed Paul over to him. ³⁴The governor read the letter and
asked what province he was from. Learning that he was from
Cilicia, ³⁵he said, "I will hear your case when your accusers
get here." Then he ordered that Paul be kept under guard in
Herod's palace.

PAUL'S TRIAL BEFORE FELIX

24 Five days later the high priest Ananias went down
to Caesarea with some of the elders and a lawyer
named Tertullus, and they brought their charges against Paul
before the governor. ²When Paul was called in, Tertullus presented his case before Felix: "We have enjoyed a long period
of peace under you, and your foresight has brought about
reforms in this nation. ³Everywhere and in every way, most
excellent Felix, we acknowledge this with profound gratitude. ⁴But in order not to weary you further, I would request
that you be kind enough to hear us briefly.

⁵"We have found this man to be a troublemaker, stirring
up riots among the Jews all over the world. He is a ringleader
of the Nazarene sect ⁶and even tried to desecrate the temple; so we seized him. [7]ª ⁸By examining him yourself you
will be able to learn the truth about all these charges we are
bringing against him."

⁹The other Jews joined in the accusation, asserting that
these things were true.

¹⁰When the governor motioned for him to speak, Paul
replied: "I know that for a number of years you have been a
judge over this nation; so I gladly make my defense. ¹¹You
can easily verify that no more than twelve days ago I went up
to Jerusalem to worship. ¹²My accusers did not find me arguing with anyone at the temple, or stirring up a crowd in the
synagogues or anywhere else in the city. ¹³And they cannot
prove to you the charges they are now making against me.
¹⁴However, I admit that I worship the God of our ancestors
as a follower of the Way, which they call a sect. I believe everything that is in accordance with the Law and that is written in the Prophets, ¹⁵and I have the same hope in God as

**What were the charges
against Paul? (24:5)**
He was said to be a troublemaker
and a ringleader of the Nazarene
sect (a name for the followers
of Jesus). To cause conflict in
the empire was treason against
Caesar, and to be a leader of an
unapproved religious sect was
illegal.

ª 6–8 Some manuscripts include here *him, and we would have judged him in
accordance with our law.* ⁷*But the commander Lysias came and took him from us
with much violence,* ⁸*ordering his accusers to come before you.*

these men themselves have, that there will be a resurrection of both the righteous and the wicked. ¹⁶So I strive always to keep my conscience clear before God and man.

¹⁷"After an absence of several years, I came to Jerusalem to bring my people gifts for the poor and to present offerings. ¹⁸I was ceremonially clean when they found me in the temple courts doing this. There was no crowd with me, nor was I involved in any disturbance. ¹⁹But there are some Jews from the province of Asia, who ought to be here before you and bring charges if they have anything against me. ²⁰Or these who are here should state what crime they found in me when I stood before the Sanhedrin— ²¹unless it was this one thing I shouted as I stood in their presence: 'It is concerning the resurrection of the dead that I am on trial before you today.'"

²²Then Felix, who was well acquainted with the Way, adjourned the proceedings. "When Lysias the commander comes," he said, "I will decide your case." ²³He ordered the centurion to keep Paul under guard but to give him some freedom and permit his friends to take care of his needs.

²⁴Several days later Felix came with his wife Drusilla, who was Jewish. He sent for Paul and listened to him as he spoke about faith in Christ Jesus. ²⁵As Paul talked about righteousness, self-control and the judgment to come, Felix was afraid and said, "That's enough for now! You may leave. When I find it convenient, I will send for you." ²⁶At the same time he was hoping that Paul would offer him a bribe, so he sent for him frequently and talked with him.

²⁷When two years had passed, Felix was succeeded by Porcius Festus, but because Felix wanted to grant a favor to the Jews, he left Paul in prison.

PAUL'S TRIAL BEFORE FESTUS

25 Three days after arriving in the province, Festus went up from Caesarea to Jerusalem, ²where the chief priests and the Jewish leaders appeared before him and presented the charges against Paul. ³They requested Festus, as a favor to them, to have Paul transferred to Jerusalem, for they were preparing an ambush to kill him along the way. ⁴Festus answered, "Paul is being held at Caesarea, and I myself am going there soon. ⁵Let some of your leaders come with me, and if the man has done anything wrong, they can press charges against him there."

⁶After spending eight or ten days with them, Festus went down to Caesarea. The next day he convened the court and ordered that Paul be brought before him. ⁷When Paul came in, the Jews who had come down from Jerusalem stood around him. They brought many serious charges against him, but they could not prove them.

⁸Then Paul made his defense: "I have done nothing wrong against the Jewish law or against the temple or against Caesar."

⁹Festus, wishing to do the Jews a favor, said to Paul, "Are you willing to go up to Jerusalem and stand trial before me there on these charges?"

¹⁰Paul answered: "I am now standing before Caesar's court, where I ought to be tried. I have not done any wrong

How was Felix acquainted with the Way? (24:22)
He could not have governed Judea and Samaria for six years without becoming familiar with the activities of the Christians.

Why did Felix think that Paul might offer a bribe? (24:26)
Felix imagined that Paul had access to considerable funds because he had heard about Paul bringing money to the Christians in Jerusalem.

How far was it from Caesarea to Jerusalem? (25:1)
This was a distance of 60 miles (97 kilometers) that required 2 days to travel.

Why did Paul want to be tried by Festus? (25:9)
As a Roman citizen, Paul had a right to a trial in a Roman court where he would probably receive fairer treatment than in a Jewish court.

to the Jews, as you yourself know very well. ¹¹ If, however, I am guilty of doing anything deserving death, I do not refuse to die. But if the charges brought against me by these Jews are not true, no one has the right to hand me over to them. I appeal to Caesar!"

¹² After Festus had conferred with his council, he declared: "You have appealed to Caesar. To Caesar you will go!"

FESTUS CONSULTS KING AGRIPPA

¹³ A few days later King Agrippa and Bernice arrived at Caesarea to pay their respects to Festus. ¹⁴ Since they were spending many days there, Festus discussed Paul's case with the king. He said: "There is a man here whom Felix left as a prisoner. ¹⁵ When I went to Jerusalem, the chief priests and the elders of the Jews brought charges against him and asked that he be condemned.

¹⁶ "I told them that it is not the Roman custom to hand over anyone before they have faced their accusers and have had an opportunity to defend themselves against the charges. ¹⁷ When they came here with me, I did not delay the case, but convened the court the next day and ordered the man to be brought in. ¹⁸ When his accusers got up to speak, they did not charge him with any of the crimes I had expected. ¹⁹ Instead, they had some points of dispute with him about their own religion and about a dead man named Jesus who Paul claimed was alive. ²⁰ I was at a loss how to investigate such matters; so I asked if he would be willing to go to Jerusalem and stand trial there on these charges. ²¹ But when Paul made his appeal to be held over for the Emperor's decision, I ordered him held until I could send him to Caesar."

²² Then Agrippa said to Festus, "I would like to hear this man myself."

He replied, "Tomorrow you will hear him."

PAUL BEFORE AGRIPPA

²³ The next day Agrippa and Bernice came with great pomp and entered the audience room with the high-ranking military officers and the prominent men of the city. At the command of Festus, Paul was brought in. ²⁴ Festus said: "King Agrippa, and all who are present with us, you see this man! The whole Jewish community has petitioned me about him in Jerusalem and here in Caesarea, shouting that he ought not to live any longer. ²⁵ I found he had done nothing deserving of death, but because he made his appeal to the Emperor I decided to send him to Rome. ²⁶ But I have nothing definite to write to His Majesty about him. Therefore I have brought him before all of you, and especially before you, King Agrippa, so that as a result of this investigation I may have something to write. ²⁷ For I think it is unreasonable to send a prisoner on to Rome without specifying the charges against him."

26 Then Agrippa said to Paul, "You have permission to speak for yourself."

So Paul motioned with his hand and began his defense: ² "King Agrippa, I consider myself fortunate to stand before

Why did Paul appeal to Caesar? (25:11)
Every Roman citizen had the right to have his case heard before Caesar or his representative. Winning such a case could have resulted in official recognition of Christianity as a religion separate from Judaism.

What was the audience room? (25:23)
This was an auditorium appropriate for a special occasion. In attendance were the king, his sister, the Roman governors, and the outstanding teachers of both the Jews and the Romans.

you today as I make my defense against all the accusations of the Jews, [3] and especially so because you are well acquainted with all the Jewish customs and controversies. Therefore, I beg you to listen to me patiently.

[4] "The Jewish people all know the way I have lived ever since I was a child, from the beginning of my life in my own country, and also in Jerusalem. [5] They have known me for a long time and can testify, if they are willing, that I conformed to the strictest sect of our religion, living as a Pharisee. [6] And now it is because of my hope in what God has promised our ancestors that I am on trial today. [7] This is the promise our twelve tribes are hoping to see fulfilled as they earnestly serve God day and night. King Agrippa, it is because of this hope that these Jews are accusing me. [8] Why should any of you consider it incredible that God raises the dead?

[9] "I too was convinced that I ought to do all that was possible to oppose the name of Jesus of Nazareth. [10] And that is just what I did in Jerusalem. On the authority of the chief priests I put many of the Lord's people in prison, and when they were put to death, I cast my vote against them. [11] Many a time I went from one synagogue to another to have them punished, and I tried to force them to blaspheme. I was so obsessed with persecuting them that I even hunted them down in foreign cities.

[12] "On one of these journeys I was going to Damascus with the authority and commission of the chief priests. [13] About noon, King Agrippa, as I was on the road, I saw a light from heaven, brighter than the sun, blazing around me and my companions. [14] We all fell to the ground, and I heard a voice saying to me in Aramaic,[a] 'Saul, Saul, why do you persecute me? It is hard for you to kick against the goads.'

[15] "Then I asked, 'Who are you, Lord?'

" 'I am Jesus, whom you are persecuting,' the Lord replied. [16] 'Now get up and stand on your feet. I have appeared to you to appoint you as a servant and as a witness of what you have seen and will see of me. [17] I will rescue you from your own people and from the Gentiles. I am sending you to them [18] to open their eyes and turn them from darkness to light, and from the power of Satan to God, so that they may receive forgiveness of sins and a place among those who are sanctified by faith in me.'

[19] "So then, King Agrippa, I was not disobedient to the vision from heaven. [20] First to those in Damascus, then to those in Jerusalem and in all Judea, and then to the Gentiles, I preached that they should repent and turn to God and demonstrate their repentance by their deeds. [21] That is why some Jews seized me in the temple courts and tried to kill me. [22] But God has helped me to this very day; so I stand here and testify to small and great alike. I am saying nothing beyond what the prophets and Moses said would happen— [23] that the Messiah would suffer and, as the first to rise from the dead, would bring the message of light to his own people and to the Gentiles."

[24] At this point Festus interrupted Paul's defense. "You are

What did it mean to "kick against the goads"? (26:14)
This was a Greek proverb for useless resistance. It described an ox kicking against the stick that was used to guide and direct oxen.

Why did Festus call Paul insane? (26:24)
The governor thought that Paul's education and reading had led him to an obsession with prophecy, and he considered the idea of resurrection ridiculous.

[a] 14 Or *Hebrew*

out of your mind, Paul!" he shouted. "Your great learning is driving you insane."

²⁵"I am not insane, most excellent Festus," Paul replied. "What I am saying is true and reasonable. ²⁶The king is familiar with these things, and I can speak freely to him. I am convinced that none of this has escaped his notice, because it was not done in a corner. ²⁷King Agrippa, do you believe the prophets? I know you do."

²⁸Then Agrippa said to Paul, "Do you think that in such a short time you can persuade me to be a Christian?"

²⁹Paul replied, "Short time or long—I pray to God that not only you but all who are listening to me today may become what I am, except for these chains."

³⁰The king rose, and with him the governor and Bernice and those sitting with them. ³¹After they left the room, they began saying to one another, "This man is not doing anything that deserves death or imprisonment."

³²Agrippa said to Festus, "This man could have been set free if he had not appealed to Caesar."

PAUL SAILS FOR ROME

27 When it was decided that we would sail for Italy, Paul and some other prisoners were handed over to a centurion named Julius, who belonged to the Imperial Regiment. ²We boarded a ship from Adramyttium about to sail for ports along the coast of the province of Asia, and we put out to sea. Aristarchus, a Macedonian from Thessalonica, was with us.

³The next day we landed at Sidon; and Julius, in kindness to Paul, allowed him to go to his friends so they might provide for his needs. ⁴From there we put out to sea again and passed to the lee of Cyprus because the winds were against us. ⁵When we had sailed across the open sea off the coast of Cilicia and Pamphylia, we landed at Myra in Lycia. ⁶There the centurion found an Alexandrian ship sailing for Italy and put us on board. ⁷We made slow headway for many days and had difficulty arriving off Cnidus. When the wind did not allow us to hold our course, we sailed to the lee of Crete, opposite Salmone. ⁸We moved along the coast with difficulty and came to a place called Fair Havens, near the town of Lasea.

⁹Much time had been lost, and sailing had already become dangerous because by now it was after the Day of Atonement.ᵃ So Paul warned them, ¹⁰"Men, I can see that our voyage is going to be disastrous and bring great loss to ship and cargo, and to our own lives also." ¹¹But the centurion, instead of listening to what Paul said, followed the advice of the pilot and of the owner of the ship. ¹²Since the harbor was unsuitable to winter in, the majority decided that we should sail on, hoping to reach Phoenix and winter there. This was a harbor in Crete, facing both southwest and northwest.

THE STORM

¹³When a gentle south wind began to blow, they saw their opportunity; so they weighed anchor and sailed along the

ᵃ 9 That is, Yom Kippur

Why did Agrippa ask if Paul could persuade him to be a Christian in a short time? (26:28)
The king was trying to avoid giving an answer to Paul about what he believed.

When was the Day of Atonement? (27:9)
This day fell in the latter part of September or in October. The usual sailing period for Jews lasted from Pentecost (May or June) to Tabernacles (five days after the fast).

shore of Crete. ¹⁴Before very long, a wind of hurricane force, called the Northeaster, swept down from the island. ¹⁵The ship was caught by the storm and could not head into the wind; so we gave way to it and were driven along. ¹⁶As we passed to the lee of a small island called Cauda, we were hardly able to make the lifeboat secure, ¹⁷so the men hoisted it aboard. Then they passed ropes under the ship itself to hold it together. Because they were afraid they would run aground on the sandbars of Syrtis, they lowered the sea anchor*ᵃ* and let the ship be driven along. ¹⁸We took such a violent battering from the storm that the next day they began to throw the cargo overboard. ¹⁹On the third day, they threw the ship's tackle overboard with their own hands. ²⁰When neither sun nor stars appeared for many days and the storm continued raging, we finally gave up all hope of being saved.

²¹After they had gone a long time without food, Paul stood up before them and said: "Men, you should have taken my advice not to sail from Crete; then you would have spared yourselves this damage and loss. ²²But now I urge you to keep up your courage, because not one of you will be lost; only the ship will be destroyed. ²³Last night an angel of the God to whom I belong and whom I serve stood beside me ²⁴and said, 'Do not be afraid, Paul. You must stand trial before Caesar; and God has graciously given you the lives of all who sail with you.' ²⁵So keep up your courage, men, for

ᵃ 17 Or the sails

Why did they pass ropes under the ship? (27:17)
The ropes were probably passed crosswise under the ship to keep it from breaking apart in the storm.

Why did they throw cargo overboard? (27:18)
They did this to lighten the ship in hopes of keeping it from sinking.

PAUL'S JOURNEY TO ROME (27:1 – 28:14)

I have faith in God that it will happen just as he told me. ²⁶Nevertheless, we must run aground on some island."

THE SHIPWRECK

²⁷On the fourteenth night we were still being driven across the Adriatic^a Sea, when about midnight the sailors sensed they were approaching land. ²⁸They took soundings and found that the water was a hundred and twenty feet^b deep. A short time later they took soundings again and found it was ninety feet^c deep. ²⁹Fearing that we would be dashed against the rocks, they dropped four anchors from the stern and prayed for daylight. ³⁰In an attempt to escape from the ship, the sailors let the lifeboat down into the sea, pretending they were going to lower some anchors from the bow. ³¹Then Paul said to the centurion and the soldiers, "Unless these men stay with the ship, you cannot be saved." ³²So the soldiers cut the ropes that held the lifeboat and let it drift away.

³³Just before dawn Paul urged them all to eat. "For the last fourteen days," he said, "you have been in constant suspense and have gone without food—you haven't eaten anything. ³⁴Now I urge you to take some food. You need it to survive. Not one of you will lose a single hair from his head." ³⁵After he said this, he took some bread and gave thanks to God in front of them all. Then he broke it and began to eat. ³⁶They were all encouraged and ate some food themselves. ³⁷Altogether there were 276 of us on board. ³⁸When they had eaten as much as they wanted, they lightened the ship by throwing the grain into the sea.

³⁹When daylight came, they did not recognize the land, but they saw a bay with a sandy beach, where they decided to run the ship aground if they could. ⁴⁰Cutting loose the anchors, they left them in the sea and at the same time untied the ropes that held the rudders. Then they hoisted the foresail to the wind and made for the beach. ⁴¹But the ship struck a sandbar and ran aground. The bow stuck fast and would not move, and the stern was broken to pieces by the pounding of the surf.

⁴²The soldiers planned to kill the prisoners to prevent any of them from swimming away and escaping. ⁴³But the centurion wanted to spare Paul's life and kept them from carrying out their plan. He ordered those who could swim to jump overboard first and get to land. ⁴⁴The rest were to get there on planks or on other pieces of the ship. In this way everyone reached land safely.

PAUL ASHORE ON MALTA

28 Once safely on shore, we found out that the island was called Malta. ²The islanders showed us unusual kindness. They built a fire and welcomed us all because it was raining and cold. ³Paul gathered a pile of brushwood and, as he put it on the fire, a viper, driven out by the heat, fastened itself on his hand. ⁴When the islanders saw the snake hanging from his hand, they said to each other, "This man

^a 27 In ancient times the name referred to an area extending well south of Italy.   ^b 28 Or about 37 meters   ^c 28 Or about 27 meters

How did Paul encourage the people on the ship to eat? (27:35)
Paul set an example by taking bread and giving thanks to God for it.

Why did the soldiers plan to kill the prisoners? (27:42)
If a prisoner escaped, the guard who was in charge of that prisoner would be killed.

Why were the islanders afraid of the viper? (28:3)
They must have known that it was poisonous.

must be a murderer; for though he escaped from the sea, the goddess Justice has not allowed him to live." [5] But Paul shook the snake off into the fire and suffered no ill effects. [6] The people expected him to swell up or suddenly fall dead; but after waiting a long time and seeing nothing unusual happen to him, they changed their minds and said he was a god.

[7] There was an estate nearby that belonged to Publius, the chief official of the island. He welcomed us to his home and showed us generous hospitality for three days. [8] His father was sick in bed, suffering from fever and dysentery. Paul went in to see him and, after prayer, placed his hands on him and healed him. [9] When this had happened, the rest of the sick on the island came and were cured. [10] They honored us in many ways; and when we were ready to sail, they furnished us with the supplies we needed.

PAUL'S ARRIVAL AT ROME

[11] After three months we put out to sea in a ship that had wintered in the island—it was an Alexandrian ship with the figurehead of the twin gods Castor and Pollux. [12] We put in at Syracuse and stayed there three days. [13] From there we set sail and arrived at Rhegium. The next day the south wind came up, and on the following day we reached Puteoli. [14] There we found some brothers and sisters who invited us to spend a week with them. And so we came to Rome. [15] The brothers and sisters there had heard that we were coming, and they traveled as far as the Forum of Appius and the Three Taverns to meet us. At the sight of these people Paul thanked God and was encouraged. [16] When we got to Rome, Paul was allowed to live by himself, with a soldier to guard him.

PAUL PREACHES AT ROME UNDER GUARD

[17] Three days later he called together the local Jewish leaders. When they had assembled, Paul said to them: "My brothers, although I have done nothing against our people or against the customs of our ancestors, I was arrested in Jerusalem and handed over to the Romans. [18] They examined me and wanted to release me, because I was not guilty of any crime deserving death. [19] The Jews objected, so I was compelled to make an appeal to Caesar. I certainly did not intend to bring any charge against my own people. [20] For this reason I have asked to see you and talk with you. It is because of the hope of Israel that I am bound with this chain."

[21] They replied, "We have not received any letters from Judea concerning you, and none of our people who have come from there has reported or said anything bad about you. [22] But we want to hear what your views are, for we know that people everywhere are talking against this sect."

[23] They arranged to meet Paul on a certain day, and came in even larger numbers to the place where he was staying. He witnessed to them from morning till evening, explaining about the kingdom of God, and from the Law of Moses and from the Prophets he tried to persuade them about Jesus. [24] Some were convinced by what he said, but others

Who were Castor and Pollux? (28:11)
These were two "sons" of the Greek god Zeus. They served as guardian gods of sailors.

Why could Paul live by himself if he was in prison? (28:16)
Paul had not committed any serious crime and was not politically dangerous, so he could live by himself with a guard assigned to him. Paul had also proved himself trustworthy.

would not believe. ²⁵They disagreed among themselves and began to leave after Paul had made this final statement: "The Holy Spirit spoke the truth to your ancestors when he said through Isaiah the prophet:

²⁶ "'Go to this people and say,
　"You will be ever hearing but never understanding;
　　you will be ever seeing but never perceiving."
²⁷ For this people's heart has become calloused;
　they hardly hear with their ears,
　and they have closed their eyes.
Otherwise they might see with their eyes,
　hear with their ears,
　understand with their hearts
and turn, and I would heal them.'*a*

²⁸"Therefore I want you to know that God's salvation has been sent to the Gentiles, and they will listen!" [29]*b*
³⁰For two whole years Paul stayed there in his own rented house and welcomed all who came to see him. ³¹He proclaimed the kingdom of God and taught about the Lord Jesus Christ—with all boldness and without hindrance!

What was Paul's key message? (28:28)
God's salvation had been sent to the Gentiles. This is the main theme of the book of Acts beginning in chapter 10.

---

a 27 Isaiah 6:9,10 (see Septuagint)　　*b* 29 Some manuscripts include here
After he said this, the Jews left, arguing vigorously among themselves.

Romans

INTRODUCTION

Who wrote this book? Paul wrote this book to the church in Rome.

Why was this book written? The book of Romans shows how Jesus' death makes us right with God and how Jesus will help us live a good life.

For whom was this book written? This book is a letter Paul sent to Christians in Rome.

What are some important teachings in this book?

Everyone sins	Romans 3:9 – 20
God saves people who believe	Romans 4:1 – 25
Jesus died for us	Romans 5:1 – 11
God's Spirit helps us to do right	Romans 8:1 – 11
God loves us forever	Romans 8:28 – 39
God shows us how to love	Romans 12:9 – 21

When did these things happen?

10 BC AD 1 10 20 30 40 50 60 70 80 90 100

JESUS' BIRTH (C. 6/5 BC)

JESUS' DEATH, RESURRECTION AND ASCENSION (C. AD 30)

PAUL'S CONVERSION (C. AD 35)

PAUL'S MISSIONARY JOURNEYS (C. AD 46 – 67)

NERO'S REIGN (AD 54 – 68)

BOOK OF ROMANS WRITTEN (C. AD 57)

PAUL'S FIRST IMPRISONMENT IN ROME (C. AD 59 – 62)

PAUL'S IMPRISONMENT AND DEATH IN ROME (C. AD 67 – 68)

DESTRUCTION OF JERUSALEM'S TEMPLE (C. AD 70)

1 Paul, a servant of Christ Jesus, called to be an apostle and set apart for the gospel of God— [2]the gospel he promised beforehand through his prophets in the Holy Scriptures [3]regarding his Son, who as to his earthly life[a] was a descendant of David, [4]and who through the Spirit of holiness was appointed the Son of God in power[b] by his resurrection from the dead: Jesus Christ our Lord. [5]Through him we received grace and apostleship to call all the Gentiles to the obedience that comes from[c] faith for his name's sake. [6]And you also are among those Gentiles who are called to belong to Jesus Christ.

[7]To all in Rome who are loved by God and called to be his holy people:

Grace and peace to you from God our Father and from the Lord Jesus Christ.

PAUL'S LONGING TO VISIT ROME

[8]First, I thank my God through Jesus Christ for all of you, because your faith is being reported all over the world. [9]God, whom I serve in my spirit in preaching the gospel of his Son, is my witness how constantly I remember you [10]in my prayers at all times; and I pray that now at last by God's will the way may be opened for me to come to you.

[11]I long to see you so that I may impart to you some spiritual gift to make you strong— [12]that is, that you and I may be mutually encouraged by each other's faith. [13]I do not want you to be unaware, brothers and sisters,[d] that I planned many times to come to you (but have been prevented from doing so until now) in order that I might have a harvest among you, just as I have had among the other Gentiles.

[14]I am obligated both to Greeks and non-Greeks, both to the wise and the foolish. [15]That is why I am so eager to preach the gospel also to you who are in Rome.

[16]For I am not ashamed of the gospel, because it is the power of God that brings salvation to everyone who believes: first to the Jew, then to the Gentile. [17]For in the gospel the righteousness of God is revealed—a righteousness that is by faith from first to last,[e] just as it is written: "The righteous will live by faith."[f]

GOD'S WRATH AGAINST SINFUL HUMANITY

[18]The wrath of God is being revealed from heaven against all the godlessness and wickedness of people, who suppress the truth by their wickedness, [19]since what may be known about God is plain to them, because God has made it plain to them. [20]For since the creation of the world God's invisible qualities—his eternal power and divine nature—have been clearly seen, being understood from what has been made, so that people are without excuse.

---

[a] 3 Or *who according to the flesh*   [b] 4 Or *was declared with power to be the Son of God*   [c] 5 Or *that is*   [d] 13 The Greek word for *brothers and sisters* (*adelphoi*) refers here to believers, both men and women, as part of God's family; also in 7:1, 4; 8:12, 29; 10:1; 11:25; 12:1; 15:14, 30; 16:14, 17.
[e] 17 Or *is from faith to faith*   [f] 17 Hab. 2:4

Why did Paul call himself a servant? (1:1)
The Greek word Paul used literally meant a slave, but it could also mean a servant who willingly serves his master.

The Church in Rome (1:7)

Did Paul think that anyone could be saved? (1:16–17)
Yes, everyone who believes can be saved. The opportunity was first offered to Jews but was extended to anyone who had faith in Jesus.

What is God's wrath like? (1:18)
God's wrath is not impulsive anger. Instead, God reveals himself to people, so that what can be known about him is clearly seen in nature and in their hearts. But when they refuse to honor and obey him, he abandons them to their wickedness.

²¹For although they knew God, they neither glorified him as God nor gave thanks to him, but their thinking became futile and their foolish hearts were darkened. ²²Although they claimed to be wise, they became fools ²³and exchanged the glory of the immortal God for images made to look like a mortal human being and birds and animals and reptiles.

²⁴Therefore God gave them over in the sinful desires of their hearts to sexual impurity for the degrading of their bodies with one another. ²⁵They exchanged the truth about God for a lie, and worshiped and served created things rather than the Creator—who is forever praised. Amen.

²⁶Because of this, God gave them over to shameful lusts. Even their women exchanged natural sexual relations for unnatural ones. ²⁷In the same way the men also abandoned natural relations with women and were inflamed with lust for one another. Men committed shameful acts with other men, and received in themselves the due penalty for their error.

²⁸Furthermore, just as they did not think it worthwhile to retain the knowledge of God, so God gave them over to a depraved mind, so that they do what ought not to be done. ²⁹They have become filled with every kind of wickedness, evil, greed and depravity. They are full of envy, murder, strife, deceit and malice. They are gossips, ³⁰slanderers, God-haters, insolent, arrogant and boastful; they invent ways of doing evil; they disobey their parents; ³¹they have no understanding, no fidelity, no love, no mercy. ³²Although they know God's righteous decree that those who do such things deserve death, they not only continue to do these very things but also approve of those who practice them.

GOD'S RIGHTEOUS JUDGMENT

2 You, therefore, have no excuse, you who pass judgment on someone else, for at whatever point you judge another, you are condemning yourself, because you who pass judgment do the same things. ²Now we know that God's judgment against those who do such things is based on truth. ³So when you, a mere human being, pass judgment on them and yet do the same things, do you think you will escape God's judgment? ⁴Or do you show contempt for the riches of his kindness, forbearance and patience, not realizing that God's kindness is intended to lead you to repentance?

⁵But because of your stubbornness and your unrepentant heart, you are storing up wrath against yourself for the day of God's wrath, when his righteous judgment will be revealed. ⁶God "will repay each person according to what they have done."ᵃ ⁷To those who by persistence in doing good seek glory, honor and immortality, he will give eternal life. ⁸But for those who are self-seeking and who reject the truth and follow evil, there will be wrath and anger. ⁹There will be trouble and distress for every human being who does evil: first for the Jew, then for the Gentile; ¹⁰but glory, honor and peace for everyone who does good: first for the Jew, then for the Gentile. ¹¹For God does not show favoritism.

ᵃ 6 Psalm 62:12; Prov. 24:12

What does "gave them over" mean? (1:26–32)
God allowed them to face the consequences of their refusal to believe and obey. As a result, they committed sexual sins and a whole range of other sins listed in verses 29–31. They did not act out of ignorance, according to Paul, because they knew what God's laws were.

What was Paul's attitude about judging others? (2:1–3)
Paul's teaching about judging agreed with Jesus' teaching. Paul pointed out that we shouldn't pass judgment on others because all of us are sinners.

¹²All who sin apart from the law will also perish apart from the law, and all who sin under the law will be judged by the law. ¹³For it is not those who hear the law who are righteous in God's sight, but it is those who obey the law who will be declared righteous. ¹⁴(Indeed, when Gentiles, who do not have the law, do by nature things required by the law, they are a law for themselves, even though they do not have the law. ¹⁵They show that the requirements of the law are written on their hearts, their consciences also bearing witness, and their thoughts sometimes accusing them and at other times even defending them.) ¹⁶This will take place on the day when God judges people's secrets through Jesus Christ, as my gospel declares.

THE JEWS AND THE LAW

¹⁷Now you, if you call yourself a Jew; if you rely on the law and boast in God; ¹⁸if you know his will and approve of what is superior because you are instructed by the law; ¹⁹if you are convinced that you are a guide for the blind, a light for those who are in the dark, ²⁰an instructor of the foolish, a teacher of little children, because you have in the law the embodiment of knowledge and truth— ²¹you, then, who teach others, do you not teach yourself? You who preach against stealing, do you steal? ²²You who say that people should not commit adultery, do you commit adultery? You who abhor idols, do you rob temples? ²³You who boast in the law, do you dishonor God by breaking the law? ²⁴As it is written: "God's name is blasphemed among the Gentiles because of you."^a

²⁵Circumcision has value if you observe the law, but if you break the law, you have become as though you had not been circumcised. ²⁶So then, if those who are not circumcised keep the law's requirements, will they not be regarded as though they were circumcised? ²⁷The one who is not circumcised physically and yet obeys the law will condemn you who, even though you have the^b written code and circumcision, are a lawbreaker.

²⁸A person is not a Jew who is one only outwardly, nor is circumcision merely outward and physical. ²⁹No, a person is a Jew who is one inwardly; and circumcision is circumcision of the heart, by the Spirit, not by the written code. Such a person's praise is not from other people, but from God.

GOD'S FAITHFULNESS

3 What advantage, then, is there in being a Jew, or what value is there in circumcision? ²Much in every way! First of all, the Jews have been entrusted with the very words of God.

³What if some were unfaithful? Will their unfaithfulness nullify God's faithfulness? ⁴Not at all! Let God be true, and every human being a liar. As it is written:

"So that you may be proved right when you speak
  and prevail when you judge."^c

What did Paul mean by being judged apart from the law or under the law? (2:12–15)
The Gentiles had not been given the law of Moses, so they would not be judged by that law. Instead, they would be judged by how well they obeyed the laws written on their heart. The Jews, however, would be judged by how well they kept the law of Moses.

How did Paul criticize the Jews? (2:17–24)
The Jews were proud that they knew the law, but Paul pointed out that knowing and teaching the law were not the same as obeying it.

What was Paul's view of circumcision? (2:25–29)
Circumcision was a sign of the covenant, and many Jews thought that circumcision was also a guarantee of God's favor. But Paul said that circumcision was meaningless unless the person also obeyed the law. In fact, if a Gentile behaved more righteously than a Jew, who had the law, the Gentile would symbolically have the sign of circumcision because of having the Holy Spirit within.

^a 24 Isaiah 52:5 (see Septuagint); Ezek. 36:20,22   ^b 27 Or who, by means of a   ^c 4 Psalm 51:4

ROMANS 3:5

[5] But if our unrighteousness brings out God's righteousness more clearly, what shall we say? That God is unjust in bringing his wrath on us? (I am using a human argument.) [6] Certainly not! If that were so, how could God judge the world? [7] Someone might argue, "If my falsehood enhances God's truthfulness and so increases his glory, why am I still condemned as a sinner?" [8] Why not say—as some slanderously claim that we say—"Let us do evil that good may result"? Their condemnation is just!

NO ONE IS RIGHTEOUS

[9] What shall we conclude then? Do we have any advantage? Not at all! For we have already made the charge that Jews and Gentiles alike are all under the power of sin. [10] As it is written:

"There is no one righteous, not even one;
[11]   there is no one who understands;
      there is no one who seeks God.
[12] All have turned away,
      they have together become worthless;
   there is no one who does good,
      not even one."[a]
[13] "Their throats are open graves;
      their tongues practice deceit."[b]
   "The poison of vipers is on their lips."[c]
[14]   "Their mouths are full of cursing and bitterness."[d]
[15] "Their feet are swift to shed blood;
[16]   ruin and misery mark their ways,
[17] and the way of peace they do not know."[e]
[18]   "There is no fear of God before their eyes."[f]

[19] Now we know that whatever the law says, it says to those who are under the law, so that every mouth may be silenced and the whole world held accountable to God. [20] Therefore no one will be declared righteous in God's sight by the works of the law; rather, through the law we become conscious of our sin.

RIGHTEOUSNESS THROUGH FAITH

[21] But now apart from the law the righteousness of God has been made known, to which the Law and the Prophets testify. [22] This righteousness is given through faith in[g] Jesus Christ to all who believe. There is no difference between Jew and Gentile, [23] for all have sinned and fall short of the glory of God, [24] and all are justified freely by his grace through the redemption that came by Christ Jesus. [25] God presented Christ as a sacrifice of atonement,[h] through the shedding of his blood—to be received by faith. He did this to demonstrate his righteousness, because in his forbearance he had left the sins committed beforehand unpunished— [26] he did it to demonstrate his righteousness at the present time, so as to be just and the one who justifies those who have faith in Jesus.

If we are saved by grace rather than works, is it okay to sin? (3:7–8)
Paul spoke out strongly against this incorrect belief. New life in Christ means putting aside our old, evil ways.

Why can no one be declared righteous by keeping the law? (3:20)
Since no one can keep the law perfectly, the law condemns us by showing us how sinful we are.

What did Paul mean by the word justified? (3:24)
Justification is what happens when someone believes in Christ. God declares the person to be not guilty and righteous. God cancels the guilt of the person's sin and credits Christ's righteousness to the person.

---

[a] *12* Psalms 14:1-3; 53:1-3; Eccles. 7:20   [b] *13* Psalm 5:9   [c] *13* Psalm 140:3
[d] *14* Psalm 10:7 (see Septuagint)   [e] *17* Isaiah 59:7,8   [f] *18* Psalm 36:1
[g] *22* Or *through the faithfulness of*   [h] *25* The Greek for *sacrifice of atonement* refers to the atonement cover on the ark of the covenant (see Lev. 16:15,16).

[27] Where, then, is boasting? It is excluded. Because of what law? The law that requires works? No, because of the law that requires faith. [28] For we maintain that a person is justified by faith apart from the works of the law. [29] Or is God the God of Jews only? Is he not the God of Gentiles too? Yes, of Gentiles too, [30] since there is only one God, who will justify the circumcised by faith and the uncircumcised through that same faith. [31] Do we, then, nullify the law by this faith? Not at all! Rather, we uphold the law.

ABRAHAM JUSTIFIED BY FAITH

4 What then shall we say that Abraham, our forefather according to the flesh, discovered in this matter? [2] If, in fact, Abraham was justified by works, he had something to boast about—but not before God. [3] What does Scripture say? "Abraham believed God, and it was credited to him as righteousness."[a]

[4] Now to the one who works, wages are not credited as a gift but as an obligation. [5] However, to the one who does not work but trusts God who justifies the ungodly, their faith is credited as righteousness. [6] David says the same thing when he speaks of the blessedness of the one to whom God credits righteousness apart from works:

[7] "Blessed are those
    whose transgressions are forgiven,
    whose sins are covered.
[8] Blessed is the one
    whose sin the Lord will never count against them."[b]

[9] Is this blessedness only for the circumcised, or also for the uncircumcised? We have been saying that Abraham's faith was credited to him as righteousness. [10] Under what circumstances was it credited? Was it after he was circumcised, or before? It was not after, but before! [11] And he received circumcision as a sign, a seal of the righteousness that he had by faith while he was still uncircumcised. So then, he is the father of all who believe but have not been circumcised, in order that righteousness might be credited to them. [12] And he is then also the father of the circumcised who not only are circumcised but who also follow in the footsteps of the faith that our father Abraham had before he was circumcised.

[13] It was not through the law that Abraham and his offspring received the promise that he would be heir of the world, but through the righteousness that comes by faith. [14] For if those who depend on the law are heirs, faith means nothing and the promise is worthless, [15] because the law brings wrath. And where there is no law there is no transgression.

[16] Therefore, the promise comes by faith, so that it may be by grace and may be guaranteed to all Abraham's offspring—not only to those who are of the law but also to those who have the faith of Abraham. He is the father of us all. [17] As it is written: "I have made you a father of many nations."[c] He is our father in the sight of God, in whom he

What is needed for salvation? (3:28)
Paul said that people gain salvation through faith alone. This was the verse that changed Martin Luther's view of salvation.

Why did Paul want to show that Abraham was justified by faith? (4:1–3)
Paul wanted to show that the Gentiles could also participate in the covenant even though they were not circumcised. Jews continued to think that because they were the descendants of Abraham only they could be saved. But in verse 11, Paul said that Abraham was the father of all who believed, not just the circumcised Jews.

Why does the law bring wrath? (4:15)
The law reveals sin, and since no one can keep the law perfectly, anyone who tries to earn salvation by keeping the law will face God's anger.

---

a 3 Gen. 15:6; also in verse 22   *b 8 Psalm 32:1,2*   *c 17 Gen. 17:5*

How did Paul compare
Abraham's faith to the faith
of Christians? (4:18–25)
Even though Abraham was
"as good as dead" and Sarah's
"womb was also dead," Abraham
believed God's promise that
they would have a son and many
descendants. Abraham believed
in a God who brought life from
the dead, and Christians are
justified by believing in the God
who raised Jesus from the dead.

How did Paul define hope?
(5:5)
Christian hope is not just
optimism or an empty wish. This
confident hope is based on God's
love, revealed by the Holy Spirit,
and demonstrated by the death
of Christ.

What did Paul have in
mind with this extended
comparison of Adam and
Christ? (5:12–21)
Paul said that just as sin and
death came into the world
through one man, Adam, righteousness and life came to the
world through one person,
Jesus Christ. Paul went on to
draw various contrasts between
the two.

believed—the God who gives life to the dead and calls into
being things that were not.

[18] Against all hope, Abraham in hope believed and so became the father of many nations, just as it had been said
to him, "So shall your offspring be."[a] [19] Without weakening
in his faith, he faced the fact that his body was as good as
dead—since he was about a hundred years old—and that
Sarah's womb was also dead. [20] Yet he did not waver through
unbelief regarding the promise of God, but was strengthened
in his faith and gave glory to God, [21] being fully persuaded
that God had power to do what he had promised. [22] This is
why "it was credited to him as righteousness." [23] The words
"it was credited to him" were written not for him alone, [24] but
also for us, to whom God will credit righteousness—for us
who believe in him who raised Jesus our Lord from the dead.
[25] He was delivered over to death for our sins and was raised
to life for our justification.

PEACE AND HOPE

5 Therefore, since we have been justified through faith,
we[b] have peace with God through our Lord Jesus
Christ, [2] through whom we have gained access by faith into
this grace in which we now stand. And we[c] boast in the hope
of the glory of God. [3] Not only so, but we[c] also glory in our
sufferings, because we know that suffering produces perseverance; [4] perseverance, character; and character, hope. [5] And
hope does not put us to shame, because God's love has been
poured out into our hearts through the Holy Spirit, who has
been given to us.

[6] You see, at just the right time, when we were still powerless, Christ died for the ungodly. [7] Very rarely will anyone
die for a righteous person, though for a good person someone might possibly dare to die. [8] But God demonstrates his
own love for us in this: While we were still sinners, Christ
died for us.

[9] Since we have now been justified by his blood, how much
more shall we be saved from God's wrath through him! [10] For
if, while we were God's enemies, we were reconciled to him
through the death of his Son, how much more, having been
reconciled, shall we be saved through his life! [11] Not only is
this so, but we also boast in God through our Lord Jesus
Christ, through whom we have now received reconciliation.

DEATH THROUGH ADAM,
LIFE THROUGH CHRIST

[12] Therefore, just as sin entered the world through one
man, and death through sin, and in this way death came to
all people, because all sinned—

[13] To be sure, sin was in the world before the law was giv-
en, but sin is not charged against anyone's account where
there is no law. [14] Nevertheless, death reigned from the time
of Adam to the time of Moses, even over those who did not
sin by breaking a command, as did Adam, who is a pattern
of the one to come.

---

[a] 18 Gen. 15:5   [b] 1 Many manuscripts *let us*   [c] 2,3 Or *let us*

¹⁵But the gift is not like the trespass. For if the many died by the trespass of the one man, how much more did God's grace and the gift that came by the grace of the one man, Jesus Christ, overflow to the many! ¹⁶Nor can the gift of God be compared with the result of one man's sin: The judgment followed one sin and brought condemnation, but the gift followed many trespasses and brought justification. ¹⁷For if, by the trespass of the one man, death reigned through that one man, how much more will those who receive God's abundant provision of grace and of the gift of righteousness reign in life through the one man, Jesus Christ!

¹⁸Consequently, just as one trespass resulted in condemnation for all people, so also one righteous act resulted in justification and life for all people. ¹⁹For just as through the disobedience of the one man the many were made sinners, so also through the obedience of the one man the many will be made righteous.

²⁰The law was brought in so that the trespass might increase. But where sin increased, grace increased all the more, ²¹so that, just as sin reigned in death, so also grace might reign through righteousness to bring eternal life through Jesus Christ our Lord.

DEAD TO SIN, ALIVE IN CHRIST

6 What shall we say, then? Shall we go on sinning so that grace may increase? ²By no means! We are those who have died to sin; how can we live in it any longer? ³Or don't you know that all of us who were baptized into Christ Jesus were baptized into his death? ⁴We were therefore buried with him through baptism into death in order that, just as Christ was raised from the dead through the glory of the Father, we too may live a new life.

⁵For if we have been united with him in a death like his, we will certainly also be united with him in a resurrection like his. ⁶For we know that our old self was crucified with him so that the body ruled by sin might be done away with,ᵃ that we should no longer be slaves to sin— ⁷because anyone who has died has been set free from sin.

⁸Now if we died with Christ, we believe that we will also live with him. ⁹For we know that since Christ was raised from the dead, he cannot die again; death no longer has mastery over him. ¹⁰The death he died, he died to sin once for all; but the life he lives, he lives to God.

¹¹In the same way, count yourselves dead to sin but alive to God in Christ Jesus. ¹²Therefore do not let sin reign in your mortal body so that you obey its evil desires. ¹³Do not offer any part of yourself to sin as an instrument of wickedness, but rather offer yourselves to God as those who have been brought from death to life; and offer every part of yourself to him as an instrument of righteousness. ¹⁴For sin shall no longer be your master, because you are not under the law, but under grace.

SLAVES TO RIGHTEOUSNESS

¹⁵What then? Shall we sin because we are not under the law but under grace? By no means! ¹⁶Don't you know that

Did Paul think that everyone would be saved? (5:18–19) Paul believed that salvation was available to everyone, but that each person needed to accept God's gift of grace by believing in Christ.

What is the significance of baptism? (6:3–4) When we were born, we became united with Adam and the sin he represented. But through baptism, we are united with Christ, and we share in his death and resurrection so that we can have new life.

ᵃ 6 Or *be rendered powerless*

when you offer yourselves to someone as obedient slaves, you are slaves of the one you obey—whether you are slaves to sin, which leads to death, or to obedience, which leads to righteousness? [17]But thanks be to God that, though you used to be slaves to sin, you have come to obey from your heart the pattern of teaching that has now claimed your allegiance. [18]You have been set free from sin and have become slaves to righteousness.

[19]I am using an example from everyday life because of your human limitations. Just as you used to offer yourselves as slaves to impurity and to ever-increasing wickedness, so now offer yourselves as slaves to righteousness leading to holiness. [20]When you were slaves to sin, you were free from the control of righteousness. [21]What benefit did you reap at that time from the things you are now ashamed of? Those things result in death! [22]But now that you have been set free from sin and have become slaves of God, the benefit you reap leads to holiness, and the result is eternal life. [23]For the wages of sin is death, but the gift of God is eternal life in[a] Christ Jesus our Lord.

RELEASED FROM THE LAW, BOUND TO CHRIST

7 Do you not know, brothers and sisters—for I am speaking to those who know the law—that the law has authority over someone only as long as that person lives? [2]For example, by law a married woman is bound to her husband as long as he is alive, but if her husband dies, she is released from the law that binds her to him. [3]So then, if she has sexual relations with another man while her husband is still alive, she is called an adulteress. But if her husband dies, she is released from that law and is not an adulteress if she marries another man.

[4]So, my brothers and sisters, you also died to the law through the body of Christ, that you might belong to another, to him who was raised from the dead, in order that we might bear fruit for God. [5]For when we were in the realm of the flesh,[b] the sinful passions aroused by the law were at work in us, so that we bore fruit for death. [6]But now, by dying to what once bound us, we have been released from the

[a] 23 Or *through*   [b] 5 In contexts like this, the Greek word for *flesh* (*sarx*) refers to the sinful state of human beings, often presented as a power in opposition to the Spirit.

What two kinds of slavery did Paul describe? (6:19–23)
He described slavery to sin and slavery to God. Slavery to sin results in death. But slavery to God is a willing acceptance of his grace and gift of eternal life.

What did Paul mean when he said that Christians had died to the law? (7:4–6)
In Romans 6:2–7, Paul said that Christians died to sin. Here he says that Christians have died to the law, which means the law no longer has any power over them. Now Christians are free to live lives guided by the Holy Spirit.

If God forgives my sins, why can't I do whatever I want?
ROMANS 6

The Bible is very clear that no one can keep God's law perfectly. Ever since Adam and Even sinned in the Garden of Eden, people have been unable to obey God and keep all of his commandments. That is why keeping the law is not the way to salvation. Instead, God sent his Son to earth to be a sacrifice for sins. Jesus paid the price for our sins, and we are saved by grace not by our good works.

Paul explained that when we are baptized, we are united with Christ and share in his death and resurrection. For us to share in Christ's death means that our old sinful natures die away. To share in his resurrection means that our new identity comes to life. This new identity is one that tries, with the help of the Holy Spirit, to live a life that pleases God. And we don't want to take this gift of forgiveness lightly or for granted. We need to continue to strive to rid our lives of sin in thankfulness and service to God.

law so that we serve in the new way of the Spirit, and not in the old way of the written code.

THE LAW AND SIN

[7]What shall we say, then? Is the law sinful? Certainly not! Nevertheless, I would not have known what sin was had it not been for the law. For I would not have known what coveting really was if the law had not said, "You shall not covet."[a] [8]But sin, seizing the opportunity afforded by the commandment, produced in me every kind of coveting. For apart from the law, sin was dead. [9]Once I was alive apart from the law; but when the commandment came, sin sprang to life and I died. [10]I found that the very commandment that was intended to bring life actually brought death. [11]For sin, seizing the opportunity afforded by the commandment, deceived me, and through the commandment put me to death. [12]So then, the law is holy, and the commandment is holy, righteous and good.

[13]Did that which is good, then, become death to me? By no means! Nevertheless, in order that sin might be recognized as sin, it used what is good to bring about my death, so that through the commandment sin might become utterly sinful.

[14]We know that the law is spiritual; but I am unspiritual, sold as a slave to sin. [15]I do not understand what I do. For what I want to do I do not do, but what I hate I do. [16]And if I do what I do not want to do, I agree that the law is good. [17]As it is, it is no longer I myself who do it, but it is sin living in me. [18]For I know that good itself does not dwell in me, that is, in my sinful nature.[b] For I have the desire to do what is good, but I cannot carry it out. [19]For I do not do the good I want to do, but the evil I do not want to do—this I keep on doing. [20]Now if I do what I do not want to do, it is no longer I who do it, but it is sin living in me that does it.

[21]So I find this law at work: Although I want to do good, evil is right there with me. [22]For in my inner being I delight in God's law; [23]but I see another law at work in me, waging war against the law of my mind and making me a prisoner of the law of sin at work within me. [24]What a wretched man I am! Who will rescue me from this body that is subject to death? [25]Thanks be to God, who delivers me through Jesus Christ our Lord!

So then, I myself in my mind am a slave to God's law, but in my sinful nature[c] a slave to the law of sin.

LIFE THROUGH THE SPIRIT

8 Therefore, there is now no condemnation for those who are in Christ Jesus, [2]because through Christ Jesus the law of the Spirit who gives life has set you[d] free from the law of sin and death. [3]For what the law was powerless to do because it was weakened by the flesh,[e] God did by sending

How did the law bring death? (7:9–12)
The law revealed sin, and death is the punishment for sin.

Was the law responsible for causing evil? (7:12–13)
Paul insisted that the law was holy. The law did not cause Paul to sin. It shone a light on the sin and made him realize that because he was sinful he would have to face the consequences.

How powerful is sin? (7:14–25)
Sin can take over, making people do what they don't want to do and keeping them from doing what they should do. Even though Christians have had their sins forgiven by Jesus, sin is still a reality in a Christian's life.

What new law does a Christian operate under? (8:2–4)
Paul used the word *law* in several ways in the book of Romans. Here he said that Christians live under the law or power of the Holy Spirit, who brings life rather than death. For Christians, the law becomes a guide for living in a way that is pleasing to God.

---

[a] 7 Exodus 20:17; Deut. 5:21   [b] 18 Or *my flesh*   [c] 25 Or *in the flesh*
[d] 2 The Greek is singular; some manuscripts *me*   [e] 3 In contexts like this, the Greek word for *flesh* (*sarx*) refers to the sinful state of human beings, often presented as a power in opposition to the Spirit; also in verses 4-13.

his own Son in the likeness of sinful flesh to be a sin offering.[a] And so he condemned sin in the flesh, [4]in order that the righteous requirement of the law might be fully met in us, who do not live according to the flesh but according to the Spirit.

[5]Those who live according to the flesh have their minds set on what the flesh desires; but those who live in accordance with the Spirit have their minds set on what the Spirit desires. [6]The mind governed by the flesh is death, but the mind governed by the Spirit is life and peace. [7]The mind governed by the flesh is hostile to God; it does not submit to God's law, nor can it do so. [8]Those who are in the realm of the flesh cannot please God.

[9]You, however, are not in the realm of the flesh but are in the realm of the Spirit, if indeed the Spirit of God lives in you. And if anyone does not have the Spirit of Christ, they do not belong to Christ. [10]But if Christ is in you, then even though your body is subject to death because of sin, the Spirit gives life[b] because of righteousness. [11]And if the Spirit of him who raised Jesus from the dead is living in you, he who raised Christ from the dead will also give life to your mortal bodies because of[c] his Spirit who lives in you.

[12]Therefore, brothers and sisters, we have an obligation—but it is not to the flesh, to live according to it. [13]For if you live according to the flesh, you will die; but if by the Spirit you put to death the misdeeds of the body, you will live.

[14]For those who are led by the Spirit of God are the children of God. [15]The Spirit you received does not make you slaves, so that you live in fear again; rather, the Spirit you received brought about your adoption to sonship.[d] And by him we cry, "Abba,[e] Father." [16]The Spirit himself testifies with our spirit that we are God's children. [17]Now if we are children, then we are heirs—heirs of God and co-heirs with Christ, if indeed we share in his sufferings in order that we may also share in his glory.

PRESENT SUFFERING AND FUTURE GLORY

[18]I consider that our present sufferings are not worth comparing with the glory that will be revealed in us. [19]For

---

[a] 3 Or flesh, for sin   [b] 10 Or you, your body is dead because of sin, yet your spirit is alive   [c] 11 Some manuscripts bodies through   [d] 15 The Greek word for adoption to sonship is a term referring to the full legal standing of an adopted male heir in Roman culture; also in verse 23.   [e] 15 Aramaic for father

---

What does it mean to be children of God? (8:14–17)
This refers to adoption. Adoption was common in Paul's time among the Greeks and Romans. An adopted child was granted all the privileges of a biological child, including the rights of inheritance. Christians are adopted by God through grace.

What are some of the ways that the Holy Spirit helps believers?

Paul talks about two kinds of people: those who live by the sinful nature and those who live by the Spirit. The sinful nature leads to death and is filled with hostility to God and rebellion against his rules. Those who belong to Christ have the Holy Spirit living in them. Their spirits are alive because of the work of the Holy Spirit, and the Holy Spirit also guarantees that they will live forever with Jesus.

Christians should be thankful for the Holy Spirit, for it is the Holy Spirit that draws them into God's family as children of God. As members of God's family, Christians will inherit the blessings of eternal life.

The Holy Spirit also helps Christians in their times of weakness and offers prayers that God will strengthen and help them.

the creation waits in eager expectation for the children of God to be revealed. [20] For the creation was subjected to frustration, not by its own choice, but by the will of the one who subjected it, in hope [21] that[a] the creation itself will be liberated from its bondage to decay and brought into the freedom and glory of the children of God.

[22] We know that the whole creation has been groaning as in the pains of childbirth right up to the present time. [23] Not only so, but we ourselves, who have the firstfruits of the Spirit, groan inwardly as we wait eagerly for our adoption to sonship, the redemption of our bodies. [24] For in this hope we were saved. But hope that is seen is no hope at all. Who hopes for what they already have? [25] But if we hope for what we do not yet have, we wait for it patiently.

[26] In the same way, the Spirit helps us in our weakness. We do not know what we ought to pray for, but the Spirit himself intercedes for us through wordless groans. [27] And he who searches our hearts knows the mind of the Spirit, because the Spirit intercedes for God's people in accordance with the will of God.

[28] And we know that in all things God works for the good of those who love him, who[b] have been called according to his purpose. [29] For those God foreknew he also predestined to be conformed to the image of his Son, that he might be the firstborn among many brothers and sisters. [30] And those he predestined, he also called; those he called, he also justified; those he justified, he also glorified.

MORE THAN CONQUERORS

[31] What, then, shall we say in response to these things? If God is for us, who can be against us? [32] He who did not spare his own Son, but gave him up for us all—how will he not also, along with him, graciously give us all things? [33] Who will bring any charge against those whom God has chosen? It is God who justifies. [34] Who then is the one who condemns? No one. Christ Jesus who died—more than that, who was raised to life—is at the right hand of God and is also interceding for us. [35] Who shall separate us from the love of Christ? Shall trouble or hardship or persecution or famine or nakedness or danger or sword? [36] As it is written:

"For your sake we face death all day long;
　　we are considered as sheep to be slaughtered."[c]

[37] No, in all these things we are more than conquerors through him who loved us. [38] For I am convinced that neither death nor life, neither angels nor demons,[d] neither the present nor the future, nor any powers, [39] neither height nor depth, nor anything else in all creation, will be able to separate us from the love of God that is in Christ Jesus our Lord.

What hope do Christians have for the future? (8:23–25) Christians have already been adopted as God's children but look forward to eternal life and the resurrection of their bodies when Christ returns.

What pattern does God follow when he works in the hearts of his people? (8:30) God chooses his people, calls them to himself, offers salvation through Christ, and promises them a glorious eternity.

Do Christians need to be afraid that God will stop loving them? (8:37–39) Paul says that there is absolutely nothing that can separate a Christian from God's love.

---

[a] 20,21 Or subjected it in hope. [21]For　　[b] 28 Or that all things work together for good to those who love God, who; or that in all things God works together with those who love him to bring about what is good—with those who　　[c] 36 Psalm 44:22　　[d] 38 Or nor heavenly rulers

What did Paul say about the descendants of Jacob, the people of Israel? (9:1–9)
Paul pointed out that even though the people of Israel were God's chosen people, not all of them believed in or followed God. They had all the advantages of God's children (vv. 4–5), but not all chose to live by faith.

PAUL'S ANGUISH OVER ISRAEL

9 I speak the truth in Christ—I am not lying, my conscience confirms it through the Holy Spirit— ²I have great sorrow and unceasing anguish in my heart. ³For I could wish that I myself were cursed and cut off from Christ for the sake of my people, those of my own race, ⁴the people of Israel. Theirs is the adoption to sonship; theirs the divine glory, the covenants, the receiving of the law, the temple worship and the promises. ⁵Theirs are the patriarchs, and from them is traced the human ancestry of the Messiah, who is God over all, forever praised!ᵃ Amen.

GOD'S SOVEREIGN CHOICE

⁶It is not as though God's word had failed. For not all who are descended from Israel are Israel. ⁷Nor because they are his descendants are they all Abraham's children. On the contrary, "It is through Isaac that your offspring will be reckoned."ᵇ ⁸In other words, it is not the children by physical descent who are God's children, but it is the children of the promise who are regarded as Abraham's offspring. ⁹For this was how the promise was stated: "At the appointed time I will return, and Sarah will have a son."ᶜ

¹⁰Not only that, but Rebekah's children were conceived at the same time by our father Isaac. ¹¹Yet, before the twins were born or had done anything good or bad—in order that God's purpose in election might stand: ¹²not by works but by him who calls—she was told, "The older will serve the younger."ᵈ ¹³Just as it is written: "Jacob I loved, but Esau I hated."ᵉ

When God chooses people for himself, is he being unfair to those he does not choose? (9:14–18)
Paul said that God has the sovereign right to grant mercy to whomever he chooses.

¹⁴What then shall we say? Is God unjust? Not at all! ¹⁵For he says to Moses,

"I will have mercy on whom I have mercy,
    and I will have compassion on whom I have
        compassion."ᶠ

¹⁶It does not, therefore, depend on human desire or effort, but on God's mercy. ¹⁷For Scripture says to Pharaoh: "I raised you up for this very purpose, that I might display my power in you and that my name might be proclaimed in all the earth."ᵍ ¹⁸Therefore God has mercy on whom he wants to have mercy, and he hardens whom he wants to harden.

What did Paul mean by the example of the potter making pottery? (9:19–21)
This was an illustration from everyday life to show that God, like a potter, is in control and has the right to make choices as a sovereign God.

¹⁹One of you will say to me: "Then why does God still blame us? For who is able to resist his will?" ²⁰But who are you, a human being, to talk back to God? "Shall what is formed say to the one who formed it, 'Why did you make me like this?'"ʰ ²¹Does not the potter have the right to make out of the same lump of clay some pottery for special purposes and some for common use?

²²What if God, although choosing to show his wrath and make his power known, bore with great patience the objects of his wrath—prepared for destruction? ²³What if he did

---

ᵃ 5 Or *Messiah, who is over all. God be forever praised!* Or *Messiah. God who is over all be forever praised!*   ᵇ 7 Gen. 21:12   ᶜ 9 Gen. 18:10,14
ᵈ 12 Gen. 25:23   ᵉ 13 Mal. 1:2,3   ᶠ 15 Exodus 33:19
ᵍ 17 Exodus 9:16   ʰ 20 Isaiah 29:16; 45:9

this to make the riches of his glory known to the objects of his mercy, whom he prepared in advance for glory— [24]even us, whom he also called, not only from the Jews but also from the Gentiles? [25]As he says in Hosea:

"I will call them 'my people' who are not my people;
    and I will call her 'my loved one' who is not my
        loved one,"[a]

[26]and,

"In the very place where it was said to them,
    'You are not my people,'
    there they will be called 'children of the living God.'"[b]

[27]Isaiah cries out concerning Israel:

"Though the number of the Israelites be like the sand
        by the sea,
    only the remnant will be saved.
[28]For the Lord will carry out
    his sentence on earth with speed and finality."[c]

[29]It is just as Isaiah said previously:

"Unless the Lord Almighty
    had left us descendants,
we would have become like Sodom,
    we would have been like Gomorrah."[d]

ISRAEL'S UNBELIEF

[30]What then shall we say? That the Gentiles, who did not pursue righteousness, have obtained it, a righteousness that is by faith; [31]but the people of Israel, who pursued the law as the way of righteousness, have not attained their goal. [32]Why not? Because they pursued it not by faith but as if it were by works. They stumbled over the stumbling stone. [33]As it is written:

"See, I lay in Zion a stone that causes people to
        stumble
    and a rock that makes them fall,
    and the one who believes in him will never be put to
        shame."[e]

10 Brothers and sisters, my heart's desire and prayer to God for the Israelites is that they may be saved. [2]For I can testify about them that they are zealous for God, but their zeal is not based on knowledge. [3]Since they did not know the righteousness of God and sought to establish their own, they did not submit to God's righteousness. [4]Christ is the culmination of the law so that there may be righteousness for everyone who believes.

[5]Moses writes this about the righteousness that is by the law: "The person who does these things will live by them."[f] [6]But the righteousness that is by faith says: "Do not say in your heart, 'Who will ascend into heaven?'"[g] (that is,

What was Israel's problem? (9:30–32)
They tried to keep the law in order to earn God's favor, not by faith but by works.

Did Paul mean that there was no longer a need for the law? (10:4)
No, Paul was saying that Christ was the completion or fulfillment of the law. Because Christ perfectly obeyed the law, Christians no longer feel burdened by its requirements. Instead, Christians follow the law out of gratitude for their salvation.

---

[a] 25 Hosea 2:23   [b] 26 Hosea 1:10   [c] 28 Isaiah 10:22,23 (see Septuagint)
[d] 29 Isaiah 1:9   [e] 33 Isaiah 8:14; 28:16   [f] 5 Lev. 18:5   [g] 6 Deut. 30:12

to bring Christ down) [7]"or 'Who will descend into the deep?'"[a] (that is, to bring Christ up from the dead). [8]But what does it say? "The word is near you; it is in your mouth and in your heart,"[b] that is, the message concerning faith that we proclaim: [9]If you declare with your mouth, "Jesus is Lord," and believe in your heart that God raised him from the dead, you will be saved. [10]For it is with your heart that you believe and are justified, and it is with your mouth that you profess your faith and are saved. [11]As Scripture says, "Anyone who believes in him will never be put to shame."[c] [12]For there is no difference between Jew and Gentile—the same Lord is Lord of all and richly blesses all who call on him, [13]for, "Everyone who calls on the name of the Lord will be saved."[d]

[14]How, then, can they call on the one they have not believed in? And how can they believe in the one of whom they have not heard? And how can they hear without someone preaching to them? [15]And how can anyone preach unless they are sent? As it is written: "How beautiful are the feet of those who bring good news!"[e]

[16]But not all the Israelites accepted the good news. For Isaiah says, "Lord, who has believed our message?"[f] [17]Consequently, faith comes from hearing the message, and the message is heard through the word about Christ. [18]But I ask: Did they not hear? Of course they did:

> "Their voice has gone out into all the earth,
>   their words to the ends of the world."[g]

[19]Again I ask: Did Israel not understand? First, Moses says,

> "I will make you envious by those who are not a
>   nation;
>   I will make you angry by a nation that has no
>   understanding."[h]

[20]And Isaiah boldly says,

> "I was found by those who did not seek me;
>   I revealed myself to those who did not ask for me."[i]

[21]But concerning Israel he says,

> "All day long I have held out my hands
>   to a disobedient and obstinate people."[j]

THE REMNANT OF ISRAEL

11 I ask then: Did God reject his people? By no means! I am an Israelite myself, a descendant of Abraham, from the tribe of Benjamin. [2]God did not reject his people, whom he foreknew. Don't you know what Scripture says in the passage about Elijah—how he appealed to God against Israel: [3]"Lord, they have killed your prophets and torn down your altars; I am the only one left, and they are trying to kill me"[k]? [4]And what was God's answer to him? "I have reserved for myself seven thousand who have not bowed the knee to

---

What is the significance of the statement "Jesus is Lord"? (10:9)
This was the earliest confession of the Christian faith, and it was probably spoken at the baptisms of believers.

Why did Paul emphasize the importance of mission work? (10:14–15)
In order for people to hear the message and believe, others have to go out and tell them the good news.

---

[a] 7 Deut. 30:13　　[b] 8 Deut. 30:14　　[c] 11 Isaiah 28:16 (see Septuagint)
[d] 13 Joel 2:32　　[e] 15 Isaiah 52:7　　[f] 16 Isaiah 53:1　　[g] 18 Psalm 19:4
[h] 19 Deut. 32:21　　[i] 20 Isaiah 65:1　　[j] 21 Isaiah 65:2　　[k] 3 1 Kings 19:10,14

Baal."*ᵃ ⁵So too, at the present time there is a remnant chosen by grace. ⁶And if by grace, then it cannot be based on works; if it were, grace would no longer be grace.

⁷What then? What the people of Israel sought so earnestly they did not obtain. The elect among them did, but the others were hardened, ⁸as it is written:

"God gave them a spirit of stupor,
　eyes that could not see
　and ears that could not hear,
to this very day."ᵇ

⁹And David says:

"May their table become a snare and a trap,
　a stumbling block and a retribution for them.
¹⁰May their eyes be darkened so they cannot see,
　and their backs be bent forever."ᶜ

INGRAFTED BRANCHES

¹¹Again I ask: Did they stumble so as to fall beyond recovery? Not at all! Rather, because of their transgression, salvation has come to the Gentiles to make Israel envious. ¹²But if their transgression means riches for the world, and their loss means riches for the Gentiles, how much greater riches will their full inclusion bring!

¹³I am talking to you Gentiles. Inasmuch as I am the apostle to the Gentiles, I take pride in my ministry ¹⁴in the hope that I may somehow arouse my own people to envy and save some of them. ¹⁵For if their rejection brought reconciliation to the world, what will their acceptance be but life from the dead? ¹⁶If the part of the dough offered as firstfruits is holy, then the whole batch is holy; if the root is holy, so are the branches.

¹⁷If some of the branches have been broken off, and you, though a wild olive shoot, have been grafted in among the others and now share in the nourishing sap from the olive root, ¹⁸do not consider yourself to be superior to those other branches. If you do, consider this: You do not support the root, but the root supports you. ¹⁹You will say then, "Branches were broken off so that I could be grafted in." ²⁰Granted. But they were broken off because of unbelief, and you stand by faith. Do not be arrogant, but tremble. ²¹For if God did not spare the natural branches, he will not spare you either.

²²Consider therefore the kindness and sternness of God: sternness to those who fell, but kindness to you, provided that you continue in his kindness. Otherwise, you also will be cut off. ²³And if they do not persist in unbelief, they will be grafted in, for God is able to graft them in again. ²⁴After all, if you were cut out of an olive tree that is wild by nature, and contrary to nature were grafted into a cultivated olive tree, how much more readily will these, the natural branches, be grafted into their own olive tree!

ALL ISRAEL WILL BE SAVED

²⁵I do not want you to be ignorant of this mystery, brothers and sisters, so that you may not be conceited: Israel has

ᵃ 4 1 Kings 19:18　　*ᵇ 8* Deut. 29:4; Isaiah 29:10　　*ᶜ 10* Psalm 69:22,23

What was the remnant? (11:5)
There was a difference between God's covenant with the entire nation of Israel and with those who truly followed him. Although many Israelites rebelled against God, some remained faithful. These were the ones God had chosen by grace.

Why did Paul preach to the Gentiles and not to his fellow Jews? (11:13–16)
Because many Jews had rejected God, Paul preached the Word to the Gentiles. Paul hoped that this would, in turn, cause many of the Jews to recognize the truth of the gospel and return to God.

What did this analogy about the olive tree mean? (11:17–21)
The olive tree represented the people of God, and the roots represented the patriarchs. Individual branches that had broken off were Jews who had turned away from God, and the branches grafted onto the tree were believers who were Gentiles.

Grafting (11:17–24)

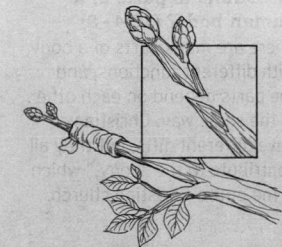

experienced a hardening in part until the full number of the Gentiles has come in, [26] and in this way[a] all Israel will be saved. As it is written:

"The deliverer will come from Zion;
  he will turn godlessness away from Jacob.
[27] And this is[b] my covenant with them
  when I take away their sins."[c]

[28] As far as the gospel is concerned, they are enemies for your sake; but as far as election is concerned, they are loved on account of the patriarchs, [29] for God's gifts and his call are irrevocable. [30] Just as you who were at one time disobedient to God have now received mercy as a result of their disobedience, [31] so they too have now become disobedient in order that they too may now[d] receive mercy as a result of God's mercy to you. [32] For God has bound everyone over to disobedience so that he may have mercy on them all.

DOXOLOGY

[33] Oh, the depth of the riches of the wisdom and[e]
      knowledge of God!
  How unsearchable his judgments,
    and his paths beyond tracing out!
[34] "Who has known the mind of the Lord?
    Or who has been his counselor?"[f]
[35] "Who has ever given to God,
    that God should repay them?"[g]
[36] For from him and through him and for him are all
      things.
  To him be the glory forever! Amen.

A LIVING SACRIFICE

12 Therefore, I urge you, brothers and sisters, in view of God's mercy, to offer your bodies as a living sacrifice, holy and pleasing to God — this is your true and proper worship. [2] Do not conform to the pattern of this world, but be transformed by the renewing of your mind. Then you will be able to test and approve what God's will is — his good, pleasing and perfect will.

HUMBLE SERVICE IN THE BODY OF CHRIST

[3] For by the grace given me I say to every one of you: Do not think of yourself more highly than you ought, but rather think of yourself with sober judgment, in accordance with the faith God has distributed to each of you. [4] For just as each of us has one body with many members, and these members do not all have the same function, [5] so in Christ we, though many, form one body, and each member belongs to all the others. [6] We have different gifts, according to the grace given to each of us. If your gift is prophesying, then prophesy in accordance with your[b] faith; [7] if it is serving, then serve; if it is teaching, then teach; [8] if it is to encourage, then give

Why did Paul compare Christians to parts of a human body? (12:4–8)
There are many parts of a body with different functions, and the parts depend on each other. In the same way, Christians have different gifts, but they all contribute to the "body," which is the entire Christian church.

---

[a] 26 Or *and so*   [b] 27 Or *will be*   [c] 27 Isaiah 59:20,21; 27:9 (see Septuagint); Jer. 31:33,34   [d] 31 Some manuscripts do not have *now.*   [e] 33 Or *riches and the wisdom and the*   [f] 34 Isaiah 40:13   [g] 35 Job 41:11   [h] 6 Or *the*

encouragement; if it is giving, then give generously; if it is to lead,[a] do it diligently; if it is to show mercy, do it cheerfully.

LOVE IN ACTION

[9] Love must be sincere. Hate what is evil; cling to what is good. [10] Be devoted to one another in love. Honor one another above yourselves. [11] Never be lacking in zeal, but keep your spiritual fervor, serving the Lord. [12] Be joyful in hope, patient in affliction, faithful in prayer. [13] Share with the Lord's people who are in need. Practice hospitality.

[14] Bless those who persecute you; bless and do not curse. [15] Rejoice with those who rejoice; mourn with those who mourn. [16] Live in harmony with one another. Do not be proud, but be willing to associate with people of low position.[b] Do not be conceited.

[17] Do not repay anyone evil for evil. Be careful to do what is right in the eyes of everyone. [18] If it is possible, as far as it depends on you, live at peace with everyone. [19] Do not take revenge, my dear friends, but leave room for God's wrath, for it is written: "It is mine to avenge; I will repay,"[c] says the Lord. [20] On the contrary:

> "If your enemy is hungry, feed him;
>   if he is thirsty, give him something to drink.
> In doing this, you will heap burning coals on his
>   head."[d]

[21] Do not be overcome by evil, but overcome evil with good.

SUBMISSION TO GOVERNING AUTHORITIES

13 Let everyone be subject to the governing authorities, for there is no authority except that which God has established. The authorities that exist have been established by God. [2] Consequently, whoever rebels against the authority is rebelling against what God has instituted, and those who do so will bring judgment on themselves. [3] For rulers hold no terror for those who do right, but for those who do wrong. Do you want to be free from fear of the one in authority? Then do what is right and you will be commended. [4] For the one in authority is God's servant for your good. But if you do wrong, be afraid, for rulers do not bear the sword for no reason. They are God's servants, agents of wrath to bring punishment on the wrongdoer. [5] Therefore, it is necessary to submit to the authorities, not only because of possible punishment but also as a matter of conscience.

[6] This is also why you pay taxes, for the authorities are God's servants, who give their full time to governing. [7] Give to everyone what you owe them: If you owe taxes, pay taxes; if revenue, then revenue; if respect, then respect; if honor, then honor.

LOVE FULFILLS THE LAW

[8] Let no debt remain outstanding, except the continuing debt to love one another, for whoever loves others has fulfilled

What does it mean to "bless those who persecute you"? (12:14)
Though sometimes it may be hard to follow, one of the basic principles Jesus taught his disciples was to treat others the way you want to be treated. This means being nice to people even when they've been unkind to you. Praying for those who have hurt us is another way to bless them and show love in action.

Why are Christians expected to obey the government authorities? (13:1–5)
A practical reason is to avoid punishment. But the more important reason is that governments are given authority by God to maintain order in society and to administer justice.

---

[a] 8 Or to provide for others   [b] 16 Or willing to do menial work
[c] 19 Deut. 32:35   [d] 20 Prov. 25:21,22

the law. ⁹The commandments, "You shall not commit adultery," "You shall not murder," "You shall not steal," "You shall not covet,"ᵃ and whatever other command there may be, are summed up in this one command: "Love your neighbor as yourself."ᵇ ¹⁰Love does no harm to a neighbor. Therefore love is the fulfillment of the law.

THE DAY IS NEAR

¹¹And do this, understanding the present time: The hour has already come for you to wake up from your slumber, because our salvation is nearer now than when we first believed. ¹²The night is nearly over; the day is almost here. So let us put aside the deeds of darkness and put on the armor of light. ¹³Let us behave decently, as in the daytime, not in carousing and drunkenness, not in sexual immorality and debauchery, not in dissension and jealousy. ¹⁴Rather, clothe yourselves with the Lord Jesus Christ, and do not think about how to gratify the desires of the flesh.ᶜ

THE WEAK AND THE STRONG

14 Accept the one whose faith is weak, without quarreling over disputable matters. ²One person's faith allows them to eat anything, but another, whose faith is weak, eats only vegetables. ³The one who eats everything must not treat with contempt the one who does not, and the one who does not eat everything must not judge the one who does, for God has accepted them. ⁴Who are you to judge someone else's servant? To their own master, servants stand or fall. And they will stand, for the Lord is able to make them stand.

⁵One person considers one day more sacred than another; another considers every day alike. Each of them should be fully convinced in their own mind. ⁶Whoever regards one day as special does so to the Lord. Whoever eats meat does so to the Lord, for they give thanks to God; and whoever abstains does so to the Lord and gives thanks to God. ⁷For none of us lives for ourselves alone, and none of us dies for ourselves alone. ⁸If we live, we live for the Lord; and if we die, we die for the Lord. So, whether we live or die, we belong to the Lord. ⁹For this very reason, Christ died and returned to life so that he might be the Lord of both the dead and the living.

¹⁰You, then, why do you judge your brother or sisterᵈ? Or why do you treat them with contempt? For we will all stand before God's judgment seat. ¹¹It is written:

"'As surely as I live,' says the Lord,
'every knee will bow before me;
    every tongue will acknowledge God.'"ᵉ

¹²So then, each of us will give an account of ourselves to God.

ᵃ *9* Exodus 20:13-15,17; Deut. 5:17-19,21   ᵇ *9* Lev. 19:18   ᶜ *14* In contexts like this, the Greek word for *flesh* (*sarx*) refers to the sinful state of human beings, often presented as a power in opposition to the Spirit.   ᵈ *10* The Greek word for *brother or sister* (*adelphos*) refers here to a believer, whether man or woman, as part of God's family; also in verses 13, 15 and 21.   ᵉ *11* Isaiah 45:23

How can Christians clothe themselves with Christ? (13:14)
Believers should not only have faith in their hearts, but they should also demonstrate that they belong to Christ by practicing Christian virtues.

Whose faith was weak? (14:1)
Paul was probably referring to Jewish Christians who were unwilling to give up some of their former religious practices, such as following the Sabbath regulations and obeying dietary rules. They were not trying to earn God's favor but were unclear if the Old Testament rules still applied to Christians.

What did Paul urge believers who had different practices or opinions? (14:4, 10–12)
He told them not to judge each other for these differences because each Christian answers to God for his behavior. Christians are not to put themselves in God's place as judge.

[13]Therefore let us stop passing judgment on one another. Instead, make up your mind not to put any stumbling block or obstacle in the way of a brother or sister. [14]I am convinced, being fully persuaded in the Lord Jesus, that nothing is unclean in itself. But if anyone regards something as unclean, then for that person it is unclean. [15]If your brother or sister is distressed because of what you eat, you are no longer acting in love. Do not by your eating destroy someone for whom Christ died. [16]Therefore do not let what you know is good be spoken of as evil. [17]For the kingdom of God is not a matter of eating and drinking, but of righteousness, peace and joy in the Holy Spirit, [18]because anyone who serves Christ in this way is pleasing to God and receives human approval.

[19]Let us therefore make every effort to do what leads to peace and to mutual edification. [20]Do not destroy the work of God for the sake of food. All food is clean, but it is wrong for a person to eat anything that causes someone else to stumble. [21]It is better not to eat meat or drink wine or to do anything else that will cause your brother or sister to fall.

[22]So whatever you believe about these things keep between yourself and God. Blessed is the one who does not condemn himself by what he approves. [23]But whoever has doubts is condemned if they eat, because their eating is not from faith; and everything that does not come from faith is sin.[a]

15 We who are strong ought to bear with the failings of the weak and not to please ourselves. [2]Each of us should please our neighbors for their good, to build them up. [3]For even Christ did not please himself but, as it is written: "The insults of those who insult you have fallen on me."[b] [4]For everything that was written in the past was written to teach us, so that through the endurance taught in the Scriptures and the encouragement they provide we might have hope.

[5]May the God who gives endurance and encouragement give you the same attitude of mind toward each other that Christ Jesus had, [6]so that with one mind and one voice you may glorify the God and Father of our Lord Jesus Christ.

[7]Accept one another, then, just as Christ accepted you, in order to bring praise to God. [8]For I tell you that Christ has become a servant of the Jews[c] on behalf of God's truth, so that the promises made to the patriarchs might be confirmed [9]and, moreover, that the Gentiles might glorify God for his mercy. As it is written:

"Therefore I will praise you among the Gentiles;
    I will sing the praises of your name."[d]

[10]Again, it says,

"Rejoice, you Gentiles, with his people."[e]

[11]And again,

"Praise the Lord, all you Gentiles;
    let all the peoples extol him."[f]

What sort of peace should Christians promote among themselves? (14:19–21) Christians should work for peaceful relationships and to build one another up. If that means honoring someone else's rules, even if you think they aren't necessary, Paul says you should do it so as not to cause a fellow Christian to violate his or her conscience.

How does Scripture help Christians? (15:4) Paul said that Scripture was written for our instruction so that as we patiently endure we will be encouraged to hold fast to our hope in Christ.

---

[a] 23 Some manuscripts place 16:25-27 here; others after 15:33.
[b] 3 Psalm 69:9   [c] 8 Greek *circumcision*   [d] 9 2 Samuel 22:50; Psalm 18:49
[e] 10 Deut. 32:43   [f] 11 Psalm 117:1

[12] And again, Isaiah says,

"The Root of Jesse will spring up,
 one who will arise to rule over the nations;
 in him the Gentiles will hope."[a]

[13] May the God of hope fill you with all joy and peace as you trust in him, so that you may overflow with hope by the power of the Holy Spirit.

PAUL THE MINISTER TO THE GENTILES

[14] I myself am convinced, my brothers and sisters, that you yourselves are full of goodness, filled with knowledge and competent to instruct one another. [15] Yet I have written you quite boldly on some points to remind you of them again, because of the grace God gave me [16] to be a minister of Christ Jesus to the Gentiles. He gave me the priestly duty of proclaiming the gospel of God, so that the Gentiles might become an offering acceptable to God, sanctified by the Holy Spirit.

[17] Therefore I glory in Christ Jesus in my service to God. [18] I will not venture to speak of anything except what Christ has accomplished through me in leading the Gentiles to obey God by what I have said and done— [19] by the power of signs and wonders, through the power of the Spirit of God. So from Jerusalem all the way around to Illyricum, I have fully proclaimed the gospel of Christ. [20] It has always been my ambition to preach the gospel where Christ was not known, so that I would not be building on someone else's foundation. [21] Rather, as it is written:

"Those who were not told about him will see,
 and those who have not heard will understand."[b]

[22] This is why I have often been hindered from coming to you.

PAUL'S PLAN TO VISIT ROME

[23] But now that there is no more place for me to work in these regions, and since I have been longing for many years to visit you, [24] I plan to do so when I go to Spain. I hope to see you while passing through and to have you assist me on my journey there, after I have enjoyed your company for a while. [25] Now, however, I am on my way to Jerusalem in the service of the Lord's people there. [26] For Macedonia and Achaia were pleased to make a contribution for the poor among the Lord's people in Jerusalem. [27] They were pleased to do it, and indeed they owe it to them. For if the Gentiles have shared in the Jews' spiritual blessings, they owe it to the Jews to share with them their material blessings. [28] So after I have completed this task and have made sure that they have received this contribution, I will go to Spain and visit you on the way. [29] I know that when I come to you, I will come in the full measure of the blessing of Christ.

[30] I urge you, brothers and sisters, by our Lord Jesus Christ and by the love of the Spirit, to join me in my struggle by praying to God for me. [31] Pray that I may be kept safe from

---

Was Paul boasting about his accomplishments? (15:17–18)
Paul was careful to give all the credit and glory to Christ, who gave him the ability to do his work.

What was Paul concerned about? (15:31)
Paul asked the Christians in Rome to pray that he would be safe in Judea. It was important for him to deliver the collection to the believers there, but he had received warnings about what might happen (see Acts 20:22–23).

---

a 12 Isaiah 11:10 (see Septuagint)   *b 21* Isaiah 52:15 (see Septuagint)

the unbelievers in Judea and that the contribution I take to Jerusalem may be favorably received by the Lord's people there, ³²so that I may come to you with joy, by God's will, and in your company be refreshed. ³³The God of peace be with you all. Amen.

PERSONAL GREETINGS

16 I commend to you our sister Phoebe, a deacon*^{a,b}* of the church in Cenchreae. ²I ask you to receive her in the Lord in a way worthy of his people and to give her any help she may need from you, for she has been the benefactor of many people, including me.

³Greet Priscilla*^c* and Aquila, my co-workers in Christ Jesus. ⁴They risked their lives for me. Not only I but all the churches of the Gentiles are grateful to them.

⁵Greet also the church that meets at their house.

Greet my dear friend Epenetus, who was the first convert to Christ in the province of Asia.

⁶Greet Mary, who worked very hard for you.

⁷Greet Andronicus and Junia, my fellow Jews who have been in prison with me. They are outstanding among*^d* the apostles, and they were in Christ before I was.

⁸Greet Ampliatus, my dear friend in the Lord.

⁹Greet Urbanus, our co-worker in Christ, and my dear friend Stachys.

¹⁰Greet Apelles, whose fidelity to Christ has stood the test.

Greet those who belong to the household of Aristobulus.

¹¹Greet Herodion, my fellow Jew.

Greet those in the household of Narcissus who are in the Lord.

¹²Greet Tryphena and Tryphosa, those women who work hard in the Lord.

Greet my dear friend Persis, another woman who has worked very hard in the Lord.

¹³Greet Rufus, chosen in the Lord, and his mother, who has been a mother to me, too.

¹⁴Greet Asyncritus, Phlegon, Hermes, Patrobas, Hermas and the other brothers and sisters with them.

¹⁵Greet Philologus, Julia, Nereus and his sister, and Olympas and all the Lord's people who are with them.

¹⁶Greet one another with a holy kiss.

All the churches of Christ send greetings.

¹⁷I urge you, brothers and sisters, to watch out for those who cause divisions and put obstacles in your way that are contrary to the teaching you have learned. Keep away from them. ¹⁸For such people are not serving our Lord Christ, but their own appetites. By smooth talk and flattery they deceive the minds of naive people. ¹⁹Everyone has heard about your obedience, so I rejoice because of you; but I want you to be wise about what is good, and innocent about what is evil.

What do we know about the people who are greeted here? (16:3–16)
Most of the people were Gentiles, freed slaves, or descendants of freed slaves. It seems that many of the early Christians came from the lower classes of society. Of the 27 people mentioned, 10 were women. It is clear that women were an important part of the ministry of the early church.

What warning did Paul give to the believers? (16:17–19)
Paul warned them to be careful about people who would try to create divisions and promote false teachings. Paul wanted the believers to be on guard so that they would not be led astray by such people.

---

^a 1 Or *servant*　　*^b 1* The word *deacon* refers here to a Christian designated to serve with the overseers/elders of the church in a variety of ways; similarly in Phil. 1:1 and 1 Tim. 3:8,12.　　*^c 3* Greek *Prisca*, a variant of *Priscilla*
^d 7 Or *are esteemed by*

²⁰The God of peace will soon crush Satan under your feet. The grace of our Lord Jesus be with you.

²¹Timothy, my co-worker, sends his greetings to you, as do Lucius, Jason and Sosipater, my fellow Jews.

²²I, Tertius, who wrote down this letter, greet you in the Lord.

²³Gaius, whose hospitality I and the whole church here enjoy, sends you his greetings.

Erastus, who is the city's director of public works, and our brother Quartus send you their greetings. [24]*a*

²⁵Now to him who is able to establish you in accordance with my gospel, the message I proclaim about Jesus Christ, in keeping with the revelation of the mystery hidden for long ages past, ²⁶but now revealed and made known through the prophetic writings by the command of the eternal God, so that all the Gentiles might come to the obedience that comes from*b* faith— ²⁷to the only wise God be glory forever through Jesus Christ! Amen.

---

a 24 Some manuscripts include here *May the grace of our Lord Jesus Christ be with all of you. Amen.*   *b* 26 Or *that is*

1 Corinthians

INTRODUCTION

Who wrote this book? Paul.

Why was this book written? Paul wrote the book of 1 Corinthians to help the Corinthians solve problems in their church.

For whom was this book written? This book is a letter that Paul sent to Christians in Corinth.

What are some important teachings in this book?

Believers must stop sinning	1 Corinthians 6:9 – 11
Each of us is important	1 Corinthians 12:14 – 31
What love is really like	1 Corinthians 13:1 – 13
Jesus is alive	1 Corinthians 15:3 – 8
We will be resurrected too	1 Corinthians 15:35 – 58

When did these things happen?

	10BC	AD1	10	20	30	40	50	60	70	80	90	100
JESUS' LIFE (C. 6/5 BC – AD 30)												
PAUL'S CONVERSION (C. AD 35)												
PAUL'S MISSIONARY JOURNEYS (C. AD 46 – 67)												
PAUL'S STAY IN CORINTH (C. AD 51 – 52)												
NERO'S REIGN (AD 54 – 68)												
BOOK OF 1 CORINTHIANS WRITTEN (C. AD 55)												
PAUL'S FIRST IMPRISONMENT IN ROME (C. AD 59 – 62)												
PAUL'S IMPRISONMENT AND DEATH IN ROME (C. AD 67 – 68)												

1 Paul, called to be an apostle of Christ Jesus by the will of God, and our brother Sosthenes,

²To the church of God in Corinth, to those sanctified in Christ Jesus and called to be his holy people, together with all those everywhere who call on the name of our Lord Jesus Christ—their Lord and ours:

³Grace and peace to you from God our Father and the Lord Jesus Christ.

THANKSGIVING

⁴I always thank my God for you because of his grace given you in Christ Jesus. ⁵For in him you have been enriched in every way—with all kinds of speech and with all knowledge— ⁶God thus confirming our testimony about Christ among you. ⁷Therefore you do not lack any spiritual gift as you eagerly wait for our Lord Jesus Christ to be revealed. ⁸He will also keep you firm to the end, so that you will be blameless on the day of our Lord Jesus Christ. ⁹God is faithful, who has called you into fellowship with his Son, Jesus Christ our Lord.

A CHURCH DIVIDED OVER LEADERS

¹⁰I appeal to you, brothers and sisters,ᵃ in the name of our Lord Jesus Christ, that all of you agree with one another in what you say and that there be no divisions among you, but that you be perfectly united in mind and thought. ¹¹My brothers and sisters, some from Chloe's household have informed me that there are quarrels among you. ¹²What I mean is this: One of you says, "I follow Paul"; another, "I follow Apollos"; another, "I follow Cephasᵇ"; still another, "I follow Christ."

¹³Is Christ divided? Was Paul crucified for you? Were you baptized in the name of Paul? ¹⁴I thank God that I did not baptize any of you except Crispus and Gaius, ¹⁵so no one can say that you were baptized in my name. ¹⁶(Yes, I also baptized the household of Stephanas; beyond that, I don't remember if I baptized anyone else.) ¹⁷For Christ did not send me to baptize, but to preach the gospel—not with wisdom and eloquence, lest the cross of Christ be emptied of its power.

CHRIST CRUCIFIED IS GOD'S POWER AND WISDOM

¹⁸For the message of the cross is foolishness to those who are perishing, but to us who are being saved it is the power of God. ¹⁹For it is written:

"I will destroy the wisdom of the wise;
the intelligence of the intelligent I will frustrate."ᶜ

²⁰Where is the wise person? Where is the teacher of the law? Where is the philosopher of this age? Has not God made foolish the wisdom of the world? ²¹For since in the

The Church in Corinth (1:2)

Why did Paul call the Christians of Corinth brothers and sisters? (1:10)

Christians have a close relationship with one another, almost like biological brothers and sisters, because of their shared belief in Christ.

Who were Apollos and Cephas? (1:12)

Apollos was a Jewish Christian who was a great public speaker and who had a thorough knowledge of the Scriptures. He worked alongside Paul during the early years of the church in Corinth. Cephas is the Aramaic word for Peter. The people in Corinth who followed Peter were probably Jewish Christians.

Who were these wise people, teachers of the law, and the philosophers? (1:20)

The wise people were probably Greek philosophers in general. The Jewish teachers of the law were the scholars of their day. The philosophers were probably a specific type of Greek philosopher who engaged in long debates and arguments.

ᵃ 10 The Greek word for *brothers and sisters* (*adelphoi*) refers here to believers, both men and women, as part of God's family; also in verses 11 and 26; and in 2:1; 3:1; 4:6; 6:8; 7:24, 29; 10:1; 11:33; 12:1; 14:6, 20, 26, 39; 15:1, 6, 50, 58; 16:15, 20.   ᵇ 12 That is, Peter   ᶜ 19 Isaiah 29:14

wisdom of God the world through its wisdom did not know him, God was pleased through the foolishness of what was preached to save those who believe. ²²Jews demand signs and Greeks look for wisdom, ²³but we preach Christ crucified: a stumbling block to Jews and foolishness to Gentiles, ²⁴but to those whom God has called, both Jews and Greeks, Christ the power of God and the wisdom of God. ²⁵For the foolishness of God is wiser than human wisdom, and the weakness of God is stronger than human strength.

²⁶Brothers and sisters, think of what you were when you were called. Not many of you were wise by human standards; not many were influential; not many were of noble birth. ²⁷But God chose the foolish things of the world to shame the wise; God chose the weak things of the world to shame the strong. ²⁸God chose the lowly things of this world and the despised things—and the things that are not—to nullify the things that are, ²⁹so that no one may boast before him. ³⁰It is because of him that you are in Christ Jesus, who has become for us wisdom from God—that is, our righteousness, holiness and redemption. ³¹Therefore, as it is written: "Let the one who boasts boast in the Lord."ᵃ

2 And so it was with me, brothers and sisters. When I came to you, I did not come with eloquence or human wisdom as I proclaimed to you the testimony about God.ᵇ ²For I resolved to know nothing while I was with you except Jesus Christ and him crucified. ³I came to you in weakness with great fear and trembling. ⁴My message and my preaching were not with wise and persuasive words, but with a demonstration of the Spirit's power, ⁵so that your faith might not rest on human wisdom, but on God's power.

GOD'S WISDOM REVEALED BY THE SPIRIT

⁶We do, however, speak a message of wisdom among the mature, but not the wisdom of this age or of the rulers of this age, who are coming to nothing. ⁷No, we declare God's wisdom, a mystery that has been hidden and that God destined for our glory before time began. ⁸None of the rulers of this age understood it, for if they had, they would not have crucified the Lord of glory. ⁹However, as it is written:

"What no eye has seen,
    what no ear has heard,
and what no human mind has conceived"ᶜ—
        the things God has prepared for those who
            love him—

¹⁰these are the things God has revealed to us by his Spirit.

The Spirit searches all things, even the deep things of God. ¹¹For who knows a person's thoughts except their own spirit within them? In the same way no one knows the thoughts of God except the Spirit of God. ¹²What we have received is not the spirit of the world, but the Spirit who is from God, so that we may understand what God has freely given us. ¹³This is what we speak, not in words taught us by

---

Why was it difficult for both Jews and Greeks to believe in Jesus? (1:23)
The Jews were looking for a political savior, not a crucified one. Greeks and Romans were sure that an honorable person would never be crucified, so they could not imagine a Savior who was a treated like a criminal.

Was Paul an effective public speaker? (2:4)
Paul's letters show that he was knowledgeable about many subjects, and he had a very effective style of writing. His speech before the Areopagus was very powerful (see Acts 17:22 – 31). His point here was that when he was trying to convince people to believe in Jesus, he did not want to rely on effective speaking but on the power of the Holy Spirit.

What is the "spirit of the world"? (2:12)
This is human wisdom that is apart from God. It is the attitude of the sinful nature (see Romans 8:6 – 7).

ᵃ 31 Jer. 9:24   ᵇ 1 Some manuscripts *proclaimed to you God's mystery*
ᶜ 9 Isaiah 64:4

human wisdom but in words taught by the Spirit, explaining spiritual realities with Spirit-taught words.[a] [14]The person without the Spirit does not accept the things that come from the Spirit of God but considers them foolishness, and cannot understand them because they are discerned only through the Spirit. [15]The person with the Spirit makes judgments about all things, but such a person is not subject to merely human judgments, [16]for,

> "Who has known the mind of the Lord
>   so as to instruct him?"[b]

But we have the mind of Christ.

THE CHURCH AND ITS LEADERS

3 Brothers and sisters, I could not address you as people who live by the Spirit but as people who are still worldly—mere infants in Christ. [2]I gave you milk, not solid food, for you were not yet ready for it. Indeed, you are still not ready. [3]You are still worldly. For since there is jealousy and quarreling among you, are you not worldly? Are you not acting like mere humans? [4]For when one says, "I follow Paul," and another, "I follow Apollos," are you not mere human beings?

[5]What, after all, is Apollos? And what is Paul? Only servants, through whom you came to believe—as the Lord has assigned to each his task. [6]I planted the seed, Apollos watered it, but God has been making it grow. [7]So neither the one who plants nor the one who waters is anything, but only God, who makes things grow. [8]The one who plants and the one who waters have one purpose, and they will each be rewarded according to their own labor. [9]For we are co-workers in God's service; you are God's field, God's building.

[10]By the grace God has given me, I laid a foundation as a wise builder, and someone else is building on it. But each one should build with care. [11]For no one can lay any foundation other than the one already laid, which is Jesus Christ. [12]If anyone builds on this foundation using gold, silver, costly stones, wood, hay or straw, [13]their work will be shown for what it is, because the Day will bring it to light. It will be revealed with fire, and the fire will test the quality of each person's work. [14]If what has been built survives, the builder will receive a reward. [15]If it is burned up, the builder will suffer loss but yet will be saved—even though only as one escaping through the flames.

[16]Don't you know that you yourselves are God's temple and that God's Spirit dwells in your midst? [17]If anyone destroys God's temple, God will destroy that person; for God's temple is sacred, and you together are that temple.

[18]Do not deceive yourselves. If any of you think you are wise by the standards of this age, you should become "fools" so that you may become wise. [19]For the wisdom of this world is foolishness in God's sight. As it is written: "He catches the wise in their craftiness"[c]; [20]and again, "The Lord knows

Why did Paul compare the Christians to crops? (3:6–9)
He wanted to show that both he and Apollos were important to the Corinthians' spiritual growth but that God was ultimately responsible. Paul had planted the seed by first preaching the gospel, and Apollos had provided the water by working among the believers. But God provided the spiritual growth.

How were the Christians like a building? (3:9–17)
Paul again wanted to show that he and Apollos had played different roles, but both were important to the building up of the church. Jesus Christ was the foundation of the church.

---

[a] 13 Or *Spirit, interpreting spiritual truths to those who are spiritual*
[b] 16 Isaiah 40:13   [c] 19 Job 5:13

that the thoughts of the wise are futile."[a] [21]So then, no more boasting about human leaders! All things are yours, [22]whether Paul or Apollos or Cephas[b] or the world or life or death or the present or the future—all are yours, [23]and you are of Christ, and Christ is of God.

THE NATURE OF TRUE APOSTLESHIP

4 This, then, is how you ought to regard us: as servants of Christ and as those entrusted with the mysteries God has revealed. [2]Now it is required that those who have been given a trust must prove faithful. [3]I care very little if I am judged by you or by any human court; indeed, I do not even judge myself. [4]My conscience is clear, but that does not make me innocent. It is the Lord who judges me. [5]Therefore judge nothing before the appointed time; wait until the Lord comes. He will bring to light what is hidden in darkness and will expose the motives of the heart. At that time each will receive their praise from God.

[6]Now, brothers and sisters, I have applied these things to myself and Apollos for your benefit, so that you may learn from us the meaning of the saying, "Do not go beyond what is written." Then you will not be puffed up in being a follower of one of us over against the other. [7]For who makes you different from anyone else? What do you have that you did not receive? And if you did receive it, why do you boast as though you did not?

[8]Already you have all you want! Already you have become rich! You have begun to reign—and that without us! How I wish that you really had begun to reign so that we also might reign with you! [9]For it seems to me that God has put us apostles on display at the end of the procession, like those condemned to die in the arena. We have been made a spectacle to the whole universe, to angels as well as to human beings. [10]We are fools for Christ, but you are so wise in Christ! We are weak, but you are strong! You are honored, we are dishonored! [11]To this very hour we go hungry and thirsty, we are in rags, we are brutally treated, we are homeless. [12]We work hard with our own hands. When we are cursed, we bless; when we are persecuted, we endure it; [13]when we are slandered, we answer kindly. We have become the scum of the earth, the garbage of the world—right up to this moment.

PAUL'S APPEAL AND WARNING

[14]I am writing this not to shame you but to warn you as my dear children. [15]Even if you had ten thousand guardians in Christ, you do not have many fathers, for in Christ Jesus I became your father through the gospel. [16]Therefore I urge you to imitate me. [17]For this reason I have sent to you Timothy, my son whom I love, who is faithful in the Lord. He will remind you of my way of life in Christ Jesus, which agrees with what I teach everywhere in every church.

[18]Some of you have become arrogant, as if I were not coming to you. [19]But I will come to you very soon, if the Lord is

[a] 20 Psalm 94:11   [b] 22 That is, Peter

Why did Paul say the Corinthians "have begun to reign"? (4:8)
Paul was being sarcastic. The new Christians were actually spiritually immature. Paul said they had become kings by themselves, implying that they were too proud to admit that their faith was a gift of God through the work of the apostles.

What did Paul mean that the apostles had become a spectacle? (4:9)
In ancient Rome, winning generals would lead parades into the arena. At the end of the line were the prisoners who were condemned to fight lions and other wild animals. Paul said the apostles had been put on display to be mocked. He was still being critical of the Corinthians, who were blind to the truth about themselves because of their pride.

How was Paul the spiritual father of the believers? (4:15)
Paul was the one who had first preached the gospel to them and who had urged them to put their faith in Christ.

willing, and then I will find out not only how these arrogant people are talking, but what power they have. [20] For the kingdom of God is not a matter of talk but of power. [21] What do you prefer? Shall I come to you with a rod of discipline, or shall I come in love and with a gentle spirit?

DEALING WITH A CASE OF INCEST

5 It is actually reported that there is sexual immorality among you, and of a kind that even pagans do not tolerate: A man is sleeping with his father's wife. [2] And you are proud! Shouldn't you rather have gone into mourning and have put out of your fellowship the man who has been doing this? [3] For my part, even though I am not physically present, I am with you in spirit. As one who is present with you in this way, I have already passed judgment in the name of our Lord Jesus on the one who has been doing this. [4] So when you are assembled and I am with you in spirit, and the power of our Lord Jesus is present, [5] hand this man over to Satan for the destruction of the flesh,[a,b] so that his spirit may be saved on the day of the Lord.

[6] Your boasting is not good. Don't you know that a little yeast leavens the whole batch of dough? [7] Get rid of the old yeast, so that you may be a new unleavened batch—as you really are. For Christ, our Passover lamb, has been sacrificed. [8] Therefore let us keep the Festival, not with the old bread leavened with malice and wickedness, but with the unleavened bread of sincerity and truth.

[9] I wrote to you in my letter not to associate with sexually immoral people— [10] not at all meaning the people of this world who are immoral, or the greedy and swindlers, or idolaters. In that case you would have to leave this world. [11] But now I am writing to you that you must not associate with anyone who claims to be a brother or sister[c] but is sexually immoral or greedy, an idolater or slanderer, a drunkard or swindler. Do not even eat with such people.

[12] What business is it of mine to judge those outside the church? Are you not to judge those inside? [13] God will judge those outside. "Expel the wicked person from among you."[d]

LAWSUITS AMONG BELIEVERS

6 If any of you has a dispute with another, do you dare to take it before the ungodly for judgment instead of before the Lord's people? [2] Or do you not know that the Lord's people will judge the world? And if you are to judge the world, are you not competent to judge trivial cases? [3] Do you not know that we will judge angels? How much more the things of this life! [4] Therefore, if you have disputes about such matters, do you ask for a ruling from those whose way of life is scorned in the church? [5] I say this to shame you. Is it possible that there is nobody among you wise enough to

---

What did yeast symbolize? (5:6–8)
Yeast usually symbolized sin or evil. When the Jews celebrated Passover, they were supposed to eat bread made without yeast (or leaven). Just a small amount of yeast can work through a large batch of dough. In the same way, just a small amount of sin among a group of believers can affect the entire group.

---

[a] 5 In contexts like this, the Greek word for *flesh* (*sarx*) refers to the sinful state of human beings, often presented as a power in opposition to the Spirit.
[b] 5 Or *of his body*   [c] 11 The Greek word for *brother or sister* (*adelphos*) refers here to a believer, whether man or woman, as part of God's family; also in 8:11, 13.   [d] 13 Deut. 13:5; 17:7; 19:19; 21:21; 22:21, 24; 24:7

judge a dispute between believers? ⁶But instead, one brother takes another to court—and this in front of unbelievers!

⁷The very fact that you have lawsuits among you means you have been completely defeated already. Why not rather be wronged? Why not rather be cheated? ⁸Instead, you yourselves cheat and do wrong, and you do this to your brothers and sisters. ⁹Or do you not know that wrongdoers will not inherit the kingdom of God? Do not be deceived: Neither the sexually immoral nor idolaters nor adulterers nor men who have sex with men*ᵃ* ¹⁰nor thieves nor the greedy nor drunkards nor slanderers nor swindlers will inherit the kingdom of God. ¹¹And that is what some of you were. But you were washed, you were sanctified, you were justified in the name of the Lord Jesus Christ and by the Spirit of our God.

SEXUAL IMMORALITY

¹²"I have the right to do anything," you say—but not everything is beneficial. "I have the right to do anything"—but I will not be mastered by anything. ¹³You say, "Food for the stomach and the stomach for food, and God will destroy them both." The body, however, is not meant for sexual immorality but for the Lord, and the Lord for the body. ¹⁴By his power God raised the Lord from the dead, and he will raise us also. ¹⁵Do you not know that your bodies are members of Christ himself? Shall I then take the members of Christ and unite them with a prostitute? Never! ¹⁶Do you not know that he who unites himself with a prostitute is one with her in body? For it is said, "The two will become one flesh."ᵇ ¹⁷But whoever is united with the Lord is one with him in spirit.ᶜ

¹⁸Flee from sexual immorality. All other sins a person commits are outside the body, but whoever sins sexually, sins against their own body. ¹⁹Do you not know that your bodies are temples of the Holy Spirit, who is in you, whom you have received from God? You are not your own; ²⁰you were bought at a price. Therefore honor God with your bodies.

ᵃ 9 The words *men who have sex with men* translate two Greek words that refer to the passive and active participants in homosexual acts.
ᵇ 16 Gen. 2:24   ᶜ 17 Or *in the Spirit*

Why did lawsuits show that the Christians had been defeated? (6:7–8)
The fact that the Corinthians took others to court showed that they lacked Christian charity and were not working to resolve their differences peacefully and prayerfully.

What did Paul mean that they had the right to do anything? (6:12)
Paul may have been quoting some of the Corinthian believers who thought they could do anything they wanted because their sins had been forgiven by God. Paul argued that even if that were true (which it was not), not everything would be beneficial or good.

Why is a Christian's body the temple of the Holy Spirit? (6:19–20)
A Christian should respect his or her body and not commit sexual sins because the Holy Spirit lives within each believer.

What does it mean to be sexually pure?   1 CORINTHIANS 6

Our culture puts a great emphasis on attractiveness and sexuality. Movies, television, popular music, and advertising are filled with images of sexuality. Many people in today's world seem to think that having sex before marriage is fine as long as no one gets hurt or gets a sexually transmitted disease. In fact, people who decide not to have sex until they are married are sometimes seen as old-fashioned and unusual.

The Bible has many passages in the Old Testament and the New Testament that talk about God's plan for human sexuality. God created human beings as sexual creatures, and sex is a good gift from God that brings pleasure to people, unites them in a relationship, and is necessary for having children. But God wants people to use this gift in the right way. That means that only people who are married should have sex. And people should not have immoral sex, such as sex with prostitutes. The Holy Spirit lives inside each of us, and we should honor and respect our bodies and not use our bodies in ways that would dishonor God.

Was Corinth an immoral city? (7:2)
Yes. For example, Corinth's temple to Aphrodite, the goddess of love, had 1,000 prostitute priestesses. Paul said that husbands and wives should be faithful to each other.

What was Paul's teaching about divorce? (7:10–11)
Paul echoed Jesus' teaching that married people should stay together rather than divorce.

Why should Christians remain married if their spouses are not Christians? (7:12–14)
Paul said that a Christian husband or wife could be a godly influence on an unbelieving spouse. The children in such a family are also influenced by the Christian parent.

Why did Paul say that each person should remain in the situation he or she was in when God called them? (7:20–23)
Paul said each person should be content to live for the Lord in whatever economic or social situation he or she was in when they became a Christian. The important thing was to have a godly attitude.

CONCERNING MARRIED LIFE

7 Now for the matters you wrote about: "It is good for a man not to have sexual relations with a woman." ²But since sexual immorality is occurring, each man should have sexual relations with his own wife, and each woman with her own husband. ³The husband should fulfill his marital duty to his wife, and likewise the wife to her husband. ⁴The wife does not have authority over her own body but yields it to her husband. In the same way, the husband does not have authority over his own body but yields it to his wife. ⁵Do not deprive each other except perhaps by mutual consent and for a time, so that you may devote yourselves to prayer. Then come together again so that Satan will not tempt you because of your lack of self-control. ⁶I say this as a concession, not as a command. ⁷I wish that all of you were as I am. But each of you has your own gift from God; one has this gift, another has that.

⁸Now to the unmarried[a] and the widows I say: It is good for them to stay unmarried, as I do. ⁹But if they cannot control themselves, they should marry, for it is better to marry than to burn with passion.

¹⁰To the married I give this command (not I, but the Lord): A wife must not separate from her husband. ¹¹But if she does, she must remain unmarried or else be reconciled to her husband. And a husband must not divorce his wife.

¹²To the rest I say this (I, not the Lord): If any brother has a wife who is not a believer and she is willing to live with him, he must not divorce her. ¹³And if a woman has a husband who is not a believer and he is willing to live with her, she must not divorce him. ¹⁴For the unbelieving husband has been sanctified through his wife, and the unbelieving wife has been sanctified through her believing husband. Otherwise your children would be unclean, but as it is, they are holy.

¹⁵But if the unbeliever leaves, let it be so. The brother or the sister is not bound in such circumstances; God has called us to live in peace. ¹⁶How do you know, wife, whether you will save your husband? Or, how do you know, husband, whether you will save your wife?

CONCERNING CHANGE OF STATUS

¹⁷Nevertheless, each person should live as a believer in whatever situation the Lord has assigned to them, just as God has called them. This is the rule I lay down in all the churches. ¹⁸Was a man already circumcised when he was called? He should not become uncircumcised. Was a man uncircumcised when he was called? He should not be circumcised. ¹⁹Circumcision is nothing and uncircumcision is nothing. Keeping God's commands is what counts. ²⁰Each person should remain in the situation they were in when God called them.

²¹Were you a slave when you were called? Don't let it trouble you — although if you can gain your freedom, do so. ²²For the one who was a slave when called to faith in the

---

a 8 Or *widowers*

Lord is the Lord's freed person; similarly, the one who was free when called is Christ's slave. [23] You were bought at a price; do not become slaves of human beings. [24] Brothers and sisters, each person, as responsible to God, should remain in the situation they were in when God called them.

CONCERNING THE UNMARRIED

[25] Now about virgins: I have no command from the Lord, but I give a judgment as one who by the Lord's mercy is trustworthy. [26] Because of the present crisis, I think that it is good for a man to remain as he is. [27] Are you pledged to a woman? Do not seek to be released. Are you free from such a commitment? Do not look for a wife. [28] But if you do marry, you have not sinned; and if a virgin marries, she has not sinned. But those who marry will face many troubles in this life, and I want to spare you this.

[29] What I mean, brothers and sisters, is that the time is short. From now on those who have wives should live as if they do not; [30] those who mourn, as if they did not; those who are happy, as if they were not; those who buy something, as if it were not theirs to keep; [31] those who use the things of the world, as if not engrossed in them. For this world in its present form is passing away.

[32] I would like you to be free from concern. An unmarried man is concerned about the Lord's affairs—how he can please the Lord. [33] But a married man is concerned about the affairs of this world—how he can please his wife— [34] and his interests are divided. An unmarried woman or virgin is concerned about the Lord's affairs: Her aim is to be devoted to the Lord in both body and spirit. But a married woman is concerned about the affairs of this world—how she can please her husband. [35] I am saying this for your own good, not to restrict you, but that you may live in a right way in undivided devotion to the Lord.

[36] If anyone is worried that he might not be acting honorably toward the virgin he is engaged to, and if his passions are too strong[a] and he feels he ought to marry, he should do as he wants. He is not sinning. They should get married. [37] But the man who has settled the matter in his own mind, who is under no compulsion but has control over his own will, and who has made up his mind not to marry the virgin—this man also does the right thing. [38] So then, he who marries the virgin does right, but he who does not marry her does better.[b]

[39] A woman is bound to her husband as long as he lives. But if her husband dies, she is free to marry anyone she wishes, but he must belong to the Lord. [40] In my judgment, she is happier if she stays as she is—and I think that I too have the Spirit of God.

---

[a] 36 Or if she is getting beyond the usual age for marriage   [b] 36-38 Or [36]If anyone thinks he is not treating his daughter properly, and if she is getting along in years (or if her passions are too strong), and he feels she ought to marry, he should do as he wants. He is not sinning. He should let her get married. [37]But the man who has settled the matter in his own mind, who is under no compulsion but has control over his own will, and who has made up his mind to keep the virgin unmarried—this man also does the right thing. [38]So then, he who gives his virgin in marriage does right, but he who does not give her in marriage does better.

What was the basis for Paul's advice? (7:26–31)
Paul was concerned about the difficulty of living a Christian life in an immoral society, and he also believed that the time for doing God's work was growing short.

CONCERNING FOOD SACRIFICED TO IDOLS

What was food that had been sacrificed to idols? (8:1) Most of the meat sold in the marketplace in Corinth was left over from animals that had been sacrificed to pagan gods. The Corinthians had written to Paul to ask if they were permitted to eat this meat.

8 Now about food sacrificed to idols: We know that "We all possess knowledge." But knowledge puffs up while love builds up. ²Those who think they know something do not yet know as they ought to know. ³But whoever loves God is known by God.ᵃ

⁴So then, about eating food sacrificed to idols: We know that "An idol is nothing at all in the world" and that "There is no God but one." ⁵For even if there are so-called gods, whether in heaven or on earth (as indeed there are many "gods" and many "lords"), ⁶yet for us there is but one God, the Father, from whom all things came and for whom we live; and there is but one Lord, Jesus Christ, through whom all things came and through whom we live.

⁷But not everyone possesses this knowledge. Some people are still so accustomed to idols that when they eat sacrificial food they think of it as having been sacrificed to a god, and since their conscience is weak, it is defiled. ⁸But food does not bring us near to God; we are no worse if we do not eat, and no better if we do.

⁹Be careful, however, that the exercise of your rights does not become a stumbling block to the weak. ¹⁰For if someone with a weak conscience sees you, with all your knowledge, eating in an idol's temple, won't that person be emboldened to eat what is sacrificed to idols? ¹¹So this weak brother or sister, for whom Christ died, is destroyed by your knowledge. ¹²When you sin against them in this way and wound their weak conscience, you sin against Christ. ¹³Therefore, if what I eat causes my brother or sister to fall into sin, I will never eat meat again, so that I will not cause them to fall.

PAUL'S RIGHTS AS AN APOSTLE

9 Am I not free? Am I not an apostle? Have I not seen Jesus our Lord? Are you not the result of my work in the Lord? ²Even though I may not be an apostle to others,

---

ᵃ *2,3* An early manuscript and another ancient witness *think they have knowledge do not yet know as they ought to know. ³But whoever loves truly knows.*

How are Christians supposed to honor the consciences of fellow believers?

1 CORINTHIANS 8

In the early church one of the things that Christians struggled with was whether to eat meat that had been sacrificed to idols. Much of the meat that was sold in the marketplace in cities like Corinth was left over from animals that had been sacrificed to pagan gods. Some Christians thought they should not eat that meat, while others thought the meat was acceptable to eat.

Paul told the people that eating the meat that had been sacrificed to idols was not wrong, because the pagan gods really did not exist. But he also told believers that they should be sensitive to the consciences of other Christians. In 1 Corinthians 10 Paul said that Christians should not eat meat that was part of a sacrifice when they had a meal with unbelievers, because that might give the idea that they agreed with the practice of pagan sacrifices.

Most Christians today do not have to decide about eating meat that has been sacrificed, but Christians should be sensitive to the consciences of other Christians and not do anything that would lead others to sin. Christians should also make sure that their behavior does not give unbelievers a reason to criticize them or their faith.

surely I am to you! For you are the seal of my apostleship in the Lord.

³This is my defense to those who sit in judgment on me. ⁴Don't we have the right to food and drink? ⁵Don't we have the right to take a believing wife along with us, as do the other apostles and the Lord's brothers and Cephas*? ⁶Or is it only I and Barnabas who lack the right to not work for a living?

⁷Who serves as a soldier at his own expense? Who plants a vineyard and does not eat its grapes? Who tends a flock and does not drink the milk? ⁸Do I say this merely on human authority? Doesn't the Law say the same thing? ⁹For it is written in the Law of Moses: "Do not muzzle an ox while it is treading out the grain."ᵇ Is it about oxen that God is concerned? ¹⁰Surely he says this for us, doesn't he? Yes, this was written for us, because whoever plows and threshes should be able to do so in the hope of sharing in the harvest. ¹¹If we have sown spiritual seed among you, is it too much if we reap a material harvest from you? ¹²If others have this right of support from you, shouldn't we have it all the more?

But we did not use this right. On the contrary, we put up with anything rather than hinder the gospel of Christ.

¹³Don't you know that those who serve in the temple get their food from the temple, and that those who serve at the altar share in what is offered on the altar? ¹⁴In the same way, the Lord has commanded that those who preach the gospel should receive their living from the gospel.

¹⁵But I have not used any of these rights. And I am not writing this in the hope that you will do such things for me, for I would rather die than allow anyone to deprive me of this boast. ¹⁶For when I preach the gospel, I cannot boast, since I am compelled to preach. Woe to me if I do not preach the gospel! ¹⁷If I preach voluntarily, I have a reward; if not voluntarily, I am simply discharging the trust committed to me. ¹⁸What then is my reward? Just this: that in preaching the gospel I may offer it free of charge, and so not make full use of my rights as a preacher of the gospel.

PAUL'S USE OF HIS FREEDOM

¹⁹Though I am free and belong to no one, I have made myself a slave to everyone, to win as many as possible. ²⁰To the Jews I became like a Jew, to win the Jews. To those under the law I became like one under the law (though I myself am not under the law), so as to win those under the law. ²¹To those not having the law I became like one not having the law (though I am not free from God's law but am under Christ's law), so as to win those not having the law. ²²To the weak I became weak, to win the weak. I have become all things to all people so that by all possible means I might save some. ²³I do all this for the sake of the gospel, that I may share in its blessings.

THE NEED FOR SELF-DISCIPLINE

²⁴Do you not know that in a race all the runners run, but only one gets the prize? Run in such a way as to get the prize. ²⁵Everyone who competes in the games goes into strict

What did Paul say about supporting the work of ministers? (9:3–11)
Paul said that Christians should support Christian workers by paying them for their work and by providing food and lodging.

What was Paul's reward for preaching the gospel? (9:18–19)
Paul gave up his right to support himself in order to preach the gospel and to win others to Christ — at no charge.

Did the Corinthians understand Paul's description of a race? (9:24–27)
Yes. The city of Corinth sponsored the Isthmian Games, which included foot races. The games took place every other year and were second only to the Olympic Games. The prize for winning a race was a wreath made of laurel or other leaves.

---

*5 That is, Peter   ᵇ 9 Deut. 25:4

training. They do it to get a crown that will not last, but we do it to get a crown that will last forever. [26]Therefore I do not run like someone running aimlessly; I do not fight like a boxer beating the air. [27]No, I strike a blow to my body and make it my slave so that after I have preached to others, I myself will not be disqualified for the prize.

WARNINGS FROM ISRAEL'S HISTORY

10 For I do not want you to be ignorant of the fact, brothers and sisters, that our ancestors were all under the cloud and that they all passed through the sea. [2]They were all baptized into Moses in the cloud and in the sea. [3]They all ate the same spiritual food [4]and drank the same spiritual drink; for they drank from the spiritual rock that accompanied them, and that rock was Christ. [5]Nevertheless, God was not pleased with most of them; their bodies were scattered in the wilderness.

[6]Now these things occurred as examples to keep us from setting our hearts on evil things as they did. [7]Do not be idolaters, as some of them were; as it is written: "The people sat down to eat and drink and got up to indulge in revelry."[a] [8]We should not commit sexual immorality, as some of them did—and in one day twenty-three thousand of them died. [9]We should not test Christ,[b] as some of them did—and were killed by snakes. [10]And do not grumble, as some of them did—and were killed by the destroying angel.

[11]These things happened to them as examples and were written down as warnings for us, on whom the culmination of the ages has come. [12]So, if you think you are standing firm, be careful that you don't fall! [13]No temptation[c] has overtaken you except what is common to mankind. And God is faithful; he will not let you be tempted[c] beyond what you can bear. But when you are tempted,[c] he will also provide a way out so that you can endure it.

IDOL FEASTS AND THE LORD'S SUPPER

[14]Therefore, my dear friends, flee from idolatry. [15]I speak to sensible people; judge for yourselves what I say. [16]Is not the cup of thanksgiving for which we give thanks a participation in the blood of Christ? And is not the bread that we break a participation in the body of Christ? [17]Because there is one loaf, we, who are many, are one body, for we all share the one loaf.

[18]Consider the people of Israel: Do not those who eat the sacrifices participate in the altar? [19]Do I mean then that food sacrificed to an idol is anything, or that an idol is anything? [20]No, but the sacrifices of pagans are offered to demons, not to God, and I do not want you to be participants with demons. [21]You cannot drink the cup of the Lord and the cup of demons too; you cannot have a part in both the Lord's table and the table of demons. [22]Are we trying to arouse the Lord's jealousy? Are we stronger than he?

What example did Paul use to warn about idolatry? (10:7) Paul referred to the story of the Israelites when they worshiped the golden calf (see Exodus 32:1–6).

What was the meaning of sharing one loaf? (10:17) This was a symbol of the unity of the Christian church, because all Christians share in the Lord's Supper and believe in Jesus, the Bread of Life.

[a] 7 Exodus 32:6   [b] 9 Some manuscripts *test the Lord*   [c] 13 The Greek for *temptation* and *tempted* can also mean *testing* and *tested*.

THE BELIEVER'S FREEDOM

²³"I have the right to do anything," you say—but not everything is beneficial. "I have the right to do anything"—but not everything is constructive. ²⁴No one should seek their own good, but the good of others.

²⁵Eat anything sold in the meat market without raising questions of conscience, ²⁶for, "The earth is the Lord's, and everything in it."*a*

²⁷If an unbeliever invites you to a meal and you want to go, eat whatever is put before you without raising questions of conscience. ²⁸But if someone says to you, "This has been offered in sacrifice," then do not eat it, both for the sake of the one who told you and for the sake of conscience. ²⁹I am referring to the other person's conscience, not yours. For why is my freedom being judged by another's conscience? ³⁰If I take part in the meal with thankfulness, why am I denounced because of something I thank God for?

³¹So whether you eat or drink or whatever you do, do it all for the glory of God. ³²Do not cause anyone to stumble, whether Jews, Greeks or the church of God— ³³even as I try to please everyone in every way. For I am not seeking my own good but the good of many, so that they may be saved. ¹Follow my example, as I follow the example of Christ.

ON COVERING THE HEAD IN WORSHIP

²I praise you for remembering me in everything and for holding to the traditions just as I passed them on to you. ³But I want you to realize that the head of every man is Christ, and the head of the woman is man,*b* and the head of Christ is God. ⁴Every man who prays or prophesies with his head covered dishonors his head. ⁵But every woman who prays or prophesies with her head uncovered dishonors her head—it is the same as having her head shaved. ⁶For if a woman does not cover her head, she might as well have her hair cut off; but if it is a disgrace for a woman to have her hair cut off or her head shaved, then she should cover her head.

⁷A man ought not to cover his head,*c* since he is the image and glory of God; but woman is the glory of man. ⁸For man did not come from woman, but woman from man; ⁹neither was man created for woman, but woman for man. ¹⁰It is for this reason that a woman ought to have authority over her own*d* head, because of the angels. ¹¹Nevertheless, in the Lord woman is not independent of man, nor is man independent of woman. ¹²For as woman came from man, so also man is born of woman. But everything comes from God.

¹³Judge for yourselves: Is it proper for a woman to pray to God with her head uncovered? ¹⁴Does not the very nature of

Why were Christians not supposed to eat meat with an unbeliever if they were told the meat had been offered to idols? (10:28–29) This might give the wrong impression that they agreed with the practice of sacrifices, and it might offend the conscience of a fellow believer.

Why were men supposed to keep their heads uncovered in worship? (11:4) During that time, men uncovered their heads in worship to show respect for God and to show their position in Christ.

Why were women supposed to keep their heads covered? (11:5–6) In the Greek culture, for women to remove their head covering in public was a sign of loose morals. Paul said that a woman who did this might as well have her hair cut or shaved. A shaved head showed that a woman had been publicly disgraced or was declaring her independence from her husband.

---

a 26 Psalm 24:1   *b 3* Or *of the wife is her husband*   *c 4-7* Or *⁴Every man who prays or prophesies with long hair dishonors his head. ⁵But every woman who prays or prophesies with no covering of hair dishonors her head—she is just like one of the "shorn women." ⁶If a woman has no covering, let her be for now with short hair; but since it is a disgrace for a woman to have her hair shorn or shaved, she should grow it again. ⁷A man ought not to have long hair*   *d 10* Or *have a sign of authority on her*

things teach you that if a man has long hair, it is a disgrace to him, [15] but that if a woman has long hair, it is her glory? For long hair is given to her as a covering. [16] If anyone wants to be contentious about this, we have no other practice—nor do the churches of God.

CORRECTING AN ABUSE OF THE LORD'S SUPPER

[17] In the following directives I have no praise for you, for your meetings do more harm than good. [18] In the first place, I hear that when you come together as a church, there are divisions among you, and to some extent I believe it. [19] No doubt there have to be differences among you to show which of you have God's approval. [20] So then, when you come together, it is not the Lord's Supper you eat, [21] for when you are eating, some of you go ahead with your own private suppers. As a result, one person remains hungry and another gets drunk. [22] Don't you have homes to eat and drink in? Or do you despise the church of God by humiliating those who have nothing? What shall I say to you? Shall I praise you? Certainly not in this matter!

[23] For I received from the Lord what I also passed on to you: The Lord Jesus, on the night he was betrayed, took bread, [24] and when he had given thanks, he broke it and said, "This is my body, which is for you; do this in remembrance of me." [25] In the same way, after supper he took the cup, saying, "This cup is the new covenant in my blood; do this, whenever you drink it, in remembrance of me." [26] For whenever you eat this bread and drink this cup, you proclaim the Lord's death until he comes.

[27] So then, whoever eats the bread or drinks the cup of the Lord in an unworthy manner will be guilty of sinning against the body and blood of the Lord. [28] Everyone ought to examine themselves before they eat of the bread and drink from the cup. [29] For those who eat and drink without discerning the body of Christ eat and drink judgment on themselves. [30] That is why many among you are weak and sick, and a number of you have fallen asleep. [31] But if we were more discerning with regard to ourselves, we would not come under such judgment. [32] Nevertheless, when we are judged in this way by the Lord, we are being disciplined so that we will not be finally condemned with the world.

[33] So then, my brothers and sisters, when you gather to eat, you should all eat together. [34] Anyone who is hungry should eat something at home, so that when you meet together it may not result in judgment.

And when I come I will give further directions.

CONCERNING SPIRITUAL GIFTS

12 Now about the gifts of the Spirit, brothers and sisters, I do not want you to be uninformed. [2] You know that when you were pagans, somehow or other you were influenced and led astray to mute idols. [3] Therefore I want you to know that no one who is speaking by the Spirit of God says, "Jesus be cursed," and no one can say, "Jesus is Lord," except by the Holy Spirit.

How were the Corinthian Christians showing disrespect for the Lord's Supper? (11:20–22)
The early church held a love feast in connection with the Lord's Supper. But some of the people gorged themselves and got drunk while others went hungry. They did not share the meal equally, and the people who arrived first did not always wait for the others to arrive before starting the meal.

[4]There are different kinds of gifts, but the same Spirit distributes them. [5]There are different kinds of service, but the same Lord. [6]There are different kinds of working, but in all of them and in everyone it is the same God at work.

[7]Now to each one the manifestation of the Spirit is given for the common good. [8]To one there is given through the Spirit a message of wisdom, to another a message of knowledge by means of the same Spirit, [9]to another faith by the same Spirit, to another gifts of healing by that one Spirit, [10]to another miraculous powers, to another prophecy, to another distinguishing between spirits, to another speaking in different kinds of tongues,[a] and to still another the interpretation of tongues.[a] [11]All these are the work of one and the same Spirit, and he distributes them to each one, just as he determines.

UNITY AND DIVERSITY IN THE BODY

[12]Just as a body, though one, has many parts, but all its many parts form one body, so it is with Christ. [13]For we were all baptized by[b] one Spirit so as to form one body—whether Jews or Gentiles, slave or free—and we were all given the one Spirit to drink. [14]Even so the body is not made up of one part but of many.

[15]Now if the foot should say, "Because I am not a hand, I do not belong to the body," it would not for that reason stop being part of the body. [16]And if the ear should say, "Because I am not an eye, I do not belong to the body," it would not for that reason stop being part of the body. [17]If the whole body were an eye, where would the sense of hearing be? If the whole body were an ear, where would the sense of smell be? [18]But in fact God has placed the parts in the body, every one of them, just as he wanted them to be. [19]If they were all one part, where would the body be? [20]As it is, there are many parts, but one body.

[21]The eye cannot say to the hand, "I don't need you!" And the head cannot say to the feet, "I don't need you!" [22]On the contrary, those parts of the body that seem to be weaker are

[a] 10 Or languages; also in verse 28   [b] 13 Or with; or in

---

What do these verses show about God? (12:4–6)
These verses show the Trinity of God by naming the Holy Spirit, the Lord Jesus, and God the Father – one God with three persons.

What is "speaking in different kinds of tongues"? (12:10)
Some people think this refers to a person's ability to speak in a human language that he or she has never learned, which is what the apostles did on Pentecost. Others think it refers to speaking in a heavenly type of language of praise and prayer when a person is overcome by the Holy Spirit.

What are spiritual gifts, and how can we know what our gifts are?
1 CORINTHIANS 12

God has given his people gifts through the Holy Spirit. The Bible says that there are a variety of gifts that God gives. These gifts may include the ability to teach, to preach, to prophesy, to heal, to give leadership, to help people in need, to serve others, to encourage others, to show love, and many others. God gives Christians spiritual gifts so that they can use them within the church. The Bible makes it clear that one gift is not more important than others. For example, the gift of preaching is not more important than the gift of showing hospitality. Within the church, believers are like the different parts of a body; each one has a role to play in cooperation with other believers.

We discover our gifts by looking at what we do well when we are working with other Christians. Parents, pastors, teachers, and fellow church members can often be helpful in identifying our strengths and talents. Once we discover our gifts, it is important for us to use them to serve God and other people both within the church and in the larger community in which we live. In this way we honor God and do his work in the world.

indispensable, [23] and the parts that we think are less honorable we treat with special honor. And the parts that are unpresentable are treated with special modesty, [24] while our presentable parts need no special treatment. But God has put the body together, giving greater honor to the parts that lacked it, [25] so that there should be no division in the body, but that its parts should have equal concern for each other. [26] If one part suffers, every part suffers with it; if one part is honored, every part rejoices with it.

[27] Now you are the body of Christ, and each one of you is a part of it. [28] And God has placed in the church first of all apostles, second prophets, third teachers, then miracles, then gifts of healing, of helping, of guidance, and of different kinds of tongues. [29] Are all apostles? Are all prophets? Are all teachers? Do all work miracles? [30] Do all have gifts of healing? Do all speak in tongues[a]? Do all interpret? [31] Now eagerly desire the greater gifts.

LOVE IS INDISPENSABLE

And yet I will show you the most excellent way.

13 If I speak in the tongues[b] of men or of angels, but do not have love, I am only a resounding gong or a clanging cymbal. [2] If I have the gift of prophecy and can fathom all mysteries and all knowledge, and if I have a faith that can move mountains, but do not have love, I am nothing. [3] If I give all I possess to the poor and give over my body to hardship that I may boast,[c] but do not have love, I gain nothing.

[4] Love is patient, love is kind. It does not envy, it does not boast, it is not proud. [5] It does not dishonor others, it is not self-seeking, it is not easily angered, it keeps no record of wrongs. [6] Love does not delight in evil but rejoices with the truth. [7] It always protects, always trusts, always hopes, always perseveres.

[8] Love never fails. But where there are prophecies, they will cease; where there are tongues, they will be stilled; where there is knowledge, it will pass away. [9] For we know in part and we prophesy in part, [10] but when completeness comes, what is in part disappears. [11] When I was a child, I talked like a child, I thought like a child, I reasoned like a child. When I became a man, I put the ways of childhood behind me. [12] For now we see only a reflection as in a mirror; then we shall see face to face. Now I know in part; then I shall know fully, even as I am fully known.

[13] And now these three remain: faith, hope and love. But the greatest of these is love.

INTELLIGIBILITY IN WORSHIP

14 Follow the way of love and eagerly desire gifts of the Spirit, especially prophecy. [2] For anyone who speaks in a tongue[d] does not speak to people but to God. Indeed, no one understands them; they utter mysteries by the Spirit. [3] But the one who prophesies speaks to people for their strengthening, encouraging and comfort. [4] Anyone

What does it mean that the church is the body of Christ? (12:27)
Paul used a comparison between the human body and the church to show that individual parts of the body (or church) play different roles, but all are important to the health of the whole body.

What did Paul mean about giving over one's body "to hardship"? (13:3)
Many early Christians suffered, even to the point of giving up their lives, for their faith. Paul said that even this sacrifice would amount to nothing if the person did not act out of love.

What were their mirrors like? (13:12)
A mirror at that time was a piece of polished metal (probably bronze) that gave only an imperfect reflection. This describes how we know God now in contrast to how we will know him when we see him face to face in heaven.

Why did Paul prefer prophecy to speaking in tongues? (14:1–5)
When people spoke prophecies, their words benefited everyone in the church. Speaking in tongues was for the benefit of the individual rather than the whole congregation.

[a] 30 Or other languages   [b] 1 Or languages   [c] 3 Some manuscripts body to the flames   [d] 2 Or in another language; also in verses 4, 13, 14, 19, 26 and 27

who speaks in a tongue edifies themselves, but the one who prophesies edifies the church. [5] I would like every one of you to speak in tongues,[a] but I would rather have you prophesy. The one who prophesies is greater than the one who speaks in tongues,[a] unless someone interprets, so that the church may be edified.

[6] Now, brothers and sisters, if I come to you and speak in tongues, what good will I be to you, unless I bring you some revelation or knowledge or prophecy or word of instruction? [7] Even in the case of lifeless things that make sounds, such as the pipe or harp, how will anyone know what tune is being played unless there is a distinction in the notes? [8] Again, if the trumpet does not sound a clear call, who will get ready for battle? [9] So it is with you. Unless you speak intelligible words with your tongue, how will anyone know what you are saying? You will just be speaking into the air. [10] Undoubtedly there are all sorts of languages in the world, yet none of them is without meaning. [11] If then I do not grasp the meaning of what someone is saying, I am a foreigner to the speaker, and the speaker is a foreigner to me. [12] So it is with you. Since you are eager for gifts of the Spirit, try to excel in those that build up the church.

[13] For this reason the one who speaks in a tongue should pray that they may interpret what they say. [14] For if I pray in a tongue, my spirit prays, but my mind is unfruitful. [15] So what shall I do? I will pray with my spirit, but I will also pray with my understanding; I will sing with my spirit, but I will also sing with my understanding. [16] Otherwise when you are praising God in the Spirit, how can someone else, who is now put in the position of an inquirer,[b] say "Amen" to your thanksgiving, since they do not know what you are saying? [17] You are giving thanks well enough, but no one else is edified.

[18] I thank God that I speak in tongues more than all of you. [19] But in the church I would rather speak five intelligible words to instruct others than ten thousand words in a tongue.

[20] Brothers and sisters, stop thinking like children. In regard to evil be infants, but in your thinking be adults. [21] In the Law it is written:

"With other tongues
    and through the lips of foreigners
I will speak to this people,
    but even then they will not listen to me,
                    says the Lord."[c]

[22] Tongues, then, are a sign, not for believers but for unbelievers; prophecy, however, is not for unbelievers but for believers. [23] So if the whole church comes together and everyone speaks in tongues, and inquirers or unbelievers come in, will they not say that you are out of your mind? [24] But if an unbeliever or an inquirer comes in while everyone is

---

[a] 5 Or *in other languages*; also in verses 6, 18, 22, 23 and 39   [b] 16 The Greek word for *inquirer* is a technical term for someone not fully initiated into a religion; also in verses 23 and 24.   [c] 21 Isaiah 28:11,12

prophesying, they are convicted of sin and are brought under judgment by all, [25] as the secrets of their hearts are laid bare. So they will fall down and worship God, exclaiming, "God is really among you!"

GOOD ORDER IN WORSHIP

[26] What then shall we say, brothers and sisters? When you come together, each of you has a hymn, or a word of instruction, a revelation, a tongue or an interpretation. Everything must be done so that the church may be built up. [27] If anyone speaks in a tongue, two — or at the most three — should speak, one at a time, and someone must interpret. [28] If there is no interpreter, the speaker should keep quiet in the church and speak to himself and to God.

[29] Two or three prophets should speak, and the others should weigh carefully what is said. [30] And if a revelation comes to someone who is sitting down, the first speaker should stop. [31] For you can all prophesy in turn so that everyone may be instructed and encouraged. [32] The spirits of prophets are subject to the control of prophets. [33] For God is not a God of disorder but of peace — as in all the congregations of the Lord's people.

[34] Women[a] should remain silent in the churches. They are not allowed to speak, but must be in submission, as the law says. [35] If they want to inquire about something, they should ask their own husbands at home; for it is disgraceful for a woman to speak in the church.[b]

[36] Or did the word of God originate with you? Or are you the only people it has reached? [37] If anyone thinks they are a prophet or otherwise gifted by the Spirit, let them acknowledge that what I am writing to you is the Lord's command. [38] But if anyone ignores this, they will themselves be ignored.[c]

[39] Therefore, my brothers and sisters, be eager to prophesy, and do not forbid speaking in tongues. [40] But everything should be done in a fitting and orderly way.

THE RESURRECTION OF CHRIST

15 Now, brothers and sisters, I want to remind you of the gospel I preached to you, which you received and on which you have taken your stand. [2] By this gospel you are saved, if you hold firmly to the word I preached to you. Otherwise, you have believed in vain.

[3] For what I received I passed on to you as of first importance[d]: that Christ died for our sins according to the Scriptures, [4] that he was buried, that he was raised on the third day according to the Scriptures, [5] and that he appeared to Cephas,[e] and then to the Twelve. [6] After that, he appeared to more than five hundred of the brothers and sisters at the same time, most of whom are still living, though some have fallen asleep. [7] Then he appeared to James, then to all the apostles, [8] and last of all he appeared to me also, as to one abnormally born.

---

[a] 33,34 Or peace. As in all the congregations of the Lord's people, [34]women
[b] 34,35 In a few manuscripts these verses come after verse 40.   [c] 38 Some manuscripts But anyone who is ignorant of this will be ignorant   [d] 3 Or you at the first   [e] 5 That is, Peter

---

How did the Christians at Corinth worship? (14:26)
Their worship included a hymn and word of instruction (which were also elements of Old Testament worship). The worship also included revelation, speaking in tongues, and interpretation. All of the parts of worship were meant to strengthen the believers' faith and commitment to the Lord.

What role did Paul think women should play in worship services? (14:34–35)
These verses have been the subject of a great deal of debate. Some think that Paul's instruction for women to not become leaders or ministers still applies today. Others think this instruction was only in keeping with the customs of the ancient world. Others think Paul was speaking about women who disrupted the worship with too many questions. Whatever the interpretation, it is clear that Paul wanted worship services to be orderly and respectful.

What is the most important message of the gospel? (15:3–4)
The core message of the gospel is that Jesus died for our sins, that he was buried, and that he rose from the dead.

⁹For I am the least of the apostles and do not even deserve to be called an apostle, because I persecuted the church of God. ¹⁰But by the grace of God I am what I am, and his grace to me was not without effect. No, I worked harder than all of them—yet not I, but the grace of God that was with me. ¹¹Whether, then, it is I or they, this is what we preach, and this is what you believed.

THE RESURRECTION OF THE DEAD

¹²But if it is preached that Christ has been raised from the dead, how can some of you say that there is no resurrection of the dead? ¹³If there is no resurrection of the dead, then not even Christ has been raised. ¹⁴And if Christ has not been raised, our preaching is useless and so is your faith. ¹⁵More than that, we are then found to be false witnesses about God, for we have testified about God that he raised Christ from the dead. But he did not raise him if in fact the dead are not raised. ¹⁶For if the dead are not raised, then Christ has not been raised either. ¹⁷And if Christ has not been raised, your faith is futile; you are still in your sins. ¹⁸Then those also who have fallen asleep in Christ are lost. ¹⁹If only for this life we have hope in Christ, we are of all people most to be pitied.

²⁰But Christ has indeed been raised from the dead, the firstfruits of those who have fallen asleep. ²¹For since death came through a man, the resurrection of the dead comes also through a man. ²²For as in Adam all die, so in Christ all will be made alive. ²³But each in turn: Christ, the firstfruits; then, when he comes, those who belong to him. ²⁴Then the end will come, when he hands over the kingdom to God the Father after he has destroyed all dominion, authority and power. ²⁵For he must reign until he has put all his enemies under his feet. ²⁶The last enemy to be destroyed is death. ²⁷For he "has put everything under his feet."ᵃ Now when it says that "everything" has been put under him, it is clear that this does not include God himself, who put everything under Christ. ²⁸When he has done this, then the Son himself will be made subject to him who put everything under him, so that God may be all in all.

²⁹Now if there is no resurrection, what will those do who are baptized for the dead? If the dead are not raised at all, why are people baptized for them? ³⁰And as for us, why do we endanger ourselves every hour? ³¹I face death every day—yes, just as surely as I boast about you in Christ Jesus our Lord. ³²If I fought wild beasts in Ephesus with no more than human hopes, what have I gained? If the dead are not raised,

"Let us eat and drink,
	for tomorrow we die."ᵇ

³³Do not be misled: "Bad company corrupts good character."ᶜ ³⁴Come back to your senses as you ought, and stop sinning; for there are some who are ignorant of God—I say this to your shame.

ᵃ 27 Psalm 8:6   ᵇ 32 Isaiah 22:13   ᶜ 33 From the Greek poet Menander

How was Christ the "firstfruits"? (15:20)
In the Old Testament, this was the first sheaf of wheat from the harvest that was given to the Lord to show that everything belonged to him and would be dedicated to him. Christ, who rose from the dead, is the guarantee that all believers will also be raised from the dead.

What was the baptism for the dead? (15:29)
It isn't clear what this practice was. Perhaps believers were being baptized on behalf of others who had died without being baptized, or Christians were being baptized as they looked forward to the resurrection of the dead. It could also have been that new Christians were being baptized and taking their place in the church to replace those who had died.

THE RESURRECTION BODY

³⁵But someone will ask, "How are the dead raised? With what kind of body will they come?" ³⁶How foolish! What you sow does not come to life unless it dies. ³⁷When you sow, you do not plant the body that will be, but just a seed, perhaps of wheat or of something else. ³⁸But God gives it a body as he has determined, and to each kind of seed he gives its own body. ³⁹Not all flesh is the same: People have one kind of flesh, animals have another, birds another and fish another. ⁴⁰There are also heavenly bodies and there are earthly bodies; but the splendor of the heavenly bodies is one kind, and the splendor of the earthly bodies is another. ⁴¹The sun has one kind of splendor, the moon another and the stars another; and star differs from star in splendor.

⁴²So will it be with the resurrection of the dead. The body that is sown is perishable, it is raised imperishable; ⁴³it is sown in dishonor, it is raised in glory; it is sown in weakness, it is raised in power; ⁴⁴it is sown a natural body, it is raised a spiritual body.

If there is a natural body, there is also a spiritual body. ⁴⁵So it is written: "The first man Adam became a living being"ᵃ; the last Adam, a life-giving spirit. ⁴⁶The spiritual did not come first, but the natural, and after that the spiritual. ⁴⁷The first man was of the dust of the earth; the second man is of heaven. ⁴⁸As was the earthly man, so are those who are of the earth; and as is the heavenly man, so also are those who are of heaven. ⁴⁹And just as we have borne the image of the earthly man, so shall weᵇ bear the image of the heavenly man.

⁵⁰I declare to you, brothers and sisters, that flesh and blood cannot inherit the kingdom of God, nor does the perishable inherit the imperishable. ⁵¹Listen, I tell you a mystery: We will not all sleep, but we will all be changed— ⁵²in a flash, in the twinkling of an eye, at the last trumpet. For the trumpet will sound, the dead will be raised imperishable, and we will be changed. ⁵³For the perishable must clothe itself with the imperishable, and the mortal with immortality. ⁵⁴When the perishable has been clothed with the imperishable, and the mortal with immortality, then the saying that is written will come true: "Death has been swallowed up in victory."ᶜ

⁵⁵"Where, O death, is your victory?
Where, O death, is your sting?"ᵈ

⁵⁶The sting of death is sin, and the power of sin is the law. ⁵⁷But thanks be to God! He gives us the victory through our Lord Jesus Christ.

⁵⁸Therefore, my dear brothers and sisters, stand firm. Let nothing move you. Always give yourselves fully to the work of the Lord, because you know that your labor in the Lord is not in vain.

THE COLLECTION FOR THE LORD'S PEOPLE

16 Now about the collection for the Lord's people: Do what I told the Galatian churches to do. ²On the first day of every week, each one of you should set aside a sum

ᵃ 45 Gen. 2:7   ᵇ 49 Some early manuscripts *so let us*   ᶜ 54 Isaiah 25:8
ᵈ 55 Hosea 13:14

What will our bodies be like in heaven? (15:42–49)
Paul said that the resurrected body will be of a different type than the earthly body. It will be far superior in every way: It will not die, it will be glorious, and it will be spiritual. He said that our resurrected bodies will be similar to Christ's glorified resurrected body.

What is the victory God gives to Christians? (15:57)
Sin brought death into the world, and people were judged under the law, which showed us our sin. But Christ paid the price for our sin by dying and rising again. Thus sin and death no longer have power over a believer.

What was the purpose of the collection? (16:1)
The collection was being taken for the Christians in Jerusalem who had become poor as a result of famine or persecution. This collection would reflect the unity of the believers and show the Jewish Christians that the Gentile Christians were sincere.

of money in keeping with your income, saving it up, so that when I come no collections will have to be made. ³Then, when I arrive, I will give letters of introduction to the men you approve and send them with your gift to Jerusalem. ⁴If it seems advisable for me to go also, they will accompany me.

PERSONAL REQUESTS

⁵After I go through Macedonia, I will come to you—for I will be going through Macedonia. ⁶Perhaps I will stay with you for a while, or even spend the winter, so that you can help me on my journey, wherever I go. ⁷For I do not want to see you now and make only a passing visit; I hope to spend some time with you, if the Lord permits. ⁸But I will stay on at Ephesus until Pentecost, ⁹because a great door for effective work has opened to me, and there are many who oppose me.

¹⁰When Timothy comes, see to it that he has nothing to fear while he is with you, for he is carrying on the work of the Lord, just as I am. ¹¹No one, then, should treat him with contempt. Send him on his way in peace so that he may return to me. I am expecting him along with the brothers.

¹²Now about our brother Apollos: I strongly urged him to go to you with the brothers. He was quite unwilling to go now, but he will go when he has the opportunity.

¹³Be on your guard; stand firm in the faith; be courageous; be strong. ¹⁴Do everything in love.

¹⁵You know that the household of Stephanas were the first converts in Achaia, and they have devoted themselves to the service of the Lord's people. I urge you, brothers and sisters, ¹⁶to submit to such people and to everyone who joins in the work and labors at it. ¹⁷I was glad when Stephanas, Fortunatus and Achaicus arrived, because they have supplied what was lacking from you. ¹⁸For they refreshed my spirit and yours also. Such men deserve recognition.

FINAL GREETINGS

¹⁹The churches in the province of Asia send you greetings. Aquila and Priscilla*a* greet you warmly in the Lord, and so does the church that meets at their house. ²⁰All the brothers and sisters here send you greetings. Greet one another with a holy kiss.

²¹I, Paul, write this greeting in my own hand.

²²If anyone does not love the Lord, let that person be cursed! Come, Lord*b*!

²³The grace of the Lord Jesus be with you.

²⁴My love to all of you in Christ Jesus. Amen.*c*

Who opposed Paul in Ephesus? (16:9)
Paul's opponents were probably the craftsmen who made shrines to Artemis and others in the city who they had stirred up against him (see Acts 19:23 – 34).

What was a holy kiss? (16:20)
A public kiss on the cheek was a common practice in the ancient world that the Christians borrowed to show their respect and love for one another. This practice may have been common in synagogues at that time, and it would have been natural for congregations with Jews and Gentiles to continue to follow the custom to greet and say farewell to each other.

---

a 19 Greek *Prisca,* a variant of *Priscilla*   *b 22* The Greek for *Come, Lord* reproduces an Aramaic expression (*Marana tha*) used by early Christians.
c 24 Some manuscripts do not have *Amen.*

2 Corinthians

INTRODUCTION

Who wrote this book?	Paul.
Why was this book written?	The book of 2 Corinthians lets the Corinthians know that Paul loves them even though their church has many problems.
For whom was this book written?	This book is a letter that was sent to Christians in Corinth.

What are some important teachings in this book?	Our prayers help leaders	2 Corinthians 1:8 – 11
	Forgive those who repent	2 Corinthians 2:5 – 11
	We are God's ministers	2 Corinthians 5:11 – 21
	Give generously	2 Corinthians 9:6 – 15
	Strength in weakness	2 Corinthians 12:7 – 10

When did these things happen?

10 BC   AD 1   10   20   30   40   50   60   70   80   90   100

JESUS' LIFE (C. 6/5 BC – AD 30)

PAUL'S CONVERSION (C. AD 35)

PAUL'S MISSIONARY JOURNEYS (C. AD 46 – 67)

COUNCIL AT JERUSALEM (C. AD 49/50)

NERO'S REIGN (AD 54 – 68)

BOOK OF 2 CORINTHIANS WRITTEN (C. AD 55)

PAUL'S FIRST IMPRISONMENT IN ROME (C. AD 59 – 62)

PAUL'S IMPRISONMENT AND DEATH IN ROME (C. AD 67 – 68)

1 Paul, an apostle of Christ Jesus by the will of God, and Timothy our brother,

To the church of God in Corinth, together with all his holy people throughout Achaia:

[2] Grace and peace to you from God our Father and the Lord Jesus Christ.

PRAISE TO THE GOD OF ALL COMFORT

[3] Praise be to the God and Father of our Lord Jesus Christ, the Father of compassion and the God of all comfort, [4] who comforts us in all our troubles, so that we can comfort those in any trouble with the comfort we ourselves receive from God. [5] For just as we share abundantly in the sufferings of Christ, so also our comfort abounds through Christ. [6] If we are distressed, it is for your comfort and salvation; if we are comforted, it is for your comfort, which produces in you patient endurance of the same sufferings we suffer. [7] And our hope for you is firm, because we know that just as you share in our sufferings, so also you share in our comfort.

[8] We do not want you to be uninformed, brothers and sisters,[a] about the troubles we experienced in the province of Asia. We were under great pressure, far beyond our ability to endure, so that we despaired of life itself. [9] Indeed, we felt we had received the sentence of death. But this happened that we might not rely on ourselves but on God, who raises the dead. [10] He has delivered us from such a deadly peril, and he will deliver us again. On him we have set our hope that he will continue to deliver us, [11] as you help us by your prayers. Then many will give thanks on our behalf for the gracious favor granted us in answer to the prayers of many.

PAUL'S CHANGE OF PLANS

[12] Now this is our boast: Our conscience testifies that we have conducted ourselves in the world, and especially in our relations with you, with integrity[b] and godly sincerity. We have done so, relying not on worldly wisdom but on God's grace. [13] For we do not write you anything you cannot read or understand. And I hope that, [14] as you have understood us in part, you will come to understand fully that you can boast of us just as we will boast of you in the day of the Lord Jesus.

[15] Because I was confident of this, I wanted to visit you first so that you might benefit twice. [16] I wanted to visit you on my way to Macedonia and to come back to you from Macedonia, and then to have you send me on my way to Judea. [17] Was I fickle when I intended to do this? Or do I make my plans in a worldly manner so that in the same breath I say both "Yes, yes" and "No, no"?

[18] But as surely as God is faithful, our message to you is not "Yes" and "No." [19] For the Son of God, Jesus Christ, who was preached among you by us — by me and Silas[c] and Timothy — was not "Yes" and "No," but in him it has always been

What troubles did Paul have to face in Asia? (1:8-11)
Paul doesn't say how he suffered here, but he thought he might die. God saved him so that he would be reminded to rely on God for all things. Later in this book, Paul lists many ways in which he suffered (see 11:23-29).

Why did Paul defend himself? (1:12-14)
Some false teachers among the Corinthian Christians had challenged Paul's teachings and claimed that he was not a true apostle. They also said that Paul's change of plans about visiting them meant that he couldn't be trusted. Paul said his conscience was clear, and he reminded the Corinthians that since he had spent time with them, they should know that his character was honorable.

---

[a] 8 The Greek word for *brothers and sisters* (*adelphoi*) refers here to believers, both men and women, as part of God's family; also in 8:1; 13:11.
[b] 12 Many manuscripts *holiness*   [c] 19 Greek *Silvanus*, a variant of *Silas*

"Yes." [20] For no matter how many promises God has made, they are "Yes" in Christ. And so through him the "Amen" is spoken by us to the glory of God. [21] Now it is God who makes both us and you stand firm in Christ. He anointed us, [22] set his seal of ownership on us, and put his Spirit in our hearts as a deposit, guaranteeing what is to come.

[23] I call God as my witness — and I stake my life on it — that it was in order to spare you that I did not return to Corinth. [24] Not that we lord it over your faith, but we work **2** with you for your joy, because it is by faith you stand firm. [1] So I made up my mind that I would not make another painful visit to you. [2] For if I grieve you, who is left to make me glad but you whom I have grieved? [3] I wrote as I did, so that when I came I would not be distressed by those who should have made me rejoice. I had confidence in all of you, that you would all share my joy. [4] For I wrote you out of great distress and anguish of heart and with many tears, not to grieve you but to let you know the depth of my love for you.

FORGIVENESS FOR THE OFFENDER

[5] If anyone has caused grief, he has not so much grieved me as he has grieved all of you to some extent — not to put it too severely. [6] The punishment inflicted on him by the majority is sufficient. [7] Now instead, you ought to forgive and comfort him, so that he will not be overwhelmed by excessive sorrow. [8] I urge you, therefore, to reaffirm your love for him. [9] Another reason I wrote you was to see if you would stand the test and be obedient in everything. [10] Anyone you forgive, I also forgive. And what I have forgiven — if there was anything to forgive — I have forgiven in the sight of Christ for your sake, [11] in order that Satan might not outwit us. For we are not unaware of his schemes.

MINISTERS OF THE NEW COVENANT

[12] Now when I went to Troas to preach the gospel of Christ and found that the Lord had opened a door for me, [13] I still had no peace of mind, because I did not find my brother Titus there. So I said goodbye to them and went on to Macedonia.

[14] But thanks be to God, who always leads us as captives in Christ's triumphal procession and uses us to spread the aroma of the knowledge of him everywhere. [15] For we are to God the pleasing aroma of Christ among those who are being saved and those who are perishing. [16] To the one we are an aroma that brings death; to the other, an aroma that brings life. And who is equal to such a task? [17] Unlike so many, we do not peddle the word of God for profit. On the contrary, in Christ we speak before God with sincerity, as those sent from God.

3 Are we beginning to commend ourselves again? Or do we need, like some people, letters of recommendation to you or from you? [2] You yourselves are our letter, written on our hearts, known and read by everyone. [3] You show that you are a letter from Christ, the result of our ministry, written

---

What were seals and deposits? (1:22)
A wax seal was used to secure a scroll; it showed ownership and security. God symbolically put his seal on his people to show that he owned them. A deposit was the first installment of a payment which guaranteed a much larger payment would be made later. The Holy Spirit was the believer's guarantee that God would fulfill his promises.

When should people in the church forgive someone who has sinned? (2:5–11)
A member of the church in Corinth had committed a serious sin, and the church had disciplined him. Now Paul said that he should be forgiven and taken back into the church because he was truly sorry for his sin. This is a good model for the church today.

What type of procession was this? (2:14)
When a Roman general was victorious, he would lead officials, musicians, soldiers, and the prisoners they had taken in a procession of celebration. Paul compared God to the general who led the procession.

Why did some teachers have letters of recommendation? (3:1)
Some of the false teachers in Corinth produced letters of recommendation to try to establish that they were true teachers. Paul said he did not need to prove he was a true apostle; the believers in Corinth were the evidence that he had been teaching God's truth.

not with ink but with the Spirit of the living God, not on tablets of stone but on tablets of human hearts.

[4] Such confidence we have through Christ before God. [5] Not that we are competent in ourselves to claim anything for ourselves, but our competence comes from God. [6] He has made us competent as ministers of a new covenant—not of the letter but of the Spirit; for the letter kills, but the Spirit gives life.

THE GREATER GLORY OF THE NEW COVENANT

[7] Now if the ministry that brought death, which was engraved in letters on stone, came with glory, so that the Israelites could not look steadily at the face of Moses because of its glory, transitory though it was, [8] will not the ministry of the Spirit be even more glorious? [9] If the ministry that brought condemnation was glorious, how much more glorious is the ministry that brings righteousness! [10] For what was glorious has no glory now in comparison with the surpassing glory. [11] And if what was transitory came with glory, how much greater is the glory of that which lasts!

[12] Therefore, since we have such a hope, we are very bold. [13] We are not like Moses, who would put a veil over his face to prevent the Israelites from seeing the end of what was passing away. [14] But their minds were made dull, for to this day the same veil remains when the old covenant is read. It has not been removed, because only in Christ is it taken away. [15] Even to this day when Moses is read, a veil covers their hearts. [16] But whenever anyone turns to the Lord, the veil is taken away. [17] Now the Lord is the Spirit, and where the Spirit of the Lord is, there is freedom. [18] And we all, who with unveiled faces contemplate[a] the Lord's glory, are being transformed into his image with ever-increasing glory, which comes from the Lord, who is the Spirit.

PRESENT WEAKNESS AND RESURRECTION LIFE

4 Therefore, since through God's mercy we have this ministry, we do not lose heart. [2] Rather, we have renounced secret and shameful ways; we do not use deception, nor do we distort the word of God. On the contrary, by setting forth the truth plainly we commend ourselves to everyone's conscience in the sight of God. [3] And even if our gospel is veiled, it is veiled to those who are perishing. [4] The god of this age has blinded the minds of unbelievers, so that they cannot see the light of the gospel that displays the glory of Christ, who is the image of God. [5] For what we preach is not ourselves, but Jesus Christ as Lord, and ourselves as your servants for Jesus' sake. [6] For God, who said, "Let light shine out of darkness,"[b] made his light shine in our hearts to give us the light of the knowledge of God's glory displayed in the face of Christ.

[7] But we have this treasure in jars of clay to show that this all-surpassing power is from God and not from us. [8] We are hard pressed on every side, but not crushed; perplexed, but

[a] 18 Or reflect   [b] 6 Gen. 1:3

What did Paul mean when he wrote about Moses' veil? (3:14)
Moses wore a veil so that people would not see the glory of his face fade after his experience with God on the mountaintop. Paul said that in a similar way a "veil" keeps people from understanding that through Christ the demands of the old covenant have been fulfilled and that he is the only way to heaven.

Who is the god of this age? (4:4)
This is the devil. Those who follow the devil have, in effect, made him their god.

Why was treasure stored in jars of clay? (4:7)
Treasure was often stored in plain clay jars so as not to attract attention to their contents. Here the treasure is the gospel, and the clay jar represents Paul and his human weaknesses.

not in despair; [9] persecuted, but not abandoned; struck down, but not destroyed. [10] We always carry around in our body the death of Jesus, so that the life of Jesus may also be revealed in our body. [11] For we who are alive are always being given over to death for Jesus' sake, so that his life may also be revealed in our mortal body. [12] So then, death is at work in us, but life is at work in you.

[13] It is written: "I believed; therefore I have spoken."[a] Since we have that same spirit of[b] faith, we also believe and therefore speak, [14] because we know that the one who raised the Lord Jesus from the dead will also raise us with Jesus and present us with you to himself. [15] All this is for your benefit, so that the grace that is reaching more and more people may cause thanksgiving to overflow to the glory of God.

[16] Therefore we do not lose heart. Though outwardly we are wasting away, yet inwardly we are being renewed day by day. [17] For our light and momentary troubles are achieving for us an eternal glory that far outweighs them all. [18] So we fix our eyes not on what is seen, but on what is unseen, since what is seen is temporary, but what is unseen is eternal.

AWAITING THE NEW BODY

5 For we know that if the earthly tent we live in is destroyed, we have a building from God, an eternal house in heaven, not built by human hands. [2] Meanwhile we groan, longing to be clothed instead with our heavenly dwelling, [3] because when we are clothed, we will not be found naked. [4] For while we are in this tent, we groan and are burdened, because we do not wish to be unclothed but to be clothed instead with our heavenly dwelling, so that what is mortal may be swallowed up by life. [5] Now the one who has fashioned us for this very purpose is God, who has given us the Spirit as a deposit, guaranteeing what is to come.

[6] Therefore we are always confident and know that as long as we are at home in the body we are away from the Lord. [7] For we live by faith, not by sight. [8] We are confident, I say, and would prefer to be away from the body and at home with the Lord. [9] So we make it our goal to please him, whether we are at home in the body or away from it. [10] For we must all appear before the judgment seat of Christ, so that each of us may receive what is due us for the things done while in the body, whether good or bad.

THE MINISTRY OF RECONCILIATION

[11] Since, then, we know what it is to fear the Lord, we try to persuade others. What we are is plain to God, and I hope it is also plain to your conscience. [12] We are not trying to commend ourselves to you again, but are giving you an opportunity to take pride in us, so that you can answer those who take pride in what is seen rather than in what is in the heart. [13] If we are "out of our mind," as some say, it is for God; if we are in our right mind, it is for you. [14] For Christ's love compels us, because we are convinced that one died for all, and therefore all died. [15] And he died for all, that those who

How did Paul remain confident? (4:16–18)
Paul looked beyond the problems he had in this world in order to look toward the glory to come in eternity.

What is the earthly tent? (5:1)
The earthly tent is a person's present body. In this section, Paul talks about the limitations and pains of the present life in contrast to the wonderful life that is to come in heaven.

[a] 13 Psalm 116:10 (see Septuagint)　　[b] 13 Or Spirit-given

live should no longer live for themselves but for him who died for them and was raised again.

¹⁶ So from now on we regard no one from a worldly point of view. Though we once regarded Christ in this way, we do so no longer. ¹⁷ Therefore, if anyone is in Christ, the new creation has come:*ᵃ* The old has gone, the new is here! ¹⁸ All this is from God, who reconciled us to himself through Christ and gave us the ministry of reconciliation: ¹⁹ that God was reconciling the world to himself in Christ, not counting people's sins against them. And he has committed to us the message of reconciliation. ²⁰ We are therefore Christ's ambassadors, as though God were making his appeal through us. We implore you on Christ's behalf: Be reconciled to God. ²¹ God made him who had no sin to be sin*ᵇ* for us, so that in him we might become the righteousness of God.

6 As God's co-workers we urge you not to receive God's grace in vain. ² For he says,

"In the time of my favor I heard you,
 and in the day of salvation I helped you."*ᶜ*

I tell you, now is the time of God's favor, now is the day of salvation.

PAUL'S HARDSHIPS

³ We put no stumbling block in anyone's path, so that our ministry will not be discredited. ⁴ Rather, as servants of God we commend ourselves in every way: in great endurance; in troubles, hardships and distresses; ⁵ in beatings, imprisonments and riots; in hard work, sleepless nights and hunger; ⁶ in purity, understanding, patience and kindness; in the Holy Spirit and in sincere love; ⁷ in truthful speech and in the power of God; with weapons of righteousness in the right hand and in the left; ⁸ through glory and dishonor, bad report and good report; genuine, yet regarded as impostors; ⁹ known, yet regarded as unknown; dying, and yet we live on; beaten, and yet not killed; ¹⁰ sorrowful, yet always rejoicing; poor, yet making many rich; having nothing, and yet possessing everything.

ᵃ 17 Or Christ, that person is a new creation.   *ᵇ 21 Or be a sin offering*
ᶜ 2 Isaiah 49:8

What are reconciled people called to do? (5:18–20)
People who have been restored to a right relationship with God through believing in Jesus as their Savior are called to be Christ's ambassadors, telling the world about God's love.

Why did Paul list the difficulties he had to face? (6:4–10)
He wanted to remind the Corinthians that even in the greatest difficulties, he always tried to live in a way that would honor God. Paul endured many hardships as God's servant, unlike the false teachers who wanted comfort and personal gain.

Why can't I wait to become a Christian until after I've had my fun?
2 CORINTHIANS 6

One very practical answer to the question is that none of us knows how long we will live. If we put off becoming a Christian until some date in the future, we could become involved in a bad accident and lose consciousness or even our life before we have accepted God's invitation to be a part of his family.

Another reason not to postpone becoming a Christian is that sin may become so powerful and so attractive that we can't give it up and in that way lose our opportunity to follow God and do his will.

Still another reason to become a Christian when God calls us is that we should not resist the Holy Spirit working in our heart. God shows great love by choosing his people. If we do not respond to his call, we are insulting God and acting as if his gift of salvation is not important.

Finally, by becoming a Christian when God calls us, we can benefit from participating with other believers as we grow in our faith and do God's work in the world. And we will learn that living life according to God's plan is the most fun life of all!

[11]We have spoken freely to you, Corinthians, and opened wide our hearts to you. [12]We are not withholding our affection from you, but you are withholding yours from us. [13]As a fair exchange—I speak as to my children—open wide your hearts also.

WARNING AGAINST IDOLATRY

[14]Do not be yoked together with unbelievers. For what do righteousness and wickedness have in common? Or what fellowship can light have with darkness? [15]What harmony is there between Christ and Belial[a]? Or what does a believer have in common with an unbeliever? [16]What agreement is there between the temple of God and idols? For we are the temple of the living God. As God has said:

> "I will live with them
>   and walk among them,
> and I will be their God,
>   and they will be my people."[b]

[17]Therefore,

> "Come out from them
>   and be separate,
>   says the Lord.
> Touch no unclean thing,
>   and I will receive you."[c]

[18]And,

> "I will be a Father to you,
>   and you will be my sons and daughters,
>   says the Lord Almighty."[d]

7 Therefore, since we have these promises, dear friends, let us purify ourselves from everything that contaminates body and spirit, perfecting holiness out of reverence for God.

PAUL'S JOY OVER THE CHURCH'S REPENTANCE

[2]Make room for us in your hearts. We have wronged no one, we have corrupted no one, we have exploited no one. [3]I do not say this to condemn you; I have said before that you have such a place in our hearts that we would live or die with you. [4]I have spoken to you with great frankness; I take great pride in you. I am greatly encouraged; in all our troubles my joy knows no bounds.

[5]For when we came into Macedonia, we had no rest, but we were harassed at every turn—conflicts on the outside, fears within. [6]But God, who comforts the downcast, comforted us by the coming of Titus, [7]and not only by his coming but also by the comfort you had given him. He told us about your longing for me, your deep sorrow, your ardent concern for me, so that my joy was greater than ever.

[8]Even if I caused you sorrow by my letter, I do not regret it. Though I did regret it—I see that my letter hurt you, but

What did Paul urge the Corinthians to avoid? (6:14)
Paul did not want them to cooperate with false teachers because they were spreading Satan's message rather than God's.

What was the effect of Paul's previous letter to the Corinthians? (7:8–10)
The letter had made them sad, but their sorrow led to repentance.

[a] 15 Greek Beliar, a variant of Belial   [b] 16 Lev. 26:12; Jer. 32:38; Ezek. 37:27   [c] 17 Isaiah 52:11; Ezek. 20:34,41   [d] 18 2 Samuel 7:14; 7:8

only for a little while— ⁹yet now I am happy, not because you were made sorry, but because your sorrow led you to repentance. For you became sorrowful as God intended and so were not harmed in any way by us. ¹⁰Godly sorrow brings repentance that leads to salvation and leaves no regret, but worldly sorrow brings death. ¹¹See what this godly sorrow has produced in you: what earnestness, what eagerness to clear yourselves, what indignation, what alarm, what longing, what concern, what readiness to see justice done. At every point you have proved yourselves to be innocent in this matter. ¹²So even though I wrote to you, it was neither on account of the one who did the wrong nor on account of the injured party, but rather that before God you could see for yourselves how devoted to us you are. ¹³By all this we are encouraged.

In addition to our own encouragement, we were especially delighted to see how happy Titus was, because his spirit has been refreshed by all of you. ¹⁴I had boasted to him about you, and you have not embarrassed me. But just as everything we said to you was true, so our boasting about you to Titus has proved to be true as well. ¹⁵And his affection for you is all the greater when he remembers that you were all obedient, receiving him with fear and trembling. ¹⁶I am glad I can have complete confidence in you.

THE COLLECTION FOR THE LORD'S PEOPLE

8 And now, brothers and sisters, we want you to know about the grace that God has given the Macedonian churches. ²In the midst of a very severe trial, their overflowing joy and their extreme poverty welled up in rich generosity. ³For I testify that they gave as much as they were able, and even beyond their ability. Entirely on their own, ⁴they urgently pleaded with us for the privilege of sharing in this service to the Lord's people. ⁵And they exceeded our expectations: They gave themselves first of all to the Lord, and then by the will of God also to us. ⁶So we urged Titus, just as he had earlier made a beginning, to bring also to completion this act of grace on your part. ⁷But since you excel in everything—in faith, in speech, in knowledge, in complete earnestness and in the love we have kindled in youᵃ—see that you also excel in this grace of giving.

⁸I am not commanding you, but I want to test the sincerity of your love by comparing it with the earnestness of others. ⁹For you know the grace of our Lord Jesus Christ, that though he was rich, yet for your sake he became poor, so that you through his poverty might become rich.

¹⁰And here is my judgment about what is best for you in this matter. Last year you were the first not only to give but also to have the desire to do so. ¹¹Now finish the work, so that your eager willingness to do it may be matched by your completion of it, according to your means. ¹²For if the willingness is there, the gift is acceptable according to what one has, not according to what one does not have.

¹³Our desire is not that others might be relieved while you are hard pressed, but that there might be equality. ¹⁴At the

How had the Christians in Macedonia reflected the grace of God? (8:2–5) Even in their hardship and poverty, they contributed generously to the collection Paul was taking for the Christians in Jerusalem. The Macedonian Christians gave themselves to the Lord and then sacrificially helped other believers.

How did Paul try to encourage the Corinthians to give generously? (8:8–14) After giving the example of the Macedonians, Paul reminded the Corinthians of Jesus' great sacrifice. He also reminded them of their earlier eagerness to give, and he described how equality was maintained among Christians.

ᵃ 7 Some manuscripts *and in your love for us*

present time your plenty will supply what they need, so that in turn their plenty will supply what you need. The goal is equality, [15] as it is written: "The one who gathered much did not have too much, and the one who gathered little did not have too little."[a]

TITUS SENT TO RECEIVE THE COLLECTION

[16] Thanks be to God, who put into the heart of Titus the same concern I have for you. [17] For Titus not only welcomed our appeal, but he is coming to you with much enthusiasm and on his own initiative. [18] And we are sending along with him the brother who is praised by all the churches for his service to the gospel. [19] What is more, he was chosen by the churches to accompany us as we carry the offering, which we administer in order to honor the Lord himself and to show our eagerness to help. [20] We want to avoid any criticism of the way we administer this liberal gift. [21] For we are taking pains to do what is right, not only in the eyes of the Lord but also in the eyes of man.

[22] In addition, we are sending with them our brother who has often proved to us in many ways that he is zealous, and now even more so because of his great confidence in you. [23] As for Titus, he is my partner and co-worker among you; as for our brothers, they are representatives of the churches and an honor to Christ. [24] Therefore show these men the proof of your love and the reason for our pride in you, so that the churches can see it.

9 There is no need for me to write to you about this service to the Lord's people. [2] For I know your eagerness to help, and I have been boasting about it to the Macedonians, telling them that since last year you in Achaia were ready to give; and your enthusiasm has stirred most of them to action. [3] But I am sending the brothers in order that our boasting about you in this matter should not prove hollow, but that you may be ready, as I said you would be. [4] For if any Mace-

[a] 15 Exodus 16:18

How did Paul guard his reputation? (8:19–21)
Paul used people of excellent character to help him gather the offering and administer it so that no one could question his honesty or integrity.

What does the Bible teach about giving money to the church and other good causes?
2 CORINTHIANS 8–9

The Bible has a lot to say about how believers should use their wealth. For example, in the Old Testament people who owned fields were supposed to leave some grain at the edges of the fields for poor people to gather. God told people to take special care of those who could not take care of themselves, such as widows and orphans. Jesus told people to be generous to individuals who need help. He said, "Give to the one who asks you, and do not turn away from the one who wants to borrow from you" (Matthew 5:42).

In this passage Paul was encouraging the Christians in Corinth to give generously to help the Christians who were struggling in Jerusalem. After giving the example of the generous Macedonians, Paul reminded the Corinthians of Jesus' great sacrifice. He also reminded them of their earlier eagerness to give, and he described the principle of equality among Christians.

Christians should give generously to the church and other good causes because everything that they have is a gift from God, and they should be eager to use their resources to support God's work. Our gifts will help other people, will reflect our gratitude to God, and will cause others who see our generosity to praise God.

donians come with me and find you unprepared, we—not to say anything about you—would be ashamed of having been so confident. ⁵So I thought it necessary to urge the brothers to visit you in advance and finish the arrangements for the generous gift you had promised. Then it will be ready as a generous gift, not as one grudgingly given.

GENEROSITY ENCOURAGED

⁶Remember this: Whoever sows sparingly will also reap sparingly, and whoever sows generously will also reap generously. ⁷Each of you should give what you have decided in your heart to give, not reluctantly or under compulsion, for God loves a cheerful giver. ⁸And God is able to bless you abundantly, so that in all things at all times, having all that you need, you will abound in every good work. ⁹As it is written:

"They have freely scattered their gifts to the poor;
  their righteousness endures forever."ᵃ

¹⁰Now he who supplies seed to the sower and bread for food will also supply and increase your store of seed and will enlarge the harvest of your righteousness. ¹¹You will be enriched in every way so that you can be generous on every occasion, and through us your generosity will result in thanksgiving to God.

¹²This service that you perform is not only supplying the needs of the Lord's people but is also overflowing in many expressions of thanks to God. ¹³Because of the service by which you have proved yourselves, others will praise God for the obedience that accompanies your confession of the gospel of Christ, and for your generosity in sharing with them and with everyone else. ¹⁴And in their prayers for you their hearts will go out to you, because of the surpassing grace God has given you. ¹⁵Thanks be to God for his indescribable gift!

PAUL'S DEFENSE OF HIS MINISTRY

10 By the humility and gentleness of Christ, I appeal to you—I, Paul, who am "timid" when face to face with you, but "bold" toward you when away! ²I beg you that when I come I may not have to be as bold as I expect to be toward some people who think that we live by the standards of this world. ³For though we live in the world, we do not wage war as the world does. ⁴The weapons we fight with are not the weapons of the world. On the contrary, they have divine power to demolish strongholds. ⁵We demolish arguments and every pretension that sets itself up against the knowledge of God, and we take captive every thought to make it obedient to Christ. ⁶And we will be ready to punish every act of disobedience, once your obedience is complete.

⁷You are judging by appearances.ᵇ If anyone is confident that they belong to Christ, they should consider again that we belong to Christ just as much as they do. ⁸So even if I boast somewhat freely about the authority the Lord gave

What is the source of generosity? (9:8)
Paul said that God's grace works in people's hearts to encourage them to be generous and to live lives characterized by good works.

How would the Corinthians' gifts benefit the church? (9:12–14)
The Corinthians' gifts would help God's people in Jerusalem, but they would also cause people in other places to thank and praise God because of their great generosity and willingness to serve.

ᵃ 9 Psalm 112:9   ᵇ 7 Or *Look at the obvious facts*

us for building you up rather than tearing you down, I will not be ashamed of it. [9]I do not want to seem to be trying to frighten you with my letters. [10]For some say, "His letters are weighty and forceful, but in person he is unimpressive and his speaking amounts to nothing." [11]Such people should realize that what we are in our letters when we are absent, we will be in our actions when we are present.

[12]We do not dare to classify or compare ourselves with some who commend themselves. When they measure themselves by themselves and compare themselves with themselves, they are not wise. [13]We, however, will not boast beyond proper limits, but will confine our boasting to the sphere of service God himself has assigned to us, a sphere that also includes you. [14]We are not going too far in our boasting, as would be the case if we had not come to you, for we did get as far as you with the gospel of Christ. [15]Neither do we go beyond our limits by boasting of work done by others. Our hope is that, as your faith continues to grow, our sphere of activity among you will greatly expand, [16]so that we can preach the gospel in the regions beyond you. For we do not want to boast about work already done in someone else's territory. [17]But, "Let the one who boasts boast in the Lord."[a] [18]For it is not the one who commends himself who is approved, but the one whom the Lord commends.

PAUL AND THE FALSE APOSTLES

11 I hope you will put up with me in a little foolishness. Yes, please put up with me! [2]I am jealous for you with a godly jealousy. I promised you to one husband, to Christ, so that I might present you as a pure virgin to him. [3]But I am afraid that just as Eve was deceived by the serpent's cunning, your minds may somehow be led astray from your sincere and pure devotion to Christ. [4]For if someone comes to you and preaches a Jesus other than the Jesus we preached, or if you receive a different spirit from the Spirit you received, or a different gospel from the one you accepted, you put up with it easily enough.

[5]I do not think I am in the least inferior to those "super-apostles."[b] [6]I may indeed be untrained as a speaker, but I do have knowledge. We have made this perfectly clear to you in every way. [7]Was it a sin for me to lower myself in order to elevate you by preaching the gospel of God to you free of charge? [8]I robbed other churches by receiving support from them so as to serve you. [9]And when I was with you and needed something, I was not a burden to anyone, for the brothers who came from Macedonia supplied what I needed. I have kept myself from being a burden to you in any way, and will continue to do so. [10]As surely as the truth of Christ is in me, nobody in the regions of Achaia will stop this boasting of mine. [11]Why? Because I do not love you? God knows I do!

[12]And I will keep on doing what I am doing in order to cut the ground from under those who want an opportunity to be considered equal with us in the things they boast about.

---

[a] 17 Jer. 9:24   [b] 5 Or *to the most eminent apostles*

[13] For such people are false apostles, deceitful workers, masquerading as apostles of Christ. [14] And no wonder, for Satan himself masquerades as an angel of light. [15] It is not surprising, then, if his servants also masquerade as servants of righteousness. Their end will be what their actions deserve.

PAUL BOASTS ABOUT HIS SUFFERINGS

[16] I repeat: Let no one take me for a fool. But if you do, then tolerate me just as you would a fool, so that I may do a little boasting. [17] In this self-confident boasting I am not talking as the Lord would, but as a fool. [18] Since many are boasting in the way the world does, I too will boast. [19] You gladly put up with fools since you are so wise! [20] In fact, you even put up with anyone who enslaves you or exploits you or takes advantage of you or puts on airs or slaps you in the face. [21] To my shame I admit that we were too weak for that!

Whatever anyone else dares to boast about — I am speaking as a fool — I also dare to boast about. [22] Are they Hebrews? So am I. Are they Israelites? So am I. Are they Abraham's descendants? So am I. [23] Are they servants of Christ? (I am out of my mind to talk like this.) I am more. I have worked much harder, been in prison more frequently, been flogged more severely, and been exposed to death again and again. [24] Five times I received from the Jews the forty lashes minus one. [25] Three times I was beaten with rods, once I was pelted with stones, three times I was shipwrecked, I spent a night and a day in the open sea, [26] I have been constantly on the move. I have been in danger from rivers, in danger from bandits, in danger from my fellow Jews, in danger from Gentiles; in danger in the city, in danger in the country, in danger at sea; and in danger from false believers. [27] I have labored and toiled and have often gone without sleep; I have known hunger and thirst and have often gone without food; I have been cold and naked. [28] Besides everything else, I face daily the pressure of my concern for all the churches. [29] Who is weak, and I do not feel weak? Who is led into sin, and I do not inwardly burn?

[30] If I must boast, I will boast of the things that show my weakness. [31] The God and Father of the Lord Jesus, who is to be praised forever, knows that I am not lying. [32] In Damascus the governor under King Aretas had the city of the Damascenes guarded in order to arrest me. [33] But I was lowered in a basket from a window in the wall and slipped through his hands.

PAUL'S VISION AND HIS THORN

12 I must go on boasting. Although there is nothing to be gained, I will go on to visions and revelations from the Lord. [2] I know a man in Christ who fourteen years ago was caught up to the third heaven. Whether it was in the body or out of the body I do not know — God knows. [3] And I know that this man — whether in the body or apart from the body I do not know, but God knows — [4] was caught up to paradise and heard inexpressible things, things that no one is permitted to tell. [5] I will boast about a man like that,

Why did Paul list all of the hardships he faced? (11:23 – 28) Paul wanted to establish that he was Christ's servant and was willing to suffer in order to preach the gospel. In contrast, the false teachers led comfortable lives.

What had happened to Paul 14 years earlier? (12:2 – 4) Early in Paul's ministry, he experienced a vision in which he came into the presence of God in the "third heaven." Most Jews at that time considered there to be three heavens: the first heaven as the atmosphere, the second above that where the moon, sun and stars reside, and the third the place where God resides. When Paul states that he was taken up to the third heaven, this was the place we normally think of as heaven.

but I will not boast about myself, except about my weaknesses. [6] Even if I should choose to boast, I would not be a fool, because I would be speaking the truth. But I refrain, so no one will think more of me than is warranted by what I do or say, [7] or because of these surpassingly great revelations. Therefore, in order to keep me from becoming conceited, I was given a thorn in my flesh, a messenger of Satan, to torment me. [8] Three times I pleaded with the Lord to take it away from me. [9] But he said to me, "My grace is sufficient for you, for my power is made perfect in weakness." Therefore I will boast all the more gladly about my weaknesses, so that Christ's power may rest on me. [10] That is why, for Christ's sake, I delight in weaknesses, in insults, in hardships, in persecutions, in difficulties. For when I am weak, then I am strong.

What was the thorn in Paul's flesh? (12:7–9)
There have been various guesses, but no one really knows what this physical or spiritual problem was.

PAUL'S CONCERN FOR THE CORINTHIANS

[11] I have made a fool of myself, but you drove me to it. I ought to have been commended by you, for I am not in the least inferior to the "super-apostles,"[a] even though I am nothing. [12] I persevered in demonstrating among you the marks of a true apostle, including signs, wonders and miracles. [13] How were you inferior to the other churches, except that I was never a burden to you? Forgive me this wrong!

[14] Now I am ready to visit you for the third time, and I will not be a burden to you, because what I want is not your possessions but you. After all, children should not have to save up for their parents, but parents for their children. [15] So I will very gladly spend for you everything I have and expend myself as well. If I love you more, will you love me less? [16] Be that as it may, I have not been a burden to you. Yet, crafty fellow that I am, I caught you by trickery! [17] Did I exploit you through any of the men I sent to you? [18] I urged Titus to go to you and I sent our brother with him. Titus did not exploit you, did he? Did we not walk in the same footsteps by the same Spirit?

Why did Paul ask to be forgiven for not being a burden? (12:13)
The false teachers had criticized Paul for not requesting payment or support from the Corinthians. Paul's apology was sarcastic.

[19] Have you been thinking all along that we have been defending ourselves to you? We have been speaking in the sight of God as those in Christ; and everything we do, dear friends, is for your strengthening. [20] For I am afraid that when I come I may not find you as I want you to be, and you may not find me as you want me to be. I fear that there may be discord, jealousy, fits of rage, selfish ambition, slander, gossip, arrogance and disorder. [21] I am afraid that when I come again my God will humble me before you, and I will be grieved over many who have sinned earlier and have not repented of the impurity, sexual sin and debauchery in which they have indulged.

Why was Paul afraid of what he might find when he got to Corinth? (12:20–21)
Since the church in Corinth was spiritually immature, Paul was afraid that the church would be divided by anger, gossip, and other sins. He also feared that some of those who had been involved in sexual and other sins had not repented.

FINAL WARNINGS

13 This will be my third visit to you. "Every matter must be established by the testimony of two or three witnesses."[b] [2] I already gave you a warning when I was with you the second time. I now repeat it while absent: On my return

---

[a] 11 Or *the most eminent apostles*   [b] 1 Deut. 19:15

I will not spare those who sinned earlier or any of the others, ³since you are demanding proof that Christ is speaking through me. He is not weak in dealing with you, but is powerful among you. ⁴For to be sure, he was crucified in weakness, yet he lives by God's power. Likewise, we are weak in him, yet by God's power we will live with him in our dealing with you.

⁵Examine yourselves to see whether you are in the faith; test yourselves. Do you not realize that Christ Jesus is in you—unless, of course, you fail the test? ⁶And I trust that you will discover that we have not failed the test. ⁷Now we pray to God that you will not do anything wrong—not so that people will see that we have stood the test but so that you will do what is right even though we may seem to have failed. ⁸For we cannot do anything against the truth, but only for the truth. ⁹We are glad whenever we are weak but you are strong; and our prayer is that you may be fully restored. ¹⁰This is why I write these things when I am absent, that when I come I may not have to be harsh in my use of authority—the authority the Lord gave me for building you up, not for tearing you down.

FINAL GREETINGS

¹¹Finally, brothers and sisters, rejoice! Strive for full restoration, encourage one another, be of one mind, live in peace. And the God of love and peace will be with you.

¹²Greet one another with a holy kiss. ¹³All God's people here send their greetings.

¹⁴May the grace of the Lord Jesus Christ, and the love of God, and the fellowship of the Holy Spirit be with you all.

Why did Paul tell the Corinthians to examine themselves? (13:5) Instead of asking Paul to prove that he was a true apostle of Christ, the people of Corinth were to look at their own lives to see if they were following Christ. If they were, Paul would not have to impose strict punishments.

Galatians

INTRODUCTION

Who wrote this book? Paul.

Why was this book written? The book of Galatians helps the Galatian believers rely on Jesus rather than on trying to keep God's law.

For whom was this book written? This book is a letter sent to several churches in the province of Galatia.

What are some important teachings in this book?

Jesus died for our sins	Galatians 1:3 – 5
Jesus saves us	Galatians 3:6 – 14
We belong to Christ	Galatians 3:26 – 29
Serve others in love	Galatians 5:13 – 14
The Spirit makes us good	Galatians 5:22 – 25
Do good to all people	Galatians 6:7 – 10

When did these things happen?

10 BC AD 1 10 20 30 40 50 60 70 80 90 100

JESUS' LIFE (C. 6/5 BC – AD 30)
PAUL'S CONVERSION (C. AD 35)
PAUL'S MISSIONARY JOURNEYS (C. AD 46 – 67)
BOOK OF GALATIANS WRITTEN (C. AD 48 – 53)
COUNCIL AT JERUSALEM (C. AD 49/50)
NERO'S REIGN (AD 54 – 68)
PAUL'S FIRST IMPRISONMENT IN ROME (C. AD 59 – 62)
PAUL'S IMPRISONMENT AND DEATH IN ROME (C. AD 67 – 68)
DESTRUCTION OF JERUSALEM'S TEMPLE (C. AD 70)

1 Paul, an apostle—sent not from men nor by a man, but by Jesus Christ and God the Father, who raised him from the dead— [2]and all the brothers and sisters[a] with me,

To the churches in Galatia:

[3]Grace and peace to you from God our Father and the Lord Jesus Christ, [4]who gave himself for our sins to rescue us from the present evil age, according to the will of our God and Father, [5]to whom be glory for ever and ever. Amen.

NO OTHER GOSPEL

[6]I am astonished that you are so quickly deserting the one who called you to live in the grace of Christ and are turning to a different gospel— [7]which is really no gospel at all. Evidently some people are throwing you into confusion and are trying to pervert the gospel of Christ. [8]But even if we or an angel from heaven should preach a gospel other than the one we preached to you, let them be under God's curse! [9]As we have already said, so now I say again: If anybody is preaching to you a gospel other than what you accepted, let them be under God's curse!

[10]Am I now trying to win the approval of human beings, or of God? Or am I trying to please people? If I were still trying to please people, I would not be a servant of Christ.

PAUL CALLED BY GOD

[11]I want you to know, brothers and sisters, that the gospel I preached is not of human origin. [12]I did not receive it from any man, nor was I taught it; rather, I received it by revelation from Jesus Christ.

[13]For you have heard of my previous way of life in Judaism, how intensely I persecuted the church of God and tried to destroy it. [14]I was advancing in Judaism beyond many of my own age among my people and was extremely zealous for the traditions of my fathers. [15]But when God, who set me apart from my mother's womb and called me by his grace, was pleased [16]to reveal his Son in me so that I might preach him among the Gentiles, my immediate response was not to consult any human being. [17]I did not go up to Jerusalem to see those who were apostles before I was, but I went into Arabia. Later I returned to Damascus.

[18]Then after three years, I went up to Jerusalem to get acquainted with Cephas[b] and stayed with him fifteen days. [19]I saw none of the other apostles—only James, the Lord's brother. [20]I assure you before God that what I am writing you is no lie.

[21]Then I went to Syria and Cilicia. [22]I was personally unknown to the churches of Judea that are in Christ. [23]They only heard the report: "The man who formerly persecuted us is now preaching the faith he once tried to destroy." [24]And they praised God because of me.

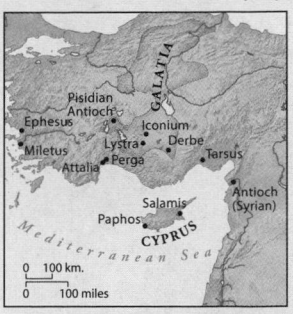

The churches in Galatia (1:2)

Who was throwing the Galatian Christians into confusion? (1:6–7)
Judaizers were Jewish Christians who thought that Christians were still required to observe some of the Old Testament rules. For example, they insisted that Gentile Christians must be circumcised. They also said that Paul was a false teacher who removed the requirements in order to make his message more appealing.

How did Paul defend himself? (1:13–17)
Paul explained that he too had been a sincere Jew who practiced all of the Jewish traditions. However, when God called him, he immediately went out to preach the gospel of Christ.

---

[a] 2 The Greek word for *brothers and sisters* (*adelphoi*) refers here to believers, both men and women, as part of God's family; also in verse 11; and in 3:15; 4:12, 28, 31; 5:11, 13; 6:1, 18.   [b] 18 That is, Peter

PAUL ACCEPTED BY THE APOSTLES

2 Then after fourteen years, I went up again to Jerusalem, this time with Barnabas. I took Titus along also. ²I went in response to a revelation and, meeting privately with those esteemed as leaders, I presented to them the gospel that I preach among the Gentiles. I wanted to be sure I was not running and had not been running my race in vain. ³Yet not even Titus, who was with me, was compelled to be circumcised, even though he was a Greek. ⁴This matter arose because some false believers had infiltrated our ranks to spy on the freedom we have in Christ Jesus and to make us slaves. ⁵We did not give in to them for a moment, so that the truth of the gospel might be preserved for you.

⁶As for those who were held in high esteem—whatever they were makes no difference to me; God does not show favoritism—they added nothing to my message. ⁷On the contrary, they recognized that I had been entrusted with the task of preaching the gospel to the uncircumcised,ᵃ just as Peter had been to the circumcised.ᵇ ⁸For God, who was at work in Peter as an apostle to the circumcised, was also at work in me as an apostle to the Gentiles. ⁹James, Cephasᶜ and John, those esteemed as pillars, gave me and Barnabas the right hand of fellowship when they recognized the grace given to me. They agreed that we should go to the Gentiles, and they to the circumcised. ¹⁰All they asked was that we should continue to remember the poor, the very thing I had been eager to do all along.

PAUL OPPOSES CEPHAS

¹¹When Cephas came to Antioch, I opposed him to his face, because he stood condemned. ¹²For before certain men came from James, he used to eat with the Gentiles. But when they arrived, he began to draw back and separate himself from the Gentiles because he was afraid of those who belonged to the circumcision group. ¹³The other Jews joined him in his hypocrisy, so that by their hypocrisy even Barnabas was led astray.

¹⁴When I saw that they were not acting in line with the truth of the gospel, I said to Cephas in front of them all, "You are a Jew, yet you live like a Gentile and not like a Jew. How is it, then, that you force Gentiles to follow Jewish customs?

¹⁵"We who are Jews by birth and not sinful Gentiles ¹⁶know that a person is not justified by the works of the law, but by faith in Jesus Christ. So we, too, have put our faith in Christ Jesus that we may be justified by faith inᵈ Christ and not by the works of the law, because by the works of the law no one will be justified.

¹⁷"But if, in seeking to be justified in Christ, we Jews find ourselves also among the sinners, doesn't that mean that Christ promotes sin? Absolutely not! ¹⁸If I rebuild what I destroyed, then I really would be a lawbreaker.

Did the apostles think that Paul was called by God? (2:7–10)
Yes, the leaders in Jerusalem believed that Paul's calling was primarily to preach the gospel to the Gentiles, while theirs was to preach the gospel to the Jews.

Why did Paul disagree with Cephas (Peter)? (2:11–14)
Peter had separated himself from Gentile Christians because he did not want to be criticized by the Jews who wanted the Gentiles to follow Jewish laws. Paul pointed out that Peter himself did not follow all of the Jewish dietary laws and asked why Peter would insist that Gentiles be circumcised.

ᵃ 7 That is, Gentiles   ᵇ 7 That is, Jews; also in verses 8 and 9   ᶜ 9 That is, Peter; also in verses 11 and 14   ᵈ 16 Or *but through the faithfulness of . . . justified on the basis of the faithfulness of*

[19]"For through the law I died to the law so that I might live for God. [20]I have been crucified with Christ and I no longer live, but Christ lives in me. The life I now live in the body, I live by faith in the Son of God, who loved me and gave himself for me. [21]I do not set aside the grace of God, for if righteousness could be gained through the law, Christ died for nothing!"[a]

FAITH OR WORKS OF THE LAW

3 You foolish Galatians! Who has bewitched you? Before your very eyes Jesus Christ was clearly portrayed as crucified. [2]I would like to learn just one thing from you: Did you receive the Spirit by the works of the law, or by believing what you heard? [3]Are you so foolish? After beginning by means of the Spirit, are you now trying to finish by means of the flesh?[b] [4]Have you experienced[c] so much in vain—if it really was in vain? [5]So again I ask, does God give you his Spirit and work miracles among you by the works of the law, or by your believing what you heard? [6]So also Abraham "believed God, and it was credited to him as righteousness."[d]

[7]Understand, then, that those who have faith are children of Abraham. [8]Scripture foresaw that God would justify the Gentiles by faith, and announced the gospel in advance to Abraham: "All nations will be blessed through you."[e] [9]So those who rely on faith are blessed along with Abraham, the man of faith.

[10]For all who rely on the works of the law are under a curse, as it is written: "Cursed is everyone who does not continue to do everything written in the Book of the Law."[f] [11]Clearly no one who relies on the law is justified before God, because "the righteous will live by faith."[g] [12]The law is not based on faith; on the contrary, it says, "The person who does these things will live by them."[h] [13]Christ redeemed us from the curse of the law by becoming a curse for us, for it is written: "Cursed is everyone who is hung on a pole."[i] [14]He redeemed us in order that the blessing given to Abraham

[a] 21 Some interpreters end the quotation after verse 14.   *[b] 3* In contexts like this, the Greek word for *flesh* (*sarx*) refers to the sinful state of human beings, often presented as a power in opposition to the Spirit.
[c] 4 Or *suffered*   *[d] 6* Gen. 15:6   *[e] 8* Gen. 12:3; 18:18; 22:18
[f] 10 Deut. 27:26   *[g] 11* Hab. 2:4   *[h] 12* Lev. 18:5   *[i] 13* Deut. 21:23

What argument did Paul make about the law? (2:19–21)
Paul's point was that the law condemned people because no person could keep the law perfectly. If it was possible to earn salvation by keeping the law, then Christ's sacrifice meant nothing.

How did Abraham become righteous? (3:6–9)
Abraham believed in God and was considered righteous. Because all believers are Abraham's spiritual children, faith is the way to salvation.

How did Christ break the curse of the law? (3:13–14)
Christ paid the price for all the sins of the world and thus accepted the curse of the law by being put to death. His sacrifice brought salvation to all who believe in him.

Does God love people of different backgrounds, races, and cultures?

GALATIANS 3

Yes. God's message is one of diversity and inclusiveness. Within the church our unity as Christians is a strong bond that makes other differences — ethnic, social, sexual, or economic — unimportant.

In the Old Testament, God's chosen people were the people of Israel, the descendants of Abraham. But when Jesus came, he ministered to Jews and to Gentiles. Paul said that the gospel "is the power of God that brings salvation to everyone who believes: first to the Jew, then to the Gentile" (Romans 1:16).

Before Jesus ascended to heaven he told his followers to go throughout the world, making disciples of all nations. On Pentecost when the Holy Spirit was given to the church, thousands of people heard the gospel message in their own language and became Christians.

God wants everyone to be close to him. A children's Bible song makes the same point: "Red and yellow, black and white, they are precious in his sight. Jesus loves the little children of the world."

might come to the Gentiles through Christ Jesus, so that by faith we might receive the promise of the Spirit.

THE LAW AND THE PROMISE

15 Brothers and sisters, let me take an example from everyday life. Just as no one can set aside or add to a human covenant that has been duly established, so it is in this case. 16 The promises were spoken to Abraham and to his seed. Scripture does not say "and to seeds," meaning many people, but "and to your seed,"*a* meaning one person, who is Christ. 17 What I mean is this: The law, introduced 430 years later, does not set aside the covenant previously established by God and thus do away with the promise. 18 For if the inheritance depends on the law, then it no longer depends on the promise; but God in his grace gave it to Abraham through a promise.

19 Why, then, was the law given at all? It was added because of transgressions until the Seed to whom the promise referred had come. The law was given through angels and entrusted to a mediator. 20 A mediator, however, implies more than one party; but God is one.

21 Is the law, therefore, opposed to the promises of God? Absolutely not! For if a law had been given that could impart life, then righteousness would certainly have come by the law. 22 But Scripture has locked up everything under the control of sin, so that what was promised, being given through faith in Jesus Christ, might be given to those who believe.

CHILDREN OF GOD

23 Before the coming of this faith,*b* we were held in custody under the law, locked up until the faith that was to come would be revealed. 24 So the law was our guardian until Christ came that we might be justified by faith. 25 Now that this faith has come, we are no longer under a guardian.

26 So in Christ Jesus you are all children of God through faith, 27 for all of you who were baptized into Christ have clothed yourselves with Christ. 28 There is neither Jew nor Gentile, neither slave nor free, nor is there male and female, for you are all one in Christ Jesus. 29 If you belong to Christ, then you are Abraham's seed, and heirs according to the promise.

4 What I am saying is that as long as an heir is underage, he is no different from a slave, although he owns the whole estate. 2 The heir is subject to guardians and trustees until the time set by his father. 3 So also, when we were underage, we were in slavery under the elemental spiritual forces*c* of the world. 4 But when the set time had fully come, God sent his Son, born of a woman, born under the law, 5 to redeem those under the law, that we might receive adoption to sonship.*d* 6 Because you are his sons, God sent the Spirit of his Son into our hearts, the Spirit who calls out, *"Abba,*e*

What was Paul's further argument about Abraham? (3:16–18)
Paul said that Abraham received God's promise that all nations would be blessed through him. The law was not given until much later, and it did not cancel out the promise God made to Abraham.

How are believers "children of God"? (3:26–29)
All who believe in Christ are called children of God. They are equal in God's sight, and all are spiritual descendants of Abraham.

---

a 16 Gen. 12:7; 13:15; 24:7   *b* 22,23 Or *through the faithfulness of Jesus . . .*
23 Before faith came   *c* 3 Or *under the basic principles*   *d* 5 The Greek word for *adoption to sonship* is a legal term referring to the full legal standing of an adopted male heir in Roman culture.   *e* 6 Aramaic for *Father*

Father." [7] So you are no longer a slave, but God's child; and since you are his child, God has made you also an heir.

PAUL'S CONCERN FOR THE GALATIANS

[8] Formerly, when you did not know God, you were slaves to those who by nature are not gods. [9] But now that you know God—or rather are known by God—how is it that you are turning back to those weak and miserable forces[a]? Do you wish to be enslaved by them all over again? [10] You are observing special days and months and seasons and years! [11] I fear for you, that somehow I have wasted my efforts on you.

[12] I plead with you, brothers and sisters, become like me, for I became like you. You did me no wrong. [13] As you know, it was because of an illness that I first preached the gospel to you, [14] and even though my illness was a trial to you, you did not treat me with contempt or scorn. Instead, you welcomed me as if I were an angel of God, as if I were Christ Jesus himself. [15] Where, then, is your blessing of me now? I can testify that, if you could have done so, you would have torn out your eyes and given them to me. [16] Have I now become your enemy by telling you the truth?

[17] Those people are zealous to win you over, but for no good. What they want is to alienate you from us, so that you may have zeal for them. [18] It is fine to be zealous, provided the purpose is good, and to be so always, not just when I am with you. [19] My dear children, for whom I am again in the pains of childbirth until Christ is formed in you, [20] how I wish I could be with you now and change my tone, because I am perplexed about you!

HAGAR AND SARAH

[21] Tell me, you who want to be under the law, are you not aware of what the law says? [22] For it is written that Abraham had two sons, one by the slave woman and the other by the free woman. [23] His son by the slave woman was born according to the flesh, but his son by the free woman was born as the result of a divine promise.

[24] These things are being taken figuratively: The women represent two covenants. One covenant is from Mount Sinai and bears children who are to be slaves: This is Hagar. [25] Now Hagar stands for Mount Sinai in Arabia and corresponds to the present city of Jerusalem, because she is in slavery with her children. [26] But the Jerusalem that is above is free, and she is our mother. [27] For it is written:

"Be glad, barren woman,
    you who never bore a child;
shout for joy and cry aloud,
    you who were never in labor;
because more are the children of the desolate woman
    than of her who has a husband."[b]

[28] Now you, brothers and sisters, like Isaac, are children of promise. [29] At that time the son born according to the flesh persecuted the son born by the power of the Spirit. It

How had the Galatians been slaves? (4:8)
When the Galatians were pagans, they thought they were worshiping real gods. When they became Christians, they were freed from this slavery to false gods.

How were they allowing themselves to become slaves again? (4:9–10)
They were once again trying to earn salvation by observing the law and doing good works. They should have recognized their freedom in Christ.

Who were Abraham's two sons? (4:22–23)
His sons were Ishmael, born to the slave woman Hagar, and Isaac, born to the free woman Sarah. Paul used Hagar to represent the law and Sarah to represent God's promise.

[a] 9 Or *principles*   [b] 27 Isaiah 54:1

is the same now. [30] But what does Scripture say? "Get rid of the slave woman and her son, for the slave woman's son will never share in the inheritance with the free woman's son."[a] [31] Therefore, brothers and sisters, we are not children of the slave woman, but of the free woman.

FREEDOM IN CHRIST

5 It is for freedom that Christ has set us free. Stand firm, then, and do not let yourselves be burdened again by a yoke of slavery.

[2] Mark my words! I, Paul, tell you that if you let yourselves be circumcised, Christ will be of no value to you at all. [3] Again I declare to every man who lets himself be circumcised that he is obligated to obey the whole law. [4] You who are trying to be justified by the law have been alienated from Christ; you have fallen away from grace. [5] For through the Spirit we eagerly await by faith the righteousness for which we hope. [6] For in Christ Jesus neither circumcision nor uncircumcision has any value. The only thing that counts is faith expressing itself through love.

[7] You were running a good race. Who cut in on you to keep you from obeying the truth? [8] That kind of persuasion does not come from the one who calls you. [9] "A little yeast works through the whole batch of dough." [10] I am confident in the Lord that you will take no other view. The one who is throwing you into confusion, whoever that may be, will have to pay the penalty. [11] Brothers and sisters, if I am still preaching circumcision, why am I still being persecuted? In that case the offense of the cross has been abolished. [12] As for those agitators, I wish they would go the whole way and emasculate themselves!

LIFE BY THE SPIRIT

[13] You, my brothers and sisters, were called to be free. But do not use your freedom to indulge the flesh[b]; rather, serve one another humbly in love. [14] For the entire law is fulfilled in keeping this one command: "Love your neighbor as yourself."[c] [15] If you bite and devour each other, watch out or you will be destroyed by each other.

[16] So I say, walk by the Spirit, and you will not gratify the desires of the flesh. [17] For the flesh desires what is contrary to the Spirit, and the Spirit what is contrary to the flesh. They are in conflict with each other, so that you are not to do whatever[d] you want. [18] But if you are led by the Spirit, you are not under the law.

[19] The acts of the flesh are obvious: sexual immorality, impurity and debauchery; [20] idolatry and witchcraft; hatred, discord, jealousy, fits of rage, selfish ambition, dissensions, factions [21] and envy; drunkenness, orgies, and the like. I warn you, as I did before, that those who live like this will not inherit the kingdom of God.

What would happen to the Galatians if they required circumcision? (5:2–6)
If they made circumcision a requirement, they would be placing themselves under the law rather than accepting salvation through the grace of God.

What did yeast symbolize? (5:9)
In the Bible, yeast often symbolized evil or a false teaching. Here it referred to the way Judaism could take over their whole life.

How can Christians overcome sinful desires? (5:16)
Living by the promptings and power of the Spirit can keep us from giving in to temptation.

---

[a] *30* Gen. 21:10   [b] *13* In contexts like this, the Greek word for *flesh* (*sarx*) refers to the sinful state of human beings, often presented as a power in opposition to the Spirit; also in verses 16, 17, 19 and 24; and in 6:8.
[c] *14* Lev. 19:18   [d] *17* Or *you do not do what*

²²But the fruit of the Spirit is love, joy, peace, forbearance, kindness, goodness, faithfulness, ²³gentleness and self-control. Against such things there is no law. ²⁴Those who belong to Christ Jesus have crucified the flesh with its passions and desires. ²⁵Since we live by the Spirit, let us keep in step with the Spirit. ²⁶Let us not become conceited, provoking and envying each other.

DOING GOOD TO ALL

6 Brothers and sisters, if someone is caught in a sin, you who live by the Spirit should restore that person gently. But watch yourselves, or you also may be tempted. ²Carry each other's burdens, and in this way you will fulfill the law of Christ. ³If anyone thinks they are something when they are not, they deceive themselves. ⁴Each one should test their own actions. Then they can take pride in themselves alone, without comparing themselves to someone else, ⁵for each one should carry their own load. ⁶Nevertheless, the one who receives instruction in the word should share all good things with their instructor.

⁷Do not be deceived: God cannot be mocked. A man reaps what he sows. ⁸Whoever sows to please their flesh, from the flesh will reap destruction; whoever sows to please the Spirit, from the Spirit will reap eternal life. ⁹Let us not become weary in doing good, for at the proper time we will reap a harvest if we do not give up. ¹⁰Therefore, as we have opportunity, let us do good to all people, especially to those who belong to the family of believers.

NOT CIRCUMCISION BUT THE NEW CREATION

¹¹See what large letters I use as I write to you with my own hand!

¹²Those who want to impress people by means of the flesh are trying to compel you to be circumcised. The only reason they do this is to avoid being persecuted for the cross of Christ. ¹³Not even those who are circumcised keep the law, yet they want you to be circumcised that they may boast about your circumcision in the flesh. ¹⁴May I never boast except in the cross of our Lord Jesus Christ, through which*ᵃ* the world has been crucified to me, and I to the world. ¹⁵Neither circumcision nor uncircumcision means anything; what counts is the new creation. ¹⁶Peace and mercy to all who follow this rule—to*ᵇ* the Israel of God.

¹⁷From now on, let no one cause me trouble, for I bear on my body the marks of Jesus.

¹⁸The grace of our Lord Jesus Christ be with your spirit, brothers and sisters. Amen.

What did Paul mean by saying that a person reaps what he or she sows? (6:7–10)
This was an analogy to farming. If a farmer plants a particular type of seed, that seed will develop into a specific type of plant. In the same way, if people live in sinful ways, there will be negative consequences. But if people live to please the Spirit, there will be positive outcomes.

What really matters? (6:15)
Paul said that neither circumcision nor uncircumcision matters. The important thing is that we become new creations in Christ.

ᵃ 14 Or *whom*   *ᵇ 16* Or *rule and to*

Ephesians

INTRODUCTION

Who wrote this book? Paul.

Why was this book written? The book of Ephesians shows that the church is not a building but people who love and obey Jesus.

For whom was this book written? This book is a letter Paul sent to the Christians in Ephesus.

What are some important teachings in this book?

What God did to save us	Ephesians 1:3 – 14
God gives life in Christ	Ephesians 2:1 – 10
Jesus gives peace	Ephesians 2:11 – 18
How to live a holy life	Ephesians 4:20 – 32
Children and parents	Ephesians 6:1 – 4

When did these things happen?

	10 BC	AD 1	10	20	30	40	50	60	70	80	90	100

JESUS' LIFE (C. 6/5 BC – AD 30)

PAUL'S CONVERSION (C. AD 35)

PAUL'S MISSIONARY JOURNEYS (C. AD 46 – 67)

COUNCIL AT JERUSALEM (C. AD 49/50)

NERO'S REIGN (AD 54 – 68)

PAUL'S FIRST IMPRISONMENT IN ROME (C. AD 59 – 62)

BOOK OF EPHESIANS WRITTEN (C. AD 60)

PAUL'S IMPRISONMENT AND DEATH IN ROME (C. AD 67 – 68)

DESTRUCTION OF JERUSALEM'S TEMPLE (C. AD 70)

1 Paul, an apostle of Christ Jesus by the will of God,

To God's holy people in Ephesus,*a* the faithful in Christ Jesus:

²Grace and peace to you from God our Father and the Lord Jesus Christ.

PRAISE FOR SPIRITUAL BLESSINGS IN CHRIST

³Praise be to the God and Father of our Lord Jesus Christ, who has blessed us in the heavenly realms with every spiritual blessing in Christ. ⁴For he chose us in him before the creation of the world to be holy and blameless in his sight. In love ⁵he*b* predestined us for adoption to sonship*c* through Jesus Christ, in accordance with his pleasure and will— ⁶to the praise of his glorious grace, which he has freely given us in the One he loves. ⁷In him we have redemption through his blood, the forgiveness of sins, in accordance with the riches of God's grace ⁸that he lavished on us. With all wisdom and understanding, ⁹he*d* made known to us the mystery of his will according to his good pleasure, which he purposed in Christ, ¹⁰to be put into effect when the times reach their fulfillment—to bring unity to all things in heaven and on earth under Christ.

¹¹In him we were also chosen,*e* having been predestined according to the plan of him who works out everything in conformity with the purpose of his will, ¹²in order that we, who were the first to put our hope in Christ, might be for the praise of his glory. ¹³And you also were included in Christ when you heard the message of truth, the gospel of your salvation. When you believed, you were marked in him with a seal, the promised Holy Spirit, ¹⁴who is a deposit guaranteeing our inheritance until the redemption of those who are God's possession—to the praise of his glory.

THANKSGIVING AND PRAYER

¹⁵For this reason, ever since I heard about your faith in the Lord Jesus and your love for all God's people, ¹⁶I have not stopped giving thanks for you, remembering you in my prayers. ¹⁷I keep asking that the God of our Lord Jesus Christ, the glorious Father, may give you the Spirit*f* of wisdom and revelation, so that you may know him better. ¹⁸I pray that the eyes of your heart may be enlightened in order that you may know the hope to which he has called you, the riches of his glorious inheritance in his holy people, ¹⁹and his incomparably great power for us who believe. That power is the same as the mighty strength ²⁰he exerted when he raised Christ from the dead and seated him at his right hand in the heavenly realms, ²¹far above all rule and authority, power and dominion, and every name that is invoked, not only in the present age but also in the one to come. ²²And God placed

The Church in Ephesus (1:1)

Do we choose God, or did God choose us? (1:4–5, 11) In his letters, Paul emphasized the fact that God chose his people. Here he said that God "chose us" (verse 4), "predestined us" (verse 5), and "we were also chosen, having been predestined" (verse 11).

What were seals and deposits? (1:13–14) A wax seal was used to seal a scroll shut. The decoration of the seal showed to whom the seal belonged. If the seal was unbroken when the scroll arrived at its destination, the letter was assumed to be unread. God put his seal on his people to show that he owned them. A deposit was the first of many payments of an inheritance. The Holy Spirit was a deposit that believers would have a glorious future with God in eternity.

---

a 1 Some early manuscripts do not have *in Ephesus.*   *b 4,5* Or *sight in love.*
⁵*He*   *c 5* The Greek word for *adoption to sonship* is a legal term referring to the full legal standing of an adopted male heir in Roman culture.
d 8,9 Or *us with all wisdom and understanding.* ⁹*And he*   *e 11* Or *were made heirs*   *f 17* Or *a spirit*

What did it mean that God placed everything under Christ's feet? (1:22)
This was an Old Testament expression that symbolized a complete conquest. Here it means that Christ is the head of the church.

What is the message of salvation? (2:8–9)
Christians have been saved by grace through faith, not through good works. Faith is the gift of God. It is not earned through anything we do.

What is the meaning of the word handiwork? (2:10)
The Greek word sometimes implies a work of art. We are God's works of art.

In what way did Jesus set aside the law? (2:15)
God's law still sets forth the moral standards and type of behavior he expects. What Jesus set aside were specific commandments and regulations that separated Jews from Gentiles.

all things under his feet and appointed him to be head over everything for the church, [23] which is his body, the fullness of him who fills everything in every way.

MADE ALIVE IN CHRIST

2 As for you, you were dead in your transgressions and sins, [2] in which you used to live when you followed the ways of this world and of the ruler of the kingdom of the air, the spirit who is now at work in those who are disobedient. [3] All of us also lived among them at one time, gratifying the cravings of our flesh[a] and following its desires and thoughts. Like the rest, we were by nature deserving of wrath. [4] But because of his great love for us, God, who is rich in mercy, [5] made us alive with Christ even when we were dead in transgressions—it is by grace you have been saved. [6] And God raised us up with Christ and seated us with him in the heavenly realms in Christ Jesus, [7] in order that in the coming ages he might show the incomparable riches of his grace, expressed in his kindness to us in Christ Jesus. [8] For it is by grace you have been saved, through faith—and this is not from yourselves, it is the gift of God— [9] not by works, so that no one can boast. [10] For we are God's handiwork, created in Christ Jesus to do good works, which God prepared in advance for us to do.

JEW AND GENTILE RECONCILED THROUGH CHRIST

[11] Therefore, remember that formerly you who are Gentiles by birth and called "uncircumcised" by those who call themselves "the circumcision" (which is done in the body by human hands)— [12] remember that at that time you were separate from Christ, excluded from citizenship in Israel and foreigners to the covenants of the promise, without hope and without God in the world. [13] But now in Christ Jesus you who once were far away have been brought near by the blood of Christ.

[14] For he himself is our peace, who has made the two groups one and has destroyed the barrier, the dividing wall of hostility, [15] by setting aside in his flesh the law with its commands and regulations. His purpose was to create in himself one new humanity out of the two, thus making peace, [16] and in one body to reconcile both of them to God through the cross, by which he put to death their hostility. [17] He came and

[a] 3 In contexts like this, the Greek word for *flesh* (*sarx*) refers to the sinful state of human beings, often presented as a power in opposition to the Spirit.

Why are some people saved and not others?   EPHESIANS 2

Since the fall of Adam and Eve, all people have been sinners—unable to keep God's law perfectly. But in his grace, God chose people to save. We are not responsible for our own salvation. In fact, if it were up to us alone, we could never be saved because we cannot keep God's laws. But God in his grace gave us the gift of faith. We should not feel proud of ourselves for being part of God's community of faith. Instead, we should thank God for the love that he showed by creating faith in our hearts so that we can live lives of service to God and to others.

preached peace to you who were far away and peace to those who were near. [18] For through him we both have access to the Father by one Spirit.

[19] Consequently, you are no longer foreigners and strangers, but fellow citizens with God's people and also members of his household, [20] built on the foundation of the apostles and prophets, with Christ Jesus himself as the chief cornerstone. [21] In him the whole building is joined together and rises to become a holy temple in the Lord. [22] And in him you too are being built together to become a dwelling in which God lives by his Spirit.

GOD'S MARVELOUS PLAN FOR THE GENTILES

3 For this reason I, Paul, the prisoner of Christ Jesus for the sake of you Gentiles—

[2] Surely you have heard about the administration of God's grace that was given to me for you, [3] that is, the mystery made known to me by revelation, as I have already written briefly. [4] In reading this, then, you will be able to understand my insight into the mystery of Christ, [5] which was not made known to people in other generations as it has now been revealed by the Spirit to God's holy apostles and prophets. [6] This mystery is that through the gospel the Gentiles are heirs together with Israel, members together of one body, and sharers together in the promise in Christ Jesus.

[7] I became a servant of this gospel by the gift of God's grace given me through the working of his power. [8] Although I am less than the least of all the Lord's people, this grace was given me: to preach to the Gentiles the boundless riches of Christ, [9] and to make plain to everyone the administration of this mystery, which for ages past was kept hidden in God, who created all things. [10] His intent was that now, through the church, the manifold wisdom of God should be made known to the rulers and authorities in the heavenly realms, [11] according to his eternal purpose that he accomplished in Christ Jesus our Lord. [12] In him and through faith in him we may approach God with freedom and confidence. [13] I ask you, therefore, not to be discouraged because of my sufferings for you, which are your glory.

A PRAYER FOR THE EPHESIANS

[14] For this reason I kneel before the Father, [15] from whom every family[a] in heaven and on earth derives its name. [16] I pray that out of his glorious riches he may strengthen you with power through his Spirit in your inner being, [17] so that Christ may dwell in your hearts through faith. And I pray that you, being rooted and established in love, [18] may have power, together with all the Lord's holy people, to grasp how wide and long and high and deep is the love of Christ, [19] and to know this love that surpasses knowledge—that you may be filled to the measure of all the fullness of God.

[20] Now to him who is able to do immeasurably more than all we ask or imagine, according to his power that is at work

What mystery was revealed? (3:6)
The mystery that previous generations had not known was that believing Gentiles and Jews would be united together in the church. This was achieved through Jesus' death and resurrection.

How do these verses reflect the Trinity? (3:14–17)
Paul prayed to the Father that the Holy Spirit would strengthen the Ephesians so that Christ would live in their hearts. All three persons of the Trinity play a part in building faith in a believer.

---

a 15 The Greek for *family* (*patria*) is derived from the Greek for *father* (*pater*).

within us, [21] to him be glory in the church and in Christ Jesus throughout all generations, for ever and ever! Amen.

UNITY AND MATURITY IN THE BODY OF CHRIST

4 As a prisoner for the Lord, then, I urge you to live a life worthy of the calling you have received. [2] Be completely humble and gentle; be patient, bearing with one another in love. [3] Make every effort to keep the unity of the Spirit through the bond of peace. [4] There is one body and one Spirit, just as you were called to one hope when you were called; [5] one Lord, one faith, one baptism; [6] one God and Father of all, who is over all and through all and in all.

[7] But to each one of us grace has been given as Christ apportioned it. [8] This is why it[a] says:

> "When he ascended on high,
>   he took many captives
>   and gave gifts to his people."[b]

[9] (What does "he ascended" mean except that he also descended to the lower, earthly regions[c]? [10] He who descended is the very one who ascended higher than all the heavens, in order to fill the whole universe.) [11] So Christ himself gave the apostles, the prophets, the evangelists, the pastors and teachers, [12] to equip his people for works of service, so that the body of Christ may be built up [13] until we all reach unity in the faith and in the knowledge of the Son of God and become mature, attaining to the whole measure of the fullness of Christ.

[14] Then we will no longer be infants, tossed back and forth by the waves, and blown here and there by every wind of teaching and by the cunning and craftiness of people in their deceitful scheming. [15] Instead, speaking the truth in love, we will grow to become in every respect the mature body of him who is the head, that is, Christ. [16] From him the whole body, joined and held together by every supporting ligament, grows and builds itself up in love, as each part does its work.

INSTRUCTIONS FOR CHRISTIAN LIVING

[17] So I tell you this, and insist on it in the Lord, that you must no longer live as the Gentiles do, in the futility of their thinking. [18] They are darkened in their understanding and separated from the life of God because of the ignorance that is in them due to the hardening of their hearts. [19] Having lost all sensitivity, they have given themselves over to sensuality so as to indulge in every kind of impurity, and they are full of greed.

[20] That, however, is not the way of life you learned [21] when you heard about Christ and were taught in him in accordance with the truth that is in Jesus. [22] You were taught, with regard to your former way of life, to put off your old self, which is being corrupted by its deceitful desires; [23] to be made new in the attitude of your minds; [24] and to put on the new self, created to be like God in true righteousness and holiness.

What is the role of leaders in the church? (4:11–12)
Leaders are not supposed to do all the work themselves but are supposed to train others and prepare them for works of service.

What is the new self? (4:24)
When someone becomes a believer, through Christ he becomes a new person. The Christian puts on this new way of life, almost like a new set of clothes.

---

[a] 8 Or *God*   [b] 8 Psalm 68:18   [c] 9 Or *the depths of the earth*

²⁵Therefore each of you must put off falsehood and speak truthfully to your neighbor, for we are all members of one body. ²⁶"In your anger do not sin"^a: Do not let the sun go down while you are still angry, ²⁷and do not give the devil a foothold. ²⁸Anyone who has been stealing must steal no longer, but must work, doing something useful with their own hands, that they may have something to share with those in need.

²⁹Do not let any unwholesome talk come out of your mouths, but only what is helpful for building others up according to their needs, that it may benefit those who listen. ³⁰And do not grieve the Holy Spirit of God, with whom you were sealed for the day of redemption. ³¹Get rid of all bitterness, rage and anger, brawling and slander, along with every form of malice. ³²Be kind and compassionate to one another, forgiving each other, just as in Christ God forgave you. ¹Follow God's example, therefore, as dearly loved children ²and walk in the way of love, just as Christ loved us and gave himself up for us as a fragrant offering and sacrifice to God.

³But among you there must not be even a hint of sexual immorality, or of any kind of impurity, or of greed, because these are improper for God's holy people. ⁴Nor should there be obscenity, foolish talk or coarse joking, which are out of place, but rather thanksgiving. ⁵For of this you can be sure: No immoral, impure or greedy person — such a person is an idolater — has any inheritance in the kingdom of Christ and of God.^b ⁶Let no one deceive you with empty words, for because of such things God's wrath comes on those who are disobedient. ⁷Therefore do not be partners with them.

⁸For you were once darkness, but now you are light in the Lord. Live as children of light ⁹(for the fruit of the light consists in all goodness, righteousness and truth) ¹⁰and find out what pleases the Lord. ¹¹Have nothing to do with the fruitless deeds of darkness, but rather expose them. ¹²It is shameful even to mention what the disobedient do in secret. ¹³But everything exposed by the light becomes visible — and everything that is illuminated becomes a light. ¹⁴This is why it is said:

> "Wake up, sleeper,
>   rise from the dead,
>   and Christ will shine on you."

¹⁵Be very careful, then, how you live — not as unwise but as wise, ¹⁶making the most of every opportunity, because the days are evil. ¹⁷Therefore do not be foolish, but understand what the Lord's will is. ¹⁸Do not get drunk on wine, which leads to debauchery. Instead, be filled with the Spirit, ¹⁹speaking to one another with psalms, hymns, and songs from the Spirit. Sing and make music from your heart to the Lord, ²⁰always giving thanks to God the Father for everything, in the name of our Lord Jesus Christ.

How can Christians follow God's example? (5:1–2)
One way is to have a forgiving spirit (4:32). The life of sacrifice Jesus lived serves as an example of how Christians should live.

How do Christians live as children of light? (5:8–14)
Christians turn away from the darkness of sin and the old way of life in order to live in the light of Christ. Christians reflect that light to the rest of the world by living lives characterized by goodness and truth.

---

^a 26 Psalm 4:4 (see Septuagint)   ^b 5 Or *kingdom of the Messiah and God*

INSTRUCTIONS FOR CHRISTIAN HOUSEHOLDS

21 Submit to one another out of reverence for Christ.

22 Wives, submit yourselves to your own husbands as you do to the Lord. 23 For the husband is the head of the wife as Christ is the head of the church, his body, of which he is the Savior. 24 Now as the church submits to Christ, so also wives should submit to their husbands in everything.

25 Husbands, love your wives, just as Christ loved the church and gave himself up for her 26 to make her holy, cleansing[a] her by the washing with water through the word, 27 and to present her to himself as a radiant church, without stain or wrinkle or any other blemish, but holy and blameless. 28 In this same way, husbands ought to love their wives as their own bodies. He who loves his wife loves himself. 29 After all, no one ever hated their own body, but they feed and care for their body, just as Christ does the church— 30 for we are members of his body. 31 "For this reason a man will leave his father and mother and be united to his wife, and the two will become one flesh."[b] 32 This is a profound mystery—but I am talking about Christ and the church. 33 However, each one of you also must love his wife as he loves himself, and the wife must respect her husband.

6 Children, obey your parents in the Lord, for this is right. 2 "Honor your father and mother"—which is the first commandment with a promise— 3 "so that it may go well with you and that you may enjoy long life on the earth."[c]

4 Fathers,[d] do not exasperate your children; instead, bring them up in the training and instruction of the Lord.

5 Slaves, obey your earthly masters with respect and fear, and with sincerity of heart, just as you would obey Christ. 6 Obey them not only to win their favor when their eye is on you, but as slaves of Christ, doing the will of God from your heart. 7 Serve wholeheartedly, as if you were serving the Lord, not people, 8 because you know that the Lord will reward each one for whatever good they do, whether they are slave or free.

9 And masters, treat your slaves in the same way. Do not threaten them, since you know that he who is both their Master and yours is in heaven, and there is no favoritism with him.

THE ARMOR OF GOD

10 Finally, be strong in the Lord and in his mighty power. 11 Put on the full armor of God, so that you can take your stand against the devil's schemes. 12 For our struggle is not against flesh and blood, but against the rulers, against the authorities, against the powers of this dark world and against the spiritual forces of evil in the heavenly realms. 13 Therefore put on the full armor of God, so that when the day of evil comes, you may be able to stand your ground, and after you have done everything, to stand. 14 Stand firm then, with the belt of truth buckled around your waist, with the breastplate

How are husbands and wives supposed to relate? (5:22–33)
Husbands and wives are to love each other and seek what is best for the other. Paul used the example of Jesus taking the church as his bride to describe the way that husbands and wives should treat each other.

How did Paul continue to develop the theme of submitting to one another? (6:1–9)
He urged children to obey their parents, but told fathers not to exasperate, meaning to anger or provoke, their children. He told slaves to obey their masters, but he also told masters to treat their slaves with kindness.

Why is it necessary to put on the armor of God? (6:10)
Only God's power is strong enough to help us withstand the devil.

[a] 26 Or *having cleansed*   [b] 31 Gen. 2:24   [c] 3 Deut. 5:16
[d] 4 Or *Parents*

of righteousness in place, [15] and with your feet fitted with the readiness that comes from the gospel of peace. [16] In addition to all this, take up the shield of faith, with which you can extinguish all the flaming arrows of the evil one. [17] Take the helmet of salvation and the sword of the Spirit, which is the word of God.

[18] And pray in the Spirit on all occasions with all kinds of prayers and requests. With this in mind, be alert and always keep on praying for all the Lord's people. [19] Pray also for me, that whenever I speak, words may be given me so that I will fearlessly make known the mystery of the gospel, [20] for which I am an ambassador in chains. Pray that I may declare it fearlessly, as I should.

FINAL GREETINGS

[21] Tychicus, the dear brother and faithful servant in the Lord, will tell you everything, so that you also may know how I am and what I am doing. [22] I am sending him to you for this very purpose, that you may know how we are, and that he may encourage you.

[23] Peace to the brothers and sisters,[a] and love with faith from God the Father and the Lord Jesus Christ. [24] Grace to all who love our Lord Jesus Christ with an undying love.[b]

A Soldier's Armor (6:11 - 17)

---

[a] 23 The Greek word for *brothers and sisters* (*adelphoi*) refers here to believers, both men and women, as part of God's family.   [b] 24 Or *Grace and immortality to all who love our Lord Jesus Christ.*

Philippians

INTRODUCTION

Who wrote this book?   Paul.

Why was this book written?   The book of Philippians thanks the people for their love and gifts and gives them instructions on how to live good Christian lives.

For whom was this book written?   This book is a letter Paul sent to Christians at Philippi.

What are some important teachings in this book?

Live as good Christians	Philippians 1:27 – 30
Live a humble life	Philippians 2:1 – 4
How Jesus was humble	Philippians 2:5 – 11
The Christian's goal	Philippians 3:12 – 16
How to be at peace	Philippians 4:4 – 7
Think about good things	Philippians 4:8 – 9

When did these things happen?

10BC AD1 10 20 30 40 50 60 70 80 90 100

JESUS' LIFE (C. 6/5 BC – AD 30)	
PAUL'S CONVERSION (C. AD 35)	
PAUL'S MISSIONARY JOURNEYS (C. AD 46 – 67)	
COUNCIL AT JERUSALEM (C. AD 49/50)	
NERO'S REIGN (AD 54 – 68)	
PAUL'S FIRST IMPRISONMENT IN ROME (C. AD 59 – 62)	
BOOK OF PHILIPPIANS WRITTEN (C. AD 61)	
PAUL'S IMPRISONMENT AND DEATH IN ROME (C. AD 67 – 68)	
DESTRUCTION OF JERUSALEM'S TEMPLE (C. AD 70)	

1 Paul and Timothy, servants of Christ Jesus,

To all God's holy people in Christ Jesus at Philippi, together with the overseers and deacons*a*:

²Grace and peace to you from God our Father and the Lord Jesus Christ.

THANKSGIVING AND PRAYER

³I thank my God every time I remember you. ⁴In all my prayers for all of you, I always pray with joy ⁵because of your partnership in the gospel from the first day until now, ⁶being confident of this, that he who began a good work in you will carry it on to completion until the day of Christ Jesus.

⁷It is right for me to feel this way about all of you, since I have you in my heart and, whether I am in chains or defending and confirming the gospel, all of you share in God's grace with me. ⁸God can testify how I long for all of you with the affection of Christ Jesus.

⁹And this is my prayer: that your love may abound more and more in knowledge and depth of insight, ¹⁰so that you may be able to discern what is best and may be pure and blameless for the day of Christ, ¹¹filled with the fruit of righteousness that comes through Jesus Christ—to the glory and praise of God.

PAUL'S CHAINS ADVANCE THE GOSPEL

¹²Now I want you to know, brothers and sisters,*b* that what has happened to me has actually served to advance the gospel. ¹³As a result, it has become clear throughout the whole palace guard*c* and to everyone else that I am in chains for Christ. ¹⁴And because of my chains, most of the brothers and sisters have become confident in the Lord and dare all the more to proclaim the gospel without fear.

¹⁵It is true that some preach Christ out of envy and rivalry, but others out of goodwill. ¹⁶The latter do so out of love, knowing that I am put here for the defense of the gospel. ¹⁷The former preach Christ out of selfish ambition, not sincerely, supposing that they can stir up trouble for me while I am in chains. ¹⁸But what does it matter? The important thing is that in every way, whether from false motives or true, Christ is preached. And because of this I rejoice.

Yes, and I will continue to rejoice, ¹⁹for I know that through your prayers and God's provision of the Spirit of Jesus Christ what has happened to me will turn out for my deliverance.*d* ²⁰I eagerly expect and hope that I will in no way be ashamed, but will have sufficient courage so that now as always Christ will be exalted in my body, whether by life or by death. ²¹For to me, to live is Christ and to die is gain. ²²If I am to go on living in the body, this will mean fruitful labor for me. Yet what shall I choose? I do not know! ²³I am

---

a 1 The word *deacons* refers here to Christians designated to serve with the overseers/elders of the church in a variety of ways; similarly in Romans 16:1 and 1 Tim. 3:8,12.   *b 12* The Greek word for *brothers and sisters* (*adelphoi*) refers here to believers, both men and women, as part of God's family; also in verse 14; and in 3:1, 13, 17; 4:1, 8, 21.   *c 13* Or *whole palace*   *d 19* Or *vindication*; or *salvation*

The Church in Philippi (1:1)

What was Paul's goal for the Philippian Christians? (1:9–11)
Paul wanted them to grow in love and in insight so that they could know what was morally superior. He wanted them to live holy lives until Christ returned, when they would be made perfect.

How did Paul's imprisonment help to spread the gospel? (1:12–14)
Everyone who knew of Paul's imprisonment realized that he was in chains not because of any crime he had committed but because he was a Christian. Others were encouraged by his example and began to speak more freely about the gospel.

Did Paul want to die? (1:21–26)
Paul was not afraid of death. He realized that if he died, he would be in heaven with Christ. But he also realized that if he lived, he could continue to do God's work by preaching the gospel. He concluded that this was what he should be doing.

torn between the two: I desire to depart and be with Christ, which is better by far; [24] but it is more necessary for you that I remain in the body. [25] Convinced of this, I know that I will remain, and I will continue with all of you for your progress and joy in the faith, [26] so that through my being with you again your boasting in Christ Jesus will abound on account of me.

LIFE WORTHY OF THE GOSPEL

[27] Whatever happens, conduct yourselves in a manner worthy of the gospel of Christ. Then, whether I come and see you or only hear about you in my absence, I will know that you stand firm in the one Spirit,[a] striving together as one for the faith of the gospel [28] without being frightened in any way by those who oppose you. This is a sign to them that they will be destroyed, but that you will be saved—and that by God. [29] For it has been granted to you on behalf of Christ not only to believe in him, but also to suffer for him, [30] since you are going through the same struggle you saw I had, and now hear that I still have.

IMITATING CHRIST'S HUMILITY

2 Therefore if you have any encouragement from being united with Christ, if any comfort from his love, if any common sharing in the Spirit, if any tenderness and compassion, [2] then make my joy complete by being like-minded, having the same love, being one in spirit and of one mind. [3] Do nothing out of selfish ambition or vain conceit. Rather, in humility value others above yourselves, [4] not looking to your own interests but each of you to the interests of the others.

[5] In your relationships with one another, have the same mindset as Christ Jesus:

[6] Who, being in very nature[b] God,
    did not consider equality with God something to be
       used to his own advantage;
[7] rather, he made himself nothing
    by taking the very nature[c] of a servant,
    being made in human likeness.
[8] And being found in appearance as a man,
    he humbled himself
    by becoming obedient to death—
       even death on a cross!

[9] Therefore God exalted him to the highest place
    and gave him the name that is above every name,
[10] that at the name of Jesus every knee should bow,
    in heaven and on earth and under the earth,
[11] and every tongue acknowledge that Jesus Christ
       is Lord,
    to the glory of God the Father.

DO EVERYTHING WITHOUT GRUMBLING

[12] Therefore, my dear friends, as you have always obeyed—not only in my presence, but now much more in my absence—continue to work out your salvation with fear and

---

a 27 Or *in one spirit*   b 6 Or *in the form of*   c 7 Or *the form*

Did Paul see persecution as a punishment? (1:29–30)
No, not at all. Paul believed that when Christians were persecuted, it was a sign that their faith was genuine. He said it was a privilege to suffer on behalf of Christ.

What type of attitude did Paul want Christians to have? (2:2–5)
Paul wanted them to look out for other people rather than selfishly looking out for their own interests. In other words, he wanted them to adopt Christ's sacrificial attitude.

Why is this section in poetic form? (2:6–11)
Some people think that this was an early Christian hymn, possibly adapted by Paul.

What did it mean to "work out your salvation with fear and trembling"? (2:12)
Paul didn't mean that Christians had to earn their salvation, which is impossible. He meant that they should seek spiritual growth and development. They were not to do this because they were frightened of God but because of their reverence and awe for him.

trembling, [13] for it is God who works in you to will and to act in order to fulfill his good purpose.

[14] Do everything without grumbling or arguing, [15] so that you may become blameless and pure, "children of God without fault in a warped and crooked generation."[a] Then you will shine among them like stars in the sky [16] as you hold firmly to the word of life. And then I will be able to boast on the day of Christ that I did not run or labor in vain. [17] But even if I am being poured out like a drink offering on the sacrifice and service coming from your faith, I am glad and rejoice with all of you. [18] So you too should be glad and rejoice with me.

TIMOTHY AND EPAPHRODITUS

[19] I hope in the Lord Jesus to send Timothy to you soon, that I also may be cheered when I receive news about you. [20] I have no one else like him, who will show genuine concern for your welfare. [21] For everyone looks out for their own interests, not those of Jesus Christ. [22] But you know that Timothy has proved himself, because as a son with his father he has served with me in the work of the gospel. [23] I hope, therefore, to send him as soon as I see how things go with me. [24] And I am confident in the Lord that I myself will come soon.

[25] But I think it is necessary to send back to you Epaphroditus, my brother, co-worker and fellow soldier, who is also your messenger, whom you sent to take care of my needs. [26] For he longs for all of you and is distressed because you heard he was ill. [27] Indeed he was ill, and almost died. But God had mercy on him, and not on him only but also on me, to spare me sorrow upon sorrow. [28] Therefore I am all the more eager to send him, so that when you see him again you may be glad and I may have less anxiety. [29] So then, welcome him in the Lord with great joy, and honor people like him, [30] because he almost died for the work of Christ. He risked his life to make up for the help you yourselves could not give me.

NO CONFIDENCE IN THE FLESH

3 Further, my brothers and sisters, rejoice in the Lord! It is no trouble for me to write the same things to you again, and it is a safeguard for you. [2] Watch out for those dogs, those evildoers, those mutilators of the flesh. [3] For it is we who are the circumcision, we who serve God by his Spirit, who boast in Christ Jesus, and who put no confidence in the flesh— [4] though I myself have reasons for such confidence.

If someone else thinks they have reasons to put confidence in the flesh, I have more: [5] circumcised on the eighth day, of the people of Israel, of the tribe of Benjamin, a Hebrew of Hebrews; in regard to the law, a Pharisee; [6] as for zeal, persecuting the church; as for righteousness based on the law, faultless.

[7] But whatever were gains to me I now consider loss for the sake of Christ. [8] What is more, I consider everything a loss because of the surpassing worth of knowing Christ Jesus my Lord, for whose sake I have lost all things. I consider them garbage, that I may gain Christ [9] and be found in him, not

[a] 15 Deut. 32:5

What was a drink offering? (2:17)
It was usually wine or oil poured out as a sacrifice. Paul may have been thinking of his entire ministry, but it is more likely that he was thinking of his imprisonment that could result in a martyr's death. In that case, his life would be poured out as an offering to God.

How was Paul legalistically faultless? (3:4–9)
Earlier in his life, Paul had conformed to the Jewish laws and kept them carefully in order to earn God's blessing. However, he now realized that righteousness could only come from a God-given faith in Christ.

having a righteousness of my own that comes from the law, but that which is through faith in[a] Christ—the righteousness that comes from God on the basis of faith. [10]I want to know Christ—yes, to know the power of his resurrection and participation in his sufferings, becoming like him in his death, [11]and so, somehow, attaining to the resurrection from the dead.

[12]Not that I have already obtained all this, or have already arrived at my goal, but I press on to take hold of that for which Christ Jesus took hold of me. [13]Brothers and sisters, I do not consider myself yet to have taken hold of it. But one thing I do: Forgetting what is behind and straining toward what is ahead, [14]I press on toward the goal to win the prize for which God has called me heavenward in Christ Jesus.

FOLLOWING PAUL'S EXAMPLE

[15]All of us, then, who are mature should take such a view of things. And if on some point you think differently, that too God will make clear to you. [16]Only let us live up to what we have already attained.

[17]Join together in following my example, brothers and sisters, and just as you have us as a model, keep your eyes on those who live as we do. [18]For, as I have often told you before and now tell you again even with tears, many live as enemies of the cross of Christ. [19]Their destiny is destruction, their god is their stomach, and their glory is in their shame. Their mind is set on earthly things. [20]But our citizenship is in heaven. And we eagerly await a Savior from there, the Lord Jesus Christ, [21]who, by the power that enables him to bring everything under his control, will transform our lowly bodies so that they will be like his glorious body.

CLOSING APPEAL FOR STEADFASTNESS AND UNITY

4 Therefore, my brothers and sisters, you whom I love and long for, my joy and crown, stand firm in the Lord in this way, dear friends!

[2]I plead with Euodia and I plead with Syntyche to be of the same mind in the Lord. [3]Yes, and I ask you, my true companion, help these women since they have contended at my

[a] 9 Or *through the faithfulness of*

What did the winner of an ancient race receive? (3:14)
The winner of a Greek race received a wreath made of leaves and sometimes a cash award. The spiritual race Paul was running would result in the rewards of heaven.

What enemies of Christianity is Paul referring to here? (3:18–19)
These were people who were the opposite of the legalists. They did not seek to follow laws but lived for their own earthly pleasures.

Is it OK for Christians to worry?

PHILIPPIANS 4

Fear and worry are normal human emotions. Christians should not feel like failures when they have worries. If a family member is traveling, we may worry about his or her safety. If a friend becomes ill, we may worry that he or she won't get better. If we are in the woods when it's getting dark, we may worry that we will get lost. But worry itself does not accomplish anything (other than possibly a headache or stomachache).

The Bible tells us that even if we start to worry, we can have confidence that God is in control of all things. Jesus said that God knows what we need and will provide for us. If we do begin to worry, Paul said, "In every situation, by prayer and petition, with thanksgiving, present your requests to God." We can be at peace because we know that God is in charge, God knows what is best for us, God has assured us that we are his children, and God has given us eternal life. Even if we still worry about things, we know that we can take our worries to God and that he will take care of us.

side in the cause of the gospel, along with Clement and the rest of my co-workers, whose names are in the book of life.

FINAL EXHORTATIONS

[4]Rejoice in the Lord always. I will say it again: Rejoice! [5]Let your gentleness be evident to all. The Lord is near. [6]Do not be anxious about anything, but in every situation, by prayer and petition, with thanksgiving, present your requests to God. [7]And the peace of God, which transcends all understanding, will guard your hearts and your minds in Christ Jesus.

[8]Finally, brothers and sisters, whatever is true, whatever is noble, whatever is right, whatever is pure, whatever is lovely, whatever is admirable—if anything is excellent or praiseworthy—think about such things. [9]Whatever you have learned or received or heard from me, or seen in me—put it into practice. And the God of peace will be with you.

THANKS FOR THEIR GIFTS

[10]I rejoiced greatly in the Lord that at last you renewed your concern for me. Indeed, you were concerned, but you had no opportunity to show it. [11]I am not saying this because I am in need, for I have learned to be content whatever the circumstances. [12]I know what it is to be in need, and I know what it is to have plenty. I have learned the secret of being content in any and every situation, whether well fed or hungry, whether living in plenty or in want. [13]I can do all this through him who gives me strength.

[14]Yet it was good of you to share in my troubles. [15]Moreover, as you Philippians know, in the early days of your acquaintance with the gospel, when I set out from Macedonia, not one church shared with me in the matter of giving and receiving, except you only; [16]for even when I was in Thessalonica, you sent me aid more than once when I was in need. [17]Not that I desire your gifts; what I desire is that more be credited to your account. [18]I have received full payment and have more than enough. I am amply supplied, now that I have received from Epaphroditus the gifts you sent. They are a fragrant offering, an acceptable sacrifice, pleasing to God. [19]And my God will meet all your needs according to the riches of his glory in Christ Jesus.

[20]To our God and Father be glory for ever and ever. Amen.

FINAL GREETINGS

[21]Greet all God's people in Christ Jesus. The brothers and sisters who are with me send greetings. [22]All God's people here send you greetings, especially those who belong to Caesar's household.

[23]The grace of the Lord Jesus Christ be with your spirit. Amen.[a]

---

[a] 23 Some manuscripts do not have *Amen*.

What is the peace of God? (4:7)
This is not just a feeling of relaxation but a deep inner contentment that comes from the knowledge that you are at peace with God because he has forgiven your sins. The image of guarding one's heart and mind is the image of a sentry standing guard.

What are two ways in which Christians can live godly lives? (4:8–9)
Paul urged believers to think pure thoughts and to follow the example of Paul's actions.

What was the fragrant offering? (4:18)
Paul compared the gifts the church had sent to an Old Testament sacrifice offered for praise and thanksgiving.

Colossians

INTRODUCTION

Who wrote this book? Paul.

Why was this book written? The book of Colossians shows that Jesus is supreme and that he saves us completely.

For whom was this book written? This book is a letter written to Christians at Colossae.

What are some important teachings in this book?

Jesus is supreme	Colossians 1:15 – 20
Jesus forgives our sins	Colossians 2:13 – 15
How to live a holy life	Colossians 3:12 – 17

When did these things happen?

	10 BC	AD 1	10	20	30	40	50	60	70	80	90	100

JESUS' LIFE (C. 6/5 BC – AD 30)

PAUL'S CONVERSION (C. AD 35)

PAUL'S MISSIONARY JOURNEYS (C. AD 46 – 67)

COUNCIL AT JERUSALEM (C. AD 49/50)

NERO'S REIGN (AD 54 – 68)

PAUL'S FIRST IMPRISONMENT IN ROME (C. AD 59 – 62)

BOOK OF COLOSSIANS WRITTEN (C. AD 60)

PAUL'S IMPRISONMENT AND DEATH IN ROME (C. AD 67 – 68)

DESTRUCTION OF JERUSALEM'S TEMPLE (C. AD 70)

1 Paul, an apostle of Christ Jesus by the will of God, and Timothy our brother,

²To God's holy people in Colossae, the faithful brothers and sisters*ᵃ* in Christ:

Grace and peace to you from God our Father.*ᵇ*

THANKSGIVING AND PRAYER

³We always thank God, the Father of our Lord Jesus Christ, when we pray for you, ⁴because we have heard of your faith in Christ Jesus and of the love you have for all God's people— ⁵the faith and love that spring from the hope stored up for you in heaven and about which you have already heard in the true message of the gospel ⁶that has come to you. In the same way, the gospel is bearing fruit and growing throughout the whole world—just as it has been doing among you since the day you heard it and truly understood God's grace. ⁷You learned it from Epaphras, our dear fellow servant,*ᶜ* who is a faithful minister of Christ on our*ᵈ* behalf, ⁸and who also told us of your love in the Spirit.

⁹For this reason, since the day we heard about you, we have not stopped praying for you. We continually ask God to fill you with the knowledge of his will through all the wisdom and understanding that the Spirit gives,*ᵉ* ¹⁰so that you may live a life worthy of the Lord and please him in every way: bearing fruit in every good work, growing in the knowledge of God, ¹¹being strengthened with all power according to his glorious might so that you may have great endurance and patience, ¹²and giving joyful thanks to the Father, who has qualified you*ᶠ* to share in the inheritance of his holy people

---

ᵃ 2 The Greek word for *brothers and sisters (adelphoi)* refers here to believers, both men and women, as part of God's family; also in 4:15.   *ᵇ 2* Some manuscripts *Father and the Lord Jesus Christ*   *ᶜ 7* Or *slave*   *ᵈ 7* Some manuscripts *your*   *ᵉ 9* Or *all spiritual wisdom and understanding*   *ᶠ 12* Some manuscripts *us*

The Church in Colossae (1:2)

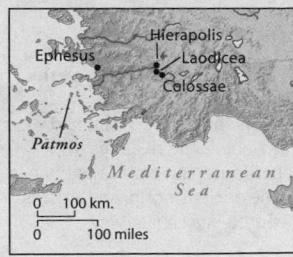

What are the three great Christian virtues? (1:5)
They are faith, hope, and love. They are listed together several times in the New Testament; the most familiar listing is in 1 Corinthians 13:13.

Why do we have to go to church?

COLOSSIANS 1

It is possible for someone to be a Christian without going to church, but there are several strong reasons why Christians should go to church.

First, in a church Christians can hear ministers and teachers explain God's Word and what it means for people's lives. If we simply read the Bible on our own, we may not understand parts of it or we may form wrong ideas. Good preaching will help us understand what the Bible really says.

Second, church is a place where people can gather to give praise and honor to God as a group. Whether it's a small church of just a few people or a huge church with several thousand members, when we join with other believers to sing and pray to God, it is a testimony of our faith.

Third, we go to church to encourage one another and build each other up in our faith. Fellow Christians can help to strengthen our faith, correct us when we make mistakes, support us when we face difficult times, and share our joys and sorrows. Fellowship with other Christians is a major benefit of church membership.

Finally, there is strength in numbers. We can serve God more effectively through evangelism and service projects by joining with other Christians than we could on our own.

God loves the church and wants his people to be active members, both for their sake and for the sake of others. Hebrews 10:24–25 says, "Let us consider how we may spur one another on toward love and good deeds, *not giving up meeting together*, as some are in the habit of doing, but encouraging one another—and all the more as you see the Day approaching."

in the kingdom of light. ¹³For he has rescued us from the dominion of darkness and brought us into the kingdom of the Son he loves, ¹⁴in whom we have redemption, the forgiveness of sins.

THE SUPREMACY OF THE SON OF GOD

¹⁵The Son is the image of the invisible God, the firstborn over all creation. ¹⁶For in him all things were created: things in heaven and on earth, visible and invisible, whether thrones or powers or rulers or authorities; all things have been created through him and for him. ¹⁷He is before all things, and in him all things hold together. ¹⁸And he is the head of the body, the church; he is the beginning and the firstborn from among the dead, so that in everything he might have the supremacy. ¹⁹For God was pleased to have all his fullness dwell in him, ²⁰and through him to reconcile to himself all things, whether things on earth or things in heaven, by making peace through his blood, shed on the cross.

²¹Once you were alienated from God and were enemies in your minds because of ^a your evil behavior. ²²But now he has reconciled you by Christ's physical body through death to present you holy in his sight, without blemish and free from accusation— ²³if you continue in your faith, established and firm, and do not move from the hope held out in the gospel. This is the gospel that you heard and that has been proclaimed to every creature under heaven, and of which I, Paul, have become a servant.

PAUL'S LABOR FOR THE CHURCH

²⁴Now I rejoice in what I am suffering for you, and I fill up in my flesh what is still lacking in regard to Christ's afflictions, for the sake of his body, which is the church. ²⁵I have become its servant by the commission God gave me to present to you the word of God in its fullness— ²⁶the mystery that has been kept hidden for ages and generations, but is now disclosed to the Lord's people. ²⁷To them God has chosen to make known among the Gentiles the glorious riches of this mystery, which is Christ in you, the hope of glory.

²⁸He is the one we proclaim, admonishing and teaching everyone with all wisdom, so that we may present everyone fully mature in Christ. ²⁹To this end I strenuously contend with all the energy Christ so powerfully works in me.

2 I want you to know how hard I am contending for you and for those at Laodicea, and for all who have not met me personally. ²My goal is that they may be encouraged in heart and united in love, so that they may have the full riches of complete understanding, in order that they may know the mystery of God, namely, Christ, ³in whom are hidden all the treasures of wisdom and knowledge. ⁴I tell you this so that no one may deceive you by fine-sounding arguments. ⁵For though I am absent from you in body, I am present with you in spirit and delight to see how disciplined you are and how firm your faith in Christ is.

What were the rights of the firstborn? (1:15)
Just as the firstborn son had the rights and privileges of inheritance and a place of honor in the ancient world, so Christ is honored in a similar way.

What was the mystery of God? (1:25–26)
Many pagan religions used the word *mystery* to refer to secret rituals and symbols that were kept hidden from ordinary people. Paul used the word to refer to God's plans that had once been hidden but were now revealed through Christ: Salvation comes to all who by grace through faith believe in him.

^a 21 Or *minds, as shown by*

SPIRITUAL FULLNESS IN CHRIST

[6] So then, just as you received Christ Jesus as Lord, continue to live your lives in him, [7] rooted and built up in him, strengthened in the faith as you were taught, and overflowing with thankfulness.

[8] See to it that no one takes you captive through hollow and deceptive philosophy, which depends on human tradition and the elemental spiritual forces[a] of this world rather than on Christ.

[9] For in Christ all the fullness of the Deity lives in bodily form, [10] and in Christ you have been brought to fullness. He is the head over every power and authority. [11] In him you were also circumcised with a circumcision not performed by human hands. Your whole self ruled by the flesh[b] was put off when you were circumcised by[c] Christ, [12] having been buried with him in baptism, in which you were also raised with him through your faith in the working of God, who raised him from the dead.

[13] When you were dead in your sins and in the uncircumcision of your flesh, God made you[d] alive with Christ. He forgave us all our sins, [14] having canceled the charge of our legal indebtedness, which stood against us and condemned us; he has taken it away, nailing it to the cross. [15] And having disarmed the powers and authorities, he made a public spectacle of them, triumphing over them by the cross.[e]

FREEDOM FROM HUMAN RULES

[16] Therefore do not let anyone judge you by what you eat or drink, or with regard to a religious festival, a New Moon celebration or a Sabbath day. [17] These are a shadow of the things that were to come; the reality, however, is found in Christ. [18] Do not let anyone who delights in false humility and the worship of angels disqualify you. Such a person also goes into great detail about what they have seen; they are puffed up with idle notions by their unspiritual mind. [19] They have lost connection with the head, from whom the whole body, supported and held together by its ligaments and sinews, grows as God causes it to grow.

[20] Since you died with Christ to the elemental spiritual forces of this world, why, as though you still belonged to the world, do you submit to its rules: [21] "Do not handle! Do not taste! Do not touch!"? [22] These rules, which have to do with things that are all destined to perish with use, are based on merely human commands and teachings. [23] Such regulations indeed have an appearance of wisdom, with their self-imposed worship, their false humility and their harsh treatment of the body, but they lack any value in restraining sensual indulgence.

LIVING AS THOSE MADE ALIVE IN CHRIST

3 Since, then, you have been raised with Christ, set your hearts on things above, where Christ is, seated at the right hand of God. [2] Set your minds on things above, not on

What false teaching was Paul addressing? (2:8)
Paul was criticizing the false teachings in Colossae that said a person had to combine faith in Christ with secret knowledge and that faith had to be combined with specific actions such as circumcision and other religious rituals.

How did Paul criticize the heresy? (2:20–23)
He said that although these practices seemed wise, they were restrictions imposed by human beings rather than God. He added that the supposed humility and strict dietary rules of these false teachers were of no value.

---

[a] 8 Or *the basic principles*; also in verse 20   [b] 11 In contexts like this, the Greek word for *flesh* (*sarx*) refers to the sinful state of human beings, often presented as a power in opposition to the Spirit; also in verse 13.
[c] 11 Or *put off in the circumcision of*   [d] 13 Some manuscripts *us*
[e] 15 Or *them in him*

earthly things. ³For you died, and your life is now hidden with Christ in God. ⁴When Christ, who is your*ᵃ* life, appears, then you also will appear with him in glory.

⁵Put to death, therefore, whatever belongs to your earthly nature: sexual immorality, impurity, lust, evil desires and greed, which is idolatry. ⁶Because of these, the wrath of God is coming.*ᵇ* ⁷You used to walk in these ways, in the life you once lived. ⁸But now you must also rid yourselves of all such things as these: anger, rage, malice, slander, and filthy language from your lips. ⁹Do not lie to each other, since you have taken off your old self with its practices ¹⁰and have put on the new self, which is being renewed in knowledge in the image of its Creator. ¹¹Here there is no Gentile or Jew, circumcised or uncircumcised, barbarian, Scythian, slave or free, but Christ is all, and is in all.

¹²Therefore, as God's chosen people, holy and dearly loved, clothe yourselves with compassion, kindness, humility, gentleness and patience. ¹³Bear with each other and forgive one another if any of you has a grievance against someone. Forgive as the Lord forgave you. ¹⁴And over all these virtues put on love, which binds them all together in perfect unity.

¹⁵Let the peace of Christ rule in your hearts, since as members of one body you were called to peace. And be thankful. ¹⁶Let the message of Christ dwell among you richly as you teach and admonish one another with all wisdom through psalms, hymns, and songs from the Spirit, singing to God with gratitude in your hearts. ¹⁷And whatever you do, whether in word or deed, do it all in the name of the Lord Jesus, giving thanks to God the Father through him.

INSTRUCTIONS FOR CHRISTIAN HOUSEHOLDS

¹⁸Wives, submit yourselves to your husbands, as is fitting in the Lord.

¹⁹Husbands, love your wives and do not be harsh with them.

²⁰Children, obey your parents in everything, for this pleases the Lord.

²¹Fathers,*ᶜ* do not embitter your children, or they will become discouraged.

²²Slaves, obey your earthly masters in everything; and do it, not only when their eye is on you and to curry their favor, but with sincerity of heart and reverence for the Lord. ²³Whatever you do, work at it with all your heart, as working for the Lord, not for human masters, ²⁴since you know that you will receive an inheritance from the Lord as a reward. It is the Lord Christ you are serving. ²⁵Anyone who does wrong will be repaid for their wrongs, and there is no favoritism.

4 Masters, provide your slaves with what is right and fair, because you know that you also have a Master in heaven.

FURTHER INSTRUCTIONS

²Devote yourselves to prayer, being watchful and thankful. ³And pray for us, too, that God may open a door for our message, so that we may proclaim the mystery of Christ, for

which I am in chains. ⁴Pray that I may proclaim it clearly, as I should. ⁵Be wise in the way you act toward outsiders; make the most of every opportunity. ⁶Let your conversation be always full of grace, seasoned with salt, so that you may know how to answer everyone.

FINAL GREETINGS

⁷Tychicus will tell you all the news about me. He is a dear brother, a faithful minister and fellow servant*ᵃ* in the Lord. ⁸I am sending him to you for the express purpose that you may know about our*ᵇ* circumstances and that he may encourage your hearts. ⁹He is coming with Onesimus, our faithful and dear brother, who is one of you. They will tell you everything that is happening here.

¹⁰My fellow prisoner Aristarchus sends you his greetings, as does Mark, the cousin of Barnabas. (You have received instructions about him; if he comes to you, welcome him.) ¹¹Jesus, who is called Justus, also sends greetings. These are the only Jews*ᶜ* among my co-workers for the kingdom of God, and they have proved a comfort to me. ¹²Epaphras, who is one of you and a servant of Christ Jesus, sends greetings. He is always wrestling in prayer for you, that you may stand firm in all the will of God, mature and fully assured. ¹³I vouch for him that he is working hard for you and for those at Laodicea and Hierapolis. ¹⁴Our dear friend Luke, the doctor, and Demas send greetings. ¹⁵Give my greetings to the brothers and sisters at Laodicea, and to Nympha and the church in her house.

¹⁶After this letter has been read to you, see that it is also read in the church of the Laodiceans and that you in turn read the letter from Laodicea.

¹⁷Tell Archippus: "See to it that you complete the ministry you have received in the Lord."

¹⁸I, Paul, write this greeting in my own hand. Remember my chains. Grace be with you.

What did it mean for conversation to be seasoned with salt? (4:6)
Salt was a preservative and added flavor to foods. A Christian's conversation should be wholesome and should influence others to seek Christ.

Why did Paul say he wrote this in his own hand? (4:18)
Paul's custom was to dictate his letters but then to add some personal greetings that he wrote himself at the end of the letter.

ᵃ 7 Or *slave*; also in verse 12   *ᵇ* 8 Some manuscripts *that he may know about your*   *ᶜ* 11 Greek *only ones of the circumcision group*

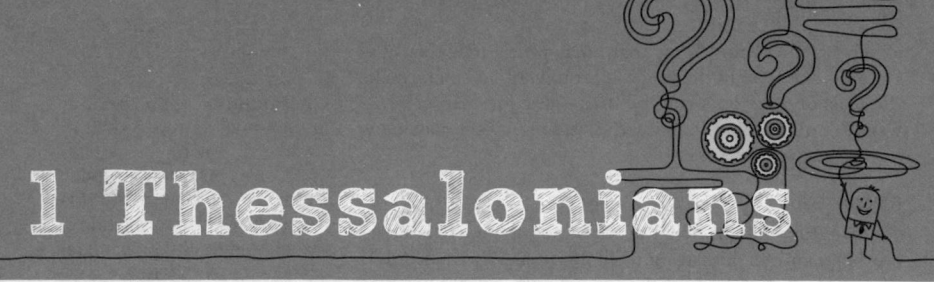

1 Thessalonians

INTRODUCTION

Who wrote this book?   Paul.

Why was this book written?   The book of 1 Thessalonians teaches the Christians in Thessalonica how to please God.

For whom was this book written?   This book is a letter Paul sent to Christians at Thessalonica.

What are some important teachings in this book?

Being Christian examples	1 Thessalonians 1:4 – 10
Living to please God	1 Thessalonians 4:3 – 12
Jesus will come again	1 Thessalonians 4:13 – 18

When did these things happen?

10 BC   AD1   10   20   30   40   50   60   70   80   90   100

JESUS' LIFE (C. 6/5 BC – AD 30)

PAUL'S CONVERSION (C. AD 35)

PAUL'S MISSIONARY JOURNEYS (C. AD 46 – 67)

COUNCIL AT JERUSALEM (C. AD 49/50)

BOOK OF 1 THESSALONIANS WRITTEN (C. AD 51)

NERO'S REIGN (AD 54 – 68)

PAUL'S FIRST IMPRISONMENT IN ROME (C. AD 59 – 62)

PAUL'S IMPRISONMENT AND DEATH IN ROME (C. AD 67 – 68)

DESTRUCTION OF JERUSALEM'S TEMPLE (C. AD 70)

1 Paul, Silas[a] and Timothy,

To the church of the Thessalonians in God the Father and the Lord Jesus Christ:

Grace and peace to you.

THANKSGIVING FOR THE THESSALONIANS' FAITH

[2] We always thank God for all of you and continually mention you in our prayers. [3] We remember before our God and Father your work produced by faith, your labor prompted by love, and your endurance inspired by hope in our Lord Jesus Christ.

[4] For we know, brothers and sisters[b] loved by God, that he has chosen you, [5] because our gospel came to you not simply with words but also with power, with the Holy Spirit and deep conviction. You know how we lived among you for your sake. [6] You became imitators of us and of the Lord, for you welcomed the message in the midst of severe suffering with the joy given by the Holy Spirit. [7] And so you became a model to all the believers in Macedonia and Achaia. [8] The Lord's message rang out from you not only in Macedonia and Achaia—your faith in God has become known everywhere. Therefore we do not need to say anything about it, [9] for they themselves report what kind of reception you gave us. They tell how you turned to God from idols to serve the living and true God, [10] and to wait for his Son from heaven, whom he raised from the dead—Jesus, who rescues us from the coming wrath.

PAUL'S MINISTRY IN THESSALONICA

2 You know, brothers and sisters, that our visit to you was not without results. [2] We had previously suffered and been treated outrageously in Philippi, as you know, but with the help of our God we dared to tell you his gospel in the face of strong opposition. [3] For the appeal we make does not spring from error or impure motives, nor are we trying to trick you. [4] On the contrary, we speak as those approved by God to be entrusted with the gospel. We are not trying to please people but God, who tests our hearts. [5] You know we never used flattery, nor did we put on a mask to cover up greed—God is our witness. [6] We were not looking for praise from people, not from you or anyone else, even though as apostles of Christ we could have asserted our authority. [7] Instead, we were like young children[c] among you.

Just as a nursing mother cares for her children, [8] so we cared for you. Because we loved you so much, we were delighted to share with you not only the gospel of God but our lives as well. [9] Surely you remember, brothers and sisters, our toil and hardship; we worked night and day in order not to be a burden to anyone while we preached the gospel of God to you. [10] You are

---

[a] 1 Greek *Silvanus*, a variant of *Silas*   [b] 4 The Greek word for *brothers and sisters* (*adelphoi*) refers here to believers, both men and women, as part of God's family; also in 2:1, 9, 14, 17; 3:7; 4:1, 10, 13; 5:1, 4, 12, 14, 25, 27.
[c] 7 Some manuscripts *were gentle*

The Church in Thessalonica (1:1)

What were three marks of conversion displayed by the Thessalonians? (1:9–10)
They turned away from idols, served God, and waited for Christ to return.

How did Paul compare himself to a parent? (2:7, 11–12)
Paul said that he was gentle like a mother when he was with them. He was also like a father who encouraged and comforted his children and urged them to live godly lives.

Why did Paul remind them of his toil and hardship? (2:9)
The Greeks disliked manual labor and thought it was only fit for slaves. However, Paul was not ashamed of doing any work that would allow him to spread the gospel. He did not want to be a burden to the believers.

witnesses, and so is God, of how holy, righteous and blameless we were among you who believed. [11]For you know that we dealt with each of you as a father deals with his own children, [12]encouraging, comforting and urging you to live lives worthy of God, who calls you into his kingdom and glory.

[13]And we also thank God continually because, when you received the word of God, which you heard from us, you accepted it not as a human word, but as it actually is, the word of God, which is indeed at work in you who believe. [14]For you, brothers and sisters, became imitators of God's churches in Judea, which are in Christ Jesus: You suffered from your own people the same things those churches suffered from the Jews [15]who killed the Lord Jesus and the prophets and also drove us out. They displease God and are hostile to everyone [16]in their effort to keep us from speaking to the Gentiles so that they may be saved. In this way they always heap up their sins to the limit. The wrath of God has come upon them at last.[a]

PAUL'S LONGING TO SEE THE THESSALONIANS

[17]But, brothers and sisters, when we were orphaned by being separated from you for a short time (in person, not in thought), out of our intense longing we made every effort to see you. [18]For we wanted to come to you — certainly I, Paul, did, again and again — but Satan blocked our way. [19]For what is our hope, our joy, or the crown in which we will glory in the presence of our Lord Jesus when he comes? Is it not you? [20]Indeed, you are our glory and joy.

3 So when we could stand it no longer, we thought it best to be left by ourselves in Athens. [2]We sent Timothy, who is our brother and co-worker in God's service in spreading the gospel of Christ, to strengthen and encourage you in your faith, [3]so that no one would be unsettled by these trials. For you know quite well that we are destined for them. [4]In fact, when we were with you, we kept telling you that we would be persecuted. And it turned out that way, as you well know. [5]For this reason, when I could stand it no longer, I sent to find out about your faith. I was afraid that in some way the tempter had tempted you and that our labors might have been in vain.

TIMOTHY'S ENCOURAGING REPORT

[6]But Timothy has just now come to us from you and has brought good news about your faith and love. He has told us that you always have pleasant memories of us and that you long to see us, just as we also long to see you. [7]Therefore, brothers and sisters, in all our distress and persecution we were encouraged about you because of your faith. [8]For now we really live, since you are standing firm in the Lord. [9]How can we thank God enough for you in return for all the joy we have in the presence of our God because of you? [10]Night and day we pray most earnestly that we may see you again and supply what is lacking in your faith.

[11]Now may our God and Father himself and our Lord Jesus clear the way for us to come to you. [12]May the Lord make your love increase and overflow for each other and for

What type of crown was this? (2:19–20)
This was not a crown worn by a king but a wreath used on festive occasions or given as a prize for winning a race. The Thessalonian Christians brought honor and joy to Paul.

What trials did the believers have to endure? (3:3)
The Christians in Thessalonica faced opposition and persecution for their beliefs. Paul said that Christians should expect troubles like this.

What good news did Timothy bring to Paul? (3:6)
Timothy reported that despite being persecuted, the believers had a strong faith in God, love for one another, and an eagerness for Paul to return.

[a] 16 Or *them fully*

everyone else, just as ours does for you. ¹³May he strengthen your hearts so that you will be blameless and holy in the presence of our God and Father when our Lord Jesus comes with all his holy ones.

LIVING TO PLEASE GOD

4 As for other matters, brothers and sisters, we instructed you how to live in order to please God, as in fact you are living. Now we ask you and urge you in the Lord Jesus to do this more and more. ²For you know what instructions we gave you by the authority of the Lord Jesus.

³It is God's will that you should be sanctified: that you should avoid sexual immorality; ⁴that each of you should learn to control your own body*a* in a way that is holy and honorable, ⁵not in passionate lust like the pagans, who do not know God; ⁶and that in this matter no one should wrong or take advantage of a brother or sister.*b* The Lord will punish all those who commit such sins, as we told you and warned you before. ⁷For God did not call us to be impure, but to live a holy life. ⁸Therefore, anyone who rejects this instruction does not reject a human being but God, the very God who gives you his Holy Spirit.

⁹Now about your love for one another we do not need to write to you, for you yourselves have been taught by God to love each other. ¹⁰And in fact, you do love all of God's family throughout Macedonia. Yet we urge you, brothers and sisters, to do so more and more, ¹¹and to make it your ambition to lead a quiet life: You should mind your own business and work with your hands, just as we told you, ¹²so that your daily life may win the respect of outsiders and so that you will not be dependent on anybody.

BELIEVERS WHO HAVE DIED

¹³Brothers and sisters, we do not want you to be uninformed about those who sleep in death, so that you do not grieve like the rest of mankind, who have no hope. ¹⁴For we believe that Jesus died and rose again, and so we believe that God will

---

a 4 Or *learn to live with your own wife,* or *learn to acquire a wife*   *b* 6 The Greek word for *brother or sister* (*adelphos*) refers here to a believer, whether man or woman, as part of God's family.

Why did Paul need to teach these Christians about remaining sexually pure? (4:3–8)
In Greek and Roman society during the first century, people generally had low moral standards about sexuality, and they thought chastity was an unreasonable requirement. Paul wanted the Christians to realize that God had called them to live holy lives.

What wrong idea did some Thessalonian Christians have about death? (4:13–18)
Some seemed to have misunderstood Paul's teaching and thought that all Christians would live until Christ returned. When some Christians died, the others wondered if they would participate in Christ's second coming. Paul said that Christians who had died would join with the living when Christ returned.

What does the Bible teach about the return of Jesus?
1 THESSALONIANS 4–5

In many churches the mystery of faith is expressed in these statements: "Christ has died, Christ is risen, Christ will come again." There are three important truths in this confession. First, Christ came to earth to give his life as a sacrifice for sin. He was crucified in order to pay the price for the sins of the world. Second, Christ rose from the dead and in that way overcame death and guaranteed that Christians would have everlasting life. Third, Christ will return to judge the world and to bring about the new earth and heaven.

The Bible gives some information about Jesus' return, but there is much that is not spelled out. For example, Paul wrote that it is not known when Jesus will come again. But Christians know that Jesus has brought salvation. Whether Jesus returns during our lifetimes or later is not important. We should not live in fear, but we should have confidence that we will live with Jesus forever because he has paid the price for sin, and we should encourage fellow Christians with this truth.

bring with Jesus those who have fallen asleep in him. [15]According to the Lord's word, we tell you that we who are still alive, who are left until the coming of the Lord, will certainly not precede those who have fallen asleep. [16]For the Lord himself will come down from heaven, with a loud command, with the voice of the archangel and with the trumpet call of God, and the dead in Christ will rise first. [17]After that, we who are still alive and are left will be caught up together with them in the clouds to meet the Lord in the air. And so we will be with the Lord forever. [18]Therefore encourage one another with these words.

THE DAY OF THE LORD

5 Now, brothers and sisters, about times and dates we do not need to write to you, [2]for you know very well that the day of the Lord will come like a thief in the night. [3]While people are saying, "Peace and safety," destruction will come on them suddenly, as labor pains on a pregnant woman, and they will not escape.

[4]But you, brothers and sisters, are not in darkness so that this day should surprise you like a thief. [5]You are all children of the light and children of the day. We do not belong to the night or to the darkness. [6]So then, let us not be like others, who are asleep, but let us be awake and sober. [7]For those who sleep, sleep at night, and those who get drunk, get drunk at night. [8]But since we belong to the day, let us be sober, putting on faith and love as a breastplate, and the hope of salvation as a helmet. [9]For God did not appoint us to suffer wrath but to receive salvation through our Lord Jesus Christ. [10]He died for us so that, whether we are awake or asleep, we may live together with him. [11]Therefore encourage one another and build each other up, just as in fact you are doing.

FINAL INSTRUCTIONS

[12]Now we ask you, brothers and sisters, to acknowledge those who work hard among you, who care for you in the Lord and who admonish you. [13]Hold them in the highest regard in love because of their work. Live in peace with each other. [14]And we urge you, brothers and sisters, warn those who are idle and disruptive, encourage the disheartened, help the weak, be patient with everyone. [15]Make sure that nobody pays back wrong for wrong, but always strive to do what is good for each other and for everyone else.

[16]Rejoice always, [17]pray continually, [18]give thanks in all circumstances; for this is God's will for you in Christ Jesus.

[19]Do not quench the Spirit. [20]Do not treat prophecies with contempt [21]but test them all; hold on to what is good, [22]reject every kind of evil.

[23]May God himself, the God of peace, sanctify you through and through. May your whole spirit, soul and body be kept blameless at the coming of our Lord Jesus Christ. [24]The one who calls you is faithful, and he will do it.

[25]Brothers and sisters, pray for us. [26]Greet all God's people with a holy kiss. [27]I charge you before the Lord to have this letter read to all the brothers and sisters.

[28]The grace of our Lord Jesus Christ be with you.

What was Paul's teaching about Christ's return? (5:4–11)
Paul said that Christians should live lives of faith, hope, and love as they wait for Christ to return. He said that God has chosen them for salvation through Jesus and that they should encourage and build one another up with this truth.

What does *sanctify* mean? (5:23)
Sanctify means to make something holy. Here it refers to the work of the Holy Spirit in a Christian helping him or her to live a godly life, to become more like Jesus.

What was a holy kiss? (5:26)
A public kiss on the cheek was a common practice in the ancient world that the Christians borrowed to show their respect and love for one another and for the Lord. It was not a romantic kiss but was used instead as a greeting or farewell.

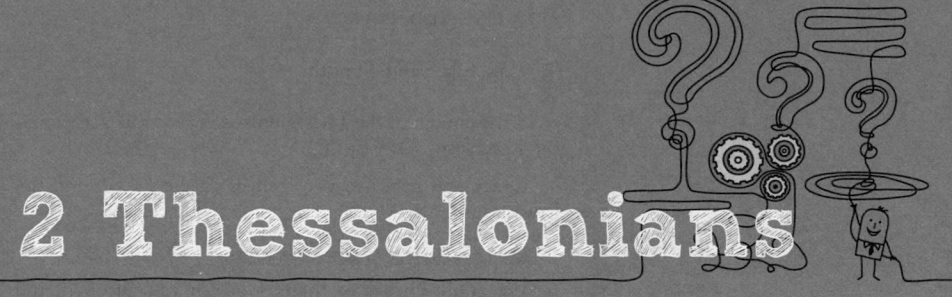

2 Thessalonians

INTRODUCTION

Who wrote this book? Paul.

Why was this book written? The book of 2 Thessalonians tells these Christians to work hard until Jesus comes again.

For whom was this book written? The book of 2 Thessalonians is a letter Paul sent to Christians at Thessalonica.

What are some important teachings in this book?

God will punish the wicked	2 Thessalonians 1:5 – 10
Everyone should work	2 Thessalonians 3:6 – 15

When did these things happen?

10 BC AD 1 10 20 30 40 50 60 70 80 90 100

JESUS' LIFE (C. 6/5 BC – AD 30) _____

PAUL'S CONVERSION (C. AD 35) _____

PAUL'S MISSIONARY JOURNEYS (C. AD 46 – 67) _____

COUNCIL AT JERUSALEM (C. AD 49/50) _____

BOOK OF 2 THESSALONIANS WRITTEN (C. AD 51 – 52) _____

NERO'S REIGN (AD 54 – 68) _____

PAUL'S FIRST IMPRISONMENT IN ROME (C. AD 59 – 62) _____

PAUL'S IMPRISONMENT AND DEATH IN ROME (C. AD 67 – 68) _____

DESTRUCTION OF JERUSALEM'S TEMPLE (C. AD 70) _____

1 Paul, Silas[a] and Timothy,

To the church of the Thessalonians in God our Father and the Lord Jesus Christ:

[2] Grace and peace to you from God the Father and the Lord Jesus Christ.

THANKSGIVING AND PRAYER

[3] We ought always to thank God for you, brothers and sisters,[b] and rightly so, because your faith is growing more and more, and the love all of you have for one another is increasing. [4] Therefore, among God's churches we boast about your perseverance and faith in all the persecutions and trials you are enduring.

[5] All this is evidence that God's judgment is right, and as a result you will be counted worthy of the kingdom of God, for which you are suffering. [6] God is just: He will pay back trouble to those who trouble you [7] and give relief to you who are troubled, and to us as well. This will happen when the Lord Jesus is revealed from heaven in blazing fire with his powerful angels. [8] He will punish those who do not know God and do not obey the gospel of our Lord Jesus. [9] They will be punished with everlasting destruction and shut out from the presence of the Lord and from the glory of his might [10] on the day he comes to be glorified in his holy people and to be marveled at among all those who have believed. This includes you, because you believed our testimony to you.

[11] With this in mind, we constantly pray for you, that our God may make you worthy of his calling, and that by his power he may bring to fruition your every desire for goodness and your every deed prompted by faith. [12] We pray this so that the name of our Lord Jesus may be glorified in you, and you in him, according to the grace of our God and the Lord Jesus Christ.[c]

THE MAN OF LAWLESSNESS

2 Concerning the coming of our Lord Jesus Christ and our being gathered to him, we ask you, brothers and sisters, [2] not to become easily unsettled or alarmed by the teaching allegedly from us — whether by a prophecy or by word of mouth or by letter — asserting that the day of the Lord has already come. [3] Don't let anyone deceive you in any way, for that day will not come until the rebellion occurs and the man of lawlessness[d] is revealed, the man doomed to destruction. [4] He will oppose and will exalt himself over everything that is called God or is worshiped, so that he sets himself up in God's temple, proclaiming himself to be God.

[5] Don't you remember that when I was with you I used to tell you these things? [6] And now you know what is holding him back, so that he may be revealed at the proper time. [7] For the secret power of lawlessness is already at work; but

Will people who have never heard of God be punished when Jesus returns? (1:8)
In this verse, Paul was writing about punishment for those who refused to believe in and follow God and accept the gospel of Jesus.

How would Jesus' name be glorified? (1:12)
In ancient times, one's name often summed up what a person was. Here Paul was praying that Jesus would receive glory for everything he did in the lives of the Thessalonian Christians.

What were the believers troubled about? (2:1–3)
Apparently they had received a forged letter claiming to be from Paul that said the day of the Lord had already come. Paul reassured them that the day of the Lord would not come until certain things had happened.

Who is the man of lawlessness? (2:3–10)
This is someone who will rebel against God and set himself up as a god. He represents the forces of Satan and evil.

---

[a] *1* Greek *Silvanus*, a variant of *Silas*   [b] *3* The Greek word for *brothers and sisters* (*adelphoi*) refers here to believers, both men and women, as part of God's family; also in 2:1, 13, 15; 3:1, 6, 13.   [c] *12* Or *God and Lord, Jesus Christ*   [d] *3* Some manuscripts *sin*

the one who now holds it back will continue to do so till he is taken out of the way. [8] And then the lawless one will be revealed, whom the Lord Jesus will overthrow with the breath of his mouth and destroy by the splendor of his coming. [9] The coming of the lawless one will be in accordance with how Satan works. He will use all sorts of displays of power through signs and wonders that serve the lie, [10] and all the ways that wickedness deceives those who are perishing. They perish because they refused to love the truth and so be saved. [11] For this reason God sends them a powerful delusion so that they will believe the lie [12] and so that all will be condemned who have not believed the truth but have delighted in wickedness.

STAND FIRM

[13] But we ought always to thank God for you, brothers and sisters loved by the Lord, because God chose you as firstfruits[a] to be saved through the sanctifying work of the Spirit and through belief in the truth. [14] He called you to this through our gospel, that you might share in the glory of our Lord Jesus Christ.

[15] So then, brothers and sisters, stand firm and hold fast to the teachings[b] we passed on to you, whether by word of mouth or by letter.

[16] May our Lord Jesus Christ himself and God our Father, who loved us and by his grace gave us eternal encouragement and good hope, [17] encourage your hearts and strengthen you in every good deed and word.

REQUEST FOR PRAYER

3 As for other matters, brothers and sisters, pray for us that the message of the Lord may spread rapidly and be honored, just as it was with you. [2] And pray that we may be delivered from wicked and evil people, for not everyone has faith. [3] But the Lord is faithful, and he will strengthen you and protect you from the evil one. [4] We have confidence in the Lord that you are doing and will continue to do the things we command. [5] May the Lord direct your hearts into God's love and Christ's perseverance.

[a] 13 Some manuscripts *because from the beginning God chose you*
[b] 15 Or *traditions*

How could Christians stay strong in their faith? (2:13–15)
Paul reminded them that they had been chosen by God to be saved through the working of the Holy Spirit in their hearts which caused them to believe in Jesus. By holding to the truth of the gospel, they could stand firm.

What are God's teachings about work?

2 THESSALONIANS 3

When God created Adam and Eve, he told them to care for the world that God had created. After Adam and Eve sinned, part of their punishment was that work often became difficult. God told Adam: "By the sweat of your brow you will eat your food" (Genesis 3:19).

The Bible tells us that work is important and that we should not be lazy. The book of Proverbs has many sayings about work, such as, "Diligent hands will rule, but laziness ends in forced labor" (Proverbs 12:24). Paul told the Thessalonians that they should not be lazy but should work hard. He used himself as an example and reminded them that he had worked hard when he was with them so that he would not have to depend on other people to provide for his living. Christians should use the talents that God has given them and should see their jobs as a way of serving God and other people. The Bible's teachings about work are summed up in Colossians 3:23: "Whatever you do, work at it with all your heart, as working for the Lord, not for human masters."

Why did Paul warn about idleness? (3:6)
The Greeks disliked manual labor and thought it was only fit for slaves. Paul had warned about idleness in his first letter to the Thessalonians (see 1 Thessalonians 4:11–12 and 5:14). Apparently the problem had continued or gotten worse.

How had Paul modeled hard work for them? (3:7–9)
Even though Paul had the right to ask the members of the church to support him, he did not do that because he did not want to be a burden to them. Instead, he worked night and day, and he urged the Thessalonians to follow his example.

WARNING AGAINST IDLENESS

⁶In the name of the Lord Jesus Christ, we command you, brothers and sisters, to keep away from every believer who is idle and disruptive and does not live according to the teaching*ᵃ* you received from us. ⁷For you yourselves know how you ought to follow our example. We were not idle when we were with you, ⁸nor did we eat anyone's food without paying for it. On the contrary, we worked night and day, laboring and toiling so that we would not be a burden to any of you. ⁹We did this, not because we do not have the right to such help, but in order to offer ourselves as a model for you to imitate. ¹⁰For even when we were with you, we gave you this rule: "The one who is unwilling to work shall not eat."

¹¹We hear that some among you are idle and disruptive. They are not busy; they are busybodies. ¹²Such people we command and urge in the Lord Jesus Christ to settle down and earn the food they eat. ¹³And as for you, brothers and sisters, never tire of doing what is good.

¹⁴Take special note of anyone who does not obey our instruction in this letter. Do not associate with them, in order that they may feel ashamed. ¹⁵Yet do not regard them as an enemy, but warn them as you would a fellow believer.

FINAL GREETINGS

¹⁶Now may the Lord of peace himself give you peace at all times and in every way. The Lord be with all of you.

¹⁷I, Paul, write this greeting in my own hand, which is the distinguishing mark in all my letters. This is how I write.

¹⁸The grace of our Lord Jesus Christ be with you all.

ᵃ 6 Or tradition

1 Timothy

INTRODUCTION

Who wrote this book? Paul.

Why was this book written? The book of 1 Timothy gives Timothy advice on his leadership role in the church.

For whom was this book written? This book is a letter Paul sent to his young helper, Timothy.

What are some important teachings in this book?

Beware of false teachers	1 Timothy 1:3 – 11
Choosing leaders	1 Timothy 3:1 – 16
Be an example	1 Timothy 4:11 – 16
The Christian family	1 Timothy 5:1 – 2
Don't love money	1 Timothy 6:3 – 10
Advice to the rich	1 Timothy 6:17 – 21

When did these things happen?

10 BC AD 1 10 20 30 40 50 60 70 80 90 100

JESUS' LIFE (C. 6/5 BC – AD 30)

PAUL'S CONVERSION (C. AD 35)

PAUL'S MISSIONARY JOURNEYS (C. AD 46 – 67)

COUNCIL AT JERUSALEM (C. AD 49/50)

NERO'S REIGN (AD 54 – 68)

PAUL'S FIRST IMPRISONMENT IN ROME (C. AD 59 – 62)

BOOK OF 1 TIMOTHY WRITTEN (C. AD 63 – 65)

PAUL'S IMPRISONMENT AND DEATH IN ROME (C. AD 67 – 68)

DESTRUCTION OF JERUSALEM'S TEMPLE (C. AD 70)

1 Paul, an apostle of Christ Jesus by the command of God our Savior and of Christ Jesus our hope,

²To Timothy my true son in the faith:

Grace, mercy and peace from God the Father and Christ Jesus our Lord.

TIMOTHY CHARGED TO OPPOSE FALSE TEACHERS

³As I urged you when I went into Macedonia, stay there in Ephesus so that you may command certain people not to teach false doctrines any longer ⁴or to devote themselves to myths and endless genealogies. Such things promote controversial speculations rather than advancing God's work—which is by faith. ⁵The goal of this command is love, which comes from a pure heart and a good conscience and a sincere faith. ⁶Some have departed from these and have turned to meaningless talk. ⁷They want to be teachers of the law, but they do not know what they are talking about or what they so confidently affirm.

⁸We know that the law is good if one uses it properly. ⁹We also know that the law is made not for the righteous but for lawbreakers and rebels, the ungodly and sinful, the unholy and irreligious, for those who kill their fathers or mothers, for murderers, ¹⁰for the sexually immoral, for those practicing homosexuality, for slave traders and liars and perjurers—and for whatever else is contrary to the sound doctrine ¹¹that conforms to the gospel concerning the glory of the blessed God, which he entrusted to me.

THE LORD'S GRACE TO PAUL

¹²I thank Christ Jesus our Lord, who has given me strength, that he considered me trustworthy, appointing me to his service. ¹³Even though I was once a blasphemer and a persecutor and a violent man, I was shown mercy because I acted in ignorance and unbelief. ¹⁴The grace of our Lord was poured out on me abundantly, along with the faith and love that are in Christ Jesus.

¹⁵Here is a trustworthy saying that deserves full acceptance: Christ Jesus came into the world to save sinners—of whom I am the worst. ¹⁶But for that very reason I was shown mercy so that in me, the worst of sinners, Christ Jesus might display his immense patience as an example for those who would believe in him and receive eternal life. ¹⁷Now to the King eternal, immortal, invisible, the only God, be honor and glory for ever and ever. Amen.

THE CHARGE TO TIMOTHY RENEWED

¹⁸Timothy, my son, I am giving you this command in keeping with the prophecies once made about you, so that by recalling them you may fight the battle well, ¹⁹holding on to faith and a good conscience, which some have rejected and so have suffered shipwreck with regard to the faith. ²⁰Among them are Hymenaeus and Alexander, whom I have handed over to Satan to be taught not to blaspheme.

What myths were the false teachers preaching? (1:3–4)
These were probably invented stories based on Old Testament history. These myths distorted the truth for the false teacher's own benefit.

Why did Paul describe his past? (1:13–14)
Paul wanted to remind Timothy of how powerful God's grace is. It changed a man who had once persecuted Christians into a missionary who led many people to Christ.

What were the prophecies made about Timothy? (1:18)
During the early church, God often revealed his will through prophets. For example, prophets played a role in sending Paul and Barnabas on their mission to the Gentiles (see Acts 13:1–3). We don't know the specific prophecies made about Timothy, but they probably pointed to his leadership role in the church.

INSTRUCTIONS ON WORSHIP

2 I urge, then, first of all, that petitions, prayers, intercession and thanksgiving be made for all people— ²for kings and all those in authority, that we may live peaceful and quiet lives in all godliness and holiness. ³This is good, and pleases God our Savior, ⁴who wants all people to be saved and to come to a knowledge of the truth. ⁵For there is one God and one mediator between God and mankind, the man Christ Jesus, ⁶who gave himself as a ransom for all people. This has now been witnessed to at the proper time. ⁷And for this purpose I was appointed a herald and an apostle—I am telling the truth, I am not lying—and a true and faithful teacher of the Gentiles.

⁸Therefore I want the men everywhere to pray, lifting up holy hands without anger or disputing. ⁹I also want the women to dress modestly, with decency and propriety, adorning themselves, not with elaborate hairstyles or gold or pearls or expensive clothes, ¹⁰but with good deeds, appropriate for women who profess to worship God.

¹¹A woman*a* should learn in quietness and full submission. ¹²I do not permit a woman to teach or to assume authority over a man;*b* she must be quiet. ¹³For Adam was formed first, then Eve. ¹⁴And Adam was not the one deceived; it was the woman who was deceived and became a sinner. ¹⁵But women*c* will be saved through childbearing—if they continue in faith, love and holiness with propriety.

QUALIFICATIONS FOR OVERSEERS AND DEACONS

3 Here is a trustworthy saying: Whoever aspires to be an overseer desires a noble task. ²Now the overseer is to be above reproach, faithful to his wife, temperate, self-controlled, respectable, hospitable, able to teach, ³not given to drunkenness, not violent but gentle, not quarrelsome, not a lover of money. ⁴He must manage his own family well and see that his children obey him, and he must do so in a manner worthy of full*d* respect. ⁵(If anyone does not know how to manage his own family, how can he take care of God's church?) ⁶He must not be a recent convert, or he may become conceited and fall under the same judgment as the devil. ⁷He must also have a good reputation with outsiders, so that he will not fall into disgrace and into the devil's trap.

⁸In the same way, deacons*e* are to be worthy of respect, sincere, not indulging in much wine, and not pursuing dishonest gain. ⁹They must keep hold of the deep truths of the faith with a clear conscience. ¹⁰They must first be tested; and then if there is nothing against them, let them serve as deacons.

¹¹In the same way, the women*f* are to be worthy of respect, not malicious talkers but temperate and trustworthy in everything.

a 11 Or *wife;* also in verse 12   *b 12* Or *over her husband*   *c 15* Greek *she*
d 4 Or *him with proper*   *e 8* The word *deacons* refers here to Christians designated to serve with the overseers/elders of the church in a variety of ways; similarly in verse 12; and in Romans 16:1 and Phil. 1:1.   *f 11* Possibly deacons' wives or women who are deacons

Why might it be surprising for Paul to urge that Christians pray for kings? (2:1–2)
During this time, Nero was the Roman emperor. He was an extremely cruel ruler, who persecuted Christians and had them killed in savage ways.

How was Christ a ransom? (2:6)
The Greek word for *ransom* usually referred to the price paid to free a slave. Jesus gave his life to free people from their sins.

Should women not wear jewelry or braid their hair? (2:9–10)
Paul didn't absolutely forbid these things. He wanted women to be modest and not simply follow the fashions of the time that emphasized extravagance and proud personal display.

Is it wrong for women to teach or preach? (2:12–14)
There are various opinions about these verses. Some think Paul was prohibiting women from teaching or exercising authority over men in all times and places. Others think he meant that women who had not been properly taught (like the women of Ephesus) should not attempt to teach. Still others think Paul was expressing an opinion that was appropriate for the culture in which he lived but that does not apply to today's world.

Who was an overseer? (3:1)
The Greek word for *overseer* described an official in a civic or religious organization. Here it refers to someone who led a church. The responsibilities of such a leader were to preach and teach, to direct the affairs of the church, and serve as a shepherd (or pastor) to God's people.

What was the role of deacons? (3:8)
The Greek word for *deacon* means "someone who serves." But in the church, the role of

the deacons was probably to provide leadership for the helping ministries of the church, such as feeding the poor and providing help to widows and orphans.

---

[12] A deacon must be faithful to his wife and must manage his children and his household well. [13] Those who have served well gain an excellent standing and great assurance in their faith in Christ Jesus.

REASONS FOR PAUL'S INSTRUCTIONS

[14] Although I hope to come to you soon, I am writing you these instructions so that, [15] if I am delayed, you will know how people ought to conduct themselves in God's household, which is the church of the living God, the pillar and foundation of the truth. [16] Beyond all question, the mystery from which true godliness springs is great:

He appeared in the flesh,
was vindicated by the Spirit,[a]
was seen by angels,
was preached among the nations,
was believed on in the world,
was taken up in glory.

4 The Spirit clearly says that in later times some will abandon the faith and follow deceiving spirits and things taught by demons. [2] Such teachings come through hypocritical liars, whose consciences have been seared as with a hot iron. [3] They forbid people to marry and order them to abstain from certain foods, which God created to be received with thanksgiving by those who believe and who know the truth. [4] For everything God created is good, and nothing is to be rejected if it is received with thanksgiving, [5] because it is consecrated by the word of God and prayer.

[6] If you point these things out to the brothers and sisters,[b] you will be a good minister of Christ Jesus, nourished on the truths of the faith and of the good teaching that you have followed. [7] Have nothing to do with godless myths and old wives' tales; rather, train yourself to be godly. [8] For physical training is of some value, but godliness has value for all things, holding promise for both the present life and the life to come. [9] This is a trustworthy saying that deserves full acceptance. [10] That is why we labor and strive, because we have put our hope in the living God, who is the Savior of all people, and especially of those who believe.

[11] Command and teach these things. [12] Don't let anyone look down on you because you are young, but set an example for the believers in speech, in conduct, in love, in faith and in purity. [13] Until I come, devote yourself to the public reading of Scripture, to preaching and to teaching. [14] Do not neglect your gift, which was given you through prophecy when the body of elders laid their hands on you.

[15] Be diligent in these matters; give yourself wholly to them, so that everyone may see your progress. [16] Watch your life and doctrine closely. Persevere in them, because if you do, you will save both yourself and your hearers.

Why did some false teachers forbid marriage and tell people not to eat certain foods? (4:3)
These rules grew out of the mistaken idea that the physical world was evil, which was a central belief in one of the heresies (false doctrines) of that time.

How old was Timothy? (4:12)
Timothy was probably in his midthirties or younger. It was rare for a person that young to have a leadership position, so some questioned his abilities.

---

[a] 16 Or *vindicated in spirit*   [b] 6 The Greek word for *brothers and sisters* (*adelphoi*) refers here to believers, both men and women, as part of God's family.

WIDOWS, ELDERS AND SLAVES

5 Do not rebuke an older man harshly, but exhort him as if he were your father. Treat younger men as brothers, [2] older women as mothers, and younger women as sisters, with absolute purity.

[3] Give proper recognition to those widows who are really in need. [4] But if a widow has children or grandchildren, these should learn first of all to put their religion into practice by caring for their own family and so repaying their parents and grandparents, for this is pleasing to God. [5] The widow who is really in need and left all alone puts her hope in God and continues night and day to pray and to ask God for help. [6] But the widow who lives for pleasure is dead even while she lives. [7] Give the people these instructions, so that no one may be open to blame. [8] Anyone who does not provide for their relatives, and especially for their own household, has denied the faith and is worse than an unbeliever.

[9] No widow may be put on the list of widows unless she is over sixty, has been faithful to her husband, [10] and is well known for her good deeds, such as bringing up children, showing hospitality, washing the feet of the Lord's people, helping those in trouble and devoting herself to all kinds of good deeds.

[11] As for younger widows, do not put them on such a list. For when their sensual desires overcome their dedication to Christ, they want to marry. [12] Thus they bring judgment on themselves, because they have broken their first pledge. [13] Besides, they get into the habit of being idle and going about from house to house. And not only do they become idlers, but also busybodies who talk nonsense, saying things they ought not to. [14] So I counsel younger widows to marry, to have children, to manage their homes and to give the enemy no opportunity for slander. [15] Some have in fact already turned away to follow Satan.

[16] If any woman who is a believer has widows in her care, she should continue to help them and not let the church be burdened with them, so that the church can help those widows who are really in need.

[17] The elders who direct the affairs of the church well are worthy of double honor, especially those whose work is preaching and teaching. [18] For Scripture says, "Do not

What was the list of widows? (5:9)
The church in Ephesus seems to have kept a list of widows that they supported. Widows who did not have relatives to support them had a difficult time providing for their own needs.

What did the Scriptures include? (5:18)
The fact that Paul quoted an Old Testament verse (Deuteronomy 25:4) and a New Testament verse (Luke 10:7) shows that parts of the New Testament were already considered to have the same authority as the Old Testament.

What is the responsibility of the church for people who have special needs?

1 TIMOTHY 5

The Bible describes the church as the body of Christ. Within the church all people are equal: the rich and the poor, the healthy and the sick, the old and the young, the strong and the weak. An important part of the church's work is caring for members who have needs.

In this passage Paul gives very detailed instructions about how the church was supposed to take care of widows. These instructions applied to the specific situation of the church at that time. It would be a mistake for people today to try to follow these instructions in detail. The emphasis throughout the Bible is that God's people should care for one another. People who have been given much by God should share with those who have needs. God has given his love generously to his people, and in a spirit of thankfulness and love, believers should give generously — time, money, or help — to others.

muzzle an ox while it is treading out the grain,"[a] and "The worker deserves his wages."[b] [19]Do not entertain an accusation against an elder unless it is brought by two or three witnesses. [20]But those elders who are sinning you are to reprove before everyone, so that the others may take warning. [21]I charge you, in the sight of God and Christ Jesus and the elect angels, to keep these instructions without partiality, and to do nothing out of favoritism.

[22]Do not be hasty in the laying on of hands, and do not share in the sins of others. Keep yourself pure.

[23]Stop drinking only water, and use a little wine because of your stomach and your frequent illnesses.

[24]The sins of some are obvious, reaching the place of judgment ahead of them; the sins of others trail behind them. [25]In the same way, good deeds are obvious, and even those that are not obvious cannot remain hidden forever.

6 All who are under the yoke of slavery should consider their masters worthy of full respect, so that God's name and our teaching may not be slandered. [2]Those who have believing masters should not show them disrespect just because they are fellow believers. Instead, they should serve them even better because their masters are dear to them as fellow believers and are devoted to the welfare[c] of their slaves.

FALSE TEACHERS AND THE LOVE OF MONEY

These are the things you are to teach and insist on. [3]If anyone teaches otherwise and does not agree to the sound instruction of our Lord Jesus Christ and to godly teaching, [4]they are conceited and understand nothing. They have an unhealthy interest in controversies and quarrels about words that result in envy, strife, malicious talk, evil suspicions [5]and constant friction between people of corrupt mind, who have been robbed of the truth and who think that godliness is a means to financial gain.

[6]But godliness with contentment is great gain. [7]For we brought nothing into the world, and we can take nothing out of it. [8]But if we have food and clothing, we will be content with that. [9]Those who want to get rich fall into temptation and a trap and into many foolish and harmful desires that plunge people into ruin and destruction. [10]For the love of money is a root of all kinds of evil. Some people, eager for money, have wandered from the faith and pierced themselves with many griefs.

FINAL CHARGE TO TIMOTHY

[11]But you, man of God, flee from all this, and pursue righteousness, godliness, faith, love, endurance and gentleness. [12]Fight the good fight of the faith. Take hold of the eternal life to which you were called when you made your good confession in the presence of many witnesses. [13]In the sight of God, who gives life to everything, and of Christ Jesus, who while testifying before Pontius Pilate made the good confession, I charge you [14]to keep this command without

---

What did Paul mean by telling Timothy not to be too hasty in the laying on of hands? (5:22)
The laying on of hands was part of the process of ordaining elders. Paul wanted to not rush this but to give people time to prove themselves before they were ordained.

Did Paul think that Christians should live in poverty? (6:6-10)
Paul said that being godly was better than being rich, and he also pointed out that the desire to become rich led some to wander from their faith and do evil deeds. He urged Christians to be content with what God had given them.

What did Paul say about the timing of Jesus' return? (6:14-15)
Paul did not know when this would happen, except that it would be at a time God chose.

---

[a] 18 Deut. 25:4   [b] 18 Luke 10:7   [c] 2 Or *and benefit from the service*

spot or blame until the appearing of our Lord Jesus Christ, [15]which God will bring about in his own time—God, the blessed and only Ruler, the King of kings and Lord of lords, [16]who alone is immortal and who lives in unapproachable light, whom no one has seen or can see. To him be honor and might forever. Amen.

[17]Command those who are rich in this present world not to be arrogant nor to put their hope in wealth, which is so uncertain, but to put their hope in God, who richly provides us with everything for our enjoyment. [18]Command them to do good, to be rich in good deeds, and to be generous and willing to share. [19]In this way they will lay up treasure for themselves as a firm foundation for the coming age, so that they may take hold of the life that is truly life.

[20]Timothy, guard what has been entrusted to your care. Turn away from godless chatter and the opposing ideas of what is falsely called knowledge, [21]which some have professed and in so doing have departed from the faith.

Grace be with you all.

What were the wealthy Christians supposed to do with their money? (6:17–19) Paul said that they should put their hope in God rather than in their riches. He also said they should be generous and share their wealth with others.

2 Timothy

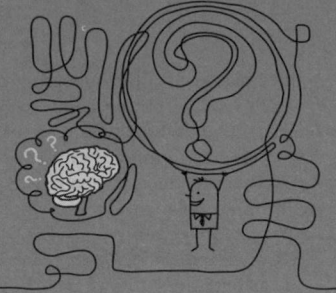

INTRODUCTION

Who wrote this book?	Paul.
Why was this book written?	This letter encourages Timothy to keep on working hard after Paul dies.
For whom was this book written?	This book is a letter Paul sent to his young helper, Timothy.

What are some important teachings in this book?		
	Teach God's truth	2 Timothy 1:8 – 15
	Teach gently	2 Timothy 2:22 – 26
	Teach faithfully	2 Timothy 4:1 – 5

When did these things happen?

	10 BC	AD 1	10	20	30	40	50	60	70	80	90	100

JESUS' LIFE (C. 6/5 BC – AD 30)

PAUL'S CONVERSION (C. AD 35)

PAUL'S MISSIONARY JOURNEYS (C. AD 46 – 67)

COUNCIL AT JERUSALEM (C. AD 49/50)

NERO'S REIGN (AD 54 – 68)

PAUL'S FIRST IMPRISONMENT IN ROME (C. AD 59 – 62)

BOOK OF 2 TIMOTHY WRITTEN (C. AD 67 – 68)

PAUL'S IMPRISONMENT AND DEATH IN ROME (C. AD 67 – 68)

DESTRUCTION OF JERUSALEM'S TEMPLE (C. AD 70)

1 Paul, an apostle of Christ Jesus by the will of God, in keeping with the promise of life that is in Christ Jesus,

[2] To Timothy, my dear son:

Grace, mercy and peace from God the Father and Christ Jesus our Lord.

THANKSGIVING

[3] I thank God, whom I serve, as my ancestors did, with a clear conscience, as night and day I constantly remember you in my prayers. [4] Recalling your tears, I long to see you, so that I may be filled with joy. [5] I am reminded of your sincere faith, which first lived in your grandmother Lois and in your mother Eunice and, I am persuaded, now lives in you also.

APPEAL FOR LOYALTY TO PAUL AND THE GOSPEL

[6] For this reason I remind you to fan into flame the gift of God, which is in you through the laying on of my hands. [7] For the Spirit God gave us does not make us timid, but gives us power, love and self-discipline. [8] So do not be ashamed of the testimony about our Lord or of me his prisoner. Rather, join with me in suffering for the gospel, by the power of God. [9] He has saved us and called us to a holy life — not because of anything we have done but because of his own purpose and grace. This grace was given us in Christ Jesus before the beginning of time, [10] but it has now been revealed through the appearing of our Savior, Christ Jesus, who has destroyed death and has brought life and immortality to light through the gospel. [11] And of this gospel I was appointed a herald and an apostle and a teacher. [12] That is why I am suffering as I am. Yet this is no cause for shame, because I know whom I have believed, and am convinced that he is able to guard what I have entrusted to him until that day.

[13] What you heard from me, keep as the pattern of sound teaching, with faith and love in Christ Jesus. [14] Guard the good deposit that was entrusted to you — guard it with the help of the Holy Spirit who lives in us.

EXAMPLES OF DISLOYALTY AND LOYALTY

[15] You know that everyone in the province of Asia has deserted me, including Phygelus and Hermogenes.

[16] May the Lord show mercy to the household of Onesiphorus, because he often refreshed me and was not ashamed of my chains. [17] On the contrary, when he was in Rome, he searched hard for me until he found me. [18] May the Lord grant that he will find mercy from the Lord on that day! You know very well in how many ways he helped me in Ephesus.

THE APPEAL RENEWED

2 You then, my son, be strong in the grace that is in Christ Jesus. [2] And the things you have heard me say in the presence of many witnesses entrust to reliable people who will also be qualified to teach others. [3] Join with me in suffering, like a good soldier of Christ Jesus. [4] No one serving

Why did Paul tell Timothy to "fan into flame the gift of God"? (1:6 – 7)
God usually does not give gifts that are fully developed. Christians have to develop their gifts through practice and use. Timothy had to overcome a lack of confidence.

What is the central theme of the gospel Paul preached? (1:9)
We are not saved by our own efforts but by the grace of God and the saving work of Jesus Christ.

as a soldier gets entangled in civilian affairs, but rather tries to please his commanding officer. ⁵Similarly, anyone who competes as an athlete does not receive the victor's crown except by competing according to the rules. ⁶The hardworking farmer should be the first to receive a share of the crops. ⁷Reflect on what I am saying, for the Lord will give you insight into all this.

⁸Remember Jesus Christ, raised from the dead, descended from David. This is my gospel, ⁹for which I am suffering even to the point of being chained like a criminal. But God's word is not chained. ¹⁰Therefore I endure everything for the sake of the elect, that they too may obtain the salvation that is in Christ Jesus, with eternal glory.

¹¹Here is a trustworthy saying:

If we died with him,
    we will also live with him;
¹²if we endure,
    we will also reign with him.
If we disown him,
    he will also disown us;
¹³if we are faithless,
    he remains faithful,
    for he cannot disown himself.

DEALING WITH FALSE TEACHERS

¹⁴Keep reminding God's people of these things. Warn them before God against quarreling about words; it is of no value, and only ruins those who listen. ¹⁵Do your best to present yourself to God as one approved, a worker who does not need to be ashamed and who correctly handles the word of truth. ¹⁶Avoid godless chatter, because those who indulge in it will become more and more ungodly. ¹⁷Their teaching will spread like gangrene. Among them are Hymenaeus and Philetus, ¹⁸who have departed from the truth. They say that the resurrection has already taken place, and they destroy the faith of some. ¹⁹Nevertheless, God's solid foundation stands firm, sealed with this inscription: "The Lord knows those who are his," and, "Everyone who confesses the name of the Lord must turn away from wickedness."

²⁰In a large house there are articles not only of gold and silver, but also of wood and clay; some are for special purposes and some for common use. ²¹Those who cleanse themselves from the latter will be instruments for special purposes, made holy, useful to the Master and prepared to do any good work.

²²Flee the evil desires of youth and pursue righteousness, faith, love and peace, along with those who call on the Lord out of a pure heart. ²³Don't have anything to do with foolish and stupid arguments, because you know they produce quarrels. ²⁴And the Lord's servant must not be quarrelsome but must be kind to everyone, able to teach, not resentful. ²⁵Opponents must be gently instructed, in the hope that God will grant them repentance leading them to a knowledge of the truth, ²⁶and that they will come to their senses and escape from the trap of the devil, who has taken them captive to do his will.

What does Paul's description of Jesus show about his nature? (2:8)
The fact that Jesus rose from the dead showed that Jesus is God. The fact that he was descended from David showed that he was human.

Why was Paul chained like a criminal? (2:9)
Apparently he was waiting to be executed.

What was God's "solid foundation"? (2:19)
In spite of the false teachings, Paul wanted Timothy to know that the church, which is God's foundation, upholds the truth. The two inscriptions show God's care for the church and the Christian's responsibility.

3 But mark this: There will be terrible times in the last days. ²People will be lovers of themselves, lovers of money, boastful, proud, abusive, disobedient to their parents, ungrateful, unholy, ³without love, unforgiving, slanderous, without self-control, brutal, not lovers of the good, ⁴treacherous, rash, conceited, lovers of pleasure rather than lovers of God— ⁵having a form of godliness but denying its power. Have nothing to do with such people.

⁶They are the kind who worm their way into homes and gain control over gullible women, who are loaded down with sins and are swayed by all kinds of evil desires, ⁷always learning but never able to come to a knowledge of the truth. ⁸Just as Jannes and Jambres opposed Moses, so also these teachers oppose the truth. They are men of depraved minds, who, as far as the faith is concerned, are rejected. ⁹But they will not get very far because, as in the case of those men, their folly will be clear to everyone.

A FINAL CHARGE TO TIMOTHY

¹⁰You, however, know all about my teaching, my way of life, my purpose, faith, patience, love, endurance, ¹¹persecutions, sufferings—what kinds of things happened to me in Antioch, Iconium and Lystra, the persecutions I endured. Yet the Lord rescued me from all of them. ¹²In fact, everyone who wants to live a godly life in Christ Jesus will be persecuted, ¹³while evildoers and impostors will go from bad to worse, deceiving and being deceived. ¹⁴But as for you, continue in what you have learned and have become convinced of, because you know those from whom you learned it, ¹⁵and how from infancy you have known the Holy Scriptures, which are able to make you wise for salvation through faith in Christ Jesus. ¹⁶All Scripture is God-breathed and is useful for teaching, rebuking, correcting and training in righteousness, ¹⁷so that the servant of God*ᵃ* may be thoroughly equipped for every good work.

4 In the presence of God and of Christ Jesus, who will judge the living and the dead, and in view of his appearing and his kingdom, I give you this charge: ²Preach the word; be prepared in season and out of season; correct,

---

ᵃ 17 Or *that you, a man of God,*

Who were Jannes and Jambres? (3:8)
These two men were two members of Pharaoh's court who went against Moses. Though they were not mentioned in the Old Testament, they were believed to be magicians.

Why is knowledge of Scripture so important? (3:14–17)
Timothy had been taught the Scripture by his mother and grandmother. Paul said that Scripture is inspired by God and contains the truths people need to know in order to gain faith in Jesus. Scripture is also useful for teaching people how to live in a way that pleases God.

Is the Bible really God's Word?   2 TIMOTHY 3

Yes. God has spoken to people through creation and through the Bible. Creation communicates in a general way who God is and what he is like. The Bible is a more specific way that God has chosen to reveal himself to people. The books of the Bible were written by many authors over several centuries, but the message of the Bible is unified. The Bible tells the story of God and his relationship with people: God created a perfect world, people disobeyed God and brought sin into the world, God sent his Son to redeem the world, and Jesus will come again to make all things new.

The Bible also contains many prophecies that have been fulfilled. For example, the prophecies about the Messiah in the Old Testament were fulfilled by Jesus. In addition, the Bible has been a life-changing book for millions of people for thousands of years.

People believe that the Bible is truly God's Word because the Holy Spirit creates faith in their hearts, allowing them to see what God has done and plans to do for his people.

What was a drink offering?
(4:6)
This was an offering of wine that was poured out at the base of the altar as part of a sacrifice. Paul saw his death as a pouring out of his life as an offering to Christ.

What did Paul mean when he said, "I was delivered from the lion's mouth"?
(4:17)
Because Paul was a Roman citizen, he could not be thrown into the amphitheater to face the lions. So this expression must have implied that he was not found guilty at the first hearing.

rebuke and encourage—with great patience and careful instruction. [3]For the time will come when people will not put up with sound doctrine. Instead, to suit their own desires, they will gather around them a great number of teachers to say what their itching ears want to hear. [4]They will turn their ears away from the truth and turn aside to myths. [5]But you, keep your head in all situations, endure hardship, do the work of an evangelist, discharge all the duties of your ministry.

[6]For I am already being poured out like a drink offering, and the time for my departure is near. [7]I have fought the good fight, I have finished the race, I have kept the faith. [8]Now there is in store for me the crown of righteousness, which the Lord, the righteous Judge, will award to me on that day—and not only to me, but also to all who have longed for his appearing.

PERSONAL REMARKS

[9]Do your best to come to me quickly, [10]for Demas, because he loved this world, has deserted me and has gone to Thessalonica. Crescens has gone to Galatia, and Titus to Dalmatia. [11]Only Luke is with me. Get Mark and bring him with you, because he is helpful to me in my ministry. [12]I sent Tychicus to Ephesus. [13]When you come, bring the cloak that I left with Carpus at Troas, and my scrolls, especially the parchments.

[14]Alexander the metalworker did me a great deal of harm. The Lord will repay him for what he has done. [15]You too should be on your guard against him, because he strongly opposed our message.

[16]At my first defense, no one came to my support, but everyone deserted me. May it not be held against them. [17]But the Lord stood at my side and gave me strength, so that through me the message might be fully proclaimed and all the Gentiles might hear it. And I was delivered from the lion's mouth. [18]The Lord will rescue me from every evil attack and will bring me safely to his heavenly kingdom. To him be glory for ever and ever. Amen.

FINAL GREETINGS

[19]Greet Priscilla[a] and Aquila and the household of Onesiphorus. [20]Erastus stayed in Corinth, and I left Trophimus sick in Miletus. [21]Do your best to get here before winter. Eubulus greets you, and so do Pudens, Linus, Claudia and all the brothers and sisters.[b]

[22]The Lord be with your spirit. Grace be with you all.

---

[a] 19 Greek *Prisca*, a variant of *Priscilla*　　[b] 21 The Greek word for *brothers and sisters* (*adelphoi*) refers here to believers, both men and women, as part of God's family.

Titus

INTRODUCTION

Who wrote this book? Paul.

Why was this book written? The book of Titus shows Titus how to be a good teacher and leader.

For whom was this book written? This book is a letter Paul sent to a young helper named Titus.

What are some important teachings in this book?

How to live a Christian life	Titus 2:1 – 15
Christians are to do good	Titus 3:3 – 8

When did these things happen?

10 BC AD 1   10   20   30   40   50   60   70   80   90   100

JESUS' LIFE (C. 6/5 BC – AD 30)

PAUL'S CONVERSION (C. AD 35)

PAUL'S MISSIONARY JOURNEYS (C. AD 46 – 67)

COUNCIL AT JERUSALEM (C. AD 49/50)

NERO'S REIGN (AD 54 – 68)

PAUL'S FIRST IMPRISONMENT IN ROME (C. AD 59 – 62)

BOOK OF TITUS WRITTEN (C. AD 63 – 65)

PAUL'S IMPRISONMENT AND DEATH IN ROME (C. AD 67 – 68)

DESTRUCTION OF JERUSALEM'S TEMPLE (C. AD 70)

1 Paul, a servant of God and an apostle of Jesus Christ to further the faith of God's elect and their knowledge of the truth that leads to godliness— [2]in the hope of eternal life, which God, who does not lie, promised before the beginning of time, [3]and which now at his appointed season he has brought to light through the preaching entrusted to me by the command of God our Savior,

[4]To Titus, my true son in our common faith:

Grace and peace from God the Father and Christ Jesus our Savior.

APPOINTING ELDERS WHO LOVE WHAT IS GOOD

[5]The reason I left you in Crete was that you might put in order what was left unfinished and appoint[a] elders in every town, as I directed you. [6]An elder must be blameless, faithful to his wife, a man whose children believe[b] and are not open to the charge of being wild and disobedient. [7]Since an overseer manages God's household, he must be blameless—not overbearing, not quick-tempered, not given to drunkenness, not violent, not pursuing dishonest gain. [8]Rather, he must be hospitable, one who loves what is good, who is self-controlled, upright, holy and disciplined. [9]He must hold firmly to the trustworthy message as it has been taught, so that he can encourage others by sound doctrine and refute those who oppose it.

REBUKING THOSE WHO FAIL TO DO GOOD

[10]For there are many rebellious people, full of meaningless talk and deception, especially those of the circumcision group. [11]They must be silenced, because they are disrupting whole households by teaching things they ought not to teach—and that for the sake of dishonest gain. [12]One of Crete's own prophets has said it: "Cretans are always liars, evil brutes, lazy gluttons."[c] [13]This saying is true. Therefore rebuke them sharply, so that they will be sound in the faith [14]and will pay no attention to Jewish myths or to the merely human commands of those who reject the truth. [15]To the pure, all things are pure, but to those who are corrupted and do not believe, nothing is pure. In fact, both their minds and consciences are corrupted. [16]They claim to know God, but by their actions they deny him. They are detestable, disobedient and unfit for doing anything good.

DOING GOOD FOR THE SAKE OF THE GOSPEL

2 You, however, must teach what is appropriate to sound doctrine. [2]Teach the older men to be temperate, worthy of respect, self-controlled, and sound in faith, in love and in endurance.

[a] 5 Or *ordain*   [b] 6 Or *children are trustworthy*   [c] 12 From the Cretan philosopher Epimenides

---

Titus's Task on Crete (1:5)

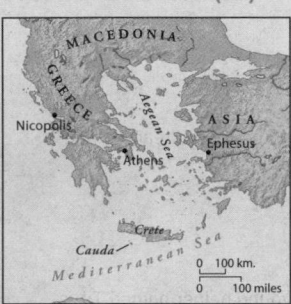

Were elders and overseers the same? (1:5–7)
Yes. The term *elder* reflects their qualifications for the office, such as maturity and wisdom. The term *overseer* reflects their task of watching over God's people.

What did these "rebellious people" teach? (1:10–14)
They taught that Christians should be circumcised. They also taught Jewish myths that weren't part of Scripture and wanted to eliminate physical pleasure from people's lives.

Was Paul saying that Christians could do anything they wanted? (1:15)
No, Paul was talking about the freedom Christians have to enjoy all the legitimate gifts of God. He was not saying that Christians could act immorally.

³Likewise, teach the older women to be reverent in the way they live, not to be slanderers or addicted to much wine, but to teach what is good. ⁴Then they can urge the younger women to love their husbands and children, ⁵to be self-controlled and pure, to be busy at home, to be kind, and to be subject to their husbands, so that no one will malign the word of God.

⁶Similarly, encourage the young men to be self-controlled. ⁷In everything set them an example by doing what is good. In your teaching show integrity, seriousness ⁸and soundness of speech that cannot be condemned, so that those who oppose you may be ashamed because they have nothing bad to say about us.

⁹Teach slaves to be subject to their masters in everything, to try to please them, not to talk back to them, ¹⁰and not to steal from them, but to show that they can be fully trusted, so that in every way they will make the teaching about God our Savior attractive.

¹¹For the grace of God has appeared that offers salvation to all people. ¹²It teaches us to say "No" to ungodliness and worldly passions, and to live self-controlled, upright and godly lives in this present age, ¹³while we wait for the blessed hope—the appearing of the glory of our great God and Savior, Jesus Christ, ¹⁴who gave himself for us to redeem us from all wickedness and to purify for himself a people that are his very own, eager to do what is good.

¹⁵These, then, are the things you should teach. Encourage and rebuke with all authority. Do not let anyone despise you.

SAVED IN ORDER TO DO GOOD

3 Remind the people to be subject to rulers and authorities, to be obedient, to be ready to do whatever is good, ²to slander no one, to be peaceable and considerate, and always to be gentle toward everyone.

³At one time we too were foolish, disobedient, deceived and enslaved by all kinds of passions and pleasures. We lived in malice and envy, being hated and hating one another. ⁴But when the kindness and love of God our Savior appeared, ⁵he saved us, not because of righteous things we had done, but because of his mercy. He saved us through the washing of rebirth and renewal by the Holy Spirit, ⁶whom he poured out on us generously through Jesus Christ our Savior, ⁷so that, having been justified by his grace, we might become heirs having the hope of eternal life. ⁸This is a trustworthy saying. And I want you to stress these things, so that those who have trusted in God may be careful to devote themselves to doing what is good. These things are excellent and profitable for everyone.

⁹But avoid foolish controversies and genealogies and arguments and quarrels about the law, because these are unprofitable and useless. ¹⁰Warn a divisive person once, and then warn them a second time. After that, have nothing to do with them. ¹¹You may be sure that such people are warped and sinful; they are self-condemned.

Why did Paul give these instructions? (2:1–10)
Paul wanted all Christians to live upright lives so that they could not be criticized by others and harm the spread of the gospel.

What effect did grace have on believers? (2:11–14)
God's grace brought salvation, and it also helped people reject worldliness and live godly lives.

What is the importance of grace? (3:3–8)
Paul again made it clear that God does not save people because of their good works. Instead, God renews people's hearts through the working of the Holy Spirit and makes them able to inherit eternal life though Jesus Christ.

How were the Christians to deal with troublemakers and false teachers? (3:10)
After warning a person twice, they were to have nothing to do with the person. The people who were spreading false doctrines were excommunicated from the church in the hope that they might repent and to protect those in the church from falsehood.

FINAL REMARKS

¹²As soon as I send Artemas or Tychicus to you, do your best to come to me at Nicopolis, because I have decided to winter there. ¹³Do everything you can to help Zenas the lawyer and Apollos on their way and see that they have everything they need. ¹⁴Our people must learn to devote themselves to doing what is good, in order to provide for urgent needs and not live unproductive lives.

¹⁵Everyone with me sends you greetings. Greet those who love us in the faith.

Grace be with you all.

Philemon

INTRODUCTION

Who wrote this book? Paul.

Why was this book written? This book asks Philemon to welcome back a runaway slave named Onesimus, who had become a Christian.

To whom was this book written? This book is a personal letter sent to a Christian named Philemon.

When did these things happen?

	10 BC	AD 1	10	20	30	40	50	60	70	80	90	100
JESUS' LIFE (C. 6/5 BC – AD 30)												
PAUL'S CONVERSION (C. AD 35)												
PAUL'S MISSIONARY JOURNEYS (C. AD 46 – 67)												
COUNCIL AT JERUSALEM (C. AD 49/50)												
NERO'S REIGN (AD 54 – 68)												
PAUL'S FIRST IMPRISONMENT IN ROME (C. AD 59 – 62)												
BOOK OF PHILEMON WRITTEN (C. AD 60)												
PAUL'S IMPRISONMENT AND DEATH IN ROME (C. AD 67 – 68)												
DESTRUCTION OF JERUSALEM'S TEMPLE (C. AD 70)												

He was a member of the church in Colossae, and he was a slave owner. Apphia was probably his wife.

[1] Paul, a prisoner of Christ Jesus, and Timothy our brother,

To Philemon our dear friend and fellow worker— [2] also to Apphia our sister and Archippus our fellow soldier—and to the church that meets in your home:

[3] Grace and peace to you[a] from God our Father and the Lord Jesus Christ.

THANKSGIVING AND PRAYER

[4] I always thank my God as I remember you in my prayers, [5] because I hear about your love for all his holy people and your faith in the Lord Jesus. [6] I pray that your partnership with us in the faith may be effective in deepening your understanding of every good thing we share for the sake of Christ. [7] Your love has given me great joy and encouragement, because you, brother, have refreshed the hearts of the Lord's people.

PAUL'S PLEA FOR ONESIMUS

[8] Therefore, although in Christ I could be bold and order you to do what you ought to do, [9] yet I prefer to appeal to you on the basis of love. It is as none other than Paul—an old man and now also a prisoner of Christ Jesus— [10] that I appeal to you for my son Onesimus,[b] who became my son while I was in chains. [11] Formerly he was useless to you, but now he has become useful both to you and to me.

What had Onesimus done? (vv. 10–18)
Onesimus, a slave of Philemon, had apparently stolen from his master and run away. He traveled to Rome, where he met Paul and became a Christian.

[12] I am sending him—who is my very heart—back to you. [13] I would have liked to keep him with me so that he could take your place in helping me while I am in chains for the gospel. [14] But I did not want to do anything without your consent, so that any favor you do would not seem forced but would be voluntary. [15] Perhaps the reason he was separated from you for a little while was that you might have him back forever— [16] no longer as a slave, but better than a slave, as a dear brother. He is very dear to me but even dearer to you, both as a fellow man and as a brother in the Lord.

What did Paul ask Philemon to do? (vv. 17–21)
Even though Philemon could have imposed almost any type of punishment on a runaway slave, Paul asked him to welcome Onesimus back as a fellow believer. Paul said he would repay him for anything Onesimus had stolen. Paul acted as a mediator, offering to pay Onesimus's debt in a similar way to Christ paying for the sins of believers.

[17] So if you consider me a partner, welcome him as you would welcome me. [18] If he has done you any wrong or owes you anything, charge it to me. [19] I, Paul, am writing this with my own hand. I will pay it back—not to mention that you owe me your very self. [20] I do wish, brother, that I may have some benefit from you in the Lord; refresh my heart in Christ. [21] Confident of your obedience, I write to you, knowing that you will do even more than I ask.

[22] And one thing more: Prepare a guest room for me, because I hope to be restored to you in answer to your prayers.

[23] Epaphras, my fellow prisoner in Christ Jesus, sends you greetings. [24] And so do Mark, Aristarchus, Demas and Luke, my fellow workers.

[25] The grace of the Lord Jesus Christ be with your spirit.

---

[a] 3 The Greek is plural; also in verses 22 and 25; elsewhere in this letter "you" is singular.   [b] 10 Onesimus means *useful.*

Hebrews

INTRODUCTION

Who wrote this book?
The author of Hebrews is unknown.

Why was this book written?
The book of Hebrews shows how the Christian faith is superior to the faith of Old Testament times.

For whom was this book written?
This book is a letter sent to Jewish Christians.

What are some important teachings in this book?

Jesus is superior to angels	Hebrews 1:1 – 14
Jesus is a real human being	Hebrews 2:5 – 18
We must believe	Hebrews 3:7 – 19
Jesus understands	Hebrews 4:14 – 16
God keeps his promises	Hebrews 6:13 – 20
The blood of Christ	Hebrews 9:11 – 28
Heroes of the faith	Hebrews 11:1 – 40
God disciplines us	Hebrews 12:1 – 13

When did these things happen?

	10 BC	AD 1	10	20	30	40	50	60	70	80	90	100

JESUS' BIRTH (C. 6/5 BC)

JESUS' DEATH, RESURRECTION AND ASCENSION (C. AD 30)

PAUL'S CONVERSION (C. AD 35)

COUNCIL AT JERUSALEM (C. AD 49/50)

NERO'S REIGN (AD 54 – 68)

BOOK OF HEBREWS WRITTEN (C. AD 60 – 70)

PAUL'S IMPRISONMENT AND DEATH IN ROME (C. AD 67 – 68)

DESTRUCTION OF JERUSALEM'S TEMPLE (C. AD 70)

GOD'S FINAL WORD: HIS SON

1 In the past God spoke to our ancestors through the prophets at many times and in various ways, ²but in these last days he has spoken to us by his Son, whom he appointed heir of all things, and through whom also he made the universe. ³The Son is the radiance of God's glory and the exact representation of his being, sustaining all things by his powerful word. After he had provided purification for sins, he sat down at the right hand of the Majesty in heaven. ⁴So he became as much superior to the angels as the name he has inherited is superior to theirs.

THE SON SUPERIOR TO ANGELS

⁵For to which of the angels did God ever say,

"You are my Son;
   today I have become your Father"[a]?

Or again,

"I will be his Father,
   and he will be my Son"[b]?

⁶And again, when God brings his firstborn into the world, he says,

"Let all God's angels worship him."[c]

⁷In speaking of the angels he says,

"He makes his angels spirits,
   and his servants flames of fire."[d]

⁸But about the Son he says,

"Your throne, O God, will last for ever and ever;
   a scepter of justice will be the scepter of your
      kingdom.
⁹You have loved righteousness and hated wickedness;
   therefore God, your God, has set you above your
      companions
   by anointing you with the oil of joy."[e]

¹⁰He also says,

"In the beginning, Lord, you laid the foundations of
   the earth,
and the heavens are the work of your hands.
¹¹They will perish, but you remain;
   they will all wear out like a garment.
¹²You will roll them up like a robe;
   like a garment they will be changed.
But you remain the same,
   and your years will never end."[f]

¹³To which of the angels did God ever say,

"Sit at my right hand
   until I make your enemies
   a footstool for your feet"[g]?

What did the Jewish people think about angels? (1:4)
The Jews had a very high respect for angels because angels had been involved in giving the law to Moses on Mount Sinai (see Deuteronomy 33:2).

How did the author prove that Jesus was superior to the angels? (1:5–14)
He proved this by quoting seven passages from the Old Testament to show that Jesus is God's Son, that angels worship him, and that he is God.

---

[a] 5 Psalm 2:7   [b] 5 2 Samuel 7:14; 1 Chron. 17:13   [c] 6 Deut. 32:43 (see Dead Sea Scrolls and Septuagint)   [d] 7 Psalm 104:4   [e] 9 Psalm 45:6,7 [f] 12 Psalm 102:25-27   [g] 13 Psalm 110:1

14 Are not all angels ministering spirits sent to serve those who will inherit salvation?

WARNING TO PAY ATTENTION

2 We must pay the most careful attention, therefore, to what we have heard, so that we do not drift away. 2 For since the message spoken through angels was binding, and every violation and disobedience received its just punishment, 3 how shall we escape if we ignore so great a salvation? This salvation, which was first announced by the Lord, was confirmed to us by those who heard him. 4 God also testified to it by signs, wonders and various miracles, and by gifts of the Holy Spirit distributed according to his will.

JESUS MADE FULLY HUMAN

5 It is not to angels that he has subjected the world to come, about which we are speaking. 6 But there is a place where someone has testified:

"What is mankind that you are mindful of them,
    a son of man that you care for him?
7 You made them a little*a* lower than the angels;
    you crowned them with glory and honor
8   and put everything under their feet."*b,c*

In putting everything under them,*d* God left nothing that is not subject to them.*d* Yet at present we do not see everything subject to them.*d* 9 But we do see Jesus, who was made lower than the angels for a little while, now crowned with glory and honor because he suffered death, so that by the grace of God he might taste death for everyone.

10 In bringing many sons and daughters to glory, it was fitting that God, for whom and through whom everything exists, should make the pioneer of their salvation perfect through what he suffered. 11 Both the one who makes people holy and those who are made holy are of the same family. So Jesus is not ashamed to call them brothers and sisters.*e* 12 He says,

"I will declare your name to my brothers and sisters;
    in the assembly I will sing your praises."*f*

13 And again,

"I will put my trust in him."*g*

And again he says,

"Here am I, and the children God has given me."*h*

14 Since the children have flesh and blood, he too shared in their humanity so that by his death he might break the power of him who holds the power of death—that is, the devil— 15 and free those who all their lives were held in slavery by

How was Jesus "lower than the angels"? (2:9)
When Jesus took on human form, he became lower than the angels, just like all human beings. But after his resurrection, he was restored to his full glory.

What relationship do believers have with God? (2:10–11)
Believers become children of God because of the sacrifice of Jesus. And Jesus becomes a brother to Christians.

---

a 7 Or *them for a little while*   *b* 6-8 Psalm 8:4-6   *c* 7,8 Or *"You made him a little lower than the angels;/ you crowned him with glory and honor/ 8 and put everything under his feet."*   *d* 8 Or *him*   *e* 11 The Greek word for *brothers and sisters* (*adelphoi*) refers here to believers, both men and women, as part of God's family; also in verse 12; and in 3:1, 12; 10:19; 13:22.
f 12 Psalm 22:22   *g* 13 Isaiah 8:17   *h* 13 Isaiah 8:18

their fear of death. [16] For surely it is not angels he helps, but Abraham's descendants. [17] For this reason he had to be made like them,[a] fully human in every way, in order that he might become a merciful and faithful high priest in service to God, and that he might make atonement for the sins of the people. [18] Because he himself suffered when he was tempted, he is able to help those who are being tempted.

JESUS GREATER THAN MOSES

3 Therefore, holy brothers and sisters, who share in the heavenly calling, fix your thoughts on Jesus, whom we acknowledge as our apostle and high priest. [2] He was faithful to the one who appointed him, just as Moses was faithful in all God's house. [3] Jesus has been found worthy of greater honor than Moses, just as the builder of a house has greater honor than the house itself. [4] For every house is built by someone, but God is the builder of everything. [5] "Moses was faithful as a servant in all God's house,"[b] bearing witness to what would be spoken by God in the future. [6] But Christ is faithful as the Son over God's house. And we are his house, if indeed we hold firmly to our confidence and the hope in which we glory.

WARNING AGAINST UNBELIEF

[7] So, as the Holy Spirit says:

> "Today, if you hear his voice,
> [8]   do not harden your hearts
> as you did in the rebellion,
>   during the time of testing in the wilderness,
> [9] where your ancestors tested and tried me,
>   though for forty years they saw what I did.
> [10] That is why I was angry with that generation;
>   I said, 'Their hearts are always going astray,
>   and they have not known my ways.'
> [11] So I declared on oath in my anger,
>   'They shall never enter my rest.'"[c]

[12] See to it, brothers and sisters, that none of you has a sinful, unbelieving heart that turns away from the living God. [13] But encourage one another daily, as long as it is called "Today," so that none of you may be hardened by sin's deceitfulness. [14] We have come to share in Christ, if indeed we hold our original conviction firmly to the very end. [15] As has just been said:

> "Today, if you hear his voice,
>   do not harden your hearts
>   as you did in the rebellion."[d]

[16] Who were they who heard and rebelled? Were they not all those Moses led out of Egypt? [17] And with whom was he angry for forty years? Was it not with those who sinned, whose bodies perished in the wilderness? [18] And to whom did God swear that they would never enter his rest if not to

---

How are believers like God's house? (3:6)
God lives with them, and they are members of his family and household.

What is the importance of holding firmly to the faith? (3:14)
Continuing in faith (persevering) rather than falling away shows that a person is truly a Christian.

Why were the Israelites who escaped from Egypt not permitted to enter Canaan? (3:16 – 19)
They had refused to believe God's promises about the promised land, and God was angry with them for their rebellion and disobedience. Only their children were allowed to enter. (See Numbers 14:26 – 35.)

---

[a] 17 Or *like his brothers*   [b] 5 Num. 12:7   [c] 11 Psalm 95:7-11
[d] 15 Psalm 95:7,8

those who disobeyed? [19] So we see that they were not able to enter, because of their unbelief.

A SABBATH-REST FOR THE PEOPLE OF GOD

4 Therefore, since the promise of entering his rest still stands, let us be careful that none of you be found to have fallen short of it. [2] For we also have had the good news proclaimed to us, just as they did; but the message they heard was of no value to them, because they did not share the faith of those who obeyed.[a] [3] Now we who have believed enter that rest, just as God has said,

"So I declared on oath in my anger,
'They shall never enter my rest.'"[b]

And yet his works have been finished since the creation of the world. [4] For somewhere he has spoken about the seventh day in these words: "On the seventh day God rested from all his works."[c] [5] And again in the passage above he says, "They shall never enter my rest."

[6] Therefore since it still remains for some to enter that rest, and since those who formerly had the good news proclaimed to them did not go in because of their disobedience, [7] God again set a certain day, calling it "Today." This he did when a long time later he spoke through David, as in the passage already quoted:

"Today, if you hear his voice,
do not harden your hearts."[d]

[8] For if Joshua had given them rest, God would not have spoken later about another day. [9] There remains, then, a Sabbath-rest for the people of God; [10] for anyone who enters God's rest also rests from their works,[e] just as God did from his. [11] Let us, therefore, make every effort to enter that rest, so that no one will perish by following their example of disobedience.

[12] For the word of God is alive and active. Sharper than any double-edged sword, it penetrates even to dividing soul and spirit, joints and marrow; it judges the thoughts and attitudes of the heart. [13] Nothing in all creation is hidden from

How do believers enter God's rest? (4:3)
The Israelites had to have faith in God's promises in order to find rest in Canaan. Believers enter God's rest today when they have faith in Jesus. As a result, Christians have rest now and in the future because of the peace of knowing that God is with them and that they will spend eternity with Jesus.

---

[a] 2 Some manuscripts *because those who heard did not combine it with faith*
[b] 3 Psalm 95:11; also in verse 5   [c] 4 Gen. 2:2   [d] 7 Psalm 95:7,8
[e] 10 Or *labor*

Does God know everything that I do or think?   HEBREWS 4

One of God's characteristics is that he is omniscient (all-knowing). God knows everything perfectly about the past, present, and future. The Bible teaches that because God is the creator of the universe, he knows all that has happened and will happen. Psalm 147:5 says, "Great is our Lord and mighty in power; his understanding has no limit." And Hebrews 4:13 says, "Nothing in all creation is hidden from God's sight."

It can be frightening to realize that God knows everything that we think and everything that we do. We cannot hide from God. When we have bad thoughts or do bad things, God knows all about it. But God loves us in spite of the things that we do that disappoint him. The fact that God knows everything can be a source of comfort for Christians because even though God can see our sins, he also sees the faith that we have in our hearts, and he knows us as his children.

God's sight. Everything is uncovered and laid bare before the eyes of him to whom we must give account.

JESUS THE GREAT HIGH PRIEST

[14] Therefore, since we have a great high priest who has ascended into heaven,[a] Jesus the Son of God, let us hold firmly to the faith we profess. [15] For we do not have a high priest who is unable to empathize with our weaknesses, but we have one who has been tempted in every way, just as we are—yet he did not sin. [16] Let us then approach God's throne of grace with confidence, so that we may receive mercy and find grace to help us in our time of need.

5 Every high priest is selected from among the people and is appointed to represent the people in matters related to God, to offer gifts and sacrifices for sins. [2] He is able to deal gently with those who are ignorant and are going astray, since he himself is subject to weakness. [3] This is why he has to offer sacrifices for his own sins, as well as for the sins of the people. [4] And no one takes this honor on himself, but he receives it when called by God, just as Aaron was.

[5] In the same way, Christ did not take on himself the glory of becoming a high priest. But God said to him,

"You are my Son;
today I have become your Father."[b]

[6] And he says in another place,

"You are a priest forever,
in the order of Melchizedek."[c]

[7] During the days of Jesus' life on earth, he offered up prayers and petitions with fervent cries and tears to the one who could save him from death, and he was heard because of his reverent submission. [8] Son though he was, he learned obedience from what he suffered [9] and, once made perfect, he became the source of eternal salvation for all who obey him [10] and was designated by God to be high priest in the order of Melchizedek.

WARNING AGAINST FALLING AWAY

[11] We have much to say about this, but it is hard to make it clear to you because you no longer try to understand. [12] In fact, though by this time you ought to be teachers, you need someone to teach you the elementary truths of God's word all over again. You need milk, not solid food! [13] Anyone who lives on milk, being still an infant, is not acquainted with the teaching about righteousness. [14] But solid food is for the mature, who by constant use have trained themselves to distinguish good from evil.

6 Therefore let us move beyond the elementary teachings about Christ and be taken forward to maturity, not laying again the foundation of repentance from acts that lead to death,[d] and of faith in God, [2] instruction about cleansing rites,[e] the laying on of hands, the resurrection of the dead, and eternal judgment. [3] And God permitting, we will do so.

How was Jesus like and unlike other human beings? (4:15)
Jesus was like other human beings because he faced every kind of temptation a person can have. But unlike any other person, he did not sin.

How was Jesus made "perfect"? (5:8–10)
Jesus was always perfect. This refers to the way that Jesus perfectly fulfilled his purpose here on earth through suffering and dying on the cross for our sins. Jesus did not give in to temptation or refuse to accept death on the cross. Unlike Adam, who fell into sin, Jesus obeyed his Father's will perfectly.

Why did the author criticize these Christians? (5:11–14)
Even though they had been Christians for some time, they were spiritually immature and needed to be reminded of the basic truths of Christianity.

[a] 14 Greek *has gone through the heavens*   [b] 5 Psalm 2:7   [c] 6 Psalm 110:4
[d] 1 Or *from useless rituals*   [e] 2 Or *about baptisms*

[4]It is impossible for those who have once been enlightened, who have tasted the heavenly gift, who have shared in the Holy Spirit, [5]who have tasted the goodness of the word of God and the powers of the coming age [6]and who have fallen[a] away, to be brought back to repentance. To their loss they are crucifying the Son of God all over again and subjecting him to public disgrace. [7]Land that drinks in the rain often falling on it and that produces a crop useful to those for whom it is farmed receives the blessing of God. [8]But land that produces thorns and thistles is worthless and is in danger of being cursed. In the end it will be burned.

[9]Even though we speak like this, dear friends, we are convinced of better things in your case—the things that have to do with salvation. [10]God is not unjust; he will not forget your work and the love you have shown him as you have helped his people and continue to help them. [11]We want each of you to show this same diligence to the very end, so that what you hope for may be fully realized. [12]We do not want you to become lazy, but to imitate those who through faith and patience inherit what has been promised.

THE CERTAINTY OF GOD'S PROMISE

[13]When God made his promise to Abraham, since there was no one greater for him to swear by, he swore by himself, [14]saying, "I will surely bless you and give you many descendants."[b] [15]And so after waiting patiently, Abraham received what was promised.

[16]People swear by someone greater than themselves, and the oath confirms what is said and puts an end to all argument. [17]Because God wanted to make the unchanging nature of his purpose very clear to the heirs of what was promised, he confirmed it with an oath. [18]God did this so that, by two unchangeable things in which it is impossible for God to lie, we who have fled to take hold of the hope set before us may be greatly encouraged. [19]We have this hope as an anchor for the soul, firm and secure. It enters the inner sanctuary behind the curtain, [20]where our forerunner, Jesus, has entered on our behalf. He has become a high priest forever, in the order of Melchizedek.

MELCHIZEDEK THE PRIEST

7 This Melchizedek was king of Salem and priest of God Most High. He met Abraham returning from the defeat of the kings and blessed him, [2]and Abraham gave him a tenth of everything. First, the name Melchizedek means "king of righteousness"; then also, "king of Salem" means "king of peace." [3]Without father or mother, without genealogy, without beginning of days or end of life, resembling the Son of God, he remains a priest forever.

[4]Just think how great he was: Even the patriarch Abraham gave him a tenth of the plunder! [5]Now the law requires the descendants of Levi who become priests to collect a tenth from the people—that is, from their fellow Israelites—even though they also are descended from Abraham.

What does it mean to "fall away"? (6:4–6)
To fall away from the faith means a believer has completely turned away from God and can never return to God. Perhaps that person was not a genuine Christian.

Did the author think these Christians had fallen away? (6:9–12)
No. He said their love and good works were evidence of their faith. He urged them to continue to live in faith so that they could be confident about their salvation.

How is hope like an anchor? (6:19)
A ship's anchor holds it safely in position. In the same way, a Christian's hope guarantees his or her eternal safety. This anchor is secured by Christ.

Who was Melchizedek? (7:1–3)
He was the king of Salem as well as a priest. He blessed Abraham after Abraham defeated the kings who had captured Lot. In return, Abraham gave him one-tenth of his belongings (see Genesis 14:18–20). Melchizedek was a symbol of the coming king and priest, Jesus.

[a] 6 Or age, [b]if they fall   [b] 14 Gen. 22:17

[6] This man, however, did not trace his descent from Levi, yet he collected a tenth from Abraham and blessed him who had the promises. [7] And without doubt the lesser is blessed by the greater. [8] In the one case, the tenth is collected by people who die; but in the other case, by him who is declared to be living. [9] One might even say that Levi, who collects the tenth, paid the tenth through Abraham, [10] because when Melchizedek met Abraham, Levi was still in the body of his ancestor.

JESUS LIKE MELCHIZEDEK

[11] If perfection could have been attained through the Levitical priesthood—and indeed the law given to the people established that priesthood—why was there still need for another priest to come, one in the order of Melchizedek, not in the order of Aaron? [12] For when the priesthood is changed, the law must be changed also. [13] He of whom these things are said belonged to a different tribe, and no one from that tribe has ever served at the altar. [14] For it is clear that our Lord descended from Judah, and in regard to that tribe Moses said nothing about priests. [15] And what we have said is even more clear if another priest like Melchizedek appears, [16] one who has become a priest not on the basis of a regulation as to his ancestry but on the basis of the power of an indestructible life. [17] For it is declared:

"You are a priest forever,
　in the order of Melchizedek."[a]

[18] The former regulation is set aside because it was weak and useless [19] (for the law made nothing perfect), and a better hope is introduced, by which we draw near to God.

[20] And it was not without an oath! Others became priests without any oath, [21] but he became a priest with an oath when God said to him:

"The Lord has sworn
　and will not change his mind:
　'You are a priest forever.'"[a]

[22] Because of this oath, Jesus has become the guarantor of a better covenant.

[23] Now there have been many of those priests, since death prevented them from continuing in office; [24] but because Jesus lives forever, he has a permanent priesthood. [25] Therefore he is able to save completely[b] those who come to God through him, because he always lives to intercede for them.

[26] Such a high priest truly meets our need—one who is holy, blameless, pure, set apart from sinners, exalted above the heavens. [27] Unlike the other high priests, he does not need to offer sacrifices day after day, first for his own sins, and then for the sins of the people. He sacrificed for their sins once for all when he offered himself. [28] For the law appoints as high priests men in all their weakness; but the oath, which came after the law, appointed the Son, who has been made perfect forever.

How was Jesus unlike the Old Testament priests?
(7:23–27)
Jesus is perfect and lives forever. He does not have to offer endless sacrifices because he offered himself as a sacrifice once and for all.

---

[a] 17,21 Psalm 110:4　　[b] 25 Or forever

THE HIGH PRIEST OF A NEW COVENANT

8 Now the main point of what we are saying is this: We do have such a high priest, who sat down at the right hand of the throne of the Majesty in heaven, [2] and who serves in the sanctuary, the true tabernacle set up by the Lord, not by a mere human being.

[3] Every high priest is appointed to offer both gifts and sacrifices, and so it was necessary for this one also to have something to offer. [4] If he were on earth, he would not be a priest, for there are already priests who offer the gifts prescribed by the law. [5] They serve at a sanctuary that is a copy and shadow of what is in heaven. This is why Moses was warned when he was about to build the tabernacle: "See to it that you make everything according to the pattern shown you on the mountain."[a] [6] But in fact the ministry Jesus has received is as superior to theirs as the covenant of which he is mediator is superior to the old one, since the new covenant is established on better promises.

[7] For if there had been nothing wrong with that first covenant, no place would have been sought for another. [8] But God found fault with the people and said[b]:

"The days are coming, declares the Lord,
  when I will make a new covenant
with the people of Israel
  and with the people of Judah.
[9] It will not be like the covenant
  I made with their ancestors
when I took them by the hand
  to lead them out of Egypt,
because they did not remain faithful to my covenant,
  and I turned away from them,
                              declares the Lord.
[10] This is the covenant I will establish with the people
        of Israel
  after that time, declares the Lord.
I will put my laws in their minds
  and write them on their hearts.
I will be their God,
  and they will be my people.
[11] No longer will they teach their neighbor,
  or say to one another, 'Know the Lord,'
because they will all know me,
  from the least of them to the greatest.
[12] For I will forgive their wickedness
  and will remember their sins no more."[c]

[13] By calling this covenant "new," he has made the first one obsolete; and what is obsolete and outdated will soon disappear.

WORSHIP IN THE EARTHLY TABERNACLE

9 Now the first covenant had regulations for worship and also an earthly sanctuary. [2] A tabernacle was set up. In its first room were the lampstand and the table with its

What did the author say about the new sanctuary? (8:5)
The author said that the earthly sanctuary of the tabernacle (the tent where God was worshiped and where sacrifices were offered in the desert) was only a shadow of the sanctuary of heaven. Heaven is the perfect tabernacle where Jesus, our perfect sacrifice, dwells in the presence of God.

What was the new covenant and what were its features? (8:10–12)
The new covenant, or new agreement, was achieved through Jesus' death and resurrection. This covenant says that we can be saved through faith, not through obeying the law. In this covenant, God's laws would become inner principles that believers live by, and God would have close fellowship with his people.

---

[a] 5 Exodus 25:40   [b] 8 Some manuscripts may be translated *fault and said to the people.*   [c] 12 Jer. 31:31-34

Why did the author devote
so much time to comparing
the old and new covenants?
(9:1–15)
The author was writing to Jewish
Christians who would have been
familiar with the Old Testament
system of sacrifices. The author
wanted to convince them that
Jesus' once and for all sacrifice
permanently and perfectly
replaced the previous system.

consecrated bread; this was called the Holy Place. ³Behind
the second curtain was a room called the Most Holy Place,
⁴which had the golden altar of incense and the gold-covered
ark of the covenant. This ark contained the gold jar of manna, Aaron's staff that had budded, and the stone tablets of the
covenant. ⁵Above the ark were the cherubim of the Glory,
overshadowing the atonement cover. But we cannot discuss
these things in detail now.

⁶When everything had been arranged like this, the priests
entered regularly into the outer room to carry on their ministry. ⁷But only the high priest entered the inner room, and
that only once a year, and never without blood, which he offered for himself and for the sins the people had committed
in ignorance. ⁸The Holy Spirit was showing by this that the
way into the Most Holy Place had not yet been disclosed as
long as the first tabernacle was still functioning. ⁹This is an
illustration for the present time, indicating that the gifts and
sacrifices being offered were not able to clear the conscience
of the worshiper. ¹⁰They are only a matter of food and drink
and various ceremonial washings—external regulations applying until the time of the new order.

THE BLOOD OF CHRIST

¹¹But when Christ came as high priest of the good things
that are now already here,ᵃ he went through the greater and
more perfect tabernacle that is not made with human hands,
that is to say, is not a part of this creation. ¹²He did not enter
by means of the blood of goats and calves; but he entered
the Most Holy Place once for all by his own blood, thus ob-
tainingᵇ eternal redemption. ¹³The blood of goats and bulls
and the ashes of a heifer sprinkled on those who are ceremonially unclean sanctify them so that they are outwardly
clean. ¹⁴How much more, then, will the blood of Christ, who
through the eternal Spirit offered himself unblemished to
God, cleanse our consciences from acts that lead to death,ᶜ
so that we may serve the living God!

¹⁵For this reason Christ is the mediator of a new covenant,
that those who are called may receive the promised eternal
inheritance—now that he has died as a ransom to set them
free from the sins committed under the first covenant.

¹⁶In the case of a will,ᵈ it is necessary to prove the death
of the one who made it, ¹⁷because a will is in force only
when somebody has died; it never takes effect while the one
who made it is living. ¹⁸This is why even the first covenant
was not put into effect without blood. ¹⁹When Moses had
proclaimed every command of the law to all the people, he
took the blood of calves, together with water, scarlet wool
and branches of hyssop, and sprinkled the scroll and all the
people. ²⁰He said, "This is the blood of the covenant, which
God has commanded you to keep."ᵉ ²¹In the same way, he
sprinkled with the blood both the tabernacle and everything
used in its ceremonies. ²²In fact, the law requires that nearly

ᵃ 11 Some early manuscripts *are to come*   ᵇ 12 Or *blood, having obtained*
ᶜ 14 Or *from useless rituals*   ᵈ 16 Same Greek word as *covenant*; also in
verse 17   ᵉ 20 Exodus 24:8

everything be cleansed with blood, and without the shedding of blood there is no forgiveness.

²³ It was necessary, then, for the copies of the heavenly things to be purified with these sacrifices, but the heavenly things themselves with better sacrifices than these. ²⁴ For Christ did not enter a sanctuary made with human hands that was only a copy of the true one; he entered heaven itself, now to appear for us in God's presence. ²⁵ Nor did he enter heaven to offer himself again and again, the way the high priest enters the Most Holy Place every year with blood that is not his own. ²⁶ Otherwise Christ would have had to suffer many times since the creation of the world. But he has appeared once for all at the culmination of the ages to do away with sin by the sacrifice of himself. ²⁷ Just as people are destined to die once, and after that to face judgment, ²⁸ so Christ was sacrificed once to take away the sins of many; and he will appear a second time, not to bear sin, but to bring salvation to those who are waiting for him.

CHRIST'S SACRIFICE ONCE FOR ALL

10 The law is only a shadow of the good things that are coming—not the realities themselves. For this reason it can never, by the same sacrifices repeated endlessly year after year, make perfect those who draw near to worship. ² Otherwise, would they not have stopped being offered? For the worshipers would have been cleansed once for all, and would no longer have felt guilty for their sins. ³ But those sacrifices are an annual reminder of sins. ⁴ It is impossible for the blood of bulls and goats to take away sins.

⁵ Therefore, when Christ came into the world, he said:

> "Sacrifice and offering you did not desire,
>   but a body you prepared for me;
> ⁶ with burnt offerings and sin offerings
>   you were not pleased.
> ⁷ Then I said, 'Here I am—it is written about me in the
>   · scroll—
>   I have come to do your will, my God.'"ᵃ

⁸ First he said, "Sacrifices and offerings, burnt offerings and sin offerings you did not desire, nor were you pleased with them"—though they were offered in accordance with the law. ⁹ Then he said, "Here I am, I have come to do your will." He sets aside the first to establish the second. ¹⁰ And by that will, we have been made holy through the sacrifice of the body of Jesus Christ once for all.

¹¹ Day after day every priest stands and performs his religious duties; again and again he offers the same sacrifices, which can never take away sins. ¹² But when this priest had offered for all time one sacrifice for sins, he sat down at the right hand of God, ¹³ and since that time he waits for his enemies to be made his footstool. ¹⁴ For by one sacrifice he has made perfect forever those who are being made holy.

¹⁵ The Holy Spirit also testifies to us about this. First he says:

Why was only one sacrifice necessary? (9:26–27) Christ, because he was sinless, only had to die once as the perfect sacrifice for all sin.

ᵃ 7 Psalm 40:6-8 (see Septuagint)

16 "This is the covenant I will make with them
    after that time, says the Lord.
I will put my laws in their hearts,
    and I will write them on their minds."[a]

17 Then he adds:

"Their sins and lawless acts
    I will remember no more."[b]

18 And where these have been forgiven, sacrifice for sin is no longer necessary.

A CALL TO PERSEVERE IN FAITH

19 Therefore, brothers and sisters, since we have confidence to enter the Most Holy Place by the blood of Jesus, 20 by a new and living way opened for us through the curtain, that is, his body, 21 and since we have a great priest over the house of God, 22 let us draw near to God with a sincere heart and with the full assurance that faith brings, having our hearts sprinkled to cleanse us from a guilty conscience and having our bodies washed with pure water. 23 Let us hold unswervingly to the hope we profess, for he who promised is faithful. 24 And let us consider how we may spur one another on toward love and good deeds, 25 not giving up meeting together, as some are in the habit of doing, but encouraging one another—and all the more as you see the Day approaching.

26 If we deliberately keep on sinning after we have received the knowledge of the truth, no sacrifice for sins is left, 27 but only a fearful expectation of judgment and of raging fire that will consume the enemies of God. 28 Anyone who rejected the law of Moses died without mercy on the testimony of two or three witnesses. 29 How much more severely do you think someone deserves to be punished who has trampled the Son of God underfoot, who has treated as an unholy thing the blood of the covenant that sanctified them, and who has insulted the Spirit of grace? 30 For we know him who said, "It is mine to avenge; I will repay,"[c] and again, "The Lord will judge his people."[d] 31 It is a dreadful thing to fall into the hands of the living God.

32 Remember those earlier days after you had received the light, when you endured in a great conflict full of suffering. 33 Sometimes you were publicly exposed to insult and persecution; at other times you stood side by side with those who were so treated. 34 You suffered along with those in prison and joyfully accepted the confiscation of your property, because you knew that you yourselves had better and lasting possessions. 35 So do not throw away your confidence; it will be richly rewarded.

36 You need to persevere so that when you have done the will of God, you will receive what he has promised. 37 For,

"In just a little while,
    he who is coming will come
    and will not delay."[e]

How can we draw near to God? (10:22)
First, a person should have a sincere heart devoted only to God. Second, a person should have full assurance of faith and no second thoughts about trusting Jesus. Third, a person should have a conscience free from guilt because of Christ's sacrifice. Fourth, a person's heart should be washed of sin as symbolized by baptism.

How had these Christians acted when they first became believers? (10:32–34)
They had stood firm in the faith and suffered insults and persecution. They also sympathized with fellow believers and willingly accepted the loss of possessions. The author encouraged them to regain their early confidence and enthusiasm.

[a] 16 Jer. 31:33   [b] 17 Jer. 31:34   [c] 30 Deut. 32:35   [d] 30 Deut. 32:36; Psalm 135:14   [e] 37 Isaiah 26:20; Hab. 2:3

³⁸And,

> "But my righteous*ᵃ* one will live by faith.
> And I take no pleasure
> in the one who shrinks back."*ᵇ*

³⁹But we do not belong to those who shrink back and are destroyed, but to those who have faith and are saved.

FAITH IN ACTION

11 Now faith is confidence in what we hope for and assurance about what we do not see. ²This is what the ancients were commended for.

³By faith we understand that the universe was formed at God's command, so that what is seen was not made out of what is visible.

⁴By faith Abel brought God a better offering than Cain did. By faith he was commended as righteous, when God spoke well of his offerings. And by faith Abel still speaks, even though he is dead.

⁵By faith Enoch was taken from this life, so that he did not experience death: "He could not be found, because God had taken him away."*ᶜ* For before he was taken, he was commended as one who pleased God. ⁶And without faith it is impossible to please God, because anyone who comes to him must believe that he exists and that he rewards those who earnestly seek him.

⁷By faith Noah, when warned about things not yet seen, in holy fear built an ark to save his family. By his faith he condemned the world and became heir of the righteousness that is in keeping with faith.

⁸By faith Abraham, when called to go to a place he would later receive as his inheritance, obeyed and went, even though he did not know where he was going. ⁹By faith he made his home in the promised land like a stranger in a foreign country; he lived in tents, as did Isaac and Jacob, who were heirs with him of the same promise. ¹⁰For he was looking forward to the city with foundations, whose architect and builder is God. ¹¹And by faith even Sarah, who was past childbearing age, was enabled to bear children because she*ᵈ* considered

Why is it impossible to please God without faith? (11:6)
If we don't have faith, we don't love God or believe in his promises. A faithless person is an enemy of God.

ᵃ 38 Some early manuscripts *But the righteous*   *ᵇ 38* Hab. 2:4 (see Septuagint)   *ᶜ 5* Gen. 5:24   *ᵈ 11* Or *By faith Abraham, even though he was too old to have children—and Sarah herself was not able to conceive—was enabled to become a father because he*

What is faith?

Faith is the response of a believer to God's revelation of himself. A person who has faith believes that everything that the Bible teaches about God is completely true and trustworthy. But faith is more than knowledge of the Bible and belief that it is true. Faith is also the assurance the Holy Spirit creates in the heart of believers that God has saved them by grace through the sacrifice of Jesus. Our faith as Christians convinces us that our sins have been forgiven and that we are part of God's family forever.

Faith is not something that we create for ourselves; it is a gift of the Holy Spirit who works in our hearts. And true faith changes the way we live. If we truly believe that Jesus has saved us from our sins, then we will accept God's promises and live lives that honor him. We will love God and our fellow human beings, and we will allow the Holy Spirit to help us become the kinds of people that God wants us to be.

him faithful who had made the promise. ¹²And so from this one man, and he as good as dead, came descendants as numerous as the stars in the sky and as countless as the sand on the seashore.

¹³All these people were still living by faith when they died. They did not receive the things promised; they only saw them and welcomed them from a distance, admitting that they were foreigners and strangers on earth. ¹⁴People who say such things show that they are looking for a country of their own. ¹⁵If they had been thinking of the country they had left, they would have had opportunity to return. ¹⁶Instead, they were longing for a better country—a heavenly one. Therefore God is not ashamed to be called their God, for he has prepared a city for them.

¹⁷By faith Abraham, when God tested him, offered Isaac as a sacrifice. He who had embraced the promises was about to sacrifice his one and only son, ¹⁸even though God had said to him, "It is through Isaac that your offspring will be reckoned."ᵃ ¹⁹Abraham reasoned that God could even raise the dead, and so in a manner of speaking he did receive Isaac back from death.

²⁰By faith Isaac blessed Jacob and Esau in regard to their future.

²¹By faith Jacob, when he was dying, blessed each of Joseph's sons, and worshiped as he leaned on the top of his staff.

²²By faith Joseph, when his end was near, spoke about the exodus of the Israelites from Egypt and gave instructions concerning the burial of his bones.

²³By faith Moses' parents hid him for three months after he was born, because they saw he was no ordinary child, and they were not afraid of the king's edict.

²⁴By faith Moses, when he had grown up, refused to be known as the son of Pharaoh's daughter. ²⁵He chose to be mistreated along with the people of God rather than to enjoy the fleeting pleasures of sin. ²⁶He regarded disgrace for the sake of Christ as of greater value than the treasures of Egypt, because he was looking ahead to his reward. ²⁷By faith he left Egypt, not fearing the king's anger; he persevered because he saw him who is invisible. ²⁸By faith he kept the Passover and the application of blood, so that the destroyer of the firstborn would not touch the firstborn of Israel.

²⁹By faith the people passed through the Red Sea as on dry land; but when the Egyptians tried to do so, they were drowned.

³⁰By faith the walls of Jericho fell, after the army had marched around them for seven days.

³¹By faith the prostitute Rahab, because she welcomed the spies, was not killed with those who were disobedient.ᵇ

³²And what more shall I say? I do not have time to tell about Gideon, Barak, Samson and Jephthah, about David and Samuel and the prophets, ³³who through faith conquered kingdoms, administered justice, and gained what was promised; who shut the mouths of lions, ³⁴quenched

Did Moses believe in Christ? (11:24–26)
Moses' understanding of the coming Messiah was limited, but he believed God's promises to redeem his people, which pointed toward the coming of Christ.

ᵃ 18 Gen. 21:12   ᵇ 31 Or unbelieving

the fury of the flames, and escaped the edge of the sword; whose weakness was turned to strength; and who became powerful in battle and routed foreign armies. [35]Women received back their dead, raised to life again. There were others who were tortured, refusing to be released so that they might gain an even better resurrection. [36]Some faced jeers and flogging, and even chains and imprisonment. [37]They were put to death by stoning;[a] they were sawed in two; they were killed by the sword. They went about in sheepskins and goatskins, destitute, persecuted and mistreated— [38]the world was not worthy of them. They wandered in deserts and mountains, living in caves and in holes in the ground.

[39]These were all commended for their faith, yet none of them received what had been promised, [40]since God had planned something better for us so that only together with us would they be made perfect.

12 Therefore, since we are surrounded by such a great cloud of witnesses, let us throw off everything that hinders and the sin that so easily entangles. And let us run with perseverance the race marked out for us, [2]fixing our eyes on Jesus, the pioneer and perfecter of faith. For the joy set before him he endured the cross, scorning its shame, and sat down at the right hand of the throne of God. [3]Consider him who endured such opposition from sinners, so that you will not grow weary and lose heart.

GOD DISCIPLINES HIS CHILDREN

[4]In your struggle against sin, you have not yet resisted to the point of shedding your blood. [5]And have you completely forgotten this word of encouragement that addresses you as a father addresses his son? It says,

"My son, do not make light of the Lord's discipline,
    and do not lose heart when he rebukes you,
[6]because the Lord disciplines the one he loves,
    and he chastens everyone he accepts as his son."[b]

[7]Endure hardship as discipline; God is treating you as his children. For what children are not disciplined by their father? [8]If you are not disciplined—and everyone undergoes discipline—then you are not legitimate, not true sons and daughters at all. [9]Moreover, we have all had human fathers who disciplined us and we respected them for it. How much more should we submit to the Father of spirits and live! [10]They disciplined us for a little while as they thought best; but God disciplines us for our good, in order that we may share in his holiness. [11]No discipline seems pleasant at the time, but painful. Later on, however, it produces a harvest of righteousness and peace for those who have been trained by it.

[12]Therefore, strengthen your feeble arms and weak knees. [13]"Make level paths for your feet,"[c] so that the lame may not be disabled, but rather healed.

Did these heroes of faith receive what they hoped for? (11:39–40)
They did not all receive what they hoped for during their lifetime, but they continued to live by faith. They believed God's promises, which God fulfilled through Christ.

Who were these witnesses? (12:1)
The image is of an athletic contest in an amphitheater. The witnesses are the heroes of faith described in the previous chapter. They are not the spectators but inspiring examples.

How did the author encourage these Christians to put up with hardship? (12:7–11)
He said that hardship was a form of discipline and that discipline can help people to become more godly (spiritually mature) and give them peace.

[a] 37 Some early manuscripts *stoning; they were put to the test;*
[b] 5,6 Prov. 3:11,12 (see Septuagint)   [c] 13 Prov. 4:26

WARNING AND ENCOURAGEMENT

[14] Make every effort to live in peace with everyone and to be holy; without holiness no one will see the Lord. [15] See to it that no one falls short of the grace of God and that no bitter root grows up to cause trouble and defile many. [16] See that no one is sexually immoral, or is godless like Esau, who for a single meal sold his inheritance rights as the oldest son. [17] Afterward, as you know, when he wanted to inherit this blessing, he was rejected. Even though he sought the blessing with tears, he could not change what he had done.

THE MOUNTAIN OF FEAR
AND THE MOUNTAIN OF JOY

[18] You have not come to a mountain that can be touched and that is burning with fire; to darkness, gloom and storm; [19] to a trumpet blast or to such a voice speaking words that those who heard it begged that no further word be spoken to them, [20] because they could not bear what was commanded: "If even an animal touches the mountain, it must be stoned to death."[a] [21] The sight was so terrifying that Moses said, "I am trembling with fear."[b]

[22] But you have come to Mount Zion, to the city of the living God, the heavenly Jerusalem. You have come to thousands upon thousands of angels in joyful assembly, [23] to the church of the firstborn, whose names are written in heaven. You have come to God, the Judge of all, to the spirits of the righteous made perfect, [24] to Jesus the mediator of a new covenant, and to the sprinkled blood that speaks a better word than the blood of Abel.

[25] See to it that you do not refuse him who speaks. If they did not escape when they refused him who warned them on earth, how much less will we, if we turn away from him who warns us from heaven? [26] At that time his voice shook the earth, but now he has promised, "Once more I will shake not only the earth but also the heavens."[c] [27] The words "once more" indicate the removing of what can be shaken — that is, created things — so that what cannot be shaken may remain.

[28] Therefore, since we are receiving a kingdom that cannot be shaken, let us be thankful, and so worship God acceptably with reverence and awe, [29] for our "God is a consuming fire."[d]

CONCLUDING EXHORTATIONS

13 Keep on loving one another as brothers and sisters. [2] Do not forget to show hospitality to strangers, for by so doing some people have shown hospitality to angels without knowing it. [3] Continue to remember those in prison as if you were together with them in prison, and those who are mistreated as if you yourselves were suffering.

[4] Marriage should be honored by all, and the marriage bed kept pure, for God will judge the adulterer and all the sexually immoral. [5] Keep your lives free from the love of money and be content with what you have, because God has said,

---

What mountain was this? (12:18–21)
This was Mount Sinai where Moses received the law from God (see Exodus 19:12–22). Just as the people were terrified in God's presence, the law of the old covenant inspired fear because people could not obey it perfectly.

When will this shaking take place? (12:26–27)
This will happen at the end of time when Christ returns to judge the world.

Why were they told to show hospitality to strangers? (13:2)
Travelers in ancient times depended on the hospitality of others who would provide them with a place to sleep and with a meal. The author reminded them that some people such as Abraham and Gideon had shown hospitality to individuals who turned out to be angels.

---

[a] 20 Exodus 19:12,13   [b] 21 See Deut. 9:19.   [c] 26 Haggai 2:6
[d] 29 Deut. 4:24

"Never will I leave you;
  never will I forsake you."[a]

⁶So we say with confidence,

"The Lord is my helper; I will not be afraid.
  What can mere mortals do to me?"[b]

⁷Remember your leaders, who spoke the word of God to you. Consider the outcome of their way of life and imitate their faith. ⁸Jesus Christ is the same yesterday and today and forever.

⁹Do not be carried away by all kinds of strange teachings. It is good for our hearts to be strengthened by grace, not by eating ceremonial foods, which is of no benefit to those who do so. ¹⁰We have an altar from which those who minister at the tabernacle have no right to eat.

¹¹The high priest carries the blood of animals into the Most Holy Place as a sin offering, but the bodies are burned outside the camp. ¹²And so Jesus also suffered outside the city gate to make the people holy through his own blood. ¹³Let us, then, go to him outside the camp, bearing the disgrace he bore. ¹⁴For here we do not have an enduring city, but we are looking for the city that is to come.

¹⁵Through Jesus, therefore, let us continually offer to God a sacrifice of praise—the fruit of lips that openly profess his name. ¹⁶And do not forget to do good and to share with others, for with such sacrifices God is pleased.

¹⁷Have confidence in your leaders and submit to their authority, because they keep watch over you as those who must give an account. Do this so that their work will be a joy, not a burden, for that would be of no benefit to you.

¹⁸Pray for us. We are sure that we have a clear conscience and desire to live honorably in every way. ¹⁹I particularly urge you to pray so that I may be restored to you soon.

BENEDICTION AND FINAL GREETINGS

²⁰Now may the God of peace, who through the blood of the eternal covenant brought back from the dead our Lord Jesus, that great Shepherd of the sheep, ²¹equip you with everything good for doing his will, and may he work in us what is pleasing to him, through Jesus Christ, to whom be glory for ever and ever. Amen.

²²Brothers and sisters, I urge you to bear with my word of exhortation, for in fact I have written to you quite briefly.

²³I want you to know that our brother Timothy has been released. If he arrives soon, I will come with him to see you.

²⁴Greet all your leaders and all the Lord's people. Those from Italy send you their greetings.

²⁵Grace be with you all.

Why was Jesus compared to the remains of sacrificed animals? (13:11–14)
The bodies of sacrificed animals were burned in a location outside of the city. Jesus was crucified outside the city and served as a sacrifice for the sins of the human race. Going to Jesus outside of the camp is a symbol of leaving Judaism behind in order to follow Christ.

Who were these leaders? (13:17)
The original Christian leaders had died (see verse 7), and new leaders had taken their place. The believers were told to respect them and follow their teaching.

---

[a] *5* Deut. 31:6   [b] *6* Psalm 118:6,7

James

INTRODUCTION

Who wrote this book? James, the brother of Jesus, wrote this book.

Why was this book written? The book of James shows Christians how to practice their faith in Jesus.

For whom was this book written? This book was written to Christians everywhere.

What are some important teachings in this book?

God does not tempt us	James 1:12 – 18
We are to do what God says	James 1:22 – 25
Don't show favoritism	James 2:1 – 13
Be careful what you say	James 3:1 – 12
Don't criticize others	James 4:11 – 12
Be patient when you suffer	James 5:7 – 11
Pray when you are sick	James 5:13 – 16

When did these things happen?

10 BC AD 1 10 20 30 40 50 60 70 80 90 100

JESUS' BIRTH (C. 6/5 BC)

JESUS' DEATH, RESURRECTION AND ASCENSION (C. AD 30)

PAUL'S CONVERSION (C. AD 35)

BOOK OF JAMES WRITTEN (C. AD 40 – 50)

COUNCIL AT JERUSALEM (C. AD 49/50)

NERO'S REIGN (AD 54 – 68)

JAMES'S DEATH (C. AD 62)

DESTRUCTION OF JERUSALEM'S TEMPLE (C. AD 70)

1 James, a servant of God and of the Lord Jesus Christ,

To the twelve tribes scattered among the nations:

Greetings.

TRIALS AND TEMPTATIONS

[2]Consider it pure joy, my brothers and sisters,[a] whenever you face trials of many kinds, [3]because you know that the testing of your faith produces perseverance. [4]Let perseverance finish its work so that you may be mature and complete, not lacking anything. [5]If any of you lacks wisdom, you should ask God, who gives generously to all without finding fault, and it will be given to you. [6]But when you ask, you must believe and not doubt, because the one who doubts is like a wave of the sea, blown and tossed by the wind. [7]That person should not expect to receive anything from the Lord. [8]Such a person is double-minded and unstable in all they do.

[9]Believers in humble circumstances ought to take pride in their high position. [10]But the rich should take pride in their humiliation — since they will pass away like a wild flower. [11]For the sun rises with scorching heat and withers the plant; its blossom falls and its beauty is destroyed. In the same way, the rich will fade away even while they go about their business.

[12]Blessed is the one who perseveres under trial because, having stood the test, that person will receive the crown of life that the Lord has promised to those who love him.

[13]When tempted, no one should say, "God is tempting me." For God cannot be tempted by evil, nor does he tempt anyone; [14]but each person is tempted when they are dragged away by their own evil desire and enticed. [15]Then, after desire has conceived, it gives birth to sin; and sin, when it is full-grown, gives birth to death.

[16]Don't be deceived, my dear brothers and sisters. [17]Every good and perfect gift is from above, coming down from the Father of the heavenly lights, who does not change like shifting shadows. [18]He chose to give us birth through the word of truth, that we might be a kind of firstfruits of all he created.

LISTENING AND DOING

[19]My dear brothers and sisters, take note of this: Everyone should be quick to listen, slow to speak and slow to become angry, [20]because human anger does not produce the righteousness that God desires. [21]Therefore, get rid of all moral filth and the evil that is so prevalent and humbly accept the word planted in you, which can save you.

[22]Do not merely listen to the word, and so deceive yourselves. Do what it says. [23]Anyone who listens to the word but does not do what it says is like someone who looks at his face in a mirror [24]and, after looking at himself, goes away and immediately forgets what he looks like. [25]But whoever looks intently into the perfect law that gives freedom, and

What was this crown? (1:12)
This was the term used for a wreath given to an athlete who won a race. The crown was made of laurel or another plant and would not last. But the crown God will award believers is a permanent one: eternal life in heaven with him.

What kind of birth is this? (1:18)
This is not the act of creation or physical birth; instead, it is the new birth God gives to believers in Christ.

How are Christians "firstfruits"? (1:18)
The first grain of a harvest was a symbol of the whole harvest that would follow. In the same way, the early Christians were a symbol of the many people throughout history who would be born again.

---

[a] 2 The Greek word for *brothers and sisters* (*adelphoi*) refers here to believers, both men and women, as part of God's family; also in verses 16 and 19; and in 2:1, 5, 14; 3:10, 12; 4:11; 5:7, 9, 10, 12, 19.

continues in it—not forgetting what they have heard, but doing it—they will be blessed in what they do.

²⁶Those who consider themselves religious and yet do not keep a tight rein on their tongues deceive themselves, and their religion is worthless. ²⁷Religion that God our Father accepts as pure and faultless is this: to look after orphans and widows in their distress and to keep oneself from being polluted by the world.

FAVORITISM FORBIDDEN

2 My brothers and sisters, believers in our glorious Lord Jesus Christ must not show favoritism. ²Suppose a man comes into your meeting wearing a gold ring and fine clothes, and a poor man in filthy old clothes also comes in. ³If you show special attention to the man wearing fine clothes and say, "Here's a good seat for you," but say to the poor man, "You stand there" or "Sit on the floor by my feet," ⁴have you not discriminated among yourselves and become judges with evil thoughts?

⁵Listen, my dear brothers and sisters: Has not God chosen those who are poor in the eyes of the world to be rich in faith and to inherit the kingdom he promised those who love him? ⁶But you have dishonored the poor. Is it not the rich who are exploiting you? Are they not the ones who are dragging you into court? ⁷Are they not the ones who are blaspheming the noble name of him to whom you belong?

⁸If you really keep the royal law found in Scripture, "Love your neighbor as yourself,"ᵃ you are doing right. ⁹But if you show favoritism, you sin and are convicted by the law as law-breakers. ¹⁰For whoever keeps the whole law and yet stumbles at just one point is guilty of breaking all of it. ¹¹For he who said, "You shall not commit adultery,"ᵇ also said, "You shall not murder."ᶜ If you do not commit adultery but do commit murder, you have become a lawbreaker.

¹²Speak and act as those who are going to be judged by the law that gives freedom, ¹³because judgment without mercy will be shown to anyone who has not been merciful. Mercy triumphs over judgment.

ᵃ *8* Lev. 19:18   ᵇ *11* Exodus 20:14; Deut. 5:18   ᶜ *11* Exodus 20:13; Deut. 5:17

What three reasons did James give for not showing favoritism to the rich? (2:5 – 13)
First, the rich oppressed those who were poor (verses 5 – 7). Second, showing favoritism was a sin that went against the law of love (verses 8 – 11). Third, God would judge those who showed favoritism (verses 12 – 13).

Are people saved by faith alone or by faith and good deeds?
JAMES 2

Ephesians 2:8 says, "For it is by grace you have been saved, through faith—and this not from yourselves, it is the gift of God." This and other passages of Scripture make it clear that it is faith alone that brings salvation, and faith is something that God creates in our hearts through the power of the Holy Spirit.

If faith is all that is necessary for salvation, why does James say that "faith by itself, if it is not accompanied by action, is dead" (2:17)? Does this mean that we need to have faith and have to do good deeds in order to be saved?

What James is saying is that if a person has faith, then he or she will demonstrate that faith by living a life that is pleasing to God. That does not mean that a Christian can obey God's laws perfectly, but it does mean that a person who truly believes in God will behave in a way that shows his or her faith. True faith is more than just agreeing that the Bible is true; it is something that changes a person's whole life. The Holy Spirit works in the heart of a believer to produce good deeds that honor God. If a person lives a life that is filled with sin, it may show that the person does not truly have faith.

FAITH AND DEEDS

[14] What good is it, my brothers and sisters, if someone claims to have faith but has no deeds? Can such faith save them? [15] Suppose a brother or a sister is without clothes and daily food. [16] If one of you says to them, "Go in peace; keep warm and well fed," but does nothing about their physical needs, what good is it? [17] In the same way, faith by itself, if it is not accompanied by action, is dead.

[18] But someone will say, "You have faith; I have deeds."

Show me your faith without deeds, and I will show you my faith by my deeds. [19] You believe that there is one God. Good! Even the demons believe that—and shudder.

[20] You foolish person, do you want evidence that faith without deeds is useless[a]? [21] Was not our father Abraham considered righteous for what he did when he offered his son Isaac on the altar? [22] You see that his faith and his actions were working together, and his faith was made complete by what he did. [23] And the scripture was fulfilled that says, "Abraham believed God, and it was credited to him as righteousness,"[b] and he was called God's friend. [24] You see that a person is considered righteous by what they do and not by faith alone.

[25] In the same way, was not even Rahab the prostitute considered righteous for what she did when she gave lodging to the spies and sent them off in a different direction? [26] As the body without the spirit is dead, so faith without deeds is dead.

TAMING THE TONGUE

3 Not many of you should become teachers, my fellow believers, because you know that we who teach will be judged more strictly. [2] We all stumble in many ways. Anyone who is never at fault in what they say is perfect, able to keep their whole body in check.

[3] When we put bits into the mouths of horses to make them obey us, we can turn the whole animal. [4] Or take ships as an example. Although they are so large and are driven by strong winds, they are steered by a very small rudder wherever the pilot wants to go. [5] Likewise, the tongue is a small part of the body, but it makes great boasts. Consider what a great forest is set on fire by a small spark. [6] The tongue also is a fire, a world of evil among the parts of the body. It corrupts the whole body, sets the whole course of one's life on fire, and is itself set on fire by hell.

[7] All kinds of animals, birds, reptiles and sea creatures are being tamed and have been tamed by mankind, [8] but no human being can tame the tongue. It is a restless evil, full of deadly poison.

[9] With the tongue we praise our Lord and Father, and with it we curse human beings, who have been made in God's likeness. [10] Out of the same mouth come praise and cursing. My brothers and sisters, this should not be. [11] Can both fresh water and salt water flow from the same spring? [12] My brothers and sisters, can a fig tree bear olives, or a grapevine bear figs? Neither can a salt spring produce fresh water.

[a] *20* Some early manuscripts *dead*   [b] *23* Gen. 15:6

Can faith and good deeds exist independently? (2:17–18)
James said that faith and deeds must accompany each other. Faith without actions is dead. When we have faith, we are eager to do good deeds.

How did Abraham serve as an example of faith and deeds? (2:20–24)
Abraham believed God's promises and obeyed God by being willing to offer his son Isaac as a sacrifice. God considered Abraham righteous because of his faith-inspired actions.

Are some people judged more strictly than others? (3:1)
James said that people who have greater responsibility and influence will be judged according to how they use that power. Because teachers or ministers can shape people's beliefs, they are held to a higher standard.

Is it really impossible to tame the tongue? (3:7–12)
The tongue is able to cause great harm. James says that cursing other people is like cursing God because people have been made in God's likeness. Because of sin, no one is able to speak or act perfectly. But when God is working in Christians' lives, they are better able to use their tongues to praise God and build up others.

What is wisdom? (3:13–18)
James said that real wisdom shows itself in good deeds, not in evil actions. The qualities of true wisdom are listed in verse 17.

TWO KINDS OF WISDOM

¹³Who is wise and understanding among you? Let them show it by their good life, by deeds done in the humility that comes from wisdom. ¹⁴But if you harbor bitter envy and selfish ambition in your hearts, do not boast about it or deny the truth. ¹⁵Such "wisdom" does not come down from heaven but is earthly, unspiritual, demonic. ¹⁶For where you have envy and selfish ambition, there you find disorder and every evil practice.

¹⁷But the wisdom that comes from heaven is first of all pure; then peace-loving, considerate, submissive, full of mercy and good fruit, impartial and sincere. ¹⁸Peacemakers who sow in peace reap a harvest of righteousness.

SUBMIT YOURSELVES TO GOD

4 What causes fights and quarrels among you? Don't they come from your desires that battle within you? ²You desire but do not have, so you kill. You covet but you cannot get what you want, so you quarrel and fight. You do not have because you do not ask God. ³When you ask, you do not receive, because you ask with wrong motives, that you may spend what you get on your pleasures.

Why does James speak so strongly against friendship with the world? (4:4)
Here *world* is not referring to the whole of creation (including human beings). Instead, it's referring to an attitude of rebellion against God and his laws. James said that becoming friendly with the sinful world is like committing adultery toward God.

⁴You adulterous people,^a don't you know that friendship with the world means enmity against God? Therefore, anyone who chooses to be a friend of the world becomes an enemy of God. ⁵Or do you think Scripture says without reason that he jealously longs for the spirit he has caused to dwell in us^b? ⁶But he gives us more grace. That is why Scripture says:

> "God opposes the proud
> 　but shows favor to the humble."^c

⁷Submit yourselves, then, to God. Resist the devil, and he will flee from you. ⁸Come near to God and he will come near to you. Wash your hands, you sinners, and purify your hearts, you double-minded. ⁹Grieve, mourn and wail. Change your laughter to mourning and your joy to gloom. ¹⁰Humble yourselves before the Lord, and he will lift you up.

What is slander, and why is it wrong? (4:11–12)
Slander is saying false things about another person. More broadly, it is speaking critically or negatively about someone behind their back. Jesus said that we are to love God and our neighbor. If we use speech in a hateful or hurtful way, we are not acting out of love.

¹¹Brothers and sisters, do not slander one another. Anyone who speaks against a brother or sister^d or judges them speaks against the law and judges it. When you judge the law, you are not keeping it, but sitting in judgment on it. ¹²There is only one Lawgiver and Judge, the one who is able to save and destroy. But you—who are you to judge your neighbor?

BOASTING ABOUT TOMORROW

Is it wrong to make plans? (4:13–15)
Planning ahead is something the Bible encourages. The problem comes if our plans don't take into account God's will. We need to realize that God is in charge, and our plans should reflect the godly way he wants us to live.

¹³Now listen, you who say, "Today or tomorrow we will go to this or that city, spend a year there, carry on business and make money." ¹⁴Why, you do not even know what will happen tomorrow. What is your life? You are a mist that appears for a little while and then vanishes. ¹⁵Instead, you ought to say, "If it is the Lord's will, we will live and do this or that." ¹⁶As it is, you boast in your arrogant schemes. All

---

^a 4 An allusion to covenant unfaithfulness; see Hosea 3:1.　　^b 5 Or *that the spirit he caused to dwell in us envies intensely*; or *that the Spirit he caused to dwell in us longs jealously*　　^c 6 Prov. 3:34　　^d 11 The Greek word for *brother or sister* (*adelphos*) refers here to a believer, whether man or woman, as part of God's family.

such boasting is evil. ¹⁷If anyone, then, knows the good they ought to do and doesn't do it, it is sin for them.

WARNING TO RICH OPPRESSORS

5 Now listen, you rich people, weep and wail because of the misery that is coming on you. ²Your wealth has rotted, and moths have eaten your clothes. ³Your gold and silver are corroded. Their corrosion will testify against you and eat your flesh like fire. You have hoarded wealth in the last days. ⁴Look! The wages you failed to pay the workers who mowed your fields are crying out against you. The cries of the harvesters have reached the ears of the Lord Almighty. ⁵You have lived on earth in luxury and self-indulgence. You have fattened yourselves in the day of slaughter.ᵃ ⁶You have condemned and murdered the innocent one, who was not opposing you.

PATIENCE IN SUFFERING

⁷Be patient, then, brothers and sisters, until the Lord's coming. See how the farmer waits for the land to yield its valuable crop, patiently waiting for the autumn and spring rains. ⁸You too, be patient and stand firm, because the Lord's coming is near. ⁹Don't grumble against one another, brothers and sisters, or you will be judged. The Judge is standing at the door!

¹⁰Brothers and sisters, as an example of patience in the face of suffering, take the prophets who spoke in the name of the Lord. ¹¹As you know, we count as blessed those who have persevered. You have heard of Job's perseverance and have seen what the Lord finally brought about. The Lord is full of compassion and mercy.

¹²Above all, my brothers and sisters, do not swear—not by heaven or by earth or by anything else. All you need to say is a simple "Yes" or "No." Otherwise you will be condemned.

THE PRAYER OF FAITH

¹³Is anyone among you in trouble? Let them pray. Is anyone happy? Let them sing songs of praise. ¹⁴Is anyone among you sick? Let them call the elders of the church to pray over them and anoint them with oil in the name of the Lord. ¹⁵And the prayer offered in faith will make the sick person well; the Lord will raise them up. If they have sinned, they will be forgiven. ¹⁶Therefore confess your sins to each other and pray for each other so that you may be healed. The prayer of a righteous person is powerful and effective.

¹⁷Elijah was a human being, even as we are. He prayed earnestly that it would not rain, and it did not rain on the land for three and a half years. ¹⁸Again he prayed, and the heavens gave rain, and the earth produced its crops.

¹⁹My brothers and sisters, if one of you should wander from the truth and someone should bring that person back, ²⁰remember this: Whoever turns a sinner from the error of their way will save them from death and cover over a multitude of sins.

ᵃ 5 Or *yourselves as in a day of feasting*

Why was James so critical of rich people? (5:1–6)
The Bible doesn't say that it's wrong to be well off. But it is full of warnings about the danger of loving money and using it selfishly. Here James criticized greedy people who exploited their workers by not paying a fair wage. This is something that God judges harshly.

Why does Paul urge the poor to be patient? (5:7)
James urged the poor who were being taken advantage of to develop patience. He wanted them to look forward to the return of Christ. Knowing that Christ is coming again makes suffering easier to bear.

Is it wrong for Christians to take an oath? (5:12)
James wasn't criticizing promises to tell the truth in court or taking an oath of office. Instead, he was speaking against the practice of making casual oaths either in God's name or in the name of something else. Christians should always speak the truth without oaths.

Will prayer always lead to healing? (5:15–16)
It is important to ask God for healing, but many Christians continue to have health problems and Christians continue to die. That doesn't mean that they didn't pray hard enough or that God didn't hear their prayers. The term James used isn't a medical term. Instead, he used a word that means *made whole* and *forgiven*. Of course we want to be healthy, but our highest goal ought to be becoming right with God. Even if God doesn't heal our bodies, he will forgive our sins if we ask in faith.

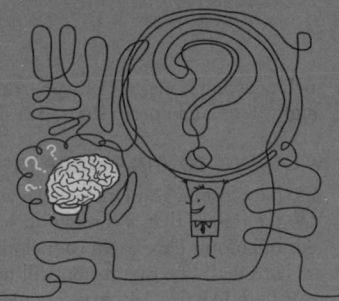

1 Peter

INTRODUCTION

Who wrote this book? Peter, the disciple of Jesus, wrote this book.

Why was this book written? The book of 1 Peter encourages Christians to live holy lives in spite of suffering.

For whom was this book written? This book is a letter sent to Christians everywhere.

What are some important teachings in this book?

Faith is precious	1 Peter 1:3 – 9
God chose us	1 Peter 2:9 – 12
Love each other	1 Peter 3:8 – 12
Suffering as Christians	1 Peter 4:12 – 19
Be humble	1 Peter 5:6 – 11

When did these things happen?

10 BC   AD 1   10   20   30   40   50   60   70   80   90   100

JESUS' BIRTH (C. 6/5 BC)

PETER BECOMES A DISCIPLE (C. AD 26)

JESUS' DEATH, RESURRECTION AND ASCENSION (C. AD 30)

PAUL'S CONVERSION (C. AD 35)

COUNCIL AT JERUSALEM (C. AD 49/50)

NERO'S REIGN (AD 54 – 68)

BOOK OF 1 PETER WRITTEN (C. AD 60 – 64)

DESTRUCTION OF JERUSALEM'S TEMPLE (C. AD 70)

1 Peter, an apostle of Jesus Christ,

To God's elect, exiles scattered throughout the provinces of Pontus, Galatia, Cappadocia, Asia and Bithynia, ²who have been chosen according to the foreknowledge of God the Father, through the sanctifying work of the Spirit, to be obedient to Jesus Christ and sprinkled with his blood:

Grace and peace be yours in abundance.

PRAISE TO GOD FOR A LIVING HOPE

³Praise be to the God and Father of our Lord Jesus Christ! In his great mercy he has given us new birth into a living hope through the resurrection of Jesus Christ from the dead, ⁴and into an inheritance that can never perish, spoil or fade. This inheritance is kept in heaven for you, ⁵who through faith are shielded by God's power until the coming of the salvation that is ready to be revealed in the last time. ⁶In all this you greatly rejoice, though now for a little while you may have had to suffer grief in all kinds of trials. ⁷These have come so that the proven genuineness of your faith—of greater worth than gold, which perishes even though refined

REGIONS PETER ADDRESSED (1:1)

Whose words did Peter echo
in this verse? (1:8)
Peter's words are like the words
spoken by Jesus to Thomas (see
John 20:29). Peter was present
when Jesus spoke these words.

by fire—may result in praise, glory and honor when Jesus
Christ is revealed. [8]Though you have not seen him, you love
him; and even though you do not see him now, you believe
in him and are filled with an inexpressible and glorious joy,
[9]for you are receiving the end result of your faith, the salvation of your souls.

[10]Concerning this salvation, the prophets, who spoke of
the grace that was to come to you, searched intently and with
the greatest care, [11]trying to find out the time and circumstances to which the Spirit of Christ in them was pointing
when he predicted the sufferings of the Messiah and the
glories that would follow. [12]It was revealed to them that they
were not serving themselves but you, when they spoke of
the things that have now been told you by those who have
preached the gospel to you by the Holy Spirit sent from
heaven. Even angels long to look into these things.

BE HOLY

[13]Therefore, with minds that are alert and fully sober, set
your hope on the grace to be brought to you when Jesus
Christ is revealed at his coming. [14]As obedient children, do
not conform to the evil desires you had when you lived in
ignorance. [15]But just as he who called you is holy, so be holy
in all you do; [16]for it is written: "Be holy, because I am holy."[a]

[17]Since you call on a Father who judges each person's work
impartially, live out your time as foreigners here in reverent
fear. [18]For you know that it was not with perishable things
such as silver or gold that you were redeemed from the empty way of life handed down to you from your ancestors, [19]but
with the precious blood of Christ, a lamb without blemish
or defect. [20]He was chosen before the creation of the world,
but was revealed in these last times for your sake. [21]Through
him you believe in God, who raised him from the dead and
glorified him, and so your faith and hope are in God.

[22]Now that you have purified yourselves by obeying the
truth so that you have sincere love for each other, love one
another deeply, from the heart.[b] [23]For you have been born
again, not of perishable seed, but of imperishable, through
the living and enduring word of God. [24]For,

"All people are like grass,
    and all their glory is like the flowers of the field;
the grass withers and the flowers fall,
[25]   but the word of the Lord endures forever."[c]

And this is the word that was preached to you.

2 Therefore, rid yourselves of all malice and all deceit, hypocrisy, envy, and slander of every kind. [2]Like newborn
babies, crave pure spiritual milk, so that by it you may grow
up in your salvation, [3]now that you have tasted that the Lord
is good.

THE LIVING STONE AND A CHOSEN PEOPLE

[4]As you come to him, the living Stone—rejected by humans but chosen by God and precious to him— [5]you also,

What does it mean to be
"redeemed"? (1:18)
To redeem means to free from
captivity. In the Greek world, a
slave could be freed by paying a
price (or ransom) to the master.
Jesus redeemed his people from
death by paying the price for
their sins with his blood, like a
lamb that was sacrificed in the
Old Testament.

[a] 16 Lev. 11:44,45; 19:2   [b] 22 Some early manuscripts *from a pure heart*
[c] 25 Isaiah 40:6-8 (see Septuagint)

like living stones, are being built into a spiritual house[a] to be a holy priesthood, offering spiritual sacrifices acceptable to God through Jesus Christ. [6]For in Scripture it says:

> "See, I lay a stone in Zion,
>   a chosen and precious cornerstone,
> and the one who trusts in him
>   will never be put to shame."[b]

[7]Now to you who believe, this stone is precious. But to those who do not believe,

> "The stone the builders rejected
>   has become the cornerstone,"[c]

[8]and,

> "A stone that causes people to stumble
>   and a rock that makes them fall."[d]

They stumble because they disobey the message—which is also what they were destined for.

[9]But you are a chosen people, a royal priesthood, a holy nation, God's special possession, that you may declare the praises of him who called you out of darkness into his wonderful light. [10]Once you were not a people, but now you are the people of God; once you had not received mercy, but now you have received mercy.

LIVING GODLY LIVES IN A PAGAN SOCIETY

[11]Dear friends, I urge you, as foreigners and exiles, to abstain from sinful desires, which wage war against your soul. [12]Live such good lives among the pagans that, though they accuse you of doing wrong, they may see your good deeds and glorify God on the day he visits us.

[13]Submit yourselves for the Lord's sake to every human authority: whether to the emperor, as the supreme authority, [14]or to governors, who are sent by him to punish those who do wrong and to commend those who do right. [15]For it is God's will that by doing good you should silence the ignorant talk of foolish people. [16]Live as free people, but do not use your freedom as a cover-up for evil; live as God's slaves. [17]Show proper respect to everyone, love the family of believers, fear God, honor the emperor.

[18]Slaves, in reverent fear of God submit yourselves to your masters, not only to those who are good and considerate, but also to those who are harsh. [19]For it is commendable if someone bears up under the pain of unjust suffering because they are conscious of God. [20]But how is it to your credit if you receive a beating for doing wrong and endure it? But if you suffer for doing good and you endure it, this is commendable before God. [21]To this you were called, because Christ suffered for you, leaving you an example, that you should follow in his steps.

[22]"He committed no sin,
    and no deceit was found in his mouth."[e]

---

[a] 5 Or *into a temple of the Spirit*   [b] 6 Isaiah 28:16   [c] 7 Psalm 118:22
[d] 8 Isaiah 8:14   [e] 22 Isaiah 53:9

In what way are Christians like "living stones"? (2:5)
The Holy Spirit lives in each Christian, and God uses Christians (like spiritual stones) to form the church, which is made up of believers. The church is like a temple where God lives.

Why did Peter use the phrase "chosen people"? (2:9)
Just as God called the people of Israel his chosen people, Christians have been chosen by God in his mercy to become part of his family.

Why are Christians supposed to obey rulers and other authorities? (2:13–15)
God is the one who allows human authority and governments to exist, so obeying rulers—as long as it doesn't conflict with God's laws—is like obeying God. Also, Christians should be good citizens as an example to others.

Why were slaves told to put up with harsh treatment? (2:18–21)
Christians are called by God to follow the example of Jesus, who suffered even though he did nothing wrong. This did not mean that Peter agreed with slavery. He wanted Christian slaves to be an example to their non-Christian masters.

23 When they hurled their insults at him, he did not retaliate; when he suffered, he made no threats. Instead, he entrusted himself to him who judges justly. 24 "He himself bore our sins" in his body on the cross, so that we might die to sins and live for righteousness; "by his wounds you have been healed." 25 For "you were like sheep going astray,"[a] but now you have returned to the Shepherd and Overseer of your souls.

3 Wives, in the same way submit yourselves to your own husbands so that, if any of them do not believe the word, they may be won over without words by the behavior of their wives, 2 when they see the purity and reverence of your lives. 3 Your beauty should not come from outward adornment, such as elaborate hairstyles and the wearing of gold jewelry or fine clothes. 4 Rather, it should be that of your inner self, the unfading beauty of a gentle and quiet spirit, which is of great worth in God's sight. 5 For this is the way the holy women of the past who put their hope in God used to adorn themselves. They submitted themselves to their own husbands, 6 like Sarah, who obeyed Abraham and called him her lord. You are her daughters if you do what is right and do not give way to fear.

7 Husbands, in the same way be considerate as you live with your wives, and treat them with respect as the weaker partner and as heirs with you of the gracious gift of life, so that nothing will hinder your prayers.

SUFFERING FOR DOING GOOD

8 Finally, all of you, be like-minded, be sympathetic, love one another, be compassionate and humble. 9 Do not repay evil with evil or insult with insult. On the contrary, repay evil with blessing, because to this you were called so that you may inherit a blessing. 10 For,

"Whoever would love life
    and see good days
must keep their tongue from evil
    and their lips from deceitful speech.
11 They must turn from evil and do good;
    they must seek peace and pursue it.
12 For the eyes of the Lord are on the righteous
    and his ears are attentive to their prayer,
but the face of the Lord is against those who do evil."[b]

13 Who is going to harm you if you are eager to do good? 14 But even if you should suffer for what is right, you are blessed. "Do not fear their threats[c]; do not be frightened."[d] 15 But in your hearts revere Christ as Lord. Always be prepared to give an answer to everyone who asks you to give the reason for the hope that you have. But do this with gentleness and respect, 16 keeping a clear conscience, so that those who speak maliciously against your good behavior in Christ may be ashamed of their slander. 17 For it is better, if it is God's will, to suffer for doing good than for doing evil. 18 For Christ also suffered once for sins, the righteous for the un-

Why were wives to be submissive to their husbands? (3:1)
This is similar to Peter's instructions about citizens submitting to governments or slaves submitting to masters. Peter said that, in this way, women who were married to unbelievers might win their husbands to faith.

How should Christians behave if they are mistreated? (3:9)
Peter said that believers should not seek revenge but should show kindness even to those who treat them poorly. His instructions are similar to many of Jesus' instructions (for example, see Luke 6:29).

a 24,25 Isaiah 53:4,5,6 (see Septuagint)   b 12 Psalm 34:12-16
c 14 Or fear what they fear   d 14 Isaiah 8:12

righteous, to bring you to God. He was put to death in the body but made alive in the Spirit. [19] After being made alive,[a] he went and made proclamation to the imprisoned spirits— [20] to those who were disobedient long ago when God waited patiently in the days of Noah while the ark was being built. In it only a few people, eight in all, were saved through water, [21] and this water symbolizes baptism that now saves you also—not the removal of dirt from the body but the pledge of a clear conscience toward God.[b] It saves you by the resurrection of Jesus Christ, [22] who has gone into heaven and is at God's right hand—with angels, authorities and powers in submission to him.

LIVING FOR GOD

4 Therefore, since Christ suffered in his body, arm yourselves also with the same attitude, because whoever suffers in the body is done with sin. [2] As a result, they do not live the rest of their earthly lives for evil human desires, but rather for the will of God. [3] For you have spent enough time in the past doing what pagans choose to do—living in debauchery, lust, drunkenness, orgies, carousing and detestable idolatry. [4] They are surprised that you do not join them in their reckless, wild living, and they heap abuse on you. [5] But they will have to give account to him who is ready to judge the living and the dead. [6] For this is the reason the gospel was preached even to those who are now dead, so that they might be judged according to human standards in regard to the body, but live according to God in regard to the spirit.

[7] The end of all things is near. Therefore be alert and of sober mind so that you may pray. [8] Above all, love each other deeply, because love covers over a multitude of sins. [9] Offer hospitality to one another without grumbling. [10] Each of you should use whatever gift you have received to serve others, as faithful stewards of God's grace in its various forms. [11] If anyone speaks, they should do so as one who speaks the very words of God. If anyone serves, they should do so with the strength God provides, so that in all things God may be praised through Jesus Christ. To him be the glory and the power for ever and ever. Amen.

SUFFERING FOR BEING A CHRISTIAN

[12] Dear friends, do not be surprised at the fiery ordeal that has come on you to test you, as though something strange were happening to you. [13] But rejoice inasmuch as you participate in the sufferings of Christ, so that you may be overjoyed when his glory is revealed. [14] If you are insulted because of the name of Christ, you are blessed, for the Spirit of glory and of God rests on you. [15] If you suffer, it should not be as a murderer or thief or any other kind of criminal, or even as a meddler. [16] However, if you suffer as a Christian, do not be ashamed, but praise God that you bear that name. [17] For it is time for judgment to begin with God's household; and if it begins with us, what will the outcome be for those who do not obey the gospel of God? [18] And,

a 18,19 Or *but made alive in the spirit,* [19] *in which also*   b 21 Or *but an appeal to God for a clear conscience*

What is baptism? (3:21)
Baptism is a symbol for the washing away of sin but also the promise of salvation through Christ. It shows a person's commitment to following Jesus.

What did Peter mean by saying that "love covers over a multitude of sins"? (4:8)
Because Christians are called to love and to keep forgiving over and over again, love is said to cover many sins.

Why did Peter say that Christians should rejoice in their sufferings for Christ? (4:12–13)
Peter was saying something similar to what Jesus said in Matthew 5:10: "Blessed are those who are persecuted because of righteousness, for theirs is the kingdom of heaven." Those who suffer for Christ can look forward to a reward in heaven.

"If it is hard for the righteous to be saved,
what will become of the ungodly and the sinner?"[a]

¹⁹So then, those who suffer according to God's will should commit themselves to their faithful Creator and continue to do good.

TO THE ELDERS AND THE FLOCK

5 To the elders among you, I appeal as a fellow elder and a witness of Christ's sufferings who also will share in the glory to be revealed: ²Be shepherds of God's flock that is under your care, watching over them—not because you must, but because you are willing, as God wants you to be; not pursuing dishonest gain, but eager to serve; ³not lording it over those entrusted to you, but being examples to the flock. ⁴And when the Chief Shepherd appears, you will receive the crown of glory that will never fade away.

⁵In the same way, you who are younger, submit yourselves to your elders. All of you, clothe yourselves with humility toward one another, because,

"God opposes the proud
but shows favor to the humble."[b]

⁶Humble yourselves, therefore, under God's mighty hand, that he may lift you up in due time. ⁷Cast all your anxiety on him because he cares for you.

⁸Be alert and of sober mind. Your enemy the devil prowls around like a roaring lion looking for someone to devour. ⁹Resist him, standing firm in the faith, because you know that the family of believers throughout the world is undergoing the same kind of sufferings.

¹⁰And the God of all grace, who called you to his eternal glory in Christ, after you have suffered a little while, will himself restore you and make you strong, firm and steadfast. ¹¹To him be the power for ever and ever. Amen.

FINAL GREETINGS

¹²With the help of Silas,[c] whom I regard as a faithful brother, I have written to you briefly, encouraging you and testifying that this is the true grace of God. Stand fast in it.

¹³She who is in Babylon, chosen together with you, sends you her greetings, and so does my son Mark. ¹⁴Greet one another with a kiss of love.

Peace to all of you who are in Christ.

Why did Peter tell elders of the church to be shepherds? (5:2–4)
Jesus, who called himself the Good Shepherd, had instructed Peter to act as a shepherd (John 21:15–17). In turn, Peter told the elders that they were to be shepherds who watched over their spiritual flocks (the people of the church).

How are Christians supposed to resist the devil? (5:8–9)
Like a lion, the devil is seeking to destroy. Christians resist the devil by being self-controlled and alert to his ways and by standing firm in their faith. Christians should pray for each other for strength to withstand temptation.

---

[a] 18 Prov. 11:31 (see Septuagint)   [b] 5 Prov. 3:34   [c] 12 Greek *Silvanus*, a variant of *Silas*

2 Peter

INTRODUCTION

Who wrote this book?   Peter, the disciple of Jesus, wrote this book.

Why was this book written?   The book of 2 Peter warns Christians against false teachers.

For whom was this book written?   This book is a letter sent to Christians everywhere.

What are some important teachings in this book?

What false teachers are like   2 Peter 2:1 – 22
How the world will end   2 Peter 3:1 – 13

When did these things happen?   10 BC   AD 1   10   20   30   40   50   60   70   80   90   100

JESUS' BIRTH (C. 6/5 BC)

JESUS' DEATH, RESURRECTION AND ASCENSION (C. AD 30)

PAUL'S CONVERSION (C. AD 35)

COUNCIL AT JERUSALEM (C. AD 49/50)

NERO'S REIGN (AD 54 – 68)

BOOK OF 2 PETER WRITTEN (C. AD 65 – 68)

PETER'S DEATH (C. AD 67 – 68)

DESTRUCTION OF JERUSALEM'S TEMPLE (C. AD 70)

1 Simon Peter, a servant and apostle of Jesus Christ,

To those who through the righteousness of our God and Savior Jesus Christ have received a faith as precious as ours:

² Grace and peace be yours in abundance through the knowledge of God and of Jesus our Lord.

CONFIRMING ONE'S CALLING AND ELECTION

³ His divine power has given us everything we need for a godly life through our knowledge of him who called us by his own glory and goodness. ⁴ Through these he has given us his very great and precious promises, so that through them you may participate in the divine nature, having escaped the corruption in the world caused by evil desires.

⁵ For this very reason, make every effort to add to your faith goodness; and to goodness, knowledge; ⁶ and to knowledge, self-control; and to self-control, perseverance; and to perseverance, godliness; ⁷ and to godliness, mutual affection; and to mutual affection, love. ⁸ For if you possess these qualities in increasing measure, they will keep you from being ineffective and unproductive in your knowledge of our Lord Jesus Christ. ⁹ But whoever does not have them is nearsighted and blind, forgetting that they have been cleansed from their past sins.

¹⁰ Therefore, my brothers and sisters,ᵃ make every effort to confirm your calling and election. For if you do these things, you will never stumble, ¹¹ and you will receive a rich welcome into the eternal kingdom of our Lord and Savior Jesus Christ.

PROPHECY OF SCRIPTURE

¹² So I will always remind you of these things, even though you know them and are firmly established in the truth you now have. ¹³ I think it is right to refresh your memory as long as I live in the tent of this body, ¹⁴ because I know that I will soon put it aside, as our Lord Jesus Christ has made clear to me. ¹⁵ And I will make every effort to see that after my departure you will always be able to remember these things.

¹⁶ For we did not follow cleverly devised stories when we told you about the coming of our Lord Jesus Christ in power, but we were eyewitnesses of his majesty. ¹⁷ He received honor and glory from God the Father when the voice came to him from the Majestic Glory, saying, "This is my Son, whom I love; with him I am well pleased."ᵇ ¹⁸ We ourselves heard this voice that came from heaven when we were with him on the sacred mountain.

¹⁹ We also have the prophetic message as something completely reliable, and you will do well to pay attention to it, as to a light shining in a dark place, until the day dawns and the morning star rises in your hearts. ²⁰ Above all, you must

Why did Peter say that God has given believers everything they need to know him? (1:3)
During that time, some people had the false belief that they needed a type of secret knowledge in order to be saved. Peter said that God had provided all the knowledge of himself that they needed.

Are some of these virtues more important than others? (1:5–8)
The order of the virtues does not mean that some are more important than others. What is important is that believers develop these virtues in increasing measure.

How could Peter be so sure of the truth of his message? (1:17–21)
He was present when Jesus was transfigured, and he heard God's voice calling Jesus his Son. Peter also said that Scripture (the Old Testament) showed that Jesus was the Messiah.

ᵃ *10* The Greek word for *brothers and sisters* (*adelphoi*) refers here to believers, both men and women, as part of God's family.   ᵇ *17* Matt. 17:5; Mark 9:7; Luke 9:35

understand that no prophecy of Scripture came about by the prophet's own interpretation of things. ²¹For prophecy never had its origin in the human will, but prophets, though human, spoke from God as they were carried along by the Holy Spirit.

FALSE TEACHERS AND THEIR DESTRUCTION

2 But there were also false prophets among the people, just as there will be false teachers among you. They will secretly introduce destructive heresies, even denying the sovereign Lord who bought them — bringing swift destruction on themselves. ²Many will follow their depraved conduct and will bring the way of truth into disrepute. ³In their greed these teachers will exploit you with fabricated stories. Their condemnation has long been hanging over them, and their destruction has not been sleeping.

⁴For if God did not spare angels when they sinned, but sent them to hell,ᵃ putting them in chains of darknessᵇ to be held for judgment; ⁵if he did not spare the ancient world when he brought the flood on its ungodly people, but protected Noah, a preacher of righteousness, and seven others; ⁶if he condemned the cities of Sodom and Gomorrah by burning them to ashes, and made them an example of what is going to happen to the ungodly; ⁷and if he rescued Lot, a righteous man, who was distressed by the depraved conduct of the lawless ⁸(for that righteous man, living among them day after day, was tormented in his righteous soul by the lawless deeds he saw and heard)— ⁹if this is so, then the Lord knows how to rescue the godly from trials and to hold the unrighteous for punishment on the day of judgment. ¹⁰This is especially true of those who follow the corrupt desire of the fleshᶜ and despise authority.

Bold and arrogant, they are not afraid to heap abuse on celestial beings; ¹¹yet even angels, although they are stronger and more powerful, do not heap abuse on such beings when bringing judgment on them fromᵈ the Lord. ¹²But these people blaspheme in matters they do not understand. They are like unreasoning animals, creatures of instinct, born only to be caught and destroyed, and like animals they too will perish.

¹³They will be paid back with harm for the harm they have done. Their idea of pleasure is to carouse in broad daylight. They are blots and blemishes, reveling in their pleasures while they feast with you.ᵉ ¹⁴With eyes full of adultery, they never stop sinning; they seduce the unstable; they are experts in greed—an accursed brood! ¹⁵They have left the straight way and wandered off to follow the way of Balaam son of Bezer,ᶠ who loved the wages of wickedness. ¹⁶But he was rebuked for his wrongdoing by a donkey—an animal

How does God deal with wicked people such as false teachers? (2:9)
Wicked people face the consequences of their actions; and if they die unrepentant, they will face judgment.

What types of feasts were these? (2:13)
These were probably love feasts that took place in connection with the Lord's Supper. The wicked behaved shamefully even at these holy celebrations.

ᵃ 4 Greek *Tartarus*   ᵇ 4 Some manuscripts *in gloomy dungeons*   ᶜ 10 In contexts like this, the Greek word for *flesh* (*sarx*) refers to the sinful state of human beings, often presented as a power in opposition to the Spirit; also in verse 18.   ᵈ 11 Many manuscripts *beings in the presence of*   ᵉ 13 Some manuscripts *in their love feasts*   ᶠ 15 Greek *Bosor*

without speech—who spoke with a human voice and restrained the prophet's madness.

[17] These people are springs without water and mists driven by a storm. Blackest darkness is reserved for them. [18] For they mouth empty, boastful words and, by appealing to the lustful desires of the flesh, they entice people who are just escaping from those who live in error. [19] They promise them freedom, while they themselves are slaves of depravity—for "people are slaves to whatever has mastered them." [20] If they have escaped the corruption of the world by knowing our Lord and Savior Jesus Christ and are again entangled in it and are overcome, they are worse off at the end than they were at the beginning. [21] It would have been better for them not to have known the way of righteousness, than to have known it and then to turn their backs on the sacred command that was passed on to them. [22] Of them the proverbs are true: "A dog returns to its vomit,"[a] and, "A sow that is washed returns to her wallowing in the mud."

THE DAY OF THE LORD

3 Dear friends, this is now my second letter to you. I have written both of them as reminders to stimulate you to wholesome thinking. [2] I want you to recall the words spoken in the past by the holy prophets and the command given by our Lord and Savior through your apostles.

[3] Above all, you must understand that in the last days scoffers will come, scoffing and following their own evil desires. [4] They will say, "Where is this 'coming' he promised? Ever since our ancestors died, everything goes on as it has since the beginning of creation." [5] But they deliberately forget that long ago by God's word the heavens came into being and the earth was formed out of water and by water. [6] By these waters also the world of that time was deluged and destroyed. [7] By the same word the present heavens and earth are reserved for fire, being kept for the day of judgment and destruction of the ungodly.

[8] But do not forget this one thing, dear friends: With the Lord a day is like a thousand years, and a thousand years are like a day. [9] The Lord is not slow in keeping his promise, as some understand slowness. Instead he is patient with you, not wanting anyone to perish, but everyone to come to repentance.

[10] But the day of the Lord will come like a thief. The heavens will disappear with a roar; the elements will be destroyed by fire, and the earth and everything done in it will be laid bare.[b]

[11] Since everything will be destroyed in this way, what kind of people ought you to be? You ought to live holy and godly lives [12] as you look forward to the day of God and speed its coming.[c] That day will bring about the destruction of the heavens by fire, and the elements will melt in the heat. [13] But in keeping with his promise we are looking forward to a new heaven and a new earth, where righteousness dwells.

What did Peter mean by calling these wicked people "springs without water"? (2:17)
If a thirsty person came to a spring looking for water but found that it was dry, he or she wouldn't be satisfied. In the same way, the false teachers promised to teach the truth, but they really had nothing to offer but lies and deception.

What type of freedom did these people promise? (2:19)
They promised freedom from rules for moral behavior, but they were actually slaves of sin.

What did the scoffers doubt? (3:3–4)
Because Jesus hadn't returned, they thought he wasn't coming back. They believed that the world would continue on in the same way and that their wicked ways would not be punished.

What did Peter say about God's view of time? (3:8–9)
Peter said that God was not bound by the human understanding of time. Because God has always been and will always be, he can patiently wait to return until more people have turned to him.

How should Christians live? (3:11–13)
Christians should live holy and godly lives as they look forward to Christ's second coming, which will bring judgment for unbelievers but life in heaven for believers.

---

[a] 22 Prov. 26:11   [b] 10 Some manuscripts *be burned up*   [c] 12 Or *as you wait eagerly for the day of God to come*

¹⁴So then, dear friends, since you are looking forward to this, make every effort to be found spotless, blameless and at peace with him. ¹⁵Bear in mind that our Lord's patience means salvation, just as our dear brother Paul also wrote you with the wisdom that God gave him. ¹⁶He writes the same way in all his letters, speaking in them of these matters. His letters contain some things that are hard to understand, which ignorant and unstable people distort, as they do the other Scriptures, to their own destruction.

¹⁷Therefore, dear friends, since you have been forewarned, be on your guard so that you may not be carried away by the error of the lawless and fall from your secure position. ¹⁸But grow in the grace and knowledge of our Lord and Savior Jesus Christ. To him be glory both now and forever! Amen.

1 John

INTRODUCTION

Who wrote this book?   John, the disciple of Jesus, wrote this book.

Why was this book written?   This book shows Christians how to live close to God and other people.

For whom was this book written?   The book of 1 John is a letter John sent to Christians everywhere.

What are some important teachings in this book?

God forgives sins	1 John 1:5 – 10
God's children love others	1 John 2:7 – 11
God's children do right	1 John 3:7 – 11
Jesus shows us what love is	1 John 3:16 – 20
Love comes from God	1 John 4:7 – 11
God gives us eternal life	1 John 5:10 – 12

When did these things happen?

10 BC   AD 1   10   20   30   40   50   60   70   80   90   100

JESUS' BIRTH (C. 6/5 BC)

JOHN BECOMES A DISCIPLE (C. AD 26)

JESUS' DEATH, RESURRECTION AND ASCENSION (C. AD 30)

NERO'S REIGN (AD 54 – 68)

DESTRUCTION OF JERUSALEM'S TEMPLE (C. AD 70)

DOMITIAN'S REIGN (C. AD 81 – 96)

BOOK OF 1 JOHN WRITTEN (C. AD 85 – 95)

JOHN'S EXILE ON PATMOS (C. AD 90 – 95)

THE INCARNATION OF THE WORD OF LIFE

1 That which was from the beginning, which we have heard, which we have seen with our eyes, which we have looked at and our hands have touched—this we proclaim concerning the Word of life. ²The life appeared; we have seen it and testify to it, and we proclaim to you the eternal life, which was with the Father and has appeared to us. ³We proclaim to you what we have seen and heard, so that you also may have fellowship with us. And our fellowship is with the Father and with his Son, Jesus Christ. ⁴We write this to make our*ᵃ* joy complete.

LIGHT AND DARKNESS, SIN AND FORGIVENESS

⁵This is the message we have heard from him and declare to you: God is light; in him there is no darkness at all. ⁶If we claim to have fellowship with him and yet walk in the darkness, we lie and do not live out the truth. ⁷But if we walk in the light, as he is in the light, we have fellowship with one another, and the blood of Jesus, his Son, purifies us from all*ᵇ* sin.

⁸If we claim to be without sin, we deceive ourselves and the truth is not in us. ⁹If we confess our sins, he is faithful and just and will forgive us our sins and purify us from all unrighteousness. ¹⁰If we claim we have not sinned, we make him out to be a liar and his word is not in us.

2 My dear children, I write this to you so that you will not sin. But if anybody does sin, we have an advocate with the Father—Jesus Christ, the Righteous One. ²He is the atoning sacrifice for our sins, and not only for ours but also for the sins of the whole world.

LOVE AND HATRED FOR FELLOW BELIEVERS

³We know that we have come to know him if we keep his commands. ⁴Whoever says, "I know him," but does not do what he commands is a liar, and the truth is not in that person. ⁵But if anyone obeys his word, love for God*ᶜ* is truly made complete in them. This is how we know we are in him: ⁶Whoever claims to live in him must live as Jesus did.

⁷Dear friends, I am not writing you a new command but an old one, which you have had since the beginning. This old command is the message you have heard. ⁸Yet I am writing you a new command; its truth is seen in him and in you, because the darkness is passing and the true light is already shining.

⁹Anyone who claims to be in the light but hates a brother or sister*ᵈ* is still in the darkness. ¹⁰Anyone who loves their brother and sister*ᵉ* lives in the light, and there is nothing in them to make them stumble. ¹¹But anyone who hates a brother or sister is in the darkness and walks around in the

Why would people claim to be without sin? (1:8)
One of the false beliefs (heresies) in the early church was called Gnosticism. Among other mistaken ideas, this view included the idea that breaking God's law was not a sin because the human body was thought to be evil anyway.

Are Christians required to obey God's laws? (2:4–5)
No one can keep God's laws perfectly, but Christians obey God's laws as a way of expressing thankfulness for his gift of salvation. Faith and good works go together.

ᵃ 4 Some manuscripts *your*   *ᵇ 7* Or *every*   *ᶜ 5* Or *word, God's love*
ᵈ 9 The Greek word for *brother or sister* (*adelphos*) refers here to a believer, whether man or woman, as part of God's family; also in verse 11; and in 3:15, 17; 4:20; 5:16.   *ᵉ 10* The Greek word for *brother and sister* (*adelphos*) refers here to a believer, whether man or woman, as part of God's family; also in 3:10; 4:20, 21.

darkness. They do not know where they are going, because the darkness has blinded them.

REASONS FOR WRITING

¹²I am writing to you, dear children,
  because your sins have been forgiven on account of
    his name.
¹³I am writing to you, fathers,
  because you know him who is from the beginning.
I am writing to you, young men,
  because you have overcome the evil one.

¹⁴I write to you, dear children,
  because you know the Father.
I write to you, fathers,
  because you know him who is from the beginning.
I write to you, young men,
  because you are strong,
  and the word of God lives in you,
  and you have overcome the evil one.

ON NOT LOVING THE WORLD

¹⁵Do not love the world or anything in the world. If anyone loves the world, love for the Father*a* is not in them. ¹⁶For everything in the world—the lust of the flesh, the lust of the eyes, and the pride of life—comes not from the Father but from the world. ¹⁷The world and its desires pass away, but whoever does the will of God lives forever.

WARNINGS AGAINST DENYING THE SON

¹⁸Dear children, this is the last hour; and as you have heard that the antichrist is coming, even now many antichrists have come. This is how we know it is the last hour. ¹⁹They went out from us, but they did not really belong to us. For if they had belonged to us, they would have remained with us; but their going showed that none of them belonged to us.

²⁰But you have an anointing from the Holy One, and all of you know the truth.*b* ²¹I do not write to you because you do not know the truth, but because you do know it and because no lie comes from the truth. ²²Who is the liar? It is whoever denies that Jesus is the Christ. Such a person is the antichrist—denying the Father and the Son. ²³No one who denies the Son has the Father; whoever acknowledges the Son has the Father also.

²⁴As for you, see that what you have heard from the beginning remains in you. If it does, you also will remain in the Son and in the Father. ²⁵And this is what he promised us—eternal life.

²⁶I am writing these things to you about those who are trying to lead you astray. ²⁷As for you, the anointing you received from him remains in you, and you do not need anyone to teach you. But as his anointing teaches you about all

---

What did John mean by the "world"? (2:15)
This did not refer to the world of people or the created world. Instead, John meant the world of sin that was controlled by Satan.

Who is the antichrist? (2:18)
John's definition of an antichrist is probably anyone who opposes Jesus Christ. Some people think that before Jesus returns, a major antichrist will appear and will be an enemy of God and his people. Already in the early church there were many "antichrists." These are people who spread false teachings about God.

---

a 15 Or *world, the Father's love*   *b* 20 Some manuscripts *and you know all things*

things and as that anointing is real, not counterfeit—just as it has taught you, remain in him.

GOD'S CHILDREN AND SIN

²⁸ And now, dear children, continue in him, so that when he appears we may be confident and unashamed before him at his coming.

²⁹ If you know that he is righteous, you know that everyone who does what is right has been born of him.

3 See what great love the Father has lavished on us, that we should be called children of God! And that is what we are! The reason the world does not know us is that it did not know him. ² Dear friends, now we are children of God, and what we will be has not yet been made known. But we know that when Christ appears,ᵃ we shall be like him, for we shall see him as he is. ³ All who have this hope in him purify themselves, just as he is pure.

⁴ Everyone who sins breaks the law; in fact, sin is lawlessness. ⁵ But you know that he appeared so that he might take away our sins. And in him is no sin. ⁶ No one who lives in him keeps on sinning. No one who continues to sin has either seen him or known him.

⁷ Dear children, do not let anyone lead you astray. The one who does what is right is righteous, just as he is righteous. ⁸ The one who does what is sinful is of the devil, because the devil has been sinning from the beginning. The reason the Son of God appeared was to destroy the devil's work. ⁹ No one who is born of God will continue to sin, because God's seed remains in them; they cannot go on sinning, because they have been born of God. ¹⁰ This is how we know who the children of God are and who the children of the devil are: Anyone who does not do what is right is not God's child, nor is anyone who does not love their brother and sister.

MORE ON LOVE AND HATRED

¹¹ For this is the message you heard from the beginning: We should love one another. ¹² Do not be like Cain, who belonged to the evil one and murdered his brother. And why did he murder him? Because his own actions were evil and his brother's were righteous. ¹³ Do not be surprised, my brothers and sisters,ᵇ if the world hates you. ¹⁴ We know that we have passed from death to life, because we love each other. Anyone who does not love remains in death. ¹⁵ Anyone who hates a brother or sister is a murderer, and you know that no murderer has eternal life residing in him.

¹⁶ This is how we know what love is: Jesus Christ laid down his life for us. And we ought to lay down our lives for our brothers and sisters. ¹⁷ If anyone has material possessions and sees a brother or sister in need but has no pity on them, how can the love of God be in that person? ¹⁸ Dear children, let us not love with words or speech but with actions and in truth.

Are Christians perfect? (3:9 – 10)
No. Even Christians sin, but overall their life should not be characterized by sin but by doing what God requires. Christians strive to please God by their actions.

Whose words did John echo here? (3:15)
Jesus said that anyone who was angry with his brother was guilty of murder (see Matthew 5:21 – 22).

ᵃ *2 Or when it is made known*   ᵇ *13 The Greek word for brothers and sisters (adelphoi) refers here to believers, both men and women, as part of God's family; also in verse 16.*

¹⁹This is how we know that we belong to the truth and how we set our hearts at rest in his presence: ²⁰If our hearts condemn us, we know that God is greater than our hearts, and he knows everything. ²¹Dear friends, if our hearts do not condemn us, we have confidence before God ²²and receive from him anything we ask, because we keep his commands and do what pleases him. ²³And this is his command: to believe in the name of his Son, Jesus Christ, and to love one another as he commanded us. ²⁴The one who keeps God's commands lives in him, and he in them. And this is how we know that he lives in us: We know it by the Spirit he gave us.

ON DENYING THE INCARNATION

4 Dear friends, do not believe every spirit, but test the spirits to see whether they are from God, because many false prophets have gone out into the world. ²This is how you can recognize the Spirit of God: Every spirit that acknowledges that Jesus Christ has come in the flesh is from God, ³but every spirit that does not acknowledge Jesus is not from God. This is the spirit of the antichrist, which you have heard is coming and even now is already in the world.

⁴You, dear children, are from God and have overcome them, because the one who is in you is greater than the one who is in the world. ⁵They are from the world and therefore speak from the viewpoint of the world, and the world listens to them. ⁶We are from God, and whoever knows God listens to us; but whoever is not from God does not listen to us. This is how we recognize the Spirit^a of truth and the spirit of falsehood.

GOD'S LOVE AND OURS

⁷Dear friends, let us love one another, for love comes from God. Everyone who loves has been born of God and knows God. ⁸Whoever does not love does not know God, because God is love. ⁹This is how God showed his love among us: He sent his one and only Son into the world that we might live through him. ¹⁰This is love: not that we loved God, but that he loved us and sent his Son as an atoning sacrifice for our sins. ¹¹Dear friends, since God so loved us, we also ought to love one another. ¹²No one has ever seen God; but if we love one another, God lives in us and his love is made complete in us.

¹³This is how we know that we live in him and he in us: He has given us of his Spirit. ¹⁴And we have seen and testify that the Father has sent his Son to be the Savior of the world. ¹⁵If anyone acknowledges that Jesus is the Son of God, God lives in them and they in God. ¹⁶And so we know and rely on the love God has for us.

God is love. Whoever lives in love lives in God, and God in them. ¹⁷This is how love is made complete among us so that we will have confidence on the day of judgment: In this world we are like Jesus. ¹⁸There is no fear in love. But perfect love drives out fear, because fear has to do with punishment. The one who fears is not made perfect in love.

^a 6 Or *spirit*

Is it possible to be saved by believing in the Father but not the Son? (3:23)
No, if we deny the Son, we do not have the Father. If we believe in Jesus, we believe also in God. God is a Trinity, three person in one: the Father, Son, and Holy Spirit.

What did it mean to test the spirits? (4:1)
John wanted the believers to listen carefully to what people said about God to see if they were filled with the Holy Spirit or if they were false teachers who were filled with spirits that were not from God. Someone with the Holy Spirit acknowledges that Jesus is God.

How can Christians be confident of their salvation? (4:17)
If Christians (people who acknowledge that Jesus is the Son of God) are like Christ in their love, this is a sign that God lives in them. Therefore they can be confident that they have the gift of salvation.

[19]We love because he first loved us. [20]Whoever claims to love God yet hates a brother or sister is a liar. For whoever does not love their brother and sister, whom they have seen, cannot love God, whom they have not seen. [21]And he has given us this command: Anyone who loves God must also love their brother and sister.

FAITH IN THE INCARNATE SON OF GOD

5 Everyone who believes that Jesus is the Christ is born of God, and everyone who loves the father loves his child as well. [2]This is how we know that we love the children of God: by loving God and carrying out his commands. [3]In fact, this is love for God: to keep his commands. And his commands are not burdensome, [4]for everyone born of God overcomes the world. This is the victory that has overcome the world, even our faith. [5]Who is it that overcomes the world? Only the one who believes that Jesus is the Son of God.

[6]This is the one who came by water and blood—Jesus Christ. He did not come by water only, but by water and blood. And it is the Spirit who testifies, because the Spirit is the truth. [7]For there are three that testify: [8]the[a] Spirit, the water and the blood; and the three are in agreement. [9]We accept human testimony, but God's testimony is greater because it is the testimony of God, which he has given about his Son. [10]Whoever believes in the Son of God accepts this testimony. Whoever does not believe God has made him out to be a liar, because they have not believed the testimony God has given about his Son. [11]And this is the testimony: God has given us eternal life, and this life is in his Son. [12]Whoever has the Son has life; whoever does not have the Son of God does not have life.

CONCLUDING AFFIRMATIONS

[13]I write these things to you who believe in the name of the Son of God so that you may know that you have eternal life. [14]This is the confidence we have in approaching God: that if we ask anything according to his will, he hears us.

---

[a] 7,8 Late manuscripts of the Vulgate *testify in heaven: the Father, the Word and the Holy Spirit, and these three are one.* [8]*And there are three that testify on earth: the* (not found in any Greek manuscript before the fourteenth century)

How does this section reflect Jesus' teaching? (4:19–21)
Jesus summarized the law of God by saying that it meant to love God above all and to love our neighbor as ourselves (see Matthew 22:37–39).

Are God's commands easy to obey? (5:3)
When John said that God's commands are not "burdensome," he did not mean that they were easy. Instead, he meant that the Holy Spirit helps Christians to do God's will.

What do the water and blood symbolize? (5:6)
The water symbolizes Jesus' baptism, and the blood symbolizes his death. In this section, John was contradicting the false teaching that Jesus was only a man until his baptism, when the Holy Spirit came over him.

Why doesn't God always answer our prayers?　　1 JOHN 5

The Bible tells us to pray continually (1 Thessalonians 5:17). The Bible also says that God will hear our prayers and will answer them. If that is true, why do people still get sick and die, and why do we not have everything that we want?

God has a plan for each person, and he knows what is best for each of us. Sometimes if we ask God for something, it seems as if God is not answering our prayer. But God may be waiting to answer us in order to teach us patience. God may also answer our prayers in ways that confuse us or make us sad. We must remember that God is perfect and that in this life we may not always understand his plans.

Before Jesus was crucified, he prayed, "Father, if you are willing, take this cup from me; yet not my will, but yours be done" (Luke 22:42). God certainly heard Jesus' prayer, but Jesus still was crucified. Jesus gives us an example of trusting God. We may pray for God to do certain things, but we must also be willing to accept the fact that God's will may not be the same as ours. Regardless, we can be sure that God loves us and cares for us.

**What sin leads to death?
(5:16)**
Denying the truth about Jesus
or continuing to commit sins
without repenting can lead
to separation from God and
spiritual death.

¹⁵And if we know that he hears us—whatever we ask—we know that we have what we asked of him.

¹⁶If you see any brother or sister commit a sin that does not lead to death, you should pray and God will give them life. I refer to those whose sin does not lead to death. There is a sin that leads to death. I am not saying that you should pray about that. ¹⁷All wrongdoing is sin, and there is sin that does not lead to death.

¹⁸We know that anyone born of God does not continue to sin; the One who was born of God keeps them safe, and the evil one cannot harm them. ¹⁹We know that we are children of God, and that the whole world is under the control of the evil one. ²⁰We know also that the Son of God has come and has given us understanding, so that we may know him who is true. And we are in him who is true by being in his Son Jesus Christ. He is the true God and eternal life.

²¹Dear children, keep yourselves from idols.

2 John

INTRODUCTION

Who wrote this book? John, the disciple of Jesus, wrote this book.

Why was this book written? The book of 2 John shows Christians how to live close to God and other people.

For whom was this book written? This book is a letter John sent to Christians everywhere.

When did these things happen?

	10BC	AD1	10	20	30	40	50	60	70	80	90	100

JESUS' BIRTH (C. 6/5 BC) _____

JOHN BECOMES A DISCIPLE (C. AD 26) _____

JESUS' DEATH, RESURRECTION AND ASCENSION (C. AD 30) _____

NERO'S REIGN (AD 54 – 68) _____

DESTRUCTION OF JERUSALEM'S TEMPLE (C. AD 70) _____

DOMITIAN'S REIGN (C. AD 81 – 96) _____

BOOK OF 2 JOHN WRITTEN (C. AD 85 – 95) _____

JOHN'S EXILE ON PATMOS (C. AD 90 – 95) _____

¹The elder,

To the lady chosen by God and to her children, whom I love in the truth—and not I only, but also all who know the truth— ²because of the truth, which lives in us and will be with us forever:

³Grace, mercy and peace from God the Father and from Jesus Christ, the Father's Son, will be with us in truth and love.

⁴It has given me great joy to find some of your children walking in the truth, just as the Father commanded us. ⁵And now, dear lady, I am not writing you a new command but one we have had from the beginning. I ask that we love one another. ⁶And this is love: that we walk in obedience to his commands. As you have heard from the beginning, his command is that you walk in love.

⁷I say this because many deceivers, who do not acknowledge Jesus Christ as coming in the flesh, have gone out into the world. Any such person is the deceiver and the antichrist. ⁸Watch out that you do not lose what we*ᵃ* have worked for, but that you may be rewarded fully. ⁹Anyone who runs ahead and does not continue in the teaching of Christ does not have God; whoever continues in the teaching has both the Father and the Son. ¹⁰If anyone comes to you and does not bring this teaching, do not take them into your house or welcome them. ¹¹Anyone who welcomes them shares in their wicked work.

¹²I have much to write to you, but I do not want to use paper and ink. Instead, I hope to visit you and talk with you face to face, so that our joy may be complete.

¹³The children of your sister, who is chosen by God, send their greetings.

What false teaching was John describing? (v. 7)
This was the false teaching that Jesus was the Son of God only after his baptism and up until his crucifixion. Jesus was both Son of God and man.

What kind of paper and ink were used for writing letters during this time? (v. 12)
Paper was made from papyrus reeds. Ink was made by mixing carbon, water, and gum or oil.

ᵃ *8 Some manuscripts* you

3 John

INTRODUCTION

Who wrote this book?   John, the disciple of Jesus, wrote this book.

Why was this book written?   The book of 3 John shows Christians how to live close to God and other people.

For whom was this book written?   This book is a letter John sent to a Christian named Gaius.

When did these things happen?

10 BC AD 1 10 20 30 40 50 60 70 80 90 100

JESUS' BIRTH (C. 6/5 BC)

JOHN BECOMES A DISCIPLE (C. AD 26)

JESUS' DEATH, RESURRECTION AND ASCENSION (C. AD 30)

NERO'S REIGN (AD 54 – 68)

DESTRUCTION OF JERUSALEM'S TEMPLE (C. AD 70)

BOOK OF 3 JOHN WRITTEN (C. AD 85 – 95)

JOHN'S EXILE ON PATMOS (C. AD 90 – 95)

¹The elder,

To my dear friend Gaius, whom I love in the truth.

²Dear friend, I pray that you may enjoy good health and that all may go well with you, even as your soul is getting along well. ³It gave me great joy when some believers came and testified about your faithfulness to the truth, telling how you continue to walk in it. ⁴I have no greater joy than to hear that my children are walking in the truth.

⁵Dear friend, you are faithful in what you are doing for the brothers and sisters,ᵃ even though they are strangers to you. ⁶They have told the church about your love. Please send them on their way in a manner that honors God. ⁷It was for the sake of the Name that they went out, receiving no help from the pagans. ⁸We ought therefore to show hospitality to such people so that we may work together for the truth.

⁹I wrote to the church, but Diotrephes, who loves to be first, will not welcome us. ¹⁰So when I come, I will call attention to what he is doing, spreading malicious nonsense about us. Not satisfied with that, he even refuses to welcome other believers. He also stops those who want to do so and puts them out of the church.

¹¹Dear friend, do not imitate what is evil but what is good. Anyone who does what is good is from God. Anyone who does what is evil has not seen God. ¹²Demetrius is well spoken of by everyone—and even by the truth itself. We also speak well of him, and you know that our testimony is true.

¹³I have much to write you, but I do not want to do so with pen and ink. ¹⁴I hope to see you soon, and we will talk face to face.

Peace to you. The friends here send their greetings. Greet the friends there by name.

What was a sign that a person was a Christian? (v. 11)
John said that if a person continually did good works, the person was from God. On the other hand, if a person continually did evil, that person was not from God.

ᵃ 5 The Greek word for *brothers and sisters* (*adelphoi*) refers here to believers, both men and women, as part of God's family.

Jude

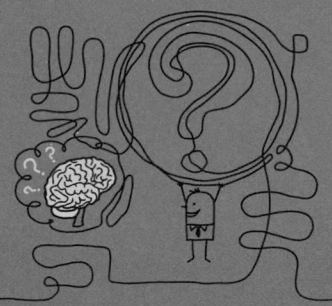

INTRODUCTION

Who wrote this book? Jude, the brother of Jesus, wrote this book.

Why was this book written? The book of Jude warns Christians about false teachers.

For whom was this book written? This book is a letter written to Christians everywhere.

When did these things happen?

	10 BC	AD 1	10	20	30	40	50	60	70	80	90	100

JESUS' BIRTH (C. 6/5 BC)

JESUS' DEATH, RESURRECTION AND ASCENSION (C. AD 30)

JUDE'S CONVERSION (C. AD 30)

PAUL'S CONVERSION (C. AD 35)

COUNCIL AT JERUSALEM (C. AD 49/50)

NERO'S REIGN (AD 54 – 68)

BOOK OF JUDE WRITTEN (C. AD 65 – 80)

DESTRUCTION OF JERUSALEM'S TEMPLE (C. AD 70)

¹Jude, a servant of Jesus Christ and a brother of James,

To those who have been called, who are loved in God the Father and kept for*a* Jesus Christ:

²Mercy, peace and love be yours in abundance.

THE SIN AND DOOM OF UNGODLY PEOPLE

³Dear friends, although I was very eager to write to you about the salvation we share, I felt compelled to write and urge you to contend for the faith that was once for all entrusted to God's holy people. ⁴For certain individuals whose condemnation was written about*b* long ago have secretly slipped in among you. They are ungodly people, who pervert the grace of our God into a license for immorality and deny Jesus Christ our only Sovereign and Lord.

⁵Though you already know all this, I want to remind you that the Lord*c* at one time delivered his people out of Egypt, but later destroyed those who did not believe. ⁶And the angels who did not keep their positions of authority but abandoned their proper dwelling—these he has kept in darkness, bound with everlasting chains for judgment on the great Day. ⁷In a similar way, Sodom and Gomorrah and the surrounding towns gave themselves up to sexual immorality and perversion. They serve as an example of those who suffer the punishment of eternal fire.

⁸In the very same way, on the strength of their dreams these ungodly people pollute their own bodies, reject authority and heap abuse on celestial beings. ⁹But even the archangel Michael, when he was disputing with the devil about the body of Moses, did not himself dare to condemn him for slander but said, "The Lord rebuke you!"*d* ¹⁰Yet these people slander whatever they do not understand, and the very things they do understand by instinct—as irrational animals do—will destroy them.

¹¹Woe to them! They have taken the way of Cain; they have rushed for profit into Balaam's error; they have been destroyed in Korah's rebellion.

¹²These people are blemishes at your love feasts, eating with you without the slightest qualm—shepherds who feed only themselves. They are clouds without rain, blown along by the wind; autumn trees, without fruit and uprooted—twice dead. ¹³They are wild waves of the sea, foaming up their shame; wandering stars, for whom blackest darkness has been reserved forever.

¹⁴Enoch, the seventh from Adam, prophesied about them: "See, the Lord is coming with thousands upon thousands of his holy ones ¹⁵to judge everyone, and to convict all of them of all the ungodly acts they have committed in their ungodliness, and of all the defiant words ungodly sinners have spoken against him."*e* ¹⁶These people are grumblers and faultfinders; they follow their own evil desires; they boast about themselves and flatter others for their own advantage.

---

a 1 Or *by;* or in   *b 4* Or *individuals who were marked out for condemnation*   *c 5* Some early manuscripts *Jesus*   *d 9* Jude is alluding to the Jewish *Testament of Moses* (approximately the first century A.D.).   *e 14,15* From the Jewish *First Book of Enoch* (approximately the first century B.C.)

How did some people "pervert the grace of our God"? (v. 4)
Some people were saying that salvation by grace gave them the right to sin because God would forgive them.

How did Jude challenge the argument that people could feel free to sin? (vv. 5–7)
He gave three examples of God punishing sin. God punished the people of Israel who did not believe his promises, the angels who rebelled, and the immoral people of Sodom and Gomorrah.

A CALL TO PERSEVERE

[17]But, dear friends, remember what the apostles of our Lord Jesus Christ foretold. [18]They said to you, "In the last times there will be scoffers who will follow their own ungodly desires." [19]These are the people who divide you, who follow mere natural instincts and do not have the Spirit.

[20]But you, dear friends, by building yourselves up in your most holy faith and praying in the Holy Spirit, [21]keep yourselves in God's love as you wait for the mercy of our Lord Jesus Christ to bring you to eternal life.

[22]Be merciful to those who doubt; [23]save others by snatching them from the fire; to others show mercy, mixed with fear—hating even the clothing stained by corrupted flesh.[a]

DOXOLOGY

[24]To him who is able to keep you from stumbling and to present you before his glorious presence without fault and with great joy— [25]to the only God our Savior be glory, majesty, power and authority, through Jesus Christ our Lord, before all ages, now and forevermore! Amen.

What was the warning of the apostles? (vv. 17–19)
The apostles warned that there would be false teachers whose teachings would divide Christians into factions.

[a] 22,23 The Greek manuscripts of these verses vary at several points.

Revelation

INTRODUCTION

Who wrote this book? John, the disciple of Jesus, wrote this book.

Why was this book written? John wrote this book to tell people about a vision he had of Jesus and about "what must soon take place."

For whom was this book written? This book was written for all Christians everywhere.

What are some important teachings in this book?

Jesus is God	Revelation 1:9 – 18
Letters to seven churches	Revelation 2 – 3
God is on his throne	Revelation 4:1 – 11
God will judge Satan	Revelation 20:7 – 10
God will judge the dead	Revelation 20:11 – 15
A new world	Revelation 21:1—22

When did these things happen?

10 BC AD 1 10 20 30 40 50 60 70 80 90 100

JESUS' BIRTH (C. 6/5 BC)

JOHN BECOMES A DISCIPLE (C. AD 26)

JESUS' DEATH, RESURRECTION AND ASCENSION (C. AD 30)

NERO'S REIGN (AD 54 – 68)

PAUL'S IMPRISONMENT AND DEATH IN ROME (C. AD 67 – 68)

DESTRUCTION OF JERUSALEM'S TEMPLE (C. AD 70)

DOMITIAN'S REIGN (C. AD 81 – 96)

JOHN'S EXILE ON PATMOS (C. AD 90 – 95)

BOOK OF REVELATION WRITTEN (C. AD 90 – 96)

PROLOGUE

1 The revelation from Jesus Christ, which God gave him to show his servants what must soon take place. He made it known by sending his angel to his servant John, [2] who testifies to everything he saw—that is, the word of God and the testimony of Jesus Christ. [3] Blessed is the one who reads aloud the words of this prophecy, and blessed are those who hear it and take to heart what is written in it, because the time is near.

GREETINGS AND DOXOLOGY

[4] John,

To the seven churches in the province of Asia:

Grace and peace to you from him who is, and who was, and who is to come, and from the seven spirits[a] before his throne, [5] and from Jesus Christ, who is the faithful witness, the firstborn from the dead, and the ruler of the kings of the earth.

To him who loves us and has freed us from our sins by his blood, [6] and has made us to be a kingdom and priests to serve his God and Father—to him be glory and power for ever and ever! Amen.

[7] "Look, he is coming with the clouds,"[b]
   and "every eye will see him,
  even those who pierced him";
   and all peoples on earth "will mourn because
     of him."[c]
              So shall it be! Amen.

[8] "I am the Alpha and the Omega," says the Lord God, "who is, and who was, and who is to come, the Almighty."

JOHN'S VISION OF CHRIST

[9] I, John, your brother and companion in the suffering and kingdom and patient endurance that are ours in Jesus, was on the island of Patmos because of the word of God and the testimony of Jesus. [10] On the Lord's Day I was in the Spirit, and I heard behind me a loud voice like a trumpet, [11] which said: "Write on a scroll what you see and send it to the seven churches: to Ephesus, Smyrna, Pergamum, Thyatira, Sardis, Philadelphia and Laodicea."

[12] I turned around to see the voice that was speaking to me. And when I turned I saw seven golden lampstands, [13] and among the lampstands was someone like a son of man,[d] dressed in a robe reaching down to his feet and with a golden sash around his chest. [14] The hair on his head was white like wool, as white as snow, and his eyes were like blazing fire. [15] His feet were like bronze glowing in a furnace, and his voice was like the sound of rushing waters. [16] In his right hand he held seven stars, and coming out of his mouth was a sharp, double-edged sword. His face was like the sun shining in all its brilliance.

---

a 4 That is, the sevenfold Spirit   *b 7* Daniel 7:13   *c 7* Zech. 12:10
d 13 See Daniel 7:13.

The Seven Churches (1:4)

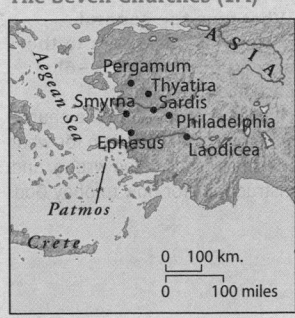

Why did God say he was the Alpha and the Omega? (1:8)
These are the first and last letters in the Greek alphabet. God is the beginning and the end.

What is the Lord's Day? (1:10)
Sunday was called the Lord's Day because that was the day Jesus rose from the dead. It was also the day Christians met for worship.

What were scrolls like? (1:11)
Scrolls were pieces of parchment or papyrus that were sewn together and rolled on a spindle or rod.

What did the number seven symbolize? (1:12)
The number seven is used 52 times in Revelation. The number seven represented completeness and perfection.

Who was the son of man? (1:13)
This was Jesus. During his time on earth, Jesus called himself the son of man many times.

¹⁷When I saw him, I fell at his feet as though dead. Then he placed his right hand on me and said: "Do not be afraid. I am the First and the Last. ¹⁸I am the Living One; I was dead, and now look, I am alive for ever and ever! And I hold the keys of death and Hades.

¹⁹"Write, therefore, what you have seen, what is now and what will take place later. ²⁰The mystery of the seven stars that you saw in my right hand and of the seven golden lampstands is this: The seven stars are the angels[a] of the seven churches, and the seven lampstands are the seven churches.

TO THE CHURCH IN EPHESUS

2 "To the angel[b] of the church in Ephesus write:

These are the words of him who holds the seven stars in his right hand and walks among the seven golden lampstands. ²I know your deeds, your hard work and your perseverance. I know that you cannot tolerate wicked people, that you have tested those who claim to be apostles but are not, and have found them false. ³You have persevered and have endured hardships for my name, and have not grown weary.

⁴Yet I hold this against you: You have forsaken the love you had at first. ⁵Consider how far you have fallen! Repent and do the things you did at first. If you do not repent, I will come to you and remove your lampstand from its place. ⁶But you have this in your favor: You hate the practices of the Nicolaitans, which I also hate.

⁷Whoever has ears, let them hear what the Spirit says to the churches. To the one who is victorious, I will give the right to eat from the tree of life, which is in the paradise of God.

TO THE CHURCH IN SMYRNA

⁸"To the angel of the church in Smyrna write:

These are the words of him who is the First and the Last, who died and came to life again. ⁹I know your afflictions and your poverty—yet you are rich! I know about the slander of those who say they are Jews and are not, but are a synagogue of Satan. ¹⁰Do not be afraid of what you are about to suffer. I tell you, the devil will put some of you in prison to test you, and you will suffer persecution for ten days. Be faithful, even to the point of death, and I will give you life as your victor's crown.

¹¹Whoever has ears, let them hear what the Spirit says to the churches. The one who is victorious will not be hurt at all by the second death.

TO THE CHURCH IN PERGAMUM

¹²"To the angel of the church in Pergamum write:

These are the words of him who has the sharp, double-edged sword. ¹³I know where you live—where Satan has his throne. Yet you remain true to my name. You

What was the general pattern in the letters to the seven churches? (2:1–6)
Each had three parts: compliments for what the church was doing well, criticism for what the church was doing wrong, and instructions for how to obey God.

What type of crown was this? (2:10)
This is probably not a royal, physical crown. It may refer to eternal life or a type of reward in heaven.

Why did Paul say the church in Pergamum lived "where Satan has his throne"? (2:13)
Pergamum was the official center of emperor worship. The first shrine to the Roman emperor was built there in 29 B.C. The people there also worshiped pagan gods such as Asclepius and Zeus.

[a] 20 Or messengers   [b] 1 Or messenger; also in verses 8, 12 and 18

did not renounce your faith in me, not even in the days of Antipas, my faithful witness, who was put to death in your city—where Satan lives.

¹⁴ Nevertheless, I have a few things against you: There are some among you who hold to the teaching of Balaam, who taught Balak to entice the Israelites to sin so that they ate food sacrificed to idols and committed sexual immorality. ¹⁵ Likewise, you also have those who hold to the teaching of the Nicolaitans. ¹⁶ Repent therefore! Otherwise, I will soon come to you and will fight against them with the sword of my mouth.

¹⁷ Whoever has ears, let them hear what the Spirit says to the churches. To the one who is victorious, I will give some of the hidden manna. I will also give that person a white stone with a new name written on it, known only to the one who receives it.

TO THE CHURCH IN THYATIRA

¹⁸ "To the angel of the church in Thyatira write:

These are the words of the Son of God, whose eyes are like blazing fire and whose feet are like burnished bronze. ¹⁹ I know your deeds, your love and faith, your service and perseverance, and that you are now doing more than you did at first.

²⁰ Nevertheless, I have this against you: You tolerate that woman Jezebel, who calls herself a prophet. By her teaching she misleads my servants into sexual immorality and the eating of food sacrificed to idols. ²¹ I have given her time to repent of her immorality, but she is unwilling. ²² So I will cast her on a bed of suffering, and I will make those who commit adultery with her suffer intensely, unless they repent of her ways. ²³ I will strike her children dead. Then all the churches will know that I am he who searches hearts and minds, and I will repay each of you according to your deeds.

²⁴ Now I say to the rest of you in Thyatira, to you who do not hold to her teaching and have not learned Satan's so-called deep secrets, 'I will not impose any other burden on you, ²⁵ except to hold on to what you have until I come.'

²⁶ To the one who is victorious and does my will to the end, I will give authority over the nations— ²⁷ that one 'will rule them with an iron scepter and will dash them to pieces like pottery'ᵃ—just as I have received authority from my Father. ²⁸ I will also give that one the morning star. ²⁹ Whoever has ears, let them hear what the Spirit says to the churches.

TO THE CHURCH IN SARDIS

3 "To the angel ᵇ of the church in Sardis write:

These are the words of him who holds the seven spiritsᶜ of God and the seven stars. I know your deeds;

Who were the Nicolaitans? (2:15)
These were people who thought that spiritual liberty gave them the right to practice idolatry and immorality.

Who was Jezebel? (2:20–23)
She was a prominent woman in the congregation who encouraged church members to join guilds (groups of people who practiced the same trade) even though the dinners held by the guilds included meals offered to pagan gods. She also promoted sexual immorality.

ᵃ 27 Psalm 2:9   ᵇ 1 Or *messenger*; also in verses 7 and 14   ᶜ 1 That is, the sevenfold Spirit

you have a reputation of being alive, but you are dead. ²Wake up! Strengthen what remains and is about to die, for I have found your deeds unfinished in the sight of my God. ³Remember, therefore, what you have received and heard; hold it fast, and repent. But if you do not wake up, I will come like a thief, and you will not know at what time I will come to you.

⁴Yet you have a few people in Sardis who have not soiled their clothes. They will walk with me, dressed in white, for they are worthy. ⁵The one who is victorious will, like them, be dressed in white. I will never blot out the name of that person from the book of life, but will acknowledge that name before my Father and his angels. ⁶Whoever has ears, let them hear what the Spirit says to the churches.

TO THE CHURCH IN PHILADELPHIA

⁷"To the angel of the church in Philadelphia write:

These are the words of him who is holy and true, who holds the key of David. What he opens no one can shut, and what he shuts no one can open. ⁸I know your deeds. See, I have placed before you an open door that no one can shut. I know that you have little strength, yet you have kept my word and have not denied my name. ⁹I will make those who are of the synagogue of Satan, who claim to be Jews though they are not, but are liars—I will make them come and fall down at your feet and acknowledge that I have loved you. ¹⁰Since you have kept my command to endure patiently, I will also keep you from the hour of trial that is going to come on the whole world to test the inhabitants of the earth.

¹¹I am coming soon. Hold on to what you have, so that no one will take your crown. ¹²The one who is victorious I will make a pillar in the temple of my God. Never again will they leave it. I will write on them the name of my God and the name of the city of my God, the new Jerusalem, which is coming down out of heaven from my God; and I will also write on them my new name. ¹³Whoever has ears, let them hear what the Spirit says to the churches.

TO THE CHURCH IN LAODICEA

¹⁴"To the angel of the church in Laodicea write:

These are the words of the Amen, the faithful and true witness, the ruler of God's creation. ¹⁵I know your deeds, that you are neither cold nor hot. I wish you were either one or the other! ¹⁶So, because you are lukewarm—neither hot nor cold—I am about to spit you out of my mouth. ¹⁷You say, 'I am rich; I have acquired wealth and do not need a thing.' But you do not realize that you are wretched, pitiful, poor, blind and naked. ¹⁸I counsel you to buy from me gold refined in the fire, so you can become rich; and white clothes to wear, so you can cover your shameful nakedness; and salve to put on your eyes, so you can see.

What type of book is this? (3:5)
The book of life is a record of all the names of those who believe in Jesus as their Lord and Savior and will live forever with God.

Why was the church in Laodicea described as lukewarm? (3:16)
"Hot" may have been a reference to the hot springs in nearby Hierapolis that people went to for healing. The church did not provide spiritual healing, nor did it supply spiritual refreshment (symbolized by a cold glass of water) for those who needed it. Christians are to be wholeheartedly devoted to the Lord.

¹⁹Those whom I love I rebuke and discipline. So be earnest and repent. ²⁰Here I am! I stand at the door and knock. If anyone hears my voice and opens the door, I will come in and eat with that person, and they with me.

²¹To the one who is victorious, I will give the right to sit with me on my throne, just as I was victorious and sat down with my Father on his throne. ²²Whoever has ears, let them hear what the Spirit says to the churches."

THE THRONE IN HEAVEN

4 After this I looked, and there before me was a door standing open in heaven. And the voice I had first heard speaking to me like a trumpet said, "Come up here, and I will show you what must take place after this." ²At once I was in the Spirit, and there before me was a throne in heaven with someone sitting on it. ³And the one who sat there had the appearance of jasper and ruby. A rainbow that shone like an emerald encircled the throne. ⁴Surrounding the throne were twenty-four other thrones, and seated on them were twenty-four elders. They were dressed in white and had crowns of gold on their heads. ⁵From the throne came flashes of lightning, rumblings and peals of thunder. In front of the throne, seven lamps were blazing. These are the seven spirits*a* of God. ⁶Also in front of the throne there was what looked like a sea of glass, clear as crystal.

In the center, around the throne, were four living creatures, and they were covered with eyes, in front and in back. ⁷The first living creature was like a lion, the second was like an ox, the third had a face like a man, the fourth was like a flying eagle. ⁸Each of the four living creatures had six wings and was covered with eyes all around, even under its wings. Day and night they never stop saying:

> "'Holy, holy, holy
> is the Lord God Almighty,'*b*
> who was, and is, and is to come."

⁹Whenever the living creatures give glory, honor and thanks to him who sits on the throne and who lives for ever and ever, ¹⁰the twenty-four elders fall down before him who sits on the throne and worship him who lives for ever and ever. They lay their crowns before the throne and say:

¹¹"You are worthy, our Lord and God,
> to receive glory and honor and power,
> for you created all things,
> and by your will they were created
> and have their being."

THE SCROLL AND THE LAMB

5 Then I saw in the right hand of him who sat on the throne a scroll with writing on both sides and sealed with seven seals. ²And I saw a mighty angel proclaiming in a loud voice, "Who is worthy to break the seals and open

Does this verse refer to unbelievers? (3:20)
No, from the context we know that this verse applies to believers who need to quit sinning and turn back to God. When they do, Jesus is waiting to fellowship with them.

Who were the 24 elders? (4:4)
These may have been representatives of the believers in heaven or they may have been a special group of angels. The number 24 could be symbolic of the 12 tribes of Israel and the 12 apostles.

Who were the four living creatures? (4:6–8)
These seem to be angelic beings who guarded the heavenly throne and who led the worship of God.

---

a 5 That is, the sevenfold Spirit   b 8 Isaiah 6:3

the scroll?" ³But no one in heaven or on earth or under the earth could open the scroll or even look inside it. ⁴I wept and wept because no one was found who was worthy to open the scroll or look inside. ⁵Then one of the elders said to me, "Do not weep! See, the Lion of the tribe of Judah, the Root of David, has triumphed. He is able to open the scroll and its seven seals."

⁶Then I saw a Lamb, looking as if it had been slain, standing at the center of the throne, encircled by the four living creatures and the elders. The Lamb had seven horns and seven eyes, which are the seven spirits*ᵃ* of God sent out into all the earth. ⁷He went and took the scroll from the right hand of him who sat on the throne. ⁸And when he had taken it, the four living creatures and the twenty-four elders fell down before the Lamb. Each one had a harp and they were holding golden bowls full of incense, which are the prayers of God's people. ⁹And they sang a new song, saying:

"You are worthy to take the scroll
    and to open its seals,
because you were slain,
    and with your blood you purchased for God
    persons from every tribe and language and people
        and nation.
¹⁰You have made them to be a kingdom and priests to
        serve our God,
    and they will reign*ᵇ* on the earth."

¹¹Then I looked and heard the voice of many angels, numbering thousands upon thousands, and ten thousand times ten thousand. They encircled the throne and the living creatures and the elders. ¹²In a loud voice they were saying:

"Worthy is the Lamb, who was slain,
    to receive power and wealth and wisdom and
        strength
    and honor and glory and praise!"

¹³Then I heard every creature in heaven and on earth and under the earth and on the sea, and all that is in them, saying:

"To him who sits on the throne and to the Lamb
    be praise and honor and glory and power,
        for ever and ever!"

¹⁴The four living creatures said, "Amen," and the elders fell down and worshiped.

THE SEALS

6 I watched as the Lamb opened the first of the seven seals. Then I heard one of the four living creatures say in a voice like thunder, "Come!" ²I looked, and there before me was a white horse! Its rider held a bow, and he was given a crown, and he rode out as a conqueror bent on conquest.

³When the Lamb opened the second seal, I heard the second living creature say, "Come!" ⁴Then another horse came out, a fiery red one. Its rider was given power to take peace

---

Who was the Lamb, and what do its horns represent? (5:6)
Jesus, the Lamb, was sacrificed for our sins and in that way is a mighty conqueror over sin and death. The horn was an ancient symbol for power or strength. Seven, a common number in the Bible, symbolizes perfection. Seven horns represent complete power.

What type of harp was this? (5:8)
This was a handheld stringed instrument used to accompany singing.

Harp

What did the four horsemen symbolize? (6:1–8)
The rider on the white horse may have symbolized military force. The rider on the red horse symbolized warfare and bloodshed; the rider on the black horse symbolized famine; and the rider on the pale horse symbolized death.

ᵃ 6 That is, the sevenfold Spirit   ᵇ 10 Some manuscripts they reign

from the earth and to make people kill each other. To him was given a large sword."

⁵When the Lamb opened the third seal, I heard the third living creature say, "Come!" I looked, and there before me was a black horse! Its rider was holding a pair of scales in his hand. ⁶Then I heard what sounded like a voice among the four living creatures, saying, "Two pounds*ᵃ* of wheat for a day's wages,*ᵇ* and six pounds*ᶜ* of barley for a day's wages,*ᵇ* and do not damage the oil and the wine!"

⁷When the Lamb opened the fourth seal, I heard the voice of the fourth living creature say, "Come!" ⁸I looked, and there before me was a pale horse! Its rider was named Death, and Hades was following close behind him. They were given power over a fourth of the earth to kill by sword, famine and plague, and by the wild beasts of the earth.

⁹When he opened the fifth seal, I saw under the altar the souls of those who had been slain because of the word of God and the testimony they had maintained. ¹⁰They called out in a loud voice, "How long, Sovereign Lord, holy and true, until you judge the inhabitants of the earth and avenge our blood?" ¹¹Then each of them was given a white robe, and they were told to wait a little longer, until the full number of their fellow servants, their brothers and sisters,*ᵈ* were killed just as they had been.

¹²I watched as he opened the sixth seal. There was a great earthquake. The sun turned black like sackcloth made of goat hair, the whole moon turned blood red, ¹³and the stars in the sky fell to earth, as figs drop from a fig tree when shaken by a strong wind. ¹⁴The heavens receded like a scroll being rolled up, and every mountain and island was removed from its place.

¹⁵Then the kings of the earth, the princes, the generals, the rich, the mighty, and everyone else, both slave and free, hid in caves and among the rocks of the mountains. ¹⁶They called to the mountains and the rocks, "Fall on us and hide us*ᵉ* from the face of him who sits on the throne and from the wrath of the Lamb! ¹⁷For the great day of their*ᶠ* wrath has come, and who can withstand it?"

144,000 SEALED

7 After this I saw four angels standing at the four corners of the earth, holding back the four winds of the earth to prevent any wind from blowing on the land or on the sea or on any tree. ²Then I saw another angel coming up from the east, having the seal of the living God. He called out in a loud voice to the four angels who had been given power to harm the land and the sea: ³"Do not harm the land or the sea or the trees until we put a seal on the foreheads of the servants of our God." ⁴Then I heard the number of those who were sealed: 144,000 from all the tribes of Israel.

⁵From the tribe of Judah 12,000 were sealed,
   from the tribe of Reuben 12,000,

ᵃ 6 Or *about 1 kilogram*   *ᵇ 6* Greek *a denarius*   *ᶜ 6* Or *about 3 kilograms*
ᵈ 11 The Greek word for *brothers and sisters* (*adelphoi*) refers here to believers, both men and women, as part of God's family; also in 12:10; 19:10.
ᵉ 16 See Hosea 10:8.   *ᶠ 17* Some manuscripts *his*

Why were the people terrified? (6:15–17)
The powerful signs in nature showed that God's judgment would be fierce for those who did not believe in him.

How were God's people going to be sealed? (7:2–4)
Ancient documents were folded and tied, and then a lump of clay was pressed over the knot. The person sending the document would press a ring or roll a cylinder seal over the clay to show that the document was genuine and to protect the contents. God's people were going to be "sealed" by having a mark placed on their foreheads.

A Sealed Scroll

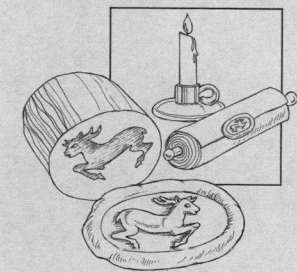

from the tribe of Gad 12,000,
⁶from the tribe of Asher 12,000,
from the tribe of Naphtali 12,000,
from the tribe of Manasseh 12,000,
⁷from the tribe of Simeon 12,000,
from the tribe of Levi 12,000,
from the tribe of Issachar 12,000,
⁸from the tribe of Zebulun 12,000,
from the tribe of Joseph 12,000,
from the tribe of Benjamin 12,000.

THE GREAT MULTITUDE IN WHITE ROBES

⁹After this I looked, and there before me was a great multitude that no one could count, from every nation, tribe, people and language, standing before the throne and before the Lamb. They were wearing white robes and were holding palm branches in their hands. ¹⁰And they cried out in a loud voice:

"Salvation belongs to our God,
    who sits on the throne,
    and to the Lamb."

¹¹All the angels were standing around the throne and around the elders and the four living creatures. They fell down on their faces before the throne and worshiped God, ¹²saying:

"Amen!
Praise and glory
and wisdom and thanks and honor
and power and strength
be to our God for ever and ever.
Amen!"

¹³Then one of the elders asked me, "These in white robes—who are they, and where did they come from?"

¹⁴I answered, "Sir, you know."

And he said, "These are they who have come out of the great tribulation; they have washed their robes and made them white in the blood of the Lamb. ¹⁵Therefore,

"they are before the throne of God
    and serve him day and night in his temple;
and he who sits on the throne
    will shelter them with his presence.
¹⁶'Never again will they hunger;
    never again will they thirst.
The sun will not beat down on them,'ᵃ
    nor any scorching heat.
¹⁷For the Lamb at the center of the throne
    will be their shepherd;
'he will lead them to springs of living water.'ᵃ
    'And God will wipe away every tear from their eyes.'ᵇ"

THE SEVENTH SEAL AND THE GOLDEN CENSER

8 When he opened the seventh seal, there was silence in heaven for about half an hour.

²And I saw the seven angels who stand before God, and seven trumpets were given to them.

ᵃ 16,17 Isaiah 49:10   ᵇ 17 Isaiah 25:8

Why were the people wearing white robes? (7:9)
This was a symbol of blessedness and purity. These faithful people wore white robes because Jesus' blood shed for their sins had made them pure, as if they had never sinned.

What does "shelter them with his presence" refer to? (7:15)
This was a reminder of the tabernacle in the Old Testament. God would dwell with them and give them shelter and protection.

³Another angel, who had a golden censer, came and stood at the altar. He was given much incense to offer, with the prayers of all God's people, on the golden altar in front of the throne. ⁴The smoke of the incense, together with the prayers of God's people, went up before God from the angel's hand. ⁵Then the angel took the censer, filled it with fire from the altar, and hurled it on the earth; and there came peals of thunder, rumblings, flashes of lightning and an earthquake.

THE TRUMPETS

⁶Then the seven angels who had the seven trumpets prepared to sound them.

⁷The first angel sounded his trumpet, and there came hail and fire mixed with blood, and it was hurled down on the earth. A third of the earth was burned up, a third of the trees were burned up, and all the green grass was burned up.

⁸The second angel sounded his trumpet, and something like a huge mountain, all ablaze, was thrown into the sea. A third of the sea turned into blood, ⁹a third of the living creatures in the sea died, and a third of the ships were destroyed.

¹⁰The third angel sounded his trumpet, and a great star, blazing like a torch, fell from the sky on a third of the rivers and on the springs of water— ¹¹the name of the star is Wormwood.ᵃ A third of the waters turned bitter, and many people died from the waters that had become bitter.

¹²The fourth angel sounded his trumpet, and a third of the sun was struck, a third of the moon, and a third of the stars, so that a third of them turned dark. A third of the day was without light, and also a third of the night.

¹³As I watched, I heard an eagle that was flying in midair call out in a loud voice: "Woe! Woe! Woe to the inhabitants of the earth, because of the trumpet blasts about to be sounded by the other three angels!"

9 The fifth angel sounded his trumpet, and I saw a star that had fallen from the sky to the earth. The star was given the key to the shaft of the Abyss. ²When he opened the Abyss, smoke rose from it like the smoke from a gigantic furnace. The sun and sky were darkened by the smoke from the Abyss. ³And out of the smoke locusts came down on the earth and were given power like that of scorpions of the earth. ⁴They were told not to harm the grass of the earth or any plant or tree, but only those people who did not have the seal of God on their foreheads. ⁵They were not allowed to kill them but only to torture them for five months. And the agony they suffered was like that of the sting of a scorpion when it strikes. ⁶During those days people will seek death but will not find it; they will long to die, but death will elude them.

⁷The locusts looked like horses prepared for battle. On their heads they wore something like crowns of gold, and their faces resembled human faces. ⁸Their hair was like women's hair, and their teeth were like lions' teeth. ⁹They had breastplates like breastplates of iron, and the sound of their wings was like the thundering of many horses and chariots

---

What signs of judgment were similar to the plagues on Egypt? (8:7–10)
These plagues included hail (seventh plague), water turning to blood (first plague), and darkness covering the land (ninth plague). (See Exodus 7–10.)

What is wormwood? (8:11)
This is a plant with a strong, bitter taste. Here it represents disaster and sadness.

What is the Abyss? (9:1)
This is thought to be the bottomless underground pit where demons live.

ᵃ *11* Wormwood is a bitter substance.

rushing into battle. ¹⁰They had tails with stingers, like scorpions, and in their tails they had power to torment people for five months. ¹¹They had as king over them the angel of the Abyss, whose name in Hebrew is Abaddon and in Greek is Apollyon (that is, Destroyer).

¹²The first woe is past; two other woes are yet to come.

¹³The sixth angel sounded his trumpet, and I heard a voice coming from the four horns of the golden altar that is before God. ¹⁴It said to the sixth angel who had the trumpet, "Release the four angels who are bound at the great river Euphrates." ¹⁵And the four angels who had been kept ready for this very hour and day and month and year were released to kill a third of mankind. ¹⁶The number of the mounted troops was twice ten thousand times ten thousand. I heard their number.

¹⁷The horses and riders I saw in my vision looked like this: Their breastplates were fiery red, dark blue, and yellow as sulfur. The heads of the horses resembled the heads of lions, and out of their mouths came fire, smoke and sulfur. ¹⁸A third of mankind was killed by the three plagues of fire, smoke and sulfur that came out of their mouths. ¹⁹The power of the horses was in their mouths and in their tails; for their tails were like snakes, having heads with which they inflict injury.

²⁰The rest of mankind who were not killed by these plagues still did not repent of the work of their hands; they did not stop worshiping demons, and idols of gold, silver, bronze, stone and wood—idols that cannot see or hear or walk. ²¹Nor did they repent of their murders, their magic arts, their sexual immorality or their thefts.

THE ANGEL AND THE LITTLE SCROLL

10 Then I saw another mighty angel coming down from heaven. He was robed in a cloud, with a rainbow above his head; his face was like the sun, and his legs were like fiery pillars. ²He was holding a little scroll, which lay open in his hand. He planted his right foot on the sea and his left foot on the land, ³and he gave a loud shout like the roar of a lion. When he shouted, the voices of the seven thunders spoke. ⁴And when the seven thunders spoke, I was about to write; but I heard a voice from heaven say, "Seal up what the seven thunders have said and do not write it down."

⁵Then the angel I had seen standing on the sea and on the land raised his right hand to heaven. ⁶And he swore by him who lives for ever and ever, who created the heavens and all that is in them, the earth and all that is in it, and the sea and all that is in it, and said, "There will be no more delay! ⁷But in the days when the seventh angel is about to sound his trumpet, the mystery of God will be accomplished, just as he announced to his servants the prophets."

⁸Then the voice that I had heard from heaven spoke to me once more: "Go, take the scroll that lies open in the hand of the angel who is standing on the sea and on the land."

⁹So I went to the angel and asked him to give me the little scroll. He said to me, "Take it and eat it. It will turn your stomach sour, but 'in your mouth it will be as sweet as

What were the horns of the altar? (9:13)
The altar made for the tabernacle had a curved horn at each of its four corners. If someone were running away from judgment, that person would be safe if he took hold of the horns (see 1 Kings 1:50 – 51).

What was the mystery of God? (10:7)
The mystery was that God had won the victory over the forces of evil and would reign forever.

honey.'[a]" [10]I took the little scroll from the angel's hand and ate it. It tasted as sweet as honey in my mouth, but when I had eaten it, my stomach turned sour. [11]Then I was told, "You must prophesy again about many peoples, nations, languages and kings."

THE TWO WITNESSES

11 I was given a reed like a measuring rod and was told, "Go and measure the temple of God and the altar, with its worshipers. [2]But exclude the outer court; do not measure it, because it has been given to the Gentiles. They will trample on the holy city for 42 months. [3]And I will appoint my two witnesses, and they will prophesy for 1,260 days, clothed in sackcloth." [4]They are "the two olive trees" and the two lampstands, and "they stand before the Lord of the earth."[b] [5]If anyone tries to harm them, fire comes from their mouths and devours their enemies. This is how anyone who wants to harm them must die. [6]They have power to shut up the heavens so that it will not rain during the time they are prophesying; and they have power to turn the waters into blood and to strike the earth with every kind of plague as often as they want.

[7]Now when they have finished their testimony, the beast that comes up from the Abyss will attack them, and overpower and kill them. [8]Their bodies will lie in the public square of the great city—which is figuratively called Sodom and Egypt—where also their Lord was crucified. [9]For three and a half days some from every people, tribe, language and nation will gaze on their bodies and refuse them burial. [10]The inhabitants of the earth will gloat over them and will celebrate by sending each other gifts, because these two prophets had tormented those who live on the earth.

[11]But after the three and a half days the breath[c] of life from God entered them, and they stood on their feet, and terror struck those who saw them. [12]Then they heard a loud voice from heaven saying to them, "Come up here." And they went up to heaven in a cloud, while their enemies looked on.

[13]At that very hour there was a severe earthquake and a tenth of the city collapsed. Seven thousand people were killed in the earthquake, and the survivors were terrified and gave glory to the God of heaven.

[14]The second woe has passed; the third woe is coming soon.

THE SEVENTH TRUMPET

[15]The seventh angel sounded his trumpet, and there were loud voices in heaven, which said:

> "The kingdom of the world has become
>   the kingdom of our Lord and of his Messiah,
>   and he will reign for ever and ever."

[16]And the twenty-four elders, who were seated on their thrones before God, fell on their faces and worshiped God, [17]saying:

Who are these witnesses? (11:3–6) They seem to be modeled on Moses and Elijah because of the types of miracles they could perform. They may symbolize believers who speak God's truth in the time before Christ returns.

Why was a trumpet sounded? (11:15) In the ancient world, when a new king took his throne, trumpets were sounded. This seventh trumpet ushered in the reign of Christ on the earth.

[a] 9 Ezek. 3:3   [b] 4 See Zech. 4:3,11,14.   [c] 11 Or *Spirit* (see Ezek. 37:5,14)

"We give thanks to you, Lord God Almighty,
　　the One who is and who was,
because you have taken your great power
　　and have begun to reign.
[18] The nations were angry,
　　and your wrath has come.
The time has come for judging the dead,
　　and for rewarding your servants the prophets
and your people who revere your name,
　　both great and small—
and for destroying those who destroy the earth."

[19] Then God's temple in heaven was opened, and within his temple was seen the ark of his covenant. And there came flashes of lightning, rumblings, peals of thunder, an earthquake and a severe hailstorm.

THE WOMAN AND THE DRAGON

12 A great sign appeared in heaven: a woman clothed with the sun, with the moon under her feet and a crown of twelve stars on her head. [2] She was pregnant and cried out in pain as she was about to give birth. [3] Then another sign appeared in heaven: an enormous red dragon with seven heads and ten horns and seven crowns on its heads. [4] Its tail swept a third of the stars out of the sky and flung them to the earth. The dragon stood in front of the woman who was about to give birth, so that it might devour her child the moment he was born. [5] She gave birth to a son, a male child, who "will rule all the nations with an iron scepter."[a] And her child was snatched up to God and to his throne. [6] The woman fled into the wilderness to a place prepared for her by God, where she might be taken care of for 1,260 days.

[7] Then war broke out in heaven. Michael and his angels fought against the dragon, and the dragon and his angels fought back. [8] But he was not strong enough, and they lost their place in heaven. [9] The great dragon was hurled down— that ancient serpent called the devil, or Satan, who leads the whole world astray. He was hurled to the earth, and his angels with him.

[10] Then I heard a loud voice in heaven say:

"Now have come the salvation and the power
　　and the kingdom of our God,
　　and the authority of his Messiah.
For the accuser of our brothers and sisters,
　　who accuses them before our God day and
　　　　night,
　　has been hurled down.
[11] They triumphed over him
　　by the blood of the Lamb
　　and by the word of their testimony;
they did not love their lives so much
　　as to shrink from death.
[12] Therefore rejoice, you heavens
　　and you who dwell in them!

What did the ark symbolize? (11:19)
In Old Testament times, the ark symbolized God's presence with his people. In the New Testament, the ark—which was lost or destroyed—was a symbol of God keeping his covenant with his people.

What did the red dragon symbolize? (12:3)
The mythologies of ancient people often included dragons. In the Old Testament, dragons often symbolized the enemies of God and his people. Here the dragon symbolizes Satan, the ultimate enemy.

Who was the son who would rule with an iron scepter? (12:5)
This was Jesus, the Messiah. Being snatched up to God refers to his ascension into heaven.

Who was Michael? (12:7)
Michael was the archangel who defeated Satan in heavenly warfare. As a result, Satan was hurled out of heaven onto the earth.

---

[a] 5 Psalm 2:9

But woe to the earth and the sea,
  because the devil has gone down to you!
He is filled with fury,
  because he knows that his time is short."

¹³When the dragon saw that he had been hurled to the
earth, he pursued the woman who had given birth to the male
child. ¹⁴The woman was given the two wings of a great eagle,
so that she might fly to the place prepared for her in the wilderness, where she would be taken care of for a time, times
and half a time, out of the serpent's reach. ¹⁵Then from his
mouth the serpent spewed water like a river, to overtake the
woman and sweep her away with the torrent. ¹⁶But the earth
helped the woman by opening its mouth and swallowing the
river that the dragon had spewed out of his mouth. ¹⁷Then
the dragon was enraged at the woman and went off to wage
war against the rest of her offspring—those who keep God's
commands and hold fast their testimony about Jesus.

THE BEAST OUT OF THE SEA

13 The dragon*ᵃ* stood on the shore of the sea. And I saw
a beast coming out of the sea. It had ten horns and
seven heads, with ten crowns on its horns, and on each head
a blasphemous name. ²The beast I saw resembled a leopard,
but had feet like those of a bear and a mouth like that of a
lion. The dragon gave the beast his power and his throne and
great authority. ³One of the heads of the beast seemed to
have had a fatal wound, but the fatal wound had been healed.
The whole world was filled with wonder and followed the
beast. ⁴People worshiped the dragon because he had given
authority to the beast, and they also worshiped the beast and
asked, "Who is like the beast? Who can wage war against it?"

⁵The beast was given a mouth to utter proud words and
blasphemies and to exercise its authority for forty-two
months. ⁶It opened its mouth to blaspheme God, and to
slander his name and his dwelling place and those who live
in heaven. ⁷It was given power to wage war against God's
holy people and to conquer them. And it was given authority
over every tribe, people, language and nation. ⁸All inhabitants of the earth will worship the beast—all whose names
have not been written in the Lamb's book of life, the Lamb
who was slain from the creation of the world.*ᵇ*

⁹Whoever has ears, let them hear.

¹⁰"If anyone is to go into captivity,
  into captivity they will go.
If anyone is to be killed*ᶜ* with the sword,
  with the sword they will be killed."*ᵈ*

This calls for patient endurance and faithfulness on the part
of God's people.

THE BEAST OUT OF THE EARTH

¹¹Then I saw a second beast, coming out of the earth. It
had two horns like a lamb, but it spoke like a dragon. ¹²It

Who was this beast?
(13:1–4)
Some think that the beast
represented the Roman Empire,
but others think the beast is
the final antichrist. (See note at
1 John 2:18.)

**Who was the beast from the
earth? (13:11–12)**
This beast may have had a
connection to emperor worship.
The dragon controlled the beast
from the sea, and the beast from
the sea controlled the beast from
the earth.

ᵃ 1 Some manuscripts *And I*   *ᵇ 8* Or *written from the creation of the world in
the book of life belonging to the Lamb who was slain*   *ᶜ 10* Some manuscripts
anyone kills   *ᵈ 10* Jer. 15:2

exercised all the authority of the first beast on its behalf, and made the earth and its inhabitants worship the first beast, whose fatal wound had been healed. [13]And it performed great signs, even causing fire to come down from heaven to the earth in full view of the people. [14]Because of the signs it was given power to perform on behalf of the first beast, it deceived the inhabitants of the earth. It ordered them to set up an image in honor of the beast who was wounded by the sword and yet lived. [15]The second beast was given power to give breath to the image of the first beast, so that the image could speak and cause all who refused to worship the image to be killed. [16]It also forced all people, great and small, rich and poor, free and slave, to receive a mark on their right hands or on their foreheads, [17]so that they could not buy or sell unless they had the mark, which is the name of the beast or the number of its name.

[18]This calls for wisdom. Let the person who has insight calculate the number of the beast, for it is the number of a man.[a] That number is 666.

THE LAMB AND THE 144,000

14 Then I looked, and there before me was the Lamb, standing on Mount Zion, and with him 144,000 who had his name and his Father's name written on their foreheads. [2]And I heard a sound from heaven like the roar of rushing waters and like a loud peal of thunder. The sound I heard was like that of harpists playing their harps. [3]And they sang a new song before the throne and before the four living creatures and the elders. No one could learn the song except the 144,000 who had been redeemed from the earth. [4]These are those who did not defile themselves with women, for they remained virgins. They follow the Lamb wherever he goes. They were purchased from among mankind and offered as firstfruits to God and the Lamb. [5]No lie was found in their mouths; they are blameless.

THE THREE ANGELS

[6]Then I saw another angel flying in midair, and he had the eternal gospel to proclaim to those who live on the earth — to every nation, tribe, language and people. [7]He said in a loud voice, "Fear God and give him glory, because the hour of his judgment has come. Worship him who made the heavens, the earth, the sea and the springs of water."

[8]A second angel followed and said, "'Fallen! Fallen is Babylon the Great,'[b] which made all the nations drink the maddening wine of her adulteries."

[9]A third angel followed them and said in a loud voice: "If anyone worships the beast and its image and receives its mark on their forehead or on their hand, [10]they, too, will drink the wine of God's fury, which has been poured full strength into the cup of his wrath. They will be tormented with burning sulfur in the presence of the holy angels and of the Lamb. [11]And the smoke of their torment will rise for ever and ever. There will be no rest day or night for

What was the meaning of the number of the beast? (13:18)
There have been many attempts to interpret the number. Some think it is a code for one of the Roman emperors. Others think it is a number symbolizing evil, since each number falls short of the perfect number, seven.

Who were the 144,000? (14:3)
There are many theories about who this group is. Some believe that after all the Christians are raptured, 144,000 Jewish single men will evangelize the world during the tribulation. Others believe the 144,000 represents the church or a remnant of the church. Still others believe the 144,000 and the "great multitude" of verse 9 are one and the same. The 144,000 may be symbolic of those who are faithful to God especially in times of tribulation.

---

[a] 18 Or is humanity's number   [b] 8 Isaiah 21:9

those who worship the beast and its image, or for anyone who receives the mark of its name." [12] This calls for patient endurance on the part of the people of God who keep his commands and remain faithful to Jesus.

[13] Then I heard a voice from heaven say, "Write this: Blessed are the dead who die in the Lord from now on."

"Yes," says the Spirit, "they will rest from their labor, for their deeds will follow them."

HARVESTING THE EARTH AND TRAMPLING THE WINEPRESS

[14] I looked, and there before me was a white cloud, and seated on the cloud was one like a son of man[a] with a crown of gold on his head and a sharp sickle in his hand. [15] Then another angel came out of the temple and called in a loud voice to him who was sitting on the cloud, "Take your sickle and reap, because the time to reap has come, for the harvest of the earth is ripe." [16] So he who was seated on the cloud swung his sickle over the earth, and the earth was harvested.

[17] Another angel came out of the temple in heaven, and he too had a sharp sickle. [18] Still another angel, who had charge of the fire, came from the altar and called in a loud voice to him who had the sharp sickle, "Take your sharp sickle and gather the clusters of grapes from the earth's vine, because its grapes are ripe." [19] The angel swung his sickle on the earth, gathered its grapes and threw them into the great winepress of God's wrath. [20] They were trampled in the winepress outside the city, and blood flowed out of the press, rising as high as the horses' bridles for a distance of 1,600 stadia.[b]

SEVEN ANGELS WITH SEVEN PLAGUES

15 I saw in heaven another great and marvelous sign: seven angels with the seven last plagues—last, be cause with them God's wrath is completed. [2] And I saw what looked like a sea of glass glowing with fire and, standing beside the sea, those who had been victorious over the beast and its image and over the number of its name. They held harps given them by God [3] and sang the song of God's servant Moses and of the Lamb:

> "Great and marvelous are your deeds,
>   Lord God Almighty.
> Just and true are your ways,
>   King of the nations.[c]
> [4] Who will not fear you, Lord,
>   and bring glory to your name?
> For you alone are holy.
> All nations will come
>   and worship before you,
> for your righteous acts have been revealed."[d]

[5] After this I looked, and I saw in heaven the temple—that is, the tabernacle of the covenant law—and it was opened.

---

[a] 14 See Daniel 7:13.   [b] 20 That is, about 180 miles or about 300 kilometers   [c] 3 Some manuscripts ages   [d] 3,4 Phrases in this song are drawn from Psalm 111:2,3; Deut. 32:4; Jer. 10:7; Psalms 86:9; 98:2.

What did it mean to harvest the earth? (14:15–16)
This was an image of a farmer harvesting grain at the end of the season and gathering it in. This scene represents preparations for the final judgment.

What was the "tabernacle of the covenant law"? (15:5)
The tabernacle was the place where God's presence dwelled when the Israelites wandered in the desert. It contained the tablets of the law that Moses brought down from Mount Sinai.

⁶Out of the temple came the seven angels with the seven plagues. They were dressed in clean, shining linen and wore golden sashes around their chests. ⁷Then one of the four living creatures gave to the seven angels seven golden bowls filled with the wrath of God, who lives for ever and ever. ⁸And the temple was filled with smoke from the glory of God and from his power, and no one could enter the temple until the seven plagues of the seven angels were completed.

THE SEVEN BOWLS OF GOD'S WRATH

16 Then I heard a loud voice from the temple saying to the seven angels, "Go, pour out the seven bowls of God's wrath on the earth."

²The first angel went and poured out his bowl on the land, and ugly, festering sores broke out on the people who had the mark of the beast and worshiped its image.

³The second angel poured out his bowl on the sea, and it turned into blood like that of a dead person, and every living thing in the sea died.

⁴The third angel poured out his bowl on the rivers and springs of water, and they became blood. ⁵Then I heard the angel in charge of the waters say:

"You are just in these judgments, O Holy One,
    you who are and who were;
⁶for they have shed the blood of your holy people and
        your prophets,
    and you have given them blood to drink as they
        deserve."

⁷And I heard the altar respond:

"Yes, Lord God Almighty,
    true and just are your judgments."

⁸The fourth angel poured out his bowl on the sun, and the sun was allowed to scorch people with fire. ⁹They were seared by the intense heat and they cursed the name of God, who had control over these plagues, but they refused to repent and glorify him.

¹⁰The fifth angel poured out his bowl on the throne of the beast, and its kingdom was plunged into darkness. People gnawed their tongues in agony ¹¹and cursed the God of heaven because of their pains and their sores, but they refused to repent of what they had done.

¹²The sixth angel poured out his bowl on the great river Euphrates, and its water was dried up to prepare the way for the kings from the East. ¹³Then I saw three impure spirits that looked like frogs; they came out of the mouth of the dragon, out of the mouth of the beast and out of the mouth of the false prophet. ¹⁴They are demonic spirits that perform signs, and they go out to the kings of the whole world, to gather them for the battle on the great day of God Almighty.

¹⁵"Look, I come like a thief! Blessed is the one who stays awake and remains clothed, so as not to go naked and be shamefully exposed."

What do the frogs represent? (16:13)
Frogs were unclean animals (see Leviticus 11:10). This image suggests the lies and deception that will lead people to follow evil in the last days.

¹⁶ Then they gathered the kings together to the place that in Hebrew is called Armageddon.

¹⁷ The seventh angel poured out his bowl into the air, and out of the temple came a loud voice from the throne, saying, "It is done!" ¹⁸ Then there came flashes of lightning, rumblings, peals of thunder and a severe earthquake. No earthquake like it has ever occurred since mankind has been on earth, so tremendous was the quake. ¹⁹ The great city split into three parts, and the cities of the nations collapsed. God remembered Babylon the Great and gave her the cup filled with the wine of the fury of his wrath. ²⁰ Every island fled away and the mountains could not be found. ²¹ From the sky huge hailstones, each weighing about a hundred pounds,^a fell on people. And they cursed God on account of the plague of hail, because the plague was so terrible.

BABYLON, THE PROSTITUTE ON THE BEAST

17 One of the seven angels who had the seven bowls came and said to me, "Come, I will show you the punishment of the great prostitute, who sits by many waters. ² With her the kings of the earth committed adultery, and the inhabitants of the earth were intoxicated with the wine of her adulteries."

³ Then the angel carried me away in the Spirit into a wilderness. There I saw a woman sitting on a scarlet beast that was covered with blasphemous names and had seven heads and ten horns. ⁴ The woman was dressed in purple and scarlet, and was glittering with gold, precious stones and pearls. She held a golden cup in her hand, filled with abominable things and the filth of her adulteries. ⁵ The name written on her forehead was a mystery:

BABYLON THE GREAT
THE MOTHER OF PROSTITUTES
AND OF THE ABOMINATIONS OF THE EARTH.

⁶ I saw that the woman was drunk with the blood of God's holy people, the blood of those who bore testimony to Jesus.

When I saw her, I was greatly astonished. ⁷ Then the angel said to me: "Why are you astonished? I will explain to you the mystery of the woman and of the beast she rides, which has the seven heads and ten horns. ⁸ The beast, which you saw, once was, now is not, and yet will come up out of the Abyss and go to its destruction. The inhabitants of the earth whose names have not been written in the book of life from the creation of the world will be astonished when they see the beast, because it once was, now is not, and yet will come.

⁹ "This calls for a mind with wisdom. The seven heads are seven hills on which the woman sits. ¹⁰ They are also seven kings. Five have fallen, one is, the other has not yet come; but when he does come, he must remain for only a little while. ¹¹ The beast who once was, and now is not, is an eighth king. He belongs to the seven and is going to his destruction.

¹² "The ten horns you saw are ten kings who have not yet received a kingdom, but who for one hour will receive

^a 21 Or about 45 kilograms

What is Armageddon? (16:16)
This is the mountain of Megiddo. Many believe Armageddon refers to a valley where a battle will be fought and where God will finally overthrow evil.

Who was the great prostitute sitting on many waters? (17:1)
This was a symbol for Babylon. Babylon was a symbol for everything that was evil and godless. Babylon was also a reference to the Roman Empire.

Who is the eighth king? (17:11)
This isn't known for sure, but some think this is the antichrist who will be defeated by God in the final battle.

authority as kings along with the beast. ¹³They have one purpose and will give their power and authority to the beast. ¹⁴They will wage war against the Lamb, but the Lamb will triumph over them because he is Lord of lords and King of kings—and with him will be his called, chosen and faithful followers."

¹⁵Then the angel said to me, "The waters you saw, where the prostitute sits, are peoples, multitudes, nations and languages. ¹⁶The beast and the ten horns you saw will hate the prostitute. They will bring her to ruin and leave her naked; they will eat her flesh and burn her with fire. ¹⁷For God has put it into their hearts to accomplish his purpose by agreeing to hand over to the beast their royal authority, until God's words are fulfilled. ¹⁸The woman you saw is the great city that rules over the kings of the earth."

LAMENT OVER FALLEN BABYLON

18 After this I saw another angel coming down from heaven. He had great authority, and the earth was illuminated by his splendor. ²With a mighty voice he shouted:

> "'Fallen! Fallen is Babylon the Great!'ᵃ
>   She has become a dwelling for demons
> and a haunt for every impure spirit,
>   a haunt for every unclean bird,
>   a haunt for every unclean and detestable animal.
> ³For all the nations have drunk
>   the maddening wine of her adulteries.
> The kings of the earth committed adultery with her,
>   and the merchants of the earth grew rich from her
>   excessive luxuries."

WARNING TO ESCAPE BABYLON'S JUDGMENT

⁴Then I heard another voice from heaven say:

> "'Come out of her, my people,'ᵇ
>   so that you will not share in her sins,
>   so that you will not receive any of her plagues;
> ⁵for her sins are piled up to heaven,
>   and God has remembered her crimes.
> ⁶Give back to her as she has given;
>   pay her back double for what she has done.
>   Pour her a double portion from her own cup.
> ⁷Give her as much torment and grief
>   as the glory and luxury she gave herself.
> In her heart she boasts,
>   'I sit enthroned as queen.
> I am not a widow;ᶜ
>   I will never mourn.'
> ⁸Therefore in one day her plagues will overtake her:
>   death, mourning and famine.
> She will be consumed by fire,
>   for mighty is the Lord God who judges her.

If Babylon is a reference to Rome, why did John not mention Rome? (18:1–3) There are many hints that he was talking about Rome here. To come out and describe Rome in such negative terms would have been like an act of treason.

ᵃ 2 Isaiah 21:9   ᵇ 4 Jer. 51:45   ᶜ 7 See Isaiah 47:7,8.

THREEFOLD WOE OVER BABYLON'S FALL

⁹"When the kings of the earth who committed adultery with her and shared her luxury see the smoke of her burning, they will weep and mourn over her. ¹⁰Terrified at her torment, they will stand far off and cry:

"'Woe! Woe to you, great city,
    you mighty city of Babylon!
In one hour your doom has come!'

¹¹"The merchants of the earth will weep and mourn over her because no one buys their cargoes anymore— ¹²cargoes of gold, silver, precious stones and pearls; fine linen, purple, silk and scarlet cloth; every sort of citron wood, and articles of every kind made of ivory, costly wood, bronze, iron and marble; ¹³cargoes of cinnamon and spice, of incense, myrrh and frankincense, of wine and olive oil, of fine flour and wheat; cattle and sheep; horses and carriages; and human beings sold as slaves.

¹⁴"They will say, 'The fruit you longed for is gone from you. All your luxury and splendor have vanished, never to be recovered.' ¹⁵The merchants who sold these things and gained their wealth from her will stand far off, terrified at her torment. They will weep and mourn ¹⁶and cry out:

"'Woe! Woe to you, great city,
    dressed in fine linen, purple and scarlet,
    and glittering with gold, precious stones and pearls!
¹⁷In one hour such great wealth has been brought
        to ruin!'

"Every sea captain, and all who travel by ship, the sailors, and all who earn their living from the sea, will stand far off. ¹⁸When they see the smoke of her burning, they will exclaim, 'Was there ever a city like this great city?' ¹⁹They will throw dust on their heads, and with weeping and mourning cry out:

"'Woe! Woe to you, great city,
    where all who had ships on the sea
    became rich through her wealth!
In one hour she has been brought to ruin!'

²⁰"Rejoice over her, you heavens!
    Rejoice, you people of God!
    Rejoice, apostles and prophets!
For God has judged her
    with the judgment she imposed on you."

THE FINALITY OF BABYLON'S DOOM

²¹Then a mighty angel picked up a boulder the size of a large millstone and threw it into the sea, and said:

"With such violence
    the great city of Babylon will be thrown down,
    never to be found again.
²²The music of harpists and musicians, pipers and
        trumpeters,
    will never be heard in you again.

What kind of cargo and merchandise is listed here? (18:11–13)
Many of these were luxurious and expensive items. For example, purple dye was costly because it had to be extracted from the murex shellfish. Citron was an expensive wood from North Africa. Marble was used to decorate public buildings and homes of the very rich. Myrrh and frankincense were used to make incense and perfume.

Why would they throw dust on their heads? (18:19)
This was an act of sorrow and grief.

What is a millstone, and what does this act symbolize? (18:21)
A large millstone required a donkey to turn it because of its size and weight. Throwing a boulder the size of a millstone into the sea was a symbol of complete destruction.

No worker of any trade
    will ever be found in you again.
The sound of a millstone
    will never be heard in you again.
23 The light of a lamp
    will never shine in you again.
The voice of bridegroom and bride
    will never be heard in you again.
Your merchants were the world's important people.
    By your magic spell all the nations were led astray.
24 In her was found the blood of prophets and of God's
        holy people,
    of all who have been slaughtered on the earth."

THREEFOLD HALLELUJAH
OVER BABYLON'S FALL

19 After this I heard what sounded like the roar of a
great multitude in heaven shouting:

"Hallelujah!
Salvation and glory and power belong to our God,
2   for true and just are his judgments.
He has condemned the great prostitute
    who corrupted the earth by her adulteries.
He has avenged on her the blood of his servants."

3 And again they shouted:

"Hallelujah!
The smoke from her goes up for ever and ever."

4 The twenty-four elders and the four living creatures fell
down and worshiped God, who was seated on the throne.
And they cried:

"Amen, Hallelujah!"

5 Then a voice came from the throne, saying:

"Praise our God,
    all you his servants,
you who fear him,
    both great and small!"

6 Then I heard what sounded like a great multitude, like
the roar of rushing waters and like loud peals of thunder,
shouting:

"Hallelujah!
    For our Lord God Almighty reigns.
7 Let us rejoice and be glad
    and give him glory!
For the wedding of the Lamb has come,
    and his bride has made herself ready.
8 Fine linen, bright and clean,
    was given her to wear."
(Fine linen stands for the righteous acts of God's holy people.)

9 Then the angel said to me, "Write this: Blessed are those
who are invited to the wedding supper of the Lamb!" And
he added, "These are the true words of God."

What does the word *Hallelujah* mean? (19:1)
Hallelujah is a combination of
two Hebrew words that mean
"Praise the Lord." The word was
used many times by the writers
of the psalms, but it only appears
four times in the New Testament,
all within the first six verses of
this chapter.

What does the bride symbolize? (19:7)
The bride represents the church,
the whole group of God's people,
who are about to enter a closer
relationship with Christ, almost
like a marriage.

¹⁰At this I fell at his feet to worship him. But he said to me, "Don't do that! I am a fellow servant with you and with your brothers and sisters who hold to the testimony of Jesus. Worship God! For it is the Spirit of prophecy who bears testimony to Jesus."

THE HEAVENLY WARRIOR DEFEATS THE BEAST

¹¹I saw heaven standing open and there before me was a white horse, whose rider is called Faithful and True. With justice he judges and wages war. ¹²His eyes are like blazing fire, and on his head are many crowns. He has a name written on him that no one knows but he himself. ¹³He is dressed in a robe dipped in blood, and his name is the Word of God. ¹⁴The armies of heaven were following him, riding on white horses and dressed in fine linen, white and clean. ¹⁵Coming out of his mouth is a sharp sword with which to strike down the nations. "He will rule them with an iron scepter."ᵃ He treads the winepress of the fury of the wrath of God Almighty. ¹⁶On his robe and on his thigh he has this name written:

KING OF KINGS AND LORD OF LORDS.

¹⁷And I saw an angel standing in the sun, who cried in a loud voice to all the birds flying in midair, "Come, gather together for the great supper of God, ¹⁸so that you may eat the flesh of kings, generals, and the mighty, of horses and their riders, and the flesh of all people, free and slave, great and small."

¹⁹Then I saw the beast and the kings of the earth and their armies gathered together to wage war against the rider on the horse and his army. ²⁰But the beast was captured, and with it the false prophet who had performed the signs on its behalf. With these signs he had deluded those who had received the mark of the beast and worshiped its image. The two of them were thrown alive into the fiery lake of burning sulfur. ²¹The rest were killed with the sword coming out of the mouth of the rider on the horse, and all the birds gorged themselves on their flesh.

THE THOUSAND YEARS

20 And I saw an angel coming down out of heaven, having the key to the Abyss and holding in his hand a great chain. ²He seized the dragon, that ancient serpent, who is the devil, or Satan, and bound him for a thousand years. ³He threw him into the Abyss, and locked and sealed it over him, to keep him from deceiving the nations anymore until the thousand years were ended. After that, he must be set free for a short time.

⁴I saw thrones on which were seated those who had been given authority to judge. And I saw the souls of those who had been beheaded because of their testimony about Jesus and because of the word of God. Theyᵇ had not worshiped the beast or its image and had not received its mark on their

Who was the rider on the white horse? (19:11–16) This was a picture of Jesus returning as Warrior, Messiah, and King.

Why were they consumed by fire? (19:20) This is similar to the picture of Gehenna in Matthew 5:22. Gehenna was a valley south of Jerusalem where human sacrifices were once offered to pagan gods. It later became a dump where fires burned constantly to destroy garbage. It became a symbol of eternal punishment.

ᵃ 15 Psalm 2:9   ᵇ 4 Or God; I also saw those who

foreheads or their hands. They came to life and reigned with Christ a thousand years. [5] (The rest of the dead did not come to life until the thousand years were ended.) This is the first resurrection. [6] Blessed and holy are those who share in the first resurrection. The second death has no power over them, but they will be priests of God and of Christ and will reign with him for a thousand years.

THE JUDGMENT OF SATAN

[7] When the thousand years are over, Satan will be released from his prison [8] and will go out to deceive the nations in the four corners of the earth—Gog and Magog—and to gather them for battle. In number they are like the sand on the seashore. [9] They marched across the breadth of the earth and surrounded the camp of God's people, the city he loves. But fire came down from heaven and devoured them. [10] And the devil, who deceived them, was thrown into the lake of burning sulfur, where the beast and the false prophet had been thrown. They will be tormented day and night for ever and ever.

THE JUDGMENT OF THE DEAD

[11] Then I saw a great white throne and him who was seated on it. The earth and the heavens fled from his presence, and there was no place for them. [12] And I saw the dead, great and small, standing before the throne, and books were opened. Another book was opened, which is the book of life. The dead were judged according to what they had done as recorded in the books. [13] The sea gave up the dead that were in it, and death and Hades gave up the dead that were in them, and each person was judged according to what they had done. [14] Then death and Hades were thrown into the lake of fire. The lake of fire is the second death. [15] Anyone whose name was not found written in the book of life was thrown into the lake of fire.

A NEW HEAVEN AND A NEW EARTH

21 Then I saw "a new heaven and a new earth,"[a] for the first heaven and the first earth had passed away, and there was no longer any sea. [2] I saw the Holy City, the new Jerusalem, coming down out of heaven from God, prepared as a bride beautifully dressed for her husband. [3] And I heard a loud voice from the throne saying, "Look! God's dwelling place is now among the people, and he will dwell with them. They will be his people, and God himself will be with them and be their God. [4] 'He will wipe every tear from their eyes. There will be no more death'[b] or mourning or crying or pain, for the old order of things has passed away."

[5] He who was seated on the throne said, "I am making everything new!" Then he said, "Write this down, for these words are trustworthy and true."

[6] He said to me: "It is done. I am the Alpha and the Omega, the Beginning and the End. To the thirsty I will give water without cost from the spring of the water of life. [7] Those who are victorious will inherit all this, and I will be their God

Who were Gog and Magog? (20:8)
These were pagan rulers in the Old Testament. Here they represent nations of the world joining together for a final assault on God.

Do people's works either save or condemn them? (20:12–13)
No, salvation is by grace alone, but the things people do reflect whether they have been saved or not.

What will the new heaven and earth be like? (21:2–22:5)
The description of the new heaven and earth combines elements of Jerusalem, the temple, and the Garden of Eden. It will be a place of perfection where people will live with God and where there will be no sorrow or death.

[a] 1 Isaiah 65:17   [b] 4 Isaiah 25:8

and they will be my children. ⁸But the cowardly, the unbelieving, the vile, the murderers, the sexually immoral, those
who practice magic arts, the idolaters and all liars—they will
be consigned to the fiery lake of burning sulfur. This is the
second death."

THE NEW JERUSALEM, THE BRIDE
OF THE LAMB

⁹One of the seven angels who had the seven bowls full of
the seven last plagues came and said to me, "Come, I will
show you the bride, the wife of the Lamb." ¹⁰And he carried
me away in the Spirit to a mountain great and high, and
showed me the Holy City, Jerusalem, coming down out of
heaven from God. ¹¹It shone with the glory of God, and its
brilliance was like that of a very precious jewel, like a jasper,
clear as crystal. ¹²It had a great, high wall with twelve gates,
and with twelve angels at the gates. On the gates were written the names of the twelve tribes of Israel. ¹³There were
three gates on the east, three on the north, three on the south
and three on the west. ¹⁴The wall of the city had twelve
foundations, and on them were the names of the twelve
apostles of the Lamb.

¹⁵The angel who talked with me had a measuring rod of
gold to measure the city, its gates and its walls. ¹⁶The city was
laid out like a square, as long as it was wide. He measured the
city with the rod and found it to be 12,000 stadia[a] in length,
and as wide and high as it is long. ¹⁷The angel measured
the wall using human measurement, and it was 144 cubits[b]
thick.[c] ¹⁸The wall was made of jasper, and the city of pure
gold, as pure as glass. ¹⁹The foundations of the city walls
were decorated with every kind of precious stone. The first
foundation was jasper, the second sapphire, the third agate,
the fourth emerald, ²⁰the fifth onyx, the sixth ruby, the seventh chrysolite, the eighth beryl, the ninth topaz, the tenth
turquoise, the eleventh jacinth, and the twelfth amethyst.[d]
²¹The twelve gates were twelve pearls, each gate made of a
single pearl. The great street of the city was of gold, as pure
as transparent glass.

---

[a] 16 That is, about 1,400 miles or about 2,200 kilometers   [b] 17 That is,
about 200 feet or about 65 meters   [c] 17 Or high   [d] 20 The precise
identification of some of these precious stones is uncertain.

What was the shape of the city? (21:16)
The city was a perfect cube, as were the Most Holy Place of the tabernacle and the temple. The entire city will be a place where believers will experience God's presence.

What will heaven be like?   REVELATION 21–22

Heaven is where God's people will live with him forever. Those who are not saved will spend eternity in hell. The Bible gives various word pictures to describe both heaven and hell, but those word pictures give only a general idea about heaven and hell because human beings are not capable of completely understanding how wonderful heaven is or how terrible hell is.

When John wrote about his vision of heaven, he described it as a place of great beauty and light. He compared it to a city that had streets of gold and that had walls covered with precious stones. Does that mean that heaven is literally a city with gold streets? Probably not. In this life, we can only imagine what God and heaven will be like, but our human imaginations are limited by what we know here on earth. Heaven will be far beyond our ability to describe in human terms. Heaven is a place where there will be no sin or sadness. It will be a place of perfection, where we will live with God and see him face to face and live with him for all of eternity.

²²I did not see a temple in the city, because the Lord God Almighty and the Lamb are its temple. ²³The city does not need the sun or the moon to shine on it, for the glory of God gives it light, and the Lamb is its lamp. ²⁴The nations will walk by its light, and the kings of the earth will bring their splendor into it. ²⁵On no day will its gates ever be shut, for there will be no night there. ²⁶The glory and honor of the nations will be brought into it. ²⁷Nothing impure will ever enter it, nor will anyone who does what is shameful or deceitful, but only those whose names are written in the Lamb's book of life.

What is the Lamb's book of life? (21:27)
This is a book listing the names of all who are members of God's kingdom.

EDEN RESTORED

22 Then the angel showed me the river of the water of life, as clear as crystal, flowing from the throne of God and of the Lamb ²down the middle of the great street of the city. On each side of the river stood the tree of life, bearing twelve crops of fruit, yielding its fruit every month. And the leaves of the tree are for the healing of the nations. ³No longer will there be any curse. The throne of God and of the Lamb will be in the city, and his servants will serve him. ⁴They will see his face, and his name will be on their foreheads. ⁵There will be no more night. They will not need the light of a lamp or the light of the sun, for the Lord God will give them light. And they will reign for ever and ever.

Why was it a blessing to see God's face? (22:4)
In ancient times, criminals were banished from the presence of the king. One of the blessings of the new heaven and earth will be the ability to see God face to face.

JOHN AND THE ANGEL

⁶The angel said to me, "These words are trustworthy and true. The Lord, the God who inspires the prophets, sent his angel to show his servants the things that must soon take place."

⁷"Look, I am coming soon! Blessed is the one who keeps the words of the prophecy written in this scroll."

Are these descriptions of the new earth and heaven true? (22:6–8)
The angel testified to John that the message was sent by God. John also testified that he heard and saw all the things recorded in Revelation.

⁸I, John, am the one who heard and saw these things. And when I had heard and seen them, I fell down to worship at the feet of the angel who had been showing them to me. ⁹But he said to me, "Don't do that! I am a fellow servant with you and with your fellow prophets and with all who keep the words of this scroll. Worship God!"

¹⁰Then he told me, "Do not seal up the words of the prophecy of this scroll, because the time is near. ¹¹Let the one who does wrong continue to do wrong; let the vile person continue to be vile; let the one who does right continue to do right; and let the holy person continue to be holy."

EPILOGUE: INVITATION AND WARNING

¹²"Look, I am coming soon! My reward is with me, and I will give to each person according to what they have done. ¹³I am the Alpha and the Omega, the First and the Last, the Beginning and the End.

¹⁴"Blessed are those who wash their robes, that they may have the right to the tree of life and may go through the gates into the city. ¹⁵Outside are the dogs, those who practice magic arts, the sexually immoral, the murderers, the idolaters and everyone who loves and practices falsehood.

¹⁶ "I, Jesus, have sent my angel to give you*ᵃ* this testimony for the churches. I am the Root and the Offspring of David, and the bright Morning Star."

¹⁷ The Spirit and the bride say, "Come!" And let the one who hears say, "Come!" Let the one who is thirsty come; and let the one who wishes take the free gift of the water of life.

¹⁸ I warn everyone who hears the words of the prophecy of this scroll: If anyone adds anything to them, God will add to that person the plagues described in this scroll. ¹⁹ And if anyone takes words away from this scroll of prophecy, God will take away from that person any share in the tree of life and in the Holy City, which are described in this scroll.

²⁰ He who testifies to these things says, "Yes, I am coming soon."

Amen. Come, Lord Jesus.

²¹ The grace of the Lord Jesus be with God's people. Amen.

ᵃ 16 The Greek is plural.

Study
Helps

Table of Weights and Measures

	Biblical Unit	Approximate American Equivalent	Approximate Metric Equivalent
Weights	talent (60 minas)	75 pounds	34 kilograms
	mina (50 shekels)	1 1/4 pounds	560 grams
	shekel (2 bekas)	2/5 ounce	11.5 grams
	pim (2/3 shekel)	1/4 ounce	7.8 grams
	beka (10 gerahs)	1/5 ounce	5.7 grams
	gerah	1/50 ounce	0.6 gram
	daric	1/3 ounce	8.4 grams
Length	cubit	18 inches	45 centimeters
	span	9 inches	23 centimeters
	handbreadth	3 inches	7.5 centimeters
	stadion (pl. stadia)	600 feet	183 meters
Capacity *Dry Measure*	cor [homer] (10 ephahs)	6 bushels	220 liters
	lethek (5 ephahs)	3 bushels	110 liters
	ephah (10 omers)	3/5 bushel	22 liters
	seah (1/3 ephah)	7 quarts	7.5 liters
	omer (1/10 ephah)	2 quarts	2 liters
	cab (1/18 ephah)	1 quart	1 liter
Liquid Measure	bath (1 ephah)	6 gallons	22 liters
	hin (1/6 bath)	1 gallon	3.8 liters
	log (1/72 bath)	1/3 quart	0.3 liter

The figures of the table are calculated on the basis of a shekel equaling 11.5 grams, a cubit equaling 18 inches and an ephah equaling 22 liters. The quart referred to is either a dry quart (slightly larger than a liter) or a liquid quart (slightly smaller than a liter), whichever is applicable. The ton referred to in the footnotes is the American ton of 2,000 pounds. These weights are calculated relative to the particular commodity involved. Accordingly, the same measure of capacity in the text may be converted into different weights in the footnotes.

This table is based upon the best available information, but it is not intended to be mathematically precise; like the measurement equivalents in the footnotes, it merely gives approximate amounts and distances. Weights and measures differed somewhat at various times and places in the ancient world. There is uncertainty particularly about the ephah and the bath; further discoveries may shed more light on these units of capacity.

Becoming a Christian

Becoming a Christian (someone who follows Jesus Christ) is simple. You can find the verses listed by using the table of contents in the front of this Bible. Read the verses and talk to God right now, right where you are. He is always happy to listen.

A ADMIT

Admit honestly to God that you are a sinner and have not obeyed him.

Romans 3:23
Romans 6:23
1 John 1:9

B BELIEVE

Believe that Jesus Christ is God's Son and died on the cross and became alive again. He died for your sins so you can be forgiven.

1 Corinthians 15:3–4
John 3:16
Acts 4:12
Romans 5:8

C CONFESS

Confess your faith in Jesus. Tell someone you know (like a pastor, parent, or other Christian). Then celebrate!

Romans 10:9–10
Romans 10:13

If you don't already attend a church, try to find one. It is important to help you grow in your new life in Christ. On a regular basis try to read the Bible and pray as these things will also play a very important part in helping you get to know God better.

If you just decided to follow Jesus, we would love to hear from you! Write to:

Zonderkidz Bible Editors
Zondervan
5300 Patterson Avenue SE
Grand Rapids, MI 49530

Reading Plans

Of all the reasons people mention for not reading the Bible, simple discouragement ranks highest. The Bible's length alone is imposing. More like a self-contained library than a book, it includes 66 different books, by several dozen authors. Little wonder people get confused and discouraged.

The three-course Reading Plan breaks the Bible into more manageable portions. If you're new to the Bible, begin with Course 1, then proceed to Course 2, and finally—if you're ambitious—tackle Course 3. Your understanding and appreciation for the Bible will gradually increase.

All three courses assign only one chapter a day, except in a few cases where the chapters are very short. The reading should take only about 10 minutes.

COURSE 1: INTRODUCTION TO THE BIBLE

Course 1 is a place to begin reading the Bible. These two-week reading courses take you quickly into passages every Christian should know. Of the 1,189 Bible chapters, why begin with these? First, they are frequently quoted or referred to elsewhere. Second, they are relatively easy to read and understand. Course 1 should whet your appetite for more.

TIME COMMITMENT: TWO WEEKS

Goal: To survey basic Biblical foundations

1. **Two Weeks on the Life and Teachings of Jesus**
   - ☐ Day 1.   Luke 1: Preparing for Jesus' Arrival
   - ☐ Day 2.   Luke 2: The Story of Jesus' Birth
   - ☐ Day 3.   Mark 1: The Beginning of Jesus' Ministry
   - ☐ Day 4.   Mark 9: A Day in the Life of Jesus
   - ☐ Day 5.   Matthew 5: The Sermon on the Mount
   - ☐ Day 6.   Matthew 6: The Sermon on the Mount
   - ☐ Day 7.   Luke 15: Parables of Jesus
   - ☐ Day 8.   John 3: A Conversation with Jesus
   - ☐ Day 9.   John 14: Jesus' Final Instructions
   - ☐ Day 10. John 17: Jesus' Prayer for His Disciples
   - ☐ Day 11. Matthew 26: Betrayal and Arrest
   - ☐ Day 12. Matthew 27: Jesus' Execution on a Cross
   - ☐ Day 13. John 20: Resurrection
   - ☐ Day 14. Luke 24: Jesus' Appearance after Resurrection

2. Two Weeks on the Life and Teachings of Paul

- ☐ Day 1.   Acts 9: The Conversion of Saul
- ☐ Day 2.   Acts 16: Paul's Macedonian Call and a Jailbreak
- ☐ Day 3.   Acts 17: Scenes from Paul's Missionary Journey
- ☐ Day 4.   Acts 26: Paul Tells His Life Story to a King
- ☐ Day 5.   Acts 27: Shipwreck on the Way to Rome
- ☐ Day 6.   Acts 28: Paul's Arrival in Rome
- ☐ Day 7.   Romans 3: Paul's Theology in a Nutshell
- ☐ Day 8.   Romans 7: Struggle with Sin
- ☐ Day 9.   Romans 8: Life in the Spirit
- ☐ Day 10. 1 Corinthians 13: Paul's Description of Love
- ☐ Day 11. 1 Corinthians 15: Thoughts on the Afterlife
- ☐ Day 12. Galatians 5: Freedom in Christ
- ☐ Day 13. Ephesians 3: Paul's Summary of His Mission
- ☐ Day 14. Philippians 2: Imitating Christ

3. Two Weeks on the Old Testament

- ☐ Day 1.   Genesis 1: The Story of Creation
- ☐ Day 2.   Genesis 3: The Origin of Sin
- ☐ Day 3.   Genesis 22: Abraham and Isaac
- ☐ Day 4.   Exodus 3: Moses' Encounter with God
- ☐ Day 5.   Exodus 20: The Gift of the Ten Commandments
- ☐ Day 6.   1 Samuel 17: David and Goliath
- ☐ Day 7.   2 Samuel 11: David and Bathsheba
- ☐ Day 8.   2 Samuel 12: Nathan's Rebuke of the King
- ☐ Day 9.   1 Kings 18: Elijah and the Prophets of Baal
- ☐ Day 10. Job 38: God's Answer to Job
- ☐ Day 11. Psalm 51: A Classic Confession
- ☐ Day 12. Isaiah 40: Words of Comfort from God
- ☐ Day 13. Daniel 6: Daniel and the Lions
- ☐ Day 14. Amos 4: A Prophet's Stern Warning

COURSE 2: A GUIDED TOUR OF THE BIBLE

Course 2 offers a kind of bird's-eye view. The daily readings consist of 180 selected passages, including at least one chapter from each of the Bible's 66 books. You can read both the chapter and its accompanying notes in 15 minutes per day.

With a few exceptions, the Biblical material appears in chronological order. You will read the psalms attributed to David as you read about David's life. You will read the prophets along with their background history. Portions from the Gospels, too, are interspersed, giving a composite picture of Jesus' life on earth; Paul's letters are scattered throughout the record of Jesus' life. This arrangement should help convey the Bible's "plot."

Since "A Guided Tour of the Bible" is arranged in 180 separate readings, most people will find it convenient to read one designated passage each day, along with the notes. If you miss a few days, don't worry. Just resume reading when you can.

TIME COMMITMENT: 180 DAYS

Goal: To understand the underlying story of the Bible

The Plot Unveiled

- ☐ Day 1.   Genesis 1: A Book of Beginnings
- ☐ Day 2.   Genesis 2: One Shining Moment
- ☐ Day 3.   Genesis 3: The Crash
- ☐ Day 4.   Genesis 4: Crouching at the Door
- ☐ Day 5.   Genesis 7: Under Water
- ☐ Day 6.   Genesis 8: The Rainbow
- ☐ Day 7.   Genesis 15: The Plan
- ☐ Day 8.   Genesis 19: A Catastrophe Sent from God
- ☐ Day 9.   Genesis 22: Final Exam
- ☐ Day 10.   Genesis 27: Jacob Gets the Blessing
- ☐ Day 11.   Genesis 28: Something Undeserved
- ☐ Day 12.   Genesis 37: Family Battles
- ☐ Day 13.   Genesis 41: Behind the Scenes
- ☐ Day 14.   Genesis 45: A Long Forgiveness

Birthing a Nation

- ☐ Day 15.   Exodus 3: Time for Action
- ☐ Day 16.   Exodus 10–11: The Ten Plagues
- ☐ Day 17.   Exodus 14: Miracle at the Red Sea
- ☐ Day 18.   Exodus 20: The Ten Commandments
- ☐ Day 19.   Exodus 32: The Dream Dies
- ☐ Day 20.   Leviticus 26: Legal Matters
- ☐ Day 21.   Numbers 11: Trials in the Desert
- ☐ Day 22.   Numbers 14: Open Mutiny
- ☐ Day 23.   Deuteronomy 4: Never Forget
- ☐ Day 24.   Deuteronomy 8: Dangers of Success
- ☐ Day 25.   Deuteronomy 28: Loud and Clear
- ☐ Day 26.   Joshua 2: New Spies, New Spirit
- ☐ Day 27.   Joshua 6: Strange Tactics
- ☐ Day 28.   Joshua 7: Slow Learners
- ☐ Day 29.   Joshua 24: Home at Last
- ☐ Day 30.   Judges 6: Unlikely Leader
- ☐ Day 31.   Judges 7: Military Upset
- ☐ Day 32.   Judges 16: Superman's Flaws
- ☐ Day 33.   Ruth 1: Tough Love

The Golden Age

- ☐ Day 34.   1 Samuel 3: Transition Team
- ☐ Day 35.   1 Samuel 16: Tale of Two Kings
- ☐ Day 36.   Psalm 23: A Shepherd's Song
- ☐ Day 37.   1 Samuel 17: Giant-Killer
- ☐ Day 38.   Psalm 19: Outdoor Lessons

☐ Day 39.   1 Samuel 20: Jonathan's Loyalty
☐ Day 40.   Psalm 27: Ups and Downs
☐ Day 41.   2 Samuel 6: King of Passion
☐ Day 42.   1 Chronicles 17: God's House
☐ Day 43.   Psalm 103: The Goodness of God
☐ Day 44.   2 Samuel 11: Adultery and Murder
☐ Day 45.   2 Samuel 12: Caught in the Act
☐ Day 46.   Psalm 51: True Confession
☐ Day 47.   Psalm 139: David's Spiritual Secret
☐ Day 48.   1 Kings 3: Raw Talent
☐ Day 49.   1 Kings 8: High-Water Mark
☐ Day 50.   Psalm 84: Home Sweet Home
☐ Day 51.   Proverbs 4: Life Advice
☐ Day 52.   Proverbs 10: One-Liners
☐ Day 53.   Proverbs 22: Sayings of the Wise
☐ Day 54.   Song of Songs 2: Love Story
☐ Day 55.   Ecclesiastes 3: A Time for Everything

The Northern Kingdom

☐ Day 56.   1 Kings 17: The Prophets
☐ Day 57.   1 Kings 18: Mountaintop Showdown
☐ Day 58.   2 Kings 5: Double Portion
☐ Day 59.   Joel 2: Word Power
☐ Day 60.   Jonah 3–4: Beloved Enemies
☐ Day 61.   Amos 4: Street-Corner Prophet
☐ Day 62.   Hosea 1, 3: Parable of Love
☐ Day 63.   Hosea 11: Wounded Lover
☐ Day 64.   2 Kings 17: Postmortem

The Southern Kingdom

☐ Day 65.   2 Chronicles 20: Meanwhile in Jerusalem
☐ Day 66.   Micah 6: Pollution Spreads
☐ Day 67.   2 Chronicles 30: Hezekiah's Festival
☐ Day 68.   Isaiah 6: Power behind the Throne
☐ Day 69.   Isaiah 25: Eloquent Hope
☐ Day 70.   2 Chronicles 32: Battlefield Lessons
☐ Day 71.   Nahum 1: Enemy Justice
☐ Day 72.   Zephaniah 3: Rotten Ruling Class
☐ Day 73.   2 Kings 22: Boy Wonder
☐ Day 74.   Jeremiah 2: National Adultery
☐ Day 75.   Jeremiah 15: Balky Prophet
☐ Day 76.   Jeremiah 31: Israel's Future
☐ Day 77.   Jeremiah 38: A Prophet's Perils
☐ Day 78.   Habakkuk 1: Debating God
☐ Day 79.   Lamentations 3: Poet in Shock
☐ Day 80.   Obadiah: No Room to Gloat

Starting Over
- ☐ Day 81.   Ezekiel 1: In Exile
- ☐ Day 82.   Ezekiel 2–3: Toughening Up
- ☐ Day 83.   Ezekiel 4: Write Large and Shout
- ☐ Day 84.   Ezekiel 37: Resurrection Time
- ☐ Day 85.   Daniel 1: Enemy Employers
- ☐ Day 86.   Daniel 3: Ordeal by Fire
- ☐ Day 87.   Daniel 5: Like Father, Like Son
- ☐ Day 88.   Daniel 6: Daniel's Longest Night
- ☐ Day 89.   Ezra 3: Home at Last
- ☐ Day 90.   Haggai 1: A Needed Boost
- ☐ Day 91.   Zechariah 8: Raising Sights
- ☐ Day 92.   Nehemiah 2: A Man for All Seasons
- ☐ Day 93.   Nehemiah 8: Mourning into Joy
- ☐ Day 94.   Esther 4: A Race's Survival
- ☐ Day 95.   Malachi 2: Low-Grade Disappointment

Cries of Pain
- ☐ Day 96.   Job 1–2: Is God Unfair?
- ☐ Day 97.   Job 38: God Speaks to Job
- ☐ Day 98.   Job 42: Happy Ending
- ☐ Day 99.   Isaiah 40: Who's in Charge?
- ☐ Day 100. Isaiah 52: The Suffering Servant
- ☐ Day 101. Isaiah 53: Wounded Healer
- ☐ Day 102. Isaiah 55: The End of It All

A Surprising Messiah
- ☐ Day 103. Luke 1: One Final Hope
- ☐ Day 104. Luke 2: No Fear
- ☐ Day 105. Mark 1: Immediate Impact
- ☐ Day 106. Mark 2: Signal Fires of Opposition
- ☐ Day 107. John 3: Late-Night Rendezvous
- ☐ Day 108. Mark 3: Miracles and Magic
- ☐ Day 109. Mark 4: Hard Soil
- ☐ Day 110. Mark 5: Jesus and Illness
- ☐ Day 111. Matthew 5: Inflammatory Word
- ☐ Day 112. Matthew 6: Sermon on the Mount
- ☐ Day 113. Matthew 13: Kingdom Tales
- ☐ Day 114. Mark 6: Contrast in Power
- ☐ Day 115. Luke 16: Of Two Worlds
- ☐ Day 116. Luke 12: Jesus on Money
- ☐ Day 117. Luke 18: Underdogs

Responses to Jesus
- ☐ Day 118. Luke 15: Master Storyteller
- ☐ Day 119. John 6: Food that Endures
- ☐ Day 120. Mark 7: Poles Apart

☐ Day 121. Matthew 18: Out of Bondage
☐ Day 122. John 10: No Secrets
☐ Day 123. Mark 8: Turning Point
☐ Day 124. Mark 9: Slow Learners
☐ Day 125. Luke 10: Mission Improbable
☐ Day 126. Mark 10: Servant Leadership
☐ Day 127. Mark 11: Opposition Heats Up
☐ Day 128. Mark 12: Baiting Jesus
☐ Day 129. Mark 13: A Day to Dread
☐ Day 130. Mark 14: A Scent of Doom

Final Days

☐ Day 131. John 14: One Final Meal Together
☐ Day 132. John 15: Vital Link
☐ Day 133. John 16: Grief into Joy
☐ Day 134. John 17: Commissioning
☐ Day 135. Matthew 26: Appointment with Destiny
☐ Day 136. Matthew 27: No Justice
☐ Day 137. Mark 15: Removing the Barrier
☐ Day 138. Matthew 28: A Rumor of Life
☐ Day 139. John 20: The Rumor Spreads
☐ Day 140. Luke 24: The Final Link

The Word Spreads

☐ Day 141. Acts 1: Departure
☐ Day 142. Acts 2: Explosion
☐ Day 143. Acts 5: Shock Waves
☐ Day 144. Acts 9: About-Face
☐ Day 145. Galatians 3: Legalism
☐ Day 146. Acts 16: Detour
☐ Day 147. Philippians 2: Downward Mobility
☐ Day 148. Acts 17: Mixed Results
☐ Day 149. 1 Thessalonians 3–4: Preparing for the End
☐ Day 150. 2 Thessalonians 2: Rumor Control
☐ Day 151. 1 Corinthians 13: The Love Chapter
☐ Day 152. 1 Corinthians 15: The Last Enemy
☐ Day 153. 2 Corinthians 4: Baked Dirt
☐ Day 154. 2 Corinthians 12: Boasting of Weakness

Paul's Legacy

☐ Day 155. Romans 3: Remedy
☐ Day 156. Romans 7: Limits of the Law
☐ Day 157. Romans 8: Spirit Life
☐ Day 158. Romans 12: When Christians Disagree
☐ Day 159. Acts 26: Unexpected Passage
☐ Day 160. Acts 27: Perfect Storm
☐ Day 161. Acts 28: Rome at Last

- ☐ Day 162. Ephesians 2: Prison Letter
- ☐ Day 163. Ephesians 3: Success Story
- ☐ Day 164. Colossians 1: Spanning the Gap
- ☐ Day 165. Philemon: A Personal Favor
- ☐ Day 166. Titus 2: Paul's Troubleshooter
- ☐ Day 167. 1 Timothy 1: Growth Pains
- ☐ Day 168. 2 Timothy 2: Final Words

Vital Letters

- ☐ Day 169. Hebrews 2: The Great Descent
- ☐ Day 170. Hebrews 11: What Is True Faith?
- ☐ Day 171. Hebrews 12: Marathon Race
- ☐ Day 172. James 1: Walk the Talk
- ☐ Day 173. 1 Peter 1: Converted Coward
- ☐ Day 174. 2 Peter 1: Hidden Dangers
- ☐ Day 175. Jude: Sounding the Alarm
- ☐ Day 176. 1 John 3: Merest Christianity
- ☐ Day 177. 2 and 3 John: Pesky Deceivers
- ☐ Day 178. Revelation 1: The Final Word
- ☐ Day 179. Revelation 12: Another Side of History
- ☐ Day 180. Revelation 21: An End and a Beginning

COURSE 3: EVERY WORD IN THE BIBLE

Course 3 takes you completely through the Bible, reading every word. Other Bible-reading plans allot only a year for this project, requiring that at least three chapters be read each day. But many readers find such a pace to be unrealistic and discouraging. For this reason, Course 3 assigns only one chapter a day. (Some short chapters have been combined, so occasionally you will read two brief chapters in a day.) In all, the reading plan works out evenly to a three-year total.

The Course 3 plan alternates between the Old Testament and New Testament. This mixing provides variety.

TIME COMMITMENT: THREE YEARS

Goal: To read all the way through the Bible with understanding

GENESIS
☐ 1 ☐ 2 ☐ 3 ☐ 4 ☐ 5 ☐ 6 ☐ 7 ☐ 8
☐ 9 ☐ 10 ☐ 11 ☐ 12 ☐ 13 ☐ 14 ☐ 15
☐ 16 ☐ 17 ☐ 18 ☐ 19 ☐ 20 ☐ 21
☐ 22 ☐ 23 ☐ 24 ☐ 25 ☐ 26 ☐ 27
☐ 28 ☐ 29 ☐ 30 ☐ 31 ☐ 32 ☐ 33
☐ 34 ☐ 35 ☐ 36 ☐ 37 ☐ 38 ☐ 39
☐ 40 ☐ 41 ☐ 42 ☐ 43 ☐ 44 ☐ 45
☐ 46 ☐ 47 ☐ 48 ☐ 49 ☐ 50

MATTHEW 1–9
☐ 1 ☐ 2 ☐ 3 ☐ 4 ☐ 5 ☐ 6 ☐ 7 ☐ 8 ☐ 9

EXODUS
☐ 1 ☐ 2 ☐ 3 ☐ 4 ☐ 5 ☐ 6 ☐ 7 ☐ 8
☐ 9 ☐ 10 ☐ 11 ☐ 12 ☐ 13 ☐ 14 ☐ 15
☐ 16 ☐ 17 ☐ 18 ☐ 19 ☐ 20 ☐ 21 ☐ 22
☐ 23 ☐ 24 ☐ 25 ☐ 26 ☐ 27 ☐ 28 ☐ 29
☐ 30 ☐ 31 ☐ 32 ☐ 33 ☐ 34 ☐ 35 ☐ 36
☐ 37 ☐ 38 ☐ 39 ☐ 40

MATTHEW 10–20
☐ 10 ☐ 11 ☐ 12 ☐ 13 ☐ 14 ☐ 15
☐ 16 ☐ 17 ☐ 18 ☐ 19 ☐ 20

LEVITICUS 1–14
☐ 1 ☐ 2 ☐ 3 ☐ 4 ☐ 5 ☐ 6 ☐ 7 ☐ 8
☐ 9 ☐ 10 ☐ 11 ☐ 12 ☐ 13 ☐ 14

MATTHEW 21–28
☐ 21 ☐ 22 ☐ 23 ☐ 24 ☐ 25 ☐ 26
☐ 27 ☐ 28

LEVITICUS 15–27
☐ 15 ☐ 16 ☐ 17 ☐ 18 ☐ 19 ☐ 20 ☐ 21
☐ 22 ☐ 23 ☐ 24 ☐ 25 ☐ 26 ☐ 27

MARK 1–8
☐ 1 ☐ 2 ☐ 3 ☐ 4 ☐ 5 ☐ 6 ☐ 7 ☐ 8

NUMBERS
☐ 1–2 ☐ 3 ☐ 4 ☐ 5 ☐ 6 ☐ 7 ☐ 8
☐ 9 ☐ 10 ☐ 11 ☐ 12 ☐ 13 ☐ 14 ☐ 15
☐ 16 ☐ 17 ☐ 18 ☐ 19 ☐ 20 ☐ 21
☐ 22 ☐ 23 ☐ 24 ☐ 25 ☐ 26 ☐ 27
☐ 28 ☐ 29 ☐ 30 ☐ 31 ☐ 32 ☐ 33
☐ 34 ☐ 35 ☐ 36

MARK 9–16
☐ 9 ☐ 10 ☐ 11 ☐ 12 ☐ 13 ☐ 14 ☐ 15
☐ 16

DEUTERONOMY 1–17
☐ 1 ☐ 2 ☐ 3 ☐ 4 ☐ 5 ☐ 6 ☐ 7 ☐ 8
☐ 9 ☐ 10 ☐ 11 ☐ 12 ☐ 13 ☐ 14 ☐ 15
☐ 16 ☐ 17

LUKE 1–8
☐ 1 ☐ 2 ☐ 3 ☐ 4 ☐ 5 ☐ 6 ☐ 7 ☐ 8

DEUTERONOMY 18–34
☐ 18 ☐ 19 ☐ 20 ☐ 21 ☐ 22 ☐ 23
☐ 24 ☐ 25 ☐ 26 ☐ 27 ☐ 28 ☐ 29
☐ 30 ☐ 31 ☐ 32 ☐ 33 ☐ 34

LUKE 9–16
☐ 9 ☐ 10 ☐ 11 ☐ 12 ☐ 13 ☐ 14 ☐ 15
☐ 16

JOSHUA
☐ 1 ☐ 2 ☐ 3 ☐ 4 ☐ 5 ☐ 6 ☐ 7 ☐ 8
☐ 9 ☐ 10 ☐ 11 ☐ 12 ☐ 13 ☐ 14 ☐ 15
☐ 16 ☐ 17 ☐ 18 ☐ 19 ☐ 20 ☐ 21
☐ 22 ☐ 23 ☐ 24

LUKE 17–24
☐ 17 ☐ 18 ☐ 19 ☐ 20 ☐ 21 ☐ 22
☐ 23 ☐ 24

JUDGES
☐ 1 ☐ 2 ☐ 3 ☐ 4 ☐ 5 ☐ 6 ☐ 7 ☐ 8
☐ 9 ☐ 10 ☐ 11 ☐ 12 ☐ 13 ☐ 14 ☐ 15
☐ 16 ☐ 17 ☐ 18 ☐ 19 ☐ 20 ☐ 21

JOHN 1–7
☐ 1 ☐ 2 ☐ 3 ☐ 4 ☐ 5 ☐ 6 ☐ 7

RUTH
☐ 1 ☐ 2 ☐ 3 ☐ 4

1 SAMUEL 1–15
☐ 1 ☐ 2 ☐ 3 ☐ 4 ☐ 5 ☐ 6 ☐ 7 ☐ 8
☐ 9 ☐ 10 ☐ 11 ☐ 12 ☐ 13 ☐ 14 ☐ 15

JOHN 8–14
☐ 8 ☐ 9 ☐ 10 ☐ 11 ☐ 12 ☐ 13 ☐ 14

1 SAMUEL 16–31
☐ 16 ☐ 17 ☐ 18 ☐ 19 ☐ 20 ☐ 21
☐ 22 ☐ 23 ☐ 24 ☐ 25 ☐ 26 ☐ 27
☐ 28 ☐ 29 ☐ 30 ☐ 31

JOHN 15–21
☐ 15 ☐ 16 ☐ 17 ☐ 18 ☐ 19 ☐ 20
☐ 21

2 SAMUEL
☐ 1 ☐ 2 ☐ 3 ☐ 4 ☐ 5 ☐ 6 ☐ 7 ☐ 8
☐ 9 ☐ 10 ☐ 11 ☐ 12 ☐ 13 ☐ 14 ☐ 15
☐ 16 ☐ 17 ☐ 18 ☐ 19 ☐ 20 ☐ 21 ☐ 22
☐ 23 ☐ 24

ACTS 1–7
☐ 1 ☐ 2 ☐ 3 ☐ 4 ☐ 5 ☐ 6 ☐ 7

1 KINGS 1–11
☐ 1 ☐ 2 ☐ 3 ☐ 4 ☐ 5 ☐ 6 ☐ 7 ☐ 8
☐ 9 ☐ 10 ☐ 11

ACTS 8–14
☐ 8 ☐ 9 ☐ 10 ☐ 11 ☐ 12 ☐ 13 ☐ 14

1 KINGS 12–22
☐ 12 ☐ 13 ☐ 14 ☐ 15 ☐ 16 ☐ 17
☐ 18 ☐ 19 ☐ 20 ☐ 21 ☐ 22

ACTS 15–21
☐ 15 ☐ 16 ☐ 17 ☐ 18 ☐ 19 ☐ 20
☐ 21

2 KINGS
☐ 1 ☐ 2 ☐ 3 ☐ 4 ☐ 5 ☐ 6 ☐ 7 ☐ 8
☐ 9 ☐ 10 ☐ 11 ☐ 12 ☐ 13 ☐ 14 ☐ 15
☐ 16 ☐ 17 ☐ 18 ☐ 19 ☐ 20 ☐ 21
☐ 22 ☐ 23 ☐ 24 ☐ 25

ACTS 22–28
☐ 22 ☐ 23 ☐ 24 ☐ 25 ☐ 26 ☐ 27
☐ 28

1 CHRONICLES 1–14
☐ 1 ☐ 2 ☐ 3 ☐ 4 ☐ 5 ☐ 6 ☐ 7 ☐ 8
☐ 9 ☐ 10 ☐ 11 ☐ 12 ☐ 13 ☐ 14

ROMANS 1–8
☐ 1 ☐ 2 ☐ 3 ☐ 4 ☐ 5 ☐ 6 ☐ 7 ☐ 8

1 CHRONICLES 15–29
☐ 15 ☐ 16 ☐ 17 ☐ 18 ☐ 19 ☐ 20
☐ 21 ☐ 22 ☐ 23–27 ☐ 28 ☐ 29

ROMANS 9–16
☐ 9 ☐ 10 ☐ 11 ☐ 12 ☐ 13 ☐ 14 ☐ 15
☐ 16

2 CHRONICLES 1–18
☐ 1 ☐ 2 ☐ 3 ☐ 4 ☐ 5 ☐ 6 ☐ 7 ☐ 8
☐ 9 ☐ 10 ☐ 11 ☐ 12 ☐ 13 ☐ 14 ☐ 15
☐ 16–17 ☐ 18

1 CORINTHIANS 1–9
☐ 1 ☐ 2 ☐ 3 ☐ 4 ☐ 5 ☐ 6 ☐ 7 ☐ 8–9

2 CHRONICLES 19–36
☐ 19 ☐ 20 ☐ 21 ☐ 22 ☐ 23 ☐ 24
☐ 25 ☐ 26–27 ☐ 28 ☐ 29 ☐ 30 ☐ 31
☐ 32 ☐ 33 ☐ 34 ☐ 35 ☐ 36

1 CORINTHIANS 10–16
☐ 10 ☐ 11 ☐ 12 ☐ 13 ☐ 14 ☐ 15
☐ 16

EZRA
☐ 1–2 ☐ 3 ☐ 4 ☐ 5 ☐ 6 ☐ 7 ☐ 8
☐ 9 ☐ 10

NEHEMIAH
☐ 1 ☐ 2–3 ☐ 4 ☐ 5 ☐ 6 ☐ 7 ☐ 8 ☐ 9
☐ 10 ☐ 11 ☐ 12 ☐ 13

2 CORINTHIANS
☐ 1 ☐ 2–3 ☐ 4 ☐ 5 ☐ 6 ☐ 7 ☐ 8–9
☐ 10 ☐ 11 ☐ 12–13

ESTHER
☐ 1 ☐ 2 ☐ 3 ☐ 4 ☐ 5 ☐ 6 ☐ 7 ☐ 8
☐ 9–10

JOB 1–21
☐ 1 ☐ 2 ☐ 3 ☐ 4 ☐ 5 ☐ 6 ☐ 7 ☐ 8
☐ 9 ☐ 10 ☐ 11 ☐ 12 ☐ 13 ☐ 14 ☐ 15
☐ 16 ☐ 17 ☐ 18 ☐ 19 ☐ 20 ☐ 21

GALATIANS
☐ 1 ☐ 2 ☐ 3 ☐ 4 ☐ 5–6

JOB 22–42
☐ 22 ☐ 23 ☐ 24 ☐ 25 ☐ 26 ☐ 27
☐ 28 ☐ 29 ☐ 30 ☐ 31 ☐ 32 ☐ 33
☐ 34 ☐ 35 ☐ 36 ☐ 37 ☐ 38 ☐ 39
☐ 40 ☐ 41 ☐ 42

EPHESIANS
☐ 1 ☐ 2 ☐ 3 ☐ 4

PSALMS 1–40
☐ 1–2 ☐ 3–4 ☐ 5 ☐ 6 ☐ 7 ☐ 8 ☐ 9
☐ 10 ☐ 11–12 ☐ 13–14 ☐ 15–16
☐ 17 ☐ 18 ☐ 19 ☐ 20–21 ☐ 22
☐ 23–24 ☐ 25 ☐ 26 ☐ 27 ☐ 28–29
☐ 30 ☐ 31 ☐ 32 ☐ 33 ☐ 34 ☐ 35
☐ 36 ☐ 37 ☐ 38 ☐ 39 ☐ 40

PHILIPPIANS
☐ 1 ☐ 2 ☐ 3 ☐ 4

PSALMS 41–80

☐ 41 ☐ 42 ☐ 43 ☐ 44 ☐ 45 ☐ 46–47
☐ 48 ☐ 49 ☐ 50 ☐ 51 ☐ 52 ☐ 53 ☐ 54
☐ 55 ☐ 56 ☐ 57 ☐ 58 ☐ 59 ☐ 60–61
☐ 62 ☐ 63–64 ☐ 65 ☐ 66 ☐ 67 ☐ 68
☐ 69 ☐ 70 ☐ 71 ☐ 72 ☐ 73 ☐ 74
☐ 75 ☐ 76 ☐ 77 ☐ 78 ☐ 79 ☐ 80

COLOSSIANS

☐ 1 ☐ 2 ☐ 3 ☐ 4

PSALMS 81–121

☐ 81 ☐ 82 ☐ 83 ☐ 84 ☐ 85 ☐ 86
☐ 87 ☐ 88 ☐ 89 ☐ 90 ☐ 91 ☐ 92–93
☐ 94 ☐ 95 ☐ 96 ☐ 97 ☐ 98–99
☐ 100–101 ☐ 102 ☐ 103 ☐ 104
☐ 105 ☐ 106 ☐ 107 ☐ 108 ☐ 109
☐ 110–111 ☐ 112 ☐ 113 ☐ 114
☐ 115 ☐ 116–117 ☐ 118 ☐ 119:1–48
☐ 119:49–96 ☐ 119:97–144
☐ 119:145–176 ☐ 120–121

1 THESSALONIANS

☐ 1–2 ☐ 3–4 ☐ 5

2 THESSALONIANS

☐ 1–2 ☐ 3

PSALMS 122–150

☐ 122–123 ☐ 124–125 ☐ 126–128
☐ 129–130 ☐ 131–132 ☐ 133–134
☐ 135–136 ☐ 137–138 ☐ 139 ☐ 140
☐ 141–142 ☐ 143 ☐ 144 ☐ 145
☐ 146 ☐ 147 ☐ 148 ☐ 149–150

PROVERBS

☐ 1 ☐ 2 ☐ 3 ☐ 4 ☐ 5 ☐ 6 ☐ 7 ☐ 8
☐ 9 ☐ 10 ☐ 11 ☐ 12 ☐ 13 ☐ 14 ☐ 15
☐ 16 ☐ 17 ☐ 18 ☐ 19 ☐ 20 ☐ 21
☐ 22 ☐ 23 ☐ 24 ☐ 25 ☐ 26 ☐ 27
☐ 28 ☐ 29 ☐ 30 ☐ 31

1 TIMOTHY

☐ 1–2 ☐ 3–4 ☐ 5 ☐ 6

ECCLESIATES

☐ 1 ☐ 2 ☐ 3 ☐ 4 ☐ 5 ☐ 6 ☐ 7 ☐ 8
☐ 9 ☐ 10 ☐ 11 ☐ 12

SONG OF SONGS

☐ 1 ☐ 2 ☐ 3 ☐ 4 ☐ 5 ☐ 6 ☐ 7 ☐ 8

2 TIMOTHY

☐ 1 ☐ 2 ☐ 3 ☐ 4

ISAIAH 1–36

☐ 1 ☐ 2 ☐ 3 ☐ 4 ☐ 5 ☐ 6 ☐ 7 ☐ 8
☐ 9 ☐ 10 ☐ 11 ☐ 12 ☐ 13 ☐ 14 ☐ 15
☐ 16 ☐ 17 ☐ 18 ☐ 19–20 ☐ 21 ☐ 22
☐ 23 ☐ 24 ☐ 25 ☐ 26 ☐ 27 ☐ 28
☐ 29 ☐ 30 ☐ 31 ☐ 32 ☐ 33 ☐ 34
☐ 35 ☐ 36

TITUS

☐ 1 ☐ 2–3

ISAIAH 37–66

☐ 37 ☐ 38 ☐ 39 ☐ 40 ☐ 41 ☐ 42
☐ 43 ☐ 44 ☐ 45 ☐ 46 ☐ 47 ☐ 48
☐ 49 ☐ 50 ☐ 51 ☐ 52 ☐ 53 ☐ 54
☐ 55 ☐ 56 ☐ 57 ☐ 58 ☐ 59 ☐ 60
☐ 61 ☐ 62 ☐ 63 ☐ 64 ☐ 65 ☐ 66

PHILEMON

☐ PHILEMON

JEREMIAH 1–27

☐ 1 ☐ 2 ☐ 3 ☐ 4 ☐ 5 ☐ 6 ☐ 7 ☐ 8
☐ 9 ☐ 10 ☐ 11 ☐ 12 ☐ 13 ☐ 14 ☐ 15
☐ 16 ☐ 17 ☐ 18 ☐ 19 ☐ 20 ☐ 21
☐ 22 ☐ 23 ☐ 24 ☐ 25 ☐ 26 ☐ 27

HEBREWS 1–7

☐ 1 ☐ 2 ☐ 3 ☐ 4 ☐ 5 ☐ 6 ☐ 7

JEREMIAH 27–52

☐ 27 ☐ 28 ☐ 29 ☐ 30 ☐ 31 ☐ 32
☐ 33 ☐ 34 ☐ 35 ☐ 36 ☐ 37 ☐ 38
☐ 39 ☐ 40 ☐ 41 ☐ 42 ☐ 43 ☐ 44–45
☐ 46 ☐ 47 ☐ 48 ☐ 49 ☐ 50 ☐ 51
☐ 52

HEBREWS 8–13
☐ 8 ☐ 9 ☐ 10 ☐ 11 ☐ 12 ☐ 13

LAMENTATIONS
☐ 1 ☐ 2 ☐ 3 ☐ 4 ☐ 5

EZEKIEL 1–24
☐ 1 ☐ 2 ☐ 3 ☐ 4 ☐ 5 ☐ 6 ☐ 7 ☐ 8
☐ 9 ☐ 10 ☐ 11 ☐ 12 ☐ 13 ☐ 14 ☐ 15
☐ 16 ☐ 17 ☐ 18 ☐ 19 ☐ 20 ☐ 21
☐ 22 ☐ 23 ☐ 24

JAMES
☐ 1 ☐ 2 ☐ 3 ☐ 4–5

EZEKIEL 25–48
☐ 25 ☐ 26 ☐ 27 ☐ 28 ☐ 29 ☐ 30
☐ 31 ☐ 32 ☐ 33 ☐ 34 ☐ 35 ☐ 36
☐ 37 ☐ 38 ☐ 39 ☐ 40 ☐ 41 ☐ 42
☐ 43 ☐ 44 ☐ 45 ☐ 46 ☐ 47 ☐ 48

1 PETER
☐ 1 ☐ 2 ☐ 3 ☐ 4–5

DANIEL
☐ 1 ☐ 2 ☐ 3 ☐ 4 ☐ 5 ☐ 6 ☐ 7 ☐ 8
☐ 9 ☐ 10 ☐ 11 ☐ 12

2 PETER
☐ 1 ☐ 2 ☐ 3

HOSEA
☐ 1 ☐ 2–3 ☐ 4 ☐ 5 ☐ 6–7 ☐ 8 ☐ 9
☐ 10 ☐ 11–12 ☐ 13–14

JOEL
☐ 1 ☐ 2 ☐ 3

AMOS
☐ 1 ☐ 2 ☐ 3 ☐ 4 ☐ 5 ☐ 6 ☐ 7 ☐ 8
☐ 9

OBADIAH
☐ OBADIAH

JONAH
☐ 1–2 ☐ 3–4

1, 2, 3 JOHN
☐ 1, 2, 3 JOHN

MICAH
☐ 1 ☐ 2 ☐ 3 ☐ 4 ☐ 5 ☐ 6 ☐ 7

NAHUM
☐ 1 ☐ 2 ☐ 3

JUDE
☐ JUDE

HABAKKUK
☐ 1 ☐ 2 ☐ 3

ZEPHANIAH
☐ 1 ☐ 2 ☐ 3

REVELATION 1–7
☐ 1 ☐ 2 ☐ 3 ☐ 4–5 ☐ 6 ☐ 7

HAGGAI
☐ 1 ☐ 2

REVELATION 8–14
☐ 8 ☐ 9 ☐ 10–11 ☐ 12 ☐ 13 ☐ 14

ZECHARIAH
☐ 1 ☐ 2 ☐ 3 ☐ 4 ☐ 5 ☐ 6 ☐ 7 ☐ 8
☐ 9 ☐ 10 ☐ 11 ☐ 12–13 ☐ 14

MALACHI
☐ 1 ☐ 2 ☐ 3–4

REVELATION 15–22
☐ 15–16 ☐ 17 ☐ 18 ☐ 19 ☐ 20 ☐ 21
☐ 22

Subject Index

Adultery Deuteronomy 22:22–25; Proverbs 5:7–14; 6:27–29; 9:17; Jeremiah 5:7–9; Ezekiel 6:9; Hosea 1:2; Matthew 5:27–30

Alcohol Deuteronomy 14:26; 1 Kings 16:9; Proverbs 23:29–35; Isaiah 5:22

Altars Genesis 12:7–8; 26:25; 33:20; Exodus 27:2; Joshua 8:31; 22:10–12; 1 Kings 1:50; 2:28–34; 2 Kings 3:2; 23:19–20; 2 Chronicles 32:12; Isaiah 17:8; Ezekiel 43:13; Acts 17:23; Revelation 9:13

Angel of the Lord Genesis 16:7; 48:16; Psalm 34:6–7

Angels Genesis 32:1–2, 24–30; Judges 2:1, 4; 6:11, 14; 2 Kings 2:11; 1 Chronicles 12:22; Job 4:18–19; Isaiah 6:2; Daniel 4:13; 10:5; 21:1; Matthew 18:10; Mark 16:5; Hebrews 1:4–14; 2:9; Revelation 12:7

Animals Genesis 1:21, 24–25; 7:2; 9:2–3; Exodus 39:34; Ecclesiastes 3:18–21

Anointed one Psalm 20:6

Anointing Exodus 29:7; Leviticus 8:10; 1 Samuel 9:16; 26:9; 1 Kings 1:39; 1 Chronicles 29:22; Psalm 2:2; 92:10; 133:2; Jeremiah 6:20; Luke 7:38

Antichrist 1 John 2:18; Revelation 13:1–4

Ark of the covenant Exodus 25:10–22; Leviticus 16:2; Numbers 4:5; 7:89; Joshua 3:4; 6:9; 1 Samuel 3:3; 4:4; 5:11; 6:9; 7:2; 14:18; 2 Samuel 6:10; 7:2; 1 Kings 8:1–6; 8:9; 1 Chronicles 13:3; 28:18; 2 Chronicles 1:4; 5:10; 35:3; Jeremiah 3:16; Revelation 11:19

Baptism Mark: 1:10–11; Acts 18:25; 22:16; Romans 6:3–4; 1 Peter 3:21; 1 John 5:6

Birthright Genesis 25:31; Deuteronomy 21:15–17; 1 Chronicles 5:1–2; 26:10; Psalm 89:27

Blasphemy Numbers 14:10; Matthew 26:65; Mark 14:64; John 5:18

Blessings Genesis 27:4; 32:26; 48:20; Numbers 23: 8, 11, 25; Ruth 4:12; 2 Samuel 7:19; 1 Chronicles 16:43; Job 42:12; Psalm 1:1; 18:37–42; 33:12; 65:4; 147:19–20; Proverbs 11:11; Ezekiel 36:11

Blood Genesis 9:4

Body Romans 12:4–8; 2 Corinthians 5:1

Book of life Revelation 3:5; 21:27

Bride Song of Songs 4:12

Bridegroom Isaiah 61:10; John 3:29

Burial Joshua 8:24; 24:32; 2 Samuel 2:5–7; 2 Chronicles 24:16; 24:25; Isaiah 14:19; Jeremiah 34:20; Ezekiel 39:14; Amos 2:1; 6:10; Matthew 8:22; Mark 5:3; 14:8; Luke 8:27; 23:56; 24:2; John 11:38; Acts 9:37

Casting lots Joshua 18:10; 1 Samuel 10:20–21; Nehemiah 10:34; Jonah 1:7; Acts 1:26

Census Exodus 30:11–12; Numbers 1:1–2; 1:3; 1:20–43; 3:15; 3:21–22; 26:2–61; 2 Samuel 24:3, 10; 1 Chronicles 21:1, 6–7; 23:3

Cherubim Genesis 3:24; Exodus 25:18; 37:16; Ezekiel 10:12; 41:18

Children Psalm 127:3–5; Proverbs 19:26;

Index to In-Text Maps and Charts

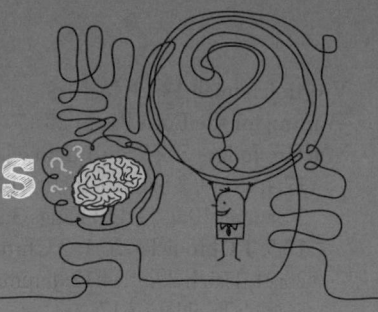

OLD TESTAMENT MAPS

NEW TESTAMENT MAPS

OLD AND NEW TESTAMENT CHARTS

The NIV Concordance, created by John R. Kohlenberger III, has been developed specifically for use with the New International Version (NIV). Like all concordances, it is a special index that contains an alphabetical listing of words used in the Bible text.

This concordance contains 2,474 word entries, with more than 10,000 Scripture references. Each word entry is followed by significant Scripture references in which that particular word is found, as well as by a brief excerpt from the surrounding context. In the context, the entry word is abbreviated by its first letter in bold print. Other forms of the entry word and related words indexed in this concordance are in parentheses.

This concordance also contains 155 biographical entries for significant people in the Bible. The descriptive phrases replace the brief context surrounding each occurrence of the name. In those instances where more than one Bible character has the same name, that name is placed under one block entry, and each person is given a number (1), (2), etc.

Two entries are marked with an asterisk (*). LORD* and LORD'S* list occurrences of the proper name of God, *Yahweh*, spelled "LORD" and "LORD's in the NIV. These entries are distinguished from LORD and LORD's, which list occurrences of the title "Lord" and "Lord's."

This concordance is a valuable tool for Bible study. While one of its key purposes is to help the reader find forgotten references to familiar verses, it can also be used to do word studies and to locate and trace biblical themes. Whenever you find a significant context, be sure to read at least the whole verse in the NIV to discover its fuller meaning in its larger context.

AARON
Priesthood of (Ex 28:1; Nu 17; Heb 5:1-4; 7), garments (Ex 28; 39), consecration (Ex 29), ordination (Lev 8).
Spokesman for Moses (Ex 4:14-16, 27-31; 7:1-2). Supported Moses' hands in battle (Ex 17:8-13). Built golden calf (Ex 32; Dt 9:20). Talked against Moses (Nu 12). Priesthood opposed (Nu 16); staff budded (Nu 17). Forbidden to enter land (Nu 20:1-12). Death (Nu 20:22-29; 33:38-39).

ABANDON
Dt   4: 31 he will not **a** or destroy you
1Ti   4:   1 in later times some will **a** the faith

ABBA
Ro   8: 15 And by him we cry, "**A**, Father."
Gal   4:   6 the Spirit who calls out, "**A**,

ABEL
Second son of Adam (Ge 4:2). Offered proper sacrifice (Ge 4:4; Heb 11:4). Murdered by Cain (Ge 4:8; Mt 23:35; Lk 11:51; 1Jn 3:12).

ABIGAIL
Wife of Nabal (1Sa 25:30); pled for his life with David (1Sa 25:14-35). Became David's wife (1Sa 25:36-42).

ABIJAH
Son of Rehoboam; king of Judah (1Ki 14:31–15:8; 2Ch 12:16–14:1).

ABILITY (ABLE)
Ezr   2: 69 According to their **a** they gave
2Co   1:   8 far beyond our **a** to endure,
         8:   3 were able, and even beyond their **a**.

ABIMELEK
1. King of Gerar who took Abraham's wife Sarah, believing her to be his sister (Ge 20). Later made a covenant with Abraham (Ge 21:22-33).
2. King of Gerar who took Isaac's wife Rebekah, believing her to be his sister (Ge 26:1-11). Later made a covenant with Isaac (Ge 26:12-31).

ABLE (ABILITY ENABLE ENABLED ENABLES)
Eze   7: 19 gold will not be **a** to deliver them

Da   3: 17   the God we serve is **a** to deliver us
Ro   8: 39   will be **a** to separate us
     14:   4   the Lord is **a** to make them stand.
     16: 25   to him who is **a** to establish you
2Co   9:   8   God is **a** to bless you abundantly,
Eph   3: 20   him who is **a** to do immeasurably
2Ti   1: 12   that he is **a** to guard what I have
     3: 15   which are **a** to make you wise
Heb   7: 25   he is **a** to save completely
Jude   : 24   To him who is **a** to keep you
Rev   5:   5   He is **a** to open the scroll and its

ABOLISH
Mt   5: 17   think that I have come to **a** the Law

ABOMINATION
Da   11: 31   set up the **a** that causes desolation.

ABOUND (ABOUNDING ABOUNDS)
2Co   9:   8   you will **a** in every good work.
Php   1:   9   your love may **a** more and more

ABOUNDING (ABOUND)
Ex   34:   6   to anger, **a** in love and faithfulness,
Ps   86:   5   **a** in love to all who call to you.

ABOUNDS (ABOUND)
2Co   1:   5   also our comfort **a** through Christ.

ABRAHAM
Covenant relation with the LORD (Ge 12:1-3; 13:14-17; 15; 17; 22:15-18; Ex 2:24; Ne 9:8; Ps 105; Mic 7:20; Lk 1:68-75; Ro 4; Heb 6:13-15).

Called from Ur, via Harran, to Canaan (Ge 12:1; Ac 7:2-4; Heb 11:8-10). Moved to Egypt, nearly lost Sarah to Pharoah (Ge 12:10-20). Divided the land with Lot (Ge 13). Saved Lot from four kings (Ge 14:1-16); blessed by Melchizedek (Ge 14:17-20; Heb 7:1-20). Declared righteous by faith (Ge 15:6; Ro 4:3; Gal 3:6-9). Fathered Ishmael by Hagar (Ge 16).

Name changed from Abram (Ge 17:5; Ne 9:7). Circumcised (Ge 17; Ro 4:9-12). Entertained three visitors (Ge 18); promised a son by Sarah (Ge 18:9-15; 17:16). Moved to Gerar; nearly lost Sarah to Abimelek (Ge 20). Fathered Isaac by Sarah (Ge 21:1-7; Ac 7:8; Heb 11:11-12); sent away Hagar and Ishmael (Ge 21:8-21; Gal 4:22-30). Tested by offering Isaac (Ge 22; Heb 11:17-19; Jas 2:21-24). Sarah died; bought field of Ephron for burial (Ge 23). Secured wife for Isaac (Ge 24). Death (Ge 25:7-11).

ABSALOM
Son of David by Maakah (2Sa 3:3; 1Ch 3:2). Killed Amnon for rape of his sister Tamar; banished by David (2Sa 13). Returned to Jerusalem; received by David (2Sa 14). Rebelled against David; seized kingdom (2Sa 15-17). Killed (2Sa 18).

ABSTAIN (ABSTAINS)
1Pe   2: 11   and exiles, to **a** from sinful desires,

ABSTAINS (ABSTAIN)
Ro   14:   6   and whoever **a** does so to the Lord

ABUNDANCE (ABUNDANT)
Lk   12: 15   not consist in an **a** of possessions."
Jude   :   2   peace and love be yours in **a**.

ABUNDANT (ABUNDANCE)
Dt   28: 11   will grant you **a** prosperity—
Ps   145:   7   They celebrate your **a** goodness
Pr   28: 19   work their land will have **a** food,
Ro   5: 17   who receive God's **a** provision

ABUSE
2Pe   2: 11   do not heap **a** on such beings

ACCEPT (ACCEPTED ACCEPTS)
Ex   23:   8   "Do not **a** a bribe, for a bribe
Pr   10:   8   The wise in heart **a** commands,
     19: 20   Listen to advice and **a** discipline,
Ro   15:   7   **A** one another, then, just as Christ
Jas   1: 21   humbly **a** the word planted in you,

ACCEPTED (ACCEPT)
Lk   4: 24   "no prophet is **a** in his hometown.

ACCEPTS (ACCEPT)
Ps   6:   9   the LORD **a** my prayer.
Jn   13: 20   whoever **a** anyone I send **a** me;

ACCOMPANY
Mk   16: 17   *these signs will* **a** *those who believe:*

ACCOMPLISH
Isa   55: 11   but will **a** what I desire and achieve

ACCORD
Nu   24: 13   not do anything of my own **a**,
Jn   10: 18   me, but I lay it down of my own **a**.

ACCOUNT (ACCOUNTABLE)
Mt   12: 36   will have to give **a** on the day
Ro   14: 12   of us will give an **a** of ourselves
Heb   4: 13   of him to whom we must give **a**.

ACCOUNTABLE (ACCOUNT)
Eze   33:   6   I will hold the watchman **a** for
Ro   3: 19   and the whole world held **a** to God.

ACCUSATION (ACCUSE)
1Ti   5: 19   not entertain an **a** against an elder

ACCUSE (ACCUSATION)
Pr   3: 30   Do not **a** anyone for no reason—
Lk   3: 14   money and don't **a** people falsely—

ACHAN
Sin at Jericho caused defeat at Ai; stoned (Jos 7; 22:20; 1Ch 2:7).

ACHE
Pr   14: 13   Even in laughter the heart may **a**,

ACKNOWLEDGE
Mt   10: 32   also **a** before my Father in heaven.
1Th   5: 12   **a** those who work hard among you,
Php   2: 11   every tongue **a** that Jesus Christ is
1Jn   4:   3   spirit that does not **a** Jesus is not

ACQUIT
Ex   23:   7   to death, for I will not **a** the guilty.

ACTION (ACTIONS ACTIVE ACTS)
Jas   2: 17   if it is not accompanied by **a**,

ACTIONS (ACTION)
Gal   6:   4   Each one should test their own **a**.
Titus   1: 16   God, but by their **a** they deny him.

ACTIVE (ACTION)
Heb   4: 12   For the word of God is alive and **a**.

ACTS (ACTION)
Ps   145: 12   people may know of your mighty **a**
     150:   2   Praise him for his **a** of power;
Isa   64:   6   all our righteous **a** are like filthy

ADAM
First man (Ge 1:26-2:25; Ro 5:14; 1Ti 2:13). Sin of (Ge 3; Hos 6:7; Ro 5:12-21). Children of (Ge 4:1-5:5). Death of (Ge 5:5; Ro 5:12-21; 1Co 15:22).

ADD
Dt   12: 32   do not **a** to it or take away from it.
Pr   30:   6   Do not **a** to his words, or he will
Lk   12: 25   by worrying can **a** a single hour
Rev   22: 18   them, God will **a** to that person

ADMIRABLE
Php   4:   8   whatever is lovely, whatever is **a**—

ADMONISH
Col   3: 16   and **a** one another with all wisdom

ADOPTION
Ro   8: 23   wait eagerly for our **a** to sonship
Eph   1:   5   he predestined us for **a** to sonship

ADORE
SS   1:   4   How right they are to **a** you!

ADORNMENT (ADORNS)
1Pe   3:   3   should not come from outward **a**,

ADORNS (ADORNMENT)
Ps   93:   5   holiness **a** your house for endless

ADULTERY
Ex   20: 14   "You shall not commit **a**.
Mt   5: 27   was said, 'You shall not commit **a**.'
     5: 28   lustfully has already committed **a**
     5: 32   a divorced woman commits **a**.
     15: 19   murder, **a**, sexual immorality, theft,

ADULTS
1Co 14: 20 but in your thinking be **a**.

ADVANCED
Job 32: 7 **a** years should teach wisdom.

ADVANTAGE
Ex 22: 22 "Do not take a **of** the widow
Dt 24: 14 Do not take **a** of a hired worker
1Th 4: 6 should wrong or take **a** of a brother

ADVERSITY
Pr 17: 17 a brother is born for a time of **a**.

ADVICE
1Ki 12: 8 Rehoboam rejected the **a** the elders
12: 14 he followed the **a** of the young men
Pr 12: 5 but the **a** of the wicked is deceitful.
12: 15 to them, but the wise listen to **a**.
19: 20 Listen to **a** and accept discipline,
20: 18 Plans are established by seeking **a**;

ADVOCATE
Jn 14: 16 he will give you another **a** to help
14: 26 But the **A**, the Holy Spirit,
1Jn 2: 1 sin, we have an **a** with the Father—

AFFECTION
2Pe 1: 7 and to godliness, mutual **a**; and to mutual **a**, love.

AFFLICTION
Ro 12: 12 patient in **a**, faithful in prayer.

AFRAID (FEAR)
Ge 26: 24 Do not be **a**, for I am with you;
Ex 3: 6 because he was **a** to look at God.
Ps 27: 1 of my life—of whom shall I be **a**?
56: 3 When I am **a**, I put my trust in
Pr 3: 24 you lie down, you will not be **a**;
Jer 1: 8 Do not be **a** of them, for I am
Mt 8: 26 of little faith, why are you so **a**?"
10: 28 Do not be **a** of those who kill
10: 31 So don't be **a**; you are worth more
Mk 5: 36 said, Jesus told him, "Don't be **a**,
Jn 14: 27 hearts be troubled and do not be **a**.
Heb 13: 6 Lord is my helper; I will not be **a**.

AGED
Job 12: 12 Is not wisdom found among the **a**?
Pr 17: 6 children are a crown to the **a**,

AGREE
Mt 18: 19 earth **a** about anything they ask for,
Ro 7: 16 want to do, I **a** that the law is good.

AHAB
Son of Omri; king of Israel (1Ki 16:28–22:40), husband of Jezebel (1Ki 16:31). Promoted Baal worship (1Ki 16:31-33); opposed by Elijah (1Ki 17:1; 18; 21), a prophet (1Ki 20:35-43), Micaiah (1Ki 22:1-28). Defeated Ben-Hadad (1Ki 20). Killed for failing to kill Ben-Hadad and for murder of Naboth (1Ki 20:35–21:40).

AHAZ
Son of Jotham; king of Judah, (2Ki 16; 2Ch 28; Isa 7).

AHAZIAH
1. Son of Ahab; king of Israel (1Ki 22:51–2Ki 1:18; 2Ch 20:35-37).
2. Son of Jehoram; king of Judah (2Ki 8:25-29; 9:14-29), also called Jehoahaz (2Ch 21:17–22:9; 25:23).

AIM
1Co 7: 34 Her **a** is to be devoted to the Lord

AIR
1Co 9: 26 not fight like a boxer beating the **a**.
Eph 2: 2 the ruler of the kingdom of the **a**,
1Th 4: 17 clouds to meet the Lord in the **a**.

ALABASTER
Mt 26: 7 him with an **a** jar of very expensive

ALERT
Jos 8: 4 far from it. All of you be on the **a**.
Mk 13: 33 Be **a**! You do not know
Eph 6: 18 be **a** and always keep on praying
1Pe 1: 13 with minds that are **a** and fully

ALIENATED
Gal 5: 4 the law have been **a** from Christ;

ALIVE (LIVE)
Ac 1: 3 convincing proofs that he was **a**.
Ro 6: 11 to sin but **a** to God in Christ Jesus.
1Co 15: 22 die, so in Christ all will be made **a**.
Heb 4: 12 the word of God is **a** and active.

ALMIGHTY (MIGHT)
Ge 17: 1 to him and said, "I am God **A**;
Job 11: 7 Can you probe the limits of the **A**?
33: 4 the breath of the **A** gives me life.
Ps 91: 1 will rest in the shadow of the **A**.
Isa 6: 3 "Holy, holy, holy is the LORD **A**;

ALTAR
Ge 22: 9 Abraham built an **a** there
Ex 27: 1 "Build an **a** of acacia wood,
1Ki 18: 30 he repaired the **a** of the LORD,
2Ch 4: 1 a bronze **a** twenty cubits long,
4: 19 the golden **a**; the tables

ALWAYS
Ps 16: 8 I keep my eyes **a** on the LORD.
26: 3 for I have **a** been mindful of your
51: 3 and my sin is **a** before me.
Mt 26: 11 The poor you will **a** have with you,
28: 20 And surely I am with you **a**,
1Co 13: 7 It **a** protects, **a** trusts, **a** hopes,
Php 4: 4 Rejoice in the Lord **a**. I will say it
1Pe 3: 15 **A** be prepared to give an answer

AMAZIAH
Son of Joash; king of Judah (2Ki 14; 2Ch 25).

AMBASSADORS
2Co 5: 20 We are therefore Christ's **a**,

AMBITION
Ro 15: 20 It has always been my **a** to preach
1Th 4: 11 make it your **a** to lead a quiet life:

AMON
Son of Manasseh; king of Judah (2Ki 21:18-26; 1Ch 3:14; 2Ch 33:21-25).

ANANIAS
1. Husband of Sapphira; died for lying to God (Ac 5:1-11).
2. Disciple who baptized Saul (Ac 9:10-19).
3. High priest at Paul's arrest (Ac 22:30–24:1).

ANCESTORS
Heb 1: 1 spoke to our **a** through the prophets

ANCHOR
Heb 6: 19 We have this hope as an **a**

ANCIENT
Da 7: 9 and the **A** of Days took his seat.

ANDREW
Apostle; brother of Simon Peter (Mt 4:18; 10:2; Mk 1:16-18, 29; 3:18; 13:3; Lk 6:14; Jn 1:35-44; 6:8-9; 12:22; Ac 1:13).

ANGEL (ANGELS ARCHANGEL)
Ps 34: 7 The **a** of the LORD encamps
Ac 6: 15 his face was like the face of an **a**.
2Co 11: 14 Satan himself masquerades as an **a**
Gal 1: 8 or an **a** from heaven should preach

ANGELS (ANGEL)
Ps 8: 5 a little lower than the **a**
91: 11 command his **a** concerning you
Mt 18: 10 that their **a** in heaven always see
25: 41 fire prepared for the devil and his **a**.
Lk 20: 36 for they are like the **a**.
1Co 6: 3 you not know that we will judge **a**?
Heb 1: 4 the **a** as the name he has inherited
1: 14 Are not all **a** ministering spirits
2: 7 them a little lower than the **a**;
13: 2 hospitality to **a** without knowing it.
1Pe 1: 12 Even **a** long to look into these
2Pe 2: 4 if God did not spare **a** when they

ANGER (ANGERED ANGRY)
Ex 32: 10 that my **a** may burn against them
34: 6 slow to **a**, abounding in love

Dt 29: 28 In furious **a** and in great wrath
2Ki 22: 13 Great is the LORD's **a** that burns
Ps 30: 5 For his **a** lasts only a moment,
Pr 15: 1 wrath, but a harsh word stirs up **a**.

ANGERED (ANGER)
Pr 22: 24 do not associate with one easily **a**,
1Co 13: 5 it is not easily **a**, it keeps no record

ANGRY (ANGER)
Ps 2: 12 he will be **a** and your way will lead
Pr 29: 22 An **a** person stirs up conflict,
Jas 1: 19 to speak and slow to become **a**,

ANOINT
Ps 23: 5 You **a** my head with oil;
Jas 5: 14 **a** them with oil in the name

ANOTHER
1Pe 3: 8 love one **a**, be compassionate

ANT
Pr 6: 6 Go to the **a**, you sluggard;

ANTICHRIST
1Jn 2: 18 have heard that the **a** is coming,
2Jn : 7 person is the deceiver and the **a**.

ANTIOCH
Ac 11: 26 were called Christians first at **A**.

ANXIETY
Pr 12: 25 **A** weighs down the heart,
1Pe 5: 7 Cast all your **a** on him because he

ANXIOUS (ANXIETY)
Php 4: 6 Do not be **a** about anything,

APOLLOS
  Christian from Alexandria, learned in the Scriptures; instructed by Aquila and Priscilla (Ac 18:24-28). Ministered at Corinth (Ac 19:1; 1Co 1:12; 3; Titus 3:13).

APOSTLES
  See also Andrew, Bartholomew, James, John, Judas, Matthew, Nathanael, Paul, Peter, Philip, Simon, Thaddaeus, Thomas.
Ac 1: 26 so he was added to the eleven **a**.
     2: 43 and signs performed by the **a**.
1Co 12: 28 placed in the church first of all **a**,
     15: 9 For I am the least of the **a** and do
2Co 11: 13 For such people are false **a**,
Eph 2: 20 built on the foundation of the **a**

APPEAR (APPEARANCE APPEARING)
Mk 13: 22 false prophets will **a** and perform
2Co 5: 10 we must all **a** before the judgment
Col 3: 4 you also will **a** with him in glory.
Heb 9: 24 now to **a** for us in God's presence.
     9: 28 he will **a** a second time,

APPEARANCE (APPEAR)
1Sa 16: 7 People look at the outward **a**,

APPEARING (APPEAR)
2Ti 4: 8 to all who have longed for his **a**.
Titus 2: 13 the **a** of the glory of our great God

APPLY
Pr 22: 17 **a** your heart to what I teach,
    23: 12 **A** your heart to instruction and

APPROACH
Eph 3: 12 we may **a** God with freedom
Heb 4: 16 then **a** God's throne of grace

APPROVED
2Ti 2: 15 to present yourself to God as one **a**,

AQUILA
  Husband of Priscilla; co-worker with Paul, instructor of Apollos (Ac 18; Ro 16:3; 1Co 16:19; 2Ti 4:19).

ARARAT
Ge 8: 4 to rest on the mountains of **A**.

ARCHANGEL (ANGEL)
1Th 4: 16 with the voice of the **a**
Jude : 9 But even the **a** Michael, when he

ARCHITECT
Heb 11: 10 whose **a** and builder is God.

ARGUING
Php 2: 14 everything without grumbling or **a**,

ARK
Ge 6: 14 So make yourself an **a** of cypress
Dt 10: 5 put the tablets in the **a** I had made,
2Ch 35: 3 "Put the sacred **a** in the temple
Heb 9: 4 This **a** contained the gold jar

ARM (ARMY)
Nu 11: 23 "Is the LORD's **a** too short?
1Pe 4: 1 **a** yourselves also with the same

ARMAGEDDON
Rev 16: 16 place that in Hebrew is called **A**.

ARMOR (ARMY)
1Ki 20: 11 his **a** should not boast like one who
Eph 6: 11 Put on the full **a** of God, so that
     6: 13 Therefore put on the full **a** of God,

ARMS (ARMY)
Dt 33: 27 underneath are the everlasting **a**.
Ps 18: 32 It is God who **a** me with strength
Pr 31: 20 She opens her **a** to the poor
Isa 40: 11 He gathers the lambs in his **a**
Mk 10: 16 And he took the children in his **a**,

ARMY (ARM ARMOR ARMS)
Ps 33: 16 king is saved by the size of his **a**;
Rev 19: 19 the rider on the horse and his **a**.

AROMA
2Co 2: 15 the pleasing **a** of Christ among
     2: 16 one we are an **a** that brings death;
     2: 16 to the other, an **a** that brings life.

ARRAYED
Ps 110: 3 **A** in holy splendor, your young
Isa 61: 10 **a** me in a robe of his righteousness,

ARROGANT
Ro 11: 20 Do not be **a**, but tremble.

ARROWS
Eph 6: 16 can extinguish all the flaming **a**

ASA
  King of Judah (1Ki 15:8-24; 1Ch 3:10; 2Ch 14-16).

ASCENDED
Eph 4: 8 "When he **a** on high, he took many

ASCRIBE
1Ch 16: 28 **A** to the LORD, all you families
     16: 28 **a** to the LORD glory and strength.
Job 36: 3 I will **a** justice to my Maker.
Ps 29: 2 **A** to the LORD the glory due his

ASHAMED (SHAME)
Lk 9: 26 Whoever is **a** of me and my words, the Son of Man will be **a** of them
Ro 1: 16 For I am not **a** of the gospel,
2Ti 1: 8 So do not be **a** of the testimony
    2: 15 worker who does not need to be **a**

ASSIGNED
Mk 13: 34 each with their **a** task, and tells
1Co 3: 5 as the Lord has **a** to each his task.
    7: 17 whatever situation the Lord has **a**

ASSOCIATE
Pr 22: 24 do not **a** with one easily angered,
Ro 12: 16 be willing to **a** with people of low
1Co 5: 11 you must not **a** with anyone who
2Th 3: 14 Do not **a** with them, in order

ASSURANCE
Heb 10: 22 and with the full **a** that faith brings,

ASTRAY
Pr 10: 17 ignores correction leads others **a**.
Isa 53: 6 have gone **a**, each of us has turned
Jer 50: 6 their shepherds have led them **a**
1Pe 2: 25 For "you were like sheep going **a**,"
1Jn 3: 7 do not let anyone lead you **a**.

ATHALIAH
  Evil queen of Judah (2Ki 11; 2Ch 23).

ATHLETE
2Ti 2: 5 competes as an **a** does not receive

ATONEMENT
Ex 25: 17 "Make an **a** cover of pure gold–
30: 10 Once a year Aaron shall make **a**
Lev 17: 11 blood that makes **a** for one's life.
23: 27 this seventh month is the Day of **A**.
Nu 25: 13 God and made **a** for the Israelites."
Ro 3: 25 presented Christ as a sacrifice of **a**,
Heb 2: 17 that he might make **a** for the sins

ATTENTION
Pr 4: 1 pay **a** and gain understanding.
5: 1 My son, pay **a** to my wisdom,
22: 17 Pay **a** and turn your ear
Titus 1: 14 and will pay no **a** to Jewish myths

ATTITUDE (ATTITUDES)
Eph 4: 23 made new in the **a** of your minds;
1Pe 4: 1 yourselves also with the same **a**,

ATTITUDES (ATTITUDE)
Heb 4: 12 the thoughts and **a** of the heart.

ATTRACTIVE
Titus 2: 10 teaching about God our Savior **a**.

AUTHORITIES (AUTHORITY)
Ro 13: 5 it is necessary to submit to the **a**,
13: 6 for the **a** are God's servants,
Titus 3: 1 to be subject to rulers and **a**,
1Pe 3: 22 **a** and powers in submission to him.

AUTHORITY (AUTHORITIES)
Mt 7: 29 he taught as one who had **a**,
9: 6 the Son of Man has **a** on earth
28: 18 "All **a** in heaven and on earth has
Ro 13: 1 for there is no **a** except
13: 2 rebels against the **a** is rebelling
1Co 11: 10 ought to have **a** over her own head,
1Ti 2: 2 for kings and all those in **a**, that we
2: 12 to teach or to assume **a** over a man;
Heb 13: 17 your leaders and submit to their **a**,

AVENGE (VENGEANCE)
Dt 32: 35 It is mine to **a**; I will repay.

AVOID
Pr 20: 3 It is to one's honor to **a** strife,
20: 19 so **a** anyone who talks too much.
1Th 4: 3 you should **a** sexual immorality;
2Ti 2: 16 **A** godless chatter, because those
Titus 3: 9 But **a** foolish controversies

AWAKE
Ps 17: 15 when I **a**, I will be satisfied
1Th 5: 6 asleep, but let us be **a** and sober.

AWE (AWESOME)
Job 25: 2 "Dominion and **a** belong to God;
Ps 119:120 of you; I stand in **a** of your laws.
Isa 29: 23 will stand in **a** of the God of Israel.
Jer 33: 9 they will be in **a** and will tremble
Hab 3: 2 I stand in **a** of your deeds, Lord.
Mal 2: 5 me and stood in **a** of my name.
Mt 9: 8 saw this, they were filled with **a**;
Lk 7: 16 They were all filled with **a**
Ac 2: 43 Everyone was filled with **a**
Heb 12: 28 acceptably with reverence and **a**,

AWESOME (AWE)
Ge 28: 17 and said, "How **a** is this place!
Ex 15: 11 majestic in holiness, **a** in glory,
Dt 7: 21 is among you, is a great and **a** God.
10: 17 God, mighty and **a**, who shows no
28: 58 revere this glorious and **a** name–
Jdg 13: 6 looked like an angel of God, very **a**.
Ne 1: 5 the great and **a** God, who keeps his
9: 32 God, mighty and **a**, who keeps his
Job 10: 16 again display your **a** power against
37: 22 God comes in **a** majesty.
Ps 45: 4 your right hand achieve **a** deeds.
47: 2 For the Lord Most High is **a**,
66: 5 has done, his **a** deeds for mankind!
68: 35 You, God, are **a** in your sanctuary;
89: 7 he is more **a** than all who surround
99: 3 praise your great and **a** name–

Ps 111: 9 holy and **a** is his name.
145: 6 tell of the power of your **a** works–
Da 9: 4 the great and **a** God, who keeps his

BAAL
1Ki 18: 25 Elijah said to the prophets of **B**,

BAASHA
King of Israel (1Ki 15:16–16:7; 2Ch 16:1-6).

BABIES (BABY)
Lk 18: 15 bringing **b** to Jesus for him to place
1Pe 2: 2 Like newborn **b**, crave pure

BABY (BABIES)
Isa 49: 15 "Can a mother forget the **b** at her
Lk 1: 44 the **b** in my womb leaped for joy.
2: 12 You will find a **b** wrapped in cloths
Jn 16: 21 **b** is born she forgets the anguish

BABYLON
Ps 137: 1 By the rivers of **B** we sat and wept

BACKSLIDING
Jer 3: 22 I will cure you of **b**."
Eze 37: 23 save them from all their sinful **b**,

BAGS
Mt 25: 15 To one he gave five **b** of gold, to another
two **b**, and to another one

BALAAM
Prophet who attempted to curse Israel (Nu 22-24; Dt 23:4-5; 2Pe 2:15; Jude 11). Killed (Nu 31:8; Jos 13:22).

BALM
Jer 8: 22 Is there no **b** in Gilead? Is there no

BANISH
Jer 25: 10 will **b** from them the sounds of joy

BANQUET
SS 2: 4 Let him lead me to the **b** hall,
Lk 14: 13 But when you give a **b**,

BAPTIZE (BAPTIZED)
Mt 3: 11 "I **b** you with water for repentance.
3: 11 He will **b** you with the Holy Spirit
Mk 1: 8 I **b** you with water, but he will **b**
1Co 1: 17 For Christ did not send me to **b**,

BAPTIZED (BAPTIZE)
Mt 3: 6 they were **b** by him in the Jordan
Mk 1: 9 and was **b** by John in the Jordan.
10: 38 be **b** with the baptism I am **b** with?"
16: 16 believes and is **b** will be saved,
Jn 4: 2 in fact it was not Jesus who **b**,
Ac 1: 5 For John **b** with water, but in a few

BARABBAS
Mt 27: 17 release to you: Jesus **B**, or Jesus

BARBS
Nu 33: 55 remain will become **b** in your eyes

BARE
Heb 4: 13 and laid **b** before the eyes of him

BARNABAS
Disciple, originally Joseph (Ac 4:36), prophet (Ac 13:1), apostle (Ac 14:14). Brought Paul to apostles (Ac 9:27), Antioch (Ac 11:22-29; Gal 2:1-13), on the first missionary journey (Ac 13-14). Together at Jerusalem Council, they separated over John Mark (Ac 15). Later co-workers (1Co 9:6; Col 4:10).

BARTHOLOMEW
Apostle (Mt 10:3; Mk 3:18; Lk 6:14; Ac 1:13). Possibly also known as Nathanael (Jn 1:45-49; 21:2).

BATH
Jn 13: 10 who have had a **b** need only

BATHSHEBA
Wife of Uriah who committed adultery with and became wife of David (2Sa 11), mother of Solomon (2Sa 12:24; 1Ki 1-2; 1Ch 3:5).

BATTLE
2Ch 20: 15 For the **b** is not yours, but God's.
Ps 24: 8 mighty, the Lord mighty in **b**.
Ecc 9: 11 to the swift or the **b** to the strong,

BEAR (BEARING BIRTH BIRTHRIGHT BORE BORN FIRSTBORN NEWBORN)
Ge   4: 13 punishment is more than I can **b**.
Ps 38: 4 me like a burden too heavy to **b**.
Isa 53: 11 many, and he will **b** their iniquities.
Da   7: 5 beast, which looked like a **b**.
Mt   7: 18 A good tree cannot **b** bad fruit,
Jn 15: 2 branch that does **b** fruit he prunes
    15: 16 so that you might go and **b** fruit–
Ro 15: 1 We who are strong ought to **b**
1Co 10: 13 tempted beyond what you can **b**.
Col 3: 13 **B** with each other and forgive one

BEARING (BEAR)
Eph 4: 2 patient, **b** with one another in love.
Col 1: 10 **b** fruit in every good work,

BEAST
Rev 13: 18 calculate the number of the **b**, for it

BEAT (BEATING)
Isa 2: 4 They will **b** their swords
Joel 3: 10 **B** your plowshares into swords

BEATING (BEAT)
1Co 9: 26 I do not fight like a boxer **b** the air.
1Pe 2: 20 if you receive a **b** for doing wrong

BEAUTIFUL (BEAUTY)
Ge   6: 2 the daughters of humans were **b**,
    12: 11 "I know what a **b** woman you are.
    12: 14 saw that Sarai was a very **b** woman.
    24: 16 The woman was very **b**, a virgin;
    26: 7 of Rebekah, because she is **b**."
    29: 17 had a lovely figure and was **b**.
Pr 11: 22 snout is a **b** woman who shows no
Ecc 3: 11 He has made everything **b** in its
Isa 4: 2 the Branch of the LORD will be **b**
    52: 11 How **b** on the mountains and rose
Eze 20: 6 and honey, the most **b** of all lands.
Zec 9: 17 How attractive and **b** they will be!
Mt 23: 27 which look **b** on the outside
    26: 10 She has done a **b** thing to me.
Ro 10: 15 "How **b** are the feet of those who

BEAUTY (BEAUTIFUL)
Ps 27: 4 to gaze on the **b** of the LORD
    45: 11 the king be enthralled by your **b**;
Pr 31: 30 is deceptive, and **b** is fleeting;
Isa 33: 17 Your eyes will see the king in his **b**
    53: 2 He had no **b** or majesty to attract
    61: 3 them a crown of **b** instead of ashes,
Eze 28: 12 full of wisdom and perfect in **b**.
1Pe 3: 4 unfading **b** of a gentle and quiet

BED
Heb 13: 4 and the marriage **b** kept pure,

BEELZEBUL
Lk 11: 15 said, "By **B**, the prince of demons,

BEER
Pr 20: 1 Wine is a mocker and **b** a brawler;

BEERSHEBA
Jdg 20: 1 all Israel from Dan to **B**

BEGINNING
Ge   1: 1 In the **b** God created the heavens
Ps 102: 25 In the **b** you laid the foundations
   111: 10 of the LORD is the **b** of wisdom;
Pr   1: 7 the LORD is the **b** of knowledge,
     4: 7 The **b** of wisdom is this:
Jn   1: 1 In the **b** was the Word,
1Jn 1: 1 That which was from the **b**,
Rev 21: 6 and the Omega, the **B** and the End.

BEHAVE (BEHAVIOR)
Ro 13: 13 us **b** decently, as in the daytime,

BEHAVIOR (BEHAVE)
Pr   1: 3 receiving instruction in prudent **b**,

BELIEVE (BELIEVED BELIEVER BELIEVERS BELIEVES BELIEVING)
Pr 14: 15 The simple **b** anything,
Mt 18: 6 those who **b** in me–

Mt 21: 22 If you **b**, you will receive whatever
Mk   1: 15 Repent and **b** the good news!"
     9: 24 the boy's father exclaimed, "I do **b**;
    16: 17 accompany those who **b**:
Lk   8: 50 just **b**, and she will be healed."
    24: 25 how slow to **b** all that the prophets
Jn   1: 7 so that through him all might **b**.
     3: 18 does not **b** stands condemned
     6: 29 to **b** in the one he has sent."
    10: 38 even though you do not **b** me,
    11: 27 "I **b** that you are the Messiah,
    14: 1 You **b** in God; **b** also in me.
    14: 11 **B** me when I say that I am
    16: 30 This makes us **b** that you came
    16: 31 "Do you now **b**?" Jesus replied.
    17: 21 the world may **b** that you have sent
    20: 27 into my side. Stop doubting and **b**."
    20: 31 may **b** that Jesus is the Messiah,
Ac 16: 31 They replied, "**B** in the Lord Jesus,
    24: 14 I **b** everything that is in accordance
Ro   3: 22 faith in Jesus Christ to all who **b**.
     4: 11 he is the father of all who **b**
    10: 9 **b** in your heart that God raised
    10: 14 how can they **b** in the one of whom
1Th 4: 14 For we **b** that Jesus died and rose
2Th 2: 11 delusion so that they will **b** the lie
1Ti 4: 10 and especially of those who **b**.
Titus 1: 6 a man whose children **b** and are
Heb 11: 6 comes to him must **b** that he exists
Jas 2: 19 You **b** that there is one God. Good! Even the
                demons **b** that–
1Jn 4: 1 Dear friends, do not **b** every spirit,

BELIEVED (BELIEVE)
Ge 15: 6 Abram **b** the LORD, and he
Jnh 3: 5 The Ninevites **b** God. A fast was
Jn   1: 12 to those who **b** in his name,
     2: 22 Then they **b** the scripture
     3: 18 already because they have not **b**
    20: 8 also went inside. He saw and **b**.
    20: 29 who have not seen and yet have **b**."
Ac 13: 48 were appointed for eternal life **b**.
Ro   4: 3 "Abraham **b** God, and it was
    10: 14 call on the one they have not **b** in?
1Co 15: 2 Otherwise, you have **b** in vain.
Gal 3: 6 So also Abraham "**b** God, and it
2Ti 1: 12 because I know whom I have **b**,
Jas 2: 23 that says, "Abraham **b** God, and it

BELIEVER (BELIEVE)
1Co 7: 12 brother has a wife who is not a **b**
2Co 6: 15 what does a **b** have in common

BELIEVERS (BELIEVE)
Ac   4: 32 All the **b** were one in heart
     5: 12 all the **b** used to meet together
1Co 6: 5 to judge a dispute between **b**?
1Ti 4: 12 set an example for the **b** in speech,
1Pe 2: 17 love the family of **b**, fear God,

BELIEVES (BELIEVE)
Mk   9: 23 is possible for one who **b**."
    11: 23 **b** that what they say will happen,
    16: 16 Whoever **b** and is baptized
Jn   3: 16 whoever **b** in him shall not perish
     3: 36 Whoever **b** in the Son has eternal
     5: 24 him who sent me has eternal life
     6: 35 and whoever **b** in me will never be
     6: 40 and **b** in him shall have eternal life,
     6: 47 you, the one who **b** has eternal life.
     7: 38 Whoever **b** in me, as Scripture has
Ro   1: 16 salvation to everyone who **b**:
     9: 33 the one who **b** in him will never be
    10: 4 righteousness for everyone who **b**.
1Jn 5: 1 Everyone who **b** that Jesus is
     5: 5 Only the one who **b** that Jesus is

BELIEVING (BELIEVE)
Jn 11: 26 whoever lives by **b** in me will never
    20: 31 by **b** you may have life in his name.

BELONG (BELONGS)
Dt 29: 29 The secret things **b** to the Lord
Job 25: 2 "Dominion and awe **b** to God;
Ps 47: 9 for the kings of the earth **b** to God;
95: 4 and the mountain peaks **b** to him.
Jn 8: 44 You **b** to your father, the devil,
15: 19 As it is, you do not **b** to the world,
Ro 1: 6 those Gentiles who are called to **b**
7: 4 that you might **b** to another, to him
14: 8 we live or die, we **b** to the Lord.
Gal 5: 24 Those who **b** to Christ Jesus have
1Th 5: 8 But since we **b** to the day, let us be

BELONGS (BELONG)
Job 41: 11 Everything under heaven **b** to me.
Ps 111: 10 To him **b** eternal praise.
Eze 18: 4 For everyone **b** to me, the parent as
Jn 8: 47 Whoever **b** to God hears what God
Ro 12: 5 each member **b** to all the others.

BELOVED (LOVE)
Dt 33: 12 "Let the **b** of the Lord rest
SS 2: 16 My **b** is mine and I am his;
7: 10 I belong to my **b**, and his desire is

BELT
Isa 11: 5 Righteousness will be his **b**
Eph 6: 14 the **b** of truth buckled around your

BENEFICIAL (BENEFIT)
1Co 10: 23 but not everything is **b**.

BENEFIT (BENEFICIAL BENEFITS)
Ro 6: 22 the **b** you reap leads to holiness,
2Co 4: 15 All this is for your **b**,

BENEFITS (BENEFIT)
Ps 103: 2 my soul, and forget not all his **b**–
Jn 4: 38 and you have reaped the **b** of their

BENJAMIN
Twelfth son of Jacob by Rachel (Ge 35:16-24; 46:19-21;
1Ch 2:2). Jacob refused to send him to Egypt, but relented
(Ge 42-45).

BEREAN
Ac 17: 11 the **B** Jews were of more noble

BESTOWS
Ps 84: 11 the Lord **b** favor and honor;

BETHLEHEM
Mt 2: 1 After Jesus was born in **B** in Judea,

BETRAY
Pr 25: 9 do not **b** another's confidence,

BIND (BINDS)
Dt 6: 8 and **b** them on your foreheads.
Pr 6: 21 **B** them always on your heart;
Isa 61: 1 He has sent me to **b**
Mt 16: 19 whatever you **b** on earth will be

BINDS (BIND)
Ps 147: 3 and **b** up their wounds.
Isa 30: 26 when the Lord **b** up the bruises

BIRDS
Mt 8: 20 "Foxes have dens and **b** have nests,

BIRTH (BEAR)
Ps 58: 3 Even from **b** the wicked go astray;
Mt 1: 18 This is how the **b** of Jesus
1Pe 1: 3 great mercy he has given us new **b**

BIRTHRIGHT (BEAR)
Ge 25: 34 up and left. So Esau despised his **b**.

BLAMELESS
Ge 17: 1 walk before me faithfully and be **b**.
Job 1: 1 This man was **b** and upright;
Ps 84: 11 from those whose walk is **b**.
119: 1 are those whose ways are **b**,
Pr 19: 1 poor whose walk is **b** than a fool
1Co 1: 8 so that you will be **b** on the day
Eph 5: 27 any other blemish, but holy and **b**.
Php 2: 15 that you may become **b** and pure,
1Th 3: 13 your hearts so that you will be **b**
5: 23 body be kept **b** at the coming of
Titus 1: 6 An elder must be **b**, faithful to his

Heb 7: 26 one who is holy, **b**, pure, set apart
2Pe 3: 14 spotless, **b** and at peace with him.

BLASPHEMES
Mk 3: 29 whoever **b** against the Holy Spirit

BLEMISH
1Pe 1: 19 Christ, a lamb without **b** or defect.

BLESS (BLESSED BLESSING BLESSINGS)
Ge 12: 3 I will **b** those who **b** you,
Ro 12: 14 **B** those who persecute you;

BLESSED (BLESS)
Ge 1: 22 God **b** them and said, "Be fruitful
2: 3 Then God **b** the seventh day
22: 18 all nations on earth will be **b**,
Ps 1: 1 **B** is the one who does not walk
2: 12 **B** are all who take refuge in him.
33: 12 **B** is the nation whose God is
41: 1 **B** are those who have regard
84: 5 **B** are those whose strength is
106: 3 **B** are those who act justly,
112: 1 **B** are those who fear the Lord,
118: 26 **B** is he who comes in the name
Pr 29: 18 **b** is the one who heeds wisdom's
31: 28 Her children arise and call her **b**;
Mt 5: 3 "**B** are the poor in spirit, for theirs
5: 4 **B** are those who mourn, for they
5: 5 **B** are the meek, for they will
5: 6 **B** are those who hunger and thirst
5: 7 **B** are the merciful, for they will
5: 8 **B** are the pure in heart, for they
5: 9 **B** are the peacemakers, for they
5: 10 **B** are those who are persecuted
5: 11 "**B** are you when people insult you,
Lk 1: 48 on all generations will call me **b**,
Jn 12: 13 "**B** is he who comes in the name
Ac 20: 35 'It is more **b** to give than
Titus 2: 13 while we wait for the **b** hope–
Jas 1: 12 **B** is the one who perseveres under
Rev 1: 3 **B** is the one who reads aloud
22: 14 "**B** are those who wash their robes,

BLESSING (BLESS)
Eze 34: 26 there will be showers of **b**.

BLESSINGS (BLESS)
Pr 10: 6 **B** crown the head of the righteous,

BLIND
Mt 15: 14 If the **b** lead the **b**, both will fall
23: 16 "Woe to you, **b** guides! You say,
Jn 9: 25 I do know. I was **b** but now I see!"

BLOOD
Ge 9: 6 "Whoever sheds human **b**, by humans shall
their **b** be shed;
Ex 12: 13 The **b** will be a sign for you
24: 8 "This is the **b** of the covenant
Lev 17: 11 For the life of a creature is in the **b**,
17: 11 it is the **b** that makes atonement
Ps 72: 14 for precious is their **b** in his sight.
Pr 6: 17 hands that shed innocent **b**,
Mt 26: 28 This is my **b** of the covenant,
Ro 3: 25 through the shedding of his **b**–
5: 9 have now been justified by his **b**,
1Co 11: 25 cup is the new covenant in my **b**;
Eph 1: 7 we have redemption through his **b**,
2: 13 brought near by the **b** of Christ.
Col 1: 20 by making peace through his **b**,
Heb 9: 12 once for all by his own **b**,
9: 22 everything be cleansed with **b**,
1Pe 1: 19 but with the precious **b** of Christ,
1Jn 1: 7 and the **b** of Jesus, his Son,
Rev 1: 5 has freed us from our sins by his **b**,
5: 9 with your **b** you purchased for God
7: 14 them white in the **b** of the Lamb.
12: 11 over him by the **b** of the Lamb

BLOT (BLOTS)
Ex 32: 32 **b** me out of the book you have
Ps 51: 1 to your great compassion **b** out my
Rev 3: 5 I will never **b** out the name

BLOTS (BLOT)
Isa 43: 25 "I, even I, am he who **b** out your

BLOWN
Eph 4: 14 and **b** here and there by every wind
Jas 1: 6 the sea, **b** and tossed by the wind.

BOAST
1Ki 20: 11 his armor should not **b** like one
Ps 44: 8 In God we make our **b** all day long,
Pr 27: 1 Do not **b** about tomorrow, for you
1Co 1: 31 "Let the one who boasts **b**
Gal 6: 14 May I never **b** except in the cross
Eph 2: 9 not by works, so that no one can **b**.

BOAZ
Wealthy Bethlehemite who showed favor to Ruth (Ru 2), married her (Ru 4). Ancestor of David (Ru 4:18-22; 1Ch 2:12-15), Jesus (Mt 1:5-16; Lk 3:23-32).

BODIES (BODY)
Ro 12: 1 to offer your **b** as a living sacrifice,
1Co 6: 15 not know that your **b** are members
6: 19 not know that your **b** are temples
Eph 5: 28 to love their wives as their own **b**.

BODY (BODIES)
Zec 13: 6 are these wounds on your **b**?'
Mt 10: 28 can destroy both soul and **b** in hell.
10: 28 be afraid of those who kill the **b**
10: 28 can destroy both soul and **b** in hell.
26: 26 "Take and eat; this is my **b**."
Jn 13: 10 their whole **b** is clean.
1Co 11: 24 "This is my **b**, which is for you;
12: 12 Just as a **b**, though one, has many
Eph 5: 30 for we are members of his **b**.

BOLD (BOLDNESS)
Pr 21: 29 The wicked put up a **b** front,
28: 1 but the righteous are as **b** as a lion.

BOLDNESS (BOLD)
Ac 4: 29 to speak your word with great **b**.

BONDAGE
Ezr 9: 9 God has not forsaken us in our **b**.

BOOK (BOOKS)
Jos 1: 8 Keep this **B** of the Law always
Ne 8: 8 They read from the **B** of the Law
Jn 20: 30 which are not recorded in this **b**.
Php 4: 3 whose names are in the **b** of life.
Rev 21: 27 are written in the Lamb's **b** of life.

BOOKS (BOOK)
Ecc 12: 12 Of making many **b** there is no end,

BORE (BEAR)
Isa 53: 4 up our pain and **b** our suffering,

BORN (BEAR)
Isa 9: 6 For to us a child is **b**, to us a son is
Jn 3: 7 my saying, 'You must be **b** again.'
1Pe 1: 23 For you have been **b** again,
1Jn 4: 7 Everyone who loves has been **b**
5: 1 that Jesus is the Christ is **b** of God,

BORROWER
Pr 22: 7 and the **b** is slave to the lender.

BOUGHT
Ac 20: 28 which he **b** with his own blood.
1Co 6: 20 you were **b** at a price.
7: 23 You were **b** at a price;
2Pe 2: 1 the sovereign Lord who **b** them—

BOUNDLESS
Eph 3: 8 the Gentiles the **b** riches of Christ,

BOW
Ps 95: 6 Come, let us **b** down in worship,
Isa 45: 23 Before me every knee will **b**;
Ro 14: 11 Lord, 'every knee will **b** before me;
Php 2: 10 name of Jesus every knee should **b**,

BRANCH (BRANCHES)
Isa 4: 2 that day the **B** of the Lord will be
Jer 33: 15 I will make a righteous **B** sprout

BRANCHES (BRANCH)
Jn 15: 5 "I am the vine; you are the **b**.

BRAVE
2Sa 2: 7 then, be strong and **b**, for Saul your

BREAD
Dt 8: 3 that man does not live on **b** alone
Pr 30: 8 riches, but give me only my daily **b**.
Isa 55: 2 spend money on what is not **b**,
Mt 4: 4 'Man shall not live on **b** alone,
6: 11 Give us today our daily **b**.
Jn 6: 35 Jesus declared, "I am the **b** of life.
21: 13 took the **b** and gave it to them,
1Co 11: 23 the night he was betrayed, took **b**,

BREAK (BREAKING BROKEN)
Nu 30: 2 he must not **b** his word but must
Jdg 2: 1 'I will never **b** my covenant
Ps 2: 9 You will **b** them with a rod of iron;
Isa 42: 3 A bruised reed he will not **b**,
Mt 12: 20 A bruised reed he will not **b**,

BREAKING (BREAK)
Jas 2: 10 just one point is guilty of **b** all of it.

BREASTPIECE (BREASTPLATE)
Ex 28: 15 "Fashion a **b** for making decisions

BREASTPLATE (BREASTPIECE)
Isa 59: 17 He put on righteousness as his **b**,
Eph 6: 14 the **b** of righteousness in place,
1Th 5: 8 putting on faith and love as a **b**,

BREATHED (GOD-BREATHED)
Ge 2: 7 **b** into his nostrils the breath of life,
Jn 20: 22 with that he **b** on them and said,

BRIBE
Ex 23: 8 "Do not accept a **b**, for a **b** blinds
Pr 6: 35 he will refuse a **b**, however great it

BRIDE
Rev 19: 7 and his **b** has made herself ready.

BRIGHTER (BRIGHTNESS)
Pr 4: 18 shining ever **b** till the full light

BRIGHTNESS (BRIGHTER)
2Sa 22: 13 Out of the **b** of his presence bolts
Da 12: 3 who are wise will shine like the **b**

BROAD
Mt 7: 13 gate and **b** is the road that leads

BROKEN (BREAK)
Ps 51: 17 My sacrifice, O God, is a **b** spirit;
Ecc 4: 12 of three strands is not quickly **b**.

BROKENHEARTED (HEART)
Ps 34: 18 The Lord is close to the **b**
109: 16 the poor and the needy and the **b**.
147: 3 He heals the **b** and binds up their
Isa 61: 1 He has sent me to bind up the **b**,

BROTHER (BROTHER'S BROTHERS)
Pr 17: 17 a **b** is born for a time of adversity.
18: 24 a friend who sticks closer than a **b**.
Mt 18: 15 "If your **b** or sister sins,
Mk 3: 35 Whoever does God's will is my **b**
Lk 17: 3 "If your **b** or sister sins against you,
1Co 8: 13 if what I eat causes my **b** or sister
1Jn 2: 10 who loves their **b** and sister

BROTHER'S (BROTHER)
Ge 4: 9 "Am I my **b** keeper?"

BROTHERS (BROTHER)
Mt 25: 40 did for one of the least of these **b**
Mk 10: 29 "no one who has left home or **b**
Heb 13: 1 Keep on loving one another as **b**

BUILD (BUILDING BUILDS BUILT)
Mt 16: 18 on this rock I will **b** my church,
Ac 20: 32 which can **b** you up and give you
1Co 3: 10 But each one should **b** with care.
14: 12 excel in those that **b** up the church.
1Th 5: 11 one another and **b** each other up,

BUILDING (BUILD)
1Co 3: 9 you are God's field, God's **b**.
2Co 10: 8 authority the Lord gave us for **b**
Eph 4: 29 only what is helpful for **b** others

BUILDS (BUILD)
Ps 127: 1 Unless the Lord **b** the house,
1Co 8: 1 puffs up while love **b** up.

BUILT (BUILD)
Mt 7: 24 is like a wise man who **b** his house
1Co 14: 26 so that the church may be **b** up.
Eph 2: 20 **b** on the foundation of the apostles
4: 12 that the body of Christ may be **b**

BURDEN (BURDENED BURDENS)
Ps 38: 4 overwhelmed me like a **b** too heavy
Mt 11: 30 my yoke is easy and my **b** is light."

BURDENED (BURDEN)
Gal 5: 1 do not let yourselves be **b** again

BURDENS (BURDEN)
Ps 68: 19 our Savior, who daily bears our **b**.
Gal 6: 2 Carry each other's **b**, and in this

BURIED
Ro 6: 4 We were therefore **b** with him
1Co 15: 4 that he was **b**, that he was raised

BURNING
Lev 6: 9 the fire must be kept **b** on the altar.
Ro 12: 20 you will heap **b** coals on his head."

BUSINESS
Da 8: 27 got up and went about the king's **b**.
1Th 4: 11 You should mind your own **b**

BUSY
1Ki 20: 40 While your servant was **b** here
2Th 3: 11 are not **b**; they are busybodies.
Titus 2: 5 pure, to be **b** at home, to be kind,

CAESAR
Mt 22: 21 give back to **C** what is Caesar's,

CAIN
Firstborn of Adam (Ge 4:1), murdered brother Abel (Ge 4:1-16; 1Jn 3:12).

CALEB
Judahite who spied out Canaan (Nu 13:6); allowed to enter land because of faith (Nu 13:30-14:38; Dt 1:36). Possessed Hebron (Jos 14:6-15:19).

CALF
Ex 32: 4 into an idol cast in the shape of a **c**,
Lk 15: 23 Bring the fattened **c** and kill it.

CALL (CALLED CALLING CALLS)
Ps 145: 18 Lord is near to all who **c** on him,
Pr 31: 28 children arise and **c** her blessed;
Isa 5: 20 Woe to those who **c** evil good
55: 6 **c** on him while he is near.
65: 24 Before they **c** I will answer;
Jer 33: 3 '**C** to me and I will answer you
Mt 9: 13 I have not come to **c** the righteous,
Ro 10: 12 richly blesses all who **c** on him,
11: 29 gifts and his **c** are irrevocable.
1Th 4: 7 For God did not **c** us to be impure,

CALLED (CALL)
1Sa 3: 5 and said, "Here I am; you **c** me."
2Ch 7: 14 my people, who are **c** by my name,
Ps 34: 6 This poor man **c**, and the Lord
Mt 21: 13 "'My house will be **c** a house
Ro 8: 30 And those he predestined, he also **c**; those he **c**, he also justified;
1Co 7: 15 God has **c** us to live in peace.
Gal 5: 13 and sisters, were **c** to be free.
1Pe 2: 9 the praises of him who **c** you

CALLING (CALL)
Jn 1: 23 voice of one **c** in the wilderness.
Ac 22: 16 your sins away, **c** on his name.'
Eph 4: 1 worthy of the **c** you have received.
2Pe 1: 10 every effort to confirm your **c**

CALLS (CALL)
Joel 2: 32 everyone who **c** on the name
Jn 10: 3 He **c** his own sheep by name
Ro 10: 13 "Everyone who **c** on the name

CALM
Pr 29: 11 but the wise bring **c** in the end.

CAMEL
Mt 19: 24 easier for a **c** to go through the eye
23: 24 strain out a gnat but swallow a **c**.

CANAAN
1Ch 16: 18 **C** as the portion you will inherit."

CANCELED
Col 2: 14 having **c** the charge of our legal

CAPITAL
Dt 21: 22 someone guilty of a **c** offense is put

CARE (CAREFUL CAREFULLY CARES CARING)
Ps 8: 4 human beings that you **c** for them?
Pr 29: 7 The righteous **c** about justice
Lk 10: 34 him to an inn and took **c** of him.
Jn 21: 16 Jesus said, "Take **c** of my sheep."
1Co 3: 10 But each one should build with **c**.
Eph 5: 29 but they feed and **c** for their body,
Heb 2: 6 a son of man that you **c** for him?
1Pe 2: 2 of God's flock that is under your **c**,

CAREFUL (CARE)
Ex 23: 13 "Be **c** to do everything I have said
Dt 6: 3 be **c** to obey so that it may go well
Jos 23: 6 be **c** to obey all that is written
23: 11 So be very **c** to love the Lord
Pr 13: 24 one who loves their children is **c**
Mt 6: 1 "Be **c** not to practice your
Ro 12: 17 Be **c** to do what is right in the eyes
1Co 8: 9 Be **c**, however, that the exercise of
Eph 5: 15 Be very **c**, then, how you live—

CAREFULLY
Pr 12: 26 righteous choose their friends **c**,

CARES (CARE)
Ps 55: 22 Cast your **c** on the Lord and he
Na 1: 7 He **c** for those who trust in him,
1Th 2: 7 Just as a nursing mother **c** for her
1Pe 5: 7 on him because he **c** for you.

CARING (CARE)
1Ti 5: 4 practice by **c** for their own family

CARRIED (CARRY)
Ex 19: 4 and how I **c** you on eagles' wings
Heb 13: 9 Do not be **c** away by all kinds
2Pe 1: 21 God as they were **c** along

CARRIES (CARRY)
Dt 32: 11 to catch them and **c** them aloft.
Isa 40: 11 arms and **c** them close to his heart;

CARRY (CARRIED CARRIES)
Lk 14: 27 whoever does not **c** their cross
Gal 6: 2 Each other's burdens, and in this
6: 5 each one should **c** their own load.

CAST
Ps 22: 18 them and **c** lots for my garment.
55: 22 **C** your cares on the Lord and he
Jn 19: 24 them and **c** lots for my garment."
1Pe 5: 7 **C** all your anxiety on him because

CATTLE
Ps 50: 10 and the **c** on a thousand hills.

CAUGHT
1Th 4: 17 are left will be **c** up together

CAUSE (CAUSES)
Pr 24: 28 against your neighbor without **c**—
Ecc 8: 3 Do not stand up for a bad **c**, for he
Mt 18: 7 the things that **c** people to stumble!
Ro 14: 21 that will **c** your brother or sister
1Co 10: 32 Do not **c** anyone to stumble,

CAUSES (CAUSE)
Isa 8: 14 he will be a stone that **c** people
Mt 18: 6 "If anyone **c** one of these little

CEASE
Ps 46: 9 He makes wars **c** to the ends

CELEBRATE
Ps 2: 11 fear and **c** his rule with trembling.

CENSER
Lev 16: 12 is to take a **c** full of burning coals

CENTURION
Mt   8:   5   Capernaum, a **c** came to him,

CERTAINTY
Lk   1:   4   you may know the **c** of the things
Jn   17:   8   They knew with **c** that I came

CHAFF
Ps   1:   4   They are like **c** that the wind blows

CHAINED
2Ti   2:   9   But God's word is not **c**.

CHAMPION
Ps   19:   5   like a **c** rejoicing to run his course.

CHANGE (CHANGED)
1Sa   15: 29   does not lie or **c** his mind;
Ps   110:   4   has sworn and will not **c** his mind:
Jer   2:   5   If you really **c** your ways and your
Mal   3:   6   "I the LORD do not **c**. So you,
Mt   18:   3   unless you **c** and become like little
Heb   7: 21   has sworn and will not **c** his mind:
Jas   1: 17   lights, who does not **c** like shifting

CHANGED (CHANGE)
1Co   15: 51   not all sleep, but we will all be **c**–

CHARACTER
Ru   3: 11   that you are a woman of noble **c**.
Pr   31: 10   A wife of noble **c** who can find?
Ro   5:   4   perseverance, **c**; and **c**, hope.
1Co   15: 33   "Bad company corrupts good **c**."

CHARGE
Ro   8: 33   will bring any **c** against those
2Co   11:   7   the gospel of God to you free of **c**?
2Ti   4:   1   and his kingdom, I give you this **c**:

CHARIOTS
2Ki   6: 17   and **c** of fire all around Elisha.
Ps   20:   7   Some trust in **c** and some in horses

CHARM
Pr   31: 30   **C** is deceptive, and beauty is

CHASE
Pr   12: 11   who **c** fantasies have no sense.

CHATTER (CHATTERING)
1Ti   6: 20   Turn away from godless **c**
2Ti   2: 16   Avoid godless **c**, because those who

CHATTERING (CHATTER)
Pr   10:   8   but a **c** fool comes to ruin.
     10: 10   grief, and a **c** fool comes to ruin.

CHEAT (CHEATED)
Mal   1: 14   "Cursed is the **c** who has
1Co   6:   8   you yourselves **c** and do wrong,

CHEATED (CHEAT)
Lk   19:   8   if I have **c** anybody out of anything,
1Co   6:   7   Why not rather be **c**?

CHEEK
Mt   5: 39   turn to them the other **c** also.

CHEERFUL (CHEERS)
Pr   15: 13   A happy heart makes the face **c**,
     15: 15   the **c** heart has a continual feast.
     17: 22   A **c** heart is good medicine,
2Co   9:   7   for God loves a **c** giver.

CHEERS (CHEERFUL)
Pr   12: 25   the heart, but a kind word **c** it up.

CHILD (CHILDHOOD CHILDLESS CHILDREN)
Pr   22: 15   Folly is bound up in the heart of a **c**,
     23: 13   not withhold discipline from a **c**;
     29: 15   but a **c** left undisciplined disgraces
Isa   9:   6   For to us a **c** is born, to us a son is
     11:   6   and a little **c** will lead them.
     66: 13   As a mother comforts her **c**, so will
Mt   18:   2   He called a little **c** to him,
Lk   1: 42   and blessed is the **c** you will bear!
     1: 80   And the **c** grew and became strong
1Co   13: 11   When I was a **c**, I talked like a **c**,
1Jn   5:   1   loves the father loves his **c** as well.

CHILDHOOD (CHILD)
1Co   13: 11   I put the ways of **c** behind me.

CHILDLESS
Ps   113:   9   settles the **c** woman in her home

CHILDREN (CHILD)
Dt   4:   9   Teach them to your **c** and to their **c**
     11: 19   Teach them to your **c**,
Ps   8:   2   Through the praise of **c** and infants
Pr   13: 24   spares the rod hates their **c**,
     17:   6   parents are the pride of their **c**.
     20: 11   Even small **c** are known by their
     22:   6   Start **c** off on the way they should
     29: 17   Discipline your **c**, and they will
     31: 28   Her **c** arise and call her blessed;
Mt   7: 11   how to give good gifts to your **c**,
     11: 25   and revealed them to little **c**.
     18:   3   change and become like little **c**,
     19: 14   said, "Let the little **c** come to me,
     21: 16   "'From the lips of **c** and infants
Mk   9: 37   these little **c** in my name welcomes
     10: 14   them, "Let the little **c** come to me,
     10: 16   And he took the **c** in his arms,
     13: 12   **C** will rebel against their parents
Lk   10: 21   and revealed them to little **c**.
     18: 16   said, "Let the little **c** come to me,
Jn   12: 36   so that you may become **c** of light."
Ro   8: 16   with our spirit that we are God's **c**.
2Co   12: 14   **c** should not have to save for
Eph   6:   1   **C**, obey your parents in the Lord,
     6:   4   Fathers, do not exasperate your **c**;
Col   3: 20   **C**, obey your parents in everything,
     3: 21   do not embitter your **c**, or they will
1Ti   3:   4   well and see that his **c** obey him,
     3: 12   and must manage his **c** and his
     5: 10   such as bringing up **c**,
Heb   12:   7   God is treating you as his **c**.
1Jn   3:   1   that we should be called **c** of God!

CHOOSE (CHOOSES CHOSE CHOSEN)
Dt   30: 19   Now **c** life, so that you and your
Jos   24: 15   **c** for yourselves this day whom you
Pr   8: 10   **C** my instruction instead of silver,
Jn   15: 16   You did not **c** me, but I chose you
Ac   15: 14   God first intervened to **c** a people

CHOOSES (CHOOSE)
Jn   7: 17   who **c** to do the will of God

CHOSE (CHOOSE)
Ge   13: 11   Lot **c** for himself the whole plain
Ps   33: 12   the people he **c** for his inheritance.
Jn   15: 16   but I **c** you and appointed you so
1Co   1: 27   But God **c** the foolish things
Eph   1:   4   For he **c** us in him before
2Th   2: 13   because God **c** you as firstfruits

CHOSEN (CHOOSE)
Isa   41:   8   whom I have **c**, you descendants
Mt   22: 14   many are invited, but few are **c**."
Lk   10: 42   Mary has **c** what is better, and it
     23: 35   if he is God's Messiah, the **C** One."
Jn   15: 19   but I have **c** you out of the world.
1Pe   1: 20   He was **c** before the creation
     2:   9   But you are a **c** people, a royal

CHRIST (CHRIST'S CHRISTIAN MESSIAH)
Jn   1: 41   found the Messiah" (that is, the **C**).
Ro   3: 22   faith in Jesus **C** to all who believe.
     5:   6   powerless, **C** died for the ungodly.
     5:   8   we were still sinners, **C** died for us.
     5: 17   life through the one man, Jesus **C**!
     6:   4   just as **C** was raised from the dead
     8:   1   for those who are in **C** Jesus,
     8:   9   does not have the Spirit of **C**, they do not belong to **C**.
     8: 35   separate us from the love of **C**?
     10:   4   **C** is the culmination of the law so
     14:   9   **C** died and returned to life so that
     15:   3   even **C** did not please himself but,
1Co   1: 23   but we preach **C** crucified.
     2:   2   while I was with you except Jesus **C**
     3: 11   one already laid, which is Jesus **C**.

1Co	5: 7	For **C**, our Passover lamb, has been
	8: 6	Jesus **C**, through whom all things
	10: 4	them, and that rock was **C**.
	10: 9	We should not test **C**, as some
	11: 1	as I follow the example of **C**.
	11: 3	that the head of every man is **C**,
	11: 3	and the head of **C** is God.
	12: 27	Now you are the body of **C**,
	15: 3	that **C** died for our sins according
	15: 14	And if **C** has not been raised,
	15: 22	die, so in **C** all will be made alive.
	15: 57	victory through our Lord Jesus **C**.
2Co	3: 3	show that you are a letter from **C**,
	4: 5	but Jesus **C** as Lord, and ourselves
	5: 10	before the judgment seat of **C**,
	5: 17	if anyone is in **C**, the new creation
	11: 2	to **C**, so that I might present you as
Gal	2: 20	I have been crucified with **C**
	3: 13	**C** redeemed us from the curse
	6: 14	in the cross of our Lord Jesus **C**,
Eph	1: 3	and Father of our Lord Jesus **C**,
	3: 8	Gentiles the boundless riches of **C**,
	4: 13	whole measure of the fullness of **C**.
	5: 2	just as **C** loved us and gave himself
	5: 23	head of the wife as **C** is the head
	5: 25	just as **C** loved the church and gave
Php	1: 21	to live is **C** and to die is gain.
	1: 27	manner worthy of the gospel of **C**.
	4: 19	to the riches of his glory in **C** Jesus.
Col	1: 27	which is **C** in you, the hope
	1: 28	present everyone fully mature in **C**.
	2: 6	as you received **C** Jesus as Lord,
	2: 17	the reality, however, is found in **C**.
	3: 15	Let the peace of **C** rule in your
2Th	2: 1	the coming of our Lord Jesus **C**
1Ti	1: 15	**C** Jesus came into the world to save
	2: 5	and mankind, the man **C** Jesus,
2Ti	2: 3	like a good soldier of **C** Jesus.
	3: 15	salvation through faith in **C** Jesus.
Titus	2: 13	our great God and Savior, Jesus **C**,
Heb	3: 14	We have come to share in **C**,
	9: 14	will the blood of **C**, who through
	9: 15	For this reason **C** is the mediator
	9: 28	so **C** was sacrificed once to take
	10: 10	of the body of Jesus **C** once for all.
	13: 8	Jesus **C** is the same yesterday
1Pe	1: 19	but with the precious blood of **C**,
	2: 21	called, because **C** suffered for you,
	3: 18	For **C** also suffered once for sins,
	4: 14	insulted because of the name of **C**,
1Jn	2: 22	whoever denies that Jesus is the **C**.
	3: 16	Jesus **C** laid down his life for us.
	5: 1	who believes that Jesus is the **C**
Rev	20: 4	reigned with **C** a thousand years.

CHRIST'S (CHRIST)

2Co	5: 14	For **C** love compels us, because we
	5: 20	We are therefore **C** ambassadors,
	12: 9	so that **C** power may rest on me.

CHRISTIAN (CHRIST)

1Pe	4: 16	if you suffer as a **C**, do not be

CHURCH

Mt	16: 18	and on this rock I will build my **c**,
	18: 17	if they refuse to listen even to the **c**,
Ac	20: 28	Be shepherds of the **c** of God,
1Co	5: 12	mine to judge those outside the **c**?
	14: 4	one who prophesies edifies the **c**.
	14: 12	excel in those that build up the **c**.
	14: 26	done so that the **c** may be built up.
Eph	5: 23	wife as Christ is the head of the **c**,
Col	1: 24	the sake of his body, which is the **c**.

CIRCUMCISED

Ge	17: 10	Every male among you shall be **c**.
Gal	2: 8	in Peter as an apostle to the **c**,

CIRCUMSTANCES

Php	4: 11	to be content whatever the **c**.
1Th	5: 18	give thanks in all **c**; for this is God's

CITIZENS (CITIZENSHIP)

Eph	2: 19	but fellow **c** with God's people

CITIZENSHIP (CITIZENS)

Php	3: 20	But our **c** is in heaven.

CITY

Heb	13: 14	here we do not have an enduring **c**,

CIVILIAN

2Ti	2: 4	a soldier gets entangled in **c** affairs,

CLAIM (CLAIMS)

Pr	25: 6	do not **c** a place among his great
1Jn	1: 6	If we **c** to have fellowship with him
	1: 8	If we **c** to be without sin,
	1: 10	If we **c** we have not sinned,

CLAIMS (CLAIM)

Jas	2: 14	if someone **c** to have faith but has
1Jn	2: 6	Whoever **c** to live in him must live
	2: 9	Anyone who **c** to be in the light

CLAP

Ps	47: 1	**C** your hands, all you nations;
Isa	55: 12	trees of the field will **c** their hands.

CLAY

Isa	45: 9	Does the **c** say to the potter,
	64: 8	We are the **c**, you are the potter,
Jer	18: 6	"Like **c** in the hand of the potter,
La	4: 2	are now considered as pots of **c**,
Da	2: 33	of iron and partly of baked **c**.
Ro	9: 21	the same lump of **c** some pottery
2Co	4: 7	this treasure in jars of **c** to show
2Ti	2: 20	and silver, but also of wood and **c**;

CLEAN

Lev	16: 30	you will be **c** from all your sins.
Ps	24: 4	one who has **c** hands and a pure
Mt	12: 44	swept **c** and put in order.
	23: 25	You **c** the outside of the cup
Mk	7: 19	this, Jesus declared all foods **c**.)
Jn	13: 10	you are **c**, though not every one
	15: 3	You are already **c** because
Ac	10: 15	impure that God has made **c**."
Ro	14: 20	All food is **c**, but it is wrong

CLING

Ps	63: 8	I **c** to you; your right hand upholds
Ro	12: 9	Hate what is evil; **c** to what is good.

CLOAK

2Ki	4: 29	"Tuck your **c** into your belt,

CLOSE (CLOSER)

Ps	34: 18	The Lord is **c**
Isa	40: 11	and carries them **c** to his heart;
Jer	30: 21	near and he will come **c** to me—

CLOSER (CLOSE)

Ex	3: 5	"Do not come any **c**," God said.
Pr	18: 24	friend who sticks **c** than a brother.

CLOTHE (CLOTHED CLOTHES CLOTHING)

Ps	45: 3	**c** yourself with splendor
Isa	52: 1	**c** Zion, **c** yourself with strength!
Ro	13: 14	**c** yourselves with the Lord Jesus
Col	3: 12	**c** yourselves with compassion,
1Pe	5: 5	**c** yourselves with humility toward

CLOTHED (CLOTHE)

Ps	30: 11	my sackcloth and **c** me with joy,
Pr	31: 25	She is **c** with strength and dignity;
Lk	24: 49	the city until you have been **c**

CLOTHES (CLOTHE)

Mt	6: 25	food, and the body more than **c**?
	6: 28	"And why do you worry about **c**?
Jn	11: 44	"Take off the grave **c** and let him

CLOTHING (CLOTHE)

Dt	22: 5	nor a man wear women's **c**,
Mt	7: 15	They come to you in sheep's **c**,

CLOUD (CLOUDS)

Ex	13: 21	them in a pillar of **c** to guide them
Isa	19: 1	the Lord rides on a swift **c** and
Lk	21: 27	of Man coming in a **c** with power
Heb	12: 1	by such a great **c** of witnesses,

CLOUDS (CLOUD)
Ps 104: 3 He makes the **c** his chariot and
Da   7: 13 man, coming with the **c** of heaven.
Mk 13: 26 Man coming in **c** with great power
1Th   4: 17 them in the **c** to meet the Lord

CO-HEIRS (INHERIT)
Ro   8: 17 heirs of God and **c** with Christ,

COALS
Pr 25: 22 will heap burning **c** on his head,
Ro 12: 20 this, you will heap burning **c** on his

COAT
Lk   6: 29 If someone takes your **c**, do not

COLD
Pr 25: 25 Like **c** water to a weary soul is
Mt 10: 42 anyone gives even a cup of **c** water
    24: 12 the love of most will grow **c**,

COMFORT (COMFORTED COMFORTS)
Ps 23: 4 your rod and your staff, they **c** me.
   119: 52 ancient laws, and I find **c** in them.
   119: 76 May your unfailing love be my **c**,
Zec   1: 17 the Lord will again **c** Zion
1Co 14: 3 strengthening, encouraging and **c**.
2Co   1: 4 that we can **c** those in any trouble
    2: 7 you ought to forgive and **c** him,

COMFORTED (COMFORT)
Mt   5: 4 who mourn, for they will be **c**.

COMFORTS (COMFORT)
Job 29: 25 I was like one who **c** mourners.
Isa 49: 13 For the Lord **c** his people
   51: 12 "I, even I, am he who **c** you.
   66: 13 As a mother **c** her child, so will I
2Co   1: 4 who **c** us in all our troubles,
    7: 6 But God, who **c** the downcast,

COMMAND (COMMANDED COMMANDING COMMANDMENT COMMANDMENTS COMMANDS)
Ex   7: 2 You are to say everything I **c** you,
Nu 24: 13 to go beyond the **c** of the Lord—
Dt   4: 2 Do not add to what I **c** you and do
  30: 16 For I **c** you today to love
  32: 46 so that you may **c** your children
Ps 91: 11 he will **c** his angels concerning you
  148: 5 for at his **c** they were created,
Pr   6: 23 For this **c** is a lamp, this teaching is
  13: 13 whoever respects a **c** is rewarded.
Ecc   8: 2 Obey the king's **c**, I say,
Joel   2: 11 mighty is the army that obeys his **c**.
Jn 13: 34 "A new **c** I give you:
  15: 12 My **c** is this: Love each other as I
1Co 14: 37 I am writing to you is the Lord's **c**.
Gal   5: 14 is fulfilled in keeping this one **c**:
1Ti   1: 5 The goal of this **c** is love,
Heb 11: 3 the universe was formed at God's **c**,
1Jn   3: 23 And this is his **c**: to believe
2Jn   : 6 his **c** is that you walk in love.

COMMANDED (COMMAND)
Ps 33: 9 came to be; he **c**, and it stood firm.
Mt 28: 20 to obey everything I have **c** you.
1Co   9: 14 way, the Lord has **c** that those who
1Jn   3: 23 and to love one another as he **c** us.

COMMANDING (COMMAND)
2Ti   2: 4 rather tries to please his **c** officer.

COMMANDMENT (COMMAND)
Jos 22: 5 be very careful to keep the **c**
Mt 22: 38 This is the first and greatest **c**.
Ro   7: 12 and the **c** is holy,
Eph   6: 2 is the first **c** with a promise—

COMMANDMENTS (COMMAND)
Ex 20: 6 those who love me and keep my **c**.
  34: 28 words of the covenant–the Ten **C**.
Dt   7: 9 those who love him and keep his **c**.
Ecc 12: 13 Fear God and keep his **c**, for this is
Da   9: 4 those who love him and keep his **c**,
Mt 22: 40 the Prophets hang on these two **c**."

COMMANDS (COMMAND)
Dt 11: 27 you obey the **c** of the Lord your
Ps 112: 1 who find great delight in his **c**.
  119: 47 in your **c** because I love them.
  119: 86 All your **c** are trustworthy;
  119: 98 Your **c** are always with me
  119:127 I love your **c** more than gold,
  119:143 me, but your **c** give me delight.
  119:172 word, for all your **c** are righteous.
Pr   3: 1 but keep my **c** in your heart,
  10: 8 The wise in heart accept **c**,
Mt   5: 19 teaches these **c** will be called great
Jn 14: 15 "If you love me, keep my **c**.
  14: 21 Whoever has my **c** and keeps them
Ac 17: 30 now he **c** all people everywhere
1Co   7: 19 Keeping God's **c** is what counts.
1Jn   5: 3 this is love for God: to keep his **c**. And his **c** are not burdensome,

COMMEND (COMMENDED COMMENDS)
Ecc   8: 15 So I **c** the enjoyment of life,
1Pe   2: 14 wrong and to **c** those who do right.

COMMENDED (COMMEND)
Ro   3: 3 do what is right and you will be **c**.
Heb 11: 39 These were all **c** for their faith,

COMMENDS (COMMEND)
2Co 10: 18 but the one whom the Lord **c**.

COMMIT (COMMITS COMMITTED)
Ex 20: 14 "You shall not **c** adultery.
Ps 37: 5 **C** your way to the Lord;
Mt   5: 27 was said, 'You shall not **c** adultery.'
Lk 23: 46 into your hands I **c** my spirit."
Ac 20: 32 "Now I **c** you to God
1Co   6: 18 We should not **c** sexual immorality,
1Pe   4: 19 to God's will should **c** themselves

COMMITS (COMMIT)
Pr   6: 32 a man who **c** adultery has no sense;
  29: 22 hot-tempered person **c** many sins.
Mt 19: 9 marries another woman **c** adultery."

COMMITTED (COMMIT)
Nu   5: 7 must confess the sin they have **c**.
1Ki   8: 61 may your hearts be fully **c**
2Ch 16: 9 those whose hearts are fully **c**
Mt   5: 28 lustfully has already **c** adultery
2Co   5: 19 And he has **c** to us the message
1Pe   2: 22 "He **c** no sin, and no deceit was

COMMON
Pr 22: 2 Rich and poor have this in **c**:
1Co 10: 13 has overtaken you except what is **c**
2Co   6: 14 and wickedness have in **c**?

COMPANION
Pr 13: 20 for a **c** of fools suffers harm.
  28: 7 a **c** of gluttons disgraces his father.
  29: 3 but a **c** of prostitutes squanders his

COMPANY
Pr 24: 1 the wicked, do not desire their **c**;
Jer 15: 17 I never sat in the **c** of revelers,
1Co 15: 33 "Bad **c** corrupts good character."

COMPARED (COMPARING)
Eze 31: 2 "'Who can be **c** with you

COMPARING (COMPARED)
Ro   8: 18 present sufferings are not worth **c**
2Co   8: 8 of your love by **c** it
Gal   6: 4 without **c** themselves to someone

COMPASSION (COMPASSIONATE COMPASSIONS)
Ex 33: 19 I will have **c** on whom I will have **c**.
Ne   9: 19 your great **c** you did not abandon
  9: 28 in your **c** you delivered them time
Ps 51: 1 to your great **c** blot out my
  103: 4 pit and crowns you with love and **c**,
  103: 13 As a father has **c** on his children,
  145: 9 he has **c** on all he has made.
Isa 49: 13 will have **c** on his afflicted ones.
  49: 15 and have no **c** on the child she has
Hos   2: 19 and justice, in love and **c**.

Hos 11: 8 all my **c** is aroused.
Jnh 3: 9 with **c** turn from his fierce anger so
Mt 9: 36 saw the crowds, he had **c** on them,
Mk 8: 2 "I have **c** for these people;
Ro 9: 15 I will have **c** on whom I have **c**."
Col 3: 12 clothe yourselves with **c**, kindness,
Jas 5: 11 The Lord is full of **c** and mercy.

COMPASSIONATE (COMPASSION)
Ne 9: 17 gracious and **c**, slow to anger
Ps 103: 8 The Lord is **c** and gracious,
112: 4 for those who are gracious and **c**
Eph 4: 32 Be kind and **c** to one another,
1Pe 3: 8 love one another, be **c** and humble.

COMPASSIONS (COMPASSION)
La 3: 22 not consumed, for his **c** never fail.

COMPEL (COMPELLED COMPELS)
Lk 14: 23 lanes and **c** them to come in,

COMPELLED (COMPEL)
Ac 20: 22 "And now, **c** by the Spirit, I am
1Co 9: 16 boast, since I am **c** to preach.

COMPELS (COMPEL)
2Co 5: 14 For Christ's love **c** us, because we

COMPETENCE (COMPETENT)
2Co 3: 5 but our **c** comes from God.

COMPETENT (COMPETENCE)
Ro 15: 14 and **c** to instruct one another.
1Co 6: 2 are you not **c** to judge trivial cases?
2Co 3: 5 Not that we are **c** in ourselves
3: 6 He has made us **c** as ministers

COMPETES
1Co 9: 25 Everyone who **c** in the games goes
2Ti 2: 5 anyone who **c** as an athlete does

COMPLACENT
Am 6: 1 Woe to you who are **c** in Zion,

COMPLETE
Jn 15: 11 in you and that your joy may be **c**.
16: 24 will receive, and your joy will be **c**.
17: 23 they may be brought to **c** unity.
Ac 20: 24 **c** the task the Lord Jesus has given
Php 2: 2 then make my joy **c** by being
Col 4: 17 it that you **c** the ministry you have
Jas 1: 4 so that you may be mature and **c**,
2: 22 faith was made **c** by what he did.

CONCEAL (CONCEALED CONCEALS)
Ps 40: 10 I do not **c** your love and your
Pr 25: 2 It is the glory of God to **c** a matter;

CONCEALED (CONCEAL)
Jer 16: 17 me, nor is their sin **c** from my eyes.
Mt 10: 26 for there is nothing **c** that will not
Mk 4: 22 whatever is **c** is meant to be

CONCEALS (CONCEAL)
Pr 28: 13 Whoever **c** their sins does not

CONCEITED
Gal 5: 26 Let us not become **c**,
1Ti 6: 4 they are **c** and understand nothing.

CONCEIVE (CONCEIVED)
Isa 7: 14 The virgin will **c** and give birth
Mt 1: 23 "The virgin will **c** and give birth

CONCEIVED (CONCEIVE)
Mt 1: 20 because what is **c** in her is
1Co 2: 9 and what no human mind has **c**"–

CONCERN (CONCERNED)
Eze 36: 21 I had **c** for my holy name,
1Co 7: 32 I would like you to be free from **c**.
12: 25 that its parts should have equal **c**
2Co 11: 28 of my **c** for all the churches.

CONCERNED (CONCERN)
Jnh 4: 10 "You have been **c** about this plant,
1Co 7: 32 An unmarried man is **c**

CONDEMN (CONDEMNATION CONDEMNED CONDEMNING CONDEMNS)
Job 40: 8 you **c** me to justify yourself?

Isa 50: 9 Who will **c** me? They will all wear
Lk 6: 37 Do not **c**, and you will not be
Jn 3: 17 Son into the world to **c** the world,
12: 48 words I have spoken will **c** them
Ro 2: 27 yet obeys the law will **c** you who,
1Jn 3: 20 If our hearts **c** us, we know that

CONDEMNATION (CONDEMN)
Ro 5: 18 just as one trespass resulted in **c**
8: 1 there is now no **c** for those who are
2Co 3: 9 that brought **c** was glorious,

CONDEMNED (CONDEMN)
Ps 34: 22 who takes refuge in him will be **c**.
Mt 12: 37 and by your words you will be **c**."
23: 33 How will you escape being **c**
Jn 3: 18 Whoever believes in him is not **c**,
16: 11 prince of this world now stands **c**.
Ro 14: 23 whoever has doubts is **c** if they eat,
1Co 11: 32 that we will not be finally **c**
Heb 11: 7 By his faith he **c** the world

CONDEMNING (CONDEMN)
Pr 17: 15 the guilty and **c** the innocent–
Ro 2: 1 you are **c** yourself, because you

CONDEMNS (CONDEMN)
Pr 14: 34 exalts a nation, but sin **c** any people
Ro 8: 34 Who then is the one who **c**?

CONDUCT
Pr 20: 11 is their **c** really pure and upright?
21: 8 but the **c** of the innocent is upright.
Ecc 6: 8 how to **c** themselves before others?
Jer 4: 18 "Your own **c** and actions have
17: 10 each person according to their **c**,
Eze 3: 1 I will judge you according to your **c**
1Ti 3: 15 how people ought to **c** themselves

CONFESS (CONFESSION)
Lev 16: 21 and **c** over it all the wickedness
26: 40 if they will **c** their sins and the sins
Nu 5: 7 **c** the sin they have committed.
Ps 38: 18 I **c** my iniquity; I am troubled by
Jas 5: 16 Therefore **c** your sins to each other
1Jn 1: 9 If we **c** our sins, he is faithful

CONFESSION (CONFESS)
2Co 9: 13 accompanies your **c** of the gospel

CONFIDENCE
Ps 71: 5 Lord, my **c** since my youth.
Pr 11: 13 A gossip betrays a **c**,
25: 9 to court, do not betray another's **c**,
31: 11 Her husband has full **c** in her
Isa 32: 17 will be quietness and **c** forever.
Jer 17: 7 in the Lord, whose **c** is in him.
Php 3: 3 and who put no **c** in the flesh–
Heb 4: 16 God's throne of grace with **c**,
10: 19 since we have **c** to enter the Most
10: 35 So do not throw away your **c**;
11: 1 Now faith is **c** in what we hope
13: 17 Have **c** in your leaders and submit
1Jn 5: 14 This is the **c** we have

CONFIRM
2Pe 1: 10 make every effort to **c** your calling

CONFLICT
Pr 6: 14 his heart–he always stirs up **c**.
6: 19 a person who stirs up **c**
10: 12 Hatred stirs up **c**, but love covers
15: 18 A hot-tempered person stirs up **c**,
16: 28 A perverse person stirs up **c**,
28: 25 The greedy stir up **c**,
29: 22 An angry person stirs up **c**,

CONFORM (CONFORMED)
Ro 12: 2 not **c** to the pattern of this world,
1Pe 1: 14 do not **c** to the evil desires you had

CONFORMED (CONFORM)
Ro 8: 29 predestined to be **c** to the image

CONQUERORS
Ro 8: 37 are more than **c** through him who

CONSCIENCE (CONSCIENCES)
Ro   13: 5 but also as a matter of **c**.
1Co   8: 7 a god, and since their **c** is weak,
      8: 12 this way and wound their weak **c**,
     10: 25 without raising questions of **c**,
     10: 29 being judged by another's **c**?
Heb 10: 22 to cleanse us from a guilty **c**
1Pe   3: 16 keeping a clear **c**, so that those who

CONSCIENCES (CONSCIENCE)
Ro   2: 15 hearts, their **c** also bearing witness,
1Ti   4: 2 whose **c** have been seared as
Titus 1: 15 their minds and **c** are corrupted.
Heb   9: 14 cleanse our **c** from acts that lead

CONSCIOUS
Ro   3: 20 through the law we become **c** of
1Pe   2: 19 unjust suffering because they are **c**

CONSECRATE (CONSECRATED)
Ex   13: 2 "**C** to me every firstborn male.
Lev 20: 7 "'**C** yourselves and be holy,

CONSECRATED (CONSECRATE)
Ex   29: 43 and the place will be **c** by my glory.
1Ti   4: 5 because it is **c** by the word of God

CONSIDER (CONSIDERATE CONSIDERED CONSIDERS)
1Sa 12: 24 **c** what great things he has done
Job 37: 14 stop and **c** God's wonders.
Ps   8: 3 When I **c** your heavens, the work
     143: 5 and **c** what your hands have done.
Lk   12: 24 **C** the ravens: They do not sow
     12: 27 "**C** how the wild flowers grow.
Php   3: 8 I **c** everything a loss because
Heb 10: 24 And let us **c** how we may spur one
Jas   1: 2 **C** it pure joy, my brothers
      1: 26 Those who **c** themselves religious

CONSIDERATE (CONSIDER)
Titus 3: 2 to be peaceable and **c**, and always
Jas   3: 17 then peace-loving, **c**, submissive,
1Pe   2: 18 only to those who are good and **c**,
      3: 7 the same way be **c** as you live

CONSIDERED (CONSIDER)
Job   1: 8 "Have you **c** my servant Job?
      2: 3 "Have you **c** my servant Job?
Ps   44: 22 we are **c** as sheep to be slaughtered.
Isa 53: 4 yet we **c** him punished by God,
Ro   8: 36 all day long; we are **c** as sheep to be

CONSIDERS (CONSIDER)
Pr   31: 16 She **c** a field and buys it; out of her
Ro   14: 5 One person **c** one day more sacred

CONSIST
Lk   12: 15 life does not **c** in an abundance

CONSOLATION
Ps   94: 19 within me, your **c** brought me joy.

CONSTRUCTIVE
1Co 10: 23 but not everything is **c**.

CONSUME (CONSUMING)
Jn   2: 17 "Zeal for your house will **c** me."

CONSUMING (CONSUME)
Dt   4: 24 For the LORD your God is a **c** fire,
Heb 12: 29 for our "God is a **c** fire."

CONTAIN
1Ki   8: 27 the highest heaven, cannot **c** you.
2Pe   3: 16 His letters **c** some things that are

CONTAMINATES
2Co   7: 1 from everything that **c** body

CONTEMPLATE
2Co   3: 18 unveiled faces **c** the Lord's glory,

CONTEMPT
Pr   14: 31 oppresses the poor shows **c** for
     17: 5 Whoever mocks the poor shows **c**
     18: 3 so does **c**, and with shame comes
Da   12: 2 others to shame and everlasting **c**.
Ro   2: 4 do you show **c** for the riches of his
Gal   4: 14 did not treat me with **c** or scorn.

1Th   5: 20 Do not treat prophecies with **c**

CONTEND
Jude :   3 urge you to **c** for the faith that was

CONTENT (CONTENTMENT)
Pr   13: 25 The righteous eat to their hearts' **c**,
Php   4: 11 to be **c** whatever the circumstances.
      4: 12 learned the secret of being **c** in any
1Ti   6: 8 clothing, we will be **c** with that.
Heb 13: 5 and be **c** with what you have,

CONTENTMENT (CONTENT)
1Ti   6: 6 But godliness with **c** is great gain.

CONTINUAL (CONTINUE)
Pr   15: 15 but the cheerful heart has a **c** feast.

CONTINUE (CONTINUAL)
Php   2: 12 **c** to work out your salvation
2Ti   3: 14 **c** in what you have learned and
1Jn   5: 18 born of God does not **c** to sin;
Rev 22: 11 let the one who does right **c** to do
     22: 11 let the holy person **c** to be holy."

CONTRITE
Ps   51: 17 a broken and **c** heart you, God,
Isa 57: 15 and to revive the heart of the **c**.
     66: 2 who are humble and **c** in spirit,

CONTROL (CONTROLLED SELF-CONTROL SELF-CONTROLLED)
1Co   7: 9 But if they cannot **c** themselves,
      7: 37 but has **c** over his own will,
1Th   4: 4 should learn to **c** your own body

CONTROLLED (CONTROL)
Ps   32: 9 understanding but must be **c** by bit

CONTROVERSIES
Titus 3: 9 But avoid foolish **c** and genealogies

CONVERSATION
Col   4: 6 Let your **c** be always full of grace,

CONVERT
1Ti   3: 6 He must not be a recent **c**, or he

CONVICTION
Heb   3: 14 we hold our original **c** firmly

CONVINCED (CONVINCING)
Ro   8: 38 I am **c** that neither death nor life,
2Ti   1: 12 am **c** that he is able to guard what I
      3: 14 have learned and have become **c** of,

CONVINCING (CONVINCED)
Ac   1: 3 and gave many **c** proofs that he was

CORNELIUS
Roman to whom Peter preached; first Gentile Christian (Ac 10).

CORNERSTONE (STONE)
Ps   118: 22 builders rejected has become the **c**;
Isa 28: 16 a precious **c** for a sure foundation;
Eph   2: 20 Christ Jesus himself as the chief **c**.
1Pe   2: 6 a chosen and precious **c**,
      2: 7 rejected has become the **c**,"

CORRECT (CORRECTING CORRECTION CORRECTS)
2Ti   4: 2 **c**, rebuke and encourage—

CORRECTING (CORRECT)
2Ti   3: 16 **c** and training in righteousness,

CORRECTION (CORRECT)
Pr   10: 17 but whoever ignores **c** leads others
     12: 1 but whoever hates **c** is stupid.
     15: 5 whoever heeds **c** shows prudence.
     15: 10 the one who hates **c** will die.

CORRECTS (CORRECT)
Job   5: 17 "Blessed is the one whom God **c**;
Pr   9: 7 Whoever **c** a mocker invites insults

CORRUPT (CORRUPTS)
Ge   6: 11 Now the earth was **c** in God's sight

CORRUPTS (CORRUPT)
Ecc   7: 7 into a fool, and a bribe **c** the heart.
1Co 15: 33 "Bad company **c** good character."
Jas   3: 6 It **c** the whole body, sets the whole

COST
Pr   4: 7 Though it **c** all you have,
Isa 55: 1 milk without money and without **c**.
Rev 21: 6 thirsty I will give water without **c**

COUNSEL (COUNSELOR)
1Ki 22: 5 "First seek the **c** of the LORD."
Pr 15: 22 Plans fail for lack of **c**,
Rev 3: 18 I **c** you to buy from me gold

COUNSELOR (COUNSEL)
Isa 9: 6 And he will be called Wonderful **C**,

COUNT (COUNTING COUNTS)
Ro   4: 8 Lord will never **c** against them."
        6: 11 **c** yourselves dead to sin but alive

COUNTING (COUNT)
2Co 5: 19 not **c** people's sins against them.

COUNTRY
Jn   4: 44 prophet has no honor in his own **c**.

COUNTS (COUNT)
Jn   6: 63 the flesh **c** for nothing.
1Co 7: 19 God's commands is what **c**.
Gal   5: 6 **c** is faith expressing itself through

COURAGE (COURAGEOUS)
Ac 23: 11 stood near Paul and said, "Take **c**!

COURAGEOUS (COURAGE)
Dt 31: 6 Be strong and **c**. Do not be afraid
Jos   1: 6 Be strong and **c**, because you will
1Co 16: 13 firm in the faith; be **c**; be strong.

COURSE
Ps 19: 5 a champion rejoicing to run his **c**.
Pr 15: 21 understanding keeps a straight **c**.

COURTS
Ps 84: 10 your **c** than a thousand elsewhere;
  100: 4 thanksgiving and his **c** with praise;

COVENANT (COVENANTS)
Ge   9: 9 "I now establish my **c** with you
Ex 19: 5 if you obey me fully and keep my **c**,
1Ch 16: 15 He remembers his **c** forever,
Job 31: 1 "I made a **c** with my eyes not
Jer 31: 31 I will make a new **c** with the people
1Co 11: 25 "This cup is the new **c** in my blood;
Gal   4: 24 One **c** is from Mount Sinai
Heb 9: 15 Christ is the mediator of a new **c**,

COVENANTS (COVENANT)
Ro   9: 4 the **c**, the receiving of the law,
Gal   4: 24 The women represent two **c**.

COVER (COVER-UP COVERED COVERS)
Ps 91: 4 He will **c** you with his feathers,
Jas   5: 20 and **c** over a multitude of sins.

COVER-UP (COVER)
1Pe 2: 16 do not use your freedom as a **c**

COVERED (COVER)
Ps 32: 1 are forgiven, whose sins are **c**.
Isa 6: 2 With two wings they **c** their faces,
Ro   4: 7 are forgiven, whose sins are **c**.
1Co 11: 4 with his head **c** dishonors his head.

COVERS (COVER)
Pr 10: 12 conflict, but love **c** over all wrongs.
1Pe 4: 8 because love **c** over a multitude

COVET
Ex 20: 17 "You shall not **c** your neighbor's
Ro 13: 9 "You shall not **c**," and whatever

COWARDLY
Rev 21: 8 But the **c**, the unbelieving, the vile,

CRAFTINESS (CRAFTY)
1Co 3: 19 "He catches the wise in their **c**";

CRAFTY (CRAFTINESS)
Ge   3: 1 the serpent was more **c** than any
2Co 12: 16 Yet, **c** fellow that I am, I caught you

CRAVE
Pr 23: 3 Do not **c** his delicacies, for that
1Pe 2: 2 babies, **c** pure spiritual milk,

CREATE (CREATED CREATION CREATOR)
Ps 51: 10 **C** in me a pure heart, O God,
Isa 45: 18 he did not **c** it to be empty,

CREATED (CREATE)
Ge   1: 1 In the beginning God **c** the heavens
        1: 21 So God **c** the great creatures
        1: 27 So God **c** mankind in his own
        1: 27 male and female he **c** them.
Ps 148: 5 for at his command they were **c**,
Ro   1: 25 and served **c** things rather than
1Co 11: 9 neither was man **c** for woman,
Col   1: 16 For in him all things were **c**:
1Ti   4: 4 For everything God **c** is good,
Rev 10: 6 who **c** the heavens and all that is

CREATION (CREATE)
Mk 16: 15 *preach the gospel to all* **c**.
Jn 17: 24 because you loved me before the **c**
Ro   8: 19 For the **c** waits in eager expectation
        8: 39 nor anything else in all **c**, will be
2Co 5: 17 is in Christ, the new **c** has come:
Col   1: 15 God, the firstborn over all **c**.
1Pe 1: 20 He was chosen before the **c**
Rev 13: 8 was slain from the **c** of the world.

CREATOR (CREATE)
Ge 14: 22 Most High, **C** of heaven and earth,
Isa 42: 5 LORD says—the **C** of the heavens,
Ro   1: 25 created things rather than the **C**—

CREATURE (CREATURES)
Lev 17: 11 For the life of a **c** is in the blood,

CREATURES (CREATURE)
Ge   6: 19 into the ark two of all living **c**,
Ps 104: 24 the earth is full of your **c**.

CREDIT (CREDITED)
Ro   4: 24 whom God will **c** righteousness—
1Pe 2: 20 it to your **c** if you receive a beating

CREDITED (CREDIT)
Ge 15: 6 and he **c** it to him as righteousness.
Ro   4: 5 their faith is **c** as righteousness.
Gal   3: 6 it was **c** to him as righteousness."
Jas 2: 23 it was **c** to him as righteousness,"

CRIED (CRY)
Ps 18: 6 I **c** to my God for help.

CRIMSON
Isa 1: 18 though they are red as **c**, they shall

CRIPPLED
Mk 9: 45 to enter life **c** than to have two feet

CRITICISM
2Co 8: 20 want to avoid any **c** of the way we

CROOKED
Pr 10: 9 whoever takes **c** paths will be
Php 2: 15 fault in a warped and **c** generation."

CROSS
Mt 10: 38 Whoever does not take up their **c**
Lk   9: 23 take up their **c** daily and follow me.
Ac   2: 23 to death by nailing him to the **c**.
1Co 1: 17 lest the **c** of Christ be emptied of
Gal   6: 14 in the **c** of our Lord Jesus Christ,
Php 2: 8 even death on a **c**!
Col   1: 20 through his blood, shed on the **c**.
        2: 14 taken it away, nailing it to the **c**.
        2: 15 triumphing over them by the **c**.
Heb 12: 2 joy set before him he endured the **c**,

CROWD
Ex 23: 2 pervert justice by siding with the **c**,

CROWN (CROWNED CROWNS)
Pr   4: 9 and present you with a glorious **c**."
      10: 6 Blessings **c** the head
      12: 4 noble character is her husband's **c**,
      17: 6 Children's children are a **c**
Isa 61: 3 on them a **c** of beauty instead
Zec 9: 16 in his land like jewels in a **c**.
Mt 27: 29 then twisted together a **c** of thorns
1Co 9: 25 to get a **c** that will last forever.

2Ti   4:   8   store for me the **c** of righteousness,
Rev   2: 10   will give you life as your victor's **c.**

CROWNED (CROWN)
Ps   8:   5   the angels and **c** them with glory
Pr   14: 18   the prudent are **c** with knowledge.
Heb   2:   7   you **c** them with glory and honor

CROWNS (CROWN)
Rev   4: 10   They lay their **c** before the throne
     19: 12   fire, and on his head are many **c.**

CRUCIFIED (CRUCIFY)
Mt   20: 19   to be mocked and flogged and **c.**
     27: 38   Two rebels were **c** with him,
Lk   24:   7   be **c** and on the third day be raised
Jn   19: 18   they **c** him, and with him two
Ac   2: 36   Jesus, whom you **c,** both Lord
Ro   6:   6   that our old self was **c** with him so
1Co   1: 23   but we preach Christ **c:**
     2:   2   you except Jesus Christ and him **c.**
Gal   2: 20   I have been **c** with Christ and I no
     5: 24   Christ Jesus have **c** the flesh with

CRUCIFY (CRUCIFIED CRUCIFYING)
Mt   27: 22   They all answered, "**C** him!"
     27: 31   Then they led him away to **c** him.

CRUCIFYING (CRUCIFY)
Heb   6:   6   their loss they are **c** the Son of God

CRUSH (CRUSHED)
Ge   3: 15   he will **c** your head, and you will
Isa   53: 10   it was the Lord's will to **c** him
Ro   16: 20   peace will soon **c** Satan under your

CRUSHED (CRUSH)
Ps   34: 18   and saves those who are **c** in spirit.
Isa   5:   5   he was **c** for our iniquities;
2Co   4:   8   pressed on every side, but not **c;**

CRY (CRIED)
Ps   34: 15   and his ears are attentive to their **c;**
     40:   1   he turned to me and heard my **c.**
   130:   1   Out of the depths I **c** to you,

CULMINATION
Ro   10:   4   Christ is the **c** of the law so

CUP
Ps   23:   5   my head with oil; my **c** overflows.
Mt   10: 42   anyone gives even a **c** of cold water
     23: 25   You clean the outside of the **c**
     26: 39   may this **c** be taken from me.
1Co   11: 25   "This **c** is the new covenant in my

CURSE (CURSED)
Dt   11: 26   you today a blessing and a **c**–
     21: 23   is hung on a pole is under God's **c.**
Lk   6: 28   bless those who **c** you,
Gal   1:   8   to you, let them be under God's **c!**
     3: 13   redeemed us from the **c** of the law by becom-
         ing a **c** for us,
Rev   22:   3   No longer will there be any **c.**

CURSED (CURSE)
Ge   3: 17   "**C** is the ground because of you;
Dt   27: 15   "**C** is anyone who makes an idol–
     27: 16   "**C** is anyone who dishonors their
     27: 17   "**C** is anyone who moves their
     27: 18   "**C** is anyone who leads the blind
     27: 19   "**C** is anyone who withholds justice
     27: 20   "**C** is anyone who sleeps with his
     27: 21   "**C** is anyone who has sexual
     27: 22   "**C** is anyone who sleeps with his
     27: 23   "**C** is anyone who sleeps with his
     27: 24   "**C** is anyone who kills their
     27: 25   "**C** is anyone who accepts a bribe
     27: 26   "**C** is anyone who does not uphold
Ro   9:   3   I could wish that I myself were **c**
Gal   3: 10   "**C** is everyone who does not

CURTAIN
Ex   26: 33   Hang the **c** from the clasps
     26: 33   The **c** will separate the Holy Place
Lk   23: 45   the **c** of the temple was torn in two.
Heb   10: 20   way opened for us through the **c,**

CYMBAL
1Co   13:   1   a resounding gong or a clanging **c.**

DANCE (DANCING)
Ecc   3:   4   a time to mourn and a time to **d,**
Mt   11: 17   the pipe for you, and you did not **d;**

DANCING (DANCE)
Ps   30: 11   You turned my wailing into **d;**
   149:   3   Let them praise his name with **d**

DANGER
Pr   27: 12   The prudent see **d** and take refuge,
Ro   8: 35   or nakedness or **d** or sword?

DANIEL
     Hebrew exile to Babylon, name changed to Belteshazzar (Da 1:6-7). Refused to eat unclean food (Da 1:8-21). Interpreted Nebuchadnezzar's dreams (Da 2; 4), writing on the wall (Da 5). Thrown into lion's den (Da 6). Visions of (Da 7-12).

DARK (DARKEST DARKNESS)
Ro   2: 19   a light for those who are in the **d,**
2Pe   1: 19   it, as to a light shining in a **d** place,

DARKEST (DARK)
Ps   23:   4   though I walk through the **d** valley,

DARKNESS (DARK)
Ge   1:   4   he separated the light from the **d.**
2Sa   22: 29   the Lord turns my **d** into light.
Job   34: 22   utter **d,** where evildoers can hide.
Jn   3: 19   but people loved **d** instead of light
2Co   6: 14   fellowship can light have with **d**?
Eph   5:   8   For you were once **d,** but now you
1Pe   2:   9   out of **d** into his wonderful light.
1Jn   1:   5   in him there is no **d** at all.
     2:   9   a brother or sister is still in the **d.**

DAUGHTERS
Joel   2: 28   Your sons and **d** will prophesy,

DAVID
     Son of Jesse (Ru 4:17-22; 1Ch 2:13-15), ancestor of Jesus (Mt 1:1-17; Lk 3:31).
     Anointed king by Samuel (1Sa 16:1-13). Musician to Saul (1Sa 16:14-23; 18:10). Killed Goliath (1Sa 17). Relation with Jonathan (1Sa 18:1-4; 19-20; 23:16-18; 2Sa 1). Disfavor of Saul (1Sa 18:6–23:29). Spared Saul's life (1Sa 24; 26). Among Philistines (1Sa 21:10-14; 27-30). Lament for Saul and Jonathan (2Sa 1).
     Anointed king of Judah (2Sa 2:1-11); of Israel (2Sa 5:1-4; 1Ch 11:1-3). Promised eternal dynasty (2Sa 7; 1Ch 17; Ps 132). Adultery with Bathsheba (2Sa 11-12). Absalom's revolt (2Sa 14-18). Last words (2Sa 23:1-7). Death (1Ki 2:10-12; 1Ch 29:28).

DAWN
Ps   37:   6   righteous reward shine like the **d,**

DAY (DAYS)
Ge   1:   5   God called the light "**d,**"
Ex   20:   8   "Remember the Sabbath **d**
Lev   23: 28   because it is the **D** of Atonement,
Nu   14: 14   them in a pillar of cloud by **d**
Jos   1:   8   meditate on it **d** and night,
Ps   84: 10   Better is one **d** in your courts than
     96:   2   proclaim his salvation **d** after **d.**
   118: 24   The Lord has done it this very **d;**
Pr   27:   1   do not know what a **d** may bring.
Joel   2: 31   great and dreadful **d** of the Lord.
Ob   : 15   "The **d** of the Lord is near for all
Lk   11:   3   Give us each **d** our daily bread.
Ac   17: 11   examined the Scriptures every **d**
2Co   4: 16   we are being renewed **d** by **d.**
1Th   5:   2   the **d** of the Lord will come like
2Pe   3:   8   With the Lord a **d** is like a thousand

DAYS (DAY)
Dt   17: 19   he is to read it all the **d** of his life so
Ps   23:   6   love will follow me all the **d** of my
     90: 10   Our **d** may come to seventy years,
Ecc   12:   1   Creator in the **d** of your youth,
Joel   2: 29   I will pour out my Spirit in those **d.**
Mic   4:   1   In the last **d** the mountain
Heb   1:   2   in these last **d** he has spoken to us
2Pe   3:   3   that in the last **d** scoffers will come,

DEACONS
1Ti 3: 8 way, **d** are to be worthy of respect,

DEAD (DIE)
Dt 18: 11 or spiritist or who consults the **d**.
Mt 28: 7 'He has risen from the **d** and is
Ro 6: 11 count yourselves **d** to sin but alive
Eph 2: 1 you were **d** in your transgressions
1Th 4: 16 and the **d** in Christ will rise first.
Jas 2: 17 is not accompanied by action, is **d**.
     2: 26 so faith without deeds is **d**.

DEATH (DIE)
Nu 35: 16 the murderer is to be put to **d**.
Ps 116: 15 of the LORD is the **d** of his faithful
Pr 8: 36 all who hate me love **d**."
    14: 12 right, but in the end it leads to **d**.
Ecc 7: 2 for **d** is the destiny of everyone;
Isa 25: 8 he will swallow up **d** forever.
    53: 12 he poured out his life unto **d**,
Jn 5: 24 but has crossed over from **d** to life.
Ro 5: 12 **d** through sin, and in this way **d**
   6: 23 For the wages of sin is **d**,
   8: 13 Spirit you put to **d** the misdeeds
1Co 15: 21 For since **d** came through a man,
    15: 31 I face **d** every day—yes, just as
    15: 55 "Where, O **d**, is your victory?
1Pe 3: 18 He was put to **d** in the body
Rev 1: 18 I hold the keys of **d** and Hades.
    20: 6 The second **d** has no power over
    20: 14 The lake of fire is the second **d**.
    21: 4 There will be no more **d**'

DEBAUCHERY
Ro 13: 13 not in sexual immorality and **d**,
Eph 5: 18 drunk on wine, which leads to **d**.

DEBORAH
    Prophetess who led Israel to victory over Canaanites (Jdg 4-5).

DEBT (DEBTORS DEBTS)
Ro 13: 8 except the continuing **d** to love

DEBTORS (DEBT)
Mt 6: 12 as we also have forgiven our **d**.

DEBTS (DEBT)
Dt 15: 1 seven years you must cancel **d**.
Mt 6: 12 And forgive us our **d**, as we

DECAY
Ps 16: 10 will you let your faithful one see **d**.
Ac 2: 27 will not let your holy one see **d**.

DECEIT (DECEIVE)
Mk 7: 22 greed, malice, **d**, lewdness, envy,
1Pe 2: 1 yourselves of all malice and all **d**,
    2: 22 and no **d** was found in his mouth."

DECEITFUL (DECEIVE)
Jer 17: 9 The heart is **d** above all things
2Co 11: 13 are false apostles, **d** workers,

DECEITFULNESS (DECEIVE)
Mk 4: 19 the **d** of wealth and the desires
Heb 3: 13 of you may be hardened by sin's **d**.

DECEIVE (DECEIT DECEITFUL DECEITFULNESS DECEIVED DECEIVES DECEPTIVE)
Lev 19: 11 "'Do not **d** one another.
Pr 14: 5 An honest witness does not **d**,
Mt 24: 5 am the Messiah,' and will **d** many.
Ro 16: 18 flattery they **d** the minds of naive
1Co 3: 18 Do not **d** yourselves. If any of you
Gal 6: 3 they are not, they **d** themselves.
Eph 5: 6 no one **d** you with empty words,
Jas 1: 22 to the word, and so **d** yourselves.
Jas 1: 26 rein on their tongues **d** themselves,
1Jn 1: 8 we **d** ourselves and the truth is not

DECEIVED (DECEIVE)
Ge 3: 13 said, "The serpent **d** me, and I ate."
Gal 6: 7 Do not be **d**: God cannot be
1Ti 2: 14 And Adam was not the one **d**; it was the woman who was **d**
2Ti 3: 13 to worse, deceiving and being **d**.
Jas 1: 16 Don't be **d**, my dear brothers

DECENCY
1Ti 2: 9 modestly, with **d** and propriety,

DECEPTIVE (DECEIVE)
Pr 31: 30 Charm is **d**, and beauty is fleeting;
Col 2: 8 through hollow and **d** philosophy,

DECLARE (DECLARED DECLARING)
1Ch 16: 24 **D** his glory among the nations,
Ps 19: 1 The heavens **d** the glory of God;
    96: 3 **D** his glory among the nations,
Isa 42: 9 taken place, and new things I **d**;
Ro 10: 9 If you **d** with your mouth, "Jesus is

DECLARED (DECLARE)
Mk 7: 19 saying this, Jesus **d** all foods clean.)
Ro 2: 13 the law who will be **d** righteous.
   3: 20 no one will be **d** righteous

DECLARING (DECLARE)
Ps 71: 8 **d** your splendor all day long.
Ac 2: 11 hear them **d** the wonders of God

DECREED (DECREES)
La 3: 37 it happen if the Lord has not **d** it?
Lk 22: 22 Son of Man will go as it has been **d**.

DECREES (DECREED)
Lev 10: 11 Israelites all the **d** the LORD has
Ps 119: 112 on keeping your **d** to the very end.

DEDICATE (DEDICATION)
Pr 20: 25 It is a trap to **d** something rashly

DEDICATION (DEDICATE)
1Ti 5: 11 sensual desires overcome their **d**

DEED (DEEDS)
Col 3: 17 whether in word or **d**, do it all

DEEDS (DEED)
1Sa 2: 3 knows, and by him **d** are weighed.
Ps 65: 5 us with awesome and righteous **d**,
   66: 3 to God, "How awesome are your **d**!
   78: 4 next generation the praiseworthy **d**
   86: 10 you are great and do marvelous **d**;
   92: 4 For you make me glad by your **d**,
   111: 3 Glorious and majestic are his **d**,
Hab 3: 2 I stand in awe of your **d**, LORD.
Mt 5: 16 that they may see your good **d**
   11: 19 wisdom is proved right by her **d**."
Ac 26: 20 their repentance by their **d**.
Jas 2: 14 claims to have faith but has no **d**?
    2: 20 that faith without **d** is useless?
1Pe 2: 12 they may see your good **d**

DEEP (DEPTH)
1Co 2: 10 things, even the **d** things of God.
1Ti 3: 9 must keep hold of the **d** truths

DEER
Ps 42: 1 As the **d** pants for streams of water,

DEFEND (DEFENSE)
Ps 74: 22 Rise up, O God, and **d** your cause;
Pr 31: 9 **d** the rights of the poor and needy.
Jer 50: 34 He will vigorously **d** their cause so

DEFENSE (DEFEND)
Ps 35: 23 Awake, and rise to my **d**!
Php 1: 16 put here for the **d** of the gospel.

DEFERRED
Pr 13: 12 Hope **d** makes the heart sick,

DEFILE (DEFILED)
Da 1: 8 Daniel resolved not to **d** himself

DEFILED (DEFILE)
Isa 24: 5 The earth is **d** by its people;

DEFRAUD
Lev 19: 13 "'Do not **d** or rob your neighbor.

DEITY
Col 2: 9 Christ all the fullness of the **D** lives

DELIGHT (DELIGHTS)
1Sa 15: 22 "Does the LORD **d** in burnt
Ps 1: 2 but whose **d** is in the law
   16: 3 noble ones in whom is all my **d**."
   35: 9 the LORD and **d** in his salvation.

Ps   37:   4 Take **d** in the Lord, and he will
     43:   4 of God, to God, my joy and my **d**.
     51: 16 You do not **d** in sacrifice,
    119: 77 I may live, for your law is my **d**.
Isa 42:   1 my chosen one in whom I **d**;
     55:   2 you will **d** in the richest of fare.
     61: 10 I **d** greatly in the Lord;
Jer   9: 24 earth, for in these I **d**,"
     15: 16 they were my joy and my heart's **d**,
Mic   7: 18 angry forever but **d** to show mercy.
Zep   3: 17 He will take great **d** in you;
Mt   12: 18 the one I love, in whom I **d**;
1Co 13:   6 Love does not **d** in evil but rejoices
2Co 12: 10 for Christ's sake, I **d** in weaknesses,

DELIGHTS (DELIGHT)
Ps   22:   8 deliver him, since he **d** in him."
     35: 27 who **d** in the well-being of his
     36:   8 them drink from your river of **d**.
Pr   3: 12 he loves, as a father the son he **d** in.
     12: 22 **d** in people who are trustworthy.
     29: 17 will bring you the **d** you desire.

DELILAH
   Woman who betrayed Samson (Jdg 16:4-22).

DELIVER (DELIVERANCE DELIVERED DELIVERER
DELIVERS)
Ps   72: 12 he will **d** the needy who cry out,
     79:   9 **d** us and forgive our sins for your
Da   3: 17 the God we serve is able to **d** us
Mt   6: 13 but **d** us from the evil one.'
2Co   1: 10 that he will continue to **d** us,

DELIVERANCE (DELIVER)
Ps   3:   8 From the Lord comes **d**.
     32:   7 and surround me with songs of **d**.
     33: 17 A horse is a vain hope for **d**;

DELIVERED (DELIVER)
Ps   34:   4 he **d** me from all my fears.
Ro   4: 25 He was **d** over to death for our sins

DELIVERER (DELIVER)
Ps   18:   2 is my rock, my fortress and my **d**;
     40: 17 You are my help and my **d**;
    140:   7 my strong **d**, you shield my head
    144:   2 stronghold and my **d**, my shield,

DELIVERS (DELIVER)
Ps   34: 17 he **d** them from all their troubles.
     34: 19 the Lord **d** him from them all;
     37: 40 The Lord helps them and **d** them;

DEMANDED
Lk   12: 20 This very night your life will be **d**
     12: 48 been given much, much will be **d**;

DEMONS
Mt   12: 27 And if I drive out **d** by Beelzebul,
Mk   5: 15 been possessed by the legion of **d**,
Ro   8: 38 life, neither angels nor **d**,
Jas   2: 19 Good! Even the **d** believe that—

DEMONSTRATE (DEMONSTRATES)
Ac   26: 20 **d** their repentance by their deeds.
Ro   3: 26 he did it to **d** his righteousness

DEMONSTRATES (DEMONSTRATE)
Ro   5:   8 God **d** his own love for us in this:

DEN
Da   6: 16 and threw him into the lions' **d**.
Mt   21: 13 but you are making it 'a **d**

DENARIUS
Mk   12: 15 "Bring me a **d** and let me look

DENIED (DENY)
1Ti   5:   8 has **d** the faith and is worse than

DENIES (DENY)
1Jn   2: 23 No one who **d** the Son has

DENY (DENIED DENIES DENYING)
Ex   23:   6 "Do not **d** justice to your poor
Job 27:   5 till I die, I will not **d** my integrity.
La   3: 35 **d** people their rights before the
Lk   9: 23 be my disciple must **d** themselves
Titus 1: 16 but by their actions they **d** him.

DENYING (DENY)
Eze 22: 29 the foreigner, **d** them justice.
2Ti   3:   5 a form of godliness but **d** its power.
2Pe   2:   1 even **d** the sovereign Lord who

DEPART (DEPARTED)
Ge   49: 10 The scepter will not **d** from Judah,
Job   1: 21 mother's womb, and naked I will **d**.
Mt   25: 41 to those on his left, '**D** from me,
Php   1: 23 I desire to **d** and be with Christ,

DEPARTED (DEPART)
1Sa   4: 21 "The Glory has **d** from Israel"—
Ps 119:102 I have not **d** from your laws,

DEPOSIT
2Co   1: 22 put his Spirit in our hearts as a **d**,
      5:   5 who has given us the Spirit as a **d**,
Eph   1: 14 who is a **d** guaranteeing our
2Ti   1: 14 Guard the good **d** that was entrusted

DEPRAVED (DEPRAVITY)
Ro   1: 28 God gave them over to a **d** mind,
2Pe   2:   7 was distressed by the **d** conduct

DEPRAVITY (DEPRAVED)
Ro   1: 29 of wickedness, evil, greed and **d**.

DEPRIVE
Dt   24: 17 Do not **d** the foreigner
Pr   18:   5 and so **d** the innocent of justice.
Isa 10:   2 to **d** the poor of their rights
     29: 21 with false testimony **d** the innocent
1Co   7:   5 Do not **d** each other except

DEPTH (DEEP)
Ro   8: 39 neither height nor **d**, nor anything
     11: 33 the **d** of the riches of the wisdom

DESERT See WILDERNESS

DESERTED (DESERTS)
Mt   26: 56 all the disciples **d** him and fled.
2Ti   1: 15 in the province of Asia has **d** me,

DESERTING (DESERTS)
Gal   1:   6 you are so quickly **d** the one who

DESERTS (DESERTED DESERTING)
Zec 11: 17 shepherd, who **d** the flock!

DESERVE (DESERVES)
Ps 103: 10 he does not treat us as our sins **d**
Jer 21: 14 I will punish you as your deeds **d**,
Mt   22:   8 those I invited did not **d** to come.
Ro   1: 32 those who do such things **d** death,

DESERVES (DESERVE)
Lk   10:   7 for the worker **d** his wages.
1Ti   5: 18 and "The worker **d** his wages."

DESIRABLE (DESIRE)
Pr   22:   1 name is more **d** than great riches;

DESIRE (DESIRABLE DESIRES)
Ge   3: 16 Your **d** will be for your husband,
Dt   5: 21 You shall not set your **d** on your
Ps   40:   6 and offering you did not **d**—
     40:   8 I **d** to do your will, my God;
     73: 25 earth has nothing I **d** besides you.
Pr   3: 15 nothing you **d** can compare
     10: 24 what the righteous **d** will be
     11: 23 The **d** of the righteous ends only
     19:   2 **D** without knowledge is not good
Isa 26:   8 and renown are the **d** of our hearts.
     53:   2 appearance that we should **d** him.
     55: 11 but will accomplish what I **d**
Hos   6:   6 For I **d** mercy, not sacrifice,
Mt   9: 13 'I **d** mercy, not sacrifice.'
Ro   7: 18 For I have the **d** to do what is good,
1Co 12: 31 Now eagerly **d** the greater gifts.
     14:   1 and eagerly **d** gifts of the Spirit,
Php   1: 23 I **d** to depart and be with Christ,
Heb 13: 18 **d** to live honorably in every way.
Jas   1: 15 after **d** has conceived, it gives birth

DESIRES (DESIRE)
Ge   4:   7 it **d** to have you, but you must rule
1Ch 29: 18 keep these **d** and thoughts

Ps	34:	12 life and **d** to see many good days,
	37:	4 will give you the **d** of your heart.
	103:	5 who satisfies your **d** with good
	145:	19 He fulfills the **d** of those who fear
Pr	11:	6 the unfaithful are trapped by evil **d**.
	19:	22 What a person **d** is unfailing love;
Mk	4:	19 and the **d** for other things come
Ro	8:	5 minds set on what the Spirit **d**.
	13:	14 how to gratify the **d** of the flesh.
Gal	5:	16 and you will not gratify the **d**
	5:	17 For the flesh **d** what is contrary
1Ti	3:	1 to be an overseer **d** a noble task.
	6:	9 harmful **d** that plunge people
2Ti	2:	22 Flee the evil **d** of youth and pursue
Jas	1:	20 the righteousness that God **d**.
	4:	1 from your **d** that battle within you?
1Pe	2:	11 to abstain from sinful **d**,
1Jn	2:	17 The world and its **d** pass away,

DESOLATE

Isa	54:	1 the children of the **d** woman than

DESPAIR

Isa	61:	3 of praise instead of a spirit of **d**.
2Co	4:	8 perplexed, but not in **d**;

DESPISE (DESPISED DESPISES)

Job	42:	6 Therefore I **d** myself and repent
Pr	1:	7 fools **d** wisdom and instruction.
	3:	11 do not **d** the LORD's discipline,
	14:	21 It is a sin to **d** one's neighbor,
	15:	32 disregard discipline **d** themselves,
	23:	22 do not **d** your mother when she is
Zec	4:	10 "Who dares **d** the day of small
Lk	16:	13 devoted to the one and **d** the other.
Titus	2:	15 Do not let anyone **d** you.

DESPISED (DESPISE)

Ge	25:	34 and left. So Esau **d** his birthright.
Isa	53:	3 He was **d** and rejected by mankind,
1Co	1:	28 of this world and the **d** things–

DESPISES (DESPISE)

Pr	15:	20 but a foolish man **d** his mother.

DESTINED (DESTINY)

Lk	2:	34 "This child is **d** to cause the falling

DESTINY (DESTINED PREDESTINED)

Ps	73:	17 then I understood their final **d**.
Ecc	7:	2 for death is the **d** of everyone;

DESTITUTE

Pr	31:	8 for the rights of all who are **d**.
Heb	11:	37 in sheepskins and goatskins, **d**,

DESTROY (DESTROYED DESTROYS DESTRUCTION)

Pr	1:	32 complacency of fools will **d** them;
	11:	9 the godless **d** their neighbors,
Mt	10:	28 of the One who can **d** both soul

DESTROYED (DESTROY)

Job	19:	26 And after my skin has been **d**,
1Co	8:	11 is **d** by your knowledge.
	15:	26 The last enemy to be **d** is death.
2Co	5:	1 if the earthly tent we live in is **d**,
Heb	10:	39 those who shrink back and are **d**,
2Pe	3:	10 the elements will be **d** by fire,

DESTROYS (DESTROY)

Pr	6:	32 whoever does so **d** himself.
	18:	9 his work is brother to one who **d**.
	28:	24 wrong," is partner to one who **d**.
Ecc	9:	18 but one sinner **d** much good.
1Co	3:	17 If anyone **d** God's temple, God will

DESTRUCTION (DESTROY)

Ps	1:	6 the way of the wicked leads to **d**.
Pr	16:	18 Pride goes before **d**, a haughty
Hos	13:	14 Where, O grave, is your **d**?
Mt	7:	13 broad is the road that leads to **d**,
Gal	6:	8 flesh, from the flesh will reap **d**;
2Th	1:	9 will be punished with everlasting **d**
1Ti	6:	9 that plunge people into ruin and **d**.
2Pe	2:	1 bringing swift **d** on themselves.
	3:	16 other Scriptures, to their own **d**.

DETERMINED (DETERMINES)

Job	14:	5 A person's days are **d**;
Isa	14:	26 This is the plan **d** for the whole
Da	11:	36 what has been **d** must take place.

DETERMINES (DETERMINED)

Ps	147:	4 He **d** the number of the stars
1Co	12:	11 them to each one, just as he **d**.

DETESTABLE (DETESTS)

Pr	21:	27 The sacrifice of the wicked is **d**–
	28:	9 even their prayers are **d**.
Isa	1:	13 Your incense is **d** to me.
Lk	16:	15 What people value highly is **d**
Titus	1:	16 They are **d**, disobedient and unfit

DETESTS (DETESTABLE)

Dt	22:	5 the LORD your God **d** anyone who
	23:	18 the LORD your God **d** them both.
	25:	16 the LORD your God **d** anyone who
Pr	11:	1 The LORD **d** dishonest scales,
	12:	22 The LORD **d** lying lips, but he
	15:	8 The LORD **d** the sacrifice
	15:	9 The LORD **d** the way
	15:	26 The LORD **d** the thoughts
	16:	5 The LORD **d** all the proud
	17:	15 the LORD **d** them both.
	20:	23 the LORD **d** differing weights,

DEVIL (DEVIL'S)

Mt	13:	39 the enemy who sows them is the **d**.
	25:	41 the eternal fire prepared for the **d**
Lk	4:	2 forty days he was tempted by the **d**.
	8:	12 then the **d** comes and takes away
Eph	4:	27 and do not give the **d** a foothold.
2Ti	2:	26 and escape from the trap of the **d**,
Jas	4:	7 Resist the **d**, and he will flee
1Pe	5:	8 Your enemy the **d** prowls around
1Jn	3:	8 who does what is sinful is of the **d**,
Rev	12:	9 that ancient serpent called the **d**,

DEVIL'S (DEVIL)

Eph	6:	11 your stand against the **d** schemes.
1Ti	3:	7 into disgrace and into the **d** trap.
1Jn	3:	8 was to destroy the **d** work.

DEVISED

2Pe	1:	16 we did not follow cleverly **d** stories

DEVOTE (DEVOTED DEVOTING DEVOTION DEVOUT)

Job	11:	13 "Yet if you **d** your heart to him
Jer	30:	21 who is he who will **d** himself to be
Col	4:	2 **D** yourselves to prayer,
1Ti	4:	13 **d** yourself to the public reading
Titus	3:	8 may be careful to **d** themselves

DEVOTED (DEVOTE)

Ezr	7:	10 For Ezra had **d** himself to the study
Ac	2:	42 They **d** themselves to the apostles'
Ro	12:	10 Be **d** to one another in love.
1Co	7:	34 Her aim is to be **d** to the Lord

DEVOTING (DEVOTE)

1Ti	5:	10 **d** herself to all kinds of good deeds.

DEVOTION (DEVOTE)

1Ch	28:	9 serve him with wholehearted **d**
1Co	7:	35 way in undivided **d** to the Lord.
2Co	11:	3 your sincere and pure **d** to Christ.

DEVOUR

2Sa	2:	26 to Joab, "Must the sword **d** forever?
Mk	12:	40 They **d** widows' houses
1Pe	5:	8 lion looking for someone to **d**.

DEVOUT (DEVOTE)

Lk	2:	25 Simeon, who was righteous and **d**.

DIE (DEAD DEATH DIED DIES)

Ge	2:	17 eat from it you will certainly **d**."
Ex	11:	5 Every firstborn son in Egypt will **d**,
Ru	1:	17 Where you **d** I will **d**, and there I
2Ki	14:	6 each will **d** for their own sin."
Pr	5:	23 For lack of discipline they will **d**,
	10:	21 many, but fools **d** for lack of sense.
	11:	7 placed in mortals **d** with them;
	15:	10 one who hates correction will **d**.

Pr 23: 13 them with the rod, they will not **d**.
Ecc 3: 2 a time to be born and a time to **d**,
Isa 66: 24 the worms that eat them will not **d**,
Eze 3: 18 wicked person will **d** for their sin,
    18: 4 one who sins is the one who will **d**.
    33: 8 wicked person will **d** for their sin,
Mt 26: 52 all who draw the sword will **d**
Jn 11: 25 in me will live, even though they **d**;
    11: 26 by believing in me will never **d**.
Ro 5: 7 Very rarely will anyone **d**
    14: 8 and if we **d**, we **d** for the Lord.
1Co 15: 22 For as in Adam all **d**, so in Christ
Php 1: 21 to live is Christ and to **d** is gain.
Heb 9: 27 as people are destined to **d** once,
Rev 14: 13 Blessed are the dead who **d**

DIED (DIE)
Ro 5: 6 Christ **d** for the ungodly.
    6: 2 We are those who have **d** to sin;
    6: 8 Now if we **d** with Christ, we believe
    14: 15 someone for whom Christ **d**.
1Co 8: 11 for whom Christ **d**, is destroyed
    15: 3 that Christ **d** for our sins according
2Co 5: 14 one **d** for all, and therefore all **d**.
Col 3: 3 For you **d**, and your life is now
1Th 5: 10 He **d** for us so that, whether we are
2Ti 2: 11 If we **d** with him, we will also live
Heb 9: 15 that he has **d** as a ransom to set
Rev 2: 8 Last, who **d** and came to life again.

DIES (DIE)
Job 14: 14 If someone **d**, will they live again?
1Co 15: 36 does not come to life unless it **d**.

DIFFERENCE (DIFFERENT)
Ro 10: 12 For there is no **d** between Jew

DIFFERENT (DIFFERENCE)
1Co 12: 4 There are **d** kinds of gifts,
2Co 11: 4 or a **d** gospel from the one you

DIGNITY
Pr 31: 25 She is clothed with strength and **d**;

DIGS
Pr 26: 27 Whoever **d** a pit will fall into it;

DILIGENCE (DILIGENT)
Heb 6: 11 show this same **d** to the very end,

DILIGENT (DILIGENCE)
Pr 21: 5 The plans of the **d** lead to profit as
1Ti 4: 15 Be **d** in these matters;

DIRECT (DIRECTS)
Ps 119: 35 **D** me in the path of your
    119:133 **D** my footsteps according to your
Jer 10: 23 it is not for them to **d** their steps.
2Th 3: 5 May the Lord **d** your hearts

DIRECTS (DIRECT)
Ps 42: 8 By day the LORD **d** his love,
Isa 48: 17 who **d** you in the way you should

DIRGE
Mt 11: 17 we sang a **d**, and you did not

DISAPPEAR
Mt 5: 18 until heaven and earth **d**,
Lk 16: 17 earth to **d** than for the least stroke

DISASTER
Ps 57: 1 your wings until the **d** has passed.
Pr 3: 25 Have no fear of sudden **d**
    17: 5 whoever gloats over **d** will not go
Isa 45: 7 I bring prosperity and create **d**;
Eze 7: 5 Unheard-of **d**! See, it comes!

DISCERN (DISCERNING)
Ps 19: 12 But who can **d** their own errors?
    139: 3 You **d** my going out and my lying
Php 1: 10 you may be able to **d** what is best

DISCERNING (DISCERN)
Pr 14: 6 knowledge comes easily to the **d**.
    15: 14 The **d** heart seeks knowledge,
    17: 10 A rebuke impresses a **d** person
    17: 24 A **d** person keeps wisdom in view,

Pr 17: 28 and **d** if they hold their tongues.
    19: 25 rebuke the **d**, and they will gain
    28: 11 and **d** sees how deluded they are.

DISCIPLE (DISCIPLES)
Mt 10: 42 of these little ones who is my **d**,
Lk 14: 27 and follow me cannot be my **d**.

DISCIPLES (DISCIPLE)
Mt 28: 19 go and make **d** of all nations,
Jn 8: 31 my teaching, you are really my **d**.
    13: 35 will know that you are my **d**, if you
Ac 11: 26 The **d** were called Christians first

DISCIPLINE (DISCIPLINED DISCIPLINES)
Ps 38: 1 your anger or **d** me in your wrath.
    39: 11 rebuke and **d** anyone for their sin,
    94: 12 Blessed is the one you **d**, LORD,
Pr 3: 11 do not despise the LORD's **d**,
    5: 12 You will say, "How I hated **d**!
    5: 23 For lack of **d** they will die,
    10: 17 Whoever heeds **d** shows the way
    12: 1 Whoever loves **d** loves knowledge,
    13: 18 Whoever disregards **d** comes
    13: 24 their children is careful to **d** them.
    15: 5 A fool spurns a parent's **d**,
    15: 32 disregard **d** despise themselves,
    19: 18 **D** your children, for in that there is
    19: 20 Listen to advice and accept **d**,
    22: 15 the rod of **d** will drive it far away.
    23: 13 Do not withhold **d** from a child;
    29: 17 **D** your children, and they will give
Heb 12: 5 do not make light of the Lord's **d**,
    12: 7 Endure hardship as **d**;
    12: 11 No **d** seems pleasant at the time,
Rev 3: 19 Those whom I love I rebuke and **d**.

DISCIPLINED (DISCIPLINE)
Jer 31: 18 'You **d** me like an unruly calf,
1Co 11: 32 we are being **d** so that we will not
Col 2: 5 delight to see how **d** you are
Titus 1: 8 upright, holy and **d**.
Heb 12: 7 For what children are not **d** by

DISCIPLINES (DISCIPLINE)
Dt 8: 5 so the LORD your God **d** you.
Pr 3: 12 because the LORD **d** those he
Heb 12: 6 the Lord **d** the one he loves,
    12: 10 but God **d** us for our good,

DISCLOSED
Lk 8: 17 nothing hidden that will not be **d**,

DISCOURAGED
Jos 1: 9 do not be **d**, for the LORD your
    10: 25 "Do not be afraid; do not be **d**.
1Ch 28: 20 Do not be afraid or **d**,
Isa 42: 4 or be **d** till he establishes justice
Col 3: 21 children, or they will become **d**.

DISCREDITED
2Co 6: 3 so that our ministry will not be **d**.

DISCRETION
1Ch 22: 12 May the LORD give you **d**
Pr 1: 4 knowledge and **d** to the young–
    2: 11 **D** will protect you,
    5: 2 that you may maintain **d** and your
    8: 12 I possess knowledge and **d**.
    11: 22 beautiful woman who shows no **d**.

DISCRIMINATED
Jas 2: 4 have you not **d** among yourselves

DISFIGURED
Isa 52: 14 his appearance was so **d** beyond

DISGRACE (DISGRACEFUL DISGRACES)
Pr 11: 2 then comes **d**, but with humility
    19: 26 is a child who brings shame and **d**.
Ac 5: 41 worthy of suffering **d** for the Name.
Heb 13: 13 the camp, bearing the **d** he bore.

DISGRACEFUL (DISGRACE)
Pr 10: 5 sleeps during harvest is a **d** son.
    17: 2 servant will rule over a **d** son

DISGRACES (DISGRACE)
Pr 28: 7 companion of gluttons **d** his father.
29: 15 left undisciplined **d** its mother.

DISGUISE
Pr 26: 24 Enemies **d** themselves with their

DISHONEST
Pr 11: 1 The Lord detests **d** scales,
29: 27 The righteous detest the **d**;
Lk 16: 10 whoever is **d** with very little will
1Ti 3: 8 wine, and not pursuing **d** gain.

DISHONOR (DISHONORS)
Lev 18: 7 "'Do not **d** your father by having
Pr 30: 9 and so **d** the name of my God.
1Co 13: 5 It does not **d** others, it is not
15: 43 it is sown in **d**, it is raised in glory;

DISHONORS (DISHONOR)
Dt 27: 16 is anyone who **d** their father

DISMAYED
Isa 41: 10 do not be **d**, for I am your God.

DISOBEDIENCE (DISOBEY)
Ro 5: 19 as through the **d** of the one man
11: 32 has bound everyone over to **d** so
Heb 2: 2 and **d** received its just punishment,
4: 6 did not go in because of their **d**,
4: 11 by following their example of **d**.

DISOBEDIENT (DISOBEY)
2Ti 3: 2 proud, abusive, **d** to their parents,
Titus 1: 6 to the charge of being wild and **d**.
1: 16 **d** and unfit for doing anything

DISOBEY (DISOBEDIENCE DISOBEDIENT)
Dt 11: 28 the curse if you **d** the commands
2Ch 24: 20 'Why do you **d** the Lord's
Ro 1: 30 of doing evil; they **d** their parents;

DISORDER
1Co 14: 33 For God is not a God of **d**
2Co 12: 20 slander, gossip, arrogance and **d**.
Jas 3: 16 there you find **d** and every evil

DISOWN
Pr 30: 9 I may have too much and **d** you
Mt 10: 33 will **d** before my Father in heaven.
26: 35 to die with you, I will never **d** you."
2Ti 2: 12 If we **d** him, he will also **d** us;

DISPLAY (DISPLAYS)
Eze 39: 21 "I will **d** my glory among
1Ti 1: 16 Christ Jesus might **d** his immense

DISPLAYS (DISPLAY)
Isa 44: 23 Jacob, he **d** his glory in Israel.

DISPUTE (DISPUTES)
Pr 17: 14 the matter before a **d** breaks out.
1Co 6: 1 If any of you has a **d** with another,

DISPUTES (DISPUTE)
Pr 18: 18 Casting the lot settles **d** and keeps

DISQUALIFIED
1Co 9: 27 I myself will not be **d** for the prize.

DISREGARD
Pr 15: 32 Those who **d** discipline despise

DISREPUTE
2Pe 2: 2 will bring the way of truth into **d**.

DISSENSION
Ro 13: 13 debauchery, not in **d** and jealousy.

DISTINGUISH
1Ki 3: 9 and to **d** between right and wrong.
Heb 5: 14 have trained themselves to **d** good

DISTORT
2Co 4: 2 nor do we **d** the word of God.
2Pe 3: 16 ignorant and unstable people **d**,

DISTRESS (DISTRESSED)
Ps 18: 6 In my **d** I called to the Lord;
Jnh 2: 2 "In my **d** I called to the Lord,
Jas 1: 27 and widows in their **d** and to keep

DISTRESSED (DISTRESS)
Ro 14: 15 sister is **d** because of what you eat,

DIVIDED (DIVISION)
Mt 12: 25 "Every kingdom **d** against itself
Lk 23: 34 **d** up his clothes by casting lots.
1Co 1: 13 Is Christ **d**? Was Paul crucified

DIVINATION
Lev 19: 26 "'Do not practice **d** or seek

DIVINE
Ro 1: 20 his eternal power and **d** nature—
2Co 10: 4 they have **d** power to demolish
2Pe 1: 4 may participate in the **d** nature,

DIVISION (DIVIDED DIVISIONS DIVISIVE)
Lk 12: 51 peace on earth? No, I tell you, but **d**.
1Co 12: 25 there should be no **d** in the body,

DIVISIONS (DIVISION)
Ro 16: 17 to watch out for those who cause **d**
1Co 1: 10 and that there be no **d** among you,
11: 18 as a church, there are **d** among you,

DIVISIVE (DIVISION)
Titus 3: 10 Warn a **d** person once,

DIVORCE (DIVORCES)
Mt 19: 3 for a man to **d** his wife for any
1Co 7: 11 a husband must not **d** his wife.

DIVORCES (DIVORCE)
Mal 2: 16 man who hates and **d** his wife,"

DOCTOR
Mt 9: 12 "It is not the healthy who need a **d**,

DOCTRINE
1Ti 4: 16 Watch your life and **d** closely.
Titus 2: 1 what is appropriate to sound **d**.

DOMINION
Ps 22: 28 for **d** belongs to the Lord and he

DOOR
Ps 141: 3 keep watch over the **d** of my lips.
Mt 6: 6 close the **d** and pray to your Father,
7: 7 and the **d** will be opened to you.
Rev 3: 20 I stand at the **d** and knock.

DOORKEEPER
Ps 84: 10 I would rather be a **d** in the house

DOUBLE-EDGED
Heb 4: 12 Sharper than any **d** sword,
Rev 1: 16 of his mouth was a sharp, **d** sword.
2: 12 of him who has the sharp, **d** sword.

DOUBLE-MINDED (MIND)
Ps 119: 113 I hate **d** people, but I love your law.
Jas 1: 8 Such a person is **d** and unstable

DOUBT
Mt 14: 31 faith," he said, "why did you **d**?"
21: 21 if you have faith and do not **d**,
Mk 11: 23 and does not **d** in their heart
Jas 1: 6 you must believe and not **d**,
Jude : 22 Be merciful to those who **d**;

DOWNCAST
Ps 42: 5 Why, my soul, are you **d**?
2Co 7: 6 who comforts the **d**, comforted us

DRAW (DRAWING DRAWS)
Mt 26: 52 "for all who **d** the sword will die
Jn 12: 32 earth, will **d** all people to myself."
Heb 10: 22 let us **d** near to God with a sincere

DRAWING (DRAW)
Lk 21: 28 your redemption is **d** near."

DRAWS (DRAW)
Jn 6: 44 the Father who sent me **d** them,

DREADFUL
Heb 10: 31 It is a **d** thing to fall into the hands

DRESS
1Ti 2: 9 want the women to **d** modestly,

DRINK (DRUNK DRUNKARDS DRUNKENNESS)
Pr 5: 15 **D** water from your own cistern,
Lk 12: 19 eat, **d** and be merry."'
Jn 7: 37 who is thirsty come to me and **d**.
1Co 12: 13 were all given the one Spirit to **d**.

DRIVES
1Jn 4: 18 But perfect love **d** out fear,

DROP
Pr 17: 14 so **d** the matter before a dispute
Isa 40: 15 Surely the nations are like a **d**

DRUNK (DRINK)
Eph 5: 18 Do not get **d** on wine, which leads

DRUNKARDS (DRINK)
Pr 23: 21 for **d** and gluttons become poor,
1Co 6: 10 the greedy nor **d** nor slanderers

DRUNKENNESS (DRINK)
Lk 21: 34 **d** and the anxieties of life,
Ro 13: 13 not in carousing and **d**,
Gal 5: 21 and envy; **d**, orgies, and the like.
1Pe 4: 3 living in debauchery, lust, **d**, orgies,

DRY
Isa 53: 2 and like a root out of **d** ground.
Eze 37: 4 bones and say to them, '**D** bones,

DUST
Ge 2: 7 a man from the **d** of the ground
Ps 103: 14 he remembers that we are **d**.
Ecc 3: 20 come from **d**, and to **d** all return.

DUTY
Ecc 12: 13 for this is the **d** of all mankind.
Ac 23: 1 I have fulfilled my **d** to God in all
1Co 7: 3 husband should fulfill his marital **d**

DWELL (DWELLING DWELLS)
1Ki 8: 27 "But will God really **d** on earth?
Ps 23: 6 I will **d** in the house of the LORD
Isa 43: 18 do not **d** on the past.
Eph 3: 17 Christ may **d** in your hearts
Col 1: 19 to have all his fullness **d** in him,
     3: 16 of Christ **d** among you richly

DWELLING (DWELL)
Eph 2: 22 built together to become a **d**

DWELLS (DWELL)
1Co 3: 16 that God's Spirit **d** in your midst?

EAGER
Pr 31: 13 and flax and works with **e** hands.
1Pe 5: 2 dishonest gain, but **e** to serve;

EAGLE'S (EAGLES)
Ps 103: 5 your youth is renewed like the **e**.

EAGLES (EAGLE'S)
Isa 40: 31 They will soar on wings like an **e**;

EAR (EARS)
1Co 2: 9 eye has seen, what no **e** has heard,
     12: 16 And if the **e** should say, "Because I

EARS (EAR)
Job 42: 5 My **e** had heard of you but now my
Ps 34: 15 and his **e** are attentive to their cry;
Pr 21: 13 Whoever shuts their **e** to the cry
2Ti 4: 3 to say what their itching **e** want

EARTH (EARTHLY)
Ge 1: 1 God created the heavens and the **e**.
Ps 24: 1 The **e** is the LORD's,
    108: 5 let your glory be over all the **e**.
Isa 6: 3 the whole **e** is full of his glory."
     51: 6 the **e** will wear out like a garment
     55: 9 the heavens are higher than the **e**,
     66: 1 throne, and the **e** is my footstool.
Jer 23: 24 "Do not I fill heaven and **e**?"
Hab 2: 20 let all the **e** be silent before him.
Mt 6: 10 will be done, on **e** as it is in heaven.
     16: 19 you bind on **e** will be bound
     24: 35 Heaven and **e** will pass away,
     28: 18 and on **e** has been given to me.
Lk 2: 14 on **e** peace to those on whom his
1Co 10: 26 for, "The **e** is the Lord's,
Php 2: 10 heaven and on **e** and under the **e**,
2Pe 3: 13 to a new heaven and a new **e**,

EARTHLY (EARTH)
Php 3: 19 Their mind is set on **e** things.
Col 3: 2 on things above, not on **e** things.

EAST
Ps 103: 12 as far as the **e** is from the west,

EASY
Mt 11: 30 For my yoke is **e** and my burden is

EAT (EATING)
Ge 2: 17 you must not **e** from the tree
Isa 55: 1 have no money, come, buy and **e**!
     65: 25 the lion will **e** straw like the ox,
Mt 26: 26 his disciples, saying, "Take and **e**;
Ro 14: 2 faith allows them to **e** anything,
1Co 8: 13 if what I **e** causes my brother
     10: 31 So whether you **e** or drink
2Th 3: 10 is unwilling to work shall not **e**."

EATING (EAT)
Ro 14: 17 kingdom of God is not a matter of **e**

EDICT
Heb 11: 23 they were not afraid of the king's **e**.

EDIFIES
1Co 14: 4 speaks in a tongue **e** themselves,

EFFECT
Isa 32: 17 its **e** will be quietness
Heb 9: 18 was not put into **e** without blood.

EFFORT
Lk 13: 24 "Make every **e** to enter through
Ro 9: 16 depend on human desire or **e**,
     14: 19 Let us therefore make every **e** to do
Eph 4: 3 Make every **e** to keep the unity
Heb 4: 11 make every **e** to enter that rest,
     12: 14 make every **e** to live in peace
2Pe 1: 5 make every **e** to add to your faith
     3: 14 make every **e** to be found spotless,

ELAH
Son of Baasha; king of Israel (1Ki 16:6-14).

ELDERLY (ELDERS)
Lev 19: 32 show respect for the **e** and revere

ELDERS (ELDERLY)
1Ti 5: 17 The **e** who direct the affairs

ELECTION
Ro 9: 11 God's purpose in **e** might stand:
2Pe 1: 10 to confirm your calling and **e**.

ELI
High priest in youth of Samuel (1Sa 1-4). Blessed Hannah (1Sa 1:12-18); raised Samuel (1Sa 2:11-26).

ELIJAH
Prophet; predicted famine in Israel (1Ki 17:1; Jas 5:17). Fed by ravens (1Ki 17:2-6). Raised Sidonian widow's son (1Ki 17:7-24). Defeated prophets of Baal at Carmel (1Ki 18:16-46). Ran from Jezebel (1Ki 19:1-9). Prophesied death of Azariah (2Ki 1). Succeeded by Elisha (1Ki 19:19-21; 2Ki 2:1-18). Taken to heaven in whirlwind (2Ki 2:11-12).
Return prophesied (Mal 4:5-6); equated with John the Baptist (Mt 17:9-13; Mk 9:9-13; Lk 1:17). Appeared with Moses in transfiguration of Jesus (Mt 17:1-8; Mk 9:1-8).

ELISHA
Prophet; successor of Elijah (1Ki 19:16-21); inherited his cloak (2Ki 2:1-18). Miracles of (2Ki 2-6).

ELIZABETH
Mother of John the Baptist, relative of Mary (Lk 1:5-58).

EMBITTER
Col 3: 21 Fathers, do not **e** your children,

EMPEROR
1Pe 2: 17 of believers, fear God, honor the **e**.

EMPTY
Mt 12: 36 for every **e** word they have spoken.
Eph 5: 6 no one deceive you with **e** words,
1Pe 1: 18 you were redeemed from the **e** way

ENABLE (ABLE)
Lk 1: 74 to **e** us to serve him without fear
Ac 4: 29 **e** your servants to speak your word

ENABLED (ABLE)
Lev 26: 13 **e** you to walk with heads held high.
Jn 6: 65 me unless the Father has **e** them."

ENABLES (ABLE)
Php   3: 21 by the power that **e** him to bring
ENCAMPS
Ps   34: 7 the Lord **e** around those who fear
ENCOURAGE (ENCOURAGEMENT ENCOURAGING)
Ps   10: 17 you **e** them, and you listen to their
Ac   15: 32 said much to **e** and strengthen
Ro   12: 8 if it is to **e**, then give
1Th   4: 18 Therefore **e** one another with these
2Ti   4: 2 correct, rebuke and **e**–
Titus 2: 6 Similarly, **e** the young men to be
Heb   3: 13 But **e** one another daily, as long as
ENCOURAGEMENT (ENCOURAGE)
Ac   4: 36 (which means "son of **e**"),
Ro   15: 4 the **e** they provide we might have
     15: 5 **e** give you the same attitude of
Heb 12: 5 completely forgotten this word of **e**
ENCOURAGING (ENCOURAGE)
1Co 14: 3 their strengthening, **e** and comfort.
Heb 10: 25 habit of doing, but **e** one another–
END
Ps 119: 33 that I may follow it to the **e**.
Pr   14: 12 right, but in the **e** it leads to death.
     19: 20 the **e** you will be counted among
     23: 32 In the **e** it bites like a snake
Ecc 12: 12 making many books there is no **e**,
Mt   10: 22 stands firm to the **e** will be saved.
Lk   21: 9 but the **e** will not come right away."
1Co 15: 24 Then the **e** will come, when he
ENDURANCE (ENDURE)
Ro   15: 4 so that through the **e** taught
     15: 5 May the God who gives **e**
2Co   1: 6 you patient **e** of the same sufferings
Col   1: 11 might so that you may have great **e**
1Ti   6: 11 faith, love, **e** and gentleness.
Titus 2: 2 and sound in faith, in love and in **e**.
ENDURE (ENDURANCE ENDURES)
Ps   72: 17 May his name **e** forever;
Pr   12: 19 Truthful lips **e** forever, but a lying
     27. 24 for riches do not **e** forever,
Ecc   3: 14 everything God does will **e** forever;
Mal   3: 2 who can **e** the day of his coming?
2Ti   2: 12 if we **e**, we will also reign with him.
Heb 12: 7 **E** hardship as discipline;
Rev   3: 10 kept my command to **e** patiently,
ENDURES (ENDURE)
Ps 112: 9 poor, their righteousness **e** forever;
     136: 1 His love **e** forever.
Da   9: 15 yourself a name that **e** to this day,
1Pe   1: 25 but the word of the Lord **e** forever."
ENEMIES (ENEMY)
Ps   23: 5 before me in the presence of my **e**.
Mic   7: 6 a man's **e** are the members of his
Mt   5: 44 love your **e** and pray for those who
Lk   20: 43 until I make your **e** a footstool
ENEMY (ENEMIES ENMITY)
Pr   24: 17 Do not gloat when your **e** falls;
     25: 21 If your **e** is hungry, give him food
     27: 6 trusted, but an **e** multiplies kisses.
1Co 15: 26 The last **e** to be destroyed is death.
1Ti   5: 14 and to give the **e** no opportunity
Jas   4: 4 of the world becomes an **e** of God.
ENJOY (JOY)
Dt   6: 2 and so that you may **e** long life.
Eph   6: 3 and that you may **e** long life
Heb 11: 25 than to **e** the fleeting pleasures
ENJOYMENT (JOY)
Ecc   4: 8 why am I depriving myself of **e**?"
1Ti   6: 17 us with everything for our **e**.
ENLIGHTENED (LIGHT)
Eph   1: 18 eyes of your heart may be **e** in
Heb   6: 4 for those who have once been **e**,
ENMITY (ENEMY)
Ge   3: 15 I will put **e** between you

ENOCH
   Walked with God and taken by him (Ge 5:18-24; Heb 11:5).
Prophet (Jude 14).
ENTANGLED (ENTANGLES)
2Ti   2: 4 soldier gets **e** in civilian affairs,
2Pe   2: 20 Jesus Christ and are again **e** in it
ENTANGLES (ENTANGLED)
Heb 12: 1 hinders and the sin that so easily **e**.
ENTER (ENTERED ENTERS ENTRANCE)
Ps 100: 4 **E** his gates with thanksgiving
Mt   5: 20 will certainly not **e** the kingdom
      7: 13 "**E** through the narrow gate.
     18: 8 It is better for you to **e** life maimed
Mk   10: 15 like a little child will never **e** it."
     10: 23 the rich to **e** the kingdom of God!"
ENTERED (ENTER)
Ro   5: 12 just as sin **e** the world through one
Heb   9: 12 he **e** the Most Holy Place once
ENTERS (ENTER)
Mk   7: 18 that nothing that **e** a person
Jn   10: 2 The one who **e** by the gate is
ENTERTAIN
1Ti   5: 19 Do not **e** an accusation against
ENTHRALLED
Ps   45: 11 Let the king be **e** by your beauty;
ENTHRONED (THRONE)
1Sa   4: 4 who is **e** between the cherubim.
Ps   2: 4 The One **e** in heaven laughs;
    102: 12 But you, Lord, sit **e** forever;
Isa 40: 22 He sits **e** above the circle
ENTICE
Pr   1: 10 if sinful men **e** you, do not give
2Pe   2: 18 they **e** people who are just escaping
ENTIRE
Gal   5: 14 For the **e** law is fulfilled in keeping
ENTRUSTED (TRUST)
1Ti   6: 20 guard what has been **e** to your care.
2Ti   1: 12 to guard what I have **e** to him until
      1: 14 good deposit that was **e** to you–
Jude : 3 once for all **e** to God's holy people.
ENVY
Pr   3: 31 Do not **e** the violent or choose any
     14: 30 to the body, but **e** rots the bones.
1Co 13: 4 It does not **e**, it does not boast,
EPHRAIM
   1. Second son of Joseph (Ge 41:52; 46:20). Blessed as
firstborn by Jacob (Ge 48).
   2. Synonymous with Northern Kingdom (Isa 7:17; Hos 5).
EQUAL
Isa 40: 25 Or who is my **e**?" says the Holy
Jn   5: 18 Father, making himself **e** with God.
1Co 12: 25 its parts should have **e** concern
EQUIP (EQUIPPED)
Eph   4: 12 to **e** his people for works of service,
Heb 13: 21 **e** you with everything good
EQUIPPED (EQUIP)
2Ti   3: 17 God may be thoroughly **e** for every
ERROR
Jas   5: 20 the **e** of their way will save them
ESAU
   Firstborn of Isaac, twin of Jacob (Ge 25:21-26). Also called
Edom (Ge 25:30). Sold Jacob his birthright (Ge 25:29-34);
lost blessing (Ge 27). Reconciled to Jacob (Gen 33).
ESCAPE (ESCAPING)
Ro   2: 3 think you will **e** God's judgment?
Heb   2: 3 how shall we **e** if we ignore so great
ESCAPING (ESCAPE)
1Co   3: 15 only as one **e** through the flames.
ESTABLISH (ESTABLISHED ESTABLISHES)
Ge   6: 18 But I will **e** my covenant with you,
1Ch 28: 7 I will **e** his kingdom forever if he is
Ro   10: 3 of God and sought to **e** their own,

ESTABLISHED (ESTABLISH)
Ps 8: 2 infants you have **e** a stronghold

ESTABLISHES (ESTABLISH)
Pr 16: 9 course, but the Lord **e** their steps.

ESTEEM (ESTEEMED)
Isa 53: 3 and we held him in low **e**.

ESTEEMED (ESTEEM)
Pr 22: 1 to be **e** is better than silver or gold.

ESTHER
Jewess who lived in Persia; cousin of Mordecai (Est 2:7). Chosen queen of Xerxes (Est 2:8-18). Foiled Haman's plan to exterminate the Jews (Est 3-4; 7-9).

ETERNAL (ETERNITY)
Ps 16: 11 with **e** pleasures at your right hand.
111: 10 To him belongs **e** praise.
119: 89 Your word, Lord, is **e**;
Isa 26: 4 the Lord himself, is the Rock **e**.
Mt 19: 16 good thing must I do to get **e** life?"
25: 41 the **e** fire prepared for the devil
25: 46 but the righteous to **e** life."
Jn 3: 15 who believes may have **e** life
3: 16 him shall not perish but have **e** life.
3: 36 believes in the Son has **e** life,
4: 14 of water welling up to **e** life."
5: 24 believes him who sent me has **e** life
6: 47 the one who believes has **e** life.
6: 68 You have the words of **e** life.
10: 28 I give them **e** life, and they shall
17: 3 Now this is **e** life: that they know
Ro 1: 20 his **e** power and divine nature—
6: 23 of God is **e** life in Christ Jesus our
2Co 4: 17 for us an **e** glory that far outweighs
4: 18 temporary, but what is unseen is **e**.
1Ti 1: 16 believe in him and receive **e** life.
1: 17 Now to the King **e**, immortal,
Heb 9: 12 thus obtaining **e** redemption.
1Jn 5: 11 God has given us **e** life, and this life
5: 13 you may know that you have **e** life.

ETERNITY (ETERNAL)
Ps 93: 2 you are from all **e**.
Ecc 3: 11 has also set **e** in the human heart;

ETHIOPIAN
Jer 13: 23 Can an **E** change his skin

EUNUCHS
Mt 19: 12 choose to live like **e** for the sake

EVANGELIST (EVANGELISTS)
2Ti 4: 5 do the work of an **e**, discharge all

EVANGELISTS (EVANGELIST)
Eph 4: 11 the **e**, the pastors and teachers,

EVE
2Co 11: 3 afraid that just as **E** was deceived
1Ti 2: 13 For Adam was formed first, then **E**.

EVEN-TEMPERED
Pr 17: 27 whoever has understanding is **e**.

EVER (EVERLASTING FOREVER)
Ex 15: 18 "The Lord reigns for **e** and **e**."
Dt 8: 19 you **e** forget the Lord your God
Ps 5: 11 you be glad; let them **e** sing for joy.
10: 16 The Lord is King for **e** and **e**;
25: 3 one who hopes in you will **e** be put
45: 6 throne, O God, will last for **e** and **e**;
52: 8 I trust in God's unfailing love for **e**
89: 33 nor will I **e** betray my faithfulness.
145: 1 I will praise your name for **e** and **e**.
Pr 4: 18 shining **e** brighter till the full light
5: 19 may you be intoxicated with her
Isa 66: 8 Who has **e** heard of such things?
Jer 31: 36 "will Israel **e** cease being a nation
Da 7: 18 possess it forever–yes, for **e** and **e**.'
12: 3 like the stars for **e** and **e**.
Mk 4: 12 "'they may be **e** seeing but never
Jn 1: 18 No one has **e** seen God, but
Rev 1: 18 now look, I am alive for **e** and **e**!
22: 5 And they will reign for **e** and **e**.

EVER-INCREASING (INCREASE)
Ro 6: 19 to impurity and to **e** wickedness,
2Co 3: 18 into his image with **e** glory,

EVERLASTING (EVER)
Dt 33: 27 and underneath are the **e** arms.
Ne 9: 5 your God, who is from **e** to **e**."
Ps 90: 2 world, from **e** to **e** you are God.
139: 24 in me, and lead me in the way **e**.
Isa 9: 6 Mighty God, **E** Father,
33: 14 of us can dwell with **e** burning?"
35: 10 **e** joy will crown their heads.
45: 17 by the Lord with an **e** salvation;
54: 8 **e** kindness I will have compassion
55: 3 I will make an **e** covenant with you,
63: 12 them, to gain for himself **e** renown,
Jer 31: 3 "I have loved you with an **e** love;
Da 9: 24 to bring in **e** righteousness, to seal
12: 2 some to **e** life, others to shame and **e** contempt.
2Th 1: 9 will be punished with **e** destruction
Jude : 6 bound with **e** chains for judgment

EVER-PRESENT
Ps 46: 1 and strength, an **e** help in trouble.

EVIDENCE (EVIDENT)
Jn 14: 11 on the **e** of the works themselves.

EVIDENT (EVIDENCE)
Php 4: 5 Let your gentleness be **e** to all.

EVIL (EVILDOER EVILDOERS)
Ge 2: 9 of the knowledge of good and **e**.
Job 1: 1 he feared God and shunned **e**.
1: 8 a man who fears God and shuns **e**."
34: 10 Far be it from God to do **e**,
Ps 23: 4 will fear no **e**, for you are with me;
34: 14 Turn from **e** and do good;
51: 4 and done what is **e** in your sight;
97: 10 those who love the Lord hate **e**,
101: 4 have nothing to do with what is **e**.
Pr 8: 13 To fear the Lord is to hate **e**;
11: 27 **e** comes to one who searches for it.
Isa 5: 20 who call **e** good and good **e**,
13: 11 I will punish the world for its **e**,
Hab 1: 13 Your eyes are too pure to look on **e**;
Mt 5: 45 He causes his sun to rise on the **e**
6: 13 but deliver us from the **e** one.'
7: 11 you are **e**, know how to give
12: 35 an **e** man brings **e** things out of the **e**
Jn 17: 15 you protect them from the **e** one.
Ro 2: 9 for every human being who does **e**:
12: 9 Hate what is **e**; cling to what is
12: 17 Do not repay anyone **e** for **e**.
16: 19 and innocent about what is **e**.
1Co 13: 6 Love does not delight in **e**
14: 20 In regard to **e** be infants, but in
Eph 6: 16 all the flaming arrows of the **e** one.
1Th 5: 22 reject every kind of **e**.
1Ti 6: 10 of money is a root of all kinds of **e**.
2Ti 2: 22 Flee the **e** desires of youth
Jas 1: 13 For God cannot be tempted by **e**,
1Pe 2: 16 your freedom as a cover-up for **e**;
3: 9 Do not repay **e** with **e** or insult
3: 9 the contrary, repay **e** with blessing,

EVILDOER (EVIL)
Pr 24: 20 for the **e** has no future hope,

EVILDOERS (EVIL)
Pr 24: 19 Do not fret because of **e** or be

EXACT
Heb 1: 3 the **e** representation of his being,

EXALT (EXALTED EXALTS)
Ps 30: 1 I will **e** you, Lord, for you lifted
34: 3 let us **e** his name together.
118: 28 you are my God, and I will **e** you.
Isa 24: 15 **e** the name of the Lord, the God
Mt 23: 12 For those who **e** themselves will be

EXALTED (EXALT)
2Sa 22: 47 **E** be my God, the Rock, my Savior!

1Ch 29: 11 you are **e** as head over all.
Ne 9: 5 and may it be **e** above all blessing
Ps 21: 13 Be **e** in your strength, Lord;
46: 10 I will be **e** among the nations,
57: 5 Be **e**, O God, above the heavens;
97: 9 you are **e** far above all gods.
99: 2 he is **e** over all the nations.
108: 5 Be **e**, O God, above the heavens;
148: 13 the Lord, for his name alone is **e**;
Isa 6: 1 high and **e**, seated on a throne;
12: 4 and proclaim that his name is **e**.
33: 5 The Lord is **e**, for he dwells
Eze 21: 26 The lowly will be **e** and the **e** will
Mt 23: 12 who humble themselves will be **e**.
Php 1: 20 now as always Christ will be **e**
2: 9 Therefore God **e** him to the highest

EXALTS (EXALT)
Ps 75: 7 He brings one down, he **e** another.
Pr 14: 34 Righteousness **e** a nation, but sin

EXAMINE (EXAMINED)
Ps 26: 2 try me, **e** my heart and my mind;
Jer 17: 10 search the heart and **e** the mind,
La 3: 40 Let us **e** our ways and test them,
1Co 11: 28 to **e** themselves before they eat
2Co 13: 5 **E** yourselves to see whether you

EXAMINED (EXAMINE)
Ac 17: 11 **e** the Scriptures every day to see

EXAMPLE (EXAMPLES)
Jn 13: 15 I have set you an **e** that you should
1Co 11: 1 Follow my **e**, as I follow the **e**
1Ti 4: 12 set an **e** for the believers in speech,
Titus 2: 7 everything set them an **e** by doing
1Pe 2: 21 leaving you an **e**, that you should

EXAMPLES (EXAMPLE)
1Co 10: 6 Now these things occurred as **e**
10: 11 things happened to them as **e**
1Pe 5: 3 to you, but being **e** to the flock.

EXASPERATE
Eph 6: 4 Fathers, do not **e** your children;

EXCEL (EXCELLENT)
1Co 14: 12 try to **e** in those that build
2Co 8: 7 you also **e** in this grace of giving.

EXCELLENT (EXCEL)
1Co 12: 31 yet I will show you the most **e** way.
Php 4: 8 if anything is **e** or praiseworthy—
1Ti 3: 13 have served well gain an **e** standing
Titus 3: 8 These things are **e** and profitable

EXCHANGED
Ro 1: 23 **e** the glory of the immortal God
1: 25 **e** the truth about God for a lie,

EXCUSE (EXCUSES)
Jn 15: 22 now they have no **e** for their sin.
Ro 1: 20 made, so that people are without **e**.

EXCUSES (EXCUSE)
Lk 14: 18 "But they all alike began to make **e**.

EXISTS
Heb 2: 10 and through whom everything **e**,
11: 6 to him must believe that he **e**

EXPECT (EXPECTATION)
Mt 24: 44 at an hour when you do not **e** him.

EXPECTATION (EXPECT)
Ro 8: 19 waits in eager **e** for the children
Heb 10: 27 but only a fearful **e** of judgment

EXPEL
1Co 5: 13 "**E** the wicked person from among

EXPENSIVE
1Ti 2: 9 or gold or pearls or **e** clothes,

EXPLOIT
Pr 22: 22 Do not **e** the poor because they are
2Co 12: 17 I **e** you through any of the men

EXPOSE
1Co 4: 5 and will **e** the motives of the heart.
Eph 5: 11 of darkness, but rather **e** them.

EXTENDS
Pr 31: 20 poor and **e** her hands to the needy.
Lk 1: 50 His mercy **e** to those who fear him,

EXTINGUISHED
2Sa 21: 17 the lamp of Israel will not be **e**."

EXTOL
Job 36: 24 Remember to **e** his work,
Ps 34: 1 I will **e** the Lord at all times;
68: 4 **e** him who rides on the clouds;
95: 2 thanksgiving and **e** him with music
109: 30 mouth I will greatly **e** the Lord;
111: 1 I will **e** the Lord with all my
115: 18 it is we who **e** the Lord,
117: 1 **e** him, all you peoples.
145: 2 and **e** your name for ever
145: 10 your faithful people **e** you.
147: 12 **E** the Lord, Jerusalem;

EXTORT
Lk 3: 14 "Don't **e** money and don't accuse

EYE (EYES)
Ex 21: 24 **e** for **e**, tooth for tooth,
Ps 94: 9 Does he who formed the **e** not see?
Mt 5: 29 If your right **e** causes you
5: 38 have heard that it was said, '**E** for **e**,
7: 3 speck of sawdust in your brother's **e**
1Co 2: 9 "What no **e** has seen, what no ear
Col 3: 22 not only when their **e** is on you
Rev 1: 7 and "every **e** will see him,

EYES (EYE)
Nu 33: 55 remain will become barbs in your **e**
Jos 23: 13 your backs and thorns in your **e**,
2Ch 16: 9 For the **e** of the Lord range
Job 31: 1 "I made a covenant with my **e** not
36: 7 not take his **e** off the righteous;
Ps 119: 18 Open my **e** that I may see
121: 1 I lift up my **e** to the mountains—
141: 8 But my **e** are fixed on you,
Pr 3: 7 Do not be wise in your own **e**;
4: 25 Let your **e** look straight ahead;
15: 3 The **e** of the Lord are
Isa 6: 5 and my **e** have seen the King,
Hab 1: 13 Your **e** are too pure to look on evil;
Jn 4: 35 open your **e** and look at the fields!
2Co 4: 18 So we fix our **e** not on what is seen,
Heb 12: 2 fixing our **e** on Jesus, the pioneer
Jas 2: 5 who are poor in the **e** of the world
1Pe 3: 12 For the **e** of the Lord are
Rev 7: 17 away every tear from their **e**."
21: 4 will wipe every tear from their **e**.

EZEKIEL
Priest called to be prophet to the exiles (Eze 1–3).

EZRA
Priest and teacher of the Law who led a return of exiles to Israel to reestablish temple and worship (Ezr 7–8). Corrected intermarriage of priests (Ezr 9–10). Read Law at celebration of Feast of Tabernacles (Neh 8).

FACE (FACES)
Ge 32: 30 "It is because I saw God **f** to **f**,
Ex 34: 29 that his **f** was radiant because he
Nu 6: 25 the Lord make his **f** shine on you
1Ch 16: 11 and his strength; seek his **f** always.
2Ch 7: 14 and seek my **f** and turn from their
Ps 4: 6 Let the light of your **f** shine on us.
27: 8 My heart says of you, "Seek his **f**!"
31: 16 Let your **f** shine on your servant;
105: 4 and his strength; seek his **f** always.
119:135 Make your **f** shine on your servant
Isa 50: 7 Therefore have I set my **f** like flint,
Mt 17: 2 His **f** shone like the sun, and his
1Co 13: 12 in a mirror; then we shall see **f** to **f**.
2Co 4: 6 glory displayed in the **f** of Christ.
1Pe 3: 12 the **f** of the Lord is against those
Rev 1: 16 His **f** was like the sun shining in all

FACES (FACE)
2Co 3: 18 unveiled **f** contemplate the Lord's

FACTIONS
Gal   5: 20   rage, selfish ambition, dissensions,

FADE
1Pe   5:   4   of glory that will never **f** away.

FAIL (FAILING FAILINGS FAILS)
1Ch 28: 20   He will not **f** you or forsake you
2Ch 34: 33   they did not **f** to follow the Lord,
Ps   89: 28   my covenant with him will never **f**.
Pr   15: 22   Plans **f** for lack of counsel,
Isa   51:   6   my righteousness will never **f**.
La   3: 22   for his compassions never **f**.
2Co 13:   5   unless, of course, you **f** the test?

FAILING (FAIL)
1Sa 12: 23   I should sin against the Lord by **f**

FAILINGS (FAIL)
Ro   15:   1   to bear with the **f** of the weak

FAILS (FAIL)
1Co 13:   8   Love never **f**. But where there are

FAINT
Isa 40: 31   weary, they will walk and not be **f**.

FAIR
Pr   1:   3   doing what is right and just and **f**;
Col   4:   1   your slaves with what is right and **f**,

FAITH (FAITHFUL FAITHFULLY FAITHFULNESS
FAITHLESS)
2Ch 20: 20   Have **f** in the Lord your God
      20: 20   have **f** in his prophets
Mt   9: 29   "According to your **f** let it be done
    17: 20   if you have **f** as small as a mustard
    24: 10   many will turn away from the **f**
Mk   11: 22   "Have **f** in God," Jesus answered.
Lk   7:   9   I have not found such great **f** even
    12: 28   will he clothe you–you of little **f**!
    17:   5   said to the Lord, "Increase our **f**!"
    18:   8   comes, will he find **f** on the earth?"
Ac   14:   9   him, saw that he had **f** to be healed
    14: 27   how he had opened a door of **f**
Ro   1: 12   encouraged by each other's **f**.
      1: 17   "The righteous will live by **f**."
      1: 17   righteousness that is by **f** from first
      3: 22   righteousness is given through **f**
      3: 25   of his blood–to be received by **f**.
      4:   5   their **f** is credited as righteousness.
      5:   1   we have been justified through **f**,
    10: 17   **f** comes from hearing the message,
    14:   1   Accept the one whose **f** is weak,
    14: 23   that does not come from **f** is sin.
    16: 26   the obedience that comes from **f**–
1Co 13:   2   have a **f** that can move mountains,
    13: 13   three remain: **f**, hope and love.
    16: 13   stand firm in the **f**; be courageous;
2Co   5:   7   For we live by **f**, not by sight.
    13:   5   to see whether you are in the **f**;
Gal   2: 16   we may be justified by **f** in Christ
      2: 20   body, I live by **f** in the Son of God,
      3: 11   "the righteous will live by **f**."
      3: 24   that we might be justified by **f**.
Eph   2:   8   you have been saved, through **f**–
      4:   5   one Lord, one **f**, one baptism;
      6: 16   take up the shield of **f**,
Col   1: 23   if you continue in your **f**,
1Th   5:   8   be sober, putting on **f** and love as
1Ti   2: 15   if they continue in **f**,
      4:   1   later times some will abandon the **f**
      5:   8   has denied the **f** and is worse than
      6: 12   Fight the good fight of the **f**.
2Ti   3: 15   salvation through **f** in Christ Jesus.
      4:   7   finished the race, I have kept the **f**.
Phm   :   6   with us in the **f** may be effective
Heb 10: 38   my righteous one will live by **f**.
    11:   1   Now **f** is confidence in what we
    11:   3   By **f** we understand that the
    11:   5   By **f** Enoch was taken from this
    11:   6   without **f** it is impossible to please
    11:   7   By **f** Noah, when warned

Heb 11:   7   By his **f** he condemned the world
    11:   8   By **f** Abraham, when called to go
    11: 17   By **f** Abraham, when God tested
    11: 20   By **f** Isaac blessed Jacob and Esau
    11: 21   By **f** Jacob, when he was dying,
    11: 22   By **f** Joseph, when his end was
    11: 24   By **f** Moses, when he had grown
    11: 31   By **f** the prostitute Rahab,
    12:   2   Jesus, the pioneer and perfecter of **f**.
Jas   2: 14   Can such **f** save them?
      2: 17   In the same way, **f** by itself, if it is
      2: 26   is dead, so **f** without deeds is dead.
2Pe   1:   5   effort to add to your **f** goodness;
1Jn   5:   4   overcome the world, even our **f**.
Jude   :   3   contend for the **f** that was once

FAITHFUL (FAITH)
Nu   12:   7   he is **f** in all my house.
Dt   7:   9   he is the **f** God, keeping his
    32:   4   A **f** God who does no wrong,
2Sa 22: 26   "To the **f** you show yourself **f**,
Ps   16: 10   will you let your **f** one see decay.
    25: 10   and **f** toward those who keep
    31: 23   Love the Lord, all his **f** people!
    33:   4   right and true; he is **f** in all he does.
    37: 28   just and will not forsake his **f** ones.
    97: 10   for he guards the lives of his **f** ones
  116: 15   is the death of his **f** servants.
  145: 13   all he promises and **f** in all he does.
  145: 17   in all his ways and **f** in all he does.
  146:   6   he remains **f** forever.
Pr   31: 26   and **f** instruction is on her tongue.
Mt   25: 21   'Well done, good and **f** servant!
    25: 21   You have been **f** with a few things;
Ro   12: 12   patient in affliction, **f** in prayer.
1Co   4:   2   been given a trust must prove **f**.
    10: 13   And God is **f**; he will not let you be
1Th   5: 24   The one who calls you is **f**, and he
1Ti   3:   2   to be above reproach, **f** to his wife,
2Ti   2: 13   he remains **f**, for he cannot disown
Heb   3:   6   Christ is **f** as the Son over God's
    10: 23   profess, for he who promised is **f**.
1Pe   4: 10   as **f** stewards of God's grace in its
      4: 19   themselves to their **f** Creator
1Jn   1:   9   he is **f** and just and will forgive us
Rev   1:   5   who is the **f** witness, the firstborn
      2: 10   Be **f**, even to the point of death,
    19: 11   whose rider is called **F** and True.

FAITHFULLY (FAITH)
Dt   11: 13   So if you **f** obey the commands
1Sa 12: 24   and serve him **f** with all your heart;
1Ki   2:   4   if they walk **f** before me with all

FAITHFULNESS (FAITH)
Ps   51:   6   you desired **f** even in the womb;
    57: 10   your **f** reaches to the skies.
    85: 10   Love and **f** meet together;
    86: 15   to anger, abounding in love and **f**.
    89:   1   make your **f** known through all
    89: 14   love and **f** go before you.
    91:   4   his **f** will be your shield
  117:   2   the **f** of the Lord endures forever.
  119: 75   and that in **f** you have afflicted me.
Pr   3:   3   Let love and **f** never leave you;
Isa   11:   5   and **f** the sash around his waist.
La   3: 23   new every morning; great is your **f**.
Hab   2:   4   righteous person will live by his **f**–
Ro   3:   3   their unfaithfulness nullify God's **f**?
Gal   5: 22   forbearance, kindness, goodness, **f**,

FAITHLESS (FAITH)
Ps   119:158   I look on the **f** with loathing,
Jer   3: 22   "Return, **f** people; I will cure you
2Ti   2: 13   if we are **f**, he remains faithful,

FALL (FALLEN FALLS)
Ps   37: 24   he will not **f**, for the Lord
    69:   9   of those who insult you **f** on me.
Pr   11: 28   who trust in their riches will **f**,
Lk   11: 17   a house divided against itself will **f**.

Jn 16: 1 you so that you will not **f** away.
Ro   3: 23 and **f** short of the glory of God,
     14: 4 own master, servants stand or **f**.

FALLEN (FALL)
2Sa 1: 19 How the mighty have **f**!
Isa 14: 12 How you have **f** from heaven,
1Co 15: 20 of those who have **f** asleep.
Gal 5: 4 you have **f** away from grace.
1Th 4: 15 precede those who have **f** asleep.
Heb 6: 6 and who have **f** away, to be brought

FALLS (FALL)
Pr 24: 17 Do not gloat when your enemy **f**;
Jn 12: 24 a kernel of wheat **f** to the ground

FALSE (FALSEHOOD FALSELY)
Ex 20: 16 shall not give **f** testimony against
    23: 1 "Do not spread **f** reports.
Pr 13: 5 The righteous hate what is **f**,
    19: 5 A **f** witness will not go unpunished,
Mt   7: 15 "Watch out for **f** prophets.
    19: 18 steal, you shall not give **f** testimony,
    24: 11 and many **f** prophets will appear
Php 1: 18 whether from **f** motives or true,
1Ti 1: 3 not to teach **f** doctrines any longer
2Pe 2: 1 there will be **f** teachers among you.

FALSEHOOD (FALSE)
Ps 119:163 and detest **f** but I love your law.
Pr 30: 8 Keep **f** and lies far from me;
Eph 4: 25 each of you must put off **f**

FALSELY (FALSE)
Lev 19: 12 "'Do not swear **f** by my name
Lk   3: 14 money and don't accuse people **f**–
1Ti 6: 20 ideas of what is **f** called knowledge,

FALTER
Pr 24: 10 If you **f** in a time of trouble,
Isa 42: 4 he will not **f** or be discouraged till

FAMILIES (FAMILY)
Ps 68: 6 God sets the lonely in **f**, he leads

FAMILY (FAMILIES)
Pr 31: 15 she provides food for her **f**
Lk   9: 61 go back and say goodbye to my **f**."
    12: 52 in one **f** divided against each other,
1Ti 3: 4 He must manage his own **f** well
     3: 5 know how to manage his own **f**,
     5: 4 practice by caring for their own **f**

FAMINE
Ge 41: 30 seven years of **f** will follow them.
Am   8: 11 I will send a **f** through the land–
Ro   8: 35 or persecution or **f** or nakedness

FAN
2Ti 1: 6 this reason I remind you to **f**

FAST
Dt 13: 4 serve him and hold **f** to him.
Jos 22: 5 to hold **f** to him and to serve him
    23: 8 to hold **f** to the LORD your God,
Ps 119: 31 I hold **f** to your statutes, LORD;
   139: 10 me, your right hand will hold me **f**.
Mt   6: 16 "When you **f**, do not look somber
1Pe 5: 12 the true grace of God. Stand **f** in it.

FATHER (FATHER'S FATHERLESS FATHERS)
Ge   2: 24 That is why a man leaves his **f**
    17: 4 You will be the **f** of many nations.
Ex 20: 12 "Honor your **f** and your mother,
    21: 15 "Anyone who attacks their **f**
    21: 17 "Anyone who curses their **f**
Lev 18: 7 "'Do not dishonor your **f**
    19: 3 must respect your mother and **f**,
Dt   5: 16 "Honor your **f** and your mother,
    21: 18 son who does not obey his **f**
Ps 27: 10 Though my **f** and mother forsake
    68: 5 A **f** to the fatherless, a defender
Pr 10: 1 A wise son brings joy to his **f**,
    23: 22 Listen to your **f**, who gave you life,
    23: 24 The **f** of a righteous child has great
    28: 7 of gluttons disgraces his **f**.

Pr 29: 3 loves wisdom brings joy to his **f**,
Isa 9: 6 Everlasting **F**, Prince of Peace.
Mt   6: 9 "'Our **F** in heaven, hallowed be
    10: 37 "Anyone who loves their **f**
    15: 4 said, 'Honor your **f** and mother'
    19: 5 this reason a man will leave his **f**
Lk 12: 53 **f** against son and son against **f**,
    23: 34 Jesus said, "**F**, forgive them,
Jn   6: 44 unless the **F** who sent me draws
     6: 46 from God; only he has seen the **F**.
     8: 44 You belong to your **f**, the devil,
    10: 30 I and the **F** are one."
    14: 6 comes to the **F** except through me.
    14: 9 who has seen me has seen the **F**.
Ro   4: 11 he is the **f** of all who believe
2Co 6: 18 And, "I will be a **F** to you, and you
Eph 6: 2 "Honor your **f** and mother"–
Heb 12: 7 are not disciplined by their **f**?

FATHER'S (FATHER)
Pr   1: 8 wise son heeds his **f** instruction,
    19: 13 A foolish child is a **f** ruin,
Lk   2: 49 know I had to be in my **F** house?"
Jn   2: 16 Stop turning my **F** house
    10: 29 can snatch them out of my **F** hand.
    14: 2 My **F** house has many rooms;

FATHERLESS (FATHER)
Dt 10: 18 He defends the cause of the **f**
    24: 17 the foreigner or the **f** of justice,
    24: 19 the foreigner, the **f** and the widow,
Ps 68: 5 A father to the **f**, a defender
Pr 23: 10 or encroach on the fields of the **f**,

FATHERS (FATHER)
Lk 11: 11 "Which of you **f**, if your son asks
Eph 6: 4 **F**, do not exasperate your children;
Col 3: 21 **F**, do not embitter your children,

FATHOM
Job 11: 7 "Can you **f** the mysteries of God?
Ps 145: 3 his greatness no one can **f**.
Ecc 3: 11 no one can **f** what God has done
Isa 40: 28 his understanding no one can **f**.
1Co 13: 2 of prophecy and can **f** all mysteries

FAULT (FAULTS)
Mt 18: 15 sins, go and point out their **f**,
Php 2: 15 of God without **f** in a warped
Jas 1: 5 generously to all without finding **f**,
Jude : 24 his glorious presence without **f**

FAULTFINDERS
Jude : 16 These people are grumblers and **f**;

FAULTS (FAULT)
Ps 19: 12 Forgive my hidden **f**.

FAVORITISM
Ex 23: 3 do not show **f** to a poor person
Lev 19: 15 to the poor or **f** to the great,
Ac 10: 34 true it is that God does not show **f**
Ro   2: 11 For God does not show **f**.
Gal 2: 6 God does not show **f**–
Eph 6: 9 heaven, and there is no **f** with him.
Col 3: 25 for their wrongs, and there is no **f**.
1Ti 5: 21 and to do nothing out of **f**.
Jas 2: 1 Lord Jesus Christ must not show **f**.
     2: 9 But if you show **f**, you sin and are

FEAR (AFRAID FEARS)
Dt   6: 13 **F** the LORD your God, serve him
    10: 12 you but to **f** the LORD your God,
    31: 12 learn to **f** the LORD your God
Ps 19: 9 The **f** of the LORD is pure,
    23: 4 the darkest valley, I will **f** no evil,
    27: 1 and my salvation–whom shall I **f**?
    91: 5 You will not **f** the terror of night,
   111: 10 The **f** of the LORD is
Pr   8: 13 To **f** the LORD is to hate evil;
     9: 10 The **f** of the LORD is
    10: 27 The **f** of the LORD adds length
    14: 27 The **f** of the LORD is a fountain
    15: 33 instruction is to **f** the LORD,

Pr   16:   6 through the **f** of the LORD evil is
      19: 23 The **f** of the LORD leads to life;
      29: 25 **F** of man will prove to be a snare,
Ecc   5:   7 Therefore **f** God.
Isa   11:   3 will delight in the **f** of the LORD.
      41: 10 So do not **f**, for I am with you;
Lk   12:   5 will show you whom you should **f**:
Php   2: 12 to work out your salvation with **f**
1Jn   4: 18 There is no **f** in love. But perfect love drives out **f**,

FEARS (FEAR)
Job   1:   8 a man who **f** God and shuns evil."
Ps   34:   4 he delivered me from all my **f**.
Pr   31: 30 a woman who **f** the LORD is to be
1Jn   4: 18 The one who **f** is not made perfect

FEED
Jn   21: 15 Jesus said, "**F** my lambs."
      21: 17 Jesus said, "**F** my sheep.
Ro   12: 20 "If your enemy is hungry, **f** him;
Jude   : 12 shepherds who **f** only themselves.

FEET (FOOT)
Ps   8:   6 you put everything under their **f**:
      22: 16 they pierce my hands and my **f**.
      40:   2 he set my **f** on a rock and gave me
     110:   1 enemies a footstool for your **f**."
     119:105 Your word is a lamp to my **f**
Ro   10: 15 "How beautiful are the **f** of those
1Co   12: 21 And the head cannot say to the **f**,
      15: 25 has put all his enemies under his **f**.
Heb   12: 13 "Make level paths for your **f**,"

FELLOWSHIP
2Co   6: 14 **f** can light have with darkness?
      13: 14 the **f** of the Holy Spirit be with you
1Jn   1:   6 If we claim to have **f** with him
       1:   7 light, we have **f** with one another,

FEMALE
Ge   1: 27 male and **f** he created them.
Gal   3: 28 nor is there male and **f**, for you are

FERVOR
Ro   12: 11 but keep your spiritual **f**,

FIDELITY
Ro   1: 31 no understanding, no **f**, no love,

FIELD (FIELDS)
Mt   6: 28 See how the flowers of the **f** grow.
      13: 38 The **f** is the world, and the good
1Co   3:   9 you are God's **f**, God's building.

FIELDS (FIELD)
Lk   2:   8 shepherds living out in the **f**
Jn   4: 35 open your eyes and look at the **f**!

FIERY (FIRE)
1Pe   4: 12 do not be surprised at the **f** ordeal

FIG (FIGS)
Ge   3:   7 so they sewed **f** leaves together

FIGHT (FOUGHT)
Ex   14: 14 The LORD will **f** for you;
Dt   1: 30 is going before you, will **f** for you,
       3: 22 the LORD your God himself will **f**
Ne   4: 20 Our God will **f** for us!"
Ps   35:   1 **f** against those who **f** against me.
Jn   18: 36 my servants would **f** to prevent my
1Co   9: 26 I do not **f** like a boxer beating
2Co   10:   4 The weapons we **f** with are not
1Ti   1: 18 them you may **f** the battle well,
       6: 12 **F** the good **f** of the faith.
2Ti   4:   7 I have fought the good **f**, I have

FIGS (FIG)
Lk   6: 44 People do not pick **f**

FILL (FILLED FILLS FULL FULLNESS FULLY)
Ge   1: 28 **f** the earth and subdue it.
Ps   16: 11 you will **f** me with joy in your
      81: 10 wide your mouth and I will **f** it.
Pr   28: 19 chase fantasies will have their **f**
Hag   2:   7 and I will **f** this house with glory,'

Jn   6: 26 you ate the loaves and had your **f**.
Ac   2: 28 you will **f** me with joy in your
Ro   15: 13 May the God of hope **f** you with all

FILLED (FILL)
Ps   72: 19 may the whole earth be **f** with his
     119: 64 The earth is **f** with your love,
Isa   11:   9 for the earth will be **f**
Eze   43:   5 glory of the LORD **f** the temple.
Hab   2: 14 For the earth will be **f**
Lk   1: 15 he will be **f** with the Holy Spirit
       1: 41 Elizabeth was **f** with the Holy Spirit.
Jn   12:   3 the house was **f** with the fragrance
Ac   2:   4 of them were **f** with the Holy Spirit
       4:   8 Then Peter, **f** with the Holy Spirit,
       9: 17 and be **f** with the Holy Spirit."
      13:   9 called Paul, **f** with the Holy Spirit,
Eph   5: 18 Instead, be **f** with the Spirit,
Php   1: 11 **f** with the fruit of righteousness

FILLS (FILL)
Nu   14: 21 of the LORD **f** the whole earth,
Ps   107:   9 and **f** the hungry with good things.
Eph   1: 23 him who **f** everything in every way.

FILTHY
Isa   64:   6 all our righteous acts are like **f** rags;
Col   3:   8 and **f** language from your lips.

FIND (FINDS FOUND)
Nu   32: 23 be sure that your sin will **f** you out.
Dt   4: 29 you will **f** him if you seek him
1Sa   23: 16 and helped him **f** strength in God.
Ps   91:   4 under his wings you will **f** refuge;
     112:   1 LORD, who **f** great delight in his
Pr   14: 22 those who plan what is good **f** love
      31: 10 wife of noble character who can **f**?
Jer   6: 16 and you will **f** rest for your souls.
Mt   7:   7 seek and you will **f**;
      11: 29 and you will **f** rest for your souls.
      16: 25 loses their life for me will **f** it.
Lk   18:   8 will he **f** faith on the earth?"
Jn   10:   9 come in and go out, and **f** pasture.

FINDS (FIND)
Ps   62:   1 Truly my soul **f** rest in God;
     119:162 promise like one who **f** great spoil.
Pr   18: 22 He who **f** a wife **f** what is good
Mt   7:   8 the one who seeks **f**; and to the one
      10: 39 Whoever **f** their life will lose it,
Lk   12: 37 whose master **f** them watching
      15:   4 go after the lost sheep until he **f** it?

FINISH (FINISHED)
Jn   4: 34 him who sent me and to **f** his work.
       5: 36 that the Father has given me to **f**–
Ac   20: 24 my only aim is to **f** the race
2Co   8: 11 Now **f** the work, so that your eager
Gal   3:   3 are you now trying to **f** by means
Jas   1:   4 Let perseverance **f** its work so

FINISHED (FINISH)
Ge   2:   2 seventh day God had **f** the work he
Jn   19: 30 the drink, Jesus said, "It is **f**."
2Ti   4:   7 the good fight, I have **f** the race,

FIRE (FIERY)
Ex   13: 21 in a pillar of **f** to give them light,
Lev   6: 12 The **f** on the altar must be kept
Isa   30: 27 and his tongue is a consuming **f**.
Jer   23: 29 "Is not my word like **f**,"
Mt   3: 11 you with the Holy Spirit and **f**.
       5: 22 will be in danger of the **f** of hell.
      25: 41 the eternal **f** prepared for the devil
Mk   9: 43 hell, where the **f** never goes out.
Ac   2:   3 to be tongues of **f** that separated
1Co   3: 13 It will be revealed with **f**, and the
Heb   12: 29 for our "God is a consuming **f**."
Jas   3:   5 what a great forest is set on **f**
2Pe   3: 10 the elements will be destroyed by **f**,
Jude   : 23 by snatching them from the **f**;
Rev   20: 14 **f**. The lake of **f** is the second death.

FIRM
Ex   14: 13 Stand **f** and you will see
2Ch 20: 17 stand **f** and see the deliverance
Ps   33: 11 plans of the LORD stand **f** forever,
     37: 23 The LORD makes **f** the steps
     40: 2 and gave me a **f** place to stand.
     89: 2 that your love stands **f** forever,
     119: 89 it stands **f** in the heavens.
Zec   8: 23 nations will take **f** hold of one Jew
Mk   13: 13 the one who stands **f** to the end
1Co 16: 13 on your guard; stand **f** in the faith;
2Co   1: 24 because it is by faith you stand **f**.
Eph   6: 14 Stand **f** then, with the belt of truth
Col   4: 12 that you may stand **f** in all the will
2Th   2: 15 stand **f** and hold fast to the teachings
2Ti   2: 19 God's solid foundation stands **f**,
Heb   6: 19 anchor for the soul, **f** and secure.
1Pe   5: 9 Resist him, standing **f** in the faith,

FIRST
Isa 44: 6 I am the **f** and I am the last;
     48: 12 I am the **f** and I am the last.
Mt   5: 24 **F** go and be reconciled to them;
      6: 33 But seek **f** his kingdom and his
      7: 5 **f** take the plank out of your own
     20: 27 wants to be **f** must be your slave—
     22: 38 This is the **f** and greatest
     23: 26 **F** clean the inside of the cup
Mk   13: 10 the gospel must **f** be preached to all
Ac   11: 26 disciples were called Christians **f**
Ro   1: 16 **f** to the Jew, then to the Gentile.
1Co 12: 28 in the church **f** of all apostles,
2Co   8: 5 They gave themselves **f** of all
1Ti   2: 13 For Adam was formed **f**, then Eve.
Jas   3: 17 comes from heaven is **f** of all pure;
1Jn   4: 19 We love because he **f** loved us.
3Jn   : 9 who loves to be **f**, will not welcome
Rev   1: 17 I am the **F** and the Last.
      2: 4 have forsaken the love you had at **f**.

FIRSTBORN (BEAR)
Ex   11: 5 Every **f** son in Egypt will die,

FIRSTFRUITS
Ex   23: 19 "Bring the best of the **f** of your soil

FISH
Mk   1: 17 I will send you out to **f** for people."
Lk   5: 10 from now on you will **f** for people."

FITTING
Ps   33: 1 it is **f** for the upright to praise him.
     147: 1 how pleasant and **f** to praise him!
Pr   19: 10 It is not **f** for a fool to live
     26: 1 in harvest, honor is not **f** for a fool.
1Co 14: 40 everything should be done in a **f**
Col   3: 18 your husbands, as is **f** in the Lord.
Heb   2: 10 to glory, it was **f** that God,

FIX (FIXING)
Dt   11: 18 **F** these words of mine in your
Pr   4: 25 **f** your gaze directly before you.
2Co   4: 18 So we **f** our eyes not on what is
Heb   3: 1 calling, **f** your thoughts on Jesus,

FIXING (FIX)
Heb 12: 2 **f** our eyes on Jesus, the pioneer

FLAME (FLAMES FLAMING)
2Ti   1: 6 you to fan into **f** the gift of God,

FLAMES (FLAME)
1Co   3: 15 only as one escaping through the **f**.

FLAMING (FLAME)
Eph   6: 16 you can extinguish all the **f** arrows

FLASH
1Co 15: 52 in a **f**, in the twinkling of an eye,

FLATTER (FLATTERING FLATTERY)
Ps   12: 2 they **f** with their lips but harbor
Job 32: 21 no partiality, nor will I **f** anyone;
Jude   : 16 **f** others for their own advantage.

FLATTERING (FLATTER)
Ps   12: 3 May the LORD silence all **f** lips
Pr   26: 28 it hurts, and a **f** mouth works ruin.

FLATTERY (FLATTER)
Ro   16: 18 **f** they deceive the minds of naive
1Th   2: 5 You know we never used **f**, nor did

FLAWLESS
2Sa 22: 31 The LORD's word is **f**;
Job 11: 4 'My beliefs are **f** and I am pure
Ps   12: 6 And the words of the LORD are **f**,
     18: 30 The LORD's word is **f**.
Pr   30: 5 "Every word of God is **f**; he is
SS   5: 2 my darling, my dove, my **f** one.

FLEE
Ps 139: 7 Where can I **f** from your presence?
1Co   6: 18 **F** from sexual immorality.
     10: 14 my dear friends, **f** from idolatry.
1Ti   6: 11 man of God, **f** from all this,
2Ti   2: 22 **F** the evil desires of youth
Jas   4: 7 the devil, and he will **f** from you.

FLEETING
Ps   89: 47 Remember how **f** is my life.
Pr   31: 30 is deceptive, and beauty is **f**;

FLESH
Ge   2: 23 bone of my bones and **f** of my **f**;
      2: 24 to his wife, and they become one **f**.
Job 19: 26 yet in my **f** I will see God;
Eze 11: 19 of stone and give them a heart of **f**.
     36: 26 of stone and give you a heart of **f**.
Mt   26: 41 spirit is willing, but the **f** is weak."
Mk   10: 8 and the two will become one **f**.'
Jn   1: 14 The Word became **f** and made his
      6: 51 bread is my **f**, which I will give
Ro   8: 4 do not live according to the **f** but
      8: 8 realm of the **f** cannot please God.
1Co   6: 16 said, "The two will become one **f**."
Gal   3: 3 trying to finish by means of the **f**?
      5: 19 The acts of the **f** are obvious:
      5: 24 crucified the **f** with its passions
Eph   5: 31 and the two will become one **f**."
      6: 12 For our struggle is not against **f**

FLOCK (FLOCKS)
Isa 40: 11 He tends his **f** like a shepherd:
Eze 34: 2 not shepherds take care of the **f**?
Zec 11: 17 shepherd, who deserts the **f**!
Mt   26: 31 the sheep of the **f** will be scattered.'
Ac   20: 28 all the **f** of which the Holy Spirit
1Pe   5: 2 of God's **f** that is under your care,

FLOCKS (FLOCK)
Lk   2: 8 keeping watch over their **f** at night.

FLOG
Ac   22: 25 **f** a Roman citizen who hasn't even

FLOODGATES
Mal   3: 10 will not throw open the **f** of heaven

FLOURISHING
Ps   52: 8 am like an olive tree **f** in the house

FLOW (FLOWING)
Nu   13: 27 and it does **f** with milk and honey!
Jn   7: 38 of living water will **f** from within

FLOWERS
Isa 40: 7 The grass withers and the **f** fall,
Lk   12: 27 "Consider how the wild **f** grow.

FLOWING (FLOW)
Ex   3: 8 a land **f** with milk and honey—

FOLDING
Pr   6: 10 a little **f** of the hands to rest—

FOLLOW (FOLLOWS)
Ex   23: 2 "Do not **f** the crowd in doing
Lev 18: 4 laws and be careful to **f** my decrees.
Dt   5: 1 Learn them and be sure to **f** them.
Ps   23: 6 love will **f** me all the days of my
Mt   16: 24 and take up their cross and **f** me.
Jn   10: 4 his sheep **f** him because they know
1Co 14: 1 **F** the way of love and eagerly desire
Eph   5: 1 **F** God's example, therefore,
Rev 14: 4 They **f** the Lamb wherever he goes.

FOLLOWS (FOLLOW)
Jn 8: 12 Whoever f me will never walk

FOOD (FOODS)
Pr 20: 13 awake and you will have f to spare.
    22: 9 for they share their f with the poor.
    25: 21 enemy is hungry, give him f to eat;
    31: 15 she provides f for her family
Da   1: 8 to defile himself with the royal f
Jn   6: 27 Do not work for f that spoils, but for f that
              endures to eternal life,
1Co 8: 8 f does not bring us near to God;
1Ti 6: 8 But if we have f and clothing,
Jas 2: 15 sister is without clothes and daily f.

FOODS (FOOD)
Mk   7: 19 this, Jesus declared all f clean.)

FOOL (FOOLISH FOOLISHNESS FOOLS)
Ps 14: 1 The f says in his heart, "There
Pr 15: 5 A f spurns a parent's discipline,
    26: 5 Answer a f according to his folly,
Mt   5: 22 And anyone who says, 'You f!'

FOOLISH (FOOL)
Pr 10: 1 a f son brings grief to his mother.
    17: 25 A f son brings grief to his father
Mt   7: 26 practice is like a f man who built
    25: 2 Five of them were f and five were
1Co 1: 27 God chose the f things of the world

FOOLISHNESS (FOOL)
1Co 1: 18 of the cross is f to those who are
     1: 25 the f of God is wiser than human
     2: 14 Spirit of God but considers them f,
     3: 19 of this world is f in God's sight.

FOOLS (FOOL)
Pr 14: 9 F mock at making amends for sin,
    17: 28 Even f are thought wise if they
    18: 2 F find no pleasure in understanding
    28: 26 who trust in themselves are f,
1Co 4: 10 We are f for Christ, but you are so

FOOT (FEET FOOTHOLD)
Jos 1: 3 every place where you set your f,
Isa 1: 6 the sole of your f to the top of your
1Co 12: 15 Now if the f should say, "Because I

FOOTHOLD (FOOT)
Eph 4: 27 and do not give the devil a f.

FORBEARANCE
Ro   3: 25 his f he had left the sins committed
Gal 5: 22 love, joy, peace, f, kindness,

FORBID
1Co 14: 39 and do not f speaking in tongues.

FOREIGNER (FOREIGNERS)
Ex 22: 21 "Do not mistreat or oppress a f,

FOREIGNERS (FOREIGNER)
1Pe 2: 11 urge you, as f and exiles, to abstain

FOREKNEW (KNOW)
Ro   8: 29 those God f he also predestined
    11: 2 not reject his people, whom he f.

FOREVER (EVER)
1Ch 16: 15 He remembers his covenant f,
    16: 34 for he is good; his love endures f.
Ps   9: 7 The Lord reigns f;
    23: 6 dwell in the house of the Lord f.
    33: 11 plans of the Lord stand firm f,
    86: 12 I will glorify your name f.
    92: 8 But you, Lord, are f exalted.
   110: 4 "You are a priest f, in the order
   119: 111 Your statutes are my heritage f;
Jn   6: 51 Whoever eats this bread will live f.
    14: 16 to help you and be with you f—
1Co 9: 25 do it to get a crown that will last f.
1Th 4: 17 And so we will be with the Lord f.
Heb 13: 8 the same yesterday and today and f.
1Pe 1: 25 the word of the Lord endures f."
1Jn 2: 17 does the will of God lives f.

FORFEIT
Lk   9: 25 and yet lose or f their very self?

FORGAVE (FORGIVE)
Ps 32: 5 And you f the guilt of my sin.
Lk   7: 42 him back, so he f the debts of both.
Eph 4: 32 other, just as in Christ God f you.
Col 2: 13 He f us all our sins,
     3: 13 Forgive as the Lord f you.

FORGET (FORGETS FORGETTING)
Dt   6: 12 that you do not f the Lord,
Ps 103: 2 my soul, and f not all his benefits—
   137: 5 If I f you, Jerusalem, may my right
Isa 49: 15 Though she may f, I will not f you!
Heb 6: 10 will not f your work and the love

FORGETS (FORGET)
Jn 16: 21 is born she f the anguish because
Jas 1: 24 immediately f what he looks like.

FORGETTING (FORGET)
Php 3: 13 F what is behind and straining

FORGIVE (FORGAVE FORGIVENESS FORGIVING)
2Ch 7: 14 and I will f their sin and will heal
Ps 19: 12 F my hidden faults.
Mt   6: 12 And f us our debts, as we also have
     6: 14 if you f other people when they sin
    18: 21 many times shall I f my brother
Mk 11: 25 anything against anyone, f them,
Lk 11: 4 F us our sins, for we also f everyone
    23: 34 "Father, f them, for they do not
Col 3: 13 F as the Lord forgave you.
1Jn 1: 9 and will f us our sins and purify

FORGIVENESS (FORGIVE)
Ps 130: 4 But with you there is f, so that we
Ac 10: 43 in him receives f of sins through
Eph 1: 7 through his blood, the f of sins,
Col 1: 14 we have redemption, the f of sins.
Heb 9: 22 the shedding of blood there is no f.

FORGIVING (FORGIVE)
Ne   9: 17 But you are a f God,
Eph 4: 32 to one another, f each other, just as

FORMED
Ge   2: 7 the Lord God f a man
Ps 103: 14 for he knows how we are f,
Isa 45: 18 be empty, but f it to be inhabited—
Ro   9: 20 what is f say to the one who f it,
1Ti 2: 13 For Adam was f first, then Eve.
Heb 11: 3 that the universe was f at God's

FORSAKE (FORSAKEN)
Jos 1: 5 I will never leave you nor f you.
    24: 16 us to f the Lord to serve other
2Ch 15: 2 you, but if you f him, he will f you.
Ps 27: 10 Though my father and mother f me,
Isa 55: 7 Let the wicked f their ways
Heb 13: 5 will I leave you; never will I f you."

FORSAKEN (FORSAKE)
Ezr 9: 9 God has not f us in our bondage.
Ps 22: 1 God, my God, why have you f me?
    37: 25 I have never seen the righteous f
Mt 27: 46 my God, why have you f me?").
Rev 2: 4 You have f the love you had at first.

FORTIFIED
Pr 18: 10 name of the Lord is a f tower;

FORTRESS
Ps 18: 2 is my rock, my f and my deliverer;
    71: 3 me, for you are my rock and my f.

FOUGHT (FIGHT)
2Ti 4: 7 I have f the good fight, I have

FOUND (FIND)
1Ch 28: 9 If you seek him, he will be f by you;
Isa 55: 6 Seek the Lord while he may be f;
Da   5: 27 on the scales and f wanting.
Lk 15: 6 I have f my lost sheep.'
    15: 9 I have f my lost coin.'
Ac   4: 12 Salvation is f in no one else,

FOUNDATION
Isa 28: 16 a precious cornerstone for a sure **f**;
1Co 3: 11 can lay any **f** other than the one
Eph 2: 20 built on the **f** of the apostles
2Ti 2: 19 God's solid **f** stands firm,

FOXES
Mt 8: 20 "**F** have dens and birds have nests,

FRANKINCENSE
Mt 2: 11 him with gifts of gold, **f** and myrrh.

FREE (FREED FREEDOM FREELY)
Ps 146: 7 The LORD sets prisoners **f**,
Jn 8: 32 truth, and the truth will set you **f**."
Ro 6: 18 You have been set **f** from sin
Gal 3: 28 neither slave nor **f**, nor is there
1Pe 2: 16 Live as **f** people, but do not use

FREED (FREE)
Rev 1: 5 has **f** us from our sins by his blood,

FREEDOM (FREE)
Ro 8: 21 brought into the **f** and glory
2Co 3: 17 the Spirit of the Lord is, there is **f**.
Gal 5: 13 But do not use your **f** to indulge
1Pe 2: 16 do not use your **f** as

FREELY (FREE)
Isa 55: 7 to our God, for he will **f** pardon.
Mt 10: 8 **F** you have received; **f** give.
Ro 3: 24 and all are justified **f** by his grace
Eph 1: 6 which he has **f** given us in the One

FRIEND (FRIENDS)
Ex 33: 11 face to face, as one speaks to a **f**.
Pr 17: 17 A **f** loves at all times, and a brother
18: 24 there is a **f** who sticks closer than
27: 6 Wounds from a **f** can be trusted,
27: 10 Do not forsake your **f** or a **f** of your
Jas 4: 4 to be a **f** of the world becomes

FRIENDS (FRIEND)
Pr 16: 28 and a gossip separates close **f**.
18: 24 who has unreliable **f** soon comes
Zec 13: 6 I was given at the house of my **f**.'
Jn 15: 13 to lay down one's life for one's **f**.

FRUIT (FRUITFUL)
Ps 1: 3 which yields its **f** in season
Pr 11: 30 The **f** of the righteous is a tree
Mt 7: 16 By their **f** you will recognize them.
Jn 15: 2 branch that does bear **f** he prunes
Gal 5: 22 But the **f** of the Spirit is love, joy,
Rev 22: 2 bearing twelve crops of **f**, yielding its **f** every month.

FRUITFUL (FRUIT)
Ge 1: 22 "Be **f** and increase in number
Ps 128: 3 wife will be like a **f** vine within
Jn 15: 2 so that it will be even more **f**.

FULFILL (FULFILLED FULFILLMENT)
Ps 116: 14 I will **f** my vows to the LORD
Mt 5: 17 to abolish them but to **f** them.
1Co 7: 3 The husband should **f** his marital

FULFILLED (FULFILL)
Pr 13: 19 A longing **f** is sweet to the soul,
Mk 14: 49 But the Scriptures must be **f**."
Ro 13: 8 whoever loves others has **f** the law.

FULFILLMENT (FULFILL)
Ro 13: 10 Therefore love is the **f** of the law.

FULL (FILL)
Ps 127: 5 Blessed is the man whose quiver is **f**
Pr 31: 11 Her husband has **f** confidence in her
Isa 6: 3 the whole earth is **f** of his glory."
Lk 6: 45 speaks what the heart is **f** of.
Jn 10: 10 may have life, and have it to the **f**.
Ac 6: 3 who are known to be **f** of the Spirit

FULLNESS (FILL)
Col 1: 19 to have all his **f** dwell in him,
2: 9 in Christ all the **f** of the Deity lives

FULLY (FILL)
1Ki 8: 61 may your hearts be **f** committed

2Ch 16: 9 whose hearts are **f** committed
Ps 119: 4 precepts that are to be **f** obeyed.
119:138 righteous; they are **f** trustworthy.
1Co 15: 58 Always give yourselves **f**

FUTURE
Ps 37: 37 a **f** awaits those who seek peace.
Pr 23: 18 There is surely a **f** hope for you,
Ro 8: 38 neither the present nor the **f**,

GABRIEL
Angel who interpreted Daniel's visions (Da 8:16-26; 9:20-27); announced births of John (Lk 1:11-20), Jesus (Lk 1:26-38).

GAIN (GAINED)
Ps 60: 12 With God we will **g** the victory,
Mk 8: 36 for someone to **g** the whole world,
1Co 13: 3 but do not have love, I **g** nothing.
Php 1: 21 me, to live is Christ and to die is **g**.
3: 8 them garbage, that I may **g** Christ
1Ti 6: 6 with contentment is great **g**.
1Pe 5: 2 not pursuing dishonest **g**, but eager

GAINED (GAIN)
Ro 5: 2 through whom we have **g** access

GALILEE
Isa 9: 1 in the future he will honor **G**

GALL
Mt 27: 34 Jesus wine to drink, mixed with **g**;

GAP
Eze 22: 30 stand before me in the **g** on behalf

GARBAGE
Php 3: 8 I consider them **g**, that I may gain

GARDENER
Jn 15: 1 true vine, and my Father is the **g**.

GARMENT (GARMENTS)
Ps 102: 26 they will all wear out like a **g**.
Mt 9: 16 the patch will pull away from the **g**,
Jn 19: 23 This **g** was seamless, woven in one
19: 24 them and cast lots for my **g**."

GARMENTS (GARMENT)
Ge 3: 21 The LORD God made **g** of skin
Isa 61: 10 For he has clothed me with **g**
63: 1 with his **g** stained crimson?

GATE (GATES)
Mt 7: 13 "Enter through the narrow **g**.
Jn 10: 9 I am the **g**; whoever enters through

GATES (GATE)
Ps 100: 4 Enter his **g** with thanksgiving
Mt 16: 18 the **g** of Hades will not overcome

GATHER (GATHERS)
Zec 14: 2 I will **g** all the nations to Jerusalem
Mt 12: 30 and whoever does not **g** with me
23: 37 longed to **g** your children together,

GATHERS (GATHER)
Isa 40: 11 He **g** the lambs in his arms
Mt 23: 37 as a hen **g** her chicks under her

GAVE (GIVE)
Ezr 2: 69 their ability they **g** to the treasury
Job 1: 21 The LORD **g** and the LORD has
Jn 3: 16 so loved the world that he **g** his
2Co 8: 5 They **g** themselves first of all
Gal 2: 20 loved me and **g** himself for me.
1Ti 2: 6 who **g** himself as a ransom for all

GAZE
Ps 27: 4 to **g** on the beauty of the LORD
Pr 4: 25 fix your **g** directly before you.

GENEALOGIES
1Ti 1: 4 themselves to myths and endless **g**.

GENERATIONS
Ps 22: 30 **g** will be told about the Lord.
102: 12 renown endures through all **g**.
145: 13 dominion endures through all **g**.
Lk 1: 48 now on all **g** will call me blessed,
Eph 3: 5 other **g** as it has now been revealed

GENEROUS
Ps 112: 5 Good will come to those who are **g**
Pr   22: 9 The **g** will themselves be blessed,
2Co   9: 5 Then it will be ready as a **g** gift,
1Ti   6: 18 and to be **g** and willing to share.

GENTILE (GENTILES)
Ro   1: 16 first to the Jew, then to the **G.**
     10: 12 no difference between Jew and **G–**

GENTILES (GENTILE)
Isa 42: 6 for the people and a light for the **G,**
Ro   3: 9 alike are all under the power
     11: 13 as I am the apostle to the **G,** I take
1Co   1: 23 block to Jews and foolishness to **G,**

GENTLE (GENTLENESS)
Pr   15: 1 A **g** answer turns away wrath,
Mt   11: 29 for I am **g** and humble in heart,
     21: 5 to you, **g** and riding on a donkey,
1Co   4: 21 I come in love and with a **g** spirit?
1Pe   3: 4 unfading beauty of a **g** and quiet

GENTLENESS (GENTLE)
2Co 10: 1 By the humility and **g** of Christ,
Gal   5: 23 **g** and self-control.
Php   4: 5 Let your **g** be evident to all.
Col   3: 12 kindness, humility, **g** and patience.
1Ti   6: 11 faith, love, endurance and **g.**
1Pe   3: 15 But do this with **g** and respect,

GETHSEMANE
Mt   26: 36 his disciples to a place called **G,**

GIDEON
Judge, also called Jerub-Baal; freed Israel from Midianites (Jdg 6-8; Heb 11:32). Given sign of fleece (Jdg 8:36-40).

GIFT (GIFTS)
Pr   21: 14 A **g** given in secret soothes anger,
Mt   5: 23 you are offering your **g** at the altar
Ac   2: 38 you will receive the **g** of the Holy
Ro   6: 23 the **g** of God is eternal life in Christ
1Co   7: 7 of you has your own **g** from God;
2Co   9: 2 the **g** is acceptable according
      9: 15 be to God for his indescribable **g!**
Eph   2: 8 yourselves, it is the **g** of God–
1Ti   4: 14 Do not neglect your **g,** which was
2Ti   1: 6 you to fan into flame the **g** of God,
Jas   1: 17 good and perfect **g** is from above,
1Pe   4: 10 should use whatever **g** you have

GIFTS (GIFT)
Ro   11: 29 for God's **g** and his call are
     12: 6 We have different **g,**
1Co 12: 4 There are different kinds of **g,**
     12: 31 Now eagerly desire the greater **g.**
     14: 1 and eagerly desire **g** of the Spirit,
     14: 12 Since you are eager for **g**

GILEAD
Jer   8: 22 Is there no balm in **G?** Is there no

GIVE (GAVE GIVEN GIVER GIVES GIVING)
Nu   6: 26 toward you and **g** you peace."
1Sa   1: 11 forget your servant but **g** her a son,
      1: 11 I will **g** him to the Lord for all
2Ch   7: 5 be strong and do not **g** up, for your
Pr   21: 26 the righteous **g** without sparing.
     23: 26 **g** me your heart and let your eyes
     28: 27 Those who **g** to the poor will lack
     30: 8 but **g** me only my daily bread.
Eze 36: 26 I will **g** you a new heart and put
Mt   6: 11 **G** us today our daily bread.
      10: 8 Freely you have received; freely **g.**
     22: 21 them, "So **g** back to Caesar what is
Mk   8: 37 what can anyone **g** in exchange
Lk   6: 38 **G,** and it will be given to you.
     11: 13 Father in heaven **g** the Holy Spirit
Jn   10: 28 I **g** them eternal life, and they shall
     13: 34 "A new command I **g** you:
Ac   20: 35 'It is more blessed to **g** than
Ro   12: 8 encourage, then **g** encouragement;
     12: 8 if it is giving, then **g** generously;
     13: 7 **G** to everyone what you owe them:

Ro   14: 12 then, each of us will **g** an account
2Co   9: 7 should **g** what you have decided
Rev 14: 7 voice, "Fear God and **g** him glory,

GIVEN (GIVE)
Nu   8: 16 Israelites who are to be **g** wholly
Ps   115: 16 but the earth he has **g** to mankind.
Isa   9: 6 a son is **g,** and the government
Mt   6: 33 all these things will be **g** to you as
      7: 7 "Ask and it will be **g** to you;
Lk   22: 19 saying, "This is my body **g** for you;
Jn   3: 27 can receive only what is **g** them
Ro   5: 5 Holy Spirit, who has been **g** to us.
1Co   4: 2 those who have been **g** a trust must
     12: 13 and we were all **g** the one Spirit
Eph   4: 7 of us grace has been **g** as Christ

GIVER (GIVE)
Pr   18: 16 ushers the **g** into the presence
2Co   9: 7 for God loves a cheerful **g.**

GIVES (GIVE)
Ps 119:130 unfolding of your words **g** light;
Pr   14: 30 A heart at peace **g** life to the body,
     15: 30 good news **g** health to the bones.
Isa 40: 29 He **g** strength to the weary
Mt   10: 42 anyone **g** even a cup of cold water
Jn   6: 63 The Spirit **g** life; the flesh counts
1Co 15: 57 He **g** us the victory through our
2Co   3: 6 the letter kills, but the Spirit **g** life.

GIVING (GIVE)
Ne   8: 8 **g** the meaning so that the people
Ps   19: 8 Lord are right, **g** joy to the heart.
Mt   6: 4 so that your **g** may be in secret.
2Co   8: 7 you also excel in this grace of **g.**

GLAD (GLADNESS)
Ps   31: 7 I will be **g** and rejoice in your love,
     46: 4 whose streams make **g** the city
     97: 1 Lord reigns, let the earth be **g;**
    118: 24 let us rejoice today and be **g.**
Zec   2: 10 "Shout and be **g,** Daughter Zion.
Mt   5: 12 Rejoice and be **g,** because great is

GLADNESS (GLAD)
Ps   45: 15 Led in with joy and **g,** they enter
     51: 8 Let me hear joy and **g;**
    100: 2 Worship the Lord with **g;**
Jer 31: 13 I will turn their mourning into **g;**

GLORIFIED (GLORY)
Jn   13: 31 "Now the Son of Man is **g** and God is **g** in him.
Ro   8: 30 those he justified, he also **g.**
2Th   1: 10 he comes to be **g** in his holy people

GLORIFY (GLORY)
Ps   34: 3 **G** the Lord with me; let us exalt
     86: 12 I will **g** your name forever.
Mt   5: 16 deeds and **g** your Father in heaven.
Jn   13: 32 God will **g** the Son in himself,
     17: 1 **G** your Son, that your Son may **g**

GLORIOUS (GLORY)
Ps   45: 13 All **g** is the princess within her
    111: 3 **G** and majestic are his deeds,
    145: 5 They speak of the **g** splendor
Isa   4: 2 the Lord will be beautiful and **g,**
     12: 5 Lord, for he has done **g** things;
     42: 21 to make his law great and **g.**
     63: 15 from your lofty throne, holy and **g.**
Mt   19: 28 Son of Man sits on his **g** throne,
Lk   9: 30 and Elijah, appeared in **g** splendor,
Ac   2: 20 of the great and **g** day of the Lord.
2Co   3: 8 of the Spirit be even more **g?**
Php   3: 21 so that they will be like his **g** body.
Jude : 24 you before his **g** presence without

GLORY (GLORIFIED GLORIFY GLORIOUS)
Ex   15: 11 awesome in **g,** working wonders?
     33: 18 said, "Now show me your **g.**"
1Sa   4: 21 "The **G** has departed from Israel"
1Ch 16: 24 Declare his **g** among the nations,
     16: 28 ascribe to the Lord **g**
     29: 11 power and the **g** and the majesty

Ps 8: 5 crowned them with **g** and honor.
19: 1 The heavens declare the **g** of God;
24: 7 that the King of **g** may come in.
29: 1 beings, ascribe to the LORD **g**
34: 2 I will **g** in the LORD;
72: 19 the whole earth be filled with his **g**.
96: 3 Declare his **g** among the nations,
Pr 19: 11 is to one's **g** to overlook an offense.
25: 2 It is the **g** of God to conceal
25: 2 a matter is the **g** of kings.
Isa 6: 3 the whole earth is full of his **g**."
42: 8 I will not yield my **g** to another
48: 11 I will not yield my **g** to another.
Eze 43: 2 and I saw the **g** of the God of Israel
Mt 24: 30 of heaven, with power and great **g**.
25: 31 the Son of Man comes in his **g**,
Mk 8: 38 in his Father's **g** with the holy
13: 26 in clouds with great power and **g**.
Lk 2: 9 and the **g** of the Lord shone around
2: 14 "**G** to God in the highest heaven,
Jn 1: 14 have seen his **g**, the **g** of the one
17: 5 your presence with the **g** I had
17: 24 and to see my **g**, the **g** you have
Ac 7: 2 God of **g** appeared to our father
Ro 1: 23 exchanged the **g** of the immortal
3: 23 and fall short of the **g** of God,
8: 18 with the **g** that will be revealed
9: 4 theirs the divine **g**, the covenants,
1Co 10: 31 you do, do it all for the **g** of God.
11: 7 since he is the image and **g** of God;
11: 7 but woman is the **g** of man.
15: 43 sown in dishonor, it is raised in **g**;
2Co 3: 10 what was glorious has no **g** now
3: 18 faces contemplate the Lord's **g**,
4: 17 us an eternal **g** that far outweighs
Php 4: 19 the riches of his **g** in Christ Jesus.
Col 1: 27 is Christ in you, the hope of **g**.
3: 4 you also will appear with him in **g**.
1Ti 3: 16 on in the world, was taken up in **g**.
Titus 2: 13 appearing of the **g** of our great God
Heb 1: 3 The Son is the radiance of God's **g**
2: 7 crowned them with **g** and honor
1Pe 1: 24 all their **g** is like the flowers
Rev 4: 11 to receive **g** and honor and power,
21: 23 for the **g** of God gives it light,

GLUTTONS
Titus 1: 12 always liars, evil brutes, lazy **g**."

GNASHING
Mt 8: 12 will be weeping and **g** of teeth."

GNAT
Mt 23: 24 You strain out a **g** but swallow

GOAL
2Co 5: 9 So we make it our **g** to please him,
Php 3: 14 on toward the **g** to win the prize

GOAT (GOATS SCAPEGOAT)
Isa 11: 6 leopard will lie down with the **g**,

GOATS (GOAT)
Nu 7: 17 five male **g** and five male lambs

GOD (GOD'S GODLINESS GODLY GODS)
Ge 1: 1 beginning **G** created the heavens
1: 2 of **G** was hovering over the waters.
1: 26 Then **G** said, "Let us make
1: 27 So **G** created mankind in his own
1: 31 **G** saw all that he had made, and it
2: 3 Then **G** blessed the seventh day
2: 22 the LORD **G** made a woman
3: 21 The LORD **G** made garments
3: 23 So the LORD **G** banished him
5: 22 walked faithfully with **G** 300 years
6: 2 sons of **G** saw that the daughters
9: 16 everlasting covenant between **G**
17: 1 to him and said, "I am **G** Almighty;
21: 33 name of the LORD, the Eternal **G**.
22: 8 "**G** himself will provide the lamb
28: 12 the angels of **G** were ascending

Ge 32: 28 because you have struggled with **G**
32: 30 "It is because I saw **G** face to face,
35: 10 **G** said to him, "Your name is
41: 51 said, "It is because **G** has made me
50: 20 me, but **G** intended it for good
Ex 2: 24 **G** heard their groaning and he
3: 6 he said, "I am the **G** of your father,
3: 6 because he was afraid to look at **G**.
6: 7 know that I am the LORD your **G**,
8: 10 is no one like the LORD our **G**.
13: 18 So **G** led the people around
15: 2 He is my **G**, and I will praise him,
17: 9 with the staff of **G** in my hands."
19: 3 Then Moses went up to **G**,
20: 2 "I am the LORD your **G**,
20: 5 the LORD your **G**, am a jealous **G**,
20: 19 But do not have **G** speak to us
22: 28 "Do not blaspheme **G** or curse
31: 18 stone inscribed by the finger of **G**.
34: 6 the compassionate and gracious **G**,
34: 14 name is Jealous, is a jealous **G**.
Lev 18: 21 not profane the name of your **G**.
19: 2 I, the LORD your **G**, am holy.
26: 12 walk among you and be your **G**,
Nu 22: 38 I must speak only what **G** puts
23: 19 **G** is not human, that he should lie,
Dt 1: 17 anyone, for judgment belongs to **G**.
3: 22 the LORD your **G** himself will
3: 24 For what **g** is there in heaven
4: 24 **G** is a consuming fire, a jealous **G**.
4: 31 the LORD your **G** is a merciful **G**;
4: 39 day that the LORD is **G** in heaven
5: 11 the name of the LORD your **G**,
5: 14 is a sabbath to the LORD your **G**.
5: 26 voice of the living **G** speaking
6: 4 The LORD our **G**, the LORD is
6: 5 Love the LORD your **G** with all
6: 13 Fear the LORD your **G**, serve him
6: 16 Do not put the LORD your **G**
7: 9 is **G**; he is the faithful **G**,
7: 12 the LORD your **G** will keep his
7: 21 is a great and awesome **G**.
8: 5 the LORD your **G** disciplines you.
10: 12 what does the LORD your **G** ask you but to fear
the LORD your **G**,
10: 14 To the LORD your **G** belong
10: 17 For the LORD your **G** is **G** of gods
11: 13 to love the LORD your **G**
13: 3 The LORD your **G** is testing you
13: 4 It is the LORD your **G** you must
15: 6 the LORD your **G** will bless you
19: 9 to love the LORD your **G**
25: 16 the LORD your **G** detests anyone
29: 29 things belong to the LORD our **G**,
30: 2 return to the LORD your **G**
30: 16 today to love the LORD your **G**,
30: 20 you may love the LORD your **G**,
31: 6 the LORD your **G** goes with you;
32: 3 Oh, praise the greatness of our **G**!
32: 4 A faithful **G** who does no wrong,
33: 27 The eternal **G** is your refuge,
Jos 1: 9 the LORD your **G** will be with you
14: 8 the LORD my **G** wholeheartedly.
22: 5 to love the LORD your **G**, to walk
22: 34 that the LORD is **G**.
23: 11 careful to love the LORD your **G**.
23: 14 the LORD your **G** gave you has
Jdg 16: 28 Please, **G**, strengthen me just once
Ru 1: 16 be my people and your **G** my **G**.
1Sa 2: 2 there is no Rock like our **G**.
2: 3 for the LORD is a **G** who knows,
2: 25 **G** may mediate for the offender;
10: 26 men whose hearts **G** had touched.
12: 12 the LORD your **G** was your king.
17: 26 defy the armies of the living **G**?
17: 46 know that there is a **G** in Israel.
30: 6 found strength in the LORD his **G**.

2Sa 14:14 But that is not what **G** desires;
22: 3 my **G** is my rock, in whom I take
22:31 "As for **G**, his way is perfect:
1Ki 4:29 **G** gave Solomon wisdom and very
8:23 there is no **G** like you in heaven
8:27 "But will **G** really dwell on earth?
8:61 committed to the LORD our **G**,
18:21 If the LORD is **G**, follow him;
18:37 are **G**, and that you are turning
20:28 think the LORD is a **g** the hills
2Ki 19:15 you alone are **G** over all
1Ch 16:35 Cry out, "Save us, **G** our Savior;
28: 2 for the footstool of our **G**, and I
28: 9 acknowledge the **G** of your father,
29:10 LORD, the **G** of our father Israel,
29:17 my **G**, that you test the heart and
2Ch 2: 4 for the Name of the LORD my **G**
5:14 the LORD filled the temple of **G**.
6:18 will **G** really dwell on earth
18:13 can tell him only what my **G** says."
20: 6 you not the **G** who is in heaven?
25: 8 for **G** has the power to help
30: 9 for the LORD your **G** is gracious
33:12 the favor of the LORD his **G**
Ezr 8:22 "The gracious hand of our **G** is
9: 6 my **G**, to lift up my face to you,
9:13 our **G**, you have punished us less
Ne 1: 5 the great and awesome **G**,
8: 8 from the Book of the Law of **G**,
9:17 But you are a forgiving **G**,
9:32 "Now therefore, our **G**, the great **G**,
Job 1: 1 he feared **G** and shunned evil.
2:10 Shall we accept good from **G**,
4:17 mortal be more righteous than **G**?
5:17 is the one whom **G** corrects;
11: 7 you fathom the mysteries of **G**?
19:26 yet in my flesh I will see **G**;
22:13 Yet you say, 'What does **G** know?
25: 4 a mortal be righteous before **G**?
33:14 For **G** does speak–now one way,
34:12 unthinkable that **G** would do wrong,
36:26 How great is **G**–
37:22 **G** comes in awesome majesty.
Ps 18: 2 my **G** is my rock, in whom I take
18:28 my **G** turns my darkness into light.
19: 1 The heavens declare the glory of **G**;
22: 1 My **G**, my **G**, why have you
29: 3 the **G** of glory thunders, the LORD
31:14 I say, "You are my **G**."
40: 3 mouth, a hymn of praise to our **G**.
40: 8 I desire to do your will, my **G**;
42: 2 My soul thirsts for **G**, for the living
42: 2 When can I go and meet with **G**?
42:11 Put your hope in **G**, for I will yet
45: 6 O **G**, will last for ever and ever;
46: 1 **G** is our refuge and strength,
46:10 "Be still, and know that I am **G**;
47: 7 For **G** is the King of all the earth;
50: 3 Our **G** comes and will not be silent
51: 1 O **G**, according to your unfailing
51:10 O **G**, and renew a steadfast spirit
51:17 sacrifice, O **G**, is a broken spirit;
62: 7 and my honor depend on **G**;
65: 5 and righteous deeds, **G** our Savior,
66: 1 Shout for joy to **G**, all the earth!
66:16 Come and hear, all you who fear **G**;
68: 6 **G** sets the lonely in families,
71:17 my youth, **G**, you have taught
71:19 Who is like you, **G**?
71:22 harp for your faithfulness, my **G**;
73:26 but **G** is the strength of my heart
77:13 What **g** is as great as our **G**?
78:19 They spoke against **G**;
81: 1 Sing for joy to **G** our strength;
84: 2 my flesh cry out for the living **G**.
84:10 the house of my **G** than dwell
86:12 you, Lord my **G**, with all my heart;

Ps 89: 7 of the holy ones **G** is greatly feared;
90: 2 to everlasting you are **G**.
91: 2 fortress, my **G**, in whom I trust."
95: 7 for he is our **G** and we are
100: 3 Know that the LORD is **G**. It is he
108: 1 My heart, O **G**, is steadfast;
113: 5 Who is like the LORD our **G**,
139:23 Search me, **G**, and know my heart;
Pr 3: 4 a good name in the sight of **G**
25: 2 It is the glory of **G** to conceal
30: 5 "Every word of **G** is flawless;
Ecc 3:11 can fathom what **G** has done
11: 5 cannot understand the work of **G**,
12:13 of the matter: Fear **G** and keep his
Isa 9: 6 Mighty **G**, Everlasting Father,
37:16 you alone are **G** over all
40: 3 in the desert a highway for our **G**.
40: 8 the word of our **G** endures forever."
40:28 The LORD is the everlasting **G**,
41:10 not be dismayed, for I am your **G**.
44: 6 apart from me there is no **G**.
52: 7 who say to Zion, "Your **G** reigns!"
55: 7 and to our **G**, for he will freely
57:21 says my **G**, "for the wicked."
59: 2 have separated you from your **G**;
61:10 my soul rejoices in my **G**.
62: 5 so will your **G** rejoice over you.
Jer 23:23 "Am I only a **G** nearby,"
31:33 I will be their **G**, and they will be
32:27 the LORD, the **G** of all mankind.
Eze 28:13 You were in Eden, the garden of **G**;
Da 3:17 the **G** we serve is able to deliver us
9: 4 the great and awesome **G**,
Hos 12: 6 But you must return to your **G**;
Joel 2:13 Return to the LORD your **G**, for he
Am 4:12 Israel, prepare to meet your **G**."
Mic 6: 8 and to walk humbly with your **G**.
Na 1: 2 is a jealous and avenging **G**,
Zec 14: 5 Then the LORD my **G** will come,
Mal 3: 8 "Will a mere mortal rob **G**?
Mt 1:23 (which means "**G** with us")
5: 8 pure in heart, for they will see **G**.
6:24 You cannot serve both **G**
19: 6 Therefore what **G** has joined
19:26 but with **G** all things are possible."
22:21 Caesar's, and to **G** what is God's."
22:37 "'Love the Lord your **G** with all
27:46 (which means "My **G**, my **G**,
Mk 12:29 The Lord our **G**, the Lord is one.
16:19 *at the right hand of **G**.*
Lk 1:37 For no word from **G** will ever fail."
1:47 my spirit rejoices in **G** my Savior,
10: 9 'The kingdom of **G** has come near
10:27 "'Love the Lord your **G** with all
18:19 "No one is good–except **G** alone.
Jn 1: 1 and the Word was with **G**, and the Word was **G**.
1:18 No one has ever seen **G**, but
1:18 who is himself **G** and is in closest
3:16 For **G** so loved the world that he
4:24 **G** is spirit, and his worshipers must
7:17 to do the will of **G** will find
14: 1 You believe in **G**;
20:28 said to him, "My Lord and my **G**!"
Ac 2:24 But **G** raised him from the dead,
5: 4 lied just to human beings but to **G**."
5:29 "We must obey **G** rather than
7:55 to heaven and saw the glory of **G**,
17:23 inscription: TO AN UNKNOWN **G**.
20:27 to you the whole will of **G**.
20:32 "Now I commit you to **G**
Ro 1:17 righteousness of **G** is revealed–
2:11 For **G** does not show favoritism.
3: 4 Let **G** be true, and every human
3:23 and fall short of the glory of **G**,
4:24 **G** will credit righteousness–
5: 8 **G** demonstrates his own love for us
6:23 the gift of **G** is eternal life in Christ

Ro   8: 28 in all things **G** works for the good
      11: 22 the kindness and sternness of **G**:
      14: 12 give an account of ourselves to **G**.
1Co   1: 20 not **G** made foolish the wisdom
       2: 9 the things **G** has prepared for those
       3: 6 it, but **G** has been making it grow.
       6: 20 Therefore honor **G** with your
       7: 24 they were in when **G** called them.
       8: 8 food does not bring us near to **G**;
      10: 13 **G** is faithful; he will not let you
      10: 31 you do, do it all for the glory of **G**.
      14: 33 For **G** is not a **G** of disorder
      15: 28 him, so that **G** may be all in all.
2Co   1: 9 not rely on ourselves but on **G**,
       2: 14 But thanks be to **G**, who always
       3: 5 our competence comes from **G**.
       4: 7 this all-surpassing power is from **G**
       5: 19 that **G** was reconciling the world
       5: 21 become the righteousness of **G**.
       6: 16 we are the temple of the living **G**.
       9: 7 for **G** loves a cheerful giver.
       9: 8 **G** is able to bless you abundantly,
Gal   2: 6 **G** does not show favoritism–
       6: 7 **G** cannot be mocked.
Eph   2: 10 **G** prepared in advance for us
       4: 6 one **G** and Father of all, who is
Php   2: 6 being in very nature **G**, did not consider equal-
             ity with **G**
       4: 19 And my **G** will meet all your needs
1Th   2: 4 not trying to please people but **G**,
       4: 7 For **G** did not call us to be impure,
       4: 9 yourselves have been taught by **G**
       5: 9 For **G** did not appoint us to suffer
1Ti   2: 5 there is one **G** and one mediator
       4: 4 For everything **G** created is good,
       5: 4 for this is pleasing to **G**.
Titus 2: 13 of the glory of our great **G**
Heb   1: 1 the past **G** spoke to our ancestors
       4: 12 For the word of **G** is alive
       6: 10 **G** is not unjust; he will not forget
      10: 31 fall into the hands of the living **G**.
      11: 6 faith it is impossible to please **G**,
      12: 10 but **G** disciplines us for our good,
      12: 29 for our "**G** is a consuming fire."
      13: 15 us continually offer to **G** a sacrifice
Jas   1: 13 For **G** cannot be tempted by evil,
       2: 19 You believe that there is one **G**.
       2: 23 "Abraham believed **G**, and it was
       4: 4 the world becomes an enemy of **G**.
       4: 8 Come near to **G** and he will come
1Pe   4: 11 who speaks the very words of **G**.
2Pe   1: 21 from **G** as they were carried along
1Jn   1: 5 him and declare to you: **G** is light;
       2: 5 love for **G** is truly made complete
       3: 20 that **G** is greater than our hearts,
       4: 7 another, for love comes from **G**.
       4: 7 has been born of **G** and knows **G**.
       4: 9 This is how **G** showed his love
       4: 11 Dear friends, since **G** so loved us,
       4: 12 No one has ever seen **G**; but if we
       4: 16 Whoever lives in love lives in **G**,
Rev   4: 8 holy is the Lord **G** Almighty,'
       7: 17 **G** will wipe away every tear
      19: 6 For our Lord **G** Almighty reigns.

GOD-BREATHED (BREATHED)
2Ti   3: 16 All Scripture is **G** and is useful

GOD'S (GOD)
2Ch   20: 15 For the battle is not yours, but **G**.
Job   37: 14 stop and consider **G** wonders.
Ps   52: 8 I trust in **G** unfailing love for ever
      69: 30 I will praise **G** name in song
Mk   3: 35 Whoever does **G** will is my brother
Jn   10: 36 because I said, 'I am **G** Son'?
Ro   2: 3 think you will escape **G** judgment?
       2: 4 that **G** kindness is intended
       3: 3 nullify **G** faithfulness?
       7: 22 my inner being I delight in **G** law;

Ro   9: 16 desire or effort, but on **G** mercy.
      11: 29 for **G** gifts and his call are
      12: 2 test and approve what **G** will is–
      13: 6 for the authorities are **G** servants,
1Co   7: 19 Keeping **G** commands is what
2Co   6: 2 now is the time of **G** favor, now is
Eph   1: 7 with the riches of **G** grace
       5: 1 Follow **G** example, therefore,
1Th   4: 3 It is **G** will that you should be
       5: 18 for this is **G** will for you in Christ
1Ti   6: 1 so that **G** name and our teaching
2Ti   2: 19 **G** solid foundation stands firm,
Titus 1: 7 an overseer manages **G** household,
Heb   1: 3 The Son is the radiance of **G** glory
       9: 24 to appear for us in **G** presence.
      11: 3 was formed at **G** command,
1Pe   2: 15 For it is **G** will that by doing good
       3: 4 which is of great worth in **G** sight.

GODLINESS (GOD)
1Ti   2: 2 quiet lives in all **g** and holiness.
       4: 8 value, but **g** has value for all things,
       6: 6 **g** with contentment is great gain.
       6: 11 and pursue righteousness, **g**, faith,

GODLY (GOD)
2Co   7: 10 **G** sorrow brings repentance
      11: 2 jealous for you with a **g** jealousy.
2Ti   3: 12 live a **g** life in Christ Jesus will be
2Pe   3: 11 You ought to live holy and **g** lives

GODS (GOD)
Ex   20: 3 shall have no other **g** before me.
Ac   19: 26 by human hands are no **g** at all.

GOLD
Job   23: 10 tested me, I will come forth as **g**.
Ps   19: 10 precious than **g**, than much pure **g**;
      119:127 love your commands more than **g**,
Pr   22: 1 esteemed is better than silver or **g**.

GOLGOTHA
Jn   19: 17 (which in Aramaic is called **G**).

GOLIATH
      Philistine giant killed by David (1Sa 17; 21:9).

GOOD
Ge   1: 4 God saw that the light was **g**,
       1: 31 he had made, and it was very **g**.
       2: 18 "It is not **g** for the man to be alone.
      50: 20 God intended it for **g**
Job   2: 10 Shall we accept **g** from God,
Ps   14: 1 there is no one who does **g**.
      34: 8 Taste and see that the LORD is **g**;
      37: 3 Trust in the LORD and do **g**;
      84: 11 no **g** thing does he withhold
      86: 5 are forgiving and **g**,
     103: 5 your desires with **g** things so
     119: 68 You are **g**, and what you do is **g**;
     133: 1 How **g** and pleasant it is
     147: 1 How **g** it is to sing praises to our
Pr   3: 4 and a **g** name in the sight of God
      11: 27 Whoever seeks **g** finds favor,
      13: 21 are rewarded with **g** things.
      17: 22 A cheerful heart is **g** medicine,
      18: 22 He who finds a wife finds what is **g**
      22: 1 A **g** name is more desirable than
      31: 12 She brings him **g**, not harm,
Isa   5: 20 Woe to those who call evil **g** and **g**
      52: 7 the feet of those who bring **g** news,
Jer   6: 16 ask where the **g** way is, and walk
Mic   6: 8 shown you, O mortal, what is **g**.
Mt   5: 45 sun to rise on the evil and the **g**,
       7: 17 Likewise, every **g** tree bears **g** fruit,
      12: 35 A **g** man brings **g** things out of the **g**
      19: 17 "There is only One who is **g**.
      25: 21 'Well done, **g** and faithful servant!
Mk   3: 4 to do **g** or to do evil, to save life
       8: 36 What **g** is it for someone to gain
Lk   6: 27 do **g** to those who hate you,
Jn   10: 11 "I am the **g** shepherd. The **g**

Ro   8: 28   for the **g** of those who love him,
     10: 15   feet of those who bring **g** news!"
     12:   9   Hate what is evil; cling to what is **g**.
1Co   10: 24   their own **g**, but the **g** of others.
     15: 33   company corrupts **g** character."
2Co   9:   8   you will abound in every **g** work.
Gal   6:   9   us not become weary in doing **g**,
     6: 10   let us do **g** to all people,
Eph   2: 10   in Christ Jesus to do **g** works,
Php   1:   6   he who began a **g** work in you will
1Th   5: 21   test them all; hold on to what is **g**,
2Th   3: 13   never tire of doing what is **g**.
1Ti   3:   7   have a **g** reputation with outsiders,
     4:   4   For everything God created is **g**,
     6: 12   Fight the **g** fight of the faith.
     6: 18   do **g**, to be rich in **g** deeds,
2Ti   3: 17   equipped for every **g** work.
     4:   7   I have fought the **g** fight, I have
Heb   12: 10   but God disciplines us for our **g**,
1Pe   2:   3   you have tasted that the Lord is **g**.
     2: 12   Live such **g** lives among the pagans

GOSPEL
Ro   1: 16   For I am not ashamed of the **g**,
     15: 16   duty of proclaiming the **g** of God,
1Co   1: 17   to baptize, but to preach the **g**–
     9: 16   Woe to me if I do not preach the **g**!
     15:   1   to remind you of the **g** I preached
Gal   1:   7   trying to pervert the **g** of Christ.
Php   1: 27   a manner worthy of the **g** of Christ.
     1: 27   as one for the faith of the **g**

GOSSIP
Pr   11: 13   A **g** betrays a confidence,
     16: 28   and a **g** separates close friends.
     18:   8   of a **g** are like choice morsels;
     26: 20   without a **g** a quarrel dies down.
2Co   12: 20   slander, **g**, arrogance and disorder.

GOVERNED
Ro   8:   6   the mind **g** by the Spirit is life

GRACE (GRACIOUS)
Ps   45:   2   lips have been anointed with **g**,
Jn   1: 17   **g** and truth came through Jesus
Ac   20: 32   to God and to the word of his **g**,
Ro   3: 24   by his **g** through the redemption
     5: 15   that came by the **g** of the one man,
     5: 17   God's abundant provision of **g**
     5: 20   increased, **g** increased all the more,
     6: 14   are not under the law, but under **g**.
     11:   6   if it were, **g** would no longer be **g**.
2Co   6:   1   you not to receive God's **g** in vain.
     8:   9   you know the **g** of our Lord Jesus
     12:   9   to me, "My **g** is sufficient for you,
Gal   2: 21   I do not set aside the **g** of God,
     5:   4   you have fallen away from **g**.
Eph   1:   7   with the riches of God's **g**
     2:   5   it is by **g** you have been saved.
     2:   7   the incomparable riches of his **g**,
     2:   8   For it is by **g** you have been saved,
Php   1:   7   all of you share in God's **g** with me.
Col   4:   6   conversation be always full of **g**,
2Th   2: 16   **g** gave us eternal encouragement
2Ti   2:   1   be strong in the **g** that is in Christ
Titus   2: 11   For the **g** of God has appeared
     3:   7   having been justified by his **g**,
Heb   2:   9   the **g** of God he might taste death
     4: 16   approach God's throne of **g**
     4: 16   **g** to help us in our time of need.
Jas   4:   6   But he gives us more **g**. That is why
2Pe   3: 18   grow in the **g** and knowledge of

GRACIOUS (GRACE)
Nu   6: 25   face shine on you and be **g** to you;
Isa   30: 18   the LORD longs to be **g** to you;

GRAIN
Ecc   11:   1   Ship your **g** across the sea;
1Co   9:   9   an ox while it is treading out the **g**."

GRANTED
Php   1: 29   For it has been **g** to you on behalf

GRASS
Ps   103: 15   The life of mortals is like **g**,
1Pe   1: 24   the **g** withers and the flowers fall,

GRAVE (GRAVES)
Pr   7: 27   Her house is a highway to the **g**,
Hos   13: 14   Where, O **g**, is your destruction?

GRAVES (GRAVE)
Jn   5: 28   are in their **g** will hear his voice
Ro   3: 13   "Their throats are open **g**;

GREAT (GREATER GREATEST GREATNESS)
Ge   12:   2   "I will make you into a **g** nation,
Dt   10: 17   gods and Lord of lords, the **g** God,
2Sa   22: 36   your help has made me **g**.
Ps   19: 11   in keeping them there is **g** reward.
     89:   1   sing of the LORD's **g** love forever;
     103: 11   so **g** is his love for those who fear
     108:   4   For **g** is your love, higher than
     119:165   **G** peace have those who love your
     145:   3   **G** is the LORD and most worthy
Pr   23: 24   father of a righteous child has **g** joy
Isa   42: 21   his righteousness to make his law **g**
La   3: 23   **g** is your faithfulness.
Mk   10: 43   become **g** among you must be your
Lk   21: 27   in a cloud with power and **g** glory.
1Ti   6:   6   with contentment is **g** gain.
Titus   2: 13   appearing of the glory of our **g** God
Heb   2:   3   if we ignore so **g** a salvation?
1Jn   3:   1   See what **g** love the Father has

GREATER (GREAT)
Mk   12: 31   is no commandment **g** than these."
Jn   1: 50   You will see **g** things than that."
     15: 13   **G** love has no one than this:
1Co   12: 31   Now eagerly desire the **g** gifts.
Heb   11: 26   as of **g** value than the treasures
1Jn   3: 20   that God is **g** than our hearts,
     4:   4   is in you is **g** than the one who is

GREATEST (GREAT)
Mt   22: 38   is the first and **g** commandment.
Lk   9: 48   least among you all who is the **g**."
1Co   13: 13   But the **g** of these is love.

GREATNESS (GREAT)
Ps   145:   3   his **g** no one can fathom.
     150:   2   praise him for his surpassing **g**.
Isa   9:   7   the **g** of his government and peace
     63:   1   forward in the **g** of his strength?

GREED (GREEDY)
Lk   12: 15   guard against all kinds of **g**;
Ro   1: 29   wickedness, evil, **g** and depravity.
Eph   5:   3   or of **g**, because these are improper
Col   3:   5   desires and **g**, which is idolatry.
2Pe   2: 14   they are experts in **g**–

GREEDY (GREED)
Pr   15: 27   The **g** bring ruin to their
1Co   6: 10   thieves nor the **g** nor drunkards
Eph   5:   5   No immoral, impure or **g** person–

GREEN
Ps   23:   2   makes me lie down in **g** pastures,

GREW (GROW)
Lk   2: 52   And Jesus **g** in wisdom and stature,
Ac   16:   5   in the faith and **g** daily in numbers.

GRIEF (GRIEVE)
Ps   10: 14   you consider their **g** and take it
Pr   14: 13   ache, and rejoicing may end in **g**.
La   3: 32   Though he brings **g**, he will show
Jn   16: 20   grieve, but your **g** will turn to joy.
1Pe   1:   6   have had to suffer **g** in all kinds

GRIEVE (GRIEF)
Eph   4: 30   do not **g** the Holy Spirit of God,
1Th   4: 13   so that you do not **g** like the rest

GROUND
Ge   3: 17   it,' "Cursed is the **g** because of you;
Ex   3:   5   where you are standing is holy **g**."
Eph   6: 13   you may be able to stand your **g**,

GROW (GREW)
Pr   13: 11 money little by little makes it **g**.
1Co   3: 6 it, but God has been making it **g**.
2Pe   3: 18 But **g** in the grace and knowledge

GRUMBLE (GRUMBLING)
1Co 10: 10 do not **g**, as some of them did–
Jas   5: 9 Don't **g** against one another,

GRUMBLING (GRUMBLE)
Jn   6: 43 "Stop **g** among yourselves,"
1Pe   4: 9 hospitality to one another without **g**.

GUARANTEEING (GUARANTOR)
2Co   1: 22 as a deposit, **g** what is to come.
Eph   1: 14 is a deposit **g** our inheritance until

GUARANTOR (GUARANTEEING)
Heb   7: 22 Jesus has become the **g** of a better

GUARD (GUARDIAN, GUARDIAN-REDEEMER)
Ps 141: 3 Set a **g** over my mouth, Lord;
Pr   4: 23 Above all else, **g** your heart,
     13: 3 Those who **g** their lips preserve
     21: 23 Those who **g** their mouths and
Isa 52: 12 God of Israel will be your rear **g**.
Mk   13: 33 Be on **g**! Be alert! You do not know
1Co 16: 13 Be on your **g**; stand firm
Php   4: 7 will **g** your hearts and your minds
1Ti   6: 20 **g** what has been entrusted to your

GUARDIAN (GUARD)
Gal   3: 25 come, we are no longer under a **g**.

GUARDIAN-REDEEMER (GUARD)
Ru   3: 9 since you are a **g** of our family."

GUIDE
Ex   13: 21 of cloud to **g** them on their way
     15: 13 In your strength you will **g** them
Ne   9: 19 cloud did not fail to **g** them on
Ps   25: 5 **G** me in your truth and teach me,
     48: 14 he will be our **g** even to the end.
     67: 4 and **g** the nations of the earth.
     73: 24 You **g** me with your counsel,
    139: 10 even there your hand will **g** me,
Pr   6: 22 When you walk, they will **g** you;
Isa 58: 11 The Lord will **g** you always;
Jn   16: 13 he will **g** you into all the truth.

GUILTY
Ex   34: 7 does not leave the **g** unpunished;
Jn   8: 46 Can any of you prove me **g** of sin?
Heb 10: 22 to cleanse us from a **g** conscience
Jas   2: 10 at just one point is **g** of breaking all

HADES
Mt   16: 18 the gates of **H** will not overcome it.
Lk   16: 23 In **H**, where he was in torment,

HAGAR
   Servant of Sarah, wife of Abraham, mother of Ishmael (Ge 16:1-6; 25:12). Driven away by Sarah while pregnant (Ge 16:5-16); after birth of Isaac (Ge 21:9-21; Gal 4:21-31).

HAGGAI
   Post-exilic prophet who encouraged rebuilding of the temple (Ezr 5:1; 6:14; Hag 1-2).

HAIR (HAIRS)
Lk   21: 18 not a **h** of your head will perish.
1Co 11: 6 for a woman to have her **h** cut off

HAIRS (HAIR)
Mt   10: 30 even the very **h** of your head are all

HALLELUJAH
Rev 19: 1, multitude in heaven shouting: "**H**!

HALLOWED (HOLY)
Mt   6: 9 Father in heaven, **h** be your name,

HAND (HANDIWORK HANDS)
Ps   16: 8 With him at my right **h**, I will not
     37: 24 the Lord upholds him with his **h**.
    139: 10 even there your **h** will guide me,
Ecc   9: 10 Whatever your **h** finds to do, do it
Mt   6: 3 not let your left **h** know what your right **h** is
                doing,
Jn   10: 28 one will snatch them out of my **h**.
1Co 12: 15 say, "Because I am not a **h**, I do not

HANDIWORK (HAND)
Eph   2: 10 For we are God's **h**,

HANDS (HAND)
Ps   22: 16 they pierce my **h** and my feet.
     24: 4 one who has clean **h** and a pure
     31: 5 Into your **h** I commit my spirit;
     31: 15 My times are in your **h**;
Pr   10: 4 but diligent **h** bring wealth.
     31: 20 and extends her **h** to the needy.
Isa 55: 12 trees of the field will clap their **h**.
     65: 2 out my **h** to an obstinate people,
Lk   23: 46 into your **h** I commit my spirit."
1Th   4: 11 business and work with your **h**,
1Ti   2: 8 lifting up holy **h** without anger
      5: 22 not be hasty in the laying on of **h**,

HANNAH
   Wife of Elkanah, mother of Samuel (1Sa 1). Prayer at dedication of Samuel (1Sa 2:1-10). Blessed (1Sa 2:18-21).

HAPPY
Ps   68: 3 may they be **h** and joyful.
Pr   15: 13 A **h** heart makes the face cheerful,
Ecc   3: 12 better for people than to be **h**
Jas   5: 13 Is anyone **h**? Let them sing songs

HARD (HARDEN HARDSHIP)
Ge   18: 14 Is anything too **h** for the Lord?
Ps 118: 5 When **h** pressed, I cried
Mt   19: 23 it is **h** for someone who is rich
1Co   4: 12 We work **h** with our own hands.
1Th   5: 12 those who work **h** among you,

HARDEN (HARD)
Ro   9: 18 he hardens whom he wants to **h**.
Heb   3: 8 do not **h** your hearts as you did

HARDHEARTED (HEART)
Dt   15: 7 do not be **h** or tightfisted toward

HARDSHIP (HARD)
Ro   8: 35 Shall trouble or **h** or persecution
2Ti   4: 5 endure **h**, do the work
Heb 12: 7 Endure **h** as discipline;

HARM
Ps 121: 6 the sun will not **h** you by day,
Pr   3: 29 not plot **h** against your neighbor,
     31: 12 good, not **h**, all the days of her life.
Ro   13: 10 Love does no **h** to a neighbor.
1Jn   5: 18 and the evil one cannot **h** them.

HARMONY
Ro   12: 16 Live in **h** with one another.
2Co   6: 15 What **h** is there between Christ

HARVEST
Mt   9: 37 "The **h** is plentiful but the workers
Jn   4: 35 at the fields! They are ripe for **h**.
Gal   6: 9 at the proper time we will reap a **h**
Heb 12: 11 it produces a **h** of righteousness

HASTE (HASTY)
Pr   21: 5 lead to profit as surely as **h** leads
     29: 20 you see someone who speaks in **h**?

HASTY (HASTE)
Pr   19: 2 how much more will **h** feet miss
Ecc   5: 2 do not be **h** in your heart to utter
1Ti   5: 22 Do not be **h** in the laying

HATE (HATED HATES HATRED)
Lev 19: 17 "'Do not **h** a fellow Israelite
Ps   5: 5 You **h** all who do wrong;
     45: 7 righteousness and **h** wickedness;
     97: 10 those who love the Lord **h** evil,
    139: 21 Do I not **h** those who **h** you,
Pr   8: 13 To fear the Lord is to **h** evil; I **h**
Am   5: 15 **H** evil, love good;
Mt   5: 43 your neighbor and **h** your enemy.'
Lk   6: 27 do good to those who **h** you,
Ro   12: 9 **H** what is evil; cling to what is

HATED (HATE)
Mt   10: 22 be **h** by everyone because of me,
Ro   9: 13 "Jacob I loved, but Esau I **h**."

Eph   5: 29 all, no one ever **h** their own body,
Heb   1: 9 righteousness and **h** wickedness;

HATES (HATE)
Pr   6: 16 There are six things the LORD **h**,
      13: 24 spares the rod **h** their children,
Mal   2: 16 "The man who **h** and divorces his
Jn   3: 20 Everyone who does evil **h** the light,
1Jn   2: 9 to be in the light but **h** a brother

HATRED (HATE)
Pr   10: 12 **H** stirs up conflict, but love covers

HAUGHTY
Pr   16: 18 destruction, a **h** spirit before a fall.

HAY
1Co   3: 12 costly stones, wood, **h** or straw,

HEAD (HEADS HOTHEADED)
Ge   3: 15 he will crush your **h**, and you will
Ps   23: 5 You anoint my **h** with oil;
Pr   25: 22 will heap burning coals on his **h**,
Isa   59: 17 the helmet of salvation on his **h**;
Mt   8: 20 of Man has no place to lay his **h**."
Ro   12: 20 will heap burning coals on his **h**."
1Co   11: 3 the **h** of every man is Christ, and the **h** of the
              woman is man, and the **h** of Christ is God.
      12: 21 And the **h** cannot say to the feet,
Eph   5: 23 the husband is the **h** of the wife as Christ is
              the **h**
2Ti   4: 5 keep your **h** in all situations,
Rev   19: 12 fire, and on his **h** are many crowns.

HEADS (HEAD)
Lev   26: 13 you to walk with **h** held high.
Isa   35: 10 everlasting joy will crown their **h**.

HEAL (HEALED HEALING HEALS)
2Ch   7: 14 their sin and will **h** their land.
Ps   41: 4 **h** me, for I have sinned against
Mt   10: 8 **H** the sick, raise the dead,
Lk   4: 23 'Physician, **h** yourself!'
       5: 17 Lord was with Jesus to **h** the sick.

HEALED (HEAL)
Isa   53: 5 him, and by his wounds we are **h**.
Mt   9: 22 he said, "your faith has **h** you."
      14: 36 and all who touched it were **h**.
Ac   4: 10 that this man stands before you **h**.
      14: 9 saw that he had faith to be **h**
Jas   5: 16 each other so that you may be **h**.
1Pe   2: 24 "by his wounds you have been **h**."

HEALING (HEAL)
Eze   47: 12 for food and their leaves for **h**."
Mal   4: 2 righteousness will rise with **h** in its
1Co   12: 9 to another gifts of **h** by that one
      12: 30 Do all have gifts of **h**? Do all speak
Rev   22: 2 the tree are for the **h** of the nations.

HEALS (HEAL)
Ex   15: 26 for I am the LORD, who **h** you."
Ps   103: 3 your sins and **h** all your diseases,
     147: 3 He **h** the brokenhearted and binds

HEALTH (HEALTHY)
Pr   3: 8 This will bring **h** to your body
      15: 30 good news gives **h** to the bones.

HEALTHY (HEALTH)
Mk   2: 17 "It is not the **h** who need a doctor,

HEAR (HEARD HEARING HEARS)
Dt   6: 4 **H**, O Israel: The LORD our God,
      31: 13 law, must **h** it and learn to fear
2Ch   7: 14 then I will **h** from heaven,
Ps   94: 9 he who fashioned the ear not **h**?
Isa   29: 18 day the deaf will **h** the words
      65: 24 they are still speaking I will **h**.
Mt   11: 15 Whoever has ears, let them **h**.
Jn   8: 47 The reason you do not **h** is that
2Ti   4: 3 what their itching ears want to **h**.

HEARD (HEAR)
Job   42: 5 My ears had **h** of you but now my
Isa   66: 8 Who has ever **h** of such things?

Mt   5: 21 "You have **h** that it was said
       5: 27 "You have **h** that it was said,
       5: 33 you have **h** that it was said
       5: 38 "You have **h** that it was said,
       5: 43 "You have **h** that it was said,
1Co   2: 9 what no ear has **h**, and what no
1Th   2: 13 which you **h** from us, you accepted
2Ti   1: 13 What you **h** from me, keep as
Jas   1: 25 not forgetting what they have **h**,

HEARING (HEAR)
Ro   10: 17 faith comes from **h** the message,

HEARS (HEAR)
Jn   5: 24 whoever **h** my word and believes
1Jn   5: 14 according to his will, he **h** us.
Rev   3: 20 If anyone **h** my voice and opens

HEART (BROKENHEARTED HARDHEARTED
HEARTS WHOLEHEARTEDLY)
Ex   25: 2 everyone whose **h** prompts them
Lev   19: 17 not hate a fellow Israelite in your **h**.
Dt   4: 29 him if you seek him with all your **h**
       6: 5 LORD your God with all your **h**
      10: 12 LORD your God with all your **h**
      15: 10 and do so without a grudging **h**;
      30: 6 you may love him with all your **h**
      30: 10 LORD your God with all your **h**
Jos   22: 5 and to serve him with all your **h**
1Sa   13: 14 sought out a man after his own **h**
      16: 7 but the LORD looks at the **h**."
2Ki   23: 3 and decrees with all his **h** and
1Ch   28: 9 for the LORD searches every **h**
2Ch   7: 16 eyes and my **h** will always be there.
Job   22: 22 and lay up his words in your **h**.
      37: 1 "At this my **h** pounds and leaps
Ps   14: 1 says in his **h**, "There is no God."
      19: 14 this meditation of my **h** be pleasing
      37: 4 will give you the desires of your **h**.
      45: 1 My **h** is stirred by a noble theme as
      51: 10 Create in me a pure **h**, O God,
      51: 17 a broken and contrite **h** you, God,
      66: 18 If I had cherished sin in my **h**,
      86: 11 give me an undivided **h**, that I may
     119: 11 in my **h** that I might not sin against
     139: 23 Search me, God, and know my **h**;
Pr   3: 5 Trust in the LORD with all your **h**
       4: 21 sight, keep them within your **h**;
       4: 23 guard your **h**, for everything you
       7: 3 write them on the tablet of your **h**.
      13: 12 Hope deferred makes the **h** sick,
      14: 13 Even in laughter the **h** may ache,
      15: 30 eyes brings joy to the **h**, and good
      17: 22 A cheerful **h** is good medicine,
      24: 17 stumble, do not let your **h** rejoice,
      27: 19 the face, so one's life reflects the **h**.
Ecc   3: 11 also set eternity in the human **h**;
       8: 5 the wise **h** will know the proper
SS   4: 9 You have stolen my **h**, my sister,
Isa   40: 11 and carries them close to his **h**;
      57: 15 and to revive the **h** of the contrite.
Jer   17: 9 The **h** is deceitful above all things
      29: 13 when you seek me with all your **h**.
Eze   36: 26 I will give you a new **h** and put
Mt   5: 8 Blessed are the pure in **h**, for they
       6: 21 treasure is, there your **h** will be
      12: 34 mouth speaks what the **h** is full of.
      22: 37 the Lord your God with all your **h**
Lk   6: 45 mouth speaks what the **h** is full of.
Ro   2: 29 is circumcision of the **h**,
      10: 10 it is with your **h** that you believe
Eph   5: 19 music from your **h** to the Lord,
       6: 6 doing the will of God from your **h**.
Col   3: 23 you do, work at it with all your **h**,
1Pe   1: 22 one another deeply, from the **h**.

HEARTS (HEART)
Dt   11: 18 Fix these words of mine in your **h**
1Ki   8: 39 do, since you know their **h** (for you
       8: 61 may your **h** be fully committed

Ps   62: 8 pour out your **h** to him, for God is
Jer   31: 33 their minds and write it on their **h**.
Lk   16: 15 of others, but God knows your **h**.
      24: 32 "Were not our **h** burning within us
Jn   14: 1 "Do not let your **h** be troubled.
Ac   15: 9 for he purified their **h** by faith.
Ro   2: 15 of the law are written on their **h**,
1Co   14: 25 the secrets of their **h** are laid bare.
2Co   3: 2 written on our **h**, known and read
       3: 3 of stone but on tablets of human **h**.
       4: 6 shine in our **h** to give us the light
Eph   3: 17 may dwell in your **h** through faith.
Col   3: 1 Christ, set your **h** on things above,
Heb   3: 8 do not harden your **h** as you did
      10: 16 I will put my laws in their **h**, and I
1Jn   3: 20 that God is greater than our **h**,

HEAT
2Pe   3: 12 and the elements will melt in the **h**.

HEAVEN (HEAVENLY HEAVENS)
Ge   14: 19 Most High, Creator of **h** and earth.
1Ki   8: 27 even the highest **h**, cannot contain
2Ki   2: 1 take Elijah up to **h** in a whirlwind,
2Ch   7: 14 then I will hear from **h**, and I will
Isa   14: 12 How you have fallen from **h**,
      66: 1 "**H** is my throne, and the earth is
Da   7: 13 man, coming with the clouds of **h**.
Mt   6: 9 "'Our Father in **h**, hallowed be
       6: 20 up for yourselves treasures in **h**,
      16: 19 you the keys of the kingdom of **h**;
      16: 19 bind on earth will be bound in **h**,
      19: 23 is rich to enter the kingdom of **h**.
      24: 35 **H** and earth will pass away, but my
      26: 64 and coming on the clouds of **h**."
      28: 18 "All authority in **h** and on earth has
Mk   16: 19 *was taken up into* **h**
Lk   15: 7 **h** over one sinner who repents
      18: 22 and you will have treasure in **h**.
Ro   10: 6 heart, 'Who will ascend into **h**?'"
2Co   5: 1 an eternal house in **h**, not built
      12: 2 ago was caught up to the third **h**.
Php   2: 10 in **h** and on earth and under
       3: 20 But our citizenship is in **h**.
1Th   1: 10 and to wait for his Son from **h**,
Heb   8: 5 a copy and shadow of what is in **h**.
       9: 24 he entered **h** itself, now to appear
2Pe   3: 13 we are looking forward to a new **h**
Rev   21: 1 I saw "a new **h** and a new earth,"

HEAVENLY (HEAVEN)
2Co   5: 2 clothed instead with our **h** dwelling,
Eph   1: 3 who has blessed us in the **h** realms
       1: 20 at his right hand in the **h** realms,
2Ti   4: 18 bring me safely to his **h** kingdom.
Heb   12: 22 of the living God, the **h** Jerusalem.

HEAVENS (HEAVEN)
Ge   1: 1 In the beginning God created the **h**
1Ki   8: 27 The **h**, even the highest heaven,
2Ch   2: 6 since the **h**, even the highest **h**,
Ps   8: 3 When I consider your **h**, the work
      19: 1 The **h** declare the glory of God;
     102: 25 the **h** are the work of your hands.
     108: 4 is your love, higher than the **h**;
     119: 89 it stands firm in the **h**.
     139: 8 If I go up to the **h**, you are there;
Isa   51: 6 the **h** will vanish like smoke,
      55: 9 "As the **h** are higher than the earth,
      65: 17 will create new **h** and a new earth.
Joel   2: 30 I will show wonders in the **h**
Eph   4: 10 ascended higher than all the **h**,
2Pe   3: 10 The **h** will disappear with a roar;

HEBREW
Ge   14: 13 and reported this to Abram the **H**.

HEEDS
Pr   13: 1 A wise son **h** his father's
      13: 18 whoever **h** correction is honored.
      15: 5 but whoever **h** correction shows
      15: 32 but the one who **h** correction gains

HEEL
Ge   3: 15 head, and you will strike his **h**."

HEIRS (INHERIT)
Ro   8: 17 **h** of God and co-heirs with Christ,
Gal   3: 29 and **h** according to the promise.
Eph   3: 6 gospel the Gentiles are **h** together
1Pe   3: 7 as **h** with you of the gracious gift

HELL
Mt   5: 22 will be in danger of the fire of **h**.
2Pe   2: 4 but sent them to **h**, putting them

HELMET
Isa   59: 17 and the **h** of salvation on his head;
Eph   6: 17 Take the **h** of salvation
1Th   5: 8 and the hope of salvation as a **h**.

HELP (HELPED HELPER HELPING HELPS)
2Sa   22: 36 You make your saving **h** my shield;
Ps   18: 6 I cried to my God for **h**.
      30: 2 called to you for **h**, and you healed
      46: 1 an ever-present **h** in trouble.
      70: 4 long for your saving **h** always say,
      79: 9 **H** us, God our Savior, for the glory
     121: 1 where does my **h** come from?
Isa   41: 10 I will strengthen you and **h** you;
Jnh   2: 2 the realm of the dead I called for **h**,
Mk   9: 24 **h** me overcome my unbelief!"
Ac   16: 9 over to Macedonia and **h** us."

HELPED (HELP)
1Sa   7: 12 "Thus far the LORD has **h** us."

HELPER (HELP)
Ge   2: 18 I will make a **h** suitable for him."
Ps   10: 14 you are the **h** of the fatherless.
Heb   13: 6 confidence, "The Lord is my **h**;

HELPING (HELP)
Ac   9: 36 always doing good and **h** the poor.
1Co   12: 28 gifts of healing, of **h**, of guidance,
1Ti   5: 10 **h** those in trouble and devoting

HELPS (HELP)
Ro   8: 26 the Spirit **h** us in our weakness.

HEN
Mt   23: 37 as a **h** gathers her chicks under her

HERITAGE (INHERIT)
Ps   127: 3 Children are a **h** from the LORD,

HEROD
1. King of Judea who tried to kill Jesus (Mt 2; Lk 1:5).
2. Son of 1. Tetrarch of Galilee who arrested and beheaded John the Baptist (Mt 14:1-12; Mk 6:14-29; Lk 3:1, 19-20; 9:7-9); tried Jesus (Lk 23:6-15).
3. Grandson of 1. King of Judea who killed James (Ac 12:2); arrested Peter (Ac 12:3-19). Death (Ac 12:19-23).

HERODIAS
Wife of Herod the Tetrarch who persuaded her daughter to ask for John the Baptist's head (Mt 14:1-12; Mk 6:14-29).

HEZEKIAH
King of Judah. Restored the temple and worship (2Ch 29-31). Sought the LORD for help against Assyria (2Ki 18-19; 2Ch 32:1-23; Isa 36-37). Illness healed (2Ki 20:1-11; 2Ch 32:24-26; Isa 38). Judged for showing Babylonians his treasures (2Ki 20:12-21; 2Ch 32:31; Isa 39).

HID (HIDE)
Ge   3: 8 they **h** from the LORD God among
Ex   2: 2 child, she **h** him for three months.
Jos   6: 17 because she **h** the spies we sent.
Heb   11: 23 faith Moses' parents **h** him for

HIDDEN (HIDE)
Ps   19: 12 Forgive my **h** faults.
     119: 11 I have **h** your word in my heart
Pr   2: 4 and search for it as for **h** treasure,
Isa   59: 2 your sins have **h** his face from you,
Mt   5: 14 A town built on a hill cannot be **h**.
      13: 44 heaven is like treasure **h** in a field.
Col   1: 26 that has been kept **h** for ages
       2: 3 in whom are **h** all the treasures
       3: 3 and your life is now **h** with Christ

HIDE (HID HIDDEN)
Ps   17: 8 **h** me in the shadow of your wings
   143: 9 Lord, for I **h** myself in you.

HIGH
Isa 57: 15 "I live in a **h** and holy place,

HILL (HILLS)
Mt   5: 14 town built on a **h** cannot be hidden.

HILLS (HILL)
Ps   50: 10 and the cattle on a thousand **h**.

HINDER (HINDERS)
1Sa 14: 6 Nothing can **h** the Lord
Mt   19: 14 do not **h** them, for the kingdom
1Co   9: 12 anything rather than **h** the gospel
1Pe   3: 7 so that nothing will **h** your prayers.

HINDERS (HINDER)
Heb 12: 1 let us throw off everything that **h**

HINT
Eph   5: 3 you there must not be even a **h**

HOLD
Ex   20: 7 Lord will not **h** anyone guiltless
Lev 19: 13 "'Do not **h** back the wages
Jos 22: 5 to **h** fast to him and to serve him
Ps   73: 23 you **h** me by my right hand.
Pr   4: 4 "Take **h** of my words with all your
Isa 54: 2 tent curtains wide, do not **h** back;
Mk   11: 25 if you **h** anything against anyone,
Php   2: 16 as you **h** firmly to the word of life.
    3: 12 which Christ Jesus took **h** of me.
Col   1: 17 and in him all things **h** together.
1Th   5: 21 test them all; **h** on to what is good,
1Ti   6: 12 Take **h** of the eternal life
Heb 10: 23 Let us **h** unswervingly to the hope

HOLINESS (HOLY)
Ex   15: 11 majestic in **h**, awesome in glory,
Ps   29: 2 the Lord in the splendor of his **h**.
   96: 9 the Lord in the splendor of his **h**;
Ro   6: 19 to righteousness leading to **h**.
2Co   7: 1 perfecting **h** out of reverence
Eph   4: 24 God in true righteousness and **h**.
Heb 12: 10 in order that we may share in his **h**.
   12: 14 without **h** no one will see the Lord.

HOLY (HALLOWED HOLINESS)
Ex   19: 6 kingdom of priests and a **h** nation.'
   20: 8 the Sabbath day by keeping it **h**.
Lev 11: 44 and be **h**, because I am **h**.
   20: 7 yourselves and be **h**, because I am
  20: 26 You are to be **h** to me because I,
  21: 8 Lord am **h**–I who make you **h**.
  22: 32 Do not profane my **h** name,
Ps   24: 3 Who may stand in his **h** place?
  77: 13 Your ways, God, are **h**. What god is
  99: 3 great and awesome name–he is **h**.
  99: 5 worship at his footstool; he is **h**.
  99: 9 for the Lord our God is **h**.
 111: 9 **h** and awesome is his name.
Isa   5: 16 the **h** God will be proved **h** by his
   6: 3 "**H, h, h** is the Lord Almighty;
  40: 25 who is my equal?" says the **H** One.
  57: 15 who lives forever, whose name is **h**:
Eze 28: 25 I will be proved **h** through them
Da   9: 24 and to anoint the Most **H** Place.
Hab   2: 20 The Lord is in his **h** temple;
Ac   2: 27 will not let your **h** one see decay.
Ro   7: 12 the law is **h**, and the commandment is **h**,
   12: 1 sacrifice, **h** and pleasing to God–
2Th   1: 10 to be glorified in his **h** people
2Ti   1: 9 saved us and called us to a **h** life–
   3: 15 you have known the **H** Scriptures,
Titus 1: 8 upright, **h** and disciplined.
1Pe   1: 15 is **h**, so be **h** in all you do;
   1: 16 "Be **h**, because I am **h**."
   2: 9 a royal priesthood, a **h** nation,
2Pe   3: 11 You ought to live **h** and godly lives
Rev   4: 8 "'**H, h, h** is the Lord God

HOME (HOMES)
Dt   6: 7 Talk about them when you sit at **h**
Ps   84: 3 Even the sparrow has found a **h**,
Pr   3: 33 he blesses the **h** of the righteous.
Mk   10: 29 "no one who has left **h** or brothers
Jn   14: 23 and make our **h** with them.
Titus 2: 5 pure, to be busy at **h**, to be kind,

HOMES (HOME)
Ne   4: 14 daughters, your wives and your **h**."
1Ti   5: 14 to manage their **h** and to give

HOMOSEXUALITY
1Ti   1: 10 for those practicing **h**, for slave

HONEST
Lev 19: 36 **h** weights, an **h** ephah and an **h** hin.
Dt   25: 15 must have accurate and **h** weights
Job 31: 6 let God weigh me in **h** scales and
Pr   12: 17 An **h** witness tells the truth,

HONEY
Ex   3: 8 a land flowing with milk and **h**–
Ps   19: 10 they are sweeter than **h**, than **h**
 119:103 taste, sweeter than **h** to my mouth!

HONOR (HONORABLE HONORABLY HONORED HONORS)
Ex   20: 12 "**H** your father and your mother,
Nu   25: 13 he was zealous for the **h** of his God
Dt   5: 16 "**H** your father and your mother,
1Sa   2: 30 Those who **h** me I will **h**, but those
Ps   8: 5 crowned them with glory and **h**.
Pr   3: 9 **H** the Lord with your wealth,
  11: 16 A kindhearted woman gains **h**,
  15: 33 and humility comes before **h**.
  20: 3 It is to one's **h** to avoid strife,
  31: 31 **H** her for all that her hands have
Mt   15: 4 '**H** your father and mother'
Ro   12: 10 **H** one another above yourselves.
1Co   6: 20 Therefore **h** God with your bodies.
Eph   6: 2 "**H** your father and mother"–
1Ti   5: 17 church well are worthy of double **h**,
Heb   2: 7 crowned them with glory and **h**
Rev   4: 9 **h** and thanks to him who sits

HONORABLE (HONOR)
1Th   4: 4 body in a way that is holy and **h**,

HONORABLY (HONOR)
Heb 13: 18 and desire to live **h** in every way.

HONORED (HONOR)
Ps   12: 8 what is vile is **h** by the human race.
Pr   13: 18 but whoever heeds correction is **h**.
1Co 12: 26 if one part is **h**, every part rejoices
Heb 13: 4 Marriage should be **h** by all,

HONORS (HONOR)
Ps   15: 4 but **h** those who fear the Lord;
Pr   14: 31 is kind to the needy **h** God.
3Jn   6 their way in a manner that **h** God.

HOOKS
Isa   2: 4 and their spears into pruning **h**.
Joel   3: 10 and your pruning **h** into spears.

HOPE (HOPES)
Job 13: 15 he slay me, yet will I **h** in him;
Ps   42: 5 Put your **h** in God, for I will yet
  62: 5 rest in God; my **h** comes from him.
 119: 74 for I have put my **h** in your word.
 130: 7 Israel, put your **h** in the Lord,
 147: 11 put their **h** in his unfailing love.
Pr   13: 12 **H** deferred makes the heart sick,
Isa 40: 31 but those who **h** in the Lord will
Ro   5: 4 and character, **h**.
   8: 24 But **h** that is seen is no **h** at all.
  12: 12 Be joyful in **h**, patient in affliction,
  15: 4 they provide we might have **h**
1Co 13: 13 three remain: faith, **h** and love.
  15: 19 for this life we have **h** in Christ,
Col   1: 27 is Christ in you, the **h** of glory.
1Th   5: 8 and the **h** of salvation as a helmet.
1Ti   6: 17 to put their **h** in God, who richly

Titus 2: 13 while we wait for the blessed **h**−
Heb 6: 19 We have this **h** as an anchor
 11: 1 faith is confidence in what we **h**
1Jn 3: 3 All who have this **h** in him purify

HOPES (HOPE)
1Co 13: 7 trusts, always **h**, always perseveres.

HORSE
Ps 147: 10 is not in the strength of the **h**,
Pr 26: 3 A whip for the **h**, a bridle
Zec 1: 8 me was a man mounted on a red **h**.
Rev 6: 2 and there before me was a white **h**!
 6: 4 Then another **h** came out, a fiery
 6: 5 and there before me was a black **h**!
 6: 8 and there before me was a pale **h**!
 19: 11 and there before me was a white **h**,

HOSANNA
Mt 21: 9 shouted, "**H** to the Son of David!"

HOSHEA
 Last king of Israel (2Ki 15:30; 17:1-6).

HOSPITABLE (HOSPITALITY)
1Ti 3: 2 respectable, **h**, able to teach,
Titus 1: 8 he must be **h**, one who loves what

HOSPITALITY (HOSPITABLE)
Ro 12: 13 people who are in need. Practice **h**.
1Ti 5: 10 showing **h**, washing the feet
Heb 13: 2 shown **h** to angels without knowing
1Pe 4: 9 Offer **h** to one another without

HOSTILE
Ro 8: 7 governed by the flesh is **h** to God;

HOT
1Ti 4: 2 have been seared as with a **h** iron.
Rev 3: 15 that you are neither cold nor **h**.

HOT-TEMPERED
Pr 15: 18 A **h** person stirs up conflict,
 19: 19 A **h** person must pay the penalty;
 22: 24 not make friends with a **h** person,
 29: 22 and a **h** person commits many sins.

HOTHEADED (HEAD)
Pr 14: 16 but a fool is **h** and yet feels secure.

HOUR
Ecc 9: 12 one knows when their **h** will come:
Mt 6: 27 worrying add a single **h** to your life?
Lk 12: 40 an **h** when you do not expect him."
Jn 12: 23 "The **h** has come for the Son
 12: 27 this very reason I came to this **h**.

HOUSE (HOUSEHOLD HOUSEHOLDS STOREHOUSE)
Ex 20: 17 shall not covet your neighbor's **h**.
Ps 23: 6 in the **h** of the LORD forever.
 84: 10 in the **h** of my God than dwell
 122: 1 "Let us go to the **h** of the LORD."
 127: 1 Unless the LORD builds the **h**,
Pr 7: 27 Her **h** is a highway to the grave,
 21: 9 of the roof than share a **h**
Isa 56: 7 my **h** will be called a **h** of prayer
Zec 13: 6 I was given at the **h** of my friends.'
Mt 7: 24 is like a wise man who built his **h**
 12: 29 can anyone enter a strong man's **h**
 21: 13 "'My **h** will be called a **h**
Mk 3: 25 If a **h** is divided against itself, that **h**
Lk 11: 17 a **h** divided against itself will fall.
Jn 2: 16 Stop turning my Father's **h**
 12: 3 the **h** was filled with the fragrance
 14: 2 My Father's **h** has many rooms;
Heb 3: 3 of a **h** has greater honor than the **h**

HOUSEHOLD (HOUSE)
Jos 24: 15 But as for me and my **h**, we will
Mic 7: 6 are the members of his own **h**.
Mt 10: 36 will be the members of his own **h**.'
 12: 25 or **h** divided against itself will not
1Ti 3: 12 manage his children and his **h** well.
 3: 15 to conduct themselves in God's **h**,

HOUSEHOLDS (HOUSE)
Pr 15: 27 The greedy bring ruin to their **h**,

HUMAN (HUMANITY)
Ge 9: 6 "Whoever sheds **h** blood,
1Sa 15: 29 for he is not a **h** being, that he
Ac 5: 29 obey God rather than **h** beings!
2Pe 1: 21 never had its origin in the **h** will,

HUMANITY (HUMAN)
Heb 2: 14 he too shared in their **h** so

HUMBLE (HUMBLED HUMILIATE HUMILIATING
HUMILITY)
2Ch 7: 14 will **h** themselves and pray and
Ps 25: 9 He guides the **h** in what is right
Pr 3: 34 favor to the **h** and oppressed.
Isa 66: 2 those who are **h** and contrite
Mt 11: 29 for I am gentle and **h** in heart,
Eph 4: 2 Be completely **h** and gentle;
Jas 4: 10 **H** yourselves before the Lord,
1Pe 5: 6 **H** yourselves, therefore,

HUMBLED (HUMBLE)
Mt 23: 12 who exalt themselves will be **h**,
Php 2: 8 he **h** himself by becoming obedient

HUMILIATE (HUMBLE)
Pr 25: 7 for him to **h** you before his nobles.

HUMILIATING (HUMBLE)
1Co 11: 22 God by **h** those who have nothing?

HUMILITY (HUMBLE)
Pr 11: 2 but with **h** comes wisdom.
 15: 33 LORD, and **h** comes before honor.
2Co 10: 1 the **h** and gentleness of Christ,
Php 2: 3 in **h** value others above yourselves,
1Pe 5: 5 with **h** toward one another,

HUNGRY
Ps 107: 9 and fills the **h** with good things.
 146: 7 oppressed and gives food to the **h**.
Pr 25: 21 If your enemy is **h**, give him food
Eze 18: 7 his food to the **h** and provides
Mt 25: 35 For I was **h** and you gave me
Lk 1: 53 has filled the **h** with good things
Jn 6: 35 comes to me will never go **h**,
Ro 12: 20 "If your enemy is **h**, feed him;

HURT (HURTS)
Ecc 8: 9 lords it over others to his own **h**.
Mk 16: 18 *it will not **h** them*
Rev 2: 11 one who is victorious will not be **h**

HURTS (HURT)
Ps 15: 4 who keeps an oath even when it **h**,
Pr 26: 28 A lying tongue hates those it **h**,

HUSBAND (HUSBAND'S HUSRANDS)
1Co 7: 3 The **h** should fulfill his marital
 7: 3 and likewise the wife to her **h**.
 7: 4 her own body but yields it to her **h**.
 7: 4 the **h** does not have authority over
 7: 10 wife must not separate from her **h**.
 7: 11 And a **h** must not divorce his wife.
 7: 13 And if a woman has a **h** who is not
 7: 39 But if her **h** dies, she is free
2Co 11: 2 I promised you to one **h**, to Christ,
Eph 5: 23 For the **h** is the head of the wife as
 5: 33 and the wife must respect her **h**.

HUSBAND'S (HUSBAND)
Pr 12: 4 of noble character is her **h** crown,

HUSBANDS (HUSBAND)
Eph 5: 22 yourselves to your own **h** as you do
 5: 25 **H**, love your wives, just as Christ
Titus 2: 4 the younger women to love their **h**
1Pe 3: 1 yourselves to your own **h** so that,
 3: 7 **H**, in the same way be considerate

HYMN
1Co 14: 26 each of you has a **h**, or a word

HYPOCRISY (HYPOCRITE HYPOCRITES)
Mt 23: 28 on the inside you are full of **h**
1Pe 2: 1 of all malice and all deceit, **h**, envy,

HYPOCRITE (HYPOCRISY)
Mt 7: 5 You **h**, first take the plank

HYPOCRITES (HYPOCRISY)
Ps 26: 4 deceitful, nor do I associate with **h**.
Mt 6: 5 do not be like the **h**, for they love

HYSSOP
Ps 51: 7 Cleanse me with **h**, and I will be

IDLE (IDLENESS)
1Th 5: 14 those who are **i** and disruptive,
2Th 3: 6 away from every believer who is **i**
1Ti 5: 13 they get into the habit of being **i**

IDLENESS (IDLE)
Pr 31: 27 and does not eat the bread of **i**.

IDOL (IDOLATRY IDOLS)
Isa 44: 17 From the rest he makes a god, his **i**;
1Co 8: 4 We know that "An **i** is nothing

IDOLATRY (IDOL)
Col 3: 5 evil desires and greed, which is **i**.

IDOLS (IDOL)
1Co 8: 1 Now about food sacrificed to **i**:

IGNORANT (IGNORE)
1Co 15: 34 there are some who are **i** of God—
Heb 5: 2 to deal gently with those who are **i**
1Pe 2: 15 good you should silence the **i** talk
2Pe 3: 16 **i** and unstable people distort,

IGNORE (IGNORANT IGNORES)
Dt 22: 1 not **i** it but be sure to take it back
Ps 9: 12 he does not **i** the cries
Heb 2: 3 escape if we **i** so great a salvation?

IGNORES (IGNORE)
Pr 10: 17 whoever **i** correction leads others

ILLUMINATED
Rev 18: 1 and the earth was **i** by his splendor.

IMAGE
Ge 1: 26 "Let us make mankind in our **i**,
1: 27 God created mankind in his own **i**, in the **i** of
God he created them;
Ro 8: 29 to be conformed to the **i** of his Son,
1Co 11: 7 since he is the **i** and glory of God;
2Co 3: 18 into his **i** with ever-increasing glory,
Col 1: 15 The Son is the **i** of the invisible
3: 10 in knowledge in the **i** of its Creator.

IMAGINE
Eph 3: 20 more than all we ask or **i**,

IMITATE (IMITATORS)
1Co 4: 16 Therefore I urge you to **i** me.
Heb 6: 12 but to **i** those who through faith
13: 7 of their way of life and **i** their faith.
3Jn : 11 do not **i** what is evil but what is

IMITATORS (IMITATE)
1Th 1: 6 You became **i** of us and of the Lord,
2: 14 became **i** of God's churches

IMMANUEL
Isa 7: 14 birth to a son, and will call him **I**.
Mt 1: 23 they will call him **I**" (which means

IMMORAL (IMMORALITY)
1Co 5: 9 to associate with sexually **i** people
5: 10 the people of this world who are **i**,
5: 11 or sister but is sexually **i** or greedy,
6: 9 Neither the sexually **i** nor idolaters
Eph 5: 5 No **i**, impure or greedy person—
Heb 12: 16 See that no one is sexually **i**, or is
13: 4 the adulterer and all the sexually **i**.
Rev 21: 8 the sexually **i**, those who practice
22: 15 arts, the sexually **i**, the murderers,

IMMORALITY (IMMORAL)
Mt 5: 32 except for sexual **i**, makes her
19: 9 except for sexual **i**, and marries
1Co 6: 13 is not meant for sexual **i**
6: 18 Flee from sexual **i**. All other sins
10: 8 We should not commit sexual **i**,
Gal 5: 19 sexual **i**, impurity and debauchery;
Eph 5: 3 must not be even a hint of sexual **i**,
1Th 4: 3 that you should avoid sexual **i**;
Jude : 4 grace of our God into a license for **i**

IMMORTAL (IMMORTALITY)
Ro 1: 23 exchanged the glory of the **i** God
1Ti 1: 17 Now to the King eternal, **i**,
6: 16 who alone is **i** and who lives

IMMORTALITY (IMMORTAL)
Ro 2: 7 and **i**, he will give eternal life.
1Co 15: 53 and the mortal with **i**.
2Ti 1: 10 and **i** to light through the gospel.

IMPERISHABLE
1Pe 1: 23 seed, but of **i**, through the living

IMPORTANCE (IMPORTANT)
1Co 15: 3 I passed on to you as of first **i**:

IMPORTANT (IMPORTANCE)
Mt 23: 23 have neglected the more **i** matters
Mk 12: 29 "The most **i** one," answered Jesus,
12: 33 as yourself is more **i** than all burnt
Php 1: 18 The **i** thing is that in every way,

IMPOSSIBLE
Mt 17: 20 Nothing will be **i** for you."
Lk 18: 27 "What is **i** with man is possible
Heb 6: 18 in which it is **i** for God to lie,
11: 6 without faith it is **i** to please God,

IMPROPER
Eph 5: 3 because these are **i** for God's holy

IMPURE (IMPURITY)
Ac 10: 15 "Do not call anything **i** that God
Eph 5: 5 No immoral, **i** or greedy person—
1Th 4: 7 For God did not call us to be **i**,
Rev 21: 27 Nothing **i** will ever enter it,

IMPURITY (IMPURE)
Ro 1: 24 hearts to sexual **i** for the degrading
Eph 5: 3 or of any kind of **i**, or of greed,

INCENSE
Ex 40: 5 Place the gold altar of **i** in front
Ps 141: 2 my prayer be set before you like **i**;

INCOME
Ecc 5: 10 is never satisfied with their **i**.
1Co 16: 2 of money in keeping with your **i**,

INCOMPARABLE
Eph 2: 7 ages he might show the **i** riches

INCREASE (EVER-INCREASING INCREASED INCREASING)
Ge 1: 22 "Be fruitful and **i** in number and
Ps 62: 10 though your riches **i**, do not set
Lk 17: 5 said to the Lord, "**I** our faith!"
1Th 3: 12 May the Lord make your love **i**

INCREASED (INCREASE)
Ac 6: 7 of disciples in Jerusalem **i** rapidly,
Ro 5: 20 where sin **i**, grace **i** all the more,

INCREASING (INCREASE)
Ac 6: 1 the number of disciples was **i**,
2Th 1: 3 all of you have for one another is **i**.
2Pe 1: 8 these qualities in **i** measure,

INDEPENDENT
1Co 11: 11 in the Lord woman is not **i** of man, nor is man **i**
of woman.

INDESCRIBABLE
2Co 9: 15 Thanks be to God for his **i** gift!

INDISPENSABLE
1Co 12: 22 body that seem to be weaker are **i**,

INEFFECTIVE
2Pe 1: 8 they will keep you from being **i**

INEXPRESSIBLE
2Co 12: 4 up to paradise and heard **i** things,
1Pe 1: 8 are filled with an **i** and glorious joy,

INFANTS
Mt 21: 16 the lips of children and **i** you, Lord,
1Co 14: 20 In regard to evil be **i**, but in your

INHERIT (CO-HEIRS HEIRS HERITAGE INHERITANCE)
Ps 37: 11 the meek will **i** the land and enjoy
37: 29 The righteous will **i** the land

Mt 5: 5 the meek, for they will **i** the earth.
Mk 10: 17 "what must I do to **i** eternal life?"
1Co 15: 50 cannot **i** the kingdom of God,

INHERITANCE (INHERIT)
Dt 4: 20 to be the people of his **i**, as you
Pr 13: 22 A good person leaves an **i** for their
Eph 1: 14 deposit guaranteeing our **i** until
    5: 5 has any **i** in the kingdom of Christ
Heb 9: 15 receive the promised eternal **i**–
1Pe 1: 4 This **i** is kept in heaven for you,

INIQUITIES (INIQUITY)
Ps 78: 38 he forgave their **i** and did not
    103: 10 or repay us according to our **i**.
Isa 59: 2 your **i** have separated you from
Mic 7: 19 hurl all our **i** into the depths

INIQUITY (INIQUITIES)
Ps 51: 2 Wash away all my **i** and cleanse me
Isa 53: 6 has laid on him the **i** of us all.

INJUSTICE
2Ch 19: 7 the LORD our God there is no **i**

INNOCENT
Pr 17: 26 a fine on the **i** is not good,
Mt 10: 16 shrewd as snakes and as **i** as doves.
    27: 4 said, "for I have betrayed **i** blood."
1Co 4: 4 clear, but that does not make me **i**.

INSCRIPTION
Mt 22: 20 image is this? And whose **i**?"

INSOLENT
Ro 1: 30 **i**, arrogant and boastful;

INSTITUTED
Ro 13: 2 is rebelling against what God has **i**,

INSTRUCT (INSTRUCTED INSTRUCTION)
Ps 32: 8 I will **i** you and teach you
Pr 9: 9 **i** the wise and they will be wiser
Ro 15: 14 and competent to **i** one another.

INSTRUCTED (INSTRUCT)
2Ti 2: 25 Opponents must be gently **i**,

INSTRUCTION (INSTRUCT)
Pr 1: 3 for receiving **i** in prudent behavior,
    1: 7 but fools despise wisdom and **i**.
    1: 8 your father's **i** and do not forsake
    4: 1 Listen, my sons, to a father's **i**;
    4: 13 Hold on to **i**, do not let it go;
    6: 23 correction and **i** are the way to life,
    8: 10 Choose my **i** instead of silver,
    8: 33 Listen to my **i** and be wise;
    13: 1 A wise son heeds his father's **i**,
    13: 13 Whoever scorns **i** will pay for it,
    16: 20 Whoever gives heed to **i** prospers,
    16: 21 and gracious words promote **i**.
    23: 12 Apply your heart to **i** and your ears
    23: 23 wisdom, **i** and insight as well.
Isa 8: 20 Consult God's **i** and the testimony
1Co 14: 6 or prophecy or word of **i**?
    14: 26 hymn, or a word of **i**, a revelation,
Eph 6: 4 in the training and **i** of the Lord.
1Th 4: 8 who rejects this **i** does not reject
2Th 3: 14 anyone who does not obey our **i**
1Ti 6: 3 sound **i** of our Lord Jesus Christ
2Ti 4: 2 with great patience and careful **i**.

INSULT (INSULTS)
Pr 12: 16 but the prudent overlook an **i**.
Mt 5: 11 are you when people **i** you,
Lk 6: 22 when they exclude you and **i** you
1Pe 3: 9 not repay evil with evil or **i** with **i**.

INSULTS (INSULT)
Pr 9: 7 corrects a mocker invites **i**;

INTEGRITY
1Ki 9: 4 walk before me faithfully with **i**
Job 2: 3 And he still maintains his **i**,
    27: 5 till I die, I will not deny my **i**.
Pr 10: 9 Whoever walks in **i** walks securely,
    11: 3 The **i** of the upright guides them,

Pr 29: 10 The bloodthirsty hate a person of **i**
Titus 2: 7 In your teaching show **i**,

INTELLIGENCE
Isa 29: 14 the **i** of the intelligent will vanish."
1Co 1: 19 the **i** of the intelligent I will

INTELLIGIBLE
1Co 14: 19 I would rather speak five **i** words

INTERCEDE (INTERCEDES INTERCESSION)
Heb 7: 25 him, because he always lives to **i**

INTERCEDES (INTERCEDE)
Ro 8: 26 the Spirit himself **i** for us through

INTERCESSION (INTERCEDE)
Isa 53: 12 and made **i** for the transgressors.
1Ti 2: 1 **i** and thanksgiving be made for all

INTEREST
Ne 5: 10 But let us stop charging **i**!

INTERESTS
1Co 7: 34 and his **i** are divided.
Php 2: 4 not looking to your own **i** but each of you to
        the **i** of the others.
    2: 21 everyone looks out for their own **i**,

INTERMARRY (MARRY)
Dt 7: 3 Do not **i** with them. Do not give

INVESTIGATED
Lk 1: 3 I myself have carefully **i** everything

INVISIBLE
Ro 1: 20 of the world God's **i** qualities–
Col 1: 15 The Son is the image of the **i** God,
1Ti 1: 17 eternal, immortal, **i**, the only God,

INVITE (INVITED INVITES)
Lk 14: 13 you give a banquet, **i** the poor,

INVITED (INVITE)
Mt 22: 14 "For many are **i**, but few are
    25: 35 I was a stranger and you **i** me in,

INVITES (INVITE)
1Co 10: 27 If an unbeliever **i** you to a meal

IRON
1Ti 4: 2 have been seared as with a hot **i**.
Rev 2: 'will rule them with an **i** scepter

IRREVOCABLE
Ro 11: 29 for God's gifts and his call are **i**.

ISAAC
Son of Abraham by Sarah (Ge 17:19; 21:1-7; 1Ch 1:28). Offered up by Abraham (Ge 22; Heb 11:17-19). Rebekah taken as wife (Ge 24). Fathered Esau and Jacob (Ge 25:19-26; 1Ch 1:34). Tricked into blessing Jacob (Ge 27). Father of Israel (Ex 3:6; Dt 29:13; Ro 9:10).

ISAIAH
Prophet to Judah (Isa 1:1). Called by the LORD (Isa 6).

ISHMAEL
Son of Abraham by Hagar (Ge 16; 1Ch 1:28). Blessed, but not son of covenant (Ge 17:18-21; Gal 4:21-31). Sent away by Sarah (Ge 21:8-21).

ISRAEL (ISRAELITES)
1. Name given to Jacob (see JACOB).
2. Corporate name of Jacob's descendants; often specifically Northern Kingdom.
Dt 6: 4 Hear, O I: The LORD our God,
1Sa 4: 21 "The Glory has departed from I"–
Isa 27: 6 I will bud and blossom and fill all
Jer 31: 10 'He who scattered I will gather
Eze 39: 23 that the people of I went into exile
Mk 12: 29 'Hear, O I: The Lord our God,
Lk 22: 30 judging the twelve tribes of I.
Ro 9: 6 all who are descended from I are I.
    11: 26 and in this way all I will be saved.
Eph 3: 6 Gentiles are heirs together with I,

ISRAELITES (ISRAEL)
Ex 14: 22 the I went through the sea on dry
    16: 35 The I ate manna forty years,
Hos 1: 10 "Yet the I will be like the sand
Ro 9: 27 number of the I be like the sand

ITCHING
2Ti   4:   3 say what their **i** ears want to hear.

JACOB
Second son of Isaac, twin of Esau (Ge 25:21-26; 1Ch 1:34). Bought Esau's birthright (Ge 25:29-34); tricked Isaac into blessing him (Ge 27:1-37). Abrahamic covenant perpetuated through (Ge 28:13-15; Mal 1:2). Vision at Bethel (Ge 28:10-22). Wives and children (Ge 29:1–30:24; 35:16-26; 1Ch 2-9). Wrestled with God; name changed to Israel (Ge 32:22-32). Sent sons to Egypt during famine (Ge 42-43). Settled in Egypt (Ge 46). Blessed Ephraim and Manasseh (Ge 48). Blessed sons (Ge 49:1-28; Heb 11:21). Death (Ge 49:29-33). Burial (Ge 50:1-14).

JAMES
1. Apostle; brother of John (Mt 4:21-22; 10:2; Mk 3:17; Lk 5:1-10). At transfiguration (Mt 17:1-13; Mk 9:1-13; Lk 9:28-36). Killed by Herod (Ac 12:2).
2. Apostle; son of Alphaeus (Mt 10:3; Mk 3:18; Lk 6:15).
3. Brother of Jesus (Mt 13:55; Mk 6:3; Lk 24:10; Gal 1:19) and Judas (Jude 1). With believers before Pentecost (Ac 1:13). Leader of church at Jerusalem (Ac 12:17; 15; 21:18; Gal 2:9, 12). Author of epistle (Jas 1:1).

JAPHETH
Son of Noah (Ge 5:32; 1Ch 1:4-5). Blessed (Ge 9:18-28).

JARS
2Co   4:   7 we have this treasure in **j** of clay

JEALOUS (JEALOUSY)
Ex   20:   5 am a **j** God, punishing the children
       34: 14 whose name is **J**, is a **j** God.
Dt   4: 24 God is a consuming fire, a **j** God.
Joel 2: 18 Then the LORD was **j** for his land
Zec   1: 14 I am very **j** for Jerusalem and Zion,
2Co 11: 2 am **j** for you with a godly jealousy.

JEALOUSY (JEALOUS)
1Co 3: 3 For since there is **j** and quarreling
2Co 11: 2 I am jealous for you with a godly **j**.
Gal 5: 20 hatred, discord, **j**, fits of rage,

JEHOAHAZ
1. Son of Jehu; king of Israel (2Ki 13:1-9).
2. Son of Josiah; king of Judah (2Ki 23:31-34; 2Ch 36:1-4).

JEHOASH
Son of Jehoahaz; king of Israel (2Ki 13-14; 2Ch 25).

JEHOIACHIN
Son of Jehoiakim; king of Judah exiled by Nebuchadnezzar (2Ki 24:8-17; 2Ch 36:8-10; Jer 22:24-30; 24:1). Raised from prisoner status (2Ki 25:27-30; Jer 52:31-34).

JEHOIAKIM
Son of Josiah; king of Judah (2Ki 23:34-24:6; 2Ch 36:4-8; Jer 22:18-23; 36).

JEHORAM
Son of Jehoshaphat; king of Judah (2Ki 8:16-24).

JEHOSHAPHAT
Son of Asa; king of Judah (1Ki 22:41-50; 2Ki 3; 2Ch 17-20).

JEHU
King of Israel (1Ki 19:16-19; 2Ki 9-10).

JEPHTHAH
Judge from Gilead who delivered Israel from Ammon (Jdg 10:6-12:7). Made rash vow concerning his daughter (Jdg 11:30-40).

JEREMIAH
Prophet to Judah (Jer 1:1-3). Called by the LORD (Jer 1). Put in stocks (Jer 20:1-3). Threatened for prophesying (Jer 11:18-23; 26). Opposed by Hananiah (Jer 28). Scroll burned (Jer 36). Imprisoned (Jer 37). Thrown into cistern (Jer 38). Forced to Egypt with those fleeing Babylonians (Jer 43).

JEROBOAM
1. Official of Solomon; rebelled to become first king of Israel (1Ki 11:26-40; 12:1-20; 2Ch 10). Idolatry (1Ki 12:25-33); judgment for (1Ki 13-14; 2Ch 13).
2. Son of Jehoash; king of Israel (1Ki 14:23-29).

JERUSALEM
2Ki 23: 27 and I will reject **J**, the city I chose,
2Ch 6: 6 now I have chosen **J** for my Name

Ne   2: 17 let us rebuild the wall of **J**,
Ps 122: 6 Pray for the peace of **J**:
   125: 2 As the mountains surround **J**,
   137: 5 If I forget you, **J**, may my right
Isa 40: 9 You who bring good news to **J**,
    65: 18 for I will create **J** to be a delight
Joel 3: 17 **J** will be holy; never again will
Zep 3: 16 On that day they will say to **J**,
Zec 2: 4 man, '**J** will be a city without walls
     8: 8 I will bring them back to live in **J**;
   14: 8 living water will flow out from **J**,
Mt 23: 37 "**J, J**, you who kill the prophets
Lk 13: 34 "**J, J**, you who kill the prophets
   21: 24 **J** will be trampled
Jn   4: 20 where we must worship is in **J**."
Ac   1: 8 and you will be my witnesses in **J**,
Gal 4: 25 to the present city of **J**,
Rev 21: 2 the new **J**, coming down

JESUS
LIFE: Genealogy (Mt 1:1-17; Lk 3:21-37). Birth announced (Mt 1:18-25; Lk 1:26-45). Birth (Mt 2:1-12; Lk 2:1-40). Escape to Egypt (Mt 2:13-23). As a boy in the temple (Lk 2:41-52). Baptism (Mt 3:13-17; Mk 1:9-11; Lk 3:21-22; Jn 1:32-34). Temptation (Mt 4:1-11; Mk 1:12-13; Lk 4:1-13). Ministry in Galilee (Mt 4:12-18:35; Mk 1:14-9:50; Lk 4:14-13:9; Jn 1:35-2:11; 4; 6), Transfiguration (Mt 17:1-8; Mk 9:2-8; Lk 9:28-36), on the way to Jerusalem (Mt 19-20; Mk 10; Lk 13:10-19:27), in Jerusalem (Mt 21-25; Mk 11-13; Lk 19:28-21:38; Jn 2:12-3:36; 5; 7-12). Last supper (Mt 26:17-35; Mk 14:12-31; Lk 22:1-38; Jn 13-17). Arrest and trial (Mt 26:36-27:31; Mk 14:43-15:20; Lk 22:39-23:25; Jn 18:1-19:16). Crucifixion (Mt 27:32-66; Mk 15:21-47; Lk 23:26-55; Jn 19:28-42). Resurrection and appearances (Mt 28; Mk 16; Lk 24; Jn 20-21; Ac 1:1-11; 7:56; 9:3-6; 1Co 15:1-8; Rev 1:1-20).

MIRACLES: Healings: official's son (Jn 4:43-54), demoniac in Capernaum (Mk 1:23-26; Lk 4:33-35), Peter's mother-in-law (Mt 8:14-17; Mk 1:29-31; Lk 4:38-39), leper (Mt 8:2-4; Mk 1:40-45; Lk 5:12-16), paralytic (Mt 9:1-8; Mk 2:1-12; Lk 5:17-26), cripple (Jn 5:1-9), shriveled hand (Mt 12:10-13; Mk 3:1-5; Lk 6:6-11), centurion's servant (Mt 8:5-13; Lk 7:1-10), widow's son raised (Lk 7:11-17), demoniac (Mt 12:22-23; Lk 11:14), Gadarene demoniacs (Mt 8:28-34; Mk 5:1-20; Lk 8:26-39), woman's bleeding and Jairus' daughter (Mt 9:18-26; Mk 5:21-43; Lk 8:40-56), blind man (Mt 9:27-31), mute man (Mt 9:32-33), Canaanite woman's daughter (Mt 15:21-28; Mk 7:24-30), deaf man (Mk 7:31-37), blind man (Mk 8:22-26), demoniac boy (Mt 17:14-18; Mk 9:14-29; Lk 9:37-43), ten lepers (Lk 17:11-19), man born blind (Jn 9:1-7), Lazarus raised (Jn 11), crippled woman (Lk 13:11-17), man with dropsy (Lk 14:1-6), two blind men (Mt 20:29-34; Mk 10:46-52; Lk 18:35-43), Malchus' ear (Lk 22:50-51). Other Miracles: water to wine (Jn 2:1-11), catch of fish (Lk 5:1-11), storm stilled (Mt 8:23-27; Mk 4:37-41; Lk 8:22-25), 5,000 fed (Mt 14:15-21; Mk 6:35-44; Lk 9:10-17; Jn 6:1-14), walking on water (Mt 14:25-33; Mk 6:48-52; Jn 6:15-21), 4,000 fed (Mt 15:32-39; Mk 8:1-9), money from fish (Mt 17:24-27), fig tree cursed (Mt 21:18-22; Mk 11:12-14), catch of fish (Jn 21:1-14).

MAJOR TEACHING: Sermon on the Mount (Mt 5-7; Lk 6:17-49), to Nicodemus (Jn 3), to Samaritan woman (Jn 4), Bread of Life (Jn 6:22-59), at Feast of Tabernacles (Jn 7-8), woes to Pharisees (Mt 23; Lk 11:37-54), Good Shepherd (Jn 10:1-18), Olivet Discourse (Mt 24-25; Mk 13; Lk 21:5-36), Upper Room Discourse (Jn 13-16).

PARABLES: Sower (Mt 13:3-23; Mk 4:3-25; Lk 8:5-18), seed's growth (Mk 4:26-29), wheat and weeds (Mt 13:24-30, 36-43), mustard seed (Mt 13:31-32; Mk 4:30-32), yeast (Mt 13:33; Lk 13:20-21), hidden treasure (Mt 13:44), valuable pearl (Mt 13:45-46), net (Mt 13:47-51), house owner (Mt 13:52), good Samaritan (Lk 10:25-37), unmerciful servant (Mt 18:15-35), lost sheep (Mt 18:10-14; Lk 15:4-7), lost coin (Lk 15:8-10), prodigal son (Lk 15:11-32), dishonest manager (Lk 16:1-13), rich man and Lazarus (Lk 16:19-31), persistent widow (Lk 18:1-8), Pharisee and tax collector (Lk 18:9-14), payment of workers (Mt 20:1-16), tenants and the vineyard (Mt 21:28-46; Mk 12:1-12; Lk 20:9-19), wedding banquet (Mt 22:1-14), faithful servant (Mt 24:45-51), ten virgins (Mt 25:1-13), talents (Mt 25:1-30; Lk 19:12-27).

DISCIPLES see APOSTLES. Call of (Jn 1:35-51; Mt 4:18-22; 9:9; Mk 1:16-20; 2:13-14; Lk 5:1-11, 27-28). Named Apostles (Mk 3:13-19; Lk 6:12-16). Twelve sent out (Mt 10; Mk 6:7-11; Lk 9:1-5). Seventy sent out (Lk 10:1-24). Defection of (Jn 6:60-71; Mt 26:56; Mk 14:50-52). Final commission (Mt 28:16-20; Jn 21:15-23; Ac 1:3-8).

Ac	2: 32	God has raised this **J** to life, and we
	9: 5	Saul asked. "I am **J**, whom you are
	15: 11	of our Lord **J** that we are saved,
	16: 31	"Believe in the Lord **J**, and you will
Ro	3: 24	redemption that came by Christ **J**.
	5: 17	life through the one man, **J** Christ!
	8: 1	for those who are in Christ **J**,
1Co	2: 2	I was with you except **J** Christ
	8: 6	and there is but one Lord, **J** Christ,
	12: 3	and no one can say, "**J** is Lord,"
2Co	4: 5	but **J** Christ as Lord, and ourselves
Gal	2: 16	of the law, but by faith in **J** Christ.
	3: 28	for you are all one in Christ **J**,
	5: 6	in Christ **J** neither circumcision
Eph	2: 10	in Christ **J** to do good works,
	2: 20	with Christ **J** himself as the chief
Php	1: 6	until the day of Christ **J**.
	2: 5	have the same mindset as Christ **J**:
	2: 10	name of **J** every knee should bow,
Col	3: 17	do it all in the name of the Lord **J**,
2Th	2: 1	the coming of our Lord **J** Christ
1Ti	1: 15	**J** came into the world to save
2Ti	3: 12	life in Christ **J** will be persecuted,
Titus	2: 13	our great God and Savior, **J** Christ,
Heb	2: 9	But we do see **J**, who was made
	3: 1	fix your thoughts on **J**, whom we
	4: 14	into heaven, **J** the Son of God,
	7: 22	**J** has become the guarantor
	7: 24	but because **J** lives forever, he has
	12: 2	fixing our eyes on **J**, the pioneer
2Pe	1: 16	of our Lord **J** Christ in power,
1Jn	1: 7	and the blood of **J**, his Son,
	2: 1	**J** Christ, the Righteous One.
	2: 6	to live in him must live as **J** did.
	4: 15	acknowledges that **J** is the Son
Rev	22: 20	Amen. Come, Lord **J**.

JEW (JEWS JUDAISM)

Zec	8: 23	take firm hold of one **J** by the hem
Ro	1: 16	first to the **J**, then to the Gentile,
	10: 12	there is no difference between **J**
1Co	9: 20	To the Jews I became like a **J**,
Gal	3: 28	There is neither **J** nor Gentile,

JEWELRY (JEWELS)

1Pe	3: 3	wearing of gold **j** or fine clothes.

JEWELS (JEWELRY)

Isa	61: 10	as a bride adorns herself with her **j**.
Zec	9: 16	in his land like **j** in a crown.

JEWS (JEW)

Mt	2: 2	who has been born king of the **J**?
	27: 11	him, "Are you the king of the **J**?"
Jn	4: 22	know, for salvation is from the **J**.
Ro	2: 29	Or is God the God of **J** only?
1Co	1: 22	**J** demand signs and Greeks look
	9: 20	To the **J** I became like a Jew, to win
	12: 13	whether **J** or Gentiles,
Rev	2: 9	claim to be **J** though they are not,

JEZEBEL

Sidonian wife of Ahab (1Ki 16:31). Promoted Baal worship (1Ki 16:32-33). Killed prophets of the LORD (1Ki 18:4, 13). Opposed Elijah (1Ki 19:1-2). Had Naboth killed (1Ki 21). Death prophesied (1Ki 21:17-24). Killed by Jehu (2Ki 9:30-37).

JOASH

Son of Ahaziah; king of Judah. Sheltered from Athaliah by Jehoiada (2Ki 11; 2Ch 22:10-23:21). Repaired temple (2Ki 12; 2Ch 24).

JOB

Wealthy man from Uz; feared God (Job 1:1-5). Righteousness tested by disaster (Job 1:6-22), personal affliction (Job 2). Maintained innocence in debate with three friends (Job

3-31), Elihu (Job 32-37). Rebuked by the LORD (Job 38-41). Vindicated and restored to greater stature by the LORD (Job 42). Example of righteousness (Eze 14:14, 20).

JOHN

1. Son of Zechariah and Elizabeth (Lk 1). Called the Baptist (Mt 3:1-12; Mk 1:2-8). Witness to Jesus (Mt 3:11-12; Mk 1:7-8; Lk 3:15-18; Jn 1:6-35; 3:27-30; 5:33-36). Doubts about Jesus (Mt 11:2-6; Lk 7:18-23). Arrest (Mt 4:12; Mk 1:14). Execution (Mt 14:1-12; Mk 6:14-29; Lk 9:7-9). Ministry compared to Elijah (Mt 11:7-19; Mk 9:11-13; Lk 7:24-35).

2. Apostle; brother of James (Mt 4:21-22; 10:2; Mk 3:17; Lk 5:1-10). At transfiguration (Mt 17:1-13; Mk 9:1-13; Lk 9:28-36). Desire to be greatest (Mk 10:35-45). Leader of church at Jerusalem (Ac 4:1-3; Gal 2:9). Elder who wrote epistles (2Jn 1; 3Jn 1). Prophet who wrote Revelation (Rev 1:1; 22:8).

3. Cousin of Barnabas, co-worker with Paul, (Ac 12:12-13:13; 15:37), see MARK.

JOIN (JOINED)

Pr	23: 20	not **j** those who drink too much
	24: 21	do not **j** with rebellious officials,
Ro	15: 30	to **j** me in my struggle by praying
2Ti	1: 8	**j** with me in suffering
2Ti	2: 3	**J** with me in suffering, like a good

JOINED (JOIN)

Mt	19: 6	Therefore what God has **j** together,
Mk	10: 9	Therefore what God has **j** together,
Eph	2: 21	the whole building is **j** together
	4: 16	body, **j** and held together by every

JOINTS

Heb	4: 12	soul and spirit, **j** and marrow;

JOKING

Eph	5: 4	foolish talk or coarse **j**, which are

JONAH

Prophet in days of Jeroboam II (2Ki 14:25). Called to Nineveh; fled to Tarshish (Jnh 1:1-3). Cause of storm; thrown into sea (Jnh 1:4-16). Swallowed by fish (Jnh 1:17). Prayer (Jnh 2). Preached to Nineveh (Jnh 3). Attitude reproved by the LORD (Jnh 4). Sign of (Mt 12:39-41; Lk 11:29-32).

JONATHAN

Son of Saul (1Sa 13:16; 1Ch 8:33). Valiant warrior (1Sa 13-14). Relation to David (1Sa 18:1-4; 19-20; 23:16-18). Killed at Gilboa (1Sa 31). Mourned by David (2Sa 1).

JORAM

1. Son of Ahab; king of Israel (2Ki 3; 8-9; 2Ch 22).

JORDAN

Nu	34: 12	boundary will go down along the **J**
Jos	4: 22	'Israel crossed the **J** on dry ground.'
Mt	3: 6	baptized by him in the **J** River.

JOSEPH

1. Son of Jacob by Rachel (Ge 30:24; 1Ch 2:2). Favored by Jacob, hated by brothers (Ge 37:3-4). Dreams (Ge 37:5-11). Sold by brothers (Ge 37:12-36). Served Potiphar; imprisoned by false accusation (Ge 39). Interpreted dreams of Pharaoh's servants (Ge 40), of Pharaoh (Ge 41:4-40). Made greatest in Egypt (Ge 41:41-57). Sold grain to brothers (Ge 42-45). Brought Jacob and sons to Egypt (Ge 46-47). Sons Ephraim and Manasseh blessed (Ge 48). Blessed (Ge 49:22-26; Dt 33:13-17). Death (Ge 50:22-26; Ex 13:19; Heb 11:22). 12,000 from (Rev 7:8).

2. Husband of Mary, mother of Jesus (Mt 1:16-24; 2:13-19; Lk 1:27; 2; Jn 1:45).

3. Disciple from Arimathea, who gave his tomb for Jesus' burial (Mt 27:57-61; Mk 15:43-47; Lk 23:50-53).

4. Original name of Barnabas (Ac 4:36).

JOSHUA

1. Son of Nun; name changed from Hoshea (Nu 13:8, 16; 1Ch 7:27). Fought Amalekites under Moses (Ex 17:9-14). Servant of Moses on Sinai (Ex 24:13; 32:17). Spied Canaan (Nu 13). With Caleb, allowed to enter land (Nu 14:6, 30). Succeeded Moses (Dt 1:38; 31:1-8; 34:9).

Charged Israel to conquer Canaan (Jos 1). Crossed Jordan (Jos 3-4). Circumcised sons of wilderness wanderings (Jos 5). Conquered Jericho (Jos 6), Ai (Jos 7-8), five kings at Gibeon (Jos 10:1-28), southern Canaan (Jos 10:29-43), northern Canaan (Jos 11-12). Defeated at Ai (Jos 7). Deceived by Gibeonites (Jos 9). Renewed covenant (Jos 8:30-35; 24:1-27). Divided land among tribes (Jos 13-22). Last words (Jos 23). Death (Jos 24:28-31).

2. High priest during rebuilding of temple (Hag 1-2; Zec 3:1-9; 6:11).

JOSIAH
Son of Amon; king of Judah (2Ki 22-23; 2Ch 34-35).

JOTHAM
Son of Azariah (Uzziah); king of Judah (2Ki 15:32-38; 2Ch 26:21–27:9).

JOY (ENJOY ENJOYMENT JOYFUL OVERJOYED REJOICE REJOICES REJOICING)
Dt	16: 15	hands, and your **j** will be complete.
1Ch	16: 27	and **j** are in his dwelling place.
Ne	8: 10	for the **j** of the LORD is your
Est	9: 22	their sorrow was turned into **j**
Job	38: 7	and all the angels shouted for **j**?
Ps	4: 7	Fill my heart with **j** when their
	21: 6	glad with the **j** of your presence.
	30: 11	sackcloth and clothed me with **j**,
	43: 4	God, to God, my **j** and my delight.
	51: 12	to me the **j** of your salvation
	66: 1	Shout for **j** to God, all the earth!
	96: 12	all the trees of the forest sing for **j**.
	107: 22	tell of his works with songs of **j**.
	119: 111	forever; they are the **j** of my heart.
Pr	10: 1	A wise son brings **j** to his father,
	10: 28	The prospect of the righteous is **j**,
	12: 20	those who promote peace have **j**.
	15: 30	in a messenger's eyes brings **j**
Isa	35: 10	everlasting **j** will crown their heads
	51: 11	Gladness and **j** will overtake them,
	55: 12	You will go out in **j** and be led
Lk	1: 44	the baby in my womb leaped for **j**.
	2: 10	will cause great **j** for all the people.
Jn	15: 11	and that your **j** may be complete.
	16: 20	grieve, but your grief will turn to **j**.
2Co	8: 2	trial, their overflowing **j** and their
Php	2: 2	then make my **j** complete by being
	4: 1	love and long for, my **j** and crown,
1Th	2: 19	our **j**, or the crown in which we
Phm	: 7	Your love has given me great **j**
Heb	12: 2	the **j** set before him he endured
Jas	1: 2	Consider it pure **j**, my brothers
1Pe	1: 8	an inexpressible and glorious **j**,
2Jn	: 4	It has given me great **j** to find some
3Jn	: 4	I have no greater **j** than to hear

JOYFUL (JOY)
Ps	100: 2	come before him with **j** songs.
Pr	23: 25	may she who gave you birth be **j**!
Hab	3: 18	I will be **j** in God my Savior.

JUDAH
1. Son of Jacob by Leah (Ge 29:35; 35:23; 1Ch 2:1). Tribe of blessed as ruling tribe (Ge 49:8-12; Dt 33:7).

2. Name used for people and land of Southern Kingdom.
Jer	13: 19	All **J** will be carried into exile,
Zec	10: 4	From **J** will come the cornerstone,
Heb	7: 14	that our Lord descended from **J**,

JUDAISM (JEW)
Gal	1: 13	of my previous way of life in **J**,

JUDAS
1. Apostle (Lk 6:16; Jn 14:22; Ac 1:13). Probably also called Thaddaeus (Mt 10:3; Mk 3:18).

2. Brother of James and Jesus (Mt 13:55; Mk 6:3), also called Jude (Jude 1).

3. Apostle, also called Iscariot, who betrayed Jesus (Mt 10:4; 26:14-56; Mk 3:19; 14:10-50; Lk 6:16; 22:3-53; Jn 6:71; 12:4; 13:2-30; 18:2-11). Suicide of (Mt 27:3-5; Ac 1:16-25).

JUDGE (JUDGED JUDGES JUDGING JUDGMENT)
Ge	18: 25	Will not the **J** of all the earth do
1Ch	16: 33	LORD, for he comes to **j** the earth.
Joel	3: 12	there I will sit to **j** all the nations
Mt	7: 1	"Do not **j**, or you too will be
Jn	7: 24	but instead **j** correctly."

Jn	12: 47	For I did not come to **j** the world,
Ac	17: 31	set a day when he will **j** the world
1Co	4: 3	indeed, I do not even **j** myself.
	6: 2	the Lord's people will **j** the world?
2Ti	4: 1	who will **j** the living and the dead,
	4: 8	the righteous **J**, will award to me
Jas	4: 12	who are you to **j** your neighbor?
Rev	20: 4	who had been given authority to **j**.

JUDGED (JUDGE)
Mt	7: 1	"Do not judge, or you too will be **j**.
Jn	5: 24	will not be **j** but has crossed over
Jas	3: 1	who teach will be **j** more strictly.
Rev	20: 12	The dead were **j** according to what

JUDGES (JUDGE)
Jdg	2: 16	Then the LORD raised up **j**,
Ps	9: 8	and **j** the peoples with equity.
	58: 11	there is a God who **j** the earth."
Ro	2: 16	God **j** people's secrets through Jesus
Heb	4: 12	it **j** the thoughts and attitudes
Rev	19: 11	With justice he **j** and wages war.

JUDGING (JUDGE)
Mt	19: 28	**j** the twelve tribes of Israel.
Jn	7: 24	Stop **j** by mere appearances,
2Co	10: 7	You are **j** by appearances.

JUDGMENT (JUDGE)
Dt	1: 17	of anyone, for **j** belongs to God.
Ps	1: 5	the wicked will not stand in the **j**,
	119: 66	Teach me knowledge and good **j**,
Ecc	12: 14	God will bring every deed into **j**,
Isa	66: 16	his sword the LORD will execute **j**
Mt	5: 21	who murders will be subject to **j**.'
	10: 15	Gomorrah on the day of **j** than
	12: 36	the day of **j** for every empty word
Jn	5: 22	but has entrusted all **j** to the Son,
	16: 8	about sin and righteousness and **j**:
Ro	14: 10	will all stand before God's **j** seat.
	14: 13	Therefore let us stop passing **j**
1Co	11: 29	eat and drink **j** on themselves.
	11: 31	we would not come under such **j**.
2Co	5: 10	we must all appear before the **j** seat
Heb	9: 27	to die once, and after that to face **j**,
	10: 27	only a fearful expectation of **j**
1Pe	4: 17	For it is time for **j** to begin
Jude	: 6	everlasting chains for **j** on the great

JUST (JUSTICE JUSTIFICATION JUSTIFIED JUSTIFY JUSTLY)
Dt	32: 4	are perfect, and all his ways are **j**.
Ps	37: 28	For the LORD loves the **j** and will
	111: 7	of his hands are faithful and **j**;
Pr	1: 3	doing what is right and **j** and fair;
	2: 8	for he guards the course of the **j**
Da	4: 37	does is right and all his ways are **j**.
Ro	3: 26	time, so as to be **j** and the one who
Heb	2: 2	received its **j** punishment,
1Jn	1: 9	he is faithful **j** and will forgive
Rev	16: 7	true and **j** are your judgments."

JUSTICE (JUST)
Ex	23: 2	do not pervert **j** by siding
	23: 6	"Do not deny **j** to your poor people
Job	37: 23	in his **j** and great righteousness,
Ps	9: 16	LORD is known by his acts of **j**;
	11: 7	the LORD is righteous, he loves **j**;
	45: 6	a scepter of **j** will be the scepter
	101: 1	I will sing of your love and **j**;
Pr	21: 15	When **j** is done, it brings joy
	29: 4	By **j** a king gives a country stability,
	29: 26	is from the LORD that one gets **j**.
Isa	9: 7	and upholding it with **j**
	28: 17	I will make **j** the measuring line
	30: 18	For the LORD is a God of **j**.
	42: 1	and he will bring **j** to the nations.
	42: 4	be discouraged till he establishes **j**
	56: 1	"Maintain **j** and do what is right,
	61: 8	"For I, the LORD, love **j**;
Eze	34: 16	I will shepherd the flock with **j**.
Am	5: 15	maintain **j** in the courts.

Am 5: 24 But let **j** roll on like a river,
Zec 7: 9 'Administer true **j**; show mercy
Lk 11: 42 you neglect **j** and the love of God.

JUSTIFICATION (JUST)
Ac 13: 39 sin, a **j** you were not able to obtain
Ro 4: 25 sins and was raised to life for our **j**.
5: 18 one righteous act resulted in **j**

JUSTIFIED (JUST)
Ro 3: 24 all are **j** freely by his grace through
3: 28 that a person is **j** by faith apart
5: 1 since we have been **j** through faith,
5: 9 Since we have now been **j** by his
8: 30 he called, he also **j**; those he **j**,
1Co 6: 11 you were **j** in the name of the Lord
Gal 2: 16 that a person is not **j** by the works
3: 11 relies on the law is **j** before God,
3: 24 came that we might be **j** by faith.

JUSTIFY (JUST)
Gal 3: 8 that God would **j** the Gentiles

JUSTLY (JUST)
Ps 106: 3 Blessed are those who act **j**,
Mic 6: 8 To act **j** and to love mercy

KEEP (KEEPER KEEPING KEEPS KEPT)
Ge 31: 49 "May the LORD **k** watch between
Ex 20: 6 love me and **k** my commandments.
Nu 6: 24 LORD bless you and **k** you;
Ps 18: 28 You, LORD, **k** my lamp burning;
19: 13 **K** your servant also from willful
121: 7 The LORD will **k** you from all
141: 3 **k** watch over the door of my lips.
Pr 4: 24 **K** your mouth free of perversity;
17: 28 are thought wise if they **k** silent,
Isa 26: 3 You will **k** in perfect peace those
Am 5: 13 Therefore the prudent **k** quiet
Mt 10: 10 staff, for the worker is worth his **k**.
Lk 12: 35 service and **k** your lamps burning,
Gal 5: 25 let us **k** in step with the Spirit.
Eph 4: 3 Make every effort to **k** the unity
1Ti 5: 22 the sins of others. **K** yourself pure.
2Ti 4: 5 you, **k** your head in all situations,
Heb 13: 5 **K** your lives free from the love
Jas 1: 26 and yet do not **k** a tight rein on
2: 8 If you really **k** the royal law found
1Jn 5: 3 love for God: to **k** his commands.
Jude : 24 To him who is able to **k** you

KEEPER (KEEP)
Ge 4: 9 "Am I my brother's **k**?"

KEEPING (KEEP)
Ex 20: 8 the Sabbath day by **k** it holy.
Ps 19: 11 in **k** them there is great reward.
Mt 3: 8 Produce fruit in **k** with repentance.
Lk 2: 8 **k** watch over their flocks at night.
1Co 7: 19 **K** God's commands is what counts.
2Pe 3: 9 Lord is not slow in **k** his promise,

KEEPS (KEEP)
1Co 13: 5 angered, it **k** no record of wrongs.
Jas 2: 10 For whoever **k** the whole law

KEPT (KEEP)
Ps 130: 3 LORD, **k** a record of sins, Lord,
2Ti 4: 7 finished the race, I have **k** the faith.
1Pe 1: 4 This inheritance is **k** in heaven

KEYS
Mt 16: 19 will give you the **k** of the kingdom

KILL (KILLS)
Mt 17: 23 will **k** him, and on the third day

KILLS (KILL)
Lev 24: 21 whoever **k** a human being is to be
2Co 3: 6 for the letter **k**, but the Spirit gives

KIND (KINDNESS KINDS)
Ge 1: 24 animals, each according to its **k**."
2Ch 10: 7 "If you will be **k** to these people
Pr 11: 17 Those who are **k** benefit themselves,
12: 25 the heart, but a **k** word cheers it up.
14: 21 blessed is the one who is **k**

Pr 14: 31 whoever is **k** to the needy honors
19: 17 Whoever is **k** to the poor lends
Da 4: 27 by being **k** to the oppressed.
Lk 6: 35 because he is **k** to the ungrateful
1Co 13: 4 Love is patient, love is **k**.
15: 35 what **k** of body will they come?"
Eph 4: 32 Be **k** and compassionate to one
2Ti 2: 24 but must be **k** to everyone,
Titus 2: 5 to be **k**, and to be subject to their

KINDNESS (KIND)
Ac 14: 17 He has shown **k** by giving you rain
Ro 11: 22 but **k** to you, provided that you continue in his **k**.
Gal 5: 22 peace, forbearance, **k**, goodness,
Eph 2: 7 expressed in his **k** to us in Christ

KINDS (KIND)
1Co 12: 4 There are different **k** of gifts,
1Ti 6: 10 of money is a root of all **k** of evil.

KING (KINGDOM KINGS)
1. Kings of Judah and Israel: see Saul, David, Solomon.
2. Kings of Judah: see Rehoboam, Abijah, Asa, Jehoshaphat, Jehoram, Ahaziah, Athaliah (Queen), Joash, Amaziah, Uzziah, Jotham, Ahaz, Hezekiah, Manasseh, Amon, Josiah, Jehoahaz, Jehoiakim, Jehoiachin, Zedekiah.
3. Kings of Israel: see Jeroboam I, Nadab, Baasha, Elah, Zimri, Tibni, Omri, Ahab, Ahaziah, Joram, Jehu, Jehoahaz, Jehoash, Jeroboam II, Zechariah, Shallum, Menahem, Pekah, Pekahiah, Hoshea.
Jdg 17: 6 In those days Israel had no **k**;
1Sa 12: 12 'No, we want a **k** to rule over us'–
12: 12 the LORD your God was your **k**.
Ps 24: 7 that the **K** of glory may come in.
Isa 32: 1 a **k** will reign in righteousness
Zec 9: 9 See, your **k** comes to you,
1Ti 6: 15 the **K** of kings and Lord of lords,
Rev 19: 16 thigh he has this name written: **K**

KINGDOM (KING)
Ex 19: 6 you will be for me a **k** of priests
1Ch 29: 11 Yours, LORD, is the **k**;
Ps 45: 6 justice will be the scepter of your **k**.
Da 4: 3 His **k** is an eternal **k**;
Mt 3: 2 for the **k** of heaven has come near."
5: 3 spirit, for theirs is the **k** of heaven.
6: 10 your **k** come, your will be done,
6: 33 But seek first his **k** and his
7: 21 Lord,' will enter the **k** of heaven,
11: 11 the **k** of heaven is greater than he.
13: 24 "The **k** of heaven is like a man who
13: 31 "The **k** of heaven is like a mustard
13: 33 "The **k** of heaven is like yeast
13: 44 "The **k** of heaven is like treasure
13: 45 the **k** of heaven is like a merchant
13: 47 the **k** of heaven is like a net that
16: 19 you the keys of the **k** of heaven;
18: 23 the **k** of heaven is like a king who
19: 24 who is rich to enter the **k** of God."
24: 7 rise against nation, and **k** against **k**.
24: 14 gospel of the **k** will be preached
25: 34 the **k** prepared for you since
Mk 9: 47 you to enter the **k** of God with one
10: 14 for the **k** of God belongs to such as
10: 23 for the rich to enter the **k** of God!"
Lk 10: 9 'The **k** of God has come near
12: 31 But seek his **k**, and these things
17: 21 is,' because the **k** of God is in your
Jn 3: 5 one can enter the **k** of God unless
18: 36 said, "My **k** is not of this world.
1Co 6: 9 wrongdoers will not inherit the **k**
15: 24 when he hands over the **k** to God
Rev 1: 6 has made us to be a **k** and priests
11: 15 "The **k** of the world has become

KINGS (KING)
Ps 2: 2 The **k** of the earth rise
72: 11 May all **k** bow down to him and all
Da 7: 24 ten horns are ten **k** who will come
1Ti 2: 2 for **k** and all those in authority,
Rev 1: 5 and the ruler of the **k** of the earth.

KISS
Ps　　2: 12　**K** his son, or he will be angry
Pr　 24: 26　An honest answer is like a **k**
Lk　 22: 48　the Son of Man with a **k**?"

KNEE (KNEES)
Isa　45: 23　Before me every **k** will bow;
Ro　 14: 11　Lord, 'every **k** will bow before me;
Php　 2: 10　name of Jesus every **k** should bow,

KNEES (KNEE)
Isa　35:　3　hands, steady the **k** that give way;
Heb　12: 12　your feeble arms and weak **k**.

KNEW (KNOW)
Job　23:　3　If only I **k** where to find him;
Jnh　 4:　2　I **k** that you are a gracious
Mt　　7: 23　tell them plainly, 'I never **k** you.

KNOCK
Mt　　7:　7　**k** and the door will be opened
Rev　 3: 20　I stand at the door and **k**.

KNOW (FOREKNEW KNEW KNOWING KNOWLEDGE
KNOWN KNOWS)
Dt　 18: 21　"How can we **k** when a message
Job　19: 25　I **k** that my redeemer lives,
　　　42:　3　things too wonderful for me to **k**.
Ps　 46: 10　says, "Be still, and **k** that I am God;
　　　73: 11　Does the Most High **k** anything?"
　　 139:　1　LORD, and you **k** me.
　　 139: 23　Search me, God, and **k** my heart;
Pr　 27:　1　you do not **k** what a day may bring.
Jer　24:　7　I will give them a heart to **k** me,
　　　31: 34　because they will all **k** me,
Mt　　6:　3　let your left hand **k** what your right
　　　24: 42　because you do not **k** on what day
Lk　　1:　4　so that you may **k** the certainty
Jn　　3: 11　you, we speak of what we **k**, and we
　　　4: 22　worship what you do not **k**;
　　　9: 25　One thing I do **k**. I was blind
　　　10: 14　I **k** my sheep and my sheep **k** me—
　　　17:　3　that they **k** you, the only true God,
　　　21: 24　We **k** that his testimony is true.
Ac　　1:　7　"It is not for you to **k** the times
Ro　　6:　6　we **k** that our old self was crucified
　　　7: 18　I **k** that good itself does not dwell
　　　8: 28　we **k** that in all things God works
1Co　 2:　2　I resolved to **k** nothing while I was
　　　6: 15　Do you not **k** that your bodies are
　　　6: 19　Do you not **k** that your bodies are
　　　8:　2　do not yet **k** as they ought to **k**.
　　　13: 12　Now I **k** in part; then I shall **k** fully,
　　　15: 58　because you **k** that your labor
Php　 3: 10　I want to **k** Christ—yes, to **k**
2Ti　 1: 12　because I **k** whom I have believed,
Jas　 4: 14　do not even **k** what will happen
1Jn　 2:　4　Whoever says, "I **k** him," but does
　　　3: 14　We **k** that we have passed
　　　3: 16　This is how we **k** what love is:
　　　5:　2　This is how we **k** that we love
　　　5: 13　may **k** that you have eternal life.

KNOWING (KNOW)
Ge　　3:　5　will be like God, **k** good and evil."
Php　 3:　8　worth of **k** Christ Jesus my Lord,

KNOWLEDGE (KNOW)
Ge　　2:　9　the tree of the **k** of good and evil.
Job　42:　3　that obscures my plans without **k**?'
Ps　 19:　2　night after night they reveal **k**.
　　 139:　6　Such **k** is too wonderful for me,
Pr　　1:　7　of the LORD is the beginning of **k**,
　　　10: 14　The wise store up **k**, but the mouth
　　　12:　1　Whoever loves discipline loves **k**,
　　　13: 16　All who are prudent act with **k**,
　　　19:　2　Desire without **k** is not good—
Isa　11:　9　the **k** of the LORD as the waters
Hab　 2: 14　will be filled with the **k** of the glory
Ro　 11: 33　riches of the wisdom and **k** of God!
1Co　 8:　1　But **k** puffs up while love builds up.
　　　8: 11　Christ died, is destroyed by your **k**.

1Co　 13:　2　can fathom all mysteries and all **k**,
2Co　 2: 14　aroma of the **k** of him everywhere.
　　　4:　6　of the **k** of God's glory displayed
Eph　 3: 19　know this love that surpasses **k**—
Col　　2:　3　all the treasures of wisdom and **k**.
1Ti　 6: 20　ideas of what is falsely called **k**,
2Pe　 3: 18　grow in the grace and **k** of our Lord

KNOWN (KNOW)
Ps　 16: 11　You make **k** to me the path of life;
　　 105:　1　make **k** among the nations what he
Isa　46: 10　I make **k** the end
Mt　 10: 26　or hidden that will not be made **k**.
Ro　　1: 19　since what may be **k** about God is
　　　11: 34　"Who has **k** the mind of the Lord?
　　　15: 20　the gospel where Christ was not **k**,
2Co　 3:　2　our hearts, **k** and read by everyone.
2Pe　 2: 21　than to have **k** it and then to turn

KNOWS (KNOW)
1Sa　 2:　3　for the LORD is a God who **k**,
Job　23: 10　But he **k** the way that I take;
Ps　 44: 21　since he **k** the secrets of the heart?
　　　94: 11　The LORD **k** all human plans; he **k**
Ecc　 8:　7　Since no one **k** the future, who can
Mt　　6:　8　your Father **k** what you need
　　　24: 36　about that day or hour no one **k**,
Ro　　8: 27　searches our hearts **k** the mind
2Ti　 2: 19　"The Lord **k** those who are his,"

LABAN
Brother of Rebekah (Ge 24:29-51), father of Rachel and
Leah (Ge 29-31).

LABOR
Ex　 20:　9　Six days you shall **l** and do all your
Isa　55:　2　your **l** on what does not satisfy?
Mt　　6: 28　They do not **l** or spin.
1Co　 3:　8　rewarded according to their own **l**.
　　　15: 58　know that your **l** in the Lord is not

LACK (LACKING LACKS)
Pr　 15: 22　Plans fail for **l** of counsel,
Col　　2: 23　but they **l** any value in restraining

LACKING (LACK)
Ro　 12: 11　Never be **l** in zeal, but keep your
Jas　　1:　4　and complete, not **l** anything.

LACKS (LACK)
Jas　　1:　5　If any of you **l** wisdom, you should

LAID (LAY)
Isa　53:　6　and the LORD has **l** on him
1Co　 3: 11　other than the one already **l**,
1Jn　 3: 16　Jesus Christ **l** down his life for us.

LAKE
Rev　19: 20　into the fiery **l** of burning sulfur.
　　　20: 14　The **l** of fire is the second death.

LAMB (LAMB'S LAMBS)
Ge　 22:　8　"God himself will provide the **l**
Ex　 12: 21　and slaughter the Passover **l**.
Isa　11:　6　The wolf will live with the **l**,
　　　53:　7　he was led like a **l** to the slaughter,
Jn　　1: 29　"Look, the **L** of God, who takes
1Co　 5:　7　our Passover **l**, has been sacrificed.
1Pe　 1: 19　a **l** without blemish or defect.
Rev　 5:　6　Then I saw a **L**, looking as if it had
　　　5: 12　"Worthy is the **L**, who was slain,
　　　14:　4　as firstfruits to God and the **L**.

LAMB'S (LAMB)
Rev　21: 27　names are written in the **L** book

LAMBS (LAMB)
Lk　 10:　3　you out like **l** among wolves.
Jn　 21: 15　Jesus said, "Feed my **l**."

LAMENT
2Sa　 1: 17　took up this **l** concerning Saul

LAMP (LAMPS)
2Sa　22: 29　You, LORD, are my **l**;
Ps　 18: 28　You, LORD, keep my **l** burning;
　　 119: 105　Your word is a **l** to my feet

Pr 31: 18 and her l does not go out at night.
Lk 8: 16 "No one lights a l and hides it
Rev 21: 23 gives it light, and the Lamb is its l.

LAMPS (LAMP)
Mt 25: 1 be like ten virgins who took their l
Lk 12: 35 service and keep your l burning,

LAND
Ge 1: 10 God called the dry ground "l,"
1: 11 said, "Let the l produce vegetation:
12: 7 your offspring I will give this l."
Ex 3: 8 a l flowing with milk and honey–
Nu 35: 33 Bloodshed pollutes the l,
Dt 34: 1 LORD showed him the whole l–
Jos 13: 2 "This is the l that remains:
14: 4 Levites received no share of the l
2Ch 7: 14 their sin and will heal their l.
7: 20 then I will uproot Israel from my l,
Eze 36: 24 bring you back into your own l.

LANGUAGE
Ge 11: 1 Now the whole world had one l
Jn 8: 44 speaks his native l, for he is a liar
Ac 2: 6 heard their own l being spoken.
Col 3: 8 slander, and filthy l from your lips.
Rev 5: 9 God persons from every tribe and l

LAST (LASTING LASTS LATTER)
2Sa 23: 1 These are the l words of David:
Isa 44: 6 I am the first and I am the l;
Mt 19: 30 But many who are first will be l,
Mk 10: 31 will be l, and the l first."
Jn 15: 16 fruit that will l–and so
Ro 1: 17 that is by faith from first to l,
2Ti 3: 1 will be terrible times in the l days.
2Pe 3: 3 in the l days scoffers will come,
Rev 1: 17 I am the First and the L.
22: 13 the First and the L, the Beginning

LASTING (LAST)
Ex 12: 14 to the LORD–a l ordinance.
Lev 24: 8 of the Israelites, as a l covenant.
Nu 25: 13 have a covenant of a l priesthood,
Heb 10: 34 had better and l possessions.

LASTS (LAST)
Ps 30: 5 For his anger l only a moment,
2Co 3: 11 greater is the glory of that which l!

LATTER (LAST)
Job 42: 12 The LORD blessed the l part

LAUGH (LAUGHS)
Ecc 3: 4 a time to weep and a time to l,

LAUGHS (LAUGH)
Ps 2: 4 The One enthroned in heaven l;
37: 13 but the Lord l at the wicked, for he

LAVISHED
Eph 1: 8 that he l on us. With all wisdom
1Jn 3: 1 See what great love the Father has l

LAW (LAWS)
Dt 31: 11 you shall read this l before them
31: 26 "Take this Book of the L and place
Jos 1: 8 Keep this Book of the L always
Ne 8: 8 from the Book of the L of God,
Ps 1: 2 delight is in the l of the LORD,
19: 7 The l of the LORD is perfect,
119: 18 may see wonderful things in your l.
119: 72 The l from your mouth is more
119: 97 Oh, how I love your l! I meditate
119:165 peace have those who love your l,
Jer 31: 33 "I will put my l in their minds
Mt 5: 17 that I have come to abolish the L
7: 12 you, for this sums up the L
22: 40 All the L and the Prophets hang
Lk 16: 17 stroke of a pen to drop out of the L.
Jn 1: 17 For the l was given through Moses;
Ro 2: 12 All who sin apart from the l will
2: 15 requirements of the l are written
5: 13 account where there is no l.
5: 20 The l was brought in so

Ro 6: 14 because you are not under the l,
7: 6 we have been released from the l so
7: 12 So then, the l is holy,
8: 3 For what the l was powerless to do
10: 4 Christ is the culmination of the l
13: 10 love is the fulfillment of the l.
Gal 3: 13 curse of the l by becoming a curse
3: 24 So the l was our guardian until
5: 3 he is obligated to obey the whole l.
5: 4 by the l have been alienated
5: 14 For the entire l is fulfilled
Heb 7: 19 (for the l made nothing perfect),
10: 1 The l is only a shadow of the good
Jas 1: 25 the perfect l that gives freedom,
2: 10 For whoever keeps the whole l

LAWLESSNESS
2Th 2: 3 occurs and the man of l is revealed,
2: 7 the secret power of l is already
1Jn 3: 4 sins breaks the law; in fact, sin is l.

LAWS (LAW)
Lev 25: 18 and be careful to obey my l,
Ps 119: 30 I have set my heart on your l.
119:120 fear of you; I stand in awe of your l.
Heb 8: 10 I will put my l in their minds
10: 16 I will put my l in their hearts, and l

LAY (LAID LAYING)
Job 22: 22 and I up his words in your heart.
Isa 28: 16 "See, I l a stone in Zion, a tested
Mt 8: 20 of Man has no place to l his head."
Jn 10: 15 and I l down my life for the sheep.
15: 13 to l down one's life for one's
1Co 3: 11 no one can l any foundation other
1Jn 3: 16 we ought to l down our lives for
Rev 4: 10 They l their crowns before

LAYING (LAY)
1Ti 5: 22 not be hasty in the l on of hands,
Heb 6: 1 not l again the foundation

LAZARUS
1. Poor man in Jesus' parable (Lk 16:19–31).
2. Brother of Mary and Martha whom Jesus raised from the dead (Jn 11:1–12:19).

LAZY
Pr 10: 4 L hands make for poverty,
Heb 6: 12 We do not want you to become l,

LEAD (LEADERS LEADS LED)
Ex 15: 13 love you will l the people you have
Ps 27: 11 l me in a straight path because
61: 2 l me to the rock that is higher than l.
139: 24 and l me in the way everlasting.
143: 10 may your good Spirit l me on level
Ecc 5: 6 Do not let your mouth l you
Isa 11: 6 and a little child will l them.
Da 12: 3 those who l many to righteousness,
Mt 6: 13 And l us not into temptation,
1Jn 3: 7 do not let anyone l you astray.

LEADERS (LEAD)
Heb 13: 7 Remember your l, who spoke
13: 17 Have confidence in your l

LEADS (LEAD)
Ps 23: 2 he l me beside quiet waters,
Pr 19: 23 The fear of the LORD l to life;
Isa 40: 11 he gently l those that have young;
Mt 7: 13 gate and broad is the road that l
Jn 10: 3 sheep by name and l them out.
Ro 14: 19 every effort to do what l to peace
2Co 2: 14 God, who always l us as captives

LEAH
Wife of Jacob (Ge 29:16–30); bore six sons and one daughter (Ge 29:31–30:21; 34:1; 35:23).

LEAN
Pr 3: 5 l not on your own understanding;

LEARN (LEARNED LEARNING)
Isa 1: 17 L to do right; seek justice.
Mt 11: 29 my yoke upon you and l from me,

LEARNED (LEARN)
Php 4: 11 I have I to be content whatever
2Ti 3: 14 know those from whom you I it,

LEARNING (LEARN)
Pr 1: 5 the wise listen and add to their I,
2Ti 3: 7 always I but never able to come

LED (LEAD)
Isa 53: 7 he was I like a lamb
Am 2: 10 I you forty years in the wilderness
Ro 8: 14 For those who are I by the Spirit

LEFT
Jos 1: 7 turn from it to the right or to the I,
Pr 4: 27 Do not turn to the right or the I,
Mt 6: 3 do not let your I hand know what
    25: 33 on his right and the goats on his I.

LEGION
Mk 5: 9 "My name is L," he replied,

LEND (LENDS)
Dt 15: 8 freely I them whatever they need.
Ps 37: 26 are always generous and I freely;
Lk 6: 34 Even sinners I to sinners,

LENDS (LEND)
Pr 19: 17 kind to the poor I to the LORD,

LENGTH (LONG)
Pr 10: 27 fear of the LORD adds I to life,

LEPROSY
2Ki 7: 3 Now there were four men with I

LETTER (LETTERS)
Mt 5: 18 not the smallest I, not the least
2Co 3: 2 You yourselves are our I,
    3: 6 not of the I but of the Spirit; for the I kills,
2Th 3: 14 not obey our instruction in this I.

LETTERS (LETTER)
2Co 3: 7 which was engraved in I on stone,
    10: 10 "His I are weighty and forceful,
2Pe 3: 16 He writes the same way in all his I,

LEVEL
Ps 143: 10 good Spirit lead me on I ground.
Isa 26: 7 The path of the righteous is I;
Heb 12: 13 "Make I paths for your feet,"

LEVI (LEVITES)
1. Son of Jacob by Leah (Ge 29:34; 46:11; 1Ch 2:1). Tribe of blessed (Ge 49:5-7; Dt 33:8-11), chosen as priests (Nu 3-4), numbered (Nu 3:39; 26:62), allotted cities, but not land (Nu 18; 35; Dt 10:9; Jos 13:14; 21), land (Eze 48:8-22), 12,000 from (Rev 7:7).
2. See MATTHEW.

LEVITES (LEVI)
Nu 1: 53 The L are to be responsible
    8: 6 "Take the L from among all
    18: 21 "I give to the L all the tithes

LEWDNESS
Mk 7: 22 malice, deceit, I, envy, slander,

LIAR (LIE)
Pr 19: 22 better to be poor than a I.
Jn 8: 44 for he is a I and the father of lies.
Ro 3: 4 be true, and every human being a I.

LIBERATED
Ro 8: 21 the creation itself will be I from its

LIE (LIAR LIED LIES LYING)
Lev 19: 11 "'Do not I. "'Do not deceive
Nu 23: 19 that he should I, not a human
Dt 6: 7 when you I down and when you
Ps 23: 2 He makes me I down in green
Isa 11: 6 the leopard will I down
Eze 34: 14 There they will I down in good
Ro 1: 25 the truth about God for a I,
Col 3: 9 Do not I to each other, since you
Heb 6: 18 which it is impossible for God to I,

LIED (LIE)
Ac 5: 4 You have not I just to human

LIES (LIE)
Ps 34: 13 evil and your lips from telling I.
Jn 8: 44 for he is a liar and the father of I.

LIFE (LIVE)
Ge 2: 7 into his nostrils the breath of I,
    2: 9 of the garden were the tree of I
    9: 11 Never again will all I be destroyed
Ex 21: 23 injury, you are to take I for I,
Lev 17: 14 because the I of every creature is its
    24: 18 must make restitution–I for I.
Dt 30: 19 Now choose I, so that you and your
Ps 16: 11 make known to me the path of I;
    23: 6 will follow me all the days of my I,
    34: 12 Whoever of you loves I and desires
    39: 4 let me know how fleeting my I is.
    49: 7 one can redeem the I of another
    104: 33 I will sing to the LORD all my I;
Pr 6: 23 and instruction are the way to I,
    7: 23 little knowing it will cost him his I.
    8: 35 For those who find me find I
    11: 30 fruit of the righteous is a tree of I,
    21: 21 righteousness and love finds I,
Eze 37: 5 enter you, and you will come to I.
Da 12: 2 some to everlasting I,
Mt 6: 25 do not worry about your I,
    7: 14 and narrow the road that leads to I,
    10: 39 whoever loses their I for my sake
    16: 25 wants to save their I will lose it,
    20: 28 to give his I as a ransom for many."
Mk 10: 45 to give his I as a ransom for many.
Lk 12: 15 I does not consist in an abundance
    12: 22 do not worry about your I,
    14: 26 yes, even their own I–
Jn 1: 4 In him was I, and that I was the light
    3: 15 who believes may have eternal I
    3: 36 believes in the Son has eternal I,
    4: 14 of water welling up to eternal I."
    5: 24 has crossed over from death to I.
    6: 35 Jesus declared, "I am the bread of I.
    6: 47 the one who believes has eternal I.
    6: 68 You have the words of eternal I.
    10: 10 I have come that they may have I,
    10: 15 and I lay down my I for the sheep.
    10: 28 I give them eternal I, and they shall
    11: 25 "I am the resurrection and the I.
    14: 6 am the way and the truth and the I.
    15: 13 lay down one's I for one's friends.
    20: 31 by believing you may have I in his
Ac 13: 48 appointed for eternal I believed.
Ro 4: 25 was raised to I for our justification.
    6: 13 have been brought from death to I;
    6: 23 God is eternal I in Christ Jesus our
    8: 38 convinced that neither death nor I,
1Co 15: 19 If only for this I we have hope
2Co 3: 6 the letter kills, but the Spirit gives I.
Gal 2: 20 The I I now live in the body, I live
Eph 4: 1 to live a I worthy of the calling you
Php 2: 16 as you hold firmly to the word of I.
Col 1: 10 you may live a I worthy of the Lord
1Th 4: 12 your daily I may win the respect
1Ti 4: 8 the present I and the I to come.
    4: 16 Watch your I and doctrine closely.
    6: 19 take hold of the I that is truly I.
2Ti 3: 12 live a godly I in Christ Jesus will be
Jas 1: 12 person will receive the crown of I
    3: 13 Let them show it by their good I,
1Pe 3: 10 "Whoever would love I and see
2Pe 1: 3 a godly I through our knowledge
1Jn 3: 14 we have passed from death to I,
    5: 11 God has given us eternal I, and this I
Rev 13: 8 written in the Lamb's book of I,
    20: 12 was opened, which is the book of I.
    21: 27 are written in the Lamb's book of I.
    22: 2 side of the river stood the tree of I,

LIFT (LIFTED LIFTING)
Ps 121: 1 I I up my eyes to the mountains–
    134: 2 L up your hands in the sanctuary
La 3: 41 Let us I up our hearts and our hands

LIFTED (LIFT)
Ps 40: 2 He I me out of the slimy pit,

Jn   3: 14 so the Son of Man must be l up,
      12: 32 I, when I am I up from the earth,

LIFTING (LIFT)
1Ti   2: 8 I up holy hands without anger

LIGHT (ENLIGHTENED)
Ge   1: 3 "Let there be I," and there was I.
2Sa 22: 29 Lord turns my darkness into I.
Job 38: 19 "What is the way to the abode of I?
Ps   4: 6 Let the I of your face shine on us.
     19: 8 are radiant, giving I to the eyes.
     27: 1 The Lord is my I and my
     56: 13 walk before God in the I of life.
     76: 4 You are radiant with I,
   104: 2 The Lord wraps himself in I as
  119:105 lamp to my feet and a I for my path.
  119:130 unfolding of your words gives I;
Isa   2: 5 let us walk in the I of the Lord.
     9: 2 in darkness have seen a great I;
   49: 6 also make you a I for the Gentiles,
Mt   4: 16 shadow of death a I has dawned."
     5: 16 way, let your I shine before others,
   11: 30 yoke is easy and my burden is I."
Jn   3: 19 L has come into the world,
     8: 12 he said, "I am the I of the world.
2Co 4: 6 made his I shine in our hearts
     6: 14 Or what fellowship can I have
   11: 14 masquerades as an angel of I.
1Ti   6: 16 and who lives in unapproachable I,
1Pe   2: 9 of darkness into his wonderful I.
1Jn   1: 5 God is I; in him there is no darkness
     1: 7 But if we walk in the I, as he is
Rev 21: 23 for the glory of God gives it I,

LIGHTNING
Da 10: 6 his face like I, his eyes like flaming
Mt 24: 27 For as I that comes from the east is
    28: 3 His appearance was like I, and his

LIKENESS
Ge   1: 26 in our I, so that they may rule over
Ps   17: 15 will be satisfied with seeing your I.
Isa 52: 14 his form marred beyond human I
Ro   8: 3 his own Son in the I of sinful flesh
Php 2: 7 a servant, being made in human I.
Jas   3: 9 who have been made in God's I.

LION
Isa 11: 7 and the I will eat straw like the ox.
1Pe   5: 8 around like a roaring I looking
Rev 5: 5 See, the L of the tribe of Judah,

LIPS
Ps   34: 1 his praise will always be on my I.
  119: 171 May my I overflow with praise,
Pr   13: 3 who guard their I preserve their
    27: 2 an outsider, and not your own I.
Isa   6: 5 For I am a man of unclean I, and I
Mt 21: 16 read, "'From the I of children
Col   3: 8 and filthy language from your I.

LISTEN (LISTENING)
Dt 30: 20 Lord your God, I to his voice,
Pr   1: 5 let the wise I and add to their
   12: 15 to them, but the wise I to advice.
Jn 10: 27 My sheep I to my voice;
Jas   1: 19 Everyone should be quick to I,
    1: 22 Do not merely I to the word,

LISTENING (LISTEN)
1Sa   3: 9 Lord, for your servant is I.'"
Pr   18: 13 To answer before I–that is folly

LIVE (ALIVE LIFE LIVES LIVING)
Ex 20: 12 that you may I long in the land
   33: 20 face, for no one may see me and I."
Dt   8: 3 that man does not I on bread alone
Job 14: 14 If someone dies, will they I again?
Ps 119:175 Let me I that I may praise you,
Isa 55: 3 come to me; listen, that you may I.
Eze 37: 3 "Son of man, can these bones I?"
Hab 2: 4 the righteous person will I by his
Mt   4: 4 'Man shall not I on bread alone,

Ac   17: 24 not I in temples built by human
    17: 28 'For in him we I and move and
Ro   1: 17 "The righteous will I by faith."
2Co 5: 7 For we I by faith, not by sight.
Gal   2: 20 The life I now I in the body,
    5: 25 Since we I by the Spirit, let us keep
Php 1: 21 me, to I is Christ and to die is gain.
1Th   5: 13 L in peace with each other.
2Ti   3: 12 who wants to I a godly life
Heb 12: 14 Make every effort to I in peace
1Pe   1: 17 I out your time as foreigners here

LIVES (LIVE)
Job 19: 25 I know that my redeemer I,
Pr   11: 30 and the one who is wise saves I.
Isa 57: 15 he who I forever, whose name is
Da   3: 28 to give up their I rather than serve
Jn 14: 17 he I with you and will be in you.
Gal   2: 20 I no longer live, but Christ I in me.
Heb 13: 5 Keep your I free from the love
2Pe 3: 11 You ought to live holy and godly I
1Jn   3: 16 to lay down our I for our brothers
    4: 16 Whoever I in love I in God,

LIVING (LIVE)
Ge   2: 7 life, and the man became a I being.
Jer   2: 13 the spring of I water, and have dug
Mt 22: 32 the God of the dead but of the I."
Jn   7: 38 said, rivers of I water will flow
Ro 12: 1 to offer your bodies as a I sacrifice.
Heb 10: 31 to fall into the hands of the I God.
Rev 1: 18 I am the L One; I was dead,

LOAD
Gal   6: 5 each one should carry their own I.

LOCUSTS
Mt   3: 4 His food was I and wild honey.

LOFTY
Ps 139: 6 for me, too I for me to attain.

LONELY
Ps 68: 6 God sets the I in families, he leads

LONG (LENGTH LONGED LONGING LONGS)
1Ki 18: 21 "How I will you waver between
Jn   9: 4 As I as it is day, we must do
Eph 3: 18 to grasp how wide and I and high
1Pe   1: 12 Even angels I to look into these

LONGED (LONG)
Mt 13: 17 righteous people I to see what you
   23: 37 how often have I have I to gather your
2Ti   4: 8 to all who have I for his appearing.

LONGING (LONG)
Pr   13: 19 A I fulfilled is sweet to the soul,
2Co 5: 2 I to be clothed instead with our

LONGS (LONG)
Isa 30: 18 Yet the Lord I to be gracious

LOOK (LOOKING LOOKS)
Job 31: 1 my eyes not to I lustfully at a young
Ps   34: 5 Those who I to him are radiant;
Pr   4: 25 Let your eyes I straight ahead;
Isa 60: 5 Then you will I and be radiant,
Hab 1: 13 Your eyes are too pure to I on evil;
Zec 12: 10 They will I on me, the one they
Mk 13: 21 is the Messiah!' or, 'L, there he is!'
Lk 24: 39 L at my hands and my feet. It is I
Jn   1: 36 by, he said, "L, the Lamb of God!"
    4: 35 open your eyes and I at the fields!
   19: 37 "They will I on the one they have
Jas   1: 27 to I after orphans and widows
1Pe   1: 12 Even angels long to I into these

LOOKING (LOOK)
Rev 5: 6 a Lamb, I as if it had been slain,

LOOKS (LOOK)
1Sa 16: 7 but the Lord I at the heart."
Lk   9: 62 puts a hand to the plow and I back
Php 2: 21 everyone I out for their own interests,

LORD (LORD'S LORDING)

Ne   4: 14 Remember the **L**, who is great
Job 28: 28 human race, "The fear of the **L**–
Ps   54: 4 the **L** is the one who sustains me.
    62: 12 and with you, **L**, is unfailing love";
    86: 5 You, **L**, are forgiving and good,
  110: 1 The Lᴏʀᴅ says to my **l**:
  147: 5 Great is our **L** and mighty in power
Isa   6: 1 died, I saw the **L**, high and exalted,
Da   9: 4 "**L**, the great and awesome God,
Mt   3: 3 'Prepare the way for the **L**,
    4: 7 'Do not put the **L** your God
    7: 21 "Not everyone who says to me, '**L**,
   22: 37 "'Love the **L** your God with all
   22: 44 "'The **L** said to my **L**: "Sit at my
Mk 12: 11 the **L** has done this, and it is
   12: 29 The **L** our God, the **L** is one.
Lk   2: 9 An angel of the **L** appeared to
    6: 46 "Why do you call me, '**L**, **L**,'
   10: 27 "'Love the **L** your God with all
Ac   2: 21 on the name of the **L** will be saved.'
   16: 31 "Believe in the **L** Jesus, and you
Ro 10: 9 "Jesus is **L**," and believe in your
   10: 13 the name of the **L** will be saved."
   12: 11 your spiritual fervor, serving the **L**.
   14: 8 we live or die, we belong to the **L**.
1Co 1: 31 the one who boasts boast in the **L**."
    3: 5 as the **L** has assigned to each his
    7: 34 to be devoted to the **L** in both body
   11: 23 The **L** Jesus, on the night he was
   12: 3 "Jesus is **L**," except by the Holy
   15: 57 victory through our **L** Jesus Christ.
   16: 22 let that person be cursed! Come, **L**!
2Co 3: 17 Now the **L** is the Spirit, and where
    8: 5 gave themselves first of all to the **L**,
   10: 17 the one who boasts boast in the **L**."
Gal   6: 14 in the cross of our **L** Jesus Christ,
Eph 4: 5 one **L**, one faith, one baptism;
    5: 10 and find out what pleases the **L**.
    5: 19 music from your heart to the **L**,
Php 2: 11 acknowledge that Jesus Christ is **L**,
    3: 1 and sisters, rejoice in the **L**!
    4: 4 Rejoice in the **L** always. I will say it
Col   2: 6 as you received Christ Jesus as **L**,
    3: 17 do it all in the name of the **L** Jesus,
    3: 23 working for the **L**, not for human
    4: 17 you have received in the **L**."
1Th 3: 12 May the **L** make your love increase
    5: 2 day of the **L** will come like a thief
    5: 23 at the coming of our **L** Jesus Christ.
2Th 2: 1 the coming of our **L** Jesus Christ
2Ti 2: 19 "The **L** knows those who are his,"
Heb 12: 14 holiness no one will see the **L**.
   13: 6 confidence, "The **L** is my helper;
Jas   4: 10 Humble yourselves before the **L**,
1Pe 1: 25 the word of the **L** endures forever."
    2: 3 you have tasted that the **L** is good.
    3: 15 in your hearts revere Christ as **L**.
2Pe 1: 16 the coming of our **L** Jesus Christ
    2: 1 sovereign **L** who bought them–
    3: 9 The **L** is not slow in keeping his
Jude : 14 the **L** is coming with thousands
Rev 4: 8 holy is the **L** God Almighty,'
    4: 11 "You are worthy, our **L** and God,
   17: 14 triumph over them because he is **L**
   22: 20 Amen. Come, **L** Jesus.

LORD'S (LORD)

Ac 21: 14 up and said, "The **L** will be done."
1Co 10: 26 "The earth is the **L**, and everything
   11: 26 you proclaim the **L** death until he
2Co 3: 18 faces contemplate the **L** glory,
2Ti 2: 24 And the **L** servant must not be
Jas 4: 15 "If it is the **L** will, we will live

LORDING (LORD)

1Pe 5: 3 not **l** it over those entrusted to you,

LORD* (LORD'S*; this is the proper name of God, *Yahweh*, spelled "Lᴏʀᴅ" in the NIV)

Ge   2: 4 when the **L** God made the earth
    2: 7 the **L** God formed a man
    3: 21 The **L** God made garments of skin
    7: 16 Then the **L** shut him in.
   15: 6 Abram believed the **L**, and he
   18: 14 Is anything too hard for the **L**?
   31: 49 "May the **L** keep watch between
Ex   3: 2 There the angel of the **L** appeared
    9: 12 But the **L** hardened Pharaoh's heart
   14: 30 That day the **L** saved Israel
   20: 2 "I am the **L** your God, who
   33: 11 The **L** would speak to Moses face
   40: 34 glory of the **L** filled the tabernacle.
Lev 19: 2 'Be holy because I, the **L** your God,
Nu   8: 5 The **L** said to Moses:
   14: 21 glory of the **L** fills the whole earth,
Dt   2: 7 The **L** your God has blessed you
    5: 9 for I, the **L** your God, am a jealous
    6: 4 The **L** our God, the **L** is one.
    6: 5 Love the **L** your God with all your
    6: 16 Do not put the **L** your God
   10: 14 **L** your God belong the heavens,
   10: 17 For the **L** your God is God of gods
   11: 1 Love the **L** your God and keep his
   28: 1 If you fully obey the **L** your God
   30: 16 you today to love the **L** your God,
   30: 20 For the **L** is your life, and he will
   31: 6 for the **L** your God goes with you;
Jos 22: 5 to love the **L** your God, to walk
   24: 15 household, we will serve the **L**."
1Sa 1: 28 So now I give him to the **L**.
    2: 2 "There is no one holy like the **L**;
    7: 12 "Thus far the **L** has helped us."
   12: 22 his great name the **L** will not reject
   15: 22 as much as in obeying the **L**?
2Sa 22: 2 "The **L** is my rock, my fortress
1Ki 2: 3 and observe what the **L** your God
    8: 11 the glory of the **L** filled his temple.
    8: 61 fully committed to the **L** our God,
   18: 21 If the **L** is God, follow him;
2Ki 13: 23 But the **L** was gracious to them
1Ch 16: 8 Give praise to the **L**, proclaim his
   16: 23 Sing to the **L**, all the earth;
   28: 9 for the **L** searches every heart
   29: 11 Yours, **L**, is the kingdom;
2Ch 5: 14 the glory of the **L** filled the temple
   16: 9 the **L** range throughout the earth
   19: 6 for mere mortals but for the **L**,
   30: 9 for the **L** your God is gracious
Ne   1: 5 "**L**, the God of heaven, the great
Job 1: 21 The **L** gave and the **L** has taken
   38: 1 the **L** spoke to Job out of the storm.
   42: 9 did what the **L** told them;
Ps   1: 2 whose delight is in the law of the **L**,
    9: 9 The **L** is a refuge for the oppressed,
   12: 6 the words of the **L** are flawless,
   16: 8 I keep my eyes always on the **L**.
   19: 7 The law of the **L** is perfect,
   19: 14 heart be pleasing in your sight, **L**,
   23: 1 The **L** is my shepherd, I lack
   23: 6 dwell in the house of the **L** forever.
   27: 1 The **L** is the stronghold of my life
   27: 4 to gaze on the beauty of the **L**
   29: 1 ascribe to the **L** glory and strength.
   32: 2 one whose sin the **L** does not count
   33: 12 is the nation whose God is the **L**,
   33: 18 the eyes of the **L** are on those who
   34: 3 Glorify the **L** with me; let us exalt
   34: 7 of the **L** encamps around those
   34: 8 Taste and see that the **L** is good;
   34: 18 The **L** is close to the brokenhearted
   37: 4 Take delight in the **L**, and he will
   40: 1 I waited patiently for the **L**;
   47: 2 For the **L** Most High is awesome,
   48: 1 Great is the **L**, and most worthy

Ps   55: 22 Cast your cares on the **L** and he
      75: 8 In the hand of the **L** is a cup full
      84: 11 For the **L** God is a sun and shield;
      86: 11 Teach me your way, **L**, that I may
      89: 5 heavens praise your wonders, **L**,
      95: 1 Come, let us sing for joy to the **L**;
      96: 1 Sing to the **L** a new song;
      98: 4 Shout for joy to the **L**, all the earth,
     100: 1 Shout for joy to the **L**, all the earth.
     103: 1 Praise the **L**, my soul; all my
     103: 8 The **L** is compassionate
     104: 1 Praise the **L**, my soul. **L** my God,
     107: 8 to the **L** for his unfailing love
     110: 1 The **L** says to my lord: "Sit at my
     113: 4 The **L** is exalted over all the nations
     115: 1 Not to us, **L**, not to us but to your
     116: 15 the sight of the **L** is the death of his
     118: 1 Give thanks to the **L**, for he is good;
     118: 24 The **L** has done it this very day;
     121: 2 My help comes from the **L**,
     121: 5 The **L** watches over you–the **L** is
     125: 2 so the **L** surrounds his people both
     127: 1 Unless the **L** builds the house,
     127: 3 Children are a heritage from the **L**,
     130: 3 If you, **L**, kept a record of sins,
     135: 6 The **L** does whatever pleases him,
     136: 1 Give thanks to the **L**, for he is good.
     139: 1 You have searched me, **L**, and you
     144: 3 **L**, what are human beings that you
     145: 3 Great is the **L** and most worthy
     145: 18 The **L** is near to all who call on him,
Pr   1: 7 The fear of the **L** is the beginning
       3: 5 Trust in the **L** with all your heart
       3: 9 Honor the **L** with your wealth,
       3: 12 because the **L** disciplines those he
       3: 19 By wisdom the **L** laid the earth's
       5: 21 your ways are in full view of the **L**,
       6: 16 There are six things the **L** hates,
      10: 27 The fear of the **L** adds length to life,
      11: 1 The **L** detests dishonest scales,
      12: 22 The **L** detests lying lips, but he
      14: 26 Whoever fears the **L** has a secure
      15: 3 The eyes of the **L** are everywhere,
      16: 2 but motives are weighed by the **L**.
      16: 4 The **L** works out everything to its
      16: 9 but the **L** establishes their steps.
      16: 33 but its every decision is from the **L**.
      18: 10 name of the **L** is a fortified tower;
      18: 22 and receives favor from the **L**.
      19: 14 but a prudent wife is from the **L**.
      19: 17 is kind to the poor lends to the **L**,
      21: 3 acceptable to the **L** than sacrifice.
      21: 30 plan that can succeed against the **L**.
      21: 31 battle, but victory rests with the **L**.
      22: 2 The **L** is the Maker of them all.
      24: 18 or the **L** will see and disapprove
      31: 30 a woman who fears the **L** is to be
Isa   6: 3 holy, holy is the **L** Almighty;
      11: 2 The Spirit of the **L** will rest on him
      11: 9 of the **L** as the waters cover the sea.
      12: 2 The **L**, the **L** himself, is my strength
      24: 1 the **L** is going to lay waste the earth
      25: 8 The Sovereign **L** will wipe away
      29: 15 to hide their plans from the **L**,
      33: 6 the fear of the **L** is the key to this
      35: 10 those the **L** has rescued will return.
      40: 5 For the mouth of the **L** has spoken.
      40: 7 because the breath of the **L** blows
      40: 10 the Sovereign **L** comes with power,
      40: 28 The **L** is the everlasting God,
      40: 31 in the **L** will renew their strength.
      42: 8 "I am the **L**; that is my name!
      43: 11 I am the **L**, and apart from me
      44: 24 I am the **L**, the Maker of all things,
      45: 5 I am the **L**, and there is no other;
      45: 21 Was it not I, the **L**? And there is no
      51: 11 Those the **L** has rescued will return

Isa   53: 6 the **L** has laid on him the iniquity
      53: 10 the will of the **L** will prosper in his
      55: 6 Seek the **L** while he may be found;
      58: 8 of the **L** will be your rear guard.
      58: 11 The **L** will guide you always;
      59: 1 the arm of the **L** is not too short
      61: 3 a planting of the **L** for the display
      61: 10 I delight greatly in the **L**;
Jer   1: 9 Then the **L** reached out his hand
       9: 24 in these I delight," declares the **L**.
      16: 19 **L**, my strength and my fortress,
      17: 7 is the one who trusts in the **L**,
La   3: 40 and let us return to the **L**.
Eze   1: 28 of the likeness of the glory of the **L**.
Hos   1: 7 but I, the **L** their God, will save
       3: 5 return and seek the **L** their God
       6: 1 "Come, let us return to the **L**.
Joel   2: 1 for the day of the **L** is coming.
       2: 11 The day of the **L** is great;
       3: 14 day of the **L** is near in the valley
Am   5: 18 you who long for the day of the **L**!
Jnh   1: 3 But Jonah ran away from the **L**
Mic   4: 2 the word of the **L** from Jerusalem.
       6: 8 what does the **L** require of you?
Na   1: 2 The **L** is a jealous and avenging
       1: 3 The **L** is slow to anger but great
Hab   2: 14 of the **L** as the waters cover the sea.
       2: 20 The **L** is in his holy temple;
Zep   3: 17 The **L** your God is with you,
Zec   1: 17 and the **L** will again comfort Zion
       9: 16 The **L** their God will save his people
      14: 5 Then the **L** my God will come,
      14: 9 On that day there will be one **L**,
Mal   4: 5 and dreadful day of the **L** comes.

LORD'S* (LORD*; this is the proper name of God,
Yahweh, spelled "LORD's" in the NIV)
Ex   34: 34 he entered the **L** presence to speak
Nu   14: 41 you disobeying the **L** command?
Dt   6: 18 is right and good in the **L** sight,
      32: 9 For the **L** portion is his people,
Jos   21: 45 all the **L** good promises to Israel
Ps   24: 1 The earth is the **L**,
      32: 10 the **L** unfailing love surrounds
      89: 1 I will sing of the **L** great love
     103: 17 the **L** love is with those who fear
Pr   3: 11 do not despise the **L** discipline,
Isa   24: 14 west they acclaim the **L** majesty.
      62: 3 a crown of splendor in the **L** hand,
Jer   48: 10 who is lax in doing the **L** work!
La   3: 22 Because of the **L** great love we are
Mic   4: 1 the mountain of the **L** temple will

LOSE (LOSES LOSS LOST)
1Sa   17: 32 "Let no one I heart on account
Mt   10: 39 Whoever finds their life will I it,
Lk   9: 25 and yet I or forfeit their very self?
Jn   6: 39 that I shall I none of all those
Heb   12: 3 will not grow weary and I heart.
      12: 5 not I heart when he rebukes you,

LOSES (LOSE)
Mt   5: 13 But if the salt I its saltiness,
Lk   15: 4 a hundred sheep and I one of them.
      15: 8 has ten silver coins and I one.

LOSS (LOSE)
Ro   11: 12 their I means riches for the Gentiles,
1Co   3: 15 the builder will suffer I but yet will
Php   3: 8 I consider everything a I because

LOST (LOSE)
Ps   73: 2 I had nearly I my foothold.
Jer   50: 6 "My people have been I sheep;
Eze   34: 4 the strays or searched for the I.
      34: 16 I will search for the I and bring
Lk   15: 4 go after the I sheep until he finds
      15: 6 I have found my I sheep.'
      15: 9 I have found my I coin.'
      15: 24 he was I and is found.'
      19: 10 came to seek and to save the I."

Php   3: 8 for whose sake I have I all things.

LOT (LOTS)
  Nephew of Abraham (Ge 11:27; 12:5). Chose to live in Sodom (Ge 13). Rescued from four kings (Ge 14). Rescued from Sodom (Ge 19:1-29; 2Pe 2:7). Fathered Moab and Ammon by his daughters (Ge 19:30-38).

Est   3: 7 the I) was cast in the presence
      9: 24 the I) for their ruin and destruction.
Pr 16: 33 The I is cast into the lap, but its
    18: 18 Casting the I settles disputes
Ecc 3: 22 their work, because that is their I.
Ac   1: 26 cast lots, and the I fell to Matthias;

LOTS (LOT)
Ps 22: 18 them and cast I for my garment.
Mt 27: 35 divided up his clothes by casting I.

LOVE (BELOVED LOVED LOVELY LOVER LOVERS LOVES LOVING)
Ge 22: 2 son, your only son, whom you I–
Ex 15: 13 In your unfailing I you will lead
    20: 6 showing I to a thousand generations
    34: 6 abounding in I and faithfulness,
Lev 19: 18 but I your neighbor as yourself.
    19: 34 L them as yourself, for you were
Nu 14: 18 abounding in I and forgiving sin
Dt   5: 10 showing I to a thousand generations
     6: 5 L the LORD your God with all
     7: 13 He will I you and bless you
   10: 12 to I him, to serve the LORD your
   11: 13 to I the LORD your God
   13: 6 or the wife you I, or your closest
   30: 6 you may I him with all your heart
Jos 22: 5 to I the LORD your God, to walk
1Ki 3: 3 Solomon showed his I
     8: 23 you who keep your covenant of I
2Ch 5: 13 his I endures forever."
Ne   1: 5 covenant of I with those who I him
Ps 18: 1 I I you, LORD, my strength.
    23: 6 I will follow me all the days of my
    25: 6 your great mercy and I, for they are
    31: 16 save me in your unfailing I.
    32: 10 LORD's unfailing I surrounds
    33: 5 the earth is full of his unfailing I.
    33: 18 whose hope is in his unfailing I,
    36: 5 Your I, LORD,
    36: 7 How priceless is your unfailing I,
    45: 7 You I righteousness and hate
    51: 1 God, according to your unfailing I;
    57: 10 For great is your I,
    63: 3 Because your I is better than life,
   66: 20 prayer or withheld his I from me!
    77: 8 his unfailing I vanished forever?
    85: 7 Show us your unfailing I, LORD,
    85: 10 L and faithfulness meet together;
    86: 13 For great is your I toward me;
    89: 1 sing of the LORD's great I forever;
    89: 33 but I will not take my I from him,
    92: 2 proclaiming your I in the morning
    94: 18 slipping," your unfailing I, LORD,
  100: 5 is good and his I endures forever;
  101: 1 I will sing of your I and justice;
  103: 4 crowns you with I and compassion,
  103: 8 slow to anger, abounding in I.
  103: 11 so great is his I for those who fear
  107: 8 to the LORD for his unfailing I
  108: 4 For great is your I, higher than
  116: 1 I I the LORD, for he heard my
  118: 1 he is good; his I endures forever.
  119: 47 your commands because I I them.
  119: 64 The earth is filled with your I,
  119: 76 May your unfailing I be my
  119: 97 Oh, how I I your law! I meditate
  119: 119 dross; therefore I I your statutes.
  119:124 your servant according to your I
  119:132 do to those who I your name.
  119:159 See how I I your precepts;
  119:163 detest falsehood but I I your law.
  119:165 peace have those who I your law,

Ps 122: 6 "May those who I you be secure.
  130: 7 for with the LORD is unfailing I
  136: 1 His I endures forever.
  143: 8 bring me word of your unfailing I,
  145: 8 slow to anger and rich in I.
  145: 20 LORD watches over all who I him,
  147: 11 put their hope in his unfailing I.
Pr   3: 3 Let I and faithfulness never leave
     4: 6 I her, and she will watch over you.
     5: 19 you ever be intoxicated with her I.
     8: 17 I I those who I me, and those who
     9: 8 rebuke the wise and they will I you.
   10: 12 but I covers over all wrongs.
   14: 22 those who plan what is good find I
   15: 17 with I than a fattened calf
   17: 9 Whoever would foster I covers
   19: 22 a person desires is unfailing I;
   20: 6 Many claim to have unfailing I,
   20: 13 Do not I sleep or you will grow
   20: 28 L and faithfulness keep a king safe;
   21: 21 righteousness and I finds life,
   27: 5 is open rebuke than hidden I.
Ecc 9: 6 Their I, their hate and their
     9: 9 whom you I, all the days of this
SS   2: 4 and let his banner over me be I.
     8: 6 for I is as strong as death,
     8: 7 Many waters cannot quench I;
Isa   5: 1 sing for the one I I a song about his
   16: 5 In I a throne will be established;
   38: 17 In your I you kept me from the pit
   54: 10 yet my unfailing I for you will not
   55: 3 my faithful I promised to David.
   61: 8 "For I, the LORD, I justice;
   63: 9 In his I and mercy he redeemed
Jer   5: 31 and my people I it this way.
   31: 3 loved you with an everlasting I;
   32: 18 You show I to thousands but bring
   33: 11 his I endures forever."
La   3: 22 of the LORD's great I we are not
     3: 32 so great is his unfailing I.
Eze 33: 32 more than one who sings I songs
Da   9: 4 covenant of I with those who I him
Hos 2: 19 and justice, in I and compassion.
     3: 1 L her as the LORD loves
   11: 4 of human kindness, with ties of I.
   12: 6 maintain I and justice, and wait
Joel 2: 13 slow to anger and abounding in I.
Am   5: 15 Hate evil, I good; maintain justice
Mic 3: 2 you who hate good and I evil;
     6: 8 to I mercy and to walk humbly
Zep 3: 17 his I he will no longer rebuke you,
Zec 8: 19 Therefore I truth and peace."
Mt   3: 17 said, "This is my Son, whom I I;
     5: 44 I your enemies and pray for those
     6: 24 will hate the one and I the other,
   17: 5 said, "This is my Son, whom I I;
   19: 19 'I your neighbor as yourself.'"
   22: 37 "'L the Lord your God with all
Lk   6: 32 "If you I those who I you,
     7: 42 which of them will I him more?"
   20: 13 I will send my son, whom I I;
Jn 13: 34 command I give you: L one another.
   13: 35 my disciples, if you I one another."
   14: 15 "If you I me, keep my commands.
   15: 13 Greater I has no one than this:
   15: 17 This is my command: L each other.
   21: 15 do you I me more than these?"
Ro 5: 5 because God's I has been poured
     5: 8 God demonstrates his own I for us
    8: 28 for the good of those who I him,
    8: 35 separate us from the I of Christ?
    8: 39 separate us from the I of God that
   12: 9 L must be sincere. Hate what is
   12: 10 Be devoted to one another in I.
   13: 8 continuing debt to I one another,
   13: 9 "L your neighbor as yourself."
   13: 10 Therefore I is the fulfillment

1Co 2: 9 prepared for those who l him–
8: 1 puffs up while l builds up.
13: 1 but do not have l, I am only
13: 2 but do not have l, I am nothing.
13: 3 but do not have l, I gain nothing.
13: 4 L is patient, l is kind. It does not
13: 4 L is patient, l is kind. It does not
13: 6 L does not delight in evil
13: 8 L never fails. But where there are
13: 13 these three remain: faith, hope and l. But the greatest of these is l.
14: 1 Follow the way of l and eagerly
16: 14 Do everything in l.
2Co 5: 14 For Christ's l compels us,
8: 8 sincerity of your l by comparing it
8: 24 show these men the proof of your l
Gal 5: 6 is faith expressing itself through l.
5: 13 serve one another humbly in l.
5: 22 But the fruit of the Spirit is l, joy,
Eph 1: 4 holy and blameless in his sight. In l
2: 4 But because of his great l for us,
3: 17 being rooted and established in l,
3: 18 high and deep is the l of Christ,
3: 19 and to know this l that surpasses
4: 2 bearing with one another in l.
4: 15 speaking the truth in l, we will
5: 2 and walk in the way of l, just as
5: 25 Husbands, l your wives, just as
5: 28 to l their wives as their own bodies.
5: 33 must l his wife as he loves himself,
Php 1: 9 that your l may abound more
2: 2 having the same l, being one
Col 1: 5 l that spring from the hope stored
2: 2 in heart and united in l,
3: 14 And over all these virtues put on l,
3: 19 l your wives and do not be harsh
1Th 3: 12 your labor prompted by l, and your
4: 9 been taught by God to l each other.
5: 8 on faith and l as a breastplate,
2Th 3: 5 Lord direct your hearts into God's l
1Ti 1: 5 The goal of this command is l,
2: 15 faith, l and holiness with propriety.
4: 12 conduct, in l, in faith and in purity.
6: 10 For the l of money is a root of all
6: 11 faith, l, endurance and gentleness.
2Ti 1: 7 us power, l and self-discipline.
2: 22 faith, l and peace, along with those
3: 10 faith, patience, l, endurance,
Titus 2: 4 women to l their husbands
Phm : 9 to appeal to you on the basis of l.
Heb 6: 10 the l you have shown him as you
10: 24 may spur one another on toward l
13: 5 your lives free from the l of money
Jas 1: 12 has promised to those who l him.
2: 5 he promised those who l him?
2: 8 "L your neighbor as yourself,"
1Pe 1: 22 you have sincere l for each other,
1: 22 you have sincere l for each other,
2: 17 everyone, the family of believers,
3: 8 be sympathetic, l one another,
3: 10 For, "Whoever would l life and see
4: 8 Above all, l each other deeply,
4: 8 because l covers over a multitude
5: 14 Greet one another with a kiss of l.
2Pe 1: 7 and to mutual affection, l.
1: 17 saying, "This is my Son, whom l l;
1Jn 2: 5 l for God is truly made complete
2: 15 Do not l the world or anything
3: 1 See what great l the Father has
3: 10 who does not l their brother
3: 11 We should l one another.
3: 14 to life, because we l each other.
3: 16 This is how we know what l is:
3: 18 let us not l with words or speech
3: 23 l one another as he commanded
4: 7 one another, for l comes from God.
4: 8 not know God, because God is l.

1Jn 4: 9 is how God showed his l among us:
4: 10 This is l: not that we loved God,
4: 11 us, we also ought to l one another.
4: 12 but if we l one another, God lives
4: 16 God is l. Whoever lives in l lives
4: 17 This is how l is made complete
4: 18 There is no fear in l. But perfect l
4: 19 We l because he first loved us.
4: 20 whoever does not l their brother
4: 21 loves God must also l their brother
5: 2 we know that we l the children
5: 3 In fact, this is l for God: to keep his
2Jn : 5 l ask that we l one another.
: 6 his command is that you walk in l.
Jude : 12 are blemishes at your l feasts,
: 21 yourselves in God's l as you wait
Rev 2: 4 You have forsaken the l you had
3: 19 Those whom l l l rebuke
12: 11 they did not l their lives so much

LOVED (LOVE)
Ge 24: 67 she became his wife, and he l her;
37: 3 Now Israel l Joseph more than any
Dt 7: 8 it was because the Lord l you
1Sa 1: 5 a double portion because he l her,
20: 17 because he l him as he l himself.
Ps 44: 3 light of your face, for you l them.
Jer 2: 2 youth, how as a bride you l me
31: 3 "I have l you with an everlasting
Hos 2: 23 to the one I called 'Not my l one.'
3: 1 though she is l by another man
9: 10 became as vile as the thing they l.
11: 1 "When Israel was a child, l l him,
Mal 1: 2 "I have l you," says the Lord.
Mk 12: 6 one left to send, a son, whom he l.
Jn 3: 16 For God so l the world that he gave
3: 19 people l darkness instead of light
11: 5 Now Jesus l Martha and her sister
12: 43 for they l human praise more than
13: 1 in the world, he l them to the end.
13: 23 the disciple whom Jesus l,
13: 34 As I have l you, so you must love
14: 21 The one who loves me will be l
15: 9 "As the Father has l me, so have l l
15: 12 Love each other as I have l you.
19: 26 disciple whom he l standing
Ro 8: 37 conquerors through him who l us.
9: 13 "Jacob l l, but Esau l hated."
9: 25 'my l one' who is not my l one,"
11: 28 they are l on account
Gal 2: 20 who l me and gave himself for me.
Eph 5: 2 just as Christ l us and gave himself
5: 25 just as Christ l the church and gave
2Th 2: 16 who l us and by his grace gave us
2Ti 4: 10 for Demas, because he l this world,
Heb 1: 9 You have l righteousness and hated
1Jn 4: 10 not that we l God, but that he l us
4: 11 since God so l us, we also ought
4: 19 We love because he first l us.

LOVELY (LOVE)
Ps 84: 1 How l is your dwelling place,
SS 2: 14 voice is sweet, and your face is l.
5: 16 sweetness itself; he is altogether l.
Php 4: 8 is pure, whatever is l, whatever is

LOVER (LOVE)
1Ti 3: 3 not quarrelsome, not a l of money.

LOVERS (LOVE)
2Ti 3: 2 People will be l of themselves,
3: 3 brutal, not l of the good,
3: 4 l of pleasure rather than l of God–

LOVES (LOVE)
Ps 11: 7 Lord is righteous, he l justice;
33: 5 The Lord l righteousness
34: 12 Whoever of you l life and desires
127: 2 for he grants sleep to those he l.
Pr 3: 12 the Lord disciplines those he l,
12: 1 Whoever l discipline l knowledge,

Pr	17: 17	A friend **I** at all times, and
	17: 19	Whoever **I** a quarrel **I** sin;
	22: 11	One who **I** a pure heart and who
Mt	10: 37	"Anyone who **I** their father
Lk	7: 47	has been forgiven little **I** little."
Jn	3: 35	The Father **I** the Son and has
	10: 17	The reason my Father **I** me is that **I**
	14: 21	The one who **I** me will be loved
	14: 23	"Anyone who **I** me will obey my
Ro	13: 8	for whoever **I** others has fulfilled
2Co	9: 7	for God **I** a cheerful giver.
Eph	5: 28	He who **I** his wife **I** himself.
	5: 33	must love his wife as he **I** himself,
Heb	12: 6	the Lord disciplines the one he **I**,
1Jn	4: 7	Everyone who **I** has been born
	5: 1	who **I** the father **I** his child
3Jn	: 9	but Diotrephes, who **I** to be first,
Rev	1: 5	To him who **I** us and has freed us

LOVING (LOVE)

Ps	25: 10	All the ways of the LORD are **I**
Heb	13: 1	Keep on **I** one another as brothers
1Jn	5: 2	by **I** God and carrying out his

LOWLY

Job	5: 11	The **I** he sets on high, and those
Pr	29: 23	low, but the **I** in spirit gain honor.
Isa	57: 15	to revive the spirit of the **I**
Eze	21: 26	The **I** will be exalted and
Mt	18: 4	whoever takes the **I** position
1Co	1: 28	God chose the **I** things of this

LUKE

Co-worker with Paul (Col 4:14; 2Ti 4:11; Phm 24).

LUKEWARM

Rev	3: 16	So, because you are **I**—

LUST

Pr	6: 25	Do not **I** in your heart after her
Col	3: 5	impurity, **I**, evil desires and greed,
1Th	4: 5	not in passionate **I** like the pagans,
1Jn	2: 16	the **I** of the flesh, the **I** of the eyes,

LYING (LIE)

Pr	6: 17	haughty eyes, a **I** tongue,
	26: 28	A **I** tongue hates those it hurts,

MACEDONIA

Ac	16: 9	a vision of a man of **M** standing

MADE (MAKE)

Ge	1: 16	God **m** two great lights—
	1: 25	God **m** the wild animals according
	2: 22	the LORD God **m** a woman
2Ki	19: 15	You have **m** heaven and earth.
Ps	95: 5	for he **m** it, and his hands formed
	100: 3	It is he who **m** us, and we are his;
	139: 14	I am fearfully and wonderfully **m**;
Ecc	3: 11	He has **m** everything beautiful in
Mk	2: 27	"The Sabbath was **m** for man,
Jn	1: 3	Through him all things were **m**;
Ac	17: 24	"The God who **m** the world
Heb	1: 2	whom also he **m** the universe.
Rev	14: 7	Worship him who **m** the heavens,

MAGI

Mt	2: 1	**M** from the east came to Jerusalem

MAGOG

Eze	38: 2	of the land of **M**, the chief prince
	39: 6	I will send fire on **M** and on those
Rev	20: 8	Gog and **M**—and to gather them

MAIMED

Mt	18: 8	It is better for you to enter life **m**

MAJESTIC (MAJESTY)

Ex	15: 6	hand, LORD, was **m** in power.
	15: 11	**m** in holiness, awesome in glory,
Ps	8: 1	**m** is your name in all the earth!
	29: 4	the voice of the LORD is **m**.
	111: 3	Glorious and **m** are his deeds,
SS	6: 10	sun, **m** as the stars in procession?
2Pe	1: 17	came to him from the **M** Glory,

MAJESTY (MAJESTIC)

Ex	15: 7	your **m** you threw down those who
Dt	33: 26	and on the clouds in his **m**.
1Ch	16: 27	Splendor and **m** are before him;
Est	1: 4	the splendor and glory of his **m**.
Job	37: 22	God comes in awesome **m**.
	40: 10	clothe yourself in honor and **m**.
Ps	45: 4	In your **m** ride forth victoriously
	93: 1	LORD reigns, he is robed in **m**;
	145: 5	the glorious splendor of your **m**—
Isa	53: 2	beauty or **m** to attract us to him,
Eze	31: 2	can be compared with you in **m**?
2Pe	1: 16	but we were eyewitnesses of his **m**.
Jude	: 25	only God our Savior be glory, **m**,

MAKE (MADE MAKER MAKES MAKING)

Ge	1: 26	"Let us **m** mankind in our image,
	2: 18	I will **m** a helper suitable for him."
	12: 2	"I will **m** you into a great nation,
Ex	22: 3	steals must certainly **m** restitution,
Nu	6: 25	the LORD **m** his face shine on you
Ps	108: 1	sing and **m** music with all my soul.
Isa	14: 14	I will **m** myself like the Most
	29: 16	formed it, "You did not **m** me"?
Jer	31: 31	"when I will **m** a new covenant
Mt	3: 3	Lord, **m** straight paths for him.'"
	28: 19	go and **m** disciples of all nations,
Lk	13: 24	"**M** every effort to enter through
Ro	14: 19	Let us therefore **m** every effort to
2Co	5: 9	So we **m** it our goal to please him,
Eph	4: 3	**M** every effort to keep the unity
Col	4: 5	**m** the most of every opportunity.
1Th	4: 11	**m** it your ambition to lead a quiet
Heb	4: 11	**m** every effort to enter that rest,
	12: 14	**M** every effort to live in peace
2Pe	1: 5	**m** every effort to add to your faith
	3: 14	**m** every effort to be found spotless,

MAKER (MAKE)

Job	4: 17	man be more pure than his **M**?
	36: 3	I will ascribe justice to my **M**.
Ps	95: 6	us kneel before the LORD our **M**;
Pr	22: 2	The LORD is the **M** of them all.
Isa	45: 9	to those who quarrel with their **M**,
	54: 5	For your **M** is your husband—
Jer	10: 16	these, for he is the **M** of all things,

MAKES (MAKE)

1Co	3: 7	but only God, who **m** things grow.

MAKING (MAKE)

Ps	19: 7	are trustworthy, **m** wise the simple.
Ecc	12: 12	Of **m** many books there is no end,
Jn	5: 18	Father, **m** himself equal with God.
Eph	5: 16	**m** the most of every opportunity,

MALE

Ge	1: 27	**m** and female he created them.
Gal	3: 28	nor free, nor is there **m** and female,

MALICE (MALICIOUS)

Ro	1: 29	envy, murder, strife, deceit and **m**.
Col	3: 8	anger, rage, **m**, slander, and filthy
1Pe	2: 1	rid yourselves of all **m** and all

MALICIOUS (MALICE)

1Ti	3: 11	not **m** talkers but temperate
	6: 4	envy, strife, **m** talk, evil suspicions

MAN (MANKIND MEN WOMAN WOMEN)

Ge	2: 7	the LORD God formed a **m**
	2: 18	not good for the **m** to be alone.
	2: 23	for she was taken out of **m**."
Dt	8: 3	does not live on bread alone
1Sa	13: 14	sought out a **m** after his own heart
Ps	127: 5	Blessed is the **m** whose quiver is
Pr	30: 19	way of a **m** with a young woman.
Isa	53: 3	by mankind, a **m** of suffering,
Mt	19: 5	this reason a **m** will leave his father
Lk	4: 4	'**M** shall not live on bread alone.'"
Ro	5: 12	entered the world through one **m**,
1Co	7: 2	**m** should have sexual relations
	11: 3	that the head of every **m** is Christ,

1Co 11: 3 and the head of the woman is **m**,
     13: 11 When I became a **m**, I put the ways
Php   2: 8 being found in appearance as a **m**,
1Ti   2: 5 and mankind, the **m** Christ Jesus,
      2: 12 or to assume authority over a **m**;

MANAGE
Jer 12: 5 how will you **m** in the thickets
1Ti   3: 4 He must **m** his own family well
      3: 12 to his wife and must **m** his children
      5: 14 to **m** their homes and to give

MANASSEH
1. Firstborn of Joseph (Ge 41:51; 46:20). Blessed (Ge 48).
2. Son of Hezekiah; king of Judah (2Ki 21:1-18; 2Ch 33:1-20).

MANGER
Lk   2: 12 in cloths and lying in a **m**."

MANKIND (MAN)
Ge   1: 26 "Let us make **m** in our image,

MANNA
Ex   16: 31 people of Israel called the bread **m**.
Dt   8: 16 He gave you **m** to eat
Jn   6: 49 Your ancestors ate the **m**
Rev   2: 17 I will give some of the hidden **m**.

MANNER
1Co 11: 27 in an unworthy **m** will be guilty
Php   1: 27 conduct yourselves in a **m** worthy

MARITAL (MARRY)
Ex   21: 10 of her food, clothing and **m** rights.
1Co   7: 3 husband should fulfill his **m** duty

MARK (MARKS)
Cousin of Barnabas (Col 4:10; 2Ti 4:11; Phm 24; 1Pe 5:13), see JOHN.
Ge   4: 15 the LORD put a **m** on Cain so
Rev 13: 16 to receive a **m** on their right hands

MARKS (MARK)
Jn   20: 25 "Unless I see the nail **m** in his
Gal   6: 17 I bear on my body the **m** of Jesus.

MARRED
Isa 52: 14 and his form **m** beyond human

MARRIAGE (MARRY)
Mt   22: 30 neither marry nor be given in **m**;
     24: 38 marrying and giving in **m**,
Heb 13: 4 **M** should be honored by all,

MARRIED (MARRY)
Ro   7: 2 by law a **m** woman is bound to her
1Co   7: 33 But a **m** man is concerned
      7: 36 is not sinning. They should get **m**.

MARRIES (MARRY)
Mt   5: 32 anyone who **m** a divorced woman
     19: 9 and **m** another woman commits
Lk   16: 18 the man who **m** a divorced woman

MARRY (INTERMARRY MARITAL MARRIAGE MARRIED MARRIES)
Mt   22: 30 people will neither **m** nor be given
1Co   7: 9 they should **m**, for it is better to **m**
1Ti   5: 14 So I counsel younger widows to **m**,

MARTHA
Sister of Mary and Lazarus (Lk 10:38-42; Jn 11; 12:2).

MARVELED
Lk   2: 33 mother **m** at what was said

MARY
1. Mother of Jesus (Mt 1:16-25; Lk 1:27-56; 2:1-40). With Jesus at temple (Lk 2:41-52), at the wedding in Cana (Jn 2:1-5), questioning his sanity (Mk 3:21), at the cross (Jn 19:25-27). Among disciples after Ascension (Ac 1:14).
2. Magdalene; former demoniac (Lk 8:2). Helped support Jesus' ministry (Lk 8:1-3). At the cross (Mt 27:56; Mk 15:40; Jn 19:25), burial (Mt 27:61; Mk 15:47). Saw angel after resurrection (Mt 28:1-10; Mk 16:1-9; Lk 24:1-12); also Jesus (Jn 20:1-18).
3. Sister of Martha and Lazarus (Jn 11). Washed Jesus' feet (Jn 12:1-8).

MASQUERADES
2Co 11: 14 for Satan himself **m** as an angel

MASTER (MASTERED MASTERS)
Mt   10: 24 teacher, nor a servant above his **m**.
     24: 46 servant whose **m** finds him doing
     25: 21 "His **m** replied, 'Well done,
Ro   6: 14 For sin shall no longer be your **m**,
      14: 4 To their own **m**, servants stand
2Ti   2: 21 useful to the **M** and prepared to do

MASTERED (MASTER)
1Co   6: 12 but I will not be **m** by anything.
2Pe   2: 19 are slaves to whatever has **m** them."

MASTERS (MASTER)
Mt   6: 24 "No one can serve two **m**.
Eph   6: 5 obey your earthly **m** with respect
      6: 9 **m**, treat your slaves in the same
Titus 2: 9 be subject to their **m** in everything,

MATTHEW
Apostle; former tax collector (Mt 9:9-13; 10:3; Mk 3:18; Lk 6:15; Ac 1:13). Also called Levi (Mk 2:14-17; Lk 5:27-32).

MATURE (MATURITY)
Eph   4: 13 of the Son of God and become **m**,
Php   3: 15 who are **m** should take such a view
Heb   5: 14 But solid food is for the **m**,
Jas   1: 4 its work so that you may be **m**

MATURITY (MATURE)
Heb   6: 1 Christ and be taken forward to **m**,

MEAL
1Co 10: 27 If an unbeliever invites you to a **m**
Heb 12: 16 single **m** sold his inheritance rights

MEANING
Ne   8: 8 and giving the **m** so that the people

MEANS
1Co   9: 22 by all possible **m** I might save some.

MEAT
Ro   14: 6 eats **m** does so to the Lord,
     14: 21 It is better not to eat **m** or drink

MEDIATOR
1Ti   2: 5 one God and one **m** between God
Heb   8: 6 which he is **m** is superior to the old
      9: 15 this reason Christ is the **m** of a new
     12: 24 to Jesus the **m** of a new covenant,

MEDICINE
Pr   17: 22 A cheerful heart is good **m**,

MEDITATE (MEDITATION)
Jos   1: 8 **m** on it day and night, so that you
Ps 119: 15 I **m** on your precepts and consider
    119: 78 but I will **m** on your precepts.
    119: 97 I **m** on it all day long.
    145: 5 I will **m** on your wonderful works.

MEDITATES (MEDITATE)
Ps   1: 2 who **m** on his law day and night.

MEDITATION (MEDITATE)
Ps   19: 14 this **m** of my heart be pleasing
    104: 34 May my **m** be pleasing to him, as I

MEDIUM
Lev 20: 27 or woman who is a **m** or spiritist

MEEK
Ps   37: 11 But the **m** will inherit the land
Mt   5: 5 Blessed are the **m**, for they will

MEET (MEETING)
Ps   85: 10 Love and faithfulness **m** together;
Am   4: 12 Israel, prepare to **m** your God."
1Th   4: 17 the clouds to **m** the Lord in the air.

MEETING (MEET)
Heb 10: 25 not giving up **m** together, as some

MELCHIZEDEK
Ge   14: 18 **M** king of Salem brought out bread
Ps 110: 4 a priest forever, in the order of **M**."
Heb   7: 11 one in the order of **M**,

MELT
2Pe   3: 12 the elements will **m** in the heat.

MEMBERS
Mic   7:   6 a man's enemies are the **m** of his
Ro   12:   4 of us has one body with many **m**,
1Co   6: 15 your bodies are **m** of Christ
Eph   4: 25 for we are all **m** of one body.
Col   3: 15 since as **m** of one body you were

MEN (MAN)
Ro   1: 27 **M** committed shameful acts with other **m**,
1Ti   2:   8 Therefore I want the **m** everywhere

MENAHEM
King of Israel (2Ki 15:17-22).

MERCIFUL (MERCY)
Dt   4: 31 the Lord your God is a **m** God;
Ne   9: 31 for you are a gracious and **m** God.
Mt   5:   7 Blessed are the **m**, for they will be
Lk   6: 36 Be **m**, just as your Father is **m**.
Heb   2: 17 in order that he might become a **m**
Jude   : 22 Be **m** to those who doubt;

MERCY (MERCIFUL)
Ex   33: 19 have **m** on whom I will have **m**,
Ps   25:   6 Lord, your great **m** and love,
Isa   63:   9 his love and **m** he redeemed them;
Hos   6:   6 For I desire **m**, not sacrifice,
Mic   6:   8 to love **m** and to walk humbly
Hab   3:   2 in wrath remember **m**.
Mt   12:   7 mean, 'I desire **m**, not sacrifice,'
   23: 23 justice, **m** and faithfulness.
Ro   9: 15 "I will have **m** on whom I have **m**,
Eph   2:   4 love for us, God, who is rich in **m**,
Jas   2: 13 **M** triumphs over judgment.
1Pe   1:   3 In his great **m** he has given us new

MESSAGE
Isa   53:   1 Who has believed our **m**
Jn   12: 38 who has believed our **m**
Ro   10: 17 faith comes from hearing the **m**,
1Co   1: 18 the **m** of the cross is foolishness
2Co   5: 19 to us the **m** of reconciliation.

MESSIAH (MESSIAH)
Mt   1: 16 of Jesus who is called the **M**.
   16: 16 "You are the **M**, the Son
   22: 42 "What do you think about the **M**?
Jn   1: 41 "We have found the **M**" (that is,
   4: 25 that **M**" (called Christ) "is coming.
   20: 31 may believe that Jesus is the **M**,
Ac   2: 36 you crucified, both Lord and **M**."
   5: 42 the good news that Jesus is the **M**.
   9: 22 by proving that Jesus is the **M**.
   17:   3 proving that the **M** had to suffer
   18: 28 the Scriptures that Jesus was the **M**.
   26: 23 that the **M** would suffer and,

MESSIAHS (MESSIAH)
Mt   24: 24 For false **m** and false prophets will

METHUSELAH
Ge   5: 27 **M** lived a total of 969 years,

MICHAEL
Archangel (Jude 9); warrior in angelic realm, protector of Israel (Da 10:13, 21; 12:1; Rev 12:7).

MIDWIVES
Ex   1: 17 The **m**, however, feared God

MIGHT (ALMIGHTY MIGHTY)
Jdg   16: 30 Then he pushed with all his **m**,
2Sa   6: 14 before the Lord with all his **m**.
Ps   21: 13 we will sing and praise your **m**.
Zec   4:   6 'Not by **m** nor by power, but by my
1Ti   6: 16 To him be honor and **m** forever.

MIGHTY (MIGHT)
Ex   6:   1 of my **m** hand he will let them go;
Dt   7:   8 he brought you out with a **m** hand
2Sa   1: 19 How the **m** have fallen!
   23:   8 the names of David's **m** warriors:
Ps   24:   8 and **m**, the Lord **m** in battle.
   50:   1 The **M** One, God, the Lord,
   89:   8 are **m**, and your faithfulness
   136: 12 a **m** hand and outstretched arm;

Ps   147:   5 Great is our Lord and **m** in power;
Isa   9:   6 Wonderful Counselor, **M** God,
Zep   3: 17 you, the **M** Warrior who saves.
Eph   6: 10 in the Lord and in his **m** power.

MILE
Mt   5: 41 If anyone forces you to go one **m**,

MILK
Ex   3:   8 a land flowing with **m** and honey–
Isa   55:   1 buy wine and **m** without money
1Co   3:   2 I gave you **m**, not solid food,
Heb   5: 12 You need **m**, not solid food!
1Pe   2:   2 crave pure spiritual **m**, so that by it

MILLSTONE (STONE)
Lk   17:   2 with a **m** tied around their neck

MIND (DOUBLE-MINDED MINDFUL MINDS MINDSET)
1Sa   15: 29 does not lie or change his **m**;
1Ch   28:   9 devotion and with a willing **m**,
Ps   26:   2 me, examine my heart and my **m**;
Mt   22: 37 all your soul and with all your **m**.'
Ac   4: 32 believers were one in heart and **m**.
Ro   7: 25 then, I myself in my **m** am a slave
   8:   7 The **m** governed by the flesh is
   12:   2 by the renewing of your **m**.
1Co   2:   9 what no human **m** has conceived"
   14: 14 spirit prays, but my **m** is unfruitful.
2Co   13: 11 another, be of one **m**, live in peace.
Php   3: 19 Their **m** is set on earthly things.
1Th   4: 11 You should **m** your own business
Heb   7: 21 sworn and will not change his **m**:

MINDFUL (MIND)
Ps   8:   4 is mankind that you are **m** of them,
Lk   1: 48 he has been **m** of the humble state
Heb   2:   6 is mankind that you are **m** of them,

MINDS (MIND)
Ps   7:   9 the righteous God who probes **m**
Isa   26:   3 peace those whose **m** are steadfast,
Jer   31: 33 "I will put my law in their **m**
Eph   4: 23 new in the attitude of your **m**;
Col   3:   2 Set your **m** on things above,
Heb   8: 10 I will put my laws in their **m**
Rev   2: 23 he who searches hearts and **m**,

MINDSET (MIND)
Php   2:   5 have the same **m** as Christ Jesus:

MINISTERING (MINISTRY)
Heb   1: 14 Are not all angels **m** spirits sent

MINISTRY (MINISTERING)
Ac   6:   4 to prayer and the **m** of the word."
2Co   5: 18 gave us the **m** of reconciliation:
2Ti   4:   5 discharge all the duties of your **m**.

MIRACLES
1Ch   16: 12 done, his **m**, and the judgments he
Ps   77: 14 You are the God who performs **m**;
Mt   11: 20 most of his **m** had been performed,
   11: 21 the **m** that were performed in you
Mk   6:   2 What are these remarkable **m** he is
Ac   2: 22 accredited by God to you by **m**,
   19: 11 did extraordinary **m** through Paul,
1Co   12: 28 then **m**, then gifts of healing,
Heb   2:   4 wonders and various **m**, and by

MIRE
Ps   40:   2 slimy pit, out of the mud and **m**;
Isa   57: 20 whose waves cast up **m** and mud.

MIRIAM
Sister of Moses and Aaron (Nu 26:59). Led dancing at Red Sea (Ex 15:20-21). Struck with leprosy for criticizing Moses (Nu 12). Death (Nu 20:1).

MIRROR
Jas   1: 23 who looks at his face in a **m**

MISERY
Ex   3:   7 "I have indeed seen the **m** of my
Jdg   10: 16 he could bear Israel's **m** no longer.
Hos   5: 15 in their **m** they will earnestly seek
Ro   3: 16 ruin and **m** mark their ways,
Jas   5:   1 because of the **m** that is coming

MISLED

1Co 15: 33 Do not be **m**:

MISS

Pr 19: 2 more will hasty feet **m** the way!

MIST

Hos 6: 4 Your love is like the morning **m**,
Jas 4: 14 You are a **m** that appears for a little

MISUSE

Ex 20: 7 "You shall not **m** the name
Dt 5: 11 "You shall not **m** the name
Ps 139: 20 your adversaries **m** your name.

MOCK (MOCKED MOCKER MOCKERS MOCKING)

Ps 22: 7 All who see me **m** me;
Pr 14: 9 Fools **m** at making amends for sin,
Mk 10: 34 who will **m** him and spit on him,

MOCKED (MOCK)

Mt 27: 29 knelt in front of him and **m** him.
27: 41 of the law and the elders **m** him.
Gal 6: 7 not be deceived: God cannot be **m**.

MOCKER (MOCK)

Pr 9: 7 corrects a **m** invites insults;
9: 12 you are a **m**, you alone will suffer.
20: 1 Wine is a **m** and beer a brawler;
22: 10 Drive out the **m**, and out goes

MOCKERS (MOCK)

Ps 1: 1 take or sit in the company of **m**,

MOCKING (MOCK)

Isa 50: 6 I did not hide my face from **m**

MODEL

1Th 1: 7 And so you became a **m** to all
2Th 3: 9 to offer ourselves as a **m** for you

MOMENT

Job 20: 5 the joy of the godless lasts but a **m**.
Ps 30: 5 For his anger lasts only a **m**, but his
Isa 66: 8 a nation be brought forth in a **m**?
Gal 2: 5 We did not give in to them for a **m**,

MONEY

Ecc 5: 10 loves **m** never has enough;
Isa 55: 1 and you who have no **m**, come,
Mt 6: 24 You cannot serve both God and **m**.
Lk 9: 3 bag, no bread, no **m**, no extra shirt.
1Co 16: 2 you should set aside a sum of **m**
1Ti 3: 3 not quarrelsome, not a lover of **m**.
6: 10 the love of **m** is a root of all kinds
2Ti 3: 2 themselves, lovers of **m**, boastful,
Heb 13: 5 your lives free from the love of **m**

MOON

Ps 121: 6 you by day, nor the **m** by night.
Joel 2: 31 the **m** to blood before the coming
1Co 15: 41 the **m** another and the stars

MORNING

Ge 1: 5 was evening, and there was **m**—
Dt 28: 67 In the **m** you will say, "If only it
Ps 5: 3 In the **m**, LORD, you hear my
2Pe 1: 19 and the **m** star rises in your hearts.
Rev 22: 16 of David, and the bright **M** Star."

MORTAL

1Co 15: 53 and the **m** with immortality.

MOSES

Levite; brother of Aaron (Ex 6:20; 1Ch 6:3). Put in basket into Nile; discovered and raised by Pharaoh's daughter (Ex 2:1-10). Fled to Midian after killing Egyptian (Ex 2:11-15). Married to Zipporah, fathered Gershom (Ex 2:16-22).

Called by the LORD to deliver Israel (Ex 3-4). Pharaoh's resistance (Ex 5). Ten plagues (Ex 7-11). Passover and Exodus (Ex 12-13). Led Israel through Red Sea (Ex 14). Song of deliverance (Ex 15:1-21). Brought water from rock (Ex 17:1-7). Raised hands to defeat Amalekites (Ex 17:8-16). Delegated judges (Ex 18; Dt 1:9-18).

Received Law at Sinai (Ex 19-23; 25-31; Jn 1:17). Announced Law to Israel (Ex 19:7-8; 24; 35). Broke tablets because of golden calf (Ex 32; Dt 9). Saw glory of the LORD (Ex 33-34). Supervised building of tabernacle (Ex 36-40).

Set apart Aaron and priests (Lev 8-9). Numbered tribes (Nu 1-4; 26). Opposed by Aaron and Miriam (Nu 12). Sent spies into Canaan (Nu 13). Announced forty years of wandering for failure to enter land (Nu 14). Opposed by Korah (Nu 16). Forbidden to enter land for striking rock (Nu 20:1-13; Dt 1:37). Lifted bronze snake for healing (Nu 21:4-9; Jn 3:14). Final address to Israel (Dt 1-33). Succeeded by Joshua (Nu 27:12-23; Dt 34). Death (Dt 34:5-12).

"Law of Moses" (1Ki 2:3; Ezr 3:2; Mk 12:26; Lk 24:44). "Book of Moses" (2Ch 25:12; Ne 13:1). "Song of Moses" (Ex 15:1-21; Rev 15:3). "Prayer of Moses" (Ps 90).

MOTHS

Mt 6: 19 where **m** and vermin destroy,

MOTHER (MOTHER'S)

Ge 2: 24 why a man leaves his father and **m**
3: 20 because she would become the **m**
Ex 20: 12 "Honor your father and your **m**,
Lev 20: 9 they have cursed their father or **m**,
Dt 5: 16 "Honor your father and your **m**,
21: 18 does not obey his father and **m**
27: 16 who dishonors their father or **m**."
1Sa 2: 19 Each year his **m** made him a little
Ps 113: 9 her home as a happy **m** of children.
Pr 23: 25 May your father and **m** rejoice;
29: 15 left undisciplined disgraces its **m**.
31: 1 utterance his **m** taught him.
Isa 49: 15 "Can a **m** forget the baby at her
66: 13 As a **m** comforts her child, so will I
Mt 10: 37 or **m** more than me is not worthy
15: 4 said, 'Honor your father and **m**'
19: 5 a man will leave his father and **m**
Mk 7: 10 'Honor your father and **m**,' and,
10: 19 honor your father and **m**.'"
Jn 19: 27 to the disciple, "Here is your **m**."

MOTHER'S (MOTHER)

Job 1: 21 "Naked I came from my **m** womb,
Pr 1: 8 do not forsake your **m** teaching.

MOTIVES

Pr 16: 2 but **m** are weighed by the LORD.
1Co 4: 5 and will expose the **m** of the heart.
Php 1: 18 way, whether from false **m** or true,
1Th 2: 3 not spring from error or impure **m**,
Jas 4: 3 because you ask with wrong **m**,

MOUNTAIN (MOUNTAINS)

Mic 4: 2 let us go up to the **m** of the LORD,
Mt 17: 20 you can say to this **m**,

MOUNTAINS (MOUNTAIN)

Isa 52: 7 beautiful on the **m** are the feet
55: 12 the **m** and hills will burst into song
1Co 13: 2 if I have a faith that can move **m**,

MOURN (MOURNING)

Ecc 3: 4 a time to **m** and a time to dance,
Isa 61: 2 of our God, to comfort all who **m**,
Mt 5: 4 Blessed are those who **m**, for they
Ro 12: 15 **m** with those who **m**.

MOURNING (MOURN)

Jer 31: 13 I will turn their **m** into gladness;
Rev 21: 4 There will be no more death' or **m**

MOUTH

Ps 19: 14 May these words of my **m** and this
40: 3 He put a new song in my **m**,
119:103 taste, sweeter than honey to my **m**!
Pr 27: 2 praise you, and not your own **m**;
Isa 51: 16 I have put my words in your **m**
Mt 12: 34 the **m** speaks what the heart is full
15: 11 but what comes out of their **m**,
Ro 10: 9 If you declare with your **m**,

MUD

Ps 40: 2 slimy pit, out of the **m** and mire;
Isa 57: 20 whose waves cast up mire and **m**.
2Pe 2: 22 returns to her wallowing in the **m**."

MULTITUDE (MULTITUDES)

Isa 31: 1 who trust in the **m** of their chariots
1Pe 4: 8 because love covers over a **m**
Rev 7: 9 there before me was a great **m**

MULTITUDES (MULTITUDE)
Joel   3: 14   **M, m** in the valley of decision!

MURDER (MURDERER MURDERERS)
Ex   20: 13   "You shall not **m.**
Mt   15: 19   **m,** adultery, sexual immorality,
Ro   13: 9   "You shall not **m,**" "You shall not
Jas   2: 11   commit adultery but do commit **m,**

MURDERER (MURDER)
Nu   35: 16   a **m;** the **m** is to be put to death.
Jn   8: 44   He was a **m** from the beginning,
1Jn   3: 15   hates a brother or sister is a **m,**

MURDERERS (MURDER)
1Ti   1: 9   kill their fathers or mothers, for **m,**
Rev   21: 8   vile, the **m,** the sexually immoral,

MUSIC
Ps   27: 6   sing and make **m** to the Lord.
  95: 2   and extol him with **m** and song.
  98: 4   burst into jubilant song with **m;**
  108: 1   sing and make **m** with all my soul.
Eph   5: 19   make **m** from your heart to the Lord,

MUSTARD
Mt   13: 31   kingdom of heaven is like a **m** seed,
  17: 20   you have faith as small as a **m** seed,

MUZZLE
Dt   25: 4   Do not **m** an ox while it is treading
Ps   39: 1   I will put a **m** on my mouth while
1Co   9: 9   Do not **m** an ox while it is treading

MYRRH
Mt   2: 11   gifts of gold, frankincense and **m.**
Mk   15: 23   offered him wine mixed with **m,**

MYSTERY
Ro   16: 25   the revelation of the **m** hidden
1Co   15: 51   Listen, I tell you a **m:** We will not
Eph   5: 32   This is a profound **m**—but I am
Col   1: 26   the **m** that has been kept hidden
1Ti   3: 16   the **m** from which true godliness

MYTHS
1Ti   4: 7   Have nothing to do with godless **m**

NADAB
Son of Jeroboam I; king of Israel (1Ki 15:25-32).

NAIL (NAILING)
Jn   20: 25   "Unless I see the **n** marks in his

NAILING (NAIL)
Ac   2: 23   him to death by **n** him to the cross.
Col   2: 14   has taken it away, **n** it to the cross.

NAKED
Ge   2: 25   Adam and his wife were both **n,**
Job   1: 21   womb, and **n** I will depart.
Isa   58: 7   you see the **n,** to clothe them,
2Co   5: 3   are clothed, we will not be found **n.**

NAME
Ex   3: 15   "This is my **n** forever, the **n** you
  20: 7   "You shall not misuse the **n**
Dt   5: 11   "You shall not misuse the **n**
  28: 58   this glorious and awesome **n**—
1Ki   5: 5   will build the temple for my **N.'**
2Ch   7: 14   people, who are called by my **n,**
Ps   34: 3   let us exalt his **n** together.
  103: 1   my inmost being, praise his holy **n.**
  147: 4   the stars and calls them each by **n.**
Pr   22: 1   A good **n** is more desirable than
  30: 4   What is his **n,** and what is the **n**
Isa   40: 26   and calls forth each of them by **n.**
  57: 15   who lives forever, whose **n** is holy:
Jer   14: 7   Lord, for the sake of your **n.**
Da   12: 1   everyone whose **n** is found written
Joel   2: 32   the **n** of the Lord will be saved;
Zec   14: 9   one Lord, and his **n** the only **n.**
Mt   1: 21   you are to give him the **n** Jesus,
  6: 9   in heaven, hallowed be your **n,**
  18: 20   where two or three gather in my **n,**
Jn   10: 3   He calls his own sheep by **n**
  16: 24   not asked for anything in my **n.**
Ac   4: 12   is no other **n** under heaven given

Ro   10: 13   on the **n** of the Lord will be saved."
Php   2: 9   the **n** that is above every **n,**
Col   3: 17   do it all in the **n** of the Lord Jesus,
Heb   1: 4   the angels as the **n** he has inherited
Rev   20: 15   whose **n** was not found written

NAOMI
Mother-in-law of Ruth (Ru 1). Advised Ruth to seek marriage with Boaz (Ru 2-4).

NARROW
Mt   7: 13   "Enter through the **n** gate.

NATHANAEL
Apostle (Jn 1:45-49; 21:2). Probably also called Bartholomew (Mt 10:3).

NATION (NATIONS)
Ge   12: 2   "I will make you into a great **n,**
Ps   33: 12   Blessed is the **n** whose God is
Pr   14: 34   Righteousness exalts a **n,** but sin
Isa   65: 1   a **n** that did not call on my name,
1Pe   2: 9   a holy **n,** God's special possession,
Rev   7: 9   could count, from every **n,** tribe,

NATIONS (NATION)
Ge   17: 4   You will be the father of many **n.**
  18: 18   and all **n** on earth will be blessed
Ex   19: 5   of all **n** you will be my treasured
Ne   1: 8   I will scatter you among the **n,**
Ps   96: 3   Declare his glory among the **n,**
Isa   40: 15   Surely the **n** are like a drop
Eze   36: 23   has been profaned among the **n,**
Hag   2: 7   what is desired by all **n** will come,
Zec   8: 23   **n** will take firm hold of one Jew
  14: 2   I will gather all the **n** to Jerusalem
Mt   28: 19   go and make disciples of all **n,**
Rev   21: 24   The **n** will walk by its light,

NATURAL (NATURE)
1Co   15: 44   it is sown a **n** body, it is raised

NATURE (NATURAL)
Php   2: 6   Who, being in very **n** God, did not

NAZARENE
Mt   2: 23   that he would be called a **N.**

NAZIRITE
Jdg   13: 7   because the boy will be a **N** of God

NECESSARY
Ro   13: 5   it is **n** to submit to the authorities,

NEED (NEEDS NEEDY)
Mt   6: 8   knows what you **n** before you ask
Ro   12: 13   the Lord's people who are in **n.**
1Co   12: 21   say to the hand, "I don't **n** you!"
1Jn   3: 17   sister in **n** but has no pity on them,

NEEDLE
Mt   19: 24   to go through the eye of a **n** than

NEEDS (NEED)
Isa   58: 11   he will satisfy your **n**
Php   4: 19   God will meet all your **n** according

NEEDY (NEED)
Pr   14: 21   is the one who is kind to the **n.**
  14: 31   is kind to the **n** honors God.
  31: 20   and extends her hands to the **n.**
Mt   6: 2   "So when you give to the **n,** do not

NEGLECT (NEGLECTED)
Ne   10: 39   "We will not **n** the house of our
Ps   119: 16   I will not **n** your word.
Ac   6: 2   for us to **n** the ministry of the word
1Ti   4: 14   not **n** your gift, which was given

NEGLECTED (NEGLECT)
Mt   23: 23   But you have **n** the more important

NEHEMIAH
Cupbearer of Artaxerxes (Ne 2:1); governor of Israel (Ne 8:9). Returned to Jerusalem to rebuild walls (Ne 2-6). With Ezra, reestablished worship (Ne 8). Prayer confessing nation's sin (Ne 9). Dedicated wall (Ne 12).

NEIGHBOR (NEIGHBOR'S)
Ex   20: 16   give false testimony against your **n.**
Lev   19: 18   people, but love your **n** as yourself.

Pr 27: 10 better a **n** nearby than a relative far
Mt 19: 19 and 'love your **n** as yourself.'"
Lk 10: 29 asked Jesus, "And who is my **n**?"
Ro 13: 10 Love does no harm to a **n**.

NEIGHBOR'S (NEIGHBOR)
Ex 20: 17 "You shall not covet your **n** house.
Dt 5: 21 "You shall not covet your **n** wife.
19: 14 not move your **n** boundary stone
Pr 25: 17 Seldom set foot in your **n** house–

NEW
Ps 40: 3 He put a **n** song in my mouth,
Ecc 1: 9 there is nothing **n** under the sun.
Isa 65: 17 I will create **n** heavens and a **n**
Jer 31: 31 I will make a **n** covenant
Eze 36: 26 I will give you a **n** heart and put a **n** spirit in you;
Mt 9: 17 they pour **n** wine into **n** wineskins,
Lk 22: 20 "This cup is the **n** covenant in my
2Co 5: 17 in Christ, the **n** creation has come:
Eph 4: 24 and to put on the **n** self,
2Pe 3: 13 to a **n** heaven and a **n** earth,
1Jn 2: 8 Yet I am writing you a **n** command;

NEWBORN (BEAR)
1Pe 2: 2 Like **n** babies, crave pure spiritual

NEWS
Isa 52: 7 the feet of those who bring good **n**,
Mk 1: 15 Repent and believe the good **n**!"
Lk 2: 10 I bring you good **n** that will cause
Ac 5: 42 proclaiming the good **n** that Jesus
17: 18 Paul was preaching the good **n**
Ro 10: 15 feet of those who bring good **n**!"

NICODEMUS
Pharisee who visited Jesus at night (Jn 3). Argued fair treatment of Jesus (Jn 7:50-52). With Joseph, prepared Jesus for burial (Jn 19:38-42).

NIGHT
Job 35: 10 Maker, who gives songs in the **n**,
Ps 1: 2 meditates on his law day and **n**.
91: 5 You will not fear the terror of **n**,
Jn 3: 2 He came to Jesus at **n** and said,
1Th 5: 2 Lord will come like a thief in the **n**.
5: 5 We do not belong to the **n**
Rev 21: 25 shut, for there will be no **n** there.

NOAH
Righteous man (Eze 14:14, 20) called to build ark (Ge 6-8; Heb 11:7; 1Pe 3:20; 2Pe 2:5). God's covenant with (Ge 9:1-17). Drunkenness of (Ge 9:18-23). Blessed sons, cursed Canaan (Ge 9:24-27).

NOBLE
Ru 3: 11 you are a woman of **n** character.
Ps 45: 1 by a **n** theme as I recite my verses
Pr 12: 4 **n** character is her husband's crown,
31: 10 wife of **n** character who can find?
31: 29 "Many women do **n** things, but
Isa 32: 8 But the **a** make **n** plans, and by **n**
Lk 8: 15 good soil stands for those with a **n**
Php 4: 8 whatever is **n**, whatever is right,

NOTHING
Ne 9: 21 they lacked **n**, their clothes did not
Jer 32: 17 **N** is too hard for you.
Jn 15: 5 apart from me you can do **n**.

NULLIFY
Ro 3: 31 we, then, **n** the law by this faith?

OATH
Dt 7: 8 and kept the **o** he swore to your

OBEDIENCE (OBEY)
2Ch 31: 21 of God's temple and in **o** to the law
Ro 1: 5 all the Gentiles to the **o** that comes
6: 16 to death, or to **o**, which leads
2Jn 6 that we walk in **o** to his commands.

OBEDIENT (OBEY)
Lk 2: 51 with them and was **o** to them.
Php 2: 8 himself by becoming **o** to death–
1Pe 1: 14 As **o** children, do not conform

OBEY (OBEDIENCE OBEDIENT OBEYED)
Ex 12: 24 "**O** these instructions as a lasting
Dt 6: 3 be careful to **o** so that it may go
13: 4 Keep his commands and **o** him;
21: 18 son who does not **o** his father
30: 2 God and **o** him with all your heart
32: 46 to **o** carefully all the words
1Sa 15: 22 To **o** is better than sacrifice,
Ps 119: 34 your law and **o** it with all my heart.
Mt 28: 20 to **o** everything I have commanded
Jn 14: 23 who loves me will **o** my teaching.
Ac 5: 29 must **o** God rather than human
Ro 6: 16 you are slaves of the one you **o**–
Gal 5: 3 he is obligated to **o** the whole law.
Eph 6: 1 **o** your parents in the Lord, for this
6: 5 heart, just as you would **o** Christ.
Col 3: 20 **o** your parents in everything,
1Ti 3: 4 and see that his children **o** him,

OBEYED (OBEY)
Ps 119: 4 precepts that are to be fully **o**.
Jnh 3: 3 Jonah **o** the word of the LORD
Jn 17: 6 to me and they have **o** your word.
Heb 11: 8 as his inheritance, **o** and went,
1Pe 3: 6 who **o** Abraham and called him

OBLIGATED
Ro 1: 14 I am **o** both to Greeks
Gal 5: 3 that he is **o** to obey the whole law.

OBSCENITY
Eph 5: 4 Nor should there be **o**, foolish talk

OBSOLETE
Heb 8: 13 "new," he has made the first one **o**;

OBTAINED
Ro 9: 30 not pursue righteousness, have **o** it,
Php 3: 12 Not that I have already **o** all this,

OFFENSE (OFFENSIVE)
Pr 17: 9 would foster love covers over an **o**,
19: 11 it is to one's glory to overlook an **o**.

OFFENSIVE (OFFENSE)
Ps 139: 24 See if there is any **o** way in me,

OFFER (OFFERED OFFERING OFFERINGS)
Ro 12: 1 **o** your bodies as a living sacrifice,
Heb 13: 15 let us continually **o** to God

OFFERED (OFFER)
Heb 7: 27 sins once for all when he **o** himself.

OFFERING (OFFER)
Ge 22: 8 provide the lamb for the burnt **o**,
Ps 40: 6 Sacrifice and **o** you did not desire
Isa 53: 10 the LORD makes his life an **o**
Mt 5: 23 if you are **o** your gift at the altar
Eph 5: 2 himself up for us as a fragrant **o**
Heb 10: 5 "Sacrifice and **o** you did not desire,

OFFERINGS (OFFER)
Mal 3: 8 we robbing you?' "In tithes and **o**.
Mk 12: 33 is more important than all burnt **o**

OFFICER
2Ti 2: 4 tries to please his commanding **o**.

OFFSPRING
Ge 3: 15 and between your **o** and hers;
12: 7 "To your **o** I will give this land."

OIL
Ps 23: 5 You anoint my head with **o**;
Isa 61: 3 the **o** of joy instead of mourning,
Heb 1: 9 by anointing you with the **o** of joy."

OLIVE (OLIVES)
Zec 4: 3 Also there are two **o** trees by it,
Ro 11: 17 though a wild **o** shoot, have been
Rev 11: 4 They are "the two **o** trees"

OLIVES (OLIVE)
Jas 3: 12 can a fig tree bear **o**, or a grapevine

OMEGA
Rev 1: 8 "I am the Alpha and the **O**,"

OMRI
King of Israel (1Ki 16:21-26).

OPINIONS
1Ki 18: 21 will you waver between two **o**?
Pr 18: 2 but delight in airing their own **o**.

OPPORTUNITY
Ro 7: 11 sin, seizing the **o** afforded
Gal 6: 10 as we have **o**, let us do good to all
Eph 5: 16 making the most of every **o**,
Col 4: 5 make the most of every **o**.
1Ti 5: 14 to give the enemy no **o** for slander.

OPPOSES
Jas 4: 6 "God **o** the proud but shows favor
1Pe 5: 5 "God **o** the proud but shows favor

OPPRESS (OPPRESSED)
Ex 22: 21 "Do not mistreat or **o** a foreigner,
Zec 7: 10 Do not **o** the widow

OPPRESSED (OPPRESS)
Ps 9: 9 The LORD is a refuge for the **o**,
Isa 53: 7 He was **o** and afflicted, yet he did
Zec 10: 2 the people wander like sheep **o**

ORDERLY
1Co 14: 40 be done in a fitting and **o** way.

ORGIES
Gal 5: 21 drunkenness, **o**, and the like.
1Pe 4: 3 lust, drunkenness, **o**,

ORIGIN
2Pe 1: 21 For prophecy never had its **o**

ORPHANS
Jn 14: 18 I will not leave you as **o**;
Jas 1: 27 to look after **o** and widows in their

OUTCOME
Heb 13: 7 Consider the **o** of their way of life
1Pe 4: 17 what will the **o** be for those who do

OUTSIDERS
Col 4: 5 wise in the way you act toward **o**;
1Th 4: 12 daily life may win the respect of **o**
1Ti 3: 7 also have a good reputation with **o**,

OUTSTANDING
SS 5: 10 and ruddy, **o** among ten thousand.
Ro 13: 8 Let no debt remain **o**,

OUTSTRETCHED
Ex 6: 6 I will redeem you with an **o** arm
Jer 27: 5 power and **o** arm I made the earth
Eze 20: 33 with a mighty hand and an **o** arm

OUTWEIGHS
2Co 4: 17 an eternal glory that far **o** them all.

OVERCOME (OVERCOMES)
Mt 16: 18 and the gates of Hades will not **o** it.
Mk 9: 24 help me **o** my unbelief!"
Jn 16: 33 But take heart! I have **o** the world."
Ro 12: 21 Do not be **o** by evil, but **o** evil
1Jn 5: 4 is the victory that has **o** the world,

OVERCOMES (OVERCOME)
1Jn 5: 4 everyone born of God **o** the world.
5: 5 Who is it that **o** the world?

OVERFLOW (OVERFLOWS)
Ps 119: 171 May my lips **o** with praise, for you
Ro 15: 13 so that you may **o** with hope
2Co 4: 15 may cause thanksgiving to **o**
1Th 3: 12 love increase and **o** for each other

OVERFLOWS (OVERFLOW)
Ps 23: 5 anoint my head with oil; my cup **o**.

OVERJOYED (JOY)
Da 6: 23 The king was **o** and gave orders
Mt 2: 10 they saw the star, they were **o**.
Jn 20: 20 disciples were **o** when they saw
Ac 12: 14 she was so **o** she ran back without
1Pe 4: 13 that you may be **o** when his glory

OVERSEER (OVERSEERS)
1Ti 3: 1 to be an **o** desires a noble task.
3: 2 Now the **o** is to be above reproach,
Titus 1: 7 Since an **o** manages God's

OVERSEERS (OVERSEER)
Ac 20: 28 the Holy Spirit has made you **o**.
Php 1: 1 together with the **o** and deacons:

OVERWHELMED
Ps 38: 4 My guilt has **o** me like a burden
65: 3 When we were **o** by sins,
Mt 26: 38 "My soul is **o** with sorrow
Mk 7: 37 People were **o** with amazement.

OWE
Ro 13: 7 Give to everyone what you **o** them:
Phm : 19 that you **o** me your very self.

OX
Dt 25: 4 Do not muzzle an **o** while it is
Isa 11: 7 the lion will eat straw like the **o**.
1Co 9: 9 "Do not muzzle an **o** while it is

PAGANS
Mt 5: 47 Do not even **p** do that?
1Pe 2: 12 such good lives among the **p** that,

PAIN (PAINFUL PAINS)
Job 33: 19 on a bed of **p** with constant distress
Jn 16: 21 to a child has **p** because her time

PAINFUL (PAIN)
Ge 3: 17 through **p** toil you will eat food
Heb 12: 11 seems pleasant at the time, but **p**.

PAINS (PAIN)
Ge 3: 16 "I will make your **p** in childbearing

PALMS
Isa 49: 16 engraved you on the **p** of my hands

PANTS
Ps 42: 1 As the deer **p** for streams of water, so my soul **p** for you,

PARADISE
Lk 23: 43 today you will be with me in **p**."
2Co 12: 4 was caught up to **p** and heard
Rev 2: 7 tree of life, which is in the **p** of God.

PARALYZED
Mk 2: 3 bringing to him a **p** man,

PARDON (PARDONS)
Isa 55: 7 and to our God, for he will freely **p**.

PARDONS (PARDON)
Mic 7: 18 like you, who **p** sin and forgives

PARENT (PARENT'S PARENTS)
Pr 17: 21 is no joy for the **p** of a godless fool.

PARENT'S (PARENT)
15: 5 A fool spurns a **p** discipline,

PARENTS
Ex 20: 5 for the sin of the **p** to the third
Pr 17: 6 **p** are the pride of their children.
Lk 18: 29 sisters or **p** or children for the sake
21: 16 You will be betrayed even by **p**,
Ro 1: 30 of doing evil; they disobey their **p**;
2Co 12: 14 not have to save up for their **p**,
Eph 6: 1 Children, obey your **p** in the Lord,
Col 3: 20 obey your **p** in everything,
2Ti 3: 2 disobedient to their **p**, ungrateful,

PARTIALITY
Dt 10: 17 who shows no **p** and accepts no
2Ch 19: 7 our God there is no injustice or **p**
Lk 20: 21 that you do not show **p** but teach

PARTICIPATION
1Co 10: 16 bread that we break a **p** in the body

PASS
Ex 12: 13 I see the blood, I will **p** over you.
La 1: 12 nothing to you, all you who **p** by?
Lk 21: 33 but my words will never **p** away.
1Co 13: 8 there is knowledge, it will **p** away.

PASSION (PASSIONS)
1Co 7: 9 to marry than to burn with **p**.

PASSIONS (PASSION)
Gal 5: 24 have crucified the flesh with its **p**
Titus 2: 12 to ungodliness and worldly **p**,

PASSOVER
Ex 12: 11 Eat it in haste; it is the Lᴏʀᴅ's **P**.
Dt 16: 1 celebrate the **P** of the Lᴏʀᴅ your
1Co 5: 7 For Christ, our **P** lamb, has been

PAST
Isa 43: 18 do not dwell on the **p**.
Ro 15: 4 was written in the **p** was written
Heb 1: 1 the **p** God spoke to our ancestors

PASTORS
Eph 4: 11 the evangelists, the **p** and teachers,

PASTURE (PASTURES)
Ps 37: 3 dwell in the land and enjoy safe **p**.
100: 3 are his people, the sheep of his **p**.
Jer 50: 7 their verdant **p**, the Lᴏʀᴅ,
Eze 34: 13 I will **p** them on the mountains
Jn 10: 9 come in and go out, and find **p**.

PASTURES (PASTURE)
Ps 23: 2 He makes me lie down in green **p**,

PATCH
Mt 9: 16 No one sews a **p** of unshrunk cloth

PATH (PATHS)
Ps 27: 11 me in a straight **p** because of my
119: 9 person stay on the **p** of purity?
119:105 to my feet and a light for my **p**.
Pr 15: 19 the **p** of the upright is a highway.
15: 24 The **p** of life leads upward
Isa 26: 7 The **p** of the righteous is level;
Lk 1: 79 guide our feet into the **p** of peace."
2Co 6: 3 no stumbling block in anyone's **p**,

PATHS (PATH)
Ps 23: 3 He guides me along the right **p**
25: 4 ways, Lᴏʀᴅ, teach me your **p**.
Pr 3: 6 and he will make your **p** straight.
Ro 11: 33 and his **p** beyond tracing out!
Heb 12: 13 "Make level **p** for your feet,"

PATIENCE (PATIENT)
Pr 19: 11 A person's wisdom yields **p**; it is
2Co 6: 6 understanding, **p** and kindness;
Col 1: 11 may have great endurance and **p**,
3: 12 humility, gentleness and **p**.

PATIENT (PATIENCE PATIENTLY)
Pr 15: 18 the one who is **p** calms a quarrel.
Ro 12: 12 Be joyful in hope, **p** in affliction,
1Co 13: 4 Love is **p**, love is kind. It does not
Eph 4: 2 be **p**, bearing with one another
1Th 5: 14 help the weak, be **p** with everyone.

PATIENTLY (PATIENT)
Ps 40: 1 I waited **p** for the Lᴏʀᴅ;
Ro 8: 25 we do not yet have, we wait for it **p**.

PATTERN
Ro 5: 14 who is a **p** of the one to come.
12: 2 not conform to the **p** of this world,
2Ti 1: 13 keep as the **p** of sound teaching,

PAUL
Also called Saul (Ac 13:9). Pharisee from Tarsus (Ac 9:11; Php 3:5). Apostle (Gal 1). At stoning of Stephen (Ac 8:1). Persecuted Church (Ac 9:1-2; Gal 1:13). Vision of Jesus on road to Damascus (Ac 9:4-9; 26:12-18). In Arabia (Gal 1:17). Preached in Damascus; escaped death through the wall in a basket (Ac 9:19-25). In Jerusalem; sent back to Tarsus (Ac 9:26-30).

Brought to Antioch by Barnabas (Ac 11:22-26). First missionary journey to Cyprus and Galatia (Ac 13-14). Stoned at Lystra (Ac 14:19-20). At Jerusalem council (Ac 15). Split with Barnabas over Mark (Ac 15:36-41).

Second missionary journey with Silas (Ac 16-20). Called to Macedonia (Ac 16:6-10). Freed from prison in Philippi (Ac 16:16-40). In Thessalonica (Ac 17:1-9). Speech in Athens (Ac 17:16-33). In Corinth (Ac 18). In Ephesus (Ac 19). Return to Jerusalem (Ac 20). Farewell to Ephesian elders (Ac 20:13-38). Arrival in Jerusalem (Ac 21:1-26). Arrested (Ac 21:27-36). Addressed crowds (Ac 22), Sanhedrin (Ac 23:1-11). Transferred to Caesarea (Ac 23:12-35). Trial before Felix (Ac 24),

Festus (Ac 25:1-12). Before Agrippa (Ac 25:13–26:32). Voyage to Rome; shipwreck (Ac 27). Arrival in Rome (Ac 28).

PAY (REPAID REPAY)
Lev 26: 43 They will **p** for their sins because
Pr 22: 17 **P** attention and turn your ear
Mt 22: 17 Is it right to **p** the imperial tax
Ro 13: 6 This is also why you **p** taxes,
2Pe 1: 19 you will do well to **p** attention to it,

PEACE (PEACEMAKERS)
Nu 6: 26 toward you and give you **p**."'
Ps 34: 14 and do good; seek **p** and pursue it.
85: 10 righteousness and **p** kiss each
119:165 Great **p** have those who love your
122: 6 Pray for the **p** of Jerusalem:
Pr 14: 30 A heart at **p** gives life to the body,
17: 1 Better a dry crust with **p** and quiet
Isa 9: 6 Everlasting Father, Prince of **P**.
26: 3 in perfect **p** those whose minds are
48: 22 "There is no **p**," says the Lᴏʀᴅ,
Zec 9: 10 He will proclaim **p** to the nations.
Mt 10: 34 I did not come to bring **p**,
Lk 2: 14 and on earth **p** to those on whom
Jn 14: 27 **P** I leave with you; my **p** I give you.
16: 33 so that in me you may have **p**.
Ro 5: 1 we have **p** with God through our
1Co 7: 15 God has called us to live in **p**.
14: 33 is not a God of disorder but of **p**–
Gal 5: 22 Spirit is love, joy, **p**, forbearance,
Eph 2: 14 For he himself is our **p**, who has
Php 4: 7 the **p** of God, which transcends
Col 1: 20 by making **p** through his blood,
3: 15 Let the **p** of Christ rule in your
1Th 5: 3 people are saying, "**P** and safety,"
2Th 3: 16 the Lord of **p** himself give you **p**
2Ti 2: 22 love and **p**, along with those who
1Pe 3: 11 they must seek **p** and pursue it.
Rev 6: 4 power to take **p** from the earth

PEACEMAKERS (PEACE)
Mt 5: 9 Blessed are the **p**, for they will be
Jas 3: 18 **P** who sow in peace reap a harvest

PEARL (PEARLS)
Rev 21: 21 each gate made of a single **p**.

PEARLS (PEARL)
Mt 7: 6 do not throw your **p** to pigs.
13: 45 like a merchant looking for fine **p**.
1Ti 2: 9 or gold or **p** or expensive clothes,
Rev 21: 21 The twelve gates were twelve **p**,

PEKAH
King of Israel (2Ki 15:25-31; Isa 7:1).

PEKAHIAH
Son of Menahem; king of Israel (2Ki 15:22-26).

PEN
Mt 5: 18 not the least stroke of a **p**,

PENTECOST
Ac 2: 1 When the day of **P** came, they were

PEOPLE (PEOPLES)
Dt 32: 9 For the Lᴏʀᴅ's portion is his **p**,
Ru 1: 16 Your **p** will be my **p** and your God
2Ch 7: 14 if my **p**, who are called by my
Ps 133: 1 it is when God's **p** live together
Jer 24: 7 They will be my **p**, and I will be
Zec 2: 11 in that day and will become my **p**.
Mt 4: 19 I will send you out to fish for **p**."
Lk 2: 10 will cause great joy for all the **p**.
Jn 12: 32 earth, will draw all **p** to myself."
Ac 15: 14 to choose a **p** for his name
Ro 5: 12 and in this way death came to all **p**,
8: 27 for God's **p** in accordance
1Co 9: 22 I have become all things to all **p** so
2Co 6: 16 their God, and they will be my **p**."
Eph 1: 18 glorious inheritance in his holy **p**,
6: 18 keep on praying for all the Lord's **p**.
1Ti 2: 4 who wants all **p** to be saved
2Ti 2: 2 entrust to reliable **p** who will also
Titus 2: 14 himself a **p** that are his very own,

Heb   9: 27 Just as **p** are destined to die once,
1Pe   2: 9 But you are a chosen **p**, a royal
Rev   5: 8 which are the prayers of God's **p**.
      19: 8 the righteous acts of God's holy **p**.)
      21: 3 They will be his **p**, and God

PEOPLES (PEOPLE)
Da   7: 14 **p** of every language worshiped him
Mic   4: 1 the hills, and **p** will stream to it.

PERCEIVING
Isa   6: 9 be ever seeing, but never **p**.'

PERFECT (PERFECTER PERFECTION)
SS   6: 9 but my dove, my **p** one, is unique,
Isa 26: 3 in **p** peace those whose minds are
Mt   5: 48 Be **p**, therefore, as your heavenly Father is **p**.
Ro   12: 2 his good, pleasing and **p** will.
2Co 12: 9 my power is made **p** in weakness."
Col   3: 14 binds them all together in **p** unity.
Heb   9: 11 more **p** tabernacle that is not made
      10: 14 he has made **p** forever those who
Jas   1: 17 good and **p** gift is from above,
      1: 25 looks intently into the **p** law
      3: 2 never at fault in what they say is **p**,
1Jn   4: 18 But **p** love drives out fear,

PERFECTER (PERFECT)
Heb 12: 2 on Jesus, the pioneer and **p** of faith.

PERFECTION (PERFECT)
Ps 119: 96 To all **p** I see a limit, but your
Heb   7: 11 If **p** could have been attained

PERFORMS
Ps   77: 14 You are the God who **p** miracles;

PERISH (PERISHABLE)
Ps 102: 26 They will **p**, but you remain;
Lk   13: 3 you repent, you too will all **p**.
Jn   10: 28 eternal life, and they shall never **p**;
Col   2: 22 that are all destined to **p** with use,
Heb   1: 11 They will **p**, but you remain;
2Pe   3: 9 you, not wanting anyone to **p**,

PERISHABLE (PERISH)
1Co 15: 42 The body that is sown is **p**, it is

PERJURERS
1Ti   1: 10 for slave traders and liars and **p**–

PERMIT
1Ti   2: 12 I do not **p** a woman to teach

PERSECUTE (PERSECUTED PERSECUTION)
Mt   5: 11 **p** you and falsely say all kinds
Jn   15: 20 persecuted me, they will **p** you
Ac   9: 4 "Saul, Saul, why do you **p** me?"
Ro   12: 14 Bless those who **p** you; bless and

PERSECUTED (PERSECUTE)
1Co   4: 12 when we are **p**, we endure it;
2Ti   3: 12 godly life in Christ Jesus will be **p**,

PERSECUTION (PERSECUTE)
Ro   8: 35 trouble or hardship or **p** or famine

PERSEVERANCE (PERSEVERE)
Ro   5: 3 we know that suffering produces **p**;
      5: 4 **p**, character; and character, hope.
Heb 12: 1 let us run with **p** the race marked
Jas   1: 3 testing of your faith produces **p**.
2Pe   1: 6 and to self-control, **p**; and to **p**,

PERSEVERE (PERSEVERANCE PERSEVERED PERSEVERES)
1Ti   4: 16 **P** in them, because if you do,
Heb 10: 36 You need to **p** so that when you

PERSEVERED (PERSEVERE)
Heb 11: 27 he **p** because he saw him who is
Jas   5: 11 count as blessed those who have **p**.
Rev   2: 3 You have **p** and have endured

PERSEVERES (PERSEVERE)
1Co 13: 7 trusts, always hopes, always **p**.
Jas   1: 12 one who **p** under trial because,

PERSUADE
2Co   5: 11 to fear the Lord, we try to **p** others.

PERVERSION (PERVERT)
Lev 18: 23 sexual relations with it; that is a **p**.
Jude : 7 up to sexual immorality and **p**.

PERVERT (PERVERSION)
Gal   1: 7 are trying to **p** the gospel of Christ.

PESTILENCE
Ps   91: 6 the **p** that stalks in the darkness,

PETER
Apostle, brother of Andrew, also called Simon (Mt 10:2; Mk 3:16; Lk 6:14; Ac 1:13), and Cephas (Jn 1:42). Confession of Christ (Mt 16:13-20; Mk 8:27-30; Lk 9:18-27). At transfiguration (Mt 17:1-8; Mk 9:2-8; Lk 9:28-36; 2Pe 1:16-18). Caught fish with coin (Mt 17:24-27). Denial of Jesus predicted (Mt 26:31-35; Mk 14:27-31; Lk 22:31-34; Jn 13:31-38). Denied Jesus (Mt 26:69-75; Mk 14:66-72; Lk 22:54-62; Jn 18:15-27). Commissioned by Jesus to shepherd his flock (Jn 21:15-23).
Speech at Pentecost (Ac 2). Healed beggar (Ac 3:1-10). Speech at temple (Ac 3:11-26), before Sanhedrin (Ac 4:1-22). In Samaria (Ac 8:14-25). Sent by vision to Cornelius (Ac 10). Announced salvation of Gentiles in Jerusalem (Ac 11; 15). Freed from prison (Ac 12). Inconsistency at Antioch (Gal 2:11-21). At Jerusalem Council (Ac 15).

PHARISEES
Mt   5: 20 surpasses that of the **P**

PHILIP
1. Apostle (Mt 10:3; Mk 3:18; Lk 6:14; Jn 1:43-48; 14:8; Ac 1:13).
2. Deacon (Ac 6:1-7); evangelist in Samaria (Ac 8:4-25), to Ethiopian (Ac 8:26-40).

PHILOSOPHY
Col   2: 8 through hollow and deceptive **p**,

PHYLACTERIES
Mt   23: 5 They make their **p** wide

PHYSICAL
1Ti   4: 8 For **p** training is of some value,
Jas   2: 16 does nothing about their **p** needs,

PIECES
Ge   15: 17 and passed between the **p**.
Jer 34: 18 two and then walked between its **p**.

PIERCE (PIERCED)
Ps   22: 16 they **p** my hands and my feet.

PIERCED (PIERCE)
Isa 53: 5 he was **p** for our transgressions,
Zec 12: 10 the one they have **p**, and they will
Jn   19: 37 will look on the one they have **p**."

PIGS
Mt   7: 6 do not throw your pearls to **p**.

PILATE
Governor of Judea. Questioned Jesus (Mt 27:1-26; Mk 15:15; Lk 22:66–23:25; Jn 18:28–19:16); sent him to Herod (Lk 23:6-12); consented to his crucifixion when crowds chose Barabbas (Mt 27:15-26; Mk 15:6-15; Lk 23:13-25; Jn 19:1-10).

PILLAR
Ge   19: 26 back, and she became a **p** of salt.
Ex   13: 21 by night in a **p** of fire to give them
1Ti   3: 15 the **p** and foundation of the truth.

PIT
Ps   40: 2 He lifted me out of the slimy **p**,
     103: 4 who redeems your life from the **p**
Mt   15: 14 the blind, both will fall into a **p**."

PITIED
1Co 15: 19 we are of all people most to be **p**.

PLAGUE
2Ch   6: 28 famine or **p** comes to the land,

PLAIN
Ro   1: 19 God has made it **p** to them.

PLAN (PLANNED PLANS)
Pr   14: 22 those who **p** what is good find love
Eph   1: 11 to the **p** of him who works

PLANK
Mt   7: 3 attention to the **p** in your own eye?
Lk   6: 41 attention to the **p** in your own eye?

PLANNED (PLAN)
Ps   40: 5 have done, the things you **p** for us.
Isa   46: 11 what I have **p**, that I will do.
Heb 11: 40 since God had **p** something better

PLANS (PLAN)
Ps   20: 4 heart and make all your **p** succeed.
       33: 11 But the **p** of the LORD stand firm
Pr   20: 18 **P** are established by seeking advice;
Isa   32: 8 But the noble make noble **p**,

PLANTED (PLANTS)
Ps   1: 3 person is like a tree **p** by streams
Mt   15: 13 Father has not **p** will be pulled
1Co   3: 6 I **p** the seed, Apollos watered it,

PLANTS (PLANTED)
1Co   3: 7 neither the one who **p** nor the one
        9: 7 Who **p** a vineyard and does not eat

PLATTER
Mk   6: 25 head of John the Baptist on a **p**."

PLAYED
Lk   7: 32 "'We **p** the pipe for you, and you
1Co   14: 7 what tune is being **p** unless there is

PLEADED
2Co   12: 8 Three times I **p** with the Lord

PLEASANT (PLEASE)
Ps   16: 6 lines have fallen for me in **p** places;
      133: 1 and **p** it is when God's people live
      147: 1 how **p** and fitting to praise him!
Heb 12: 11 No discipline seems **p** at the time,

PLEASE (PLEASANT PLEASED PLEASES PLEASING
PLEASURE PLEASURES)
Pr   20: 23 and dishonest scales do not **p** him.
Jer   6: 20 your sacrifices do not **p** me."
Jn   5: 30 for I seek not to **p** myself but him
Ro   8: 8 realm of the flesh cannot **p** God.
      15: 2 Each of us should **p** our neighbors
1Co   7: 32 how he can **p** the Lord.
      10: 33 even as I try to **p** everyone in every
2Co   5: 9 So we make it our goal to **p** him,
Gal   1: 10 If I were still trying to **p** people,
1Th   4: 1 you how to live in order to **p** God,
2Ti   2: 4 tries to **p** his commanding officer.
Heb 11: 6 faith it is impossible to **p** God,

PLEASED (PLEASE)
Mt   3: 17 with him I am well **p**."
1Co   1: 21 God was **p** through the foolishness
Col   1: 19 God was **p** to have all his fullness
Heb 11: 5 commended as one who **p** God.
2Pe   1: 17 with him I am well **p**."

PLEASES (PLEASE)
Ps   135: 6 The LORD does whatever **p** him,
Pr   15: 8 the prayer of the upright **p** him.
Jn   3: 8 The wind blows wherever it **p**.
        8: 29 alone, for I always do what **p** him."
Col   3: 20 in everything, for this **p** the Lord.
1Ti   2: 3 is good, and **p** God our Savior,
1Jn   3: 22 his commands and do what **p** him.

PLEASING (PLEASE)
Ps   104: 34 May my meditation be **p** to him,
Ro   12: 1 living sacrifice, holy and **p** to God
Php   4: 18 an acceptable sacrifice, **p** to God.
Heb 13: 21 he work in us what is **p** to him,

PLEASURE (PLEASE)
Ps   147: 10 His **p** is not in the strength
Pr   21: 17 loves **p** will become poor;
Eze   18: 32 For I take no **p** in the death
Eph   1: 5 in accordance with his **p** and will–
        1: 9 of his will according to his good **p**,
2Ti   3: 4 lovers of **p** rather than lovers

PLEASURES (PLEASE)
Ps   16: 11 with eternal **p** at your right hand.
Heb 11: 25 than to enjoy the fleeting **p** of sin.
2Pe   2: 13 reveling in their **p** while they feast

PLENTIFUL
Mt   9: 37 "The harvest is **p** but the workers

PLOW (PLOWSHARES)
Lk   9: 62 "No one who puts a hand to the **p**

PLOWSHARES (PLOW)
Isa   2: 4 They will beat their swords into **p**
Joel   3: 10 Beat your **p** into swords and your

PLUNDER
Ex   3: 22 And so you will **p** the Egyptians."

POINT
Jas   2: 10 yet stumbles at just one **p** is guilty

POISON
Mk   16: 18 *and when they drink deadly* **p**,
Jas   3: 8 It is a restless evil, full of deadly **p**.

POLLUTE (POLLUTED)
Nu   35: 33 "'Do not **p** the land where you
Jude   8 these ungodly people **p** their own

POLLUTED (POLLUTE)
Ezr   9: 11 is a land **p** by the corruption
Pr   25: 26 a **p** well are the righteous who give
Ac   15: 20 to abstain from food **p** by idols,
Jas   1: 27 oneself from being **p** by the world.

PONDER
Ps   64: 9 of God and **p** what he has done.
      119: 95 me, but I will **p** your statutes.

POOR (POVERTY)
Dt   15: 4 need be no **p** people among you,
      15: 11 There will always be **p** people
Ps   34: 6 This **p** man called, and the LORD
      82: 3 uphold the cause of the **p**
      112: 9 freely scattered their gifts to the **p**,
Pr   13: 7 another pretends to be **p**, yet has
      14: 31 oppresses the **p** shows contempt
      19: 1 Better the **p** whose walk is
      19: 17 Whoever is kind to the **p** lends
      22: 2 Rich and **p** have this in common:
      22: 9 they share their food with the **p**.
      28: 6 Better the **p** whose walk is
      31: 20 She opens her arms to the **p**
Isa   61: 1 to proclaim good news to the **p**.
Mt   5: 3 "Blessed are the **p** in spirit,
      11: 5 good news is proclaimed to the **p**.
      19: 21 your possessions and give to the **p**,
      26: 11 The **p** you will always have
Mk   12: 42 a **p** widow came and put in two
Ac   10: 4 and gifts to the **p** have come up as
1Co   13: 3 If I give all I possess to the **p**
2Co   8: 9 yet for your sake he became **p**,
Jas   2: 2 and a **p** man in filthy old clothes

PORTION
Dt   32: 9 For the LORD's **p** is his people,
2Ki   2: 9 "Let me inherit a double **p** of your
La   3: 24 to myself, "The LORD is my **p**;

POSSESS (POSSESSING POSSESSION POSSES-
SIONS)
Nu   33: 53 for I have given you the land to **p**.

POSSESSING (POSSESS)
2Co   6: 10 nothing, and yet **p** everything.

POSSESSION (POSSESS)
Ge   15: 7 give you this land to take **p** of it."
Nu   13: 30 go up and take **p** of the land,
Eph   1: 14 of those who are God's **p**–

POSSESSIONS (POSSESS)
Lk   12: 15 not consist in an abundance of **p**."
2Co   12: 14 because what I want is not your **p**
1Jn   3: 17 If anyone has material **p** and sees

POSSIBLE
Mt   19: 26 but with God all things are **p**."
Mk   9: 23 "Everything is **p** for one who
      10: 27 all things are **p** with God."
Ro   12: 18 If it is **p**, as far as it depends on you
1Co   9: 22 by all **p** means I might save some.

POT (POTSHERDS POTTER POTTERY)
2Ki   4: 40 of God, there is death in the **p**!"
Jer   18: 4 the potter formed it into another **p**,

POTSHERDS (POT)
Isa   45:   9 but **p** among the **p** on the ground.

POTTER (POT)
Isa   29: 16 Can the pot say to the **p**,
      45:   9 Does the clay say to the **p**,
      64:   8 We are the clay, you are the **p**;
Jer   18:   6 do with you, Israel, as this **p** does?"
Ro   9: 21 Does not the **p** have the right

POTTERY (POT)
Ro   9: 21 of clay some **p** for special purposes

POUR (POURED)
Ps   62:   8 **p** out your hearts to him, for God
Joel   2: 28 I will **p** out my Spirit on all people.
Mal   3: 10 **p** out so much blessing that there
Ac   2: 17 I will **p** out my Spirit on all people.

POURED (POUR)
Ac   10: 45 the Holy Spirit had been **p** out
Ro   5:   5 because God's love has been **p**

POVERTY (POOR)
Pr   14: 23 but mere talk leads only to **p**.
      21:   5 profit as surely as haste leads to **p**.
      30:   8 give me neither **p** nor riches,
Mk   12: 44 she, out of her **p**, put in everything
2Co   8:   2 their extreme **p** welled up in rich
       8:   9 you through his **p** might become

POWER (POWERFUL POWERS)
1Ch   29: 11 greatness and the **p** and the glory
2Ch   32:   7 for there is a greater **p** with us than
Job   36: 22 "God is exalted in his **p**. Who is
Ps   63:   2 and beheld your **p** and your glory.
      68: 34 Proclaim the **p** of God,
     147:   5 Great is our Lord and mighty in **p**;
Pr   24:   5 The wise prevail through great **p**,
Isa   40: 10 Sovereign LORD comes with **p**,
Zec   4:   6 'Not by might nor by **p**, but by my
Mt   22: 29 the Scriptures or the **p** of God.
      24: 30 of heaven, with **p** and great glory.
Ac   1:   8 you will receive **p** when the Holy
       4: 33 With great **p** the apostles
      10: 38 with the Holy Spirit and **p**,
Ro   1: 16 because it is the **p** of God
1Co   1: 18 us who are being saved it is the **p**
      15: 56 is sin, and the **p** of sin is the law.
2Co   12:   9 so that Christ's **p** may rest on me.
Eph   1: 19 his incomparably great **p** for us
Php   3: 10 to know the **p** of his resurrection
Col   1: 11 strengthened with all **p** according
2Ti   1:   7 us timid, but gives us **p**,
Heb   7: 16 of the **p** of an indestructible life.
Rev   4: 11 to receive glory and honor and **p**,
      19:   1 glory and **p** belong to our God,
      20:   6 second death has no **p** over them,

POWERFUL (POWER)
Ps   29:   4 The voice of the LORD is **p**;
Lk   24: 19 **p** in word and deed before God
2Th   1:   7 in blazing fire with his **p** angels.
Heb   1:   3 sustaining all things by his **p** word.
Jas   5: 16 prayer of a righteous person is **p**

POWERLESS
Ro   5:   6 when we were still **p**, Christ died
       8:   3 what the law was **p** to do because it

POWERS (POWER)
Ro   8: 38 present nor the future, nor any **p**,
1Co   2: 10 to another miraculous **p**,
Col   1: 16 whether thrones or **p** or rulers
       2: 15 And having disarmed the **p**

PRACTICE
Lev   19: 26 "'Do not **p** divination or seek
Mt   23:   3 for they do not **p** what they preach.
Lk   8: 21 hear God's word and put it into **p**."
Ro   12: 13 who are in need. **P** hospitality.
1Ti   5:   4 put their religion into **p** by caring

PRAISE (PRAISED PRAISES PRAISING)
Ex   15:   2 and I will **p** him, my father's God,

Dt   32:   3 Oh, **p** the greatness of our God!
Ru   4: 14 "**P** be to the LORD, who this day
2Sa   22: 47 **P** be to my Rock!
1Ch   16: 25 the LORD and most worthy of **p**;
2Ch   20: 21 to **p** him for the splendor of his
Ps   8:   2 Through the **p** of children
      33:   1 it is fitting for the upright to **p** him.
      40:   1 his **p** will always be on my lips.
      40:   3 mouth, a hymn of **p** to our God.
      48:   1 and most worthy of **p**, in the city
      68: 19 **P** be to the Lord, to God our Savior,
      89:   5 The heavens **p** your wonders,
     100:   4 give thanks to him and **p** his name.
     105:   2 Sing to him, sing **p** to him;
     106:   1 **P** the LORD. Give thanks
     119:175 Let me live that I may **p** you,
     139: 14 I **p** you because I am fearfully
     145: 21 Let every creature **p** his holy name
     146:   1 **P** the LORD. **P** the LORD, my soul.
     150:   2 **p** him for his surpassing greatness.
     150:   6 Let everything that has breath **p** the LORD. **P**
                 the LORD.
Pr   27:   2 Let someone else **p** you, and not
      27: 21 but people are tested by their **p**.
      31: 31 let her works bring her **p** at the city
Mt   21: 16 Lord, have called forth your **p**'?"
Jn   12: 43 they loved human **p** more than **p** from God.
Eph   1:   6 to the **p** of his glorious grace,
       1: 12 might be for the **p** of his glory.
       1: 14 to the **p** of his glory.
Heb   13: 15 offer to God a sacrifice of **p**—
Jas   5: 13 Let them sing songs of **p**.

PRAISED (PRAISE)
1Ch   29: 10 David **p** the LORD in the presence
Ne   8:   6 Ezra **p** the LORD, the great God;
Da   2: 19 Then Daniel **p** the God of heaven
Ro   9:   5 who is God over all, forever **p**!
1Pe   4: 11 God may be **p** through Jesus Christ

PRAISES (PRAISE)
2Sa   22: 50 I will sing the **p** of your name.
Ps   47:   6 Sing **p** to God, sing **p**; sing **p**
     147:   1 good it is to sing **p** to our God,
Pr   31: 28 her husband also, and he **p** her:

PRAISING (PRAISE)
Ac   10: 46 speaking in tongues and **p** God.
1Co   14: 16 when you are **p** God in the Spirit,

PRAY (PRAYED PRAYER PRAYERS PRAYING)
Dt   4:   7 our God is near us whenever we **p**
1Sa   12: 23 the LORD by failing to **p** for you.
2Ch   7: 14 will humble themselves and **p**
Job   42:   8 My servant Job will **p** for you,
Ps   122:   6 **P** for the peace of Jerusalem:
Mt   5: 44 and **p** for those who persecute you,
       6:   5 for they love to **p** standing
       6:   9 "This, then, is how you should **p**:
      26: 36 here while I go over there and **p**."
Lk   6: 28 you, **p** for those who mistreat you,
      18:   1 them that they should always **p**
      22: 40 them, "**P** that you will not fall
Ro   8: 26 not know what we ought to **p** for,
1Co   14: 13 in a tongue should **p** that they may
1Th   5: 17 **p** continually,
Jas   5: 13 Let them **p**. Is anyone happy?
       5: 16 **p** for each other so that you may be

PRAYED (PRAY)
1Sa   1: 27 I **p** for this child, and the LORD
Jnh   2:   1 From inside the fish Jonah **p**
Mk   14: 35 and **p** that if possible the hour

PRAYER (PRAY)
2Ch   30: 27 for their **p** reached heaven, his holy
Ezr   8: 23 about this, and he answered our **p**.
Ps   6:   9 the LORD accepts my **p**.
      86:   6 Hear my **p**, LORD; listen to my
Pr   15:   8 the **p** of the upright pleases him.
Isa   56:   7 house will be called a house of **p**
Mt   21: 13 house will be called a house of **p**,'

Mk 11: 24 whatever you ask for in **p**,
Jn 17: 15 My **p** is not that you take them
Ac   6: 4 will give our attention to **p**
Php 4: 6 every situation, by **p** and petition,
Jas 5: 15 the **p** offered in faith will make
1Pe 3: 12 and his ears are attentive to their **p**,

PRAYERS (PRAY)
1Ch 5: 20 He answered their **p**, because they
Mk 12: 40 and for a show make lengthy **p**.
1Pe 3: 7 so that nothing will hinder your **p**.
Rev 5: 8 which are the **p** of God's people.

PRAYING (PRAY)
Mk 11: 25 And when you stand **p**, if you hold
Jn 17: 9 I am not **p** for the world,
Ac 16: 25 Silas were **p** and singing hymns
Eph 6: 18 always keep on **p** for all the Lord's

PREACH (PREACHED PREACHING)
Mt 23: 3 they do not practice what they **p**.
Mk 16: 15 and **p** the gospel to all creation.
Ac   9: 20 At once he began to **p**
Ro 10: 15 how can anyone **p** unless they are
    15: 20 to **p** the gospel where Christ was
1Co 1: 17 to baptize, but to **p** the gospel—
     1: 23 but we **p** Christ crucified:
     9: 14 that those who **p** the gospel should
     9: 16 Woe to me if I do not **p** the gospel!
2Co 10: 16 so that we can **p** the gospel
Gal 1: 8 heaven should **p** a gospel other
2Ti 4: 2 **P** the word; be prepared in season

PREACHED (PREACH)
Mk 13: 10 the gospel must first be **p** to all
Ac   8: 4 who had been scattered **p** the word
1Co 9: 27 so that after I have **p** to others,
    15: 1 remind you of the gospel I **p** to you
2Co 11: 4 a Jesus other than the Jesus we **p**,
Gal 1: 8 a gospel other than the one we **p**
Php 1: 18 false motives or true, Christ is **p**.
1Ti 3: 16 angels, was **p** among the nations,

PREACHING (PREACH)
Ro 10: 14 can they hear without someone **p**
1Co 9: 18 in **p** the gospel I may offer it free
1Ti 4: 13 of Scripture, to **p** and to teaching.
     5: 17 especially those whose work is **p**

PRECEPTS
Ps 19: 8 The **p** of the LORD are right,
   111: 7 all his **p** are trustworthy.
   111: 10 all who follow his **p** have good
   119: 40 How I long for your **p**!
   119: 69 I keep your **p** with all my heart.
   119:104 I gain understanding from your **p**;
   119:159 See how I love your **p**; preserve my

PRECIOUS
Ps 19: 10 They are more **p** than gold,
   116: 15 **P** in the sight of the LORD is
Pr   8: 11 for wisdom is more **p** than rubies,
Isa 28: 16 stone, a **p** cornerstone for a sure
1Pe 1: 19 but with the **p** blood of Christ,
     2: 6 a chosen and **p** cornerstone,
2Pe 1: 4 us his very great and **p** promises,

PREDESTINED (DESTINY)
Ro   8: 29 **p** to be conformed to the image
     8: 30 And those he **p**, he also called;
Eph 1: 5 he **p** us for adoption to sonship
     1: 11 been **p** according to the plan

PREDICTION
Jer 28: 9 LORD only if his **p** comes true."

PREPARE (PREPARED)
Ps 23: 5 You **p** a table before me
Am   4: 12 to you, Israel, **p** to meet your God."
Jn 14: 2 that I am going there to **p** a place

PREPARED (PREPARE)
Mt 25: 34 the kingdom **p** for you since
1Co 2: 9 the things God has **p** for those who
Eph 2: 10 which God **p** in advance for us

2Ti 4: 2 be **p** in season and out of season;
1Pe 3: 15 Always be **p** to give an answer

PRESENCE (PRESENT)
Ex 25: 30 Put the bread of the **P** on this table
Ezr 9: 15 not one of us can stand in your **p**."
Ps 31: 20 the shelter of your **p** you hide them
    89: 15 who walk in the light of your **p**,
    90: 8 secret sins in the light of your **p**.
   139: 7 Where can I flee from your **p**?
Jer 5: 22 "Should you not tremble in my **p**?
Heb 9: 24 now to appear for us in God's **p**.
Jude : 24 before his glorious **p** without fault

PRESENT (PRESENCE)
2Co 11: 2 that I might **p** you as a pure virgin
Eph 5: 27 and to **p** her to himself as a radiant
2Ti 2: 15 Do your best to **p** yourself to God

PRESERVES
Ps 119: 50 Your promise **p** my life.

PRESS (PRESSED PRESSURE)
Php 3: 14 I **p** on toward the goal to win

PRESSED (PRESS)
Lk   6: 38 A good measure, **p** down,

PRESSURE (PRESS)
2Co 1: 8 We were under great **p**, far beyond
    11: 28 I face daily the **p** of my concern

PREVAILS
1Sa 2: 9 "It is not by strength that one **p**;

PRICE
Job 28: 18 the **p** of wisdom is beyond rubies.
1Co 6: 20 you were bought at a **p**.
     7: 23 You were bought at a **p**;

PRIDE (PROUD)
Pr   8: 13 I hate **p** and arrogance,
    16: 18 **P** goes before destruction,
Da   4: 37 those who walk in **p** he is able
Gal 6: 4 can take **p** in themselves alone,
Jas 1: 9 to take **p** in their high position.

PRIEST (PRIESTHOOD PRIESTS)
Heb 4: 14 a great high **p** who has ascended
     4: 15 do not have a high **p** who is unable
     7: 26 Such a high **p** truly meets our need
     8: 1 We do have such a high **p**, who sat

PRIESTHOOD (PRIEST)
Heb 7: 24 lives forever, he has a permanent **p**.
1Pe 2: 5 a spiritual house to be a holy **p**,
     2: 9 people, a royal **p**, a holy nation,

PRIESTS (PRIEST)
Ex 19: 6 you will be for me a kingdom of **p**
Rev 5: 10 a kingdom and **p** to serve our God,

PRINCE
Isa 9: 6 Everlasting Father, **P** of Peace.
Jn 12: 31 now the **p** of this world will be
Ac   5: 31 him to his own right hand as **P**

PRISON (PRISONER)
Isa 42: 7 blind, to free captives from **p**
Mt 25: 36 I was in **p** and you came to visit
Rev 20: 7 Satan will be released from his **p**

PRISONER (PRISON)
Ro   7: 23 making me a **p** of the law of sin
Eph 3: 1 the **p** of Christ Jesus for the sake

PRIVILEGE
2Co 8: 4 for the **p** of sharing in this service

PRIZE
1Co 9: 24 Run in such a way as to get the **p**.
Php 3: 14 on toward the goal to win the **p**

PROCLAIM (PROCLAIMED)
1Ch 16: 23 **p** his salvation day after day.
Ps 19: 1 the skies **p** the work of his hands.
    50: 6 the heavens **p** his righteousness,
    68: 34 **P** the power of God, whose majesty
   118: 17 will **p** what the LORD has done.
Zec 9: 10 He will **p** peace to the nations.

Ac 20: 27 I have not hesitated to **p** to you
Ro 10: 8 concerning faith that we **p**:
1Co 11: 26 cup, you **p** the Lord's death until

PROCLAIMED (PROCLAIM)
Ro 15: 19 I have fully **p** the gospel of Christ.
Col 1: 23 has been **p** to every creature under

PRODUCE (PRODUCES)
Mt 3: 8 **P** fruit in keeping with repentance.
3: 10 does not **p** good fruit will be cut

PRODUCES (PRODUCE)
Pr 30: 33 so stirring up anger **p** strife."
Ro 5: 3 that suffering **p** perseverance;
Heb 12: 11 it **p** a harvest of righteousness

PROFANE
Lev 22: 32 Do not **p** my holy name, for I must

PROFESS
1Ti 2: 10 for women who **p** to worship God.
Heb 4: 14 let us hold firmly to the faith we **p**.
10: 23 unswervingly to the hope we **p**,

PROMISE (PROMISED PROMISES)
1Ki 8: 20 Lord has kept the **p** he made:
Ac 2: 39 The **p** is for you and your children
Gal 3: 14 faith we might receive the **p**
1Ti 4: 8 holding **p** for both the present life
2Pe 3: 9 Lord is not slow in keeping his **p**,

PROMISED (PROMISE)
Ex 3: 17 I have **p** to bring you up out of
Dt 26: 18 his treasured possession as he **p**,
Ps 119: 57 I have **p** to obey your words.
Ro 4: 21 had power to do what he had **p**.
Heb 10: 23 we profess, for he who **p** is faithful.
2Pe 3: 4 say, "Where is this 'coming' he **p**?

PROMISES (PROMISE)
Jos 21: 45 of all the Lord's good **p** to Israel
Ro 9: 4 law, the temple worship and the **p**.
2Pe 1: 4 us his very great and precious **p**,

PROMPTED
1Th 1: 3 by faith, your labor **p** by love,
2Th 1: 11 and your every deed **p** by faith.

PROPHECIES (PROPHESY)
1Co 13: 8 But where there are **p**, they will
1Th 5: 20 Do not treat **p** with contempt

PROPHECY (PROPHESY)
1Co 14: 1 gifts of the Spirit, especially **p**.
2Pe 1: 20 that no **p** of Scripture came

PROPHESY (PROPHECIES PROPHECY PROPHESY-
ING PROPHET PROPHETS)
Joel 2: 28 Your sons and daughters will **p**,
Mt 7: 22 did we not **p** in your name
1Co 14: 39 be eager to **p**, and do not forbid

PROPHESYING (PROPHESY)
Ro 12: 6 If your gift is **p**, then prophesy

PROPHET (PROPHESY)
Dt 18: 18 for them a **p** like you from among
Am 7: 14 neither a **p** nor the son of a **p**,
Mt 10: 41 Whoever welcomes a **p** as a **p** will
Lk 4: 24 "no **p** is accepted in his hometown.

PROPHETS (PROPHESY)
Ps 105: 15 do my **p** no harm."
Mt 5: 17 come to abolish the Law or the **P**;
7: 12 for this sums up the Law and the **P**.
24: 24 messiahs and false **p** will appear
Lk 24: 25 believe all that the **p** have spoken!
Ac 10: 43 All the **p** testify about him
1Co 12: 28 apostles, second **p**, third teachers,
14: 32 The spirits of **p** are subject
Eph 2: 20 foundation of the apostles and **p**,
Heb 1: 1 ancestors through the **p** at many
1Pe 1: 10 the **p**, who spoke of the grace

PROSPER (PROSPERITY PROSPERS)
Pr 28: 25 who trust in the Lord will **p**.

PROSPERITY (PROSPER)
Ps 73: 3 when I saw the **p** of the wicked.

PROSPERS (PROSPER)
Ps 1: 3 whatever they do **p**.

PROSTITUTE (PROSTITUTES)
1Co 6: 15 of Christ and unite them with a **p**?

PROSTITUTES (PROSTITUTE)
Mt 21: 31 **p** are entering the kingdom of God
Lk 15: 30 your property with **p** comes home,

PROSTRATE
Dt 9: 18 again I fell **p** before the Lord

PROTECT (PROTECTS)
Ps 32: 7 you will **p** me from trouble
Pr 2: 11 Discretion will **p** you,
Jn 17: 11 **p** them by the power of your name,

PROTECTS (PROTECT)
1Co 13: 7 It always **p**, always trusts,

PROUD (PRIDE)
Pr 16: 5 The Lord detests all the **p**
Ro 12: 16 Do not be **p**, but be willing
1Co 13: 4 envy, it does not boast, it is not **p**.

PROVE
1Co 4: 2 been given a trust must **p** faithful.

PROVIDE (PROVIDED PROVIDES)
Ge 22: 8 "God himself will **p** the lamb
Isa 43: 20 because I **p** water in the wilderness
1Ti 5: 8 Anyone who does not **p** for their

PROVIDED (PROVIDE)
Jnh 1: 17 Now the Lord **p** a huge fish
4: 6 the Lord God **p** a leafy plant
4: 7 dawn the next day God **p** a worm,
4: 8 rose, God **p** a scorching east wind,

PROVIDES (PROVIDE)
1Ti 6: 17 who richly **p** us with everything
1Pe 4: 11 do so with the strength God **p**,

PROVOKED
Ecc 7: 9 Do not be quickly **p** in your spirit,

PRUDENT
Pr 14: 15 the **p** give thought to their steps.
19: 14 but a **p** wife is from the Lord.
Am 5: 13 Therefore the **p** keep quiet in such

PRUNING
Isa 2: 4 and their spears into **p** hooks.
Joel 3: 10 and your **p** hooks into spears.

PSALMS
Eph 5: 19 speaking to one another with **p**,
Col 3: 16 with all wisdom through **p**,

PUBLICLY
Ac 20: 20 have taught you **p** and from house

PUFFS
1Co 8: 1 knowledge **p** up while love builds

PUNISH (PUNISHED)
Ex 32: 34 to **p**, I will **p** them for their sin."
Pr 23: 13 if you **p** them with the rod,
Isa 13: 11 I will **p** the world for its evil,
1Pe 2: 14 by him to **p** those who do wrong

PUNISHED (PUNISH)
La 3: 39 should the living complain when **p**
2Th 1: 9 They will be **p** with everlasting
Heb 10: 29 to be **p** who has trampled the Son

PURE (PURIFIES PURIFY PURITY)
2Sa 22: 27 to the **p** you show yourself **p**,
Ps 24: 4 who has clean hands and a **p** heart,
51: 10 Create in me a **p** heart, O God,
Pr 20: 9 can say, "I have kept my heart **p**;
Isa 52: 11 Come out from it and be **p**,
Hab 1: 13 Your eyes are too **p** to look on evil;
Mt 5: 8 Blessed are the **p** in heart, for they
2Co 11: 2 I might present you as a **p** virgin
Php 4: 8 whatever is **p**, whatever is lovely,
1Ti 5: 22 the sins of others. Keep yourself **p**.
Titus 1: 15 To the **p**, all things are **p**,
2: 5 to be self-controlled and **p**, to be
Heb 13: 4 all, and the marriage bed kept **p**,

1Jn 3: 3 purify themselves, just as he is **p**.

PURGE
Pr 20: 30 and beatings **p** the inmost being.

PURIFIES (PURE)
1Jn 1: 7 of Jesus, his Son, **p** us from all sin.

PURIFY (PURE)
Titus 2: 14 to **p** for himself a people that are
1Jn 1: 9 and **p** us from all unrighteousness.
3: 3 this hope in him **p** themselves,

PURITY (PURE)
Ps 119: 9 person stay on the path of **p**?
2Co 6: 6 in **p**, understanding,
1Ti 4: 12 conduct, in love, in faith and in **p**.

PURPOSE
Pr 19: 21 it is the LORD's **p** that prevails.
Isa 55: 11 achieve the **p** for which I sent it.
Ro 8: 28 been called according to his **p**.

PURSES
Lk 12: 33 Provide **p** for yourselves that will

PURSUE
Ps 34: 14 and do good; seek peace and **p** it.
2Ti 2: 22 of youth, and **p** righteousness, faith,
1Pe 3: 11 they must seek peace and **p** it.

QUALITIES (QUALITY)
2Pe 1: 8 if you possess these **q** in increasing

QUALITY (QUALITIES)
1Co 3: 13 and the fire will test the **q** of each

QUARREL (QUARRELSOME)
Pr 15: 18 the one who is patient calms a **q**.
17: 14 Starting a **q** is like breaching a dam
17: 19 Whoever loves a **q** loves sin;

QUARRELSOME (QUARREL)
Pr 19: 13 **q** wife is like the constant dripping
1Ti 3: 3 gentle, not **q**, not a lover of money.
2Ti 2: 24 the Lord's servant must not be **q**

QUENCH
1Th 5: 19 Do not **q** the Spirit.

QUICK-TEMPERED
Titus 1: 7 not **q**, not given to drunkenness,

QUIET (QUIETNESS)
Ps 23: 2 he leads me beside **q** waters,
Lk 19: 40 "if they keep **q**, the stones will cry
1Ti 2: 2 peaceful and **q** lives in all godliness
1Pe 3: 4 beauty of a gentle and **q** spirit,

QUIETNESS (QUIET)
Isa 30: 15 in **q** and trust is your strength,
32: 17 its effect will be **q** and confidence
1Ti 2: 11 woman should learn in **q** and full

QUIVER
Ps 127: 5 Blessed is the man whose **q** is full

RACE
Ecc 9: 11 The **r** is not to the swift or
1Co 9: 24 that in a **r** all the runners run,
2Ti 4: 7 I have finished the **r**, I have kept
Heb 12: 1 with perseverance the **r** marked

RACHEL
Daughter of Laban (Ge 29:16); wife of Jacob (Ge 29:28); bore two sons (Ge 30:22-24; 35:16-24; 46:19).

RADIANCE (RADIANT)
Heb 1: 3 The Son is the **r** of God's glory

RADIANT (RADIANCE)
Ex 34: 29 that his face was **r** because he had
Ps 34: 5 Those who look to him are **r**;
SS 5: 10 My beloved is **r** and ruddy,
Isa 60: 5 Then you will look and be **r**,
Eph 5: 27 her to himself as a **r** church,

RAIN (RAINBOW)
Mt 5: 45 and sends **r** on the righteous

RAINBOW (RAIN)
Ge 9: 13 I have set my **r** in the clouds, and it

RAISED (RISE)
Ro 4: 25 was **r** to life for our justification.
10: 9 your heart that God **r** him
1Co 15: 4 he was **r** on the third day according

RAN (RUN)
Jnh 1: 3 But Jonah **r** away from the LORD

RANSOM
Mt 20: 28 to give his life as a **r** for many."
Heb 9: 15 he has died as a **r** to set them free

RAVENS
1Ki 17: 6 The **r** brought him bread and meat
Lk 12: 24 Consider the **r**: They do not sow

READ (READS)
Jos 8: 34 Joshua **r** all the words of the law–
Ne 8: 8 understood what was being **r**.
2Co 3: 2 hearts, known and **r** by everyone.

READS (READ)
Rev 1: 3 is the one who **r** aloud the words

REAL (REALITY)
Jn 6: 55 For my flesh is **r** food and my blood is **r** drink.

REALITY (REAL)
Col 2: 17 the **r**, however, is found in Christ.

REAP (REAPS)
Job 4: 8 evil and those who sow trouble **r** it.
2Co 9: 6 generously will also **r** generously.

REAPS (REAP)
Gal 6: 7 A man **r** what he sows.

REASON
1Pe 3: 15 asks you to give the **r** for the hope

REBEKAH
Sister of Laban, secured as bride for Isaac (Ge 24). Mother of Esau and Jacob (Ge 25:19-26). Taken by Abimelek as sister of Isaac; returned (Ge 26:1-11). Encouraged Jacob to trick Isaac out of blessing (Ge 27:1-17).

REBEL
Mt 10: 21 children will **r** against their parents

REBUKE (REBUKING)
Pr 9: 8 **r** the wise and they will love you.
27: 5 Better is open **r** than hidden love.
Lk 17: 3 or sister sins against you, **r** them;
2Ti 4: 2 correct, **r** and encourage–
Rev 3: 19 Those whom I love I **r**

REBUKING (REBUKE)
2Ti 3: 16 and is useful for teaching, **r**,

RECEIVE (RECEIVED RECEIVES)
Ac 1: 8 you will **r** power when the Holy
20: 35 more blessed to give than to **r**.' "
2Co 6: 17 no unclean thing, and I will **r** you."
Rev 4: 11 to **r** glory and honor and power,

RECEIVED (RECEIVE)
Mt 6: 2 they have **r** their reward in full.
10: 8 Freely you have **r**; freely give.
1Co 11: 23 For I **r** from the Lord what I
Col 2: 6 just as you **r** Christ Jesus as Lord,
1Pe 4: 10 should use whatever gift you have **r**

RECEIVES (RECEIVE)
Mt 7: 8 For everyone who asks **r**;
Ac 10: 43 who believes in him **r** forgiveness

RECKONING
Isa 10: 3 What will you do on the day of **r**,

RECOGNIZE (RECOGNIZED)
Mt 7: 16 By their fruit you will **r** them.

RECOGNIZED (RECOGNIZE)
Mt 12: 33 be bad, for a tree is **r** by its fruit.
Ro 7: 13 in order that sin might be **r** as sin,

RECOMPENSE
Isa 40: 10 him, and his **r** accompanies him.

RECONCILE (RECONCILED RECONCILIATION)
Eph 2: 16 and in one body to **r** both of them

RECONCILED (RECONCILE)
Mt 5: 24 First go and be **r** to them;

Ro   5: 10 were **r** to him through the death
2Co   5: 18 who **r** us to himself through Christ

RECONCILIATION (RECONCILE)
Ro   5: 11 whom we have now received **r**.
       11: 15 For if their rejection brought **r**
2Co   5: 18 and gave us the ministry of **r**:
       5: 19 committed to us the message of **r**.

RECORD
Ps 130:   3 you, Lᴏʀᴅ, kept a **r** of sins, Lord,

RED
Isa   1: 18 though they are **r** as crimson,

REDEEM (REDEEMED REDEEMER REDEMPTION)
2Sa   7: 23 out to **r** as a people for himself,
Ps   49:   7 No one can **r** the life of another
Gal   4:   5 to **r** those under the law, that we

REDEEMED (REDEEM)
Gal   3: 13 Christ **r** us from the curse of the law
1Pe   1: 18 you were **r** from the empty way

REDEEMER (REDEEM)
Job 19: 25 I know that my **r** lives,

REDEMPTION (REDEEM)
Ps 130:   7 love and with him is full **r**.
Lk   21: 28 because your **r** is drawing near."
Ro   8: 23 to sonship, the **r** of our bodies.
Eph   1:   7 we have **r** through his blood,
Col   1: 14 in whom we have **r**, the forgiveness
Heb   9: 12 blood, thus obtaining eternal **r**.

REFUGE
Nu   35: 11 some towns to be your cities of **r**,
Dt   33: 27 The eternal God is your **r**,
Ru   2: 12 wings you have come to take **r**."
Ps   46:   1 God is our **r** and strength,
     91:   2 "He is my **r** and my fortress,

REHOBOAM
   Son of Solomon (1Ki 11:43; 1Ch 3:10). Harsh treatment of subjects caused divided kingdom (1Ki 12:1-24; 14:21-31; 2Ch 10-12).

REIGN (REIGNS)
Ro   6: 12 not let sin **r** in your mortal body
1Co   15: 25 he must **r** until he has put all his
2Ti   2: 12 if we endure, we will also **r** with
Rev 20:   6 **r** with him for a thousand years.

REIGNS (REIGN)
Ex   15: 18 "The Lᴏʀᴅ **r** for ever and ever."

REJECTED (REJECTS)
Ps 118: 22 stone the builders **r** has become
Isa   53:   3 was despised and **r** by mankind,
1Ti   4:   4 nothing is to be **r** if it is received
1Pe   2:   4 **r** by humans but chosen by God
      2:   7 stone the builders **r** has become

REJECTS (REJECTED)
Lk   10: 16 whoever **r** me **r** him who sent me."
Jn   3: 36 whoever **r** the Son will not see life,

REJOICE (JOY)
Ps   66:   6 come, let us **r** in him.
    118: 24 let us **r** today and be glad.
Pr   5: 18 you **r** in the wife of your youth.
Lk   10: 20 but **r** that your names are written
      15:   6 together and says, 'R with me;
Ro   12: 15 **R** with those who **r**;
Php   4:   4 **R** in the Lord always. I will say it again: **R**!

REJOICES (JOY)
Isa   61: 10 my soul **r** in my God.
Lk   1: 47 and my spirit **r** in God my Savior,
1Co   12: 26 is honored, every part **r** with it.
      13:   6 delight in evil but **r** with the truth.

REJOICING (JOY)
Ps   30:   5 night, but **r** comes in the morning.
Lk   15:   7 the same way there will be more **r**
Ac   5: 41 **r** because they had been counted

RELIABLE
2Ti   2:   2 entrust to **r** people who will also be

RELIGION
1Ti   5:   4 of all to put their **r** into practice
Jas   1: 27 **R** that God our Father accepts as

REMAIN (REMAINS)
Nu   33: 55 you allow to **r** will become barbs
Jn   15:   7 If you **r** in me and my words **r**
Ro   13:   8 Let no debt **r** outstanding,
1Co   13: 13 And now these three **r**:

REMAINS (REMAIN)
Ps 146:   6 he **r** faithful forever.
2Ti   2: 13 if we are faithless, he **r** faithful,
Heb   7:   3 Son of God, he **r** a priest forever.

REMEMBER (REMEMBERS REMEMBRANCE)
Ex   20:   8 "**R** the Sabbath day by keeping it
1Ch   16: 12 **R** the wonders he has done,
Ecc   12:   1 **R** your Creator in the days of your
Jer   31: 34 and will **r** their sins no more."
Gal   2: 10 we should continue to **r** the poor,
Php   1:   3 I thank my God every time I **r** you.
Heb   8: 12 and will **r** their sins no more."

REMEMBERS (REMEMBER)
Ps 103: 14 are formed, he **r** that we are dust.
    111:   5 he **r** his covenant forever.
Isa   43: 25 own sake, and **r** your sins no more.

REMEMBRANCE (REMEMBER)
1Co   11: 24 is for you; do this in **r** of me."

REMIND
Jn   14: 26 will **r** you of everything I have said

REMOVED
Ps   30: 11 you **r** my sackcloth and clothed me
    103: 12 so far has he **r** our transgressions
Jn   20:   1 that the stone had been **r**

RENEW (RENEWED RENEWING)
Ps   51: 10 and **r** a steadfast spirit within me.
Isa   40: 31 in the Lᴏʀᴅ will **r** their strength.

RENEWED (RENEW)
Ps 103:   5 that your youth is **r** like the eagle's.
2Co   4: 16 yet inwardly we are being **r** day

RENEWING (RENEW)
Ro   2:   2 transformed by the **r** of your mind.

RENOUNCE (RENOUNCES)
Da   4: 27 **R** your sins by doing what is right,

RENOUNCES (RENOUNCE)
Pr   28: 13 confesses and **r** them finds mercy.

RENOWN
Isa   63: 12 to gain for himself everlasting **r**,
Jer   32: 20 have gained the **r** that is still yours.

REPAID (PAY)
Lk   14: 14 you will be **r** at the resurrection
Col   3: 25 Anyone who does wrong will be **r**

REPAY (PAY)
Dt   32: 35 It is mine to avenge; I will **r**.
Ru   2: 12 May the Lᴏʀᴅ **r** you for what you
Ro   12: 19 I will **r**," says the Lord.
1Pe   3:   9 the contrary, **r** evil with blessing,

REPENT (REPENTANCE REPENTS)
Job 42:   6 I despise myself and **r** in dust
Jer   15: 19 "If you **r**, I will restore you that you
Mt   4: 17 time on Jesus began to preach, "**R**,
Lk   13:   3 But unless you **r**, you too will all
      17:   3 and if they **r**, forgive them.
Ac   2: 38 Peter replied, "**R** and be baptized,
      17: 30 all people everywhere to **r**.

REPENTANCE (REPENT)
Lk   3:   8 Produce fruit in keeping with **r**.
      5: 32 call the righteous, but sinners to **r**."
Ac   26: 20 demonstrate their **r** by their deeds.
2Co   7: 10 Godly sorrow brings **r** that leads

REPENTS (REPENT)
Lk   15: 10 of God over one sinner who **r**."

REPROACH
1Ti   3:   2 Now the overseer is to be above **r**,

REPUTATION
1Ti   3:   7 also have a good **r** with outsiders,

REQUESTS
Ps   20:   5 May the Lᴏʀᴅ grant all your **r**.
Php   4:   6 present your **r** to God.

REQUIRE
Mic   6:   8 what does the Lᴏʀᴅ **r** of you?

RESCUE (RESCUES)
Da   6: 20 been able to **r** you from the lions?"
2Pe   2:   9 the Lord knows how to **r** the godly

RESCUES (RESCUE)
1Th   1: 10 who **r** us from the coming wrath.

RESIST
Jas   4:   7 **R** the devil, and he will flee
1Pe   5:   9 **R** him, standing firm in the faith,

RESOLVED
Da   1:   8 Daniel **r** not to defile himself
1Co   2:   2 For I **r** to know nothing while I

RESPECT (RESPECTABLE)
Lev 19:   3 of you must **r** your mother
      19: 32 show **r** for the elderly and revere
Mal   1:   6 a master, where is the **r** due me?"
1Th   4: 12 that your daily life may win the **r**
1Ti   3:   4 do so in a manner worthy of full **r**.
1Pe   2: 17 Show proper **r** to everyone,
        3:   7 them with **r** as the weaker partner

RESPECTABLE (RESPECT)
1Ti   3:   2 self-controlled, **r**, hospitable,

REST
Ex   31: 15 seventh day is a day of sabbath **r**,
Ps   91:   1 the Most High will **r** in the shadow
Jer   6: 16 and you will find **r** for your souls.
Mt   11: 28 burdened, and I will give you **r**.

RESTITUTION
Ex   22:   3 who steals must certainly make **r**,
Lev   6:   5 must make **r** in full, add a fifth

RESTORE
Ps   51: 12 **R** to me the joy of your salvation
Gal   6:   1 by the Spirit should **r** that person

RESURRECTION
Mt   22: 30 the **r** people will neither marry nor
Lk   14: 14 be repaid at the **r** of the righteous."
Jn   11: 25 said to her, "I am the **r** and the life.
Ro   1:   4 in power by his **r** from the dead:
1Co 15: 12 say that there is no **r** of the dead?
Php   3: 10 yes, to know the power of his **r**
Rev 20:   5 This is the first **r**.

RETRIBUTION
Jer 51: 56 For the Lᴏʀᴅ is a God of **r**;

RETURN
2Ch 30:   9 If you **r** to the Lᴏʀᴅ, then your
Ne   1:   9 but if you **r** to me and obey my
Isa   55: 11 It will not **r** to me empty, but will
Hos   6:   1 "Come, let us **r** to the Lᴏʀᴅ.
Joel   2: 12 "**r** to me with all your heart,

REVEALED (REVELATION)
Dt   29: 29 but the things **r** belong to us
Isa   40:   5 the glory of the Lᴏʀᴅ will be **r**,
Mt   11: 25 and **r** them to little children.
Ro   1: 17 the righteousness of God is **r**−
        8: 18 with the glory that will be **r** in us.

REVELATION (REVEALED)
Gal   1: 12 I received it by **r** from Jesus Christ.
Rev   1:   1 The **r** from Jesus Christ,

REVENGE (VENGEANCE)
Lev 19: 18 "'Do not seek **r** or bear a grudge
Ro   12: 19 Do not take **r**, my dear friends,

REVERE (REVERENCE)
Ps   33:   8 all the people of the world **r** him.

REVERENCE (REVERE)
Lev 19: 30 and have **r** for my sanctuary.
Ps   5:   7 in **r** I bow down toward your holy

Col   3: 22 of heart and **r** for the Lord.
1Pe   3:   2 see the purity and **r** of your lives.

REVIVE
Ps   85:   6 Will you not **r** us again, that your
Isa   57: 15 to **r** the spirit of the lowly and to **r**

REWARD (REWARDED)
Ps   19: 11 in keeping them there is great **r**.
    127:   3 the Lᴏʀᴅ, offspring a **r** from him.
Pr   19: 17 he will **r** them for what they have
        25: 22 head, and the Lᴏʀᴅ will **r** you.
Jer   17: 10 to **r** each person according to their
Mt   5: 12 because great is your **r** in heaven,
        6:   5 they have received their **r** in full.
      16: 27 he will **r** each person according
1Co   3: 14 the builder will receive a **r**.
Rev 22: 12 My **r** is with me, and I will give

REWARDED (REWARD)
Ru   2: 12 May you be richly **r** by the Lᴏʀᴅ,
Ps   18: 24 The Lᴏʀᴅ has **r** me according
Pr   14: 14 and the good **r** for theirs.
1Co   3:   8 and they will each be **r** according

RICH (RICHES)
Pr   23:   4 Do not wear yourself out to get **r**;
Jer   9: 23 or the **r** boast of their riches,
Mt   19: 23 for someone who is **r** to enter
2Co   6: 10 poor, yet making many **r**;
        8:   9 his poverty might become **r**.
1Ti   6: 17 Command those who are **r** in this

RICHES (RICH)
Ps   119: 14 statutes as one rejoices in great **r**.
Pr   30:   8 give me neither poverty nor **r**,
Isa   10:   3 Where will you leave your **r**?
Ro   9: 23 to make the **r** of his glory known
      11: 33 the depth of the **r** of the wisdom
Eph   2:   7 he might show the incomparable **r**
        3:   8 to the Gentiles the boundless **r**
Col   1: 27 among the Gentiles the glorious **r**

RID
Ge   21: 10 "Get **r** of that slave woman and her
1Co   5:   7 Get **r** of the old yeast, so that you
Gal   4: 30 "Get **r** of the slave woman and her

RIGHT (RIGHTS)
Ge   18: 25 not the Judge of all the earth do **r**?"
Ex   15: 26 God and do what is **r** in his eyes,
Dt   5: 32 do not turn aside to the **r**
Ps   16:   8 With him at my **r** hand, I will not
      19:   8 The precepts of the Lᴏʀᴅ are **r**,
      63:   8 your **r** hand upholds me.
    110:   1 "Sit at my **r** hand until I make your
Pr   4: 27 Do not turn to the **r** or the left;
      14: 12 There is a way that appears to be **r**,
Isa   1: 17 Learn to do **r**; seek justice.
Jer 23:   5 do what is just and **r** in the land.
Hos 14:   9 The ways of the Lᴏʀᴅ are **r**;
Mt   6:   3 know what your **r** hand is doing,
Jn   1: 12 he gave the **r** to become children
Ro   9: 21 Does not the potter have the **r**
      12: 17 careful to do what is **r** in the eyes
Eph   1: 20 and seated him at his **r** hand
Php   4:   8 whatever is **r**, whatever is pure,

RIGHTEOUS (RIGHTEOUSNESS)
Ps   34: 15 eyes of the Lᴏʀᴅ are on the **r**,
      37: 25 yet I have never seen the **r** forsaken
    119:137 You are **r**, Lᴏʀᴅ, and your laws
    143:   2 no one living is **r** before you.
Pr   3: 33 but he blesses the home of the **r**.
      11: 30 The fruit of the **r** is a tree of life,
      18: 10 the **r** run to it and are safe.
Isa 64:   6 all our **r** acts are like filthy rags;
Hab   2:   4 but the **r** person will live by his
Mt   5: 45 and sends rain on the **r**
        9: 13 For I have not come to call the **r**,
      13: 49 and separate the wicked from the **r**
      25: 46 but the **r** to eternal life."
Ro   1: 17 "The **r** will live by faith."

Ro   3: 10 "There is no one **r**, not even one;
1Ti   1: 9 that the law is made not for the **r**
Jas   2: 24 is considered **r** by what they do
1Pe 3: 18 for sins, the **r** for the unrighteous,
1Jn 3: 7 is right is **r**, just as he is **r**.
Rev 19: 8 (Fine linen stands for the **r** acts

RIGHTEOUSNESS (RIGHTEOUS)

Ge 15: 6 and he credited it to him as **r**.
1Sa 26: 23 rewards everyone for their **r**
Ps   9: 8 He rules the world in **r** and judges
     45: 7 You love **r** and hate wickedness;
     85: 10 **r** and peace kiss each other.
     89: 14 **R** and justice are the foundation
   111: 3 deeds, and his **r** endures forever.
Pr 14: 34 **R** exalts a nation, but sin
     21: 21 Whoever pursues **r** and love finds
Isa 59: 17 He put on **r** as his breastplate,
Eze 18: 20 The **r** of the righteous will be
Da   9: 24 to bring in everlasting **r**, to seal
     12: 3 and those who lead many to **r**,
Mal 4: 2 the sun of **r** will rise with healing
Mt   5: 6 those who hunger and thirst for **r**,
     5: 20 you that unless your **r** surpasses
     6: 1 practice your **r** in front of others
     6: 33 seek first his kingdom and his **r**,
Ro   3: 25 He did this to demonstrate his **r**,
     4: 3 and it was credited to him as **r**."
     4: 9 faith was credited to him as **r**.
     6: 13 to him as an instrument of **r**.
2Co 5: 21 we might become the **r** of God.
Gal 2: 21 **r** could be gained through the law,
     3: 6 and it was credited to him as **r**."
Eph 6: 14 with the breastplate of **r** in place,
Php 3: 9 not having a **r** of my own
2Ti 3: 16 correcting and training in **r**,
     4: 8 is in store for me the crown of **r**,
Heb 11: 7 and became heir of the **r** that is
2Pe 2: 21 not to have known the way of **r**,

RIGHTS (RIGHT)

La   3: 35 deny people their **r** before the Most

RISE (RAISED)

Isa 26: 19 their bodies will **r**–let those who
Mt 27: 63 'After three days I will **r** again.'
Jn   5: 29 who have done what is good will **r**
1Th 4: 16 and the dead in Christ will **r** first.

ROAD

Mt   7: 13 gate and broad is the **r** that leads

ROBBERS

Jer   7: 11 Name, become a den of **r** to you?
Lk 19: 46 you have made it 'a den of **r**.'"
Jn 10: 8 come before me are thieves and **r**,

ROCK

Ps 18: 2 The Lord is my **r**, my fortress
     40: 2 he set my feet on a **r** and gave me
Mt   7: 24 man who built his house on the **r**.
     16: 18 on this **r** I will build my church,
Ro   9: 33 and a **r** that makes them fall,
1Co 10: 4 them, and that **r** was Christ.

ROD

Ps 23: 4 your **r** and your staff, they comfort
Pr 13: 24 Whoever spares the **r** hates their
     23: 13 if you punish them with the **r**,

ROOM (ROOMS)

Mt   6: 6 go into your **r**, close the door
Lk   2: 7 there was no guest **r** available
Jn 21: 25 the whole world would not have **r**

ROOMS (ROOM)

Jn 14: 2 My Father's house has many **r**;

ROOT

Isa 53: 2 and like a **r** out of dry ground.
1Ti   6: 10 the love of money is a **r** of all kinds

ROYAL

Jas   2: 8 If you really keep the **r** law found
1Pe 2: 9 are a chosen people, a **r** priesthood,

RUIN (RUINS)

Pr 18: 24 unreliable friends soon comes to **r**,
     19: 3 person's own folly leads to their **r**,
1Ti   6: 9 desires that plunge people into **r**

RUINS (RUIN)

2Ti 2: 14 value, and only **r** those who listen.

RULE (RULER RULERS RULES)

1Sa 12: 12 'No, we want a king to **r** over us'–
Ps 119:133 to your word; let no sin **r** over me.
Zec 9: 10 His **r** will extend from sea to sea
Col   3: 15 peace of Christ **r** in your hearts,
Rev 2: 27 that one 'will **r** them with an iron

RULER (RULE)

Eph 2: 2 of the **r** of the kingdom of the air,
1Ti   6: 15 the blessed and only **R**, the King

RULERS (RULE)

Ps   2: 2 and the **r** band together against
     8: 6 You made them **r** over the works
Col   1: 16 or powers or **r** or authorities;

RULES (RULE)

Ps 103: 19 heaven, and his kingdom **r** over all.
Lk 22: 26 and the one who **r** like the one who
2Ti 2: 5 by competing according to the **r**.

RUMORS

Mt 24: 6 You will hear of wars and **r** of wars,

RUN (RAN)

Isa 40: 31 they will **r** and not grow weary,
1Co 9: 24 **R** in such a way as to get the prize.
Heb 12: 1 let us **r** with perseverance the race

RUTH

    Moabitess; widow who went to Bethlehem with mother-in-law Naomi (Ru 1). Gleaned in field of Boaz; shown favor (Ru 2). Proposed marriage to Boaz (Ru 3). Married (Ru 4:1-12); bore Obed, ancestor of David (Ru 4:13-22), Jesus (Mt 1:5).

SABBATH

Ex 20: 8 "Remember the **S** day by keeping it
Dt   5: 12 "Observe the **S** day by keeping it
Col   2: 16 New Moon celebration or a **S** day.

SACKCLOTH

Mt 11: 21 would have repented long ago in **s**

SACRED

Mt   7: 6 "Do not give dogs what is **s**;
1Co 3: 17 for God's temple is **s**, and you

SACRIFICE (SACRIFICED)

Ge 22: 2 **S** him there as a burnt offering
Ex 12: 27 'It is the Passover **s** to the Lord,
1Sa 15: 22 To obey is better than **s**,
Ps 51: 17 My **s**, O God, is a broken spirit;
Hos 6: 6 not **s**, and acknowledgment of God
Mt   9: 13 'I desire mercy, not **s**.'
Ro 12: 1 to offer your bodies as a living **s**,
Heb 9: 26 away with sin by the **s** of himself.
     13: 15 offer to God a **s** of praise–
1Jn 2: 2 He is the atoning **s** for our sins,

SACRIFICED (SACRIFICE)

1Co 5: 7 our Passover lamb, has been **s**.
     8: 1 Now about food **s** to idols:
Heb 9: 28 so Christ was **s** once to take away

SADDUCEES

Mk 12: 18 Then the **S**, who say there is no

SAFE (SAVE)

Ps 37: 3 in the land and enjoy **s** pasture.
Pr 18: 10 the righteous run to it and are **s**.

SAFETY (SAVE)

Ps   4: 8 alone, Lord, make me dwell in **s**.
1Th 5: 3 "Peace and **s**," destruction will

SAINTS See FAITHFUL, [GOD'S, LORD'S] PEOPLE,

SAKE

Ps 44: 22 your **s** we face death all day long;
Php 3: 7 consider loss for the **s** of Christ.
Heb 11: 26 disgrace for the **s** of Christ as

SALT

Ge 19: 26 back, and she became a pillar of **s**.
Mt 5: 13 "You are the **s** of the earth.

SALVATION (SAVE)

Ex 15: 2 he has become my **s**.
1Ch 16: 23 proclaim his **s** day after day.
Ps 27: 1 The LORD is my light and my **s**—
51: 12 Restore to me the joy of your **s**
62: 2 Truly he is my rock and my **s**;
85: 9 Surely his **s** is near those who fear
96: 2 proclaim his **s** day after day.
Isa 25: 9 let us rejoice and be glad in his **s**."
45: 17 the LORD with an everlasting **s**;
51: 6 But my **s** will last forever,
59: 17 and the helmet of **s** on his head;
61: 10 has clothed me with garments of **s**
Jnh 2: 9 '**S** comes from the LORD.'"
Lk 2: 30 For my eyes have seen your **s**,
Jn 4: 22 we do know, for **s** is from the Jews.
Ac 4: 12 **S** is found in no one else, for there
13: 47 that you may bring **s** to the ends
Ro 11: 11 **s** has come to the Gentiles to make
2Co 7: 10 brings repentance that leads to **s**
Eph 6: 17 Take the helmet of **s** and the sword
Php 2: 12 to work out your **s** with fear
1Th 5: 8 and the hope of **s** as a helmet.
2Ti 3: 15 make you wise for **s** through faith
Heb 2: 3 we escape if we ignore so great a **s**?
6: 9 the things that have to do with **s**.
1Pe 1: 10 Concerning this **s**, the prophets,
2: 2 by it you may grow up in your **s**,

SAMARITAN

Lk 10: 33 But a **S**, as he traveled, came where

SAMSON

Danite judge. Birth promised (Jdg 13). Married to Philistine (Jdg 14). Vengeance on Philistines (Jdg 15). Betrayed by Delilah (Jdg 16:1-22). Death (Jdg 16:23-31). Feats of strength: killed lion (Jdg 14:6), 30 Philistines (Jdg 14:19), 1,000 Philistines with jawbone (Jdg 15:13-17), carried off gates of Gaza (Jdg 16:3), pushed down temple of Dagon (Jdg 16:25-30).

SAMUEL

Ephraimite judge and prophet (Heb 11:32). Birth prayed for (1Sa 1:10-18). Dedicated to temple by Hannah (1Sa 1:21-28). Raised by Eli (1Sa 2:11, 18-26). Called as prophet (1Sa 3). Led Israel to victory over Philistines (1Sa 7). Asked by Israel for a king (1Sa 8). Anointed Saul as king (1Sa 9-10). Farewell speech (1Sa 12). Rebuked Saul for sacrifice (1Sa 13). Announced rejection of Saul (1Sa 15). Anointed David as king (1Sa 16). Protected David from Saul (1Sa 19:18-24). Death (1Sa 25:1). Returned from dead to condemn Saul (1Sa 28).

SANCTIFIED (SANCTIFY)

Ac 20: 32 among all those who are **s**.
Ro 15: 16 to God, **s** by the Holy Spirit.
1Co 6: 11 you were **s**, you were justified
7: 14 husband has been **s** through his
Heb 10: 29 blood of the covenant that **s** them,

SANCTIFY (SANCTIFIED SANCTIFYING)

1Th 5: 23 peace, **s** you through and through.

SANCTIFYING (SANCTIFY)

2Th 2: 13 be saved through the **s** work

SANCTUARY

Ex 25: 8 "Then have them make a **s** for me,

SAND

Ge 22: 17 sky and as the **s** on the seashore.
Mt 7: 26 man who built his house on **s**.

SANDALS

Ex 3: 5 "Take off your **s**, for the place
Jos 5: 15 "Take off your **s**, for the place

SANG (SING)

Job 38: 7 while the morning stars **s** together
Rev 5: 9 And they **s** a new song, saying:

SARAH

Wife of Abraham, originally named Sarai; barren (Ge 11:29-31; 1Pe 3:6). Taken by Pharaoh as Abraham's sister;
returned (Ge 12:10-20). Gave Hagar to Abraham; sent her away in pregnancy (Ge 16). Name changed; Isaac promised (Ge 17:15-21; 18:10-15; Heb 11:11). Taken by Abimelek as Abraham's sister; returned (Ge 20). Isaac born; Hagar and Ishmael sent away (Ge 21:1-21; Gal 4:21-31). Death (Ge 23).

SATAN

Job 1: 6 and **S** also came with them.
Zec 3: 2 to **S**, "The LORD rebuke you, **S**!
Mk 4: 15 **S** comes and takes away the word
2Co 11: 14 **S** himself masquerades as an angel
12: 7 a messenger of **S**, to torment me.
Rev 12: 9 or **S**, who leads the whole world
20: 2 **S**, and bound him for a thousand
20: 7 **S** will be released from his prison

SATISFIED (SATISFY)

Isa 53: 11 he will see the light of life and be **s**;

SATISFIES (SATISFY)

Ps 103: 5 **s** your desires with good things

SATISFY (SATISFIED SATISFIES)

Isa 55: 2 and your labor on what does not **s**?

SAUL

1. Benjamite; anointed by Samuel as first king of Israel (1Sa 9-10). Defeated Ammonites (1Sa 11). Rebuked for offering sacrifice (1Sa 13:1-15). Defeated Philistines (1Sa 14). Rejected as king for failing to annihilate Amalekites (1Sa 15). Soothed from evil spirit by David (1Sa 16:14-23). Sent David against Goliath (1Sa 17). Jealousy and attempted murder of David (1Sa 18:1-11). Gave David Michal as wife (1Sa 18:12-30). Second attempt to kill David (1Sa 19). Anger at Jonathan (1Sa 20:26-34). Pursued David: killed priests at Nob (1Sa 22), went to Keilah and Ziph (1Sa 23), life spared by David at En Gedi (1Sa 24) and in his tent (1Sa 26). Rebuked by Samuel's spirit for consulting witch at Endor (1Sa 28). Wounded by Philistines; took his own life (1Sa 31; 1Ch 10).

2. See PAUL

SAVE (SAFE SAFETY SALVATION SAVED SAVIOR)

Isa 63: 1 proclaiming victory, mighty to **s**."
Mt 1: 21 because he will **s** his people
16: 25 wants to **s** their life will lose it,
Lk 19: 10 came to seek and to **s** the lost."
Jn 3: 17 but to **s** the world through him.
1Ti 1: 15 came into the world to **s** sinners—
Jas 5: 20 of their way will **s** them from death

SAVED (SAVE)

Ps 34: 6 he **s** him out of all his troubles.
Isa 45: 22 "Turn to me and be **s**, all you ends
Joel 2: 32 the name of the LORD will be **s**;
Mk 13: 13 stands firm to the end will be **s**.
16: 16 *believes and is baptized will be* **s**,
Jn 10: 9 enters through me will be **s**.
Ac 4: 12 mankind by which we must be **s**."
16: 30 "Sirs, what must I do to be **s**?"
Ro 9: 27 the sea, only the remnant will be **s**.
10: 9 him from the dead, you will be **s**.
1Co 3: 15 will suffer loss but yet will be **s**—
15: 2 By this gospel you are **s**, if you hold
Eph 2: 5 it is by grace you have been **s**.
2: 8 For it is by grace you have been **s**,
1Ti 2: 4 who wants all people to be **s**

SAVIOR (SAVE)

Ps 89: 26 Father, my God, the Rock my **S**.'
Isa 43: 11 and apart from me there is no **s**.
Hos 13: 4 no God but me, no **S** except me.
Lk 1: 47 and my spirit rejoices in God my **S**,
2: 11 town of David a **S** has been born
Jn 4: 42 that this man really is the **S**
Eph 5: 23 his body, of which he is the **S**.
1Ti 4: 10 God, who is the **S** of all people,
Titus 2: 10 about God our **S** attractive.
2: 13 the glory of our great God and **S**,
3: 4 and love of God our **S** appeared,
1Jn 4: 14 his Son to be the **S** of the world.
Jude : 25 to the only God our **S** be glory,

SCALES

Lev 19: 36 Use honest **s** and honest weights,
Da 5: 27 You have been weighed on the **s**

SCAPEGOAT (GOAT)
Lev 16: 10 it into the wilderness as a **s.**

SCARLET
Isa 1: 18 "Though your sins are like **s,**

SCATTERED
Jer 31: 10 'He who **s** Israel will gather them
Ac 8: 4 who had been **s** preached the word

SCEPTER
Rev 19: 15 "He will rule them with an iron **s.**"

SCHEMES
2Co 2: 11 For we are not unaware of his **s.**
Eph 6: 11 your stand against the devil's **s.**

SCOFFERS
2Pe 3: 3 that in the last days **s** will come,

SCORPION
Rev 9: 5 of the sting of a **s** when it strikes.

SCRIPTURE (SCRIPTURES)
Jn 10: 35 and **S** cannot be set aside–
1Ti 4: 13 yourself to the public reading of **S,**
2Ti 3: 16 All **S** is God-breathed and is useful
2Pe 1: 20 that no prophecy of **S** came

SCRIPTURES (SCRIPTURE)
Lk 24: 27 in all the **S** concerning himself.
Jn 5: 39 You study the **S** diligently because
Ac 17: 11 examined the **S** every day to see

SCROLL
Eze 3: 1 eat what is before you, eat this **s;**

SEA
Ex 14: 16 the Israelites can go through the **s**
Isa 57: 20 the wicked are like the tossing **s,**
Mic 7: 19 iniquities into the depths of the **s.**
Jas 1: 6 who doubts is like a wave of the **s,**
Rev 13: 1 I saw a beast coming out of the **s.**

SEAL (SEALS)
Jn 6: 27 God the Father has placed his **s**
2Co 1: 22 set his **s** of ownership on us,
Eph 1: 13 you were marked in him with a **s,**

SEALS (SEAL)
Rev 5: 2 "Who is worthy to break the **s**
6: 1 opened the first of the seven **s.**

SEARCH (SEARCHED SEARCHES SEARCHING)
Ps 4: 4 beds, **s** your hearts and be silent.
139: 23 **S** me, God, and know my heart;
Pr 2: 4 and **s** for it as for hidden treasure,
Jer 17: 10 "I the LORD **s** the heart
Eze 34: 16 I will **s** for the lost and bring back
Lk 15: 8 and **s** carefully until she finds it?

SEARCHED (SEARCH)
Ps 139: 1 You have **s** me, LORD, and you

SEARCHES (SEARCH)
Ro 8: 27 who **s** our hearts knows the mind
1Co 2: 10 The Spirit **s** all things, even the

SEARCHING (SEARCH)
Am 8: 12 east, **s** for the word of the LORD,

SEARED
1Ti 4: 2 whose consciences have been **s** as

SEASON
2Ti 4: 2 be prepared in **s** and out of **s;**

SEAT (SEATED SEATS)
Da 7: 9 and the Ancient of Days took his **s.**
2Co 5: 10 all appear before the judgment **s**

SEATED (SEAT)
Ps 47: 8 God is **s** on his holy throne.
Isa 6: 1 high and exalted, **s** on a throne;
Col 3: 1 Christ is, **s** at the right hand of God.

SEATS (SEAT)
Lk 11: 43 you love the most important **s**

SECRET (SECRETS)
Dt 29: 29 The **s** things belong to the LORD
Jdg 16: 6 "Tell me the **s** of your great
Ps 90: 8 you, our **s** sins in the light of your

Pr 11: 13 but a trustworthy person keeps a **s.**
Mt 6: 4 so that your giving may be in **s.**
2Co 4: 2 we have renounced **s** and shameful
Php 4: 12 have learned the **s** of being content

SECRETS (SECRET)
Ps 44: 21 since he knows the **s** of the heart?
1Co 14: 25 as the **s** of their hearts are laid bare.

SECURE (SECURITY)
Ps 112: 8 Their hearts are **s,** they will have
Heb 6: 19 an anchor for the soul, firm and **s.**

SECURITY (SECURE)
Job 31: 24 or said to pure gold, 'You are my **s,**'

SEED (SEEDS)
Lk 8: 11 The **s** is the word of God.
1Co 3: 6 I planted the **s,** Apollos watered it,
2Co 9: 10 he who supplies **s** to the sower
Gal 3: 29 you are Abraham's **s,** and heirs
1Pe 1: 23 again, not of perishable **s,**

SEEDS (SEED)
Jn 12: 24 But if it dies, it produces many **s.**
Gal 3: 16 Scripture does not say "and to **s,**"

SEEK (SEEKS SELF-SEEKING)
Dt 4: 29 you will find him if you **s** him
1Ch 28: 9 If you **s** him, he will be found
2Ch 7: 14 pray and **s** my face and turn
Ps 119: 10 I **s** you with all my heart; do not let
Isa 55: 6 **S** the LORD while he may be
65: 1 found by those who did not **s** me.
Mt 6: 33 But **s** first his kingdom and his
Lk 19: 10 For the Son of Man came to **s**
Ro 10: 20 found by those who did not **s** me;
1Co 7: 27 Do not **s** to be released.

SEEKS (SEEK)
Jn 4: 23 the kind of worshipers the Father **s.**

SEER
1Sa 9: 9 of today used to be called a **s.**)

SELF-CONTROL (CONTROL)
1Co 7: 5 tempt you because of your lack of **s.**
Gal 5: 23 gentleness and **s.**
2Pe 1: 6 and to knowledge, **s;** and to **s,**

SELF-CONTROLLED (CONTROL)
1Ti 3: 2 his wife, temperate, **s,** respectable,
Titus 1: 8 what is good, who is **s,** upright,
2: 2 worthy of respect, **s,** and sound
2: 5 to be **s** and pure, to be busy
2: 6 encourage the young men to be **s.**
2: 12 to live **s,** upright and godly lives

SELF-INDULGENCE
Mt 23: 25 inside they are full of greed and **s.**

SELF-SEEKING (SEEK)
1Co 13: 5 it is not **s,** it is not easily angered,

SELFISH
Ps 119: 36 statutes and not toward **s** gain.
Pr 18: 1 unfriendly person pursues **s** ends
Gal 5: 20 fits of rage, **s** ambition, dissensions,
Php 1: 17 preach Christ out of **s** ambition,
2: 3 Do nothing out of **s** ambition
Jas 3: 14 envy and **s** ambition in your hearts,
3: 16 you have envy and **s** ambition,

SEND (SENDING SENT)
Isa 6: 8 And I said, "Here am I. **S** me!"
Mt 9: 38 to **s** out workers into his harvest
Jn 16: 7 but if I go, I will **s** him to you.

SENDING (SEND)
Jn 20: 21 the Father has sent me, I am **s** you."

SENSES
Lk 15: 17 "When he came to his **s,** he said,
1Co 15: 34 Come back to your **s** as you ought,
2Ti 2: 26 that they will come to their **s**

SENSUAL
Col 2: 23 value in restraining **s** indulgence.

SENT (SEND)
Isa 55: 11 achieve the purpose for which I **s** it.

Mt 10: 40 me welcomes the one who **s** me.
Jn 4: 34 "is to do the will of him who **s** me
Ro 10: 15 anyone preach unless they are **s**?
1Jn 4: 10 **s** his Son as an atoning sacrifice

SEPARATE (SEPARATED SEPARATES)
Mt 19: 6 has joined together, let no one **s**."
Ro 8: 35 Who shall **s** us from the love
1Co 7: 10 A wife must not **s** from her
2Co 6: 17 "Come out from them and be **s**,

SEPARATED (SEPARATE)
Isa 59: 2 your iniquities have **s** you from

SEPARATES (SEPARATE)
Pr 16: 28 and a gossip **s** close friends.

SERPENT
Ge 3: 1 Now the **s** was more crafty than
Rev 12: 9 that ancient **s** called the devil,

SERVANT (SERVANTS)
1Sa 3: 10 "Speak, for your **s** is listening."
Mt 20: 26 great among you must be your **s**,
25: 21 'Well done, good and faithful **s**!
Php 2: 7 by taking the very nature of a **s**,
2Ti 2: 24 And the Lord's **s** must not be

SERVANTS (SERVANT)
Lk 17: 10 do, should say, 'We are unworthy **s**;
Jn 15: 15 I no longer call you **s**,

SERVE (SERVICE SERVING)
Dt 10: 12 to **s** the Lord your God with all
Jos 22: 5 and to **s** him with all your heart
24: 15 household, we will **s** the Lord."
Mt 4: 10 Lord your God, and **s** him only.'"
6: 24 "No one can **s** two masters.
6: 24 You cannot **s** both God and money.
20: 28 but to **s**, and to give his life as
Eph 6: 7 **S** wholeheartedly, as if you were

SERVICE (SERVE)
1Co 12: 5 There are different kinds of **s**,
Eph 4: 12 to equip his people for works of **s**,

SERVING (SERVE)
Ro 12: 11 your spiritual fervor, **s** the Lord.
Eph 6: 7 as if you were **s** the Lord,
Col 3: 24 It is the Lord Christ you are **s**.
2Ti 2: 4 No one **s** as a soldier gets entangled

SEVEN (SEVENTH)
Ge 7: 2 Take with you **s** pairs of every kind
Jos 6: 4 march around the city **s** times,
1Ki 19: 18 Yet I reserve **s** thousand in Israel–
Pr 6: 16 hates, **s** that are detestable to him:
24: 16 though the righteous fall **s** times,
Isa 4: 1 that day **s** women will take hold
Da 9: 25 comes, there will be **s** 'sevens,'
Mt 18: 21 sins against me? Up to **s** times?"
Lk 11: 26 takes **s** other spirits more wicked
Ro 11: 4 myself **s** thousand who have not
Rev 1: 4 To the **s** churches in the province
1: 4 from the **s** spirits before his throne,
6: 1 Lamb opened the first of the **s** seals.
8: 2 I saw the **s** angels who stand before
8: 2 and **s** trumpets were given to them.
10: 4 And when the **s** thunders spoke,
15: 7 to the **s** angels **s** golden bowls filled

SEVENTH (SEVEN)
Ge 2: 2 so on the **s** day he rested from all
Ex 23: 12 but on the **s** day do not work,

SEX (SEXUAL SEXUALLY)
1Co 6: 9 nor men who have **s** with men

SEXUAL (SEX)
Mt 5: 32 except for **s** immorality, makes her
19: 9 except for **s** immorality,
1Co 6: 13 is not meant for **s** immorality,
6: 18 Flee from **s** immorality.
7: 1 a man not to have **s** relations
10: 8 should not commit **s** immorality,
Eph 5: 3 not be even a hint of **s** immorality,
1Th 4: 3 you should avoid **s** immorality;

SEXUALLY (SEX)
1Co 5: 9 associate with **s** immoral people–
6: 18 but whoever sins **s**, sins against

SHADOW
Ps 36: 7 take refuge in the **s** of your wings.
Heb 10: 1 The law is only a **s** of the good

SHALLUM
King of Israel (2Ki 15:10-16).

SHAME (ASHAMED)
Ps 22: 5 they trusted and were not put to **s**.
34: 5 faces are never covered with **s**.
Pr 13: 18 discipline comes to poverty and **s**,
Heb 12: 2 scorning its **s**, and sat down

SHARE (SHARED)
Ge 21: 10 that woman's son will never **s**
Lk 3: 11 who has two shirts should **s**
Gal 4: 30 the slave woman's son will never **s**
6: 6 the word should **s** all good things
Eph 4: 28 they may have something to **s**
1Ti 6: 18 to be generous and willing to **s**.
Heb 12: 10 order that we may **s** in his holiness.
13: 16 to do good and to **s** with others,

SHARED (SHARE)
Heb 2: 14 he too **s** in their humanity so

SHARON
SS 2: 1 I am a rose of **S**, a lily

SHARPER
Heb 4: 12 **S** than any double-edged sword,

SHED (SHEDDING)
Ge 9: 6 by humans shall their blood be **s**;
Col 1: 20 through his blood, **s** on the cross.

SHEDDING (SHED)
Heb 9: 22 without the **s** of blood there is no

SHEEP
Ps 100: 3 are his people, the **s** of his pasture.
119:176 I have strayed like a lost **s**.
Isa 53: 6 We all, like **s**, have gone astray,
Jer 50: 6 "My people have been lost **s**;
Eze 34: 11 I myself will search for my **s**
Mt 9: 36 helpless, like **s** without a shepherd.
Jn 10: 3 He calls his own **s** by name
10: 15 and I lay down my life for the **s**.
10: 27 My **s** listen to my voice;
21: 17 Jesus said, "Feed my **s**.
1Pe 2: 25 For "you were like **s** going astray,"

SHELTER
Ps 61: 4 take refuge in the **s** of your wings.
91: 1 in the **s** of the Most High will rest

SHEM
Son of Noah (Ge 5:32; 6:10). Blessed (Ge 9:26). Descendants (Ge 10:21-31; 11:10-32).

SHEPHERD (SHEPHERDS)
Ps 23: 1 The Lord is my **s**, I lack nothing.
Isa 40: 11 He tends his flock like a **s**:
Jer 31: 10 will watch over his flock like a **s**.'
Eze 34: 12 a **s** looks after his scattered flock
Zec 11: 17 "Woe to the worthless **s**,
Mt 9: 36 and helpless, like sheep without a **s**.
Jn 10: 11 "I am the good **s**. The good **s** lays
10: 16 there shall be one flock and one **s**.
1Pe 5: 4 And when the Chief **S** appears,

SHEPHERDS (SHEPHERD)
Jer 23: 1 "Woe to the **s** who are destroying
Lk 2: 8 there were **s** living out in the fields
Ac 20: 28 Be **s** of the church of God,
1Pe 5: 2 Be **s** of God's flock that is under

SHIELD
Ps 28: 7 Lord is my strength and my **s**;
Eph 6: 16 take up the **s** of faith,

SHINE (SHONE)
Ps 4: 6 Let the light of your face **s** on us,
80: 1 between the cherubim, **s** forth
Isa 60: 1 "Arise, **s**, for your light has come,

Da 12: 3 are wise will **s** like the brightness
Mt   5: 16 let your light **s** before others,
    13: 43 the righteous will **s** like the sun
2Co 4: 6 made his light **s** in our hearts
Eph 5: 14 the dead, and Christ will **s** on you."

SHIPWRECK (SHIPWRECKED)
1Ti 1: 19 so have suffered **s** with regard

SHIPWRECKED (SHIPWRECK)
2Co 11: 25 three times I was **s**, I spent a night

SHONE (SHINE)
Mt 17: 2 His face **s** like the sun, and his
Lk   2: 9 glory of the Lord **s** around them,
Rev 21: 11 It **s** with the glory of God, and its

SHORT
Isa 59: 1 of the Lord is not too **s** to save,
Ro   3: 23 and fall **s** of the glory of God,

SHOULDERS
Isa 9: 6 the government will be on his **s**.
Lk 15: 5 finds it, he joyfully puts it on his **s**

SHOWED
1Jn 4: 9 This is how God **s** his love among

SHREWD
Mt 10: 16 Therefore be as **s** as snakes and as

SHUN
Job 28: 28 and to **s** evil is understanding."
Pr   3: 7 fear the Lord and **s** evil.

SICK
Pr 13: 12 Hope deferred makes the heart **s**,
Mt   9: 12 who need a doctor, but the **s**.
    25: 36 I was **s** and you looked after me,
Jas 5: 14 Is anyone among you **s**?

SICKLE
Joel 3: 13 Swing the **s**, for the harvest is ripe.

SIDE
Ps 91: 7 A thousand may fall at your **s**,
   124: 1 the Lord had not been on our **s**—
2Ti 4: 17 Lord stood at my **s** and gave me

SIGHT
Ps 90: 4 years in your **s** are like a day
   116: 15 in the **s** of the Lord is the death
2Co 5: 7 For we live by faith, not by **s**.
1Pe 3: 4 which is of great worth in God's **s**.

SIGN (SIGNS)
Isa 7: 14 the Lord himself will give you a **s**:

SIGNS (SIGN)
Mt 24: 24 and perform great **s** and wonders
Mk 16: 17 these **s** will accompany those who
Jn   3: 2 could perform the **s** you are doing
     9: 16 can a sinner perform such **s**?"
    20: 30 Jesus performed many other **s**
1Co 1: 22 Jews demand **s** and Greeks look

SILENT
Pr 17: 28 are thought wise if they keep **s**,
Isa 53: 7 as a sheep before its shearers is **s**,
Hab 2: 20 let all the earth be **s** before him.
1Co 14: 34 Women should remain **s**

SILVER
Pr 25: 11 of **s** is a ruling rightly given.
Hag 2: 8 'The **s** is mine and the gold is
1Co 3: 12 on this foundation using gold, **s**,

SIMON
    1. See PETER.
    2. Apostle, called the Zealot (Mt 10:4; Mk 3:18; Lk 6:15; Ac 1:13).
    3. Samaritan sorcerer (Ac 8:9-24).

SIN (SINFUL SINNED SINNER SINNERS SINNING SINS)
Nu   5: 7 and must confess the **s** they have
    32: 23 sure that your **s** will find you out.
Dt 24: 16 each will die for their own **s**.
1Ki 8: 46 there is no one who does not **s**—
2Ch 7: 14 I will forgive their **s** and will heal
Ps   4: 4 Tremble and do not **s**; when you

Ps 32: 2 is the one whose **s** the Lord does
    32: 5 And you forgave the guilt of my **s**.
    51: 2 iniquity and cleanse me from my **s**.
    66: 18 If I had cherished **s** in my heart,
   119: 11 that I might not **s** against you.
   119:133 to your word; let no **s** rule over me.
Isa 6: 7 taken away and your **s** atoned for."
Mic 7: 18 you, who pardons **s** and forgives
Jn   1: 29 who takes away the **s** of the world!
     8: 34 everyone who sins is a slave to **s**.
Ro   5: 12 just as **s** entered the world through
     5: 20 But where **s** increased,
     6: 11 count yourselves dead to **s** but alive
     6: 23 For the wages of **s** is death,
    14: 23 that does not come from faith is **s**.
2Co 5: 21 God made him who had no **s** to be **s**
Gal 6: 1 if someone is caught in a **s**,
Heb 9: 26 to do away with **s** by the sacrifice
    11: 25 to enjoy the fleeting pleasures of **s**.
    12: 1 and the **s** that so easily entangles.
1Pe 2: 22 "He committed no **s**, and no deceit
1Jn 1: 8 If we claim to be without **s**,
     3: 4 in fact, **s** is lawlessness.
     3: 5 away our sins. And in him is no **s**.
     3: 9 is born of God will continue to **s**,
     5: 18 born of God does not continue to **s**;

SINCERE
Ro 12: 9 Love must be **s**. Hate what is evil;
Heb 10: 22 us draw near to God with a **s** heart

SINFUL (SIN)
Ps 51: 5 Surely I was **s** at birth,
    51: 5 Surely I was **s** at birth,
Ro   7: 5 the **s** passions aroused by the law
1Pe 2: 11 to abstain from **s** desires,

SINFUL NATURE see FLESH

SING (SANG SINGING SONG SONGS)
Ps 30: 4 **S** the praises of the Lord, you his
    47: 6 **S** praises to God, **s** praises; **s** praises
    59: 16 in the morning I will **s** of your love
    89: 1 I will **s** of the Lord's great love
   101: 1 I will **s** of your love and justice;
Eph 5: 19 **S** and make music from your heart

SINGING (SING)
Ps 63: 5 **s** lips my mouth will praise you.
Ac 16: 25 were praying and **s** hymns to God,

SINNED (SIN)
2Sa 12: 13 "I have **s** against the Lord."
Job 1: 5 "Perhaps my children have **s**
Ps 51: 4 have I **s** and done what is evil
Da   9: 5 we have **s** and done wrong.
Mic 7: 9 Because I have **s** against him, I will
Lk 15: 18 I have **s** against heaven and against
Ro   3: 23 for all have **s** and fall short
1Jn 1: 10 If we claim we have not **s**, we make

SINNER (SIN)
Ecc 9: 18 war, but one **s** destroys much good.
Lk 15: 7 heaven over one **s** who repents
    18: 13 said, 'God, have mercy on me, a **s**.'
Jas 5: 20 Whoever turns a **s** from the error
1Pe 4: 18 become of the ungodly and the **s**?"

SINNERS (SIN)
Ps   1: 1 stand in the way that **s** take or sit
Pr 23: 17 Do not let your heart envy **s**,
Mt   9: 13 come to call the righteous, but **s**."
Ro   5: 8 While we were still **s**, Christ died
1Ti 1: 15 came into the world to save **s**—

SINNING (SIN)
Ex 20: 20 be with you to keep you from **s**."
1Co 15: 34 senses as you ought, and stop **s**;
Heb 10: 26 If we deliberately keep on **s** after
1Jn 3: 6 one who lives in him keeps on **s**.
     3: 9 they cannot go on **s**, because they

SINS (SIN)
Ezr 9: 6 because our **s** are higher than our
Ps 19: 13 your servant also from willful **s**;

Ps   32:   1 are forgiven, whose **s** are covered.
     103:   3 who forgives all your **s** and heals
     130:   3 Lᴏʀᴅ, kept a record of **s**, Lord,
Pr   28: 13 Whoever conceals their **s** does not
Isa   1: 18 "Though your **s** are like scarlet,
      43: 25 and remembers your **s** no more.
      59:   2 your **s** have hidden his face
Eze   18:   4 The one who **s** is the one who will
Mt   1: 21 will save his people from their **s**."
      18: 15 "If your brother or sister **s**,
Lk   11:   4 Forgive us our **s**, for we also forgive everyone
                who **s** against us.
      17:   3 your brother or sister **s** against you,
Ac   22: 16 be baptized and wash your **s** away,
1Co   15:   3 Christ died for our **s** according
Eph   2:   1 dead in your transgressions and **s**,
Col   2: 13 He forgave us all our **s**,
Heb   1:   3 he had provided purification for **s**,
       7: 27 He sacrificed for their **s** once for all
       8: 12 will remember their **s** no more."
      10: 12 for all time one sacrifice for **s**,
Jas   5: 16 Therefore confess your **s** to each
       5: 20 and cover over a multitude of **s**.
1Pe   2: 24 so that we might die to **s** and live
       3: 18 For Christ also suffered once for **s**,
1Jn   1:   9 If we confess our **s**, he is faithful
       1:   9 will forgive us our **s** and purify us
Rev   1:   5 freed us from our **s** by his blood,

SITS
Ps   99:   1 he **s** enthroned between
Isa   40: 22 He **s** enthroned above the circle
Mt   19: 28 Son of Man **s** on his glorious throne,
Rev   4:   9 thanks to him who **s** on the throne

SKIN
Job   19: 20 escaped only by the **s** of my teeth.
      19: 26 And after my **s** has been destroyed,
Jer   13: 23 Can an Ethiopian change his **s**

SLAIN (SLAY)
Rev   5: 12 who was **s**, to receive power

SLANDER (SLANDERED SLANDERERS)
Lev   19: 16 spreading **s** among your people.
1Ti   5: 14 the enemy no opportunity for **s**.
Titus 3:   2 to **s** no one, to be peaceable

SLANDERED (SLANDER)
1Co   4: 13 when we are **s**, we answer kindly.

SLANDERERS (SLANDER)
Ro   1: 30 **s**, God-haters, insolent,
1Co   6: 10 nor drunkards nor **s** nor swindlers
Titus 2:   3 not to be **s** or addicted to much

SLAUGHTER
Isa   53:   7 he was led like a lamb to the **s**,

SLAVE (SLAVERY SLAVES)
Ge   21: 10 "Get rid of that **s** woman and her
Mt   20: 27 wants to be first must be your **s**—
Jn   8: 34 everyone who sins is a **s** to sin.
1Co   12: 13 whether Jews or Gentiles, **s** or free
Gal   3: 28 Jew nor Gentile, neither **s** nor free,
       4: 30 the **s** woman's son will never share

SLAVERY (SLAVE)
Gal   4:   3 in **s** under the elemental spiritual

SLAVES (SLAVE)
Ro   6:   6 we should no longer be **s** to sin—
       6: 22 and have become **s** of God,
2Pe   2: 19 for "people are **s** to whatever has

SLAY (SLAIN)
Job   13: 15 Though he **s** me, yet will I hope

SLEEP (SLEEPING)
Ps   121:   4 Israel will neither slumber nor **s**.
1Co   15: 51 We will not all **s**, but we will all be

SLEEPING (SLEEP)
Mk   13: 36 do not let him find you **s**.

SLOW
Ex   34:   6 and gracious God, **s** to anger,

Jas   1: 19 **s** to speak and **s** to become angry,
2Pe   3:   9 The Lord is not **s** in keeping his

SLUGGARD (SLUGGARDS)
Pr   6:   6 Go to the ant, you **s**;

SLUGGARDS (SLUGGARD)
Pr   20:   4 **S** do not plow in season;

SLUMBER
Ps   121:   3 he who watches over you will not **s**;
Pr   6: 10 little **s**, a little folding of the hands
Ro   13: 11 for you to wake up from your **s**,

SNAKE (SNAKES)
Nu   21:   8 "Make a **s** and put it up on a pole;
Pr   23: 32 In the end it bites like a **s**
Jn   3: 14 lifted up the **s** in the wilderness,

SNAKES (SNAKE)
Mt   10: 16 Therefore be as shrewd as **s** and as
Mk   16: 18 *they will pick up* **s**

SNATCH (SNATCHING)
Jn   10: 28 no one will **s** them out of my hand.

SNATCHING (SNATCH)
Jude   : 23 save others by **s** them from the fire;

SNOW
Ps   51:   7 me, and I will be whiter than **s**.

SOAR
Isa   40: 31 They will **s** on wings like eagles;

SODOM
Ge   19: 24 rained down burning sulfur on **S**
Ro   9: 29 we would have become like **S**,

SOIL
Ge   4:   2 kept flocks, and Cain worked the **s**.
Mt   13: 23 the seed falling on good **s** refers

SOLDIER
1Co   9:   7 Who serves as a **s** at his own
2Ti   2:   3 like a good **s** of Christ Jesus.

SOLE
Dt   28: 65 resting place for the **s** of your foot.
Isa   1:   6 From the **s** of your foot to the top

SOLID
2Ti   2: 19 God's **s** foundation stands firm,
Heb   5: 12 You need milk, not **s** food!

SOLOMON
Son of David by Bathsheba; king of Judah (2Sa 12:24; 1Ch 3:5, 10). Appointed king by David (1Ki 1); adversaries Adonijah, Joab, Shimei killed by Benaiah (1Ki 2). Asked for wisdom (1Ki 3; 2Ch 1). Judged between two prostitutes (1Ki 3:16-28). Built temple (1Ki 5-7; 2Ch 2-5); prayer of dedication (1Ki 8; 2Ch 6). Visited by Queen of Sheba (1Ki 10; 2Ch 9). Wives turned his heart from God (1Ki 11:1-13). Jeroboam rebelled against (1Ki 11:26-40). Death (1Ki 11:41-43; 2Ch 9:29-31).
Proverbs of (1Ki 4:32; Pr 1:1; 10:1; 25:1); psalms of (Ps 72; 127); song of (SS 1:1).

SON (SONS)
Ge   22:   2 said, "Take your **s**, your only **s**,
Ex   11:   5 Every firstborn **s** in Egypt will die,
Dt   21: 18 rebellious **s** who does not obey his
Ps   2:   7 He said to me, "You are my **s**;
       2: 12 Kiss his **s**, or he will be angry
Pr   10:   1 A wise **s** brings joy to his father,
Isa   7: 14 will conceive and give birth to a **s**,
Hos   11:   1 and out of Egypt I called my **s**.
Mt   2: 15 "Out of Egypt I called my **s**."
       3: 17 said, "This is my **S**, whom I love;
      11: 27 knows the **S** except the Father,
      11: 27 knows the Father except the **S**
      16: 16 Messiah, the **S** of the living God."
      17:   5 said, "This is my **S**, whom I love;
      20: 18 the **S** of Man will be delivered over
      24: 30 appear the sign of the **S** of Man
      24: 44 because the **S** of Man will come
      27: 54 "Surely he was the **S** of God!"
      28: 19 and of the **S** and of the Holy Spirit,
Mk   10: 45 even the **S** of Man did not come
      14: 62 you will see the **S** of Man sitting

Lk   9: 58 the **S** of Man has no place to lay his
       18: 8 when the **S** of Man comes, will he
       19: 10 For the **S** of Man came to seek
Jn   3: 14 so the **S** of Man must be lifted up,
        3: 16 that he gave his one and only **S**,
       17: 1 Glorify your **S**, that your **S** may
Ro   8: 29 conformed to the image of his **S**,
        8: 32 He who did not spare his own **S**,
1Co   15: 28 the **S** himself will be made subject
Gal   4: 30 for the slave woman's **s** will never
1Th   1: 10 and to wait for his **S** from heaven,
Heb   1: 2 days he has spoken to us by his **S**,
       10: 29 punished who has trampled the **S**
1Jn   1: 7 Jesus, his **S**, purifies us from all sin.
        4: 9 only **S** into the world that we might
        5: 5 believes that Jesus is the **S** of God.
        5: 11 eternal life, and this life is in his **S**.

SONG (SING)
Ps   40: 3 He put a new **s** in my mouth,
       96: 1 Sing to the Lord a new **s**;
      149: 1 Sing to the Lord a new **s**,
Isa   49: 13 burst into **s**, you mountains!
       55: 12 hills will burst into **s** before you,
Rev   5: 9 And they sang a new **s**, saying:
       15: 3 sang the **s** of God's servant Moses

SONGS (SING)
Job   35: 10 Maker, who gives **s** in the night,
Ps   100: 2 come before him with joyful **s**.
Eph   5: 19 hymns, and **s** from the Spirit.
Jas   5: 13 Let them sing **s** of praise.

SONS (SON)
Joel   2: 28 **s** and daughters will prophesy,
2Co   6: 18 you will be my **s** and daughters,

SORROW
Jer   31: 12 garden, and they will **s** no more.
Ro   9: 2 I have great **s** and unceasing
2Co   7: 10 Godly **s** brings repentance that

SOUL (SOULS)
Dt   6: 5 and with all your **s** and with all
       10: 12 all your heart and with all your **s**,
Jos   22: 5 all your heart and with all your **s**."
Ps   23: 3 he refreshes my **s**. He guides me
       42: 1 of water, so my **s** pants for you,
       42: 11 Why, my **s**, are you downcast?
      103: 1 Praise the Lord, my **s**;
Pr   13: 19 A longing fulfilled is sweet to the **s**,
Mt   10: 28 of the One who can destroy both **s**
       16: 26 the whole world, yet forfeit their **s**?
       22: 37 with all your **s** and with all your
Heb   4: 12 it penetrates even to dividing **s**

SOULS (SOUL)
Jer   6: 16 and you will find rest for your **s**.
Mt   11: 29 and you will find rest for your **s**.

SOUND
1Co   14: 8 the trumpet does not **s** a clear call,
       15: 52 the trumpet will **s**, the dead will
2Ti   4: 3 will not put up with **s** doctrine.

SOVEREIGN
Da   4: 25 Most High is **s** over all kingdoms

SOW (SOWS)
Job   4: 8 and those who **s** trouble reap it.
Mt   6: 26 they do not **s** or reap or store away
2Pe   2: 22 "A **s** that is washed returns to her

SOWS (SOW)
2Co   9: 6 and whoever **s** generously will

SPARE (SPARES)
Ro   8: 32 He who did not **s** his own Son,
       11: 21 God did not **s** the natural branches,

SPARES (SPARE)
Pr   13: 24 Whoever **s** the rod hates their

SPEARS
Isa   2: 4 and their **s** into pruning hooks.
Joel   3: 10 and your pruning hooks into **s**.
Mic   4: 3 and their **s** into pruning hooks.

SPECTACLE
1Co   4: 9 have been made a **s** to the whole
Col   2: 15 he made a public **s** of them,

SPIN
Mt   6: 28 They do not labor or **s**.

SPIRIT (SPIRITS SPIRITUAL)
Ge   1: 2 the **S** of God was hovering over
        6: 3 said, "My **S** will not contend
2Ki   2: 9 inherit a double portion of your **s**,"
Job   33: 4 The **S** of God has made me;
Ps   31: 5 Into your hands I commit my **s**;
       51: 10 and renew a steadfast **s** within me.
       51: 11 or take your Holy **S** from me.
       51: 17 My sacrifice, O God, is a broken **s**;
      139: 7 Where can I go from your **S**?
Isa   57: 15 to revive the **s** of the lowly
       63: 10 rebelled and grieved his Holy **S**.
Eze   11: 19 heart and put a new **s** in them;
       36: 26 a new heart and put a new **s** in you;
Joel   2: 28 I will pour out my **S** on all people.
Zec   4: 6 but by my **S**,' says the Lord
Mt   1: 18 to be pregnant through the Holy **S**.
        3: 11 He will baptize you with the Holy **S**
        3: 16 he saw the **S** of God descending
        4: 1 led by the **S** into the wilderness
        5: 3 "Blessed are the poor in **s**, for
       26: 41 The **s** is willing, but the flesh is
       28: 19 and of the Son and of the Holy **S**,
Lk   1: 80 child grew and became strong in **s**;
       11: 13 in heaven give the Holy **S** to those
Jn   4: 24 God is **s**, and his worshipers must worship in
                 the **S**
        7: 39 that time the **S** had not been given,
       14: 26 the Holy **S**, whom the Father will
       16: 13 But when he, the **S** of truth, comes,
       20: 22 and said, "Receive the Holy **S**.
Ac   1: 5 will be baptized with the Holy **S**."
        2: 4 tongues as the **S** enabled them.
        2: 38 will receive the gift of the Holy **S**.
        6: 3 who are known to be full of the **S**
       19: 2 "Did you receive the Holy **S**
Ro   8: 9 if indeed the **S** of God lives in you.
        8: 26 the **S** helps us in our weakness.
1Co   2: 10 God has revealed to us by his **S**.
        2: 10 The **S** searches all things,
        2: 14 without the **S** does not accept
        3: 1 as people who live by the **S** but as
        6: 19 bodies are temples of the Holy **S**,
       12: 1 Now about the gifts of the **S**,
       12: 13 we were all baptized by one **S**
       12: 13 and we were all given the one **S**
       14: 1 and eagerly desire gifts of the **S**,
2Co   3: 6 the letter kills, but the **S** gives life.
        5: 5 who has given us the **S** as a deposit,
Gal   5: 16 say, walk by the **S**, and you will not
        5: 22 But the fruit of the **S** is love, joy,
        5: 25 Since we live by the **S**, let us keep
Gal   6: 1 who live by the **S** should restore
Eph   1: 13 with a seal, the promised Holy **S**,
        4: 30 do not grieve the Holy **S** of God,
        5: 18 Instead, be filled with the **S**,
        5: 19 hymns, and songs from the **S**.
        6: 17 of salvation and the sword of the **S**,
1Th   5: 19 Do not quench the **S**.
2Th   2: 13 the sanctifying work of the **S**
Heb   4: 12 even to dividing soul and **s**,
1Pe   3: 4 beauty of a gentle and quiet **s**,
2Pe   1: 21 were carried along by the Holy **S**.
1Jn   4: 1 do not believe every **s**, but test

SPIRITS (SPIRIT)
1Co   12: 10 another distinguishing between **s**,
       14: 32 The **s** of prophets are subject
1Jn   4: 1 but test the **s** to see whether they

SPIRITUAL (SPIRIT)
Ro   12: 11 but keep your **s** fervor,
1Co   2: 13 the Spirit, explaining **s** realities

1Co 15: 44 a natural body, it is raised a **s** body.
Eph   1: 3 realms with every **s** blessing
      6: 12 against the **s** forces of evil
1Pe   2: 2 crave pure **s** milk, so that by it you
      2: 5 offering **s** sacrifices acceptable

SPLENDOR
1Ch 16: 29 the Lord in the **s** of his holiness.
     29: 11 glory and the majesty and the **s**,
Job 37: 22 of the north he comes in golden **s**;
Ps   29: 2 the Lord in the **s** of his holiness.
     45: 3 clothe yourself with **s** and majesty.
     96: 6 **S** and majesty are before him;
     96: 9 the Lord in the **s** of his holiness;
    104: 1 you are clothed with **s** and majesty.
    145: 5 of the glorious **s** of your majesty—
Isa 61: 3 the Lord for the display of his **s**.
     63: 1 robed in **s**, striding forward
Lk   9: 30 Elijah, appeared in glorious **s**,
2Th   2: 8 and destroy by the **s** of his coming.

SPOIL
Ps 119:162 promise like one who finds great **s**.

SPOTLESS
2Pe   3: 14 make every effort to be found **s**,

SPREAD (SPREADING)
Ac   12: 24 the word of God continued to **s**
     19: 20 way the word of the Lord **s** widely

SPREADING (SPREAD)
1Th   3: 2 in God's service in **s** the gospel

SPRING
Jer   2: 13 forsaken me, the **s** of living water,
Jn   4: 14 in them a **s** of water welling
Jas   3: 12 can a salt **s** produce fresh water.

SPUR
Heb 10: 24 how we may **s** one another

SPURNS
Pr   15: 5 A fool **s** a parent's discipline,

STAFF
Ps   23: 4 your rod and your **s**, they comfort

STAKES
Isa 54: 2 your cords, strengthen your **s**.

STAND (STANDING STANDS)
Ex   14: 13 **S** firm and you will see
2Ch 20: 17 **s** firm and see the deliverance
Ps   1: 5 Therefore the wicked will not **s**
     40: 2 rock and gave me a firm place to **s**.
    119:120 fear of you; I **s** in awe of your laws.
Eze 22: 30 **s** before me in the gap on behalf
Zec 14: 4 day his feet will **s** on the Mount
Mt   12: 25 divided against itself will not **s**.
Ro   14: 10 we will all **s** before God's judgment
1Co 15: 58 dear brothers and sisters, **s** firm.
Eph   6: 14 **S** firm then, with the belt of truth
2Th   2: 15 firm and hold fast to the teachings
Jas   5: 8 be patient and **s** firm,
Rev   3: 20 I **s** at the door and knock.

STANDING (STAND)
Ex   3: 5 where you are **s** is holy ground."
Jos   5: 15 the place where you are **s** is holy."
1Pe   5: 9 Resist him, **s** firm in the faith,

STANDS (STAND)
Ps   89: 2 that your love **s** firm forever,
    119: 89 it **s** firm in the heavens.
2Ti   2: 19 God's solid foundation **s** firm,

STAR (STARS)
Nu   24: 17 A **s** will come out of Jacob;
Rev 22: 16 David, and the bright Morning **S**."

STARS (STAR)
Da   12: 3 like the **s** for ever and ever.
Php   2: 15 you will shine among them like **s**

STEADFAST
Ps   51: 10 and renew a **s** spirit within me.
Isa 26: 3 peace those whose minds are **s**,
1Pe   5: 10 and make you strong, firm and **s**.

STEAL
Ex   20: 15 "You shall not **s**.
Mt   19: 18 you shall not **s**, you shall not give
Eph   4: 28 has been stealing must **s** no longer,

STEP (STEPS)
Gal   5: 25 let us keep in **s** with the Spirit.

STEPS (STEP)
Pr   16: 9 but the Lord establishes their **s**.
Jer 10: 23 it is not for them to direct their **s**.
1Pe   2: 21 that you should follow in his **s**.

STICKS
Pr   18: 24 there is a friend who **s** closer than

STIFF-NECKED
Ex   34: 9 Although this is a **s** people,

STILL
Ps   46: 10 "Be **s**, and know that I am God;
Zec   2: 13 Be **s** before the Lord,

STIRS
Pr   6: 19 a person who **s** up conflict
     10: 12 Hatred **s** up conflict, but love
     15: 1 wrath, but a harsh word **s** up anger.
     29: 22 An angry person **s** up conflict,

STONE (CAPSTONE CORNERSTONE MILLSTONE)
1Sa 17: 50 the Philistine with a sling and a **s**;
Isa   8: 14 and Judah he will be a **s** that causes
Eze 11: 19 remove from them their heart of **s**
Mk   16: 3 "Who will roll the **s** away
Lk   4: 3 God, tell this **s** to become bread."
Jn   8: 7 the first to throw a **s** at her."
2Co   3: 3 not on tablets of **s** but on tablets

STORE
Pr   10: 14 The wise **s** up knowledge,
Mt   6: 19 "Do not **s** up for yourselves

STOREHOUSE (HOUSE)
Mal   3: 10 Bring the whole tithe into the **s**,

STRAIGHT
Pr   3: 6 and he will make your paths **s**.
      4: 25 Let your eyes look **s** ahead;
     15: 21 understanding keeps a **s** course.
Jn   1: 23 'Make **s** the way for the Lord.'"

STRAIN
Mt   23: 24 You **s** out a gnat but swallow

STRANGER
Mt   25: 35 I was a **s** and you invited me in,
Jn   10: 5 But they will never follow a **s**;

STRAPS
Mk   1: 7 **s** of whose sandals I am not worthy

STREAMS
Ps   1: 3 person is like a tree planted by **s**
     46: 4 a river whose **s** make glad the city
Ecc   1: 7 All **s** flow into the sea, yet the sea is

STRENGTH (STRONG)
Ex   15: 2 "The Lord is my **s** and my
Dt   6: 5 all your soul and with all your **s**.
2Sa 22: 33 It is God who arms me with **s**
Ne   8: 10 the joy of the Lord is your **s**."
Ps   28: 7 The Lord is my **s** and my shield;
     46: 1 God is our refuge and **s**,
     96: 7 ascribe to the Lord glory and **s**.
    118: 14 The Lord is my **s** and my
    147: 10 pleasure is not in the **s** of the horse,
Isa 40: 31 in the Lord will renew their **s**.
Mk   12: 30 all your mind and with all your **s**.'
1Co   1: 25 of God is stronger than human **s**.
Php   4: 13 this through him who gives me **s**.
1Pe   4: 11 do so with the **s** God provides,

STRENGTHEN (STRONG)
2Ch 16: 9 to **s** those whose hearts are fully
Ps 119: 28 **s** me according to your word.
Isa 35: 3 **S** the feeble hands, steady the
     41: 10 I will **s** you and help you;
Eph   3: 16 of his glorious riches he may **s** you
2Th   2: 17 and **s** you in every good deed
Heb 12: 12 **s** your feeble arms and weak knees.

STRIFE
Pr　20:　3　It is to one's honor to avoid **s**,
　　22: 10　out the mocker, and out goes **s**;

STRIKE
Ge　　3: 15　your head, and you will **s** his heel."
Zec　13:　7　"**S** the shepherd, and the sheep will
Mt　26: 31　"'I will **s** the shepherd,

STRONG (STRENGTH STRENGTHEN)
Dt　31:　6　Be **s** and courageous. Do not be
1Ki　　2:　2　"So be **s**, act like a man,
Pr　31: 17　her arms are **s** for her tasks.
SS　　8:　6　for love is as **s** as death, its jealousy
Lk　　2: 40　And the child grew and became **s**;
Ro　15:　1　We who are **s** ought to bear
1Co　　1: 27　things of the world to shame the **s**.
　　16: 13　in the faith; be courageous; be **s**.
2Co　12: 10　For when I am weak, then I am **s**.
Eph　　6: 10　be **s** in the Lord and in his mighty

STRUGGLE
Ro　15: 30　join me in my **s** by praying to God
Eph　　6: 12　For our **s** is not against flesh
Heb　12:　4　In your **s** against sin, you have not

STUDY
Ezr　　7: 10　Ezra had devoted himself to the **s**
Ecc　12: 12　end, and much **s** wearies the body.
Jn　　5: 39　You **s** the Scriptures diligently

STUMBLE (STUMBLING)
Ps　37: 24　though he may **s**, he will not fall,
　　119:165　law, and nothing can make them **s**.
Isa　　8: 14　be a stone that causes people to **s**
Jer　31:　9　a level path where they will not **s**,
Eze　 7: 19　for it has caused them to **s** into sin.
1Co　10: 32　Do not cause anyone to **s**,
1Pe　　2:　8　"A stone that causes people to **s**

STUMBLING (STUMBLE)
Ro　14: 13　your mind not to put any **s** block
1Co　　8:　9　rights does not become a **s** block
2Co　　6:　3　We put no **s** block in anyone's path,

SUBDUE
Ge　　1: 28　fill the earth and **s** it.

SUBJECT (SUBJECTED)
1Co　14: 32　of prophets are **s** to the control
　　15: 28　the Son himself will be made **s**
Titus　2:　5　and to be **s** to their husbands,
　　2:　9　slaves to be **s** to their masters
　　3:　1　Remind the people to be **s** to rulers

SUBJECTED (SUBJECT)
Ro　　8: 20　the creation was **s** to frustration,

SUBMISSION (SUBMIT)
1Co　14: 34　but must be in **s**, as the law says.
1Ti　　2: 11　learn in quietness and full **s**.

SUBMISSIVE (SUBMIT)
Jas　　3: 17　considerate, **s**, full of mercy

SUBMIT (SUBMISSION SUBMISSIVE SUBMITS)
Ro　13:　5　necessary to **s** to the authorities,
1Co　16: 16　to **s** to such people and to everyone
Eph　　5: 21　**S** to one another out of reverence
Col　　3: 18　**s** yourselves to your husbands, as is
Heb　12:　9　How much more should we **s**
　　13: 17　leaders and **s** to their authority,
Jas　　4:　7　**S** yourselves, then, to God.
1Pe　　2: 18　reverent fear of God **s** yourselves

SUBMITS (SUBMIT)
Eph　　5: 24　Now as the church **s** to Christ,

SUCCESSFUL
Jos　　1:　7　that you may be **s** wherever you go.
2Ki　18:　7　he was **s** in whatever he undertook.
2Ch　20: 20　in his prophets and you will be **s**."

SUFFER (SUFFERED SUFFERING SUFFERINGS
　　　SUFFERS)
Isa　53: 10　to crush him and cause him to **s**,
Mk　　8: 31　Son of Man must **s** many things
Lk　24: 26　the Messiah have to **s** these things

Lk　24: 46　The Messiah will **s** and rise
Php　　1: 29　believe in him, but also to **s** for him,
1Pe　　4: 16　if you **s** as a Christian, do not be

SUFFERED (SUFFER)
Heb　　2:　9　and honor because he **s** death,
　　2: 18　Because he himself **s** when he was
1Pe　　2: 21　called, because Christ **s** for you,

SUFFERING (SUFFER)
Isa　53:　3　a man of **s**, and familiar with pain.
Ac　　5: 41　been counted worthy of **s** disgrace
2Ti　　1:　8　join with me in **s** for the gospel,

SUFFERINGS (SUFFER)
Ro　　8: 17　if indeed we share in his **s** in order
　　8: 18　that our present **s** are not worth
2Co　　1:　5　share abundantly in the **s** of Christ,
Php　　3: 10　and participation in his **s**,

SUFFERS (SUFFER)
Pr　13: 20　for a companion of fools **s** harm.
1Co　12: 26　If one part **s**, every part **s** with it;

SUFFICIENT
2Co　12:　9　said to me, "My grace is **s** for you,

SUITABLE
Ge　　2: 18　I will make a helper **s** for him."

SUN
Ecc　　1:　9　there is nothing new under the **s**.
Mal　　4:　2　the **s** of righteousness will rise
Mt　　5: 45　He causes his **s** to rise on the evil
　　17:　2　His face shone like the **s**, and his
Rev　　1: 16　His face was like the **s** shining in
　　21: 23　The city does not need the **s**

SUPERIOR
Heb　　1:　4　as the name he has inherited is **s**
　　8:　6　he is mediator is **s** to the old one,

SUPREMACY
Col　　1: 18　in everything he might have the **s**.

SURE
Nu　32: 23　you may be **s** that your sin will find
Dt　　6: 17　Be **s** to keep the commands
　　14: 22　Be **s** to set aside a tenth of all
Isa　28: 16　cornerstone for a **s** foundation;

SURPASS (SURPASSES SURPASSING)
Pr　31: 29　noble things, but you **s** them all."

SURPASSES (SURPASS)
Mt　　5: 20　that unless your righteousness **s**
Eph　　3: 19　to know this love that **s** knowledge

SURPASSING (SURPASS)
Ps　150:　2　praise him for his **s** greatness.
2Co　　3: 10　in comparison with the **s** glory.
　　9: 14　of the **s** grace God has given you.
Php　　3:　8　a loss because of the **s** worth

SURROUNDED
Heb　12:　1　since we are **s** by such a great cloud

SUSPENDS
Job　26:　7　he **s** the earth over nothing.

SUSTAINING (SUSTAINS)
Heb　　1:　3　**s** all things by his powerful word.

SUSTAINS (SUSTAINING)
Ps　18: 35　shield, and your right hand **s** me;
　　146:　9　the foreigner and **s** the fatherless
　　147:　6　The LORD **s** the humble but casts
Isa　50:　4　to know the word that **s** the weary.

SWALLOWED
1Co　15: 54　"Death has been **s** up in victory."
2Co　　5:　4　so that what is mortal may be **s**

SWEAR
Mt　　5: 34　I tell you, do not **s** an oath at all:

SWORD (SWORDS)
Ps　45:　3　Gird your **s** on your side,
Mt　10: 34　not come to bring peace, but a **s**.
　　26: 52　all who draw the **s** will die by the **s**.
Lk　　2: 35　a **s** will pierce your own soul too."
Ro　13:　4　for rulers do not bear the **s** for no

Eph 6: 17 of salvation and the **s** of the Spirit,
Heb 4: 12 Sharper than any double-edged **s**,
Rev 1: 16 was a sharp, double-edged **s**.

SWORDS (SWORD)
Pr 12: 18 words of the reckless pierce like **s**,
Isa 2: 4 They will beat their **s**
Joel 3: 10 Beat your plowshares into **s**

SYMPATHETIC
1Pe 3: 8 be **s**, love one another,

SYNAGOGUE
Lk 4: 16 the Sabbath day he went into the **s**,
Ac 17: 2 Paul went into the **s**, and on three

TABERNACLE
Ex 40: 34 the glory of the LORD filled the **t**.

TABLE (TABLES)
Ps 23: 5 You prepare a **t** before me

TABLES (TABLE)
Ac 6: 2 word of God in order to wait on **t**.

TABLET (TABLETS)
Pr 3: 3 write them on the **t** of your heart.
7: 3 write them on the **t** of your heart.

TABLETS (TABLET)
Ex 31: 18 Sinai, he gave him the two **t**
Dt 10: 5 put the **t** in the ark I had made,
2Co 3: 3 not on **t** of stone but on **t** of human

TAKE (TAKEN TAKES TAKING TOOK)
Dt 12: 32 do not add to it or **t** away from it.
31: 26 "**T** this Book of the Law and place
Job 23: 10 But he knows the way that I **t**;
Ps 49: 17 for they will **t** nothing with them
51: 11 or **t** your Holy Spirit from me.
Mt 10: 38 Whoever does not **t** up their cross
11: 29 **T** my yoke upon you and learn
16: 24 deny themselves and **t** up their cross

TAKEN (TAKE)
Lev 6: 4 they have stolen or **t** by extortion,
Isa 6: 7 your guilt is **t** away and your sin
Mt 24: 40 one will be **t** and the other left.
Mk 16: 19 *them, he was* **t** *up into heaven*
1Ti 3: 16 on in the world, was **t** up in glory.

TAKES (TAKE)
1Ki 20: 11 not boast like one who **t** it off.'"
Jn 1: 29 who **t** away the sin of the world!
Rev 22: 19 if anyone **t** words away from this

TAKING (TAKE)
Php 2: 7 nothing by **t** the very nature

TALENT See BAGS

TAME
Jas 3: 8 no human being can **t** the tongue.

TASK
Mk 13: 34 each with their assigned **t**, and tells
Ac 20: 24 complete the **t** the Lord Jesus has
1Co 3: 5 the Lord has assigned to each his **t**.
2Co 2: 16 And who is equal to such a **t**?

TASTE (TASTED)
Ps 34: 8 **T** and see that the LORD is good;
Col 2: 21 Do not **t**! Do not touch!"?
Heb 2: 9 God he might **t** death for everyone.

TASTED (TASTE)
1Pe 2: 3 you have **t** that the Lord is good.

TAUGHT (TEACH)
Mt 7: 29 because he **t** as one who had
1Co 2: 13 but in words **t** by the Spirit,
Gal 1: 12 it from any man, nor was I **t** it;

TAX (TAXES)
Mt 22: 17 to pay the imperial **t** to Caesar

TAXES (TAX)
Ro 13: 7 you owe them: If you owe **t**, pay **t**;

TEACH (TAUGHT TEACHER TEACHERS TEACHES TEACHING)
Ex 33: 13 **t** me your ways so I may know you

Dt 4: 9 **T** them to your children and to
8: 3 to **t** you that man does not live
11: 19 **T** them to your children,
1Sa 12: 23 I will **t** you the way that is good
Ps 32: 8 **t** you in the way you should go;
51: 13 I will **t** transgressors your ways,
90: 12 **T** us to number our days, that we
143: 10 **T** me to do your will, for you are
Jer 31: 34 longer will they **t** their neighbor,
Lk 11: 1 "Lord, **t** us to pray, just as John
Jn 14: 26 will **t** you all things and will
1Ti 2: 12 I do not permit a woman to **t**
3: 2 respectable, hospitable, able to **t**,
Titus 2: 1 **t** what is appropriate to sound
Heb 8: 11 longer will they **t** their neighbor,
Jas 3: 1 that we who **t** will be judged more
1Jn 2: 27 you do not need anyone to **t** you.

TEACHER (TEACH)
Mt 10: 24 "The student is not above the **t**,
23: 8 for you have one **T**, and you are
Jn 13: 14 your Lord and **T**, have washed

TEACHERS (TEACH)
1Co 12: 28 prophets, third **t**, then miracles,
Eph 4: 11 the evangelists, the pastors and **t**,
Heb 5: 12 by this time you ought to be **t**,

TEACHES (TEACH)
1Ti 6: 3 If anyone **t** otherwise and does not

TEACHING (TEACH)
Pr 1: 8 and do not forsake your mother's **t**.
Mt 28: 20 **t** them to obey everything I have
Jn 7: 17 out whether my **t** comes from God
14: 23 who loves me will obey my **t**.
1Ti 4: 13 of Scripture, to preaching and to **t**,
2Ti 3: 16 is God-breathed and is useful for **t**,
Titus 2: 7 In your **t** show integrity,

TEAR (TEARS)
Rev 7: 17 God will wipe away every **t**

TEARS (TEAR)
Ps 126: 5 Those who sow with **t** will reap
Php 3: 18 and now tell you again even with **t**,

TEETH (TOOTH)
Mt 8: 12 will be weeping and gnashing of **t**."

TEMPERATE
1Ti 3: 2 reproach, faithful to his wife, **t**,
3: 11 not malicious talkers but **t**
Titus 2: 2 Teach the older men to be **t**,

TEMPEST
Ps 55: 8 shelter, far from the **t** and storm."

TEMPLE (TEMPLES)
1Ki 8: 27 How much less this **t** I have built!
Hab 2: 20 The LORD is in his holy **t**;
1Co 3: 16 that you yourselves are God's **t**
2Co 6: 16 For we are the **t** of the living God.

TEMPLES (TEMPLE)
Ac 17: 24 does not live in **t** built by human
1Co 6: 19 your bodies are **t** of the Holy Spirit,

TEMPT (TEMPTATION TEMPTED)
1Co 7: 5 Satan will not **t** you because of

TEMPTATION (TEMPT)
Mt 6: 13 lead us not into **t**, but deliver us
26: 41 pray so that you will not fall into **t**.
1Co 10: 13 No **t** has overtaken you except

TEMPTED (TEMPT)
Mt 4: 1 the wilderness to be **t** by the devil.
1Co 10: 13 not let you be **t** beyond what you
Heb 2: 18 he himself suffered when he was **t**,
2: 18 able to help those who are being **t**.
4: 15 but we have one who has been **t**
Jas 1: 13 For God cannot be **t** by evil,

TEN (TENTH TITHE TITHES)
Ex 34: 28 the **T** Commandments.
Ps 91: 7 side, **t** thousand at your right hand,
Mt 25: 28 give it to the one who has **t** bags.
Lk 15: 8 suppose a woman has **t** silver coins

TENTH (TEN)
Dt   14: 22 Be sure to set aside a **t** of all

TERRIBLE (TERROR)
2Ti   3: 1 There will be **t** times in the last

TERROR (TERRIBLE)
Ps   91: 5 You will not fear the **t** of night,
Lk   21: 26 People will faint from **t**,
Ro   13: 3 rulers hold no **t** for those who do

TEST (TESTED TESTS)
Dt   6: 16 your God to the **t** as you did
Ps 139: 23 **t** me and know my anxious
Ro   12: 2 you will be able to **t** and approve
1Co   3: 13 the fire will **t** the quality of each
1Jn   4: 1 **t** the spirits to see whether they are

TESTED (TEST)
Ge   22: 1 Some time later God **t** Abraham.
Job 23: 10 when he has **t** me, I will come forth
Pr   27: 21 but people are **t** by their praise.
1Ti   3: 10 They must first be **t**;

TESTIFY (TESTIMONY)
Jn   5: 39 These are the very Scriptures that **t**

TESTIMONY (TESTIFY)
Isa   8: 20 instruction and the **t** of warning.
Lk   18: 20 you shall not give false **t**,
2Ti   1: 8 be ashamed of the **t** about our Lord

TESTS (TEST)
Pr   17: 3 for gold, but the LORD **t** the heart.
1Th   2: 4 people but God, who **t** our hearts.

THADDAEUS
   Apostle (Mt 10:3; Mk 3:18); probably also known as Judas
son of James (Lk 6:16; Ac 1:13).

THANKFUL (THANKS)
Heb 12: 28 let us be **t**, and so worship God

THANKS (THANKFUL THANKSGIVING)
Ne   12: 31 assigned two large choirs to give **t**.
Ps 100: 4 give **t** to him and praise his name.
1Co 15: 57 But **t** be to God! He gives us
2Co   2: 14 But **t** be to God, who always leads
      9: 15 **T** be to God for his indescribable
1Th   5: 18 give **t** in all circumstances,

THANKSGIVING (THANKS)
Ps   95: 2 Let us come before him with **t**
    100: 4 Enter his gates with **t** and his
Php   4: 6 **t**, present your requests to God.
1Ti   4: 3 to be received with **t** by those who

THIEF (THIEVES)
1Th   5: 2 of the Lord will come like a **t**
Rev 16: 15 "Look, I come like a **t**!

THIEVES (THIEF)
1Co   6: 10 nor **t** nor the greedy nor drunkards

THINK (THOUGHT THOUGHTS)
Ro   12: 3 Do not **t** of yourself more highly
Php   4: 8 **t** about such things.

THIRST (THIRSTY)
Ps   69: 21 food and gave me vinegar for my **t**.
Mt   5: 6 hunger and **t** for righteousness,
Jn   4: 14 the water I give them will never **t**.

THIRSTY (THIRST)
Isa 55: 1 all you who are **t**,
Jn   7: 37 "Let anyone who is **t** come to me
Rev 22: 17 Let the one who is **t** come;

THOMAS
   Apostle (Mt 10:3; Mk 3:18; Lk 6:15; Jn 11:16; 14:5; 21:2; Ac
1:13). Doubted resurrection (Jn 20:24-28).

THORN (THORNS)
2Co 12: 7 I was given a **t** in my flesh,

THORNS (THORN)
Nu   33: 55 in your eyes and **t** in your sides.
Mt   27: 29 twisted together a crown of **t** and
Heb   6: 8 land that produces **t** and thistles is

THOUGHT (THINK)
Pr   14: 15 the prudent give **t** to their steps.
1Co 13: 11 I talked like a child, I **t** like a child,

THOUGHTS (THINK)
Ps 139: 23 test me and know my anxious **t**.
Isa 55: 8 "For my **t** are not your **t**, neither
Heb   4: 12 it judges the **t** and attitudes

THREE
Ecc   4: 12 of **t** strands is not quickly broken.
Mt   12: 40 the Son of Man will be **t** days and **t** nights in
                 the heart of the earth.
     18: 20 where two or **t** gather in my name,
     27: 63 said, 'After **t** days I will rise again.'
1Co 13: 13 And now these **t** remain:
     14: 27 or at the most—should speak,
2Co 13: 1 testimony of two or **t** witnesses."

THRESHING
2Sa 24: 18 altar to the LORD on the **t** floor

THRONE (ENTHRONED)
2Sa   7: 16 your **t** will be established
Ps   45: 6 Your **t**, O God, will last for ever
     47: 8 God is seated on his holy **t**.
Isa   6: 1 high and exalted, seated on a **t**;
     66: 1 "Heaven is my **t**, and the earth is
Heb   4: 16 then approach God's **t** of grace
     12: 2 at the right hand of the **t** of God.
Rev   4: 10 They lay their crowns before the **t**
     20: 11 I saw a great white **t** and him who
     22: 3 The **t** of God and of the Lamb will

THROW
Jn   8: 7 the first to **t** a stone at her."
Heb 10: 35 So do not **t** away your confidence;
     12: 1 let us **t** off everything that hinders

THWART
Isa 14: 27 has purposed, and who can **t** him?

TIBNI
   King of Israel (1Ki 16:21-22).

TIME (TIMES)
Est   4: 14 royal position for such a **t** as this?"
Da   7: 25 be delivered into his hands for a **t**, times and
                 half a **t**.
Hos 10: 12 for it is **t** to seek the LORD,
Ro   9: 9 "At the appointed **t** I will return,
Heb   9: 28 and he will appear a second **t**,
     10: 12 had offered for all **t** one sacrifice
1Pe   4: 17 For it is **t** for judgment to begin

TIMES (TIME)
Ps   9: 9 a stronghold in **t** of trouble.
     31: 15 My **t** are in your hands;
     62: 8 Trust in him at all **t**, you people;
Pr   17: 17 A friend loves at all **t**,
Am   5: 13 in such **t**, for the **t** are evil.
Mt   18: 21 sins against me? Up to seven **t**?"
Ac   1: 7 "It is not for you to know the **t**
Rev 12: 14 care of for a time, **t** and half a time,

TIMID
2Ti   1: 7 God gave us does not make us **t**,

TIMOTHY
   Believer from Lystra (Ac 16:1). Joined Paul on second
missionary journey (Ac 16-20). Sent to settle problems at
Corinth (1Co 4:17; 16:10). Led church at Ephesus (1Ti 1:3). Co-
writer with Paul (1Th 1:1; 2Th 1:1; Phm 1).

TIRE (TIRED)
2Th   3: 13 never **t** of doing what is good.

TIRED (TIRE)
Ex   17: 12 When Moses' hands grew **t**,
Isa 40: 28 He will not grow **t** or weary,

TITHE (TEN)
Lev 27: 30 "'A **t** of everything
Dt   12: 17 your own towns the **t** of your grain
Mal   3: 10 Bring the whole **t**

TITHES (TEN)
Mal   3: 8 "In **t** and offerings.

TITUS
   Gentile co-worker of Paul (Gal 2:1-3; 2Ti 4:10); sent to
Corinth (2Co 2:13; 7-8; 12:18), Crete (Titus 1:4-5).

TODAY
Mt 6: 11 Give us **t** our daily bread.
Lk 23: 43 **t** you will be with me in paradise."
Heb 3: 13 as long as it is called "T,"
13: 8 Christ is the same yesterday and **t**

TOIL
Ge 3: 17 through painful **t** you will eat food

TOLERATE
Hab 1: 13 then do you **t** the treacherous?
Rev 2: 2 that you cannot **t** wicked people,

TOMB
Mt 27: 65 make the **t** as secure as you know
Lk 24: 2 the stone rolled away from the **t**,

TOMORROW
Pr 27: 1 not boast about **t**, for you do not
Isa 22: 13 drink," you say, "for **t** we die!"
Mt 6: 34 do not worry about **t**, for **t**
Jas 4: 13 "Today or **t** we will go to this

TONGUE (TONGUES)
Ps 39: 1 my ways and keep my **t** from sin;
Pr 12: 18 but the **t** of the wise brings healing.
1Co 14: 2 who speaks in a **t** does not speak
14: 4 speaks in a **t** edifies themselves,
14: 13 one who speaks in a **t** should pray
14: 19 than ten thousand words in a **t**.
Php 2: 11 and every **t** acknowledge that Jesus
Jas 3: 8 no human being can tame the **t**.

TONGUES (TONGUE)
Isa 28: 11 strange **t** God will speak to this
Mk 16: 17 *they will speak in new* **t**;
Ac 2: 4 other **t** as the Spirit enabled them.
10: 46 For they heard them speaking in **t**
19: 6 they spoke in **t** and prophesied.
1Co 12: 30 Do all speak in **t**? Do all interpret?
14: 18 I speak in **t** more than all of you.
14: 39 and do not forbid speaking in **t**.
Jas 1: 26 rein on their **t** deceive themselves,

TOOK (TAKE)
1Co 11: 23 the night he was betrayed, **t** bread,
Php 3: 12 which Christ Jesus **t** hold of me.

TOOTH (TEETH)
Ex 21: 24 eye for eye, **t** for **t**, hand for hand,
Mt 5: 38 was said, 'Eye for eye, and **t** for **t**.'

TORMENTED
Rev 20: 10 They will be **t** day and night

TORN
Gal 4: 15 you would have **t** out your eyes
Php 1: 23 I am **t** between the two: I desire

TOUCH (TOUCHED)
Ps 105: 15 "Do not **t** my anointed ones;
Lk 24: 39 **T** me and see; a ghost does not
2Co 6: 17 **T** no unclean thing, and I will
Col 2: 21 Do not taste! Do not **t**!"?

TOUCHED (TOUCH)
1Sa 10: 26 men whose hearts God had **t**.
Mt 14: 36 cloak, and all who **t** it were healed.

TOWER
Ge 11: 4 a **t** that reaches to the heavens,
Pr 18: 10 name of the LORD is a fortified **t**;

TOWN (TOWNS)
Mt 5: 14 **t** built on a hill cannot be hidden.

TOWNS (TOWN)
Nu 35: 2 to give the Levites **t** to live
35: 15 These six **t** will be a place of refuge

TRACING
Ro 11: 33 and his paths beyond **t** out!

TRADITION
Mt 15: 6 word of God for the sake of your **t**.
Col 2: 8 which depends on human **t**

TRAINING
1Co 9: 25 in the games goes into strict **t**.
2Ti 3: 16 correcting and **t** in righteousness,

TRAMPLED
Lk 21: 24 Jerusalem will be **t**
Heb 10: 29 to be punished who has **t** the Son

TRANCE
Ac 10: 10 was being prepared, he fell into a **t**.

TRANSCENDS
Php 4: 7 God, which **t** all understanding,

TRANSFIGURED
Mt 17: 2 There he was **t** before them.

TRANSFORM (TRANSFORMED)
Php 3: 21 will **t** our lowly bodies so that they

TRANSFORMED (TRANSFORM)
Ro 12: 2 be **t** by the renewing of your mind.
2Co 3: 18 are being **t** into his image

TRANSGRESSION (TRANSGRESSIONS TRANSGRESSORS)
Isa 53: 8 **t** of my people he was punished.
Ro 4: 15 where there is no law there is no **t**.

TRANSGRESSIONS (TRANSGRESSION)
Ps 32: 1 is the one whose **t** are forgiven,
51: 1 great compassion blot out my **t**.
103: 12 so far has he removed our **t** from
Isa 53: 5 But he was pierced for our **t**,
Eph 2: 1 you were dead in your **t** and sins,

TRANSGRESSORS (TRANSGRESSION)
Ps 51: 13 Then I will teach **t** your ways,
Isa 53: 12 and was numbered with the **t**.
53: 12 and made intercession for the **t**.

TREADING
Dt 25: 4 Do not muzzle an ox while it is **t**
1Co 9: 9 "Do not muzzle an ox while it is **t**

TREASURE (TREASURED TREASURES)
Isa 33: 6 of the LORD is the key to this **t**.
Mt 6: 21 where your **t** is, there your heart
2Co 4: 7 But we have this **t** in jars of clay

TREASURED (TREASURE)
Dt 7: 6 to be his people, his **t** possession.
Lk 2: 19 But Mary **t** up all these things

TREASURES (TREASURE)
Mt 6: 19 store up for yourselves **t** on earth,
Col 2: 3 in whom are hidden all the **t**
Heb 11: 26 of greater value than the **t** of Egypt,

TREAT
Lev 22: 2 sons to **t** with respect the sacred
1Ti 5: 1 **T** younger men as brothers,
1Pe 3: 7 **t** them with respect as the weaker

TREATY
Dt 7: 2 Make no **t** with them, and show

TREE
Ge 2: 9 of the garden were the **t** of life
2: 9 and the **t** of the knowledge of good
Ps 1: 3 is like a **t** planted by streams
Mt 3: 10 every **t** that does not produce good
12: 33 for a **t** is recognized by its fruit.
Rev 22: 14 may have the right to the **t** of life

TREMBLE (TREMBLING)
1Ch 16: 30 **T** before him, all the earth!
Ps 114: 7 **T**, earth, at the presence of the Lord,

TREMBLING (TREMBLE)
Ps 2: 11 fear and celebrate his rule with **t**.
Php 2: 12 out your salvation with fear and **t**,

TRESPASS
Ro 5: 17 if, by the **t** of the one man,

TRIALS
1Th 3: 3 one would be unsettled by these **t**.
Jas 1: 2 whenever you face **t** of many kinds,
2Pe 2: 9 how to rescue the godly from **t**

TRIBES
Ge 49: 28 All these are the twelve **t** of Israel,
Mt 19: 28 judging the twelve **t** of Israel.

TRIBULATION
Rev 7: 14 who have come out of the great **t**;

TRIUMPHAL (TRIUMPHING)
Isa 60: 11 their kings led in **t** procession.
2Co   2: 14 as captives in Christ's **t** procession

TRIUMPHING (TRIUMPHAL)
Col   2: 15 of them, **t** over them by the cross.

TROUBLE (TROUBLED TROUBLES)
Job 14:   1 are of few days and full of **t**.
Ps   46:   1 strength, an ever-present help in **t**.
    107: 13 they cried to the Lord in their **t**,
Pr   24: 10 If you falter in a time of **t**,
Mt   6: 34 Each day has enough **t** of its own.
Jn   16: 33 In this world you will have **t**.
Ro   8: 35 Shall **t** or hardship or persecution

TROUBLED (TROUBLE)
Jn   14:   1 "Do not let your hearts be **t**.
    14: 27 Do not let your hearts be **t** and do

TROUBLES (TROUBLE)
1Co   7: 28 those who marry will face many **t**
2Co   1:   4 who comforts us in all our **t**,
     4: 17 momentary **t** are achieving for us

TRUE (TRUTH)
Dt   18: 22 does not take place or come **t**,
1Sa   9:   6 and everything he says comes **t**.
Ps 119:160 All your words are **t**; all your
Jn   17:   3 the only **t** God, and Jesus Christ,
Ro   3:   4 Let God be **t**, and every human
Php   4:   8 whatever is **t**, whatever is noble,
Rev 22:   6 These words are trustworthy and **t**.

TRUMPET
1Co 14:   8 if the **t** does not sound a clear call,
    15: 52 twinkling of an eye, at the last **t**.

TRUST (ENTRUSTED TRUSTED TRUSTWORTHY)
Ps   20:   7 we **t** in the name of the Lord our
    37:   3 **T** in the Lord and do good;
    56:   4 in God I **t** and am not afraid.
    119: 42 taunts me, for I **t** in your word.
Pr   3:   5 **T** in the Lord with all your heart
Isa 30: 15 in quietness and **t** is your strength,
1Co   4:   2 been given a **t** must prove faithful.

TRUSTED (TRUST)
Ps   26:   1 I have **t** in the Lord and have not
Isa 25:   9 we **t** in him, and he saved us.
Da   3: 28 They **t** in him and defied the king's
Lk   16: 10 "Whoever can be **t** with very little

TRUSTWORTHY (TRUST)
Ps 119:138 are righteous; they are fully **t**.
Pr   11: 13 but a **t** person keeps a secret.
Rev 22:   6 to me, "These words are **t** and true.

TRUTH (TRUE TRUTHFUL TRUTHS)
Isa 45: 19 I, the Lord, speak the **t**;
Zec   8: 16 Speak the **t** to each other,
Jn   4: 23 the Father in the Spirit and in **t**,
     8: 32 Then you will know the **t**, and the **t**
     8: 32 Then you will know the **t**, and the **t**
    14:   6 "I am the way and the **t** and the life.
    16: 13 he will guide you into all the **t**.
    18: 38 "What is **t**?" retorted Pilate.
Ro   1: 25 They exchanged the **t** about God
1Co 13:   6 in evil but rejoices with the **t**.
2Co 13:   8 against the **t**, but only for the **t**.
Eph   4: 15 Instead, speaking the **t** in love,
     6: 14 belt of **t** buckled around your waist,
2Th   2: 10 because they refused to love the **t**
1Ti   2:   4 to come to a knowledge of the **t**.
     3: 15 the pillar and foundation of the **t**.
2Ti   2: 15 correctly handles the word of **t**.
     3:   7 to come to a knowledge of the **t**.
Heb 10: 26 received the knowledge of the **t**,
1Pe   1: 22 by obeying the **t** so that you have
2Pe   2:   2 and will bring the way of **t**
1Jn   1:   6 we lie and do not live out the **t**.
     1:   8 ourselves and the **t** is not in us.

TRUTHFUL (TRUTH)
Jn   3: 33 it has certified that God is **t**.

TRUTHS (TRUTH)
1Ti   3:   9 keep hold of the deep **t** of the faith
Heb   5: 12 teach you the elementary **t** of God's

TRY (TRYING)
Ps   26:   2 and **t** me, examine my heart and
Isa   7: 13 Will you **t** the patience of my God
1Co 14: 12 **t** to excel in those that build
2Co   5: 11 the Lord, we **t** to persuade others.

TRYING (TRY)
2Co   5: 12 We are not **t** to commend ourselves
1Th   2:   4 We are not **t** to please people

TURN (TURNED TURNS)
Ex   32: 12 **T** from your fierce anger;
Dt   5: 32 do not **t** aside to the right
    28: 14 Do not **t** aside from any
Jos   1:   7 do not **t** from it to the right
2Ch   7: 14 face and **t** from their wicked ways,
    30:   9 He will not **t** his face from you
Ps   78:   6 they in **t** would tell their children.
Pr   22:   6 they are old they will not **t** from it.
Isa 29: 16 You **t** things upside down,
    30: 21 Whether you **t** to the right
    45: 22 "**T** to me and be saved, all you ends
    55:   7 Let them **t** to the Lord, and he
Eze 33: 11 they **t** from their ways and live.
Mal   4:   6 He will **t** the hearts of the parents
Mt   5: 39 **t** to them the other cheek also.
    10: 35 to **t** "'a man against his father,
Jn   12: 40 understand with their hearts, nor **t**
Ac   3: 19 and **t** to God, so that your sins may
    26: 18 and **t** them from darkness to light,
1Ti   6: 20 **T** away from godless chatter
1Pe   3: 11 must **t** from evil and do good;

TURNED (TURN)
Ps   30: 11 You **t** my wailing into dancing;
    40:   1 he **t** to me and heard my cry.
Isa 53:   6 each of us has **t** to our own way;
Hos   7:   8 Ephraim is a flat loaf not **t** over.
Joel 2: 31 The sun will be **t** to darkness
Ro   3: 12 All have **t** away, they have together

TURNS (TURN)
2Sa 22: 29 the Lord **t** my darkness
Pr   15:   1 A gentle answer **t** away wrath,
Isa 44: 25 of the wise and **t** it into nonsense,
Jas   5: 20 Whoever **t** a sinner from the error

TWELVE
Ge   49: 28 All these are the **t** tribes of Israel,
Mt   10:   1 Jesus called his **t** disciples to him

TWINKLING
1Co 15: 52 a flash, in the **t** of an eye, at the last

UNAPPROACHABLE
1Ti   6: 16 immortal and who lives in **u** light,

UNBELIEF (UNBELIEVER UNBELIEVERS UNBELIEVING)
Mk   9: 24 help me overcome my **u**!"
Ro   11: 20 they were broken off because of **u**,
Heb   3: 19 able to enter, because of their **u**.

UNBELIEVER (UNBELIEF)
1Co   7: 15 But if the **u** leaves, let it be so.
    10: 27 If an **u** invites you to a meal
    14: 24 if an **u** or an inquirer comes in
2Co   6: 15 have in common with an **u**?
1Ti   5:   8 the faith and is worse than an **u**.

UNBELIEVERS (UNBELIEF)
1Co   6:   6 and this in front of **u**!
2Co   6: 14 Do not be yoked together with **u**.

UNBELIEVING (UNBELIEF)
1Co   7: 14 the **u** husband has been sanctified
     7: 14 and the **u** wife has been sanctified
Rev 21:   8 But the cowardly, the **u**, the vile,

UNCERTAIN
1Ti   6: 17 which is so **u**, but to put their hope

UNCHANGEABLE
Heb   6: 18 that, by two **u** things in which it is

UNCIRCUMCISED
1Sa 17: 26 Who is this **u** Philistine that he
Col   3: 11 or Jew, circumcised or **u**,

UNCIRCUMCISION
1Co   7: 19 is nothing and **u** is nothing.
Gal   5: 6 neither circumcision nor **u** has any

UNCLEAN
Isa   6: 5 For I am a man of **u** lips, and I live
Ro   14: 14 Jesus, that nothing is **u** in itself.
2Co   6: 17 Touch no **u** thing, and I will

UNCONCERNED
Eze 16: 49 were arrogant, overfed and **u**;

UNCOVERED
Heb   4: 13 Everything is **u** and laid bare

UNDERSTAND (UNDERSTANDING UNDERSTANDS)
Job 42: 3 Surely I spoke of things I did not **u**,
Ps   73: 16 When I tried to **u** all this,
      119:125 that I may **u** your statutes.
Lk   24: 45 so they could **u** the Scriptures.
Ac   8: 30 "Do you **u** what you are reading?"
Ro   7: 15 I do not **u** what I do. For what I
1Co   2: 14 and cannot **u** them because they
Eph   5: 17 but **u** what the Lord's will is.
2Pe   3: 16 some things that are hard to **u**,

UNDERSTANDING (UNDERSTAND)
Ps   119: 32 for you have broadened my **u**.
      119:104 I gain **u** from your precepts;
     147: 5 in power; his **u** has no limit.
Pr   3: 5 heart and lean not on your own **u**;
       4: 7 Though it cost all you have, get **u**.
      10: 23 a person of **u** delights in wisdom.
      11: 12 one who has **u** holds their tongue.
      15: 21 but whoever has **u** keeps a straight
      15: 32 one who heeds correction gains **u**.
Isa 40: 28 and his **u** no one can fathom.
Da   5: 12 a keen mind and knowledge and **u**,
Mk   4: 12 and ever hearing but never **u**;
      12: 33 with all your **u** and with all your
Php   4: 7 which transcends all **u**, will guard

UNDERSTANDS (UNDERSTAND)
1Ch 28: 9 every heart and **u** every desire

UNDIVIDED
1Ch 12: 33 to help David with **u** loyalty–
Ps   86: 11 give me an **u** heart, that I may fear
Eze 11: 19 I will give them an **u** heart and put
1Co   7: 35 in a right way in **u** devotion

UNDOING
Pr   18: 7 The mouths of fools are their **u**,

UNDYING
Eph   6: 24 Lord Jesus Christ with an **u** love.

UNFADING
1Pe   3: 4 the **u** beauty of a gentle and quiet

UNFAILING
Ps   33: 5 the earth is full of his **u** love.
     119: 76 May your **u** love be my comfort,
     143: 8 bring me word of your **u** love, for I
Pr   19: 22 What a person desires is **u** love;
La   3: 32 compassion, so great is his **u** love.

UNFAITHFUL
Lev   6: 2 is **u** to the LORD by deceiving
1Ch 10: 13 Saul died because he was **u**
Pr   13: 15 but the way of the **u** leads to their

UNFOLDING
Ps   119:130 The **u** of your words gives light;

UNGODLINESS
Titus 2: 12 It teaches us to say "No" to **u**

UNITED (UNITY)
Ro   6: 5 For if we have been **u** with him
Php   2: 1 from being **u** with Christ, if any
Col   2: 2 encouraged in heart and **u** in love,

UNITY (UNITED)
Ps   133: 1 God's people live together in **u**!
Eph   4: 3 keep the **u** of the Spirit through

UNIVERSE
Heb   1: 2 through whom also he made the **u**.

UNKNOWN
Ac   17: 23 with this inscription: TO AN **u** GOD.

UNLEAVENED
Ex   12: 17 "Celebrate the Festival of **U** Bread,

UNPROFITABLE
Titus 3: 9 because these are **u** and useless.

UNPUNISHED
Ex   34: 7 Yet he does not leave the guilty **u**;
Pr   19: 5 A false witness will not go **u**,

UNREPENTANT
Ro   2: 5 stubbornness and your **u** heart,

UNRIGHTEOUS
Zep   3: 5 not fail, yet the **u** know no shame.
Mt   5: 45 rain on the righteous and the **u**.
1Pe   3: 18 the righteous for the **u**, to bring
2Pe   2: 9 to hold the **u** for punishment

UNSEARCHABLE
Ro   11: 33 How **u** his judgments, and his

UNSEEN
2Co   4: 18 temporary, but what is **u** is eternal.

UNSTABLE
Jas   1: 8 double-minded and **u** in all they
2Pe   2: 14 they seduce the **u**; they are experts
       3: 16 ignorant and **u** people distort,

UNTHINKABLE
Job 34: 12 It is **u** that God would do wrong,

UNVEILED
2Co   3: 18 with **u** faces contemplate the Lord's

UNWORTHY
Job 40: 4 "I am **u**–how can I reply to you?
Lk   17: 10 do, should say, 'We are **u** servants;

UPRIGHT
Job   1: 1 This man was blameless and **u**;
Pr   2: 7 He holds success in store for the **u**,
      15: 8 but the prayer of the **u** pleases him.
Titus 1: 8 who is self-controlled, **u**,
       2: 12 **u** and godly lives in this present

UPROOTED
Jude   : 12 autumn trees, without fruit and **u**

USEFUL
2Ti   2: 21 **u** to the Master and prepared to do
       3: 16 God breathed and is **u** for teaching

USELESS
1Co 15: 14 our preaching is **u** and so is your
Jas   2: 20 that faith without deeds is **u**?

UZZIAH
Son of Amaziah; king of Judah also known as Azariah (2Ki 15:1-7; 1Ch 6:24; 2Ch 26).

VAIN
Ps   33: 17 A horse is a **v** hope for deliverance;
Isa 65: 23 They will not labor in **v**, nor will
1Co 15: 2 Otherwise, you have believed in **v**.
      15: 58 your labor in the Lord is not in **v**.
2Co   6: 1 you not to receive God's grace in **v**.

VALLEY
Ps   23: 4 I walk through the darkest **v**,
Isa 40: 4 Every **v** shall be raised up,
Joel   3: 14 LORD is near in the **v** of decision.

VALUABLE (VALUE)
Lk   12: 24 how much more **v** you are than

VALUE (VALUABLE)
Mt   13: 46 When he found one of great **v**,
1Ti   4: 8 For physical training is of some **v**, but godliness has **v** for all things,
Heb 11: 26 as of greater **v** than the treasures

VEIL
Ex   34: 33 to them, he put a **v** over his face.
2Co   3: 14 to this day the same **v** remains

VENGEANCE (AVENGE REVENGE)
Isa 34: 8 For the LORD has a day of v,

VICTORIES (VICTORY)
Ps 18: 50 He gives his king great v;
21: 1 great is his joy in the v you give!

VICTORIOUS (VICTORY)
Zec 9: 9 king comes to you, righteous and v,
Rev 2: 7 To the one who is v, I will give
2: 11 The one who is v will not be hurt
2: 17 To the one who is v, I will give
2: 26 To the one who is v and does my
3: 5 The one who is v will, like them,
3: 12 The one who is v I will make
3: 21 To the one who is v, I will give
21: 7 Those who are v will inherit all

VICTORIOUSLY (VICTORY)
Ps 45: 4 In your majesty ride forth v

VICTORY (VICTORIES VICTORIOUS VICTORIOUSLY)
Ps 60: 12 With God we will gain the v,
1Co 15: 54 has been swallowed up in v."
15: 57 He gives us the v through our Lord
1Jn 5: 4 This is the v that has overcome

VINDICATED
1Ti 3: 16 in the flesh, was v by the Spirit,

VINE
Jn 15: 1 "I am the true v, and my Father is

VINEGAR
Mk 15: 36 filled a sponge with wine v, put it

VIOLATION
Heb 2: 2 every v and disobedience received

VIOLENCE
Isa 60: 18 No longer will v be heard in your
Eze 45: 9 Give up your v and oppression

VIPERS
Ro 3: 13 "The poison of v is on their lips."

VIRGIN
Isa 7: 14 The v will conceive and give birth
Mt 1: 23 "The v will conceive and give birth
2Co 11: 2 I might present you as a pure v

VIRTUES
Col 3: 14 And over all these v put on love,

VISION
Ac 26: 19 disobedient to the v from heaven.

VOICE
Ps 95: 7 if only you would hear his v,
Isa 30: 21 your ears will hear a v behind you,
Jn 5: 28 are in their graves will hear his v
10: 3 him, and the sheep listen to his v.
Heb 3: 7 "Today, if you hear his v,
Rev 3: 20 If anyone hears my v and opens

VOMIT
Pr 26: 11 As a dog returns to its v, so fools
2Pe 2: 22 "A dog returns to its v," and,

VOW
Nu 30: 2 a man makes a v to the LORD

WAGES
Lk 10: 7 you, for the worker deserves his w.
Ro 4: 4 w are not credited as a gift but as
6: 23 the w of sin is death, but the gift

WAILING
Ps 30: 11 You turned my w into dancing;

WAIST
2Ki 1: 8 had a leather belt around his w."
Mt 3: 4 he had a leather belt around his w.

WAIT (WAITED WAITS)
Ps 27: 14 W for the LORD; be strong
130: 5 I w for the LORD, my whole being
Isa 30: 18 Blessed are all who w for him!
Ac 1: 4 w for the gift my Father promised,
Ro 8: 23 groan inwardly as we w eagerly
1Th 1: 10 and to w for his Son from heaven,
Titus 2: 13 while we w for the blessed hope—

WAITED (WAIT)
Ps 40: 1 I w patiently for the LORD;

WAITS (WAIT)
Ro 8: 19 the creation w in eager expectation

WALK (WALKED)
Dt 11: 19 and when you w along the road,
Ps 1: 1 Blessed is the one who does not w
23: 4 though I w through the darkest
89: 15 w in the light of your presence,
Isa 2: 5 let us w in the light of the LORD.
30: 21 saying, "This is the way; w in it."
40: 31 weary, they will w and not be faint.
Jer 6: 16 and w in it, and you will find rest
Da 4: 37 those who w in pride he is able
Am 3: 3 Do two w together unless they
Mic 6: 8 and to w humbly with your God.
Mk 2: 9 say, 'Get up, take your mat and w'?
Jn 8: 12 Whoever follows me will never w
1Jn 1: 7 But if we w in the light, as he is
2Jn 6 his command is that you w in love.

WALKED (WALK)
Ge 5: 24 Enoch w faithfully with God;
Jos 14: 9 which your feet have w will be
Mt 14: 29 w on the water and came toward

WALL
Jos 6: 20 gave a loud shout, the w collapsed;
Ne 2: 17 let us rebuild the w of Jerusalem,
Rev 21: 12 a great, high w with twelve gates,

WALLOWING
2Pe 2: 22 returns to her w in the mud."

WANT (WANTED WANTING WANTS)
1Sa 8: 19 they said. "We w a king over us.
Lk 19: 14 say, 'We don't w this man to be our
Ro 7: 15 For what I w to do I do not do,
Php 3: 10 I w to know Christ—yes, to know

WANTED (WANT)
1Co 12: 18 of them, just as he w them to be.

WANTING (WANT)
Da 5: 27 weighed on the scales and found w.
2Pe 3: 9 with you, not w anyone to perish,

WANTS (WANT)
Mt 20: 26 whoever w to become great among
Mk 8: 35 For whoever w to save their life
Ro 9: 18 on whom he w to have mercy,
9: 18 he hardens whom he w to harden.
1Ti 2: 4 who w all people to be saved

WAR (WARS)
Isa 2: 4 nor will they train for w anymore.
Da 9: 26 W will continue until the end,
2Co 10: 3 we do not wage w as the world
Rev 19: 11 justice he judges and wages w.

WARN (WARNED WARNINGS)
Eze 3: 19 if you do w the wicked person
33: 9 if you do w the wicked person

WARNED (WARN)
Ps 19: 11 By them your servant is w;

WARNINGS (WARN)
1Co 10: 11 and were written down as w for us,

WARS (WAR)
Ps 46: 9 He makes w cease to the ends
Mt 24: 6 will hear of w and rumors of w,

WASH (WASHED WASHING)
Ps 51: 7 w me, and I will be whiter than
Jn 13: 5 and began to w his disciples' feet,
Ac 22: 16 be baptized and w your sins away,
Rev 22: 14 are those who w their robes,

WASHED (WASH)
1Co 6: 11 But you were w, you were
Rev 7: 14 they have w their robes and made

WASHING (WASH)
Eph 5: 26 the w with water through the word,
Titus 3: 5 saved us through the w of rebirth

WATCH (WATCHES WATCHING WATCHMAN)
Ge 31: 49 the Lord keep **w** between you
Jer 31: 10 them and will **w** over his flock like
Mt 24: 42 "Therefore keep **w**, because you do
26: 41 "**W** and pray so that you will not
Lk 2: 8 keeping **w** over their flocks at night
1Ti 4: 16 **W** your life and doctrine closely.

WATCHES (WATCH)
Ps 1: 6 For the Lord **w** over the way
121: 3 he who **w** over you will not

WATCHING (WATCH)
Lk 12: 37 servants whose master finds them **w**

WATCHMAN (WATCH)
Eze 3: 17 I have made you a **w** for the people

WATER (WATERED WATERS)
Ps 1: 3 like a tree planted by streams of **w**,
22: 14 I am poured out like **w**, and all my
Pr 25: 21 if he is thirsty, give him **w** to drink.
Isa 49: 10 and lead them beside springs of **w**,
Jer 2: 13 broken cisterns that cannot hold **w**.
Zec 14: 8 On that day living **w** will flow
Mk 9: 41 anyone who gives you a cup of **w**
Jn 4: 10 he would have given you living **w**."
7: 38 rivers of living **w** will flow
Eph 5: 26 washing with **w** through the word,
1Pe 3: 21 this **w** symbolizes baptism that
Rev 21: 6 thirsty I will give **w** without cost

WATERED (WATER)
1Co 3: 6 I planted the seed, Apollos **w** it,

WATERS (WATER)
Ps 23: 2 he leads me beside quiet **w**,
Isa 58: 11 like a spring whose **w** never fail.
1Co 3: 7 nor the one who **w** is anything,

WAVE (WAVES)
Jas 1: 6 the one who doubts is like a **w**

WAVES (WAVE)
Isa 57: 20 whose **w** cast up mire and mud.
Mt 8: 27 the winds and the **w** obey him!"
Eph 4: 14 tossed back and forth by the **w**,

WAY (WAYS)
Dt 1: 33 to show you the **w** you should go.
2Sa 22: 31 "As for God, his **w** is perfect:
Job 23: 10 But he knows the **w** that I take;
Ps 1: 1 stand in the **w** that sinners take
37: 5 Commit your **w** to the Lord;
139: 24 and lead me in the **w** everlasting.
Pr 14: 12 is a **w** that appears to be right,
22: 6 off on the **w** they should go,
Isa 30: 21 behind you, saying, "This is the **w**;
53: 6 of us has turned to our own **w**;
Mt 3: 3 'Prepare the **w** for the Lord,
Jn 14: 6 "I am the **w** and the truth
1Co 10: 13 provide a **w** out so that you can
12: 31 will show you the most excellent **w**.
Heb 4: 15 who has been tempted in every **w**,
9: 8 the **w** into the Most Holy Place had
10: 20 living **w** opened for us through

WAYS (WAY)
Ex 33: 13 teach me your **w** so I may know
Ps 25: 10 All the **w** of the Lord are loving
51: 13 I will teach transgressors your **w**,
Pr 3: 6 in all your **w** submit to him, and he
16: 17 who guard their **w** preserve their
Isa 55: 7 Let the wicked forsake their **w**
55: 8 neither are your **w** my **w**,"
Jas 3: 2 We all stumble in many **w**.

WEAK (WEAKER WEAKNESS)
Mt 26: 41 spirit is willing, but the flesh is **w**."
Ro 14: 1 Accept the one whose faith is **w**,
1Co 1: 27 chose the **w** things of the world
8: 9 a stumbling block to the **w**.
9: 22 To the **w** I became **w**, to win the **w**.
2Co 12: 10 For when I am **w**, then I am strong.
Heb 12: 12 your feeble arms and **w** knees.

WEAKER (WEAK)
1Co 12: 22 seem to be **w** are indispensable,
1Pe 3: 7 them with respect as the **w** partner

WEAKNESS (WEAK)
Ro 8: 26 way, the Spirit helps us in our **w**.
1Co 1: 25 **w** of God is stronger than human
2Co 12: 9 my power is made perfect in **w**."
Heb 5: 2 since he himself is subject to **w**.

WEALTH
Pr 3: 9 Honor the Lord with your **w**,
Mk 10: 22 away sad, because he had great **w**.
Lk 15: 13 and there squandered his **w** in wild

WEAPONS
2Co 10: 4 The **w** we fight with are not the **w**

WEARIES (WEARY)
Ecc 12: 12 and much study **w** the body.

WEARY (WEARIES)
Isa 40: 31 they will run and not grow **w**,
Mt 11: 28 all you who are **w** and burdened,
Gal 6: 9 not become **w** in doing good,

WEDDING
Mt 22: 11 who was not wearing **w** clothes.
Rev 19: 7 For the **w** of the Lamb has come,

WEEP (WEEPING WEPT)
Ecc 3: 4 a time to **w** and a time to laugh,
Lk 6: 21 Blessed are you who **w** now, for

WEEPING (WEEP)
Ps 30: 5 **w** may stay for the night,
126: 6 Those who go out **w**, carrying seed
Mt 8: 12 where there will be **w** and gnashing

WELCOMES
Mt 18: 5 **w** one such child in my name **w** me.
2Jn : 11 Anyone who **w** them shares in

WELL
Lk 17: 19 your faith has made you **w**."
Jas 5: 15 faith will make the sick person **w**;

WEPT (WEEP)
Ps 137: 1 and **w** when we remembered Zion.
Jn 11: 35 Jesus **w**.

WEST
Ps 103: 12 as far as the east is from the **w**,

WHIRLWIND (WIND)
2Ki 2: 1 to take Elijah up to heaven in a **w**,
Hos 8: 7 They sow the wind and reap the **w**.
Na 1: 3 His way is in the **w** and the storm,

WHITE (WHITER)
Isa 1: 18 scarlet, they shall be as **w** as snow;
Da 7: 9 His clothing was as **w** as snow;
Rev 1: 14 hair on his head was **w** like wool,
3: 4 dressed in **w**, for they are worthy.
20: 11 I saw a great **w** throne and him

WHITER (WHITE)
Ps 51: 7 wash me, and I will be **w** than snow.

WHOLE
Mt 16: 26 for someone to gain the **w** world,
24: 14 in the **w** world as a testimony to all
Jn 13: 10 their **w** body is clean.
21: 25 even the **w** world would not have
Ac 20: 27 proclaim to you the **w** will of God.
Ro 3: 19 and the **w** world held accountable
8: 22 the **w** creation has been groaning
Gal 5: 3 he is obligated to obey the **w** law.
Eph 4: 13 attaining to the **w** measure
Jas 2: 10 For whoever keeps the **w** law
1Jn 2: 2 but also for the sins of the **w** world.

WHOLEHEARTEDLY (HEART)
Dt 1: 36 he followed the Lord **w**."
Eph 6: 7 Serve **w**, as if you were serving

WICKED (WICKEDNESS)
Ps 1: 1 does not walk in step with the **w**
1: 5 Therefore the **w** will not stand
73: 3 when I saw the prosperity of the **w**.

Pr   10: 20   the heart of the **w** is of little value.
       11: 21   The **w** will not go unpunished,
Isa   53: 9   was assigned a grave with the **w**,
       55: 7   Let the **w** forsake their ways
       57: 20   But the **w** are like the tossing sea,
Eze   3: 18   that **w** person will die for their sin,
       18: 23   any pleasure in the death of the **w**?
       33: 14   And if I say to a **w** person,

WICKEDNESS (WICKED)
Eze   28: 15   you were created till **w** was found

WIDE
Isa   54: 2   stretch your tent curtains **w**, do not
Mt   7: 13   For **w** is the gate and broad is
Eph   3: 18   to grasp how **w** and long and high

WIDOW (WIDOWS)
Dt   10: 18   cause of the fatherless and the **w**,
Lk   21: 2   saw a poor **w** put in two very small

WIDOWS (WIDOW)
Jas   1: 27   orphans and **w** in their distress

WIFE (WIVES)
Ge   2: 24   and mother and is united to his **w**,
      24: 67   So she became his **w**, and he loved
Ex   20: 17   shall not covet your neighbor's **w**,
Dt   5: 21   shall not covet your neighbor's **w**.
Pr   5: 18   you rejoice in the **w** of your youth.
     12: 4   A **w** of noble character is her
     18: 22   who finds a **w** finds what is good
     19: 13   quarrelsome **w** is like the constant
     31: 10   A **w** of noble character who can
Mt   19: 3   for a man to divorce his **w** for any
1Co   7: 2   sexual relations with his own **w**,
      7: 33   how he can please his **w**—
Eph   5: 23   head of the **w** as Christ is the head
      5: 33   must love his **w** as he loves himself,
      5: 33   the **w** must respect her husband.
1Ti   3: 2   faithful to his **w**, temperate,
Rev   21: 9   you the bride, the **w** of the Lamb."

WILD
Lk   15: 13   squandered his wealth in **w** living.
Ro   11: 17   and you, though a **w** olive shoot,

WILL (WILLING WILLINGNESS)
Ps   40: 8   I desire to do your **w**, my God;
   143: 10   Teach me to do your **w**, for you are
Isa   53: 10   Yet it was the Lord's **w** to crush
Mt   6: 10   kingdom come, your **w** be done,
     26: 39   Yet not as I **w**, but as you **w**."
Jn   7: 17   chooses to do the **w** of God will find
Ac   20: 27   to you the whole **w** of God.
Ro   12: 2   test and approve what God's **w** is—
1Co   7: 37   but has control over his own **w**,
Eph   5: 17   understand what the Lord's **w** is.
Php   2: 13   for it is God who works in you to **w**
1Th   4: 3   It is God's **w** that you should be
      5: 18   for this is God's **w** for you in Christ
Heb   9: 16   In the case of a **w**, it is necessary
     10: 7   I have come to do your **w**,
Jas   4: 15   "If it is the Lord's **w**, we **w** live
1Jn   5: 14   ask anything according to his **w**,
Rev   4: 11   by your **w** they were created

WILLING (WILL)
Ps   51: 12   salvation and grant me a **w** spirit,
Da   3: 28   were **w** to give up their lives rather
Mt   18: 14   Father in heaven is not **w** that any
     23: 37   her wings, and you were not **w**.
     26: 41   The spirit is **w**, but the flesh is

WILLINGNESS (WILL)
2Co   8: 12   For if the **w** is there, the gift is

WIN
Php   3: 14   on toward the goal to **w** the prize
1Th   4: 12   your daily life may **w** the respect

WIND (WHIRLWIND)
Jas   1: 6   the sea, blown and tossed by the **w**.

WINE
Pr   20: 1   **W** is a mocker and beer a brawler;
Isa   55: 1   buy **w** and milk without money

Mt   9: 17   Neither do people pour new **w**
Lk   23: 36   They offered him **w** vinegar
Ro   14: 21   drink **w** or to do anything else
Eph   5: 18   Do not get drunk on **w**, which

WINESKINS
Mt   9: 17   people pour new wine into old **w**.

WINGS
Ru   2: 12   under whose **w** you have come
Ps   17: 8   hide me in the shadow of your **w**
Isa   40: 31   They will soar on **w** like eagles;
Lk   13: 34   gathers her chicks under her **w**,

WIPE
Rev   7: 17   God will **w** away every tear

WISDOM (WISE)
1Ki   4: 29   God gave Solomon **w** and very
Ps   111: 10   the Lord is the beginning of **w**;
Pr   31: 26   She speaks with **w**, and faithful
Jer   10: 12   he founded the world by his **w**
Mt   11: 19   **w** is proved right by her deeds."
Lk   2: 52   And Jesus grew in **w** and stature,
Ro   11: 33   the depth of the riches of the **w**
Col   2: 3   are hidden all the treasures of **w**
Jas   1: 5   If any of you lacks **w**, you should

WISE (WISDOM WISER)
1Ki   3: 12   I will give you a **w** and discerning
Job   5: 13   He catches the **w** in their craftiness,
Ps   19: 7   trustworthy, making **w** the simple.
Pr   3: 7   Do not be **w** in your own eyes;
      9: 8   rebuke the **w** and they will love
     10: 1   A **w** son brings joy to his father,
     11: 30   and the one who is **w** saves lives.
     13: 20   Walk with the **w** and become **w**,
     17: 28   Even fools are thought **w** if they
Da   12: 3   Those who are **w** will shine like
Mt   11: 25   hidden these things from the **w**
1Co   1: 27   things of the world to shame the **w**;
2Ti   3: 15   make you **w** for salvation through

WISER (WISE)
1Co   1: 25   of God is **w** than human wisdom,

WITHER (WITHERS)
Ps   1: 3   and whose leaf does not **w**—

WITHERS (WITHER)
Isa   40: 7   The grass **w** and the flowers fall,
1Pe   1: 24   the grass **w** and the flowers fall,

WITHHOLD
Ps   84: 11   no good thing does he **w** from
Pr   23: 13   Do not **w** discipline from a child;

WITNESS (WITNESSES)
Jn   1: 8   he came only as a **w** to the light.

WITNESSES (WITNESS)
Dt   19: 15   by the testimony of two or three **w**.
Ac   1: 8   and you will be my **w** in Jerusalem,

WIVES (WIFE)
Eph   5: 22   **W**, submit yourselves to your own
      5: 25   love your **w**, just as Christ loved
1Pe   3: 1   **W**, in the same way submit

WOE
Isa   6: 5   "**W** to me!" I cried. "I am ruined!

WOLF
Isa   65: 25   The **w** and the lamb will feed

WOMAN (MAN)
Ge   2: 22   the Lord God made a **w**
      3: 15   put enmity between you and the **w**,
Lev   20: 13   with a man as one does with a **w**,
Dt   22: 5   A **w** must not wear men's clothing,
Ru   3: 11   that you are a **w** of noble character.
Pr   31: 30   a **w** who fears the Lord is to be
Mt   5: 28   lustfully has already committed
Jn   8: 3   brought in a **w** caught
Ro   7: 2   by law a married **w** is bound to her
1Co   11: 3   and the head of the **w** is man,
     11: 13   Is it proper for a **w** to pray to God
1Ti   2: 11   A **w** should learn in quietness

WOMEN (MAN)
Lk 1:42 "Blessed are you among **w**,
1Co 14:34 **W** should remain silent
1Ti 2:9 I also want the **w** to dress modestly,
Titus 2:3 teach the older **w** to be reverent
1Pe 3:5 the way the holy **w** of the past

WOMB
Job 1:21 I came from my mother's **w**,
Jer 1:5 I formed you in the **w** I knew you,
Lk 1:44 the baby in my **w** leaped for joy.

WONDERFUL (WONDERS)
Job 42:3 things too **w** for me to know.
Ps 119:18 that I may see **w** things in your law.
119:27 I may meditate on your **w** deeds.
119:129 statutes are **w**; therefore I obey
139:6 Such knowledge is too **w** for me,
Isa 9:6 he will be called **W** Counselor,
1Pe 2:9 out of darkness into his **w** light.

WONDERS (WONDERFUL)
Job 37:14 stop and consider God's **w**.
Ps 17:7 Show me the **w** of your great love,
31:21 for he showed me the **w** of his love
Joel 2:30 I will show **w** in the heavens
Ac 2:19 I will show **w** in the heavens

WOOD
Isa 44:19 Shall I bow down to a block of **w**?"
1Co 3:12 costly stones, **w**, hay or straw,

WORD (WORDS)
Dt 8:3 but on every **w** that comes
2Sa 22:31 The LORD's **w** is flawless;
Ps 119:9 By living according to your **w**.
119:11 I have hidden your **w** in my heart
119:105 Your **w** is a lamp to my feet
Pr 12:25 the heart, but a kind **w** cheers it up.
30:5 "Every **w** of God is flawless; he is
Isa 55:11 so is my **w** that goes out from my
Jn 1:1 In the beginning was the **W**, and the **W** was
with God, and the **W** was God.
1:14 The **W** became flesh and made his
2Co 2:17 we do not peddle the **w** of God
4:2 nor do we distort the **w** of God.
Eph 6:17 of the Spirit, which is the **w** of God.
Php 2:16 as you hold firmly to the **w** of life.
2Ti 2:15 and who correctly handles the **w**
Heb 4:12 the **w** of God is alive and active.
Jas 1:22 Do not merely listen to the **w**,

WORDS (WORD)
Dt 11:18 Fix these **w** of mine in your hearts
Ps 119:103 How sweet are your **w** to my taste,
119:130 unfolding of your **w** gives light;
119:160 All your **w** are true; all your
Pr 30:6 Do not add to his **w**, or he will
Jer 15:16 When your **w** came, I ate them;
Mt 24:35 but my **w** will never pass away.
Jn 6:68 You have the **w** of eternal life.
15:7 in me and my **w** remain in you,
1Co 14:19 rather speak five intelligible **w**
Rev 22:19 if anyone takes **w** away from this

WORK (HANDIWORK WORKER WORKERS WORKING WORKMAN)
Ex 23:12 but on the seventh day do not **w**,
Nu 8:11 be ready to do the **w** of the LORD.
Dt 5:14 On it you shall not do any **w**,
Jer 48:10 who is lax in doing the LORD's **w**!
Jn 6:27 Do not **w** for food that spoils,
9:4 is coming, when no one can **w**.
1Co 3:13 test the quality of each person's **w**.
Php 1:6 he who began a good **w** in you will
2:12 continue to **w** out your salvation
Col 3:23 you do, **w** at it with all your heart,
1Th 5:12 those who **w** hard among you,
2Th 3:10 is unwilling to **w** shall not eat."
2Ti 3:17 equipped for every good **w**.
Heb 6:10 he will not forget your **w**

WORKER (WORK)
Lk 10:7 for the **w** deserves his wages.

1Ti 5:18 and "The **w** deserves his wages."
2Ti 2:15 a **w** who does not need to be

WORKERS (WORK)
Mt 9:37 is plentiful but the **w** are few.
1Co 3:9 For we are **c** in God's service;

WORKING (WORK)
Col 3:23 all your heart, as **w** for the Lord,

WORKS (WORK)
Pr 31:31 her **w** bring her praise at the city
Ro 8:28 in all things God **w** for the good
Eph 2:10 to do good **w**, which God prepared
4:12 to equip his people for **w** of service,

WORLD (WORLDLY)
Ps 50:12 for the **w** is mine, and all that is
Isa 13:11 I will punish the **w** for its evil,
Mt 5:14 "You are the light of the **w**.
16:26 for someone to gain the whole **w**,
Mk 16:15 "Go into all the **w** and preach
Jn 1:29 who takes away the sin of the **w**!
3:16 God so loved the **w** that he gave his
8:12 he said, "I am the light of the **w**.
15:19 but I have chosen you out of the **w**. That is why
the **w** hates you.
16:33 I have overcome the **w**."
18:36 said, "My kingdom is not of this **w**.
Ro 3:19 and the whole **w** held accountable
1Co 3:19 the wisdom of this **w** is foolishness
2Co 5:19 that God was reconciling the **w**
10:3 For though we live in the **w**, we do
1Ti 6:7 For we brought nothing into the **w**,
1Jn 2:2 but also for the sins of the whole **w**.
2:15 not love the **w** or anything in the **w**.
Rev 13:8 slain from the creation of the **w**.

WORLDLY (WORLD)
Titus 2:12 to ungodliness and **w** passions,

WORMS
Mk 9:48 where "'the **w** that eat them do

WORRY (WORRYING)
Mt 6:25 I tell you, do not **w** about your life,
10:19 do not **w** about what to say or how

WORRYING (WORRY)
Mt 6:27 you by **w** add a single hour to your

WORSHIP
1Ch 16:29 **W** the LORD in the splendor of his
Ps 95:6 let us bow down in **w**, let us kneel
Mt 2:2 it rose and have come to **w** him."
Jn 4:24 his worshipers must **w** in the Spirit
Ro 12:1 this is your true and proper **w**.

WORTH (WORTHY)
Job 28:13 No mortal comprehends its **w**;
Pr 31:10 She is **w** far more than rubies.
Mt 10:31 you are **w** more than many
Ro 8:18 sufferings are not **w** comparing
1Pe 1:7 of greater **w** than gold,
3:4 which is of great **w** in God's sight.

WORTHLESS
Pr 11:4 Wealth is **w** in the day of wrath,
Jas 1:26 themselves, and their religion is **w**.

WORTHY (WORTH)
1Ch 16:25 is the LORD and most **w** of praise;
Eph 4:1 live a life **w** of the calling you have
Php 1:27 in a manner **w** of the gospel
Rev 5:2 "Who is **w** to break the seals

WOUNDS
Pr 27:6 **W** from a friend can be trusted,
Isa 53:5 and by his **w** we are healed.
Zec 13:6 'What are these **w** on your body?'
1Pe 2:24 "by his **w** you have been healed."

WRATH
2Ch 36:16 at his prophets until the **w**
Ps 2:5 anger and terrifies them in his **w**,
76:10 Surely your **w** against mankind
Pr 15:1 A gentle answer turns away **w**,
Jer 25:15 cup filled with the wine of my **w**

Ro   1: 18 The **w** of God is being revealed
        5: 9 saved from God's **w** through him!
1Th 5: 9 God did not appoint us to suffer **w**
Rev 6: 16 and from the **w** of the Lamb!

WRESTLED
Ge 32: 24 a man **w** with him till daybreak.

WRITE (WRITING WRITTEN)
Dt   6: 9 **W** them on the doorframes of your
Pr   7: 3 **w** them on the tablet of your heart.
Heb 8: 10 minds and **w** them on their hearts.

WRITING (WRITE)
1Co 14: 37 what I am **w** to you is the Lord's

WRITTEN (WRITE)
Jos   1: 8 be careful to do everything **w** in it.
Da 12: 1 everyone whose name is found **w**
Lk 10: 20 that your names are **w** in heaven."
Jn 20: 31 these are **w** that you may believe
1Co 4: 6 "Do not go beyond what is **w**."
2Co 3: 3 **w** not with ink but with the Spirit
Heb 12: 23 whose names are **w** in heaven.

WRONG (WRONGDOING WRONGED WRONGS)
Ex 23: 2 not follow the crowd in doing **w**.
Nu   5: 7 restitution for the **w** they have
Job 34: 12 unthinkable that God would do **w**,
1Th 5: 15 that nobody pays back **w** for **w**,

WRONGDOING (WRONG)
Job 1: 22 not sin by charging God with **w**.

WRONGED (WRONG)
1Co 6: 7 Why not rather be **w**?

WRONGS (WRONG)
Pr 10: 12 conflict, but love covers over all **w**.
1Co 13: 5 angered, it keeps no record of **w**.

YEARS
Ps 90: 4 A thousand **y** in your sight are like
      90: 10 Our days may come to seventy **y**,
2Pe 3: 8 the Lord a day is like a thousand **y**,

Rev 20: 2 and bound him for a thousand **y**.

YESTERDAY
Heb 13: 8 Jesus Christ is the same **y** and today

YOKE (YOKED)
Mt 11: 29 Take my **y** upon you and learn

YOKED (YOKE)
2Co 6: 14 Do not be **y** together

YOUNG (YOUTH)
Ps 119: 9 can a **y** person stay on the path
1Ti 4: 12 down on you because you are **y**,

YOUTH (YOUNG)
Ps 103: 5 your **y** is renewed like the eagle's.
Ecc 12: 1 your Creator in the days of your **y**,
2Ti 2: 22 Flee the evil desires of **y** and

ZEAL
Jn   2: 17 **Z** for your house will consume me.
Ro 12: 11 Never be lacking in **z**, but keep

ZECHARIAH
   1. Son of Jeroboam II; king of Israel (2Ki 15:8-12).
   2. Post-exilic prophet who encouraged rebuilding of temple (Ezr 5:1; 6:14; Zec 1:1).
   3. Father of John the Baptist (Lk 1:13; 3:2).

ZEDEKIAH
   Mattaniah, son of Josiah (1Ch 3:15), made king of Judah by Nebuchadnezzar (2Ki 24:17–25:7; 2Ch 36:10-14; Jer 37-39; 52:1-11).

ZERUBBABEL
   Descendant of David (1Ch 3:19; Mt 1:3). Led return from exile (Ezr 2-3; Ne 7:7; Hag 1-2; Zec 4).

ZIMRI
   King of Israel (1Ki 16:9-20).

ZION
Ps 137: 3 "Sing us one of the songs of **Z**!"
Jer 50: 5 They will ask the way to **Z** and
Ro 9: 33 I lay in **Z** a stone that causes people
   11: 26 "The deliverer will come from **Z**;

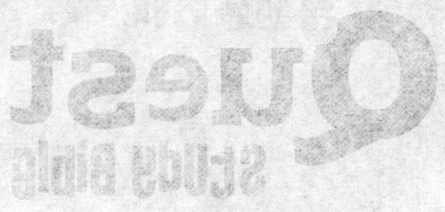

Quest Study Bible

Project Management and Editorial	Carol Postma
Proofreading	Peachtree Editorial and Proofreading Service
Theological Review	Terry Fisher, Master of Arts in Theology Fuller Seminary
Production Management	Phil Heich
Art Direction	Ron Huizinga
Cover and Interior Design	Ron Huizinga
Typesetting Management	Mark Sheeres

NEW INTERNATIONAL VERSION

youth Quest study Bible

Project Management and Editorial	Carol Postma
Proofreading	Peachtree Editorial and Proofreading Service
Theological Review	Terry Fisher, Master of Arts in Theology, Fuller Seminary
Production Management	Phil Herich
Art Direction	Ron Huizinga
Cover and Interior Design	Ron Huizinga
Typesetting Management	Mark Sheeres

WORLD OF THE PATRIARCHS

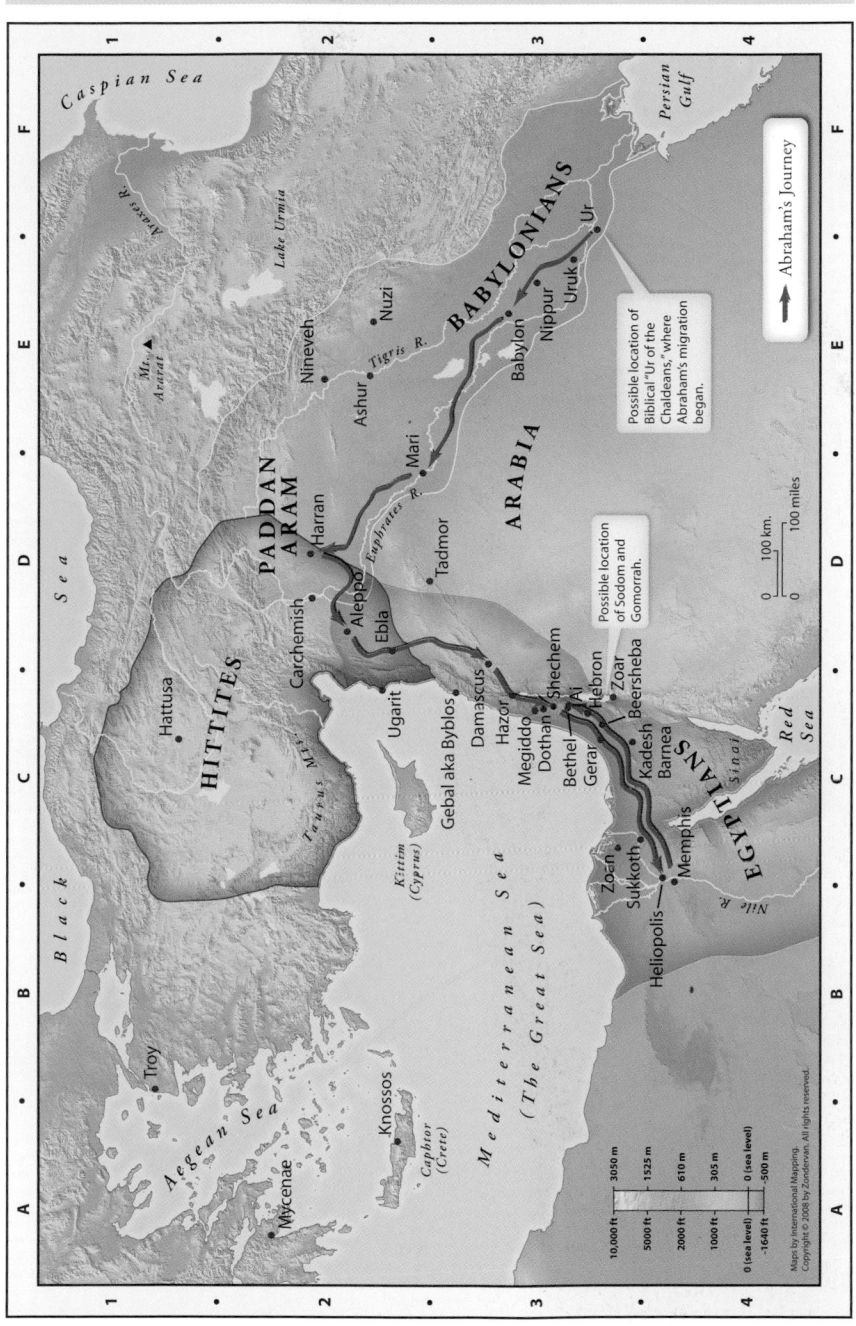

Possible location of Biblical "Ur of the Chaldeans," where Abraham's migration began.

Possible location of Sodom and Gomorrah.

Abraham's Journey

Caspian Sea

Black Sea

Aegean Sea

Mediterranean Sea (The Great Sea)

Red Sea

Persian Gulf

Araxes R.

Lake Urmia

Mt. Ararat

Tigris R.

Euphrates R.

Nile R.

Taurus Mts.

Kittim (Cyprus)

Capthor (Crete)

Sinai

BABYLONIANS

ARABIA

PADDAN ARAM

HITTITES

EGYPTIANS

Troy
Mycenae
Knossos
Hattusa
Carchemish
Ugarit
Gebal aka Byblos
Aleppo
Ebla
Damascus
Hazor
Megiddo
Dothan
Shechem
Bethel
Ai
Gerar
Hebron
Zoar
Beersheba
Kadesh Barnea
Zoan
Sukkoth
Memphis
Heliopolis
Harran
Tadmor
Mari
Ashur
Nineveh
Nuzi
Babylon
Nippur
Uruk
Ur

100 km.
100 miles

10,000 ft. / 3050 m
5000 ft. / 1525 m
2000 ft. / 610 m
1000 ft. / 305 m
0 (sea level) / 0 (sea level)
-1640 ft. / -500 m

EXODUS AND CONQUEST OF CANAAN

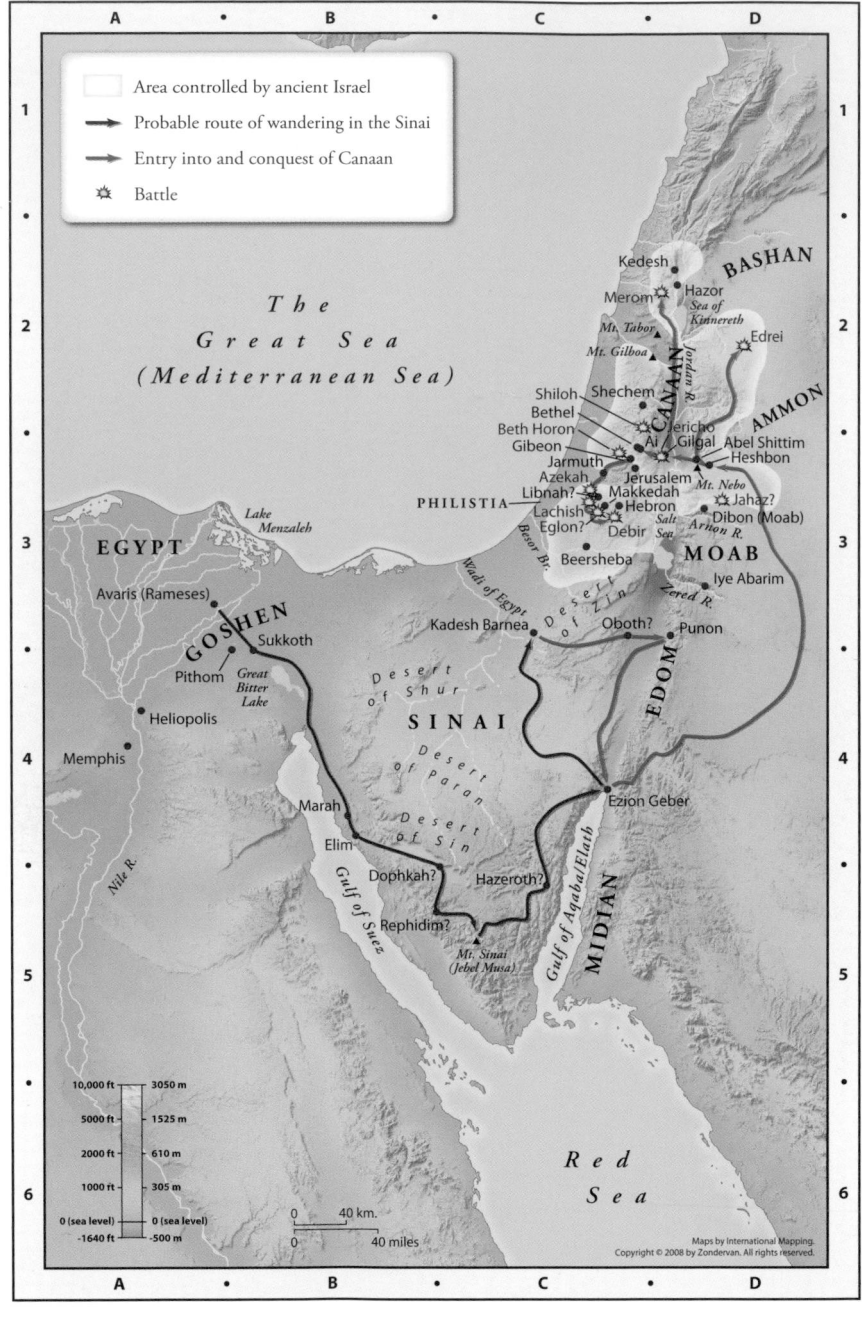

A   B   C   D

☐ Area controlled by ancient Israel

→ Probable route of wandering in the Sinai

→ Entry into and conquest of Canaan

✹ Battle

The
Great Sea
(Mediterranean Sea)

Kedesh

Merom ✹   Hazor   BASHAN
    Sea of
Mt. Tabor   *Kinnereth*
Mt. Gilboa ▲   Edrei ✹

Shiloh   Shechem
Bethel
Beth Horon   ✹Jericho
Gibeon   Ai   Gilgal   Abel Shittim
Jarmuth   Heshbon
Azekah   Jerusalem   *Mt. Nebo*
Libnah?   Makkedah   ✹Jahaz?
PHILISTIA   Lachish   Hebron   Dibon (Moab)
   Eglon?   Debir   *Salt*   *Arnon R.*
         Sea

CANAAN   *Jordan R.*   AMMON

Beersheba   MOAB

Wadi of Egypt   *Besor Br.*   Iye Abarim

EGYPT

Avaris (Rameses)
GOSHEN
Sukkoth

Pithom   *Great*
Bitter
Heliopolis   *Lake*

Memphis

Lake
Menzaleh

Kadesh Barnea   Oboth?   Punon
    Desert
of Shur   *of Zin*
      Zered R.
Desert
of Paran
SINAI   EDOM

Desert
of Sin
Marah   Ezion Geber

Elim
Dophkah?   Hazeroth?
    Gulf of Aqaba/Elath
Rephidim?   MIDIAN
Mt. Sinai
(Jebel Musa)

Gulf of Suez

Nile R.

Red
Sea

10,000 ft   3050 m
5000 ft   1525 m
2000 ft   610 m
1000 ft   305 m
0 (sea level)   0 (sea level)
-1640 ft   -500 m

0   40 km.
0   40 miles

LAND OF THE TWELVE TRIBES

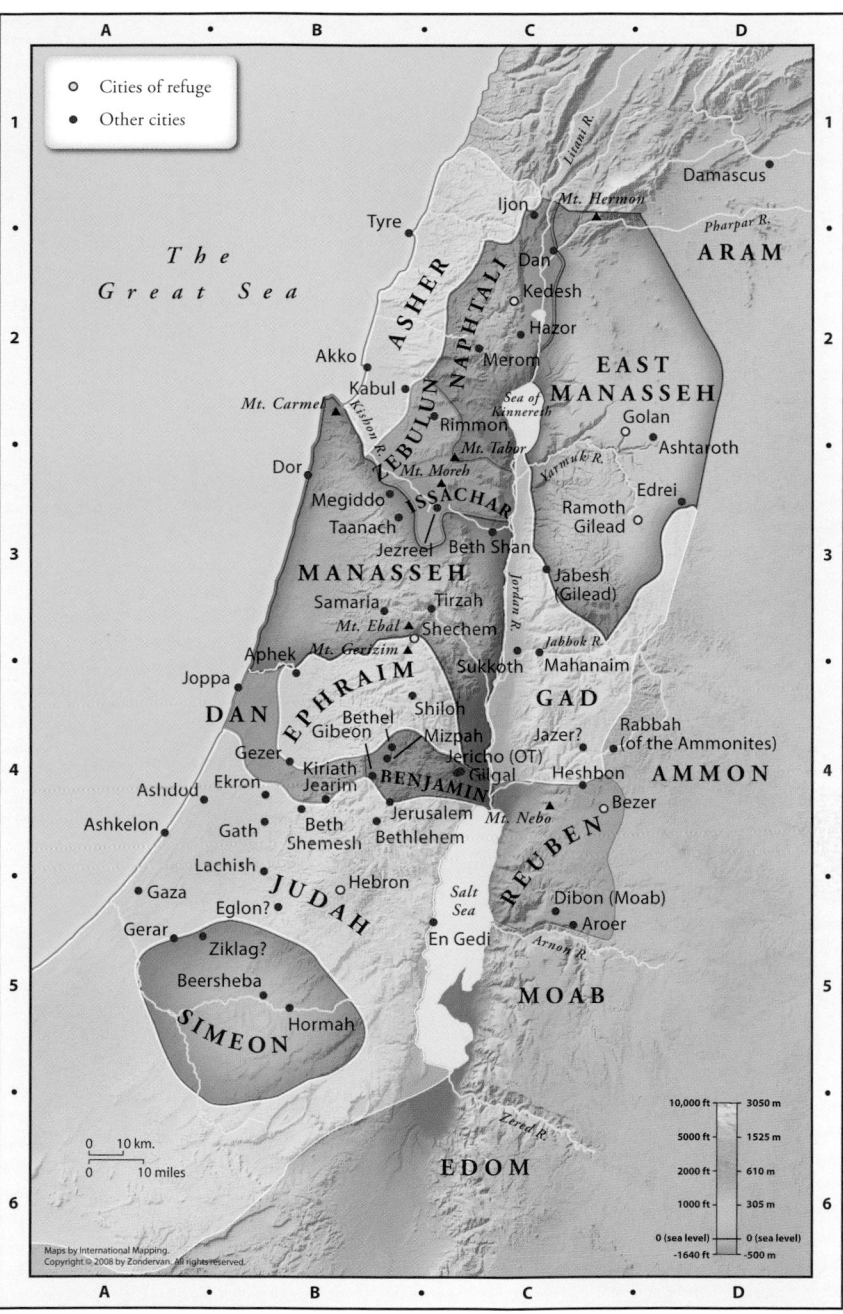

○ Cities of refuge
● Other cities

The Great Sea

Damascus

Tyre
Ijon · *Mt. Hermon* ▲
Pharpar R.
ARAM

ASHER
Dan
Kedesh ○
Hazor
Merom

Akko
Kabul
Mt. Carmel ▲
Rimmon

NAPHTALI
ZEBULUN
Sea of Kinnereth

EAST MANASSEH
Golan ●
Ashtaroth ●

Dor
Mt. Tabor ▲
Mt. Moreh ▲
ISSACHAR
Yarmuk R.
Edrei ○

Megiddo
Taanach
Jezreel
Beth Shan

Ramoth Gilead ○

MANASSEH
Samaria
Tirzah ○
Mt. Ebal ▲
Shechem
Mt. Gerizim ▲

Jordan R.

Jabesh (Gilead)

Aphek
Joppa

EPHRAIM
Sukkoth
Mahanaim
Jabbok R.

DAN
Bethel
Gibeon
Shiloh
Mizpah
Jazer?

GAD
Rabbah (of the Ammonites)

Gezer
Kiriath Jearim
BENJAMIN
Jericho (OT)
Gilgal
Heshbon
AMMON

Ashdod
Ekron
Jerusalem
Mt. Nebo
Bezer ○

Ashkelon
Gath
Beth Shemesh
Bethlehem
REUBEN

Lachish
Hebron
Salt Sea
Dibon (Moab)

Gaza
Eglon?
JUDAH
En Gedi
Aroer
Arnon R.

Gerar
Ziklag?
Beersheba
SIMEON
Hormah

MOAB

Zered R.

EDOM

0   10 km.
0   10 miles

	10,000 ft	3050 m
	5000 ft	1525 m
	2000 ft	610 m
	1000 ft	305 m
	0 (sea level)	0 (sea level)
	-1640 ft	-500 m

KINGDOM OF DAVID AND SOLOMON

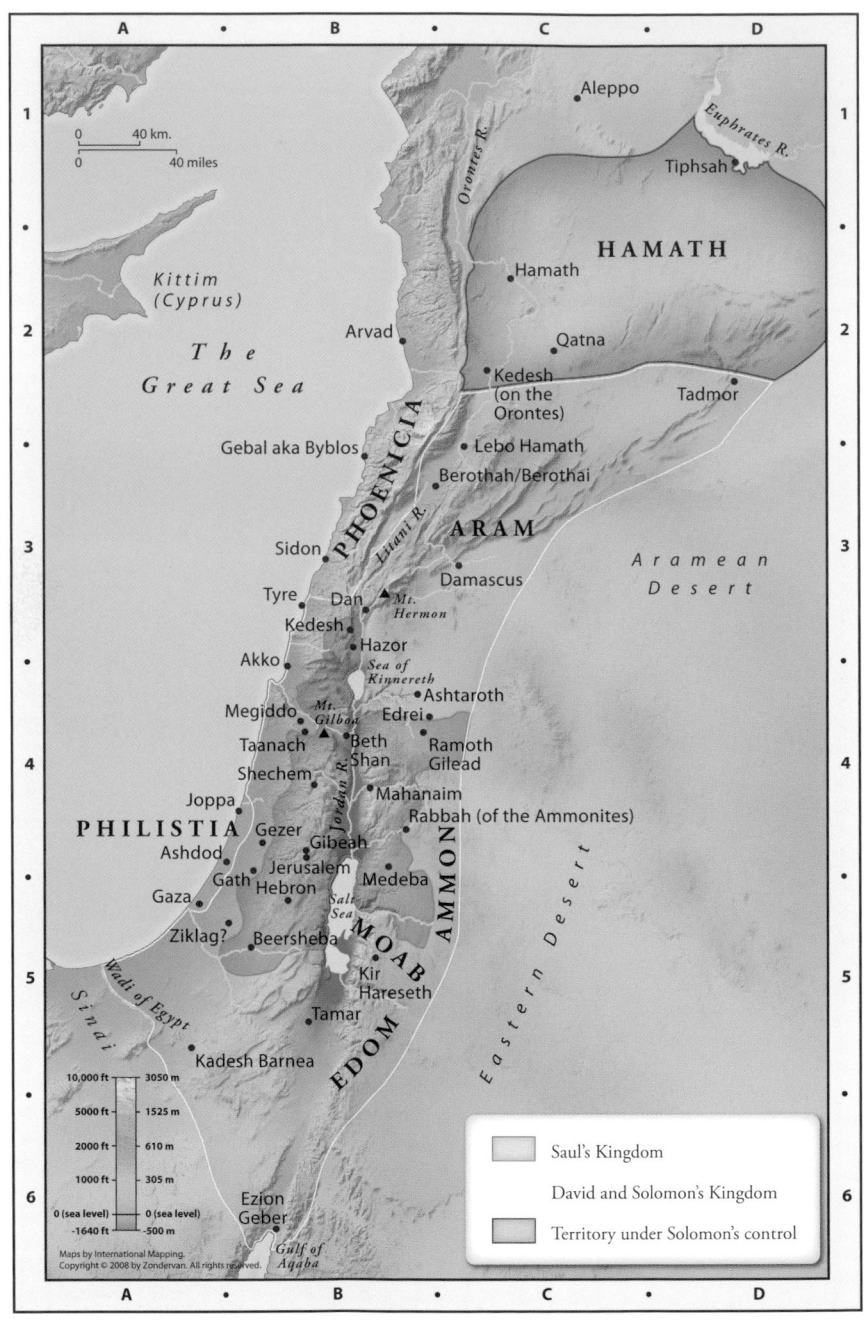

Maps by International Mapping.
Copyright © 2008 by Zondervan. All rights reserved.

Saul's Kingdom

David and Solomon's Kingdom

Territory under Solomon's control

JESUS' MINISTRY

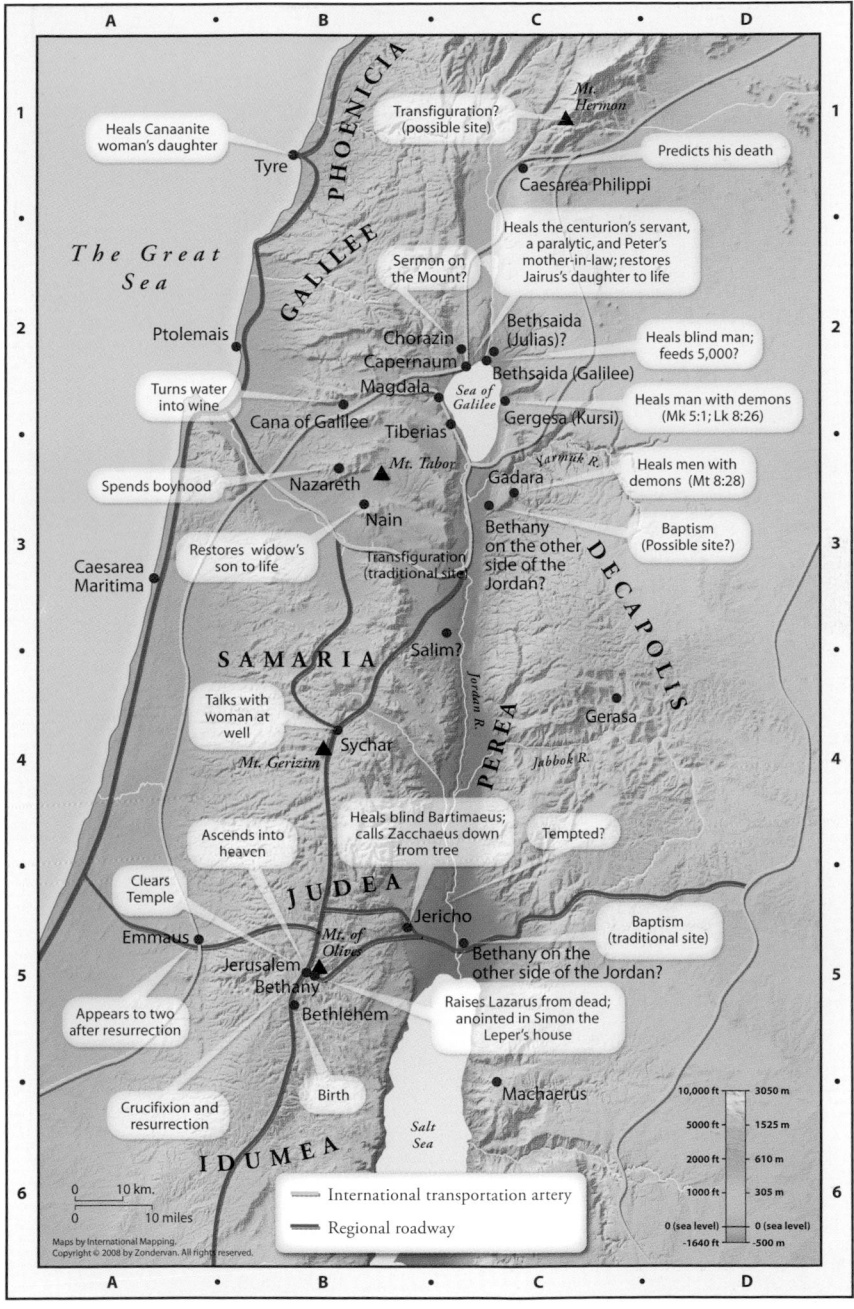

Heals Canaanite woman's daughter

Tyre

PHOENICIA

Transfiguration? (possible site)

Mt. Hermon

Predicts his death

Caesarea Philippi

GALILEE

The Great Sea

Sermon on the Mount?

Heals the centurion's servant, a paralytic, and Peter's mother-in-law; restores Jairus's daughter to life

Ptolemais

Chorazin

Bethsaida (Julias)?

Heals blind man; feeds 5,000?

Capernaum

Bethsaida (Galilee)

Magdala

Sea of Galilee

Turns water into wine

Cana of Galilee

Tiberias

Gergesa (Kursi)

Heals man with demons (Mk 5:1; Lk 8:26)

Yarmuk R.

Spends boyhood

Mt. Tabor

Nazareth

Gadara

Heals men with demons (Mt 8:28)

Nain

Restores widow's son to life

Transfiguration (traditional site)

Bethany on the other side of the Jordan?

Baptism (Possible site?)

DECAPOLIS

Caesarea Maritima

SAMARIA

Salim?

Jordan R.

Talks with woman at well

Sychar

Mt. Gerizim

Gerasa

PEREA

Jabbok R.

Heals blind Bartimaeus; calls Zacchaeus down from tree

Tempted?

Ascends into heaven

Clears Temple

JUDEA

Emmaus

Jericho

Baptism (traditional site)

Jerusalem

Mt. of Olives

Bethany

Bethany on the other side of the Jordan?

Appears to two after resurrection

Bethlehem

Raises Lazarus from dead; anointed in Simon the Leper's house

Crucifixion and resurrection

Birth

Salt Sea

Machaerus

IDUMEA

	10,000 ft	3050 m
	5000 ft	1525 m
	2000 ft	610 m
	1000 ft	305 m
	0 (sea level)	0 (sea level)
	-1640 ft	-500 m

0   10 km.
0   10 miles

International transportation artery

Regional roadway

PAUL'S MISSIONARY JOURNEYS

First Missionary Journey (A.D. 46–48)
Second Missionary Journey (A.D. 49–52)
Third Missionary Journey (A.D. 53–57)
Trip to Rome (A.D. 59–60)

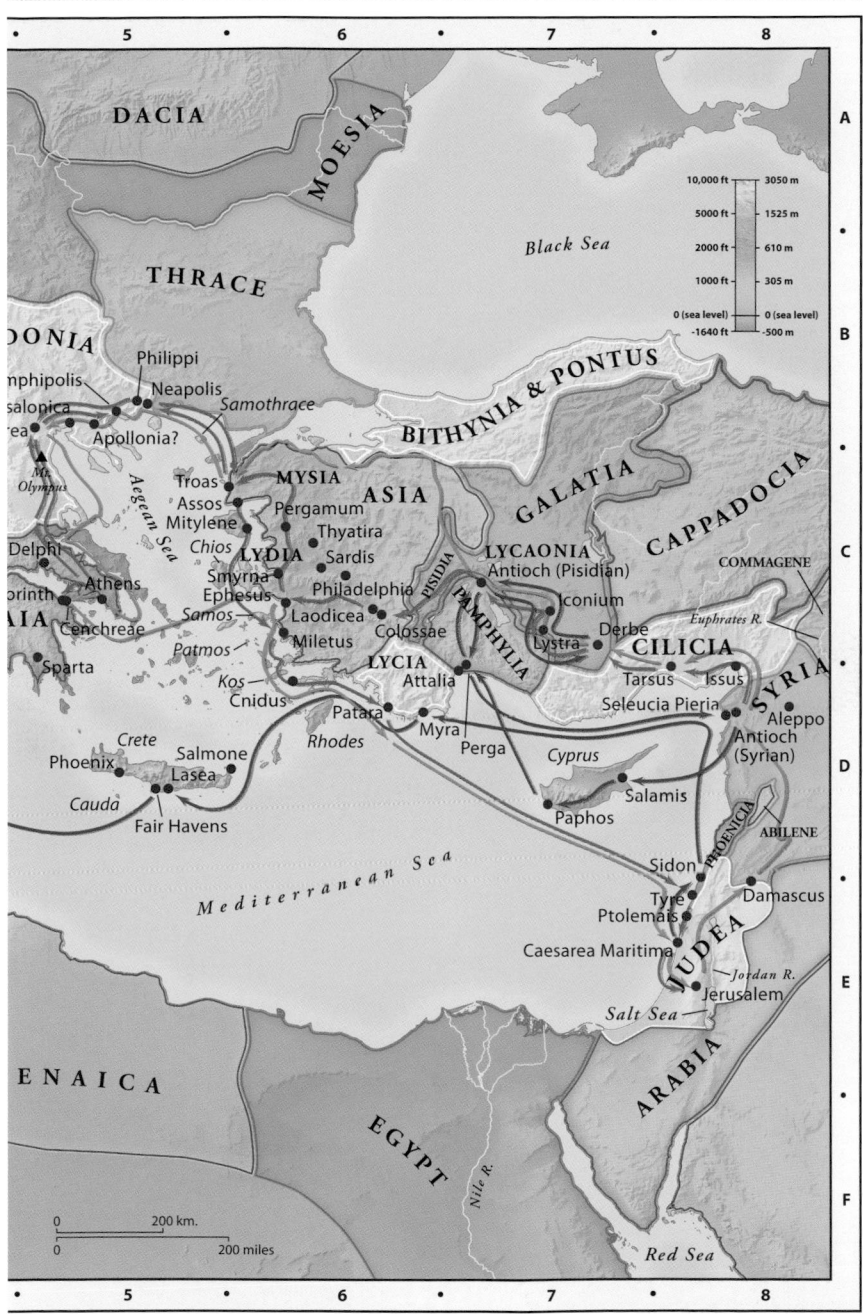

DACIA

MOESIA

THRACE

Black Sea

10,000 ft — 3050 m
5000 ft — 1525 m
2000 ft — 610 m
1000 ft — 305 m
0 (sea level) — 0 (sea level)
-1640 ft — -500 m

BITHYNIA & PONTUS

GALATIA

CAPPADOCIA

Philippi
Neapolis
Amphipolis
Samothrace
ssalonica
rea
Apollonia?
Mt.
Olympus

MACEDONIA

MYSIA
ASIA

Troas
Assos
Mitylene
Pergamum
Thyatira
Chios
Sardis
LYDIA
Smyrna
Ephesus
Philadelphia
Samos
Laodicea
Colossae
Miletus

PISIDIA
LYCAONIA
Antioch (Pisidian)
Iconium
Lystra
Derbe

COMMAGENE

Euphrates R.

CILICIA

Delphi
orinth
Athens
AIA
Cenchreae
Sparta
Patmos

Aegean
Sea

Kos
Cnidus

LYCIA
Attalia
PAMPHYLIA

Tarsus
Issus
Seleucia Pieria

SYRIA

Aleppo
Antioch
(Syrian)

Patara
Myra
Perga
Rhodes

Cyprus

Crete
Phoenix
Salmone
Lasea
Cauda
Fair Havens

Salamis
Paphos

PHOENICIA

ABILENE

Sidon
Tyre
Ptolemais

Damascus

Mediterranean Sea

Caesarea Maritima

JUDEA

Jordan R.

Jerusalem

Salt Sea

ENAICA

EGYPT

Nile R.

ARABIA

Red Sea

0   200 km.
0   200 miles

JERUSALEM IN THE TIME OF JESUS

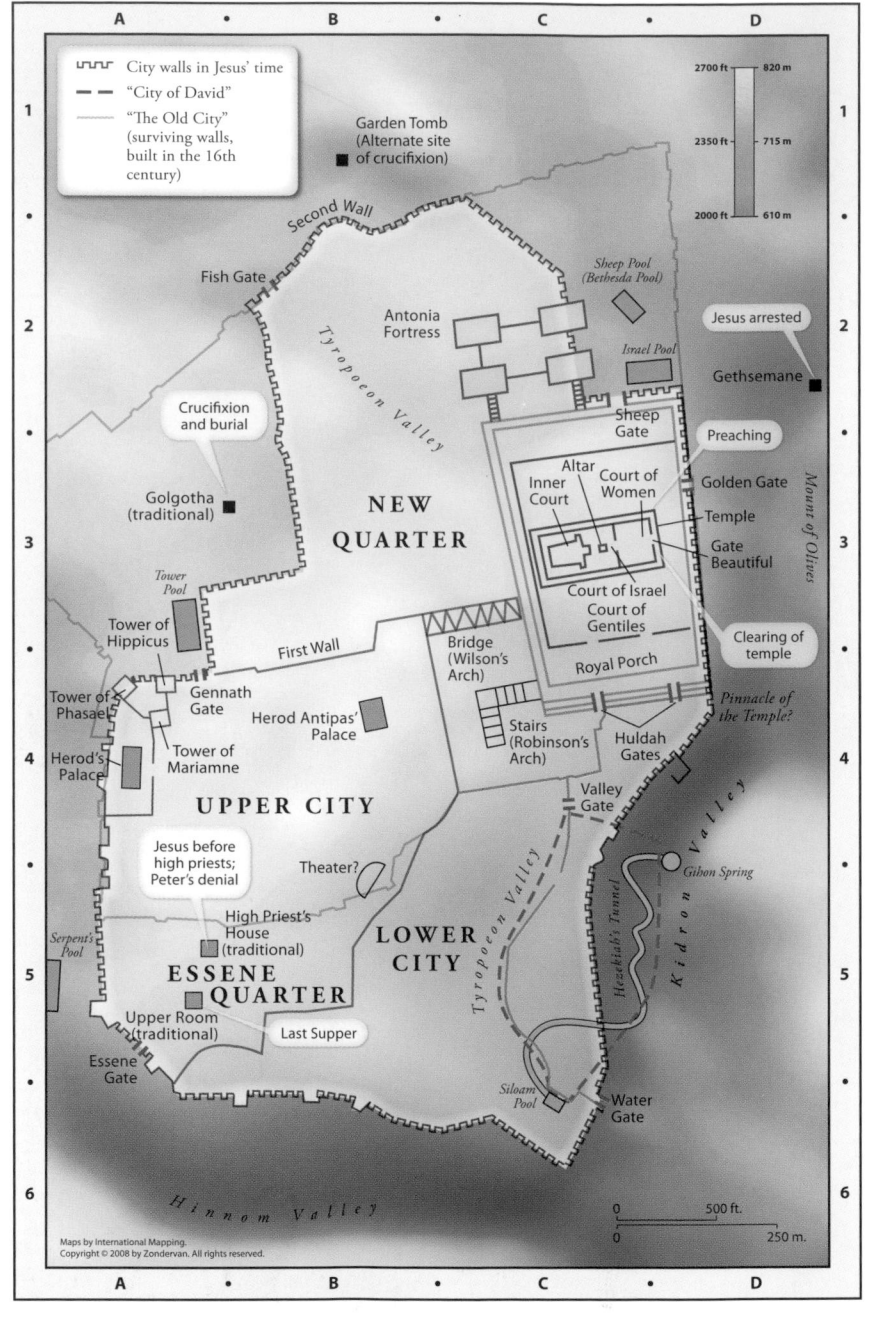

Legend:
- City walls in Jesus' time
- "City of David"
- "The Old City" (surviving walls, built in the 16th century)

2700 ft — 820 m
2350 ft — 715 m
2000 ft — 610 m

Garden Tomb (Alternate site of crucifixion)

Second Wall

Fish Gate

Sheep Pool (Bethesda Pool)

Antonia Fortress

Israel Pool

Jesus arrested

Gethsemane

Tyropoeon Valley

Crucifixion and burial

Golgotha (traditional)

NEW QUARTER

Sheep Gate

Altar
Inner Court
Court of Women

Preaching

Golden Gate

Temple

Gate Beautiful

Mount of Olives

Court of Israel
Court of Gentiles

Clearing of temple

Tower Pool

Tower of Hippicus

First Wall

Bridge (Wilson's Arch)

Royal Porch

Pinnacle of the Temple?

Tower of Phasael

Gennath Gate

Herod Antipas' Palace

Stairs (Robinson's Arch)

Huldah Gates

Herod's Palace

Tower of Mariamne

UPPER CITY

Valley Gate

Kidron Valley

Jesus before high priests; Peter's denial

Theater?

High Priest's House (traditional)

LOWER CITY

Gihon Spring

Serpent's Pool

ESSENE QUARTER

Tyropoeon Valley

Hezekiah's Tunnel

Upper Room (traditional)

Last Supper

Essene Gate

Siloam Pool

Water Gate

Hinnom Valley

0   500 ft.
0   250 m.